Compendium of Historical Sources

The How and Where of American Genealogy

by
Ronald A. Bremer

Published by:
Mr. & Mrs. Carl L. Bremer

This book retails for
one-hundred dollars
and is available from Ron Bremer,
Post Office Box 16422, Salt Lake City, UT 84116

"I do not think it is worth while for me to ask you to make any further researches. As I am now in my eighty-first year, I shall soon be able to make personal enquiries from any of my forerunners who happen to have gone in whatever direction I am going."

—Proceedings of the
Huguenot Society of London

All of the various notekeeping forms, and census forms, in this book, as well as other special forms and charts are available from the Genealogy Book Club, Post Office Box 4064, Wofford Heights, California 93285. Send one dollar for their latest catalog.

"You must know that there is nothing higher and stronger and more wholesome and good for life in the future than some good memory, especially a memory of childhood, or home. People talk to you a great deal about your education, but some good sacred memory, preserved from childhood, is perhaps the best education. If a man carries many such memories with him into life, he is safe to the end of his days. And if one has only one good memory left in one's heart, even that may sometime be the means of saving him."

The Brothers Karamazov
By Feodor Dostoyevsky
1966, Norton Publishers
500 Fifth Ave.
New York, NY 10110

As one does research, it becomes clear that mistakes are commonplace, that records change or are moved, and new sources are always being found. Therefore, if you find errors in this book, or additional sources, please write to me at P.O. Box 16422, Salt Lake City, Utah 84116.

ACKNOWLEDGEMENTS

The author expresses his gratitude to Mrs. Arlene H. Eakle, Salt Lake City, Utah; Mr. Robert J. Tarte, Ashland, Massachusetts; Mr. Michael J. Smyth, Marianna, Florida; Mr. C. Christian Larsen, Salt Lake City, Utah; Mr. and Mrs. Ray D. Kell, Princeton, New Jersey; Col. Paul K. Brown, USA (Ret.), Bryn Mawr, Pennsylvania; Mr. and Mrs. Jonny Blumhagen, Salt Lake City, Utah; Mrs. Zelma Bickmore, Twenty-Nine Palms, California; Mr. Louis M. Breithaupt, Salt Lake City, Utah; Mr. and Mrs. Colin James, Denver, Colorado; Mr. and Mrs. Carl L. Bremer, Bellflower, California; Mr. and Mrs. Michael Andrus, Salt Lake City, Utah; Mrs. Kay Davenport, Orem, Utah; Mr. and Mrs. Curt Jones, Taft, California; Mr. and Mrs. Moli Tupai, West Jordan, Utah; Mr. Robert E. Carlberg, Anaheim, California; Mrs. Marian McConnell, Stockton, California; Mr. and Mrs. David C. Chamberlain, Tigard, Oregon; Mr. Jimmy B. Parker and Mr. Thomas E. Daniels, both of the Genealogical Society, Salt Lake City, Utah; Mr. and Mrs. Garland D. Asbel, Bellflower, California; Mrs. Mabel DeHaven, Westlake Village, California, and especially to Joan E. Coltrain, Salt Lake City, Utah.

THIS BOOK IS LOVINGLY
DEDICATED TO ALL
THE
L. O. L. I. T. S.

The Author

RONALD ALLAN BREMER, professional genealogist, author, lecturer, and historian, was born at South Gate, Los Angles County, California, on the second of May 1937. He first became interested in the facinating endeavor of genealogy at the early age of thirteen. His mother was a genealogist and taught genealogical research. His family has been tracing their roots for over one hundred years! His father's family descends from German, Dutch and English ancestry, and his mother's family descends from German, English, Scotch-Irish, and Jewish ancestry.

He has attended Cerritos College in California; American University in Washington, D.C.; and Brigham Young University in Provo, Utah. He also attended the Eleventh Annual Genealogical Institute sponsored by the National Archives.

Early in his career, Ron Bremer became dissatisfied with the old and often stodgy approach to genealogical research. It wasn't long before he started looking for better methods and faster ways to do genealogy. He soon discovered that an enormous quantity of important records existed in the United States that were either unknown or ignored by most genealogists. One of his most important contributions to genealogical research has been the location and identification of these little-known but extremely valuable record sources.

Mr. Bremer has lectured before the major genealogical societies in America. He is presently Editor for the *Roots Digest* magazine. A contributor to numerous genealogical periodicals and in constant demand as a motivational speaker, every year he conducts an average of forty all-day genealogical seminars or workshops. Mr. Bremer has personally visited the major genealogical record centers in every state and in Washington, D.C.

TABLE OF CONTENTS

INTRODUCTION

To find and understand the life of your ancestors, you must discover the records that tell you about them. To help you find these records and to make your research more productive and enjoyable, I have traveled over 100,000 miles in all 50 states, crisscrossing the country 37 times, and visited almost every city, town and hamlet. I have visited the National Archives, the Library of Congress, the libraries of the Daughters of the American Revolution and of the Sons of the American Revolution, the Supreme Court, the Federal Records Centers, and the presidential libraries have been fully consulted for the preparation of this work. In each of the states, the capitol, the office of the Secretary of State, the state archives, the state library, the office of the Adjutant-General, the state university, the state historical society, the state land offices, the state law library, the state genealogical society, and special collections were inventoried to amass our data. Moreover, the municipal archives of every major city in the nation were exhausted.

I have also conducted more than a thousand workshops and seminars and have listened to thousands of people raise questions about genealogy.

From these experiences we have put together this book which will answer the most often asked genealogy questions (see below) and contains approximately ninety percent of all the resources you should need to locate your American ancestors.

1. Is there a system I should follow to guarantee the most success in my research?
2. What is the best way of keeping records?
3. Which is the best way to file my records?
4. What sources are the most valuable?
5. Where can I find church records?
6. How can I make the best use of the public library?
7. What records exist on the federal level?
8. How can I locate old university or college records?
9. What can I expect to find on my lines in Salt Lake City?
10. Did most immigrants come to America under the sponsorship of an alliance?
11. Are there records of those who were Masons?
12. How can I find the various special collections in America?
13. Which are the most important reference works for the genealogists?
14. Are court records the very best genealogical source?

15. Why are land records so very important?
16. How can I determine a maiden name from a deed?
17. When did registration of vital records begin in each state?
18. Which federal forms do I need to use when I write to Washington, D.C.?
19. Where can I find a description of all the American migration trails?
20. How do I use the Library of Congress?
21. Exactly what is in the National Archives for the family historian?
22. Is the D.A.R. Library open to all researchers?
23. Where are all the service and pension records located?
24. Are there passenger lists for every port of entry?
25. How do I determine the overseas home of my immigrant ancestor?
26. Where is the record of naturalization for my great-grandfather?
27. Are there any records for those who worked on the early railroads?
28. How can I locate a place that has changed its name?
29. Is there a listing of all the political townships in America?
30. Do insurance companies keep records of genealogical importance?
31. How can I know all the federal, territorial, and state censuses?
32. Why is the W.P.A. Inventory the "key" to the county courthouse?
33. Are the unpublished W.P.A. Inventories available to researchers?
34. Where can I locate the most updated information on all the counties?
35. What are the records of importance in Canadian genealogical research?
36. What do the initials "D.D." mean?
37. How can I locate materials on inter-library loan?
38. Are copies of out-of-print books available anywhere?
39. Is there a simple, easy-to-understand way of determining relationships?
40. Where can I locate an old map of the county where my ancestors lived?
41. What is the best way of locating an old family cemetery?

Before you proceed there is a warning:

"Genealogy Pox (Very Contagious to Adults)—Symptoms: Continual complaint as to need for names, dates, and places. Patient has blank expression, sometimes deaf to spouse and children. Has no taste for work of any kind, except feverishly looking through records at libraries and courthouses. Has compulsion to write letters. Swears at mailman when he doesn't leave mail. Frequents strange places such as cemeteries, ruins, and remote desolate country areas. Makes secret night calls. Hides phone bills from spouse and mumbles to self. Has strange faraway look in eyes.
"No Known Cure.
"Treatment: Medication is useless. Disease is not fatal, but gets progressively worse. Patient should attend genealogy workshops, subscribe to genealogical magazines and be given corner in the house where he or she can be alone.
"Remarks: The unusual nature of this disease is — the sicker the patient gets, the more he or she enjoys it." — Anonymous

Section I
RESEARCH

CHAPTER 1

GENERAL PRINCIPLES OF GENEALOGY RESEARCH

Before you begin your search, there are a few things you should know about the general principles of research.

1. Genealogical Research Methods

LINEAGE: The purpose of this research is to prove parentage and heritage;

PEDIGREE: The purpose of this research is to link people together in families with a minimum number of research sources.

WHOLISTIC: The purpose of this approach is to understand people, their lifestyle, and their environment. This approach demands a great many more sources and information.

The greater the number and variety of sources the better and more interesting your information will be; the better the information, the more accurate your pedigree.

The researcher should always weigh the quality and extent of information desired against the time and cost of such research. For example:

If there were 50 documents in ten different locations that would help you to understand your ancestor better:

the wholistic research would try to use all 50 documents;

the pedigree researcher may use ten documents in one or two locations;

the lineage researcher may use one or two documents which may be a vital record or census schedule, which are most readily accessible.

WARNING: Name-gathering may be hazardous to your pedigree!

2. Jurisdictional Record Gathering — To find the proper records you must know who caused the record to be made and what its purpose was, who preserved the record, and who has custody (jurisdiction) of them at the present time.

3. You may want to refresh your knowledge of American History to make the task of research more logical.

4. Organization. The best way to do accurate research is to presume you will die before completing your research. We are not trying to intimidate the beginner, but rather to stress the importance of orderliness. It is surprizing how many people have plowed the same field (genealogically speaking) over and over because they did not keep accurate records.

Most people keep records like this:

However, if someone else will have to finish your research, he will save time and money if he starts where you left off. The more accurate and trustworthy your research, the more success he will experience.

In our notekeeping section we will explain exactly how to keep your records.

5. Directional Research. An axiom of genealogical research is "never start work on an ancestor unless you know when and where he/she died". All Orientals read from back to front. The same is true of genealogy. You should never start with the birth of a person and work toward his death. It is more accurate to start with the death of a person and collect all of the documents you can find working backward to his birth. When you work the other way, you often build walls that block your success.

6. Impasses. Whenever you come up against an impasse (stone wall), it is because you have cheated your sources. You haven't explored all of the sources available to you. You have used too many shortcuts. Using the jurisdictional concept, accumulate all of the records that time and money will allow. A useful axiom is that you should never work on a state unless you know the county your ancestor lived in, and you should never search for an ancestor unless you know when and where he died.

7. Define the Borders. When I was a young boy I put 1000-piece puzzles together while listening to the radio. I found that if I tried to start in the middle I had little success, but if I built the border first it was much easier. If you build the border of your search well, the family puzzle will be much easier to put together. The borders for genealogy are surname, locality (jurisdiction), time (date), sources available (documents).

8. General vs. Particular Research. When you are doing research you are looking for a particular person (particular search). This is the best way to search most records but when searching county records make a general search; that is, check all the people with the same surname. Most researchers get stuck because they start out by looking for a particular person. This can often lead to wrong assumptions and stall your research. For example, in the current Salt Lake City telephone directory, there are 42 John Smith's and nine of them are John W. Smith. Which one would be the right one. In any one county there can be more than one person with the same name who is married to a woman with the same name. A general search means you would take all the people in a county jurisdiction with the same surname and then narrow it down to the right person. One good professional genealogist I know who uses this approach has never had her work challenged.

9. **One family group sheet(see forms) per source or document.** Since all sources will not give the same information (some women and men lie about their age) you should keep a family group sheet on each document you search (more help will be given in the notekeeping secton). Each group sheet then becomes a part of the family puzzle.

A good search of a given family (father, mother, and children) should have about 24 family group sheets. If you only have 12, you probably have not done as much homework as you should.

10. **Evaluation of Sources.** Since not all sources are of equal value, when you are analyzing which one you want to rely on you need to know which ones are of most value.

Remember, most people tend to be more honest when they are in court than when they are in a parlor game. Here is a list of what I have found to be the most accurate and useful.

The most reliable record sources are:

1. Judicial court records

2. Property Records
   Deeds
   Mortgages
   Plat maps
   Tax lists
3. Probate Records
   Testate (with a will)
   Intestate (without a will)
4. Vital Records
   Birth
   Marriage
   Death
5. Church Records
   Christening
   Marriage
   Burial
   Yearbooks

6. Fraternal Records
7. Alliances
8. Life Insurance Companies

The eight least reliable sources:

1. Family tradition
2. Printed family histories
3. Lineage books
4. Printed vital records
5. Tombstone inscriptions
6. Death certificates
7. Federal census
8. Salt Lake archives

Interesting Fact:
    The number of people having common grandparents is 25.
    The number of people having common grandparents (gr-gr) is 625
    The number of people having gr-gr-gr-gr grandparents is 15,625
    By the time you go back ten generations, the number of people having the common ancestral couple rises to a phenomenal 9,725,625!

CHAPTER 2

NOTE KEEPING

Doing genealogical research is like building a house — you must start with a sound foundation then add a strong super structure to complete the project.

Note Keeping & Organization

More researchers have stalled, failed, got frustrated, and lost time and money because of improper notekeeping than any other single cause. Without a sound foundation of notekeeping, everything else becomes more difficult and the accuracy of the information is brought into question.

The following record keeping system has been found to be the easiest and most accurate way of doing research: (Some people prefer to keep records on a vertical sheet and some prefer the horizontal sheet. Both are included).

1. Family File (see page 24)

(You can use a manila folder or envelope or you can order a special genealogy family folder from Genealogy Forms). One family folder should be kept on each family (father, mother, children) with the family name on the outside. Keep all records and documents pertaining to that family in their family file folder. You might want to obtain two copies of all documents — one for the file when the person is a child and one when the same person is a parent.

You can file these in one of two ways: Either in alphabetical order or by pedigree chart using the chart number and the position number.

2. Family Group Sheet (see pages 25 and 27)

This is the key notekeeping instrument, you should keep all of your research on these sheets. They are designed to organize your research and to help you focus on the information you need to obtain. As indicated previously, it is important that one family group sheet be kept on each document. Only the information from that document should be put on that sheet. You should record all of the information from each document, even if it is a duplication of previous sources.

Any interesting facts, anecdotes, historical or biographical information should be recorded on the back of the family group sheet. Blank family group sheets become your worksheets and blank sheets should be taken with you on every research outing. These sheets, along with the original documents, copies or photographs of them become the heart of the family file.

Note: In working with your family group sheets in the Source section, there is some important information needed:

a) Researcher — who did the research. Put your name and addresses in this space;

b) Date — The date you looked at the document or did the interview; or received the letter.

c) Condition of Document — Describe the document, what it is, i.e. birth certificate, death record, census, tombstone, etc. or person you interviewed, and its condition;

d) Location — describe the location of the document in detail — 5th floor of county courthouse, second floor of Genealogical Library, family Bible at grandmother's house;

e) Address of document or person contacted;

f) Call or film number;

g) Pedigree chart number.

3. Pedigree Chart (see pages 29 and 30)

This is your road map or index to your family file and should exist in the front of all your files, or you may want to keep your pedigree charts in a separate binder. I have found this the best way to organize files. Example: The father of the family you are working on may be on chart 3, position 10. It can be abbreviated 3-10 so it can be easily found.

4. The Research Organization (see pages 31 and 33)

Often people go to repositories without any idea of what they expect to accomplish. Many people become extremely frustrated because they seem to experience little success. Before you leave home you need to know who you are looking for and what records you are going to look at and where they are to be found. The research organizer helps you plan your research trip. Never put more than one problem on a page.

(1) Objective Line. What you want to accomplish (need to be very specific, i.e. birth certificate, death record, marriage certificate, census, etc.;

(2) Name of ancestor. Who you are looking for.

(3) Document. In this column you should write down every source you think you could possibly find to answer your question and then keep track of every attempt you make to solve the problem if it is successful or not. The deadends are often as important to your ultimate success as when you find an interesting ancester. Write a separate entry for each document you search: the Family Bible, Microfilm, County History Book, etc.

(4) Date of Document. The date or time period you are looking for i.e. 1880 census etc.

(5) Location (file number, film number). Where the document is located; name and address of person to be contacted, Masonic Grand Lodge, Jefferson City, Missouri, etc.

(6) Search Method. What are you going to do to locate the information, i.e. personal visit, letter, telephone call, etc.;

(7) Date completed.

Build the Super Structure

Now that you are familiar with notekeeping, you need to build a sound super structure.

1. Preliminary Survey

The first thing you need to know is what has already been done on you lines by any previous researcher.

(a) Home Sources. Search the records in your own possession and those of other relatives, especially the extended family (distant relatives);

(b) Mormon Library in Salt Lake City or one of its many branch libraries, 50 East North Temple, Salt Lake City, UT 84150. There may be a branch near you. Request a copy of their TOIR (Temple Ordinance Index Request form).

(c) Computerized Genealogy Library. (The world's largest collection of linked pedigrees), P.O. Box 27193, Salt Lake City, UT 84127;

(d) National Union Catalog of Manuscript Collection. This multi-volume reference work is available in most large libraries;

(e) Photo Duplication Service. The Library of Congress will send you a copy of all the cards (DCC) for books published on any given surname.

(f) First Decennial Digest (Vol. 21 through 25). This is an alphabetical listing by plaintiff surname of all the reported appellate court cases in the United States from 1658 to 1911. This is usually located in most county courthouses and law libraries.

(g) Contact or join the local genealogical society in your area. (Your public library can tell you how to contact them);

(h) Hire a professional genealogist (care must be taken to ensure quality research). Contact the Association of Professional Genealogists, P.O. Box 11601, Salt Lake City, UT 84174.

2. Pre-Search Analysis

After you find out what has already been done on your line, you need to find out what records exist that will be of value to you in your search and what must be done to gain access to those records.

The purpose of this entire book is to help you solve this part of your family search. Good luck in your efforts to find your ancestors.

3. Actual Research

Using the research organizer (calender), plan your search so that you will conserve time, energy and money.

4. Post-Search Analysis

When the search is completed, you need to evaluate the different sources as to their accuracy. (Use the list in Chapter One). Create a final family group sheet that reflects this evaluation. However, always keep your eyes open for new information.

5. Re-Survey

Now you are ready to start a new line.

Are you building a chicken coop or a cathedral?

RELATIONSHIPS

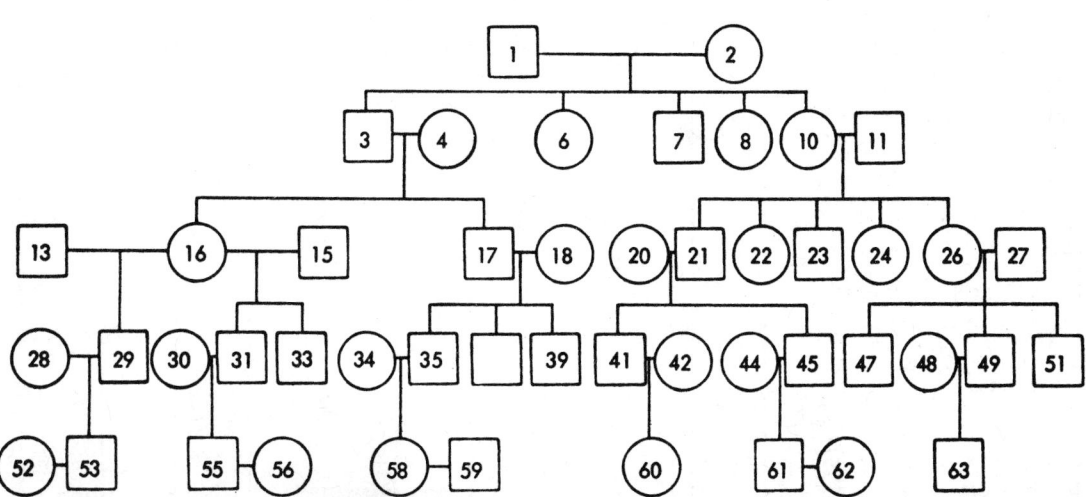

The purpose of this chart is to illustrate relationships as they are pointed out and to furnish a basis for exercises in finding and expressing relationships. All males are indicated by odd numbers and by squares; all females, by even numbers and by circles. A horizontal line connecting male and female indicates marriage. The children of a couple are joined to them by a perpendicular line from the line connecting the couple. Five generations are shown.

All other persons represented are descendants or descendants-in-law of the couple No. 1 and No. 2. One daughter-in-law is shown, No. 4, and one son-in-law, No. 11. Grandsons-in-law are Nos. 13, 15, and 27; granddaughters-in-law are Nos. 18 and 20. No. 10 is a sister of 3, and a sister-in-law of 4; 3 is a brother of 10 and a brother-in-law of 11. Nos. 4 and 11 may be regarded as "double-in-laws," as they are related through two marriages. The two husbands of No. 16 provide for "half relationships," No. 29 being a half brother of No. 31; and No. 53 and No. 55, half cousins. Nos. 17 and 21 are first cousins. Nos. 35 and 41 are second cousins. Nos. 26 and 58 are first cousins, twice removed. No. 53 is a lineal relative of Nos. 1 and 2. No. 53 is a collateral relative to No. 63.

Rules concerning cousins:

1. "Descendants of cousins in any degree remain that same degree of relationship to you. However, in addition they are designated as removed according to the number of generations each is removed from that cousin."

2. "Cousins in any degree to any of your progenitors are that same degree of cousin relationship to you. But, in addition, you are designated as removed according to the number of generations you are removed from that progenitor.

FAMILY NAME
(Father's Name)

PEDIGREE
CHART #

INDEX OF CONTENTS:

FAMILY GROUP SHEET

HUSBAND Occupation

Born	Place	
Chr.	Place	
Marr.	Place	
Died	Place	
Bur.	Place	
Father	Mother	
Other Wives		

WIFE

Born	Place	
Chr.	Place	
Died	Place	
Bur.	Place	
Father	Mother	
Other Husbands		

Children	Sex	DATE BORN / PLACE BORN	DATE DIED / PLACE DIED	DATE MARRIED & PLACE TO WHOM
1				
2				
3				
4				
5				
6				
7				
8				
9				
10				
11				
12				
13				
14				
15				

SOURCES		Other Marriages
Researcher	Date	
Document		
Location of Document		
Address		
Call or Film #		
Pedigree Chart # (PCN)		

Historical & Biographical Notes

FAMILY GROUP SHEET

HUS.

OCCUPATION(S)

		SOURCES
BORN	PLACE	
CHR.	PLACE	
MARR.	PLACE	
DIED	PLACE	Researcher
BUR.	PLACE	Date
FATHER		Document
MOTHER	OTHER WIVES	Location of Document

WIFE

		Address
BORN	PLACE	
CHR.	PLACE	
DIED	PLACE	
BUR.	PLACE	Call or Film #
FATHER	OTHER HUSBANDS	Pedigree Chart # (PCN)
MOTHER		

CHILDREN	DATE BORN	DATE MARRIED	PLACE	DATE DIED
SEX	PLACE BORN	TO		PLACE DIED
1				
2				
3				
4				
5				
6				
7				
8				
9				
10				

Historical & Biographical Notes

PEDIGREE CHART

CHART NO. _____

NO. 1 ON THIS CHART IS

THE SAME PERSON AS NO. _____

ON CHART NO. _____

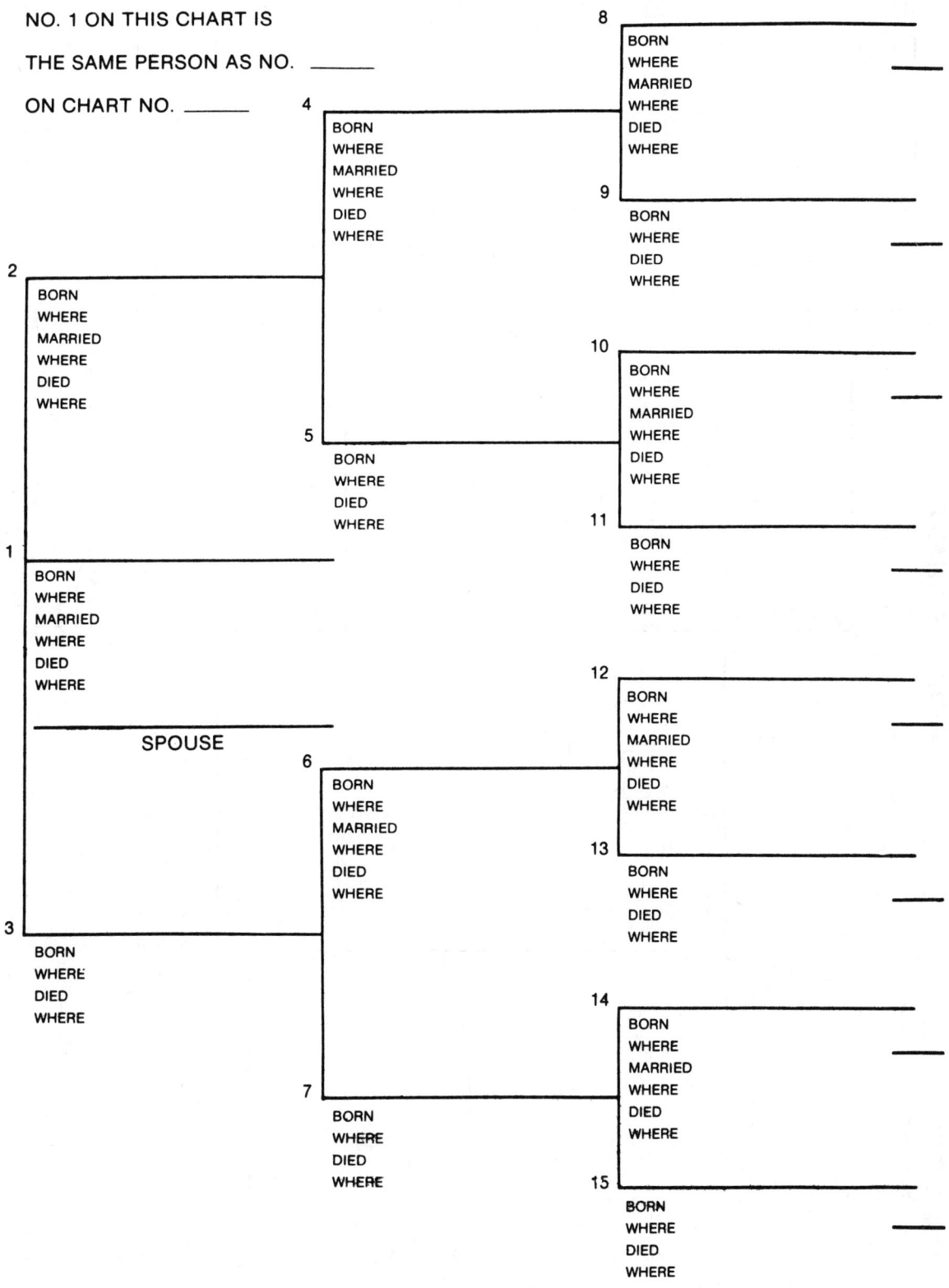

4
BORN
WHERE
MARRIED
WHERE
DIED
WHERE

8
BORN
WHERE
MARRIED
WHERE
DIED
WHERE

9
BORN
WHERE
DIED
WHERE

2
BORN
WHERE
MARRIED
WHERE
DIED
WHERE

5
BORN
WHERE
DIED
WHERE

10
BORN
WHERE
MARRIED
WHERE
DIED
WHERE

11
BORN
WHERE
DIED
WHERE

1
BORN
WHERE
MARRIED
WHERE
DIED
WHERE

SPOUSE

12
BORN
WHERE
MARRIED
WHERE
DIED
WHERE

6
BORN
WHERE
MARRIED
WHERE
DIED
WHERE

13
BORN
WHERE
DIED
WHERE

3
BORN
WHERE
DIED
WHERE

7
BORN
WHERE
DIED
WHERE

14
BORN
WHERE
MARRIED
WHERE
DIED
WHERE

15
BORN
WHERE
DIED
WHERE

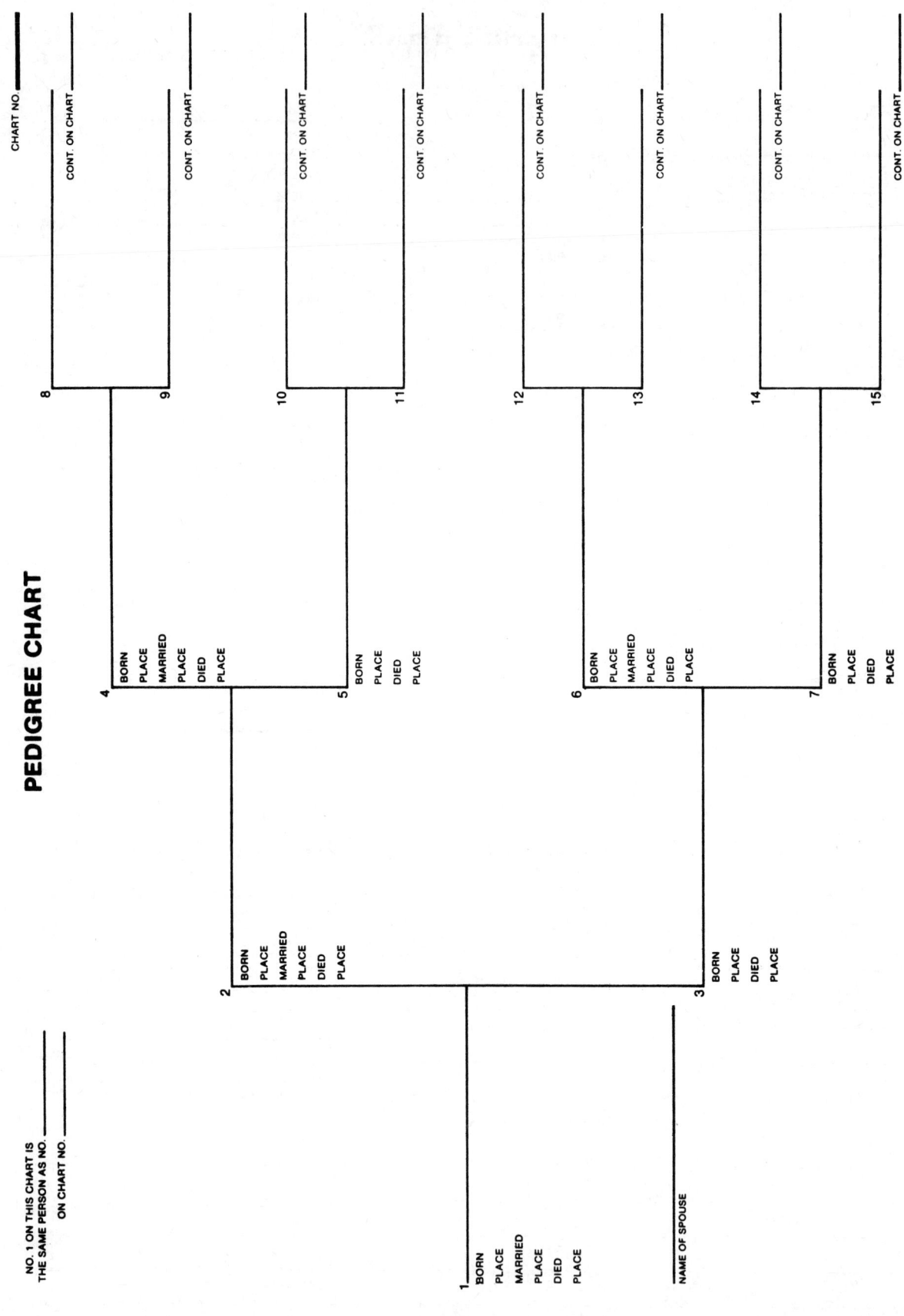

PEDIGREE CHART

CHART NO. ▬▬▬

NO. 1 ON THIS CHART IS
THE SAME PERSON AS NO. ▬▬▬
ON CHART NO. ▬▬▬

1
BORN
PLACE
MARRIED
PLACE
DIED
PLACE

NAME OF SPOUSE

2
BORN
PLACE
MARRIED
PLACE
DIED
PLACE

3
BORN
PLACE
DIED
PLACE

4
BORN
PLACE
MARRIED
PLACE
DIED
PLACE

5
BORN
PLACE
DIED
PLACE

6
BORN
PLACE
MARRIED
PLACE
DIED
PLACE

7
BORN
PLACE
DIED
PLACE

8
CONT. ON CHART ▬▬▬

9
CONT. ON CHART ▬▬▬

10
CONT. ON CHART ▬▬▬

11
CONT. ON CHART ▬▬▬

12
CONT. ON CHART ▬▬▬

13
CONT. ON CHART ▬▬▬

14
CONT. ON CHART ▬▬▬

15
CONT. ON CHART ▬▬▬

RESEARCH ORGANIZER
(Calendar)

Researched By   Name of Ancestor

Objective:

DOCUMENT DESIRED	DATE DOCUMENT WAS PRODUCED	PRESENT LOCATION OF DOCUMENT	SEARCH METHOD	RESULTS

HOME SOURCES:

Personal & Family Records:
____Personal Knowledge
____Personal Interview
____Family Bible
____Journals, Diaries
____Biography
____Letters
____Scrapbooks
____Baby Book
____Wedding Book
____Legal Papers
____Funeral Program
____Pedigrees
____Family Group Sheets
____Family Histories
____Heirlooms
____Farm Records
____Health Records
____Military Records
____Economic Records

Health Records:
____Xrays
____Insurance Papers
____Hospital Records
____Medical Records
____Immunizations

Certificates:
____Birth
____Marriage
____Death
____Divorce
____Adoption
____Graduation
____Christening
____Blessing
____Baptism
____Confirmation
____Ordination
____Transfer
____Ministerial
____Mission Release
____Membership
____Apprenticeship
____Achievement
____Award

School Records:
____Diplomas
____Report Cards
____Honor Roll
____Awards
____Transcripts
____Yearbooks
____Publications
____Elementary
____Secondary
____College
____Scholarship

Insurance:
____Life
____Marine
____Fire
____Automobile
____Accident
____Health

OTHER SOURCES:

**Genealogical Society
of Utah Indexes:**
____Computer File Index
____Family Group Archive
____Temple Index Bureau

Computer Lists:
____
____
____

U.S. Federal Censuses
____Indexes
____1790   ____1860
____1800   ____1870
____1810   ____1880
____1820   ____1900
____1830   ____1910
____1840   ____1920
____1850   ____1930
____Mortality Schedules
____Agriculture

State Censuses:
____
____

Local Histories:
____
____

City Directories:
____
____

Newspapers:
____Indexes
____Births
____Deaths
____Marriages
____Anniversaries
____Obituaries
____Advertisements
____Specific Dates
____Announcements
____Society Page
____Business Page
____Genealogical
____Historical
____Gossip
____Local News

Church Records:
____Birth
____Christening
____Baptism
____Confirmation
____Ordination
____Marriage
____Banns
____Divorce
____Annulment
____Death
____Burial
____Membership Lists
____Ministers Records
____Minutes
____Mission Reports

Marriage Records:
____Banns
____Applications
____Licenses
____Returns

Employment Records:
____Indentures
____Apprenticeships
____Applications
____Transfers
____Termination
____Disciplinary
____Licenses
____Pensions
____Service Awards
____Personnel
____Social Security
____Retirement
____Union

Military Records:
____Service
____Pension
____Disability
____Discharge
____National Guard
____Selective Service
____Bounty Award
____Service Medals
____Ribbons
____Sword
____Firearms
____Uniform
____Citations
____Separation Papers
____
____
____

Cemetery Records:
____Sextons
____Family Bibles
____Tombstones
____Memorials
____Gifts

Land Records:
____Deeds
____Mortgages
____Surveys
____Patents, Grants
____Maps
____Land Grants
____Leases
____Water Rights

Probate Records:
____Wills
____Administrations
____Inventories
____Bonds
____Settlements
____Packets
____Guardianships

Legal Papers:
____Bonds
____Loans
____Contracts
____Summons
____Subpoena
____Tax Notices
____Guardian Papers
____Abstracts of Title
____Auctions
____Divorce
____Bankruptcies
____Convictions

Court Records:
____Dockets
____Minutes
____Orders, Decrees
____Judgments
____Case Files

Court-Related Records:
____Sheriff
____Police
____Jail
____Jury
____Lawyers Briefs
____Justice of Peace

Licenses:
____Business
____Occupation
____Professional
____Hunting
____Firearms
____Drivers
____Motor Vehicle
____
____
____

Tax Records:
____Poll Tax
____Personal Property
____Real Estate
____School
____Poor Rate
____Income Tax

Immigrant Records:
____Passenger Lists
____Passports
____Visas
____Vaccination
____Protocols
____Letterbooks
____Crew Lists
____Register of Seamen
____Logbooks
____Naturalizations
____Citizenship Papers
____Customs Records
____Immigrant Aid Societies
____Deportment
____Alien Registration

Institutional Records:
____Charities
____Hospitals
____Convents
____Seminaries
____Libraries
____Historical Societies
____Genealogical Societies
____Mission Societies

Collections:
____Indexes
____Newspapers
____Personal Papers
____Correspondence
____Surname Files
____Biographies
____Inscriptions
____DAR

RESEARCH ORGANIZER

(Calendar)

Researched By _____   Name of Ancestor _____

Objective _____

DOCUMENT DESIRED (See Reverse Side)	DATE DOCUMENT WAS PRODUCED	PRESENT LOCATION OF DOCUMENT	SEARCH METHOD	RESULTS

HOME SOURCES:

Personal & Family Records:
___Personal Knowledge
___Personal Interview
___Family Bible
___Publications
___Journals, Diaries
___Biography
___Letters
___Scrapbooks
___Baby Book
___Wedding Book
___Legal Papers
___Funeral Program
___Pedigrees
___Family Group Sheets
___Family Histories
___Heirlooms
___Farm Records
___Health Records
___Military Records
___Economic Records

Health Records:
___Xrays
___Insurance Papers
___Hospital Records
___Medical Records
___Immunizations

Certificates:
___Birth
___Marriage
___Death
___Divorce
___Adoption
___Graduation
___Christening
___Blessing
___Baptism
___Confirmation
___Ordination
___Transfer
___Ministerial
___Mission Release
___Membership
___Apprenticeship
___Achievement
___Award

School Records:
___Diplomas
___Report Cards
___Honor Roll
___Awards
___Transcripts
___Yearbooks
___Publications
___Elementary
___Secondary
___College
___Scholarship

Insurance:
___Life
___Marine
___Fire
___Automobile
___Accident
___Health

OTHER SOURCES:

Genealogical Society of Utah Indexes:
___Computer File Index
___Family Group Archive
___Temple Index Bureau

Computer Lists:
___
___

Local Histories:
___
___
___

City Directories:
___
___

Newspapers:
___Indexes
___Births
___Deaths
___Marriages
___Anniversaries
___Obituaries
___Advertisements
___Specific Dates
___Announcements
___Society Page
___Business Page
___Genealogical
___Historical
___Gossip
___Local News

Church Records:
___Birth
___Christening
___Baptism
___Confirmation
___Ordination
___Marriage
___Banns
___Divorce
___Annulment
___Death
___Burial
___Membership Lists
___Ministers Records
___Minutes
___Mission Reports

Marriage Records:
___Banns
___Applications
___Licenses
___Returns

Licenses:
___Business
___Occupation
___Professional
___Hunting
___Firearms
___Drivers
___Motor Vehicle

Court Records:
___Dockets
___Minutes
___Orders, Decrees
___Judgments
___Case Files

Court-Related Records:
___Sheriff
___Police
___Jail
___Jury
___Lawyers Briefs
___Justice of Peace

Land Records:
___Deeds
___Mortgages
___Surveys
___Patents, Grants
___Maps
___Land Grants
___Leases
___Water Rights

State Censuses:
___
___

U.S. Federal Censuses:
___Indexes
___1790 ___1860
___1800 ___1870
___1810 ___1880
___1820 ___1900
___1830 ___1910
___1840 ___1920
___1850 ___1930
___Mortality Schedules
___Agriculture

Probate Records:
___Wills
___Administrations
___Inventories
___Bonds
___Settlements
___Packets
___Guardianships

Legal Papers:
___Bonds
___Loans
___Contracts
___Summons
___Subpoena
___Tax Notices
___Guardian Papers
___Abstracts of Title
___Auctions
___Divorce
___Bankruptcies
___Convictions

Employment Records:
___Indentures
___Apprenticeships
___Applications
___Transfers
___Termination
___Disciplinary
___Licenses
___Pensions
___Service Awards
___Personnel
___Social Security
___Retirement
___Union

Institutional Records:
___Charities
___Hospitals
___Convents
___Libraries
___Seminaries
___Historical Societies
___Genealogical Societies
___Mission Societies

Tax Records:
___Poll Tax
___Personal Property
___Real Estate
___School
___Poor Rate
___Income Tax

Immigrant Records:
___Passenger Lists
___Passports
___Visas
___Vaccination
___Protocols
___Letterbooks
___Crew Lists
___Register of Seamen
___Logbooks
___Naturalizations
___Citizenship Papers
___Customs Records
___Immigrant Aid Societies
___Deportment
___Alien Registration

Military Records:
___Service
___Pension
___Disability
___Discharge
___National Guard
___Selective Service
___Bounty Award
___Service Medals
___Ribbons
___Sword
___Firearms
___Uniform
___Citations
___Separation Papers

Collections:
___Indexes
___Newspapers
___Personal Papers
___Correspondence
___Surname Files
___Biographies
___Inscriptions
___DAR

Cemetery Records:
___Sextons
___Family Bibles
___Tombstones
___Memorials
___Gifts

CHAPTER 3

CORRESPONDENCE

When writing letters for genealogical information the most important thing to remember is to keep your correspondence short and simple. Most of these people are very busy and don't have time to read or write long letters. Usually one paragraph is enough. If you send more than one piece of paper you probably won't receive an answer.

Never ask for a specific name, most agencies will not do your research for you. You will do better to ask for a whole family. (Remember General vs. Particular Research).

Genealogical Correspondence

CAVEAT! (Warning!) Try not to write to the various county officials. This is very important. I suggest that you hire an agent as explained elsewhere in this book. (See Miscellaneous Information)

Sometimes federal and state agencies and officials either refuse to respond to your request or they put you off for a long time. Happily, this is not the general situation. However, if this happens to you, you may wish to contact the particular agency or office concerned and state that you are requesting this information under The Freedom of Information Act. This will usually produce the desired response. (See Freedom of Information Act in Miscellaneous.)

When writing to non-government agencies it is suggested that you always include a self-addressed, stamped envelope or a one dollar bill in with you letter. And this is done as a courtesy to your recipients as well as a measure to increase your letter response success. Remember many people will not take the time and effort to answer your letters if they have to pay for the postage.

If you find that your letters are not being answered, then instead of writing a second follow-up letter, it is suggested that you merely send a small edible gift as a subtle reminder. This could be in the form of a jar of jam; cheese; candy; etc. This is especially effective in communist countries.

Correspondence	
Subject	**Letter Substance**
Genealogical Society	Would you please check your indexes to see if you have any information of the _____ family who lived in _____ county?
Public Libraries	Would you please check your indexes to see if you have any information on the _____ family who lived in _____ County?

Subject	Letter Substance
Colleges or Universities	Would you please check your indexes to see if you have any information on the _____ family who lived in _____ county?
Church Officials	Would you please check your indexes to see if you have any information on the _____ family who lived in _____ county?
Alliances	Would you please check your indexes to see if you have any information on _____, who came to this country about ____ and who later resided in _____?
Fraternal Organizations	Would you please check your indexes to see if you have any information on _____ who was from _____ county?
Historical Society	Would you please check your indexes to see if you have any information on the _____ family who lived in _____ county?
Adjt. General	Would you please check your indexes to see if you have any information on _____ who was from _____ county?
County Clerk	Would you please check your indexes to see if you have any information on the _____ surname(s)?
Probate Clerk	Do you have any testate or intestate proceedings for the _____ surname(s)?
Clerk of the Court	Would you please check your indexes to see if you have information on the _____ surname(s)?
Phone Company	May I order a copy of the most recent edition of your local phone directory?
Museum	Would you please check your indexes to see if you have any information on the _____ family who lived in _____ county?
State Library	Would you please check your indexes to see if you have any information on the _____ family who lived in _____ county?
Newspapers	Would you please place the folowing ad in the personal column of your newspaper and bill me for same?
Vital Records	Would you please check your indexes to see if you have any information on _____, who was born (or died) on _____, at _____?
Life Insurance Companys	Would you please check your records to see if you have any information on _____, who died _____, at _____, and is believed to have been insured by your fine company?
Department of Motor Vehicles	Would you please check your records to see if you have any information on _____, and who lived in _____ county?
Secretary of State	Would you please check your indexes to see if you have any information on _____ who was from _____?
Sexton	Would you please check your indexes to see if you have any information on _____, who died _____ and is believed to be

buried in your cemetery?

Railroad Companies — Would you please check your records to see if you have any information on _____, who died _____, at _____, and is believed to have been employed by your fine company?

Postal Maps — Would you please send me the Geographic Site Location Report for the _____ post office which was located in _____ county?

Undertaker — Would you please check your indexes to see if you have any information on _____, who died _____, at _____, and is believed to have been serviced by your fine company?

Relatives — Do you have any information or old records on the following family members?

Magazine Quiries — Would you please place the following quiry in your fine magazine and bill me for same?

Old Maps — Would you please check your indexes to see if you have any kind of a map for _____ county, for the approximate time period of _____?

Title & Abstract Company — Would you please send me a cost estimate for running a chain of title for the following property located in your county?

Genealogists — Would you please tell me if you are a wholistic researcher and a registered genealogist?

Addresses and Salutations

Title	Envelope and Inside Address	Salutation(s)	Title	Envelope and Inside Address	Salutation(s)
Abbot	The Right Reverend	Right Reverend Abbot:		name, organization, fort or base. city	(All officers below rank of Captain are addressed as Dear Mr. Doe.
Adjt. Gen.	Adjt. General	Dear General			
Ambassador (American)	His Excellency The American Ambassador to Sweden	Sir: Your Excellency: Dear Mr. Ambassador	Bishop (Anglican)	The Right Reverend the Lord Bishop of Chester or, The Lord Bishop of Chester (Specific postal Address)	My Lord: My Lord Bishop
	The American Embassy Stockholm, Sweden		Bishop (Methodist)	Reverend Bishop John Doe (Specific postal address)	Dear Sir: My Dear Bishop:
Ambassador (Foreign, in U.S.A.)	His Excellency The French Ambassador The French Embassy Washington, D.C.	Sir: Excellency: Your Excellency:	Bishop (Port. Episcopal)	To the Right Reverend John Doe Bishop of Richmond (Specific postal address)	My Dear Bishop: Right Reverend and Dear Sir
Archbishop (Anglican)	The Most Reverend His Grace The Lord Archbishop of York (Specific postal Address)	Your Grace: My Lord Bishop:	Bishop (Roman Catholic)	The Lord Bishop of Wichita or The Most Reverend John Doe Bishop of Wichita (Specific postal address)	My Lord: My Lord Bishop Your Excellency
Archbishop (Roman Catholic)	The Most Reverend John Doe Archbishop of New York Specific postal address)	Your Excellency:			
Army and Navy Officers	Address according to rank (omitting qualifying adjectives, such as "Lt." in "Lt. Col.")	Sir: Dear Colonel: Dear Mr. Doe:	Clergyman	The Reverend John Doe (Complete postal address)	Dear Sir: Reverend Sir:

Title	Envelope and Inside Address	Salutation(s)	Title	Envelope and Inside Address	Salutation(s)
Clerk (Co.)	County Clerk	Dear Co. Clerk	Partnership	Doe & Doe	Gentlemen:
Clerk (Court)	Clerk of the Court	Dear Clerk		(Complete postal address)	(men)
Consul	The American Consul at Vienna	Sir:			Mesdames
	The American Embassy	Dear Sir:			or (women)
	Vienna, Austria or	My Dear Sir:			Ladies:
	The British Consul at San Fran.		President of	The President	Sir:
	The British Consulate		the U.S.A.	The White House	Mr. President:
	San Francisco, California			Washington, D.C.	Dear Mr.
Deacon	The Reverend Deacon Doe	Reverend Sir:			President
(Anglican &	(Complete postal address)		Pres. (Hist.	President	Dear President
Prot.)			S o c i e t y)		
Dean	The Very Reverend the	Sir:	Pres. (Gen.		
(Anglican)	Dean of Bocking	Very Reverend	Society)		
	(Complete postal address)	Sir:	Priest	The Reverend John Doe	Dear Father:
Editor	Editor		(Roman	St. Mary's Church	Reverend Father
Governor of	His Excellency	Sir:	Catholic)	(Complete postal address)	Dear Father Doe
a State	The Governor of Utah	Dear Sir:	Rabbi	Rabbi John Doe or	Dear Sir:
	Salt Lake City, Utah or	Dear Governor:		The Reverend John Doe	My dear Sir:
	The Honorable John Doe	Your Excellency:		(Specific postal address)	Reverend Sir:
Grand Sec.	Grand Secretary	Dear Grand Sec.			
(Masons)			Represen-	The Honorable John Doe	Sir:
Judge	The Honorable John Doe	Dear Sir:	tative (U.S.)	The House of Representatives	Dear Sir:
	(Name of Court) City, State	Dear Judge:		Washington, D. C.	Dear Congress-
Librarian	Librarian	Dear Librarian:			man Doe:
					Dear Sir:
Legislator of	The Honorable John Doe	Dear Sir:	Sec. of State	Secretary of State	Dear Sir:
A State	Utah Legislature	Dear Mr. Doe:			
	Salt Lake City, Utah		Senator	The Honorable John Doe	Sir:
			(U.S.)	The United States Senate	Dear Sir:
Mayor	His Honor the Mayor or	Dear Sir:		Washington, D. C.	My Dear
	The Honorable John Doe	Dear Mr. Mayor			Senator:
	Mayor's Office	Dear Mayor Doe	Undertaker	(Firm name)	Dear Sir:
	Salt Lake City, Utah		(Mortician)		

Section II
REPOSITORIES

CHAPTER 4

THE PUBLIC LIBRARY

Most novice genealogists walk into the local library or archive with an arm load of pedigree charts and family group sheets or only a single surname and say to the receptionist, "I'm ready to go to work, where do I start?" or "Give me all you have on my ancestors." The Librarian is overwhelmed as to where to begin, so you need to have specific questions in mind about what you want to know. Remember in Chapter 2 we indicated that you begin by finding out what others have done on your line. This information will usually be found in the genealogy section of the repository. But even if you use the world's largest genealogy collection in Salt Lake City you would still only find about 10% if the material you need, to write an accurate and interesting genealogy.

Most of the important research, therefore, is original research that you do yourself. It also follows that the genealogy section of the library is not the most important section for genealogy research, unless there happens to be a specific book on your particular line.

There are other institutions in the city and other parts of the library that contain records of inestimable value to the serious researcher:

Other Institutions

County Courthouse	Seminaries	Insurance Companies
Law Libraries	Military Installations	Railroad Headquarters
Historical Societies	Business Libraries	Telephone Companies
Masonic Grand Lodge	Patriotic Societies	Government Agencies
College or University Libraries	Professional Organizations	Private Collections
Federal Courthouse	Municipal Reference Libraries	Local Museums

Many of these sources are explained in other parts of this book.

Sections of the Library or Archive Resource Center

Usually larger libraries have available the following sections or departments that contain useful information for the genealogist.

1. **Reference Section.** (The most useful section). Look for books that will help with your research (see our reference section for specific titles). They may be found in different sections in larger libraries. Probably the best way to examine the reference section is to browse.

2. **Periodical Section.** What you are looking for are Federal, Regional, State and

Local Historical Society publications and quarterlies. Some specific places to start are.

   a. Genealogy Periodical Annual Index
   b. Ulriches Periodical Index
   c. Directory of Genealogical Periodicals
   d. Genealogy and Local History books in print

To show you the value of this tool, the Genealogy Library in Salt Lake City subscribes to more than 2,000 related periodicals.

3. **Map Section (Cartographic).**

4. **Government Documents Section.** The United States has designated many libraries across the nation as Federal Government Documents Depositories. Most states have a similar program. These centers can be especially rich in resources.

   a. See special index under Military Section of this book.
   b. Search Schmeckebier, Lawrence, and Eastin, Roy B. *Government Publications and Their Use.* Washington, D.C., Brookings Institution, 1949.

5. **Manuscripts Section.** Manuscripts are defined as unpublished works such as letters, diaries, Bibles, photos etc. Libraries often act as repositories for such documents.

   a. The best general source is National Union catalog of Manuscript Collections (NUCMC)
   b. Directory of Archives and Manuscript Repositories.

6. **Business and Science Section.** You can find information on associations, Incorporations, Insurance companies etc.

   a. Encyclopedia of Associations
   b. Insurance Almanac
   c. Moody's Investors Service Inc.

7. **Newspaper Section.** This section often has a collection of current and old newspapers available. The three books of most value are:

   a. from 1936 — N. W. Ayers and Sons, Director of Newspapers and Periodicals, list all of the newspapers in the U.S. and Canada.
   b. from 1821 to 1936 use Gregory, Winifred. *American Newspapers, 1821-1936: A Union List of Files Available in the United States and Canada.* New York: H. W. Wilson Company, 1937.
   c. from 1690-1820 — Brigham, Clarence Saunders. *History and Bibliography of American Newspapers, 1690-1820.* Hamden, Connecticut: Archon, 1962 (Two volumes). 1947 reprint.

The last two do not include current newspapers. Some states publish their own guide which is in most state libraries. These books will tell you the name of the newspaper, the years it was issued, its present location and if it was microfilmed or not.

Some large newspapers are indexed so you can look up a specific surname, in others, you will want to look at the vital statistics sections, birth, wedding announcements, marriages, and obituaries.

How to Obtain Genealogical Books Through Interlibrary Loan

by Fred L. Heidenreich, M.L.S.
University of Arizona

"Reprinted with permission from the Arizona State Genealogical Society's *Copper State Bulletin*, Vol. XI, issue #1, Spring 1976."

This article will discuss possible ways of obtaining genealogical materials through interlibrary loan. Thousands of American libraries provide interlibrary loan services to their users. If patrons ask for a book not in a library collection, the libraries which participate in interlibrary loan (I.L.L.) may offer to borrow a copy for the patron, from another participating library which does own the book. A small percentage of libraries will, if requested, actually include genealogical materials in these interlibrary lending and borrowing arrangements. A proper understanding of interlibrary loan policies and procedures will enable the genealogist to gain access to a host of published genealogical materials which he might otherwise never be able to see.

First let me say that interlibrary loan may not be the best approach to every genealogical problem. Sometimes it is easier, quicker, cheaper, or at least wiser, to seek alternate means for obtaining the information or material desired. In fact, there are some rather formidable obstacles that genealogists must overcome when attempting to use interlibrary loan as a research tool.

Section V.2e of the National Interlibrary Loan Code; 1968, Annotated, specifies that librarians should not ordinarily ask to borrow genealogical, heraldic, or similar materials. (Sarah K. Thompson, *Interlibrary Loan Procedure Manual*, Chicago: American Library Association, 1970, p. 2) Probably a majority of American libraries are not willing to accept interlibrary loan requests for genealogical materials. There are many reasons for this. Most public libraries having special genealogical collections will not circulate these materials even to their own local patrons. Usually genealogy books must be used within the library and in some cases may not even leave the "genealogy or local history room" where they are kept. Traditionally, genealogical and heraldry materials have been considered to be rare, irreplaceable, or expensive. Librarians sometimes consider the genealogical collection to be especially vulnerable to the rip-off artist, who would think nothing of clipping out the article about his family or defacing a valuable healdry book for his *very own* "Jones coat-of-arms". Another reason for not lending genealogical materials is the fact that many of the books are clearly reference type sources having a wide appeal to local genealogists. For example, the absence from the library collection for three or four weeks of an important state-wide index to something like cemetery records (such as the one our Society is compiling), could impose a serious inconvenience on the numerous people who might need to consult the book. Nevertheless, a majority of the genealogy books are probably not in such demand that they could not be lent to someone doing serious research.

"Serious research" is the key. It is the stated purpose of interlibrary loan services to "make available for *research*, materials not owned by a given library, in the belief that the furtherance of knowledge is in the general interest." (Ibid.) I have always believed that most academic and public libraries discriminate against genealogists. Librarians often do not regard genealogy as serious research.[1] Their opinions are sometimes reinforced by the neophytes who make naive requests or even unreasonable demands. What is the librarian to think of the person like this? After glancing momentarily at the index to a recently obtained interlibrary loan volume, Mr. Jones shoves the book back at the librarian with the comment, "I guess these aren't my Joneses after all." Is this serious research? Or what about the eager lady who appears at the reference desk with not one, but a dozen or more hastily copied interlibrary loan requests at a time? She obviously has no appreciation for the amount of money and staff time involved in processing such requests. Librarians are not favorably impressed by this kind of research. Perhaps another reason we as genealogists are largely ignored or not taken seriously is because librarians rarely have any training or background in genealogical methods and sources themselves. Genealogy is one topic which is seldom touched upon in professional schools of library science.

If I have painted a discouraging picture of the interlibrary loan scene for genealogists, let me add a few bright touches. Not all libraries adhere to the National Interlibrary Loan Code's prohibition against the lending of genealogical materials. Many regional, state, and local libraries have adopted more liberalized provisions which modify restrictions of the national code. In fact a great number of academic and public libraries *do* loan genealogical materials. There are also a few select genealogical libraries which will loan or "rent" their books under certain conditions (usually for a fee). This paper however is limited to a discussion of obtaining genealogical books from major public and academic libraries with multi-disciplinary collections, through regular established policies. I have a four point formula for genealogical interlibrary loans which I feel will bring success to the genealogist and which, if followed carefully, will impress the librarian with the seriousness of our research intents. These are the four steps: (1) Assess and be prepared to justify your need for the book. (2) Verify the citation completely and accurately in an acceptable bibliographic source. (3) Determine which libraries own the book. (4) of those libraries owning a copy of the book, find out in advance which one will lend it. Few librarians will ask their patrons to go to such extents or to pay attention to such details. This is normally the work which they must do. But if these procedures are followed, success is virtually assured. I will attempt to explain the four steps in greater detail.

Do I Really Need to See the Book?

Do not use interlibrary loan for books containing quick factual type information that could be obtained easily through correspondence. Don't use interlibrary loan when requests for photocopies of a few pages would suffice.

How else might the book be more easily obtained? If a genealogist lives near one of the branch libraries of the L.D.S. Genealogical Society, he should use its facilities for obtaining *microfilmed* books rather than going to the public library for an interlibrary loan. The L.D.S. Genealogical Society will not lend the actual books however; nor will they furnish microfilm or paper photocopies of recently copyrighted materials. Recently copyrighted materials which are still in print might well be purchased rather than borrowed, especially if they are inexpensive and likely to be of lasting value to one's research. Unfortunately few of us can afford to purchase even a fraction of the published materials relating to our personal research.

Do not request reference type books, as they will not be lent, even by those libraries who normally do loan other genealogical materials. Reference materials might be defined as those books having a wide appeal to large numbers of people—things such as directories, bibliographies and indexes, encyclopedic works, guides and handbooks, catalogs, dictionaries and compendiums, etc. Do not request multivolume sets unless it is known which volume has the desired information. Lastly do not request a genealogical book on the basis of casual interest. Be able to justify your serious research purpose in requesting *that* particular book.

What is the Correct Citation and Where is it Listed in Print?

Verifying the correct citation means locating it in an authoritative bibliography, preferably in the published catalog of a major library, or in a standard indexing source. All, or as much as possible, of the following information should be supplied. For books give the author (full name), title, edition, place, published, date, and series (when applicable). For periodicals or serials give the title of the serial, volume, and date, author and title of the article, and inclusive pagination. Also indicate fully the source of verification or where the reference is cited, giving title, volume, date and page number. In other words, tell *where* the reference is listed in print and show exactly *how* it is listed in print.

What are some of the sources which can be used to verify references? A first choice would be one of the author catalogs of the *Library of Congress-National Union Catalog* series. It should be understood that this catalog is not limited just to books held or cataloged by the Library of Congress, but includes items cataloged by hundreds of other libraries as well. A union catalog is one which lists the holdings of not one, but of many libraries. Because of its immensity, this source may not be available in every library. University libraries would be most likely to have a complete set of the *National Union Catalogs*. Many other sources would be equally acceptable as sources of verification. I will list a few well-known sources as examples: *American Genealogical Index*, and its successor the *American Genealogical-Biographical Index* (available at the Arizona State Library); the *Genelogical Periodical Annual;* Donald Lines Jacobus' *Index to Genealogical Periodicals; The Genealogical Index* of the Newberry library in Chicago; *American and English Genealogies in the Library of Congress* or its successors; O. William Filby's *American and British Genealogy and Healdry; a Select List of Books,* published by the American Library Association; or even the microfilmed card catalog of the L.D.S. Genealogical Society. If none of these sources are available or if they do not contain the desired reference, then explain in as much detail as possible how you know that such a book exists. As a minimum, you should have in hand a published reference to the book you want to borrow.

The importance of verification cannot be minimized. Many libraries flatly refuse to process interlibrary loans for materials that cannot be verified in an acceptable source. If you do not provide the verification yourself, then the librarians must take their time to verify the reference, which they may or may not do, depending on their attitude toward genealogical requests.

Who Owns the Book?

The next step is more difficult. Before a book can be borrowed, it must be determined which libraries own copies of the book. Some librarians will attempt to do this for you, but your chances of successfully obtaining the items through interlibrary loan are greatly enhanced if you can do this yourself. Some libraries may not go to the trouble of determining the location of a book, but will blindly send the request to some larger library, or they may refer the request through a chain of libraries in a pre-determined pattern or network until it finally reaches a library that has the book you want and is willing to send it. This referral process can be very slow and time consuming, taking months to eventually get back to you. Thus you can see the advantage of pre-determining the location of a book before you even request it.

How does one go about doing this? If you can get access to the *National Union Catalog,* and the book you want is listed there, you can usually determine what libraries have the books. Locations have been listed in the *National Union Catalogs* since 1953. More recent editions of the *N.U.C.* list many locations. In fact the *National Union Catalog* (N.U.C.) is supplemented by a *Register of Additional Locations* which may list dozens of libraries holding the book that is wanted.

As an example, suppose I wanted to borrow the book: *Early Germans of New Jersey: Their History, Churches & Genealogies,* by Theodore F. Chambers, a 1969 reprint of the 1895 edition. First I would check the *National Union Catalog, 1968-1972 Cumulation.* There I would see a minature Library of Congress printed card for the Chambers book which would look something like this:

Chambers, Theodore Frelinghuysen, 1948-1916.
The early Germans of New Jersey; their history, churches, and genealogies. With a new forward by Kenn Stryker-Rodda. Baltimore, Genealogical Pub. Co., 1969.
xiii, 667p. illus., maps (part fold.), ports. 23 cm.
1. Germans in New Jersey. 2. New Jersey — Genealogy. I. Title.
F145.G3C4 1969   917.4'09'743   78-85697

The numbers at the bottom of each entry are, from left to right, the recommended Library of Congress classification number, the recommended Dewey decimal classification number, and the LC (Library of Congress) *card number.* The LC card number is always given in the lower right corner. Symbols for the libraries which own copies are listed in the lower left corner on the line just below the LC classification number. In this case no symbols of other libraries are listed. The next step is to check the *National Union Catalog — Register of Additional Locations, 1968-1972.* Under the LC card number for the Chambers book, 78-85697, I would find the following:

78-85697 (Chambers) IEG ICN NN NjR IaAS N InU IaU

By consulting a table of abbreviations entitled *Symbols of American Libraries,*[2] (Washington, D.C.: Library of Congress, 1969), I can translate the above to mean that all of the following libraries own the Chambers book.[3]

Garrett Theological Seminary, Evanston, Illinois
Newberry Library, Chicago
New York Public Library
Rutgers, New Brunwick, New Jersey
Iowa State University, Ames, Iowa
New York State Library, Albany
Indiana University, Bloomington
University of Iowa, Iowa City

Hundreds of other libraries undoubtedly also own copies of the Chambers book, but we know for sure that at least the Library of Congress plus the eight libraries listed here own the book we want to borrow.

At this point perhaps I should mention that many large libraries (including the Tucson Public Library) now have access to vast on-line computer databases of nation-wide cataloging information such as O.C.L.C. (abbreviation for Ohio College Library Center's on-line union catalog computer network) which also contain locations for the items listed.

If one is *unable* to find the location of a book that is wanted, perhaps the librarian could be of help. Nevertheless, I still firmly believe the genealogist will be better off if he can first pre-determine by himself the location of a volume before requesting it through interlibrary loan. If the *National Union Catalog* and its *Register of Additional Locations* are not available, then the genealogist would do well to correspond with some library known to lend genealogical materials. It would be a simple matter to write, asking a particular library if the book that is wanted is owned and if it is available through interlibrary loan. The names and addresses of American libraries can be found in the *American Library Directory,* available in most libraries. Reference books such as Lee Ash's *Subject Collections* (New York: R. R. Bowker, 1974) or the *Directory of Special Libraries and Information Centers* (M. L. Young, H. C. Young and A. T. Kruzas. Detroit: Gale, 1974) actually list and describe the collections, services, and lending policies of many libraries specializing in genealogy. Corresponding with one of these libraries about the book that is wanted is the most fool-proof way of determining its location. It is also the surest way of finding out if a book will be lent.

Who Will Lend the Book?

I have explained how to verify a reference to a book, and how to determine who owns a copy of a book. The most important question of all, "Who will lend the book?" now needs to be examined. In her recent publication *Interlibrary Loan Policies Directory* (Chicago: American Library Association, 1975), Sarah K. Thompson estimates that in 1972-73, approximately 194,000 interlibrary loan requests were not filled because the borrowing library, in ignorance, requested non-circulating materials contrary to the I.L.L. lending policies of the lending libraries. She goes on to state that these unfilled requests probably cost the borrowing and lending libraries over $400,000 in wasted manpower, besides disappointing readers who waited in vain for their materials. Much of this waste could be prevented if a library's lending policies were checked in advance before sending requests. *Subject Collections,* and the *Directory of Special Libraries and Information Centers* mentioned in the preceeding paragraph both discuss the lending policies of thousands of American libraries. The American Library Association's *Interlibrary Loan Policies Directory* also displays the lending policies of 276 major libraries in the U.S. In addition, it outlines interlibrary loan charges where photocopies are sent in lieu of the original volumes. If a periodical article is requested, it is most likely that a photocopy, rather than the original, will be sent. This directory specifically states whether or not genealogical materials will be lent, and if so, under what conditions.

Always keep in mind that the definition of "genealogical materials" is subject to local interpretation. What one library labels or classifies as "genealogy", another library may classify as "biography" or "history". For example the Chambers book discussed earlier, *Early Germans of New Jersey: Their History, Churches and Genealogies,* contains a wealth of genealogical information, yet neither the recommended Dewey decimal number nor the Library of Congress number classify the book as "Genealogy". It is therefore possible that one might even be able to get the Chambers book from a library which does *not* lend genealogical materials.

Continuing with the same example, I learn from the *Interlibrary Loan Policies Directory* that of the eight libraries owning a copy of the book, one library listed will lend the book. That one library is the University of Iowa Library in Iowa City.[3]

Armed with (1) my justifications for borrowing the book, (2) my verification from the *National Union Catalog* or some other source, (3) my locations identified by correspondence or in the *Register of Additional Locations,* and (4) my assurance that the University of Iowa Library will lend the book, I am now prepared to face the reference librarian with my request. It is a request so well prepared, so well thought out, and so indicative of my serious research intent, that my chances for success are greatly multiplied.

A list compiled from the *Interlibrary Loan Policies Directory,* of libraries known to lend genealogical materials is given below. Keep in mind that this list only reflects the policies of those 276 major libraries surveyed. Undoubtedly hundreds of other libraries in this country also lend genealogical materials. Also remember that, though exceptions may not be specified in the directory, even these libraries will probably *not* lend reference materials, very old or very rare items, manuscripts, or materials in special non-circulating collections within the library.

N.U.C. Library Symbol	Name of Library	Comments
Ak	Alaska Division of State Libraries	small collection
ArU	University of Arkansas	

Symbol	Name of Library	Comments
AzTeS	Arizona State University	
CLSU	University of Southern California	
CLU	University of California-Los Angeles	
C-S	California State Library	lent from Sutro Library (only within the State of Calif.)
CU-A	University of California, Davis	
CtU	University of Connecticut	
CtW	Wesleyan University	
CtY	Yale University	
FU	University of Florida Libraries	
G	Georgia Library Information Network	
GEU	Emory University	
GU	University of Georgia	
IEN	Northwestern University Library	
IaU	University of Iowa	
KMK	Kansas State University	
KyU	University of Kentucky Library	
MU	University of Massachusetts	
MiDW	Wayne State University	
MiEM	Michigan State University	
Mo	Missouri State Library	send requests to: Director, State Historical Society Columbia, MO 65201
MoU	University of Missouri Library	
Ms	Mississippi Library Commission	
Mt	Montana State Library	
NNC	Comumbia University Library	
NSySU	Syracuse University	
NcRS	North Carolina State University'	
NhD	Dartmouth'	
NhU	University of New Hampshire	
MjP	Princeton University Library	
OO	Oberlin College Library	
OU	Ohio State University	
Or	Oregon State Library	
PBL	Lehigh University	
PPAP	American Philosophical Society Library	
PPT	Temple University	
ScU	University of South Carolina	Send requests to the South Carolina Library only
TU	University of Tennessee	
TxHU	University of Houston Libraries	
TxU	University of Texas at Austin'	
Vt	Vermont Department of Libraries	census not lent
WyU	University of Wyoming	
WaPS	Washington State University Library	
WaU	University of Washington	

The following libraries lend only on a selective basis. See comments.

CU	University of California-Berkeley	-occasionally lent
MW	Worcester Public Library	-lent at discretion of

Symbol	Name of Library	Comments
		subject specialist, in-library use restriction recommended.
K	Kansas State University	-some lent
NIC	Cornell University Library	-depends on usage
OClW	Case Western Reserve Library	-some lent
OKentU	Kent State University	-lent subject to exceptions
PU	University of Pennsylvania	-lent selectively
WU	University of Wisconsin	-some lent
WaS	Seattle Public Library	-occasionally lent with permission

The following libraries lend only if duplicates are available in their collections:

Symbol	Name of Library
Ct	Connecticut State Library
I	Illinois State University
PP	Free Library of Philadelphia
T	Tennessee State Library
Tx	Texas State Library
ViU	University of Virginia

Special comments or special restrictions:

Symbol	Name of Library	Comments
AU	University of Alabama	2^c copies if available
ICRL	Center for Research Libraries	Lends on unrestricted basis to Center members—non-members will be served no more than 12 times per year.
Me	Maine State Library	Will lend books for in-library use only. No census on microfilm.
MnU	University of Minnesota	Lent for academic, not genealogical research.
OHi	Ohio Historical Society	Only the newspapers on microfilm are available on loan.
OAU	Ohio University Library	U.S. National Archives Census schedules lent, other materials generally lent, but may photocopy.
WvU	West Virginia University	Will lend monographs (exception: West Virginia materials not lent unless duplicates available)

Readers are invited to submit their experiences with interlibrary loan. Perhaps other libraries can be added to this list.

Notes

1. William A. Katz, professor Library Science at the State University of New York in Albany writes: "The importance of genealogy ... sometimes escapes the general librarian. He is more inclined to dismiss the whole business as somewhat snobbish, smacking of the D.A.R., European nobility, and little old ladies in search of elusive

family roots." *(Introduction to Reference Work. Volume II, Reference Services.* New York: McGraw Hill, 1969)

2. These standardized abbreviations for American libraries may also be found in the introduction to editions of the *National Union Catalog* in most union lists of serials.

3. If this approach does not work, I can then check the *National Union Catalog of Pre-1956 Imprints.* (In progress), for the original 1895 edition. Fourteen additional libraries owning copies of the book, two of which definitely lend genealogical materials, are listed here. The *National Union Catalog of Pre-1956 Imprints* will be one of the most monumental national bibliographies ever compiled. At this writing, May 1976, the Library of Congress has completed 444 volumes so far covering A through P. The rest of the alphabet has yet to be completed.

*The author would like to hear from other readers regarding their own experiences with Interlibrary Loans. Contact Mr. Fred Heidenreich, 1518 South Brown Place, Tucson, Arizona 85710.

The Dewey Decimal System

929	Genealogy Heraldry	974.8	Pennsylvania	977.3	Illinois
929.1	Genealogy	974.9	New Jersey	977.4	Michigan
929.2	Family histories			977.5	Wisconsin
929.3	Immigration	975	Southeastern States	977.6	Minnesota
929.4	Personal names	975.1	Delaware	977.7	Iowa
929.6	Heraldry	975.2	Maryland	977.8	Missouri
929.7	Peerage, Royalty	975.3	District of Columbia		
929.8	Heraldic design	975.4	West Virginia	978	Western States
		975.5	Virginia	978.1	Kansas
940	General Europe	975.6	North Carolina	978.2	Nebraska
941	Scotland	975.7	South Carolina	978.3	South Dakota
941.5	Ireland	975.8	Georgia	978.4	North Dakota
942	England	975.9	Florida	978.6	Montana
943	Germany			978.7	Wyoming
971	Canada	976	South Central States	978.8	Colorado
		976.1	Alabama	978.9	New Mexico
973	United States of America	976.2	Mississippi		
		976.3	Louisiana	979	Pacific States
974	Northeastern States	976.4	Texas	979.1	Arizona
974.1	Maine	976.6	Oklahoma	979.2	Utah
974.2	New Hampshire	976.7	Arkansas	979.3	Nevada
974.3	Vermont	976.8	Tennessee	979.4	California
974.4	Massachusetts	976.9	Kentucky	979.5	Oregon
974.5	Rhode Island			979.6	Idaho
974.6	Connecticut	977	North Central States	979.7	Washington
974.7	New York	977.1	Ohio	979.8	Alaska
		977.2	Indiana		

CHAPTER 5

SALT LAKE CITY: GENEALOGICAL CENTER OF THE WORLD

The Genealogical Department of The Church of Jesus Christ of Latter-day Saints (Mormon) has the largest library of its kind in the world. This is due primarily to its world-wide microfilming program. (There are many libraries which have a larger collection of books, newspapers, & periodicals.) Another unique feature of this library is its massive computer program. Briefly, they are attempting to index most of the records which they have microfilmed. However, they are not filming all of the records in each of the countries nor are they filming all of the records in any given area. Hence, only a part of the records you may need to be successful in your research are available at this fine facility. The records which they have not filmed will still have to be searched. It is impossible to do it all, in Salt Lake City!

Hopefully, before you visit this library, you will have already done your homework and are ready to commence actual research. Experience tells us that most researchers show up without this important preparation. This initial preparation is necessary whether you are visiting this library, the national archives, or a local county courthouse. Failure to do so may result in much frustration.

What should you be doing first? You need to conduct a Preliminary Survey. Or, in other words, discover what has already been done on your ancestral lines. Here are the basic steps for an American line. (There are comparable European steps.)

The International Genealogical Index
(I. G. I.)

INTRODUCTION

The International Genealogical Index (IGI), formerly known as the Computer File Index or CFI, lists names found in the computer of the Genealogical Society of Utah. It does not include all information known about an individual, but it uniquely identifies each person and gives a batch number that can be traced to the original input source.

The IGI can be used for at least four purposes:

1. To find genealogical information
2. To avoid duplication in reasearch.
3. To determine if someone else is researching a given line. This is done by noting the batch number, in the last two columns. (The name may have been simply extracted as part of an indexing project.)
4. For LDS Church members, to determine the dates that temple ordinances for

those persons may have been performed during their lifetime or by proxy after their death. They may have been performed at any time from the 1840's to the date printed on top of the microfiche. (The IGI is limited to names of deceased persons. The records of living LDS Church members are kept by the Church Membership Department. For information on living LDS Church members, you must check with them personally. If they do not have the information, they will need to check with their present ward clerk.

USING THE IGI

You can search the IGI personally at the Genealogical Society Library in Salt Lake City, Utah, and at most LDS branch genealogical libraries; or you can send a completed Temple Ordinance Indexes Request form (stock no. PFGS0073) and $1.00 for each name to the Genealogical Society. Request forms are available from the LDS Church Distribution Center, 1999 West 1700 South, Salt Lake City, Utah 84104 (or the distribution center nearest you) and from most branch libraries. The request *must* include a name, date, and place (see below).

To use the IGI, you need the following information about a person: (1) *name;* (2) a *date* of an event in the person's life, such as a birth, christening, or marriage (the date may be approximate); and (3) the *place* of the event (at least a state in the United States, a county in England and the Scandinavian countries, and a province in Canada; for Germany you must know at least the name of the kingdom or duchy as it existed in 1918 such as Baden, Bavaria, or Prussia).

You may have to look under every jurisdiction to which a place belonged at any time. For example, West Virginia was a part of Virginia until 1863. Earlier entries for that area should be found under "Virginia." However, if an entry was submitted that said that the person was born in 1790 in West Virginia, the person's name will appear in the IGI under "West Virginia." The changing boundaries of the German countries make incorrect jurisdictions an especially troublesome problem in the IGI.

When using the IGI, follow these steps:

1. Obtain the correct microfiche.

    Names are filed under the *place* of the identifying event. The microfiche are arranged by geographical regions (such as North America, England, Southern Europe). Within each region, names are arranged alphabetically by surname. (Those for Norway and Iceland are arranged by given names. For Wales and Monmouthshire, England, there are two sets of Microfiche — one arranged by given name and one by surname.)

    The region, locality, and first name on the microfiche are printed at the top of each microfiche (see example). Thus, if you were looking for a Mary Ash in Lincolnshire, England, you would look on microfiche C 0002

C0001	ENGLAND LINCOLN	LINCOLN	
			AS OF DEC 1980
C0002	ENGLAND ARNOLD SARAH	LINCOLN	AS OF DEC 1980
C0003	ENGLAND BANNISTER MARY	LINCOLN	AS OF DEC 1980

2. Place the microfiche in the reading machine.

3. Locate the surname. Surnames are arranged according to standard spellings, so they may not appear to be in strict alphabetical order. Entries with the same surname are arranged alphabetically by given name.

4. Search for the given name desired. Look under all spelling variations. Entries with the same name are arranged chronologically by event date.

Forms for extracting information, in the IGI format, are available from the Genealogical Society (stock no. PFGS0368). Photocopies may be made of individual pages in the IGI.

FINDING THE ORIGINAL INPUT SOURCE

The last two columns of the IGI give a reference number that you can use to find the original source of input. The reference number is made up of the batch number and the serial/sheet number.

The major sources of information indexed in the IGI are:

1. Extraction programs. Names were extracted from original or printed sources such as vital records of births and marriages. Entries from extraction programs have batch numbers that begin with C, E, P, J, K, M (except M17 and M18), 725, 744, 745, and 754. To trace these batch numbers, use *Parish and Vital Records Listings in Batch Sequence,* available on microfiche wherever copies of the IGI are found.

2. Forms submitted by LDS Church members. Entries submitted by Church members have all-digit batch numbers with the third digit smaller than 4, such as 7108514-67. The batch number can be traced to a microfilmed copy of the form, which will give the name and address of the person who submitted it and may give additional information about the entry, such as the original source of the information. Use the *IGI Batch Number Index — Numberical* to determine the correct film number, and use the sheet number to find the correct form on the film. The batch number index is available on microfiche wherever copies of the IGI are found.

3. Marriage sealing records taken from LDS temple records. Batch numbers for these entries begin with *A, M17,* or *M18.* An *A* batch number with sealing date between 1942 and 1970 may be traced to an Archive Records in the Family Group Records Archive at the Genealogical Society Library. You may use the Temple Ordinance Indexes Request form to request searches of the archive. An *A* batch number with a sealing date earlier than 1942 can only be traced through the original temple record by direct descendants of the person listed. The descendant must personally do this research or have it done by an agent, such as a professional genealogist with access to the Genealogical Society Library in Salt Lake City.

Other batch numbers can be traced to other input sources. For more information, see *How to Trace CFI Batch Numbers.* Genealogical Research Papers, series F, no. 5, on microfiche at LDS branch genealogical libraries and at the main library.

Tracing the IGI Batch Numbers

Q. What are the sources(s) for the names in the International Genealogical Index IGI)?

A. There are a number of sources of input into the computer. The key to determining how a specific name got there is the *batch number* (the last two columns on each page of the IGI).

The batch number usually can be traced to obtain additional information. The way to trace a batch number is determined by the prefix — the first letter or first three digits of the batch number.

Q. How can I trace the batch numbers of the IGI?

A. Each batch number requires a different approach to trace it. An all digit batch number with the 3rd digit smaller than 4, as

7525320-56

Means the name was submitted by a member of the LDS Church on an Entry Form, Marriage Entry Form, or if an acceptable census or probate record was used, A Family Group record form. These are called "patron submitted" entries. The batch number can be traced to a microfilmed copy of the form submitted — which will tell you:

1. The name and address of the person submitting the form.
2. The relationship of the person submitting the form.
3. The exact source used by the patron.
4. Other genealogical data on the form.
5. Perhaps other names submitted at the same time.

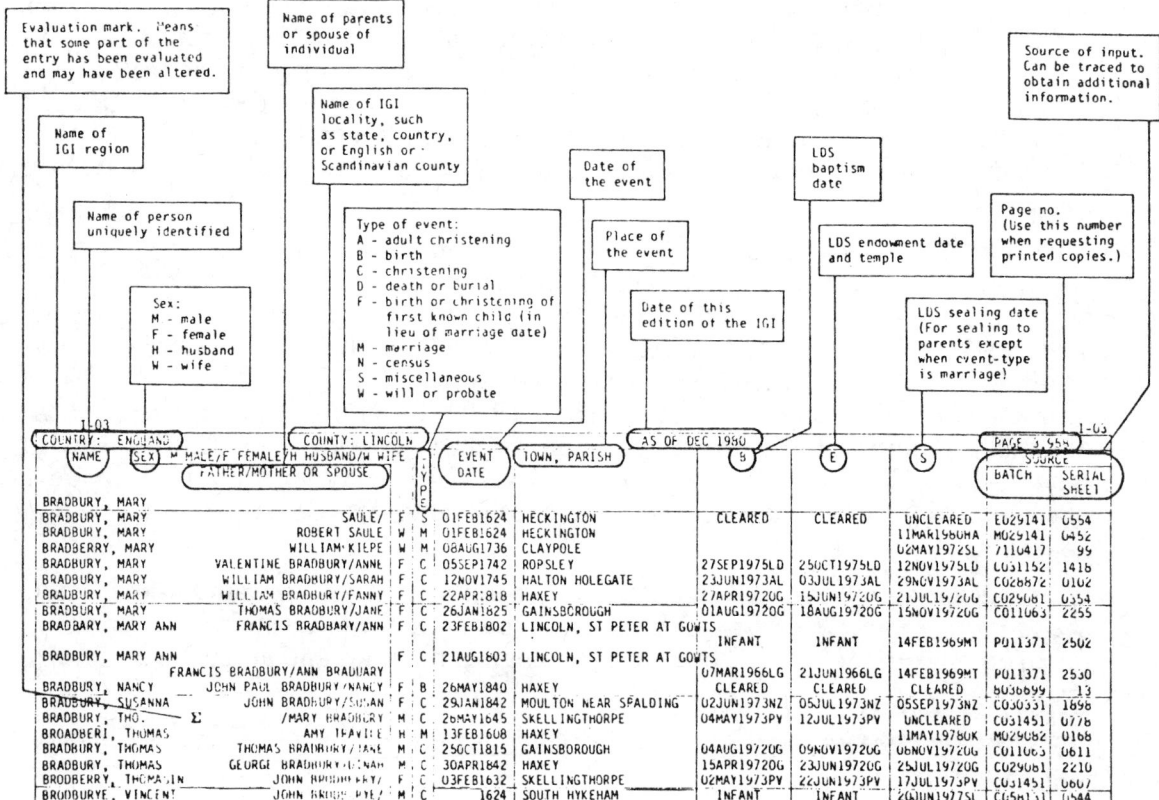

Q. How do I trace a patron-submitted batch number such as 7525320-56?

A. 1. Write down the batch number and sheet number.

2. Locate the "Batch Number Index." This is on microfiche on each floor and is filed with the other microfiche. The batch number index for patron sheets for all geographical areas is combined into one "batch number index." (Branch Libraries may have this on microfilm).

3. Locate your batch number on the "Batch Number Index." These are arranged numberically. You will *not* find the sheet number (last two digits) on the Batch Number Index. (You will need those two digits later).

Example:

Batch Number	Patron Sheets
7525320	884,601

4. Write down the microfilm number in the second column (marked "patrons sheets")

5. *Go to the LDS Records Collection.* Locate the proper microfilm cabinet and help yourself to the film. *(Branch Libraries need to order the desired film.)*

6. *The forms on the microfilm have the "batch number" and "sheet number" stamped at the top of each form.*

Example:

75   253   2056

ENTRY FORM

There will be 99 forms with the same basic batch number. There will be *only one* with the batch number plus the specific *sheet number.* When you find that, you have the sheet you are looking for.

Q. How can I trace a batch number beginning with an "A" or "MI"?

A. A prefix of *A* or *MI* means the "sealing conversion program" or extractions from the original temple records.

The way these batch numbers are traced depends on the DATE OF SEALING.

The Genealogical Department, as a special project, went through the temple sealing records and where there was enough information (date and place of original marriage), extracted all sealings of wives to husbands. Entries for deceased persons or those married more than 95 years ago appear in the IGI.

IGI batch numbers that begin with the *prefix A and have a proxy sealing date later than 1942* should have an Archive Records showing the entire family as it was submitted.

1. Look in the main section of the Family Group Records Archive under the name of the husband. (Temple Ordinance Indexes Request, PFGS 0073).

2. If the sheet is not found in the archives binder, check the microfilm copy of the main section. These films are on the 4th floor in the cabinets with orange labels. The film register is near the microfilm cabinets. Locate the section in the register entitled "main section."

3. If the sheet is not on the film, an Archive Record is no longer available. A copy of the family group records may be found in the temple records. (see below)

IGI batch numbers that begin with *"A" or "MI" and have a sealing date earlier than 1942* must be traced by using the original temple records. There will not be family group records on these persons.

Be sure to write down from the IGI the date of sealing, the temple where sealed, and the batch number. Go to the Special Collections Room

Use of the temple records is limited to searches for those persons whose names appear on your pedigree chart and their children. To personally use these records, one must have a current LDS temple recommend.

TIB cards may also be requested on these individuals to obtain additional information. There is a charge for the TIB searches. Ask at the counter on the fourth floor.

The 1976 edition of the IGI does not contain names of living persons.

Q. How can I trace a batch number beginning with *P, C, M,* or *725, 745,* or *754?*

A. All of these prefixes indicate "Controlled Extraction Program." This means that the name was extracted from a parish register or town vital record by employees of the Genealogical Department. (Research Paper Series F. No. 3, (PRGS 0670)

Additional information may be found by going to the correct *geographical area in the Library.* It may be in the form of a printout, a book, or a microfilm. The annual publication *Parish and Vital Records Listings* tells the areas and time periods extracted as part of this program and lists film numbers.

For other batch number, consult the Instruction book (Research Paper Series F. No. 5, (PRGS 1436). (Also check the Main Section Archive Records and Temple Records Index Bureau (TIB) for ordinance dates not found in the IGI).

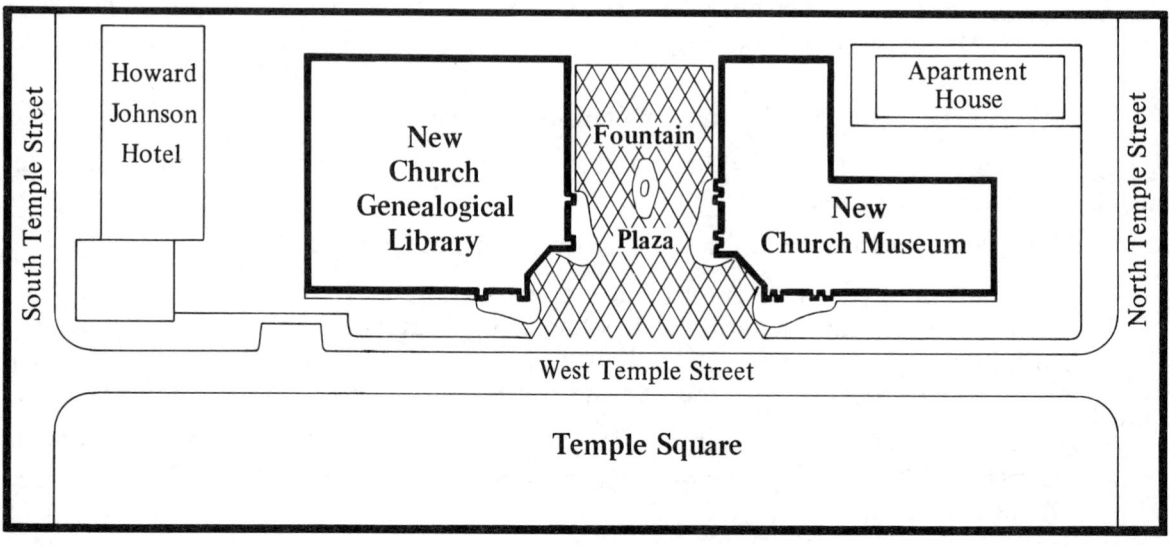

CHAPTER 6

THE LIBRARY OF CONGRESS

REFERENCE SERVICES AND FACILITIES OF THE
LOCAL HISTORY AND GENEALOGY ROOM

The Local History and Genealogy (LH&G) Reading Room is on the second floor of the Thomas Jefferson Building, Room 244.

In addition to the local history and genealogy publications in the Library's general collections, there is a reference collection of some 6,000 volumes in the LH&G Room. The reference collection contains various indexes, guides, and other works conveniently arranged for the use of readers. In general, books on genealogy and U.S. local history may be used only in the LH&G Room.

Special catalogs and indexes, most of them arranged by family name, are also accessible to readers working in the LH&G Room. Readers should be aware that most of the reference collections and catalogs in the LH&G Room are intended to facilitate research in U.S. rather than foreign local history and genealogy. Readers interested in foreign genealogy or local history should begin their research at the Main Catalog in the Thomas Jefferson Building before coming to LH&G. To learn what material, if any, is available at the Library, they should check appropriate subject headings, e.g., GERMANY-GENEALOGY; HERALDRY-POLAND: REGISTERS OF BIRTHS, ETC.-DUBLIN.

1. The staff of the Library of Congress cannot undertake research in family history or heraldry. In order to perform work of this nature satisfactorily, it is necessary to identify the particular branch of the family concerned, and, because of the time and effort involved, searches for this kind of information usually require the services of a professional genealogist or heraldic searcher.

2. Readers who have never undertaken genealogical research are urged to study the subject before coming to the Library.

3. A complete transcript of the Family Name Index in the LH&G Room, as of December 1971, was published in two volumes in 1972 by the Magna Carta Book Company, 5502 Magnolia Avenue, Baltimore, Maryland 21215. Entitled *Genealogies in the Library of Congress, a Bibliography*, and edited by Marion J. Kaminkow, it lists over 20,000 genealogies, including many in foreign languages. A one-volume supplement, issued by the same publisher in 1977, lists about 3,000 works added to the Library's collections from January 1972 to July 1976. This work is available in many public libraries.

4. *United States Local Histories in the Library of Congress, a Bibliography*, also edited by Marion J. Kaminkow and published by the Magna Carta Book Company in 1975, lists in five volumes some 90,000 works, arranged according to the Library's classification for U.S. local history, which is primarily geographical (regional, subdivided by State and further subdivided by period, county, and city). Many of the works listed in

the bibliography provide information on early settlers, the establishment of local government, churches, schools, industry, and trade, and biographical sketches of community leaders. This compendium may also be available in large libraries.

5. Genealogical books in the Library's collections are represented in its catalogs by cards filed under the names of the principal families concerned, e.g., DEAN FAMILY, HUNTER FAMILY, RUSSELL FAMILY. (These file *after* entries for all authors with those surnames.) The cards provide details such as the name of the author, the title, place and date of publication, name of the publisher, number of pages, size, and the Library's call number for the items described. Genealogical information does not appear on these cards. Files of such cards from the Library's Main Catalog can be photocopied to order.

6. The Library does not permit its books on genealogy, heraldry, and U.S. local and State history to circulate on interlibrary loan.

Bibliographies

The General Reading Rooms Division distributes free upon request three short bibliographies: *Guides to Genealogical Research, a Selected List* of publications that tell how to trace ancestors; *Surnames, a Selected List of References* on family names of many national origins, and *Immigrant Arrivals, a Short Guide to Published Sources* that may be helpful in identifying ships and passenger lists.

Reference Guides

LIBRARY OF CONGRESS
GENERAL READING ROOMS DIVISION

GUIDES TO GENEALOGICAL RESEARCH
A Selected List

General; United States

American Genealogical Research Institute. How to trace your family tree; a complete and easy to understand guide for the beginner. [Arlington, Va., C1973] 197 p. CS16.A48 1973
    Bibliography: p. [194]-197.

American Society of Genealogists. Genealogical research. Washington, 1960+ port. CS16.A5

Arizona Temple District Genealogical Library, *Mesa Ariz.* Practical research in genealogy; a compliation of genealogical research data, compiled by Gladys Busby & Evelyn Fish. Mesa, C1955. 150 p. maps. CS47.A75
    Includes bibliographical references.

Basic course in genealogy; instruction to help beginners in genealogical research. [Hampton, Va., Thomas Nelson Community College, [1972] 109 p. CS16.B34
    Includes bibliographical references.

Bennett, Archibald F. Advanced genealogical research. Salt Lake City, Bookcraft [1959] 256 p. illus. CS16.B38

Bennett, Archibald F. Finding your forefathers in America. Salt Lake City, Bookcraft, 1957. 444 p. illus. CS47.B4

Bennett, Archibald F. A Guide for genealogical research. [Salt Lake City] Genealogical Society of the Church of Jesus Christ of Latter-Day Saints, 1951. 338 p. illus., facsims., ports. CS16.B4
    Bibliography: p. 286-294.

Bennett, Archibald F. Searching with success; a genealogical text. Salt Lake City, Deseret Book Co., 1962. 262 p. Illus. CS16.B42

Blockson, Charles L., *and* Ron Fry. Black genealogy. Englewood Cliffs, N.J., Prentice-Hall [1977] 232 p. facsims. CS21.B55
    Bibliography: p. 220-228.

Cache Genealogical Library, *Logan, Utah.* Handbook for genealogical correspondence. John F. Vallentine, editor. Salt Lake City, Bookcraft, 1963. 273 p. illus. CS16.C3

Colket, Meredith B., *and* Frank E. Bridgers. Guide to genealogical records in the National Archives. Washington, National Archives, National Archives and Records Service, General Services Administration, 1964. 145 p. (National Archives publication no. 64-8) CS15.C6

Dauthers of the American Revolution. *Genealogical Advisory Committee to the Registrar General.* Is that lineage right? A training manual for the examiner of lineage papers, with helpful hints for the beginner in genealogical research. [Washington] National Society of the Daughters of the American Revolution [1965] 55 p.   CS15.D3 1965
   Bibliography: p. 43-46

Doane, Gilbert H. Searching for your ancestors; the how and why of genealogy. [4th ed.] Minneapolis, University of Minnesota Press [1973] 212 p. illus.   CS16.D6 1973
   Bibiographies: p. 171-192
   "A bibliography of lists, registers, rolls, and rosters of Revolutionary War soldiers": p. 200-205.

Everton, George B. The handy book for genealogists. 6th ed., rev. and enl. Logan, Utah, Everton Publishers, 1971. 298 p. maps
                                        CS16.E85 1971
   Bibliography: p. 293-297.

Everton, George B. The how book for genealogists. 7th ed. Logan, Utah, Everton Publishers [1973, C1971] xv, 237 p. illus.   CS16.E9 1973

Filby, P. William. American & British genealogy & heraldry; a selected list of books. 2d ed. Chicago, American Library Association, 1975. xxi, 467 p.   Z5311.F55 1975

Fudge, George H., *and* Frank Smith. LDS genealogist's handbook; modern procedures and systems. Salt Lake City, Bookcraft, 1972. xiv, 186 p.   CS16.F8

Gardner, Dave E., *and others.* A basic course in genealogy. Salt Lake City, Bookcraft, 1958. 2. v.   CS9.G3
   Contents: v. 1. An introduction to record keeping and research, by D.E. Gardner, D. Harland, and F. Smith (339 p.).—v. 2. Research procedure and evaluation of evidence, by D. Harland (404 p.).

Genealogical Associates. Genealogical address list. Evanston, Ill., C1964. a v. (unpaged)
                                        CS44.G48
   Supplements the authors' *Genealogy and Local History,* published in 1962.

Genealogical Associates. Genealogy and local history; and archival and bibliographical guide. 2d rev. ed. Evanston, Ill., C1962. 125 leaves.
                                        CS16.G37 1962

Gobble, John R. What to say in your genealogical letters; do's and dont's in genealogical correspondence. [Idaho Falls, Idaho, 1967] 25 p. illus.   CS15.G6

Greenwood, Val D. The researcher's guide to American genealogy. With an introd. by Milton Rubincam. Baltimore, Genealogical Pub. Co., 1973. xv, 535 p. illus.   CS47.G73
   Includes bibliographical references.

Groene, Bertram H. Tracing your Civil War ancestor. Winston-Salem, N.C., J. F. Blair [1973] 124 p. illus.   CD3047.G76
   Bibliography: p. [112]-118.

Hilton, Suzanne. Who do you think you are? Digging for your family roots. Philadelphia, Westminster Press [1976] 189 p. illus.
                                        CS16.G54
   Bibliography: p. 179-183.

Hopkins, Garland E. Your Family tree, a hobby handbook. Richmond, Dietz Press [1949] 58 p.
                                        CS16.G65

Jacobus, Donald L. Genealogy as pastime and profession. 2d ed. rev. With an introd. By Milton Rubincam. Baltimore, Genealogical Pub. Co., 1968. 120 p.   CS16.J3 1968

Jones, Vincent L., Arlene H. Eakle, *and* Mildred H. Christensen. Genealogical research; a jurisdictional approach. Rev. ed. [Woods Cross, Utah, Genealogical Copy Service] 1972. 326 p.   CS9.J63 1972
   Includes bibliographies.

Kirkham, E. Kay. The abc's of American genealogical research. [3d ed., rev.] Salt Lake City, Deseret Book Co., 1955. 123 p. illus.
                                        CS16.K5 1955

Kirkham, E. Kay. How to read the handwriting and records of early America. For researchers in American genealogy. [Salt Lake Ctiy, Kay Pub. Co., 1961] 37 p. facsims.
                                        Z113.K5

Kirkham, E. Kay. The land records of America and their genealogical value. [Washington, 1963] 60 p. facsims., maps.   HD197 1963

Kirkham, E. Kay. Making the genealogical record; an explanation of the O-Kay system of recordkeeping. Salt Lake City, Deseret Book Co. [1959] 43 p. illus. (The Columbia series in genealogy)   CS24.K5

Kirkham, E. Kay. Photography in genealogy; an explanation of the O-Kay system of record keeping. [Salt Lake City, 1959] 47 p. illus. (The Columbia series in genealogy)   CS16.K52

Kirkham, E. Kay. Research in American genealogy; a practical approach to genealogical research. [Salt Lake City, 1956] 477 p. maps, port.   CS16.K53
   Includes bibliographies.

Kirkham, E. Kay. Simplified genealogy for Americans. Salt Lake City, Deseret Book Co., 1968. 172 p. illus., maps.   CS16.K54

Kirkham, E. Kay. Some of the military records of America, before 1900; their use and value in genealogical and historical research. [Washington? 1963] 35 p. fllus.   CS49.K49

Kirkahm, E. Kay. A survey of American census schedules; an explanation and description of our Federal census enumerations 1790 to

1950. Salt Lake City, Deseret Book Co. [1959] 102 p. illus. (The Columbia series in genealogy) CS49.K5

Konrad, J. A directory of genealogical periodicals. Munroe Falls, Ohio, Summit Publications [1975] 61 p. CS1.K66

Lancour, Harold. A bibliography of ship passenger lists, 1538-1825; being a guide to published lists of early immigrants to North America. 3d ed., rev. and enl. by Richard J. Wolfe. With a list of passenger arrival records in the National Archives by Frank E. Bridges. New York, New York Public Library, 1963. 137p. Z7164.I3L2 1963

Nichols, Elizabeth L. Help is available. [Logan, Utah, Everton Publishers, 1972] 168 p. (A simplified step by step instruction book for the beginner in genealogy, no. 2) CS16.N53

Phillimore, William P. W. How to write the history of a family; a guide for the genealogist. 2d ed. London, E. Stock, 1888. 207 p. CS16.P54

Radewald, Bette M. The library handbook; simplified methods and terms for the genalogist. Riverside, Calif., RE:Genealogy, 1974. 94 p. illus. Z710.R3
Bibliography: p. 89-90

Skalka, Lois M. Tracing, charting, and writing your family history. New York, Pilot Books [1975] 48 p. CS16.S56
Includes bibliographical references.

Stetson, Oscar F. The art of ancestor hunting; a guide to ancestral research and genealogy. Brattleboro, Vt., Stephen Daye Press, 1936. 276 p. forms. CS16.S8

Stevenson, Noel C. Genealogical evidence; a practical system for judging the reliability of records. Los Angeles [1973] 22 leaves. CS14.S74

Stevenson, Noel C., ed The genealogical reader; a collection of articles. Salt Lake City, Deseret Book Co., 1958. 188 p. illus., facsims. CS3.S75

Stevenson, Noel C. Search and research, the researcher's handbook; a guide to official records and library sources for investigators, historians, genealogists, lawyers, and librarians. Rev. ed. Salt Lake City, Deseret Book Co., 1959. 364 p. Z5313.U5S8 1959

U.S. *Library of Congress.* Genealogies in the Lirary of Congress, a bibliography. Edited by Maricn J. Kaminkow. Baltimore, Md., Magna Carta Book Co., 1972. 2 v. Z5319.U53

Williams, Ethel W. Know your ancestors; a guide to genealogical research. Rutland, Vt., C. E. Tuttle Co. [1961, ᶜ1960] 313 p. illus. CS16.W53 1961

Wright, Norman E. Building An American pedigree; a study in genealogy. Provo, Utah, Brigham Young University Press [1974] xvi, 639 p. illus. CS47.W68
Bibliography: p. [629]-639.

Wright, Norman E., *and* David H. Pratt. Genealogical research essentials. Salt Lake City, Bookcraft [1967] 318 p. illus. CS9.W7
Includes bibliographies.

Zabriskie, George O. Climbing our family tree systematically. Salt Lake City, Parliament Press, 1969. 222 p. CS16.Z3 1969

U.S. Regions, States, Counties

Bowen, Richard L. Massachusetts records; a handbook for genealogists, historians, lawyers, and other researchers. Rehoboth, Mass., 1957. 66 p. illus. CD3291.B6

Bryan, Evelyn M. F. Hunting your ancestors in South Carolina, a guide for amateur genealogists. [2d ed., rev. & enl. Jacksonville, Fla., Florentine Press] 1974. 42 p. CS16.B79 1974
Bibliography: p. 37-40.

Douthit, Ruth L. Ohio resources for genealogists. With some references for genealogical searching in Ohio. [Rev. Detroit] Detroit Society for Genealogical Research, 1971 [ᶜ1972] 136 p. F490.D68 1971

Draughon, Wallace R. *and* William P. Johnson North Carolina genealogical reference; a research guide for all genealogists both amateur and professional. New ed. Durham, N.C., 1966. 571 p. maps. Z5313.U6N63 1966

Hathaway, Beverly W. Genealogy research sources in Tennessee. West Jordan, Utah, Allstates Research Co., 1972. 107 p. maps. F435.H3
Bibliography: p. 107.

Hathaway, Beverly W. Primer for Georgia genealogical research. West Jordan, Utah, Printed by Allstates Research Co. (ᶜ1973] 27 leaves. maps. CS16.H37

Hoenstine, Floyd G. Guide to genealogical and historical research in Pennsylvania. 2d ed., rev. and enl. Hollidaysburg, Pa., 1966. 439 p. map. Z1329.H73 1966

Jaussi, Laureen R., *and* Gloria D. Chaston. Genealogical records of Utah. Salt Lake City, Deseret Book Co., 1974 xxxi, 312 p. illus. CD3541.J38 1974

Kirkahm, E. Kay. The counties of the United States. For researchers in American genealogy and history. [Salt Lake City, Kay Pub. Co., 1961] 77 p. E180.K5

Kirkham, E. Kay. A survey of American church records; for the period before the Civil War, east of the Mississippi River. Salt Lake City, Deseret Book Co., 1959-60. 2 v. CS3065.K52
Includes bibliographies.
Contents: v. 1. Major denominations.—v.

2. Minor denominations; including a special treatise on the Huguenots of France in America and religious migrations and immigrations in the United States.

McCay, Betty L. Sources for genealogical searching in Indiana. Indianapolis, 1969. 24 leaves. map.　　　　　　　　F525.5.M3

McCay, Betty L. Sources for genealogical searching in Kentucky. Rev. Indianapolis, 1969. 15 leaves. maps (1 on cover)　F450.2.M3 1969

McCay, Betty L. Sources for genealogical searching in Maryland. [Indianapolis? ᶜ1972] 21 leaves. map.　　　　　　　CS3281.M3

McCay, Betty L. Sources for genealogical searching in North Carolina. Indianapolis, 1969. 10 leaves. map.　　　　　　　CS47.M33

McCay, Betty L. Sources for genealogical searching in Ohio. Rev. Indianapolis, 1973. 15 leaves.　　　　　　　　CD3441.M32 1973

McCay, Betty L. Sources for genealogical searching in Pennsylvania. [Indianapolis?] 1968. 20 leaves. maps.　　　　　Z5313.U6P46
　　　Includes bibliographies.

McCay, Betty L. Sources for genealogical searching in Tennessee. Indianapolis, 1970. 15 leaves. map.　　　　　　　CS16.M3

McCay, Betty L. Sources for genealogical searching in Virginia and West Viginia. Indianapolis, 1971. 30 leaves. map.
　　　　　　　　　　　Z5313.U6V78

Meyer, Mary K. Genealogical research in Maryland; a guide. Rev. and enl. Baltimore, Maryland Historical Society, 1976. 109 p.
　　　　　　　　　　Z1293.M485 1976
　　　Bibliography: p. 61-108.

New Jersey. *Bureau of Archives and History*. Genealogical research; a guide to source materials in the Archives and History Bureau of the New Jersey State Library. [New Brunswick] Genealogical Society of New Jersey, 1971. 36 p.　Z5313.U5N52 1971

North American genealogical sources. Compiled Norman Edgar Wright. Provo, Utah, Brigham Young University [1968]+　CD3000.N6
　　　Contents: [1] Southern States.—[2] Middle Atlantic States and Canada.—[3] Midwestern States.—[4] Southwestern States.—

Passano, Eleanor P. An index of the source records of Maryland: genealogical, biographical, historical. With a new introd. by P. W. Filby. Baltimore, Genealogical Pub. Co., 1967. 478 p.
　　　　　　　　　　　Z1293.P3 1967
　　　Originally published in 1940.
　　　Bibliography: p. 363-478.

Peterson, Clarence S. Consolidated bibliography of county histories in fifty States in 1961, consolidated 1935-1961. Baltimore, Genealogical Pub. Co., 1973 [ᶜ1961] 186 p.
　　　　　　　　　　　Z1250.P47 1973

St. Louis Genealogical Society. Tracing family trees in eleven States: Missouri, Illinois, Kentucky, Virginia, Georgia, Ohio, North Carolina, South Carolina, Tennessee, Indiana, Pennsylvania. Brentwood, Mo., 1970. 290 p. maps.　　　　　　　　CS51.S2

Stryker-Rodda, Kenn. New Jersey: digging for ancestors in the Garden State. [Detroit] Detroit Society for Genealogical Research, 1970. 38 p. illus., map.　　　　　　　CS16.S86
　　　Bibliography: p. 21-37.

Swem, Earl G., *comp*. Virginia historical index. Roanoke, Va., Stone Print. and Manufacturing Co., 1934-36. 2 v.　F221.S93

Tennessee. State Library and Archives, *Nashville*. Tennessee county data for historical and genealogical research. [Compiled by Robert M. McBride] Nashville [pref. 1966] 50 p.
　　　　　　　　　　　F443.A15A57

U.S. *Library of Congress* United States local Histories in the Library of Congress, a bibliography. Edited by Marion J. Kaminkow. Baltimore, Md., Magna Carta Book Co., 1975. 5 v.　　　　　　　Z1250.U59 1975
　　　Contents: V. 1. Atlantic States, Maine to New York.—v. 2. Atlantic States, New Jersey to Florida.—v. 3. Middle West, Alaska, Hawaii.—v. 4. The West.—v. 5. Supplement and index.

Waters, Margaret R. Genealogical sources available at the Indiana State Library for all Indiana counties. [Indianapolis?] ᶜ1946. 37 leaves.　　　　　　　　F525.W3
　　　"Supplement no. 1, June 15, 1949": leaf inserted.

Williams, Jacqueline H., *and* Betty H. Williams. Resources for genealogical research in Missouri. [Warrensburg? Mo., 1969] 60 p. maps.　　　　　　　　CS16.W534

Wright, Norman E. Genealogical reader: Northeastern United States and Canada. Provo, Utah, Brigham Young University [1973] 209 p.　　　　　　　CS47.W69
　　　Includes bibliographical references.

Wright, Norman E. Genealogy in America. Salt Lake City, Desert Book Co., 1968+ maps.
　　　　　　　　　　　CS47.W7
　　　Bibliographical footnotes.
　　　Contents: v. 1. Massachusetts, Connecticut, and Maine.—

British Isles

Camp, Anthony J. Tracing your ancestors. New, corr. ed. Baltimore, Genealogical Pub. Co., 1971 [ᶜ1964] 78 p.　　CS415.C3 1971

Falley, Margaret D. Irish and Scotch-Irish ancestral research; a guide to the genealogical records, methods and sources in Ireland. Evanston, Ill. [1962] 2 v.　　CS483.F32
　　　Contents: V. 1. Repositories and

records.— v. 2. Bibliography and family index.

Gardner, David E. *and* Frank Smith. Genealogical research in England and Wales. Salt Lake City, Bookcraft [1956-64] 3 v. illus., facsims., forms, maps, port.   CS414.G3
    Bibliographical footnotes.

Gibson, Jeremy S. W. Wills and where to find them. Baltimore, Genealogical Pub. Co., 1974. xxii, 210 p. maps.   CS1068.A2G5 1974

Hamilton-Edwards, Gerald K. S. In search of British ancestry. 3d ed. Baltimore, Genealogical Pub. Co., 1974. 293 p. illus., facsims., geneal. table, map, plates.
                           CS9.H27 1974
    Bibliography: p. 233-283.

Hamilton-Edwards, Gerald K. S. In search of Scottish ancestry. Baltimore, Genealogical Pub. Co., 1972. 252 p. illus., facsims., geneal. tables, map.   CS463.H35 1972
    Bibliograpy: p. 233-283.

Iredale, David. Discovering your family tree: a pocket guide to tracing your English ancestors. [Rev. ed. Aylesbury, Bucks.] Shire Publications [1973] 72 p. illus., facsims., geneal. tables, port.   CS415.I74 1973

Kaminkow, Marion J. A new bibliography of British genealogy with notes. Baltimore, Magna Charta Book Co., 1965. xvii, 170 p.
                           Z5313.G69K3

McCay, Betty L. Seven lesson course in Irish research and sources. [Indianapolis? ᶜ1972] 36 leaves. map.   CS483.M3

Matthews, Constance M. C. Your family history and how to discover it. Guildford, Lutterworth Press [1976] 144 p. illus., facsims.   CS16.M37
    Bibliography: p. [117]-120.

Pine, Leslie G. The genealogist's encyclopedia. New York, Weybright and Talley [1969] 360 p. illus.   CS9.P48 1969b

Pine, Leslie G. Teach yourself heraldry and genealogy. Illustrated by W. J. Hill. London, English Universities Press [1958] 192 p. coats of arms. (The Teach yourself books)   CR23.P6

Pine, Leslie G. Trace your ancestors. [2d ed., rev.] London, Evans Bros. [1954] 144 p. illus.
                           CS9.P5 1954

Pine, Leslie G. Your family tree; a guide to genealogical sources. [Rev. and expanded] London, H. Jenkins [1962] 191 p. illus. CS415.P56 1962

Rye, Walter. Records and record searching; a guide to the genealogist and topographer. 2d ed. London, G. Allen, 1897. 253 p. illus.
                         CS415.R8 1897
    Includes bibliographical references.

Society of Genealogists. Genealogists' handbook. Edited by Peter Spufford and Anthony J.

Camp. [5th ed. London] 1969. 43 p.
                           CS415.S6 1969
    Bibliography: p. 6-7.

Unett, John. Making a pedigree. 2d ed., with new pref. and bibliography. Baltimore, Genealogical Pub. Co., 1971. 137 p.
                         CS15.U5 1971
    Bibliography: p. [128]-130.

Wagner, *Sir* Anthony R. English genealogy. 2d ed., enl. Oxford, Clarendon Press, 1972. 461 p. geneal. tables.   CS414.W3 1972
    Bibliographical footnotes.

Willis, Arthur J. Genealogy for beginners. 2d ed., rev. London, Phillimore [1970] 183 p. illus., coat of arms, facsims., geneal. tables, map, plates.   CS16.W55 1970
    Includes bibliographical references.

Other Foreign Countries

Friederichs, Heinz F. How to find my German ancestors and relatives. Neustadt, Degener, 1969. 16 p. map.   CS614.F7

Kennedy, Patricia. How to trace your Loyalist ancestors: the use of the Loyalist sources in the Public Archives of Canada. [Ottawa] Ontario Genealogical Society, 1971. 13 p. (Ontario Genealogical Society. Ottawa Branch. Publication 71-3)   CD3624.K46

Norway. *Kontoret for kulturelt samkvem med utlandet.* How to trace your ancestors in Norway. [Manuscript by Jan H. Olstad and Gunvald Boe. 3d ed. Oslo, royal Ministry of Foreign Affairs. Dept. of Cultural Relations, 1971] 7 p.   CS912.N67 1971
    "Norway no. 316."

Nova Scotia. *Public Archives.* Tracing your ancestors in Nova Scotia. [Halifax] 1967. 13 p.
                           CS88.N64A5

Olsson, Nils W. Tracing your Swedish ancestry. [Stockhom, royal Swedish Ministry of Foreign Affairs, 1963] 19 p. facsims., maps.
                           CS922.O4

Pine, Leslie G. American origins. Baltimore, Genealogical Pub. Co., 1967 [ᶜ1960] 357 p.
                         CS16.P55 1967
    Includes bibliographical references.

Public Archives of Canada. Tracing your ancestors in Canada. Ottawa, 1972. 20 p.   CS82.P8 1972
    Includes bibliographical references.

Rottenberg, Dan. Finding our fathers; a guidebook to Jewish genealogy. New york, Random House [1977] xiv, 401 p. illus.   CS21.R58
    Bibliography: p. 376-401

Smith, Clifford N., *and* Anna P. Smith. Encyclopedia of German-American genealogical research. New York, R. R. Bowker Co., 1976. 273 p.   E184.G3S66
    Includes bibliographical references.

Wallauer, Maralyn A. A guide to foreign genealogical research; a selected bibliography of printed material with addresses. Milwaukee, Wis. [1973] 78 p.   Z5311.W44

Wijnaendts van Resandt, Willem. Searching for your ancestors in the Netherlands. The Hague, Centraal Bureau voor Genealogie, 1972. 16 p. map.   CS813.W55

SURNAMES
A Selected List of References

Note: Publications on this list can be consulted in the Library of Congress; they are not, however, available on interlibrary loan. Some of them may be in the collections of a library to which you have access.

Bibliography

Smith, Elsdon C. Personal Names; a bibliography. New York, New York Public Library, 1952. 226 p.   Z6824.S55
> Surnames: items 2910-3306.
> Reprinted from the *Bulletin* of the New York Public Library, 1950-51.

Periodicals

Beiträge zur Namenforschung. 1.-16. Jahrg., 1949/50-65; n.F., Bd. 1+ 1966+ Heidelberg, C. Winter. 4 no. a year.   P769.B45
> —Beiheft. 1+ Heidelberg, C. Winter, 1969+   P769.B46

Names. v. 1+ mar. 1953+ Berkeley, University of California Press. quarterly.   P769.N3
> Journal of the American Name Society.

Onoma. Bulletin d'information et de bibliographie. bibliographical and information bulletin. v. 1+ 1950+ Louvain, International Centre of Onomastics. annual.   P323.O6

Revue internationadle d'onomastique. t. 1+ mars/ juin 1949+ Paris, Editions d'Artrey. maps. quarterly.   CS2300.R4

General

Baring—Gould, Sabine. Family names and their story. Baltimore, Genealogical Pub. Co., 1968. 431 p.   CS2501.B35 1968
> Reprint of the 1910 ed.
> Bibliographic footnotes.

Brown, Samuel L. Surnames are the fossils of speech. [St. Paul, North Central Pub. Co., C1967] 350 p.   CS2385.B7
> An etymological dictionary of surnames.

Cottle, Basil. The Penguin dictionary of surnames. [Harmondsworth] Penguin Books [1967] 333 p. (penguin reference books, R32) CS2505.C67
> Bibliography: p. 333-[334].

Dellquest, Augustus W. These names of ours, a book of surnames. New York, T. Y. Crowell Co. [C1938] xxiii, 296 p.   CS2505.D45

Ferguson, Robert. Surnames as a science. London, New York, G. Routledge, 1883. 235 p.
                                            CS2465.F45
> "List of the principal works consulted": p. [213]-214.

Hassall, William O. History through surnames. Oxford, New York, Pergamon Press [1967] xv, 224 p. illus.   CS2385.H3 1967

Hughes, Pennethorne. How you got your name; the origin and meaning of surnames. [Rev. ed.] London, Phoenix House [1961] 159 p.
                                        CS2505.H83 1961
> "Authorities": p. [143]-146

Hughes, Pennethorne. Is thy name Wart? London, Phoenix House [1965] 128 p.   CS2505.H84

Hughes, Pennethorne. Your book of surnames. London, Faber and Faber [1967] 59 p. illus., plates.   CS2505.H86
> "Suggestions for further reading": p.59.

Lambert, Eloise, *and* Mario A. Pei. Our names, where they came from and what they mean. New York, Lothrop, Lee & Shepard (1960) 192 p.   CS2303.L35

Pine, Leslie G. The story of surnames. Rutland, Vt., C. E. Tuttle Co. [1967, C1965] 152 p.
                                          CS2385.P5 1967
> "Sources and suggestions for further reading": p. 134-141.

Smith, Elsdon C. American surnames. Philadelphia, Chilton Book Co. [1969] xx, 370 p.
                                            CS2485.S63
> Bibliography: p. 327-329.

Smith, Elsdon C. New dictionary of American family names. New York, Harper & Row [1972, C1973] xxix, 570 p.   CS2481.S55 1973

Vroonen, Eug® ene. Encyclop.edie des noms des personnes; .etude par groupes linguistiques. Paris, .Editions universitaires [C1973] 743 p. (Encyclop.edie universitaire)   CS2305.V75
> Continuation of the author's *Les Noms des personnes dans le monde.*
> Includes bibliographic references.

Vroonen, Eug® ene. Les noms des personnes dans le monde. Anthroponymie universelle compar.ee. Bruxelles, .Editions de la Librairie encyclop.edique, 1967. 495 p.
                                            CS2305.V76
> Bibliography: p. 5-13.
> Includes information on surnames.

Weekley, Ernest. Surnames [3d ed.] New York, E. P. Dutton [1937] xxii, 360 p. CS2505.W5 1937
> Bibliography: p. xvi-xx.

Belgian

Carnoy, Albert J. Origines des noms de familles en Belgique. Louvain, .Editions Universitas, 1953. 408 p.   CS2940.B4C3

Debrabandere, Frans. Studie van de persoonsnamen in de kasselrij Kortrijk,

1350-1400. Handzame, Familia et Patria, 1970. 558 p. 2 fold maps. CS2529.C63D43 1970
Bibliography: p. 21-34.
Glossary of surnames: p. 39-496.

Vroonen, Eug® ene. Les noms de famille de Belgique; essai d'anthroponymie belge. Bruxelles, D. Dessart [1957] 2 v. CS2940.B4V7

British

Bannister, John. A glossary of Cornish names, ancient and modern, local, family, personal, &c.; 20,000 Celtic and other names, now or formerly in use in Cornwall; with derivations and significations. London, Williams & Norgate [1871] xx, 212 p.   CS2401.B3

Bardsley, Charles W. E. A dictionary of English and Welsh surnames, with special American instances. Rev. for the press by his widow. London, New York, H. Frowde, 1901. xvi, 847 p.
CS2505.B3 1901
"List of references and key to abbreviations": p. [xiii]-xvi.

Bardsley, Charles W. E. English surnames; their sources and significations. New introd. by L. G. Pine. [Newton Abbot] David & Charles Reprints [1969] xxxv, 612 p. CS2505.B33 1969
Reprint of 1875 ed.

Black, George F. The surnames of Scotland; their orgin, meaning, and history. New York, New York Public Library, 1946. lxxi, 838 p. port.
CS2435.B55
Bibliography: p. lix-lxxi.
Reprinted from the *Bulletin* of the New York Public Library, Aug. 1943-Sept. 1946.

Dolan, J. R. English ancestral names, the evolution of the surname from medieval occupations. New York, C. N. Potter; distributed by Crown Publishers [1972] xvi, 381 p.   CS2505.D65 1972
Bibliography: 363-365.

Ewen, Cecil Henry L'Estrange. A guide to the origin of British surnames. London, J. Gifford [1938] 206 p.   CS2505.E78
"Sources® and literature": p. 176-181. Bibliographic footnotes.

Ewen, Cecil Henry L'Estrange. A history of surnames in the British Isles; a concise account of their origin, evolution, etymology, and legal status. London, K. Paul, Trench, Trubner, 1931. Detroit, Gale Research Co., 1968. xx, 508 p.   CS2505.E8 1968
Bibliography: p. 429-436.
— — Additions and corrections. Paignton, Devon, 1946. 11 p.   CS2505. E8 Add.

Fransson, Gustav. Middle English surnames of occupation, 1100-1350, with an excursus on toponymical surnames. London, Williams & Norgate [1935] 217 p. (Lund studies in English, 3)   CS2505.F7
Bibliography: p. [8]-14.

Freeman, John W. Discovering surnames. [Rev. ed. Aylesbury, Bucks.] Shire Publications [1973] 70 p. (Discovering series, 35)
CS2385.F7 1973
"A pocket guide to 1,000 surnames with special chapters on Irish, Scottish and Welsh names."

Guppy, Henry B. Homes of family names in Great Britain. London, Harrison, 1980. lxv, 601 p. map.   CS2505.G85
Bibliographic footnotes.

Harrison, Henry. Surnames of the United Kingdom; a concise etymological dictionary. Assisted by Gyda Pulling. Baltimore, Genealogical Pub. Co., 1969. 2 v. in 1.
CS2505.H32
Reprint of the 1912-18 ed.

Kneen, John J. The personal names of the Isle of Man. London, Oxford University Press, H. Milford, 1937. lx, 295 p.   CS2509.I8K6
Bibliography: p. [lviii]-lx.

Lower, Mark A. Patronymica britannica. a dictionary of the family names of the United Kingdom. London, J. R. Smith, 1860. xxxix, 443 p. port.   CS2505.L63

Matthews, Constance M. C. English surnames. New York, C. Scribner's Sons [1967] 367 p.
CS2505.M3 1967
Bibliography: p. 321-324.

Moore, Arthur W. Manx names; or, The surnames and place-names of the Isle of Man. 2d ed., rev. London, E. Stock, 1903. xvi, 261 p. CS2421.M6

The Norman people and their existing descendants in the British dominions and the United States of America. London, H. S. King, 1874. xvi, 484 p.   CS432.N7N7 1874
Includes bibliographic references.

Reaney, Percy H. A dictionary of British surnames. 2d ed., with corrections and additions, by R. M. Wilson. London, Boston, Routledge & K. Paul [1976] lxiv, 398 p. CS2505.R39 1976

Reaney, Percy H. The origin of English surnames. New York, Barnes & Noble [1967] xix, 415 p.
CS2505.R4
Bibliography: p. xvii-xix

Weekley, Ernest. The romance of names. London, J. Murray, 1914. xiv, 250 p.   CS2505.W4

White, George Pawley. A handbook of Cornish surnames. Camborne [Cornwall] 1972. 70 p.
CS2405.W47

Danish

Knudsen, Gunnar, Marius Kristensen, *and* Rikard Hornby. Danmarks gamle personnavne. 2. Tilnavne. Kobenhavn, I kommission hos G. E. C. Gads Forlag, 1949-64. 2 v. (1292 columns)
CS2573.K5
Contents: 1. A-K.—2. L-O.

Dutch

Hekket, B. J. Oost Nederlandse familienamen; hun onstaan en betekenis. Enschede, Twents-Gelderse Uitg. W. G. Witkam, 1975. 181 p.
CS2525.H44
Bibliography: p. 24-25

Huizinga, A. Encyclopedie van namen, een vraagbaak over de afkomst van onze Nederlandse en Vlaamse familie- en geslachtsnamen. Amsterdam, A. J. G. Strengholt [1955] 328 p.
PF576.H8
Bibliography: p. [4].

Swaen, Adriaan E. H. Nederlandsche geslachtsnamen. Zutphen, W. J. Thieme, 1942. 162 p.
CS2525.S9
Bibliographic footnotes.

Winkler, Johan. De Nederlandsche geslachtsnamen in oorsprong, geschiedenis en beteekenis. Haarlem, H. D. Tjeenk Willink, 1885. 2 v.
CS2525.W5

Winkler, Johan. Studiën in Nederlandsche namenkunde. Haarlem, H. D. Tjeenk Willink, 1900. 328. p.
DJ14.W5

French & French-Canadian

Blanche, Pierre. Dictionnaire et armorial des noms de famille de France. [Paris] Fayard [1974] xlvi, 249 p.
CR1798.B55

Chapuy, Paul. Origine des noms patronymiques français (donnant l'étymologie de 10,000 noms de famille) suivi d'une étude sur les noms de famille basques. Paris, Dorbon-aîné [1934] 350 p.
CS2695.C5
Bibliography: p. [5]-6.

Dauzat, Albert. Dictionnaire étymologique des noms de famille et prénoms de France. 3.éd. rev. et augm. par Marie Thérèse Morlet. Paris, Larousse [1967] xxii, 624 p.
CS2691.D3 1967
Bibliography: p. [xxv].

Dauzat, Albert. Les noms de famille de France; traité d'anthroponymie française. Paris, Payot, 1945. 454 p. maps. (Bibliothèque scientifique)
CS2695.D3
Bibliography: p. [397]-400.

Dionne, Narcisse E. Les Canadiens-Français. Origine des familles émigrées de France, d'Espagne, de Suisse, etc., pour venir se fixer au Canada, depuis la fondation de Québec jusqu'á ces derniers temps, et signification de leurs noms. Québec, Garneau, 1914. xxxiii, 611 p.
CS2700.D5

Gourvil, Francis. Noms de famille bretons d'origine toponymique. Quimper, Société archéologique du Finistère, 1970. xlviii, 330 p.
CS2398.G63
Bibliography: p. xlv-xlviii.

German & Austrian

Bach, Adolf. Die deutschen Personennamen. 2., stark erw. Aufl. Heidelberg, C. Winter, 1952-53. 2 v. (His Deutsche Namenkunde, Bd. I, 1-2)
PF3576.B33, v. I, 1-2
Includes bibliographies.

Bahlow, Hans. Deutsches Namenlexikon; Familienund Vornamen nach Ursprung und Sinn erklärt. München, Keysersche Verlagsbuchhandlung [1967] 588 p. (Keysers Nachschlagewerke)
CS2541.B3
Bibliography: p. 588.

Bahlow, Hans, Liegnitzer Namenbuch; Familiennamen, gedeutet aus den Quellen des Mittelalters. Lorch/Württ., G. Weber [1975] 158 p. facsim. (Beiträge zur Liegnitzer Geschichte, 5. Bd.)
CS2549.L43B33

Bahlow, Hans. Niederdeutsches Namenbuch. [Walluf bei Wiesbaden] M. Sändig [1972] 572 p.
CS2545.B33
Bibliography: p. 557-560.

Brechenmacher, Josef K. Deutsches Namenbuch. 2. Aufl. Stuttgart, E. Klett [193-] 388 p. (His Deutsche Sprachkunde, 3. Bd.)
CS2545.B68 1930z
Bibliography: p. [327]-334.

Brechenmacher, Josef K. Etymologisches Wörterbuch der deutschen Familiennamen. 2., von Grund auf neugearb. Aufl der Deutschen Sippennamen (Bde. 5-9 der Sippenbücherei). Limburg a.d. Lahn, C. A. Starke-Verlag [1957-63] 2 v.
CS2545.B73
Bibliography: v. 1, p. [xix]-xxxvii.

Finsterwalder, Karl. Die Familiennamen in Tirol und Nachbargebieten und die Entwicklung des Personennamens im Mittelalter. Mit einem urkundlichen Nachschlagswerk für 4100 Familienund Hofnamen. Innsbruck, Wagner, 1951. xxiv, 418 p. (Schlern-Schriften, 81)
CS2549.T9F5
Includes bibliographic references.

Fleischer, Wolfgang. Die deutschen Personennamen; Geschichte, Bildung und Bedeutung. 2., durchgesehene und ergänzte Aufl. Berlin, Akademie-Verlag, 1968. 242 p. (Wissenschaftliche Taschenbücher, Bd. 20)
CS2541.F56 1968
"Nachweis wichtiger Fachliteratur zur Namenkunde": p. 194-201.

Gottschald, Max. Deutsche Namenkunde; unsere Familiennamen nach ihrer Entstehung und Bedeutung. 4. Aufl., mit einem Nachwort und einem bibliographischen Nachtrag von Rudolf Schützeichel. Berlin, W. de Gruyter, 1971. 646 p.
CS2545.G6 1971
"Nachwort und bibliographischer Nachtrag": p. 631-646.

Heintze, Albert. Die deutschen Familiennamen, geschichtlich, geographisch, sprachlich [von]

Heintze-Cascorbi. 7., sehrverb. und verm. Aufl. hrsg. von Paul Cascorbi. Halle/S., Buchhandlung des Waisenhauses, 1933. xii, 536 p.   CS2545.H4 1933
Bibliography: p. [vii]-ix.

Linnartz, Kaspar. Unsere Familiennamen; zehntausend Berufsnamen im ABC erklärt. Berlin, F. Dümmler, 1936. 169 p.   CS2545.L5
Bibliography: p. [15]-16

Linnartz, Kaspar. Unsere Familiennamen; aus deutschen und fremden vornamen im ABC erklärt. Bonn, F. Dümmler, 1939. xxiii, 140, 145 p.   CS2545.L52
Supplements the preceding.

Pott, August F. Die Personennamen, insbesondere die Familiennamen und ihre Entstehungsarten; auch unter Berücksichtigung der Ortsnamen. 2., durch ein Register verm. Ausg. Wiesbaden, M. Sändig [1968] xvi, 721, 156 p.
CS2303.P6 1968

Schwarz, Ernst. Sudetendeutsche Familiennamen des 15. und 16. Jahrhunderts. München, R. Lerche, 1973. 356 p. maps. (Handbuch der sudetendeutschen Kulturgeschichte, 6. Bd.)
CS2549.C95S38
Bibliography: p. 9-16

Zoder, Rudolf. Familiennamen in Ostfalen. Hildesheim, G. Olms, 1968. 2 v.   CS2549.S2Z6
Bibliography: v. 1, p. 11-24
Contents: A-K.—2. L-Z.

Zschaetzsch, Karl G. Uralte Sippen- und Familiennamen. 5., bearb. und erw. Aufl. Berlin, Arier-Verlag, 1940. 703 p.   CS2545.Z8 1940

Hispanic & Basque

Almerich Sellarés, Luis. Origen i definició dels cognoms catalans. Barcelona, Editorial Millá, 1968. 207 p. (Biblioteca popular catalana vell i nou)   CS2770.C3A4

Alvarez, Grace de Jesús C. Topónimos en apellidos hispanos. Garden City, N.Y., Estudios de Hispanófila, Adelphi University [1968] 587 p. facsims., maps, ports. (Estudios de Hispanófila, 7)   DP13.A45
Bibliography: p. [579]-584.

Clapés y Corbera, Juan. Els cognoms catalans; origen i evolució (més de 7.000 exemples). Barcelona, Llibreria Catalònia, 1929. 291 p. (Collecció històrica i literària)
CS2770.C3C6

López de mesa, Luis. Rudimentos de onomatologá. Bogotá, Impr. del Banco de la República, 1961. 713 p.   CS2303.L6

Maduell, Charles R. The romance of Spanish surnames. [New Orleans?] 1967. xiii, 221, xiv-xxii p.   CS2745.M3
Bibliography: p. 220-221.

Michelena, Luis. Apellidos vascos. 3. ed, aum. y

corr. San Sebastián, Txertoa [1973] 250 p. (Editorial Txertoa. [Publicaciones] no. 8)
CS2940.B37M52 1973

Moll y Cassanovas, Francisco de B. Els llinatges catalans (Catalunya, Païs Valenciá, Illes Balers); assaig de divulgació lingüística. Palma de Mallorca, Editorial Moll [1959] 3 v. (445 p.) Biblioteca Raixa, 40-42) CS2770.C3M6
Bibliography: v. 1, p. [12]-16.

Querexeta, Jaime de. Diccionario onomástico y heráldico vasco; más de 25.000 apellidos vascos, con su significación, casa solar, pruebas de hidalguía y escudos de armas. Bilbao [Editorial "La Gran Enciclopedia Vasca"] 1970-75. 6 v. coats of arms (part col.), facsims. (part col.) Biblioteca de La Gran Enciclopedia Vaca. Biblioteca magna de la Gran Enciclopedia Vasca, 9)   CR2157.B3Q46

Tibón, Gutierre. Onomástica hispanoamericana; índice de siete mil nombres y apellidos castellanos, vascos, árabes, judíndice toponímico. México, Union tipográfica Editorial Hispano Americana [1961] 360 p. illus.   CS2745.T5

Youmans, Charles L. Diccionario de apellidos castellanos, origen y significado [por] ruiz Arquero [pseud.] Habana, 1955. 152 p.
CS2741.Y6

Irish

Kelly, Patrick. Irish family names, with origins, meanings, clans, arms, crests, and mottoes. Collected from the living Gaelic and from authoritative books, mss., and public documents. 2d ed. [n.p.] 1958. 136 p.
CS2415.K4 1958

Mac Giolla Domhnaigh, Padraig. Some Ulster surnames. [New ed.] with foreword by Edward McLysaght. Baile Atha Cliath [Dublin] Clódhanna Teo. [1974?] 64, [5] p.
CS2419.U37M3 1975
First published in 1923 under title Some Anglicised Surnames in Ireland.

MacLysaght, Edward. A guide to Irish surnames. [2d ed., rev. and enl.] Dublin, Helicon [1965], ᶜ1964] 256 p.   CS2415.M23 1965
"Bibliography of irish family history": p. 207-247.

MacLysaght, Edward. Irish families; their names, arms, and origins. Illustrated by Myra Maguire. [3d ed., rev.] New York, Crown Publishers [1972] 365 p. illus. CS498.M3 1972
Bibliography: p.316-336
—More Irish families. Galway [Ire.] O'Gorman, 1960. 320 p. col. coats or arms.
CS498.M32
Bibliography: p. 285-290.
—Supplement to Irish families. Baltimore, Genealogical Book Co. [1964] 163 p.
CS498.M33
"Additional notes on names dealt with in

Irish Families and *More Irish Families*": p. 157-163.

MacLysaght, Edward. The surnames of Ireland. [Dublin] Irish University Press [1973] xxi, 377 p. maps.   CS2411.M25 1973
"Bibliography of Irish family history": p. 305-368

Woulfe, Patrick. Sloinnte Gaedheal is Gall: Irish names and surnames, collected and edited with explanatory and historical notes. Dublin, M. H. Gill, 1923. xlvi, 696 p.   CS2411.W6

Italian

Fucliia, Joseph G. Our Italian surnames. Evanston, Ill., Chandler's, 1949. 299 p.
Includes bibliographies.   CS2715.F8

Pinguentini, Gianni. I nostri cognomi. [Trieste, Stab. tip. nazionale, 1971] 152 p.   CS2715.P56

Jewish

Kessler, Gerhard. Die Familiennamen der Juden in Deutschland. Leipzig, Zentralstelle für Deutsche Personen- und Familiengeschichte, 1935. 151 p. (Mitteilungen der Zentralstelle für Deutsche Personen- und Familiengeschichte. Quellen und Darstellungen aus dem Gebiete der Genealogie und verwandter Wissenschaften, 53. Heft)   CS610.Z4, Heft 53
Bibliography: p. [116]-120

Lévy, Paul. Les noms des Israélites en France; histoire et dictionnaire. Paris, Presses universitaires de France, 1960. 210 p.
Bibliography: p. [3]-6   CS3010.L5

Oriental

Bauer, Wolfgang. Der chinesische Personenname; die Bildungsgesetze und hauptsächlichsten Bedeutungsinhalte von Ming, Tzu und Hsiao-Ming. Wiesbaden, O. Harrassowitz, 1959. 406 p. illus. (Asiatische Forschungen; Monographienreihe zur Geschichte, Kultur und Sprache der Völker Ostund Zentralasiens, Bd. 4)   CS2990.B3
Bibliography: p. [390]-406

Vroonen, Eugéne. Les noms de personnes en Orient et spécialement en Egypte. Noms musulmans: arabes, turcs. Noms chrétiens: arméniens, coptes, grecs, libanais et syriens, maltais. Noms israélites. Le Caire, Le Scribe égyptien, 1946. xvi, 191 p.   CS2950.V7
Bibliographic footnotes.
Includes information on surnames.

Weig, Johann. Die chinesischen Familiennamen nach dem Büchlein [Bei dja sing] nebst Anhang enthaltend Anagaben über berühmte Persönlichkeiten der chinesischen Geschichte. Tsingtau, Missionsdruckerei, 1931. 285 p. illus.   CS2990.W4

Portuguese & Brazilian

Guérios, Rosário F. M. Dicionário etimologico de nomes e sobrenomes. 2. ed. rev. e ampliada. Sao Paulo, Editora Ave Maria, 1973. 231 p.   CS2761.G8 1973
Bibliography: p. 225-230.

Liete de Vasconcellos Pereira de Mello, José. Antroponimia portuguesa. Lisboa, Imprensa Nacional, 1928. xix, 659 p.   CS2761.L4
Bibliography: p. [595]-615.

Nascentes, Antenor. Dicionário etimológico da língua portuguêsa. t. 2. Nomes próprios. Rio de Janeiro, F. Alves, 1952. xxvii, 389 p.
          PC5305.N3, v.2
Bibliography p. [xiii]-xxvii.
Includes information on surnames.

Romanian

Constantinescu, N. A. Dictionar onomastic romî-nesc. [Bucuresti] Editura Academiei Republicii Populare Romîne, 1963. lxxvii, 468 p. (Academia Republicii Populare Romîne. Comisia pentru Studiul Formarii Limbii si Poporului Romîn. [Publicatiile] 5)   CS2731.C6
Bibliography: p. lxvii-lxxv.

Slavic

Benes, Josef. O ceských prıjmenıch. Praha, Nakl. Ceskoslovenské akademie ved, 1962. 355 p. (Ceskoslovenska akademie ved. Studie a prameny, sv. 14)   CS2830.B4
Bibliography: p. 327-332.
—Rejstriky. Sest. Vera Dolezalová. Revidoval Miroslav Frydrich. Zvláštnı priloha zpravodaje Mıstopisné komise CSAV. Praha, 1970. 203 p.   CS2830.B4 Suppl.

Bubak, Józef. Nazwiska ludności dawnego starostwa nowotarskiego. Wroclaw, Zaklad Narodowy im. Ossolińskich, 1970-71. 2 v. map. (Komitet Jezykoznawstwa Polskiej Akademii Nauk. Prace onomastyczne, 14)   PG6576.B8
Bibliography: v. 2, p. [108]-185

Fedosiuk, IUrii A. Russkie familii. Popularnyi etimologicheskii slovar. Moskva, Detskaia literatura, 1972. 222 p. (Shkolnaia biblioteka)
          CS2815.F43

Golebiowska, Teresa. Antroponimia Orawy. Kraków, Nakl. Uniwersytetu Jagiellońskiego, 1971. 160 p. (Zeszyty naukowe Uniwersytetu Jagiellońskiego, 256)   PG6014.K732, zesz. 34
Prace jezykoznawcze, zesz. 34
Studia orawskie, nr. 6.
Summary in French.
Bibliography: p. [151]-155

Ilchev, Stefan. Rechnik na lichnite i familini imena u bulgarite. Sofiia, Izd-vo na Bulgarskata Akademiia na naukite, 1969. 626 p.
          CS2860.B8R4
At head of title: Bulgarska akademiia na

naukite. Institut za bulgarski ezik.
Includes bibliographies.

Jacknow, Helmut. Die slavischen Personennamen in Berlin bis zur tschechischen Einwanderung im 18. Jahrhundert; eine onomastisch-demographische Untersuchung. Berlin [Osteuropa-Institut]; Wiesbaden, In Kommission bei O. Harrassowitz, 1970. 244 p. (Veröffentlichungen der Abteilung für Slavische Sprachen und Literaturen des Osteuropa-Instituts (Slavisches Seminar) an der Freien Universität Berlin, Bd. 37)
CS2805.J3

> Bibliography: p. 1-17
> "Etymologisches Namenbuch": p. 79-211.

Maczyński, Jan. Nazwiska lodzian (XV-XIX wiek). Lodź, 1970. 278 p. (Lódzkie Towarzystwo Naukowe. Prace Wydzialu 1. Jezykoznawstwa, Nauki o Literaturze i Filozofii, nr. 71)
CS2840.M3

> Includes bibliographic references.

Neumann, Johann. Tschechische Familiennamen in Wien; eine namenskundliche Dokumentation. 14 000 Familiennamen, interpretiert bzw. übersetzt von berufenen Slawisten, Häufigkeitszahl und Quellennachweis bei jedem Namen. Wien, Verlag A. Holzhausens Nfg., 1972. 269. p.
CS2830.Z9V45

> "Quellenverzeichnis": p. [268]-269.

Rospond, Stanislaw. Slownik nazwisk śląskich. Wroclaw, Zaklad Narodowy im. Ossolińskich, 1967+
CS2840.R62

> At head of title: Instytut Slaski w Opolu.
> Bibliography: v. 1, p. [xlv]-xlvi.
> Contents: cz. 1. A-F.—cz. 2. G-K.—

Unbegaun, Boris O. Russian surnames. Oxford, Clarendon Press, 1972. xvii, 529 p. PG2576.U5

> Bibliography: p. [415]-424.

South African

Rosenthal, Eric. South African surnames. Cape Town, H. Timmins, 1965. 262 p. CS3080.S6R6

> Bibliography: p. 261-262.

Swiss

Familiennamenbuch der Schweiz. Répertoire des noms de famille suisses. Repertorio dei nomi di famiglia svizzeri. 2., erw. Aufl. Zürich, Polygraphischer Verlag, 1968-71. 6 v.
CS2625.F34

> Contents: Bd. 1. A-C.—Bd. 2. D-G.—Bd. 3. H-L.—Bd. 4. M-R.—Bd. 5. S.—Bd. 6. T-Z.

June 1977

IMMIGRANT ARRIVALS
A Short Guide to Published Sources

For one who is tracing the arival of an ancestor, the published sources may prove disappointing. Too often, it seems, they do not contain the specific names and details that are sought. For this information one must usually turn to records and documents such as those held in the National Archives

Study of the published sources may be valuable, however, if the general knowledge gained provides clues for further search or ties together fragments gleaned earlier. For example, awareness of immigration patterns and the dispersal of ethnic groups throughout the country may serve to focus one's search on a particular time frame and geographic region. Similarly, a knowledge of changing ship design and construction through the years may illuminate some scrap of information that family legend has reported about an ancestor's travel. With this thought in mind, the following list has been compiled to include material somewhat broader than the immediate question of arrivals.

Ship Records

Cutler, Carl C. Queens of the western ocean; the story of America's mail and passenger sailing lines. With a foreword by Chester W. Nimitz. Annapolis, U.S. Naval Institute [1961] xxi, 672 p. illus., maps (on lining papers), plans, ports. HE745.C8

> Bibliographic references included in "Notes" (p. 360-367). "Index to ships' names": p. 579-613.

Dunn, Laurence. Famous liners of the past, Belfast built. Illustrated by Laurence Dunn. London, A. Coles [1964] 238 p. illus. HE565.G7D8

> Descriptions arranged by steamship line. Many of the ships included were built in the 20th century.

Gibbs, Charles R. V. British passenger liners of the five oceans, a record of the British passenger lines and their liners from 1838 to the present day. London, Putnam [1963] 559 p. illus.
HE565.G7G5

> "North Atlantic section": p. 173-321.

Gibbs, Charles R. V. Passenger liners of the western ocean; a record of the North Atlantic steam and motor passenger vessels from 1838 to the present day. 2d ed. [completely rev.] London,

— 68 —

Staples Press [1957] 434 p. illus., maps.

VM18.G5 1957

Lloyd's register of shipping. London, Wyman. annual. HE565.A3L7

"Founded 1760."

Descriptive details are arranged alphabetically by ship. Before 1834 only ships in ports of the United Kingdom were surveyed. The survey was gradually extended to foreign ports so that the register is now international. Its history and the development of its classification scheme are described in the *Annals of Lloyd's Register,* centenary ed. ([London, Lloyd's Register, 1934] 251 p. HE565.H3L8 1934)

Macpherson, Arthur G. H. Mail and passenger steamships of the nineteenth century. Philadelphia, J. B. Lippincott Co. [1929?] xxvii, 324 p. plates (part col.)   VK19.M3 1929

Morton Allan directory of European passenger steamship arrivals for the years 1890 to 1930 at the port of New York and for the years 1904 to 1926 at the ports of New York, Philadelphia, Boston and Baltimore. New York, Immigration Information Bureau [ᶜ1931] 268 p. HE945.A2D5 1931

An earlier edition was published in 1928 *as Directory Relating to Record of Arrival of Passenger Steamships at the ports of New York, Philadelphia, Boston and Baltimore 1904 to 1926 Inclusive* (136 p. HE945.A2D5) and reprinted in San Francisco by R and E Research Associates in 1972 (HE565.U7D57 1972).

Smith, Eugene W. Trans-Atlantic passenger ships, past and present. Boston, G. H. Dean Co. [1947] 350 p. illus. HE565.A3S5

Includes alphabetic list and brief description of "Principal North Atlantic passenger ships built between 1840 and 1940."

Tute, Warren. Atlantic conquest; the ships and the men of the North Atlantic passenger services, 1816-1961. London, Cassell [1962] 247 p. illus., map, ports. VK18.T8 1962

Bibliography: p. 238.

A general history of shipping with an emphasis on passenger transport.

The Immigration Experience; Descriptions of the Crossing and Arrival

Coleman, Terry. Going to America. New York, Pantheon Books [1972] 317 p. illus.

JV7618.N7C58 1972

London edition has title *Passage to America; a History of Emigrants from Great Britain and Ireland to America in the Mid-nineteenth Century.*

Bibliography: p. [251]-286.

Greenhill, Basil. The great migration; crossing the Atlantic under sail. London, National Maritime Museum, H. M. Stationery Off.,

1968. 32 p. illus., facsims., maps. JV6451.G73

Includes sketches of shipboard life reproduced from the *Illustrated London News.*

Guillet, Edwin C. The great migration; the Atlantic crossing by sailing-ship since 1770. [2d ed. Toronto] University of Toronto Press [ᶜ1963] 284, 16 p. illus. JV6451.G8 1963

"Supplement . . . including two notable diaries not used in the original book" (16 p.) at end.

Bibliography: p. 257-274.

Jones, Maldwyn A. Destination America. London, Weidenfeld and Nicolson [1975] 256 p. illus.

JV6450.J62 1976

"Notes on sources": p. 248-250. "Further reading": p. 251-252.

Novotny, Ann. Strangers at the door; Ellis Island, Castle Garden, and the great migration to America. Riverside, Conn., Chatham Press [1971] 160 p. illus. JV6450.N6

Bibliography: p. 152-153.

Includes four "picture essays."

Turner, Thomas J. The hygiene of emigrant ships. Read before the American Public Health Association, December, 1880. Boston, Franklin Press: Rand, Avery, 1881. 71 p.

Bibliography: p. 71. JV6518.T9

U.S. *Congress. Senate. Select Committee on Sickness and Mortality on Board Emigrant Ships.* Report of the Select Committee on the Senate of the United States on the sickness and mortality on board emigrant ships. August 2, 1854. Washingotn, B. Tucker, Senate Printer, 1854. 147 p. JV6518.A4 1854 Rare Bk. Coll.

Reprinted in New York by Arno Press in 1977 (JV6518.U54 1977).

Passenger Records

Lists of early immigrant were often published in local history and genealogical journals or as small monographs. A bibliography first compiled by Harold Lancour gives the locations of many of these lists. The third edition, *A Bibliography of Ship Passenger Lists, 1538-1825; Being a Guide to Published Lists of Early Immigrants to North America,* revised and enlarged by Richard J. Wolfe, was published in 1963 by the New York Public Library (137 p. Z7164.I3L2). Appendixes include "Published Lists of Ship Passengers and Immigrants after 1825" (p. 87-91) and "Passenger Arrival Records in the National Archives" (p. 93-99). The book is obtainable from the publisher, the New York Public Library, for $10.00. The order number is ISBN O-87104-023-9. There is no index to the family names that appear in the vaious lists, but publication of such a list, compiled by P. William Filby for Gale Research Co., is expected.

Items that appear in the Lancour bibliography are not included in the list that follows, except in instances where they have been reprinted in a more accessible form.

Dickson, R. J. Ulster emigration to colonial America, 1718-1775. London, Routledge & K. Paul [1966] xiv, 320 p. map. (Ulster-Scot historical series, no. 1)   E184.S4D47

Bibliography: p. 208-311.

Appendixes contain data on ships, emigrants, and ports.

Ellis, Eilish. Emigrants from Ireland, 1847-1852: state-aided emigration schemes from crown estates in Ireland. Baltimore, Genealogical Pub. Co., 1977. 68 p.   JV7711.E37 1977

Reprint of the 1960 edition published in *Analecta Hibernica* (Dublin) no. 22 under the title "State-Aided Emigration Schemes From Crown Estates in Ireland, c. 1850."

Includes bibliographic references and lists of emigrants.

Emigrants to Pennsylvania, 1641-1819. A consolidation of ship passenger lists from the *Pennsylvania Magazine of History and Biography*. Edited by Michael Tepper. Baltimore, Genealogical Pub. Co., 1975. 292 p.   E148.E5 1975

Index of ships: p. 263. Index of names: p. 265-292.

Pertinent items were chosen from Lancour's bibliography and reprinted here.

Immigrants to the middle colonies: a consolidation of ship passenger lists and associated data from the *New York Genealogical and Biographical Record*. Edited by Michael Tepper. Baltimore, Genealogical Pub. Co., 1978. 178 p.   F106.I47

Index of names: p. 155-178.

McCracken, George E. The *Welcome* claimants proved, disproved and doubtful with an account of some of their descendants. With a foreword by Walter Lee Sheppard, Jr. Baltimore, Genealogical Pub. Co., 1970. xv, 660 p. facsims., plates. (Publications of the Penn's colony, v. 2. Welcome Society of Pennsylvania, no. 2)   F148.W45 no. 2

The *Welcome* brought William Penn and other passengers to Pennsylvania in 1682.

Massachusetts. *Superintendent of Alien Passengers*. A list of alien passengers, bonded from January 1, 1847, to January 1, 1851, for the use of the overseers of the poor in the Commonwealth. Prepared under the direction of the Auditor of Accounts by J. B. Munroe, Superintendent of Alien Passengers for the Port of Boston. Baltimore, Genealogical Pub. Co., 1971. 99 p.   JV6518.M37 1971

"Originally published in Boston, 1851."

Olsson, Nils W. Swedish passenger arrivals in New York, 1820-1850. Chicago, Swedish Pioneer Historical Society, 1967. xx, 391 p. illus., facsims., fold col. plate, ports.   E184.S23O43

Passengers to America: a consolidation of ship passenger lists from the *New England Historical and Genealogical Register*. Edited by Michael Tepper. Baltimore, Genealogical Pub. Co., 1977. 554 p.   CS68.P37 1977

Index of names: p. 481-550. Index of ships: p. 551-554.

Pertinent items listed in Lancour's bibliography are reprinted here with a new introduction.

Port arrivals and immigrants to the City of Boston. 1715-1716 and 1762-1769. Compiled under the direction of William H. Whitmore. With a reconstructed index. Baltimore, Genealogical Pub. Co., 1973. 111 p.

F73.25.P67

An excerpt (p. 229-317 inclusive) from *A Volume of Records Relating to the Early History of Boston Containing Miscellaneous Papers*, prepared by the Registry Dept. of Boston and published in 1900.

Rasmussen, Louis J. San Francisco ship passenger lists. Baltimore, Genealogical Pub. Co., 1978. xvi, 273 p.   CS68.R37

Originally published in Colma, Calif. 1965.

"This volume is the first in a series of volumes which will reflect the names of passengers arriving by vessels in the Port of San Francisco during the period of 1850 to 1875." Arrivals from 1850 to 1864 are included in this volume.

Surname index: p. 174-264.

Sheppard, Walter L., *comp*. Passengers and ships prior to 1684. Reprints of articles with corrections, additions and new materials. Baltimore, Genealogical Pub. Co., 1970. 245 p. illus., plans (part fold.) (Publications of the Penn's colony, v. 1. Welcome Society of Pennsylvania, no. 1)   F148.W45 no. 1

Includes bibliographic references.

Index of vessels: p. [211]-212. Index of names: p. [213]-245.

Contents: The real *Welcome* passengers, by Marion R. Balderston.—William Penn's twenty-three ships, with notes on some of their passengers, by M. R. Balderston.—The *Lyon* of Liverpool in the Chester port books, 1682, by M. R. Balderston.—Pennsylvania's 1683 ships and some of their passengers, M. R. Balderston.—Digest of ship and passenger arrivals in the Delaware, by W. L. Sheppard, Jr.—Goods to start a colony, by M. R. Balderston.—Early shipping to the Jersey shore of the Delaware, by W. L. Sheppard, Jr., and M. R. Balderston.—John West and the *Welcome*, by W. L. Sheppard, Jr.—Mrs. Thomas Wynne of Philadelphia and her family, by Francis J. Dallett.—The Philadelphia and Bucks County registers of arrivals compared, corrected and retranscribed by Hannah B. Roach.—Passengers on the *Friends' Adventure* and the *Endeavor*, by J. H. Battle.—The names of the early settlers of

Darby Township, Chester County, Pennsylvania, by Morgan Bunting.—The sailing of the ship *Submission* in the year 1682, with a true copy of the vessel's log, by L. Taylor Dickson, with corrections by H. B. Roach.—the first purchasers of Pennsylvania, by H. B. Roach.

Ship passenger lists: national and New England, 1600-1825. Edited and indexed by Carl Boyer, 3rd. Newhall, Calif., Boyer, 1977. 270 p.
CS68.S53

Index of ship names: p. 203-204. Index of place names: p. 204-215. Index of personal names: p. 216-267.

Contains many of the lists and abstracts of some of the articles from items 1-71 of Lancour's bibliography. "A second volume, covering lists numbered 72 to 115, for New York and New Jersey, is in preparation, and materials for a third volume, lists 116 to 197, for Pennsylvania and Delaware, are being collected. A fourth volume would deal with the Southern lists. Depending on demand additional cross-index volumes and lists subsequent to 1825 will be considered."

Whyte, Donald. A dictionary of Scottish emigrants to the U.S.A. Baltimore, Magna Carta Book Co., 1972. 504 p.　E184.S3W49

Bibliography: p. 467-472. Index of places of origin: p. 493-504.

Names of over 6,000 immigrants alphabetically arranged.

Immigrants in America

The body of material published about individual ethnic groups is far too extensive to be listed here. By way of introduction a few general histories of American immigration (some of which contain lengthy bibliographies) are described.

Bromwell, William J. History of immigration to the United States, exhibiting the number, sex, age, occupation, and country of birth, of passengers arriving in the United States by sea from foreign countries, from September 30, 1819 to December 31, 1855; compiled entirely from official date: with an introductory review of the progress and extent of immigration to the United States prior to 1819, and an appendix, containing the naturalization and passenger laws of the United States. New York, Redfield, 1856. 225 p.　JV4643.B8

Reprinted in New York by Arno Press and A. M. Kelley (1969).

Statistical data are presented in yearly tables. No passenger names are included.

Davie, Maurice R. World immigration, with special reference to the United States. New York, Macmillan Co., 1936. 588 p. illus., maps (part fold.)　JV6032.D3

"Bibliographic notes" at end of each chapter.

Hansen, Marcus L. The Atlantic migration, 1607-1860; a history of the continuing settlement of the United States. Edited with a foreword by Arthur M. Schlesinger. Cambridge Mass., Harvard University Press, 1940. xvii, 391 p. illus.　JV6451.H3

"Bibliography and notes": p. [309]-371.

Jones, Maldwyn A. American immigration. [Chicago] University of Chicago Press [1960] 359 p. illus. (The Chicago history of American civilization)　JV6450.J6

Bibliography: p. 325-341.

OUT-OF-PRINT MATERIALS AND REPRINTED PUBLICATIONS

Dealers

Classified telephone directories usually list booksellers who specialize in out-of-print publications. The *New York Times Book Review* and general literary periodicals like the *Atlantic Monthly* often carry advertisements of out-of-print dealers and book-search services.

The collections of most large libraries contain several reference sources listing booksellers. Among these are the *American Book Trade Directory,* which gives names, addresses, and specialties of U.S. booksellers by place, and a list of Canadian booksellers, and *AB Bookman's Yearbook,* which provides a list of U.S. and Canadian dealers arranged by subject specialty. The *ABAA Membership List,* a directory of booksellers arranged by name, geographic area, and specialty; the *Directory of American Book Specialists* (New York, Continental Pub. Co [1974] 187 p.), listing U.S. and Canadian booksellers by specialty; *Book Dealers in North America; a Directory of Dealers in Secondhand and Antiquarian Books in Canada and the United States of America* (London, Sheppard Press, 1954/55+), with listings by name, place, and specialty; and *The Antiquarian Booktrade, an International Directory of Subject Specialists* (Metuchen, N.J., Scarecrow Press, 1972. 176 p.), by B. Donald Grose, which lists by specialty nearly 2,000 antiquarian booksellers throughout the world, may also be available in these libraries. Upon request (accompanied by a self-addressed, stamped envelope), the Antiquarian Booksellers' Association of America, Inc. (Shop 2, Concourse, 630 Fifth Avenue, New York, N.Y. 10020), will send a folder containing an alphabetical list of its members, with their addresses and specialties, and a statement entitled "When Books Are Sold or Appraised — Useful Guidelines."

Reprints

Many scarce books and periodicals of all kinds are now being brought back into print by publishers specializing in this type of production, such as the Johnson Reprint Corporation and the Kraus Reprint Company. Most of these firms issue catalogs of their publications, some of which are included in the *Publishers' Trade List Annual,* also available in nearly all large libraries. Among the general guides to this type of reprint are:

Announced reprints. v. 1+ Feb. 1696+ Washington, Microcard Editions. quarterly.

Bulletin of reprints. v. 11+ 1974+ M†unchen, Verlag Dokumentation. quarterly.

Catalog of reprints in series. 21st ed. Robert M. Orton, editor. Metuchen, N.J., Scarecrow Press, 1972. 922 p.

Guide to reprints. 1967+ Kent, Conn., Guide to Reprints, Inc. annual.

International bibliography of reprints. Edited by Christa Gnirss. New York, R. R. Bowker Co., 1976+
    Contents: v. 1. Books and serials.—

Ostwald, Renate. Nachdruckverzeichnis von Einzelwerken, Serien und Zeitschriften aus allen Wissensgebieten (Reprints). Wiesbaden, G. Nobis, 1965+

Reprint bulletin — book reviews. v. 1+ June 1955+ Dobbs Ferry, N.Y., Oceana Publications. bimonthly.

Reprint review. v. 1+ Nov. 1969+ [London, Garratt Freeman Associates] quarterly.

Williams, Sam P. Reprints in print — serials, 1969,covering reprints of scholarly serials and monographs in series in print and available as of December 31, 1969. [2d ed.] Dobbs Ferry, N.Y., Oceana Publications, 1970. 577 p.

Photographic Reproduction

Some out-of-print publications can be difficult or time-consuming to locate on the antiquarian market and may not have been reprinted. In such cases, copies may sometimes by obtainable through various methods of photographic reproduction.

Full-size paper copies of books, magazine articles, and other materials can be obtained by use of the electrostatic process. The Library of Congress Photoduplication Service can produce Xerox and other types of copies from materials in the Library's collections, subject to copyright or other restrictions. Further details, including rates, are obtainable upon request from the Library of Congress, Photoduplication Service, Washington D.C. 20540.

There are also several commercial organizations which specialize in producing electrostatic copies of scarce books. Among them are University Microfilms International, 300 North Zeeb Road, Ann Arbor, Michigan 48106, and Micro Photo Division, Bell & Howell Company, Old Mansfield Road, P.O. Box 774, Wooster, Ohio 44691. They produce fullsize copies of out-of-print books, provided they can locate a copy of the book and obtain permission from the copyright holder where needed. Information of the charges for these services is available upon application to these companies. Many libraries have electrostatic or other copiers, which can produce full-size paper copies of pages from books, periodicals, and other materials in their collections, subject to copyright or other restrictions.

Many scarce materials are copied on 35-mm. roll microfilm, microfiche (small sheets of film, similar in appearance to snapshot negatives), or opaque microform (cards on which the material is printed in extremely small size). However, publications reproduced in these forms can be used only with special reading machines. If such devices are available in a nearby library or other facility, a librarian may be able to help you determine the organizations to which you can turn for microcopies. Many of the materials available in microform are listed in the *Guide to Microforms in Print* (Westport, Conn., Microform Review, 1961+ annual), the *Subject Guide to Microforms in Print* (Westport, Conn., Microform Review, 1962+ annual, Eva M. Tilton's *Union List of Publications in Opaque Microforms*, 2d ed. (New York, Scarecrow Press, 1964. 744p.), the *National Register of Microform Masters* (Washington, Library of Congress, Sept. 1965+ annual), and *Newspapers in Microform* (Washington, Library of Congress, 1948+). A list of libraries with facilities for copying materials in their collections can be found in Joseph Z. Nitecki's *Directory of Library Reprographic Services, a World Guide,* 6th ed. ([Weston, Conn.] Published for the Reproduction of Library materials Section, RTSD-American Library Association, by Microform Review, Inc., [c1976] 178 p.). The *American Library Directory* (New York, R. R. Bowker Co., 1923+ biennial) indicates the availability of microfilming facilities and reading machines for various types of microforms in the libraries listed.

CHAPTER 7

NATIONAL ARCHIVES

The National Archives has custody of millions of records relating to persons who have had dealings with the Federal Government. The National Archives is unable to make extensive searches but, given enough identifying information, will try to find a record about a specific person. Most of the records, subject to some restrictions, may be freely consulted at the National Archives in Washington D.C. or the General Archives Division in Suitland MD, and at the Regional Archives Branches.

Censuses

The National Archives has microfilmed all of the available census schedules and the indexes to them. A positive microfilm copy of these schedules is available at a moderate cost per roll. The rolls are arranged alphabetically by State and thereunder alphabetically by county.(See Census.)

Mortality Schedules

Whenever possible, the National Archives is acquiring microfilm copies of the mortality schedules of the 1850-1880 censuses from the various depositories where they are held. The schedules show the name, the month and the cause of death, and the State, territory or country of birth of each person who died during the year that preceded the taking of each of the censuses.

The National Archives has some or all of the available mortality schedules on microfilm for the following States: Arizona, Colorado, District of Columbia, Delaware, Georgia, Illinois, Kansas, Kentucky, Louisiana, Massachusetts, Minnesota, Montana, Nebraska, New Jersey, North Carolina, North Dakota, South Carolina, Tennesee, Texas, Utah, Vermont, Virginia, and Washington.

Records for the District of Columbia

Records for the District of Columbia are found in the General Archives Division, Suitland MD. They include naturalization records, copies of wills, 1801-1888; Records relating to the administration of estates, 1801-1878. A search of these records requires the name of the person in question, the type of records involved, and the approximate date of the transaction.

Indian Records

Indian Records kept in the National Archives are arranged by tribes, from 1830 to 1940. They include lists of Indians (mostly Cherokee, Chickasaw, Choctaw, and Creek) who moved west during the period 1830-1846; annuity pay rolls, 1841-1949; annual census rolls, 1885-1940 and Eastern Cherokee claims, 1902-1910.

Land Records

The land records (dated 1800-1974) in the General Archives Division include bounty land warrant files, donation land entry files, homestead application files, and private land claims files relating to the entry of individual settlers on land in the public land states. There are no land records for the Thirteen Original States and Maine, Vermont, West Virginia, Kentucky, Tennessee, Texas, and Hawaii. Records for these States are maintained by the States (see Land Records).

The General Archives Division has a name index to land entries in Alabama, Alaska, Arizona, Florida, Louisiana, Nevada, and Utah for the period 1800-1908, and will search the index if the full name of the applicant and the name of the State or territory is given. A search of the records for all other public lands requires the applicant's full name, a description of the land, the name of the land office, type of entry, and certificate number. The General Archives Division has a name index of land entries after 1908 for all public land states.

Naturalization Records

The General Archives Division has naturalization proceedings of the District of Columbia courts 1802-1926. The National Archives has photocopies of indexes of naturalization documents 1887-1906 filed by the courts in Maine, Massachusetts, New Hampshire and Rhode Island. A search of these records will be made for information before September 27, 1906, if given the full name of the petitioner and the approximate date of naturalization.

Passenger Lists

The National Archives has incomplete series of customs passenger lists and immigration passenger lists of ships arriving from abroad at Atlantic and Gulf of Mexico ports. These lists very from port to port from 1800 to 1952. The National Archives will search the customs passenger lists if, in addition, the name of the passenger and the name of the port of entry, the name of the vessel and the approximate date of arrival or the port of embarkation is given or the exact date of arrival. The National Archives will search the immigration passenger lists that are over 50 years old if an inquirer can give the full name and age of the passenger and names and ages of accompanying passengers, the name of the port of entry, the name of the vessel and the exact date of arrival.

Passport Applications

The National Archives has passport applications and related papers, 1791-1926, of U.S. citizens who intended to travel abroad and will make a limited search for age and citizenship information in such of these records as are at least 75 years old. The name of the person who applied for a passport and the place and approximate date of application should be supplied.

Claims for Pensions and Bounty Lands

Under numerous laws passed since the Revolutionary War, money and land have been awarded to Army, Navy, and Marine veterans and their widows and other dependents. Each claim—whether for bounty land or pension, whether submitted by the veteran, or whether approved—is filed under the name of the veteran on whose service the applicant based his claim. The National Archives has bounty land warrant application files based on service in wartime between 1775 and 1855 and pension application files based on military service between 1775 and 1916. Records of service in the Confederate States of America are not available in the National Archives. Special forms must be used to secure land bounty and pension information. (see Federal Forms)

Service Records — Army

Records relating to service in the U.S. Regular Army of officers (1789-1916) and enlisted men (1787-1912) during both war and peacetime as well as those persons serving during wartime in volunteer units raised by States and mustered into Federal Service (1775-1903) are in the National Archives. There are some records of soldiers for the Confederate Army. Form NATF Form 26 must be used to obtain information.

Service Records — Naval and Marine

The National Archives has records relating to American Naval and Marine service in the Revolutionary War (1775-1783) in the U.S. Navy (for officers, 1798-1902, and enlisted men 1798-1885) and in the U.S. Marine Corps (1798-1895). There are also some records for persons who served in the Confederate Navy and Marine Corps.

Only those requests for information about naval and marine service during the Revolutionary War and about service in the Confederate Navy and Marine Corps should be sent on GSA Form 6751. All other requests regarding naval and marine service records should be by letter. The request should include the mans name and the name of the war in which he served or the dates of his service. For enlisted men the name of at least one vessel on which he served (with approximate dates) must also be given and if possible, his place of enlistment.

Coast Guard Records

The Coast Guard was created by an act on January 28, 1915, which consolidated the former Revenue-Cutter and Life-Saving Services of the Department of the Treasury. The Bureau of Lighthouses of the Department of Commerce became a part of the U.S. Coast Guard on July 1, 1939. Revenue-Cutter Service vessels were manned by military personnel.

The National Archives has record books of Revenue-Cutter Service officer personnel. 1791-1919 which are indexed by name of officer. There are also record copies of officers commissions, 1791-1909; applications for cadet appointments and officers commissions 1832-1914; and muster rolls and payrolls of revenue cutters 1832-1914.

Vital Statistics

The National Archives has records of birth, marriages, and deaths at U.S. Army facilities, 1884-1912, with some records dated as late as 1928. It will search these records if provided with the following: birth records—name of child, names of his parents, place of birth, and month and year of birth; marriage records—names of contracting parties; death records—name, date, place and rank of deceased.

The National Archives also has some records of births and marriages, through 1941, and reports of some deaths through 1949, of American citizens abroad, registered at Foreign Service posts.

For a listing of various branches of the National Archives, see chapter on State Resource Centers.

List of Record Groups Arranged By Record Group Number
Found in the National Archives

The records in the National Archives are kept in groups and are assigned a number for easier access. For example, the census records are in Group 29. Below is a numerical listing of all the Record Groups in the National Archives. Following this listing is a bar graph showing the dates that each record group covers. If you look at the bar graph for the census records (Group 29) you will see that is spans from 1790 to 1960, the last year recorded before the publication of the book *Guide to the National Archives of the United States,* from which the information comes.

1 Records of the War Labor Policies Board............

2 Records of the National War Labor Board (World War I)................................

3 Records of the U.S. Housing Corporation............

4 Records of the U.S. Food Adminsitration............

5 Records of the U.S. Grain Corporation..............

6 Records of the U.S. Sugar Equalization Board, Inc......................................

7 Records of the Bureau of Entomology & Plant Quarantine......................................

8 Records of the Bureau of Agricultural Engineering.....

9 Records of the National Recovery Administration.....

10 Records of the National Commission on Law Observance and Enforcement................................

11 General Records of the U.S. Government.............

12 Records of the Office of Education.................

13 Records of the National Mediation Board............

14 Records of the U.S. Railroad Administration.........

15 Records of the Veterans Adminsitration..............

16 Records of the Office of the Secretary of Agriculture...

17 Records of the Bureau of Animal Industry...........

18 Records of the Army Air Forces....................

19 Records of the Bureau of Ships....................

20 Records of the Office of the Special Adviser to the President on Foreign Trade.......................

21 Records of District Courts of the U.S................

22 Records of the Fish and Wildlife Service.............

23 Records of the Coast and Geodetic Survey...........

24 Records of the Bureau of Naval Personnel............

25 Records of the National Labor Relations Board.......

26 Records of the U.S. Coast Guard...................

27 Records of the Weather Bureau....................

28 Records of the Post Office Department..............

29 Records of the Bureau of the Census...............

30 Records of the Bureau of Public Roads..............

31 Records of the Federal Housing Administration.......

32 Records of the U.S. Shipping Board.................

33 Records of the Federal Extension Service............

34 Records of the Federal Deposit Insurance Corporation ....

35 Records of the Civilian Conservation Corps..........

36 Records of the Bureau of Customs.................

37 Records of the Hydrographic Office.................

38 Records of the Office of the Chief of Naval Operations................................

39 Records of the Bureau of Accounts (Treasury)........

40 General Records of the Department of Commerce.....

41 Records of the Bureau of Marine Inspection and Navigation......................................

42 Records of the Office of Public Buildings and Grounds......................................

43 Records of International Conferences, Commissions, and Expositions................................

44 Records of the Office of Government Reports.........

45 Naval Records Collection of the Office of Naval Records and Library...............................

46 Records of the U.S. Senate........................

47 Records of the Social Security Administration........

48 Records of the Office of the Secretary of the Interior ....

49 Records of the Bureau of Land Management..........

50 Records of the Treasurer of the U.S.................

51 Records of the Bureau of the Budget................

52 Records of the Bureau of Medicine and Surgery.......

53 Records of the Bureau of the Public Debt............

54 Records of the Bureau of Plant Industry, Soils, and Agricultural Engineering......................

55 Records of the Government of the Virgin Islands......

56 General Records of the Department of the Treasury....

57 Records of the Geological Survey...................

58 Records of the Internal Revenue Service..............

59 General Records of the Department of State..........

60 General Records of the Department of Justice.........

61 Records of the War Industries Board.................

62 Records of the Council of National Defense..........

63 Records of the Committee on Public Information......

64 Records of the National Archives and Records Service......................................

65 Records of the Federal Bureau of Investigation........

66 Records of the Commission of Fine Arts.............

67 Records of the U.S. Fuel Administration.............

68 Records of the U.S. Coal Commission...............

69 Records of the Work Projects Administration.........

70 Records of the Bureau of Mines...................

71 Records of the Bureau of Yards and Docks...........

72 Records of the Bureau of Aeronautics...............

73 Records of the President's Organization on Unemployment Relief..............................

74 Records of the Bureau of Ordnance.................

75 Records of the Bureau of Indian Affairs..............

76 Records of Boundary and Claims Commissions and Arbitrations....................................

77 Records of the Office of the Chief of Engineers........

78 Records of the Naval Observatory...................

79 Records of the National Park Service................

80 General Records of the Department of the Navy.......

81 Records of the U.S. Tariff Commission..............

82 Records of the Federal Reserve System...............

83 Records of the Bureau of Agricultural Economics.....

84 Records of the Foreign Service Posts of the Department of State..............................

85 Records of the Immigration & Naturalization Service...

86 Records of the Women's Bureau...................

87 Records of the U.S. Secret Service.................

88 Records of the Food and Drug Administration........

89 Records of the Federal Fuel Distributor.............

DATE SPAN OF ACCESSIONED RECORDS BY RECORD GROUP

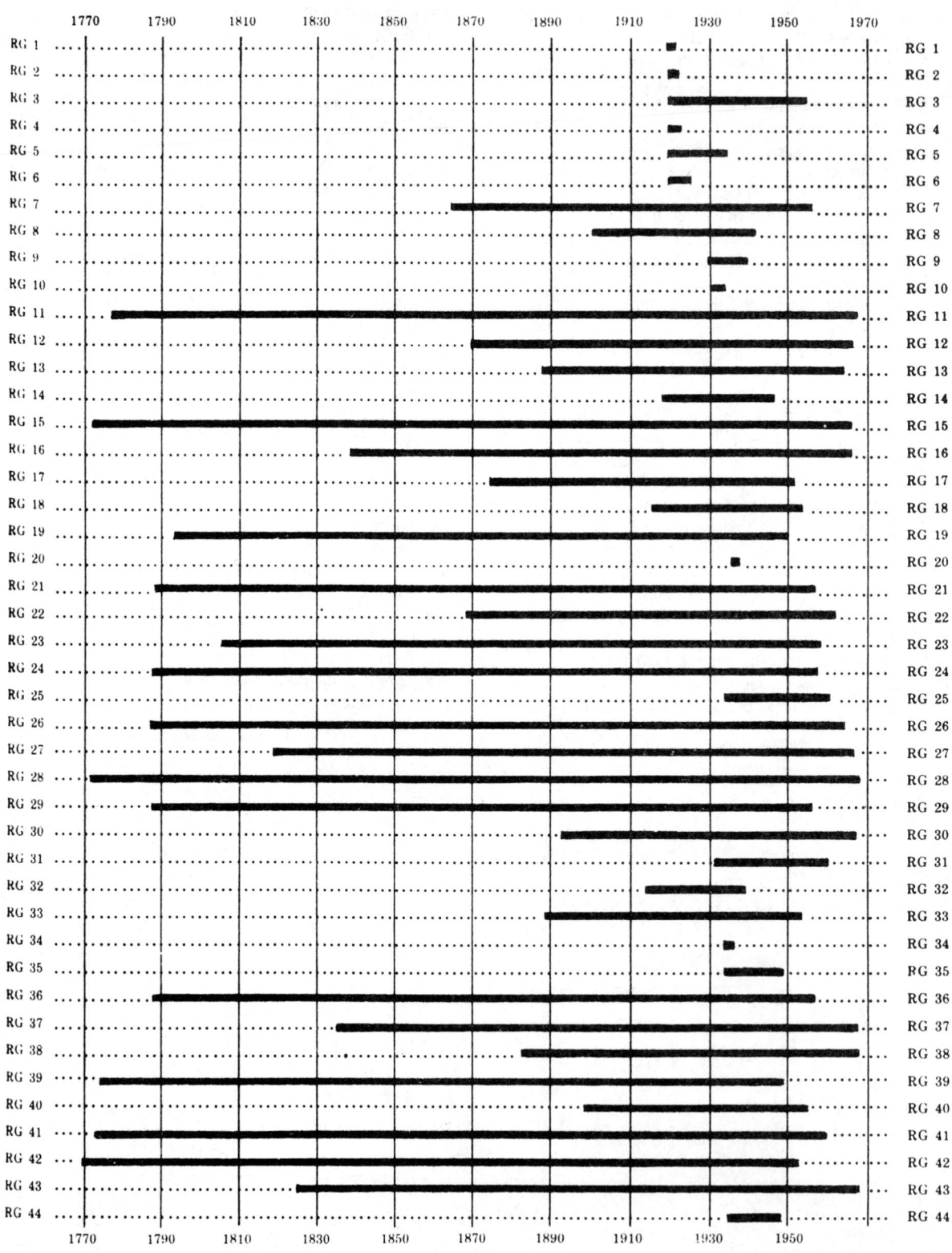

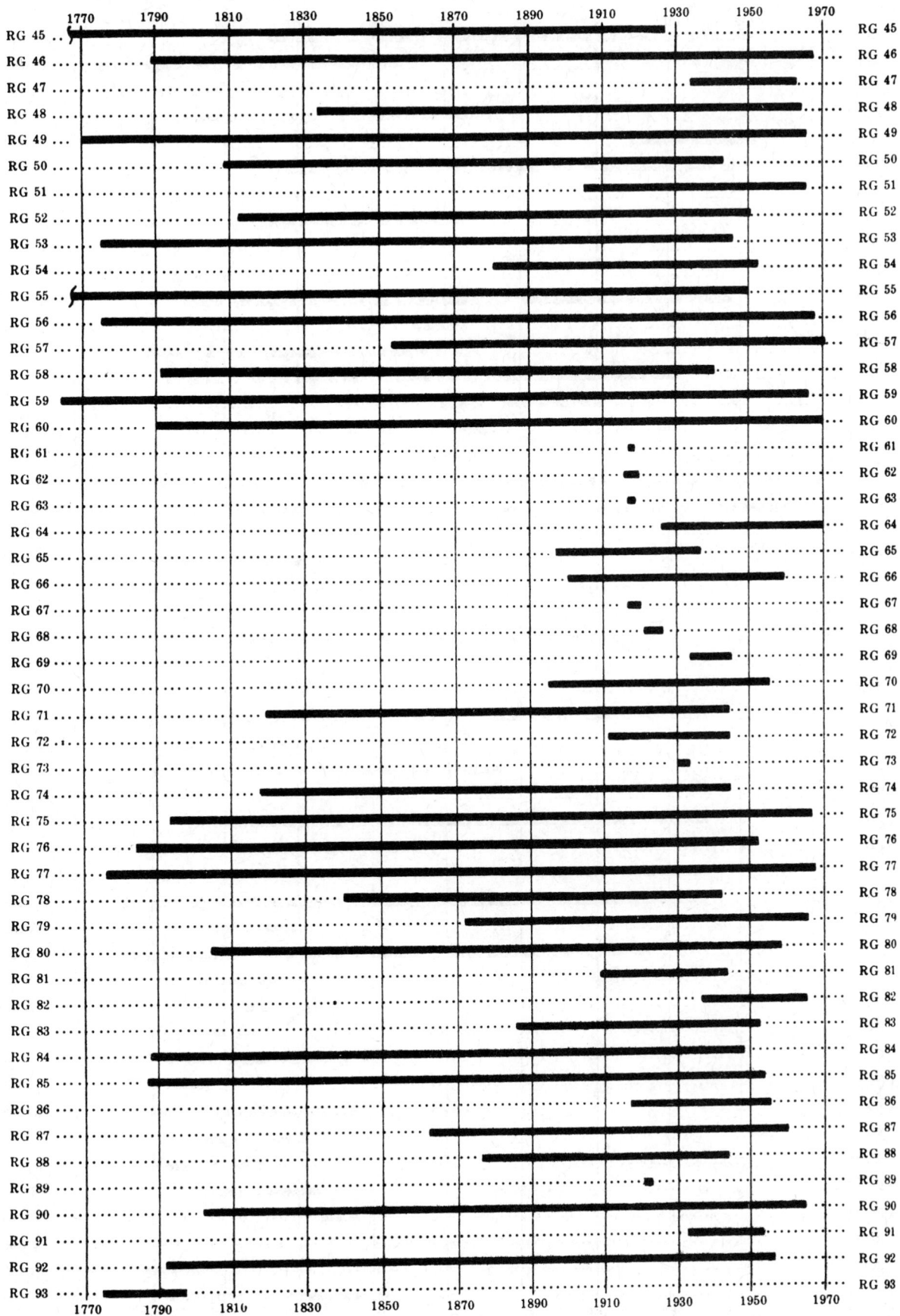

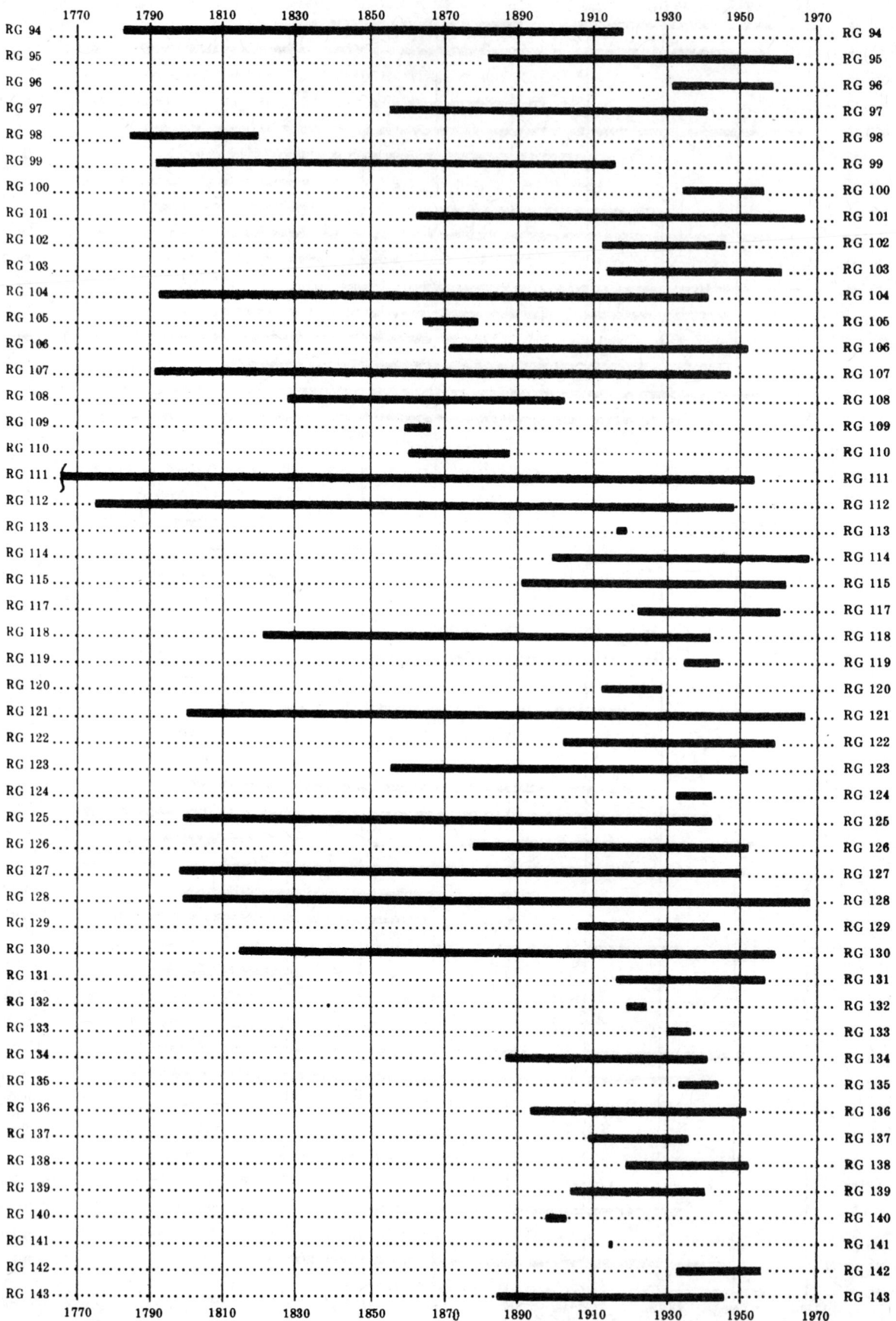

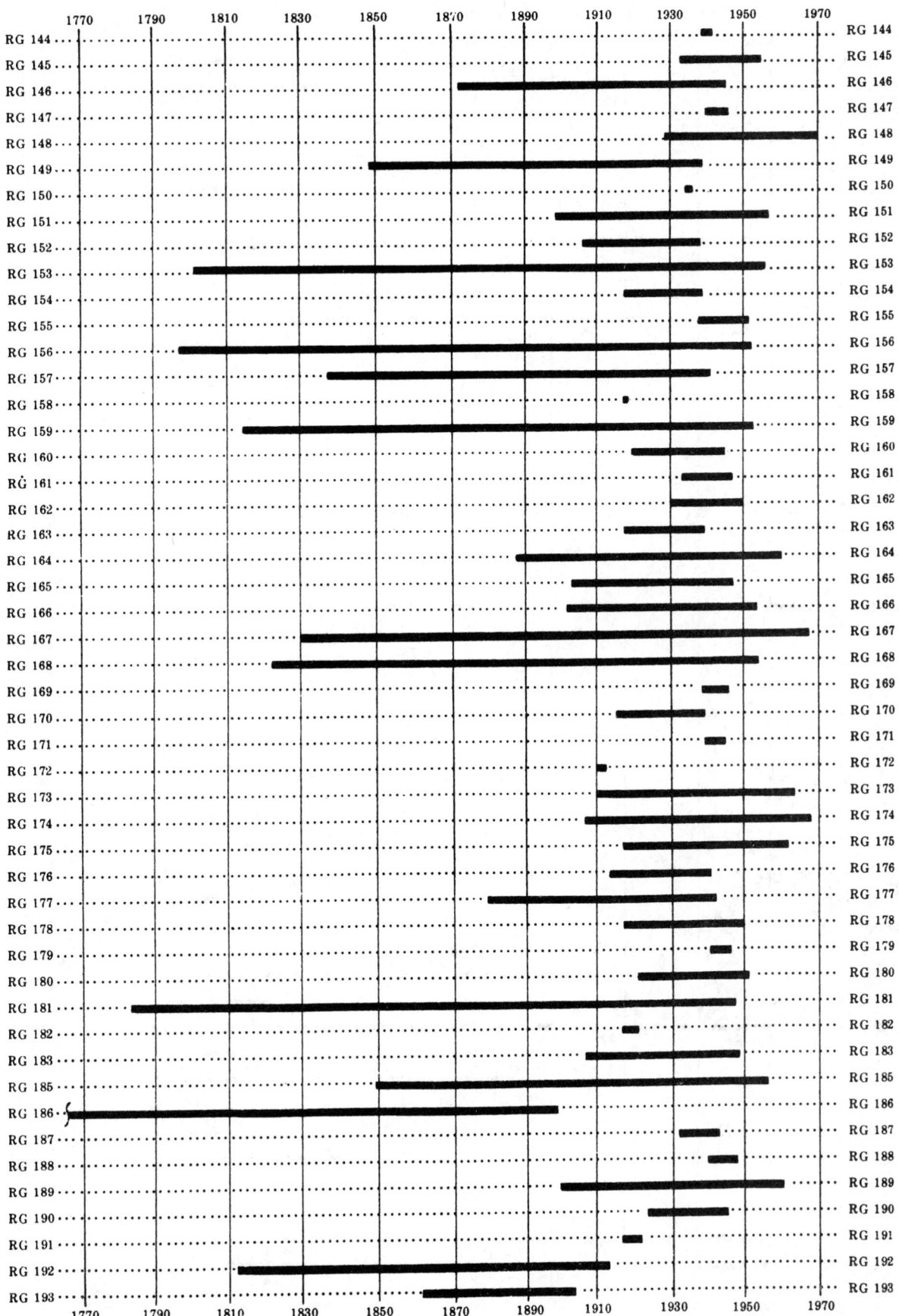

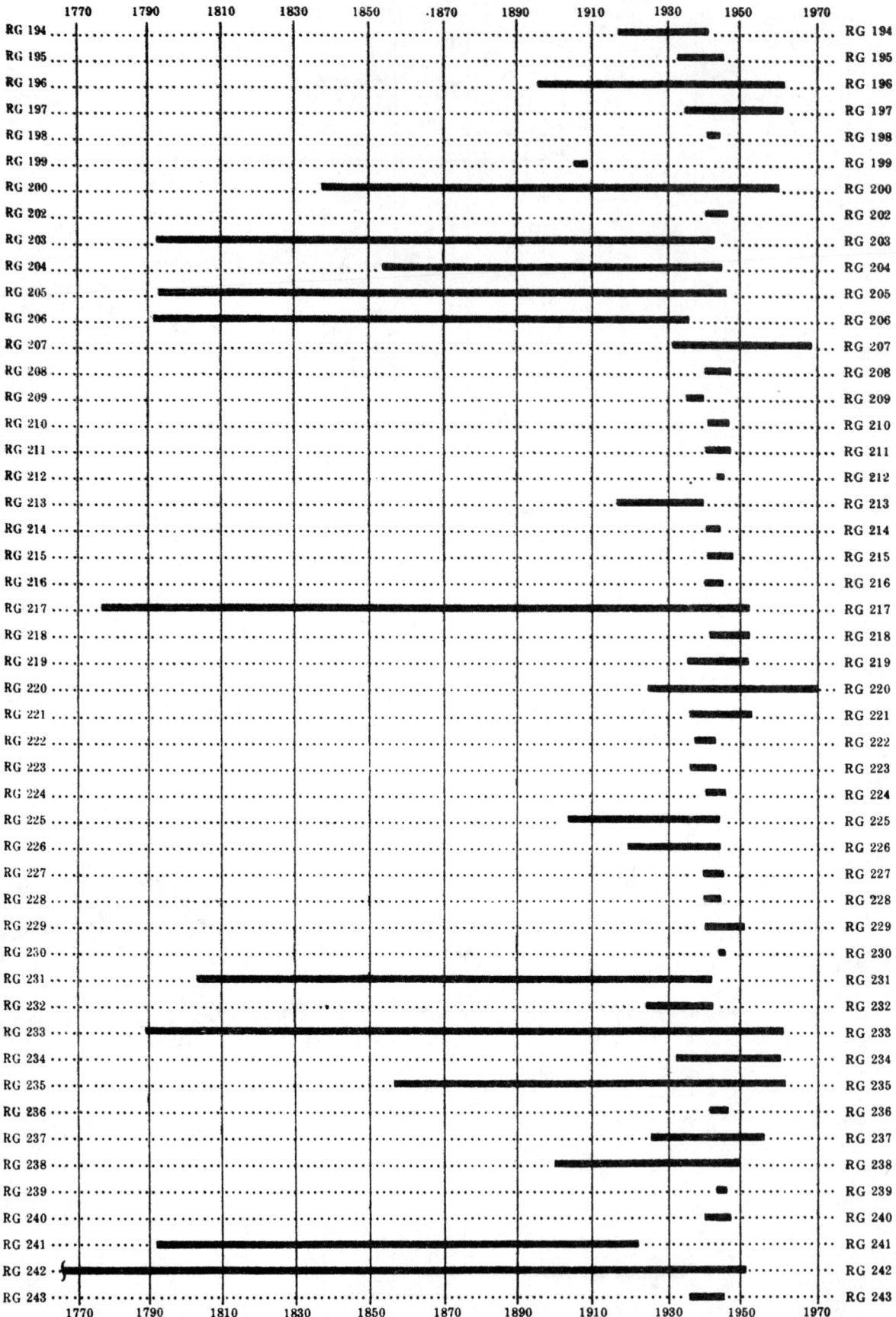

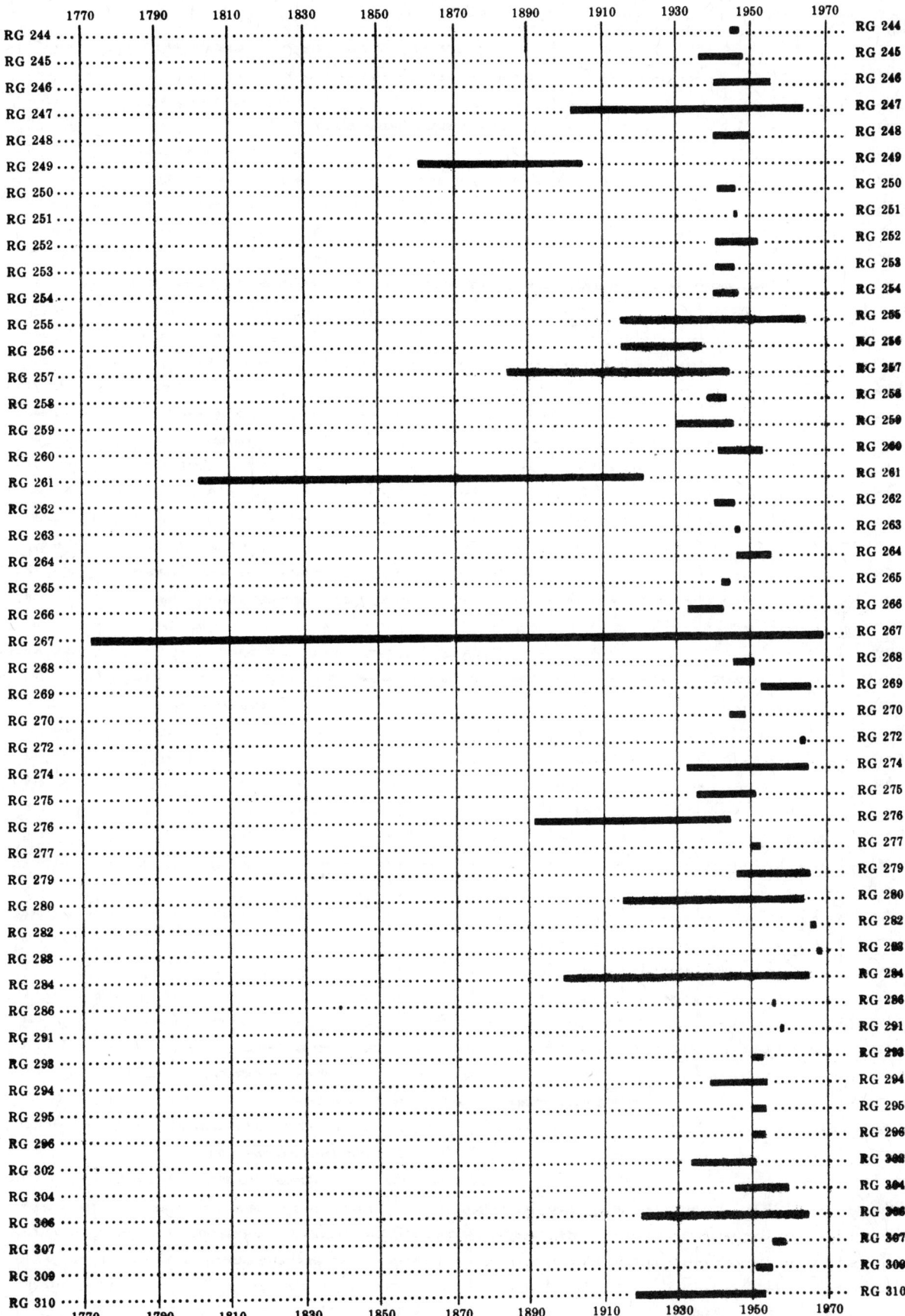

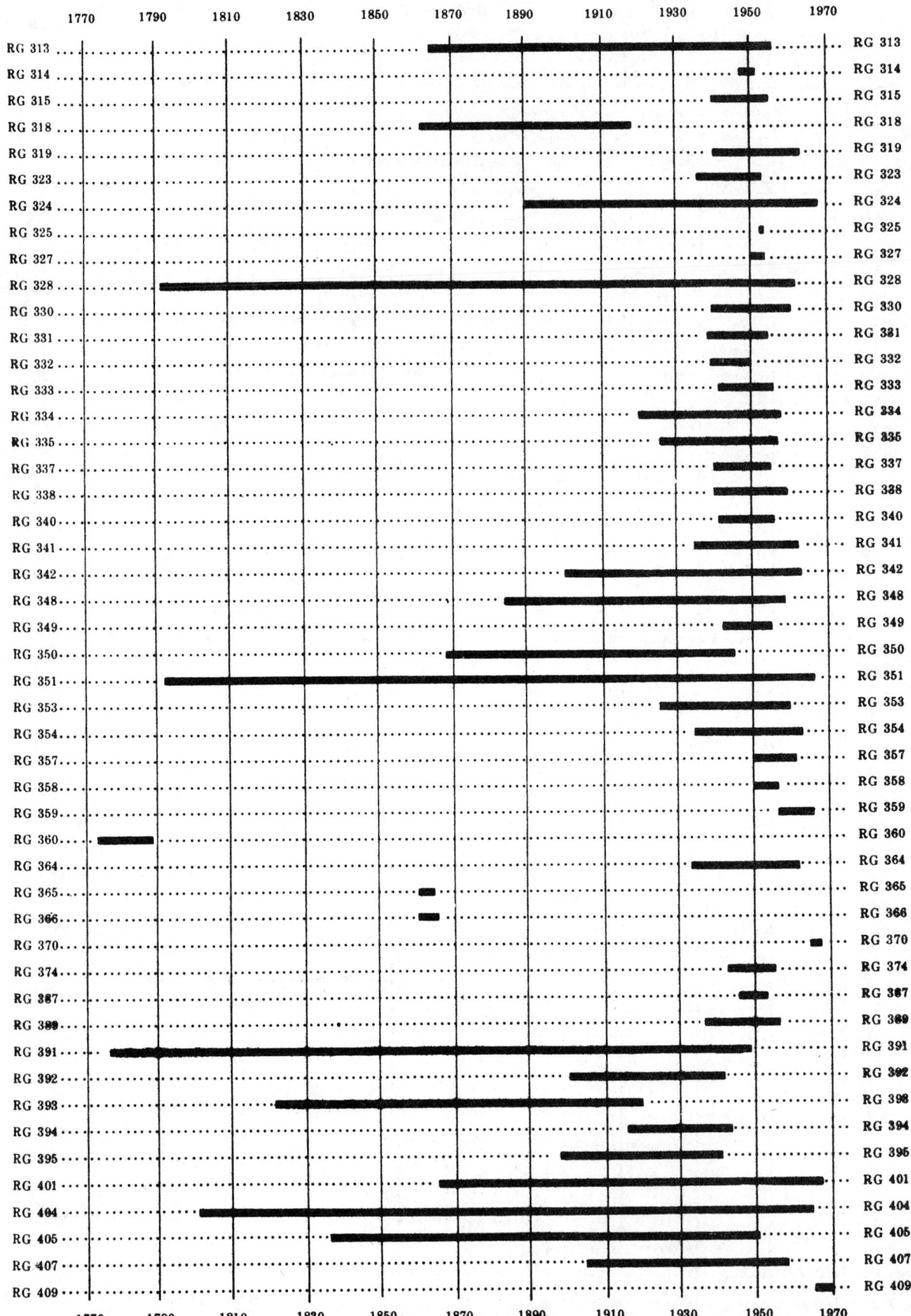

CHAPTER 8

D.A.R. LIBRARY

The Daughters of the American Revolution Library in Washington D.C. has a collection that is of great value to the genealogist. However, there are two important things to remember about this library. First, the D.A.R. Library does not maintain a genealogical research service, and second it is strictly a reference library. Therefore, no materials can leave the library and either you must do the research yourself or hire someone to check their records for you. However, their library is designed to help the patron with his research. (See instruction following)

Records of Value in the D.A.R. Library

A. Local records (one of the best collections)

1. The D.A.R. Library acts as the Archives for many of the Thirteen Original States
2. State, County and Local Histories
3. Land Records and County deeds
4. County Census and Taxpayer lists
5. City Records
6. Church Records
7. Abstracts of Wills
8. Cemetery Inscriptions
9. Sexton Records
10. Inventories of Estates
11. Published Vital Records
12. Oaths of Allegiance

B. Personal Records

1. Journals
2. Family Bible Records
3. Family Histories
4. Biographies
5. Early Settlers
6. Photographs and Photostats

C. War Records and Rosters

1. Abstracts of Revolutionary War Pensions
2. Abstracts of Revolutionary War Pensioners who served from New Hampshire
3. Patriot Index

D. Other Records

1. Collections of the Maryland Genealogical Records Committee
2. County Records of Various Tennessee Counties

3. County Records of Various West Virginia Counties
4. Miscellaneous records of various Alabama Counties.
5. D.A.R. Linage Books of Membership
6. Barbour Collection of Connecticut Vital Records to 1850
7. Early New York Records
8. Maryland Parish Records
9. Miscellaneous Court Records

E. Mortality Schedules 1850 to 1880 many of the original schedules are in the D.A.R. Library

Introduction To The NSDAR Library

Beginning Your Research:

Begin your research with the card catalogs. These catalogs are a guide to the material available in the Library collection. Each book is represented by at least one Subject Card and by an Author Card; some books also have a Title Card. You should start your research by using the most specific information on your search problem that you already have—such as the name of a person or a city. Look in the card catalogs for these specific subjects, such as the name of a person or city, or for the author or title of a particular book you wish to use. If you do not find any cards on these specific subjects—or if you wish to locate additional related material—then check the catalogs for cards on broader subjects such as a family name, a county, or a state. (Example: Look first for SMITH, JOHN; then SMITH FAMILY or SMITH FAMILY, PENNSYLVANIA). You will usually find other specific subjects as subdivisions of a geographical area. (Example: DUTCHESS CO., NEW YORK—CEMETERY RECORDS.)

How To Use The Catalogs:

There are several separate sections of the card catalog, each containing a different kind of information. It is important that you check all the relevant sections. Please note that subject headings and filing order vary between various sections of the card catalog. If you have difficulty finding things in the card catalog, please ask the person at the Reference Desk for assistance.

I. *The New Catalog* begins immediately to the right of the Reference Desk. It contains all of the cards being produced in the course of the Librarian General's Reclassification Project. There is a "Call Number" (or address) in the upper left hand corner of each card, which matches a label on the spine of the book described. This Call Number tells you where to find the book on the shelves. (Please read the section "Locating a Specific Book", and consult the map of the book stacks.)

There are three separate sections of the New Catalog, each identified by a different color of label on the drawer:

The *PINK* section contains Subject Cards about specific *individuals and families*. These cards are in alphabetical order by surname. If there are several cards with the *same surname*, the cards for individuals come before those for families. (Example of filing order: JOHNSON, JOHN, comes first, followed by JOHNSON FAMILY and JOHNSTON FAMILY-ALABAMA.

The *GREEN* section contains the rest of the Subject Cards, including those which refer to specific geographical locations as well as those covering more general subjects such as EMIGRANTS, U.S. CENSUS, etc. These cards are in strict alphabetical order, word by word. (Example: JOHNSON CO., MISSOURI comes before JOHNSON TOWNSHIP, INDIANA.)

The *YELLOW* section contains the Author and Title Cards. These are also arranged, word by word, in alphabetical order.

II. *The Old Catalog* is arranged in a *single alphabetical sequence;* that is, Subject, Author and Title Cards are all interfiled. In this section of the catalog, Subject Cards for specific locations (city or county) and for family names will follow cards for specific people with the same name. (Example: SMITH, HAROLD comes first, followed by SMITH CO., TEXAS and SMITH FAMILY.

Since these cards do not have Call Numbers on them you must find a clue to the location of the book described from the other information on the card. (Please read the section "Locating a Specific Book" for suggestions.)

In addition to the Subject, Author and Title Cards (many of which will be duplicated in the New Catalog sections) there are other special cards found only in the *Old Catalog:*

If you find a card in the Old Catalog that has *parentheses* within the body of the card, it is an ANALYTICAL CARD. This means that there is information about the subject you are researching in the book that is listed within the parentheses. The underlined word refers to the Author of the book. Example:

       King family   Louisiana

    Kendall, J. S.
        King family (in *his* History of
New Orleans. 1922. v.3, p. 1166)

This card indicates that there is some information about the King family of Louisiana on page 1166 of the third volume of a book by J. S. Kendall titled *History of New Orleans.* All of the information given on the analytical card is necessary to locate the book. It may also help to check the Author Card for the cited work in the YELLOW section of the New Catalog to see if a Call Number has been assigned to the book.

Special Procedures

If a card is marked L.C. (Locked Case), F.C. (File Case) or Special File, someone will locate the material for you. Please fill out a request slip with all the information shown on the card and take it to the Reference Desk. As a security measure, we will ask that you leave some form of positive identification at the desk while you are using this material. If a card from the new catalog reads "poor condition; kept in office" follow this same procedure to have someone get the book for you to use. These books cannot be photocopied.

Locating A Specific Book:

The Library stacks are open, and you may get the books yourself. Please do not take more than THREE books to your desk at any one time.

PLEASE DO NOT RESHELVE YOUR BOOKS!!! Leave the books that you are no longer using on your table. Staff members will circulate through the Library to pick up books that are no longer being used.

The DAR *Patriots' Index* is on a central desk with two lamps in front of the card catalogs. the DAR Lineage books and back issues of the DAR Magazine are located on Stack One. Research Aids are shelved on the small bookcase directly behind the visitor's register.

We do not have a numbering system for the Libary.

Books of a general nature that are not limited to a specific location or family or which have a call number beginning with GEN will be in the GENERAL SECTION of the Library (Stacks 1-3). The books in this section are arranged in alphabetical order by subject categories such as CENSUS, EMIGRANTS, etc. Collections of family histories will be found in this section with a call number beginning GEN/FAMILIES. The GENERAL SECTION is also the location of the set of volumes of Pension Records containing any pensions claimed by every DAR Patriot ancestor who was established prior to 1965. The access to these books is by a special card file located at the far right of the card catalog.

Books which deal with a specific geographic location or which have a call number beginning with the name of a state will be found in the STATE AND LOCAL HISTORY SECTION of the Library (Stacks 3-21 and the North Balcony*). These books are arranged alphabetically in sections by the name of the state*. Within each state section, the books are arranged in three divisions. The first division contains books on specific cities or counties within the state, arranged alphabetically by city or county name. (In Massachusetts, New York, Pennsylvania and the newly reclassified states, cities and counties are arranged separately.) The next division contains books on miscellaneous topics which pertain to the state as a whole. These books are arranged alphabetically by author. (In the newly reclassified states and Georgia, this division is arranged by categories similar to those used in the General section.) The last division of each state contains the Genealogical Records Committee (G.R.C.) Reports. These are arranged by some combination of chronology and volume number which varies from state to state.

*Books about the following states are located on the North Balcony: Alaska, Arizona, California, Colorado, Florida, Hawaii, Idaho, Kansas, Louisiana, Minnesota, Montana, Nebraska, Nevada, New Mexico, North Dakota, Oklahoma, South Dakota, Texas, Utah Washington and Wisconsin.

Family histories and genealogies of specific families will be in the FAMILY SECTION (Stacks 22-37). These books have call numbers beginning with the word FAMILIES. The books in this section are arranged alphabetically by surname.

REQUEST FORM FOR COPIES OF ANCESTOR/MEMBERS APPLICATIONS

Record Copy Department
Office of the Registrar General, NSDAR

Only those who fall into one of the categories listed below (as written in the Executive Board Ruling, 1967) may receive copies of applications of active members:

_____ a. Members of the NSDAR
_____ b. Prospective members of the NSDAR
_____ c. Genealogist of the C.A.R.
_____ d. Official Registrar and/or Official Genealogist of the S.A.R.
_____ e. Official Registrar of the S.R.

(PLEASE CHECK CATEGORY ABOVE)

REVOLUTIONARY ANCESTOR REQUESTED

Full name of Revolutionary Ancestor _____

Date of Birth_____ Date of Death_____

Name of wife or wives_____
(Ancestor card does not state which wife the children are through.)

State served during the Revolution_____. Name of child through whom descent

is claimed_____. If line through child requested is not established, will accept

through any child: Yes ☐ No ☐

DAR MEMBERSHIP APPLICATION REQUESTED

Full name of member requested:

First name	Maiden name	Married name

National No._____ (if known) Living_____ Deceased_____

Chapter/State affiliation _____

Revolutionary Ancestor credited to above member _____

If you are requesting copies of more than one ancestor, list information on back
along with any additional information.

★ ★ ★REQUEST FOR INFORMATION OTHER THAN RECORD COPY ON THIS FORM WILL NOT BE HONORED ★ ★ ★

NAME AND ADDRESS OF PERSON REQUESTING COPY:

_____

_____

_____

Fee per copy is $2.00. Make checks payable fo: "TREASURER GENERAL, NSDAR" and mail to OFFICE OF THE REGISTRAR GENERAL, NSDAR, 1776 D Street N.W., Washington, D.C. 20006.

NATIONAL SOCIETY DAUGHTERS OF THE AMERICAN REVOLUTION
Administration Building, 1776 D Street, N.W.
Washington, D.C. 20006

Record Copy Department
Office of the Registrar General

Date _____

Dear _____.

Only those who fall into one of the categories listed below (as written in the Executive Board Ruling, 1967) may receive copies of applications of active members:
  a. Members of the NSDAR (give national number)
  b. Prospective members of the NSDAR (give chapter name)
  c. Genealogist of the C.A.R.
  d. Official Registrar and/or Official Genealogist of the S.A.R.
  e. Official Registrar of the S.R.

THE FEE IS $4.00 PER COPY

This office regrets that assistance is not available to you at this time for the following reasons:

_____ The files have been checked and there is no record of service for the ancestor at this time, which means that no member has established that particular line for membership. This would not preclude the possibility of acceptance.

_____ Revolutionary War service for more than one _____ has been accepted. Specific information must be provided so that the files may be checked.

_____ No members have established lines through the child/children in whom you are interested. If you wish, a copy of the most recent open paper on this ancestor will be sent to you.

_____ The ancestor files do not state which wife the children are through.

_____ Since the acceptance of this record, it has come to the attention of this office that there is an error in earlier accepted records. To send out copies and further perpetuate inaccurate information is not to the best interest of the Society.

_____ This ofice does NO ORIGINAL research. The files pertain only to Revolutionary ancestors whose lines have been established by members and to the Revolutionary period.

_____ WE DO NOT send out copies of application papers that have been CLOSED by the member.

_____ This office does not send out names and addresses of members.

_____ Your check for $_____ is returned herewith.

_____ Your check for $_____ is being returned in lieu of the exact amount.

_____ Enclosed is a bill for your convenience.

_____ Other:

Record Copy Department
Office of the Registrar General, NSDAR

CHAPTER 9

NATIONAL & STATE RECORD CENTERS

American Antiquarian Society
185 Salisbury St.
Worcester, Mass.

The American Antiquarian Society has the largest single collection of printed source materials peretaining to the first 250 years of American history in the United States. Their collection includes:

a. The largest collection of printed genealogies;
b. The largest collection of colonial and early federal newspapers;
c. The largest collection of published county histories;
d. The largest collection of City Directories;
e. Early New England Diaries, family correspondence, etc.;
f. Private papers of important figures.

Other National Research Centers:

Bancroft Library
University of California
Berkeley, Calif. 94720

Western America, Newspapers, Diaries, Journals, Pacific Northwest, Bay Area, Wagon Trains, Overland Journeys, Miners, Railroads, Territorial, Bibles, Photographs, Church Records, Homesteading, Indians, Miscellaneous.

Federal Archives and Records Center
7358 Pulaski Road
Chicago, IL 60629

Court Records, Naturalizations, Bankruptcy.

Federal Archives and Records Center
1557 St. Joseph Avenue
East Point, GA 30044

Court Records, Naturalizations, Bankruptcy, WW 1 Draft Registration.

Federal Archives and Records Center
2306 East Bannister Road
Kansas City, MO 64131

Court Records, Naturalizations, Bankruptcy.

Federal Archives and Records Center
Military Ocean Terminal
Bayonne, NY 07002

Court Records, Naturalizations, Bankruptcy, Naturalization Index.

Genealogical Society of Pennsylvania
1300 Locust St.
Philadelphia, PA 19107

Printed Family Histories, County Histories, City Directories, Newspapers, Church Records, Manuscripts, Maps, Vital Records, Delaware Valley, Penn. German Quakers, Scotch-Irish, Mennonite, Censuses.

The Genealogical Society
50 East North Temple
Salt Lake City, UT 84150

Printed Family Histories, County Histories, City Directories, Church Records, Foreign Records, Vital Records, Censuses, Property Records, Probate Records, Court Records, International Genealogical Index, Family Group Sheets, Major Source Papers.

New England Historic-Genealogical Society
101 Newbury St.
Boston, Mass. 02116

Printed Family Histories, Published Vital Records, Manuscripts, County Histories, Newspapers, Church Records, Coats of Arms, Censuses.

New York Genealogical & Biographical Society
122 East 58th St.
New York, NY 10022

Printed Family Histories, County Histories, Vital Records, Dutch Records, Newspapers, Church Records, Manuscripts, Censuses.

New York Public Library
5th Ave. and 42nd St.
New York, NY 10018

Printed Family Histories, County Histories, City Directories, Newspapers, Church Records, Manuscripts, Ethnic Records, Maps, Vital Records, Censuses.

Newberry Library
60 West Walton Street
Chicago, IL 60610

Printed Family Histories, County Histories, Coats of Arms, Newspapers, Diaries, Journals, City Directories, Northwest Territory, Great Lkes, Migrations, Public Domain States, Railroads, Miscel., Censuses.

Virginia Historical Society
428 North Boulevard

Richmond, VA 23221

Printed Family Histories, County Histories, City Directories, Newspapers, Church Records, Manuscripts, Maps, Censuses, Civil War, The South.

Washington National Records Center
Federal Office Building
Suitland, Maryland 21668

Court Records, Property Records, Naturalizations.

Western Reserve Historical Society
10825 East Boulevard
Cleveland, OH 44106

Printed Family Histories, County Histories, City Directories, Newspapers, Church Records, Manuscripts, Shakers, Maps, Vital Records, Northwest Territory, Ohio Valley, Western Pennsylvania, Lake Erie, Censuses.

Wilson Library
University of North Carolina
Chapel Hill, NC 27514

Manuscripts, Newspapers, Church Records, Maps, Civil War, The South, City Directories, Censuses.

Major State Research Centers

In every state there are repositories (Libraries & Archives) that have extensive genealogy collections or reference materials that are valuable to the genealogist. We have listed the six repositories in each state that we have found to provide you with the greatest amount of genealogy help. Obviously in large states like New York and California there are many more good repositories.

These Genealogy Repositories may not contain the largest genealogy collection, but do in our opinion contain the largest collections of original resource materials.

To help you know what to expect when visiting a certain repository we have put a "G" after those libraries that have an excellent Genealogy Collection and a "R" after those that have excellent reference materials, (at these libraries you will need to know which references you wish to search). If the library has both there will be a "G" and an "R" after their name.

Statewide Genealogical Centers

G = General   R = Reference   G,R = Both

Alabama

Alabama Department of Archives "G"
    and History
624 Washington Avenue
Montgomery, AL 36104

Special Collection Division G,R
Mobile Public Library
701 Government Street
Mobile, AL 36602

Southern Historical Collection G,R
Birmingham Public and Jefferson
    County Free Library
2020 7th Avenue, N
Birmingham, AL 35203

Special Collections R
Amelia Gayle Gorgas Library
University of Alabama
University, AL 35486

Special Collections **R**
Ralph Brown Draughon Library
Auburn University
Auburn, AL 36830

Federal Archives and Records **G**
  Center
1557 St. Joseph Avenue
East Point, GA 30044

Alaska

Archives and Records Management **G**
450 Whittier Street
Juneau, AK 99801

Archives and Manuscripts **R**
Elmer E. Rasmuson Library
University of Alaska
Fairbanks, AK 99701

Alaska Historical Library **R**
Alaska Division of State Libraries
State Office Building
Juneau, AK 99801

Special Collections **R**
Sheldon Jackson College Library
Sitka, AK 99835

Adjutant General **G**
National Guard
Anchorage, AK 99501

Federal Archives and Records **G**
  Center
6125 Sant Point Way
Seattle, WA 98115

Arizona

Department of Administration **G,R**
Library, Archives, and Public
  Records
Capitol Building, Third Floor
Phoenix, AZ 85007

Special Collections **R**
University of Arizona Library
Tucson, AZ 85721

Arizona Historical Foundation **R**
Charles Trumbull Hayden Library
Arizona State University
Tempe, AZ 85281

Arizona Historical Society **G**
949 East Second Street
Tucson, AZ 85719

Special Collections **R**
Tucson Public Library
200 South 6th
Tucson, AZ 85701

Federal Archives and Records **G**
  Center
24000 Avila Road
Laguna Niquel, CA 92677

Arkansas

Arkansas History Commission **G**
300 West Markham Street
Little Rock, AR 72201

Special Collections **R**
University of Arkansas Library
Fayetteville Campus
Fayetteville, AR 72701

Department of State Lands **G**
State Capitol
Little Rock, AR 72201

Arkansas Collection **R**
Ft. Smith Public Library
61 South 8th
Ft. Smith, AR 72901

Special Collections **R**
University of Arkansas at Little
  Rock Library
University Avenue at 33rd Street
Little Rock, AR 72204

Federal Archives and Records **G**
  Center
4900 Hemphill Street
Fort Worth, TX 76115

California

Bancroft Library **G,R**
University of California
Berkeley, CA 94720

California State Archives **G**
1020 "O" Street
Sacramento, CA 95814

Los Angeles County Museum **G**
OF Natural History
900 Exposition Boulevard
Los Angeles, CA 90007

Special Collections **R**
Stanford University Library
Stanford, CA 94305

Sutro Library **G**
2130 Fulton Street
San Francisco, CA 94117

Federal Archives and Records **G**
  Center
24000 Avila Road
Laguna Niquel, CA 92677

Federal Archives and Records **G**
  Center
1000 Commodore Drive
San Bruno, CA 94066

Colorado

Colorado State Archives **G**
  and Public Records
1313 Sherman Street, 1-B20,
Denver CO 80203

State Historical Society of G
    Colorado
Documentary Resources Dept.
200 14th Avenue
Denver, CO 80203

Western Historical Collection R
Norlin Library
University of Colorado
Boulder, CO 80302

Western History Department G,R
Denver Public Library
1357 Broadway
Denver, CO 80203

Special Collections R
Charles Leaming Tutt Library
Colorado College
Colorado Springs, CO 80903

Federal Archives and Records G
    Center
Bldg 48, Denver Federal Center
Denver, CO 80225

Connecticut

Connecticut State Library G
231 Capitol Avenue
Hartford, CT 06115

Connecticut Historical Society G
1 Elizabeth Street
Hartford, CT 06105

Special Collections R
Yale University Library
120 High Street
New Haven, CT 06520

Department of Special Collections R
Wilbur L. Cross Library
University of Connecticut
Storrs, CT 06268

New Haven Colony Historical G
    Society
114 Whitney Avenue
New Haven, CT 06510

Federal Archives and Records G
    Center
380 Trapelo Road
Waltham, MA 02154

Delaware

Historical and Cultural Affairs G
Hall of Records
Dover, DE 19901

Historical Society of Delaware G
505 Market Street
Wilmington, DE 19801

Eleutherian Mills Historical Library R
Greenville
Wilmington, DE 19807

Special Collections R
Hugh M. Morris Library
University of Delaware
Newark, DE 19711

Genealogical Society of G
    Pennsylvania
1300 Locust Street
Philadelphia, PA 19107

Federal Archives and Records G
    Center
5000 Wissahickon Avenue
Phildelphia, PA 19144

District of Columbia

Department of Public Health G
Vital Records Division
300 Indiana Avenue, NW
Washington, D.C. 20001

Recorder of Deeds G
6th and D Streets, NW
Washington, D.C. 20004

Register of Wills G
5th and E Streets, NW
Washington, D.C. 20001

Columbia Historical Society G
1307 New Hampshire Avenue, NW
Washington, D.C. 20036

Central Reference Division (NNC) G
National Archives (GSA)
Washington, D.C. 20408

Washington National Records G
    Center
Federal Office Building
Suitland, MD 21668

Florida

Bureau of Archives and Records G
    Management
401 East Gaines Street
Tallahassee, FL 32304

State Land Office G
Elliot Building
Tallahassee, FL 32304

P. K. Yonge Library of Florida R
    History
University of Florida Library
Gainesville, FL 32611

Tampa—Hillsborough County G
    Public Library
900 North Ashley Street
Tampa, FL 33602

Polk County Historical G
    Commission
511 Court House
Bartow, FL 33830

Federal Archives and Records G

Center
1557 St. Joseph Avenue
East Point, GA 30044

Georgia

Georgia Department of Archives **G**
and History
Central Research Division
330 Capitol Avenue, SE
Atlanta, GA 30334

Special Collections **R**
Ilah Dunlap Little Memorial
Library
University of Georgia
Athens, GA 30602

Washington Memorial Library **G,R**
1180 Washington Avenue
Macon, GA 31201

Georgia Historical Society **G**
501 Whitaker Street
Savannah, GA 31401

Surveyor General Department **G**
Archives and Records Building
Atlanta, GA 30334

Federal Archives and Records **G**
Center
1557 St. Joseph Avenue
East Point, GA 30044

Hawaii

Hawaiian Historical Society **G**
560 Kawaiahao Street
Honolulu, HI 96813

Public Archives **G**
Iolani Palace Grounds
Honolulu, HI 96813

State Library Branch **R**
Hawaii State Library
478 South King Street
Honolulu, HI 96813

Special Collections **R**
Gregg M. Sinclair Library
University of Hawaii
Honolulu, HI 96822

Special Collections **R**
Ralph E. Woolley Library
B.Y.U.—Hawaii
Laie, HI 96762

Federal Archives and Records **G**
Center
1000 Commodore Drive
San Bruno, CA 94066

Idaho

Idaho State Archives **G**
325 West State Street
Boise, ID 83702

Idaho State Historical Society **G**
325 West State Street
Boise, ID 83706

Boise Branch Genealogical Library **G**
325 West State Street
Boise, ID 83706

Special Collections **R**
University of Idaho Library
Moscow, ID 83843

Special Collections **R**
David O. McKay Library
Ricks College
Rexburg, ID 83440

Federal Archives and Records **G**
Center
6125 Sand Point Way
Seattle, WA 98115

Illinois

State Archives **G**
Archives Building
Springfield, IL 62706

Illinois State Historical Library **G**
Old State Capitol
Springfield, IL 62706

Newberry Library **G,R**
60 West Walton Street
Chicago, IL 60610

Special Collections **R**
Champaign Library
University of Illinois at Urbana
Urbana, IL 61801

Adjutant General **G**
State Armory
Springfield, IL 62706

Federal Archives and Records **G**
Center
7358 Pulaski Road
Chicago, IL 60629

Indiana

Indiana State Library **G**
315 West Ohio Street
Indianapolis, IN 64202

Indiana Historical Society **G**
315 West Ohio Street
Indianapolis, IN 46202

Archives Division, Indiana State **G**
Library
315 West Ohio Street
Indianapolis, IN 46202

Genealogical Department **G**
Public Library of Ft. Wayne and
Allen County
900 Webster Street
Ft. Wayne, IN 46802

Lily Library **R**
Indiana University Universities
10th Street and Jordan Avenue
Bloomington, IN 47401

Federal Archives and Records **G**
  Center
7358 Pulaski Road
Chicago, IL 60629

Iowa

Iowa State Department of History **G**
  and Archives
Historical Building
Des Moines, IA 50319

State Historical Society of Iowa **G**
Iowa and Gilbert Streets
Iowa City, IA 52240

Special Collections **R**
University of Iowa Libraries
Iowa City, IA 52242

Davenport Museum **G**
1717 West 12th Street
Devenport, IA 52804

Special Collections **R**
Marshalltown Community
  College Library
113 North First Avenue
Marshalltown, IA 50158

Federal Archives and Records **G**
  Center
2306 East Bannister Road
Kansas City, MO 64131

Kansas

Kansas State Archives **G**
120 West 10th Street
Topeka, KS 66612

Kansas State Historical Society **G**
120 West 10th Street
Topeka, KS 66612

Topeka Genealogical Workshop **G**
2110 North Topeka Avenue
Topeka, KS 66609

Spencer Research Library **R**
University of Kansas Libraries
Lawrence, KS 66045

Kansas Genealogical Society **G**
700 Avenue G
Dodge City, KS 67801

Federal Archives and Records **G**
  Center
2306 East Bannister Road
Kansas City, MO 64131

Kentucky

Bureau of State Archives and **G**
  Records

851 East Main Street
Frankfort, KY 40601

Kentucky Historical Society **G**
Old State House
Frankfort, KY 40601

Special Collections **R**
Margaret I. King Library
University of Kentucky
Lexington, KY 40506

Filson Club Library **G**
118 West Breckinridge Street
Louisville, KY 40203

Kentucky Library and Museum **G,R**
Western Kentucky University
Bowling Green, KY 42101

Federal Archives and Records **G**
  Center
1557 St. Joseph Avenue
East Point, GA 30044

Louisiana

State Archives and Records **G**
  Commission
Capitol Station
Baton Rouge, LA 70804

State Land Office **G**
Capitol Station
Baton Rouge, LA 70804

Louisianna Historical Society **G**
Gallier Hall
545 St. Charles Avenue
New Orleans, LA 70130

Louisiana State Museum **G**
751 Chartres Street
New Orleans, LA 70116

Department of Archives and **R**
  History
Louisiana State University Library
Baton Rouge, LA 70803

Federal Archives and Records **G**
  Center
4900 Hemphill Street
Fort Worth, TX 76115

Maine

Maine State Archives **G**
State Capitol
Augusta, ME 04330

Bangor Public Library **R**
145 Harlow Street
Bangor, ME 04401

Maine Historical Society **G,R**
485 Congress Street
Portland, ME 04111

State Forestry Department **G**
State Capitol

Augusta, Maine 04330

Special Collections R
Raymond H. Fogler Library
University of Maine at Orono
Orono, ME 04473

Federal Archives and Records G
Center
380 Trapelo Road
Waltham, MA 02154

Maryland

Hall of Records G
St. John's Street and College Ave.
Annapolis, MD 21404

Maryland Historical Society G
201 West Monument Street
Baltimore, MD 21201

Peabody Library R
17 East Mount Vernon Place
Baltimore, MD 21202

Special Collections R
Blackwell Library
Salisbury State College
Camden and College Avenues
Salisbury, MD 21801

Maryland Collection R
McKeldin Library
University of Maryland
College Park, MD 20742

Washington National Records G
Center
Federal Office Building
Suitland, MD 21668

Massachusetts

Archives of the Commonwealth G
State House
Boston, MA 02133

New England Historic Genealogical G
Society
101 Newbury Street
Boston, MA 02116

American Antiquarian Society G,R
185 Salisbury Street
Worcester, MA 01609

The Houghton Library R
Harvard University Library
Cambridge, MA 02138

Registrar of Vital Statistics G
272 State House
Boston, MA 02133

Federal Archives and Records G
Center
380 Trapelo Road
Waltham, MA 02154

Michigan

Michigan State Archives G
3405 North Logan Street
Lansing, MI 48918

Michigan Historical Collections G,R
Bentley Historical Library
University of Michigan
Ann Arbor, MI 48104

Michigan State Library R
735 East Michigan Avenue
Lansing, MI 48913

Burton Collection G,R
Detroit Public Library
5201 Woodward Avenue
Detroit, MI 48202

Historical Society of Michigan G
2117 Washtenaw Avenue
Ann Arbor, MI 48104

Federal Archives and Records G
Center
7358 Pulaski Road
Chicago, IL 60629

Minnesota

Minnesota State Archives G
Commission
117 University Avenue
St. Paul, MN 55101

Minnesota Historical Society G
690 Cedar Street
St. Paul, MN 55101

Special Collections R
Centennial Hall Learning
Resources Center
St. Cloud State College
St. Cloud, MN 56301

Special Collections R
O. Meredith Wilson Library
University of Minnesota
Minneapolis, MN 55455

Special Collections R
Memorial Library
Mankato State College
Mankato, MN 56001

Federal Archives and Records G
Center
7358 Pulaski Road
Chicago, IL 60629

Mississippi

Mississippi Department of G
Archives and History
Archives and History Building
Capitol Green
Jackson, MS 39205

Mississippi Historical Society **G**
Archives and History Building
Capitol Green
Jackson, MS 39205

Museum Library **G**
Old Court House
Vicksburg, MS 39180

Special Collections **R**
Evans Memorial Library
Aberdeen, MS 39730

Special Collections **R**
Mitchell Memorial Library
Mississippi State University
State College, MS 39762

Federal Archives and Records **G**
    Center
1557 St. Joseph Avenue
East Point, GA 30044

Missouri

Records Management and **G**
    Archives Service
1011 Industrial Drive
Jefferson City, MO 65101

Headquarters
Office of the Adjutant General **G**
Jefferson City, MO 65101

Missouri Historical Society **G**
Lindell and DeBaliviere Avenue
St. Louis, MO 63112

State Historical Society of **G**
    Missouri
Hitt and Lowry Streets
University Library Building
Columbia, MO 65201

Federal Archives and Records **G**
    Center
2306 East Bannister Road
Kansas City, MO 64131

Miissouri Valley Room
Kansas City Public Library
311 East 12th Street
Kansas City, MO 64106

Montana

Montana Historical Society **G**
225 North Roberts Street
Helena, MT 59601

Department of Military Affairs **G**
Office of the Adjutant General
Helena, MT 59601

Department of State Lands **G**
State Capitol
Helena, MT 59601

Special Collections **R**
University Library

Montana State University
Bozeman, MT 59715

Special Collections **R**
University Library
University of Montana
Missoula, MT 59801

Federal Archives and Records **G**
    Center
Blgd. 48, Denver Federal Center
Denver, CO 80225

Nebraska

Nebraska State Historical Society **G**
1500 R Street
Lincoln, NE 68508

Rare Books Room **R**
Don L. Love Memorial Library
University of Nebraska
Lincoln, NE 68508

Special Collections **R**
Calvin T. Ryan Library
Kearney State College
Kearney, NE 68847

Spencer D.A.R. Collection **G**
Edith Abbott Memorial Library
211 North Washington
Grand Island, NE 68801

Special Collections **R**
North Platte Public Library
120 West Fourth Street
North Platte, NE 69101

Federal Archives and Records **G**
    Center
2306 East Bannister Road
Kansas City, MO 64131

Nevada

State Archives **G**
Capitol Building
Carson City, NV 89701

Nevada Historical Society **G**
1650 North Virginia Street
Reno, NV 89504

Special Collections **R**
Noble H. Getchell Library
University of Nevada
Reno, NV 89507

Special Collections **R**
James R. Dickinson Library
University of Nevada at Las Vegas
4505 Maryland Parkway
Las Vegas, NV 89154

Federal Archives and Records **G**
    Center
24000 Avila Road
Laguna Niquel, CA 92677

Federal Archives and Records **G**
Center
1000 Commodore Drive
San Bruno, CA 94066

New Hampshire

New Hampshire Historical Society **G**
30 Park Street
Concord, NH 03301

Records and Archives Center **G**
71 South Fruit Street
Concord, NH 03301

Bureau of Vital Statistics **G**
61 South Spring Street
Concord, NH 03301

History Room **G**
Dover Public Library
73 Locust Street
Dover, NH 03820

New Hampshire State Library **G,R**
20 Park Street
Concord, NH 03301

Federal Archives and Records **G**
Center
380 Trapelo Road
Waltham, MA 02154

New Jersey

New Jersey State Library **R**
185 West State Street
Trenton, NJ 08625

Special Collections **G,R**
Rutgers University Library
College Avenue
New Brunswick, NJ 08901

New Jersey Historical Society **G**
230 Broadway
Newark, NJ 07104

Special Collections **G,R**
Savitz Learning Resource Center
Glassboro State College
Glassboro, NJ 08028

Department of Rare Books and **R**
Special Collections
Harvey S. Firestone Memorial
Library
Princeton University
Princeton, NJ 08540

Federal Archives and Records **G**
Center
Military Ocean Terminal
Bayonne, NJ 07002

New Mexico

New Mexico State Records Center **G**
and Archives

404 Montezuma Street
Santa Fe, NM 87501

Special Collections **G**
Museum of New Mexico
Santa Fe, NM 87501

Speical Collections **R**
Zimmerman Library
University of New Mexico
Albuquerque, NM 87106

New Mexico State Library **R**
300 Don Gaspar
Santa Fe, NM 87501

Special Collections **R**
Center for Learning and Infor-
mation Resources
University of Albuquerque
St. Joseph Place
Albuquerque, NM 87124

Federal Archives and Records **G**
Center
4900 Hemphill Street
Fort Worth, TX 76115

New York

Manuscripts and History **G,R**
New York State Library
Washington Avenue
Albany, NY 12225

Miscellaneous Records Division **G**
162 Washington Avenue
Albany, NY 12225

*(The index to these records is located at the
Bureau of Surplus Real Property, Old State
Office Building, Albany, NY 12225.)*

Special Collections **G**
New York Historical Society
170 Central Park W
New York, NY 10024

The University of the State of New York **G**
The State Education Department
New York State Archives
Albany, NY 12230

Division of Military and Naval **G**
Affairs
War Records
Bldg 22, New York State Campus
Albany, NY 12226

Federal Archives and Records **G**
Center
Military Ocean Terminal
Bayonne, NJ 07002

North Carolina

Division of Archives and Records **G**
Management
109 East Jones Street
Raleigh, NC 27602

Manscripts Department **G,R**
Louis Round Wilson Library
University of North Carolina
Chapel Hill, NC 27514

Manuscripts **G,R**
William R. Perkins Library
Duke University
Durham, NC 27706

Carolina Room **G,R**
Rowan Public Library
201 West Fisher Street
Salisbury, NC 28144

North Carolina Room **G,R**
Pack Memorial Public Library
One S. Pack Square
Asherville, NC 28801

Federal Archives and Records **G**
 Center
1557 St. Joseph Avenue
East Point, GA 30044

North Dakota

State Historical Society of **G**
 North Dakota
Liberty Memorial Building
Bismarck, ND 58501

State Land Department **G**
Capitol Building
Bismarck, ND 58501

Orin G. Libby Mansucript **R**
 Collection
Chester Fritz Library
University of North Dakota
Grand Forks, ND 58201

Speical Collections **R**
University Library
North Dakota State University
Fargo, ND 58102

Speical Collections **R**
Memorial Library
Minot State College
Minot, ND 58701

Federal Archives and Records **G**
 Center
Bldg 48, Denver Federal Center
Denver, CO 80225

Ohio

Ohio Historical Society **G**
Ohio History Center
Columbus, OH 43211

Auditor of State **G**
State Capitol
Columbus, OH 43215

Western Reserve Historical Society **G**
10825 East Boulevard
Cleveland, OH 44106

Special Collections **R**
Vernon Alden Library
Ohio University
Athens, OH 45701

The Cincinnati Historical Society **G**
Eden Park
Cincinnati, OH 45202

Federal Archives and Records **G**
 Center
7358 Pulaski Road
Chicago, IL 60629

Oklahoma

Oklahoma Historical Society **G**
Historical Building
Oklahoma City, OK 73105

Division of Archives and Records **G**
109 State Capitol
Oklahoma City, OK 73105

Genealogy Department **G,R**
Tulsa City—County Library
400 CivicCenter
Tulsa, OK 74103

Library **R**
Thomas Gilcrease Institute
2501 West Newton, R.R.6
Tulsa, OK 74127

Special Collection **R**
William Bennett Bizzell Memorial
 Library
University of Oklahoma
401 West Brooks
Norman, OK 73069

Federal Archives and Records **G**
 Center
4900 Hemphill Street
Fort Worth, TX 76115

Oregon

Oregon State Archives **G**
Oregon State Library
State Library Building
Salem, OR 97310

Oregon State Library **R**
State Library Building
Salem, OR 97310

Special Collections **R**
Memorial Library
University of Oregon
Eugene, OR 97403

Oregon Historical Soceity **G**
1230 SW Park Avenue
Portland, OR 97205

Special Collections **R**
Willamette University Library
900 State Street
Salem, OR 97301

Federal Archives and Records G
  Center
6125 Sand Point Way
Seattle, WA 98115

Pennsylvania

Pennsylvania Historical and G
  Museum Commission
William Penn Memorial Museum
  and Archives Building
Harrisburg, PA 17108

Historical Society of Pennsylvania G,R
1300 Locust Street
Philadelphia, PA 19107

Genealogy and Local History G,R
  Section
Pennsylvania State Library
Education Building
Harrisburg, PA 17108

Special Collections R
University of Pennsylvania Library
3420 Walnut Street
Philadelphia, PA 19104

Bureau of Land Records G
South Office Building, Room 123
Commonwealth Avenue
Harrisburg, PA 15222

Federal Archives and Records G
  Center
5000 Wissahickon Avenue
Philadelphia, PA 19144

Rhode Island

Rhode Island State Archives G
Room 314, State House
Providence, RI 02903

Records Center G
Veterans Memorial Building
83 Park Street
Providence, RI 02903

The Rhode Island Historical G
  Society
121 Hope Street
Providence, RI 02906

Special Collections R
University of Rhode Island Library
Kingston, RI 02881

Newport Historical Society G
82 Touro Street
Newport, RI 02840

Federal Archives and Records G
  Center
380 Trapelo Road
Waltham, MA 02154

South Carolina

South Carolina Department of G

Archives and History
1430 Senate Street
Columbia, SC 29211

South Caroliniana Library G
University of South Carolina
Columbia, SC 29208

Charleston Library Society G,R
164 King Street
Charleston, SC 29401

South Carolina Historical Society G
Fireproof Building
Charleston, SC 29401

The South Carolina Historical G,R
  Room
Greenville County Library
300 College Street
Greenville, SC 29601

Federal Archives and Records G
  Center
1557 St. Joseph Avenue
East Point, GA 30044

South Dakota

South Dakota State Historical G
  Society
Soldiers and Sailors Memorial
  Building
Pierre, SD 57501

Special Collections R
I.D. Weeks Library
University of South Dakota
Vermillion, SD 57069

Secretary of State G
State House
Pierre, SD 57501

Public Lands G
State House
Pierre, SD 57501

South Dakota Collection R
South Dakota State Library
  Commission
322 South Fort Street
Pierre, SD 57501

Federal Archives and Records G
  Center
Bldg 48, Denver Federal Center
Denver, CO 80225

Tennessee

Tennessee State Library and G
  Archives
403 7th Avenue North
Nashville, TN 37219

Special Collections G,R
John Willard Brister Library
Memphis State University

Southern and Patterson
Memphis, TN 38152

Special Collections G,R
James D. Hoskins Library
University of Tennessee
Knoxville, TN 37916

Historical Collection R
Chattanooga Public Library
601 McCallie Avenue
Chattanooga, TN 37403

Historical Collection G,R
Knoxville—Knox Public Library
500 West Church Avenue
Knoxville, TN 37902

Federal Archives and Records G
    Center
1557 St. Joseph Avenue
East Point, GA 30044

Texas

Archives Division G
Texas State Library
Capitol Station
Austin, TX 78711

General Land Office G
Texas State Library
Capitol Station
Austin, Texas 78711

Texas Historical Center G
Mirabeau B. Lamar Library
University of Texas
Austin, TX 78712

Special Collections R
University of Texas Library
P.O. Box 19218,
Arlington, TX 76019

Center For Genealogical Research G
Clayton Library
5300 Caroline Street
Houston, TX 77004

Federal Archives and Records G
    Center
4900 Hemphill Street
Fort Worth, TX 76115

Utah

State Archives and Records Service
State Capitol Building
Salt Lake City, UT 84114

Daughters of Utah Pioneers
    Library
Pioneer Memorial Museum
300 North Main Street
Salt Lake City, UT 84116

Utah State Historical Society
300 Rio Grande
Salt Lake City, UT 84101

Special Collections
Marriott Library
University of Utah
Salt Lake City, UT 84112

The Historical Department
The Church of Jesus Christ of
    Latter-day Saints
50 East North Temple
Salt Lake City, UT 84150

Federal Archives and Records
    Center
Bldg 48, Denver Federal Center
Denver, CO 80225

Vermont

Public Records Division G
The Pavilion
Montpelier, VT 05602

Vermont Historical Society G
The Pavilion
Montpelier, VT 05602

Special Collections R
Guy W. Bailey Memorial Library
University of Vermont
Burlington, VT 05401

Genealogical Library G,R
Bennington Museum
West Main Street
Bennington, VT 05201

Miscellaneous Records Division G
162 Washington Avenue
Albany, NY 12225

*(The index to these records is located at the
Bureau of Surplus Real Property, Old State
Office Building, Albany, NY 12225.)*

Federal Archives and Records G
    Center
380 Trapelo Road
Waltham, MA 02154

Virginia

Virginia State Library G,R
12th and Capitol Streets
Richmond, VA 23219

Virginia Historical Society G,R
428 North Boulevard
Richmond, VA 23221

Special Collections G,R
Earl Gregg Swem Library
College of William and Mary
Williamsburg, VA 23185

Special Collections G,R
Adlerman Library
University of Virginia
Charlottesville, VA 22901

Special Collections G,R
Cyrus Hall McCormick Library
Washington and Lee University
Lexington, VA 24450

Washington National Records G
    Center
Federal Office Building
Suitland, MD 21668

Washington

Division of Archives and Records G
    Management
Washington State Archives and
    Records Center
12th and Washington
Olympia, WA 98501

Washington State Historical G
    Society
315 North Stadium Way
Tacoma, WA 98403

Special Collections R
University of Washington Library
Seattle, WA 98105

Washington—Northwest Room R
Washington State Library
Olympia, WA 98504

Special Collections R
Washington State University
    Library
Pullman, WA 99163

Federal Archives and Records G
    Center
6125 Sand Point Way
Seattle, WA 98115

West Virginia

Department of Archives and G
    History
State Capitol Building
Charleston, WV 25305

Land Division G
State Capitol Building
Charleston, WV 25305

West Virginia Collection G,R
West Virginia University Library
Morgantown, WV 26506

Secretary of State G
State Capitol Building
Charleston, WV 25305

Special Collections R
Cabell County Public Library
900 5th Avenue
Huntington, WV 25701

Washington National Records G
    Center

Federal Office Building
Suitland, MD 21668

Wisconsin

Division of Archives and G
    Manuscripts
816 State Street
Madison, WI 53706

State Historical Society of G
    Wisconsin
816 State Street
Madison, WI 53706

Special Collections R
University of Wisconsin Library
2311 East Hartford Avenue
Milwaukee, WI 53201

Military Affairs G
3020 Wright Street
Madison, WI 53704

Special Collections R
William D. McIntyre Library
University of Wisconsin
105 Garfield Avenue
Eau Claire, WI 54701

Federal Archives and Records G
    Center
7358 South Pulaski Road
Chicago, IL 60652

Wyoming

Wyoming Archives and Historical G
    Department
State Office Building
Cheyenne, WY 82001

Wyoming State Historical Society G
State Office Building
Cheyenne, WY 82001

Wyoming State Library R
Supreme Court and Library Building
Cheyenne, WY 82002

Division of Rare Books and Special R
    Collections
William Robertson Coe Library
University of Wyoming
13th and Ivinson
Laramie, WY 82071

Special Collections G,R
Laramie County Library
2800 Central Avenue
Cheyenne, Wyoming 82001

Federal Archives and Records G
    Center
Gldg 48, Denver Federal Center
Denver, CO 80225

Roots Digest
12 exciting issues each year

- *ROOTS DIGEST* is the only monthly genealogy magazine in the country and features information, articles and stories from the common heritage we all share. It summarizes the best material from hundreds of periodicals worldwide.

- *ROOTS DIGEST* peeks into the lives of the famous and the infamous. A valuable tool for the arm chair researcher. Be in the know!

- *ROOTS DIGEST* seeks to fill the need created by the millions who are presently tracing their roots. These represent just about every ethnic group, young and old alike.

- *ROOTS DIGEST* has over two-dozen contributing editors and is the voice of the Genealogical Community. Both for the novice and expert!

Inside the Magazine

- **Foreign Research**
- **Ethnic Sources**
- **Coats of Arms**
- **Adoptions**
- **Calendar of Events**
- **Computers**
- **Analysis**
- **Civil War**
- **Immigration**
- **Newspapers**

- **Feature Articles**
- **Research Sources**
- **Book Reviews**
- **Seminar Information**
- **Little Known Sources**
- **Personalities**
- **Celebrities**
- **Family Associations**
- **Maritime**
- **Railroads**
- **Convention Information**

- **Questions & Answers**
- **Library Research**
- **Archives & Repositories**
- **Famous Women**
- **Salt Lake Library**
- **Surnames**
- **Denominations**
- **History**
- **Maps**
- **Travel**

Subscribe Now!

You are invited to subscribe to the Roots Digest Magazine.
$18⁰⁰ for 1 year, $30⁰⁰ for 2 years, $45⁰⁰ for 3 years

Name _____ **Date** _____

Address _____

City _____ **State** _____ **Zip** _____

Visa or M.C.# _____ **Exp. Date** _____ **Signature** _____

Complete and Mail To

Roots Digest Magazine
P.O. Box 2101
Glenwood Springs, CO 81602

Section III
RECORDS

CHAPTER 10

COURT RECORDS

Court records are by far the best source of accurate genealogy information and need not be difficult for the genealogist. Most people have been honest and religious and when they put their hand on the Bible they would tell the truth to the best of their ability. They would be more honest in court than almost any other situation.

Historically the average American would appear in court as an average three times in twenty years for a multitude of reasons. Some of the various reasons for litigation are: contract disputes, estate probates, property disputes, orphan records, accidents, vital records, bastardy proceedings, taxes, claims, dwellings, family matters, heirs, religious freedom, gambling, indecency, legacy, liens, mental conditions, water rights, neglect, passengers, political matters, prostitution, removals, rent, right of way, schools, servitude, ships, sickness, suits, indictments, trespassing, horse stealing, naturalization, oaths, apprenticeship, roads, and any other miscellaneous matters deemed by the courts as needed or sworn testimony or evidentiary proofs.

The Court Systems

1. There are two distinct court systems in the United States: *Federal Courts* and *State Courts.* Each has its own jurisdiction and each state has its own court structure.

2. Both court systems have two levels of courts: *Trial Courts* and *Appellate Courts.* Trial courts have original jurisdiction and therefore, these records are of the most value to the genealogist. Appellate Courts only hear cases from trial courts and no new information is added. They are only of value when the Trial Court records are not available.

3. Both court systems try two kinds of cases: *Criminal* and *Civil.* Some States have separate courts for each kind of case; however, most states try both cases in the same court.

4. Probably the court records that are of most value to the genealogist are the probate records. Probate Courts handle estate matters. Some terms used in probate courts that may be useful are:

Testate—with a will
Intestate—without a will
Incompetent's estate—mentally incompetent
Guardianship—for the estate of those under legal age
Heirs—those who inherit if the deceased left no will
Beneficiaries—those mentioned in a will
Legatee—one who receives personal property
Devisee—one who receives real property

5. Understanding court records of value to the genealogist (name may differ from state to state):

    a. *Case file*—all documents related to a case are found here.

    b. *Docket*—(register of actions) cases are identified by number and are usually indexed. There is one page for each case with a listing of all material related to the case.

    c. *Minute book—Court Order book*—summary of actions of the court arranged chronologically.

    d. *Judgement Book*—a listing of civil judgements that are indexed by the name of the defendants. (Most useful to genealogists.)

Court records can best be researched by hiring a researcher to do the work for you. If this is impossible you will need to make a personal visit.

The Court System Important to the Genealogist

STATE COURTS
State Courts are known by various names (See chart pp. 208).

STATE SUPREME COURT
Indexed in the Dicennial Digest.
(First Dicennial Digest, vol. 21 to 25—An index of all appellate and supreme court cases from 1658-1911 by plaintiff only for all 50 states and the original colonies. Available in most law libraries and many courthouses.)

APPELLATE COURT
Indexed in Dicennial Digest.

COUNTY COURTS
Also called Circuit, Superior, District, etc.
(Available in the courthouse or in the state repositories.)

FEDERAL COURTS

U.S. SUPREME COURT
Indexed in Supreme Court Digest (available in law libraries and large public libraries).

CIRCUIT COURT OF APPEALS
Began in 1891. Indexed in the Federal Digest available in most law libraries.

DISTRICT COURTS
89 in 50 states from 1789 to present. Indexed in appropriate Federal Record Center.

OLD CIRCUIT COURTS
1789 to 1912. Most early federal cases and naturalization took place in these courts. Indexed in appropriate Federal Record Center.

General Procedure For Settling An Estate

Testate
(Proving the Will)

1. Making the will
2. Codicil(s) (additions to the will
3. Death
4. Petition for probate

5. Admission to probate
6. Will is recorded (list of beneficiaries)
7. Executor is bonded (not in every case)
8. Inventory is taken

9. Caveats (Contesting a will, might list more heirs)
10. Final Settlement

Intestate

1. Death
2. Petition for probate (list of heirs)
3. Notice of hearing
4. Hearing and appointment of an administrator
5. Administrator is bonded
6. Determination of heirship
7. Inventory is taken

8. Claims filed by relatives, creditors and/or widows (gives names, dates and places)
9. Final settlement

Federal Judicial Circuit in Which Each State Is Located

State	Circuit	State	Circuit
Alabama	Fifth Circuit	Nebraska*	Eighth Circuit
Alaska	Ninth Circuit	Nevada*	Ninth Circuit
Arizona*	Ninth Circuit	New Hampshire*	First Circuit
Arkansas	Eighth Circuit	New Jersey*	Third Circuit
California	Ninth Circuit	New Mexico*	Tenth Circuit
Colorado*	Tenth Circuit	New York	Second Circuit
Connecticut*	Second Circuit	North Carolina	Fourth Circuit
Delaware*	Third Circuit	North Dakota*	Eighth Circuit
Florida	Fifth Circuit	Ohio	Sixth Circuit
Georgia	Fifth Circuit	Oklahoma	Tenth Circuit
Hawaii	Ninth Circuit	Oregon*	Ninth Circuit
Idaho*	Ninth Circuit	Pennsylvania	Third Circuit
Illinois	seventh Circuit	Puerto Rico	First Circuit
Indiana	Seventh Circuit	Rhose Island*	First Circuit
Iowa	Eighth Circuit	South Carolina	Fourth Circuit
Kansas*	Tenth Circuit	South Dakota*	Eighth Circuit
Kentucky	Sixth Circuit	Tennessee	Sixth Circuit
Louisiana	Fifth Circuit	Texas	Fifth Circuit
Maine*	First Circuit	Utah*	Tenth Circuit
Maryland*	Fourth Circuit	Vermont	Second Circuit
Massachusetts*	First Circuit	Virginia	Fourth Circuit
Michigan	Sixth Circuit	Washington	Ninth Circuit
Minnesota*	Eighth Circuit	West Virginia	Fourth Circuit
Mississippi	Fifth Circuit	Wisconsin	Seventh Circuit
Missouri	Eighth Circuit	Wyoming*	Tenth Circuit
Montana*	Ninth Circuit		

*Only one district court.

JURISDICTION OF STATE COURTS

STATE	Court of Last Resort	Intermediate Appellate Court	Major Trial Courts	Jurisdiction of Wills (Probate)
ALABAMA	Supreme Court	Court of Criminal Appeals	Circuit Courts	Probate Courts
ALASKA	Supreme Court	Court of Civil Appeals	Superior Courts	Superior Courts
ARIZONA	Supreme Court	Court of Appeals	Superior Courts	Superior Courts
ARKANSAS	Supreme Court	Court of Appeals	Circuit Courts	Chancery and Probate Courts
CALIFORNIA	Supreme Court	Court of Appeals	Superior Courts	Superior Courts
COLORADO	Supreme Courts	Court of Appeals	District Courts	District Courts
CONNECTICUT	Supreme Court	None	Superior Courts	Probate Courts
DELAWARE	Supreme Court	None	Court of Chancery Superior Court	Register Courts
FLORIDA	Supreme Court	District Courts of Appeal	Circuit Courts	Judge's Courts
GEORGIA	Supreme Court	Court of Appeals	Superior Courts	Ordinary Courts
HAWAII	Supreme Court	Intermediate Appellate Courts	Circuit Courts	Circuit Courts
IDAHO	Supreme Court	Court of Appeals	District Courts	District Courts
ILLINOIS	Supreme Court	Appellate Court	Circuit Courts	Circuit Courts
INDIANA	Supreme Court	Court of Appeals	Superior Court Circuit Court	Probate Courts
IOWA	Supreme Court	Court of Appeals	District Courts	District Courts
KANSAS	Supreme Court	Court of Appeals	District Courts	Probate Courts
KENTUCKY	Supreme Court	Court of Appeals	Circuit Courts	County Courts
LOUISIANA	Supreme Court	Court of Appeals	District Courts	District Courts
MAINE	Supreme Judicial	None	Superior Courts	Probate Courts
MARYLAND	Court of Appeals	Court of Special Appeals	Circuit Court of Counties	County Orphans Courts
MASSACHUSETTS	Supreme Judicial Court	Appeals Court	Trial Courts	Probate Courts
MICHIGAN	Supreme Court	Court of Appeals	Circuit Courts	Probate Courts
MINNESOTA	Supreme Court	None	District Courts	Probate Courts
MISSISSIPPI	Supreme Court	None	Circuit Courts, Chancery Courts	Probate Courts
MISSOURI	Supreme Court	Court of Appeals	Circuit Courts	Probate Courts
MONTANA	Supreme Court	None	District Courts	District Courts
NEBRASKA	Supreme Court	None	District Courts	County Courts
NEVADA	Supreme Court	None	District Courts	District Courts
NEW HAMPSHIRE	Supreme Court	None	Superior Courts	Probate Courts
NEW JERSEY	Suprme Court	Appellate Division of Superior Court	Superior Courts	Surrogate of Probate
NEW MEXICO	Supreme Court	Court of Appeals	District Courts	Probate Courts
NEW YORK	Court of Appeals	Appellate Division of Superior Court	Superior Courts	Surrogate of Probate
NORTH CAROLINA	Supreme Court	Court of Appeals	Superior Courts	Superior Courts
NORTH DAKOTA	Supreme Court	None	District Courts	County Courts
OHIO	Supreme Court	Court of Appeals	District Courts	County Courts
OKLAHOMA	Court of Criminal Appeals	Court of Appeals	District Courts	County Courts
OREGON	Supreme Court	Court of Appeals	Circuit Courts	Circuit Courts
PENNSYLVANIA	Supreme Court	Superior Court, Commonwealth Court	Courts of Common Pleas	County Register of Wills
RHODE ISLAND	Supreme Court	None	Superior Courts	Town Probate Courts
SOUTH CAROLINA	Supreme Court	None	Circuit Courts	Probate Courts
SOUTH DAKOTA	Supreme Court	None	Circuit Courts	County Courts
TENNESSEE	Supreme Court	Court of Appeals	Chancery Courts	Probate Courts
TEXAS	Supreme Court and Court of Criminal Appeals	Court of Civil Appeals	District Court	County and Probate Courts
UTAH	Supreme Court	None	District Courts	District Courts
VERMONT	Supreme Court	None	Superior Courts	District Courts
VIRGINIA	Supreme Court	None	Circuit Courts	Circuit Courts
WASHINGTON	Supreme Court	Court of Appeals	Superior Courts	Superior Courts
WEST VIRGINIA	Supreme Court of Appeals	None	Circuit Courts	County Courts
WISCONSIN	Supreme Court	Court of Appeals	Circuit Courts	Probate Courts
WYOMING	Supreme Court	None	District Courts	District Courts
WASHINGTON, D.C.	Court of Appeals	None	Superior Court	Probate Courts

PRESENT SYSTEM
THE UNITED STATES COURT SYSTEM

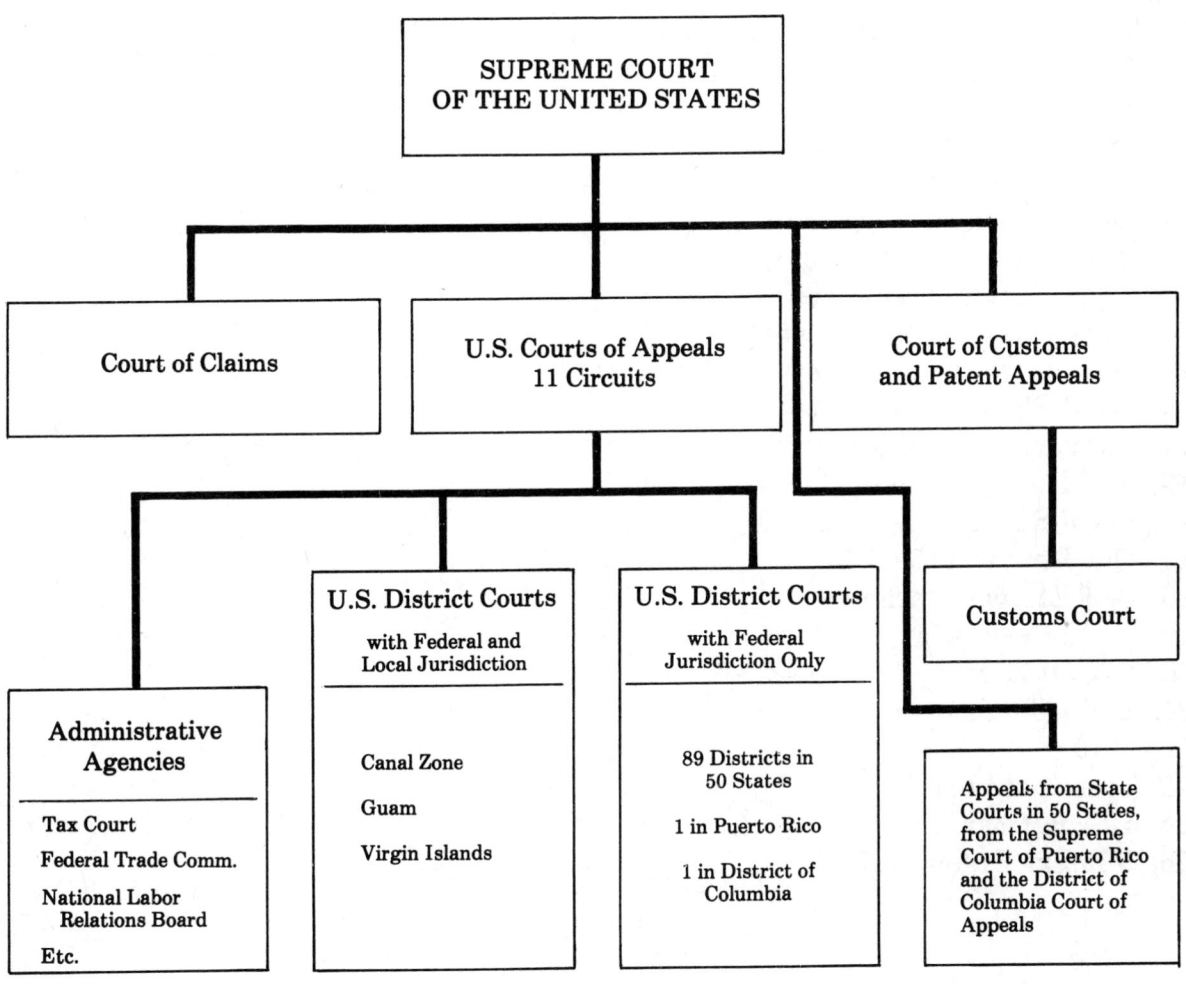

SUPREME COURT
OF THE UNITED STATES

Court of Claims

U.S. Courts of Appeals
11 Circuits

Court of Customs
and Patent Appeals

Administrative
Agencies

Tax Court

Federal Trade Comm.

National Labor
Relations Board

Etc.

U.S. District Courts

with Federal and
Local Jurisdiction

Canal Zone

Guam

Virgin Islands

U.S. District Courts

with Federal
Jurisdiction Only

89 Districts in
50 States

1 in Puerto Rico

1 in District of
Columbia

Customs Court

Appeals from State
Courts in 50 States,
from the Supreme
Court of Puerto Rico
and the District of
Columbia Court of
Appeals

Is There Life After the Courthouse?

After you have exhausted the many records usually deposited in the ancestral county courthouse, what other sources or facilities should also be checked in that same county? Here are just a few suggestions:

1. Published County History
2. Official County Atlas
3. The Main Public Library
4. Local College or University
5. The County Museum
6. County Historical Society
7. Oldest Mortuary
8. Local Monument Maker
9. Old Weekly Newspapers
10. Local Genealogical Society
11. Soil Conservation District
12. The Current Newspaper
13. Local Phone Book
14. Title or Abstract Company
15. Site Location Reports
16. Local Researcher/Historian
17. Old Timers in the Area
18. Special Local Facilities
19. Local Cemeteries
20. Sexton Records
21. Local Churches
22. "Mug" Books
23. Fraternal Lodge
24. D.A.R. Chapter
25. Military Organizations

CHAPTER 11

LAND RECORDS

In searching for the records of your ancestors the acquisition and disposition of land can provide valuable information. The first sentence of the first deed usually tells you where the person is from. Along with the general information that you would expect to find in such records, deeds provide one of the best sources for maiden names. They also generally let you know when a person moved into an area or turned 21 and when they left or when they died.

It is important to know that in considering land records there are two kinds; State Land States and Public Domain States. State Land States are the thirteen original states and states created out of those states plus Texas and Hawaii and a small part of Ohio. (See map on pp. 213) All of the other states are Public Domain States which means that the original owner of the land was the federal government. The chart that follows will tell you where the records can be found in each State Land State.

State Land States

ORIGINAL AND SUBSEQUENT LAND TITLES

Chart by: Vincent L. Jones,
taken from his book *Stamp Out Chaos: Eliminate Confusion.* (Reprinted with permission.)

STATES	DOCUMENTS OF ORIGINAL TITLE (Land Grants)	DOCUMENTS OF TITLE EXCHANGE (Deeds, Bills of Sale, Leases)	PROBATE	COURT	MARRIAGE
30 Public Domain States	National Archives	Counties	Counties	Co.	Co.
Maine & Massachussetts	Town Clerk	Co.	Co.	Co.	Town Clerk
Rhode Island	Town Clerk	Town Clerk	Town Clerk	Co.	Town Clerk
New Hampshire bef. 1769 New Hampshire aft. 1769 *****	Town Clerk County	Aft. 1769 Co.	Aft. 1769 Co.	Aft. 1769 Co.	Town Clerk Town Clerk
Vermont and Connecticut	Town Clerk	Town Clerk	Probate Dist.	Co.	Town Clerk
**New York	State Archives at Albany	Co.'s	N.Y. Co. Ct. Hs., Manhattan, Since Rev. in Co.	Co.	Township Clerk 1880
*New Jersey	East Jersey Perth Amboy West Jersey Burlington	Few deeds State House at Trenton, use church records.	St. House, Trenton, before Revo.; counties after war.	Co.	Colonial St. House Trenton; Co. aft. war.
Delaware & Pennsylvania	State Land Office Dover or Harrisburg	Co.	Co.	Co.	Use church; Co. aft. 1885

Maryland	Hall of Records	Co.	Co.	Co.	aft. 1951 Co.
Virginia West Virginia Kentucky	State Archives; W. Va. aft 1864 Ky. aft. 1791; all prior at Richmond, Va.	Co.	Co.		Co.*** Co.
North Carolina	Archives at Raleigh; also some in co.'s	Co.	Co.	Co.	Co.
Tennessee	State Archives Nashville	Co.	Co.	Co.	aft. 1838 Co.
South Carolina ****	Archives at Columbia	bef. 1783 Charleston Co.; aft. 1783 large Jud. Dist.	bef. 1785 Charleston Co. aft. 1785 sm. Jud. Dist.	****	Co. aft. about 1886
Georgia (Ask for pamphlet on Georgia land lotteries.)	Archives at Atlanta	Co.	Co.	Co.	Co.
Texas Rep. of Texas 1836	State Land Office Austin, Texas	Co.	Co.	Co.	Co.

*New Jersey was divided into the proprietory of East and West at one time. And deeds didn't need to be recorded so many were not.

**New York sold their land to foreign banks and the banks mortgaged the land to individuals so they have very early mortgage records.

***There are many Jefferson (Ky.) Co. land grants at Louisville.

****South Carolina before 1769 Charleston Co. had all records, they created 6 "large" Judicial Dists., later they created "small" Jud. Dist. and records were kept in Sm. Dist. with old "large" court house (1772), in 1798 the large abandoned, since 1798 kept in small dist. Old large J.D. records in small J.D. that got court house, after 1868 probate in counties (same as sm. Jud. Dists.) Note: 3 of the large Court houses (96 Addyville, Georgetown and Orangeburg) have burned.

*****Prior to 1769 all New Hampshire records were in central colonial office at Dover, N.H. (now part of State Archives).

Property Qualifications In the Colonies

Connecticut:	40 shillings freehold, or, after 1715, £4 personalty.
Delaware:	50 acres freehold, of which 12 must be improved, or £40 personalty.
Georgia:	50 acres freehold
Maryland:	50 acres or £40 personalty within the county.
Massachusetts:	40 acres freehold or £50 personalty.
New Hampshire:	40 acres free hold or £50 personalty.
New York:	A freehold of the value of £40.
North Carolina:	50 acres freehold.
Pennsylvania:	50 acres, of which 10 must be cleared, or £50 personalty.
Rhode Island:	Freehold of the value of £40 or of 40 shillings per annum.
South Carolina:	100 acres or £60 personalty.
Virginia:	100 acres or 25 acres with a house (after 1736).

Public Domain States

In 1785 the Continental Congress developed a system of describing land for legal purposes. The system is generally known as the "Township and Range Survey System." All territory that wasn't already inhabited was surveyed by this system. That includes all Public Domain States. The system paid little attention to the natural contours and features of the land. Instead it is as though someone placed a giant grid over the land and all parcels were recorded according to where they fell on the grid. The

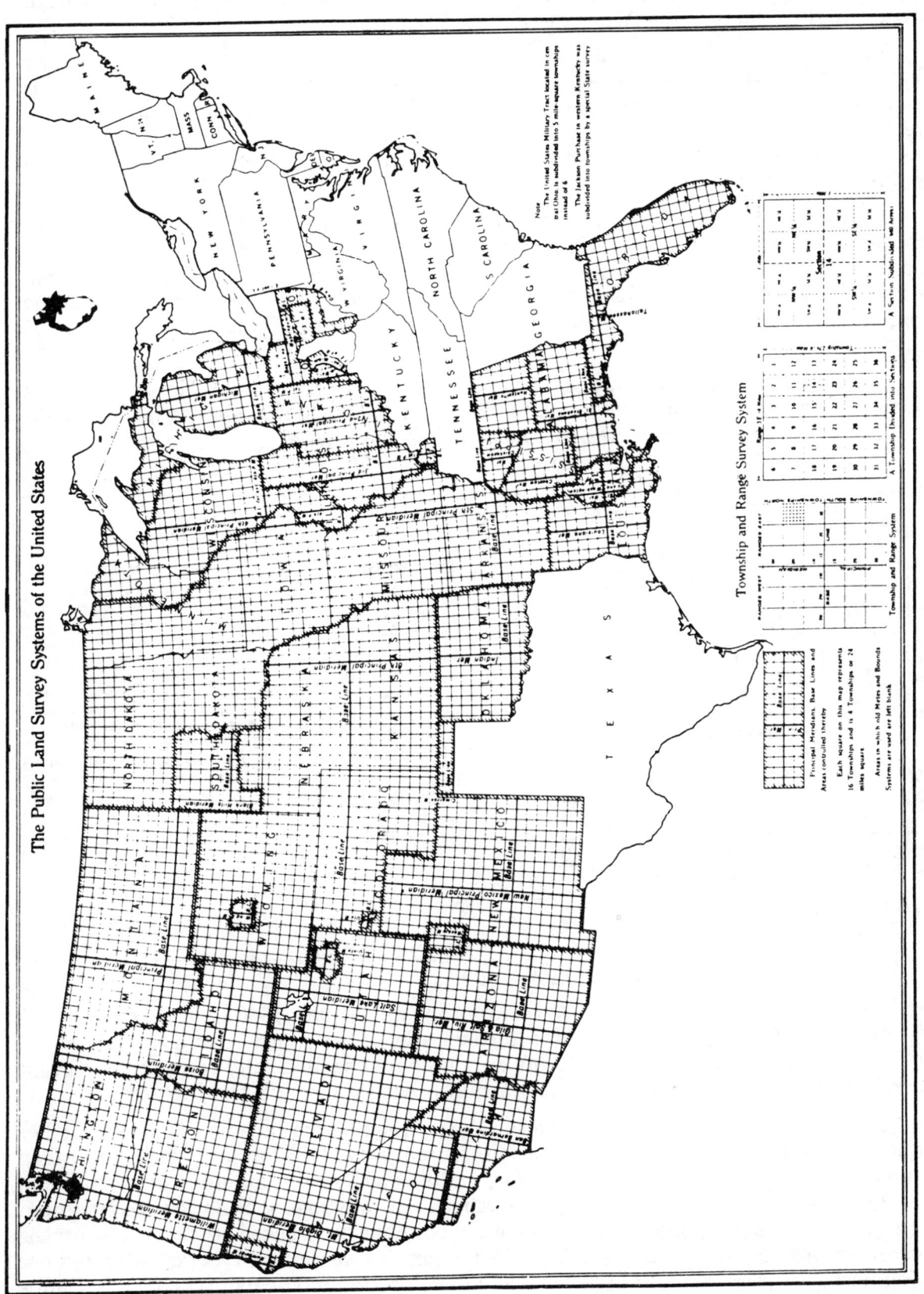

The Public Land Survey Systems of the United States

Township and Range Survey System

initial point on this system was determined by astronomical observation and from these a meridian and a base line was formed.

A *principal meridian* runs through the point from north to south, and a *base line* (that is, a line parallel to the equator) runs through the point from east to west. Because of the curvature of the planet, additional lines called *guide meridians* are run every 24 miles east and west of the principal meridians, and *standard parallels* are run every 24 miles north and south of the base lines. These guide meridians and standard parallels are also known as *guide lines*.

Beginning at the principal meridian, points are marked out at intervals of 6 miles east and west on the base line. Lines running north-south are then run through these points, creating 6-mile-wide strips called *ranges*. The same is done upon the principal meridian, beginning at the base line; these 6-mile-wide east-west strips tartan the ranges; the squares are called *townships*. Each township is 6 miles on a side, or 36 square miles in area.

The first township north of the base line is called Township 1 North; the third township south of the base line is called Township 3 South; and similar numbering is used for the ranges east and west of the principal meridians.

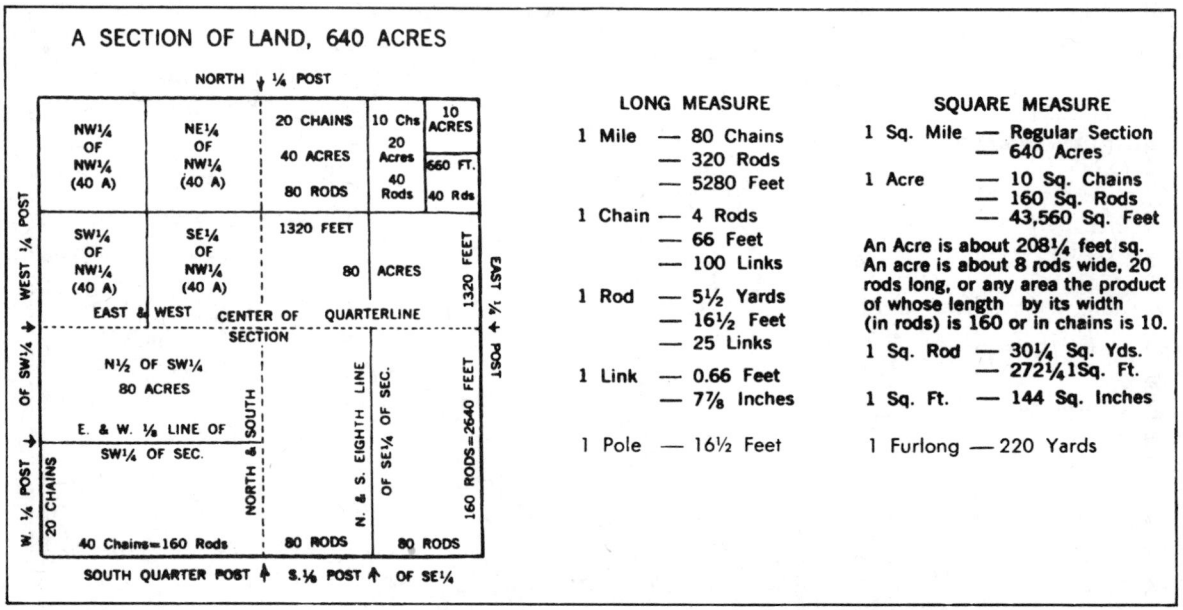

Each township is divided into 36 *sections* one mile square (640 acres). These are set out by running through the townships lines parallel to the southern and eastern edges, at intervals of one mile. The 36 sections are numbered sequentially from the northeast corner, proceeding westward and eastward alternately through the township.

The sections are the smallest tracts the law requires to be surveyed, but further subdivisions are made by dividing sections into quarters (160 acres). These are called the northeast quarter, northwest quarter, and so on. Due to planetary curvature and unavoidable errors, sections along the northern and western boundaries are irregular. The quarters along the northern and western boundaries of these sections take up the excess or shortage in the township. The *quarter quarters* (40 acres) along those boundaries are given *lot* numbers, such as Lot 2, Section 5, Township 42 North, Range 12 East. A lot is an irregular area less than 40 acres.

Your Public Lands (BLM)
Excerpted From The Biggest Land Title Office in the World
By William J. "Doc" Dorasavage and Paul Herndon

The Continental Congress passed the Land Ordinance Act of May 20, 1785, authorizing the Treasury Department to survey and sell public domain land as a source of revenue. The public domain is defined as all the land originally acquired by the United States for purposes of National expansion. The Act also established the policy of "survey before settlement"—a policy that continues to this day.

Today, the BLM Eastern States Office maintains a complete set of field notes and township plats covering thirteen public domain States within its 31-State area of jurisdiction. The field notes are filed by State in 1,745 bound volumes; and over 30,000 plats are filed by State, township and range.

When the public lands were sold, "patents" were issued. In this case, patents are deeds that transfer land ownership from a sovereign (the United States Government) to a buyer. Patents are the best form of warrenty deed, and are often the first record in a chain of title to a piece of property.

Today the BLM Eastern States Office houses 8,978 bound volumes, containing over five million patent documents. Some patents issued before 1908 are filed by State and name of the land office where the certificate originated. Others are filed according to the act of Congress under which they were issued, regardless of geographical location. Since 1908, all patents have been assigned consecutive serial numbers and filed numerically.

The new Act provided for credit sales of public land, reduced the minimum size of individual tracts that could be sold to 320 acres, and set a $2 per acre minimum price for public lands. It retained the provision that all public lands be sold at public auction.

The tract book system of recording land transactions was established about that time. The tract books began simply as listings of all the transactions involving surveyed public lands—by State or territory, meridian, township, range, section and subdivision. Now, the tract books are used as the basic index for public land title research in the eastern States.

Today there are 1,582 original General Land Office tract books at the Eastern States Office, showing how, when, and to whom title to public domain lands passed from the United States—in the States of Alabama, Arkansas, Florida, Illinois, Indiana, Iowa, Louisiana, Michigan, Minnesota, Missouri, Mississippi, Ohio and Wisconsin. An additional 2,325 tract books covering the western public domain States are also filed at the office on microfilm. For day-to-day management, the western BLM State Offices use the Master Title Plat system instead of tract books.

On April 25, 1812, by an Act of Congress, the General Land Office was created within the Treasury Department. It was the first bureau to be created with a department.

Two years after its creation, the General Land Office was destroyed by British troops invading Washington. Fire again destroyed the two-story wooden building in 1833, but all records were rescued and carried to the safety of nearby private homes.

In 1946, after a major reorganization, the General Land Office became a part of the new Bureau of Land Management within the Interior Department.

After 1950, reorganization—and more moves for the public land records—became commonplace. In 1954, the Bureau abolished regional offices in favor of State offices;

and old Region VI became the Eastern State Office, Eastern States Office later merged with the Washington office Branch of Field Services and became a Division of Field Services within the BLM headquarters. In 1964, another Bureau reorganization changed the Division back to the Eastern States Office.

Due to the age and wear from frequent use, the records are slowly and continuously losing their readability. Since they are the original records and there are no duplicate sets.

Homestead Act Records

The Homestead Act of May 20, 1862, permitted settlers to acquire free land provided they would take up residence on it and improve it. Only a small registration fee was charged. The available land was located in the vast territories known as the public domain which had been surveyed by the Government and offered to settlers as an inducement to move westward from the Atlantic Coast states. These public lands were in the states generally west of the Alleghenies, but did not include Kentucky, West Virginia or Tennessee. Most of Texas was also excluded. To qualify for a homestead under the Act, the applicant had to be an American Citizen or show that he had declared his intention to become an American.

If it is known that an immigrant ancestor applied for a homestead a search of the records might turn up a copy of his *Declaration of Intention.* Information about homestead grants might be obtained from the courthouse of the county in which the land is located. When the legal description of the homestead land is acquired (from tax receipts, deeds or other county records), it is then possible to locate the actual application and other papers related to the claim. These papers are in the custody of the National Archives and Records Service and are stored in the Washington National Records Center. To locate the homestead file it is necessary first to ascertain the "land entry number." This can be supplied by the Federal Bureau of Land Management, Eastern States Land Office, 7981 Eastern Avenue, Silver Spring, Maryland, if the legal discription is known.

Contact the Bureau of Land Management, giving them the legal description of the land involved. They will supply copies of the Patent for 50c per page, payment to be made in advance. Addresses for district offices and the states for which they maintain records follow:

ALABAMA, ARKANSAS, FLORIDA, ILLINOIS, INDIANA, IOWA, LOUISIANA, MICHIGAN, MINNESOTA, MISSISSIPPI, MISSOURI, OHIO AND WISCONSIN
350 South Pickett St., Alexandria, VA 22304

ALASKA
555 Cordova St., Anchorage, AK 99501

ARIZONA
2400 Valley Bank Center, Phoenix, AZ 85073

CALIFORNIA
Federal Building, Room E-2841, 2800 Cottage Way, Sacramento, CA 95825

COLORADO
Colorado State Bank Building, 1600 Broadway, Denver, CO 80202

IDAHO
P.O. Box 042, Boise, ID 83724

MONTANA, NORTH DAKOTA and SOUTH DAKOTA
P.O. Box 30157, Billings, MT 59107

NEVADA
Federal Building, Room 3008, 300 Booth St., Reno, NV 89509

NEW MEXICO, OKLAHOMA and TEXAS
P.O. Box 1449, Santa Fe, NM 87501

OREGON and WASHINGTON
P.O. Box 2965, Portland, OR 97208

UTAH
University Club Building, 136 East South Temple, Salt Lake City, UT 84111

WYOMING, KANSAS and NEBRASKA
P.O. Box 1828, Cheyenne, WY 82001

Lastly, write the National Archives, giving all pertinent information: name of person filing, legal description of land, patent number, date of patent, and land office of issuance. With continuing changes at the National Archives, their current fee for supplying copies of patent files is not known. Their address is:

Reference Branch
General Archives Division
Washington, DC 20409

If the land entry number cannot be determined it still may be possible to locate the homestead record if the researcher knows the approximate date of the claim and the approximate location of the property. A visit to the Washington National Records Center would probably be necessary in this instance, and it may take some time to locate the papers. Once the journal entry or abstract entry is located at the Center, the land entry number will be given, and the original documents may then be obtained with little difficulty.

Land Offices In the States Were Opened As Follows:

This section shows the date that the first government land office opened in each of the areas indicated. This enables the researcher to know the date from which the earliest land records were recorded. Seldom will you find land records for those residents who were in a given area prior to the opening of a land office. Examples of those who would have been in the area earlier are squatters, miners, bandits, pioneers, scouts, trappers, Indians, etc. Individuals who preceded the opening of a land office who did indeed own land usually made a record of same after the land office was opened. This may have been in the form of a homestead, squatter's claim, preemptive right, adverse possession, petition, litigation, etc.

1779	First State land office opened in Virginia
1784	Massachusetts—established a State land office in Boston
1800	Ohio—established the first office at Steubenville, a second one at Marietta
1801	Ohio—District offices at Chillicothe and Cincinnati
1804	Louisiana—New Orleans, Opelousas and Ouchite
1806	Alabama—St. Stephens
1807	Indiana—Vincennes
1809	Tennessee—Nashville
1818	Missouri—St. Louis and Franklin

1821	Arkansas—Little Rock
1825	Florida—Tallahasee
1834	Wisconsin—Mineral Point
1838	Iowa—Dubuque and Burlington
1849	Minnesota—Stillwater
1853	California—Los Angeles and Henicia
1854	Washington—Olympia
1855	Nebraska—Omaha
1855	Oregon—Winchester and Oregon City
1855	Kansas—Lecompton
1858	New Mexico—Santa Fe
1861	Dakota—Vermillion
1863	Colorado—Golden City
1864	Nevada—Carson City
1867	Montana—Helena
1868	Idaho—Boise
1868	Utah—Salt Lake City
1870	Arizona—Prescott
1870	Wyoming—Cheyenne
1885	Alaska—Sitka

United States Land Offices, 1869

This section shows the various federal government land offices as they existed in the year 1869. You will notice that in some states the state government is now disposing of all property. Hence, many of the old land offices are closed down. Also, many newer ones were opened up shortly after the Civil war. Remember that this list would be very different for the years say 1850 and 1880. Sometimes individuals not only had to purchase their land from clear across the state but often in another state altogether.

Illinois
Springfield

Missouri
Booneville
Ironton
Springfield

Alabama
Mobile
Huntsville
Montgomery

Mississippi
Jackson

Louisiana
New Orleans
Monroe
Natchitoches

Michigan
Detroit
East Saginaw
Ionia
Marquette
Traverse City

Arkansas
Little Rock
Washington
Clarksville

Florida
Tallahassee

Iowa
Fort Des Moines
Council Bluffs
Fort Dodge
Sioux City

Wisconsin
Menasha
Falls of St. Croix
Stevens' Point
La Crosse
Bayfield
Eau Claire

California
San Francisco
Marysville
Humboldt
Stockton
Visalia
Sacramento

Indiana
Indianapolis

Nevada
Carson City
Austin
Belmont

Washington T.
Olympia
Vancouver

Minnesota
Taylor's Falls
St. Cloud
Winnebago City
St. Peter
Greenleaf
Du Luth

Ohio
Chillicothe

Montana T.
Helena

Arizona T.
Prescott

Oregon
Oregon City
Roseburg
Le Grand

Kansas
Topeka
Junction City
Humboldt

Nebraska
Omaha City
Brownsville
Nebraska City
Dakota City

New Mexico T.
Santa Fe

Dakota T.
Vermilion

Colorado T.
Denver City
Fair Play

Idaho T.
Boise City
Lewiston

Directory Of State Land Officials

This section shows the present land offices in each of the states. Researchers who have any question about any property within any given state should contact the state land office concerned. Usually these state offices can tell you where a certain piece of land may have been purchased at a given date. If you have any problems in this regard, suggest you consult the reference chapter under "Title Companies."

The following is a list of officials who should be addressed concerning State and other lands outside the jurisdiction of the Bureau of Land Management.

ALABAMA	Secretary of State, Montgomery 36104
ALASKA	Director, Division of Lands, Department of Natural Resources, Anchorage 99501
ARIZONA	State Land Commissioner, Phoenix 85007
ARKANSAS	Commissioner of State Lands, Little Rock 72201
CALIFORNIA	Division of State Lands, Sacramento 95814
COLORADO	State Board of Land Commissioners, Denver 80203
CONNECTICUT	The State Treasurer, Hartford 06515
DELAWARE	Chairman, State Park Commission, Dover 19901
FLORIDA	Commissioner of Agriculture, Tallahassee 32301
GEORGIA	Secretary of State, Atlanta 30334
HAWAII	Department of Public Lands, State Office Building, Honolulu 96810
IDAHO	State Land Commissioner, Boise 83702
ILLINOIS	State, Archives, Springfield 62706
INDIANA	Auditor of State, Indianapolis 46204
IOWA	Secretary of State, Des Moines 50319
KANSAS	Auditor of State and Register of State Lands, Topeka 66603
KENTUCKY	Commissioner of Finance, Department of Fincance, Frankfort, regarding land sales, Secretary of State, Frankfort, regarding old land records 40601
LOUISIANA	Register, State Land Office, Baton Rouge 70804
MAINE	State Land Agent and Forest Commissioner, State House, Augusta 04330
MARYLAND	Hall of Records Commission, P.O. Box 828, Annapolis 21401
MASSACHUSETTS	Department of Conservation, State House, Boston 02202
MICHIGAN	Auditor General, Tax Division, State Capitol Building, Lansing 48933
MINNESOTA	Director, Division of Lands & Minerals, St. Paul 55101
MISSISSIPPI	Land Commissioner, Jackson 39201
MISSOURI	Secretary of State, Jefferson City 65101
MONTANA	Commissioner of State Lands & Investments, Helena 59601
NEBRASKA	Board of Educational Lands and Funds, Lincoln 68508
NEVADA	State Land Register, Carson City 89701
NEW HAMPSHIRE	State Forester, Concord 03301
NEW JERSEY	Department of Conservation and Economic Development, Trenton 08625
NEW MEXICO	Commissioner of Public Lands, Santa Fe 87501
NEW YORK	Board of Commissioners of Land Office, Albany: (for forest lands) Director of Lands and Forests, Conservation Department, Albany 12207

NORTH CAROLINA	Secretary of State, Raleigh 27601
NORTH DAKOTA	State Land Commissioner, Bismarck 58501
OHIO	Auditor of State, Columbus 43215
OKLAHOMA	Secretary, Commissioner of the Land Office Oklahoma City 73105
OREGON	Clerk of State Land Board, Salem 97301
PENNSYLVANIA	Secretary of Internal Affairs, Harrisburg 17120
RHODE ISLAND	No state land
SOUTH CAROLINA	South Carolina Archives Department, 1430 Senate Street, Columbia, South Carolina 29201
SOUTH DAKOTA	Commissioner of School and Public Lands, Pierre 57501
TENNESSEE	Tennessee State Library & Archives Building, 403-7th Avenue North, Nashville, Tennessee 37201
TEXAS	Commissioner, General Land Office, Austin 78701
UTAH	Executive Secretary, State Land Board, Salt Lake City 84114
VIRGINIA	State Librarian, Virginia State Library, Richmond 23219
VERMONT	State Forester, Montpelier 05602
WASHINGTON	Commissioner, Department of Public Lands, Olympia 98501
WEST VIRGINIA	State Tax Commissioner, or State Auditor, Charleston 25301
WISCONSIN	The Commissioners of the Public Lands, Madison 53702
WYOMING	Commissioner of Public Lands, Cheyenne 82001

MISCELLANEOUS

CANADA	Northern Administration & Lands Branch, Department of Northern Affiars & National Resources, Ottawa, Canada
MEXICO	Secretary of Agriculture, Mexico City, Mexico
PANAMA	Secretary of the Treasury, Panama, Republic of Panama
PUERTO RICO	Office of Puerto Rico, 2210 R Street, N.W., Washington D.C. 20008
VIRGIN ISLANDS	Governor, St. Thomas, Virgin Islands, U.S.A.

Land Records

The land records (dated chiefly 1800-1950) in the Washington Records Center include bounty-land warrant files, donation land entry files, homestead application files, and private land claim files relating to the entry of individual settlers on land in the public land States. There are no land records for the Thirteen Original States and Maine, Vermont, West Virginia, Kentucky, Tennessee, Texas, and Hawaii. Records for these States are maintained by State officials, usually in the State capital. The donation land entry files and homestead application files show, in addition to the name of the applicant, the location of the land and the date he acquired it, his residence or post office address, his age or date and place of birth, his marital status, and, if applicable, the given name of his wife or the size of his family. If an applicant for homestead land was of foreign birth, his application file contains evidence of his naturalization or of his intention to become a citizen. Supporting documents show the immigrant's country of birth and sometimes the date and port of arrival. Genealogical information in records relating to private land claims varies from the mention of the claimant's name and location of the land to such additional information as the claimant's place of residence when he made the claim and the names of his relatives, both living and dead.

The Washington National Records Center, Washington, D.C. 20409, will search these land records for Alabama, Alaska, Arizona, Florida, Louisiana, Nevada, or Utah for the period 1800-July 1, 1908, if the full name of the applicant and the name of the State or Territory in which the land was located are given. A search of the records for all other public land States or Territories, 1800-1950, requires in addition to the applicant's name, (1) the number of the land entry file or a description of the land by township, range, section, and fraction of section or (2) the name of the land office and either the date when the original application was filed or the date of the final certificate. An inquirer may be able to obtain the legal description of land by writing to the county recorder of deeds in the county seat of the county in which the land was located.

How To Determine Maiden Names

It is usually easier to trace the male lines than the female. This is because of the laws and traditions which reduced a woman to that of almost a possession of her husband. And while there are often various records which may help us to determine a maiden name, there is one document which is by far the most important in this regard. It is the deed or property record.

As an average, a couple usually bought land six times in their life time. Then there should be six deeds or records of this conveying of land ownership. Typically, there are four signatures on each deed which represent the witness to this event or legal instrument. Tradition says that the signatures of the first two witnesses will probably be from the husband's side of the family and that the last two signatures will be from the wife's side of the family.

Hence, if the researcher will make note of all the individuals who sign on the deeds, he will usually find a clue to the wife's maiden name. While this is not positive proof, it is nevertheless a good tool. And with this information, a researcher can often search other supportive records, such as probates, plat maps, etc., and determine if in fact this is the maiden name of the wife.

This principal works about ninety percent of the time in the colonial period and the early federal period. It begins to become less effective after the Civil War with the advent of the railroad and the moving of people rapidly across the country, often away from their families.

However, in the earlier pre-railroad days, most families usually traveled together to find new land. This is also true of entire church groups and towns.

If we don't know where an individual comes from, we may find out where in the first sentence of the 1st deed in the new locality.

CHAPTER 12

COUNTIES

The states and territories of the United States are composed of counties, except in Louisiana they are called parishes. In Alaska they are called boroughs. A number of cities such as New York, Philadelphia, San Francisco, and New Orleans embrace the entire county within the city limits. The cities of Baltimore and St. Louis are independent of the surrounding or adjacent county.

Many counties have more than one courthouse, even though they had only one county seat (shire-town). Some counties have as many as five courthouses. You will need to search all of them to find the one that has your family records. Some records may be in more than one courthouse.

The distance between courthouses was decided by the family cow. Most families would not travel any further than they could go and return between the morning and evening milking. If it was too far they would not register or vote, pay taxes, register their deeds, etc. The county officials were forced to divide the county or build another courthouse.

Research Rule: Never search in a state unless you know the county you are looking for.

County Subdivisions in Each State in the (1880's)

In the District of Columbia the county and municipal organizations were abandoned in 1874 and the cities of Washington and Georgetown and the county of Washington thereupon ceased to exist. The District is now governed as a unit (by a Board of Commissioners appointed by the President of the United States), except that certain laws passed before the present form of government was established have not been adjusted to present conditons, and they are applicable only in portions of the District more or less distinct at the time of their enactment.

Alaska still remains without county divisions, and Indian territory is anomalous in its status. The censuses of these two territories were spearate from that of the general population, and they are not included in the following analysis of population by minor civil divisions.

The conditions of the secondary political organizations within the states are constantly changing as new counties are created or others are organized out of old ones or consolidations take place, especially in those portions of the recently admitted states not yet fully occupied by settlers.

The compact masses of population that receive special authority for organizing as chartered cities, towns, villages, or boroughs, increase in number every year with the growth of communities, requiring special provisions for police and sanitary regulations.

In New England, and in a portion of the country strongly affected by New England migration, the town has many of the powers which in the south pertain to the county. To a great extent the citizens of a chartered municipality within such town continue to participate in town government and are subject to town regulations, while in some states the city is more or less independent of the town, as previously stated.

The usual subdivision of the city is the ward, a geographical division for representative, executive, or magisterial purposes but without any legislative functions except such as are shared by other wards in the city council or board of aldermen.

A fuller explanation than this of the municipal relations of the civil divisions of the states and territories would be beyond the limits of the present purpose, which is to make clear what units were utilized for census purposes in the several states and territories, and for what units population has been separately returned by the census enumerators, as set forth in the following summary:

ALABAMA.—The county subdivisions are known as election precincts. The municipal incorporations are included in one or more precincts, or are coextensive with them. The city of Mobile forms an exception to this rule.

ARKANSAS.—The primary divisions of the county are know as townships. The municipal incorporations form essential parts of the townships, and the people participate in the township government.

CALIFORNIA.—The counties are divided into what are known as judicial townships. San Bernardino and San Diego counties are returned by precincts. The municipal incorporations are included in one or more townships or precincts, or are coextenxive with them. San Franciso city and San Francisco county are coextensive.

COLORADO.—The counties are divided into election precincts. The cities, towns, and incorporated villages form essential parts of the precincts, or comprise one or more of them.

CONNECTICUT.—The county division is the town. Cities usually form parts of the towns in which they are located. Hartford city and Hartford town are coextensive. Another class of municipal incorporations, known as boroughs, are also comprised in the towns in which they are located.

DELAWARE.—The divisions of the counties are known as hundreds. Incorporated cities and towns form constituent parts of the hundreds in which they are located.

DISTRICT OF COLUMBIA.—The county and municipal organizations were abandoned in 1874, and the cities of Washington and Georgetown and the county of Washington thereupon ceased to exist, except in the operation of certain laws not yet harmonized with present conditions.

FLORIDA.—The country subdivisions are known as election precincts. The municipal incorporations are included in the precincts, or each comprises one or more precincts.

GEORIGA.—The county subdivisions are known as militia districts. The municipal incorporations are comprised in the militia districts, or each embraces one or more districts.

IDAHO.—The counties are divided into precincts. The cities, towns, and chartered villages form essential parts of the precincts.

ILLINOIS.—There are 87 counties divided into townships, and 15 counties (mainly in the southern part) divided into precincts. Municipal incorporations, whether cities, towns, or villages, are included within these townships and precincts. The people in the municipalities in townships participate in the township government.

INDIANA.—County subdivisions are known as townships. The municipal incorporations are embraced in the townships, and the people of the municipalities participate in township government.

IOWA.—The counties are subdivided into townships. Incorporated cities, towns, and villages form constituent parts of the townships in which they are located. A number of cities and towns are coextensive with the townships and the governments are coexistent.

KANSAS.—The county subdivisions are townships. Cities of the first and second classes; that is, those having a population of more than 2,000, are independent of the townships and form principal divisions of the counties. The people in cities of the third class, which correspond to incorporated villages in most states, participate in the government of the townships in which they are located.

KENTUCKY.—Counties are divided into magisterial districts and voting precincts. Municipal incorporations, with few exceptions, are included in the districts or precincts, or comprise one or more of them.

LOUISIANA.—The subdivisions of the parish are known as police jury wards. The municipal incorporations are included in these wards and form parts of them, except in the case of Orleans parish, which is coextensive with the city of New Orleans.

MAINE.—The usual divisions of the county are known as towns; besides these there are cities, which are, in effect, merely towns under a slightly different form of government, and plantations, gores, and townships. The last three classes are, as a rule, sparsely settled; the form of government granted to plantations is very simple and gives to the organization but little power. Gores and townships are, as a rule, unincorporated, and are simply tracts of land laid off by the state authorities.

MARYLAND.—The divisions of the county are known as election districts. The whole territory of the county, regardless of municipal organizations, is divided into these subdivisions, incorporated cities and villages being included in election districts, or each comprising one or more election districts. The city of Baltimore is independent of Baltimore county, and may be regarded as forming a county by itself.

MASSACHUSETTS.—The several divisions of the county are towns and cities, the cities differing from the towns only in the character of their government.

MIGHIGAN.—The divisions of the county are townships. Cities are independent of the townships, while the people in incorporated villages participate in the township government.

MINNESOTA.—The divisions of the county are townships, although they are frequently known as towns, cities and villages, with few exceptions, and the boroughs are independent of the townships and form principal divisions of the counties. Municipalities are chartered by special act.

MISSISSIPPI.—The county subdivisions are known as beats, or supervisors' districts. The municipal incorporations are comprised within one or more beats, or are coextensive with them. Many of the larger beats are divided into town or more election precincts.

MISSOURI.—The divisions of the county are known as townships. The municipal incorporations are included within the townships. In 1876 the city of St. Louis was taken out of the county of the same name; it now maintains municipal organization; independent of the county.

MONTANA.—The counties are divided into townships. Under the law, townships may be divided into election precincts. Cities, towns, and incorporated villages are included in the townships and precincts, or are each coextensive with one or more of them.

NEBRASKA.—The county subdivisions are townships or election precincts. Most of the cities, and all the towns and incorporated villages are comprised within one or more townships or election precincts, or are coextensive with them. Precincts may be formed in this state with municipal functions, embracing as many as four sparsely populated congressional townships.

NEVADA.—The counties are divided into election precincts. Cities and incorporated villages are included within the election precincts, or each may include one or more precincts.

NEW HAMPSHIRE.—The usual divisions of the county are known as towns; besides these there are cities which are, in effect, merely towns under a slightly different form of government, and locations, grants, purchases, and townships. The last four classes are, as a a rule, unorganized, and are simply tracts of land laid off by the state authorities.

NEW JERSEY.—Townships are the divisions of the county. Cities are, as a rule, independent of the townships. Minor municipal organizations, known as towns and boroughs, are incorporated under the state laws, and, with few exceptions, form constituent parts of townships.

NEW YORK.—The divisions of the county are known as towns. Cities and villages are incorporated, the former being independent of the towns from which they were taken, while the latter remain in the towns and form component parts of them. New York city and New York county are coextensive.

NORTH CAROLINA.—The divisions of the county are known as townships. Municipal incorporations are included within the townships and form parts of them.

NORTH DAKOTA.—In North Dakota the census returns have been largely made by townships, which are the congressional townships, or townships organized from congressional townships. Some counties have not been returned by subdivisions.

OHIO.—The counties are divided into townships. Municipal incorporations, with the exception of a few cities, are included in the townships, and the people of the municipalities participate in township government.

OREGON.—The counties are divided into election precincts. The cities, towns, and incorporated villages are comprised within the elction precincts, or each may comprise one or more election precincts.

PENNSYLVANIA.—The county divisions are known as townships, cities, and boroughs. The boroughs are incorporated towns or villages. Villages, before incorporation, are included in the townships. Philadelphia city and Philadelphia county are coextensive.

RHODE ISLAND.—The several divisions of the counties are towns and cities, the cities differing from the towns only in the character of their government.

SOUTH CAROLINA.—The divisions of the county are known as townships. The municipal incorporations, with the exception of Charleston, which is independent, form essential parts of the townships in which they are located.

SOUTH DAKOTA.—In South Dakota the census returns have been largely made by townships, which are the congressional townships, or townships organized from congressional townships. Some counties have not been returned by subdivisions.

TENNESSEE.—The counties are divided into civil districts. The municipal incorporations each comprise one or more civil districts or parts of civil districts.

TEXAS.—The counties are divided into, first, four commissioners' precincts; second, into a certain number of justices' precincts; and third, into a certain, and generally much larger, number of election precincts. The population of counties has been returned by justices' precincts, except for Bandera county, which is given by commissioners' precincts. The municipal incorporations from parts of the commissioners' precincts or justices' precincts, or are coextensive with the justices' precincts.

VERMONT.—The ordinary civil divisions of the county are town and cities. There are also several unorganized subdivisions known as gores. Under the laws of this state villages are incorporated, forming constituent parts of the towns in which they are located.

VIRGINIA.—The usual subdivisions of the counties are called magisterial districts, a division which corresponds very nearly to a township of the middle states. Cities (with some exceptions), towns, and villages form essential parts of magisteral districts. Some cities maintain municipal organization independent of counties, but Petersburg is the only one officially reported to this office.

WASHINGTON.—The counties are divided into precincts, and municipalities from component parts of these precincts, or each municipality may comprise one or more precincts.

WEST VIRGINIA.—The counties are divided into magisterial districts, as in Virginia. Cities, towns, and villages form component parts of magisterial districts.

WISCONSIN.—The divisions of the county are towns. Most of the cities and several of the incorporated villages are independent of the towns and form principal divisions of the counties. In most of the villages, however, and several of the cities, the people still participate in the government of the towns in which they are located.

WYOMING.—The counties are divided into precincts, and municipalities form component parts of these precincts, or each municipality may comprise one or more precincts.

THE TERRITORIES.—The counties in the territories of Arizona, New Mexico, Oklahoma, and Utah are divided into election precincts. Municipal incorporations are comprised in these precincts, or each comprises one or more precincts.

Many States have counties with the same or similar names. The following is a list of those names with their spelling. Make sure you search the proper county.

Counties With the Same Name or Similar Name

Allegany in Maryland and New York

Alleghany in North Carolina and Virginia

Allegheny in Pennsylvania

Andrew in Missouri

Andrews in Texas

Aransas in Texas

Arkansas in Arkansas

Barber in Kansas

Barbour in Alabama and West Virginia

Brevard in Florida

Broward in Florida

Brooke in West Virginia

Brooks in Georgia and Texas

Brown in all States

Bulloch in Georiga

Bullock in Alabama

Burnet in Texas

Burnett in Wisconsin

Cheboygan in Michigan; Sheboygan in Wisconsin

Clarke in Alabama, Georgia, Iowa, Mississippi,
   and Virginia; all others Clark

Coffee in Alabama, Georgia, and Tennessee

Coffey in Kansas

Coal in Oklahoma

Cole in Missouri

Coles in Illinois

Cook in Illinois and Minnesota

Cooke in Texas

Davidson in North Carolina and Tennessee

Davie in North Carolina

Daviess in Indiana, Kentucky, and Missouri

Davis in Iowa and Utah

Davison in South Dakota

Dickenson in Virginia

Dickinson in Iowa, Kansas, and Michigan

Dickson in Tennessee

Douglas in all States

Forrest in Mississippi; Forest in others

Glascock in Georgia

Glasscock in Texas

Green in Kentucky and Wisconsin; all others
   Greene

Harford in Maryland

Hartford in Connecticut

Huntingdon in Pennsylvania

Huntington in Indiana

Johnston in North Carolina and Oklahoma; all
   others Johnson

Kanabec in Minnesota

Kennebec in Maine

Kearney in Nebraska

Kearny in Kansas

Lawrence in all States

Linn in Iowa, Kansas, Missouri, and Oregon

Lynn in Texas

Loudon in Tennessee

Loudoun in Virginia

Manatee in Florida

Manistee in Michigan

Merced in California; Mercer elsewhere

Morton
Norton both in Kansas

Muscogee in Georgia

Muskogee in Oklahoma

Park in Colorado and Montana

Parke in Indiana

Pottawatomie in Kansas and Oklahoma

Pottawattamie in Iowa

Sanders in Montana

Saunders in Nebraska

Smyth in Virginia; all others Smith

Stafford in Virginia

Strafford in New Hampshire

Stanley in South Dakota

Stanly in North Carolina

Stark in Illinois, North Dakota, and Ohio

Starke in Indiana

Stephens in Georgia, Oklahoma, and Texas

Stevens in Kansas, Minnesota, and Washington

Storey in Nevada

Story in Iowa

Terrell in Georgia and Texas

Tyrrell in North Carolina

Tooele in Utah

Toole in Montana

Vermillion in Indiana; all others Vermilion

Woods in Oklahoma; all others Wood

Wyandot in Ohio

Wyandotte in Kansas

Every State produces a work known as the Blue Book. It is called by various names as shown in the following list. The value of the Blue Book is two fold: (1) It lists all the officials of the government from governor to county dog catcher; (2) It usually indicates all those counties that have more than one courthouse per county.

Many times the records you want are in the county courthouse but not in the county seat.

Alabama Official and Statistical Register

Alaska Blue Book

Arizona Blue Book: A Guide to the State of Arizona

Arkansas Almanac; the Encyclopedia of Arkansas

California Blue Book

Colorado Year Book

Connecticut Register and Manual

Delaware State Manual

Directory of Florida Government

Georgia Official and Statistical Register

Guide to Government in Hawaii

Idaho Blue Book

Illinois Blue Book

Roster of State and Local Officials of the State of Indiana

Iowa Official Register

Kansas Directory

State Directory of Kentucky

Louisiana Roster of Officials

Maine Register, State Yearbook and Legislative Manual

Maryland Manual

[Massachusetts] Manual for the General Court

Michigan Manual

Minnesota Legislative Manual

Mississippi Official and Statistical Register

Official Manual, State of Missouri

Montana Manual of State and Local Government

Nebraska Blue Book

Legislative Manual, State of Nevada

New Hampshire Manual for the General Court

New Jersey Legislative Manual

New Mexico Blue Book

Legislative Manual, New York

North Carolina Manual

North Dakota Decision Makers

[Ohio] Official Roster

Directory and Manual of the State of Oklahoma

Oregon Blue Book

Pennsylvania Manual

Rhode Island Manual

South Carolina Legislative Manual

South Dakota Legislative Manual

Tennessee Blue Book

Texas Almanac and State Industrial Guide

Utah Official Roster

Vermont Legislative Directory and State Manual

[Virginia] Report of the Secretary of the Commonwealth

Legislative Manual, State of Washington

West Virginia Blue Book

Wisconsin Blue Book

Wyoming Official Directory

When the Courthouse Burns Downs: And You Are Out Of Marshmallows What Do You Do?

A researchers greatest problem is not so much what records do I search next but where are they? Being able to consult the original records is thus his greatest single problem. This is beautifully expressed by Sylvestre Bonnard, "And why, I asked myself, why should I have learned that this precious book exists if I am never to possess it—never even to see it? I would go to seek it in the burning heart of Africa, or in the icy regions of the pole, if I knew it were there. But I do not know where it is."

The average American ancestor resided in several dozen jurisdictions or spheres of authority. Some of which are: federal, state, county, town, church, fraternal, family, professional, etc.; experienced researchers have long learned that the most important jurisdiction is the county (where property transactions were recorded.) We call this the basic jurisdiction. Hence, the various county courthouses are presently the target for millions of researchers!

In this regard, it is usually all the local county officials can do just to keep up with their current responsibilities much less take the time to search the older records of their respective counties.

Many have in fact been flooded with these type of requests. Almost as if in retaliation these officials seem to be manufacturing excuses as to why the older records are missing. The most popular excuse seems to be that the courthouse burned. In a recent survey, out of the 159 counties of Georgia, 43 were burned during the civil war. However, of these only nine completely destroyed the records. Oftentimes the records were moved prior to a fire, as was the case of Chambersburg, Pennsylvania.

The second biggest excuse seems to be a lack of knowledge concerning the older records by the newer county officials. While this is certainly a very valid reason, it is nevertheless, very frustrating to researchers. A case in point. A researcher recently traveled to a courthouse in up-state New York and asked for the Lis Pendens and Dower Books. The Surrogate Judge stated that he never heard of such records. Later, this same researcher located the records in question behind the boiler in the furnace room. Another researcher was conducting a records survey in the state of Kentucky, and after working all day in search of a particular record asked the officials in desperation where this particular record was located. They reluctantly informed him that it was in the women's restroom.

And Yet, there are times when the record or records have indeed been destroyed. In one Ohio county the officials decided that the courthouse was just too full and they auctioned off many of their older records. Several years ago, shortly after an exhaustive microfilming program, an official in a Parish in Louisiana stated, "I am glad that everything has been microfilmed. Now I can throw out all these old books."

Besides checking with their predecessors and just snooping around the courthouse, there is one very effective way for most county officials to ascertain not only exactly what records and for what years should be deposited there, but also their exact location.

There is an inventory or index to the county courthouses of America. We refer to it as the W.P.A. county inventories. Not only will this work make the county officials look much more knowledgeable but it will often save researchers countless hours of fruitless research when they are looking for records which may have never existed or were destroyed. (See section on W.P.A. Section.)

Researchers do not have the right to expect a newly elected county official to be totally familiar with all the records which have ever existed in his particular courthouse. Conversely, researchers should do all they can to learn more about these older records *before* they visit the courthouse. What is really needed is a current inventory of each county courthouse which may be purchased by interested researchers. Admittedly, this might be a monumental project in most instances but county officials could contact their local genealogical/historical society who usually would be most enthusiastic about engaging in such a project. By so doing, researchers would know what records were available and county officials could better serve them and their own constituents, thereby saving much time and frustration.

Courthouse Burned?

1. **Records Are Not All Burned!** have you ever tried to burn a book? If you have, you will know how difficult it is to completely burn a book. While considerable damage does often result from a fire, in many instances, the bulk of the actual records have survived, In more than one county in America where this has happened, the charred remains were deposited with the local historical society or given to some private individual. Our problem is to locate the reamins of these records. (Note that a flood often did more damage than a fire because of mold, mildew, and fungus destroying wherever remained.)

2. **A New Broom Sweeps Clean.** Sometimes a county clerk will state that no records exist for a particular time period and that they were presumably destroyed by fire. In not a few cases, he is merely telling you what he has been told. It could be that he is a newly-elected official and really does not have any firsthand experience with the old records. His predecessors may have simply "dumped" the old records. This actually happened in Columbiana County, Ohio, where the clerk sold all the loose papers and probate packets! Another possibility is that the clerk has stored all the old records in the attic and simply does not want to be bothered.

3. **W.P.A. Inventories.** Often, a clerk will tell you that the records were destroyed many years ago by "Sherman's Bummers," or some similar catastrophe. Do not accept this as the final authority! Many times, this type of story is used as an excuse to discourage researchers. Check the W.P.A. Inventory (either published or unpublished) for that county and you may be able to tell the clerk, for example, that the records you are after were in the basement vault in 1943.

4. **Reconstituted or Re-recorded Records.** Usually after records were destroyed, the county officials attempted to reconstruct the missing information. In this case, county residents were urged to bring any documents or evidences of previous transactions and events, into the county office so they could again be recorded. Be sure and ask for these newer records if you are told the original records were all destroyed. The officials may not mention these alternate records.

5. **Title and Abstract Companies.** In most states, you find these companies often have a set of records that are similar in many respects to the property records found in the local county courthouse. While they are usually in a condensed or abstracted form, they are, nevertheless, a great help to the researcher.

6. **Alternative Records.** In those counties where the records have been destroyed, there are often alternative or supplemental records in existence. Genealogists need to contact the local researchers and organizations to find out exactly what records they should use under this circumstance.

7. **Legal Records.** Occasionaliy, it is possible to find a partial equivalent to probate records for a county by locating the private papers of attorneys who practiced law in that county. You can usually find out the names of these attorneys by consulting the city and business directories or the state bar association records for that time period. Once this information is secured, researchers can often find these collections through the local or state historical society. Sometimes, these papers are in the special collections of the university for that state.

8. **Multiple Courthouses.** In many, many counties, there exists more than one courthouse. This is true all over the county. For example, St. Louis County in Minnesota has two while Berkshire County in Massachusetts has three! Your county, ancestrally speaking, may have had more than one "shire" town. Be sure and search all the various courthouses in the county.

9. **Changed Residences.** Remember, the average ancestor moved at least six times in his lifetime. Seldom did they live and die in the same area. Researchers usually know where people lived after a fire and it is very often possible to learn where they lived before coming to that particular county. Search the records of these earlier and later counties.

10. **Adjacent Counties.** History has shown that many persons who lived in one county also owned land in one or more neighboring counties. It was often much easier to go down the river 30 miles to another county seat than to go ten miles over a mountain or through a dense forest to the local county seat. Be aware of these economic, social, and geographical situations.

11. **Decennial Digest.** Some of your ancestors may have appealed their court cases to a higher or appellate court. Most of these reported appellate cases have been indexed in *The Decennial Digest*, volumes 21-15. This work covers the years from 1658 to 1906 and is found in most law libraries.

12. **Federal Courts.** if the local (state) county court records are missing and there are no records in the appellate (state) court, you should check the Federal court records. The actual records have generally been deposited in the regional Federal Records Center for that state. These Federal court records usually cover the period from about 1790 to 1930.

13. **Printed or Microfilmed Records.** Many early records have been published. An example would be the

records of the famed Plymouth Colony. In many other instances, the records may have been abstracted by a private researcher. Some of these transcriptions were later published, but most still exist in manuscript form. They are usually in the possession of private individuals or local historical societies. In more recent times, the records may have been microfilmed prior to their destruction.

14. **Parent County.** Whenever a new county was formed, it became necessary for the new county to set up its own record-keeping system. Initially, they might either retain the original records from the parent county, or, more often, they would create a duplicate set of records. Hence, it is often possible to find some of the very early records for a county in its parent county.

15. **Removed Records.** Sometimes, the original records for a county were literally "carried off," especially in times of war. For example, many county records for Maine are located in Worcester, Massachusetts. Some early Virginia records are located in Washington County, Pennsylvania. Many, many early records for the state of Vermont are located in Albany County, New York. Many southern records have been deposited north of the Mason-Dixon Line and some are even located in Americana, Brazil!

16. **Search Jurisdictionally.** Sometimes, researchers falsely assume that because the courthouse has burned, they will be unable to overcome or solve a particular problem. Our ancestors usually lived within several jurisdictions or spheres of authority during their lifetime. Granted that many records have been destroyed, but usually not all of them. For example, what about church records, fraternal records, life insurance records, business records, employment records, family records, newspaper records, military records, undertaker records, sexton records, tombstone records, and school records, etc.?

Areas Identified As Counties and County Equivalents

Not all areas designated as counties have county governments. The following detailed classification of county-type areas, as distinguished from county governments, shows the distribution of the 3,141 "counties." This classification is primarily from Bureau of the Census, 1967 Census of Governments, Vol. 1, *Governmental Organization,* Washington, D.C., 1968, but takes account of subsequent changes.

Total of all county-type areas in the United States 3,141

Areas with an independently organized county government . . . .[1]3,047

County-type areas without an independently organized county government 104

    A. Areas with governments legally designated as city-county and operating primarily as cities 3

        (1) California: City and county of San Francisco
        (2) Colorado: City and county of Denver
        (3) Hawaii: City and county of Honolulu

    B. Areas designated as metropolitan governments and operating primarily as cities . . . 1

        Tennessee: Metropolitan government of Nashville and Dividson County

    C. Areas having certain types of county offices, but as part of another government (city, township) 12

        (1) Florida: County of Duval (City of Jacksonville)
        (2) Indiana: County of Marion (city of Indianapolis)
        (3) Louisiana: Parish of Orleans (city of New Orleans)
            and parish of East Baton Rouge (city of Baton Rouge)
        (4) Massachusetts: County of Nantucket (town of Nantucket)
            and county of Suffolk (City of Boston)
        (5) New York: Counties of Bronx, Kings, New York, Queens,
            and Richmond (all city of New York)
        (6) Pensylvania: County of Philadelphia (city of Philadelphia)

    D. Cities located outside of any "county area and administering functions elsewhere commonly performed by counties 42

        (1) District of Columbia: Washington
        (2) Maryland: Baltimore city (distinct from Baltimore County)
        (3) Missouri: St. Louis city (distinct from St. Louis County)
        (4) Nevada: Carson City city

(5) Virginia: Alexandria, Bedford, Bristol, Buena Vista,
Charlottesville, Chesapeake, Clifton Forge, Colonial Heights,
Covington, Danville, Emporia, Fairfax, Falls Church, Franklin,
Fredericksburg, Galax, Hampton, Harrisonburg, Hopewell, Lexington,
Lynchburg, Martinsville, Newport News, Norfolk, Norton, Petersburg,
Portsmouth, Radford, Richmond, Roanoke, Salem, South Boston, Staunton,
Suffolk, Virginia Beach, Waynesboro, Williamsburg, and Winchester.

E. Unorganized areas bearing county designations 16

(1) Connecticut (county areas with no county government):
Fairfield, Hartford, Litchfield, Middlesex, New Haven, New London,
Tolland, and Windham
(2) Rhode Island (county areas with no county government): Bristol,
Kent, Newport, Providence, and Washington
(3) South Dakota (county areas attached to other counties for
government purposes): Shannon, Todd, and Washabaugh

F. Other unorganized county-type areas 30

(1) Alaska: 29 census divisions
(2) Montana: Area of Yellowstone National Park (areas located in
Idaho and Wyoming are included in county areas in those States).

[1]Includes 10 organized boroughs in Alaska, not included in the total of 3,141 county-type areas in the
U.S. The 10 boroughs are either coextensive with or fall within census divisions in Alaska.

County Register

How to use the county register that follows.

Suppose you were working in Wright County, Missouri in 1888. You would look under Missouri and then Wright County. Since Hartville is the county seat, your records should be in the courthouse in Hartville. However, you will note that Wright County was formed in 1841, so if you were searching prior to that date the register indicates that Pulaski County is the parent county of Wright County, and you would need to search the records of the courthouse in Wayneville, the county seat of Pulaski County. Since Pulaski County was formed from Crawford County in 1833, you would look there for earlier records. So, even though your ancestors may have lived in the same house for many generations, the county jurisdiction may have changed several times.

County Name	County Seat	Parent County	Year Created
ALABAMA			
Autauga	Prattville	Montgomery	1818
Baldwin	Bay Minette	Washington	1809
Barbour	Clayton & Eufaula	Creek Cession 1832	1832
Bibb	Centerville	Monroe, Montgomery	1818
Blount	Oneonta	Cherokee Cession, Montgomery	1818
Bullock	Union Springs	Barbour, Macon, Montgomery, Pike	1866
Butler	Greenville	Conecuh, Montgomery	1819
Calhoun	Anniston	Creek Cession 1832	1832
Chambers	LaFayette	Creek Cession 1832	1832
Cherokee	Centre	Cherokee Cession 1835	1836
Chilton	Clanton	Autauga, Bibb, Perry, Shelby	1868
Choctaw	Butler	Sumter, Washington	1847
Larke	Grove Hill	Washington	1812
Clay	Ashland	Randolph, Talladega	1866
Cleburne	Heflin	Calhoun, Randolph, Talladega	1866
Coffee	Elba & Enterprise	Dale	1841
Colbert	Tuscumbia	Franklin	1867
Conecuh	Evergreen	Monroe	1818
Coosa	Rockford	Creek Cession 1832	1832
Covington	Andalusia	Henry	1821
Crenshaw	Luverne	Butler, Coffee, Covington, Lowndes, Pike	1866
Cullman	Cullman	Blount, Morgan, Winston	1877
Dale	Ozark	Covington, Henry	1824
Dallas	Selma	Montgomery	1818
DeKalb	Fort Payne	Cherokee Cession 1835	1836
Elmore	Wetumnpka	Autauga, Coosa, Montgomery, Tallapoosa	1866
Escambia	Brewton	Baldwin, Conecuh	1868
Etowah	Gadsden	Blount, Calhoun, Cherokee, DeKalb, Marshall, St. Clair	1866
Fayette	Fayette	Marion, Pickens, Tuscaloosa	1824
Franklin	Russelville	Cherokee & Chickasaw Cession of 1816	1818
Geneva	Geneva	Dale, Henry, Coffee	1868
Greene	Eutaw	Marengo, Tuscaloosa	1819
Hale	Greensboro	Green, Marengo, Perry, Tuscaloosa	1819
Hale	Greensboro	Greene, Marengo, Perry, Tuscaloosa	1867
Henry	Abbeville	Conecuh	1819
Houston	Dothan	Dale, Geneva, Henry	1903
Jackson	Scottsboro	Cherokee Cession of 1816	1819
Jeferson	Birmingham	Blount	1819
Lamar	Vernon	Marion, Fayette, Pickens	$867
Lauderdale	Florence	Cherokee & Chickasaw Cession in 1816	1818
Lawrence	Moulton	Cherokee & Chickasaw Cession 1816	1818
Lee	Opelika	Chambers, Macon, Russell, Tallapoosa	1866
Limestone	Athens	Cherokee & Chickasaw Cession 1816	1818
Lowndes	Hayneville	Butler, Dallas, Montgomery	1830
Macon	Tuskegee	Creek Cession of 1832	1832
Madison	Huntsville	Cherokee & Chickasaw Cession 1806-7	1808
Marengo	Linden	Choctaw Cession 1816	1818
Marion	Hamilton	Tuscaloosa	1818
Marshall	Guntersville	Blount, Cherokee Cession 1835, Jackson	1836
Mobile	Mobile	West Florida	1812
Monroe	Monroeville	Creek Cession 1814, Washington	1815
Montgomery	Montgomery	Monroe	1816
Morgan	Decatur	Cherokee Turkeytown Cession	1818
Perry	Marion	Montgomery	1819
Pickens	Carrollton	Tuscaloosa	1820
Pike	Troy	Henry, Montgomery	1821
Randolph	Wedowee	Creek Cession 1832	1832
Russell	Phenix City	Creek Cession 1832	1832
St. Clair	Ashville & Pell City	Shelby	1818
Shelby	Columbiana	Montgomery	1818
Sumter	Livingston	Choctaw Cession 1830	1832
Talladega	Talladega	Creek Cession 1832	1832
Tallapoosa	Dadeville	Creek Cession 1832	1832
Tuscaloosa	Tuscaloosa	Cherokee & Choctaw Cession 1816	1818
Walker	Jasper	Marion, Tuscaloosa	1823
Washington	Chatom	Mississippi Terr., Baldwin	1800
Wilcox	Camden	Monroe, Dallas	1819
Winston	Double Springs	Walker	1850
ARIZONA			
Apache	St. Johns	Yavapai	1879
Cochise	Bisbee	Pima	1881
Coconino	Flagstaff	Yavapai	1891
Gila	Globe	Maricopa	1881
Graham	Safford	Apache, Pima	1881
Greenlee	Clifton	Graham	1909
Maricopa	Phoenix	Yavapai	1871
Mohave	Kingman	Original county	1864
Navajo	Holbrook	Apache	1895

County Name	County Seat	Parent County	Year Created
Pima	Tucson	Original county	1864
Pinal	Florence	Pima	1875
Santa Cruz	Nogales	Pima	1899
Yavapai	Prescott	Oringial county	1864
Yuma	Yuma	Original county	1864

ARKANSAS

County Name	County Seat	Parent County	Year Created
Arkansas	Stuttgart & DeWitt	Oringial county	1813
Ashley	Hamburg	Chicot, Union, Drew	1848
Baxter	Mountain Home	Fulton, Izard, Marion & Searcy	1873
Benton	Bentonville	Washington	1836
Boone	Harrison	Carrol, Madison	1869
Bradley	Warren	Union	1840
Calhoun	Hampton	Dallas, Ouachita	1850
Carroll	Berryville & Eureka Springs	Izard	1833
Chicot	Lake Village	Arkansas	1823
Clark	Arkadelphia	Arkansas	1818
Clay	Corning & Pigott	Randolph, Green	1873
Cleburne	Heber Springs	White, Van Buren, Independence	1883
Cleveland	Rison	Dallas, Bradley, Jefferson, Lincoln	1873
Columbia	Magnolia	Lafayette, Hempstead, Ouachita	1852
Conway	Morrilton	Pulaski	1825
Craighead	Jonesboro & Lake City	Mississippi, Greene, Poinsett	1859
Crawford	Van Buren	Pulaski	1820
Crittenden	Marion	Phillips	1825
Cross	Wynne	Crittenden, Poinsett, St. Francis	1862
Dallas	Fordyce	Clark, Bradley	1845
Desha	Arkansas City	Arkansas, Chicot	1838
Drew	Monticello	Arkansas, Bradley	1846
Faulkner	Conway	Pulaski, Conway	1873
Franklin	Charleston & Ozark	Crawford	1837
Fulton	Salem	Izard	1842
Garland	Hot Springs N.P.	Montgomery, Hot Springs, Saline	1873
Grant	Sheridan	Jefferson, Hot Springs, Saline	1869
Greene	Paragould	Lawrence	1833
Hempstead	Hope	Arkansas	1818
Hot Springs	Malvern	Clark	1829
Howard	Nashville	Pike, Hempstead, Polk, Sevier	1873
Independence	Batesville	Laurence, Arkansas	1820
Izard	Melbourne	Independence, Fulton	1825
Jackson	Newport	Woodruff	1829
Jefferson	Pine Bluff	Arkansas, Pulaski	1829
Johnson	Clarksville	Pope	1833
Lafayette	Lewisville	Hempstead	1827
Lawrence	Powhatan	New Madrid, Mo.	1815
Lee	Marianna	Phillips, Monroe, Crittenden, St. Francis	1873
Lincoln	Star City	Arkansas, Bradley, Desha, Drew, Jefferson	1871
Little River	Ashdown	Hempstead	1867
Logan	Booneville & Paris	Pope, Franklin, Johnson, Scott, Yell	1871
Lonoke	Lonoke	Pulaski, Prairie	1873
Madison	Huntsville	Washington	1836
Marion	Yellville	Izard	1835
Miller	Texarkana	Abolished 1836 & ret. to Arkansas Re-established 1874	1820

County Name	County Seat	Parent County	Year Created
Mississippi	Blytheville & Osceola	Crittenden	1833
Monroe	Clarendon	Phillips, Arkansas	1829
Montgomery	Mount Ida	Hot Springs	1842
Nevada	Prescott	Hempstead, Columbia, Ouachita	1871
Newton	Jasper	Carroll	1842
Ouachita	Camden	Union	1842
Perry	Perryville	Conway	1840
Phillips	Helena	Arkansas, Hempstead	1820
Pike	Murfreesboro	Clark, Hempstead	1833
Poinsett	Harrisburg	Greene, St. Francis	1838
Polk	Mena	Sevier	1844
Pope	Russellville	Crawford	1829
Prairie	Des Arc & De Valls Bluff	Pulaski	1846
Pulaski	Little Rock	Arkansas	1818
Randolph	Pocahontas	Lawrence	1835
St. Francis	Forrest City	Phillips	1827
Saline	Benton	Pulaski, Hempstead	1835
Scott	Waldron	Pulaski, Crawford, Pope	1833
Searcy	Marshall	Marion	1835
Sebastian	Fort Smith & Greenwood	Scott, Polk, Crawford	1851
Sevier	DeQueen	Hempstead, Miller	1828
Sharp	Evening Shade & Hardy	Laurence	1868
Stone	Mountain View	Izard, Independence, Searcy, Van Buren	1873
Union	El Dorado	Hempstead, Clark	1829
Van Buren	Clinton	Independence, Conway, Izard	1833
Washington	Fayetteville	Crawford	1828
White	Searcy	Pulaski, Jackson	1835
Woodruff	Augusta	Jackson, St. Francis	1862
Yell	Danville & Dardanelle	Pope, Scott	1840

CALIFORNIA

County Name	County Seat	Parent County	Year Created
Alameda	Oakland	Contra Costa & Santa Clara	1853
Alpine	Markleeville	Eldorado, Amador, Calaveras	1864
Amador	Jackson	Calaveras	1854
Butte	Oroville	Original county	1850
Calaveras	San Andreas	Original county	1850
Colusa	Colusa	Original county	1850
Contra Costa	Martinez	Original county	1850
Del Norte	Crescent City	Klamath	1857
El Dorado	Placerville	Original county	1850
Fresno	Fresno	Merced, Mariposa	1856
Glenn	Willows	Colusa	1891
Humboldt	Eureka	Trinity	1853
Imperial	El Centro	San Diego	1907
Inyo	Independence	Tulare	1866
Kern	Bakersfield	Tulare, Los Angeles	1866
Kings	Hanford	Tulare	1893
Lake	Lakeport	Tuolumne	1861
Lassen	Susanville	Plumas, Shasta	1864
Los Angeles	Los Angeles	Original county	1850
Madera	Madera	Fresno	1843
Marin	San Rafael	Original county	1893
Mariposa	Mariposa	Original county	1850
Mendocino	Ukiah	Original county	1850
Merced	Merced	Mariposa	1855
Modoc	Alturas	Siskiyou	1874
Mono	Bridgeport	Calaveras, Fresno	1861

County Name	County Seat	Parent County	Year Created
Monterey	Salinas	Original county	1850
Napa	Napa	Original county	1850
Nevada	Nevada City	Yuba	1851
Orange	Santa Ana	Los Angeles	1889
Placer	Auburn	Yuba, Sutter	1851
Plumas	Quincy	Butte	1854
Riverside	Riverside	San Diego, San Bernardino	1893
Sacramento	Sacramento	Original county	1850
San Benito	Hollister	Monterey	1874
San Bernardino	San Bernardino	Los Angeles	1853
San Diego	San Diego	Original county	1850
San Francisco	San Francisco	Original county	1850
San Joaquin	Stockton	Original county	1850
San Luis Obispo	San Luis Obispo & Templeton	Original county	1850
San Mateo	Redwood City	San Francisco	1856
Santa Barbara	Santa Barbara	Original county	1850
Santa Clara	San Jose	Original county	1850
Santa Cruz	Santa Cruz	Original county	1850
Shasta	Redding	Original county	1850
Sierra	Downieville	Yuba	1852
Siskiyou	Yreka	Shasta, Klamath	1852
Solano	Fairfield	Original county	1850
Sonoma	Santa Rosa	Original county	1850
Stanislaus	Modesto	Tuolumne	1854
Sutter	Yuba City	Original county	1850
Tehama	Red Bluff	Colusa, Butte, Shasta	1856
Trinity	Weaverville	Original county	1850
Tulare	Visalia	Mariposa	1852
Tuolumne	Sonora	Original county	1850
Ventura	Ventura	Santa Barbara	1872
Yolo	Woodland	Original county	1850
Yuba	Marysville	Original county	1850

COLORADO

County Name	County Seat	Parent County	Year Created
Adams	Brighton	Arapahoe	1901
Alamosa	Alamosa	Costilla, Conejos	1913
Arapahoe	Littleton	Original county	1861
Archuleta	Pagosa Springs	Conejos	1885
Baca	Springfield	Las Animas	1889
Bent	Las Animas	Greenwood	1870
Boulder	Boulder	Original county	1861
Chaffee	Salida	Lake	1861
Cheyenne	Cheyenne Wells	Bent, Elbert	1889
Clear Creek	Georgetown	Original county	1861
Conejos	Conejos	Original county	1861
Costilla	San Luis	Original county	1861
Crowley	Ordway	Bent, Otero	1911
Custer	Westcliffe	Fremont	1877
Delta	Delta	Gunnison	1883
Denver, City & Co.	Denver	Arapahoe	1901
Dolores	Dove Creek	Ouray	1881
Douglas	Castle Rock	Original county	1861
Eagle	Eagle	Summit	1883
Elbert	Kiowa	Douglas, Greenwood	1874
El Paso	Colorado Springs	Original county	1861
Fremont	Canon City	Original county	1861
Garfield	Glenwood Springs	Summit	1883
Gilpin	Central City	Original county	1861
Grand	Hot Sulphur Spr.	Summit	1874
Gunnison	Gunnison	Lake	1877
Hinsdale	Lake City	Conejos	1874
Huerfano	Walsenburg	Original county	1861

County Name	County Seat	Parent County	Year Created
Jackson	Walden	Grand, Larimer	1909
Jefferson	Golden	Original county	1861
Kiowa	Eads	Cheyenne, Bent	1889
Kit Carson	Burlington	Elbert	1889
Lake	Leadville	Original county	1861
La Plata	Durango	Conejos, Lake	1874
Larimer	Fort Collins	Original county	1861
Las Animas	Trinidad	Huerfano	1866
Lincoln	Hugo	Elbert	1889
Logan	Sterling	Weld	1887
Mesa	Grand Junction	Gunnison	1883
Mineral	Creede	Hinsdale	1893
Moffatt	Craig	Routt	1911
Montezuma	Cortez	La Plata	1889
Montrose	Montrose	Gunnison	1883
Morgan	Fort Morgan	Weld	1889
Otero	La Junta	Bent	1889
Ouray	Ouray	Hinsdale, San Juan	1877
Park	Fairplay	Original county	1861
Phillips	Holyoke	Logan	1889
Pitkin	Aspen	Gunnison	1881
Prowers	Lamar	Bent	1889
Pueblo	Pueblo	Original county	1861
Rio Blanco	Meeker	Summit	1889
Rio Grande	Del Norte	Conejos, Costilla	1874
Routt	Steamboat Springs	Grand	1877
Saguache	Saguache	Costilla	1866
San Juan	Silverton	La Plata	1876
San Miguel	Telluride	Ouray	1861
Sedgwick	Julesburg	Logan	1889
Summit	Breckenridge	Original county	1861
Teller	Cripple Creek	El Paso	1899
Washington	Akron	Weld, Arapahoe	1887
Weld	Greeley	Original county	1861
Yuma	Wray	Washington, Arapahoe	1889

CONNECTICUT

County Name	County Seat	Parent County	Year Created
Fairfield	Bridgeport	Original county	1666
Hartford	Hartford	Original county	1666
Litchfield	Litchfield & Winsted	Hartford, Fairfield	1751
Middlesex	Middletown	Hartford, New London, New Haven	1785
New Haven	Waterbury & New Haven	Original county	1666
New London	New London & Norwich	Original county	1666
Tolland	Rockville	Windham	1785
Windham	Putnam & Willimantic	Hartford, New London	1726

DELAWARE

County Name	County Seat	Parent County	Year Created
Kent	Dover	St. Jones, Name changed to Kent 1682	1682
New Castle	Wilmington	Original county	1673
Sussex	Georgetown	Early 17th Century Horrekill District	1682

FLORIDA

County Name	County Seat	Parent County	Year Created
Alachua	Gainesville	Duval, St. John	1824
Baker	Macclenny	New River	1861
Bay	Panama City	Calhoun, Washington	1913
Bradford	Starke	New River up to 1861	1858
Brevard	Titusville	St. Lucas up to 1855	1844
Broward	St. Lauderdale	Dade, Palm Beach	1915
Calhoun	Blountstown	Franklin, Washington, Jackson	1838
Charlotte	Punta Gorda	De Soto	1921

County Name	County Seat	Parent County	Year Created
Citrus	Inverness	Hernando	1887
Clay	Green Cove Springs	Duval	1858
Collier	Naples	Lee, Monroe	1923
Columbia	Lake City	Alachua	1832
Dade	Miami	Monroe, St. Lucie (1855)	1836
De Soto	Arcadia	Manatee	1887
Dixie	Cross City	Lafayette	1921
Duval	Jacksonville	St. John	1822
Escambia	Pensacola	One of two original counties	1822
Flagler	Bunnell	St. John, Volusia	1917
Franklin	Apalachicola	Jackson	1832
Gadsden	Quincy	Jackson	1823
Gilchrist	Trenton	Alachua	1925
Glades	Moore Haven	De Soto	1921
Gulf	Port St. Joe	Calhoun	1925
Hamilton	Jasper	Duval	1827
Hardee	Wauchula	De Soto	1921
Hendry	La Belle	Lee	1923
Hernando	Brooksville	Alachua (formerly Benton)	1843
Highlands	Sebring	De Soto	1921
Hillsborough	Tampa	Alachua, Monroe	1834
Holmes	Bonifay	Walton, Washington, Calhoun	1848
Indian River	Vero Beach	St. Lucie	1925
Jackson	Marianna	Escambia	1822
Jefferson	Monticello	Leon	1827
Lafayette	Mayo	Madison	1856
Lake	Tavares	Orange, Sumter	1887
Lee	Ft. Myers	Monroe	1887
Leon	Tallahassee	Gadsden	1824
Levy	Bronson	Alachua, Marion	1845
Liberty	Bristol	Franklin, Gadsden	1855
Madison	Madison	Jefferson	1827
Manatee	Bradenton	Hillsboro	1855
Marion	Ocala	Alachua, Hillsborough, Mosquito	1844
Martin	Stuart	Palm Beach, St. Lucie	1925
Monroe	Key West	St. Johns	1823
Nassau	Fernandina Beach	Duval	1824
Okaloosa	Crestview	Santa Rosa, Walton	1915
Okeechobee	Okeechobee	Osceola, Palm Beach, St. Lucie	1917
Orange	Orlando	changed from Mosquito, 1845 Sumter 1871	1824
Osceola	Kissimmee	Brevard, Orange	1887
Palm Beach	West Palm Beach	Dade	1909
Pasco	Dade City	Hernando	1887
Pinellas	Clearwater	Hillsboro	1911
Polk	Bartow	Brevard, Hillsborough	1861
Putnam	Palatka	Alachua, Marion, Orange, St. Johns	1849
St. Johns	St. Augustine	One of two original counties	1822
St. Lucie	Fort Pierce	Brevard	1905
Santa Rosa	Milton	Escambia	1842
Sarasota	Sarasota	Manatee	1921
Seminole	Sanford	Orange	1913
Sumter	Bushnell	Marion	1853
Suwannee	Live Oak	Columbia	1858
Taylor	Perry	Madison	1856
Union	Lake Butler	Bradford	1921
Volusia	De Land	St. Lucas	1854
Wakulla	Crawfordville	Leon	1843
Walton	De Funiak Springs	Jackson	1824
Washington	Chipley	Jackson, Walton	1825

GEORIGA

County Name	County Seat	Parent County	Year Created
Appling	Baxley	Creek Indian Lands	1818
Atkinson	Pearson	Coffee, Clinch	1917
Bacon	Alma	Appling, Pearce, Ware	1914
Baker	Newton	Early	1825
Baldwin	Milledgeville	Creek Indian Lands	1803
Banks	Homer	Franklin, Habersham	1858
Barrow	Winder	Jackson, Walton, Guinett	1914
Bartow	Cartersville	Changed from Cass 1861	1832
Ben Hill	Fitzgerald	Irwin, Wilcox	1906
Berrien	Nashville	Lowndes, Coffee, Irwin	1856
Bibb	Macon	Jones, Monroe, Twiggs, Houston	1822
Bleckley	Cochran	Pulaski	1912
Brantley	Nahunta	Charlton, Pierce, Wayne	1920
Brooks	Quitman	Lowndes, Thomas	1858
Bryan	Pembroke	Effingham, Liberty	1793
Bulloch	Statesboro	Franklin	1796
Burke	Waynesboro	St. George Parrish	1777
Butts	Jackson	Henry, Monroe	1825
Calhoun	Morgan	Baker & Early	1854
Camden	Woodbine	St. Mary, St. Thomas	1777
Campbell	Merged Fulton 1926 and 1932	Carroll, Coweta	1828
Candler	Metter	Bulloch, Emauel, Tattnall	1914
Carroll	Carrollton	Indian Lands	1826
Cattoosa	Ringgold	Walker, Whitfield	1853
Charlton	Folkston	Camden, Ware	1854
Chatham	Savannah	St. Phillip, Christ Church Parish	1777
Chattahoochee	Cusseta	Muscogee, Marion	1854
Chattooga	Summerville	Floyd, Walker	1838
Cherokee	Canton	Cherokee Lands, Habersham, Hall	1831
Clarke	Athens	Jackson, Green	1801
Clay	Ft. Gaines	Early Randolph	1854
Clayton	Jonesboro	Fayette, Henry	1858
Clench	Homerville	Ware, Lowndes	1850
Cobb	Marietta	Cherokee	1832
Coffee	Douglas	Clinch, Irwin, Ware, Telfair	1854
Colquitt	Moultrie	Lowndes, Thomas	1856
Columbia	Appling	Richmond	1790
Cook	Adel	Berrien	1918
Coweta	Newman	Indian Lands	1826
Crawford	Knoxville	Houston, Marion, Talbot, Macon	1822
Crisp	Cordele	Dooly	1905
Dade	Trenton	Walker	1837
Dawson	Dawsonville	Lumpkin, Gilmer	1857
Decatur	Bainbridge	Early	1823
De Kalb	Decatur	Fayette, Gwinett, Newton, Henry	1822
Dodge	Eastman	Montgomery, Pulaski, Telfair	1870
Dooly	Vienna	Indian Lands	1821
Dougherty	Albany	Baker	1853
Douglas	Douglasville	Carroll, Campbell	1870
Early	Blakely	Creek Indian Lands	1818
Echols	Statenville	Clinch, Lowndes	1858
Effingham	Springfield	St. Mathews, St. Phillips	1777
Elbert	Elberton	Wilkes	1790
Emanuel	Swainsboro	Montgomery, Bulloch	1812
Evans	Claxton	Bulloch, Tattnall	1914
Fannin	Blue Ridge	Gilmer, Union	1854

County Name	County Seat	Parent County	Year Created
Fayette	Fayetteville	Indian Lands, Henry	1821
Floyd	Rome	Cherokee, Chattooga, Palding	1832
Forsyth	Cumming	Cherokee, Lumpkin	1832
Franklin	Carnesville	Cherokee Lands	1784
Fulton	Atlanta	De Kalb, Campbell	1853
Gilmer	Ellijay	Cherokee	1832
Glascock	Gibson	Warren Jefferson	1857
Glynn	Brunswick	St. David, St. Patrick	1777
Gordon	Calhoun	Cass, Floyd	1850
Grady	Cairo	Decatur, Thomas	1905
Greene	Greensboro	Washington, Oglethorpe, Wilkes	1786
Gwinnett	Lawrenceville	Cherokee Lands, Jackson	1818
Habersham	Clarkesville	Cherokee Lands, Franklin	1818
Hall	Gainesville	Cherokee Lands, Jackson, Franklin	1818
Hancock	Sparta	Greene, Washington	1793
Haralson	Buchanan	Carroll, Polk	1856
Harris	Hamilton	Muscogee, Troup	1827
Hart	Hartwell	Elbert, Franklin	1853
Heard	Franklin	Carroll, Coweta, Troup	1830
Henry	McDonough	Indian Lands, Walton	1821
Houston	Perry	Indian Lands	1821
Irwin	Ocilla	Indian Lands, Coffee, Telfair	1818
Jackson	Jefferson	Franklin	1796
Jasper	Monticello	Baldwin	1807
Jeff Davis	Hazelhurst	Appling, Coffee	1905
Jefferson	Louisville	Burke, Warren	1796
Jenkins	Millen	Bullock, Burke, Emanuel, Screven	1905
Johnson	Wrightsville	Emanuel, Laurens, Washington	1858
Jones	Gray	Baldwin, Bibb, Putnam	1807
Lamar	Barnesville	Monroe, Pike	1920
Lanier	Lakeland	Berrien, Lowndes, Clinch	1919
Laurens	Dublin	Montgomery, Washington, Wilkinson	1807
Lee	Leesburg	Indian Lands	1826
Liberty	Hinesville	St. Andrew, St. James, St. Johns	1777
Lincoln	Lincolnton	Wilkes	1796
Long	Ludowici	Liberty	1920
Lowndes	Valdosta	Irwin	1825
Lumpkin	Dahlonega	Cherokee, Habersham, Hall	1832
Macon	Oglethorpe	Houston, Marion	1837
Madison	Danielsville	Clarke, Elbert, Franklin, Jackson, Oglethorpe	1811
Marion	Buena Vista	Lee, Muscogee, Stewart	1870
McDuffie	Thomson	Columbia, Warren	1870
McIntosh	Darien	Liberty	1793
Meriwether	Greenville	Troup	1827
Miller	Colquitt	Baker, Early	1856
Mitchell	Camilla	Baker	1857
Monroe	Forsyth	Indian Lands	1821
Montgomery	Mt. Vernon	Washington, Laurens, Tattnall, Telfair	1793
Morgan	Madison	Baldwin, Jasper	1807
Murray	Chatsworth	Cherokee	1832
Muscogee	Columbus	Creek Lands, Harris, Lee, Marion	1826
Newton	Covington	Henry, Jasper, Morgan, Walton	1821
Oconee	Watkinsville	Clarke	1875
Oglethorpe	Lexington	Clarke, Green, Wilkes	1793
Paulding	Dallas	Cherokee Lands, Carroll, Cobb	1832
Peach	Fort Valley	Houston, Macon	1924
Pickens	Jasper	Cherokee, Gilmer	1853
Pierce	Blackshear	Appling, Ware	1857
Pike	Zebulon	Monroe	1822
Polk	Cedartown	Paulding	1851
Pulaski	Hawkinsville	Laurens, Wilkinson	1808
Putnam	Eatonton	Baldwin	1807
Quitman	Georgetown	Randolph, Stewart	1858
Rabun	Clayton	Cherokee Lands, Habersham	1819
Randolph	Cuthbert	Baker, Lee	1828
Richmond	Augusta	St. Paul Parish	1777
Rockdale	Conyers	Henry, Newton	1870
Schley	Ellaville	Marion, Sumter	1857
Screven	Sylvania	Burke, Effingham	1793
Seminole	Donalsonville	Decatur, Early	1920
Spalding	Griffin	Fayette, Henry, Pike	1851
Stephens	Toccoa	Franklin, Habersham	1905
Stewart	Lumpkin	Randolph	1830
Sumter	Americus	Lee	1831
Talbot	Talbotton	Crawford, Harris, Marion, Macon, Muscogee	1827
Taliaferro	Crawfordville	Green, Hancock, Oglethorpe, Warren, Wilkes	1825
Tattnall	Reidsville	Montgomery, Liberty	1801
Taylor	Butler	Marion, Talbot	1852
Telfair	McRae	Wilkinson, Appling	1807
Terrell	Dawson	Lee, Randolph	1856
Thomas	Thomasville	Baker, Decatur, Irwin, Lowndes	1825
Tift	Tifton	Berrien, Irwin, Worth	1905
Toombs	Lyons	Emanuel, Tattnall, Montgomery	1917
Towns	Hiawassee	Rabun, Union	1856
Treutlen	Soperton	Emanuel, Montgomery	1917
Troup	LaGrange	Indian Lands	1826
Turner	Ashburn	Dooly, Irwin, Wilcox, Worth	1905
Twiggs	Jeffersonville	Wilkinson	1809
Union	Blairsville	Cherokee Lands, Lumpkin	1832
Upson	Thomaston	Crawford, Pike	1824
Walker	LaFayette	Murray	1833
Walton	Monroe	Cherokee Lands	1818
Ware	Waycross	Appling	1824
Warren	Warrenton	Columbia, Richmond, Wilkes	1793
Washington	Sandersville	Indian Lands	1784
Wayne	Jesup	Indian Lands, Appling, Glynn, Camden	1803
Webster	Preston	Changed from Kinchafoonee 1856	1853
Wheeler	Alamo	Montgomery	1912
White	Cleveland	Habersham	1857
Whitfield	Dayton	Murray, Walker	1851
Wilcox	Abbeville	Dooly, Irwin, Pulaski	1857
Wilkes	Washington	Washington	1777
Wilkinson	Irwinton	Creek Cession	1803
Worth	Sylvester	Dooly, Irwin	1853

HAWAII

County Name	County Seat	Parent County	Year Created
Hawaii	Hilo		
Honolulu	Honolulu		
Kalawao	Kalaupapa		
Kauai	Lihue		
Maui	Wailuku		

County Name	County Seat	Parent County	Year Created
IDAHO			
Ada	Boise	Boise	1864
Adams	Council	Washington	1911
Bannock	Pocatello	Oneida, Bear Lake	1893
Bear Lake	Paris	Oneida	1875
Benewah	St. Maries	Kootenai	1915
Bingham	Blackfoot	Oneida	1885
Blaine	Hailey	Alturas	1895
Boise	Idaho City	Original county	1864
Bonner	Sandpoint	Kootenai	1907
Booneville	Idaho Falls	Bingham	1911
Boundary	Bonners Ferry	Bonner	1915
Butte	Arco	Bingham, Blaine, Jefferson	1917
Camas	Fairfield	Blaine	1917
Canyon	Caldwell	Owyhee, Ada	1891
Caribou	Soda Springs	Bannock, Oneida	1919
Cassia	Burley	Oneida	1879
Clark	Dubois	Fremont	1919
Clearwater	Orofino	Nez Perce	1911
Custer	Challis	Alturas	1881
Elmore	Mountain Home	Alturas, Ada	1889
Franklin	Preston	Oneida	1913
Fremont	St. Anthony	Bingham	1893
Gem	Emmett	Boise, Canyon	1915
Gooding	Gooding	Lincoln	1913
Idaho	Grangeville	Original county	1864
Jefferson	Rigby	Fremont	1913
Jerome	Jerome	Gooding, Lincoln	1919
Kootenai	Coeur d'Alene	Nez Perce	1864
Latah	Moscow	Nez Perce	1864
Lewis	Nez Perce	Nez Perce	1911
Lincoln	Shoshone	Alturas	1895
Madison	Rexburg	Fremont	1913
Minidoka	Rupert	Lincoln	1913
Nez Perce	Lewiston	Original county	1864
Oneida	Malad City	Original county	1864
Owyhee	Murphy	Original county	1863
Payette	Payette	Canyon	1917
Power	American Falls	Bingham, Blaine, Oneida	1913
Shoshone	Wallace	Original county	1864
Teton	Driggs	Madison, Fremont, Bingham	1915
Twin Falls	Twin Falls	Cassia	1907
Valley	Cascade	Boise, Idaho	1917
Washington	Weiser	Boise	1879
ILLINOIS			
Adams	Quincy	Pike	1825
Alexander	Cairo	Johnson	1819
Bond	Greenville	Madison	1817
Boone	Belvidere	Winnebago	1837
Brown	Mt. Sterling	Schuyler	1839
Bureau	Princeton	Putnam	1837
Calhoun	Hardin	Pike	1825
Carroll	Mt. Carroll	Jo Daviess	1839
Cass	Virginia	Morgan	1837
Champaign	Urbana	Vermillion	1833
Christian	Taylorville	Sangamon, Shelby	1839
Clark	Marshall	Crawford	1819
Clay	Louisville	Wayne, Lawrence, Fayette	1824
Clinton	Carlyle	Washington, Bond, Fayette, Crawford	1824
Coles	Charleston	Clark, Edgar	1830
Cook	Chicago	Putnam	1831
Crawford	Robinson	Edwards	1816
Cumberland	Toledo	Coles	1843
De Kalb	Sycamore	Kane	1837
De Witt	Clinton	Macon, McLean	1839
Douglas	Tuscola	Coles	1859
DuPage	Wheaton	Cook	1839
Edgar	Paris	Clark	1823
Edwards	Albion	Madison, Gallatin	1814
Effingham	Effingham	Fayette, Crawford	1831
Fayette	Vandalia	Bond, Wayne, Clark, Jefferson	1821
Ford	Paxton	Clark	1859
Franklin	Benton	White, Gallatin	1818
Fulton	Lewistown	Pike	1823
Gallatin	Shawneetown	Randolph	1812
Greene	Carrollton	Madison	1821
Grundy	Morris	LaSalle	1841
Hamilton	McLeansboro	White	1821
Hancock	Carthage	Pike, Unorg. Terr.	1825
Hardin	Elizabethtown	Pope	1839
Henderson	Oquawka	Warren	1841
Henry	Cambridge	Fulton	1825
Iroquois	Watseka	Vermillion	1833
Jackson	Murphysboro	Randolph, Johnson	1816
Jasper	Newton	Clay, Crawford	1831
Jefferson	Mt. Vernon	Edwards, White	1819
Jersey	Jerseyville	Greene	1839
Jo Daviess	Galena	Henry, Mercer, Putnam	1827
Johnson	Vienna	Randolph	1822
Kane	Geneva	LaSalle	1836
Kankakee	Kankakee	Iroquois, Will	1853
Kendall	Yorkville	LaSalle, Kane	1841
Knox	Galesburg	Fulton	1825
Lake	Waukegan	McHenry	1829
LaSalle	Ottawa	Putnam, Vermillion	1831
Lawrence	Lawrenceville	Crawford, Edwards	1821
Lee	Dixon	Ogle	1839
Livingston	Pontiac	LaSalle, McLean	1837
Logan	Lincoln	Sangamon	1839
Macon	Decatur	Shelby	1829
Macoupin	Carlinville	Madison, Greene	1829
Madison	Edwardsville	St. Clair	1812
Marion	Salem	Fayette, Jefferson	1823
Marshall	Lacon	Putnam	1839
Mason	Haivana	Tazewell	1841
Massac	Metropolis	Pope, Jefferson	1843
McDonough	Macomb	Schuyler	1826
McHenry	Woodstock	Cook	1836
McLean	Bloomington	Tazewell, Unorg. Terr.	1830
Menard	Petersburg	Sangamon	1839
Mercer	Aledo	Unog. Terr., Pike	1825
Monroe	Waterloo	Randolph, St. Clair	1816
Montgomery	Hillsboro	Bond, Madison	1821
Morgan	Jacksonville	Sangamon	1823
Moultrie	Sullivan	Shelby, Macon	1843
Ogle	Oregon	Jo Daviess	1836
Peoria	Peoria	Fulton	1825
Perry	Pinckneyville	Randolph, Jackson	1827
Piatt	Monticello	De Witt, Macon	1841
Pike	Pittsfield	Madison, Bond, Clark	1821
Pope	Golconda	Gallatin, Johnson	1816
Pulaski	Mound City	Johnson	1843

County Name	County Seat	Parent County	Year Created
Putnam	Hennepin	Fulton	1825
Randolph	Chester	N.W. Territory, St. Clair	1795
Richland	Olney	Clay, Lawrence	1841
Rock Island	Rock Island	Jo Daviess	1831
St. Clair	Belleville	N.W. Territory	1790
Saline	Harrisburg	Gallatin	1847
Sangamon	Springfield	Bond, Madison	1821
Schuyler	Rushville	Pike, Fulton	1825
Scott	Winchester	Morgan	1839
Shelby	Shelbyville	Fayette	1827
Stark	Toulon	Knox, Putnam	1839
Stephenson	Freeport	Jo Daviess, Winnebago	1837
Tazewell	Pekin	Sangamon	1827
Union	Jonesboro	Johnson	1818
Vermilion	Danville	Unorg. Terr., Edgar	1826
Wabash	Mt. Carmel	Edwards	1824
Warren	Monmouth	Pike	1825
Washington	Nashville	St. Clair	1818
Wayne	Fairfield	Edwards	1819
White	Carmi	Gallatin	1815
Whiteside	Morrison	Jo Daviess, Henry	1836
Will	Joliet	Cook, Iroquois	1836
Williamson	Marion	Franklin	1839
Winnebago	Rockford	Jo Daviess	1836
Wooford	Eureka	Tazewell, McLean	1841

INDIANA

County Name	County Seat	Parent County	Year Created
Adams	Decatur	Allen, Randolph	1835
Allen	Fort Wayne	Unorg. Terr., Randolph	1823
Bartholomew	Columbus	Unorg. Terr., Jackson	1821
Benton	Fowler	Jasper	1840
Blackford	Hartford City	Jay	1838
Boone	Lebanon	Hendricks, Marion	1830
Brown	Nashville	Monroe, Bartholomew, Jackson	1836
Carroll	Delphi	Unorg. Terr.,	1826
Cass	Logansport	Carroll	1828
Clark	Jeffersonville	Knox	1801
Clay	Brazil	Owen, Putnam, Vigo, Sullivan	1825
Clinton	Frankfort	Tippecanoe	1830
Crawford	English	Orange, Harrison, Perry	1818
Daviess	Washington	Knox	1816
Dearborn	Lawrenceburg	Clark	1803
Decatur	Greensburg	Unorg. Terr.	1821
DeKalb	Auburn	Allen, Lagrange	1835
Delaware	Muncie	Randolph	1827
Dubois	Jasper	Pike	1817
Elkhart	Goshen	Allen, Cass	1830
Fayette	Connersville	Wayne, Franklin	1818
Floyd	New Albany	Harrison, Clarke	1819
Fountain	Covington	Montgomery, Parke	1825
Franklin	Brookville	Clark, Dearborn, Jefferson	1810
Fulton	Rochester	Allen, Cass, St. Joseph	1835
Gibson	Princeton	Knox	1813
Grant	Marion	Delaware	1831
Greene	Bloomfield	Daviess, Sullivan	1821
Hamilton	Noblesville	Unorg. Terr., Marion	1823
Hancock	Greenfield	Madison	1827
Harrison	Corydon	Knox, Clark	1808
Hendricks	Danville	Unorg. Terr. Putnam	1823
Henry	New Castle	Unorg. Terr.	1821

County Name	County Seat	Parent County	Year Created
Howard	Kokomo	Carroll, Cass, Miami, Grant, Hamilton	1844
Huntington	Huntington	Allen, Grant	1832
Jackson	Brownstown	Washington, Clark, Jefferson	1815
Jasper	Rensselaer	White, Warren	1835
Jay	Portland	Randolph, Delaware	1835
Jefferson	Madison	Dearborn, Clark	1810
Jennings	Vernon	Jefferson, Jackson	1816
Johnson	Franklin	Unorg. Terr.	1822
Knox	Vincennes	Northwest Territory	1790
Kosciusko	Warsaw	Elkhart, Cass	1835
Lagrange	Lagrange	Elkhart, Allen	1832
Lake	Crown Point	Pointer, Newton	1836
LaPorte	LaPorte	St. Joseph	1832
Lawrence	Bedford	Orange	1818
Madison	Anderson	Unorg. Terr., Marion	1823
Marion	Indianapolis	Unorg. Terr.	1822
Marshall	Plymouth	St. Joseph, Elkhart	1835
Martin	Shoals	Daviess, Dubois	1820
Miami	Peru	Cass	1832
Monroe	Bloomington	Orange	1818
Montgomery	Crawfordsville	Parke, Putnam	1822
Morgan	Martinsville	Unorg. Terr.	1821
Newton	Kentland	Jasper	1835
Noble	Albion	Elkhart, Lagrange, Allen	1835
Ohio	Rising Sun	Dearborn	1844
Orange	Paoli	Washington, Knox, Gibson	1815
Owen	Spencer	Daviess, Sullivan	1818
Parke	Rockville	Unorg. Terr., Vigo	1821
Perry	Cannelton	Warrick, Gibson	1814
Pike	Petersburg	Gibson, Perry	1816
Porter	Valparaiso	St. Joseph	1835
Posey	Mount Vernon	Warrick	1814
Pulaski	Winamac	Cass, St. Joseph	1835
Putnam	Greencastle	Unorg. Terr., Vigo, Owen	1821
Randolph	Winchester	Wayne	1818
Ripley	Versailles	Dearborn, Jefferson	1816
Rush	Rushville	Unorg. Terr.	1821
Saint Joseph	South Bend	Cass	1830
Scott	Scottsburg	Clark, Jefferson, Jennings	1820
Shelby	Shelbyville	Unorg. Terr.	1821
Spencer	Rockport	Warrick, Perry	1818
Starke	Knox	St. Joseph	1835
Steuben	Angola	LaGrange	1835
Sullivan	Sullivan	Knox	1816
Switzerland	Vevay	Dearborn, Jefferson	1814
Tippecanoe	Lafayette	Unorg. Terr., Parke	1826
Tipton	Tipton	Hamilton, Cass, Miami	1844
Union	Liberty	Wayne, Franklin, Fayette	1821
Vanderburgh	Evansville	Gibson, Posey, Warrick	1818
Vermillion	Newport	Parke	1824
Vigo	Terre Haute	Sullivan	1818
Wabash	Wabash	Cass, Grant	1832
Warren	Williamsport	Fountain	1827
Warrick	Boonville	Knox	1813
Washington	Salem	Clark, Harrison, Jefferson	1813
Wayne	Richmond	Clark, Dearborn	1810
Wells	Bluffton	Allen, Delaware	1835
White	Monticello	Carroll	1834
Whitley	Columbia City	Elkhart, Allen	1835

County Name	County Seat	Parent County	Year Created
IOWA			
Adair	Greenfield	Cass	1851
Adams	Corning	Taylor	1851
Allamakee	Waukon	Clayton	1847
Appanoose	Centerville	Davis	1843
Audubon	Audubon	Cass, Black Hawk	1851
Benton	Vinton	Indian Land Purchase	1837
Black Hawk	Waterloo	Delaware	1843
Boone	Boone	Polk	1846
Bremer	Waverly	Winnebago, Indian Reserve	1851
Buchanan	Independence	Delaware	1837
Buena Vista	Storm Lake	Sac. Clay	1851
Butler	Allison	Buchanan, Black Hawk	1851
Calhoun	Rockwell City	Formerly Fox County	1851
Carroll	Carroll	Guthrie	1851
Cass	Atlantic	Pottawattamie	1851
Cedar	Tipton	Wisconsin Territory	1837
Cerro Gordo	Mason City	Floyd	1851
Cherokee	Cherokee	Crawford	1851
Chickasaw	New Hampton	Fayette	1851
Clarke	Osceola	Lucas	1846
Clay	Spencer	Indian Lands	1851
Clayton	Elkader	Dubuque	1837
Clinton	Clinton	Dubuque	1837
Crawford	Denison	Shelby	1851
Dallas	Adel	Polk	1846
Davis	Bloomfield	Van Buren	1843
Decatur	Leon	Appanoose	1846
Delaware	Manchester	Debuque	1837
Des Moines	Burlington	Wisconsin Territory	1834
Dickinson	Spirit Lake	Kossuth	1851
Dubuque	Dubuque	Michigan Territory	1834
Emmett	Estherville	Kossuth, Dickinson	1851
Fayette	West Union	Clayton	1837
Floyd	Charles City	Chickasaw	1851
Franklin	Hampton	Chickasaw	1851
Fremont	Sidney	Pottawattamie	1847
Greene	Jefferson	Dallas	1851
Grundy	Grundy Center	Black Hawk	1851
Guthrie	Guthrie Center	Jackson	1851
Hamilton	Webster City	Webster	1856
Hancock	Garner	Wright	1851
Hardin	Eldora	Black Hawk	1851
Harrison	Logan	Pottawattamie	1851
Henry	Mount Pleasant	Wisconsin Territory	1836
Howard	Cresco	Chickasaw, Floyd	1851
Humboldt	Dakota City	Webster	1851
Ida	Ida Grove	Cherokee	1851
Iowa	Marengo	Washington	1843
Jackson	Maquoketa	Wisconsin Terr.	1837
Jasper	Newton	Mahaska	1846
Jefferson	Fairfield	Indian Land Purchase	1839
Johnson	Iowa City	Des Moines	1837
Jones	Anamosa	Wisconsin Territory	1837
Keokuk	Sigourney	Washington	1837
Kossuth	Algona	Webster	1851
Lee	Ft. Madison & Keokuk	Des Moines	1836
Linn	Cedar Rapdis	Wisconsin Territory	1837
Louisa	Wapello	Des Moines	1836
Lucas	Chariton	Monroe	1846
Lyon	Rock Rapids	Woodbury	1851
Madison	Winterest	Polk	1844
Mahaska	Oskaloosa	Fox, Sac Indian Purchase	1843
Marion	Knoxville	Washington	1845
Marshall	Marshalltown	Jasper	1846
Mills	Glenwood	Pottawattie	1851
Mitchell	Osage	Chickasaw	1851
Monona	Onawa	Harrison	1851
Monroe	Albia	Wapello	1843
Montgomery	Red Oak	Polk	1851
Muscatine	Muscatine	Des Moines	1836
O'Brien	Primghar	Cherokee	1851
Osceola	Sibley	Woodbury	1851
Page	Clarinda	Pottawattamie	1847
Palo Alto	Emmetsburg	Kossuth	1851
Plymouth	Le Mars	Woodbury	1851
Pocahontas	Pocahontas	Humboldt	1851
Polk	Des Moines	Indian Lands	1846
Pottawattamie	Council Bluffs	Indian Lands	1851
Poweshiek	Montezuma	Mesquakie Indian Lands	1843
Ringgold	Mount Ayr	Taylor	1847
Sac	Sac City	Greene	1851
Scott	Davenport	Wisconsin Territory	1837
Shelby	Harlan	Cass	1851
Sioux	Orange City	Plymouth	1851
Story	Nevada	Jasper, Polk, Boone	1846
Tama	Toledo	Boone, Benton	1843
Taylor	Bedford	Page	1847
Union	Creston	Clarke	1851
Van Buren	Keosauqua	Des Moines	1836
Wapello	Ottumwa	Indian Lands	1843
Warren	Indianola	Polk	1846
Washington	Washington	Wisconsin Territory	1837
Wayne	Corydon	Appanoose	1846
Webster	Fort Dodge	Yell, Risley	1851
Winnebago	Forest City	Kossuth	1847
Winneshiek	Decorah	Indian Lands	1847
Woodbury	Sioux City	Indian Lands	1851
Worth	Northwood	Mitchell	1851
Wright	Clarion	Webster	1851
KANSAS			
Allen	Iola	Original county	1855
Anderson	Garnett	Original county	1855
Atchison	Atchison	Original county	1855
Barber	Medicine Lodge	Harper	1867
Barton	Great Bend	Ellsworth	1867
Bourbon	Fort Scott	Original county	1855
Brown	Hiawatha	Original county	1855
Butler	El Dorado	Original county	1855
Chase	Cottonwood Falls	Butler	1859
Chautauqua	Sedan	Howard	1875
Cherokee	Columbus	Unorg. Terr.	1855
Cheyenne	Saint Francis	Kirwin Land District	1873
Clark	Ashland	Ford	1885
Clay	Clay Center	Original county	1857
Cloud	Concordia	Formerly Shirley County	1860
Coffey	Burlington	Original county	1855
Comanche	Coldwater	Kiowa	1867
Cowley	Winfield	Formerly Hunter	1867
Crawford	Girard	Bourbon	1867
Decatur	Oberlin	Norton	1873
Dickinson	Abilene	Original county	1855

County Name	County Seat	Parent County	Year Created
Doniphan	Troy	Original county	1855
Douglas	Lawrence	Original county	1855
Edwards	Kinsley	Kiowa	1874
Elk	Howard	Howard	1875
Ellis	Hays	Unorg. Terr.	1867
Ellsworth	Ellsworth	Saline	1867
Finney	Garden City	Arapahoe, Foote, Sequoyah	1883
Ford	Dodge City	Unorg. Terr.	1873
Franklin	Ottawa	Original county	1855
Geary	Junction City	Davis Co. 1875 to 1888, Riley	1855
Gove	Gove	Unorg. Terr.	1868
Graham	Hill City	Rooks	1867
Grant	Ulysses	Finney, Kearney	1873
Gray	Cimarron	Finney, Ford	1887
Greeley	Tribune	Hamilton	1873
Greenwood	Eureka	Original county	1855
Hamilton	Syracuse	Unorg. Terr.	1873
Harper	Anthony	Kingman	1867
Harvey	Newton	McPherson, Sedgwich, Marion	1872
Haskell	Sublette	Finney	1887
Hodgeman	Jetmore	Indian Lands	1873
Jackson	Holton	See Calhoun	1855
Jefferson	Oskaloosa	Original county	1855
Jewell	Mankato	Mitchell	1867
Johnson	Olathe	Original county	1855
Kearny	Lakin	Finney	1873
Kingman	Kingman	Unorg. Terr.	1886
Kiowa	Greensburg	Comanche, Edwards	1886
Labette	Oswego	Neosho	1867
Lane	Dighton	Finney	1873
Leavenworth	Leavenworth	Original county	1855
Lincoln	Lincoln	Ellsworth	1867
Linn	Mound City	Original county	1855
Logan	Oakley	Wallace (changed from St. John 1887)	1881
Lyon	Emporia	Madison	1857
Marion	Marion	Chase	1855
Marshall	Marysville	Original county	1855
McPherson	McPherson	Unorg. Terr.	1867
Meade	Meade	Unorg. Terr.	1885
Miami	Paola	Formerly Lykins	1855
Mitchell	Beloit	Kirwin Land District	1867
Montgomery	Independence	Labette	1867
Morris	Council Grove	Madison	1855
Morton	Elkhart	Stanton	1886
Nemaha	Seneca	Original county	1855
Neosho	Erie	Original county	1855
Ness	Ness City	Hodgeman	1867
Norton	Norton	Unorg. Terr.	1867
Osage	Lyndon	Formerly Weller	1855
Osborne	Osborne	Mitchell	1867
Ottawa	Minneapolis	Saline	1860
Pawnee	Larned	Rush, Stafford	1867
Phillips	Phillipsburg	Kirwin Land District	1867
Pottawatomie	Westmoreland	Riley, Calhoun	1857
Pratt	Pratt	Stafford	1867
Rawlins	Atwood	Kirwin Land District	1873
Reno	Hutchinson	Sedgwick, McPherson	1867
Republic	Belleville	Washington, Cloud	1860
Rice	Lyons	Reno	1867
Riley	Manhattan	Unorg. Terr., Wabaunsee	1855

County Name	County Seat	Parent County	Year Created
Rooks	Stockton	Kirwin Land District	1867
Rush	La Crosse	Unorg. Terr.	1867
Russell	Russell	Ellsworth	1867
Saline	Salina	Original county	1860
Scott	Scott City	Finney	1873
Sedgwick	Wichita	Butler	1867
Seward	Liberal	Indian Lands	1855
Shawnee	Topeka	Original county	1855
Sheridan	Hoxie	Unorg. Terr.	1873
Sherman	Goodland	Kirwin Land District	1873
Smith	Smith Center	Unorg. Terr.	1867
Stafford	Saint John	Unorg. Terr.	1867
Stanton	Johnson	Reorganized	1873
Stevens	Hugoton	Indian Lands	1873
Sumner	Wellington	Cowley	1867
Thomas	Colby	Kirwin Land District	1873
Trego	Wakeeney	Ellis	1867
Wabaunsee	Alma	Riley, Morris	1855
Wallace	Sharon Springs	Indian Lands	1868
Washington	Washington	Original county	1855
Wichita	Leoti	Indian Lands	1873
Wilson	Fredonia	Original county	1855
Woodson	Yates Center	Original county	1855
Wyandotte	Kansas City	Original county	1859

KENTUCKY

County Name	County Seat	Parent County	Year Created
Adair	Columbia	Green	1801
Allen	Scottsville	Barren, Warren	1815
Anderson	Lawrenceburg	Franklin, Mercer, Washington	1827
Ballard	Wickliffe	Hickman, McCracken	1842
Barren	Glasgow	Green, Warren	1798
Bath	Owingsville	Montgomery	1811
Bell	Pineville	Knox, Harlan	1867
Boone	Burlington	Campbell	1798
Bourbon	Paris	Fayette	1785
Boyd	Catlettsburg	Carter, Lawrence, Greenup	1860
Boyle	Danville	Mercer, Lincoln	1842
Bracken	Brooksville	Campbell, Mason	1796
Breathitt	Jackson	Clay, Estill, Perry	1839
Breckinridge	Hardinsburg	Hardin	1799
Bullitt	Shepherdsville	Jefferson, Nelson	1796
Butler	Morgantown	Logan, Ohio	1810
Caldwell	Princeton	Livingston	1809
Calloway	Murray	Hickman	1821
Campbell	Alexandria & Newport	Harrison, Mason, Scott	1794
Carlisle	Bardwell	Ballard	1886
Carroll	Carrollton	Gallatin, Henry, Trimble	1838
Carter	Grayson	Greenup, Lawrence	1838
Casey	Liberty	Lincoln	1806
Christian	Hopkinsville	Logan	1796
Clark	Winchester	Bourbon, Fayette	1792
Clay	Manchester	Madison, Floyd, Knox	1806
Clinton	Albany	Wayne, Cumberland	1836
Crittenden	Marion	Livingston	1842
Cumberland	Burkesville	Green	1798
Daviess	Owensboro	Ohio	1815
Edmonson	Brownsville	Grayson, Hart, Warren	1825
Elliott	Sandy Hook	Carter, Lawrence, Morgan	1869
Estill	Irvine	Clark, Madison	1808
Fayette	Lexington	Kentucky Co. Virginia	1780
Fleming	Flemingsburg	Mason	1798

County Name	County Seat	Parent County	Year Created
Floyd	Prestonsburg	Fleming, Mason, Montgomery	1799
Franklin	Frankfort	Woodford, Mercer, Shelby	1794
Fulton	Hickman	Hickman	1845
Gallatin	Warsaw	Franklin, Shelby	1798
Garrard	Lancaster	Madison, Lincoln, Mercer	1796
Grant	Williamstown	Pendleton	1820
Graves	Mayfield	Hickman	1821
Grayson	Leitchfield	Hardin, Ohio	1810
Green	Greensburg	Lincoln, Nelson	1792
Greenup	Greenup	Mason	1803
Hancock	Hawesville	Daviess, Ohio, Breckinridge	1829
Hardin	Elizabethtown	Nelson	1792
Harlan	Harlan	Knox	1819
Harrison	Cynthiana	Bourbon, Scott	1793
Hart	Mumfordville	Hardin, Barren, possibly Green	1819
Henderson	Henderson	Christian	1798
Henry	New Castle	Shelby	1798
Hickman	Clinton	Caldwell, Livingston	1821
Hopkins	Madisonville	Henderson	1806
Jackson	McKee	Rockcastle, Owsley, Madison, Clay, Estill, Laurel	1858
Jefferson	Louisville	Kentucky Co. Virginia	1780
Jessamine	Nicholasville	Fayette	1798
Johnson	Paintsville	Floyd, Morgan, Lawrence	1843
Kenton	Independence	Campbell	1840
Knott	Hindman	Perry, Breathitt, Floyd, Letcher	1884
Knox	Barbourville	Lincoln	1799
Larue	Hodgenville	Hardin	1843
Laurel	London	Whitley, Clay, Knox, Rock-Castle	1825
Lawrence	Louisa	Floyd, Greenup	1821
Lee	Beattyville	Owsley, Breathitt, Wolfe, Estill	1870
Leslie	Hyden	Clay, Harlan, Perry	1878
Letcher	Whitesburg	Perry, Harlan	1842
Lewis	Vanceburg	Mason	1806
Lincoln	Stanford	Kentucky Co., Virginia	1780
Livingston	Smithland	Christian	1798
Logan	Russellville	Lincoln	1792
Lyon	Eddyville	Caldwell	1854
Madison	Richmond	Lincoln	1785
Magoffin	Salyersville	Floyd, Johnson, Morgan	1860
Marion	Lebanon	Washington	1834
Marshall	Benton	Callaway	1842
Martin	Inez	Laurence, Floyd, Pike, Johnson	1870
Mason	Maysville	Bourbon	1788
Mc Cracken	Paducah	Hickman	1824
Mc Creary	Whitley City	Wayne, Pulaski, Whitley	1912
McLean	Calhoun	Muhlenburg, Daviess, Ohio	1854
Meade	Brandenburg	Hardin, Breckinridge	1823
Menifee	Frenchburg	Powell, Wolfe, Bath, Morgan Montgomery	1869
Mercer	Harrodsburg	Lincoln	1785
Metcalfe	Edmonton	Monroe, Adair, Barren, Cumberland, Green	1860
Monroe	Tompkinsville	Barren, Cumberland	1820
Montgomery	Mount Sterling	Clark	1796
Morgan	West Liberty	Floyd, Bath	1822
Muhlenberg	Greenville	Christian, Logan	1798
Nelson	Bardstown	Jefferson	1784
Nicholas	Carlisle	Bourbon, Mason	1799
Ohio	Hartford	Hardin	1798
Oldham	LaGrange	Henry, Shelby, Jefferson	1823
Owen	Owenton	Scott, Franklin, Gallatin, Pendleton	1819
Owsley	Booneville	Clay, Estill, Breathitt	1843
Pendleton	Falmouth	Bracken, Campbell	1787
Perry	Hazard	Clay, Floyd	1820
Pike	Pikeville	Floyd	1821
Powell	Stanton	Clark, Estill, Montgomery	1852
Pulaski	Somerset	Green, Lincoln	1798
Robertson	Mt. Olivet	Nicholas, Bracken, Mason, Fleming, Harrison	1867
Rockcastle	Mount Vernon	Pulaski, Lincoln, Madison	1810
Rowan	Morehead	Fleming, Morgan	1856
Russell	Jamestown	Cumberland, Adair, Wayne, Pulaski	1825
Scott	Georgetown	Woodford	1792
Shelby	Shelbyville	Jefferson	1792
Simpson	Franklin	Allen, Logan, Warren	1819
Spencer	Taylorsville	Shelby, Bullitt, Nelson	1824
Taylor	Campbellsville	Green	1848
Todd	Elkton	Christian, Logan	1819
Trigg	Cadiz	Christian, Caldwell	1820
Trimble	Bedford	Henry, Oldham, Gallatin	1837
Union	Morganfield	Henderson	1811
Warren	Bowling Green	Logan	1796
Washington	Springfield	Nelson	1792
Wayne	Monticello	Pulaski, Cumberland	1800
Webster	Dixon	Hopkins, Union, Henderson	1860
Whitley	Williamsburg	Knox	1818
Wolfe	Campton	Owsley, Breathitt, Powell, Morgan	1860
Woodford	Versailles	Fayette	1788

LOUISIANA

County Name	County Seat	Parent County	Year Created
Acadia	Crowley	St. Landry	1805
Allen	Oberlin	Calcasieu	1912
Ascension	Donaldsonville	St. James	1807
Assumption	Napoleonville	Original Parish	1807
Avoyelles	Marksville	Original Parish - reorg. 1873	1807
Beauregard	DeRidder	Calcasieu	1912
Bienville	Arcadia	Claiborne	1848
Bossier	Benton	Claiborne	1843
Caddo	Shreveport	Natchitoches	1838
Calcasieu	Lake Charles	St. Landry	1840
Caldwell	Columbia	Catahoula, Ouachita	1838
Cameron	Cameron	Calcasieu, Vermillion	1870
Catahoula	Harrisonburg		1808
Claiborne	Homer	Natchitoches	1828
Concordia	Vidalia	Avoyelles	1805
De Soto	Mansfield	Natchitoches	1843
East Baton Rouge	Baton Rouge	Original Parish	1810
East Carroll	Lake Providence	Carroll	1877
East Feliciana	Clinton	Seceded from Feliciana	1824
Evangeline	Ville Platte	St. Landry	1910
Franklin	Winnsboro	Catahoula, Ouachita, Madison	1843
Grant	Colfax	Rapides, Winn	1869
Iberia	New Iberia	St. Martin, St. Mary	1868
Iberville	Plaquemine	Assumption, Ascension	1805
Jackson	Jonesboro	Claiborne, Ouachita, Union	1845
Jefferson	Gretna	Orleans	1825
Jefferson Davis	Jennings	Calcasieu	1912
Lafayette	Lafayette	St. Martin	1823
Lafourche	Thibodaux		1805

County Name	County Seat	Parent County	Year Created
La Salle	Jena	Catahoula	1908
Lincoln	Ruston	Bienville, Jackson, Union, Claiborne	1873
Livingston	Livingston	St. Helena	1832
Madison	Tallulah	Concordia	1838
Morehouse	Bastrop	Ouachita	1844
Natchitoches	Natchitoches	Original Parish	1805
Orleans	New Orleans	Original Parish	1805
Ouachita	Monroe	Original Parish	1805
Plaquemines	Point a la Hache	Orleans	1807
Pointe Coupe	New Reads	Feliciana, Avoyelles	1805
Rapids	Alexandria	Original Parish	1805
Red River	Coushatta	Caddo, Bossier, Bienville, Natchitoches, De Soto	1848
Richland	Rayville	Ouachita, Carroll, Franklin Morehouse	1852
Sabine	Many	Natchitoches	1843
St. Bernard	Chalmette	Original Parish	1807
St. Charles	Hahnville	Original Parish	1807
St. Helena	Greensburg	Livingston	1810
St. James	Convent	Original Parish	1807
St. John the Baptist	Edgard	Original Parish	1807
St. Landry	Opelousas	Avoyelles, Rapides	1807
St. Martin	St. Martinville	Original Parish	1807
St. Mary	Franklin	Assumption	1811
St. Tammany	Covington	St. Helena, Orleans	1810
Tangipahoa	Amite	Livingston, St. Tammany, Washington	1869
Tensas	St. Joseph	Concordia	1843
Terrebonne	Houma	La Fourche	1822
Union	Farmerville	Ouachita	1839
Vermillion	Abbeville	Lafayette	1844
Vernon	Leesville	Natchitoches, Rapides, Sabine	1871
Washington	Franklinton	St. Tammany	1819
Webster	Minden	Claibourne, Bienville, Bossier	1871
West Baton Rouge	Port Allen	Baton Rouge	1807
West Carroll	Oak Grove	Carroll	1877
West Feliciana	Saint Francisville	Feliciana	1824
Winn	Winnfield	Natchitoches, Catahoula, Rapides	1852

MAINE

County Name	County Seat	Parent County	Year Created
Androscoggin	Auburn	Cumberland, Oxford, Kennebec	1854
Aroostook	Houlton	Washington	1839
Cumberland	Portland	York	1760
Franklin	Farmington	Cumberland	1838
Hancock	Ellsworth	Lincoln	1789
Kennebec	Augusta	Lincoln	1799
Knox	Rockland	Lincoln, Waldo	1860
Lincoln	Wiscasset	York	1760
Oxford	So. Paris	York, Cumberland	1805
Penobscot	Bangor	Hancock	1816
Piscataquis	Dover-Foxcroft	Penobscot, Somerset	1838
Sagadahoc	Bath	Lincoln	1854
Somerset	Skowhegan	Kennebec	1809
Waldo	Belfast	Hancock, Lincoln, Kennebec	1827
Washington	Machias	Lincoln	1789
York (shire)	Alfred	Original county reorg. 1658	1652

MARYLAND

County Name	County Seat	Parent County	Year Created
Allegany	Cumberland	Washington	1789
Ann Arundel	Annapolis	Original county	1650
Baltimore	Towson	Original county	1659
Baltimore City	Baltimore	Baltimore	1729
Calvert	Prince Frederick	Original county	1654
Caroline	Denton	Dorchester, Queen Annes	1773
Carroll	Westminster	Baltimore, Frederick	1837
Cecil	Elkton	Kent	1674
Charles	La Plata	Original county	1658
Dorchester	Cambridge	Original county	1668
Frederick	Frederick	Prince Georges	1748
Garrett	Oakland	Allegany	1872
Harford	Bel Air	Baltimore	1774
Howard	Ellicott City	Baltimore, Anne Arundel	1851
Kent	Chestertown	Original county	1642
Montgomery	Rockville	Frederick	1776
Prince Georges	Upper Marlboro	Charles, Calvert	1695
Queen Annes	Centreville	Talbot	1706
Saint Mary's	Leonardtown	Original county	1637
Somerset	Princess Anne	Original county	1666
Talbot	Easton	kent	1662
Washington	Hagerstown	Frederick	1776
Wicomico	Salisbury	Somerset, Worcester	1867
Worcester	Snow Hill	Somerset	1742

MASSACHUSETTS

County Name	County Seat	Parent County	Year Created
Barnstable	Barnstable & West Harwick	New Plymouth Colony	1685
Berkshire	Pittsfield	Hampshire	1760
Bristol	Taunton, New Bedford, Fall River	New Plymouth Colony	1685
Dukes	Edgartown	(Martha's Vineyard)	1695
Essex	Laurence, Newburyport, Salem	Original county	1643
Franklin	Greenfield	Hampshire	1811
Hampden	Springfield	Hampshire	1812
Hampshire	Northampton	Middlesex	1662
Middlesex	Cambridge & Lowell	Original county	1643
Nantucket	Nantucket	Original county	1695
Norfolk	Dedham	Suffolk	1793
Plymouth	Plymouth	New Plymouth Colony	1685
Suffolk	Boston	Original county	1643
Worcester	Worcester	Suffolk, Middlesex	1731

MICHIGAN

County Name	County Seat	Parent County	Year Created
Alcona	Harrisville	Alpena, Cheboygan	1840
Alger	Munising	Scoolcraft	1885
Allegan	Allegan	Kalamazoo	1831
Alpena	Alpena	Cheboygan	1840
Antrim	Bellaire	Grand Traverse	1840
Arenac	Standish	Bay, Saginaw	1831
Baraga	L'Anse	Houghton	1875
Barry	Hastings	St. Joseph, Kalamazoo	1829
Bay	Bay City	Saginaw, Midland	1857
Benzie	Beulah	Grand Traverse, Leelanau	1863
Berrien	St. Joseph	Cass	1829
Branch	Coldwater	St. Joseph, Lenawee	1829
Calhoun	Marshall	St. Joseph, Kalamazoo	1829
Cass	Cassopolis	Lenawee	1829
Charlevoix	Charlevoix	Emmet	1840
Cheboygan	Cheboygan	Mackinac	1840
Chippewa	Sault Ste. Marie	Mackinac	1826
Clare	Harrison	Isabella, Midland, Mecosta	1840
Clinton	St. Johns	Shiawssee, Kent	1831
Crawford	Grayling	Cheboygan, Antrim, Kalkaska	1840
Delta	Escanaba	Mackinac	1843
Dickinson	Iron Mountain	Marquette, Menominee	1891
Eaton	Charlotte	St. Joseph, Kalamazoo, Calhoun	1829

County Name	County Seat	Parent County	Year Created
Emmett	Petoskey	Mackinac	1840
Genessee	Flint	Oakland	1835
Gladwin	Gladwin	Saginaw, Midland	1831
Gogebic	Bessemer	Ontonagon	1887
Grand Traverse	Traverse City	Mackinac	1840
Gratiot	Ithaca	Saginaw, Clinton	1831
Hillsdale	Hillsdale	Lenawee	1829
Houghton	Houghton	Chippewa	1845
Huron	Bad Axe	Saginaw, St. Clair, Sanilac	1840
Ingham	Mason	Washtenaw	1829
Ionia	Ionia	Kent	1831
Iosco	Tawas City	Saginaw, Cheboygan	1840
Iron	Crystal Falls	Marquette, Menominee	1885
Isabella	Mt. Pleasant	Saginaw, Midland	1831
Jackson	Jackson	Washtenaw	1829
Kalamazoo	Kalkaska	Grand Traverse, Antrim	1840
Kent	Grand Rapids	Kalamazoo	1831
Keweenaw	Eagle River	Houghton	1861
Lake	Baldwin	Oceana, Mason, Newaygo	1840
Lapeer	Lapeer	Oakland	1822
Leelanau	Leland	Grand Traverse	1840
Lenawee	Adrian	Wayne	1822
Livingston	Howell	Shiawassee, Washtenaw	1833
Luce	Newberry	Chippewa, Mackinac	1887
Mackinac	St. Ignace	Wayne and the French	1818
Macomb	Mt. Clemens	Wayne	1818
Manistee	Manistee	Mackinac, Ottawa, Oceana, Grand Traverse	1840
Marquette	Marquette	Chippewa, Houghton	1843
Mason	Ludington	Ottawa, Oceana	1840
Mecosta	Big Rapids	Kent, Newaygo	1840
Menominee	Menominee	Marquette	1861
Midland	Midland	Saginaw	1831
Missaukee	Lake City	Antrim, Grand Traverse	1840
Monroe	Monroe	Wayne	1817
Montcalm	Stanton	Ionia	1831
Montmorency	Atlanta	Cheboygan, Alpena	1840
Muskegon	Muskegon	Ottawa	1859
Newaygo	White Cloud	Kent, Muskegon, Oceana	1840
Oakland	Pontiac	Wayne	1819
Oceana	Hart	Ottawa	1831
Ogemaw	West Branch	Cheboygan, Midland, Iosco	1840
Ontonagon	Ontonagon	Chippewa, Houghton	1843
Osceola	Reed City	Mason, Newaygo, Mecosta	1840
Oscoda	Mio	Cheboygan, Alpena, Alcona	1840
Otsego	Gaylord	Mackinac, Alpena, Cheboygan, Antrim	1840
Ottawa	Grand Haven	Kent	1831
Presque Isle	Rogers City	Mackinac	1840
Roscommon	Roscommon	Cheboygan, Midland	1830
Saginaw	Saginaw	Oakland	1822
St. Clair	Port Huron	Wayne	1820
St. Joseph	Centreville	Wayne	1829
Sanilac	Sandusky	Oakland, St. Clair, Lapeer	1822
Schoolcraft	Manistique	Chippewa, Houghton, Marquette	1843
Shiawassee	Corunna	Oakland, Genesee	1822
Tuscola	Caro	Saginaw	1840
Van Buren	Paw Paw	Cass	1829
Washtenaw	Ann Arbor	Wayne	1822
Wayne	Detroit	Original county	1815
Wexford	Cadillac	Manistee	1840

MINNESOTA

County Name	County Seat	Parent County	Year Created
Aitkin	Aitkin	Cass, Itasca	1857
Anoka	Anoka	Ramsey	1857
Becker	Detroit Lakes	Indian Lands	1858
Baltrami	Bemidji	Unorg. Terr.,	1866
Benton	Foley	Original county	1849
Big Stone	Ortonville	Pierce	1862
Blue Earth	Mankato	Unorg. Terr.,	1853
Brown	New Ulm	Nicollect, Blue Earth	1855
Carlton	Carlton	Pine, St. Louis	1857
Carver	Chaska	Hennepin	1855
Cass	Walker	Original county	1851
Chippewa	Montevideo	Pierce	1862
Chisago	Center City	Washington	1851
Clay	Moorhead	Formerly Breckenridge	1858
Clearwater	Bagley	Beltrami	1902
Cook	Grand Marais	Lake	1874
Cottonwood	Windom	Brown	1857
Crow Wing	Brainerd	Cass, Aitkin	1857
Dakota	Hastings	Original county	1849
Dodge	Mantorville	Olmstead	1855
Douglas	Alexandria	Todd	1858
Faribault	Blue Earth	Blue Earth	1855
Fillmore	Preston	Wabasha	1853
Freeborn	Albert Lea		1855
Goodhue	Red Wing	Wabasha	1853
Grant	Elbow Lake	Stearns	1868
Hennepin	Minneapolis	Dakota	1852
Houston	Caledonia	Fillmore	1854
Hubbard	Park Rapids	Cass	1883
Isanti	Cambridge	Anoka	1857
Itasca	Grand Rapids	Original county	1849
Jackson	Jackson	Unorg. Terr.	1857
Kanabec	Mora	Pine	1858
Kandiyohi	Willmar	Meeker	1858
Kittson	Hallock	Unorg. Terr., formerly Pembina	1862
Koochiching	International Falls	Itasca	1906
Lac qui Parle	Madison	Toombs	1871
Lake	Two Harbors	Formerly Doty	1856
Lake of the Woods	Baudette	Beltrami	1922
La Sueur	Le Center	Unorg. Terr.,	1853
Lincoln	Ivanhoe	Lyon	1866
Lyon	Marshall	Redwood	1868
Mahnomen	Mahnomen	Becker, Norman	1906
Marshall	Warren	Kittson	1879
Martin	Fairmont	Faribault, Brown	1857
McLeod	Glencoe	Carver	1856
Meeker	Litchfield	Wright, Stearns	1856
Mille Lacs	Milaca	Kanabec	1857
Morrison	Little Falls	Benton, Stearns	1856
Mower	Austin	Fillmore, Freeborn	1855
Murray	Slayton	Lyon	1857
Nicollet	Saint Peter	Unorg. Terr.,	1853
Nobles	Worthington	Jackson	1857
Norman	Ada	Polk	1881
Olmsted	Rochester	Unorg. Terr.,	1855
Otter Tail	Fergus Falls	Pembina, Cass	1858
Pennington	Thief River Falls	Red Lake	1910
Pine	Pine City	Unorg. Lands	1856
Pipestone	Pipestone	Murray	1857

County Name	County Seat	Parent County	Year Created
Polk	Crookston	Indian Lands	1858
Pope	Glenwood	Pierce	1862
Ramsey	Saint Paul	Original county	1849
Red Lake	Red Lake Falls	Polk	1896
Redwood	Redwood Falls	Brown	1862
Renville	Olivia	Unorg. Terr.	1855
Rice	Faribault	Original county	1853
Rock	Luverne	Nobles as Unorg. Co. Brown	1857
Roseau	Roseau	Kittson	1894
Saint Louis	Duluth	Doty (now Lake)	1855
Scott	Shakopee	Dakota	1853
Sherburne	Elk River	Benton	1856
Sibley	Gaylord	Unorg. Terr.,	1853
Stearns	Saint Cloud	Indian Lands	1855
Steele	Owatonna	Unorg. Terr., Dodge	1855
Stevens	Morris	Pierce, Big Stone	1862
Swift	Benson	Chippewa, Unorg. Lands	1870
Todd	Long Prairie	Stearns	1855
Traverse	Wheaton	Toombs	1862
Wabasha	Wabasha	Original county	1849
Wadena	Wadena	Cass, Todd	1858
Waseca	Waseca	Steele	1857
Washington	Stillwater	Original county	1849
Watonwan	Saint James	Brown	1860
Wilkin	Breckenridge	Cass, Tommbs, Johnson	1858
Winona	Winona	Unorg. Terr.,	1854
Wright	Buffalo	Hennepin	1855
Yellow Medicine	Granite Falls	Redwood	1871

MISSISSIPPI

County Name	County Seat	Parent County	Year Created
Adams	Natchez	Natchez District	1799
Alcorn	Corinth	Tippaw, Tishomingo, Wilkinson	1870
Amite	Liberty	Wilkinson	1809
Attala	Kosciusko	Choctaw Cession	1833
Benton	Ashland	Marshall, Tippah	1870
Bolivar	Rosedale & Cleveland	Choctaw Cession	1836
Calhoun	Pittsboro	Lafayette, Valobusha	1852
Carroll	Carrollton & Vaiden	Choctaw Cession	1833
Chickasaw	Houston & Okolona	Chickasaw Cession of 1832	1836
Chawtaw	Ackerman	Chickasaw Cession of 1832	1833
Claiborne	Port Gibson	Jefferson	1802
Clarke	Quitman	Choctaw Cession	1812
Clay	West Point	Chickasaw, Lowndes, Monroe, Oktibbeha	1871
Coahoma	Clarksdale	Chickasaw Cession 1836	1836
Copiah	Hazelhurst	Hinds	1823
Covington	Collins	Laurence, Wayne	1819
De Soto	Hernando	Indian Lands	1836
Forrest	Hattiesburg	Perry	1906
Franklin	Meadville	Adams	1809
George	Lucedale	Greene, Jackson	1910
Greene	Leakesville	Amita, Franklin, Wayne	1811
Grenada	Grenada	Carroll, Yalobusha, Choctaw, Talahatchie	1870
Hancock	Bay St. Louis	Mobile District	1812
Harrison	Gulfport	Hancock, Jackson	1841
Hinds	Jackson & Raymond	Choctaw Cession 1820	1821
Holmes	Lexington	Yazoo	1833
Humphreys	Belzoni	Holmes, Washington, Yazoo, Sunflower	1918
Issaquena	Mayersville	Washington	1844
Itawamba	Fulton	Chickasaw Cession 1832	1836

County Name	County Seat	Parent County	Year Created
Jackson	Pascagoula	Mobile District	1812
Jasper	Bay Springs & Paulding	Indian Lands	1833
Jefferson	Fayette	Natchez, Originally Pickering	1799
Jefferson Davis	Prentiss	Covington, Lawrence	1906
Jones	Ellisville & Laurel	Covington, Wayne	1826
Kemper	DeKalb	Choctaw Cession 1832	1833
Lafayette	Oxford	Chickasaw Cession	1836
Lamar	Purvis	Marion, Pearl River	1904
Lauderdale	Meridian	Choctaw Cession	1833
Lawrence	Monticello	Marion	1814
Leake	Carthage	Choctaw Cession	1833
Lee	Tupelo	Itawamba, Pontotoc	1866
Leflore	Greenwood	Carroll, Sunflower, Tallahatchie	1871
Lincoln	Brookhaven	Franklin, Lawrence, Copiah, Pike, Amite	1870
Lowndes	Columbus	Monroe	1830
Madison	Canton	Yazoo	1828
Marion	Columbia	Amite, Wayne, Franklin	1811
Marshall	Holly Springs	Chickasaw Cession 1832	1836
Monroe	Aberdeen	Chickasaw Cession 1821	1821
Montgomery	Winona	Carroll, Choctaw	1871
Neshoba	Philadelphia	Choctaw Cession 1830	1833
Newton	Decatur	Neshoba	1836
Noxubee	Macon	Choctaw Cession 1830	1833
Oktibbeha	Starkville	Choctaw Cession 1830	1833
Panola	Batesville & Sardis	Chickasaw Cession 1832	1836
Pearl River	Poplarville	Hancock, Marion	1890
Perry	New Augusta	Greene	1820
Pike	Magnolia	Marion	1815
Pontotoc	Pontotoc	Chickasaw Cession 1832	1836
Prentiss	Booneville	Tishomingo	1870
Quitman	Marks	Panola, Coahoma	1877
Rankin	Brandon	Hinds	1828
Scott	Forest	Choctaw Cession 1832	1833
Sharkey	Rolling Fork	Warren, Washington, Issaquena	1876
Simpson	Mendenhall	Choctaw Cession 1820	1824
Smith	Raleigh	Choctaw Cession 1820	1833
Stone	Wiggins	Harrison	1916
Sunflower	Indianola	Bolivar	1844
Tallahatchie	Charleston & Sumner	Choctaw Cession 1820	1833
Tate	Senatobia	Marshall, Tunica, De Soto	1873
Tippah	Ripley	Chickasaw Cession 1832	1836
Tishomingo	Iuka	Chickasaw Cession 1832	1836
Tunica	Tunica	Chickasaw Cession 1832	1836
Union	New Albany	Pontotoc, Tippah	1870
Walthall	Tylertown	Marion, Pike	1910
Warren	Vicksburg	Natchez District	1809
Washington	Greenville	Warren, Yazoo	1827
Wayne	Waynesboro	Washington	1809
Webster	Walthall	Montgomery, Chickasaw, Choctaw, Oktibbeha	1874
Wilkinson	Woodville	Adams	1802
Winston	Louisville	Choctaw Cession 1830	1833
Yalobusha	Coffeyville & Water Valley	Choctaw Cession 1830	1833
Yazoo	Yazoo City	Hinds	1823

MISSOURI

County Name	County Seat	Parent County	Year Created
Adair	Kirksville	Macon	1841
Andrew	Savannah	Platte Purchase	1841
Atchison	Rockport	Holt	1843

County Name	County Seat	Parent County	Year Created
Audrain	Mexico	Monroe	1831
Barry	Cassville	Greene	1835
Barton	Lamar	Jasper	1855
Bates	Butler	Jackson	1841
Benton	Warsaw	Pettis, St. Clair	1835
Bollinger	Marble Hill	Cape Girardeau, Stoddard, Wayne	1851
Boone	Columbia	Howard	1820
Buchanan	Saint Joseph	Platte Purchase	1838
Butler	Poplar Bluff	Wayne	1849
Caldwell	Kingston	Ray	1836
Callaway	Fulton	Montgomery	1820
Camden	Camdenton	Benton, Pulaski	1841
Cape Girardeau	Jackson	Original District	1812
Carroll	Carrollton	Ray	1833
Carter	Van Buren	Ripley, Shannon	1859
Cass	Harrisonville	Jackson	1835
Cedar	Stockton	Dade, St. Clair	1845
Chariton	Keytesville	Howard	1820
Christian	Ozark	Greene, Taney, Webster	1859
Clark	Kahoka	Lewis	1836
Clay	Liberty	Ray	1822
Clinton	Plattsburg	Clay	1833
Cole	Jefferson City	Cooper	1820
Cooper	Boonville	Howard	1818
Crawford	Steelville	Gasconade	1829
Dade	Greenfield	Greene	1841
Dallas	Buffalo	Polk	1841
Daviess	Gallatin	Ray	1836
De Kalb	Maysville	Clinton	1845
Dent	Salem	Crawford, Shannon	1851
Douglas	Ava	Ozark, Taney	1857
Dunklin	Kennett	Stoddard	1845
Franklin	Union	St. Louis	1818
Gasconade	Hermann	Franklin	1820
Gentry	Albany	Clinton	1841
Greene	Springfield	Crawford	1833
Grundy	Trenton	Livingston	1841
Harrison	Bethany	Daviess	1845
Henry	Clinton	Lafayette	1834
Hickory	Hermitage	Benton, Polk	1845
Holt	Oregon	Platte Purchase	1841
Howard	Fayette	St. Charles, St. Louis	1816
Howell	West Plains	Oregon, Ozark	1857
Iron	Ironton	Dent, Madison, Reynolds, St. Francis, Washington, Wayne	1857
Jackson	Independence	Lafayette	1826
Jasper	Carthage	Newton	1841
Jefferson	Hillsboro	Ste. Genevieve, St. Louis	1818
Johnson	Warrensburg	Lafayette	1834
Knox	Edina	Scotland	1845
Laclede	Lebanon	Camden, Pulaski, Wright	1849
Lafayette	Lexington	Cooper	1820
Lawrence	Mount Vernon	Barry, Dade	1845
Lewis	Monticello	Marion	1833
Lincoln	Troy	St. Charles	1818
Linn	Linneus	Chariton	1837
Livingston	Chillicothe	Carroll	1837
Macon	Macon	Randolph	1837
Madison	Fredericktown	Cape Girardeau, Ste. Genevieve	1818
Maries	Vienna	Osage, Pulaski	1855
Marion	Palmyra	Ralls	1822
McDonald	Pineville	Newton	1849
Mercer	Princeton	Grundy	1845
Miller	Tuscumbia	Cole	1837
Mississippi	Charleston	Scott	1845
Moniteau	California	Cole, Morgan	1845
Monroe	Paris	Ralls	1831
Montgomery	Montgomery City	St. Charles	1818
Morgan	Versailles	Cooper	1833
New Madrid	New Madrid	Original district	1812
Newton	Neosho	Barry	1838
Nodaway	Maryville	Andrew	1841
Oregon	Alton	Ripley	1845
Osage	Linn	Gasconade	1841
Ozark	Gainesville	Taney	1841
Pemiscot	Caruthersville	New Madrid	1851
Perry	Perryville	Ste. Genevieve	1820
Pettis	Sedalia	Cooper, Saline	1833
Phelps	Rolla	Crawford, Pulaski, Maries	1857
Pike	Bowling Green	St. Charles	1818
Platte	Platte City	Platte Purchase	1838
Polk	Bolivar	Greene	1835
Pulaski	Waynesville	Crawford	1833
Putnam	Unionville	Linn	1843
Ralls	New London	Pike	1820
Randolph	Huntsville	Chariton	1829
Ray	Richmond	Howard	1820
Reynolds	Centerville	Shannon	1845
Ripley	Doniphan	Wayne	1833
St. Charles	St. Charles	Original district	1812
St. Clair	Osceola	Rives	1841
St. Francis	Farmington	Jefferson, Ste. Genevieve, Washington	1821
St. Louis	Clayton	Original district	1812
Ste. Genevieve	Ste. Genevieve	Original district	1812
Saline	Marshall	Cooper, Howard	1820
Schuyler	Lancaster	Adair	1845
Scotland	Memphis	Lewis	1841
Scott	Benton	New Madrid	1821
Shannon	Eminence	Ripley, Washington	1841
Shelby	Shelbyville	Marion	1835
Stoddard	Bloomfield	Cape Girardeau	1835
Stone	Galena	Taney	1851
Sullivan	Milan	Linn	1843
Taney	Forsyth	Greene	1837
Texas	Houston	Shannon, Wright	1845
Vernon	Nevada	Bates	1851
Warren	Warrenton	Montgomery	1833
Washington	Potosi	Ste. Genevieve	1813
Wayne	Greenville	Cape Girardeau	1818
Webster	Marshfield	Greene, Wright	1855
Worth	Grant City	Gentry	1861
Wright	Hartville	Pulaski	1841

MONTANA

County Name	County Seat	Parent County	Year Created
Beaverhead	Dillion	Original county	1865
Big Horn	Hardin	Rosebud, Yellowstone	1913
Blaine	Chinook	Chouteau, Hill	1912
Broadwater	Townsend	Jefferson, Meagher	1897
Carbon	Red Lodge	Park, Yellowstone	1895
Carter	Ekalaka	Custer	1917
Cascade	Great Falls	Chouteau, Meagher	1887
Chouteau	Fort Benton	Original county	1865
Custer	Miles City	Original county	1865

County Name	County Seat	Parent County	Year Created
Daniels	Scobey	Valley, Sheridan	1920
Dawson	Glendive	Original county	1869
Deer Lodge	Anaconda	Original county	1865
Fallon	Baker	Custer	1913
Fergus	Lewistown	Meagher	1885
Flathead	Kalispell	Missoula	1893
Gallatin	Bozeman	Original county	1865
Garfield	Jordan	Valley, McCone	1919
Glacier	Cut Bank	Teton	1919
Golden Valley	Ryegate	Musselshell	1920
Granite	Philipsburg	Deer Lodge	1893
Hill	Havre	Chouteau	1912
Jefferson	Boulder	Original county	1865
Judith Basin	Stanford	Fergus, Cascade	1920
Lake	Polson	Flathead, Missoula	1923
Lewis & Clark	Helena	Original county	1865
Liberty	Chester	Chouteau, Hill	1920
Madison	Virginia City	Original county	1865
McCone	Circle	Dawson, Richland	1919
Meagher	White Sulpher Springs	Original county	1867
Mineral	Superior	Missoula	1914
Missoula	Missoula	Original county	1865
Musselshell	Roundup	Fergus, Yellowstone	1911
Park	Livingston	Gallatin	1887
Petroleum	Winnett	Fergus, Garfield	1924
Phillips	Malta	Valley	1915
Pondera	Conrad	Chateau	1919
Powder River	Broadus	Custer	1919
Powell	Deer Lodge	Missoula	1901
Prairie	Terry	Custer	1915
Ravalli	Hamilton	Missoula	1893
Richland	Sidney	Dawson	1914
Roosevelt	Wolf Point	Valley, Richland	1919
Rosebud	Forsyth	Dawson	1901
Sanders	Thompson Falls	Missoula	1905
Sheridan	Plentywood	Custer	1913
Silver Bow	Butte	Deer Lodge	1881
Stillwater	Columbus	Sweet Grass, Yellowstone, Carbon	1913
Sweet Grass	Big Timber	Meagher, Park, Yellowstone	1895
Teton	Choteau	Chouteau	1893
Toole	Shelby	Teton	1914
Treasure	Hysham	Big Horn	1919
Valley	Glasgow	Dawson	1893
Wheatland	Harlowton	Meagher, Sweet Grass	1917
Wibaux	Wibaux	Dawson	1914
Yellowstone	Billings	Gallatin, Meagher, Custer, Carbon	1883

NEBRASKA

County Name	County Seat	Parent County	Year Created
Adams	Hastings	Clay	1867
Antelope	Neligh	Pierce	1871
Arthur	Arthur	Unorg. Terr.	1887
Banner	Harrisburg	Cheyene	1888
Blaine	Brewster	Custer	1885
Boone	Albion	Platte	1871
Box Butte	Alliance	Unorg. Terr.	1887
Boyd	Butte	Holt	1891
Brown	Ainsworth	Unorg. Terr.	1883
Buffalo	Kearney	Original county	1855
Burt	Tekamah	Original county	1854
Butler	David City	Unorg. Terr.	1856
Cass	Plattsmouth	Original county	1854
Cedar	Hartington	Original county	1857
Chase	Imperial	Unorg. Terr.	1873
Cherry	Valentine	Unorg. Terr.	1883
Cheyenne	Sidney	Unorg. Terr.	1867
Clay	Clay Center	Original county	1855
Colfax	Schuyler	Dodge	1869
Cuming	West Point	Burt	1855
Custer	Broken Bow	Unorg. Terr.	1877
Dakota	Dakota City	Original county	1855
Dawes	Chadron	Sioux	1885
Dawson	Lexington	Buffalo	1860
Deuel	Chappell	Cheyenne	1888
Dixon	Ponca	Original county	1856
Dodge	Fremont	Original county	1854
Douglas	Omaha	Original county	1854
Dundy	Benkelman	Unorg. Terr.	1873
Fillmore	Geneva	Unorg. Terr.	1856
Franklin	Franklin	Kearney Org. 1871	1867
Frontier	Stockville	Unorg. Terr.	1872
Furnas	Beaver City	Unorg. Terr.	1873
Gage	Beatrice	Original county	1855
Garden	Oshkosh	Unorg. Terr.	1909
Garfield	Burwell	Wheeler	1884
Gosper	Elwood	Unorg. Terr.	1873
Grant	Hyannis	Unorg. Terr.	1887
Greeley	Greeley	Boone	1871
Hall	Grand Island	Original county	1858
Hamilton	Aurora	York	1867
Harlan	Alma	Unorg. Terr.	1871
Hayes	Hayes Center	Unorg. Terr.	1877
Hitchcock	Trenton	Unorg. Terr.	1873
Holt	O'Neill	Knox	1860
Hooker	Mullen	Unorg. Terr.	1889
Howard	Saint Paul	Hall	1871
Jefferson	Fairbury	Gage	1856
Johnson	Tecumseh	Original county	1855
Kearney	Minden	Original county	1860
Keith	Ogallala	Lincoln	1873
Keya Paha	Springview	Brown, Rock	1884
Kimball	Kimball	Cheyenne	1888
Knox	Center	See L'Eau Qui Court & Emmet	1857
Lancaster	Lincoln	Original county	1855
Lincoln	North Platte	Unorg. Terr.	1860
Logan	Stapleton	Custer	1885
Loup	Taylor	Unorg. Terr.	1855
Madison	Madison	Platte	1856
McPherson	Tryon	Lincoln, Keith	1887
Merrick	Cen'ral City	Original county	1858
Morrill	Bridgeport	Cheyenne	1908
Nance	Fullerton	Merrick	1879
Nemaha	Auburn	Original county	1854
Nuckolls	Nelson	Clay	1860
Otoe	Nebraska City	Original county	1854
Pawnee	Pawnee City	Original county	1855
Perkins	Grant	Keith	1887
Phelps	Holdrege	Unorg. Terr.	1873
Pierce	Pierce	Madison	1856
Platte	Columbus	Original county	1856
Polk	Osceola	Original county	1856
Red Willow	McCook	Frontier	1873
Richardson	Falls City	Original county	1854

County Name	County Seat	Parent County	Year Created
Rock	Bassett	Brown	1857
Saline	Wilber	Gage, Lancaster	1855
Sarpy	Papillion	Original county	1857
Saunders	Wahoo	Sarpy, Douglas	1856
Scotts Bluff	Gering	Cheyenne	1881
Seward	Seward	Lancaster	1855
Sheridan	Rushville	Sioux	1885
Sherman	Loup City	Buffalo	1871
Sioux	Harrison	Unorg. Terr.	1877
Stanton	Stanton	Dodge	1855
Thayer	Hebron	Jefferson	1856
Thomas	Thedford	Blaine	1887
Thurston	Pender	Burt	1889
Valley	Ord	Unorg. Terr.	1871
Washington	Blair	Original county	1854
Wayne	Wayne	Thurston	1871
Webster	Red Cloud	Unorg. Terr.	1867
Wheeler	Bartlett	Boone	1877
York	York	Original county	1855

NEVADA

County Name	County Seat	Parent County	Year Created
Churchill	Fallon	Original county	1861
Clark	Las Vegas	Lincoln	1909
Douglas	Minden	Original county	1861
Elko	Elko	Lander	1869
Esmeralda	Goldfield	Original county	1861
Eureka	Eureka	Lander	1873
Humboldt	Winnemucca	Original county	1861
Lander	Austin	Original county	1862
Lincoln	Pioche	Nye	1866
Lyon	Yerington	Original county	1861
Mineral	Hawthorne	Esmeralda	1911
Nye	Tonopah	Esmeralda	1864
Ormsby	Carson City	Original county	1861
Pershing	Lovelock	Humboldt	1919
Storey	Virginia City	Original county	1861
Washoe	Reno	Original county	1861
White Pine	Ely	Lincoln	1869

NEW HAMPSHIRE

County Name	County Seat	Parent County	Year Created
Belknap	Laconia	Strafford, Merrimac	1840
Carroll	Ossipee	Strafford	1840
Cheshire	Keene	Original county	1769
Coos	Lancaster	Grafton	1803
Grafton	Woodsville	Original county	1769
Hillsboro	Nashua	Original county	1769
Merrimack	Concord	Rockingham, Hillsboro	1823
Rockingham	Exeter	Original county	1769
Stafford	Dover	Original county	1769
Sullivan	Newport	Cheshire	1827

NEW JERSEY

County Name	County Seat	Parent County	Year Created
Atlantic	Mays Landing	Gloucester	1837
Bergen	Hackensack	Prov. East Jersey	1683
Burlington	Mt. Holly	Original county	1694
Camden	Camden	Gloucester	1844
Cape May	Cape May C.H.	Cumberland	1692
Cumberland	Bridgeton	Salem	1748
Essex	Newark	Prov. East Jersey	1683
Gloucester	Woodbury	Original county	1686
Hudson	Jersey City	Bergen	1840
Hunterdon	Flemington	Burlington	1714
Mercer	Trenton	Somerset, Middlesex, Hunterdon, Burlington	1838
Middlesex	New Brunswick	Prov. East Jersey	1683
Monmouth	Freehold	Prov. East Jersey	1683
Morris	Morristown	Hunterdon	1739
Ocean	Toms River	Monmouth	1850
Passaic	Paterson	Bergen, Essex	1837
Salem	Salem	Original county	1694
Somerset	Somerville	Middlesex	1688
Sussex	Newton	Morris	1753
Union	Elizabeth	Essex	1857
Warren	Belvidere	Sussex	1824

NEW MEXICO

County Name	County Seat	Parent County	Year Created
Bernalillo	Albuquerque	Original county	1852
Catron	Reserve	Socorro	1921
Chaves	Roswell	Lincoln	1889
Colfax	Raton	Mora	1869
Curry	Clovis	Quay, Roosevelt	1909
DeBaca	Fort Sumner	Chaves, Guadalupe, Roosevelt	1917
Dona Ana	Las Cruces	Original county	1852
Eddy	Carlsbad	Lincoln	1889
Grant	Silver City	Socorro	1868
Guadalupe	Santa Rosa	Lincoln, San Miguel	1891
Harding	Mosquero	Mora, Union	1921
Hidalgo	Lordsburg	Grant	1919
Lea	Lovington	Chaves, Eddy	1917
Lincoln	Carrizoza	Socorro	1869
Los Alamos	Los Alamos	Sandoval, Santa Fe	1949
Luna	Deming	Dona Ana, Grant	1901
McKinley	Gallup	Bernalillo, Valencia, San Juan, Rio Arriba	1899
Mora	Mora	San Miguel	1860
Otero	Alamogordo	Dona Ana, Lincoln, Socorro	1899
Quay	Tucumcari	Chaves	1903
Rio Arriba	Tierra Amarilla	Original county	1852
Roosevelt	Portales	Chaves	1903
Sandoval	Bernalillo	Rio Arriba	1903
San Juan	Aztec	Rio Arriba	1887
San Miguel	Las Vegas	Original county	1852
Santa Fe	Santa Fe	Original county	1852
Sierra	Truth or Consequences	Socorro	1884
Socorro	Socorro	Original county	1852
Taos	Taos	Original county	1852
Torrance	Estancia	Lincoln, San Miguel, Socorro, Santa Fe, Valencia	1903
Union	Clayton	Colfax, Mora, San Miguel	1893
Valencia	Los Lunas	Original county	1852

NEW YORK

County Name	County Seat	Parent County	Year Created
Albany	Albany	Original county	1683
Allegany	Belmont	Genesee	1806
Bronx	Bronx	New York	1912
Broome	Binghamton	Tioga	1806
Cattaraugus	Little Valley	Genesee	1808
Cayuga	Auburn	Onondaga	1799
Chautauqua	Mayville	Genesee	1808
Chemung	Elmira	Tioga	1836
Chenango	Norwich	Herkimer, Tioga	1798
Clinton	Plattsburg	Washington	1788
Columbia	Hudson	Albany	1786
Cortland	Cortland	Onondaga	1808
Delaware	Delhi	Ulster, Otsego	1797
Dutchess	Poughkeepsie	Original county	1683
Erie	Buffalo	Niagara	1821
Essex	Elizabethtown	Clinton	1799

County Name	County Seat	Parent County	Year Created	County Name	County Seat	Parent County	Year Created
Franklin	Malone	Clinton	1808	Carteret	Beaufort	Bath	1722
Fulton	Johnstown	Montgomery	1838	Caswell	Yanceyville	Orange	1777
Genesee	Batavia	Ontario	1802	Catawba	Newton	Lincoln	1842
Greene	Catskill	Ulster, Albany	1800	Chatham	Pittsboro	Orange	1770
Hamilton	Lake Pleasant	Montgomery	1816	Cherokee	Murphy	Macon	1839
Herkimer	Herkimer	Montgomery	1791	Chowan	Edenton	Prec. Albermarle	1670
Jefferson	Watertown	Oneida	1805	Clay	Hayesville	Cherokee	1861
Kings	Brooklyn	Original county	1683	Cleveland	Shelby	Rutherford, Lincoln	1841
Lewis	Lowville	Chenango	1805	Columbus	Whiteville	Bladen, Brunswick	1808
Livingston	Genesee	Genesee, Ontario	1821	Craven	New Bern	Prec. Bath Co.	1705
Madison	Wampsville	Chenango	1806	Cumberland	Fayetteville	Bladen	1754
Monroe	Rochester	Genesee, Ontario	1821	Currituck	Currituck	Albermarle	1670
Montgomery	Fonda	Albany	1772	Dare	Manteo	Currituck, Tyrell, Hyde	1870
Nassau	Mineola	Queens	1898	Davidson	Lexington	Rowan	1822
New York	New York	Original county	1683	Davie	Mocksville	Rowan	1836
Niagara	Lockport	Genesee	1808	Duplin	Kenansville	New Hanover	1749
Oneida	Rome & Utica	Herkimer	1798	Durham	Durham	Orange, Wake	1881
Onondaga	Syracuse	Herkimer	1794	Edgecombe	Tarboro	Bertie	1741
Ontario	Canandaigua	Montgomery	1789	Forsyth	Winston-Salem	Stokes	1849
Orange	Goshen	Original county	1683	Franklin	Louisburg	Bute	1778
Orleans	Albion	Genesee	1824	Gaston	Gastonia	Lincoln	1846
Oswego	Oswego, & Pulaski	Oneida, Onondaga	1816	Gates	Gatesville	Chowan, Hertford	1778
Otsego	Cooperstown	Montgomery	1791	Graham	Robbinsville	Cherokee	1872
Putnam	Carmel	Dutchess	1812	Granville	Oxford	Edgecombe, Orig. Glasgow	1746
Queens	Jamaica	Original county	1683	Greene	Snox Hill	Dobbs, or Glasgow	1799
Rensselaer	Troy	Albany	1791	Guilford	Greensboro	Rowan, Orange	1770
Richmond	St. George	Original county	1683	Halifax	Halifax	Edgecombe	1754
Rockland	New City	Orange	1798	Harnett	Lillington	Cumberland	1855
St. Lawrence	Canton	Clinton, Herkimer, Montgomery	1802	Haywood	Waynesville	Buncombe	1808
				Henderson	Henderson	Buncombe	1838
Saratoga	Ballston Spa	Albany	1791	Hertford	Winton	Bertie, Chowan, Northampton	1754
Schenectady	Schenectady	Albany	1809	Hoke	Raeford	Cumberland, Robeson	1911
Schoharie	Schoharie	Albany, Ostego	1795	Hyde	Swanquarter	Wickham, Prec. Bath Co.	1705
Schuyler	Watkins Glen	Tompkins, Steuben, Chemung	1854	Iredell	Statesville	Rowan	1788
Seneca	Ovid & Waterloo	Cayuga	1804	Jackson	Sylva	Haywood, Macon	1851
Steuben	Bath	Ontario	1796	Johnston	Smithfield	Craven	1746
Suffolk	Riverhead	Original county	1683	Jones	Trenton	Craven	1778
Sullivan	Monticello	Ulster	1809	Lee	Sanford	Chatham, Harnett, Moore	1907
Tioga	Owego	Montgomery	1791	Lenoir	Kinston	Dobbs	1791
Tompkins	Ithaca	Cayuga, Seneca	1817	Lincoln	Lincolnton	Tryon	1778
Ulster	Kingston	Original county	1683	Macon	Franklin	Haywood	1828
Warren	Lake George	Washington	1813	Madison	Marshall	Buncombe, Yancey	1851
Washington	Hudson Falls	Albany	1772	Martin	Williamston	Halifax, Tyrell	1774
Wayne	Lyons	Ontario, Seneca	1823	Mc Dowell	Marion	Burke, Rutherford	1842
Westchester	White Plains	Original county	1683	Mecklenburg	Charlotte	Anson	1762
Wyoming	Warsaw	Genesee	1841	Mitchell	Bakersville	Burke, Caldwell, Mc Dowell Watauga	1861

NORTH CAROLINA

County Name	County Seat	Parent County	Year Created	County Name	County Seat	Parent County	Year Created
Alamance	Graham	Orange	1849	Montgomery	Troy	Anson	1778
Alexander	Taylorsville	Iredell, Caldwell & Wilkes	1847	Moore	Carthage	Cumberland	1784
Alleghany	Sparta	Ashe	1859	Nash	Nashville	Edgecombe	1777
Anson	Wadesboro	Bladen	1749	New Hanover	Wilmington	Craven	1729
Ashe	Jefferson	Wilkes	1799	Northampton	Jackson	Bertie	1741
Avery	Newland	Caldwell, Mitchell, Watauga	1911	Onslow	Jacksonville	Preceding Bath	1734
Beaufort	Washington	Bath	1705	Orange	Hillsboro	Bladen, Granville, Johnston	1752
Bertie	Windsor	Chowan, Bath	1722	Pamlico	Bayboro	Beaufort, Craven	1872
Bladen	Elizabethtown	New Hanover, Bath	1734	Pasquotank	Elizabeth City	Prec. Albemarle	1670
Brunswick	Southport	New Hanover, Bladen	1764	Pender	Bergaw	New Hanover	1875
Buncombe	Asheville	Burke, Rutherford	1791	Perquimans	Hertford	Prec. Albermarle	1670
Burke	Morganton	Rowan	1777	Person	Roxboro	Caswell	1791
Cabarrus	Concord	Mecklenburg	1792	Pitt	Greenville	Beaufort	1760
Caldwell	Lenoir	Burke, Wilkes	1841	Polk	Columbus	Henderson, Rutherford	1847
Camden	Camden	Pasquotank	1777	Randolph	Asheboro	Guilford	1778

County Name	County Seat	Parent County	Year Created	County Name	County Seat	Parent County	Year Created
Richmond	Rockingham	Anson	1779	Pembina	Cavalier	Indian Lands	1867
Robeson	Lumberton	Bladen	1786	Pierce	Rugby	DeSmet	1887
Rockingham	Wentworth	Guilford	1785	Ramsey	Devils Lake	Pembina	1873
Rowan	Salisbury	Anson	1753	Ransom	Lisbon	Pembina	1873
Rutherford	Rutherfordton	Burke, Tyron	1779	Renville	Mohall	Ward	1873
Sampson	Clinton	Duplin, New Hanover	1784	Richland	Wahpeton	Original county	1873
Scotland	Laurinburg	Richmond	1899	Rolette	Rolla	Buffalo	1873
Stanly	Albemarle	Montgomery	1841	Sargent	Forman	Ransom	1883
Stokes	Danbury	Surry	1789	Sheridan	McClusky	McLean	1873
Surry	Dobson	Rowan	1770	Sioux	Fort Yates	Standing Rock Reservation	1915
Swain	Bryson City	Jackson, Macon	1871	Slope	Amidon	Billings	1915
Transylvania	Brevard	Henderson, Jackson	1861	Stark	Dickinson	Unorg. Terr.	1879
Tyrrell	Columbia	Bertie, Chowan, Currituck, Pasquotank	1729	Steele	Finley	Grand Forks, Griggs	1883
				Stutsman	Jamestown	Pembina	1873
Union	Monroe	Anson, Meckelenburg	1842	Towner	Cando	Rolette, Cavalier	1883
Vance	Henderson	Franklin, Granville, Warren	1881	Traill	Hillsboro	Grand Forks, Burbank, Cass	1875
Wake	Raleigh	Cumberland, Johnston, Orange	1770	Walsh	Grafton	Grand Forks	1881
Warren	Warrenton	Bute	1779	Ward	Minot	Renville	1885
Washington	Plymouth	Tyrrell	1799	Wells	Fessenden	Sheridan	1873
Watauga	Boone	Ashe, Caldwell, Wilkes, Yancey	1849	Williams	Williston	Buford, Flannery	1873
Wayne	Goldsboro	Craven, Dobbs	1779	**OHIO**			
Wilkes	Wilkesboro	Burke, Surry	1777	Adams	West Union	Hamilton	1797
Wilson	Wilson	Edgecombe, Johnston, Nash, Wayne	1855	Allen	Lima	Shelby	1820
Yadkin	Yadkinville	Surry	1850	Ashland	Ashland	Wayne, Richland, Huron, Lorain	1846
Yancey	Burnsville	Buncombe, Burke	1833	Ashtabula	Jefferson	Trumbull, Geauga	1807
NORTH DAKOTA				Athens	Athens	Washington	1805
Adam	Hettinger	Stark, comprising part of old Hettinger	1885	Auglaize	Wapakoneta	Allen, Mercer	1848
				Belmont	St. Clairsville	Jefferson, Washington	1801
Barnes	Valley City	Cass	1875	Brown	Georgetown	Adams, Clermont	1817
Benson	Minnewaukan	Ramsey	1833	Butler	Hamilton	Hamilton	1803
Billings	Medora	Unorg. Terr.	1879	Carroll	Carrollton	Columbiana, Stark, Harrison Jefferson	1832
Bottineau	Bottineau	Unorg. Terr.	1873	Champaign	Urbana	Greene, Franklin	1805
Bowman	Bowman	Billings	1883	Clark	Springfield	Champaign, Madison, Greene	1817
Burke	Bowbells	Ward	1910	Clermont	Batavia	Hamilton	1800
Burleigh	Bismarck	Buffalo	1873	Clinton	Wilmington	Highland, Warren	1810
Cass	Fargo	Original county	1873	Columbiana	Lisbon	Jefferson, Washington	1803
Cavalier	Langdon	Pembina	1873	Coshocton	Coshocton	Muskingum, Tuscarawas	1810
Dickey	Ellendale	LaMoure	1881	Crawford	Bucyrus	Delaware	1820
Divide	Crosby	Williams	1910	Cuyahoga	Cleveland	Geauga	1808
Dunn	Manning	Stark, Mercer	1883	Darke	Greenville	Miami	1809
Eddy	New Rockford	Foster	1885	Defiance	Defiance	Williams, Henry, Paulding	1845
Emmons	Linton	Unorg. Terr.	1879	Delaware	Delaware	Franklin	1808
Foster	Carrington	Pembina	1873	Erie	Sandusky	Huron, Sandusky	1838
Golden Valley	Beach	Billings	1912	Fairfield	Lancaster	Ross, Washington	1800
Grand Forks	Grand Forks	Pembina	1873	Fayette	Washington C.H.	Ross, Highland	1810
Grant	Carson	Morton	1916	Franklin	Columbus	Ross, Wayne Co. Mich.	1803
Griggs	Cooperstown	Foster, Burbank, Traill	1881	Fulton	Wauseon	Lucas, Henry, Williams	1850
Hettinger	Mott	Stark	1883	Gallia	Gallipolis	Washington, Adams	1803
Kidder	Steele	Buffalo	1873	Geauga	Chardon	Trumbull	1805
La Moure	La Moure	Pembina	1873	Greene	Xenia	Hamilton, Ross	1803
Logan	Napoleon	Buffalo	1873	Guernsey	Cambridge	Belmont, Muskingum	1810
McHenry	Towner	Buffalo	1873	Hamilton	Cincinnati	Original county	1790
McIntosh	Ashley	Logan	1883	Hancock	Findlay	Logan	1820
McKenzie	Watford City	Billings, Stark	1883	Hardin	Kenton	Logan	1820
McLean	Washburn	Stevens	1883	Harrison	Cadiz	Jefferson, Tuscarawas	1813
Mercer	Stanton	Original county	1875	Henry	Napoleon	Shelby	1820
Morton	Mandan	Original county	1873	Highland	Hillsboro	Ross, Adams, Clermont	1805
Mountrail	Stanley	Ward	1873	Hocking	Logan	Athens, Ross, Fairfield	1818
Nelson	Lakota	Foster, Grand Forks	1883	Holmes	Millersburg	Coshocton, Wayne, Tuscarawas	1824
Oliver	Center	Mercer	1885				

County Name	County Seat	Parent County	Year Created
Huron	Norwalk	Portage, Cuyahoga	1809
Jackson	Jackson	Scioto, Gallia, Athen, Ross	1816
Jefferson	Steubenville	Washington	1797
Knox	Mt. Vernon	Fairfield	1808
Lake	Painesville	Geauga, Cuyahoga	1840
Lawrence	Ironton	Gallia, Scioto	1815
Licking	Newark	Fairfield	1808
Logan	Bellefontaine	Champaign	1817
Lorain	Elyria	Huron, Cuyahoga, Medina	1822
Lucas	Toledo	Wood, Sandusky, Henry	1835
Madison	London	Franklin	1810
Mahoning	Youngstown	Columbiana, Trumbull	1846
Marion	Marion	Delaware	1820
Medina	Medina	Portage	1812
Meigs	Pomeroy	Gallia, Athens	1819
Mercer	Celina	Darke	1820
Miami	Troy	Montgomery	1807
Monroe	Woodsfield	Belmont, Wash., Guernsey	1813
Montgomery	Dayton	Hamilton, Wayne Co., Mich.	1803
Morgan	McConnelsville	Washington, Guernsey, Muskingum	1817
Morrow	Mt. Gilead	Knox, Marion, Delaware, Richland	1848
Muskingum	Zanesville	Washington, Fairfield	1804
Noble	Caldwell	Monroe, Washington, Morgan, Guernsey	1851
Ottawa	Port Clinton	Erie, Sandusky, Lucas	1840
Paulding	Paulding	Darke	1820
Perry	New Lexington	Washington, Fairfield, Muskingum	1817
Pickaway	Circleville	Ross, Fairfield, Franklin	1810
Pike	Waverly	Ross, Scioto, Adams	1815
Portage	Ravenna	Trumbull	1807
Preble	Eaton	Montgomery, Butler	1808
Putnam	Ottawa	Shelby	1820
Richland	Mansfield	Fairfield	1808
Ross	Chillicothe	Adams, Washington	1798
Sandusky	Fremont	Huron	1820
Scioto	Portsmouth	Adams	1803
Seneca	Tiffin	Huron	1820
Shelby	Sidney	Miami	1819
Stark	Canton	Columbiana	1808
Summit	Akron	Portage, Medina, Stark	1840
Trumbull	Warren	Jefferson, Wayne Co., Mich.	1800
Tuscarawas	New Philadelphia	Muskingum	1808
Union	Marysville	Franklin, Madison, Logan, Delaware	1820
Van Wert	Van Wert	Darke	1820
Vinton	McArthur	Gallia, Athens, Ross, Jackson Hocking	1850
Warren	Lebanon	Hamilton	1803
Washington	Marietta	Original county	1788
Wayne	Wooster	Columbiana	1786
Williams	Bryan	Darke	1820
Wood	Bowling Green	Logan	1820
Wyandot	Upper Sandusky	Marion, Crawford, Hardin, Hancock	1845

OKLAHOMA

County Name	County Seat	Parent County	Year Created
Adair	Stilwell	Cherokee Lands	1907
Alfalfa	Cherokee	Woods	1907
Atoka	Atoka	Choctaw Lands	1907
Beaver	Beaver	Original county	1907
Beckham	Sayre	Roger Mills	1907
Blaine	Watonga	Original county	1907
Bryan	Durant	Choctaw Lands	1907
Caddo	Anadarko	Original Lands	1907
Canadian	El Reno	Original county	1907
Carter	Ardmore	Chickasaw Lands	1907
Cherokee	Tahlequah	Cherokee Lands	1907
Choctaw	Hugo	Choctaw Lands	1907
Cimarron	Boise City	Beaver	1907
Cleveland	Norman	Unassigned Lands	1907
Coal	Coalgate	Choctaw Lands	1907
Comanche	Lawton	Kiowa, Comanche, Apache Lands	1907
Cotton	Walters	Comanche	1912
Craig	Uinita	Cherokee Lands	1907
Creek	Sapulpa	Creek Lands	1907
Custer	Arapaho	Cheyenne, Arapaho Lands	1907
Delaware	Jay	Cherokee	1907
Dewey	Taloga	Orig. county (Cheyenne, Arapaho Lands)	1907
Ellis	Arnett	Day, Woodward	1907
Garfield	Enid	Orig. "O" changed to Garfield 1901 (Cherokee Outlet)	1907
Garvin	Pauls Valley	Chickasaw Lands	1907
Grady	Chickasha	Caddo, Comanche	1907
Grant	Medford	Original county	1907
Greer	Mangum	Org. by Texas, to Okla. by court decision	1907
Harmon	Hollis	Greer, Jackson	1909
Harper	Buffalo	Indian Lands, Woods, Woodward	1907
Haskell	Stigler	Choctaw Lands	1907
Hughes	Holdenville	Creek Lands	1907
Jackson	Altus	Greer	1907
Jefferson	Waurika	Comanche	1907
Johnston	Tishomingo	Chickasaw Lands	1907
Kay	Newkirk	Orig. county (Cherokee Outlet)	1907
Kingfisher	Kingfisher	Original county	1907
Kiowa	Hobart	Original county	1907
Latimer	Wilburton	Choctaw Lands	1907
Le Flore	Poteau	Choctaw Lands	1907
Lincoln	Chandler	Original county	1907
Logan	Guthrie	Original county	1907
Love	Marietta	Chickasaw Lands	1907
Major	Fairview	Woods	1907
Marshall	Madill	Chickasaw Lands	1907
Mayes	Pryor	Indian Lands	1907
McClain	Purcell	Chickasaw Lands	1907
McCurtain	Idabel	Choctaw Lands	1907
McIntosh	Eufaula	Indian Lands	1907
Murray	Sulphur	Chickasaw Lands	1907
Muskogee	Muskogee	Creek	1907
Noble	Perry	cherokee Outlet	1907
Nowata	Nowata	Cherokee Lands	1907
Okfuskee	Okemah	Creek Lands	1907
Oklahoma	Oklahoma City	Original county	1907
Okmulgee	Okmulgee	Creek Lands	1907
Osage	Pawhuska	Osage Indian Lands	1907
Ottawa	Miami	Cherokee Nation	1907
Pawnee	Pawnee	Cherokee Outlet	1907
Payne	Stillwater	Original county	1907
Pittsburg	McAlester	Choctaw Lands	1907
Pontotoc	Ada	Chickasaw Lands	1907
Pottawatomie	Shawnee	Original county	1907

County Name	County Seat	Parent County	Year Created
Pushmataha	Antlers	Choctaw Lands	1907
Roger Mills	Cheyenne	Cheyenne, Arapaho Lands	1907
Rogers	Claremore	Cherokee Nation	1907
Seminole	Wewoka	Seminole Indian Lands	1907
Sequoyah	Sallisaw	Cherokee Indian Lands	1907
Stephens	Duncan	Comanche County	1907
Texas	Guymon	Beaver	1907
Tillman	Frederick	Comanche Indian Lands	1907
Tulsa	Tulsa	Creek Lands	1907
Wagoner	Wagoner	Creek Lands	1907
Washington	Bartlesville	Cherokee Lands	1907
Washita	Cordell	Cheyenne, Arapaho Lands	1907
Woods	Alva	Cherokee Outlet	1907
Woodward	Woodward	Cherokee Outlet	1907

OREGON

County Name	County Seat	Parent County	Year Created
Baker	Baker	Wasco	1862
Benton	Corvallis	Polk	1847
Clackamas	Oregon City	Original county	1843
Clatsop	Astoria	Twality	1844
Columbia	St. Helens	Washington	1854
Coos	Coquille	Umpqua, Jackson	1853
Crook	Prineville	Wasco	1882
Curry	Gold Beach	Coos	1855
Deschutes	Bend	Crook	1916
Douglas	Roseburg	Umpqua 1852 & 1862	1852
Gilliam	Condon	Wasco	1885
Grant	Canyon City	Wasco, Umatilla	1864
Harney	Burns	Grant	1889
Hood River	Hood River	Wasco	1908
Jackson	Medford	Umpqua	1852
Jefferson	Madras	Crook	1914
Josephine	Grants Pass	Jackson	1856
Klamath	Klamath Falls	West part of Lake Co.	1882
Lake	Lakeview	Jackson, Wasco	1874
Lane	Eugene	Linn, Umpqua	1851
Lincoln	Newport	Benton, Polk	1893
Linn	Albany	Champoeg	1847
Malheur	Vale	Baker	1887
Marion	Salem	Orig. Co. name changed from Champoeg	1843
Morrow	Heppner	Umatilla	1885
Multnomah	Portland	Washington, Clackamas	1854
Polk	Dallas	Yamhill	1845
Sherman	Moro	Wasco	1889
Tillamook	Tillamook	Clatsop, Polk, Yamhill	1853
Umatilla	Pendleton	Wasco	1862
Union	La Grande	Baker	1864
Wallowa	Enterprise	Union	1887
Wasco	The Dalles	Clackamas, Marion, Linn, Lane, Douglas, Jackson	1854
Washington	Hillsboro	Orig. Co. formerly Twality	1843
Wheeler	Fossil	Crook, Gilliam, Grant	1899
Yamhill	McMinnville	Original county	1843

PENNSYLVANIA

County Name	County Seat	Parent County	Year Created
Adams	Gettysburg	York	1800
Allegheny	Pittsburgh	Westmoreland, Washington	1788
Armstrong	Kittanning	Allegheny, Indiana, Clarion, Butler, Jefferson, Westmoreland	1800
Beaver	Beaver	Allegheny, Washington	1800
Bedford	Bedford	Cumberland	1771
Berks	Reading	Bucks, Chester, Lancaster, Philadelphia	1751
Blair	Hollidaysburg	Huntingdon, Bedford	1846
Bradford	Towanda	Luzerne, Lycoming	1810
Bucks	Doylestown	Original county	1682
Butler	Butler	Allegheny	1800
Cambria	Edensburg	Somerset, Bedford, Huntingdon	1804
Cameron	Emporium	Clinton, Elk, McKean, Potter	1860
Carbon	Jim Thorpe	Northampton, Monroe	1843
Centre	Bellefonte	Lycoming, Mifflin, Northumberland, Huntingdon	1800
Chester	W. Chester	Original county	1682
Clarion	Clarion	Venango, Armstrong	1804
Clearfield	Clearfield	Huntingdon, Lycoming	1804
Clinton	Lock Haven	Lycoming, Centre	1839
Columbia	Bloomsburg	Northumberland	1813
Crawford	Meadville	Allegheny	1800
Cumberland	Carlisle	Lancaster	1750
Dauphin	Harrisburg	Lancaster	1785
Delaware	Media	Chester	1789
Elk	Ridgway	Jefferson, McKean, Clearfield	1843
Erie	Erie	Allegheny	1800
Fayette	Uniontown	Westmoreland	1783
Forest	Tionesta	Jefferson, Venango	1848
Franklin	Chambersburg	Cumberland	1784
Fulton	McConnellsburg	Bedford	1850
Greene	Waynesburg	Washington	1796
Huntingdon	Huntingdon	Bedford	1787
Indiana	Indiana	Westmoreland, Lycoming	1803
Jefferson	Brookville	Lycoming	1804
Juniata	Mifflintown	Mifflin	1831
Lackawanna	Scranton	Luzerne	1878
Lancaster	Lancaster	Chester	1728
Lawrence	New Castle	Beaver, Mercer	1849
Lebanon	Lebanon	Dauphin, Lancaster	1813
Lehigh	Allentown	Northampton	1812
Luzerne	Wilkes-Barre	Northumberland	1786
Lycoming	Williamsport	Northumberland	1795
McKean	Smethport	Lycoming	1804
Mercer	Mercer	Allegheny	1800
Mifflin	Lewistown	Cumberland, Northumberland	1789
Monroe	Stroudsburg	Pike, Northampton	1836
Montgomery	Norristown	Philadelphia	1784
Montour	Danville	Columbia	1850
Northampton	Easton	Bucks	1751
Northumberland	Sunbury	Lancaster, Bedford, Berks, Northampton	1772
Perry	New Bloomfield	Cumberland	1820
Philadelphia	Philadelphia	Original County	1682
Pike	Milford	Northampton	1814
Potter	Coudersport	Lycoming	1804
Schuylkill	Pottsville	Berko, Northampton	1811
Snyder	Middleburg	Union	1855
Somerset	Somerset	Bedford	1795
Sullivan	Laporte	Lycoming	1847
Susquehanna	Montrose	Luzerne	1810
Tioga	Wellsboro	Lycoming	1804
Union	Lewisburg	Northumberland	1813
Venango	Franklin	Allegheny, Lycoming	1800
Warren	Warren	Allegheny, Lycoming	1800
Washington	Washington	Westmoreland	1781
Wayne	Honesdale	Northampton	1798
Westmoreland	Greensboro	Bedford	1773

County Name	County Seat	Parent County	Year Created
Wyomning	Tunkhannock	Luzerne	1842
York	York	Lancaster	1748

RHODE ISLAND

County Name	County Seat	Parent County	Year Created
Bristol	Bristol, Warren & Barrington		1746-7
Kent	E. Greenwich	Providence	1750
Newport	Newport	Original County	1703
Providence	Providence	Original County	1703
Washington	S. Kingston	Newport	1729

SOUTH CAROLINA

County Name	County Seat	Parent County	Year Created
Abbeville	Abbeville	District 96	1785
Aiken	Aiken	Edgefield, Orangeburg, Barnwell, Lexington	1871
Allendale	Allendale	Pendleton District	1826
Bamberg	Bamberg	Barnwell	1897
Barnwell	Barnwell	Orangeburg District	1798
Beaufort	Beaufort	Original District	1785
Berkeley	Moncks Corner	Charleston	1882
Calhoun	St. Matthews	Lexington, Orangeburg	1908
Charleston	Charleston	Original District	1785
Cherokee	Gaffney	Union, York, Spartanburg	1897
Chester	Chester	Craven, Camden District	1785
Chesterfield	Chesterfield	Cheraws District	1785
Clarendon	Manning	Sumter District	1785
Colleton	Waterboro	Charleston District	1785
Darlington	Darlington	Cheraws District	1785
Dillion	Dillion	Marion	1910
Dorchester	St. George	Berkeley, Colleton	1897
Edgefield	Edgefield	District 96	1785
Fairfield	Winnsboro	Camden District	1785
Florence	Florence	Marion, Darlington, Clarendon, Williamsburg	1888
Georgetown	Georgetown	Original District	1785
Greenville	Greenville	Washington District	1786
Greenwood	Greenwood	Abbeville, Edgefield	1897
Hampton	Hampton	Beaufort	1878
Horry	Conway	Georgetown District	1801
Jasper	Ridgeland	Beaufort, Hampton	1912
Kershaw	Camden	Camden District	1791
Lancaster	Lancaster	Camden District	1785
Laurens	Laurens	District 96	1785
Lee	Bishopville	Darlington, Sumter, Kershaw	1902
Lexington	Lexington	Orangeburg District	1785
Marion	Marion	Georgetown District	1785
Marlboro	Bennettsville	Cheraws District	1785
McCormick	McCormick	Greenwood, Abbeville	1916
Newberry	Newberry	District 96	1785
Oconee	Wahalla	Pickens	1768
Orangeburg	Orangeburg	Original District	1785
Pickens	Pickens	Pendleton District	1826
Richland	Columbia	Kershaw District	1785
Saluda	Saluda	Edgefield	1896
Spartanburg	Spartanburg	District 96	1785
Sumter	Sumter	Camden District	1785
Union	Union	District 96	1785
Williamsburg	Kingtree	Georgetown District	1785
York	York	Camden, Pickney District	1785

SOUTH DAKOTA

County Name	County Seat	Parent County	Year Created
Aurora	Plankinton	Brule	1879
Beadle	Huron	Spink, Clark	1879
Bennett	Martin	Indian Lands	1909
Bon Homme	Tyndall	Charles Mix	1862
Brookings	Brookings	Unorganized Territory	1862
Brown	Aberdeen	Beadle	1879
Brule	Chamberlain	Old Buffalo	1875
Buffalo	Gannvalley	Territorial County	1873
Butte	Belle Fourche	Harding	1883
Campbell	Mound City	Buffalo	1873
Charles Mix	Lake Andes	Original District	1862
Clark	Clark	Hanson	1873
Clay	Vermillion		1862
Codington	Watertown	Indian Lands	1877
Corson	McIntosh	Boreman, Dowey	1909
Custer	Custer	Indian Lands	1875
Davison	Mitchell	Hanson	1873
Day	Webster	Clark	1879
Devel	Clear Lake	Brookings	1862
Dewey	Timber Lake	Indian Reservation, Armstrong	1873
Douglas	Armour	Charles Mix	1873
Edmunds	Ipswich	Buffalo	1873
Fall River	Hot Springs	Custer	1883
Faulk	Faulkton		1873
Grant	Milbank	Codington, Devel	1873
Gregory	Burke	Yankton	1862
Haakon	Philip	Stanley	1914
Hamlin	Hayti	Devel	1873
Hand	Miller	Buffalo	1873
Hanson	Alexander	Buffalo, Devel	1871
Harding	Buffalo	Unorganized Territory	1909
Hughes	Pierre	Buffalo	1873
Hutchinson	Olivet	Unorganized Territory	1862
Hyde	Highmore	Buffalo	1873
Jackson	Kodoka	Stanley	1914
Jerauld	Wessington Springs	Aurora	1883
Jones	Murdo	Lyman	1916
Kingsbury	DeSmet	Hanson	1873
Lake	Madison	Brookings, Hanson	1873
Lawrence	Deadwood	Unorganized Territory	1875
Lincoln	Canton	Minnehaha	1862
Lyman	Kinnebec	Unorganized Territory	1873
Marshall	Britton	Day	1885
McCook	Salem	Hanson	1873
McPherson	Leola	Buffalo	1873
Meade	Sturgis	Lawrence	1889
Mellette	White River	Lyman	1909
Miner	Howard	Hanson	1873
Minnehaha	Sioux Falls	Territorial County	1862
Moody	Flandreau	Brookings, Minnehaha	1873
Pennington	Rapid City	Unorganized Territory	1875
Perkins	Bison	Harding, Butte	1909
Potter	Gettysburg	Buffalo	1875
Roberts	Sisseton	Grant	1883
Sanborn	Woonsocket	Miner	1883
Shannon	Attached to Fall River County	Territorial County	1875
Spink	Redfield	Hanson	1873
Stanley	Ft. Pierce	Unorganized Territory	1873
Sully	Onida	Potter	1873
Todd		Attached to Tripp Co.	1909
Tripp	Winner	Unorganized Territory	1873
Turner	Parker	Lincoln	1871
Union	Elk Point	Unorganized Territory	1862
Walworth	Selby	Buffalo	1873

County Name	County Seat	Parent County	Year Created	County Name	County Seat	Parent County	Year Created
Washabaugh		Attached to Jackson Co.	1883	Macon	Lafayette	Smith, Sumner	1842
Yankton	Yankton	Unorganized Territory	1862	Madison	Jackson	Western District	1821
Ziebach	Dupree	Schnasse, Sterling, Armstrong	1911	Marion	Jasper	Indian Lands	1817
				Marshall	Lewisburg	Bedford, Lincoln, Giles, Maury	1836

TENNESSEE

County Name	County Seat	Parent County	Year Created	County Name	County Seat	Parent County	Year Created
Anderson	Clinton	Knox	1801	Maury	Columbia	Williamson	1807
Bedford	Shelbyville	Rutherford	1807	McMinn	Athens	Indian Lands	1819
Benton	Camden	Henry, Humphreys	1835	McNairy	Selmer	Hardin	1823
Bledsoe	Pikeville	Roane	1807	Meigs	Decatur	Hamilton, McMinn, Rhea	1836
Blount	Maryville	Knox	1795	Monroe	Madisonville	Roane	1819
Bradley	Cleveland	Indian Lands	1836	Montgomery	Clarksville	Tennessee	1796
Campbell	Jacksboro	Anderson, Claiborne	1806	Moore	Lynchburg	Bedford, Franklin	1871
Cannon	Woodbury	Coffee, Warren, Wilson	1836	Morgan	Wartburg	Roane	1817
Carroll	Huntington	Western District	1821	Obion	Union City	Western District	1823
Carter	Elizabethton	Washington	1796	Overton	Livingston	Jackson	1806
Cheatham	Ashland City	Davidson, Dickson, Montgomery	1856	Perry	Linden	Hickman	1821
Chester	Henderson	Hardeman, Madison, Henderson, McNairy	1879	Pickett	Byrdstown	Fentress, Overton	1879
				Polk	Benton	Bradley, McMinn	1839
Claiborne	Tazewell	Grainger, Hawkins	1801	Putnam	Cookeville	White, Jackson, Overton, DeKalb	1842
Clay	Celina	Jackson, Overton	1870				
Cocke	Newport	Jefferson	1797	Rhea	Dayton	Roane	1807
Coffee	Manchester	Franklin, Warren, Bedford	1836	Roane	Kingston	Knox, Blount	1801
Crockett	Alamo	Dyer, Madison, Gibson, Haywood	1845	Robertson	Springfield	Tennessee	1796
Cumberland	Crossville	Bledsoe, Morgan, Roane	1855	Rutherford	Murfreesboro	Davidson	1803
Davidson	Nashville	Washington	1783	Scott	Huntsville	Fentress, Morgan, Anderson	1849
Decatur	Decaturville	Perry	1845	Sequatchie	Dunlap	Hamilton	1857
DeKalb	Smithville	Cannon, Warren, White	1837	Sevier	Sevierville	Jefferson	1794
Dickson	Charlotte	Montgomery, Robertson	1803	Shelby	Memphis	Hardin	1819
Dyer	Dyersburg	Western District	1823	Smith	Carthage	Sumner	1799
Fayette	Somerville	Shelby, Hardeman	1824	Stewart	Dover	Montgomery	1803
Fentress	Jamestown	Morgan, Overton	1823	Sullivan	Blountville	Washington	1779
Franklin	Winchester	Bedford, Warren	1807	Sumner	Gallatin	Davidson	1786
Gibson	Trenton	Western District	1823	Tipton	Covington	Western District	1823
Giles	Pulaski	Maury	1809	Trousdale	Hartsville	Macon, Smith, Wilson	1870
Grainger	Rutledge	Hawkins, Knox	1796	Unicoi	Erwin	Carter, Washington	1875
Greene	Greenville	Washington	1783	Union	Maynardville	Anderson, Campbell, Claiborne, Grainger, Knox	1797
Grundy	Altamont	Coffee, Warren	1844				
Hamblen	Morristown	Grainger, Hawkins	1870	Van Buren	Spencer	Bledsoe, Warren, White	1840
Hamilton	Chattanooga	Rhea	1819	Warren	McMinnville	White	1807
Hancock	Sneedville	Claiborne, Hawkins	1844	Washington	Jonesboro	Covered present state. Many counties from section	1777
Hardeman	Bolivar	Western District	1823	Wayne	Waynesboro	Hickman	1817
Hardin	Savannah	Western District	1819	Weakley	Dresden	Western District	1823
Hawkins	Rogersville	Sullivan	1786	White	Sparta	Overton, Jackson, Smith	1806
Haywoood	Brownsville	Western District	1823	Williamson	Franklin	Davidson	1799
Henderson	Lexington	Western District	1821	Wilcox	Lebanon	Sumner	1799
Henry	Paris	Western District	1821				
Hickman	Centerville	Dickson	1807	**TEXAS**			
Houston	Erin	Dickson, Stewart	1871	Anderson	Palestine	Houston	1846
Humphreys	Waverly	Stewart, Smith	1809	Andrews	Andrews	Bexar	1876
Jackson	Gainesboro	Smith	1801	Angelina	Lufkin	Nacogdoches	1846
Jefferson	Dandridge	Green, Hawkins	1792	Aransas	Rockport	Refugio	1871
Johnson	Mountain City	Carter	1836	Archer	Archer City	Fannin	1858
Knox	Knoxville	Greene, Hawkins	1792	Armstrong	Claude	Bexar	1876
Lake	Tiptonville	Obion	1870	Atascosa	Jourdanton	Bexar	1856
Lauderdale	Ripley	Dyer, Tipton	1835	Austin	Bellville	Old Mexican Municipality	1836
Lawrence	Lawrenceburg	Hickman, Maury	1817	Bailey	Muleshoe	Bexar	1876
Lewis	Hohenwald	Hickman, Maury, Wayne, Lawrence	1843	Bandera	Bandera	Uvalde, Bexar	1856
Lincoln	Fayetteville	Bedford	1809	Bastrop	Bastrop	Old Mexican Municipality	1836
Loudon	Loudon	Blount, Monroe, Roane, McMinn	1870	Baylor	Seymour	Fannin	1858
				Bee	Beeville	Goliad, Refugio, Live Oak, San Patricio	1857
				Bell	Belton	Milam	1850

County Name	County Seat	Parent County	Year Created	County Name	County Seat	Parent County	Year Created
Bexar	San Antonio	Old Mexican Municipality est. 1718	1836	Fannin	Bonham	Red River	1837
				Fayette	La Grange	Bastrop, Colorado	1837
Blanco	Johnson City	Gillespie, Comal, Burnet, Hays	1858	Fisher	Roby	Bexar	1876
				Floyd	Floydada	Bexar	1876
Borden	Gail	Bexar	1876	Foard	Crowell	Hardman, Knox, King, Cottle	1891
Bosque	Meridian	McLennan, Milam District	1854	Fort Bend	Richmond	Austin	1837
Bowie	Boston	Red River	1840	Franklin	Mt. Vernon	Titus	1875
Brazoria	Angelton	Old Mexican Municipality	1836	Freestone	Fairfield	Limestone	1850
Brazos	Bryan	Washington, Robertson	1841	Frio	Pearsall	Atascosa, Bexar, Uvalde	1858
Brewster	Alpine	Presidio	1887	Gaines	Seminole	Bexar	1876
Briscoe	Silverton	Bexar	1876	Galveston	Galveston	Brazoria	1838
Brooks	Falfurrias	Starr, Zapata, Hidalgo	1911	Garza	Post	Bexar	1876
Brown	Brownwood	Travis, Comanche	1856	Gillespie	Fredericksburg	Bexar, Travis	1848
Burleson	Caldwell	Milam, Washington	1842	Glasscock	Garden City	Tom Green	1887
Burnet	Burnet	Travis, Bell, Williamson	1852	Goliad	Goliad	Old Mexican Municipality	1836
Caldwell	Lockhart	Gonzales	1848	Gonzales	Gonzales	Old Mexican Municipality	1836
Calhoun	Port Lavaca	Victoria, Matagorda, Jackson	1846	Gray	Pampa	Bexar	1876
Callahan	Baird	Bexar, Travis, Bosque	1858	Grayson	Sherman	Fannin	1846
Cameron	Brownsville	Nueces	1848	Gregg	Longview	Rusk, Upshur	1873
Camp	Pittsburg	Upshur	1874	Grimes	Anderson	Montgomery	1846
Carson	Panhandle	Bexar	1876	Guadalupe	Seguin	Bexar, Gonzales	1846
Cass	Linden	Boxie	1846	Hale	Plainview	Bexar	1876
Castro	Dimmitt	Bexar	1876	Hall	Memphis	Bexar, Young	1876
Chambers	Anahuac	Jefferson, Liberty	1858	Hamilton	Hamilton	Bosque, Comanche, Lampasas, Coryell	1842
Cherokee	Rusk	Nacogdoches	1846	Hansford	Spearman	Bexar, Young	1876
Childress	Childress	Bexar, Youngland District	1876	Hardeman	Quanah	Fannin	1858
Clay	Henrietta	Cooke	1857	Hardin	Kountze	Jefferson, Liberty	1858
Cochran	Morton	Bexar	1876	Harris	Houston	Formerly Harrisburg Municipality	1836
Coke	Robert Lee	Tom Green	1889				
Coleman	Coleman	Travis, Brown	1858	Harrison	Marshall	Shelby	1839
Collin	McKinney	Fannin	1846	Hartley	Channing	Bexar, Young	1876
Collingsworth	Wellington	Bexar, Youngland District	1876	Haskell	Haskell	Fannin, Milam	1858
Colorado	Columbus	Old Mexican Municipality	1836	Hays	San Marcos	Travis	1848
Comal	New Braunfels	Bexar, Gonzales, Travis	1846	Hemphill	Canadian	Bexar, Young	1876
Comanche	Comanche	Bosque, Coryell	1856	Henderson	Athens	Houston, Nacogdoches	1846
Concho	Paint Rock	Bexar	1858	Hidalgo	Edinburgh	Cameron	1852
Cooke	Gainesville	Frannin	1848	Hill	Hillsboro	Navarro	1853
Coryell	Gatesville	Bell	1854	Hockley	Levelland	Bexar, Young	1876
Cottle	Paducah	Fannin	1876	Hood	Granbury	Johnson	1865
Crane	Crane	Tom Green	1887	Hopkins	Sulphur Springs	Lamar, Nacogdoches	1846
Crockett	Ozona	Bexar	1875	Houston	Crockett	Nacogdoches	1837
Crosby	Crosbyton	Bexar District	1876	Howard	Big Spring	Bexar, Young	1876
Culberson	Van Horn	El Paso	1911	Hudspeth	Sierra Blanca	El Paso	1917
Dallam	Dalhart	Bexar	1876	Hunt	Greenville	Fannin, Nacogdoches	1846
Dallas	Dallas	Nacogdoches, Robertson	1846	Hutchinson	Stinnett	Bexar District	1876
Dawson	Lamesa	Bexar (org. 1905)	1858	Irion	Mertzon	Tom Green	1889
Deaf Smith	Hereford	Bexar	1876	Jack	Jacksboro	Cooke	1856
Delta	Cooper	Hopkins, Lamar	1870	Jackson	Edna	Old Mexican Municipality	1836
Denton	Denton	Fannin	1846	Jasper	Jasper	Old Mexican Municipality	1836
DeWitt	Cuero	Goliad, Gonzales, Victoria	1846	Jeff Davis	Fort Davis	Presidio	1887
Dickens	Dickens	Bexar	1876	Jefferson	Beaumont	Old Mexican Municipality	1836
Dimmit	Carrizo Springs	Uvalde, Bexar, Maverick, Webb	1858	Jim Hogg	Hebbronville	Brooks, Duval	1913
				Jim Wells	Alice	Nueces	1911
Donley	Clarendon	Jack	1876	Johnson	Cleburne	Ellis, Hill, Navarro	1854
Duval	San Diego	Live Oak, Starr, Neuces	1858	Jones	Anson	Bexar, Bosque	1858
Eastland	Eastland	Bosque, Coryell, Travis	1858	Karnes	Karnes City	Bexar	1854
Ector	Odessa	Tom Green	1887	Kaufman	Kaufman	Henderson	1848
Edwards	Rocksprings	Bexar	1858	Kendall	Boerne	Kerr, Blanco	1862
Ellis	Waxahachie	Navarro	1849	Kenedy	Sarita	Willacy, Hidalgo, Cameron	1921
El Paso	El Paso	Bexar	1850	Kent	Jayton	Bexar, Young	1876
Erath	Stephenville	Bosque, Coryell	1856	Kerr	Kerrville	Bexar	1856
Falls	Marlin	Limestone, Milam	1850				

County Name	County Seat	Parent County	Year Created	County Name	County Seat	Parent County	Year Created
Kimble	Junction	Bexar	1858	Real	Leakey	Bandera, Kerr, Edwards	1913
King	Guthrie	Bexar	1876	Red River	Clarksville	Old Mexican Municipality	1836
Kinney	Brackettville	Bexar	1850	Reeves	Pecos	Pecos	1883
Kleberg	Kingsville	Nueces	1913	Refugio	Refugio	Old Mexican Municipality	1836
Knox	Benjamin	Young, Bexar	1858	Roberts	Miami	Bexar	1876
Lamar	Paris	Red River	1840	Robertson	Franklin	Milam	1837
Lamb	Littlefield	Bexar	1876	Rockwell	Rockwell	Kaufman	1873
Lampasas	Lampasas	Bell, Travis	1856	Runnels	Ballinger	Bexar, Travis	1858
LaSalle	Cotulla	Bexar, Webb	1858	Rusk	Henderson	Nacogdoches	1843
Lavaca	Hallettsville	Colorado, Victoria, Jackson, Gonzales	1846	Sabine	Hemphill	Old Mexican Municipality	1836
				San Augustine	San Augustine	Old Mexican Municipality	1836
Lee	Giddings	Bastrop, Burleston, Washington, Fayette	1874	San Jacinto	Coldspring	Liberty, Polk, Montgomery, Walker	1870
Leon	Centerville	Robertson	1846	San Patricio	Sinton	Old Mexican Municipality	1836
Liberty	Liberty	Old Spanish Municipality	1836	San Saba	San Saba	Bexar	1856
Limestone	Groesbeck	Robertson	1846	Schleicher	Eldorado	Crockett	1887
Lipscomb	Lipscomb	Bexar	1876	Scurry	Snyder	Bexar	1876
Live Oaks	George West	Nueces, San Patricio	1856	Shackelford	Albany	Bosque	1858
Llano	Llano	Bexar	1856	Shelby	Center	Old Mexican Municipality	1836
Loving	Mentone	Tom Green	1887	Sherman	Stratford	Bexar	1876
Lubbock	Lubbock	Bexar, Crosby	1876	Smith	Tyler	Nacogdoches	1846
Lynn	Tahoka	Bexar	1876	Somervell	Glen Rose	Hood, Johnson	1875
Madison	Madisonville	Leon, Grimes, Walker	1842	Starr	Rio Grande City	Nueces	1848
Marion	Jefferson	Cass	1860	Stephens	Breckenridge	Bosque	1858
Martin	Stanton	Bexar	1876	Sterling	Sterling City	Tom Green	1891
Mason	Mason	Gillespie	1858	Stonewall	Aspermont	Bexar	1876
Matagorda	Bay City	Old Mexican Municipality	1836	Sutton	Sonora	Crockett	1887
Maverick	Eagle Pass	Kenedy	1856	Swisher	Tulia	Bexar, Young	1876
McCulloch	Brady	Bexar	1856	Tarrant	Fort Worth	Navarro	1849
McLennan	Waco	Milam	1850	Taylor	Abilene	Bexar, Travis	1858
McMullen	Tilden	Bexar, Live Oak, Atascosa	1858	Terrell	Sanderson	Pecos	1905
Medina	Hondo	Bexar	1848	Terry	Bexar attached to Martin from 1889		1876
Menard	Menard	Bexar	1858				
Midland	Midland	Tom Green	1885	Throckmorton	Throckmorton	Fannin	1858
Milam	Cameron	Old Mexican Municipality	1836	Titus	Mt. Pleasant	Red River, Bowie	1846
Mills	Goldthwaite	Comanche, Brown, Hamilton, Lampasas	1887	Tom Green	San Angelo	Bexar	1874
				Travis	Austin	Bastrop	1840
Mitchell	Colorado City	Bexar	1876	Trinity	Groveton	Houston	1850
Montague	Montague	Cooke	1857	Tyler	Woodville	Liberty	1846
Montgomery	Conroe	Washington	1837	Upshur	Gilmer	Harrison, Nacogdoches	1846
Moore	Dumas	Bexar	1876	Upton	Rankin	Tom Green	1887
Morris	Daingerfield	Titus	1875	Uvalde	Uvalde	Bexar	1850
Motley	Matador	Bexar	1876	Val Verde	Del Rio	Crockett, Kinney, Pecos	1885
Nacogdoches	Nacogdoches	Old Mexican Municipality	1836	Van Zandt	Canton	Henderson	1848
Navarro	Corsicana	Robertson	1846	Victoria	Victoria	Old Mexican Municipality	1836
Newton	Newton	Jasper	1846	Walker	Huntsville	Montgomery	1846
Nolan	Sweetwater	Young, Bexar	1876	Waller	Hempstead	Austin, Grimes	1873
Nueces	Corpus Christi	San Patricio	1846	Ward	Monahans	Tom Green	1887
Ochiltree	Perryton	Bexar	1876	Washington	Brenham	Texas Municipality	1836
Oldham	Vega	Bexar	1876	Webb	Laredo	Bexar	1848
Orange	Orange	Jefferson	1852	Wharton	Wharton	Matagorda, Jackson	1846
Palo Pinto	Palo Pinto	Navarro, Bosque	1856	Wheeler	Wheeler	Bexar, Young	1876
Panola	Carthage	Harrison, Shelby	1846	Wichita	Wichita Falls	Youngland District	1858
Parker	Weatherford	Bosque, Navarro	1855	Wilbarger	Vernon	Bexar	1858
Parmer	Farwell	Bexar	1876	Willacy	Raymondville	Hidalgo, Cameron	1911
Pecos	Fort Stockton	Presidio	1871	Williamson	Georgetown	Milam	1848
Polk	Livingston	Liberty	1846	Wilson	Floresville	Bexar, Karnes	1860
Potter	Amarillo	Bexar	1876	Winkler	Kermit	Tom Green	1887
Presidio	Marfa	Bexar	1850	Wise	Decatur	Cooke	1856
Rains	Emory	Hopkins, Hunt, Wood	1870	Wood	Quitman	Van Zandt	1850
Randall	Canyon	Bexar	1876	Yoakum	Plains	Bexar	1876
Reagan	Big Lake	Tom Green	1903	Young	Graham	Bosque, Fannin	1856

County Name	County Seat	Parent County	Year Created
Zapata	Zapata	Starr, Webb	1858
Zavala	Crystal City	Uvalde, Maverick	1858

UTAH

County Name	County Seat	Parent County	Year Created
Beaver	Beaver	Iron, Millard	1856
Box Elder	Brigham City	Unorg. Terr.	1856
Cache	Logan	Unorg. Terr.	1856
Carbon	Price	Emery	1894
Daggett	Manila	Uintah	1919
Davis	Farmington	Salt Lake	1852
Duchesne	Duchesne	Wasatch	1913
Emery	Castle Dale	Sanpete, Sevier	1880
Garfield	Panquitch	Iron, Sevier, Kane	1882
Grand	Moab	Emery, Uintah	1890
Iron	Parowan	Unorg. Terr.	1850
Juab	Nephi	Original county	1852
Kane	Kanab	Washington, Unorg. Terr.	1864
Millard	Fillmore	Juab	1851
Morgan	Morgan	Davis, Summit	1862
Piute	Junction	Sevier	1865
Rich	Randolph	Formerly Richland	1864
Salt Lake	Salt Lake City	Original county	1852
San Juan	Monticello	Kane	1880
Sanpete	Manti	Original county	1852
Sevier	Richfield	Sanpete	1865
Summit	Coalville	Salt Lake	1854
Tooele	Tooele	Original county	1852
Uintah	Vernal	Wasatch	1880
Utah	Provo	Original county	1852
Wasatch	Heber	Summit	1862
Washington	St. George	Unorg. Terr.	1852
Wayne	Loa	Piute	1892
Weber	Ogden	Original county	1852

VERMONT

County Name	County Seat	Parent County	Year Created
Addison	Middlebury	Rutland	1785
Bennington	Bennington	Original county	1779
Caladonia	St. Johnsbury	Newly Organized Terr.	1792
Chittenden	Burlington	Original county	1787
Essex	Guildhall	Unorg. Terr.	1792
Franklin	St. Albans	Chittenden	1792
Grand Isle	North Hero	Franklin	1802
Lamoille	Hyde Park	Chittenden, Orleans, Franklin	1835
Orange	Chelsea	Original county	1781
Orleans	Newport	Original county	1792
Rutland	Rutland	Original county	1781
Washington	Montpelier	Addison, Orange	1810
Windham	Newfane	Bennington	1781
Windsor	Woodstock	Original county	1781

VIRGINIA

County Name	County Seat	Parent County	Year Created
Accomack	Accomac	Northampton	1634
Albemarle	Charlottesville	Goochland, Louisa	1744
Alexandria	Alexandria	Fairfax	1801
Alleghany	Covington	Bath, Botetourt, Monroe	1822
Amelia	Amelia C.H.	Brunswick, Prince George	1734
Amherst	Amherst	Albemarle	1758
Appomattox	Appomattox	Buckingham, Campbell, Charlotte, Prince Edward	1845
Arlington	Arlington	Fairfax	1847
Augusta	Staunton	Orange	1738
Bath	Warm Springs	Augusta, Botetourt, Greenbrier	1790
Bedford	Bedford	Albemarle, Lunenburg	1752
Bland	Bland	Giles, Tazewell, Wythe	1861
Botetourt	Fincastle	Augusta	1769
Brunswick	Laurenceville	Prince George, Isle of Wight Surry	1720
Buchanan	Grundy	Russell, Tazewell	1858
Buckingham	Buckingham	Albemarle, Appomattox	1758
Campbell	Rustburg	Bedford	1781
Caroline	Bowling Green	Essex, King and Queen, King William	1727
Carroll	Hillsville	Grayson, Patrick	1842
Charles City	Charles City	Original Shire	1634
Charlotte	Charlotte Court House	Lunenburg	1764
Chesapeake	Chesapeake	Norfolk 1810-80	1764
Chesterfield	Chesterfield	Henrico	1749
Clarke	Berryville	Frederick	1836
Craig	New Castle	Botetourt, Giles, Roanoke, Monroe, Alleghany, Montgomery	1851
Culpeper	Culpepper	Orange	1748
Cumberland	Cumberland	Goochland	1855
Dickenson	Clintwood	Buchanan, Russell, Wise	1880
Dinwiddie	Dinwiddie	Prince George	1634
Elizabeth City	Hampton	Original Shire	1634
Essex	Tappahannock	Old Rappahannock	1692
Fairfax	Fairfax	Prince William, Loudoun	1742
Fauquier	Warrenton	Prince William	1758
Floyd	Floyd	Montgomery, Franklin	1831
Fluvanna	Palmyra	Albemarle	1777
Franklin	Rocky Mount	Bedford, Henry, Patrick	1785
Frederick	Winchester	Orange, Augusta	1738
Giles	Pearisburg	Montgomery, Monroe, Tazewell, Craig, Mercer, Wythe	1806
Gloucester	Gloucester	York	1651
Goochland	Goochland	Henrico	1727
Grayson	Independence	Wythe, Patrick	1792
Greene	Stanardsville	Orange	1838
Greensville	Emporia	Brunswick, Sussex	1780
Halifax	Halifax	Lunenburg	1752
Hanover	Hanover	New Kent	1720
Henrico	Richmond	Original Shire	1634
Henry	Martinsville	Pittsylvania, Patrick	1776
Highland	Montgomery	Bath, Pendleton	1847
Isle of Wight	Isle of Wight	Original Shire	1634
James City	Williamsburg	Original Shire	1634
King & Queen	King & Queen C.H.	New Kent	1691
King George	King George	Richmond, Westmoreland	1720
King William	King William	King and Queen	1700
Lancaster	Lancaster	Northumberland, York	1652
Lee	Jonesville	Russell, Scott	1792
Loudoun	Leesburg	Fairfax	1757
Louisa	Louisa	Hanover	1742
Lunenburg	Lunenburg	Brunswick	1745
Lynchburg	Lynchburg	Ind. City	
Madison	Madison	Culpeper	1792
Mathews	Mathews	Gloucester	1790
Mecklenburg	Boydton	Lunenburg	1764
Middlesex	Saluda	Lancaster	1674
Montgomery	Christiansburg	Fincastle, Botetourt, Pulaski	1776
Nansemond	Suffolk	Upper Norfolk	1637
Nelson	Lovingston	Amherst	1807
New Kent	New Kent	York	1654
Northampton	Eastville	Original Shire	1634
Northumberland	Heathsville	Indian District of Chickacoan	1648
Nottoway	Nottoway	Amelia	1788

County Name	County Seat	Parent County	Year Created
Orange	Orange	Spotsylvania	1734
Page	Luray	Rockingham, Shenandoah	1831
Patrick	Stuart	Henry	1790
Pittsylvania	Chatham	Halifax	1766
Powhatan	Powhatan	Cumberland, Chesterfield	1777
Prince Edward	Farmville	Amelia	1752
Prince George	Prince George	Charles City	1700
Prince William	Manassas	King George, Stafford	1727
Princess Anne	Princess Anne	Lower Norfolk	1691
Pulaski	Pulaski	Montgomery, Wythe	1839
Rappahannock	Washington	Culpeper	1833
Richmond	Warsaw	Rappahannock	1692
Roanoke	Salem	Botetourt, Montgomery	1838
Roanoke	Roanoke	Ind. City	
Rockbridge	Lexington	Augusta, Botetourt	1777
Rockingham	Harrisonburg	Augusta	1777
Russell	Lebanon	Washington	1785
Scott	Gate City	Lee, Russell, Washington	1814
Shenandoah	Woodstock	Frederick	1772
Smyth	Marion	Washington, Wythe	1832
Southampton	Courtland	Isle of Wight, Nansemond	1749
Spotsylvania	Spotsylvania	Essex, King and Queen, King William	1720
Stafford	Stafford	Westmoreland	1666
Staunton	Staunton	Ind. City	
Suffolk	Suffolk	Ind. City	
Surry	Surry	James City	1652
Sussex	Sussex	Surry	1752
Tazewll	Tazewell	Russell, Wythe	1799
Virginia Beach	Virginia Beach	Ind. City	
Warren	Front Royal	Frederick, Shenandoah	1836
Washington	Abingdon	Fincastle, Montgomery	1776
Westmoreland	Montross	Northunberland	1653
Williamsburg	Williamsburg	Ind. City	
Wise	Wise	Lee, Russell, Scott	1856
Wythe	Wytheville	Montgomery	1789
York	Yorktown	Original Shire	1634

WASHINGTON

County Name	County Seat	Parent County	Year Created
Adams	Ritzville	Whitman	1883
Asotin	Asotin	Garfield	1883
Benton	Prosser	Yakima, Klickitat	1905
Chelan	Wenatchee	Kittitas, Okanogan	1899
Clallam	Port Angeles	Jefferson	1854
Clark	Vancouver	Original county	1844
Columbia	Dayton	Walla Walla	1875
Cowlitz	Kelso	Lewis	1854
Douglas	Waterville	Lincoln	1883
Ferry	Republic	Stevens	1899
Franklin	Pasco	Whitman	1883
Garfield	Pomeroy	Columbia	1881
Grant	Ephrata	Douglas	1909
Gray's Harbor	Montesano	Organized as Chelalis	1854
Island	Coupeville	Original county	1853
Jefferson	Port Townsend	Original county	1852
King	Seattle	Original county	1852
Kitsap	Port Orchard	King	1857
Kittitas	Ellensburg	Yakima	1883
Klickitat	Goldendale	Walla Walla	1859
Lewis	Chehalis	Original county	1845
Lincoln	Davenport	Spokane	1883
Mason	Shelton	Thurston	1854
Okanogan	Okanogan	Stevens	1888

County Name	County Seat	Parent County	Year Created
Pacific	South Bend	Original county	1851
Pend Oreille	Newport	Stevens	1911
Pierce	Tacoma	Original county	1852
San Juan	Friday Harbor	Whatcom	1873
Skagit	Mount Vernon	Whatcom	1883
Skamania	Stevenson	Clark	1854
Snohomish	Everett	Island	1861
Spokane	Spokane	Walla Walla	1858
Stevens	Colville	Walla Walla	1863
Thurston	Olympia	Original county	1852
Wahkiakum	Cathlamet	Lewis	1854
Walla Walla	Walla Walla	Original county	1854
Whatcom	Bellingham	Original county	1854
Whitman	Colfax	Stevens	1871
Yakima	Yakima	Walla Walla	1865

WEST VIRGINIA

County Name	County Seat	Parent County	Year Created
Barbour	Philippi	Harrison, Lewis, Randolph	1843
Berkeley	Martinsburg	Frederick	1772
Boone	Madison	Kanawha, Cabell, Logan	1847
Braxton	Sutton	Kanawha, Lewis, Nicholas	1836
Brooke	Ohio	Wellsburg	1796
Cabell	Huntington	Kanawha	1809
Calhoun	Grantsville	Gilmer	1856
Clay	Clay	Braxton, Nicholas	1858
Doddridge	W. Union	Harrison, Tyler, Ritchie, Lewis	1845
Fayette	Fayetteville	Kanawha, Greenbrier, Logan	1831
Gilmer	Glenville	Lewis, Kanawha	1845
Grant	Petersburg	Hardy	1866
Greenbrier	Lewisburg	Montgomery	1777
Hampshire	Romney	Frederick	1752
Hancock	New Cumberland	Brooke	1848
Hardy	Moorefield	Hampshire	1785
Harrison	Clarksburg	Monongalia	1784
Jackson	Ripley	Kanawha, Mason, Wood	1831
Jefferson	Charles Town	Berkeley	1801
Kanawha	Charleston	Greenbrier, Montgomery	1788
Lewis	Weston	Harrison	1816
Lincoln	Hamlin	Boone, Cabell, Kanawha	1867
Logan	Logan	Kanawha, Cabell, Giles	1824
Marion	Fairmont	Harrison, Monongalia	1842
Marshall	Moundsville	Ohio	1835
Mason	Point Pleasant	Kanawha	1804
McDowell	Welch	Tazewell	1858
Mercer	Princeton	Giles, Tazewell	1837
Mineral	Keyser	Hampshire	1866
Mingo	Williamson	Logan	1895
Monongalia	Morgantown	Dist. of W. Augusta	1776
Monroe	Union	Greenbrier	1799
Morgan	Berkeley Springs	Berkeley, Hampshire	1820
Nicholas	Summersville	Greenbrier, Kanawha	1818
Ohio	Wheeling	Dist. of W. Augusta	1776
Pendleton	Franklin	Augusta, Hardy	1787
Pleasants	St. Marys	Ritchie, Tyler, Wood	1851
Pocahontas	Marlinton	Pendleton, Randolph and Bath all Virginia	1821
Preston	Kingwood	Monongalia	1818
Putnam	Winfield	Kanawha, Mason, Cabell	1848
Raleigh	Beckley	Fayette	1850
Randolph	Elkins	Harrison	1786
Ritchie	Harrisville	Harrison, Lewis, Wood	1843
Roane	Spencer	Kanawha, Jackson, Gilmer	1856
Summers	Hinton	Greenbrier, Monroe, Mercer	1871

County Name	County Seat	Parent County	Year Created
Taylor	Grafton	Barbour, Harrison, Marion, Preston	1844
Tucker	Parsons	Randolph	1856
Tyler	Middlebourne	Ohio	1814
Upshur	Buckhannon	Randolph, Barbour, Lewis	1851
Wayne	Wayne	Cabell	1842
Webster	Webster Springs	Braxton, Nicholas	1860
Wetzel	New Martinsville	Tyler	1846
Wirt	Elizabeth	Wood, Jackson	1848
Wood	Parkersburg	Harrison	1798
Wyoming	Pineville	Logan	1850

WISCONSIN

County Name	County Seat	Parent County	Year Created
Adams	Friendship	Portage	1848
Ashland	Ashland	Unorg. Terr.,	1860
Barron	Barron	Formerly Dallas & Polk	1859
Bayfield	Washburn	Ashland, Orig. La Pointe	1845
Brown	Green Bay	Territorial county	1818
Buffalo	Alma	Trempealeau	1853
Burnett	Grantsburg	Polk	1856
Calumet	Chilton	Territorial county	1836
Chippewa	Chippewa Falls	Crawford	1845
Clark	Neillsville	Crawford	1853
Columbia	Portage	Portage	1846
Crawford	Prairie du Chien	Territorial county	1818
Dane	Madison	Territorial county	1836
Dodge	Juneau	Territorial county	1836
Door	Sturgeon Bay	Brown	1851
Douglas	Superior	Unorg. Terr.,	1854
Dunn	Menomonie	Chippewa	1854
Eau Claire	Eau Claire	Chippewa	1856
Florence	Florence	Marinette, Oconto	1882
Fond du Lac	Fond du Lac	Territorial county	1836
Forest	Crandon	Langlade, Oconto	1885
Grant	Lancaster	Territorial county	1836
Green	Monroe	Territorial county	1836
Green Lake	Green Lake	Marquette District	1858
Iowa	Dodgeville	Territorial county	1829
Iron	Hurley	Ashland, Oneida	1893
Jackson	Black River Falls	La Crosse	1853
Jefferson	Jefferson	Milwaukee	1836
Juneau	Mauston	Adams	1856
Kenosha	Kenosha	Racine	1850
Kewaunee	Kewaunee	Manitowoc	1852
La Crosse	La Crosse	Unorg. Terr.,	1851
Lafayette	Darlington	Iowa	1846
Langlade	Antigo	Lincoln, Oconto	1879
Lincoln	Merrill	Marathon	1874
Manitowoc	Manitowoc	Territorial county	1836
Marathon	Wausau	Portage	1850
Marinette	Marinette	Oconto	1879
Marquette	Montello	Marquette District	1836
Menominee	Keshena	Menominee Indian Reservation	1961
Milwaukee	Milwaukee	Territorial county	1834
Monroe	Sparta	La Crosse	1854
Oconto	Oconto	Unorg. Terr.,	1851
Oneida	Rhinelander	Lincoln	1885
Outagamie	Appleton	Brown	1851
Ozaukee	Port Washington	Milwaukee	1853
Pepin	Durand	Dunn	1858
Pierce	Ellsworth	St. Croix	1853
Polk	Balsam Lake	St. Croix	1853
Portage	Stevens Point	Territorial county	1836

County Name	County Seat	Parent County	Year Created
Price	Phillips	Chippewa, Lincoln	1879
Racine	Racine	Territorial county	1836
Richland	Richland Center	Iowa	1842
Rock	Janesville	Territorial county	1836
Rusk	Ladysmith	Chippewa	1901
St. Croix	Hudson	Territorial county	1840
Sauk	Baraboo	Territorial county	1840
Sawyer	Hayward	Ashland, Chippewa	1883
Shawano	Shawano	Oconta	1853
Sheboygan	Sheboygan	Territorial county	1836
Taylor	Medford	Clark, Lincoln, Marathon, Chippewa	1875
Trempealeau	Whitehall	Crawford, La Crosse	1854
Vernon	Viroqua	Richland, Crawford	1851
Vilas	Eagle River	Oneida	1893
Walworth	Elkhorn	Territorial county	1836
Washburn	Shell Lake	Burnett	1883
Washington	West Bend	Territorial county	1836
Waukesha	Waukesha	Milwaukee	1846
Waupaca	Waupaca		1851
Waushara	Wautoma	Marquette	1851
Winnebago	Oshkosh	Territorial county	1840
Wood	Wisconsin Rapids	Portage	1856

WYOMING

County Name	County Seat	Parent County	Year Created
Albany	Laramie	Original county	1868
Big Horn	Basin	Fremont, Johnson	1890
Campbell	Gillette	Crook, Weston	1911
Carbon	Rawlins	Original county	1868
Converse	Douglas	Laramie, Albany	1888
Crook	Sundance	Pease	1875
Fremont	Lander	Sweetwater	1884
Goshen	Torrington	Platte, Laramie	1911
Hot Springs	Thermopolis	Fremont	1911
Johnson	Buffalo	Pease	1875
Laramie	Cheyenne	Original county	1867
Lincoln	Kemmerer	Uinta	1911
Natrona	Casper	Carbon	1888
Niobrara	Lusk	Converse	1911
Park	Cody	Big Horn	1909
Platte	Wheatland	Laramie	1911
Sheridan	Sheridan	Johnson	1888
Sublette	Pinedale	Fremont	1921
Sweetwater	Green River	Original county	1867
Teton	Jackson	Lincoln	1921
Uinta	Evanston	Original county	1869
Washakie	Worland	Big Horn, Fremont	1911
Weston	Newcastle	Crook	1890

County Name Changes

Counties that have changed their name or ceased to exist.

County Name Changes

Accawmack, Virginia was Northampton prior to 1642

Aishcum, Michigan changed to Lake 1843

Albemarle, North Carolina discontinued 1739

Alcona, Michigan (Mar. 8, 1843, act 67); Neewaygo (Apr. 1, 1840, Act 119)

Allen, Missouri changed to Atchison 1845

Allred, North Dakota — See McKenzie

Alpena, Michigan (Mar. 8, 1843, act 67); Anamickee (Apr. 1, 1840, act 119)

Alturas, Idaho original county; discontinued

Anamickee, Michigan changed to Alpena 1843

Andy Johnson, Minnesota changed from Toombs 1858 and to Wilkin 1868

Antrim, Michigan (Mar. 8, 1843, act 67); Meegisee (Apr. 1, 1840, act 119)

Arapahoe, Kansas discontinued

Arehdale, North Carolina changed to Beaufort 1712

Arkansas, Missouri — New Madrid

Arlington, Virginia (Mar. 16, 1920, chap. 241); Alexandria (Mar. 13, 1847, Chap. 53)

Armstrong, South Dakota merged with Dewey

Ashley, Missouri changed to Texas 1845

Atchison, Missouri (Feb. 14, 1845, unnumbered); Allen (Feb. 23, 1843, unnumbered)

Attakaps, Louisiana original Parrish — discontinued

—B—

Bad Ax, Wisconsin — See Vernon

Baker, Alabama — See Chilton

Barbour, Virginia — See West Virginia

Barron, Wisconsin (Mar. 4, 1869, chap. 75); Dallas (Mar. 19, 1859, chap. 191)

Bartow, Georgia (Dec. 6, 1861, act 97); Cass (Dec. 3, 1832, unnumbered)

Bath, North Carolina discontinued 1739

Baton Rouge, Louisiana

Bayfield, Wisconsin (Apr. 12, 1866, chap. 146); La Pointe (Feb. 19, 1845 unnumbered)

Beaufort, North Carolina (1712); Pamptecough (1705)

Benton, Alabama — See Calhoun

Benton, Florida, Alachua (Now Hernando)

Berkeley, South Carolina discontinued

Berkeley, Virginia — See West Virginia

Bibb, Alabama (Dec. 4, 1820, act 24); Cahaba (Feb. 7, 1818, unnumbered)

Billings, Kansas — See Norton

Blackbird, Nebraska — See Thurston

Blaine, Alabama abolished 1867, changed to Etowah 1868

Bleeker, Michigan changed to Menominee 1863

Boone, Virginia — See West Virginia

Bradford, Florida (Dec. 6, 1861, chap. 1,300); New River (Dec. 21, 1858, chap. 895)

Bradford, Pennsylvania (Mar. 24, 1812, chap. 109); Ontario Feb. 21, 1810, chap. 30)

Branciforte, California changed to Santa Cruz 1850

Braxton, Virginia — See West Virginia

Brazos, Texas (Jan. 28, 1842, unnumbered); Navasoto (Jan. 30, 1841, unnumbered)

Breckenridge, Kansas — See Lyon

Breckenridge, Minnesota — See Clay, Toombs and Wilkin

Brevard, Florida (Jan. 6, 1855, chap. 651); St. Lucie (Mar. 14, 1844, unnumbered)

Brooke, Virginia — See West Virginia

Buchanan, Michigan discontinued

Buchanan, Texas changed to Stephens 1861

Buffalo, North Dakota disorganized 1873

Buncombe, Iowa changed to Lyon 1862

Burbank, North Dakota disorganized and transferred to Trail and Giggs.

Bute, North Carolina discontinued 1779

—C—

Cabela, Alabama — See Bibb

Cabell, Virginia — See West Virginia

Calhoun, Alabama (Jan. 29, 1858, act 306); Benton (Dec. 18, 1832, act 11)

Calhoun, Kansas name chnaged to Jackson after Civil War

Calhoun, Nebraska changed to Saunders 8 Jan. 1862

Calhoun, Virginia — See West Virginia

Calhoun, Iowa (Jan. 12, 1853, chap. 12); Fox (Jan 15, 1851, chap. 9)

Camden, Missouri (Feb. 23, 1843, unnumbered); Kinderhook (Jan. 29, 1841, unnumbered)

Camden Dist, South Carolina original dist discontinued

Carbonate, Colorado original name of Lake Co.

Carroll, Louisiana — See East and West Carroll

Carson, Nevada discontinued

Carter, Wyoming changed to Sweetwater 1869

Carteret Dist, South Carolina name changed to Granville 1700

Cass, Georgia changed to Bartow 1861

Cass, Missouri (Feb. 19, 1849, unnumbered); Van Buren (Mar. 3, 1835 unnumbered)

Cass, Texas (May 16, 1871, chap. 95); Davis (Dec. 17, 1861, chap. 14); Cass (Apr. 25, 1846, unnumbered)

Chaffee, Colorado (Feb. 10, 1879, unnumbered); Lake (Nov. 1, 1861, unnumbered)

Champoeg, Oregon original co. (name changed to Marion)

Charles River, Virginia — See York

Charlevoix, Michigan (Mar. 8, 1843, act 67); Reshkauko (Apr. 1, 1840, act 119)

Charlotte, New York Albany (renamed Washington 1784)

Chehalis, Washington original co. — now Grays Harbor changed 1915

Cheonoquet, Michigan changed to Montmorency 1843

Cheraws Dist, South Carolina original dist. discontinued

Cherokee, Kansas (Feb. 18, 1860, chap. 30); McGee (Aug. 39, 1855, chap. 30)

Chilton, Alabama (Dec. 17, 1874, act 72); Baker (Dec. 30, 1868, act 142)

Christian, Illinois (Feb. 1, 1840, unnumbered); Dane (Feb. 15, 1839, unnumbered)

Clare, Michigan (Mar. 8, 1843, act 67); Kaykakee (Apr. 1, 1840, act 119)

Claremont, South Carolina

Clark, Missouri (Old), Arkansas

Clark, Oregon Now part of state of Washington

Clark, Washington (Sept. 3, 1849, unnumbered); Vancouver (June 27, 1844, unnumbered)

Clay, Arkansas (Dec. 6, 1875, act 42); Clayton (Mar. 24, 1873, act 27)

Clay, Minnesota (Mar. 6, 1862, chap. 33); Breckin ridge (Mar. 18, 1858, chap. 34)

Clay, Mississippi (Apr. 10, 1876, chap. 103); Colfax (May 12, 1871, chap. 430)

Clay Virginia — See West Virginia

Cleveland, Arkansas (Mar. 5, 1885; act 38); Dorsey (Apr. 17, 1873, act 58)

Cloud Kansas (Feb. 26, 1867, chap 40); Shirley (Feb. 27, 1860, chap 43)

Colletcon, (Old), South Carolina discontinued

Conejos, Colorado (Nov. 7, 1861, unnumbered); Guadalupe (Nov. 1, 1861, unnumbered)

Cotaco, Alabama — See Morgan

Covington, Alabama (Oct. 10, 1868, act 39); Jones (Aug. 6, 1868, unnumbered); Covington (Dec. 7, 1821, unnumbered)

Craven, North Carolina (1712); Archdale (Dec. 3, 1705)

Craven, (Old), South Carolina discontinued

Crawford, Michigan (Mar. 8, 1843, act 67); Shawano (Apr. 1, 1840, act 119)

Custer, Montana (Feb. 16, 1877, unnumbered); Big Horn (Feb. 2, 1865, unnumbered)

—D—

Dallas, Missouri (Dec. 16, 1844, unnumbered); Niangua (Jan. 29, 1841, unnumbered)

Dallas, Wisconsin changed to Barron

Dane, Illinois name changed in 1840 to Christian County

Davis, Kansas, Riley — See Geary, Junction City

Davis, Texas changed to Cass 1871

Day, Oklahoma Cheyenne — Arapho Lands disc. 1906

Des Moines, Michigan disorganized

Dewey, South Dakota (Mar. 9, 1883, chap. 17); Rusk (Jan. 8, 1873, chap. 19)

Dobbs, North Carolina Johnston, discontinued 1791

Doddridge, Virginia — See West Virginia

Dodge, Missouri — Putnam

Dorn, Kansas — See Nesho

Dorsey, Arkansas — See Cleveland

Doty, Minnesota — See St. Louis and Lake

Dunmore, Virginia — See Shenandoah

Dunn, North Dakota formed from part Howard (disc. in 1883 and annexed to Stark in 1897)

—E—

Emmet, Michigan (Mar. 8, 1843, act 67); Tonedagana (Apr. 1, 1840, act 119)

Encinal, Texas discontinued

Etowah, Alabama (Dec. 1, 1868, act 20); Baine (Dec. 7, 1866, act 92)

—F—

Fayette, Virginia — See West Virginia

Feliciana, Louisiana

Fincastle, Virginia Botetourt discontinued 1777

Finney, Kan. (Feb. 21, 1883, chap. 71); Sequoyah (Mar. 6, 1873, chap. 72)

Foote, Kansas — See Gray

Fox, Iowa — See Calhoun

—G—

Garfield, Kansas annexed to Finney 1893

Gates, Wisconsin — See Rusk

Geary, Kansas (Feb. 28, 1889, chap. 132); Davis (Aug. 30, 1855, chap. 30)

Gilmer, Virginia — See West Virginia

Glasgow, North Carolina discontinued 1799

Godfrey, Kansas changed to Seward 1861

Grays Harbor, Washington (Mar. 15, 1915, chap. 77); Chehalis (Apr. 14, 1854, unnumbered)

Greenbrier, Virginia — See West Virginia

Greene, Nebraska changed to Seward 3 Jan. 1862

Gringras, North Dakota name changed to Wells 1881

Guadalupe, Colorado original name of Conejose Co.

—H—

Hampshire, Virginia — See West Virginia

Hancock, Alabama — See Winston

Hancock, Virginia — See West Virginia

Hardy, Virginia — See West Virginia

Harris, Texas (Dec. 28, 1839, joint resolution); Harrisburg (Mar. 17, 1836 Tex. const.)

Harrison, Virginia — See West Virginia

Hempstead, Missouri Arkansas

Henry, Missouri (Feb. 15, 1841, unnumbered); Rives (Dec. 13, 1834, unnumbered)

Hernando, Florida (Dec. 24, 1850, chap. 415); Benton (Mar. 6, 1844); Hernando (Feb. 24, 1843, chap. 51)

Holt, Missouri (Feb. 15, 1841, unnumbered); Nodaway (Jan. 29, 1841, unnumbered)

Holt, Nebraska (Jan. 9, 1862, unnumbered); West (Jan. 13, 1860, unnumbered)

Howard, Indiana (Dec. 28, 1846, chap. 168); Richardville (Jan. 15, 1844, chap. 3)

Howard, Kansas taken to form Elk and Chautauqua

Hunter, Kansas — See Cowley

Hyde, North Carolina (1712,); Wickham (Dec. 3, 1705)

—I—

Illinois, Virginia discontinued 1784

Iosco, Michigan (Mar. 8, 1843, act 67); Kanotin (Apr. 1, 1840, act 119)

Iron, Utah (Dec. 3, 1850, unnumbered); Little Salt Lake County, (Jan 31, 1850)

Isle of Wight, Virginia (1637); Warrosquoyoake (1634)

Isle Royal, Michigan disorganized 1897

Izard, Nebraska changed to Stanton

—J—

Jackson, Kansas (Feb. 11, 1859, chap. 99); Calhoun (Aug. 30, 1855, chap. 30)

Jackson, Nebraska

Jackson, Virginia — See West Virginia

Jasper, Georgia (Dec. 10, 1812, unnumbered); Randolph (Dec. 10, 1807, unnumbered)

Jefferson, Mississippi (Jan. 11, 1802, unnumbered); Pickering (Apr. 2, 1799)

Jefferson, Nebraska (Oct. 23, 1865); Jones (Jan. 26, 1856, unnumbered)

Jefferson Virginia — See West Virginia

Johnson Minnesota — See Wilkin

Johnson, Wyoming (Dec. 13, 1879, chap 31); Pease (Dec. 8, 1875, unnumbered)

Jones, Nebraska

Josh Bell, Kentucky

—K—

Kalkaska, Michigan (Mar. 8, 1843, act 67); Wabasee (Apr. 1, 1840, act 119)

Kanawah, Virginia — See West Virginia

Kanotin, Michigan changed to Iosco 1843

Kautawaubet, Michigan changed to Wexford, 1843

Kaykakee, Michigan changed to Clare, 1843

Kent, Delaware (1683); St. Jones (1682)

Kentucky, Virginia discontinued 1780

Kinchafoonee, Georgia Stewart, changed to Webster 1856

Kinderhook, Missouri - Benton, Pulaski

Kishkekosh, Iowa changed to Monroe 1846

Kitsap, Washington (July 13, 1857, unnumbered); Slaughter (Jan. 16, 1857, unnumbered)

Knox, Nebraska (Feb. 21, 1873); L'eau Qui Court, (Feb. 10, 1857, unnumbered)

—L—

Lafayette, Missouri (Feb. 16, 1825, chap. 1); Lillard (Nov. 16, 1820, chap. 10)

Lake, Colorado (Feb. 10, 1879, unnumbered); Carbonate (Nov. 1, 1861, unnumbered)

Lake, Michigan (Mar. 8, 1843, act 67); Aishcum (Apr. 1, 1840, act 119)

Lamar, Alabama (Feb. 8, 1877, act 205); Sanford (Oct. 8, 1868, act 13); Jones (Feb. 4, 1867, act 298)

Langlade, Wisconsin (Feb. 19, 1880, chap. 19); New (Feb. 27, 1879, chap. 114)

La Pointe, Wisconsin — See Bayfield

Lawrence, Missouri New Madrid abolished 1818

L'Eau Qui Court, Nebraska — See Knox and Emmet

Lewis, Oregon now part of state of Washington

Lewis, Virginia — See West Virginia

Lewis and Clark, Montana (Dec. 20, 1867, unnumbered; eff. Mar. 1, 1868); Edgerton (Feb. 2, 1865, unnumbered)

Liberty, South Carolina

Lillard, Missouri Cooper

Lincoln, Minnesota; Rock (Mar. 23, 1857, chap. 14)

Lincoln, Nebraska (Dec. 11, 1861, unnumbered); Shorter (Jan. 7, 1860 unnumbered)

Lincoln, Virginia — See West Virginia

Logan, Arkansas (Dec. 14, 1875, act 62); Sarber (Mar. 22, 1871, act 25)

Logan, Kansas (Feb. 24, 1887, chap. 173); St. John (Mar. 4, 1881, chap. 48)

Logan, Virginia — See West Virginia

Loudon, Tennessee (July 7, 1870, chap. 77); Christiana (June 2, 1870, chap. 2)

Lovely, Arkansas abolished 1828

Lower Norfolk, Virginia - New Norfolk

Lykins, Kansas — See Miami

Lyon, Iowa (Sept. 11, 1862, chap. 23); Buncombe (Jan. 15, 1851, chap. 9)

Lyon, Kansas (Feb. 5, 1862, chap 61); Breckenridge (Feb. 17, 1857, unnumbered)

—M—

Madison, Kansas divided to Morris & Lyon Counties

Manitou, Michigan disbanded 1895

Mankahta, Minnesota discontinued

Mackinac, Michigan (Mar. 9, 1843, chap. 89); Michilimackinac (Oct. 26, 1818, procl.)

Marion Arkansas (Sept. 29, 1836, unnumbered); Searcy (Nov. 3, 1835, unnumbered)

Marion, Oregon (Sept. 3, 1849, unnumbered); Champoick (July 5, 1843, unnumbered)

Marion Virginia — See West Virginia

Marshall, Virginia — See West Virginia

Mason, Michigan (Mar. 8, 1843, act 67); Notipekago Apr. 1, 1840, act 119)

Mason Virginia — See West Virginia

Mason, Washington (Jan 8, 1864, unnumbered); Sawamish (Mar. 13, 1854)

McDowell, Virginia — See West Virginia

McGhee, Kansas — See Cherokee

Meegisee, Michigan changed to Antrim 1843

Menominee, Michigan (Mar. 19, 1863, act 163); Bleeker (Mar. 15, 1861, act 213)

Mercer, Virginia — See West Virginia

Miami, Kansas (June 3, 1861, chap. 18); Lykins (Aug. 30, 1855, chap. 30)

Michilimackinac, Michigan changed to Mackinac 1843

Mikenauk, Michigan changed to Roscommon 1843

Milton, Georgia, Cobb, Cherokie, Forsyth merged Fulton 1911

Monongalia, Minnesota discontinued

Monongalia, Virginia — See West Virginia

Monroe, Iowa (Jan 19, 1846); Kishkekosh (Feb. 17, 1843, chap. 34)

Monroe, Virginia — See West Virginia

Montgomery, New York (Apr. 2, 1784, chap. 17); Tryon (Mar. 12, 1772, chap. 613)

Montmorency, Michigan (Mar. 8, 1843, act 67); Chednoquet (Apr. 1, 1840, act 119)

Morgan, Alabama (June 14, 1821, unnumbered); Cotaco (Feb. 6, 1818, unnumbered)

Morgan, Virginia — See West Virginia

Morris, Kansas (Feb. 11, 1859, chap. 60); Wise (Aug. 30, 1855, chap. 30)

Mosquito, Florida changed to Orange 1845

—N—

Nansemond, Virginia (1645); Upper Norfolk 1637

Navasota, Texas name changed to Brazos in 1842

Neewago, Michigan changed to Alcoma 1843

Nemaha, Nebraska (Nov. 23, 1854 procl.); Forney

Neosho, Kansas (June 3, 1861, chap. 18); Dorn (Aug. 30, 1855, chap. 30)

New, Wisconsin — See Langlade

New Norfolk, Virginia - Elizabeth City

Newport, Rhode Island (June 16, 1729); Rhode Island (June 22, 1703)

New River, Florida changed to Bradford 1861

Niangua, Missouri - Polk

Nicholas, Virginia — See West Virginia

Ninety-Six Dist, South Carolina; Original district (discontinued)

Norfolk, Virginia; Lower Norfolk changed to Cheaspeak City 1963

Northampton, Virginia (1642); Accawmack (1634)

Norton, Kansas (Feb. 19, 1874, chap. 55); Billings (Mar. 6, 1873, chap. 72); Norton (Feb. 26, 1867)

Notipekago, Michigan changed to Mason 1843

—O—

Ohio, Virginia — See West Virginia

Okkuddo, Michigan changed to Otsego 1843

Orange, Florida (Jan. 30, 1845, chap. 31); Mosquito (Dec. 29, 1824, unnumbered)

Orange, South Carolina

Osage, Kansas (Feb. 11, 1859, chap. 100); Weller (1855, chap. 30)

Osceola, Michigan (Mar. 8, 1843, act 67); Unwattin (Apr. 1, 1840, act 119)

Otoe, Kansas

Otoe, Nebraska; Pierce

Otsego, Michigan (Mar. 8, 1843, act 67); Okkuddo (Apr. 1, 1840, act 119)

Ouray, Colorado (Mar. 2, 1883, unnumbered); Uncompahgre (Feb. 27, 1883, unnumbered)

Ozark, Missouri (Mar. 24, 1845, unnumbered); Decatur (Feb. 22, 1843, unnumbered); Ozark (Jan. 29, 1841, unnumbered)

—P—

Pah Ute, Arizona disolved 1895 returned to Mohave

Pahute, Nevada discontinued

Patuxent, Maryland changed to Colvert 1658

Pease, Wyoming changed to Johnson 13 Dec. 1879

Pembina, Minnesota changed to Kittson 1878

Pendleton, South Carolina; Washington District discontinued 1826

Pendleton, Virginia — See West Virginia

Pickering, Mississippi changed to Jefferson 1802

Pickney District, South Carolina original district discontinued

Pierce, Minnesota disorganized

Pierce, Nebraska; Otoe

Pleasants, Virginia — See West Virginia

Pocahontas, Virginia — See West Virginia

Providence, Rhode Island (June 16, 1729); Providence Plantations (June 22, 1703

Pulaski, Missouri; Franklin

Putnam, Virginia — See West Virginia

—R—

Raleigh, Virginia — See West Virginia

Randolph, Georgia changed to Jasper 1812

Randolph, Virginia — See West Virginia

Reshkauko, Michigan changed to Charlevoix 1843

Rich, Utah (Jan. 29, 1868, chap. 2); Richland (Jan. 16, 1864, unnumbered)

Richardson, Kansas changed to Wabaunsee 1859

Richardville, Indiana — See Howard

Ritchie, Virginia — See West Virginia

Risley, Iowa changed to Webster 1853

Rives, Missouri - Lafayette

Roane, Virginia — See West Virginia

Roop, Nevada discontinued

Roscommon, Michigan (Mar. 8, 1843, act 67); Mikenauk (Apr. 1, 1840, act 119)

Rusk, South Dakota name changed to Dewey in 1883; Dewey organized 1910

Rusk, Wisconsin (June 19, 1905, chap. 463); Gates (May 15, 1901, chap. 469)

—S—

Salem, South Carolina

Salt Lake, Utah (Jan. 29, 1868, chap. 3); Great Salt Lake (Mar. 3, 1852, unnumbered)

Sanford, Alabama — See Lamar

San Miguel, Colorado (Mar. 2, 1883, unnumbered); Ouray (Nov. 1, 1861, unnumbered)

Santa Cruz, California

Saunders, Nebraska (Jan 8, 1862, unnumbered); Calhoun (Jan. 26, 1856, unnumbered)

Sawamish, Washington — See Mason

Sequoyah, Kansas — See Gray and Finney

Seward, Kansas

Seward, Nebraska

Shawano, Michigan changed to Crawford 1843

Shenanhoah, Virginia

Shirley, Kansas — See Cloud

Shorter, Nebraska changed to Lincoln 11 Dec. 1861

Slaughter, Iowa changed to Washington 1839

St. John, Kansas — See Logan

St. Jones, Delaware changed to Kent County 1682

St. Louis, Minnesota (Mar. 3, 1855, chap. 22); Superior (Feb. 20, 1855, chap. 6)

St. Lucas, Florida changed to Brevard 1855

St. Mary's Nevada discontinued

Stanton, Nebraska; Izard (Mar. 6, 1855 unnumbered)

Stephens, Texas (Dec. 17, 1861, chap. 4); Buchanan (Jan. 22, 1858, chap. 55)

Sumner, Mississippi changed to Webster 1882

Superior, Minnesota changed to Saint Louis 1855

Sussex, Delaware (1683); Deal (1682)

Sweetwater, Wyoming (Dec. 13, 1869, chap 35); Carter (Dec. 27, 1867, chap 35)

—T—

Taylor, Nebraska

Taylor, Virginia — See West Virginia

Tennessee, Tennessee

Texas, Missouri (Feb. 14, 1845, unnumbered); Ashley (Feb. 17 1843, unnumbered)

Thayer, Nebraska (Oct. 30, 1871); Jefferson

Tonedagana, Michigan changed to Emmet 1843

Toombs, Minnesota changed to Andy Johnson Co. 1858 changed to Wilkin Co. 1868

Tryon, New York; Albany (renamed Montgomery 1784)

Tryon, North Carolina discontinued 1779

Tucker, Virginia — See West Virginia

Twality, Oregon changed to Washington 1849

Tyler, Virginia — See West Virginia

Umpqua, Oregon; Benton and Linn (absorbed by Douglas 1863)

Uncompahgre, Colorado changed to Ouray 1883

Union, South Dakota (Jan. 7, 1864, chap. 14); Cole (Apr. 10, 1862, chap. 14)

Union, Tennessee (Jan. 28, 1846, chap. 123); Cooke (Oct. 9, 1797, chap. 8)

Unwattin, Michigan changed to Osceola 1843

Upper Norfolk, Virginia; New Norfolk (see Nansemond)

Upshur, Virginia — See West Virginia

—V—

Vernon, Wisconsin (Mar. 22, 1862, chap. 137); Bad Axe (Mar. 1, 1851, chap. 131)

—W—

Wabassee, Michigan changed to Kalkaska 1843

Wabaunsee, Kansas (Feb. 11, 1859, chap. 49); Richardson (Aug. 30, 1855, chap. 30)

Wahkaw, Iowa changed to Woodbury 1853

Wahnata, Minnesota disorganized

Wallace, North Dakota — See McKenzie

Warrosquoyacke, Virginia changed to Isle of Wight 1637

Warwick, Virginia; discontinued 1953 rec. in Newport News

Washington, Iowa (Jan 25, 1839, unnumbered); Slaughter (Jan. 16, 1837)

Washington, New York (Apr. 2, 1784, chap. 17); Charlotte (Mar. 12, 1772, chap. 613)

Washington, Oregon (Sept. 3, 1849, unnumbered); Twality (July 5, 1843)

Washington, Rhode Island (Oct. 29, 1781); King's (June 16, 1729)

Washington, South Dakota

Washington, Vermont (Nov. 8, 1814, chap. 79); Jefferson (Nov. 1, 1810, chap. 74)

Washington Dist., South Carolina original district discontinued

Wayne, Tennessee abolished 1788

Wayne, Virginia — See West Virginia

Webster, Georgia (Feb. 21, 1856, act 367); Kinchafoonee (Dec. 16, 1853, act 227)

Webster, Iowa (Jan 12, 1853, chap. 12); Risley (Jan. 15, 1851, chap. 9)

Webster, Mississippi (Jan. 30, 1882, chap. 132); Sumner (Apr. 6, 1874, chap. 112)

Webster, Virginia — See West Virginia

Weller, Kansas — See Osage

Wells, North Dakota (Feb. 26, 1881, chap. 53); Gingras (Jan 4, 1873, chap. 18)

West, Nebraska changed to Holt Jan. 1862

Wetzel, Virginia — See West Virginia

Wexford, Michigan (Mar. 8, 1843, act 67); Kautawaubet (Arp. 1, 1840, act 119)

Wilkin, Minnesota (Mar. 6, 1868, chap. 115); Andy Johnson (Mar. 8, 1862, chap. 25)

Winnebago, Indian Reservation, Nebraska

Winston, Alabama (Jan. 22, 1858, act 322); Hancock (Feb. 12, 1850, act 58)

Winyaw, South Carolina

Wirt, Virginia — See West Virginia

Wise, Kansas — See Morris

Wood, Virginia — See West Virginia

Woodbury, Iowa (Jan 12, 1853, chap. 12); Wahkaw (Jan. 15, 1851, chap. 9)

Wyoming, Virginia — See West Virginia

—Y—

Yohogania, Virginia discontinued 1786

York, Virginia (1642); Charles River (1634)

COUNTIES WITH MULTIPLE COURTHOUSES
(A Partial Listing)

ALABAMA
Barbour - Clayton and Eufaula
Coffee - Elba and Enterprise

ARKANSAS
Arkansas - DeWitt and Stuttgart
Carroll - Berryville and Eureka Springs
Clay - Piggott and Corning
Craighead - Jonesboro and Lake City
Franklin - Ozark and Charleston
Logan - Paris and Booneville
Mississippi - Osceola and Blytheville
Prairie - Des Arc and De Valls Bluff
Sebastian - Fort Smith and Greenwood
Yell - Danville and Dardanelle

CALIFORNIA:
Riverside - Riverside and Indio
Ventura - Ventura and ?

CONNECTICUT
Litchfield - Litchfield and Winstead
New Haven - Waterbury and New Haven
New London - New London and Norwich
Windham - Putnam and Willimantic

IOWA
Lee - Fort Madison and Keokuk

MASSACHUSETTS
Barnstable - Barnstable and West Harwich
Berkshire - Pittsfield, No. Adams, & Great Barrington
Essex - Lawrence, Newburyport, and Salem
Middlesex - Cambridge and Lowell

MISSISSIPPI
Bolivar - Cleveland and Rosedale
Carroll - Carrollton and Vaiden
Chichasaw - Houston and Okolona
Choctaw - Ackerman and Chester
Coahoma - Clarksdale and Friar Point
Hinds - Jackson and Raymond
Jasper - Bay Springs and Paulding
Jones - Ellisville and Laurel
Panola - Batesville and Sardis
Tallahatchie - Charleston and Sumner
Yalobusha - Coffeville and Water Valley

MISSOURI
Jackson - Independence and Kansas City

NEW HAMPSHIRE
Hillsboro - Nashua and Manchester

NEW YORK
Catteraugus - Little Valley and ?
Oneida - Rome and Utica
Oswego - Oswego and Pulaski

RHODE ISLAND
Bristol - Warren and Barrington

VERMONT
Bennington - Bennington and Manchester

Selected County Historical Societies and County Histories

ARIZONA

COCONINO COUNTY
Society—North Arizona Pioneers Historical Society, Inc., Fort Valley Rd., Flagstaff, AZ 86002

MOHAVE COUNTY
Society—Mohave Pioneers Historical Society, Inc., Beale Plaza, Kingman, AZ 86401

PIMA COUNTY
Society—Arizona Pioneers Historical Society Research Library, 949 E. 2nd St., Tucson, AZ 85719

PINAL COUNTY
Published History—Pinal Drill, May 1880

YAVAPAI COUNTY
Society—Prescott Historical Society, West Gourley St., Prescott, AZ 86301
Published History—Arizona Gazette, 1866

ARKANSAS

ARKANSAS COUNTY
Published History—Halliburton, William Henry, A Topographical Description: History of Arkansas Co. Ark. From 1541 to 1875

ASHLEY COUNTY
Published History—Etheridge, Young Williams, History of Ashley Co., Ark. Van Buren, 1959 (Ark. Hist. Series, No. 8).

BAXTER COUNTY
Published History—Shiras, Frances H. History of Baxter Co., Ark., Mountain Home, AR

BENTON COUNTY
Society—Bentonville, AR

BOONE COUNTY
Published History—Rea, Ralph Randolph, Boone Co. and its people, Van Buren, 1955 (Ark. Hist. Series Vol. 4)

BRADLEY COUNTY
Society—Southern Arkansas Biographical and Historical Memoirs, Goodspeed Publishing Co. Chicago, 1890

CALHOUN COUNTY
Society—Southern Arkansas Biographical and Historical Memoirs, Goodspeed Publishing Co. Chicago, 1890

CARROLL COUNTY
Society—Carroll County Historical Society, 106 Ada St., Berryville, AR
Published History—Mills, Nellie Alice, Early Days at Eureka Springs, Monett, Mo. 1949

CHICOT COUNTY
Published History—Southern Arkansas Biographical and Historical Memoirs, Goodspeed Publishing Co., Chicago, 1890

CLARK COUNTY
Published History—Butler, Laura Scott, History of Clark Co., In Ark History Assoc. Publications, (Little Rock, 1906-1917)

CLAY COUNTY
Published History—Webb, Robert T. History and Traditions of Clay Co., Mountain Home, 1933

CLEVELAND COUNTY
Published History—Southern Arkansas Biographical and Historical Memoirs, Goodspeed Publishing Co., Chicago, 1890

COLUMBIA COUNTY
Published History—Kilgore, Nettie Hicks, History of Columbia Co., Magnolia, 1947

CONWAY COUNTY
Published History—Historical Reminiscenses and Biographical Memoirs of Conway Co. Ark., Little Rock, AR; Facimile Reprint by Press-Argus, Van Buren (Ark. Series #10, Nov. 1960)

CRAIGHEAD COUNTY
Published History—Stuck, Charles Albert, The Story of Craighead Co., Jonesburo, 1960

CRAWFORD COUNTY
Society—Crawford County Historical Society, Public Library, Van Buren, AR
Published History—Eno, Clara Bertha, History of Crawford Co. Ark., Van Buren, 1951

CRITTENDEN COUNTY
Published History—Eastern Arkansas Biographical and Historical Memoirs, Goodspeed Publishing Co., Chicago, 1890

CROSS COUNTY
Published History—Chowning, Robert W., History of Cross Co. Ark., 1955; A Narrative Historical Edition, Wynne, 1955

DALLAS COUNTY
Published History—Smith, Jonathan Kennon, The Romance of Tulip, Memphis, Tenn. 1965

DESHA COUNTY
Published History—Southern Arkansas Biographical and Historical Memoirs, Goodspeed Publishing Co., Chicago, 1890

DREW COUNTY
Published History—Southern Arkansas Biographical and Historical Memoirs, Goodspeed Publishing Co., Chicago, 1890

FAULKNER COUNTY
Society—Faulkner County Historical Society, P.O. Box 731, Conway, AR 72032
Published History—Gatewood, Robert L., Faulkner Co. Arkansas 1778-1964, Conway, AR 1964

FRANKLIN COUNTY
Published History—History of Northwest Arkansas, Goodspeed Publishing Co., Chicago 1889

GARLAND COUNTY
Society—Garland County Historical Society, 1030 Park St., Hot Springs, AR
Published History—Hot Springs Ark. and Hot Springs Nat'l Park, Little Rock Pioneer Press, 1966

GRANT COUNTY
Published History—Central Arkansas Biographical and Historical Memoirs, Goodspeed Publishing Co., Chicago, 1889

GREENE COUNTY
Published History—Goodspeed's History of Green Co. Ark. w/foreward by High Park, Van Buren, 1963 (Ark. Hist. Series #13)

HEMPSTEAD COUNTY
Published History—Carrigan, Alfred Holt, Reminiscences of Hempstead Co., Hist. Assoc. Publications, Vol 2, p. 114-121

HOT SPRING COUNTY
Published History—Central Arkansas Biographical and Historical Memoirs, Goodspeed Publishing Co., Chicago 1890

HOWARD COUNTY
Published History—Southern Ark. Biographical and Historical Memoirs, Goodspeed Publishing Co., Chicago, 1890

INDEPENDENCE COUNTY
Society—Independence County Historical Society, P.O. Box 1412, Batesville, AR
Published History—Neil, Robert, Reminiscences of Independence Co. Ark., Hist. Assoc., Vol 3, P. 332-356

IZARD COUNTY
Published History—Shannon, Karr, A History of Izard Co. Ark., Little Rock, 1947

JACKSON COUNTY
Society—Jackson County Historical Society, Billingsley Memorial Library, 213 Walnut St., Newport, AR
Published History—Berens, W. E., Makers of Jackson Co., Jackson Co. Hist., n. d.

JEFFERSON COUNTY
Society—Jefferson County Historical Society, P.O. Box 593, Pine Bluff, AR
Published History—Central Arkansas Biographical and Historical Memoirs, Goodspeed Publishing Co., Chicago, 1889

JOHNSON COUNTY
Published History—Langford, Ella Malloy, Johnson County Arkansas The First Hundred Years, Clarksville Ark. 1921

LAFAYETTE COUNTY
Published History—Southern Arkansas Biographical and Historical Memoirs, Goodspeed Publishing Co., Chicago, 1890

LAWRENCE COUNTY
Published History—McLeod, Walter E., Centennial Memorial History of Lawrence Co., Russellvill, AR 1936

LEE COUNTY
Published History—Eastern Arkansas Biographical and Historical Memoirs, Goodspeed Publishing Co., Chicago, 1890

LINCOLN COUNTY
Published History—Southern Arkansas Biographical and Historical Memoirs, Goodspeed Publishing Co., Chicago, 1889

LITTLE RIVER COUNTY
Published History—Southern Arkansas Biographical and Historical Memoirs, Goodspeed Publishing Co., Chicago, 1890

LONOKE COUNTY
Published History—Young, R. L., History of Lonoke County Ark., Lonoke, 1924

MADISON COUNTY
Published History—History of Northwest Ark., Goodspeed Publishing Co., Chicago, 1889

MILLER COUNTY
Published History—Chandler, Barbara and Howe, J. Ed, History of Texarkana and Bowie and Miller Counties, Texas-Arkansas, Texarkana, 1939

MISSISSIPPI COUNTY
Published History—Edrington, Mable, History of Mississippi County

MONROE COUNTY
Published History—Eastern Arkansas Biographical and Historical Memoirs, Goodspeed Publishing Co., Chicago, 1890

NEVADA COUNTY
Published History—Southern Arkansas Biographical and Historical Memoirs, Goodspeed Publishing Co., Chicago, 1890

NEWTON COUNTY
Published History—History of Newton County, By Walter F. Lackey, Zions Printing and Publishing Co., Independence 1940

Published History—Southern Arkansas Biographical and Historical Memoirs, Goodspeed Publishing Co., Chicago, 1890

OUACHITA COUNTY
Published History—Southern Arkansas Biographical and Historical Memoirs, Goodspeed Publishing Co., Chicago, 1890

PERRY COUNTY
Published History—Central Arkansas Biographical and Historical Memoirs, Goodspeed Publishing Co., Chicago, 1889

PHILLIPS COUNTY
Published History—Eastern Arkansas Biographical and Historical Memoirs, Goodspeed Publishing Co., Chicago, 1890

PIKE
Published History—Southern Arkansas Biographical and Historical Memoirs, Goodspeed Publishing Co., Chicago, 1890

POPE COUNTY
Society—Arkansas Valley Historical Society, 2801 W. Main, Russellville, AR

Published History—West, David Porter, D. Porter West's Early History of Pope County, Russellville, 1905

PRAIRIE COUNTY
Published History—Eastern Arkansas Biographical and Historical Memoirs, Goodspeed Publishing Co., Chicago, 1890

PULASKI COUNTY
Society—Pulaski County Historical Society, Little Rock Univ., Little Rock, AR

Published History—Central Arkansas Biographical and Historical Memoirs, Goodspeed Publishing Co., Chicago, 1890

RANDOLPH COUNTY
Published History—Dalton, Lawrence, History of Randolph County, Little Rock, 1957

ST. FRANCIS COUNTY
Published History—Chowing, Robert W., History of St. Francis County Arkansas, A Narrative History Edition, Forrest City, N.D.

SALINE COUNTY
Published History—Central Arkansas Biographical and Historical Memoirs, Goodspeed Publishing Co., Chicago, 1889

SCOTT COUNTY
Published History—Goodner, Norman, A History of Scott County, Arkansas, Siloam Springs, AR, 1941

SEARCY COUNTY
Published History—McInturff, Orville J., Searcy County My Dear; A History of Searcy County, Ark., Marshall, 1963

SEBASTIAN COUNTY
Published History—DuVal, Benjamin T., History of Sebastain Co. Ark., (Historical Address Delivered at Fort Smith, Ark., 4 July 1876) Fort Smith, 1877

SEVIER COUNTY
Published History—Ray, W. S., Early Days in Sevier County (Ark. Hist. Pub., Vol 4, pp. 170-203, 1806-1907)

UNION COUNTY
Published History—Green, Juanita Whitaker, The History of Union Co., Ark. 1954

WASHINGTON COUNTY
Society—Arkansas Historical Society, Fayetteville, AR

Published History—Lemke, Walter John, Historic Washington County Arkansas, Fayetteville, 1952

WHITE COUNTY
Society—White County Historical Society, 110 E. Center St., Searcy, AR

Published History—Orr, W. E., That Judsonia, Judsonia, 1957

WOODRUFF COUNTY
Published History—Eastern Arkansas Biographical and Historical Memoirs, Goodspeed Publishing Co., Chicago, 1890

YELL COUNTY
Published History—Banks, Wayne, History of Yell County Arkansas, Van Buren 1959

CALIFORNIA

ALAMEDA COUNTY
Published History—History of Alameda County, By M. W. Wood

ALPINE COUNTY
Published History—Memorial and Biographical History of Northern California, Lewis Publishing Co., Chicago, 1891

AMADOR COUNTY
Published History—Memorial and Biographical History of Northern California, Lewis Publishing Co., (Amador Co., pp. 100-106) Chicago, 1891

BUTTE COUNTY
Published History—History of Butte County, By George C. Mansfield, Historical Record Co., Los Angeles, 1918

CALAVERAS COUNTY
Published History—History of State of Calif. and Biographical Record of the Sacramento Valley, By J. M. Guinn, Chapman Publishing Co., 1906

CALUSA COUNTY
Published History—History of Calusa Co., By Justus H. Rogers, Orlando, 1891

CONTRA COSTA COUNTY
Published History—History of Contra Costa Co., Historical Record Co., Los Angeles, CA 1926

DEL NORTE COUNTY
Society—Del Norte County Historical Society, 710 H Street, Cresent City, CA 95531

Published History—History of Del Norte Co., By Esther Ruth Smith, Holmes Book Co., Oakland, 1953

FRESNO COUNTY
Society—Fresno County Historical Society, 1177 Fulton St., Fresno, CA 93721

Published History—History of Fresno, Tulare and Kern Co., Lewis Publishing Co., Chicago, 1892

GLENN COUNTY
Published History—History of State of Calif. Biographical Records of the Sacramento Valley, Chapman Publishing Co., Chicago, 1908

HUMBOLT COUNTY
Society—Humbolt County Historical Society, P.O. Box 882, Eureka, CA

Published History—History of Humbolt Co., By Leigh Irvine, Historic Record Co., Los Angeles, CA 1915

IMPERIAL COUNTY
Published History—History of Imperial Co., By F. C. Farr, Elms and Frank, Berkley, 1918

KERN COUNTY
Society—Kern County Historical Society, 3801 Chester Ave., Bakersfield, CA 93301

Published History—History of Kern Co., By Wallace Morgan, Historical Record Co., Los Angeles, 1914

KINGS COUNTY
Published History—History of Tulane and Kings Co., By Menefee and Dodge, Historical Record Co., Los Angeles, CA 1913

LAKE COUNTY
Published History—History of Napa and Lake Counties, Slocum, Bowen and Co., San Francisco, 1881

LASSEN COUNTY
Published History—Fairfields Pioneer History of Lasson County, Asa Merrill Fairfield, H. S. Crocker Co., San Francisco, 1916

LOS ANGELES COUNTY
Published History—An Illustrated History of Southern Calif., Lewis Publishing Co., Chicago. 1890

MENDOCINO COUNTY
Historical and Discriptive Sketchbook of Napa, Sonoma, Lake and Medocino Counties, By C. A. Menefec, Reporters Publishing House, Napa City, 1873

MERCED COUNTY
Published History—History of Merced County, By John Outcalt, Hist. Record Co., Los Angeles, 1925

MONTEREY COUNTY
Published History—History of State of Calif., Record of Santa Cruz, San Benito, Monterey and San Luis Obispo Counties, By J. M. Guinn, Chapman Publishing Co., Chicago, 1903

NAPA COUNTY
Published History—Historical and Discriptive Sketchbook of Napa, Sonoma, Lake and Mendocino Counties, Slocum, Bowen and Co., San Francisco, 1881

PLACER COUNTY
Society—Placer County Historical Society, 205 Summit St., Auburn, CA

SAN BERNADINO COUNTY
Society—San Bernadino County Historical Society, 10039 Ave., Bloomington, CA

SANTA BARBARA COUNTY
Society—Carpinteria Valley Historical Society, Route 1, Box 150, Carpinteria, CA

SHASTA COUNTY
Society—Fort Crook Historical Society, Highway 229, Fall River Mills, CA

COLORADO

ARAPAHOE COUNTY
Society—Littleton Area Historical Society, Littleton, CO

Published History—History of City of Denver and Arapahoe County, 1880, Chicago

BENT COUNTY
Published History—History of Arkansas Valley, O. L. Baskin and Co., Chicago, 1880

BOULDER COUNTY
Society—Boulder Historical Society, 1655 Broadway, Boulder, CO
Published History—History of Clear Creek and Boulder Valley, O. L. Baskin and Co., Chicago, 1880

CHAFFEE COUNTY
Published History—History of Arkansas Valley, O. L. Baskin and Co., Chicago, 1881

CHEYENNE COUNTY
Society—Eastern Colorado Historical Society, Cheyenne Wells, CO

CLEAR CREEK COUNTY
Published History—History of Clear Creek and Boulder Counties, O. L. Baskins and Co., Chicago, 1880

CUSTER COUNTY
Published History—History of Arkansas Valley, O. L. Baskin and Co., Chicago, 1881

DENVER COUNTY
Society—State Historical Society of Colorado, Colorado State Museum, 200-14th Ave., Denver, CO 80203
Published History—Portrait and Biographical Record of Denver and Vicinity, Chapman Publishing Co., 1898, Chicago

EL PASO COUNTY
Published History—History of Pikes Peak, P.O. Box 2524, Colorado Springs, CO 80902
Published History—History of Arkansas Valley, O. L. Baskin and Co., Chicago, 1881

FREMONT COUNTY
Published History—History of Arkansas Valley, O. L. Baskin and Co., Chicago, 1881

CONNECTICUT

FAIRFIELD COUNTY
Published History—History of Fairfield County, By D. Hamilton Hurd, D. W. Lewis and Co., Philadelphia, 1881

HARTFORD COUNTY
Published History—Hartford County, By J. Hammond Trumbull, Edward L. Osgood Publisher, Boston 1886

GILPIN COUNTY
Published History—History of Clear Creek and Boulder Valleys, O. L. Baskins and Co., Chicago, 1880

JEFFERSON COUNTY
Published History—History of Clear Creek and Boulder Valleys, O. L. Baskin and Co., Chicago, 1880

LAKE COUNTY
Published History—History of Arkansas Valley, O. L. Baskin and Co., Chicago, 1881

LARIMER COUNTY
Published History—History of Larimer County, Ansils Watrons, Courier Printing and Publishing Co., Fort Collins, 1911

LOGAN COUNTY
Society—Logan Historical Society, 1320 South 4th Ave., Sterling, CO

PITKIN COUNTY
Society—Aspen Historical Society, P.O. Box 1323, Aspen, CO 81611

PUEBLO COUNTY
Published History—History of Arkansas Valley, O. L. Baskin and Co., Chicago, 1881

WELD COUNTY
Published History—History of Greenley and the Union Colony of Colorado, Greenley Tribune Press, Greenley, 1890

LITCHFIELD COUNTY
Society—Litchfield Historical Society, P.O. Box 384, Litchfield, CT

NEW HAVEN COUNTY
Published History—History of New Haven County, By J. L. Rockey, W. W. Preston and Co., New York, 1892

NEW LONDON COUNTY
Published History—History of New London County, By D. Hamilton Hurd, J. W. Lewis Publishing Co., Philadelphia, 1882

WINDHAM COUNTY
Published History—History of Windham County, By Ellwn, D. Larned, Charles Hamilton, Worcester, 1874

DELAWARE

NEW CASTLE COUNTY
Society—Historical Society of Delaware, Library, Old Town Hall, 509 Market St., Wilmington, DE 19801

FLORIDA

BROWARD COUNTY
Society—History Society of Fort Lauderdale, Inc., 315 S.E. 6th St., Fort Lauderdale, FL 33301

DUVAL COUNTY
Society—Jacksonville Historical Society, Public Library, 101 E. Adams St., Jacksonville, FL 32202

ESCAMBIA COUNTY
Society—Pensacola Historical Society, 405 S. Adams St., Pensacola, FL 32501

HILLSBORO COUNTY
Society—Florida Historical Society, University of Southern Florida Library, Tampa, FL

LAKE COUNTY
Society—Lake County Historical Society, 315 New Hampshire Ave., Tavares, FL

ST. JOHNS COUNTY
Society—St. Augustine Historical Society, Library, 271 Charlotte St., St. Augustine, FL 32084

GEORGIA

BALDWIN COUNTY
Published History—History of Baldwin County, By: Anna Marie G. Cook, Keys-Hearn Printing Co., Anderson, SC, 1925

BARTOW COUNTY
Published History—History of Bartow, By: Lucy J. Cuayas, Tribune Publishing Co., Cartersville, GA, 1933

BIBB COUNTY
Published History—Hist. Collections of Georgia, By: George White, Pudney and Russell, New York, 1854

BLECKLEY COUNTY
Published History—History of Pulaski and Bleckley Counties, D.A.R. Hawkinsville Chapter, Macon, GA, 1957-58

BURKE COUNTY
Published History—History and Pictures of Burke County, By: Neil H. Baldwin and A. M. Hillhouse, Filmed by Man Film Lab., Waynesboro, GA, 1960

CAMDEN COUNTY
Published History—History of Camden County, Reprints, Kingsland, GA, The Southeast Georgian, 1967

CASS COUNTY
Published History—Historical Collections of Georgia, By: Geo. William White, Pudney and Russell, New York, 1854

CATOOSA COUNTY
Published History—Official History of Catoosa County, Ringsgold, GA, 1953

CHARLTON COUNTY
Published History—History of Charlton County, Stein Printing Co., Atlanta, GA, 1932

CHATHAM COUNTY
Published History—Historical Collections of Georgia, By: Geo. William White, Pudney and Russell, New York, 1854

CHATTAHOOCHEE COUNTY
Published History—History of Chattahoochee County, By: Norma K. Rogers, Columbus Office Supply, Columbus, GA, 1933

CHEROKEE COUNTY
Published History—The History of Cherokee County, By: Lloyd G. Marlin, Walter W. Brown Pub. Co., Atlanta, GA, 1932

CLARKE COUNTY
Published History—Clarke County Georgia, By: Charles N. Strahan, Athens, GA, 1893

CLINCH COUNTY
Published History—History of Clinch County, By: Folks Huxford, The J. W. Burke Co., Macon, GA, 1916

COBB COUNTY
Published History—The First Hundred Years, By: Sarah B. G. Temple, Walter W. Brown Pub. Co., Atlanta, GA, 1935

COFFEE COUNTY
Published History—Ward's History of Coffee County, By: Warren P. Ward, Press of Foote and Davis Co., Atlanta, GA, 1930

COLQUITT COUNTY
Published History—History of Colquitt County, By: W. A. Covington, Foote and Davis Co., Atlanta, GA, 1937

COWETA COUNTY
Published History—Coweta County Chronicles For One Hundred Years, By: Mary G. Jones, The Stein Printing Co., Atlanta, GA, 1920

CRISP COUNTY
Published History—Crisp County Historical Sketches, Ham Printing Co., Caroela, GA, 1932

DE KALB COUNTY
Published History—History by De Kalb Historical Society, Georgia Papers, Decatur, GA

DODGE COUNTY
Published History—History of Dodge County, By: Addie D. Cobb, Foote and Davis Co., Atlanta, 1932

IDAHO

ADA COUNTY
Society—Idaho Historical Society, 610 North Julia Davis Dr., Boise, ID

IDAHO COUNTY
Society—Idaho County Historical Society, Grangeville, 83530

LATAH COUNTY
Society—The Latah County, Pioneer Assoc. Inc., 403 North Washington St., Moscow, ID 83843

LEMHI COUNTY
Society—Lemhi County Historical Society, Salmon, ID 83467

OWYHEE COUNTY
Society—Owyhee County Historical Society Inc., Murphy, ID 83650

ILLINOIS

ADAMS COUNTY
Society—Historical Society of Quincy and Adams County, 1515 Jersey St., Quincey, IL 62301
Published History—History of Adams County, Murray, Williamson and Phelps, Chicago, 1879

ALEXANDER COUNTY
Published History—History of Alexander County, Union and Pulaski Counties, By: Wm. Henry Perrin, Baskin, 1883

BOND COUNTY
Society—Bond County Historical Society, 211 East Vine St., Greenville, IL 62246
Published History—History of Bond and Montgomery Counties, By: William Perrin, O. L. Baskin and Co., Chicago, 1882

BOONE COUNTY
Society—Boone County Historical Society, 934 So. State Street, Belvidere, IL 61008
Published History—Past and Present Boone County, H. F. Kett Co., Chicago, 1877

BROWN COUNTY
Published History—History of Brown, Schuyler, W. R. Brink and Co., Philadelphia, 1882

BEREAU COUNTY
Society—Bereau County Historical Society, 109 Park Ave. West, Princeton, IL 61356
Published History—Reminiscenes of Bereau County, By: N. Matson, Republican Book & Job Office, Prinston, 1872

CALHOUN COUNTY
Society—Calhoun County Historical Society, Godfrey, IL 62035
Published History—Portrait and Biographical Album of Pike and Calhoun, Biog. Pub. Co., Chicago, 1891

CARROLL COUNTY
Published History—History of Carroll County, H. F. Kett and Co., Chicago, 1878

CASS COUNTY
Society—Cass County Historical Society, Cass County Courthouse, Virginia, IL 62691
Published History—History of Cass County, By: William H. Perrin, O. L. Baskin and Co., Chicago, 1882

CHAMPAIGN COUNTY
Society—Champaign County Historical Society, 201 So. Race St., Urbana, IL 61801
Published History—Portrait and Biographical Album of Champaign County, Chapman Bros., Chicago, 1887

CHRISTIAN COUNTY
Published History—Historical Encyclopedia and History of Christian County, By: Henry L. Fowkes, Chicago, 1918

CLARK COUNTY
Society—Clark County Historical Society, Box 207, Marshall, IL 62441
Published History—History of Crawford and Clark Counties, By: W. H. Perrin, O. L. Baskin and Co., Chicago, 1883

CLAY COUNTY
Society—Clay County Historical Society, Box 297, Louisville, IL 62858
Published History—History of Wayne and Clay Counties, Globe Pub. Co., Chicago, 1884

CLINTON COUNTY
Published History—History of Marion and Clinton Counties, Brink, McDonough and Co., Phila., 1881

COLES COUNTY
Society—Coles County Historical Society, 46 Circle Drive, Charleston, IL 61920
Published History—History of Coles County, W. M. LaBarron Jr. and Co., Chicago, 1879

COOK COUNTY
Society—Chicago Historical Society, North Ave and Clarke St., Chicago, IL 60614
Society—Ravenswood-Lakeview Historical Assoc., Hild Regional Branch Library, 4544 North Lincoln St., Chicago, IL 60625
Society—West Side Historical Society, Legler Regional Branch Library, 115 So. Pulaski Rd., Chicago, IL 60624
Published History—History of Cook County, By: Alfred T. Andreas, Chicago, 1884

CRAWFORD COUNTY
Society—Crawford County Historical Society, Robinson, IL 62454
Published History—History of Crawford and Clark Counties, O. L. Baskin and Co., Chicago, 1883

CUMBERLAND COUNTY
Society—Cumberland County Historical Society, Cumberland High School, Toledo, IL 62468
Published History—Cumberland County, Taylor Printshop, Olney, IL, 1968

DE KALB COUNTY
Published History—Portrait and Biographical Album of DeKalb County, Chapman Bros., Chicago, 1885

DE WITT COUNTY
Published History—History of DeWitt County, W. R. Brink and Co., Phila., 1882

DOUGLAS COUNTY
Society—Douglas County Historical Society, 501 East Sales, Tuscola, IL 61953
Published History—Historical and Biographical Record of Douglas County, By: J. Gresham, Wilson, Humphreys and Co., Logansport, 1900

DU PAGE COUNTY
Society—DuPage County Historical Society, 102 East Wesley, Wheaton, IL 60187
Published History—Portrait of Biographical Record of Cook and DuPage, Lake City Publishing Co., Chicago, 1894

EGAR COUNTY
Published History—History of Egar County, Wm. Lebaron Jr. and Co., Chicago 1879

EDWARDS COUNTY
Society—Edwards County Historical Society, 212 West Main Street, Albion, IL 62806
Published History—History of English Settlers in Edwards County, By: George Flower, Fergus Printing Co., Chicago, 1882

EFFINGHAM COUNTY
Published History—History of Effingham County, By: W. H. Perrin, O. L. Baskin and Co., Chicago, 1883

FAYETTE COUNTY
Society—Valdalia Historical Society, 215 West Randolph St., Vandalia, 62471

FORD COUNTY
Published History—Portrait and Biographical Record of Ford County, Lake City Publishing Co., Chicago, 1892

FRANKLIN COUNTY
Published History—History of Gallitan, Saline, Hamilton, Franklin, and Williamson Counties, Goodspeed Publishing Co., Chicago, 1887

FULTON COUNTY
Society—Fulton County Historical Society, 45 No. Park Dr., Canton, IL 61520
Published History—History of Fulton County, Charles C. Chapman and Co., Peoria, IL, 1879

GALLATIN COUNTY
Society—Gallatin County Historical Society, Shawneetown, IL 62984
Published History—History of Gallatin, Saline, Hamilton, Franklin, and Williamson Counties, Goodspeed Publishing Co., Chicago, 1887

GREENE COUNTY
Society—Greene County Historical Society, Sixth St., Carrollton, IL
Published History—History of Greene County, Donnelley, Gassette, and Loyd, Chicago, 1877

GRUNDY COUNTY
Society—Grundy County Historical Society, Morris, IL 60450
Published History—History of Grundy County, O. L. Baskin and Co., Chicago, 1882

HAMILTON COUNTY
Society—Hamilton County Historical Society, McLeansboro, IL 62859
Published History—History of Gallatin, Saline, Hamilton, Franklin, and Williamson Counties, Chicago, 1887

HANCOCK COUNTY
Published History—History of Hancock County, T. H. Gregg, Charles C. Chapman and Co., Chicago, 1880

HARDIN COUNTY
Published History—Biographical Review of Johnson, Massac, Pope and Hardin Counties, Chicago, 1893

HENDERSON COUNTY
Published History—History of Mercer and Henderson Counties, H. H. Hill and Co., Chicago, 1882

HENRY COUNTY
Society—Henry County Historical Society, P.O. Box 14, Cambridge, IL 61238
Published History—History of Henry County, H. F. Kett and Co., Chicago, 1877

IROQUOIS COUNTY
Society—Iroquois County Historical Society, 301 So. Poplar, Onarga, IL 60955
Published History—History of Iroquois County, By: W. W. Beckwith, H. H. Hill and Co., Chicago, 1880

JACKSON COUNTY
Published History—Portrait and Biographical Record, of Randolph, Jackson, Perry and Monroe Counties, Biographical Pub. Co., Chicago, 1894

JASPER COUNTY
Published History—Portrait and Biographical Record of Effingham, Jasper and Richland Counties, Lake City Pub. Co., Chicago, 1893

JEFFERSON COUNTY
Published History—History of Jefferson County, By: W. H. Perrin, Globe Publishing Co., Chicago, 1883

JERSEY COUNTY
Society—Jersey County Historical Society, 708 So. Washington, St., Jerseyville, IL 62052
Published History—History of Green and Jersey Counties, Cont. Hist. Company, Springfield, 1885

JO DAVIESS COUNTY

Society—The Galena Historical Society, 305 Bouthillier St., Galena, IL 61036

Published History—Portrait and Biographical Record of Jo Daviess County, Chapman Bros., Chicago, 1889

JOHNSON COUNTY

Society—Johnson County Historical Society, Vienna, IL 62995

Published History—History of Johnson County, Mrs. P. T. Chapman, The Herrin News, 1925

KANE COUNTY

Society—Geneva Historical Society, 228 South 2nd St., Geneva, IL 60134

Published History—Commemorative Biographical and Historical Record of Kane County; Beers, Leggett and Co., Chicago, 1888

KANKAKEE COUNTY

Society—Kankakee County Historical Society, Eighth Ave. and Water St., Kankakee, IL 60901

Published History—Portrait and Biographical Record of Kankakee County, Lake City Pub. Co., Chicago, 1893

KENDALL COUNTY

Published History—History of Kendall County, By: Rev. E. W. Hicks, Knickerbocker and Hodder, Aurora, 1877

KNOX COUNTY

Published History—History of Knox County, Charles C. Chapman and Co., Chicago, 1878

LAKE COUNTY

Society—Lake County Historical Society, P.O. Box 847, Lake Forest, IL 60045

Published History—Past and Present of Lake County, By: Wm. LeBaron and Co., Chicago, 1877

LA SALLE COUNTY

Society—LaSalle County Historical Society, P.O. Box 577, Ottawa, IL 61350

Published History—Past and Present of LaSalle County, H. F. Kett and Co., Chicago, 1877

LEE COUNTY

Society—Lee County Historical Society, 513 2nd St., Dixon, IL 61021

Published History—History of Lee County, H. H. Hill and Co., Chicago, 1881

LIVINGSTON COUNTY

Society—Livingston County Historical Society, 412 Bank of Pontiac Bldg., Pontiac, IL 61764

Published History—History of Livingston County, Wm. LeBaron Jr. and Co., Chicago, 1878

LOGAN COUNTY

Society—Logan County Historical Society, Lincoln, IL 62656

Published History—History of Logan County, Donnelley, Loyd and Co., Chicago, 1878

McDONOUGH COUNTY

Society—McConough County Historical Society, 739 So. Pearl, Macomb, IL 61455

Published History—History of McDonough County, By: D. W. Lusk, S. J. Clark Pub. Co., Springfield, 1878

McHENRY COUNTY

Society—McHenry County Historical Society, P.O. Box 526, Woodstock, IL 60098

Published History—History of McHenry County, Inter-state Pub. Co., Chicago, 1885

McLEAN COUNTY

Society—McLean County Historical Society, 201 East Grove St., Bloomington, IL 61701

Published History—The Good Old Times in McLean County, By: E. Duis, Leader Pub. & Printing House, Bloomington, 1874

MACON COUNTY

Society—Macon County Historical Comm., Macon County Court House, Decatur, IL 62523

Society—Macon County Historical Society, 33 Eastmoreland Dr., Decatur, IL 62521

Published History—Portriat and Biographical Record of Macon County, Lake City Pub. Co., Chicago, 1893

MACOUPIN COUNTY

Published History—History of Macoupin County, Brink, McDonough and Co., Phila., 1879

MADISON COUNTY

Society—Land of Goshen Historical Society, Park Drive, Edwardsville, IL 62025

Society—Madison County Historical Society, 715 No. Main, Edwardsville, IL 62025

Published History—History of Madsion County, W. R. Brink and Co., Edwardsville, 1882

MARION COUNTY

Published History—Brinkerhoff's History of Marion County, B. F. Bowen and Co., Indianapolis, 1909

MARSHALL COUNTY

Society—Marshall County Historical Society, 310 So. Prairie St., Lacon, IL 61540

Published History—Record of the Olden Times, By: Spencer Ellsworth, Home Journal Steam Printing, Lacon, 1880

MASON COUNTY

Published History—History of Menard and Mason Counties, O. L. Baskin and Co., Chicago, 1879

MASSAC COUNTY

Published History—History of Massac County, O. J. Page, Metropolis, 1900

MENARD COUNTY

Society—Menard County Historical Society, Greenview, IL 62642

Published History—History of Menard and Mason Counties, O. L. Baskin and Co., Chicago, 1879

MERCER COUNTY

Society—Mercer County Historical Society, S.E. Second Ave., Aledo, IL 61231

Published History—History of Mercer and Henderson Counties, H. H. Hill and Co., Chicago, 1882

MONROE COUNTY

Society—Monroe County History Society, 604 Morrison Ave., Waterloo, IL 62298

Published History—History of Randolph, Monroe, and Perry Counties, J. L. McDonough and Co., Phila., 1883

MONTGOMERY COUNTY

Society—Historical Society of Montgomery County, 904 So. Main St., Hillsboro, IL 62049

Published History—History of Bond and Montgomery Counties, By: Wm. Henry Perrin, O. L. Baskin and Co., Chicago, 1882

MORGAN COUNTY

Society—Morgan County Historical Society, 247 Webster Ave., Jacksonville, IL 62650

Published History—History of Morgan County, It's Past and Present, Donnelly, Loyd, and Co., Chicago, 1878

MOULTRIE COUNTY

Society—Moultrie County Historical Society, Bethany, IL 61914

Published History—History of Moultrie and Shelby Counties, Brink, McDonough and Co., Chicago, 1881

OGLE COUNTY

Society—Ogle County Historical Society, Oregon, IL 61061

Published History—History of Ogle County, H. F. Kett and Co., Chicago, 1878

PEORIA COUNTY

Society—Peoria Historical Society, 1212 West Moss Ave., Peoria, IL 61602

Published History—History of Peoria County, Johnson and Co., Chicago, 1880

PERRY COUNTY

Society—Perry County Historical Society, Pinckenyville, IL 62274

Published History—History of Randolph, Monroe, and Perry Counties, J. L. McDonough and Co., Phila., 1883

PIATT COUNTY

Society—Piatt County Historical Society, 907 Longview Road, Monticello, 61856

Published History—History of Piatt County, By: Emma Piatt, Shepard and Johnson, Chicago, 1883

PIKE COUNTY

Society—Pike County Historical Society, P.O. Box 91, Pittsfield, IL 62363

Published History—History of Pike County, Charles C. Chapman and Co., Chicago, 1880

POPE COUNTY

Society—Pope County Historical Society, Golconda, IL 62938

PULASKI COUNTY

Published History—History of Alexander, Union and Pulaski Counties, O. L. Baskin and Co., Chicago, 1883

PUTNAM COUNTY

Published History—Record of Olden Times, Home Journal Steam Printing, Lacon, 1880

RANDOLPH COUNTY

Society—Randolph County Historical Society, P.O. Box 5, Steeleville, IL 62288

Published History—History of Randolph, Monroe, and Perry Counties, J. L. McDonough and Co., Phila., 1883

RICHLAND COUNTY

Society—Richland County Historical Society, 405 North West Street, Olney, IL 62450

Published History—Biographical and Portrait of Effingham, Jasper, and Richland Counties, Lake Pub. Co., Chicago, 1893

ROCK ISLAND COUNTY

Society—Rock Island County Historical Society, 822 11th Ave., Moline, IL 61265

Published History—Past and Present of Rock Island County, H. F. Kett and Co., Chicago, 1877

ST. CLAIR COUNTY

Society—St. Clair County Historical Society, 701 East Washington St., Belleville, IL 62221

Published History—History of St. Clair County, Brink, McDonough and Co., Phila., 1881

SALINE COUNTY

Society—Saline County Historical Society, Saline County Museum, Harrisburg, IL 62946

Published History—History of Gallatin, Saline, Hamilton, Franklin, and Williamson Counties, Goodspeed Pub. Co., Chicago, 1887

SANGAMON COUNTY
Society—Illinois State Historical Society, Centennial Bld., Springfield, IL 62706

Society—Sangamon County Historical Society, Room 1018, Ridgely Bld., Springfield, IL 62706

Published History—History of Sangamon County, Portrait and Biog., Chicago, 1881

SCHUYLER COUNTY
Published History—History of Schuyler and Brown Counties, W. R. Brink and Co., Phila., 1882

SCOTT COUNTY
Published History—Portrait and Biographical Review of Morgan and Scott Counties, Chapman Bros., Chicago, 1889

SHELBY COUNTY
Society—Shelby County Historical Society, P.O. Box 393, Shelbyville, IL 62565

Published History—Portrait and Biographical Record of Shelby and Moultrie Counties, Biographical Pub. Co., Chicago, 1891

STARK COUNTY
Published History—Stark County and It's Pioneers, By: Mrs. E. H. Shallenberger, B. W. Seaton, Prairie Chief Office, 1876

STEPHENSON COUNTY
Society—Stephenson County Historical Society, 1440 So. Carroll Ave., Freeport, IL 61032

Published History—History of Stephenson County, Western History Co., Chicago, 1880

TAZEWELL COUNTY
Society—Tazewell County Historical Assoc., County Clerk, Pekin, IL 61554

Published History—Portrait and Biographical Record of Tazewell, Mason Biographical Pub. Co., Chicago, 1894

UNION COUNTY
Published History—History of Alexander, Union and Pulaski Counties, O. L. Baskin and Co., Chicago, 1883

VERMILION COUNTY
Society—Illiana Historical Society, P.O. Box 207, Danville, IL 61832

Published History—History of Vermilion County, By: H. W. Beckwith, H. H. Hill and Co., Chicago, 1879

WABASH COUNTY
Society—Wabash County Historical Society, 120 East 5th St., Mt. Carmel, IL 62863

Published History—Wabash County Illinois Historical Encyclopedia, N. Bateman, Chicago, 1911

WARREN COUNTY
Society—Warren County Historical Society, Alexis, IL 61412

Published History—Portrait and Biographical Album of Warren County, Chapman Bros., Chicago, 1886

WASHINGTON COUNTY
Society—Historical Society of Washington County, P.O. Box 247, Nashville, IL 62263

WAYNE COUNTY
Society—Wayne County Historical Society, 300 S.E. 2nd St., Fairfield, IL 62837

Published History—History of Wayne and Clay Counties, Globe Pub. Co., Chicago, 1884

WHITE COUNTY
Society—White County Historical Society, 223 East Main St., Carmi, IL 62821

Published History—History of White County, Inter-state Pub. Co., Chicago, 1883

WHITESIDE COUNTY
Published History—History of Whiteside County, By: Charles Bent Morrison, 1877

WILL COUNTY
Published History—History of Will County, Wm. LaBaron and Co., Chicago, 1878

WILLIAMSON COUNTY
Society—Williamson County Historical Society, Marion Carnegie Library, South Market St., Marion, IL

Published History—History of Gallatin, Saline, Hamilton, and Williamson Counties, Goodspeed Pub. Co., Chicago, 1887

WINNEBAGO COUNTY
Society—Rockford Historical Society, 1325 Casper Ave., Rockford, IL 61107

Published History—History of Winnebago County, H. F. Kett and Co., Chicago, 1877

WOODFORD COUNTY
Published History—Past and Present of Woodford County, Wm. LeBaron and Co., Chicago, 1878

INDIANA

ADAMS COUNTY
Published History—Biographical and Historical Record of Adams and Wells Counties, Lewis Pub. Co., Chicago, 1887

ALLEN COUNTY
Published History—History of Allen County, By: Thomas Helm, Kingman Bros., Chicago, 1880

BARTHOLOMEW COUNTY
Published History—History of Bartholomew County, Brant and Fuller, Chicago, 1880

BENTON COUNTY
Published History—Counties of Warren, Benton, Jasper and Newton. F. A. Battey and Co., Chicago, 1883

BLACKFORD COUNTY
Society—Blackford County Historical Society, P.O. Box 1, Hartford City, IN 47348

Published History—Biographical and Historical Record of Jay and Blackford Counties, Lewis Pub. Co., Chicago, 1887

BOONE COUNTY
Published History—History of Boone County, Hardin and Spaliz Pub. Co., 1887

BROWN COUNTY
Published History—Historical and Biographical Sketchs of Morgan, Monroe and Brown Counties, By: Charles Blancherd, F. A. Battey and Co., Chicago, 1884

CARROLL COUNTY
Published History—Recollections of the Early Carroll County, By: Dr. James Hervey Stewart, Hitchcock and Walden, Cinn. 1872

CASS COUNTY
Society—Cass County Historical Society, 1004 E. Market St., Logansport, IN 46947

Published History—History of Cass County, By: Thomas B. Helm, Brant and Fuller, Chicago, 1886

CLARK COUNTY
Published History—Biographical and Historical Souvenir for Clark, Harrison, Floyd, Jefferson, Jennings, Colt and Washington, John M. Gresham and Co., Chicago, 1889

CLAY COUNTY
Published History—Clay and Owen Counties, By Richard Blanchard, F. A. Battey and Co., Chicago, 1884

CLINTON COUNTY
Published History—History of Clinton County, By: Hon. Joseph Claybaugh, A. W. Bowen and Co., 1913

CRAWFORD COUNTY
Published History—History of Crawford County, By: Hazen Hayes Pleasent, Wm. Mitchell Printing Co., Greenfield, 1926

DAVIESS COUNTY
Published History—History of Knox and Daviess County, The Goodspeed Pub. Co., Chicago, 1886

DEARBORN COUNTY
Published History—History of Dearborn and Ohio Counties, F. F. Weakley and Co., Chicago, 1885

DECATUR COUNTY
Published History—History of Decatur County, By: Lewis A. Harding, B. F. Bowen, Indianapolis, 1915

DE KALB COUNTY
Published History—History of DeKalb County, Inter-State Pub. Co., Chicago, 1885

DELAWARE COUNTY
Published History—History of Delaware County, By: Frank D. Haimbaugh, Historical Pub. Co., Indianapolis, 1924

DU BOIS COUNTY
Published History—History of Pile and DuBois County, Goodspeed Pub., Chicago, 1885

ELKHART COUNTY
Published History—History of Elkhart County, Chas C. Chapman and Co., Chicago, 1881

FAYETTE COUNTY
Published History—History of Fayette County, By: Fredrick I. Barrows, B. F. Bowen and Co., Indianapolis, 1917

FLOYD COUNTY
Published History—Biographical and Historical Souvenir, Clark, Crawford, Harrison, Floyd, Jefferson, Jennings, Scott, and Washington; John M. Gresham and Co., Chicago, 1889

FOUNTAIN COUNTY
Published History—History of Fountain County, By: H. W. Beckwith, H. H. Hill and Co., Chicago, 1881

FRANKLIN COUNTY
Published History—History of Wayne, Fayette, Union and Franklin Counties, Lewis Pub. Co., Chicago, 1899

FULTON COUNTY
Published History—An Account of Fulton County From It's Origin, Henry A. Barnhart, Dayton Hist. Pub. Co., Dayton, Ohio, 1923

GIBSON COUNTY
Published History—History of Gibson County, By G. L. R. Stormont, B. F. Bowen and Co., Indianapolis, 1914

GRANT COUNTY
Published History—Briographical Memiors of Grant County, A. W. Bowen and Co., Chicago, 1901

GREENE COUNTY
Published History—History of Green County and Sullivan County, Goodspeed Bros. and Co., Chicago, 1884

HAMILTON COUNTY
Published History—History of Hamilton County, Kingman Bros., Chicago, 1880

HANCOCK COUNTY
Published History—History of Hancock County, By: Geo. J. Richman, Federal Pub. Co., Indianapolis, 1916

HARRISON COUNTY
Published History—Biographical and Historical Souvenir, Clark, Crawford, Floyd, Harrison, Jefferson, Jennings, Scott and Washington; John M. Gresham and Co., Chicago, 1888

HENDRICKS COUNTY
Published History—History of Hendricks County, Inter-State Pub. Co., Chicago, 1885

HENRY COUNTY
Published History—History of Henry County, Inter-State Pub. Co., Chicago, 1884

HOWARD COUNTY
Published History—Historical and Biographical Records of Howard and Tipton Counties, By: Charles Blanchard, F. A. Battey and Co., Chicago, 1883

HUNTINGTON COUNTY
Published History—History of Huntington County, Brant and Fuller, Chicago, 1887

JACKSON COUNTY
Published History—History of Jackson County, Brant and Fuller, Chicago, 1886

JASPER COUNTY
Society—Jasper County Historical Society, Rensselaer, IN 47978
Published History—County Histories of Benton, Jasper, and Newton, F. A. Battey and Co., Chicago, 1883

JAY COUNTY
Published History—Biographical and Historical Record of Jay and Blackford Counties, Lewis Pub. Co., Chicago, 1887

JEFFERSON COUNTY
Published History—Biographical and Historical Souvenir, Counties of Clark, Crawford, Floyd, Harrison, Jefferson, Jennings, Scott and Washington, John M. Gresham and Co., Chicago, 1889

JENNINGS COUNTY
Published History—Biographical and Historical Souvenir, Counties of Clark, Crawford, Floyd, Harrison, Jefferson, Jennings, Scott and Washington, John M. Gresham and Co., Chicago, 1889

JOHNSON COUNTY
Published History—History of Johnson County, Brant and Fuller, Chicago, 1888

KNOX COUNTY
Published History—History of Old Vincennes and Knox Counties, S. J. Clark Pub. Co., Chicago, 1911

KOSCIUSKO COUNTY
Published History—Biographical and Historical Record of Kosciusko, Lewis Pub. Co., Chicago, 1887

LAKE COUNTY
Published History—LaGrang and Noble Counties, F. A. Battey and Co., Chicago, 1882

La PORTE COUNTY
Published History—History of LaPorte County, Chas C. Chappman and Co., Chicago, 1880

LAWRENCE COUNTY
Published History—History of Lawrence County, Orange and Washington, Goodspeed Bros. and Co., Chicago, 1884

MADISON COUNTY
Published History—Centennial History of Madison County, 1823-1923, By: J. J. Netterville, Historians Assoc., Anderson, 1925

MARION COUNTY
Published History—History of Marion County and Indianapolis, By: B. R. Sulgrove, L. H. Everts and Co., Philidelphia, 1884

MARSHALL COUNTY
Published History—History of Indiana—Special Edition for Marshall County, Brant and Fuller Co., Madison, 1890

MARTIN COUNTY
Published History—Living Leaders, Encyclopedia of Bio. Daviess and Martin Counties, American Pub. Co., 1897

MIAMI COUNTY
Published History—History of Miami County, Brant and Fuller Co., 1887

MONROE COUNTY
Published History—Counties of Morgan, Monroe and Brown, F. A. Battey and Co., Chicago, 1884

MONTGOMERY COUNTY
Published History—History of Montgomery County, H. H. Hill and N. Iddings, Chicago, 1881

MORGAN COUNTY
Published History—Counties of Morgan, Monroe and Brown, F. A. Battey and Co., Chicago, 1884

NEWTON COUNTY
Published History—Counties of Warren, Benton, Jasper and Newton, F. A. Battey and Co., Chicago, 1883

NOBLE COUNTY
Published History—Counties of LaGrange and Noble, F. A. Battey and Co., Chicago, 1882

OHIO COUNTY
Published History—History of Dearborn and Ohio Counties, F. E. Weakley and Co., Chicago, 1885

ORANGE COUNTY
Published History—History of Lawrence, Orange and Washington Counties, Goodspeed Bro's. and Co., Chicago, 1884

OWEN COUNTY
Published History—Clay and Owen Counties, F. A. Battey and Co., Chicago, 1884

PARKE COUNTY
Published History—History of Vigo and Parke Counties, H. H. Hill and N. Iddings, Chicago, 1880

PERRY COUNTY
Published History—History of Warrick, Spencer and Perry Counties, Goodspeed Bro's. and Co., Chicago, 1885

PIKE COUNTY
Published History—History of Pike and Dubois Counties, Goodspeed Bro's. and Co., Chicago, 1885

PORTER COUNTY
Published History—Counties of Porter and Lake, F. A. Battey and Co., Chicago, 1882

POSEY COUNTY
Published History—History of Posey County, Goodspeed Bro's. and Co., Chicago, 1886

PULASKI COUNTY
Published History—Counties of White and Pulaski, F. A. Battey and Co., Chicago, 1883

PUTMAN COUNTY
Published History—Biographical and Historical Record of Putman County, Lewis Pub. Co., Chicago, 1887

RANDOLPH COUNTY
Published History—History of Randolph County, A. L. Kingman, Chicago, 1882

RIPLEY COUNTY
Published History—History and Directory of Ripley County, Republican Print, Versailles, 1888

RUSH COUNTY
Published History—History of Rush County, Brant and Fuller, Chicago, 1888

ST. JOSEPH COUNTY
Published History—History of St. Joseph County, C. C. Chapman, Chicago, 1880

SCOTT COUNTY
Published History—Biographical and Historical Souvenir, for Counties of Clark, Crawford, Harrison, Floyd, Jefferson, Jennings, Scott and Washington; John Gresham, Chicago, 1889

SHELBY COUNTY
Published History—History of Shelby County, Brant and Fuller, Chicago, 1887

SPENCER COUNTY
Published History—History of Warrick, Spencer and Perry Counties, Goodspeed Bro's., Chicago, 1885

STARKE COUNTY
Published History—Pictorial and Biographical Record of LaPorte, Porter, Lake and Starke Counties, Goodspeed Bro's., Chicago, 1894

STEUBEN COUNTY
Published History—History of Steuben County, Inter-State Pub. Co., Chicago, 1885

SULLIVAN COUNTY
Published History—History of Greene and Sullivan Counties, Goodspeed Bro's., Chicago, 1884

SWITZERLAND
Published History—History of Dearborn, Ohio and Switzerland Counties, F. E. Weakley and Co., Chicago, 1885

TIPPECANOE COUNTY
Published History—Biography and Portrait Album of Tippecanoe County, Lewis Pub. Co., Chicago, 1888

TIPTON COUNTY
Published History—Counties of Howard and Tipton, F. A. Battey, Chicago, 1883

UNION COUNTY
Society—Union County Historical Society, 26 West Union, Liberty, IN 47353
Published History—Biography and General History of Wayne, Fayette, Union and Franklin Counties, Lewis Pub. Co., Chicago, 1899

VANDERBURGH COUNTY
Published History—History of Vanderburgh County, Brant and Fuller, Madison, WI, 1889

VERMILLION COUNTY
Published History—Biographical and Historical Record of Vermillion County, Lewis Pub., Chicago, 1888

VIGO COUNTY
Published History—History of Vigo and Parke Counties, H. H. Hill and N. Iddings, Chicago, 1888

WABASH COUNTY
Published History—History of Wabash County, John Morris Print., Chicago 1884

WARREN COUNTY
Published History—Warren, Benton, Jasper and Newton Counties, F. A. Battey and Co., Chicago, 1883

WARRICK COUNTY
Published History—History of Warrick, Spencer and Perry Counties, Goodspeed Bro's., Chicago, 1885

WASHINGTON COUNTY
Published History—History of Lawrence, Orange and Washington Counties, Goodspeed Bro's. and Co., Chicago, 1884

WAYNE COUNTY
Published History—History of Wayne County, 2 Vols.; Inter-State Pub. Co., Chicago, 1884

WELLS COUNTY
Published History—Briographical and Historical Record of Adams and Wells Counties, Lewis Pub. Co., Chicago, 1887

WHITE COUNTY
Published History—White and Pulaski Counties, F. A. Battey and Co., Chicago, 1883

WHITLEY COUNTY
Published History—Whitley and Noble Counties, F. A. Battey and Co., Chicago, 1882

IOWA

ADAIR COUNTY
Published History—History of Adair and Guthrie Counties, Continental Hist. Co., Springfield, 1884

ALLAMAKEE COUNTY
Published History—History of Winneshiek and Allamakee Counties, By: W. E. Alexander, Western Pub. Co., Sioux City, 1882

APPANOOSE COUNTY
Published History—Biographical and Historical Record of Wayne and Appanoose Counties, By: S. Thomas, Lewis Pub. Co., Chicago, 1903

AUDUBON COUNTY
Published History—Biographical and Historical of Shelby and Audubon Counties, W. S. Dunbar and Co., Chicago, 1889

BENTON COUNTY
Published History—History of Benton County, Western Historical Co., Chicago, 1878

BLACKHAWK COUNTY
Published History—History of Blackhawk County, Western Historical Co., Chicago, 1878

BOONE COUNTY
Published History—The History of Boone County and It's Cities and Towns, Union Historical Co., Birdsall, Williams, and Co., Des Moines, 1880

BREMER COUNTY
Society—Bremer County Historical Society, 402 West Bremer Ave., Waverly, IA 50677
Published History—History of Butler and Bremer Counties, Union Pub. Co., Springfield, 1883

BUCHANAN COUNTY
Published History—History of Buchanan County, William Bro's., Cleveland, 1881

BUENA VISTA COUNTY
Published History—Past and Present of Buena Vista County, S. J. Clark Pub. Co., Chicago, 1909

BUTLER COUNTY
Published History—History of Butler and Bremer Counties, Union Publishing Co., Springfield, 1883

CALHOUN COUNTY
Published History—Biographical Record of Calhoun County, S. J. Clark Pub. Co., Chicago, 1902

CASS COUNTY
Published History—History of Cass County, Continental History Co., Springfield, 1884

CEDAR COUNTY
Society—Cedar County Historical Society, Tipton, IA 52772
Published History—History of Cedar County, Western Historical Co., Chicago, 1878

CERRO GORDO COUNTY
Published History—History of Franklin and Cerro Gordo, Union Pub. Co., Springfield, 1883

CHEROKEE COUNTY
Published History—Briographical History of Cherokee County, W. S. Dunbar and Co., Chicago, 1889

CHICKASAW COUNTY
Published History—History of Chickasaw and Howard Counties, By: W. E. Alexander, Western Pub. Co., Decorah, 1883

CLARKE COUNTY
Published History—Biographical and Historical Record, Lewis Publishing Co., Chicago, 1886

CLAY COUNTY
Society—Parker Historical Society, 127 East Third Street, Spencer, IA
Published History—History of Clay County, By: Samuel Gillespie, S. J. Clark Pub. Co., Chicago, 1909

CLAYTON COUNTY
Published History—History of Clayton County, By: Realto E. Price, Robert O. Law Comp., Chicago, 1916

CLINTON COUNTY
Published History—History of Clinton County, Western Historical Co., Chicago, 1879

CRAWFORD COUNTY
Published History—Biographical History of Crawford, Ida and Sac Counties, Lewis Pub. Co., Chicago, 1893

DALLAS COUNTY
Published History—Past and Present of Dallas County, By: R. F. Wood, S. J. Clark Pub. Co., Chicago, 1907

DAVIS COUNTY
Published History—History of Davis County, State Hist. Co., Des Moines, 1882

DECATUR COUNTY
Published History—Biographical and Historical Record of Ringgold and Decatur Counties, Lewis Pub. Co., Chicago, 1887

DELAWARE COUNTY
Published History—History of Delaware County and It's People, By: Captain John F. Merry, S. J. Clark Pub. Co., Chicago, 1914

DES MOINES COUNTY
Published History—History of Des Moines and It's People, By: Augustine M. Antrobus, S. J. Clark Pub. Co., Chicago, 1915

DICKENSON COUNTY
Published History—A History of Dickenson County, By: R. A. Smith, Keynon Printing and Mfg. Co., Des Moines, 1902

DUBUQUE COUNTY
Published History—History of Dubuque County, By: Western A. Goodspeed and K. C. Goodspeed, Goodspeed Historical Assoc.

EMMET COUNTY
Published History—History of Emmet and Dickenson Counties, Pioneer Pub. Co., Chicago, 1917

FAYETTE COUNTY
Published History—Past and Present of Fayette County, By: B. F. Bowen and Co., Indianapolis, 1910

FLOYD COUNTY
Published History—History of Floyd County, Inter-State Pub. Co., Chicago, 1882

FRANKLIN COUNTY
Published History—History of Franklin County, By: I. L. Stuart, S. J. Clark Pub. Co., Chicago, 1914

FREMONT COUNTY
Published History—History of Fremont County, By: L. Lingenfelter, Sidney Steam Printing Co., St. Joseph, 1877

GREENE COUNTY
Published History—Past and Present of Greene County, By: E. B. Stillman, Chicago, 1907

JOHNSON COUNTY
Society—State Historical Society of Iowa, 402 Iowa Ave., Iowa City, IA 52240

POLK COUNTY
Society—Polk County Historical Society, 317 S.W. 42nd St., Des Moines, IA 50312

WAYNE COUNTY
Society—Wayne County Historical Society, Corydon, IA 50060

KANSAS

ALLEN COUNTY
Society—Allen County Historical Society, Courthouse, Iola, KS 66749

ANDERSON COUNTY
Published History—History of Anderson County, By: Johnson, 1877

ATCHISON COUNTY
Published History—History of Atchinson County, By: Ingalls

BOURBON COUNTY
Society—Bourbon County Historical Society, Fort Scott, KS 66701

BROWN COUNTY
Published History—History of Brown County, By: Ruley

BUTLER COUNTY
Society—Butler County Historical Society, P.O. Box 11, El Dorado, KS 67042

CHEROKEE COUNTY
Published History—History of Cherokee County, By: Allison, 1904

CLAY COUNTY
Published History—Portrait and Biography of Washington, Clay and Riley Counties, By: Chapman

COWLEY COUNTY
Society—Cowley County Historical Society, 1011 Mansfield, St., Winfield, KS 67156

CRAWFORD COUNTY
Published History—Historical and Biographical Record of Crawford County, 1905

DICKINSON COUNTY
Society—Dickinson County Historical Society, 4th St. and So. Olive St., Abilene, KS 67410

DONIPHAN COUNTY
Published History—Doniphan County History for 50 Years, By: Gray, 1905

FORD COUNTY
Society—Ford County Historical Society, 803 Third Ave., Dodge City, KS 67801

FRANKLIN COUNTY
Society—Franklin County Historical Society, P.O. Box 145, Ottawa, KS 66067

JOHNSON COUNTY
Published History—History of Johnson County, By: Gregg

LABETTE COUNTY
Published History—History of Labette County, By: Case, 1893

LANE COUNTY
Society—Lane County Historical Society, Dighton, KS 67839

LEAVENWORTH COUNTY
Published History—Leavenworth County, By: Andreas, 1883

LINCOLN COUNTY
Published History—History of Lincoln County, By: Barr, 1908

LINN COUNTY
Society—Linn County Historical Society, Mound City, KS 66056

MARION COUNTY
Society—Marion County Historical Society Inc., County Court House, Marion, KS 66861

MARSHALL COUNTY
Published History—History of Marshall County, By: Porter

McPHERSON COUNTY
Published History—Pioneer McPherson County, By: Sullivan Co.

MONTGOMERY COUNTY
Published History—History of Montgomery County, By: Duncan, 1913

NEMAHA COUNTY
Published History—Nemaha County History, By: Tennal, 1916

NEOSHO COUNTY
Published History—Neosho County History, By: Graves

NORTON COUNTY
Published History—Norton County History, By: Bowers, 1872-1942

OSAGE COUNTY
Society—Osage County Historical Society, Lyndon, KS 66451

PAWNEE COUNTY
Society—Pawnee County Historical Society, Cummins Memorial Library, Larned, KS 67550

POTTAWATOMIE COUNTY
Published History—Early History of Pottawatomie County, 1854-1954

RAWLINS COUNTY
Society—Rawlins County Historical Society, 308 State St., Atwood, KS 67730

REPUBLIC COUNTY
Published History—History of Republic County, By: Savage, 1883

RICE COUNTY
Published History—Early Rice County, By: Jones, 1928

RUSSELL COUNTY
Society—Russell County Historical Society, 331 Kansas St., Russell, KS 67665

SALINE COUNTY
Published History—Portrait and Biography; Dickinson, Saline, McPherson and Marion Counties, 1893, By: Chapman

SEWARD COUNTY
Society—Seward County Historical Society, Coronado Museum, Liberal, KS 67901

WABAUNSEE COUNTY
Published History—Early History of Wabaunsee County, By: Thomson, 1901

WILSON COUNTY
Published History—History of Neosho and Wilson Counties, By: Duncan, 1902

WOODSON COUNTY
Society—Woodson County Historical Society, 411 No. State St., Yates Center, KS 66783

KENTUCKY

ADAIR
Published History—History of Adair County

ANDERSON COUNTY
Society—Anderson County Historical Society, 110 Center, Lawrencebury, KY 40842

BARREN COUNTY
Published History—History of Barren County

BOONE COUNTY
Published History—Boone County Kentucky and It's People, By: Rea

BOURBON COUNTY
Published History—History of Bourbon, Scott, Harrison and Nicholas, Counties, 1882, By: Perrin and Peter

BOYLE COUNTY
Published History—History of Boyle County

BRACKEN COUNTY
Published History—A Glimpse of Old Bridgeport and It's Environs in the Bluegrass of Kentucky, 1774-1899, Kentucky Historical Society

BRECKENRIDGE COUNTY
Published History—History of Breckenridge

CALDWELL COUNTY
Published History—History of Caldwell County, By: Baker

CAMPBELL COUNTY
Published History—History of Campbell County, 1876, By: Jones

CASEY COUNTY
Published History—Casey County Lore, 1939, By: Watkins

CHRISTIAN COUNTY
Published History—County of Christian, 1884, By: Perrin

DAVIESS COUNTY
Published History—Daviess County History, 1883, Inter-State Pub. Co., Chicago

FAYETTE COUNTY
Published History—History of Fayette County, 1882, By: Perrin

FLEMING COUNTY
Published History—History of Fleming County, 1908

FLOYD COUNTY
Published History—Historic Floyd, 1800-1950, By: Scalf

FRANKLIN COUNTY
Society—Kentucky Historical Society, Broadway, Frankfort, KY 40601

GARRARD COUNTY
Published History—History of Garrard County, Kentucky and It's Churches, 1947, By: Dalico

GRANT COUNTY
Published History—History of Grant County, Kentucky, 1876, By: Elliston

GREENUP COUNTY
Published History—History of Greenup County, Kentucky, By: Biggs and MacKay

HADIN COUNTY
Published History—Who Was Who in Hadin County, County Historical Society

HARLAN COUNTY
Published History—History of Harlan County, By: Middleton

HARRISON COUNTY
Published History—History of Harrison County

HART COUNTY
Published History—History of Hart County

HENRY COUNTY
Published History—Henry County, By: Drane

HICKMAN COUNTY
Published History—History of Hickman County

JEFFERSON COUNTY
Published History—Louisville and Jefferson Counties, 1896, By: Johnson

JESSAMINE COUNTY
Published History—Jessamine and Jefferson Counties, By: Jenny

JOHNSON COUNTY
Published History—Johnson County, By: Hall

KENTON COUNTY
Published History—Kenton County, By: Christopher

LITCHER COUNTY
Published History—History of Litcher County

LEWIS COUNTY
Published History—History of Lewis County, 1912, By Ragan

LIVINGSTON COUNTY
Published History—History of Livingston County

LOGAN COUNTY
Published History—Russellville and Logan Counties, By: Finley

MADISON COUNTY
Society—Madison County Historical Society Inc., 120 West Main St., Richmond, KY 40475

MARSHALL COUNTY
Published History—History of Marshall County, By: Freeman

MASON COUNTY
Published History—History of Mason County, By: Lee

MERCER COUNTY
Published History—History of Mercer County

METCALFE COUNTY
Published History—History of Metcalfe County, Kentucky

MONTGOMERY COUNTY
Published History—Montgomery County, By: Reid

MUBLENGER COUNTY
Published History—History of Mublenberg County, By: Rothert

NELSON COUNTY
Published History—History of Irvine and Nelson Counties, By: Pack

NICHOLAS COUNTY
Published History—History of Bourbon, Scott, Harrison and Nicholas Counties, By: Perrin

OHIO COUNTY
Published History—History of Ohio County, By: Taylor

PENDLETON COUNTY
Published History—History of Pendleton County

PERRY COUNTY
Published History—History of Perry County, By: Johnson

PULASKI COUNTY
Published History—History of Pulaski County, By: Romey, University of Kentucky

RUSSELL COUNTY
Society—Russell County Historical Society, Jamestown, KY 42629

SCOTT COUNTY
Published History—History of Scott County, 1904, By: Baines

SHELBY COUNTY
Published History—History of Shelby County, By: Willis, Hist. Socy. Com. on Ph.

TAYLOR COUNTY
Published History—Early Taylor County, Kentucky History, By: Nesbitt

TODD COUNTY
Published History—Early Todd County, By: Kennedy

UNION COUNTY
Published History—Union County, 1886, Evansville

WARREN COUNTY
Published History—History of Warren County

WASHINGTON COUNTY
Published History—Early Washington County, By: Baylor

WAYNE COUNTY
Published History—History of Wayne County

WOLFE COUNTY
Published History—Early and Modern History of Wolfe County

WOODFORD COUNTY
Society—Woodford County Historical Society Inc., 232 Montgomery Ave., Versailles, KY 10383

LOUISIANA

ASSUMPTION COUNTY
Published History—Place Names of Assumption Parish, By: Alleman, 1936

AVOYELLES COUNTY
Published History—History of Avoyelles Parish, Saucier; 1943

BEAUREGARD COUNTY
Published History—Early Annals of Beauregard Parish, Fraser, 1933

CALCASIEU COUNTY
Published History—Econ. and Sec. Deu Calcasieu Parish, Ulman; 1840

CLAIBORNE COUNTY
Published History—History of Claiborne Parish, 1828-1885; Harris

EAST BATON ROUGE COUNTY
Published History—Annual of the Parish of East Baton Rouge, 1933; Booth

EAST FELICIANA COUNTY
Published History—East Feliciana, Past and Present, 1893; Shipwith

EVANGELINE COUNTY
Published History—History of Evangeline Parish, 1941; Gahn

LAFAYETTE COUNTY
Published History—Early Days of Lafayette Parish, 1931; Buchanan

La SALLE COUNTY
Published History—History of La Salle Parish, Taylor; 1959

LINCOLN COUNTY
Published History—History of Lincoln Parish, Mondy; 1934

MOREHOUSE COUNTY
Published History—Memorier of Early Settlement of Morehouse Parish, Davenport; 1911

NATCHITOCHES COUNTY
Published History—Places Names of Natchitoches, 1935; Berry

ST. MARTIN COUNTY
Society—Attakapas Historical Assoc., P.O. Box 107, St. Martinsville, LA 70582

ST. TAMMANY COUNTY
Published History—History of St. Tammany County, By: Burns

TANGIPAHOA COUNTY
Published History—History of Tangipahoa Parish, By: Lanier

TERREBONNE COUNTY
Published History—History of Terrebonne Parish, 1861, By: Watkins

WASHINGTON COUNTY
Published History—History of Washington Parish, By: Carter

MARYLAND

ALLEGANY COUNTY
Society—Allegany County Historical Society, 218 Washington St., Cumberland, MD 21502

CAROLINE COUNTY
Published History—History of Caroline County, By: Noble

CARROLL COUNTY
Published History—Hundred Years of Carroll County, 1837-1937, By: Lynch

CECIL COUNTY
Society—Historical Society of Cecil County, Cecil County Library Bldg., Elkton, MD 21921

CHARLES COUNTY
Published History—D.A.R. Charles County Tombstone and Bible Records, Washington, DC

DORCHESTER COUNTY
Society—Dorchester Historical Society, Cambridge, MD 21613

FREDERICK COUNTY
Society—Historical Society of Frederick County, Frederick, MD 21701

GARRETT COUNTY
Society—Garrett County Historical Society, Center St., Oakland, MD 21550

HARFORD COUNTY
Society—Historical Society of Harford County, 324 Kenmore Ave., Bel Air, MD 21210

HOWARD COUNTY
Society—Howard County Historical Society, Ellicott City, MD 21043

KENT COUNTY
Published History—History of Kent County, 1630-1916, By: Usilton

MONTGOMERY COUNTY
Society—Montgomery County Historical Society, 103 W. Montgomery Ave., Rockville, MD 20850

QUEEN ANNE'S COUNTY
Society—Queen Anne's County Historical Society, So. Commerce St., Centerville, MD 21617

TALBOT COUNTY
Society—Historical Society of Talbot County, 29 So. Washington, St., Easton, MD 21601

WASHINGTON COUNTY
Society—Washington County Historical Society, 135 W. Washington St., Hayestown, MD 21740

WICOMICO COUNTY
Society—Wicomico Historical Society, 309 Gay St., Salisbury, MD 21801

WORCESTER COUNTY
Published History—Counties of Maryland, By: Mathews

MAINE

ANDROSCOGGIN COUNTY
Society—Androscoggin Historical Society, 2 Furner St., Auburn, ME 04210
Published History—History of Androscoggin County, By: Georgia D. Merrill, W. A. Fergerson and Co., Boston, 1891

AROOSTOOK COUNTY
Published History—History of Aroostook, By: Edward Wiggin, The Star Herarld Press, 1922

CUMBERLAND COUNTY
Society—Maine Historical Society, 485 Congress St., Portland, ME 04111
Published History—History of Cumberland County, By: Clayton W. Woodford, Everts and Perk, Phila., 1880

KENNEBEC COUNTY
Society—Kennebec Historical Society, Lithgrow Library Bldg., Augusta, ME 04330
Published History—Illustrated History of Kennebec County, By: Henry O. Kingsbury, H. W. Blake and Co., 1892, New York

KNOX COUNTY
Published History—Chronicles of Knox County, By: R. B. Filmore, 1922

LINCOLN COUNTY
Published History—The History of Acient, Shepscot and Newcastle, By: David Q. Cushman, Bath E. Upton and Son Printers, 1882

OXFORD COUNTY
Published History—Saco Valley Settlement and Families, By: Gideon Tibbets, Portland, ME, 1895

PENOBSCOT COUNTY
Society—Bangor Historical Society, 159 Union St., Bangor, ME 04401
Published History—History of Penobscot County, Chase and Co., 1882

PICATAQUIS COUNTY
Published History—History of Picataquis County, Portland, ME, Hoyt-Fogg-Donham, 1880

SAGADAHOC COUNTY
Published History—Memorial Volume of the Popham Celebration, By: Rev. Edward Ballard, Bailey and Noyes, Portland, 1863

WASHINGTON COUNTY
Published History—The Narraguagus Valley, By: James A. Milliken, A. J. Huston, Portland, 1910

YORK COUNTY
Published History—History of York County, By: Clayton W. Woodford, Philadelphia, PA, Everts and Peck, 1880

MASSACHUSETTS

BARNSTABLE
Society—Historical Society of the Town of Barnstable, Main St., Barnstable, MA 02630
Published History—History of Cape Cod, By: Frederick Freeman, Pub. by: W. H. Piper and Co., Boston, MA 1869

BERKSHIRE COUNTY
Society—Berkshire County Historical Society, 113 E. Housatomic St., Pittsfield, MA 01201
Published History—History of Berkshire County, New York, J. B. Beers and Co., 1885

BRISTOL COUNTY
Published History—History of Bristol County, By: Duane Hamilton Hurd, Pub by: J. W. Lewis and Co., 1883, Phila.

DUKES COUNTY
Society—Dukes County Historical Society, School and Cooke St., Egartown, MA 02539
Published History—The Story of Martha's Vineyard, By: Charles Gilbert Hine, Pub by: Hine Bro's., 1908, New York

ESSEX COUNTY
Society—Historical Society of Old Newbury, 98 High St., Newbury Port, MA 01950
Published History—Standard History of Essex County, C. F. Jewett and Co., Boston, MA 1878

FRANKLIN COUNTY
Society—Historical Society of Greenfield, Church St., Greenfield, MA 01301

HAMPDEN COUNTY
Published History—Hampden County, 1636-1936, By: Johnson

HAMPSHIRE COUNTY
Society—Northhampton Historical Society, 58 Bridge St., Northhampton, MA 01060

MIDDLESEX COUNTY
Society—Cambridge Historical Society, 159 Brottle St., Cambridge, MA 02138
Published History—History of Middlesex County, Pub By: Estes and Lauriat, Boston, MA 1880

NANTUCKET COUNTY
Society—Nantucket Historical Assoc., Old Town Bldg, Union St., Nantucket, MA 02554
Published History—The History of Nantucket, By: Macy Obed, Mansfield, MA 1880

NORFOLK COUNTY
Society—Dedham Historical Society, 612 High St., Dedham, MA 02026
Published History—History of Norfolk County, By: Duane Hamilton Hurd, Phila., J. W. Lewis and Co., 1884

PLYMOUTH COUNTY
Published History—History of Plymouth County, By: Duane Hamilton Hurd, Phila., J. W. Lewis and Co., 1884

SUFFOLK COUNTY
Society—Massachusetts Historical Society, 1154 Boylestown St., Boston, MA 02215
Published History—The Memorial History of Boston, By: Justin Winsor, J. R. Osgood and Co., Boston 1882

WORCESTER COUNTY
Society—Fitchburg Historical Society, 50 Grove St., Fitchburg, MA 01420
Published History—The History of the County of Worcester, By: Whitney Peter, Worcester, MA 1793

MICHIGAN

ALLEGAN COUNTY
Published History—History of Allegan and Barry Counties, By: Johnson, 1880

ALPENA COUNTY
Published History—Alpena County Cent. By: Oliver

BARAGA COUNTY
Society—Baraga County Historical Society, L'anse, MI 49946

BARRY COUNTY
Published History—History of Barry County, By: Potter, 1912

BAY COUNTY
Published History—Bay County Michigan, Past and Present, By: Butterfield, 1957

BERRIEN COUNTY
Published History—History of Berrien and Van Buren Counties, By: Ellis

BRANCH COUNTY
Published History—History of Branch County, By: Johnson, 1879

CALHOUN COUNTY
Published History—Portrait and Biography of Calhoun County, By: Chapman, 1891

CHEBOYGAN COUNTY
Published History—History of Cheboygan and Mackinac Counties, By: Van Fleet, 1873

CHIPPEWA COUNTY
Society—Chippewa County Historical Society, 400 Hudson Dr., Sault Ste. Marie, MI 49783

CLINTON COUNTY
Published History—Past and Present of Clinton County, By: Daboll and Kelly, 1906

DICKINSON COUNTY
Society—Iron County Historical Society, Iron Mountain, MI 49801

EATON COUNTY
Published History—Past and Present of Eaton County, By: Williams

GENESSE COUNTY
Published History—History of Genesse County, By: Ellis, 1879

GRAND TRAVERSE COUNTY
Published History—Grand Traverse and Leelanau Counties, By: Sprauge and Smith, 1913

GRATIOT COUNTY
Published History—Portrait and Biography of Gratiot County, By: Chapman, 1884

HILLSDALE COUNTY
Society—Hillsdale County Historical Society, 122 Orchard Ridge, Hillsdale, MI 49242

INGHAM COUNTY
Published History—Pioneer History of Ingham County, By: Adams, 1953

IONIA COUNTY
Published History—History and Directory of Ionia County, By: Dillenback, 1872

IOSCO COUNTY
Society—Iosco County Historical Society, Tawas City, MI 48763

ISABELLE COUNTY
Published History—Portrait and Biography Album of Isabelle County, By: Chapman, 1884

JACKSON COUNTY
Society—Jackson County Historical Society, 1113 First St., Jackson, MI 49203

KALAMAZOO COUNTY
Society—Kalamazoo County Historical Society, 315 So. Rose St., Kalamazoo, MI 49006

KENT COUNTY
Society—Grand Rapids Historical Society, 929 Edna St., Grand Rapids, MI 49507

LENAWEE COUNTY
Society—Lenawee Historical Society Inc., 4380 Evergreen Dr., Adrian, MI 49221

MACKINAC COUNTY
Published History—History of Cheboygan and Mackinac Counties, By: Van Fleet, 1873

MACOMB COUNTY
Published History—History of Macomb County, By: Leeson, 1882

MARQUETTE COUNTY
Society—Marquette County Historical Society, 213 No. Front St., Marquette, MI 49855

MASON COUNTY
Society—Mason County Historical Society, 409 Filer St., Ludington, MI 49431

MECOSTA COUNTY
Society—Mecosta Historical Society, Big Rapids, MI 49307

MENOMINEE COUNTY
Published History—Cent. History of Menominee County, By: Ingalls, 1876

MIDLAND COUNTY
Published History—Portrait and Biography of Midland County, 1883

MONTCALM COUNTY
Published History—History of Montcalm County, By: Dosef, 1916

MUSKEGON COUNTY
Published History—Muskegon County, By: Page, 1882

OAKLAND COUNTY
Society—Oakland County Pioneer and Historical Society, 405 Oakland Ave., Pontiac, MI 48058

OCEANA COUNTY
Published History—Oceana County and Cities, By: Hartwick and Zuller, 1890

OSCEOLA COUNTY
Published History—Portrait and Biography of Osceola County, 1884

SAGINAW COUNTY
Society—Saginaw Historical Society, Cherry St., Saginaw, MI 48607

ST. CLAIR COUNTY
Society—St. Clair County Historical Society, 115 6th St., Port Huron, MI 48060

ST. JOSEPH COUNTY
Published History—History of St. Joseph County, 1827-77

VAN BUREN COUNTY
Published History—History of Van Buren County, By: Johnson

WASHTENAW COUNTY
Society—Historical Society of Michigan, 2117 Washtenaw, Anne Arbor, MI 48104

WAYNE COUNTY
Society—Detroit Historical Comm., 5401 Woodward Ave., Detroit, MI 40202

MINNESOTA

ANOKA COUNTY
Society—Anoka County Historical Society, Court House, Anoka, MN 55303

BECKER COUNTY
Society—Becker County Historical Society, County Court House, Detroit Lakes, MN 56501

BELTRAMI COUNTY
Society—Beltrami County Historical Society, Third and Bemidji Sts., Bemidji, MN 56601

BIG STONE COUNTY
Published History—Big Stone County History, By: Wulff

BLUE EARTH COUNTY
Published History—History of Blue Earth County, By: Hughes

BROWN COUNTY
Society—Brown County Historical Society

CARLTON COUNTY
Society—Carlton County Historical Society, 315 Court House, Carlton, MN 55718

CARVER COUNTY
Published History—Carver County, Today and Yesterday

CHIPPEWA COUNTY
Society—Chippewa County Historical Society, Highways 7 and 59, Montevideo MN 56265

CLAY COUNTY
Society—Clay County Historical Society, 11th Street No., Moorhead, MN 56560

CLEARWATER COUNTY
Society—Clearwater County Historical Society, Bagley, MN 56621

COOK COUNTY
Society—Cook County Historical Society Inc., Broadway, Grand Marais, MN 55604

COTTONWOOD COUNTY
Society—Cottonwood County Historical Society, 9th St. and 5th Ave., Windom, MN 56101

CROW WING COUNTY
Society—Crow Wing County Historical Society, c/o Courthouse, Brainerd, MN 56401

DAKOTA COUNTY
Published History—History of Dakota County, By: Rev. Edward D. Neill

DODGE COUNTY
Society—Dodge County Historical and Old Settlers Society, Mantorville, MN 55955

DOUGLAS COUNTY
Published History—History of Douglas and Grant Counties, By: Larsen

FARIBAULT COUNTY
Society—Faribault County Historical Society, 405 East 6th St., Blue Earth, MN 56013

FILLMORE COUNTY
Published History—History of Fillmore County, 1858, By: Bishop

FREEBORN COUNTY
Society—Freeborn County Historical Society, Box 105, Bridge Ave., Albert Lea, MN 56007

GOODHUE COUNTY
Society—Goodhue County Historical Society, 1166 Oak St., Red Wing, MN 55066

GRANT COUNTY
Society—Grant County Historical Society, Elbow Lake, MN 5631?

HENNEPIN COUNTY
Society—Hennepin County Historical Society, 2303-3rd Ave. So., Minneapolis, MN 55404

HOUSTON COUNTY
Published History—History of Houston County, 1882, Minneapolis Hist. Co., Minneapolis

HUBBARD COUNTY
Society—Hubbard County Historical Society

ITASCA COUNTY
Published History—The Itasca Story, 1959, By: Debie

JACKSON COUNTY
Published History—History of Jackson County, 1910, By: Rose, Northern Hist. Pub. Co., Jackson

KANDIYOHI COUNTY
Society—Kandiyohi County Historical Society, 610 Highway 717 North East, Willmar, MN 56201

KITTSON COUNTY
Published History—W.P.A. Kittson County, County Historical Society, 1940

LAC QUI PARLE COUNTY
Society—Lac Qui Parle County Historical Society, City Hall, 404-6th Ave., Madison, MN 56256

LAKE COUNTY
Society—Lake County Historical Society, Depot Bldg., Two Harbors, MN 55616

Le SUEUR COUNTY
Published History—History of LeSueur County, By: Gresham

LINCOLN COUNTY
Published History—Early History of Lincoln County, 1936, By: Tasker, Lake Benton News Print, Lake Benton

LYON COUNTY
Society—Lyon County Historical Society, Marshall Library Bldg., Marshall, MN 56258

McLEOD COUNTY
Published History—History of McLeod County, 1917, By: Curtiss-Wedge

MARSHALL COUNTY
Society—Marshall County Historical Society, Warren, MN 56762

MARTIN COUNTY
Published History—History of Martin County, 1897, By: Budd

MEEKER COUNTY
Society—Meeker County Historical Society, 318 No. Marshall, Litchfield, MN 55355

MORRISON COUNTY
Published History—History of Morrison and Todd Counties, By: Fuller

MOWER COUNTY
Published History—Early History of Mower County, 1876, By: Paden, Hitchkiss, Austin

MURRAY COUNTY
Society—Murray County Historical Society, Slayton, MN 56172

NICOLLET COUNTY
Society—Nicollet County Historical Society, 100 W. Nassau, St. Peter, MN 56082

NOBLES COUNTY
Society—Nobles County Historical Society, 416-12th St., Worthington, MN 56187

NORMAN COUNTY
Published History—A Short History of Norman County

OLMSTEAD COUNTY
Society—Olmstead County Historical Society, 214-3rd Ave. S.W., Rochester, MN 55901

OTTER TRAIL COUNTY
Society—Otter Tail County Historical Society, Court House, Fergus Falls, MN 56537

PENNINGTON COUNTY
Society—Pennington County Historical Society, County Courthouse, First and Main, Thief River Falls, MN 56701

PIPESTONE COUNTY
Published History—History of Rock and Pipestone Counties, By: Rose, 1911

POLK COUNTY
Published History—History and Biography of Polk County, 1916, By: Holcombe

POPE COUNTY
Society—Pope County Historical Society

REDWOOD COUNTY
Published History—History of Redwood County, 1916, By: Curtiss-Wedge

RENVILLE COUNTY
His Published History—History of Renville County, 1916, By: Curtiss-Wedge

RICE COUNTY
Society—Rice County Historical Society, 12 N.E. First Ave., Faribault, MN 55021

ST. LOUIS COUNTY
Society—St. Louis County Historical Society, 2228 E. Superior St., Duluth, MN 55812

SCOTT COUNTY
Society—Scott County Historical Society, So. Holmes St., Shakopee, MN 55379

STEARNS COUNTY
Published History—History of Stearns County, By: Mitchell

STEELE COUNTY
Published History—History of Steele County, 1868, By: Mitchell

STEVENS COUNTY
Society—Branch of Minneapolis Historical Society, St. Paul, MN

SWIFT COUNTY
Society—Swift County Historical Society, Benson, MN 56215

TODD COUNTY
Published History—History of Morrison and Todd Counties, 1915, By: Fuller

TRAVERSE COUNTY
Published History—History of Traverse County, 1881, By: Barrett, Browns Valley, MN

WABASHA COUNTY
Published History—Wabasha County, 1870, By: Mitchell

WASECA COUNTY
Society—Waseca County Historical Society, Corner 4th St. and 2nd Ave. N.E., Waseca, MN 56093

WASHINGTON COUNTY
Society—Washington County Historical Society

WATONWAN COUNTY
Published History—History of Cottonwood and Watonwan Counties, By: Brown

WILKIN COUNTY
Society—Wilkin County Historical Society, Saint Francis Home, Breckenridge, MN 56520

WINONA COUNTY
Society—Winona County Historical Society Inc., 125 West 5th St., Winona, MN 55987

WRIGHT COUNTY
Published History—History of Wright County, 1915, By: Curtiss-Wedge

YELLOW MEDICINE COUNTY
Published History—History of Yellow Medicine County, 1914, By: Rose, Northern Hist. Pub. Co., Marshall

MISSISSIPPI

BOLIVAR COUNTY
Published History—Bolivar County, By: W. F. Gray, 1923

CALHOUN COUNTY
Published History—History of Calhoun County, By: J. S. Ryan and T. M. Murphree

CLAIBORNE COUNTY
Society—Port Gibson-Claiborne County Historical Society, Town Hall, 1001 College St., Port Gibson, MS 39150

CLAY COUNTY
Published History—Gravestone Records, Clay County, By: A. E. Miller

COPIAH COUNTY
Published History—Marriage Records, Copiah County, Marie Luter Upton, 1823-43

HANCOCK COUNTY
Published History—History of Hancock County, By: Claiborne, 1876

HINDS COUNTY
Published History—History of Hinds County, By: Rowland, 1821-1922

JACKSON COUNTY
Published History—Four Centuries in the Pascagouda, By: Cain

MONROE COUNTY
Published History—History of Aberdine and Monroe Counties, By: Rollins, 1821-1900

NEWTON COUNTY
Published History—History of Newton County, By: A. J. Brown, 1834-1894

WASHINGTON COUNTY
Published History—Papers of Washington County, Mississippi Historical Society

MISSOURI

ADAIR COUNTY
Published History—History of Adair County, By: E. M. Violette and C. N. Tolman, Denslow History Co., 1911

AUDRAIN COUNTY
Society—Audrain County Historical Society, 501 So. Muldrow, Mexico, MO 65265

BARRY COUNTY
Society—Barry County Historical Society, 516 Central Ave., Cassville, MO 65625

BARTON COUNTY
Published History—History of Polk, Cedar, Dade and Barton Counties, Goodspeed Pub. Co., 1889

BATES COUNTY
Published History—History of Bates County, By: W. O. Atkeson, Hist. Publishing Co., Topeka, 1918

BOONE COUNTY
Society—State Historical Society of Missouri, Corner Hitt and Lowry Sts., Columbia, MO 65201

BUCHANAN COUNTY
Society—St. Joseph Historical Society, 402 Felix St., St. Joseph, MO 64501
Published History—History of Buchanan County, Union Historical Co., St. Joseph 1881

CALDWELL COUNTY
Published History—History of Caldwell and Livingston Counties, Nat'l Historical Co., St. Louis, 1886

CALLAWAY COUNTY
Published History—History of Callaway County, National Historical Co., St. Louis, 1884

CASS COUNTY
Published History—History of Cass County, By: Allen Glenn, Historical Pub. Co., Topeka, 1917

CEDAR COUNTY
Society—Dade County Historical Society, Rt. #4, Stockton, MO 65785

CHARITON COUNTY
Published History—History of Chariton and Howard Counties, By: T. Berry Smith, Pearl S. Gehrig, Historical Pub. Co., 1923

CLAY COUNTY
Published History—History of Clay and Platte Counties, Nat'l Historical Co., St. Louis 1885

CLINTON COUNTY
Published History—History of Clinton County, Nat'l Historical Co., St. Louis, 1881

DAVIESS COUNTY
Published History—History of Daviess and Gentry Counties, By: John C. Leopard and Buel Leopard, R. M. McGammon and Mary Hillman McGammon, Historical Pub. Co., Topeka, 1922

DENT COUNTY
Published History—History of Laclede, Camden, Dallas, Webster, Wright, Texas, Pulaski, Phelps, and Dent Counties, Goodspeed Pub. Co., Chicago, 1889

GASCONADE COUNTY
Published History—History of Franklin, Jefferson, Washington, Crawford, and Gasconade Counties, Goodspeed Pub. Co., Chicago 1888

GENTRY COUNTY
Published History—History of Gentry and Worth Counties, National Historical Co., St. Joseph, 1882

GREENE COUNTY
Society—Greene County Historical Society Inc., 397 E. Central, Springfield, MO 65802
Published History—History of Greene County, Western Historical Co., St. Louis, 1883

GRUNDY COUNTY
Published History—History of Grundy County, Birdsall and Dean, Kansas City, 1881

HARRISON COUNTY
Society—Harrison County Historical Society
Published History—History of Harrison County, By: Geo. W. Wanamaker, Historical Pub. Co., Topeka, 1921

HENRY COUNTY
Published History—History of Henry and St. Clair Counties, National Historical Co., St. Joseph, 1883

HICKORY COUNTY
Society—Hickory County Historical Society, Hermitage, MO 65668
Published History—History of Hickory, Polk, Cedar, Dade, and Barton Counties, Goodspeed Pub. Co., Chicago, 1889

HOWARD COUNTY
Published History—History of Howard and Cooper Counties, National Hist. Co., St. Louis, 1883

JACKSON COUNTY
Published History—History of Jackson County, Union Historical Co., Kansas City, 1881

JEFFERSON COUNTY
Published History—History of Franklin, Jefferson, Washington, Crawford, and Gasconade Counties, Goodspeed Pub. Co., Chicago, 1888

JOHNSON COUNTY
Society—Johnson County Historical Society
Published History—History of Johnson County, By: Ewing Cockrell, Historical Pub. Co., Topeka 1918

KNOX COUNTY
Society—Knox County Historical Society
Published History—History of Lewis, Clark, Knox, and Scotland Counties, Goodspeed Pub. Co., St. Louis, 1887

LAFAYETTE COUNTY
Published History—Young's History of Lafayette County, By: Hon. William Young, B. F. Bowen and Co., Indianapolis, 1910

LEWIS COUNTY
Published History—History of Lewis, Clark, Knox, and Scotland Counties, Goodspeed Publishing Co., Chicago 1887

LINN COUNTY
Published History—History of Linn County, Birdsall and Dean, Kansas City, 1882

LIVINGSTON COUNTY
Published History—History of Caldwell and Livingston Counties, National Historical Co., St. Louis, 1886

MACON COUNTY
Published History—General History of Macon County, Henry Taylor and Co., Chicago, 1910

MARIES COUNTY
Published History—History of Cole, Moniteau, Morgan, Benton, Miller, Maries and Osage Counties, Goodspeed Publishing Co., Chicago, 1889

MERCER COUNTY
Society—Mercer County Historical Society, 902 E. Oak St., Princeton, MO 64673

MILLER COUNTY
Published History—History of Cole, Moniteau, Morgan, Benton, Miller, Maries and Osage Counties, Goodspeed Publishing Co., Chicago, 1889

MISSISSIPPI COUNTY
Society—Mississippi County Historical Society, 200 E. Commercial St., Charleston, MO 63834

MONROE COUNTY
Society—Monroe County Historical Society, Paris, MO 65275
Published History—History of Monroe County and Shelby County, National Hist. Co., St. Louis, 1884

MONTGOMERY COUNTY
Society—Morgan County Historical Society, Versailles, MO 65582

NEWTON COUNTY
Published History—History of Newton, Lawrence, Barry and McDonald Counties, Goodspeed Pub. Co., Chicago, 1888

OSAGE COUNTY
Published History—History of Cole, Moniteau, Morgan, Benton, Miller, Maries, and Osage Counties, Goodspeed Publishing Co., Chicago, 1889

PETTIS COUNTY
Published History—History of Pettis County, F. A. North, 1882

POLK COUNTY
Published History—History of Hickory, Polk, Cedar, Dade and Benton Counties, Goodspeed Publishing Co., Chicago, 1889

PULASKI COUNTY
Published History—History of Laclede, Camden, Dallas, Webster, Wright, Texas, Pulaski, Phelps and Dent Counties, Goodspeed Pub. Co., Chicago, 1889

PUTNAM COUNTY
Published History—History of Adair, Sullivan, Putnam, and Schuyler Counties, Goodspeed Publishing Co., Chicago, 1888

RALLS COUNTY
Published History—Portrait and Biographical Records of Ralls, Marion and Pike Counties, C. O. Owens and Co., Chicago, 1895

RANDOLPH COUNTY
Published History—History of Randolph and Macon Counties, National Hist. Co., St. Louis, 1884

ST. CHARLES COUNTY
Society—St. Charles County Historical Society, P.O. Box 455, St. Charles, MO 63301

ST. LOUIS COUNTY
Published History—St. Louis; The Fourth City, By: Walter B. Stevens, S. J. Clark Publishing Co., St. Louis, 1909

SALINE COUNTY
Society—Saline County Historical Society, P.O. Box 428, Marshall, MO 65340
Published History—History of Saline County, Missouri Historical Co., St. Louis, 1881

SCHUYLER COUNTY
Published History—History of Adair, Sullivan, Putnam and Schuyler Counties, Goodspeed Publishing Co., Chicago, 1880

SCOTLAND COUNTY
Published History—History of Lewis, Clark, Knox and Scotland Counties, Goodspeed Publishing Co., St. Louis, 1887

SHELBY COUNTY
Published History—History of Monroe and Shelby Counties, National Historical Co., St. Louis, 1884

SULLIVAN COUNTY
Published History—History of Adair, Sullivan, Putnam, and Schuyler Counties, Goodspeed Publishing Co., Chicago, 1888

VERNON COUNTY
Published History—History of Vernon County, Brown and Co., St. Louis, 1887

WARREN COUNTY
Published History—Portrait and Biographical Records of St. Charles, Lincoln and Warren Counties, Chapman Publishing Co., Chicago, 1885

MONTANA

DAWSON COUNTY
Society—Frontier Gateway Museum Assoc., P.O. Box 1181, Glendive, 59330

FERGUS COUNTY
Society—Central Montana Museum, East Main St., Lewiston, MT 59457

LEWIS and CLARK COUNTY
Society—Montana Historical Society, Roberts at Fifth Ave., Helena, MT 59601

NEBRASKA

ADAMS COUNTY
Published History—Past and Present of Adams County, By: Judge Wm. Barton and David J. Lewis, S. J. Clark Pub. Co., Chicago, 1916

ANTELOPE COUNTY
Published History—A History of Antelope County, By: A. J. Leach, R. R. Donnelley and Sons, Chicago 1909

ARTHUR COUNTY
Society—Arthur County Historical Society, Arthur, NE 69121

BOONE COUNTY
Published History—Biographical Souvenir of the Counties of Buffalo, Kearney, and Phelps, F. A. Battey and Co., Chicago, 1890

BUFFALO COUNTY
Published History—History of Buffalo County and It's People, By: Samuel Clay Bassett, S. J. Clark Pub. Co., Chicago, 1916

CASS COUNTY
Published History—Portrait and Biographical Album of Otoe and Cass Counties, Chapman Bros., Chicago, 1889

CHERRY COUNTY
Society—Cherry County Historical Society, Main St. and Highway 20, Valentine, NE 69201

CHEYENNE COUNTY
Society—Cheyenne County Historical Society, 740 Illinois St., Sidney, NE 69162

CLAY COUNTY
Published History—Biographical and Historical Memoirs of Adam, Clay, Webster and Nuckolls Counties, Goodspeed Pub. Co., Chicago, 1890

DAKOTA COUNTY
Published History—Warner's History of Dakota County, By: M. M. Warner, Lyons Mirror Job Office, Dakota City, 1893

DAWSEN COUNTY
Society—Dawsen County Historical Society, Taft St., Lexington, NE 68850

DUNDY COUNTY
Society—Dundy Historical Society, Benkleman, NE 69021

FRANKLIN COUNTY
Society—Franklin County Historical Society, Franklin, NE 68939

GARDEN COUNTY
Society—Historical Society of Garden County, West Ind. and G St., Oshkosh, NE 69514

GARFIELD COUNTY
Society—Garfield County Historical Society, Burwell, NE 68823

GRANT COUNTY
Society—Grant County Historical Society, Courthouse, Hyannis, NE 69350

HALL COUNTY
Society—Hall County Historical Society, 721 West Koeing St., Grand Island, NE 68801

HITCHCOCK
Society—Hitchcock County Historical Society, Trenton, NE 69044

JOHNSON COUNTY
Society—Johnson County Historical Society, 180 No. Fifth St., Tecumseh, NE 68450

KEARNEY COUNTY
Society—Kearney County Historical Society, Minden, NE 68959

KEITH COUNTY
Society—Keith County Historical Society, 1004 Spruce St., Box 92, Ogallala, NE 69153

KIMBALL COUNTY
Society—Plains Historical Society, Kimball, NE 69145

LANCASTER COUNTY
Society—Nebraska State Historical Society, 1500 R, Lincoln, NE 68508

PAWNEE COUNTY
Society—Pawnee City Historical Society, Pawnee City, NE 68420

PERKINS COUNTY
Society—Perkins County Historical Society, Grant, NE 69140

PHELPS COUNTY
Society—Phelps County Historical Society, 512 East Ave., Holdrege, NE 68949

RICHARDSON COUNTY
Society—Richardson County Historical Society, Falls City, NE 68355

SCOTTS BLUFF COUNTY
Society—North Platte Valley Historical Society, 1349-10th St., Bering, NE 69341

SHERIDAN COUNTY
Society—Sheridan County Historical Society, U.S. Highway 20, Rushville, NE 69360

VALLEY COUNTY
Society—Loup Valley Historical Assoc., Ord, NE 68862

WAYNE COUNTY
Society—Wayne County Historical Society, Wayne, NE 68787

YORK COUNTY
Society—York County Historical Assoc., Rt. #1, York, NE 68467

NEVADA

DOUGLAS COUNTY
Society—Carson Valley Historical Society

WASHOE COUNTY
Society—Nevada Historical Society, 1650 No. Virginia St., P.O. Box 1129, Reno, NV 89504

NEW HAMPSHIRE

BELKNAP COUNTY
Society—Laconia Historical Society Inc., P.O. Box 267, Laconia, NH 03246
Published History—History of Merrimack and Belknap Counties, J. W. Lewis Co., Philadelphia, 1885

CARROLL COUNTY
Published History—Saco Valley Settlements and Families, By: Gideon T. Ridlon, Portland, 1895

CHESHIRE COUNTY
Society—Historical Society of Cheshire County, Keene Public Library, 79 W. Street, Keene, NH 03431
Published History—History of Cheshire and Sullivan Counties, J. S. Lewis and Co., Philadelphia, 1886

COOS COUNTY
Society—Lancaster Historical Society, 226 Main St., Lancaster, NH 03584
Published History—History of Coos County, W. A. Fergerson and Co., Syracuse, 1888

HILLSBOROUGH COUNTY

Society—Manchester Historical Assoc., 129 Amherst St., Manchester, NH 03104

MERRIMACK COUNTY

Society—New Hampshire Historical Society, 30 Park St., Concord, NH 03301

Published History—History of Merrimack and Belknap Counties, J. S. Lewis and Co., Philadelphia, 1885

ROCKINGHAM COUNTY

Published History—History of Rockingham County, Richmond-Arnold Pub. Co., Chicago, 1915

STAFFORD COUNTY

Published History—History of Stafford County, By: J. Scales, Chicago, 1914

NEW JERSEY

CAMDEN COUNTY

Society—Camden County Historical Society, Park Blvd. and Euclid Ave., Camden, NJ 08103

CAPE MAY COUNTY

Society—Cape May Historical Society

ESSEX COUNTY

Society—New Jersey Historical Society, 230 Broadway, Newark, NJ 07104

GLOUCESTER COUNTY

Society—Gloucester County Historical Society, 58 No. Broad St., Woodbury, NJ 08906

MONMOUTH COUNTY

Society—Monmouth County Historical Assoc., 70 Court St., Freehold, NJ 07728

OCEAN COUNTY

Society—Ocean County Historical Society, Court House, Washington, St., Toms River, NJ 08753

PASSAIC COUNTY

Society—Passaic County Historical Society, P.O. Box 1729, Paterson, NJ 07509

SALEM COUNTY

Society—Salem County Historical Society, 78-93 Market St., Salem, NJ 08079

SOMERSET COUNTY

Society—Somerset County Historical Society, County Courthouse, Somerville, NJ 08876

SUSSEX COUNTY

Society—Sussex County Historical Society, 82 Main St., Newton, NJ 07860

NEW MEXICO

BERNALILLO COUNTY

Society—Historical Society of New Mexico, University Hill, N.E., Albuquerque, NM

SANTA FE COUNTY

Society—Historical Society of New Mexico, Palace Ave., Santa Fe, NM

TAOS COUNTY

Society—Taos County Historical Society, Kit Carson St., Taos, NM 87571

NEW YORK

ALBANY COUNTY

Society—The Albany Historical Assoc., 9 Ten Broeck Place, Albany, NY 12210

Published History—History of Albany, Gregg, Arthur B., The Atmont Enterprise, 1936

ALLEGANY COUNTY

Published History—Allegany and It's People, (G.S.) Allred, NY, W. A. Fergusson and Co., 1896

BRONX COUNTY

Society—Bronx County Historical Society, 3266 Bainbridge Ave., Bronx, NY 10467

Published History—New York, (G.S.) Wells, James Lee, The Lee Historical Pub. Co., 1927

BROOME COUNTY

Society—Broome County Historical Society, 30 Frount Street, Binghamton, NY 13905

Published History—Wilkinson, J. G. (G.S.) Pub. in Binghamton, The Times Assoc., 1872

CATTARAUGUS COUNTY

Published History—Ellis, Franklin, Philadelphia, By: L. H. Everts, 1879

CAYUGA COUNTY

Society—Cayuga County Historical Society, 203 Genesee St., Auburn, NY 13021

Published History—Storke, Elliot G. (G.S.) Syracuse, NY, D. Mason, 1879

CHAUTAUQUA

Published History—Young, Andrew White (G.S.) Buffalo, NY, Printing House of Matthews and Warren, 1875

CHEMUNG COUNTY

Society—Chemung County Historical Society, 304 Williams St., Elmira, NY 14901

Published History—Peirce, Henry B. (G.S.) Philadelphia, PA, Everts and Ensign, 1879

CHENANGO COUNTY

Society—Chenango County Historical Society, Rexford St., Norwich, NY 13815

Published History—Smith, James Hadden (G.S.) Syracuse, NY, Mason and Co., 1880

CLINTON COUNTY

Society—Clinton County Historical Assoc., 179 East Brooks Road, Platts Borg, NY 14534

COLUMBIA COUNTY

Published History—History of Columbia County (G.S.), Philadelphia, Everts and Ensign, 1878

CORTLAND COUNTY

Society—Cortland County Historical Society, 25 Homer Ave., Cortland, NY 13045

Published History—Goodwin, Hermon C. (G.S.), Pioneer History, New York, A. B. Burdick, 1859

DELAWARE COUNTY

Society—Delaware County Historical Society, 155 Main St., Delhi, NY 13753

Published History—Monroe, John D. (G.S.), History of Delaware County, Delaware County Historical Assoc., 1949

DUTCHESS COUNTY

Published History—Helen W. Reynolds, New York, Payson and Clark, L.T.D. 1929

ERIE COUNTY

Society—Erie County Historical Society, Supreme Court Law Library, Erie County Hall, Buffalo, NY 14202

Published History—Smith, H. Perry, Syracuse, New York, D. Mason and Co., 1884

ESSEX COUNTY

Society—Essex County Historical Society, Adirondack Center Museum, Elizabeth, NY 12932

Published History—Watson, Winslow C. (G.S.), Albany, New York, J. Munsell, 1863

FRANKLIN COUNTY

Society—Franklin County Historical and Museum Society, Elm Society, Malone, NY 12953

Published History—Hough, Franklin B. (G.S.), Baltimore, Reginal Publishing Co., 1970

FULTON

Society—Johnstown Historical Society, 17 North Williams St., Johnstown, NY 12095

GENESEE COUNTY

Society—Historical Society of Early American Decoration, 145 Union St., Batavia, NY 14020

Published History—North, Safford E., Boston, The Boston History Co. Publishers 1899

GREENE COUNTY

Published History—History of Green County, New York, (G.S.), J. R. Berrs and Co., 1884

HAMILTON COUNTY

Society—Hamilton County Historical Society, Lake Pleasant, NY 12108

Published History—Aber, Ted, History of Hamilton County, Lake Pleasant, NY, Great Wilderness Books, 1965

HERKIMER COUNTY

Society—Herkimer County Historical Society, 400 North Main St., Box 727, Herkimer, NY 13350

Published History—Benton, Nathaniels, (G.S.), A History of Herkimer County, Albany New York, J. Munsell, 1856

JEFFERSON COUNTY

Society—Jefferson County Historical Society, 228 Washington St., Watertown, NY 13601

Published History—Haddock, John A., The History of Jefferson County, Albany New York, Weed, Parsons Printing Co., 1895

KINGS COUNTY

Society—Long Island Historical Society, 128 Pierepont St., Brooklyn, NY 11201

LEWIS COUNTY

Society—Lewis County Historical Society, Lowville, NY 13367

Published History—History of Lewis County, By: Frank B. Hough, Pub. by: Munsell and Rowland, Albany, 1860

LIVINGSTON COUNTY

Society—Livingston County Historical Society, 30 Center St., Geneseo, NY 14454

Published History—History of Livingston County, By: Edward E. Doty, Edward E. Doty, Geneseo, 1876

MADISON COUNTY

Published History—History of Chenango and Madison Counties, Pub. by: D. Mason and Co., Syracuse, 1880

MONROE COUNTY

Society—American Baptist Historical Society, 1106 So. Goodman St., Rochester, NY

Published History—History of Monroe County, Pub. by: Everts, Ensign and Everts, Phila., 1877

MONTGOMERY COUNTY

Published History—History of Montgomery and Fulton Counties, F. W. Beers and Co., New York, 1878

NASSAU COUNTY

Published History—History of Long Island, By: D. Peter Ross, Lewis Publishing Co., New York, 1902, Vol. 1 and 2

NEW YORK COUNTY

Society—The New York Historical Society, 170 Central Park West, New York, NY 10024,

Published History—History of New York, By: John W. Leonard, 1910

NIAGARA COUNTY

Society—Niagara County Historical Society Inc., 215 Niagara St., (Mail): 118 Cottage St., Lockport, NY 14094

ONEIDA COUNTY

Society—Oneida Historical Society, 318 Genesee St., Utica, NY 13502

ONONDAGA COUNTY

Society—Onondaga Historical Assoc., 311 Montgomery St., Syracuse, NY 13202

Published History—History of Onondaga County, By: W. W. Clayton, D. Mason and Co., Syracuse, 1878

ONTARIO COUNTY

Society—Ontario County Historical Society, 55 North Main St., Canandaigua, NY 14424

Published History—History of Ontario County, By: George S. Conover and Lewis Cass Aldrich, 1893, D. Manson and Co., Syracuse

ORANGE COUNTY

Society—Goshen Library and Historical Society, 203 Main St., Goshen, NY 10924

Published History—History of Orange County, By: E. M. Ruttenber and L. H. Clark, Everts and Peck, Philadelphia, 1881

ORLEANS COUNTY

Society—Cobblestone Society, Albion, NY 14411

Published History—Pioneer History of Orleans County, By: Arad Thomas, H. A. Bruner, Orleans American Steam Press Print., 1871, Albion

OSWEGO COUNTY

Society—Oswego County Historical Society, 135 East 3rd St., Oswego, NY 13126

Published History—History of Oswego County, L. H. Everts and Co., Philadelphia, 1877

OTSEGO COUNTY

Society—New York Historical Assoc., Lake Road, Copperstown, NY 13326

Published History—Biographical Review of Otsego County, Biographical Review Publishing Co., 1893, Boston

PUTNAM COUNTY

Published History—History of Putnam, By: William J. Blake, Baker and Scribner, New York, 1849

QUEENS COUNTY

Society—King Manor Assoc., 162-05 89th Ave., Jamaica, NY 11432

Published History—Portrait and Biographical Record of Queens County, Chapman Publishing Co., New York, 1896

RENSSELAER COUNTY

Society—Rensselaer County Historical Society, 59 Second St., Troy, NY 12180

Published History—History of Rensselaer County, By: Nathaniel Bartlett Sylvester, Everts and Park, Philadelphia, 1880

RICHMOND COUNTY

Published History—History of Richmond County, By: Richard M. Bayles, L. E. Preston and Co., New York, 1887

ROCKLAND COUNTY

Published History—History of Rockland County, J. B. Beers and Co., New York, 1884

ST. LAWRENCE COUNTY

Society—St. Lawrence County Historical Assoc., P.O. Box 43, Canton, NY 13617

SARATOGA COUNTY

Society—Ballston Spa Area Historical Society, 36 Church St., Ballston Spa, NY 12020

Published History—History of Saratoga County, By: Nathaniel Bartlett Sylvester, Everts and Ensign, 1878 Philadelphia

SCHENECTADY COUNTY

Society—Schenectady County Historical Society, 32 Washington Ave., Schenectady, NY 12305

Published History—History of Albany and Schenectady, W. W. Munsell and Co., 1662-1886, New York, Schnectady, Albany 1886

SCHOHARIE COUNTY

Society—Schoharie County Historical Society, Old Stone Fort Museum, Schoharie, 12157

SENECA COUNTY

Society—Waterloo Library and Historical Society, 31 East Williams St., Waterloo, NY

Published History—Gazette—May 28, 1817

SUFFOLK COUNTY

Society—Suffolk County Historical Society, P.O. Box 689, Riverhead, NY 11901

SULLIVAN COUNTY

Society—Sullivan County Historical Society, 11 Bank St., Monticello, NY 12701

TIOGA COUNTY

Society—Tioga County Historical Society, 122 Front St.

TOMPKINS COUNTY

Society—Dewitt Historical Society of Tompkins County, 121 East Court St., Ithaca, NY 14850

ULSTER COUNTY

Society—Ulster County Historical Society, Rt. 209, Road 3, Kingston, NY 12401

WARREN COUNTY

Society—Lake George Historical Assoc., Lake George, NY 12845

WASHINGTON COUNTY

Society—Washington County Historical Society, 8 McDowell St., Hudson Falls, NY 12839

WAYNE COUNTY

Society—Wayne County Historical Society, 21 Butternut St., Lyons, NY 14489

WESTCHESTER COUNTY

Society—The Manuscript Society, 270 Martin Ave., White Plains, NY 10601

WYOMING COUNTY

Society—Warsaw Historical Society, P.O. Box 245, Warsaw, NY 14569

YATES COUNTY

Society—Yates County Genealogical and Historical Society, 200 Main St., Penn. Yan, NY 14527

NORTH CAROLINA

ANSON COUNTY

Society—Anson County Historical Society Inc., 210 E. Wade St., Wadeshow, NC 28170

YADKIN COUNTY

Society—Yadkin County Historical Society, Yadkinville, NC 27055

ASHE COUNTY

Published History—Western North Carolina—A History 1730-1913, Asheville 1914, By: John Preston Arthur; Edward Buncombe Chapter of The D.A.R.

AVERY COUNTY

Published History—Western North Carolina—A History 1730-1913, By: John Preston Arthur; Edward Buncombe Chapter of the D.A.R.

CALDWELL COUNTY

Society—Caldwell County Historical Society

CATAWBA COUNTY

Society—Catawba County Historical Society

CHEROKEE COUNTY

Published History—Western North Carolina—A History 1730-1913, Asheville 1914, By: John Preston Arthur; Edward Buncombe Chapter of the D.A.R.

CLAY COUNTY

Published History—Western North Carolina—A History 1730-1913, By: John Preston Arthur, Asheville 1918, Edward Buncombe Chapter of the D.A.R.

CRAVEN COUNTY

Society—New Bern Historical Society Foundation Inc., P.O. Box 119, New Bern, NC 28560

EDGECOMBE COUNTY

Published History—History of Edgecombe County, By: J. Kelly Turner and John L. Bridgers Jr., Edward and Broughton Printing Co., Raleigh, 1920

HALIFAX COUNTY

Published History—History of Halifax County, By: N. C. Allen, Cornhill Co., Boston, 1918

MOORE COUNTY

Society—Moore County Historical Assoc., Carthage, NC 28327

NEW HANOVER COUNTY

Society—Lower Cape Fear Historical Inc., 118 So. 4th St., Wilmington, NC 28401

ORANGE COUNTY

Society—Orange County Historical Society

PITT COUNTY

Society—Edenton and Chawan County Historical Comm., 117 W. 5th St., Greenville, NC 27932

RANDOLPH COUNTY

Society—Randolph County Historical Society, 167 No. Fayetteville St., Asheboro, NC 27203

WAKE COUNTY

Society—North Carolina State Department of Archives and History, 109 E. Jones St., Raleigh, NC 27602

WATAUGA COUNTY

Society—Southern Appalachian Historical Assoc., Boone, NC 28607

NORTH DAKOTA

BARNES COUNTY

Society—Barnes County Historical Society

BURLEIGH COUNTY

Society—North Dakota State Histocial Society

DIVIDE COUNTY

Society—Divide County Historical Society, Crosby, ND 58730

EDDY COUNTY

Society—Eddy County Historical Society, New Rockford, ND 58356

HETTINGER COUNTY

Society—Hettinger County Historical Society, Mott, ND 58646

PEMBINA COUNTY

Society—Pembina County Historical Society, Cavalier, ND 58220

RICHLAND COUNTY

Society—Richland County Historical Society

STUTSMAN COUNTY

Society—Fort Seward Historical Society Inc., 321-3rd Ave. S.E., Janestown, ND 58401

TRAILL COUNTY
Society—Traill County Historical Society, Hillsboro, ND 58045

WELLS COUNTY
Society—Wells County Historical Society, Fessenden, ND 58438

OHIO

ADAMS COUNTY
Published History—History of Adams County, By: E. B. Stivers, West Union, OH, 1900

ALLEN COUNTY
Society—Allen County Historical Society, Lima, OH 45802
Published History—History of Allen County, Ohio, Warner, Beers and Co., Chicago, 1885

ASHLAND COUNTY
Published History—History of Ashland County, By: Geo. W. Hill, Cleveland, Williams Bros., 1880

ASHTABULA COUNTY
Society—Ashtabula County Historical Society, P.O. Box 193, Jefferson, OH 44067
Published History—History of Ashtabula County, William Bro's., Philadelphia, 1878

ATHENS COUNTY
Published History—Historical and Biographical Memiors of Early Pioneer Settlers of Ohio, By: S. P. Hildreth, H. W. Derby and Co., Cinn. 1854

AUGLAIZE COUNTY
Published History—History of Auglaize County, By: Robert Sutton, Wapakoueta, 1880

BELMONT COUNTY
Published History—History of Belmont and Jefferson Counties, By: J. A. Caldwell, Wheeling W. Va., Hist. Pub. Co., 1888

BROWN COUNTY
Published History—History of Brown County, By: D. J. Lake and B. N. Griffing, W. H. Beers and Co., Philadelphia, 1883

BUTLER COUNTY
Published History—Historical and Biographical Cyclopedia of Butler County, Western Biog. Pub. Co., Cinn., 1882

CARROLL COUNTY
Society—Carroll County Historical Society, Public Square, Carrollton, OH 44615
Published History—Commemorative Biographical Record of Harrison and Carroll Counties, J. H. Beers and Co., Chicago, 1891

CHAMPAIGN COUNTY
Published History—History of Champaign and Logan Counties, By: Joshua Antrim, Press Printing Co., Bellefontaine, OH 1872

CLARK COUNTY
Society—Clark County Historical Society, Memorial Hall, 300 West Main St., Springfield, OH 45504
Published History—History of Clark County, W. H. Beers and Co., Chicago, 1881

CLERMONT COUNTY
Society—Clermont County Historical Society, P.O. Box 14, Batavia, OH 45103

CLINTON COUNTY
Society—The Clinton County Historical Society, 149 E. Locust St., Wilmington, OH 45177
Published History—History of Clinton County, W. H. Beers and Co., Chicago, 1882

COLUMBIANA COUNTY
Society—Lisbon Historical Society, 100 East Washington St., Lisbon, OH 44432
Published History—History of Columbiana County, I. W. Ensign Co., Philadelphia 1879

COSHOCTON COUNTY
Society—Coshocton County Historical Society
Published History—History of Coshocton, By: N. N. Hill, Newark, OH, A. A. Graham and Co., 1881

CRAWFORD COUNTY
Published History—History of Crawford County, Baskin and Battey, Chicago, 1881

CUYAHOGA COUNTY
Society—The Early Settlers Assoc. of the Western Reserve, Cleveland, OH
Society—Great Lakes Historical Society, 320 Republic Bldg. Cleveland, OH
Society—Lakewood Historical Society, 14710 Lakewood Ave., Cleveland, OH
Society—The Western Reserve Historical Society, 10325 East Blvd., Cleveland, OH 44106
Published History—History of Cuyahoga County, By: Johnson, Gresfield, D. W. Ensign and Co., Phila. 1879

DARKE COUNTY
Society—Darke County Historical Society and Garst Museum, 205 North Broadway, Greenville, OH
Published History—History of Darke County, W. H. Beers and Co., 1880

DEFIANCE COUNTY
Society—Defiance County Historical Society, Fort St., Defiance, OH 43512
Published History—History of Defiance County, Warner, Beers and Co., Chicago, 1883

DELAWARE COUNTY
Society—Delaware County Historical Society, 157 East William St., Delaware, OH 43015
Published History—History of Delaware County, O. L. Baskin and Co., Chicago, 1880

ERIE COUNTY
Society—Erie County Historical Society, c/o Sandusky Library, Sandusky, OH 44870
Published History—History of the Firelands, Comprising Huron and Erie Counties, W. W. Williams, Cleveland, 1879

FAIRFIELD COUNTY
Published History—Complete History of Fairfield County, Ohio—1795-1876, By: Hervey Scott, Siebert and Lilley, Columbus, OH, 1877

FAYETTE COUNTY
Published History—History of Fayette County, By: R. S. Dills, Odell and Mayer, Dayton, OH, 1881

FRANKLIN COUNTY
Society—Franklin County Historical Society and Museum, 280 E. Broad St., Columbus, OH 43215
Published History—History of Franklin and Pickaway Counties, Ohio, Williams Bro's., Cleveland, OH, 1880

FULTON COUNTY
Society—Fulton County Historical Society, Courthouse, South Fulton St., Wauseon, OH 43567

GALLIA COUNTY
Published History—Historical Hand Atlas, accomp. by History of Lawrence and Gallia Counties, Chicago and Toledo, H. H. Hardesty and Co., 1882

GEAUGA COUNTY
Published History—History of Geauga and Lake Counties, William Bro's., 1878 and Pioneer and General History of Geauga County, Ohio, 1880

GREEN COUNTY
Society—The Greene County Historical Society, 74 West Church, Xenia, OH 45385
Published History—History of Greene County, R. S. Dills, Dayton, Odell and Mayer Pub., 1881

GUERNSEY COUNTY
Published History—History of Guernsey County, 2 Vols., B. F. Bowen and Co., Indianapolis, 1911

HAMILTON COUNTY
Society—Cinncinnati Historical Society, Eden Park, Cinncinnati, OH 45202
Published History—History of Hamilton County, By: H. A. Ford and K. B. Ford, Cleveland, 1881, L. A. Williams and Co.

HANCOCK COUNTY
Published History—History of Hancock County, D. B. Beardsley, Springfield, Ohio, Republic Printing Co., 1881

HARDIN COUNTY
Published History—History of Hardin County, Ohio, Warner, Beers and Co., Chicago, 1883

HARRISON COUNTY
Published History—Commemorative Biographical Records of Counties of Harrison and Carroll, J. H. Beers and Co., Chicago, 1891

HENRY COUNTY
Published History—History of Henry and Fulton Counties, Syracuse, New York, 1888, D. Mason and Co.,

HIGHLAND COUNTY
Society—Highland County Historical Society, East Main St., Hillsboro, OH 45133
Published History—History of Ross and Highland Counties, William Bro's., Cleveland, 1880

HOCKING COUNTY
Society—Hocking County Historical Society, 56 W. Main St., Logan, OH 43138
Published History—History of Hocking County, Inter-State Pub. Co., Chicago, 1883

HOLMES COUNTY
Society—Holmes County Historical Society, Millersburg, OH 44654
Published History—Commemorative Biographical Record of Counties of Wayne and Holmes, J. H. Beers and Co., 1889

HURON COUNTY
Society—Firelands Historical Society
Published History—History of Firelands, Comprising Huron and Erie Counties, W. W. Williams, Cleveland, 1879

JACKSON COUNTY
Published History—History of Jackson County, D. W. Williams, Jackson, OH 1900, and Atlas of Jackson County, Simmons and Titles, 1875, Phila.

JEFFERSON COUNTY
Published History—History of Belmont and Jefferson Counties, J. A. Caldwell, Wheeling W. Va. Hist. Pub. Co., 1880

KNOX COUNTY
Society—Knox County Historical Society
Published History—History of Knox County, N. N. Hill Jr. Comp., Mt. Vernon, Ohio, A. A. Graham and Co., 1881

LAKE COUNTY
Published History—History of Geauga and Lake Counties, Williams Bro's., Phila., 1878

LAWRENCE COUNTY
Published History—History of Lawrence and Gallia Counties, H. H. Hardesty and Co.. Chicago. 1882

LICKING COUNTY
Society—Licking County Historical Society, P.O. Box 535, Newark, OH 43055
Published History—History of Licking County, N. N. Hill Comp., A. A. Graham and Co., Newark, OH, 1881

LOGAN COUNTY
Society—Logan County Historical Society, 400 Linden St., Bellefontaine, OH 43311
Published History—History of Champaign and Logan Counties, Joshua Antrim, Press Printing Co., Bellefontaine, OH, 1872

LORAIN COUNTY
Society—Lorain County Historical Society, 331 Fifth St., Elyria, OH 44035
Published History—History of Lorain County, Williams Bro's., 1879, Phila.

LUCAS COUNTY
Published History—History of the City of Toledo and Lucas County, Ohio, New York and Toledo, 1888, Munsell and Co.,

MADISON COUNTY
Published History—History of Madison County, W. H. Beers and Co., Chicago, 1883

MAHONING COUNTY
Society—Mahoning Valley Historical Society
Published History—History of Trumbull and Mahoning Counties, 2 Vols., H. Z. Williams and Bro's., Cleveland, 1882

MARION COUNTY
Published History—History of Marion, Laggett, and Conaway Counties, Chicago, 1883

MEDINA COUNTY
Society—Medina County Historical Society
Published History—History of Medina County, Ohio, Baskin and Battey, Chicago, 1881

MEIGS COUNTY
Society—Meigs County Pioneer and Historical Society, Courthouse and 2nd St., Pomeroy, OH 45769
Published History—Historical and Geographical Encyclopedia—Containing History of Meigs County, H. H. Hardesty and Co., Chicago and Toledo, 1883

MERCER COUNTY
Society—Mercer County Historical Society, 605 Johnson Ave., Celina, OH 45822
Published History—History of Van Wert and Mercer Counties, R. Sutton and Co., Wapakoneta, OH 1882

MIAMI COUNTY
Society—Troy Historical Society, 2816 Troy Urbana Rd., Troy, OH 45373
Published History—History of Miami County, W. H. Beers and Co., Chicago 1880

MONROE COUNTY
Published History—Historical Hand Atlas and History of Monroe County, H. H. Hardesty and Co., Chicago and Toledo, 1882

MONTGOMERY COUNTY
Society—Montgomery County Historical Society, Old Courthouse, Dayton, OH 45402
Published History—History of Montgomery County, W. H. Beers, Chicago, 1882

MORGAN COUNTY
Published History—History of Morgan County, L. H. Watkins and Co., Chicago, 1886

MORROW COUNTY
Published History—History of Morrow County, O. L. Baskin and Co., Chicago, 1880

MUSKINGUM COUNTY
Society—Pioneer and Historical Society of Muskingum County, 612 Larzelers Ave., Zanesville, OH 43701
Published History—History of Muskingum County, J. F. Everhart and Co., Columbus, OH, 1882

NOBLE COUNTY
Published History—History of Noble County, L. H. Watkins and Co., Chicago, 1887

OTTAWA COUNTY
Published History—Commemorative Biographical Record of the Counties of Sandusky and Ottawa, J. H. Beers and Co., Chicago, 1896

PAULDING COUNTY
Published History—Representative Citizens of Paulding, W. S. Hardesty, Toledo, OH, 1902

PERRY COUNTY
Published History—History of Fairfield and Perry Counties, W. H. Beers and Co., Chicago, 1883

PICKAWAY COUNTY
Published History—History of Franklin and Pickaway Counties, William Bro's. Pub., Cleveland, 1880

PIKE COUNTY
Published History—Beaver Valley Pioneers, Pike County—1880-1947, H. E. Brill, Oklahoma City, 1947

PORTAGE COUNTY
Society—Portage County Historical Society, 6459 No. Chestnut, Revenna, OH 44266
Published History—History of Portage County, Warner, Beers and Co., Chicago, 1885

PREBLE COUNTY
Published History—History of Preble County, H. Z. Williams and Bro's., Cleveland, 1881

PUTNAM COUNTY
Published History—Historical Hand Atlas, Containing History of Putnam County, H. H. Hardesty and Co., Chicago, 1880

RICHLAND COUNTY
Society—Ohio Genealogical Society, 454 Park Ave., Mansfield, OH 44906
Published History—History of Richland County, A. A. Graham and Co., Mansfield, OH, 1880

ROSS COUNTY
Society—Ross County Historical Society Inc., 45 West 5th St., P.O. Box 344, Chillicothe, OH 45601
Published History—History of Ross and Highland Counties, William Bro's., 1880, Cleveland

SANDUSKY COUNTY
Published History—History of Sandusky County, H. Z. Williams and Bro's., Cleveland, OH, 1882

SCIOTO COUNTY
Published History—Pioneers of Scioto County, James Keyes, Portsmith, OH, 1880

SENECA COUNTY
Published History—History of Seneca County, Warner, Beers and Co., Chicago, 1886

SHELBY COUNTY
Published History—History of Shelby County, R. Sutton and Co., Philadelphia, 1883

STARK COUNTY
Society—Stark County Historical Society
Published History—History of Stark County, Wm. H. Perrin, Baskin and Battey, Chicago, 1881

TRUMBULL COUNTY
Society—Trumbull County Historical Society, 444 High St. N.E., Warren, OH 44481
Published History—History of Trumbull and Mahoning Counties, 2 Vols., H. Z. Williams and Bro's., Cleveland, OH, 1880

TUSCARAWAS COUNTY
Society—Tuscarawas County Historical Assoc., 114 E. High, New Philadelphia, OH 44663
Published History—History of Tuscarawas County, Warner, Beers and Co., Chicago, 1884

UNION COUNTY
Society—Union County Historical Society, 246 West 6th St., Marysville, OH 43040
Published History—History of Union County, W. H. Beers and Co., Chicago, 1883

VAN WERT COUNTY
Society—Van Wert Historical Society, 602 No. Washington St., Van Wert, OH 45891
Published History—History of Van Wert and Mercer Counties, Wapokoneta, 1882, R. Sutton

VINTON COUNTY
Published History—History of Vinton County, M. C. Arthur, Lew Ogan, 1954

WARREN COUNTY
Society—Warren County Historical Society
Published History—History of Warren County, W. H. Beers and Co., Chicago, 1882

WASHINGTON COUNTY
Published History—History of Washington County, H. Z. Williams and Bro's., Cleveland, 1881

WAYNE COUNTY
Society—Wayne County Historical Society
Published History—History of Wayne County, R. Douglass, Indianapolis, 1878

WILLIAMS COUNTY
Published History—County of Williams, W. A. Goodspeed and Charles Branchard, F. A. Battey and Co., Chicago, 1882

WOOD COUNTY
Society—Wood County Historical Society, 301 Sand Ridge Rd., Bowling Green, OH 43402
Published History—Commemmorative Historical and Biographical Record of Wood County, J. H. Beers and Co., Chicago, 1897

WYANDOT COUNTY
Society—Wyandot County Historical Society, 130 So. 7th St., Upper Sandusky, OH 43351
Published History—History of Wyandot County, A. J. Hare, Philadelphia, 1879

OKLAHOMA

CARTER COUNTY
Society—Chickasaw Historical Society of Southern Oklahoma, P.O. Box 1328, Ardmore, OK 73401

CHEROKKE COUNTY
Society—Cherokee National Historical Society, P.O. Box 515, Tahlequah, OK 74464

COMANCHE COUNTY
Society—Southwestern Oklahoma Historical Society, 916½ B Ave., Lawton, OK 73501

CRAIG COUNTY
Published History—Muskogee and Northeastern Oklahoma, By: John D. Benedict, S. J. Clark Pub. Co., Chicago, 1922

DELAWARE COUNTY
Published History—Muskogee and Northeastern Oklahoma, By: John D. Benedict, S. J. Clark Pub. Co., Chicago, 1922

LINCOLN COUNTY

Society—Lincoln County Historical Society, Chandler, OK 74834

NOBLE COUNTY

Society—Cherokee Strip Historical Society, West Ditch Witch, Perry, OK 73077

OKLAHOMA COUNTY

Society—Oklahoma Historical Society, Historical Bldg., Oklahoma City, OK 73105

OREGON

BAKER COUNTY

Society—Baker County Historical Society, 1655-1st City Hall, Baker, OR 97814

CLATSOP COUNTY

Society—Clatsop County Historical Society, 441-8th St., Astoria, OR 97103

DOUGLAS COUNTY

Society—Douglas County Historical Society, 544 S.E. Douglas Ave., Roseburg, OR 97470

MULTNOMAH COUNTY

Society—Oregon Historical Society, 1230 S.W. Park Ave., Portland, OR 97205

WASHINGTON COUNTY

Society—Washington County Historical Society and Museum, 25845 N.W. Brogden Ave., Hillsboro, OR 97123

PENNSYLVANIA

ADAMS COUNTY

Society—Adams County Historical Society, P.O. Drawer A, Old Dorm, Seminary Campus, Gettysburg, PA 17325

ALLEGHENY COUNTY

Society—Historical Society of Western Pennsylvania, 4338 Bigelow Blvd., Pittsburg, PA 15213
Published History—History of Allegheny County; A. Warner and Co., Chicago, 1889, (1548 Pages)

ARMSTRONG COUNTY

Society—Kittanning Public Library, Kittanning, PA
Published History—History of Armstrong County, By: Robert Walter Smith; Walterman, Walkins and Co., Chicago, 1883

BEAVER COUNTY

Published History—History of Beaver County, By: Rev. Joseph H. Bausman; 2 Vols.

BEDFORD COUNTY

Published History—History of Bedford and Somerset Counties, By: Hon. William H. Koontz; Lewis Pub. Co., New York, 1906

BERKS COUNTY

Society—Historical Society of Berks County, 940 Centre, Ave., Reading, PA 19601
Published History—History of Berks County; Everts, Peck, and Richards, Philadelphia, 1886

BLAIR COUNTY

Society—Blair County Historical Society, P.O. Box 1083, Altoona, PA 16603
Published History—Biographical and Portrait Cyclopedia of Blair County, By: Samuel T. Wiley and W. Scott Garver; 1892

BRADFORD COUNTY

Society—Bradford Historical Society, Court St., Towanda, PA 18848
Published History—History of Bradford County, By: H. C. Bradsby; S. B. Nelson and Co., Chicago, 1891

BUCKS COUNTY

Society—Bucks County Historical Society, Pine and Ashland Sts., Doylestown, PA 18901
Published History—History of Bucks County, By: J. H. Battle; A. Warner and Co., Philadelphia, 1887

BUTLER COUNTY

Society—Butler County Historical Society, P.O. Box 88, Slippery Rock, PA 16057
Published History—History of Butler County; R. C. Brown and Co., 1895

CAMBRIA COUNTY

Society—Cambria County Historical Society, 201 West Sample St., Ebensburg, PA 15931
Published History—History of Cambria County, By: Henry Wilson; Storey, 3 Vols.

CAMERON COUNTY

Society—Cameron County Historical Society, 325 Oak St., Emporium, PA 15834

CARBON COUNTY

Published History—History of Lehigh and Carbon Counties, Alfred Mathews and Austin N. Hungerford; Evert and Richards Pub., Phila., 1884

CENTRE COUNTY

Published History—History of Centre and Clinton Counties, By: John Blair Linn; Louis H. Everts Co., Phila., 1883

CHESTER COUNTY

Society—Chester County Historical Society, 225 North High St., West Chester, PA 19380

CLARION COUNTY

Society—Clarion County Historical Society, 64 North 5th Ave., Clarion, PA 16214

CLEARFIELD COUNTY

Society—Clearfield County Historical Society, 104 East Pine St., Clearfield, PA 16830
Published History—History of Clearfield County, With Illustrations and Biographical Sketches; By: Lewis Cass Aldrich, 1887

CLINTON COUNTY

Society—Clinton County Historical Society, Loch Haven, PA 17745

COLUMBIA COUNTY

Society—Columbia County Historical Society, 353 East Main St., Bloomsburg, PA 17815
Published History—History of Columbia and Montour Counties; By: J. H. Battle

CRAWFORD COUNTY

Society—Crawford County Historical Society, 848 North Main St., Meadville, PA 16335

CUMBERLAND COUNTY

Society—Cumberland County Historical Society, 21 N. Pitt St., Carlisle, PA 17013
Published History—History of Cumberland County; By: Conway P. Wing, 1879

DAUPHIN COUNTY

Society—Historical Society of Dauphin County, 219 South Front St., Harrisburg, PA 17104
Published History—Centenary Memorial, County of Dauphin; By: William Henry Egle, 1886

DELAWARE COUNTY

Society—Delaware County Historical Society, 410 Market St., Chester, PA 19016

ELK COUNTY

Society—Elk County Historical Society, P.O. Box 361, Ridgway, PA 15853

ERIE COUNTY

Society—Erie County Historical Society, 407 State St., Erie, PA 16501
Published History—History of Erie County; Warner, Beers and Co., 1884

FAYETTE COUNTY

Society—Westmoreland-Fayette Historical Society, West Overton, Scottsdale, PA 15638
Published History—History of Fayette County, By: Franklin Ellis; Everts and Co. Pub., Phila., 1882

FRANKLIN COUNTY

Society—Kittochtinny Historical Society, Chambersburg, PA
Published History—History of Franklin County; By: Samuel D. Bates; Warner, Beers and Co., Chicago, 1887

FULTON COUNTY

Society—Fulton County Historical Society, McConnellsburg, PA 17233

GREENE COUNTY

Society—Greene County Historical Society, North Morgan St., Waynesburg, PA 15370

HUNTINGDON COUNTY

Society—Huntingdon County Historical Society, P. O. Box 182, 109-4th St., Huntingdon, PA 16652
Published History—History of Huntingdon County; By: Milton Scott Lytle, 1876

INDIANA COUNTY

Society—Historical and Genealogical Society of Indiana County, Memorial Hall, Indiana, PA 15701
Published History—Indiana County, Her People Past and Present; By: J. T. Stewart; J. H. Beers and Co., Chicago, 1913

JUANITA COUNTY

Society—Juanita County Historical Society, Port Royal, PA 17082

LACKAWANNA COUNTY

Society—Lackawanna Historical Society, 232 Monroe Ave., Scranton, PA 18510
Published History—History of Luzrene, Lackawanna and Wyoming Counties; W. M. Munsell and Co., 1880

LANCASTER COUNTY

Society—Lancaster County Historical Society, Willson Bldg., 230 N. President Ave , Lancaster, PA 17603
Published History—History of Lancaster County; By: Franklin Ellis and Samuel Evans, 1883

LAWRENCE COUNTY

Society—Lawrence County Historical Society, New Castle, PA 16101

LEBANON COUNTY

Society—Lebanon County Historical Society, 6th and Walnut Sts., Lebanon, PA 17042
Published History—History of Dauphin and Lebanon Counties; Everts and Peck, Phila., 1883

LEHIGH COUNTY

Society—Lehigh County Historical Society, 414 Walnut St., Allentown, PA 18102
Published History—History of Lehigh and Carbon Counties; Alfred Mathews and Austin N. Hungeford; Everts and Richards, Phila., 1884

LUZERNE COUNTY

Society—Wyoming Historical and Genealogical Society, 69 South Franklin St., Wilkes-Barre, PA 18701
Published History—History of Luzerne, Lackawanna, and Wyoming Counties; W. M. Munsell and Co., 1880

LYCOMING COUNTY

Society—Lycoming County Historical Society, 858 West 14th St., Williamsport, PA 17701
Published History—History of Lycoming County; By: John F. Meginness; Brown, Runk and Co., Chicago, 1892

McKEAN COUNTY

Society—McKean County Historical Society, Smethport, PA 16749

Published History—Mckean, The Governors Counties; By Rufus Barrett Stone, 1926

MERCER COUNTY

Society—Mercer County Historical Society, 119 South Pitt St., Mercer, PA 16137

MIFFLIN COUNTY

Society—Mifflin County Historical Society, Lewiston Municipal Bldg., Third and Main Sts., Lewiston, PA 17044

Published History—History of Mifflin County; By: Joseph Cochran, 1879

MONROE COUNTY

Society—Monroe County Historical Society, 205 Analomink St., Stroudsburg, PA 18360

Published History—History of North Hampton, LeHigh, Carbon and Schuylkill Counties; By: I. Daniel Rupp, 1845

MONTGOMERY COUNTY

Society—Historical Society of Montgomery, 1654 DeKalb St., Norristown, PA 19406

Published History—The Montgomery County Story; By: E. Gordon Alderfer, 1951

MONTOUR COUNTY

Society—Montour County Historical Society, 709 Bloom St., Danville, PA 17821

Published History—History of Columbia and Montour Counties; By: J. H. Battle, 1887

NORTH HAMPTON COUNTY

Society—North Hampton County Historical and Genealogical Society, 101 South 4th St., Easton, PA 18042

Published History—History of North Hampton, LeHigh, Monroe, Carbon and Schuylkill Counties; By: I Daniel Rupp, 1845

NORTHUMBERLAND COUNTY

Society—Northumberland County Historical Society, 1019 Susquehanna Ave., Sunbury, PA 17801

Published History—History of Northumberland County; By: Herbert C. Bell; Brown, Runk and Co., Chicago, 1891

PERRY COUNTY

Society—Historical Society of Perry County, Newport, PA 17074

Published History—History of Perry County; By: H. H. Hain, 1922

PHILADELPHIA COUNTY

Society—Historical and Genealogical Society of Pennsylvania, 1300 Locust St., Philadelphia, PA 19107

PIKE COUNTY

Society—Pike County Historical Society, Milford, PA 18337

POTTER COUNTY

Society—Potter County Historical Society, 308 North Main St., Coudersport, PA 16915

SCHUYLKILL COUNTY

Society—Historical Society of Schuylkill County, 14 North 3rd St., Pottsville, PA 17901

Published History—History of Schuylkill County; W. W. Munsell and Co., New York, 1881

SNYDER COUNTY

Society—Snyder County Historical Society, 224 East Main St., Middleburg, PA 17842

Published History—The Story of Snyder County; By: George Frankun; Dunkel Berger, 1948

SOMERSET COUNTY

Society—Historical and Genealogical Society of Somerset County, P.O. Box 533, Somerset, PA 15501

Published History—Early Somerset County; By: Frederic Doyle, 1945

SULLIVAN COUNTY

Society—Sullivan County Historical Society, Laporte, PA 18626

SUSQUEHANNA COUNTY

Society—Susquehanna County Historical Society and Free Library Assoc., Montrose, PA 18801

Published History—Centennial History of Susquehanna County; By: Rhamanthus M. Stocher, Phila., 1887

TIOGA COUNTY

Society—Tioga County Historical Society, Knoxville, PA 16928

UNION COUNTY

Society—Union County Historical Society, 306 St. George St., Lewisburg, PA 17837

VENANGO COUNTY

Society—Venango County Historical Society, P.O. Box 101, Franklin, PA 16323

Published History—History of Venango County; By: J. H. Newton, 1879

WARREN COUNTY

Society—Warren County Historical Society, P.O. Box 427, 210-4th Ave., Warren, PA 16365

WASHINGTON COUNTY

Society—Washington County Historical Society, 49 East Maiden St., Washington, PA 15301

Published History—City of Washington and Washington County; By: Joseph F. McFarland, 1910

WAYNE COUNTY

Society—Wayne County Historical Society, 810 Main St., P.O. Box 446, Honesdale, PA 18431

WESTMORELAND COUNTY

Society—Westmoreland County Historical Society, 221 North Main St., Greensburg, PA 15601

Published History—History of Westmoreland County; By: John N. Boucher, 1906

WYOMING COUNTY

Society—Wyoming County Historical Society, 116 Warren St., Tunkhannock, PA 18657

Published History—History of Luzrene, Lackawanna and Wyoming Counties; W. M. Munsell and Co., 1880

YORK COUNTY

Society—Historical Society of York County, 250 East Market St., York, PA 17403

RHODE ISLAND

BRISTOL COUNTY

Society—Bristol Historical Society, 48 Court St., Bristol, RI 02809

KENT COUNTY

Published History—History of Washington and Kent Counties; By: J. R. Cole; W. W. Preston and Co., New York, 1889

NEWPORT COUNTY

Society—Newport Historical Society, 82 Touro St., Newport, RI 02840

PROVIDENCE COUNTY

Society—Western Rhode Island Civic and Historical Society, 365 Plainfield St., Providence, RI 02909

Society—Rhode Island Historical Society, 52 Powell St., Providence, RI 02906

Published History—History of Providence County; By: Richard M. Bayles; W. W. Preston and Co., New York, 1891

WASHINGTON COUNTY

Published History—History of Washington and Kent Counties; By: J. R. Cole; W. W. Preston and Co., New York, 1889

SOUTH CAROLINA

ANDERSON COUNTY

Society—Anderson County Historical Society, P.O. Box 102, Anderson, SC 29621

BARNWELL COUNTY

Society—Barnwell County Historical Society, Barnwell, SC 29812

BEAUFORT COUNTY

Society—Beaufort County Historical Society, Beaufort, SC 29902

COLLETON COUNTY

Society—Colleton County Historical Society, P.O. Box 325, Walterboro, SC 29488

DARLINGTON COUNTY

Society—Darlington County Historical Society, P.O. Box 206, Darlington, SC 29532

EDGEFIELD COUNTY

Society—Edgefield County Historical Society, 320 Norris St., Edgefield, SC 29829

FAIRFIELD COUNTY

Society—Fairfield County Historical Society, Hudson and Walnut Sts., Winnsboro, SC 29180

GEORGETOWN COUNTY

Society—Georgetown County Historical Society, P.O. Box 314, Georgetown, SC 29440

GREENVILLE COUNTY

Society—Greenville County Historical Society, 420 No. Main St., Greenville, SC 29601

GREENWOOD COUNTY

Society—Greenwood County Historical Society, North Main St., Greenwood, SC 29646

KERSHAW COUNTY

Society—Kershaw County Historical Society, 1709 Fair St., Camden, SC 29020

LANCASTER COUNTY

Society—Lancaster County Historical Society, 601 Marion Sims Dr., Lancaster, SC 29720

LEE COUNTY

Society—Lee County Historical Comm., Main St., Bishopville, SC

LEXINGTON COUNTY

Society—Lexington County Historical Society, 210 West Main St., Lexington, SC 29072

MARION COUNTY

Published History—History of Marion County; W. W. Sellers; R. L. Bryan Co., Columbia, 1902

MARLBORO COUNTY

Society—Marlboro Historical Society, 506 West Main St., Bennettsville, 29512

NEWBERRY COUNTY

Published History—Annals of Newberry County; By: John Belton O'Neall and John Chapman; Newberry, 1892

ORANGEBURG COUNTY

Published History—History of Orangeburg County; By: A. S. Salley; R. Lewis Berry; Orangeburg, 1898

RICHLAND COUNTY

Society—Historic Columbia Foundation, Columbia Museum of Art and Science, 1527 Senate St., Columbia, SC

SUMTER COUNTY
Society—Sumter County Historical Society, 26 So. Magnolia St., Sumter, SC 29150

YORK COUNTY
Society—York County Historical Society, 949 Beverly Dr., Rock Hill, SC 29732

SOUTH DAKOTA

BROOKINGS COUNTY
Society—Brookings County Historical Society, County Courthouse, Brookings, SD 57006

HUGHES COUNTY
Society—South Dakota State Historical Society, Memorial Bldg., Capitol Bldg., Pierre, SD 57501

LAKE COUNTY
Society—Lake County Historical Society, General Beadle State College, Madison, SD 57042

PENNINGTON COUNTY
Society—Minnilusa Pioneer Assoc., 1002 St. Joseph St., Rapid City, SD 57701

SPINK COUNTY
Society—Spink County Historical Society, Frankfort, SD 57440

STANLEY COUNTY
Society—Stanley County Historical Society, Verendrye Museum, Fort Pierre, SD 57532

YANKTON COUNTY
Society—Yankton County Historical Society, P.O. Box 588, Yankton, SD

TENNESSEE

ANDERSON COUNTY
Published History—History of Anderson County; University of Tennessee

BEDFORD COUNTY
Published History—Bedford County; By: H. L. Davidson

BENTON COUNTY
Published History—History of Benton County—to 1900, Memphis

BLEDSOE COUNTY
Published History—Bledsoe County; University of Tennessee; Duggan, Brown and Miser, 1927

BLOUNT COUNTY
Published History—History of Blount County War Trails to Landing Strip—1795-1955; Nashville Historical Comm.

BRADLEY COUNTY
Published History—A History of Bradley County; Post 81 American Legion; John M. Wooten, 1949

CAMPBELL COUNTY
Published History—History of Campbell County; Dr. G. L. Ridenour, Lafayette, 1941

CANNON COUNTY
Published History—History of Woodbury Funeral Home; Woodbury, TN

CARROLL COUNTY
Published History—Early History of Carter County—1760-1861, E. Tenn. Historical Society, Knoxville, 1950

CHESTER COUNTY
Published History—History of Chester County, Tennessee; S. E. Raid, Jackson, 1924

CLAY COUNTY
Published History—Historical Sketeches of Clay County, Tennessee; Wm. Curtis Stone, Sr., Nashville, 1962

COCKE COUNTY
Published History—Over the Misty Blue Hills; Ruth W. Odell, Newport, 1951

COFFEE COUNTY
Published History—History of Coffee County; L. Ewell, Manchester, 1936

CROCKETT COUNTY
Published History—History of Tennessee, Historical and Biographical Sketch of Louderdale, Tipton, Haywood, and Crockett Counties, Nashville, 1887

CUMBERLAND COUNTY
Published History—Cumberland County First 100 Years; Crossville Cent. Comm., 1956

DAVIDSON COUNTY
Society—Tennessee Historical Society, (State Library and Archives), 403-7th Ave. No., Nashville, TN 37219
Published History—History of Davidson County, Biographical Sketches of Prominent Pioneers; Nashville, 1971

DECATUR COUNTY
Published History—A Note on Decatur County; D. Hawkin; Tennessee Folklore Soceity, Bull. Vol. 19, Sept., 1953

De KALB COUNTY
Published History—History of DeKalb County; W. T. Hale, Nashville, 1915

DICKSON COUNTY
Published History—History of Dickson County; Robert E. Corlew, Nashville Historical Comm., 1956

DYER COUNTY
Published History—History of Tennessee, With Sketches of Gibson, Obion, Weakly, Lake and Dyer Counties; Goodspeed Pub. Co., Nashville, 1887

FENTRESS COUNTY
Published History—History of Fentress County; A. R. Hogue, Nashville, 1916, 1920

FRANKLIN COUNTY
Published History—Brief History of Franklin County; T. F. Rhoton, University of Tenn., 1941

GIBSON COUNTY
Published History—History of Tennessee, Sketches of Gibson, Obion, Weakley, Dyer and Lake Counties; Goodspeed Pub. Co., Nashville, 1887

GILES COUNTY
Published History—Giles County Tennessee; J. B. Kellebrew, Nashville, 1871

HAMBLEN COUNTY
Published History—Hemblen County Cent. Cel., "Historic Hamblen" 1870-1970; Movistown, 1970

HAMILTON COUNTY
Published History—History of Hamilton County; Zella Armstrong, Chattanooga, 1931

HARDEMAN COUNTY
Published History—Early Hardeman County; W. W. Clift; M.A. Thesis Peadoby, Nashville, 1930

HARDIN COUNTY
Published History—History of Hardin County; B. G. Brozelton, Nashville, 1885

HAWKINS COUNTY
Published History—Historical Sketches of Hawkins County, Tennessee; James Woods Rogan, Newspaper Clippings, 1959

HAYWOOD COUNTY
Published History—History of Tennessee, Historical and Biographical Sketches of Lauderdale, Tipton, Haywood and Crockett Counties; Goodspeed Pub. Co., Nashville, 1887

HENDERSON COUNTY
Published History—History of Henderson County; N. J. Bolen, Murfreesboro, 1922

HENRY COUNTY
Published History—History of Henry County; E. H. Reynolds, Jacksonville, 1904

HICKMAN COUNTY
Published History—History of Hickman County; W. D. Spence and David Jerome, Nashville, 1900

HOUSTON COUNTY
Published History—History of Houston County Tennessee; (N.P.) Iris McClain, 1966 (B.H.)

HUMPHREYS COUNTY
Published History—History of Humphreys County; Jill K. Garrett, Columbia, 1963

LAKE COUNTY
Published History—History of Tennessee, Sketches of Gibson, Obion, Weakly, Dyer and Lake Counties; Goodspeed Pub. Co., Nashville, 1887

LAUDERDALE COUNTY
Published History—Lauderdale County Tennessee, From Earliest Times; Kate Johnston Peters, Ripley, 1957

LAWRENCE COUNTY
Published History—Brief History of Early Lawrence County; John F. Movison, Jr., 1968

MADISON COUNTY
Published History—Jackson and Madison Counties; A. F. Kuhlman; Jackson, McKaran Arc., 1920

MARION COUNTY
Published History—History of Marion County; Gertrude Bible Link; Mid. Tenn. St. Coll., 1953

MAURY COUNTY
Published History—History of Maury County; Wm. Bruce Turner, Nashville, 1955

McMINN COUNTY
Society—McMinn County Chapter, E. Tennessee Historical Society, Courthouse, Athens, TN 37303

McNAIRY COUNTY
Published History—Rem. of Early Settlement and Early Settlers of McNairy County; M. J. Wright, Washington, DC, 1882

MEIGS COUNTY
Published History—Rhea and Meigs Counties; (N.A.), J. C. Allen, 1908

MONROE COUNTY
Published History—Early Days in Monroe County; Worth S. Ray

MONTGOMERY COUNTY
Published History—History of Montgomery County; Ursula Beach, Nashville 1964

MORGAN COUNTY
Published History—History of Morgan County; Ethel Ott and G. K. Freytag, 1971

OBION COUNTY
Published History—History of Tennessee, Sketches of Gibson, Obion, Weakley, Dyer and Lake Counties; Goodspeed Pub. Co., Nashville, 1887

OVERTON COUNTY
Published History—Overton County Tennessee; A. V. Goodpast, Livingston, 1876

PICKETT COUNTY
Published History—Pickett County Tennessee; Thesis, Vanderbit Univ., C. G. Smith, 1928

POLK COUNTY
Published History—History of Polk County; (N.P.), E. R. Hayes, 1937

PUTNAM COUNTY
Published History—History of Putnam County; W. S. McClain, Cookeville, 1925

RHEA COUNTY
Published History—Rhea and Meigs Counties; (N.P.), J. C. Allen, 1908

ROANE COUNTY
Published History—History of Roane County—1801-70; Emma Wells, Chattanooga, 1927

ROBERTSON COUNTY
Published History—Chronicles of Robertson County; (N.P.), Mrs. Archie Thomas, 1902

RUTHERFORD COUNTY
Published History—History of Rutherford County; (N.P.), E. C. Sims, 1947

SCOTT COUNTY
Published History—Scott County Tennessee; (N.P.), A. P. Foster, 1923

SEVIER COUNTY
Published History—History of Sevier County; J. Hammer, 1876

SHELBY COUNTY
Published History—History of Shelby County; J. R. Williams, Memphis, 1897

SMITH COUNTY
Published History—History of Smith County; (N.P., N.D.), J. W. Bowen

STEWART COUNTY
Published History—History of Stewart County; Iris H. McClain, Columbia, 1965

SULLIVAN COUNTY
Published History—History of Sullivan County; Jay Guy Cisco, Bristol 1909

SUMNER COUNTY
Published History—Historic Sumner County; J. G. Cisco, Nashville, 1909

TIPTON COUNTY
Published History—History of Tennessee, Historical and Biographical Sketch of Lauderdale, Tipton, Haywood, and Crockett Counties; Goodspeed Pub. Co., 1887

TROUSDALE COUNTY
Published History—Trousdale, A Constitutional County; J. C. McMurty, (N.P., N.D.)

WARREN COUNTY
Published History—Early History of Warren County, Tennessee; William Thomas Hale, McMinnville, 1930

WEAKLEY COUNTY
Published History—History of Tennessee, Sketches of Gibson, Obion, Weakley, Dyer and Lake Counties; Goodspeed Pub. Co., Nashville, 1887

WHITE COUNTY
Published History—History of White County; (N.P.), Rev. Monroe Seals, 1935

WILSON COUNTY
Published History—History of Wilson County; Difon Meritt, Lebanon, 1961

TEXAS

ANDERSON COUNTY
Published History—Centennial History of Anderson County; By: Pauline Buck Hohes; Naylor Co., San Antonio, 1936

ARCHER COUNTY
Society—Archer County Historical Society, Courthouse, Main Square, Archer City, TX 76351

BANDERA COUNTY
Published History—Pioneer History of Bandera County; By: J. Marvin Hunter; Hunter's Printing House

BASTROP COUNTY
Society—Bastrop County Historical Society, South Main St., Bastrop, TX 78602

BELL COUNTY
Society—Bell County Historical Society, P.O. Box 536, Baylor Station, Belton, TX 76513

BURLESON COUNTY
Published History—History of Texas, Together With A Biographical History of Williamson, Bastrop, Travis, Lee, and Burleson Counties; Lewis Pub. Co., Chicago, 1893

CAMERON COUNTY
Society—Lower Rio Grande Valley Historical Society, 504 East Tyler St., Harlingen, TX 78550

CORYELL COUNTY
Published History—Memorial and Biographical History of McLennan Falls, Bell, and Coryell Counties; Lewis Pub. Co., Chicago, 1893

CROCKETT COUNTY
Society—Crockett County Historical Society, P.O. Drawer B., Ozona, TX 76943

DALLAS COUNTY
Society—Dallas Historical Society, Hall of State, Fair Park, Dallas, TX 75226
Published History—Memorial and Biographical History of Dallas County; Lewis Pub. Co., Chicago, 1892

ECTOR COUNTY
Society—Permian Historical Society, 622 No. Lee, Odessa, TX 79760

EL PASO COUNTY
Society—El Paso County Historical Society, P.O. Box 28, El Paso, TX 79930

GALVESTON COUNTY
Society—Galveston Historical Foundation, P.O. Box 3296, Galveston, TX 77550

GILLESPIE COUNTY
Society—Gillespie County Historical Society, P.O. Box 765, Fredericksburg, TX 78624

GRAYSON COUNTY
Society—Grayson County Historical Society, 1035 So. Travis St., Sherman, TX 75090

HARRIS COUNTY
Society—Harris County Historical Society, 2305 Claremont Lane, Houston, TX 77019

HARRISON COUNTY
Society—Harrison County Historical Society, Old County Courthouse, Marshall, TX 75670

Jeff Davis COUNTY
Society—Fort Davis Historical Society, P.O. Box 258, Fort Davis, TX 79734

JEFFERSON COUNTY
Society—Texas Gulf Historical Society, 2595 Gladys St., Beaumont, TX 77702

MARION COUNTY
Society—Jefferson Historical Society, 223 West Austin, Jefferson, TX 75657

MIDLAND COUNTY
Society—Midland County Historical Society, 2102 Community Lane, Midland, TX 79701

NAVARRO COUNTY
Society—Navarro County Historical Society, Corsicana Nat'l Bank, Corsicana, TX 75110

PECOS COUNTY
Society—Fort Stockton Historical Society, 1101 North Young St., Fort Stockton, TX 79735

RANDALL COUNTY
Society—Panhandle-Plains Historical Society, P.O. Box 786, West Texas Station, Canyon, TX 79015

SMITH COUNTY
Society—Smith County Historical Society, 624 North Broadway, Tyler, TX 75701

STARR COUNTY
Society—Starr County Historical Society, 801 East Main St., Rio Grande City, TX 78572

TARRANT COUNTY
Society—Tarrant County Historical Society, 4736 Crestline Rd., Fort Worth, TX 76107

WEBB COUNTY
Society—Laredo Historical Society, 1018 Market St., Laredo, TX 78040

UTAH

BOX ELDER COUNTY
Published History—Tullidge's History; By: Edward W. Tullidge; Press of Juvenile Instructor, Salt Lake City, UT, 1889

CACHE COUNTY
Society—Cache Valley Chapter, Utah State Historical Society, Utat State University, Logan, UT 84321
Published History—Utah Gazetteer and Directory of Logan, Ogden, Provo, and S.L.C.; By: Robert W. Sloan; Herald Printing and Pub. Co., S.L.C., UT, 1884

DAVIS COUNTY
Published History—Tullidge's History; By: Edward W. Tullidge; Press of Juvenile Instructor, Salt Lake City, UT, 1889

EMERY COUNTY
Published History—History of Sanpete and Emery Counties; By: W. H. Lever, Ogden, UT, 1898

IRON COUNTY
Society—Iron County Historical Society, Special Collections, College of Southern Utah Library, Cedar City, UT 84720

MORGAN COUNTY
Published History—Tullidge's Histories; By: Edward W. Tullidge; Press of Juvenile Instructor, Salt Lake City, 1889

PIUTE COUNTY
Published History—Tullidge's Histories; By: Edward W. Tullidge; Press of Juvenile Instructor, Salt Lake City, 1889

RICH COUNTY
Published History—Tullidge's Histories; By: Edward W. Tullidge; Press of Juvenile Instructor, Salt Lake City, 1889

SALT LAKE COUNTY
Society—Salt Lake Valley Chapter, Utah State Historical Society, 300 Rio Grande, Salt Lake City, UT 84101

SEVIER COUNTY
Society—Sevier Valley Chapter, Utah State Historical Society, Richfield, UT 84701

UTAH COUNTY
Society—Utah Valley Chapter, Utah State Historical Society, Department of History, Brigham Young University, Provo, UT 84601

WEBER COUNTY
Society—Weber County Chapter, Utah State Historical Society, 1456-24th St., Ogden, UT 84401

VERMONT

ADDISON COUNTY
Society—Sheldon Art Museum, Archaeological and Historical Society, 1 Park St., Middlebury, VT
Published History—Histori of Addison County; By: H. P. Smith; D. Mason and Co., Syracuse, 1886

CALEDONIA COUNTY
Published History—Gazzetteer of Caledonia and Essex Counties; By: Hamilton Child; The Syracuse Jounral Co., 1887

CHITTENDEN COUNTY
Society—Chittenden County Historical Society, University of Vermont, Burlington, VT 05401
Published History—History of Chittenden Counties; By: W. S. Rann; D. Mason and Co., Syracuse, 1886

ESSEX COUNTY
Published History—Gazetteer of Caledonia and Essex Counties; By: Hamilton Child, Syracuse, 1887

FRANKLIN COUNTY
Society—St. Albans Historical Society, St. Albans, VT 05478
Published History—History of Franklin and Grand Isle Counties; By: Lewis C. Alorich; D. Mason and Co., 1891

GRAND ISLE COUNTY
Society—Grand Isle County Historical Society, Grand Isle, VT 05458
Published History—History of Franklin and Grand Isle Counties; By: Lewis C. Alorich; D. Mason and Co., 1891

ORANGE COUNTY
Society—Chelsea Historical Society, Chelsea, VT 05038
Published History—Gazetteer of Orange County; By: Hamilton Child; Syracuse Journal Co., 1888

ORLEANS COUNTY
Society—Orleans County Historical Society, Old Stone House, Orleans, VT 05860
Published History—Successful Vermonters; By: William H. Jeffrey; The Hist. Pub. Co., East Burk, 1904

RUTLAND COUNTY
Published History—History of Rutland County; By: H. P. Smith and W. S. Rann; D. Mason and Co., Syracuse, 1886

WASHINGTON COUNTY
Published History—Gazetteer of Washington County; By: Hamilton Child; Syracuse Co., Syracuse, 05641

WINDHAM COUNTY
Society—Historical Society of Windham County, Newfane, VT 05345

WINDSOR COUNTY
Society—Woodstock Historical Society, 26 Elm St., Woodstock, VT 05091
Published History—History of Windsor County; By: Lewis Cass Aldrich and Frank R. Holmes; D. Mason and Co., Syracuse, 1891

VIRGINIA

ALLEGHANY COUNTY
Society—Alleghany County Historical Society, Covington, VA 24426

ARLINGTON COUNTY
Society—Arlington Historical Society, 1318-24th St. So., Arlington, VA 22202

CAROLINE COUNTY
Published History—History of Caroline County; By: Marshall Wingfield: Trevet Christian and Co., Richmond, 1924

CULPEPER COUNTY
Society—Culpeper Historical Society, P.O. Box 790, Culpeper, VA 22701

FREDERICK COUNTY
Society—Winchester-Frederick County Historical Society, Winchester, VA 22601

GOOCHLAND COUNTY
Society—Goochland County Historical Society, c/o Secretary, County Courthouse, Goochland, VA 23063

HENRICO COUNTY
Society—Virginia Historical Society, 428 No. Blvd., Richmond, VA 23221

KING AND QUEEN COUNTY
Society—King and Queen County Historical Society, King and Queen Courthouse, King and Queen, VA 23085
Published History—King and Queen County History; By: Rev. Alfred Bagby; Neale Pub. Co., Washington, 1908

LOUISA COUNTY
Society—Louisa County Historical Society, P.O. Box 111, Louisa, VA 23093
Published History—History of Louisa County; By: Malcolm H. Harris; Peitz Press, Richmond, 1936

MATHEWS COUNTY
Society—Mathews County Historical Society Inc., P.O. Box 426, Mathews, VA 23109

PATRICK COUNTY
Published History—History of Patrick and Henry Counties; By: Virginia G. and Lewis G. Pedigo; Stone Print and Manufact. Co., Roanoke, 1933

PRINCE WILLIAM COUNTY
Society—Prince William County Historical Society, 405 No. W. St., Manassas, VA 22110

RAPPAHANNOCK
Society—Rappahannock County Historical Society, Aven Hall, Washington, VA 22747

ROCKBRIGDE COUNTY
Society—Rockbridge County Historical Society, 6 Randolph St., Lexington, VA 24450
Published History—History of Rockbridge County; By: Oren F. Morton; McClure Co., Staunton, 1920

ROCKINGHAM COUNTY
Society—Rockingham County Historical Society, 345 So. Main St., Harrisonburg, VA 22801
Published History—History of Rockingham County; By: John W. Wayland; Ruebush-Elkins Co., Dayton, 1912

SHANANDOAH COUNTY
Published History—History of Shanandoah County; By: John W. Wayland; Shanandoah, Pub. Co., Strasburg, 1927

SMYTH COUNTY
Society—Smyth County Historical Society, 230 No. Church St., Marion, VA 24354

SOUTHAMPTON COUNTY
Society—Southampton County Historical Society, Courtland, VA 23827

SPOTSYLVANIA COUNTY
Society—Spotsylvania Historical Assoc., P.O. Box 64, Spotsylvania, VA 22534

TAZEWELL COUNTY
Published History—History of Tazewell County; By: William C. Pendleton; W. C. Hill Pub. Co., Richmond, 1920

WASHINGTON COUNTY
Society—Historical Society of Washington County Virginia, Washington County Courthouse, Abingdon, VA 24210

WASHINGTON

ADAMS COUNTY
Society—Adams County Historical Society, G. Hayes Phillips Bld., Lind, WA 99341

CHELAN COUNTY
Society—Chelan County Historical Society, Willis Carey History Museum, Cashmere, WA 98815

CLALLAM COUNTY
Society—Clallam County Historical Society, Pioneer Memorial Museum, Port Angeles, WA 98362

CLARK COUNTY
Society—Fort Vancouver Historical Society, P.O. Box 1834, Vancouver, WA 98663

COWLITZ COUNTY
Society—Cowlitz County Historical Society, 511-25th Ave., Longview, WA 98620

FRANKLIN COUNTY
Society—Franklin County Historical Society, P.O. Box 1033, Pasco, WA 99301

GRANT COUNTY
Society—Grant County Historical Society, 529 D St. S.W., Ephrata, WA 98823

GRAYS HARBOR COUNTY
Society—Grays Harbor County Historical Society, 308 West 6th St., Aberdeen, WA 98520

ISLAND COUNTY
Society—Island County Historical Society, Coupeville, WA 98239

JEFFESON COUNTY
Society—Jefferson County Historical Society, City Hall, Port Townsend, WA 98368

KING COUNTY
Society—Seattle Historical Society, 2161 East Hamlin, Seattle, WA 98102

KITSAP COUNTY
Society—Kitsap County Historical Society, 837-4th St., Bremerton, WA 98310

KITTITAS COUNTY
Society—Kittitas County Historical Society, Olnstead Place, Rt. 5, Ellensburg, WA 98925

KLICKITAT COUNTY
Society—Klickitat County Historical Society, 127 W. Broadway, Goldendale, WA 98620

LEWIS COUNTY
Society—Lewis County Historical Society and Museum, 1070 Washington, Chechalis, WA 98532

MASON COUNTY
Society—Mason County Historical Society, Shelton, WA 98594

OKANOGAN COUNTY
Society—Okanogan County Historical Society, P.O. Box 553, Omak, WA 98841

PACIFIC COUNTY
Society—Pacific County Historical Society, P.O. Box 384, Raymond, WA 98577

PIERCE COUNTY
Society—Washington State Historical Society, 215 N. Stadium Way, Tacoma, WA 98403

SKAGIT COUNTY
Society—Skagit County Historical Society, P.O. Box 424, Mount Vernon, WA 98273

SKAMANIA COUNTY
Society—Skamania County Historical Society, Rt. 1, Box 46, Stevenson, WA 98646

SNOHOMISH COUNTY
Society—Snohomish County Historical Assoc., Bryan Park, Everett, WA 98201

SPOKANE COUNTY
Society—Eastern Washington State Historical Society, 216 West 1st Ave., Spokane, WA 99204

STEVENS COUNTY
Society—Stevens County Historical Assoc., North 137 Wynne St., Colville, WA 99114

THURSTON COUNTY
Society—State Capitol Historical Assoc., 211 West 21st Ave., Olympia, WA 98501

WAHKIAKUM COUNTY
Society—Wahkiakum County Historical Society, P.O. Box 236, Cathlamet, WA 98612

WALLA WALLA COUNTY
Society—Walla Walla Valley Pioneer and Historical Society, P.O. Box 1616, Walla Walla, WA 99362

WHATCOM COUNTY
Society—Whatcom County Historical Society, City Hall, Bellingham, WA 98225

YAKIMA COUNTY
Society—Yakima Valley Museum and Historical Society, 2105 Tieton Drive, Yakima, WA 98902

WEST VIRGINIA

BARBOUR COUNTY
Society—Barbour County Historical Society, Philippi, WV 26416

BERKELEY COUNTY
Society—Berkeley County Historical Society, 102 West King St., Martinsburg, WV 25401
Published History—History of Berkeley County; By: Willis F. Evans, 1928

BROOKE COUNTY
Society—Brooke County Historical Society, 1200 Pleasant Ave., Wellsburg, WV 26070
Published History—Northern West Virginia Panhandle, Ohio, Marshall and Hancock Counties; By: Peter Boyd; Historical Pub. Co., Indianapolis, 1927

CABEL COUNTY
Published History—Annals and Families of Cabel County; By: George Seldon Wallace; Garret and Massie Pub., Richmond, 1935

FAYETTE COUNTY
Society—Fayette County Historical Society, P.O. Box 828, Oakhill, WV 25901

GILMER COUNTY
Society—Gilmer County Historical Society, Glenville, WV 26351

GREENBRIER COUNTY
Society—Greenbrier Historical Society, Lewisburg, WV 24901

HAMPSHIRE COUNTY
Published History—History of Hampshire County; Hu Maxwell and H. L. Swisher; A. Brown, B. Dughner Printer, Morgantown, 1897

HANCOCK COUNTY
Society—Hancock County Historical Society, of West Virginia, 102 Sedgewick St., New Cumberland, WV 26047

HARRISON COUNTY
Society—Harrison County Historical Society, 300 St. Clair St., Clarksburg, WV 26301

JACKSON COUNTY
Published History—History of Upper Ohio Valley; Brant and Fuller, Madison, 1891

JEFFERSON COUNTY
Society—Jefferson County Historical Society, South George St., Charlestown, WV 25414
Published History—History of Upper Ohio Valley; Brant and Fuller, Madison, 1891

KANAWHA COUNTY
Society—Kanawha County Historical Society, 408-13th St., Dunbar, WV 25064
Published History—History of the Great Kanawha Valley; Brant, Fuller and Co., Madison, 1891

MARION COUNTY
Society—Marion County Historical Society, 319 Monroe St., Fairmont, WV 26555

MARSHALL COUNTY
Published History—Northern West Virginia Panhandle, Ohio, Marshall, Brooke and Hancock Counties; By: Peter Boyd; Historical Pub. Co., Indianapolis, 1927

MASON COUNTY
Society—Mason County Historical Society, Southside, WV 25187
Published History—History of the Great Kanawha Valley: Brant, Fuller and Co., Madison, 1891

MINGO COUNTY
Society—Mingo County Historical Society, Elm St., Kermit, WV 25674

MONONGALIA COUNTY
Published History—History of Mongahela County; By: Samuel T. Wiley; Preston Pub. Co., Kingwood, 1883

MONROE COUNTY
Society—Monroe County Historical Society, Union, WV 24983
Published History—History of Monroe County; By: Orem F. Morton; McClure Pub. Co., Stanton, 1916

OHIO COUNTY
Society—Wheeling Area Historical Society, Wheeling Ohio County Library, Wheeling, WV 26003

PENDLETON COUNTY
Published History—History of Pendleton County; Orem F. Martin Pub., Franklin 1910

PLEASANTS COUNTY
Published History—History of Pleasants County; By: Robert L. Pemberton; Oracle Press, St. Marys 1929

POCAHONTAS COUNTY
Society—Pocahontas County Historical Society, P.O. Box 51, Marlinton, WV 24954
Published History—Historical Sketches of Pocahontas County; By: William T. Price; Price Bro's. Pub., Marlington, 1901

RANDOLPH COUNTY
Society—Randolph County Historical Society, P.O. Box 1164, Elkins, WV 26241
Published History—History of Randolph County; By: Hu Maxwell; Acme Pub. Co., Morgantown, 1898

RITCHIE COUNTY
Published History—History of Ritchie County; By: Minnie Kendall Lowther; Wheeling News Litho Co., Wheeling 1911

ROANE COUNTY
Published History—History of Roane County; By: William H. Bishop, Spencer, 1927

Summers COUNTY
Published History—History of Summers County; By: James H. Miller, Hinton, 1908

TAYLOR COUNTY
Society—Taylor County Historical Society, Grafton, WV 26354

TUCKER COUNTY
Published History—History of Tucker County; By Hu Maxwell; Preston Pub. Co., Kingwood, 1884

TYLER COUNTY
Published History—History of Upper Ohio Valley; By: Brant and Fuller, Madison, 1891

UPSHUR COUNTY
Society—Upshur County Historical Society, 35 Hart Ave., Buckhannon, WV
Published History—History of Upshur County; By: W. B. Cutright, 1907

WETZEL COUNTY
Published History—History of Upper Ohio Valley; Brant and Fuller, Madison 1891

WOOD COUNTY
Society—West Augusta Historical and Genealogical Society, 498 Reed St., Parkersburg, WV 26102

WISCONSIN

ADAMS COUNTY
Society—Friendship Rural School Historical Society, Logansville, WI

BARRON COUNTY
Society—Barron Historical Society, 231 West LaSalle Ave., Barron, WI 54812
Published History—History of Barron County; By: Gorden S. Newton and Franklin Curtiss; H. C. Cooper, Jr. and Co., Minneapolis, 1922

BROWN COUNTY
Society—Brown County Historical Society, South Monroe Ave., Greenbay, WI 54301
Published History—History of Brown County, Past and Present; S J. Clark Pub. Co., Chicago, 1913

BUFFALO COUNTY
Published History—History of Buffalo County; By: L. Kessinger, Alma, 1888

BURNETT COUNTY
Society—Burnett County Historical Society, Webster, WI 54893

CALUMET COUNTY
Society—Calumet County Historical Society, P.O. Box 204, Chilton, WI 53014

CLARK COUNTY
Society—Clark County Historical Society, Merrillan, WI 54754
Published History—Biographical History of Clark and Jackson Counties; Lewis Pub. Co., Chicago, 1891

COLUMBIA COUNTY
Published History—History of Columbia County; Western Hist. Co., Chicago, 1880

CRAWFORD COUNTY
Society—Crawford County Historical Society, Prairie Du Chien, WI 53821
Published History—History of Crawford and Richland Counties, Union Pub. Co., Springfield, 1884

DANE COUNTY
Society State Historical Society of Wisconsin; 816 State St., Madison, WI 53706

DODGE COUNTY
Society—Dodge County Historical Society, 127 So. Springs St., Beaver Dam, WI 53915
Published History—History of Dodge County; Western Hist. Co., Chicago, 1880

DOOR COUNTY
Society—Door County Historical Society, 110 N. 4th Ave., Sturgeon Bay, WI 54238
Published History—History of Door County; By: Charles J. Matin; Expositor Job Printer, Sturgeon Bay, 1881

DOUGLAS COUNTY
Society—Douglas County Historical Society, 906 East 2nd St., Superior, WI 54880

DUNN COUNTY
Society—Dunn County Historical Society, 1020-9th St., Menomonie, WI 54751

FLORENCE COUNTY
Published History—Commemorative Biographical Record of Western Shore of Greenbay; J. H. Beers and Co., Chicago, 1896

FOND DU LAC COUNTY
Society—Fond du Lac County Historical Society, P.O. Box 131, Fond du Lac, WI 54935

FOREST COUNTY
Society—Forest County Historical Society, 204 N. Prospect, Crandon, WI 54520

GREEN COUNTY
Published History—History of Green County; By: Helen M. Bingham; Burdick and Armitage, Milwaukee, 1877

IOWA COUNTY
Published History—Commemorative Briographical Record of Rock, Green, Grant, Iowa, and Lafayette Counties; J. H. Beers and Co., Chicago, 1901

IRON COUNTY
Society—Iron County Historical Society, Montreal, WI 54550

JACKSON COUNTY
Society—Jackson County Historical Society, Black River Falls, WI 54615
Published History—Biographical History of Clark and Jackson Counties; Lewis Pub. Co., Chicago, 1891

JEFFERSON COUNTY
Society—Lake Mills-Aztalan Historical Society, Jefferson, WI 53549

JUNEAU COUNTY
Society—Juneau County Historical Society, 211 No. Union St., Mauston, WI 53948
Published History—Biographical History of LaCrosse, Monroe and Juneau Counties; Lewis Pub. Co., Chicago, 1892

KENOSHA COUNTY
Society—Kenosha County Historical Society, 527-74th Ave., Kenosha, WI 53140
Published History—Portriat and Biographical Album of Racine and Kenosha Counties; By: Frank H. Lyman; S. J. Clark Pub. Co., Chicago, 1916

La CROSSE COUNTY
Society—LaCrosse County Historical Society, 429 N. 7th St., LaCrosse, WI 54601

LAGLADE COUNTY
Society—Laglade County Historical Society, 1418 Clermont St., Antigo, WI 54409

LINCOLN COUNTY
Society—Lincoln County Historical Society, 1204-6th St., Merrill, WI 54452

MANITOWOC COUNTY
Society—Manitowoc County Historical Society, 1115 North 18th St., Manitowoc, WI 54220

MARATHON COUNTY
Society—Marathon County Historical Society, 403 McIndoe St., Wausau, WI 54401

MARINETTE COUNTY
Society—Marinette County Historical Society, P.O. box 262, Marinette, WI 54143

OCONTO COUNTY
Society—Oconto County Historical Society, 917 Park Ave., Oconto, WI 54153

OUTAGAMIE COUNTY
Society—Outagamie County Historical Society, 116 East Franklin, Appleton, WI 54912

OZAUKEE COUNTY
Society—Ozaukee County Historical Society, P.O. Box 201, Cedarburg, WI 53012

PIERCE COUNTY
Society—Pierce County Historical Society, Chalmer Davee Library, Wisconsin State University, River Falls, WI 54022

POLK COUNTY
Society—Polk County Historical Society, Balsam Lake, WI 54810

PORTAGE COUNTY
Society—Portage County Historical Society, Stevens Point, WI 54481

PRICE COUNTY
Society—Price County Historical Society, 556-4th Ave. So., Park Falls, WI 54022

RACINE COUNTY
Society—Racine County Historical Society, 701 So. Main St., Racine, WI 53403

ROCK COUNTY
Society—Rock County Historical Society, P.O. Box 896, Janesville, WI 53545

RUSK COUNTY
Society—Rusk County Historical Society, P.O. Box 391, Ladysmith, WI 54848

ST. CROIX COUNTY
Society—St. Croix County Historical Society, 1004-3rd St., Hudsen, WI 54016

SAUK COUNTY
Society—Sauk County Historical Society, 908 Ash St., Baraboo, WI 53913

SHAWANO COUNTY
Society—Shawano County Historical Society, 1003 South Main St., Shawano, WI 54166

SHEBOYGAN COUNTY
Society—Sheboygan County Historical Society, 3110 Erie Ave., Sheboygan, WI 53081

TAYLOR COUNTY
Society—Taylor County Historical Society, Medford, WI 54451

WALWORTH COUNTY
Society—Walworth County Historical Society, 9 East Rockwell St., Elkhorn, WI 53121

WASHINGTON COUNTY
Society—Washington County Historical Society, 815 So. 7th Ave., West Bend, WI 53098

WAUKESHA COUNTY
Society—Waukesha County Historical Society, 916 North East Ave., Waukesha, WI 53186

WAUPACA COUNTY
Society—Waupaca Historical Society, Hutchinson House, South Park, Waupaca, WI 54981

WAUSHARA COUNTY
Society—Waushara County Historical Society, Wautoma, WI 54982

WINNEBAGO COUNTY
Society—Winnebago County Historical and Archeological Society, 833 Prospect Ave., Oshkosh, WI 54901

WYOMING

BIG HORN COUNTY
Society—Big Horn County Historical Society, P.O. Box 308, Basin, WY 82410

CAMPBELL COUNTY
Society—Campbell Historical Society, Gillette, WY 82716

CARBON COUNTY
Society—Carbon County Historical Chapter, Wyoming State Historical Society, Rawlins, WY 82301

CROOK COUNTY
Society—Crook County Historical Society, Sundance, WY 82729

FREMONT COUNTY
Society—Fremont County Historical Chapter, Wyoming State Historical Society, 123 West Fremont Ave., Riverton, WY 82501

GOSHEN COUNTY
Society—Goshen County Historical Society, Torrington, WY 82240

UNITED STATES

Alabama

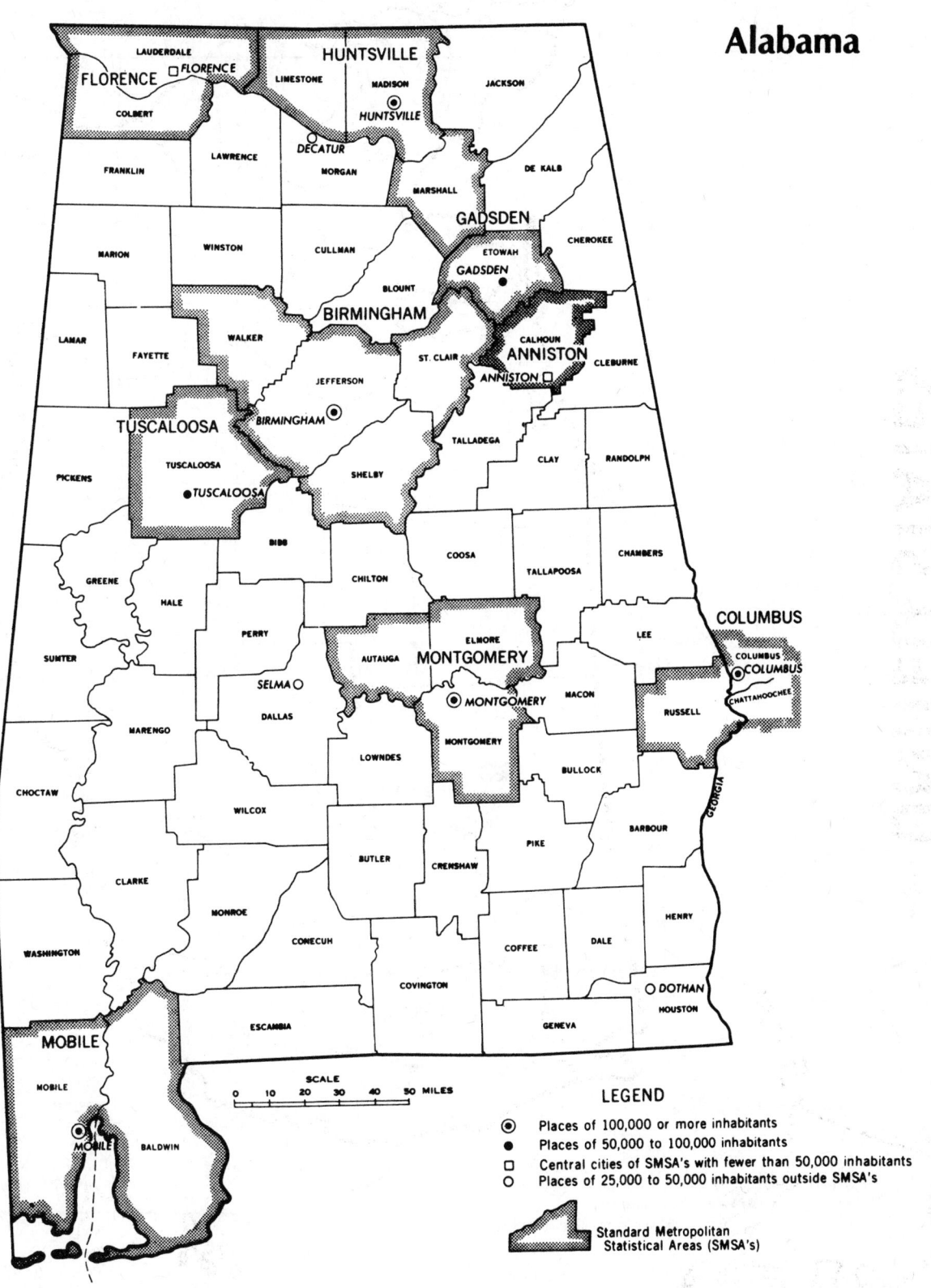

LEGEND

- ⊙ Places of 100,000 or more inhabitants
- ● Places of 50,000 to 100,000 inhabitants
- □ Central cities of SMSA's with fewer than 50,000 inhabitants
- ○ Places of 25,000 to 50,000 inhabitants outside SMSA's

Standard Metropolitan Statistical Areas (SMSA's)

SCALE
0 10 20 30 40 50 MILES

U.S. DEPARTMENT OF COMMERCE

BUREAU OF THE CENSUS

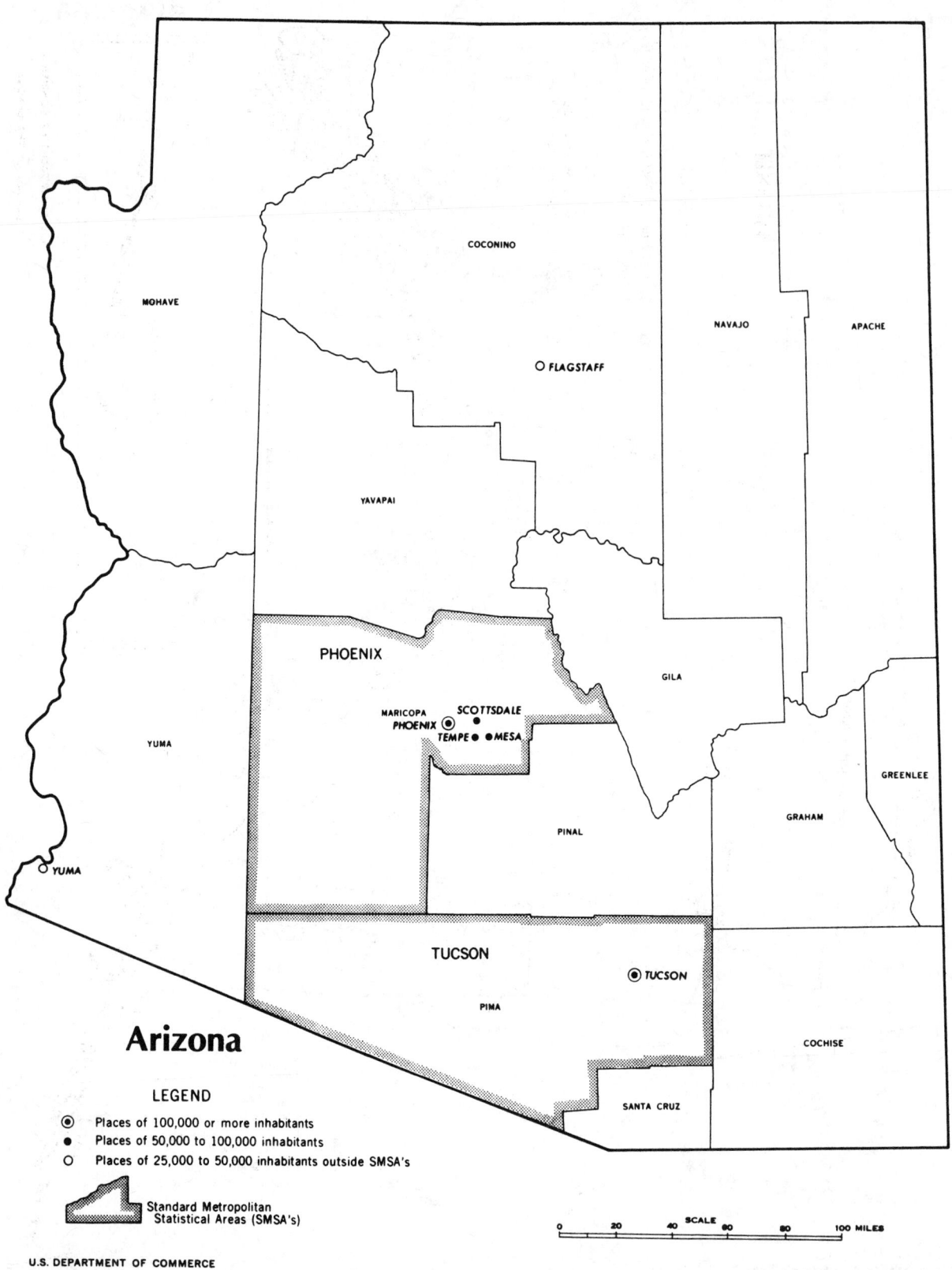

Arizona

LEGEND

- ◉ Places of 100,000 or more inhabitants
- ● Places of 50,000 to 100,000 inhabitants
- ○ Places of 25,000 to 50,000 inhabitants outside SMSA's

Standard Metropolitan Statistical Areas (SMSA's)

SCALE
0   20   40   60   80   100 MILES

U.S. DEPARTMENT OF COMMERCE

BUREAU OF THE CENSUS

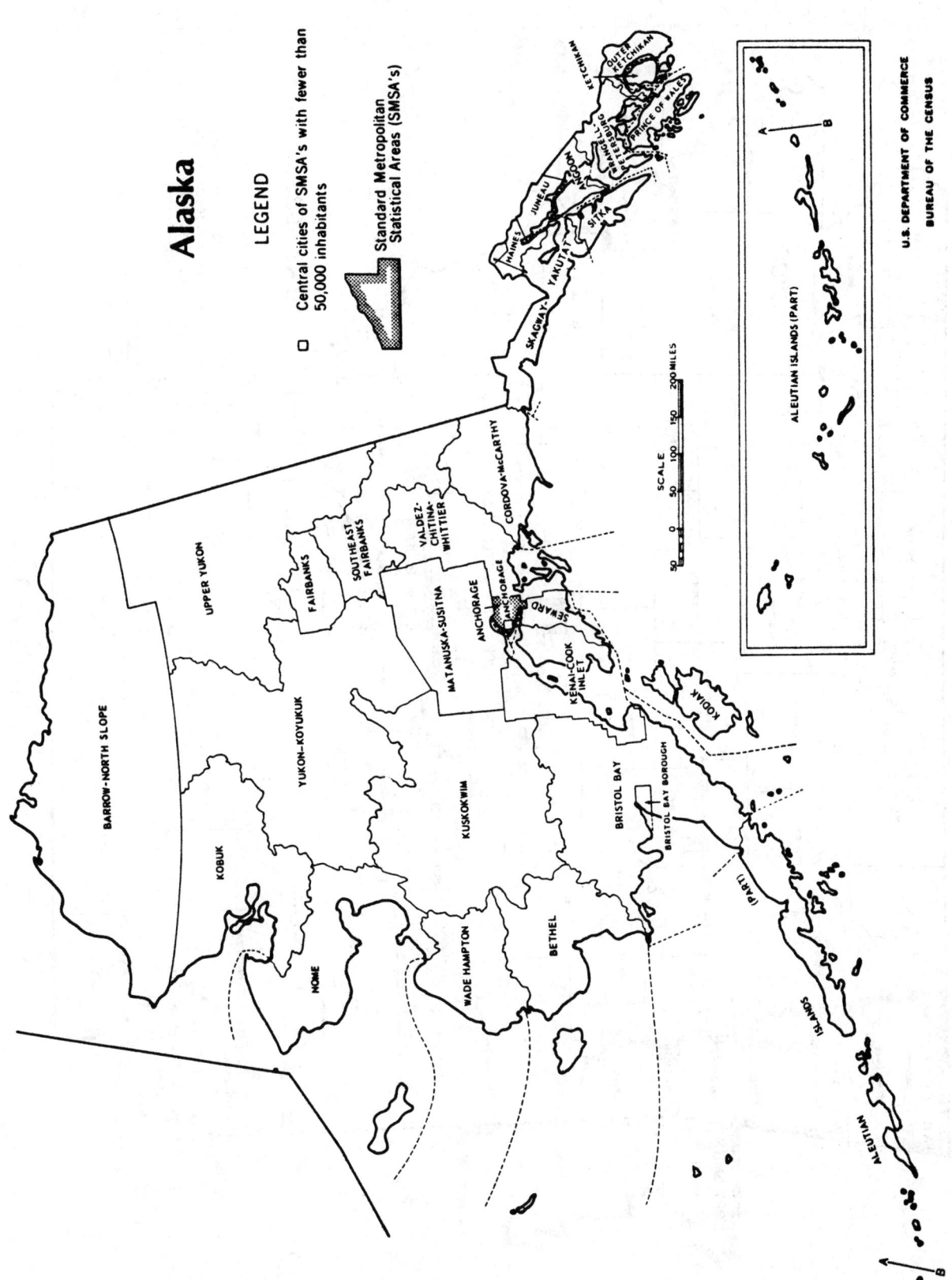

Alaska

LEGEND

□ Central cities of SMSA's with fewer than 50,000 inhabitants

Standard Metropolitan Statistical Areas (SMSA's)

SCALE
50 0 50 100 150 200 MILES

U.S. DEPARTMENT OF COMMERCE
BUREAU OF THE CENSUS

ALEUTIAN ISLANDS (PART)

BARROW-NORTH SLOPE

KOBUK

UPPER YUKON

FAIRBANKS

SOUTHEAST FAIRBANKS

VALDEZ-CHITINA-WHITTIER

CORDOVA-McCARTHY

YUKON-KOYUKUK

MATANUSKA-SUSITNA

ANCHORAGE

SEWARD

KENAI-COOK INLET

KODIAK

NOME

KUSKOKWIM

WADE HAMPTON

BETHEL

BRISTOL BAY

BRISTOL BAY BOROUGH

ALEUTIAN ISLANDS (PART)

SKAGWAY-YAKUTAT

HAINES

JUNEAU

SITKA

ANGOON

WRANGELL-PETERSBURG

PRINCE OF WALES

OUTER KETCHIKAN

KETCHIKAN

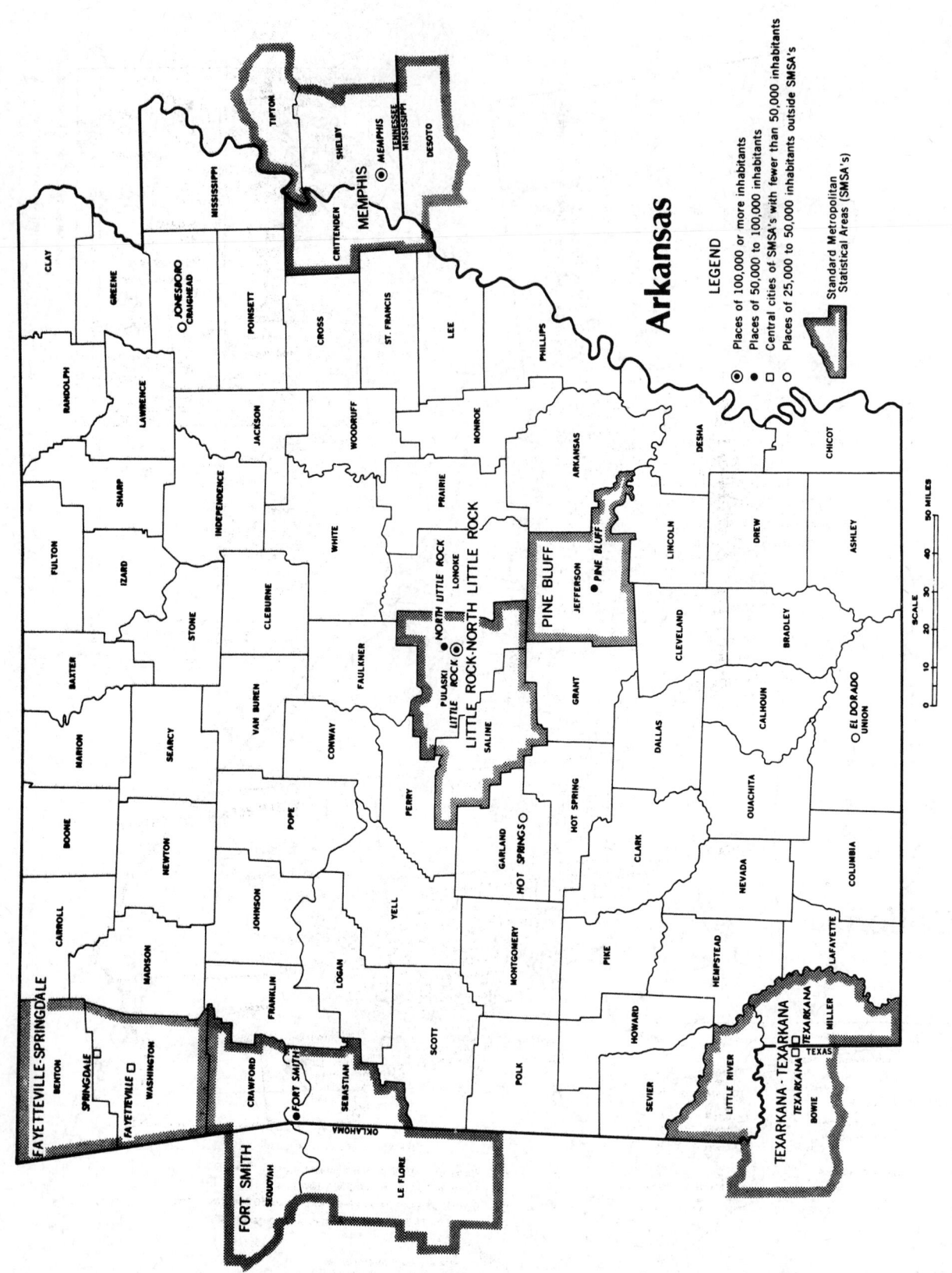

Arkansas

LEGEND

- ⊙ Places of 100,000 or more inhabitants
- ● Places of 50,000 to 100,000 inhabitants
- □ Central cities of SMSA's with fewer than 50,000 inhabitants
- ○ Places of 25,000 to 50,000 inhabitants outside SMSA's

Standard Metropolitan
Statistical Areas (SMSA's)

California

LEGEND

◉ Places of 100,000 or more inhabitants

● Places of 50,000 to 100,000 inhabitants

□ Central cities of SMSA's with fewer than 50,000 inhabitants

○ Places of 25,000 to 50,000 inhabitants outside SMSA's

Standard Metropolitan Statistical Areas (SMSA's)

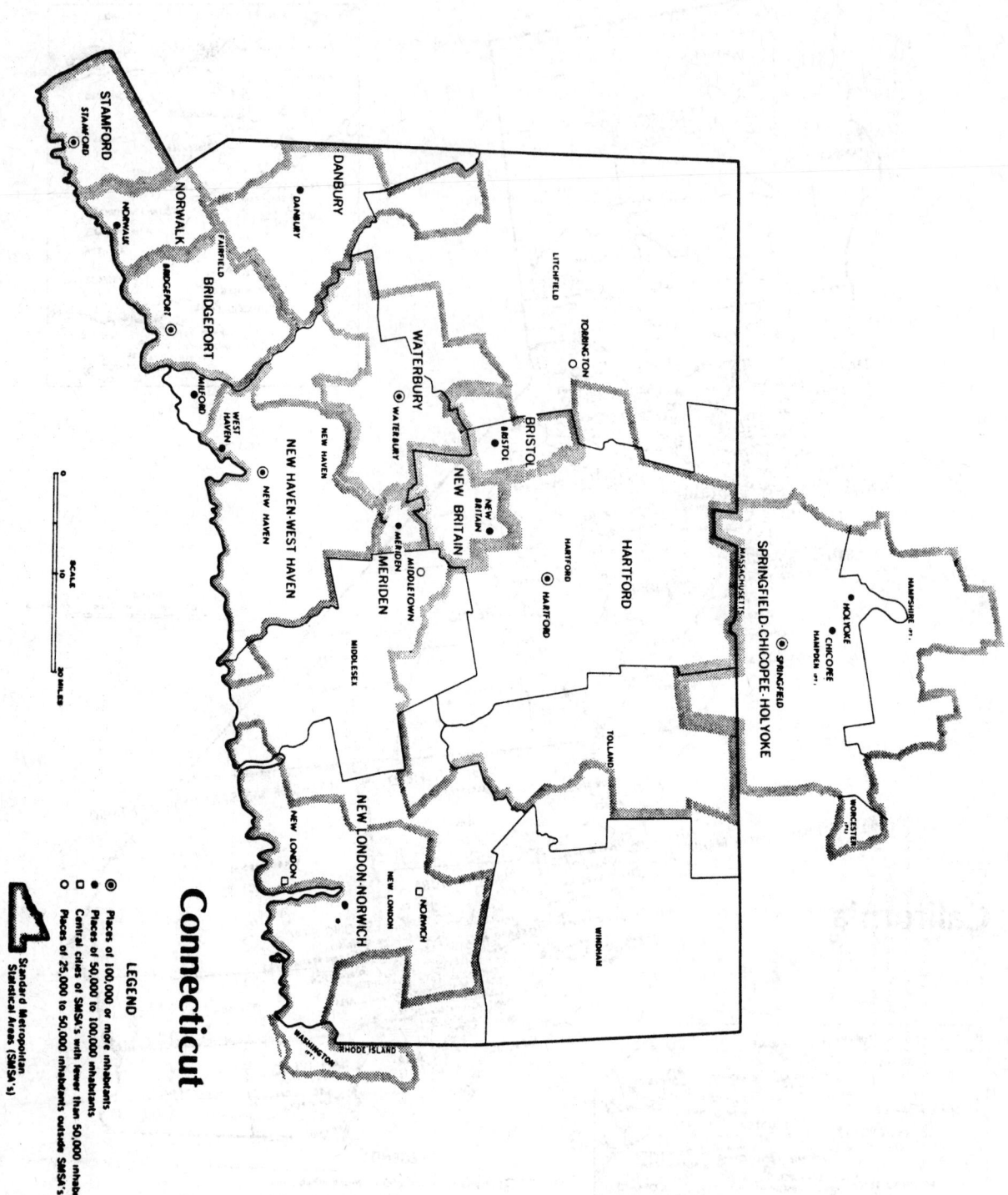

Connecticut

LEGEND

- ◉ Places of 100,000 or more inhabitants
- ● Places of 50,000 to 100,000 inhabitants
- ◻ Central cities of SMSA's with fewer than 50,000 inhabitants
- ○ Places of 25,000 to 50,000 inhabitants outside SMSA's

Standard Metropolitan
Statistical Areas (SMSA's)

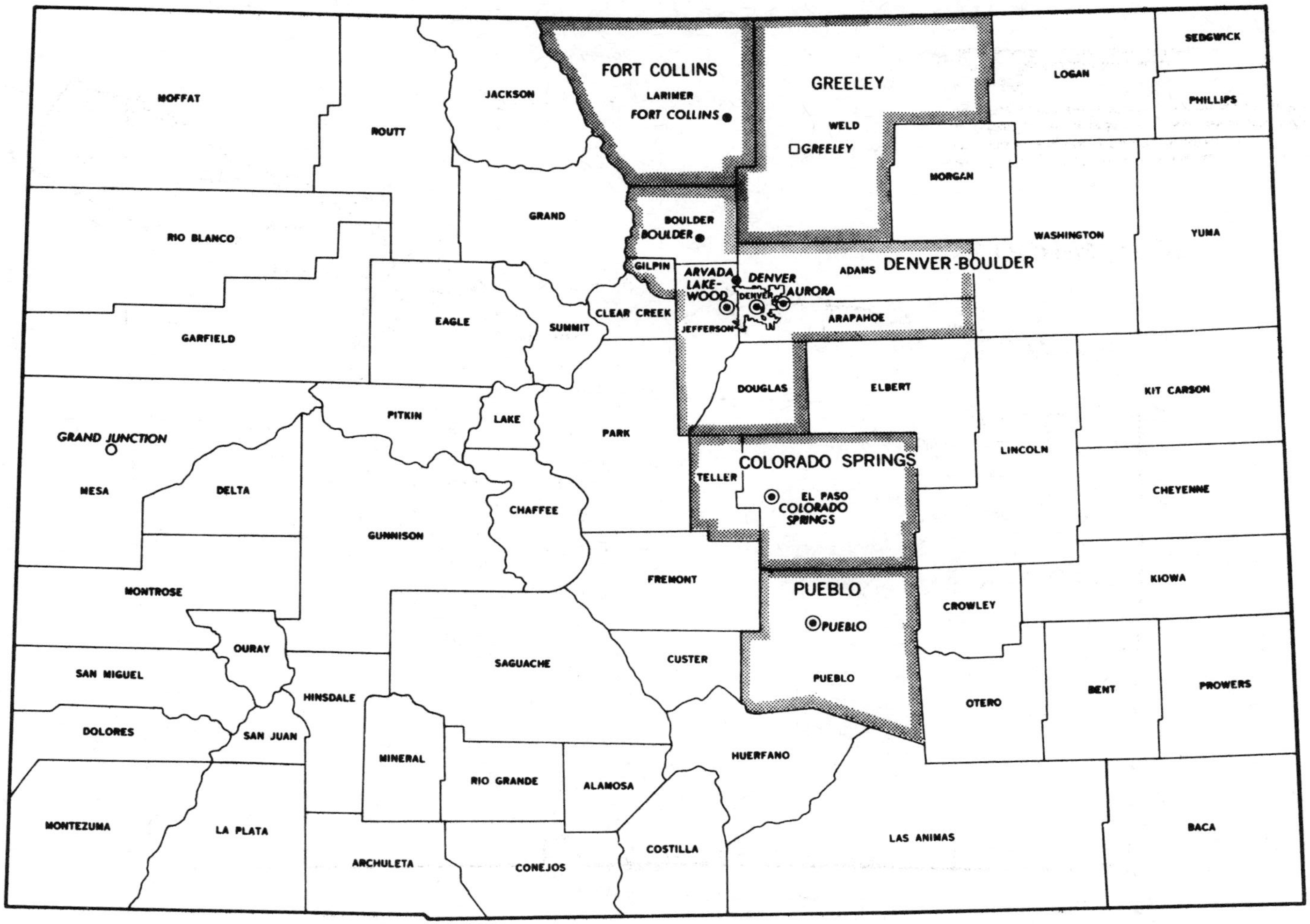

SCALE
0 10 20 30 40 50 MILES

Colorado

LEGEND

- ◉ Places of 100,000 or more inhabitants
- ● Places of 50,000 to 100,000 inhabitants
- □ SMSA central cities with fewer than 50,000 inhabitants
- ○ Places of 25,000 to 50,000 inhabitants outside SMSA's
- Standard Metropolitan Statistical Areas (SMSA's)

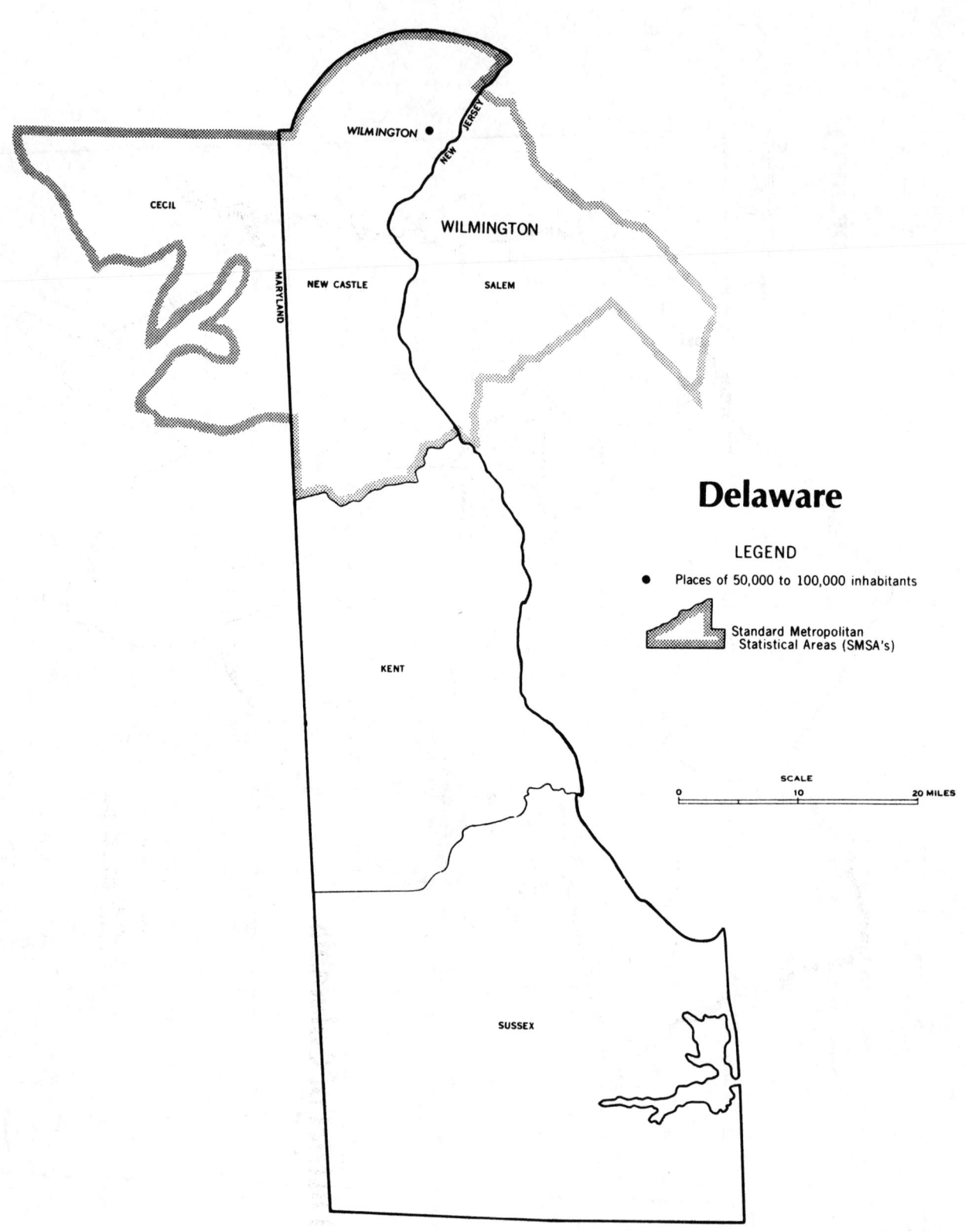

Delaware

LEGEND

● Places of 50,000 to 100,000 inhabitants

Standard Metropolitan
Statistical Areas (SMSA's)

SCALE

0   10   20 MILES

CECIL

WILMINGTON ●

NEW JERSEY

MARYLAND

WILMINGTON

NEW CASTLE

SALEM

KENT

SUSSEX

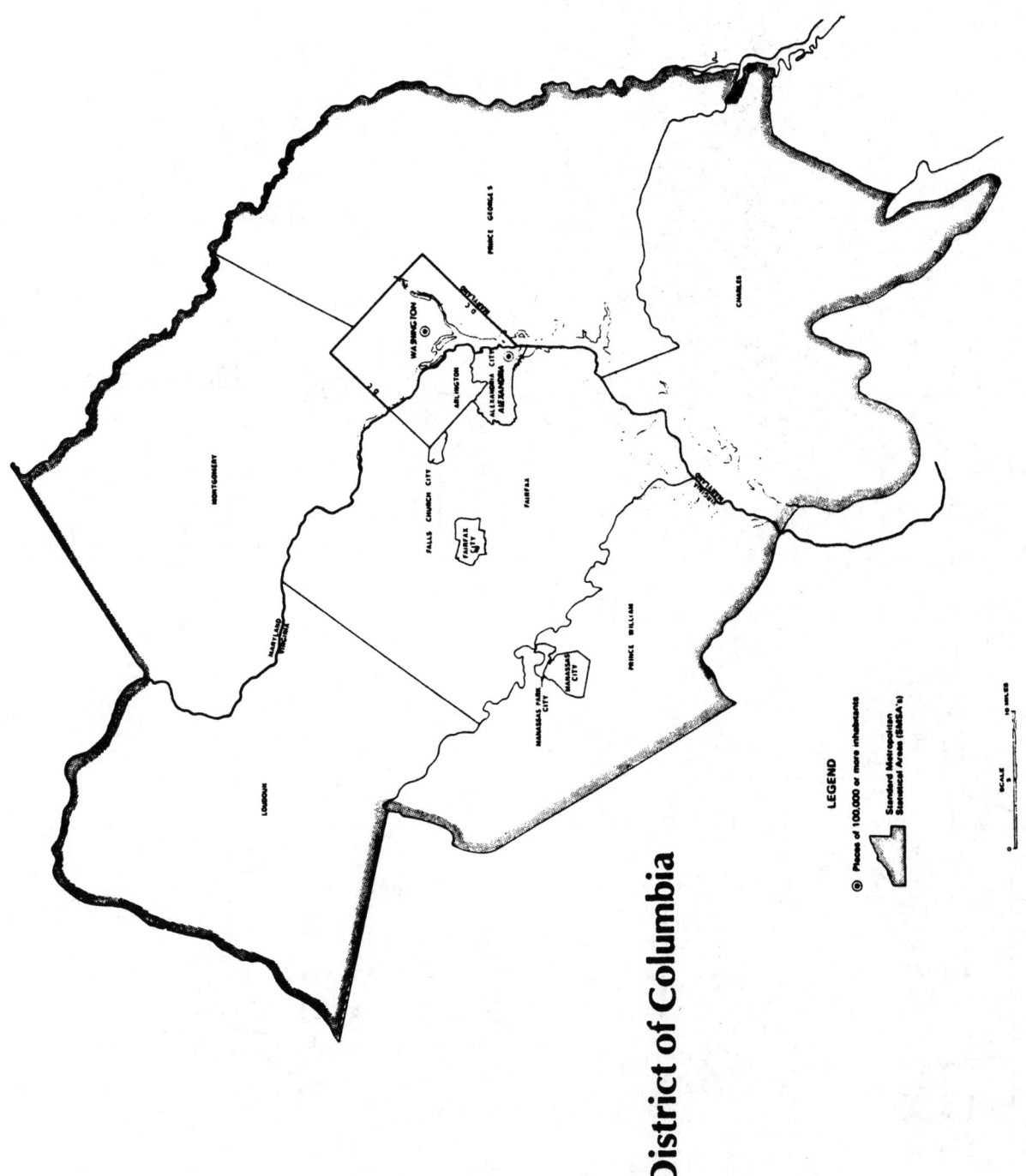

District of Columbia

LEGEND

⊙ Places of 100,000 or more inhabitants

▽ Standard Metropolitan Statistical Areas (SMSA's)

SCALE

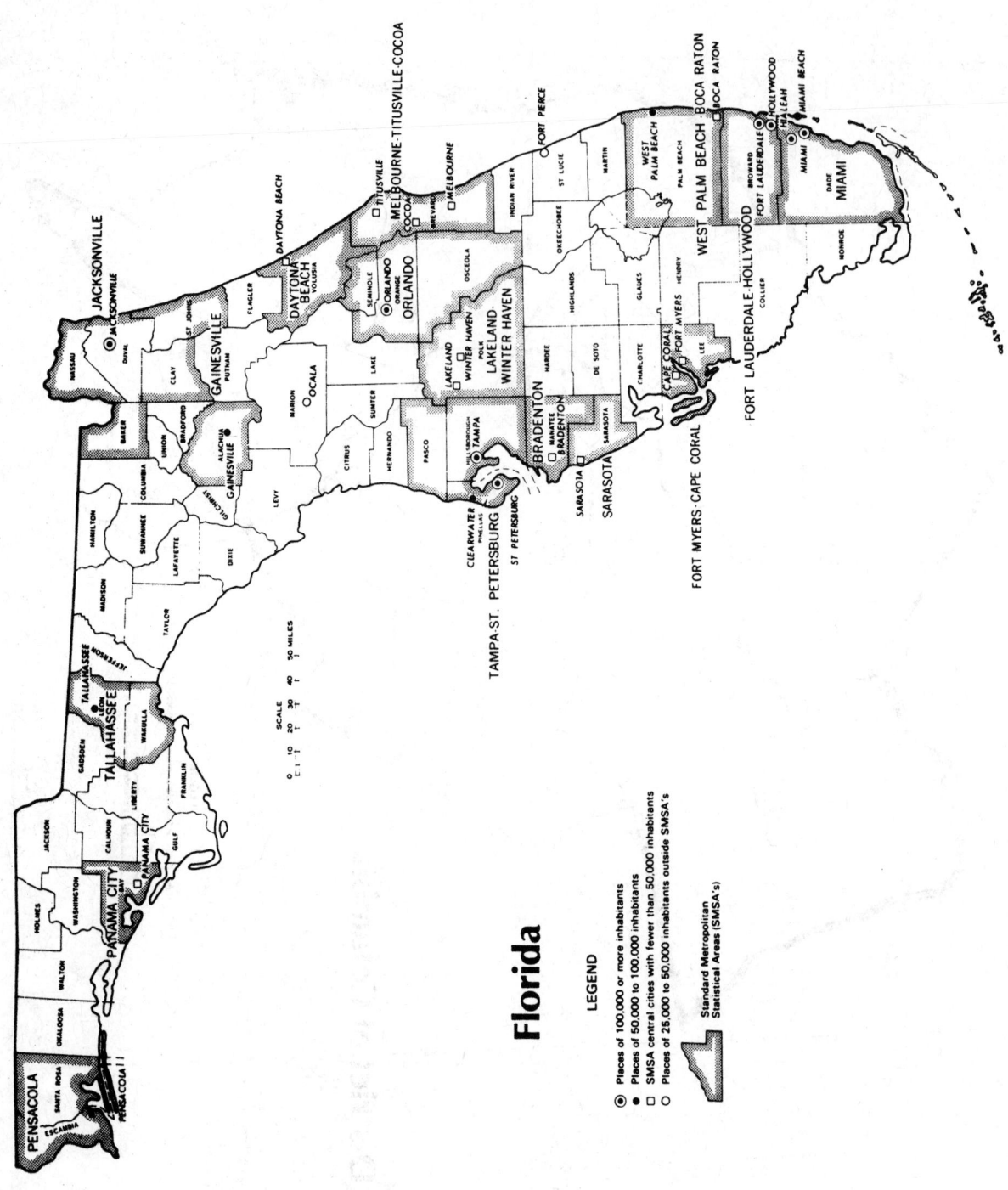

Florida

LEGEND

- ⊙ Places of 100,000 or more inhabitants
- ● Places of 50,000 to 100,000 inhabitants
- □ SMSA central cities with fewer than 50,000 inhabitants
- ○ Places of 25,000 to 50,000 inhabitants outside SMSA's

Standard Metropolitan
Statistical Areas (SMSA's)

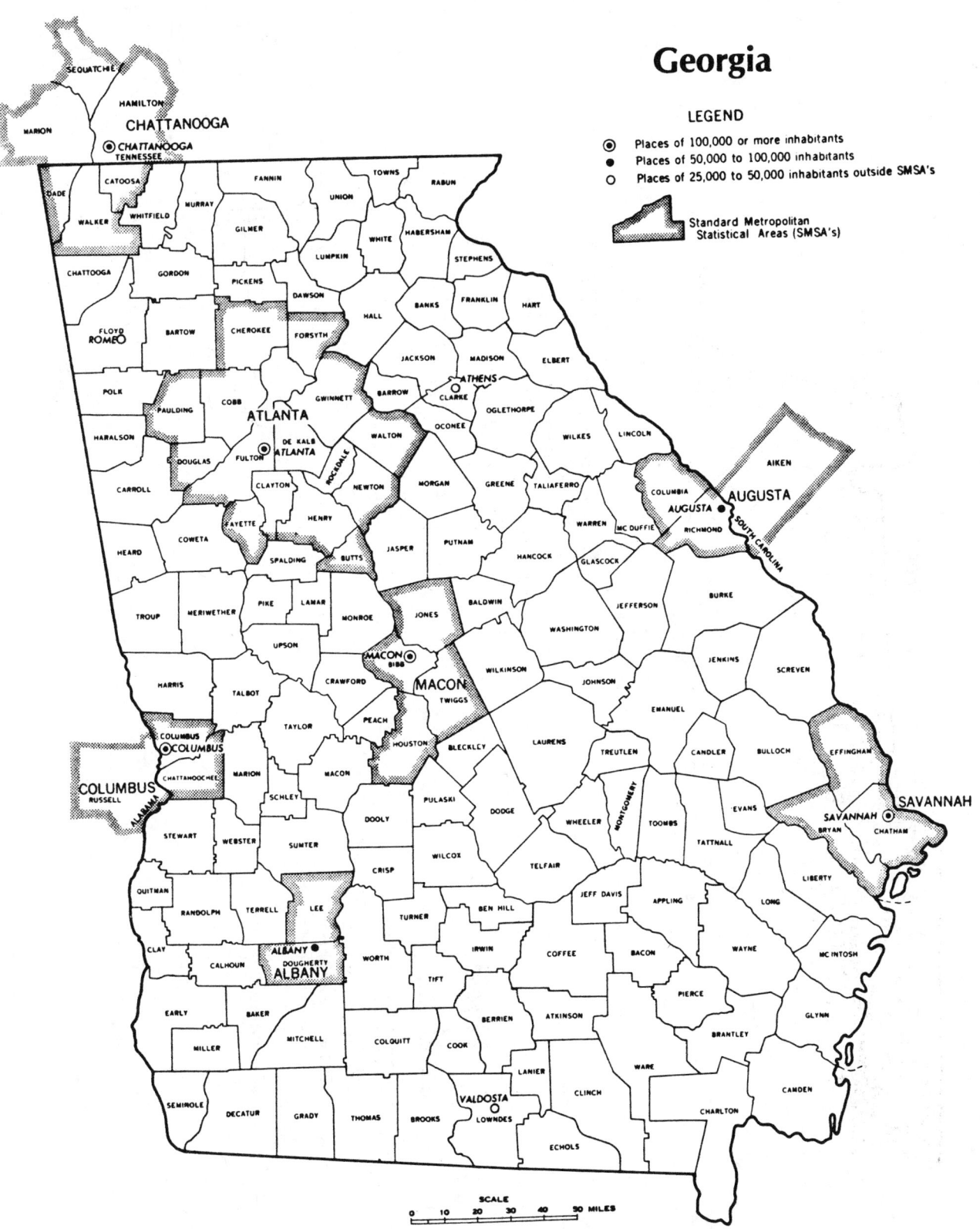

Georgia

LEGEND

⊙ Places of 100,000 or more inhabitants

● Places of 50,000 to 100,000 inhabitants

○ Places of 25,000 to 50,000 inhabitants outside SMSA's

Standard Metropolitan Statistical Areas (SMSA's)

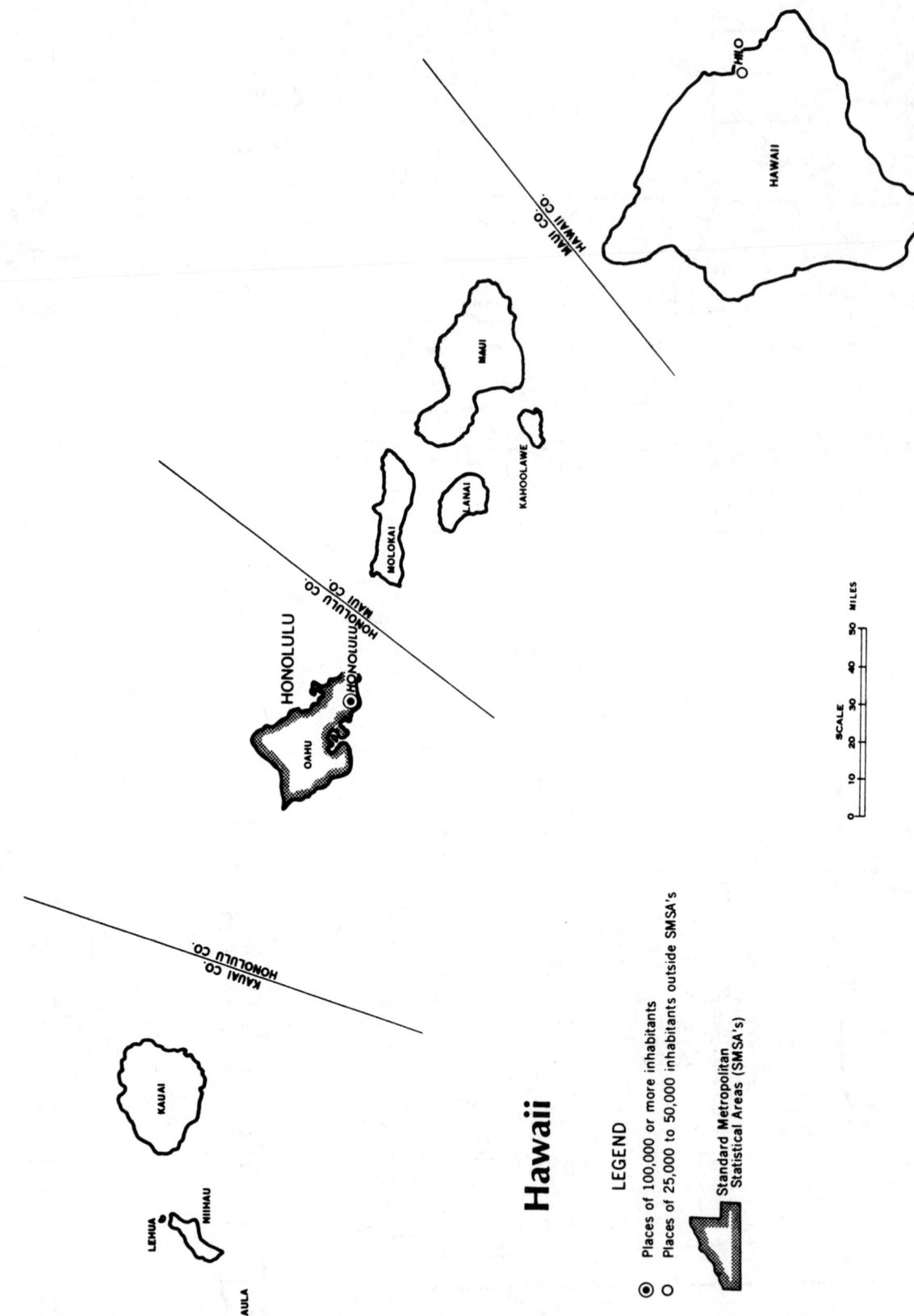

Hawaii

LEGEND

⊙ Places of 100,000 or more inhabitants

○ Places of 25,000 to 50,000 inhabitants outside SMSA's

Standard Metropolitan
Statistical Areas (SMSA's)

KAUAI CO.
HONOLULU CO.

KAUAI

NIIHAU

LEHUA

KAULA

HONOLULU CO.
MAUI CO.

HONOLULU

OAHU

HONOLULU

MOLOKAI

MAUI

LANAI

KAHOOLAWE

MAUI CO.
HAWAII CO.

HILO

HAWAII

SCALE
0 10 20 30 40 50 MILES

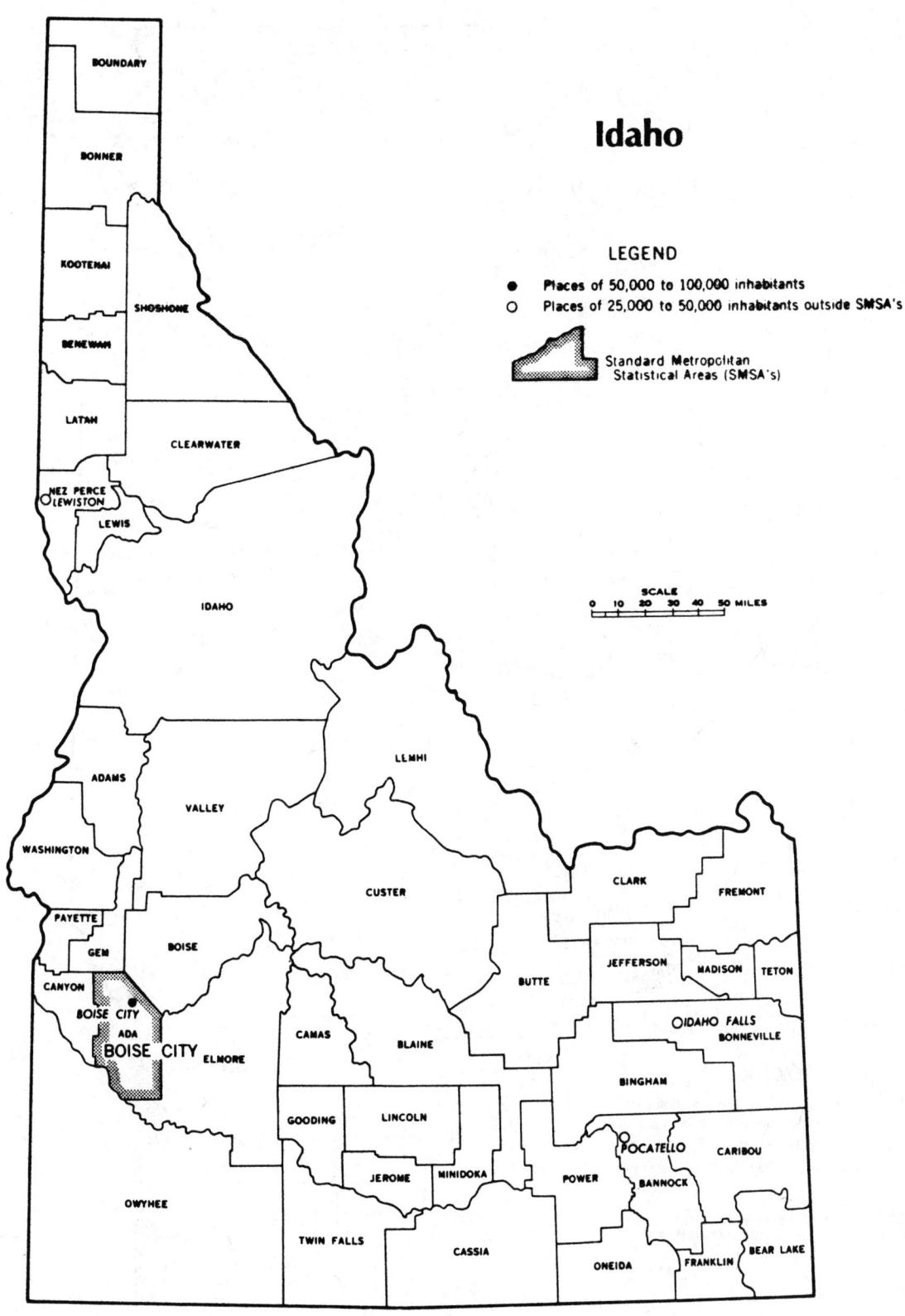

Idaho

LEGEND

●   Places of 50,000 to 100,000 inhabitants

○   Places of 25,000 to 50,000 inhabitants outside SMSA's

Standard Metropolitan Statistical Areas (SMSA's)

SCALE
0 10 20 30 40 50 MILES

BOUNDARY

BONNER

KOOTENAI

SHOSHONE

BENEWAH

LATAH

CLEARWATER

NEZ PERCE
○ LEWISTON

LEWIS

IDAHO

ADAMS

VALLEY

LEMHI

WASHINGTON

CLARK

FREMONT

PAYETTE

GEM

BOISE

CUSTER

JEFFERSON

MADISON

TETON

CANYON

BUTTE

○ IDAHO FALLS

BONNEVILLE

● BOISE CITY

ADA

BOISE CITY

ELMORE

CAMAS

BLAINE

BINGHAM

GOODING

LINCOLN

○ POCATELLO

CARIBOU

JEROME

MINIDOKA

POWER

BANNOCK

OWYHEE

TWIN FALLS

CASSIA

ONEIDA

FRANKLIN

BEAR LAKE

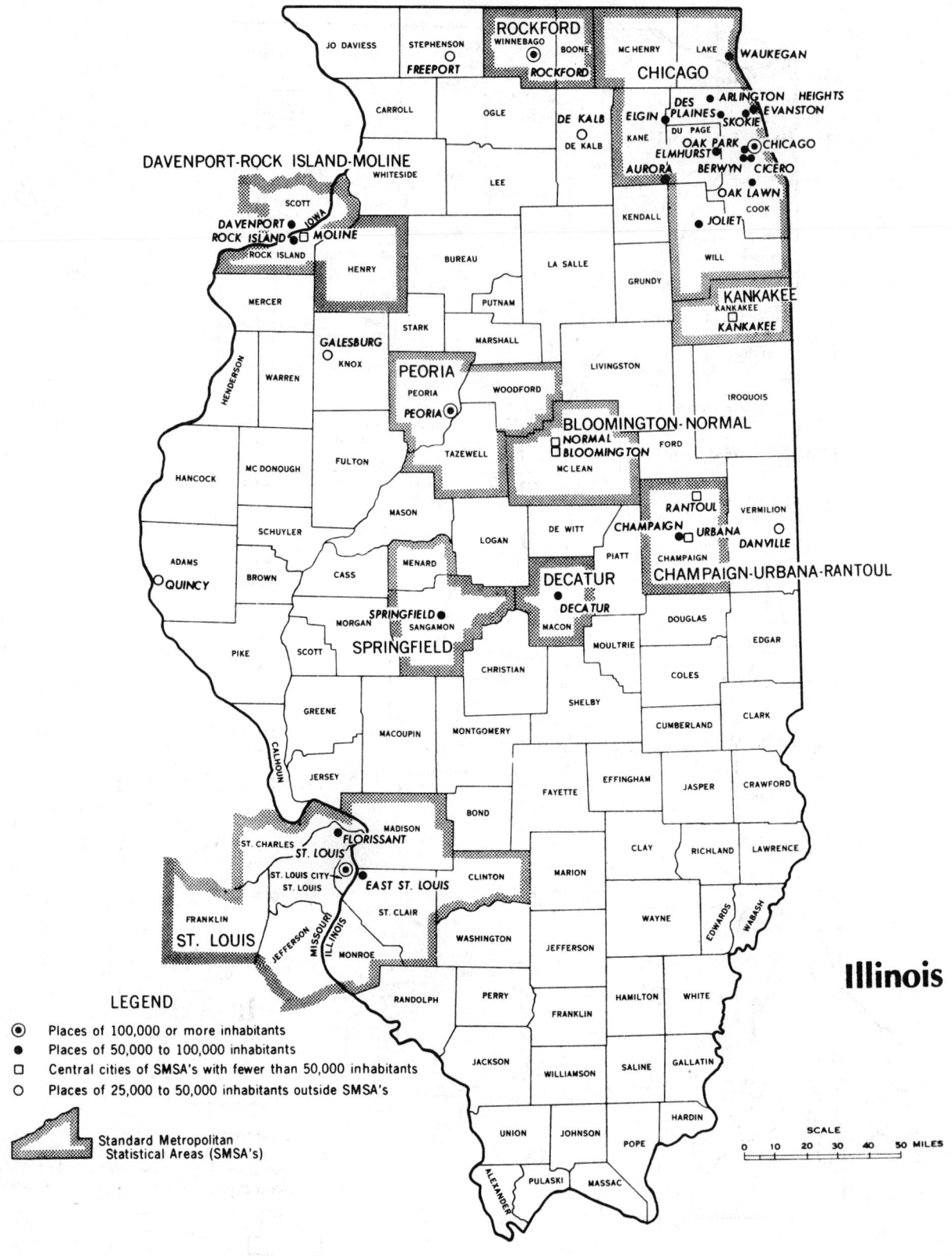

Illinois

LEGEND

⊙   Places of 100,000 or more inhabitants

●   Places of 50,000 to 100,000 inhabitants

□   Central cities of SMSA's with fewer than 50,000 inhabitants

○   Places of 25,000 to 50,000 inhabitants outside SMSA's

Standard Metropolitan Statistical Areas (SMSA's)

SCALE

0   10   20   30   40   50 MILES

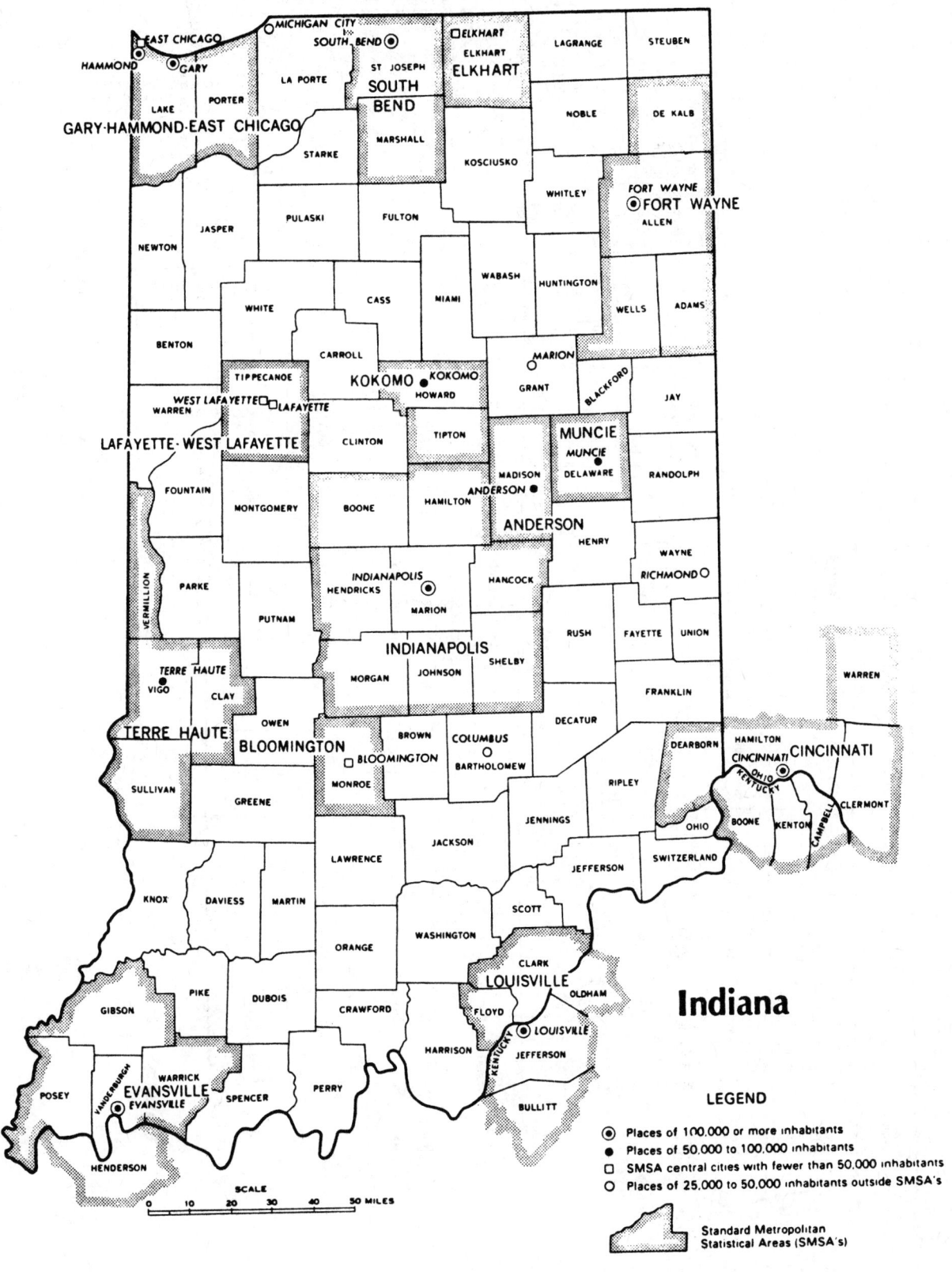

Indiana

LEGEND

⊙ Places of 100,000 or more inhabitants
● Places of 50,000 to 100,000 inhabitants
□ SMSA central cities with fewer than 50,000 inhabitants
○ Places of 25,000 to 50,000 inhabitants outside SMSA's

Standard Metropolitan
Statistical Areas (SMSA's)

SCALE
0   10   20   30   40   50 MILES

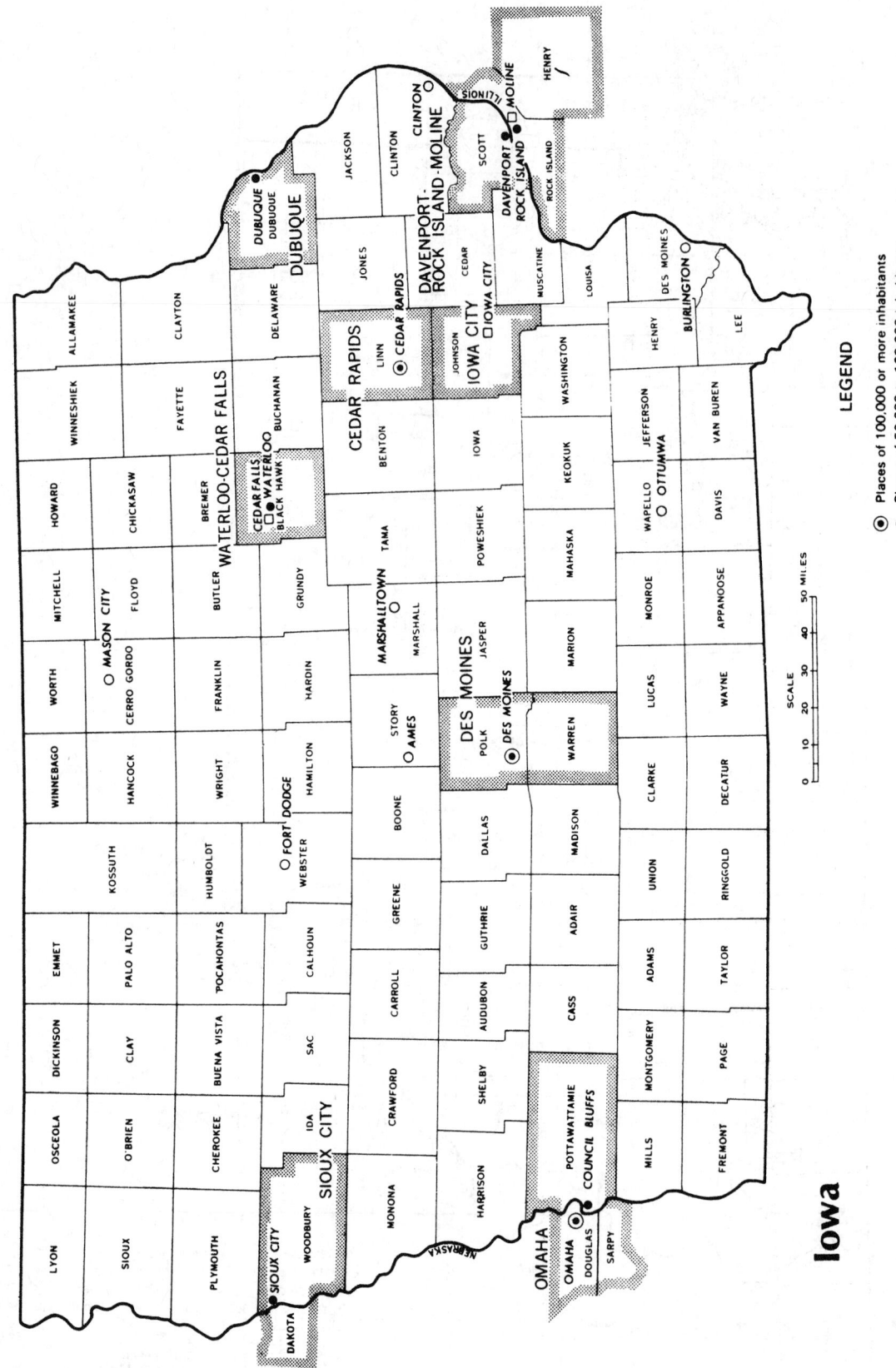

Iowa

SCALE

0   10   20   30   40   50 MILES

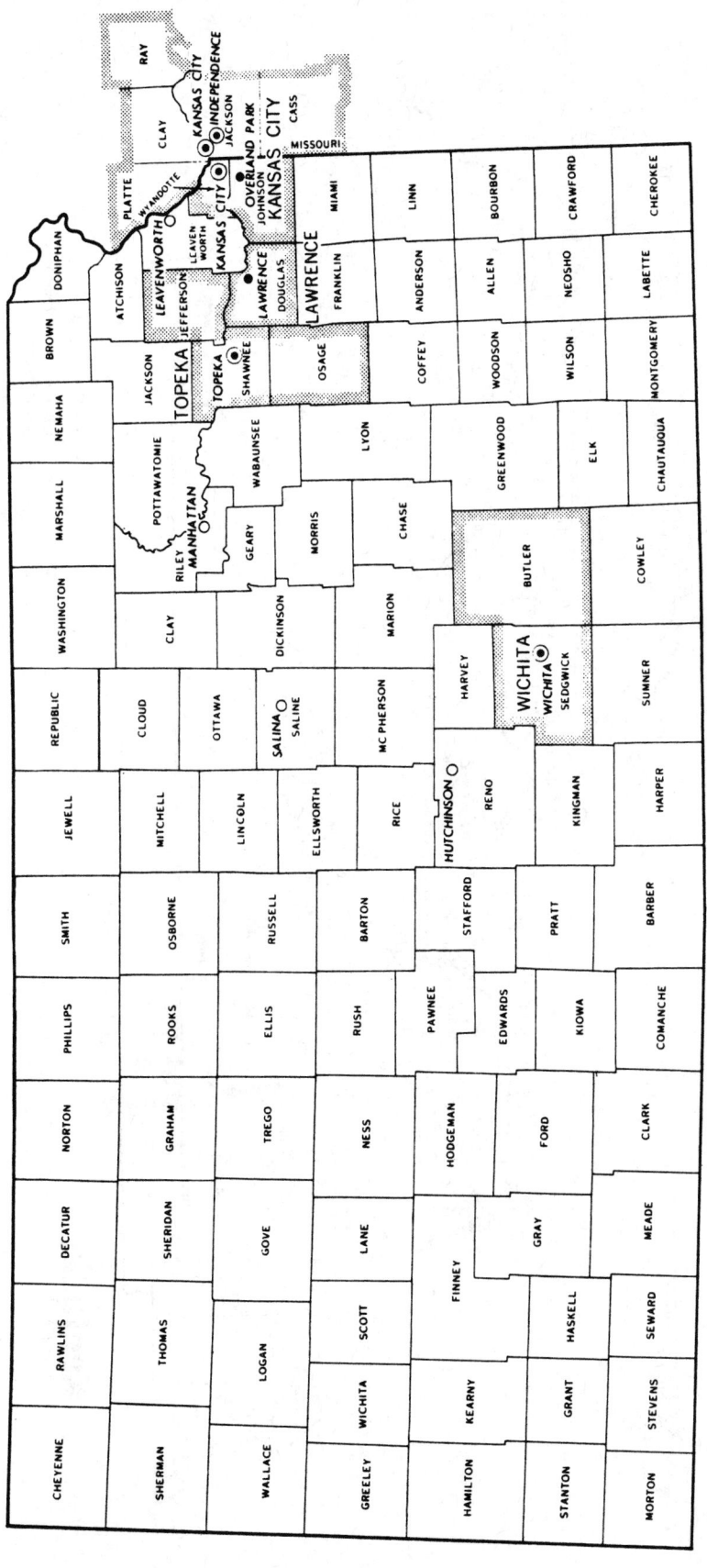

Kansas

LEGEND

◉ Places of 100,000 or more inhabitants

● Places of 50,000 to 100,000 inhabitants

○ Places of 25,000 to 50,000 inhabitants outside SMSA's

Standard Metropolitan Statistical Areas (SMSA's)

SCALE

0 10 20 30 40 50 MILES

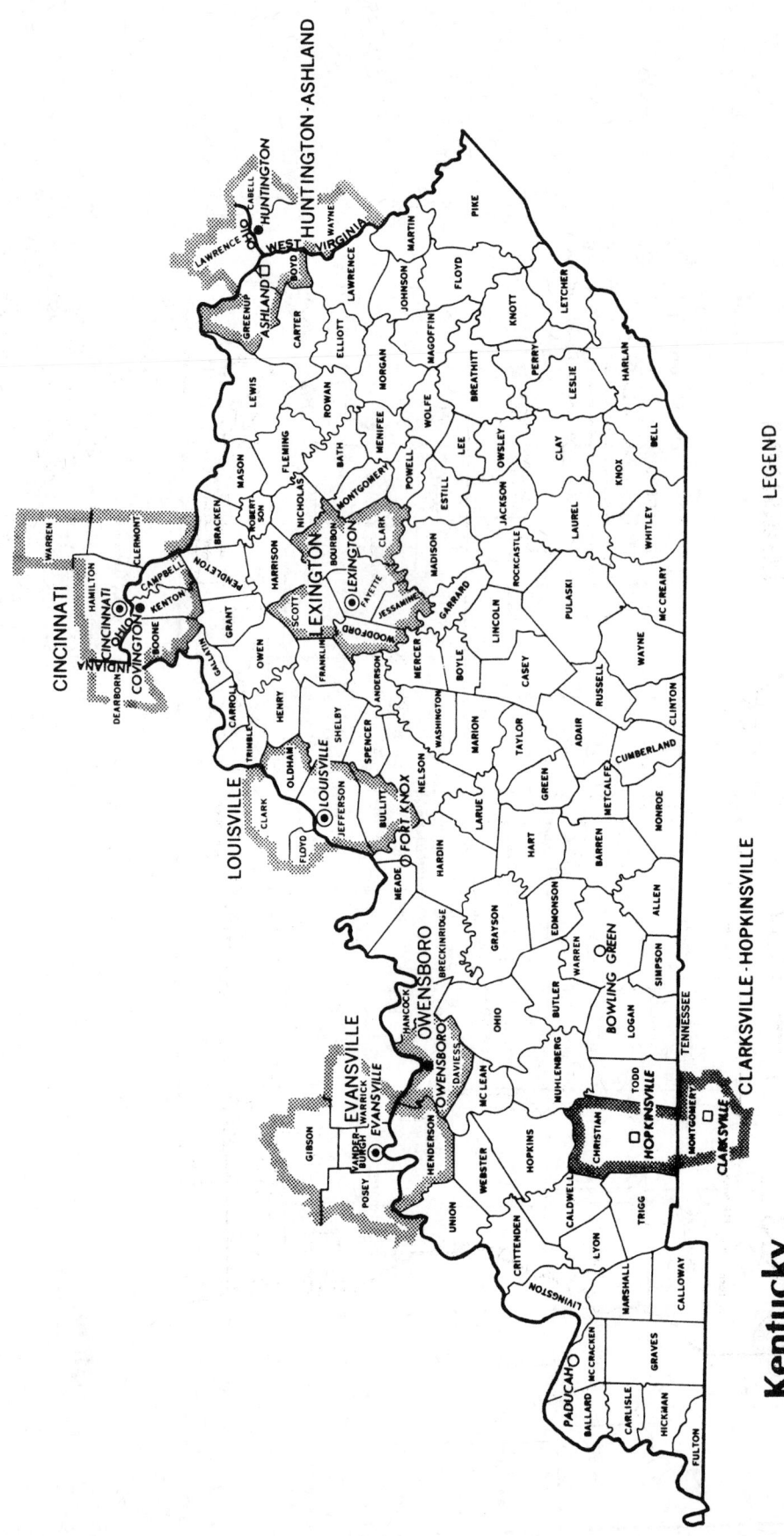

Kentucky

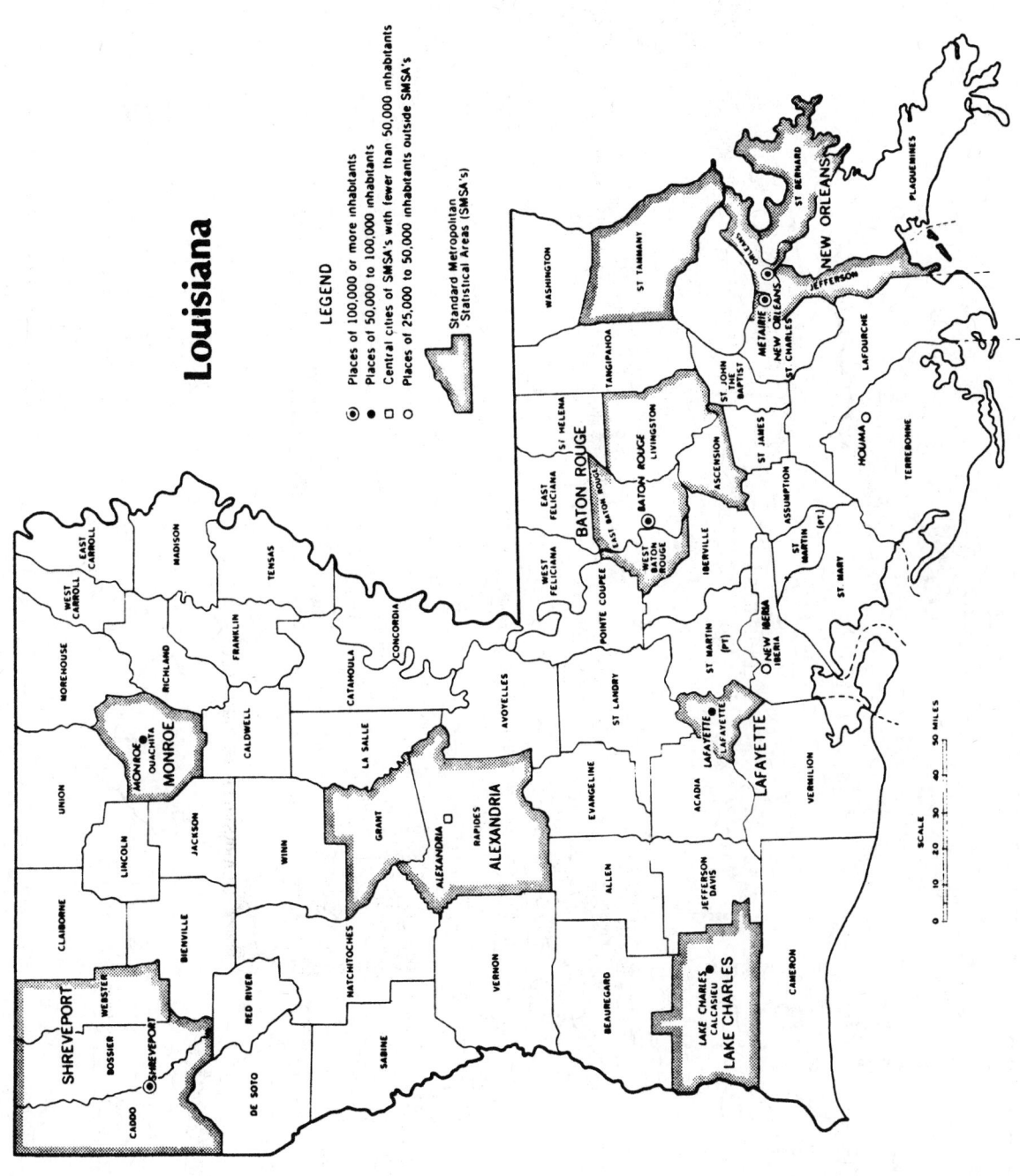

Louisiana

LEGEND

⊙ Places of 100,000 or more inhabitants
● Places of 50,000 to 100,000 inhabitants
□ Central cities of SMSA's with fewer than 50,000 inhabitants
○ Places of 25,000 to 50,000 inhabitants outside SMSA's

▱ Standard Metropolitan
Statistical Areas (SMSA's)

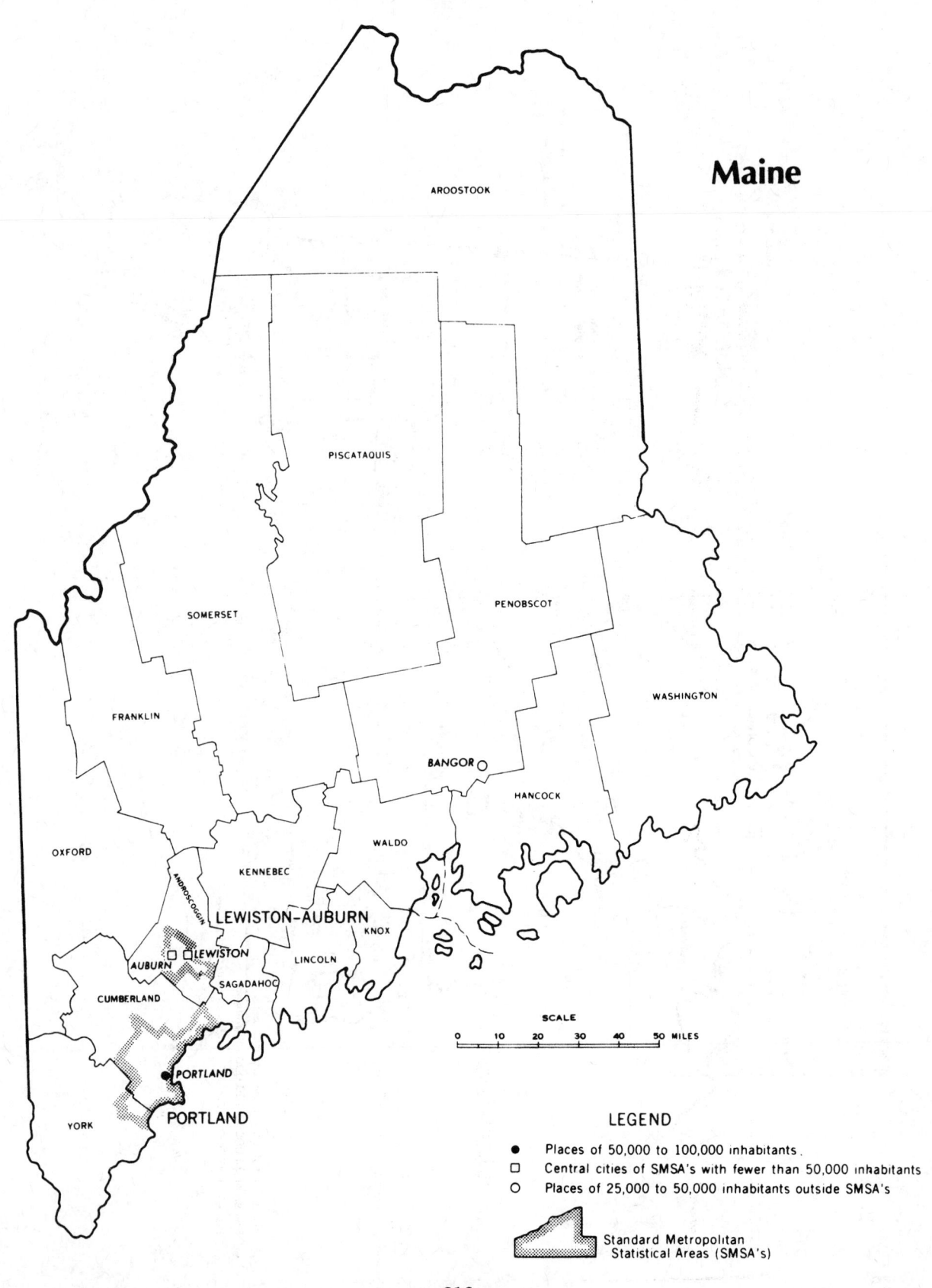

Maine

AROOSTOOK

PISCATAQUIS

SOMERSET

PENOBSCOT

FRANKLIN

WASHINGTON

BANGOR ○

HANCOCK

OXFORD

KENNEBEC

WALDO

ANDROSCOGGIN

LEWISTON-AUBURN

KNOX

□ □ LEWISTON

AUBURN

LINCOLN

SAGADAHOC

CUMBERLAND

SCALE

0   10   20   30   40   50 MILES

● PORTLAND

YORK

PORTLAND

LEGEND

●   Places of 50,000 to 100,000 inhabitants.

□   Central cities of SMSA's with fewer than 50,000 inhabitants.

○   Places of 25,000 to 50,000 inhabitants outside SMSA's

Standard Metropolitan
Statistical Areas (SMSA's)

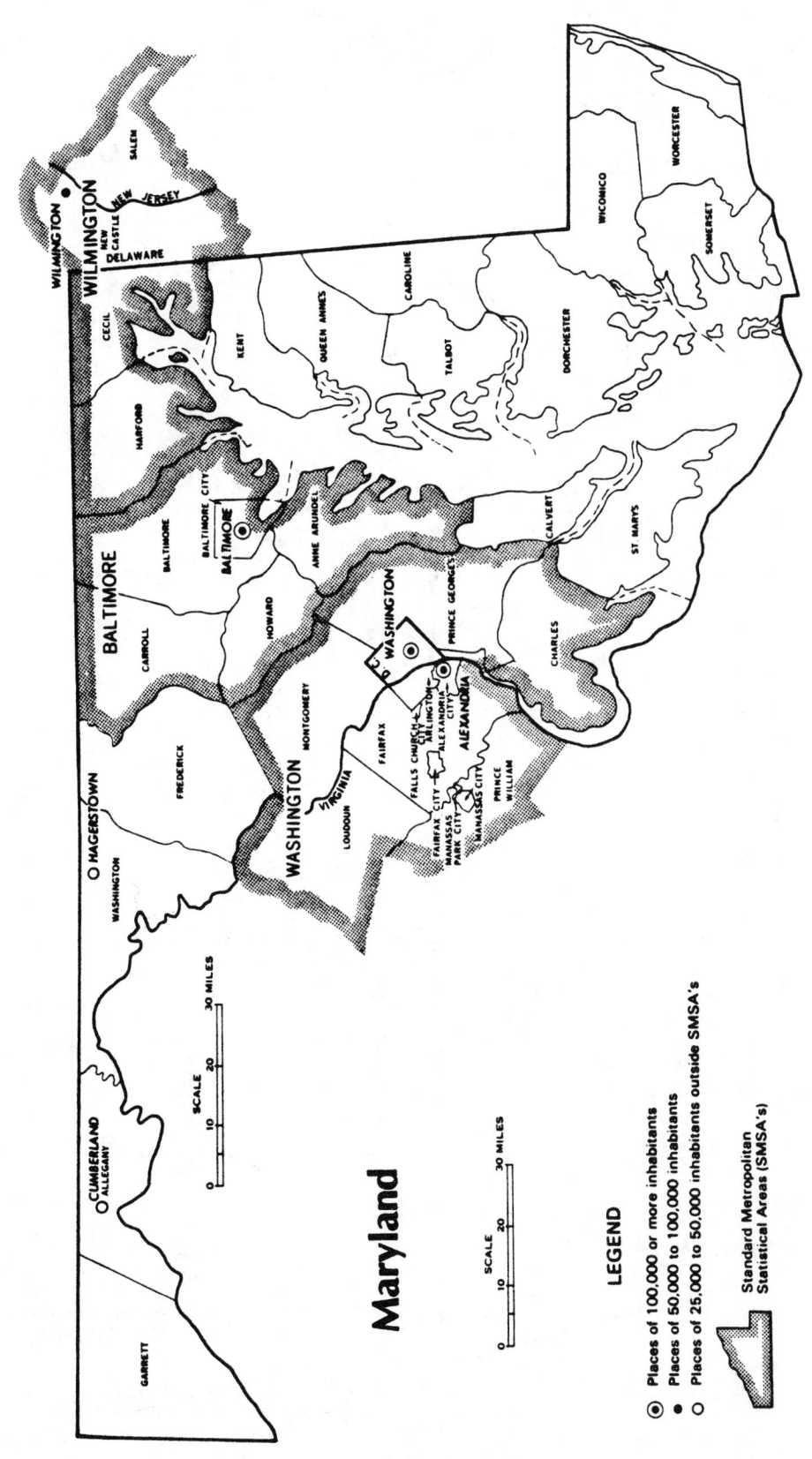

Maryland

LEGEND

⊙ Places of 100,000 or more inhabitants

● Places of 50,000 to 100,000 inhabitants

○ Places of 25,000 to 50,000 inhabitants outside SMSA's

Standard Metropolitan
Statistical Areas (SMSA's)

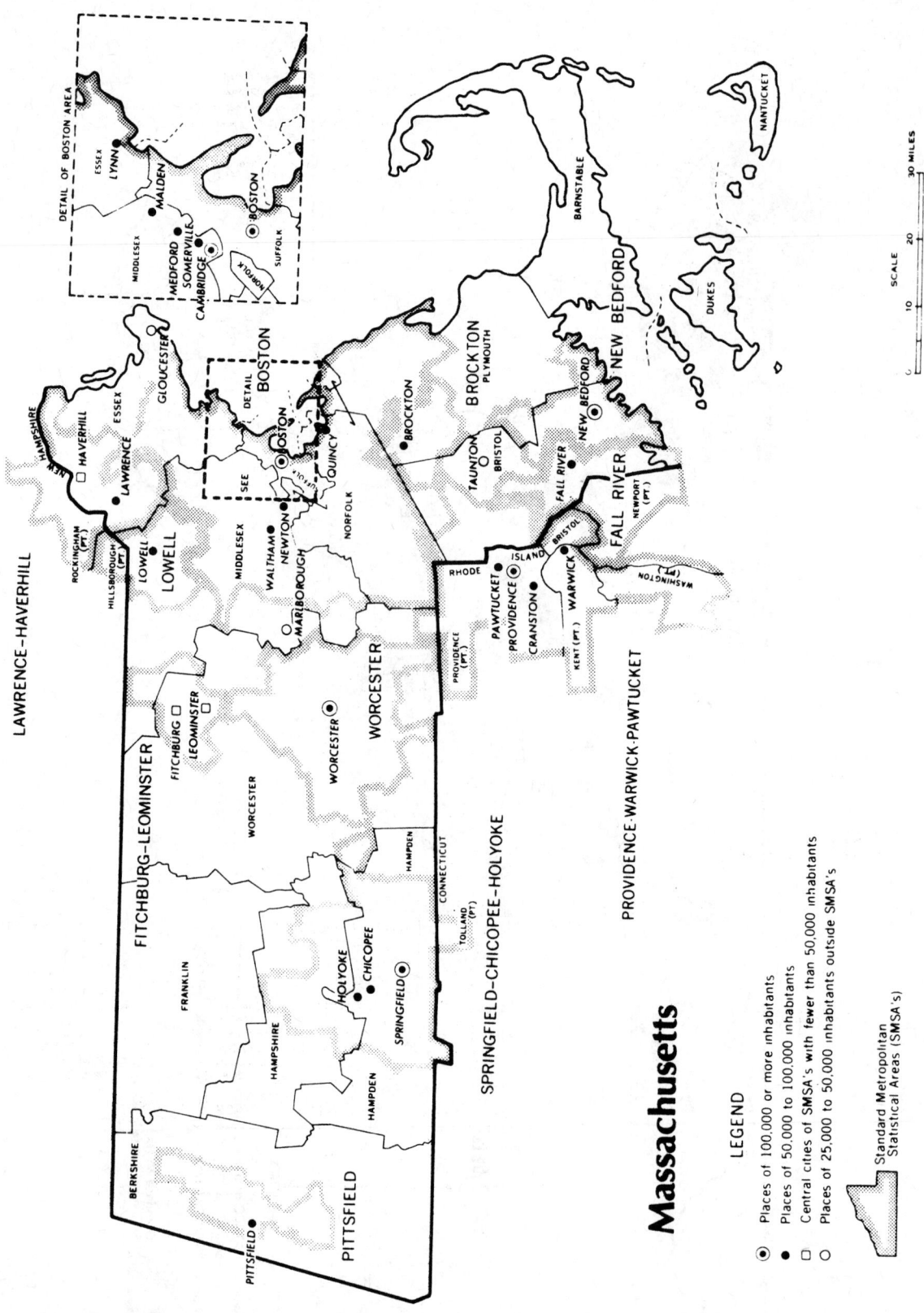

Massachusetts

LEGEND

⊙ Places of 100,000 or more inhabitants

● Places of 50,000 to 100,000 inhabitants

□ Central cities of SMSA's with fewer than 50,000 inhabitants

○ Places of 25,000 to 50,000 inhabitants outside SMSA's

Standard Metropolitan
Statistical Areas (SMSA's)

Michigan

LEGEND

- ⊙ Places of 100,000 or more inhabitants
- ● Places of 50,000 to 100,000 inhabitants
- ☐ SMSA central cities with fewer than 50,000 inhabitants
- ○ Places of 25,000 to 50,000 inhabitants outside SMSA's

Standard Metropolitan
Statistical Areas (SMSA's)

1. DEARBORN HEIGHTS
2. PONTIAC
3. ROSEVILLE
4. ROYAL OAK
5. ST. CLAIR SHORES
6. SOUTHFIELD
7. STERLING HEIGHTS
8. TAYLOR
9. WESTLAND
10. FARMINGTON HILLS
11. TROY

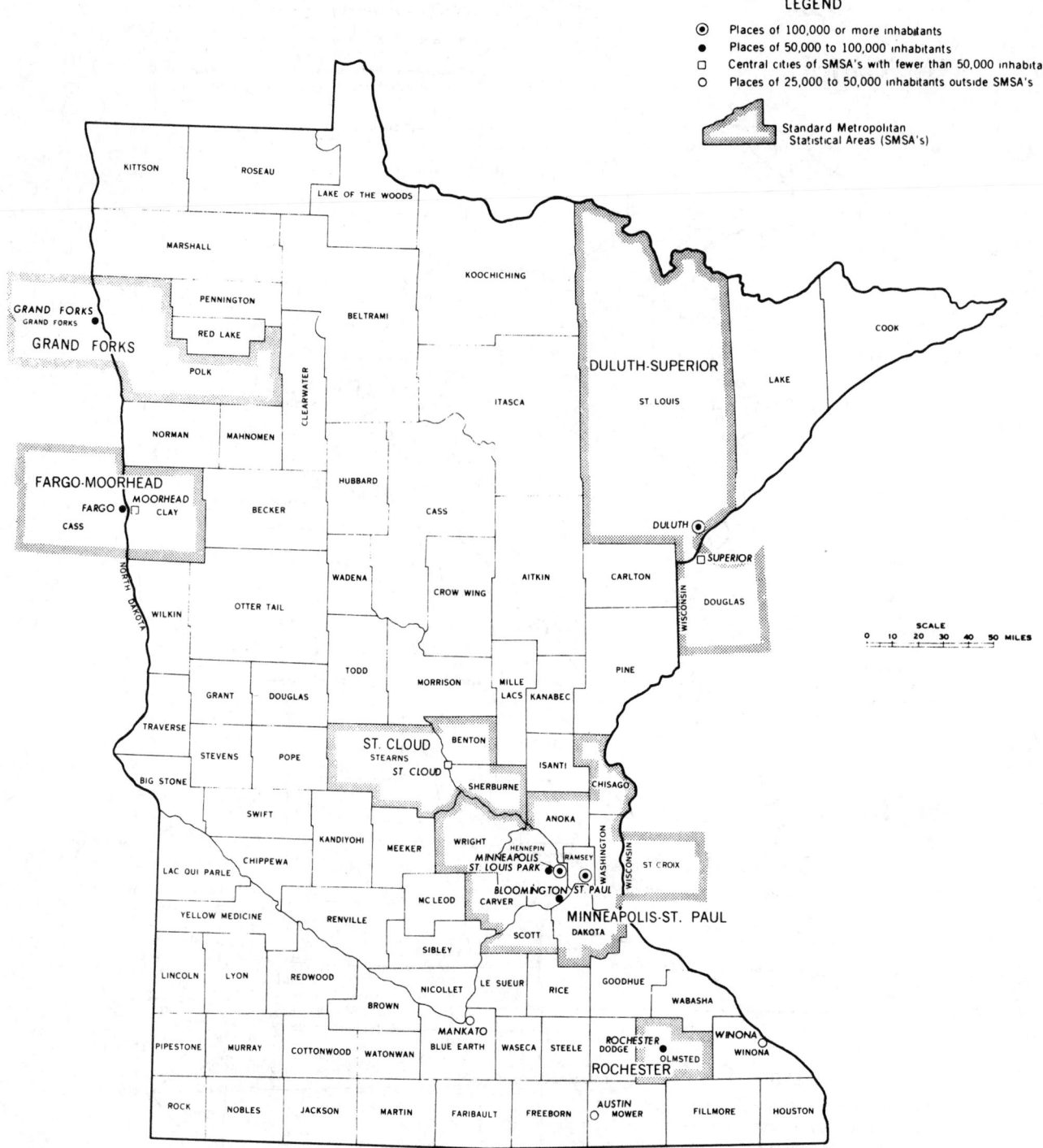

Minnesota

LEGEND

⊙ Places of 100,000 or more inhabitants
● Places of 50,000 to 100,000 inhabitants
□ Central cities of SMSA's with fewer than 50,000 inhabitants
○ Places of 25,000 to 50,000 inhabitants outside SMSA's

Standard Metropolitan
Statistical Areas (SMSA's)

KITTSON
ROSEAU
LAKE OF THE WOODS
MARSHALL
KOOCHICHING
PENNINGTON
BELTRAMI
RED LAKE
GRAND FORKS
GRAND FORKS
GRAND FORKS
POLK
COOK
DULUTH-SUPERIOR
CLEARWATER
LAKE
ST LOUIS
NORMAN
MAHNOMEN
ITASCA
HUBBARD
BECKER
CASS
FARGO-MOORHEAD
MOORHEAD
FARGO
CLAY
CARLTON
CASS
WADENA
DULUTH
WILKIN
OTTER TAIL
CROW WING
AITKIN
SUPERIOR
DOUGLAS
NORTH DAKOTA
WISCONSIN
TODD
PINE
TRAVERSE
GRANT
DOUGLAS
MORRISON
MILLE LACS
KANABEC
STEVENS
POPE
BENTON
BIG STONE
ST. CLOUD
STEARNS
ST CLOUD
ISANTI
SWIFT
SHERBURNE
CHISAGO
ANOKA
KANDIYOHI
WASHINGTON
MEEKER
WRIGHT
HENNEPIN
MINNEAPOLIS
ST LOUIS PARK
RAMSEY
ST CROIX
LAC QUI PARLE
CHIPPEWA
BLOOMINGTON
ST PAUL
MC LEOD
CARVER
YELLOW MEDICINE
RENVILLE
MINNEAPOLIS-ST. PAUL
SCOTT
DAKOTA
SIBLEY
LINCOLN
LYON
REDWOOD
NICOLLET
LE SUEUR
RICE
GOODHUE
WABASHA
BROWN
MANKATO
PIPESTONE
MURRAY
COTTONWOOD
WATONWAN
BLUE EARTH
WASECA
STEELE
ROCHESTER
DODGE
WINONA
OLMSTED
WINONA
ROCHESTER
ROCK
NOBLES
JACKSON
MARTIN
FARIBAULT
FREEBORN
AUSTIN
MOWER
FILLMORE
HOUSTON

SCALE
0 10 20 30 40 50 MILES

Mississippi

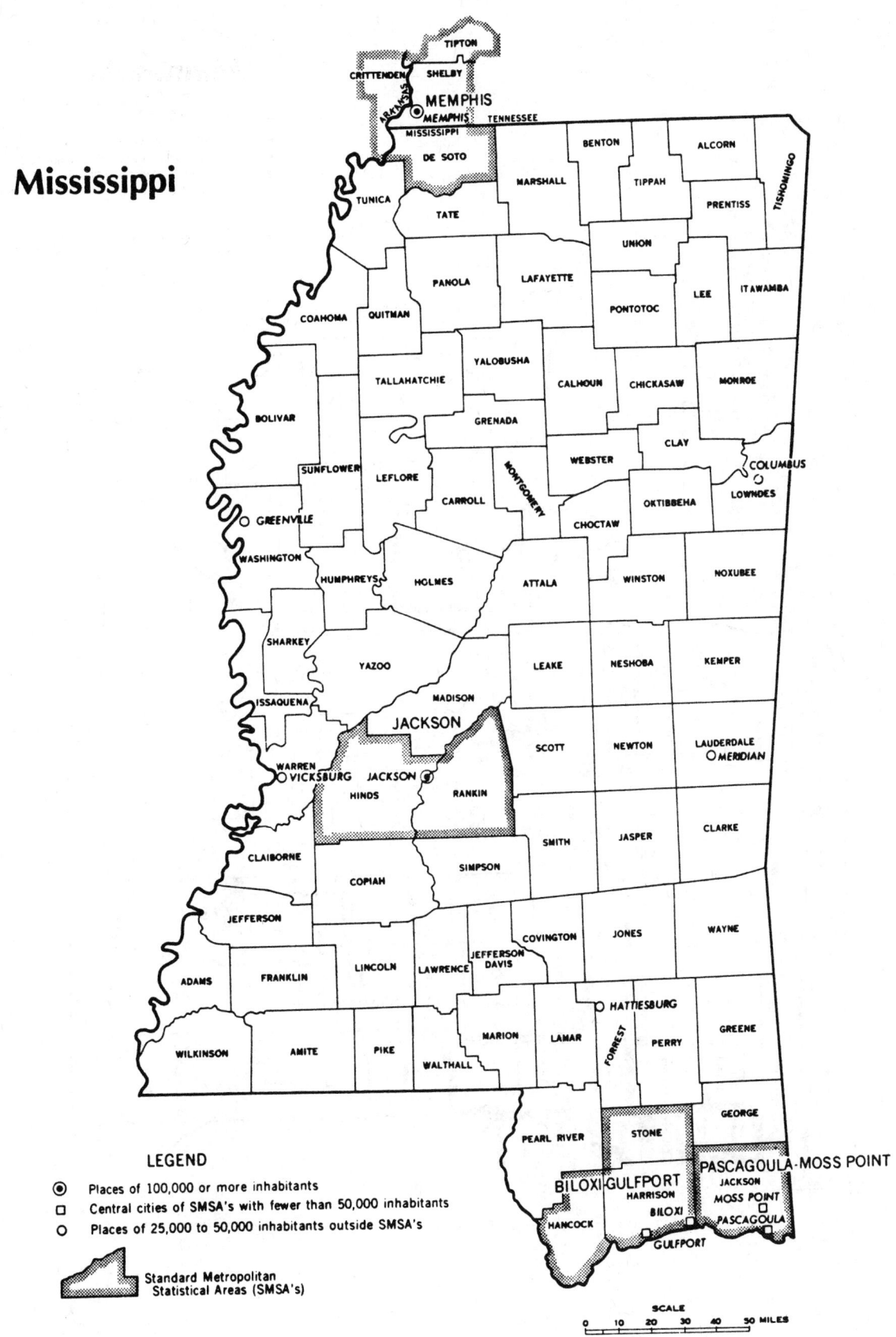

LEGEND

- ⊙ Places of 100,000 or more inhabitants
- □ Central cities of SMSA's with fewer than 50,000 inhabitants
- ○ Places of 25,000 to 50,000 inhabitants outside SMSA's

Standard Metropolitan
Statistical Areas (SMSA's)

SCALE

0   10   20   30   40   50 MILES

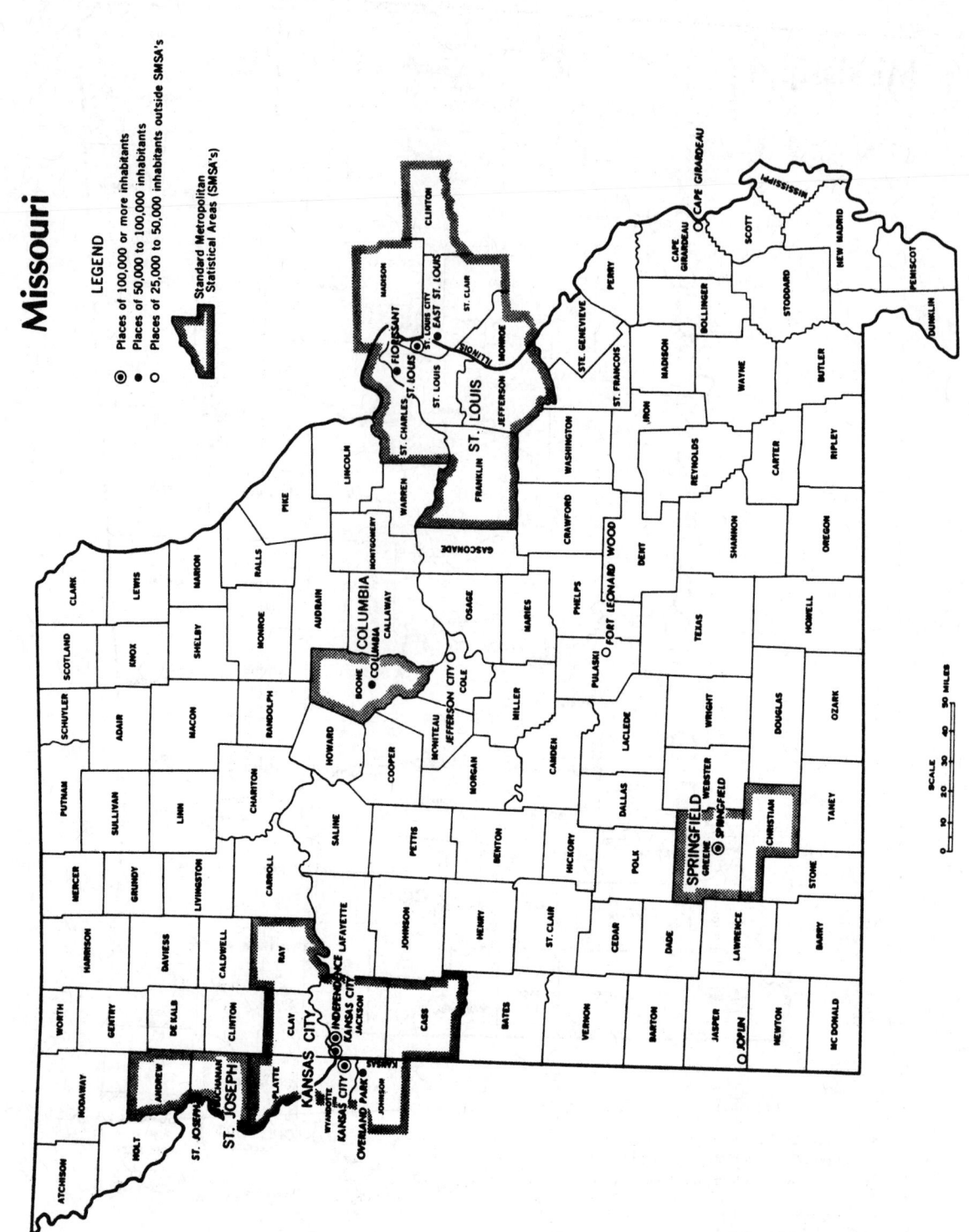

Missouri

LEGEND

◉ Places of 100,000 or more inhabitants
● Places of 50,000 to 100,000 inhabitants
○ Places of 25,000 to 50,000 inhabitants outside SMSA's

Standard Metropolitan
Statistical Areas (SMSA's)

SCALE

0   10   20   30   40   50 MILES

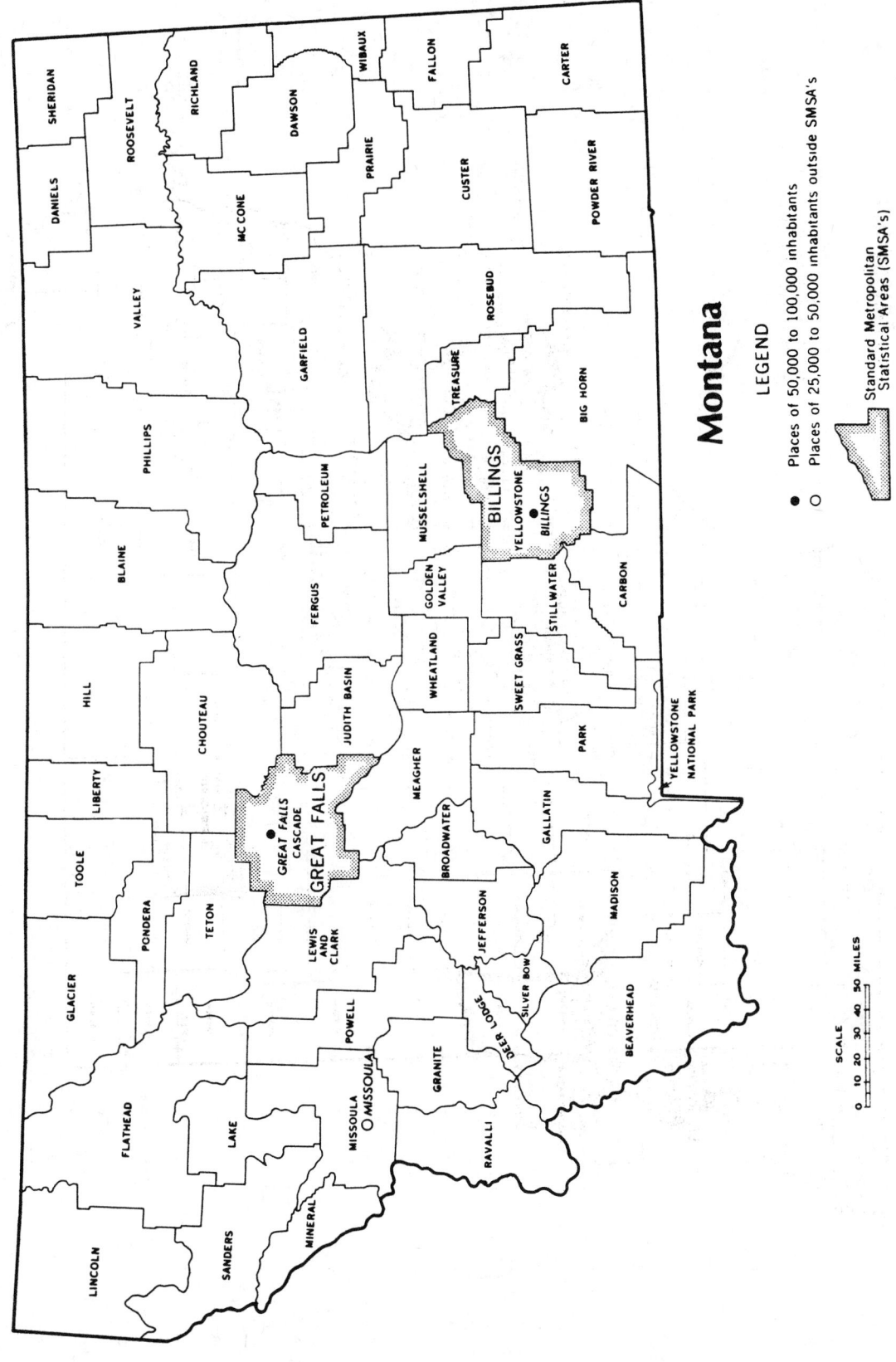

Montana

LEGEND

- ● Places of 50,000 to 100,000 inhabitants
- ○ Places of 25,000 to 50,000 inhabitants outside SMSA's

Standard Metropolitan
Statistical Areas (SMSA's)

SCALE

0 10 20 30 40 50 MILES

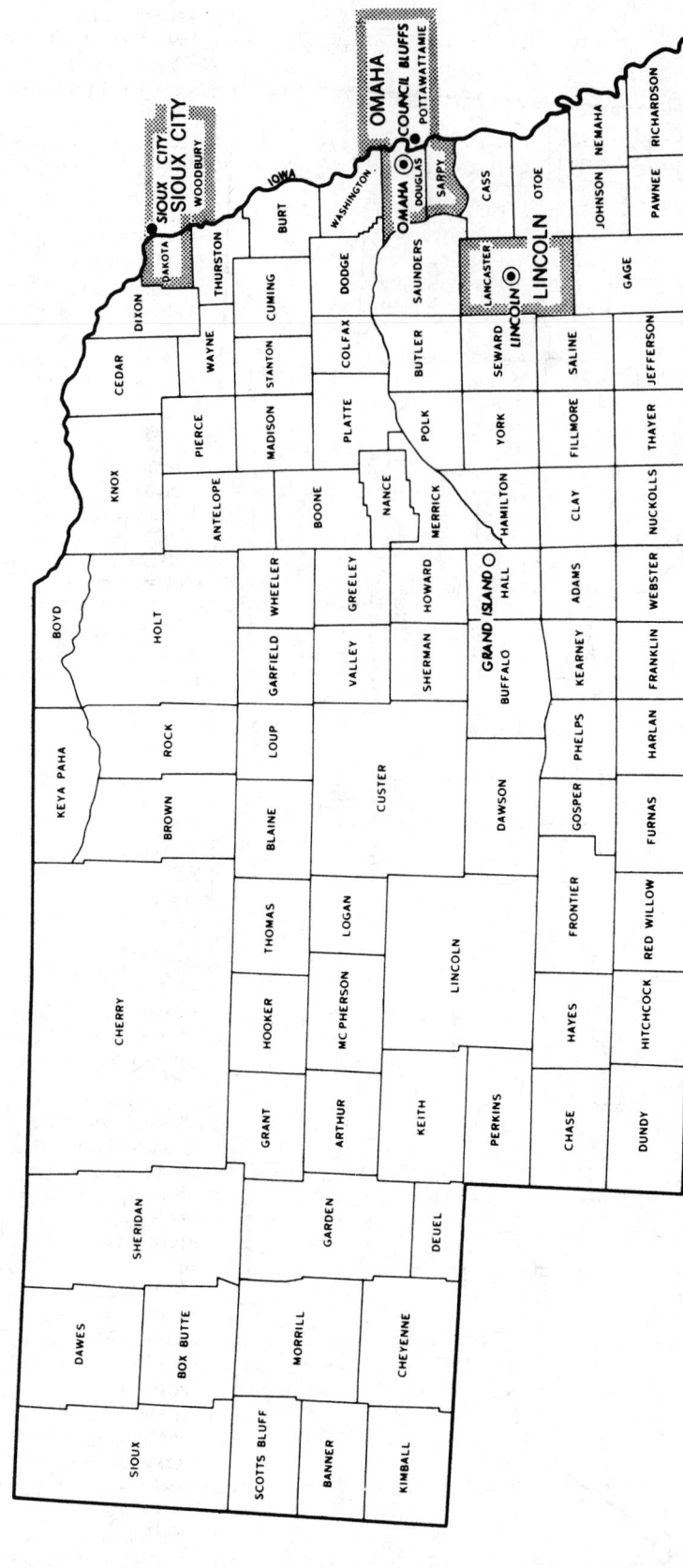

Nebraska

LEGEND

⊙ Places of 100,000 or more inhabitants

● Places of 50,000 to 100,000 inhabitants

○ Places of 25,000 to 50,000 inhabitants outside SMSA's

Standard Metropolitan
Statistical Areas (SMSA's)

SCALE

0 10 20 30 40 50 MILES

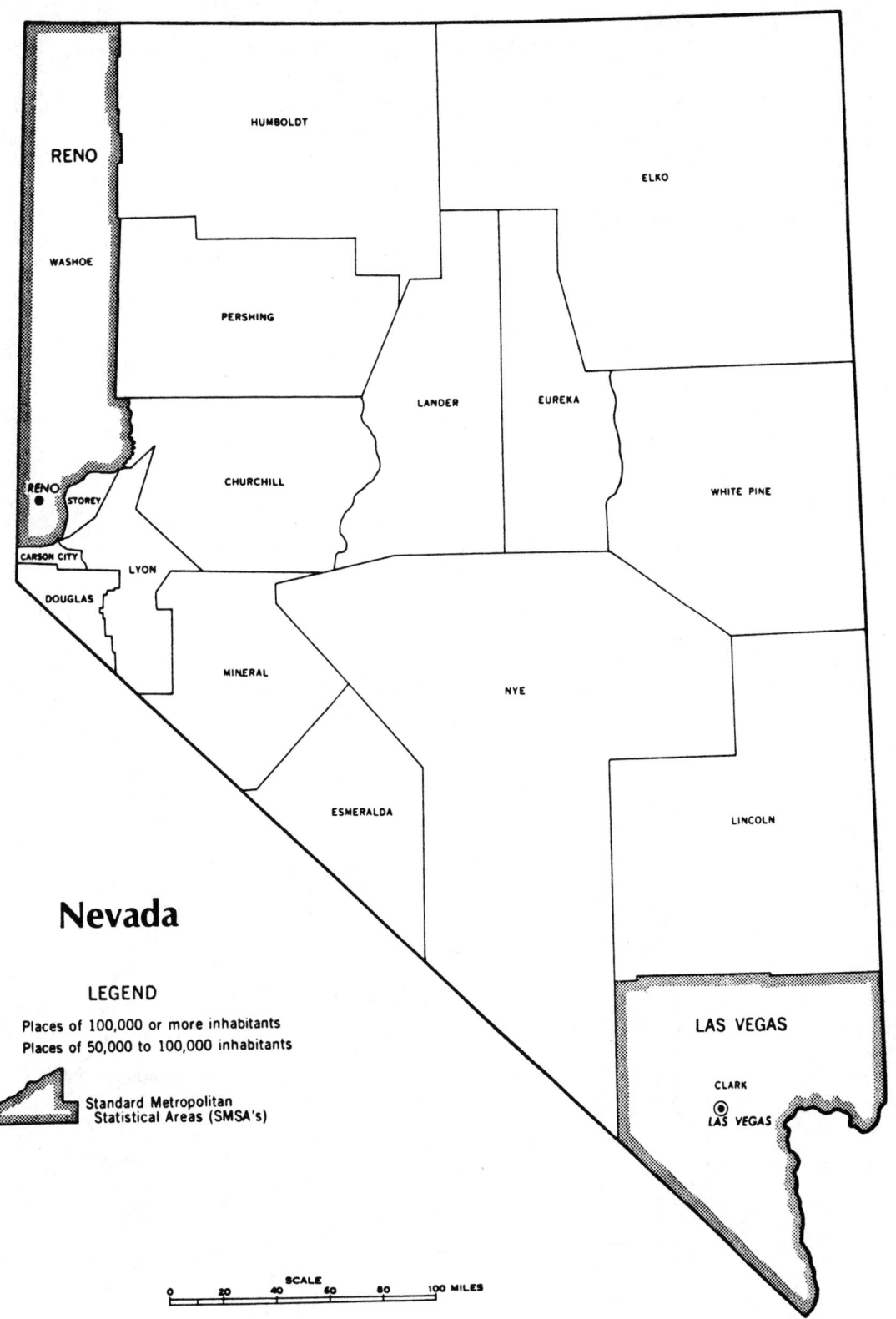

HUMBOLDT

RENO

ELKO

WASHOE

PERSHING

LANDER

EUREKA

RENO
● STOREY

CHURCHILL

WHITE PINE

CARSON CITY

LYON

DOUGLAS

MINERAL

NYE

Nevada

ESMERALDA

LINCOLN

LEGEND

⊙ Places of 100,000 or more inhabitants
● Places of 50,000 to 100,000 inhabitants

Standard Metropolitan
Statistical Areas (SMSA's)

LAS VEGAS

CLARK

⊙
LAS VEGAS

SCALE
0   20   40   60   80   100 MILES

New Hampshire

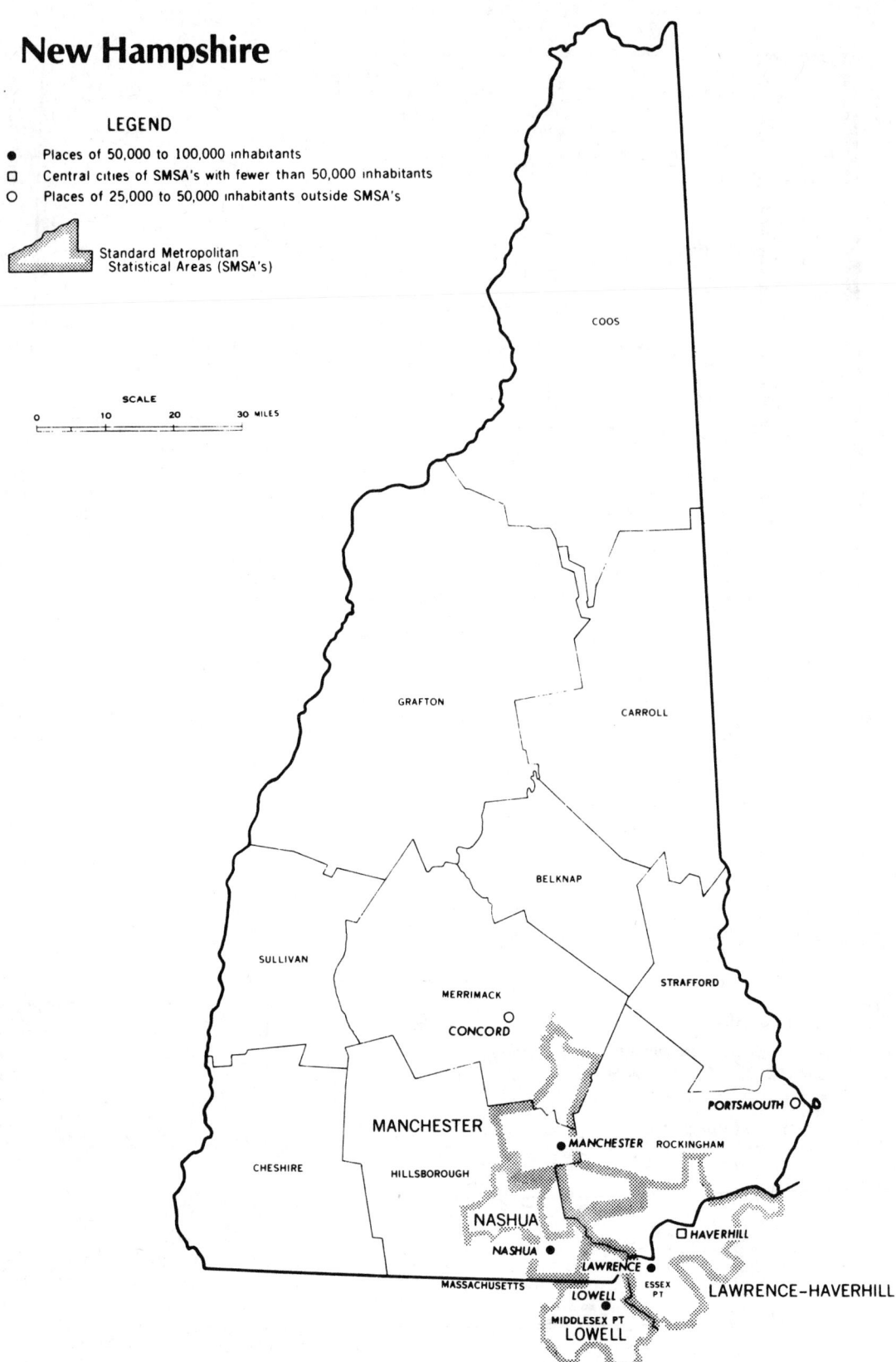

LEGEND

- ●   Places of 50,000 to 100,000 inhabitants
- □   Central cities of SMSA's with fewer than 50,000 inhabitants
- ○   Places of 25,000 to 50,000 inhabitants outside SMSA's

Standard Metropolitan
Statistical Areas (SMSA's)

SCALE

0   10   20   30 MILES

COOS

GRAFTON

CARROLL

BELKNAP

SULLIVAN

MERRIMACK

STRAFFORD

CONCORD

PORTSMOUTH

MANCHESTER

MANCHESTER

ROCKINGHAM

CHESHIRE

HILLSBOROUGH

NASHUA

HAVERHILL

NASHUA

LAWRENCE

MASSACHUSETTS

ESSEX PT

LAWRENCE-HAVERHILL

LOWELL

MIDDLESEX PT

LOWELL

New Jersey

LEGEND

⊚ Places of 100,000 or more inhabitants

● Places of 50,000 to 100,000 inhabitants

□ Central cities of SMSA's with fewer than 50,000 inhabitants

○ Places of 25,000 to 50,000 inhabitants outside SMSA's

Standard Metropolitan
Statistical Areas (SMSA's)

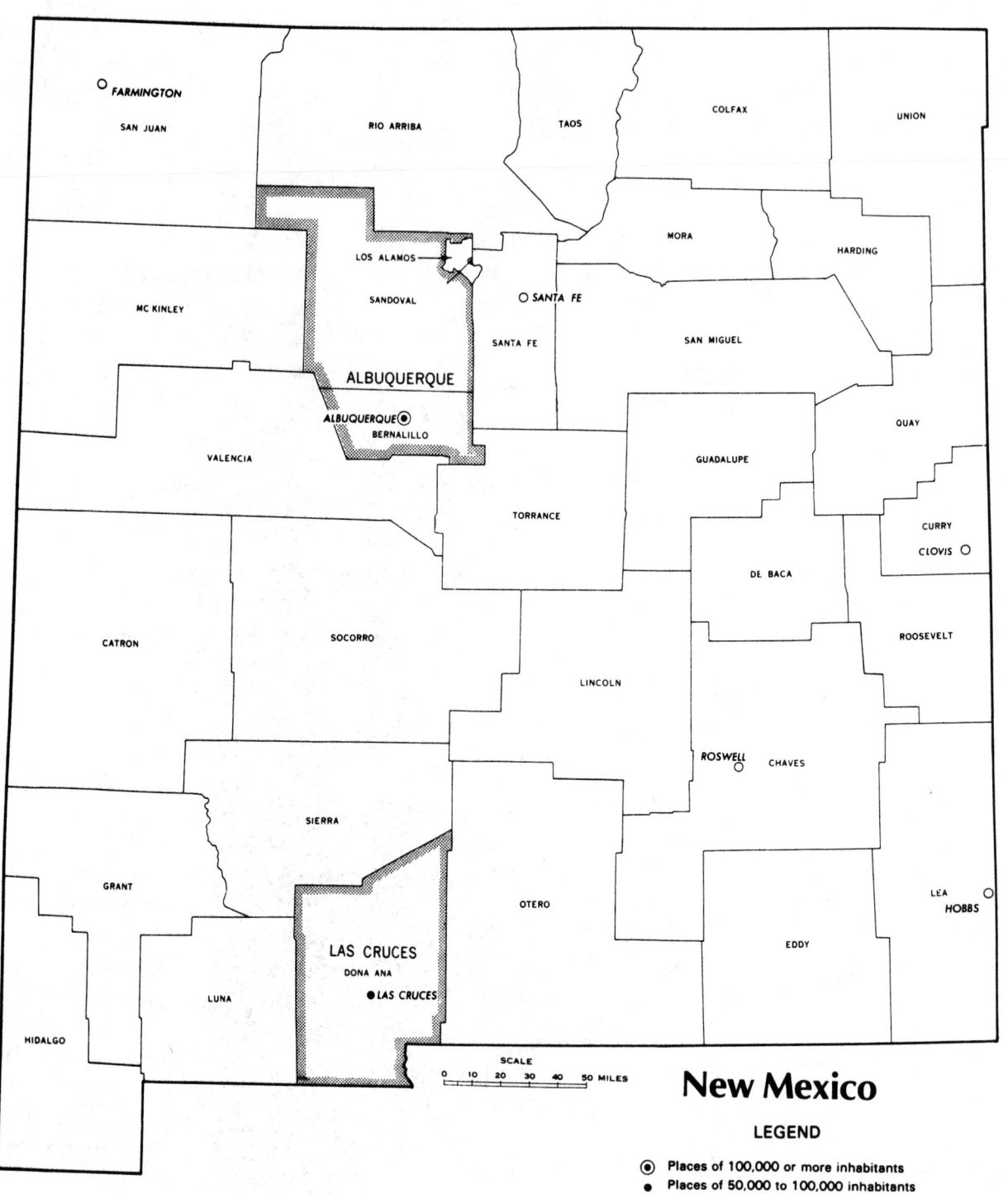

O FARMINGTON

SAN JUAN

RIO ARRIBA

TAOS

COLFAX

UNION

MORA

HARDING

LOS ALAMOS

MC KINLEY

SANDOVAL

O SANTA FE

SANTA FE

SAN MIGUEL

ALBUQUERQUE

ALBUQUERQUE⊙

BERNALILLO

QUAY

VALENCIA

GUADALUPE

CURRY

CLOVIS O

TORRANCE

DE BACA

CATRON

SOCORRO

ROOSEVELT

LINCOLN

ROSWELL
O
CHAVES

SIERRA

GRANT

LEA
O
HOBBS

OTERO

EDDY

LAS CRUCES

DONA ANA

●LAS CRUCES

LUNA

SCALE

0 10 20 30 40 50 MILES

HIDALGO

New Mexico

LEGEND

⊙ Places of 100,000 or more inhabitants

● Places of 50,000 to 100,000 inhabitants

O Places of 25,000 to 50,000 inhabitants outside SMSA's

Standard Metropolitan
Statistical Areas (SMSA's)

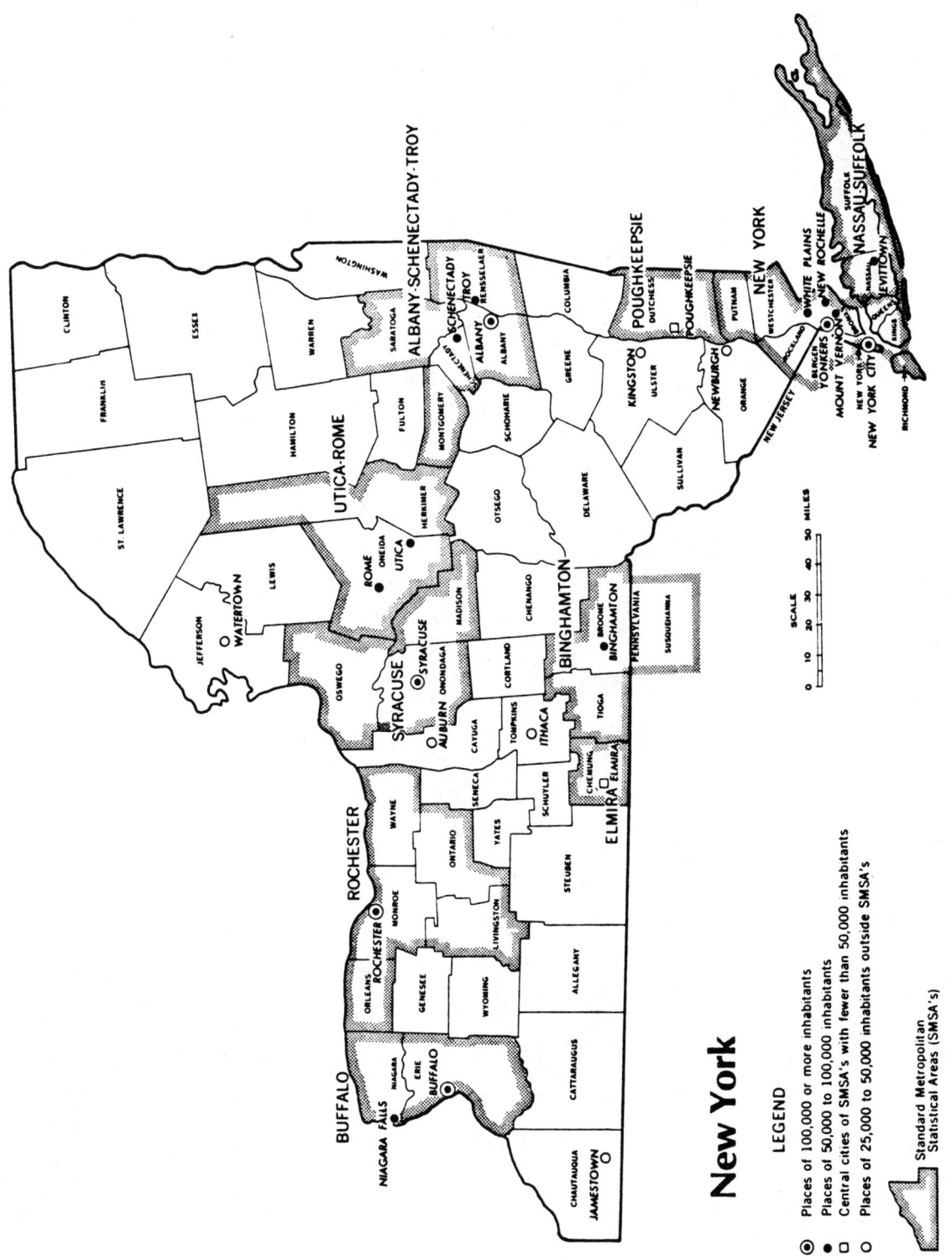

New York

LEGEND

⊙ Places of 100,000 or more inhabitants

● Places of 50,000 to 100,000 inhabitants

□ Central cities of SMSA's with fewer than 50,000 inhabitants

○ Places of 25,000 to 50,000 inhabitants outside SMSA's

Standard Metropolitan
Statistical Areas (SMSA's)

SCALE

0 10 20 30 40 50 MILES

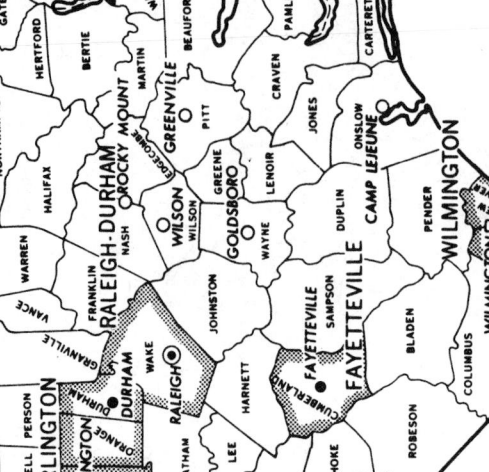

North Carolina

LEGEND

⊙ Places of 100,000 or more inhabitants

● Places of 50,000 to 100,000 inhabitants

☐ Central cities of SMSA's with fewer than 50,000 inhabitants

○ Places of 25,000 to 50,000 inhabitants outside SMSA's

 Standard Metropolitan Statistical Areas (SMSA's)

SCALE

0 10 20 30 40 50 MILES

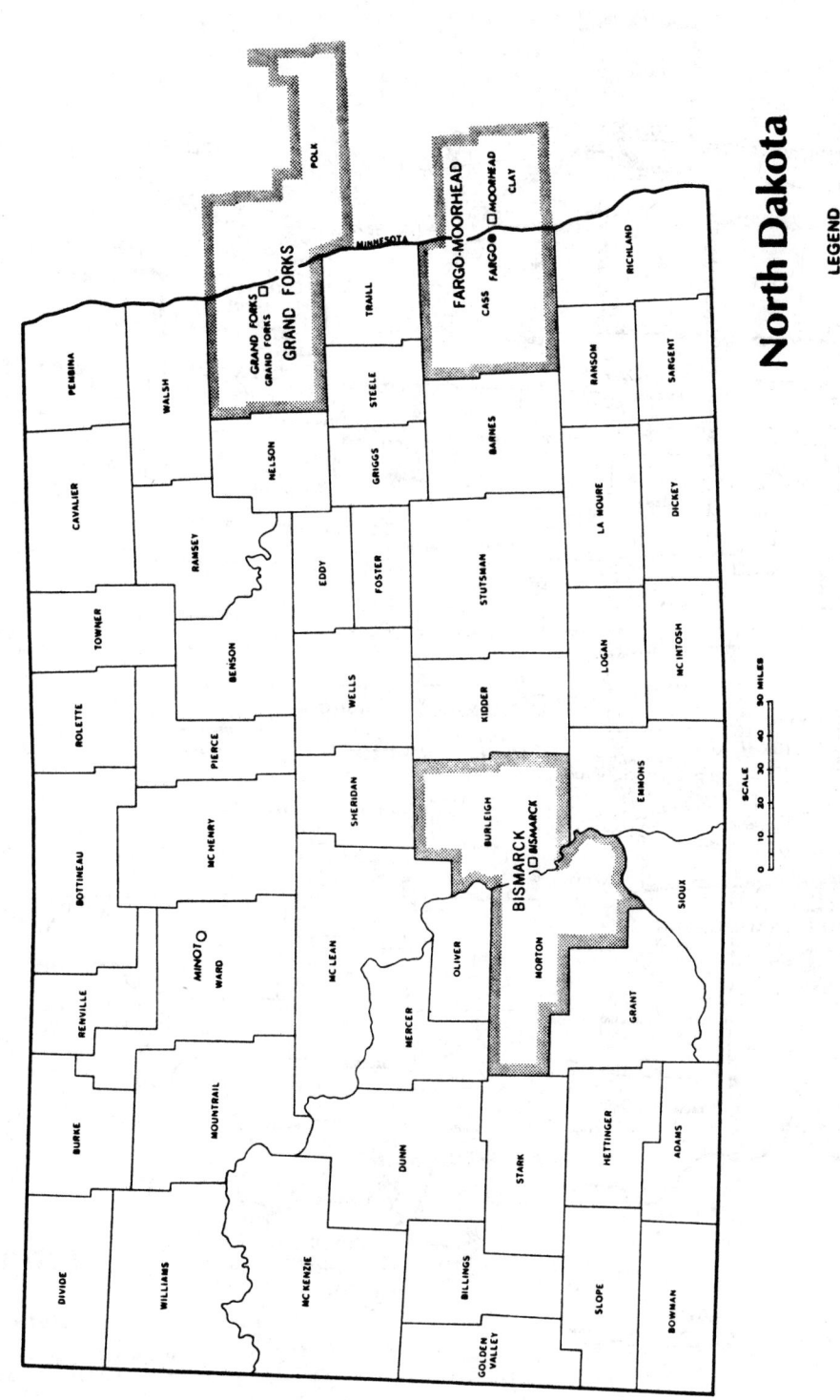

North Dakota

LEGEND

- ● Places of 50,000 to 100,000 inhabitants
- □ SMSA central cities with fewer than 50,000 inhabitants
- ○ Places of 25,000 to 50,000 inhabitants outside SMSA's

Standard Metropolitan
Statistical Areas (SMSA's)

Ohio

LEGEND

- ⊙ Places of 100,000 or more inhabitants
- ● Places of 50,000 to 100,000 inhabitants
- □ SMSA central cities with fewer than 50,000 inhabitants
- ○ Places of 25,000 to 50,000 inhabitants outside SMSA's

Standard Metropolitan
Statistical Areas (SMSA's)

SCALE

0   10   20   30   40   50 MILES

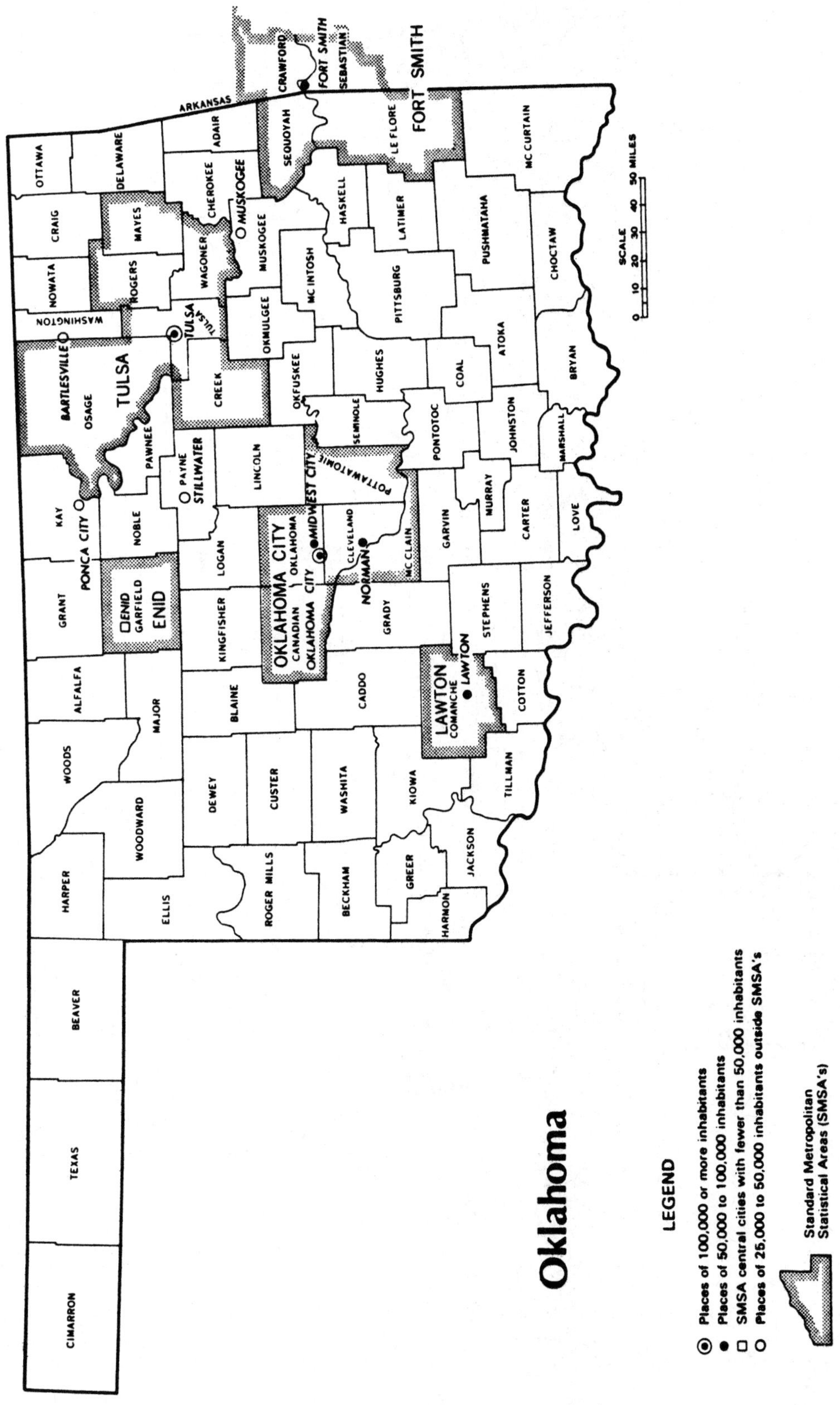

Oklahoma

LEGEND

⊙ Places of 100,000 or more inhabitants

● Places of 50,000 to 100,000 inhabitants

□ SMSA central cities with fewer than 50,000 inhabitants

○ Places of 25,000 to 50,000 inhabitants outside SMSA's

Standard Metropolitan
Statistical Areas (SMSA's)

CIMARRON

TEXAS

BEAVER

HARPER

WOODS

ALFALFA

GRANT

KAY

OSAGE

WASHINGTON

NOWATA

CRAIG

OTTAWA

DELAWARE

MAYES

ROGERS

CHEROKEE

ADAIR

SEQUOYAH

MUSKOGEE

WAGONER

WOODWARD

MAJOR

GARFIELD

NOBLE

PAWNEE

PAYNE

CREEK

TULSA

MCINTOSH

HASKELL

LE FLORE

ELLIS

DEWEY

BLAINE

KINGFISHER

LOGAN

LINCOLN

OKFUSKEE

OKMULGEE

MCCLAIN

OKLAHOMA

CANADIAN

CLEVELAND

SEMINOLE

HUGHES

PITTSBURG

LATIMER

PUSHMATAHA

ROGER MILLS

CUSTER

WASHITA

CADDO

GRADY

POTTAWATOMIE

PONTOTOC

COAL

ATOKA

BECKHAM

GREER

KIOWA

COMANCHE

STEPHENS

GARVIN

MURRAY

JOHNSTON

MARSHALL

CARTER

LOVE

BRYAN

CHOCTAW

MCCURTAIN

HARMON

JACKSON

TILLMAN

COTTON

JEFFERSON

ARKANSAS

CRAWFORD

FORT SMITH

SEBASTIAN

BARTLESVILLE

TULSA

PONCA CITY

ENID

STILLWATER

OKLAHOMA CITY

MIDWEST CITY

NORMAN

LAWTON

MUSKOGEE

FORT SMITH

SCALE

0 10 20 30 40 50 MILES

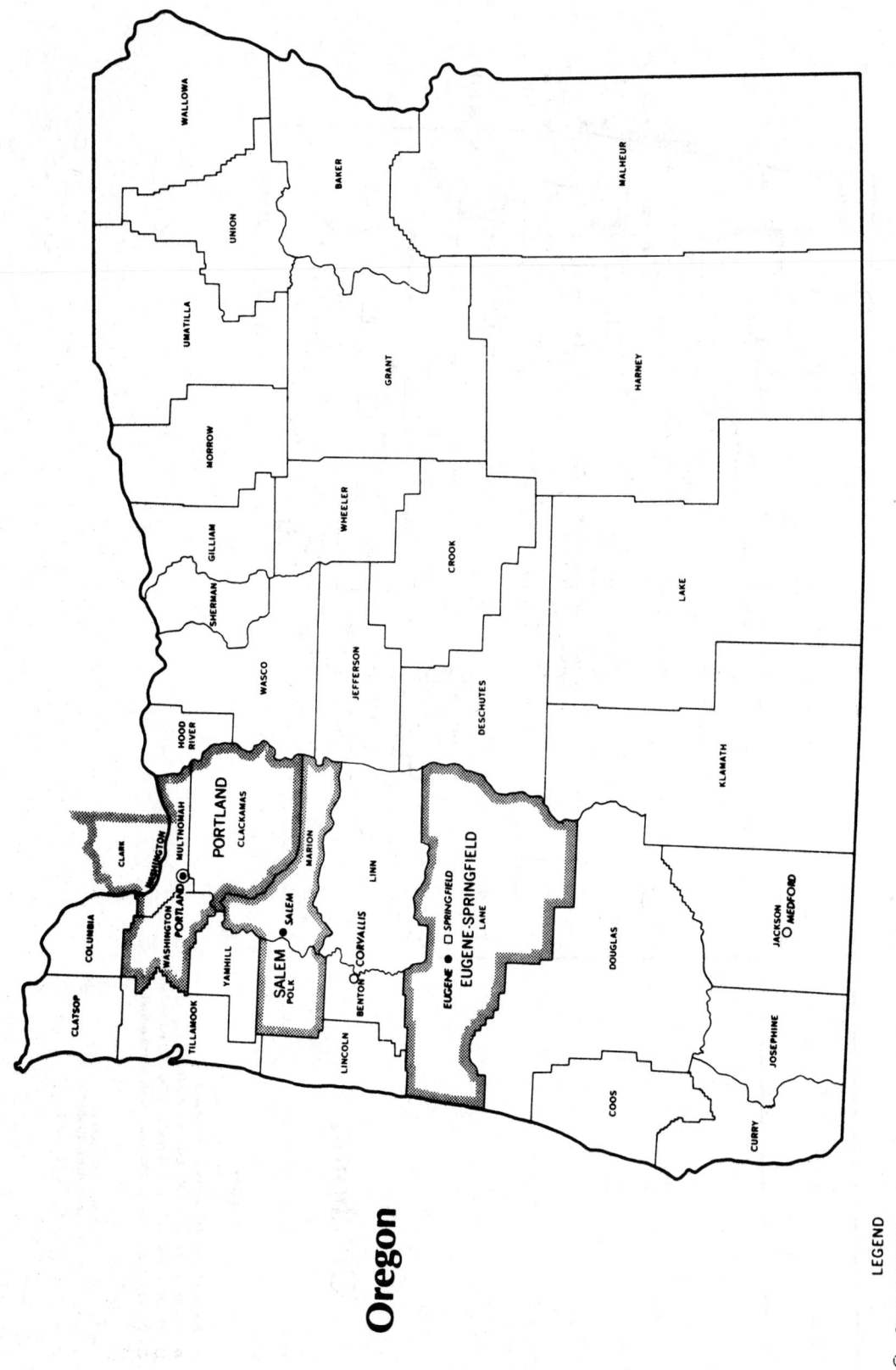

Oregon

LEGEND

◉ Places of 100,000 or more inhabitants
● Places of 50,000 to 100,000 inhabitants
□ Central cities of SMSA's with fewer than 50,000 inhabitants
○ Places of 25,000 to 50,000 inhabitants outside SMSA's

⬡ Standard Metropolitan
Statistical Areas (SMSA's)

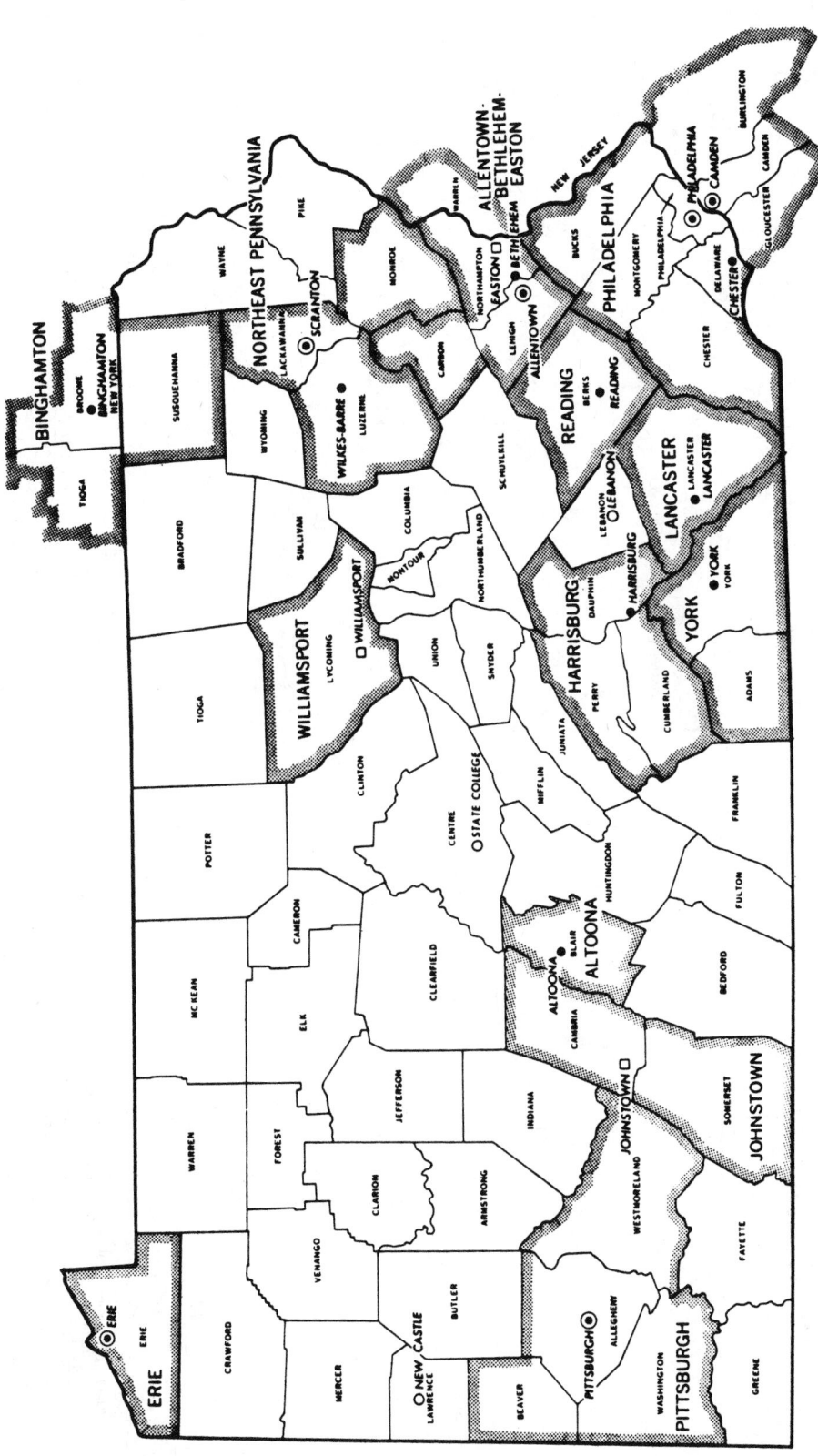

Pennsylvania

LEGEND

⊙ Places of 100,000 or more inhabitants

● Places of 50,000 to 100,000 inhabitants

▢ Central cities of SMSA's with fewer than 50,000 inhabitants

○ Places of 25,000 to 50,000 inhabitants outside SMSA's

Standard Metropolitan
Statistical Areas (SMSA's)

SCALE

0   10   20   30   40   50 MILES

Rhode Island

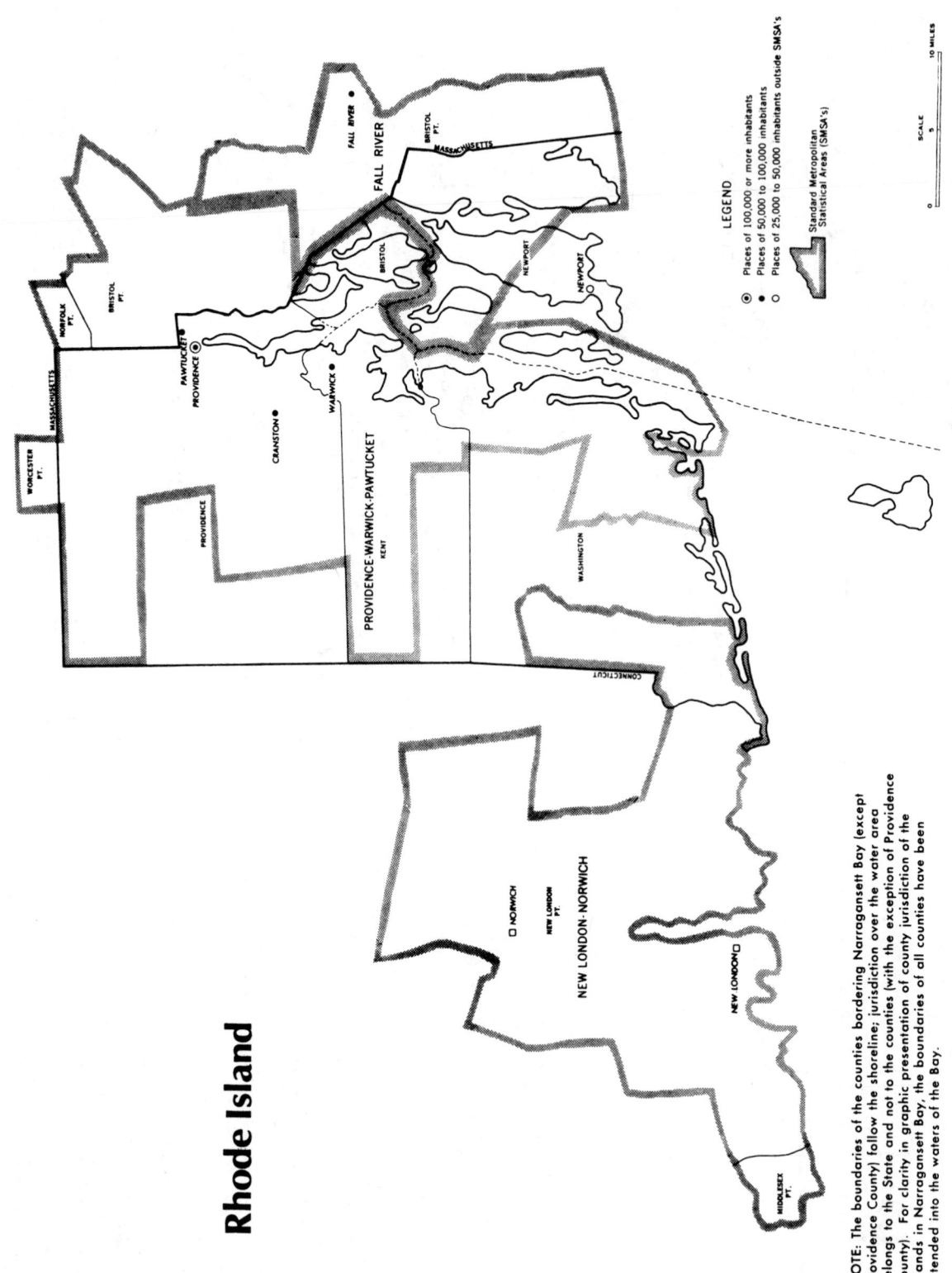

NOTE: The boundaries of the counties bordering Narragansett Bay (except Providence County) follow the shoreline; jurisdiction over the water area belongs to the State and not to the counties (with the exception of Providence County). For clarity in graphic presentation of county jurisdiction of the islands in Narragansett Bay, the boundaries of all counties have been extended into the waters of the Bay.

LEGEND

◉ Places of 100,000 or more inhabitants
● Places of 50,000 to 100,000 inhabitants
○ Places of 25,000 to 50,000 inhabitants outside SMSA's

Standard Metropolitan Statistical Areas (SMSA's)

SCALE

0   5   10 MILES

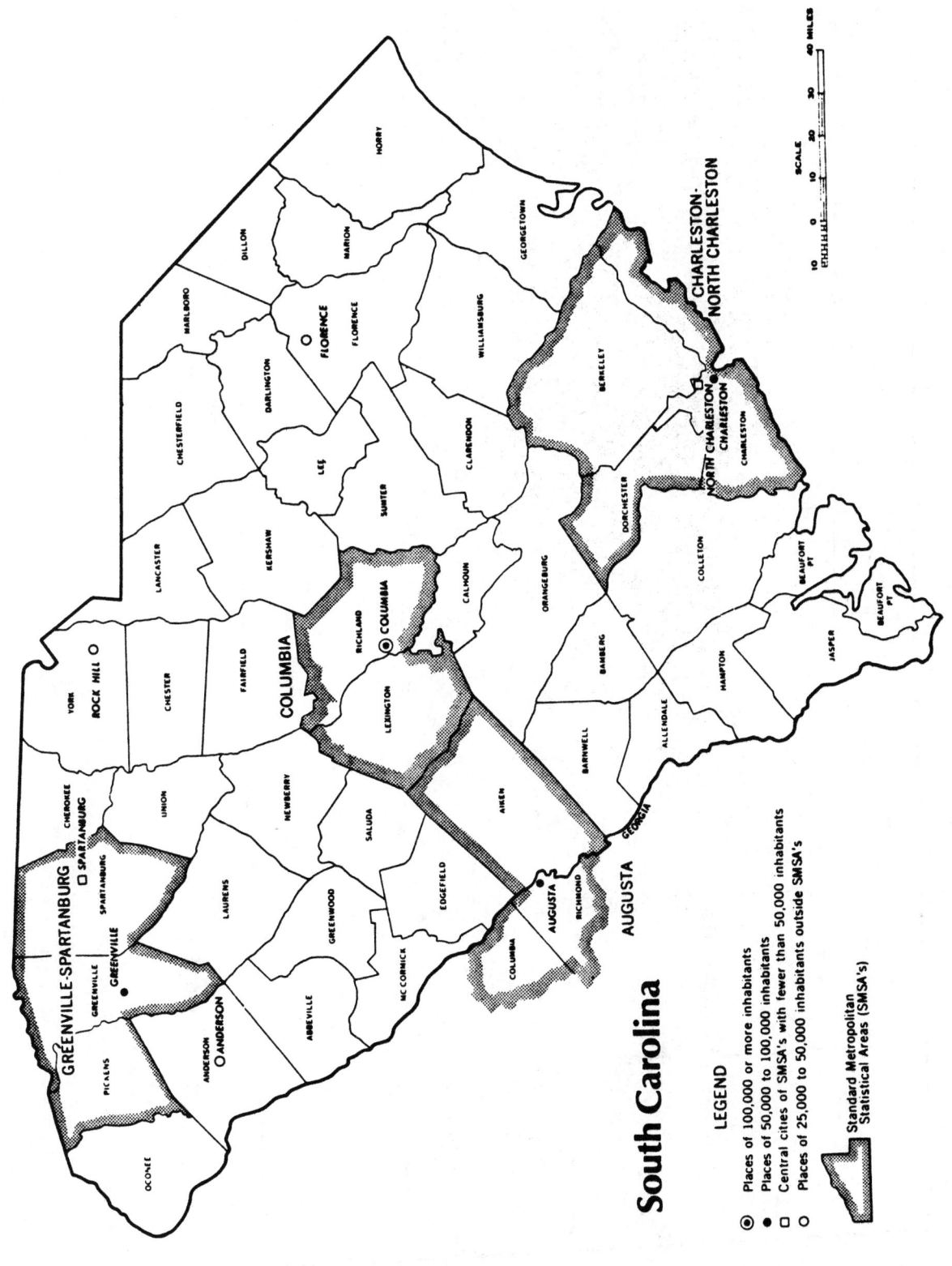

South Carolina

LEGEND

⊙ Places of 100,000 or more inhabitants
● Places of 50,000 to 100,000 inhabitants
□ Central cities of SMSA's with fewer than 50,000 inhabitants
○ Places of 25,000 to 50,000 inhabitants outside SMSA's

Standard Metropolitan
Statistical Areas (SMSA's)

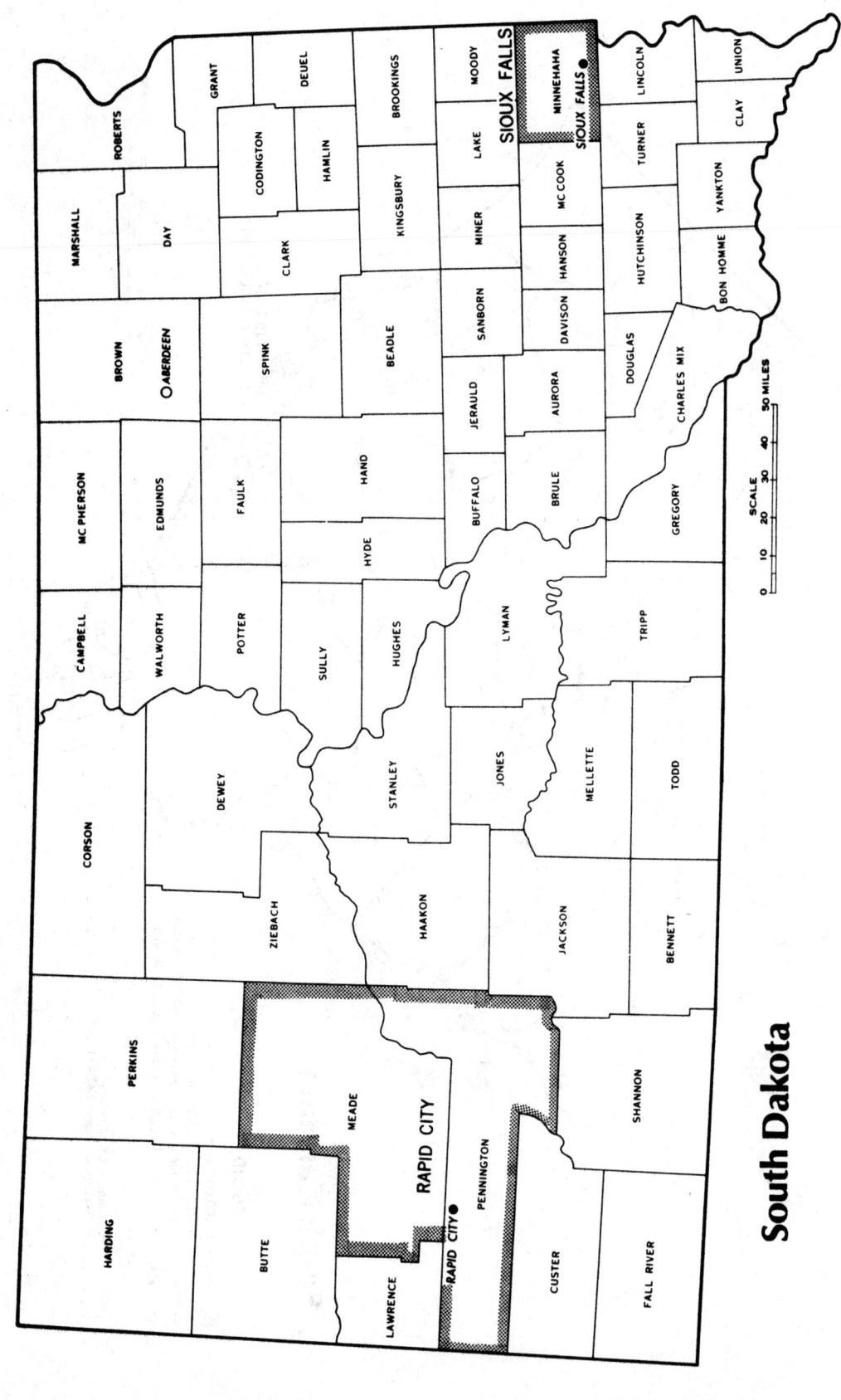

South Dakota

LEGEND

- ● Places of 50,000 to 100,000 inhabitants
- ○ Places of 25,000 to 50,000 inhabitants outside SMSA's

Standard Metropolitan
Statistical Areas (SMSA's)

SCALE

0 10 20 30 40 50 MILES

Tennessee

JOHNSON CITY-KINGSPORT-BRISTOL

CLARKSVILLE-HOPKINSVILLE

NASHVILLE DAVIDSON

MEMPHIS

KNOXVILLE

CHATTANOOGA

LEGEND

- ⦿ Places of 100,000 or more inhabitants
- ⦿ Places of 25,000 to 50,000 inhabitants outside SMSA's
- ☐ Central cities of SMSA's with fewer than 50,000 inhabitants

Standard Metropolitan
Statistical Areas (SMSA's)

SCALE
0 10 20 30 40 50 MILES

KENTUCKY
VIRGINIA
GEORGIA
MISSISSIPPI
ARKANSAS
DADE
WALKER
CATOOSA
DESOTO

LAKE, OBION, WEAKLEY, HENRY, STEWART, MONTGOMERY, ROBERTSON, SUMNER, MACON, CLAY, PICKETT, FENTRESS, SCOTT, CAMPBELL, CLAIBORNE, HANCOCK, CLAY, HAWKINS, SULLIVAN, WASHINGTON, CARTER, JOHNSON, UNICOI, GREENE, HAMBLEN, GRAINGER, UNION, ANDERSON, MORGAN, CUMBERLAND, OVERTON, JACKSON, SMITH, TROUSDALE, WILSON, DAVIDSON, CHEATHAM, DICKSON, HOUSTON, HUMPHREYS, BENTON, CARROLL, GIBSON, DYER, LAUDERDALE, CROCKETT, HAYWOOD, TIPTON, SHELBY, FAYETTE, HARDEMAN, MCNAIRY, CHESTER, MADISON, HENDERSON, DECATUR, PERRY, HICKMAN, WILLIAMSON, RUTHERFORD, CANNON, DE KALB, WHITE, PUTNAM, ROANE, KNOX, JEFFERSON, COCKE, SEVIER, BLOUNT, LOUDON, MONROE, MCMINN, MEIGS, RHEA, BLEDSOE, VAN BUREN, WARREN, COFFEE, BEDFORD, MARSHALL, MAURY, LEWIS, WAYNE, HARDIN, LAWRENCE, GILES, LINCOLN, FRANKLIN, MOORE, GRUNDY, SEQUATCHIE, MARION, HAMILTON, BRADLEY, POLK

CRITTENDEN

HOPKINSVILLE, CLARKSVILLE, KINGSPORT, BRISTOL, JOHNSON CITY, CHRISTIAN

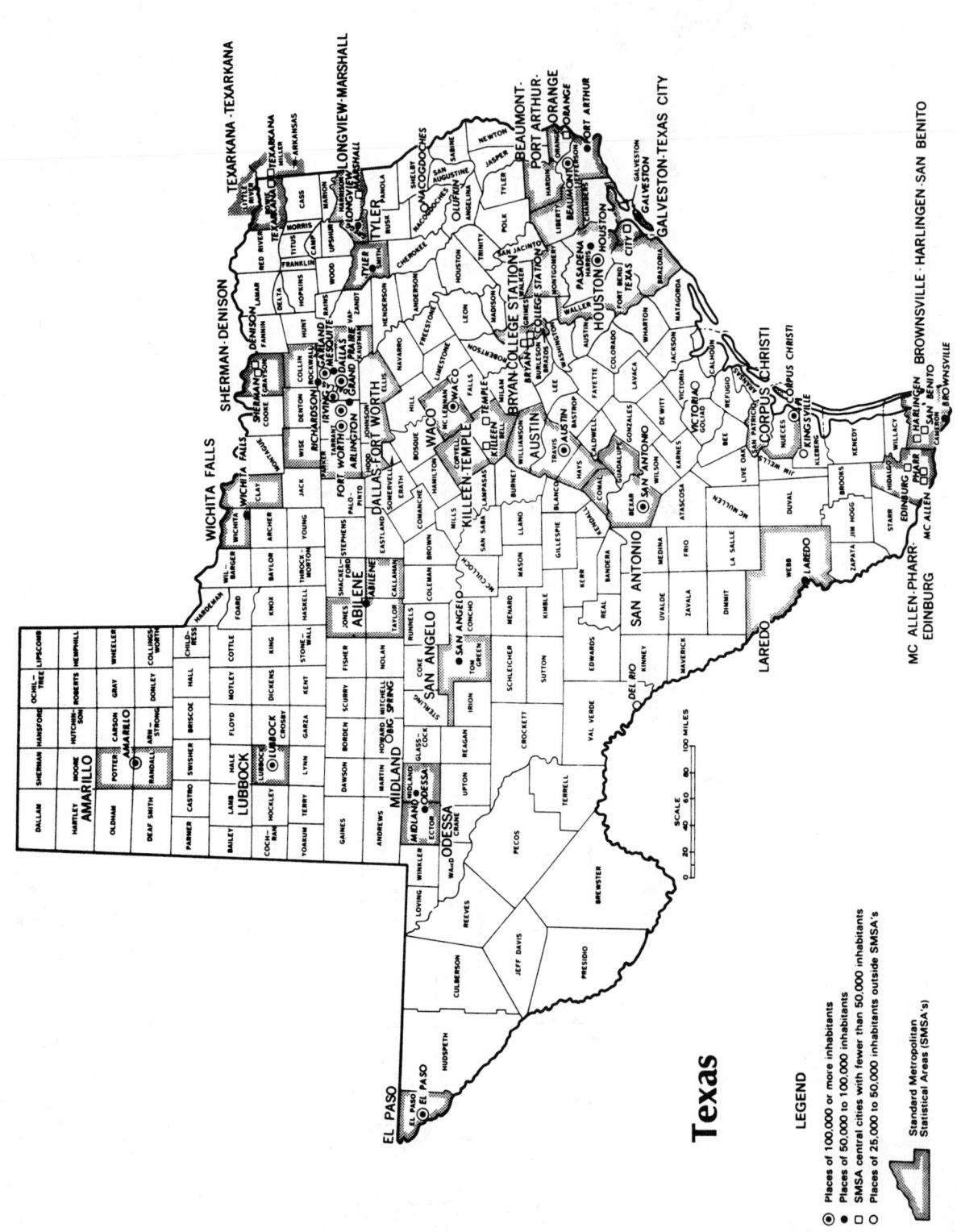

Texas

LEGEND

◉ Places of 100,000 or more inhabitants

● Places of 50,000 to 100,000 inhabitants

□ SMSA central cities with fewer than 50,000 inhabitants

○ Places of 25,000 to 50,000 inhabitants outside SMSA's

Standard Metropolitan
Statistical Areas (SMSA's)

Utah

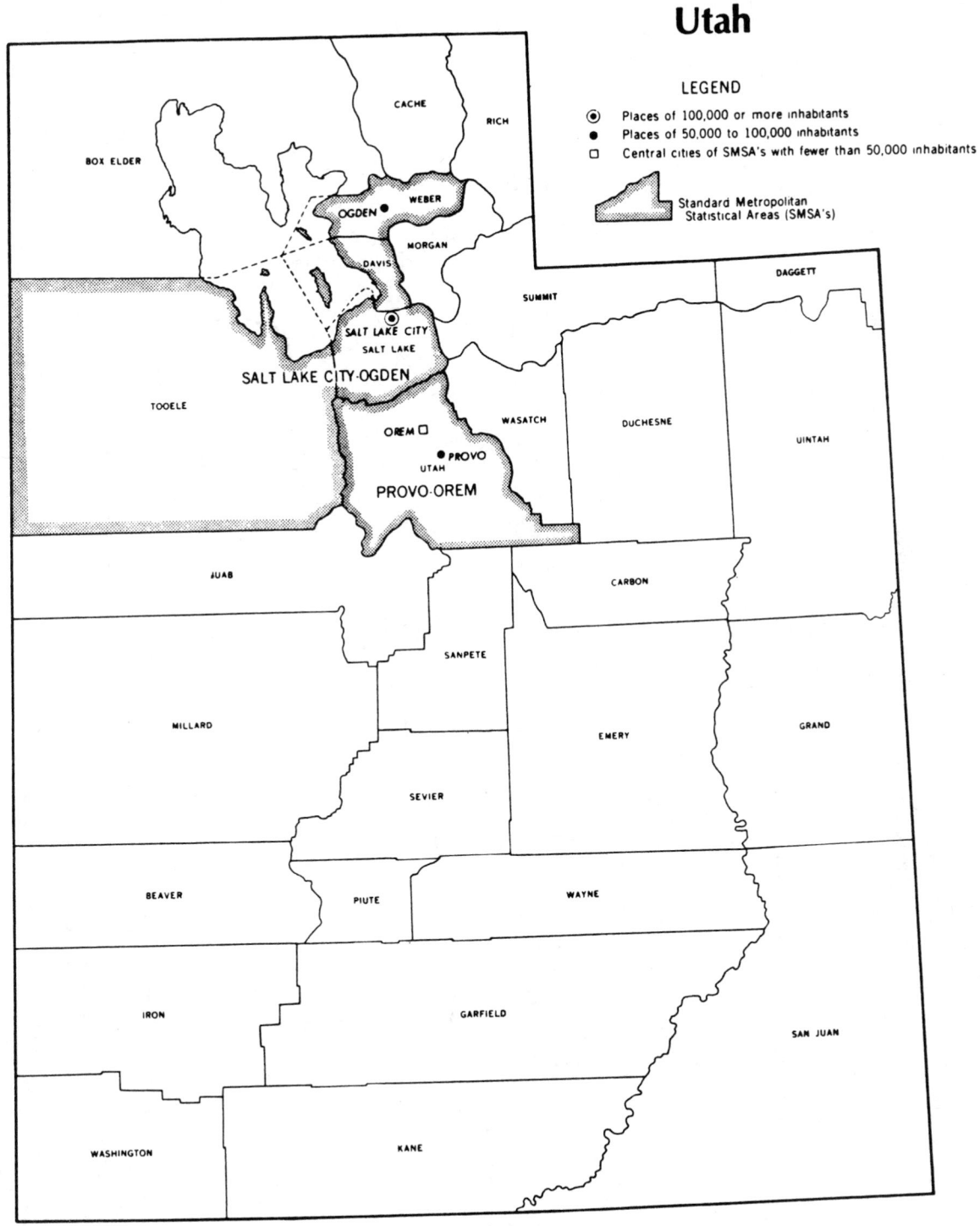

LEGEND

⊙ Places of 100,000 or more inhabitants

● Places of 50,000 to 100,000 inhabitants

□ Central cities of SMSA's with fewer than 50,000 inhabitants

Standard Metropolitan Statistical Areas (SMSA's)

SCALE

0 10 20 30 40 50 MILES

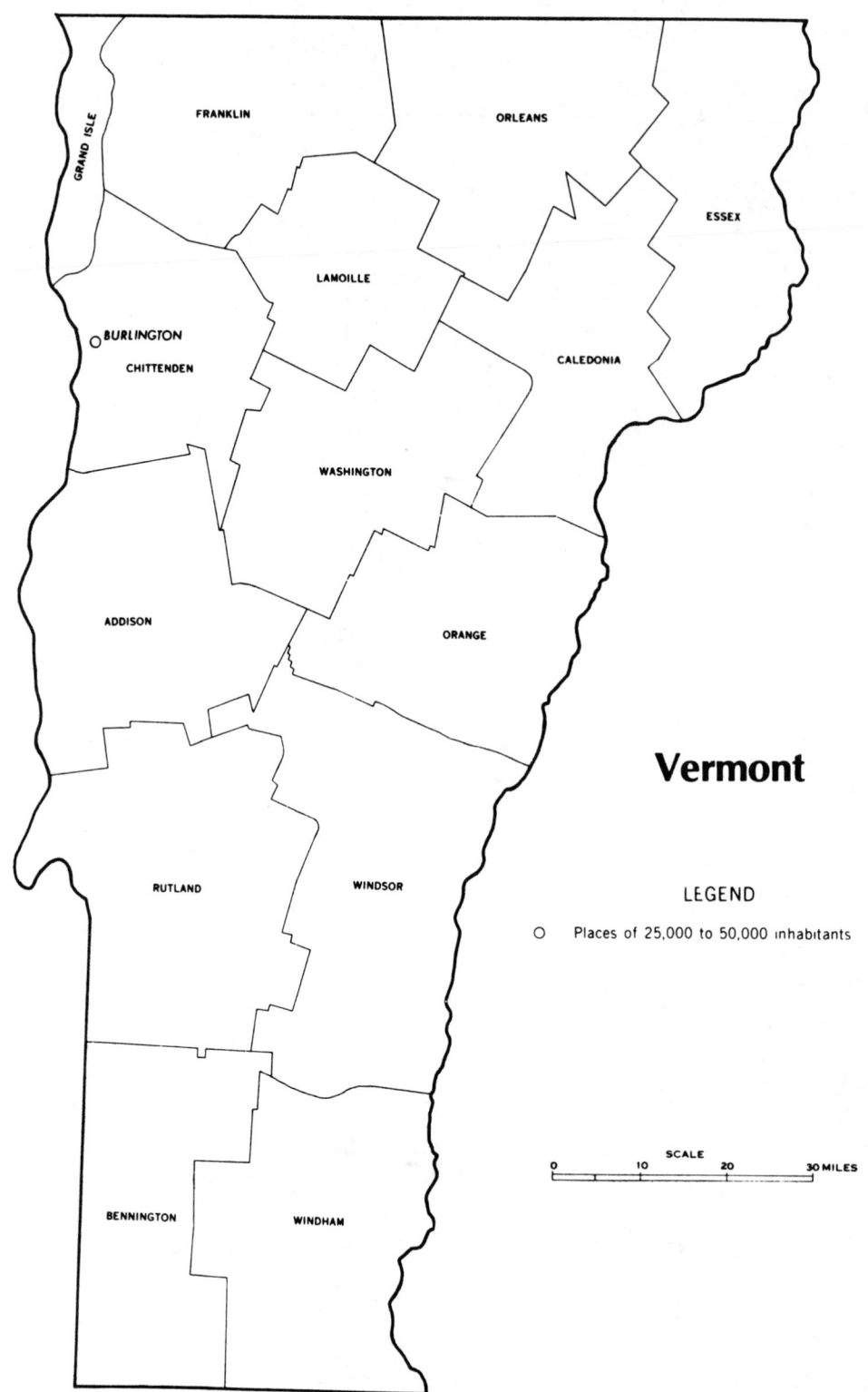

Vermont

LEGEND

○   Places of 25,000 to 50,000 inhabitants

SCALE

0   10   20   30 MILES

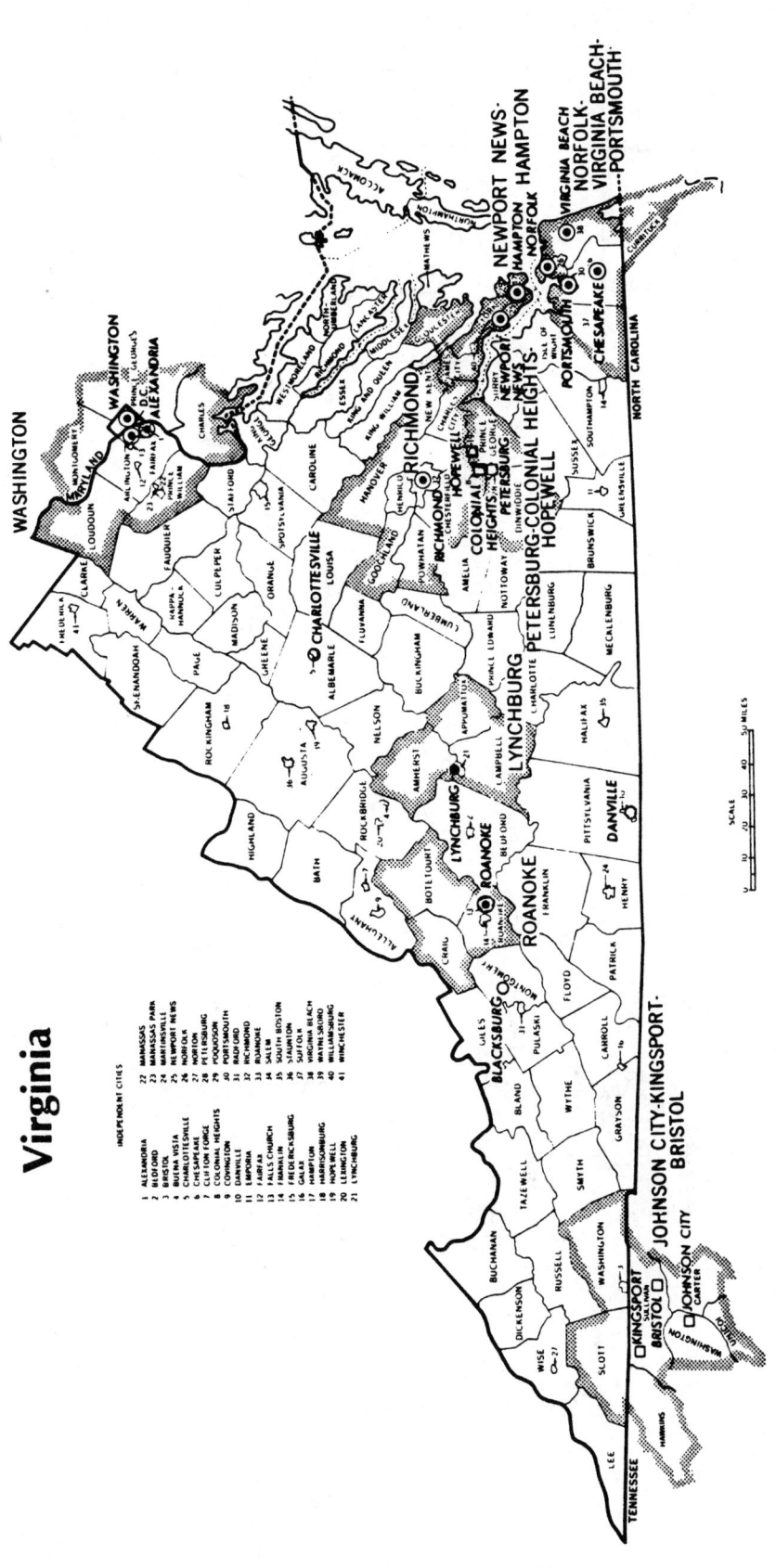

Virginia

INDEPENDENT CITIES

1 ALEXANDRIA
2 BEDFORD
3 BRISTOL
4 BUENA VISTA
5 CHARLOTTESVILLE
6 CHESAPEAKE
7 CLIFTON FORGE
8 COLONIAL HEIGHTS
9 COVINGTON
10 DANVILLE
11 EMPORIA
12 FAIRFAX
13 FALLS CHURCH
14 FRANKLIN
15 FREDERICKSBURG
16 GALAX
17 HAMPTON
18 HARRISONBURG
19 HOPEWELL
20 LEXINGTON
21 LYNCHBURG
22 MANASSAS
23 MANASSAS PARK
24 MARTINSVILLE
25 NEWPORT NEWS
26 NORFOLK
27 NORTON
28 PETERSBURG
29 POQUOSON
30 PORTSMOUTH
31 RADFORD
32 RICHMOND
33 ROANOKE
34 SALEM
35 SOUTH BOSTON
36 STAUNTON
37 SUFFOLK
38 VIRGINIA BEACH
39 WAYNESBORO
40 WILLIAMSBURG
41 WINCHESTER

LEGEND

- ◉ Places of 100,000 or more inhabitants
- ● Places of 50,000 to 100,000 inhabitants
- ◻ SMSA central cities with fewer than 50,000 inhabitants
- ○ Places of 25,000 to 50,000 inhabitants outside SMSA's

Standard Metropolitan Statistical Areas (SMSA's)

SCALE

0   10   20   30   40   50 MILES

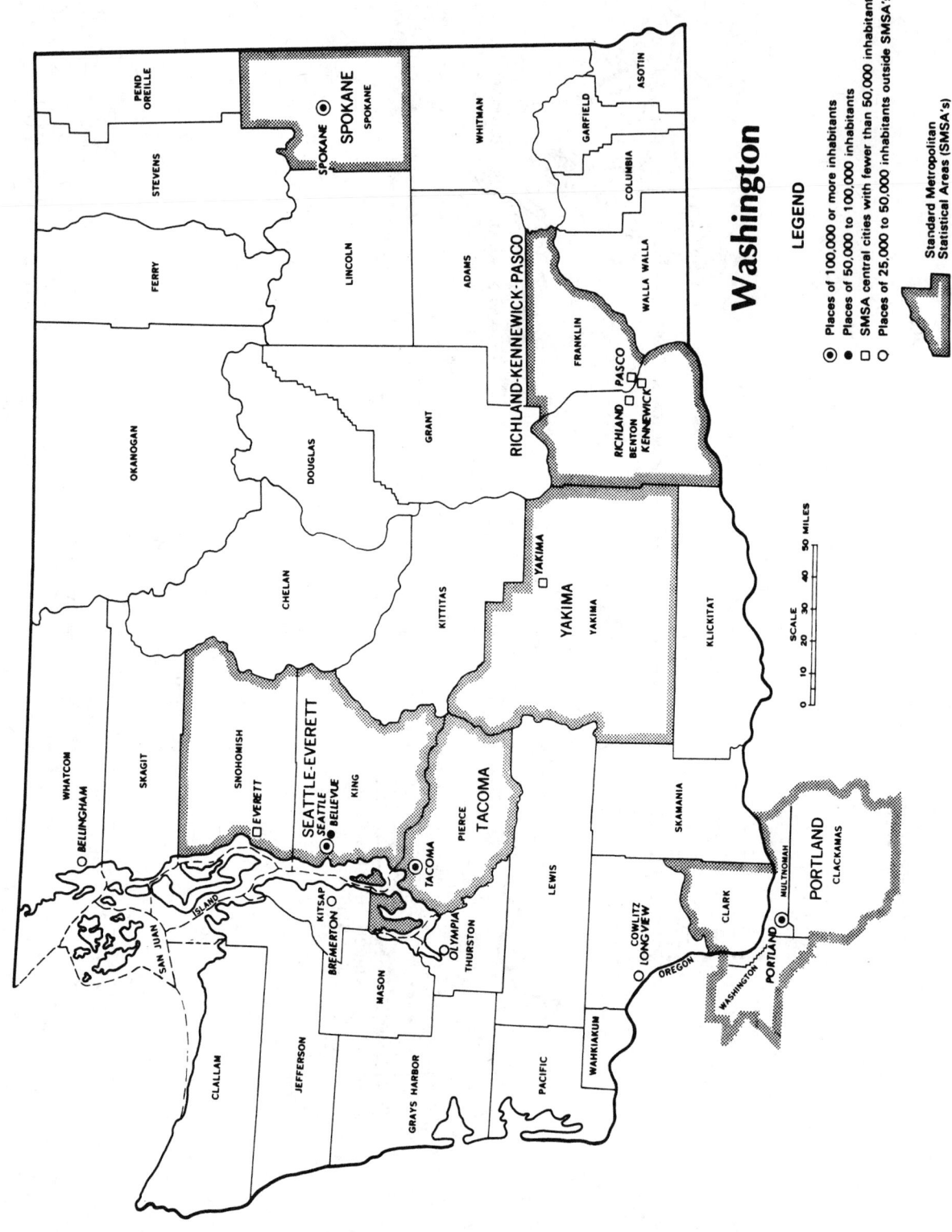

Washington

LEGEND

⊚ Places of 100,000 or more inhabitants

● Places of 50,000 to 100,000 inhabitants

□ SMSA central cities with fewer than 50,000 inhabitants

○ Places of 25,000 to 50,000 inhabitants outside SMSA's

Standard Metropolitan
Statistical Areas (SMSA's)

SCALE

0 10 20 30 40 50 MILES

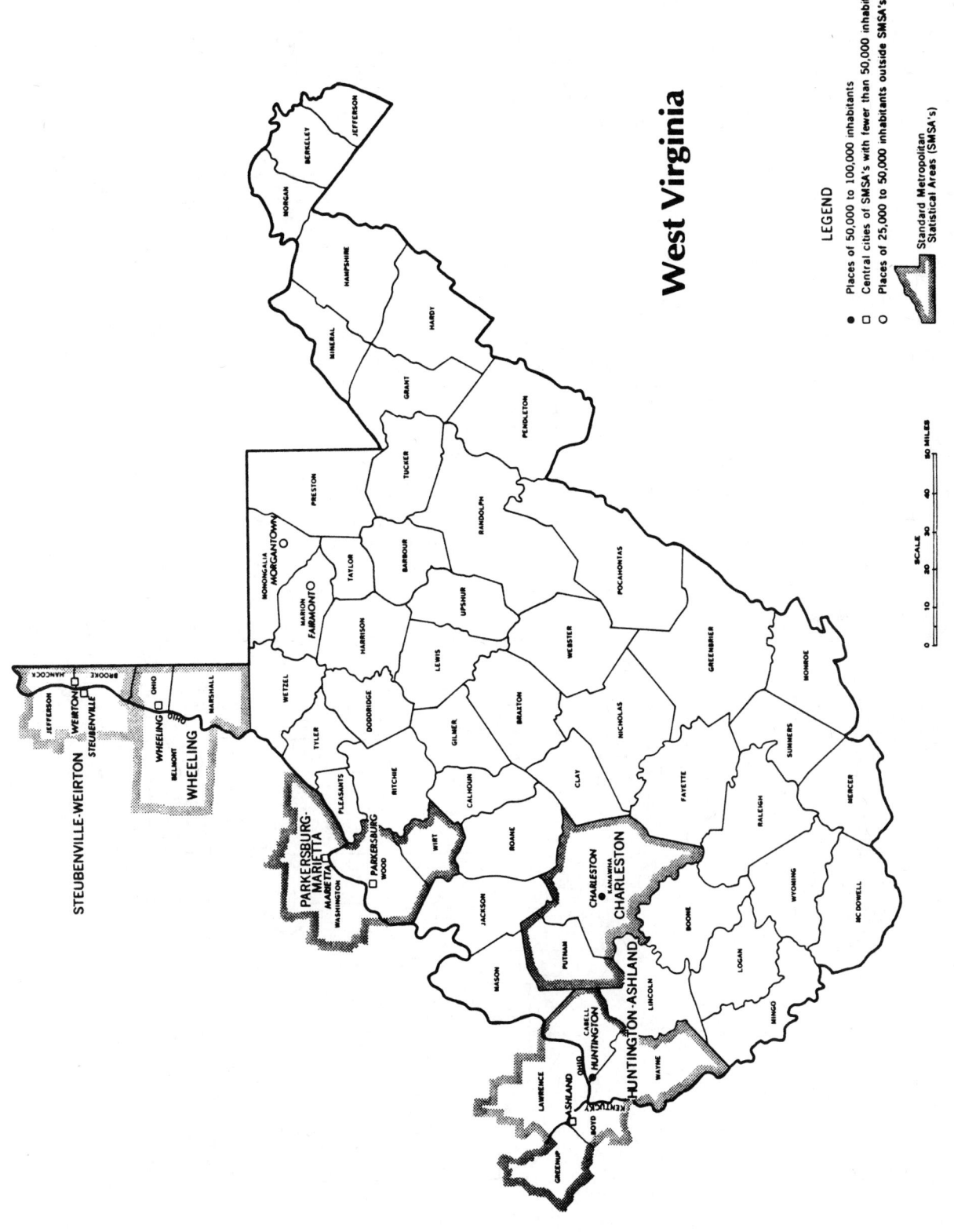

West Virginia

LEGEND

● Places of 50,000 to 100,000 inhabitants

□ Central cities of SMSA's with fewer than 50,000 inhabitants

○ Places of 25,000 to 50,000 inhabitants outside SMSA's

Standard Metropolitan
Statistical Areas (SMSA's)

SCALE

0 10 20 30 40 50 MILES

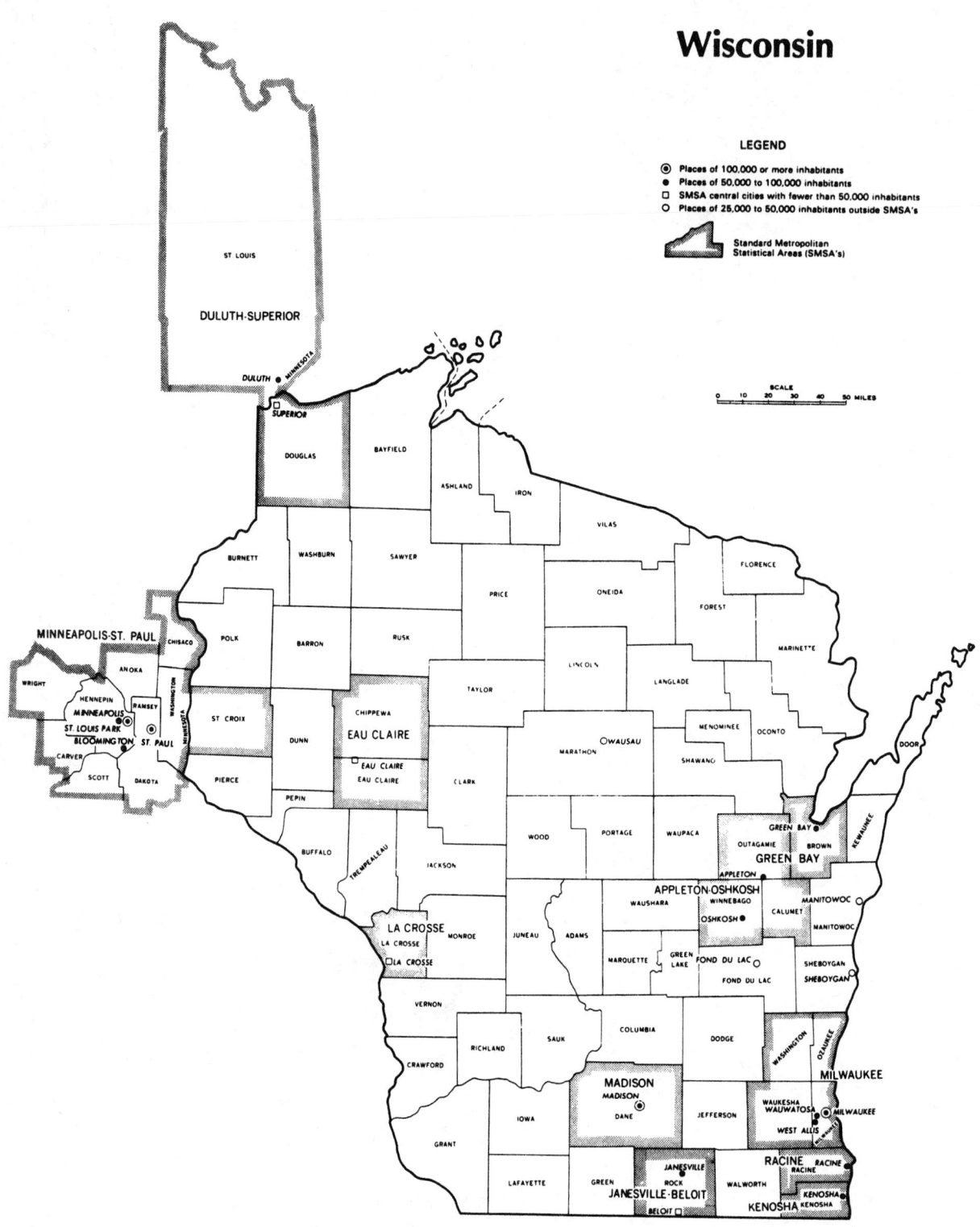

Wisconsin

LEGEND

⊙ Places of 100,000 or more inhabitants
● Places of 50,000 to 100,000 inhabitants
□ SMSA central cities with fewer than 50,000 inhabitants
○ Places of 25,000 to 50,000 inhabitants outside SMSA's

Standard Metropolitan
Statistical Areas (SMSA's)

SCALE
0 10 20 30 40 50 MILES

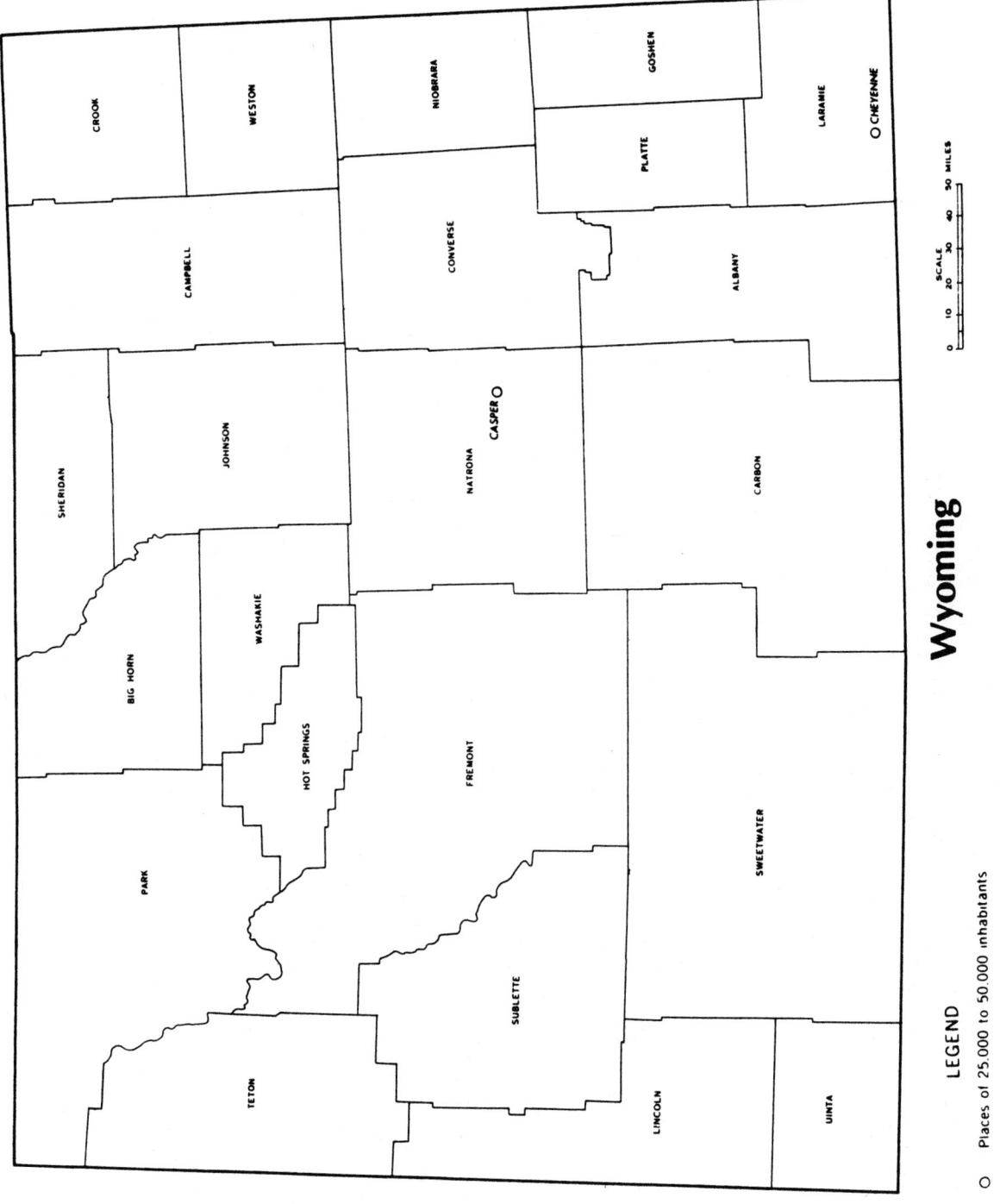

Wyoming

LEGEND

O Places of 25,000 to 50,000 inhabitants

CHAPTER 13

WPA INVENTORIES — PUBLISHED — UNPUBLISHED

W. P. A. County Inventories

One of the important projects of the W.P.A. during the great depression was the "Historical Records Survey Program." In this program people were hired by the W.P.A. to inventory all records both public and private, that were of historical value. The project was never completed, and not all of the records that were inventoried are of value to the genealogist. However, where an inventory of the county records was completed, they can be very useful. Where the county inventories exist they will list all records from the inception of the county until the time of inventory. Some of the inventories were published and some were not. The following is a list of the Published W.P.A. County Inventories, followed by a list of the Unpublished County W.P.A. Inventories.

W.P.A. Published

This section is a listing of those various county inventories published by the W.P.A. Hopefully your ancestral county is listed under the state concerned so that you will probably know the exact location of the records. If not, then you would want to order a copy of the largest or thickest inventory published under that state. This will tell you what ought to be in every county in that state. When ordering, you need not concern yourself about the W.P.A. number to the left of the county title.

Hence, once you have located a book you would like, you can usually obtain a copy from the appropriate state library or through inter-library loan. For example, if you wanted to order an inventory of Alabama and the county you wanted was not listed, you would need to order a large county WPA Inventory such as Lowndes County which was printed in 1939 and is probably available from the State Library in Montgomery, because it contains approximately the same kinds of information as all other counties in Alabama. From these records, therefore, you could determine what kind of records to ask for in the appropriate county.

The WPA Inventories are your "key" to the county courthouses of America because they tell you what kind of records were kept in each county.

Published   W. P. A.   County Inventories

Re: W.P.A. = 40 states, all except—Conn., Del., Maine, Maryland, Ohio, Penn., S.C., Vt., Alaska and Hawaii.

Inventories of County Archives	Date of Inventory

ALABAMA:

No.	14.	Clay	December 1941
No.	17.	Clobert	May 1939
No.	18.	Conecuh	May 1938
No.	22.	Cullman	December 1941
No.	32.	Greene	Feb. 1942
		Prelim. Edition	
No.	33.	Hale	July 1940
No.	39.	Lauderdale	June 1942
		Prelim. edition	
No.	43.	Lowndes	November 1939
No.	45.	Madison	June 1942
		Prelim. edition	
No.	46.	Marengo	August 1940
No.	60.	Sumter	August 1940
No.	61.	Talladega	April 1940
No.	66.	Wilcox	Feb. 1942
		Prelim. edition	
No.	67.	Winston	December 1941
		Prelim. edition	

ARIZONA:

No.	7.	Maricopa	August 1940
No.	10.	Pima	July 1938
No.	12.	Santa Cruz	November 1941

ARKANSAS:

No.	3.	Baxter	February 1942
No.	4.	Benton	December 1941
No.	8.	Carroll	May 1942
No.	12.	Cleburne	March 1939
No.	13.	Cleveland	April 1941
No.	19.	Cross	July 1940
No.	23.	Faulkner	December 1939
No.	30.	Hot Srpings	March 1940
No.	33.	Izard	March 1942
No.	34.	Jackson	October 1941
No.	44.	Madison	May 1942

No.	48.	Monroe	April 1942
No.	49.	Montgomery	April 1942
No.	57.	Polk	January 1942
No.	62.	Saline	May 1942
No.	63.	Scott	March 1942
No.	65.	Searcy	June 1940

CALIFORNIA, NORTHERN:

No.	1.	Alameda: Vol. 11	February 1942
No.	10.	Fresno	July 1940
No.	15.	Kern: Vol. II	June 1941
No.	22.	Marin	December 1937
No.	27.	Mono	April 1940
No.	29.	Napa	March 1941
No.	36.	San Benito	February 1940
No.	39.	San Francisco: Vol. II	May 1940
No.	41.	San Luis Obispo	November 1939
No.	42.	San Mateo	June 1938
No.	44.	Santa Clara	April 1939

CALIFORNIA, SOUTHERN:

No.	20.	Los Angeles	January 1940
		Tax Collector's Office—Assessor's Office	
No.	37.	San Bernardino	August 1940
		Title-Line Inventory of.	
No.	38.	San Diego	January 1941
		Vol. III Tax and Financial Offices	
No.	42.	Santa Barbara	January 1941
		Title-Line Inventory of.	
No.	57.	Ventura	August 1940
		Title-Line Inventory of.	
No.	20.	Los Angeles	1943
		County Clerks's Office—County and Municipal Special Districts	

COLORADO:

No.	2.	Alamosa	June 1942
No.	3.	Arapahoe	February 1939
No.	6.	Bent	June 1938

No. 11. Conejos .... October 1938
No. 12. Costilla .... May 1938
No. 22. Fremont .... January 1938
No. 23. Garfield .... June 1941
No. 27. Hinsdale .... October 1939
No. 35. Larimer .... October 1941
No. 38. Logan .... April 1940
No. 44. Morgan .... September 1939
No. 48. Phillips .... March 1941
No. 50. Prowers 1941
No. 57. San Miguel .... January 1941
No. 61. Washington ...... January 1941
No. 63. Yuma .... February 1941

DELAWARE:

No. 1. New Castle 1941

FLORIDA:

No. 8. Charlotee .... November 1938
No. 10. Clay .... January 1941
No. 11. Collier .... March 1938
No. 16. Duval .... February 1938
No. 18. Flagler .... August 1938
No. 25. Hardee .... June 1939
No. 26. Hendry .... June 1938
No. 37. Leon .... December 1941
No. 46. Okaloosa .... May 1939
No. 54. Pinellas .... June 1940
No. 58. Sarasota .... May 1939
No. 65. Wakulla .... March 1942

GEORGIA:

No. 25. Chatham .... March 1938
No. 32. Clinch .... September 1940
No. 37. Cook .... August 1941
No. 47. Dougherty .... January 1941
No. 50. Echols .... September 1940
No. 81. Jefferson .... May 1940
No. 88. Lee .... June 1942
        Vol I-Historical Sketch—Vol. II-
        Records Entries
No. 106. Muscogee .... January 1941
No. 121. Richmond .... April 1939

IDAHO:

        County Government in Idaho:
        Supplementing Inventories of
        County Archives ...... June 1942
No. 6. Bingham .... May 1942
No. 11. Boundary .... February 1939
No. 17. Clark .... March 1940
No. 28. Kootenai .... October 1939
No. 30. Lemhi .... May 1938
No. 34. Minidoka .... September 1937
No. 35. Nez Perce .... June 1939
No. 39. Power .... April 1941
No. 41. Teton .... December 1940

ILLINOIS:

No. 1. Adams .... April 1939
No. 5. Brown .... February 1938
No. 8. Carroll .... December 1937
No. 10. Champaign .... January 1938

No. 12. Clark .... June 1938
No. 18. Cumberland .... April 1938
No. 20. Dewitt .... October 1941
No. 21. Douglas .... November 1939
No. 25. Effingham ...... September 1940
No. 26. Fayette .... September 1939
No. 28. Franklin .... January 1941
No. 39. Jackson .... March 1939
No. 43. Jo Daviess .... February 1938
No. 48. Knox .... September 1938
No. 53. Livingston .... June 1940
No. 54. Logan .... July 1938
        Governmental Organization and
        Records System, Macon County,
        Illinois .... December 1938
No. 56. Macoupin .... July 1939
No. 65. Manard .... April 1941
No. 68. Montgomery ... October 1939
No. 69. Morgan .... June 1939
No. 70. Moultrie .... November 1941
No. 71. Ogle .... August 1940
No. 72. Peoria .... January 1942
No. 74. Piatt .... August 1940
No. 75. Pike .... March 1938
No. 81. Rock Island ..... December 1939
No. 82. Saline .... February 1941
No. 83. Sangamon .... April 1939
No. 85. Scott .... May 1938
No. 86. Shelby .... January 1940
No. 88. St. Clair ..... September 1939
No. 89. Stephenson .... June 1938
No. 92. Vermilion .... March 1940

INDIANA:

No. 2. Allen .... September 1939
No. 5. Blackford 1936
No. 6. Boone 1937
No. 11. Clay .... June 1939
No. 18. Delaware .... March 1940
No. 25. Fulton .... May 1942
No. 28. Greene .... October 1938
No. 34. Howard .... September 1939
No. 38. Jay .... July 1940
No. 46. LaPorte .... May 1939
No. 49. Marion .... June 1938
No. 50. Marshall .... June 1941
No. 53. Monroe .... July 1940
No. 55. Morgan .... February 1941
No. 65. Posey .... June 1940
No. 71. St. Joseph .... April 1939
No. 73. Shelby .... July 1940
No. 79. Tippecanoe .... August 1941
No. 80. Tipton .... September 1941
No. 82. Vanderburgh ..... February 1939
No. 87. Warrick ...... January 1940
No. 90. Wells .... September 1941

IOWA

No. 14. Carroll .... July 1940
No. 18. Cherokee .... May 1939
No. 25. Dallas .... August 1938
No. 31. Dubuque .... February 1938
No. 47. Ida .... May 1938

No. 50. Jasper . . . . December 1938
No. 69. Montgomery . . . . . December 1941
No. 77. Polk . . . . January 1942
No. 81. Sac . . . . July 1940
No. 87. Taylor . . . . August 1941
No. 97. Woodbury . . . . May 1940

KANSAS:

No. 6. Bourbon . . . . July 1940
No. 11. Cherokee . . . . April 1940
No. 30. Franklin . . . . August 1939
No. 32. Gove . . . . December 1941
No. 33. Graham . . . . December 1939
No. 35. Gray . . . . August 1939
No. 37. Greenwood . . . . May 1938
No. 46. Johnson . . . . July 1937
No. 63. Montgomery . . . . . September 1938
No. 64. Morris . . . . June 1942
No. 70. Osage . . . . April 1941
No. 74. Phillips . . . . September 1941
No. 88. Seward . . . . December 1938
No. 89. Shawnee . . . . December 1940

KENTUCKY:

No. 3. Anderson . . . . . . September 1941
No. 14. Breckinridge . . . . . September 1940
No. 20. Carlisle . . . . June 1938
No. 34. Fayette . . . . August 1937
No. 57. Jessamine . . . . February 1940
No. 61. Knox . . . . December 1937
No. 63. Laurel . . . . December 1938
No. 74. McCreary . . . . February 1938
No. 82. Meade . . . . January 1941

LOUISIANA: (Parish Archives)

Title-Line Inventory of the Parish Archives
of Louisiana Parts 1 and 2, Acadia Through
Winn. . . . . December 1939)
No. 2. Allen . . . . June 1938
No. 4. Assumption . . . . March 1942
No. 6. Beauregard . . . . October 1940
No. 8. Bossier . . . . August 1940
No. 10. Calcasieu . . . . March 1938
No. 22. Grant . . . . April 1940
No. 26. Jefferson . . . . January 1940
No. 26. Jefferson . . . . April 1940
A Brief History
No. 28. Lafayette . . . . February 1943
No. 29. Lafourche . . . . March 1942
No. 34. Marehouse . . . . March 1942
No. 35. Natchitoches . . . . September 1938
No. 36. Orleans . . . . June 1939
Preliminary Inventory of Notarial
Records
No. 37. Ouachita . . . . March 1942
No. 38. Plaquemines . . . . August 1939
No. 43. Sabine . . . . January 1942
No. 44. St. Bernard . . . . . . December 1938
No. 45. St. Charles . . . . . . November 1937
No. 55. Terrebonne . . . . May 1941
No. 59. Washington . . . . March 1940
No. 60. Webster . . . . March 1942

MARYLAND:

No. 1. Allegany . . . . September 1937
No. 2. Anne Arundel . . . . December 1941
No. 6. Carroll . . . . March 1940
No. 11. Garrett . . . . June 1938
No. 13. Howard . . . . March 1939
No. 15. Montgomery . . . . . . February 1939
No. 21. Washington . . . . . December 1937
No. 22. Wicomicc . . . . September 1940

MASSACHUSETTS:

No. 5. Essex . . . . December 1937

MICHIGAN:

No. 2. Alger . . . . March 1941
No. 4. Alpena . . . . May 1938
Revised edition . . . . April 1942
No. 7. Baraga . . . . November 1937
No. 9. Bay . . . . November 1940
No. 13. Calhoun . . . . May 1941
No. 16. Cheboygan . . . . . . December 1938
No. 25. Genesee . . . . March 1940
No. 35. Iosco . . . . May 1938
No. 36. Iron . . . . June 1938
No. 38. Jackson . . . . June 1941
No. 52. Marquette . . . . May 1940
No. 61. Muskegon . . . . . . December 1941

MINNESOTA:

No. 1. Atkin . . . . March 1942
No. 2. Anoka . . . . February 1942
No. 4. Beltrami . . . . November 1941
No. 5. Benton . . . . March 1940
No. 6. Big Stone . . . . August 1941
No. 7. Blue Earth . . . . August 1937
No. 11. Cass . . . . February 1941
No. 12. Chippewa . . . . . . September 1940
No. 19. Dakota . . . . May 1940
No. 20. Dodge . . . . September 1941
No. 21. Douglas . . . . March 1941
No. 22. Fairbault . . . . October 1938
No. 23. Fillmore . . . . January 1942
No. 24. Freeborn . . . . August 1937
No. 25. Goodhue . . . . August 1941
No. 26. Grant . . . . November 1939
No. 28. Houston . . . . December 1941
No. 29. Hubbard . . . . April 1941
No. 32. Jackson . . . . April 1940
No. 33. Kanabec . . . . May 1941
No. 41. Lincoln . . . . June 1941
No. 45. Marshall . . . . December 1939
No. 46. Martin . . . . October 1939
No. 47. Meeker . . . . November 1940
No. 48. Mille Lacs . . . . February 1942
No. 49. Morrison . . . . April 1940
No. 51. Murray . . . . June 1941
No. 52. Nicollet . . . . May 1938
No. 53. Nobles . . . . December 1939
No. 55. Olmsted . . . . April 1939
No. 56. Otter Tail . . . . November 1940
No. 59. Pipestone . . . . August 1939
No. 64. Redwood . . . . October 1941

No. 65. Renville .... December 1940
No. 66. Rice .... September 1940
No. 67. Rock .... September 1940
No. 70. Scott .... January 1939
Governmental Organization and
Record System—Scott County,
Minnesota .... January 1939
Reprinted from No. 70 Scott County
No. 71. Sherburne ...... September 1940
No. 73. Stearns .... May 1940
No. 78. Traverse .... October 1938
No. 79. Wabasha .... April 1939
No. 82. Washington .... October 1938
No. 86. Wright .... September 1940
No. 87. Yellow Medicine .... October 1941
General Legislation Concerning
Counties in Minnesota

MISSISSIPPI:

No. 3. Amite .... September 1937
No. 18. Forrest .... June 1938
No. 22. Grenada .... April 1940
No. 27. Humphreys .... August 1941
No. 37. Lamar .... July 1939
No. 55. Pearl River ...... February 1938
No. 70. Tippah .... June 1942
Prelim. edition
No. 72. Tunica .... June 1942
Prelim edition
No. 74. Walthall .... June 1942
Prelim. edition
No. 55. Pearl River 1936
Prelim. edition

MISSOURI:

No. 19. Cass .... April 1941
Historical sketch of Cass County,
Missouri 1941
No. 26. Cole .... November 1938
No. 30. Dallas .... November 1940

No. 42. Henry .... October 1940
Historical sketch of Henry County
Missouri .... October 1940
No. 51. Johnson .... October 1941
No. 58. Linn .... December 1938
No. 60. McDonald .... February 1942
No. 61. Macon County ...... August 1941
Historical Sketch
No. 64. Marion .... January 1941
Historical sketch of Marion County
Missouri .... March 1941
No. 73. Jasper .... January 1940
Historical sketch of Jasper County,
Missouri 1941
Governmental Organization and
Records System, Jasper County
Missouri .... February 1940
No. 80. Pettis .... June 1939
No. 82. Pike .... November 1937
No. 90. Reynolds .... June 1938
No. 91. Ripley .... May 1938
No. 102. Shelby .... March 1939

MONTANA:

No. 1. Beaverhead ...... November 1939
No. 5. Carbon, Gallatin, Park, Stillwater,
Sweet Grass .... January 1942
No. 15. Flathead, Mineral, Lake, Ravalli,
Lincoln, Sanders .. November 1940
No. 16. Gallatin .... (See No. 5)
No. 24. Lake .... (See No. 15)
No. 27. Lincoln .... See No. 15)
No. 28. Madison .... May 1940
No. 31. Mineral .... (See No. 15)
No. 32. Missoula .... September 1938
No. 34. Park .... (See No. 5)
No. 41. Ravalli .... (See No. 15)
No. 45. Sanders .... (See No. 15)
No. 47. Silver Bow .... July 1939
No. 48. Stillwater .... (See No. 5)
No. 49. Sweet Grass .... (See No. 5)
No. 51. Toole .... October 1938

NEBRASKA:

No. 37. Gosper .... June 1940
No. 39. Greeley .... May 1941
No. 47. Howard .... December 1941
No. 58. Loup .... May 1941
No. 61. Merrick .... February 1942
No. 80. Seward .... June 1939
No. 91. Webster .... March 1942

NEVADA:

No. 3. Douglas .... November 1937
No. 4. Elko .... December 1938
No. 6. Eureka .... October 1939
No. 11. Mineral .... March 1941
No. 12. Nye .... September 1940
No. 13. Ormsby .... March 1940
No. 14. Washoe .... September 1938

NEW HAMPSHIRE:

No. 1. Belnap .... June 1938
No. 2. Carroll .... February 1939
No. 3. Cheshire .... August 1939
No. 4. Coos .... February 1940
No. 5. Grafton .... April 1940
No. 7. Merrimack ...... December 1936
Prelim. edition.

NEW JERSEY:

No. 2. Bergen 1939
No. 14. Morris .... September 1937
Prelim. edition.
No. 15. Ocean .... August 1940
No. 16. Passaic .... January 1940
No. 19. Sussex .... December 1941

NEW MEXICO:

No. 1. Bernalillo .... September 1938
No. 4. Colfax .... November 1937
No. 7. Dona Ana ...... November 1940
No. 8. Eddy .... May 1939
No. 9. Grant .... December 1941
No. 12. Hidalgo 1941

No. 15. Luna . . . . April 1942
No. 17. Mora . . . . November 1941
No. 18. Otero . . . . October 1939
No. 23. Sandoval . . . . January 1939
No. 24. San Niguel . . . . February 1941
No. 26. Sierra . . . . June 1942
No. 29. Torrance . . . . April 1939
No. 30. Union . . . . June 1940
No. 31. Valencia . . . . July 1940

NEW YORK STATE:

No. 1. Albany . . . . October 1937
No. 3. Broome . . . . July 1938
No. 4. Cattaraugus . . . . . February 1939
No. 6. Chautauqua . . . . October 1938
No. 7. Chemung . . . . January 1939
No. 51. Ulster—Part II . . . . . October 1940

NEW YORK CITY:

No. 1. Bronx . . . . February 1940
No. 2. Kings . . . . January 1942
No. 5. Richmond Burough and County
. . . . August 1939

NORTH CAROLINA:

Vol. 1. Alamance through Columbus
. . . . March 1938
Vol. 2. Craven through Moore . . Aug. 1938
Vol. 3. Nash through Yancey . . . Oct. 1939

NORTH DAKOTA:

No. 17. Golden Valley . . . . July 1941
No. 29. Mercer . . . . March 1941
No. 53. Williams . . . . April 1938

OHIO:

No. 1. Adams . . . . December 1938
No. 2. Allen . . . . December 1936
No. 3. Ashlan 1942
No. 5. Athens . . . . May 1939
No. 8. Brown . . . . June 1938
No. 15. Columbiana . . . . July 1942
No. 18. Cuyahoga . . . . April 1937
No. 22. Fayette . . . . July 1940
No. 25. Franklin . . . . May 1942
No. 28. Geuga . . . . August 1942
No. 31. Hamilton . . . . October 1937
No. 32. Hancock . . . . December 1941
No. 40. Jackson . . . . January 1942
No. 42. Knox . . . . April 1939
No. 43. Lake . . . . October 1943
No. 47. Lorain 1941
No. 48. Lucas . . . . April 1937
No. 49. Madison . . . . August 1941
No. 57. Montgomery . . . . . December 1941
No. 66. Pike . . . . May 1942
No. 71. Ross . . . . June 1939
No. 73. Scioto . . . . August 1938
No. 74. Seneca . . . . April 1942
No. 76. Stark . . . . January 1940
No. 77. Summit . . . . May 1941
No. 78. Trumbull . . . . April 1937
No. 84. Washington . . . . April 1938

No. 7. Belmont . . . . May 1942

OKLAHOMA:

No. 3. Atoka . . . . February 1941
No. 5. Beckham . . . . March 1939
No. 11. Cherokee . . . . August 1941
No. 13. Cimarron . . . . January 1938
No. 31. Haskell . . . . July 1940
No. 41. Lincoln . . . . January 1940
Prelim. edition
No. 46. McIntosh . . . . June 1938
No. 49. Mayes . . . . May 1937
No. 51. Muskogee . . . . December 1937
No. 61. Pittsburgh . . . . May 1940
No. 64. Pushmataha . . . . May 1938

OREGON:

No. 2. Benton . . . . April 1942
No. 4. Clatsop . . . . September 1940
No. 6. Coos . . . . May 1942
No. 14. Hood River . . . . . . December 1939
No. 17. Josephine . . . . November 1939
Essay of County Governmental
Organization in Oregon . Dec. 1939
No. 18. Klamath . . . . October 1941
No. 22. Linn . . . . May 1939
No. 25. Morrow . . . . October 1937
No. 26. Multnomah, Vol. I. . . . . . June 1940
Vol. II . . . . May 1940
Governmental Organization,
Multnomah County. An Abstract
from No. 26 Multnomah County
Vol. I. . . . . May 1940
Historical sketch and Governmental
Organization Multnomah County
Oregon, Vol. I. . . . . March 1941
No. 29. Tillamook . . . . April 1940
History, Governmental Organ-
ization and Records System of
Tillamook County . . . . . Sept. 1940
No. 30. Umatilla . . . . January 1942
No. 33. Wasco . . . . February 1941
No. 34. Washington . . . . . . November 1940

PENNSYLVANIA:

County Government and Archives
in Pennsylvania 1942
No. 1. Adams . . . . August 1941
No. 4. Beaver . . . . April 1942
No. 6. Berks . . . . August 1941
No. 7. Blair . . . . May 1941
No. 8. Bradford 1942
No. 23. Delaware . . . . August 1939
Revised edition . . . . . October 1941
No. 25. Erie . . . . August 1940
No. 26. Fayette . . . . May 1940
No. 27. Forest . . . . October 1940
No. 8. Bradford 1946
No. 11. Cambria 1950
No. 39. Lehigh 1946
No. 30. Greene . . . . November 1940
No. 36. Lancaster . . . . February 1941
No. 37. Lawrence . . . . January 1942

No. 40. Luzerne .... December 1938
No. 62. Warren .... February 1942
No. 63. Washington .... May 1941
No. 64. Wayne .... July 1939
No. 65. Westmoreland ..... January 1942

SOUTH CAROLINA:

No. 1. Abbeville .... April 1938
No. 2. Aiken .... December 1938
No. 3. Allendale .... August 1938
No. 4. Anderson .... August 1939
No. 11. Cherokee .... February 1941
No. 17. Dillon .... December 1938
No. 21. Florence .... August 1938
No. 27. Jasper .... October 1938
No. 31. Lee .... January 1937
No. 35. McCormick .... June 1940
No. 37. Oconee .... June 1939
No. 39. Pickens .... June 1941
No. 40. Richland .... April 1940
No. 41. Saluda .... October 1940

SOUTH DAKOTA:

No. 3. Bennett .... October 1940
No. 8. Buffalo .... December 1937
No. 12. Clark .... March 1941
No. 24. Faulk .... April 1942
No. 27. Haakon .... January 1941
No. 35. Jackson & Washabaugh . Nov. 1941
No. 47. Millette .... December 1940
No. 48. Miner .... July 1941
No. 53. Loudon .... March 1941

TENNESSEE:

No. 1. Anderson .... July 1941
No. 2. Bedford .... May 1940
No. 5. Blount .... April 1941
No. 6. Bradley .... January 1941
No. 11. Cheatham ...... November 1941
No. 17. Crockett .... August 1940
No. 33. Hamilton .... November 1937
No. 38. Haywood .... March 1939
No. 53. Loudon .... March 1941
No. 75. Rutherford .... March 1938
No. 82. Sullivan .... March 1942
No. 84. Tipton .... July 1941
No. 95. Wilson .... September 1938

TEXAS:

No. 10. Bandera .... June 1940
No. 11. Bastrop .... June 1941
No. 25. Brown .... May 1940
No. 28. Caldwell .... November 1941
No. 29. Calhoun .... January 1941
No. 61. Danton .... August 1937
No. 62. DeWitt .... January 1940
No. 75. Fayette .... December 1940
No. 86. Gillespie .... October 1941
No. 92. Gregg .... August 1940
No. 94. Guadalupe .... December 1939
No. 105. Hays .... January 1940
No. 111. Hood .... March 1940
No. 120. Jackson .... December 1940

No. 158. Marion .... March 1940
No. 166. Milam .... June 1941
No. 167. Mills .... April 1940
No. 181. Orange .... December 1941
No. 198. Robertson .... March 1941
No. 199. Rockwall .... February 1940
No. 202. Sabine .... June 1939
No. 213. Sommervell .... March 1940
No. 232. Uvalde .... May 1941
No. 247. Wilson .... November 1939

UTAH:

No. 2. Box Elder .... December 1938
Historical sketch and Governmental
Organization of Box Elder County
.... February 1939
No. 4. Carbon .... July 1940
No. 5. Daggett .... August 1939
No. 8. Emery .... March 1941
No. 10. Grand .... April 1938
No. 15. Morgan .... August 1937
No. 20. Sanpete .... October 1941
No. 23. Tooele .... June 1939
No. 24. Uintah .... November 1940
No. 25. Utah .... September 1940
No. 26. Wasatch .... July 1938
No. 29. Weber .... January 1940

VERMONT:

Vol. 7   Lamoille .... December 1936

VIRGINIA:

No. 4. Amelia .... February 1940
No. 13. Brunswick .... January 1943
No. 21. Chesterfield .... August 1938
No. 27. Dinwiddie .... July 1939
No. 47. Isle of Wight ...... April 1940
No. 60. Middlesex .... May 1939
No. 73. Powhatan .... August 1939
No. 75. Prince George ..... October 1941
No. 88. Southampton .... March 1940

WASHINGTON:

No. 1. Adams .... June 1939
No. 2. Asotin .... December 1938
No. 3. Benton .... June 1939
No. 4. Chelan .... April 1942
No. 8. Cowlitz ...... September 1942
No. 12. Garfield ...... November 1941
No. 17. King .... August 1941
Part 2. Judicial Officers
No. 21. Lewis .... April 1941
No. 22. Lincoln .... January 1942
No. 26. Pend Oreille .... September 1937
No. 29. Skagit .... March 1938
No. 31. Snohomish .... March 1942
Historical sketch and Government
Organization and Records System.
Prelim, edition.
No. 32. Spokane .... March 1941
No. 33. Stevens ...... February 1942
No. 39. Yakima .... July 1940

WEST VIRGINIA:

No. 11. Gilmer .... March 1942
No. 12. Grant .... May 1938
No. 22. Lincoln .... March 1938
No. 24. Marion .... February 1941
No. 28. Mineral .... January 1941
No. 31. Monroe .... November 1938
No. 36. Pendleton .... January 1939
No. 38. Pocahontas ..... December 1937
No. 40. Putnam .... April 1941
No. 42. Randolph ...... November 1938
No. 43. Ritchie .... September 1938
No. 44. Roane .... August 1941
No. 46. Taylor .... April 1939

WISCONSIN:

County Government in Wisconsin
Vol. 1. 1942
Vol. II. 1942
Vol. III. 1942
No. 3. Barron .... March 1939
No. 6. Buffalo .... September 1940
No. 9. Chippewa ...... April 1941
No. 10. Clark .... July 1941
No. 16. Douglas 1942
No. 17. Dunn .... June 1941

No. 18. Eau Claire .... January 1942
No. 22. Grant 1942
No. 27. Jackson .... Novebmer 1941
No. 32. LaCrosse .... June 1939
No. 37. Marathon .... August 1940
No. 41. Monroe .... February 1941
No. 43. Oneida .... April 1941
No. 45. Pepin .... August 1941
No. 48. Polk 1941
No. 54. Rusk .... June 1939
No. 55. St. Croix .... October 1940
No. 58. Shawano 1942
No. 59. Sheboygan ...... December 1937
No. 60. Taylor .... September 1941
No. 61. Trempealeall .... September 1940
No. 62. Vernon .... February 1942
No. 69. Waushapa ...... February 1941

WYOMING:

No. 8. Goshen .... June 1940
No. 11. Laramie .... July 1938
No. 12. Lincoln .... May 1941
No. 15. Park .... January 1942
No. 16. Platte .... December 1939
No. 19. Sweetwater .... March 1939
No. 3. Campbell Co. ..... February 1942

Unpublished W.P.A. Records

Many of the WPA Records were not published. These unpublished records provide a valuable source of information for the genealogist. The following is a list of the counties whose records were not published. They are listed by state.

In each state there are one or more repositories of these records. You will find the name of the institution that have these records at the beginning of each state. The full address may be found in the State Repositories Section .

Unpublished W.P.A. County Inventories

ALABAMA— Alabama Department of Archives & History, Montgomery, AL

Autauga	Baldwin	Barbour	Bibb	Blount	Bullock
Butler	Calhoun	Chambers	Cherokee	Chilton	Choctaw
Clarke	Clay	Cleburne	Coffee	Colbret	Conecutt
Coosa	Covington	Crenshaw	Cullman	Dale	Dallas
DeKalb	Elmore	Escambia	Etowah	Fayette	Franklin
Geneva	Greene	Hale	Haney	Houston	Jackson
Jefferson	Lamar	Lauderdale	Lawrence	Lee	Limestone
Lowndes	Macon	Madison	Marengo	Marion	Marshall
Mobile	Monroe	Montgomery	Morgan	Parry	Pickens
Pike	Randolph	Russell	St. Clair	Shelby	Sumter
Talladega	Tallapossa	Tuscaloosa	Walker	Washington	Wilcox
Winston					

ARKANSAS— University of Arkansas, Fayetteville, Arkansas

Arkansas	Ashley	Baxter	Benton	Boone	Bradley
Calhoun	Carroll	Chicot	Clark	Clay	Cleburne
Cleveland	Columbia	Conway	Craighead	Crawford	Crittenden
Cross	Dallas	Desha	Drew	Faulkner	Franklin
Fulton	Garland	Grant	Greene	Hempstead	Hot Springs
Howard	Independence	Izard	Jackson	Jefferson	Johnson
Lafayette	Lawrence	Lee	Lincoln	Little River	Logan
Lonoke	Madison	Marion	Miller	Mississippi	Monroe
Montgomery	Nevada	Newton	Ouachita	Parry	Phillips
Pulaski	Randolph	St. Francis	Saline	Scott	Searcy
Sebastian	Sevier	Sharp	Stone	Union	Van Buren
Washington	White	Woodruff	Yell		

CALIFORNIA, SOUTHERN—L. A. County Museum of Natural History, Los Angeles California

Los Angeles	San Bernardino	San Diego	Santa Barbara	Ventura

COLORADO— Colorado State Archives & Public Records Division, Denver, Colorado

Adams	Archuleta	Baca	Boulder	Chaffee	Cheyenne
Clear Creek	Crowley	Custer	Delta	Denver	Dolores
Douglas	Eagle	Elbert	El Paso	Gilpin	Grand
Gunnison	Huerfano	Jackson	Jefferson	Kiowa	Kit Carson
Lake	La Plate	Las Animas	Lincoln	Mesa	Mineral
Moffat	Montezuma	Montrose	Morgan	Otero	Ouray
Park	Pitkin	Pueblo	Rio Blanco	Rio Grande	Routt
Saguache	San Juan	Sedgwick	Summit	Teller	Washington
Weld					

DELAWARE— Delaware Division of Historical & Cultural Affairs, Dover, Delaware

Rehoboth	Sussex

GEORGIA— University of Georiga, Athens Georiga

Appling	Atkinson	Bacon	Baker	Baldwin	Banks
Barron	Bartown	Ben Hill	Berrien	Bibb	Bleckley
Brantley	Brooks	Bryan	Bullock	Burke	Butts
Calhoun	Camden	Candler	Carroll	Catoosa	Charlton
Chatham	Chattahoochee	Chattooga	Cherokee	Clarke	Clay
Clayton	Clinch	Cobb	Coffee	Colquilt	Columbia
Cook	Coweta	Crawford	Crisp	Dade	Dawson
Decatur	DeKalb	Dodge	Dooly	Dougherty	Douglas
Early	Echols	Effingham	Elbert	Emanuel	Evans
Fannin	Fayette	Floyd	Forsyth	Franklin	Fulton
Gilmer	Glascock	Glynn	Gordon	Grady	Greene
Gwinnett	Habersham	Hall	Hancock	Haralson	Harris
Hart	Heard	Henry	Houston	Irwin	Jackson
Jasper	Jeff Davis	Jefferson	Jenkins	Johnson	Jones
Lamar	Lanier	Laurens	Lee	Liberty	Lincoln
Long	Lowndes	Lumpkin	McDuffie	McIntosh	Macon
Madison	Marion	Meriwether	Miller	Mitchell	Monroe
Montgomery	Morgan	Murray	Muscogee	Newton	Oconee
Oglethorpe	Paulding	Peach	Pickens	Pierce	Pike
Polk	Pulaski	Putnam	Quitman	Raburn	Randolph
Richmond	Rockdale	Schley	Screven	Seminole	Spalding
Stephens	Stewart	Sumter	Talbot	Taliaferro	Tattnall
Taylor	Telfair	Terrell	Thomas	Tift	Toombs
Towns	Treutlen	Troup	Truner	Twiggs	Union
Upson	Walker	Walton	Ware	Warren	Washington
Wayne	Webster	Wheeler	White	Wilcox	Wilkes
Wilkinson	Worth				

ILLINOIS— Illinois State Archives, Springfield, Illinois

Alexander	Bond	Boone	Bureau	Calhoun	Christian
Clay	Clinton	Coles	Cook	Crawford	De Kalb
Du Page	Edgar	Edwards	Ford	Fulton	Gallatin
Greene	Grundy	Hamilton	Hancock	Hardin	Henderson
Henry	Iroquois	Jasper	Jefferson	Johnson	Kane
Kankakee	Kendall	Lake	La Salle	Lawrence	Lee
McDonough	McHenry	McLean	Macon	Madison	Marion
Marshall	Mason	Massal	Mercer	Monroe	Perry
Pope	Pulaski	Putnam	Randolph	Richland	Schuyler
Stark	Tazewell	Union	Wabash	Warren	Washington
Wayne	White	Whiteside	Will	Williamson	Winnebago
Woodford					

INDIANA— Indiana State Library, Indianapolis, Indiana

Adams	Allen	Bartholomew	Benton	Blackford	Boone
Brown	Carroll	Cass	Clark	Clinton	Crawford
Daviess	Dearborn	Decatur	De Kalb	Delaware	Debois
Elkhart	Fayette	Floyd	Fountain	Franklin	Fulton
Gibson	Grant	Greene	Hamilton	Harrison	Hendricks
Henry	Howard	Huntington	Jackson	Jasper	Jay
Jefferson	Jennings	Johnson	Knox	Kosciusko	Lagrange
Lake	Laporte	Lawrence	Madison	Marion	Marshall
Martin	Miami	Monroe	Montgomery	Morgan	Newton
Noble	Ohio	Orange	Owen	Parke	Perry
Pike	Porter	Posey	Pulaski	Putnam	Randolph
Ripley	Rush	St. Joseph	Scott	Shelby	Spencer
Starke	Steuben	Sullivan	Switzerland	Tippecanoe	Tipton
Union	Vanderburgh	Vermillion	Vigo	Wabash	Warren
Warrick	Washington	Wells	White	Whitley	

KANSAS— Kansas State Historical Society, Topeka, Kansas

Allen	Anderson	Atchison	Barber	Barton	Bourbon
Brown	Butler	Chase	Chautauqua	Cherokee	Cheyenne
Clark	Clay	Cloud	Coffey	Comanche	Cowley
Crawford	Decatur	Dickinson	Doniphan	Douglas	Edwards
Elk	Ellis	Ellsworth	Finney	Ford	Franklin
Geary	Gore	Graham	Grant	Gray	Greeley
Greenwood	Hamilton	Harper	Harvey	Haskell	Hodgeman
Jackson	Jefferson	Jewell	Johnson	Kearney	Kiowa
Labette	Lane	Leavenworth	Lincoln	Linn	Logan
Lyon	McPherson	Marion	Marshall	Miami	Mitchell
Montgomery	Morris	Neosho	Ness	Norton	Osage
Osborne	Ottawa	Pawnee	Phillips	Pottawatomie	Pratt
Rawlins	Reno	Rice	Riley	Rooks	Rush
Russell	Saline	Scott	Sedgwick	Seward	Shawnee
Sheridan	Sherman	Smith	Stafford	Stevens	Sumner
Thomas	Trego	Wabaunsee	Wallace	Washington	Wichita
Wilson	Woodson	Wyandotte			

KENTUCKY— Kentucky Department of Libraries & Archives, Frankfort, Kentucky

Adair	Allen	Anderson	Ballard	Barren	Bath
Bell	Boone	Bourbon	Boyd	Boyle	Bracken
Breathitt	Breckinridge	Bullitt	Butler	Caldwell	Calloway
Campbell	Carroll	Carter	Casey	Christian	Clark
Clay	Clinton	Crittenden	Cumberland	Daviess	Edmonson
Elliot	Estill	Fayette	Fleming	Floyd	Franklin
Fulton	Gallatin	Garrard	Grant	Graves	Grayson
Green	Greenup	Hancock	Hardin	Harrison	Hart
Henderson	Henry	Hickman	Hopkins	Jackson	Jefferson
Jessamine	Johnson	Kenton	Knott	Knox	Larue
Laurel	Lawrence	Lee	Leslie	Letcher	Lewis
Lincoln	Livingston	Logan	Lyon	McCracken	McLean
Madison	Magoffin	Marion	Marshall	Martin	Mason
Meade	Menifee	Mercer	Metcalfe	Monroe	Montgomery
Morgan	Muhlenburg	Nelson	Nicholas	Ohio	Oldham
Owen	Owsley	Pendleton	Perry	Pike	Powell
Pulaski	Robertson	Rockcastle	Rowan	Russell	Scott
Shelby	Simpson	Spencer	Taylor	Todd	Trigg
Trimble	Union	Warren	Washington	Wayne	Webster
Whitley	Wolfe	Woodford			

MARYLAND— Maryland Hall of Records, Annapolis, Maryland

Anne Arundel	Baltimore	Calvert	Caroline	Cecil	Charles
Dorchester	Frederick	Hartford	Kent	Prince George's	Queen Anne's
St. Mary's	Somerset	Talbot	Worcester		

MASSACHUSETTS— Massachusetts State Library, Boston, Massachusetts

Barnstable	Berkshire	Bristol	Dukes	Franklin	Hampden
Hampshire	Nantucket	Norfolk	Plymouth	Suffolk	Worcester

MICHIGAN— University of Michigan, Ann Arbor, Michigan

Alcona	Alger	Allegan	Alpena	Antrim	Arenac
Baraga	Barry	Bay	Benzie	Berrien	Branch
Calhoun	Cass	Charlevoix	Cheboygan	Chippewa	Clare
Clinton	Crawford	Delta	Dickinson	Eaton	Emmet
Genesee	Gladwin	Gogebic	Grand Traverse	Gratiot	Hillsdale
Houghton	Huron	Ingham	Ionia	Iosco	Iron
Isabella	Jackson	Kalamazoo	Kalkaska	Kent	Keweenaw
Lake	Lapeer	Leelanaw	Livingston	Mackinac	Macomb
Manistee	Marquette	Mason	Mecosta	Menominee	Midland
Missaukee	Monroe	Montcalm	Montmorency	Muskegon	Newaygo
Oakland	Oceana	Ogemaw	Ontonagon	Osceola	Oscoda
Otsego	Ottawa	Presque Isle	Roscommon	Saginaw	St. Clair
St. Joseph	Sanilac	Schoolcraft	Shiawassee	Tuscola	Van Buren
Washtenaw	Wayne	Wexford			

MINNESOTA— Minnesota Historical Soceity, St. Paul, Minnesota

Aitkin	Anoka	Becker	Beltrami	Benton	Big Stone
Blue Earth	Brown	Carlton	Carver	Cass	Chippewa
Chisago	Clay	Clearwater	Columbia	Cook	Cottonwood
Crow Wing	Hennepin	Hubbard	Isanti	Itasca	Jackson
Kanabec	Kandiyohi	Kittson	Koochiching	Lac qui Parle	Lake
Lake of the Woods	Le Sueur	Lincoln	Lyon	McLeod	Mahnomen
Meeker	Mower	Nobles	Norman	Olmsted	Otter Tail

Pennington	Pine	Polk	Pope	Ramsey	Red Lake
Roseau	St. Louis	Sibley	Steele	Stevens	Swift
Todd	Wabasha	Wadena	Waseca	Watonwan	Wilkin
Winona					

MISSISSIPPI— Mississippi Department of Archives & History, Jackson, Mississippi

Adams	Amite	Attala	Clarke	Covington	George
Greene	Harrison	Issaquena	Jefferson	Lafayette	Lamar
Lauderdale	Leake	Lee	Leflore	Lowndes	Marshall
Monroe	Noxubee	Oktibbeha	Panola	Pearl River	Perry
Pike	Pontotoc	Prentiss	Quitman	Sharkey	Stone
Sunflower	Tallahatchie	Tate	Tippah	Tishomingo	Tunica
Union	Walthall	Warren	Washington	Wayne	Webster
Winston	Yalobusha	Yazoo			

MISSOURI— Western Historical Manuscript, Columbia, Missouri

Adair	Andrew	Atchison	Audrain	Barry	Barton
Bates	Benton	Bollinger	Boone	Buchanan	Butler
Caldwell	Callaway	Camden	Cape Girardeau	Carroll	Carter
Cass	Cedar	Chariton	Christian	Clark	Clay
Clinton	Cole	Cooper	Crawford	Dade	Dallas
Daviess	De Kalb	Dent	Douglas	Dunklin	Franklin
Gasconade	Gentry	Greene	Grundy	Harrison	Henry
Hickory	Holt	Howard	Howell	Iron	Jackson
Jasper	Jefferson	Johnson	Knox	Laclede	Lafayette
Lawrence	Lewis	Lincoln	Linn	Livingston	McDonald
Macon	Madison	Maries	Marion	Mercer	Miller
Mississippi	Moniteau	Monroe	Montgomery	Morgan	New Madrid
Newton	Nodaway	Oregon	Osage	Ozark	Pemiscot
Perry	Pettis	Phelps	Pike	Platte	Polk
Pulaski	Putnam	Ralls	Randolph	Ray	Reynolds
Ripley	St. Charles	St. Clair	St. Francois	St. Louis	Ste. Genevieve
Saline	Schuyler	Scotland	Scott	Shannon	Shelby
Stoddard	Stone	Sullivan	Taney	Texas	Vernon
Warren	Washington	Wayne	Webster	Worth	Wright

MONTANA— Montana Historical Society, Helena, Montana

Beaverhead	Big Horn	Blaine	Broadwater	Carbon	Carter
Cascade	Chouteau	Custer	Daniels	Dawson	Deer Lodge
Fallon	Fergus	Flathead	Gallatin	Garfield	Glacier
Golden Valley	Granite	Hill	Jefferson	Judith Basin	McCone
Meagher	Mineral	Missoula	Musselshell	Park	Petroleum
Phillips	Pondera	Powder River	Powell	Prairie	Ravalli
Richland	Roosevelt	Rosebud	Sanders	Sheridan	Silver Bow
Stillwater	Sweet Grass				

NEBRASKA— Nebraska State Historical Society, Lincoln, Nebraska

Adams	Boone	Box Butte	Boyd	Brown	Buffalo
Burt	Butler	Cass	Cherry	Cheyenne	Clay
Colfax	Cuming	Custer	Dakota	Dawes	Dawson
Dodge	Douglas	Franklin	Frontier	Furnas	Gage
Gosper	Greeley	Hall	Hamilton	Harlan	Hitchcock
Holt	Howard	Johnson	Kearney	Lancaster	Lincoln
Loup	Merrick	Morrill	Nance	Nemaha	Nuckolls
Otoe	Pierce	Platte	Red Willow	Saunders	Scotts Bluff
Stanton	Thurston	Washington	Webster	Wheeler	York

NEVADA— Nevada Historical Society, Reno, Nevada

Churchill	Clark	Douglas	Elko	Esmeralda	Eureka
Humboldt	Lander	Lincoln	Lyon	Nye	Ormsby
Pershing	Storey	Washoe	White Pine		

NEW HAMPSHIRE— University of New Hampshire, Durham, New Hampshire

| Hillsborough | Merrimack | Rockingham | Strafford | Sullivan |

NEW JERSEY— New Jersey State Library, Trenton, New Jersey

Atlantic	Bergen	Burlington	Camden	Cape May	Cumberland
Essex	Gloucester	Hudson	Hunterdon	Mercer	Middlesex
Monmonth	Morris	Ocean	Passaic	Salem	Somerset
Sussex	Union	Warren			

NEW YORK— New York State Archives, Albany, New York

Albany	Allegany	Broome	Cattaraugus	Cayuga	Chautauqua
Chemung	Chenango	Clinton	Columbia	Cortland	Delaware
Dutchess	Erie	Essex	Franklin	Fulton	Genesee
Greene	Hamilton	Herkimer	Jefferson	Lewis	Livingston

Madison	Monroe	Montgomery	Nassau	Niagara	Oneida
Onondaga	Ontario	Orange	Orleans	Oswego	Otsego
Putnam	Rensselaer	Rockland	St. Lawrence	Saratoga	Schenectady
Schoharie	Schuyler	Seneca	Steuben	Suffolk	Sullivan
Tioga	Tompkins	Ulster	Warren	Washington	Wayne
Westchester	Wyoming	Yates			

NEW YORK CITY— N.Y.C. Department of Records & Information Services, N.Y.C., New York

Bronx	Brooklyn	Manhattan	Queens	Richmond

NORTH DAKOTA— State Historical Society of North Dakota, Bismarck, North Dakota

Adams	Benson	Billings	Bottineau	Bowman	Burke
Burleigh	Cass	Cavalier	Dickey	Divide	Dunn
Eddy	Emmons	Foster	Grand Forks	Grant	Griggs
Hettinger	Kidder	La Moure	Logan	McHenry	McIntosh
McKenzie	McLean	Mercer	Morton	Mountrail	Nelson
Oliver	Pembina	Pierce	Ramsey	Ransom	Sheridan
Sioux	Slope	Stark	Stutsman	Towner	Walsh
Wells					

OHIO— Ohio Historical Society, Columbus, Ohio

Adams	Allen	Ashland	Ashtabula	Auglaize	Belmont
Brown	Butler	Carroll	Champaign	Clark	Clermont
Clinton	Columbiana	Coshocton	Crawford	Cuyahoga	Darke
Defiance	Delaware	Erie	Fairfield	Fayette	Franklin
Fulton	Gallia	Geauga	Greene	Guernsey	Hamilton
Hancock	Hardin	Harrison	Henry	Highland	Hocking
Holmes	Huron	Jackson	Jefferson	Knox	Lake
Lawrence	Licking	Logan	Lorain	Lucas	Madison
Mahoning	Marion	Medina	Meigs	Mercer	Miami
Monroe	Montgomery	Morgan	Morrow	Muskingum	Noble
Ottawa	Paulding	Perry	Pickaway	Pike	Portage
Preble	Putnam	Richland	Sandusky	Scioto	Seneca
Shelby	Stark	Summit	Trumbull	Tuscarawas	Union
Van Wert	Vinton	Warren	Washington	Wayne	Williams
Wood	Wyandot				

OHIO— Ohio University, Athens, Ohio

Athens	Belmont	Carroll	Gallia	Guernsey	Harrison
Hocking	Holmes	Jefferson	Lawrence	Meigs	Miami
Monroe	Morgan	Muskingum	Noble	Perry	Tuscarawas
Vinton	Washington				

OKLAHOMA— Oklahoma Department of Libraries, Oklahoma City, Oklahoma

Adair	Alfalfa	Atoka	Beaver	Beckham	Blaine
Bryan	Choctaw	Cleveland	Coal	Comanche	Cotton
Craig	Creek	Custer	Delaware	Dewey	Ellis
Garfield	Garvin	Grady	Grant	Greer	Harmon
Harper	Haskell	Hughes	Jackson	Jefferson	Johnston
Kay	Kingfisher	Kiowa	Lincoln	Logan	Love
McClain	McCurtain	McIntosh	Major	Marshall	Mayes
Murray	Muskogee	Noble	Nowata	Okfuskec	Oklahoma
Okmulgee	Osage	Ottawa	Pawnee	Payne	Pittsburgh
Pontotoc	Pottawatomie	Pushmataha	Roger Mills	Rogers	Seminole
Sequoyah	Stephens	Texas	Tillman	Tulsa	Wagoner
Washington	Washita	Woods	Woodward		

OREGON— Oregon State Library, Salem, Oregon

Benton	Clatsop	Coos	Hood River	Josephine	Linn
Morrow	Multnomah	Tillamook	Umatilla	Union	Wasco
Washington					

PENNSYLVANIA— Pennsylvania Historical & Museum Commission, Harrisburg, PA

Adams	Allegheny	Armstrong	Beaver	Bedford	Berks
Blair	Bradford	Cambria	Cameron	Carbon	Centre
Chester	Clarion	Clearfield	Clinton	Columbia	Crawford
Cumberland	Dauphin	Delaware	Elk	Erie	Fayette
Forest	Franklin	Fulton	Greene	Huntington	Indiana
Jefferson	Lackawanna	Lawrence	Lebanon	Lehigh	Lycoming
Mckean	Mercer	Mifflin	Monroe		

SOUTH CAROLINA— South Carolina Department of Archives & History, Columbia, SC

Abbeville	Aiken	Allendale	Anderson	Barnwell	Beaufort
Berkeley	Calhoun	Charleston	Cherokee	Chester	Chesterfield
Clarendon	Colleton	Darlington	Dillon	Dorchester	Edgefield
Fairfield	Florence	Georgetown	Greenville	Greenwood	Hampton
Horry	Jasper	Kershaw	Lancaster	Laurens	Lee
Lexington	McCormick	Marion	Marlboro	Newberry	Oconee
Orangeburg	Pickens	Richland	Saluda	Spartanburg	Sumter
Union	Williamsburg	York			

SOUTH DAKOTA— University of South Dakota, Vermillion, South Dakota

Armstrong	Aurora	Beadle	Bennett	Bon Homme	Brookings
Brown	Brule	Campbell	Charles Mix	Clark	Clay
Codington	Corson	Custer	Davison	Day	Deuel
Dewey	Douglas	Edmunds	Fall River	Faulk	Grant
Gregory	Haakon	Hamlin	Harding	Hughes	Hutchinson
Hyde	Jackson	Jerauld	Jones	Kingsburg	Lake
Lincoln	Lyman	McCook	McPherson	Marshall	Meade
Mellette	Miner	Minnehaha	Moody	Pennington	Perkins
Potter	Roberts	Stanley	Sully	Todd	Tripp
Turner	Union	Walworth	Washabaugh	Washington	Yankton

TENNESSEE— Chattanooga-Hamilton County Bicentennial Library, Chattanooga, TN

Anderson	Bledsoe	Blount	Bradley	Campbell	Carter
Claiborne	Cocke	Coffee	Cumberland	Davidson	Grainger
Greene	Grundy	Hamblen	Hamilton	Hawkins	Jackson
Jefferson	Knox	Lincoln	Loudon	McMinn	Marion
Meigs	Monroe	Morgan	Polk	Putnam	Rhea
Roane	Robertson	Rutherford	Scott	Sequatchie	Sevier
Shelby	Smith	Sullivan	Union	Van Buren	Washington
White	Wilson				

TENNESSEE— State Library & Archives, Nashville, Tennessee

Anderson	Bedford	Benton	Bledsoe	Blount	Bradley
Campbell	Cannon	Carroll	Carter	Cheatham	Chester
Claiborne	Clay	Cocke	Coffee	Crockett	Davidson
Decatur	Dyer	Fayette	Franklin	Gibson	Giles
Grundy	Hamblen	Hamilton	Hardeman	Hardin	Hawkins
Henderson	Henry	Hickman	Houston	Humphreys	James
Knox	Lauderdale	Lawrence	Lewis	Lincoln	Loudon
McMinn	McNairy	Macon	Madison	Marion	Marshall
Maury	Meigs	Monroe	Montgomery	Obion	Overton
Perry	Polk	Putnam	Rhea	Roane	Robertson
Rutherford	Sequatchie	Shelby	Smith	Stewart	Sullivan
Sumner	Tipton	Trousdale	Unicoi	Van Buren	Warren
Washington	White	Williamson	Wilson		

TEXAS— University of Texas at Austin, Austin, Texas

Anderson	Andrews	Angelina	Aransas	Archer	Armstrong
Atascosa	Austin	Bailey	Bandera	Bastrop	Bee
Bell	Bexar	Blanco	Borden	Bosque	Brazoria
Brazos	Brewster	Briscoe	Brooks	Brown	Burleson
Burnet	Caldwell	Calhoun	Callahan	Cameron	Camp
Carson	Cass	Castro	Chambers	Cherokee	Childress
Clay	Cochran	Coke	Coleman	Collin	Collingsworth
Colorado	Comal	Comanche	Concho	Cooke	Coryell
Cottle	Crane	Crockett	Crosby	Culberson	Dallas
Dawson	Deaf Smith	Delta	Denton	De Witt	Dickens
Dimmit	Donley	Duval	Eastland	Edwards	Ellis
El Paso	Erath	Falls	Fannin	Fayette	Fisher
Floyd	Foard	Fort Bend	Franklin	Freestone	Frio
Gaines	Galveston	Garza	Gillespie	Glasscock	Goliad
Gonzales	Gray	Grayson	Gregg	Grimes	Guadalupe
Hale	Hall	Hamilton	Hansford	Hardeman	Hardin
Harrison	Hartley	Haskell	Hays	Hemphill	Henderson
Hidalgo	Hill	Hockley	Hood	Hopkins	Houston
Howard	Hudspeth	Hunt	Hutchinson	Irion	Jack
Jackson	Jasper	Jeff Davis	Jefferson	Jim Hogg	Jim Wells
Johnson	Jones	Karnes	Kaufman	Kendall	Kenedy
Kent	Kerr	Kimble	King	Kinney	Kleburg
Knox	Lamar	Lamb	Lampasas	La Salle	Lavaca
Lee	Leon	Liberty	Limestone	Lipscomb	Live Oak
Llano	Loving	Lubbock	Lynn	McCulloch	McLennan
McMullen	Madison	Marion	Martin	Mason	Matagorda
Maverick	Medina	Menard	Midland	Millam	Mills
Mitchell	Montague	Montgomery	Moore	Morris	Motley

Nacogdoches	Navarro	Newton	Nolan	Nueces	Ochiltree
Oldham	Orange	Palo Pinto	Panola	Parker	Parmer
Pecos	Polk	Potter	Presidio	Rains	Randall
Reagan	Real	Red River	Reeves	Refugio	Roberts
Robertson	Rockwall	Runnels	Rusk	Sabine	San Augustine
San Jacinto	San Patricio	San Saba	Schleicher	Scurry	Shackleford
Shelby	Sherman	Smith	Somervell	Starr	Stephens
Sterling	Stonewall	Sutton	Swisher	Tarrant	Taylor
Terrell	Terry	Throckmorton	Titus	Tom Green	Travis
Trinity	Tyler	Upshur	Upton	Uvalde	Val Verde
Van Zante	Victoria	Walker	Waller	Ward	Washington
Webb	Wharton	Wheeler	Wichita	Wilbarger	Willacy
Williamson	Wilson	Winkler	Wise	Wood	Yoakum
Young	Zapata	Zavala			

UTAH— Utah State Historical Society, Salt Lake City, Utah

Beaver	Cache	Carson	Cedar	Davis	Duchesne
Emery	Garfield	Grand	Greasewood	Humboldt	Iron
Juab	Kane	Millard	Morgan	Piute	Rich
Rio Virgen	St. Mary's	Salt Lake	San Juan	Sanpete	Sevier
Shambip	Summit	Tooele	Wasatch	Washington	Wayne
Weber					

VERMONT— Vermont Public Records Division, Montpelier, Vermont

Bennington	Caledonia	Chittenden	Essex	Franklin	Orange
Orleans	Rutland	Washington	Windham	Windsor	

VIRGINIA— Virginia State Library Archive & Record Division, Richmond, Virginia

Accomack	Albemarle	Alleghany	Amherst	Appomattox	Arlington
Augusta	Bath	Bedford	Bland	Botetourt	Brunswick
Buchanan	Buckingham	Campbell	Caroline	Carroll	Charles City
Clarke	Craig	Culpeper	Cumberland	Dickenson	Elizabeth City
Essex	Fairfax	Fauquier	Floyd	Fluvanna	Franklin
Giles	Grayson	Greene	Halifax	Hanover	Henrico
Henry	Highland	Isle of Wight	James City	King and Queen	King George
King William	Lancaster	Lee	Loudoun	Louisa	Lunenberg
Madison	Mathews	Middlesex	Montgomery	Nansemond	Nelson
New Kent	Northumberland	Nottoway	Page	Pittsylvania	Prince Edward
Prince William	Princess Anne	Pulaski	Rappahannock	Richmond	Roanoke
Rockingham	Russell	Scott	Shenandoah	Smyth	Southampton
Spotsylvania	Stafford	Sussex	Tazewell	Warren	Warwick
Washington	Westmoreland	Wise	Wythe		

WEST VIRGINIA— West Virginia University, Morgantown, West Virginia

Barbour	Berkeley	Boone	Braxton	Brooke	Cavell
Calhoun	Clay	Doddridge	Fayette	Gilmer	Grant
Greenbrier	Hampshire	Hancock	Hardy	Harrison	Jefferson
Kanawha	Lewis	Lincoln	Logan	McDowell	Marion
Marshall	Mason	Mercer	Mineral	Mingo	Monongalia
Monroe	Morgan	Ohio	Pendleton	Pleasants	Pocahontas
Preston	Putnam	Raleigh	Randolph	Ritchie	Roane
Summers	Taylor	Tucker	Tyler	Upshur	Wayne
Webster	Wetzel	Wirt	Wood	Wyoming	

WISCONSIN— State Historical Society of Wisconsin, Madison, Wisconsin

Adams	Ashland	Bayfield	Brown	Burnett	Calumet
Columbia	Crawford	Dane	Door	Florence	Fond du Lac
Forest	Green	Green Lake	Iowa	Iron	Jackson
Juneau	Kenosha	Kewaunee	Lafayette	Langlade	Lincoln
Manitowoc	Marinette	Marquette	Milwaukee	Oconto	Outgagamie
Ozaukee	Pierce	Portage	Price	Racine	Richland
Rock	Sauk	Sawyer	Vilas	Walworth	Washburn
Washington	Waukesha	Waupaca	Winnebago	Wood	

WYOMING— Wyoming State Archives & Historical Department, Cheyenne, Wyoming

Albany	Big Horn	Campbell	Carbon	Converse	Crook
Fremont	Goshen	Hot Springs	Johnson	Laramie	Lincoln
Natrona	Niobrara	Park	Platte	Sheridan	Sublette
Sweetwater	Teton	Uinta	Washakie	Weston	

**MANY OF THE OLD DEFUNCT COUNTIES THAT DO NOT EXIST TODAY
ARE LISTED IN THE UNPUBLISHED W.P.A. CHAPTER.**

CHAPTER 14

VITAL RECORDS

Vital records (birth and death) are usually kept on a state level and until recently most marriage and divorce records were kept on a county level (usually nearest courthouse).

JURISDICTIONS OF DIVORCE ACTIONS FOR EACH STATE IN THE UNITED STATES

Names of county courts that keep marriage and divorce records:

NAME OF STATE	COURT OF JURISDICTION	NAME OF STATE	COURT OF JURISDICTION
Alabama	County Court	Mississippi	Chancery Court
Alaska	U.S. District Court	Missouri	Circuit Court
Arizona	Superior Court	Montana	District Court
Arkansas	County Court or Chancery Court	Nebraska	District Court
		Nevada	County Clerk
California	Superior Court	New Hampshire	Superior Court
Colorado	District Court or County Court	New Jersey	Superior Court, Chancery Division
Connecticut	Superior Court	New Mexico	District Court
Delaware	Prothonotary	New York	County Clerk
District of Columbia	U.S. District Court	North Carolina	Superior Court
Florida	Circuit Court	North Dakota	District Court
Georgia	Superior Court	Ohio	Court of Common Pleas
Hawaii	U.S. District Court or Circuit Court	Oklahoma	County Clerk
		Oregon	County Clerk
Idaho	County Recorder	Pennsylvania	Prothonotary
Illinois	Circuit Court or Superior Court or City Courts	Rhode Island	Superior Court
		South Carolina	County Court
Indiana	County Clerk	South Dakota	County Court
Iowa	County Clerk	Tennesee	County Court
Kansas	District Court	Texas	District Court
Kentucky	District Court or Circuit Court	Utah	District Court
		Vermont	County Court
Louisiana	Parish Clerk	Virginia	County or City Court
Maine	Superior Court	Washington	County Clerk
Maryland	Circuit Court	West Virginia	Circuit Court, Chancery Side
Massachusetts	Superior Court or Probate Court		
		Wisconsin	County Clerk
Michigan	County Clerk	Wyoming	District Court
Minnesota	District Court		

WHERE TO WRITE FOR BIRTH AND DEATH RECORDS
UNITED STATES AND OUTLYING AREAS

Division of Vital Statistics
State Dept. of Public Health
Montgomery, Ala. 36130   1908

State of Alaska Dept. of Health and
    Social Services
Bureau of Vital Statistics
Pouch H-02G
Juneau, Alaska 99811   1960

Division of Vital Records
State Dept. of Health
P.O. Box 3887
Phoenix, Ariz. 85030   1909

Division of Vital Records
Arkansas Dept. of Health
4815 West Markham St.
Little Rock, Ark. 72201   1914

Vital Statistics Branch
Dept. of Health Services
410 N St.
Sacramento, Calif. 95814   1905

Records and Statistics Section
Colorado Dept. of Health
4210 East 11th Ave.
Denver, Colo. 80220   1907

Public Health Statistics Section
State Dept. of Health
79 Elm St., Hartford, Conn. 06115   1893

Bureau of Vital Statistics
Division of Public Health
Dept. of Health and Social Services,
    State Health Bldg.
Dover, Del. 19901   1913

Vital Records Section
615 Pennsylvania Ave., N.W.
Room 100
Washington, D.C. 20004   1854

Dept. of Health and Rehabilitative Services
Center Operations Services
Office of Vital Statistics
P.O. Box 210
Jacksonville, Fla. 32231   1899

Vital Records Unit
State Dept. of Human Resources
Room 217-H
47 Trinity Ave., S.W.
Atlanta, Ga. 30334   1919

Research and Statistics Office
State Dept. of Health
P.O. Box 3378
Honolulu, Hawaii 96801   1847

Bureau of Vital Statistics
State Dept. of Health and Welfare, Statehouse
Boise, Idaho 83720   1911

Office of Vital Records
State Dept. of Public Health
535 West Jefferson St.
Springfield, Ill. 62761   1916

Division of Vital Records
State Board of Health
1330 West Michigan St.
Indianapolis, Ind. 46206   1907

Division of Records and Statistics
State Dept. of Health
Des Moines, Iowa 50319   1880

Bureau of Registration and Health Statistics
Kansas State Dept. of Health and Environment
6700 South Topeka Ave.
Topeka, Kansas 66620   1911

Office of Vital Statistics
Dept. of Human Resources
275 East Main St.
Frankfort, Ky. 40621   1911

Division of Vital Records
Office of Health Services and
    Environmental Quality
P.O. Box 60630
New Orleans, La. 70160   1918

Office of Vital Records
Human Services Bldg.
State House
Augusta, Maine 04333   1892

Division of Vital Records
State Dept. of Health and Mental Hygiene
State Office Bldg.
P.O. Box 13146, 201 W. Preston St.
Baltimore, Md. 21203   1898

Registrar of Vital Statistics
McCormack Bldg., Room 103
1 Ashburton Pl.
Boston, Mass. 02108   1841

Office of Vital and Health Statistics
Michigan Dept. of Public Health
3500 North Logan St.
Lansing, Mich. 48914   1906

Minnesota Dept. of Health
Section of Vital Statistics
717 Delaware St., S.E.
Minneapolis, Minn. 55440   1908

Vital Records
State Board of Health
P.O. Box 1700
Jackson, Miss. 39205   1912

Division of Health
Bureau of Vital Records
State Dept. of Health and Welfare
Jefferson City, Mo. 65101   1910

Bureau of Records and Statistics
State Dept. of Health and Enviromental Sciences
Helena, Mont. 59601   1907

Bureau of Vital Statistics
State Dept. of Health
301 Centennial Mall So.
P.O. Box 95007
Lincoln, Nebr. 68509   1904

Division of Health — Vital Statistics,
Capitol Complex
Carson City, Nev. 89701   1911

Bureau of Vital Records
health and Welfare Bldg.
Hazen Drive
Concord, N.H. 03301   1883

State Dept. of Health
Bureau of Vital Statistics
P.O. Box 1540
Trenton, N.J. 06825   1878

Vital Statistics Bureau
New Mexico Health Services Division,
P.O. Box 968
Santa Fe, N. Mex. 87503   1920

Bureau of Vital Records
State Dept. of Health
Empire State Plaza, Tower Bldg.
Albany, N.Y. 12237   1915

Dept. of Human Resources
Division of Health Services
Vital Records Branch
P.O. Box 2091
Raleigh, N.C. 27602   1913

Division of Vital Records
State Dept. of Health
Office of Statistical Services
Bismarck, N. Dak. 58505   1907

Division of Vital Statistics
Ohio Dept. of Health
G-20 Ohio Depts. Bldg.
65 South Front St.
Columbus, Ohio 43215   1908

Vital Records Section
State Dept. of Health
Northeast 10th St. & Stonewall
P.O. Box 53551
Oklahoma City, Okla. 73105   1917

Oregon State Health Division
Vital Statistics Section
P.O. Box 116
Portland, Oreg. 97207   1903

Division of Vital Statistics
State Dept. of Health
101 South Mercer St.
P.O. Box 1528
New Castle, Pa. 16103   1906

Division of Vital Statistics State Dept. of Health,
Cannon Bldg.,
Room 101, 75 Davis St.
Providence, R.I. 02908   1896

Division of Vital Records
Bureau of Health Measurement
Office of Vital Records and Public Health Services
Dept. of Health Analysis and
        Environmental Control
2600 Bull St.
Columbia, S.C. 29201   1915

State Dept. of Health
Health Statistics Program
Joe Foss Office Bldg.
Pierre, S. Dak. 57501   1920

Division of Vital Records
State Dept. of Public Health
Cordell Hull Bldg.
Nashville, Tenn. 37219   1914

Bureau of Vital Statistics
Texas Dept. of Health
1100 West 49th St.
Austin, Tex. 78756   1903

Bureau of Vital Statistics
Utah State Dept. of Health
150 West North Temple
P.O. Box 2500
Salt Lake City, Utah 84110   1905

Public Health Statistics Division
Dept. of Health, 115 Colchester Ave.
Burlington, Vt. 05401   1919

Bureau of Vital Records and Health Statistics
State Dept. of Health
James Madison Bldg., P.O. Box 1000
Richmond, Va. 23208   1912

Registrar of Vital Statistics
Charles Harwood Memorial Hospital
St. Croix, Virgin Islands 00820

Vital Records LB-11
P.O. Box 9709
Olympia, Wash. 98504   1907

Division of Vital Statistics
State Dept. of Health
State Office Bldg. No. 3
Charleston, W. Va. 25305   1925

Bureau of Health Statistics
Wisconsin Division of Health
P.O. Box 309
Madison, Wis. 53701   1907

Vital Records Services
Division of Health and Medical Services,
Hathaway Bldg.
Cheyenne, Wyo. 82002   1909

COMMON LAW MARRIAGES

Many of our Ancestors forgot to get married — This is known as Common Law Marriage. — Common Law Marriage is recognized by court decisions in the following states and territories:

Alabama	Montana
Colorado	Ohio
Connecticut	Oklahoma
Florida	Pennsylvania
Georgia	Rhode Island
Idaho	South Carolina
Indiana	South Dakota
Iowa	Tennessee
Kansas	Texas
Maine	Washington
Michigan	District of Columbia
Mississippi	Alaska

Exceptions — date when suspended:

They are recognized in:

Minnesota —if entered into prior to April 26, 1941
Missouri — If entered into prior to March 31, 1921

Nebraska — if entered into prior to 1923
Nevada — if entered into prior to March 29, 1943
New Jersey
— if entered into prior to November 30, 1939
New York — if entered into prior to April 20, 1933

Common Law Marriages are prohibited by statute in the following States:

Arizona	North Carolina
Arkansas	North Dakota
California	Oregon
Delaware	Utah
Illinois	Vermont
Kentucky	Virginia
Louisiana	West Virginia
Maryland	Wisconsin
Massachusetts	Wyoming
New Hampshire	Hawaii
New Mexico	Puerto Rico

It is interesting to note that many Colonial Marriage Records contained the abbreviation "c.f." or "con. for." beside the entries, indication that the parties concerned are confessed fornicators.

CHAPTER 15

CENSUS RECORDS

There are two kinds of census records; 1) Population schedules—the counting of the people, 2) Non-population schedules—gathering information other than just people, i.e., manufacturing, industry and agriculture. Also in some years mortality schedules, or a record of the people who died the previous year, were kept.

Population Schedules

Schudules began in 1790 and have continued every 10 years since that time. The National Archives is the repository for most of these records. All that are available have been microfilmed and are available in the National Archives in Washington, D.C., and their regional centers. The "Index of United States Census Records" which follows will give you the microfilm file number and the roll numbers for each year by state. The schedules are arranged by census year and then alphabetically by state and then with few exceptions by county. It is therefore imperative that the researcher know the county of the subject of research during the cecsus year and in some cases may need to know the exact address.

Census microfilm for most schedules are not only available in the National Archives and their regional branches, but also in the LDS Library in Salt Lake City and their more than 400 branches. They are also available from the Census Microfilm Rntal Program, P.O. Box 2940, Hyattsville, MD 20784, and from the American Genealogy Lending Library, P.O. Box 244, Bountiful, UT 84010.

Schedules after 1910

To protect the privacy of the living, population schedules are restricted for 72 years after the census is taken and are, therefore, not available to researchers during that time. The 1920 census will not be available in the National Archives until 1992. However, if you are a direct descendant of the person you are looking for, or you have the permission of that individual, those records are available at: Personal Census Service Branch, Bureau of the Census, Pittsburg, KS 66762.

INDEX OF UNITED STATES CENSUS RECORDS

1. The number in the first row is the National Archives microfilm number for each census schedule. The number is the same for every state for that census year.
2. The numbers are the microfilm roll numbers for each state.
3. A second number beginning in 1880 is the Soundex Number for each state. The number starting with a "T" (ex.: T623) is the microfilm number, and the second number ending with "r" (ex.: 74r) is the number of rolls of film for that state.
4. Because the records for 1890 were destroyed, there are only a few states with the number "3" that are census schedules; the rest which are indicated with an "sv" after the number (ex.: 1-3sv) is a special veterans census.

STATE	1790	1800	1810	1820	1830	1840	1850	1860	1870	1880	1890	1900	1910
Archives Microfilm Number	M36	M32	M252	M33	M19	M704	M432	M653	M593	T9	M407	T623	T624
Alabama	--	--	--	--	1-4	1-16	1-24	1-36	1-45	1-35 T734-74r	--	1-44 T1038-180r	1-37 T1259-140r
Alaska	--	--	--	--	--	--	--	--	--	--	--	1828-32 T1031-15r	1748-50
Arizona	--	--	--	--	--	--	--	--	46	36-37 T735-2r	--	45-48 T1032-22r	38-42
Arkansas	--	--	--	--	5	17-20	25-32	37-54	417-67	38-60 T736-48r	--	49-80 T1033-132r	43-68 T1260-139r
California	1							55-72	68-93	61-86 T737-34r	--	81-116 T1034-198r	69-111 T1261-272r
Connecticut	1	1-3	1-3	1-3	6-11	21-32	37-51	73-93	96-117	94-110 T739-25r	--	131-152 T1036-107r	127-144
Delaware	--	4	4	4	12-13	33-34	52-55	95-100	119-122	116-120 T741-9r	--	153-157 T1037-21r	145-148
Washington, D.C.	--	--	5	5	14	35	56-57	101-105	123-127	121-124 T742-9r	--	158-164 T1038-42r	149-155
Florida	--	--	--	--	15	36	58-60	106-110	128-133	125-132 T743-16r	--	165-177 T1039-59r	156-169 T1262-84r
Georgia	--	--	--	6-10	16-21	37-53	61-96	111-153	134-184	133-172 T744-86r	--	178-230 T1040-214r	170-220 T1263-174r
Hawaii												1833-1837 T1041-30r	1751-1755
Idaho	--	--	--	--	--	--	--	--	185	173 T745-2r	--	231-234 T1042-2r	221-228
Illinois	--	--	--	11-12	22-25	54-73	97-134	154-241	186-295	174-262 T746-143r	3	235-356 T1043-479r	229-337 T1264-491r
Indiana	--	--	--	13-15	26-32	74-100	135-181	242-309	296-373	263-324 T747-98r	--	357-414 T1044-257r	338-389
Iowa	--	--	--	--	--	101-102	182-189	310-345	374-427	325-371 T748-78r	--	415-468 T1045-215r	390-430
Kansas	--	--	--	--	--	--	--	346-352	428-443	372-400 T1479-51r	--	469-505 T1046-215r	431-461 T1265-145r
Kentucky	--	--	--	--	--	--	--	--	--	401-446 T750-83r	1-3s-v	506-555 T1047-200r	462-506 T1266-194r
Louisiana	--	--	10	30-32	43-45	127-135	229-247	407-431	505-535	447-474 T751-55r	4-5 sv	556-586 T1048-146r	507-535 T1267-132r
Maine	2	6-8	11-12	33-39	46-52	136-155	248-276	432-455	536-565	475-492 T752-29r	6-7 sv	587-603 T1049-80r	536-548
Maryland	--	9-12	13-16	40-46	55-58	156-172	277-302	456-485	566-599	493-518 T753-47r	8-10 sv	604-630 T1050-127r	549-570
Massachussetts	3	13-19	17-22	47-55	59-68	173-202	303-345	486-534	600-659	519-568 T754-70r	11-16 sv	631-697 T1051-314r	571-633
Michigan	4	--	--	56	69	203-212	346-366	535-566	660-715	569-614 T755-73r	17-21 sv	698-755 T1052-257r	634-688 T1268-253r
Minnesota	--	--	--	--	--	--	367	567-576	717-719	615-638 T756-37r	3 22-25 sv	756-798 T1053-180r	689-730

INDEX OF UNITED STATES CENSUS RECORDS (Continued)

STATE	1790	1800	1810	1820	1830	1840	1850	1860	1870	1880	1890	1900	1910
Mississippi	--	--	--	57-58	70-71	213-219	368-390	577-604	720-754	639-670 / T757-69r	26 sv	799-835 / T1054-155r	731-765 / T1269-118r
Missouri	--	--	--	--	72-73	220-233	391-424	605-664	755-826	671-741 / T758-114r	27-34 sv	836-908 / T1055-300r	766-828 / T1270-285r
Montana	--	--	--	--	--	--	--	--	827	742 / T759-2r	35 sv	909-915 / T1056-40r	829-837
Nebraska	--	--	--	--	--	--	--	665	828-833	743-757 / T760-22r	36-38 sv	916-942 / T1057-107r	838-857
Nevada	--	--	--	--	--	--	--	--	834-835	758-759 / T761-3r	39 sv	943 / T1058-7r	858-859
New Hampshire	5	20	23-25	59-61	74-78	234-246	425-441	666-681	836-850	760-769 / T762-13r	40 sv	944-952 / T1059-52r	860-866
New Jersey	--	--	--	--	79-83	247-262	442-466	682-711	851-892	770-801 / T763-49r	41-43 sv	953-998 / T1060-203r	867-912
New Mexico	--	--	--	--	--	--	467-470	712-716	893-897	802-804 / T764-6r	44 sv	999-1003 / T1061-23r	913-919
New York	6	21-28	26-37	62-79	84-117	263-353	471-518	717-855	898-1120	805-949 / T765-187r	45-57 sv	1004-1179 / T1062-768r	920-1094
North Carolina	7	29-34	38-43	80-85	118-125	354-374	619-656	856-927	1121-1166	950-988 / T766-79r	58 sv	1180-1225 / T1063-168r	1095-1137 / T1271-178r
North Dakota	--	--	--	--	--	--	--	94	118	111-115 / T740-6r	59 sv[3]	1226-1234 / T1064-36r	1138-1149
Ohio	--	--	--	86-95	126-142	375-434	657-741	928-1054	1167-1284	989-1079 / T767-143r	60-75 sv	1235-1334 / T1065-397r	1150-1241 / T1272-418r
Oklahoma	--	--	--	--	--	--	--	--	--	--	76 sv	1335-1344 / T1066-42r	1242-1277 / T1273-143r
Oregon	--	--	--	--	--	--	742	1055-1056	1285-1288	1080-1084 / T768-8r	77 sv	1345-1353 / T1067-54r	1278-1291
Pennsylvania	8-9	35-44	44-57	96-114	143-166	435-503	743-840	1057-1201	1289-1470	1085-1208 / T769-168r	78-91 sv	1354-1503 / T1068-612r	1292-1435 / T1274-688r
Rhode Island	10	45-46	58-59	115-117	167-168	504-506	841-847	1202-1211	1471-1480	1209-1216 / T770-11r	92 sv	1504-1513 / T1069-49r	1436-1445
South Carolina	11	47-50	60-62	118-121	169-173	507-516	848-868	1212-1238	1481-1512	1217-1243 / T771-54r	93 sv	1514-1545 / T1070-124r	1446-1474 / T1275-93r
South Dakota	--	--	--	--	--	--	--	94	118	111-115 / T740-6r	94 sv[3]	1546-1556 / T1071-44r	1475-1489
Tennessee	--	--	63	122-125	174-182	517-537	869-907	1239-1286	1513-1572	1244-1287 / T772-86r	95-98 sv	1557-1606 / T1072-188r	1490-1526 / T1276-142r
Texas	--	--	--	--	--	--	908-918	1287-1312	1573-1609	1288-1334 / T773-77r	99-102 sv[3]	1607-1681 / T1073-286r	1527-1601 / T1277-262r
Utah	--	--	--	--	--	--	919	1313-1314	1610-1613	1336-1339 / T774-7r	103 sv	1682-1688 / T1074-29r	1602-1611
Vermont	12	51-52	64-65	126-128	183-188	538-548	920-931	1315-1329	1614-1629	1340-1350 / T775-15r	105 sv	1689-1696 / T1075-41r	1612-1618
Virginia	--	--	66-71	129-142	189-201	549-579	932-993	1330-1397	1630-1682	1351-1395 / T776-82r	106-107 sv	1697-1740 / T1076-174r	1619-1652 / T1278-183r
Washington	--	--	--	--	--	--	--	1398	1683	1396-1398 / T777-4r	--	1741-1754 / T1077-69r	1653-1675
West Virginia	--	--	--	--	--	--	--	--	1684-1702	1399-1416 / T778-32r	111-116 sv	1755-1776 / T1078-92r	1676-1699 / T1279-108r
Wisconsin	--	--	--	--	--	580	994-1009	1399-1438	1703-1747	1417-1453 / T779-31r	117 sv	1777-1825 / T1079-188r	1700-1744
Wyoming	--	--	--	--	--	--	--	--	1748	1454 / T780-1r	--	1826-1827 / T1080-15r	1745-1747

ALABAMA

1820: The extant part of the Alabama territorial census for 1820 is in the Alabama Department of Archives and History, Montgomery. The National Archives has a copy.

ALASKA

The only available census before 1900 is the Special Census of Sitka, Alaska, taken by the War Department, printed in 1871 as 42nd Cong., 1st sess. H. Ex. Doc. 5, pp. 13-26.

ARIZONA

1850, 1860. The schedules for 1850 and 1860 that relate to the present state of Arizona are included among the schedules for New Mexico.

1864. The National Archives has photostats in two volumes and typed and mimeographed copies of the Arizona schedules of 1864. The schedules are arranged by judicial district and thereunder by minor subdivision. For each person in a household, an entry shows name, age, sex, and matital status; number of years and months of residence in Arizona; brief naturalization data if appropriate; place of residence of the family; occupation; and value of real and personal estate.

1866, 1867, 1869. Photostate of Arizona schedules of 1866, 1867, and 1869 are available in one volume. The schedules are arranged by county. For each person in a household, an entry shows name; place of residence; whether head of family; and whether under 10, 10 but under 21, or over 21. The following list identifies by census year the name of the counties for which schedules are available.

1866. Pahute, Mohave, Pime, Yuma, and Yavapai
1867. Mohave, Pima, and Yuma
1869. Yavapai

1870. *Federal Census—Territory of New Mexico and Territory of Arizona*

ARKANSAS

1860. The 1860 schedules for little River County are missing.

CALIFORNIA

1850. The 1850 schedules for Contra Costa, San Francisco, and Santa Clara Counties are missing from the schedules at the National Archives

COLORADO

1860. The 1860 schedules relating to the present state of Colorado are included in the 1860 schedules for Kansas.

DELAWARE

1790. The Missing 1790 census has been reconstructed from local real estate tax lists and published as *Reconstructed 1790 Census of Delaware*. Entries for each hundred of each county are arranged alphabetically.

WASHINGTON D.C.

1790. Schedules that relate to the parts of Montgomery and Prince Georges Counties that now form the present District of Columbia are among the schedules of Maryland for 1790. Schedules for that part of Virginia that was formerly a part of the District of Columbia were enumerated as part of the schedules of Virginia; however, the 1790 census schedules for Virginia are not extant.

1800. Entries for the extant 1800 schedules have been alphabetized and printed in Artemas C. Harmon's, "U.S. Census of the District of Columbia in Maryland for the Year 1800,"

1820, 1830, and 1840. Schedules include Alexandria County, the part of the District of Columbia that was retroceded to Virginia in 1846. For the location of the ward boundaries of Washington City and Georgetown for each of the decennial years 1820-70.

FLORIDA

1825. The National Archives has photostatic copies of two pages of the territorial census for Leon County, 1825. The originals are in the Florida State Library, Tallahassee.

GEORGIA

1790-1820. Tax lists for various years for a few of the counties have been published in *Some Early Tax Digests of Georgia*, edited by Ruth Blair, 2 vols. (Atlanta: Georgia Department of Archives and History, 1926). This publication is used as a substitute for missing 1790, 1800, 1810, and 1820 schedules. Also available is *Substitute for Georgia's Lost 1790 Census* (Albany, Ga: Delwyn Associates, 1975). Wills, deeds, tax digests, court minutes, voter lists, and newspapers were searched to compile this list.

1800. The only schedules known to exist are for Oglethorpe County. These have been published in *1800 Census of Oglethorpe County, Georgia* by Mary B. Warren (Athens, Ga., 1965).

1820. The 1820 schedules for Franklin, Rabun, and Twiggs Counties are missing.

ILLINOIS

1810. Some of the 1810 schedules together with 1818 schedules for Illinois territory, were transcribed and published in *Illinois Census Returns, 1810, 1818, Collections of the Illinois State Historical Library*, vol. 24, edited by Margaret Cross Norton (Springfield, Ill. 1935). This volume has been reprinted by the Genealogical Publishing Co., Baltimore, 1969

1820. The 1820 state schedules, which differ slightly from the 1820 federal schedules, have been published in *Illinois Census Returns, 1820, Collection of the Illinois State History Library*, vol. 26, edited by Margaret Cross Norton (Springfield, Ill., 1934). This volume has been reprinted by the Genealogical Publishing Co., Baltimore, 1969.

1850. The 1850 schedules for Edgar County show the county of birth of each person enumerated. See O. Kenneth Baker's "Virginia (and West Virginia) Origins of Settlers in Edgar Co., Illinois, as Revealed by the 1850 Census," *National Genealogical Society Quarterly* 36 (Sept. 1948): 73-76, and his "Migration From Virginia to Edgar County, Illinois, as Revealed by the 1850 Census Schedules for 200 Families," *National Genealogical Society Quarterly* 38 (Mar. 1950): 1-5, (June 1950): 41-46.

IOWA

1836. The National Archives has an index published as *Iowa 1836 Territorial Census*.

1844, 1846. The National Archives has an electrostatic copy of the Iowa Territorial Census for Keokuk County, 1844 and for Louisa, Polk, and Wapello Counties, 1846 (all bound in one volume).

1850-80. The Archives Branch, FARC Kansas City, has nonpopulation schedules on microfilm A1156, 61 rolls.

KANSAS

1855, 1856, 1857, 1858, 1859. Schedules of these Kansas territorial censuses are in the Kansas State Historical Society, Topeka. The National Archives has microfilm copies on GR28, 3 rolls, and the Archives Branch, FARC Kansas City, has microfilm copies on XC-1, XC-2, and XC-3, 1 roll each.

1860. The Archives Branch, FARC Kansas City, has a microfilm copy of the schedules of the 1860 Kansas territorial census on XC-4, 5 rolls.

1865. The Archives Branch, FARC Kansas City, has a microfilm copy of the 1865 Kansas state census on XC 5, 8 rolls.

1875. The Archives Branch, FARC Kansas City, has a microfilm copy of the 1875 Kansas State census on XC-6, 20 rolls.

KENTUCKY

1790, 1800. Schedules for 1790 and 1800 have been reconstructed from local tax returns. Entries have been alphabetized and printed in two separate volumes: *"First Census"* of *Kentucky, 1790*, by Charles Brunk Heinemann and Gaius Marcus Brumbaugh (Washington: G. M. Brumbaugh, 1940), and *"Second Census"* of *Kentucky, 1800*, compiled by Garrett Glenn Clift (Frankfort, 1954). Both volumes have been reprinted by the Genealogical Publishing Co. of Baltimore, the first in 1965, and the second in 1966.

MAINE

1800. Some of the 1800 schedules for York County are missing.

MARYLAND

1830. The 1830 schedules for Montgomery, Prince Georges, St. Marys, Queen Anne's, and Somerset Counties are missing.

MINNESOTA

1849. The National Archives has a copy of the 1849 census of the Territory of Minnesota, published as Appendix D of the *Journal of the House of Representatives, First Session of the Legislative Assembly of the Territory of Minnesota* (St. Paul, 1850).

1857. The 1857 schedules for Minnesota Territory are arranged alphabetically by county, and thereunder by minor subdivision. The enumeration was taken as of 21 September 1857. For each inhabitant of a household, an entry shows name; age; sex; color; state, territory, or country of birth; if a voter, whether native or naturalized; and occupation.

1870. A large part of the 1870 schedules formerly in the possession of the Bureau of the Census was destroyed by fire in 1921; others that were damaged were destroyed by authorization of Congress in 1933. The destroyed schedules pertain to the counties with names running alphabetically from Aitkin to Sibley. National Archives Microfilm Publication T132, 13 rolls, is a copy of the duplicate set of the 1870 schedules in the custody of the Minnesota Historical Society, St. Paul.

MISSISSIPPI

1816. The Mississippi Department of Archives and History, Jackson, has the territorial schedules for 1816 and some other years. The National Archives has a copy of the 1816 schedules.

1830. The 1830 schedules for Pike County are missing.

1860. The 1860 schedules for free and slave inhabitants for Hancock and Washington Counties and the 1860 schedules for free inhabitants for Tallahatchie County are missing.

MONTANA

1860. The 1860 schedules that relate to the eastern part of the present state of Montana are included in the volume for the unorganized part of Nebraska Territory; those for the western part are included in the schedules of Washington Territory.

NEBRASKA

1854, 1855, 1856. These territorial censuses were published as *1854-1856 Nebraska State Census,* by Evelyn M. Cox (Ellensburg, Wash., 1973).

1880.

1885. Nebraska was one of five states and territories to elect to take in 1885 census. The unbound population and mortality schedules are in the National Archives and have been microfilmed on M352, 56 rolls.

NEVADA

1860. The 1860 schedules that relate to the present state of Nevada are included among the schedules for Utah.

NEW HAMPSHIRE

1800. Some of the 1800 schedules for Rockingham and Strafford Counties are missing.

1820. The 1820 schedules for Grafton County are missing.

NEW JERSEY

1790. Susbstitues for the missing 1790 census of New Jersey are *New Jersey in 1793: An Abstract and Index to the 1793 Militia Census of the State of New Jersey, By James S. Norton (Salt Lake City; Institute of Family Research, 1973), and Revolutionary Census of New Jersey,* by Ken Stryker-Rodda (New Orleans: Polyanthos, 1972), which covers 1773-84.

1800-1820. No population schedules for New Jersey in these years have survived.

NEW MEXICO

1790, 1823, 1845. *Spanish and Mexican Colonial Census of New Mexico, 1790, 1823, 1845,* by Virginia L. Olmsted (Albuquerque, 1975) is the best record of New Mexico's early censuses.

1885. New Mexico was one of five states and territories to elect to take in 1885 census. The unbound population and mortality schedules are in the National Archives and have been microfilmed on M846, 6 rolls.

NEW YORK

Information about state schedules, 1825-1925, for New York is available as *An Inventory of New York State and Federal Census Records,* revised edition, compiled by Edna L. Jacobson (Albany: New York State Library, 1956).

1870. Two separate enumerations were taken for New York City in 1870. Both have been filmed on M593, the first enumeration on rolls 975-1013 and the second enumeration on rolls 1014-1053.

NORTH CAROLINA

1790. The 1790 schedules for Caswell, Granville, and Orange Counties are not extant. As a substitute in the published 1790 index, local tax records were used.

1810. The 1810 schedules for Craven, Greene, New Hanover, and Wake Counties are missing.

1820. The 1820 schedules for Currituck, Franklin, Martin, Montgomery, and Wake Counties are missing.

NORTH DAKOTA

1885. Dakota was one of five states and territories to elect to take an 1885 census. The schedules are in depositories in North and South Dakota. Those for the present state of North Dakota have been reproduced in *Collections of the State Historical Society of North Dakota* 4 (1913): 338-448; the names of enumerated persons are in a general index to the volume. There are special veterans' schedules for North and South Dakota which have been microfilmed on GR27, roll 5.

1900. Schedules for the first time were designated "North Dakota" and "South Dakota," rather than "Dakota."

OHIO

1800. The National Archives has a microfilm copy of the 1800 and 1803 censuses for Washington County on GR4, 1 roll.

1810. The National Archives has a microfilm copy of the 1810 census for Washington County on GR3, 1 roll.

OKLAHOMA

1860. The 1860 schedules that relate to the present state of Oklahoma are included with schedules for Arkansas. They arrpear on roll 52 of M653. The persons enumerated were living on Indian lands.

1890. The National Archives has a microfilm copy of the 1890 territorial census schedules for Logan, Oklahoma, Cleveland, Canadian, Kingfisher, Payne, and Beaver Counties on GR24, 1 roll.

1900. The 1900 schedules are the first to list Oklahoma.

1907. For Seminole County, special agents were employed to take a census as of 1 July 1907. The schedules contain name, age, sex, color, and relationship to head of the family for each person enumerated.

SOUTH CAROLINA

1820-50. The schedules for Clarendon County for 1820, 1830, 1840, and 1850 are missing.

SOUTH DAKOTA

1895. Some schedules of an 1895 census are

microfilmed on rolls 4 and 5 of GR27, obtained from the South Dakota State Historical Society, Included are age, sex, and nationality.

TENNESSEE

1800. Some of the 1800 schedules have been reconstructed from local tax recrods. see *Early East Tennessee Tax Payers*, compiled by Pollyana Creekmore (Easley, S.C.: Southern Historical Press, 1980), which is a reprint of material originally published by the East Tennessee Historical Society.

1810. The National Archives has the 1810 schedules for Rutherford County. The 1810 schedules for Grainger County have been transcribed and published in *Grainger County, Tennessee Federal Census of 1810, Population Schedule (Third Census) and County Tax Lists for 1810*, edited by Pollyana Creekmore (Knoxville: Lawson McGhee, 1956).

1820. The National Archives has the 1820 schedules for twenty-six of the forty-eight counties.

TEXAS

1829-36. The Texas State Archives, Asutin, has extant Texas census schedules, 1829-36. These were published as *The First Census of Texas, 1829-1836*, NGS Special Publication 22, by Marion Day Mullins (Washington: National Genealogical Society, 1976).

VIRGINIA

1790. The 1790 schedules have been reconstructed and published in two volumes that supplement each other: *Heads of Families at the First Census of the United States Taken in the Year 1790: Records of the State Enumerations, 1782 to 1785, Virginia* (Washington: Bureau of the Census, 1908), and Augusta B. Fothergill and John Mark Naugle, *Virginia Tax Payers, 1782-87, Other Than Those Published by the United States Census Bureau* (Richmond, 1940). The first volume has been reprinted by the Reprint Co., Spartanburg, S.C., 1961 and by The Genealogical Publishing Co., Baltimore, 1966 and 1970. The Fothergill and Naugle volume was reprinted by the Genealogical Publishing Co., in 1966.

1810. The 1810 schedules for the following counties are missing: Grayson, Greenbrier, Halifax, Hardy, Henry, James City, King William, Louisa, Mecklenburg, Nansemond, Northampton, Orange, Patrick, Pittsylvania, Russell, and Tazewell. T1019 reproduces a card index for 1810 census schedules for Virginia.

1820, 1830, 1840. Schedules for Alexandria County are included with schedules for the District of Columbia.

WASHINGTON

1860. The 1860 schedules for Benton, Columbia, San Juan, and Snohomish Counties are missing.

1870. The 1870 schedules for Benton and Columbia Counties are missing.

WISCONSIN

1820, 1830. The schedules of 1820 and 1830 are included in the schedules for Michigan.

1836-42, 1846, 1847. The National Archives has a microfilm copy of these Wisconsin territorial censuses on GR20, 3 rolls. Original schedules are in the State Historical Society of Wisconsin, Madison, WI 53706.

WYOMING

1860. The 1860 schedules for present-day Wyoming are among the schedules for Nebraska.

Problems With Census Records

1. At best, even using todays methods, only about 70% of the population is counted.

2. Many people for religious reasons, example; (the Lord sent the plague on Israel because King David did a census count), would give false information.

3. Human nature has not changed over the years. So people would make up information to make them look good. For example; great-grandmother was 39 in the 1850 census and in the 1860 census she was 41.

4. There was no universal agreement on what the question meant. In different ethnic groups, sections of the country, or religious groups would have different meanings for the same words. Words like; uncle, aunt, cousin, etc., may mean something different in each case.

5. Often the information was not provided by the family itself, but rather by a neighbor whose knowledge was questionable at best.

6. Another very important problem with census records is the lack of standardization of spelling, and translation of names and information. This is particulary true, before the Civil War. Often the same family would live on the same farm for 50 to 100 years; yet each census would have a totally different spelling.

7. *Warning*—The biggest mistake that researchers make, in using censuses, is in doing a particular rather than general search (see Chapter 2). You may find someone in what appears to be the right location with the right name but who may not be your ancestor, and it will lead you down entirely the wrong path.

Also remember that finding the state of your ancestor is not enough. You must not do anything until you find the county of origin.

In this section you will find out what is available in each census, what records are available, how to use the soundex system, where to find the records, and a copy of the census schedules, with what information is available on each.

Content of Schedules

The chart "Content of Census Schedules" in this chapter will explain what information is available in each schedule.

A copy of the information on each schedule has been reduced to 8½ by 11 so that you can use them while doing research.

Contents of Census Schedules, 1790-1840 and 1850-1910

1790-1840

Yes = X

	1790	1800	1810	1820	1830	1840
Name of head of family and number of free white males (within specified age groups) and free white females (age groups unspecified in each household)	X	X	X	X	X	X
Number of free white females, within specified age groups, in each household	-	X	X	X	X	X
Name of slaveowner and number of slaves owned by each owner	X	X	X	X	X	X
Number of male and female slaves, within specified age groups, owned by each owner	-	-	-	X	X	X
Number of foreigners, in each household, not naturalized	-	-	-	X	X	-
Number of deaf, dumb, and blind persons, within specified categories, in each household	-	-	-	-	X	X
Name and age of each person receiving a federal military pension	-	-	-	-	-	X
Number of persons in each household attending specified classes at school	-	-	-	-	-	X

1850-1910
(free inhabitants of each household)

	1850	1860	1870	1880	1885*	1890	1900	1910
Name and age	X	X	X	X	X	X	X	X
Name of street and number of house	-	-	-	X	X	X	X	X
Relationship to head of family	-	-	-	X	X	X	X	X
Month of birth, if born within the year	-	-	X	X	X	-	X	-

Category							
Sex, color, birthplace, and occupation................	X	X	X	X	X	X	X	X
Whether naturalized or whether naturalization papers had been taken out......................	-	-	-	-	-	X	X	X
Number of years in the United States.................	-	-	-	-	-	X	X	X
Value of personal estate............................	-	X	X	-	-	-	-	-
Value of real estate...............................	X	X	X	-	-	-	-	-
Whether home and farm free of mortgage.............	-	-	-	-	-	X	X	X
Marital status.....................................	-	-	-	X	X	X	X	X
Whether married within the year......................	X	X	X	X	X	X	-	-
Month of marriage, if married within the year.......	-	-	X	-	-	-	-	-
Whether temporarily or permanently disabled.......	-	-	-	X	X	-	-	-
Whether suffering from acute or chronic disease.....	-	-	-	-	-	X	-	-
Whether crippled, maimed, or deformed..............	-	-	-	X	X	X	-	-
Time unemployed during the census year.............	-	-	-	X	X	X	X	X
Whether deaf, dumb, blind, or insane.................	X	X	X	X	X	X	-	X
Whether a pauper..................................	X	X	-	-	-	X	-	-
Whether a prisoner or homeless child..................	-	-	-	-	-	X	-	-
Whether a convict.................................	X	X	-	-	-	X	-	-
Whether able to speak English.........................	-	-	-	-	-	X	X	X
Whether able to read and write and whether attended school within the year......................	X	X	X	X	X	X	X	X
Birthplaces of father and mother.......................	-	-	-	X	X	X	X	X
Whether father or mother of foreign birth.............	-	-	X	X	X	X	X	X
Number of living children, if a mother.................	-	-	-	-	-	X	X	X
Whether soldier, sailor, or marine during the Civil War (U.S. or Conf.), or widow of such person......	-	-	-	-	-	X	X	X
Number of years in present marriage...................	-	-	-	-	-	-	X	X
Number of children born.............................	-	-	-	-	-	-	X	X
Mother tongue.....................................	-	-	-	-	-	-	-	X

*Five states and territories (Colorado, Florida, Nebraska, New Mexico, and Dakota Territory) chose to take an 1885 census with federal assistance.

Census Age Group/Birth Year Guide

Until 1850 the head of household indicated his/her age by age group rather than birth date. To help you determine the approximate year of his/her birth the following chart is provided.

The chart below is useful in determining the age of the head of household when working with the early census records prior to 1850. For example, if you find your ancestor's name listed as head of household in the column marked "45 and over," in the 1810 census, you can immediately refer to this chart and find that he was probably born before 1765. This saves a lot of time in figuring birth dates, especially when there are several listings for the same name, and you are trying to find the one with the right age.

1790 Census

Age	Born
16 & UP	Before 1774
Under 16	1775-1790

1800 Census

Age	Born
Under 10	1790-1800
10 not yet 16	1785-1790
16 not yet 26	1775-1784
26 not yet 45	1756-1774
45 and over	Before 1755

1810 Census

Age	Born
Under 10	1800-1810
10 not yet 16	1795-1800
16 not yet 26	1785-1794
26 not yet 45	1766-1784
45 and over	Before 1765

1820 Census

Age	Born
Under 10	1810-1820
10 not yet 16	1805-1810
16-18	1802-1804
16 not yet 26	1795-1804
26 not yet 45	1776-1794
45 and over	Before 1775

1830 Census

Age	Born
Under 5	1825-1830
5 not yet 10	1821-1825
10 not yet 15	1816-1820
15 not yet 20	1811-1815
20 not yet 30	1801-1810
30 not yet 40	1791-1800
40 not yet 50	1781-1790
50 not yet 60	1771-1780
60 not yet 70	1761-1770
70 not yet 80	1751-1760
80 not yet 90	1741-1750
90 not yet 100	1731-1740
100 and over	Before 1730

1840 Census

Age	Born
Under 5	1835-1840
5 not yet 10	1831-1835
10 not yet 15	1826-1830
15 not yet 20	1821-1825
20 not yet 30	1811-1820
30 not yet 40	1801-1810
40 not yet 50	1791-1800
50 not yet 60	1781-1790
60 not yet 70	1771-1780
70 not yet 80	1761-1770
80 not yet 90	1751-1760
90 not yet 100	1741-1750
100 and over	Before 1740

Index to the Eleventh Census of the United States — 1890

These 6,160 entries comprise the index to all of the surviving portion of the population census of 1890. The records for the balance of the population were destroyed by fire in 1921. The surviving fragments, consisting of 1,233 pages or pieces, include enumeration for:

Alabama
District of Columbia
Georgia
Illinois
Minnesota
New Jersey
New York
North Carolina
Ohio
South Dakota
Texas

Mortality Schedules

In the census of 1850, 1860, 1870, 1880, 1885, a special mortality of death census was taken of all individuals who died the year previous to the census year, i.e., 1849, 1859, 1869, 1879, 1884. This in effect is a death record for ten percent of the nation, for this particular time period. Although later mortality schedules were taken they are of little genealogical value.

Mortality Census Schedule Microfilm

ARIZONA
T655
1870	Mohave County—Yuma County	Roll 1
1880	Apache County—Yuma County	Roll 2

COLORADO
T655
1870	Arapahoe County—Weld County	Roll 3
1870	Arapahoe County—Weld County	Roll 4

DISTRICT OF COLUMBIA
T655
1850	Indexas and Schedules	Roll 5
1860	Indexes and Schedules	Roll 5
1870	Indexes and Schedules	Roll 5
1800	Indexas and Schedules	Roll 5

GEORGIA
T655
1850	Appling County—Wilkinson County	Roll 7
1860	Appling County—Worth County	Roll 8
1870	Appling County—Worth County	Roll 9
	(Rolls 7-9 include both indexes and Schedules)	
1880	Appling County—Franklin County	Roll 10
1880	Fulton County—Pulaski County	Roll 11
1800	Putnam County—Worth County	Roll 12
	(Rolls 10-12 contain Schedules only)	

ILLINOIS
T1133
1850	Adams County—Woodford County	Roll 58
1860	Adams County—Kendall County	Roll 58
1860	Knox County—Woodford County	Roll 59
1870	Adams County—Ogle County	Roll 59
1870	Ogle County—Woodford County	Roll 60
1880	Adams County—Clinton County	Roll 60
1880	Coles County—Cook County	Roll 61
1800	Crawford County—Livingston County	Roll 62
1800	Livingston County—Sangamon County	Roll 63
1800	Sangamon County—Woodford County	Roll 64

IOWA
T1156
1850	Appanoose County—Washington County	Roll 54
1860	Adair County—Wright County	Roll 55
1870	Adair County—Hancock County	Roll 56
1870	Hardin County—Shelby County	Roll 57
1870	Sioux County—Wright County	Roll 58
1880	Adair County—Des Moines County	Roll 59
1880	Dickinson County—Linn County	Roll 60
1880	Louisa County—Van Buren County	Roll 61
1880	Wapello County—Wright County	Roll 62

KANSAS
T1130
1860	Allen County—Wyandotte County	Roll 1
1870	Allen County—Wyandotte County	Roll 3
1880	Allen County—Lyons County	Roll 6
1880	Marion County—Wyandotte County	Roll 7

KENTUCKY
T655
1850	Pendleton County—Woodford County	Roll 13
1860	Adair County—Woodford County	Roll 14

1870	Adair County—Woodford County	Roll 15
	(Rolls 13-15 include Indexes & Schedules)	
1880	A—Mere	Roll 16
1880	Meri—Z	Roll 17
	(Rolls 16 & 17 contain Index & Abstracts for 1880)	
1880	Adair County—Jackson County	Roll 18
1880	Jefferson County—Mason County	Roll 19
1880	Meade County—Woodford County	Roll 20
	(Rolls 18-20 contain Schedules)	

LOUISIANA
T655
1850	Ascension Parish—Vermilion Parish	Roll 21
1860	Ascension Parish—Winn Parish	Roll 22
1870	Ascension Parish—Winn Parish	Roll 23
	(Rolls 21-23 Contain Indexes & Schedules)	
1880	Ascension Parish—Natchitoches Parish	Roll 24
1880	Orleans Parish—Winn Parish	Roll 25
	(Rolls 24 & 25 Contain Schedules)	

MASSACHUSETTS
T1204
1850	Barnstable County—Plymouth County	Roll 9
1850	Suffolk County—Worcester County	Roll 10
1860	Barnstable County—Worcester County	Roll 17
1870	Barnstable County—Middlesex County	Roll 22
1870	Nantucket County—Worcester County	Roll 23
1880	Barnstable County—Newburyport, Essex County	Roll 37
1880	Salem, Essex County—Hampshire County	Roll 38
1880	Middlesex County—Norfolk County	Roll 39
1880	Plymouth County—Worcester County	Roll 40

MICHIGAN
T1163
1850	Allegan County—Wayne County	Roll 1

T1164
1860	Allegan County—Wayne County	Roll 15
1870	Alcona County—Livingston County	Roll 26
1870	Mackinac County—Wexford County	Roll 27
1880	Alcona County—Gratiot County	Roll 74
1880	Hillsdale County—Lenawee County	Roll 75
1880	Livingston County—Roscommon County	Roll 76
1880	Saginaw County—Wexford County	Roll 77

MONTANA
GR6
1870	Bears Head—Missoula	Roll 1
1800	Missoula—Jefferson County	Roll 1

NEBRASKA
T1128
1860	Burt County—Shorter County	Roll 2
1870	Buffalo County—York County	Roll 3
1880	Adams County—Saunders County	Roll 14
1880	Seward County—Unorganized County	Roll 15

NEW JERSEY
GR21
1850	Atlantic County—Warren County	Roll 1
1860	Atlantic County—Warren County	Roll 1
1870	Atlantic County—Middlesex County	Roll 1
1870	Middlesex County—Warren County	Roll 2
1880	Hunterdon County—Union County	Roll 2
1880	Union County—Warren County	Roll 3

1880	Atlantic County—Hudson County	Roll 3
1880	Hudson County, Cont.	Roll 4

NORTH CAROLINA
GR1

1850	Alamance County—Yancey County	Roll 1
1860	Alamance County—Yancey County	Roll 2
1870	Alamance County—Yancey County	Roll 3
1880	Alamance County—Pitt County	Roll 4
1880	Polk County—Yancey County	Roll 5

OHIO
T1159

1850	Hamilton County—Marion County	Roll 14
1850	Medina County—Wyandot County	Roll 15
1860	Adams County—Huron County	Roll 29
1860	Jackson County—Wyandot County	Roll 30
1880	Adams County—Clinton County	Roll 102
1880	Columbia County—Darke County	Roll 103
	Defiance County—Geauga County	Roll 104

PENNSYLVANIA
T956

1850	Adams County, Berwick Township— Philadelphia County, 6th Ward, Kensington	Roll 14
1850	Philadelphia County, 7th Ward, Kensington—York County, Shrewsbury Township	Roll 15
1860	Adams County, Araban Township— Potter County, West Branch Township	Roll 16
1860	Schuykill County, Ashland Township— York County, North Codens Township	Roll 17
1870	Adams County—Erie County, 4th Ward	Roll 18
1870	Erie County—Philadelphia, 89th District	Roll 19
1870	Philadelphia—York County	Roll 20
1880	Adams County, Franklin Township— Centre County, Boggs Township	Roll 21
1880	Centre County, Union Township— Lancaster County, West Lampeter Township	Roll 22
1880	Lancaster County, Lancaster Township— Philadelphia	Roll 23
1800	Philadelphia—York County, Rock Belton Township	Roll 24

SOUTH CAROLINA
GR22

1850	Abbeville County—Willaimsburg County	Roll 1
1860	Abbeville County—York County	Roll 1
1870	Abbeville County—York County	Roll 2
1880	Abbeville County—York County	Roll 3

TENNESSEE
T655

1850	Anderson County—Wilson County	Roll 26
1860	Anderson County—Wilson County	Roll 27
	(Rolls 26 & 27 include Indexes & Schedules)	
1880	Anderson County—Greene County	Roll 28
1880	Grundy County—Moore County	Roll 29
1880	Morgan County—Wilson County	Roll 30
	(Rolls 28-30 Contain Schedules only)	

TEXAS
T1134

1850	Anderson County—Camal County	Roll 53
	(Roll 53 also contains the 1880 Sechedule for Defective, Dependent, and Delinquent Classes, 1880)	
1850	Camal County—Wharton County	Roll 54
1860	Anderson County—Titus County	Roll 54
1860	Titus County—Zapata County	Roll 55
1870	Anderson County—Menard County	Roll 55
1870	Menard County—Zavala County Texas	Roll 56
1870	Beaver County—Iron County, Utah	Roll 56
1880	Anderson County—Cherokee County	Roll 56
1880	Cherokee County—Grayson County	Roll 57
1880	Grayson County—McLennan County	Roll 58
1880	Upshur County—Zavala County	Roll 59
1880	McLennan County—Upshur County	Roll 60

UTAH
GR7

1870	Beaver County—Weber County	Roll 1

UTAH
T1134

1870	Beaver County—Iron County	Roll 56

VERMONT
GR7

1870	Addison County—Windsor County	Roll 1

VIRGINIA
T1132

1850	Accomack County—York County	Roll 1
1860	Accomack County—York County	Roll 5
1870	Accomack County—York County	Roll 10
1880	Accomack County—Henrico County	Roll 18
1880	Henrico County—York County	Roll 19

WASHINGTON
T1154

1860	Clark County—Walla Walla County	Roll 3
1870	Chehalis (Grays Harbor)—Yakima County	Roll 3
1880	Chehalis (Grays Harbor)—Yakima County	Roll 3

Schedules for 1820, 1830, and 1840 censuses were filed with the federal district or superior courts. The duplicate sets for 1850, 1860, and 1870 were filed with county courts. Many schedules filed with county courts have been deposited in state libraries or state archives. The original 1880 schedules were so fragile that they were transferred to various nonfederal depositories in 1956 after they were microfilmed.

As mentioned above, mortality schedules and some of the other nonpopulation schedules—agriculture, industry, and social statistics—were also transferred to nonfederal depositories. These depositories are identified in the discussions of the schedules by state.

Many state and local libraries have sets of the published 1790 schedules and microfilm copies of some of the population and mortality schedules. Some of these institutions are identified in Special List 24, *Federal Population and Mortality Census Schedules, 1790-1910* (Washington: National Archives and Records Service, 1982).

Microfilm Copies of Census Schedules

The National Archives has reproduced as microfilm publications all of the available federal population census schedules. They can be used in the Microfilm Research Room in the National Archives building and in the research rooms of the regional archives branches in the Federal Archives and Records Centers. The microfilm publication numbers are cited in this chapter as the schedules are discussed by census year. Researchers are required to use the microfilm for their research, although they may be permitted to use the original schedules (or photostats) in bound volumes if the microfilm copy is illegible.

Positive microfilm copies of the schedules are also available for sale from the National Archives. Information about the cost and contents of each roll of the various microfilm publications is given in each of the three federal census microfilm catalogs listed in table 3 above. Buying the microfilm, however does not guarantee that the researcher will find the entries he or she is seeking.

STATE	PUBLISHED CENSUS INDEXES
ALABAMA	1830, 1850
ARIZONA	1860 1864, & 1870 (all in one volume)
ARKANSAS	1830 "Territory", 1840 (2), 1850, 1860 "Surname"
CALIFORNIA	1850
CONNECTICUT	1790, 1880, 1810, 1830
DELAWARE	1800, 1810, 1830, 1840
D.C.	1800, 1820, 1830
FLORIDA	1830 (2), 1840 (2), 1850
GEORGIA	1790 "Substitute for Lost Census", 1820, 1830 (2), 1850, 1840 1850 "Mortality Schedules"
IDAHO	1870, 1880 "Idaho Territory Federal Population and Mortality Schedules"
ILLINOIS	1830
INDIANA	1820, 1830
IOWA	1836 "Territorial Census", 1840, 1850
KANSAS	1855 "Territorial Census"
KENTUCKY	1810, 1820, 1830, 1850
LOUISIANA	1810, 1810-1820 (2 vols.), 1820, 1830
MAINE	1790, 1800, 1810, 1820, 1830
MARYLAND	1790, 1800, 1810, 1820, 1830, 1850
MASSACHUSETTS	1800, 1810, 1820, 1830
MICHIGAN	"Early Michigan Census Records", 1830 "Territory of Michigan and a Guide to Ancestral Trails in Michigan", 1830, 1840, (2) 1850
MINNESOTA	1850 "Territorial Census"
MISSISSIPPI	1810 & 1816 "Natchez District", 1820, 1830 (2), 1840 (2 vols.), 1850 (2), 1850 "Mortality Schedule"
MISSOURI	1830, 1840
NEBRASKA	1860 "Territorial Census"
NEW HAMPSHIRE	1790, 1800, 1810, 1820, 1830
NEW JERSEY	1790 "Revolutionary Census", 1793, 1800, 1830, 1850
NEW MEXICO	"Spanish & Mexican Colonial Censuses for 1790, 1823, and 1845" (all in one volume), 1850 "Territorial Census" (4 vols.)
NEW YORK	1790, 1800, 1810, 1820, 1850 "City of New York", 1850 (2 vols.)
NORTH CAROLINA	1790, 1800 (2), 1810, 1820 (2), 1830, 1840, 1850
OHIO	1790 "Early Ohio Census", 1830, 1840, 1850
PENNSYLVANIA	1790, 1800 (2 vols.) 1810, 1820, 1830, 1850 (2 vols.)
RHODE ISLAND	1790, 1800, 1810, 1820, 1830, 1850
SOUTH CAROLINA	1790, 1800, 1810, 1820, 1830, 1850, 1840
TENNESSEE	1820, 1830 (3 vols.), 1840, 1850 (8 vols., Vol. 3 missing), 1830

TEXAS	1850, 1850 Census (in printed form, 5 vols.)
VERMONT	1790, 1810, 1820, 1830
VIRGINIA	1790, 1880 "Accomack County", 1810, 1820, 1830, 1850
WASHINGTON	1860 "Territorial Census"
WISCONSIN	1836 "Territorial Census"

Colonial, Territorial, and State Census Records

ALABAMA
1801, 1808, 1810, 1818, 1820, 1821, 1823, 1832, 1838, 1840, 1844, 1850, 1855, 1866, 1875

ALASKA
1870, 1876, 1878, 1880, 1881, 1885, 1887, 1889, 1890, 1891, 1892, 1893, 1894, 1895, 1904, 1905, 1906, 1907

ARIZONA
1790, 1796, 1864, 1866, 1867, 1869

ARKANSAS
1823, 1827, 1829, 1854

CALIFORNIA
1790, 1798, 1836, 1852, 1855, 1865, 1875, 1885, 1895, 1897, 1905, 1915, 1925, 1935

COLORADO
1861, 1866, 1885

CONNECTICUT
1636, 1756, 1762, 1774, 1798

DELAWARE
1776, 1798

DISTRICT OF COLUMBIA
1798, 1803, 1807, 1818, 1867, 1878, 1885, 1888, 1897, 1905, 1906, 1907, 1908, 1909, 1912, 1913, 1915, 1919

FLORIDA
1790, 1825, 1837, 1845, 1855, 1865, 1875, 1885, 1895, 1905, 1915, 1925, 1935, 1945, 1955

GEORGIA
1738, 1740, 1750, 1753, 1756, 1810, 1817, 1824, 1829, 1831, 1838, 1845, 1852, 1859

IDAHO
1863

ILLINOIS
1787, 1793, 1810, 1818, 1820, 1825, 1830, 1835, 1840, 1845, 1855, 1865

INDIANA
1801, 1815, 1820, 1825, 1830, 1835, 1840, 1845, 1850, 1865, 1871, 1877, 1883, 1889, 1895, 1901, 1907, 1917, 1921

IOWA
1836, 1838, 1840, 1844, 1846, 1847, 1849, 1851, 1852, 1854, 1856, 1859, 1862, 1863, 1865, 1867, 1869, 1873, 1875, 1885, 1895, 1905, 1915, 1925

KANSAS
1855, 1859, 1865, 1875, 1885, 1895, 1905, 1915, 1925

KENTUCKY
1792, 1798, 1799, 1803, 1807, 1811, 1815, 1819, 1823, 1827, 1831, 1835, 1839, 1843, 1847, 1851, 1859, 1867, 1875, 1883, 1891, 1899

LOUISIANA
1790, 1805, 1806, 1811, 1813, 1817, 1821, 1825, 1829, 1833, 1837, 1841, 1845, 1863, 1858

MAINE
1798, 1837

MARYLAND
1701, 1704, 1708, 1710, 1712, 1755, 1762, 1776, 1778

MASSACHUSETTS
1754, 1764, 1783, 1785-6, 1793, 1798, 1837, 1840, 1850, 1855, 1860, 1865, 1870, 1875, 1885, 1895, 1905, 1915, 1925, 1935, 1945

MINNESOTA
1830, 1849, 1857, 1865, 1875, 1885, 1895, 1905

MISSISSIPPI
1774, 1788, 1789, 1792, 1801, 1805, 1808, 1810, 1816, 1820, 1822, 1823, 1824, 1825, 1830, 1837, 1840-1, 1845, 1850-3, 1866, 1800

MISSOURI
1789, 1790, 1796, 1803, 1814, 1817, 1821, 1824, 1828, 1832, 1836, 1840, 1844, 1848, 1852, 1856, 1860, 1864, 1868, 1876

MONTANA
1864

NEBRASKA
1854, 1855, 1856, 1861, 1874, 1875, 1876, 1877, 1878, 1879, 1882, 1883, 1884, 1885

NEVADA
1861, 1863, 1865, 1867, 1875

NEW HAMPSHIRE

1767, 1773, 1774, 1775, 1786, 1798

NEW JERSEY

1726, 1737, 1738, 1745, 1772, 1798, 1855, 1875, 1885, 1895, 1905, 1915

NEW MEXICO

1790, 1823, 1845, 1864, 1865, 1885, 1895, 1905, 1915

NEW YORK

1698, 1793, 1712, 1714, 1723, 1731, 1737, 1746, 1749, 1756, 1771, 1795, 1798, 1801, 1804, 1807, 1814, 1821, 1825, 1835, 1845, 1855, 1865, 1875, 1880, 1885, 1892, 1895, 1905, 1915, 1925

NORTH CAROLINA

1784, 1785, 1786, 1787, 1798

NORTH DAKOTA

1885, 1895, 1905, 1915, 1925

OHIO

1790, 1801, 1802, 1807, 1811, 1815, 1819, 1823, 1827, 1831, 1835, 1839, 1843, 1847, 1851, 1855, 1859, 1863, 1867, 1871, 1875, 1879, 1883, 1887, 1891, 1895, 1899, 1903, 1907, 1911, 1915

OKLAHOMA

1860, 1890, 1896, 1907

OREGON

1845, 1849, 1851, 1852, 1856, 1857, 1865, 1875, 1895, 1905

PENNSYLVANIA

1776, 1798

RHODE ISLAND

1708, 1730, 1745, 1749, 1755, 1774, 1782, 1798, 1865, 1875, 1885, 1895, 1905, 1915, 1925, 1935

SOUTH CAROLINA

1798, 1868, 1875

SOUTH DAKOTA

1885, 1895, 1905, 1915, 1925, 1935, 1945

TENNESSEE

1798

TEXAS

1790, 1815, 1829, 1836, 1847, 1848, 1858

UTAH

1851, 1856, 1895

VERMONT

1765, 1771, 1776, 1798

VIRGINIA

1623, 1624, 1625, 1634, 1699, 1701, 1703, 1779, 1798

WASHINGTON

1871, 1883, 1885, 1889, 1892

WEST VIRGINIA

Part of Virginia until 1863

WISCONSIN

1830, 1836, 1838, 1842, 1846, 1847, 1855, 1865, 1875, 1885, 1895, 1905

WYOMING

1905, 1915, 1925

Nonpopulation Schedules, 1850-80, on Microfilm in the National Archives
These Are Census of Things Other Than Living People

State or Territory	Types of Schedules
Arizona	1870-80 mortality
Colorado	1870-80 mortality
District of Columbia	1850-80 mortality
	1850-70 agriculture, industry, and social statistics
	1880 agriculture, for D.C., Mont., Nev., and Wyo.
	1880 manufactures and supplemental
Georgia	1850-80 mortality
	1850-80 agriculture
	1850-70 social statistics
	1880 manufactures
	1880 supplemental
Kentucky	1850-80 mortality
	1850-80 agriculture
	1850-70 industry
	1850-70 social statistics
	1880 manufactures
	1880 supplemental
Louisiana	1850-80 mortality
	1850-80 agriculture
	1850-70 social statistics
	1880 manufactures
	1880 supplemental
Maryland	1850-60 agriculture and industry and industry and 1850 social statistics for Baltimore City and County
Massachusetts	1850-70 mortality, 1860-70 agriculture and industry, and 1860 social statistics
Montana	1870 mortality, social statistics, agriculture, and industry; and

	1880 mortality, supplemental, and manufactures For Montana 1880 agriculture schedules, see under D.C.	Texas	1880 manufactures 1880 supplemental 1850-80 mortality (The 1870 roll contains 1870 mortality sched- for Utah and Vermont also.) 1850-80 agriculture, 1850-70 social statistics, 1850-70 indus- try, 1880 manufactures, and 1880 social statistics
Nevada	For Nevada 1880 agriculture schedules, see under D.C.		
North Carolina	1850 mortality, agriculture, social statistics, and industry 1860 mortality, industry, agri- culture, and social statistics 1870 mortality, agriculture, industry, and social statistics 1880 mortality, agriculture, manufactures, and supplemental	Utah	1870 mortality See under Texas
		Vermont	1850-70 agriculture and 1850- 70 industry 1870 mortality See under Texas
Tennesee	1850-60, 1880 mortality 1850-80 agriculture 1850-70 industry 1850-70 social statistics	Virginia	1860 Halifax County free inhab- itants, mortality, agriculture, industry, and social statistics
		Wyoming	For 1880 agriculture, see under D.C.

Guide to the Soundex System

The Soundex filing system, alphabetic for the first letter of surname and numeric thereunder as indicated by divider cards, keeps together names of the same and similar sounds but of variant spellings.

To search for a particular name, you must first work out the code number for the surname of the individual. No number is assigned to the first letter of the surname. If the name is Kuhne, for example, the index card will be in the "K" segment of the index. The code number for Kuhne, worked out accoring to the system below, is 500

Soundex Coding Guide

Code	Key Letters and Equivalents		
1	b, p, f, v	4	l
2	c, s, k, g, j, q, x, z	5	m, n
3	d, t	6	r

The letters a, e, i, o, u, y, w, and h are *not* coded.

The first letter of a surname is *not* coded.

Every Soundex number must be a 3-digit number. A name yielding no code numbers, as Lee, would thus be L000; one yielding only one code number would have two zeros added, as Kuhne, coded as K500; and one yielding two code numbers would have one zero added, as Ebell, coded as E140. Not more than three digits are used, so Ebelson would be coded as E142, *not* E1425.

When two key letters or equivalents appear together, or one key letter immediately follows or precedes an equivalent, the two are coded as one letter, by a single number, as follows: Ke*ll*y, coded as K400; Buer*ck*, coded as B620; *LL*oyd, coded as L300; and S*ch*aefer, coded as S160.

If several surnames have the same code, the cards for them are arrnaged alphabetically by given name. There are divider cards showing most code numbers, but not all. For instance, one divider may be numbered 350 and the next one 400. Between the two divider cards there may be names coded 353, 350, 360, 365, and 355, but instead of being in numberical order they are interfiled alphatbetically by given name.

Such prefixes to surnames as "van," "Von," "Di," "de," "le," "Di," "D'," "dela," or "du" are sometimes disregarded in alphabetizing and in coding.

The following names are examples of Soundex coding and are given only as illustrations.

Name	Letters Coded	Code No.
Allricht	l,r,c	A462
Eberhard	b,r,r	E166
Engebrethson	n,g,b	E521
Heimbach	m,b,c	H512
Hanselmann	n,s,l	H524
Henzelmann	n,z,l	H524
Hildebrand	l,d,b	H431
Kavanagh	v,n,g	K152
Lind, Van	n,d	L530
Lukaschowsky	k,s,s	L222
McDonnell	c,d,n	M235
McGee	c	M200
O'Brien	b,r,n	O165
Opnian	p,n,n	O155
Oppenheimer	p,n,m	O155
Riedemanas	d,m,n	R355
Zita	t	Z300
Zitzmeinn	t,z,m	Z325

Native Americans, Orientals, and Religious Nuns

Researchers using the Soundex system to locate religious nuns or persons with American Indian or oriental names should be aware of the way such names were coded. Variations in coding differed from the normal coding system.

Phonetically spelled oriental and Indian names were sometimes coded as if one continuous name, or, if a distinguishable surname was given, the names were coded in the normal manner. For example, the American Indian name Shinka-Wa-Sa may have been coded as "Shinka" (S520) or "Sa" (S000). Researchers should investigate the various possibilities of coding such names.

Religious nun names were coded as if "Sister" was their surname, and they appear in each State's Soundex under the code "S236." Within the State's Soundex Code S236, the names are not necessarily in alphabetical order.

Abbreviations Used in the Soundex
(Relationships to head of household)

A	Aunt	GD	Granddaughter	Ni	Niece	Si	Sister
AdD	Adopted daughter	GF	Grandfather	Nu	Nurse	SiL	Sister-in-law
AdS	Adopted son	GGF	Great-grandfather			SL	Son-in-law
At	Attendant	GGM	Great-grandmother	O	Officer	SM	Step-mother
		GGGF	Great-great-grandfather	P	Patient	SML	Step-mother-in-law
B	Brother	GGGM	Great-great-grandmother	Pa	Partner(share	SS	Step-son
BL	Brother-in-law	GM	Grandmother		common abode)	SSi	Step-sister
Bo	Boarder	GN	Grand nephew	Pr	Prisoner	SSiL	Step-sister-in-law
C	Cousin	GNi	Grand Niece	Pri	Principal	SSL	Step-son-in-law
		GS	Grandson	Pu	Pupil	Su	Superintendent
D	Daughter	GU	Great Uncle	R	Roomer	U	Uncle
DL	Daughter-in-law			S	Son		
F	Father	Hh	Hired hand	SB	Step-brother	W	Wife
FB	Foster brother	Hm	Hired man	SBL	Step-brother-in-law	WA	Warden
FF	Foster father	I	Inmate	SD	Step-daughter		
FL	Father-in-law	L	Lodger	SDL	Step-daughter-in-law	**Citizenship Status**	
FM	Foster mother	M	Mother	Se	Servant	A	Alien
FSi	Foster Sister	ML	Mother-in-law	SF	Step-father	NA	Naturalized
GA	Great Aunt	N	Nephew	SFL	Step-father-in-law	PA	First papers filed

HEADS OF FAMILIES AT THE FIRST CENSUS OF THE UNITED STATES TAKEN IN THE YEAR 1790

STATE _____ COUNTY _____ TOWN OR DISTRICT _____

REFERENCES/REMARKS _____

NAME OF HEAD OF FAMILY	FREE WHITE MALES OF 16 YEARS AND UPWARDS, INCLUDING HEADS OF FAMILIES	FREE WHITE MALES UNDER 16 YEARS	FREE WHITE FEMALES, INCLUDING HEADS OF FAMILIES	ALL OTHER FREE PERSONS	SLAVES	REMARKS

HEADS OF FAMILIES AT THE SECOND CENSUS OF THE UNITED STATES TAKEN IN THE YEAR 1800

STATE_____ COUNTY_____ TOWN OR DISTRICT_____

REFERENCES/REMARKS_____

NAMES OF HEADS OF FAMILIES	FREE WHITE MALES					FREE WHITE FEMALES					All Other Free Persons Except Indians Not Taxed	Slaves	REMARKS
	Under 10 Years of Age	Of 10 Years and under 16	Of 16 and under 26 including Heads of Families	Of 26 and under 45 including Heads of Families	Of 45 and upwards including Heads of Families	Under 10 Years of Age	Of 10 Years and under 16	Of 16 and under 26 including Heads of Families	Of 26 and under 45 including Heads of Families	Of 45 and upwards including Heads of Families			

HEADS OF FAMILIES AT THE THIRD CENSUS OF THE UNITED STATES TAKEN IN THE YEAR 1810

STATE_____ COUNTY_____ TOWN OR DISTRICT_____

REFERENCES/REMARKS_____

NAMES OF HEADS OF FAMILIES	FREE WHITE MALES					FREE WHITE FEMALES					All Other Free Persons Except Indians Not Taxed	Slaves	REMARKS
	Under 10 Years of Age	Of 10 Years and under 16	Of 16 and under 26 including Heads of Families	Of 26 and under 45 including Heads of Families	Of 45 and upwards including Heads of Families	Under 10 Years of Age	Of 10 Years and under 16	Of 16 and under 26 including Heads of Families	Of 26 and under 45 including Heads of Families	Of 45 and upwards including Heads of Families			

HEADS OF FAMILIES AT THE FOURTH CENSUS OF THE UNITED STATES TAKEN IN THE YEAR 1820

STATE _____ COUNTY _____ TOWN OR DISTRICT _____

REFERENCES/REMARKS _____

NAMES OF HEADS OF FAMILIES	FREE WHITE MALES						FREE WHITE FEMALES					Foreigners not Naturalized.	Number of persons engaged in Agriculture.	Number of persons engaged in Commerce.	Number of persons engaged in Manufactures.	All other free persons except Indians not taxed.	REMARKS
	Under 10 years of age.	Of 10 years and under 16.	Between 16 and 18 years of age.	Of 16 and under 26 including Heads of Families.	Of 26 and under 45 including Heads of Families.	Of 45 and upwards, including Heads of Families.	Under 10 years of age.	Of 10 years and under 16.	Of 16 and under 26 including Heads of Families.	Of 26 and under 45 including Heads of Families.	Of 45 and upwards, including Heads of Families.						

HEADS OF FAMILIES AT THE FIFTH CENSUS OF THE UNITED STATES TAKEN IN THE YEAR 1830

STATE _____ COUNTY _____ TOWN OR DISTRICT _____

REFERENCES/REMARKS _____

NAMES OF HEADS OF FAMILIES	FREE WHITE PERSONS (Males top line, Females bottom line)															Persons who are deaf and dumb, under 14 years of age	Persons who are deaf and dumb, of the age of 14 and under 25	Persons who are deaf and dumb, of 25 and upwards	Persons who are blind.	Aliens — Foreigners not naturalized	REMARKS
	Under 5 years of age	Of 5 and under 10	Of 10 and under 15	Of 15 and under 20	Of 20 and under 30	Of 30 and under 40	Of 40 and under 50	Of 50 and under 60	Of 60 and under 70	Of 70 and under 80	Of 80 and under 90	Of 90 and under 100	Of 100 and upwards							

HEADS OF FAMILIES AT THE SIXTH CENSUS OF THE UNITED STATES TAKEN IN THE YEAR 1840

STATE _____ COUNTY _____ TOWN OR DISTRICT _____

REFERENCES/REMARKS _____

NAMES OF HEADS OF FAMILIES

FREE WHITE PERSONS (Males top line, Females bottom line)

- Under 5 years of age
- Of 5 and under 10
- Of 10 and under 15
- Of 15 and under 20
- Of 20 and under 30
- Of 30 and under 40
- Of 40 and under 50
- Of 50 and under 60
- Of 60 and under 70
- Of 70 and under 80
- Of 80 and under 90
- Of 90 and under 100
- Of 100 and upwards

Total (of all persons, white & black)

Number of Persons in each family employed in:
- Mining.
- Agriculture.
- Commerce.
- Manufacturer and Trader.
- Navigation of the ocean.
- Navigation of canals, lakes, and rivers.
- Learned Professionals and Engineers.

If there are pensioners for Military service living in this family, indicate with an * and list on supplementary sheet.

Deaf & dumb, blind & Insane white persons.

Deaf & Dumb
- Under 14
- 14 and under 25
- 25 and upwards

Blind

Blind & Insane
- Insane and idiots at Public Charge.
- Insane and idiots at Private Charge.

Number of white persons over 20 years of age in each family who cannot read & write.

REMARKS

— 289 —

POPULATION SCHEDULES OF THE SEVENTH CENSUS OF THE UNITED STATES TAKEN IN THE YEAR 1850

STATE _____ COUNTY _____ MINOR CIVIL DIVISION _____

REFERENCES/REMARKS _____

Dwelling houses numbered in the order of visitation.	Families numbered in the order of visitation.	The name of every person whose usual place of abode on the first day of June, 1850, was in this family.	DESCRIPTION			Profession, Occupation, or Trade of each Male Person over 15 years of age.	Value of Real Estate owned.	Place of Birth, Naming the State, Territory, or Country.	Married within the year.	Attended School within the year.	Persons over 20 years of age who cannot read or write.	Whether deaf and dumb, blind, insane, idiotic, pauper, or convict.	REMARKS
			Age	Sex	Color, White, black, or mulatto								

POPULATION SCHEDULES OF THE EIGHTH CENSUS OF THE UNITED STATES TAKEN IN THE YEAR 1860

STATE_____ COUNTY_____ MINOR CIVIL DIVISION_____ POST OFFICE_____

REFERENCES/REMARKS_____

Dwelling houses numbered in the order of visitation.	Families numbered in the order of visitation.	The name of every person whose usual place of abode on the first day of June, 1860, was in this family.	DESCRIPTION			Profession, Occupation, or Trade of each Person, Male and Female, over 15 years of age.	VALUE OF ESTATE OWNED		Place of Birth, Naming the State, Territory, or Country.	Married within the year.	Attended School within the year.	Persons over 20 years of age who cannot read or write.	Whether deaf and dumb, blind, insane, idiotic, pauper, or convict.	REMARKS
			Age	Sex	Color, White, black, or mulatto		Value of Real Estate	Value of Personal Estate						

— 291 —

POPULATION SCHEDULES OF THE NINTH CENSUS OF THE UNITED STATES TAKEN IN THE YEAR 1870

STATE _____ COUNTY _____ TOWN OR DISTRICT _____

REFERENCES/REMARKS _____

Dwelling houses numbered in the order of visitation.	Families numbered in the order of visitation.	The name of every Person whose place of abode on the first day of June, 1870, was in this family.	Age at last birthday.	Sex — Male(M), Female(F).	Color—White(W), Black(B), Mulat-{to(M)}, Chinese(C), Indian(I).	Profession, Occupation, or Trade of each Person, Male or Female.	Value of Real Estate.	Value of Personal Estate.	Place of birth, naming the State or Territory of the United States, or the Country, if of foreign birth.	Father of foreign birth.	Mother of foreign birth.	If born or married within the year, state the month.	Attended School within the year.	Cannot read(R), cannot write(W), neither(N).	Whether deaf and dumb, blind, insane, or idiotic.	Male U.S. citizens of 21 & upwards.	Male U.S. citizens of 21 & upwards whose right to vote is denied.	REMARKS

POPULATION SCHEDULES OF THE TENTH CENSUS OF THE UNITED STATES TAKEN IN THE YEAR 1880

STATE_____ COUNTY_____ TOWN OR DISTRICT_____

REFERENCES/REMARKS_____

Dwelling houses numbered in the order of visitation.	Families numbered in the order of visitation.	The name of each Person whose place of abode on the first day of June, 1880, was in this family.	PERSONAL DESCRIPTION					OCCUPATION		HEALTH					NATIVITY			REMARKS
			Age at last birthday.	Sex—Male(M), Female(F).	Color (White(W), Black(B), Mulatto(M), Chinese(C), Indian(I).	If born within the census year, give the month.	Relationship of this person to the head of this family — whether wife, son, daughter, servant, boarder, or other. Single(S), Married(M), Widowed(W), Divorced(D); if married within the census year (Mc).	Profession, Occupation, or trade of each person, male or female.	Number of months unemployed during the census year.	Is the person sick or temporarily disabled on this day?	Is the person blind(B), deaf and dumb(D), idiotic(Id), or insane(I), Is the person crippled, bedridden, or otherwise disabled?	Attended School within the year.	Cannot read(R), cannot write(W), neither one(N).	Place of Birth of this person, naming State or Territory of the United States, or the Country, if of foreign birth.	Place of Birth of the Father of this person, naming State or Territory of the United States, or the Country, if of foreign birth.	Place of Birth of the Mother of this person, naming State or Territory of the United States, or the Country, if of foreign birth.	

POPULATION SCHEDULES OF THE ELEVENTH CENSUS OF THE UNITED STATES TAKEN IN THE YEAR 1890

UNITED STATES 1890 CENSUS
SPECIAL SCHEDULE

State _____
County _____
City _____
Town _____
Twp. _____

Page Line	House number	Family number	Names of surviving Soldiers, Sailors, Marines and Widows	Rank	Company	Name of regiment or vessel	Date of enlistment	Date of discharge	Length of service yrs. mos. days

Line	Post Office address	Disability incurred	Remarks

STATE_____ COUNTY_____

TOWN OR DISTRICT_____

REFERENCES/REMARKS_____

_____

_____

_____

_____

_____

	LOCATION			NAME	RELATION	PERSONAL DESCRIPTION									Place of birth of each person United States, give the *State*
	IN CITIES			of each person whose place of abode on June 1, 1900, was in this family					DATE OF BIRTH							
	Street	House Number	Number of dwelling house, in the order of visitation	Number of family, in the order of visitation	Enter surname first, then the given name and middle initial, if any INCLUDE every person living on June 1, 1900 OMIT children born *since* June 1, 1900	Relationship of each person to the head of the family	Color or race	Sex	Month	Year	Age at last birthday	Whether single, married, widowed, or divorced	Number of years married	Mother of how many children	Number of these children living	Place of birth of this PERSON
			1	2	3	4	5	6	7		8	9	10	11	12	13
1																
2																
3																
4																
5																
6																
7																
8																
9																
10																
11																
12																
13																
14																
15																
16																
17																
18																
19																
20																
21																
22																
23																
24																
25																

TWELFTH CENSUS OF THE UNITED STATES

SCHEDULE No. 1—POPULATION

NATIVITY		CITIZENSHIP			OCCUPATION, TRADE, OR PROFESSION		EDUCATION				OWNERSHIP OF HOME				
and parents of each person enumerated. If born in the or *Territory*; if of foreign birth, give the *Country* only					of each person TEN YEARS of age and over											
Place of birth of FATHER of this person	Place of birth of MOTHER of this person	Year of immigration to the United States	Number of years in the United States	Naturalization	OCCUPATION	Months not employed	Attended school (in months)	Can read	Can write	Can speak English	Owned or rented	Owned free or mortgaged	Farm or house	Number of farm schedule	
14	15	16	17	18	19	20	21	22	23	24	25	26	27	28	
															1
															2
															3
															4
															5
															6
															7
															8
															9
															10
															11
															12
															13
															14
															15
															16
															17
															18
															19
															20
															21
															22
															23
															24
															25

POPULATION SCHEDULES OF THE THIRTEENTH CENSUS OF THE UNITED STATES TAKEN IN THE YEAR 1910

STATE _____ COUNTY _____ TOWN OR DISTRICT _____

REFERENCES/REMARKS

LOCATION.			NAME	RELATION.	PERSONAL DESCRIPTION.							NATIVITY.		
Street, avenue, road, etc.	House number (in cities or towns).	Number of dwelling house in order of visitation.	Number of family in order of visitation.	of each person whose place of abode on April 15, 1910, was in this family. Enter surname first, then the given name and middle initial, if any. Include every person living on April 15, 1910. Omit children born since April 15, 1910.	Relationship of this person to the head of the family.	Sex.	Color or race.	Age at last birthday.	Whether single, married, widowed, or divorced.	Number of years of present marriage.	Mother of how many children. Number born.	Number now living.	Place of birth of each person and parents of each person enumerated. If of foreign birth, give the state or territory.	
												Number born.	Number now living.	Place of birth of this Person.	Place of birth of Father of this person.
	1	2		3	4	5	6	7	8	9	10	11	12	13
1														
2														
3														
4														
5														
6														
7														
8														
9														
10														
11														
12														
13														
14														
15														
16														
17														
18														
19														
20														
21														

A census enumeration schedule form (blank), showing columns 14 through 32.

	CITIZENSHIP			OCCUPATION					EDUCATION			OWNERSHIP OF HOME.						
Place of birth of Mother of this person.	Year of immigration to the United States.	Whether naturalized or alien.	Whether able to speak English; or, if not, give language spoken.	Trade or profession of, or particular kind of work done by this person, as spinner, salesman, laborer, etc.	General nature of industry, business, or establishment in which this person works, as cotton mill, dry goods store, farm, etc.	Whether an employer, employee, or working on own account.	Whether out of work on April 15, 1910.	If an employee—Number of weeks out of work during year 1909.	Whether able to read.	Whether able to write.	Attended school any time since September 1, 1909.	Owned or rented.	Owned free or mortgaged.	Farm or house.	Number of farm schedule.	Whether a survivor of the Union or Confederate Army or Navy.	Whether blind (both eyes).	Whether deaf and dumb.
14	15	16	17	18	19	20	21	22	23	24	25	26	27	28	29	30	31	32

d. If born in the United States, give the country.

Row numbers: 1, 2, 3, 4, 5, 6, 7, 8, 9, 10, 11, 12, 13, 14, 15, 16, 17, 18, 19, 20, 21

STATE _____ COUNTY _____ TOWN OR DISTRICT _____

REFERENCES/REMARKS _____

PLACE OF ABODE.				NAME	RELATION.	TENURE.		PERSONAL DESCRIPTION.				CITIZENSHIP.			EDUCATION.			PERSON	
Street, avenue, road, etc.	House number of farm, etc. (See instructions.)	Number of dwelling house in order of visitation.	Number of family in order of visitation.	of each person whose place of abode on January 1, 1920, was in this family. Enter surname first, then the given name and middle initial, if any. Include every person living on January 1, 1920. Omit children born since January 1, 1920.	Relationship of this person to the head of the family.	Home owned or rented.	If owned, free or mortgaged.	Sex.	Color or race.	Age at last birthday.	Single, married, widowed, or divorced.	Year of immigration to the United States.	Naturalized or alien.	If naturalized, year of naturalization.	Attended school any time since Sept. 1, 1919.	Whether able to read.	Whether able to write.	Place of birth. Place of birth of each person	
1	2	3	4	5	6	7	8	9	10	11	12	13	14	15	16	17	18	19	
																			1
																			2
																			3
																			4
																			5
																			6
																			7
																			8
																			9
																			10
																			11
																			12
																			13
																			14
																			15
																			16
																			17
																			18
																			19
																			20

NATIVITY AND MOTHER TONGUE.

t and parents of each person enumerated. If born in the United States, give the state or territory. If of foreign birth, give the place of birth and, in addition, the mother tongue. (See instructions.)

	FATHER.		MOTHER.		Whether able to speak English.	OCCUPATION.			Number of farm schedule.
	Place of birth.	Mother tongue.	Place of birth.	Mother tongue.		Trade, profession, or particular kind of work done, as spinner, salesman, laborer, etc.	Industry, business, or establishment in which at work, as cotton mill, dry goods store, farm, etc.	Employer, salary or wage worker, or working on own account.	
Mother tongue.									
20	21	22	23	24	25	26	27	28	29
									1
									2
									3
									4
									5
									6
									7
									8
									9
									10
									11
									12
									13
									14
									15
									16
									17
									18
									19
									20

STATE_____ COUNTY_____

TOWN OR DISTRICT_____

REFERENCES/REMARKS_____

PLACE OF ABODE				NAME	RELATION	HOME DATA				PERSONAL DESCRIPTION					EDUCATION		PLACE OF BIRTH
Street, avenue, road, etc.	House number (in cities or towns)	Number of dwelling house in order of visitation	Number of family in order of visitation	of each person whose *place of abode* on April 1, 1930, was in this family. Enter surname first, then the given name and middle initial, if any. Include every person living on April 1, 1930. Omit children born since April 1, 1930	Relationship of this person to the head of the family	Home owned or rented	Value of home, if owned, or monthly rental, if rented	Radio set	Does this family live on a farm?	Sex	Color or race	Age at last birthday	Marital condition	Age at first marriage	Attended school or college any time since Sept. 1, 1929	Whether able to read and write	Place of birth of each person enumerated and of his father and mother. If born in the United States, give State or Territory. If of foreign birth, give country in which birthplace is now situated. (See Instructions.) Distinguish Canada-French from Canada-English, and Irish Free State (Ireland) from Northern Ireland.
																	PERSON — FATHER
1	2	3	4	5	6	7	8	9	10	11	12	13	14	15	16	17	18 — 19

OCCUPATION AND INDUSTRY

BIRTH	MOTHER TONGUE (OR NATIVE LANGUAGE) OF FOREIGN BORN					CITIZENSHIP, ETC.			OCCUPATION AND INDUSTRY				EMPLOYMENT		VETERANS		
and of his or her parents. If born in [...]. If of foreign birth, give country in [...] instructions.) Distinguish Canada-Free State from Northern Ireland MOTHER 20	Language spoken in home before coming to the United States 21	CODE (For office use only. Do not write in these columns) State or N. T. A	Country B	Nativity C		Year of immigration to the United States 22	Naturalization 23	Whether able to speak English 24	OCCUPATION Trade, profession, or particular kind of work, as spinner, salesman, riveter, teacher, etc. 25	INDUSTRY Industry or business, as cotton mill, dry-goods store, shipyard, public school, etc. 26	CODE (For office use only. Do not write in this column) D	Class of worker 27	Whether actually at work yesterday (or the last regular working day) Yes or No 28	If not, line number on Unemployment Schedule 29	Whether a veteran of U. S. military or naval forces Yes or No 30	What war or expedition? 31	Number of farm schedule 32
																	1
																	2
																	3
																	4
																	5
																	6
																	7
																	8
																	9
																	10
																	11
																	12
																	13
																	14
																	15
																	16
																	17
																	18
																	19
																	20
																	21

POPULATION SCHEDULES OF THE SIXTEENTH CENSUS OF THE UNITED STATES TAKEN IN THE YEAR 1940

STATE _____ COUNTY _____ TOWN OR DISTRICT _____

REFERENCES/REMARKS _____

Line No.	LOCATION		HOUSEHOLD DATA			NAME	RELATION		PERSONAL DESCRIPTION				EDUCATION			PLACE OF BIRTH		CITIZENSHIP	RES
	Street, avenue, road, etc.	House number (in cities and towns)	Number of household in order of visitation	Home owned (O) or rented (R)	Value of home, if owned, or monthly rental, if rented	Does this household live on a farm? (Yes or No)	Name of each person whose usual place of residence on April 1, 1940, was in this household. BE SURE TO INCLUDE: 1. Persons temporarily absent from household. Write "Ab" after names of such persons. 2. Children under 1 year of age. Write "Infant" if child has not been given a first name. Enter ⊗ after name of person furnishing information.	Relationship of this person to the head of the household, as wife, daughter, father, mother-in-law, grandson, lodger, lodger's wife, servant, hired hand, etc.	CODE (Leave blank)	Sex—Male (M), Female (F)	Color or race	Age at last birthday	Marital status—Single (S), Married (M), Widowed (Wd), Divorced (D)	Attended school or college any time since March 1, 1940? (Yes or No)	Highest grade of school completed	CODE (Leave blank)	If born in the United States, give State, Territory, or possession. If foreign born, give country in which birthplace was situated on January 1, 1937. Distinguish Canada-French from Canada-English and Irish Free State (Eire) from Northern Ireland.	CODE (Leave blank)	Citizenship of the foreign born	IN WHAT PLACE ? For a person who, on April 1, 1 Col. 17 "Same house," and 1 town, enter, "Same place," 1 For a person who lived in a d directed in the Instructions. mail address.) City, town, or village having 2,500 or more inhabitants. Enter "R" for all other places.
	1	2	3	4	5	6	7	8	A	9	10	11	12	13	14	B	15	C	16	17
1																				
2																				
3																				
4																				
5																				
6																				
7																				
8																				
9																				
10																				
11																				
12																				
13																				
14																				
15																				
16																				

PERSONS 14 YEARS OLD AND OVER—EMPLOYMENT STATUS

RESIDENCE, APRIL 1, 1935

DID THIS PERSON LIVE ON APRIL 1, 1935

1935, was living in the same house as at present, enter in [this col.]
or one living in a different house but in the same city or
leaving Cols. 18, 19, and 20 blank, in both instances.

[Dif]ferent place, enter city or town, county, and State, which may differ from
(Enter actual place of residence, which may differ from

OCCUPATION, INDUSTRY, AND CLASS OF WORKER

For a person at work, assigned to public emergency work, or with a job ("Yes" in Col. 21, 22, or 24), enter present occupation, industry, and class of worker.

For a person seeking work ("Yes" in Col. 23): (a) If he has previous work experience, enter last occupation, industry, and class of worker; or (b) If he does not have previous work experience, enter "New worker" in Col. 28, and leave Col. 29 and 30 blank.

Col.	Heading
18	COUNTY
19	STATE (or Territory or foreign country)
20	On a farm? (Yes or No)
D	CODE (Leave blank.)
21	Was this person AT WORK for pay or profit in private or nonemergency work during week of March 24–30? (Yes or No)
22	If not at work, was he on, or assigned to, public EMERGENCY WORK (WPA, NYA, CCC, etc.) during week of March 24–30? (Yes or No)
23	Was this person SEEKING WORK? (Yes or No)
24	If not seeking work, did he HAVE A JOB, business, etc.? (Yes or No)
25	For persons answering "No" to quest. 21, 22, 23, and 24 — Indicate whether engaged in home housework (H), in school (S), unable to work (U), or other (O) [CODE E]
26	Number of hours worked during week of March 24–30, 1940
27	Duration of unemployment up to March 30, 1940—in weeks
28	OCCUPATION — Trade, profession, or particular kind of work, as— frame spinner, salesman, laborer, rivet heater, music teacher
29	INDUSTRY — Industry or business, as— cotton mill, retail grocery, farm, shipyard, public school
30	Class of worker
F	CODE (Leave blank.)
31	Number of weeks worked in 1939 (Equivalent full-time weeks)
32	INCOME IN 1939 (12 months ending December 31, 1939) Amount of money wages or salary received (including commissions)
33	Did this person receive income of $50 or more from sources other than money wages or salary? (Yes or No)
34	Number of Farm Schedule

Line No. 1, 2, 3, 4, 5, 6, 7, 8, 9, 10, 11, 12, 13, 14, 15, 16

POPULATION SCHEDULES OF THE SEVENTEENTH CENSUS OF THE UNITED STATES TAKEN IN THE YEAR 1950

STATE _____ COUNTY _____ TOWN OR DISTRICT _____

REFERENCES/REMARKS _____

LINE NUMBER	FOR HEAD OF HOUSEHOLD						FOR ALL PERSONS							
	Name of street, avenue, or road	House (and apartment) number	Serial number of dwelling unit	Is this house on a farm (or ranch)? (Yes or No)	If No in item 4 — Is this house on a place of three or more acres? (Yes or No)	Agriculture Questionnaire Number	NAME. What is the name of the head of this household? What are the names of all other persons who live here? List in this order: The head, His wife, Unmarried sons and daughters (in order of age), Married sons and daughters and their families, Other relatives, Other persons, such as lodgers, roomers, maids or hired hands who live in, and their relatives. (Last name first)	RELATIONSHIP. Enter relationship of person to head of the household, as Head, Wife, Daughter, Grandson, Mother-in-law, Lodger, Lodger's wife, Maid, Hired hand, Patient, etc.	LEAVE BLANK	RACE. White (W), Negro (Neg), American Indian (Ind), Japanese (Jap), Chinese (Chi), Filipino (Fil), Other race—spell out	SEX. Male (M), Female (F)	How was he on his last birthday? (If under one year of age, enter month of birth as April, May, Dec., etc.)	Is he now married, widowed, divorced, separated, or never married? (Mar, Wd, D, Sep, Nev)	What State (or foreign country) was he born in? If born outside Continental United States, enter name of Territory, possession, or foreign country. Distinguish Canada-French from Canada-other	If foreign born— Is he naturalized? (Yes, No, or AP for born abroad of American parents) LEAVE BLANK
	1	2	3	4	5	6	7	8	A	9	10	11	12	13	14
SAMPLE LINE 1															
2															
3															
4															
5															
SAMPLE LINE 6															
7															
8															
9															

FOR PERSONS 14 YEARS OF AGE AND OVER

	15	16	17	18	19	20a (Occupation)	20b (Industry)	20c (P, G, O, or NP)	LEAVE BLANK	LINE NUMBER
	What was this person doing most of last week — working, keeping house, or something else? (Wk, H, Ot, or U for unable to work)	If H or Ot in item 15— Did this person do any work at all last week, not counting work around the house? (Include work for pay, in own business, profession, on farm, or unpaid family work) (Yes or No)	If No in item 16— Was this person looking for work? (Yes or No)	If No in item 17— Even though he didn't work last week, does he have a job or business? (See Special Cases below) (Yes or No)	If Wk in item 15 or Yes in item 16— How many hours did he work last week? (Include unpaid work on family farm or business) (Number of hours)	1. If employed (Wk in item 15, or Yes in item 16 or item 18), describe job or business held last week 2. If looking for work (Yes in item 17), describe last job or business 3. For all other persons, leave blank What kind of work was he doing? For example: Nails heels on shoes. Chemistry professor. Farmer. Farm helper. Armed forces. Never worked.	What kind of business or industry was he working in? For example: Shoe factory. State university. Farm. Farm.	Class of worker For PRIVATE employer (P) For GOVERNMENT (G) In OWN business (O) WITHOUT PAY on family farm or business (NP)	C	
① ASK QUES. BELOW										1
										2
										3
										4
										5
⑥ ASK QUES. BELOW										6
										7
										8
										9

— 306 —

POPULATION SCHEDULES OF THE EIGHTEENTH CENSUS OF THE UNITED STATES TAKEN IN THE YEAR 1960

STATE _____ COUNTY _____ TOWN OR DISTRICT _____

REFERENCES/REMARKS _____

FIRST—Copy sample key and address from listing sheet to P1, H1, and H2.

SECOND—Determine if more than 1 HU.

If ACR: Review Sec. B,1

If no ACR ask: Does more than 1 family live in this home? If "Yes"—Do they live and eat with the family, or do they have separate quarters?

THIRD—List names in P2; mark relationship in P3. Before listing "other relatives" or "nonrelatives," find out if they have separate quarters.

If ACR: Review Sec. B,2 and B,3. Then copy final list from Sec. A.

If no ACR ask: What is the name of the head of this household? What are the names of all other persons who live here?

FOURTH—If no ACR, check listing. Ask: Is there anyone else who usually lives here but is temporarily away? Is there anyone staying here now who has no usual residence elsewhere? I have ...... names now. Is that right?

P1. Sample key

Fill for:
- Household heads — A B C D
- Persons listed out of order
- All "GQ" persons — GQ
- Vacant units

P2. Name—Enter last name first.

List persons in this order:
- The head
- His wife
- Unmarried sons and daughters (in order of age)
- Married sons and daughters and their families
- Other relatives
- Other persons, such as lodgers, maids, or hired hands who live in and their relatives living in

P3. What is his relationship to the head of the household?

Head / Wife of head / Son or daughter / Other relative / Nonrelative / Inmate

(Hd Wif S/D Rel Non Inm)

P4. Sex

Male / Female

(M F)

P5. Color or race

White / Negro / American Indian / Japanese / Chinese / Filipino / Other — Specify other

(Wh Neg Ind Jp Chi Fil Other)

P6. What

Jan–Mar A

Jan / Feb / Mar

FOURTH—*If no ACR check listing.* Ask:
Is there anyone else who usually lives here but is temporarily away?
Is there anyone staying here now who has no usual residence elsewhere?
I have ...... names now. Is that right?

FIFTH—Fill P4–P7 for each person.

SIXTH—*Check for visitors.* Fill Individual Census Report if no one to report for visitor at his home.
If ACR ask:
Review Sec. C.
Did any visitor stay here overnight Thurs., Mar. 31?

SEVENTH—Fill H3–H13 (except in GQ's). For "unit," "apartment," or "rooms," use "house," as appropriate.

EIGHTH—*Check for other units.*
If no ACR ask:
Review Sec. E.1 and E.2.
Does anyone else live in this building or elsewhere on this property?
Are there any vacant apartments or any vacant rooms for rent?

NINTH—*Ask about next unit:*
Name?
No. of people?
When home?
If vacant.—
Whom to see?

Line No.

P7. MARITAL STATUS—
Is he now:
Married — Widowed — Divorced — Separated — Never married

P6. What is the month and year of his birth? (*If only age is known, use age conversion table to obtain date of birth*)

Mark 3 circles—1 for month, 1 for decade, and 1 for specific year

Specific year of birth
0 1 2 3 4 5 6 7 8 9

Decade of birth
—18— '50 '60 '70 '80 '90
—19— '00 '10 '20 '30 '40 '50 '60

Month of birth
Jan Apr Jul Oct
Feb May Aug Nov
Mar Jun Sep Dec

x race
Japanese
Chinese
Filipino
Other
Jp Chi Fil Other — Specify other

CHAPTER 16

IMMIGRATION, NATURALIZATION & PASSENGER LISTS

All but the original Americans are immigrants or are descendants of immigrants. Therefore, immigration and naturalization records are of great value to the Genealogy Researcher.

To understand how people immigrated to America, you should read the book *Puritan Village* by Powell (see Reference Chapter). Even though the book tells about immigrating from England to America, it will teach you the techniques and sources you need to follow to trace your immigrant ancestors.

As we indicated earlier in this book, you should never try to locate an immigrant ancestor in the country of origin (until you have exhausted the U.S. sources) because you may end up with a person with the right name but who is not your ancestor. Instead you should always begin with a general search in the county of destination.

NATURALIZATION RECORDS

Citizenship

Citizenship was a prerequisite of property rights in the American Colonies as it was in England. Only citizens could own, transfer and bequeath property rights. Three classes of citizenship were recognized:

1. Aliens—those born outside of the British Empire and not entitled to the legal rights of Englishmen.

2. Denizens—persons born outside of the British Empire, but entitled to civil (though usually not political) rights of Englishmen by virtue of naturalization processes. This means that they could own, inherit, transfer property, but could not hold public office nor vote.

3. Native-born-subjects of the British Crown by virtue of being born in any part of the British Empire or on any British vessel.

Each Colony in America provided its own procedures for the naturalization of aliens: some Colonies granted citizenship (denizenship) by special legislative act; some issued patents of naturalization through the Proprietor or Governor, others passed general laws which applied to those petitioning for citizenship. Some Colonies provided procedures whereby deceased aliens could become naturalized so their heirs could inherit. Several times special acts of Colonial Assemblies would naturalize entire groups of people without listing them by individual names. The naturalization of a citizen in one Colony, however, was not necessarily regarded as valid in another.

In 1709, Parliament passed a law that naturalization could by obtained by taking an oath of allegiance to the British Crown and partaking of the sacrament of the

Church of England before witnesses. In 1740, a general law was passed requiring only an oath of allegiance to the Crown.

With the Declaration of Independence in 1776, all aliens living in America were automatically naturalized and no formal record resulted. This law remained in effect until after the Revolutionary War. During the War, oaths of allegiance were required of all citizens and aliens within the borders of the Colonies and were recorded in the county of residence.

The first federal Naturalization Act was passed in 1789. One could be naturalized in "any court of record," federal or state. Most of the early records are found in both state and federal courts. Most people went to the most accessible court. This was almost always true until the formation of the Immigration and Naturalization Service in 1890.

Requirements for Citizenship

1. Residence Requirements. (1790) Could apply for citizenship before any court of record—state or federal—after only two years residence. In 1795, this was increased to five years, at least one of which had been spent within the state where the application was filed, and at least 3 years after a declaration of intention had been filed with the court. This procedure remained standard until 1906.

2. AGE & Racial requirements. At first only free white persons over 21 years of age were granted naturalization. Then in 1870, Negroes were permitted to become citizens; American Indians were included in 1940, Chinese in 1943 and Filipinos and natives of India in 1946. Under the Immigration and Nationality Act of 1952, all racial discrimination was removed and the applicant need be only 18 years of age to apply.

3. WIVES & Dependent Children of Citizens. Prior to 1922, wives and children of naturalized or native-born citizens automatically become citizens. Single women over the age of 21 had to go through the formal process of naturalization. Since 1922, all alien women must file for citizenship regardless of marital status; however, if her husband is a citizen, only 3 years residence is required.

4. PROCEDURE. Before 1906, an alien had to appear before a court of record—state or federal—and file a declaration of intention to become a citizen (take out first papers) at least three years prior to filing formal application for citizenship. He then could apply, be interviewed by the court as to his loyalities, literacy, etc., and finally take the oath of allegiance to the United States and its laws. A certificate of citizenship would then be issued to him. Under the Naturalization Act of 1906, three steps were outlined 1) petition, 2) investigation and interview and 3) final hearing before the court in public session, administration of oath of allegiance and awarding of certificate.

Records

Records. Prior to 1906, two copies were made and preserved; the one kept by the court handling the proceeding and copy given to applicant as proof of his naturalization. (Frequently only record concerning naturalization granted by the court will be found entered in the regular court minutes or orders.) Since 1906, three copies are prepared; one kept by the court, one given to the applicant and one forwarded to the bureau of Immigration and Naturalization. Copies to the Bureau are closed to the public, those retained by the court are public records and may be searched and copied.

To find naturalization records, your first search should be in the court records in the county of destination. The records created through naturalization processes may be found recorded among the regular court records: dockets, minutes, orders, case files, and judgments. In many jurisdictions, they were recorded in separate volumes labeled naturalization or citizenship. If the court records are not available, check alliance/fraternal records (most people were sponsored as immigrants by an alliance or fraternal organization). Many alliances also owned insurance companies who sold the imigrants insurance. If you know where he spent the last few years of life, but cannot find his naturaliation records, you may want toa check insurance records, voting lists and poll tax lists in that county.

There are three documents of naturalization that are of value to the genealogist.
a. Declaration of Intention (called first papers). Many people never got past this stage.This is especially true of Germans from Russia who settled in the midwest.
b. Naturalization Petition (called second papers). One had to live in the United States at least 5 years and have taken out Declaration of Intention papers at least 3 years prior to this petition.
c. Naturalization Certificate—which was received by the immigrant at the time the Oath of Allegiance is administered. These are generally very scarce, usually found in family collections.

The Contents of the naturalization records will vary with the time period, document, and locality. In general, later records contain more information. The information listed below is typical of what may be found in naturalization documents.

Declaration of Intention

(first papers)
name of individual
address
occupation
birthplace of
nationality
country from which emigrated
birthdate or age
personal description
date of intention
marital status
last foreign residence
port of entry
name of ship
date of entry
date of document

Petition

(second or final papers)
name
address
occupation
date emigrated
birthplace
country from which emigrated
birthdate or age
time in the U.S.
date of intention
name and age of spouse
birthplace of spouse
names of children
ages of children
last foreign residence
port and mode of entry
name of ship
date of entry
names of witnesses
date of document
address of spouse

Certificate of Naturalization

name
address
birthplace or nationality
country from which emigrated
birthdate or age
personal description
marital status
name of spouse
age or birthdate of spouse
address of spouse
names, ages and addresses of children
date of document

Oath of Allegiance

date
name
renounce allegiance to any foreign government

Copying Naturalization Records

Please be advised that the Immigration and Nationality Act (U.S. Code 1454e) limiting the certification and reproduction of naturalization records was amended in 1963. This amendment allows uncertified copies of naturalization records to be issued. The government printed a form (M-154) which summarized the main points of the naturalization laws.

The Form apprises clerks of court of the restrictions applicable to the issuance of copies and information from naturalization records. As stated in the Form, unless the court has issued an order in an individual case directing the making and issuance of certification of any part of the naturalization records, clerks of court are prohibited by law from making and issuing such certifications. However, the law authorizes this Service to make and issue such certifications upon application made to this Service. Persons requiring such certifications should follow the instructions outlined in Form M-154.

The revision of the Form has been occasioned by a change in policy respecting the making and issuance of *uncertified copies* and information from naturalization records by clerks of court. Until now, clerks of court have been restricted to furnishing such information orally only. This restriction has been removed, and clerks of court may now furnish uncertified copies of information in writing, by printing, by photocopy or by any other reproducitve process, as well as orally, in accordance with the rules of court. Clerks of court do not require the consent or approval of this Service for the making and issuance of such uncertified copies or information.

A facsimile reproduction of Form M-154 is shown below.

Clerks of court are prohibited by law from making and issuing certifications of a naturalization record or any part thereof, except upon order of the Court. The Immigration and Naturalization Service is authorized by law to make such certifications when needed in any judicial proceeding, or to comply with a State or Federal statute. Persons requiring such certifications should be advised to submit application Form N-585 to the appropriate Service office. A supply of Form N-585 is available to clerks of court or to other interested persons from the Immigration and Naturalization Service.

The Prohibition against the issuance of certifications by clerks of court does not extend to the furnishing of uncertified information. Clerks of court may furnish such information orally, in writing, by printing, or by photocopy or other reproductive process, in accordance with the rules of court, without consent of or approval by the Immigration and Naturalization Service.

Form M-154
(Rev. 12-5-72)N

GPO 951-675

Chronology of Principal Immigration Restrictions by Public Law

1612	VA. Co. Charter
1639	Colonial restrictions against criminals and pauper immigrants. Religious and physical fitness tests.
1681	Royal Denizations
1700	Order-in-Council (halted colonial denizations)
1709	Gen. Nat. Act (foreign protestents)
1740	Act of Parliament (non-Catholics)
1761	Act of Parliament
1773	Act banning local naturalizations
1789	State laws restricting admission of "convicted malefactors." The U.S. Constitution gives Congress power over immigration.
1798	The Temporary Alien and Sedition deportation statute and requirement that ship captains identify arriving alien passengers.
1819	First permanent federal immigration legislation requires listing of immigrants landing.

1875	Congress ends period of free immigration and restricts Chinese.
1882	First general federal immigration restriction law bars convicts, lunatics, idiots and paupers.
1885	Alien contract labor is restricted.
1891	Congress expands the list of excludable aliens on mental, moral, economic and physical grounds.
1903	Congress expands, codifies immigration restrictions. Anarchists excluded.
1907	Congress lays the foundation for a Gentlemen's Agreement with Japan. Congress creates Commission to Investigate Immigration.
1913	The Immigration Commission recommends restrictions be made quantitative as well as qualitative and suggests a literacy test.
1917	Congress again expands and codifies immigration restrictions but provides 10 exceptions thereto.
1921	The first federal quota restrictions
1924	Japanese exclusion legislation. Congress further restricts immigration by tighter quotas. The national origins plan emerges. The qualitative restrictions of the 1917 act are preserved and extended.
1929	National Origins Quota Plan becomes effective.
1940	The Alien Registration Act.
1943	Chinese exclusion acts are repealed. Temporary alien contract labor is permitted.
1945-46	The War Brides Act and Alien Fiancees or Fiances Act.
1947	Special exceptions are provided for aliens assigned to the United Nations. U.S. Senate authorizes investigation of immigration.
1948	Information and Educational Exchange Act. The Displaced Persons Act.
1950	Internal Security Act. Report No. 1515 of the Senate Judiciary Subcommittee on Immigration lays foundation for 1952 law.
1952	Immigration and Nationality (McCarran-Walter) Act preserves previous restriction principles including national origins plan; creates preference for skilled aliens; broadens classes of nonquota immigrants; all races are made eligible for immigration and naturalization; security provisions and those for procedural review are strengthened; broad structural changes in enforcement agencies and in grounds for exclusion and deportation are adopted. This is the most important revision and codification of immigration law in the nation's history.
1953	Refugee Relief Act authorizes entry of 214,000 nonquota immigrants outside the national origins restrictions.
1957	Refugee-Escapee Act further relaxes immigration restrictions; admits orphans; encourages waivers and status adjustment for the excludable and deportable and waives quota mortgages imposed by the Displaced Persons Act of 1948.
1960	World Refugee Year Law in an effort to stimulate international cooperation in resettlement of refugees.
1961	Nonquota status for alien orphan immigrants is made permanent; qualitative restrictions are relaxed; judicial review in exclusion and deportation cases is limited and defined; the quota ceiling is removed from the Asia-Pacific Triangle and adjusted for former colonial dependencies; race and ethnic records eliminated on visas.

America Is a Nation of Immigrants

A total of 46,712,725 people immigrated to the United States between 1820 and 1974. Here is a list of the Countries with the number of immigrants in millions.

Germany	6.95
Italy	5.26
Great Britain	4.84
Ireland	4.72
Austria & Hungary	4.31
Canada	4.04
Russia	3.36
Mexico	1.85
Central America	1.59
Sweden	1.27
Norway	.85
France	.74
Greece	.62
South America	.58
Poland	.50
Portugal	.40
Denmark	.36
Netherlands	.36
Switzerland	.35
Austrailia	.11
Africa	.10
Other Countries	1.42

PASSENGER LISTS

A law passed by congress in 1819 required that customs officers keep a list of all passengers arrving in the United States. Prior to that time passenger lists are very fragmented and what is available is mostly baggage lists, cargo manifests, or ships logs. (Some are available in the National Archives). From 1820 to 1945 extensive records are available.

Some Limitations of Passengers Lists

1. Passenger lists are not available for every place of arrival. During the 19th century, no law required passenger records to be kept for persons entering the United States from Canada and Mexico. Aside from the major ports of Boston, New York, Philadelphia, Baltimore, and New Orleans the records are vary sparce.

2. Not all of the lists are complete. Most of the records for most ports are incomplete.

3. The passenger lists were written by many different people over many years and they appear on National Archive microfilm in various stages of repair.

4. The tremendous volume of records, especially for New York and Philadelphia make a general search almost impossible.

5. The lists originally were maintained at the port of entry. Therefore, some were destroyed, others were lost by fire or negligence.

By Port

Baltimore

1. Only fragments of the original passenger lists exist.

2. Only eleven original lists prior to 1833, nine of these are cargo manifests.

3. In 1833 Maryland passed a law to keep track of passengers for reimbursement purposes, they are known as the "City Lists."

4. "City Lists" only required name, age and occuaption, sometimes included place of nativity, residence and destination.

Boston

1. Early records were destroyed in a fire in 1894.

2. Original lists are available from 1833 to 1891.

3. For the period 1820 to 1874 only copies of the orignal lists are available.

New Orleans

1. With the help of cargo manifests the lists are fairly complete from 1820 to 1902, especially where one uses the five volumes entitled "Passenger Lists Taken from Manifests of the Customs Service Port of New Orleans, 1813-1867." They contain the passenger's name, the name of the ship, the port of embarkation and the date of arrival.

New York

The original lists are largely complete from 1820 to 1897 and seem to follow the 1918 law most closely.

Philadelphia

Cargo manifests begin as early as 1800. Passenger lists are available from 1820 to 1899, however, microfilm copies are only available to 1882.

San Francisco

Lists were destroyed by fire in 1851 and 1940 and only some lists for 1920 are available. Some lists are available in the book "Ship N' Rail" a multi-volume series by Louis Ramussen.

Cargo Manifests (Sometimes called baggage lists)

In 1799 a law was passed requiring the names of passengers with baggage. Cargo manifests are a helpful supplement to passenger lists. These manifests give the passenger name, the name of the ship, date of arrival and sometimes the passenger's age, occupation, and former place of residence.

Copies and Abstracts

Customs officers were to send records to the Secretary of State once a quarter. Some sent copies and some sent abstracts. The Secretary of State then reported to Congress. From 1820 to 1870 these reports were part of the Congressional Record.

There are many more ports, covered by copies and abstracts than original lists cover. Lists are available for the following ports, with some gaps:

Baltimore	1820-1869
Boston	1820-1874
New Orleans	1820-1875
New York	1820-1874
Philadelphia	1820-1854

State Department Transcripts

The State Department made transcripts of records they received from 1819 until 1832. There were originally nine volumes but volume two is now missing. Entires are arranged by quarter—year of arrival and by district, or port, name of vessel, and name of passenger.

A typical entry shows the name of the vessel, quarter—year of arrival, name of master, name of district or port, passenger name, age, sex, occupation, name of country of emigration and country of intended settlement.

Passenger Arrival Records

1. Passenger arrival records are important to the genealogist because they contain

   a. information on names of individuals and places connected with them,

   b. ages and occuptations of individuals and sometimes relationships,

   c. dates of arrival or of death, if death occurred en route, and

   d. changes of residence.

A. Passenger Arrival Records Available

2. Passenger arrival records in the National Archives consist of the following types:

   a. *Customs passenger lists, 1819-1902:*

   The congressional act of March 2, 1819, required masters of vessels to furnish collectors of customs with lists of all passengers coming aboard at a foreign port and required collectors of customs to submit copies of such lists to the Secretary of State, who was to furnish statements on incoming passengers to the Congress at each of its sessions. An act of May 7, 1874, required the collectors of customs to submit "returns" from passenger lists to the Secretary of the Treasury, who was to prepare statements about them for publication. The customs passenger lists consist of original lists, 1820-1902; copies of lists, 1820-74; abstract of lists, 1820-75; and State Department transcripts, 1819-32.

   b. *Microfilm copies of immigration passenger lists, 1883-1945:*

   These film copies are copies of lists that were created as a result of a congressional act of August 3, 1882, under which the Secretary of the Treasury was made responsible for handling immigration activities in the United States, and later acts.

   c. *Customs cargo manifests, ca. 1800-19:*

   Customs cargo manifests, which were submitted in accordance with the congressional act of March 2, 1799, sometimes contain the names of passengers bringing in baggage.

   d. *Customs lists of aliens, 1798-1800:*

Salem and Beverly, Massachusetts. Customs lists of aliens relate only to the ports of Salem and Beverly. The lists which were required under the congressional act of June 25, 1798, were submitted by the masters of vessels to the collectors of customs, the latter being also required to submit copies of the lists to the Department of State. The whereabouts of the original lists of other ports and of the copies submitted to the Department of State is unknown. The Salem and Beverly lists have been published in the *New England Historical and Genealogical Register,* vol. 106, pp. 203-209, July 1952.

e. *Abstracts of lists of arrivals:*

New Orleans, 1813-67. The abstracts were prepared by the Work Projects Administration from records of the United States Customs Service in New Orleans. They were typed and bound into six volumes; Volume 5, however, is missing. Each volume is indexed alphabetically by names of passengers, vessels, and masters, except volume 1 which is indexed alphabetically by names of passengers and masters.

The ports or districts for which the National Archives has passenger lists and the dates covered by each type of list, the New Orleans typed abstracts excepted, will be found in Appendix A.

3. Passenger lists or copies of them outside the National Archives include those for the following ports (see also Appendix C):

   a. *Baltimore:*

      (1) The Maryland Historical Society, Baltimore, has passenger lists for the period October 30, 1891-1919, presented to the Society by the National Archives.

      (2) The Records Management Officer, City Hall, Baltimore, has passenger lists for the period 1833-66. These lists have been collated with those in the National Archives and the National Archives microfilm copy includes reproductions of lists from the Baltimore City Hall that were not in Federal custody.

   b. *Boston:*

      The Archives Division, Office of the Secretary of the Commonwealth of Massachusetts, Boston, has passenger lists for the period January 1, 1848 - July 31, 1891. These lists were created as a result of an act of May 10, 1848, of the Commonwealth of Massachusetts. The Boston Public Library, Boston 17, has microfilm copies of passenger lists, September 25, 1820 - July 29, 1891, produced by the National Archvies.

   c. *Galveston:*

      The Archives Division, Texas State Library, Capitol Station, Austin, has lists of passenger arrivals, 1839-46 (chiefly for the port of Galveston). The Houston Public Library, Houston, Texas, and the Rosenberg Library Association, Galveston, Texas, have microfilm copies of quarterly abstracts of passenger lists, 1846-71.

   d. *Gloucester (Massachusetts):*

      The Archives Division, Office of the Secretary of the Commonwealth of Massachusetts, Boston, has passenger lists for the period May 27, 1869 - November 16, 1871.

e. *Lewes (Delaware):*

The Public Archives Commission, State of Delaware, Dover, has lists of passengers arriving December 1, 1836 - April 13, 1841. These lists will be found in "Record Book of the Customs House at Lewes, Delaware."

f. *Lynn (Massachusetts):*

The Archives Division, Office of the Secretary of the Commonwealth of Massachusetts, Boston, has passenger lists for the period November 2, 1869 - August 21, 1871.

g. *Marblehead (Massachusetts);*

The Archives Division, Office of the Secretary of the Commonwealth of Massachusetts, Boston has passenger lists for the period April 19, 1870 - October 31, 1871.

h. *New Amstel (New Castle, Delaware);*

(1) The Historical Society of Delaware, Old Town Hall, Wilmington, has a microfilm copy of manuscript records in Dutch which include three lists of passengers arriving in 1661 and 1662. The original records are on deposit in the Archives of the City of Amsterdam.

(2) Publication of passenger lists as follows:

The three reproduced Dutch passenger lists, 1661 and 1662, in the Historical Society of Delaware have been published in *Delaware History*, vol. VIII, No. 3, pp. 310-311, Wilmington, March 1959. A. R. Dunlap is the transcriber.

i. *New Bedford (Massachusetts):*

The Archives Division, Office of the Secretary of the Commonwealth of Massachusetts, Boston, has passenger lists for the period May 25, 1869 - September 27, 1871.

j. *Newburyport (Massachusetts):*

The Archives Division, Office of the Secretary of the Commonwealth of Massachusetts, Boston, has passenger lists for the period November 5, 1869 - May 1871.

k. *New Orleans:*

The New Orleans Public Library, 219 Loyola Avenue, New Orleans 40, Louisiana, and the Genealogical Society of the Church of Jesus Christ of Latter Day Saints, 107 South Main Street, Salt Lake City 11, Utah, have microfilm copies of passenger lists, January 1, 1820 - January 31, 1903, and of quarterly abstracts of passenger lists, January 1, 1820 -June 30, 1875.

l. *New York:*

The Genealogical Society of the Church of Jesus Christ of Latter-day Saints, Salt Lake City, Utah, has microfilm copies of passenger lists, January 7, 1820 - December 30, 1876. The National Library of Ireland, Kildare Street, Dublin, has microfilm copies of passenger lists, January 7, 1820 - February 29, 1860.

m. *Philadelphia:*

(1) The Division of Public Records, Pennsylvania Historical and Museum

Commission, Harrisburg, has lists of passengers, 1727 - 1808.

(2) The Historical Society of Pennsylvania, 1300 Locust Street, Philadelphia, lists in its *Guide to the Manuscript Collection . . .,* 2d edition, Philadelphia, 1949, the following items:

    (a) Item 237. Harrold E. Gillingham Papers, 1792-1855. Includes list of alien passengers, 1798-1829.

    (b) Item 425. Miscellaneous Collection of The Historical Society of Pennsylvania, 1661-1931. This collection includes papers relating to Palatines and redemptioners, 1768-1803.

    (c) Item 1228. *Britannia.* Ship, Mustering Book, 1773. 1 vol. This book contains a list of passengers who embarked from Rotterdam.

(3) Publications of passenger lists as follows:

    (a) Passenger lists for the period 1727-1808 which are on deposit in the Division of Public Records, Pennsylvania Historical and Museum Commission, have been completely published in Ralph Beaver Strassburger, *Pennsylvania German Pioneers, a Publication of the Original Lists of Arrivals in the Port of Philadelphia from 1727 to 1808,* edited by William John Hinke, 3 vols., Norristown, Pennsylvania, 1934.

    (b) Passenger lists for the period 1727-75 are published in *Pennsylvania Archives,* 2d series, volume 17, Harrisburg, 1890, and in I. Daniel Rupp, *A Collection of Upwards of Thirty Thousand Names of German, Swiss, Dutch, French and Other Immigrants in Pennsylvania from 1727 to 1776,* 2d edition, Philadelphia, 1876.

    (c) Passenger lists for the period 1786-1808 are published in *Pennsylvania Archives,* 2d series, vol. 17, Harrisburg, 1890.

    (d) Items 425 and 1228 cited in the *Guide* of the Historical Society of Pennsylvania are printed in Strassburger's *Pennsylvania German Pioneers.*

n. *Provincetown (Massachusetts);*

The Archives Divison, Office of the Secretary of the Commonwealth of Massachusetts, Boston, has passenger lists for the period June 30, 1870 - April 18, 1871.

o. *Salem (Massachusetts):*

The Archives Division, Office of the Secretary of the Commonwealth of Massachusetts, Boston, has passenger lists for the period May 18, 1869 - March 18, 1872.

p. *San Francisco:*

The California Historical Society, 2090 Jackson Street, San Francisco 9, has lists of passenger arrivals, chiefly 1820-69. These lists were compiled by the Society from newspapers and other sources. The Society also has an alphabetical name and index to these lists.

q. *Savannah:*

(1) The University Libraries, The University of Georgia, Athens, Georgia,

has a list of passenger arrivals, 1732-41; the list is arranged alphabetically by name of passenger.

(2) Publication of passenger list as follows:

The list of passenger arrivals, 1732-41, has been published in E. Merton Coulter and Albert B. Saye, *A List of the Early Settlers of Georgia,* Athens, The University of Georgia Press, 1949. In 1959 the publication was out of print.

r. *Wareham (Massachusetts):*

The Archives Division, Office of the Secretary of the Commonwealth of Massachusetts, Boston, has passenger lists for the period June 30, 1870 - May 17, 1871.

4. European passenger lists or copies of passenger lists outside the National Archives include those for the following countries:

a. *England:* The Public Record Office in London has lists of persons who left England for America in the 17th and 18th centuries which have been published. Such printed lists will be found in John Camden Hotten, *The Original Lists of Persons of Quality . . . Who Went from Great Britain to the American Plantations, 1600-1700 . . . ,* London, 1874, and in Gerald Fothergill, "Emigrants from England" [1773-76], *New England Historical and Genealogical Register,* vol. 62. pp. 242-253, 320-332; vol. 63. pp. 16-31, 134-146, 234-244, 342-355; vol. 64, pp. 18-25, 106-115, 214-227, 314-326; and vol. 65, pp. 20-35, 116-132, and 232-251, Boston, 1908-11.

b. *Ireland:* The Department of Manuscripts, Britism Museum, London, England, has lists of Irish passengers to America, 1803-6. For information about these lists see Margaret D. Falley, "Genealogical Research in Ireland, a Survey Made in Ireland in 1951, *"The American* Genealogist, Whole No. 112, vol. 28, No. 4, pp. 243-244, New Haven, Connecticut, October 1952. Lists of Irish passengers, 1803-6, have been published in "Early Irish Emigrants to America, 1803-1806," *The Recorder,* vol. 3, No. 5, pp. 19-23, New York, June 1926, and in Gerald Fothergill, "Passenger Lists to America" [1803-4], *New England Historical and Genealogical Register,* vol. 60, pp. 23-28, 160-; 64, 240-243, 346-349; vol. 61, pp. 133-139, 265-270, 347-353; vol. 62, pp. 78-81, 168-171; and vol. 66, pp. 30-32, 306-308, Boston; 1906-12. The Public Record Office of Northern Ireland in Belfast prepared six typed leaflets containing the names of persons who emigrated in 1833-35 to the United States and Canada from various parishes in County Londonderry, Ireland. Copies of the leaflets are available in the library of the National Archives.

c. *France:* The Louisiana Historical Society in New Orleans has transcripts of lists of passengers leaving France for Louisiana, 1718-24, some of which have been translated and published in *The Louisiana Historical Quarterly,* vols. 14 (1931), 15(1932), and 21 (1938).

d. *Germany:* The Public Record Office, London, England, has lists of emigrants who left the Palatinate, 1708-12, and came to America via London. The lists have been published in Walter Allen Knittle, *Early Eighteenth Century Palatine Emigration . . . ,* Philadelphia, 1937. The Manuscript Division, Library of Congress, has microfilm copies of lists of immigrants from Hamburg, Germany, and related indexes, 1850-73. For further information concerning these lists see Marion Dexter Learned, *Guide to the Manuscript Materials Relating to American History in the German State Archives,* p. 274, Washington, 1912.

e. *Spain:* The Archivo General de Indias in Seville has records of passengers leaving Spain for the Indies and Florida and Louisiana, 1509-1790, of which those for 1509-59 have been published in *Catalogo de Pasajeros a Indias durante los Siglos XVI, XVII, y XVIII,* 3 vols., 1940-46, Seville, Spain.

f. *Switzerland:* The State Archives of Zurich has lists of Swiss emigrants who came to Carolina and Pennsylvania, 1733-44. These lists have been published in Albert Bernhardt Faust, *List of Swiss Emigrants in the Eighteenth Century to the American Colonies,* vol. 1, Washington, 1920. The State Archives of Bern and Basel have records about Swiss emigrants who came to America, 1706-95 and 1734-94, respectively. Lists compiled from these records have been published in Volume 2 of Faust's *List of Swiss Emigrants . . . ,* Washington, 1925.

5. Other passenger arrival materials:

a. The Maine Historical Society, 485 Congress Street, Portland, Maine. has passenger lists, 1862-64, and 1866-76. The Society has not been able to verify that the arrivals relate to Portland. The lists are not indexed.

b. The New York Historical Society, 170 Central Park West, New York 24, New York, has "a ten-page typescript entitled 'A List of Irish Immigrants who came to South Carolina in 1768' [copied by] Janie Revill [Columbia, South Carolina 1937]."

c. Information on other source materials about passenger arrivals including some of those already mentioned can be found in *A Bibliography of Ship Passenger Lists 1538-1825 Being a Guide to Published lists of Early Immigrants to North America,* compiled by Harold Lancour, Third Edition, revised and enlarged by Richard J. Wolfe, New York, The New York Public Library, 1963.

B. Using Passenger Arrival Records

6. In *Using* passenger arrival records in the National Archives the following points should be noted:

a. *Information needed:*

In addition to the *name* of the *passenger* and the *name of* the *port of entry,* the following information should be supplied: The *name of* the *vessel* and the *approximate date of arrival* or *the name of* the *port of embarkation* and the *exact date of arrival.* Where specific information cannot be furnished a search of the indexes can be made if in addition to the name of the passenger the name of the port of entry and the supposed year of arrival are given.

b. *Indexes available in the National Archives:*

Indexes to the customs and immigration passenger lists and the dates covered by these indexes are listed by port in Appendix B.

(1) *Customs passenger lists:*

The card indexes are arranged alphabetically by name of passenger. There are two separate indexes for the port of Baltimore, which are arranged according to the soundex system. One is an index to the names of the lists created under Federal legislation and covers the period 1832-97, with a few entries as early as 1820. The other is an index to the names on the lists created under the Maryland Act of March 22, 1833, and covers arrivals for the period 1833-66. Both indexes are arranged alphabetically to the first letter of the surname, thereunder by a code number, and thereunder alphabetically by given name.

(2) *Immigration passenger lists:*

The indexes consist of two types, card indexes and book indexes.

(a) *Card indexes*

The card indexes are arranged alphabetically by name of passenger. Three of the indexes, those relating to the ports of Baltimore; New York, July 1, 1902, - June 30, 1948; and Philadelphia, are arranged according to the soundex system, which is described in (1) above.

(b) *Book indexes:*

The book indexes are arranged, with some variation, by name of steamship line, then by date of vessel arrival, and then alphabetically to the first letter of the surname of the passenger.

c. *Indexes available outside the Nation Archives* (see also Appendix C):

Microfilm copies of the card index to the names on lists of arrivals at the port of Boston, 1848-91, filed with the Archives Division, Office of the Secretary of the Commonwealth, Boston, Massachusetts, are available at the Boston Public Library and at the Genealogical Society of the Church of Jesus Christ of Latter Day Saints, Salt Lake City, Utah. Microfilm copies of the card index to the New York Passenger lists, 1820-46, can be examined in the New York Public Library, New York, New York.

d. *Related materials useful in locating passenger arrival records:*

(1) *In the National Archives:*

Records of Vessel entrances for the following ports: Baltimore, 1782-1934; Boston, 1879-99, New Orleans, 1812-1903; New York, 1789-1919; and Philadelphia, 1789-1900. There are gaps in the date span of these records. These records, which are in annual volumes, show by calendar year the following information: the name of each vessel, the name of its captain, the name of the port of embarkation, and the exact date of arrival. For some ports the records of vessel entrances are in two series, one arranged alphabetically by name of vessel and the other chronologically by date of arrival. From these records can be ascertained (1) the date of arrival of a specific vessel, and (2) the names of all vessels departing from a particular foreign port to a particular American port in a given year.

Naturalization records of the District of Columbia, 1802-1926, and of Maine, Massachusetts, New Hampshire, and Rhode Island, 1787-1906: In addition to the name of the petitioner, the records normally contain his date of arrival and the name of the port at which he arrived and sometimes the name of the vessel on which he arrived.

Homestead application files, 1862-1950: If an applicant for homestead land was other than native-born, his file may include evidence of the date of his arrival and the name of the port at which he arrived.

The Atlantic Migration, 1607-1860, a History of the Continuing Settlement of the United States by Marcus Lee Hansen, Cambridge, 1941. Ports of embarkation in Europe and of arrival in the United States in the 19th century are discussed for various nationalities on pages 172-198.

The Morton Allen Directory of European Steamship Arrivals . . . , New York, 1931. This publication includes information concerning the arrivals of vessels at the ports of New York, 1890-1930, and of Baltimore, Boston, and Philadelphia, 1904-26. It lists by year, name of steamship company, and exact date the names of vessels arriving at those ports for the periods indicated.

(2) *Outside the National Archives:*

Records of naturalization proceedings outside the District of Colubmia: Such records are to be found with those of the Federal, State, or other court of record that issued the naturalization certificate if it was issued before September 27, 1906. For information concerning the locations of naturalization records see Sargent B. Child and Dorothy P. Holmes, *Check list of Historical Records Survey Publication,* revised 1943, Federal Works Agency, Work Projects Administration, Washington, DC. This publication includes citations to inventories that have been prepared on Federal, State, and county records. The whereabouts of naturalization records may also be learned by examining various published guides to manuscript collections. The lists of voters in an immigrant's county of residence in a few instances may include information concerning the court in which naturalization took place.

Family Records sometimes provide information that will be helpful in identifying passenger arrival records.

The public library of Fort Wayne and Allen County, Indiana, has microfilm copies of passenger lists for the following ports:

1. Baltimore: September 2, 1820 — December 28, 1891
2. New York: January 7, 1820 - June 30, 1821; January 2, 1847
3. Boston: September 25, 1820 - May 19, 1848

The library also has a microfilm copy of the index to the New York passenger lists, 1820-46.

Ports or Districts for which the National Archives has Passenger Lists, showing dates for each type of list.

Name of port or district[1]	Customs passenger lists[2]			Immigration passenger lists[3]
	Originals	Copies and abstracts	State Department transcripts	
Alexandria, VA.[2]	---	1820-52	1820-31	---
Annapolis, MD.	---	1849	---	
Apalachicola, FL	---	---	---	Sept. 4, 1918
Baltimore, MD	1820-91	1820-69	1820, 1822-27, 1829	Dec. 12, 1891-Nov. 30, 1909
Bangor, ME	---	1848	---	---
Barnstable, MA	---	1820-26	1820-26	
Bath, ME	---	1825-32, 1867	---	---
Beaufort, NC	---	1865	---	---
Balfast, ME	---	1820-31, 1851	1820, 1822-24, 1827, 1829, 1831	---
Boca Grande, FL	---	---	---	Oct. 28, 1912-Aug. 16, 1935
Boston and Charlestown, MA[4] ..	1883-99	1820-74	1820-27	Aug. 1, 1891-Dec. 1943
Bridgeport, CT	---	1870	---	---
Bridgetown, NJ	---	1828	1828	---
Bristol and Warren, RI	---	1820-24, 1828, 1843-71	1820-28	
Brunswick, GA	---	---	---	Nov. 22, 1901-Nov. 27, 1939
Cape May, NJ	---	1828	---	---
Carabelle, FL	---	---	---	Nov. 7, 1915
Charleston, SC[5]	---	1820-29	1820-29	Apr. 9, 1906-Dec. 3, 1945
Darien, GA	---	1823, 1825	---	
Delaware (see also entry for Wilmington)	---	---	1820	---
Dighton, MA	---	1820-36	1819, 1823, 1826, 1828	---
East River, VA	---	1830	1830	---
Edenton, NC	---	1820	1820	---
Edgartown, MA	---	1820-70	1820-28, 1831-32	---
Fairfield, CT	---	1820-21	1820	---
Fall River, MA	---	1837-65	---	---
Fernandina, FL	---	---	---	Aug. 29, 1904-Oct. 7, 1932
Frenchman's Bay, ME	---	1821, 1826, 1827	1822, 1825-27	---
Galveston, TX	---	1846-71	---	---
Georgetown, DC	---	1820-21	1820	---
Georgetown, SC	---	---	---	June 17, 1923-Oct. 24, 1939
Gloucester, MA	---	1820, 1832-39 1867-70	---	Oct, 1906-June 1923 Feb. 1, 1930-Dec. 1943
Gulfport, MS	---	---	---	Aug. 1904-Sept. 1944
Hampton, VA	---	1821	---	---
Hartford, CT	---	1832	---	Feb. 1929-Dec. 1943
Havre de Grace, MD	---	1820	---	---
Hingham, MA	---	1852	---	---
Jacksonville, FL[6]	---	---	---	Jan. 18, 1904-Dec. 17, 1945
Kennebunk, ME	---	1820-27, 1842	1820, 1822-25, 1827	---
Key West, FL	---	1837-68	---	Nov. 1898-Dec. 1945
Knights Key, FL	---	---	---	Feb. 7, 1908-Jan. 20, 1912
Little Egg Harbor (port of Tuckerton), NJ	---	1831	---	---
Marblehead, MA	---	1820-52	1821-23, 1825-27	---
Mayport, FL[6]	---	---	---	Nov. 16, 1907-Apr. 13, 1916
Miami, FL	---	---	---	Oct. 1899-Dec. 1945
Millville, FL	---	---	---	July 4, 1916
Mobile, AL	1820-62	1832, 1849-52	---	Apr. 3, 1904-Dec. 24, 1945
Nantucket, MA	---	1820-62	1820, 1822-25, 1829, 1831	---
Newark, NJ	---	1836	---	---
New Bedford, MA	1823-99	1826-52	1822, 1825-27 1830-31	July 1, 1902-July 1942
New Bern, NC	---	1820-45, 1865	1820-30	---
Newburyport, MA	---	1821-39	1821-31	---

| Name of port or district[1] | Customs passenger lists[2] | | | Immigration passenger lists[3] |
	Originals	Copies and abstracts	State Department transcripts	
New Haven, CT	---	1820-73	1822-31	---
New London, CT	---	1820-47	1820, 1823-27 1829, 1831	---
New Orleans, LA	1820-1902	1820-75	1820-27	Jan. 1903-Dec. 1945
Newport, RI	1820-75	1820-57	1820-28, 1830-31	---
New York, NY	1820-97	1820-74	1820-27	June 16, 1897-1942
Norfolk and Portsmouth, VA ...	---	1820-57	1820-32	---
Oswegatchie, NY	---	1821-23	1821-23	---
Panama City, FL	---	---	---	Nov. 10, 1927-Dec. 12, 1939
Pascagoula, MS	---	---	---	July 15, 1903-May 21, 1935
Passamaquoddy, ME	---	1820-59	1822-26, 1831	---
Penobscot, ME	---	1851	---	---
Pensacola, FL	---	---	---	May 12, 1900-July 16, 1945
Perth Amboy, NJ	---	1820, 1829-32	1829	---
Petersburg, VA	---	1820-21	1819-20, 1822	---
Philadelphia, PA[2]	1820-99	1820-54	1820-22, 1824-27, 1829	Jan, 1883-Dec. 31, 1945
Plymouth, MA	---	1821-43	1822, 1824, 1826-27, 1829-30	---
Plymouth NC	---	1820, 1825, 1840	1820, 1823	---
Port Everglades, FL	---	---	---	Feb. 15, 1932-Dec. 10, 1945
Port Inglis, FL	---	---	---	Mar. 29, 1912, Jan 2, 1913
Portland and Falmouth ME[4]	---	1820-68, 1873	1820-32	Nov. 1893-Mar. 1943
Port Royal, SC	---	1865	---	---
Portsmouth, NH	---	1820-61	1820, 1822, 1824-31	---
Port St. Joe, FL	---	---	---	Jan. 12, 1923-Oct. 13, 1939
Providence, RI	---	1820-67	1820, 1822-31	June 1911-June 1943
Richmond, VA	---	1820-44	1820-24, 1828, 1830	---
Rochester, NY	---	1866	---	---
Sag Harbor, NY	---	1829-34	1829	---
St. Andrews, FL	---	---	---	Jan. 2, 1916-May 13, 1926
St. Augustine, FL	---	1821-27, 1870	1822-24, 1827	---
St. Johns, FL	---	1865	---	---
St. Petersburg, FL	---	---	---	Dec. 15, 1926-March 1, 1941
Salem and Beverly, MA[2]	---	1865-66	1823	---
Sandusky, OH	---	1820	1820	---
Savannah, GA	---	1820-68	1820-23, 1825-26, 1831	June 5, 1906-Dec. 6, 1945
Saybrook, CT	---	1820	---	---
Tampa, FL	---	---	---	Nov. 1898-Dec. 1945
Waldoboro, ME	---	1820-33	1820-21	---
Washington, NC	---	1820-48	1828-29, 1831	---
West Palm Beach, FL	---	---	---	Sept. 8, 1920-Nov. 21, 1945
Wilmington, DE (see also entry for Delaware)	---	1820-48	---	---
Wiscasset, ME	---	---	1819, 1829	---
Yarmouth, ME	---	1820	---	---

Footnotes

1. A Customs district is a geographical area under the jurisdiction of a collector of customs. There may be one or more ports of entry within a district.

2. The National Archives also has among its customs arrival records lists of aliens, 1798-1800, for Salem and Beverly, Mass., and cargo manifests, ca. 1800-19, for Alexandria, VA, and Philadelphia and fragmentary manifests for a few other ports for the same period.
   The customs passenger lists have been microfilmed. Quarterly abstracts of passenger lists for Galveston, 1846-71, and New Orleans, 1820-75, have also been microfilmed.

3. Positive prints of negative microfilm rolls containing copies of immigration passenger lists over 50 years old have been prepared.

4. There are lists of arrivals at Charlestown, Mass., among the copies and abstracts and among the State Department transcripts for Boston. Likewise there are lists of arrivals at Falmouth, Maine, among the copies and abstracts and among the State Department transcripts for Portland.

5. Sometimes shown in the customs records as the District of South Carolina.

6. The Mayport, FL, copies of immigration passenger lists include at least one for Jacksonville, FL, that of February 24, 1916.

Indexes to the Passenger Lists in the National Archives

Name of port	Customs passenger lists[1]	Immigration passenger lists[2]	
	Card indexes	Card indexes	Book indexes
Baltimore, MD	1820-97	1897-July 1952	---
Boston, MA	1848-91	1902-Dec. 31, 1920	Apr. 1, 1899-Sept. 14, 1940
Gulfport, MS	---	Aug. 27, 1904-Aug. 28, 1954	---
Miami, FL	---	Dec. 30, 1929-Feb. 23, 1942	---
New Bedford, MA	1875-99	July 1, 1902-Nov. 18, 1954	---
New Orleans, LA	1853-1902	Oct. 1900-1952	---
New York, NY	1820-46	June 16, 1897-Dec. 31, 1943	Jan 1, 1906-Dec. 31, 1942
Pascagoula, MS	---	July 15, 1903-May 21, 1935	---
Philadelphia, PA	1820-1906[1]	Jan. 1, 1883-June 28, 1948	May 14, 1906-June 17, 1926
Portland, ME	---	Jan. 29, 1893,-Nov. 22, 1954	Apr. 1907-Apr. 6, 1930
Providence, RI	---	June 18, 1911-Oct. 5, 1934	Dec. 13, 1911-June 26, 1934
Miscellaneous ports in AL, FL, GA, and SC	---	1890-1924	---
Miscellaneous ports, not including New York	1820-74	---	---

Footnotes

1. Includes entries for the names of passengers found on cargo manifests, 1800-19, and later.

2. Both the card indexes and book indexes have been microfilmed. These indexes are available for examination provided all entries on each roll relate to lists over 50 years old.

Passenger and Immigration Lists

By P. William Filby

While assisting genealogists at the Peabody Library and later at the Maryland Historical Society, one of my main questions has been the existence of passenger lists.

Normally, I referred the researcher to Lancour's *Bibliography of Ship Passenger Lists* (Rev. 1962), where each source was arranged chronologically under general and then state headings. If the researcher wanted an immigrant who came to Pennsylvania in 1762, he had only to check Lancour, to see if any list covering this period existed. If it did, the researcher had to find the source suggested.

But this edition, produced by Richard J. Wolfe, brought us to 1962, and already we were in the 1970s, so I felt that an update was vital.

Gunther Pohl of the New York Public Library, with similar ideas, had kept a list of all passengers noticed since 1962, taken from the many periodicals kept by NYPL; Mrs. Mary K. Meyer also had such a list; Dorothy M. Lower at Allen County Public library, Fort Wayne, had also taken interest in such sources, and when they knew of my intentions, they gladly and unselfishly submitted at least 200 sources.

When my intentions were announced publicly, lists began descending upon me daily, so that within a year Lancour's 262 sources had increased to almost 1,000. By 1980 it was time to present a completely new list of passenger sources to librarians and researchers.

With the encouragement of Gale Research Co., *Passenger and Immigration Lists Bibliography, 1538-1900*, was published. By the end of 1981 the list had swelled to over 1300 sources.

Since then I have spoken throughout the country, appealing for details of any passenger lists which appeared in periodicals, books, or newspapers.

As ever, my host of friends responded with many new lists. Dorothy M. Lower, with her very complete current periodical list, seldom fails to send less than three lits a week, and from Canada, Terrence M. Punch and George Hancocks, with Eric Jonasson, have been very faithful. With this wonderful response there have been over 200 additions in 1982.

Then, after a National Genealogical Society talk at the National Archives, Michael Cassady informed me that he was continually transcribing passenger lists from National Archives copies, and that those would all be available.

To my delight, Sylvia Nimmo, 6201 Kentucky Rd., Rt. 21, Papillion, Nebraska 68133, will be publishing these lists containing well over 10,000 names, in the next two or three months.

Happily, these are not the only appearances of new lists. Two Delaware firms, the Genealogical Publishing Co., Baltimore, and Scholarly Resources, Wilmington, have for many months now been preparing lists not formerly available to the public.

CHAPTER 17

CHURCH RECORDS

Religious Distribution, 1775

Church members	74% of the population			Jersey, Delaware
Congregationalists	30.9 New England	Baptists	1.3	Rhode Island, Pennsylvania, New
Anglicans	26.9 New York, South			Jersey, Delaware
Presbyterians	22.0 Frontier			
German churches Incl. Lutherans)	10.7 Pennsylvania	Roman Catholics	1.3	Maryland, Pennsylvania
Dutch Reformed	4.0 New York, New Jersey	Methodists	0.2	Scattered
		Jews	0.1	New York, Rhode Island
Quakers	2.1 Pennsylvania, New			

Headquarters of Denominations

(Addresses of denominational headquarters are given wherever possible; otherwise, the names of chief and preferably permanent officals are listed.)

From *A Handbook of Denominations*, 7th Edition by Frank S. Mead. Copyright © 1980 by Abingdon. Reproduced by permission.

Adventists:

Seventh Day Adventists
6840 Eastern Avenue
Washington, D.C. 20012

Church of God
(General Conference)
Oregon, IL 61061

Primitive Advent Christian Church
Sec., Hugh W. Good,
Elkview, WV 25071

African Orthodox Church
122 West 129th Street
New York, NY 10027

Amana Church Society
Pres., Charles L. Selzer
Homestead, IA 52236

American Ethical Union
2 West 64th Street
New York, NY 10023

American Evangelical Christian

Churches
Pineland, FL 33945

American Rescue Workers
2827 Frankford Avenue
Philadelphia, PA 19134

Anglican Orthodox Church
Bishop James Parker Dees
323 East Walnut Street
Statesville, NC 28677

Apostolic Christian Church (Nazarean)
P.O. Box 151
Tremont, IL 61568

Apostolic Christian Church of America
Elder Roy L. Sauder
3528 North Linden Lane
Peoria, IL 61604

Apostolic Faith
Northwest Sixth and Burnside
Portland, OR 97209

Apostolic Overcoming Holy Church
of God

Secretary, Mrs. Juanita R. Arrington
514 10th Avenue
Birmingham, AL 35204

Armenian Churches
St. Varton Cathedral
630 Second Avenue
New York, NY 10016

Baha'i
536 Sheridan Road
Wilmette, IL 60091

Baptists:

American Baptist Churches
in the U.S.A.
Valley Forge, PA 19481

Southern Baptist Convention
460 James Robertson Parkway
Nashville, TN 37209

National Baptist Convention U.S.A. Inc.
Secretary, Rev. T. J. Jemison
915 Spain Street
Baton Rouge, LA 70872

National Baptist Convention of America
Secretary, Rev. Billy H. Wilson
2620 South Marsallis Avenue
Dallas, TX 77020

American Baptist Association
4605 North State Line Avenue
Texarkana, TX 755011

Baptist Bible Fellowship International
730 East Kearny
Springfield, MO 65800

Baptist General Conference
1233 Central Street
Evanston, IL 60201

Baptist Missionary Association
of America
Secretary, Rev. Ralph Cottrell
P.O. Box 2866
Texarkana, AR 75501

Bethel Ministerial Assn.
Box 5353
Evansville, IN 47715

Central Baptist Association
Dana M. Crawford
726 Hollis Street
Kingsport, TN 37660

Conservative Baptist Association
of America
P.O. Box 66
Wheaton, IL 60187

Duck River (and Kindred)
Association of Baptists
Clerk, Marvin Davenport
Auburntown, TN 37061

Free Will Baptists

1134 Murfreesboro Road
Nashville, TN 37202

General Association of Regular
Baptist Churches
1300 North Meacham Road
Schaumburg, IL 60185

General Baptists
Poplar Bluff, MO 63901

General Conference of the
Evangelical Baptist Church Inc.
Kevetter Bldg.
2400 East Ash Street
Goldsboro, NC 27530

Landmark Baptists
Dr. I. K. Cross
P.O. Box 848
Bellflower, CA 90706

National Baptist Evangelical and
Soul Saving Assembly of U.S.A.
441 Monroe Avenue
Detroit, MI 48226

National Primitive Baptist
Convention, U.S.A.
P.O. Box 2355
Tallahassee, FL 32301

North American Baptist Conference
1 South 210 Summit Avenue
Oakbrook Terrace, IL 60181

Primitive Baptists
Elder W. H. Cayce
South Second Street
Thornton, AR 71766

Reformed Baptists
Gene Rice
1919 Division Street
Nashville, TN 37203

Separate Baptists in Christ
Floyd Wilson
59 Greenspring Street
Indianapolis, IN 46224

Seventh Day Baptist
General Conference
510 Watchung Avenue
Box 868
Plainfield, NJ 07061

United Free Will
Baptist Church
Kinston College
1000 University Street
Kinston, NC 18501

Berean Fundamental Church
North Platte, NB 69101

Bible Protestant Church
84 Clementon Road
Gibbsboro, NJ 08206

Bible Way Church, World Wide
1130 New Jersey Avenue NW
Washington, DC 20001

Brethren (Dunkers):

Brethren Church
524 College Avenue
Ashland, OH 44805

Church of the Brethren
1451 Dundee Avenue
Elgin, IL 60120

Fellowship of Grace Brethren Churches
1108 Chestnut Avenue
Winona Lake, IN 46590

Old Baptist German Brethren
Elder Clement Skiles
Route 1, Box 140
Bringhurst, IN 46903

Plymouth Brethren
P.O. Box 294
218 West Willow
Wheaton, IL 60187

River Brethren:

Brethren in Christ Church
Secretary Arthur M. Climenhaga
4208 Southest Jennings Avenue
Portland, OR 97222

United Zion Church
Sec., The Rev. J. Paul Martin
Box 212 D, Route 1
Annville, PA 17003

United Brethren:

Church of the United Brethren
  in Christ
302 Lake Street, P.O. Box 650
Huntington, IN 46750

United Christian Church
Elden Henry C. Heagy
Lebanon, R.D. 4
Lebanon County, PA 17042

Buddhist Churches of America
1710 Octavia Street
San Francisco, CA 94109

Christadelphians
H.P. Zilmer
1002 Webster Lane
Des Plaines, IL 60016

Christian and Missionary Alliance
250 North Highland Avenue
Nyack, NY 10960

Christian Catholic Church
Dowie Memorial Drive
Zion, IL 60099

Christian Church

(Disciples of Christ)
222 South Downey Avenue
Indianapolis, IN 46206

Christian Church of North America
1818 State Street
Sharon, PA 16146

Christian Churches and
  Churches of Christ
3533 Epley Road
Cincinnati, OH 45231

Christian Congregation
Supt., The Rev Ora Wilbert Eads
708 South Bragg Street
Monroe, NC 28110

Christian Nation Church
Gen. Sec., The Rev. W. F. Clark
345 Cedar Drive
Loveland, OH 45140

Christian Union
P.O. Box 38
Excelsior Springs, MO 64024

Christ's Sanctified Holy Church
South Cutting Avenue &
East Spencer Street
Jennings, LA 70546

Church of Christ (Holiness)
  U.S.A.
329 East Monument Street
Jackson, MS 39202

Church of Christ, Scientist
Christian Science Center
Boston, MA 02115

Church of God:

Church of God
  (Anderson, IN)
Box 2420
Anderson, IN 46011

Church of God (Apostolic)
St. Peter's Church of God (Apostolic)
11th & Hickory Street
Winston Salem, NC 27101

Church of God
  (Cleveland, TN)
Keith Street at 25th NW
Cleveeland, TN 37311

Church of God
  (Seventh Day, Denver, CO)
P.O. Box 2370
Denver, CO 80201

Church of God
  (Seventh Day, Salem, WV)
79 Water Street
Salem, WV 26426

Church of God
  (New Testament Judaism)

P.O. Box 1207
Jerusalem Acres
Cleveland, TN 37311

Church of God (Tomlinson)
2504 Arrow Wood Drive
Huntsville, AL 35803

Church of God
  and Saints of Christ
Belleville
Portsmouth, VA 23704

Church of God by Faith
3220 Haines Street
Jacksonville, FL 32206

Church of God in Christ
938 Mason Street
Memphis, TN 38126

Church of God in Christ
  (International)
1905 Columbia Avenue
Philadelphia, PA 19121

Church of God of Prophecy
Bible Place
Cleveland, TN 37311

(Original) Church of God
P.O. Box 3086
Chattanooga, TN 37404

Church of Illumination
Beverly Hall
Clymer Road
Quakertown, PA 18951

Church of Jesus Christ
Cleveland, TN 37311

Church of Jesus Christ of
  Latter-day Saints
50 East North Temple Street
Salt Lake City, UT 84111

Reorganized Church of Jesus Christ
  of Latter-day Saints
Saints Auditorium
Independence, MO 64051

Church of Jesus Christ
  (Bickertonites)
Sixth and Lincoln
Monongahela, PA 15063

Church of Jesus Christ of
  Latter-day Saints (Strangites)
Elder Vernon D. Swift
P.O. Box 522
Artesia, NM 88210

Church of Jesus Christ
  (Temple Lot)
Temple Lot
Independence, MO 64000

Church of Our Lord Jesus
  Christ of the Apostolic Faith, Inc.

2081 7th Avenue
New York, NY 10027

Church of the Nazarene
6401 The Paseo
Kansas City, MO 64131

Churches of Christ
Ed., J. Roy Vaughan Gospel Advocate
1006 Elm Hill Road
Nashville, TN 37210

Churches of Christ in
  Christian Union
459 East Ohio Street
Box 30
Circleville, OH 43113

Church of God
  General Conference
P.O. Box 926
Findlay, OH 45840

Church of God, Holiness
170 Ashby Street NW
Atlanta, GA 30314

Churches of the Living God:

Church of the Living God
  (Christian Workers for Fellowship)
Bishop F. C. Scott
801 NE 17th Street
Oklahoma City, OK 73105

House of God, Which Is the
  Living God
Bishop A. H. White
6107 Cobbs Creek Parkway
Philadelphia, PA 19143

Congregational Christian Churches
  Natioal Assn. of
P.O. Box 1620
Oak Creek, WI 53154

Congregational Holiness Church
Route 1, Box 325
Griffin, GA 30223

Conservative Congregational
  Christian Conference
25 West 626 Street, Charles Road
Wheaton, Il 60187

Divine Science
1819 East 14th Avenue
Denver, CO 80218

Eastern Churches

Albanian Churches
54 Burroughs Street
Jamaica Plain, MA 02130

American Carpatho-Russian Orthodox
  Greek Catholic Church
Johnstown, PA 15906

American Holy Orthodox Catholic

Apostolic Eastern Church
His Holiness Patriarch Clement
247 East 126th Street
New York, NY 10035

Antiochian Orthodox Christian
  Archdiocese of North America
358 Mountain Road
Englewood, NJ 07631

Bulgarian Eastern Orthodox Church
312 West 101 Street
New York, NY 10025

Eastern Orthodox Catholic
  Church in America
1914 Highway 17-92
Fern Park, FL 32730

Greek Orthodox Archdiocese of
  North and South America
8-10 East 79th Street
New York, NY 10021

Holy Apostolic and Catholic Church
  of the East (Assyrians)
554 Arball Drive
San Francisco, CA 94132

Holy Orthodox Church in America
  (Eastern Catholic and Apostolic)
See House, 321 West 101st Street
New York, NY 10025

Romanian Orthodox Episcopate
  of America
2522 Grey Tower Road
Jackson, MI 49201

Russian Orthodox Church
  in the U.S.A.
St. Nicholas Patriarchal Cathedral
15 East 97th Street
New York, NY 10029

Russian Orthodox Church
  Outside Russia
75 East 93rd Street
New York, NY 10028

Serbian Eastern Orthodox Church
  in the U.S.A. and Canada
5701 North Redwood Drive
Chicago, IL 60656

Syrian Orthodox Church
  of Antioch
292 Hamilton Place
Hackensack, NJ 07601

Ukranian Orthodox Churches
South Bound Brook, NJ 08880

Episcopal Church
815 Second Avenue
New York, NY 10017

Reformed Episcopal Church
Sec., The Rev. D. Ellsworth Raudenbush

560 Fountain Street
Havre de Grace, MD 21078

Evangelical Church of North America
Supt., Dr. V. A. Ballantyne
8719 John Drive
Indianapolis, IN 46234

Evangelical Congregational Church
100 West Park Avenue
Myerstown, PA 17067

Evangelical Covenant Church
  of America
5101 North Francisco Avenue
Chicago, IL 60625

Evangelical Free Baptist Church Inc.
P.O. Box 529
Addison, IL 60101

Evangelical Free Church of America
1515 East 66th Street
Minneapolis, MN 55423

Federated Churches, National
  Council of Community Churches
89 East Wilson Bridge Road
Worthington, OH 43085

Fire Baptized Holiness
  Church (Wesleyan)
600 College Agenue
Independence, KS 67301

Free Christian Zion
  Church of Christ
1315 Hutchinson Street
Nashville, AR 71852

Friends:

Friends General Conference
1520-B Race Street
Philadelphia, PA 19102

Friends United Meeting
Gen. Sec., Lorton G. Heusel
101 Quaker Hill Drive
Richmond, IN 47374

Religious Society of
  Friends (Conservative)
George C. Parker
North Carolina Yearly Meeting
Route 1, Box 10
Woodland, NC 27897

General Convention of the
  Swedenborgian Church
Pretty Prairie, KS 67570

Grace Gospel Fellowship
1011 Aldon Street SW
Grand Rapids, MI 49509

Independent Churches: See Federated Churches

Independent Fundamental Churches
  of America

1860 Mannheim Road
Westchester, IL 60153

International Church of the
  Foursquare Gospel
1100 Glendale Boulevard
Los Angeles, CA 90026

Jehovah's Witnesses
117 Adams Street
Brooklyn, NY 11201

Jewish Congregations
  American Jewish Committee
165 East 56th Street
New York, NY 10022

Kodesh Church of Immanuel
1509 S Street NW
Washington, DC 20009

Liberal Catholic Church
Krotona 62
Ojai, CA 93023

Lutherans:

American Lutheran Church
422 South 5th Street
Minneapolis, MN 55415

American Lutheran Church
422 South 5th Street
Minneapolis, MN 55415

Lutheran Church in America
231 Madison Avenue
New York, NY 10016

Apostolic Lutheran Church
  of America
Secretary James Johnson
Route 2, Box 99
L'Anse, MI 40016

Church of the Lutheran
  Brethren of America
Fergus Falls, MN 56537

Church of the Lutheran
  Confession
Markesan, WI 53946

Evangelical Lutheran Synod
The Rev. Alf Merseth
106 13th Street
Northwood, IA 50459

Free Lutheran Congregations
3110 East Medicine Lake Boulevard
Minneapolis, MN 55441

Lutheran Church (Missouri Synod)
500 North Broadway
St. Louis, MO 63102

Protestant Conference (Lutheran)
Sec., The Rev. Gerald Hinz
Shiocton, WI 54170

Wisconsin Evangelical

Lutheran Synod
Pres., The Rev. Oscar Nauman
3512 West North Avenue
Milwaukee, WI 53208

Mennonites:

Beachy Amish Mennonite Churches
Ervin N. Hershberger
R.D. 1,
Meyersdale, PA 15552

Church of God in Christ
  (Mennonite)
420 Wedel Street
Moundridge, KS 67107

Conservative Mennonite Conference
Secretary Daniel Yutzy
Two Rod Road
Marilla, NY 14102

Evangelical Mennonite Brethren
  Conference
5800 South 14th Street
Omaha, NE 68107

Evangelical Mennonite Church, Inc.
1420 Kerrway Court
Fort Wayne, IN 46805

General Conference Mennonite Church
722 Main Street
Newton, KS 67114

Hutterian Brethren
Joseph J. Waldner
P.O. Box 628
Havre, MT 59501

Mennonite Brethren Church
  of North America
Dr. Frank C. Peters
Winnipeg, Man., Canada

Mennonite Church
528 East Madison Street
Lombard, IL 60148

Old Order Amish Mennonite Church
c/o Raber's Book Store
Baltic, OH 43804

Old Order (Wisler)
  Mennonite Church
Henry W. Riehl
Route 1
Columbiana, OH 44408

Reformed Mennonites
Bishop Earl Basinger
1036 Lincoln Heights Avenue
Ephrata, PA 17522

Unaffiliated Mennonites
Dr. J. C. Wenger
Goshen Biblical Seminary
3003 Benham Avenue
Elkhart, IN 46514

Methodists:

United Methodist Church
475 Riverside Drive
New York, NY 10027

African Methodist Episcopal Church
Sec., The Rev. Richard A. Chappelle
3526 Dodier
St. Louis, MO 63107

African Methodist Episcopal
  Zion Church
Secretary Herman L. Anderson
P.O. Box 1401
Charlotte, NC 28232

Christian Methodist Espiscopal
  Church
564 East Frank Avenue
Memphis, TN 38006

Congregational Methodist Church
Sec., The Rev. A. F. O'Connor
P.O. Box 555
Florence, MS 39073

Cumberland Methodist Church
Pres., The Rev. Charles A. Shadrick
Whitwell, TN 37397

Evangelical Methodist Church
3036 North Meridian
Wichita, KS 67204

Free Methodist Church of
  North America
901 College Avenue
Winona Lake, IN 46590

Fundamental Methodist Church, Inc.
1034 North Broadway
Springfield, MO 65801

Primitive Methodist Church U.S.A.
Sec., The Rev. G. Kenneth Tyson
7202 Jonquil Drive
Orlando, FL 32808

Reformed Methodist Union
  Episcopal Church
Charleston, SC 29407

Reformed Zion Union
  Apostolic Church
Deacon James C. Feggins
416 South Hill Avenue
South Hill, VA 23907

Southern Methodist Church
Pres., The Rev. J. B. Gamble
P.O. Box 132
Orangeburg, SC 29115

Union American Methodist
  Episcopal Church
The Rev. David M. Harmon
774 Pine Street
Camden, NJ 08123

Metropolitan Church Association
333 Broad Street
Lake Geneva, WI 53147

Missionary Church
3901 South Wayne Avenue
Fort Wayne, IN 46807

Moravians:

Moravian Church in America
  (Unitas Fratrum)
69 West Church Street
P.O. Box 1245
Bethlehem, PA 18018

Unity of the Brethren
Pres., The Rev. Milton Maly
2205 Carnation Lane
Temple, TX 76501

Muslims, The Islamic
  Center of Washington
2551 Missachusetts Avenue NW
Washington, DC 20008

New Apostolic Church of
  North America
3753 North Troy Street
Chicago, IL 60618

Old Catholic Churches:

American Catholic Church
Archdiocese of New York
Most Rev. James Francis Lashley
457 West 144th Street
New York, NY 10030

American Catholic Church
  (Syro-Antiochian)
St. Peter's Cathedral
1811 NW 4th Court
Miami, FL 33136

Mariavite Old Catholic Church
2803 10th Street
Wyandotte, MI 48192

North American Old Roman
  Catholic Church
236 Wyona Street
Brooklyn, NY 11207

Open Bible Standard Churches, Inc.
Secretary O. Ralph Isbil
P.O. Box 1737
Des Moines, IA 50306

Pentecostal Bodies:

Assemblies of God
  (General Council of)
1445 Boonville Avenue
Springfield, MO 65802

Elim Fellowship
Carlton Spencer, Elim Fellowship
Lima, NY 14485

Emmanuel Holiness Church
Secretary J. Robert Hicks
Route 3
Anderson, SC 29621

Independent Assemblies of God—
  International
3840 Fifth Avenue
San Diego, CA 92103

International Pentecostal Assemblies
892 Berne Street
Atlanta, Ga 30316

Pentecostal Assemblies of the World
3040 North Illinois Street
Indianapolis, IN 46208

Pentecostal Church of Christ
Box 263
London, OH 43140

Pentecostal Church of God
221 Main Street
Joplin, MO 64801

Pentecostal Fire-Baptized
  Holiness Church
Taccoa, GA 30577

Pentecostal Free Will
  Baptist Church, Inc.
P.O. Box 1081
Dunn, NC 28334

Pentecostal Holiness Church
P.O. Box 12609
Oklahoma City, OK 73157

United Pentecostal Church
  International
8855 Dunn Road
Hazelwood, MO 63042

Pillar of Fire
Zarepath, NJ 08890

Polish National Catholic
  Church of America
529 East Locust Street
Scranton, PA 18505

Presbyterians:

United Presbyterian Church
  in the U.S.A.
475 Riverside Drive
New York, NY 10027

Presbyterian Church in the
  United States
341 Ponce de Leon Avenue, NE
Atlanta, GA 30308

Presbyterian Church in America
P.O. Box 256
Clinton, MS 39056

Associate Reformed
  Presbyterian Church

300 University Ridge, Ste. 206
Greenville, SC 29601

Bible Presbyterian Church
Haddon Avenue and Cuthbert Boulevard
Collingswood, NJ 08108

Cumberland Presbyterian Church
1978 Union Avenue
Memphis, TN 38401

Second Cumberland Church
  in the U.S.
Clerk, The Rev. R. E. Thomas
1404 North Grand Avenue
Tyler, TX 75701

Orthodox Presbyterian Church
7401 Old York Road
Philadelphia, PA 19126

Reformed Presbyterian Church,
  Evangelical Synod
Clerk, Dr. Paul R. Gilchrist
107 Haedy Road
Lookout Mountain, TN 37350

Reformed Presbyterian Church
  Of North America
Clerk, Louis D. Hutmire
7418 Penn Avenue
Pittsburgh, PA 15208

Reformed Bodies:

Reformed Church in America
475 Riverside Drive
New York, NY 10027

Christian Reformed Church
Stated Clerk William P. Brink
2850 Kalamazoo Avenue, SE
Grand Rapids, MI 49508

Hungarian Reformed Church
  in America
Bishop Dezso Abraham
18700 Midway Avenue
Allen Park, MI 48101

Netherlands Reformed Congregations
Pres. of Synod, The Rev. W. C. Lamain
2115 Romence Drive, NE
Grand Rapids, MI 49503

Protestant Reformed Churches
  in America
16515 South Park Avenue
South Holland, IL 60473

Reformed Church in the U.S.
Clerk, The Rev. D. W. Treick
2604 West 8th Street
Hastings, NE 68901

Roman Catholic Church
  U.S. Catholic Conference
1312 Massachusetts Avenue, NW
Washington, DC 20005

Salvation Army
120-130 West 14th Street
New York, NY 10011

Schwenkfelder Church
Pennsburg, PA 18073

Social Brethren
The Rev. John Bailey
R.R. 1, Box 122
Simpson, IL 62985

Spiritualists:

International General Assembly
of Spiritualists
1809 East Bayview Boulevard
Norfolk, VA 23503

National Spiritual Alliance
of the U.S.A.
Lake Pleasant, MA 01347

National Spiritual Association
of Church
Sec. The Rev. Alice M. Hull
P.O. Box 128
Cassadaga, FL 37206

Theosophy
Theosophical Publishing House
306 West Geneva Road
Wheaton, IL 60187

Triumph the Church and Kindgom
of God in Christ (International)
213 Farrington Avenue
Atlanta, GA 30318

Unitarian Universalist Association
25 Beacon street
Boston, MA 02108

United Church of Christ
297 Park Avenue, South
New York, NY 10010

United Holy Church
of America, Inc.
159 West Coulter Street
Philadelphia, PA 19144

Unity School of Christianity
Unity Village, MO 64063

Vedanta Society
34 West 71st Street
New York, NY 10023

Volunteers of America
340 West 85th Street
New York, NY 10024

Wesleyan Church
Gen. Sec., The Rev. D. Wayne Brown
P.O. Box 2000
Marion, IN 46952

CHAPTER 18

COLLEGES & UNIVERSITIES, PRE-1900

Many of your ancestors may have gone to college, seminaries, etc. This is particularly true if he was a professional man or a minister. Almost everyone has a minister or priest somewhere in their family. The institutions of higher learning not only kept records of their students in the local repository, but they kept records of individuals affiliated with religious denominations or associations. So even if your ancestors did not go to school, but belonged to the church or organization that sponsored that school their local records may be found at that college. For example if your ancestors were Quakers in Kansas, after you have looked in the normal Quaker records you may find some valuable information at the Friends University in Wichita. This could be true of any affiliation.

The following is a list of all known Universities and Colleges pre-1900. The weakness of this list is that it excludes the post-1900 groups who created their own schools such as the Italians and Lithuanians. Later Institutions can be found in the book *Patterson's American Education* (see Reference Section) in the reference section of your local library. We have not always used the official or even the current name of an institution. Some have gone through several name changes, but we have chosen the most popular or common name for easy access. You will note that the school is listed alphebetically by state. The second column gives the year the school was founded, chartered, established or when instruction commenced. The third column tells you the school's affiliation whether government, private or religious. The fourth column will usually tell you the original name of the school or seminary.

Universities and Colleges — Pre- 1900

Name and Address	Date Founded	Affiliation	Also Known As
ALABAMA			
Alabama Agricultural & Mechanical College, Normal, AL	1873	Blacks	Huntsville State Normal School
Alabama College, Montevallo, AL	1893	Women	AL Girls Indust. School
Alabama Polytechnic Institute, Auburn, AL	1872	State	AL Agri. & Mech. College
Athens, College, Athens, AL	1822	Women-Methodist	Athens Female Academy
Birmingham-Southern College, Birmingham, AL	1856	Methodist	Southern University
Howard College, Birmingham, AL	1841	Baptist	
Huntingdon College, Montgomery, AL	1854	Methodist	Tuskegee Female College
Judson College, Marion, AL	1838	Baptist	Judson Female Institute
Spring Hill College, Mobile, AL	1830	Catholic	
State Teachers College, Florence, AL	1830	State	LaGrange, College

Institution	Founded	Affiliation	Former Name
State Teachers College, Jacksonville, AL	1883	State	State Normal School
State Teachers College, Livingston, AL	1840	State	Livingston Female Academy
State Teachers College, Troy, AL	1887	State	
Stillman College, Tuscaloosa, AL	1876	Presbyterian	Tuscaloosa Institute
Talladega College, Talladega, AL	1867	Congregational-Christian	
Tuskee Institute, Tuskegee Institute, AL	1881	Private	Tuskegee Normal & Indus. Institute
University of Alabama, University, AL	1820	State	

ARIZONA

Institution	Founded	Affiliation	Former Name
Arizona State College, Flagstaff, AZ	1899	State	Northern AZ Normal School
Arizona State College, Tempe, AZ	1885	State	AZ Territorial Normal School
University of Arizona, Tucson, AZ	1885	State	

ARKANSAS

Institution	Founded	Affiliation	Former Name
Agricultural Mechanical & Normal College, Pine Bluff, AR	1873	Black	Land-Grant Branch Normal College
College of the Ozarks, Clarksville, AR	1834	Presbyterian	Cane Hill College
Hendrix College, Conway, AR	1876	Methodist	Central Collegiate Institute
Ouachita Baptist College, Arkedelphia, AR	1886	Baptist	
Philander Smith College, Little Rock, AR	1868	Methodist	Walden Seminary
University of Arkansas, Fayetteville, AR	1871	State	Arkansas Industrial University

CALIFORNIA

Institution	Founded	Affiliation	Former Name
California Institute of Technology, Pasadena, CA	1891	Private	Throop Polytechnic Institute
College of the Pacific, Stockton, CA	1851	Methodist	Calif. Wesleyan University
Dominican College of San Rafael, San Rafael, CA	1850	Catholic	Dominican College
Golden Gate College, San Francisco, CA	1880	Private	YMCA
La Verne College, La Verne, CA	1891	Brethren	Lordsburg College
Mills College, Oakland, CA	1852	Private	Young Ladies Seminary
Pomnona College, Claremont, CA	1887	Congregational	
St. Mary's College of California, St. Mary's Coll. CA	1863	Catholic	
St. Patrick's Seminary, Menlo Park, CA	1898	Catholic	
San Deigo State College, San Diego, CA	1897	State	San Diego State Normal School
University of California, Berkeley, CA	1868	State	Contra Costa Academy
University of San Francisco, San Francisco, CA	1855	Catholic	St. Ignatius College
University of Santa Clara, Santa Clara, CA	1851	Catholic	Santa Clar Mission
University of Southern California, Los Angeles, CA	1880	Private	
Whittier College, Whittier, CA	1891	Friends	Broadoaks School

COLORADO

Institution	Founded	Affiliation	Former Name
Colorado Agricultural & Mechanical College, Fort Collins, CO	1870	State	Agricultural Coll. of Colo.
Colorado College, Colorado College, Colorado Springs, CO	1874	Private	
Colorado State College of Education, Greeley, CO	1889	State	State Normal School
Regis College, Denver, CO	1887	Catholic	Sacred Heart College
University of Colorado, Boulder, CO	1861	State	University of Boulder
University of Denver, Denver, CO	1864	Methodist	Colorado Seminary

CONNECTICUT

New Haven State Teachers College, New Haven, CT	1893	State	New Haven Normal School
Teachers College of Connecticut, New Britain, CT	1849	State	New Britain Normal School
Trinity College, Hartford, CT	1823	Episcopal	Washington College
United States Coast Guard Academy, New London, CT	1870	Federal	Revenue Cutter Service School
University of Connecticut, Storrs, CT	1881	State	Stoors Agricultural School
Wesleyan University, Middletown, CT	1831	Women	
Willimantic State Teachers College, Willimantic, CT	1889	State	Willimantic State Normal Sch.
Yale University, New Haven, CT	1701	Men	Collegiate School

DELAWARE

University of Delaware, Newark DE	1743	Presbyterian	Newark Academy

DISTRICT OF COLUMBIA

Catholic University of America, Washington, D.C.	1887	Catholic	School of Sacred Theology
George Washington University, Washington, D.C.	1821	Private	Columbian College
Georgetown University, Washington, D.C.	1789	Catholic	
Howard University, Washington, DC	1867	Private	
Trinity College, Washington, DC	1897	Catholic	

FLORIDA

Bethune-Cookman College, Daytona Beach, FL	1872	Methodist	Cookman Institute
Florida Agricultural & Mechanical Univ., Tallahassee, FL	1887	Black	Normal & Indust. School for Negro youth
Florida Normal and Industrial Memorial Coll., St. Augustine	1892	Baptist	Florida Baptist Academy
Florida Southern College, Lakeland, FL	1885	Methodist	
Florida State University, Tallahassee, Fl	1851	State	State College for Women
Rollins College, Winter Park, FL	1885	Congregational	
Stetson University, De Land, FL	1883	Baptist	De Land Academy
University of Florida, Gainesville, FL	1853	State	East Florida Seminar

GEORGIA

Agnes Scott College, Decatur, GA	1889	Presbyterian	Decatur Female Seminary
Atlanta University, Atlanta, GA	1865	Baptist	Morehouse College
Brenau College, Gainesville, GA	1878	Private	Georgia Female Institute
Clark College, Atlanta,GA	1869	Methodist	Clark University
Emory University, Atlanta, GA	1836	Methodist	Emory College
Fort Valley State College, Fort Valley, GA	1895	Black	Fort Valley High & Indus. School
Georgia Institute of Technology, Atlanta, GA	1885	State	Georgia School of Technology
LaGrange College, LaGrange, GA	1831	Methodist	LaGrange Female Academy
Mercer University, Macon, GA	1833	Baptist	Mercer Institute
Morris Brown College, Atlanta, GA	1881	A.M.E.	Morris Brown University
North Georgia College, Dahlonega, GA	1873	State	
Oglethorpe University, Oglethorpe University, GA	1835	Private	
Paine College, Augusta, GA	1882	Black	Paine Institute
Savannah State College, Savannah, GA	1892	Black	Indus. Coll. for Colored Youth
Shorter College, Rome, GA	1873	Baptist	Cherokee Baptist Female Coll.
University of Georgia, Athens, GA	1785	State	
Wesleyan College, Macon, GA	1836	Methodist	Georgia Female College

IDAHO

College of Idaho, Caldwell, ID	1891	Presbyterian	
University of Idaho, Moscow, ID	1889	State	

ILLINOIS

Augustana College, Rock Island, IL	1860	Lutheran	Augustana Seminary
Aurora College, Aurora, IL	1893	Advent-Christian	Mendota College
Blackburn College, Carlinville, IL	1857	Presbyterian	Blackburn Theological Sem.
Bradley University, Peoria, IL	1896	Private	Bradley Polytechnic Institute
Carthage College, Carthage, IL	1846	United Lutheran	Hillsboro College
Chicago Teachers College, Chicago, IL	1869	City	Cook County Normal School
College of St. Francis, Joliet, IL	1874	Catholic	Assisi Junior College
De Paul University, Chicago, IL	1898	Catholic	St. Vincent's College
Eastern Illinois State College, Charleston, IL	1895	State	E. Ill. State Normal School
Elmhurst College, Elmhurst, IL	1865	E. & R.	Elmhurst Pro-Seminary
George Williams College, Chicago, IL	1890	YMCA	Training School YMCA
Greenville College, Greenville, IL	1855	Methodist	Almira College
Illinois College, Jacksonville, IL	1829	P & C	
Illinois State Normal University, Normal, IL	1857	State	Ill. St. Normal Univ.
Illinois Wesleyan University, Bloomington, IL	1850	Methodist	
Knox College, Galesburg, IL	1836	Private	Prairie College
Lake Forest College, Lake Forest, IL	1857	Presbyterian	Lind University
Loyola University, Chicago, IL	1870	Catholic	St. Ignatius College
McMurray College, Jacksonville, IL	1846	Methodist	Illinois Conf. Female College
Monmouth College, Monmouth, IL	1853	United Presbyterian	Monmouth Academy
North Central College, Naperville, IL	1861	E. U. Brethren	Plainfield College
Northern Illinois State College, De Kalb, IL	1895	State	N. Ill. State Normal School
Principia College, Elsah, IL	1898	Christ. Science	Principia Corporation
Quincy College, Quincy, IL	1860	Catholic	St. Francis Solanus College
Rockford College, Rockford, IL	1847	Private	Rockford Female Seminary
St. Xavier College, Chicago, IL	1846	Catholic	St. Francis Xavier Academy
School of the Art Institute of Chicago, Chicago, IL	1866	Private	
Southern Illinois University, Carbondale, IL	1869	State	So. Ill. Normal University
University of Chicago, Chicago, IL	1890	Baptist	
University of Illinois, Urbana, IL	1867	State	Ill. Industrial University
Western Illinois State College, IL	1899	State	W. Ill. State Normal School
Wheaton College, Wheaton, IL	1853	Private	Illinois Institute

INDIANA

Butler University, Indianapolis, IN	1850	Disciples	N.W. Christian University
DePaul University, Greencastle, IN	1832	Methodist	Indiana Asbury University
Earlham College, Richmond, IN	1847	Friends	Friends Boarding School
Evansville College, Evansville, IN	1854	Methodist	Moores Hill Male & Female College Institute
Franklin College of Indiana, Franklin, IN	1834	Baptist	
Goshen College, Goshen, IN	1894	Mennonite	Elkhart Institute
Hanover College, Hanover, IN	1827	Presbyterian	Long College for Women
Indiana State Teachers College, Terre Haute, IN	1865	State	Ind. State Normal School
Indiana University, Bloomington, IN	1820	State	Indiana Seminary
Manchester College, North Manchester, IN	1889	Brethren	Manchester College & Bible School
Purdue University, West Lafayette, IN	1865	State	Indiana Agricultural College

Rose Polytechnic Institute, Terre Haute, IN	1874	Private	Terre Haute School of Indus. Science
St. Joseph's College, Collegeville, IN	1889	Catholic	
St. Mary-of-the-Woods College, St. Mary-of-the-Woods, IN	1840	Catholic	
St. Mary's College, Norte Dame, IN	1853	Catholic	St. Mary's Academy
Taylor University, Upland, IN	1846	Private	Fort Wayne Female College
University of Notre Dame, Notre Dame, IN	1843	Catholic	
Valparaiso University, Valparaiso, IN	1859	Lutheran	Valparaiso Male & Female Academy
Wabash College, Crawfordsville, IN	1832	Private	Wabash Teachers Sem. and Manual Labor College

IOWA

Buena Vista College, Storm Lake, Iowa	1891	Presbyterian	
Central College, Pella, IA	1853	Reformed	
Clarke College, Dubuque, IA	1843	Catholic	St. Joseph Academy
Coe College, Cedar Rapids, IA	1851	Presbyterian	Cedar Rapids Collegiate Inst.
Cornell College, Mount Vernon, IA	1852	Methodist	Iowa Conference Seminary
Drake University, Des Moines, IA	1881	Disciples	
Grinnel College, Grinnel, IA	1847	C. & E.	Iowa College
Iowa State College of Agriculture and Mechanic Arts, Ames IA	1858	State	
Iowa State Teachers College, Cedar Falls, IA	1876	State	Iowa State Normal School
Iowa Wesleyan College, Mount Pleasant, IA	1842	Methodist	Mt. Pleasant Literary Institute
Loras College, Dubuque, IA	1839	Catholic	St. Raphael's Seminary
Luther College, Decorah, IA	1861	E. Luth.	
Morningside College, Sioux City, IA	1889	Methodist	University of the Northwest
Parsons College, Fairfield, IA	1875	Presbyterian	
St. Ambrose College, Davenport, IA	1882	Catholic	St. Ambrose Seminary
Simpson College, Indianola, IA	1860	Methodist	Indianola Male & Fem. Sem.
State University of Iowa, Iowa City, IA	1847	State	
University of Dubuque, Dubuque, IA	1852	Presbyterian	German Theo. School N.W.
Upper Iowa University, Fayette, IA	1857	Private	
Wartburg College, Waverly, IA	1852	A. Luth.	Wartburg Normal College
Westman College, Le Mars, IA	1890	E.U. Brethern	Western Union College

KANSAS

Baker University, Baldwin, KS	1858	Methodist	
Bethany College, Lindsborg, KS	1881	Aug. Luth.	Bethany Academy
Bethel College, North Newton, KS	1887	Mennonite	
College of Emporia, Emporia, KS	1882	Presbyterian	
Friends University, Wichita, KS	1888	Friends	Garfield University
Kansas State College of Agriculture and Applied Science, Manhattan, KS	1863	State	Ks. St. Agricultural College
Kansas State Teachers College, Emporia, KS	1863	State	Ks. St. Normal School
McPherson College, McPherson, KS	1887	Brethren	McPherson Coll. & Indus. Inst.
Mount St. Scholastic College, Atchison, KS	1863	Catholic	Mt. St. Scholastica Academy
Municipal University of Wichita, Wichita, KS	1892	City	Fairmount Institute
Ottawa University, Ottawa, KS	1865	Baptist	
St. Benedict's College, Atchison, KS	1859	Catholic	
St. Mary College, Xavier, KS	1882	Catholic	St. Mary's Academy
Southwestern College, Winfield, KS	1885	Methodist	South West College
University of Kansas, Lawrence, KS	1864	State	
Washburn University of Topeka, Topeka, KS	1865	City	Lincoln College

KENTUCKY

Asbury College, Wilmore, KY	1890	Private	
Berea College, Berea, KY	1869	Black	
Centre College, of Kentucky, Danville, KY	1819	Presbyterian	Central University
Georgetown College, Georgetown, KY	1787	Baptist	Rittenhouse Academy
Kentucky State College, Frankfort, KY	1886	Black	St. Normal School for Colored Persons
Kentucky Wesleyan College, Owensboro, KY	1860	Methodist	
Transylvania College, Lexington, KY	1780	D. of C.	Transylvania Seminary
Union College, Barbourville, KY	1879	Methodist	
University of Kentucky, Lexington, KY	1865	State	A. of M. Col. of Ky. Univ.
University of Louisville, Louisville, KY	1789	City	Jefferson Seminary

LOUISIANA

Centenary College of Louisiana, Shreveport, LA	1825	Methodist	College of Louisiana
Louisiana Polytechnic Institute, Ruston, LA	1894	State	La. Ind. Inst. and College
Louisiana State Univ. & Agricultural & Mech. Coll. Baton Rouge, LA	1845	State	Ls. St. Seminary of Learning
Loyola University, New Orleans, LA	1849	Catholic	Coll. of Immaculate Conception
Newcomb College, New Orleans, LA	1886	Private	
Northwestern State College of Louisiana, Natchitoches, LA	1884	State	La. State Normal School
Southern Univ. & Agricultural & Mech. Coll. Baton Rouge, LA	1880	State	Southern University
Southwestern Louisiana Institute, Lafayette, LA	1898	State	S.W. La. Industrial Institute
Tulane University, New Orleans, LA	1834	Private	Medical College of Louisiana

MAINE

Bates College, Lewiston, ME	1864	A. Bapt.	
Bowdoin College, Brunswick, ME	1794	Men	
Colby College, Waterville, ME	1813	Private	Ma. Liet. & Theo. Institution
University of Maine, Orono, ME	1865	State	Ma. St. Coll. of Agricultural and Mech. Arts

MARYLAND

College of Notre Dame of Maryland, Baltimore, MD	1848	Catholic	
Goucher College, Balrtimore, MD	1885	Women	Woman's College of Baltimore City
Hood College, Frederick, MD	1893	E. & R.	Woman's Coll. of Frederick Maryland
Johns Hopkins University, Baltimore, MD	1867	Men	
Loyola College, Baltimore, MD	1852	Catholic	
Maryland State College, Princess Anne, MD	1886	State	Delaware Conference Academy
Morgan State College, Baltimore, MD	1867	State	Centenary Biblical Institute
Mount St. Agnes College, Baltimore, MD	1867	Catholic	Mt. St. Agnes Academy
Mount St. Mary's College, Emmitsburg, MD	1808	Catholic	
Peabody Conservatory of Music, Baltimore, MD	1857	Private	
St. John's College, Annapolis, MD	1696	Private	King William's School
St. Joseph College, Emmitsburg, MD	1809	Catholic	

St. Mary's Seminary and University Baltimore, MD	1791	Catholic	
State Teachers College at Towson, Baltimore, MD	1865	State	Md. State Normal School
United States Naval Academy, Annapolis, MD	1845	Federal	
University of Maryland, College Park, MD	1807	State	Maryland Agricultural College
Washington College, Chestertown, MD	1706	Private	Kent County School
Western Maryland College, Westminster, MD	1867	Methodist	
Woodstock College, Woodstock, MD	1869	Catholic	

MASSACHUSETTS

American International College, Springfield, MA	1885	Private	French Protestant College
Amherst College, Amherst, MA	1821	Private	
Atlantic Union College, South Lancaster, MA	1882	S.D.A.	South Lancaster Academy
Clark University, Worcester, MA	1887	Private	
College of the Holy Cross, Worcester, MA	1843	Catholic	
Emerson College, Boston, MA	1880	Private	Boston Conservatory of Oratory
Harvard University, Cambridge, MA	1636	Men	
Lowell Technological Institute, Lowell, MA	1895	State	Lowell Textile School
Massachusetts Institute of Technology, Cambridge, MA	1859	Private	
Mount Holyoke College, South Hadley, MA	1836	Women	Mount Holyoke Famale Sem.
New England Conservatory of Music, Boston, MA	1867	Private	
Radcliffe College, Cambridge, MA	1879	Women	Soc. Collegiate Instruction of Women
Simmons College, Boston, MA	1899	Women	Simmons Female College
Smith College, Northampton, MA	1871	Private	Smith Coll. Sch. for Social Work
Springfield College, Springfield, MA	1885	Private	Sch. for Christian Workers
State Teachers College, Bridgewater, MA	1840	State	State Normal School
State Teachers College, Fitchburg, MA	1894	State	State Normal School
State Teachers College, Framingham, MA	1839	State	Normal School at Lexington
State Teachers College, Lowell, MA	1894	State	Ma. St. Normal Sch. at Lowell
State Teachers College, North Adams, MA	1894	State	State Normal School
State Teachers College, Salem, MA	1854	State	State Normal School
State Teachers College, Worcester, MA	1871	State	St. Normal Sch. at Worcester
State Teachers College at Boston, Boston, MA	1852	State	Boston Normal School
Tufts University, Medford, MA	1852	Univ.	Tufts College
University of Massachusetts, Amherst, MA	1863	State	Mass. Agricultural College
Wellesley College, Wellesley, MA	1870	Women	
Wheaton College, Norton, MA	1834	Women	Wheaton Female Seminary
Wheelock College, Boston, MA	1889	Women	Wheelock School
Williams College, Williamstown, MA	1785	Men	Free School
Worcester Polytechnic Institute, Worcester, MA	1864	Men	Wor. Co. Free Inst. Industrial Science

MICHIGAN

Albion College, Albion, MI	1835	Methodist	Wesleyan Seminary at Albion
Alma College, Alma, MI	1886	Presbyterian	
Calvin College, Grand Rapids, MI	1876	C.R. Church	Theo. Sem Christian Reformed Church
Central Michigan College, Mount Pleasant, MI	1892	State	Cen. Mich. Normal School Business Instit.
Emmanuel Missionary College, Berrien Springs, MI	1874	S.D.A.	Battle Creek. Coll. at Battle Creek
Hillsdale College, Hillsdale, MI	1844	A. Bapt.	Michigan Central College
Hope College, Holland, MI	1851	R. Church	
Kalamazoo College, Kalamazoo, MI	1833	Baptist	Mich. & Huron Institute
Michigan College of Mining & Technology, Houghton, MI	1885	State	Michigan Mining School
Michigan State Normal College, Ypsilanti, MI	1849	State	Mich. State Normal School
Mich. State Univ. of Agriculture and Applied Science, E. Lansing, MI	1855	State	Mich. Agricultural College
Nazareth College, Nazareth, MI	1897	Catholic	
Northern Michigan College, Marquette, MI	1899	State	Northern St. Normal School
University of Detroit, Detroit, MI	1877	Catholic	Detroit College
University of Michigan, Ann Arbor, MI	1817	State	Catholepistemiad

MINNESOTA

Augsburg College & Theological Seminary, Minneapolis, MN	1869	Lutheran	Augsburg Seminary
Carleton College, Northfield, MN	1866	Private	Northfield College
College of St. Thomas, St. Paul, MN	1885	Catholic	St. Thomas Seminary
Concordia College, Moorhead, MN	1891	E. Lutheran	
Gustavus Adolphus College, St. Peter MN	1862	A.E. Lutheran	Ansgar's Academy
Macalester College, St. Paul, MN	1885	Presbyterian	
St. John's University, Collegeville, MN	1857	Catholic	St. John's Seminary
St. Olaf College, Northfield, MN	1874	E. Lutheran	St. Olaf's School
St. Paul Seminary, St. Paul, MN	1896	Catholic	
State Teachers College, Mankato, MN	1866	State	
State Teachers Collge, Moorhead, MN	1887	State	
State Teachers College, St. Cloud, MN	1869	State	Third State Normal School
State Teachers College, Winona, MN	1858	State	Winona State Normal School
University of Minnesota, Minneapolis, MN	1851	State	
University of Minnesota, Duluth, MN	1895	State	State Normal School

MISSISSIPPI

Alcorn Agricultural & Mechanical College, Lorman, MS	1871	Black	Alcorn University
Belhaven College, Jackson, MS	1894	Presbyterian	
Blue Mountain College, Blue Mountain, MS	1873	Baptist	Blue Mountain Female Inst.
Jackson College for Negro Teachers, Jackson, MS	1877	State	Natchez Seminary
Millsaps College, Jackson, MS	1890	Methodist	
Mississippi College, Clinton, MS	1826	Baptist	Hempstead Academy
Mississippi State College, State College MS	1878	State	Ms. Agri. & Mech. College
Mississippi State College for Women, Columbus, MS	1884	State	Ms. Indus. Institute & College
Rust College, Holly Springs, MS	1866	Methodist	Rust University

Tougaloo Southern Christian College, Tougaloo, MS	1869	Black	Tougaloo University
University of Mississippi, University, MS	1844	State	

MISSOURI

Central College, Fayette, MO	1854	Methodist	Howard-Payne, Scarritt-Morrisville
Central Missouri State College, Warrensburg, MO	1870	State	State Normal School No. 2
College of St. Teresa, Kansas City, MO	1867	Catholic	St. Teresa's Academy
Culver-Stockton College, Canton, MO	1853	D. of C.	Christian University
Drury College, Springfield, MO	1873	Cong. Chruch	Springfield, College
Harris Teachers College, St. Louis, MO	1857	State	St. Louis Normal School
Lincoln University, Jefferson City, MO	1866	State	Lincoln Institute
Lindenwood College, St. Charles, MO	1827	Presbyterian	
Maryville College, St. Louis, MO	1846	Catholic	
Missouri Valley College, Marshall, MO	1888	Presbyterian	
Northeast Missouri State Teachers College, Kirksville, MO	1867	State	N. Mo. Normal School and Commericla College
Park College, Parkville, MO	1875	Presbyterian	
St. Louis University, St. Louis, MO	1818	Catholic	
Southern Missouri State College, Cape Girardeau, MO	1873	State	Mo. Normal School 3rd District
Tarkio College, Tarkio, MO	1883	U. Presbyterian	Tarkio Valley Coll. & Normal Institute
University of Missouri, Columbia, MO	1839	State	Missouri State University
Washington University, St. Louis, MO	1853	Private	Eliot Seminary
Westminster College, Fulton, MO	1851	Presbyterian	Fulton College
William Jewell College, Liberty, MO	1849	Baptist	

MONTANA

Montana School of Mines, Butte, MT	1893	State	
Montana State College, Bozeman, MT	1893	State	Agricultural College, State of Montana
Montana State University, Missoula, MT	1893	State	University of Montana
Rocky Mountain College, Billings, MT	1883	C.M.&P.(3)	Montana Wesleyan
Western Montana College of Education Dillon, MT	1893	State	State Normal School

NEBRASKA

Concordia Teachers College, Seward, NE	1894	Lutheran	
Creighton University, Omaha, NE	1878	Catholic	Creighton College
Doane College, Crete, NE	1872	Congrea.	Fontenelle College
Duchesne College, Omaha, NE	1881	Catholic	Academy of the Sacred Heart
Hastings College, Hastings, NE	1882	Presbyterian	
Midland College, Fremont, NE	1887	United Lutheran	
Nebraska State Teachers College, Peru, NE	1867	State	Mt. Vernon College
Nebraska State Teachers College, Wayne, NE	1891	State	Nebraska Normal College
Nebraska Wesleyan University, Lincoln, NE	1887	Methodist	
Union College, Lincoln, NE	1891	S.D.A.	
University of Nebraska, Lincoln, NE	1869	State	

NEW HAMPSHIRE

University of Nevada, Reno, NV	1874	State	

Dartmouth College, Hanover, NH	1769	Private	
Plymouth Teachers College, Plymouth, NH	1870	State	State Normal School
St. Anselm's College, Manchester, NH	1889	Catholic	
University of New Hampshire, Durham, NH	1866	State	NH Coll. Agri. & Mech. Arts

NEW JERSEY

College of St. Elizabeth, Convent Station, NJ	1899	Catholic	
Drew University, Madison, NJ	1867	Methodist	Drew Theological Seminary
New Jersey State Teachers College, Newark, NJ	1855	City	Newark Normal School
New Jersey State Teachers College, North Haledon, NJ	1855	State	Paterson City Normal School
New Jersey State Teachers College, Trenton, NJ	1855	State	NJ St. Normal & Model Schools
Newark College of Engineering, Newark NJ	1881	State	Co-Indus. College of Technology
Princeton University, Princeton, NJ	1746	Private	College of New Jersey
Rider College, Trenton, NJ	1865	Private	Trenton Business College
Rutgers University, New Brunswick, NJ	1766	Private	Queen's College
St. Peter's College, Jersey City, NJ	1872	Catholic	
Seton Hall University, South Orange, NJ	1856	Catholic	Seton Hall College
Stevens Institute of Technology, Hoboken, NJ	1870	Private	
Upsala College, East Orange, NJ	1893	Aug. Lutheran	

NEW MEXICO

New Mexico College of Agriculture & Mechanic Arts, State Coll., NM	1889	State	Las Cruces College
New Mexico Highlands University, Las Vegas, NM	1893	State	New Mexico Normal School
New Mexico Institute of Mining & Tech. Cocorro, NM	1889	State	New Mexico School of Mines
New Mexico Military Institute, Roswell, NM	1891	State	
New Mexico Western College, Silver City, NM	1893	State	Territorial Normal School
University of New Mexico, Albuquerque, MN	1889	State	

NEW YORK

Adelphi College, Garden City, NY	1896	Private	
Alfred University, Alfred, NY	1836	Private	
Bard College, Annandale-on-Hudson, NY	1860	Episcopal	St. Stephen's College
Barnard College, New York, NY	1889	Private	
Canisius College, Buffalo, NY	1870	Catholic	
City College, New York, NY	1847	City	Free Academy
Clarkson College of Technology, Potsdam, NY	1896	Private	Thos. Clarkson Sch. Tech.
Colgate University, Hamilton, NY	1819	Private	Hamilton Literary & Theo. Institute
College of Mount St. Vincent, New York, NY	1847	Catholic	Academy of Mount St. Vincent
Columbia University, New York, NY	1754	Private	King's College

Cooper Union, New York, NY	1859	Private	
Cornell University, Ithaca, NY	1865	State	
Elmire College, Elmire, NY	1855	Private	Elmire Female College
Fordham University, New York, NY	1841	Catholic	St. John's College
Hamilton College, Clinton, NY	1793	Private	Hamilton-Oneida Academy
Hobart College, Geneva, NY	1822	Episcopal	Geneva College
Houghton College, Houghton, NY	1883	Wes. Meth.	Houghton Wesleyan Meth. Seminary
Hunter College of the City of New York, New York, NY	1870	City	Normal College
Ithaca College, Ithaca, NY	1892	Private	Ithaca Conservatory of Music
Jewish Theological Seminary of America New York, NY	1887	Jewish	Rabbinical School
Keuka College, Keuka Park, NY	1892	Am. Bapt.	Keuka Institute
Manhattan College, New York, NY	1853	Catholic	Academy of Holy Infancy
Manhattanville College of the Sacred Heart, Purchase, NY	1841	Catholic	Manhattanville Academy
Niagara University, Niagara University NY	1856	Catholic	Sem. of Our Lady of Angels
Polytechnic Institute of Brooklyn, New York, NY	1854	Private	Brooklyn Collegiate & Pol. Institute
Pratt Institute, New York, NY	1887	Private	
Rensselaer Polytechnic Institute, Troy NY	1824	Private	Rensselaer School
St. Bonaventure University, St. Bonaventure, NY	1856	Catholic	St. Bonaventure College
St. Lawrence University, Canton, NY	1856	Universalist	
State University College for Teachers, Albany, NY	1844	State	State Normal School
State University Teachers College, Brockport, NY	1866	State	State Normal School
Syracuse University, Syracuse, NY	1870		
Union College and University, Albany, NY	1795	Private	Schenectady Academy
United States Military Academy, West Point, NY	1802	Federal	
University of Buffalo, Buffalo, NY	1846	Private	
University of Rochester, Rochester, NY	1850	Private	
Vassar College Poughkeepsie, NY	1861	Private	Vassar Female College
Wagner Lutheran College, New York, NY	1883	Uni. Lutheran	Rochester Luth. Proseminary
Webb Institute of Naval Architecture, Glen Cove, NY	1889	Men	Webb's Academy and Home for Shipbuilders
Wells College, Aurora, NY	1868	Private	Wells Seminary for the Higher Education of Young Women
Yeshiva University, New York, NY	1886	Jewish	

NORTH CAROLINA

Agricultural & Technical College of North Carolina, Greensboro, NC	1891	Black	A. & M. College for the Colored Race
Barber-Scotia College, Concord, NC	1867	Black	Scotia Seminary
Bennett College, Greensboro, NC	1873	Methodist	
Catawba College, Salisbury, NC	1851	E. & R.	
Davidson College, Davidson, NC	1836	Presbyterian	
Duke University, Durham, NC	1838	Methodist	Union Instit. in Randolph Co.
Elizabeth City State Teachers College, Elizabeth City, NC	1891	Black	Elizabeth City Normal School
Elon College, Elon College, NC	1889	Cong. Chris.	
Fayetteville State Teachers College, Fayetteville, NC	1867	Black	State Colored Normal School
Flora MacDonald College, Red Springs, NC	1896	Presbyterian	So. Presb. Coll. & Conservatory of Music

Greensboro College, Greensboro, NC	1838	Methodist	Greensboro Female College
Guilford College, Guilford College, NC	1834	Friends	New Garden Boarding School
Johnson C. Smith University, Charlotte, NC	1867	Presbyterian	Biddle Mem. Institute
Lenoir-Rhyne College, Hickory, NC	1891	U.E. Luth.	Lenoir College
Livingston College, Salisbury, NC	1879	A.M.E.	Zion Wesley Institute
Meredith College, Raleigh, NC	1891	Baptist	Baptist Female University
No. Carolina State Coll. of Agri. & Engineering, Raleigh, NC	1887	State	
Pembroke State College, Pembroke, NC	1887	State	Indian Normal School Robeson County
Queens College, Charlotte, NC	1857	Presbyterian	Charlotte Female Institute
St. Augustine's College, Raleigh, NC	1867	Prot. Epis.	
Salem College, Winston-Salem, NC	1772	Moravian	Salem Female Academy
Shaw University, Raleigh, NC	1865	Baptist	Shaw Collegiate Institute
University of North Carolina, Chapel Hill, NC	1789	State	
Wake Forest College, Winston-Salem, NC	1833	Baptist	Wake Forest Institute
Western Carolina College, Cullowhee, NC	1889	State	Cullowhee High School
Winston-Salem Teachers College, Winston-Salem, NC	1892	Black	Slater Industrial Academy
Woman's College of the Univ. of No. Carolina, Greensboro, NC	1891	State	State Normal & Industrial Sch.

NORTH DAKOTA

Jamestown College, Jamestown, ND	1884	Presbyterian	
North Dakota Agricultural College, Fargo, ND	1889	State	
State Normal & Industrial College, Ellendale, ND	1889	State	Industrial School
State Teachers College, Mayville, ND	1889	State	Normal School
State Teachers College, Valley City, ND	1889	State	State Normal School
University of North Dakota, Grand Forks, ND	1883	State	

OHIO

Antioch College, Yellow Springs, OH	1852	Private	
Ashland College, Ashland, OH	1878	Brethren	Ashland University
Baldwin-Wallace College, Berea, OH	1845	Methodist	German-Wallace College
Capital University, Columbus, OH	1830	Am. Lutheran	
Case Institute of Technology, Cleveland OH	1880	Private	
Central State College, Wilberforce, OH	1887	State	Normal & Indust. Department
College of Wooster, Wooster, OH	1866	Presbyterian	
Denison University, Granville, OH	1832	Baptist	Granville Lit. & Theo. Instit.
Fenn College, Cleveland, OH	1881	Private	Cleveland YMCA School
Heidelberg College, Tiffin, OH	1850	Evan. & Ref.	Heidelberg University
Hiram College, Hiram, OH	1849	D. of Christ.	West. Reserve Electric Instit.
John Caroll University, Cleveland, OH	1886	Catholic	St. Ignatius College
Kenyon College, Gambier, OH	1824	Prot. Episcopal	
Lake Erie College, Painesville, OH	1856	Private	Lake Erie Female Seminary
Marietta College, Marietta, OH	1797	Cong. Chris.	Muskingum Academy
Mary Manse College, Toledo, OH	1873	Catholic	Ursuline Convent Sacred Heart
Miami University, Oxford, OH	1809	State	
Mount Union College, Alliance, OH	1846	Methodist	Mount Union Seminary
Muskingum College, New Concord, OH	1837	Unit. Presbyterian	
Oberlin College, Oberlin, OH	1833	Private	Oberlin Collegiate Institute
Ohio State University, Columbus, OH	1864	State	Ohio Agri. & Mech. College

Ohio University, Athens, OH	1804	State	
Ohio Wesleyan University, Delaware, OH	1841	Methodist Episcopal	Ohio Wesleyan Female College
Otterbein College, Wasterville, OH	1847	Evan. United Brethren	
University of Akron, Akron, OH	1870	Universalist	Buchtel College
University of Cincinnati, Cincinnati, OH	1819	State	Cincinnati College
University of Dayton, Dayton, OH	1850	Catholic	St. Mary's School for Boys
University of Toledo, Toledo, OH	1872	City	Toledo University
Western College for Women, Oxford, OH	1853	Private	Western Female Seminary
Western Reserve University, Cleveland OH	1826	Private	Western Reserve College
Wilmington College, Wilmington, OH	1863	Friends	Franklin College
Wittenberg College, Springfield, OH	1845	United Lutheran	
Xavier University, Cincinnati, OH	1831	Catholic	Athenaeum

OKLAHOMA

Central State College, Edmund, OK	1890	State	Central State Normal School
Langston University, Langston, OK	1897	Black	Colored Agri. Normal Univ.
Northeastern State College, Tahlequah, OK	1846	State	Cherokee Nat. Female Seminary
Northwest State College, Alva, OK	1897	State	N.W. Terr. Normal
Oklahoma Agri. & Mech. College, Stillwater, OK	1890	State	
University of Oklahoma, Norman, OK	1890	State	

OREGON

Lewis and Clark College, Portland, OR	1867	Presbyterian	Albany College
Linfield College, McMinnville, OR	1849	Amer. Bapt.	Bapt. Coll. at McMinnville
Marylhurst College, Marylhurst, OR	1893	Catholic	St. Mary's College
Mount Angel Seminary, St. Benedict OR	1887	Catholic	Mount Angel College
Oregon College of Education, Monmouth, OR	1856	State	Christian School
Oregon State College, Corvallis, OR	1858	State	Corvallis College
Pacific University, Forest Grove, OR	1849	Congregational	Tualatin Academy
University of Oregon, Eugene, OR	1872	State	
Wilamette University, Salem, OR	1842	Methodist	Oregon Institute

PENNSYLVANIA

Academy of the New Church, Bryn Athyn, PA	1877	Gen. Church of New Jerusalem	
Albright College, Reading, PA	1856	Evan. United Brethren	Union Seminary
Allegheny College, Meadville, PA	1815	Methodist	
Beaver College, Jenkintown, PA	1853	Presbyterian	Beaver Female Seminary
Bryn Mawr College, Bryn Mawr, PA	1880	Friends	
Bucknell University, Lewisburg, PA	1846	Baptist	Univ. of Lewisburg
Cedar Crest College, Allentown, PA	1868	Evan. & Ref.	Allentown Coll. for Women
Chatham College, Pittsburgh, PA	1869	Private	Penn. Female College
Chestnut Hill College of the Sister of St. Joseph, Philadelphia, PA	1858	Catholic	Mout St. Joseph College
Dickinson College, Carlisle, PA	1773	Methodist	Grammar School
Drexel Institute of Technology, Phila. PA	1891	Private	
Duquesne University, Pittsburgh, PA	1878	Catholic	Pitts. Cath. Coll. of the Holy Ghost

Elizabethtown College, Elizabethtown, PA	1899	Brethren	
Franklin and Marshall College, Lancaster, PA	1787	Evan. & Ref.	Franklin College
Geneva College, Beaver Falls, PA	1848	Ref. Presbyterian	
Gettysburg College, Gettysburg, PA	1832	Unit. Lutheran	Penn. College
Grove City College, Grove City, PA	1876	Presbyterian	Pine Grove Normal Academy
Haverford College, Haverford, PA	1833	Friends	
Juniata College, Huntingdon, PA	1876	Brethren	Brethren's Normal School
Lafayette College, Easton, PA	1826	Presbyterian	
La Salle College, Philadelphia, PA	1863	Catholic	
Lebanon Valley College, Annville, PA	1866	Evan. United Brethren	
Lehigh University, Bethlehem, PA	1865	Private	
Lincoln University, Lincoln University, PA	1854	Presbyterian	Ashmun Institute
Lycoming College, Williamsport, PA	1812	Methodist	Williamsport Academy
Mercyhurt College, Erie, PA	1871	Catholic	St. Joseph's Academy
Moravian College, Bethlehem, PA	1742	Moravian	Mor. Sem. & Coll. for Women
Muhlenberg College, Allentown, PA	1848	Lutheran	Allentown Seminary
Pennsylvania Military College, Chester, PA	1821	Private	Bullock School
Pennsylvania State University, University Park, PA	1855	State	Famers' High School
Philadelphia Textile Institute, Philadelphia, PA	1883	Private	Phila. Textile School
St. Francis College, Loretto, PA	1847	Catholic	St. Francis Academy
St. Joseph's College, Philadelphia, PA	1851	Catholic	
St. Vincent College, Latrobe, PA	1846	Catholic	
Seton Hill College, Greensburg, PA	1883	Catholic	
State Teachers College, Bloomsburg, PA	1839	State	Literary Institute
State Teachers College, California, PA	1852	State	So. Western Normal College
State Teachers College, Cheyney, PA	1837	Black	Institute for Colored Youth
State Teachers College, Clarion, PA	1866	State	Carrier Seminary
State Teachers College, East Stroudsburg, PA	1893	State	State Normal School
State Teachers College, Edinboro, PA	1857	State	State Normal School
State Teachers College, Indiana, PA	1871	State	Ind. State Normal School
State Teachers College, Kutztown, PA	1860	State	Keystone State Normal School
State Teachers College, Lock Haven, PA	1870	State	Central State Normal School
State Teachers College, Mansfield, PA	1854	State	Mansfield Classical Seminary
State Teachers College, Millersville, PA	1854	State	Millersville Academy
State Teachers College, Shippensburg, PA	1871	State	State Normal School
State Teachers College, Slippery Rock, PA	1889	State	State Normal School
State Teachers College, West Chester, PA	1812	State	West Chester Academy
Susquehanna University, Selinsgrove, PA	1858	United Lutheran	Miss. Institute Evan. Lutheran Brethren
Swarthmore College, Swarthmore, PA	1864	Friends	
Temple·University, Philadelphia, PA	1884	Private	Temple College
Thiel College, Greenville, PA	1866	United Lutheran	
University of Pennsylvania, Philadelphia, PA	1740	Private	Coll. & Academy of Phila.
University of Pittsburgh, Pittsburgh, PA	1787	Private	Pittsburgh Academy
University of Scranton, Scranton, PA	1888	Catholic	College of St. Thomas
Ursinus College, Collegeville, PA	1869	Evan. & Ref.	Todd's School
Villanova University, Villanova, PA	1842	Catholic	Villanova College
Washington & Jefferson College, Washington, PA	1787	Men	Washington Academy

College	Year	Affiliation	Former Name
Waynesburg College, Waynesburg, PA	1850	Presbyterian	
Westminster College, New Wilmington, PA	1852	United Presbyterian	West. Collegiate Institute
Wilson College, Chambersburg, PA	1869	Presbyterian	Wilson Female College

RHODE ISLAND

College	Year	Affiliation	Former Name
Brown University, Providence, RI	1764	Baptist	
Rhode Island College of Education, Providence, RI	1854	State	Rhode Island Normal School
Rhode Island School of Design, Providence, RI	1877	Private	
University of Rhode Island, Kingston, RI	1892	State	Rhode Island College

SOUTH CAROLINA

College	Year	Affiliation	Former Name
Allen University, Columbia, SC	1870	A.M.E.	Paine Institute
Benedict College, Columbia, SC	1870	Blacks	Benedict College Institute
Citadel (Military Coll. of So. Carolina) Charleston, SC	1842	Men	
Claflin University, Orangeburg, SC	1869	Blacks	
Clemson Agricultural College, Clemson, SC	1889	State	
Coker College, Hartsville, SC	1894	Women	Welsh Neck High School
Columbia College, Columbia, SC	1854	Methodist	Columbia Female College
Converse College, Spartanburg, SC	1889	Women	
Erskine College, Due West, SC	1839	Ref. Presbyterian	Erskine Theo. Seminary
Furman University, Greenville, SC	1825	Baptist	Furman Acad. & Theo. Instit.
Lander College, Greenwood, SC	1872	Private	Williamston Female College
Limestone College, Gaffney, SC	1845	Women	
Newberry College, Newberry, SC	1856	United Lutheran	
Presbyterian College, Clinton, SC	1880	Presbyterian	Clinton College
South Carolina State College, Orangeburg, SC	1895	State	State Normal, Indus. Argi. Mech. College
University of South Carolina, Columbia, SC	1801	State	
Winthrop College, Rock Hill, SC	1886	Women	Winthrop Training School for Teachers
Wofford College, Spartanburg, SC	1851	Methodist	

SOUTH DAKOTA

College	Year	Affiliation	Former Name
Augustana College, Sioux Falls, SD	1860	Evan. Lutheran	Augustana Seminary
Black Hills Teachers College, Spearfish, SD	1883	State	Dakota Normal School
Dakota Wesleyan University, Mitchell, SD	1883	Methodist	Dakota University
General Beadle State Teachers College, Madison, SD	1881	State	Madison State Normal School
Huron College, Huron SD	1883	Presbyterian	Pierre University
South Dakota School of Mines and Technology, Rapid City, SD	1885	State	Dakota School of Mines
South Dakota State College of Agri. & Mech. Arts, Brookings, SD	1883	State	Dakota Agricultural College
Southern State Teachers College, Springfield, SD	1881	State	Springfield State Normal School
University of South Dakota, Vermillion, SD	1882	State	University of Dakota
Yankton College, Yankton, SD	1881	Congregational	

TENNESSEE

College	Year	Affiliation	Former Name
Bethel College, McKenzie, TN	1842	Cumberland Presbyterian	Bethel Seminary

College	Founded	Affiliation	Former Name
Carson-Newman College, Jefferson City TN	1851	Baptist	Mossy Creek Mission Baptist Seminary
David Lipscomb College, Nashville, TN	1891	Church of Christ	Nashville Bible School
Fisk University, Nashville, TN	1865	Private	Fisk School
George Peabody College for Teachers Nashville, TN	1875	Private	Davidson Academy Cumberland College
King College, Knoxville, TN	1863	Blacks	Mckee School
Lambuth College, Jackson, TN	1843	Methodist	
Lane College, Jackson, TN	1882	Christ. Methodist Episcopal	
LeMoyne College, Memphis, TN	1871	Congregational-Christian	
Lincoln Memorial University, Harrogate, TN	1897	Private	Cumberland Gap Tenn. High School
Maryville College, Maryville, TN	1819	Presbyterian	So. & West. Theo. Seminary
Southern Missionary College, Collegedale, TN	1893	S.D.A.	Southern Training School
Southwestern at Memphis, Memphis, TN	1848	Presbyterian	Montgomery Masonic College
Tusculum College, Greeneville, TN	1794	Presbyterian	Greenville College
Union University, Jackson, TN	1825	Baptist	Jackson Male Academy
University of Chattanooga, Chattanooga, TN	1886	Methodist	U.S. Grant University
University of the South, Sewanee, TN	1858	Prot. Episcopal	
University of Tennessee, Knoxville, TN	1794	State	Blount College
Vanderbilt University, Nashville, TN	1872	Methodist-Episc.	Central University

TEXAS

College	Founded	Affiliation	Former Name
Agricultural & Mechanical College of Texas, College Station TX	1871	State	
Austin College, Sherman, TX	1849	Presbyterian	
Baylor University, Waco, TX	1845	Baptist	
Bishop College, Marshall, TX	1880	Blacks	Bishop Baptist College
East Texas State Teachers College, Commerce, TX	1889	State	East Texas Normal College
Hardin-Simmons University, Abilene, TX	1891	Baptist	Abilene Baptist College
Howard Payne College, Brownwood, TX	1889	Baptist	
Huston-Tillotson College, Austin, TX	1877	Congregational & Methodist	
Incarnat Word College, San Antonio, TX	1881	Catholic	
Mary Hardin-Baylor College, Belton, TX	1845	Baptist	
North Texas State College, Denton, TX	1890	State	Texas Normal College
Our Lady of the Lake College, San Antonio, TX	1896	Catholic	
Prairie View Agri. & Mech. College, Prairie View, TX	1876	Blacks	Normal School for Colored Teachers
Rice Institute, Houston, TX	1891	Private	
St. Mary's University of San Antonio, San Antonio, TX	1852	Catholic	St. Mary's College
Sam Houston State Teachers College, Huntsville, TX	1879	State	
Southwest Texas State Teachers College, San Marcos, TX	1899	State	S.W. Texas State Normal School
Southwestern University, Georgetown, TX	1840	Methodist	Ruterville College
Texas Christian University, Fort Worth, TX	1873	Dis. of Christ	Add-Ran Male & Fem. College
Texas College, Tyler, TX	1894	Colored Meth. Episcopal	Phillips University
Texas Lutheran College, Seguin, TX	1891	Amer. Lutheran	

Texas Wesleyan College, Fort Worth, TX	1890	Methodist	Polytechnic College
Trinity University, San Antonio, TX	1869	Presbyterian	
University of Texas, Austin, TX	1881	State	
Wiley College, Marshall, TX	1873	Blacks	Wiley University

UTAH

Brigham Young University, Provo, UT	1875	Mormons	Brigham Young Academy
College of Southern Utah, Cedar City, UT	1897	State	Branch Normal School
University of Utah, Salt Lake City, UT	1850	State	University of Deseret
Utah State Agricultural College, Logan, UT	1888	State	Utah Agricultural College
Westminster College, Salt Lake City, UT	1875	Presbyterian & Methodist	Salt Lake Collegiate Institute

VERMONT

Middlebury College, Middlebury, VT	1800	Private	
Norwich University, Northfield, VT	1819	Private	American Lit. Science & Military Academy
University of Vermont, Burlington, VT	1791	State	State Agricultural College

VIRGINIA

Bridgewater College, Bridgewater, VA	1880	Brethren	Spring Creek Normal School
College of William & Mary, Williamsburg, VA	1693	State	
Emory & Henry College, Emory, VA	1838	Methodist	
Hampden-Sydney College, Hampden-Sydney, VA	1775	So. Presbyterian	Hampden-Sydney Academy
Hampton Institute, Hampton, VA	1868	Private	Hampton Normal & Agri. Institute
Hollins College, Hollins College, VA	1842	Private	Valley Union Seminary
Longwood College, Farmville, VA	1884	Women	State Female Normal School
Mary Baldwin College, Staunton, VA	1842	Presbyterian	Augusta Female Seminary
Randolph-Macon College, Ashland, VA	1830	Methodist	
Randolph-Macon Woman's College, Lynchburg, VA	1891	Methodist	
Roanoke College, Salem, VA	1842	Lutheran	Virginia Institute
St. Paul's Polytechnic Institute, Lawrenceville, VA	1888	Prot. Episcopal	St. Paul's School
University of Richmond, Richmond, VA	1830	Baptist	Dunlora Academy
University of Virginia, Charlottesville, VA	1819	State	
Virginia Military Institute, Lexington, VA	1839	Men	
Virginia Polytechnic Institute, Blacksburg, VA	1872	State	Vir. Agricultural & Mech. Coll.
Virginia State College, Petersburg, VA	1882	State	Vir. Normal & Collegiate Instit.
Virginia Union University, Richmond, VA	1865	Blacks	Richmond Theo. School for Freedmen
Washington & Lee University, Lexington, VA	1749	Private	Augusta Academy

WASHINGTON

Central Washington College of Education, Ellensburg, WA	1890	State	Wash. State Normal School
College of Puget Sound, Tacoma, WA	1888	Methodist	Puget Sound University
Eastern Washington College of Education, Cheney, WA	1890	State	Wash. State Normal
Gonzaga University, Spokane, WA	1894	Catholic	Gonzaga College

Pacific Lutheran College, Parkland, WA	1894	Lutheran	Pacific Lutheran University
St. Martin's College, Olympia, WA	1895	Catholic	
Seattle Pacific College, Seattle, WA	1891	Free Methodist	Seattle Seminary
Seattle University, Seattle, WA	1891	Catholic	Seattle College
State College of Washington, Pullman, WA	1890	State	Wash. State Agri. College
University of Washington, Seattle, WA	1861	State	Terr. Univ. of Washington
Walla Walla College, College Place, WA	1892	S.D.A.	
Western Washington College of Education, Bellingham, WA	1893	State	Wash. State Normal School
Whitman College, Walla Walla, WA	1859	Private	
Whitworth College, Spokane, WA	1890	Presbyterian	

WEST VIRGINIA

Bethany College, Bethany, WV	1840	Dis. of Christ.	
Bluefield State College, Bluefield, WV	1895	Blacks	Bluefield Colored Institute
Concord College, Athens, WV	1872	State	W.V. State Normal School
Fairmont State College, Fairmont, WV	1867	State	W.V. State Normal
Glenville State College, Glenville, WV	1872	State	Glenville Branch
Marshall College, Huntington, WV	1837	State	Marshall Academy
Shepherd College, Shepherdstown, WV	1872	State	State Normal School
West Liberty State College, West Liberty, WV	1837	State	West Liberty Academy
West Virginia State College, Institute, WV	1891	State	W.V. Collegiate Institute
West Virginia University, Morgantown, WV	1867	State	Agri. College of West Virginia
West Virginia Wesleyan College, Buckhannon, WV	1890	Methodist	W.V. Conference Seminary

WISCONSIN

Alverno College, Milwaukee, WI	1887	Catholic	
Beloit College, Beloit, WI	1846	Congregational & Presbyterian	
Carroll College, Waukesha, WI	1840	Presbyterian	Prairieville Academy
Lawrence College, Appleton, WI	1847	Private	Lawrence Institute
Marquette University, Milwaukee, WI	1857	Catholic	St. Aloysious Academy
Milwaukee-Downer College, Milwaukee, WI	1851	Women	Milwaukee College
Mount Mary College, Milwaukee, WI	1872	Catholic	St. Mary's Institute
Ripon College, Ripon, WI	1851	Private	Brockway College
St. Norbert College, West DePere, WI	1898	Catholic	
University of Wisconsin, Madison, WI	1836	State	
Wisconsin State College, Milwaukee, WI	1880	State	State Normal School
Wisconsin State College, Oshkosh, WI	1871	State	State Normal School
Wisconsin State College, Platteville, WI	1866	State	Platteville State Normal School
Wisconsin State College, River Falls, WI	1874	State	State Normal School
Wisconsin State College, Stevens Point, WI	1894	State	Stevens Point Normal School
Wisconsin State College, Superior, WI	1893	State	Superior Normal School
Wisconsin State College, Whitewater, WI	1866	State	Whitewater State Normal School

WYOMING

University of Wyoming, Laramie, WY	1886	State	

CHAPTER 19

FRATERNAL SOCIETIES AND ALLIANCES

Most of our ancestors belonged to a fraternal order or an alliance. (They are virtually the same thing.) Popular orders were the Masons, the Odd Fellows, Woodmen of the World, Knights of Pythias, and the Grange.

By far the Masons were the most popular and most fraternal groups were patterned after the Masons.

Some of these fraternal orders were open to everyone and some were limited to certain specific special interest groups. For example, some fraternal orders were composed of members from a certain religious persuasion and some were composed of members of certain ethnic groups.

What fraternal group did the Irish join? The Ancient Order of Hibernians in America. What about the Lithuanians? They joined The Lithuanian Alliance of America. What about the Blacks? They joined The Prince Hall Freemasonry.

Since the Germans were the largest single ethnic group to come to America, they generated many fraternal orders. These were not only created for social reasons, but for life insurance, and most importantly to sponsor immigration. Some of the most popular German organizations in America Were:

> Alliance of Transylvania Saxons
> Baptist Life Association
> Bavarian National Association of North America
> Catholic Aid Association
> Catholic Knights of St. George
> Ancient Order of Freesmiths
> Greater Beneficial Union of Pittsburgh
> German Order of Harugari
> Improved Order of Knights of Pythias
> Order of Red Eagles
> Independent Order of Red Men
> Order of the Sons of Herman
> Workmen's Benefit Fund of the United States of America
> American Turners (Turn Verein, Turngemeinde, or Turnbund)
> German American National Congress

Since the Masons were the largest group, the following list shows the state masonic grand lodge for each state. It is important to remember that there were usually local lodges located in a state before the establishment of a grand lodge. For example, the masonic grand lodge for Ohio was established in 1808. Hence, to locate lodge records prior to that date, you would need to either search the Pennsylvania grand lodge or the grand lodge from the state of origin.

Remember, too, that these are private and not public records. Even though a local lodge usually sends its old records to the state grand lodge, this does not mean that they all did. Also, not every lodge published a social history and not every grand lodge has an index. Always offer to pay for any and all services.

MASONIC GRAND LODGES

ADDRESS   DATE ESTABLISHED

Grand Secretary
P.O. Box 6195
Montgomery, Alabama 36106 1821

Grand Secretary
P.O. Box 6668
Anchorage, Alaska 99502 1858

Grand Secretary
Masonic Temple
4th Avenue at Monroe
Phoenix, Arizona, 85003 1882

Grand Secretary
Albert Pike Memorial Temple
Little Rock Arkansas 72201 1838

Grand Secretary
1111 California Street
San Francisco, California, 94108 1850

Grand Secretary
300 Masonic Temple
1614 Welton Street
Denver, Colorado 80202 1861

Grand Secretary
P.O. Box 250
Wallingford, Connecticut 06492 1739

Grand Secretary
Masonic Temple
818 Market Street
Wilmington, Delaware 19801 1806

Grand Secretary
Masonic Temple
801 13th Street, N.W.
Washington, D. C. 20005 1811

Grand Secretary
220 Ocean Street
Jacksonville, Florida 32202 1830

Grand Secretary
Masonic Temple
811 Mulberry St.
Macon, Georgia 31201 1735

(Hawaii) Grand Secretary
1111 California Street
San Franisco, California 94108 . . . .

Grand Secretary
P.O. Box 1677
Boise, Idaho 83701 1867

Grand Secretary
P.O. Box 110
Rushville, Illinois 62681 1840

Grand Secretary
Masonic Temple
525 North Illinois Street
Indianapolis, Indiana 46204 1818

Grand Secretary
P.O. Box 279
Cedar Rapids, Iowa 52406 1844

ADDRESS   DATE ESTABLISHED

Grand Secretary
P.O. Box 1217
Topeka, Kansas 66601 1856

Grand Secretary
1000 South 4th Street
Louisville, Kentucky 40203 1800

Grand Secretary
1300 Masonic Temple
333 St. Charles Street
New Orleans, Louisiana, 70130 1812

Grand Secretary
Masonic Temple
415 Congress Street
Portland, Maine 04111 1820

Grand Secretary
Masonic Temple
225 North Charles Street
Baltimore, Maryland 21201 1787

Grand Secretary
186 Tremont Street
Boston, Massachusetts 02111 1733

Grand Secretary
Masonic Temple
Grand Rapids, Michigan 49502 1826

Grand Secretary
Masonic Temple
St. Paul, Minnesota 55102 1853

Grand Secretary
P.O. Box 1030
Meridian, Mississippi 39301 1813

Grand Secretary
Masonic Temple
3681 Lindell Blvd.
St. Louis, Missouri 63108 1821

Grand Secretary
P.O. Box 1158
Helena, Montana, 59601 1866

Grand Secretary
401 Masonic Temple
Omaha, Nebraska 68102 1857

Grand Secretary
P.O. Box 186
Gardnerville, Nevada 89410 1865

Grand Secretary
Box 299
Concord, Ne Hampshire 03301 1789

Grand Secretary
P.O. Box 544
Burlington, NJ 08016 1786

Grand Secretary
P.O. Box 1805
Albuquerque, NM 87103 1877

Grand Secretary
Masonic Hall
71 West 23 Street
New York, New York 10010 1781

Grand Secretary
P.O. Box 6506
Raleigh, North Carolina 27608 1787

Grand Secretary
P.O. Box 1269
Fargo, ND 58102 1889

Grand Secretary
Grand Lodge Office Bulding
634 High Street, P.O. Box 629
Worthington, Ohio 43085 1808

Grand Secretary
301 East Oklahoma
Guthrie, Oklahoma 73044 1873

Grand Secretary
P.O. Box 96
Forest Grove, Oregon 97116 1851

Grand Secretary
Masonic Temple
One North Broad Street
Philadelphia, Pennsylvania 19107 1786

Grand Secretary
Plaridel Masonic Temple
1440 San Marcelino
Manila, Philippine Islands . . . .

Grand Secretary
Apartado 8385
Santurce, Puerto Rico 00910 1885

Grand Secretary
127 Dorrance Street
Providence, Rhode Island 02903 1791

Grand Secretary
1401 Senate Street
Columbia, South Carolina 29201 1737

Grand Secretary
P.O. Box 468
Sioux Falls, South Dakota 57101 1875

Grand Secretary
P.O. Box 216
Nashville, Tennessee 37202 1813

Grand Secretary
P.O. Box 446
Waco, Texas 76703 1837

Grand Secretary
Masonic Temple
650 East South Temple Street
Salt Lake City, Utah 84102 1872

Grand Secretary
P.O. Box 443
Burlington, Vermont 05402 1794

Grand Secretary
P.O. Box 12064
Richmond, Virginia 23219 1778

Grand Secretary
Masonic Temple
47 St. Helen's Avenue
Tacoma, Washington 98402 1858

Grand Secretary
P.O. Box 2346
Charleston, West Virginia 25328 1865

Grand Secretary
1123 North Astor Street
Milwaukee, Wisconsin 53202 1843

Grand Secretary
P.O. Box 459
Casper, Wyoming 82602 1874

FOREIGN GRAND LODGE ORGANIZATION DATES:

England 1717
Canada 1762
Denmark 1745
Finland 1924
France 1725
Germany 1736
Holland 1756
Prussia 1746
Russia 1731
Scotland 1736
Switzerland 1844
Venezuela 1824

SELECTED AMERICAN FRATERNAL SOCIETIES

There were hundreds of fraternal societies or organizations in America. Some of have long since ceased to exist. And many of them are still going.

The list that follows gives the names of the organization, the date established in America, the headquarters or where founded, and the type of membership.

Under membership, I have tried to determine the most important designation. Usually, they are given one of the the following types of designation:

   general — open to men and women
   men — open to males only

women — open to women only
church — open to members of that denomination
ethnic — open to that nationality only
fraternal — associated with that fraternal society
occupation — limited to that profession only

It is important to remember that a man could belong to a fraternal organization under any one of the above catogories. Hopefully, you will know the name of the particular organization from his personal papers, an obituary, or a county history.

Organization	Inc. in America	Hdqtrs. or Where Founded	Membership Designation
Aegis, Order of	1892		Pythias
Ahvas Israel	1890	New York, NY	Mason
Ahepa, The Order of	1922		Greek
Aid Association for Lutherans	1899	Appleton, WI.	Lutheran
Alhambra, International Order of	1904	Baltimore, MD	Catholic
Alliance of Poles, The	1895	Cleveland, OH	Poles
Alliance of Transylvanian Saxons	1902	Cleveland, OH	Germans
Allied Masonic Degrees of the United States, The grand Council of	1932	Charlotte, NC	Masons
Amaranth, The Order of	1873	Westfield, NJ	Masons
American Benefit Society	1893	Boston, MA	General
American Brotherhood	1844	New York, NY	Men
American Brotherhood, U.S.A.	1915	Chicago, IL	General
American Fraternal Congress	1898	Omaha, NE	General
American Fraternal Union	1898	Ely MN	Slovaics
American Home Watchmen	1909	Pittsburgh, PA	Presbyterians
American Hungarian Catholic Society	1894	Cleveland, OH	Hungarian
American Insurance Union	1884	Columbus, OH	General
American Knights of Protection	1894	Baltimore, MD	General
American Krusaders	1923	Arkansas	K.K.K.
American Legion of Honor	1878	Boston MA	General
American Order of United Catholics	1896	New York, NY	Catholic
American Postal Workers Accident Benefit Association	1898	Portsmouth, NH	
American Protective Association	1887	Clinton, IA	General
American Protestant Association	1849	Pittsburgh, PA	General
American Slovenian Catholic Union	1894	Joliet, IL	Slovaics
American Stars of Equity	1903	Freeport, IL	General
American Union, Order of the	1873	New York, NY	General
American Woodmen, The Supreme Camp of the	1901	Denver, CO	Men
American Workmen	1908	Washington, DC	General
Ancient and Accepted Scottish Rite of Freemasonry for the Northern Masonic Jurisdiction of the United States of America	1813	Boston, MA	Masons
Ancient and Accepted Scottish Rite of Freemasonry for the Southern Jurisdiction of the United States of America, The Supreme Council 33°, Mother Supreme Council of the World	1801	Washington, DC	Masons
Ancient Oaks, Order of	1912		Men
Anona, Degree of	1952		Pocahontas
Anti-Poke-Noses, Order of	1923		Anti K.K.K.
Antlers, The	1922		Elks
Arctic Brotherhood	1899		Prospectors
Artisans Order of Mutual Protection	1867	Philadelphia, PA	General
Associated Fraternities of America	1901		General
Association Canado-Americaine	1896	Manchester, NH	French

Bagmen of Bagdad, Ancient Mystic Order of	1895		Masons
Baptist Life Association	1883	Buffalo, NY	Germans
Bavarian National Association of North America	1884	Buffalo, NY	Bavarians
Beauceant, Social Order of the	1890	Calimesa, CA	Knights Templar
Beavers, Fraternal Order of	1911	Philadelphia, PA	Men
Beavers National Mutual Benfit, The	1916	Madison, WI	Men
Beavers Reserve Fund Fraternity	1902	Madison, WI	
Ben Hur Life Association	1894	Crawfordsville, IN	General
Bereans, Benevolent Order of	1847	Philadelphia, PA	General
B'nai B'rith International	1843	Washington, DC	Jewish
Bnai Zion	1908	New York, NY	Jewish
B'rith Abraham, Independent Order of	1859	New York, NY	Jewish
B'rith Abraham, Order of	1859	New York, NY	Jewish
Brith Sholom	1905	Philadelphia, PA	Jewish
Brotherhood of America	1890	Philadelphia, PA	General
Brotherhood of the Union	1850	Philadelphia, PA	Men
Buffaloes, Benevolent Order of	1881	New York, NY	Men
Buffaloes, Loyal Order of	1911	Newark, NJ	Men
Bugs, Order of	1912	Massachusetts	Men
Builders, Order of the	1921	New Castle, PA	Masons

Camels, Order of	1920	Milwaukee, WI	Men
Canadian Foresters Life Insurance Society	1879	Brantford, Ontario	Men
Canadian Fraternal Association, The	1891	Toronto, Ontario	General
Canadian Order of Chosen Friends	1887	Hamilton, Ontario	General
Catholic Aid Association, The	1878	St. Paul, MN	German
Catholic Association of Foresters	1879	Boston, MA	Catholic
Catholic Daughters of America	1903	New York, NY	Catholic
Catholic Family Life Insurance	1868	Milwaukee, WI	Catholic
Catholic Fraternal League. See Union Fraternal League			
Catholic Knights and Ladies of Illinois	1884	Belleville, IL	Catholic
Catholic Knights Insurance Society	1885	Milwaukee, WI	Catholic
Catholic Knights of America	1877	St. Louis, MO	Catholic
Catholic Knights of Ohio, The	1891	Lakewood, OH	Catholic
Catholic Knights of St. George	1881	Pittsburgh, PA	German
Catholic Women's Fraternal of Texas K.J.Z.T.	1894	Austin, TX	Czech
Catholic Workman	1891	New Prague, MN	Czech
Chaldeans, Modern Order of	1888	Brownsburg, IN	General
Chosen Friends, Independent Order of	1897	California	General
Chosen Friends, Order of	1879	Indianapolis, IN	General
Clansmen, American Order of	1923	San Francisco, CA	General
Clover Leaves, Fraternal Order of	1911	Missouri	General
Columbian League	1896	Detroit, MI	
Columbian Squires	1922	New Haven, CT	Catholic
Concordia Mutual Life Association	1908	Chicago, IL	Lutherans
Continental Fraternal Union, Order of the	1890	Richmond, IN	General
Corks, Ye Ancient Order of	1868		Elks
Court of Honor	1895	Springfield, IL	General
Cowboy Rangers, National Order of	1914	Denver, CO	Western
Croatian Catholic Union of the United States of America	1921	Hobart, IN	Croatian
Croatian Fraternal Union of America	1894	Pittsburgh, PA	Croatian
Czech Catholic Union	1867	Cleveland, OH	Czech
Czechoslovak Society of America	1854	Berwyn, IL	Czech

Dames of Malta	1896	Pittsburgh, PA	Knights of Malta
Danish Brotherhood in America, The	1881	Omaha, NB	Danish

Danish Sisterhood, The	1881	Chicago, IL	Danish
Daughters of America	1870	Harrisburg, OH	Women
Daughters of Isabella	1897	New Haven, CT	Catholic
Daughters of Isis	1910	Ft. Wayne, IN	Black
Daughters of Mokanna	1919	Rochester, NY	Mystic Order
Daughters of the Nile, Supreme Temple	1913	Seattle, WA	Women
Daughters of Scotia, The Order of the	1895	Troy, MI	Scottish
Daughters of Scotland	1899	Ohio	Scottish
Deer, Improved Order of	1913	Seattle, WA	
Degree of Hiawatha, See Hiawatha, Degree of .			United Workmen
Degree of Honor Protective Association	1873	St. Paul MN	
Degree of Pocahontas. See Pocahontas, Degree of			
De Molay, The Order of	1919	Kansas City, MO	Masons
Desoms, Order of	1946	Washington State	Masons
Does, Benevolent and Protective Order of the ..			Women
Druids, American Order of	1888	Fall River, MA	
Druids, United Ancient Order of	1839	New York, NY	Men

—E—

Eagles, Fraternal Order of	1898	Columbus, Oh	Men
Eastern Star, Daughters of the	1925	New York, NY	Women
Eastern Star, Order of	1876	Washington, DC	Masons
Eastern Star, Prince Hall Grand Chapter of the	1946		Blacks
Elks, Benevolent and Protective Order of	1867	Chicago, IL	Men
Elks, The Benevolent and Protective Order of, of Canada	1912	Regina, Saskatchawan	Men
Elks, Daughters of Independent, Benevolent, Protective Order of, of the World	1902	Winton, NC	Black
Elks, Improved Benevolent and Protective Order of	1897	Winton, NC	Black
Elks Mutual Benefit Association	1878		Elks
Emblem Club of the United States of America, Supreme	1917	Rutherford, NJ	Elks
Equitable Aid Union of America	1879	Pennsylvania	Masons
Equitable Reserve Association	1897	Neenah, WI	Men
Equity, Order of	1889	Indianapolis, IN	Men

—F—

Federation Life Insurance of America	1911	Milwaukee, WI	Polish
Federation of Masons of the World	1957	Austin, TX	Masons
First Catholic Slovak Ladies Association	1892	Beachwood, OH	Slovak
First Catholic Slovak Union of the United States of America and Canada	1889	Cleveland, OH	Slovak
Foresters, Ancient Order of	1832	San Francisco, CA	Men
Foresters, Catholic Order of	1883	Chicago, IL	Catholic
Foresters, Independent Order of	1874	Toronto, Ontario	Men
Fraternal Aid Union	1890	Lawrence, KS	General
Fraternal Legion	1881	Baltimore, MD	
Fraternal Mystic Circle	1885	Philadelphia, PA	Men
Fraternal Tribunes	1897	Rock Island, IL	Men
Free and Regenerated Palladium	1730	Charleston, SC	Masonic
Freemasonry, Ancient Free and Accepted Masons	1733	Boston, MA	
Freemen's Protective Silver Federation	1894	Spokane, WA	Silver
Freesmiths, Ancient Order of	1865	Baltimore, MD	German
Free Sons of Israel, The	1849	New York, NY	Jewish

—G—

Galilean Fishermen, Grand United Order of ...	1856	Washington, DC	Black

George Washington Masonic National Memorial Association	1911	Alexanderia, VA	Masons
Gleaner Life Insurance Society, The	1894	Birmingham, MI	General
Golden Chain, Order of	1929	West Caldwell, NJ	Masons
Golden Circle, Order of	1886		Black
Golden Cross, United Order of	1876	Lewiston, ME	General
Golden Key, Order of	1925	Norman, OK	Masons
Golden Links, Order of	1905	Wheeling, WV	General
Golden Rod, Order of the	1894	Detroit, MI	Men
Golden Star Fraternity	1881	Newark, NJ	General
Good Fellows, Royal Society of	1882	New York, NY	General
Good Samaritans and Daughters of Samaria, Independent Order of	1847	Washington, DC	Black
Good Templars, International Order of	1851	Utica, NY	Men
Grand College of Rites of the United States of America, The	1932	Chesapeake, VA	Masons
Grand Fraternity	1885	Philadelphia, PA	Masons
Grand Masters of Masons in North America, Conference of	1909	Towson, MD	
Greater Beneficial Union of Pittsburgh	1892	Pittsburgh, PA	Germans
Greek Catholic Union of the United States of America	1892	Minhall PA	Greek
Grottoes of North America, Supreme Council	1889	Chicago, IL	Masons

—H—

Harugari, German Order of	1847	South Ozone Park, NY	Germans
Haymakers' Association, National	1879		General
Heptasophs, Improved Order of	1878	Baltimore, MD	Men
Heptasophs, Order of the	1852	New Orleans, LA	Men
Heroes of '76	1923	Alexandria, VA	Men
Heroines of Jericho	1820		Women
Heroines of Jericho			Blacks
Hiawatha, Degree of	1952		Red Men
Hibernians in America, Ancient Order of	1836	Staten Island, NY	Irish
High Twelve International	1921	St. Louis, MO	Masons
Holy Order of Knights Beneficent of the Holy City	1934	Syracuse, NY	Masons
Homebuilders, Order of	1890	Philadelphia, PA	General
Home Circle, The	1879	Boston, MA	General
Home Forum Benefit Order	1892	Illinois	Masons
Home Palladium	1891	Kansas City, MO	General
Homesteaders, The	1906	Des Moines, IA	General
Hoo-Hoo, International Order of	1892	Norwood, MA	Lumbermen
Hooded Ladies of the Mystic Den	1923	Baltimore, MD	K.K.K.
Houn' Dawgs, Order of	1912	Cabool, MO	
Hungarian Reformed Federation of America	1896	Washington, DC	Hungarian

—I—

Imperial Mystic Legion	1896	Omaha, NB	
International Geneva Association	1904	New York, NY	
International Supreme Council of World Masons, Inc.	1948	Detroit, MI	Masons
Iowa Legion of Honor	1879	Iowa	
Iron Hall, Order of	1881	Indianapolis, IN	General
Iroquois, Order of	1898	Buffalo, NY	Men
Italo American National Union	1895	Chicago, IL	Italian

—J—

Jesters, Royal Order of	1911	Des Moines, IA	Masons
Job's Daughters, International Order of	1921	Omaha, NB	Masons

Junior Catholic Daughters of America	1925		Catholic
Junior Order of United American Mechanics of the United States of North America, Inc., National Council of the	1853	Willow Grove, PA	General
Junior Stars, Order of the Constellation of	1952		Masons

—K—

Kamelia	1923	Oklahoma	K.K.K.
Knight Masons, Order of	1923	Dover, DE	Masons
Knights and Daughters of Tabor, International Order of Twelve	1872	Independence, MO	Black
Knights and Ladies of Azar	1893	Chicago, IL	General
Knights and Ladies of Honor	1873	Indianapolis, IN	Women
Knights and Ladies of Security	1892	Kansas	General
Knights and Ladies of the Golden Rule	1879	Louisville, KY	General
Knights and Ladies of the Golden Star	1884	Newark, NJ	General
Knights of Columbus	1882	New Haven, CT	Catholic
Knights of Equity	1895	Cleveland, OH	Catholic
Knights of Honor	1873	Louisville, KY	Men
Knights of Jericho	1850	Utica, NY	Men
Knights of Khorassan, Dramatic Order of	1894	Des Moines, IA	Pythias
Knights of Liberty	1923	New York, NY	Anti K.K.K.
Knights of Luther	1912	Des Moines, IA	Protestants
Knights of Malta, The Ancient and Illustrious Order	1870	Reading, PA	Men
Knights of Peter Claver	1909	New Orleans, LA	Blacks
Knights of Pythias	1864	Stockton, CA	Men
Knights of Pythias, Improved Order of	1895	Indianapolis, IN	German
Knights of Pythias of North America, Europe, Asia, and Africa	1869	Richmond, VA	Black
Knights of St. John	1879	Parma, OH	Catholic
Knights of St. John, Supreme Ladies' Auxiliary	1900	Rochester, NY	Women
Knights of the Ancient Essenic Order	1888	Olympia, WA	
Knights of the Blue Cross of the World	1888	Homer, MI	
Knights of the Flaming Circle	1923	Pennsylvania	Men
Knights of the Globe	1889	Chicago, IL	General
Knights of the Golden Eagle	1872	North Wales, PA	Men
Knights of the Invisible Colored Kingdom	1923	Tennessee	Blacks
Knights of the Loyal Guard	1895	Flint, MI	General
Knights of the Mystic Chain, Ancient Order of	1871	Reading, PA	Masons
Knights of the Red Cross	1879		
Knights of the Red Cross of Constantine	1783	Chicago, IL	Masons
Knights of the York Cross of Honour, the Convent General	1930	Hastings-on-Hudson, NY	Masons
Knights Templar, Grand Encampment of the United States	1789	Chicago, IL	Masons
Ku Klux Klan, Knights of the	1865	Pulaski, TN	K.K.K.

—L—

Ladies Oriental Shrine of North America	1914		Masons
Ladies' Pennsylvania Slovak Catholic Union	1898	Wilkes-Barre, PA	Slovak
Lady Elks			Elks
Legion of the Red Cross	1885	Maryland	Men
Lions, Royal Order of	1911	Evansville, IN	Men
Lithuanian Alliance of America	1886	New York, NY	Lithuanian
Lithuanian Catholic Alliance	1889	Wilkes-Barre, PA	Lithuanian
Lithuanian Workers, Association of	1930	Ozone Park, NY	Lithuanian
Locomotive Engineers Mutual Life and Accident Insurance Association, The	1867	Cleveland, OH	Engineers
Loyal American Life Association	1896	Springfield, IL	General
Loyal Christian Benefit Association	1890	Titusville, PA	Catholic

— 362 —

Loyal Knights of America	1890	Wilkes-Barre, PA	Protestants
Loyal Knights and Ladies	1881	Boston, MA	General
Loyal Ladies of the Royal Arcanum	1923	Bridgeport, CT	Women
Loyal Mystic Legion of America	1892	Hastings, NB	
Loyal Orange Association [Canada]	1830	Toronto, Ontario	Irish
Loyal Order of Buffaloes. See Buffaloes, Loyal Order of			
Loyal Sons of America	1920		Men
Loyal Women of American Liberty	1888	Boston, MA	Protestants
Lutheran Brotherhood	1917	Minneapolis, MN	Norwegians

—M—

Maccabees, The	1878	Southfield, MI	Men
Maccabees, Ladies of the, of the World	1885	Muskegon, MI	Women
Maids of Athena, The	1930	Washington, DC	Women
Masonic Life Association	1872		Masons
Masonic Relief Association of the United States and Canada	1885	Sioux Falls, SD	Masons
Masonic Service Association	1919	Silver Spring, MD	Masons
Mechanical Order of the Sun, League of Friendship		Meadville, PA	Men
Mechanics, Independent Order of	1868	Baltimore, MD	Men
Mennonite Mutual Aid Association	1945	Goshen, IN	Mennonites
Modern American Fraternal Order	1896		
Modern Brotherhood of America	1897	Tipton, IA	
Modern Knights' Fidelity League	1881	Kansas City, KS	General
Modern Knights of St. Paul		Detroit, MI	Boys
Modern Romans	1904	Manistee, MI	General
Modern Samaritans, The	1897	Duluth, MN	
Modern Woodmen of America	1883	Rock Island, IL	Men
Moose, The Loyal Order of	1888	Mooseheart, IL	Men
Moose, Women of the	1914	Mooseheart, IL	Women
Mosaic Templars of America	1883	Little Rock, AR	Blacks
Muscovites, Imperial Order of	1894	Cincinnati, OH	(Odd Fellows)
Mutual Benefit Association of Rail Transportation Emoloyees, Inc.	1913	Philadelphia, PA	Railroad
Mutual Guild of Grand Secretaries	1900	San Francisco, CA	Masons
Mystic Brothers, Independent Order of	1882	Boston, MA	
Mystic Workers of the World	1892	Fulton, IL	General

—N—

National Association of Haymakers. See Haymakers, National Association of			
National Benefit Society	1894	Kansas City, MO	
National Defenders	1919	Knoxville, TN	Men
National Federated Craft	1929	Anderson, IN	Masons
National Fraternal Congress of America	1886	Chicago, IL	General
National Fraternal League	1902		
National Fraternal Union	1889	Cincinnati, OH	Masons
National Fraternal Society of the Deaf	1901	Mount Prospect, IL	Masons
National Fraternity	1893	Philadelphia, PA	General
National Home Guard	1907	Pennsylvania	General
National League of Masonic Clubs, The	1905	Hicksville, NY	Masons
National Mutual Benefit	1902	Madison, WI	
National Order of Videttes	1886	Texas	Farmers
National Protective Life Association	1891	Waverly, NY	Masons
National Slovak Society of the U.S.A.	1888	Pittsburgh, PA	Slovaks
National Sojourners, Inc.	1907	Washington, DC	Masons
National Union Assurance Society	1881	Toledo, OH	General
Native Daughters of the Golden West	1886	San Francisco, CA	Women
Native Sons of the Golden West	1875	San Francisco, CA	Men

Neighbors of Woodcraft	1897	Portland, OR	Western States
New England Order of Protection	1887	Massachuetts	General
New Era Association	1897	Grand Rapids, MI	Mich. & Ill.
North American Benefit Association	1892	Port Huron, MI	Women
North American Swiss Alliance	1865	Cleveland, OH	Swiss
North American Union Life Assurance Society	1893	Chicago, IL	General
North Star Benefit Association	1899	Moline, IL	General
Northwestern Legion of Honor	1884	Iowa	General

—O—

Occidental Mutual Benefit Association	1896	Salina, KS	General
Odd Fellows, Grand United Order of, in America	1844	Philadelphia, PA	Blacks
Odd Fellows, Independent Order of	1819	Baltimore, MD	
Odd Fellows, Junior Lodge	1921		
Order Knights of Friendship	1859	Reading, PA	General
Order of Americus	1897	Greensburg, PA	General
Order of the Bath of the United States of America	1921	Glassboro, NJ	Masons
Order of the Little Red School House	1895	Boston, MA	General
Order of Mutual Protection	1878	St. Louis, MO	General
Oriental Order of Humility and Perfection	1924		Odd Fellows
Orioles, the Fraternal Order	1910	Reading, PA	Owls
Owls, Independent International Order of	1890	St. Louis, MO	Masonic
Owls, Order of	1904	South Bend, IN	General

—P—

Pancretan Association of America	1916	Ceres, CA	Cretans
Patriarchal Circle of America	1880	Milwaukee, WI	Odd Fellows
Patriotic and Protective Order of Stags of the World	1911	St. Louis, MO	General
Patrons of Husbandry, Order of	1867	Washington, DC	Grange
Penelope, Daughters of	1929	Washington, DC	Greeks
Pennsylvania Slovak Catholic Union	1895	Wilkes-Barre, PA	Slovaks
Pente, Order of	1888	Philadelphia, PA	General
P.E.O. Sisterhood	1870	Nevada, MO	Women
Philalethes Society, The	1928	Columbia, MD	Masons
Pilgrim Fathers, United Order of	1878	Lawrence, MA	General
Pioneer Fraternal Association	1892	Winnipeg, Manitoba	General
Pocahontas, Degree of	1885	Oakley, CA	Women
Police and Fireman's Insurance Association	1913	Indianapolis, IN	Police & Firemen
Police, Fraternal Order of	1915	Indianapolis, IN	Police
Polish Beneficial Association, The	1899	Philadelphia, PA	Poles
Polish Falcons of America	1894	Pittsburgh, PA	Poles
Polish National Alliance of Brooklyn, U.S.A.	1903	Brooklyn, NY	Poles
Polish National Alliance of the United States of North America	1880	Chicago, IL	Poles
Polish National Union of America	1908	Scranton, PA	Poles
Polish Roman Catholic Union of America	1873	Chicago, IL	Poles
Polish Union of America	1890	Buffalo, NY	Poles
Polish Women's Alliance	1898	Park Ridge, IL	Poles
Portuguese Continental Union of the United States of America	1925	Boston, MA	Portuguese
Portuguese Union of the State of California	1880	San Leandro, CA	Portuguese
Praetorians, Modern Order of	1898	Dallas, TX	General
Presbyterian Beneficial Union	1901	Philadelphia, PA	Presbyterians
Prince Hall Freemasonry	1775		Blacks
Princes of Syracuse, Junior Order of			
Protected Home Circle	1886	Sharon, PA	General
Protestant Knights of America	1895	St. Louis, MO	Protestants

Providence Association of Ukrainian Catholics in America	1912	Philadelphia, PA	Catholics
Prudent Patricians of Pompeii of the United States of America	1897	Saginaw, MI	General
Puritans, Independent Order of		Pittsburgh, PA	
Pyramids, Ancient Order of	1895	Springfield, MO	General
Pythian Sisters	1888	Lonaconing, PA	Women

—R—

Rainbow Girls, International Order of	1922	McAlester, OK	Masons
Rathbone Sisters of the World	1888	Warsaw, IN	Pythians
Rebekah Assemblies, International Association of	1851	Minneapolis, KS	Odd Fellows
Rechabites, Independent Order of	1842	Washington, DC	Men
Red Eagles, Order of	1912	Kalamazoo, MI	Germans
Red Men, Improved Order of	1834	Waco, TX	Men
Red Men, Independent Order of	1850		Germans
Rosicrucian Fraternity	1858	San Jose, CA	General
Rosicrucian Order, The	1938	San Jose, CA	General
Royal Arcanum	1877	Boston, MA	General
Royal Arch Masons, International General Grand Chapter of	1797	Lexington, KY	Masons
Royal Benefit Society	1893	New York, NY	General
Royal Highlanders	1896	Lincoln, NB	General
Royal League	1883	Chicago, IL	Men
Royal Neighbors of America	1888	Rock Island, IL	Women
Royal Order of Lions. See Lions, Royal Order of			
Royal Order of Scotland, The	1878	Kensington, MD	Masons
Royal Purple, Order of, Auxiliary of the B.P.O. Elks of Canada	1915	Brandon, Manitoba	Men
Royal and Select Masters, International General Grand Council of	1872	New York, NY	Masons
Royal Society of Good Fellows. See Good Fellows, Royal Society of			
Royal Templars of Temperance, The	1870	Buffaclo, NY	General
Royal Tribe of Joseph	1894	Sedalia, MO	General
Russian Brotherhood Organization of the U.S.A.	1900	Philadelphia, PA	Russian
Russian Independent Mutual Aid Society	1931	Chicago, IL	Russian
Russian Orthodox Catholic Mutual Aid Society of the U.S.A.	1895	Wilkes-Barre, PA	Russian
Russian Orthodox Catholic Women's Mutual Aid Society	1907	Pittsburgh, PA	Russian

—S—

Saint John of Jerusalem, Sovereign Order of	1908	Shickshinny, PA	Catholics
St. Patrick's Alliance of America	1868	Newark, NJ	Catholics
Samaritans, Ancient Mystic Order of	1924	Morgantown, WV	Odd Fellows
Sanhedrims, Ancient Order of	1895	Richmond, VA	General
Sciots, Ancient Egyptian Order of	1905	Sacramento, Ca	Masons
Scottish Clans, Order of	1878	Boston, MA	Scottish
Serb National Federation	1901	Pittsburgh, PA	Serbian
Sexennial League	1888	Philadelphia, PA	General
Shepherds, Ancient Order of	1902	Chicago, IL	General
Shepherds of Bethlehem, Order of	1896	Camden, NJ	General
Shield of Honor, Order of	1877	Baltimore, MD	Men
Shrine, Ancient Arabic Order of the Nobles of the Mystic	1872	Chicago, IL	Masons
Shrine, Ancient Egyptian Arabic Order of Nobles of the	1893	Detroit, MI	Blacks
Shrine Directors Association of North America	1919	Jacksonville, FL	Masons

Slavonic Benevolent Order of the State of Texas	1896	Temple, TX	Czechs
Sloga Fraternal Life Insurance Society	1908	Milwaukee, WI	Slavic
Slovak Catholic Sokol	1905	Passaic, NJ	Slavic
Slovak Gymnastic Union Sokol of the United States of America	1896		Slavic
Slovene National Benefit Society	1904	Burr-Ridge, IL	Slovene
Social Order of the Beauceant. See Beauceant, Social Order of the			
Sociedade Portuguesa Rainha Santa Isabel	1898	Oakland, CA	Portuguese
Societas Rosicruciana in Civitatibus Foederatis	1880	Summit, NJ	Masons
Society of Blue Friars, The	1932	Franklin, IN	Masons
Society Espirito Santo of the State of California	1895	Santa Clara, CA	Portuguese
Sons and Daughters of Protection, The	1896	Lincoln, NB	General
Sons of Abraham, Independent Order of	1892	New York, NY	General
Sons of Adam	1879	Parsons, KS	Men
Sons of Benjamin, Independent Order of	1877	New York, NY	Jewish
Sons of Hermann, Order of	1840	San Antonio, TX	Germans
Sons of Italy, Order of	1905	Philadelphia, PA	Italians
Sons of Norway	1895	Minneapolis, MN	Norwegians
Sons of Pericles, The Order of	1926	Washington, DC	Greek
Sons of Poland, Association of the	1903	Jersey City, NJ	Poles
Sons of St. George, Order of	1871	Chicago, IL	English
Sons of Scotland Benevolent Association	1876	Toronto, Ontario	Scottish
Sons of Temperance	1842	New York, NY	
Sparta, Order of	1879	Philadelphia, PA	Men
Star of Bethlehem, Ancient and Illustrious	1849	Detroit, MI	General
Sunshine Girls			Pythian
Svithiod, Independent Order of	1831	Freeport, IL	Swedish

—T—

Tall Cedars of Lebanon of the United States of America	1902	Harrisburg, PA	Masons
Templars of Honor and Temperance	1845		
Templars of Liberty	1881	Newark, NJ	General
Temple of Fraternity	1896	Syracuse, NY	General
Theta Rho Clubs			Rebekah
Travelers Protective Association of America, The	1882	St. Louis, MO	Travelers
True Kindred, Supreme Conclave	1905		
True Reformers, The Grand United Order of	1881	Richmond, VA	Blacks
True Sisters, United Order of, Inc.	1846	New York, NY	Jewish

—U—

Ukrainian National Aid Association of America	1914	Pittsburgh, PA	Ukrainian
Ukrainian National Association	1894	Jersey City, NJ	Ukrainian
Ukrainian Workingmen's Association, The	1910	Scranton, PA	Ukrainian
Union Fraternal League	1893	Massachusetts	General
Union of Polish Women in America	1920	Philadelphia, PA	Polish
Union Saint-Jean Baptiste	1900	Woonsocket, RI	French
United American Mechanics	1845	Philadelphia, PA	General
United Americans, Order of	1844	New York, NY	General
United Brothers of Friendship	1861	Jefferson City, MO	Blacks
United Commercial Travelers of America, The Order of	1888	Columbus, OH	Travelers
United Daughters of Rechab	1845	Boston, MA	Women
United Friends of Michigan	1889		
United Lutheran Society	1893	Ligonier, PA	Slovak

United National Life Insurance Society	1868	Oakland, CA	Portuguese
United Societies of the United States	1903	McKeesport, PA	Greek
Unity, Order of	1889	Philadelphia, PA	General
Universal Craftsmen Council of Engineers	1894	Chicago, IL	Masons

—V—

Vasa Order of America	1896	Landisville, PA	Swedish
Verhovay Fraternal Insurance Association	1886	Pittsburgh, PA	Men
Vikings, Independent Order of	1896	Chicago, IL	Swedes

—W—

Western Bees	1905		
Western Catholic Union	1877	Quincy, IL	Catholic
Western Fraternal Life Association	1897	Cedar Rapids, IA	Czecks
Western Samaritans Life Association	1922		General
Western Slavonic Association	1908	Denver, CO	Slavic
White Shrine of Jerusalem, Order of the	1894	Romulus, MI	Masons
William Penn Association	1886	Pittsburgh, PA	General
Woodmen Circle — (Woodmen of the World			
Woodmen of the World	1890	Denver, CO	General
Woodmen of the World Life Insurance Society	1890	Omaha, NB	General
Workmen, Ancient Order of United	1868	Washington	General
Workmen's Benefit Fund of the United States of America	1884	Brooklyn, NY	Germans
Workmen's Circle, The	1900	New York, NY	Jewish

—Y—

Yellow Dogs, Order of	1923		
Yeomen, Brotherhood of American	1897	Des Moines, IA	General

—Z—

Zivena Beneficial Society	1891	Ligonier, PA	Hungarian

ALLIANCES

(Arranged by Subject of Affiliation)

Albania
Free Albania Organization (Albanian)
397 B W. Broadway
South Boston, MA 02127

American Legion
American Legion
700 N. Pennsylvania St.
Indianapolis, IN 46206

Forty and Eight
777 N. Meridian St.
Indianapolis, IN 46204

Ancient and Honorable Artillery Company
National Society Women Descendants of the
Ancient and Honorable Artillery Company
9027 S. Damen Ave.
Chicago, IL 60620

Arabian
National Association of Arab
Americans
1825 Connecticut Ave., N.W., No. 211

Washington, DC 20009

Ark and the Dove
Society of the Ark and the Dove (Colonial)
c/o The Maryland Historical Society
201 W. Monument St.
Baltimore, MD 21201

Armenian
Armenian General Benevolent Union of
America
585 Saddle River Rd.
Saddle Brook, NJ 07662

Armenian Relief Society
212 Stuart St.
Boston, MA 02116

Army and Navy Union
Army and Navy Union, U.S.A.
P.O. Box 537
1391 Main St.
Lakemore, OH 44250

Artisans
Artisans Order of Mutual Protection
2233 Spring Garden St.
Philadelphia, PA 19130

Asian Indian
Association of Indians in America
663 Fifth Ave.
New York, NY 10022

Australian-New Zealand
Australian-New Zealand Society of New York
41 E. 42d St., Rm 700
New York, NY 10017

Austrian
Oesterreichisch-Amerikanische Gesellschaft
Stallbrugasse 2
A-1610 Vienna, Austria

Aztec Club
Aztec Club of 1847
5225 Westpath Way
Washington, DC 20016

Bagmen
Ancient Mystic Order of Bagmen of
Bagdad Imperial Guild
c/o Earl F. Smith
2150 Washington Ave.
Evansville, IN 47714

Baltic
Polish Nobility Association
Villa Anneslie
529 Dunkirk Rd.
Anneslie, MD 21212

Sovereign Hospitaller Order of Saint John
Villa Anneslie
529 Dunkirk Rd.
Anneslie, MD 21212

Union of Polish Women in America
2636-38 E. Allegheny Ave.
Philadelphia, PA 19134

Baltic Women's Council
24 Central Ave.
Ridgefield Park, NJ 07660

Baptist
Baptist Life Association
8555 Main St.
Buffalo, NY 14221

Bastards
International Brotherhood of Old Bastards
2330 S. Brentwood Blvd.
St. Louis, MO 63144

Belgian
Belgian-American Association
13, rue Brederode
B-1000 Brussels, Belgium

Ben Hur
Ben Hur Life Association
227 E. Main St.

Crawfordsville, IN 47933

Black Elks
Improved Benevolent Protective Order
of Elks of The World
P.O. Box 159
Winton, NC 27986

Black Women
Girl Friends
c/o Dr. Christine Shack
16255 W. Nine Mile Rd.
Southfield, MI 48075

Blue Goose
Honorable Order of the Blue Goose,
International
P.O. Box 915
West Bend, WI 53095

British
St. George's Society of New York
71 W. 23d St., Rm. 1609
New York, NY 10010

Bulgarian
American Bulgarian League
c/o George Obreshkow
35 Sutton Pl.
New York, NY 10022

Byelorussian
Byelorussian-American Association
in the U.S.A.
166-34 Gothic Dr.
Jamaica, NY 11432

Byelorussian Congress
Committee of America
85-26 125th St.
Queens, NY 11415

California Pioneers
Society of California Pioneeers
456 McAllister St.
San Francisco, CA 94102

Canadian
Canadian Foresters Life Insurance
Society
P.O. Box 850
Brantford, ON, Canada N3T 5S3

Carpatho-Russian
Lemko Association
556 Yonkers Ave.
Yonkers, NY 10704

Catholic
Catholic Aid Association
49 W. Ninth St.
St. Paul, MN 55102

Catholic Association of Foresters
347 Commonwealth Ave.
Boston, MA 02115

Catholic Family Life Insurance
1572 E. Capitol Dr.

Milwaukee, WI 53211

Catholic Knights Insurance Society
1100 W. Wells
Milwaukee, WI 53233

Catholic Knights of America
3525 Hampton Ave.
St. Louis, MO 63139

Catholic Knights of St. George
709 Brighton Rd.
Pittsburgh, PA 15233

Catholic Life Insurance Union
1635 N.E. Loop 410
San Antonio, TX 78209

Catholic Order of Foresters
305 W. Madison St.
Chicago, IL 60606

Knights of Columbus
Columbus Plaza
New Haven, CT 06507

Knights of Peter Claver
1825 Orleans Ave.
New Orleans, LA 70116

Knights of St. John
6517 Charles Ave.
Parma, OH 44129

Knights of St. John Supreme Commandery
c/o Salvatore LaBianca
6517 Chalres Ave.
Parma OH 44129

National Catholic Society of
    Foresters
35 E. Wacker Dr.
Chicago, IL 60601

Order of the Alhambra
4200 Leeds Ave.
Baltimore, MD 21229

Supreme Ladies Auxiliary Knights of St. John
11 Christian Dr.
Cheektowaga, NY 14225

Western Catholic Union
506 Maine St.
Quincy, IL 62301

Catholic War Veterans
Catholic War Veterans of the U.S.A.
Two Massachusetts Ave., N.W.
Washington, DC 20001

Celtic
Celtic League
Naor Bothar Cnoc Sion
Baile Atha Cliath 9, Ireland

Children of the American Revolution
National Society of the Children of the
    American Revolution
1776 D. St. N.W.

Washington, DC 20006

Children of the Confederacy
Children of the Confederacy
328 North Blvd.
Richmond, VA 23220

Chinese
Chinese American Citizens Alliance
415 Bamboo Ln.
Los Angeles, CA 90012

Chinese Consolidated Benevolent
    Association
62 Mott St.
New York, NY 10013

Christian
Dames of Malta
4127 Brownsville Rd.
Pittsburgh, PA 15227

Colonial Clergy
Society of the Descendants of the
    Colonial Clergy
c/o Mrs. Robert H. Lubker
30 Leewood Rd.
Wellesley, MA 02181

Colonial Dames
Colonial Dames of America
421 E. 61st St.
New York, NY 10021

National Society of Colonial Dames
    of America
Dumbarton House
2715 Q St., N.W.
Washington, DC 20007

National Society Colonial Dames
    XVII Century
1300 New Hamshire Ave., N.W.
Washington, DC 20036

Colonial Daughters
National Society Colonial Daughters of the
    17th Century
10909 Maple Grove
Oklahoma City, OK 73120

Colonial Wars
General Society of Colonial Wars
840 Woodbine Ave.
Glendale, OH 45246

Companions
Companions of the Forest of America
250 W. 57th St.
New York, NY 10107

Coptic Egyptians
American Coptic Association
P.O. Box 9119 G.L.S.
Jersey City, NJ 07304

Croatian
Croatian Academy of America
P.O. Box 1767, Grand Central Station

New York, NY 10017

Croatian Catholic Union of the USA
One W. Old Ridge Road
Hobart, IN 46342

Croatian Fraternal Union of America
100 Delaney Dr.
Pittsburgh, PA 15235

Culinary
Societe Culinaire Philanthropique
250 West 57th Street, Room 1532
New York, NY 10019

Czech
American Sokol Educational and Physical
Culture Organization
6426 W. Cermak Road
Berwyn, IL 60402

Catholic Workman
P.O. Box 47
New Prague, MN 56071

Czech Catholic Union
5349 Dolloff Road
Cleveland, OH 44127

Czechoslovak Society of America
2701 S. Harlem Ave.
Berwyn, IL 60402

National Alliance of Czech Catholics
2657 - 59 S. Lawnsdale Ave.
Chicago, IL 60623

Slavonic Benevolent Order of the State
of Texas
P.O. Box 100
Temple, TX 76501

Sloga Fraternal Life Insurance Society
2538 W. National Avenue
Milwaukee, WI 53204

Western Fraternal Life Association
1900 First Ave. N.E.
Cedar Rapids, IA

Dames of the Loyal Legion
Dames of the Loyal Legion of the
United States
7809 Navajo St.
Philadelphia, PA 19118

Danish
Danish Brotherhood in America
P.O. Box 31728
3717 Harney Street
Omaha, NE 68131

Supreme Lodge of the Danish Sister-
hood of America
3438 N. Opal Avenue
Chicago, IL 60634

Daughters of 1812
National Society, United States Daughters
˗of 1812

1461 Rhode Island Avenue, N.W.
Washington, DC 20005

Daughters of America
National Council, Daughters of America
P.O. Box 154
Harrisburg, OH 43126

Daughters of American Colonists
National Society, Daughters of the American
Colonists
2205 Massachusetts Ave., N.W.
Washington, DC 20008

Daughters of the American Revolution
National Society, Daughters of the American
Revolution
1776 D Street, N.W.
Washington, DC 20006

Daughters of the Barons of Runnemede
National Society, Daughters of the Barons of
Runnemede
4530 Connecticut Ave., N.W.
Washington, DC 20008

Daughters of Founders & Patriots
National Society Daughters of Founders and
Patriots of America
1307 New Hampshire Ave., N.W.
Washington, DC 20036

Daughters of the Cincinnati
Daughters of the Cincinnati
122 E. 58th Street
New York, NY 10022

Daughters of the Nile
Daughters of the Nile, Supreme Temple
c/o Geraldine Neely
9832 Watts Branch Dr.
Rockville, MD 20850

Daughters of the Republic of Texas
Daughters of the Republic of Texas
112 E. 11th Street
Austin, TX 78701

Daughters of Union Veterans
Daughters of Union Veterans of the Civil
War 1861-1865
503 S. Walnut Street
Springfield, IL 62704

Daughters of Utah Pioneers
National Society Daughters of Utah Pioneers
300 N. Main
Salt Lake City, UT 84103

Degree
Degree of Honor Protective Association
325 Cedar
St. Paul, MN 55101

Descendants of the Signers
Descendants of the Signers of the
Declaration of Independence
c/o Mrs. Hans Bielenstein
50 Riverside Drive

New York, NY 10024

Disabled American Veterans
Disabled American Veterans
3725 Alexandria Pike
Cold Spring, KY 41076

Dutch
Netherlands — America Community
Association
c/o Netherlands Consulate
One Rockefeller Plaza
New York, NY 10020

Netherland Club of New York
Ten Rockefeller Plaza
New York, NY 10020

Eagles
Grand Aerie, Fraternal Order of Eagles
2401 W. Wisconsin Ave.
Milwaukee, WI 53233

Eastern Star
General Grand Chapter, Order of the the
Eastern Star
1618 New Hampshire Ave., N.W.
Washington, DC 20009

Ecuadorean
Ecuadorean American Association
115 Broadway
New York, NY 10006

Elks
Benevolent and Protective Order of Elks
2750 Lake View Ave.
Chicago, IL 60614

Entertainment
Showmen's League of America
300 W. Randolph St.
Chicago, IL 60606

Theatrical Mutual Association
c/o New York Lodge No. One
211 West 53d Street
New York, NY 10019

Equitable
Equitable Reserve Association
P.O. Box 448
Neenah, WI 54956

Estonian
Eastonian Aid
P.O. Box 357, Cooper Station
New York, NY 10276

Estonian Student Association in the
United States of America
342 E. 34th Street
New York, NY 10016

Federation
Federation Life Insurance of America
2335 South 13th Street
Milwaukee, WI 53215

Finnish
Finnish-American Historial Society of the West
P.O. Box 5522
Portland, OR 97208

Finnish-American League for
Democracy
P.O. Box 600
147 Elm Street
Fitchburg, MA 01420

League of Finnish-American Societies
Mechelininkatu 10
SF-00100 Helsinki 10, Finland

First Families
Order of First Families of Virginia, 1607-1624/5
c/o Mrs. Charles Marbury Seaman, Sr.
5055 Seminary Road, No. 439
Alexandria, VA 22311

Foreign Wars
Military Order of Foreign Wars
of the United States
c/o Col Jonathan Eben
165 E. 83d Street
New York, NY 10021

Foresters
Ancient Order of Foresters of California
2780 Mission Street
San Francisco, CA 94110

Independent Order of Foresters
Forester House
789 Don Mills Road
Don Mills, ON, Canada M3C1T9

Founders & Patriots
Order of the Founders and Patriots of America
c/o H. Carroll Parish
633 - 24th Street
Santa Monica, CA 90402

French
Union Saint-Jean-Baptiste
Box F
One Social Street
Woonsocket, RI 02895

French-Canadian
Association Canado Americaine
52 Concord Street
Manchester, NH 03101

Georgia Russian
Georgian Association in U.S.A.
c/o Sandro Baratheli
164 Burns Street
Forest Hills Gardens
New York, NY 11375

German
Alliance of Transylvanian Saxons
5393 Pearl Road
Cleveland, OH 44129

American Turners — Detroit
16284 Carlisle

Detroit, MI 48205

German-American National Congress
999 Elmhurst Road, Suite 33
Mt. Prospect, IL 60056

German Order of Harugari
1570 Clarkson Street
Denver, CO 80218

German Society of the City of New
    York
150 Fifth Avenue
New York, NY 10011

Schlaraffia Nordamerika
c/o Dr. Karl Hormann
987 Memorial Drive
Cambridge, MA 02138

Steuben Society of America
6705 Fresh Pond Road
Ridgewood, NY 11285

Gleaner
    Gleaner Life Insurance Society
    1600 N. Woodward Ave.
    Birmingham, MI 48012

Greek
    American Hellenic Congress
    c/o Peter Chumbris
    4200 Catherdral Ave., N.W.
    Washington, DC 20016

    Daughters of Penelope
    1422 K Street, N.W.
    Washington, DC 20005

    Evrytanian Association of America
    121 Greenwich Road
    Charlotte, NC 28211

    Greek American Progressive Association
    3600 Fifth Avenue
    Pittsburgh, PA 15213

    Greek Catholic Union of the U.S.A.
    502 E. Eighth Avenue
    Munhall, PA 15120

    Hungarian Reformed Federation of
        America
    11428 Rockville Pike
    Rockville, MD 20852

    Order of AHEPA
    1422 K Street, N.W.
    Washington, DC 20005

    Pancretan Association of America
    c/o Gus S. Pallios
    2521 Acron Lane
    Ceres, CA 95307

    Society of Kastorians "Omonoia"
    246 Eighth Avenue
    New York, NY 10011

Hereditary Order

Hereditary Order of Descendants of the
    Loyalists and Patriots of the
    American Revolution
5500 Burling Ct.
Bethesda, MD 20034

Haitian
    Haitian Unity Council, Inc.
    P.O. Box 152
    Canal Street Station
    New York, NY 10013

Holland Dames
    Society of Daughters of Holland Dames
    c/o Mrs. William Conrad Kopper
    P.O. Box 456
    Ridgefield, CT 06877

Holland Society
    Holland Society of New York
    122 East 58th Street
    New York, NY 10022

Hood's Texas Brigade
    Hood's Texas Brigade Association
    Confederate Research Center
    P.O. Box 619
    Hillsboro, TX 76645

Hungarian
    American Hungarian Federation
    c/o John Taba
    10195 Lee Highway
    Fairfax, VA 22030

    Hungarian Catholic League of
        America
    30 East 30th Street
    New York, NY 10016

    William Penn Association
    429 Forbes Ave, Fifth Avenue
    Pittsburgh, PA 15219

Hungarian Jews
    World Federation of Hungarian Jews
    136 East 39th Street
    New York, NY 10016

India
    Friends of India Society International
    Eight—D Sunflower Road
    Maple Shade, NJ 08052

Irish
    Ancient Order of Hibernians in America
    Box 700, Riverdale Station
    Bronx, NY 10471

Irish
    Knights of Equity and Friendly Sons
        of St. Patrick
    16 Southern Parkway
    Rochester, NY 14618

Irish
    Society of the Friendly Sons of St. Patrick
        in the City of New York

80 Wall Street, Room 1112
New York, NY 10005

Italian
American Italian Congress
111 Columbia Heights
Brooklyn, NY 11201

Italian
Amita
P.O. Box 140
Whitestone, NY 11357

Italian Catholic Federation Central Council
1801 Van Ness Ave., Suite 330
San Francisco, CA 94109

Italian Charities of America
83-20 Queens Boulevard
Elmhurst, NY 11373

Italian Welfare League
250 W. 57th Street, Suite 1131
New York, NY 10019

Italo American National Union
1400 Winston Plaza
Melrose Park, IL 60160

Order Sons of Italy in America Supreme
    Lodge
1520 Locust Street
Philadelphia, PA 19102

Unico National
72 Burroughs Pl.
Bloomfield, NJ 07003

Jamestowne Society
Jamestowne Society
P.O. Box 7389
Richmond, VA 23221

Japan
Japanese American Citizens League
1765 Sutter Street
San Francisco, CA 94115

Nippon Club
145 W. 57th Street
New York, NY 10010

Jewish
American Federation of Polish Jews
c/o Yechiel Dobekirer
United Jewish Appeal of N.Y.
130 E. 59th Street
New York, NY 10022

Association of Yugoslav Jews in the U.S.A.
247 W 99th Street
New York, NY 10025

Free Sons of Israel
932 Broadway
New York, NY 10010

Labor Zionist Alliance
575 Sixth Avenue
New York, NY 10011

United Order True Sisters
150 W. 85th Street
New York, NY 10024

Workmen's Circle
45 E. 33d Street
New York, NY 10016

Job's Daughters
International Order of Job's Daughters,
    Supreme Guardian Council
119 S 19th Street, Room 402
Omaha, NE 68102

Knife and Fork
Knife and Fork Club Inter national
One Townsite Plaza
Topeka, KS 66603

Knights of Khorassan
Dramatic Order Knights
    of Khorassan
313 E. Fifth Street, Suite 3
Des Moines, IA 50309

Knights of Malta
Ancient and Illustrious Order Knights of Malta
249 E. Liberty
East Canton, OH 44730

**Knights of PythiasSupreme Lodge Knights of
Pythias**
Pythian Building, Room 201
47 N. Grant
Stockton, CA 95202

Korean
Korean National Association
1368 W. Jefferson Blvd.
Los Angeles, CA 90007

Ladies of the Grand Army
Ladies of the Grand Army of the Republic
c/o Evelyn P. Krantz
R.R. 2
Hartwell, GA 30643

Latvian
American Latvian Association in the
    United States
P.O. Box 432
400 Hurley Ave.
Rockville, MD 20850

Lebanese
American Lebanese League
P.O. Box 57163
Washington, DC 20037

Legion of Valor
Legion of Valor of the United States
    of America
621 S. Taylor Street
Arlington, VA 22204

Letter Carriers
U.S. Letter Carriers Mutual Benefit
    Association
100 Indiana Ave., N.W.

Washington, DC 20001

Life Insurance
Life Insurance Society of American
254 W. Valley Ave.
Birmingham, AL 35209

Lithuanian
American Lithuanian Catholic Federation
    Ateitis
One S. 561 Cotuit
Glen Ellyn, IL 61037

Association of Lithuanian Workers
104-07 102d St.
Ozone Park, NY 11419

Knights of Lithuania (Lithuanian)
2455 W. 47th St.
Chicago, IL 60632

Lithuanian Alliance of America
307 W. 30th St.
New York, NY 10001

Lithuanian-American Community
    of the U.S.A.
c/o Vytautas Kutkus
6940 Hartwell
Dearborn, MI 48126

Lithuanian Catholic Alliance
P.O. Box 32
Wilkes-Barre, PA 18703

Lithuanian Roman Catholic
    Federation of America
c/o Lithuanian Catholic Center
4545 W. 63 St.
Chicago, IL 60629

United Lithuanian Relief Fund of America
Lithuanian Plaza Ct.
2558 W. 69th St.
Chicago, IL 60629

Locomotive Engineers
Locomotive Engineers Mutual Life and
    Accident Insurance Association
1026 B. of L.E. Bldg.
Cleveland, OH 44114

Loyal Christian
Loyal Christian Benefit Association
305 W. Sixth St.
Erie, PA 16512

Loyal Legion
Military Order of the Loyal Legion of
    the United States
War Library and Museum
1805 Pine St.
Philadelphia, PA 19103

Lumbermen
International Order of Hoo-Hoo
1420 Providence Hwy.
Norwood, MA 20262

Lutherans
Aid Association of Lutherans
Appleton, WI 54919

Concordia Mutual Life Association
20 N. Wacker Dr.
Chicago, IL 60606

Lutheran Benevolent Association
P.O. Box 228
Alma, MO 64001

Lutheran Fraternities of America
728 Penabscot Building
Detroit, MI 48226

Maccabees
The Maccabees
25800 Northwestern Highway
Southfield, MI 48037

Macedonian
Macedonian Patriotic
    Organization of U.S. and Canada
c/o Macedonian Tribune
542 S. Meridian Street
Indianapolis, IN 46225

Pan-Macedonian Association
370 Seventh Avenue
New York, NY 10001

Maltese
Maltese-American Benevolent Society
1832 Michigan Avenue
Detroit, MI 48216

Manx
North American Manx Association
P.O. Box 716
Williams St.
Liverpool, NS, Canada B0T 1K0

Masons
Ancient Egyptian Arabic Order Nobles
    of the Mystic Shrine
65 Cadillac Sq., No. 3111
Detroit, MI 48226

Ancient Egyptian Order of Sciots
Sciots Supreme Pyramid
3333 Watt Ave., Suite 204
Sacramento, CA 95821

Heroes of '76
8301 E. Boulevard Dr.
Alexandria, VA 22308

High Twelve International
Masonic Temple Building
3681 Lindell Blvd.
St. Louis, MO 63108

Imperial Council of the Ancient Arabic
    Order of the Nobles of the Mystic Shrine for
    North America
2900 Rocky Point Dr.
Tampa, FL 33607

International Supreme Council of

World Masons
1775 W. Forest Ave.
Detroit, MI 48206

Knights Templar, Grand Encampment,
U.S.A.
14 E. Jackson Blvd., Suite 1700
Chicago, IL 60604

Ladies Oriental Shrine of North
America
1009 Bevan Ct.
Englewood, OH 45322

Masonic Relief Association of U.S.A.
and Canada
32613 Seidel Dr.
Burlington, WI 53105

Masonic Service Association of the
United States
8120 Fenton Street
Silver Springs, MD 20910

Most Worshipful National Grand
Lodge Free and Accepted Ancient York
Masons
26070 Tryon Road
Oakwood Village, OH 44146

National Sojourners
8301 E. Boulevard Dr.
Alexandria, VA 22308

Order of the Golden Chain
584 Bloomfield Ave., Apt. 10-B
West Caldwell, NJ 07006

Philalethes Society
5449 Ring Dove Ln.
Columbia, MD 21044

Red Cross of Constantine-United
Imperial Council
14 E Jackson Blvd., Suite 1700
Chicago, IL 60604

Royal Order of Scotland
1904 White Oak Drive
Alexandria, VA 22036

Supreme Assembly, International Order of
Rainbow for Girls
P.O. Box 788
McAlester, OK 74501

Supreme Caldron, Daughters of Mokanna
23 Alexis Street
Rochester, NY 14609

Supreme Council, Ancient Accepted
Scottish Rite of Free-Masonry
33 Marrett Road
Lexington, MA 02173

Supreme Council 33rd Degree, Ancient
and Accepted Scottish Rite of Freemasonry
1733 - 16th Street, N.W.
Washington, DC 20009

Supreme Council, Mystic Order Veiled
Prophets of Enchanted Realm
6161 Busch Blvd.
Colombus, OH 43229

Supreme Council Order of the
Amaranth
1511 Farrell Ln.
Richland, WA 99352

Supreme Shrine of the Order of the
White Shrine of Jerusalem
36878 Goddard Road
Romulus, MI 48174

Tall Cedars of Lebanon of North
America
4751 Lindle Road, Suite 134
Harrisburg, PA 17111

Mayflower Descendants
General Society of Mayflower Descendants
Four Winslow Street
Plymouth, MA 02360

Montserrat
Montserrat Progressive Society of New York
207 West 137th Street
New York, NY 10030

Moose
Loyal Order of Moose
Mooseheart, IL 60539

National Fraternal Congress
National Fraternal Congress of America
230 W. Monroe St., Suite 720
Chicago, IL 60606

National Mutual Benefit
National Mutual Benefit
119 Monona Ave.
Madison, WI 53703

Neighbors of Woodcraft
Neighbors of Woodcraft
1410 S.W. Morrison Street
Portland, OR 97205

New England Women
National Society of New England Women
c/o Mrs. James D. Borland
9754 Riviera Drive
Sun City, AZ 85351

New York
St. Nicholas Society of the City of New York
122 E. 58th Street
New York, NY 10022

North American Benefit Association
North American Benefit Association
NABA Building
Port Huron, MI 48060

North American Union
North American Union Life Assurance Society
185 N. Wabash Ave.
Chicago, IL 60601

Norwegian
Sons of Norway
1455 W. Lake Street
Minneapolis, MN 55408

Norwegian
Norsemen's Federation
Radhusgaten 23B
N-1 Oslo, Norway

Odd Fellows
Ancient Mystic Order of Samaritans
974 Willey Street
Morgantown, WV 26505

Grand United Order of Odd Fellows
262 South 12th Street
Philadelphia, PA 19107

Independent Order of Odd Fellows
Sovereign Grand Lodge, I.O.O.F.
16 W. Chase Street   *422 Trade St.*
Baltimore, MD 21201 *Winston-Salem*
                     N. C. 27101

Z. B.
11/14/84

Order of the Crown
Order of the Crown in America
c/o Mrs. Richard Lindsay Roberts
444 Ridgewood Pl.
Ft. Thomas, KY 41075

Orioles
Fraternal Order of Orioles
c/o Pearson S. Stough
119 N. Ninth Street
Reading, PA 19601

Owls
Order of Owls
Home Nest
495 Maple
Hartford, CT 06114

Pennsylvania German Society
Pennsylvania German Society
P.O. Box 97
Breinigsville, PA 18031

Pilgrim Society
Pilgrim Society
Pilgrim Hall Museum
Plymouth, MA 02360

Pioneer Rivermen
Sons and Daughters of Pioneer Rivermen
c/o Frederick Way, Jr.
121 River Ave.
Sewickely, PA 15143

Pocahontas
Degree of Pocahontas, Improved Order of
Red Men
P.O. Box 683
Waco, TX 76703

Police
Fraternal Order of Police, Grand Lodge
3136 Pasadena Ave.
Flint, MI 48504

Police and Firemen
Police and Firemen's Insurance Association
3550 N. Washington Blvd.
Indianapolis, IN 46205

Polish
Alliance of Poles of America
6966 Broadway
Cleveland, OH 44105

Association of the Sons of Poland
665 Newark Ave.
Jersey City, NJ 07306

Northern Fraternal Life Insurance
1202 W. Oklahoma Ave.
Milwaukee, WI 53215

Polish Alma Mater of America
4842 W. Fullerton
Chicago, IL 60639

Polish Beneficial Association
2595 Orthodox
Philadelphia, PA 19137

Polish Falcons of America
97-99 S. 18th Street
Pittsburgh, PA 15203

Polish National Alliance of Brooklyn,
U.S.A.
155 Noble Street
Brooklyn, NY 11222

Polish National Alliance of the United
States of North America
6100 N. Cicero
Chicago, IL 60646

Polish National Union of America
1002 Pittston Ave.
Scranton, PA 18505

Polish Roman Catholic Union of America
984 Milwaukee Ave.
Chicago, IL 60622

Polish Union of America
761 Fillmore Ave.
Buffalo, NY 14212

Union of Poles in America
6501 Lansing Ave.
Cleveland, OH 44105

Polish Union of the United States of
North America
53-59 N. Main Street
Wilkes-Barre, PA 18701

Polish Women's Alliance of America
205 S. Northwest Highway
Park Ridge, IL 60068

Portuguese
Luso-American Fraternal Federation
1951 Webster Street
Oakland, CA 94612

Portuguese Continental Union of
the United States of America
899 Boylston St.
Boston, MA 02115

Portuguese Society Queen St. Isabel
3031 Telegraph Ave.
Oakland, CA 94609

United National Life Insurance Society
1951 Webster Street
Oakland, CA 94612

Pythian Sisters
Supreme Temple Order Pythian Sisters
c/o Evelyn M. Carter
Rt. 2, Box 533
Buckhannon, WV 26201

Rebekah
International Association of Rebekah
Assemblies, I.O.O.F.
P.O. Box 153
Minneapolis, KS 67467

Red Men
Great Council of U.S. Improved Order
of Red Men
P.O. Box 683
Waco, TX 76703

Restaurant
International Geneva Association
435 Fifth Avenue
New York, NY 10016

Romanian
Iuliu Maniu American Romanian
Relief Foundation
P.O. Box 1151, Gracie Station
New York, NY 10028

Romanian National Council
P.O. Box A-lll, Radio City Station
New York, NY 10019

Union and League of Romanian
Societies of America
720 Williamson Building
215 Euclid
Cleveland, OH 44114

Rosicrucian
Rosicrucian Fraternity
Beverly Hall
P.O. Box 220
Quakertown, PA 18951

Rosicrucian Order
Rosicrucian Park
San Jose, CA 95191

Royal Arcanum
Supreme Council of the Royal Arcanum
61 Batterymarch Street
Boston, MA 02110

Royal Bastards
Descendants of the Illegitimate Sons and

Daughters of the Kings of Britain
c/o Herman Nickerson, Jr.
107 Lake Lane Rock Creek
Jacksonville, NC 28540

Russian
American Russian Aid Association
349 West 86th Street
New York, NY 10024

Congress of Russian Americans
P.O. Box 5025
Long Island City, NY 11105

Russian Brotherhood Organization of
the U.S.A.
1733 Spring Garden Street
Philadelphia, PA 19130

Russian Independent Mutual Aid
Society
917 N. Wood Street
Chicago, IL 60622

Russian Orthodox Catholic Mutual Aid Society
of U.S.A.
100 Hazle Street
Wilkes-Barre, PA 18701

Russian Orthodox Catholic Women's
Mutual Aid Society
975 Greentree Road
Pittsburgh, PA 15220

Russian Orthodox Fraternity LUBOV
c/o Stephen Shust
212 Bacon Street
Jermyn, PA 18433

Tolstoy Foundation
250 W. 57th Street, Room 1101
New York, NY 10107

United Russian Orthodox Brotherhood
of America
333 Boulevard of the Allies
Pittsburgh, PA 15222

Sailor and Pilots
The Associated Turtles
c/o The New York Yacht Club
P.O. Box 66
37 West 44th Street
New York, NY 10036

Scandinavian
Augustana Historical Society
Augustana College
Rock Island, IL 61201

Independent Order of Svithiod
5518 W. Lawrence Ave.
Chicago, IL 60630

Scandinavian Fraternity of America
1350 N. Howard Street
Akron, OH 44310

Scotch-Irish
Scotch-Irish Society of the United States

of America
13 Thompson Drive
Havertown, PA 19083

Scots

American Scottish Foundation
P.O. Box 537, Lenox Hill Station
New York, NY 10021

Council of Scottish Clan Associations
Seven Wyndmoor Dr., Convent Station
Morristown, NJ 07961

Daughters of Scotia
c/o Lillian McDonald
228 Morrison Avenue
Somerville, MA 02144

Scottish Heritage USA
281 Park Ave. S., 5th Fl.
New York, NY 10010

Sons of Scotland Benevolent Association
19 Richmond Street, W.
Toronot, ON, Canada M5H 1Y9

St. Andrew's Society of the State of
New York
281 Park Ave., S.
New York, NY 10010

Serbian

Serb National Federation
3414 Fifth Ave.
Pittsburgh, PA 15213

Serbian National Defense Council
3909 W. North Street
Chicago, IL 60647

Silesians

World Association of Upper Silesians
c/o Karol Sitko
R.D. No. 2
Dalton, PA 18414

Slavic

Ethnic American Coalition
523 S. Wolfe Street
Baltimore, MD 21231

First Catholic Slovak Ladies Association
24950 Chagrin Blvd.
Beachwood, OH 44122

First Catholic Slovak Union of the
U.S.A, and Canada
3289 E. 55th Street
Cleveland, OH 44127

National Slovak Society of the United
States of America
2325 E. Carson Street
Pittsburgh, PA 15203

Slavic American National Association
918 F St., N.W., Suite 410
Washington, DC 10004

Slovak Catholic Federation

c/o Rev. Joseph V. Adamec
1515 Cass Ave.
Bay City, MI 48706

Slovak Catholic Sokol
205 Madison Street
Passaic, NJ 07055

Slovak League of America
870 Rifle Camp Rd.
West Paterson, NJ 07424

Slovak Relief Fund
1065 National Press Blvd.
Washington, DC 20045

Sokol U.S.A.
P.O. Box 189
276 Prospect St.
East Orange, NJ 07017

Slavonic

American Fraternal Union
P.O. Box 59
Ely, MN 55731

Western Slavonic Association
5809 W. 38th Ave.
Denver, CO 80212

Slovenian

American Mutual Life Association
6401 St. Clair Ave.
Cleveland, OH 44103

Slovene National Benefit Society
116 Shore Drive
Burr Ridge, IL 60521

Slovenian Women's Union
431 N. Chicago St.
Joliet, IL 60432

Society of the Cincinnati

Society of the Cincinnati
2118 Massachusetts Ave., N.W.
Washington, DC 20008

Son and Daughters of Liberty

National Council, Sons and Daughters of
Liberty
c/o Kathryn S. Knox
422 Stokes Mill Rd.
Stroudsburg, PA 18360

Sons of America

Patriotic Order Sons of
America
P.O. Box 1847
Valley Forge, PA 19481

Sons of Confederate Veterans

Sons of Confederate Veterans
P.O. Box 5164, Southern Station
Hattiesburg, MS 39401

Sons of Hermann

Grand Lodge Order of the
Sons of Hermann in Texas
P.O. Box 1941

San Antonio, TX 78297

Sons of the American Revolutions
National Society, Sons of the American
Revolution (SAR)
1000 S. Fourth St.
Louisville, KY 40203

Sons of the Revolution
General Society, Sons of the Revolution
Fraunces Tavern Museum
54 Pearl St.
New York, NY 10004

Sons of Sherman's March
Sons of Sherman's March to the Sea
1725 Farmer Ave.
Tempe, AZ 85281

Sons of Union Veterans
Auxiliary to Sons of Union Veterans
of the Civil War
c/o Viola Bremme
4724 N. Mascher St.
Philadelphia, PA 19120

Sons of Union Veterans of the Civil War
P.O. Box 24
Gettysburg, PA 17325

Sons of Utah Pioneers
National Society of the Sons of Utah Pioneers
3299 Louise Ave.
Salt Lake City, UT 84109

Sourdough
International Sourdough Reunion
c/o Eleanor Merkley
2601 W. Manor Pl., No. 223
Seattle, WA 98199

Spanish
Legionarios Del Trabajo in America
Grand Lodge
2154 S. San Joaquin St.
Stockton, CA 95206

Spanish Benevolent Society "La
Nacional"
239 W. 14th St.
New York, NY 10011

Union Espanola Benefica De California
827 Broadway
San Francisco, CA 94115

Spanish American War
Sons of Spanish American War Veterans
c/o Jack Dempsey
646 Scott St.
Redwood City, CA 94063

Spanish War Veterans
United Spanish War Veterans
P.O. Box 1915
Washington, DC 20013

St. Luke
Independent Order of St. Luke

902 St. James St.
Richmond, VA 23220

Star and Bars
Military Order of the Stars and Bars
P.O. Box 5164, Southern Station
Hattiesburg, MS 39401

Swedish
United Swedish Societies
c/o Gustave W. Kvalden
535 Fifth Ave., Room 3106
New York, NY 10017

Vasa Order of America
3720 Daryl Dr.
Landisville, PA 17538

American-Swiss Association
60 E. 42d St.
New York, NY 10017

North American Swiss Alliance
33 Public Sq.
Cleveland, OH 44113

Swiss Benevolent Society of New York
37 W. 67th St.
New York, NY 10023

Templars
National Council of the United States,
International Organization of Good
Templars
Good Templar Center
2922 Cedar Ave. S.
Minneapolis, MN 55407

Travelers Protective
Travelers Protective Association of America
3755 Lindell Blvd.
St. Louis, MO 63108

Trench Rats
National Order of Trench Rats
10224 LaReina Ave.
Downey, CA 90241

Turkish
Turkish-American Associations
147 W. 42d St.
New York, NY 10036

Ukrainian
League of Americans of Ukrainian
841 N. Western Ave.
Chicago, IL 60622

Plast, Ukrainian Youth Organization
140 Second Ave.
New York, NY 10003

Providence Association of Ukrainian
Catholics in America
817 N. Franklin Street
Phildelphia, PA 19123

Ukrainian American League
c/o Ukranian News
85 E. Fourth Street

New York, NY 10003

Ukrainian Fraternal Association
440 Wyoming Ave.
Scranton, PA 18503

Ukrainian Life Cooperative
    Association
2348 W. Cortez
Chicago, IL 60622

Ukrainian National Aid Association
    of America
527 Second Ave.
Pittsburgh, PA 15219

Ukrainian National Association
30 Montgomery St.
Jersey City, NJ 07302

United Commercial Travelers
Order of United Commercial Travelers
    of America
632 N. Park Street
Columbus, OH 43215

United Daughters of the Confederacy
United Daughters of the Confederacy
328 North Blvd.
Richmond, VA 23220

United Societies
United Societies of the United States
    of America
613 Sinclair St.
McKeesport, PA 15132

United Workmen
Ancient Order United Workmen
23003 Pacific Hwy. S.
Seattle, WA 98188

Veterans of Foreign Wars
Veterans of Foreign Wars of the U.S.A.
V.F.W. Bldg.
Kansas City, MO 64111

Vikings
Independent Order of Vikings
200 E. Ontario St. Room 505
Chicago, IL 60611

War of 1812
General Society of the War 1812
1307 New Hampshire Ave. N.W.
Washington, DC 20036

Society of the War of 1812 in the
    Commonwealth of Pennsylvania
1501 Monticello Dr.
Gladwyne, PA 19035

Veteran Corps of Artillery, State of New York,
    and the Military Society of the War of 1812
Seventh Regiment Armory

643 Park Ave.
New York, NY 10021

Welsh
St. David's Society of the State of New York
71 W. 23d St.
New York, NY 10010

Welsh National Gymanfa Ganu Association
4034 Southern Blvd.
Youngstown, OH 44512

Welsh Society
450 Broadway
Camden, NJ 08103

Whiskey Rebellion
Society of the Whiskey Rebellion of 1794
Dallowgill
3311 Columbia Pike
Lancaster, PA 17603

Women's Clubs
General Federation of Women's Clubs
1734 N St., N.W.
Washington, DC 20036

Woman's Relief Corps.
National Woman's Relief Corps, Auxiliary to
    the Grand Army of The Republic
629 S. Seventh
Springfield, IL 62703

Woodmen
Supreme Camp of the American
2100 Downing St.
Denver, CO 80205

Woodmen of the World
Canadian Woodmen of the World
Eight Wilson St., W.
Perth, ON, Canada K7H 2M5

Modern Woodmen of America
1701 First Ave.
Rock Island, IL 61201

Royal Neighbors of America
230 - 16th Street
Rock Island, IL 61201

Woodmen of the World
1450 Speer Blvd.
Denver, CO 80204

Woodmen of the World
    Life Insurance Society
Woodmen Tower
1700 Farnam St.
Omaha, NE 68102

Workmen's Benefit Fund
Workmen's Benefit Fund of the U.S.A.
Drawer 73
One Old County Rd.
Carle Place, NY 11514

CHAPTER 20

MILITARY RECORDS

Military Records

Wars have produced an incredible number of records on millions of people that are of inestimable genealogical value. Not only will they be useful in extending your pedigree, but they also contain valuable historical information.

There are two kinds of Military Records; Service Records and Pension Records. Generally the Service Records give only mimimal information. On the other hand, Pension Records often contain a great deal of information of interest to the genealogist.

Records relating to wars prior to the Revolutionary War, are mostly historical and are of little genealogical value. There were no official national records before that time. There are, however, a few Colonial and local Militia records, mainly rolls and rosters. The information is extremely limited. What is available can be found in Val Greenwood's *"Researchers Guide to American Genealogy"* and E. Kay Kirkham's *"Military Records of America"*.

During the colonial and early federal period each state had it's own army called the State Milita. Often they would have special nicknames such as the "Squirrel Hunters" or "Corn Huskers Brigade". In 1824 the names of all state militias were changed to the National Guard.

It is important to note that there may be as many as eight times more military information, that is of value to the genealogist, on the state and local level as there is at the Federal level. However, since there is more information available in one place at the federal level it should be checked first. For records prior to 1900 check the National Archives in Washington D.C. Since 1900 the Military records have been kept in the National Record Center in St. Louis, MO. After checking these two locations check the appropriate state records.

DESCRIPTIONS OF EARLY MILITARY ORGANIZATIONS

Understanding the ranks and organization of the Army can assist you in understanding the part your ancestors may have played in the war.

The following general descriptions of pre-1900 military organizations, grades, and terms have been compiled through the courtesy of James B. Gerrity, President, Illinois Military Historical Society, 409 North 6th Street, Auburn, Illinois 62615.

The U.S. Army consisted of National Troops, raised directly by the Federal Government, and State Troops, raised by each state and available for Federal service. The basic law covering State troops was the militia Act of 8 May 1792. This law remained in effect until the passage of the National defense act of 1916.

The basic organization of the Army was as follows:

Name	Size	Commanded By
Company or Battery (Artillery)	50-100 men	Lt. or Captain
Squadron (Cavalry)	2 Companies	Captain or Major
Battalion	4-10 Companies	Major or Lt. Colonel
Battalion (Cavalry)	2 Squadron	Major or Lt. Colonel
Regiment	2 or more Battalions	Lt. Colonel or Colonel
Brigade	2 or more Regiments	Brigadier Geneiral
Division	2 or more Brigades	Brigadier or Major General
Corps	2 or more Divisions	Major General
Army	2 or more Corps	Major General or Lt. Gen. (Lt. General after 1864

During the Revolution, Army organization was very fluid. Due to short term enlistments, the Continental Congress would reorganize the Army almost annually. In addition, the Congress could only request that the states abide by the wishes of Congress. As a result the states could, and frequently did, organize their troops as they thought best. As a general rule Continental and State forces were organized and fought as battalions. Some were called regiments, but their size was the same as the battalions. As far as the Revolution is concerned, we can say that the terms battalion and regiment are synonymous.

Wars following the Revolution were fought by National troops with a 2-battalion regiment and by state troops with a 1-battalion regiment. The 10-company regiment with no battalions was mandatory for state troops under the Militia Act of 1772.

The Army was divided into two groups. Arms and Services:

ARMS (These did the fighting or furnished close support).

Infantry: The foot soldier.

Artillery: Field Artillery went with the Infantry. Heavy Artillery manned guns in permanent fortifications.

Cavalry: Mounted troops.

Engineers: Built bridges, drew maps, planned fortifications.

Signals: Provided communications by flag, telegraph, etc.

SERVICES (Took care of supply, administration, etc.).

Quartermaster: Responsible for all supplies except arms.

Ordnance: Furnished and maintained weapons.

Medical: Took care of the sick and wounded.

Adjutant-General: Issued orders for the Commander and did paperwork.

Paymaster: Paid the troops.

Judge Advocate: The Army lawyer

Provost Marshal: The Army policeman.

There are other specialist services in addition to the main ones listed.

The officer grade structure was basically the same as it is now, with most of the titles unchanged.

2nd Lt.: Also known during the Revolution as Ensign, or Cornet (Cavalry)

1st Lt.: Both grades of Lieutenant also called Subaltern.

Captain Lt.: This grade was used during the Revolution and indicated the senior 1st Lt. in the Battalion.

Major, Lieutenant Colonel, Colonel, Brigadier General, Major General, Lieutenant General and General. During the Quasi War with France in 1798-9, Congress raised a large army on paper and appointed George Washington as Lt. General. To keep from outranking Washington no one was promoted above Major General until 1864 when the grade of Lt. General was reopened for U. S. Grant.

Officers are divided into three groups: Company Grade, Field Grade, and General Grade. Company Grade officers (Lt. & Capt.) were in direct command of the troops, while field grade (Major through Colonel) commanded other officers. These two grades were always of one Arm or Service. General Grade officers, (Brigadier General through

RECORDS RELATING TO SERVICE IN THE U.S. ARMY

*Required by law for the year 1816 only.

Period	Pension File	Bounty-Land Appln. File	Volunteers: Consol. Index	Volunteers: State Index	Volunteers: Record	Enlisted Men: Enlistment Paper	Enlisted Men: Enlistment Register	Officer: Consol. File	Officer: Military Academy File	Officer: Historical Register	Birth Record	Death or Burial Record
1775-1783 Revolutionary War	★	★	★	★	★							★
1784-1788 Post Revolutionary War Period	★	★	★		★							★
1789-1811	★	★	★		★	★	★		★	★		★
1812-1815 War of 1812	★	★	★	★	★	★	★		★	★		★
1816-1845	★	★		★	★	★	★		★	★	★*	★
1846-1848 Mexican War	★	★	★		★	★	★		★	★		★
1849-1860	★	★				★	★		★	★		★
1861-1866 Civil War — Union	★			★	★	★	★	★	★	★		★
1861-1866 Civil War — CSA	★			★	★							★
1867-1897	★					★	★	★	★	★		★
1898-1912 Spanish-American War / Philippine Insurrection / Boxer Rebellion	★		★	★	★	★	★	★	★	★		★
1903-1912	★					★	★	★	★	★		★
1913-1916	★							★	★	★		★

General) commanded large organizations including several Arms and Services.

The enlisted grade structure was much simpler than today. But once again we are still using most of the titles. They are:

Private; also Private 2nd Class (Ordnance), Matross (Artillery) and Rifleman (Rifle Battalion or Regiment).
Private 1st Class, Ordnance only
Corporal
Sergeant
First Sergeant. The Senior Sergeant of the company.

In addition, some staff positions were filled by the Sergeant Major, Quartermaster Sergeant, Hospital Steward, etc.

Two terms commonly encountered are line and staff. Line troops, commissioned and enlisted, were those who were actually on the firing line. During the Revolution the term "line" was frequently used to refer to the Army. National troops were the Continental Line, while State troops were the State Line, or Massachusetts Line, Pennsylvania Line, etc. Staff positions are usually found beginning with the regiment. An organization as large as a regiment is too big for the commander to take care of all the details. These commanders would have a group of assistants, called his staff, who would take care of matters of supply, administration, etc. in the commander's name.

Another area of possible confusion is the difference between enlist and muster-in, and discharge and muster-out. When a soldier joined a state regiment he was enlisted. When his regiment was taken into Federal service, he was mustered-in. If at any time he left the service while his regiment was on active duty, he was discharged. If he was still with the regiment when it was released from Federal service, he was mustered out.

Odds and Ends

SUTLER: A man who followed a regiment to sell necessary items to the soldiers. They were unofficial arrangements by each regimental commander until Congress made sutlers official on 19 March 1862. Replaced by the Post Exchange after the Civil War.

ZOUAVE: A special type of Infantry copied from a French North African regiment. Zouaves were noted for their precision drill, fast marching pace and gaudy uniforms.

SAPPERS and PIONEERS: Specialized forms of Engineer Troops.

RIFLEMAN: Until the Mexican War our Infantry was armed with the smoothbore musket, with selected men armed with a rifle and in special companies. After 1846 all infantry had a rifle, but some regiments kept the title Rifle Regiment as a mark of distinction.

BREVET: An officer who distinguished himself would be awarded a Brever promotion. Medals did not exist for many years. A Captain could be a Brevet Major or Lt. Col. while serving as a Captain. Such a Captain would outrank all other Captains without a Brevet, thus giving him a slight edge on future promotions.

Military Chronology

If you know approximately the years your ancestor would have been of military age, you can look at the following chart to find out in which war he might have participated.

Many people received pensions and other remuneration for services other than military and are considered a veteran of that war. He may have donated a mule or a load of hay or protected the cross roads near his home without firing a shot.

Many of the conscientious objectors, like Quakers, Mennonites, etc., would show up for a muster call because they were loyal citizens, even though they wouldn't fight. They were also considered veterans of that war.

American Wars and Engagements Before 1900

WAR	DATES	AREA	WAR	DATES	AREA
French-Spanish	1565-67	Florida	Texan	1835-36	Texas
English-French	1613-29	Canada	Indian Stream	1835-36	New Hamphire
Anglo-French	1629	St. Lawrence River	Creek Indian	1836-37	Georgia and Alabama
Pequot War	1636-37	New England	Florida (Seminole)	1835-42	Florida, Georgia and Alabama
	1640-45	New Netherland			
Iroquois	1642-53	New England; Acadia	Sabine or Southwestern Indian	1836-37	Louisiana
Anglo-Dutch	July 1653	New Netherland			
Bacon's Rebellion	1675-76	Virginia	Cheirokee	1836-38	
King Philip's	1675-76	New England	Osage Indian	1837	Missouri
War in the North	1676-78	Maine	Heatherly Disturbance	1836	Missouri
Culpepper's Rebellion	1677-80	Carolinas	Mormon	1838	Misisouri
Leisler's Rebellion	1688-91	New England	Aroostook	1839	Maine
Revolution in Maryland	1689	Maryland	Door's Rebellion	1842	Rhode Island
Glorious Revolution	1689	New England	Mormon	1844	Illinois
King William's War	1689-97	Canada	Mexican	1846-48	Mexico
Queen Anne's	1702-13	New England	Cayuse Indian	1847-48	Oregon
Tuscorora	1711-12	Virginia	Texas and New Mexico Indian	1849-55	
Jenkin's Ear	1739-42	Florida			
King George's	1740	Georgia and Virginia	California Indian	1851-52	
Louisbourg	1745	New England	Utah Indian	1850-53	
Fort Necessity	1754	Ohio	Rogue River Indian	1851, 1853, 1856	Oregon
Anglo-French	1755-58	Canada			
French and Indian	1754-63	New England, Virginia	Oregon Indian	1854	Oregon
Seige of Quebec	1759	Canada	Nicaraguan	1854-58	Naval
American Revolution	1775-83		Kansas Troubles	1854-59	Kansas
Wyoming Valley	1782-87	Pennsylvania	Yakima Indian	1855	Local
Shay's Rebellion	Dec. 1786-Jan. 1787	Massachusetts	Klamath & Salmon River Indian	1855	Oregon and Idaho
Whiskey Insurrection	1794	Pennsylvania	Florida Indian	1855-58	Florida
Northwestern Indian	1790-95	Ohio	John Brown's Raid	1859	Virginia
War with France (Naval)	1798-1800		War of the Rebellion	1860-65	General
War with Tripoli (Naval)	1801-05	North Coast of Africa	Cheyenne	1861-64	Local
Burr's Insurrection	1806-07	Southern Mississippi Valley	Sioux	1862-63	Minnesota
			Indian Campaign	1865-68	Oregon, Idaho, Calif.
Chesapeake (Naval)	1807	Virginia	Fenian Invasion of Canada	1866	from New England
Northwestern Indian	1811	Indiana			
Florida Seminole Indian	1812	Florida (Georgia Volunteers)	Indian Campaign	1867-69	Kansas, Colorado and Indian Territory
War of 1812	1812-15	General	Modac Indian	1872-73	Oregon
Peoria Indian	1813	Illinois	Apaches	1873	Arizona
Creek Indian	1813-14	South	Indian Campaigns	1874-75	Kansas, Colorado, Texas, Indian Terr. & New Mexico
Lafitte's Pirates	1814	Local			
Barbary Powers	1815	Africa's North Coast			
Seminole Indian	1817-18	Florida and Georgia	Cheyenne and Sioux	1876-77	Dakota
Arickaree (Rickaree) Indian	1823	Missouri River, Dakota Territory	Nez Perce	1877	Utah
			Bannock	1878	Idaho, Washington Terr. and Wyoming Territory
Fever River Indian	1827	Illinois			
Winnebago Indian	1827	Wisconsin	White River (Ute Indians)	1879	Utah and Colorado
Sac and Fox Indian	1831	Illinois	Cheyenne	1878-79	Dakota and Montana
Black Hawk	1832	Illinois and Wisconsin	Spanish-American	1898-99	Cuba
Toledo	1835-36	Ohio and Michigan	Philippine Insurrection	1899-1902	

Records Relating to Military Service

Micro film records in the National Archives (See the federal forms section for request form needed, to purchase the film or you can read it at your nearest Federal Record Center).

The left hand column gives you the National Archives Microfilm Number and then the description of what is on the film.

M-233 Register of Enlistments in the U.S. Army, 1798-1914

T-516 Index to Compiled Service Records of Revolutionary War Naval Personnel

M-694 Index to Compiled Service Records of Volunteer Soldiers Who Served From 1784-1811

T-316 Old War Index to Pension Files, 1815-1926

T-318 Index to Indian Wars Pension Files, 1892-1926

Indexes to Compiled Service Records of Volunteers from the state of:

War of 1812 . . . . .M-250 North Carolina   M-652 South Carolina

Florida War, 1835-1842 . . . . .M-245 Alabama   M-239 Louisiana

Creek War, 1813-1814 . . . . .M-244 Alabama

Cherokee Removal, 1836-39:
M-243 Alabama   M-907 Georgia   M-256 North Carolina
M-908 Tennessee

Patriot War, 1839:   M-630 Michigan

Mexican War: M-351 Mormon Organizations
                          T-317 Index to Mexican War Pension Files

Civil War, Union:
M-263 Alabama   M-540 Indiana   M-548 Nevada
M-532 Arizona Territory   M-541 Iowa   M-413 North Carolina
M-533 California   M-542 Kansas   M-552 Ohio
M-534 Colorado Territory   M-388 Maryland   M-553 Oregon
M-536 Dakota Territory   M-545 Michigan   M-554 Pennsylvania
M-537 Delaware   M-546 Minnesota   M-556 Utah
M-264 Florida   M-389 Mississippi   M-558 Washington
M-385 Georgia   M-390 Missouri   M-507 West Virginia
M-539 Illinois   M-547 Nebraska   M-559 Wiconsin

Civil War. Confederate:
M-374 Alabama   M-226 Georgia   M-380 Missouri
M-375 Arizona Territory   M-377 Kentucky   M-230 North Carolina
M-381 California   M-379 Maryland   M-231 Tennessee
M-225 Florida   M-232 Mississippi   M-382 Virginia

M-818 Index to Compiled Service Records of Confederate Soldiers Who Served In Organizations Raised Directly by the Confederate Government and of Confederate General and Staff Officers and Non-Regimental Enlisted

M-836 Confederate States Army Casualties: Lists and Narrative Reports

M-918 Register of Confederate Soldiers, Sailors, and Citizens who Died in Federal Prisons and Military Hospitals in the North

T-515 General Index to Compiled Military Service Records of Revolutionary War Soldiers

T-246 Revolutionary War Rolls, 1775-1783
(These are NOT compiled service records.)

The National Personnel Records Center

The National Personnel Records Center (NPRC), a branch of the National Archives and Records Service (NARS) is the official government repository for personnel records of former members of the U. S. military and former civilian employees of the government. The facility housing military records (MPR) is located at 9700 Page Boulevard, St. Louis, MO 63132.

The major mission of NPRC is to maintain and provide reference service on military and civilian personnel records. Requests for service pour in at the rate of 40,000 per week at MPR. Most requests pertain to proof of honorable military service in order to qualify individuals for a variety of benefits, for academic records, for individual medical files and for a variety of other purposes, both individual and organizational. These requests come mainly from the veterans themselves and their survivors, or from the VA, in order to provide educational, medical, housing and other benefits to veterans. They also come from other government agencies, potential employers, funeral directors, and police and courts. In addition to requests regarding individual files, the center also receives and responds to requests for historical information from a variety of researchers.

The enormous holdings of NPRC may sometimes be overwhelming to the uninitiated. MPR maintains almost 13 million Army personnel jackets, over four million Air Force jackets, well over 22 million Navy personnel and medical folders, approximately three million Marine Corps personnel and medical records, and over 600,000 Coast Guard folders. These 43 million official personnel records occupy more than one million cubic feet of shelf space. The records are arranged according to a computer registry number system, essentially by date of arrival in the building. The only exceptions are pre-1963 Navy personnel and medical records, which are arranged by time period and thereunder alphabetically. Almost all the folders consist of paper records; only in the last few years have certain branches of the military begun to send in records of discharged personnel on microfiche. All military records at NPRC remain in the legal custody of the branches of service, even though they are in the physical custody of the records center.

Military organizational records comprise the majority of other holdings of the Military Records Center. There are two types of organizational records. The first consists of personnel-related records such as academic records, clinical records, orders relating to individual military personnel. The second contains material on military organizations, mainly Army and Air Force field command records from the 1950s, and includes historical files, operations and planning records, budget files, publications, and the like. These records contain some material of historical value, which is currently being appraised and gradually transferred to the National Archives in Washington and opened for research.

The records center gained national attention in July 1973 when it was devastated by a tragic fire which destroyed approximately 16 million personnel records and damaged countless more. Army personnel records from 1912 to 1959 were almost totally ruined as were half the Air Force's holdings of personnel records. The center made a remarkable recovery, initiating new methods in the treatment of water-damaged records and setting up a Records Reconstruction Branch to rebuild individual personnel folders from Veterans Administration (VA) holdings, state veterans' records, Army morning reports, pay records, and similar material. The center has survived the ravages of the fire and continues to provide excellent reference service.

The records center also provides genealogical information to requesters, although this service is of low priority, especially in times of reduced work force and declining budgets. In addition, the Freedom of information Act and the Privacy Act limit the data that may be released to the general public with the veteran's authorization. The information that can be given out includes name, date of birth, duty assignments, decorations and awards, rank and grade, education, and dependents.

The primary concerns of NPRC are records maintenance and reference service. The highest priority is given those requests relating to the providing of benefits to veterans. The records center continues to serve those who have served our country.

(For information on how to use the Center, see Special Form in Federal Forms)

Data Necessary To Start The Reconstruction Process

Of course, the key to reconstructing military data is to get enough specific information from the veteran to allow our Center personnel to search the available alternate sources. The information normally required is:

1) full name used during service,
2) branch of service,
3) approximate dates of service,
4) service number,
5) place of discharge,
6) last unit of assignment, and
7) place of entry into service.

(For information on how to use the Center, see Special Form in Federal Forms)

State Adjutant Generals

In many states military records, like all other records, may have been transferred from the military to the appropraite record keeping agency or archives. Sometimes these records will move back and forth depending on who is in the Governor's seat. These records will therefore be in one of two places; 1) In some state records repository which may vary from state to state or, 2) write the military archivist in care of the Adjutant General's Office listed below:

Adjutant Generals Offices

The Adjutant General
P.O. Box 1311
64 N. Union Street
Montgomery, Alabama 36102

The Adjutant General,
Pouch 7-1914
Anchorage, Alaska 99501

The Adjutant General
747 W. Van Buren Street
Phoenix, Arizona 85007

The Adjutant General
P.O. Box 678
Little Rock, Arkansas 72203

The Adjutant General
P.O. Box 214334
2520 Marconi Avenue
Sacramento, California 95821

The Adjutant General
300 Logan Street
Denver, Colorado 80203

The Adjutant General
State Armory
Hartford, Connecticut 06106

The Adjutant General,
State Armory
Wilmington, Delaware 19899

The Adjutant General
District of Columbia
National Guard Armory
Washington, D. C., 20003

The Adjutant General
State Arsenal
St. Augustine, Florida 32084

The Adjutant General
959 E.Confederate Avenue SE
Atlanta, Georgia 30312

The Adjutant General
Fort Ruger
Oahu, Hawaii 96816

The Adjutant General
P.O. Box 1098
Boise, Idaho 83701

The Adjutant General
State Armory
Springfield, Illinois 62706

The Adjutant General
Millitary Department of Indiana
Stout Field
Indianapolis, Indiana 46241

The Adjutant General
P.O. Box 616
Des Moines, Iowa 50303

The Adjutant General
State Capitol
Topeka, Kansas 66612

The Adjutant General
State Capitol
Frankfort, Kentucky 40601

The Adjutant General
Jackson Barracks
New Orleans, Louisiana 70140

The Adjutant General
Camp Keyes
Augusta, Maine 04330

The Adjutant General
Fifth Regiment Armory
Baltimore, Maryland 21201

The Adjutant General
905 Commonwealth Avenue
Boston Massachusetts 02215

The Adjutant General
P.O. Box 210
Lansing, Michigan 48901

The Adjutant General
State Capitol
Sts. Paul Minnesota 55101

The Adjutant General
P.O. Box 331
Jackson, Mississippi 39205

The Adjutant General
1717 Industrial Drive
Jefferson City, Missouri 65101

The Adjutant General
State Arsenal
Helena, Montana 59601

The Adjutant General
1300 Military Road
Lincoln, Nebraska 68308

The Adjutant General
P.O. Box 1120
Carson City, Nevada 89701

The Adjutant General
State Military Reservation
Concord, New Hampshire 03301

Chief of Staff
Armory
Trenton, New Jersey 08610

The Adjutant General
P.O. Box 4277

Santa Fe, New Mexico 87501

Chief of Staff to the Governor
Division of Military & Naval Affairs
112 State Street
Albany, New York 12207

The Adjutant General
Justice Building
Raleigh, North Carolina 27605

The Adjutant General
P.O. Box 1817
Bismarck, North Dakota 58501

The Adjutant General
Fort Hayes
Columbus, Ohio 43218

The Adjutant General
2205 N. Central
Oklahoma City, Oklahoma 73105

The Adjutant General
Military Department
State of Oregon
Salem, Oregon 97310

The Adjutant General
RFD #2
Annville, Pennsylvania 17003

The Adjutant General
P.O. Box 3786
San Juan, Puerto Rico 00904

The Adjutant General
1051 N. Main Street
Providence, Rhode Island 02904

The Adjutant General
235 Wade Hampton State Office Building
Columbia, South Carolina 29201

The Adjutant General
Camp Rapid
Rapid City, South Dakota 75504

The Adjutant General
National Guard Armory
Sidco Drive
Nashville, Tennessee 37203

The Adjutant General
West Austin Station
P.O. Box 5218
Austin, Texas 78703

The Adjutant General
P.O. Box 2691
Fort Douglas, Utah 84113

The Adjutant General
Camp Johnson
Winooski, Vermont 05404

The Adjutant General
State Office Building
Richmond, Virginia 23219

The Adjutant General
Camp Murray
Tacoma, Washington 98433

The Adjutant General
State House
Charleston, West Virginia 25305

The Adjutant General
P.O. Box 328
Madison Wisconsin 53701

The Adjutant General
P.O. Box 395
Cheyenne, Wyoming 82001

Draft Records

CIVIL WAR

Draft records for the Civil War are only available for the Northern Army. Soldiers were drafted from the congressional district in which they lived. His military record can be found in the National Archives by congressional district. To find the congressional district search the Congressional Directory of the Second Session of the 38th Congress. This is usually located in any federal Government Documents Depository found in most large universities. At least one university library is designated as such in each state.(See National & State Record Center Section.) Some states have as many as twelve centers.

WORLD WAR I

Registration for the WWI Draft did not include men already in active Military Service. Not everyone who served registered for the draft and, obviously, not everyone who registered served.

There were three registrations, June 1917 and June and September 1918, and approximately 24 million men registered.

A great deal of paper work was created by the system. The draft cards themselves and a limited amount of the other paper work are available. Some of the peripheral material has been destroyed. None of the draft cards, which are used heavily for genealogy, have been destroyed. They are all available in the Federal Archives & Records Center, 1557 St. Joseph Ave., East Point, GA 30044.

WORLD WAR II

Draft records for World War II are found in the Regional Federal Records Center (See State Gen. Rec. Centers to decide what region your ancestor's state is in). They are recorded according to the place of registration. If your ancestor registered in Jackson, Tenn., those records would be in the Federal Records Center in East Point, GA.

There are draft records for other wars but they are so sparce and inaccurate as to be of little value.

Veterans Administration

The Veterans Administration will help you locate post 1900 Veterans records under the following conditions:

The Veterans Administration advises us that an individual upon request may gain access to his records or to any information which is contained in the V.A. record system. The V.A. will not disclose any records to any person or agency except by written request of, or prior written consent of the individual to whom the records pertains.

Information of a genealogical nature when its disclosure will not be detrimental to the memory of the veteran and not prejudicial to the interests of any living person or to the interests of the Government may be released.

Any person desiring a copy or to review any records in the custody of the V.A. must make a written request to the V.A. Regional Office having custody of the records. When requesting information from the V.A. records system, the following identifying data should be furnished:

1. Veteran's full name
2. V.A. claim number
3. Social security number
4. Service number
5. Date entered service
6. Date of separation
7. Date of birth
8. Date of death
9. V.A. Insurance file number

Beneficiary Identification and Records Locator System

This application provides all V.A. stations with direct and rapid access to the veterans index and locator information and other related data. Critical requests are sent directly into the computer via teleprocessing lines and the responses are routed back to the stations within a few seconds.

Locating devise: C number plus Social Security number will enable the V.A. to locate the exact Service number.

If you have any question contact your nearest V.A. center.

Veterans Administration Centers

If the address and/or phone number listed below has changed for any Vet Center, please contact your local telephone operator or the nearest VA office.

ALABAMA

2145 Highland Ave., Suite 250
Birmingham 35205
(205)933-0500

ALASKA

550 West 8th Ave. Rm. 101
Anchorage 99501
(907)277-1501

515 7th Ave.
Room 230
Fairbanks 99701
(907)456-4238

905 Cook St.
P.O. Box 1883
Kenai 99611
(907)283-5205

Box 957 Mile ½ Knik Rd.
Wasilla 99687
(907)376-4318

ARIZONA

807 N. 3rd St.
Phoenix 85004
(602)261-4769

727 N. Swan
Tucson 85711
(602)323-3271

ARKANSAS

813 West 3rd St.
Little Rock 72201
(501)378-6395

CALIFORNIA

859 S. Harbor Blvd.
Anaheim 92805
(714)776-0161

1899 Clayton Rd.
Suite 140
Concord 94520
(415)680-4529

1340 Van Ness Ave.
Fresno 93721
(209)487-5660

251 W. 85th Place
Los Angeles 90003
(213)753-1391/2/3

2449 W. Beverly Blvd.
Montebello 90640
(213)728-9984/9999
(213)728-9966/7

18924 Roscoe Blvd.
Northridge 91335
(213)993-8862

616 16th St.
Oakland 94612
(415)763-3904

4954 Arlington Ave.
Riverside 92504
(213)993-8862

1520 State St., Suite 110
San Diego 92101
(714)235-9728

1708 Waller St.
San Francisco 94117
(415)386-6726/7/8

2989 Mission St.
San Francisco 94110
(415)824-5111/2

1648 W. Santa Clara St.
San Jose 95116
(408)258-5600

361 S. Monroe St., Suite 605
San Jose 95128
(408)249-1643

1406 Pacific Ave.
Venice 90291
(213)392-4124/5/6

COLORADO

875 W. Moneno Ave.
Colorado Springs 80905
(303)633-2902

1820 Gilpin St.
Denver 80218
(303)861-9281/7521

CONNECTICUT

370 Market St.
Hartford 06120
(203)278-1290

363 Whalley Ave.
New Haven 06510
(203)624-7234/0355

DELAWARE

Van Buren Medical Center
1411 N. Van Buren St.
Wilmington 19806
(302)571-8277

DISTRICT OF COLUMBIA

709 8th Street, S.E.
Washington 20003
(202)745-8401/8403

FLORIDA

400 N.E. Prospect Road
Ft. Lauderdale 33334
(305)563-2992/3

228 Pearl St.
Jacksonville 32202
(904)358-1232

2615 Biscayne Blvd.
Miami 33137
(305)573-8830/1/2

333 North Orange
Orlando 32801
(813)420-6151/6152

250 31st St., South
St. Petersburg 33712
(813)821-3344

1507 W. Sligh Ave.
Tampa 33610
(813)821-3355

GEORGIA

65 11th St., N.E.
Atlanta 30309
(404)881-7264

HAWAII

1370 Kapiolani Blvd.
Suite 201
Honolulu 96814
(808)546-3743

IDAHO

103 W. State St.
Boise 83702
(208)342-3612

ILLINOIS

547 W. Roosevelt Rd.
Chicago 60607
(312)829-4400

VA Medical Center/Lakeside
Chicago Heights 60304
(312)943-6600

155 South Oak Park Avenue
Oak Park 60302
(312)383-3225

605 N.E. Monroe Street
Peoria 61615
(309)671-7300/1

INDIANA

101 N. Kentucky Ave.
Evansville 47711
(812)425-6496

528 W. Berry St.
Fort Wayne 46802
(219)423-9456

811 Massachusetts Ave.
Indianapolis 46204
(317)269-2838

IOWA

3619 6th Avenue
Des Moines 50313
(515)284-6119/6120

706 Jackson
Sioux City 51101
(712)233-3200

KANSAS

310 S. Laura St.
Wichita 67211
(316)265-3260

KENTUCKY

249 West Short St.
Lexington 40507
(606)231-8387

821 S. 2nd St.
Louisville 40203
(502)589-1981

LOUISIANA

1529 N. Claiborne
New Orleans 70116
(504)943-8386

MAINE

96 Harlow St.
Bangor 04401
(207)947-3391/2

175 Lancaster St. Rm. 213
Portland 04101
(207)780-3584

MARYLAND

1420 W. Patapsco Ave.
Patapsco Plaza Shopping Ctr.
Baltimore 21230
(301)355-8592

1153 Mondawmin Concourse
Mondawmin Shopping Ctr.
Baltimore 21215
(301)728-8924

7 Elkton Commercial Plaza
Elkton 21921
(301)398-0171

8121 Georgia Ave.
Suite 500
Silver Spring 20910
(202)745-8400

MASSACHUSETTS

480 Tremont St.
Boston 02116
(617)451-0171/2/3

362 Washington St.
Brighton 02135
(617)783-1343/4

15 Bolton Place
Brockton 02401
(617)580-2720

1985 Main St.
Northgate Plaza
Springfield 01103
(413)737-5167

MICHIGAN

5514 Woodward Ave.
Detroit 48202
(313)871-3233

18411 W. Seven Mile Rd.
Detroit 48219
(313)535-3333/4

1940 Eastern, S.E.
Grand Rapids 49508

MINNESOTA

2480 University Ave.
St. Paul 55114
(612)644-4002/5601

MISSISSIPPI

522 North State St.
Jackson 39201
(601)353-4912

MISSOURI

3600 Broadway, Suite 19
Kansas City 6411
(816)753-1866/1974

2345 Pine St.
St. Louis 63103
(314)231-1260/1/2

MONTANA

2708 Montana Ave.
Billings 59101
(406)657-6071

NEBRASKA

1240 N. 10th St.
Lincoln 68508
(402)476-9736

5123 Levenworth Street
Omaha 68106
(402)553-2068

NEVADA

214 S. 8th St.
Las Vegas 89101
(702)385-2212/3

341 S. Arlington St.
Reno 89501
(702)323-1294

NEW HAMPSHIRE

14 Pearl St.
Manchester 03104
(603)668-7060

NEW JERSEY

626 Newark Ave.
Jersey City 07306
(201)656-6986/7484

601 Broad St.
Newark 07102
(201)622-6940

318 East State St.
Trenton 08608
(609)989-2260/1

NEW MEXICO

4603 4th St., N.W.
Albuquerque 87107
(505)345-8366/8877

211 West Mesa
Gallup 87301
(505)722-3821/2

NEW YORK

875 Central Ave.
West Mall Office Plaza
Albany 12206
(518)438-2505

226 E. Fordham Rd.
Rooms 216,217
Bronx 10458
(212)367-3500

165 Cadman Plaza, East
Brooklyn 11201
(212)330-2825

114 Elmwood Ave.
Buffalo 14201
(716)882-0505

166 W. 75th St.
Manhattan 10023
(212)944-2917

148-43 Hillside Ave.
Queens 11435
(212)658-6767/8

200 Hamilton Ave.
White Plains Mall
White Plains 10601
(914)684-0570

NORTH CAROLINA

#4 Market Square
Fayetteville 28301
(919)323-4908

NORTH DAKOTA

1300 S. 13½ St.
Fargo 58103
(701)237-0942

108 Burdick Expressway
Minot 58701
(701)852-0177

OHIO

31 E. 12th St., 4th Floor
Cincinnati 45202
(513)241-9420

11511 Lorain Ave.
Cleveland 44111
(216)671-8530/1/2

4959 N. High St.
Columbus 43214
(614)436-0300

438 Wayne Ave.
Dayton 45410
(513)461-9150

14206 Euclid Ave.
East Cleveland 44112
(216)451-3200

OKLAHOMA

4111 North Lincoln Blvd., #10
Oklahoma City 73105
(405)521-9308

1605 South Boulder
Tulsa 74119
(918)581-7105

OREGON

1247 Villard
Eugene 97403
(503)687-6918

2450 S.E. Belmont
Portland 97214
(503)231-1586

PENNSYLVANIA

127 State St.
Harrisburg 17101
(717)782-3954

4328 Old William Penn. Hwy.
Monroeville 15146
(412)372-8627/8

1107 Arch St.
Philadelphia 19107
(215)627-0238

5601 Broad St.
Philadelphia 19107
(215)627-0238

954 Penn. Ave.
Pittsburgh 15222
(412)765-1193

PUERTO RICO

Suite LC 8-A/9
Medical Center Plaza
La Rivera Rio Piedras
San Juan 00921
(809)783-8269

RHODE ISLAND

172 Pine St.
Pawtucket 02860
(401)728-9501

SOUTH CAROLINA

904 Pendleton St.
Greenville 29601
(803)271-2711

3366 Rivers Ave.
No. Charleston 29405
(803)747-8387

SOUTH DAKOTA

610 Kansas City St.
Rapid City 57701
(605)348-0077

100 W. 6th St., Suite 101
Sioux Falls 57102
(605)332-0856

TENNESSEE

1515 E. Magnolia Ave.
Suite 201
Knoxville 37917
(615)971-5866

Sterick Bldg.
8 North 3rd St.
Memphis 38103
(901)521-3506

TEXAS

500-A Lancaster-Kiest Ctr.
Dallas 75216
(214)371-0490

2121 Wyoming St.
El Paso 79903
(915)542-2851/2/3

Seminary South Office Bldg.
Suite 10
Fort Worth 76115
(817)921-3733

3121 San Jacinto St.
Suite 106
Houston 77004
(713)522-5354/5376

717 Corpus Christi
Laredo 78040
(512)723-4680

107 Lexington Ave.
San Antonio 78205
(512)229-4025

1916 Fredericksburg Rd.
San Antonio 78201
(512)229-4120

UTAH

216 E. 5th St., South
Salt Lake City 84102
(801)584-1294

VERMONT

75 Woodstockd Rd.
White River Junction 05001
(802)295-2908

RFD #652, *Tafts Corners*
Williston 05495
(802)878-3371

VIRGIN ISLANDS

Havensight Mall
St. Thomas 00802
(809)774-6674

VIRGINIA

7450½ Tidewater Dr.
Norfolk 23505
(804)587-1338

Gresham Court
1030 West Franklin St.
Richmond 23220
(804)355-8958

WASHINGTON

1322 E. Pike St.
Seattle 98122
(206)442-4706

North 1611 Division
Spokane 99208
(509)326-6970

3591 South D. St.
Tacoma 98408
(206)473-0731/2

WEST VIRGINIA

1014 6th Ave.
Huntington 25701
(304)523-8387

1191 Pineview Dr.
Morgantown 26505
(304)291-4001/2

WISCONSIN

147 South Butler St.
Madison 53703
(608)264-5342/3

3400 W. Wisconsin Ave.
Milwaukee 53202
(414)344-5504/5815

WYOMING

641 East Second St.
Casper 82601
(307)235-8010

1810 Pioneer St.
Cheyenne 82001
(307)788-2660

Confederate Records

A unique Confederate Records Repository is The Museum Of The Confederacy in Richmond, Virginia. Their records contain the following:

Official Records of the Union and Confederate Armies during the War of the Rebellion: "OR"
is a compilation of official reports and correspondence submitted by both armies during the war. The 128 volume collection is accessed by a two volume index. The "OR" may be used for tracing unit movements or individual's names in various rosters and reports.

Official Records of the Union and Confederate Navies during the War of the Rebellion:
is a 30 volume set which offers similar information for naval officers and sailors as found in the "OR".

Southern Historical Society Papers:
is a set of articles, memoirs, and parole lists, and rosters published by the Southern Historical Society. A 2 volume index provides access to the 52 volume set. As with the "OR", the "SHSP" may be used for tracing units and individual names.

Roll of Honor:
is a 345 volume set of bound application forms which were distributed among veterans and their families from the mid 1890's to the mid-1930's. Each form gives the applicant's name and unit; some give other data such as date of enlistment, parole date, date and place where wounds were received, imprisoned, or killed. A few even contain comments about the applicant's service experiences. The "RH" is indexed through the letter "S".

Other Important Confederate Repositories

1. The National Archives—have the largest single collection of Confederate Records.

2. Virginia Historical Society
   428 North Boulevard
   Richmond, VA 23221

3. Southern Historical Collection
   Manuscripts Dept.
   Louis Round Wilson Library
   Univeristy of North Carolina
   Chapel Hill, NC 27514

4. Confederate Research Center
   Hill Junior College
   Hillsboro, TX

How to Find Confederate Military And Pension Records

The following is a list of sources you can contact for information regarding Confederate Military and Pension Records.

CONFEDERATE STATES MILITARY SERVICE RECORDS (1861-1865)
Military Service Records (NNCC), National Archives (GSA), Washington, D.C. 20408. See Federal Order Forms Section, form GSA 6751.

CONFEDERATE STATES MILITARY SERVICE RECORDS INDEX (1861-1865)
The Latter-day Saint Temple Genealogical Library, 10471 West Santa Monica Blvd., West Los Angeles. The library has a military service records index for the Confederate states for the years 1861-1865. It is under microfilm series number M253.

CONFEDERATE VETERANS AND WIDOWS PENSIONS

Alabama State of Alabama Department of Archives & History, Montgomery, Alabama 36130

Arkansas	Arkansas History Commission, 300 West Markham Street, Little Rock, Arkansas 72201
Florida	Department of State, Division of Archives & History, The Capitol, Tallahassee, Florida 32304
Georgia	Georgia Department of Archives & History, Atlanta, Georgia 30334
Kentucky	Kentucky Historical Society, Old State House, P.O. Box H, Frankfort, Kentucky 40601
Louisiana	Secretary of State, Archives & Records Service, P.O. Box 44125, Capitol Station, Baton Rouge, Louisiana 70804
Mississippi	Mississippi Department of Archives & History, War Memorial Building, 120 North State Street, Jackson, Mississippi 39201
Missouri	Office of the Adjutant General, Headquarters Missouri National Guard, 1717 Industrial Ave., Jefferson City, Missouri 65101
North Carolina	North Carolina State Department of Archives & History, Raleigh, North Carolina 27601
Oklahoma	Archives Division, Oklahoma State Library, Okalhoma City, Oklahoma 73105
South Carolina	South Carolina Comptroller General's Office, Columbia, South Carolina 29201
Tennessee	Tennessee State Library & Archives, Nashville, Tennessee 37219
Texas	Texas State Library, Texas Archives & Library Building, Box 12927, Capitol Station, Austin, Texas 78711
Virginia	Virginia State Library, Archives Division, Richmond, Virginia 23219

Pension records are almost always more valuable genealogically than the military service records. You can order Confederate Military Service Records from the National Archives in Washington, D.C. Some state agencies also have them.

GOVERNMENT INDEXES

For one reason or another many service men did not receive a pension from the regular Federal, State or Colonial sources and therefore applied directly to congress for relief. Because of this, their records are not found in the National Archives. Instead the congressional pensions are in special indexes (listed below) and are available in most Federal Government Document Depositories (for listing see pp. ____).

If for example you were looking for pension records of an ancestor who fought in the Revolutionary War you would search the first five indexes.

Government Indexes

1.	Poore's	1775-1881
2.	CIS	1789-1857
3.	Greely	1789-1817
4.	Checklist	1789-1909
5.	Tables of and Annotated Index	1789-1893
6.	Ames	1881-1893
7.	Document Catalog	1893-1940
8.	Document Index	1895-1933
9.	Numerical Lists	1933-Present

10. Price Lists	1893-Present
11. Monthly Catalog	1895-Present
12. Congressional Index	1937-Present
13. Pierce's Register	1775-1782

Pierce's Register

The pay records (certificates) of every person who served in the Continental Army (except those from South Carolina, who paid their own) (and those who served in state militas), are found in *Pierce's Register*. John Pierce was Paymaster General and Commissioner of Army Accounts in 1783. The Register is available in most large public libraries.

One of the finest sources of military information is the:

United States Army Military History Institute
Carlisle Barracks, Pennsylvania 17013

The Military History Institute collects, preserves, and provides to researchers source materials of American military history. The Institute is housed in Upton Hall. Upton Hall became the home for the U.S. Army Military History Research Collection in July 1967. The Research Collection, renamed the Military History Institute in April 1977, holds more than one million cataloged items relating to military history. No other agency has as extensive a collection of materials relating exclusively to the role of the military in the development of the United States.

The nucleus of the Institute's holdings came from three sources: The U.S. Army War College, the National War College, and the U.S. Army Command and General Staff College. These three schools collectively transferred more than 120,000 volumnes to the Institute. Some of these books date from the fifteenth century and provide the historical background from which the American Army came.

The Military History Institute receives books and periodicals from libraries throughout the Army as well as from many individual donors. In addition to purely military matters, these volumes include coverage of many allied fields, such as: law, science and technology, sociology, medicine, religion, exploration, economics, geography, and political science. Many relate to military and diplomatic affairs of foreign nations, for the military history of the United States has been closely intertwined with that of other nations.

Original source materials are a vital part of the Military History Institute's holdings. Diaries, letters, photographs, art work, and personal records provide intimate insights to the past. The Institute's holdings include the original handwritten manuscript of Upton's *Military Policy of the United States;* the personal papers of numerous prominent generals, and the papers of thousands of junior officers and enlisted men and women whose services contributed to American Military History from the colonial period to the present.

The Institute has over 300,000 volumes; 60,000 periodicals; 500,000 photographs; 40,000 audio/visual items; 75,000 military artifacts; 3,000,000 personal manuscripts, diaries and letters; and about 100,000 classified and unclassified documents.

The institute cannot conduct extensive research for scholars but will gladly provide research and reference assistance. This assistance includes explanation of the various finding aids, reference help both in person at the Institute and via correspondence, and assistance in locating material.

a. **Circulation.** The U.S. Army Military History Institute is not a circulating library. Books and other items may not be withdrawn by individuals other than members of the Carlisle Barracks community.

b. **Interlibrary Loans.** Published books may be borrowed through interlibrary loan.

John J. Slonaker, Chief of the historical reference branch at the Military Institute states that many genealogical researchers have found our sources on American wars particularly helpful. For example, available here are published regimental histories and state adjutant general reports that include unit rosters and provide some personal data on soldiers. Also useful are country and state histories and a few reprinted pension lists. If the researcher has the time, he or she may find nuggets of information in our large periodical collection and in such standard military publication as U.S. War Department *Special Orders* and annual *Army Registers*.

There are 10,000 boxes of personal papers in the archives. Expecially noteworthy in the archives are the letters and diaries of Civil War soldiers and similar material collected through our Spanish-American war, Philippine Insurrection and World War I veterans surveys. Also there are 400,000 photographic stills and colections of 20th century motion picture film and audio tape.

A visit to this fine facility is suggested for the Serious genealogy researcher. Hours of Operation: 8:00 a.m. to 4:30 p.m. (Except Federal holidays). Inquiries concerning the Military History Institue, its holdings and use of its facilities should be sent to: U.S. Army Military History Institute, Carlisle Barrack, PA 17013, Telephone (717)245-3611; AUTOVON 242-3611.

Special Bibliographic Series
U.S. Army Military History Institute
Carlisle Barracks, Pennsylvania 17013

This series consists of some twenty-one subject bibliographies relating solely to collections of materials held at the USAMHI.

These items are available for sale from the Superintendent of Documents, US Government Printing Office, Washington, D.C. 20402; price and stock numbers are indicated. GPO Prices subject to change.

** These items are available for sale from the AG Publication Center; order by CMH Pub Number.

* These items are out of stock. Loan copies are available from repository libraries or the US Army Military History Institute through the interlibrary loan program.
Unmarked items are available from the US Army Military History Institute.

1. *The US Army and Domestic Disturbances* (w/1 Supplement) by John Slonaker. (1970, 66 pp.).
2. *The US Army and the Negro* (w/2 Supplements) by John Slonaker. (1971, 102 pp.).
*3. *Language Dictionaries with an Emphasis on Military Dictionaries* by Barbara Wrinkle. (1971, 83 pp.).
#4. *US Army Unit Histories*, Vol. I (Revised), by George S. Pappas, Elizabeth Snoke, and Alexandra Campbell. (1978, 197 pp.), GPO Stock No. 008-029-00104-7. Price $4.00.
4. *US Army Unit Histories*, Vol. II (Revised), by George S. Pappas, Elizabeth Snoke, and Alexandra Campbell. (1978, 431 pp.).
5. *The Volunteer Army* by John Slonaker. (1972, 98 pp.).
6. *Manuscript Holdings of the US Army Military History Research Collection*, Vol I, by Richard J. Sommers. (1972, 168 pp.).
6. *Manuscript Holdings of the US Army Military History Research Collection*, Vol II, by Richard J. Sommers. (1975, 260 pp.).
6. (Vol. III, to be published).
7. *The Mexican War*, by Elizabeth Snoke, (1973, 107 pp.).

*8. *A Suggested Guide to the Curricular Archives of the US Army War College, 1907-1940*, by Benjamin Franklin Cooling. (1973, 95 pp.). Will be reprinted and available through AG Pub. Center.

*9. *The US Army and the Spanish-American War Era, 1895-1910.* Vol. I, by Thomas Kelly III. 1974, 151 pp.). Will be reprinted and available through AG Pub. Center.

*9. *The US Army and the Spanish-American War Era, 1895-1919,* Vol. II, by Thomas Kelly III. (1974, 56 pp.).

10. *Pennsylvania Military History* by John B. B. Trussell, Jr. (1975, 91 pp.).

**11. *Era of the Civil War, 1820-1876,* By Louise Arnold (Revised) (1982, 704 pp.). (CMH Pub. 102-3).

12. *The Armies of Austria-Hungary and Germany, 1740-1914,* Vol. I, by Laszlo M. Alfoldi. (1975, 277 pp.).

13. *Oral History/Audio Archives,* Vol. I, by Roy Barnard. (1976, 99 pp.).

*13. *Oral History/Audio Archives,* Vol. II, by Roy Barnard. (1977, 69 pp.). GPO Stock No. 008-029-00100-4. Price: $2.40.

14. *Colonial America and the War for Independence,* by Joyce Eakin. (1976, 301 pp.).

15. *Military Forces of France,* by John Cornelius. (1977, 287 pp.).

16. World War II, Vol I (General Histories), by Roy Barnard, Duane Ryan and William Burns. (1977, 185 pp.).

#16. *World War II,* Vol. II (Pacific War), by Duane Ryan. (1978, 81 pp.), GPO Stock No. 008-029-00103-9. Price: $2.50.

*16. *World War II,* Vol. III (Eastern and Balkan Fronts), by Laszlo M. Alfoldi. (1978, 196 pp.). Will be reprinted and available through AG Pub Center.

*16. *World War II,* Vol. IV (Western Europe-Meditteranean), by Louise Arnold. (1979, 299 pp.). Will be reprinted and available through AG Pub. Center.

17. *The United States Army and the Indian Wars in the Trans-Mississippi West, 1860-1898,* by Bruce Reber. (1978, 186 pp.).

#18. *God Save the Queen — A Bibliography of the British and Commonwealth Holdings* by Lawrence Lentz. (Undated, GPO Stock No. 008-029-00110-1. Price: $5.25.).

19. *Audio Visual Archives.*
   **Vol I (Phonodisc Collection), by Robert C. Boots and Thomas Allen. (1981, 381 pp.). CMH Pub 102-4.*
   Vol II (Tape Library). To be published; will be available through the AG Pub. Center.
   Vol. III (Films). To be published; will be available through AG Pub. Center.

20. *Special Collections,* Vol. I, by Michael Winey and Randy Hackenburg. To be published; will be available through AG Pub. Center.

21. *Master List of Periodicals,* by Mathilde Carter. To be published; will be available through AG Pub. Center.

**Special Publications Series
US Army Military History Institute
Carlisle Barracks, Pennsylvania 17013**

** *Combined Operations in Peace and War,* by John Hixson and Benjamin Franklin Cooling. (1982 Revised edition, 434 pp., maps, charts, appendices, bibliography.) CMH Pub 102-2.
A study oif operations by military coalitions during peace and war in the Twentieth Century.
Essays in Some Dimensions of Military History, 5 volumes, Benjamin

Franklin Cooling and Don Rickey, editors. (1972-1977, 778 pp. total)

Anthology of lectures by prominent military historians delivered to Army War College seminars in miliotary history.

The Consequences of Defeat (tentative title):

Proceedings of the 1982 International Military History Symposium, Carlisle Barracks, Pennsylvania, 1-4 August 1982. Charles R. Shrader, editor (1983). To be published during FY 1983; available through AG Pub. Center.

Lectures and discussion by international scholars concerning the impact on military institutions of unsuccessful campaigns, 1860-1980.

Vignettes of Military History. Richard J. Sommers, editor.

\# Vol. I (1976, 60 pp.). GPO Stock No. 008-029-0096-2 Price $4.50
\# Vol. II (1978, 76 pp.). GPO Stock No. 008-029-00108-0. Price $4.75.
** Vol. III (1982, 95 pp). CMH Pub 102-1.

"Slices of Life" and other sketches of topics in American Military History; written principally by Military History institute staff, and Army War College students and faculty.

Bibliography of Published Military Sources

Adams, James N. *Index to the Transactions of the Illinois State Historical Society and Other Publications.* Springfield: Ill. State Historical Library, 1953.

Adams, James N. *General Index to Journal of the Illinois State Historical Society, Vols. I to XXV, April 1908 to Janurary 1933.* Springfield. State of Illinois.

Ainsworth, Mary Bouvier. "Recently Discovered Records Relating to Revolutionary War Veterans Who Applied for Pensions under the Act of 1792." *National Genealogical Society Quarterly* 46, (March and June 1958).

Beers, Henry P. *Guide to the Archives of the Government of the Confederate States of America.* National Archives Pub. No. 68-15. Washington: GSA, 1968.

Bodge, George Madison. *Soldiers in King Philip's War, 3rd Ed.* Baltimore: The Genealogical Publishing Company, 1967.

Cift, Garrett Glenn. *List of Officers of the Illinois Regiment, and of Crockett's Regiment Who Have Received Land for Their Services.* Frankfort, Ill.: SAR, 1962.

Colket, Meredith B., Jr. and Frank E. Bridgers. *Guide to Genealogical Records in the National Archives,* Washington, D.C.: The National Archives, 1964.

Confederate Veteran Magazine Index, Vols. I-XL. Dayton, Ohio: Morningside Bookshop, 1972.

Critz, Lalla Campbell, ed. "Bibliography of the American Revolution," *Magazine of Bibliographies,* Vol. 1, No. 4, 1973.

Cullum, George. *Biographical Register of the Officers and Graduates of the U.S. Military Academy at West Pont, N.Y.,* 9 vols. Boston: Houghton, Mifflin, & Co., 1891.

Cunningham, S. A. *The Confederate Veteran,* Vols. 1-40. Nashville, Tenn., 1893-1932.

Doane, Gilbert H. *Searching for Your Ancestors.* Minneapolis: Univ. of Minnesota Press, 1960.

Dornbusch, Charles E. *Military Bibliography of the Civil War.* 3 vols. New York: The New York Public Library, 1961-1072.

Dyer, Frederick H. *A Compendium of the War of the Rebellion.* Des Moines, Iowa: Dyer Publishing Co., 1908 (reprint), 3 vols. New York: Thomas Yoseloff, 1959.

Eby, Cecil. *That Disgraceful Affair of the Black Hawk War.* New York: W. W. Norton Co., 1973.

Evans, Clement A. *Confederate Military History,* 12 vols. Atlanta, Ga.: Confederate Publishing Company, 1899.

Foster, Olive S. and Hempstead, Mary C. *The Revolutionary War Period, 1763-1787 in Publications of the Illinois State Historical Library and Society.* Springfield, Illinois, Bicentennial Committee, 1973.

Gambrill, Georgia. *Genealogical Materials and Local Histories in the St. Louis Public Library.* St. Louis Public Library, 1965.

Greenwood, Val D. *The Researchers' Guide to American Genealogy.* Baltimore: The Genealogical Publishing Company, Inc., 1973.

Groene, Bertram Hawthorne. *Tracing Your Civil War Ancestors.* Winston-Salem, N.C.: John F. Blair Pub., 1973.

Hamersly, Lewis R. & Co. Publisher. *Records of Lviing Officers of the U.S. Army. Philadelphia, 1884.*

Hamersly, Thomas H. S. Complete Regular Army Register of the U.S.: For 100 Years (1779-1879). Washington: Thomas H. S. Hamersly Co., 1880.

Heitman, Francis. *Historical Register of Officers of the Continental Army.* 2nd ed. Baltimore: The Genealogical Publishing Company, 1967.

Heitman, Francis B. *Historical Register & Dictionary of the U.S. Army from Its Organization, Sept. 29, 1789 to March 2, 1903.* Washington: Gov't Printing Office, 1903. (Reprint Urbana, Ill.: Univ. of Illinois Press, 1965.

House, Charles J. *Names of Soldiers of the American Revolution Who Applied for State Bounty under Resolves of March 17, 1835, March 24, 1836, as Appears of Records in the Land Office.* Baltimore: Genealogical Pub. Co., 1967.

Howard, Robert P. Illinois, *A History of the Prairie State.* Grand Rapids, Mich.: Wm. B. Erdman's Publishing Company, 1972.

Hoyt, Max Ellsworth. *Index of Revolutionary War Pension Applications.* Washington, D.C.: The National Genealogical Society, 1966.

Kaminkow, Marion and Jack. *Mariners of the American Revolution.* Baltimore: Magna Carta Book Company, 1967.

Kirkham, E. Kay. *Some of the Military Records of America.* Salt Lake City: Deseret Book Company, 1964.

Meyer, Virginia M. *Roster of Revolutionary War Soldiers and Widows Who Lived in Illinois Counties.* Chicago: Illinois D.A.R., 1962.

Munden, Kenneth W. and Beers, Henry P. *Guide to Federal Archives Relating to the Civil War.* National Archives Pub. No. 63-1. Washington: G.S.A., 1962.

Nevins, Allan: Robertson, James I., Jr.: and Wiley, Bell I. *Civil War Boks—A Critical Bibliography,* 2 vols. Baton Rouge: La. State Univ. Press, 1967.

Official Army Register for 1861-1865. Washington: U.S. Adj. Gen. Off. 1861-1865.

Official Army Register of the Volunteer Force of the U.S. Army for the Years 1861-1865. Washington: U.S. Adjutant General's Office, 1861-1865.

Peterson, Clearence Stewart. *Known Military Dead During the American Revolutionary War 1775-1783.* Baltimore: The Genealogical Publishing Company, 1967.

Powell, William Henry. *List of Officers of the Army of the United States from 1779-1900.* Detroit: Gale Research Company, 1967.

Reece, J. N. *Report of the Adjutant General of the State of Illinois.* Vols. 1-9. Springfield: Phillips Brothers, 1900-1902.

St. Louis Public Library. *Genealogical Materials and Local Histories in the St. Louis Public Library, First Supplement.* St. Louis: St. Louis Pub. Lib., 1971.

Smith, Cynthia H. *Cumulative Index Journal of the Illinois State Historical Society, Vols. LI thru LX, Spring 1958 I Winter 1967.* Springfield: Ill. State Historical Library, 1971.

Smith, James B. *Adjutant General's Report Containing the Complete Muster-Out Rolls of the Illinois Volunteers Who Served in the Spanish-American War 1898-1899.* Springfield: Phillips Brothers, 1802, Vols. 1-4.

Smith, Myron J. *American Civil War Names: A Bibliography.* Metuchen, New Jersey: The Scarecrow Press, 1972.

Stevens, Frank E. "Illinois in the War of 1812-1814," *Transactions of the Illinois State Historical Society for the Year 1904.* No. 9. Springfield: Phillips Brothers, 1904.

Sylvester, H. M. *Indian Wars of New England.* 1910.

Thwaites, R. G. and Kellogg, L. P., eds. *Frontier Defense on the Upper Ohio 1777-1778.* 1912.

U.S. Bureau of Census. *A Census of Pensioners for Revolutionary of Military Services.* Baltimore: The Genealogical Publishing Company, 1967.

U.S. Congress House. *Digested Summary and Alphabetical List of Private Claims.* Baltimore: The Genealogical Publishing Company, 1970.

U.S. War Department. *Official Records of the Union and Confederate Armies in the War of the Rebellion,* 128 vols. Washington: U.S. Gov't Printing Office, 1901.

U.S. War Department. *Official Records of the Union and Confederate Navies in the War of the Rebellion,* 31 vols. Washington: U.S. Gov't Printing Off., 1897-1927.

Walker, Harriet J. *Revolutionary Soldiers Buried in Illinois.* Reprint. Baltimore: Genealogical Publishing Company, 1967.

Walker, Homer A. *Illinois Pensioners Lists of the Revolution, 1812, and Indian Wars.* Washington, D.C., 1955.

Walker, James D. *U.S. Military Service and Pension Records Housed at the National Archives.* Salt Lake City: The Genealogical Society, 1969.

Whitney, Ellen M. *The Black Hawk War. Vol. I, Illinois Volunteers.* Springfield: Illinois State Historical Library, 1970.

Williams, Ethel W. *Know Your Ancestors, A Guide to Genealogical Research.* Rutland, Vermont: Charles E. Tuttle Company, 1960.

Wright, Norman E. *Building an American Pedigree.* Provo, Utah: Brigham Young University Press, 1974.

Service and Maritime Academies

West Point, New York — 1802 — U.S. Military Academy — 10996

Annapolis, Maryland — 1845 — U.S. Naval Academy

U.S.A.F. Academy, Colorado — 1954 — U.S. Air Force Academy 80840

New London, Connecticut — 1876 — U.S. Coast Guard Academy — 06320

Kings Point, New York — 1938 — U.S. Merchant Marine Academy — 11024

Massachusetts Maritime Academy — 1891
(Formerly)
Massachusetts Nautical Training School
Buzzards Bay, Massachusetts 02532

Martime College or New York State — 1874
Fort Schuyler
Bronx, New York 10465

California Maritime Academy — 1929
(Formerly)
California Nautical School
P.O. Box 1392
Vallejo, California 94590

Texas Maritime Academy — 1962
Moody College of Marine Sceience
and Maritime Resources
Galveston, TX 77550

Marine Maritime Academy — 1941
Castine, Maine 04421

Great Lakes Maritime Academy — 1965
Northwestern Michigan College
1701 East Front Street
Traverse City, Michigan 49684

"Those Who Served"
(Source) Veterans Administration

American Revolution (1775-1784)
    Participants . . . 290,000 Deaths in Service . . . 4,000
    Last Veteran, Daniel F. Blakeman, died 5 May 1869, age 109
    Last Widow, Catherine S. Damon, died 1 November 1906, age 92
    Last Dependent, Phoebe M. Palmeter, died 25 April 1911, age 90

War of 1812 (1812-1815)
    Participants . . . 287,000 Deaths in Service . . . 2,000
    Last Veteran, Hiram Cronk, died 13 May 1905, age 105
    Last Widow, Carolina King, died 28 June 1936, age ?
    Last Dependent, Esther A. H. Morgan, died 12 March 1946, age 89

Mexican War (1846-1848)
    Participants . . . 79,000 Deaths in Service . . . 13,000
    Last Veteran, Owen Thomas Edgar, died 3 Spetember 1929, age 98
    Last Widow, Lena James Theobald, died 20 June 1963, age 89
    Last Dependent, Jesse G. Bivens, died 1 November 1962, age 94

Indian Wars (Approximately 1817-1898)
    Participants . . . 106,000 Deaths in Service . . . 1,000
    Last Veteran, Frederick Fraske, died 18 June 1973, age 101

Spanish Amnerican War (1898-1902)
    Participants . . . 392,000 Deaths in Service . . . 11,000
    Living Veterans in 1981 . . . 296

Civil War (1861-1865)
Participants . . . (Union) 2,213,000 (Confederate) 1,000,000
Deaths in Service . . . (Union) 364,000 (Confederate) 133,821 (Total) 597,821
Last Union Veteran, Albert Woolson, died 2 August 1956, age 109
LastConfederate Veteran, Walter W. Williams, died 19 December 1959, age 117

World War I (1917-1918)
Participants . . . 4,744,000 Deaths in Service . . . 116,000
Living Veterans in 1981 . . . 667,000

World War II (1940-1947)
Participants . . . 16,535,000 Deaths in Service . . . 406,000
Living Veterans in 1981 . . . 12,902,000

Korean Conflict (1950-1955)
Participants . . . 6,807,000 Deaths in Service 55,000
Living Veterans in 1981 . . . 5,897,000

Vietnam Era (1964-1975)
Participants . . . 9,834,000 Deaths in Service (Hostile Action) 47,000
(Other Causes) 62,000
Living Veterans in 1981 . . . 8,734,000

National Cemeteries

Cemeteries marked * are still active and accepting interments. Cemeteries marked ** were at press time still under construction and not ready to accept interments. Cemeteries marked *** will accept only cremated remains.

Alabama
** Fort Mitchell National Cemetery
Phenix City, AL

Mobile National Cemetery
1202 Virginia Street
Mobile, AL 36604
(205) 690-2858

Alaska
* Sitka National Cemetery
P.O. Box 1965
Sitka, AK 99835
(907) 747-3263

Arizona
Prescott National Cemetery
VA Medical Center
Prescott, AZ 86313
(602) 455-4860, Ext. 280

Arkansas
* Fayetteville National Cemetery
700 Government Ave.
Fayetteville, AR 72701
(501) 433-4301, Ext. 584

* Fort Smith National Cemetery
522 Garland Ave. at S. 6th St.
Fort Smith 72901
(501) 783-5345

Little Rock National Cemetery
2523 Confederate Boulevard
Little Rock, AR 72206
(501) 374-8011

California
Fort Rosecrans National Cemetery
Pont Loma, P.O. Box 6237
San Diego, CA 92106
(714) 225-7447

Golden Gate National Cemetery
1300 Sneath Lane
San Bruno, CA 94066
(415) 589-7737

Los Angeles National Cemetery
950 S. Sepulveda Boulevard
Los Angeles, CA 90049
(213) 824-4311, Ext. 5264

* Riverside National Cemetery
22495 Van Buren Boulevard
Riverside, CA 92508
(714) 653-8417 or 8418

San Francisco National Cemetery
P.O. Box 29012
Presidio of San Francisco
San Francisco, CA 94129
(415) 561-2008 or 2986

Colorado
* Fort Logan National Cemetery
3698 S. Sheridan Boulevard
Denver, CO 80235

(303) 761-0117

* Fort Lyon National Cemetery
VA Medical Center
For Lyon, CO 81038
(303) 456-1260, Ext. 231

Florida
* Barrancas National Cemetery
Naval Air Station
Pensacola, FL 32508
(904) 452-3357 or 4196

Bay Pines National Cemetery
VA Medical Center
Bay Pines, FL 33504
(813) 391-9644, Ext. 541

St. Augustine National Cemetery
104 Marine Street
St. Augustine, FL 32084
(904) 829-2661

Georgia
Marietta National Cemetery
500 Washington Avenue
Marietta, GA 30060
(404) 428-5631

Hawaii
* National Memorial Cemetery
  of the Pacific
2177 Puowaina Drive
Honolulu, HI 96813
(808) 546-3190

Illinois
Alton National Cemetery
600 Pearl St.
Alton, IL 62003
(618) 465-8553

* Camp Butler National Cemetery
R.F.D. #1
Springfield, IL 62707
(217) 522-5764

* Danville National Cemetery
1900 East Main St.
Danville, IL 61832
(217) 442-8000, Ext. 391

* Mound City National Cemetery
Junction-Highway 37 & 51
Mound City, IL 62963
(618) 748-9343

* Quincy National Cemetery
36th & Maine Street
Quincy, IL
(Call Keokuk National Cemetery,
  Keokuk, Iowa, for information)

Indiana
Crown Hill National Cemetery
3402 Boulevard Place
Indianapolis, IN 46208
(317) 925-8231

* Marion National Cemetery
VA Medical Center
Marion, IN 46952
(317) 674-3321, Ext. 392

New Albany National Cemetery
1943 Ekin Avenue
New Albany, IN 47150
(812) 288-3385

Iowa
* Keokuk National Cemetery
18th & Ridge Streets
Keokuk, IA 52632
(319) 524-1304

Kansas
* Fort Leavenworth National Cemetery
Fort Leavenworth, KS 66027
(913) 684-5451 or 5452

* Fort Scott National Cemetery
P.O. Box 917
Fort Scott, KS 66701
(316) 223-2840

* Leavenworth National Cemetery
VA Medical Center
Leavenworth, KS
(Call Fort Leavenworth National
  Cemetery, Kansas, for information)

Kentucky
* Camp Nelson National Cemetery
R.R. No. 3
Nicholasville, KY 40356
(606) 885-5727

Cave Hill National Cemetery
701 Baxter Avenue
Louisville, KY
(Call Zachary Taylor National
  Cemetery, Kentucky, for information)

Danville National Cemetery
377 North First Street
Danville, KY
(Call Camp Nelson National Cemetery,
  Kentucky, for information)

* Lebanon National Cemetery
Lebanon, KY 40033
(502) 692-3390

Lexington National Cemetery
833 West Main Street
Lexington, KY
(Call Camp Nelson National Cemetery,
  Kentucky, for information)

* Mill Springs National Cemetery
Rural Route #1
Nancy, KY 42544
(606) 636-6470

Zachary Taylor National Cemetery
4701 Brownsboro Road
Louisville, KY 40207
(502) 893-3852

Louisiana
* Alexandria National Cemetery
209 Shamrock Avenue
Pineville, LA 71360
(318) 442-5029

Baton Rouge National Cemetery
220 North 19th Street
Baton Rouge, LA 70806
(504) 389-0323

* Port Hudson National Cemetery
Route No. 1, Box 185
Zachary, LA 70791
(504) 654-4757

Maine
Togus National Cemetery
VA Medical and Regional Office Center
Togus, ME 04330
(207) 623-8411

Maryland
Annapolis National Cemetery
800 West Street
Annapolis, MD 21401
(301) 269-1224

Baltimore National Cemetery
5501 Frederick Avenue
Baltimore, MD 21228
(301) 644-9696 or 9697

Loudon Park National Cemetery
3445 Frederick Avenue
Baltimore, MD
(Call Baltimore Nationl Cemetery,
   Maryland, for information)

Massachusetts
* Massachusetts National Cemetery
Bourne, MA 02532
(617) 563-7113

Michigan
* Fort Custer National Cemetery
Battle Creek, MI

Minnesota
* Fort Snelling National Cemetery
7601 34th Avenue South
Minneapolis, MN 55450
(612) 726-1127 or 1128

Mississippi
* Biloxi National Cemetery
VA Medical Center
Biloxi, MS 39531
(601) 388-5541

* Corinth National Cemetery
1551 Horton Street
Corinth, MS 38834
(601) 286-5782

* Natchez National Cemetery
61 Cemetery Road
Natchez, MS 39120
(601) 445-4981

Missouri
* Jefferson Barracks National Cemetery
101 Memorial Drive
St. Louis, MO 63125
(314) 263-8691 or 8692

Jefferson City National Cemetery
1024 East McCarty Street
Jefferson City, MO 65101
(314) 636-6404

* Springfield National Cemetery
1702 East Seminole Street
Springfield, MO 65804
(417) 881-9499

Nebraska
* Fort McPherson National Cemetery
Maxwell, NE 69151
(308) 582-4433

New Jersey
Beverly National Cemetery
Beverly, NJ 08010
(609) 877-5460

Finn's Point National Cemetery
R.F.D. No. 3, Fort Mott Road
Salem, NJ 08079
(609) 935-3628

New Mexico
* Fort Bayard National Cemetery
Fort Bayard, NM 88036
(505) 537-3686

* Santa Fe National Cemetery
P.O. Box 88
Santa Fe, NM 87501
(505) 988-6400

New York
* Bath National Cemetery
VA Medical Center
Bath, NY 14810
(607) 776-2111, Ext. 293

* Calverton National Cemetery
Route 25
P.O. Box 144
Calverton, NY 11933
(516) 727-5410 or 5412

Cypress Hills National Cemetery
625 Jamaica Avenue
Brooklyn, NY 11208
(212) 277-7145

Long Island National Cemetery
Farmingdale, L.I. NY 11735
(516) 249-7300 or 7301-7302

Woodlawn National Cemetery
1825 Davis Street
Elmira, NY 14901
(607) 732-5411

North Carolina
* New Bern National Cemetery

1711 National Avenue
New Bern, NC 28560
(919) 637-2912

* Raleigh National Cemetery
501 Rock Quarry Road
Raleigh, NC 27610
(919) 832-0144

* Salisbury National Cemetery
202 Government Road
Salisbury, NC 28144
(704) 636-2661

* Wilmington National Cemetery
2011 Market Street
Wilmington, NC 28403
(919) 762-7213

Ohio
* Dayton National Cemetery
VA Medical Center
4100 West Third Street
Dayton, OH 45428
(513) 268-6511, Ext. 106

Oklahoma
* Fort Gibson National Cemetery
Fort Gibson, OK 74434
(918) 478-2334

Oregon
Roseburg National Cemetery
VA Medical Center
Roseburg, OR 97470
(503) 672-4411

* White City National Cemetery
2763 Riley Road
Eagle Point, OR 97524
(503) 826-2111, Ext. 351

* Willamette National Cemetery
P.O. Box 66147
11800 S.E. Mt. Scott Boulevard
Portland, OR 97266
(503) 761-4188

Pennsylvania
Philadelphia National Cemetery
Haines Street and Limekiln Pike
Philadelphia, PA 19138
(215) 924-6083

** Indiantown Gap National Cemetery
Annville, PA 17003

South Carolina
* Beaufort National Cemetery
1601 Boundary Street
Beaufort, SC 29902
(803) 524-3925

* Florence National Cemetery
803 East National Cemetery Road
Florence, SC 29501
(803) 669-8783

South Dakota

* Black Hills National Cemetery
P.O. Box 640
Sturgis, SD 57785
(605) 347-3830

Fort Meade National Cemetery
VA Medical Center
Fort Meade, SD
(Call Black Hills National Cemetery
     South Dakota, for information)

Hot Springs National Cemetery
VA Medical Center
Hot Springs, SD 57747
(605) 745-4101

Tennessee
* Chattanooga National Cemetery
1200 Bailey Avenue
Chattanooga, TN 37404
(615) 698-4981

Knoxville National Cemetery
939 Tyson Street, N.W.
Knoxville, TN 37917
(615) 522-8820

* Memphis National Cemetery
3568 Townes Avenue
Memphis, TN 38122
(901) 386-8311

* Mountain Home National Cemetery
P.O. Box 8
Mountain Home, TN 37684
(615) 929-7891

* Nashville National Cemetery
1420 Gallatin Road, South
Madison, TN 37115
(615) 865-0741

Texas
* Fort Bliss National Cemetery
P.O. Box 6342
Fort Bliss, TX 79906
(915) 568-3705

* Fort Sam Houston National Cemetery
1520 Harry Wurzbach Road
San Antonio, TX 78209
(512) 221-2136 or 2137

* Houston National Cemetery
10410 Stuebner Airline Road
Houston, TX 77038
(713) 447-8686

Kerrville National Cemetery
VA Medical Center
Spur Rt. 100
Kerrville, TX 78028
(512) 896-2020

San Antonio National Cemetery
517 Paso Hondo Street
San Antonio, TX
(Call Fort Sam Houston National
     Cemetery, Texas, for information

Virginia
Alexandria National Cemetery
1450 Wilkes Street
Alexandria, VA 22314
(703) 836-5214

Balls Bluff National Cemetery
Leesburg, VA
(Call Winchester National Cemetery,
   Virginia, for information)

City Point National Cemetery
10th Avenue & Davis Street
Hopewell, VA
(Call Richmond National Cemetery,
   Virginia, for information)

Cold Harbor National Cemetery
R.F.D. No. 4, Box 155
Mechanicsville, VA
(Call Richmond National Cemetery,
   Virginia, for information)

* Culpeper National Cemetery
305 U.S. Avenue
Culpeper, VA 22701
(703) 825-0027

Danville National Cemetery
721 Lee Street
Danville, VA 24541
(804) 792-9284

Fort Harrison National Cemetery
R.F.D. No. 5, Box 174
Varina Road
Richmond, VA
(Call Richmond National Cemetery,
   Virginia, for information)

Glendale National Cemetery
R.F.D. No. 5, Box 272
Richmond, VA
(Call Richmond National Cemetery,
   Virginia, for information)

Hampton National Cemetery
Cemetery Road at Marshall Avenue
Hampton, VA 23669
(804) 723-7104

Hampton National Cemetery
VA Medial Center
Hampton, VA
(Call Hampton National Cemetery,
   Virginia, for information)

** Quantico National Cemetery
Quantico, VA

Richmond National Cemetery
1701 Williamsburg Road
Richmond, VA 23231
(804) 222-1490 or 1494

Seven Pines National Cemetery
400 East Williamsburg Road
Sandston, VA

(Call Richmond National Cemetery,
   Virginia, for information)

Staunton National Cemetery
901 Richmond Avenue
Staunton, VA 24401
(703) 886-2641

Winchester National Cemetery
401 National Avenue
Winchester, VA 22601
(703) 662-8535

West Virginia
Grafton National Cemetery
431 Walnut Street
Grafton, WV 26354
(304) 265-2044

Wisconsin
* Wood National Cemetery
VA Medical Center
5000 W. National Avenue
Wood, WI 53193
(414) 384-2000, Ext. 2776

Puerto Rico
* Puerto Rico National Cemetery
Box 1298
Bayamon, PR 00619
(809) 785-7281

DEPARTMENT OF THE ARMY NATIONAL CEMETERIES

District of Columbia
Soldiers' Home National Cemetery
21 Harewood Road, N.W.
Washington, DC 20011

Virginia
* Arlington National Cemetery
Arlington, VA 22211
(703) 695-3250

DEPARTMENT OF THE INTERIOR NATIONAL CEMETERIES

District of Columbia
Battleground National Cemetery
6625 Georgia Avenue, N.W.
(Between Whittier & Van Buren Street)
Washington, DC 20012

Georgia
* Andersonville National Historic Site
Andersonville, GA 31711
(912) 924-0343

Louisiana
Chalmette National Historical Park
St. Bernard Highway
Chalmette, LA 70043
(504) 271-2412

Maryland
Antietam National Battlefield Site
Box 158
Sharpsburg, MD 21782

(301) 432-5124

Mississippi
Vicksburg National Military
   Park
Box 349
Vicksburg, MS 39180
(601) 636-0583

Montana
Custer Battlefield National
   Monument
P.O. Box 39
Crow Agency, MT 59022
(406) 638-2622

Pennsylvania
Gettysburg National Military
   Park
P.O. Box 70
Gettysburg, PA 17325
(717) 334-1124

Tennessee
* Andrew Johnson National
   Historic Site
Depot Street
Greeneville, TN 37743
(615) 638-3551

* Fort Donelson National
Military Park
P.O. Box F
Dover, TN 37058
(615) 232-5348

* Shiloh National Military Park
Shiloh, TN 38376
(901) 689-3410

Stones River National Battlefield
Rt. 10, Box 401, Old Nashville
   Highway
Murfreesboro, TN 37130
(615) 893-9501

Virginia
Fredericksburg and Spotsylvania
   County Battlefields Memorial
   National Military Park
1013 Lafayette Boulevard
P.O. Box 679
Fredericksburg, VA 22401
(703) 373-4461

Poplar Grove National Cemetery
Petersburg National Battlefield
P.O. Box 549
Petersburg, VA 23803
(804) 732-3531

Yorktown Battlefield
Colonial National Historical
   Park
Box 210
Yorktown, VA 23690
(804) 898-3400

HOW TO FIND CONFEDERATE MILITARY AND PENSION RECORDS

The following is a list of sources you can contact for information regarding Confederate Military and Pension Records.

CONFEDERATE STATES MILITARY SERVICE RECORDS (1861-1865)
Military Service Records (NNCC), National Archives (GSA), Washington, D.C. 20408. Ask for order form GSA 6751.

CONFEDERATE STATES MILITARY SERVICE RECORDS INDEX (1861-1865)
The Latter-day Saint Temple Genealogical Library, 10471 West Santa Monica Blvd., West Los Angeles. The library has a military service records index for the Confederate states for the years 1861-1865. It is under microfilm series number M253.

CONFEDERATE VETERANS AND WIDOWS PENSIONS

Alabama	State of Alabama Department of Archives & History, Montgomery, Alabama 36130
Arkansas	Arkansas History Commission, 300 West Markham Street, Little Rock, Arkansas 72201
Florida	Department of State, Division of Archives & History, The Capitol, Tallahassee, Florida 32304
Georgia	Georgia Department of Archives & History, Atlanta, Georgia 30334
Kentucky	Kentucky Historical Society, Old State House, P.O. Box H, Frankfort, Kentucky 40601
Louisiana	Secretary of State, Archives & Records Service, P.O. Box 44125, Capitol Station, Baton Rouge, Louisiana 70804
Mississippi	Mississippi Department of Archives & History, War Memorial Building, 120 North State Street, Jackson, Mississippi 39201
Missouri	Office of the Adjutant General, Headquarters Missouri National Guard, 1717 Industrial Ave., Jefferson City, Missouri 65101
North Carolina	North Carolina State Department of Archives & History, Raleigh, North Carolina 27601
Oklahoma	Archives Division, Oklahoma State Library, Oklamhoma City, Oklahoma 73105
South Carolina	South Carolina Comptroller General's Office, Columbia, South Carolina 29201
Tennessee	Tennessee State Library & Archives, Nashville, Tennessee 37219
Texas	Texas State Library, Texas Archives & Library Building, Box 12927, Capitol Station, Austin, Texas 78711
Virginia	Virginia State Library, Archives Division, Richmond, Virginia 23219

Pension records are almost always more valuable genealogically then the military service records. You can order Confederate Military Service Records from the National Archives in Washington, D.C. Some state agencies also have them.

CHAPTER 21

INSURANCE COMPANIES

In the last 200 years it is estimated that over sixty percent of our ancestors took out life insurance at least once in their lifetime (some think that in New England may be as much as 90%). These records are a rich source of information to the genealogists. Most of these records are still located in the home office of that particular company or its successor.

Basically, there are three main types of records: (1) applications, (2) certificates, and (3) loan cards. The following information is usually found in these records: full name, place of birth, marital status, occupation, parents and siblings, age at death, beneficiary, relation to beneficiary, and general health conditions.

Generally speaking, these old records are not in any order or system. This situation makes the retrieval of information very difficult. However, to the genealogists with persistence and determination, it is worth the effort it takes to locate the needed records. Few records are as rich in genealogical information.

A list of the various Life Insurance companies liscensed to operate in the United States prior to the year 1866 are listed below. This information has been adapted from Stalson, J. Owen's *Marketing Life Insurance: Its History in America.* Cambridge: Harvard University Press, 1942. For Additional information check in the Reference Section of your library under Insurance.

United States Life Companies
Arranged by Date of Origin 1759-1865

Year of Origin	Year Terminated	Company
1759		Presbyterian Min.
1769		Episcopal Corp.
1787	1791	Baltimore Fire
1794	1798	Ins. Co. of State Pa.
1794	1798	Ins. Co. of No. Am., Pa.
1798	1802	United Ins. Co., N.Y.
1798	1802	N.Y. Ins. Co.
1812	1872	Penn Co. for I. on L.
1812	1813	N.Y. Mechanics L & F
1814	1818	Dutchess County FML
1818	1867	Mass. Hospital Life
1818	1840	Union Ins., N.Y.
1820	1853	Aetna Ins. Co.
1822	1843	Farmers L & T, N.Y.
1830	1867	Baltimore Life
1830	1865	N.Y. L & T
1832	1836	Lawrenceburg Ins. Co., Ind.
1833	1837	Mississippi Ins. Co.
1833	1837	Protection Ins. Co., Miss.
1834	1857	Ohio L & T
1835		N.E. Mutual, Mass.
1835	1839	Ocean Mutual, La.
1836	1840	Southern L & T, Ala.
1836	1840	American L & T, Md.
1836	1894	Girard L., A & T, Pa.
1837	1841	Missouri L & T
1837	1857	Globe L & T, Pa.
1840	1857	Odd Fellows L & T, Pa.
1841	1852	Nat'l. S & T (Equit.), Pa.
1842		Mutual Life, N.Y.
1843		New York Life
1844		State Mutual, Mass.
1845		Mutual Benefit, N.J.
1845	1857	Mutual Life, Md.

1846		Connecticut Mutual	1853	1900	Covenant Mutual, Mo.
1846	1853	Hope Mutual, Conn.	1853	1865	Greenboro Mutual, N.C.
1847		Penn Mutual	1854	1868	Southern Mutual, S.C.
1847	1873	American Mutual, Conn.	1854	1856	Susquehanna Mutual, Pa.
1847	1853	Eagle L. & Health, N.J.	1855	1856	Kentucky Mut., Louisville
1847	1856	Southern Mutual, Ga.	1857		St. Louis Mut. (German),
1847	1852	Trenton M. L & F, N.J.			Missouri
1848		National Life, Vermont	1857		Northwestern Mut., Wis.
1848		Union Mutual, Maine	1857	1873	St. Louis Mutual, Mo.
1848	1852	Equitable L & T, Pa.	1859		Equitable Life, N.Y.
1848	1852	Philadelphia, Pa.	1859	1873	Guardian Mutual, N.Y.
1848	1852	Pennsylvania Life	1860		Guardian (Germania), N.Y.
1849	1850	Crescent Mutual, La.	1860		Home Life, N.Y.
1849	1855	Hartford L & H, Conn.	1860	1875	North American Mut., Pa.
1849	1852	Merchants & Planters, La.	1860	1896	State Ins. Co., Pa.
1849	1853	No. Amn. (Spring Garden),	1860	1908	Washington, N.Y.
		Penn.	1861	1864	Chicago Mutual, Ill.
1849	1862	North Carolina	1862		John Hancock, Mass.
1849	1853	Mutual Benfit, La.	1862	1887	Continental, Conn.
1849	1851	Phoenix, Mo.	1862	1875	North America, N.Y.
1849	1853	Morris County, N.J.	1862	1880	Piedmont & Arlington, Va.
1850		Manhattan Life, N.Y.	1862	1876	Security L & A, N.Y.
1850		U.S. Life, N.Y.	1862	1866	Peninsular M.L., Mich.
1850	1890	American L & T (L & H),	1863		New Jersey Mutual
		Penn.	1863	1873	Nat'l. Union L. & Limb,
1850	1886	Charter Oak, Conn.			New York
1850	1858	Jefferson Life, Ohio	1864		Maryland Life
1850	1867	Kentucky Mut., Covington	1864	1901	Brooklyn Life, N.Y.
1850	1870	Keystone Mutual, Pa.	1864	1879	Globe Mutual, N.Y.
1850	1882	Knickerbocker, N.Y.	1864	1871	Widows and Orphans, N.Y.
1850	1853	Southern Mutual, La.	1865		Connecticut General
1850	1862	U.S.L.A. & Trust, Pa.	1865		Provident Mut. (L & T), Penn.
1850	1851	U.S.A. & L., Conn.	1865	1870	Great Western Mut., N.Y.
1851		Phoenix Mut. (Am. Temp.),	1865	1876	Mutual Life, Ill.
		Conn.	1865	1874	National Life, Ill.
1851		Berkshire Life, Mass.	1865	1866	National L & H, Mich.
1851		Mass. Mutual	1865	1867	Provident L & Invest., Ill.
1851	1855	Nashville Mut. Protection	1865	1877	Universal, N.Y.
1852	1856	Howard Life, N.Y.	1865	1869	Central L & A, N.J.
1853		Aetna Life, Conn.	1865	1869	General L & A, N.J.

United States Branches of English Companies
Arranged by Date of Entry Into This Country

Year Entered U.S.	Year Ceased Entirely In U.S.	Company	Year Entered U.S.	Year Ceased Entirely In U.S.	Company
1807	1810	Pelican	1848	1869	British Commercial
1842	1881	Royal	1854	1862	Colonial Life
1844	1915	Eagle & Albion	1853	1881	Liverpool & London
1844	1869	Int. (Nat. Ln. Fd.)	1865	1867	No. British & Mercentile

Abbreviations in the names of companies are as follows: F = Fire; M = Marine; T = Trust; H = Health; L = Life.

State Officials having Charge of Insurance Affairs

Address and Postal Zone	Official Title
Alabama, Montgomery 36130	Commissioner of Ins.
Alaska, Juneau 99801	Director of Insurance
Arizona, Phoenix 85007	Director of Insurance
Arkansas, Little Rock 72204	Ins. Commissioner

California, San Francisco 94102 ....Ins. Commissioner
Colorado, Denver 80203 ....Commissioner of Ins.
Connecticut, Hartford 06115 ....Ins. Commissioner
Delaware, Dover 19901 ....Ins. Commissioner
D. of C., Washington 20001 ....Acting Supt. of Ins.
Florida, Tallahassee 32301 ....Ins. Commissioner
Georgia, Atlanta 30334 ....Ins. Commissioner
Guam, Agana 96910 ....Ins. Commissioner
Hawaii, Honolulu 96811 ....Ins. Commissioner
Idaho, Boise 83702 ....Director of Insurance
Illinois, Springfield 62767 ....Director of Insurance
Indiana, Indianapolis 46204 ....Ins. Commissioner
Iowa, Des Moines 50319 ....Commissioner of Ins.
Kansas, Topeka 66612 ....Ins. Commissioner
Kentucky, Frankfort 40601 ....Ins. Commissioner
Louisiana, Baton Rouge 70804 ....Commissioner of Ins.
Maine, Augusta 04333 ....Supt. of Insurance
Maryland, Baltimore 21202 ....Ins. Commissioner
Massachusetts, Boston 02202 ....Commissioner of Ins.
Michigan, Lansing 48909 ....Comm. of Insurance
Minnesota, St. Paul 55101 ....Ins. Commissioner
Mississippi. Jackson 39205 ....Commissioner of Ins.
Missouri, Jefferson City 65102 ....Dir. of Insurance
Montana, Helena 59601 ....Commissioner of Ins.
Nebraska, Lincoln 68509 ....Director of Insurance
Nevada, Carson City 89701 ....Commissioner of Ins.
New Hampshire, Concord 03301 ....Ins. Commissioner
New Jersey, Trenton 08625 ....Commissioner of Ins.
New Mexico, Santa Fe 87501 ....Supt. of Insurance
New York, Albany 12210 ....Supt. of Insurance
North Carolina, Raleigh 27611 ....Commissioner of Ins.
North Dakota, Bismarck 58501 ....Commissioner of Ins.

Ohio, Columbus 43215 ....Director of Insurance
Oklahoma, Oklahoma City 73105 ....Ins. Commissioner
Oregon, Salem 97310 ....Ins. Commissioner
Pennsylvania, Harrisburg 17120 ....Ins. Commissioner
Puerto Rico, San Juan 00904 ....Ins. Commissioner
Rhode Island, Providence 02903 ....Ins. Commissioner
South Carolina, Columbia 29204 ....Chief Ins. Comm.
South Dakota, Pierre 57501 ....Director of Insurance
Tennessee, Nashville 37219 ....Commissioner of Ins.
Texas, Austin 78786 ....Commissioner of Ins.
Utah, Salt Lake City 84102 ....Commissioner of Ins.
Vermont, Montpelier 05602 ....Commissioner of Ins.
Virginia, Richmond 23209 ....Ins. Commissioner
Virgin Islands, St. Thomas 00801 ....Commissioer of Ins.
Washington, Olympia 98501 ....Ins. Commissioner
West Virginia, Charleston 25305 ....Ins. Commissioner
Wisconsin, Madison 53702 ....Commioner of Ins.
Wyoming, Cheyenne 82002 ....Ins. Commissioner

Canada

Alberta, Edmonton T5J 3B1 ....Supt. of Insurance
British Columbia, Vancouver V6E 3S7 .Supt. of Brok., Ins & R.E.
Gov't of Canada, Ottawa K1A 0H2 ....Supt. of Insurance
Manitoba, Winnipeg R3C 3L6 ....Supt. of Insurance
New Brunswick, Fredericton E3B 5H1 ....Supt. of Insurance
Newfoundland, St. Johns ....Supt. of Insurance
Nova Scotia, Halifax B3J 2L6 ....Supt. of Insurance
Ontario, Toronto M7A 2H6 ....Supt. of Insurance
Prince Ed. Is., Charlottetown C1A 7N8 ....Supt. of Insurance
Quebec, Quebec City ....Supt. of Insurance
Saskatchewan, Regina S4P 3V7 ....Supt. of Insurance

1982 Index to U. S. Life Insurance Companies

A A A Life Ins. Co., Washington DC
AFIA Worldwide Life Ins. Co., Wilmington, DE
AFSC Ins. Co. Inc. (Ind.), Irving, TX
AICC Life Insurance Company, Phoenix, AZ
AIG Life Ins. Co. (Pa.), Wilmington, DE

A M Life Ins. Co., Wakefield, MA
Abraham Lincoln Ins. Co. (Ill.), North Kansas City, MO
Abundant Life Ins. Co., Tulsa, OK
Acacia Mutual Life Ins. Co., Washington, DC
Acacia National Life Insurance Co. (Va.), Washington, DC

Academy Life Ins. Co. (Colo.), Valley Forge, PA
Acceleration Life Ins. Co., Dublin, OH
Acceration Life Ins. Co., Indianapolis, IN
Acceleration Life Ins. Co. of Pa. (Pa.), Dublin, OH
Accredited Trust Life Ins. Co. (Mo.), Phoenix, AZ

Admiral Life Ins. Co. of America (Ariz.), Minneapolis, MN
Aetna Life Ins. and Annuity Co., Hartford, CT
Aetna Life Ins. and Annuity-Sep. Acct., Hartford, CT
Aetna Life Ins. Co., Hartford CT
Aetna Life Ins. Co.-Sep. Acct., Hartford, CT

Aetna Life Ins. Co. of Illinois, Chicago, IL
Afro-American Life Ins. Co., Jacksonville, FL
Agway Life Ins. Co., Dewitt, NY
Aid Association for Lutherans, Appleton, WI
Aid Life Insurance Company, Des Moines, IA

Aksarben Life Ins. Co., Phoenix, AZ
Alamo Life Insurance Company, Phoenix, AZ
Alexander Hamilton Life Ins. of Amer., Farmington Hills, MI
Alexander National Life of Amer., Phoenix, AZ
All American Assur. Co., Charlotte, NC

All American Life Ins. Co., Chicago, IL
All America Life Ins. Co. Consolidated, Chicago, IL
Allee-Newman Life Insurance Company, Phoenix, AZ
Allen-Russell Life Insurance Company, Phoenix, AZ
Alliance Life Ins. Co., McPherson, KS

Allianz Minnesota Life Ins. Co., Minneapolis, MN
Allied Bankers Life Ins. Co., Dallas, TX
Allied Life Ins. Co., Des Moines, IA
Allied Life Insurance Co. of Tex., Houston, TX
Allnation Life Ins. Co., Wilmington, DE

Allnation Life Ins. Co. of Pa., Lansdowne, PA
Allstate Life Ins. Co., Northbrook, IL
Allstate Life Ins. Co. of Canada, Willowdale, Ontario, Can.
Amalgamated Labor Life Ins. Co. (Ill.), Kansas City, MO
Amalgamated Life & Health Ins. Co., Chicago, IL

Amalgamated Life Ins. Co. Inc., New York, NY
American Agency Life Ins. Co., Atlanta, GA
American-Amicable Life Ins. Co., Waco, TX
American Annuity Life Ins. Co., Grand Rapids, MI
American Bankers Ins. Co., Waco, TX

American Bankers Life Assur. Co., Miami, FL
American Benefit Life Ins. Co., Decatur, AL
American Capital Life Ins. Co., Washington, DC
American Capitol Ins. Co., Houston, TX
American Central Investors Life Ins., Hato Rey, P.R.

American Citizens Life Ins. Co., Washington, DC
American Colonial Life Ins. Co., Montgomery, AL
American Community Mutual Ins. Co., Plymouth, MI
American Consumers Life Ins. Co., Phoenix, AZ
American Consumers Life Ins. Co., Atlanta, GA

American Dealers Life Insurance Co., Phoenix, AZ
American Defender Life Ins. Co., Raleigh, NC
American Educators Life Ins. Co., Birmingham, AL
American Equitable Life Ins. Co., Lufkin, TX
American Estate Life Ins. Co., Phoenix, AZ

American Exchange Life Ins. Co., Dallas, TX
American Express Life Ins. Co., San Rafael, CA
American Family Life Assur. of Columb., Columbus, GA
American Family Life Ins. Co., Madison, WI
American Family Security Ins. Co., Lexington, KY

American Farmers Mutual Life Ins. Co., Urbandale, IA
American Fidelity Assurance Co., Oklahoma, City, OK
American Fidelity Assur. Co.-Sep. Acct., Oklahoma City, OK
American Fidelity Life Ins. Co., Pensacola, FL
American Financial Life Insurance Co., North Palm Beach, FL

American Foundation Life Insurance Co., Birmingham, AL
American Founders Life Ins. Co., Austin, TX
American General Life Ins. Co., Houston, TX
American General Life Ins. Co.-Sep. Acct., Houston, TX
American General Life Ins. Co. of Dela. (Del.), Houston, TX

American General Life Ins. Co.-Sep. Acct., Wilmington, DE
American General Life Ins. Co. of NY, Syracuse, NY
American General Life Ins. Co.-Sep. Acct., Syracuse, NY
American General Life Ins. Co. of Okla., Oklahoma City, OK
American Guaranty Life Ins. Co., Portland, OR

American Guardian Life Assur. Co., Jenkintown, PA
American Health and Life Ins. Co., Baltimore, MD
American Health & Life Ins. of NY, Poughkeepsie, NY
American Heritage Life Ins. Co., Jacksonville, FL
American Heritage Life of TX, Dallas, TX

American Home Life Ins. Co., Topeka, KS
American Home Security Life Ins. Co., Artesia, NM
American Income Life Ins. Co. (Ind.), Waco, TX
American Independent Life Ins., Philadelphia, PA
American Insurance Company of Texas, Dallas, Texas

American International Life Assur. Co., New York, NY
American International Life Ins. Co., Santurce, P.R.
American Investors Assurance Co., Salt Lake City, UT
American Investors Life Ins. Co. Inc., Topeka, KS
American Liberty Life Ins. Co., Birmingham, AL

American Liberty Life Ins. Co., Baton Rouge, LA
American Life & Accident Ins. Co., Grand Prairie, TX
American Life & Acc. Ins. Co., St. Louis, MO
American Life Assurance Corp. Montgomery, AL
American Life & Casualty Ins. Co., Fargo, ND

American Life & Casualty Ins.-Sep. Act., Fargo, ND
American Life Ins. Co., Wilmington DE
American Life Ins. Co. of New York, New York, NY

American Mayflower Life of New York, New York, NY
American Medical Ins. Co. Hicksville, NY

American Merchants Life Ins. Co., Minneapolis, MN
American Mid States Life Ins. Co., Burr Ridge, IL
American Modern Life Insurance Co., Scottsdale, AZ
American Mutual Life Ins. Co., Des Moines, IA
American National Ins. Co., Galveston, TX

American National Ins. Co.-Sep. Acct., Galveston, TX
American National Life Ins. Co. of TX, Galveston, TX
American Pacific Life Ins. Co. of Calif., San Rafael, CA
American Patriot Health Ins. Co, (NY), Trevose, PA
American Pioneer Life Ins Co., Orlando, FL

American Pioneer Life Ins. Co., Columbus, OH
American Progressive Life and Health, Brewster, NY
American Progressive Life, Nashville, TN
American Public Life Ins. Co., Jackson, MS
American Republic Ins. Co., Des Moines, IA

American Republic Life Ins. Co. of NY, New York, NY
American Reserve Life Ins. Co., Boise, ID
American Reserve Life Ins. Co., Tulsa, OK
American Savings Life Ins. Co., Phoenix, AZ
American Security Life Ins. Co., San Antonio, TX

American Sentinel Life Ins. Co., Columbia, SC
American Service Life Ins. Co., Fort Smith, AR
American Service Life Insurance Co., Fort Worth, TX
American Shield Ins. Co., Phoenix, AZ
American Standard Life & Acc. Ins. Co., Enid, OK

American States Life Ins. Co.-Sep. Acct., Indianapolis, IN
American States Life Ins. Co., Indianapolis, IN
American Sun Life Ins. Co., Winter Park, FL
American Teachers Life Insurance Co., Houston, TX
American Transcontinental Life, Phoenix, AZ

American Travellers Life Ins. Co., Warminster, PA
American Trust Life Ins. Co., Dallas, TX
American Trustee Life Corp. Oklahoma City, OK
American Underwriters Life Ins. Co., Phoenix, AZ
American Union Life Ins. Co., Bloomington, IL

American United Life Ins. Co., Indianapolis, IN
American United Life Ins. Co.-Sep. Acct., Indianapolis, IN
American Variable Ann Life Assur. Co. (Del.), Worcester, MA
American Variable Ann Life-Sep. Acct., Dover, DE
American Way General Ins. Co., Scottsdale, AZ

American Way Life Ins. Co., Southfield, MI
American Western Life Ins. Co. (Utah), Boise, ID
American Woodmens Life Ins. Co., Denver, CO
American World Life Ins. Co., Houston, TX
Americana Life Ins. Co., Dublin, OH

Amica Life Ins. Co., Providence, RI
Ammest Life Ins. Co. (Ariz.), Valley Forge, PA
Amoco Life Insurance Company, Omaha, NE
Anchor Life Ins. Co., Phoenix, AZ
Anchor National Life Ins. Co. (Cal.), Phoenix, AZ

Ancorp Insurance Company, Phoenix, AZ
Andrew Jackson Life Ins. Co., Jackson, MS
Annapolis Life Ins. Co. (MD), Los Angeles, CA
Apache Life Ins. Co., Phoenix, AZ
Apollo Life Ins. Co., Phoeniz, AZ

Apollo National Life Ins. Co., Lake Bluff, IL
Appalachian Life Ins. Co., Huntington, WV
Appalachian National Life Ins. Co., Knoxville, TN
Arbor Life Ins. Co., Phoenix, AZ
Arcadia National Life Inc. Co., Phoenix, AZ

Argus Life Ins. Co., Columbia, SC
Arista Insurance Company, New York, NY
Arkansas Bankers Life Ins. Co., Phoenix, AZ
Armour Life Insurance Co., Kansas City, MO
Army Mutual Aid Association, Arlington, VA

Associated Bankers Assurance Company, Oklahoma City, OK
Associated Bankers Life Ins. Of, Denton, TX
Associated Doctors Health & Life Ins., Birmingham, AL
Associatged General Life Company, Detroit, MI
Associated Home Life Ins. Co., Scottsdale, AZ

Associated Investors Life Ins. Co., Phoenix, AZ
Assoicated Life Ins. Co., Chicago, IL
Associates Financial Life Ins. Co., Reno, NV
Associates Life Ins. Co., Indianapolis, IN
Association Life Ins. Co. Inc., Milwaukee, WI

Assumption Mutual Life Ins. Co., Moncton, New Brunswick, Can.
Assured Investors Life Co. (Calif.), Denver, CO
Assured Investors Life Ins. Co., Birmingham, AL
Astro Life Ins. Co., Phoenix, AZ
Atlanta Life Ins. Co., Atlanta, GA

Atlantic American Life Ins. Co., Atlanta, GA
Atlantic Coast Life Ins. Co., Charleston, SC
Atlantic Mutual Life Assur. Co., Moncton New Brunswick, Can.
Atlantic and Pacific Ins. Co., Denver, CO
Atlantic & Pacific Life Ins. of Amer. Atlanta, GA

Atlantic Phoenix Life Ins. Co., Phoenix, AZ
Atlantic Security Life Ins. Co., Phoenix, AZ
Atlantic Southern Ins. Co., Rio Piedras, P.R.
Atlas Life Ins. Co., Tulsa, OK
Atlas Life Ins. Co., New Orleans, LA

Audubon Life Ins. Co., Baton Rouge, LA
Auto-Owners Life Ins. Co., Lansing, MI
Auto-Tex. Life Insurance Company, Phoenix, AZ
Avon Life Ins. Co., Phoenix, AZ
Aztec Life Insurance Co. of Texas, San Antonio, TX

—B—

BA Insurance Company Inc., San Francisco, CA
BU Life Insurance Company, Cincinnati, OH
Baltimore Life Ins Co., Baltimore, MD
Banco Credit Life Ins. Co., Phoenix, AZ
Bank of Oklahoma Inc., Tulsa, OK

Bankers Commercial Life Ins. Co., Dallas, TX
Bankers Credit Life Ins. Co., Montgomery, AL
Bankers Fidelity Life Ins. Co., Phoenix, AZ
Bankers Fidelity Life Ins. Co., Atlanta, GA
Bankers Life & Casualty Co., Chicago, IL

Bankers Life and Casualty Co. of NY, Hempstead, L.I., NY
Bankers Life Company, Des Moines, IA
Bankers Life Company-Sep. Acct., Des Moines, IA
Bankers Life Ins. Co. of America, Dallas, TX
Bankers Life Insurance Co. of Florida, St. Petersburg, FL

Bankers Life Ins. Co. of Nebraska, Lincoln, NE

Bankers Life Ins. Co. of Neb.-Sep. Acct., Lincoln, NE
Bankers Life of Louisiana, Ruston, LA
Bankers Mutual Life Ins. Co., Freeport, IL
Bankers National Life Ins. Co., Parsippany, NJ

Bankers Reserve Life Ins. Co., Englewood, CO
Bankers Security Life Ins. (NY), Washington, DC
Bankers Security Life Ins.-Sep. Acct., New York, NY
Bankers' Service Life Insurance Co., Knoxville, TN
Bankers Union Life Ins. Co., Englewood, CO

Bankers United Life Assurance Co., Cedar Rapids, IA
Barrington Insurance Company, Scottsdale AZ
Bay Colony Life Ins. Co. of Az. (Ariz.), Springfield, MA
Bay Colony Life Ins. Co. of Md. (Md.), Springfield, MA
Bay Colony Life Ins. Co. of Vt. Inc. (Vt.), Springfield, NA

Ben Hur Life Association, Crawfordsville, IN
Beneficial Assurance Co., Phoenix, AZ
Beneficial Life Ins. Co., Salt Lake City, UT
Beneficial Life Ins. Co.-Sep. Acct., Salt Lake City, UT
Beneficial Reinsurance Company (Del.), Los Angeles, CA

Beneficial Standard Life Ins. Co., Los Angeles, CA
Benefit Trust Life Ins. Co., Chicago, IL
Benevolent Life Ins. Co. Inc., Shreveport, LA
Berglund Life Insurance Company, Scottsdale, AZ
Berkshire Life Ins. Co.-Sep. Acct., Pittsfield, MA

Berkshire Life Ins. Co., Pittsfield, MA
Best Life Assur. Co. of, Newport Beach, CA
Betal Life Ins. Co., Phoenix, AZ
Bnai Zion, New York, NY
Boatmen's Life Insurance Company, Phoenix, AZ

Bonneville Life Ins. Co., Salt Lake City, UT
Booker T. Washington Ins. Co. Inc., Birmingham, AL
Boston Mutual Life Ins. Co., Canton, MA
Boston Mutual Life Ins. Co.-Sep. Acct., Canton, MA
Bradford National Life Ins. Co., Lexington, KY

Brazos Security Life Insurance Co., Carrollton, TX
Brazos Valley Life Insurance Company, Phoenix, AZ
Broadway Life Ins. Co., Wichita Falls, TX
Brookings International Life Ins. Co., Brookings, SD
Buckeye National Life Insurance Co., Scottsdale, AZ

Buckeye State Insurance Co., Phoenix, AZ
Builders Life Ins. Co. (Ariz.), Omaha, NE
Business Men's Assurance Co. of Amer., Kansas City, MO

—C—

C & C Life Ins. Co. Inc. (Ariz.), Knoxville, TN
CBI Insurance Company, Phoenix, AZ
C N Life Ins. Co. Phoenix, AZ
CNA Life and Annuity Company, Chicago, IL
Cal-Farm Life Ins. Co., Sacramento, CA

California Casualty & Life Ins. Co., San Mateo, CA
California Casualty & Life-Sep. Acct., San Mateo, CA
California Federal Life Ins. Co., Phoenix, AZ
California Life Ins. Co., Los Angeles, CA
California Pacific Life Ins. Co., San Rafael, CA

California Physicians' Ins. Corp., San Francisco, CA
California-Western States Life-Sep. Acc., Sacramento, CA
California-Western States Life, Sacramento, CA
Cameron Life Ins. Co., Phoenix, AZ

Canada Life Assurance Co., Toronto, Ontario, Can.

Canada Life Ins. Co. of NY, New York, NY
Canyon State Life Ins. Co., Phoenix, AZ
Capital Assurance Life Ins. Co., Phoenix, AZ
Capital City Ins. Co. Inc., Phoenix, AZ
Capital Investors Life Insurance Co., Winter Park, FL

Capital Reserve Life Ins. Co., Jefferson City, MO
Capital Security Life Ins. Co. (N.M.), Oklahoma City, OK
Capitol American Life Ins. Co. (Ariz.), Cleveland, OH
Capitol Bankers Life Ins. Co., Minneapolis, MN
Capitol Life Ins. Co., Denver, CO

Capitol Life Ins. Co.-Sep. Acct., Denver, CO
Capitol Life Ins. Co. of NY, New York, NY
Capitol Mutual Ins. Co., Jackson, MS
Capitol Old Line Ins. Co., Helena, AR
Cardinal Insurance Incorporated, Phoenix, AZ

Carnegie Life Ins. Co. of Amer., Indianapolis, IN
Carolina American Life Ins. Co., Charleston, SC
Catholic Family Life Ins., Shorewood, WI
Catholic Knights of America, St. Louis, MO
Catholic Knights Insurance Society, Milwaukee, WI

Catholic Life Insurance Union, San Antonio, TX
Catholic Order of Foresters, Chicago, IL
Cattlemens' Life Ins. Co., Oklahoma City, OK
Cedar Springs Life Ins. Co., Phoenix, AZ
Celestial Life Insurance Company, Phoenix, AZ

Celina National Life Ins. Co., Celina, OH
Celtic Life Insurance Company (R.I.), Hartford, CT
Celtic Life Ins. Co. of Il., Chicago, IL
CENCO Insurance Company, Phoenix, AZ
Centennial Life Ins. Co., Overland Park, KS

Central American Life Ins. Co., West Monroe, LA
Central Credit Life Ins. Co., Jackson, MS
Central Guardian Life Ins. Co., Jackson, MS
Central Hawkeye Life Ins. Co., Phoenix, AZ
Central Investors Life Ins. Co. of Ill., Peoria, IL

Central Life Assurance Co., Des Moines, IA
Central Life Ins. Co. of Florida, Tampa, FL
Central National Life Ins. Co., Jacksonville, IL
Central National Life Ins. Co. of Omaha (Neb.), Morristown, NJ
Central Penn Life Ins. Co., Wilmington, DE

Central Plains Life Ins. Co. Inc., Hutchinson, KS
Central Plains Life of NA Ins. Co., Berea, OH
Central Security Life Ins. Co., Fort Worht, TX
Central State Life Ins. Co., Alexandria, LA
Central States Health & Life of Omaha, Omaha, NE

Central United Life Ins. Co., Sioux City, IA
Centurion Life Ins. Co. (Mo.), Des Moines, IA
Century Credit Life Insurance Co., Tupelo, MS
Century Life Ins. Co. of Michigan, Phoenix, AZ
Certified Life Ins. Co., Sherman Oaks, CA

Champions Life Ins. Co., Dallas, TX
Chapparal Life Ins. Co. (Ariz.), Dallas, TX
Charlotte Liberty Mutual Ins. Co., Charlotte, NC
Charlotte Liberty Mutual Ins.-Sep. Acct., Charlotte, NC
Charter Group Life Ins. Co., Scottsdale, AZ

Charter Indemnity Company (N.Y.), Louisville, KY
Charter National Life Ins. Co., St. Louis, MO
Charter Oak Life Ins. Co., Phoenix, AZ
Charter Security Life Ins. Co. (N.J.), Jacksonville, FL
Charter Security Life Ins. Co. (La.), Jacksonville, FL

Charter Security Life Ins. Co. (NY), New York, NY
Chase National Life Ins. Co., Springfield, MO
Cherokee National Life Ins. Co., Macon, GA
Chesapeake Life Ins. Co., Baltimore, MD
Chesapeake Life Ins. Co.-Sep. Acct., Baltimore, MD

Chevold Ins. Co., Phoenix, AZ
Chicago Central Natl. Ins. Co., Scottsdale, AZ
Chicago Metropolitan Mutual Assur. Co., Chicago, IL
Christian Fidelity Life Ins. Co., Waxahachie, TX
Christian Heritage Life Ins. Co., Phoenix, AZ

Christian Mutual Life Ins. Co., Concord, NH
Chrysler Life Ins. Co., Troy, MI
Chrysler Life Ins. Co. of Can., Mississauga, Ontario, Can.
Chubb/Colonial Life Ins. Co. of Amer., Dover, DE
Chubb Life Ins. Co. of America, Concord, NH

Church Life Ins. Corporation, New York, NY
Churchill Life Ins. Co., Phoenix, AZ
Cimarron Life Insurance Company, Cimarron, KS
Citadel Life Ins. Co., Charlotte, NC
Citadel Life Ins. Co., Columbia, SC

Citizens Accident and Health Ins. Co., Phoenix, AZ
Citizens Fidelity Ins. Co., Waco, TX
Citizens Home Ins. Co. Inc., Richmond, VA
Citizens Insurance Co. of Amer., Austin, TX
Citizens National Life Ins. Co., Scottsdale, AZ

Citizens Security Life Ins. Co., Frankfort, KY
Citizens & Southern Life Ins. Co., Atlanta, GA
Citizens & Southern Life Ins. Co., Houston, TX
Citizens Universal Life Ins. Co., Minneapolis, MN
City Life Ins. Co., Phoenix, AZ

Civil Service Employees Life Ins. Co., San Francisco, CA
Coast Life Ins. Co., Phoenix, AZ
Coast South Western Life Ins. Co. (Ariz.), Oklahoma City, OK
Coastal State Life Ins. Co., Atlanta, GA
College Life Ins. Co. of America, Indianapolis, IN

Cologne Life Reinsurance Co., Stamford, CT
Colonia Life Insurance Company, Toronto, Ontario, Can.
Colonial American Life Ins. Co., New Orleans, LA
Colonial Life and Accident Ins. Co., Columbia, SC
Colonial Life Ins. Co. of America, Parsippany, NJ

Colonial Penn Life Ins. Co., Philadelphia, PA
Colonial Penn Life Ins. Co.-Sep. Acct., Philadelphia, PA
Colonial Security Life Ins. Co., Dallas, TX
Colony Charter Life Ins. Co., Los Angeles, CA
Colorado Bankers Life Insurance Co., Denver, CO

Columbia Life Ins. Co., Bloomsburg, PA
Columbia National Life Ins. Co., Columbus, OH
Columbian Mutual Life Ins. Co., Binghamton, NY
Columbus Mutual Life Ins. Co., Columbus, OH
Columbus Security Life Insurance Co., Columbus, OH

Combined American Ins. Co., Dallas, TX
Combined Ins. Co. of America, Chicago, IL

Combined Ins. Co. of Wisconsin, Fond du Lac, WI
Combined Life Ins. Co. of New York, Albany, NY
Combined Underwriters Life Ins. Co., Tyler, TX

Commercial Bankers Life Ins. Co., Newport Beach, CA
Commercial Bankers Life Ins. Co. of Ind., Fort Wayne, IN
Commercial Life Assurance Co. of Can., Toronto M4T 1X1,
 Ontario, Can.
Commercial National Life Insurance Co., Scottsdale, AZ
Commercial Resources Ins. Co., Phoenix, AZ

Commercial State Life Ins. Co., St. Louis, MO
Commerical Travelers Life Ins. Co., Dallas, TX
Commercial Travelers Mutual Insurance, Utica, NY
Commerical Union Life Ins. Co. America (Del.), Boston, MA
Commodore Life Ins. Co., Dallas, TX

Commonwealth Life & Accident Ins. Co., St. Louis, MO
Commonwealth Life Ins. Co., Louisville, KY
Commonwealth Life Ins. Co.-Sep. Acct., Louisville, KY
Commonwealth National Life Ins. Co., Cleveland, MS
Community Life Ins. Co., Worthington, OH

Community Service Life Ins. Co., Phoenix, AZ
Companion Life Ins. Co., New York, NY
Companion Life Ins. Co., Columbia, SC
Companion Life Ins. Co., Dallas, TX
Concord General Life Ins. Co. Inc., Concord, NH

Concord Life Ins. Co., Phoenix, AZ
Concord National Life Ins., Munster, IN
Concordia Mutual Life Association, Chicago, IL
Confederation Life Ins. Co.,Toronto, Can.
Conger Life Ins. Co., Miami, FL

Congregation Life Ins. Co., Angola, IN
Congress Life Ins. Co. (Ariz.), Santa Ana, CA
Connecticut General Life Ins. Co., Bloomfield, CT
Connecticut General Life Ins.-Sep. Acct., Bloomfield, CT
Connecticut Mutual Life Ins. Co., Hartford, CT

Connecticut Mutual Life-Sep. Acct., Hartford, CT
Connecticut Savings Bank Life-System, Hartford, CT
Connell Life Insurance Company, Phoenix, AZ
Conqueror Life Insurance Company, Phoenix, AZ
Consolidated American Life Ins. Co., Jackson, MS

Consolidated Bankers Life Ins. Co., Shreveport, LA
Consolidated General Life Ins. Co., Dallas, TX
Consolidated Investors Life Assur., Coral Gables, FL
Consolidated National Life Ins. Co., Indianapolis, IN
Constitution Life Ins. Co., Park Ridge, IL

Consumer Benefit Life Insurance Co., Nashville, TN
Consumer Life Ins. Co. (Ariz.), Atlanta, GA
Consumers Life Ins. Co. (Del.), Camp Hill, PA
Consumers Life Ins. Co. (N.C.), Camp Hill, PA
Consumers National Life Ins. Co., Phoenix, AZ

Consumers Protective Life Ins. Co., Phoenix, AZ
Consumers United Ins. Co. (Del.), Washington, DC
Continental American Life Ins. Co., Wilmington, DE
Continental Amer. Life Ins. Co.-Sep. Acct., Wilmington, DE
Continental Assurance Co., Chicago, IL

Continental Assurance Co.-Sep. Acct., Chicago, IL
Continental Bankers Life Ins. (Minn.), Kansas City, MO
Continental Bankers Life Ins. Co., Jackson, TN

Continental General Ins. Co., Omaha, NE
Continental Guaranty Life Ins. Co., Phoenix, AZ

Continental Investors Life Ins. Co. Inc., Englewood, CO
Continental Life & Accident Co., Boise, ID
Continental Life Ins. Co., Havertown, PA
Continental Life Ins. Co., Fort Worth, TX
Continental Life Ins. Co. of S.C., Columbia, SC

Continental National Life Ins., Oklahoma City, OK
Continental Security Life Ins. Co., Jefferson City, MO
Continental Service Life & Health Ins. Baton Rouge, LA
Continental Trust Life Ins. Co., Owensboro, KY
Continental Western Life Ins. Co., West Des Moines, IA

Cooperativa de Seguros de Vida de, Hato Rey, P.R.
Co-Operative Life Ins. Co., Regina, Saskatchewan, Can.
Corona National Life Ins. Co., Phoenix, AZ
Corporate Life Ins. Co., Biglerville, PA
Corporate Profits Life Ins. Co., Phoenix, AZ

Cosmopolitan Life Ins. Co., Los Angeles, CA
Cotton States Life and Health Ins. Co., Atlanta, GA
Country Life Ins. Co., Bloomington, IL
Country Life Ins. Co.-Sep. Acct., Bloomington, IL
Covenant Life Ins. Co. (N.J.), Hartford, CT

Credit Life Corp. of America, Oklahoma City, OK
Credit Life Insurance Company, Springfield, OH
Credit Life Ins. Company-Sep. Acct., Springfield, OH
Creon Life Insurance Company, Chicago, IL
Croatian Fraternal Union of America, Pittsburgh, PA

Crown Bancshares Life Insurance Co., Phoenix, AZ
Crown Life Ins. Co., Toronto, Ontario, Can.
Cudis Insurance Society Inc., Madison, WI
Cumberland Life Ins. Co. of Tx., Irving, TX
Cumberland Life Ins. Co. (Tenn.), Irving, TX

Cumis Life Insurance Company, Burlington, Ontario, Can.
Cuna Mutual Ins. Society, Madison, WI
Customers Life Insurance Corp., Phoenix, AZ
Czechoslovak Society of America, Berwyn, IL

—D—

D Patrick Life Ins. Co., Phoenix, AZ
D S F Insurance Inc., Phoenix, AZ
Dakota National Life Ins. Co., Rapid City, SD
Dearborn Life Ins. Co., Scottsdale, AZ
Dee-Gee Life Insurance Company, Scottsdale, AZ

Degree of Honor Protective Assoc., St. Paul, MN
Del Pueblo Life Insrance Company, Espanola, NM
Delaware American Life Ins. Co. (Del.), New York, NY
Delaware National Life Insurance Co., Dover, DE
Delta Life and Annuity Company, Memphis, TN

Delta Life Ins. Co., Phoenix, AZ
Delta Life Ins. Co., New Orleans, LA
Delta National Life Insurance Co., Baton Rouge, LA
Dependable Life Insurance Company, Jacksonville, FL
Dependable Life Ins. Co., Waco, TX

Desert Sun Life Ins. Co., Phoenix, AZ
Directors Life Ins. Co., Pasadena, CA
Diversified Life Ins. Co., Phoenix, AZ
Dixie National Life Ins. Co., Jackson, MS
Doctors Life Insurance Company, Santa Monica, CA

Dominion Life Assurance Co., Waterloo, Ontario, Can.
Dorchester Life Ins. Co., Scottsdale, AZ
Dun & Bradstreet Life Insurance Co., Phoenix, AZ
Durham Life Ins. Co., Raleigh, NC
Durham Life Ins. Co.-Sep. Acct., Raleigh, NC

—E—

E F Hutton Life Ins. Co., La Jolla, CA
EJ Life Insurance Company, Phoenix, AZ
Eagle Life Ins. Co., San Antonio, TX
Early American Life Ins. Co., St. Paul, MN
Eastern States Life Ins. Co., Wilmington, DE

Education and Retirement Life Ins. Co. (Ala.), Clearwater, FL
Educators Life Ins. Co. of America (Cal.), Springfield, IL
Educators Life Ins. Co.-Sep., Acct., Los Angeles, CA
Educators Mutual Life Ins. Co., Lancaster, PA
Elna Ins. Co., Phoenix, AZ

Empire General Life Ins. Co., Birmingham, AL
Empire Life Ins. Co., Kingston, Ontario, Can.
Empire Life Ins. Co., Omaha, NE
Empire State Mutual Life Ins. Co., Jamestown, NY
Employees Life Co. (Mutual), Lake Bluff, IL

Employees Life Insurance Co., San Antonio, TX
Employees Mutual Ben. Assoc. Saintpaul, St. Paul, MN
Employers Life Ins. Co., Birmingham AL
Employers Life Ins. Co. of Wausau, Wausau, WI
Employers Life Ins. of Wausau-Sep. Acct., Wausau, WI

Employers Modern Life Co., Des Moines, IA
Employers National Life Ins. Co., Dallas, TX
Enterprise Insurance Corporation, Oklahoma City, OK
Enterprise Life Ins. Co., Dallas, TX
Enumclaw Life Ins. Co., Enumclaw, WA

Equiban Life Ins. Co., Phoenix, AZ
Equitable American Life Insurance Co., Des Moines, IA
Equitable Life Assurance Soc. U.S., New York, NY
Equitable Life Assur. Soc. U.S.-Sep. Acct., New York, NY
Equitable Life and Casualty Ins. Co., Salt Lake City, UT

Equitable Life Ins. Co., McLean, VA
Equitable Life Ins. Co. of Canada, Waterloo, Ontario, Can.
Equitable Life Ins. Co. of Iowa, Des Moines, IA
Equitable Life Ins. Co. of Iowa-Sep. Acct., Des Moines, IA
Equitable Life Ind. Co. of Iowa Cons., Des Moines IA

Equitable Reserve Association, Neenah, WI
Equitable Variable Life Ins. Co., New York, NY
Equities International Life Ins. Co., Fort Worth, TX
Equity Benefit Life Ins. Co., Blackwell, OK
Equity Life & Annuity Co., Greenville, SC

Equity National Life Ins. Co. (Ga.), Little Rock, AR
Erie Family Life Ins. Co., Erie, PA
Estate Life Ins. Co. of America (Va.), Tampa, FL
Eureka Life Ins. Co. of America, Wichita Falls, TX
Evangeline Life Ins. Co. Inc., New Iberia, LA

Excel National Life Ins. Co., Oklahoma City, OK
Excelsior Life Ins. Co., Toronto, Ontario, Can.
Exchange National Life Ins. Co. (Ariz.), Dallas, TX
Executive Fund Life Ins. Co., Lincoln, NE
Executive Life Ins. Co., Beverly Hills, CA

Executive Life Ins. Co. of Arizona, (Ariz.), Beverly Hills, CA

Executive Life Ins. Co. of New York, Jericho, NY
Executive National Life Ins. Co., Rosemont, IL

—F—

FB Annuity Company, Lansing MI
FBL Insurance Company, West Des Moines, IA
FCB Life Insurance Ltd., Phoenix, AZ
FN Life Insurance Co., Cincinnati, OH
FTS Life Ins. Co., Dallas, TX

Fair Financial Life Insurance Co., Phoenix, AZ
Fairfield Life Ins. Co. (Del.), Greenwich, CT
Family Benefit Life Ins. Co., Jefferson City, MO
Family Guardian Life Ins. Co. (Ariz.), St. Louis, MO
Family Insurance Corp., Shawano, WI

Family Life Ins. Co., Seattle, WA
Family Life Ins. Co.-Sep. Acct., Seattle, WA
Family Service Life Ins. Co., Houston, TX
Farm Bureau Life Ins. Co., West Des Moines, IA
Farm Bureau Life Ins. Co. of Michigan, Lansing, MI

Farm Bureau Life Ins. Co. of Missouri, Jefferson City, MO
Farm Family Life Ins. Co., Glenmont, NY
Farm and Home Life Ins. Co., Phoenix, AZ
Farm & Ranch Life Ins. Co. Inc., Wichita, KS
Farmers New World Life Ins. Co., Mercer Island, WA

Farmers New World Life Ins. Co.-Sep. Acct., Mercer Island, WA
Farmers and Ranchers Life Ins. Co., Oklahoma City, OK
Farmer and Traders Life Ins. Co., Syracuse, NY
Farmland Life Ins. Co., Des Moines, IA
Farwest American Assur. Co., Portland, OR

Federal Bankers Life Insurance Co., Phoenix, AZ
Federal Home Life Ins. Co. (Ind.), Battle Creek, MI
Federal Kemper Life Assurance Co., Long Grove, IL
Federal Kemper Life Assur. Co.-Sep. Acct., Long Grove, IL
Federal Life Ins. Co. (Mutual), Glenview, IL

Federal Life Ins. Co. (Mutual) Cons., Glenview, IL
Federal Life Ins. Co. (Mutual)-Sep. Acct., Glenview, IL
Federated American Life Ins. Co., Seattle, WA
Federated Guaranty Life Ins. Co., Montgomery, AL
Federated Life Ins. Co., Owatonna, MN

Fidelity American Life Assur. (Ariz.), North Salt Lake City, UT
Fidelity Bankers Life Ins. Co., Richmond, VA
Fidelity And Guaranty Life Ins. Co., Baltimore, MD
Fidelity Interstate Life Ins. Co. (Pa.), Los Angeles, CA
Fidelity Life Assoc. A Mut. Legal Res., Long Grove, IL

Fidelity Life Ins. Co., Houma, LA
Fidelity Mutual Life Ins. Co., Philadelphia, PA
Fidelity Mutual Life Ins. Co.-Sep. Acct., Philadelphia, PA
Fidelity National Life Ins. Co., Scottsdale, AZ
Fidelity Security Life Ins. Co., Kansas City, MO

Fidelity Union Life Ins. Co., Dallas, TX
Fiduciary Insurance Co. of America, New York, NY
Financial Assurance Inc. (Colo.), Kansas City, MO
Financial Credit Life Ins. Co., Phoenix, AZ
Financial Fidelity Life Ins. Co., Shreveport, LA

Financial Investors Life, Troy, MI
Financial Life Assur. Co. of Canada, Edmonton, Alberta, Can.
Financial Life Ins. Co., Houston, TX

Financial Management Life Ins. Co., Carmel, IN
Financial Protection Ins. Co. of Tex., Dallas, TX

Financial Security Ins. Co. Ltd., Honolulu, HI
Financial Security Life Ins. Co., Moline, IL
Financial Security Life of LA, Shreveport, LA
Financial Security Life of Miss. (Miss.), Shreveport, LA
Financial Service Life Ins. Co., Fort Worth, TX

Fireman's Fund American Life Ins. Co., San Rafael, CA
Fireman's Fund American Life Ins.-Cons., San Rafael, CA
Fireman's Fund Amer. Life Ins. of NY, New York, NY
Fireside Commercial Life Ins. Co., Aiexandria, LA
First Alabama Life Ins. Co., Phoenix, AZ

First City Life Ins. Co., Carrollton, TX
First Colony Life Ins. Co., Lynchburg, VA
First Columbia Life Ins. Co. (Iowa), Columbia, MO
First Commonwealth Life Ins. Co., Richmond, VA
First Continental L & A Ins. Co. Salt Lake City, UT

First Equity Life Ins. Co. of Mo., Jefferson City, MO
First Equity Security Life Ins. Co., Indianapolis, IN
First Family Life Ins. Company, Oklahoma City, OK
First Farwest Life Ins. Co., Portland, OR
First Federated Life Ins. Co., Baltimore, MD

First Federated Life Ins. Co.-Sep. Acct., Baltimore, MD
First Fidelity Life Ins. Co., Lincoln, NE
First Fidelity Life Ins. Co., Houston, TX
First Financial Life Insurance Co., Phoenix, AZ
First International Bancshares Ins. Co., Carrollton, TX

First International Ins. Co., Carrollton, TX
First Investors Life Ins. Co., New York, NY
First Investors Life Ins. Co.-Sep. Acct., New York, NY
First Kansas Life Ins. Co., Newton, KS
First Life Assurance Co., Oklahoma City, OK

First Life Assurance Co.-Sep. Acct., Oklahoma City, OK
First Life Ins. Co., Arlington, TX
First Missouri Insurance Group, Phoenix, AZ
First National Credit Ins., Colubmia, SC
First National Life Ins. Co., Montgomery, AL

First National Life Ins. Co. of Amer. (Ga.), Birmingham, AL
First National Life Ins. Co. of the USA, Lincoln, NE
First of Groves Life Insurance Co., Beaumont, TX
First Pacific Life Ins. Co. (Ariz.), Burbank, CA
First Penn-Pacific Life Ins. Co., Harrisburg, PA

First Protection Life Ins. Co., Raleigh, NC
First Pyramid Life Ins. Co. of America, Little Rock, AR
First Service Life Ins. Co., El Paso, TX
First Southern Life Ins. Co., Phoenix, AZ
First Southwest Life Ins. Co., Kansas City, MO

First Standard Life Insurance Co., Phoenix, AZ
First United Life Ins. Co., Gary, IN
First Variable Life Ins. Co., Little Rock, AR
First Variable Life Ins. Co.-Sep. Acct., Little Rock, AR
First Virginia Life Ins. Co., Falls Chruch, VA

Firstmark Life Insurance Co. of Ariz., Phoenix, AZ
Firstmark Life Ins. Co. of Indiana, Indianapolis, IN
Florida Farm Bureau Life Ins. Co., Gainesville, FL
Florida General Life Ins. Co., Coral Gables, FL
Florida Life Insurance Co., Miami, FL

Florists' Life Ins. Co., Edwardsville, IL
Foley Reserve Life Ins. Co., Houston, TX
Ford Life Ins. Co., Dearborn, MI
Foremost Life Ins. Co., Grand Rapids, MI
Forrest Life of Chattanooga, Scottsdale, AZ

Fort Dearborn Life Ins. Co., Chicago, IL
Fort Sam Life Ins. Co., Dallas, TX
Fortune Life Ins. Co. (Ariz.), Jacksonville, FL
Fortune National Life Ins. Co., Pittsburgh, PA
Foundation Life Ins. Co. of America, Chatham, NJ

Founders Life Assurance Co. of Florida, Tampa, FL
Founders Security Life Ins. Co. (Tenn.), Springfield, MO
Frandisco Life Insurance Company, Phoenix, AZ
Franklin Life Ins. Co., Springfield, IL
Franklin Life Ins. Co.-Sep. Acct., Springfield, IL

Franklin National Life Ins. Co., Fort Wayne, IN
Franklin United Life Ins. Co., Garden City, NY
Frankona American Life Reassur. Co., Kansas City, MO
Frontier Ins. Co., Jefferson City, MO
Futural Life Ins. Co., Phoenix, AZ

—G—

G. I. C. Life Ins. Co., San Antonio, TX
G & J Life Company, Phoenix, AZ
Garden State Life Ins. Co., Newark, NJ
Gem State Mutual Life Ins. Pocatello, ID
General American Life Ins. Co., St. Louis, MO

General American Life Ins.-Sep. Acct., St. Louis, MO
General Fidelity Life Ins. Co., Richmond, VA
General Financial Life Ins. Co., Phoenix, AZ
General Life & Accident Ins. Co., Fort Worth, TX
General Life Ins. Corp. of Wisconsin, Milwaukee, WI

General Reassurance Corp., Greenwich, CT
General Security Life Co., Seattle, WA
General Security Life Ins. Co., Bryan, TX
General Services Life Ins. Co., Washington, DC
General United Life Ins. Co., West Des Moines, IA

Geneva Life Insurance (Pa.), Chicago, IL
George Washington Life Ins. Co. (W.Va.), Jacksonville, FL
George Washington Life Ins. Co. of CA, San Jose, CA
Georgetown Life Ins. Co., Peoria, IL
Georgia International Life Ins. Co., Atlanta, GA

Georgia Life & Health Ins. Co., Hapeville, GA
Georgia Peoples Life Insurance Co., Phoenix, AZ
Gerber Life Ins. Co., White Plains, NY
Gerling Global Life Ins. Co., Toronto, Can.
Germantown Life Ins. Co., Philadelphia, PA

Gertrude Geddes Willis Life Ins. Co., New Orleans, LA
Gibraltar Life Ins. Co. of Amer. (Ala.), Fort Worth, TX
Gibson National Life Insurance Co., Seagoville, TX
Gleaner Life Ins. Society, Birmingham, MI
Global Life Ins., Phoenix, AZ

Globe Life and Accident Ins. Co. (Del.), Oklahoma City, OK
Globe Life and Accident Ins. Co., Oklahoma City, OK
Globe Life Ins. Co., Chicago, IL
Gold Eagle Life Ins. Co., Phoenix, AZ
Golden Eagle Mutual Life Ins. Corp., Brooklyn, NY

Golden Rule Ins. Co., Lawrenceville, IL

Golden State Mutual Life Ins. Co., Los Angeles, CA
Good Life Insurance Company, Phoenix, AZ
Government Employees Life Ins. Co. (D.C.), Rockville, MD
Government Employees Life-Sep. Acct., Washington, DC

Government Employees Life Ins. of (N.Y.), Rockville, MD
Government Personnel Mutual Life Ins., San Antonio, TX
Graham National Life Ins. Co., Scottsdale, AZ
Grand Life Ins. Co. (Ariz.), Cincinnati, OH
Grand Pacific Life Ins. Co. Ltd., Honolulu, HI

Grange Life Ins. Co., Columbus, OH
Grange Mutual Life Co., Nampa, ID
Grant Life Insurance Company, Phoenix, AZ
Great American Life Ins. Co., Hutchinson, KS
Great American Life Ins. Co. (N.J.), Los Angeles, CA

Great American Reserve Ins. Co., Dallas, TX
Great Atlantic Life Ins. Co., West Palm Beach, FL
Great Central Life Ins. Co., Oakdale, LA
Great Century Life Insurance Company, Scottsdale, AZ
Great Coast Life Ins. Co., San Antonio, TX

Great Commonwealth Life Ins. Co., Dallas, TX
Great Eastern Life Ins. Co. (S.C.), Greensboro, NC
Great Fidelity Life Ins. Co., Evansville, IN
Great Lake Ins. Co. (Ill.), Richmond, VA
Great Lakes Life Insurance Company, Phoenix, AZ

Great Life Ins. Co., Dallas, TX
Great National Life Insurance Co., Dallas, TX
Great Republic Life Ins. Co., Phoenix, AZ
Great Republic Life Ins. Co., Newport Beach, CA
Great Republic Life Ins. Co., Seattle, WA

Great Southeastern Life Ins., Shreveport, LA
Great Southern Life Ins. Co., Houston, TX
Great-West Life Assurance Co., Winnipeg, Manitoba, Can.
Great Western Ins. Co., Phoenix, AZ
Great Western Life Ins. Co., Bozeman, MT

Great Western Life Ins. Co., San Antonio, TX
Greater Beneficial Union of Pittsburg, Pittsburgh, PA
Greater Carolinas Life Insurance Co., Columbia, SC
Greater Ohio Life Ins. Co., Columbus, OH
Greenfield Life Ins. Co., Greenfield, IN

Grinnell Mutual Life Ins. Co., Grinnell, IA
Grosvenor Life Insurance Ltd., Phoenix, AZ
Group Life and Health Ins. Co., Richardson, TX
Group Life and Health Ins. Co.-Sep. Acct., Dallas, TX
Guarantee Mutual Life Co., Omaha, NE

Guarantee Mutual Life Ins. Co., Pleasantville, NJ
Guarantee Reserve Life Ins. Co. (Ind.), Calumet City, IL
Guarantee Security Life Ins. Co., Miami, FL
Guarantee Security Life Ins. Co. of AZ, Phoenix, AZ
Guarantee Trust Life Ins. Co., Chicago, IL

Guaranty Income Life Ins. Co., Baton Rouge, LA
Guaranty Life Insurance Co. of Am., (Del.), Morristown, NJ
Guaranty National Life Ins. Co., Lubbock, TX
Guard Life Ins. Co., Phoenix, AZ
Guardian Ins. & Annutiy Co. Inc. (Del.), New York, NY

Guardian Ins. & Annuity Co. Inc.-Sep. Acct., Wilmington, DE
Guardian Life Ins. Co. of America, New York, NY
Guardsman Life Ins. Co., West Des Moines, IA

Gulf Atlantic Life Ins. Co. (Texas), San Francisco, CA
Gulf Capital Life Ins. Co., Phoenix, AZ

Gulf Financial Life Ins. Co., Phoenix, AZ
Gulf Guaranty Life Ins. Co., Jackson, MS
Gulf Life Group Insurance Company, Jacksonvill, FL
Gulf Life Ins. Co., Jacksonville, FL
Gulf National Life Ins. Co., Biloxi, MS

Gulf Republic Life Ins. Co., Phoenix, AZ
Gulf States Life Ins. Co. Inc., Bossier City, LA
Gulf & Western Life Ins. Co., Phoenix, AZ
Gulfco Life Ins. Co., Marksville, LA

—H—

HAAB Security Life Insurance Co., Shreveport, LA
H B A Life Ins. Co., Phoenix, AZ
Halleen National Life Insurance Co., Phoenix, AZ
Hampton Life Insurance Company, Scottsdale, AZ
Harleysville Life Ins. Co., Harleysville, PA

Harleysville Life Ins. Co.-Sep. Acct., Harleysville, PA
Hartford Life & Accident Ins. Co., Hartford, CT
Hartford Life Ins. Co., Hartford, CT
Hartford Life Ins. Co.-Sep. Acct., Hartford, CT
Hartford Variable Annuity Life Ins. Co., Hartford, CT

Hartford Variable Ann. Life-Sep. Acct., Hartford, CT
Harvest Life Ins. Co., Middleburg Heights, OH
Hawaiian Life Ins. Co. Ltd., Honolulu, HI
Hawaiian Life Ins. Co. Ltd.-Sep. Acct., Honolulu, HI
Hawkeye Life Ins. Group Ins., Des Moines, IA

Hawkeye National Life Ins. Co., Des Moines, IA
Health Insurance of Vermont, Burlington, VT
Health Service Incorporated, Chicago, IL
Health & Welfare Life Ins. Assoc. Inc., New York, NY
Heights Life Insurance Company, Phoenix, AZ

Herald Life Ins. Co., Jacksonville, FL
Heritage Life Ins. Co. (Ariz.), Los Angeles, CA
Hermitage Health and Life Ins. Co., Brentwood, TN
Hill Country Life Ins. Co., Austin, TX
Hill Country Life Ins. Co. of Texas, Austin, TX

Holiday Life Ins. Co. (Neb.), Dallas, TX
Holston Valley Life Insurance Co., Phoenix, AZ
Home Beneficial Life Ins. Co., Richmond, VA
Home Life Ins. Co., New York, NY
Home Life Ins. Co.-Sep. Acct., New York, NY

Home Life Ins. Co. of America (Del.), Washington, DC
Home Mutual Life Ins. Co., Baltimore, MD
Home Owners Life Ins. Co., Chicago, IL
Home Owners Life Ins. Co.-Sep. Acct., Chicago, IL
Home Security Life Ins. Co., Durham, NC

Home Security Life Ins. Co., Pauls Valley, OK
Home State Life Ins. Co., Wichita, KS
Homeco Life Ins. Co. Inc., Appleton, WI
Homesteaders Life Co., Des Moines, IA
Horace Mann Life Ins. Co., Springfield, IL

Horace Mann Life Ins. Co.-Sep. Acct., Springfield, IL
Howard Life Ins. Co., Denver, CO
Huffman National Ins. Co., Phoenix, AZ
Hujopaca Life Insurance Company, Phoenix, AZ

—I—

IDS Life Ins. Co., Minneapolis, MN
IDS Life Ins. Co.-Sep. Acct., Minneapolis, MN
I D S Life Ins. Co. of New York, Albany, NY
INA International Ins. Co., Wilmington, DE
INA Life Ins. Co. (Cal.), Philadelphia, PA

INA Life Ins. Co. of New York, NY
ISI National Life Insurance Company, Phoenix, AZ
ITT Life Ins. Copr., Thorp, WI
ITT Lyndon Life Insurance Company, St. Louis, MO
Illinois Commercial Mens Association, LaGrange, IL

Illinois Dealers Life Ins. Co., Phoenix, AZ
Illinois Life Assurance Co., Chicago, IL
Illinois Life Assurance Co.-Sep. Acct., Chicago, IL
Illinois Midstates Life Ins. Co., Belleville, IL
Illinois Mutual Life and Casualty Co., Peoria, IL

Illinois Traveling Men's Health Assoc., LaGrange, IL
Imperial International Life Ins. Co., Macon, GA
Imperial Life Assurance Co. of Canada, Toronto, Can.
Independence Life and Accident Ins. Co., Louisville, KY
Independent Liberty Life Ins. Co., Grand Rapids, MI

Independent Life and Accident Ins. Co., Jacksonville, FL
Independent Order of Foresters, Don Mills, Ontario, Can.
Independent Standard Ins. Co., Dallas, TX
Indianapolis Life Ins. Co., Indianapolis, IN
Individual Assur. Co. Life Health & Acc., Kansas City, MO

Industrial Casualty Ins. Co., Chicago, IL
Industrial Indemnity Life Ins. Co., San Francisco, CA
Industrial Life Ins. Co., Sillery, Quebec, Can.
Industrail Life Ins. Co., Dallas, TX
Insuramerica Corporation, Wichita, KS

Insurance Co. of American, Austin, TX
Insurance Investors Life, Fort Worth, TX
Integon Life Ins. Corporation, Winston-Salem, NC
Integrity Life Ins. Co., Phoenix, AZ
Integrity Life Insurance Inc., Appleton, WI

Integrity National Life Ins. Co., Philadelphia, PA
Inter-American Ins. Co., Dover, DE
Intercontinental Life Ins. Co., Elizabeth, NJ
Intercontinental Life Ins. Co. of Pr., Hato Rey, P.R.
International General Ins. Corp., Milwaukee, WI

International General Ins.-Sep. Acct., Milwaukke, WI
International Reinsurance Co., New Orleans, LA
International Service Life Ins. Co., Fort Worth, TX
Inter-Ocean Ins. Co. (Ind.), Cincinnati, OH
Interservice Life Ins. Co., Phoenix, AZ

Inter-State Assurance Co. A Mutual Co., Des Moines, IA
Interstate Life Assurance Co., Chicago, IL
Intramerica Life Ins. Co., New York, NY
Investment Life & Trust Co., Mullins, SC
Investment Trust & Assurance Co., Phoenix, AZ

Investors Consolidated Ins. Co., Durham, NC
Investors Equity Life Ins. of Hawaii, Honolulu, HI
Investors Fidelity Life Assur. Corp., Columbus, OH
Investors Fidelity Life Ins. Co., Birmingham AL
Investors Growth Life Ins. Co., Phoenix, AZ

Investors Guaranty Life Ins. Co., Los Angeles, CA

Investors Heritage Life Inc. Co., Frankfort, KY
Investors Heritage Life of the South, Columbia, SC
Investors Insurance Corporation, Tigard, OR
Investors Life of Florida Ins. Co., Winter Park, FL

Investors Life Ins. Co. of America (Ariz.), Canoga Park, CA
Investors Life Ins. Co. of Nebraska, Sioux Falls, SD
Investors Life Ins. Co. of North Amer., Philadelphia, PA
Investors Life Ins. Co. of North Amer., Philadelphia, PA
Investors National Life Ins. Co., Columbia, SC

Investors Security Insurance Company, Oklahoma City, OK
Investors Trust Assurance Company, Indianapolis, IN
Inwood Life Ins. Co., Phoenix, AZ
Iowa-Midwest Insurance Company, Phoenix, AZ
Iowa State Travelers Mutual Assur. Co., West Des Moines, IA

Irwin Union Credit Insurance Corp., Phoenix, AZ

—J—

J. C. Penney Life Ins. Co. (Vt.), Dallas, TX
J. C. Penney Reinsurance Company, Phoenix, AZ
Jackson National Life Ins. Co., Lansing, MI
Jefferson National Life Ins. Co., Indianapolis, IN
Jefferson Standard Life Ins. Co., Greensboro, NC

Jefferson Standard Life Ins. Co., Greensbobo, NC
John Adams Life Ins. Co. of America, Los Angeles, CA
John Alden Life Ins. Co. (Minn.), Coral Gables, FL
John Alden Life Ins. Co.-Sep. Acct., St. Louis Park, MN
John Alden Life Ins. Co. of NY, New York, NY

John Hancock Mutual Life Ins. Co., Boston, MA
John Hancock Mutual Life Ins.-Sep. Acct., Boston, MA
John Hancock Variable Life, Boston, MA
Jordan Life Insurance Company, Phoenix, AZ
Justice Life Ins. Co., Dallas, TX

—K—

Kanawha Insurance Company, Lancaster, SC
Kansas Bancshares Life Insurance Co., Phoenix, AZ
Kansas City Life Ins. Co., Kansas City, MO
Kansas City Ins., Kansas City, MO
Kansas Farm Life Ins. Co. Inc., Manhattan, KS

Kemper Investors Life Ins. Co. (Cal.), Chicago, IL
Kemper Investors Life Ins. Co.-Sep. Acct., Los Angeles, CA
Kemper Investors Life of Illinois, Chicago, IL
Ken Gardner Life Insurance Company, Phoenix, AZ
Kennedy National Life Ins. Co. of Amer., Fort Wayne, IN

Kennesaw Life and Accident Ins. Co., Atlanta, GA
Kent Life Ins. Co., Phoenix, AZ
Kentucky Central Life Ins. Co., Lexington, KY
Kentucky Home Mutual Life Ins. Co., Louisville, KY
Key Life Ins. Co. of South Carolina, Colubmia, SC

Keystone Life Ins. Co., Philadelphia, PA
Keystone Life Ins. Co. of Texas, Carrollton, TX
Keystone Massachusetts Life (Del.), Boston, MA
Keystone Provident Life Ins. Co. (R.I.), Boston, MA
Keystone Provident Life Ins.-Sep. Acct., Providence, RI

Kiamichi Life Insurance Company, Phoenix, AZ
Kilpatrick Life Ins. Co. of La., Shreveport, LA
Kinder Life Insurance Company, Montgomery, AL
Knickerbocker Life Ins. Co., Austin, TX

Knickerbocker Life Ins. Co. of Ind., Indianapolis, IN

Knights of Columbus, New Haven, CT
Kokomo National Life Ins. Co., Kokomo, IN

—L—

L Life Insurance Company, Phoenix, AZ
Lafayette Life Ins. Co., Lafayette, IN
Lafourche Life Ins. Co., Raceland, LA
Lake Life Insurance Company, Del.
Lake States Life Ins. Co., Scottsdale, AZ

Lakeland Assurance Inc. (Ariz.), Southfield, MI
Lamar Life Ins. Co., Jackson, MS
Laymen Life Ins. Co., Anderson, IN
League Life Ins. Co., Southfield, MI
League Life Ins. Co.-Sep. Acct., Southfield, MI

Lee National Life Ins. Co. of Louisiana, Shreveport, LA
Legal Security Life Ins. Co., Dallas, TX
Liberty American Assurance Co., Lincoln, NE
Liberty General Life Ins. Co., Carrollton, TX
Liberty Investors Life Ins. Co., Oklahoma City, OK

Liberty Life Assurance Co. of Boston, Boston, MA
Liberty Life Assur. of Boston-Sep. Acct., Boston, MA
Liberty Life, Health & Acc. Ins. Co., Reading, PA
Liberty Life Ins. Co., Greenville, SC
Liberty National Life Ins. Co., Birmingham, AL

Life Assurance Co of America, Oak Brook, IL
Life Assurance Co. of Pennsylvania, Chicago, IL
Life and Casualty Ins. Co. of Tenn., Nashville, TN
Life General Security Ins. Co., Harvey, LA
Life and Health Ins Co of Amer., Philadelphia, PA

Life Insurance Associates Inc., Phoenix, AZ
Life Insurance Co. of Alabama, Gadsden, AL
Life Insurance Co. of Alaska, Anchorage, AK
Life Insurance Co. of America Inc., Oklahoma City, OK
Life Insurance Company of Cincinnati, Cincinati, OH

Life Insurance Co. of Connecticut, Danbury, CT
Life Insurance Co. of Georgia, Atlanta, GA
Life Insurance Co. of Georgia-Sep. Acct., Atlanta, GA
Life Insurance Co. of Illinois, Glenview, IL
Life Insurance Co. of Kansas Inc., Wichita, KS

Life Insurance Co. of Minnesota, Bloomington, MN
Life Ins. Co. of Mississippi, Jackson, MS
Life Insurance Co. of North America, Philadelphia, PA
Life Insurance Co. of No. Amer.-Sep. Acct., Philadelphia, PA
Life Ins. Co. of North America-Consol., Philadelphia, PA

Life Insurance Co. of the Northwest, Spokane, WA
Life Insurance Co. of the South, Metairie, LA
Life Insurance Co. of the Southwest, Dallas, TX
Life Insurance Co. of Virginia, Richmond, VA
Life Insurance Co. of Virginia-Sep. Acct., Richmond, VA

Life Investors Ins. Co. of America, Cedar Rapids, IA
Life Investors Ins. Co. of Amer.-Comb., Cedar Rapids, IA
Life of America Ins. Co. Houston, TX
Life of America Ins. Corp. of Boston, Malden, MA
Life of Indiana Insurance Company, Indianapolis, IN

Life of Mid-America Ins. Co., Dubuque, IA
Life of Montana Ins. Co., Bozeman, MT

Life of Nebraska Insurance Company, Lincoln, NE
Life Protection Ins. Co., Dallas, TX
Lifetime Security Life Ins. Co., Louisville, KY

Lincoln American Life Ins. Co., Memphis, TN
Lincoln Benefit Life Co., Lincoln, NE
Lincoln Heritage Life Ins. Co. (Ill.), Phoenix, AZ
Lincoln Income Life Ins. Co., Louisville, KY
Lincoln Liberty Life Ins. Co., Lincoln, NE

Lincoln Life and Casualty Co., Lincoln, NE
Lincoln Life Ins. Co., Scottsdale, AZ
Lincoln Mutual Life & Casualty Ins. Fargo, ND
Lincoln Mutual Life Ins. Co., Lincoln, NE
Lincoln National Life Ins. Co., Fort Wayne, IN

Lincoln National Life Ins. Co.-Sep. Acct., Fort Wayne, IN
Lincoln National Pension Ins. Co., Fort Wayne, IN
Lincoln Standard Life Insurance Co., Chicago, IL
Lincolnshire Life Insurance Company, Phoenix, AZ
Loanpay Life Ins. Co., Phoenix, AZ

London Life Ins. Co., London, Ontario, Can.
Lone Star Life Ins. Co., Dallas, TX
Long Life Insurance Company, Scottsdale, AZ
Louisiana Life Ins. Co., Sulphur, LA
Louisiana National Life Ins. Co., New Orleans, LA

Loyal American Life Ins. Co., Mobile, AL
Loyalty Life Insurance Company, Southfield, MI
Lumbermens Life Ins., Indianapolis, IN
Lutheran Brotherhood, Minneapolis, MN
Lutheran Mutural Life Ins. Co., Waverly, IA

Lyndon Insurance Company (Wisc.), St. Louis, MO

—M—

MAES Life Insurance Company, Phoenix, AZ
MBL Life Assurance Corp., Cincinnati, OH
M F A Life Ins. Co., Columbia, MO
MGIC Life Ins. Corp. (Ill.), Milwaukee, WI
MIC Life Insurance Company, Wilmington, DE

M M L Pension Insurance Co. (Del.), Springfield, MA
MONY Life Ins. Co. of Canada, Don Mills, Ontario, Can.
MRS Life Ins. Co., Phoenix, AZ
Maccabees Mutual Life Ins. Co., Southfield, MI
Maccabees Mutual Life Ins. Co.-Sep. Acct., Southfield, MI

Madison Natl. Life Ins. Co. Inc., Middleton, WI
Madison National Life Ins. Co. Inc., Canton, OH
Magnolia Life Ins. Co., Lake Charles, LA
Main Life Ins. Co. (Ariz.), Cincinnati, OH
Maine Fidelity Life Ins. Co. (Me.), Keene, NH

Maine National Life Ins. Co. (Me.), Berea, OH
Majestic Life Ins. Co., New Orleans, LA
Mammoth Life and Accident Ins. Co., Louisville, KY
Manchester Life Ins. Co., St. Louis, MO
Manhattan Life Ins. Co., New York, NY

Manhattan Mutual Life Ins. Co., Manhattan, KS
Manufacturers Life Ins. Co., Toronto, Ontario, Can.
Maritime Life Assurance Co., Halifax, Nova Scotia, Can.
Mark Twain Life Insurance Corp., Oklahoma City, OK
Marquette Indemnity Life Ins. Co., Phoenix, AZ

Marquette National Life Ins. Co., Chicago, IL

Massachusetts Casualty Ins. Co., Boston, MA
Massachusetts General Life Ins. Co. (Mass.), Englewood, CO
Massachusetts Indemnity & Life Ins. Boston, MA
Massachusetts Mutual Life Ins. Co., Springfield, MA

Massachusetts Mutual Life Ins.-Sep. Acct., Springfield, MA
Massachusetts Savings Bank Life Ins. Boston, MA
Master Life Ins. Co. (Ariz.), Philadelphia, PA
Mayflower National Life Ins. Co., Lafayette, IN
Medical Life Insurance Company, Cleveland, OH

Medico Life Ins. Co., Omaha, NE
Melancon Life Ins. Co., Carencro, LA
Mellon Life Ins. Co. (Del.), Oakbrook, IL
Member Service Life Insurance Co., Tulsa, OK
Memberlife Insurance Co. of Michigan, Dearborn, MI

Members Life Ins. Co., Farmers Branch, TX
Menlo Union Life Ins. Co., Phoenix, AZ
Mercantile & General Reins Co. Ltd. (Eng.), Toronto, Can.
Merchants Life Ins. Co., Wilmington, DE
Merchants Life Ins. Co., Buffalo, NY

Mercury National Life Ins. Co., Norman , OK
Meridian Life Ins. Co., Indianapolis, IN
Merit Life Ins. Co., Evansville, IN
Mesa Life Ins. Co., Phoenix, AZ
Metroplex Life Insurance Co., Fort Worth, TX

Metropolitan Ins. & Annuity Company (Del.), New York, NY
Metropolitan Life Ins. Co., New York, NY
Metropolitan Life Ins. Co.-Sep. Acct., New York, NY
Michigan Life Ins. Co., Southfield, MI
Mid-America Life Assurance Co., Saginaw, MI

Midamerica Mutual Life Ins. Co., Minneapolis, MN
Mid-Continent Life Insurance Co., Oklahoma City, OK
Midland Mutual Life Ins. Co., Columbus, OH
Midland Mutual Life Ins. Co.-Sep. Acct., Columbus, OH
Midland National Life Ins. Co., Sioux Falls, SD

Midland National Life-Consolidated, Sioux Falls, SD
Mid South Ins. Co., Fayetteville, NC
Mid-South Life Ins. Co., Jackson, MS
Mid-States Ins. Co. of America (Fla.), Evanston, IL
Midwest Ins. Co., Phoenix, AZ

Midwest International Life Ins. Co., Fargo, ND
Midwest Life Ins. Co. (Neb.), Minneapolis, MN
Mid-West National Life Ins. of Tenn., Nashville, TN
Midwestern Credit Ins. Co. (Ariz.), Columbus, OH
Mid-Western Life Ins. Co., Enid, OK

Mid-Western Life Ins. of Texas, Dallas, TX
Midwestern National Insurance Corp., La Crosse, WI
Midwestern National Life Ins. of Ohio, Cleveland, OH
Midwestern United Life Ins. Co., Fort Wayne, IN
Millers Life Ins. Co. of Texas, Fort Worth, TX

Milwaukee Life Ins. Co., Milwaukee, WI
Milwaukee Life Ins. Co.-Sep. Acct., Milwaukee, WI
Ministers Life, A Mutual Life Ins. Co., Minneapolis, MN
Minnehoma Life Ins. Co., Tulsa, OK
Minnesota Mutual Life Ins. Co., St. Paul, MN

Minnesota Mutual Life Ins. Co.-Sep. Acct., St. Paul, MN
Minnesota Protective Life Ins. Co., Eden Prairie, MN
Minnesota Protective Life Ins. Co. Cons., Eden Prairie, MN

Mission Life Ins. Co., Houston, TX
Mississippi American Life Ins. Co., Jackson, MS

Mississippi Valley Life Ins. Co., Phoenix, AZ
Missouri National Life Ins. Co., Kansas City, MO
Modern American Life Ins. Co., Sprinfield, MO
Modern Income Life Ins. Co., Decatur, IL
Modern Pioneers' Life Ins. Co., Phoenix, AZ

Modern Security Life Ins. Co., Kansas City, MO
Modern Woodmen of America, Rock Island, IL
Monarch Life Assurance Co., Winnipeg, Manitoba, Can.
Monarch Life Ins. Co., Springfield, MA
Monitor Life Insurance Co., Utica, NY

Montana National Life Ins. Co., Billings, MT
Montgomery Ward Life Ins. Co., Chicago, IL
Montreal Life Ins Co., Montreal, Quebec, Can.
Monument Life Ins. Co. (Ariz.), Indianapolis, IN
Monumental Life Ins. Co., Baltimore, MD

Monumental Life Ins. Co.-Sep. Acct., Baltimore, MD
Mortgage Bankers Life Ins. Co., Fort Worth, TX
Mothe Life Ins. Co., Gretna, LA
The Motor Life Ins. Co. (Del.), Jacksonville, FL
Motorists Life Ins. Co., Columbus, OH

Mountain Life Ins. Co., Maryville, TN
Mountain States Life Ins. Co. of Amer. (Co.), Albuquerque, NM
Munich American Ressurance Co., Atlanta, GA
Municipal Ins. Co. of America, Elgin, IL
Mutual Benefit Life Ins. Co., Newark, NJ

Mutual Benefit Life Ins. Co.-Sep. Acct., Newark, NJ
Mutual Investors Assurance, Phoenix, AZ
Mutual Life Assurance Co. of Canada, Waterloo, Ontario, Can.
Mutual Life Ins. Co. of New York, New York, NY
Mutual Life Ins. Co. of NY-Sep. Acct., New York, NY

Mutual Life Ins. Co. of Washington DC, Washington, DC
Mutual of Detroit Ins. Co., Plymouth, MI
Mutual of Mid-Amer. Life Ins. Co., Speedway, IN
Mutual of Omaha Ins. Co., Omaha, NE
Mutual Savings Life Ins. Co., Decatur, AL

Mutual Security Life Ins. Co., Fort Wayne, IN
Mutual Security Life Ins. Co.-Sep. Acct., Fort Wayne, IN
Mutual Service Life Ins. Co., Arden Hills, MN
Mutual Service Life Ins. Co.-Sep. Acct., Arden Hills, MN
Mutual Trust Life Ins. Co., Oak Brook, IL

La Mutuelle-Vie des Fonctionnaires, Quebec, Can

—N—

NBD Insurance Company (Ariz.), Detroit, MI
N I C O Inc. Co., Phoenix, AZ
NN Investors Life Ins. Co. Inc., Cedar Rapids, IA
NN Providence Life Ins. Co., Johnston, RI
N R G America Reassurance Corp., Wilmington, DE

NTA Life Insurance Company, Dallas, TX
Nanseekay Life Insurance Company, Scottsdale, AZ
National Alliance Life Ins. Co., Bossier City, LA
National American Life Ins. Co. of Cal., Los Angeles, CA
National Assurance Life Ins. Co., Tulsa, OK

National Atlas Life Ins. Co., Houston, TX
National Auto Dealers Ins. Co., Phoenix, AZ

National-Ben Franklin Life Ins. Corp. (Wisc.), Chicago, IL
National-Ben Franklin Corp.-Sep. Acct., Milwaukee, WI
National Benebit Life Ins. Co., New York, NY

National Benefit Life Ins. Co., Fort Worth, TX
National Benefit Life Ins. Co.-Sep. Acct., New York, NY
National Capital Life Insurance Co., Oklahoma City, OK
National Catholic Soc. of Foresters, Chicago, IL
National City Life Insurance Company, Phoenix, AZ

National Coaches Annuity Ins. Co., Little Rock, AR
National Commerce Life Ins. Co., Phoenix, AZ
National Continental Life Ins. Co., Hye, Texas
National Crown Life Insurance Co., Scottsdale, AZ
National Equity Life Ins. Co. Inc., Hononlulu, HI

National Farm Life Ins. Co., Fort Worth, TX
National Farmers Union Life Ins. Co., Denver, CO
National Fidelity Life Ins. Co. (Mo.), Overland Park, KS
National Foundation Life Ins. Co., Oklahoma City, OK
National General Ins. Co., Jackson, MS

National Guardian Life Ins. Co.,Madison, WI
National Health Insurance Company, Dallas, TX
National Health & Welfare Mutual, New York, NY
National Health & Welfare-Sep. Acct., New York, NY
National Home Life & Accident, Indianapolis, IN

National Home Life Assurance Co., Jefferson City, MO
National Home Life Assur. Co. of NY, Binghamton, NY
National Investors Life Ins. Co., Little Rock, AR
National Investors Pension Ins., Little Rock, AR
National Liberty Life Ins. of America, Valley Forge, PA

National Liberty Life Ins. Co., Frazer, PA
National Life & Accident Ins. Co., Nashville, TN
National Life Assurance Co. of Canada, Toronto, Ontario, Can.
National Life Ins. Co., Hato Rey, P.R.
National Life Ins. Co., Montpelier, VT

National Life Ins. Co.-Sep. Acct., Montpelier, VT
National Life Ins. Co. of Texas, Dallas, TX
National Masonic Provident Assoc., Columbus, OH
National Motor Club Life & Accident, Dallas, TX
National Mutual Benefit, Madison, WI

National Old Line Ins. Co., Little Rock, AR
National Public Service Ins. Co., Seattle WA
National Reserve Life Ins. Co. (S.D.), Topeka, KS
National Retirement Ins. Co., Madison Heights, MI
National Safety Life Ins. Co., Philadelphia, PA

National Savings Life Ins. Co., Little Rock, AR
National Savings Life Ins. Co., Murfreesboro, TN
National Security Ins. Co., Elba, AL
National Security Life & Accident, Dallas, TX
National Standard Life Ins. Co., Orlando, FL

National States Ins. Co., University City, MO
National Travelers Life Company, Des Moines, IA
National Union Life Ins. Co. (Ala.), Birmingham, AL
National United Life Ins. Co. (Ariz.), Kansas City, MO
National Western Life Ins. Co. (Colo.), Austin, TX

Nationwide Life Ins. Co., Columbus, OH
Nationwide Life Ins. Co.-Sep. Acct., Columbus, OH
Navajo Life Ins. Co. (Ariz.), Houston, TX
Neighbors of Woodcraft, Portland, OR
New American Life Ins. Co., Colubmia, MO

New Century Life Ins. Co., La Jolla, CA
New England General Life Ins. Co. (Del.), Boston, MA
New England Mutual Life Ins. Co., Boston, MA
New England Mutual Life Ins.-Cep. Acct., Boston, MA
New England National Life Ins. Co. (Del.), Boston, MA

New England Pension & Annuity Co. (Del.), Boston, MA
New Jersey Life Ins. Co., Saddle Brook, NJ
New Mexico Investors Life Ins. Co., Albuquerque, NM
New Southland National Ins. Co., Tuscaloosa, AL
New York Life Ins. & Annuity Corp., (Del.), New York, NY

New York Life Ins. Co., New york, NY
New York Life Ins. Co.-Sep. Acct., New York, NY
New York Savings Bank Life Ins., New York, NY
Nichols National Life Ins. Co., Phoenix, AZ
Norlen Life Ins. Co., Phoenix, AZ

North America Life Insurance Company, Houston, TX
North American Benefit Assoc., Port Huron, MI
North American Co. For Health, New York, NY
North American Co. of Life & Health, Chicago, IL
North American Equitable Life Assur., Columbus, OH

North America Insurance Co., Richmond, VA
North American Life Assurance Co., Toronto, Ontario, Can.
North American Life and Casualty Co., Minneapolis, MN
North American Reassurance Co., New York, NY
North American Reassur. Co.-Sep. Acct., New York, NY

North American Union Life Assur. Soc., Chicago, NY
North Atlantic Life Ins. Co. of Amer., Jericho, NY
North Carolina Mutual Life Ins. Co., Durham, NC
North Central Life Ins. Co., St. Paul, MN
North Coast Life Ins. Co., Spokane, WA

North West Life Assur. Co. of Canada, Vancouver, B.C., Can.
Northbrook Life Ins. Co., Northbrook, IL
Northern Great Lakes Ins. Co., Phoenix, AZ
Northern Life Assurance Co. of Canada, London, Ontario, Can.
Northern Life Ins. Co., Seattle, WA

Northern Life Ins. Co.-Sep. Acct., Seattle, WA
Northern National Life Ins. Co., Bismarck, ND
Northland Life Ins. Co., Grand Forks, ND
Northwestern Mutual Life Ins. Co., Milwaukee, WI
Northwestern Mutual Life Ins.-Sep. Acct., Milwaukee, WI

Northwestern National Life Ins. Co., Minneapolis, MN
Northwestern National Life-Sep. Acct., Minneapolis, MN
Northwestern Natl. Life Ins. Co. Cons., Minneapolis, MN
Northwestern Security Life Ins. Co. (Ariz.), Wilkesboro, NC
Norton Life Ins. Co., Phoenix, AZ

Norwood Life Ins. Co. (Ariz.), Chicago, IL

—O—

Oak Life Insurance Company, Scottsdale, AZ
Occidental Life Ins. Co. of California, Los Angeles, CA
Occidental Life Ins. Co.-Sep. Acct., Los Angeles, CA
Occidental Life Ins. Co. of Canada, Toronto, Can.
Occidental Life Ins. Co. of Illinois, Chicago, IL

Occidental Life Ins. Co. of NC, Raleigh, NC
Occidental Life Ins. Co. of Texas, Hye, Texas
Ocoee Life Insurance Company, Phoenix, AZ
Ohio Life Ins. Co., Hamilton, OH
Ohio National Life Assur. Corp., Cincinnati, OH

Ohio National Life Ins. Co., Cincinnati, OH
Ohio National Life Ins. Co.-Sep. Acct., Cincinnati, OH
Ohio State Life Ins. Co., Columbus, OH
Oklahoma Credit Life Ins. Co. (Okla.), Springfield, OH
Oklahoma National Life Ins. Co., Oklahoma City, OK

Old Alliance Life Ins. Co., Phoenix, AZ
Old American Ins. Co., Kansas City, MO
Old Colony Life Ins. Co., Jackson, MS
Old Colony Life Insurance Company, (R.I.), Atlanta, GA
Old Equity Mutual Life Ins. Co., Evanston, IL

Old Faithful Life Ins. Co., Cheyenne, WY
Old Financial Trust Life Ins. Co., Phoenix, AZ
Old Line Life Ins. Co. of America, Milwaukee, WI
Old National Life Insurance Company, Phoenix, AZ
Old Reliance Ins. Co., Phoenix, AZ

Old Republic Life Ins. Co., Chicago, IL
Old Republic Life Ins. Co. of New York, Buffalo, NY
Old Republic Life of Oklahoma, (Okla.), Chicago, IL
Old Republic Life Ins. Co. of Texas, Dallas, TX
Old South Life Ins. Co., Louisville, KY

Old South Life Ins. Co. Jonesboro, LA
Old Southern Life Ins. Co., Montgomery, AL
Old Spartan Life Ins. Co., Phoenix, AZ
Old Surety Life Ins. Co., Alva, OK
Old United Life Ins. Co. (Ariz.), Shawnee-Mission, KS

Old Western Life Ins. Co., Kansas City, MO
Olinger Life Ins. Co., Denver, CO
Omaha Financial Life Ins. Co., Minneapolis, MN
Oneida Life Ins. Co., Scottsdale, AZ
Opportunity Life Insurance Company, Scottsdale, AZ

Orange State Life Ins. Co., Largo, FL
Orleans Ins. Co., New Orleans, LA
Orono Life Ins. Co., Phoenix, AZ
Osage Life Ins. Co., Scottsdale, AZ
Oxford Life Ins. Co., Phoenix, AZ

Ozark National Life Ins. Co., Little Rock, AR
Ozark National Life Ins. Co., Kansas City, MO

—P—

P. A. T. Life Insurance Company, Phoenix, AZ
P H A Life Ins. Co., Portland, OR
PHF Life Ins. Co., Battle Creek, MI
PM Life Ins. Co., Armonk, NY
Pacific Bankers Life Assurance Co., Phoenix, AZ

Pacific Empire Life Ins. Co., Boise, ID
Pacific Fidelity Life Ins. Co., Pasadena, CA
Pacific Fidelity Life Ins. Co.-Sep. Acct., Los Angeles, CA
Pacific Guaranty Life Insurance Co. (Ariz.), Newport Beach, CA
Pacific Guardian Life Ins. Co. Ltd., Honolulu, HI

Pacific Life Ins Co. (Ariz.), Columbus, OH
Pacific Mutual Life Ins. Co., Newport Beach, CA
Pacific Mutual Life Ins. Co.-Sep. Acct., Newport Beach, CA
Pacific Northwest Life Ins. Co., Portland, OR
Pacific Standard Life Ins. Co., Phoenix, AZ

Pacific Standard Life Ins. Co. of Tex., Austin, TX
Pacific Union Assurance Co., San Francisco, CA
Pan-American Life Ins. Co., New Orleans, LA
Pan-Western Life Ins. Co., Columbus, OH

Paramount Life Ins. Co., Little Rock, AR

Paramount Life Ins. Co., Calgary Alberta, Can.
Paramount National Life Ins. Co., Dallas, TX
Parliament Life Ins. Co., King of Prussia, PA
Paso Del Norte Life Ins. Co., Phoenix, AZ
Patrick Henry Life Ins. Co., Phoenix, AZ

Patriot General Life Ins. Co., Concord, MA
Paul Revere Life Ins. Co., Worcester, MA
Paul Revere Protective Life Ins. Co. (Del.), Worcester, MA
Paul Revere Variable Annuity Ins. Co., Worcester, MA
Paul Revere Variable Annuity-Sep. Acct., Worcester, MA

Pecos Life Ins. Co., Phoenix, AZ
Peerless Life and Casualty Co., Phoenix, AZ
Pekin Life Ins. Co., Pekin, IL
Pemco Life Ins. Co., Seattle, WA
Peninsular Life Ins. Co., Jacksonville, FL

Penn Mutual Life Ins. Co., Philadelphia, PA
Penn Mutual Life Ins. Co.-Sep. Acct., Philadelphia, PA
Penn Treaty Life Ins. Co., Allentown, PA
Pennsylvania Life Ins. Co. (Pa.), Santa Monica, CA
Pennsylvania National Life Ins. Co., Harrisburg, PA

Pension Life Insurance Co. of America (N.J.), Valley Forge, PA
People Accident Ins. Co., Lincoln, NE
Peoples Life Ins. Co., Tyler, TX
Peoples Life Ins. Co. of S.C., Greenville, SC
People Life Ins. Co., Washington, DC

Personal Indemnity Mutual Ins. Co., Milwaukee, WI
Personal Life Ins. Co., St. Louis, MO
Personal Life Ins. Co.-Sep. Acct., St. Louis, MO
Petroleum State Ins. Co. (La.), Madison, NJ
Pharmacists Life Ins. Co., Algona, IA

Philadelphia American Life Ins. Co., DE
Philadelphia Life Ins. Co., Philadelphia, PA
Philadelphia Life Ins. Co.-Sep. Acct., Philadelphia, PA
Philadelphia-United Life Ins. Co., Philadelphia, PA
Philadelphia-United Life Ins.-Sep. Acct., Philadelphia, PA

Philanthropic Mutual Life Ins. Co., Rosemont, PA
Philanthropic Mut. Life Ins.-Sep. Acct., Rosemont, PA
Phoenix Life Ins. Co. (Del.), Hartford, CT
Phoenix Mutual Life Ins. Co., Hartford, CT
Phoenix Mutual Life Ins. Co.-Sep. Acct., Hartford, CT

Physicians Life Ins. Co., Omaha, NE
Physicians Mutual Insurance Company, Omaha, NE
Pico Life Insurance Company, Pickerington, OH
Piedmont Ins. Co., Marion, SC
Pierce National Life Ins. Co., Los Angeles, CA

Pikeman's Protective Life Ins. Co., Carrollton, TX
Pilgrim Health and Life Ins. Co., Augusta, GA
Pilgrim Life Ins. Co., Folcroft, PA
Pilgrim Life Ins. Co. of America, Wilmington, DE
Pilot life Ins. Co., Greensboro, NC

Pilot Life Ins. Co.-Sep. Acct., Greensboro, NC
Pine Top Life Company, Phoenix, AZ
Pioneer American Ins. Co., Waco, TX
Pioneer Annuity Life Ins. Co., Phoenix, AZ
Pioneer Life Assurance Co., Regina, Saskatchewan, Can.

Pioneeer Life Ins. Co., Wyncote, PA

Pioneer Life Ins. Co. of Illinois, Rockford, IL
Pioneer Mutual Life Ins. Co., Fargo, ND
Pioneer National Life Ins. Co., Topeka, KS
Pioneer Security Life Ins. Co., Phoenix, AZ

Pioneer Security Life Ins. Co., Houston, TX
Planters Life Insurance Company, Phoenix, AZ
Polish National Alliance of U S N A, Chicago, IL
Polish Roman Catholic Union America, Chicago, IL
Pony Express Life Ins. Co., Phoenix, AZ

Praetorian Mutual Life Ins. Co., Dallas, TX
Prairie States Life Ins. Co., Rapid City, SD
Preferred Life Ins. Co., Montgomery, AL
Preferred Life Ins. Co. (Ariz.), Dallas, TX
Preferred Risk Life Ins. Co. (Colo.), West Des Moines, IA

Premiere Life Insurance Company, Shreveport, LA
Presbyterian Ministers' Fund, Philadelphia, PA
Presbyterian Ministers' Fund-Sep. Acct., Philadelphia, PA
Presidential Life Ins. Co., Nyack, NY
Presidential Life Ins. Co. of Amer., Oklahoma City, OK

Presidents Life Insurance Company, Phoenix, AZ
Princeton Life Ins. Co., Lancaster, PA
Professional Ins. Corporation, Jacksonville, FL
Professional Investors Life Ins. Co., Tulsa, OK
Progress Life and Accident Ins. Co., Oklahoma City, OK

Progressive American Life Ins. Co., Mayfield Village, OH
Progressive Bankers Life, Scottsdale, AZ
Progressive Life Ins. Co., Red Bank, NJ
Progressive National Life Ins. Co., Kansas City, MO
Proprietors Life Assur. Co., Delaware, OH

Protected Home Mutual Life Ins. Co., Sharon, PA
Protection Life Insurance Company, Phoenix, AZ
Protective Industrial Ins. Co. of Al., Birmingham, AL
Protective Life Ins. Co., Birmingham, AL
Protective Life Ins. Co.-Sep. Acct., Birmingham, AL

Protective Service Life Ins. Co., Jackson, MS
Provident Alliance Life Ins. Co., Newport Beach, CA
Provident American Ins. Co., Dallas, TX
Provident Indemnity Life Ins. Co., Norristown, PA
Provident Life and Accident Ins. Co., Chattanooga, TN

Provident Life & Accident Ins.-Sep. Acct., Chattanooga, TN
Provident Life and Casualty Ins. Co., Chattanooga, TN
Provident Life Ins. Co., Bismarck, ND
Provident Mutual Life Ins. Co. of Phila., Philadelphia, PA
Provident Mut. Life of Phila.-Sep. Acct., Philadelphia, PA

Provident National Assur. Co., Chattanooga, TN
Provident National Assur. Co.-Sep. Acct., Chattanooga, TN
Providential Life Ins. Co., North Little Rock, AR
Providers Benefit Life Ins. Co., Bala Cynwyd, PA
Pruco Life Ins. Co., Phoenix, AZ

Prudential Ins. Co. of America, Newark, NJ
Prudential Ins. Co. of America-Sep. Acct., Newark, NJ
Public Fidelity Life Ins. Co. (Del.), Bala Cynwyd, PA
Public Investors Life Ins. Co., Alexandria, LA
Public Safety Officers Life Ins. Co. (Ariz.), Chicago, IL

Public Savings Life Ins. Co., Charleston. SC
Public Service Life Ins. Co., Sioux City, IA
Purdue National Ins. Co., Phoenix, AZ

Puritan Life Ins. Co., Johnston, RI
Purple Shield Life Ins. Co., Baton Rouge, LA

Pyramid Life Ins. Co., Shawnee Mission, KS

—Q—

Quaker Life Ins. Co., Tulsa, OK

—R—

Reliable Life and Casualty Co., Madison, WI
Reliable Life Ins. Co., Hamilton, Ontario, Can.
Reliable Life Insurance Co., Webster Groves, MO
Reliable Reinsurers Company Ltd., Phoenix, AZ
Reliance Life Ins. Co., Philadelphia, PA

Reliance Standard Life Ins. Co. (Ill.), Philadelphia, PA
Republic Bankers Life Ins. Co., Dallas, TX
Republic National Life Group Ins. Co., Dallas, TX
Republic National Life Ins. Co., Dallas, TX
Republic-Vanguard Life Ins. Co., Dallas, TX

Reserve Life Ins. Co., Dallas, TX
Reserve National Ins. Co., Oklahoma City, OK
Resources Life Ins. Co. (Del.), New York, NY
Rhea Insurance Company Inc., Phoenix, AZ
Rio Grande Life Ins. Co., Phoenix, AZ

Ritter Life Ins. Co., Huntington Valley, PA
Riverside Life Ins. Co., New Orleans, LA
Riverside Life Ins. Co. of America, Little Rock, AR
Rockford Life Ins. Co., Rockford, IL
Rocky Mountain Life Ins. Co. of Colo., Denver, CO

Roosevelt National Life Ins. of Amer., Springfield, IL
Royal Arcanum Supreme Council of The, Boston, MA
Royal-Key Life Ins. Co., Scottsdale, AZ
Royal Life Ins. Co. of America, Hartford, CT
Royal Life Ins. Co. of New York, New York, NY

Royal Neighbors of America, Rock Island, IL
Royal Oak Life Ins. Co., King of Prussia, PA
Royal State National Ins. Co., Honolulu, HI
Rumford Life Ins. Co., Providence, RI
Rural Security Life Ins. Co., Madison, WI

Rushmore Mutual Life Ins. Co., Rapid City, SD

—S—

S & H Life Ins. Co., Phoenix, AZ
S F C Insurance Company, Phoenix, AZ
St. Barnabas Life Ins. Co., Scottsdale, AZ
St. Paul Life Ins. Co., St. Paul, MN
St. Paul Life Ins. Co.-Sep. Acct., St. Paul, MN

Sabine Life Ins. Co., Many, LA
Safeco Life Ins. Co., Seattle, WA
SAFECO National Life Ins. Co., Seattle, WA
Safety Indust. Life & Sick Ben. Assoc., New Orleans, LA
Sagamore Life Insurance Company, Phoenix, AZ

Savings Bank Life Ins. Co., Hartford, CT
Savings Life Ins. Co., Shreveport, LA
Savings Life Ins. Co.-Consolidated, Shreveport, LA
Savings Life Insurance Co. of Oklahoma, Oklahoma City, OK
Savings Life Ins. Co. of Texas, Dallas, TX

Scenic City Life Insurance Company, Phoenix, AZ
Schoen Life Ins. Co. Inc., New Orleans, LA

Scor Re Life Insurance Company, Irving, TX
Scott Life Ins. Co., Phoenix, AZ
Seaboard Life Ins. Co., Vancouver, British Columbia, Can.

Seafirst Life Ins. Co., Seattle, WA
Second Gulf Financial Life Insurance, Phoenix, AZ
Securance Life Insurance Company, Phoenix, AZ
Security of America Life Ins. Co., Reading, PA
Security Assurance Co. (Ariz.), Omaha, NE

Security Atlantic Life Ins. Co., Phoenix, AZ
Security Benefit Life Ins. Co., Topeka, KS
Security Benefit Life Ins. Co.-Sep. Acct., Topeka, KS
Security Connecticut Ins. Corp., Avon, CT
Security-Connecticut Life Ins. Co., Avon, CT

Security First Life Ins. Co., Wilmington, DE
Security General Life Ins. Co., Oklahoma City, OK
Security Guaranty Life Ins. Co. (Ala.), Englewood, CO
Security Industrial Ins. Co. Inc., Donaldsonville, LA
Security International Ins. Co., Fargo, ND
Security Life and Accident Co., Denver, CO
Security Life Ins. Co. of America, Minneapolis, MN
Security Life Ins. Co. of Amer. (Cons.), Minneapolis, MN
Security Life Ins. Co. of Georgia, Macon, GA
Security Life Ins. Co. of the South, Jackson, MS

Security Mutual Life Ins. Co., Lincoln, NE
Security Mutual Life Ins. Co.-Sep. Acct., Lincoln, NE
Security Mutual Life of NY, Binghamton, NY
Security Mutual Life of NY-Sep. Acct., Binghamton, NY
Security National Life Ins. Co., Salt Lake City, UT

Security National Life Ins. Co. of P.R., Hato Rey, P.R.
Security Savings Life Ins. Co., Fort Worth, TX
Security Southwest Life Ins. Co., El Paso, TX
Senate Ins. Co. (Ariz.), Schenectady, NY
Sentinel Life Ins. Co. (Cal.), Portland, OR

Sentinel National Life Ins. Co. (Ariz.), Dallas, TX
Sentinel Security Life Ins. Co., Salt Lake City, UT
Sentry Life Ins. Co., Stevens Point, WI
Sentry Life Ins. Co.-Sep. Acct., Steven Point, WI
Sentry Life Ins. Co. of New York, Syracuse, NY

Service Life & Casualty Ins. Co., Austin, TX
Service Life Ins. Co. of Omaha, Omaha, NE
Shannon Life Ins. Co., Fort Worth, TX
Shawnee Life Insurance Company, Phoenix, AZ
The Shelby Life Ins. Co. of Shelby, Shelby, OH

Shenandoah Life Ins. Co., Roanoke, VA
Shenandoah Life Ins. Co.-Sep. Acct., Roanoke, VA
Sierra General Life Ins. Co., Reno, NV
Sierra Life Ins. Co., Twin Falls, ID
Sierra Pacific Life Ins. Co. (Ariz.), San Francisco, CA

Sierra Western Life Insurance Company, Phoenix, AZ
Slovene National Benefit Society, Burr Ridge, IL
Smoky Mountain Life Insurance Company, Phoenix, AZ
Society Life Insurance Company, Phoenix, AZ
Society National Life Ins. Co., Indianapolis, IN

Sons of Norway, Minneapolis, MN
Sooner Life Ins. Co., Ponca City, OK
South Atlantic Life Ins. Co., Charleston, SC
Southeast Life Ins. Co. of Fla., Miami, FL
Southeastern General Life Ins. Co., Winter Park, FL

Southeastern Life Ins. Co., Phoenix, AZ
Southern Aid Life Ins. Co., Richmond, VA
Southern Bankers Life Insurance Co., Phoenix, AZ
Southern Bankers Life Ins. Co., Shreveport, LA
Southern Commercial Life Insurance Co., Phoenix, AZ

Southern Educators Life Ins. Co., Norcross, GA
Southern Educators Life Ins. Co., Baton Rouge, LA
Southern Farm Bureau Life Ins. Co., Jackson, MS
Southern Fidelity Life Ins. Co., Marshall, TX
Southern Heritage Life Ins. Co., Alexandria, LA

Southern Life and Health Ins. Co., Birmingham, AL
Southern Life Ins. Co., Greensboro, NC
Southern National Life Insurance Co., Phoenix, AZ
Southern National Life Ins. Co., Dallas, TX
Southern Protective Life, Jacksonville, FL

Southern Provident Life Ins. Co., Phoenix, AZ
Southern Security Life Ins. Co., Altamonte Springs, FL
Southern States Life Insurance Co., Phoenix, AZ
Southern United Life Ins. Co., Montgomery, AL
Southland Life Ins. Co., Dallas, TX

Southwest Bancshares Life Ins. Co., Houston, TX
Southwest Capital Life Insurance Co., Norman, OK
Southwest Home Life Ins. Co., Houston, TX
Southwest Industrial Life Ins. Co., Phoenix, AZ
Southwest Pioneer Life Ins. Co. (Ariz.), Dallas, TX

Southwestern General Life Ins. Co., Dallas, TX
Southwestern Life Ins. Co., Dallas, TX
Southwestern Life Ins. Co.-Sep. Acct., Dallas, TX
Southwestern Security Life Ins. Co., Oklahoma City, OK
Sovereign Life Ins. Co. of California, Santa Barbara, CA
Springfield Life Ins. Co. Inc. (Vt.), Springfield, MA
Standard of America Life Ins. Co., Park Ridge, IL
Standard Ins. Co., Portland, OR
Standard Ins. Co.-Sep. Acct., Portland, OR
Standard Life and Accident Ins. Co., Oklahoma City, OK

Standard Life & Casualty Ins. Co., Rock Hill, SC
Standard Life Ins. Co., Jackson, MS
Standard Life Ins. Co. of Indiana, Indianapolis, IN
Standard Mutual Life Ins. Co., Lawrence, KS
Standard Security Insurance Company (Del.), New York, NY

Standard Security Life Ins. Co. of NY, New York, NY
Standard Security Life of NY-Sep. Acct., New York, NY
Stanford Life Ins. Co., Phoenix, AZ
State Bond and Mortgage Life Ins. Co., New Ulm, MN
State Farm Life & Accident Assur. Co., Bloomington, IL

State Farm Life Ins. Co., Bloomington, IL
State Life Ins. Co., Indianapolis, IN
State Life Insurance Fund of Wisc., Madison, WI
State Mutual Ins. Co. (Fla.), Rome, GA
State Mutual Life Assur. Co. of America, Worcester, MA

State Mutual Life of America-Sep. Acct., Worcester, MA
State National Life Ins. Co., Baton Rouge, LA
State Reserve Life Ins. Co., Fort Worth, TX
States General Life Ins. Co., Dallas, TX
Statesman Life Ins. Co., Des Moines, IA

Statesman National Life Ins. Co., Houston, TX
Steakley Life Ins. Co., Phoenix, AZ
Sterling Investors Life Ins. Co., Lakeland, FL

Sterling Life Ins. Co. (Ariz.), Springfield, OH
Sterling National Life Ins. Co., Palos Hills, IL

Stonewall Life Ins. Co., Birmingham AL
Sturdivant Life Ins. Co., North Wilkesboro, NC
Stuyvesant Life Ins. Co., Allentown, PA
Stuyvesant Life Ins. Co.-Sep. Acct., Allentown, PA
Summit National Life Ins. Co., Akron, OH

Summit Security Life Insurance Co., Phoenix, AZ
Sun Burst Life Insurance Company, Phoenix, AZ
Sun Life Assur. Co. of Canada, Toronto, Ontario, Can.
Sun Life Assur. Co. of Can. (US), (Del.), Wellesley Hills, MA
Sun Life Assur. of Can. (US)-Sep. Acct., Wilmington, DE

Sun Life Ins. Co. of America, Baltimore, MD
Sun Life Ins. Co. of America-Sep. Acct., Baltimore, MD
Sun States Life Ins. Co., Phoenix, AZ
Sunark Insurance Company, Phoenix, AZ
Sunbelt Life Ins. Co., Atlanta, GA

Sunbelt Life Ins. Co., Shreveport, LA
Sunland Life Ins. Co., Cisco, TX
Sunset Life Ins. Co. of America, Olympia, WA
Sunshine Life Insurance Company, Phoenix, AZ
Superior Life Ins. Co., Florence, SC

Supreme Life Ins. Co. of America, Chicago, IL
Surety Life Ins. Co., Salt Lake City, UT
Survivors' Benefit Ins. Co., St. Louis, MO
Sweeney National Life Insurance Co., Scottsdale, AZ
SwissRe Life Ins. Co. (Del.), New York, NY

—T—

Tandy Life Ins. Co., Fort Worth, TX
Tara Life Ins. Co. of America (Del.), King of Prussia, PA
Teachers Ins. & Annuity Assoc. of Amer., New York, NY
Teachers Protective Mutual Life Ins., Lancaster, PA
Tecumseh Ins. Co., Phoenix, AZ

Teledyne Life Ins. Co., Los Angeles, CA
Tempco Life Ins. Co., Phoenix. AZ
Tennessee Credit Life Ins. Co., Memphis, TN
Tennessee Farmers Life Ins. Co., Columbia, TN
Tennessee Valley Life Ins. Co., Phoenix, AZ

Teton National Ins. Co., Cheyenne, WY
Texas Central Life Ins. Co., Lancaster, TX
Texas Credit Life Insurance Co., Carrollton, TX
Texas Life Ins. Co., Waco, TX
Texas Savings Life Ins. Co., Waskom, TX

Texas South Life Insurance Company, La Grange, TX
Texas State Life Ins. Co. (Ariz.), Dallas, TX
Thomas Jefferson Life Ins. Co., New York, NY
Tidewater Life Insurance Company, Scottsdale, AZ
Time Ins. Co., Milwaukee, WI

Time Life Ins. Co. (Ariz.), Dallas, TX
Tom Benson Life Insurance Company, Phoenix, AZ
Tower Life & Accident Ins. Co. (Ill.), Indianapolis, IN
Tower Life Ins. Co., San Antonio, TX
Trans-City Life Ins. Co., Phoenix, AZ

Trans-General Life Ins. Co., Chevy Chase, MD
Trans-National Life Ins. Co., Houston, TX
Trans-Oceanic Life Ins. Co., Caparra, P.R.
Trans Pacific Life Ins. Co., Santa Monica, CA

Trans-State Life Ins. Co., Tucson, AZ

Trans World Assurance Co., San Mateo, CA
Trans-World Life Ins. Co., Shreveport, LA
Trans World Life Ins. Co. of NY, New York, NY
TransAm Assurance Company, Phoenix, AZ
Transamerica Assurance Company, Los Angeles, CA

Transamerica Ins. Corporation of Calif., Los Angeles, CA
Transamerica Life Ins. and Annuity Co., Los Angeles, CA
Transamerica Life Ins. & Ann.-Sep. Acct., Los Angeles, CA
Transport Life Ins. Co., Fort Worth, TX
Transport Life Insurance-Consolidated, Fort Worth, TX

Travelers Insurance Co., Hartford, CT
Travelers Insurance Co.-Sep. Acct., Hartford, CT
Travelers Ins. Co. of Ill. (Ill.), Hartford, CT
The Travelers Life and Annuity Co., Hartford, CT
Travelers Life Ins. Co., Hartford, CT

Travelers Life Ins. Co. of Canada, Toronto, Ontario, Can.
Trend Life Ins. Co., Oklahoma City, OK
Triad Life Ins. Corporation, Winston-Salem, NC
Trust Life Ins. Co., Scottsdale, AZ
Twentieth Century Life Ins. Co. (N.C.), St. Louis, MO

Twin Life Ins. Co., Scottsdale, AZ

—U—

UNLIC Life Ins. Co., Springfield, IL
USAA Annuity and Life Ins. Co., San Antonio, TX
USAA Life Ins. Co., San Antonio, TX
USLIFE Credit Life Ins. Co., Schaumburg, IL
USLIFE Life Ins. Co. of California, Pasadena, CA

U S National Life Ins. Co., Phoenix, AZ
Underwriters National Assurance Co., Indianapolis, IN
Unified Investors Life Ins. Co. (Ariz.), Lumberton, NC
Unigard Olympic Life Ins. Co., Bellevue, WA
UniLife Insurance Co. (Ariz.), San Antonio, TX

Union Bankers Ins. Co., Dallas, TX
Union Casualty Company, Omaha, NE
Union Central Life Ins. Co., Cincinnati, OH
Union Central Ins. Co.-Sep. Acct., Cincinnati, OH
Union Fidelity Life Ins. Co., Trevose, PA

Union Labor Life Ins. Co. (Md.), New York, NY
Union Labor Life Ins. Co.-Sep. Acct., Baltimore, MD
Union Life Ins. Co., Little Rock, AR
Union Mutual Life Ins. Co., Portland, ME
Union Mutual Life Insurance Co.-Consol., Portland, ME

Union Mutual Life Ins. Co.-Sep. Acct., Portland, ME
Union National Life Ins. Co., Baton Rouge, LA
Union National Life Ins. Co., Houston, TX
Union Security Life Ins. Co., Atlanta, GA
Unionmutual Pension & Ins. Corp., Portland, ME

Unionmutual Stock Life Ins. of Amer., Portland, ME
Unionmutual Stock Life Ins. Co. of NY, Elmsford, NY
United Agents Life Ins. Co, of Amer., Shreveport, LA
United American Ins. Co., Dallas, TX
United Bankers Life Insurance Company, Phoenix, AZ

United Bankers Life Ins. Co., Dallas, TX
United Benefit Life Ins. Co., Omaha, NE
United Benefit Life Ins. Co.-Sep. Acct., Omaha, NE

Order of United Commercial Travelers, Columbus, OH
United Companies Life Ins. Co., Baton Rouge, LA

United Educators Life Insurance Co., Framingham, MA
United Employees Life Ins. Co., Phoenix, AZ
United Equitable Life Ins. Co., Skokie, IL
United Equity Life Ins. Co., Oklahoma City, OK
United Family Life Ins. Co., Atlanta, GA

United Farm Bureau Family, Indianapolis, IN
United Farm Bureau Family-Sep. Acct., Indianapolis, IN
United Fidelity Life Ins. Co., Dallas, TX
United Founders Life Ins. Co., Oklahoma City, OK
United Founders Life Ins. Co. of Ill., Rosemont, IL

United General Life Ins. Co., Dallas, TX
United General Rein. Co. of Arizona, Phoenix, AZ
United Home Life Ins. Co., Greenwood, IN
United Insurance Co. of America, Chicago, IL
United International Life Ins. Co., Salt Lake City, UT

United Investors Life Ins. Co., Kansas City, MO
United Jersey Credit Life Ins. Co., Phoenix, AZ
United Liberty Life Ins. Co., Cincinnati, OH
United Life and Accident Ins. Co., Concord, NH
United Life Ins. Co., Cedar Rapids, IA

United Life of North America, Phoenix, AZ
United Mutual Life Ins. Co., New York, NY
United National Life Ins. Co. (Ariz.), Cherry Hill, NJ
United National Life Ins. Co. of Amer., Springfield, IL
United Pacific Life Ins. Co., Federal Way, WA

United Preferred Life Ins. Co., Phoenix, AZ
United Presidential Life Ins. Co., Kokomo, IN
United Republic Life Ins. Co., Harrisburg, PA
United Savings Life Ins. Co., Hinsdale, IL
United Security Life Insurance Co., Taylor, AZ

United Security Life Ins. Co. of Il., Palos Hills, IL
United Services General Life Co. (Okla.), Washington, DC
United Services Life Ins. Co., Washington, DC
United Services Life Ins. Co.-Consol., Washington, DC
United Societies of U S A, McKeesport, PA

United Standard Assurance Co., Indianapolis, IN
United States Life Ins. Co. City of NY, New York, NY
United Sun Life Insurance Co., Mulberry, FL
United Transportation Union Ins. Assoc., Cleveland, OH
Unity Mutual Life Ins. Co., Syracuse, NY

Universal Assurors Life Ins. Co., Omaha, NE
Universal Fidelity Life Ins. Co., Duncan, OK
Universal Guaranty Life Ins. Co., Phoenix, AZ
Universal Guaranty Life Ins. Co., Colubmus, OH
Universal Life Ins. Co., Memphis, TN

Universal Reserve Life Insurance Co., Atlanta, GA
Universal Security Life Ins., Kirkland, WA
Universal Underwriters Life Ins. Co., Kansas City, MO
Universe Life Ins. Co., Carson City, NV
University Life Ins. Co. of America, Indianapolis, IN

Upper Cumberland Life Insurance Co., Phoenix, AZ
Upper Northwest Life Ins. Co., Phoenix, AZ
The Urbaine Life Reinsurance Company, New York, NY
Utah Farm Bureau Mutual Life Ins. Co., Salt Lake City, UT
Utah Farm Bureau Mutual Life-Sep. Acct., Salt Lake City, UT

Utica National Life Insurance Co., New Hartford, NY

—V—

V I P Insurance Company, Scottsdale, AZ
Val Ford Life Insurance Company, Phoenix, AZ
Valley Forge Life Ins. Co. (Pa.), Chicago, IL
Valley Life & Casualty Ins. Co., Phoenix, AZ
Vanderblit Life Ins. Co., Phoenix, AZ

Variable Annuity Life Ins. Co., Houston, TX
Variable Annuity Life Ins. Co.-Sep. Acct., Houston, TX
Veterans Life Ins. Co. (Ill.), Valley Forge, PA
Victoria Life Insurance Company, Scottsdale, AZ
Victory Life Ins. Co., Topeka, KS

Vista Life Insurance Company (La.), Phoenix, AZ
Vista Life Insurance Company, Dearborn, MI
Volunteer State Life Ins. Co., Chattanooga, TN
Voyager Life Ins. Co., Jacksonville, FL
Voyager Life Ins. Co.-Sep. Acct., Jacksonville, FL

Voyager Life Ins. Company of SC, Colubmia, SC
Vulcan Life Ins. Co., Birmingham, AL

—W—

Wabash Life Ins. Co., Indianapolis, IN
Washington Life Ins. Co. (D.C.), Fort Wayne, IN
Washington Life Ins. Co. of Amer., Lafayette, LA
Washington National Ins. Co., Evanston, IL
Washington National Ins. Co.-Sep. Acct., Evanston, IL

Washington National Life Ins. Co., New York, NY
Washington Square Life Ins. Co. (Pa.), Pompano Beach, FL
Wausau Life Insurance Company, Wausau, WI
Wausau Underwriters Life Ins. Co. (Ind.), Wausau, WI
Webster Life Ins. Co., Spirit Lake, IA

West Coast Life Ins. Co., San Franciso, CA
West States Ins. Co. (Cal.), Phoenix, AZ
Western American Life Ins. Co., Dallas, TX
Western American Life Ins. Co., Salt Lake City, UT
Western Benefit Life Insurance Co., Tucson, AZ

Western Diversified Life Insurance Co., Northbrook, IL
Western Farm Bureau Life Ins. Co., Denver, CO
Western Fraternal Life Association, Cedar Rapids, IA
Western General Life Ins. Co., Houston, TX
Western Heritage Life Ins. Co., Madill, OK

Western Investors Life Ins. Co., Albuquerque, NM
Western Life Assurance Co., Hamilton, Ontario, Can.
Western Life Ins. Co., St. Paul, MN
Western Life Ins. Co. of America (Mo.), Rockford, IL
Western Mutual Life and Casualty Co., Rapid City, SD

Western National Life Ins. Co., Amarillo, TX
Western Pioneer Life Ins. Co., Louisville, KY
Western Reserve Life Assur. of Ohio (Ohio), Clearwater, FL
Western Reserve Life Ins. Co., Grand Junction, CO
Western Security Life Ins. Co., Phoenix, AZ

Western and Southern Life Ins. Co., Cincinnati, OH
Western States Life Ins. Co., Fargo, ND
Western Surety Life Insurance Company, Sioux Falls, SD
Western United Life Assur. Co., Spokane, WA
Westfield Life Ins. Co., Westfield Center, OH

Westland Life Ins. Co., San Francisco, CA

Westlane Ins. Co., Carrollton, TX
Westward Life Ins. Co., Phoenix, AZ
White Life Ins. Co., Wichita Falls, TX
Wichita National Life Ins. Co., Lawton, OK

William Penn Association, Pittsburgh, PA
William Penn Life Ins. Co. of New York, Great Neck, NY
Williams-Progressive L & A Ins. Co., Opelousas, LA
Willoughby Life & Dental Ins. Co. of NA., Oak Park, IL
Windsor Life Ins. Co. of America, New York, NY

Winnfield Life Ins. Co., Natchitoches, LA
Winston Mutual Life Ins. Co., Winston-Salem, NC
Winters National Life Insurance Co., Phoenix, AZ
Wisconsin Employers Ins. Co., Green Bay, WI
Wisconsin Employers Ins. Co.-Sep. Acct., Green Bay, WI

Wisconsin Life Ins. Co., Madison, WI
Wisconsin National Life Ins. Co., Oshkosh, WI
Wolverine Life Insurance Company, Phoenix, AZ
Woodbridge Life Ins. Co., Phoenix, AZ
Woodmen Accident and Life Co., Lincoln, NE

Woodmen of the World, Denver, CO

Woodmen of the World Life Ins. Society, Omaha, NE
Woodstock Life Ins. Co., Phoenix, AZ
Workmen's Benefit Fund of the U S A, Carle Place, NY
Workmen's Life Ins. Co., Phoenix, AZ

World Book Life Ins. Co., Chicago, IL
World Book Life Ins. Co.-Sep. Acct., Chicago, IL
World Insurance Company, Omaha, NE
World Life & Health Ins. Co. of Penn., King of Prussia, PA
World Service Life Ins. Co., Englewood, CO

World Service Life Ins. Co.-Sep. Acct., Englewood, CO
World Service Life Insurance Company, Fort Worth, TX
Wright Mutual Ins. Co., Detroit, MI

—Y—

Yankee Life Ins. Co., Phoenix, AZ

—Z—

Zale Life Ins. Co. (Ariz.), Dallas, TX
Zurich American Life Ins. Co., Schaumburg, IL
Zurich Life Ins. Co. (N.Y.), Schaumburg, IL
Zurich Life Ins. Co. of Canada, Toronto, Can.

CHAPTER 22

RAILROADS

Railroads played a significant role in the migration of people westward after the Civil War. A great number of people worked their way west on the railroad. Many people provided goods and services to the railroads and others purchased land from them.

Enclosed you will find a list of all current Railroads, their home office and the states they serve. Remember that railroads are private companies and do not have to give you access to their records. You will probably do better if you hire a researcher to represent you. In any case you are at their mercy. So be kind and gentle.

Probably less than 10% of the population worked for a railroad. But for those who did and whose retirement was after the mid 1930's the Railroad Retirement Board may be of some value. Enclosed you will find a statement provided by that board that may help you secure some information.

Information and Addresses of Railroads

For exact addresses and other information on Railroads see: Moody's Investors Service Inc., Moody's Transportation Manuel, 99 Church Street, New York, NY 10007.

Railroad Information Table

Abbreviation	Railroad Name	Home Office	Miles of Railroad	States Served
A.	Alaska Railroad	Anchorage, Alaska	536	Alaska
A.	Alexander	Taylorsville, N.C.	18	N.C.
A.	Apache	Phoenix, Ariz.	75	Ariz.
A. & A.	Arcade and Attica	Arcade, N.Y.	15	N.Y.
A. & E.C.	Atlantic and East Carolina	New Bern, N.C.	94	N.C.
A. & L.M.	Arkansas & Louisiana Mo.	Monroe, La.	54	Ark., La
A. & M.R.	Arcata and Mad River	Blue Lake, Calif.	8	Calif.
A. & N.	Albany & Northern	Albany, Ga.	36	Ga.
A. & N.R.	Angelina & Neches River	Keltys, Tex.	9	Tex.
A. & R.	Aberdeen and Rockfish	Aberdeen, N.C.	47	N.C.
A. & S.	Abilene & Southern	Dallas, Tex.	54	Tex.
A. & S.AB.	Atlanta & St. Andrews Bay	Dothan, Ala.	81	Ala., Fla.
A. & W.	Ahnapee and Western	Green Bay, Wis.	34	Wis.
A. & W.	Atlantic and Western	Sanford, N.C.	5	N.C.
A. & W. P.	Atlanta and West Point	Atlanta, Ga.	90	Ga.
A.A.	Ann Arbor	Dearborn, Mich.	292	Mich., Ohio
A.C.	Amador Central	Martell, Calif.	12	Calif.
A.C. & Y.	Akron, Canton & Youngstown	Akron, Ohio	170	Ohio
A.D. & N.	Ashley, Drew & Northern	Crossett, Ark.	41	Ark.

Abbreviation	Railroad Name	Home Office	Miles of Railroad	States Served
AL.	Almanor	Chester, Calif.	13	Calif.
A.N.	Apalachicola Northern	Port St. Joe, Fla.	96	Fla.
A.T. & N.	Ala., Tennessee & Northern	Mobile, Ala.	214	Ala.
A.T. & S.F. . . .	Atchison, Topeka & Santa Fe	Chicago, Ill.	12,961	Ariz., Calif., Colo., Ill., Iowa, Kans., La., Mo., Neb., N.M., Okla., Tex.
A.V.	Aroostook Valley	Presque Isle, Me.	42	Me.
A.W.	Arkansas Western	Kansas City, Mo.	56	Ark., Okla.
A.W. & W. . . .	Algers, Winslow & Western	Indianapolis, Inc.	16	Ind.
B.	Belton	Denison, Tex.	7	Tex.
B. & A.	Baltimore and Annapolis	Glen Burnie, Md.	28	Md.
B. & A.	Bangor and Aroostook	Bangor, Me.	559	Me.
B. & E.	Baltimore and Eastern	Philadelphia, Pa.	88	Md.
B. & H.	Bath and Hammondsport	Hammondsport, N.Y.	11	N.Y.
B. & H.S.	Bonhomie & Hattiesburg So.	Fernwood, Miss.	27	Miss.
B. & L.E.	Bessemer and Lake Erie	Pittsburgh, Pa.	203	Ohio, Pa.
B. & M.	Beaufort and Morehead	Beaufort, N.C.	17	N.C.
B. & M.	Boston and Maine	Boston, Mass.	1,529	Maine, Mass., N.H., N.Y., Vt.
B. & M. L. . . .	Belfast & Moosehead Lake	Belfast, Me.	33	Me.
B. & N.	Bauxite and Northern	East St. Louis, Ill.	19	Ark.
B. & O.	Baltimore & Ohio	Baltimore, Md.	5,870	D.C., Del., Ill., Ind., Ky., Md., Mich., Mo., N.Y., Ohio. Pa., Va., W. Va.
B. & O.C.T. . . .	Baltimore & Ohio Chicago Terminal	Baltimore, Md.	361	Ill., Ind.
B. & S.	Bevier and Southern	Bevier, Mo.	10	Mo.
B.A. & P.	Butte, Anaconda & Pacific	Anaconda, Mont.	116	Mont.
B.C.	Bellefonte Central	Bellefonte, Pa.	18	Pa.
B.M.	Beech Mountain	Elkins, W. Va.	10	W. Va.
B.M. & E. . . .	Beaver, Meade & Englewood	Denison, Tex.	105	Okla.
B.N.	Burlington Northern	St. Paul Minn.	26,500	Calif., Colo., Idaho, Ill., Iowa, Kansas, Ky., Minn.,Mo., Mont., Nebr.,N.D., Oregon, S.D.,Wash., Wis.,Wyo.
B.R.C.	Belt Railway of Chicago	Bedford Park, Ill.	27	Ill.
B.S.	Birmingham Southern	Fairfield, Ala.	44	Ala.
C.	Cliffside	Cliffside, N.C.	5	N.C.
C. & C.	Claremont and Concord	Boston, Mass.	14	N.H.
C. & C.	Corinth and Counce	Counce, Tenn.	19	Miss., Tenn.
C. & E. I. . . .	Chicago & Eastern Illinois	Chicago Hts., Ill.	862	Ill., Ind.
C. & G.	Columbus & Greenville	Columbus, Miss.	168	Miss.
C. & I.	Cambria and Indiana	Bethlehem, Pa.	62	Pa.
C. & I.M.	Chicago & Illinois Midland	Springfield, Ill.	121	Ill.
C. & I.W.	Chicago & Illinois Western	Chicago, Ill.	12	Ill.
C. & L.C.	Cadillac & Lake City	Lake City, Mich.	21	Mich.
C. & N.W. . . .	Chicago & North Western	Chicago, Ill.	11,401	Ill., Iowa, Kans., Mich., Minn., Mo., Neb., N.D., S.D., Wis., Wyo.
C. & NW.	Carolina & Northwestern	Charlotte, N.C.	284	N.C., S.C., Va.
C. & O.	Chesapeake and Ohio	Cleveland, Ohio	5,133*	D.C., Ill., Ind., Ky., Mich., N.Y., Ohio, Va., W. Va., Wis.
C. & P.	Clarendon & Pittsford	Proctor, Vt.	20	Vt.
C. & P.A.	Coudersport & Port Allegany	Flushing, N.Y.	26	Pa.

Abbreviation	Railroad Name	Home Office	Miles of Railroad	States Served
C. & S.	Colorado and Southern	Denver, Colo.	712	Colo., N.M., Wyo.
C. & W.	Colorado & Wyoming	Denver, Colo.	118	Colo., Wyo.
C. & W.I.	Chicago & Western Indiana	Chicago, Ill.	147	Ill.
CA.	Carrollton	Carrollton, Ky.	11	Ky.
CAD.	Cadiz	Cadiz, Ky.	10	Ky.
CA. P.	Camas Prairie	Lewiston, Ida.	258	Ida., Wash.
C.C.	Carbon County	Salt Lake City, Utah	11	Utah
C.C.T.	Central California Traction	Stockton, Calif	54	Calif.
C.F.	Cape Fear	Fort Bragg, N.C.	42	N.C.
C. OF G.	Central of Georgia	Savannah, Ga.	1,744	Ala., Ga., Tenn.
CH. R.	Chestnut Ridge	Palmerton, Pa.	7	Pa.
C.I.	Central Indiana	Anderson, Ind.	43	Ind.
C.I.	Chattahoochee Industrial	Cedar Springs, Ga.	15	Ga.
C.K. & S.	Condon, Kinzua & Southern	Kinzua, Ore.	24	Ore.
C.L.	Camp LeJeune	New Bern, N.C.	30	N.C.
CLIN.	Clinchfield	Erwin, Tenn.	306	Ky., N.C., S.C., Tenn., Va.
C.M.S.P. & P.	Chicago, Milwaukee, St. Paul and Pacific	Chicago, Ill.	10,540	Ida., Ill., Ind., Iowa, Kans., Mich., Minn., Mo., Mont., Neb., N.D., S.D., Wash., Wis.
C.N.	Canadian National	Montreal, Que.	23,076*	Minn.
C.N. & L.	Columbia, Newberry and Laurens	Jacksonville, Fla.	75	S.C.
C.N.J.	Central of New Jersey	Jersey City, N.J.	576	N.J., N.Y., Pa.
C.O.P.	City of Prineville	Prineville, Ore.	19	Ore.
C.P.	Canadian Pacific	Montreal, Que.	16,726*	Me., Mich., Vt.
C.P. & L.T.	Camino, Placerville & Lake Tahoe	Camino, Calif.	8	Calif.
C.P.-F.	Cotton Plant-Fargo	Cotton Plant, Ark.	5	Ark.
C.R.	Copper Range	Houghton, Mich.	67	Mich.
C.R. & I.C.	Cedar Rapids & Iowa City	Cedar Rapids, Iowa	27	Iowa
C.R.I. & P.	Chicago Rock Island & Pacific	Chicago, Ill.	7,793	Ark., Colo., Ill., Iowa, Kans., La., Minn., Mo., Neb., N.M., Okla., S. D., Tenn., Tex.
C.S.S. & S.B.	Chicago, South Shore & South Bend	Michigan City, Ind.	90	Ill., Ind.
C.V.	Central Vermont	St. Albans, Vt.	367*	Conn., Mass., N.H., N.Y., Vt.
C.V.	Chattahoochee Valley	West Point, Ga.	28	Ala., Ga.
C.W.	California Western	Fort Bragg, Calif.	48	Calif
C.W.	Carolina Western	Sumter, S.C.	5	S.C.
C.W.	Chesapeake Western	Harrisonburg, Va.	52	Va.
D. & H.	Delaware and Hudson	Albany, N.Y.	744	N.Y., Pa., Vt.
D. & M.	Detroit and Mackinac	Tawas City, Mich.	235	Mich.
D. & M.M.	Dansville & Mount Morris	Dansville, N.Y.	9	N.Y.
D. & NE.	Duluth & Northeastern	Cloquet, Minn.	11	Minn.
D. & R.	Dardanelle & Russellville	Dardanelle, Ark.	5	Ark.
D. & R.G.W.	Denver & Rio Grande Western	Denver, Colo.	2,128	Colo., N.M., Utah
D. & S.	Durham and Southern	Durham, N.C.	59	N.C.
D. & T.S.L.	Detroit & Toledo Shore Line	Detroit, Mich.	59	Mich., Ohio
C.M. & C.I.	Des Moines & Central Iowa	Boone, Iowa	22	Iowa
D.M. & I.R.	Duluth, Missabe & Iron Range	Duluth, Minn.	528	Minn., Wis.
D.O.	Delaware Otsego	Oneonta, N.Y.	3	N.Y.
D.Q. & E.	De Queen and Eastern	De Queen, Ark.	45	Ark.
D.T. & I.	Detroit, Toledo and Ironton	Dearborn, Mich.	464	Mich., Ohio
D.V. & S.	Delta Valley & Southern	Wilson, Ark.	2	Ark.

Abbreviation	Railroad Name	Home Office	Miles of Railroad	States Served
D.W. & P.	Duluth Winnipeg & Pacific	Montreal, Que.	174*	Minn.
E. & L.S.	Escanaba and Lake Superior	Wells, Mich.	87	Mich.
E. & M.	Edgemoor & Manetta	Lando, S.C.	3	S.C.
E.D. & W.	El Dorado and Wesson	El Dorado, Ark.	6	Ark.
E.J. & E.	Elgin, Joliet and Eastern	Chicago, Ill.	205	Ill., Ind.
E.L.	Erie Lackawanna	Cleveland, Ohio	7,016	Ill., Ind., N.J., N.Y., Ohio, Pa.
E.T. & W.N.C.	East Tenn. & Western N.C.	Johnson City, Tenn.	10	Tenn.
E.W.	East Washington	Seat Pleasant, Md.	4	D.C., Md.
F. & C.	Frankfort & Cincinnati	Boston, Mass.	25	Ky.
F.B.	Fort Benning (U.S.G.)	Fort Benning, Ga.	4	Ga.
FBL	Federal Barge Lines	St. Louis, Mo.	20	Ala.
F.C. & G.	Fernwood, Columbia & Gulf	Fernwood, Miss.	44	Miss.
F.D.D.M. & S.	Ft. Dodge, Des Moines & Southern	Boone, Iowa	120	Iowa
F. del P.	Ferrocarril del Pacifico	Guadalajara, Mex.	1,342*	
F.E.C.	Florida East Coast	St. Augustine, Fla.	572	Fla.
FERD	Ferdinand	Ferdinand, Ind.	7	Ind.
F.J. & G.	Fonda, Johnstown & Gloversville	Gloversville, N.Y.	20	N.Y.
F.R.	Fore River	New York, N.Y.	7	Mass.
F.S. & V.B.	Fort Smith & Van Buren	Kansas City, Mo.	21	Okla.
F.W. & D.	Fort Worth and Denver	Fort Worth, Tex.	1.037	Tex.
G.	Georgetown	Georgetown, Tex.	10	Tex.
G. & F.	Georgia & Florida	Augusta, Ga.	305	Ga., S.C.
G. & J.	Greenwich & Johnsonville	Albany, N.Y.	17	N.Y.
G. & N.	Greenville & Northern	Boston, Mass.	15	S.C.
G. & U.	Grafton & Upton	Hopedale, Mass.	15	Mass.
G. & W.	Genesee and Wyoming	Retsof, N.Y.	12	N.Y.
GA.	Georgia	Atlanta, Ga.	320	Ga.
G.A.S. & C.	Georgia, Ashburn, Sylvester & Camilla	Moultrie, Ga.	51	Ga.
G.B. & W.	Green Bay and Western	Green Bay, Wis.	257	Minn., Wis.
G.C.	Graham County	Robbinsville, N.C.	12	N.C.
G.C.W.	Garden City Western	Garden City, Kans.	15	Kans.
G.H. & H.	Galveston, Houston & Henderson	Galveston, Tex.	49	Tex.
G.M.	Gainesville Midland	Richmond, Va.	40	Ga.
G.M.	Green Mountain	Bellows Falls, Vt.	52	Vt.
G.M. & O.	Gulf, Mobile and Ohio	Mobile, Ala.	2,744	Ala., Ill., Ky., La., Miss., Mo., Tenn.
G.N.	Georgia Northern	Moultrie, Ga.	68	Ga.
G.N. & A.	Graysonia, Nashville & Ashdown	Denver, Colo.	27	Ark.
G. S.W.	Great Southwest	Grand Prairie, Tex.	11	Tex.
G.T.	Grand Trunk	Montreal, Que.	221	Me., N.H., N.Y., Vt.
G.T.W.	Grand Trunk Western	Detroit, Mich.	946	Ill., Ind., Mich., Wis.
G.W.	Great Western	Denver, Colo.	63	Colo.
H.	Hartwell	Hartwell, Ga.	10	Ga.
H. & B.	Hampton & Branchville	Hampton, S.C.	17	S.C.
H. & E.	Hollis & Eastern	Denison, Tex.	38	Okla.
H. & NE.	Hillsboro & North Eastern	Hillsboro, Wis.	5	Wis.
H. & S.	Hartford & Slocomb	Hartford, Ala.	22	Ala.
H.I.	Holton Inter-Urban	San Francisco, Calif.	10	Calif.
H.P.T. & D.	High Point, Thomasville & Denton	High Point, N.C.	34	N.C.
H.T. & W.	Hoosac Tunnel & Wilmington	Boston, Mass.	11	Mass., Vt.
I.C.	Illinois Central	Chicago, Ill.	6,786	Ala., Ark., Ill., Ind., Iowa, Ky., La., Minn., Miss., Mo., Neb.,

Abbreviation	Railroad Name	Home Office	Miles of Railroad	States Served
				S.D., Tenn., Wis.
I.H.B.	Indiana Harbor Belt	Hammond, Ind.	275	Ill., Ind.
I.N.	Illinois Northern	Chicago, Ill.	19	Ill.
INT.	Interstate	Andover, Va.	54	Va.
I.T.	Illinois Terminal	St. Louis, Mo.	339	Ill., Mo.
I.T.	Iowa Terminal	Mason City, Iowa	26	Iowa
K. & T.	Kentucky & Tennessee	Stearns, Ky.	11	Ky.
K.C.	Kanawha Central	Charleston, W. Va.	5	W. Va.
K.C. & NW. . . .	Kelleys Creek & Northwestern	Cleveland, Ohio	7	W. Va.
K.C.S.	Kansas City Southern	Kansas City, Mo.	863	Ark., Kans., La., Mo., Okla., Tex.
K.N.	Klamath Northern	Gilchrist, Ore.	11	Ore.
L. & A.	Louisiana & Arkansas	Kansas City, Mo.	755	Ark., La., Tex.
L. & B.R.	Lowville & Beaver River	Lowville, N.Y.	10	N.Y.
L. & C.	Lancaster and Chester	Lancaster, S.C.	30	S.C.
L. & H.R.	Lehigh & Hudson River	Warwick, N.Y.	76	N.J., N.Y.
L. & N.	Laona & Northern	Laona, Wis.	12	Wis.
L. & N.	Louisville and Nashville	Louisville, Ky.	5,662	Ala., Fla., Ga., Ill., Ind., Ky., La., Miss., Mo., N.C., Ohio, Tenn., Va.
L. & N.	Ludington & Northern	Saginaw, Mich.	4	Mich.
L. & N.E.	Lehigh and New England	Jersey City, N.J.	62	Pa.
L. & N.W. . . .	Louisiana and North West	Homer, La.	62	Ark., La.
L. & S.	Laurinburg and Southern	Laurinburg, N.C.	28	N.C.
L. & W.	Louisville and Wadley	Louisville, Ga.	10	Ga.
L. & W.V.	Lackawanna & Wyoming Valley	Scranton, Pa.	19	Pa.
L.A.L.	Livonia, Avon & Lakeville	Livonia, N.Y.	12	N.Y.
L.E.F. & C. . . .	Lake Erie, Franklin & Clarion	Clarion, Pa.	25	Pa.
L.I.	Long Island	Jamaica, N.Y.	340	N.Y.
L.N.A. & C. . . .	Louisville, New Albany & Corydon	Corydon, Ind.	11	Ind.
L.O.P. & G. . . .	Live Oak, Perry & Gulf	Perry, Fla.	58	Fla.
L.P. & N.	Longview, Portland & Northern	Longview, Wash.	42	Ore., Wash.
L.S.	Louisiana Southern	New Orleans, La.	21	La.
L.S. & I.	Lake Superior & Ishpeming	Marquette, Mich.	135	Mich.
L.V.	Lehigh Valley	Bethlehem, Pa.	1,083	N.J., N.Y., Pa.
M.	Montour	Pittsburgh, Pa.	51	Pa.
M. & B.	Marianna & Blountstown	Blountstown, Fla.	37	Fla.
M. & B.	Meridian and Bigbee	Meridian, Miss.	51	Ala., Miss.
M. & B.	Montpelier & Barre	Boston, Mass.	14	Vt.
M. & E.	Modesto & Empire Traction	Modesta, Calif.	5	Calif.
M. & E.	Morristown & Erie	Whippany, N.J.	11	N.J.
M.&G.	Mobile & Gulf	Louisville, Ky.	11	Ala.
M. & H.M.	Marquette & Huron Mountain	Marquette, Mich.	13	Mich.
M. & N.F.	Morehead & North Fork	Clearfield, Ky.	4	Ky.
M. & N.J.	Middletown & New Jersey	Middletown, N.Y.	15	N.Y.
M. & P.	Maryland & Pennsylvania	York, Pa.	38	Md., Pa.
M. & P.P.	Manitou & Pikes Peak	Colo. Springs, Colo.	9	Colo.
M. & S.V.	Mississippi & Skuna Valley	Bruce, Miss.	21	Miss.
M.A.	Magma Arizona	Superior, Ariz.	28	Ariz.
M.C.	Maine Central	Portland, Me.	936	Me., N.H., Vt.
M.C. & S.A. . . .	Moscow, Camden & San Augustine	Camden, Tex.	7	Tex.
M. CO.	Midland Continental	Jamestown, N.D.	69	N.D.
MC. R.	McCloud River	McCloud, Calif.	96	Calif.
M.D. & W.	Minnesota, Dakota & Western	Boise, Idaho	33	Minn.
M.EX.	Mississippi Export	Moss Point, Miss.	42	Miss.

Abbreviation	Railroad Name	Home Office	Miles of Railroad	States Served
M.F.	Middle Fork	Ellamore, W.Va.	13	W.Va.
M.H.	Mount Hood	Hood River, Ore.	22	Ore.
M.H.M.	Mount Hope Mineral	Jersey City, N.J.	4	N.J.
M.I.	Missouri-Illinois	St. Louis, Mo.	172	Ill., Mo.
MID.	Midway	Columbus, Ohio	4	Ohio
MISS.	Mississippian	Amory, Miss.	24	Miss.
M.K.T.	Missouri-Kansas-Texas	Dallas, Tex.	2,871	Kans., Mo., Okla., Tex.
M.N. & S.	Minneapolis, Northfield & Southern	Minneapolis, Minn.	77	Minn.
MON.	Monongahela	Brownsville, Pa.	261	Pa., W.Va.
MONON	Monon	Chicago, Ill.	573	Ind.
M.P.	Missouri Pacific	St. Louis, Mo.	9,292	Ark., Colo., Kans., La., Miss., Mo., Neb., Okla., Tex.
M.T. & W. . . .	Marinette, Tomahawk & Western	Tomahawk, Wis.	14	Wis.
M.V.	Moshassuck Valley	Saylesville, R.I.	2	R.I.
N.	Nezperce	Nezperce, Ida.	14	Ida.
N. & B.	Northampton and Bath	Pittsburgh, Pa.	7	Pa.
N. & S.L.	Norwood & St. Lawrence	New York, N.Y.	18	N.Y.
N. & W.	Norfolk & Western	Roanoke, Va.	7,800*	Ill., Ind., Iowa, Ky., Md., Mich., Mo., N.Y., N.C., Ohio, Pa., Tenn., Va. W.Va.
N.F. & D.	Norfolk, Franklin & Danville	Suffolk, Va.	204	N.C., Va.
N.H.& I.	New Hope & Ivyland	New Hope, Pa.	17	Pa.
N.J.	Napierville Junction	Albany, N.Y.	27*	N.Y.
N.L. & G.	North Louisiana & Gulf	Hodge, La.	40	La.
N.N.	Nevada Northern	East Ely, Nev.	192	Nev.
N.O. & L.C. . .	New Orleans & Lower Coast	St. Louis, Mo.	72	La.
N.P.	Narragansett Pier	Peace Dale, R.I.	6	R.I.
N.S.	Norfolk Southern	Raleigh, N.C.	624	N.C., Va.
NW.P.	Northwestern Pacific	San Francisco, Calif.	328	Calif.
N.Y. & L.B. . .	New York & Long Branch	Jersey City, N.J.	38	N.J.
N.Y.S. & W. . .	New york, Susquehanna & Western	Edgewater, N.J.	72	N.J.
O. & N.	Oregon & Northwestern	Hines, Ore.	51	Ore.
O.C. & E.	Oregon, California & Eastern	Reno, Nev.	65	Ore.
O.E.	Oregon Electric	Portland, Ore.	201	Ore.
O.P. & E.	Oregon, Pacific & Eastern	Portland, Ore.	30	Ore.
O.T.	Oregon Trunk	Portland, Ore.	152	Ore., Wash.
P. & E.	Peoria & Eastern	Indianapolis, Ind.	202	Ill., Ind.
P. & I.	Paducah & Illinois	Paducah, Ky.	19	Ill., Ky.
P. & L.E.	Pittsburgh & Lake Erie	New York, N.Y.	216	Ohio, Pa.
P. & N.	Prescott & Northwestern	Prescott, Ark.	32	Ark.
P. & S.	Pittsburg & Shawmut	Kittanning, Pa.	97	Pa.
P. & S.R.	Petaluma & Santa Rosa	San Francisco, Calif.	30	Calif.
P.C.	Pacific Coast	Seattle, Wash.	57	Wash.
P.C.	Penn Central	New York, N.Y. Philadelphia, Pa.	21,322	Conn., Del., D.C., Ill., Ind., Ky., Mass., Md., Mich., Mo., N.J., N.Y., Ohio, Pa., R.I., Va., W.Va.
P.C. & N.	Point Comfort & Northern	Pittsburgh, Pa.	12	Tex.
P.H. & D.	Port Huron & Detroit	Port Huron, Mich.	19	Mich.
PIC.	Pickens	Pickens, S.C.	9	S.C.
P.L.	Parish Line	Kinder, La.	6	La.
P.R.S.	Pennsylvania-Reading Seashore	Camden, N.J.	336	N.J.

Abbreviation	Railroad Name	Home Office	Miles of Railroad	States Served
P.R.V.	Pearl River Valley	Picayune, Miss.	4	Miss.
P.T.	Portland Traction	Portland, Ore.	36	Ore.
P.T.	Port Townsend	Seattle, Wash.	12	Wash.
P.V.S.	Pecos Valley Southern	Pecos, Tex.	40	Tex.
Q.	Quincy	Quincy, Calif.	5	Calif.
Q.A. & P.	Quanah, Acme & Pacific	Quannah, Tex.	120	Tex.
Q.C.	Quebec Central	Sherbrooke, Que.	335*	Vt.
READ.	Reader	Shreveport, La.	24	Ark.
READ.	Reading	Philadelphia, Pa.	1,286	Del., N.J., Pa.
R.F. & P.	Richmond, Fredericksburg and Potomac	Richmond, Va.	246	Va.
ROCK.	Rockingham	Rockingham, N.C.	19	N.C.
R.R.	Raritan River	South Amboy, N.J.	18	N.J.
R.S. & P.	Roscoe, Snyder & Pacific	Roscoe, Tex.	30	Tex.
R.S. & S.	Rockdale, Sandow & Southern	Pittsburg, Pa.	6	Tex.
R.V.	Rahway Valley	Kenilworth, N.J.	13	N.J.
S.	Sandersville	Sandersville, Ga.	9	Ga.
S.	Sierra	Jamestown, Calif.	57	Calif.
S.	Strasburg	Strasburg, Pa.	5	Pa.
S. & A.	Savannah & Atlanta	Savannah, Ga.	168	Ga.
S. & C.	Sumter & Choctaw	Ballamy, Ala.	4	Ala.
S.-B.C.	Sonora-Baja California	Mexicali, Mex.	331*	
S.C.L.	Seaboard Coast Line	Jacksonville, Fla. Richmond, Va.	9,280	Ala., Fla., Ga., N.C., S.C., Va.
S.D. & A.E.	San Diego & Arizona Eastern	San Francisco, Calif.	136	Calif.
S.G.	South Georgia	Perry, Fla.	76	Fla., Ga.
S.I.	Southern Indiana	Indianapolis, Ind.	5	Ind.
S.I.	Southern Industrial	Centerville, Iowa	18	Iowa
S.I.	Spokane International	Omaha, Neb.	148	Ida., Wash.
S.I.R.T.	Staten Island Rapid Transit	Baltimore, Md.	29	N.J., N.Y.
S.J. & L.C.	St. Johnsbury & Lamoille County	Morrisville, Vt.	96	Vt.
S.L.	Soo Line	Minneapolis, Minn.	4,692	Ill., Mich., Minn., Mont., N.D., S.D., Wis.
S.L.C.	San Luis Central	Denver, Colo.	13	Colo.
S.L.G. & W.	Salt Lake, Garfield & Western	Salt Lake City, Utah	14	Utah
S.L.S.F.	St. Louis-San Francisco	St. Louis, Mo.	5,106	Ala., Ark., Fla., Kans., Miss., Mo., Okla., Tenn., Tex.
S.L.S.W.	St. Louis Southwestern	Tyler, Tex.	1,554	Ark., Ill., La., Mo., Tenn., Tex.
S.M.	St. Marys	New York, N.Y.	11	Ga.
SMA	San Manuel Arizona	San Manuel, Ariz.	30	Ariz.
S.M.V.	Santa Maria Valley	Santa Maria, Calif.	26	Calif.
S.N.	Sacramento Northern	San Francisco, Calif.	328	Calif.
S.N.Y.	Southern New York	West Oneonta, N.Y.	3	N.Y.
SOU.	Southern	Washington, D.C.	6,274	Ala., D.C., Fla., Ga., Ill., Ind., Ky., Miss., N.C., S.C., Tenn., Va.
S.P.	Southern Pacific	San Francisco, Calif.	12,098	Ariz., Calif., La., Nev., N.M., Ore., Tex., Utah
S.P. & S.	Spokane, Portland & Seattle	Portland, Ore.	583	Ore., Wash.
S.R. & N.	Sabine River and Northern	Orange, Tex.	32	Tex.
S.S.	Sand Springs	Sand Springs, Okla.	35	Okla.
S.S.	South Shore	Amite, La.	17	La.
S.S.L.	Skaneateles Short Line	Skaneateles, N.Y.	5	N.Y.
S.S.L.V.	Southern San Luis Valley	Blanca, Colo.	1	Colo.

Abbreviation	Railroad Name	Home Office	Miles of Railroad	States Served
S.T.	Springfield Terminal	Springfield, Vt.	6	Vt.
S.U.	State University	Washington, D.C.	10	N.C.
S.T. & E.	Stockton Terminal & Eastern	Stockton, Calif.	14	Calif.
STEW.	Stewartstown	Stewartstown, Pa.	7	Pa.
SUN.	Sunset	Chicago, Ill.	46	Calif.
T. & N.	Texas and Northern	Dallas, Tex.	7	Tex.
T. & P.	Texas and Pacific	Dallas, Tex.	2,348	Ark., Kans., La., N.M., Okla., Tex.
T. & T.	Tijuana and Tecate	Mexicali, Mex.	44*	
T.A. & G.	Tennessee, Alabama & Georgia	Chattanooga, Tenn.	90	Ala., Ga., Tenn.
T.A. & W.	Toledo, Angola & Western	Cleveland, Ohio	8	Ohio
T.C.	Texas Central	Dublin, Tex.	65	Texas
T.C. & G.B.	Tucson, Cornelia & Gila Bend	Douglas, Ariz.	44	Ariz.
TENN.	Tennessee	Oneida, Tenn.	45	Tenn.
T.M.	Texas Mexican	Laredo, Tex.	161*	Tex.
T.N.M.	Texas-New Mexico	Dallas, Tex.	112	N.M., Tex.
T.O. & E.	Texas, Oklahoma & Eastern	De Queen, Ark.	41	Okla.
T.P. & W.	Toledo, Peoria & Western	East Peoria, Ill.	239	Ill., Ind., Iowa
T.P.T.	Trenton-Princeton Traction	Philadelphia, Pa.	5	N.J.
TRONA	Trona	Los Angeles, Calif.	31	Calif.
T.S.	Tidewater Southern	San Francisco, Calif.	48	Calif.
T.S.E.	Texas South-Eastern	Diboll, Tex.	54	Tex.
T.S.U.	Tulsa-Sapulpa Union	Sapulpa, Okla.	12	Okla.
T.VA.	Tooele Valley	Tooele, Utah	12	Utah
U.	Utah	Salt Lake City, Utah	95	Utah
UN.	Union R.R. Of Oregon	Union, Ore.	3	Ore.
U.P.	Union Pacific	Omaha, Neb.	9,397	Calif., Colo., Ida., Iowa, Kans., Mo., Mont., Neb., Nev., Ore., Utah, Wash., Wyo.
U.S.G.	United States Government	Washington, D.C.		
U.T.	Union Transportation	New Egypt, N.J.	19	N.J.
V. & S.	Valley & Siletz	Independence, Ore.	41	Ore.
V.B.R.	Virginia Blue Ridge	Piney River, Va.	15	Va.
V.C.	Ventura County	Oxnard, Calif.	11	Calif.
V.C.	Virginia Central	Fredericksburg, Va.	1	Va.
V.E.	Visalia Electric	San Francisco, Calif.	34	Calif.
V.S.	Valdosta Southern	Clyattville, Ga.	28	Fla., Ga.
VT.	Vermont	Burlington, Vt.	122	Vt.
W.	Warwick	Edgewood, R.I.	1	R.I.
W.	Waterloo	Waterloo, Iowa	67	Iowa
W.	Winifrede	Winifrede, W.Va.	7	W.Va.
W. & N.	Wharton & Northern	Jersey City, N.J.	15	N.J.
W. & O.V.	Warren & Ouachita Valley	Little Rock, Ark.	16	Ark.
W. & S.R.	Warren and Saline River	Warren, Ark.	17	Ark.
W. & T.	Wrightsville & Tennille	Dublin, Ga.	36	Ga.
W. & W.	Waynesburg & Washington	Pittsburgh, Pa.	29	Pa.
W. & W.	Winchester & Western	Winchester, Va.	18	Va.
W.A. & G.	Wellsville, Addison & Galeton	Flushing, N.Y.	77	N.Y., Pa.
WAR.	Warrenton	Warrenton, N.C.	3	N.C.
W.I. & M.	Washington Idaho & Montana	Potlatch, Ida.	49	Ida., Wash.
WIN.	Winfield	West Winfield, Pa.	13	Pa.
W.M.	Western Maryland	Baltimore, Md.	742	Md., Pa., W.Va.
W.M.W. & NW.	Weatherford, Mineral Wells and Northwestern	Dallas, Tex.	22	Tex.
W.P.	Western Pacific	San Francisco, Calif.	1,193	Calif., Nev., Utah
W.P. & Y.	White Pass & Yukon	Vancouver, B.C.	110*	Alaska
W.R.A.	Western Ry. of Alabama	Atlanta, Ga.	138	Ala.

W.S.	Ware Shoals	Ware Shoals, S.C.	5	S.C.
W.S.S.	Winston-Salem Southbound	Jacksonville, Fla.	99	N.C.
W.S.S. & Y.P. .	White Sulphur Springs & Yellowstone Park	White Sulphur Springs Mont.	18	Mont.
W.V.N.	West Virginia Northern	Kingwood, W.Va.	17	W.Va.
W.W.V.	Walla Walla Valley	St. Paul, Minn.	19	Ore., Wash.
Y.	Yancey	Burnsville, N.C.	13	N.C.
Y. & S.	Yakutat & Southern	Bellingham, Wash.	15	Alaska
Y. & S.	Youngstown & Southern	Pittsburgh, Pa.	48	Ohio, Pa.
Y.V.T.	Yakima Valley Transportation	Yakima, Wash.	26	Wash.
Y.W.	Yreka Western	Yreka, Calif.	11	Calif.

* . . . . Includes Canada or Mexico.

U.S. Railroad Retirement Board

The U.S. Railroad Retirement Board administers Federal retirement-survivor and unemployment-sickness benefit programs covering the nation's railroad workers and their families, and assists in the administration of other railroad employee protection laws. The records it maintains deal primarily with the administration and payment of these benefits. In many cases, the Board will provide information from these records on individual *deceased* railroaders for the purpose of genealogical research and there is generally no charge for this service. The Board will not release information from the records of annuitants who are still living.

Individuals covered under the railroad retirement system are those in the service of an "employer" as defined in the Railroad Retirement Act. These "employers" include express and sleeping-car companies and carriers by railroad subject to certain provisions of the Interstate Commerce Act. Also included are railway labor organizations national in scope, and certain other organizations controlled and maintained by one or more "employers" and engaged in services incidental to the transportation of passengers or property by railroad.

The Railroad Retirement Board did not begin operations until the mid-1930's, and the first benefit payments were made in 1936. Therefore, our records are limited to individuals who were either associated with the rail industry at or since that time, or who were receiving a private rail pension which the Board assumed after it began operations. If a person was not in one of these categories we would have no records on him. Also, some old records that we did maintain have subsequently been destroyed according to the Board's record retention schedule.

In the event that a person was in one of these categories then the most useful piece of information for locating any records on him, or her, would be the person's social security number or Railroad Retirement Board claim number.

However, if this information is not available, then as much of the following information as possible should be included:

* The employee's full name, including middle initial.
* The month and year of birth.
* The year last worked in the rail industry.
* The year of death.
* The railroad worked for.

Requests of this type should be sent directly to the U.S. Railroad Retirement Board, Division of Public Affairs, 844 Rush Street, Chicago, Illinois 60611.

CHAPTER 23

CANADA

Public Archives of Canada

Upper Canada is Ontario and Lower Canada is Quebec. The Public Archives of Canada was founded in 1872 as a repository of federal records and documents. Genealogical services of the Archives is limited to the identification of source material. (Staff is limited, it is more effective to use a professional researcher, the Archives maintains a list of such people but does not guarantee their work). They can not respond to general questions or determine specific family relationships. In otherwords, they will not do your research for you.

Records Available in the Public Archives at Canada Census Records

Censuses prior to 1851 contain either aggregate (only numbers in various age groups, religious affiliation, country of origin and location) or lists the head of household (name of head of household, size of family, acreage owned, or occupation). From 1851 to 1881, the name of each individual is listed with their age, sex, country or province of birth, religion, race, occupation, marital status, education, and physical disabilities if any.

There are some agricultural and industrial census available on microfilm. The agricultural records include head of household, lot and concession number, acreage under cultivation etc.

A catalogue of census returns is available from Printing and Publishing, Supply and Services, Canada. Mail Order Service, 45 Sacre Coeur Quebec, Canada K1A 059.

Marriage Records

The Archives has marriage licence records (names of couple, residence and date of marriage) for Quebec 1779 and 1818 to 1867 and Ontario 1803 to 1845.

Cemetery Records

The Archives have copies of headstone inscriptions donated by Genealogical Societies. When you are inquiring, give the name of the town or township you seek and where possible, the religious affiliation.

Acadian Records

Acadian records (not to be confused with French Canadians) are found in a work compiled by Placide Gaudet called Gaudet's Notes, the bulk of which are available in the Archives.

Indian Records

Records of the British Indian Department dating back to the mid 1700's as well as the agencies responsible for Indian Affairs since confederation are available, from the mid 1800's. They include band membership lists and treaty pay lists.

Land Records

The federal government only maintains the original petitions for land grants submitted to the Executive Council in Upper and Lower Canada prior to 1867; Quebec and Lower Canada from 1764 to 1841; Upper Canada and the United Provinces from 1791 to 1867; and the original grants issued in western lands from 1869 to 1930. The petitions contain information on the petitioner's family, ancestors, military service and country of origin.

Military Records

Detailed Personnel Records of the Canadian Armed Forces was not kept until the 20th century. All personnel files for World War I, World War II and Korea are housed in the Public Archives.

Some earlier records are available such as:

1. Records of the Office of the Commander of Forces, British North America; dates from after the American Revolution. They contain some muster rolls of some Loyalists Units and some Canadian Units raised during the War of 1812.

2. Records of the Provincial Marine and Admirality Lake Service.

3. Records accumulated by the Adjutants General of Militia in Upper and Lower Canada and by the Department of Militia and Defence, after Confederation, including pay lists for service during the War of 1812 and from 1855 to 1914. The pay lists are by regimental unit so that must be known to find the records.

4. Medal Registers for the War of 1812, the Fenian Raids, Red River and Northwest Rebellions, and the South African (Boer) War; covering the period 1866 to 1902.

5. Losses Claims for the War of 1812, Insurrection of 1837-38, and the Fenian Raids.

6. The Department of Veterans Affairs has records for the South African War.

Immigration Records

Only a few widely scattered immigration lists are available prior to 1865. An index of those lists for the years 1817 to 1831 are available in the Public Archives. French passenger lists are almost non-existent, and none are indexed.

Passenger manifests for ships arriving at the following ports:

Quebec City	1865-1908
Halifax	1880-1908
Saint John	1900-1908
Victoria	1905-1908
U.S. Ports	1905-1908

To use these records you must know the passenger's name at the time of arrival; the exact date and port of arrival; and the ship's name.

The Canada Employment and Immigration Commission Department has comprehensive records of immigrants arriving at Canadian ports after 1908.

Naturalization Records

Before 1947 all British subjects were equal in status and had no need for naturalization. Very few records were kept prior to 1865 and those between 1865 and 1917 have been destroyed. For access to records since 1917 you need the full name, the date, and birth place of your ancestor. Contact: The Citizenship Registration Branch, Secretary of State Department, 15 Eddy Street, Hull, Quebec, K1A 0M5, (there is a charge).

Loyalist Records

Loyalist (people loyal to England during the American Revolution) are of special genealogical interest. Several important sources are available in the Archives.

Ontario is the sole Province for which a Loyalist List was maintained. The list was begun in 1796. One list was kept by the Crownlands Office and another list by the Executive Council with some discrepancies between them. These lists are available in the Public Archives.

Some claims for compensation are available in the Public Record Office in London, but not many.

Several volumes of Sir Frederick Haldimand's paper in the British Library containing provisions lists and muster rolls with the name of Loyalists and some dependants is available in the Archives, as are other muster rolls in such collection as the *Ward Chipman Papers.*

Canadian Genealogical Checklist

	MAJOR ARCHIVES	VITAL STATISTICS OFFICES	MAJOR GENEALOGICAL SOCIETIES
Canada	*Public Archives of Canada*, 395 Wellington St., Ottawa, Ontario K1A 0N3. (see also their booklet *Tracing Your Ancestors in Canada* for other general information on genealogical sources in Canada).	Not applicable. Registration of births, marriages and deaths in Canada is a provincial responsibility. Contact the Vital Statistics office in the appropriate province.	No national organization. Some related groups: *Heraldry Society of Canada*, 125 Lakeway Dr., Ottawa K1L 5A9; *United Empire Loyalist Assn.*, 30-344 Bloor Street West, Toronto M5R 1B2, *American-Canadian Genealogical Soc.*, Box 668, Manchester, NH, USA 03105
Alberta	*Provincial Archives of Alberta*, 12845-102 Ave., Edmonton T5N 0M6; also see *Glenbow-Alberta Institute*, 9th Ave. and 1st St. S.E., Calgary T2G 0P3.	*Division of Vital Statistics*, 10405-100 Ave., Edmonton T5J 0A6. (b from 1887, md from 1898).	*Alberta Genealogical Society*, Box 12015, Edmonton T5J 3L2; *Alberta Family Histories Society*, Box 30270, Station B, Calgary T2M 4P1.
British Columbia	*Provincial Archives of British Columbia*, Parliament Bldgs., Victoria V8V 1X4.	*Division of Vital Statistics*, Ministry of Health, Parliament Bldgs., Victoria V8V 1X4. (bmd from 1872).	*British Columbia Genealogical Society*, Box 94371, Richmond V6Y 2A8.
Manitoba	*Provincial Archives of Manitoba*, 200 Vaughan St., Winnipeg R3C 0P8.	*Office of Vital Statistics*, 104 Norquay Bldg., 401 York Ave., Winnipeg R3C 0V8 (bmd from 1882).	*Manitoba Genealogical Society*, Box 2066, Winnipeg R3C 3R4.
New Brunswick	*Provincial Archives of New Brunswick*, Box 6000, Fredericton E3B 5H1.	*Registrar General of Vital Statistics*, Box 6000, Fredericton E3B 5H1 (bmd from 1888 - incomplete before 1920).	*New Brunswick Genealogical Society*, Box 3235, Station B, Fredericton E3A 2W0.
Newfoundland	*Provincial Archives of Newfoundland and Labrador*, Colonial Bldg., Military Rd., St. John's A1C 5E2.	*Registrar, Vital Statistics Division*, Dept. of Public Health, Confederation Bldg., St. John's A1C 5T7 (bmd from 1892).	None. Contact: *Maritime History Group*, Memorial University of Newfoundland, St. John's A1C 5S7.
Nova Scotia	*Public Archives of Nova Scotia*, 6016 University Ave., Halifax B3H 1W4.	*Deputy Registrar General*, Dept. of Public Health, Box 157, Halifax B3J 2M9 (bd from 1908 and 1864-76, m from 1864).	*Genealogical Committee*, Royal Nova Scotia Historical Society, Box 1276, Wolfville B0P 1X0.
Ontario	*Archives of Ontario*, 77 Grenville St., Queen's Park, Toronto M7A 2K9.	*Office of the Registrar General*, Macdonald Block, Parliament Bldgs., Queen's Park, Toronto M7A 1Y5 (bmd from 1869).	*Ontario Genealogical Society*, Box 66, Station Q, Toronto M4T 2L7
Prince Edward Island	*Public Archives of P.E.I.*, P.O. Box 1000, Charlottetown C1N 7M4; see also *P.E.I. Heritage Foundation*, P.O. Box 922, Charlottetown C1A 2L9.	*Division of Vital Statistics*, Dept. of Health, P.O. Box 3000, Charlottetown C1A 7P1 (bmd from 1906 - incomplete m from 1787, incomplete b from 1800).	*P.E.I. Genealogical Society*, c/o Box 922, Charlottetown C1A 2L9.
Québec	*Archives nationales du Québec.* Central address: C.P. 10450, Ste-Foy G1V 4N1. Regional archives centres have also been established at Chicoutimi, Hull, Montréal, Noranda, Rimouski, Sherbrooke, and Trois-Rivières (an archives centre for Côte-Nord is pending). Contact the central archives for regional addresses.	*Régistre de la Population*, Ministère des Affaires Sociales, 845 ave. Joffre, Québec G1S 0A6 (bmd from 1926). Church records as early as 1621 can be found in local judicial archives. The addresses of judicial archives are available from Ministère de la Justice, 175 St-Jean, Québec G1R 2X6, or from the Archives nationales in Ste-Foy.	*Société Généalogique Canadienne-Française*, C.P. 335, Place d'Armes, Montréal H2X 3H1; *Société de Généalogie de Québec*, C.P. 2234, Québec G1K 7N8; *Quebec Family History Society*, Box 1026, Pointe Claire P.O., Pointe Claire H9S 4H9. (For names of other societies, see publications under *Canada* and *Québec*)
Saskatchewan	*Saskatchewan Archives Board* - at two locations: Library Bldg., University of Regina, Regina S4S 0A2; and Murray Memorial Bldg., University of Saskatchewan, Saskatoon S7N 0W0.	*Division of Vital Statistics*, Dept. of Health, 3475 Albert Street, Regina S4S 0A6 (bmd from 1889 - incomplete before 1920).	*Saskatchewan Genealogical Society*, Box 1894, Regina S4P 0A0.
Northwest Territories	*The Archives*, Prince of Wales Northern Heritage Centre, Yellowknife X1A 2L9.	*Registrar General of Vital Statistics*, Yellowknife X0E 1H0 (bmd since circa 1940).	None.
Yukon Territory	*Archives of the Yukon Territory*, P.O. Box 2703, Whitehorse Y1A 2C6.	*Registrar General of Vital Statistics*, P.O. Box 2703, Whitehorse Y1A 2C6 (b from 1895; md from 1899).	None.

wheatfield press

box 205, st. james postal station, winnipeg, manitoba R3J 3R4

Originally compiled in June 1980 by

Eric Jonasson

author of
The Canadian Genealogical Handbook
2nd Revision, September 1981

GOVERNMENT INFORMATION SERVICE	MAJOR GENEALOGICAL GUIDES	SOME GENEALOGICAL PUBLISHERS
Information Services, Government of Canada, 300 Slater St., Ottawa, Ontario K1A 0C8	Eric Jonasson: *The Canadian Genealogical Handbook*, Winnipeg 1978 (this is regarded as the standard textbook on Canadian genealogy - has sections on each province); and Angus Baxter: *In Search of Your Roots*, Toronto 1978.	*Wheatfield Press*, Box 205, St. James Postal Station, Winnipeg, Manitoba R3J 3R4 (publishers of *The Canadian Genealogical Handbook*).
Public Affairs Bureau, Petroleum Plaza, 9945 - 108th St., Edmonton T5K 2G6	Eric Jonasson "Family History Resources of Western Canada."	*Éditions Élysée*, PB 188, Station Côte-Saint-Luc, Montréal, Québec H4V 2Y4.
Communications Branch, Ministry of the Provincial Secretary and Travel Industry, 1117 Wharf St., Victoria V8W 2Z2	None. See publications under *Canada* and *Alberta*.	*Everton Publishers, Inc.*, Box 368, Logan, Utah, USA 84321.
Citizen's Inquiry Service, 511 - 401 York Ave., Winnipeg R3C 0P8	Eric Jonasson *"Genealogical Sources in the Province of Manitoba"* in *Genealogical Journal* 8:2 (Utah Genealogical Assn., Salt Lake City) 1979.	*Genealogical Publishing Co.*, 111 Water St., Baltimore, Maryland, USA 21202.
N.B. Information Service, Box 6000, Fredericton E3B 5H1	Robert F. Fellows: *Researching Your Ancestors in New Brunswick, Canada*, Fredericton 1979.	*Generation Press*, 172 King Henrys Blvd., Agincourt, Ontario M1T 2V6.
Newfoundland Information Service, Confederation Bldg., St. John's A1C 5T7	None. See publications under *Canada*.	*Mika Publishing Co.*, Box 536, Belleville, Ontario K8N 5B2.
N.S. Communications and Information Centre, Box 2206, Halifax B3J 3C4	Terrence M. Punch: *Genealogical Research in Nova Scotia*, Halifax 1978.	**INDEPENDENT PERIODICALS** "Acadian Genealogy Exchange", 863 Wayman Branch Rd., Covington, Kentucky, USA 41015.
Citizens' Inquiry Branch, Ministry of Culture and Recreation, 77 Bloor St. West, 6th Floor, Toronto M7A 2R9	Marion Keffer and Robert and Audrey Kirk: *Some References and Sources for the Family Historian in the Province of Ontario*, Toronto 1976; and Don Wilson (comp.): *Ontario Genealogical Sources*, Toronto 1979, reprint Winnipeg 1982.	"The Canadian Genealogist", see Generation Press, above. "Early Canadian Life", 591 Argus Road, Oakville, Ontario L6J 3J4. "The French Canadian and Acadian Genealogical Review", Box 845, Upper Town, Québec, Québec.
Island Information Service, Box 2000, Charlottetown C1A 7N8	Family History in Prince Edward Island: *A Genealogical Research Guide*, Charlottetown.	"The Genealogical Helper", see Everton Publishers, above. "Lost in Canada?", 1020 Central Ave., Sparta, Wisconsin, USA 54656.
Communications gouvernementales, Ministère des Communications, Cité parlementaire, Ediface G, Québec G1A 1G6 (generally of limited value to genealogists).	Jeanne Gregoire: *Guide du généalogiste à la recherche de nos ancêtres*, Montréal 1974; and Michel Langlois: *Cherchons nos ancêtres*, Montréal 1980. (Titles of other guides can be obtained from the genealogical societies or from the Archives nationales in Ste-Foy).	**GENEALOGICAL COURSES** Genealogical Studies, Sheridan College Trafalgar Rd., Oakville, Ontario L6H 2L1. **OTHER GENEALOGICAL ORGANIZATIONS** *Canadian Ancestral Research Institute* 1275 Markham Road, Winnipeg, Manitoba R3T 4B1.
Information Services, Legislative Bldg., Regina S4S 0B3	None. See publications under *Canada*.	*Genealogical Research Library*, Centennial House, 520 Wellington St., London, Ontario N6A 3P9
N.W.T. Dept. of Information, Yellowknife X1A 2L9	None. See publications under *Canada*.	*Genealogical Society of Utah*, 50 East North Temple, Salt Lake City, Utah, USA 84150.
Information Services Division, Dept. of Information Resources, Box 2703, Whitehorse Y1A 2C6	None. See publications under *Canada*.	*Institut Généalogique Drouin*, 4184 St-Denis, Montréal, Québec H2W 2M6. *International Genealogy Consumer Organization*, 4329 S. Stafford Way, Salt Lake City, Utah, USA 84119.

Canadian Ancestral Research Institute

1275 Markham Road, Winnipeg, Manitoba R3T 4B1

reprinted by permission

Section IV
SOURCES

DO YOU WANT A REALLY SUCCESSFUL SEMINAR?

Mr. Ronald A. Bremer will insure success! Not only does he speak enthusiastically so that everyone can easily hear but he also is a master at the use of visual aids. Since he has had years of first-hand experience and has traveled to virtually every major genealogical center in the country, he is able to lecture on a wide variety of subjects. Here are some suggested topics:

1. Introduction to Genealogy
2. Notekeeping and Organization
3. Research by Correspondence
4. Little-Known Sources
5. American Migrational Patterns
6. European Genealogical Research
7. Tracing the Immigrant Ancestor
8. American Genealogical Research
9. American Judicial Court Records
10. Solving 'Stone-Wall' Problems
11. Post-1900 Genealogical Sources
12. American Church Records
13. New England States Research
14. Southern States Research
15. Mid-Atlantic States Research
16. Mid-West States Research
17. Western States Research
18. Salt Lake City Library
19. Genealogical Reference Works
20. Fraternal/Alliance Research
21. Life Insurance Companies
22. Lakes, Canals, Rivers
23. American Newspaper Research
24. Burned Courthouses!
25. American Railroad Records
26. Determining Maiden Names
27. American Military Records
28. American Land Records
29. Printed Family Histories
30. Locating Family Collections
31. Genealogy & Photography
32. Computers & Genealogy
33. Motivating/Inspiring Stories
34. Questions & Answers
35. Tombstone Epitaphs
36. Other?

RONALD A. BREMER
Professional Genealogist, Author, and Lecturer

Mr. Bremer has the ability to lecture, with short breaks, for the entire day, therefore, you may choose any five of the above topics. However, the first topic 'Introduction to Genealogy' is his most popular lecture and includes a little of *all* the others. Remember, Mr. Bremer will be speaking for at least five full hours.!

Probably the one characteristic above all others that makes Mr. Bremer so in demand and such a delight to listen to, is his ability to answer questions from his audiences. In this manner, he not only makes the seminars more personal but is often able to help each individual in attendance. And he encourages tape recording.

BIOGRAPHICAL INFORMATION

Born and raised in Southern California, Mr. Bremer first became interested in the fascinating endeavor of genealogy at the age of thirteen. Hence, he now has over thirty years experience as a genealogist. He attended Brigham Young University, and in 1961, attended the Eleventh Annual Genealogical Institute, sponsored by the National Archives and American University.

Former Research Specialist for the Genealogical Society in Salt Lake City, and Founder of the Federation of Genealogical Societies, author of *Compendium of Historical Sources,* Editor of the *Roots Digest Magazine,* are among a few of his credits and achievements.

Mr. Bremer has personally visited the major genealogical record centers in *every* state and Washington, D.C. He is presently one of the most popular and sought-after genealogical speakers in the country, having lectured to most of the various genealogical societies in the nation.

A modern Demosthenes, he seldom uses a microphone and is in constant demand as a motivational speaker. His lectures are not only most informative but also very entertaining. Lauded as the finest speaker of his time, Mr. Bremer consistently captivates, motivates, entertains, and instructs his audiences.

WHICH KIND OF A SEMINAR WOULD YOU LIKE?

You may choose from the thirty-six suggested topics or, let him come and explain all the new sources and techniques contained in his new book! Whichever . . . Remember, Mr. Bremer pays all his own travel expenses. There is absolutely no charge to your organization from him. All you need to do is provide the meeting place, the publicity, a large screen, and an overhead transparency projector. How about it? Please write:

Ronald A. Bremer, Post Office Box 16422, Salt Lake City, Utah 84116

CHAPTER 24

SPECIAL INFORMATION

A List of Miscelleanous Items You Might Find Useful In Your Genealogy Research

1. Federal Agencies with Genalogy Information
2. GPO—Government Printing Office
   Sup. Docs.—The Superintendent of Documents
   NTIS—National Technical Information Service
   CIS—Congressional Information Service Inc.
3. Federal Information Centers
4. Useful State Information
5. Where To Write For Information on States and Cities
6. Department of Motor Vehicles
7. Orphan Voyage of Florida
8. National Adoptive Search Registry Inc.
9. Canals
10. Waterways
11. American Geographical Society Collection
12. The Congregational Library
13. The Durrett Collection
14. The Draper Microfilms Collection
15. New York Municipal Building
16. Books on Demand
17. Continental Book Search
18. Genealogical and Local History Books in Print
19. Roman Numerals
20. International Soundex Reunion Registry
21. Social Security Number Area Allocations
22. Freedom of Information Act
23. Period Approximation Chart
24. Proxy Research
25. New York Public Library Form
26. Suggestions For an All Day Genealogy Seminar
27. Computerized Genealogy Library
28. Telephone Directories
29. Government Bookstores
30. Locating Cemeteries
31. Rivermen and Their Boats

Federal Agencies

The list below attempts to list the more important government agencies or bureaus. It is not complete. For a more complete listing see the *United States Government Manual,* which also provides information on existing agencies, and on abolished agencies, or those which have been transferred, terminated, or changed in name.

This section may be useful to the researcher in various ways. If, for example, your ancestor worked for the Postal Service in the 1850's, or was an Assistant Federal Marshall in the 1890's, then the records of these agencies may prove helpful. Or, if your father may have applied for a loan from the Federal Housing Administration or perhaps he worked as a Civilian Conservation Corps volunteer in 1939, then the records agencies concerned may also prove helpful.

It seems that sooner or later, most of our relatives were involved in one way or another with the Federal Government. Those researching present-day information may want to contact the appropriate agency. While those researching the first seventy or so years of the 20th century should need to contact the Civilian Personnel Records Center, 111 Winnebago St., St. Louis, Missouri 63118. And those searching Federal Records pre-1900, should contact the National Archives in Washington, DC.

Some Federal records are not in St. Louis or Washington, D.C. Check the section entitled Sources and Repositories for their location.

It is important to remember that your ancestors are often listed in Federal Records not only because they may have worked for the Federal Government, but because they were merely using some of the products, services, or benefits offered. Or, they may have even been involved in a law suit which was under the jurisdiction of the Federal District Court or the old Circuit Court. Also, most of the agencies listed below are listed in their modern name or title. Hence, for example, the Work Projects Administration was previously known at the Works Progress Administration. And in most cases, the date organized, refers to the date the predecessor organization was established.

Federal Government Agencies

Abbreviation	Full Name	Date Organized
USDA	Department of Agriculture	1862
CAB	Civil Aeronautics Board	1938
CSC	Civil Service Commission	1883
USDC	Department of Commerce	1913
NBS	National Bureau of Standards	1901
NOAA	National Oceanic & Atmospheric Admin.	1970
CCR	Commission on Civil Rights	1957
DOD	Department of Defense	1949
EPA	Environmental Protection Agency	1970
FCA	Farm Credit Administration	1933
FCC	Federal Communications Commission	1934
FDIC	Federal Deposit Insurance Corp.	1933

FHLBB	Federal Home Loan Bank Board	1932
FMC	Federal Maritime Commission	1961
FPC	Federal Power Commission	1920
FRS	Federal Reserve System	1913
FTC	Federal Trade Commission	1914
GSA	General Services Administration	1949
GPO	Government Printing Office	1860
HEW	Health, Education & Welfare	1953
OE	Office of Education	1867
PHS	Public Health Service	1798
FDA	Food and Drug Aministration	1953
SRS	Social and Rehibilatation Service	1967
AOA	Administration on Aging	1965
CSA	Community Services Administration	1969
MSA	Medical Services Administration	1967
RSA	Rehibilition Services Administration	1920
YDDPA	Youth Development and Deliquency Prevention Administration	1968
SSA	Social Security Administration	1935
HUD	Housing and Urban Development	1965
USDI	Department of the Interior	1849
ICC	Interstate Commerce Commission	1887
USDJ	Department of Justice	1870
DOL	Department of Labor	1913
NCUA	Nationa Credit Union Administration	1970
OCA	Office of Consumer Affairs	1971
OEO	Office of Economic Opportunity	1964
USPS	Postal Service	1829
SEC	Securities and Exchange Commission	1934
SI	Smithsonian Institution	1846
STATE	Department of State	
DOT	Department of Transportation	1967
FAA	Federal Aviation Administration	1967
FHA	Federal Highway Administration	1894
USDT	Department of the Treasury	1789
VA	Veterans Administration	1930
CCC	Civilian Conservation Corps	1937
CDMB	Civil and Defense Mobilization Board	1938
CWCC	Civil War Centennial Commission	1957
CPA	Civilian Production Administration	1945
CMA	Coal Mines Administration	1943
USGS	Coast and Geodetic Survey	1807
FFLB	Federal Farm Loan Bureau	1916
FFMC	Federal Farm Mortgage Corporation	1934
FFC	Federal Fire Council	1939
FHLBS	Federal Home Loan Bank System	1939
FHA	Federal Housing Administration	1934
FNMA	Federal National Mortgage Assoc.	1938
WAAC	Women's Army Auxillary Corps	1942
WAC	Women's Army Crops	1943
WR	Women's Reserve	1942
WPA	Work Projects Administration	1935
TVA	Tennessee Valley Authority	1933

What is the difference between NTIS and GPO, or SupDocs? This is a question often asked of these agencies.

Each strives to offer the best possible public access to collections of information, although their basic missions and the complexity of their information varies widely.

The GOVERNMENT PRINTING OFFICE (GPO) is the principal printing agency of the Federal Government GPO is part of the Legislative Branch and derives its authority and direction from Congress. Its primary products and services are the printing and distribution of the Congressional Record. The Federal Register, and the Weekley Compilation of Presidential Documents. In addition, important and quick turn-around printing jobs are done within GPO and others are contracted out commercially. GPO printing and binding operations are paid for by direct appropriations or by reimbursements from the Federal agencies requisitioning printing services.

THE SUPERINTENDENT OF DOCUMENTS is responsible for:

1. The compilation of catalogs and indexes of Government publications.
2. The administration of the Federal Depository Library System. Some 1200 such libraries receive free Federal publications of their choice for the public. These are funded by a direct appropriation from Congress.
3. Distribution of, by-law, publications specifically authorized by law or Congressional Resolution.
4. The sales program which offers 25,000 popular titles and over 400 Federal subscriptions to domestic and foreign customers. The sales program is self-sustaining and receives no Congressional appropriations. The price of each publication and subscription includes domestic postage. Overseas customers are charged an additional 25 percent to cover handling charges. Twenty-six Government bookstores located in 20 cities within the U.S., sell many popular publications directly to customers. A list of locations is available from SupDocs.

The NATIONAL TECHNICAL INFORMATION SERVICE (NTIS) is a central permanent source of specialized (i.e., business, economic, scientific, social) information of varied origins. NTIS's information is always available; single copies of any of its million titles are printed to order when not in stock. Its customers are mostly business people and professional accustomed to locating and applying specialized information to problem solving. NTIS titles are promoted through a wide variety of media. NTIS is self-sustaining. Its payroll, production materials, promotion and physical plant are paid for from sales income.

Congressional Information Service, Inc.

CIS is a commercial organization that provides reference and retrieval services for information published by federal, state, municipal, and foreign government sources. Services include: the *CIS/Index* to current Congressional publications, the *CIS/Microfiche Library,* and the *CIS/Congressional Bills, Resolutions, and Laws on Microfiche;* the *CIS US Serial Set Index* and *Microfiche, 1789-1969;* the *American Statistics Index* to current federal statistical publications, and *ASI Microfiche Library; State Constitutional Conventions, since 1776* and *State Labor Reports* on microfiche; the *Index to Current Urban Documents* and *Urban Documents Microfiche Collection;* and, *Current National Statistical Compendiums* of foreign government on microfiche.

Federal Information Centers

If you have questions about any program or agency in the Federal government you may want to call the Federal Information Center (FIC) nearest you. FIC staffs are prepared to help consumers find needed information or locate the right agency—usually Federal but sometimes state or local—for help with problems. Each city listed below has and FIC or a tieline—a toll-free local number connecting to an FIC elsewhere.

ALABAMA
Birmingham (205)322-8591
Mobile (205)438-1421

ALASKA
Anchorage (907)271-3650

ARIZONA
Phoenix (602)261-3313
Tucson (602)622-1511

ARKANSAS
Little Rock (501)378-6177

CALIFORNIA
Los Angeles (213)688-3800
Sacramento (916)440-3344
San Diego (714)293-6030
San Francisco (415)556-6600
San Jose (408)275-7422
Santa Ana (714)836-2386

COLORADO
Colorado Springs (303)471-9491
Denver (303)234-7181
Pueblo (303)544-9523

CONNECTICUT
Hartford (203)527-2617
New Haven (203)624-4720

FLORIDA
St. Petersburg (813)893-3495
Tampa (813)229-7911
Other locations (800)282-8556

GEORGIA
Atlanta (404)221-6891

HAWAII
Honolulu (808)546-8620

ILLINOIS
Chicago (312)353-4242

INDIANA
Gary/Hammond (219)883-4110
Indianapolis (317)269-7373

IOWA
Des Moines (515)284-4448
Other locations (800)532-1556

KANSAS
Topeka (913)295-2866
Other locations (800)432-2934

KENTUCKY
Louisville (502)582-6261

LOUISIANA
New Orleans (504)589-6696

MARYLAND
Baltimore (301)962-4980

MASSACHUSETTS
Boston (617)223-7121

MICHIGAN
Detroit (313)226-7016
Grand Rapids (616)451-2628

MINNESOTA
Minneapolis (612)349-5333

MISSOURI
Kansas City (816)374-2466
St. Louis (314)425-4106
Other locations within area code
314 (800)392-7711
Other locations within area codes
816 and 417 (800)892-5808

NEBRASKA
Omaha (401)221-3353
Other locations (800)642-8383

NEW JERSEY
Newark (201)645-3600
Paterson/Passaic (201)523-0717
Trenton (609)396-4400

NEW MEXICO
Albuquerque (505)766-3091
Santa Fe (505)983-7743

NEW YORK
Albany (518)463-4421
Buffalo (716)846-4010
New York (212)264-4464
Rochester (716)546-5075
Syracuse (315)476-8545

NORTH CAROLINA
Charlotte (704)376-3600

OHIO
Akron (216)375-5638
Cincinnati (513)684-2801
Cleveland (216)522-4040
Columbus (614)221-1014
Dayton (513)223-7377
Toledo (419)241-3223

OKLAHOMA
Oklahoma City (405)231-4868
Tulsa (918)584-4193

OREGON
Portland (503)221-2222

PENNSYLVANIA
Allentown/
 Bethlehem (215)821-7785
Philadelphia (215)597-7042
Pittsburgh (412)644-3456
Scranton (717)346-7081

RHODE ISLAND
Providence (401)331-5565

TENNESSEE
Chattanooga (615)265-8231
Memphis (901)521-3285
Nashville (615)242-5056

TEXAS
Austin (512)472-5494
Dallas (214)767-8585
Fort Worth (817)334-3624
Houston (713)229-2552
San Antonio (512)224-4471

UTAH
Ogden (801)399-1347
Salt Lake City (801)524-5353

VIRGINIA
Newport News (804)244-0480
Norfolk (804)441-3101
Richmond (804)643-4928
Roanoke (703)982-8591

WASHINGTON
Seattle (206)422-0570
Tacoma (206)383-5230

WISCONSIN
Milwaukee (414)271-2273

Where to Write for Information on States, Cities

One good way to obtain current information on special events and new attractions at a vacation destination is to write for free literature available from state or local travel bureaus. When writing to a travel bureau, allow 10 days to two weeks for a response. Request maps of the area. Historical booklets and inforamtion.

Alabama Bureau of Publicity, Information
403 State Highway Bldg.
Montgomery, AL 36104.

Alabama Travel Council
660 Adams
Montgomery, AL 36104

Alaska Travel Division
Pouch E
Juneau, AK 99801

Arizona Visitor Development Section
3003 N. Central
Phoenix, AZ 85012*

Scottsdale Chamber of Commerce
Scottsdale, AZ 85282*

Arkansas Department of Parks/Tourism
Capitol
Little Rock, AR 72201

California Office of Tourism
1400 Tenth
Sacramento, CA 95814

Disneyland
Anaheim, CA 92803*

Palm Springs Visitors Bureau
Municipal Airport
Palm Springs, CA 92262

San Francisco Visitors Bureau
Fox Plaza
San Francisco, CA 94102*

Southern California Visitors Council
705 W. Seventh
Los Angeles, CA 90017*

Colorado Division of Commerce
Capitol Annex
Denver, CO 80203*

Connecticut Development Commission
Box 865
Hartford, CT 06115

Delaware Travel Bureau
45 The Green
Dover, DE 19901

East Michigan Tourist Association
Bay City, MI 48706

West Michigan Tourist Association
136 E. Fulton
Grand Rapids, MI 49502

Minnesota Department of
 Economic Development
51 E. Eighth
St. Paul, MN 55101

Visitors Bureau
1129-20th St. NW
Washington, DC 20036*

Florida Department of Commerce
107 W. Gaines
Tallahassee, FL 32304*

Brevard Economic Development Council
Holiday Office Center
Cocoa Beach, FL 32931

Florida Attactions
Box 1568
St. Augustine, FL 32084

Miami Beach Tourist Authority
1700 Washington
Miami Beach, FL 33139*

Miami-Metro Publicity Department
499 Biscayne
Miami, FL 33132*

Walt Disney World
Box 40
Lake Buena Vista, FL 32830*

Georgia Tourist Division
Box 38097
Atlanta, GA 30334*

Hawaii Visitors Bureau
2270 Kalakaua
Honolulu, HI 96815

Idaho Department of Commerce
State House
Boise, ID 83707

Illinois Division of Tourism
222 S. College
Springfield, IL 62706

Chicago Tourism Bureau
322 S. Michigan
Chicago, IL 60604*

Indiana Division of Tourism
State House
Indianapolis, IN 46204

New York City Visitors Bureau
90 E. 42nd St.
New York, NY 10017*

Chamber of Commerce
45 Falls St.
Niagara Falls, NY 14303

North Carolina Travel Division
Box 27687
Raleigh, NC 27611*

Iowa Tourism Division
Jewett Bldg.
Des Moines, IA 50309

Department of Economic Development
State Office Bldg.
Topeka, KS 66612

Kentucky Department of Public Information
Capitol Annex
Frankfort, Ky 40601

Louisville Visitors Bureau
Founders Square
Louisville, KY 40202

Louisiana Tourist Commission
Box 44291
Baton Rouge, LA 70804

New Orleans Convention Commission
400 Royal
New Orleans, LA 70130*

Maine Department of Commerce
 and Industry
Augusta, ME 04330

Maryland Tourism Division
2525 Riva Road
Annapolis, MD 21401

Town of Ocean City
Ocean City, MD 21842

Southern Maryland
 Tri-County Council
Waldorf, MD 20601

Massachusetts Division of Tourism
100 Cambridge
Boston, MA 02202*

Cape Code Chamber of Commerce
Hyannis, MA 02601*

Michigan Tourist Council
300 S. Capitol
Lansing, MI 48926

Gatlinburg Chamber of Commerce
Gatlinburg, TN 37738*

Travel Division
Texas Highway Department
Austin, TX 78701

East Texas
 Chamber of Commerce
Longview, TX 75601

Minneapolis Visitors Bureau
15 S. Fifth
Minneapolis, MN 55402

Mississippi Agricultural/
 Industrial Board
Jackson, MS 39205

Missouri Tourism Commission
308 E. High
Jefferson City, MO 65101

Lake Ozarks Association
Lake Ozark, MO 65049

St. Louis Tourist Board
911 Locust
St. Louis, MO 63101

Montana Highway Commission
Helena, MT 59601

Nebraska Department of
 Economic Development
Capitol
Lincoln, NE 68509

Nevada Tourism Division
Carson City, NV 89701

Las Vegas Convention Authority
Box 14006
Las Vegas, NV 89114*

Reno Chamber of Commerce
Box 2109
Reno, NV 89505

New Hampshire Division
 of Economic Development
Concord, NH 03301

New Jersey Division
 of Labor and Industry
Box 2766
Trenton, NJ 08625

County of Cape May
Cape May Courthouse
Cape May, NJ 08210

New Mexico Tourist Division
113 Washington
Santa Fe, NM 87501

New York Travel Bureau
112 State
Albany, NY 12207

Chamber of Commerce
Lake Placid, NY 12946*

North Dakota Highway Department
Capitol
Bismarck, ND 58501

Ohio Tourist Bureau
Box 1001
Columbus, OH 43216

Cincinnati Visitors Bureau
200 W. Fifth
Cincinnati, OH 45202

Tourism Division
500 Will Rogers Bldg.
Oklahoma City, OK 73105

Oregon Travel Section
State Highway Bldg.
Salem, OR 97310

Pennsylvania Travel Bureau
South Office Bldg.
Harrisburg, PA 17120

Bucks County Historical Commission
Fallsington, PA 19054*

Laurel Highlands, Inc.
120 E. Main
Ligonier, PA 15658

Tourism Bureau
1525 J. F. Kennedy Blvd.
Philadelphia, PA 19102*

Poconos Vacation Bureau
1004 Main
Stroudsburg, PA 18360

Rhoda Island Tourist Division
Roger Williams Bldg.
Providence, RI 02908

South Carolina Tourism Division
Columbia, SC 29202

South Dakota Department
 of Highways
Pierre, SD 57501

Black Hills, Badlands
 Lakes Association
Sturgis, SD 57785

Tennessee Tourist Division
2611 West End
Nashville, TN 37203

Visitors Bureau
399 McCallie
Chattanooga, TN 37402

Highland Lakes Association
Box 1967
Austin, TX 78767

Visitors Bureau
Box 2277
San Antonio, TX 78206

Utah Travel Council
Capitol
Salt Lake City, UT 84114

Vermont Travel Division
61 Elm
Montpelier, VT 05602

Virginia Travel Service
911 E. Broad
Richmond, VA 23219*

Alexandria Tourist Council
221 King
Alexandria, VA 22314*

Colonial Williamsburg
Williamsburg, VA 23185*

City of Virginia Beach
Civic Center
Virginia Beach, VA 23458

Washington Tourist Division
General Administration Bldg.
Olympia, WA 95801

West Virginia Travel Division
1900 Washington St. E.
Charleston, WV 25305

Wisconsin Division of Tourism
Box 450
Madison, WI 53701

Visitors Bureau
828 N. Broadway
Milwaukee, WI 53202

Chamber of Commerce
Wisconsin Dells, WI 58965

Wyoming Travel Commission
Capitol
Cheyenne, WY 82001

Pureto Rico Tourism Co.
San Juan, Puerto Rico 00936

Virgin Islands Department
 of Commerce
Box 1692
Charlotte Amalie
St. Thomas, VI 00801

State Information

It is often important to know what state, territory, or country a state belonged to before it was known by its present name. Researchers may also find it helpful to know the first settlement in a state and when it was settled. In personal correspondence a state is often referred to by the nick-name of the state or it's people. Knowing what political subdivisions are, called can also be helpful. The chart on the following page should help you with this information.

STATE	ORIGINAL SETTLEMENT	WHEN SETTLED	BY WHOM	CAPITAL	SOURCE OF STATE LANDS	Date Organized as Territory	Date Admitted to Union	ORDER IN UNION	NO. OF COUNTIES	NO. OF CITIES	NO. OF TOWNS	NO. OF VILLAGES	NO. OF BOROUGHS	UNINCOR. PLACES	Old Popular Name of State	Old Popular Name of People
Alabama	Mobile Bay	1702	French	Montgomery	Mississippi Territory 1798	Mar. 3, 1817	Dec. 14, 1819	22	67	102	288	-	-	18	Cotton	Lizards
Alaska	Kodiak	1783	Russians	Juneau	Purchased from Russia 1867	Aug. 12, 1912	Jan. 3, 1950	49	-	94	-	-	-	19	-	-
Arizona	Tucson	1776	Spanish	Phoenix	Ceded by Mexico 1848	Feb. 24, 1863	Feb. 14, 1912	48	14	28	35	-	-	24	-	-
Arkansas	Arkansas Post	1685	French	Little Rock	Louisiana Purchase 1803	March 2, 1819	June 15, 1836	25	75	196	277	-	-	3	Bear	Toothpicks
California	San Diego	1769	Spanish	Sacramento	Ceded by Mexico 1848	-	Sept. 9, 1850	31	57	388	16	-	-	285	Golden	Gold Hunters
Colorado	Auraria	1859	Americans	Denver	Louisiana Purchase 1803	Feb. 28, 1861	Aug. 1, 1876	38	62	53	209	-	-	16	Centennial	Rovers
Connecticut	Windsor	1633	English	Hartford	Royal Charter 1662	-	Jan. 9, 1788	5	-	22	-	-	12	41	Nutmeg	Wooden Nutmegs
Delaware	Wilmington	1638	Swedes	Dover	Swedish Charter 1638 English Charter 1683	-	Dec. 7, 1787	1	3	8	43	-	-	8	Blue Hen	Blue Hen's Muskrats
Florida	St. Augustine	1565	Spanish	Tallahassee	Ceded by Spain 1819	March 30, 1822	March 3, 1845	27	67	205	166	18	-	166	Peninsular	Fly-Up-the-Creeks
Georgia	Savannah	1733	English	Atlanta	Royal Charter 1732	-	Jan. 2, 1748	4	159	276	287	10	-	25	Empire State of the South	Crackers
Hawaii	Honolulu	1820	Americans	Honolulu	Annexed 1898	June 14, 1900	Aug. 21, 1959	50	3	27	28	33	-	-	-	-
Idaho	Coeur d'Alene	1842	Americans	Boise	Treaty With Britain 1846	March 4, 1863	July 3, 1890	43	44	198	-	-	-	2	-	-
Illinois	Kaskaskia	1700?	French	Springfield	Northwest Territory 1787	March 4, 1863	July 3, 1890	21	102	295	18	950	-	38	Prairie Sucker	Suckers
Indiana	Vincennes	1727	French	Indianapolis	Northwest Territory 1787	May 7, 1800	Dec. 11, 1816	19	92	111	432	-	-	13	Hoosier	Hoosiers
Iowa	Dubuque	1833	Americans	Des Moines	Louisiana Purchase 1803	June 12, 1838	Dec. 28, 1846	29	99	134	816	-	-	2	Hawkeye	Hawkeyes
Kansas	Leavenworth	1854	Americans	Topeka	Louisiana Purchase 1803	May 30, 1854	Jan. 29, 1861	34	105	624	-	-	-	8	Garden of the West	Jayhawkers
Kentucky	Boonesboro	1775	English	Frankford	Part of Virginia	-	June 1, 1792	15	120	399	-	-	-	10	Blue Grass	Corncrackers
Louisiana	New Orleans	1718	French	Baton Rouge	Louisiana Purchase 1803	March 26, 1804	April 30, 1812	18	62	39	125	118	-	39	Creole-Pelican	Creoles
Maine	Saco Monhegan	1622?	English	Augusta	Part of Massachusetts	-	Mar. 15, 1820	23	16	22	-	-	-	81	Pine Tree	Lumber Foxes
Maryland	St. Mary's	1634	English	Annapolis	Royal Charter 1632	-	April 28, 1788	7	23	20	128	3	-	104	-	Grawthumpers
Massachusetts	Plymouth	1620	English	Boston	Royal Charter 1629	-	Feb. 6, 1788	6	12	39	-	-	-	132	Bay-Old Bay	Beaneaters
Michigan	Sault Ste. Marie	1668	French	Lansing	Northwest Territory 1787	Jan. 11, 1805	Jan. 26, 1837	26	83	255	-	273	-	60	Wolverine	Wolverines
Minnesota	St. Paul	1838	Americans	St. Paul	Northwest Territory 1787	Mar. 3, 1845	May 11, 1858	32	87	112	-	740	1	-	North Star-Gopher	Gophers
Mississippi	Biloxi	1699	French	Jackson	Mississippi Territory	April 7, 1798	Dec. 10, 1817	20	82	59	175	42	-	15	Bayou	Tadpoles
Missouri	St. Genevieve	1735	French	Jefferson City	Louisiana Purchase 1803	June 4, 1812	Aug. 10, 1821	24	114	165	365	99	-	9	Iron	-

STATE	ORIGINAL SETTLEMENT	WHEN SETTLED	BY WHOM	CAPITAL	SOURCE OF STATE LANDS	Date Organized as Territory	Date Admitted to Union	ORDER IN UNION	NO. OF COUNTIES	NO. OF CITIES	NO. OF TOWNS	NO. OF VILLAGES	NO. OF BOROUGHS	UNINCOR. PLACES	Old Popular Name of State	Old Popular Name of People
MOntana	Yellowstone River	1809	Americans	Helena	Louisiana Purchase 1803	May 26, 1864	Nob. 8, 1889	41	56	48	78	--	--	9	Mountain	Bug-eaters
Nebraska	Bellevue	1847	Americans	Lincoln	Louisiana Purchase 1803	May 30, 1854	Mar. 1, 1867	37	93	124	--	414	--	2	Black Water	--
Nevada	Genoa	1850	Americans	Carson City	Ceded by Mexico	Mar. 2, 1861	Oct. 31, 1864	36	17	13	--	--	--	41	Silver	Sage Hens
New Hampshire	Portsmouth	1623	English	Concord	For New England Grants From Council 1622	--	June 21, 1788	9	10	13	--	--	--	41	Granite	Granite Boys
New Jersey	Elizabethtown	1617	Dutch	Trenton	Dutch Settlement 1618	--	Dec. 18, 1787	3	21	53	21	4	257	47	Garden	Jersey Blues
New Mexico	San Gabriel	1598	Spanish	Santa Fe	Ceded by Mexico 1848	Sept. 9, 1850	Jan. 6, 1912	47	32	29	18	41	--	17	--	--
New York	New York	1613	Dutch	Albany	Dutch Settlement 1623	--	July 26, 1788	11	57	62	--	356	--	258	Empire	Knickerbockers
North Carolina	Albemarre Sound	1653	English	Raleigh	Royal Charter 1663	--	Nov. 21, 1789	12	100	45	420	5	--	68	Turpentine	Tarheels
North Dakota	Pembina	1859	Americans	Bismarck	Louisiana Purchase 1803	Mar. 2, 1861	Nov. 7, 1889	39	53	143	163	1	--	5	Sioux	--
Ohio	Marietta	1788	Americans	Columbus	Northwest Territory 1787	--	Mar. 1, 1803	17	88	200	--	736	--	46	Buckeye	Buckeyes
Oklahoma	Guthrie	1889	Americans	Oklahoma City	Louisiana Purchase 1803	May 2, 1890	Nov. 16, 1907	46	77	146	411	2	--	1	--	--
Oregon	Astoria	1811	Americans	Salem	Treaty With England 1846	Aug. 14, 1848	Feb. 14, 1859	36	172	57	--	--	--	18	Beaver	Web Feet
Pennsylvania	Chester	1638	Swedes	Harrisburg	Royal Grant 1651	--	Dec. 12, 1887	2	66	52	1	--	959	158	Keystone	Leatherheads Pennanites
Rhode Island	Providence	1636	English	Providence	Royal Charter 1663	--	May 29, 1790	13	--	8	--	--	--	12	Little Rhody	Gun-Flints
South Carolina	Ashley River	1670	English	Columbia	Royal Charter 1663	--	May 23, 1788	8	46	32	231	--	--	50	Palmetto	Weasels
South Dakota	Southeastern Part	1839	Americans	Pierre	Louisiana Purchase 1803	Mar. 2, 1861	Nov. 2, 1889	40	164	143	163	1	--	5	--	--
Tennessee	Watauga	1769	Americans	Nashville	Port of North Carolina	--	June 1, 1796	16	95	79	224	--	--	24	Volunteer	Butternuts
Texas	San Antonio	1692	Spanish	Austin	Republic of Texas 1815	April 1845	Dec. 29, 1845	28	254	544	363	33	--	49	Lone Star	Beef-heads
Utah	Salt Lake City	1847	Americans	Salt Lake City	Ceded by Mexico 1848	Sept. 9, 1850	Jan. 4, 1896	45	29	95	121	--	--	11	--	--
Vermont	St. Anne	1665	French	Montpelier	Port of New Hampshire and New York	--	Mar. 4, 1791	14	14	8	--	55	--	12	Green Mountain	Green Mountain Boys
Virginia	Jamestown	1607	English	Richmond	Royal Charter 1609	--	June 25, 1788	10	98	38	195	--	--	49	Old Dominion	Bendles
Washington	Columbia River	1811	English	Olympia	Oregon Territory 1848	Mar. 2, 1853	Nov. 11, 1889	42	39	96	170	--	--	37	Evergreen	--
West Virginia	Berkeley County	1726	Americans	Charleston	Part of Virginia	--	June 20, 1863	35	55	60	157	8	--	24	Panhandle	Panhandlers
Wisconsin	Green Bay	1745	French	Madison	Northwest Territory 1787	Apr. 20, 1836	May 29, 1818	30	72	185	--	385	--	24	Badger	Badgers
Wyoming	Cheyenne	1867	Americans	Cheyenne	Louisiana Purchase 1803	July 25, 1868	July 10, 1890	44	23	12	77	--	--	5	--	--

State Government Telephone Information Numbers and Addresses

For telephone numbers or addresses of state agencies or units not listed in this volume, please call the general information numbers or write to the addresses given below:

ALABAMA	State Capitol, Montgomery 36130	(205) 832-6011
ALASKA	State Capitol, 120-4th St., Juneau 99811	(907) 465-2111
ARIZONA	State Capitol, 1700 W. Washington St., Phoenix 85007	(602) 271-4900
ARKANSAS	State Capitol, 5th and Woodlane, Little Rock 72201	(501) 371-3000
CALIFORNIA	State Capitol, 10th and L Sts., Sacramento 95814	(916) 322-9900
COLORADO	State Capitol, 200 E. Colfax Ave., Denver 80203	(303) 839-5000
CONNECTICUT	State Capitol, 210 Capitol Ave., Hartford 06115	(203) 566-2211
DELAWARE	State Capitol, Dover 19901	(302) 678-4000
DISTRICT OF COLUMBIA	District Bldg., 14th and E Sts., N.W., Washington 20004	(202) 628-6000 and (202) 727-1000
FLORIDA	New Capitol, Monroe St., Tallahassee 32304	(904) 488-1234
GEORIGA	State Capitol, Capitol Sq., S.W., Atlanta 30334	(404) 656-2000
HAWAII	State Capitol, 415 S. Beretania St., Honolulu 96813	(808) 548-2211
IDAHO	Statehouse, 700 W. Jefferson St., Boise 83720	(208) 384-2411
ILLINOIS	State Capitol, Springfield 62706	(217) 782-2000
INDIANA	State House, 200 W. Washington St., Indianapolis 46204	(317) 633-4000
IOWA	Capitol Bldg., 10th and Grand, Des Moines 50319	(515) 281-5011
KANSAS	State House, 10th and Harrison Sts., Topeka 66612	(913) 296-0111
KENTUCKY	New State Capitol, Frankfort 40601	(Depts.) (502) 564-2500 (Individuals) (502) 564-3130
LOUISIANA	State Capitol, 900 Riverside N., Baton Rouge 70804	(504) 342-6600
MAINE	State House, Augusta 04330	(207) 289-1110
MARYLAND	State House, State Cir., Annapolis 21401	(301) 269-6200
MASSACHUSETTS	State House, Beacon St., Boston 02133	(617) 727-2121
MICHIGAN	Capitol Bldg., Lansing 48933	(517) 373-1837
MINNESOTA	State Capitol, Aurora Ave., & Park St., St. Paul 55155	(612) 296-6013
MISSISSIPPI	New Capitol Bldg., Jackson 39205	(601) 354-7011
MISSOURI	State Capitol, Jefferson City 65101	(314) 751-2151
MONTANA	Capitol Bldg., Helena 59601	(406) 449-2511
NEBRASKA	State Capitol, 1445 K St., Lincoln 68509	(402) 471-2311
NEVADA	State Capitol, Carson City 89710	(702) 885-5000
NEW HAMPSHIRE	State House, 107 N. Main St., Concord 03301	(603) 271-1110
NEW JERSEY	State House, Trenton 08625	(609) 292-2121
NEW MEXICO	State Capitol, Santa Fe 87503	(505) 827-4011
NEW YORK	State Capitol, Albany 12224	(518) 474-2121
NORTH CAROLINA	State Capitol, Raleigh 27603	(919) 733-1110
NORTH DAKOTA	State Capitol, Bismarck 58505	(701) 224-2000
OHIO	State House, Broad & High Sts., Columbus 43215	(614) 466-2000
OKLAHOMA	State Capitol, Lincoln Blvd., Oklahoma City 73105	(405) 521-2011
OREGON	State Capitol, Salem 97310	(503) 378-3131
PENNSYLVANIA	Main Capitol Bldg., Harrisburg 17120	(717) 787-2121
RHODE ISLAND	State House, 82 Smith St., Providence 02903	(401) 277-2000
SOUTH CAROLINA	State House, Columbia 29211	(803) 758-0221
SOUTH DAKOTA	Capitol Bldg., Pierre 57501	(605) 773-3011
TENNESSEE	State Capitol, Nashville 37219	(615) 741-3011
TEXAS	State Capitol, Austin 78711	(512) 475-2323
UTAH	State Capitol, Salt Lake City 84114	(801) 533-4000
VERMONT	State House, State St., Montpelier 05602	(802) 828-1110
VIRGINIA	State Capitol, Capitol Sq., Richmond 23219	(804) 786-0000
WASHINGTON	State Capitol, Olympia 98504	(206) 753-5000
WEST VIRGINIA	State Capitol, 1800 Kanawha Blvd., E., Charleston 25305	(304) 348-3456
WISCONSIN	State Capitol, Capitol Sq., Madison 53702	(608) 266-2211
WYOMING	State Capitol, Capitol Ave. at 24th St., Cheyenne 82002	(307) 777-7011

Most states have Driver's License Records going back to about 1920. These often contain some genealogical information. A few states will not release this information and in these cases you would have to request this data through your local police department. I suggest you always first try writing directly to the respective state agency. If they are not willing to work with you then a second letter to them should state: "I am requesting this information under the 'Freedom of Information Act,'" usually this will bring the desired results. When these two steps fail, then the third step is your local police Department. They can (if they will) request this data for you as a matter of routine business.

Motor Vehicle Addresses and Telephones Numbers

STATE OF ALABAMA
Motor Vehicle Division
State Administrative Building
P.O. Box 1331
Montgomery, Alabama 36102
(205)832-6740

STATE OF ALASKA
Department of Motor Vehicles
P.O. Box 960
Anchorage, Alaska 99510
(907)272-1581

STATE OF ARIZONA
Arizona Highway Department
Motor Vehicle Division
1739 West Jackson Street
Phoenix, Arizona 85007
(602)261-7531

STATE OF ARKANSAS
Motor Vehicle Department
Joel Y. Ledbetter Building
7th & Wolfe Streets
P.O. Box 1272
Little Rock, Arkansas 72203
(501)371-1885

STATE OF CALIFORNIA
Department of Motor Vehicles
P.O. Box 1319
Sacramento, California 95806
(916)456-7861

STATE OF COLORADO
Motor Vehicle Division
140 West 6th Avenue
Denver, Colorado 80204
(303)892-3095

STATE OF CONNECTICUT
Department of Motor Vehicles
60 State Street
Wethersfield, Connecticut 06109
(203)566-2640

STATE OF DELAWARE
Motor Vehicle Division
P.O. Box 698

Dover, Delaware 19901
(302)678-4421

DISTRICT OF COLUMBIA
Department of Motor Vehicles
301 C Street, N.W.
Washington, D.C. 20001
(202)629-3751

STATE OF FLORIDA
Motor Vehicle Department
Neil Kirkman Bldg.
Apalachee Parkway
Tallahassee, Florida 32304
(904)488-4374

STATE OF GEORGIA
Department of Motor Vehicles
126 Trinity-Washington Building
Atlanta, Georgia 30334
(404)656-4157

STATE OF HAWAII
City and County of Honolulu
Department of Motor Vehicles
1455 S. Beretania Street
Honolulu, Hawaii 96814
(808)941-2255

STATE OF IDAHO
Department of Motor Vehicles
P.O. Box 34
Boise, Idaho 83731
(208)384-2711

STATE OF ILLINOIS
Motor Vehicle Division
Centennial Building
Springfield, Illinois 62706
(217)782-2996

STATE OF INDIANA
Bureau of Motor Vehicles
State Office Building
Indianapolis, Indiana 46204
(317)633-4828

STATE OF IOWA
Department of Public Safety

Motor Vehicle Registration
  Division
Lucas Building
Des Moines, Iowa 50319
(515)281-5818

STATE OF KANSAS
Motor Vehicle Department
State Office Building
Topeka, Kansas 66626
(913)296-3621

STATE OF KENTUCKY
Department of Public Safety
Division of Motor Vehicles
New State Office Building
Frankfort, Kentucky 40601
(502)564-3780—564-4540

STATE OF LOUISIANA
Motor Vehicle Division
So. Foster Drive
P.O. Box 66196
Baton Rouge, Louisiana 70821
(504)389-7503

STATE OF MAINE
Department of Motor Vehicles
242 State Street
Augusta, Maine 04330
(207)289-3556

STATE OF MARYLAND
Department of Motor Vehicles
6601 Ritchie Highway, N.E.
Glen Burnie, Maryland 21061
(301)768-7000

STATE OF MASSACHUSETTS
Registry of Motor Vehicles
100 Nashua Street
Boston, Massachusetts 02114
(617)727-3794

STATE OF MICHIGAN
Michigan Department of State
Motor Vehicle Department
Lansing, Michigan 48918
(517)373-2480

STATE OF MINNESOTA
Department of Motor Vehicles
State Highway Building
St. Paul, Minnesota 55155
(612)296-6911

STATE OF MISSISSIPPI
Motor Vehicle Comptroller
P.O. Box 1383
Jackson, Mississippi 39205
(601)354-7414

STATE OF MISSOURI
Motor Vehicle Registry
Jefferson Building
100 East Capitol
Jefferson City, Missouri 65101
(314)751-2577

STATE OF MONTANA
Registrar of Motor Vehicles
923 Main Street
Deer Lodge, Montana 59722
(406)846-1320

STATE OF NEBRASKA
Dept. of Motor Vehicles
State Capitol
P.O. Box 94789
Lincoln, Nebraska 68509
(402)471-2281

STATE OF NEVADA
Department of Motor Vehicles
555 Wright Way
Carson City, Nevada 89701
(702)882-7301

STATE OF NEW HAMPSHIRE
Department of Public Safety
Division of Motor Vehicles
John O. Morton Building
Concord, New Hampshire 03301
(603)271-2484

STATE OF NEW JERSEY
Department of Motor Vehicles
25 South Montgomery
Trenton, New Jersey 08666
(609)292-7044

STATE OF NEW MEXICO
Department of Motor Vehicles
Bataan Memorial Building
Santa Fe, New Mexico 87501
(505)827-2936

STATE OF NEW YORK
Department of Motor Vehicles
Empire State Plaza
Albany, New York, 12228
(518)474-2121

Department of Motor Vehicles
Box 629
Raleigh, North Carolina 27602
(919)829-7453

STATE OF NORTH DAKOTA
Department of Motor Vehicles
State Office Building
Bismarck, North Dakota 58501
(701)224-2725

STATE OF OHIO
Bureau of Motor Vehicles
4300 Kimberly Parkway
P.O. Box 1199
Columbus, Ohio 43216
(614)466-2130

STATE OF OKLAHOMA
Department of Motor Vehicles
2501 Lincoln Blvd.
Oklahoma City, Oklahoma 73194
(405)521-3216

STATE OF OREGON
Department of Motor Vehicles
1905 Lana Ave., N.E.
Salem, Oregon 97310
(503)378-6947

STATE OF PENNSYLVANIA
Bureau of Motor Vehicles
Transportation & Safety Building
Harrisburg, Pennsylvania 17122
(717)787-3130

STATE OF RHODE ISLAND
Registry of Motor Vehicles
State Office Building
Providence, Rhode Island 02903
(401)277-3007

STATE OF SOUTH CAROLINA
Motor Vehicle Division
Drawer 1498
Columbia, South Carolina 29206
(803)758-3204

STATE OF SOUTH DAKOTA
Department of Motor Vehicles

118 West Capital
Pierre, South Dakota 57501
(605)224-3541

STATE OF TENNESSEE
Motor Vehicle Department
500 Deaderick Street
Nashville, Tennessee 37242
(615)741-2477

STATE OF TEXAS
Motor Vehicle Division
40th and Jackson
Austin, Texas 78779
(512)452-8111

STATE OF UTAH
Department of Motor Vehicles
1095 Motor Ave.
Salt Lake City, Utah 84116
(801)533-5312

STATE OF VERMONT
Department of Motor Vehicles
State Street
Montpelier, Vermont 05602
(802)828-2121

STATE OF VIRGINIA
Division of Motor Vehicles
2220 W. Broadstreet
Richmond, Virginia 23269
(703)770-3344

STATE OF WASHINGTON
Department of Motor Vehicles
Highways & Licenses Building
Olympia, Washington 98504
(206)753-6918

STATE OF WEST VIRGINIA
Department of Motor Vehicles
1800 Washington Street
Charleston, West Virginia 25305
(304)348-2737

STATE OF WISCONSIN
Motor Vehicle Department
State Office Building
Madison, Wisconsin 53702
(608)266-1466

STATE OF WYOMING
Department of Motor Vehicles
2200 Carey Avenue
Cheyenne, Wyoming 82001
(307)777-7271

Orphan Voyage of Florida

Genealogists, tracers of missing persons, family members separated over many years, those seeking long lost one-time close friends, and others involved in name research frequently have need for specific surname and address listing of persons across the U.S. Now such service is available.

Orphan Voyage of Florida (OVF) has developed a connection with a national marketing firm which has all current U.S. telephone directories on computer tape which can be used to extract specific surnames (or surname and one initial only). There are nearly 5,000 telephone directories across the U.S. and the computer tape carries more than 60 million names. Even if all directories were placed in one room, screening and listing of any single name would take hundreds of hours. Some telephone directories carry as many as nine or ten alphabetical sections (for each incorporated town in the area). Even the Bell and Howell Phonefiche listing used by many public libraries carries only about 700 telephone directories—or less than one-sixth of all directories published.

OVF is a chapter of Orphan Voyage, a national adoptee support non-profit group founded in 1953 by Jean Paton and now based in Colorado. It has served adoptees, adoptive parents, and those relinquishing children to adoption for over a quarter of a century.

For free details on the surname listing (which average cost will be $150) send a self-addressed stamped envelope to: OVF, 13906 Pepperrell Dr., Tampa, Fl 33624.

Tampa Bay Chapter of Orphan Voyage of Florida

In the many searches we have been involved in, it often occurs that a searcher knows the name of the person being sought, but has no idea of where to look. We have located a national firm which has all persons listed in *current* U.S. telephone directories on computer tape; the company provides mailing list and marketing information to several well-known companies. We were first advised that a single run would cost $20,000, which was later reduced to about one-third, and finally to submit 60-70 names to be extracted in a single run. As a result we estimate a single surname check will cost $150. Each additional name will cost $50 plus printing cost. We will collect the 60-70 name requests.

In requesting a surname check, one should keep in mind how common or uncommon the name is. (We have a 1967 frequency of name study conducted by the Social Security Administration listing the 2,000 most common names indicating the number of files they have for each name.) The computer can accept one surname or one surname plus one initial only for each search. Someone looking for Frank Smith, for example, would request a check for F. Smith, but the numbers of names listed would almost certainly be unworkable. On the other hand if you were looking for Xavier Smith, a listing request for X. Smith would probably be worthwhile. This service has highest potential with less common names.

Interested persons must submit $150 in check or money order (plus $50 for each additional name) which will be deposited in the Orphan Voyage of Florida account. The request for surname check may be cancelled at any time UNTIL the list is forwarded to the national organization for the computer run. If such request to cancel the surname listing is received prior to submission to the company, all money (less $2.50 service charge) will be returned,

The enclosed form on page ____ of this book can be used, and if three self-addressed stamped envelopes are enclosed we will advise you of each step (1) that we have received your request, (2) the date forward the list to the computer company, and (3) receipt of the list from the company which we must break down, print, and mail. Only volunteer help will be used by OVF to perform tasks involved.

Make Checks Payable to Orphan Voyage of Florida/Tampa Bay, 13906 Pepperrell Drive, Tampa, Fl 33624

NASR—We'll help bring you together.

We understand the search can be long and frustrating. We wish there was an easy answer. Unfortunately, there isn't.

But now there's hope. NASR . . . The National Adoptive Search Registry, Inc. A new and truly unique service run by leading professional consultants with years of experience in adoptee-birthparent searches.

NASR offers you a better chance to make your match. That's because we've pioneered and developed a special approach to matching family members. A systematic approach that's been absent from coventional search methods.

We developed this system because of a void that existed in virtually every method used by search agencies. We studied the approaches used by others and weighed the alternatives. And finally developed what is, without a doubt, the best, most modern method available in the United State today.

It's a computerized registry system. A system that runs every case through a sophisticated computer bank. Therefore, we can conduct your search on a nationwide basis, instead of a local one. This computerized approach permits us to match more variables, more information, more data, and literally, thousands of identifying features. And the search can be run in a matter of minutes, rather then days or weeks.

After we arrive at a match, we'll pull the data from the computer and an expert will perform an in-depth analysis to ensure even greater accuracy.

The fact of the matter is, there is simply no better search method. The computer is faster, more accurate and more thorough than any human can be.

And that means NASR offers you the best way to get in touch . . . especially during those times when you may feel just too frustrated to continue the search on your own. NASR will be there to continue it for you.

And NASR offers you still more. Because of our affiliation with a regional private investigation firm that specializes in private adoptee, birthparent investigations, we are continually provided with more names to match in the computer banks. Our registry also receives scores of applications sent in from adoption Triad groups around the country on a regular basis.

What Happens When You Register?

In order to initiate your search, all you have to do is complete the enclosed application and return it to NASR. Once you do, your name and background information will be immediately entered into our National Register and a search will begin.

Your application will be checked and cross referenced against our existing register. Thousands of pieces of information will be referenced and analyzed.

If there is a match, you will be notified immediately. If not, your information will be held in the computer and analyzed against every piece of new information and every new application that comes in during the future—for as long as it takes to find a match.

Note: You must be at least eighteen years of age to register with NASR.

What Makes NASR Different?

We combine a personal commitment with sophisticated computer services to give you the fastest, most accurate tracking methods available.

NATIONAL ADOPTIVE SEARCH REGISTRY, INC.

FACTUALLY COMPLETE AS FULLY AS POSSIBLE
PLEASE USE REVERSE SIDE FOR ADDITIONAL INFORMATION

DATE OF REGISTRATION_____

SEARCHER'S PRESENT NAME_____
ADDRESS:_____
        STREET   CITY   STATE   ZIP
MAILING ADDRESS (if different)_____
HOME TELEPHONE#_____ BUSINESS#_____
YOUR STATUS: ADOPTEE_____
               ADOPTIVE PARENTS_____
               BIRTH PARENT_____
               BIOLOGICAL RELATIVE_____
               OTHER_____

NAME @ BIRTH_____ SEX_____ RACE_____
DATE OF BIRTH_____ TIME OF BIRTH_____am/pm
PLACE OF BIRTH_____ TOWN_____
        COUNTY_____ STATE_____
SINGLE OR MULTIPLE BIRTH?_____ PREVIOUS BIRTHS TO MOTHER?_____
BIRTH CERTIFCATE#_____AMENDED_____FILED_____
ATTENDING PHYSICIAN:_____
BIRTH MOTHER'S MAIDEN NAME_____
   "   "   NAME/NICKNAMES/ALIAS_____
   "   "   DATE OF BIRTH_____ AGE @ BIRTH_____
   "   "   PLACE OF BIRTH_____
   "   "   MARITAL STATUS_____ RELIGION_____
   "   "   EDUCATIONAL LEVEL_____OCCUPATION_____
   "   "   PARENTS'NAMES_____/_____

BIRTH FATHER'S NAME/NICKNAME/ALIAS_____
   "   "   DATE OF BIRTH_____ AGE @ BIRTH_____
   "   "   PLACE OF BIRTH_____
   "   "   MARITAL STATUS_____ RELIGION_____
   "   "   EDUCATIONAL LEVEL_____OCCUPATION_____
   "   "   MILITARY SVCE._____YEARS_____
   "   "   PARENTS'NAMES_____/_____

KNOWN SIBLINGS BY BIRTH MOTHER_____/_____
   "   "   BY BIRTH FATHER_____/_____

NAMES OF ADOPTIVE PARENTS_____/_____
CHILD'S NAME BY ADOPTION_____
COURT OF JURISDICTION (actual)_____
   CITY_____COUNTY_____STATE_____
ATTORNEY OF RECORD_____CASE#/DECREE_____
FILED_____
PLACING AGENCY_____CASE WORKER_____

I,_____ hereby give my permission to NASR, The
National Adoptive Search Registry, to release this vital information to
the person(s) for whom this search is conducted. I understand this
permission is necessary for verification of identity and my relationship to the missing person.

SIGNED_____DATE_____

— 461 —

And that's important. Because with over 500,000 known adoptees alone in the United States today, there are literally thousands upon thousands of individuals looking for each other, coast to coast, at any given time. Conventional methods of logging, storing and cross-matching by hand are simply inadequate to meet the task.

NASR's computerized approach is designed to meet it. It provides you with the best chance of finding an individual match . . . and new hope for successful conclusion to your search.

One Low Fee

A membership fee of just $50.00 enrolls you as a lifetime member of NASR. This is a one-time fee only. There are no other additional charges—no matter how long it takes to complete your search.

To initiate your search, simply complete the enclosed application as fully as possible and return it in the enclosed envelope provided.

We look forward to helping.

NASR—We understand the longing of a searching adoptee, sibling and birthparent.

NASR, P.O. Box 2051, Great Neck, New York 11022, (516)466-4140

Canals

Three useful sources of Canal records:

1. Research Canal Boats, *American Canals,* No. 25, May 1978, pp.2-3

2. *Merchant Vessels of the United States, Government Printing Office 1868 to present.*

3. *Look up federal papers for Interstate Commerce in Industrial and Social Branch—National Archives.*

Canals

Canals	When Completed	Miles	No. Locks	No. of Feet†	Location
Albemarle and Chesapeake, . . .	1860	44	1	7½	Norfolk, VA, to Currituck Sound, NC
Augusta, ...	1847	9		11	Savannah River, GA, to Augusta, GA
Black River, ...	1849	35	109	4	Rome, NY, to Lyons Falls, NY
Cayuga & Seneca,	1839	25	11	7	Montezuma, NY, to Cayuga & Seneca Lakes, NY
Champlain, ...	1822	81	32	6	Whitehall, NY to West Troy, NY
Chesapeake and Delaware, ...	1829	14	3	9	Chesapeake City, MD, to Delaware City, Delaware
Chesapeake and Ohio, ...	1850	184	73	6	Cumberland, MD to Washington, DC
Companys, ...	1847	22	1	6	Mississippi River, LA, to Bayou Black, LA
Dalles-Celilo, ...	1915	8½	5	8	Columbia River, from Big Eddy to Celilo Falls, Oregon
Delaware and Raritan, ...	1838	66	14	8-9	New Brunswick, NJ, to Bordentown, NJ
Delaware Division, ...	1830	60	33	6	Easton, PA, to Bristol, PA

Name	Year				Location/Description
Des Moines Rapids, ...	1877	7½	3	5	At Des Moines Rapids, Mississippi River
Dismal Swamp, ..	1822	22	7	6	Connects Chesapeake Bay with Albemarle Sound
Erie, ...	1825	363	72	7	Albany, NY to Buffalo, NY
Fairfield, ...		4½	None		Alligator River to Lake Mattimuskeet, NC
Galveston and Brazos, ...	1851	38		3½	Galveston, TX, to Brazos River, TX
Hocking, ...	1843	42	26	4	Carroll, OH, to Nelsonville, OH
Illinois and Michigan, ...	1848	102	15	6	Chicago, IL, to La Salle, IL
Illinois and Mississippi, ...	1895	75	3	7	Around lower rapids of Rock River, IL, connects with Mississippi River
Lake Washington, ...	1917	8½	2	36	Seattle, WA, connects Puget Sound and Lake Washington
Lehigh Coal and Navigation Co., .	1821	108	57	6	Coalport, PA, to Easton, PA
Louisville and Portland	1872	2½	2		At Falls of Ohio River, Louisville, KY
Miami & Erie, ...	1835	274	93	5½	Cincinnati, OH, to Toledo, Oh
Morris, ...	1836	103	33	5	Easton, PA to Jersey City, NJ
Muscle Shoals and Elk River Shoals, ...	1889	16	11		Big Muscle Shoals, TN, to Elk River Shoals, TN
Newbern and Beaufort, ...		3	None		Clubfoot Creek to Harlow Creek, NC
N.Y. State Barge Canal System..	1918	800	57	12	Connects Lakes Erie, Ontario, Champlain, Cayuga, and Seneca with Hudson River.
Ogeechee, ...	1840	16	5	3	Savannah River, GA to Ogeechee River, GA
Ohio, ...	1835	317	150	4	Cleveland, OH, to Portsmouth, OH
Oswego, ...	1828	38	18	7	Oswego, NY, to Syracuse, NY
Pennsylvania, ...	1839	193	71	6	Columbia, Northumberland, Wilkesbarre, Huntingdon, PA.
Portage Lake and Lake Superior, ..	1873	25	None	15	From Keweenaw Bay to Lake Superior
Port Arthur, ...	1899	7		26	Port Arthur, TX, to Gulf of Mexico
Santa Fe, ...	1880	10		5	Waldo, FL, to Melrose, FL
Schuylkill Navigation Co., .	1826	108	71	6¼	Mill Creek, PA to Philadelphia, PA
Sturgeon Bay and Lake Michigan.	1881	1¼	None	15	Between Green Bay and Lake Michigan
St. Mary's Falls ..	1896	1 1/3	1	21	Connects Lake Superior and Huron at Sault Ste. Marie, Michigan
Susquehanna and Tidewater, ...	1840	45	32	5½	Columbia, PA, to Havre de Grace, MD
Walhonding, ...	1843	25	11	4	Rochester, OH, to Roscoe, OH

*And improvements. †Navigable depth.

The Harlem River Ship Canal, connecting the Hudson River and Long Island Sound, by way of Spuyten Duyvil Creek and Harlem River, was opened for traffic on June 17, 1895, and cost about $2,700,000.

Waterways

	Name	Section (Miles)	From	To	No. of Locks	Navigation Season
1	Atlantic Intracostal Waterway & Ext.	1129	Norfolk, VA	Miami, FL	2	All year

2	Chesapeake Bay	200	Baltimore, MD	Capes of VA	0	All year
3	Delaware River	129	Trenton, NJ	Delaware Bay	0	All year
4	Hudson River	155	Upper Bay, NY (Near N.Y.C.)	Waterford, NY junction with N.Y.S. Barge Canal	0	All year except 8-month season in north April-Nov.
5	New York State Barge Canal	522	Niagara River at Tonowanda, NY	Champlain Inlet at Whitehall, NY	58	
6	Potomac River	113	Key Bridge, Wash, DC	Chesapeake Bay, 80 miles from the Atlantic	0	All year
7	Allegheny River	72	East Brady, PA	Ohio River	9	All year
8	Monongahela River	129	Fairmont, WV	Pittsburgh, PA	10	All year
9	James River	89	Richmond, VA	Hampton Roads at Newport News, VA	0	All year
10	Kanawha River	91	Deepwater, WV	Ohio River near Point Pleasant, WV	3	All year
11	Ohio River	981	Pittsburgh, PA	Mississippi River at Cairo, IL	19	All year
12	Kentucky River	259	Beattyville, KY	Ohio River near Carrollton, KY	14	All year
13a	Green River	150	Woodburn, KY	Ohio River near Evansville, IN	4	All year
13b	Barren River	30	Bowling Green, KY	Green River at Woodburn, KY	1	All year
14	Cumberland River	317	Carthage, TN	Ohio River at Smithland, KY	4	All year
15	Gulf Intracostal Waterway	1113	Apalachee Bay (St. Marks, FL)	Brownsville, TX	9	All year
16	Apalachicola-Chattahoochee and Flint River System	297	Apalachicola Bay	Columbus and Bainbridge, GA	3	All year
17	Tennessee River	652	Knoxville, TN	Ohio River at Paducah, KY	10	All year
18	Black Warrior-Tombigbee Waterway	466	Mobile, AL	Brimingham Port, Alabama	6	All year
19a	Mississippi River: Upper	663	Minneapolis, MN	Mouth of Missouri River near St. Louis	30	March-Dec.
19b	Mississippi River: Lower	1174	Mouth of Missouri River near St. Louis	Gulf of Mexico	0	All year
20	Illinois Waterway (including Calumet-Sag Channel and the Chicago Sanitary and Ship Canal)	354	Grafton, IL	Turning basin at Calumet River in Chicago area	0	All year
21	Houston Ship Canal	50	Galveston Harbor, Texas	Houston, TX	0	All year
22	Missouri River	732	Sioux City Iowa	Mississippi River	4	April-mid-Nov.
23	Columbia River	317	Mouth of Snake River, east of Pasco, Washington	Pacific Ocean	4	All year
24a	Sacramento River	145	Colusa, CA	Suisun Bay, 48 miles NE of San Francisco	1	All year
24b	San Joaquin River	127	Stockton, CA	Suisun Bay, 48 miles NE of San Francisco	0	All year

The Golda Meir Library
The University of Wisconsin—Milwaukee

On July 26, 1978, a justice of the New York State Supreme Court signed a court order approving the American Geopraphical Society's petition to move the Society's library and map collections from New York City to The University of Wisconsin—Milwaukee. With this final legal step, Wisconsin became the custodian of a national treasure, an international resource. The magnitude of the AGS Collection, its sheer breadth and scope, is breathtaking. It is a two-fold treasure: a collection of rare and precious historic items and a current source of essential research information.

A Priceless Treasure

Prior to its transfer to UMN, the AGS Collection was described as the largest privately owned geographical research collection in the Western Hemisphere, with 180,000 volumes, 350,000 maps, 33,000 pamphlets, 5,500 atlases, 45,000 photographs, and 67 rare and special globes. Its total value has been estimated at more than $30 million by a leading rare books dealer, but its unique, irreplaceable treasures make the Collection a priceless intellectual resource. Its greatest value is found in its structural integrity, its unity, and its availability as a single, complete, and fully cataloged resource for the scholar, the researcher, and the interested layman.

The Collection includes materials that have not only played a major role in the development of the United States but are also significant to the cultural history of Western civilization. Collection holdings reflect such strengths as the achievements of the Age of Exploration, with works by and about such men as Lewis and Clark, Stanley and Livingstone, Roald Amundsen, Robert E. Peary, and Richard E. Byrd.

Collection is Center of Information

The Collection is also a vital source of information which can be used for current research and business needs. Much of the material is unavailable in a single resource elsewhere in the world. Unique to the Collection are maps reflecting the development of cartography in virtually every country in the world; unusually strong and complete sets of international geographical periodicals; and rare, early landscape views of the American West by such photographers as Carleton Watkins, Eadweard J. Muybridge, and Timothy H. O'Sullivan. Reflecting contemporary concerns are an atlas of twentieth-century deseases, a ski guide to the Northeast, and the most recent volumes on urban planning. It is a living, growing Collection, and the blending of historic resources and modern publications greatly enhances its research value. The bibliographic journal, *Current Geographical Publications,* now published by the Golda Meir Library, provides a monthly report on new acquisitions.

The American Geographical Society Collection is first and foremost a working, scholarly library, encompassing all aspects of geography and related disciplines from the past to the present. Its resources are available to scholars, researchers, business, industry, and the general public. A national trust, a wealth of information resources, and a priceless legacy for the future are the hallmarks of the American Geographical Society Collection of the University of Wisconsin—Milwaukee.

User Access

The AGS Collection is located on the third floor, East Wing of UWM's Golda Meir Library (Building No. 21 on campus map). Enter through the West Wing main entrance and take the stairway or elevator to the third floor. The Collection is open every weekday from 8:00 a.m. to 5:00 p.m. and on Saturday from 8:00 a.m. to 12:00 noon.

Resources

Current religious books published in America and England are purchased each week. The fields represented include biblical studies, theology and philosophy, preaching and worship, history, education, church organization and missions, social problems, world perspectives, church music and art, literature (chiefly biography), and the natural and social sciences as they affect religion. The Library also subscribes to a large number of religious periodicals.

Reference Materials

The many rare books and pamphlets, acquired during more than a century and a quarter, make the Congregational Library a center of research for scholars. Among the 225,000 books and pamphlets are special collections of Congregational Councils, local church histories, town histories, church architecture, theological works of five centuries, sermons, Bibles, hymnals, etc.

How to Borrow Books

In order to borrow a book simply send a letter or postcard listing author and title. It is well to request several, for if only one or two are ordered, they may be out on loan. Many readers send a fairly long list. State the number of books to be sent at one time and how frequently (one every two weeks, or three each month, for example). If books on a specific subject are desired, define subject area clearly and state needs as plainly as possible so that a satisfactory selection may be made. Specify how many titles are wanted.

In Case of Delay

The Library has a follow-up system for mailing books from a list. Those which are out on loan are automatically reserved to be sent as soon as available. Readers are asked to write the Library whenever books have not been received and more are needed.

Loan Period

Books are loaned for four weeks. Because of varying distances from Boston the lending period is counted from the day the book is received by the reader. The due date stamped in the back of the book is thus approximate. Books should be returned promptly.

Renewal

Books not in current demand may be renewed. In order to renew send a postcard before the due date. If no other readers are waiting for the book, renewal will be granted without the necessity of a reply.

Mailing Instructions

When returning books readers are requested to wrap them carefully so that they may be received in good condition. The same mailing envelope or wrapping materials may be used whenever possible. A return address label is sent with each package. No charge is made for sending books, but a small envelope is provided for a donation toward mailing costs if you wish to contribute. Special library rates are currently

1st Pound .21—each additional pound .08

Summer Reading

Non-current books may be borrowed for vacation reading for the entire summer, to be returned promptly before September 10th.

However, new books in current demand may be borrowed only for the usual period of lending. Note the due date stamped in the back of the book.

Change of Address

Any change of address should be reported to the library as promptly as possible.

Visiting the Library

The Library is open Monday through Friday from 9-4:30, with the exception of holidays. Leaders are invited to bring adult groups or young people from church schools, youth fellowships or confirmation classes to visit the Congregational Library. When arrangements are made in advance, the Librarian will prepare an exhibit of some interesting rare treasures illustrating Congregational history, and a talk on our heritage will be given. Some groups may want to see early manuscripts and Bibles such as the Chained Bible (1480 A.D.) and John Eliot's Indian Bible. Individuals and families are also cordially invited to visit and become acquainted with the Library.

The Bulletin

Issued three times a year, each issue of the *Bulletin* includes a list of the new books purchased during the preceding four months, an article of interest to readers, special book lists and reviews.

The *Bulletin* is sent to the Library's annual donors at no further cost; others may subscribe at the rate of $3.00 a year (three issues).

The Proprietor of the Library is The American Congregational Association, founded in 1853, to maintain, in the City of Boston, a Congregational House, to care for and perpetuate a library of books, pamphlets, and manuscripts, and a collection of portraits and relics of the past; to promote friendly intercourse and cooperation among Congregational ministers and churches, and with other denominations; and to do whatever else—within the limits of its charter—shall serve to illustrate Congregational history and promote the general interests of the Congregational tradition.

The address of the Congregational Library is: Congregational House, 14 Beacon St., Boston, Mass. 02108 (617) 523-0470

The Library is located diagonally across from the Massachusetts State House, on Beacon Street near the corner of Park Street.

Parking is available at the Boston Common Garage on Charles Street, a five-minute walk from the Library.

Persons preferring to park in the suburbs and travel by MBTA should take the subway to Park Street Station, a three-minute walk from the Library.

The services of the Library are available to ministers and lay people of all denominations.

The Durrett Collection

The University of Chicago; The Joseph Regenstein Library, Special Collections, 1100 East 57th Street, Chicago, Illinois 60637.

In his attempt to collect the surviving historical records of Kentucly, Col. Reuben T. Durrett accumulated many individual documents and groups of papers which taken together do not constitute a homogeneous grouping except in their relation to the history of the state and the area of the Ohio River Valley. The collection has a considerable number of important and varied manuscripts, including correspondence, deeds, petitions, land warrants, surveys, account books, etc. Most of the papers pertain to the late 18th and early 19th centuries, although the manuscripts cover a period from 1674 to the time of Durrett's death in 1913. During the period of early settlement and political development, there are original and copies of letters and records relating to men of national importance such as Washington, Jefferson, Hamilton, Clark, Wilkinson and Boone, as well as many Kentuckians of local fame.

The collection, comprising some 3,000 items, also contains a substantial number of documents relating to individuals, families, and localities. Among the most extensive are the papers of Mann Butler (1806-1845), Kentucky historian; Richard H. Collins (1870-1890), Kentucky historian; Joel Tanner Hart (1823-1876), Kentucky sculptor and poet; George Nicholas (1789-1799), Virginia and Kentucky political leader and attorney general of Kentucky; John Lewis Family (1784-1835); papers of Edmund Lyne's estate and Harry Innes, Executor (1774-1804); Joshua Lacy Wilson (1807-1846), Ohio Presbyterian clergyman and professor of philosophy at Cincinnati college; as well as miscellaneous papers of Isaac Shelby, Kentucky's first governor, and the Shelby family.

Unfortunately we have no brochure or detailed guide available to send to you. Perhaps this brief description will give you a better idea of whether there are apt to be materials here which match your specific interests. We do have a large card-file index of the correspondence in the collection.

The Draper Manuscripts

The 491 volumes of *The Draper Manuscripts* primarily reflect Lyman Copeland Draper's interest in the trans-Allegheny West, a region embracing the western areas of the Carolinaes and Virginia; portions of Georgia and Alabama; the entire Ohio River Valley; and portions of the Mississippi River Valley. Some volumes reflect Draper's early research interest in New York and New England.

Particular emphasis is placed on the period of the American Revolution. Included are correspondence, questionaries, collected reminiscences, and transcripts gathered from 1840 to 1891. Original documents, dating from 1740 to 1830, are also included.

The entire collection of Draper Manuscripts has been microfilmed. A listing of same follows. A complete description of the collection is in the book, *A Guide to the Draper Manuscripts* by Josephine L. Harper, compiler. Madison: State Historical Society of Wisconsin, 1982.

Libraries Holding Complete Sets of Draper Microfilms

ALABAMA
Birmingham Pulbic Library, Birmingham
University of Alabama, Tuscaloosa

ARKANSAS
University of Arkansas, Fayetteville

CALIFORNIA
Huntington Library & Art Gallery, San Marino
University of California, Berkeley
University of California, Santa Barbara
University of Southern California, Los Angeles

COLORADO
Denver Public Library, Denver

FLORIDA
Florida State University, Tallahassee

GEORGIA
Emory University, Atlanta
University of Georgia, Athens

ILLINOIS
Illinois State Historical Library, Springfield
Newberry Library, Chicago

INDIANA
Ball State University, Muncie
Indiana State Library, Indianapolis
Indiana University, Bloomington
Public Library of Fort Wayne and
    Allen County, Fort Wayne
Purdue University, Lafayette
Vincennes Public Library, Vincennes

IOWA
State Historical Society of Iowa, Iowa City

KANSAS
University of Kansas, Lawrence

KENTUCKY
Filson Club, Louisville
Kentucky Historical Society, Frankfort
Kentucky State Department of
Libraries, Frankfort
Murray State University, Murray
University of Kentucky, Lexington
Western Kentucky State University,
Bowling Green

LOUISIANA
Louisiana State University, Baton Rouge

MASSACHUSETTS
Harvard College Library, Cambridge

MICHIGAN
Wayne State University, Detroit

MINNESOTA
Minnesota Historical Society, Saint Paul

MISSISSIPPI
Mississippi Department of Archives
and History, Jackson
Mississippi State University, State College

MISSOURI
Southwest Missouri State College, Springfield
State Historical Society of Missouri, Columbia

NEBRASKA
University of Nebraska, Lincoln

NEW JERSEY
Princeton University, Princeton

NEW MEXICO
University of New Mexico, Albuquerque

NORTH CAROLINA
Duke University, Durham
University of North Carolina, Chapel Hill,
each have about half of the series, a planned
acquisition which totals a complete set.

OHIO
Ohio University, Athens
Public Library of Cincinnati
and Hamilton County, Cincinnati

OKLAHOMA
University of Oklahoma, Norman

PENNSYLVANIA
East Stroudsburg State University,
East Stroudsburg
Mansfield State College, Mansfield

SOUTH CAROLINA
South Carolina Department of
Archives and History, Columbia
Winthrop College, Rock Hill

TENNESSEE
Cossitt Library, Memphis
East Tennessee State University, Johnson City
Knoxville—Knox County Public Library,
Knoxville

Memphis State University, Memphis
Tennessee Polytechnic Institute, Cookeville
Tennessee State Library and Archives,
Nashville
University of Tennessee, Knoxville

TEXAS
Dallas Public Library, Dallas
Houston Public Library, Houston
Rice University, Houston
West Texas State University, Canyon

UTAH
Utah Genealogical Society (L.D.S.),
Salt Lake City

VIRGINIA
University of Virginia, Charlottesville
Virginia Polytechnic Institute, Blacksburg
Virginia State Library, Richmond
Washington and Lee University, Lexington

WEST VIRGINIA
Marshall University, Huntington
Surveyor of Lands of Berkeley
County, Martinsburg
West Virginia Institute of Technology,
Montgomery
West Virginia University, Morgantown

WISCONSIN
State Historical Society of Wisconsin, Madison
University of Wisconsin—Milwaukee,
Milwaukee

DISTRICT OF COLUMBIA
Library of Congress, Washington

New York City Municipal Building

New York City Municipal Building, Williams Street, New York City, New York

Some time ago, I received a newspaper clipping from the Long Island Branch Librarian, Doris F. Neaman. The article referred to the recent activities and findings in the sub-basement of the Municipal Building in New York City.

I went to this building and attempted to secure permission to examine the afore mentioned records. This being Earth Day, most of the city officials were away on city business. After spending almost two hours trying to locate someone in authority who could give me the permission I sought, I decided to try and go directly to the basement.

I was told by everyone in the building that there was no basement and there definitely were no records stored in this building. Just as I was about to leave, thinking I had been misinformed, a clerk told me to try the boiler room and perhaps the men down there could help me. I pushed a button in a dark corridor and a voice asked, "Who's there?"

I told the voice in the little speaker that I was here to evaluate their records and see if they are suitable for microfilming. He told me to come down two flights of stairs to the end of a long corridor. Here I met the head boilerman and his assistant.

I explained my purpose in being there and they offered to show me the records. Each of us carried a flashlight and started walking single file down through corridors, passageways, stairways and dark, damp rooms.

The boilerman said that I was one of only two outside visitors in many years. The last visitor was a professor and he removed most of the documents relating to the civil war. He was unable to recall this gentlemen's name or what institution he represented.

There are literally tons and tons of documents of all types in this catacomb-like archive. There are records in every room and in every corner. Some of the rooms were a full forty feet in height.

The records are in very bad condition generally. The basement is cold and damp and many of the pipes overhead are leaking. Much of the material has been either thrown or knocked down onto the floor or the aisleway.

As near as I can tell, the records start at about the time of the Revolution and go down to the 1930's. The bulk of the records seem to cover the period from 1860 to about 1930. However, a more thorough examination would be necessary to determine both the exact content and years covered.

We spent several hours in this great maze. The building appears to be divided into two main areas or basements, with the subway running on two sides.

Altogether, I think I visited a dozen or so large rooms which were filled to capacity. Some records were located on large structural beams high above the basement floor. Long extension ladders would be needed to gain access to them.

Some of the rooms could only be entered by ducking low or crawling on hands and knees. Because of the great amount of dust in the whole area, respirators or protective masks would be necessary to undertake any extensive evaluation.

These two afore mentioned gentlemen assisted me in locating many records for the early and middle eighteen hundreds. Some of the records that I examined were city payroll receipts, various civil war records, corporate and real estate bonds, police and firemen's records, tax lists, street records, etc. Some document were written in Dutch.

Books on Demand

Frequently Asked Questions

University Microfilms International, 300 N. Zeeb Road, Ann Arbor, MI 48106 USA 313-761-4700 and University Microfilms International, 18 Bedford Row, London WC1R 4EJ, England 01-242-9485

What is meant by Books on Demand or demand reprint program?

Books on Demand is the name of University Microfilms' on-demand book publishing and reprinting program. Unlike conventionally printed editions, books published or reprinted on demand are produced in direct response to customer orders, not in anticipation of future sales. Hence, no inventory is maintained. Only a microfilm master is kept from which xeropraphic or microfilm copies are produced each time an order is received. This unique publishing method allows University Microfilms to keep thousands of titles perpetually available. Once added to the Books on Demand program, a title is never out of print.

What types of books are available?

Academic and scholarly resource materials are the primary focus of the Books on Demand program. Originally published by university presses, learned societies, and trade book publishers around the world, these titles represent every subject area from the sciences to the humanities, and every genre from fiction to reference works—with imprints that date back to the 15th century or that are as recent as the 1970's

What does a demand reprint look like?

Both xerographic and microfilm demand reprints may be purchased. Xerographic demand reprints are usually reproduced from microfilm by printing each page on a continuous roll of paper in full, eye-legible size. Since only one side of the sheet is printed, it is folded to give the appearance of having printing on both sides, but it puts odd-numbered pages in a left-hand position instead of on the right. Printed text and line-drawing illustrations reproduce well on the durable, lightweight, opaque paper, creating a book which closely resembles the original printed publication in size, thickness and readability. Half-tones (photographs) generally do not reproduce well; however, high quality silver print reproductions of pictorial matter can be supplied at an additional price per page. A book ordered with soft cover comes with perfect (glued) binding and a 65-lb. paper cover, with an author-title label on the front cover. A book with library binding comes with a heavy buckram cover and author and title stamped in gold on the spine.

Microfilm demand reprints are produced on 35mm silver halide roll microfilm manufactured to archival standards. Both text and photographs look exactly like the original work—only in reduced form. Microfilm must be used with a microfilm viewer so that the reduced image may be enlarged to eye-legible size for reading.

How are new titles added?

Titles are added to the Books on Demand program through the acquisition of rare books listed in authoritative bibliographies and through the submission of scholarly titles by cooperating publishers and authors. More than 300 publishers now add titles on a continuing basis as they go out of print. Individual authors who hold the copyright to their previously published books may also participate by signing a standard agreement, supplying a non-returnable copy of each book, and paying a modest fee. Cooperating publishers and authors welcome the opportunity to refer their customers to a source for demand reprints of their out of print books and look forward to the royalties they receive on sales.

Are catalogs available?

A comprehensive catalog (Books on Demand 1976) listing more than 100,000 titles may be purchased for $6.95. Subject catalogs are prepared periodically and are usually available free of charge. Some catalogs now available include the following: genealogies and family histories ($1.00), religion, philosophy, law enforcement, psychology, energy, African history, anthropology and folklore, Hispano-American history, geography,

Slavic titles, and sociology.

How are prices determined for demand reprints?

Demand reprint pricing is based on the length of a particular book as well as on the unique requirements of one-at-a-time demand reprinting. If only one copy of a title is ordered, one copy is produced especially for that customer. Because of the custom production required for each book, prices are usually higher than the price of the original book.

The minimum price for a xerographic paper bound copy is $10.00 and the average price for a 260 page volume is $30.00. Cloth bindings are available on the xerographic reprint for $3.00 extra per volume. The size of a single volume is limited to 600 pages, so if a book contains more than 600 pages, an additional binding charge is required for each 600-page increment. Microfilm is approximately one-third of the xerographic price with a minimum of $6.00. For delivery outside of the United States prices are 10% higher in Mexico and Canada, and 15% higher in the rest of the world. Billing is done in U.S. dollars worldwide with the exception of the United Kingdom where billing is done in pound sterling.

What is the ordering procedure?

Please specify the following information for each book you would like to order—author, title, and order number. If the order number is not known, please supply as much information as possible including the author, complete title, original publisher, copyright date, country of publication, series note, and your reference of referral for the title. Since three formats are offered, be sure to indicate the type of copy desired. The following abbreviations may be used—M for 35mm microfilm, X for a xerographic paperbound reprint, or LB for a xerographic library-bound (cloth) reprint.

Individuals must send payment with orders. Only institutions may submit formal purchase orders for billing. Shipping and handling charges are extra. U.S. customers must add state sales tax unless a tax exemption number is on file. Since these books are custom produced only when an order is received, they are non-returnable. Delivery to points within the United States and Canada takes three to four weeks, with approximately one additional week required for delivery of library bound copies. Delivery to the rest of the world may take five to eight weeks or longer depending on the shipping method chosen.

Request For Free Book Search

Please find the following books and notify me of publication details, condition, and price. No obligation.

	AUTHOR	TITLE
1.	....	....
2.	....	....
3.	....	....
4.	....	....
5.	....	....

Name ....

Address ....

City .... State .... Zip ....

Continental Book Search

Bookfinder service—Out-of-Print Books bought and sold. Catalogues issued. Continental Book Search, Alvin M. Katz, GPO Box 2080, New York, New York 10116 (212) 254-8719

A Bookfinder Service For All Subject Categories

Search orders welcomed from libraries, private collectors, scholars, and from the general public.

We can assist you in locating the hard-to-find out-of-print books you want. No fee or obligation.

When we find your book you will be notified and given descriptive details such as publisher, date of publication, physical condition, and tendered price. Then you decide: either to send a buy order, if you desire, or not. It's up to you.

A substantial stock of out-of-print books is on hand.

Send specific wants: author and/or title, or areas of collecting and/or subject interest.

Replies to all inquiries.

Genealogical and Local History Books in Print

Genealogical and local history books in print. Comp. by Netti Schreiner—Yantis, 3d ed. Springfield, VA 22105, 6818 Springfield Dr., Genealogical Books in Print, 1981. 1,000p. 22cm. cloth $20 plus $1 postage and handling unless prepaid; paper $15 plus $1 postage and handling unless prepaid.

016.929'1 U.S.—Genealogy—Bibliography—Periodicals. U.S.—History, Local—Bibliography—Periodicals. Genealogy—Bibliography—Periodicals [CIP]5-4225

Netti Schreiner-Yantis, experienced genealogist, compiled the first edition of *Genealogical Books in Print*, which was published in 1975 (RSBR, March 15, 1976). It listed more than 5,000 entries in 311 pages of text and was published by the small press Genealogical Books in Print. In 1976, the second edition, which contained 41 pages of new listings, was published under the revised title, *Genealogical and Local History Books in Print*. A fourth edition is planned for 1984. The compiler still does not reveal how she went about preparing the work, sources used, etc.

This title provides resource data on innumerable titles for those interested in local history and genealogy. The book is in five parts. First comes a directory of names and addresses of 1,459 vendors. The entries are arranged in random order by vendor numbers, and each entry contains the name and mailing address of the vendor. This directory of vendors is a valuable asset in itself, although 549 of the entries give *Genealogical Books in Print* for addresses.

The next section is called "General Reference"; it covers materials of general or national scope. Listed in these 117 pages are directories of periodicals and of organizations, textbooks, publishers, genealogical forms, families, geographical tools, census material, books on Afro-Americans, Indians, religious and ethnic groups, the military, heraldry, and other categories—57 in all. Entries are arranged alphabetically by author or publisher and contain bibliographic information, annotations (for most but not all entries), cloth-cover prices, paper-cover prices, and vendor numbers. Lesser-known works as well as known reference works are cited. Interspersed in appropriate categories are ads placed by publishers, researchers, or material suppliers. In general, the "General Reference" section contains the material that does not fit into the locality or family sections which follow.

The "Research Sources By Locality" section is the largest, with 597 pages of material on the U.S. States and particular regions, e.g., the Old Northwest, Mississippi Valley. The state divisions are arranged alphabetically with each state divided into statewide references and alphabetical county subdivisions. The statewide references subdivision is broken into segments dealing with a variety of form and subject categories. Individual entries are arranged alphabetically under the general division or county subdivisions and contain the same information as the general reference section entries.

The section on "Localities Other Than the United States" fills 20 pages and covers Barbados, Canada, England, Europe, Ireland, Mexico, Scotland, and Wales. This section follows the arrangement of the previous locality section with entry format remaining the same.

The "Family Genealogy Section" lists 1,277 entries in 182 pages. This section includes family newsletters and biographies, early diaries, and publications about Indian captivity as well as family genealogies; all the authors or Indian prisoners' names are indexed. These genalogical works are arranged arbitrarily, but there are surname index numbers that act as the keys to the Index. The type of information contained in each entry remains consistent with that in the other sections except that the surnames found in the genealogies are listed and underlined to enhance the indexing. Most of the entires cover one surname and its descendants, but there are some compilations of biblical records that include data on hundreds of ???lated families.

The volume concludes with the Index to the family genealogy section: it cites more than 5,000 surnames. Names that are not major names in the titles of genealogies are easy to find by skimming through the names underlined in the annotations.

Roman Numerals

A repeated letter repeats its value; a letter placed after one of greater value adds to it; a letter placed before one of greater value subtracts from it; a dashline over a letter denotes multiplied by 1,000.

I 1	XXIX 29	LXXV 75	DC 600
II 2	XXX 30	LXXIX 79	DCC 700
III 3	XXXV 35	LXXX 80	DCCC 800
IV 4	XXXIX 39	LXXXV 85	CM 900
V 5	XL 40	LXXXIX 89	M 1,000
VI 6	XLV 45	XC 90	MD 1,500
VII 7	XLIX 49	XCV 95	MM 2,000
VIII 8	L 50	XCIX 99	MMM 3,000
IX 9	LV 55	C 100	MMMM
X 10	LIX 59	CL 150	or MV 4,000
XV 15	LX 60	CC 200	V 5,000
XIX 19	LXV 65	CCC 300	M̄ 1,000,000
XX 20	LXIX 69	CD 400	
XXV 25	LXX 70	D 500	

LOCATED AND MAINTAINED AT CARSON CITY, NEVADA by its innovator and Registrar, Emma May Vilardi. This endeavor is the largest multi-group participation project of its kind now in effect. In the spirit of unity, it seeks only to serve and support by solidifying a mutual goal: A CENTRAL REUNION REGISTRY.

WHO DOES IT SERVE? Any individual person seeking a reunion with next-of-kin by birth, and knowledge of their personal heritage; and/or any private or public institution, organization, association or group representing such persons.

PEOPLE SEEKING REUNIONS are adult persons who were separated in the past from family members by birth through acts of adoption, foster care, war, orphaned, foundlings, as wards of state, institutionalization and divorce.

FUNDING. The I.S.R.R. is funded solely by Emma May Vilardi. All printing costs of Soundex Forms utilized by participating organizations must be borne by that group.

IN THE EVENT OF A REGISTRY MATCH, the individual registrant or their designated organizational representative will be notified. NO PREFERENCE WILL BE GIVEN.

SORRY, SINCE OVER THREE HUNDRED REGISTRATIONS A MONTH ARE NOW BEING RECEIVED, PLEASE DO NOT REQUEST SEARCH ASSISTANCE FROM YOUR SOUNDEX REGISTRAR, NOR ASK FOR AN ACKNOWLEDGEMENT OF RECEIPT OF YOUR REGISTRATION!

BECAUSE OF THE TIME INVOLVED AND THE FINANCIAL BURDEN, THE SOUNDEX FORMS WILL NO LONGER BE RETURNED TO THE REPRESENTATIVE GROUPS AFTER SOUNDEXING.

REGISTRATIONS BY INDIVIDUALS. Write to the address shown and enclose a S.A.S.E. (self-addressed stamped envelope) with your request for a Soundex Form. You must be willing to bear this cost on your own behalf.

ORGANIZATIONS wishing to participate in the registry on behalf of their membership, request a master copy of the Soundex Form together with a S.A.S.E. Full address and organizational name is requested. Do list coordinator or representative telephone contact and number.

NOTE* The registration by two persons in this registry resulting in a match will be regarded as mutual legal consent for contact. No individuals or organizations will be allowed to mediate contacts or reunions through this registry. No "Blanket Registrations" will be accepted in the future by this registry through submission of code lines only. Representative organizations will be responsible for notifying their members of a match.

ALL ORGANIZATIONS WILL USE THE SAME SOUNDEX FORM AND WILL NOT ALTER OR DELETE PORTIONS OF THIS FORM IN ANY RESPECT.

REGISTRATION FEES OR CHARGES. There is NO ENTRY FEE OR REGISTRATION CHARGE to any individual person or organization wishing to participate in the INTERNATIONAL SOUNDEX REUNION REGISTRY.

HOW DOES THE I.S.R.R. FUNCTION? The basic data supplied by the person in search is codified by the use of Soundex (conversion of the alphabet to six numerals) for the entry classification, file number and the single code line into the Soundex Ledgers. This code line is capable of seven points of match and enables the registrar to check over 1,000 entries in about five minutes. In its present form, it is computer ready.

All data contained on the Soundex Form is then transmitted to a file card coded by the searcher's present identity as the file number. This is reference for further comparison if a match occurs in the Soundex Ledgers. Three or more points of match will result in the individual file cards being pulled.

EXCEPTION IN REGISTRATIONS. Any registration of a search pertaining to any person under 18 years of age will be placed in a HOLD FILE. Those entries will be checked monthly and will be activated only on the 18th birthday anniversary of the person concerned. NO EXCEPTION WILL BE MADE TO THIS RULE!

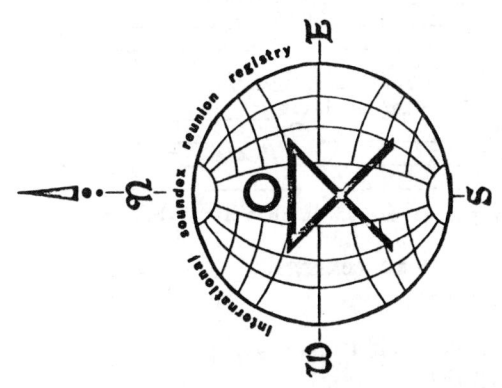

international soundex reunion registry

UNITED TODAY FOR THE
REUNIONS OF TOMORROW

EMMA MAY VILARDI
P. O. BOX 2312
CARSON CITY, NEVADA 89701

INTERNATIONAL SOUNDEX REUNION REGISTRY

'NO FEE IS CHARGED FOR REGISTRATION'

MAIL THIS FORM DIRECTLY TO:

EMMA MAY VILARDI, ISRR
POST OFFICE BOX 2312
CARSON CITY, NEVADA 89701

STATE OF _____
SECTION _____ ONE _____ TWO _____
FILE NUMBER _____

SOUNDEX ENTRY _____

CODE LINE _____

PLEASE DO NOT WRITE ABOVE THIS LINE

****

SEARCHER'S PRESENT NAME _____
ADDRESS _____/_____/_____/_____
       Street Address   Town   State   Zip Code
TELEPHONE NUMBER (AREA CODE _____)/SOCIAL SECURITY _____
IF MEMBER OF TRIAD ORGANIZATION, SHOW NAME OF, _____
      CHAPTER, OR AREA _____
DATE OF REGISTRATION _____ REFERRED BY, _____

YOU ARE: ADOPTEEE _____/ADOPTIVE PARENT _____/FOSTER CHILD _____
      FOSTER PARENT _____/DIVORCED PARENT _____/CHILD OF DIVORCE _____
      FOUNDLING _____/ORPHAN _____/OTHER _____
      BIRTH PARENT _____/OTHER NEXT-OF-KIN BY BIRTH _____

FILL OUT THE FOLLOWING COMPLETELY AS POSSIBLE IN RESPECT TO THE ADOPTEE, OR FOSTER CHILD
AS FACTS WERE KNOWN WHEN SEPARATION OCCURED

Name at Birth _____/Sex, ___ Male ____ Female ____
Date of Birth _____/Time of Birth, if known _____ AM __ PM __
Place of Birth (Hospital or other) _____
    City, or Town _____/County_____/State _____
Name of Attending Physician, or Other _____
Birth Certificate # _____/Filed _____ Amended _____
Was this a Single Birth ? _____/Plural Birth ? _____
    If a Plural Birth, Separated from each other by adoption ? _____
    Male___Female___/Name(s) _____/_____

Birth Mother's Maiden Name _____/Age at birth _____
Name used by Mother, at birth of this child _____/Nickname _____
Name used by Parent at time of Relinquishment, or Consent _____
Mother's Date of Birth _____/_____/_____
Mother's Parents _____ Town _____ County _____ State
    _____/_____

Mother's Marital Status _____/Religion _____/Occupation _____
    Educational Level _____/Military Service _____
    — Married to Birth Father? _____/Height _____/Weight_____/Hair _____/Eyes _____

Name of Birth Father _____/Nickname _____
Father's Date of Birth _____/_____/_____
Father's Parents _____ Town _____ County _____ State
    _____/_____

Father's Age at time of birth _____/Marital Status _____/Religion _____
    Educational Level _____/Occupation _____
    Military Service _____/Height _____/Weight _____/Hair _____/Eyes _____

Adoptee, Siblings by birth ? _____/_____/
    By Mother ? _____/By Father ? _____

Child's Name by Adoption _____/Nickname _____
Court of Jurisdiction (By Name) _____/Town _____
    County _____/State _____
Petitioners _____/_____
    Adoptive Mother   Adoptive Father
Attorney of Record _____/Guardian-ad-litem _____
Case number, or Decree _____/Filed _____/Final _____
Placing Agency _____/Town _____/State _____
Social Worker , or Intermediary _____/_____

QUESTION, If a match occurs in registry, may you be called collect at number shown ?
    YES   NO

THANK YOU, ADDITIONAL COMMENTS,
OR UPDATES WELCOME

COPYRIGHT 1979
EMMA MAY VILARDI

CONFIDENTIAL

— 476 —

Social Security Number Area Allocations

Although the area (first three digits) of a social security number does show the state in which it was issued, as below, it does not necessarily indicate where the individual lived, either when he applied for his number or at any later time. A person may obtain a number from any Social Security District Office. Thus a resident of one state may get a number from a nearby state or some state he is just passing through. Also, once a number is assigned to a person, he uses that number from then on, wherever he may live or work. However, generally speaking, a social security number does indicate either the state of birth, or residence.

Social Security Number Area Allocations

001-003	New Hampshire	449-467	Texas
004-007	Maine	468-477	Minnesota
008-009	Vermont	478-485	Iowa
010-034	Massachusetts	486-500	Missouri
035-039	Rhode Island	501-502	North Dakota
040-049	Connecticut	503-504	South Dakota
050-134	New York	505-508	Nebraska
135-158	New Jersey	509-515	Kansas
159-211	Pennsylvania	516-517	Montana
212-220	Maryland	518-519	Idaho
221-222	Delaware	520	Wyoming
223-231	Virginia	521-524	Colorado
232	West Virginia & North Carolina	525	New Mexico
233-236	West Virginia	526-527	Arizona
237-246	North Carolina	528-529	Utah
247-251	South Carolina	530	Nevada
252-260	Georgia	531-539	Washington
261-267	Florida	540-544	Oregon
268-302	Ohio	545-573	California
303-317	Indiana	574	Alaska
318-361	Illinois	575-576	Hawaii
362-386	Michigan	577-579	District of Columbia
387-399	Wisconsin	580	Virgin Islands & Puerto Rico
400-407	Kentucky	581-584	Puerto Rico
408-415	Tennessee	585	New Mexico
416-424	Alabama	586	Guam
425-428	Mississippi	586	Philippine Islands
429-432	Arkansas	586	American Samoa
433-439	Louisiana	587	Mississippi
440-448	Oklahoma	700-728	R.R. Retirement Bd. (All States)

The Freedom of Information Act:

What It Is And How To Use It

The federal government is a vast storehouse of untapped information. This information is useful to individuals for two reasons. The first is to provide facts that can be personally helpful to individual citizens. Regulatory agencies, for instance, have a large amount of data such as inspection reports, consumer complaints, and product tests on a broad spectrum of goods and services: interstate moving companies and bus lines, the efficacy of drugs, the nutritional content of processed foods, corporate marketing and merchandising practices, the on-time performance and safety records of airlines, and so forth.

So, too, do many of the executive departments. The Department of Health, Education and Welfare makes inspections of federally supported nursing homes. Agriculture has data on pesticides and the purity and quality of meat and poultry. HUD makes FHA mortgage appraisals and monitors the practices of many large housing developers. The National Highway Traffic Safety Administration has safety and efficiency information on all makes of cars. The General Services Administration tests a wide variety of consumer products that are used by government agencies.

The second reason is that information is necessary to determine whether the government is protecting the public interest. Access to such information is the lifeblood of a democracy, and if it does not flow to the citizenry, democracy withers. The list of facts that are being withheld by government agencies is too long and too obvious for specification. It runs from defense and foreign policy to the safety of nuclear generators and the management of our national forests and grazing lands.

In order to provide the public with a tool to pry information out of the Government, the federal Freedom of Information Act was passed in 1966 and amended in 1974 and 1976. The Act provides that any person has the right of access to and can receive copies of any document, file, or other record in the possession of any Executive agency of the *Federal* Government, subject to nine specific exemptions. Government employees face the possibility of sanctions if they arbitrarily or capriciously withhold information. In addition, the Act permits agencies to disclose records, even though they fall within an exemption, when there is no compelling public interest for withholding. While the federal Act does not apply to state governments, many states have their own freedom of information acts which do apply to records held by state and local government bodies.

What follows is a general description of the federal Freedom of Information law and some specific guidelines on how it can be used most effectively.

How To Make A Request

The first step is to determine what you want, since the law says your request must "reasonably describe" the records you seek. You do not need to specify a document by name or title. What you must do is provide a reasonable enough description to allow a government employee who is familiar with the agencies' files to locate the records you seek. For example, if you want information on nursing homes in your area, it is enough to state that the government requires annual surveys to be conducted of nursing homes, and that you want to see the surveys.

Your request need only state that it is being made pursuant to the Freedom of Information Act (5 U.S.C. Sec. 552). It may help to write "Freedom of Information Request" (or Appeal) on the envelope and on the top of the letter. With one exception (as noted later), you do not have to explain the reasons for your demand, and government employees do not have any right to ask. Be statute, the only ground an agency has for refusing your demand is proof that the documents are specifically covered by one of the exemptions. The requester does *not* have to prove that he tried to obtain the documents elsewhere and found them unavailable.

An appeal within an agency or department is usually necessary if an initial denial is received. An appeal letter should be addressed to the head of the agency and should detail the request and the denial, and state that an appeal is being made of the agency's initial denial. This may be only a two- or three-sentence letter. The government has 20 working days to reply to an appeal

Going To Court

The Act is designed to make litigation as simple as possible. If your appeal is denied, you may sue in the United States District Court where you live, where the documents are located, *or* in the District of Columbia: the choice of Court is yours. If the government cannot prove that the requested documents fall within one of nine exemptions from the Act's mandatory disclosure requirement, then the Court will order the agency to give the documents to you. The trend among federal judges is to interpret the exemptions narrowly, thus making it increasingly difficult for the government to use them frivolously. If you win, the Court may require the government to pay your attorney's fees.

Guidelines

There are, of course, many ways in which agencies avoid disclosing information even when the information is not specifically covered by one of the nine enumerated exemptions. Delay is common. However, the law sets specific deadlines for replying to Freedom of Information requests: 10 working days on the initial request and 20 working days on the administrative appeal. Only in exceptional circumstances may an agency receive a time extension. Remember that the more precise you make your request, the less room you provide an agency to delay while it seeks "clarification". On the other hand, a request including "other related documents" is sometimes appropriate, because agencies seldom volunteer knowledge of other valuable information on the same subject which they possess. Moreover, prompter results may be had if you follow up written requests with phone calls. If agencies are aware that you know your rights, they will sometimes move more quickly.

Another barrier to access is cost. The law permits agencies to charge only the direct costs of searching for and copying documents. Agencies cannot lawfully charge you for the time they spend in determining which portions of documents must be disclosed and which portions may be withheld under the nine exemptions. To save money on reproduction expenses, ask to see the documents themselves instead of having copies sent. If you do ask for copies, insist that any charges be directly related to the cost of providing them. Fifty cents per page for copying, or $4.00 for fifteen minutes of search time is excessive. It may help if you state in you letter that you will pay any costs up to a stated amount but would like to be promptly advised of costs in excess of that amount. The advantages of including this statement are: (1) you do not incur large unexpected costs, and (2) if the costs are less than the stated amount it avoids the stall tactic used by some agencies of asking you whether you will pay the copying charges before they even look for the documents. Furthermore, if you are indigent or believe that disclosure of the records you seek will primarily benefit the general public, you should request the agency to waive or reduce its fees.

Type of Documents Available From the Federal Government

The following is a partial list of documents to which citizens have gained access by claiming their rights under the Freedom of Information Act:

* Nursing Home Reports
* Meat Inspection Reports
* Reports on the Fat Content of Hot Dogs
* Atomic Energy Commission Reports on the Safety of Nuclear Generators
* Civil Rights Compliance Documents
* Internal Revenue Service Agents' Manuals
* Reports on the Level of Radioactivity in the Buildings of a Particular City
* Documents Relating to the Establishment of Political Intelligence Programs by the FBI and the IRS

* Personnel Files and Dossiers
* Reports on Treatment of Prisoners of War in South Vietnam

State Laws

All States except Mississippi and Rhode Island have Freedom of Information Acts.

As stated earlier, the Freedom of Information Act applies only to federal administrative agencies and not to state agencies. However, many states do have fairly effective laws. To find out about state laws, look them up in the state code or write the Attorney General of your state. Many of the more recent laws are modeled after the federal law. The guidelines presented in this pamphlet are also generally applicable to the states. The state laws have been used even less than the federal law. Only through citizen use will these laws become effective tools for access to information on the state and local level. If your state does not have an effective law, we can provide you with copies of a model state freedom of information statute. Just send us a post card and ask for the model statute.

Sample Request Letter

Freedom of Information Unit
(Name and Address of Government Agency)
  Re: Freedom of information Request

Dear Sir or Madam:

Pursuant to the Freedom of Information Act, 5 U.S.C. 522, I hereby request access to (or a copy of) *(describe the document containing the information that you want)* _____.

If any expenses in excess of $_____ are incurred in connection with this request, please inform me of all such charges prior to their being incurred for may approval. If you do not grant my request within 10 working days, I will deem my request denied.

Thank you for your prompt attention to this matter.

          Very Truly Yours,

          _____

Sample Appeal Letter

(Name and Address of Head of Government Agency)
  Re: Freedom of Information Appeal

Dear Secretary_____:

By letter dated (month) (day), (year), I requested access to *use same description as in request letter*_____. By letter dated (month) (day), (year), Mr./Mrs. _____of the Office of Public Information (usually) of your agency denied my request. Pursuant to the Freedom of Information Act, 5 U.S.C. 552, I hereby appeal that denial. I have inclosed a copy of my request letter and the denial that I have received.

If you do not act upon my appeal with 20 working days I will deem my request denied.

          Very Truly Yours,

          _____

If you would like additional copies of this leaflet, please write the Clearinghouse and enclose 10 cents for each additional copy to cover mailing and handling.

Freedom of Information Clearinghouse, P.O. Box 19367, Wahington, D.C. 20036

Period Approximation Chart

Date Wanted	Known Information	Formula
Birth	Age at dated event	Substract age from date Add 5 years to each side Search 11 year period
Birth	Marriage Date	Substract 16 years from date Subtract 40 years from date Search period between dates
Birth	Birth or Christening of child: Female--only child	Subtract 16 years from date Subtract 50 years from date Search period between dates

Birth	Female--several children	Subtract 16 years from date
		    of first child
		Subtract 50 years from date
		    of last child
		Search period between dates

Birth	Male--only child	Subtract 16 years from date Subtract 70 years from date Search period between dates

Birth	Male--several children	Subtract 16 years from date
		    of first child
		Subtract 70 years from date
		    of last child
		Search period between dates

Marriage	Age at dated event	Calculate age 15 Add 25 years to date Search period between dates
Marriage	Birth or Christening of child: Only child	Subtract 34 years from date Add 1 year to date Search period between dates

Marriage	Several children	Subtract 34 years from date
		    of last child
		Add 1 year to date of first
		    child
		Search period between dates

Death		Calculate birth date
		Add 90 years
		Search period between date
		    last known alive and 90th
		    year

Adapted from Basic Course to Genealogy, Vol. II by Derek Harland (Salt Lake City: Bookcraft, 1958), 104-117. (Reissued in 1963 as Genealogical Research Standards.)

Used by Permission: Genealogical Institute, 57 W. South Temple, Suite 255, Salt Lake City, Utah 84101

Most researchers cannot usually spend the time or money necessary to travel to the ancestral home. It is interesting to note that the Genealogical Society in Salt Lake City, Utah, and other similar agencies or institutions, probably do not have more than ten percent of the records needed for thorough research. However, most of the data you need can usually be obtained through correspondence.

Please be informed that most record custodians do not have the time or necessary staff to answer your request. Honestly, it is all they can do to even keep up with their current business, much less finding the time to both conduct research and answer letters. We are a vast army of genealogical enthusiasts, and as such, are often times our own worst enemy. Whenever possible, avoid writing directly to local officials unless it is absolutely necessary. Much of the so-called "anti-genealogical" attitude among local officials is of our own making.

The best procedure is to employ a field agent to extract the data for you. However, do not just tell your agent to: "Do my genealogy." An agent is used to merely perform the mechanics of making the searches that you would, if you were there. Keep your requests simple and to the point. Be sure your agent places everything he or she finds directly onto family group records, or sends you a complete copy. This is important! Remember that you must direct these searches, so really, just how much the agent finds is up to you. You may wish to employ any of the following:

- A friend or relative

- A local official

- A genealogist

- A student

It is often possible to locate cousins or distant relatives in the ancestral area. They will usually be more interested in your request because it is their family too. Sometimes it is possible to secure the services of an official. There are two general problems when you hire a genealogist. First, they are usually very expensive and secondly, they are often very reluctant to take orders from you.

A student is the best type of field agent you can hire. Most are usually willing to follow instructions, and they will work for an average wage of about two dollars an hour. This applies to students in foreign countries as well. The following letter is a suggested example for employing a student as a field researcher:

To the High School or College Librarian:

Dear Sir or Madam:

I would like to employ a student to do part-time historical research in your local area. Do you know of a student who is majoring in history and who would be interested in this type of work? If so, please forward this letter to the student. Also, it would help if the student would indicate the hourly rate desired.

Sincerely,

PHOTOCOPY ORDER FORM

Electrostatic ☐   Dep. Acc't. No. _____   Date _____ Your Order No. _____

Photostat ☐   Direct Positive ☐

Photograph:

8 × 10 ☐ Color 4 × 5 ☐ 8 × 10 ☐ 35mm ☐

Neg ☐   Mat ☐   Enlarged ☐   Call ☐

Pos ☐   Glossy ☐   Reduced ☐   Mail ☐

I certify that I require the photoduplication for the purpose of private study, research, criticism or review and I undertake not to sell or further reproduce the copy supplied without permission. I further certify that I have checked and found a copy of this work is not available through normal trade channels.

Signature _____

Mail to (if to other than requester)

Attention _____   Attention _____

PLEASE TYPE OR PRINT ONE CITATION PER SPACE — THANK YOU!

Film neg. (8 × 10) _____ @ $10.00 $_____   Service charge _____ @ $3.00 $_____
Film neg. (8 × 10) _____ @ 15.00 _____   Electrostatic _____ @ .25 _____
Film neg. (8 × 10) _____ @ 25.00 _____   Mat stat to 18 × 24 _____ @ 2.50 _____
Print   8 × 10 _____ @ 4.00 _____   Glossy stat to 11 × 14 _____ @ 3.00 _____
Color 4 × 5 ☐ 8 × 10 ☐ __ @ ____ _____   D. P. to 18 × 24 _____ @ 3.50 _____
Color 35mm ☐ _____ @ 5.00 _____ $_____
Other charges (see over) _____ @ ____ _____   CARRY OVER $_____
                                    $_____   TOTAL $_____
                                                          10% SURCHARGE $_____

THE NEW YORK PUBLIC LIBRARY   Postage and mailing (min. $.50) _____
Photographic Service
Fifth Avenue & 42nd Street   GRAND TOTAL $_____
New York, N. Y. 10018   AMOUNT RECEIVED $_____

TAKEN BY	D.A.	REF	C.E. BY	MKD. BY	MADE BY	DIV. OK	CHECKED	DELIV. BY	DUE / REFUND	FINAL REVISION

Suggestions For A Successful All-Day Genealogical Seminar

Seven Seminar Steps:

1. Appoint one person as seminar chairperson.
2. Start publicity one year in advance.
3. Bring in only one speaker.
4. Choose topics which everyone enjoys.
5. Pick a convenient and comfortable location.
6. Seminar price should include lunch.
7. Invite exhibitors and have a 'freebie' table.

Seminar Schedule:

9:00 A.M. — Commence registration

10:00 A.M. — State the seminar!

        A. Pledge of Allegience

        B . National Anthem

        C . Opening Prayer

10:15 A.M. — Presidents' Welcoming Address

10:25 A.M. — Introduction of Speaker

11:15 A.M. — Mid-morning break

11:59 A.M. — Lunch

1:00 P.M. — (Movie) 'For The Strength of The Hills' This 23 minute, 16mm, sound, color movie explains the world-wide microfilming program of the Genealogical Society of Utah, and rents for $12.00 from: Audio-Visual Services, 290 Harold R. Clark Bldg., Brigham Young University, Provo, Utah 84602.

1:30 P.M. — Speak again

2:15 P.M. — Mid-afternoon break

2:30 P.M. — (Movie) 'Monument to the Dream' This 30 minute, 16mm, sound, color movie explains the great westward migration across America and rents free from: Jefferson National Expansion Memorial, 11 North Fourth Street, St. Louis, Missouri 63102.

3:00 P.M. — Speaker again

4:00 P.M. — Conclusion of Seminar (Important) Be sure and present the speaker with a Certificate of Appreciation!

Computerized Genealogy Library

Computerized Genealogy Library, 1864 South State Street, Suite 100, Post Office Box 27193, Salt Lake City, Utah 84127

There are currently over 300,000 entries in our Genealogy program. They are all linked so that as soon as one of your ancestors is found it will show you all of the people in the program that are related to your ancestors.

What CGL Can Do For You

Free Input

Send us a copy (not originals) of your pedigree charts and Family Group Sheets (no other records please) and we will match them with the information in the computer. (It is advantageous to you to send your payment along with your materials.)

$10.00 to search the files for your ancestors. (Ancestral Route Members receive a 20% discount)

You will receive a print-out showing the number of people in the computer you are linked to, an indication of how much your information will cost, and a list of the nearest persons in your pedigree that are in the computer.

30c per name

You will receive a pedigree of all the names in the computer file that are related to you along with an alphabetical listing of those names.

For $5.00 with order ($25.00) when ordered seperately)

You receive a descendency chart of ancestors in your lines that are linked to lines of other researchers, showing their relationship and giving their most recent address.

For $3.00 Each

You can obtain a family group sheet on all those not known.

Example

Dave sent the library a pedigree with 150 names on it along with $10.00. He received a note telling him that there were 1635 in the file who were related to him, along with the names of his nearest relatives already in the file and that if he wanted them the pedigree would be sent to him at a cost of 30¢ x 1635=$490.50.

Dave sent the $495.90 plus $5.00 for the descendency chart. He received back 350 pages of pedigree plus the descendency chart showing that there were three living people doing research on one line and two on another along with their name and address.

Dave saved approximately 1500 hours of research and $1,000.00. This does not include the new relative he met and new lines to work on.

Telephone Directories

Genealogists will want a Telephone Directory of the area in which they are doing research. It is packed with address and phone numbers of:

Associations	Newspapers
Book Dealers	Nursing homes
Cemeteries	Photographers
Churches	Radio Stations
Clubs	Schools
Colleges	Similar Surnames
Doctors	Societies, etc.
Government Offices	Sororities
Libraries	Television Stations
Mortuaries	Universities

Books from the Bell System may be obtained by calling your local Bell System Business Office. There are numerous small independent companies.

City and Town Directories
In The Library of Congress

City or Town	Earliest Year	City or Town	Earliest Year	City or Town	Earliest Year
Aberdeen, SD	1887	Ashtabula, OH	1898	Ballston Spa, NY	1898
Adams, MA	1887	Astoria, OR	1890	Baltimore, MD	1814
Akron, OH	1890	Atchison, KS	1865	Bangor, ME	1864
Albany, NY	1813	Athens, GA	1889	Barnstable, MA	1895
Alexandria, VA	1876	Athens, PA	1897	Barre, VT	1890
Allentown, PA	1885	Athol, MA	1897	Bath, ME	1867
Alpena, MI	1887	Atlanta, GA	1882	Baton Rouge, LA	1890
Altoona, PA	1873	Atlantic City, NJ	1882	Battle Creek, MI	1874
Amherst, MA	1884	Atlantic Highlands, NJ	1896	Bay City, MI	1883
Amsterdam, NY	1880	Attleboro, MA	1889	Beaver Falls, PA	1888
Andover, MA	1891	Auburn, ME	1872	Belfast, ME	1890
Ann Arbor, MI	1895	Auburn, NY	1862	Belleville, IL	1887
Ansonia, CT	1888	Augusta, GA	1859	Beloit, MI	1889
Asbury Park, NJ	1886	Augusta, ME	1867	Bennington, VT	1891
Asheville, NC	1886			Berwyn, IL	1896
Ashland, WI	1888			Bethel, CT	1898

City or Town	Earliest Year	City or Town	Earliest Year	City or Town	Earliest Year
Bethlehem, PA	1897	Cumberland, MD	1873	Fresno, CA	1886
Beverly, MA	1875				
Biddeford, ME	1866				
Big Rapids, MI	1884	Dallas, TX	1883	Gainesville, TX	1887
Binghamton, NY	1869	Danbury, CT	1885	Galesburg, IL	1889
Birmingham, AL	1888	Danvers, MA	1875	Galveston, TX	1872
Bloomington, IL	1870	Danville, IL	1889	Glens Falls, NY	1874
Boston, MA	1789	Danville, VA	1888	Gloucester, MA	1869
Bowling Green, KY	1892	Davenport, IA	1858	Gloversville, NY	1888
Braddock, PA	1896	Dayton, OH	1856	Grand Forks, ND	1891
Branford, CT	1895	Decatur, IL	1889	Grand Rapids, MI	1868
Brattleboro, VT	1874	Dedham, MA	1885	Green Bay, MI	1894
Bridgeport, CT	1867	Denison, TX	1887	Greenfield, MA	1899
Bridgewater, MA	1872	Denver, CO	1881	Greensburg, PA	1899
Briston, CT	1882	Derby, CT	1883		
Bristol, RI	1876	Des Moines, IA	1871		
Brockton, MA	1874	Detroit, MI	1846	Hackensack, NJ	1894
Brookline, MA	1880	Dorchester, MA	1885	Hagerstown, MD. (See Cumberland)	1884
Brooklyn, NY	1840	Dover, NH	1833		
Buffalo, NY	1832	Dubuque, IA	1867	Hamilton, OH	1866
Burlington, IA	1890	Duluth, MN	1883	Harrisburg, PA	1867
Burlington, VT	1865	Dunkirk, NY	1887	Harrison, NJ	1893
Butte, MT	1884	Durham, NC	1887	Hartford, CT	1844
				Harvey, IL	1895
				Hastings, NE	1893
Cairo, IL	1864	East Liverpool, OH	1896	Haverhill, MA	1860
Calais, ME	1896	Easton, PA	1883	Hazleton, PA	1886
Cambridge, MA	1848	East St. Louis, IL	1889	Helena, MT	1890
Camden, ME	1894	Eastport, ME	1888	Hingham, MA	1894
Camden, NJ	1869	East Providence, RI	1890	Hollidaysburg, PA	1888
Canandaigua, NY	1890	East Saginaw, MI	1883	Holyoke, MA	1869
Canton, OH	1888	Eau Claire, WI	1884	Hoosick Falls, NY	1898
Cape May, NJ	1889	Elgin, IL	1889	Hornellsville, NY	1875
Carbondale, PA	1895	Elizabeth, NJ	1866	Houlton, ME	1895
Cedar Rapids, IA	1876	Elkhart, IN	1890	Houston, TX	1882
Chambersburg, PA	1884	Ellsworth, ME	1886	Hudson, NY	1862
Charleston, SC	1803	Elmire, NY	1857	Huntingdon, PA	1876
Charleston, WV	1889	El Paso, TX	1893	Hyde Park, IL	1883
Charleston, MA	1834	Emporia, KS	1870	Hyde Park, MA	1874
Charlotte, NC	1889	Essex, CT	1896		
Chelsea, MA	1847	Evanston, IL	1888		
Chester, PA	1859	Evansville, IN	1866	Indianapolis, IN	1855
Chicago, IL	1843	Everett, MA	1895	Ipswich, MA	1896
Chillicothe, OH	1888	Everett, WA	1866	Ithaca, NY	1883
Cincinnati, OH	1829				
Circleville, OH	1859				
Cleveland, OH	1850	Fall River, MA	1848	Jackson, MI	1869
Clinton, MA	1883	Fargo, ND	1891	Jacksonville, FL	1870
Coldwater, MI	1882	Findlay, OH	1889	Jacksonville, IL (See Springfield)	1866
Colorado Springs, CO	1879	Fitchburg, MA	1853	Jamaica, NY	1897
Columbus, OH	1842	Flint, MI	1888	Jersey City, NJ	1849
Concord, MA	1896	Flushing, NY	1889	Johnston, RI	1890
Concord, NH	1834	Fon du Lac, WI	1874	Johnstown, NY	1889
Corning, NY	1893	Fort Scott, KS	1879	Johnstown, PA	1882
Corsicana, TX	1889	Fort Smith, AR	1897	Joliet, IL	1885
Cortland, NY	1891	Fort Wayne, IN	1866	Jonesville, WI	1889
Cottage City, MA (Martha's Vineyard)	1885	Fort Worth, TX	1885	Joplin, MO	1899
		Frederick, MD	1886		
Council Bluffs, IA	1876	Freeport, IL	1888		
Covington, KY	1866	Fremont, NE	1885		
Creston, IA	1889	Fremont, OH	1889	Kalamazoo, MI	1869

City or Town	Earliest Year	City or Town	Earliest Year	City or Town	Earliest Year
Pueblo, CO	1879	Skowhegan, ME	1888	Webster, MA	1887
		Somerville, MA	1869	West Chester, PA	1857
		South Bend, IN	1885	Westerly, RI	1884
Quincy, IL	1878	Southington, CT	1882	Weymouth, MA	1870
Quincy, MA	1873	South Omaha, NE	1892	Wheeling, WV	1898
		Spokane, WA	1889	Whitman, MA	1895
		Springfield, IL	1866	Wichita, KS	1888
Racine, WI	1883	Springfield, MA	1851	Wilkes-Barre, PA	1871
Raleigh, NC	1891	Springfield, MO	1890	Williamsburg, NY	1852
Ravenna, OH	1896	Springfield, OH	1889	Williamsport, PA	1866
Reading, PA	1856	Staunton, VA	1888	Willimantic, CT	1873
Red Bank, NJ	1889	Sterling, IL	1890	Wilmington, DE	1857
Richmond, IN	1857	Steubenville, OH	1875	Wilmington, NC	1875
Richmond, VA	1852	Stevens Point, WI	1893	Winona, MN	1866
Roanoke, VA	1888	Stillwater, MN	1890	Winsted, CT	1883
Rochester, NY	1844	Stockton, CA	1876	Winston-Salem, NC	1889
Rockford, IL	1866	Superior, WI	1889	Woburn, MA	1868
Rockland, ME	1868	Swampscott, MA	1895	Woonsocket, RI	1877
Rockville, CT	1883	Syracuse, NY	1851	Worcester, MA	1844
Rome, NY	1857				
Roxbury, MA	1848				
Rutland, VT	1867	Tacoma, WA	1889	Yonkers, NY	1885
		Taunton, MA	1850	York, PA	1877
		Thomasville, GA	1886	Youngstown, OH	1880
Saco, ME See Biddeford)	1866	Tiffin, OH	1890		
Sacramento, CA	1870	Titusville, PA	1866		
Saginaw, MI (See East-		Toledo, OH	1876	Zanesville, OH	1883
Saginaw)	1883	Tonawanda, NY	1887		
St. Albans, VT	1886	Topeka, KS	1870		
St. Cloud, MN	1894	Torrington, CT	1883	**County Residential Directories**	
St. Johnsbury, VT	1897	Trenton, NJ	1857		
St. Joseph, MO	1882	Tucson, AZ	1881		
St. Louis, MO (Rare Book-				County	Earliest year
Room	1847			Adams Co., NE	1893
St. Paul, MN	1863	Upton, MA	1888	(See Hastings)	
Salem, MA	1842	Utica, NY	1843	Albany Co., NY	1884
Salem, NJ	1890			Allegany Co., MD	1890
Salem, OH	1889			(See Cumberland)	
Salt Lake City, UT	1867	Van Wert, OH	1895	Allegheny Co., PA	1897
San Antonio, TX	1881	Vincennes, IN	1888	Alpena Co., MI	1887
San Diego, CA	1899	Virginia City, VA	1864	Androscoggin Co., ME	1894
Sandusky, OH	1855			Ashtabula Co., OH	1898
Sanford, ME	1893				
San Francisco, CA	1850	Waco, TX	1888		
San Jose, CA	1870	Wakefield, MA	1869		
Santa Barbara, CA	1886	Walla Walla, WA	1894	Bates Co., MO	1884
Santa Cruz, CA	1887	Wallingford, CT	1883	Bergen Co., NJ	1885
Saratoga, NY	1872	Waltham, MA	1869	Berkshire Co., MA	1874
Sault Ste. Marie, MI	1888	Ware, MA	1892	Berrien Co., MI	1892
Savannah, GA	1871	Warren, OH	1889	Blue Earth Co., MN	1888
Schenectady, NY	1860	Washington, DC	1846	(See Mankato)	
Scranton, PA	1867	Waterbury, CT	1876	Bristol Co., MA	1867
Seattle, WA	1879	Waterford, NY	1884	Bucks Co., PA	1884
Selma, AL	1880	Waterloo, IA	1888	Burlington Co., NJ	1881
Shamokin, PA	1884	Watertown, NY	1877		
Sharon, PA	1891	Watertown, WI	1895		
Sheboygan, WI	1889	Waterville, ME	1885	California Upper Country	1866
Sherman, TX	1888	Watsonville, CA	1873	Cortland Co., NY	1891
Shreveport, LA	1888	Waukegan, IL	1895	Crawford Co., PA	1874
Sioux City, IA	1884	Waukeshaw, WI	1899	Cumberland Co., ME	1892
Sioux Falls, SD	1888	Wausau, WI	1888	Cumberland Co., NJ	1881

City or Town	Earliest Year	City or Town	Earliest Year	City or Town	Earliest Year
Cumberland Valley, PA	1890	Oneida Co., NY	1878	Arkansas	1884
		Ontario Co., NY	1888	Arizona	1881
Dutchess Co., NY	1870	(See Seneca Co.)			
		Orange Co., NY	1871	Barnstable Co., MA	1873
Essex Co., NJ	1889	Orleans Co., NY	1895	(See Plymouth Co.)	
		Otsego Co., NY	1872		
Fairfield Co., CT	1881	Oxford Co., ME	1896	California (Pacific Coast)	1883
Fond du Lac Co., WI	1890			Camden Co., NJ	1886
Frederick Co., MD	1886	Pawtuxet Valley, RI	1892	(See Gloucester Co.)	
				Colorado	1878
Genesee Co., MI	1886	Rensselaer Co., NY	1878	Connecticut	1865
(See Flint)		Richland Co., ND	1891	Connecticut River	1867
		Ross Co., OH	1888	(CT, MA, NH, VT)	
Hamilton Co., OH	1887	(See Chillicothe)			
Herkimer Co., NY	1888			Dakota	1887
Huntingdon Co., PA	1876	Saginaw Co., MI	1893	Delaware	1859
Huntington Co., IN	1899	St. Clair Co., MI	1885	Dodge Co., NE	1885
		(See Port Huron)		(See Fremont)	
Ingham Co., MI	1883	San Benito Co., CA	1875	Dutchess Co., NY	1867
(See Lansing)		(See Santa Clara Co.)			
		Sandusky Co., OH	1897	Essex Co., MA	1866
Jefferson Co., IN	1887	(See Fremont)		Essex Co., NJ	1859
		Sangamon Co., IL	1866		
Kalamazoo Co., MI	1869	San Joaquin Co., CA	1878	Florida	1883
Kennebec Co., ME	1899	San Mateo Co., CA	1875		
		(See Santa Clara Co.)		Georgia	1876
Lancaster Co., PA	1869	Santa Clara Co., CA	1875	Gloucester Co., NJ	1886
La Porte Co., IN	1897	Santa Cruz Co., CA	1875		
Labanon Co., PA	1880	(See Santa Clara Co.)		Hampden Co., MA	1872
Lehigh Co., PA	1885	Schenectady Co., NY	1888	Hampshire & Franklin Cos.	1890
(See Allentown)		Schuylkill Co., PA	1890	(See Hampden Co.)	
Lenawee Co., MI	1893	Seneca Co., NY	1888	Hillsboro Co., NH	1891
Licking Co., OH	1889	Sheboygan Co., WI	1889	Hudson Co., NJ	1859
(See Newark)		Snohomish Co., WA	1893	(See Essex Co.)	
Long Island, NY	1865	(See Everett)			
Los Angeles Co., CA	1883	Sonoma Co., CA	1885		
		Staten Island, NY	1882	Illinois	1854
McLean Co., IL	1887	Strafford Co., NH	1892	Indiana	1858
Mahoning and Shenango		(See Dover)		Iowa	1868
Valleys, PA	1875	Sullivan Co., NY	1883		
Manistee Co., MI	1895			Jackson Co., MI	1869
Marion Co., OH	1889	Tioga Co., PA	1899		
(See Salem)		Tolland Co., CT	1887	Kansas	1866
Mecosta Co., MI	1884	Trumbull Co., OH	1889	Kentucky	1859
(See Big Rapids)		(See Warren)			
Mercer Co., PA	1898	Tulare Co., CA	1888	Louisiana	1870
Miami Co., OH	1898				
(See Piqua)		Waukesha Co., WI	1899	Maine	1871
Minnehaha Co., SD	1898	Wayne Co., IN	1890	Maryland	1871
(See Sioux Falls)		(See Richmond)		Massachusetts	1853
Monroe Co., NY	1888	Westchester Co., NY	1866	Merrimac River	1872
(See Rochester)				(MA and NH)	
Monterey Co., CA	1875	York Co., PA	1886	Michigan	1856
(See Santa Clara Co.)				Middlesex Co., MA	1871
Morgan Co., IL	1891			Mississippi	1870
(See Jacksonville)		**Regional State and County**		(See Louisiana)	
Morris Co., NJ	1883	**Business Directories**		Missouri	1854
				(See Illinois)	
		Region	Earliest Year	Montana	1884
Nevada Co., CA	1871			Morgan Co., IL	1891
Niagara Co., NY	1887	Alabama	1881	(See Jacksonville)	
(See Lockport)					

City or Town	Earliest Year	City or Town	Earliest Year	City or Town	Earliest Year
Nebraska	1866	Puget Sound, WA	1872	Tennessee	1871
(See Kansas)				Texas	1878
New England	1835	Red River, AR	1893		
New Hampshire	1868	Rhode Island	1860	Union Co., NJ	1859
New Jersey	1850	(See Providence)		(See Essex Co.)	
New York State	1859	Rockingham Co., NH	1891	United States	1875
New York State (Central)	1861			Utah (Salt Lake City)	1874
New York State (Western)	1880	St. Louis, MO, to-			
North Carolina	1867	Denver, CO	1870	Vermont	1855
		South Carolina	1890	Virginia	1852
Ohio	1857	Southern States	1851		
Oregon	1873	(MD, DE, VA, NC, & DC)		West Coast	1882
		Southwestern States	1889	West Virginia	1877
Pacific Coast	1867	Strafford Co., NH	1891	Williams Co., OH	1857
Pennsylvania	1854	(See Rockingham Co.)		Wisconsin	1872
Plymouth Co., MA	1873			Worcester Co., MA	1866

Directories Transferred To Rare Book Room
(From the card catalog in Rare Book Room,
October, 1975)

Albany, NY: 1813, 1815
Albany & Rensselair, NY: 1813, 1815
Augusta, GA: 1859
Baltimore, MD: 1802, 1810, 1814, 1819, 1822
Biddeford, ME & Saco, ME: 1849
Boston, MA: 1789, 1796, 1798, 1807, 1836-1859, 1833, 1789-181?
Brooklyn, NY: 1825, 1829, 1841, 1842 etc.
Buffalo, NY: 1832, 1836, 1837, 1840, 1844, 1847-1849
Charleston, SC: 1803, 1819, 1840, 1841
Chicago, IL: 1844
Cincinnati, OH: 1819, 1825, 1829, 1831, 1834, 1836/7, 1840, 1842, 1843, 1846
Cleveland, OH: 1837, 1845, 1846/7
Concord, ?: 1830
Dayton, OH: 1850
Denver, CO: 1866, 1871
Detroit, MI: 1837
Galveston, TX: 1868/9
Georgetown, DC: 1830, 1834
Harrisburg, PA: 1843, 1839-1919
Hartford, CT: 1838, 1839, 1840 etc.
Helena, MT: 1868
Hillsdale, MI: 1870-1871
Lawrence, ?: 1848, 1851
Lexington, KY & Fayette Co: 1838
Montrial, ?: 1820
Morrisania, NY & Tremont: 1853, 1854
New Bedford, MA: 1839

Newburgh, NY: 1858-9
New Orleans, LA: 1822
New York, NY: 1786, 1789, 1797, 1798, 1800-1815, 1822, 1825
Norfolk, VA: 1806, 1807
Ogden, UT & Weber Co: (no yr)
Ohio City & Cleveland, OH: 1837-8
Oshkosh, WI: 1857
Peoria, IL: 1844
Philadelphia, PA: 1785, 1750?, 1826?, 1837
Pittsburgh, PA: 1815
Portland, ME: 1823, 1831
Portsmouth, NH: 1834-1839/40
Poughkeepsie, NY: 1843, 1845
Providence, RI: 1824
Richmond, VA: 1819, 1850 etc.
Rochester, ?: 1827
Sacramento, CA: 1856-1858, 1866-1871, 1879, 1888
San Francisco, CA: 1850, 1852, 1853
Schenectady, NY: 1841/2
St. Louis, MO: 1838, 1842, 1847, 1848
Stocton, CA 1856
Syracuse, NY: 1851/2
Truckee, CA: 1883
Utica, NY: 1828, 1829, 1839-40
Washington, DC: 1822, 1827-1830, 1834, 1841, 1843, 1846, 1850, 1853
Wheeling, WV: 1839
Worcester, MA: 1829

Major Map Collection Repositories
(Collections Of Over 100,000 Maps)

Repository	Number of Maps	Repository	Number of Maps
1. Library of Congress	3,350,000	4. Tennessee Valley Authority	625,000
2. U.S. Army Topographical Command	1,600,000	5. U.S. Bureau of the Census	400,000
		6. Boston Public Library	320,000
3. National Archives	1,500,000	7. American Geographical Society	310,000

Repository	Number of Maps		Repository	Number of Maps
8. New York Public Library	287,202		24. Indiana University	125,000
9. University of Illinois	249,800		25. University of Florida	125,000
10. U.C.L.A.	220,000		26. University of Michigan	122,000
11. University of Chicago	211,684		27. Indiana State University	120,000
12. U.S. Aeronautical Chart and Information	200,000		28. University of Kansas	120,000
13. University of Washington	182,000		20. Detroit Public Library	119,000
14. Louisiana State University	180,000		30. University of California-Berkely	117,000
15. University of Georgia	175,000		31. Free Library of Philadelphia	116,000
16. San Fernando Valley State College	165,000		32. Southern Illinois University	115,000
17. University of Minnesota	160,000		33. University of Wisconsin	113,250
18. Kentucky Dept. of Commerce	158,152		34. United States Geographic Survey	100,000
19. Harvard University	150,000		35. Princeton University	100,000
20. Yale University	150,000		36. Kent State University	100,000
21. Columbia University	150,000			
22. Southern Methodist University	127,200			
23. Pennsylvania State University	126,000			

Source: *Map Collection in the U.S. and Canada: A Directory,* 2nd ed., Special Libraries Association, New York, 1970.

Government Bookstores

GPO operates 26 bookstores all around the country where you can browse through the shelves and take your books home with you. Naturally, these stores can't stock all of the nearly 20,000 titles in our inventory, but they do carry the ones you're most likely to be looking for. And they'll be happy to special order any Government book currently offered for sale. All of our bookstores accept Visa, MasterCard, and Superintendent of Documents deposit account order.

Alabama
Roebuck Shopping City
9220-B Parkway East
Brimingham, AL 35206
(205)254-1056

California
ARCO Plaza, C-Level
505 South Flower Street
Los Angeles, CA 90071
(213)688-5841

Room 1023, Federal Building
450 Golden Gate Avenue
San Francisco, CA 94102
(415)566-0643

Colorado
Room 117, Federal Building
1961 Stout Street
Denver, CO 80294
(303)847-3964

World Savings Building
720 North Main Street
Pueblo, CO 81003
(303)544-3142

District of Columbia
U.S. Government Printing Office
710 North Capitol Street
Washington, DC 20402
(201)275-2091

Commerce Department
Room 1604, 1st Floor
14th & E Streets, NW
Washington, DC 20230
(202)377-3527

Dept, of Health and Human Services
Room 1528, North Building
330 Independence Avenue, SW
Washington, DC 20201
(202)472-7478

State Department
Room 2817 North Lobby
21st and C Streets, NW
Washington, DC 20520
(202)632-1437

U.S. Information Agency
1776 Pennsylvania Avenue, NW
Washington, DC 20547
(202)724-9928

Pentagon
Room 2E172
Main Concourse, South End
Washington, DC 20310
(703)557-1821

Florida
Room 158, Federal Building
400 W. Bay Street

Jacksonville, FL 32202
(904)791-3801

Georgia
Room 100, Federal Building
275 Peachtree Street, NE
Atlanta, GA 30303
(404)221-6947

Illinois
Room 1365, Federal Building
219 S. Dearborn Street
Chicago, IL 60604
(312)353-5133

Massachusetts
Room G25, Federal Building
Sudbury Street
Boston, MA 02203
(617)223-6071

Michigan
Suite 160, Federal Building
477 Michigan Avenue
Detroit, MI 48226
(313)226-7816

Missouri
Room 144, Federal Building
601 East 12th Street
Kansas City, MO 64106
(816)374-2160

New York

Room 110
26 Federal Plaza
New York, NY 10278
(212)264-3825

Ohio
1st Floor, Federal Building
1240 E. 9th Street
Cleveland, OH 44199
(216)522-4922

Room 207, Federal Building
200 N. High Street
Columbus, OH 43215
(614)469-6956

Pennsylvania
Room 1214, Federal Building

600 Arch Street
Philadelphia, PA 19106
(215)597-0677

Room 118, Federal Building
1000 Liberty Avenue
Pittsburgh, PA 15222
(412)644-2721

Texas
Room 1C50, Federal Building
1100 Commerce Street
Dallas, TX 75242
(214)767-0076

45 College Center
9319 Gulf Freeway
Houston, TX 77017

(713)229-3515

Washington
Room 194, Federal Building
915 Second Avenue
Seattle, WA 98174
(206)442-4270

Wisconsin
Room 190, Federal Building
517 E. Wisconsin Avenue
Milwaukee, WI 53202
(414)291-1304

Retail Sales Outlet
8660 Cherry Lane
Laurel, MD 20707
(301)953-7974

Locating Cemeteries

Ideally there should exist a nationwide or national index to all cemeteries. Obviously, this is not practical. About the only kind of national index is the index to graves of Revolutionary War Soldiers in the Lee Library, Brigham Young University, Provo, Utah.

Some states have attempted this same kind of a project or index. Indiana and Rhode Island are good examples. Some states have even tried to compile a state-wide index to cemeteries. Such is the case in New York.

One of the best ways to locate a cemetery in a certain area is to request a map of the county concerned from the state highway department. These maps are often very detailed and show the small streams and even private cemeteries. Please see list of these various state agencies following.

Probably the very best source for locating a cemetery within a known county area is the water conservation district. Their maps are usually the most detailed and most often list every know cemetery in the county. Please see list of these various state agencies following.

These state agencies usually have a map for each of the local conservation districts. Hence, you would write to the appropriate state agency for a particular county map.

State Highway Departments

Department of Highways
11 S. Union St.
Montgomery, AL 36130

Dept. of Trans. & Pub.
 Utilities
Pouch Z
Juneau, AK 99811

Dept. of Transportation
206 S. 17th Ave.
Phoenix, AZ 85007

Dept. of Highway &
 Transportation
P.O. Box 2261
Little Rock, AR 72203

Dept. of Transportation
1120 N. St.
Sacramento, CA 95814

Dept. Of Highways
4201 E. Arkansas Ave.
Denver, CO 80222

Dept. of Transportation
24 Wolcott Hill Rd.
Wethersfield, CT 06109

Dept of Transportation
Highway Administration Center
Dover, DE 19901

Dept. of Transportation

Burns Bldg.
Tallahassee, FL 32301

Dept of Transportation
Two Capitol Square, SW
Atlanta, GA 30334

Dept. of Transportation
869 Punch Bowl St.
Honolulu, HI 96813

Dept. of Transportation
3311 W. State St.
Boise, ID 83703

Dept. of Transportation
2300 S. Dirksen Pkwy.

Springfield, IL 62764

State Highway Comm.
State Off. Bldg., Rm. 1101
Indianapolis, IN 46204

Dept. of Transportation
800 Lincoln Way
Ames, IA 50010

Dept. of Transportation
State Off. Bldg.
Topeka, KS 66612

Dept. of Transportation
State Off. Bldg.
Frankfort, KY 40601

Dept. of Transportation & Dev.
P.O. Box 44245
Baton Rouge, LA 70804

Dept. of Transportation
State House, Station #16
Augusta, ME 04333

Dept. of Transportation
300 W. Preston St.
Baltimore, MD 21203

Dept. of Public Works
100 Nashua St., Rm. 426
Boston, MA 02114

Dept. of Transportation
P.O. Box 30050
Lansing, MI 48909

Dept. of Transportation
Transportation Bldg.
St. Paul, MN 55155

Dept. of Highways
P.O. Box 1850
Jackson, MS 39205

Dept. of Hwys. & Trans.
P.O. Box 270
Jefferson City, MO 65102

Dept. of Highways
Highway Bldg., Rm. A261
2701 Prospect Ave.
Helena, MT 59620

Dept. of Roads
P.O. Box 94759
Lincoln, NE 68509

Dept. of Transportation
1263 S. Stewart St.
Carson City, NV 89710

Dept. of Pub. Works & Highways
John O. Morton Bldg.
85 Loudon Rd.
Concord, NH 03301

Dept. of Transportation
1035 Parkway Ave.
Trenton, NJ 08625

Dept. of Highways
P.O. Box 1149
1120 Cerrillos Rd., Rm. 119
Santa Fe, NM 87503

Dept. of Transportation
State Campus, Bldg. 5
Albany, NY 12232

Dept. of Transportation
One S. Wilmington St.
Raleigh, NC 27611

Dept. of Highways
Highway Bldg.
Bismarck, ND 58505

Dept. of Transportation
25 S. Front St.
Columbus, OH 43215

Dept. of Transportation
200 NE 21st St.
Oklahoma City, OK 73105

Dept. of Transportation
140 Transportation Bldg.
Salem, OR 97310

Dept. of Transportation
1014 Trans. & Safety Bldg.
Harrisburg, PA 17120

Dept. of Transportation
150 Washington St.
Providence, RI 02903

Dept. of Hwy. & Pub. Trans.
P.O. Box 191
Columbia, SC 29202

Dept. of Transportation
Transportation Bldg.
Pierre, SD 57501

Dept. of Transportation
James K. Polk Bldg., #700
Nashville, TN 37219

Dept. of Highways & Pub. Trans.
Highway Bldg.
11th & Brazos St.
Austin, TX 78701

Dept. of Transportation
State Off. Bldg.
Salf Lake City, UT 84114

Agcy. of Transportation
State Administration Bldg.
Montpelier, VT 05602

Dept. of Highways & Trans.
1221 E. Broad St.
Richmond, VA 23219

Dept. of Transportation
Highway Administration Bldg.
Olympia, WA 98504

Dept. of Highways

Capitol Complex #5, Rm. 1009
Charleston, WV 25305

Dept. of Transportation
951 Hill Farms State Off. Bldg.
Madison, WI 53702

Dept. of Highways
5300 Bishop Rd.
Cheyenne, WY 82001

State Conservation Headquarters

Soil & Water Conservation
P.O. Box 3336
Montgomery, AL 36193

Dept. of Natural Resources
Pouch A
Wasilla, AK 99687

Soil & Water Conservation
1818 W. Capitol Ave.
Little Rock, AR 72202

Dept. of Conservation
1416 Ninth St., Rm. 1326
Sacramento, CA 95814

Soil Conservation Board
1313 Sherman St., #615
Denver, CO 80203

Dept. of Envir. Protection
165 Capitol Ave., Rm. 117
Hartford, CT 06106

Water & Soil Conservation
P.O. Box 1401

Soil & Water Conservation
P.O. Box 1269
Gainesville, FL 32602

Soil & Water Conservation
P.O. Box 8024
Athens, GA 30603

Land & Natural Resources
P.O. Box 621
Honolulu, HI 96809

Soil Conservation
801 Capitol Blvd.
Boise, ID 83720

Div. of Natural Resources
State Fairgrounds
Springfield, IL 62706

Soil Conservation Service
5610 Crawford, Rd. #2200
Indianapolis, IN 46224

Dept. of Soil Conservation
Wallace State Office Bldg.
Des Moines, IA 50319

State Conservation Comm.
535 Kansas Ave., Rm. 1014
Topeka, KS 66603

Dept. of Natural Resources
Capital Tower Plaza
Frankfort, KY 40601

Transportation & Develop.
P.O. Box 44155
Baton Rouge, LA 70804

Soil and Water Conservation
State House Station 28
Augusta, ME 04333

Dept. of Agriculture
Parole Plaza Bldg.
Annapolis, MD 21401

Conservation Services
100 Cambridge St.
Boston, MA 02202

Div. of Soil Conservation
P.O. Box 30017
Lansing, MI 48909

Soil & Water Conservation
P.O. Box 19
St. Paul, MN 55155

Soil & Water Conservation
P.O. Box 23005
Jackson, MS 39205

Soil & Water Conservation
P.O. Box 1368
Jefferson City, MO 65102

Div. of Conservation
25 S. Ewing
Helena, MT 59620

Natural Resources

301 Centennial Mall, S.
Lincoln, NE 68509

Conservation & Nat. Resources
210 S. Fall St.
Carson City, NV 89710

Soil Conservation
Rt. #2, Box 354 D. Clinton
Concord, NH 03301

Soil Conservation
CN-330
Trenton, NJ 08625

Soil & Water Conservation
1418 Luisa St., #2
Santa Fe, NM 87503

Soil & Water Conservation
State Campus
Albany, NY 12235

Soil & Water Conservation
512 N. Salisbury St.
Raleigh, NC 27611

Soil Conservation
State Capitol, 18th Fl.
Bismarck, ND 58505

Soil & Water Districts
Fountain Square
Columbus, OH 43224

Conservation Commission
20 State Capitol Bldg.
Oklahoma City, OK 73105

Soil & Water Conservation
635 Capitol, N.E.
Salem, OR 97310

Soil & Water Conservation
P.O. Box 2357

Harrisburg, PA 17120

Soil Conservation
Pole 95, Stillwater Rd.
Esmond, RI 02917

Land Resources Conservation
2221 Devine St., #222
Columbia, SC 29205

Div. of Conservation
304 Anderson Bldg.
Pierre, SD 57501

Div. of Conservation
4721 Trousdale Dr.
Nashville, TN 37211

Soil & Water Conservation
P.O. Box 658
Temple, TX 76503

Dept. of Agriculture
350 N. Redwood Rd.
Salt Lake City, UT 84116

Soil & Water Conservation
203 Governor St., #206
Richmond, VA 23219

Conservation Commission
Mail Stop PV-11
Olympia, WA 98504

Soil Conservation
Guthrie Agricultural Center
Charleston, WV 25305

Soil & Water Conservation
1815 University Ave.
Madison, WI 53706

Conservation Commission
2219 Carey Ave.
Cheyenne, WY 82001

Genealogical Research
On Rivermen and Their Boats

Sandra Rae Miller

With the recent increased interest in genealogy, certain areas of history previously unnoticed are now in the limelight. The history of the inland river system, its steamboats, and people who worked and traveled on them is one such area. When the title "Captain" or the occupation "river man" shows up on a census record, a whole new world opens up for the researcher. But where do you go from there? When an ancestor's occupation took him from Pittsburgh to New Orleans in a few short weeks, a monumental job faces the researcher.

First, let us clear up a misconception. The term "Captain" is an honorary title, bestowed upon those in command of a vessel. This could be the owner, master, pilot, or even a mate. The following positions are licensed by the Federal Government:

The master is the person in charge of the entire boat. He may also be the owner.

The pilot actually steers the boat, and there is usually more than one on board, unless the boat is operating less than twelve hours a day. Pilots are licensed for a particular portion of the river; consequently, if the boat is going to travel a great distance, the master would employ several pilots for the trip.

There are several mates on each boat. The first mate ranks above the others. The mates keep the boat clean and in working order, and supervise loading the freight, handling the lines, and landing the boat.

The engineer, of course, is in charge of the engines, boilers, and all machinery aboard.

Since the middle 1800's it has been required by law that these officers pass an examination before they are licensed. The procedure of getting a pilot's license, such as described in Mark Twain's *Life on the Mississippi*, is a fairly accurate description of what was involved.

There are other important positions on a steamboat that do not require a license. The agent oversees freight and passenger movement, though he is not on the boat. He usually has an office in town or on a wharfboat. The clerk handles the freight and passengers on board, while the purser takes care of financial matters. There are also deckhands and roustabouts who work under the supervision of the first mate and the firemen who are under the engineer's authority.

On a packet, where the crew has to cater to passengers, it is necessary to employ cooks, housekeepers, barkers, bartenders, and even shoeshine boys. The more elaborate the services are the larger the crew.

In the past, most of these unlicensed employees were referred to as "rivermen," so beware! The only people who can be verified by government records are those who were licensed.

Licenses were obtained through the Steamboat Inspection Service, which was established as early as 1838. However, records were not officially kept until 1856, and then only for the pilots and engineers. In 1871 licenses were required for the masters and mates. These records were kept in the form of an annual list, and they are available through the National Archives, Washington, D.C.

If you know the approximate date when and location where your ancestor received his license, the National Archives can verify these facts for you. But the only additional information the National Archives & Record Service can give you will be the license number.

Steamboats

River people are only one aspect of steamboating that you will want to research. Each steamboat has its own fascinating history, and extensive research can be cone on each boat. If you are fortunate enough to know the name of the boat and the approximate year and location it was in service, you can write to the National Archives for the "Inspection Papers." These are comparable to a birth certificate and can supply you with much information about a boat and its owners.

Keep in mind that there have been more than sixteen thousand steamboats since 1811 and many had the same name. The first steamboat to travel the inland rivers was the NEW ORLEANS. River travel before steamboats was done by keelboats and flatboats. These boats were used even after the civil War; however, they were not licensed and it is difficult to locate information about their activities.

The different types of steamboats are often confusing. They are basically categorized by their type of trade.

The packet boat carried both freight and passengers. The famous racers the NATCHES and the ROB'T. E. LEE were both packets.

Towboats push barges, which carry cargo. Modern diesel-powered towboats of today carry on this 130-year-old practice.

An excursion boat handles outings for passengers. These boats offer sightseeing and dancing for those who pay to take trips aboard. These boats are not equipped to handle overnight guests. Two good examples of this type of steamboat are the JULIA BELLE SWAIN and the BELLE OF LOUISVILLE.

On the other hand, there are overnight passenger boats, such as the DELTA QUEEN and the MISSISSIPPI QUEEN, These boats offer overnight sleeping accomodations and other facilities that one would expect at a hotel.

Showboats provided entertainment; however, their performances were held at the shore, and they were always towed from place to place by another boat.

Ferryboats are still used today and travel back and forth across the river with foot passengers and cars. Ferryboats were not all steam powered. The path of their travel usually did not vary.

The wharfboat is not a steamboat. A wharfboat houses the offices of a company or boat line, and is usually moored to the river bank. One wharfboat in use today is the former CITY OF BATON ROUGE at Peoria, on the Illinois River, The steamboat JULIA BELLE SWAIN Loads her passengers from this wharfboat.

River History

You will want to do some reading about river history to familiarize yourself with the river trade, the period, and the conditions. River books are often scarce and may be difficult to locate.

One of the most complete libraries dealing with river history is the Inland River Library at the Public Library of Cincinnati and Hamilton County. This is a private collection which is open to the public.

There are two excellent books with extensive listings of boat names: (1) the *Merchants Steam Vessels of the U.S. 1790-1868* by William Lytle and Forrest Holdcamper; and (2) the *Canadian Coastal and Inland Steam Vessel 1809-1930* by John Mills. These two books have been published by the Steamship Historical Society. The boat is listed by name, giving the year and place built, the home port, and when and where the boat was lost or destroyed.

Two over valuable books are the *Directory of Western River Packets* and the *Western River Towboat Directory*, both by Capt. Frederick Way, Jr. They were published in the 1950's and are now very scarce. These books give a brief history of each boat listed but are by no means complete. Capt. Way is presently revising these books, and they should be in print within the next few years.

Biographies and autobiographies of rivermen are limited and often deal only with notable river people. A few examples are *The Autobiography of Jon Fitch, The Story of James B. Eads, Master of the Mississippi*, which is a story of Capt. Henry Shreve, and *Stephen H. Long.*

Paddle Wheels to Propellers (a publication of the Indiana Historical Society) is the story of the Howard family and its shipyard. Along with the history of the shipyard, there is a list of the boats built at the Howard Yards.

Some of the best general river history books are, E. W. Gould's *History of River Navigation*, Louis C. Hunter's *Steamboats on the Western Rivers*, and James Lloyd's *Steamboat Directory and Disasters on the Western Waters*.

Zodak Cramer's *The Navigator* was used by travelers from about 1800 to 1820 as a guide in their river travels. Then Cumming's *The Western Pilot* supplanted Cramer and was published periodically until about 1840. Today's answer to these books is the Navigation Charts prepared by the Corps of Engineers.

Within the past few years the Corps of Engineers has published a history of each district. Some of these are excellent and well researched, while others are not. Each one pertains to a particular district, and all are available from the Government Printing Office.

There are many other books pertaining to certain rivers or particular aspects of river travel, such as keelboating and showboating.

There are three helpful periodicals available. The *S&D Reflector,* is published quarterly by the Sons and Daughters of Pioneer Rivermen. (Mrs. J. W. Rutter, secretary, 964 Worthington, Birmingham, Michigan 48009.) There are sixteen volumes, and it is currently being indexed. Most back issues are available at major libraries.

Steamboat Bill is published quarterly by the Steamship Historical Society. (Mrs. Alice Wilson, secretary, 414 Pelton Avenue, Staten Island, New York 10310.) It pertains to ocean-going vessels more than the inland river system; however, many back issues contain excellent articles about steamboats. This publication has been in print for over forty years and is indexed.

The *Waterways Journal* is a weekly publication dealing with the river of today. It has weekly columns on old boats and on events of twenty and forty years ago. This publication dates back to 1887, but it has not been indexed. The address is 666 Security Building, 319 North Fourth Street, St. Louis, Missouri 63102.

As soon as you know a little about river history and you have a boat name, officer's name, and the approximate dates and locations of their trade, then you can start reading the "river columns" in the local newspapers of that day. They can be found at the local library or through interlibrary loan. Many can also be purchased on microfilm through Bell & Howell. By using the newspapers you might even be able to piece together a day-by-day account of your captain's life on the river. The river columns contained abundant personal information as well as business details. The amount of river news in a newspaper varied over the years and depended upon the importance of the river business in the area.

Another facet of river history is the travelers themselves. If your ancestors traveled by boat to their new homes, their names may be listed in a log, or you may be able to locate information about their particular voyage in a newspaper and learn more about the people they traveled with and the circumstances of the trip.

Remember, your family history is not simply a matter of birth and death certificates. Rather, it involves where your family members lived and what they did to support themselves in this new and growing country. For every family, there is much untouched history waiting to be discovered, especially if rivers and steamboats are involved.

Early Files of Courts
And
Miscellaneous Papers

This collection of papers is made up from what were once the files of the various courts of the Colony and Province of Massachusetts Bay held in the county of Suffolk; of the Superiour Court of Judicature held in the several counties; and of the Supreme Jucicial Court prior to the present century; together with some miscellaneous papers and records.

The greater portion of this collection, numbering some two hundred and fifty thousand papers, has been floating about for a century and a half, from one place of deposit to another—cellars, attics, chests, drawers, and other places in various public buildings—becoming, in the course of years, utterly confused and much injured by neglect and careless handling. In this way large numbers of papers have undoubtedly been lost or destroyed.

Still, what now remains constitutes an accumulation of material for historical, genealogical and topographical inquiry unequalled by any other, unless it be the State Archives at the State House. Various papers have been discovered among them which have been unsuccessfully sought for both here and abroad for years.

Perhaps one of the most valuable features of this collection is the direct and varied light which the papers throw upon the methods of procedure and the forms of process used in different periods of our early history, and the construction put upon the laws by counsel of eminence. Here are preserved, in copies or originals, judgments of the courts, special verdicts, reasons of appeal, pleadings, and various other papers, which, in many cases, may furnish the only means of knowledge in this direction, and must of necessity prove of great interest and value to students of jurisprudence.

In this respect the collection is unique, in that it forms a nearly complete and consecutive series covering the Colonial and Provincial times.

I
From 1629 to 1730

All the papers previous to 1730 have been almost completely restored to their original file arrangement, and where this has been impossible they have been arranged chronologically. They have been repaired, restored and mounted in bound volumes, making a collection of two hundred and sixteen volumes of Files, two of Plans, and one of Births, Marriages and Deaths, comprising, in all, about eighty thousand papers, as catalogued below.

The numbers given represent cases and not individual papers.

Vol. 1.   April, 1629—June, 1654.   Nos. 1—199.

Vol. 2.   July, 1654—March, 1659-60.   Nos. 200—346

Vol. 3.   March, 1659-60—October, 1662.   Nos. 347—447.

Vol. 4.   October, 1662—October, 1663.   Nos. 478—577.

Filmed by Genealogy Society in Salt Lake City

CHAPTER 25

MUSEUMS

Museums are often a rich source of genealogical material. They occasionally become the repository for old county records. Many museums, especially in the Northeast, are sponsored by the local historical society and specialize in local history and genealogy.

Doing research in museums may take a little extra effort because most of their records are not indexed by family name, so you will need to explore records for the information you seek.

The following is a list of some museums that seem to be the most useful to the genealogist. They arranged by state and then by city. The museums will wary is size and amount of volumes available. Also, some volumes are available through inter-library loan and some are only available on the premises by appointment. You should check with the museum before making a visit.

The Official Museum Directory is available in most large libraries and museums and can be a very helpful source on the content, focus, and amount of material available in most museums.

ALABAMA

Bessemer Hall of History, (M), 1830 4th Ave. North, Bessemer, AL. 35020.

Thomas E. McMillan Museum, (M), Jefferson Davis College, Alco Drive, Brewton, AL. 36426.

Horseshoe Bend National Military Park, Rte. 1, Box 103, Daviston, AL. 36256.

Kennedy-Douglass Center for the Arts, (M), 217 E. Tuscalossa St., Florence, AL. 35630.

Lee County Historical Society, P.O. Box 206, Loachapoka, AL. 36865.

Historic Mobile Preservation Society, (M), 300 Oakleigh Place, Mobile, AL. 36604.

Museums of the City of Mobile 355 Government St., Mobile, AL. 36602.

Monroe, County Museum and Historical Society, Alabama & Clayborn Sts., P.O. Box 765, Monroeville, AL. 36460.

Alabama Department of Archives and History (M), 624 Washington Ave., Montgomery, AL. 36130.

Lurleen B. Wallace Museum, 725 Monroe St., Montgomery, AL. 36130.

Blount County Memorial Museum, Box 87, Oneonta, AL. 35121.

ALASKA

Anchorage Historical and Fine Arts Museum, (M), 121 W. Seventh Ave., Anchorage, AK. 99501.

Cook Inlet Historical Society, 121 W. 7th Ave., Anchorage, AK. 99501.

Circle District Historical Society Inc., Museum, P.O. Box 1893, Central, AK. 99730.

University of Alaska Museum, (M), University of Alaska, 907 Yukon Dr., Fairbanks, AK. 99701.

Alaska State Museum, (M), Subport, Pouch F.M., Juneau, AK. 99811.

Kenai Historical Society & Museum, (M), P.O. Box 1348, Kenai, AK 99611.

Tongass Historical Society Museum, (M), 629 Dock St., Ketchikan, AK. 99901.

Baranof Museum Erskine House, Box 61, Kodiak, AK. 99615.

Duncan Cottage Museum, P.O. Box 282, Metlakatla, AK. 99926. Resurrection Bay Historical Society Museum, P.O. Box 871, Seward, AK. 99664.

Sitka Historical Society Museum, Box 2414 Sitka, AK. 99835.

Talkeetna Historical Society & Museum, Box 76, Talkeetna, AK. 99676.

Valdez Historical Society, Inc., P.O. Box 6, Valdez, AK 99686.

Wrangell Museum, P.O. Box 1050, Wrangell, AK. 99929.

ARIZONA

Bisbee Civic Center and Mining Historical Museum, (M), P.O. Box 451, Bisbee, AK. 85603.

Casa Grande Valley Historical Society, (M), 110 W. Florence Blvd., Casa Grande, AZ 85222.

Chandler Historical Society, P.O. Box 926, Chandler, AZ. 85224.

The Amerind Foundation, Inc., (M), P.O. Box 248, Dragoon, AZ. 85609.

Museum of Northern Arizona, (M), Fort Valley Rd., Route 4, Flagstaff, AZ. 86001.

Northern Arizona Pioneers' Historical Society, Inc., (M), P.O. Box 1968, Fort Valley Rd., Flagstaff, AZ. 86001.

Pinal County Historical Society and Museum, P.O. Box 851, Florence, AZ. 85232.

Glendale Arizona Historical Society, 7141 N. 59th Ave., Glendale, AZ. 85301.

Mohave Museum of History and Arts, (M), 400 W. Beale, Kingman, AZ. 86401.

Pimeria Alta Historical Society, P.O. Box 2281, Nogales, AZ. 85621.

Arizona Capitol Museum, 1700 W. Washington, Phoenix, AZ. 85007.

Central Arizona Museum of History, (M), 1242 N. Central, Phoenix, AZ. 85004.

The Heard Museum, (M), 22 E. Monte Vista Rd., Phoenix, AZ. 85004.

Sharlot Hall Museum, Sharlot Hall Historical Society, Prescott Historical Society, 415 West Gurley St., Prescott, AZ. 86301.

Graham County Historical Society, 808 8th Ave., Safford, AZ. 85546.

Tempe Historical Museum, (M), P.O. Box 27394, Tempe, AZ. 85282.

Arizona Heritage Center, 949 E. 2nd St., Tucson, AZ. 85719.

Arizona State P.O. Museum, (M), University of Arizona, Tucson, AZ. 85721.

ARKANSAS

Carrol County Heritage Center, Old 1880 Court House, Berryville, AR. 72616.

Desha County Museum, Hwy. 54 East, Dumas, AR. 71639.

University of Arkansas Museum, (M), University of Arkansas, Fayetteville, AR. 72701.

Old Fort Museum (M), 320 Rogers Ave., Fort Smith, AR. 72901.

Arkansas Post County Museum, Hwy. #1-The Great River Rd., Gillett, AR. 72055.

Jacksonport Courthouse Museum, Jacksonport State Park, Jacksonport, AR. 72075.

Arkansas State University Museum, (M), Learning Resources Center, Jonesboro, AR. 72401.

Arkansas History Commission. (M), 1 Capitol Mall, Little Rock, AR. 72201.

Drew County Historical Museum, 402 S. Main, Monticello, AR. 71655.

Logan County Museum, 204 North Vine, Paris, AR. 72855.

Pioneer Village, Box 426, Rison, AR. 71665.

Rogers Historical Museum, (M), 114 S. First St., Rogers, AR. 72756.

Old Washington Historic State Park, (M), Washington, AR. 71862.

CALIFORNIA

Placer County Museum, (M), 175 Fulweiler Ave., Auburn, CA. 95603.

Catalina Island Museum Society, Inc., Box 366, Avalon, CA 90704.

Kern County Museum, (M), 3801 Chester Ave., Bakersfield, CA. 93301.

San Luis Rey Historical Society, 2855 Carlsbad Blvd. CA. 92008.

Carpinteria Valley Historical Society and Museum of History, (M), 956 Maple Ave., Carpinteria, CA. 93013.

Sherman Library and Gardens 2647 E. Coast Hwy., Corona del Mar, CA. 92625.

Del Norte County Historical Society, 577 H St., Crecent City, CA 95531.

Sierra County Museum, P.O. Box 224, Downieville, CA. 95936.

El Monte Historical Museum, 3150 N. Tyler Ave., El Monte, CA 91731.

Fillmore Historical Museum, Inc. 447 Main St., Fillmore, CA. 93105.

Fresno City and County Historical Society, (M), 7160 W. Kearney Blvd., Fresno, CA. 93706.

Eastern California Museum, (M), Box 206, Independence, CA. 93526.

La Puente Valley Historical Society, P.O. Box 522, La Puente, CA. 91747.

San Joaquin County Historical Museum, (M), P.O. Box 21, Lodi, CA. 95240.

History Center, California Historical Society, 5300 Wilshire Blvd., Los Angeles, CA. 90048.

Natural History Museum of Los Angeles County (M), 900 Exposition Blvd., Los Angeles, CA. 90007.

Southwest Museum, Box 128 Highland Park Station, Los Angeles, CA. 90042.

Los Gatos Museum, P.O. Box 1904. Los Gatos, CA 94031.

Madera County Historical Society, P.O. Box 478, Madera, CA. 93639.

Mariposa County Historical Society-Historical Center, P.O. Box 606, Mariposa, CA. 95338.

San Fernando Valley Historical Society, Inc., 10940 Sepulveda Blvd., Mission Hills, CA. 91345.

Colton Hall, (M), Civic Center, Pacific St., Monterey, CA. 93940.

Morro Bay State Park Museum of Natural History, State Park Rd., Morro Bay, CA. 93442.

Nevada County Historical Society, Inc., P.O. Box 1300, Nevada City, CA. 95959.

East Bay Negro Historical Society, Inc., 4519 Grove St., Oakland, CA. 94509.

The Oakland Museum, (M), 1000 Oak St., Oakland, CA. 94607.

Pasadena Historical Society Museum, 470 W. Walnut St., Pasadena, CA. 91103.

Porterville Museum, P.O. Box 488, Porterville, CA. 93257.

Plumas County Museum, Box 776, Quincy, CA. 95971.

Shasta College Museum and Research Center, P.O. Box 6006, Redding, CA. 96099.

Rialto Historical Society, Box 413, Rialto, CA. 92376.

Riverside Municipal Museum, (M), 3720 Orange St., Riverside, CA. 92501.

Sacramento Museum and History Commission, 1931 K St. Sacramento, CA. 95814.

The Silverado Museum, (M), Box 409, St. Helena, CA. 94574.

Calaveras County Museum and Archives, (M), P.O. Box 1281, San Andreas, CA. 95249.

Mission San Diego De Alcala, 10818 San Diego Mission Rd., San Diego, CA. 92018.

San Diego Historical Society, (M), P.O. Box 81825, Presidio Park, San Diego, CA. 92138.

San Francisco African American Historical and Cultural Society, Inc., (M), 680 McAllister St., San Francisco, CA. 94102.

San Luis Obispo County Historical Museum, 696 Monterey St., San Luis Obispo, CA. 93401.

Huntington Library, Art Gallery and Botanical Gardens, 1151 Oxford Rd., San Marino, CA. 91180.

San Mateo County Historical Association, (M), 1700 W. Hillsdale Blvd., San Mateo CA. 94402.

Marin County Historical Society, 1125 B. St. at Mission, San Rafael, CA. 94901.

The Santa Barbara Historical Society, P.O. Box 578, Santa Barbara, CA. 93102.

Santa Cruz County Historical Museum, 118 Cooper St., Santa Cruz, CA. 95060.

Santa Maria Valley Historical Society, Inc., P.O. Box 584, Santa Maria, CA. 93456.

Sonoma Valley Historical Society's Depot Park Museum, P.O. Box 861, Sonoma, CA. 95476.

Sunnyvale Historical Museum, P.O. Box 61301, Sunnyvale, CA. 94088.

Tulare County Museum, 27000 Mooney Blvd., Visalia, CA. 93277.

J. J. Jackson Memorial Museum, Box 333, Weaverville, CA. 96093.

Siskiyou County Museum, 910 S. Main St., Yreka, CA. 96097.

Community Memorial Museum of Sutter County, (M), P.O. Box 1555, Yuba City, CA. 96992.

COLORADO

Washington County Museum, Henry Rt. Box 24, Akron, CO. 80720.

Aspen Historical Society Museum, 620 W. Bleeker, Aspen, CO. 81611.

Aurora History Center, 1633 Florence St. Aurora, CO. 80010.

Melvin Schoolhouse Museum-Library, 16815 E. Costilla Ave., Aurora, CO. 80016.

Boulder Historical Society Museum, 1655 Broadway at Arapahoe, Boulder, CO. 80302.

Gilpin County Historical Museum, P.O. Box 244, Central City, CO. 80427.

Moffat County Museum, Court House, Craig, CO. 81625.

Delta County Historical Society, Box 125, Delta, CO. 81416.

Colorado Historical Society, (M), 1300 Broadway, Denver, CO. 80203.

The Summit Historical Society, P.O. Box 747, Dillon, CO. 80435.

Estes Park Area Historical Museum, Box 1691, Estes Park, CO. 80517.

Fleming Historical Society, 310 W. Denver, Fleming, CO. 80728.

Florence Pioneer Museum Historical Society, 1099 County Road 95, Florence, CO. 81226.

Fort Collins Museum, 200 Mathews, Fort Collins, CO. 80524.

Museum of Western Colorado, (M), 4th and Ute Sts., Grand Junction, CO. 81501.

Grand Lake Area Historical Society, Box 656, Grand Lake, CO. 80447.

Clear Creek Canyon Historical Society of Chaffee County, P.O. Box 2181, Granite, CO. 81228.

Greeley Municipal Museum, (M), 919 7th St., Greeley, CO. 80631.

Gunnison County Pioneer and Historical Society, 315 W. Ohio, Gunnison, CO. 81230.

Phillips County Museum, 109 S. Campbell,Holyoke, CO. 80734.

Grand County Museum, Box 168, Hot Sulphur Springs, CO. 80451.

Lincoln County Museum, P.O. Box 626, Hugo, CO. 80821.

Clear Creek Historic Mining and Milling Museum, P.O. Box 1498, Idaho Springs, CO. 80452.

Kit Carson Historical Society, Kit Carson, CO. 80825.

Belmar Museum of the City of Lakewood, 797 S. Wadsworth Blvd., Lakewood, CO. 80226.

Littleton Historical Museum, (M), 6028 S. Gallup, Littleton, CO. 80120.

Longmont Pioneer Museum, (M), 375 Kimbark, Longmont, CO. 80501.

The Lyons Redstone Museum, (M), 340 High St., Box 9, Lyons, CO. 80540.

Miramont Castle Museum, (M), 9 Capitol Hill Ave., Manitou Springs, CO. 80829.

Montrose County Historical Society, Main & Rio Grande, Box 1882, Montrose, CO. 81401.

Rimrock Historical Museum of W. Montrose County, Box 305, Nucla, CO. 81424.

Nederland Historical Society, Box 427, Nederland, CO. 80466.

Palmer Lake Historical Society, Box 662, Palmer Lake, CO. 80133.

Pueblo Metropolitan Museum (M), 419 W. 14th St., Pueblo, CO 81003.

Rocky Ford Public Museum, Museum Bldg., c/o City Hall, Rocky Ford, CO. 81067.

Saguache County Museum, Hwy. 285, Saguache, CO. 81149.

Silver Cliff Museum, Silver Cliff, CO. 81249.

San Juan County Historical Society Museum, Box 154, Silverton, CO. 81433.

Comanche Crossing Historical Society & Museum, Rte. 1, Box 75, Strasburg, CO. 80136.

San Miguel Historical Society, Telluride, CO. 81435.

CONNECTICUT

Cornwall Historical Society, Cornwall, CT. 06753.

Danbury Scott-Fanton Museum and Historical Society, Inc., 43 Main St., Danbury, CT. 06810.

Bates-Scofield Homestead, The Darien Historical Society, 45 Old King's Hwy. No., Darien, CT. 06820.

Essex Historical Society, Inc., P.O. Box 123, Essex, CT. 06426.

Fairfield Historical Society, (M), 636 Old Post Rd., Fairfield, CT. 06430.

Goshen Historical Society, Old Middle Rd., Goshen, CT. 05756.

Salmon Brook Historical Society, Inc., 208 Salmon Brook St., Granby, CT. 06035.

Putnam Cottage, 243 E. Putnam Ave., Greenwich, CT. 06830.

Henry Whitfield Museum, P.O. Box 210, Guilford, CT. 06437.

Connecticut Historical Society, 1 Elizabeth St., Hartford, CT. 06105.

Stowe-Day Foundation, (M), 77 Forest St., Hartford, CT. 06105.

Madison Historical Society, P.O. Box 17, Madison, CT. 06443.

Meriden Historical Society, Inc., P.O. Box 2025, Meriden, CT. 06450.

Middlesex County Historical Society, 151 Main St., Middletown, CT. 06457.

Eels-Stow House, Milford Historical Society, 34 High St., Milford, CT. 06460.

Monroe Historical Society, P.O. Box 212, Monroe, CT. 06468.

New Canaan Historical Society, 13 Oenoke Ridge, New Canaan, CT. 06840.

New Haven Colony Historical Society, 114 Whitney Ave., New Haven, CT. 06510.

New Milford Historical Society, 6 Aspetuck Ave., New Milford, CT. 06776.

Norfolk Historical Society, Inc., Village Green, Norfolk, CT. 06058.

Faith Trumbull Chapter, Daughters of the American Revolution, Inc., Museum and Chapter House, 42 Rockwell St., Norwich, CT. 06360.

Academy Hall Museum of the Rocky Hill Historical Society, Inc., P.O. Box 185, Rocky Hill, CT. 06067.

Stamford Historical Society, Inc., 713 Bedford St., Stamford, CT. 06901.

Mansfield Historical Society Museum, P.O. Box 145, Storrs, CT. 06268.

The Stratford Historical Society, (M), P.O. Box 382, Stratford, CT. 06497.

Wallingford Historical Society, Inc., P.O. Box 73, Wallingford, CT. 06492.

Scantic Academy Museum, East Windsor Historical Society, Inc., P.O. Box 232, Warehouse Point, CT. 06088.

Historical Museum of the Gunn Memorial Library, Wykeham Rd., Washington, CT. 06793.

The Mattatuck Museum of the Mattatuck Historical Society, (M), 119 W. Main St., Waterbury, CT. 06702.

Watertown Historical Society, Inc., 22 DeForest St., Watertown, CT. 06795.

Noah Webster Foundation and Historical Society of West Hartford, (M), 227 S. Main St., West Hartford, CT. 06107.

The Wethersfield Historical Society, 150 Main St., Wethersfield, CT. 06109.

Wilton Heritage Museum, (M), 249 Danbury Rd., Wilton, CT. 06897.

Amity and Woodbridge Historical Society, 1907 Litchfield Turnpike, Woodbridge, CT. 06525.

Woodstock Historical Society, Inc., Box 65, Woodstock, CT. 06281.

DELAWARE

State of Delaware, Division of Historical & Cultural Affairs, (M), Bureau of Museums and Historic Sites, Hall of Records, Dover, DE. 19901.

Milford Historical Society, P.O. Box 352, Milford, DE. 19963.

New Castle Historical Society, 2 E. 4th St., New Castle, DE. 19720.

Historical Society of Delaware, 505 Market St., Wilmington, DE. 19801.

DISTRICT OF COLUMBIA

Anderson House, Headquarters and Museum of the Society of the Cincinnati, (M), 2118 Massachusetts Ave., N.W., Washington DC. 20008.

Daughters of the American Revolution Museum, (M), 1776 D St., N.W., Washington DC. 20006.

Dumbarton Oaks Research Library and Collection, (M), 1703 32nd St., N.W., Washington DC. 20007.

Howard University Museum, Moorland Spingarn Research Center, (M), 500 Howard Place, N.W., Washington DC. 20059.

Library of Congress, 10 First St., S.E., Washington DC. 20540.

The National Archives, Pennsylvania Ave. and 8th St., N.W., Washington DC. 20408.

National Trust for Historic Preservation, 1785 Massachusetts Ave., N.W., Washington DC. 20036.

Smithsonian Institution, (M), 1000 Jefferson Dr., S.W., Washington DC. 20560.

Truxtun-Decatur Naval Museum, (M), 1610 H St., N.W., Washington DC. 20006.

FLORIDA

South Florida Museum and Bishop Planetarium, 201 10th St., W., Bradenton, FL. 33505.

Cedar Key State Museum, P.O. Box 538, Cedar Key, FL. 32625.

Pioneer Florida Museum, P.O. Box 335, Dade City, FL. 33525.

Halifax Historical Museum, P.O. Box 5051, Daytona Beach, FL. 32018.

Dunedin Historical Society, 94 Diane Dr., Dunedin, FL. 33528.

Broward County Historical Commission, (M), 100-B South New River Dr., E. Fort Lauderdale, FL. 33301.

Fort Lauderdale Historical Museum, (M), P.O. Box 14043, Ft. Lauderdale, FL. 33301.

Florida State Museum, (M), University of Florida, Gainesville, FL. 32611.

Pinellas County Historical Museum-Heritage Park, (M), 11909-125 St., No., Largo, FL. 33540.

Historical Museum of Southern Florida, (M), 3280 S. Miami Ave., Bldg. B, Miami, FL. 33129.

Orange County Historical Museum, (M), 812 E. Rollins St., Orlando, FL. 32803.

Historical Society of Palm Beach County, P.O. Box 1147, Palm Beach, FL. 33480.

Historic Pensacola Preservation Board, (M), 205 E. Zaragoza St., Pensacola, FL. 32501.

Pensacola Historical Museum, 405 S. Adams St., Pensacola, FL. 32501.

T. T. Wentworth, Jr. Museum, P.O. Box 806, Pensacola, FL. 32594.

St. Augustine Historical Society, 271 Charlotte St., St. Augustine, FL. 32084.

Museum of Florida History, (M), R.A. Gray Bldg., Tallahassee, FL. 32301.

Hillsborough County Historical Commission Museum, County Court House, Tampa, FL. 33602.

Historical Society Museum, (M), P.O. Box 488, Valparaiso, FL. 32580.

GEORGIA

Thronateeska Heritage Foundation, Inc., (M), 100 Roosevelt Ave., Albany, GA. 31701.

Atlanta Historical Society, (M), 3101 Andrews Drive, N.W., Atlanta, GA. 30305.

Augusta Richmond County Museum, (M), 540 Telfair St., Augusta, GA. 30901.

White County Historical Society, P.O. Box 281, Cleveland, GA. 30528.

Columbus Museum of Arts and Sciences, Inc., (M), 1251 Wynnton Rd., Columbus, GA. 31906.

American Camellia Society, P.O. Box 1217, Fort Valley, GA. 31030.

Middle Georgia Historical Society, Inc., 935 High St., Macon, GA. 31201.

Museum of Coastal History, (M), P.O. Box 1151, St. Simons Island, GA. 31522.

Georgia Historical Society, 501 Whitaker St., Savannah, GA. 31499.

Georgia Salzburger Society Museum, 9375 Whitfield Ave., Savannah, GA. 31406.

Washington-Wilkes Historical Museum, 308 E. Robert Tommbs Ave., Washington, GA. 30673.

Carter-Coile County Doctors Museum, 223 S. Church St., Winterville, GA. 30683.

HAWAII

Bernice Pauahi Bishop Museum, (M), P.O. Box 19000-A, Honolulu, HI. 96819.

IDAHO

Idaho State Historical Museum, (M), 610 N. Julia Davis Dr., Boise, ID. 83702.

St. Gertrude's Museum, Box 107, Cottonwood, ID. 83522.

Twin Falls County Historical Society, Inc., Rte. #2, Filer, ID. 83328.

South Bannock County Historical Center, P.O. Box 387, Lava Hot Springs, ID. 83246.

Nez Perce County Historical Society, Inc., Third & C Sts., Lewiston, ID. 83501.

Daughters of Utah Pioneer Relic Hall, 430 Clay St., Montpelier, ID. 83254.

Latah County Historical Society, 110 S. Adams, Moscow, ID. 83843.

Owyhee County Historical Museum, Murphy ID, 83650.

Clearwater Historical Society Museum, P.O. Box 1454, Orofino, ID. 83544.

Upper Snake River Valley Historical Society, Box 244, Rexburg, ID. 83440.

Bonner County Historical Museum, P.O. Box 1063, Sandpoint, ID. 83864.

ILLINOIS

Essley-Noble Museum, Mercer County Historical Society, 1406 S.E. 2nd Ave., Aledo, IL. 61231.

Andover Historical Society, Box 100, Andover, IL. 61233.

Historical Society and Museum of Arlington Heights, 500 N. Vail Ave., Arlington Heights, IL. 60004.

Barrington Historical Society Inc., 111 W. Station St., Barrington, IL. 60010.

Batavia Historical Society, 203 N. Washington, Batavia, IL. 60510.

University Museum, (M), Southern Illinois University, Faner 2459, Carbondale, IL. 62901.

White County Historical Society, 216 E. Main St., Carmi, IL. 62821.

Hancock County Historical Society, Courthouse, Carthage, IL. 62321.

Champaign County Historical Museum, (M), 709 W. University Ave., Champaign, IL. 61820.

Balzekas Museum of Lithuanian Culture, 4012 S. Archer Ave., Chicago, IL. 60632.

Chicago Historical Society, (M), Clark Street at North Ave., Chicago, IL. 60614.

Field Museum of Natural History, (M), Roosevelt Rd. at Lake Shore Dr., Chicago, IL. 60605.

International Museum of Surgical Sciences and Hall of Fame, 1524 N. Lake Shore Dr., Chicago, IL. 60610.

Maurice Spertus Museum of Judaica, (M), 618 S. Michigan Ave., Chicago, IL. 60605.

Morton B. Weiss Museum of Judaica, 1100 Hyde Park Blvd., Chicago, IL. 60615.

Polish Museum of America, 984 N. Milwaukee Ave., Chicago, IL. 60622.

Swedish Pioneer Historical Society, Inc., 5125 N. Spaulding Ave., Chicago, IL. 60625.

Vermilion County Museum Society, 116 N. Gilbert St., Danville, IL. 61832.

Historical Society of Des Plaines, (M), 789 Pearson, Des Plaines, IL. 60016.

Dundee Township Historical Society, Inc. 426 Highland Ave., Dundee, IL. 60118.

Madison County Historical Museum, 715 N. Main St., Edwardsville, IL. 62025.

Elmhurst Historical Museum, 120 E. Park, Elmhurst, IL. 60126.

Village of Elsah Museum, Rte. 1-4 Dogwood Lane, Ilsah, IL. 62028.

Evanston Historical Society, (M), 225 Greenwood St., Evanston, IL. 60201.

Levere Memorial Temple, P.O. Box 1856, Evanston, IL. 60204.

Stephenson County Historical Society, 1440 S. Carroll Ave., Freeport, IL. 61032.

Galena Museum, (M), 221 S. Bench St., Galena, IL. 61036.

Glenview Area Historical Society, 1121 Waukegan Rd., Glenview, IL. 60025.

Bond County Historical Society, RR #2, Box 44, Greenville, IL. 62246.

Greater Harvard Area Historical Society, P.O. Box 5277, Harvard, IL. 60033.

Highland Park Historical Society, P.O. Box 56, Highland Park, IL. 60035.

Kankakee County Historical Society Museum, 8th Ave. & Water St., Kankakee, IL. 60901.

Libertyville-Mundelein Historical Society, Inc., 413 N. Milwaukee Ave., Libertyville, IL. 60048.

Williamson County Historical Society, 105 S. Van Buren, Marion, IL. 62959.

Clark County Museum, P.O. Box 207, Marshall, IL. 62441.

Rock Island County Historical Society, P.O. Box 632, Moline, IL. 61265.

Nauvoo Historical Society Museum, P.O. Box 337, Nauvoo, IL. 62354.

Edgar County (ILL.) Historical Museum, 705 N. Main, Paris, IL. 61944.

Ford County Historical Society, 145 W. Center St., Paxton, IL. 60957.

Peoria Historical Society, 942 N.E. Glen Oak Ave., Peoria, IL. 61603.

Sandwich Historical Society, R #1 Box 117-1, Creek Rd., Plano, IL. 60545.

Bureau County Historical Society, 109 Park Ave., W., Princeton, IL. 61356.

Historical Society of Quincy and Adams County, 425 So. 12th St., Quincy, IL. 62301.

Burpee Museum of Natural History, 813 N. Main St., Rockford, IL. 61103.

South Holland Historical Society, Box 48, South Holland, IL. 60473.

Illinois State Museum, (M), Corner Spring and Edwards Sts., Springfield, IL. 62706.

State of Illinois, Department of Conservation, Division of Land and Historic Sites, 605 Stratton Office Bldg., 400 S. Spring St., Springfield, IL. 62706.

Sterling-Rock Falls Historical Society, P.O. Box 65, Sterling, IL. 61081.

McHenry County Historical Museum, McHenry County Historical Society, P.O. Box 434, Union, IL. 60180.

LaSalle County Historical Society Museum, P.O. Box 577, Ottowa, IL. 61350.

Iroquois County Historical Society Museum, (M), Old Courthouse, 2nd & Cherry, IL. 60970.

Waukegan Historical Society, 1017 N. Sheridan Rd., Waukegan, IL. 60085.

Western Springs Historical Society, 740 Hillgrove Ave., Western Springs, IL. 60558.

Dupage County Historical Museum, 102 E. Wesley St., Wheaton, IL. 60187.

Wilmette Historical Museum, 565 Hunter Rd., Wilmette, IL. 60091.

Zion Historical Society, P.O. Box 333, Zion, IL. 60099.

INDIANA

Hillforest Historical Foundation, Inc., P.O. Box 127, Aurora, IN. 44001.

Lawrence County Historical Museum, Court House, Bedford, IN. 47421.

Indiana University Museum, (M), Student Building 209, Indiana University, Bloomington, IN. 47405.

Monroe County Historical Society Museum, 202 E. Sixth St., Bloomington, IN. 47401.

Wells County Historical Museum, 420 W. Market St., Bluffton, IN. 46714.

Elkhart County Historical Society, Inc., Museum, P.O. Box 434, Bristol, IN. 46507.

Whitley County Historical Museum, 108 W. Jefferson, Columbia City, IN. 46725.

Bartholomew County Historical Society, 524 Third St., Columbus, IN. 47201.

Adams County Historical Museum, 515 W. Jefferson, Decatur, IN. 46733.

Allen County-Fort Wayne Historical Society Museum, (M), 312 E. Berry St., Fort Wayne, IN. 46802.

Louis A. Warren Lincoln Library Museum, P.O. Box 1110, Fort Wayne, IN. 46801.

Clinton County Museum, 301 E. Clinton St., Frankfort, IN. 46041.

Johnson County Historical Museum, RFD 2, Box 99, Franklin, IN. 46131.

Hammond Historical Society, 564 State St., Hammond, IN. 46320.

Hobart Historical Society Museum, P.O. Box 24, Hobart, IN. 46342.

Huntington County Historical Society Museum, Hunting County Court House, Huntington, IN. 46750.

Indiana Historical Society, 315 W. Ohio St. Rm. 350, Indianapolis, IN. 46202.

Indiana State Museum, (M), 202 N. Alabama St., Indianapolis, IN. 46204.

President Benjamin Harrison Memorial Home, (M), 1230 N. Delaware St., Indianapolis, IN. 46202.

Clark County Historical Society Howard Steamboat Museum, Inc., (M), P.O. Box 606, Jeffersonville, IN. 47130.

Newton County Historical Society, P.O. Box 103, Kentland, IN. 47951.

Howard County Historical Museum, 1200 W. Sycamore St., Kokomo, IN. 46901.

LaGrange County Historical Society, Inc., R. 1, LaGrange, IN. 46761.

La Porte County Historical Museum, La Porte County Complex, Court House Square, La Porte, IN. 46350.

Tippecanoe County Historical Museum, 909 South St., Lafayette, IN. 47901.

Cass County Historical Society, 1004 E. Market St., Logansport, IN. 46947.

Grant County Historical Society Museum, 2400 S. Washington St., Marion, IN. 46952.

Old Lighthouse Museum, P.O. Box 512, Michigan City, IN. 46360.

White County Historical Society Museum, P.O. Box 884, Monticello, IN. 47960.

Delaware County Historical Society, 4813 Petty Rd., Muncie, IN. 47302.

Brown County Historical Society, P.O. Box 668, Nashville, IN. 47448.

Floyd County Museum, 201 E. Spring St., New Albany, IN. 47150.

Henry County Historical Society, 606 S. 14th St., New Castle, IN. 47362.

Historic New Harmony, Inc., (M), P.O. Box 248, New Harmony, IN. 47631.

Conner Prairie Pioneer Settlement, (M), 13400 Allisonville Rd., Nobelsville, IN. 46060.

The Snite Museum of Art, University of Notre Dame, (M), O'Shaughnessy Hall, University of Notre Dame, Notre Dame, IN. 46556.

Miami County Historical Museum, 4th Court House, Junction, U.S. 24 and Business U.S. 31, Peru, IN. 46970.

Marshall County Historical Museum, Inc., 317 W. Monroe, Plymouth, IN. 46563.

Fulton County Historical Society Museum, (M), 7th and Pontiac Sts., Rochester, IN. 46975.

Rush County Historical Society, 619 N. Perkins, Rushville, IN. 46173.

Washington County Historical Society, Inc., 307 E. Market St., Salem, IN. 47167.

The Northern Indiana Historical Society, (M), 112 S. Lafayette Blvd., South Bend, IN. 46601.

Historical Museum of the Wabash Valley, 1411 S. 6th St., Terre Haute, IN. 47802.

Historical Society of Porter County Old Jail Museum, Old Jail Building, 153 Franklin St., Valparaiso, IN. 46383.

Ripley County Historical Society Museum, P.O. Box 224, Versailles, IN. 47042.

Switzerland County Historical Society Museum, Main & Market Sts., Vevay, IN. 47043.

George Rogers Clark National Historical Park, 401 S. Second St., Vincennes, IN. 47591.

Wm. H. Harrison Museum, 'Grouseland', 3 W. Scott St., Vincennes, IN. 47591.

IOWA

Butler County Historical Society, 303 - 6th St., Allison, IA. 50602.

Cedar Falls Historical Society Museum, 303 Clay St., Cedar Falls, IA. 50613.

Iowa Masonic Library and Museum, P.O. Box 279, Cedar Rapids, IA. 52406.

Floyd County Historical Society, 500 Gilbert St., Charles City, IA. 50616.

Wayne County Historical Society, Corydon, IA. 50060.

Union County Historical Complex, 1101 N. Vine, Creston, IA. 50801.

Vesterheim, Norwegian-American Museum, 502 W. Water St., Decorah, IA. 52101.

Iowa State Historical Department Division of Historical Museum & Archives, (M), E. 12th and Grand Ave., Des Moines, IA. 50319.

Salisbury House, 4025 Tonawanda Dr., Des Moines, IA. 50312.

Emmet County Historical Society, Inc., P.O. Box 101, Estherville, IA. 51334.

Audubon County Historical Society, Exira, IA. 50076.

Fairfield Public Library Museum, Court and Washington Sts., Fairfield, IA. 52556.

Pioneer Historical Society, Inc., Farmington, IA. 52626.

Garnavillo Historical Museum, Garnavillo, IA. 52049.

Mills County Historical Society and Museum, 406 3rd, Glenwood, IA. 51534.

Humboldt County Historical Association, Humboldt, IA. 50548.

State Historical Society of Iowa, 402 Iowa Ave., Iowa City, IA. 52240.

Van Buren County Historical Society, Keosauqua, IA. 52565.

Jackson County Historical Museum, P.O. Box 1245, Maquoketa, IA. 52060.

Kinney Pioneer Museum and Historical Society of North Iowa, P.O. Box 421, Mason City, IA. 50401.

Community Historical Museum, Maxwell, IA. 50161.

Chickasaw County Historical Society Museum, East on Highway 346, Nashua, IA. 50658.

Mitchell County Historical Museum, Rte. 4, Osage, IA. 50461.

Wapello County Historical Museum, 620 Lamhorn St., Ottumwa, IA. 52501.

Pella Historical Village, 507 Franklin, Pella, IA. 50219.

Calhoun County Historical Society, 626-8 St., Rockwell City, IA. 50579.

Sioux City Public Museum, (M), 2901 Jackson St., Sioux City, IA. 51104.

Parker Historical Society of Clay County Museum, 1820 2nd Ave., E., Spencer, IA. 51301.

Tama County Historical Society, Broadway & State Sts., Toledo, IA. 52342.

Grout Museum of History and Science, (M), 503 South St., Waterloo, IA. 50701.

Fayette County Historical Center, (M), 101 N. Walnut St., West Union, IA. 52175.

KANSAS

Dickinson County Historical Society, P.O. Box 506, Abilene, KS. 67410.

Pioneer Museum, 430 W. 4th, Ashland, KS. 67831.

Rawlins County Historical Society, 700 Vine, Atwood, KS. 67730.

Wyandotte County Museum (M), 631 N. 126th St., Bonner Springs, KS. 66012.

Chetopa Historical Museum, 5th and Maple Sts., Chetopa, KS. 67336.

Thomas County Historical Society and Museum, (M), 1525 W. 4th St., Colby, KS. 67701.

Cloud County Historical Museum, Seventh & Broadway, Concordia, KS. 66901.

Lane County Historical Museum, (M), P.O. Box 821, Dighton, KS. 67839.

Boot Hill Museum, Inc., 500 W. Wyatt Earp, Dodge City, KS. 67801.

Douglass Historical Museum, 314-316 S. Forest, Douglass, KS. 67039.

Lanesfield Historical Society, R.R. 1, Box 156, Gardner, KS. 66021.

Hodgen House Museum, 104 W. Main St., Ellsworth, KS. 67439.

Lyon County Historical Society, P.O. Box 1224, Emporia, KS. 66801.

Fort Leavenworth Historical Society, 34 Summer Place, Fort Leavenworth, KS. 66027.

Wilson County Historical Society Museum, 420 N. 7th, Fredonia, KS. 66736.

Finney County Historical Society, Inc., Box 59, Garden City, KS. 67846.

Anderson County Historical Museum, Fifth & Main Sts., Garnett, KS. 66032.

Harper City Historical Society, P.O. Box 275, Harper, KS. 67058.

Reno County Historical Society, 126 W. 12th, Hutchinson, KS. 67501.

Allen County Historical Society, 207 N. Jefferson, Iola, KS. 66749.

Haun Museum, Box 676, Jetmore, KS. 67854.

Kingman County Historical Society, 242 Ave. A West, Kingman, KS. 67068.

Edwards County Historical Museum, Half Way Park, Kinsley, KS. 67547.

Santa Fe Trail Center, (M), Rte. 3, Larned, KS. 67550.

Watkins Community Museum, 1047 Massachusetts St., Lawrence, KS. 66044.

McPherson County Old Mill Museum and Park, P.O. Box 94, Lindsborg, KS. 67456.

Osage County Historical Society, P.O. Box 361, Lyndon, KS. 66451.

Rice County Historical Museum, 221 E. Ave. S., Lyons, KS. 67554.

Riley County Historical Museum, (M), 2309 Claflin Rd., Manhattan, KS. 66502.

Jewell County Historical Museum, Main St., Mankato, KS. 66956.

Marion County Historical Society, Inc., 405 Locust, Marion, KS. 66861.

McPherson Museum, 1130 E. Euclid, McPherson, KS. 67460.

Meade County Historical Society Museum, 200 E. Carthage, Meade, KS. 67864.

Harvey County Historical Society Library and Museum, P.O. Box 4, Newton, KS. 67114.

Mennonite Library and Archives, North Newton, KS. 67117.

Old Jefferson Town, Jefferson County Historical Society, Oskaloosa, KS. 66066.

Franklin County Historical Society, Inc., Box 145, Ottawa, KS. 66067.

Crawford County Museum, 610 W. 2nd St., Pittsburg, KS. 66762.

Linn County Museum, P.O. Box 137, Pleasanton, KS. 66075.

Butterfield Trail Historical Museum, P.O. Box 216, Brewster, KS. 67732.

Albany Historical Society, Inc., Rt. 3, Sabetha, KS. 66534.

Smoky Hill Historical Museum, (M), 635 W. South, Salina, KS. 67401.

Gallery of Fine Arts-Topeka Public Library, (M), 1515 W. 10th, Topeka, KS. 66604.

Kansas State Historical Society Museum, (M), 120 W. 10th St., Topeka, KS. 66612.

Chisholm Trail Museum, (M), 502 N. Washington, Wellington, KS. 67152.

Old Cowtown Museum, (M), 1871 Sim Park Dr., Wichita, KS. 67203.

Wichita-Sedgwick County Historical Museum Assoc., (M), 204 S. Main, Wichita, KS. 67202.

The Cowley County Historical Society, 1714 E. 11th, Winfield, KS. 67156.

Woodson County Historical Society, 208 W. Mary, Yates Center, KS. 66783.

KENTUCKY

The Kentucky Museum, (M), Western Kentucky University, Bowling Green, KY. 42101.

Kentucky Historical Society, (M), Broadway at the St. Clair Mall, Box H, Frankfort, KY. 40602.

Liberty Hall Museum, 173 Arrowhead Rd., Louisville, KY. 40207.

Morgan Row House and Museum, P.O. Box 316, Harrodsburg, KY. 40330.

Shakertown at Pleasant Hill, Kentucky, (M), Rte. 4, Harrodsburg, KY. 40330.

The Lexington Cemetery, 833 W. Main St., Lexington, KY. 40508.

Waveland State Shrine, Higbee Mill Rd., Lexington, KY. 40503.

Eisenberg Museum, Southern Baptist Theological Seminary, 2825 Lexington Rd., Louisville, KY. 40280.

The Filson Club, 118 W. Breckinridge St., Louisville, KY. 40203.

Mason County Museum, 215 Sutton Street, Maysville, KY. 41056.

Jonathan Truman Dorris Museum, (M), Eastern Kentucky University, Perkins Bldg., Richmond, KY. 40475.

LOUISIANA

Bayou Folk Museum, Cloutierville, LA. 71416.

Imperial Calcasieu Museum, Inc., 204 W. Salleir St., Lake Charles, LA. 70601.

Mansfield State Commemorative Area, Rte. 2, Box 252, Mansfield, LA. 71052.

The Historic New Orleans Collection, (M), 533 Royal St., New Orleans, LA. 70130.

Louisiana State Museum, (M), 751 Chartres St., New Orleans, LA. 70116.

The R.W. Norton Art Gallery, (M), 4747 Creswell Ave. Shreveport, LA. 71106.

MAINE

Androscoggin Historical Society, 2 Turner St., Auburn, ME. 04210.

Maine State Museum, (M), LMA Bldg., Station 83, Augusta, ME. 04333.

Bangor Historical-Penobscot Heritage Museum, 159 Union St., Bangor, ME. 04401.

Bar Harbor Historical Society, 34 Mt. Desert St., Bar Harbor, ME. 04609.

Islesford Museum, Acadia National Park, Rte. 1, Box 1, Bar Harbor, ME. 04646.

Maine Maritime Museum, (M), 963 Washington St., Bath, ME. 04530.

Dr. Moses Mason House Museum, P.O. Box 12, Bethel, ME. 04217.

Boothbay Region Historical Society, Box 272, Boothbay Harbor, ME. 04538.

Bridgton Historical Society and Museum, Inc., P.O. Box 317, Bridgton, ME. 04009.

Pejepscot Historical Society, 11 Lincoln St., Brunswick, ME. 04011.

Bucksport Historical Society, Inc., P.O. Box 798, Bucksport, ME. 04416.

Stewart M. Lord Memorial Historical Society, Inc., Box 33, Burlington, ME. 04417.

Camden-Rockport Historical Society, Camden, ME. 04843.

Nylander Museum, Caribou, ME. 04736.

Wilson Museum, Perkins St., Castine, ME. 04421.

Chapman-Hall House Preservation Society, Inc., Main St., Damariscotta, ME. 04543.

Deer Isle-Stonington Historical Society, Deer Isle, ME. 04627.

Dexter Historical Society Museum, Main St., Dexter, ME. 04930.

Islesboro Historical Society, Box 134, County Rd., Islesboro, ME. 04848.

Brick Store Museum, (M), P.O. Box 177, Kennebunk, ME. 04043.

Kennebunkport Historical Society, P.O. Box 405, Kennebunkport, ME. 04046.

Parsonsfield-Porter Historical Society, RFD Box 102, Kezar Falls, ME. 04047.

Burnham Tavern, 60 Court, Machias, ME. 04654.

Gates House, Machiasport Historical Society, Machiasport, ME. 04655.

New Sweden Historical Society, Rte. 161, New Sweden, ME. 04762.

Orland Historical Society, P.O. Box 435, Orland, ME. 04472.

Colonial Pemaquid, Pemaquid Beach, Pemaquid Harbor, ME. 04560.

Phillips Historical Society, Pleasant St., Phillips, ME. 04966.

Phippsburg Historical Society, Inc., Phippsburg, ME. 04562.

The Shaker Museum, Sabbathday Lake, Poland Spring, ME. 04274.

Maine Historical Society, 485 Congress St., Portland, ME. 04101.

Shore Village Museum, 104 Limerock St., Rockland, ME. 04841.

York Institute Museum, 375 Maine St., Saco, ME. 04072.

Scarborough Historical Museum, P.O. Box 156, Scarborough, ME. 04074.

Penobscot Marine Museum, (M), Church St., Searsport, ME. 04974.

Sedgwick-Brooklin Historical Society, (M), Rt. 1, Box 73, Sedgwick, ME. 04676.

Mount Desert Island Historical Society, Somesville, ME. 04660.

Stockholm Historical Society Museum, Main & Lake Sts., Stockholm, ME. 04783.

The Vinalhaven Historical Society, Box 387, Vinalhaven, ME. 04863.

Warren Historical Society, Warren, ME. 04864.

Lincoln County Museum, and Old Jail, Federal St., Wiscasset, ME. 04578.

Yarmouth Historical Society, (M), P.O. Box 107, Yarmouth, ME. 04096.

OldGoal Museum, (M), Box 188, York, ME. 03909.

MARYLAND

National Colonial Farm, (M), 3400 Bryan Point Rd., Accokeek, MD. 20607.

Maryland Hall of Records Commission, P.O. Box 828, Annapolis, MD. 21404.

Lovely Lane Museum, (M), 2200 St. Paul St., Baltimore, MD. 21218.

Masonic Museum of the Grand Lodge of Ancient Free and Accepted Masons of Maryland, 225 N. Charles St., Baltimore, MD. 21201.

Mount Clare Museum, Carroll Park, Baltimore, MD. 21230.

Museum and Library of Maryland History, Maryland Historical Society, 201 W. Monument St., Baltimore, MD. 21201.

Historical Society of Kent County, Inc., P.O. Box 665, Chestertown, MD. 21620.

Baltimore County Historical Society, 9811 Van Buren Lane, Cockeysville, MD. 21030.

Allegany County Historical Society, Inc., 218 Washington St., Cumberland, MD. 21502.

Historical Society of Talbot County, 25 S. Washington St., Easton, MD. 21601.

Historical Society of Cecil County, P.O. Box 442, Elkton, MD. 21921.

Washington County Historical Society, Box 1281, Hagerstown, MD. 21740.

The Montgomery County Historical Society, 103 W. Montgomery Ave., Rockville, MD. 20580.

Chesapeake Bay Maritime Museum, (M), P.O. Box 636, St. Michaels, MD. 21663.

The Maryland National Capital Park and Planning Commission, 8787 Georgia Ave., Silver Spring, MD. 20907.

Calvert Marine Museum, (M), P.O. Box 97, Solomons, MD. 20688.

The Old Bohemia Historical Society, Inc., P.O. Box 61, Warwick, MD. 21912.

MASSACHUSETTS

Dyer Memorial Library, Centre Ave., Abington, MA. 02351.

Andover Historical Society, 97 Main St., Andover, MA. 01810.

The Arlington Historical Society, 7 Jason St., Arlington, MA. 02174.

Ashburnham Historical Society, Inc., 10 High Street, Ashburnham, MA. 01430.

Ashland Historical Society, Box 321, Ashland, MA. 01721.

The Sturgis Library, Box 606, Barnstable, MA. 02630.

Donald G. Trayser Memorial Museum, Main St., Barnstable, MA. 02630.

Barre Historical Society, Inc., Common St., Barre, MA. 01005.

Belchertown Historical Association, Maple St., Belchertown, MA. 01007.

Berlin Art and Historical Collections, 51 South St., Berlin, MA. 01503.

Beverly Historical Society and Museum, 117 Cabot St., Beverly, MA. 01915.

Bolton Historical Society, Inc., P.O. Box 24, Bolton, MA. 01740.

Boston Athenaeum, 10½ Beacon St., Boston, MA. 02108.

Boston Public Library, Copley Square, Boston, MA. 02117.

Massachusetts Historical Society, 1154 Boylston St., Boston, MA. 02215.

New England Methodist Historical Society, 745 Commonwealth Ave., Boston, MA. 02215.

Unitarian Universalist Historical Society, 25 Beacon St., Boston, MA. 02108.

Brookline Historical Society, 347 Harvard St., Brookline, MA. 02146.

Burlington Historical Society, Inc., P.O. Box 336, Burlington, MA. 01803.

Longfellow National Historic Site, 105 Brattle St., Cambridge, MA. 02138.

Canton Historical Society, P.O. Box 540, Canton, MA. 02021.

Chatham Historical Society, P.O. Box 381, Chatham, MA. 02633.

Chelmsford Historical Society, 40 Byam Rd., Chelmsford, MA. 01824.

Concord Antiquarian Society, (M), P.O. Box 146, Concord, MA. 01742.

Historical Society of Santuit and Cotuit, Inc., P.O. Box 1484, Cotuit, MA. 02635.

Danvers Historical Society, Box 381, Danvers, MA. 01923.

Dedham Historical Society, Box 215, Dedham, MA. 02026.

Memorial Hall Museum, Pocumtuck Valley Memorial Assn., Memorial St., Deerfield, MA. 01342.

Duxbury Rural and Historical Society, Box 176, Snug Harbor Station, Duxbury, MA. 02332.

Dukes County Historical Society, (M), Box 827, Edgartown, MA. 02539.

Fall River Historical Society, (M), 451 Rock St., Fall River, MA. 02720.

Falmouth Historical Society, P.O. Box 174, Falmouth, MA. 02541.

Fitchburg Historical Society, P.O. Box 953, Fitchburg, MA. 01420.

Framingham Historical and Natural History Society, P.O. Box 2032, Framingham, MA. 01701.

Cape Ann Historical Association, (M), 27 Pleasant St., Gloucester, MA. 01930.

Historical Society of Greenfield, P.O. Box 415, Greenfield, MA. 01302.

Groton Historical Society, Box 212, Groton, MA. 01450.

Hardwick Historical Society, On Hardwick Common, Hardwick, MA. 01037.

Haverhill Historical Society, 240 Water St., Haverhill, MA. 01830.

Old Ordinary, 21 Lincoln St., Hingham, MA. 02043.

Ipswich Historical Society, 53 S. Main St., Ipswich, MA. 01938.

Lexington Historical Society, P.O. Box 514, Lexington, MA. 02173.

Museum of our National Heritage, P.O. Box 519, Lexington, MA. 02173.

Longmeadow Historical Society, Storrs Library, 693 Longmeadow St., Longmeadow, MA. 01106.

Lynn Historical Society, Inc., 125 Green St., Lynn, MA. 01902.

Manchester Historical Society, Union St., Manchester, MA. 01944.

Marblehead Historical Society, 161 Washington St., Marblehead, MA. 01945.

Peter Rice Homestead, Home of Marlborough Historical Society, Inc., P.O. Box 513, Marlborough, MA. 01752.

Mattapoisett Museum and Carriage House, P.O. Box 535, Mattopoisett, MA. 02739.

Middleborough Historical Association, Inc., Jackson St., Middleborough, MA. 02346.

Nantucket Historical Association, Box 1016, Nantucket, MA. 02554.

Historical Society of Old Newbury, Cushing House Museum, 98 High St., Newburyport, MA. 01950.

Jackson Homestead, 527 Washington St., Newton, MA. 02158.

North Andover Historical Society, 153 Academy Rd., North Andover, MA. 01845.

Northampton Historical Society, 46-66 Bridge St., Northampton, MA. 01060.

Northborough Historical Society, Inc., P.O. Box 661, Northborough, MA. 01532.

Osterville Historical Society, Inc., P.O. Box 3, Osterville, MA. 02655.

Pembroke Historical Society, Inc., Center St., Pembroke, MA. 02359.

Petersham Historical Society, Inc., N. Main St., Petersham, MA. 01366.

Berkshire County Historical Society, Inc., (M), 780 Holmes Road, Pittsfield, MA. 02101.

Mayflower Society House, 4 Winslow St., Plymouth, MA. 02360.

Adams National Historical Site, P.O. Box 531, Quincy, MA. 02269.

Quincy Historical Society, Adams Academy Bldg., 3 Adams St., Quincy, MA. 02169.

Reading Antiquarian Society, 103 Washington St., Reading, MA. 01867.

Sandy Bay Historical Society and Museum, Inc., 40 King St., Rockport, MA. 01966.

The Helen McCarthy Memorial Museum of the Rowe Historical Society, Zoar Road, Hwy., Rowe, MA. 01367.

Rowley Historical Society, Box 41, Rowley, MA. 01969.

Roxbury Historical Society, Dudley Station Box 5, Roxbury, MA. 02114.

Essex Institute, (M), 132 Essex St., Salem, MA. 01970.

Peabody Museum of Salem, (M), East India Square, Salem, MA. 01970.

Scituate Historical Society, 121 Maple St., Scituate, MA. 02066.

Historical, Natural History and Library Society of Natick, Bacon Free Library Bldg., Eliot St., South Natick, MA. 01760.

Cape Cod National Seashore, South Wellfleet, MA. 02663.

Connecticut Valley Historical Museum, (M), 194 State St., Springfield, MA. 01103.

Harvard Historical Society, Inc., Still River Rd., Still River, MA. 01467.

Historical Room, Stockbridge Library, Stockbridge, MA. 01262.

Stoughton Historical Society, Box 542, Stoughton, MA. 02072.

Swampscott Historical Society, 99 Paradise Rd., Swampscott, MA. 01907.

Swansea Historical Society, Inc., P.O. Box 67, Swansea, MA. 02777.

Old Colony Historical Society, 66 Church Green, Taunton, MA. 02780.

Narragansett Historical Society, Inc., The Common, Templeton, MA. 01468.

Topsfield Historical Society, 27 Prospect St., Topsfield, MA. 01983.

Wakefield Historical Society, 21 Chestnut St., Wakefield, MA. 01880.

American Jewish Historical Society, 2 Thornton Rd., Waltham, MA. 02154.

Waltham Historical Society, Inc., 190 Robbins St., Waltham, MA. 02154.

Wayland Historical Society, Inc., 12 Cochituate Rd., Wayland, MA. 01778.

Wellesley Historical Society, Inc., 229 Washington St., Wellesley Hills, MA. 02181.

Wenham Historical Association and Museum, Inc., (M), 132 Main St., Wenham, MA. 01984.

Ramapogue Historical Society, Box 286, West Springfield, MA. 01090.

Edwin Smith Historical Museum, 6 Elm St., Westfield, MA. 01085.

Atheneum Society of Wilbraham, Inc., P.O. Box 294, Wilbraham, MA. 01095.

Chapin Library of Rare Books, Box 426, Williamstown, MA. 01267.

Winchendon Historical Society, Pleasant St., Winchendon, MA. 01475.

American Antiquarian Society, 185 Salisbury St., Worcester, MA. 01609.

Worcester Historical Museum, (M), 39 Salisbury St., Worcester, MA. 01608.

Historical Society of Old Yarmouth, Box 11, Yarmouth Port, MA. 02675.

MICHIGAN

Lenawee County Historical Museum, P.O. Box 511, Adrian, MI. 49221.

Gardner House Museum, 509 S. Superior St., Albion, MI. 49224.

Allegan County Historical Museum, 433 River St., Allegan, MI. 49010.

Museum of the Great Lakes, (M), 1700 Center Ave., Bay City, MI. 48706.

Berrien Springs Courthouse, (M), P.O. Box 261, Berrien Springs, MI. 49103.

Mecosta County Historical Museum, Elm and Stewart, Big Rapids, MI. 49307.

Clawson Historical Museum, 425 N. Main, Clawson, MI. 48017.

Shiawassee County Historical Society, 699 S. Norton, Corunna, MI. 48817.

Dearborn Historical Museum, (M), 915 Brady St., Dearborn, MI. 48124.

Bernard Historical Society and Museum, 7135 W. Delton Rd., Delton, MI. 49046.

Detroit Historical Museum, 5401 Woodward Ave., Detroit, MI. 48202.

Dossin Great Lakes Museum, Belle Isle, Detroit, MI. 48207.

Drummond Island Historical Museum, Drummond Island, MI. 49726.

Delta County Historical Society, P.O. Box 1776, Escanaba, MI. 49829.

Sloan Museum, (M), 1221 E. Dearsley St., Flint, MI. 48503.

Frankenmuth Historical Museum, 613 S. Main, Frankenmuth, MI. 48734.

Tri-Cities Historical Society Museum, P.O. Box 234, Grand Haven, MI. 49417.

Grand Rapids Public Museum, (M), 54 Jefferson, Grand Rapids, MI. 49503.

Coe House Museum, P.O. Box 53, Grass Lake, MI. 49240.

Charlton Park Village and Museum, (M), 2545 S. Charlton Park Rd., Hastings, MI. 49058.

Netherlands Museum, (M), 3 E. 12th St., Holland, MI. 49423.

Isle Royale National Park, 87 N. Ripley St., Houghton, MI. 49931.

Kalamazoo Public Museum, (M), 315 S. Rose St., Kalamazoo, MI. 49007.

Kalkaska County Museum, Route 3, Box 10, Kalkaska Rd., Kalkaska, MI. 49646.

Houghton County Historical Museum Society, Hwy. M-26, Lake Linden, MI. 49945.

Michigan Historical Museum, Michigan History Div., (M), 528 N. Capitol Ave., Lansing, MI. 48918.

Lincoln Park Historical Museum, 1382 Cleophus, Loncoln Park, MI. 48146.

Manistee County Historical Museum, 425 River St., Manistee, MI. 49660.

Imogene Herbert Historical Museum, P.O. Box 284, Manistique, MI. 49854.

Marquette County Historical Society, 213 N. Front St., Marquette, MI. 49855.

Honolulu House Museum, P.O. Box 68, Marshall, MI. 49068.

Mayville Historical Museum, P.O. Box 242, Mayville, MI. 48744.

Menominee County Historical Museum, P.O. Box 151, Menominee, MI. 49858.

Midland County Historical Society, 1801 W. Andrews Dr., Midland, MI. 48640.

Monroe County Historical Museum, 126 S. Monroe St., Monroe, MI. 48161.

Montague Museum & Historical Association, Church & Meade Sts., Montague, MI. 49437.

Macomb County Historical Society, (M), 15 Union St., Mount Clemens, MI. 48043.

Alger County Historical Museum, P.O. Box 201, Munising, MI. 49862.

Fort St. Joseph Museum, 508 E. Main St., Niles, MI. 49120.

Mill Race Historical Village, P.O. Box 71, Northville, MI. 48167.

Ontonagon County Historical Society Museum, P.O. Box 7, Ontonagon, MI. 49953.

Northeast Oakland Historical Society, P.O. Box 311, Oxford, MI. 48051.

Little Traverse Regional Historical Society, P.O. Box 162, Petoskey, MI. 49770.

Plymouth Historical Museum, (M), 155 S. Main St., Plymouth, MI. 48170.

Oakland County Pioneer and Historical Society, 405 Oakland Ave., Pontiac, MI. 48058.

Museum of Arts and History, 1115 Sixth St., Port Huron, MI. 48060.

Sanilac Historical Museum, 228 S. Ridge St., Port Sanilac, MI. 48469.

Beaver Island Historical Society, St. James, MI. 49782.

Troy Museum and Historic Village, 60 W. Wattles Rd., Troy, MI. 48098.

Wayne Historical Museum, (M), 1 Town Square, Wayne, MI. 48184.

Wyandotte Historical Commission, 2610 Biddle Ave., Wyandotte, MI. 48192.

Ypsilanti Historical Society, Inc., 220 N. Huron St., Ypsilanti, MI. 48197.

MINNESOTA

Freeborn County Historical Society, Box 105, Bridge Ave., Albert Lea, MN. 56007.

Anoka County Historical/Genealogical Society, 1900 Third Ave. So., Anoka, MN. 55303.

Pine County Historical Society, Askov, MN. 55704.

Clearwater County Historical Society, Bagley, MN. 56621.

Beltrami County Historical Society, P.O. Box 683, Bemidji, MN. 56601.

Swift County Historical Society, Rte. 2, Box 401, Benson, MN. 56215.

Crow Wing County Historical Society, P.O. Box 722, Brainerd, MN. 56401.

Wilkin County Historical Society, P.O. Box 212, Breckenridge, MN. 56520.

Carlton County Historical Society, Dental Bldg., Carlton, MN. 55718.

Polk County Historical Society, P.O. Box 214, Crookston, MN. 56716.

Becker County Historical Society, Courthouse, 915 Lake Ave., Detroit Lakes, MN. 56501.

The St. Louis County Historical Society, (M), 506 W. Michigan St., Duluth, MN. 55802.

Excelsior-Lake Minnetonka Historical Society, P.O. Box 305, Excelsior, MN. 55331.

Martin County Historical Society Museum, 304 E. Blue Earth Ave., Fairmont, MN. 56031.

Rice County Historical Society, P.O. Box 5, Faribault, MN. 55021.

Otter Tail County Historical Society, (M), 1110 Lincoln Ave. W., Fergus Falls, MN. 56537.

Pope County Historical Society Museum, South Hwy. 104, Glenwood, MN. 56334.

Yellow Medicine County Historical Museum, P.O. Box 160, Granite Falls, MN 56241.

Sibley County Historical Society, P.O. Box 486, Arlington, MN. 55307.

Koochiching County Historical Society Museum, P.O. Box 1147, International Falls, MN. 56649.

Jackson County Historical Museum, Box 211, Lakefield, MN. 56150.

G.A.R. Hall and Museum Meeker County Historical Society, 318 N. Marshall, Litchfield, MN. 55355.

Lac Qui Parle County Historical Society, Hwy. No. 75 So., Madison, MN. 56256.

Blue Earth County Historical Society Museum, 606 S. Broad St., Mankato, MN. 56001.

Lyon County Historical Society, Old Courtroom, Lyon County Courthouse, Marshall, MN. 56258.

Commission on Archives and History, Minnesota Annual Conference, The United Methodist Church, 122 W. Franklin Ave., Minneapolis, MN. 55404.

Hennepin County Historical Society Museum, 2303 3rd Ave., Minneapolis, MN. 55404.

Chippewa County Historical Society, Jct. 59 & State Hwy. 7, Montevideo, MN. 56265.

Stevens County Historical Museum, 207 W. Seventh St., Morris, MN. 56267.

Norwegian-American Historical Association, Library of St. Olaf College, Northfield, MN. 55057.

Goodhue County Historical Society, 1166 Oak St., Red Wing, MN. 55066.

Redwood County Historical Society, R.R. #3, Redwood Falls, MN. 56283.

Olmsted County Historical Society, Historical Center and Museum, Box 6411, Rochester, MN. 55903.

Roseau County Historical Museum and Interpretive Center, Roseau, MN. 56751.

Stearns County Historical Society, (M), P.O. Box 702, St. Cloud, MN. 56302.

Catholic Historical Society of St. Paul, 2260 Summit Ave., St. Paul, MN. 55105.

Minnesota Historical Society, 690 Cedar St., St. Paul, MN. 55101.

Nicollet County Historical Society, Grace & 3rd St., St. Peter, MN. 56082.

Dakota County Historical Museum, 130 3rd Ave., N., South St. Paul, MN. 55075.

Spring Valley Community Historical Society, 909 S. Broadway, Spring Valley, MN. 55975.

Washington County Historical Museum, 602 N. Main St., Stillwater, MN. 55082.

Lake County Historical Society and Railroad Museum, Depot Bldg., Two Harbors, MN. 55616.

Carver County Historical Society, 119 Cherry St., Waconia, MN. 55387.

Marshall County Historical Society, Box 103, Warren, MN. 56762.

Waseca County Historical Society, P.O. Box 314, Waseca, MN. 56093.

Kandiyohi County Historical Society, 610 Hwy. 71, N.E., Willmar, MN. 56201.

Cottonwood County Historical Society, 812 Fourth Ave., Windom, MN. 56101.

Winona County Historical Museum, (M), 160 Johnson St., Winona, MN. 55987.

Nobles County Historical Society, P.O. Box 213, Worthington, MN. 56187.

MISSISSIPPI

Biloxi Art and History Authority, 216 Lameuse St., Biloxi, MS. 39530.

Mississippi Baptist Historical Commission, P.O. Box 51, Clinton, MS. 39056.

The Columbus and Lowndes County Historical Society Museum, 316 7th No., Columbus, MS. 39701.

Webster County Museum, Rte. 3, Box 14, Europa, MS. 39744.

North Delta, Box 92, Friars Point, MS. 38631.

Marshall County Historical Museum, P.O. Box 806, Holly Springs, MS. 38635.

Mississippi State Historical Museum, (M), Box 571, Jackson, MS. 39205.

Lauren Rogers Library and Museum of Art, (M), P.O. Box 1108, Laurel, MS. 39440.

Mississippi Society Daughters of the American Revolution "Rosalie," 100 Orleans St., Natchez, MS. 39120.

Heritage Museum Foundation of Tate County, Inc., 103 N. Ward, Senatobia, MS. 38668.

Oktibbeha County Heritage Museum, Rt. 1, Box 56, Starkville, MS. 39759.

Watkins Museum, (M), Box 529, Taylorsville, MS. 39168.

Vicksburg National Military Park, Box 349, Vicksburg, MS. 39180.

Historic Jefferson College, (M), P.O. Box 100, Washington, MS. 39190.

Rosemont Plantation, Rosemont Plantation, Woodsville, MS. 39669.

MISSOURI

Mississippi County Historical Society, (M), 403 N. Main, Charleston, MO. 63834.

George W. Somerville Historical Library, Livingston County Memorial Library, 450 Locust, Chillicothe, MO. 64601.

State Historical Society of Missouri, Elmer Ellis Library Bldg., Corner Hitt and Lowry Sts., Columbia, MO. 65201.

Knox County Historical Museum, Edina, MO. 63537.

Florissant Valley Historical Society, P.O. Box 298, Florissant, MO. 63032.

Historic Hermann Museum, Box 88, Hermann, MO. 65041.

Hickory County Historical Society, Hermitage, MO. 65668.

Cole County Historical Museum, 109 Madison, Jefferson City, MO. 65101.

Kansas City Museum of History and Science, (M), 3218 Gladstone Blvd., Kansas City, MO. 64123.

Clay County Historical Museum, 14 N. Main, Liberty, MO. 64068.

Jesse James Bank Museum, 104 E. Franklin St., Liberty, MO. 64068.

Saline County Historical Society, P.O. Box 428, Marshall, MO. 65340.

Audrain County Historical Society, (M), P.O. Box 3, Mexico, MO. 65265.

Mercer County Missouri Historical Society, 601 Grant St., Princeton, MO. 64673.

St. Charles County Historical Society, Inc., P.O. Box 455, St. Charles, MO. 63301.

St. Joseph Museum, (M), 11th and Charles, St. Joseph, MO. 64501.

Concordia Historical Institute, 801 DeMun Ave., St. Louis, MO. 63105.

Missouri Historical Society, (M), Jefferson Memorial Bldg./Forest Park, St. Louis, MO. 63112.

Pettis County Historical Society, c/o Sedalia Public Library, Third & Kentucky, Sedalia, MO. 65301.

Johnson County Historical Society Museum, Main & Gay Sts., Warrensburg, MO. 64093.

MONTANA

O'Fallon Historical Society, P.O. Box 527, Baker, MT. 59313.

Blaine County Museum, P.O. Box 927, Chinook, MT. 59523.

McCone County Museum, P.O. Box 393, Circle, MT. 59215.

Beaverhead County Museum, P.O. Box 830, Dillon, MT. 59725.

Rosebud County Pioneer Museum, 1300 Main St., Forsyth, MT. 59327.

Cascade County Historical Society, 1400 1st Ave. No., Great Falls, MT. 59401.

Montana Historical Society, (M), 225 N. Roberts, Helena, MT. 59601.

Park County Museum, 118 W. Chinook, Livingston, MT. 59047.

Fort Missoula Historical Museum, Bldg. 322, Fort Missoula, Missoula, MT. 59801.

Musselshell Valley Historical Museum, 524 First W., Roundup, MT. 59072.

Marias Museum of History and Art, P.O. Box 787, Shelby, MT. 59474.

J.K. Ralston Museum & Art Center, P.O. Box 50, Sidney, MT. 59270.

Mineral Co. Museum and Historical Society, P.O. Box 282, Superior, MT. 59872.

Meagher County Historical Association Museum, P.O. Box 47, White Sulphur Springs, MT. 59645.

Wolf Point Area Historical Society, Inc., P.O. Box 977, Wolf Point, MT. 59201.

NEBRASKA

Dixon County Historical Society, Allen, NE. 68710.

Furnas County Museum, Arapahoe, NE. 68922.

Gage County Historical Museum, P.O. Box 793, Beatrice, NE. 68310.

Homestead National Monument, R.R. 3, Beatrice, NE. 68310.

Sarpy County Historical Museum, (M), 2402 Clay St., Bellevue, NE. 68005.

Dundy County Historical Society, Benkelman, NE. 69021.

Custer County Museum and Library, 225 S. 10th Ave., Broken Bow, NE. 68822.

Brownville Historical Society Museum, Main St., Brownville, NE. 68321.

Garfield County Historical Museum, Box 517, Burwell, NE. 68823.

Clarkson Historical Museum, Clarkson, NE. 68629.

Fort Robinson Museum, (M), Box 304, Crawford, NE. 69339.

Saline County Historical Society, Inc., Dorchester, NE. 68343.

Washington County Historical Museum, 14th and Monroe Sts., Fort Calhoun, NE. 68023.

Perkins County Historical Society, Box 174, Grant, NE. 69140.

Hastings Museum, (M), 1330 N. Burlington, Hastings, NE. 68901.

Phelps County Historical Society, P.O. Box 215, Holdrege, NE. 68949.

Grant County Historical Society, Hyannis, NE. 69350.

Dawson County Historical Society, 805 N. Taft St., Lexington, NE. 68850.

Museum of American Historical Society of Germans from Russia, 631 D St., Lincoln, NE. 68502.

Nebraska Conference United Methodist Historical Center, Lucas Bldg., Nebraska Wesleyan University, 50th and St. Paul Sts., Lincoln, NE. 68504.

Nebraska State Historical Society, (M), 1500 "R" St., Loncoln, NE. 68508.

High Plains Museum, 423 Norris Ave., McCook, NE. 69001.

Kearney County Historical Museum, 129 S. Kearney Ave., Minden, NE. 68959.

Antelope County Historical Museum, Box 22, Neligh, NE. 68756.

Great Plains Black Museum, 2213 Lake St., Omaha, NE. 68110.

Western Heritage Museum, (M), 801 S. 10th St., Omaha, NE. 68108.

Polk County Historical Museum, South end of Hawkey St., Osceola, NE. 68651.

Pawnee City Historical Society and Museum, Inc., Pawnee City, NE. 68420.

Cass County Historical Society Museum, 644 Main St. Plattsmouth, NE. 68048.

Webster County Historical Museum, 721 W. 4th Ave., Red Cloud, NE. 68970.

Sheridan County Historical Society, Inc., P.O. Box 86, Rushville, NE. 69360.

Otoe County Museum, Syracuse, NE. 68446.

Table Rock Historical Society and Museums, Table Rock, NE. 68447.

Johnson County Historical Society, Inc., Third and Lincoln Sts., Tecumseh, NE. 68450.

Tobias Community Historical Society, Tobias, NE. 68453.

Cherry County Historical Society, P.O. Box 284, Valentine, NE. 69201.

Valley Community Historical Society, Inc., P.O. Box 685, Valley, NE. 68064.

Anna Bemis Palmer Museum, P.O. Box 507, York, NE. 68467.

NEVADA

The Nevada State Museum, (M), Capitol Complex, Carson City, NV. 89710.

Northeastern Nevada Museum, (M), P.O. Box 503, Elk., NV. 89801.

Churchill County Museum and Archive, 1050 S. Maine St., Fallon, NV. 89406.

Clark County Southern Nevada Museum, 1830 S. Boulder Hwy., Henderson, NV. 89015.

Nevada Historical Society, (M), 1650 N. Virginia St., Reno, NV. 89503.

NEW HAMPSHIRE

Sandwich Historical Society, (M), Maple St., Center Sandwich, NH. 03227.

The Claremont, New Hampshire Historical Society, Inc., 26 Mulberry St., Claremont, NH. 03743.

New Hampshire Historical Society, (M), 30 Park St., Concord, NH. 03301.

Durham Historic Association Museum, 28 Mill Rd., Durham, NH. 03824.

Tuck Memorial Museum, 40 Park Ave., Hampton, NH. 03842.

New Hampshire Antiquarian Society, Main St., Hopkinton, NH. 03301.

Colony House Museum, 104 West St., Keene, NH. 03431.

Lancaster Historical Society, 226 Main St., Lancaster, NH. 03584.

Manchester Historic Association, 129 Amherst St., Manchester, NH. 03104.

New London Historical Society, Little Sunapee Rd., New London, NH. 03257.

Peterborough Historical Society, P.O. Box 58, Peterborough, NH. 03458.

Portsmouth Athenaeum, NR, 9 Market Square, Portsmouth, NH. 03801.

Strawberry Banke, Inc., (M), P.O. Box 300, Portsmouth, NH. 03801.

Salisbury Historical Society, Salisbury, NH. 03268.

Effingham Historical Society, P.O. Box 33, South Effingham, NH. 03882.

Wolfeboro Historical Society, 8 Lake St., Wolfeboro, NH. 03894.

NEW JERSEY

Environmental Education Center, Somerset County Park Commission, 190 Lord Stirling Rd., Basking Ridge, NJ. 07920.

Historical Society of Bloomfield New Jersey, 90 Broad St., Bloomfield, NJ. 07003.

Bordentown Historical Society, Old City Hall, Crosswicks St., Bordentown, NJ. 08505.

Burlington County Historical Society, 457 High St., Burlington, NJ. 08016.

Camden County Historical Society, Park Blvd. & Euclid Ave., Camden, NJ. 08103.

Cape May County Historical Museum, Rte. 9-R.D. #1, Cape May Court House, NJ. 08210.

Cranbury Historical and Preservation Society, 6 Park Place, Cranbury, NJ. 08512.

New Jersey Society, Sons of the American Revolution, 1045 E. Jersey St., Elizabeth, NJ. 07201.

Doric House, 114 Main St., Flemington, NJ. 08822.

Monmouth County Historical Association, (M), 70 Court St., Freehold, NJ. 07728.

Cumberland County Historical Society, Ye Greate St., Greenwich, NJ. 08323.

"The Hermitage" National Landmark, 335 N. Franklin Turnpike, Ho-Ho-Kus, NJ. 07423.

Hope Historical Society, P.O. Box 52, Hope, NJ. 07844.

Hopewell Museum, 28 E. Broad St., Hopewell, NJ. 08525.

Lake Hopatcong Historical Museum, P.O. Box 668, Landing, NJ. 07850.

Mahwah Historical Society, 1871 Old Station Lane, Mahwah, NJ. 07430.

Ralston Historical Association, John Ralston Museum, Rte. 24, Mendham, NJ. 07945.

Wheaton Historical Association, (M), Wheaton Village, Millville, NJ. 08332.

Montclair Historical Society, P.O. Box 322, Monclair, NJ. 07042.

Montville Township Historical Museum, 84 Main Rd., Montville, NJ. 07045.

Morris County Historical Society-Acorn Hall, (M), P.O. Box 170M, Morristown, NJ. 07960.

Morristown National Historical Park, Washington Pl., Morristown, NJ. 07960.

Neptune Historical Museum, 25 Neptune Blvd., Neptune, NJ. 07753.

The New Jersey Historical Society, (M), 230 Broadway, Newark, NJ. 07104.

The Newark Museum, (M), P.O. Box 540, Newark, NJ. 07101.

Sussex County Historical Society, 82 Main St., Newton, NJ. 07860.

Ocean City Historical Museum, 409 Wesley Ave., Ocean City, NJ. 08226.

Pascack Historical Society, 19 Ridge Ave., Park Ridge, NJ. 07656.

Passaic County Historical Society, (M), Lambert Castle, Valley Rd., Paterson, NJ. 07503.

Kearny Cottage Historical Society, 63 Catalpa Ave., Perth Amboy, NJ. 08861.

Seventh Day Baptist Historical Society, P.O. Box 868, Plainfield, NJ. 07061.

Historical Society of Princeton, 158 Nassau St., Princeton, NJ. 08540.

Bergen County Historical Society, P.O. Box 55, River Edge, NJ. 07661.

Meadowlands Museum, 91 Crane Ave., Rutherford NJ. 07070.

Salem County Historical Society, 79-83 Market St., Salem, NJ. 08079.

Atlantic County Historical Society, 907 Shore Rd., Somers Point, NJ. 08244.

Springfield Historical Society, 126 Morris Ave., Springfield, NJ. 07081.

Ocean County Historical Society, 26 Hadley Ave., Toms River, NJ. 08753.

New Jersey State Museum, (M), 205 W. State St., Trenton, NJ. 08625.

Trenton City Museum, Ellarslie, In Cadwalader Park, Trenton, NJ. 08618.

Van Riper-Hopper House-Wayne Museum, 533 Berdan Ave., Wayne, NJ. 07470.

Yesteryear Museum, 20 Harriet Dr., Whippany, NJ. 07981.

Wildwood Historical Commission, 4400 New Jersey Ave., Wildwood, NJ. 08260.

Gloucester County Historical Society, P.O. Box 409, Woodbury, NJ. 08096.

NEW MEXICO

Tularosa Basin Historical Society Museum, P.O. Box 518, Alamogordo, NM. 88310.

Albuquerque Museum, P.O. Box 1293, Albuquerque, NM. 87103.

Artesia Historical Museum and Art Center, 505 Richardson Ave., Artesia, NM. 88210.

Farmington Historical Museum, 220 No. Orchard, Farmington, NM. 87401.

Old Lincoln County Courthouse Museum, Lincoln State Monument, Lincoln, NM. 88338.

Los Alamos County Historical Museum, P.O. Box 43, Los Alamos, NM. 87544.

Chaves County Historical Museum, 200 N. Lea Ave., Roswell, NM. 88201.

Museum of New Mexico, (M), P.O. Box 2087, Santa Fe, NM. 87501.

Geronimo Springs Museum, P.O. Box 1029, Truth or Consequences, NM. 87901.

NEW YORK

Albany Institute of History and Art, (M), 125 Washington Ave., Albany, NY. 12210.

New York State Museum, (M), Cultural Education Center, Empire State Plaza, Albany, NY. 12230.

Alden Historical Society, Inc., 299 Exchange St., Alden, NY. 14004.

Almond Historical Society, Inc., P.O. Box 98, Almond, NY. 14804.

Walter Elwood Museum, 300 Guy Park Ave., Amsterdam, NY. 12010.

North Castle Historical Society, 26 Rd., Thornewood Rd., Armonk, NY. 10504.

Cayuga Museum of History and Art, 203 Genesee St., Auburn, NY. 13021.

Baldwin Historical Society, 1980 Grand Ave., Baldwin, L.I. NY. 11510.

Saratoga County Museum, Brookside, Ballston Spa, NY. 12020.

The Holland Land Office Museum, 131 W. Main St., Batavia, NY. 14020.

Bear Mountain Trailside Museums, Bear Mountain State Park, Bear Mountain, NY. 10911.

Museum of the Bedford Historical Society, Village Green, Bedford, NY. 10506.

Allegany County Museum, Court House, Court St., Belmont, NY. 14813.

Bergen Museum of Local History, 6833 Pocock Rd., Bergen, NY. 14416.

Boome County Historical Society, (M), 30 Front St., Binghamton, NY. 13905.

Adirondack Museum, (M), Blue Mountain Lake, NY. 12812.

The Bronx County Historical Society, (M), 3266 Bainbridge Ave., Bronx, NY. 10467.

The Long Island Historical Society, 128 Pierrepoint St., Brooklyn, NY. 11201.

Buffalo and Erie County Historical Society, (M), 25 Nottingham Ct., Buffalo, NY. 14216.

Big Springs Museum, East Main St., 6515 Searls Rd., Byron, NY. 14422.

Canaan Historical Society, Inc., Rte. 22, R.F.D., Canaan, NY. 12029.

Ontario County Historical Society, (M), 55 N. Main St., Canadaigua, NY. 14424.

Research/History Center of St. Lawrence County, 3½ E. Main St., Canton, NY. 13617.

Cape Vincent Historical Rooms, Community House, Market St., Cape Vincent, NY. 13618.

Castile Historical House, 17 E. Park Rd., Castile, NY. 14427.

Cattaraugus Area Historical Center, Lover's Lane Rd., Cattaraugus, NY. 14719.

Lorenzo State Historic Site, Ledyard Ave., R.D. 2, Cazenovia, NY. 13035.

Chappaqua Historical Society Museum, New Castle Town Hall, 200 S. Greeley Ave., Chappaqua, NY. 10514.

Cherry Valley Museum, 49 Main St., Cherry Valley, NY. 13320.

Historical Society of the Town of Clarence, Main St., Clarence, NY. 14031.

Putnam County Historical Society, 63 Chestnut St., Cold Spring, NY. 10516.

New York State Historical Association, (M), Fenimore House, Lake Rd., Cooperstown, NY. 13326.

The Benjamin Patterson Inn, (M), 59 W. Pulteney St., Corning, NY. 14830.

Cortland County Historical Society, Inc., 25 Homer Ave., Cortland, NY. 13045.

Davenport Historical Society, Davenport Town Hall, Davenport Center, NY. 13751.

Aurora Historical Society, Inc., 5 So. Grove St., East Aurora, NY. 14052.

Historical Society of the Town of East Bloomfield, South Ave., East Bloomfield, NY. 14443.

Eastchester Historical Society, Marble School House, P.O. Box 37, Eastchester, NY. 10709.

Eden Historical Society, Inc., 2577 West Church St., Eden, NY. 14057.

Adirondack Center Museum, Court St., Elizabethtown, NY. 12932.

Chemung County Historical Society, Inc., 415 E. Water St., Elmira, NY. 14901.

Sterling Historical Society Museum, Victory St., Fair Haven, NY. 13064.

Fairport Historical Museum, 13 Perrin St., Fairport, NY. 14450.

Wan Wyck Homestead Museum, Rte. 9, Fishkill, NY. 12524.

The Bowne House Historical Society, 37-01 Bowne St., Flushing, NY. 11354.

Montgomery County Historical Society, N.Y. Rte. 5, Fort Johnson, NY. 12070.

Ischua Valley Historical Society, Inc., 24 Howard St., Franklinville, NY. 14737.

Historical Museum of the D.R. Barker Library, 20 E. Main St., Fredonia, NY. 14063.

Geneva Historical Society and Museum, (M), 543 S. Main St., Geneva, NY. 14456.

The Chapman Historical Museum, (M), 348 Glen St., Glens Falls, NY. 12801.

Fulton County Museum, 237 N. Kingsboro Ave., Gloversville, NY. 12078.

Orange County Community of Museums and Galleries, (M), 101 Main St., Box 527, Goshen, NY. 10924.

Gouverneur Museum, Route 2, Leadmine Rd., Gouverneur, NY. 13642.

The Gravesend Historical Society, P.O. Box 1643 Gravesend Station, Gravesend, NY. 11223.

Glenn H. Curtiss Museum of Local History, (M), Lake and Main Sts., Hammondsport, NY. 14840.

Herkimer County Historical Society, 400 N. Main St., Herkimer, NY. 13350.

Sachem Historical Society, 288 Gillette Ave., Bayport, NY. 11742.

Huntington Historical Society, (M), 2 High St., Huntington, NY. 11743.

Sullivan County Historical Society, Inc., P.O. Box 247, Hurleyville, NY. 12747.

Interlaken Historical Society, Main St., Interlaken, NY. 14847.

DeWitt Historical Society of Tompkins County, 116 N. Cayuga St., Ithaca, NY. 14850.

Fenton Historical Society, (M), 67 Washington St., Jamestown, NY. 14701.

Johnstown Historical Society, 17 N. William St., Johnstown, NY. 12095.

Columbia County Historical Society, Inc., 16 Broad St., Kinderhook, NY. 12106.

Senate House State Historic Site, 312 Fair St., Kingston, NY. 12401.

Fort William Henry Museum, Canada St., Lake George, NY. 12845.

Lake Placid-North Elba Historical Society, Averyville Rd., Lake Placid, NY. 12946.

LeRoy House, 23 E. Main St., LeRoy, NY. 14482.

Old Village Hall Museum, P.O. Box 296, Lindenhurst, NY. 11757.

Little Falls Historical Museum, 77 Petrie St., Little Falls, NY. 13365.

The Niagara County Historical Center, 215 Niagara St., Lockport, NY. 14094.

Wayne County Historical Society, Inc., 21 Butternut St., Lyons, NY. 14489.

Lewis County Historical Society Museum, Box 306, Lyons Falls, NY. 13368.

Macedon Historical Society, Inc., 103 Quaker Rd., Macedon, NY. 14502.

Franklin House of History, 51 Milwaukee St., Malone, NY. 12953.

Manilius Museum, Box 173, Manilius, NY. 13104.

Historical Society of Middletown and the Wallkill Precinct, Inc., 25 East Ave., Middletown, NY. 10940.

Schuyler County Historical Society, Inc., Montour Falls, NY. 14865.

Cayuga Owasco Lakes Historical Society, P.O. Box 241, Moravia, NY. 13188.

Genesee Country Museum, (M), Box 1819, Rochester, NY. 14603.

Fryer Memorial Library/Museum, West Peterboro St., Munnsville, NY. 13409.

Historical Society of Rockland County, 20 Zukor Rd., New York, NY. 10956.

New Hartford Historical Society, P.O. Box 238, New Hartford, NY. 13413.

Huguenot Historical Society, 6 Brodhead Ave., New Paltz, NY. 12561.

American Museum of Natural History, (M), 79th St. & Central Park West, New York, NY. 10024.

Hispanic Society of America, (M), 155th St. and Broadway, New York, NY. 10032.

The New York Public Library, Astor, Lenox, and Tilden Foundations, 5th Ave. & 42nd St., New York, NY. 10018.

The New York Historical Society, (M), 170 Central Park West, New York, NY. 10024.

The Parish of Trinity Church Museum, 74 Trinity Place, New York, NY. 10006.

Seamen's Church Institute of N.Y., (M), 15 State St., New York, NY. 10004.

Washington's Headquarters State Historic Site, 84 Liberty St., Newburgh, NY. 12550.

Northport Historical Society, Inc., (M), Box 545, Northport, NY. 11768.

Chenango County Historical Society Museum, Rexfort St., Norwich, NY. 13815.

Norwood Historical Association and Museum, 39 N. Main St., Norwood, NY. 13668.

Madison County Historical Society, (M), P.O. Box 415, Oneida, NY. 13421.

Orchard Park Historical Society, 5800 Armor Rd., Orchard Park, NY. 14127.

Museums of the Oysterponds Historical Society, Village Lane, Orient, Long Island, NY. 11957.

Ossining Historical Society Museum, 196 Croton Ave., Ossining, NY. 10562.

Oswego County Historical Society, (M), 135 E. 3rd St., Oswego, NY. 13126.

Tioga County Historical Society Museum, 110 Front St., Owego, NY. 13827.

Erwin Museum, 108 Hamilton St., Painted Post, NY. 14870.

Yates County Genealogical and Historical Society, Inc., (M), 200 Main St., Penn Yan, NY. 14527.

Historical Society of Greater Port Jefferson, Box 586, Port Jefferson, NY. 11777.

Cow Neck Peninsula Historical Society, 336 Port Washington Blvd., Port Washington, NY. 11050.

Potsdam Public Museum, (M), Civic Center, Potsdam, NY. 13676.

Dutchess County Historical Society, P.O. Box 88, Poughkeepsie, NY. 12602.

Suffolk County Historical Society, (M), 300 W. Main St., Riverhead, NY. 11901.

American Baptist Historical Society, 1106 S. Goodman St., Rochester, NY. 14620.

Dar-Hervey Ely House, Livingston Park, Rochester, NY. 14608.

Rochester Historical Society, (M), 485 East Ave., Rochester, NY. 14607.

Rome Historical Society, (M), 200 Church St., Rome, NY. 13440.

The Rye Historical Society Museum, (M), One Purchase St., Rye, NY. 10580.

Historical Society of Saratoga Springs Museum, Walworth Memorial Museum, (M), Box 216, Saratoga Springs, NY. 12866.

Sayville Historical Society, Box 658, Sayville, NY. 11782.

Schenectady County Historical Society, 32 Washington Ave., Schenectady, NY. 12305.

Old Stone Fort Museum & William W. Badgley Historical Museum, (M), N. Main St., Schoharie, NY. 12157.

Town of Bethlehem Historical Association, (M), Clapper Rd. and Rte. 144, Selkirk, NY. 12158.

Seneca Falls Historical Society, 55 Cayuga St., Seneca Falls, NY. 13148.

Sidney Historical Association, Box 217, Sidney, NY. 13838.

Smithtown Historical Society, P.O. Box 69, Smithtown, NY. 11787.

Somers Historical Society, P.O. Box 336, Somers, NY. 10589.

Southold Historical Society and Museum, Main Rd. & Maple Lane, Southold, NY. 11971.

Ogden Historical Society, Inc., 568 Colby Rd., Spencerport, NY. 14559.

Concord Historical Society, Warner Museum, 13153 Mortons Corners Rd., Springville, NY. 14141.

Staten Island Historical Society, (M), 441 Clarke Ave., Staten Island, NY. 10306.

Nassau County Museum, Division of Museum Services & Department of Recreation & Parks, Muttontown Rd., Syosset, NY. 11791.

Canal Museum, (M), Weighlock Building, Erie Blvd., E., Syracuse, NY. 13202.

Onondaga Historical Association, (M), 311 Montgomery St., Syracuse, NY. 13202.

Tappantown Historical Society, Box 71, Tappan, NY. 10983.

The Historical Society of the Tarrytowns, Inc., 1 Grove St., Tarrytown, NY. 10591.

Fort Ticonderoga, Box 390, Ticonderoga, NY. 12883.

Historical Society of the Tonawandas, Inc., 113 Main St., Tonawanda, NY. 14150.

Renesselaer County Historical Society, (M), 59 2nd St., Troy, NY. 12180.

Oneida Historical Society, (M), 318 Genesee St., Utica, NY. 13502.

Historical Society of Walden & Wallkill Valley, Montgomery St., Walden, NY. 12586.

Warwick Historical Society, P.O. Box 353, Warwick, NY. 10990.

Waterford Historical Museum and Cultural Center, Inc., P.O. Box 175, Waterford, NY. 12188.

Waterloo Library and Historical Society, 31 E. Williams St., Waterloo, NY. 13165.

Jefferson County Historical Society, (M), 228 Washington St., Watertown, NY. 13601.

Old Brutus Historical Society, 8943 North Seneca St., Weedsport, NY. 13166.

History Center and Museum, P.O. Box 173, Westfield, NY. 14787.

Wilson Historical Society Museum, Rt. 425, Wilson, NY. 14172.

Middlebury Historical Society Museum, 15 Durtee Rd., Wyoming, NY. 14591.

The Hudson River Museum, (M), Trevor Park-on-Hudson, Yonders, NY. 10701.

Town of Yorktown Museum, 1974 Commerce St., Torktown Heights, NY. 10598.

NORTH CAROLINA

Western North Carolina Heritage Center, P.O. Box 5456, Asheville, NC. 28803.

Blockade Runners of the Confederacy Museum, P.O. Drawer Q., Highway 421 South, Carolina Beach, NC. 28428.

Mountain Heritage Center, (M), Western Carolina University, Cullowhee, NC. 28723.

Gaston County Art and History Museum, (M), P.O. Box 429, Dallas, NC. 28034.

Edenton Historical Commission, P.O. Box 474, Edenton, NC. 27932.

Greensboro Historical Museum, (M), 130 Summit Ave., Greensboro, NC. 27401.

Heritage Center, N.C.A. & T. State University, Greensboro, NC. 27411.

High Point Historical Society, Inc., (M), 1805 E. Lexington Ave., High Point, NC. 27262.

Orange County Historical Museum, Rt. 3, Box 390, Hillsborough, NC. 27278.

World Methodist Commission on Archives and History, The United Methodist Church, P.O. Box 518, Lake Junaluska, NC. 28745.

Davidson County Historical Museum, Old Courthouse on the Square, Lexington, NC. 27292.

The Historical Foundation of the Presbyterian and Reformed Churches, Inc., (M), Box 847, Montreat, NC. 28757.

Cherokee County Historical Museum, Inc., Peachtree St., Murphy, NC. 28906.

Catawba County Historical Museum, 1716 S. College Dr., Hwy. 321, Newton, NC. 28658.

Carson House Restoration Inc., Rt. 1, Box 179, Old Fort, NC. 28762.

North Carolina Division of Archives and History, (M), 109 E. Jones St., Raleigh, NC. 27611.

North Carolina Museum of History, 109 E. Jones St., Raleigh, NC. 27611.

Cleveland County Historical Museum, P.O. Box 1335, Shelby, NC. 28150.

Anson County Historical Society, Inc., 210 E. Wade St., Wadesboro, NC. 28170.

Lower Cape Fear Historical Society, Inc., P.O. Box 813, Wilmington, NC. 28402.

Historic Bethabara, 2147 Bethabara Rd., Winston-Salem, NC. 27106.

Old Salem, Inc., Drawer F., Salem Station, Winston-Salem, NC. 27108.

Yadkin County Historical Society, P.O. Box 1250, Yadkinville, NC. 27055.

NORTH DAKOTA

State Historical Society of North Dakota, (M), North Dakota Heritage Center, Bismark, ND. 58505.

Divide County Museum-Historical Society, Crosby, ND. 58730.

Buffalo-Trails Museum, Epping, ND. 58843.

Wells County Museum, 55 4th Ave. North, Fessenden, ND. 58438.

Steele County Historical Society, Finley, ND. 53230.

Ransom County Historical Society, Fort Ransom, ND. 38033.

Hatton-Eielson Museum, 720 Jersey Ave., Hatton, ND. 58240.

Traill County, North Dakota Historical Society, Hillsboro, ND. 58045.

Steele County Historical Society, Hope, ND. 58046.

Fort Seward Historical Society, Inc., P.O. Box 1002, Jamestown, ND. 58401.

Renville County Historical Society, Inc., P.O. Box 515, Mohall, ND. 58761.

Hettinger County Historical Society, P.O. Box 176, Regent, ND. 58650.

Barnes County Historical Museum, P.O. Box 188, Valley City, ND. 58072.

Richland County Historical Museum, Rt. 1, Wahpeton, ND. 58075.

McLean County Historical Society Museum, Washburn, ND. 58577.

Frontier Museum, R.R. 2, Box 9, Williston, ND. 58801.

OHIO

Summit County Historical Society, (M), 550 Copley Rd., Akron, OH. 44320.

Ehrhart Museum, City Hall, N. Main St., Antwerp, OH. 45813.

Ashtabula County Historical Society, P.O. Box 219, Ashtabula, OH. 44004.

Aurora Historical Society, Inc., P.O. Box 241, Aurora, OH. 44202.

Clermont County Historical Society, P.O. Box 14, Batavia, OH. 45103.

Rose Hill Museum, 27715 Lake Rd., Bay Village, OH. 44140.

Bedford Historical Society, P.O. Box 282, Bedford, OH. 44146.

Logan County Historical Museum, P.O. Box 296, Bellefontaine, OH. 43311.

Bexley Historical Society, 2242 E. Main St., Bexley, OH. 43209.

Wood County Historical Society, 13660 County Home Rd., Bowling Green, OH. 43402.

Brooklyn Historical Society, 4442 Ridge Rd., Brooklyn, OH. 44144.

Bucyrus Historical Society, P.O. Box 493, Bucyrus, OH. 44820.

Geauga County Historical Society Century Village, P.O. Box 153, Burton, OH. 44021.

McKinley Museum of History, Science & Industry, (M), P.O. Box 483, Canton, OH. 44701.

Carrol County Historical Society, P.O. Box 174, Carrollton, OH. 44615.

Mercer County Historical Museum, The Riley Home, 130 E. Market, Celina, OH. 45883.

Chagrin Falls Historical Society, P.O. Box 15, Chagrin Falls, OH. 44022.

Ross County Historical Society, Inc., 45 W. 5th St., Chillicothe, OH. 45601.

Cincinnati Historical Society, Eden Park, Cincinnati, OH. 45202.

Dunham Tavern Museum, 3915 Northampton Rd., Cleveland Heights, OH. 44121.

St. Mary's Ethnic Museum, 3256 Warren Rd., Cleveland, OH. 44111.

Ukrainian Museum-Archives, Inc., 1202 Kenilworth Ave., Cleveland, OH. 44113.

Western Reserve Historical Society, (M), 10825 East Blvd., Cleveland, OH. 44106.

Columbiana & Fairfield Township Historical Society, 115 Stanton Ave., Columbiana, OH. 44408.

Center of Science and Industry of the Franklin County Historical Society, (M), 280 E. Broad St., Columbus, OH. 43215.

Ohio Historical Center, 1932 Velma Ave., Columbus, OH. 43211.

The Montgomery County Historical Society, (M), 7 North Main St., Dayton, OH. 45402.

Dover Historical Society, 325 E. Iron Ave., Dover, OH. 44622.

The Hickories Museum of the Lorain County Historical Society, Inc., 509 Washington Ave., Elyria, OH. 44035.

Heritage Cottage, 955 Bucyrus Rd., Galion, OH. 205 N. Broadway, Greenville, OH. 45331.

Butler County Museum, 327 N. 2nd St. Hamilton, OH. 45011.

Highland County Historical Society, 151 E. Main St., Hillsboro, OH. 45133.

Hudson Library and Historical Society, 22 Aurora St., Hudson, OH. 44236.

Putnam County Historical Society Museum, Box 26, Kalida, OH. 45853.

Hardin County Relic Room, Hardin County Court House, Kenton, OH. 43326.

Lakewood Historical Society, 1200 Andrews Ave., Lakewood, OH. 44107.

Warren County Historical Society Museum, 105 S. Broadway, Box 223, Lebanon, OH. 45036.

Allen County Museum, (M), 620 W. Market St., Lima, OH. 45801.

Lisbon Historical Society, 100 E. Washington St., Lisbon, OH. 44432.

Campus Martius Museum, 601 2nd St., Marietta, OH. 45750.

Sedgewick Historical Museum, 300 N. Seventh St., Martins Ferry, OH. 43935.

The Union County Historical Society, P.O. Box 303, Marysville, OH. 43040.

Munson House, Medina County Historical Society, P.O. Box 306, Medina, OH. 44258.

Lake County Historical Society, (M), 3095 Mentor Ave., Mentor, OH. 44060.

Milford Area Museum, 32 Main St., Milford, OH. 45150.

Holmes County Historical Society, 233 N. Washington St., Millersburg, OH. 44654.

Williams County Historical Museum, 120 South East Ave., Monpelier, OH. 43543.

Sherwood-Davidson House, P.O. Box 785, 6th St. Park, Newark, OH. 43055.

Newcomerstown Historical Society, 221 W. Canal St., Newcomerstown, OH. 43832.

Historical Society of Olde Northfield, Box 99, Northfield, OH. 44067.

Firelands Historical Society Museum, 4 Case Ave., Norwalk, OH. 44857.

Oregon Jerusalem Historical Museum, 3464 Starr Ave., Oregon, OH. 43616.

Meigs County Museum, Box 145, Pomeroy, OH. 45769.

Portage County Historical Society, P.O. Box 257, Ravenna, OH. 44266.

Salem Historical Society, 208 South Broadway Ave., Salem, OH. 44460.

Follett House Museum, Sandusky Library Assoc., West Adams & Columbus Ave., Sandusky, OH. 44870.

Shaker Historical Museum, 16740 S. Park Blvd., Shaker Heights, OH. 44120.

Clark County Historical Society, 300 W. Main St., Springfield, OH. 45504.

The Jefferson County Historical Assoc., 426 Franklin Ave., Steubenville, OH. 43952.

Seneca County Museum, (M), Clay St., Tiffin, OH. 44883.

Troy-Hayner Cultural Center, 301 W. Main St., Troy, OH. 45373.

Wyandot County Historical Society, Box 111, McCtchenville, OH. 44844.

Champaign County Historical Museum, (M), 480 Main St., Vermillion, OH. 44089.

John Stark Edwards House, 309 South S E., Warren, OH. 44483.

Orange Johnson House, 50 W. New England Ave., Worthington, OH. 43085.

Greene County Historical Society, 74 W. Church St., Xenia, OH. 45385.

OKLAHOMA

Cherokee Strip Museum, 901 14th St., Alva, OK. 73717.

Woolaroc Museum, (M), Route 3, Bartlesville, OK. 74003.

Lincoln County Historical Society Museum of Pioneer History, 717 Manvel Ave., Chandler, OK. 74834.

Stephens County Historical Museum, Hwy. 81 and Beach, Box 1294, Duncan, OK. 73533.

Canadian County Historical Museum, 600 W. Wade, El Reno, OK. 73036.

No Man's Land Historical Museum, Sewel St., Goodwell, OK. 73939.

Oklahoma State Capital Newspaper & Publishing Museum, (M), 301 W. Harrison Ave., Guthrie, OK. 73044.

Oklahoma Territorial Museum of the Oklahoma Historical Society, 402-406 E. Oklahoma Ave., Guthrie, OK. 73044.

Choctaw Museum, 124 N. Broadway, Hugo, OK. 74743.

Museum of the Great Plains, (M), P.O. Box 68, Lawton, OK. 73502.

Grant County Museum, Corner of Main & Cherokee Sts., Medford, OK. 73759.

Norman's Cleveland County Historical Museum, (M), P.O. Box 260, Norman, OK. 73070.

Nowata County Historical Society Museum, 121 S. Pine St., Nowata, OK. 74048.

The State Museum of Oklahoma, (M), Historical Building, Oklahoma City, OK. 73105.

Creek Council House Museum, (M), Creek Council House, Okmulgee, OK. 74447.

Cherokee Strip Historical Museum and Henry S. Johnston Library, Rt. 2 Box, 81-A, Perry, OK. 73077.

Thomas Gilcrease Institute of American History and Art, (M), 1400 North 25 West Ave., Tulsa, OK. 74127.

OREGON

Clatsop County Historical Society, 441 Eighth St., Astoria, OR. 97103.

Oregon High Desert Museum, (M), P.O. Box 5035, Bend, OR. 97701.

Harney County Historical Museum, 18 W. D St., Burns, OR. 97720.

Herman & Eliza Oliver Historical Museum, 101 S. Canyon City Blvd., Hwy. 395, Canyon City, OR. 97820.

Lane County Museum, 740 W. 13th Ave., Eugene, OR. 97402.

Eastern Oregon Museum, Rte. 1, Box 109, Haines, OR. 97833.

Jacksonville Museum, (M), P.O. Box 480, Jacksonville, OR. 97530.

Klamath County Museum, 1451 Main St., KlamathFalls, OR. 97601.

Schminck Memorial Museum, 128 S. " E" St., Lakeview, OR. 97630.

Coos County Historical Society Museum, (M), Simpson Park, North Bend, OR. 97479.

Oregon Historical Society, 1230 S.W. Park Ave., Portland, OR. 97205.

Douglas County Historical Society, 544 S. E. Douglas Ave., Roseburg, OR. 97470.

Douglas County Museum, Box 1550, County Fairgrounds, Roseburg, OR. 97470.

Columbia County Historical Society Museum, Old Court House Museum, St. Helens, OR. 97051.

Tillamook County Pioneer Museum, (M), 2106 Second St., Tillamook, OR. 97141.

Union County Museum, 311 S. Main St., Union, OR. 97883.

PENNSYLVANIA

Lehigh County Historical Museums, Lehigh County Court House, 5th & Hamilton Sts., Allentown, PA. 18101.

Lehigh County Historical Society, Old Court House, Hamilton atFifth St., Allentown, PA. 18101.

Tioga Point Museum, P.O. Box 143, Athens, PA. 18810.

Centre County Library and Historical Museum, 203 N. Allegheny St., Bellefont, PA. 16823.

Annie S. Kemerer Museum, (M), 427 N. New St., Bethlehem, PA. 18018.

Moravian Museum of Bethlehem, (M), 66 W. Church St., Bethlehem, PA. 18018.

Cumberland County Historical Society and the Hamilton Library, P.O. Box 626, Carlisle, PA. 17013.

Unites States Army Military History Institute, Carlisle Barracks, PA. 17013.

The Clarion County Historical Society, 18 Grant St., Clarion, PA. 16214.

Clearfield County Historical Society, 104 E. Pine St., Clearfield, PA. 16830.

Museum of the Historical Society of Trappe, Pennsylvania, Main St., Trappe, Collegevile, PA. 19426.

Corry Area Historical Society, Box 107, Corry, PA. 16407.

Potter County Historical Society, 308 N. Main St., Coudersport, PA. 16915.

Mercer Museum of the Bucks County Historical Society, (M), Pine and Ashland Sts., Doylestown, PA. 18901.

Northampton County Historical Society, 101 S. 4th St., Easton, PA. 18042.

Cambria County Historical Society, 521 West High St., Ebensburg, PA. 15931.

Shelter House Society, S. 4th St. Exension, Box 254, Emmaus, PA. 18049.

Historical Society of the Cocalico Valley, 249 W. Main St., Ephrata, PA. 17522.

Cashier's House, 417 State Street, Erie, PA. 16501.

Erie County Historical Society, 417 State St., Erie, PA. 16501.

Erie Historical Museum, (M), 356 W. Sixth St., Erie, PA. 16507.

Fort Necessity National Battlefield, The National Pike, Farmington, PA. 15437.

Historical Society of Fort Washington, 473 Bethlehem Pike, Fort Washington, PA. 19034.

Adams County Historical Society, Drawer A, Gettysburg, PA. 17325.

Coschenhoppen Folklife Library and Museum, Box 476, Green Lane, PA. 18054.

The Historical Society of Dauphin County, 219 S.Front St., Harrisburg, PA. 17104.

Pennsylvania Historical and Museum Commission, (M), P.O. Box 1026, Harrisburg, PA. 17120.

William Penn Memorial Museum, Box 1026, Harrisburg, PA. 17120.

Haverford Township Historical Society, Box 825, Havertown, PA. 19083.

Wayne County Historical Society, P.O. Box 446, Honesdale, PA. 18431.

Huntingdon County Historical Society, P.O. Box 305, Huntingdon, PA. 16652.

Historical and Genealogical Society of Indiana County, S. 6th & Wayne Ave., Indiana, PA. 15701.

Old York Road Historical Society, Jenkintown Library, York & Vista Rds, Jenkintown, PA. 19046.

Heritage Center of Lancaster County, Inc., Center Square, Box 997, Lancaster, PA. 17604.

Lancaster County Historical Society, 230 N. President Ave., Lancaster, PA. 17603.

Lebanon County Historical Society, 924 Cumberland St., Lebanon, PA. 17042.

Pennsylvania Dutch Folk Culture Society, Inc., Lenhartsville, PA. 19534.

Union County Historical Society, Box 154, Laurelton, PA. 17835.

Mifflin County Historical Society, Inc., 17 N. Main St., Lewistown, PA. 17044.

Baldwin-Reynolds House Museum, 848 N. Main St., Meadville, PA. 16335.

Mercer County Historical Society, 119 S. Pitt St., Mercer, PA. 16137.

The Snyder County Historical Society, Inc., P.O. Box 276, Middleburg, PA. 17842.

Susquehanna County Historical Society and Free Library Association, Monument Square, Montrose, PA. 18801.

Columbia County Historical Society, P.O. Box 197, Orangeville, PA. 17859.

American Catholic Historical Society, P.O. Box 84, Philadelphia, PA. 19105.

American Swedish Historical Foundation-- Museum, (M), 1900 Pattison Ave., Philadelphia, PA. 19145.

The Genealogical Society of Pennsylvania, 1300 Locust St., Philadelphia, PA. 19107.

Germantown Historical Society, 5214 Germantown Ave., Philadelphia, PA. 19144.

Historical Society of Pennsylvania, 1300 Locust St., Philadelphia, PA. 19107.

Independence National Historical Park, 313 Walnut St., Philadelphia, PA. 19106.

Library Company of Philadelphia, (M), 1314 Locust St., Philadelphia, PA. 19107.

Presbyterian Historical Society, 425 Lombard St., Philadelphia, PA. 19147.

Robert W. Ryerss Library & Museum, Burholme Park, Cottman & Central Aves., Philadelphia, PA. 19111.

The Rosenback Museum and Library, (M), 2010 Delancey Place, Philadelphia, PA. 19103.

St. George's United Methodist Church, 235 N. Fourth St., Philadelphia, PA. 19106.

Historical Society of Western Pennsylvania, 4338 Bigelow Blvd., Pittsburg, PA. 15213.

The Old Post Office, Pittsburg History & Landmarks Museum, (M), One Landmarks Square, Pittsburg, PA. 15212.

Historical Society of Berks County, 940 Centre Ave., Reading, PA. 19601.

Historical Society of St. Marys and Benzinger Township, P.O. Box 584, St. Marys, PA. 15857.

Historic Schaefferstown, Inc., N. Market St., Schaefferstown, PA. 17088.

Shippensburg Historical Society Museum, West King St., Library Building, Shippensburg, PA. 17257.

Historical and Genealogical Society of Somerset County, Box 533, Somerset, PA. 15501.

Bradford County Historical Society, R.D. 2, Troy, PA. 16947.

The Valley Forge Historical Society, Valley Forge, PA. 19481.

Washington County Historical Society, Le Moyne House, 49 E. Maiden St., Washington, PA. 15301.

Fort LeBoeuf, 123 S. High St., Waterford, PA. 16441.

Radnor Historical Society, 113 W. Beech Tree Lane, Wayne, PA. 19087.

Greene County Historical Society, R.D. 2, Waynesburg, PA. 15370.

Chester County Historical Society, (M), 225 N. High St., West Chester, PA. 19380.

Wyoming Historical and Genealogical Society, 49 S. Franklin St., Wilkes-Barre, PA. 18701.

Lycoming County Historical Society and Museum, (M), 858 W. 4th St., Williamsport, PA. 17701.

The Historical Society of York County, (M), 250 E. Market St., York, PA. 17403.

RHODE ISLAND

Bristol Historical and Preservation Society, 48 Court St., Bristol, RI. 02809.

Pettaquamscutt Historical Society, P.O. Box 59, Kingston, RI. 02881.

Blackstone Valley Historical Society, North Gate Louisquisset Pike, Lincoln, RI. 02863.

Little Compton Historical Society, West Rd., Little Compton, RI. 02837.

Newport Historical Society, (M), 82 Touro St., Newport, RI. 02840.

Portsmouth Historical Society, P.O. Box 37, Portsmouth, RI. 02871.

Rhode Island Black Heritage Society, One Hilton St., Providence, RI. 02905.

Rhode Island Historical Society, 52 Power St., Providence, RI. 02906.

Rhode Island State Archives, Rm 43, State House, Smith St., Providence, RI. 02903.

Western Rhode Island Civic Historical Society, 1 Station St., Washington, RI. 02816.

SOUTH CAROLINA

Aiken County Historical Museum, (M), 226 Chesterfield, Aiken, SC. 29801.

Barnwell County Museum, P.O. Box 395, Barnwell, SC. 29812.

Marlboro County Historical Museum, 119 S. Marlboro, SC. 29512.

Camden District Heritage Foundation, Historic Camden, (M), P.O. Box 710, Camden, SC. 29020.

Charleston Museum, (M), 360 Meeting St., Charleston, SC. 29403.

The Old Slave Mart Museum, (M), P.O. Box 446, Sullivan's Island, SC. 29482.

Waring Historical Library, Medical University of South Carolina, 171 Ashley Ave., Charleston, SC. 29425.

South Carolina Confederate Relic Room and Museum, (M), World War Memorial Building, 920 Sumter St., Columbia, SC. 29201.

South Carolina Department of Archives and History, P.O. Box 11669, Columbia, SC. 29211.

Horry County Museum, 438 Main St., Conway, SC. 29526.

Limestone College, Gaffney, SC. 29340.

Hampton County Historical Society Museum, 104 Mulberry St., Hampton, SC. 29924.

Pendleton District Historical and Recreational Commission, 125 E. Queen St., Pendleton, SC. 29670.

Calhoun County Museum, (M), 303 Butler St., St. Matthews, SC. 29135.

Museum-Archives of the Sumter County Historical Society, Inc., P.O. Box 1456, Sumter, SC. 29150.

Union County Historical Museum, P.O. Drawer 220, Union, SC. 29379.

Fairfield County Museum, South Congress St., Winnsboro, SC. 29180.

SOUTH DAKOTA

Dacotah Prairie Museum, P.O. Box 395, Aberdeen, SD. 57401.

Douglas County Museum, Armour, SD. 57313.

Custer County 1881 Courthouse Museum, West of Custer, Custer, SD. 57730.

Fall River County Historical Museum, Box 529, Hot Springs, SD. 57747.

Mount Rushmore National Memorial, Keystone, SD. 57751.

The Center for Western Studies, Augustana College 29th, & S. Summit, Sioux Falls, SD. 57197.

Siouxland Heritage Museums, (M), 200 W. 6th SiouxFalls, SD. 57102.

Brookings County Historical Society Museum, Volga, SD. 57071.

TENNESSEE

Chattanooga Museum of Regional History, 176 S. Crest Rd., Chattanooga, TN. 37404.

Red Clay State Historical Area, Rte. 6, Box 733, Cleveland, TN. 37311.

Jonesboro History Museum, (M), P.O. Box 375, Jonesboro, TN. 37659.

Confederate Memorial Hall "Bleak House," 3148 Kingston Pike, S.W., Knoxville, TN. 37919.

Frank H. McClung Museum, (M), University of Tennessee, Circle Park Dr., Knoxville, TN. 37916.

Memphis Pink Palace Museum, (M), 3050 Central Ave., Memphis, TN. 38111.

American Association for State and Local History, 1400 Eighth Ave., South, Nashville, TN. 37203.

Baptist Museum of Dargan-Carver Library, 127 9th Ave., N., Nashville , TN. 37234.

Historic Landmarks Association, (M), P.O. Box 15312, Nashville, TN. 37215.

The Public Library of Nashville and Davidson County, 8th Ave. N. & Union, Nashville, TN. 37203.

Tennessee Historical Commission, 4721 Trousdale Dr., Nashville, TN. 37219.

Upper Room Chapel Devotional Library and Museum, P.O. Box 189, Nashville, TN. 37202.

Rocky Mount, (M), Rte. 2, Box 70, Piney Flats, TN. 37686.

Shiloh National Military Park and Cemetery, Shiloh, TN. 38376.

TEXAS

Neill-Cochran Museum House, 2310 San Gabriel St., Austin, TX. 78705.

Texas Confederate Museum, 112 E. 11th, Austin, TX. 78701.

Texas State Library, Box 12927, Austin, TX. 78711.

Big Bend National Park, Big Bend, TX. 79834.

Hutchinson County Museum, Boom Town Revisited, 618 N. Main, Box 325, Borger, TX. 79007.

Texas Baptist Historical Center Museum, Rte. 5, Box 222, Brenham, TX. 77833.

Burleson County Historical Museum, Burleson County Courthouse, Caldwell, TX. 77836.

Panhandle-Plains Historical Museum, (M), 2401 Fourth Ave., Canyon, TX. 79015.

Chappell Hill Historical Society Museum, Chappell Hill, TX. 77426.

Childress County Heritage Museum, Corner of Main & Ave. F. N. W., Childress, TX. 79201.

Navarro County Historical Society, Pioneer Village, 912 W. Park Ave., Corsicana, TX. 75110.

Crosby County Pioneer Memorial Museum, (M), P.O. Box 386, Crosbyton, TX. 79322.

DeWitt County Historical Museum, P.O. Box 745, Cuero, TX. 77954.

Dallas Historical Society, (M), P.O. Box 26038, Dallas, TX. 75226.

Wise County Heritage Museum, P.O. Box 427, Decatur, TX. 76234.

Whitehead Memorial Museum, 1308 S. Main St., Del Rio, TX. 78840.

Hidalgo County Historical Museum, (M), P.O. Box 482, Edinburg, TX. 78539.

Texana Museum, P.O. Box 401, Edna, TX. 77957.

El Paso Museum of History, 12901 Gateway West, El Pase, TX. 79927.

Freestone County Historical Museum, Box 524, Fairfield, TX. 75840.

The Heritage Museum at Falfurrias, Inc., P.O. Box 86, Falfurrias, TX. 78355.

Log Cabin Village Historical Complex, 2301 Rogers Rd., Ft. Worth, TX. 76109.

Morton Museum of Cooke County, (M), P.O. Box 150, Gainesville, TX. 76240.

Galveston County Museum, P.O. Box 1047, Galveston, TX. 77553.

Howard-Dickinson House Museum, P.O. Box 501, Henderson, TX. 75652.

Harris County Heritage Society, (M), 1100 Bagby, Houston, TX. 77002.

Texas Gulf Coast Historical Association, University of Houston, Houston, TX. 77004.

Jefferson Historical Society and Museum, 223 Austin, Jefferson, TX. 75657.

Harrison County Historical Museum, Old Courthouse, Peter Whetstone Square, Marshall, TX. 75670.

Midland County Historical Museum, 301 W. Missouri, Midland, TX. 79701.

Hoya Memorial Library and Museum, 211 S. Lanana St., Nacogdoches, TX. 75961.

Crockett County Museum, P.O. Drawer B, Ozona, TX. 76943.

Fort Bend County Museum, P.O. Box 251, Richmond, TX. 77469.

Central Texas Area Museum, Inc., Main andFront Sts., Salado, TX. 76571.

San Antonio Conservation Society, 107 King William St., San Antonio, TX. 78204.

Los Nogales Museum, 425 S. River, Seguin, TX. 78155.

Edwin Wolters Memorial Museum and Library, P.O. 161, 409 E. 13th St., Shiner, TX. 77984.

Scurry County Museum, (M), P.O. Box 696, Snyder, TX. 79549.

Martin County Historical Museum, P.O. Box 929, Stanton, TX. 79782.

Texarkana Historical Society and Museum, (M), Box 2343, Texarkana, TX. 75504.

Culberson County Historical Museum, (M), Box 127, Van Horn, TX. 79855.

Ellis County Museum, Inc., P.O. Box 706, Waxahachie, TX. 75165.

UTAH

Territorial Statehouse, P.O. Box 57, Fillmore, UT. 84631.

Daughters of Utah Pioneers, 300 N. Main St., Salt Lake City, UT. 84103.

Utah State Historical Society, (M), 300 Rio Grande St., Salt Lake City, UT. 84101.

VERMONT

Franklin County Museum, P.O. Box 334, St. Albans, VT. 05478.

Barnet Historical Society, RFD, Barnet, VT. 05821.

Rockingham Free Public Library and Museum, 65 Westminster St., BellowsFalls, VT. 05101.

Community Historical Museum of the Town of Mount Holly, Box 235, East Wallingford, VT. 05742.

Bennington Museum, (M), W. Main St., Bennington, VT. 05201.

Bradford Historical Society, Brook Rd., Bradford, VT. 05033.

Historical Society of Brookfield, Inc., Brookfield Center, VT. 05036.

Castleton Historical Society, Main St., Castleton, VT. 05735.

Holland Historical Society Museum, RF.D., Derby, VT. 05829.

Fairfax Historical Society, Box 105, Fairfax, VT. 05454.

Grafton Historical Society, Inc., Grafton, VT. 05146.

Jericho Historical Society, Box 35, Jericho, VT. 05465.

Black River Academy Museum, Box 16, Ludlow, VT. 05149.

Marlboro Historical Society, Marlboro, VT. 05349.

Cabot Historical Society, Inc., RFD Lower Cabot, Marshfield, VT. 05658.

Vermont Museum, (M), Pavilion Bldg., Montpelier, VT. 05602.

Missisquoi Valley Historical Society, P.O. Box 237, North Troy, VT. 05859.

Center School Museum-Northfield Historical Society, 37 S. Main St., Northfield, VT. 05663.

East Poultney Museum, Box 57, Poultney, VT. 05764.

Putney Historical Society, R.D. 2, Box 53, Putney, VT. 05346.

Randolph Historical Society, Inc., Box 15, Randolph Center, VT. 05061.

Reading Historical Society, Reading, VT. 05062.

Readsboro Historical Society, Rts. 8 & 100 Heartwellville, Readsboro, VT. 05350.

Royalton Historical Society, Royalton, VT. 05068.

Shaftsbury Historical Society, Inc., R.R. 1, Box 101, Shaftsbury, VT. 05262.

Thetford Historical Society Library and Museum, Thetford, VT. 05074.

Vernon Historians, Inc., Rd. #1 Silverlane, VT. 05354.

Woodstock Historical Society, Inc., (M), 26 Elm St., Woodstock, VT. 05091.

VIRGINIA

Jacob Simpson Payton Library, 5001 Echols Ave., Alexandria, VA. 22311.

Ramsay House Visitors Center, 211 King St., Alexandria, VA. 22314.

Amherst County Historical Museum, P.O. Box 741, Amherst, VA. 24521.

Arlington Historical Museum, P.O. Box 402, Arlington, VA. 22270.

Southwest Virginia Museum, Box 742, Big Gap, VA. 24219.

Sherwood Forest Plantation, P.O. Box 8, Charles City, VA. 23020.

Blue Ridge Institute, Ferrum, VA. 24088.

Virginia Institute of Marine Science, Box 358, Gloucester Point, VA. 23062.

Goochland County Historical Society, County Jail, Goochland, VA. 23063.

Hanover Historical Society Museum, Rt. 4, Box 182, Ashland, VA. 23005.

Harrisonburg-Rockingham Historical Society, (M), 301 S. Main St., Harrisonburg, VA. 22801.

Foundation for Historic Christ Church, Inc., P.O. Box 24, Irvington, VA. 22480.

Mary Ball Washington Museum and Library, Inc., Box 97, Lancaster, VA. 22503.

Rockbridge Historical Society, P.O. Box 514, Lexington, VA. 24450.

Manassas Museum, 9406 Main St., Manassas, VA. 22018.

Smyth County Historical and Museum Society, Inc., P.O. Box 574, Marion, VA. 24354.

Belle Grove, Box 137, Middletown, VA. 22645.

Norfolk Historical Society, P.O. Box 9472, Norfolk, VA. 23505.

Agecroft Hall, 4305 Sulgrave Rd., Richmond, VA. 23221.

Valentine Museum, (M), 1015 E. Clay St., Richmond, VA. 23219.

Virginia Historic Landmarks Commission, 221 Governor St., Richmond, VA. 23219.

Virginia Historical Society, P.O. Box 7311, Richmond, VA. 23221.

Roanoke Valley Historical Society, Box 1904, Roanoke, VA. 24008.

Spotsylvania Historical Association, Inc., P.O. Box 64, Spotsylvania County, VA. 22553.

Historic Crab Orchard Museum, P.O. Box 12, Tazewell, VA. 24651.

Colonial Williamsburg, (M), Goodwin Building, Williamsburg, VA. 23185.

Winchester-Frederick County Historical Society, Inc., Box 58, Winchester, VA. 22601.

Colonial National Historical Park, P.O. Box 210, Yorktown, VA. 23690.

WASHINGTON

Chelon County Historical Museum, 105 Parkhill St., Cashmere, WA. 98815.

Wahkiakum County Historical Society, Rte. 2, Box 392, Cathlamet, WA. 98612.

Lewis County Historical Museum, 599 NW Front St., Chehalis, WA. 98532.

Lincoln County Historical Museum, P.O. Box 585, Davenport, WA. 99122.

Edmonds South Snohomish County Historical Society, Inc., P.O. Box 52, Edmonds, WA. 98020.

Grant County Museum, Box 1141, Ephrata, WA. 98823.

Klickitat County Historical Society, P.O. Box 86, Goldendale, WA. 98620.

Cowlitz County Historical Museum, 405 Allen St., Kelso, WA. 98626.

Snoqualmie Valley Historical Museum, P.O. Box 179, North Bend, WA. 98045.

Port Gamble Historical Museum, P.O. Box 217, Port Gamble, WA. 98364.

Jefferson County Historical Society, (M), City Hall, Port Townsend, WA. 98368.

Benton County Museum & Historical Society, Inc., P.O. Box 591, Prosser, WA. 99350.

Museum of History and Industry, (M), 2161 E. Hamlin St., Seattle, WA. 98112.

Shaw Island Library & Historical Society, Shaw Island, WA. 98286.

Kitsap County Historical Society Museum, 3343 N.W. Byron St., Silverdale, WA. 98383.

Pacific County Historical Society, P.O. Box P, South Bend, WA. 98586.

Eastern Washington State Historical Society, Cheney Cowles Memorial Museum, (M), W. 2316First Ave., Spokane, WA. 99204.

Steilacoom Historical Museum Association, P.O. Box 16, Steilacoom, WA. 98388.

Skamania County Historical Society, (M), P.O. Box 396, Stevenson, WA. 98648.

Washington State Historical Society, (M), 315 N. Stadium Way, Tacoma, WA. 98403.

Clark County Historical Museum, 1511 Main St., Vancouver, WA. 98660.

Yakima Valley Museum and Historical Association, 2015 Tieton Dr., Yakima, WA. 98902.

WEST VIRGINIA

West Virginia Dept. of Culture & History, Capitol Complex, Charleston, WV. 25305.

Harpers Ferry National Historical Park, P.O. Box 65, HarpersFerry, WV. 25425.

Pocahontas County Museum, Seneca Trail, Marlinton, WV. 24954.

Oglebay Institute-Mansion Museum, (M), Oglebay Park, Wheeling, WV. 26003.

WISCONSIN

Polk County Museum, 14 Polk County Center Building, Balsam Lake, Wi. 54810.

Sauk County Historical Museum, 133-11th St., Baraboo, WI. 53913.

Bartlett Memorial Historical Museum, 2149 St. Lawrence Ave., Beloit, WI. 53511.

Jackson County Historical Society, 223 N. 4th St., Black RiverFalls, WI. 54615.

Rusk County Historical Society, Bruce, WI. 54819.

Burlington Historical Society, 432 Rose Ann Dr., Burlington, WI. 53105.

Ozaukee County Historical Society Village, P.O. Box 206, Cedarburg, WI. 53012.

Calumet County Historical Society, Inc., 1½ Miles South of Chilton on Hwy. 57, Chilton, WI. 53014.

Clear Lake Area Historical Museum, Box 242, Clear Lake, WI. 54005.

White Pillars, De Pere Historical Society, 403 N. Broadway, De Pere, WI. 54115.

Chippewa Valley Museum, Inc., (M), Box 1204, Eau Claire, WI. 54701.

Albion Academy Historical Museum, R #1, Hwy. A. #1129, Edgerton, WI. 53534.

Webster House Museum, 9 E. Rockwell, Elkhorn, WI. 53121.

Price County Historical Society, Flambeau Ave.,Fifield, WI. 54524.

Galloway House and Village, 332 14th St., Fond Du Lac, WI. 54935.

Hoard Historical Museum, (M), 409 Merchant Ave.,Fort Atkinson, WI. 53538.

Fox Lake Historical Museum, Inc., Corner of Cordelia St. & S. College Ave.,Fox Lake, WI. 53933.

Heritage Hill State Park, (M), 2640 S. Webster Ave., Green Bay, WI. 54301.

High Cliff Historical Society, P.O. Box 1, Sherwood, WI. 54169.

Hillsboro Area Historical Society, Albert Field Memorial Park, Hillsboro, WI. 54634.

Horicon Historical Society, 322 Winter St., Horicon, WI. 53032.

The Octagon House, 1004 Third St., Hudson, WI. 54016.

Rock County Historical Society, (M), P.O. Box 896, Janesville, WI. 53547.

Kenosha County Historical Society, Inc., 6300 3rd Ave., Kenosha, WI. 53140.

Kewaunee County Museum and Old Jail, Court House Square, Kewaunee, WI. 54216.

Northland Historical Society, Inc., P.O. Box 325, Lake Tomahawk, WI. 54539.

State Historical Society of Wisconsin, (M), 816 State St., Madison, WI. 53706.

North Wood County Historical Society Museum, 212 W. 3rd St., Marshfield, WI. 54449.

The Old Manse, 118 Monroe St., Mauston, WI. 53948.

Mayville Historical Society, Inc., 254 Grand Blvd., Mayville, WI. 53050.

Mazomanie Historical Society, 502 W. Hudson St., Mazomanie, WI. 53560.

McFarland Historical Society, Box 62, McFarland, WI. 53558.

Milton House Museum, (M), Box 245, Milton, WI. 53563.

Greenfield Historical Society, 3438 S. 92nd Street, Apt. 1, Milwaukee, WI. 53227.

Milwaukee County Historical Society, (M), 910 N. Third St., Milwaukee, WI. 53203.

Milwaukee Public Museum, (M), 800 W. Wells St., Milwaukee, WI. 53233.

The New Berlin Historical Society, 19765 W. National Ave., New Berlin, WI. 53151.

New Holstein Historical Society, 2025 Randolph Ave., New Holstein, WI. 53061.

Oak Creek Historical Society - Pioneer Village, 8680 Market Place, Oak Creek, WI. 53154.

Oshkosh Public Museum, (M), 1331 Algoma Blvd., Oshkosh, WI. 54901.

Racine County Historical Museum, Inc., 701 S. Main St., Racine, WI. 53403.

Ripon Historical Society, 508 Watson St., P.O. Box 274, Ripon, WI. 54971.

St. Croix Valley Historical Research Center, Chalmer Davee Library, University of Wisconsin, River Falls, WI. 54022.

Sauk Prairie Historical Society, Inc., P.O. Box 104, Sauk City, WI. 53583.

Seymour Community Museum, 421 Keune St., Seymour, WI. 54165.

Shawano County Historical Society, Inc., 1003 S. Main St., Shawano, WI. 54166.

Sheboygan County Historical Museum, 3110 Erie Ave., Sheboygan, WI. 53081.

Washburn County Historical Museum, P.O. Box 359, Shell Lake, WI. 54871.

Stoughton Historical Society, 101 S. 4th St., Stoughton, WI. 53589.

Door County Historical Museum, 18-4th and Michigan, Sturgeon Bay, WI. 54235.

Sun Prairie Historical Library & Museum, 115 E. Main St., Sun Prairie, WI. 53590.

Douglas County Historical Museum, 906 E. 2nd St., Superior, WI. 54880.

Vernon County Historical Museum, West Broadway, Viroqua, WI. 54665.

Watertown Historical Society, (M), 919 Charles St., Watertown, WI. 53094.

Waukesha County Historical Museum, (M), 101 W. Main St., Waukesha, WI. 53186.

Hutchinson House, P.O. Box 173, Waupaca, WI. 54981.

Marathon County Historical Society, 3128 10th St., Wausau, WI. 54401.

Burnett County Historical Museum, P.O. Box 108, Webster, WI. 54893.

West Allis Historical Society, 8405 W. National Ave., West Allis, WI. 53227.

Washington County Historical Library and Museum, 506 Third Ave., West Bend, WI. 53095.

Marquette County Historical Society Museum, 213 Lawrence St., Westfield, WI. 53964.

South Wood County Historical Corp., 540 Third St. South, Wisconsin Rapids, WI. 54494.

WYOMING

Wyoming State Museum, (M), Barrett Building, 22nd & Central Ave., Cheyenne, WY. 82002.

Fremont County Museums, Dubois Branch, P.O. Box 896, Dubois, WY. 82513.

Rockpile Museum, P.O. Box 922, Gillette, WY. 82716.

Sweetwater County Historical Museum, (M), P.O. Box 25, Green River, WY. 82935.

Jackson Hole Historical Museum, 101 N. Glenwood, Jackson, WY. 83001.

Laramie Plains Museum, 603 Ivinson, Laramie, WY. 82070.

Trail End Historic Center, P.O. Box 186, Sheridan, WY. 82801.

CHAPTER 26

SOURCES AND REPOSITORIES

There are many records that are stored in many places in the United States that are of great value to the genealogist but are often hard to locate. This chapter contains a list of over 2,400 of such sources. The sources are arranged in alphabetical order by subject, with the address of the location of the source.

Examine the subjects carefully. You may find some valuable sources for additional information to help in your research.

The bold type is the subject and should not be included in the address when writing to the source.

Abbott Collection
Library
Bowdoin College
Bruswick, Maine 04011

**Abbot-Downing Truck
and Body Co.** (Built Wagon)
New Hempshire Historical Society
30 Park Street
Concord, NH 03301

Abondoned Military Posts
Council on Abondoned Military
Posts-USA
Box 171
Arlington, VA 20374

Acadian
Acadian Museum
University of Moncton
Moncton Canada E1A 3E9

Acadian
Acadian Genealogy Exchange
863 Wayman Branch Road
Covington, KY 41015

Acadian
Acadian Genealogical and Historical
Association of New England
P.O. Box 668
Manchester, NH 03105

Acadian
German-Acadian Coast
Hist. & Gen. Soc.
P.O. Box 517
Destrehan, LA 70048

Acadians
St. Martin Parish Library
P.O. Box 79
Martinville, LA 70582

Acadian
French Canadian and Acadian
Genealogical Review
Box 845, Haute Ville
Quebec, G1R 4S7 Canada

Accredited, Certified & Fellow
American College of Genealogists
P.O. Box 354
Ottawa, IL 61350

Accredited Genealogists
Genealogical Department
50 East North Temple
Salt Lake City, UT 84150

Adams County Nebraska Court Records
State Historical Society
1500 R Street
Lincoln, NB 68508

Adams County, PA Cemetery Records
Adams County Historical Society
Confederate Ave.
Gettysburg, PA 17325

Adams County, PA County Records
Adams County Historical Society
Confederate Ave.
Gettysburg, PA 17325

Adams County, PA Newspaper Index
Adams County Historical Society
Confederate Ave.
Gettysburg, PA 17325

Addison County, VT County Records
Swift Research Center
1 Park Street
Middlebury, VT 05753

Addresses
National Directory of Addresses
and Telephone Numbers
240 Fencl Lane
Hillside, IL 60162

Adoptives
International Soundex Reunion
Registry
Post Office Box 2312
Carson City, NV 89701

Adoptives
American Adoption Congress
Box 23641 L'Enrant Plaza
Washington, DC 20024

Adoptives
Reunion Registry
P.O. Box 2312
Carson City, NV 89701

Adoptives
Almatch
P.O. Box 154
Washington Bridge Station
New York, NY 10033

Adoptives
ALMA International Reunion Registry
P.O. Box 154

Washington Bridge Station
New York, NY 10033

Adoptive Library
Tri-Adoption Library
7571 Westminster Ave.
Westminster, CA 92683

Adoptives
National Adoptive Search Registry
P.O. Box 2051
Great Neck, NY 11022

The Adoptions Searchbook
Triadoption Library
7571 Westminster Ave.
Westminster, CA 92683

Adorers of the Blood of Christ
Adores of the Blood of Christ
Province of Ruma
Red Bud, IL 62278

Adventist Christian Church
Library
Aurora College,
Aurora, IL 60507

**African Methodist Episcopal
  Zion Church**
Carnegie Library
Livingstone College
Salisbury, NC 28144

African Methodist Episcopal
Carnegie Library
Wilberforce University
Wilberforce, OH 45384

Agee Alabama Map Collection
Birmingham Public Library
2020 7th Ave., N.
Birmingham. AL 35203

Agricultural History
Agricultural Historical Society
University of California
Davis, CA 95616

Agricultural (Societies)
Agricultural Historical Society
Economic Research Services
U.S. Department of Agriculture
Washington, DC 20250

Air Corps Tactical School
Historical Research Center
Building 1405
Maxwell AFB, AL 36112

Alabama Baptist
Mobile College
P.O. Box 13220
Mobile, AL 36613

Alabama Census of Pensioners
Department of Arch. & Hist.
624 Washington Ave.
Montgomery, AL 36104

Alabama Cemetery Collection
Department of Arch. & Hist.

624 Washington Ave.
Montgomery, AL 36104

Alabama Cities & Towns Collection
Bowling Library
Judson College
Marion, AL 36756

1921 Alabama Confederate Census
Department of Arch. & Hist.
Montgomery, AL 36130

1907 Alabama Confederate Census
Department of Arch. & Hist.
Montgomery, AL 36130

Alabama County Books
Department of Arch. & Hist.
624 Washington AVe.
Montgomery, AL 36104

Alabama County Newspapers
Andalusia Public Library
212 S. Three Notch Street
Andalusia, AL 36420

Alabama Church Records
Department of Arch. & Hist.
624 Washington Ave.
Montgomery, AL 36104

Alabama Family Collection
Department of Arch. & Hist.
624 Washington Ave.
Montgomery, AL 36104

Alabama Genealogy Collection
Draughon Library
Auburn University
Auburn, AL 36849

Alabama Genealogy Collection
Gorgas Library
University of Alabama
University, AL 35486

Alabama Federal Land Index
Department of Arch. & Hist.
624 Washington Ave.
Montgomery, AL 36104

Alabama Historical Collection
Collier Library
University of North Alabama
Florence, AL 35630

Alabama Methodist
Birmingham-Southern College
800 Eighth Ave.
Birmingham, AL 35254

Alabama Methodist
Rush Learning Center
Birmingham-Southern College
Birmingham, AL 35204

Alabama Newspaper Index
Department of Arch. & Hist.
624 Washington Ave.
Montgomery, AL 36104

Alabama Special Collections
University of Alabama

Boldface indicates subject; DO NOT include it as part of the address.

P.O. Box 5
University, AL 35486

Alabama Supreme Court
Estate Records
Department of Arch. & Hist.
624 Washington Ave.
Montgomery, AL 36104

Alabama Territorial Records
Alabama Dept. of Arch. & Hist.
624 Washington Ave.
Montgomery, AL 36104

Alaska (History)
Western Research Library
1821 East 9th Street
The Dalles, OR 97058

Alaska Newspaper Index
State Library
State Office Building
Juneau, AK 99801

Alaska Russian Orthodox
Saint Herman's Theo. Seminary
Box 728
Kodiak, AK 99615

Alaska Territorial & Federal
Records
Alaska Historical Library
333 Willoughby Ave.
Juneau, AK 99811

Alaska Territorial and
Federal Records
Alaska State Archives
Pouch C
Juneau, AK 99801

Alaskan Territorial Government
Record Group 348
National Archives
Washington, DC 20408

Albany, NY Area Records
McKinney Library
125 Washington Ave.
Albany, NY 12210

Albany, NY City Records
City Archives and Records
402 Washington, Ave.
Albany, NY 12207

Albany County, WY Court Records
University of Wyoming
13th and Ivinson
Laramie, WY 82071

Alderman Collection (Many Families)
Dayton Public Library
215 East 3rd Street
Dayton, OH 45402

Allason Collection (Many Families)
Virginia State Library
12th and Capitol Streets
Richmond, VA 23219

Allegheny County, PA Collection
Archives of Indus. Soc.
363 Hillman
University of Pittsburgh
Pittsburgh, PA 15260

Allegheny County, PA County Records
Archives of Industrial Society
University of Pittsburgh
Pittsburgh, PA 15260

Allegheny County, PA Platt Books
Darlington Memorial Library
University of Pittsburgh
Pittsburgh, PA 16213

Allegheny Portage Railroad
Johnstown Flood Museum
304 Washington Street
Johnstown, PA 15901

Allen Collection (Many Families)
Knoxville Public Library
500 W. Church Ave.
Knoxville, TN 37902

American Antiquarian Society
American Antiquarian Society
185 Salisbury Street
Worcester, MA 01609

American Baptist Foreign Missions
Internation Ministries Library
American Baptist Churches
Valley Forge, PA 19481

American Colonization Society
Manuscripts Division
Library of Congress
Washington, DC 20540

American Evangelical Lutheran
Lutheran School of Theo.
1100 East 55th Street
Chicago, IL 60615

American Express Collection
Wells College Library
Main Street
Aurora, NY 13026

American Families Index
Illinois Room
Hayner Public Library
Alton, IL 62002

American Federation of Teachers
Library
Wayne State University
Detroit, MI 48202

American Fur Company
Bayliss Public Library
541 Library Drive
Sault Ste. Marie, MI 49783

American Gen.-Biographical Index
Godfrey Mem. Library
134 Newfield Street
Middletown, CT 06457

American Geographical Soc.
Collection
University of Wisconsin
2311 East Hartford Ave.
Milwaukee, WI 53201

American Home Missionary Society
Amistad Research Center
2601 Gentilly Blvd.
New Orleans, LA 70122

American Hospital Assoc.
American Hospital Assoc.
840 N. Lake Shore Drive
Chicago, IL 60611

American Indians
Indian Archives
State Historical Society
Oklahoma City, OK 73105

American Indian
American Indian Historical Society
1451 Masonic Ave.
San Francisco, CA 94117

American Indian Collection
National Indian Training Center
P.O. Box 66
Brigham City, UT 84302

American Indians
Record Group 75
National Archives
Washington, DC 20408

American Indians
Society of American
Indian Studies
Box 443
Hurst, TX 76053

American-Italian Archives
San Francisco Public Library
Civic Center
San Francisco, CA 94102

American Jewish Archives
American Jewish Archives
Hebrew Union College
Cincinnati, OH 45220

American Legion
American Legion
700 N. Penn. St.
Indianapolis, IN 46206

American Library Directory
R.R. Bowker Co.
1180 Ave. of the Americas
New York, NY 10036

American Lutheran
Lutheran Theo. Seminary
2375 Como Ave., W.
St. Paul, MN 55108

American Missionary Assoc.
Amistad Research Center
2601 Gentilly Blvd.

New Orleans, LA 70122

American Red Cross
National Archives & Records Service
Washington, DC

American Restoration Movement
York College
York, NE 67467

American Revolution
American Antiquarian Society
185 Salisbury Street
Worcester, MA 01609

American Shortline Railroad Assoc.
Library
Cornell University
Itaaca, NY 14850

American Sunday-School Union
Library of Phila.
Logan Square
Phila, PA 19103

American Theological Library Assoc.
Board of Microtext
P.O. Box 111
Princeton, NJ 08540

Amish
Mennonite Historical Library
Bluffton College
Bluffton, OH 45817

Amoskeag Manufacturing
Manchester Historic Assoc.
129 Amherst Street
Manchester, NH 03102

Anabaptists
Mennonite Historical Library
Bluffton College
Bluffton, OH 45817

Anglican
General Theological Seminary
175 Ninth Ave.
New York, NY 10011

Anonymous Families
Anonymous Families History Project
Clark University
Worcester, MA 01610

Apostolic Christian
Mennonite Historical Library
Bluffton College
Bluffton, OH 45817

Appalachia
Morrow Library
Marshall University
Huntington, WV 25705

Appalachia
Library
West Virginia University
Morgantown, WV 26505

Appalachian Collection

Appalachian State University
Boone, NC 28607

Archivists
Society of American Archivists
330 South Wells Street, Suite 810
Chicago, IL 60606

Archives of Virginia
Virginia State Library
12th and Capitol Streets
Richmond, VA 23219

Arizona Biographical Index
Arizona Library, Archives and
 Pulbic Records
Capitol Bldg., 3rd Floor
Phoenix, AZ 85007

Arizona Index
Mesa Public Library
464 East First Ave.
Mesa, AZ 85204

Arizona Index
Marriott Library
University of Utah
Salt Lake City, UT 84112

Arizona Newspaper Index
Arizona Library, Archives and
 Public Records
Capitol Bldg., 3rd Floor
Phoenix, AZ 85007

Arkansas Baptist
Ouachita Baptist University
410 Ouachita
Arkadelphia, AR 71923

Arkansas Biographical Index
Arkansas Historical Comm.
300 W. Markham Street
Little Rock, AR 72201

Arkansas Cemetery Index
Arkansas Historical Comm.
300 W. Markham Street
Little Rock, AR 72201

Arkansas Civil War Pensions
Arkansas Historical Comm.
300 W. Markham Street
Little Rock, AR 72201

1911 Arkansas Confederate Census
Arkansas Historical Commission
Old State House
Little Rock, AR 72201

Arkansas Federal Court Records
Library
University of Arkansas
Fayetteville, AR 72701

Arkansas Federal Court Records
Federal Archives and
 Records Center
4900 Hemphill Street
Fort Worth, TX 76115

Arkansas Forfeited Lands
Department of State Lands
State Capitol
Little Rock, AR 72201

Arkansas Gazette News
Arkansas Gazette News
P.O. Box 1821
Little Rock, AR 72203

Arkansas Masonic Records
Arkansas Historical Commission
300 W. Markham Street
Little Rock, AR 72201

Arkansas Methodist
Hendrix College
Washington and Front Streets
Conway, AR 72032

Arkansas Military Index
Arkansas Historical Commission
300 W. Markham Street
Little Rock, AR 72201

Armenian
Armenian Library and Museum
392 Concord Ave.
Belmont, MA 02178

Armenian
University of California
405 Hilgard Ave.
Los Angeles, CA 90024

Arminian-Wesleyan Holiness
Library
Asbury Theological Seminary
Wilmore, KY 40390

Armchair Research
Roots Digest
P.O. Box 2101
Glenwood Springs, CO 81602

Armchair Research
Stagecoach Library
14419 Stagecoach Road
Magnolia, TX 77355

Arnold Vital Records Collection
Knight Memorial Library
275 Elmwood Ave.
Providence, RI 02907

Ashbury Collection (Many Families)
Austin State University
Box 13055, SFA Sta.
Nacodoches, TX 75961

Ashland County, OH
 County Records
Bierce Library
University of Akron
Akron, OH 44325

Ashtabula County, OH
 County Records
Henderson Mem. Library

54 E. Jefferson Street
Jefferson, OH 44047

Ashtabula County, OH
 Vital Records
Henderson Mem. Library
54 E. Jefferson Street
Jefferson, OH 44047

Associate Presbyterian
Historical Foundation
Box 847
Montreat, NC 28757

Associated Reformed Presbyterian
McCain Library
Erskine College
Due West, SC 29639

Atlantic County, NJ
 County Records
Atlantic County Historical Society
Box 301
Somers Point, NJ 08244

Atlantic & Great Western Railway
Allegheny College
North Main Street
Meadville, PA 16335

Atlantic & St. Lawrence Railroad
Library
Bowdoin College
Brunswick, MA 04011

Atascosito District
Sam Houston Library
Farm Road 1011
Liberty, TX 77575

Auglaize County, OH
 County Records
Library
Wright State University
Dayton, OH 45431

Augustana Lutheran
Archives
Gustavus Adolphus College
St. Peter, MN 56082

1866 Austro-Prussian War Records
Library of Congress
Washington, DC 20540

—B—

Bartholomew County, IN
 County Records
Bartholomew County Historical Society
524 Third Street
Columbus, IN 47201

Baillil Collection (Many Families)
State Archives & Records Commission
Capitol Station
Baton Rouge, LA 70804

Balkan
Balkan & East European—American

Genealogical & Historical Society
4843 Mission Street
San Francisco, CA 94112

Baltic
Widener Library
Harvard University
Cambridge, MA 02138

Baltimore City Plat Maps
Peale Museum
225 Holliday Street
Baltimore, MD 21202

Baltimore City Tax Books
Records Management Division
Rm. 201, 211 E. Pleasant Street
Baltimore, MS 21202

Baltimore County Cemetery Records
Baltimore County Historical Society
9811 Van Buren Lane
Cockeysville, MD 21030

Baltimore County Alms House
Baltimore County Historical Soceity
9811 Van Buren Lane
Cockeysville, MD 21030

Baltimore Marriage Index
Hall of Records
St: John's St. & College Ave.
Annapolis, MD 21402

Baltimore & Ohio Railraod
Library
University of Maryland
College Park, MD 20742

Baltimore & Ohio Railroad
Maryland Historical Society
201 W. Monument Street
Baltimore, MD 21201

Baltimore Transit Co.
Transit Research Center
1901 Falls Road
Baltimore, MD 21218

Baptist Geographical File
American Baptist Historical Society
1106 South Goodman Street
Rochester, NY 14620

Baptist Master File Index
American Baptist Historical Society
1106 South Goodman Street
Rochester, NY 14620

Barbour Collection
Connecticut State Library
231 Capitol Ave.
Hartford, CT 06115

Barclay Collection (Many Families)
Maine Historical Society
485 Congress Street
Portland, MA 04111

Barges

Boldface indicates subject; DO NOT include it as part of the address.

Cinncinnati, Public Library
800 Vine Street
Cincinnati, OH 45202

Bartlett's Colonial Records
Rhode Island State Archives
State House
Providence, RI 02903

Basque Collection
Getchell Library
University of Nevada
Reno, NV 89507

Basque
University of Idaho
Moscow, ID 83843

Bath County, VA
 County Records
Bath County Historical Society
Box 212
Warm Springs, VA 24484

Battle Abbey (Genealogy Center)
Virginia Historical Society
428 North Blvd.
Richmond, VA 23221

Battle of New Orleans
Historic New Orleans Collection
533 Royal Street
New Orleans, LA 70130

Bayers Collection (Many Families)
State Library
State Office Bldg.
Juneau, AK 99801

Bergen County, NJ
 County Records
Johnson Public Library
P.O. Box 61
River Edge, NJ 07661

Bed & Breakfast
Visiting Friends
P.O. Box 231
Lake Jackson, TX 77566

Belgium
Belgian Researchers
8 Wycoff Ave.
Holyoke, MA 01040

Belgians
University of Wisconsin
Green Bay, WI 54302

Belgian-American Collection
Library
University of Wisconsin
Green Bay, WI 54302

Benton County, KS
 Justice of the Peace Dockets
Spencer Library
University of Kansas
Lawrence, KS 66044

Bering Sea Patrol
Coast Guard Museum
1519 Alaskan Way So.
Seattle, WA 98134

Bexar Archives
Texas History Center
P.O. Box P
Austin, TX 78712

Bible Christians
Evergreen Manor
1130 N. Westfield Blvd.
Oshkosh, WI 54901

Big Bend (Texas)
Archives of the Big Bend
Sul Ross State University
Alpine, Tx 79830

Big Bend
Big Bend National Park
Big Bend National Park, TX 79834

Big Horn Basin
Pioneer Museum
7th & Broadway
Thermopolis, WY 82443

Biographical Collection
Chattanooga Public Library
601 McCallie Ave.
Chattanooga, TN 37403

Biographical Folders
Archives
University of Pennsylvania
Philadelphia, PA 19174

Bisbee City, AZ
 Newspapers
Cooper Queen Library
Box 1857
Bisbee, AZ 85603

Blacks
Assoc. For Study of Afro-Americans
 Life and History
1401 14th Street N.W.
Washington, DC 20005

Blacks
Heartman Negro Collection
Texas Southern University
Houston, TX 77004

Blacks
Black Archives of Mid-America
1824 Paseo
Kansas City, MO 64108

Blacks
Library
East Texas State University
Commerce, TX 75428

Blacks
Black Heritage Research Center
412 Station 14 St.
Sullivan's Island, SC 29482

Blacks
Howard University
500 Howard Pl., N.W.
Washington, DC 20059

Blacks
Amistad Research Center
2601 Gentilly Blvd.
New Orleans, LA 70122

Blacks
Afro-American Historical and
  Genealogical Society
P.O. Box 13006
T Street Station
Washington, DC 20009

Blacks
Johnston Mem. Library
Virginia State College
Petersburg, VA 23803

Blacks
Library
Radford College
Radford, VA 24142

Blacks
Schomburg Center
103 West 135th Street
New York, NY 10030

Blacks
African Studies and American
  Negro Collection
Livingstone College
Salisbury, NC 28144

Black Baptist
Museum of African American Life
Bishop College
Dallas, TX 75341

Black Baptist
Baptist History Collection
Wake Forest University
Winston-Salem, NC 27109

Black Seventh-Day Adventist
Dykes Library
Oakwood College
Huntsville, AL 35896

Black Hawk War
Hoard Historical Museum
407 Merchants Ave.
Fort Atkinson, WI 53538

Black Hawk War
State Historical Library
Old State Capitol
Springfield, IL 62706

Black Hawk War
Augustana College
Rock Island, IL 61201

Black Hills
Devereaux Library

South Dakota School of Mines
Rapid City, SD 57701

Black Hills
South Dakota School of Mines
Rapid City, SD 57701

Blake Collection (Many Families)
Austin State University
Box 13055, SFA Station
Nacodoches, TX 75961

Bledsoe-Kelly Collection (Many Families)
Samford University
800 Lakshore Drive
Birmingham AL 35209

Blewett Collection (Many Families)
Lowndes County Library System
314 North 7th Street
Columbus, MS 39701

Blind
Genealogical Center Library
15 Dunwoody Park Road, Suite 130
Atlanta, GA 30336

Boltwood Collection
Jones Library
43 Amity Street
Amherst, MA 01002

Bonded Genealogists
Association of
Professional Genealogy
P.O. Box 11601
Salt Lake City, UT 84147

Books in Print
Genealogical Books in Print
6818 Lois Drive
Springfield, VA 22150

Book Rentals
Stagecoach Library
14419 Stagecoach Road
Magnolia, TX 77355

Book Search
Continental Book Search
GPO Box 2080
New York, NY 10116

Book Sales
Stagecoach Library
14419 Stagecoach Road
Magnolia, TX 77355

Borel Collection (Many Families)
Stanford University Libraries
Stanford University
Stanford, CA 94305

Boston City Records
Boston Public Library
Copley Square
Boston, MA 02117

Boston China Trade
Museum of the American-China Trade

Boldface indicates subject; **DO NOT** include it as part of the address.

215 Adams Street
Milton, MA 02186

Bohemians
University of Nebraska
303 Love Library
Lincoln, NE 68588

Brethren
Fellowship of Brethren
 Genealogists
518 Miller Drive
Elgin, IL 60120

Brethren in Christ
Mennonite Historical Library
Bluffton College
Bluffton, OH 45817

Brewer Collection (Many Families)
Austin State University
Box 13055, SFA Station
Nacodoches, TX 75961

British
International Society for British
 Genealogy and Family History
P.O. Box 20425
Cleveland, OH 44120

British Regimental Histories
Georgetown University
37 & O Streets, N.W.
Washington, DC 20057

British West Indies
Island Resources Foundation
Post Office 4187
St. Thomas, VI 00801

Bronx County, NY
 County Records
Bronx County Historical Society
3266 Bainbridge Ave.
New York, NY 10467

Brooklyn, NY City Records
St. Francis College
180 Remsen Street
Brooklyn, NY 11201

Brooklyn Collection
Brooklyn Public Library
Grand Army Plaza
Brooklyn, NY 11238

Broome County Medical Society
University of New York
Vestal Parkway East
Binghamton, NY 13901

Brotherhood of Locomotive Firemen
Debs Museum and Library
451 North 8th Street
Terra Haute, IN 47808

Brough Collection (Many Families)
Library
University of Arkansas
Fayetteville, AR 72701

Brown County, WI
 County Records
Area Research Center
University of Wisconsin
Green Gay, WI 54302

Browne Collection (Many Families)
Department Archives and History
330 Capitol Ave., S.E.
Atlanta, GA 30334

Buffalo, NY Area Death Records
Buffalo & Erie County Historical Society
25 Nottingham Court
Buffalo, NY 14216

Buffalo, NY Area Newspaper Index
Buffalo & Erie County Historical Society
25 Nottingham Court
Buffalo, NY 14216

Bureau of the Census
Bureau of the Census
Personal Census Service Branch
Pittsburg, KS 66762

Bureau of Customs
Federal Archives & Record Center
1000 Commodore Drive
San Bruno, CA 94066

Bureau of Indian Affairs
Federal Archives and Records Center
4900 Hemphill Street
Fort Worth, TX 76115

Bureau of Mines Publications
Library
University of Texas
El Paso, TX 79968

Burlington County, NJ
 County Records
Burlington County Historical Society
457 High Street
Burlington, NJ 08016

Burlington County, NJ
 County Records
Mount Holly Library
307 High Street
Mount Holly, NJ 08060

Burlington Railroad
Newberry Library
60 West Walton Street
Chicago, IL 60610

Burton Historical Collection
Detroit Public Library
5201 Woodward Ave.
Detroit, MI 48202

Business
Research Library
Route 20
Sturbridge, MA 01566

Business

Conn. Valley Hist. Museum
Wm. Pynchon Mem. Bldg.
Springfield, MA 01103

Business
Industrial Archives
320 Washington Street
North Easton, MA 02356

Business History
Center For Bus. Hist. Studies
Tulane University
New Orleans, LA 70118

Butte County, CA
Library
California State University
Chico, CA 95929

Byelorussian
Cleveland Public Library
325 Superior Ave.
Cleveland, OH 44114

Byelorussia
Pilsudski Institute
381 Park Ave. So.
New York, NY 10016

Byelorussian
Byelorussian-American Assoc.
166-34 Gothic Drive
Jamaica, NY 11432

—C—

Cabarrus County, NC Vital Records
Cannon Mem. Library
27 Union Street, N.
Concord, NC 28025

Caddo Cemetery Collection
Shreve Memorial Library
400 Edwards Street
Shreveport, LA 71120

Camp Fire Club
Camp Fire Club of America
230 Camp Fire Road
Chappaqua, NY 10514

Carpatho-Rusyn
Carpatho-Rusyn Research Center
355 Delano Place
Fairview, NJ 07022

Chicago, Burlington, & Quincy Railroad
Nebraska State Historical Society
15 & R Streets
Lincoln, NE 68508

Cajuns
Assoc. Canado-American
52 Concord Street
Manchester, NH 03101

California Terr. and Dist. Courts
Federal Arch. & Records Center
24000 Avila Road
Laguna Niguel, CA 92677

Caligraphy
Hunt Manufacturing Co.
Statesville, NC 28677

Calligraphy Kits
Pentalic Corporation
132 West 22nd Street
New York, NY 10011

Calumet Region
Calumet Region Archives
3400 Broadway
Gary, IN 46408

Camden County, NJ County Records
Camden County Historical Society
Park Ave. & Euclid Ave.
Camden, NJ 08103

Cameron County, PA Cemetery Records
Cameron County Public Library
1 E. 4th St.
Emporium, PA 15834

Cameron County TX County Records
Library
Pan American University
Edinburg, TX 78539

Cameron Collection
Princeton Historial Society
158 Nassau Street
Princeton, NJ 08540

Camp Lewis
Tacoma Public Library
1102 Tacoma Ave., So.
Tacoma, WA 98402

Canada
American-Canadian Gen. Society
P.O. Box 668
Manchester, NH 03105

Canada
Lost in Canada?
1020 Central Ave.
Sparta, WI 54656

Canadian
Canadian Genealogist
172 King Henry's Blvd.
Aigincourt, Ont. M1T 2V6
Canada

Canadian-American Assoc.
Canadian-American Assoc.
52 Concord Street
Manchester, NH 03101

Canadian Indians
Indian & Inuit Affairs Program
17 Fl., Les Terrasses de la Chaudiere
Ottawa, Ontario, Canada K1A 0H4

Canadian Postal Codes
Mail Collection & Delivery Branch
Postal Coding Division
Canada Post
Ottawa, Ontario K1A 0B1

Boldface indicates subject; DO NOT include it as part of the address.

Canada

Canals
Transportation Library
University of Michigan
Ann Arbor, MI 48104

Canals
American Antiquarian Society
185 Salisbury Street
Worcester, MA 01609

Canals
Harvard University Library
Soldiers Field
Boston, MA 02163

Canals
Canal Society of New Jersey
P.O. Box 737
Morristown, NJ 07960

Canals
Canal Museum
200 S. Delaware Drive
Easton, PA 18042

Canals
Wyoming Historical Society
49 South Franklin Street
Wilkes-Barre, PA 18701

Canals
Canal Museum
315 East Water Street
Syracuse, NY 13202

Canals
American Canal Center
Glen Echo, MD 20768

Canals
American Canal & Transportation Center
809 Rathton Road
York, PA 17403

Canals
American Canal Society
P.O. Box 842
Shepherdstown, WV 25443

Canal Boat Captains
Industrial & Social Branch
National Archives & Records Service
Washington, DC 20408

Cape Ann
Annisquam Historical Society
Walnut Street Annisquam
Gloucester, MA 01930

Cape Cod
Falmouth Historical Society
Palmer Ave. & The Village Green
Falmouth, MA 02541

Cape Cod
Sturgis Library
Route 6A
Barnstable, MA 02630

Caribbean
Caribbean Library
P.O. Box 21927, Univ. Sta.
San Juan, PR 00931

Caribbean
Yale University Library
New Haven, CT 06520

Caribbean Islands
Bureau of Libraries & Museums
P.O. Box 390
Charlotte Amalie
St. Thomas, VI 00801

Carlton County, MN County Records
Carlton County Historical Society
Carlton, MN 55718

Catholic Americana
St. Francis Seminary
3257 S. Lake Drive
Milwaukee, WI 53207

Catholic History
American Catholic Hist. Society
St. Charles Borromeo Seminary
Philadelphia, PA 19151

Catskill-Canajoharie Railroad
Durham Center Museum
Route 145
East Durham, NY 12423

Catskill Mountains
Green County Historical Society
R.D.
Coxsackie, NY 12051

Cattlemen
Colorado Historical Society
1300 Broadway
Denver, CO 80203

Cayuga County, NY County Records
Cayuga County Historical
  Research Center
County Office Bldg.
Auburn, NY 13021

C.B. & Q. Railroad
Nebraska State Historical Society
15 & R Streets
Lincoln, NE 68508

Celtic Collection
College of St. Thomas
2115 Summit
St. Paul MN 55105

Cemeteries
Genealogical Department
50 East North Temple
Salt Lake City, UT 84150

Cemeteries
American Cemetery Association
5201 Leesburg Pike
Falls Church, VA 22041

Cemeteries
American Cemetery Assoc.
250 East Town Street
Columbus, OH 43215

Cemeteries
Daughters of the American Revolution
1776 D Street, N.W.
Washington, DC 20006

Nebraska Cemetery Records
(Dodge & Washington Counties)
Keene Mem. Library
1030 N. Broad Street
Fremont, NE 68025

Census Microfilm Rental Program
Census Microfilm Rental Program
P.O. Box 2940
Hyattsville, MD 20784

Central IL, County Records
Milner Library
Illinois State University
Normal, IL 61761

Central IL, County Records
Library
Sangamon State University
Springfield, IL 62708

Central Pacific
Library
Stanford University
Stanford, CA 94305

Certificates in Calligraphy
Unicorn Galleries
P.O. Box 22G
Elm Grove, WI 53122

Central-Eastern NM,
 Cemetery Collection
Clovis Public Library
115 W. 8th
Clovis, NM 88101

Certified Genealogists
Board of Certification
 of Genealogists
P.O. Box 19165
Washington, DC 20036

Chambers County, TX County Records
Sam Houston Library
Farm Road 1011
Liberty, TX 77575

Champaign County, OH County Records
Library
Wright State University
Dayton, OH 45431

Champlain Canal
Saratoga County Historian's Office
31 Woodlawn Ave.
Saratoga Springs, NY 12866

Champlain Valley

State University of New York
153 Hawkins Hall
Plattsburgh, NY 12901

Charlotte County, VA County Records
Virginia Historical Society
428 North Blvd.
Richmond, VA 23221

Chautauquas
Special Collections
University of Iowa
Iowa City, IA 52242

Chautauqua County, NY County Records
Patterson Library
40 South Portage Street
Westfield, NY 14787

Chelsea Cemetery File
McKune Mem. Library
221 South Main
Chelsea, MI 48118

Cherokee
Research Division
125 E. Queen Street
Pendleton, SC 29670

Cherokee
Cherokee National Museum
P.O. Box 515
Tahlequah, OK 74464

Cherokee County, IA County Records
Cherokee County Historical Society
Main Street
Cherokee, IA 51012

Cherokee Strip
Cherokee Strip Living Museum
P.O. Box 230
Arkansas City, KS 67005

Chesaning Cemetery Records
Chesaning Public Library
227 E. Broad Street
Chesaning, MI 48616

Chesapeake Bay
Maryland Historical Society
201 W. Monument Street
Baltimore, MD 21201

Chesapeake Bay
Library
University of Maryland
College Park, MD 20742

Chesapeake Bay
Archives & Museum Department
University of Maryland
College Park, MD 20742

Chesapeake & Delaware Canal
Historical Society of Delaware
505 Market Street Mall
Wilmington, DE 19801

Chesapeake & Ohio Canal

Boldface indicates subject; DO NOT include it as part of the address.

Record Group 79
National Archives
Washington, DC 20408

Chicago
University of Chicago
1100 E. 57th Street
Chicago, IL 60637

Chicago Ancestor File
Chicago Ancestor File
8851 N. Lavergne
Skokie, IL 60077

Chicago & North Western Railroad
Mid-Continent Railway Historical Society
Mid-Continent Railway Museum
North Freedon, WI 53951

Chikasaw Guard
Memphis Public Library
1850 Memphis Ave.
Memphis, TN 38104

China Trade
Stonington Historical Society
Whitehall Ave.
Stonington, CT 06378

Chinese-Americans
Libraries
University of Washington
Seattle, WA 98195

Chinese Historical Society
San Francisco Public Library
Civic Center
San Francisco, CA 94102

Chinese in Hawaii
Hawaii Chinese Hist. Center
Rm. 410, 111 N. King Street
Honolulu, HI 96817

Chippewa Valley
Chippewa Valley Museum
Box 1204
Eau Clair, WI 54701

Chisholm Trail
Chisholm Trail Museum
605 Zellers Ave.
Kingfisher, OK 73750

Christian Church
Lynchburg College
Lynchburg, VA 24501

Christian Reformed
Dordt College
498 4th Ave. N.E.
Sioux Center, IA 51250

Christ's Church
Midwest Christian College
6600 N. Kelley Ave.
Oklahoma City, OK 73111

Christianburg Institute
Library
Radford College

Radford, VA 24142

Church Books
Congregational Library
14 Beacon Street
Boston, MS 02106

Church of the Brethren
Mack Library
Bridgewater College
Bridgewater, VA 22812

Church of the Brethren
Zug Mem. Library
Elizabethtown College
Elizabethtown, PA 17022

Church of the Brethren
Manchester College
North Manchester, IN 46962

Church of Christ
Disciples of Christ
  Historical Society
1101 19th Ave. So.
Nashville, TN 37212

Church of God
Azusa Pacific College
Citrus & Alosta
Azusa, CA 91702

Church of the New Jerusalem
New Church Library
5008 Whetsel Ave.
Cincinnati, OH 45227

Church of the New Jerusalem
Archives
2815 Huntingdon Pike
Bryn Athyn, PA 19009

Churches
Institute For Study of
  American Religion
Box 1311
Evanston, IL 60201

Circus
Circus Worlds Museum
415 Lynn Street
Baraboo, WI 53913

Circus Performers
Milner Library
Illinois State University
Normal, IL 61761

Cities
National League of Cities
1301 Pewnnsylvania Ave., N.W.
Washington, DC 20006

Cities
National Municipal League
47 East 68th Street
New York, NY 10021

City Directories
Stack & Reader Division

Library of Congress
Washington, DC 20540

City Ward Maps
Geogra   ıy & Map Division
Library of Congress
Washington, DC 20540

Civil War
Department of Archives & History
Capitol Complex
Charleston, WV 25305

Civil War
University of Chicago
1100 E. 57th Street
Chicago, IL 60637

Civil War
Cooper Library
University of South Carolina
Columbia, SC 29208

Civil War
Carnegie Library
Lincoln Memorial University
Harrogate, TN 37752

Civil War
Southern College
P.O. Box 629
Collegedale, TN 37315

Civil War
University of Tennessee
Vine Street
Chattanooga, TN 37402

Civil War
Sam Houston State University
P.O. Box 2179
Huntsville, TX 77340

Civil War
Alexandria Library
220 N. Washington Street
Alexandria, VA 22314

Civil War
Library
Stanford University
Stanford, CA 94305

Civil War
Huntington Library
1151 Oxford Road
San Marino, CA 91108

Civil War
Library of Congress
Washington, DC 20540

Civil War Collection
Chicago Public Library
78 E. Washington Street
Chicago, IL 60602

Civil War Collection
University of Tennessee
Chattanooga, TN 37401

Civil War Medical Records
Otis Historical Archives
Alaska Ave. & 14th St., N.W.
Washington, DC 20306

Civil War Photograph Collection
Prints & Photographs Division
Library of Congress
Washington, DC 20540

Civil War Regimental Histories
Pattee Library
Pennsylvania State University
University Park, PA 16802

Civil War Troop Lists
Records Group 110
National Archives
Washington, DC 20408

Civilian Conservation Corps
National Assoc. Civilian
  Conservation Corps
7245 Arlington Blvd., #318
Falls Chruch, VA 22042

Civilian Conservation Corps
Library
Bandelier National Monument
Los Alamos, NM 87544

Civilian Conservation Corps
National Forests in North Carolina
50 S. French Broad Ave.
Asheville, NC 28802

Civilian Conservation Corps
Green Mountain National Forest
P.O. Box 519
Rutland, VT 05701

Civilian Conservation Corps
Center for Research Libraries
5721 Cottage Grove
Chicago, IL 60637

Civilian Conservation Corps
Federal Archives & Records Center
Bldg. 48, Denver Federal Center
Denver, CO 80225

Civilian Conservation Corps
Records and Library Section
4200 Smith School Road
Austin, TX 78744

**Civilian Conservation Corpse-
  Indian Division**
Record Group 75
National Archives
Washington, DC 20408

Civilian Personnel Records
Civilian Personnel Records
111 Winnebago Street
St. Louis, MO

Clark Collection (Many Families)
Princeton Historical Society
158 Nassau Street

Boldface indicates subject; **DO NOT** include it as part of the address.

Princeton, NJ 08540

Clark Collection (Many Families)
Soceity of Cincinnati
2118 Mass. Ave. N.W.
Washington, DC 20008

Clark County, OH County Records
Library
Wright State University
Dayton, OH 45431

Clark County, WA County Records
Clark Co' nty Hist. Museum
1511 Main Street
Vancouver, WA 98660

Class Collection (Many Families)
Museum of Western Colorado
Fourth & Ute
Grand Junction, CO 81501

Clawson Collection (Many Families)
Marriott Library
University of Utah
Salt Lake City, UT 84112

Clay County, MO County Records
Library and Archives
14 North Main
Liberty, MO 64068

Cleveland Archives
Cleveland Public Library
601 Lakeside Ave., N.E.
Cleveland, OH 44114

Cleveland Newspaper Obituary Index
Cleveland Public Library
325 Superior Ave.
Cleveland, OH 44114

Cleveland, OH Obituary File
Library
1801 Superior Ave.
Cleveland, OH 44114

Clipper Ships
Ludlow Mem. Library
P.O. Box 99346
San Francisco, CA 94109

Coast Guard
Oral Hist. Office
U.S. Naval Institute
Annapolis, MD 21402

Coats of Arms
Vernon R. Nickerson
P.O. Box 1776
N. Chattham, MA 02650

Cobb Memorial Archives
Chambers County Library
Highway 29
Shawmut, AL 36876

Cold Spring Whaling Co.
Whaling Museum Society

Main Street
Cold Spring Harbor, NY 11724

Cole Collection (Many Families)
Folgler Library
University of Maine
Orono, ME 04473

Coles County, IL Cemetery Index
Coles County Historical Society
Court House
Charleston IL 61920

Collateral Cousins or Relatives
Computerized Genealogy Library
P.O. Box 27193
Salt Lake City, UT 84127

Collins Company
Canton Historical Society
11 Front Street
Collinsville, CT 06022

Colonial Dames
Colonial Dames of America
2715 Q Street, N.W.
Washington, DC 20036

Colonial Index
Massachusetts State Archives
State House
Boston, MA 02133

Colonial Library
American Antiquarian Society
185 Salisbury Street
Worcester, MA 01609

Colonial Maps
Rare Book Division
New York Public Library
New York, NY 10018

Colonial New Jersey
New Jersey Historical Society
230 Broadway
Newark, NJ 07104

Colonial Origins Collection
Calvin College
3207 Burton Street, S.E.
Grand Rapids, MI 49506

Colonial Philadelphia History
Library Company of Philadelphia
1314 Locust Street
Philadelphia, PA 19107

Colonial Records
Records and Archives Center
71 South Fruit Street
Concord, NH 03301

Colonial Swiss
The Lost Palatine Magazine
Rt. 1, Box 1160
Estero. FL 33928

Colonial Virginia
Virginia Historical Society

428 North Blvd.
Richmond, VA 23221

Colonial Virginia
Swem Library
College of William and Mary
Williamsburg, VA 23185

Colonial Virginia
Colonial Williamsburg
Francis and South Henry Streets
Williamsburg, VA 23185

Colorado
Western Historical Collections
University of Colorado
Boulder, CO 80302

Colorado Biographical File
State Historical Society
200 14th Ave.
Denver, CO 80203

Colorado Farmers Union
Western Historical Collection
University of Colorado
Boulder, CO 80302

**Colorado Justice of the
  Peace Records**
State Archives & Public Records
1313 Sherman Street
Denver, CO 80210

Colorado Mines
Bartle Library
State University of New York
Binghamton, NY 13901

Colorado Pioneer Society
Denver Public Library
1357 Broadway
Denver, CO 80203

Colorado Supreme Court Records
State Archives & Public Records
1313 Sherman Street
Denver, CO 80210

Columbia River Basin
Library
Washington State University
Pullman, WA 99163

Columbiana County, OH Probate Packets
William McIntosh
P.O. Box 98
Clinton, OH 44216

Commonwealth of Virginia
Swem Library
College of William & Mary
Williamsburg, VA 23185

Compiled Military Service Records
Record Group 94
National Archives
Washington, DC 20408

Complaints or Misunderstandings

Association of
Professional Genealogy
P.O. Box 11601
Salt Lake City, UT 84147

**Complete Handbook of Personal
  Computer Communications**
St. Martin's Press
175 Fifth Avenue
New York, NY 10010

Computer Search For Family Connections
Computerized Genealogy Library
P.O. Box 27193
Salt Lake City, UT 84127

Computer Supplies & Accessories
Misco
404 Timber Lane
Marlboro, NJ 07746

Computer Time Sharing
Genealogical Time Sharing
1822 Harding Ave.
Abington, PA 19001

Computers
Genealogical Computing
5102 Pommeroy Drive
Fairfax, VA 22032

Confederate
Confederate Descendants Society
P.O. Box 233
Athens, Ga 35611

Confederate
McCain Graduate Library
University of Southern Mississippi
Hattiesburg, MS 39401

Confederate
Confederate Descendants Society
P.O. Box 233
Athens, GA 35611

Confederate Bureau at Vicksburg
Museum Library
Old Court House
Vicksburg, MS 39180

Confederate Cemetery Index
Museum Library
Old Court House
Vicksburg, MS 39180

Confederate Civil War Papers
Brown University
Annmary Brown Mem.
Providence, RI 02912

Confederate Collection
Mobile City Museum
355 Government Street
Mobile, AL 36602

Confederate Customs Service
Civil Archives Division
National Archives & Records Service

Boldface indicates subject; **DO NOT** include it as part of the address.

Washington, DC 20408

Confederate Historical Assoc.
Memphis State University
Southern & Patterson
Memphis, TN 38152

Confederate Library
Museum of the Confederacy
1201 E. Clay Street
Richmond, VA 23219

Confederate Prison
Fort Delaware Museum
Pea Patch Island
Delaware City, DE 19803

Confederate Prisoners in Federal Prisons
Record Group 249
National Archives
Washington, DC 20408

Confederate Records
Record Group 109
National Archives
Washington, DC 20408

Confederate Records
Record Group 365
National Archives
Washington, DC 20408

Confederate States of America Collection
Rare Book & Special Collections Division
Library of Congress
Washington, DC 20540

Confederate States Muster Rolls
Charleston Library Society
164 King Street
Charleston, SC 29401

Confederate Veteran Magazine Index
Memphis Public Library
1850 Memphis Ave.
Memphis, TN 38104

Congregational Christian
Connecticut Conference
125 Sherman Street
Hartford, CT 06105

Congregational Society
Gloversville Free Library
58 East Fulton Street
Gloversville, NY 12078

Congress of Industrial Organizations
Library
Catholic University
Washington, DC 20064

Congressional Information Service Inc.
Congressional Information Service Inc.
4520 East West Highway, Suite 800
Washington, DC 20014

Connecticut County Atlases
Connecticut State Library
231 Capitol Avenue
Hartford, CT 06115

Connecticut Episcopal
Episcopal Diocese
1335 Asylum Ave.
Hartford, CT 06105

Connecticut Family File
Connecticut Historical Society
1 Elizabeth Street
Hartford, CT 06105

Connecticut Farms Area
Caldwell Parsonage Museum
909 Caldwell Ave.
Union, NJ 07083

Connecticut Home Guard
Salmon Brook Historical Society
208 Salmon Brook Street
Granby, CT 06035

Connecticut Land Co.
Geauga County Historical Society
Box 153
Burton, OH 44021

Connecticut Methodist
Wesleyan University
Church Street
Middletown, CT 06457

Connecticut Surname Catalog
New Haven Colony Historical Society
114 Whitney Avenue
New Haven, CT 06510

Connecticut Valley
Historic Deerfield
Box 53
Deerfield, MA 01342

Consular Posts Vital Records
Record Group 84
National Archives
Washington, DC 20408

Convillon Collection (Many Families)
State Archives & Records Commission
Capitol Station
Baton, Rouge, LA 70804

Cook Collection (Many Families)
Public Archives
Iolani Palace Grounds
Honolulu, HI 96813

Cook County, IL Property Records
Chicago Title & Trust
111 W. Washington
Chicago, IL 60602

Copper Country Collection
Library
Michigan Tech. University
Houghton, MI 49931

Copyright
Copyright Clearence Center
P.O. Box 8891
Boston, MA 02650

Copyright
Copyright Office
Library of Congress
Washington, DC 20540

Cornell Collection (Many Families)
Los Angeles Museum of Natural History
900 Exposition Blvd.
Los Angeles, CA 90007

Cornish
Newberry Library
60 W. Walton Street
Chicago, IL 60610

Cornstalk Militia
Military Records & Research Library
Boone National Guard Center
Frankfort, KY 40601

Cotton Mills
Industrial University
Seventh Street
Bloomington, IN 47401

Cottonwood County, MN County Records
Cottonwood County Historical Society
812 Fourth Ave.
Windom, MN 56101

Coshocton County, OH County Records
Bierce Library
University of Akron
Akron, Oh 44325

Cossacks
University of Wisconsin
728 State Street
Madison, WI 53706

Counties
National Assoc. of Counties
1735 New York Ave., N.W.
Washington, DC 20006

County Boundary Data File
Newberry Library
60 W. Walton Street
Chicago, IL 60610

County Histories
American Antiquarian Society
185 Salisbury Street
Worcester, MA 01609

County Histories or 'Mug' Books
Photoduplication Service
Library of Congress
Washington, DC 20540

County Maps
Geography & Map Division
Library of Congress
Alexandria, VA 22304

County Records
Stagecoach Library
14419 Stagecoach Road
Magnolia, TX 77355

Court-Martial Records
Record Group 153
National Archives
Washington, DC 20408

Courts-Martial Records
Record Group 125
National Archives
Washington, DC 20408

Cowlitz, Chehalis, & Cascade Railroad
Lewis County Historical Society
78 N.E. Washington Ave.
Chehalis, WA 98532

Coy CA-Place-Name Catalog
Los Angeles Museum of Natural History
900 Exposition Blvd.
Los Angeles, CA 90007

Crane Collection
Hardin-Simmons University
Abilene, TX 79601

Crawford County, OH Court Records
O. G. S. Library
419 West Third Street
Mansfield, OH 44906

Creek Indian
Creek Indian Museum
Okmulgee, OK 74447

Croatia
Stanford University Libraries
Stanford, CA 94305

Croation
Croation-Slovenian-Serbian
  Genealogical Society
936 Industrial Avenue
Palo Alto, CA 94070

Crockett Collection (Many Families)
Austin State University
Box 13055, SFA Sta.
Nacodoches, TX 75961

Croton Aqueduct
Jervis Public Library
613 N. Washington Street
Rome, NY 13440

CSA Collection
Mobile City Museum
355 Government Street
Mobile, AL 36602

Cumberland County, PA County Records
Hamilton Library Assoc.
21 N. Pitt Street
Carlisle, PA 17013

Cumberland County, PA Court Records

Boldface indicates subject; DO NOT include it as part of the address.

Historical Society
219 S. Front Street
Harrisburg, PA 17104

Cumberland Presbyterian
Bethel College
Cherry Ave.
McKenzie, TN 38201

Cumberland Presbyterian
Historical Foundation
Box 847
Montreat, NC 28757

Cumberland Presbyterian
Memphis Theological Seminary
168 East Parkway South
Memphis, TN 38104

Cumberland Presbyterian Church
Agnes Scott College
E. College Ave.
Decatur, GA 30030

Cumberland Presbyterian Church
Spencer Library
University of Kansas
Lawrence, KS 66044

Cumberland Presbyterian Church
Library
University of Arkansas
Fayetteville, AR 72701

Cumberland Presbyterian
Library
Bethel College
McKenzie, TN 38201

Curious Counsin
Computerized Genealogy Library
P.O. Box 27193
Salt Lake City, UT 84127

Custom Family Trees
Calli-Crafts
1701 N. Spencer Ave.
Indianapolis, IN 46218

Custom's House Books
Kennebunkport Historical Society
North Street
Kennebunkport, ME 04046

Customs House Books
Deer Isle Stonington
  Historical Society
Deer Isle, ME 04627

Custom House Records
Dukes County Historical Society
School & Cooke Streets
Edgartown, MA 02539

Customs Records
Essex Institute
132 Essex Street
Salem, MA 01970

Cuyahoga County, OH Cemetery Index

Cleveland Public Library
325 Superior Ave.
Cleveland, OH 44114

Czechs
University of Nebraska
303 Love Library
Lincoln, NE 68588

Czech
Stanford University Libraries
Stanford, CA 94305

Czechosolvakia
Pilsudski Institute
381 Park Ave., So.
New York, NY 10016

Czechoslovakian
Czechoslovak Society of America
2138 South 61st Street
Cicero, IL 60650

Czech-Jewish
Society for the History of
  Czechoslovak Jews
25 Mayhew Ave.
Larchmont, NY 10538

—D—

Dakota Newspaper Index
Fritz Library
University of North Dakota
Grand Forks, ND 58201

Danbury City Records
West Connecticut State College
181 White Street
Danbury, CT 06810

Danes
Dana-Life Library
Dana College
Blair, NE 68008

Danish
Danish Brotherhood in America
3717 Harney Street
Omaha, NE 68171

Danish Lutheran
Lutheran School of Theo.
1100 East 55th Street
Chicago, IL 60615

Darke County, OH County Records
Library
Wright State University
Dayton, OH 45431

Darlington Collection (Many Families)
University of Pittsburgh
601 Cathedral of Learning
Pittsburgh, PA 15260

Data Base
Computerized Genealogical Library
P.O. Box 27193
Salt Lake City, UT 84127

Databases Worldwide
Inc. Information Service
38 Commercial Wharf
Boston, MA 02110

DAR Library
Daughters of the American Revolution
1776 D Street, N.W.
Washington, DC 20006

Daughters of Charity
East Central Province
9400 New Harmony Road
Evansville, IN 47712

Daughters of Hawaii
Daughters of Hawaii
2913 Pali Highway
Honolulu, HI 96817

Daughters of Utah Pioneers
300 North Main Street
Salt Lake City, UT 84103

Davenport, IA Historical File
Davenport Museum
1717 West 12th Street
Davenport, IA 52804

Dean Collection (Many Families)
Museum of Western Colorado
Fourth and Ute
Grand Junction, CO 81501

Dearborn Files
Henry Ford Centennial Library
16301 Michigan Avenue
Dearborn, MI 48126

Deep South
University of Alabama
P.O. Box CS
University, AL 35486

Deists
Unitarian & Universalist
 Genealogical Society
10605 Lakespring Way
Cockeysville, MD 21030

Delaware Cemetery Index
Historical Society of Delaware
Market Street
Wilmington, DE 19801

Delaware Colonial Records
Vault
Hall of Records
Dover, DE 19901

Delaware County, IN County Records
Library
Ball State University
Muncie, IN 47306

Delaware & Hudson Canal
Library Bldg.
138 Pike Street
Port Jervis, NY 12771

Delaware & Hudson Canal
Ellenville Public Library
126 Canal Street
Ellenville, NY 12428

Delaware Valley
Philadelphia Maritime Museum
321 Chestnut Street
Philadelphia, PA 19106

Delaware Valley
Gloucester County Historical Society
17 Hunter Street
Woodbury, NJ 08096

Delaware Vital Records
Historical and Cultural Affairs
Hall of Records
Dover, DE 19901

Dallas City Records
Secretary
200 City Hall
Dallas, TX 75201

Delta Review Index
Memphis Public Library
1850 Memphis Ave.
Memphis, TN 38104

Dent Collection (Many Families)
Troy State University
Troy, AL 36081

Dental
School of Dental Medicine
University of Pennsylvania
Philadelphia, PA 19104

Deserts
Desert Research Institute
Stead Campus
Reno, NV 89507

Detroit United Railway
University of Michigan
312 Undergraduate Library Bldg.
Ann Arbor, MI 48109

Detroit Medical College
Library
Wayne State University
Detroit, MI 48202

Deutscher Pioneer Index
St. Louis Public Library
1301 Olive Street
St. Louis, MO 63103

Devalle Spanish Collection
Los Angeles County Museum
 of Natural History
900 Expositon Blvd.
Los Angeles, CA 90007

Directory of Online Databases
Cuadra Assoc., Inc.
2001 Wilshire Blvd., Suite 305
Santa Monica, CA 90403

Boldface indicates subject; DO NOT include it as part of the address.

Disciples of Christ
Disciples of Christ Hist. Society
1101 19th Ave., So.
Nashville, TN 37212

Disciples of Christ
Emmanuel School of Religion
Rte. 6, Box 500
Johnson City, TN 37601

Dissertation Abstracts
University Microfilms International
300 North Zeeb Road
Ann Arbor, MI 48106

District of Columbia
Record Group 351
National Archives
Washington, DC 20408

District of Columbia Court Records
Record Group 21
National Archives
Washington, DC 20408

**Documents of the First
  Fourteen Congresses**
Rare Book & Special Collections
  Division
Library of Congress
Washington, DC 20540

Document or Photo Enhancement
Central Research of Utah
60 South 500 West
Bountiful, UT 84010

Document Preservation
New England Document
  Conservation Center
800 Massachusetts Ave.
North Andover, MA 01845

Dornan Collection (Many Families)
Library
Rutgers University
New Brunswick, NJ 08901

Draper Collection (Many Families)
State Historical Society
816 State Street
Madison, WI 53706

Dresbach Collection (Many Families)
Library
University of Arkansas
Fayetteville, AR 72701

Driscoll Piracy Collection
Wichita Public Library
223 South Main
Wichita, KS 67202

Duke Collection
University of Oklahoma
401 West Brooks
Norman, OK 73069

Dunbar Travel Collection

Museum of Science & Industry
57th Street & Lake Shore Drive
Chicago, IL 60637

Durrett Collection (Many Families)
Regenstein Library
100 East 57th Street
Chicago, IL 60637

Dutch
Holland Society of New York
122 East 58th Street
New York, NY 10022

Dutch
Colonial Origins Collection
3207 Burton Street, S.E.
Grand Rapids, MI 49506

Dutch
Dutch Heritage Collection
101 7th Street, S.W.
Orange City, IA 51041

Dutch
Learning Resource Center
Central College
Pella, IA 50219

Dutch
Dordt College
498 4th Ave., N.E.
Sioux Center, IA 51250

Dutch Collection
Herrick Public Library
300 River Avenue
Holland, MI 49423

Dutch East India Co.
Indiana University
Seventh Street
Bloomington, IN 47401

Dutch Names Index
New York Genealogy and
  Biographical Society
122 East 58th Street
New York, NY 10022

Dutch Reformed
Collegiate Reformed Dutch Church
45 John Street
New York, NY 10038

Dutch Remonstrant Movement
Point Loma College
3900 Lomaland Drive
San Diego, CA 92106

Dutchess County, NY Mansucripts
Roosevelt Library
Hyde Park, NY 12538

Duxbury Plantation
Bridgewater Public Library
15 South Street
Bridgewater, MA 02324

Eardsley Collection
Ferguson Library
96 Broad Street
Stamford, CT 06901

Early American Railroads
American Antiquarian Society
185 Salisbury Street
Worcester, MA 01609

Early American Statutory Law College
Law Library
Library of Congress
Washington, DC 20540

East Anglia
Vancouver Public Library
750 Burrard Street
Vancouver, B.C. V6Z 1X5 Canada

East Central Europe
Institute of East Central Europe
420 West 118th Street
New York, NY 10027

East European Collection
University of Illinois
Urbana, IL 61801

East European Jewish Communities
Wiener Oral History Library
165 East 56th Street
New York, NY 10022

East India Co.
Cleveland Public Library
325 Superior Ave.
Cleveland, OH 44114

East India Co.
Spencer Library
University of Kansas
Lawrence, Kansas 66044

East India Co.
Indiana University
Seventh Street
Bloomington, In 47401

East Texas
East Texas Hist. Assoc.
Steen Library
Austin State University
Nacogdoches, TX 75962

Eastern European
Leo Baeck Institute
129 East 73rd Street
New York, NY 10021

Eastern Europe
Balkan & East European-
American Genealogical and
Historical Society
4843 Mission Street
San Francisco, CA 94112

Eastern Europe

Eastern European Genealogist
1510 Cravens Avenue
Torrance, CA 90501

Eastern European Maps
Jewish Gen. Society
5819 W. Keeny Street
Morton Grove, IL 60053

Eastern New Jersey
Proprietary House Assoc.
272 High Street
Perth Amboy, NJ 08862

Eastern Ohio
Morgantown Public Library
373 Spruce Street
Morgantown, WV 26505

Eastern States Marriage Index
L. I. Br. Genealogical Library
160 Washington Avenue
Plainview, NY 11803

Eastern Ohio
Youngstown Public Library
305 Wick Street
Youngstown, OH 44503

Eastern Oregon
Pierce Library
Eastern Oregon State College
La Grande, OR 97850

Eastern Washington
Library
Washington State University
Pullman, WA 99163

Early Federal Period
American Antiquarian Society
185 Salisbury Street
Worcester, MA 01609

Early Midwest Immigrants
Chicago Hist. Society
Clark St. at North Ave.
Chicago, IL 60614

Early Newspapers
American Antiquarian Society
185 Salisbury Street
Worcester, MA 01609

Early Ohio
Cincinnati Hist. Society
Eden Park
Cincinnati, Oh 45202

Early Ohio
Greene County Library
76 E. Market St.
Xenia, OH 45385

Early State Records Collection
Library of Congress
Washington, DC 20540

Early Town Records
New Hampshire State Library

Boldface indicates subject; DO NOT include it as part of the address.

20 Park Street
Concord, NH 03301

Early Virginians
Dr. Ransom B. True
APVA
Jamestown, VA 23081

Eckman Church Collection
Historical Society of Delaware
Market Street
Wilmington, DE 19801

Eckstom Collection
Folgler Library
University of Maine
Orono, ME 04473

Electric Railroads
Electric Railroaders Assoc.
4 West 40th Street
New York, NY 10018

Elizabeth City County, VA
  County Records
Hampton Assoc.
22 Wine Street
Hampton, VA 23669

Ellis Island Records
Federal Archives & Records Center
Military Ocean Terminal
Bayonne, NJ 07002

Elmhurst City Records
Elmhurst Hist. Museum
104 S. Kenilworth Ave.
Elmhurst, IL 60126

El Paso & Northeastern Railroad
Library
University of Texas
El Paso, TX 79968

El Paso & Southwestern Railroad
Library
University of Texas
El Paso, TX 79968

Emhart Industries
Hartford Division Library
123 Day Hill Road
Windsor, CT 06101

English Evangelical Lutheran
Archives
Gustavus Adolphus College
St. Peter, MN 56082

Ephrata Community
Seventh-Day Baptist Hist. Society
510 Watchung Ave.
Plainfield, NJ 07061

Episcopal Church
General Theological Seminary
175 Ninth Ave.
New York, NY 10011

Episcopal Church

University of Wyoming
13th & Ivinson
Laramie, WY 82071

Epstein Russian Collection
California Institute of Technology
1201 East California Blvd.
Pasadena, CA 91125

Estonians
Balzekas Museum
4012 Archer Ave.
Chicago, IL 60632

Estonian
World Assoc. of Estonians
243 East 34th Street
New York, NY 10016

Ethnic
Ethnic Genealogical Center
153-57 61st Road
Flushing, NY 11367

Ethicists
Unitarian & Universalist Gen. Society
10605 Larkespring Way
Cockeysville, MD 21030

Ethnic Groups
Immigration Historical Research Center
826 Berry Street
St. Paul MN 55114

Ethnic Groups
Balch Institute
108-114 Arch Street
Philadelphia, PA 19106

Evangelical Association
Evangelical Association
Duke University
Durham, NC

Evangelical Association
Evergreen Manor
1130 N. Westfield Blvd.
Oshkosh, WI 54901

Evangelical Church
Evergreen Manor
1130 N. Westfield Blvd.
Oshkosh, WI 54901

Evangelical Covenant
Archives & History Library
5125 N. Spaulding Ave.
Chicago, IL 60625

Evangelishe Gemeinschaft
Evergreen Manor
1130 N. Westfield Blvd.
Oshkosh, WI 54901

Evangelical Lutheran
Lutheran School of Theo.
1100 East 55th Street
Chicago, IL 60615

Evangelical United Brethren
Evergreen Manor
1130 N. Westfield Blvd.
Oshkosh, WI 54901

Evangelical United Brethren
Indiana Central University
1400 East Hanna Ave.
Indianapolis, IN 46227

Evangelical United Brethren
Iliff School of Theo.
2233 S. University Blvd.
Denver, CO 80210

Evangelical United Brethren
Shipman Library
Adrian College
Adrian, MI 49221

Evansville City Records
Indiana State University
8600 University Blvd.
Evansville, IN 47712

Evansville Suburban Railroad
Indiana State University
8600 University Blvd.
Evansville, IN 47712

Ex-Slave Narrative Collection
Rare Books & Special Collections
Library of Congress
Washington, DC 20540

—F—

Family Genealogies in Print
Stagecoach Library
14419 Stagecoach Road
Magnolia, TX 77355

Family Group Sheet Collection
Chesaning Public Library
227 East Broad Street
Chesaning, MI 48616

Family Group Sheet Collection
Baltimore County Historical Society
9811 Van Buren Lane
Cockeysville, MD 21030

Family Indexes
Chattanooga Public Library
601 McCallie Ave.
Chattanooga, TN 37403

Family Group Records Collection
Genealogical Society
50 East North Temple
Salt Lake City, UT 84150

Family Histories
American Antiquarian Society
185 Salisbury Street
Worcester, MA 01609

Family Name Index
Library of Congress

Washington, DC 20540

Family Name Index
New Jersey State Library
185 W. State Street
Trenton, NJ 08625

Family Organizations
National Index of Family
 Organizations and Periodicals
3638 Philadelphia Street
Chino, CA 91710

Family Organization Kit
Family Organization Kit
4247 Wade Way
West Valley City, UT 84119

Family Records Collection
New Hampshire Historical Society
20 Park Street
Concord, NH 03301

Family Reunions
Reunion News & Views
P.O. Box 14566
Baton Rouge, LA 70898

Family Surname Card File
Prince George's County Library
6532 Adelphi Road
Hyattsville, MD 20782

Family Tradition
Primate Center
3705 Erwin Road
Durham, NC 27705

Family Tree Placemats
Mesquite Hist. & Gen. Society
P.O. Box 165
Mesquite, TX 75049

Farm Security Admin. Collection
Prints & Photographs Division
Library of Congress
Washington, DC 20540

Farmers Union Central Exchange
Information Center
1185 N. Concord Street
South St. Paul, MN 55164

Farmington Canal
Salmon Brook Historical Society
208 Salmon Brook Street
Granby, CT 06035

Farmington Canal Co.
New Haven Colony Historical Society
114 Whitney Ave.
New Haven, CT 06510

Fauquier County, VA County Records
Virginia Historical Society
428 North Blvd.
Richmond, VA 23221

Fayette County, TN
Oral History Research Office

Boldface indicates subject; DO NOT include it as part of the address.

Memphis State University
Memphis, TN 38152

F.B.I. Records
U.S. Department of Justice
Federal Bureau of Investigation
Washington, DC 20535

Federal Information
Washington Service Bureau
1225 Connecticut Ave., N.W.
Washington, DC 20036

Federal Information
Roadmap Program
U.S. Department of Comm.
Office of Business Liason
Rm. 58998-C
Washington, DC 20230

Federal Land Offices
Washington National Records Center
Federal Office Bldg.
Suitland, MD 21668

Federal Land Records
(West of Mississippi River,
 Ala., Fl., La.)
General Archives Division
Washington National Records Center
Suitland, MD 20409

Federal Land Records
(East of Mississippi River and
 West of 13 Colonies)
Bureau of Land Management
7981 Eastern Ave.
Silver Spring, MD 20910

Federal Museum
Smithsonian Museum
1000 Jefferson Drive, S.W.
Washington, DC 20560

Federal Publications
Superintendant of Documents
Government Printing Office
Washington, DC 20402

**Federal Prisoners in
 Confederate Prisons**
Record Group 249
National Archives
Washington, DC 20408

Federal Records
National Archives & Records Service
General Services Administration
Washington, DC 20908

Filipino-Americans
Libraries
University of Washington
Seattle, WA 98195

Finish
Finnish-American Hist. Society
P.O. Box 3515
Porland, OR 97208

Finnish
League of Finnish-
 American Societies
151 West 51st Street
New York, NY 10019

Finnish
Library
Suomi College
Hancock, MI 49931

Finnish Lutheran
Lutheran School of Theo.
1100 East 55th Street
Chicago, IL 60615

Fire Fighters
Insurance Library Assoc.
1 Beacon Street
Boston, MA 02108

Fire & Marine Insurance
Archives
1600 Arch Street
Philadelphia, PA 19101

Fisk Icelandic Collection
Olin Library
Cornell University
Ithaca, NY 14853

First Corps of Cadets
Boston University
771 Commonwealth Ave.
Boston, MA 02215

Fletcher Collection
Library
University of Arkansas
Fayetteville, AR 72701

Floods
Johnstown Flood Museum
304 Washington Street
Johnstown, PA 15901

Florida
Strozier Library
Florida State University
Tallahassee, FL 32306

Florida Lutheran
Florida Synod
3838 W. Cypress Street
Tampa, FL 33607

Florida Methodist
Library
Florida So. College
Lakeland, FL 33802

Florida Patents & Tract Books
State Land Office
Elliot Building
Tallahassee, FL 32304

Florida Surname Index
Tampa Public Library
900 Ashley Street

Tampa, FL 33602

Florida Territory & State Records
Florida State Archives
The Capitol
Tallahassee, FL 32304

Forbes Collection
Mobile Public Library
701 Government Street
Mobile, AL 36602

Foreign Language Forms/Sheets
Distribution Center
1999 West 1700 South
Salt Lake City, UT 84104

Foreign Manuscripts on Microfilm
Stack & Reader Division
Library of Congress
Washington, DC 20540

Folklore
Folklore Archives
504 North Fess
Bloomington, IN 47401

Fort Belvoir
Army Engineer Museum
16th Street & Belvoir Road
Fort Belvoir, VA 22060

Fort Laramie
Fort Laramie National
 Historic Site
Fort Laramie, WY 82212

Fort La Presentation
Archives
622 Washington Street
Ogdensburg, NY 13669

Fort Larned
Fort Larned National Historic Site
Rt. 3
Larned, KS 67550

Fort Lewis
Fort Lewis Military Museum
Bldg. 4320
Fort Lewis, WA 98433

Fort McHenry
Library
Fort McHenry National Mon.
Baltimore, MD 21230

Fort Monroe
Fort Monroe Casemate Museum
P.O. Box 341
Fort Monroe, VA 23651

Fort Niagara
Old Fort Niagara Assoc.
P.O. Box 248
Youngstown, NY 14174

Fort Ouiatenon
Tippecanoe County Historical Assoc.

909 South State
Lafayette, IN 47901

Fort Pitt Militia Records
Western Pennsylvania Historical Society
4338 Bigelow Blvd.
Pittsburg, PA 15213

Fort Reno
Carnegie Library
215 East Wade
El Reno, OK 73036

Fort Ticonderoga
Fort Ticonderoga Museum
Box 390
Ticonderoga, NY 12883

Fort Walla Walla
Fort Walla Walla Museum
P.O. Box 1616
Walla Walla, WA 99362

Fort Wilkins
Fort Wilkins State Park
Copper Harbor, MI 49918

4-H
4-H Program
SeA Extension
U.S. Department of Agricultural
Washington, DC 20250

Fox Collection
Riley County, Kansas
 Genealogical Society
2005 Claflin Road
Manhatten, KS 66502

Fraternal Societies
Immigration History Research Center
826 Berry Street
St. Paul MN 55114

Fredonia Academy
Historical Museum
20 East Main Street
Fredonia, NY 14063

Free Church
Seventh-Day Baptist
 Historical Society
510 Watchung Ave.
Plainfield, NJ 07061

Free Methodist
Seattle Pacific University
3307 Third Ave., W.
Seattle, WA 98119

Free Methodist Church
Historical Center Library
901 College Street
Winona Lake, IN 46590

Free Thinkers
Unitarian & Universalist
 Genealogical Society
10605 Lakespring Way

Boldface indicates subject; **DO NOT** include it as part of the address.

Cockeysville, MD 21030

Free Will Baptist
Hillsdale Free Will Baptist College
Box 6343
Moore, OK 73160

Free Will Baptist
Moye Library
Mount Olive College
Mount Olive, NC 28365

Freebies
Freebies Magazine
P.O. Box 20283
Santa Barbara, CA 93120

Freebies
Stagecoach Library
14419 Stagecoach Road
Magnolia, TX 77355

Freedmen's Aid Society
Interdenominational Theo. Center
671 Beckwith Street, S.W.
Atlanta, GA 30314

Freedmen Records (Blacks)
Record Group 105
National Archives
Washington, DC 20408

Freedom of Information
Access Reports
1301 Pennsylvania Ave., N.W.
Washington, DC 20004

Freedom of Information
Freedom of Information Clearinghouse
P.O. Box 19367
Washington, DC 20036

Freedom of Information
Freedom of Information Center
223 Walter Williams Hall
Columbia, MO 65201

French
French Institute
Assumption College
Worcester, MA 01609

French-American
American-French Genealogical Society
P.O. Box 2113
Pawtucket, RI 02861

French-Canadian Immigrant File
Stanley E. Moore
26 Hazelwood Terr.
Pittsfield, MA 01201

French-Canadian
French-Canadian Genealogical Society
215 Adams Street
Manchester, CT 06040

French-Canadian
La Societe Canadienne-
  Francaise de Minn.

1401 Circle Terrace
Minneapolis, MN 55421

French-Canadian
French-Canadian Heritage
  Society of Michigan
P.O. Box 15134
Lansing, MI 48901

French-Canadian
Northwest Territory French and
  Canadian Heritage Institute
P.O. Box 26372
St. Louis Park, MN 55426

French Canadian
French Canadian and Acadian
  Genealogical Review
Box 845, Haute Ville
Quebec, G1R 4S7 Canada

French-Canadian Collection
McGill University
3475 Peel Street
Montreal, H3A 1W7 Canada

French Canada
Assoc. Canado-Americane
52 Concord Street
Manchester, NH 03101

French Huguenots
The Lost Palatine Magazine
Rt. 1, Box 1160
Estero, FL 33928

French in American Revolution
Society of Cincinnati
2118 Massachusetts Ave., N.W.
Washington, DC 20008

French & Indian War
Vermont Historical Society
Pavilion Bldg.
Montpelier, VT 05602

French & Indian War
American Antiquarian Society
185 Salisbury Street
Worcester, MA 01609

French Institute
Assumption College
500 Salisbury Street
Worcester, MA 01609

French Protestantism
University of Wisconsin
728 State Street
Madison, WI 53706

Fresno County, CA County Records
Fresno Historical Society
7160 W. Kearney Blvd.
Fresno, CA 93706

Fresno County, CA Court Records
Fresno County Historical Society
7160 W. Kearney Blvd.

Fresno, CA 93706

Frisian
Frisian Roundtable
2885 Roosevelt Ave.
Bronx, NY 10465

Frontier Religion
Brute Library
203 Church Street
Vincenmes, IN 47591

Frontier Religion Collection
Agnes Scott College
East College Ave.
Decatur, GA 30030

Frontier Religion
McCain Library
Agnes Scott College
Decatur, GA 30030

Frontier Sciences
World University
711 E. Blacklidge Drive
Tucson, AZ 85719

Fuller Family
Library
Kent State University
Kent, OH 44242

Fulton County, OH Court Records
Swanton Public Library
95 North Main Street
Swanton, OH 43558

Furman's Quaker Bibliography
Historical Society of Pennsylvania
1300 Locust Street
Philadelphia, PA

—G—

Galesburg City Records
College Archives
Knox College
Galesburg, IL 61401

California Central Valley
Library
University of The Pacific
Stockton, CA 95211

Galveston City Records
Rosenberg Library
2310 Sealy Ave.
Galveston, TX 77550

Gardner Collection
Library
Rutgers University
New Brunswick, NJ 08901

Genealogy Books
Geanealogical Books in Print
6818 Lois Drive
Springfield, VA 22150

Genealogical Society
Genealogical Department
50 East North Temple
Salt Lake City, UT 84150

Genealogical Card File
Western Reserve Historical Society
10825 East Boulevard
Cleveland, OH 44106

Genealogy Catalog
Sutro Library
2130 Fulton Street
San Francisco, CA 94117

Genealogy Collection
Ector County Library
321 West Fifth Street
Odessa, TX 79761

Genealogy Consultants
Consulting Organizations Directory
Gale Research Company
Detroit, MI 48226

Genealogical Editors
Association of Genealogical Editors
P.O. Box 16422
Salt Lake City, UT 84116

Genealogical Information
Roots Digest
P.O. Box 2101
Glenwood Springs, CO 81602

Genealogy Newspaper
Genealogy Today
2815 Clearview Pl. #400
Atlanta, Ga 30340

Genealogy Newspaper
Tri-State Trader
P.O. Box 90
Knightstown, IN 46148

Genealogical Societies
Federation of Genealogical Societies
P.O. Box 220
Davenport, IA 52805

Genealogical Society of Pennsylvania
Genealogical Society of Pennsylvania
1300 Locust Street
Philadelphia, PA 19107

**Genealogical Seminar Tapes
and Transcripts**
Carlos E. Elliott, Sr.
5807 Darnel
Houston, TX 77074

General Land Office Records
Washington National Records Center
Federal Office Bldg.
Suitland, MD 21668

Genesee County, NY County Records
Holland Land Office Museum
131 West Main Street

Boldface indicates subject; **DO NOT** include it as part of the address.

Batavia, NY 10420

Genesee River Valley
Milne Library
College of Geneseo
Geneseo, NY 14454

Genesee Valley Canal
Rochester Museum
657 East Avenue
Rochester, NY 14603

Genesee Valley Canal
Milne Library
State University of New York
Geneseo, NY 14454

General Land Office
Federal Archives & Record Center
Bldg. 48, Denver Federal Center
Denver, CO 80225

Geographic Site Location Reports
Social & Economic Records Division
National Archives and Records Service
Washington, DC 20408

Georgia
Library
University of Georgia
Athens, GA 30602

Georgia Collection
Atlanta Public Library
One Margaret Mitchell Sq., N.W.
Atlanta, GA 30303

Georgia Colonial Records
Georgia Historical Society
501 Whitaker Street
Savannah, GA 31401

Georgia Confederate Index
Georgia Historical Society
501 Whitaker Street
Savannha, Ga 31401

Georgia Confederate Pension Index
Department Archives and History
330 Capitol Ave., S.E.
Atlanta, GA

Georgia Family File
Washington Memorial Library
1180 Washington Ave.
Macon, GA 31201

Georgia Grants & Surveys
Surveyor General Department
330 Capitol Ave., S.E.
Atlanta, GA 30334

Georgia Genealogical Card File
R. J. Taylor, Jr. Foundation
P.O. Box 38176, Capitol Hill Sta.
Atlanta, GA 30334

Georgia Methodist
Pitts Theo. Library

Emory University
Atlanta, GA 30322

Georgia WWI Induction Cards
Military Division
P.O. Box 4839
Atlanta, GA 30302

German Reformed Church
Library
Ursinus College
Collegeville, PA 19426

Germans From Russia
Germans From Russia Heritage Society
P.O. Box 1671
Bismarck, ND 58502

Germans From Russia
American Historical Society of
  Germans from Russia
615 D Street
Lincoln, NE 68502

Germans From Russia
Regional Oral History Office
486 The Bancroft Library
Berkeley, CA 94720

Germans From Russia
Germans From Russia
Colorado State University
Fort Collins, CO 80523

German-Russian Mennonites
Mennonite Library and Archives
Bethel College
North Newton, KS 67117

Germans From Russia
  Heritage Collection
Institute For Regional Studies
North Dakota State University
Fargo, ND 58105

German Society of Pennsylvania
Horner Library
611 Spring Garden Street
Philadelphia, PA 19144

Germantown Friends School
Friends Free Library
5418 Germantown Ave.
Philadelphia, PA 19144

Germantown, PA Cemetery Records
Germantown Historical Society
5214 Germantown Ave.
Germantown, PA 19144

Gloucester County, NJ County Records
Gloucester County Historical Society
17 Hunter Street
Woodbury, NJ 08096

Gold Rush
Society of California Pioneers
456 McAllister Street
San Francisco, CA 94102

Gordon Family
Pleasant Valley Preservation Society
Box 102
Holmdel, NJ 07733

Gordon Collection
Kentucky Library
Western Kentucky University
Bowling Green, KY 42101

Gorman Civil War Collection
Morris Harvey College
2300 MacCorkle Ave., S.E.
Charleston, WV 25304

Gould Steamboat Index
St. Louis Public Library
1301 Olive Street
St. Louis, MO 63103

German
German-Acadian Coast Historical
  and Genealogical Society
P.O. Box 517
Destrehan, LA 70048

German
German-American Club
5251 E. Outer Drive
Detroit, MI 48200

German
F.A.C.G.D.
460 Chapman Street
Irvington, NJ 07111

German
German American National Congress
4740 N. Western Ave.
Chicago, IL 60625

German
German Society of the
 City of New York
150 Fifth Ave.
New York, NY

German
Steuben Society of America
369 Lexington Ave., #2003
New York, NY 10017

German
Society of German American Studies
204 Franklin Drive
Berea, OH 44017

German (MD)
Society for the History of
 Germans in Maryland
231 St. Paul Pl.
Baltimore, MD 21202

Germans
German Society
611 Spring Garden Street
Philadelphia, PA

Germans

German-Texas Heritage Society
Rt. 2, Box 239-A
Buda, TX 78610

German-American
Society for German-American Studies
St. Olaf College
Northfield, MN 55057

**German-American Research and
 Documentation Center**
University of Wisconsin Foundation
702 Langdon Street
Madison, WI 53706

German-Canadian
German-Canadian Historical Assoc.
139 Wildwood Park
Winnipeg R3T 0E2 Canada

German-Frakturs
Free Library of Philadelphia
Logan Square
Philadelphia, PA 19103

German Hessians
Schwaum Historical Association
4983 South Sedgewick Road
Lynhurst, OH 44124

German Methodist Episcopal
Cincinnati Historical Society
Eden Park
Cincinnatti, OH 45202

Graham Collection
Indiana Historical Society
140 N. Senate Ave.
Indianapolis, IN 46204

Grand Army of the Republic
Grand Army of the Republic
78 E. Washington Street
Chicago, IL 60602

Grand Army of the Republic Records
Northern Indiana Historical Society
112 South Lafayette Blvd.
South Bend, IN 46601

Grange Records
Ohlin Library
Cornell University
Ithaca, NY 14850

Grant County, NM County Records
Silver City Museum
312 W. Broadway
Silver City, NM 88061

Grant County, OK County Records
Grant County Museum
124½ N. Main Street
Medford, OK 73759

Great Lakes
Great Lakes Historical Society
480 Main Street
Vermillion, OH 44089

Boldface indicates subject; **DO NOT** include it as part of the address.

Great Lakes
International Assoc. for
 Great Lakes Research
1300 Elmwood Ave.
Buffalo, NY 14222

Great Lakes
Dossin Great Lakes Museum
Belle Isle
Detroit, MI 48207

Great Lakes
Lake Superior State College
College Drive
Sault Ste. Marie, MI 49783

Great Lakes
Cleveland Public Library
325 Superior Ave.
Cleveland, OH 44114

Great Lakes
Museum of the Great Lakes
1700 Center Ave.
Bay City, MI 48706

Great Lakes
Library
Michigan Technological University
Houghton, MI 49931

Great Lakes
Mackinac Island State Park
Box 30028
Lansing, MI 48909

Great Lakes
Buffalo & Erie County
 Historical Society
25 Nottingham Court
Buffalo, NY 14216

Great Lakes
Milwaukee Public Library
814 W. Wisconsin Ave.
Milwaukee, WI 53233

Great Lakes
Library
Lake Superior State College
Sault Ste. Marie, MI 49783

Great Lakes
Record Group 36
National Archives
Wasington, DC 20408

Great Lakes Chart Catalog
Lake Survey Center
630 Federal Bldg.
Detroit, MI 48226

Great Lake Collections
Library
Bowling Green State University
Bowling Green, OH 43403

Great Lakes Collection
Hayes Library

1337 Hayes Ave.
Fremont, OH 43420

Great Lakes Collection
Great Lakes Research Center
Bowling Green State University
Bowling Green, OH 43403

Great Lakes Marine Collection
Milwaukee Public Library
814 W. Wisconsin Ave.
Milwaukee, WI 53233

Great Lakes Marine Collection
Hayes Library
1337 Hayes Ave.
Femont, OH 43420

Great Lakes Shipping
Library
Michigan Tech. University
Houghton, MI 49931

Great Lakes Shipping
Mackinac Island State Park
Box 30028
Lansing, MI 48909

**Great Lakes-St. Lawrence
 Tidewater Assoc.**
St. Louis County Historical Society
506 W. Michigan Street
Duluth, MN 55802

Great Northern Railway
Hill Reference Library
Fourth Street at Market Street
St. Paul, MN 55106

Great Northern Railway
Hill Reference Library
80 W. Fourth Street
St. Paul, MN 55102

Greece
Widener Library
Harvard University
Cambridge, MA 02138

Greek
Greek American Progressive Assoc.
3600 Fifth Ave.
Pittsburgh, PA 15213

Green Bay Area WWI Draft Records
Neville Public Museum
129 S. Jefferson Street
Green Bay, WI 54301

Green Collection
Kentucky Library
Western Kentucky University
Bowling Green, KY 42101

The Green Tree (Insurance)
Mutual Assurance Co.
240 South 4th Street
Philadelphia, PA 19106

Greenbrier Valley

Greenbrier Historical Society
100 Church Street
Lewisburg, WV 24901

Greene County, NY County Records
Greene County Historical Society
Rural Delivery
Coxsackie, NY 12051

Greene County, OH County Records
Library
Wright State University
Dayton, OH 45431

Greenville, SC Newspaper Index
Greenville, County Library
300 College Street
Greenville, SC 29601

Guide to the Draper Manuscripts
State Historical Society
816 State Street
Madison WI 53706

**Guide to Genealogical Research
in the National Archives**
Genealogical Guide
P.O. Box 111
National Archives
Washington, DC 20408

Gulf Coast Region
Woodson Research Center
Rice University
Houston, TX 77001

Gypsies
Cleveland Public Library
325 Superior Ave.
Cleveland, OH 44114

Gypsies
Gypsy Lore Society
Centenary College
Hackettstown, NJ 07840

—H—

Haiti
University of Florida
University Ave.
Gainesville, FL 32611

Hale Newspaper Collection
Connecticut State Library
231 Capitol Ave.
Hartford, CT 06115

Hall Collection
Davenport Museum
1717 West 12th Street
Davenport, IA 52804

Hairbaugh Collection
Indiana Historical Society
140 N. Senate Ave.
Indianapolis, IN 46204

Hancock County, IN Vital Records
Greenfield Public Library

98 West North Street
Greenfield, IN 46140

Handicapped
Genealogical Center Library
15 Dunwoody Park Road, Suite 130
Atlanta, GA 30336

Hardin County, TX County Records
Sam Houston Library
Farm Road 1011
Liberty, TX 77575

Harmon Collection
Maine Historical Society
485 Congress Street
Portland, ME 04111

Harmony Society
Indiana University
Seventh Street
Bloomington, IN 47401

Harmony Society
Old Economy
14th & Church Streets
Ambridge, PA 15003

Harris Civil War Collection
Providence Public Library
150 Empire Street
Providence, RI 02903

Harris Collection
Carnegie Library
607 Broad Street
Rome, GA 30161

Hartford Seminary Foundation
Hartford Seminary Foundation
55 Elizabeth Street
Hartford, CT 06105

Harvard Medical Archives
Count Way Library
10 Shattuck Street
Boston, MA 02115

Harvard University Students
Pusey Library
Harvard University
Cambridge, MA 02138

Hawaii
Hawaiian Mission Children's Society
553 King Street
Honolulu, HI 96813

Hawaiian Territorial Records
State Archives
Iolani Palace Grounds
Honolulu, HI 96813

Hawkins County, TN Cemetery Index
Stamps Memorial Library
415 West Main Street
Rogersville, TN 37857

Hawkins County, TN Family Files
Stamps Memorial Library

Boldface indicates subject; DO NOT include it as part of the address.

415 West Main Street
Rogersville, TN 37857

Hayward Tax Records
Hayward Area Historical Society
22701 Main Street
Haywood, CA 94543

Heir Searchers
Genealogists International
970 East Logan Ave.
Salt Lake City, UT 84105

Hendricks County, IN County Records
Plainfield Public Library
1120 Stafford, Road
Plainsfield, IN 46168

Heritage Collection
Huntsville Public Library
P.O. Box 443
Huntsville, AL 35804

Herrington Collection
Westfield Memorial Library
425 East Broad Street
Westfield, NJ 07090

Hicksite Quakers
Unitarian & Universalist Gen. Society
10605 Lakespring Way
Cockeysville, MD 21030

Hildago County, TX County Records
Library
Pan American University
Edinburg, TX 78539

Hillsdale County, MI
Mitchell Public Library
22 North Manning Street
Hillsdale, MI 49242

Hinshaw Quaker Index
Friends Historical Library
Swarthmore College
Swarthmore, PA 19081

Hinson Collection
Charleston Library Society
164 King Street
Charleston, SC 29401

Hinson Condederate Collection
Charleston Library Society
164 King Street
Charleston, SC 29401

Hispanic
Hispanic Society of America
613 West 155th Street
New York, NY 10032

Historical Societies
American Assoc. for State
 and Local History
1400 8th Ave. South
Nashville, TN 37203

Holiness Movement

Point Loma College
3900 Lamaland Drive
San Diego, CA 92106

Holmes County, OH County Records
Bierce Library
University of Akron
Akron, OH 44325

Holland Land Company
Crawford County Historical Society
848 North Main Street
Meadville, PA 16335

The Holland Purchase
Holland Purchase Museum
131 West Main Street
Batavia, NY 14020

Holland Purchase
Holland Land Office Museum
131 West Main Street
Batavia, NY 10420

Holy Spirit Church
Central Bible College
3000 North Grant
Springfield, MD 65802

Home Copiers
Duprox Copier Co.
655 Amboy Ave.
Woodbridge, NJ 07095

Home Computers
Computerland
161 East 200 South
Salt Lake City, UT 84111

Homeowners Loan Corporation
Federal Archives & Records Center
Military Ocean Terminal
Bayonne, NJ 07002

Hooker Collection
Takoma Park Maryland Library
101 Philadelphia Ave.
Tokoma Park, MD 20012

Hospital Sisters of Third Order
St. Francis Convent
P.O. Box 42
Springfield, IL 62705

Hotel Dieu Hospital
Library
2021 Perdido Street
New Orleans, LA 70161

Howard Ship Yards & Dock Co.
Lilly Library
Indiana University
Bloomington, IN 47401

Hudson's Bay Co.
Hudson's Bay Co.
77 Main Street
Winnipeg, Man. R3C 2R1 Canada

Hudson's Bay Company

Oregon Historical Society
1230 S.W. Park Ave.
Portland, OR 97205

Hudson River Day Line
Library
University of Baltimore
1420 Maryland Ave.
Baltimore MD 21201

Hudson River Valley
Clemont State Historic Park
R.D. One
Germantown, NY 12526

Hudson Valley, NY Church Records
State University of New York
College of New Paltz
New Paltz, NY 12561

Huegely Mill
Museum of Science & Industry
57th Street & Lake Shore Drive
Chicago, IL 60637

Huguenot
Hufeland Memorial Library
983 North Ave.
New Rochelle, NY 10804

Huguenot
Library
Huguenot Historical Society
New Paltz, NY 12561

Huguenot
National Huguenot Society
1307 New Hampshire Ave., N.W.
Washington, DC 20036

Huguenot
Huguenot Society of South Carolina
25 Chalmers Street
Charleston, SC 29401

Hungarian
American Hungarian Library
 and Historical Society
215 East 82nd Street
New York, NY 10028

Hungarian-Jewish
World Federation of Hungarian Jews
136 East 39th Street
New York, NY 10016

Hungarian Reformed Church
Bethlehem Home
P.O. Box 657
Ligonier, PA 15658

Hyde-Wilder Civil War Collection
University of Tennessee
601 McCallie Ave.
Chattanooga, TN 37403

—I—

Icarian
Center For Icarian Studies

University Libraries
Macomb, IL 61455

Icelandic
Icelandic-American Society
P.O. Box 7051
Reykjavik, Iceland

Icelandic
Icelandic-Canadian Magazine
890 Valour Road,
Winnipeg, Man. R3J 3B4 Canada

Illinois
Illinois State Historical Library
Old State Capitol
Springfield, IL 62706

Illinois
University of Illinois
19 Library
Urbana, IL 61801

Illinois Central Railroad
Newberry Library
60 West Walton Street
Chicago, IL 60610

Illinois Episcopal
Episcopal Diocese
821 South 2nd Street
Springfield, IL 62704

Illinois Historical Society
Illinois Historical Society
University of Illinois
Urbana, IL 61801

Illinois & Michigan Canal
Illinois State Archives
Archives Bldg.
Springfield, IL 62756

Illinois Militia
Military & Naval Department
Armory Bldg.
Springfield, IL 62706

Illinois Military
Illinois State Historical Society
Old State Capitol
Springfield, IL 62706

Illinois Property Index
Information Services/Reference
Illinois State Archives
Springfield, IL 62756

Illinois Sons of Temperance
Evansville Museum
411 S.E. Riverside Drive
Evansville, IN 47713

Illinois United Methodist
Conference Historical Society
1211 N. Park Street
Bloomington, IL 61701

Immigration
Immigration History Research Center

Boldface indicates subject; DO NOT include it as part of the address.

826 Berry Street
St. Paul, MN 55114

Immigration
Center for Migration Studies
209 Flagg Pl.
Staten Island, NY 10304

Immigration Historical Society
690 Cedar Street
St. Paul, MN 55103

Immigration Registration
Jonathan Sheppard Books
Box 2020, Plaza Station
Albany, NY 12220

Imperial Russian Secret Police
Hoover Institution on War
Stanford University
Stanford, CA 94305

Indentures
Martin-Mitchell Museum
Aurora Ave.
Naperville, IL 60540

Indentures
Georgia College
231 W. Hancock Street
Milledgeville, GA 31061

Independent Christian Churches
Midway College
Midway, KY 40347

Independent Order of Odd Fellows
University of Baltimore
846 N. Howard Street
Baltimore, MD 21201

**Index to American Revolution
  Soldiers Graves**
Lee Library
Brigham Young University
Provo, UT 84604

Index to Cutler's History of Kansas
Wichita Public Library
223 South Main
Wichita, KS 67202

**Index to U.S. Federal Appellate
  Court Cases**
Record Group 267
National Archives
Washington, DC 20408

Index to WWI Participants
Michigan State Library
735 E. Michigan Ave.
Lansing, MI 48913

Indiana
Lilly Library
Indiana University
Bloomington, IN 47401

Indiana Baptist
Library

Franklin College
Franklin, IN 46131

Indiana Catholics
Archdiocese of Indianapolis
1350 N. Penn. Street
Indianapolis, IN 46202

Indiana County, PA County Records
Historical and Genealogical Society
6th Street & Wayne Ave.
Indiana, PA 15701

Indiana Jewish
Indiana Jewish Historical Society
215 East Berry Street, Rm. 303
Fort Wayne, IN 46802

Indiana Land Company
Washington & Jefferson College
Lincoln & Wheeling Streets
Washington, PA 15301

Indiana Lutherans
Concordia Theo. Seminary
6600 No. Clinton
Fort Wayne, IN 46825

Indiana Lutheran
Lutheran Church in America
3733 N. Meridian Street
Indianapolis, IN 46208

Indiana Pioneers Collection
Indiana State Historical Society
140 N. Senate Ave.
Indianapolis, IN 46204

Indiana Presbyterian
Duggan Library
Hanover College
Hanover, IN 47243

Indiana United Methodist
West Library
DePauw University
Greencastle, IN 46135

Indians
Indian Archives
Historical Bldg.
Oklahoma City, OK 73105

Indian Archives
Oklahoma Historical Society
Historical Bldg.
Oklahoma City, OK 73105

Indian Depredations
Record Group 75
National Archives
Washington, DC 20408

Indian Depredation Cases
Record Group 123
National Archives
Washington, DC 20408

Indian Reservation Maps
Record Group 48

National Archives
Washington, DC 20408

Indian Scout Companies (Army)
Record Group 391
National Archives
Washington, DC 20408

Indian Territory
Record Group 48
National Archives
Washington, DC 20408

**Indian Territory Federal
  Court Records**
Oklahoma Historical Society
Historical Bldg.
Okalhoma City, OK 73105

Insurance Company Records
State University of New York
1400 Washington Ave.
Albany, NY 12222

Insurance Maps Collection (Sanborn Fire)
Geography and Map Division
Library of Congress
Washington, DC 20540

Inter-Library Loan
Orlando Public Library
10 N. Rosalind Ave.
Orlando, FL 32801

Inter-Library Loan
National Center for State Courts
300 Newport Avenue
Williamsburg, VA 23185

Inter-Library Loan
Shawnee Library System
Rt. 2, Box 136A
Carterville, IL 62918

Inter-Library Loan
Congregational Library
14 Beacon Street
Boston, MA 02106

Intermountain States
Library
University of Utah
Salt Lake City, UT 84112

Internal Revenue Assessment Lists
Civil Archives Division
National Archives & Records Services
Washington, DC 20408

International Genealogical Index
Genealogical Department
50 East North Temple
Salt Lake City, UT 84150

International New Thought Alliance
Library
Unity School of Christianity
Unity Village, MO 64065

Inferior Court of Common Pleas

Social Law Library
1200 Courthouse
Boston, MA 02108

Iowa Catholics
Diocese of Sioux City
1821 Jackson Street
Sioux City, IA 51102

Iowa Grand Army Republic Records
Department of History & Archives
Hist. Building
Des Moines, IA 50319

Iowa Methodist Episcopal
Dunn Library
Simpson College
Indianola, IA 50125

Iowa Reformed
Dutch Heritage Collection
101 7th Street, S.W.
Orange City, IA 51041

Iowa State Land Office Records
Secretary of State
State House
Des Moines, IA 50319

Irish
Ireland of the Welcomes
P.O. Box 2744
Boulder, CO 80321

Irish
Gaelic Gleanings
611 Miller Valley Road, Ste. #59
Prescott, AZ 86301

Irish
Celtic League
P.O. Box 4663
Toledo, OH 43620

Irish
Irish American Cultural Assoc.
9933 S. Western, Suite 3
Chicago, IL 60643

Irish
Irish American Heritage Center
410 S. Michigan Ave., Suite 941
Chicago, IL 60605

Irish
American Irish Historical Society
991 Fifth Ave.
New York, NY 10028

Irish
Bertrand Library
Bucknell University
Lewisburg, PA 17837

Irish
Gwynedd-Mercy College
Sumneytown Pike
Gwynedd Valley, PA 19437

Irish

Boldface indicates subject; DO NOT include it as part of the address.

Irish Genealogical Digest
9411 Hunters Creek
Dallas, TX 75243

Irish
Chicago Irish Ancestry
P.O. Box A66218
Chicago, IL 60666

Irish
Irish Family Research Assoc. Inc.
9411 Hunters Creek Drive
Dallas, TX 75243

Irish
Irish Family History Society
173 Tremont Street
Newton, MA 02158

Irish
Irish Family Name Society
Box 2095
La Mesa, CA 92041

Irish
Gaelic Gleanings
3721 S. Timber Street
Santa Ana, CA 92707

Irish Collection
Bapst Library
Boston College Libraries
Chestnut Hill, MA 02167

Irish Collection
Genealogy Division
Library of Congress
Washington, DC 20540

Irish Loyal & Patriotic Union
California State University
18111 Nordhoff Street
Northridge, CA 91324

Iroquis County, IL County Records
Genealogy Library
130 W. Cherry Street
Watseka, IL 60970

Italian
Italian Genealogist
1510 Cravens Ave.
Torrance, CA 90501

Italian
American Italian Hist. Assoc.
209 Flagg Place
Staten Island, NY 10305

Italian
Italian Cultural Institute
686 Park Ave.
New York, NY 10021

Italian
Italian Americana
State University of Buffalo
Buffalo, NY 14222

Italian-American

Center for Italian-American Studies
Brooklyn College
Brooklyn, NY 11210

Italian-Americans
Center for Migration Studies
209 Flagg Pl.
Staten Island, NY 10304

—J—

Jackson Purchase
Puducah Public Library
555 Washington Street
Puducah, KY 42001

Jamestown, Virginia
University Library
University of Louisville
Louisville, KY 40208

Japanese
Japan American Society
125 Weller Street
Los Angeles, CA 90012

Jasper County, TX County Records
Sam Huston Library
Farm Road 1011
Liberty, TX 77575

Jefferson County, KY County Records
Jefferson County Archives and
 Records Service
404 Jefferson County Courthouse
Louisville, KY 40202

Jefferson County, TX County Records
Sam Houston Library
Farm Road 1011
Liberty, TX 77575

Jefferson County, WA County Records
Research Center
City Hall
Port Townsend, WA 98368

Jemison Collection
Birmingham Public Library
2020 Seventh Ave., N.
Birmingham, AL 35203

Jericho Plank Road Co.
Hempstead Public Library
115 Nichols Ct.
Hempstead, NY 11550

Jewish
Yeshiva University
500 West 185th Street
New York, NY 10033

Jewish
Goldstein Library
2911 Russell Street
Berkeley, CA 94705

Jewish
Jewish Theo. Seminary
3080 Broadway

New York, NY 10027

Jewish
Jewish Historical Assoc.
130 Sessions Street
Providence, RI 02906

Jewish
Philadelphia Jewish Archvies Center
625 Walnut Street
Philadelphia, PA 19106

Jewish
Jewish Genealogy Society
5819 W. Keeny Street
Morton Grove, IL 60053

Jewish
American Jewish Historical Society
2 Thornton Road
Waltham, MA 02154

Jewish
Canadian Jewish Congress
1590 McGregor Ave.
Montreal, H3G 1C5
Quebec, Canada

Jewish
Yivo Institute
1048 Fifth Avenue
New York, NY 10028

Jewish
Jewish Genealogy Society of
 Greater Washington
10 Buckspark Ct.
Potomac, MD 20854

Jewish
Jewish Genealogy Society
300 East 71st Street
New York, NY 10021

Jewish
Toledot
155 East 93rd Street, Suite 3C
New York, NY 10028

Jewish
Chicago Jewish Archives
618 S. Michigan Ave.
Chicago, IL 60605

Jim Hogg County, TX County Records
Library
Pan American University
Edinburg, TX 78539

Johnson County, IN Burial Records
Franklin-Johnson County Public Library
Madison at Home Ave.
Franklin, IN 46131

Johnson County, KS Cemetery Inscriptions
Johnson County Genealogical Society
P.O. Box 8057
Shawnee Mission, KS 66208

Jones Collection
Huntsville Public Library
108 Fountain
Huntsville, AL 35804

Jones Collection
Library
Rutgers University
New Brunswick, NJ 08901

Jones-Gandrud Collection
Department of Archives & History
624 Washington Ave.
Montgomery, AL 36104

Josephine County, OR Court Records
Josephine County Historical Society
716 Northwest A Street
Grants Pass, OR 97526

**Journal of American Indian
 Family Research**
Histree
P.O. Box 687
Lawton, OK 73502

Journal of the Early Republic
Indiana University
925 W. Michigan Street
Indianapolis, IN 46202

Jubilees or Centennials
Photoduplication Service
Library of Congress
Washington, DC 20540

—K—

Kalamazoo County Agricultural Society
Kalamazoo Public Library
315 South Rose Street
Kalamazoo, MI 49006

Kandiyohi County, MN County Records
Kandiyohi County Historical Society
North Highway 71
Willmar, MN 56201

Kansas Baptists
Myers Library
Ottawa University
Ottawa, KS 66067

Kansas Congregationalists
Washburn University
1700 College
Topeka, KS 66621

Kansas County Territorial Petitions
Secretary of State
State House
Topeka, KS 66612

Kansas G.A.R. Index
State Historical Society
120 West 10th Street
Topeka, KS 66612

Kansas Guerilla War Claims
Secretary of State

Boldface indicates subject; **DO NOT** include it as part of the address.

State House
Topeka, KS 66612

Kansas Index of Fraternal Organizations
State Historical Society
120 West 10th Street
Topeka, KS 66612

Kansas Notary Records
Secretary of State
State House
Topeka, KS 66612

**Kansas Territorial Supreme
Court Records**
Kansas Supreme Court Law Library
310 W. Tenth
Topeka, KS 66612

Kansas Township Organizations
Secretary of State
State House
Topeka, KS 66612

Kansas United Church of Christ
Washburn University
1700 College
Topeka, KS 66621

Kansas United Methodist
Kansas West Conference
South Western College
Winfield, KS 67156

Kendall Society
Massillon Public Library
208 Lincoln Way E.
Massillon, OH 44646

Kenosha County, WI County Records
Area Research Center
University of Wisconsin
Kenosha, WI 53140

Kent County, MI County Records
Grand Rapids Public Library
Library Plaza, N.E.
Grand Rapids, MI 49503

Kentucky
University of Louisville
Belknap Campus
Louisville, KY 40208

Kentucky
Filson Club
118 W. Breckinridge Street
Louisville, KY 40203

Kentucky
University of Chicago
1100 East 57th Street
Chicago, IL 60637

Kentucky Civil War Records
Military Records & Research Center
Boone National Guard Center
Frankfort, KY 40601

Kentucky County Records
Lincoln National Life Foundation
1300 S. Clinton Street
Fort Wayne, IN 46801

Kentucky Family File
Kentucky Historical Society
P.O. Box H
Frankfort, KY 40601

Kentucky Family Files
Filson Club Library
118 W. Breckinridge Street
Louisville, KY 40203

Kentucky Family History Charts
Waveland State Shrine
Higbee Mill Road
Lexington, KY 40503

Kentucky Family Name File
Special Collections
Murray State University
Murray, KY 42071

Kentucky Lutheran
Lutheran Church in America
3733 N Meridian Street
Indianapolis, IN 46208

Kentucky National Guard Records
Military Records & Research Library
Boone National Guard Center
Frankfort, KY 40601

Kentucky United Methodist
Kentucky Conference
1018 New Circle Road
Lexington, KY 40342

Kentucky Mexican War Records
Military Records & Research Library
Boone National Guard Center
Frankfort, KY 40601

Kentucky Spanish-American War Records
Military Records & Research Library
Boone National Guard Center
Frankfort, KY 40601

Kentucky War of 1812 Records
Military Records & Research Library
Boone National Guard Center
Frankfort, KY 40601

Key System Railroad
California Railway Museum
Star Rte. 283, Box 150
Suisan City, CA 94585

Kings County, NY County Records
St. Francis College
180 Remsen Street
Brooklyn, NY 11201

Kittson County, MN County Records
Kittson County Historical Society
Lake Bronson, MN 56734

Klondike
Library
Washington State University
Pullman, WA 99163

Knights of Malta
Mullen Library
Catholic University of America
Washington, DC 20064

Knights of Labor
Library
Catholic University
Washington, DC 20064

Knights of Labor
Library
Michigan State University
East Lansing, MI 48824

**Knox County, TN Birth and
 Death Indexes**
Knoxville Public Library
500 W. Church Ave.
Knoxville, TN 37902

Knox County, TN County Records
McGhee Library
500 W. Church Ave.
Knoxville, TN 37902

Knox County, TN Deed Book
Knoxville Public Library
500 W. Church Ave.
Knoxville, TN 37902

Ku Klux Klan
American Pilitical Items Collectors
1008 Bonsella
Walla Walla, WA 99362

Ku Klux Klan
Ball State University
University Ave.
Muncie, IN 47306

Ku Klux Klan
Libraries
Texas A & M University
College Station, TX 77843

—L—

Labor History
Library
Catholic University
Washington, DC 20064

La Crosse County, WI County Records
Area Research Center
University of Wisconsin
La Crosse, WI 54601

Lake Collection
Fort Worth Public Library
300 Taylor Street
Fort Worth, TX 76102

Lake Champlain Valley
College at Plattsburgh

State University of New York
Plattsburgh, NY 12901

Lake Erie
Erie Museum
356 West 6th Street
Erie, PA 16507

Lake Erie Collection
Libraries
Case Western Reserve University
Cleveland, OH 44106

Lake Erie-Ohio River Canal
Youngstown Public Library
305 Wick Street
Youngstown, OH 44503

Lake Long Island Collection
Princeton Historical Society
158 Nassau Street
Princeton, NJ 08540

Lambert Collection
Marriott Library
University of Utah
Salt Lake City, UT 84112

Lane County, OR County Records
Lane County Pioneer Museum
740 West 13th Ave.
Eugene, OR 97402

Lake County, OH Cemetery Records
Morley Library
184 Phelps Street
Painsville, OH 44077

Lancaster County, PA Court Records
Historical Society
219 S. Front Street
Harrisburg, PA 17104

Land of Goshen Historical Society
Madison County Historical Society
715 N. Main Street
Edwardsville, IL 62025

Language Tapes
Dunn-Donnelly Pub. Co.
666 Fifth Avenue
New York, NY 10019

Laredo Archives
Archives Division
1201 Brazos Street
Austin, TX 78711

Lasseter Confederate Collection
Emory University
Oxford College
Oxford, GA 30267

Latin American Collection
University of Texas
P.O. Box P
Austin, TX 78712

Latitudinarian Anglicans
Unitarian & Universalist Genealogy Society

Boldface indicates subject; **DO NOT** include it as part of the address.

10605 Lakespring Way
Cockeysville, MD 21030

Latvia
Pilsudski Institute
381 Park Ave. So.
New York, NY 10016

Latvians
Balzekas Museum
4012 Archer Ave.
Chicago, IL 60632

Latvian
American Latvian Assoc.
P.O. Box 432
Rockville, MD 20859

Law
Los Angeles County Law Library
301 W. First Street
Los Angeles, CA 90012

Lawrence Collection
Learning Resources Center
Southwest Texas State University
San Marcos, TX 78666

Leavenworth, Kansas Cemetery Records
Leavenworth Public Library
5th & Walnut Streets
Leavenworth, KS 66048

Le Claire Collection
Davenport Museum
1717 West 12th Street
Davenport, IA 52804

Legislative Drafting
Legislative Drafting Research Fund
435 West 116th Street
New York, NY 10027

Lehigh County, PA County Records
Archives of Lehigh County
5th and Hamilton Streets
Allentown, PA 18101

Librarians
American Library Assoc.
50 East Huron Street
Chicago, IL 60611

Library of Congress
Genealogy & Local History
Library of Congress
Washington, DC 20540

Library of Congress
Reference & Bibliographic Section
Library of Congress
Washington, DC 20559

Liberty County, TX Country Records
Sam Houston Library
Farm Road 1011
Liberty, TX 77575

Lighthouses
Portsmouth Public Library

601 Court Street
Portsmouth, VA 23704

Lighthouses
Records Group 26
National Archives
Washington, DC 20408

Lighthouse Logbooks
Great Lakes Historical Society
480 Main Street
Vermillion, OH 44089

Lists of Federal Civil War Deserters
Record Group 110
National Archives
Washington, DC 20408

List of Soldiers in Continental Service
Library
Valley Forge State Park
Valley Forge, PA 19481

Lists of Kansas County Officers
Secretary of State
State House
Topeka, KS 66612

Lithuania
Pilsudski Institute
381 Park Ave. So.
New York, NY 10016

Lithuania
Balzekas Museum
4012 S. Archer Ave.
Chicago, IL 60632

Lithuanian
Balzekas Museum
4012 Archer Ave.
Chicago, IL 60632

Lithuanian
American Lithuanian Council
2606 West 63rd Street
Chicago, IL 60629

Lithuanian
Lithuanian-American Community
42 South 15th Street, #1004
Philadelphia, PA 19102

Lithuanian
National Lithuanian Society
87-80 96th Street
Woodhaven, NY 11421

Little Nine Partners Grant
Library
Little Nine Partners Historical Society
Pine Plains, NY 12567

Llano Estacado Area
Van Howeling Memorial Library
Wayland Baptist College
Plainview, TX 79072

LLoyd's Register of Shipping
San Francisco Maritime Museum

Foot of Polk
San Francisco, CA 94109

Local Histories
New York Public Library
Fifth Ave. & 42 Street
New York, NY 10018

Local Researchers
Family Tree Newsletter
450 Potter Street
Wauseon, OH 43567

Logan County, KY County Records
Kentucky Library
Western Kentucky University
Bowling Green, KY 42101

Logan County, OH County Records
Library
Wright State University
Dayton, OH 45431

Logging Railroads
Donnelley Library
Lake Forest College
Lake Forest, IL 60045

Logging Railroads
Georgia-Pacific Archives
900 S.W. 5th
Portland, OR 97204

Long Island
Nassau County Museum
Eisenhower Park
East Meadow, NY 11554

Long Island Collection
East Hampton Free Library
159 Main Street
East Hampton, NY 11937

Long Island Genealogical Collection
Huntington Historical Society
New York Ave. & Hight Street
Huntington, NY 11743

Long Island Railroad
Melville Library
State University of New York
Stony Brook, NY 11794

Long Island Vital Records Index
Queens Borough Public Library
89-11 Merrick Blvd.
Jamaica, NY 11432

Loomis Michigan County Historical Index
Michigan State Library
735 E. Michigan Ave.
Lansing, MI 48913

Lorain County, OH Agricultural Society
Herrick Memorial Library
Public Square
Wellington, OH 44090

Los Angeles Area Great Registers
Los Angeles County Museum of

Natural History
900 Exposition Blvd.
Los Angeles, CA 90007

Los Angeles County, CA
Assessment Books
Los Angeles County Museum of
Natural History
900 Exposition Blvd.
Los Angeles, CA 90007

Lost Palatine Magazine
Gail Breitbard
Rt. 1, Box 1160
Estero, FL 33928

Louisiana Catholics
Chancery Archives
7887 Walmsley Ave.
New Orleans, LA 70125

Louisiana Collection
New Orleans Public Library
219 Loyola Ave.
New Orleans, LA 70140

Louisiana Colonial Archives
Louisiana State Museum
751 Chartres Street
New Orleans, LA 70116

Louisiana Confederate Census (1911)
Archives and Records Service
P.O. Box 44125
Baton Rouge, LA 70804

Louisiana Confederate Collection
State Archives & Records Commission
Capitol Station
Baton Rouge, LA 70804

Louisiana Confederate Records
Louisiana State Museum
751 Chartres Street
New Orleans, LA 70116

Louisiana Family History File
Louisiana State Library
760 Riverside Mall
Baton Rouge, LA 70821

Louisiana Methodist
Magale Library
Centenary College
Shreveport, LA 71104

Louisiana & Mississippi
Tulane University
7001 Freret Street
New Orleans, LA 70118

Louisiana Newspaper Index
New Orleans Public Library
219 Loyola Ave.
New Orleans, LA 70140

Louisiana Federal Court Records
Federal Archives & Records Center
4900 Hemphill Street

Boldface indicates subject; **DO NOT** include it as part of the address.

Fort Worth, TX 76115

Louisiana Purchase
Missouri Historical Society
Lindell & Debaliviere Ave.
St. Louis, MO 63112

Lowell Collection
Lowell City Library
401 Merrimack Street
Lowell, MA 01852

Lower Canada
Societe de Genealogie de Quebec
C.P. 2234. G1K 7N8
Quebec, Canada

Lower Columbia River Newspapers
Astoria Public Library
450 Tenth Street
Astoria, OR 97103

Lower Naugatuck Valley
Derby Historical Society
37 Elm Street
Ansonia, CT 06418

Loyal Legion
Chicago Historical Society
Clark Street at North Ave.
Chicago, IL 60614

Loyal Legion Records
Maine Historical Society
485 Congress Street
Portland, ME 04111

Loyalist
Canadian Committee
University of New Brunswick
Fredericton, N.B.
Canada

Loyalists
Dominion Headquarters
23 Prince Arthur Ave.
Toronto, Ont. M5R 1B2 Canada

Lutheran
Wagner College
631 Howard Ave.
Staten Island, NY 10301

Lutheran
California & Nevada Archives
465 Woolsey Street
San Francisco, CA 94134

Lutheran
Concordia History Institute
801 DeMun Ave.
St. Louis, MO 63105

Lutheran
Lutheran Theological Seminary
7301 Germantown Ave.
Philadelphia, PA 19119

Lutheran
Lutheran School of Theo.

1100 East 55th Street
Chicago, IL 60615

Luzerne County, PA County Records
Wyoming Historical Society
49 South Franklin Street
Wilkes-Barre, PA 18701

—M—

Madison County, IN County Records
Madison County Historical Society
30 West 11th Street
Anderson, IN 46015

Magna Charta 8 Volume Index
Helen M. Blumhagen
970 Logan Avenue
Salt Lake City, UT 84105

Mahoney Collection
Mississippi Room
University of So. Mississippi
Hattiesburg, MS 39401

Mahoning Valley
Arms Museum
648 Wick Ave.
Youngstown, OH 44502

Maine
Maine Historical Society
485 Congress Street
Portland, ME 04111

Maine Cemetery Collection
Maine Historical Society
485 Congress Street
Portland, ME 04111

Maine Cemetery Inscriptions
State Library
State Capitol
Augusta, ME 04330

Maine Civil War Indexes
Maine State Archives
State Capitol
Augusta, ME 04330

Maine County Records
State Archives
Augusta, ME

Maine Country Records
Maine Historical Society
485 Congress Street
Portland, ME 04111

Maine Platt Maps
State Forestry Department
State House
Augusta, ME 04301

Maine Town Records
States Archives
Augusta, ME

Maine Town Records
Maine Historical Society

Massachusetts G.A.R.
Memorial Shrine
Room 27, State House
Boston, MA 02133

Massachusetts State Censuses
 (1855 & 1865)
Archives of the Commonwealth
State House
Boston, MA 02133

Massachusetts Town Maps
Massachusetts Historical Society
1154 Boyleston Street
Boston, MA 02215

Massachusetts Tax Lists Catalog
Archives of the Commonwealth
State House
Boston, MA 02133

Massachusetts Veterans Graves
 Registration
Archives of the Commonwealth
State House
Boston, MA 02133

Maumee Valley
Toledo Public Library
325 Michigan Street
Toledo, OH 43624

McClung Historical Collection
McGhee Library
500 W. Church Ave.
Knoxville, TN 37902

McCubbins Collection
Rowan Public Library
201 W. Fisher Street
Salisbury, NC 28144

McElroy Collection
Kentucky Library
Western Kentucky University
Bowling Green, KY 42101

McGregor Collection
Alderman Library
University of Virginia
Charlettsville, VA 22901

McMurin Collection
Marriott Library
University of Utah
Salt Lake City, UT 84112

Mecklenburg County, NC Vital Records
Cannon Memorial Library
27 Union Street, N.
Concord, NC 28025

Medicine
Medical Archives
1300 York Ave.
New York, NY 10021

Medicine
University of Chicago

1126 East 59th Street
Chicago, IL 60637

Medicine
American Philosophical Society
105 S. Fifth Street
Philadelphia, PA 19106

Medicine
Library
East Texas State University
Commerce, TX 75428

Medicine
National Academy of Sciences
2101 Constitution Ave., N.W.
Washington, DC

Medicine
Brown University
20 Prospect Street
Providence, RI 02912

Medicine
Countway Library
10 Shattuck Street
Boston, MA 02115

Medicine
Fake Library
245 N. & 15th Street
Philadelphia, PA 19102

Medical
College of Physicians of Philadelphia
19 South 22nd Street
Philadelphia, PA 19103

Medical
Archives
University of Pennsylvania
Philadelphia, PA 19174

Medical
Thomas Jefferson University
1020 Walnut Street
Philadelphia, PA 19107

Medical
Cleveland Health Sciences Library
11000 Euclid Ave.
Cleveland, OH 44106

Medical
University of Cinncinati
610 Main Library
Cincinnati, OH 45221

Medical
Albany Medical College
New Scotland Ave.
Albany, NY 12208

Medical
Yale University
333 Cedar Street
New Haven, CT 06510

Medical
Hartford Medical Society

230 Scarborough Street
Hartford, CT 06105

Medical
National Library of Medicine
8600 Rockville Pike
Bethesda, MD 20014

Medical
University of Kansas
Rainbow Blvd. at 39th
Kansas City, KS 66103

Medical
Biomedical Library
University of California
Los Angeles, CA 90024

Medical
University of Texas
5323 Harry Hines Blvd.
Dallas, TX 75235

Medical Collection (Pre-1865)
Transylvania University
300 North Broadway
Lexington, KY 40508

Medical Men
Toner Collection
Library of Congress
Washington, DC 20540

Medical & Surgical Registers
Photoduplication Service
Library of Congress
Washington, DC 20540

Meigs County, OH County Records
Meigs County Museum
144 Butternut Ave.
Pomeroy, OH 45769

Memphis City Records
Memphis Public Library
1850 Peabody Ave.
Memphis, TN 38104

Memphis, TN Newspaper Index
Memphis Public Library
1850 Peabody Ave.
Memphis, TN 38104

Mennonite
Mennonite Family History
Box 171
Elverson, PA 19520

Mennonite
Schwenkfelder Library
Seminary and Perkiomen School
Pennsburg, PA 18073

Mennonite
Mennonite Historical Library
Bluffton College
Bluffton, OH 45817

Mennonites
Lancaster Mennonite Historical Society
2215 Millstream Road
Lancaster, PA 17602

Mennonites
Tabor College
401 S. Jefferson
Hillsboro, KS 67063

Mennonites
Pacific College
1717 So. Chestnut
Fresno, CA 93702

Mennonites
Library
Eastern Mennonite College
Harrisonburg, VA 22801

Mennonite Obituary Index
Goshen College
1700 South Main Street
Goshen, IN 46526

Mennonite Yearbook
Mennonite Publishing House
Scottdale, PA 15683

Mercer County, OH County Records
Library
Wright State University
Dayton, OH 45431

Merchant Families
Baker Library
Harvard University
Boston, MA 02163

Merchant Marine
International Marine Archives
21 Orange Street
Nantucket, MA 02554

Merchant Marine
American Merchant Marine
  Library Assoc.
One World Trade Center, #2601
New York, NY 10048

Merchant Marine Casualty Index
Coast Guard
New London, CT 06320

Merchant Marine
Photographic Library
U.S. Naval Institute
Annapolis, MD 21402

Merchant Marine Logbooks
Record Group 41
National Archives
Washington, DC 20408

Merchant Shipping
Stonington Historical Society
Whitehall Ave.
Stonington, CT 06378

Merchant Vessels
San Francisco Maritime Museum
Foot of Polk

485 Congress Street
Portland, ME 04111

Manuscript Catalogs
Columbia University Libraries
535 West 114th Street
New York, NY 10027

Manuscript Collection Card Catalog
American Antiquarian Society
185 Salisbury Street
Worcester, MA 01609

Maps
Geography & Map Division
Library of Congress
Washington, DC 20540

Map Collection (America)
Geogrpahy & Map Division
Library of Congress
Washington, DC 20540

Marine Accidents
Chicago Historical Society
Clark Street at North Ave.
Chicago, IL 60614

Marine
Suffolk Marine Museum
Montauk Highway
West Sayville, NY 11796

Marine
Library
Roosevelt Library
Hyde Park, NY 12538

Marine Muster Rolls
Marine Corps Historical Center
Washington Navy Yard
Washington, DC 20374

Marines
Commandant of the Marine Corps
Headquarters, U.S. Marine Corps
Washington, DC 20380

Marion County, IA County Records
Learning Resource Center
Central College
Pella, IA 50219

Maritime
Evangelical Covenant Church
5125 N. Spaulding Library
Chicago, IL 60625

Maritime
McLean County Historical Society
112 E. Front Street
Bloomington, IL 61701

Maritime
University of Delaware
So. College Ave.
Newark, NJ 19711

Maritime
Stonington Historical Society

Whitehall Ave.
Stonington, CT 06378

Maritime
New Haven Colony Historical Society
114 Whitney Ave.
New Haven, CT 06510

Maritime
Library
Lundeborg School of Seamanship
Piney Point, MD 20674

Maritime
Brown University
20 Prospect Street
Providence, RI 02912

Maritime
Library
University of Baltimore
1420 Maryland Ave.
Baltimore, MD 21201

Maritime
Library
Calvert Marine Museum
Solomons, MD 20688

Maritime
International Marine Archives
21 Orange Street
Nantucket, MA 02554

Maritime
Northwest Seaport
218-B Kirkland Ave.
Kirkland, WA 98033

Maritime
Museum of History & Industry
2161 E. Hamlin
Seattle, WA 98112

Maritime
Whaling Museum Society
Main Street
Cold Spring Harbor, NY 11724

Maritime
Library
Bowdoin College
Brunswick, ME 04011

Maritime
Essex Institute
132 Essex Street
Salem, MA 01970

Maritime
Foulger Museum
Broad Street
Nantucket, MA 02554

Maritime
South Street Seaport Museum
205 Front Street
New York, NY 10038

Maritime

New York Historical Society
170 Central Park West
New York, NY 10024

Maritime
Herkimer Home
Route 169
Little Falls, NY 13365

Maritime Data
Society of California Pioneers
456 McAllister Street
San Francisco, CA 94102

Maritime Data
Mystic Seaport Museum
Mystic, CT 06355

Maritime Data
National Maritime Museum
Foot of Polk Street
San Francisco, CA 94109

Maritime Data
Mariners Museum
Museum Drive
Newport News, VA 23606

Maritime Provinces
University of Maine
South Stevens Hall
Orono, ME 04473

Maritime Provinces
Boston Public Library
666 Boylston Street
Boston, MA 02117

Marks-Sherwood Collection
Dr. Louis S. Marks
40 Oakland Terrace
Bala-Cynwyd, PA 19004

Marshall Cousins Papers
Area Research Center
University of Wisconsin
Eau Claire, WI 54701

Martin County, MN County Records
Pioneer Museum
304 E. Blue Earth Ave.
Fairmont, MN 56039

Mary Adams Rolfe's Genealogical Papers
Historical Society of Old Newbury
98 High Street
Newburyport, MA 01950

Maryland
Library
University of Maryland
College Park, MD 20742

Maryland Civil War Index
Hall of Records
St. John's Street & College Ave.
Annapolis, MD 21402

Maryland Colonial Census Index
Hall of Records

St. John's Street & College Ave.
Annapolis, MD 21402

Maryland Colonial Proprietors
Maryland Historical Society
201 W. Monument Street
Baltimore, MD 21201

Maryland Colonial Records
Hall of Records
St. John's Street & College Ave.
Annapolis, MD 21402

Maryland Colonial War Index
Hall of Records
St. John's Street & College Ave.
Annapolis, MD 21402

Maryland County Records
Maryland Historical Society
201 W. Monument Street
Baltimore, MD 21201

Maryland Germans
Society for the Study of
  Germans in Maryland
17 Commerce Street
Baltimore, MD 21202

Maryland Jewish
Jewish Historical Society
5800 Park Heights Ave.
Baltimore, MD 21215

Maryland Probate Index
Hall of Records
St. John's Street & College Ave.
Annapolis, MD 21402

Maryland Revolution War Index
Hall of Records
St. John's Street & College Ave.
Annapolis, MD 21402

Maryland State Colonization Records
Maryland Historical Society
201 W. Monument Street
Baltimore, MD 21201

Masons
Northern Masonic Jurisdiction
33 Marrett Road
Lexington, MA 02173

Masons
Supreme Council
1733 16th Street, N.W.
Washington, DC 20009

Massachusetts
Massachusetts Historical Society
1154 Boylston Street
Boston, MA 02215

Massachusetts Dir. Tax (1798)
N.E. Historical-Genealogical Society
101 Newbury Street
Boston, MA 02116

San Francisco, CA 94109

Merchant Vessels
Industrial & Social Branch
National Archives & Records Service
Washington, DC 20408

Merrimack River
University of Lowell
One University Ave.
Lowell, MA 01854

Methodist
Iliff School of Theo.
2233 S. University Blvd.
Denver, CO 80210

Methodist
Museum and Library
235 N. 4th Street
Philadelphia, PA 19106

Methodist Episcopal
Duke University
Durham, NC

Methodist Episcopal
Evergreen Manor
1130 N. Westfield Blvd.
Oshkosh, WI 54901

Methodist Episcopal
Shipman Library
Adrian College
Adrian, MI 49221

Methodist Episcopal (CA & NV)
Library
University of the Pacific
Stockton, CA 95211

Methodist Episcopal South
Duke University
Durham, NC

Methodist Preachers
Wofford College
N. Church Street
Spartanburg, SC 29301

Methodist Preachers
Garrett-Evangelical Theo. Seminary
2121 Sheridan Road
Evanston, IL 60201

Methodist Protestant
Shipman Library
Adrian College
Adrian, MI 49221

Methodist Protestant
Wesley Theo. Seminary
4400 Massachusetts Ave., N.W.
Washington, DC 20016

Metrolina, Region
Atkins Library
University of North Carolina
Charlotte, NC 28223

Mexican Archives
State Records Center
404 Montezuma
Santa Fe, NM 87503

Mexican Texas
Daughters of the Republic of Texas
The Alamo
San Antonio, TX 78299

Mexican War Collection
Mobile City Museum
355 Government Street
Mobile, AL 36602

Miami-Erie Canal
Middletown Public Library
1320 First Ave.
Middletown, OH 45042

Miami County, OH Cemetery Index
Troy Public Library
419 W. Main Street
Troy, OH 45373

Miami County, OH County Records
Library
Wright State University
Dayton, OH 45431

Miami County, OH Pioneer Index
Troy Public Library
419 W. Main Street
Troy, OH 45373

Miami Purchase Assoc.
Miami Purchase Assoc.
812 Dayton Street
Cincinnati, OH 45214

Miami Valley
Greater Miami Valley Research Center
Wright State University
Dayton, OH 45431

Miami Valley, OH Genealogical Index
Dayton Public Library
215 East 3rd Street
Dayton, OH 45402

Michigan
Bentley Historical Library
1150 Beal Ave.
Ann Arbor, MI 48105

Michigan Baptist
Kalamazoo College
Thompson & Academy Streets
Kalamazoo, MI 49007

Michigan Biographical Files
Michigan State Library
735 E. Michigan Ave.
Lansing, MI 48913

Michigan Mining
Library
Michigan Technological University
Houghton, MI 49931

Boldface indicates subject; DO NOT include it as part of the address.

**Michigan Masonic Grand
 Lodge Records**
Bentley Historical Library
University of Michigan
Ann Arbor, MI 48104

Michigan Methodist
Shipman Library
Adrian College
Adrian, MI 49221

Michigan Pioneer Record
Michigan State Library
735 E. Michigan Ave.
Lansing, MI 48913

Microcomputer Market Place
Dekotek, Inc.
2248 Broadway
New York, NY 10024

Microfiche Publications
Lost Cause Press
750-56 Starks Blvd.
Louisville, KY 40202

Microfilm Collection
Genealogical Society
50 East North Temple
Salt Lake City, UT 84150

Microfilm Sources
Microfilm Publishing
Box 313, Wykage Street
New Rochelle, NY 10804

Microfilm Your Records
Gray Photography
#3-615 West Grand
Hot Springs, AR 71913

Microfilming Movie (G.S.)
Audio-Visual Services
290 HRC, Brigham Young University
Provo, UT 84602

Microforms
Meckler Publishing
520 Riverside Avenue
Westport, CT 06880

Microforms
Research Publications, Inc.
12 Lunar Drive
Woodbridge, CT 06525

Mid-Atlantic Methodist
Lovely Lane Museum
2200 St. Paul Street
Baltimore, MD 21218

Mid-Atlantic States
Library
Eleutherian Mills
Greenville, DE 19807

Mid-Hudson Dutch
Van Wyck Homestead Museum
Routes 9 and I84
Fishkill, NY 12524

Mid-Hudson Region
Greene County Historical Society
R.D.
Coxsackie, NY 12051

Mid-West Christian Reformed
Colonial Origins Collection
3207 Burton Street, S.E.
Grand Rapids, MI 49506

Mid-West Congregational
Chicago Theo. Seminary
5757 S. University Ave.
Chicago, IL 60637

Mid-West Episcopal
Indiana State Library
Indianapolis, In 46208

Mid-West Episcopal
Episcopal Diocese
65 East Huron Street
Chicago, IL 60611

Mid-West Evangelical & Reformed
Chicago Theo. Seminary
5757 S. University Ave.
Chicago, IL 60637

Mid-West Families
Newberry Library
60 West Walton Street
Chicago, IL 60610

Mid-West Lutherans
Indiana Dist. Archives
1145 S. Barr Street
Fort Wayne, IN 46802

Midwest Manuscripts Collection
Newberry Library
60 West Walton Street
Chicago, IL 60610

Mid-West
Garrett-Evangelical Theo. Seminary
2121 Sheridan Road
Evanston, IL 60201

Middlesex Canal
University of Lowell
One University Ave.
Lowell, MA 01854

Migrations
Center for Migration Studies
209 Flagg Street
New York, NY 10304

Millie Worcester Papers
Rochester Public Library
65 South Main Street
Rochester, NH 03867

Military
American Legion
700 N. Penn. Street
Indianapolis, IN 46206

Military Forts
Carter Museum
P.O. Box 2365
Fort Worth, TX 76101

Military Graves
Graves Registration Unit
46 Aborn Street
Providence, RI 02900

Military Graves
State Archives
State Capitol
Augusta, ME 04330

Military History
U.S. Army Military Hist. Insti.
Carlisle Barrack, PA 17013

Military Historical Society
Boston University
771 Commonwealth Ave.
Boston, MA 02215

Military Personnel Records
National Personnel Records Center
9700 Page Street
St. Louis, MO 63132

Milwaukee City Court Records
Milwaukee County Historical Society
910 North 3rd Street
Milwaukee, WI 53203

Milwaukee City Records
Legislative Reference Bureau
200 E. Wells Street
Milwaukee, WI 53202

Milwaukee City Records
Milwaukee Public Library
814 West Wisconsin Ave.
Milwaukee, WI 53233

Milwaukee County, WI County Records
Area Research Center
University of Wisconsin
Milwaukee, WI 53201

Milwaukee County, WI County Records
Legislative Reference Bureau
200 E. Wells Street
Milwaukee, WI 53202

Milwaukee County, WI Records
Milwaukee County Historical Society
910 North 3rd Street
Milwaukee, WI 53203

Mine Map Depository
Deveraux Library
South Dakota School of Mines
Rapid City, SD 57701

Mining
Western Historical Research Center
University of Wyoming
Laramie, WY 82070

Mining Disrict Maps

Record Group 48
National Archives
Washington, DC 20408

Mining Industry
Western Historical Collections
University of Colorado
Boulder, CO 80302

Miners
Western History Research Center
University of Wyoming
Laramie, WY 82070

Miners
Mines Library
University of Nevada
Reno, NV 89557

Miners
Western Historical Collections
University of Colorado
Boulder, CO 80302

Miners
Library
Montana State University
Bozeman, MT 59717

Minicomputers
Assoc. of Minicomputer Users
Two Frederick Street
Framingham, MA 01701

Minnesota Valley
Brown County Historical Society
27 North Broadway
New Ulm, MN 56073

Miscellaneous Fortification
File (forts)
Record Group 77
National Archives
Washington, DC 20408

Missing Persons
Salvation Army
30840 Hawthorne Blvd.
Palos Verdes, CA 90274

Missing Persons
Child Find, Inc.
P.O. Box 277
New Paltz, NY 12561

Missing Persons
International Tracing Service
D 3548 Arolsen
Federal Republic of Germany

Missing Persons
Military Locators, Inc.
P.O. Box 5369
Orlando, FL 32855

Missing Persons
Everton Publishers, Inc.
P.O. Box 368
Logan, UT 84321

Boldface indicates subject; **DO NOT** include it as part of the address.

Missing Persons
Social & Rehabilitation Service
Room 5004, Switzer Building
Washington, DC 20201

Missing Persons
Orphan Voyage of Florida (Computer)
13906 Pepperrell Drive
Tampa, FL 33624

Missing Persons Located
Missing Persons
P.O. Box 195
Great Kills, NY 10308

Mississippi
Mitchell Memorial Library
Mississippi State University
Mississippi State, MS 39762

Mississippi Baptist
Mississippi Baptist
 Historical Commission
P.O. Box 51
Clinton, MS 39056

Mississippi Confederate Index
Mississippi Department of
 Archives & History
Capitol Green
Jackson, MS 39205

**Mississippi Confederate
 Pension Index**
Department of Archives & History
Capitol Green
Jackson, MS 39205

Mississippi Delta
Roberts Library
Delta State University
Cleveland, MS 38733

Mississippi Marriage Collection
Department of Archives & History
Capitol Green
Jackson, MS 39205

Mississippi Marriage Index
Mississippi Room
Bolivar County Library
Cleveland, MS 38732

Mississippi Methodist
Millsaps-Wilson Library
Millsaps College
Jackson, MS 39210

Mississippi River
Winona County Historical Society
160 Johnson Street
Winona, MN 55987

Mississippi River
University of Wisconsin
1631 Pine Street
La Crosse, WI 54601

Mississippi River Plantation Maps

Record Group 56
Natinal Archives
Washington, DC 20408

Mississippi Valley
Torreyson Library
University of Central Arkansas
Conway, AR 72032

Mississippi Valley
Illinois Historical Survey
University of Illinois
Urbana, IL 61801

Mississippi Valley Collection
Memphis State University
Southern & Patterson
Memphis, TN 38152

**Mississippi & Alabama Territorial
Land Records**
Gorgas Library
University of Alabama
University, AL 35486

Missouri
Missouri Historical Society
Jefferson Memorial Bldg.
St. Louis, MO 63112

Missouri Genealogy Index
St. Louis Public Library
1301 Olive Street
St. Louis, MO 63103

Missouri Confederate
Records and Archives
1717 Industrial Drive
Jefferson City, MO 65101

Missouri-Kansas-Texas Railroad
Midwestern State University
3400 Taft Street
Wichita Falls, TX 76308

Missouri Methodist
Smiley Library
Central Methodist College
Fayette, MO 65248

Missouri Militia
Records and Archives
1717 Industrial Drive
Jefferson City, MO 65101

Missouri Place-Name File
Missouri State Historical Society
Hitt & Lowry Streets
Columbia, MO 65201

Missouri River
Missouri River Historical Museum
1500 R Street
Lincoln, NE 68508

Missouri United Methodist Church
Smiley Memorial Library
Central Methodist College
Fayette, MO 65248

Missouri Valley
Kansas City Public Library
311 East 12th Street
Kansas City, MO 64106

Mobile City & County Records
Museum of the City of Mobile
355 Government Street
Mobile, AL 36602

Mobile Alabama Collection
Mobile Public Library
701 Government Street
Mobile, AL 36602

Mobile, AL Naturalization Index
Mobile City Archives
Mobile, AL

Mobile, AL Passenger Lists
Mobile City Archives
Mobile, AL

Modesto, CA Newspaper Index
Stanislaus County Library
1500 I Street
Modesto, CA 95354

Molly Maguires
Washington & Jefferson College
Lincoln & Wheeling Streets
Washington, PA 15301

Monmouth County, NJ County Records
Moss Archives
39 Rumson Road
Rumson, NJ 07760

Monongalia County, WV
Morgantown Public Library
373 Spruce Street
Morgantown, WV 26505

Monroe County, NY Biography File
Rundel Library
115 South Avenue
Rochester, NY 14604

Monroe County, NY Place Name Index
Rundel Library
115 South Avenue
Rochester, NY 14604

Monroe County, MI County Records
Archives
126 S. Monroe Street
Monroe, MI 48161

**Montana Certificate of
 Purchase Book**
Department of State Lands
State Capitol
Helena, MT 59601

Montana Deed File
Department of State Lands
State Capitol
Helena, MT 59601

Montana Farm Loan Abstract Book

Department of State Lands
State Capitol
Helena, MT 59601

Montana Farm Loan Pouch Files
Department of State Lands
State Capitol
Helena, MT 59601

Montana Methodist
Rocky Mountain College
1511 Poly Drive
Billings, MT 59102

Montana Original Land Register
Department of State Lands
State Capitol
Helena, MT 59601

Montana Territorial Records
Courthouse
Virginia City, MT

Montgomery County, NY County Records
Department of History & Archives
Old Court House
Fonda, NY 12068

Montgomery County, OH County Records
Library
Wright State University
Dayton, OH 45431

Monuments
American Monument Assoc.
6902 N. High
Worthington, OH 43085

Moravian
Historic Bethlehem
516 Main Street
Bethlehem, PA 18018

Moravian
Moravian Archives
43 West Locust Street
Bethlehem, PA 18018

Moravian
Moravian Historical Society
214 E. Center Street
Nazareth, PA 18064

Morgan Collection
Wells College Library
Main Street
Aurora, NY 13026

Morley Collection
California Institute of Technology
1201 E. California Blvd.
Pasadena, CA 91125

Mormons
Genealogical Society
50 East North Temple
Salt Lake City, UT 84150

Mormons
Library

Boldface indicates subject; **DO NOT** include it as part of the address.

Princeton University
Princeton, NJ 08540

Mormons
Smith Library
Graceland College
Lamoni, IA 50140

Mormons
Utah State Historical Society
207 W. Second South
Salt Lake City, UT 84101

Mormons
Library
University of Utah
Salt Lake City, UT 84112

Mormons
Church Library-Archives
50 East North Temple
Salt Lake City, UT 84150

Mormon History Archives
Lee Library
Brigham Young University
Provo, UT 84602

Mormon Pioneers
Lee Library
Brigham Young University
Provo, UT 84602

Mormon Pioneers
Daughters of Utah Pioneers
300 North Main Street
Salt Lake City, UT 84103

Morris County, NJ County Records
Morris County Free Library
30 East Hanover Ave.
Whippany, NJ 07891

Morse Whaling Collection
Brown University
20 Prospect Street
Providence, RI 02912

Moultrie County, IL Vital Records
Moultrie County Historical
  and Genealogical Society
117 East Harrison Street
Sullivan, IL 61951

Mountain Men
Washington State University
Pullman, WA 99164

Museums
American Assoc. of Museums
1055 Thomas Jefferson St., N.W.
Washington, DC 20007

Museum Register
National Register Publishing Co.
5201 Old Orchard Road
Skokie, IL 60077

Mutual Assurance Co.
Mutual Assurance Co.

240 South 4th Street
Philadelphia, PA 19106

—N—

Nacogdoches Archives
Archives Division
1201 Brazos Street
Austin, TX 78711

Namegathering
Center for Death Education
1167 Social Science Bldg.
Minneapolis, MN 55455

Nase Dejiny (Our History)
Doug Kubiska
Box 45
Hallettsville, TX 77964

National Archives
National Archives & Records Service
General Services Administration
Washington, DC 20408

National Archives Magazine
Prologue
National Archives & Records Service
Washington, DC 20408

National Assoc.
American Hist. Assoc.
400 A Street, S.E.
Washington, DC 20003

National Farmers Union
Western Hist. Collections
University of Colorado
Boulder, CO 80302

National Guard
National Guard Assoc.
1 Mass. Ave., N.W.
Washington, DC 20001

National Negro Insurance Assoc.
National Insurance Assoc.
2400 S. Michigan Ave.
Chicago, IL 60616

National Organization
National Genealogical Society
1921 Sunderland Place, N.W.
Washington, DC 20036

National Organization
American Family Records Assoc.
311 East 12th Street
Kansas City, MO 64106

National Organization
Federation of Genealogical Societies
P.O. Box 220
Davenport, IA 52805

**National Woman's Christian
  Temperance Union**
Williard Memorial Library
1730 Chicago Ave.
Evanston, IL 60201

National Zip Code Directory
Superintendent of Documents
U.S. Government Printing Office
Washington, DC 20402

Naturalization Index
Federal Archives & Records Center
7358 S. Pulaski Road
Chicago, Il 60629

Naturalizations (post-1906)
Immigration & Naturalization Service
425 Eye Street, N.W.
Washington, DC 20503

Naval Discharges and Desertions
Record Group 24
National Archives
Washington, DC 20408

Naval History
Nimitz Library
U.S. Naval Academy
Annapolis, MD 21402

Naval Historical Foundation
  Collection
Manuscript Division
Library of Congress
Washington, DC 20540

Naval Officers
Historical Collection & Museum
U.S. Naval War College
Newport, RI 02840

Naval Records Collection
Record Group 45
National Archives
Washington, DC 20408

Naval Shipyard Work Logs
Federal Records Center
Building 308
Mechanicsburg, PA 17055

Naval Vessels, Stations
  and Hospitals
Record Group 52
National Archives
Washington, DC 20408

Nazarene
Point Loma College
3900 Lomaland Drive
San Diego, CA 92106

Nebraska Federal Land Records
State Historical Society
1500 R Street
Lincoln, NE 68508

Nebraska G.A.R. Records
State Historical Society
1500 R Street
Lincoln, NE 68508

Nebraska Place-Name Index
State Historical Society

1500 R Street
Lincoln, NE 68508

Nebraska State Gazeteer Index (1886)
State Historical Society
1500 R Street
Lincoln, NE 68508

Nebraska United Methodist
Nebraska Wesleyan University
50th & St. Paul
Lincoln, NE 68504

Nelson Collection
Austin State University
Box 13055, SFA Sta.
Nacodoches, TX 75961

Nelson County, KY County Records
Kentucky Library
Western Kentucky University
Bowling Green, KT 42101

Nevada Biographical Index
Getchell Library
University of Nevada
Reno, NV 89507

Nevada Mining
Library
University of Nevada
Reno, NV 89507

Nevada Mining Camps (Northeastern)
Northeastern Nevada Museum
1515 Idaho Street
Elko, NV 89801

Nevada State Census (1875)
State Archives
Capitol Bldg.
Carson City, NV 89701

Nevada Territorial Records
Nevada Historical Society
1650 N. Virginia Street
Reno, NV 89503

New Bedford Seamen's Card File
Free Public Library
Pleasant Street
New Bedford, MA 02741

New Brunswick
New Brunswick Genealogical Society
Box 3235, Sta. B
Fredericton, E3B 2W0 Canada

New Castle & Frenchtown Railroad
Historical Society of Delaware
505 Market Street Mall
Wilmington, DE 19801

New England Colonial Court Records
Supreme Judicial Court
Room 1404, Courthouse
Boston, MA 02108

New England Emigrant Aid Company
Brown University

Boldface indicates subject; DO NOT include it as part of the address.

20 Prospect Street
Providence, RI 02912

New England Historic-
Genealogical Society
New England Historic-
Genealogical Society
101 Newberry Street
Boston, MA 02116

The New England Homestead Magazine
Inquirer and Mirror, Inc.
113 Chestnut Street
Springfield, MA 01103

New England Maritime
Peabody Museum
E. India Square
Salem, MA 01970

New England Methodist
New England Methodist
Historical Society
745 Commonwealth Ave.
Boston, MA 02215

New England Quakers
Newport Historical Society
82 Touro Street
Newport, RI 02840

New England Quakers
New England Quaker Research Library
Box 655
North Amherst, MA 01059

New England Quakers Collection
Rhode Island Historical Society
121 Hope Street
Providence, RI 02906

New England States
Naturalization Index
National Archives & Records Service
General Services Administration
Washington, DC 20408

New Gloucester Proprietor's Records
New Gloucester Historical Society
New Gloucester, ME 04260

New Hampshire
New Hampshire Historical Society
30 Park Street
Concord, NH 03301

New Hampshire Colonial Records
Division of Records Management
and Archives
71 S. Fruit Street
Concord, NH 03301

New Hampshire County/Town Records
Dimond Library
University of New Hampshire
Durham, NH 03824

New Hampshire Court Records
Division of Records Management
and Archives
71 S. Fruit Street
Concord, NH 03301

New Hampshire Gazette Index
Boston Public Library
666 Boyleston Street
Boston, MA 02117

New Hampshire Militia
Division of Records Management
and Archives
71 S. Fruit Street
Concord, NH 03301

New Hampshire Quakers
Dover Public Library
73 Locust Street
Dover, NH 03820

New Haven City/County Records
New Haven Colony Historical Society
114 Whitney Ave.
New Haven, CT 06510

New Jersey Cemetery Index
Library
Rutgers University
New Brunswick, NJ 08901

New Jersey Lyceum
Mount Holly Library
307 High Street
Mount Holly, NJ 08060

New Jersey Quakers
Savitz Learning Resource Center
Glassboro State College
Glassboro, NJ 08028

New Jersey Records
Fairleigh Dickinson University
207 Montross Ave.
Rutherford, NJ 07070

New Madrid, MO Colonial Records
Missouri Historical Society
Jefferson Memorial Bldg.
St. Louis MO 63112

New Madrid, MO Land Grants
Memphis State University
Southern & Patterson
Memphis, TN 38152

New Mexico County Records
State Records Center
404 Montezuma
Sante Fe, NM 87503

New Mexico Military Records
State Records Center
404 Montezuma
Santa Fe, NM 87503

New Mexico Territorial Archives
New Mexico State Records
Center and Archives
404 Montezuma St.

Santa Fe, NM 87503

New Netherland
New York State Library
Washington Ave.
Albany, NY 12234

New Orleans Cemetery Index
Louisiana State Museum
751 Chartres Street
New Orleans, LA 70116

New Orleans City Directories
Louisiana State Museum
751 Chartres Street
New Orleans, LA 70116

New Orleans City Records
New Orleans Public Library
219 Loyola Ave.
New Orleans, LA 70140

New Orleans Collection
Archives-Manuscripts Division
533 Royal Street
New Orleans, LA 70130

New Orleans Index
New Orleans Public Library
219 Loyola Ave.
New Orleans, LA 70140

New Orleans Newspapers
Louisiana State Museum
751 Chartres Street
New Orleans, LA 70116

New Orleans Obituary File
New Orleans Public Library
219 Loyola Ave.
New Orleans, LA 70140

New York
St. Francis College
180 Remsen Street
Brooklyn, NY 11201

New York
New York Gen. & Bio. Society
122 East 58th Street
New York, NY 10022

New York Cemetery Index
Division of Cemeteries
162 Washington Avenue
Albany, NY 12225

New York City Assessment Rolls
Historical Documents Collection
Queens College
Flushing, NY 11367

New York City Board of Education
Teachers College
525 West 120th Street
New York, NY 10027

New York City 1821 Census
Historical Documents Collection
Queens College

Flushing, NY 11367

New York City Court Records
Municipal Archives
23 Park Row
New York, NY 10038

New York City Records
Hall of Records
31 Chambers Street
New York, NY

**New York City Criminal
  Court Records**
College of Criminal Justice
445 West 59th Street
New York, NY 10019

New York City Directory
City Record Distribution & Sales
31 Chambers Street
New York, NY 10007

New York City Naturalization Index
Federal Archives & Records Center
Military Ocean Terminal
Bayonne, NJ 07002

**New York City Perris
  Insurance Maps**
New York Historical Society
170 Central Park W.
New York, NY 10024

New York City & State Court Records
Historical Documents Collection
Queens College
Flushing, NY 11367

New York City Records
Municipal Archives
23 Park Row
New York, NY 10038

New York Community Data
Community Affairs Library
162 Washington Ave.
Albany, NY 12231

New York Deposition of Resident Aliens
Manuscript and History Section
New York State Library
Albany, NY

New York Genealogical-Biographical
New York Genealogical-Biographical
122 East 58th Street
New York, NY 10022

New York Port of Customs
Whaling Museum
Main Street
Sag Harbor, NY 11963

New York State Canals
New York State Library
Washington Ave.
Albany, NY 12224

New York State Censuses

Boldface indicates subject; **DO NOT** include it as part of the address.

New York State Archives
Empire State Plaza
Albany, NY 12230

New York Colonial Records
New York State Archives
Empire State Plaza
Albany, NY 12230

New York, Ontario, & Western Railway
Library
Cornell University
Ithaca, NY 14850

New York & Pennsylvania Railway
Library
Cornell University
Ithaca, NY 14850

Newburgh
Indiana State University
8600 University Blvd.
Evansville, IN 47712

Newgate Prison
Salmon Brook Historical Society
208 Salmon Brook Street
Granby, CT 06035

Newspapers
Serial Division
Library of Congress
Washington, DC 20540

Newspaper Query, Columns Directory
Stagecoach Library
14419 Stagecoach Road
Magnolia, TX 77355

Newport, City Records
Newport Historical Society
82 Touro Street
Newport, RI 02840

Newton County, TX County Records
Sam Houston Library
Farm Road 1011
Liberty, TX 77575

Niagara Frontier
Buffalo & Erie County
 Historical Society
25 Norringham Court
Buffalo, NY 14216

Niagara Frontier Index
Buffalo & Erie County
 Historical Society
25 Nottingham Court
Buffalo, NY 14216

Nicholson Whaling Collection
Providence Public Library
150 Empire Street
Providence, RI 02903

19th Century County Land
 Ownership Maps
Geography & Map Division

Library of Congress
Washington, DC. 20540

19th Century Virginia Family
 Papers Collection
Alderman Library
University of Virginia
Charlottesville, VA 22901

No Man's Land
Historical Museum
Sewell Street
Goodwell, OK 73939

Nordic Collections
Claremont Colleges
Ninth & Dartmouth
Claremont, CA 91711

Norfolk County, VA County Records
Portsmouth Public Library
601 Court Street
Portsmouth, VA 23704

Norfolk Naval Shipyard
Portsmouth Public Library
601 Court Street
Portsmouth, VA 23704

North American Land Company
Washington & Jefferson College
Lincoln & Wheeling Streets
Washington, PA 15301

North Carolina Ancestor Index
North Carolina Genealogical Society
Box 5895, Ardmore Sta.
Winston-Salem, NC 27103

North Carolina Baptist
North Carolina Baptist Hist. Collection
P.O. Box 7777, Reynolds Sta.
Winston-Salem, NC 27109

North Carolina Collection
Library
University of North Carolina
Chapel Hill, NC 27514

North Carolina Confederate
 Cemetery Index
North Carolina, Division of
 Archives and History
109 East Jones Street
Raleigh, NC 27611

North Carolina Confederate
 Index (Moore)
North Carolina, Division of
 Archives and History
109 East Jones Street
Raleigh, NC 27611

North Carolina Confederate
 Pension Index
North Carolina, Division of
 Archives & History
109 East Jones Street
Raleigh, NC 27611

**North Carolina Confederate
Soldiers' Home Index**
North Carolina, Division of
  Archives and History
109 East Jones Street
Raleigh, NC 27611

North Dakota Naturalization Register
Historical Society of North Dakota
Liberty Memorial Bldg.
Bismarck, ND 58501

North Dakota Pioneer Index
Historical Society of North Dakota
Liberty Memorial Bldg.
Bismarck, ND 58501

North Dakota Railroad Stations Index
Historical Society of North Dakota
Liberty Memorial Bldg.
Bismarck, ND 58501

North Dakota Rural P.O. Index
Historical Society of North Dakota
Liberty Memorial Bldg.
Bismarck, ND 58501

North Shore
Annisquam Historical Society
Walnut Street, Annisquam
Gloucester, MA 01930

North-East Lutherans
Concordia College
52-40 39th Drive
Woodside, NY 11377

Northeastern Ohio
Western Reserve Historical Society
10825 East Blvd.
Cleveland, OH 44106

Northeastern Minnesota
Library
University of Minnesota
Duluth, MN 55812

Norwegian
Sons of Norway
1455 West Lake Street
Minneapolis, MN 55408

Northeastern Pennsylvania
Farley Library
Wilkes College
Wilkes-Barre, PA 18703

Northern Arizona Colonization
Northern Arizona University
Box 6022
Flagstaff, AZ 86001

Northern Arizona Pioneers
Northern Arizona University
Box 6022
Flagstaff, AZ 86001

Northern Electric
California Railway Museum

Star Rte. 283, Box 153
Suisan City, CA 94585

Northern Illinois
Northern Illinois Regional
  History Center
Northern Illinois University
DeKalb, IL 60115

Northern Mexico
University of Texas
P.O. Box P
Austin, TX 78712

Northern Neck
Washington Museum & Library
Box 97
Lancaster, VA 22503

Northern Pacific Railroad
Tacoma Public Library
1102 Tacoma Ave., South
Tacoma, WA 98402

Northern Pacific Railroad
Hill Reference Library
80 West Fourth Street
St. Paul, MN 55102

Northwestern Ohio
University Library
Bowling Green State University
Bowling, Green, OH 43403

**Northwest Ohio Biographical
  Scrapbooks**
Toledo Public Library
325 Michigan Street
Toledo, OH 43624

Northwest Ohio Name Index
Toledo Public Library
325 Michigan Street
Toledo, OH 43624

Northwest Railroad
Cordova Historical Society
P.O. Box 391
Cordova, AK 99574

**Northwest Regional Manuscripts
  Collection**
Libraries
University of Washington
Seattle, WA 98195

Northwest Territory
Dawes Memorial Library
Marietta College
Marietta, OH 45750

Norwegian
Vesterheim Genealogical Center
4909 Sherwood Road
Madison, WI 53711

Norwegian Lutheran
Lutheran Theo. Seminary
2375 Como Ave. W.

Boldface indicates subject; DO NOT include it as part of the address.

St. Paul, MN 55108

Nova Scotia
Royal Nova Scotia
 Historical Society
Box 895
Armdale, Halifax B3N 1E3 Canada

—O—

O.G.S. Library
Ohio Genealogical Society Library
419 West Third Street
Mansfield, Ohio 44903

Oakland Antioch & Eastern Railway
California Railway Museum
Star Rte. 283, Box 150
Suisan City, CA 94585

Oakland County, MI County Records
Patterson House Museum
502 Maple Street
Holly, MI 48442

Oakland, CA Local History Index
Oakland Public Library
125 14th Street
Oakland, CA 94612

Oceanic Navigation Research
Oceanic Navigation Research Society
P.O. Box 8005
Universal City, CA 91608

Ohio
Ohio Historical Society
I-71 and 17th Ave.
Columbus, OH 43211

Ohio Company of Associates
Dawes Memorial Library
Marietta College
Marietta, OH 45750

Ohio County Records
Ohio Historical Society
I-71 and 17th Ave.
Columbus, OH 43211

Ohio Documents of Original Title
State of Ohio
Office of Auditor of State
Columbus, OH 43216

Ohio Notary Records
Secretary of State
30 East Broad Street
Columbus, OH 43215

Ohio Presbyterians
Library
Muskingum College
New Concord, OH 43762

Ohio Quakers
Massillon Public Library
208 Lincoln Way, E.
Massillon, OH 44646

Ohio Quakers
Wilmington College
Box 1227
Wilmington, OH 45177

Ohio River
Brooke County Historical Society
County Courthouse
Wellsburg, WV 26070

Ohio River
Indiana State University
8600 University Blvd.
Evansville, IN 47712

Ohio River
Ohio River Museum
Ohio Historical Society
Marietta, OH 45750

Ohio Valley
University of Chicago
1100 East 57th Street
Chicago, IL 60637

Ohio Valley
King Library
University of Kentucky
Lexington, KY 40506

Ohio Valley Catholics
Archdiocese of Baltimore
320 Cathedral Street
Baltimore, MD 21201

Oklahoma Biographical File
Oklahoma State Historical Society
Historical Bldg.
Oklahoma City, OK 73105

Oklahoma County Records
Oklahoma Historical Society
Historical Bldg.
Oklahoma City, OK 73105

Oklahoma Federal Court Records
Oklahoma Historical Society
Historical Bldg.
Oklahoma City, OK 73105

Oklahoma Federal Townsite Index
Washington National Records Center
Federal Office Bldg.
Suitland, MD 21668

Oklahoma Panhandle
Historical Museum
Sewell Street
Goodwell, OK 73939

Oklahoma Territorial Records
Archives and Records Division
200 Northeast 18th Street
Oklahoma City, OK 73105

Oklahoma Territory
Oklahoma Territorial Museum
402-406 E. Oklahoma Ave.
Guthrie, OK 73044

Oklahoma Town Lot Funds
Record Group 48
National Archives
Washington, DC 20408

Old Colony
Old Colony Historical Society
66 Church Green
Taunton, MA 02780

Old Genealogy Catalog
Genealogical Society of Pennsylvania
1300 Locust Street
Philadelphia, PA 19107

Old Federal Court Index
U.S. District Court
Courthouse, Foley Square
New York, NY 10007

Old Postal Guides
Post Office Department Library
12th & Penn. Avenue, N.W.
Washington, DC 20260

Old Maps (copies)
Map Division
New York Public Library
Fifth Avenue & Forty-Second Street
New York, NY 10018

Old Militia Records
Vermont Department of Administration
Public Records Division
Montpelier, VT 05602

Old Northwest
Detroit Public Library
5201 Woodward Ave.
Detroit, MI 48202

Old Northwest Territory
Brute Library
203 Church Street
Vincennes, IN 47591

Old Northwest Territory
Lansing Public Library
401 South Capitol Ave.
Lansing, MI 48914

Old Point Comfort
Fort Monroe Casemate Museum
P.O. Box 341
Fort Monroe, VA 23651

Old Southwest
McGhee Library
500 West Church Ave.
Knoxville, TN 37902

Old West Jersey
Savitz Learning Resource Center
Glassboro State College
Glassboro, NJ 08028

Old York Road
Alverthorpe Manor
515 Meeting House Road

Jenkintown, PA 19046

Olden Collection
Princeton Historical Society
158 Nassau Street
Princeton, NJ 08540

110 Crossing
Osage County Historical Society
Osage County Museum
Lyndon, KS 66451

Onondaga Newspaper Index
Onondaga Historical Assoc.
311 Montgomery Street
Syracuse, NY 13202

Oral History
Oral History Assoc.
Box 13734, NTSU Sta.
Denton, TX 76203

Oral History Kit
Family Chronicles
P.O. Box 84283
Los Angeles, CA 90073

Orange County, California
Library
University of California
Irvine, CA 92664

Ord Collection
Stanford University Libraries
Stanford University
Stanford, CA 94305

Orders and Decorations
American Numismatic Assoc.
818 North Cascade Ave.
Colorado Springs, CO 80903

Oregon County Records
Archives & Records Center
1005 Broadway, N.E.
Salem, OR 97310

Orange County, TX County Records
Sam Houston Library
Farm Road 1011
Liberty, TX 77575

Oregon Military Records
Archives & Records Center
1005 Broadway, N.E.
Salem, OR 97310

Oregon Pioneer File
Oregon Historical Society
1230 S.W. Park Ave.
Portland, OR 97205

Oregon Territory
Oregon Historical Society
1230 S.W. Park Ave.
Portland, OR 97205

Oregon Territory
Rosenbach Foundation
2010 Delancey Pl.

Philadelphia, PA 19103

Oregon Territorial Records
Archives & Records Center
1005 Broadway, N.E.
Salem, OR 97310

Oregon Territorial Records
Oregon Historical Society
1230 S.W. Park Ave.
Portland, OR 97205

Oregon Trail
Pierce Library
Eastern Oregon State College
La Grande, OR 97850

Orphan Trains
Orphan Register
5843 Grant Street
Omaha, NE 68104

Orphanages, Asylums, and Hospitals
Record Group 29
National Archives
Washington, DC 20408

Original Pennsylvania Land Titles
Bureau of Land Records
Room 123, So. Office Bldg.
Harrisburg, PA 17120

Orthodox Church
Department of History & Archives
Route 25A, Box 675
Syosset, NY 11791

Osage Trading Post Ledgers
Spencer Library
University of Kansas
Lawrence, KS 66045

Otter Tail County, MN
 Cemetery Records
Otter Tail County Historical Society
1110 Lincoln Ave., W.
Fergus Falls, MN 56537

Out of Print Books
University Microfilms International
300 North Zeeb Road
Ann Arbor, MI 48106

Overland Diaries
Spencer Library
University of Kansas
Lawrence, KS 66044

Overland Journeys
Kearney State College
Kearney, NE 68847

Overland Journeys
Oregon Historical Society
1230 S.W. Park Ave.
Portland, OR 97205

Overland Journeys
Huntington Library
1151 Oxford Road

San Marino, CA 91108

Overland Records
Society of California Pioneers
456 McAllister Street
San Francisco, CA 94102

Overland Trail Immigrants
Fort Laramie National Historic Site
Fort Lamramie, WY 82212

Ozark
Izark County Historical Society
Dolph, AR 72528

Ozarks
School of the Ozarks
Ralph Foster Museum
Point Lookout, MD 65726

Ozarks
Library
University of Arkansas
Fayetteville, AR 72701

—P—

Pacific Electric
California Railway Museum
Star Rte. 283, Box 150
Suisan City, CA 94585

Pacific Northwest
Library
University of Oregon
Eugene, OR 97403

Pacific Northwest
Umatilla National Forest
2517 S.W. Hailey Ave.
Pendleton, OR 97801

Pacific Northwest
Libraries
University of Washington
Seattle, WA 98195

Pacific North-West Collection Index
Special Collections
University of Washington
Seattle, WA 98105

Pacific Northwest Immigrants
Tacoma Public Library
1102 Tacoma Ave., So.
Tacoma, WA 98402

Pacific Northwest Military History
Fort Lewis Military Museum
Bldg. 4320
Fort Lewis, WA 98433

Pacific Northwest Missionaries
Whitman College
345 Boyer Street
Walla Walla, WA 99362

Pacific Northwest Photographers
Historical Photography Collection
University of Washington
Seattle, WA 98195

**Pacific Northwest Spanish
Mission Records**
Archives of the Jesuit Order
Gonzaga University
Spokane, WA 99258

Pacific Steamship Co.
Claremont College
Eight & Dartmouth
Claremont, CA 91711

Painters & Paper Hangers Union
Pennsylvania State University
University Park, PA 16802

Palatines
Palatines to America
P.O. Box 21112
Columbus, OH 43221

Palatines
National Society Palatines to America
106 November Drive
Camp Hill, PA 17011

Palatines
Palatines to America
1492 Guilford Road
Columbus, OH 43221

Palmer Regional History Collection
Kingsport Public Library
Broad & New Streets
Kingsport, TN 37660

Palos Park, IL Property Records
Palos Park Historical Society
127 and Southwest Highway
Palos Park, IL 60464

Pantheists
Unitarian & Universalist
 Genealogical Society
10605 Lakespring Way
Cockeysville, MD 21030

Parham Collection
Knoxville Public Library
500 W. Church Ave.
Knoxville, TN 37902

Passenger Arrivals (series)
Gen. Publishing Co.
Baltimore, MD

Passenger Lists
Cincinnati Public Library
800 Vine Street
Cincinnati, OH 45202

Passports (pre-1900)
Diplomatic Records Branch
National Archives & Records Service
Room 5E
Washington, DC 20408

Passports (post-1900)
Passport Office
1425 K Street, N.W.

Washington, DC 20520

Patriot Index
Daughters of the American Revolution
1776 D Street, N.W.
Washington, DC 20006

Patterson's Schools Classified
Educational Directory
P.O. Box 199
Mt. Prospect, IL 60056

Patuxent River
Library
Calvert Marine Museum
Solomon, MD 20688

Pawnee County, KS County Records
Santa Fe Trail Center
Route #3
Larned, KS 67550

Peabody Library
Peabody Library
17 East Mount Vernon Pl.
Baltimore, MD 21202

Pendleton Farmer's Society
Library
Clemson University
Clemson, SC 29631

Penea-Chereno Collection
Austin State University
Box 13055, SFA Sta.
Nacodoches, TX 75961

**Pennsylvania Area Grand Army
 of the Republic**
GAR Memorial Hall
4278-80 Griscom Street
Philadelphia, PA 19124

Pennsylvania Bureau of Customs
Federal Archives and Records Center
5000 Wissahickon Ave.
Philadelphia, PA 19144

**Pennsylvania County,
 Church Histories**
Carnegie Library
4400 Forbes Avenue
Pittsburgh, PA 15213

Pennsylvania Dutch
Pennsylvania Dutch Folk
 Culture Society
Lenhartsville, PA 19534

Pennsylvania Dutch
Pennsylvania Folklife
P.O. Box 1053
Lancaster, PA

Pennsylvania Family Records
Pennsylvania State Library
Walnut & Commonwealth Ave.
Harrisburg, PA 17108

Pennsylvania German

German Society of Pennsylvania
771 E. Shawmont Ave.
Philadelphia, PA 19128

Pennsylvania German
Library
Ursinus College
Collegeville, PA 19426

Pennsylvania German
Franklin & Marshall College
College Ave.
Lancaster, PA 17604

Pennsylvania Germans
Germantown Historical Society
5208 Germantown Ave.
Philadelphia, PA 19144

Pennsylvania Germans
Pennsylvania German Society
Rt. 1, Box 469
Breinigsville, PA 18031

**Pennsylvania Industries and
 Organizations**
Archives of Industrial Society
University of Pittsburgh
Pittsburgh, PA 15213

Pennsylvania Main Line Canal
Johnstown Flood Museum
304 Washington Street
Johnstown, PA 15901

Pennsylvania Maps
Department of Transportation
Publication Sales Section, Rm. 117A
Harrisburg, PA 17120

Pennsylvania Military Land Grants
Bureau of Land Records
Room 123, So. Office Bldg.
Harrisburg, PA 17120

Pennsylvania Military Records
Retired Records Section
Indiantown Gap Military
 Reservation
Annville, PA 17003

Penobscot Bay Region
Penobscot Marine Museum
Church Street
Searsport, ME 04974

Pension and Bounty Land Claims
Record Group 15
National Archives
Washington DC 20408

Pentecostal
Lee College
N. Ocoee Street
Cleveland, TN 37311

Periodicals
Serial Division
Library of Congress
Washington, DC 20540

Peter Force Library
Manuscript Division
Library of Congress
Washington, DC 20540

Pharmacy
State Historical Society
816 State Street
Madison, WI 53706

Pharmacy
University of Wisconsin
425 N. Charter Street
Madison, WI 53706

Philadelphia Area
Library
Temple University
Philadelphia, PA 19122

Philadelphia City Records
City Archives
522 City Hall Annex
Philadelphia, PA 19107

Philadelphia County Marriage Bonds
Pennsylvania State Archives
Harrisburg, PA

Philadelphia County, PA County Records
City Archives
522 City Hall Annex
Philadelphia, PA 19107

Philadelphia Guide Book
Philadelphia City Archives
790 City Hall
Philadelphia, PA 19107

Philadelphia Metropolitan Area
Urban Archives Center
Temple University
Philadelphia, PA 19122

Philadelphia Naturalization Index
Federal Court Building
9th & Chestnut Streets
Philadelphia, PA

Philadelphia Vital Records
City Archives
Philadelphia, PA

Photochemical Tombstone Etching
Central Research of Utah
60 South 500 West
Bountiful, UT 84010

Photos Copied
Leslie H. Weber
27361 Sierra Highway, #159
Canyon Country, CA 91351

Phrenology
Countway Library
10 Shattuck Street
Boston, MA 02115

Pilgrims
Duxbury Rural & Historical Society
King Caesar Road
Duxbury, MA 02332

Pilgrims
Pilgrim Society
75 Court Street
Plymouth, MA 02360

Pioneer Family Collection
Shreve Memorial Library
400 Edwards Street
Shreveport, LA 71120

Pioneer Index
Syracuse Public Library
335 Montgomery Street
Syracuse, NY 13202

Pioneer Index
State Historical Society
1500 R Street
Lincoln, NE 68508

Pioneers
Pioneer America Society
University of Akron
Akron, OH 44325

Pioneers
Library
Washington State University
Pullman, WA 99164

Pioneers of Alaska Collection
Rasmuson Library
University of Alaska
Fairbanks, AK 99701

Pioneer Anesthesiologists
American Society of Anesthesiologists
515 Busse Highway
Park Ridge, IL 60068

Pioneer Settlements
Indiana State Library
Indianapolis, IN 46208

Piracy
Bapst Library
Boston College
Chestnut Hill, MA 02167

Pittsburgh City Records
Archives of Industrial Society
University of Pittsburgh
Pittsburgh, PA 15260

Place Names
Place Name Society of the U.S.
Eastern Texas State University
Commerce, TX 75428

Place Names
Board of Geographic Names
Room 1040, GSA Building
Washington, DC 20242

Plantation Records

Louisiana State Museum
751 Chartres Street
New Orleans, LA 70116

Plantation Records
Georgia College
231 W. Hancock Street
Milledgeville, GA 31061

Plimoth Plantation
Plimoth Plantation
P.O. Box 1620
Plymouth, MA

Plymouth Colony
Plimoth Plantation
Box 1620
Plymouth, MA 02360

Plymouth Colony Records
Dennis Historical Society
Whig. Street & Nobscusset Road
Dennis, MA 02660

Plymouth Colony Records
Law Library
Barnstable County Courthouse
Barnstable, MA 02630

Plymouth Proprietors Records
Maine Historical Society
485 Congress Street
Portland, ME 04111

Poland
Pilsudski Institute
381 Park Ave., So.
New York, NY 10016

Polish
Polish Genealogical Society, Inc.
984 N. Milwaukee Ave.
Chicago, IL 60622

Polish
Polish Nobility Assoc.
529 Denkirk Road
Anneslie, MD 21212

Polish
Polish Genealogical Society
of Michigan
5201 Woodward Ave.
Detroit, MI 48203

Polish
Polish Museum of America
984 N. Milwaukee Ave.
Chicago, IL 60622

Polish
Polish Historical Commission
4291 Stanton Ave.
Pittsburgh, PA 15201

Polish
Holy Family College
Grant & Frankford Ave.
Philadelphia, PA 19114

Boldface indicates subject; DO NOT include it as part of the address.

Polish
Polish Institute
59 East 66th Street
New York, NY 10021

Polish
Polish Museum
P.O. Box 12207
Hamtramck, MI 48212

Polish
Centre of Polish Research
5214 Park Ave.
Montreal, PQ, Canada H2V 4G7

Polish Geographical History File
Stan Schmidt
106 S. Hill Street
Roselle, IL 60172

Polk County, TX County Records
Sam Houston Library
Farm Road 1011
Liberty, TX 77575

Pomona Valley
Pomona Public Library
625 S. Garey Ave.
Pomona, CA 91766

Pony Express
Pony Express Stables Museum
11th & Charles
St. Joseph, MO 64501

Population Library
Carolina Population Center
University Square E.
Chapel Hill, NC 27514

Port Mackinac
Bayliss Public Library
541 Library Drive
Sault Ste. Marie, MI 49783

Port of Maryland
Maryland Historical Society
201 W. Monument Street
Baltimore, MD 21201

**Portable Microfilm/Microfiche
  Reader**
Anacomp
5140 W. Amelia Earhart Drive
Salt Lake City, UT 84125

Portraits in Pastels
Dampson D. Sanger
Loomis Road
Liberty, NY 12754

Portuguese
American Portuguese Cultural Society
29 Broadway
New York, NY 10006

Portuguese
Cape Verdian League
23 West 124th Street
New York, NY 10027

Portuguese Manuscript Collection
Manuscript Division
Library of Congress
Washington, DC 20540

Portuguese
American-Portuguese Genealogical
  Society
P.O. Box 644
Taunton, MA 02780

Post-1910 Federal Censuses
Personal Census Service Branch
Bureau of the Census
Pittsburg, KS 66762

Post Offices (Table of)
Post Office Department Library
12th & Pennsylvania Ave., N.W.
Washington, DC 20260

Post Office County Histories
Post Office Department Library
12th & Pennsylvania Ave., N.W.
Washington, DC 20260

Postal Maps
Post Office Department Library
12th & Pennsylvania Ave., N.W.
Washington, DC 20260

Preble County, OH County Records
Library
Wright State University
Dayton, OH 45431

Preliminary Analysis
Computerized Genealogy Library
P.O. Box 27193
Salt Lake City, UT 84127

Presbyterian
Hist. Foundation
Box 847
Montreat, NC 28757

Prescott Collection
Museum of Western Colorado
Fourth & Ute
Grand Junction, CO 81501

Preserving Your Personal Records
Computerized Genealogy Library
P.O. Box 27193
Salt Lake City, UT 84127

Price Collection
Austin State University
Box 13055, SFA Sta.
Nacodoches, TX 75961

Prince Edward Island
Prince Edward Island Heritage
  Foundation
Box 922, C1A 7L9, Charlottetown
Prince Edward Island, Canada

Printed Genealogies

American Antiquarian Society
185 Salisbury Street
Worcester, MA 01609

Printed Genealogies
Photoduplication Service
Library of Congress
Washington, DC 20540

Privacy Laws
Privacy Journal
P.O. Box 8844
Washington, DC 20003

Professional Genealogist
Association of Professional
 Genealogists
P.O. Box 11601
Salt Lake City, UT 84147

Prologue Mag.
Neps-Rm-G-6
National Archives
Washington, DC 20408

Protestant Episcopal Church
duPont Library
University of the South
Sewanee, TN 37375

Proust Collection
University of Alabama
917 South 13th Street, Univ. Sta.
Birmingham, AL 35294

Prussion Army Lists
Metropolital Library
789 Yonge Street
Toronto, Ont. M4W 2G8 Canada

Public Debt or Old Loans
Civil Archives Division
National Archives & Records Service
Washington, DC 20408

Public Domain States
Federal Bureau of Land Management
7981 Eastern Ave.
Silver Springs, MD 20904

Publish Your Family Newsletter
N. Burr Coryell
P.O. Box 662
Santa Barbara, CA 93102

Pullman Corporation
Newberry Library
60 W. Walton Street
Chicago, IL 60610

Putnam County, IN County Records
West Library
DePauw University
Greencastle, IN 46135

Pyper Collection
Marriott Library
University of Utah
Salt Lake City, UT 84112

—Q—

Quabbin Dam Town Valuation Lists
Library
University of Massachusetts
Amherst, MA 01003

Quabbin Reservoir
Massachusetts Metro. Dist. Comm.
20 Somerset Street
Boston, MA 02108

Quaker
Friends Historical Library
Swarthmore College
Swarthmore, PA 19081

Quakers
Historical Society of Pennsylvania
1300 Locust Street
Philadelphia, PA 19107

Quakers
Western Yearly Meeting
105 South East Street
Plainfield, IN 46168

Quakers
Henry County Historical Museum
614 South 14th Street
New Castle, IN 47362

Quakers
Wardman Library
Whittier College
Whittier, CA 90608

Quakers
New York Yearly Meeting
15 Rutherford Pl.
New York, NY 10003

Quaker Collection
Lilly Library
Earlham College
Richmond, IN 47374

Quaker Genealogical Index
Friends Historical Library
Swarthmore College
Swarthmore, PA 19081

Questions & Answers
Genealogy Digest Magazine
P.O. Box 15861
Salt Lake City, UT 84115

—R—

Railroad
Library
Stanford University
Stanford, CA 94305

Railroad
Van Howeling Memorial Library
Wayland Baptist College
Plainview, TX 79072

Racine County, WI County Records

Boldface indicates subject; DO NOT include it as part of the address.

Area Research Center
University of Wisconsin
Kenosha, WI 53140

Railroads
Lee Library
Brigham Young University
Provo, UT 84602

Railroads
Assoc. of American Railroads
American Railroad Bldg.
Washington, DC 20036

Railroads
Transportation Library
University of Michigan
Ann Arbor, MI 48104

Railroads
Southern Methodist University
Box 396, SMU Sta.
Dallas, TX 75275

Railroads
Harvard University Library
Soldiers Field
Boston, MA 02163

Railroads
Bennett Studio
215 Broadway
Wisconsin Dells, WI 53965

Railroads
Mid-Continent Railway
  Historical Society
Mid-Continent Railway Museum
North Freedom, WI 53951

Railroads
Camp Five Foundation Museum
Box 847
Wausau, WI 54401

Railroads
Fort Lewis College
College Heights
Durango, CO 81301

Railroads
Occidental College
1600 Campus Road
Los Angeles, CA 90041

Railroads
Baker Library
Harvard University
Boston, MA 02163

Railroads
Railroad & Pioneer Museum
710 Jack Baskin Street
Temple, TX 76501

Railroads
Carter Museum
3501 Camp Bowie Blvd.
Fort Worth, TX 76101

Railroads
DeGolyer Library
Southern Methodist University
Dallas, TX 75275

Railroads
Library
East Texas State University
Commerce, TX 75428

Railroads
Wyoming Historical Society
49 South Franklin Street
Wilkes-Barre, PA 18701

Railroads
Railroad Museum
P.O. Box 15
Strasburg, PA 17579

Railroads
Altoona Public Library
1600 Fifth Ave.
Altoona, PA 16602

Railroads
Railroad House Historical Assoc.
P.O. Box 519
Sanford, NC 27330

Railroads
Folsom Library
Rensselaer Polytechnic Institute
Troy, NY 12181

Railroads
Jervis Public Library
613 N. Washington Street
Rome, NY 13440

Railroads
Catskill Center
College Hall, Rm. 202E
New Paltz, NY 12561

Railroads
State University of New York
1400 Washington Ave.
Albany, NY 12222

Railroad Companies
National Archives & Records Service
Pennsylvania Ave. & Eighth Street, N.W.
Washington, DC 20408

Railway
National Railway Historical Society
Box 2051
Philadelphia, PA 19103

Railway
Railway and Locomotive
  Historical Society
Box 1194
Boston, MA 02103

**Railway and Locomotive
  Historical Society**
Cunningham Memorial Library

Indiana State University
Terra Haute, IN 47809

Randolph Collection
Memphis Public Library
1850 Memphis Ave.
Memphis, TN 38104

Red Cross Collection
 (American National)
Prints & Photo. Division
Library of Congress
Washington, DC 20540

Reconditioned Microfilm Equipment
National Microsales Corp.
45 Seymour Street
Stratford, CT 06497

Records of Collection Districts
 or Customhouses
Record Group 36
National Archives
Washington, DC 20408

Red River Valley
Red River Valley Historical Assoc.
Southeastern Oklahoma State University
Durant, OK 74701

Red River Valley
Library
North Dakota State University
Fargo, ND 58102

Red River Valley Assoc.
Louisiana State University
8515 Youree Drive
Shreveport, LA 71105

Reformation Church
Rose Memorial Library
Drew University
Madison, NJ 07940

Reformed Church
Historical Foundation
Box 847
Montreat, NC 28757

Reformed Church
Dutch Heritage Collection
101 7th Street, S.W.
Orange City, IA 51041

Reformed Jewish
Unitarian & Universalist
 Genealocial Society
10605 Lakespring Way
Cockeysville, MD 21030

Regional English
Dictionary of American Regional
 English Project
600 N. Park Street
Madison, WI 53706

Registered Genealogist
International Genealogy Consumer

Organization
369 East 900 South
Salt Lake City, UT 84111

Registers of Vessels
Federal Archives & Records Center
380 Trapelo Road
Waltham, MA 02154

Remmel Collection
Library
University of Arkansas
Fayetteville, AR 72701

Republic of Texas
Star of the Republic Museum
Washington State Historical Park
Washington, TX 77880

Republic of Texas
Daughters of the Republic of Texas
The Alamo
San Antonio, TX 78299

Republic of Texas
Archives Division
1201 Brazos Street
Austin, TX 78711

Revolutionary War Grave Sites
Vermont State Capitol
State House
Montpelier, VT 05602

Revolutionary War Officers
Society of Cincinnati
2118 Massachusetts Ave., N.W.
Washington, DC 20008

Revolutionary War Pensions
Lu & Neumann
Box 4276, Sta. A
Dallas, TX 75208

Research Exchange File
Genealogical Society
50 East North Temple
Salt Lake City, UT 84150

Research Library
Western Reserve Historical Society
10825 East Boulevard
Cleveland, OH 44106

Research Library
Seattle Public Library
1000 Fourth Ave.
Seattle, WA 98104

Research Library
State Historical Society
816 State Street
Madison, WI 53706

Research Library
Clayton Library
5300 Caroline Street
Houston, TX 77004

Research Library

Boldface indicates subject; DO NOT include it as part of the address.

New York Public Library
5th Avenue & 42nd Street
New York, NY 10018

Research Library
Kansas City Public Library
311 East 12th Street
Kansas City, MO 64106

Research Library
New York Genealogical and
 Biographical Society
122 East 58th Street
New York, NY 10022

Research Library
Detroit Public Library
5201 Woodward Ave.
Detroit, MI 48202

Research Library
Boston Public Library
666 Boylston Street
Boston, MA 02117

Research Library
Peabody Library
17 East Mount Vernon Pl.
Baltimore, MD 21202

Research Library
Fort Wayne Public Library
900 Webster Street
Fort Wayne, IN 46802

Researcher Recommendations
Roots Digest
P.O. Box 2101
Glenwood Springs, CO 81602

Restoration Movement
Johnson Bible College
Kimberlin Heights Sta.
Knoxville, TN 37920

Revenue Cutter Service
Coast Guard Museum
1519 Alaskan Way So.
Seattle, WA 98134

Revenue-Cutter Service
Record Group 26
National Archives
Washington, DC 20408

Rhine Valley Immigrants
The Lost Palatine Magazine
Rt. 1, Box 1160
Estero, FL 33928

Rhode Island Census (1755)
Library
University of Rhode Island
Kingston, RI 02881

Rhode Island State Censuses
Archives Division
Smith Street
Providence, RI 02903

Richland County, OH Cemetery File
Richland County Museum
51 West Church Street
Lexington, OH 44904

Richland County, OH County Records
Bierce Library
University of Akron
Akron, OH 44325

Richland County, OH Court Records
O.G.S. Library
419 West Third Street
Mansfield, OH 44906

Richmond County, NY County Records
Staten Island Institute
51 Stuyvesant Pl.
Staten Island, NY 10301

Richmond, Virginia
Valentine Museum
1015 E. Clay Street
Richmond, VA 23219

Ring Collection
Marriott Library
University of Utah
Salt Lake City, UT 84112

Riley County, KS County Records
Riley County Hist. Museum
2309 Claflin Road
Manhattan, KS 66502

Rio Grande Valley
Library
Pan American University
Edinburg, TX 78539

River Disasters
Great Lakes Historical Society
480 Main Street
Vermillion, OH 44089

River Captains
Cincinnati Public Library
800 Vine Street
Cincinnati, OH 45202

Riverboats
St. Louis Public Library
1301 Olive Street
St. Louis, MO 63103

Riverboats
University of Wisconsin
1631 Pine Street
La Crosse, WI 54601

Riverboats
Louisiana State University
8515 Youree Drive
Shreveport, LA 71105

Riverboats
Lilly Library
Indiana University
Bloomington, IN 47401

Roads
Transportation Library
University of Michigan
Ann Arbor, MI 48104

Roanoke-Chowan Region
Roberts Village Center
P.O. Box 3
Murfreesboro, NC 27855

Robertson Collection
Marriott Library
University of Utah
Salt Lake City, UT 84112

Robertson Colony
Library
University of Texas
Arlington, TX 76019

Rochester Newspaper Index
Rochester Public Library
115 South Avenue
Rochester, NY 14604

Rochester, NY Coroner's Records
Rochester Museum
657 East Avenue
Rochester, NY 14603

Rock Island Railroad
Library
University of Iowa
Iowa City, IA 52242

Rockwell Collection
Museum of Western Colorado
Fourth & Ute
Grand Junction, CO 81501

Rocky Mountain Newspaper
Denver Public Library
1357 Broadway
Denver, CO 80203

Rocky Mountain Fur Trade
Fort Laramie National
 Historic Site
Fort Laramie, WY 82212

Roman Law Collection
Law Library
Library of Congress
Washington, DC 20540

Romanian
Romanian Library
200 East 38th Street
New York, NY 10016

Romanian Catholics
Assoc. of Romanian Catholics
4309 Olcott Ave.
East Chicago, IL 46312

Roseau County, MN County Records
Roseau County Museum
108 2nd Ave., N.E.
Roseau, MN 56751

Rosicrucians
Research Library
Rosicrucian Park
San Jose, CA 95191

Rosicrucians
Bacon Library
655 N. Dartmouth Ave.
Claremont, CA 91711

Rotarians
I. G. F. R.
5721 Antietam Drive
Sarasota, FL 33581

Royal Pedigrees
Genealogists International
970 Logan Ave.
Salt Lake City, UT 84105

Russia
Archive of Russian and
 East European History
420 West 118th Street
New York, NY 10027

Russian
Russian Historical and
 Genealogical Society
971 First Avenue
New York, NY 10022

Russian Collection
Alaska Hist. Library
State Office Bldg.
Juneau, AK 99811

Russian and East European
Stanford University Libraries
Stanford, CA 94305

**Russian Jewish Persecution Records
 (1882)**
Library of Congress
Washington, DC 20540

—S—

Sacramento Northern
California Railway Museum
Star Rte. 283, Box 150
Suisan City, CA 94585

Saginaw Valley
Museum of the Great Lakes
1700 Center Ave.
Bay City, MI 48706

Sailing Ships
Maritime College
Fort Schuyler
New York, NY 10465

St. Charles, MO Colonial Records
Missouri Historical Society
Jefferson Memorial Bldg.
St. Louis MO 63112

St. Charles County, MO County Records
St. Charles County Historical Society

Boldface indicates subject; DO NOT include it as part of the address.

117 Jefferson Street
St. Charles MO 63301

St. Clair County Records
St. Clair County Library
210 McMorran Blvd.
Port Huron, MI 48060

St. Clair County, MI Obituary File
St. Clair County Library
201 McMorran Blvd.
Port Huron, MI 48060

St. Croix River Valley
Area Research Center
University of Wisconsin
River Falls, WI 54022

St. Croix River Valley
Stillwater Public Library
223 N. 4th Street
Stillwater, MN 55082

St. Lawrence County, NY
  County Records
St. Lawrence County Historical Center
3½ E. Main Street
Canton, NY 13617

St. Lawrence River
St. Lawrence County Hist. Center
3½ E. Main Street
Canton, NY 13617

St. Lawrence River
Dossin Great Lakes Museum
Belle Isle
Detroit, MI 48207

St. Lawrence River Area
Young Library
St. Lawrence University
Canton, NY 13617

St. Lawrence River Area
Cleveland Public Library
325 Superior Ave.
Cleveland, OH 44114

St. Louis, MO Colonial Records
Missouri Historical Society
Jefferson Memorial Bldg.
St. Louis MO 63112

Salt Lake Library
  Card Catalog Search
Genealogical Institute
57 West South Temple
Salt Lake City, Utah 84101

Salzburgers
Salzburgers Society
Box 1141, Rt. 1
Rincon, GA 31326

San Bernardino County
Smiley Public Library
125 W. Vine Street
Redlands, CA 92373

San Diego & Arizona Railroad
Library
University of California
La Jolla, CA 92093

San Francisco Bay Area
Vallejo Naval & History Museum
734 Marin Street
Vallejo, CA 94590

San Francisco City Records
San Francisco Public Library
Civic Center
San Francisco, CA 94102

San Francisco Custom House Records
San Francisco Public Library
Civic Center
San Francisco, CA 94102

San Francisco Newspaper Index
California Historical Society
2090 Jackson Street
San Francisco, CA 94109

San Francisco Records
Society of California Pioneers
456 McAllister Street
San Francisco, CA 94102

San Jacinto County, TX County Records
Sam Houston Library
Farm Road 1011
Liberty, TX 77575

San Joaquin Valley
Pioneer Museum
1201 N. Pershing Ave.
Stockton, CA 95203

Sanborn Fire Insurance Maps
Geography & Map Division
Library of Congress
Alexandria, VA 22304

Sandusky Valley
Hayes Library
1337 Hayes Ave.
Fremont, OH 43420

Santa Fe Trail
Osage County Historical Society
Osage County Museum
Lyndon, KS 66451

Santa Fe Trail
Santa Fe Trail Center
Rte. 3
Larned, KS 67550

Saratoga County, NY County Records
Saratoga County Historian's Office
31 Woodlawn Ave.
Saratoga Springs, NY 12866

Satterthwaite Quaker Collection
Savitz Library
Glassboro State College
Glassboro, NJ 08028

Scandinavian
Scandinavian-American Genealogical Society
P.O. Box 16006
St. Paul MN 55105

Scandinavian
Schofield Memorial Library
127 East 73rd Street
New York, NY 10021

Scandinavian
University of Wisconsin
728 State Street
Madison, WI 53706

Scandinavian
Viking Kinfolk
114 Trevathan Ave.
Santa Cruz, CA 95062

Scandinavian-Americans
Libraries
University of Washington
Seattle, WA 98195

Scandinavian Collection
North Park College
5125 N. Spaulding Ave.
Chicago, IL 60625

Scottish
The Highlander
P.O. Box P440444
Chicago, IL 60644

Scottish
Scottish Hist. and Research
  Society of the Delaware Valley
2137 MacLarie Lane
Broomall, PA 19008

Scottish
The Highlander
Box 397
Barrington, IL 60010

Scottish Girls Books
Manchester Historic Association
129 Amherst Street
Manchester, NH 03102

Scotch-Irish
Gaelic Gleanings
611 Miller Valley Road, Ste. #59
Prescott, AZ 86301

Scott County, IA Civil War Enlistments
Davenport Museum
1717 West 12th Street
Davenport, IA 52804

Sea Captain Data
American Merchant Marine
U.S. Custom House
One Bowling Green
New York, NY 10004

Seamen Lists
Record Group 84

National Archives
Washington, DC 20408

Seattle Pioneers
Museum of History & Industry
2161 E. Hamlin
Seattle, WA 98112

Seilhamer Collection
Pennsylvania State Library
Walnut & Commonwealth Ave.
Harrisburg, PA 17108

Self Employed
Mind Your Own Business At Home
2520 N. Lincoln Ave., #60
Chicago, IL 60614

Self-Employed Organization
National Assoc. for the Self-Employed
P.O. Box 345749
Dallas, TX 75234

Seminar Publicity
Federation of Genealogical Societies
2827 Ashland
St. Joseph, MO 64506

Seminar Movie
National Park Service
11 North Fourth Street
St. Louis MO 63102

Seminar Publicity
Meeting Planners International
3201 Barbara Drive
Middletown, OH 45042

Seminar Publicity
Genealogy Digest
3201 Barbara Drive
Middletown, OH 45042

Seminar Publicity
World Convention Dates
79 Washington Blvd.
Hempstead, NY 11550

Seminar Speakers
Genealogy Digest
P.O. Box 16422
Salt Lake City, UT 84116

Seminole
Seminole National Museum
P.O. Box 1079
Wewoka, OK 74884

Serbian
Croation-Slovenian-Serbian
  Genealogical Society
936 Industrial Avenue
Palo Alto, CA 94070

Settlement Houses
Social Welfare History Archives
2520 Broadway Drive
Lauderdale, MN 55455

Seventh-Day Adventist

Boldface indicates subject; DO NOT include it as part of the address.

Loma Linda University
La Sierra Campus
Riverside, CA 92515

Seventh-Day Baptist
Seventh-Day Baptist Historical Society
510 Watchung Ave.
Plainfield, NJ 07061

Shaker
Library
Winterthur Museum
Winterthur, DE 19735

Shaker
Warren County Historical Society
105 South Broadway
Lebanon, OH 45036

Shakers
New York State Library
State Education Bldg. Annex
Albany, NY 12224

Shakers
Shaker Museum
Shaker Museum Road
Old Chatham, NY 12136

Shakers
Western Reserve Historical Society
10825 East Blvd.
Cleveland, OH 44106

Shakers
Warren County Historical Society
105 So. Broadway
Lebanon, OH 45036

Shakers
Shaker Community
P.O. Box 898
Pittsfield, MA 01201

Shakers
Kentucky Library
Western Kentucky University
Bowling Green, KY 42101

Shaker Membership File
Western Reserve Historical Society
10825 East Boulevard
Cleveland, OH 44106

Shelby County, OH County Records
Library
Wright State University
Dayton, OH 45431

Shelby County, TN County Records
Memphis Public Library
1850 Peabody Ave.
Memphis, TN 38104

Shenandoah Valley
McCormick Library
Washington & Lee University
Lexington, VA 24450

Shenandoah Valley

Historical Library/Archives
Eastern Mennonite College
Harrisonburg, VA 22801

Ship Crew Lists
Free Public Library
Pleasant Street
New Bedford, MA 02741

Ship Listings
Mystic Seaport Museum
Mystic, CT 06355

Ship Logs
Suffolk Marine Museum
Montauk Highway
Wast Sayville, NY 11796

Ship Logbooks
Smithtown Historical Society
P.O. Box 69
Smithtown, NY 11787

Ship Logbooks
Documents Committee
Shelter Island Public Library
Shelter Island, NY 11964

Ship Logbooks
Long Island Antiquities
93 North Country Road
Setauket, NY 11733

Ship Logbooks
Whaling Museum
Main Street
Sag Harbor, NY 11963

Ship Logbooks
New York Public Library
Fifth Ave. & 42nd Street
New York, NY 10018

Ship Logbooks
Whaling Museum Society
Main Street
Cold Spring Harbor, NY 11724

Ship Logbooks
Black Heritage Research Center
412 Station 14 St.
Sullivan's Island, SC 29482

Ship Logbooks
Tillamook County Pioneer Museum
2106 Second Street
Tillamook, OR 97141

Ship Logbooks
Swansea Public Library
Main Street
Swansea, MA 02777

Ship Logbooks
Kendall Whaling Museum
P.O. Box 297
Sharon, MA 02067

Ship Logbooks
Peabody Museum

East India Sq.
Salem, MA 01970

Ship Logbooks
Essex Institute
132 Essex Street
Salem, MA 01970

Ship Logbooks
Foulger Museum
Broat Street
Nantucket, MA 02554

Ship Logbooks
Atlantic County Historical Society
907 Shore Road
Somers Point, NJ 08244

Ship Logbooks
Bell Library
University of Minnesota
Minneapolis, MN 55455

Ship Logbooks
University of Minnesota
S-10 Wilson Library
Minneapolis, MN 55455

Ship Logbooks
Lake Superior State College
1000 College Drive
Sault Ste. Marie, MI 49783

Ship Logbooks
Museum
1 North Harbor Ave.
Grand Haven, MI 49417

Ship Logbooks
South Bend Public Library
122 W. Wayne Street
South Bend, IN 46601

Ship Logbooks
Plainfield Public Library
1120 Stafford Road
Plainfield, IN 46168

Ship Logbooks
East Central Province
9400 New Harmony Road
Evansville, IN 47712

Ship Logbooks
Fogler Library
University of Maine
Orono, ME 04473

Ship Logbooks
Dyer-York Library & Museum
371-75 Main Street
Saco, ME 04072

Ship Logbooks
Library
University of Baltimore
1420 Maryland Ave.
Baltimore, MD 21201

Ship Logbooks

Beverly Historical Society
117 Cabot Street
Beverly, MA 01915

Ship Logbooks
Longyear Historical Society
120 Seaver Street
Brookline, MA 02146

Ship Logbooks
Dennis Historical Society
Whig Street & Nobscusset Road
Dennis, MA 02660

Ship Logbooks
Dighton Historical Society
1217 Williams Street
Dighton, MA 02715

Ship's Logs
Newport Historical Society
82 Touro Street
Newport, RI 02840

Ship's Logs
Camden-Rockport Historical Society
Cramer Museum
Camden, ME 04843

Ship's Logs
Archives Department
Wilson Museum
Castine, ME 04421

Ship's Logs
Acadia National Park
Islesford History Museum
Islesford, ME 04646

Ship's Logs
Lincoln County Museum
Federal Street
Wiscasset, ME 04578

Ship's Logs
Library
Calvert Marine Museum
Solomons, MD 20688

Ship's Logs
Centerville Historical Society
513 Main Street
Centerville, MA 02632

Ship's Logs
Dukes County Historical Society
School & Cooke Streets
Edgartown, MA 02539

Ship's Logs
Annisquam Historical Society
Walnut Street Annisquam
Gloucester, MA 01930

Ship's Logs
Research Center
City Hall
Port Townsend, WA 98368

Ship's Logs

Boldface indicates subject; DO NOT include it as part of the address.

Museum of History & Industry
2161 East Hamlin
Seattle, WA 98112

Ship's Log Book & Journal File
Mystic Seaport, Inc.
Mystic, CT 06355

Ship Registers
Washington Navy Yard
11th & M Streets, S.E. Stop 314
Washington, DC 20374

Ships That Sank in Great Lakes
Chicago Historical Society
Clark Street at North Ave.
Chicago, IL 60614

Shipwrecks
Suffolk Marine Museum
Montauk Highway
West Sayville, NY 11796

Sheboygan County, WI County Records
Sheboygan County Historical Society
3110 Erie Ave.
Sheboygan, WI 53081

Simmerman Collection
Gallipolis Public Library
651 Second Ave.
Gallipolis, OH 45631

Slavic
SOKOL U.S.A.
P.O. Box 189
East Orange, NJ 07017

Slavic
Slovak League of America
870 Rifle Camp Road
West Paterson, NJ 07424

Slavic
University of Wisconsin
728 State Street
Madison, WI 53706

Slavic & East European Collection
University of California
Berkeley, CA 94720

Slovenian
Slovenian Research Center
29227 Eddy Road
Willoughby Hills, OH 44092

Slovenian
Croation-Slovenian-Serbian
 Genealogical Society
936 Industrial Avenue
Palo Alta, CA 94070

Slavonic Collection
New York Public Library
5th Ave. & 42nd Street
New York, NY 10018

Smith Collection
Marriott Library

University of Utah
Salt Lake City, UT 84112

Smith Collection
Rowan Public Library
201 West Fisher Street
Salisbury, NC 28144

Smock Collection
Indiana Historical Society
140 N. Senate Ave.
Indianapolis, IN 46204

Social Security Data
Social Security Administration
6401 Security Blvd.
Baltimore, MD 21235

Society of Black Hills Pioneers
Deadwood Public Library
435 Williams Street
Deadwood, SD 57732

Society of Brethren
Hills Library
169 Herrick Road
Newton Center, MA 02159

Society of Cincinnati
Society of Cincinnati
2118 Massachusetts Ave. N.W.
Washington, DC 20008

Society For Establishing
 Useful Manufactures
Paterson Public Library
250 Broadway
Paterson, NJ 07501

Society of Inquiry
Hills Library
169 Herrick Road
Newton Centre, MA 02159

Society of Jesus
Georgetown University
37 & O Streets, N.W.
Washington, DC 20057

Society of Tammany
Columbia University
535 West 114 Street
New York, NY 10027

SAR Library
Sons of the American Revolution
1000 South 4th Street
Louisville, KY 40203

Sons of the Revolution
Sons of the Revolution
600 S. Central Ave.
Glendale, CA 91204

Sons of Union Veterans
4278-80 Griscom Street
Philadelphia, PA 19124

South Bend, IN City Records
Northern Indiana Historical Society

112 South Lafayette Blvd.
South Bend, IN 46601

South Carolina Agricultural Societies
Library
Clemson University
Clemson, SC 29631

South Carolina Aud. Gen's.
Soldier Accounts
South Carolina Department of
Archives and History
1430 Senate Street
Columbia, SC 29211

South Carolina Baptist
Furman University
Duke Bldg.
Greenville, SC 29613

South Carolina Biographical Index
South Caroliniana Library
University of South Carolina
Columbia, SC 29208

South Carolina Citizenship Index
South Carolina Department of
Archives and History
1430 Senate Street
Columbia, SC 29211

South Carolina Colonial Records
Department of Archives and History
1430 Senate Ave.
Columbia, SC 29211

South Carolina Confederate
Pension Records
South Carolina Department of
Archives and History
1430 Senate Street
Columbia, SC 29211

South Carolina Confederate War File
South Carolina Department of
Archives and History
1430 Senate Street
Columbia, SC 29211

South Carolina County Records
Department of Archives and History
1430 Senate Ave.
Columbia, SC 29211

South Carolina Confederate Home Index
South Carolina Department of
Archives and History
1430 Senate Street
Columbia, SC 29211

South Carolina Confederate Pension Index
South Carolina Department of
Archives and History
1430 Senate Street
Columbia, SC 29211

South Carolina General Files
South Carolina Historical Society
Fire Proof Bldg.

Charleston, SC 29401

South Carolina Loyalist List
South Carolina Department of
Archives and History
1430 Senate Street
Columbia, SC 29211

South Carolina Lutherans
Wessels Library
Newberry College
Newberry, SC 29108

South Carolina Marriage
Settlements Index
South Carolina Department of
Archives and History
1430 Senate Street
Columbia, SC 29211

South Carolina Mexican Border Index
Adjutant General
1225 Bluff Road
Columbia, SC 29201

South Carolina Mexican War Index
South Carolina Department of
Archives and History
1430 Senate Street
Columbia, SC 29211

South Carolina Mills District Atlas
South Carolina Department of
Archives and History
1430 Senate Street
Columbia, SC 29211

South Carolina Miscellaneous
Records Indexes
South Carolina Department of
Archives and History
1430 Senate Street
Columbia, SC 29211

South Carolina Name File
Greenville County Library
300 College Street
Greenville, SC 29601

South Carolina Physicians
Waring Hist. Library
80 Barre Street
Charleston, SC 29401

South Carolina Spanish-
American Index
Adjutant General
1225 Bluff Road
Columbia, SC 29201

South Carolina Revolutionary
War Index
South Carolina Department of
Archives and History
1430 Senate Street
Columbia, SC 29211

South Carolina State
Grange Collection

Boldface indicates subject; **DO NOT** include it as part of the address.

Library
Clemson University
Clemson, SC 29631

South Carolina United Methodist
Library
University of South Carolina
Spartanburg, SC 29303

South Carolina War of 1812 Index
South Carolina Department of
  Archives and History
1430 Senate Street
Columbia, SC 29211

South Carolina WWI Index
Adjutant General
1225 Bluff Road
Columbia, SC 29201

South Dakota County Records
Archives Resource Center
Records Management Bldg.
Pierre, SD 57501

South Dakota Election Returns
Secretary of State
State House
Pierre, SD 57501

South Dakota Notary Records
Secretary of State
State House
Pierre, SD 57501

South Dakota Territorial Papers
Devereaux Library
South Dakota School of Mines
Rapid City, SD 57701

South Dakota Territorial Records
Secretary of State
State House
Pierre, SD 57501

South England
Cornish American
353 Ann Street, N.E.
Grand Rapids, MI 49505

South Jersey
Gloucester County Historical Society
17 Hunter Street
Woodbury, NJ 08096

South Pacific
Library
University of California
Santa Cruz, CA 95064

South Union Society
Kentucky Library
Western Kentucky University
Bowling Green, KY 42101

Southeast KS Obituary Index
Pittsburg Public Library
211 West Fourth Street
Pittsburg, KS 66762

Southeast Ohio
Library
Ohio University
Athens, OH 45701

Southeastern Pennsylvania
Mennonite Historical Society
2215 Millstream Road
Lancaster, PA 17602

Southeastern Texas
Sam Houston Library
Farm Road 1011
Liberty, TX 77575

Southern Claims Commission Index
Record Group 39
National Archives
Washington, DC 20408

Southern Baptist
Southeast Baptist Theo. Seminary
P.O. Box 752
Wake Forest, NC 27587

Southern Baptist
Baptist History Collection
Wake Forest University
Winston-Salem, NC 27109

Southern California Newspaper
  Collection
Los Angeles Museum of
  Natural History
900 Exposition Blvd.
Los Angeles, CA 90007

Southern Connecticut Town Records
Attic
Connecticut State Library
Hartford, CT 06115

Southern Historical Collection
Wilson Library
University of North Carolina
Chapel Hill, NC 27514

Southern Illinois
Morris Library
Southern Illinois University
Carbondale, IL 62901

Southern Illinois Methodist
Holman Library
McKendree College
Lebanon, IL 62254

Southern Lutherans
Southeastern District
5121 Colorado Ave., N.W.
Washington, DC 20011

Southern Ohio
Carnegie Public Library
127 S. North Street
Washington Court House, OH 43160

Southern Pacific
Library

Stanford University
Stanford, CA 94305

Southern Pacific
California Railway Museum
Star Rte. 283, Box 150
Suisan City, CA 94585

Southern Pacific Railroad
Library
University of Texas
El Paso, TX 79968

Southern Pacific Railroad
Roseville Public Library
557 Lincoln Street
Roseville, CA 95678

Southern Presbyterianism
Reformed Theological Seminary
5422 Clinton Blvd.
Jackson, MS 39209

Southern States Direct Tax
Civil Archives Division
National Archives & Records Service
Washington, DC 20408

Southern Society Collection
University Club
One West 54th Street
New York, NY 10019

Southern Texas
Conner Museum
Texas A & I University
Kingsville, TX 78363

Southern Tenant Farmers Union
Oral History Research Office
Memphis State University
Memphis, TN 38152

Southwest
Southwest Collection
Box 4090, Tech Sta.
Lubbock, TX 79409

Southwest Collection
Texas Tech University
West Broadway
Lubbock, TX 79409

Southwest Collection
El Paso Public Library
501 N. Oregon
El Paso, TX 79901

Southwest Michigan Family Collection
Niles Communtiy Library
620 East Main Street
Niles, MI 49120

Southwestern Minnesota
Southwest Minnesota History Center
Southwest State University
Marshall, MN 56258

Southwestern Ohio

Cincinnati Historical Society
Eden Park
Cincinnati, OH 45202

Southwestern Pennsylvania
Morgantown Public Library
373 Spruce Street
Morgantown, WV 26505

Southwestern Virginia
Library
Radford College
Radford, VA 24142

Southwestern Virginia
Newman Library
Virginia Polytechnic
Blacksburg, VA 24061

Spanish
Spanish American Genealogist
1510 Cravens Ave.
Torrance, CA 90501

Spanish Archives
New Mexico State Records & Archives
404 Montezuma Street
Santa Fe, NM 87501

Spanish Southwest
University of Texas
P.O. Box P
Austin, TX 78712

Speakers Bureau
National Speakers Assoc.
1324 North 22nd Ave.
Phoenix, AZ

Special Magazine
No Stone Unturned
40959 North 15th Street, W.
Palmdale, CA 93550

Spencer Collection
New York State Historical Society
Cooperstown, NY

Spring Collection
University of Wyoming
13th & Ivinson
Laramie, WY 82071

Spencer Family Collection
Library
New York State Historical Assoc.
Cooperstown, NY 13326

Spokane County, WA County Records
Spokane Public Library
West 906 Main Ave.
Spokane, WA 99201

Stark County, OH County Records
Bierce Library
University of Akron
Akron, OH 44325

Starr County, TX County Records
Library

Boldface indicates subject; DO NOT include it as part of the address.

Pan American University
Edinburg, TX 78539

State Cemetery Index
Vermont Historical Society
Montpelier, VT 05602

State Conservation Organizations
National Assoc. of Conservation
1025 Vermont Ave., N.W.
Washington, DC 20005

State House Index
Vermont State Capitol
State House
Montpelier, VT 05602

Steam and Diesel Locomotives
Schaffer Library
Union College
Schenectady, NY 12301

Steamboats
University of Wisconsin
1631 Pine Street
La Crosse, WI 54601

Steamboats
Bennett Studio
215 Broadway
Wisconsin Dells, WI 53965

Steamboats
Oshkosh Public Museum
1331 Algoma Blvd.
Oshkosh, WI 54901

Steamboats
Area Research Center
University of Wisconsin
La Crosse, WI 54601

Steamboats
Kentucky Library
Western Kentucky University
Bowling Green, KY 42101

Steamboats
University of Wisconsin
1631 Pine Street
La Crosse, WI 54601

Steamboats
Winona County Historical Society
160 Johnson Street
Winona, MN 55987

Steamboats
State Historical Society of Missouri
University of Missouri
Columbia, MO 65201

Steamboats
Dawes Memorial Library
Marietta College
Marietta, OH 45750

Steamboats
Cincinnati Public Library
800 Vine Street
Cincinnati, OH 45202

Steamboats
Record Group 41
National Archives
Washington, DC 20408

Steamboat Collection
Mobile City Museum
355 Government Street
Mobile, AL 36602

Steamboat Collection
Memphis Public Library
1850 Memphis Ave.
Memphis, TN 38104

Steamboat File
Davenport Museum
1717 West 12th Street
Davenport, IA 52804

Steamships
Steamship Historical Society
P.O. Box 2074
Ventnor City, NJ 08406

Steamships
Steamship Historical Society
of America
345 Blackstone Blvd.
Providence, RI 02906

Steamships
Library
University of Baltimore
1420 Maryland Ave.
Baltimore, MD 21201

**Steamship Historical Society
Collection**
Library
University of Baltimore
1420 Maryland Ave.
Baltimore, MD 21201

Sterling Potter Dutch Collection
Miss Edith Potter Dressel
273 Williams Street
Longmeadow, MA 01106

Stetson Collection
Florida History
University of Florida
Gainsville, FL 32601

Stevens Michigan Pioneer Collection
Kalamazoo Public Museum
315 South Rose Street
Kalamazoo, MI 49006

Stewart Collection
Savitz Library
Glassboro State College
Glassboro, NJ 08028

Stewart Collection
Museum of Western Colorado
Fourth and Ute

Grand Junction, CO 81501

Streeter Transportation Collection
American Antiquarian Society
185 Salisbury Street
Worcester, MA 01609

Strong Collection (Regimental Histories)
New York Public Library
Fifth Ave. & 42nd Street
New York, NY 10018

Studebaker Bros. Manufacturing Co.
Research Library
120 S. St. Joseph Street
South Bend, IN 46601

Suffolk County, New York
Smithtown Public Library
1 North Country Road
Smithtown, NY 11787

Summit County, OH Country Records
Bierce Library
University of Akron
Akron, OH 44325

Surname Index
Kentucky Room
Davies County Public Library
Owensboro, KY 42301

Surname Search
Orphan Voyage of Florida
13906 Pepperell Drive
Tampa, FL 33624

Surname Index (Analytical)
Library of Congress
Washington, DC 20540

Susquehanna Turnpike
Durham Center Museum
Route 145
East Durham, NY 12423

Sussex County, NJ County Records
Centenary College for Women
400 Jefferson Street
Hackettstown, NJ 07840

Swaigert Church Collection
Pennsylvania State Library
Walnut & Commonwealth Ave.
Harrisburg, PA 17108

Swedish
American Swedish Institute
2601 Oakland Ave.
Minneapolis, MN 55407

Swedish
American Swedish Institute
2600 Park Ave.
Minneapolis, MN 55407

Swedish
Swedish Pioneer Historical Society
5125 N. Spaulding Ave.
Chicago, IL 60625

Swedish
Swedish-American Genealogist
P.O. Box 2186
Winter Park, FL 32790

Swedish Baptist History
Bethel Theological Seminary
3949 Bethel Drive
New Brighton, MN 55112

Swedish Baptist
Bethel Theo. Seminary
3949 Bethel Drive
St. Paul, MN 55112

Swedish Collection
American-Swedish Institute
2600 Park Ave.
Minneapolis, MN 55407

Swedish Lutheran
Lutheran School of Theo.
1100 East 55th Street
Chicago, IL 60615

Sweetwater County, WY County Records
Sweetwater County Historical Museum
County Courthouse
Green River, WY 82935

Swinnerton Collection
Library
University of Arkansas
Fayetteville, AR 72701

Swiss
Swiss American Historical Society
216 East 39th Street
Norfolk, VA 23504

—T—

Tatnall Cemetery Collection
Division of History & Cultural Affairs
Hall of Records
Dover, DE 19901

Taylor Collection
Austin State University
Box 13055, SFA Sta.
Nacodoches, TX 75961

Telephone Companies
Telephone Publishing Co.
55 East Jackson Blvd.
Chicago, IL 60604

Telephone Directories
New York Public Library
Fifth Ave. & 42nd Street
New York, NY 10018

Telephone Directories
Research Library
195 Broadway
New York, NY 10007

Temple Spanish Collection
Los Angeles County Museum of

Boldface indicates subject; DO NOT include it as part of the address.

Natural History
900 Exposition Blvd.
Los Angeles, CA 90007

Tennessee Biographical File
Knoxville Public Library
500 West Church Ave.
Knoxville, TN 37902

Tennessee Biographical Index
Nashville Public Library
Eight Ave. No. & Union
Nashville, TN 37203

Tennessee Biographical Index
Memphis Public Library
1850 Peabody Ave.
Memphis, TN 38104

Tennessee Confederate Index
Tennessee State Archives & Library
403 7th Ave., No.
Nashville, TN 37219

Tennessee Confederate Pension Index
Tennessee State Archives and Library
403 7th Ave., No.
Nashville, TN 37219

Tennessee Confederate Questionaire (1920)
Tennessee State Archives and Library
403 7th Ave., No.
Nashville, TN 37219

Tennessee Confederate Muster Roll Index
Tennessee State Archives and Library
403 7th Ave., No.
Nashville, TN 37219

**Tennessee Confederate Soldier's
 Home Applications**
Tennessee State Archives and Library
403 7th Ave., No.
Nashville, TN 37219

**Tennessee County Biographical
 Dir. of Tennessee Gen. Assembly**
Bolivar Library
Bolivar, TN 38008

Tennessee County Hist. Series
University Press
Memphis State
Memphis, TN 38152

Tennessee Genealogy Collection
Knoxville Public Library
500 West Church Ave.
Knoxville, TN 37902

Tennessee Genealogical Index
Memphis Public Library
1850 Peabody Ave.
Memphis, TN 38104

Tennessee History
Hoskins Library
University of Tennessee
Knoxville, TN 37916

Tennessee History
Tusculum College
Box 87
Greenville, TN 37743

Tennessee Land Grants
State Library and Archives
403 7th Ave., No.
Nashville, TN 37219

Tennessee Methodist Episcopal
Tennessee Wesleyan College
P.O. Box 40
Athens, TN 37303

Tennessee Notarial Records
Secretary of State
State Capitol
Nashville, TN 37219

Tennessee Presbyterian
King Library
King College
Bristol, TN 37620

Tennessee State Histories Index
Knoxville Public Library
500 West Church Ave.
Knoxville, TN 37902

Tennessee State Supreme Court Index
State Library and Archives
403 7th Ave., No.
Nashville, TN 37219

Tennessee Tax Records Index
State Library and Archives
403 7th Ave., No.
Nashville, TN 37219

Territory of Deseret
Archives and Records Service
State Capitol
Salt Lake City, UT 84114

Territorial Surveys
Devereaux Library
South Dakota School of Mines
Rapid City, SD 57701

Texas
Library
University of Texas
Arlington, TX 76019

Texas
Research Center
Fair Park
Dallas, TX 75226

Texas Baptist
Southwestern Baptist Theo. Seminary
2001 W. Seminary Drive
Fort Worth, TX 76122

Texas Biographical Card File
Dallas Public Library
1954 Commerce Street
Dallas, TX 75201

see p. 618

Library
Huguenot Historical Society
New Paltz, NY 12561

Underwood Collection
Kentucky Library
Western Kentucky University
Bowling Green, KY 42101

Unger Collection
Evangelical and Reformed
Historical Society
555 West James Street
Lancaster, PA 17603

Union Pacific
Library
University of Iowa
Iowa City, IA 52242

Union Cemetery Index
Museum Library
Old Courthouse
Vicksburg, MS 39180

Union Soldiers Buried at Gettysburg
Historian
Gettysburg National Military Park
Gettysburg, PA 17325

Unitarian
Unitarian and Universalist
 Genealogical Society
10605 Lakespring Way
Cockeysville, MD 21030

Unitarian
Divinity School
45 Francis Ave.
Cambridge, MA 02138

United Brethren
Library
Otterbein College
Westerville, OH 43081

United Brethren
Indiana Central University
1400 East Hanna Ave.
Indianapolis, IN 46227

United Brethren in Christ
Evergreen Manor
1130 N. Westfield Blvd.
Oshkosh, WI 54901

United Brethren in Christ
Duke University
Durham, NC 27706

United Church of Christ
Connecticut Conference
125 Sherman Street
Hartford, CT 06105

United Church of Christ
Pacific School of Religion
1798 Scenic Ave.
Berkeley, CA 94709

United Church of Christ
State Historical Society
816 State Street
Madison, WI 53706

United Daughters of the Confederacy
United Daughters of the Confederacy
328 North Boulevard
Richmond, VA 23220

United Empire Loyalist
Chatham Public Library
120 Queen Street
Chatham, Ont. N7M 2GB Canada

United Evangelical
Perkins Library
Duke University
Durham, NC 27706

United Lutheran
Lutheran School of Theo.
1100 East 55th Street
Chicago, IL 60615

United Methodist
Perkins Library
Duke University
Durham, NC 27706

United Methodist Church
Shipman Library
Adrian College
Adrian, MI 49221

United Methodist
Shipman Library
Adrian College
Adrian, MI 49221

United Methodist
Baker University
Eighth Street
Baldwin, KS 66006

United Methodist
Indiana Central University
1400 East Hanna Ave.
Indianapolis, IN 46227

United Methodist Church
Huntingdon College
1500 E. Fairview Ave.
Montgomery, AL 36106

United Methodist
Pacific School of Religion
1798 Scenic Ave.
Berkeley, CA 94709

United Methodist
Iliff School of Theo.
2233 S. University Blvd.
Denver, CO 80210

United Presbyterian
Pittsburgh Theo. Seminary
616 N. Highland Ave.
Pittsburgh, PA 15206

Boldface indicates subject; **DO NOT** include it as part of the address.

United Railroads of San Francisco
Library
Stanford University
Stanford, CA 94305

United Railways & Electric Co.
Transit Research Center
1901 Falls Road
Baltimore, MD 21218

U.S. Appellate Courts
Law Library
Library of Congress
Washington, DC 20540

U.S. Coast Guard
Record Group 26
National Archives
Washington, DC 20408

U.S. Gealogical Survey Publications
Library
University of Texas
El Paso, TX 79968

U.S. Gazetteer Index
Los Angeles Temple Genealogy Library
10741 Santa Monica Blvd.
Los Angeles, CA 90025

U.S. Land Office
Bureau of State Lands
401 S. Monroe Street
Tallahassee, FL 32304

U.S. Marine Corps
Record Group 127
National Archives
Washington, DC 20408

U.S. Naval Academy
Record Group 405
National Archives
Washington, DC 20408

U.S. Naval Muster Rolls
Record Group 24
National Archives
Washington, DC 20408

U.S. Pension Fund
Civil Archives Division
National Archives & Records Service
Washington, DC 20408

U.S. Soldier's Home
Record Group 231
National Archives
Washington, DC 20408

U.S. Supreme Court
Law Library
Library of Congress
Washington, DC 20540

U.S. Surname File
Fort Wayne Public Library
900 Webster Street
Fort Wayne, IN 46802

United Society of Believers
Research Library
Syracuse University
Syracuse, NY 13210

United Transportation Union
Library
Cornell University
Ithaca, NY 14850

Universalist
Divinity School
45 Francis Ave.
Cambridge, MA 02138

Universalist Historical Society
Universalist Historical Society
25 Beacon Street
Boston, MA

Universalist Church
Harvard University
45 Francis Ave.
Cambridge, MA 02138

Universalist
Unitarian and Universalist
 Genealogical Society
10605 Lakespring Way
Cockeysville, MD 21030

University Recruits
Museum
Upper Iowa University
Fayette, IA 52142

Upper Canada
Ontario Genealogical Society
Box 66 Sta. Q
Toronto, M4T 2L7 Canada

Upper Great Lakes
Bayliss Public Library
541 Library Drive
Sault Ste. Marie, MI 49783

Upper Mississippi Valley
Augustana College
Rock Island, IL 61201

Upper Mississippi Valley Index
National Archives and Records Service
Washington, DC 20408

Upper Mississippi River Valley
Area Research Center
University of Wisconsin
La Crosse, WI 54601

Upstate New York Church Records
Cornell University
101 Olin Library
Ithaca, NY 14853

Upstate New York Church Records
State University of New York
Vestal Parkway East
Binghamton, NY 13901

Texas Collection
Baylor University
P.O. Box 6369
Waco, TX 76706

Texas Confederate Index
Archives Division
Texas State Library
Austin, TX 78711

Texas Confederate Pension Applications
Archives Division
Texas State Library
Austin, TX 78711

Texas Confederate Pension Index
Archives Division
Capitol Station
Austin, TX 78711

Texas County Records
Archives Division
1201 Brazos Street
Austin, TX 78711

Texas Episcopal
Episcopal Diocese
111 Torcido
San Antonio, TX 78209

Texas Episcopal Church
Rosenburg Library
2310 Sealy Ave.
Galveston, TX 77550

Texas Family Papers
Rice University
6100 South Main Street
Houston, TX 77001

Texas Federal Court Records
Federal Archives and Records Center
4900 Hemphill Street
Fort Worth, TX 76115

Texas Medical History
University of Texas
5323 Harry Hines Blvd.
Dallas, TX 75235

Texas-Mexican War
Peace Library
University of Texas
San Antonio, TX 78285

Texas Panhandle
Amarillo Public Library
413 East 4th Street
Amarillo, TX 79105

Texas Panhandle
Panhandle-Plains Hist. Museum
2401 4th Ave.
Canyon, TX 79016

Texas Territory
Archives Division
1201 Brazos Street
Austin, TX 78711

Theosophy
Theosophical University
2416 N. Lake Ave.
Pasadena, CA 91001

Thwing Boston Land Collection
Massachusetts Historical Society
1154 Boyleston Street
Boston, MA 02215

Ticonderoga-Champlain Valley
Ticonderoga Historical Society
Moses Circle
Ticonderoga, NY 12883

Tippecanoe County, IN County Records
Tippecanoe County Historical Society
909 South Street
Lafayette, IN 47901

Toledo Blade Obituray Index
Toledo Public Library
325 Michigan Street
Toledo, OH 43624

Topographic Maps
Geography and Map Division
Library of Congress
Washington, DC

Township Map Collection
Fort Wayne Public Library
900 Webster Street
Fort Wayne, IN 46802

Township Maps
Andriot Assoc.
P.O. Box 195
McLean, VA 22101

Townships
National Assoc. of Towns & Townships
1521 16th Street, N.W.
Washington, DC 20036

Trans-Mississippi History
Spencer Library
University of Kansas
Lawrence, KS 66044

Trans-Mississippi West
Missouri Historical Society
Jefferson Memorial Bldg.
St. Louis, MO 63112

Trans-Mississippi West
Washington University
6600 Millbrook Blvd.
St. Louis, MO 63130

Trans-Pecos Texas
El Paso Public Library
501 North Oregon
El Paso, TX 79901

Transcendentalists
Unitarian and Universalist
Genealogical Society
10605 Lakespring Way

Boldface indicates subject; DO NOT include it as part of the address.

Cockeysville, MD 21030

Transportation
University of Michigan
312 Undergraduate Library Bldg.
Ann Arbor, MI 48109

Transportation
Smithsonian Institution
12th & Constitution Ave., N.W.
Washington, DC 20560

Transportation Collection
Mobile City Museum
355 Government Street
Mobile, AL 36602

Trains (steam)
Empire State Railway Museum
P.O. Box 666
Middletown, NY 10940

Travis County Collection
Austin Public Library
P.O. Box 2287
Austin, TX 78768

Trinity Development Co.
Western Washington University
High Street
Bellingham, WA 98225

Tucson, Arizona City Directories
Arizona Daily Star
4850 South Park Ave.
Tucson, AZ 85726

Turner Collection
Division of History and
  Cultural Affairs
Hall of Records
Dover, DE 19901

Toner, Joseph Meredith Collection
Manuscript Division
Library of Congress
Washington, DC 20540

Turkish
American Turkish Society
380 Madison Ave.
New York, NY 10016

Turnpikes
American Antiquarian Society
185 Salisbury Street
Worcester, MA 01609

Tuscarawas County, OH County Records
Bierce Library
University of Akron
Akron, OH 44325

Tutwiler Collection
Birmingham Public Library
2020 Park Pl.
Birmingham, AL 35203

TVA Cemetery Records

Maps and Surveys Branch
200 Haney Bldg.
Chattanooga, TN 37401

TVA Cemetery Relocation Index
Tennessee Valley Authority
311 Broad Street #207
Chattanooga, TN 37401

TVA Oral Histories
Memphis State University
Southern and Patterson
Memphis, TN 38152

TVA Platt Maps
Mr. I. M. Pitts
505 Lupton Bldg.
Chattanooga, TN 37401

Tyler County, TX County Records
Sam Houston Library
Farm Road 1011
Liberty, TX 77575

—U—

Ukraine
Pilsudski Institute
381 Park Ave. So.
New York, NY 10016

Ukraine
Ukrainian Center
2453 W. Chicago Ave.
Chicago, IL 60622

Ukrainian
Ukrainian Institute of America
2 East 79th Street
New York, NY 10021

Ukrainian
Ukrainian Museum
203 Second Ave.
New York, NY 10003

Ukrainian
League of Americans of
  Ukrainian Descent
841 N. Western Ave.
Chicago, IL 60622

Ukrainian
Ukrainian National Assoc.
P.O. Box 76
Jersey City, NJ 07303

Ukrainian
Ukrainian Genealogical and
  Heraldic Society
573 N.E. 102nd Street
Miami Shores, FL 33138

Ukrainian
Ukrainian Museum
1202 Kenilworth Ave.
Cleveland, OH 44109

Ulster County, NY County Records

see p 616

Upstate New York Church Records
State University of New York
1400 Washington Ave.
Albany, NY 12222

Upstate New York Church Records
Arents Research Library
Syracuse University
Syracuse, NY 13210

Upstate New York Church Records
Rhees Library
University of Rochester
Rochester, NY 14627

Upper Ohio Valley
Library
West Virginia University
Morgantown, WV 26505

Upper Ohio River Valley
Washington & Jefferson College
Lincoln and Wheeling Streets
Washington, PA 15301

Upper Perkiomen Valley
Schwenkfelder Library
Pennsburg, PA 18073

Upper Susquehanna
Historical Museum
11 Ford Ave.
Oneonta, NY 13820

Upper Tombigbee Valley
University of Alabama
P.O. Box CS
University, AL 35486

Utah Biographical Files
Utah State Historical Society
300 Rio Grande
Salt Lake City, UT 84101

Utah County Records
Archives and Records Service
State Capitol
Salt Lake City, UT 84114

Utah Territory
Archives and Records Service
State Capitol
Salt Lake City, UT 84114

Utah War, 1857
Tulane University
7001 Freret Street
New Orleans, LA 70118

Utah and the West Archives
Lee Library
Brigham Young University
Provo, UT 84602

—V—

Vail Collection
Rhees Library
University of Rochester
Rochester, NY 14627

Valley Forge Orderly Books
Valley Forge Historical Society
Valley Forge, PA 19481

**Vanderburgh County, IN
County Records**
Willard Library
21 First Ave.
Evansville, IN 47710

Vermont
Genealogical Library
Bennington Museum
Bennington, VT 05201

Vermont
Bailey Library
University of Vermont
Burlington, VT 05401

Vermont Censuses
Law and Documents Unit
Vermont Department of Libraries
Montpelier, VT 05602

Vermont Town Records
Vermont Historical Society
Pavilion Bldg.
Montpelier, VT 05602

Vessel Registers
Center for Archival Collections
Bowling Green State University
Bowling Green, OH

Victoria Mining Co.
Museum
233 River Street
Ontonagon, MI 49953

Virgin Islands
Bureau of Libraries and Museums
P.O. Box 390
Charlotte Amalie
St. Thomas, VI 00801

Virginia
Virginia Historical Society
428 North Blvd.
Richmond, VA 23221

Virginia
Library
University of Virginia
Charlottesville, VA 22901

Virginia Bible Collection
Virginia Historical Society
428 North Blvd.
Richmond, VA 23221

Virginia Collection
Arlington Public Library
1015 N. Quincy Street
Arlington, VA 22201

Virginia Company of London
Manuscripts Division
Library of Congress
Washington, DC 20540

Boldface indicates subject; DO NOT include it as part of the address.

Virginia County Records
Virginia Historical Society
428 North Blvd.
Richmond, VA 23221

Virginia Court Records for Southwestern Pennsylvania
Washington & Jefferson College
Lincoln & Wheeling Streets
Washington, PA 15301

Virginia Confederate Index
Virginia State Library

Virginia Confederate Pension Index
Virginia State Library

Virginia Confederate Service Records Index
Virginia State Library

Virginia Family Papers
Swem Library
College of William and Mary
Williamsburg, VA 23185

Virginia Federal St. and Conf. Courts
Virginia State Library
12th and Capitol Streets
Richmond, VA 23219

Virginia Gazette Index
Greenwood Public Library
408 W. Washington
Greenwood, MS 38930

Virginia Military Institute
Library
Virginia Military Institute
Lexington, VA 24450

Virginia Military Institute
New Market Battlefield Park
George Collins Parkway
New Market, VA 22844

Virginia Newspaper Collection
Virginia Historical Society
428 North Blvd.
Richmond, VA 23221

Virginia Revolutionary War Land Entries and Surveys
State of Ohio
Office of Auditor of State
Columbus, OH 43216

Vital Record Index
New Hampshire Antiquarian Society
Hopkinton, NH 03229

—W—

Wagon Roads
Record Group 48
National Archives
Washington, DC 20408

Wagontrains
San Francisco Historic Records

1204 Nimitz Drive
Colma, CA 94105

Walen Collection
Mississippi Room
University of Southern Mississippi
Hattiesburg, MS 39401

Wall Index
Newberry Library
60 West Walton Street
Chicago, IL 60610

Wallace Memorial Collection
Chesapeake Public Library
300 Cedar Road
Chesapeake, VA 23324

Walloon Belgians
Area Research Center
University of Wisconsin
Green Bay, WI 54302

Wallowa Country
Enterprise Public Library
Enterprise, OR 97828

War of 1812 British Prisoners
Record Group 45
National Archives
Washington, DC 20408

War of 1812 Collection
Lily Library
University of Indiana
Bloomington, IN 47401

Ward Census Maps
Map Division
New York Public Library
Fifth Avenue and 42nd Street
New York, NY

Warren County, KY County Records
Kentucky Library
Western Kentucky University
Bowling Green, KY 42101

Warren County, OH Cemetery Index
Warren County Historical Society
105 South Broadway
Lebanon, OH 45036

Warren County, OH County Records
Museum
105 South Broadway
Lebanon, OH 45036

Warren County, OH Vital Record Index
Warren County Historical Society
105 South Broadway
Lebanon, OH 45036

Warren County, NJ County Records
Centenary College For Women
400 Jefferson Street
Hackettstown, NJ 07840

Washington Canal Co.
Record Group 351

National Archives
Washington, DC 20408

Washington, D.C.
George Washington University
2130 H Street, N.W.
Washington, DC 20052

Washington State Biographical Index
Washington Northwest Room
Washington State Library
Olympia, WA 98504

Washington State County Records
Archives and Records Management
12th and Washington Streets
Olympia, WA 98504

Washington Settlers Notebooks
Seattle Public Library
1000 4th Ave.
Seattle, WA 98104

Washington Territory
Washington State Library
Olympia, WA 98504

Waterville City Records
Waterville Historical Society
64 Silver Street
Waterville, ME 04901

Waterways
Inland River Library
Cincinnati Public Library
Cincinnati, OH 45202

Waukesha County, WI County Records
Waukesha County Museum
101 West Main Street
Waukesha, WI 53186

Waves
Oral Hist. Office
U.S. Naval Institute
Annapolis, MD 21402

Wayne County, IN County Records
Wayne County Hist. Musuem
1150 North A Street
Richmond, IN 47374

Wayne County OH County Records
Bierce Library
University of Akron
Akron, OH 44325

Wayne County, OH Court Records
Wayne County Historical Society
546 East Bowman Street
Wooster, OH 44691

Webb County, TX County Records
Library
Pan American University
Edinburg, TX 78539

Weisiger Collection
Victoria College
2200 East Red River

Victoria, TX 77901

Wellfleet Marine Benevolent Society
Wellfleet Historical Society
Main Street
Wellfleet, MA 02667

Wells Fargo
Wells Fargo Bank Library
475 Sansome Street
San Francisco, CA 94144

Wells Fargo Collection
Wells College Library
Main Street
Aurora, NY 13026

Wesleyan
Archives and Historical Library
Highway 37 and 50th Street
Marion, IN 46952

West Virginia
Morgantown Public Library
373 Spruce Street
Morgantown, WV 26505

West Virginia Cemetery Index
West Virginia Collection
West Virginia University Library
Morgantown, WV 26506

West Virginia Collection
Morgantown Public Library
373 Spruce Street
Morgantown, WV 26505

West Virginia Collection
Library
West Virginia University
Morgantown, WV 26506

West Virginia County Records
Department of Archives and History
Capitol Complex
Charleston, WV 25305

West Virginia County Records
Library
West Virginia University
Morgantown, WV 26505

West Virginia Election Returns
Secretary of State
State Capitol Bldg.
Charleston, WV 25305

West Virginia Notary Records
Secretary of State
State Capitol Bldg.
Charleston, WV 25305

West Virginia United Methodist
Pfeiffer Library
West Virginia Wesleyan College
Buckhannon, WV 26201

Western Americana
Bancroft Library
University of California

Boldface indicates subject; **DO NOT** include it as part of the address.

Berkeley, CA 94720

Western Federation of Miners
Western Historical Collections
University of Colorado
Boulder, CO 80302

Western Michigan Methodist Records
Michigan State Library
735 E. Michigan Ave.
Lansing, MI 48913

Westward Expansion Movie
Jefferson National Expansion Memorial
11 North Fourth Street
St. Louis, MO 63102

Western Historical Collections
University of Colorado
Boulder, CO 80302

Western History Collections
University of Oklahoma
630 Parrington Oval
Norman, OK 73019

Western History Manuscript
  Collection
University of Missouri
4825 Troost Ave.
Kansas City, MO 64110

Western Massachusetts
Berkshire Athenaeum
1 Wendell Ave.
Pittsfield, MA 01201

Western Maryland
Morgantown Public Library
373 Spruce Street
Morgantown, WV 26505

Western New York
Holland Land Office Museum
131 West Main Street
Batavia, NY 10420

Western New York Church Records
State University of New York
1300 Elmwood Ave.
Buffalo, NY 14222

Western Pacific
California Railway Museum
Star Rte. 283, Box 150
Suisan City, CA 94585

Western Pennsylvania
Archives Office
Community Center
Villa Maria, PA 16155

Western Pennsylvania
Carnegia Library
4400 Forbes Ave.
Pittsburgh, PS 15213

Western Pennsylvania
  Biographical Index
Carnegie Library

4400 Forbes Avenue
Pittsburgh, PA 15213

Western Pioneers
Washington State University
Pullman, WA 99164

Western Reserve
Western Reserve Historical Society
10825 East Blvd.
Cleveland, OH 44106

Western Reserve Pioneers
Library
Hiram College
Hiram, OH 44234

Western Reserve Region
Library
Kent State University
Kent, OH 44242

Western Transportation Archives
Lee Library
Brigham Young University
Provo, UT 84602

Western Tennessee
Library
Murray State University
Murray, KY 42071

Western Texas County Records
Library
University of Texas
El Paso, TX 79968

Western Township, IL
  Property Records
Western Township Public Library
1111 4th Street
Orion, IL 61273

Western Wisconsin
Winona County Historical Society
160 Johnson Street
Winona, MN 55987

Westward Migration
Library
Washington and Jefferson College
Washington, PA 15301

Whaling
International Marine Archives
21 Orange Street
Nantucket, MA 02554

Whaling
Dukes County Historical Society
School and Cooke Streets
Edgartown, MA 02539

Whaling
Foulger Museum
Broad Street
Nantucket, MA 02554

Whaling
Kendall Whaling Museum

P.O. Box 297
Sharon, MA 02067

Whaling
Providence Public Library
150 Empire Street
Providence, RI 02903

Whaling
Brown University
20 Prospect Street
Providence, RI 02912

Whaling
Stonington Historical Society
Whitehall Ave.
Stonington, CT 06378

Whaling
Lahaina Restoration Foundation
Front and Dickenson Streets
Lahaina, HI 96761

Whaling
Whaling Museum Society
Main Street
Cold Spring Harbor, NY 11724

Whaling
East Hampton Free Library
159 Main Street
East Hampton, NY 11937

Whaling
Queens Borough Public Library
89-11 Merrick Blvd.
Jamaica, NY 11432

Whaling
Whaling Museum
Main Street
Sag Harbor, NY 11963

Whaling
Whaling Museum Society
Main Street
Cold Spring Harbor, NY 11724

Whaling
Old Dartmouth Historical Society
18 Johnny Cake Hill
New Bedford, MA 02740

Whaling
Free Public Library
Box C-902
New Bedford, MA 02741

Whaling Collection
Free Public Library
Box C-902
New Bedford, MA 02741

Whiskey Rebellion
Washington and Jefferson College
Lincoln and Wheeling Streets
Washington, PA 15301

Whiskey Rebellion
Library

Washington and Jefferson College
Washington, PA 15301

Whitaker Collection
Marriott Library
University of Utah
Salt Lake City, UT 84112

White River Bad Lands
Devereaux Library
South Dakota School of Mines
Rapid City, SD 57701

Wild West Shows
Circus World Museum
415 Lynne Street
Baraboo, WI 53913

Will County, IL Property Records
Will County Historical Society
803 S. State Street
Lockport, IL 60441

Will County, IL Surname File
Will County Historical Society
803 S. State Street
Lockport, Il 60441

Willacy County, TX County Records
Library
Pan American University
Edinburg, TX 78539

Willett Collection
Samford University
800 Lakeshore Drive
Birmingham, AL 35209

Willet Family
Willet Stained Glass Studios
10 E. Moreland Ave.
Philadelphia, PA 19118

William Bacon Evans Collection
The Quaker Collection
Haverford College Library
Haverford, PA 19041

Wilson Collection
Austin State University
Box 13055, SFA Sta.
Nacodoches, TX 75961

Wilton Tax Records
Goodspeed Memorial
104 Main Street
Wilton, ME 04294

Wisconsin County Records
State Historical Society
816 State Street
Madison, WI 53706

Wisconsin County Records
McIntyre Library
University of Wisconsin
Eau Claire, WI 54701

**Wisconsin Grand Army
of the Republic**

Boldface indicates subject; DO NOT include it as part of the address.

Memorial Hall Museum
Capitol 419 North
Madison, WI 53702

Wisconsin River Raftsmen
Bennett Studio
215 Broadway
Wisconsin Dells, WI 53965

Women
Women's Hist. Research Center
2325 Oak Street
Berkeley, CA 94708

Women
Center For Research On Women
Wellesley College
Wellesley, MA 02181

Women
College Archives
Smith College
Northampton, MA 01060

Woman's Missionary Society
Library
Anderson College
Anderson, IN 46011

Woods Collection
Mississippi Room
University of Southern Mississippi
Hattiesburg, MS 39401

World's Columbian Exposition 1893
Chicago Public Library
78 E. Washington Street
Chicago, IL 60602

World Conference on Records Papers
Genealogical Department
50 East North Temple
Salt Lake City, UT 84150

World's Funniest Epitaphs
Ancestral Routes
P.O. Box 11745
Salt Lake City, UT 84111

World War I
Veterans of World War I
237 Madison Ave.
New York, NY 10016

World War I Draft Cards
Federal Records Center
1557 St. Joseph Avenue
East Point, GA 30044

**World War II Selective
  Service Records**
Washington National Records Center
Federal Office Bldg.
Suitland, MD 21668

Wortham Collection
Austin State University
Box 13055, SFA Sta.
Nacodoches, TX 75961

WPA Biographical Index
Archives Division
Texas State Library
Austin, TX 78711

Wright Collection
Georgia Historical Society
501 Whitaker Street
Savannah, GA 31401

Wyoming Cattlemen's Records
University of Wyoming
13th and Ivinson
Laramie, WY 82071

Wyoming Valley
Scranton Public Library
Vine Street and Washington Ave.
Scranton, PA 18503

Wyoming Valley
Wyoming Historical Society
49 South Franklin Street
Wilkes-Barre, PA 18701

Wyoming Valley
King's College
14 W. Jackson Street
Wilkes-Barre, PA 18711

—Y—

Yazoo Land Claims
Record Group 76
National Archives
Washington, DC 20408

Y.M.C.A.
Y.M.C.A. Hist. Library
291 Broadway
New York, NY 10007

Y.M.C.A.
George Williams College
555 31st Street
Downes Grove, IL 60515

York County, PA County Records
York County Historical Society
250 E. Market Street
York, PA 17403

York County, ME County Records
Dyer-York Library and Museum
371-75 Main Street
Saco, ME 04072

Yugoslavian
Yugoslav Press and Cultural Center
488 Madison Ave.
New York, NY 10022

—Z—

Zanesville Street Railway
Hayes Library
1337 Hayes Ave.
Fremont, OH 43420

Zapata County, TX, County Records
Library
Pan American University
Edinburg, TX 78539

Zeamer Collection
Pennsylvania State Library
Walnut and Commonwealth Ave.
Harrisburg, PA 17108

Zeitler Civil War Collection
Huntsville Public Library
P.O. Box 443
Huntsville, AL 35804

Zeitler Collection
Huntsville Public Library
P.O. Box 443
Huntsville, AL 35804

CHAPTER 27

BASIC REFERENCE SOURCES

This section contains those references most often consulted by American genealogical researchers. Seldom will you find your ancestry in these works. This is not a listing of printed or published family histories. Rather, these are the special works which help the researcher consult the original sources. These reference works are seldom found in a typical genealogical collection or library. They are usually located in the reference section of your public or university library.

In the left-hand column is an alphabetical listing of subjects (sources) important to the Genealogist, and in the right-hand column is a reference work that will help you understand the subject. For example, if a researcher wanted to find out if a particlar newspaper was published in say 1915 in Mansfield, Wright County, Missouri, he could run down the left hand column until he came to newspapers. Then, because of the date in question, he would know that he wanted to search Gregory's work. By searching this work, he would find that the newspaper in question was the Mansfield Mirror which is on microfilm and is available free from Columbia on Inter-library loan.

SUBJECT	REFERENCE
Adoption Periodical	O'Dell, Robert, *Open Arms Quarterly*, North Platte, NE, 1981.
Abstract Companies	American Land Title Association. *Directory: American Land Title Association.* Washington, D.C.: American Land Title Association, Annual.
Almanacs	Drake, Milton. *Almanacs of the United States.* New York: Scarecrow Press, two volumes.
Archives — National	*Guide to Genealogical Research in the National Archives,* The National Archives, Washington, D.C., 1982 (new edition).
State	*Directory of State Archives in the United States.* Society of American Archivists, Ann Arbor, Mich., 1980.
Associations	*Encyclopedia of American Associations.* Detroit: Gale Research Company. Annual.
Atlases	Library of Congress, Map Division. *A List of Geographical Atlases in the Library of Congress, Volume 1—, 1909—.* Washington, D.C: Reprinted (Volumes 1-11). New York: Paladin Press, 1968.
	United States Department of the Interior, Geological Survey. *The National Atlas of the United States of America.* Washington, D.C.: United States Government Printing Office, 1972.
	LeGear, C.E., *U.S. Atlases,* Library of Congress, Washington, D.C. (vol. 1) 1950, (vol 2) 1953.
	Fire Insurance Maps in the Library of Congress, Library of Congress, Washington, D.C., 1981.

SUBJECT	REFERENCE

Autobiography — Kaplan, Louis, et al. *A Bibliography of American Autobiographies.* Madison: University of Wisconsin Press, 1961.

Biographies — O'Neill, Edward H. *Bibliography by Americans, 1658-1936: A subject Bibliography.* Philadelphia: Milford, 1939.

Books in Print — Schreiner, Yantis, *Genealogical and Local History Books in Print,* Springfield, VA, 1981.

Business
Archives — Society of American Archivists. *Directory of Business Archives in the United States and Canada.* Ann Arbor: Society of American Archivists, 1969

History — Larson, Henrietta Melia. *Guide to Business History: Materials for the Study of American Business History and Suggestions for Their Use,* Cambridge: Harvard University Press, 1948.

Calendar — Watkins, Harold. *Time Counts: The Story of the Calendar.* New York: Philosophical Library, 1954

Canada — Jonasson, Eric, *The Canadian Genealogical Handbook,* Wheatfield Press, Winnipeg, Manitoba, Canada, 1981.

Census
Federal — *Guide to Genealogical Research in the National Archives,* The National Archives, Washington, D.C., 1982 (new edition).

General — Stemmons, Jack, ed. *The Census Compendium.* Salt Lake City: The Institute of Family Research, 1973

Mortality — *Guide to Genealogical Research in the National Archives,* The National Archives, Washington, D.C., 1982 (new edition).

Chamber of Commerce — *World Wide Chamber of Commerce Directory.* Loveland, Colorado: Johnson Publishing Company, Inc., annual.

Church
Agencies — Jacquet, Constant H., Jr., ed. *Yearbook of American And Canadian Churches.* Nashville: Abingdon Press, Annual.

Archives — Sueflow, August R. *A Preliminary Guide to Church Records Repositories.* Ann Arbor: Society of American Archivists, 1969.

Atlases — Gaustad. Edwin Scott. *Historical Atlas of Religion in America.* New York: Harper and Row, 1962.

Histories — Mean, Frank S. *Hankbook of Denominations in the United States.* Nashville: Abingdon Press, 1980.

Libraries — Rodda, Dorothy and Harvey, John. *Directory of Church Libraries.* Philadelphia: Drexel Press, 1967.

Records — Kirkham, E. Kay. *Survey of American Church Records.* Salt Lake City: Deseret Book Company, 1969, two volumes.

Schools — *American Association of Theological Schools Directory.* Dayton: American Association of Theological Schools, annual

Yearbooks — DeGroot, A. T. *Library of American Church Records.* Ecumenism Research Agency, (Microfilm in two series.)

City Directory — *Cities and Counties, Counties and County Seats of the United States,* A. C. Publications, McPherson, KS. n.d.

City Records — Kirkham, E. Kay. *A Handy Guide to Record-searching in the Larger Cities of the United States: Including a Guide to Their Vital Records and Some Maps with Street Indexes with Other Information of Genealogical Value.* Logan, Utah: Everton Publishers, Inc., 1974.

Coats of Arms — Moncreiffe, Iain and Pottinger, Don. *Simple Heraldry: Cheerfully Illustrated.* London: Thomas Nelson and Sons Limited, 1971.

Colleges — Elliott, Norman R., ed. *Patterson's American Education.* Mt. Prospect, Ill.: Educational Directories, Inc., annual.

Archives — Society of American Archivists. *College and University Archives in the United States and Canada.* Ann Arbor: University of Michigan, 1972.

Fraternities	Baird, William Raimond, ed. *Baird's Manual of American College Fraternities.* Menaha, Wisconsin: G. Banta Company, 1968.
Newspapers	*Editor and Publisher Yearbook.* New York: The Editor and Publisher Company, annual.
County Bibliography	Haywood, Charles. *A Bibliography of North American Folklore and Folksong.* New York: Dover Publications, Inc., 1961, Volume 1.
Formation	Kane, Joseph N. *The American Counties.* New York: Scarecrow Press, 1972.
Government	Wager, Paul W., ed. *County Government Across the Nation.* Chapel Hill: The University of North Carolina Press, 1950.
Historical Survey (W.P.A.)	Child, Sargent B. and Holmes, Dorothy P. *Check List of Historical Records Survey Publications: Bibliography of Research Projects Reports,* 1943. Baltimore: Genealogical Publishing Company, 1969, Reprint.)
Historical Survey (Unpublished)	Hefner, Loretta L. *The WPA Historical Records Survey: A Guide to the Unpublished Inventories, Indexes and Transcripts.* Society of American Archivists. Chicago, 1980.
History	Peterson, Clarence Stewart. *Consolidated Bibliography of County Histories in Fifty States in 1961.* Baltimore: The Genealogical Publishing Co., 1963.
Court Appellate	*Decennial Edition of the American Digest: A Complete Table of American Cases From 1658-1906.* St. Paul: West Publishing Company, 1911, Volumes 21-25.
Organization	Pound, Roscoe. *Organization of Courts.* Boston: Little, Brown and Company, 1940
	United States Department of Justice, *State Court Organization, 1980,* National Center for State Courts, Williamsburg, VA, 1981.
Diaries	Matthews, William and Pearce, Roy Harvey. *American Diaries: An Annotated Bibliography of American Diaries Written Prior to the Year 1861.* Berkeley: University of California Press, 1945.
	Matthews, William. *American Diaries in Manuscript, 1580-1950: A Descriptive Bibliography.* Athens: University of Georgia Press, 1974.
Directories	Klein, Bernard, ed. *Guide to American Directories.* New York: B. Klein and Company, 1972.
Ethnic	*Bibliography of American Ethnology.* B. Klein Publishing, Coral Springs, FL, 1976.
	Schatz, Walter, *Directory of Afro-American Resources.* R. R. Bowker & Co., New York, 1970.
	Thornstrom, Stephen, *Harvard Encyclopedia of American Ethnic Groups,* Belknap Press, Cambridge, 1980.
	Wasserman, Paul, *Ethnic Information Sources of the United States,* Gale Research Co., Detroit, MI, 1976.
Family Encyclopedia	Dalby, Barbara M. *Bechtel Family Encyclopedia.* 1974. (Volume 1) [Note: This work is cited as an example only.]

SUBJECT	REFERENCE
Organization	Wallace, Arthur. *Successful Family Organization.* Los Angeles: Los Angeles Temple Genealogical Library, 1965.
Social History	Calhoun, Arthur W. *A Social History of the American Family from Colonial Times to the Present.* New York: Barnes and Noble, 1945
Fraternal	Ferguson, Charles W. *Fifty Million Brothers: A panorama of American Lodges and Clubs.* New York: Farrar and Rhinehart, 1937.
	Grand Lodge of Massachusetts. *List of Lodges Masonic.* Bloomington, Ill.: Pantagraph Printing and Stationery Company, annual
	Baird, William Raimond, ed. *Baird's Manual of American College Fraternities.* Menasha, Wisconsin: G. Banta Company, 1968.
	Fraternal Monitor Staff. *Statistics of Fraternal Benefit Societies: Containing Statistical Information About Benefit Societies in the United States and Canada.* Indianapolis: The Fraternal Monitor, 1973.
Genealogy Correspondence	Cache Genealogical Library. *Handbook For Genealogical Correspondence.* Logan, Utah: The Everton Publishers, Inc., 1974.
General	Greenwood, Val D. *The Researcher's Guide to American Genealogy.* Baltimore: The Genealogical Publishing Company, Inc., 1973.
Jurisdictions	Jones, Vincent L., Eakle, Arlene H., And Christensen, Mildred H. *Family History for Fun and Profit.* Salt Lake City: Genealogical Institute, 1972. [Formerly entitled *Genealogical Research: A Jurisdictional Approach.]*
Maps	The Map Division. *Dictionary Catalog of the Map Division.* Boston: G. K. Hall, 1971, ten volumes.
Periodicals	Bremer, Ronald A. (ed.), *Roots Digest,* Roots Digest, P.O. Box 2101, Glenwood Springs, CO 81602.
Printed Works (Family Histories)	Kiminkow, Marion. *Genealogies in the Library of Congress: A Bibliography.* Baltimore: Magna Carta, 1972, two volumes.
	Sperry, Kip, *A Survey of American Genealogical Periodicals and Periodical Indexes,* Gale Research Co., Detroit, MI, 1978.
Published Genealogies	*American Genealogical Index,* Godfrey Memorial Library, Middleton, CT, 1952.
Research	American Society of Genealogists. *Genealogical Research: Methods and Sources.* Washington, D.C.: American Society of Genealogists, 1960, (Volume 1) and 1971 (Volume 2).
Societies	Meyer, Mary K., *Directory of Genealogical Societies in the United States and Canada,* Meyer, Pasadena, MD, 1982.
Standards	Harland, Derek. *Genealogical Research Standards.* Salt Lake City: Bookcraft, 1963. [Formerly entitled *A Basic Course in Genealogy, Volume II: Research Procedure and Evaluation of Evidence.]*
German	Friederich, Hernz F., *How to Find My German Ancestors and Relatives,* Verlag Degener & Co., Neustadt, W.G., 1969.
	Smith, Clifford Neal and Anna Smith, *Encyclopedia of German America Genealogical Research,* R. R. Bowker Co., New York, 1976.
Handwriting	Kirkham, E. Kay. *How to Read the Handwriting and Records of Early America.* Salt Lake City: Deseret Book Company, 1965.
	Nakanish, Akirp, *Writing Systems of the World: Alphabets, Syllabaries, Pictograms,* Charles E. Tuttle Co., Rutland, VT, 1980.
Heraldry	Moncreiffe, Iain and Pottinger, Don. *Simple Heraldry: Cheerfully Illustrated.* London: Thomas Nelson and Sons Limited, 1971.
Immigration	Buenker, John D., et. al., *Immigration and Ethnicity: A Guide to Information Sources,* Gale Resources Co., Detroit, MI, 1977.
	Hansen, Marcus Lee. *The Atlantic Migration, 1607-1860: A History of the Continuing Settlement of the United States.* Cambridge: Harvard University Press, 1940.

Morton, Allen, *Directory of European Passenger Steamship Arrivals, 1890-1930*, G.P. Co., Baltimore, MD, 1980.

Powell, Sumner Chilton. *Puritan Village: The Formation of a New England Town*. Middleton, Conn.: Wesleyan University Press, 1970.

Filby, P. William. *Passenger and Immigration Lists Index, 1538-1900*. Detroit: Gale Research Co., 1982.

Stephenson, Jean. *Scotch-Irish Migration to South Carolina, 1772: Rev. William Martin and his Five Shiploads of Settlers.* Strasburg, Va.: Shenandoah Publishing House, 1971.

Neagles, J. C. and Lila Lee Neagles, *Locating Your Immigrant Ancestor*, Everton Publishers, Logan, UT, 1975.

Indians	*Guide to Genealogical Research in the National Archives*, The National Archives, Washington, D.C., 1982 (new edition).
	Curtis, Edward S. North American Indian: Being a Series of Volumes Picturing and Descirbing the Indians of the United States and Alaska. New York: Johnson Reprint Corporation, 1970, 20 volumes, 1907 reprint.
Insurance Fraternal	Fraternal Monitor Staff. *Statistics of Fraternal Benefit Societies: Containing Statistical Information About Benefit Societies in the United States and Canada.* Indianapolis: The Fraternal Monitor, 1973.
Life	Hay, Natalie A., ed. *The Insurance Almanac: Who, What, When, and Where In Insurance: An Annual of Insurance Facts.* New York: The Underwriting Printing and Publishing Company, 1972.
Irish	O'Lauglin, Michael C., *The Complete Book for Tracing Your Irish Ancestors*, Irish Genealogical Foundation, Kansas City, MO, 1980.
Labor	Stroud, Gene S. and Donahue, Gilbert E. *Labor History in the United States: A General Bibliography*. Urbana: University of Illinois Institute of Labor and Industrial Relations, 1961.
Law Dictionary	Black, Henry Campbell. *Black's Law Dictionary*. St. Paul: West Publishing Company, 1951.
Introduction	Coughlin, George G. *Your Introduction to Law*. New York: Barnes and Noble, Inc., 1971.
Legal Secretary	Krogfoss, Robert B., ed. *Manual for the Legal Secretarial Profession*. St. Paul: West Publishing Company, 1965.
Libraries Church	Rodda, Dorothy and Harvey, John. *Directory of Church Libraries*. Philadelphia: Drexel Press, 1967.
Federal	Benton, Mildred. *Federal Library Resources: A User's Guide to Research Collections*. New York: Science/International, Inc., 1973.
General	Jaques Cattell Press, *American Library Directory*. New York: R. R. Bowker Company, biennial.
Law	American Association of Law Libraries. *Directory of Law Libraries*. New York: R. R. Bowker Company, 1970.
Special	Kruzas, Anthony T., ed. *Directory of Special Libraries and Information Centers*. Detroit: Gale Research, 1968.
Manuscripts	Library of Congress. *The National Union Catalog of Manuscript Collection*. Washington, D.C.: The Library of Congress, 1959—.
	National Historical Publications and Records Commission, *Directory of Archives and Manuscript Repositories in the United States*. National Archives and Records Service, Washington, D.C.: 1978.
Maps	Shelley, M. H., *Ward Maps of the U.S. Cities*, Library of Congress, Washington, D.C., 1975.
	Special Libraries Association. *Map Collections in the United States and Canada*. New York: The Special Libraries Association, 1954.

SUBJECT	REFERENCE
Foreign	*Foreign Language Press of America.* New York: Waxelbaum Advertising Company.
Indexes	Brayer, Herbert O. "Preliminary Guide to Indexed Newspapers in the United States, 1850-1900." *Mississippi Valley Historical Review, Volume 32, No. 2 (September 1946).*
Recent	*N. W. Ayer and Son's Directory of Newspapers and Periodicals.* Philadelphia: N. W. Ayer, annual.
Notekeeping	Jones, Vincent L., Eakle, Arlene H., and Christensen, Mildred H. *Family History for Fun and Profit.* Salt Lake City: Genealogical Institute, 1972. [Formerly entitled *Genealogical Research: A Jurisdictional Approach.*]
Occupations	Wilson, Everett B. *Early America at Work: A Pictorial Guide to Our Vanishing Occupations.* New York: A. S. Barnes and Company, 1963
Organizations Charity	Watson, Frank D. *The Charity Organization Movement in the United States: A Study in American Philanthropy.* New York: The MacMillan Co., 1932.
Fraternal	Ferguson, Charles W. *Fifty Million Brothers: A Panorama of American Lodges and Clubs.* New York: Farrar and Rhinehart, 1937.
	Grand Lodge of Massachusetts. *List of Lodges Masonic.* Bloomington, Ill.: Pantagraph Printing and Stationery Company, annual.
Secret	Whalen, William J. *Handbook of Secret Organization.* Milwaukee: The Bruce Publishing Company, 1966.
Passenger Lists Colonial	Filby, P. William. *Passenger and Immigration Lists Index, 1538-1900.* Detroit: Gale Research Co., 1982.
Federal	*Guide to Genealogical Research in the National Archives,* The National Archives, Washington, D.C., 1982 (new edition).
Periodicals	Russell, George E., ed. *Genealogical Periodical Annual Index, Volume 1—, 1963—.* Bladensburg, Maryland: Genealogical Recorders, annual.
	Towle, Laird C., *Genealogical Periodical Annual Index,* Heritage Books, Inc., Bowie, MD, 1950.
Place Names Early	Sealock, Richard Burl and Seely, Pauline Augusta, *Bibliography of Place-name Literature: United States and Canada.* Chicago: American Library Association, 1967.
Recent	*Bullinger's Postal and Shippers Guide for the United States and Canada: Containing Post Offices and Railroad Stations with the Railroad or Steamer Line on Which Every Place, or the Nearest Communication Point is Located, and the List of Railroads and Water Lines with Their Terminal Points.* Westwood, New Jersey: Bullinger's Guides, Inc., annual.
Polynesian Bibliography	Taylor, C.R.H. *A Pacific Bibliography: Printed Matter Relating to the Native Peoples of Polynesia, Melanesia, and Micronesia.* Oxford: At the Clarendon Press, 1965.
Post Office	*Directory of Post Offices.* Washington, D.C.: United States Government Printing Office, annual.
Reference Sources	Sheehy, Eugene P. *Guide to Reference Works.* Chicago: American Library Association, 1976.
Research (Foreign)	Pine, Leslie G. *American Origins.* Baltimore: Genealogical Publishing Company, 1967.
Revolutionary War	Pierce, John, *Pierce's Register,* Genealogical Publishing Co., Baltimore, MD, 1979.
Schools Church	*American Association of Theological Schools Directory.* Dayton: American Association of Theological Schools, annual.
Private	Sargent, Porter E. *The Handbook of Private Schools: An Annual Descriptive Survey of Independent Education.* Boston: Porter E. Sargent, annual.

Public	Elliott, Norman R., ed. *Patterson's American Education.* Mt. Prospect, Ill.: *Educational Directories, Inc., 1972.*
Societies Hereditary	Johnson, Charles O., ed. *The Hereditary Register of the United States of America.* Washington, D.C.: United States Hereditary Register, Inc., 1972.
Historical	Craig, Tracey L. *Directory of Historical Societies and Agencies in the United States and Canada.* Nashville: American Association for State and Local History, annual.
Sources	Bremer, Ronald A. *Compendium of Historical Sources,* P.O. Box 16422, Salt Lake City, Utah 84116.
State Archives	*Directory of State and Provincial Archivists.* Nashville: Society of American Archivists, 1971.
Blue Books	*State Blue Books and Reference Publications: A Selected Bibliography.* Lexington, Kentucky: Council of State Governments, 1983.
History	Beers, Henry P. *Bibliographies in American History: A Guide to Materials for Research.* Paterson, N.J.: Pageant Books, Inc., 1959.
Public Domain	Ashbury and Dickens. *The American State Papers.* Washington, D.C.: House of Representatives, 1800.
	Carter, Clarence Edwin, Jr., ed. *Territorial Papers of the United States.* Washington, D.C.: United States Government Printing Office, 1934—.
	McMullin, Phillip W., ed. *Grassroots of America.* Salt Lake City: Gendex Corporation [now the Institute for Family Research], 1972.
Social History	Haywood, Charles. *A Bibliography of North American Folklore and Folksong.* New York: Dover Publications, Inc., 1961, Volume 1.
Surnames	Hook, J. N., *Family Names: How Our Surnames Came to America,* Macmillan Publishing Co., Inc., New York, 1982.
Tax Records	Stevenson, Noel C. *Search and Research.* Salt Lake City: Deseret Book Company, 1977.
Telephone	Telephony Publishing Corporation. *Directory of Telephone Industry,* Chicago, 1982.
Textbook	Greenwood, Val D., *The Researcher's Guide to American Genealogy,* Genealogical Publishing Co., Baltimore, MD, 1973.
Title Companies	*Directory: American Land Title Association.* Washington, D.C.: American Land title Association, annual.
Town History	Powell, Sumner Chilton. *Puritan Village: The Formation of a New England Town.* Middletown, Conn.: Wesleyan University Press, 1970.
Transportation	Meyer, Balthasar, H., ed. *History of Transportation in the United States before 1860.* Washington, D.C.: Carnegie Institution of Washington, 1917.
Undertakers	*American Blue Book.* New York: Kates-Boyleston Publications, 1983.
United States Boundaries	Van Zandt, Franklin K. Boundaries of the United States and the Several States. Washington, D.C.: United States Government Printing Office, 1966.
Federal Research	Babbel, June A., comp. *Lest We Forget: A Guide to Genealogical Research in the Nation's Capitol.* Annandale, Va.: Potomac Stake of the Church of Jesus Christ of Latter-day Saints (new), 1976.
Government Publications	Schmeckebier, Laurence and Eastin, Roy B. *Government Publications and Their Use.* Washington, D.C.: Brookings Institution, 1969.
Historical Sources	Burnette, O. Lawrence, Jr. *Beneath the Footnote: A Guide to the Use and Preservation of American Historical Sources.* Madison: Society Press, 1970.
	Poulton, Helen J. *The Historian's Handbook: A Descriptive Guide to Reference Works.* Norman, Oklahoma: University of Oklahoma Press, 1972.
History	Barck, Oscar Theodore, Jr. and Lefler, Hugh Talmage. *Colonial America.* New York: The MacMillan Company, 1968.

Billington, Ray A. and Hedges, James B. *Westward Expansion: A History of the American Frontier*. New York: The MacMillan Company, 1974.

Krout, John A. *United States to 1877*. New York: Barnes and Noble, 1971.

Wesley, Edgar B. *Our United States: Its History in Maps*. Chicago: Denoyer-Geppert Company, 1956.

Imprints   Nilon, Charles H. *Bibliography of Bibliographies in American Literature*. New York: R. R. Bowker Company, 1970.

Migration   Waitley, Douglas. *Roads of Destiny: The Trails that Shaped a Nation*. Washington, D.C.: Robert B. Luce, Inc., 1970.

Naturalization   *Guide to Genealogical Research in the National Archives*, The National Archives, Washington, D.C., 1982 (new edition).

Social Security   Rogers, Thomas O. *What Social Security owes You and How to Get It*. Atlanta: Droke House/Hallux, 1973.

University Archives   *The Directory of College and University Archives in the United States and Canada*, Chicago Society of American Archivists, 1980.

Vital Records
Births/Deaths   Department of Health, Education and Welfare. *Where to Write for Birth and Death Records (PHS No. 630A)*. Washington, D.C.: United States Government Printing Office.

Divorces   Department of Health, Education and Welfare. *Where to Write for Divorce Records (PHS No. 630C)*. Washington D.C.: United States Government Printing Office.

Marriages   Department of Health, Education and Welfare. *Where to Write for Marriage Records (PHS No. 630B)*. Washington, D.C.: United States Government Printing Office.

TRAVEL
TOURS
RESEARCH TRIPS

- Salt Lake City
- The South
- Eastern States
- British Isles
- River Cruises

- New England
- Washington D.C.
- Canada
- Europe
- Guided Tours

Wm. E. Stebbing
2558 W. Kiva Ave.
Mesa, AZ 85202

CHAPTER 28

PLACE NAMES IN 1870's

Often the researcher will find the name of the place where an ancestor lived and not be able to find the county of residence. This may happen because the place has changed its name or it has been incorporated into another town or city.

To help solve this problem, the following is an alphabetical listing of most places, including railroad stops and post offices, in America in the 1870's. This listing is a great value to the researcher because it not only includes place names not listed in the standard gazeteer or atlas but it also lists the county and state of the place. If all you know is the name of the place of birth or death, etc., you can find the county where the records are kept.

If you are not able to find the place you are looking for in this listing, you might check the modern townships in the Township chapter.

PLACE NAMES OF THE UNITED STATES

PLACE	COUNTY	STATE	PLACE	COUNTY	STATE	PLACE	COUNTY	STATE
Aaron	Switzerland	IN	Abilene (c.h.)	Dickinson	KS	Acme	Grand Traverse	MI
Aaronsburgh	Centre	PA	Abingdon	Knox	IL	Acomb	McLennan	TX
Aaron's Run	Montgomery	KY	Abingdon	Jefferson	IA	Acorn Hill	Fredrick	VA
Abbeville (c.h.)	Henry	AL	Abingdon	Harford	MD	Acra	Greene	NY
Abbeville (c.h.)	ilcox G A		Abingdon	Washington	VA	Acron	Hale	AL
Abbeville (c.h.)	Vermillion	LA	Abingdon	Windham	CN	Acron	Marion	IN
Abbeville	Lafayette	MI	Abington	Wayne	IN	Acton	York	ME
Abbeville	Abbeville	SC	Abington	Plymouth	MA	Acton	Middlesex	MS
Abbeyville	Medina	OH	Abington	Montgomery	PA	Acton	Hood	TX
Abbot	Piscataquis	ME	Abiqui	Rio Arriba	NM	Acushnet	Bristol	MS
Abbott	Hardin	IA	Aboite	Allen	IN	Acworth	Cobb	GA
Abbottsburgh	Bladen	NC	Abscota	Calhoun	MI	Acworth	Sullivan	NH
Abbott's Corners	Erie	NY	Absecom	Atlantic	NJ	Ada	Kent	MI
Abbott's Creek	Davidson	NC	Academia	Juniata	PA	Ada	Choctaw	MI
Abbottstown	Adams	PA	Academy	Ontario	NY	Ada	Ray	MO
Abbot Village	Piscataquis	ME	Academy	Pocahontas	WV	Ada	Hardin	OH
Abb's Valley	Tazewell	VA	Acasto	Clarke	MO	Ada	Sheboygan	WI
Abbyville	Mecklenburgh	VA	Accident	Alleghany	MD	Adair	McDonough	IL
Aberdeen	Monroe	AK	Accokeek	Prince George's	MD	Adair	Adair	IA
Aberdeen	Ohio	IN	Accokeek	Stafford	VA	Adairsville	Bartow	VA
Aberdeen	Butler	KY	Accomack(c.h.)	Accomack	VA	Adairville	Logan	KY
Aberdeen	Harford	MD	Accord	Ulster	NY	Adaline	Marshall	WV
Aberdeen (c.h.)	Monroe	MS	Accotink	Fairfax	VA	Adams	Wilcox	GA
Aberdeen	Brown	OH	Acherson	Jefferson	IA	Adams	Adams	IL
Aberdeen	Smith	TX	Acker	Perry	PA	Adams	Decatur	IN
Aberdeen Junction	Monroe	MI	Ackermanville	Northampton	PA	Adams	Berkshire	MA
Aberfoil	Bullock	AL	Ackerville	Washington	WI	Adams	Mower	MI
Abernathy	Perry	MO	Ackley	Hardin	IA	Adams	Jefferson	NY
Abe Spring	Calhoun	FL	Ackworth	Warren	IA	Adams	Seneca	OH

PLACE	COUNTY	STATE
Addison	Du Page	IL
Addison	Humboldt	IA
Addison	Lenawee	MI
Addison	Stenben	NY
Addison	Gallia	OH
Addison	Somerset	PA
Addison	Addison	VT
Addison	Washington	WI
Addison Hill	Stenben	NY
Adams	Armstrong	PA
Adams	Walworth	WI
Adams' Basin	Monroe	NY
Adamsburgh	Jefferson	AK
Adamsburgh	Westmoreland	PA
Adams Centre	Jefferson	NY
Adams Centre	Adams	WI
Adams'Mill	Pulaski	KY
Adams'Mill	Muskingum	OH
Addison Point	Washington	ME
Adel (c.h.)	Dallas	IA
Adelante	Napa	CA
Adalaseat	Union	DK
Adeline	Ogle	OR
Adell	Sheboygan	OR
Adelphi	Polk	IA
Adelphi	Ross	OH
Adena	Jefferson	OH
Adkins' Mills	Wayne	WV
Adrian	Hancock	IL
Adrian (c.h.)	Lenawee	MI
Adrian	Steuben	NY
Adrian	Seneca	OH
Adrian	Armstrong	PA
Adriance	Dutchess	NY
Advance	Guthrie	IA
Advance	Charlevoix	MI
Advance	Washington	NE
⌣⌣⌣⌣le	P.A	
Adyeville	Perry	IN
Aerial	Marion	SC
Aetna	Newaygo	MI
Afton	Scott	IN
Afton (c.h.)	Union	IA
Afton	Washington	MN
Afton	Chenango	NY
Afton	Clermont	OH
Afton	Nelson	VA
Afton	Rock	WI
Agatha	Vinton	OH
Agawam	Hampden	jA
Agency City	Wapello	IA
Agnes City	Lyon	KS
Agnews' Mill	Venango	PA
Agricola	Mahaska	IA
Agricultural College	Prince George's	MD
Agricultural College Centre		PA
Ahnapee	Kewaunee	WI
Ai	Fulton	OH
Aid	Lawrence	OH
Aiden Lair	Essex	NY
Aidenville	Siskiyou	CA
Aiken	Barnwell	SC
Aiken	Bell	TX
Ainsworth	Washington	IA
Ainsworth Station	Cook	IL
Airey's	Dorchester	MD
Air Hill	Montgomery	OH
Air Line	Hart	GA
Air Mount	Yalabusha	MS
Airville	York	PA
Airy Dale	Huntingdon	PA
Aken	Richland	WI
Akersville	Fulton	PA
Akin	Franklin	IL
Akron	Peoria	IL
Akron	Fulton	IN
Akron	Tuscola	MI
Akron	Harrison	MO
Akron	Erie	NY
Akron (c.h.)	Summit	OH
Akron	Laneaster	PA
Alabama	Genesee	NY
Alabama	Houston	TX
Alabama	Polk	WI
Alabaster	Iosco	MI
Alafia	Hillsborough	FL
Alameda	Alameda	CA
Alamo	Contra Costa	CA
Alamo	Montgomery	IN
Alamo	Kalamozoo	MI
Alamode	Reynolds	MO
Alanthus Grove	Gentry	MO
Alanthus Hill	Hancock	TN
Alaska	Morgan	IN
Alaska	Kent	MI
Alaska	Kewaunee	WI
Alba	Fillmore	MI
Alba	Jasper	MO
Alba	Bradford	PA
Albanville	Monroe	WI
Albany (c.h.)	Dougherty	GA
Albany	Whitesides	IL
Albany	Deleware	IN
Albany	Davis	IA
Albany	Nemaha	KS
Albany(c.h.)	Clinton	KY
Albany (c.h.)	Oxford	ME
Albany (c.h.)	Gentry	MO
Albany (c.h.)	Albany (c.h.)	NY
Albany	Tuscarawas	OH
Albany (c.h.)	Linn	OR
Albany	Stearns	MN
Albany	Saline	NE
Albany	Berks	PA
Albany	Henry	TN
Albany	Orleans	VT
Albany	Green	WI
Albany Centre	Orleans	VT
Albemarle	Assumption	LA
Albermarle (c.h.)	Stanley	NC
Albert Lea (c.h.)	Freeborn	MN
Alberton	Howard	MD
Alberton's	Duplin	NC
Albia	Washington	AK
Albia	Monroe	IA
Albion	Mendocino	CA
Albion (c.h.)	Edward's	IL
Albion (c.h.)	Noble	IN
Albion	Marshall	IA
Albion	Republic	KS
Albion	Kennebec	ME
Albion	Calhoun	MI
Albion	Wright	MN
Albion (c.h)	Orleans	NY
Albion	Ashland	OH
Albion	Erie	PA
Albion	Providence	RI
Albion	Dane	WI
Albrightsville	Carbon	PA
Albuquerque	Bernalilo	NM
Alburgh	Grand Isle	VT
Alburgh Centre	Grand Isle	VT
Alburgh Springs	Grand Isle	VT
Alburtis	Lehigh	PA
Alcona	Alcona	MI
Alcony	Miami	OH
Alden	McHenry	IL
Alden	Hardin	IA
Alden	Freeborn	MN
Alden	Erie	NY
Alden	Polk	WI
Alden Centre	Erie	NY
Alden's Corners	Dane	WI
Aldenville	Wayne	PA
Alder Creek	Oneida	NY
Alderley	Dodge	WI
Aldie	Loudoun	VA
Aledo (c.h.)	Mercer	IL
Aleman	Socorro	NM
Aleppo	Greene	PA
Alert	Decatur	IN
Alert	Riley	KS
Alert	Butler	OH
Alexander	Morgan	IL
Alexander	Washington	ME
Alexander	Genesee	NY
Alexanderville	Sonoma	CA
Alexandria	Merceed	CA
Alexandria	Warren	IL
Alexandria	Madison	IN
Alexandria	Campbell	KY
Alexandria (c.h.)	Rapides	LA
Alexandria (c.h.)	Douglas	MN
Alexandria	Clarke	MO
Alexandria	Grafton	NH
Alexandria	Jefferson	NY
Alexandria	Licking	OH
Alexandria	Huntingdon	PA
Alexandria	De Kalb	TN
Alexandria (c.h.)	Alexandria	VA
Alfonte	Madison	IN
Alford	Berkshire	MA
Alfordsville	Davies	IN
Alfred (c.h.)	York	ME
Alfred	Allegany	NY
Alfred	Meigs	OH
Alfred Centre	Allegany	NY
Algansee	Branch	MI
Algiers	Orleans	LA
Algodon	Ionia	MI
Algodones	Santa Ana	NM
Algona (c.h.)	Kossuth	IA
Algonac	St. Clair	MI
Algonquin	McHenry	IL
Algonquin	Carroll	OH
Alhambra	Madison	IL
Alhambra	Trempealeau	WI
Alice	Grundy	IA
Alice	Oceana	MI
Alice	Cedar	MO
Aliceton	Boyle	KY
Alida	Davis	KS
Alkire's Mills	Lewis	WV
Allamakee	Allamakee	IA
Allamuchy	Warren	NJ
Allandale	Banks	GA
Allard's Corners	Orange	NY
Allatoona	Bartow	GA
Allbright	Preston	WV
Allegan(c.h.)	Allegan	MI
Allegany	Cattaraugus	NY
Allegany	Sierra	CA
Allegany Spring	Montgomery	VA
Alleghany Station	Alleghany	VA
Allegheny	Allegheny	PA
Allegeny Bridge	McKeanf	PA
Allemance	Guilford	NC
Alleman's	Clearfield	PA
Allen	La Salle	IL

PLACE	COUNTY	STATE	PLACE	COUNTY	STATE	PLACE	COUNTY	STATE
Allen	Miami	IN	Alna	Lincoln	ME	Amanda	Fairfield	OH
Allen	Lyon	KS	Alonzaville	Shenandoah	VA	Amandaville	Hart	GA
Allen	Hillsdale	MI	Alpena(c.h.)	Alpena	MI	Amandaville	Cumberland	KY
Allen	Allegany	NY	Alpha	Scott	IN	Amazonia	Andrew	MO
Allen	Cumberland	Pa	Alpha	Clinton	KY	Amber	Mason	MI
Allen Centre	Allegany	NY	Alpha	Grundy	MO	Amber	Martin	MN
Allen Creek	Oceana	MI	Alpha	Green	OH	Amber	Onondaga	NY
Allendale	Wabash	IL	Alpha	Halifax	VA	Amberson's Valley	Franklin	Pa
Allendale	Green	KY	Alpharetta(c.h.)	Milton	GA	Amboy	Lee	IL
Allendale	Ottawa	MI	Alpine	Fayette	IN	Amboy	Miami	IN
Allendale	Worth	Mo	Alpine	Bergen	NJ	Amboy	Jasper	IA
Allendale	Bergen	NJ	Alpine	Wpello	IA	Amboy	Hillsdale	MI
Allendale	Barnwell	SC	Alpine	Kent	MI	Amboy	Ashtabula	OH
Allenport	Washington	PA	Alpine	Schuyler	NY	Amboy Centre	Oswego	NY
Allen's	Richmond	GA	Alpine	York	PA	Ambrose	Indiana	PA
Allen's	Eaton	MI	Alpine City	Utah	UT	Amelia	Clermont	OH
Allen's	Miami	OH	Alpine Depot	Morgan	WV	Amelia	Amelia	VA
Allen's Creek	Amhearst	VA	Alps	Rensselaer	NY	Amenia	Dutchess	NY
Allen's Factory	Marion	AL	Alquina	Fayette	IN	Amenia Union	Dutchess	NY
Allen's Fork	Jackson	WV	Alsace	Berks	PA	America	Wabash	IN
Allen's Fresh	Charles	MD	Alstead	Cheshire	NH	America City	Nemaha	KS
Allen's Grove	Scott	IA	Alstead Centre	Cheshire	NH	American Fork	Utah	UT
Allen's Grove	Walworth	WI	Ashton	Fairfield	SC	American Ranch	Shasha	CA
Allen's Hill	Ontario	NY	Alta	Buena Vista	IA	Americus(c.h.)	Sumter	GA
Allen's Mills	Carroll	GA	Alta	Placer	CA	Americus	Tippecanoe	IN
Allen Springs	Allen	KY	Altamont	Effingham	IL	Americus	Lyon	KS
Allen's Springs	Pope	IL	Altamont	Shelby	IA	Americus(c.h.)	Jackson	MS
Allen's Station	Stenben	NY	Altamont	Alleghany	MD	Americus	Montgomery	MO
Allen's Store	Prentiss	MS	Altamont(c.h.)	Grundy	TN	Ames	Story	IA
Allenstown	Merrimack	NH	Alta Vista	Daviess	MO	Ames	Montgomery	MO
Allensville	Todd	DY	Alta Vista	Russell	VA	Amesbury	Essex	MA
Allensville	Person	NC	Alty	Scjiu;er	NY	Amesville	Athens	OH
Allensville	Vinton	OH	Altenburgh	Perry	MO	Amherst	Hancock	ME
Allensville	Miffin	PA	Altha	Stoddard	MO	Amherst	Hampshire	MA
Allenton	Wilcox	AL	Alto	Richland	LA	Amherst	Fillmore	MN
Allenton	St. Louis	MO	Alto	Howard	IN	Amherst(c.h.)	Hillsborough	NH
Allenton	Washington	RI	Alto	Kent	MI	Amherst	Washington	NE
Allen Town	fKnox	IN	Alto	Franklin	Tn	Amherst	Lorain	OH
Allentown	Monmouth	NJ	Alto	Cherokee	TX	Amherst	Portage	WI
Allentown(c.h.)	Leigh	PA	Alton	Madison	IL	Amherst(c.h.)	Amherst	VA
Allenville	Cape Girardeau	MO	Alton	Crawford	IN	Amish	Johnson	IA
Allertown	Wayne	IA	Alton	Macon	TN	Amissville	Rappahannock	VA
Alleyton	Colorado	TX	Alton	Penobscot	MO	Amite City(c.h.)	Tangipahoa	LA
Alliance	Stark	OH	Alton	Kent	MI	Amity	Clark	AR
Allis Hollow	Bradford	PA	Alton(c.h.)	Oregon	MO	Amity	Livingston	IL
Allison	Dubuque	IA	Alton	Belknap	NH	Amity	Johnson	IN
Allison Creek	York	SC	Alton	Wayne	NY	Amity	Scott	IA
Allisonville	Tyler	TX	Alton	Franklin	OH	Amity	Aroostook	ME
Alloa	Columbit	WI	Alton	McKean	PA	Amity	Orange	NY
Allowaystown	Salem	NJ	Altona	Knox	IL	Amity	Van Hill	OR
Allstown	fMiddlesex	MA	Altona	Marshall	KY	Amity	Washington	PA
Alma	Crawford	AK	Altona	Bates	MO	Amity Hill	Tredell	NC
Alma	Marion	IL	Altona	Clinton	NY	Amityville	Suffolk	NY
Alma	Whitley	IN	Alton Bay	Bilknap	NH	Amo	Hendricks	IN
Alma(c.h.)	Wabaunsee	KS	Alton Junction	Madison	IL	Amoskeag	Hillsborough	NH
Alma	Gratiot	MI	Altoona	Wilson	KS	Amsden	Montealm	MI
Alma	Allegany	NY	Altoona	Blair	PA	Amsterdam	Cass	IN
Alma	Ross	OH	Alum Bank	Bedford	PA	Amwell	Wayne	OH
Alma	Rusk	TX	Alum Creek	Delaware	OH	Anacosta	Washington	DC
Alma	Weber	UT	Alum Creek	Bastrop	TX	Anaheim	Los Angeles	CA
Alma	Page	VA	Alum Rock	Clarion	PA	Anahuac	Chambers	TX
Alma(c.h.)	Buffalo	WI	Alum Springs	Rockbridge	VA	Analomink	Monroe	PA
Alma City	Waseca	MN	Alum Well	Hawkins	TN	Anamosa(c.h.)	Jones	IW
Alma City	Harlan	NE	Alva	Aroostook	ME	Anadale	Dutchess	NY
Almeda	Newton	MO	Alvarado	Alameda	CA	Anadale	Butler	PA
Almena	Van Buren	MI	Alvarado	Steuben	IN	Anawank	Le Sueur	MN
Almira	Benzie	MI	Alvarado	Johnson	TX	Anchorage	Buffalo	WA
Almond	Randolph	AL	Alvarado	Ingham	MI	Ancona	Livingston	IL
Almond	Allegany	NY	Alvira	Union	PA	Ancora	Camden	NJ
Almond	Portage	WI	Alviso	Santa Clara	CA	Amcram Centre	Columbia	NY
Almont	Lapeer	MI	Avon	Greenbrier	WV	Ancram Centre	Columbia	NY
Almont Station	Clinton	KY	Amador City	Amador	CA	Ancram Lead Mines	Columbia	NY
Almoral	Delaware	IA	Amadore	Sniffolk	NY	Andausia	Sanford	AL

PLACE	COUNTY	STATE	PLACE	COUNTY	STATE	PLACE	COUNTY	STATE
Andalusia	Rock Island	IL	Antelope	Marion	KS	Arbuckle	Mason	WV
Andalusia	Bucks	PA	Antelope	Jefferson	NE	Arcade	Wyoming f.	NY
Anderson	Mendocino	CA	Antelope	Wasco	OR	Arcadia	Morgan	IL
Anderson(c.h.)	Madison	IN	Antes Fort	Wyoming	PA	Arcadia	Hamilton	IN
Anderson	Pope	MN	Antestown	Blair	PA	Arcadia	Carroll	IA
Anderson	Alcorn	MS	Anthony	Delaware	IN	Arcadia	Crawford	KS
Anderson	Clinton	MO	Anthony	Hunterdon	NJ	Arcadia	Bienville	LA
Anderson	Ross	OH	Anthony	Kent	RI	Arcadia	Iron	MO
Anderson(c.h.)	Grimes	TX	Anthony House	Nevada	CA	Arcadia	Wayne	NY
Anderson	Burnett	WI	Antioch	Pickens	AL	Arcadia	Davidson	NC
Anderson(c.h.)	Anderson	SC	Antioch	Troup	GA	Arcadia	Hancock	OH
Anderson	Franklin	TN	Antioch	Lake	IL	Arcadia	Washington	RI
Andersonburg	Perry	PA	Antioch	Huntingdon	IN	Arcadia	Sullivan	TN
Anderson's Mills	Butler	PA	Antioch	Washington	KY	Arcadia	Trempealeau	WI
Anderson's Mills	Pickens	SC	Antioch	Alcorn	MS	Arcadia	Grant	IN
Anderson's Store	Caswell	NC	Antioch	Robeson	NC	Arcana	Grant	IN
Andersontown	Caroline	MD	Antioch	Monroe	OH	Arcanum	Darke	OH
Andersonville	Pickens	AL	Antioch	York	SC	Arcata	Humbolt	CA
Andersonville	Sumter	GA	Antioch	Gibson	TN	Archbald	Luzerne	PA
Andersonville	Franklin	IN	Antioch	Lavaca	TX	Archbold	Fulton	OH
Andes	Delaware	NY	Antoine	Clark	AK	Archer	Alachua	FL
Andover	Tolland	CT	Antreville	Abbeville	SC	Archer	Harrison	OH
Andover	Henry	IL	Antrim	Watonwan	MN	Archerville	Campbell	TN
Andover	Oxford	ME	Antrim	Hillsborough	NH	Arch Spring	Blair	PA
Andover	Essex	MA	Antrim	Guernsey	OH	Arcola	Douglas	IL
Andover	Merrimack	NY	Antrim City	Antrim	MI	Arcola	Allen	IN
Andover	Sussex	NJ	Antwerp	Jefferson	NY	Arcola	Monona	IA
Andover	Allegany	NY	Antwerp	Paulding	OH	Arcola	Cowley	KS
Andover	Ashtabula	OH	Apache Pass	Pima	AZ	Arcola	St. Helena	LA
Andover	Windsor	VT	Apalachicola(c.h.)	Franklin	FL	Arcola	Bergen	LA
Andrew(c.h.)	Jackson	IA	Apalachin	Tioga	NY	Arcola	Loudoun	VA
Andrew Chapel	Madison	TN	Apex	Wake	NC	Arena	Iowa	WI
Andrews	Morrow	OH	Aplin	Perry	AK	Arenac	Bay	MI
Andrews	Spottsylavania	VA	Aplington	Butler	IA	Arendahl	Fillmore	MN
Andrusville	Franklin	NY	Apollo	Armstrong	PA	Arendsville	Adams	PA
Andy	Monongalia	WV	Apopka	Orange	FL	Arenzville	Cass	IL
Angelica(c.h.)	Allegany	NY	Appanoose	Hancock	IL	Argenta	Beaver Head	MT
Angelica	Shawinaw	WI	Appanoose	Franklin	KS	Argenta	Lander	NV
Angel's Camp	Calaveras	CA	Apperson's	Charles City	VA	Argentine	Genesee	MI
Angerona	Jackson	WV	Applebachville	Bucks	PA	Argo	Jefferson	AL
Angola	Sussex	DE	Apple Creek	Wayne	OH	Argo	Carroll	IL
Angola(c.h.)	Steuben	IN	Applegate	Jackson	OR	Argo	Lucas	IA
Angola	New Hanover	NC	Apple Grove	Marion	AL	Argo	Crawford	MO
Angola	Erie	NY	Apple Grove	Meigs	OH	Argus	Marshall	IN
Angola	New Hanover	NC	Apple Grove	York	PA	Argus	Crenshaw	AL
Angola	Clermont	OH	Apple Grove	Louisa	VA	Argusville	Schohario	NY
Anita	Cass	IA	Apple River	Jo Daviess	IL	Argyle	Winnebago	IL
Anna	Union	IL	Appleton	Bourbon	KS	Argyle	Penobscot	ME
Anna	Shelby	OH	Appleton	Knox	ME	Argyle	Cumberland	NC
Annandale	Hunterdon	NJ	Appleton	Cape Giradeau	MO	Argyle	Washington	NY
Annapolis	Crawford	IL	Appleton	Licking	OH	Argyle	La Fayette	WI
Annapolis	Parke	IN	Appleton	Lawrence	TN	Arica	De Kalb	MO
Annapolis(c.h.)	Anne Arundel	MD	Appleton(c.h.)	Outagamie	WI	Ariel	Wayne f.	PA
Annapolis	Jefferson	OH	Applewood	Caroline	VA	Arington	Atichison	KS
Annapolis	Iron	MO	Appling(c.h.)	Columbia	GA	Arion	Cloud	KS
Annapolis Junction	Anne Arundel	MD	Appomattox(c.h.)	Appomattox	VA	Arispie	Pottawatomie	KS
Ann Arbor(c.h.)	Washtenaw	MI	Aptos	Santa Cruz	CA	Arizona	Burt	NE
Annaton	Grant	WI	Apulia	Anondaga	NY	Arizona City	Yuma	AZ
Annawan	Henry	IL	Aquasco	Prince Geor e's	MD	Arizona	Claiborne	LA
Annieville	Clay	IA	Aquashicola	Carbon	PA	Arkabutla	De Soto	MS
Annin Creek	McKean	PA	Aquilla	Franklin	GA	Arkada	Mason	WA
Annisquaam	Essex	MA	Aquone	Macon	NC	Arkadelphia	Walker	AL
Annville	Lebanon	PA	Arabia	Lawrence	OH	Arkadelphia	Clark	AK
Anoka	Cass	IN	Arago	Richardson	Ne	Arkansas City	Cowley	KS
Anoka(c.h.)	Anoka	MN	Aransas	Bee	TX	Arkansas Post	Arkansas	AK
Anoqua	Victoria	TX	Ararat	Susquehanna	PA	Arkansaw	Pepin	WI
Anson	Somerset	ME	Ararat	Patrick	VA	Arkdale	Adams	WI
Ansonia	New Haven	CT	Arba	Randolph	IN	Arkport	Steuben	NY
Ansonville	Clearfield	PA	Arbela	Tuscola	MI	Arkwright Summit	Chautauqua	NY
Ansonville	Auson	NC	Arbela	Scotland	MO	Arland	Jackson	MI
Ansonia	Darke	OH	Arbor Hill	Adair	IA	Arlington	Bureau	IL
Antelope	Yolo	CA	Arbor Hill	Augusta	VA	Arlington	Osborne	KS
Antelope	Charles Mix	DK	Arbor Vitae	Bullock	AL			

PLACE NAMES OF THE UNITED STATES

PLACE	COUNTY	STATE	PLACE	COUNTY	STATE	PLACE	COUNTY	STATE
Arlington	Middlesex	MA	Ash Grove	Tippecanoe	IN	Athens	Limestone	AL
Arlington	Van Buren	MI	Ash Grove	Green	MO	Athens	Clarke	GA
Arlington	Sibley	MN	Ashippen	Walonwan	MN	Athens	Menard	IL
Arlington	Phelps	MO	Ashippen	Dodge	WI	Athens	Jewell	KS
Arlington	Hancock	OH	Ashkum	Iroquois	IL	Athens	Fayette	KY
Arlington	Wayne	PA	Ashland(c.h.)	Clay	AL	Athens	Claiborne	LA
Arlington	Bennington	VT	Ashland	Cass	IL	Athens	Somerset	ME
Arlington	Alexandria	VA	Ashland	Henry	IN	Athens	Calhoun	MI
Arlington	Columbia	WI	Ashland	Wapello	IA	Athens	Monroe	MS
Armada	Macomb	MI	Ashland	Boyd	KY	Athens	Clarke	MO
Armagh	Daviess	IN	Ashland	Aroostook	ME	Athens	Richardson	NE
Armagh	Indiana	PA	Ashland	Middlesex	MA	Athens	Greene	NY
Armenia	Juneau	WI	Ashland	Newaygo	MI	Athens	Athens	OH
Armiesburgh	Parke	IN	Ashland	Dodge	MN	Athens	Bradford	PA
Armington	Tazewell	IL	Ashland(c.h.)	Benton	MS	Athens	McMinn	TN
Armonk	Westchester	NY	Ashland	Boone	MO	Athens	Windham	VT
Armstrong	Vanderburgh	IN	Ashland(c.h.)	Saunders	NE	Athensville	Monroe	MI
Armstrong	Walbash	IL	Ashland	Grafton	NH	Athlone	Monroe	MI
Armstng's Corners	Fond du Lae	WI	Ashland	Greene	NY	Athol	Worcester	MA
Armstrong's Grove	Emmett	IA	Ashland	Ashland	OH	Athol	Warren	NY
Armstrong's Mills	Belmont	OH	Ashland	Jackson	OR	Athol	Jackson	WI
Armuchee	Floyd	GA	Ashland	Schuylkill	PA	Atkinson	Henry	IL
Arnaudville	St. Landry	LA	Ashland	Hanover	VA	Atkinson	Piscatapuis	ME
Arnettsville	Monongalia	WV	Ashland City(c.h.)	Cheatham	TN	Atkinson	Rockingham	NH
Arney	Owen	IN	Ashland Mills	Jackson	OR	Atkinson Depot	Rockingham	NH
Arneytown	Barlington	NJ	Ashley	Washington	IL	Atkinson's Mills	Mifflin	PA
Arnheim	Brown	OH	Ashley	Kent	MI	Atkinsonville	Owen	IN
Arno	Douglas	MO	Ashley	Pike	MO	Atkin's Tank	Smyth	VA
Arnold	Crawford	KS	Ashley	Delaware	OH	Atlanta	Columbia	AK
Arnoldsburg	Calhoun	WV	Ashley	Luzerne	PA	Atlanta(c.h.)	Fulton	GA
Arnold's Mills	Pickens	SC	Ashley Falls	Berkshire	MA	Atlanta	Alturas	ID
Arnold's Store	Anne Arundel	MD	Ashley Mills	Pulaski	AK	Atlanta	San Joaquin	CA
Arnold's Store	Bedford	TN	Ashley's Point	Phillips	AK	Atlanta	Logan	IL
Arnoldsville	Buchanan	MO	Ashleyville	Hampden	MS	Atlanta	Buchanan	IA
Arnoldton	Campbell	VA	Ashlick	Randolph	WV	Atlanta	Montgomery	KS
Arnot	Tioga	PA	Ashmore	Cole	IL	Atlanta	Winn	LA
Aroma	Kankakee	IL	Ash Ridge	Massac	IL	Atlanta	Macon	MO
Aroma	Dickinson	KS	Ash Ridge	Richland	WI	Atlanta	Pickaway	OH
Arrington	Nelson	VA	Ashtabula		O H	Atlantic	Cass	IA
Arrow Rock	Saline	MO	Ashton	Lee	IL	Atlantic City	Atlantic	NJ
Arrowxic	Sagadahoc	ME	Ashton	Clarke	MO	Atlantic City	Sweet Water	WY
Arroyo	Elk	PA	Ashton	Providence	RI	Atlantieville	Monmouth	NJ
Arroyo Grande	San Louis Obispo	CA	Ashton	San Augustine	TX	Atlantieville	Suffolk	NY
Artesia	Loundes	MS	Ashton	Dane	WI	Atlas	Pike	IL
Arthursburgh	Dutchess	NY	Ashville	Cheshire	NH	Atlas	Genesee	MI
Arvada	Jefferson	CO	Ashville(c.h.)	St. Clair	AL	Atlas	Belmont	OH
Arvonia	Osage	KS	Ashwood	Tensas	LA	Atlee's Station	Hanover	VA
Asbury	La Salle	IL	Askeaton	Brown	WI	Atoka	Choctaw Nation	IN
Asbury	Greenbrier	WV	Askew	Phillips	AK	Atoy	Cherokee	TX
Asbury	Warren	NJ	Aspen Grove	Pendleton	KY	Atsion	Burlington	NJ
Ascension	Sullivan	IN	Aspen Hills	Giles	TN	Attalaville	Attala	MS
Ascutneyville	Windsor	VT	Aspen Well	Charlotte	VA	Attanam	Yakima	WA
Ashawa	Polk	IA	Asper	Livingston	MO	Attica	Fountain	IN
Ashaway	Washington	RI	Asperville	Daviess	MO	Attica	Marion	IA
Ashborough	Clay	IN	Aspin Grove	Rockingham	NC	Attica	Ellsworth	KS
Ashborough	Randolph	NC	Aspinwall	Nemaha	NE	Attica	Lapeer	MI
Ashburn	Pike	MO	Aspinwall	Bradford	PA	Attica	Saunders	ME
Ashburnham	Worcester	MA	Assabet	Middlesex	MA	Attica	Wyoming	NY
Ashburnham Depot	Worcester	MS	Assamoosick	Southampton	VA	Attica	Seneca	OH
Ashby	Middlesex	MA	Assumption	Christian	IL	Attica	Greene	WI
Ashbysburgh	Hopkins	KY	Assumption	Assumption	LA	Attila	Williamson	IL
Ashby's Mills	Montgomery	IN	Assyria	Barry	MI	Attinsville	Montgomery	KS
Ash Creek	Rock	MN	Astoria	Fulton	IL	Attleborough	Bristol	MA
Ash Creek	Oktrbbeha	MS	Astoria	Wright	MO	Attleborough	Bucks	PA
Ashepoo	Colleton	SC	Astoria	Queens	NY	Attlebury	Dutchess	NY
Asherville	Mitchell	KS	Astoria	Clatsop	OR	Atwater	Kandiyohi	MN
Asheville(c.h.)	Buncombe	NC	Asylum	Bradford	PA	Atwater	Portage	OH
Ashfield	Franklin	MA	Atalissa	Muscatine	IA	Atwater Centre	Portage	OH
Ash Flat	Lawrence	AR	Atalla	Etowah	AL	Atwood	Koscinusko	IN
Ashford	Windham	CT	Atchison	Atchison	KS	Atwood	Antrim	MI
Ashford	Cattaraugus	NY	Atchison	Washington	PA	Atwood	Armstrong	Pa
Ashford	Fond du Lac	WI	Atco	Camden	NJ	Aubrey	Johnson	KS
Ash Grove	Iroquois	IL	Athalia	Lawrence	OH	Auburn	Lee	AL

PLACE NAMES OF THE UNITED STATES

PLACE	COUNTY	STATE	PLACE	COUNTY	STATE	PLACE	COUNTY	STATE
Auburn	Lincoln	AK	Austen	Preston	WV	Bach Grove	Wright	IA
Auburn(c.h.)	Placer	CA	Austerlitz	Kent	MI	Bachman	Montgomery	OH
Auburn	Gwinnett	GA	Austerlitz	Columbia	NY	Bachman's Mills	Carroll	MD
Auburn	Sangamon	IL	Austin	Prairie	AR	Back Creek Valley	Frederick	VA
Auburn(c.h.)	De Kalb	IN	Austin	Cook	IL	Backville	Brown	MN
Auburn	Mahaska	IA	Austin	Scott	IN	Bacon	Coshocton	OH
Auburn	Shawnee	KS	Austin	Oakland	MI	Bacon Creek	Hart	KP
Auburn	Logan	KY	Austin(c.h.)	Mower	MI	Bacon Hill	Saratoga	NY
Auburn	Audroscoggin	ME	Austin(c.h.)	Tunica	MS	Bacon's Castle	Surrey	VA
Auburn	Worcester	MA	Austin	Cass	MO	Bad Axe	Huron	MI
Auburn	Lincoln	MO	Austin	Lander	NV	Baden	Kcocuc	OH
Auburn	Rockingham	NH	Austin	Wilson	TN	Baden	St. Louis	MI
Auburn	Salem	NJ	Austin(c.h.)	Travis	TX	Baden	Gage	NE
Auburn(c.h.)	Cayuga	NY	Austinburgh	Ashtabula	OH	Baden	Beaver	PA
Auburn	Wake	NC	Austin's Mills	Hwkins	TN	Badger	Portage	WI
Auburn	Geauga	OH	Austinville	Bradford	PA	Badger Hill	Tama	IA
Auburn	Baker	OR	Australia	Bolivar	MS	Badito(c.h.)	Huerfano	CO
Auburn	Schuylkill	PA	Autaugaville	Autauga	AL	Bad River	Gratiot	MI
Auburn	Cannon	TN	Ava	Jackson	IL	Bagdad	Smith	TN
Auburn	Montgomery	VA	Ava	Oneida	NY	Bagdad	Shelby	KY
Auburn Centre	Susquehanna	PA	Ava	Noble	OH	Bagdad	Williamson	TX
Auburn Dale	Middlesex	MA	Ava	Buchanan	VA	Baggetsville	Robertson	TN
Auburn Four Corner	Susquehanna	PA	Avalanche	Vernon	WI	Bahala	Copiah	MS
Audenried	Carbon	PA	Averill's Station	Midland	MI	Bailey Hollow	Luzerne	PA
Audubon	Audubon	IA	Avery	Jo Daviess	IL	Bailey's Creek	Osage	MO
Aughwick Mills	Huntingdon	PA	Avery	Monroe	IA	Bailey's Harbor	Door	WI
Auglaize	Van Wert	OH	Avery	Berrien	MI	Bailey's Mill	Leon	FL
Au Gres	Ray	MI	Averysborough	Harnett	NC	Bailey's Mill	Belmont	OH
Augusta(c.h.)	Woodruff	AR	Avery's Creek	Buncombe	NC	Bailey's Store	Shelby	KY
Agusta(c.h.)	Richmond	GA	Avilla	Noble	IN	Baileyville	Ogle	IL
Agusta	Hancock	IL	Avilla	Jasper	MO	Baileyville	Washington	ME
Agusta	Des Moines	IA	Aviston	Clinton	IL	Bainbridge(c.h.)	Decatur	GA
Agusta	Butler	KS	Avoca	Lawrence	AL	Bainbridge	Putnam	IN
Agusta	Bracken	KY	Avoca	Lawrence	IN	Bainbridge	Christian	KY
Agusta(c.h.)	Kennebeck	ME	Avoca	Pottawattomie	IA	Bainbridge	Berrien	MI
Agusta	Kalamazoo	MI	Avoca	Jackson	KS	Bainbridge	Clinton	MO
Agusta	Kalamazoo	MI	Avoca	Cass	NE	Bainbridge	Chenango	NY
Agusta(c.h.)	Perry	MS	Avoca	Steuben	NY	Bainbridge	Ross	OH
Agusta	St. Charles	MO	Avoca	Iowa	WI	Bainbridge	Lancaster	PA
Agusta	Sussex	NJ	Avola	Vernon	MO	Bairdstown	Oglethorpe	GA
Agusta	Oneida	NY	Avon	Hartford	CN	Bairdstown	Sullivan	MO
Agusta	Carroll	OH	Avon	Fulton	IL	Baiting Hollow	Suffolk	NY
Agusta	Union	OR	Avon	Hendricks	IN	Baker	Jefferson	IA
Agusta	Northumberland	PA	Avon	Polk	IA	Baker	St. Clair	MO
Agusta	Houston	TX	Avon	Coffey	KS	Baker City(c.h.)	Baker	OR
Agusta	Ean Claire	WS	Avon	Franklin	ME	Baker's Basin	Mercer	NJ
Agusta Station	Marion	IN	Avon	St. Genevieve	MO	Bakersfield	Kern	CA
Auman's Hill	Montgomery	NC	Avon	Livingston	NY	Bakersfield	Franklin	VT
Aumsville	Marion	GA	Avon	Lorain	OH	Baker's Gap	Johnson	TN
Auraria	Lumpkin	GA	Avon	Lebanon	PA	Baker's Grove	Barton	MO
Aurdale	Otter Tail	MN	Avon Centre	Rock	WI	Baker's Run	Hardy	WV
Aurelia	Cherokee	IA	Avondale	Chester	PA	Bakerstown	Allegheny	PA
Aurelius	Ingham	MI	Avondale	Polk	WI	Bakersville	Litchfield	CN
Aurelius	Cayuga	NY	Avonia	Erie	PA	Bakersville	Washington	MD
Auriesville	Montgomery	NY	Avon Lake	Lorain	OH	Bakersville(c.h.)	Mitchell	NC
Aurora	Etowah	AL	Aydelott	Benton	IN	Bakersville	Coshocton	OH
Aurora	Kane	IL	Ayer	Middlesex	MA	Bakersville	Somerset	PA
Aurora	Dearborn	IN	Ayer's Hill	Potter	PA	Bakerville	Henry	AK
Aurora	Keokuk	IA	Ayer's Point	Washington	IL	Bala	Riley	KS
Aurora	Jewell	KS	Ayer's Village	Essex	MA	Balaka	Randolph	IN
Aurora	Marshall	KY	Ayerville	Putnam	MO	Balbeck	Jay	IN
Aurora	Hancock	ME	Ayersville	Stokes	NC	Balcony Falls	Rockbridge	VA
Aurora	Steele	MN	Ayersville	Difiance	OH	Bald Creek	Yancy	NC
Aurora	Lawrence	MO	Aylett's	King William	VA	Bald Eagle	York	PA
Aurora	Wright	MO	Ayr	Goodhue	MN	Bald Hill	Clearfield	PA
Aurora(c.h.)	Esmeralda	NV	Azalia	Bartholomew	IN	Bald Knob	Taney	MO
Aurora	Caynga	NY	Azalan	Jefferson	WI	Bald Knob	Boone	WV
Aurora	Portage	OH	Babcock Hill	Opeida	NY	Bald Mount	Luzerne	PA
Aurora	Washington	WI	Babylon	Hampshire	MA	Bald Mountain	Gilpin	CO
Aurorahville	Waushara	WI	Babylon	Suffolk	NY	Baldwin	Duval	FL
Aurora Mills	Marion	MI	Bacchus	Hopkins	TX	Baldwin	St. Mary's	LA
Au Sable	Iosco	MI	Batchelor's Hall	Pittsylvania	VA	Baldwin	Dunn	WI
Au Sable Forks	Essex	NY	Bachelor's Retreat	Oconee	SC	Baldwin City	Douglas	KS

PLACE NAMES OF THE UNITED STATES

PLACE	COUNTY	STATE	PLACE	COUNTY	STATE	PLACE	COUNTY	STATE
Baldwin's Mills	Jacksonn	MI	Bardstown	Nelson	KY	Barry	Clay	MO
Baldwinsville	Edgar	IL	Bardwell's Ferry	Franklin	MA	Barry	Cuyahoga	OH
Baldwinsville	Worchester	MA	Bareville	Lancaster	PA	Barry	Schuylkill	PA
Baldwinsville	Onondaga	NY	Barfield	Mississippi	AR	Barrytown	Dutchess	NY
Baldwyn	Lee	MS	Bargaintown	Atlantic	NJ	Barryville	Delaware	IA
Bale's Mills	Lee	VA	Barhamsville	New Kent	VA	Barryville	Barry	MI
Ballards	Santa Barbara	CO	Baring	Washington	ME	Barryville	Sullivan	NY
Ballard's Falls	Washington	KS	Barkada	Drew	AR	Barryville	Stark	OH
Ballard Vale	Essex	MA	Bark Camp Mills	Whitley	KY	Bart	Lancaster	PA
Ballardsville	Boone	WV	Barkersville	Saratoga	NY	Bartholomew	Drew	AR
Ball Camp	Knox	TN	Barkeyville	Venango	PA	Bartlett	Fremont	IA
Ballena	San Diego	CA	Barkhamstead	Litchfield	CN	Bartlett	Carroll	NH
Ball Play	Etowah	AL	Barleywood	Spartanburg	SC	Bartlett	Oneida	NY
Ball Play	Monroe	TN	Barlow	Washington	OH	Bartlett	Washington	OH
Ball's Pond	Fairfield	CN	Barlow	Clackamas	OR	Bartlett	Shelby	TN
Ballston(c.h.)	Saratoga	NY	Bar Mills	York	ME	Bartley	Gallatin	IL
Ballston Centre	Saratoga	NY	Barnard	Linn	KS	Barton	Colbert	AL
Ballstown	Ripley	IN	Barnard	Piscataquis	ME	Barton	Alleghany	MD
Ballsville	Powhatan	VA	Barnard	Charlevoix	MI	Barton	Newaygo	MI
Ballwin	St. Louis	MO	Barnard	Nodaway	MO	Barton	Barton	MO
Ballyclough	Dubnque	IA	Barnard	Windsor	VT	Barton	Tioga	NY
Balm	Blount	AL	Barnard's	Armstrong	PA	Barton	Anderson	TX
Balm	Mercer	PA	Barnardsville	Roane	TN	Barton	Orleans	VT
Balmoral	Otter Tail	MN	Barnegat	Ocean	NJ	Barton	Washington	WI
Baltic	New London	CN	Barnerville	Schoharie	NY	Bartonia	Randolph	IN
Baltimore	Baltimore	MD	Barnes'	Richland	OH	Barton Landing	Orleans	VT
Baltimore	Barry	MI	Barnes' Corners	Lewis	NY	Bartonsville	Monroe	PA
Baltimore	Fairfield	OH	Barnes' Cross Roads	Dale	AL	Bartonsville	Windham	VT
Bamberg	Barnwell	SC	Barnes' Store	Tishemingo	MS	Bartow	Jefferson	GA
Bamberg	Sheboygan	WI	Barneston	Chester	PA	Bartramville	Lawrence	OH
Bancroft	Aroostook	ME	Barnesville	Pike	GA	Bartville	Lancaster	PA
Bancroft	Berkshire	MS	Barnesville	Montgomery	MD	Basco	Hancock	IL
Bancroft	Freeborn	MN	Barnesville	Clinton	MO	Bascobel	Jackson	GA
Bancroft	Daviess	MO	Barnesville	Belmont	OH	Bascom	Seneca	OH
Bandera(c.h.)	Bandera	TX	Barnesville	Schuylkill	PA	Base Lake	Washtenaw	MI
Bangall	Dutchess	NY	Barnesville	Charlotte	Va	Base Line	Crawford	KS
Bangor	Marshall	IA	Barnet	Caledonia	VT	Basham's Gap	Morgan	AL
Bangor	Morgan	KY	Barnhart's Mills	Butler	PA	Bashau	Meigs	OH
Bangor(c.h.)	Penobscot	ME	Barnhill	Wayne	IL	Basil	Fairfield	OH
Bangor	Van Buren	MI	Barnsborough	Gloucester	NJ	Bason Spring	Williamson	TN
Bangor	Franklin	NY	Barnstable(c.h.)	Barnstable	MA	Basking Ridge	Somerset	NJ
Bangor	Northampton	PA	Barnstead	Belknap	NH	Basnettsville	Marion	WV
Bangor	La Crosse	WI	Barnum	Adams	WI	Bassett's Mills	El Paso	CO
Gank Liek	Kenton	KY	Barnumsville	Bennington	VT	Bassett's Station	Kenosha	WI
Bank's	Bay	MI	Barnumton	Camden	MO	Bass Lake	Faribault	MN
Banks	Faribault	MN	Barnwell	Barnwell	SC	Bass Station	Jackson	AL
Bankston	Saline	IL	Barracksville	Marion	WV	Bass Wood	Richland	WI
Bankston	Dubuque	IA	Barre	Worcester	MA	Bastinville	Hickman	TN
Bankston	Choctaw	MS	Barre	Washington	VT	Bastrop(c.h.)	Morehouse	LA
Banksville	Fairfield	CN	Barre Centre	Orleans	NY	Bastrop(c.h.)	Bastrop	TX
Banksville	Banks	GA	Barre Forge	Huntingdon	PA	Bastross	Lycoming	PA
Bannack City(c.h.)	BeaverHead	MT	Barre Mils	La Crosse	WI	Batavia	Solano	CA
Banner	Jackson	KS	Barren	Harrison	IN	Batavia	Kane	IL
Banner	Calhoun	MS	Barren Creek Sprngs	Wicomico	MD	Batavia	Branch	MI
Banner	Fond du Lac	WI	Barren Hill	Montgomery	PA	Batavia(c.h.)	Genesee	NY
Bannerville	Snyder	PA	Barren Plain	Robertson	TN	Batavia(c.h.)	Clermont	OH
Banquete	Nucces	TX	Barren Springs	Fentress	TN	Batchellerville	Saratoga	NY
Banta	San Joaquin	CA	Barre Plains	Worcester	MA	Baterlor's Rest	Pendleton	KY
Bantam	Clermont	OH	Barret's Station	St. Louis	MO	Batcham	Sullivan	IN
Bantam Falls	Litchfield	CN	Barrett	Marshall	Ks	Bates	Sangamon	IL
Baptistown	Hunterdon	NJ	Barrettsville	Hampshire	WV	Bates	Osceola	MI
Baptist Valley	Tazewell	VA	Barreville	McHenry	IL	Batesville(c.h.)	Independence	AR
Baraboo(c.h.)	Sauk	WI	Barrington	Stafford	NH	Batesville	Ripley	IN
Baraga	Houghton	MI	Barrington	Yates	NY	Batesville	Panola	MS
Barber	Faribaul	MN	Barrington	Bristol	RI	Batesville	Noble	OH
Barber's Mills	Wells	IN	Barrington Centre	Bristol	RI	Batesville	Spartanburgh	SC
Barbersville	Jefferson	IN	Barrington Station	Cook	IL	Batesville	Albemarle	VA
Barbour's Mills	Lycoming	PA	Barrittsville	Dawson	GA	Bath	Placer	CA
Barboursville	Knox	KY	Barron(c.h.)	Barron	WI	Bath	Mason	IN
Barboursville	Delaware	NY	Barrow	Greene	IL	Bath(c.h.)	Sagadahoe	ME
Barclay	Black Hawk	IA	Barre's Store	Macoupin	IL	Bath	Clinton	MI
Barclay	Bradford	PA	Barry	Pike	IL	Bath	Grafton	NH
Bardolph	McDonough	IL	Barry	Frederick	MD	Bath(c.h.)	Steugen	NY

PLACE NAMES OF THE UNITED STATES

PLACE	COUNTY	STATE	PLACE	COUNTY	STATE	PLACE	COUNTY	STATE
Bath	Beaufort	NC	Bear Branch	Ohio	IN	Beaver Head Rock	Madison	MT
Bath	Summit	OH	Bear Branch	Linn	MO	Beaver Kill	Sullivan	NY
Bath	Northampton	PA	Bear Branch	Richmond	NC	Beaver Meadows	Carbon	PA
Bath	Edgefield	SC	Bear Canyon	Douglas	CO	Beaver Pond	Lexington	SC
Bath(c.h.)	Bath	VA	Bear Creek	Searcy	AR	Beaver Ridge	Knox	TN
Bath Alum	Bath	VA	Bear Creek	Henry	GA	Beaver Run	Sussex	NJ
Baton Rouge(c.h.)	East Baton Rouge	LA	Bear Creek	Jay	IN	Beaver Springs	Snyder	PA
Batten's Mill	Gilmer	WV	Bear Ceek	Hinds	MS	Beaverton	Sanford	AL
Battenville	Washington	NY	Bear Creek	Cedar	MO	Beavertown	Snyder	PA
Battleborough	Edgecombe	NC	Bear Creek	Luzerne	PA	Beaver Valley	St. Clair	AL
Battle Creek	Tehama	CA	Bear Creek	Waupace	WI	Beaver Valley	New Castle	DE
Battle Creek	Calhoun	MI	Beard's Station	Oldham	KY	Beaver Valley	Columbia	PA
Battle Creek	Madison	NE	Beardstown(c.h.)	Cass	IL	Beaverville	Iroquois	IL
Battle Creek Mines	Marion	TN	Beardstown	Perry	TN	Bechtelsville	Berks	PA
Battle Ground	Tippecanoe	IN	Bear Gap	Northumberland	PA	Becker	Sherburne	MI
Battle Ground	Clarke	WA	Bear Grove	Guthrie	IA	Beckersville	Berks	PA
Battle Mound	Tulare	CA	Bear Lake	Manistee	MI	Becket	Berkshire	MA
Battle Mountain	Humboldt	NV	Bear Lake	Warren	PA	Becket Centre	Berkshire	MA
Bauff	Taney	MO	Bear Lake Mills	Van Buren	MI	Becket's Store	Pickaway	OH
Baughman	Wayne	OH	Bear River	Emmett	MI	Beckettsville	Baltimore	MD
Baugh's Station	Logan	KY	Bear River City	Box Elder	UT	Beckleysville	Baltimore	MD
Baumstown	Berks	PA	Bearsville	Ulster	NY	Beck's Creek	Shelby	IL
Bavington	Washington	PA	Beartown	Deer Lodge	MT	Beck's Grove	Brown	IN
Baxter Springs	Cherokee	KS	Beartown	Lancaster	PA	Beck's Mills	Washington	IN
Bay	Gasconade	MO	Bear Valley	Mariposa	CA	Beck's Mills	Holmes	OH
Bayard	Columbiana	OH	Bear Valley	Wabashaw	MN	Beck's Mills	Washington	PA
Bayborough	Horry	SC	Bear Valley	Richland	WI	Beckville	Panola	TX
Bay City(c.h.)	Bay	MI	Bear Wallow	Henderson	NC	Beckwith	Plumas	CA
Bay City	Pierce	WI	Beasley's Fork	Adams	OH	Beddington	Washington	ME
Bay Creek	Gwinnett	GA	Beatrice(c.h.)	Gage	NE	Bedford	Pike	IL
Bayfield(c.h.)	Bayfield	WI	Beattie	Marshall	KS	Bedford(c.h.)	Lawrence	IN
Bay Hill	Walsworth	WI	Beattie's Ford	Lincoln	NC	Bedford(c.h.)	Taylor	IA
Bay Hundred	Talbot	MD	Beatty	Westmoreland	PA	Bedford(c.h.)	Trimble	KY
Bay Minette	Baldwin	AK	Beattyville	Lee	KY	Bedford	Middlesex	MA
Baynesville	Westmoreland	VA	Beatyestown	Warren	NJ	Bedford	Calhoun	MI
Bayonne	Hudson	NJ	Beaty's Mill	Marion	WV	Bedford	Livingston	MO
Bayon Barbary	Livingston	LA	Beaucoup	Washington	IL	Bedford	Hillsborough	NH
Bayon Boeuf	St. Landry	LA	Beauford Blue	Earth	MN	Bedford(c.h.)	Westchester	NY
Bayon Chicot	St. Landry	LA	Beaufort	Franklin	MO	Bedford	Cuyahga	OH
Bayon Goula	Iberville	LA	Beaufort(c.h.)	Carteret	NC	Bedford(c.h.)	Bedford	PA
Bayou Metoe	Pulaski	GA	Beaufort(c.h.)	Beaufort	SC	Bedford	Bedford	TN
Bayou Tunica	West Feliciana	LA	Beaumont(c.h.)	Jefferson	TX	Bedford Springs	Bedford	PA
Bay Port	Hernando	FL	Beaver	Winona	MN	Bedford Station	Westchester	NY
Bayport	Suffolk	NY	Beaver	Douglas	MO	Bedias	Grimes	TX
Bay Ridge	Kings	NY	Beaver	Pike	OH	Bedminister	Bucks	PA
Bay River	Craven	NC	Beaver	Clackamas	OR	Bed Rock	Klamath	CA
Bay Settlement	Brown	WI	Beaver(c.h.)	Beaver	PA	Beebe Plain	Orleans	VT
Bay Shore	Suffolk	NY	Beaver	Anderson	TX	Bee Branch	Van Burren	AR
Bay Side	Queens	NY	Beaver(c.h.)	Beaver	UT	Bee Caves	Travis	TX
Bay Springs	Prentiss	MS	Beaver	Thurston	WA	Beech	Licking	OH
Bay View	Cecil	MD	Beaver Bay(c.h.)	Lake	MN	Beech Creek	Ashley	AR
Bay View	Essex	MS	Beaver Brook	Sullivan	NY	Beech Creek	Clinton	PA
Bayview	Milwaukee	WI	Beaver Centre	Crawford	PA	Beecher	Will	IL
Bayville	Ocean	NJ	Beaver City	Newton	IN	Beech Fork	Washington	KY
Bazaar	Chase	KS	Beaver Creek	Dale	AL	Beech Grove	Coffee	TN
Bazetta	Trumbull	OH	Beaver Creek	Pueblo	CO	Beech Hill	Mason	WV
Beach Haven	Luzerne	PA	Beaver Creek	Bond	IL	Beechland	Washington	KY
Beach Pond	Wayne	PA	Beaver Creek	Cloud	KS	Beech Spring	Lee	VA
Beach Ridge	Niagara	NY	Beaver Creek	Washington	MD	Beech Wood	Sullivan	NY
Beacon	Ogle	IL	Beaver Creek	Gratiot	MI	Beech Wood	Cameron	PA
Beacon	Mahaska	IA	Beaver Creek	Jefferson	TN	Beech Woods	Newton	AR
Beacon Falls	New Haven	CN	Beaver Ceek	Jackson	WI	Beechy Mire	Union	IN
Bealeton	Fauquier	VA	Beaver Crossing	Seward	NE	Bee Creek	Pike	IL
Beall's Mills	Gilmer	WV	Beaver Dam	Kosciusko	IN	Bee Creek	Taney	MO
Beallsville	Montgomery	MD	Beaver Dam	Ohio	KY	Bee Creek	Bledsoe	TN
Beallsville	Monroe	OH	Beaver Dam	Union	NC	Beekman	Dutchess	NY
Beallsville	Washington	PA	Beaver Dam	Allen	OH	Beekmantown	Clinton	NY
Beamsville	Darke	OH	Beaver Dam	Dodge	WI	Beeler's Station	Marshall	WV
Bean Blossom	Brown	IN	Beaver Dam Depot	Hanover	VA	Bee Lick	Lincoln	KY
Bean's Corners	Franklin	ME	Beaver Dams	Schuyler	NY	Beemerville	Sussex	NJ
Bean's Station	Grainger	TN	Beaver Falls(c.h.)	Renville	MN	Bee Ridge	Knox	MO
Beantown	Charles	MD	Beaver Falls	Lewis	NY	Beers	Allegheny	PA
Bear	Richland	WI	Beaver Falls	Beaver	PA	Beershebe Springs	Grundy	TN

PLACE NAMES OF THE UNITED STATES

PLACE	COUNTY	STATE	PLACE	COUNTY	STATE	PLACE	COUNTY	STATE
Besson.	Richie	WV	Belle Vernon	Fayette	PA	Beloit	Rock	WI
Bee Spring	Edmonson	KY	Belleview	Caalhoun	IL	Belpassi	Marion	OR
Beetown	Grant	WI	Belleview	Christian	KY	Belpre	Washington	OH
Beetrace	Appanoose	IA	Belleview	Iron	MO	Belton	Anderson	SC
Beeville(c.h.)	Bee	TX	Belleview	Davidson	TN	Belton(c.h.)	Bell	TX
Belair	Richmond	GA	Belleview	Rusk	TS	Beltsville	Prince George's	MD
Bel Air	Plaquemine	LA	Belleville	Conecuh	Al	Belvidere(c.h.)	Boone	IL
Bel Air(c.h.)	Harford	MD	Belleville(c.h.)	St. Clair	IL	Belvidere	Monona	IA
Belair	Lancaster	SC	Belleville	Hendricks	IN	Belvidere	Warren	NJ
Belbend	Luzerne	PA	Belleville	Talbot	GA	Belvidere	Allegany	NY
Belcher	Washington	NY	Belleville	Repulic	KS	Belvidere	Perquimons	NC
Belchertown	Hampshire	MA	Belleville	Wayne	MI	Belvidere	Franklin	TN
Belden	Wabash	IN	Belleville	Fillmore	MN	Belvidere	Lamoille	VT
Belden	Broome	NY	Belleville	Essex	NJ	Belvidere Corners	Lamiolle	VT
Beldenville	Pierce	WI	Belleville	Jefferson	NY	Belvoir	Douglas	KS
Belew Creek Mills	Forsyth	NC	Belleville	Richland	OH	Belvue	Pottawatomie	KS
Belew's Creek	Jefferson	MO	Belleville	Mifflin	PA	Bem	Green	WI
Belfast	Grant	AR	Belleville	Wood	WV	Bement	Piatt	IL
Belfast	Lee	IA	Belleville	Dane	WI	Bemus Heights	Saratoga	NY
Belfast(c.h.)	Waldo	ME	Bellevoir	Chatham	NC	Bemus Point	Chautanqua	NY
Belfast	Baltimore	MD	Bellevue	Dallas	AL	Ben	Chicot	AR
Belfast	Allegany	NY	Bellevue	Jackson	IA	Benaja	Rockingham	KS
Belfast	Clermont	OH	Bellevue(c.h.)	Bossier	LA	Benbow	Marion	MO
Belfast	Northampton	PA	Bellevue	Eaton	MI	Bendersville	Adams	PA
Belfast Mills	Russell	VA	Bellevue(c.h.)	Spary	NE	Benela	Calhoun	MS
Belgium	Ozaukee	WI	Bellevue	Huron	OH	Benevola	Washington	MD
Belgrade	Kennebec	ME	Bellevue	Yam Hill	OR	Benezett	Elk	PA
Belgrade	Washington	MO	Bellevue	Washington	UT	Benford's Store	Somerset	PA
Belgrade Mills	Kennebec	ME	Bellevue	Bedford	VA	Ben Franklin	Delta	TX
Belinda	Lucas	IA	Bell Factory	Madison	AL	Bengal	Clinton	MI
Belington	Barbour	WV	Bellfair Mills	Stafford	VA	Benham's Store	Ripley	IN
Belknap	Davis	IA	Bellingham	Norfolk	MS	Benicia	Solano	CA
Belknap	Armstrong	PA	Bellmore	Parke	IN	Benjamin	Lewis	MO
Bell	Leavenworth	KS	Bellona	Yates	NY	Ben Lomond	Sevier	AR
Bell	Highland	OH	Bellota	San Joaquin	CA	Bennet's Corners	Madison	NY
Bell Air	Crawford	IL	Bellows Falls	Windham	VT	Bennet's Station	Lancaster	NE
Bell Air	Cooper	MO	Bell Plain	Marshall	IL	Bennett	Allegheny	PA
Bell Air	Hardin	Tn	Bellport	Suffolk	NY	Bennettsburgh	Schuyler	NY
Bellaire	Belmont	OH	Bell's Bridge	Shasta	CA	Bennett's Corners	Medina	OH
Bellasylva	Wyoming	PA	Bell's Cross-Roads	Louisa	VA	Bennett's Creek	Steuben	NY
Bellbrook	Green	OH	Bell's Depot	Haywood	TN	Bennett's Landing	Tunica	MS
Bellbuckle	Bedford	TN	Bell's Landing	Monroe	AL	Bennett's Mills	Ocean	NJ
Bell Centre	Crawford	WI	Bell's Mills	Cleburne	AL	Bennett's River	Fulton	AR
Belle Air	Johnson	IA	Bell's Mills	Jefferson	PA	Bennett's Station	Sumter	AL
Belle Branch	Atascosa	TX	Bell's Mines	Crittenden	KY	Bennett's Switch	Miami	IN
Belle Centre	Logan	Oh	Bell's Store	Nevada	AR	Bennettstown	Christian	KY
Belle Creek	Goodhue	MI	Bell's Valley	Rockbridge	VA	Bennettsville	Etowah	AL
Belle Creek	Washington	NE	Bellton	Marshall	WV	Bennettsville	Clarke	IN
Bellefontaine	Choctaw	MS	Belltown	Monroe	TN	Bennettsville	Chenango	NY
Bellefontaine	St. Louis	MO	Bellvale	Orange	NY	Bennettsville	Marlborough	SC
Bellefontaine(c.h.)	Logan	OH	Bellview	Lebanan	PA	Bennington	Edwards	ILL
Bellefontaine	Carroll	AR	Bellville	Hamilton	FL	Bennington	Switzerland	IN
Bellefontaine	Jackson	AL	Bellville	Austin	TX	Bennington	Ottawa	KS
Bellefontaine	Pulaski	MO	Bellwood	Wilson	TN	Bennington	Shinwassee	MI
Bellefontaine(c.h.)	Centre	PA	Belmond	Wright	IA	Bennington	Hillsborough	NH
Belle Fountain	Mahaska	IA	Belmont	Crawford	AR	Bennington	Wyoming	NY
Bellefountain	Columbia	WI	Belmont	San Mateo	CA	Bennington	Morrow	OH
Belle Grove	Greenwood	KS	Belmont	Woodson	KS	Bennington	Bennington	VT
Belle Haven	Accomack	VA	Belmont	Bullitt	KY	Bennington Centre	Bennington	VT
Belle Isle	Onondago	NY	Belmont	Waldo	ME	Bennington Furnace	Blair	PA
Bellemont	Warren	IA	Belmont	Middlesex	MA	Benona	Oceana	MI
Bellemonte	Lancaster	PA	Belmont	Kent	MI	Bensalem	Bucks	PA
Belle Plain	Cumberland	NJ	Belmont	Mississippi	MO	Benson	Franklin	KY
Belle Plaine	Benton	IA	Belmont(c.h.)	N V		Benson	Swift	MN
Belle Plaine	Shawanaw	WI	Belmont(c.h.)	Belknap	NH	Benson	Hamilton	NY
Belle Point	Delaware	OH	Belmont(c.h.)	Allegany	NY	Benson	Rutland	VT
Belle Prairie	Hamilton	IL	Belmont	Belmont	OH	Benson Centre	Hamilton	Ny
Belle Prairie	Morrison	MN	Belmont	Gonzales	TX	Benson Grove	Winnebago	IA
Belle River	St. Clair	MI	Belmont	La Fayette	WI	Benson Landing	Rutland	VT
Belle Union	Putman	IN	Belmont	Putnam	OH	Ben's Run	Tyler	WV
Belle Vale	West Baton Rouge	LA	Beloit	Lyon	IA	Bent Branch	Pike	KY
Belle Valley	Erie	Pa	Beloit	Mitchell	KS	Bent Creek	Appomattox	VA
Belle Vernon	Wyandot	OH	Beloit	Mahoning	OH	Bentivoglio	Albemarle	VA

PLACE NAMES OF THE UNITED STATES

PLACE	COUNTY	STATE	PLACE	COUNTY	STATE	PLACE	COUNTY	STATE
Bentley's Springs	Baltimore	MD	Berlin	Steel	MN	Bethel	Morgan	IL
Bentleyville	Washington	PA	Berlin	Camden	NJ	Bethel	Wayne	IN
Bently	Hancock	IL	Berlin	Rensselaer	NY	Bethel	Fayette	IA
Bent Mountain	Roanoke	VA	Berlin	Holmes	OH	Bethel	Marion	KS
Benton	Lowndes	Al	Berlin	Somerset	PA	Bethel	Bath	KY
Benton(c.h.)	Saline	AR	Berlin	Marshall	TN	Bethel	Oxford	ME
Benton	Mono	CA	Berlin	Washington	TX	Bethel	Branch	MI
Benton	Columbia	FL	Berlin	Washington	VT	Bethel	Anoka	MN
Benton(c.h.)	Franklin	IL	Berlin	Southampton	VA	Bethel	Shelby	MO
Benton	Elkhart	IN	Berlin	Green Lake	WI	Bethel	Sullivan	NY
Benton	Mills	IA	Berlin Centre	Mahoning	OH	Bethel	Clermont	OH
Benton(c.h.)	Mashall	KY	Berlin Centre	Wayne	PA	Bethel	Polk	OR
Benton	Bassier	LA	Berlin Cross Roads	Jackson	WY	Bethel	Berks	PA
Benton	Kennebec	ME	Berlin Falls	Coos	NH	Bethel	York	SC
Benton	Washtenaw	MI	Berlin Heights	Erie	OH	Bethel	Giles	TN
Benton	Carver	MN	Berlin Station	Erie	OH	Bethel	Anderson	TX
Benton	Yazoo	MS	Berlinsville	Northampton	PA	Bethel	Windsor	VT
Benton	Scott	MO	Berlinville	Erie	OH	Bethel	Mercer	WV
Benton	Saunders	NE	Bermudian	Adams	PA	Bethel Corners	Caynga	NY
Benton	Grafton	NH	Bernadotte	Fulton	IL	Bethel Springs	McNairy	TN
Benton	Holmes	OH	Bernadotte	Nicollet	MI	Bethesda	Montgomery	MD
Benton	Columbia	PA	Bernalillo	Bernalillo	NM	Bethesda	Belmont	OH
Benton(c.h.)	Polk	TN	Bernard	Chicot	AR	Bethesda	Lancaster	PA
Benton	La Fayette	WI	Bernard	Brunswick	NC	Bethesda	Williamson	TN
Benton Centre	Benton	IA	Bernard Station	Wharton	TX	Bethlehem	Litchfield	CN
Benton City	Audrian	MO	Bernardston	Franklin	MA	Bethlehem	Clarke	IN
Benton Harbor	Barrien	Mi	Berne	Camden	GA	Bethlehem	Wayne	IA
Benton Ridge	Hancock	OH	Berne	Dodge	MN	Bethlehem	Henry	KY
Benton's Ferry	Livingston	LA	Berne	Albany	NY	Bethlehem	Caroline	MD
Benton's Ferry	Marion	WV	Berne	Noble	OH	Bethlehem	Benton	MS
Benton's Port	Van Buren	IA	Bernhard's Bay	Oswego	NY	Bethlehem	Gratton	NH
Benton Station	Benton	TN	Bernice	Sullivan	PA	Bethlehem	Hunterdon	NJ
Bentonville(c.h.)	Benton	AR	Bernville	Berks	PA	Bethlehem	Horthampton	PA
Bentonville	Fayette	IN	Bero	Cherokee	KS	Bethlehem	Clarendon	SC
Bentonville	Adams	OH	Berrien Centre	Berrien	MI	Bethlehem Centre	Albany	NY
Bentonville	Warren	VA	Berrien Springs(c.h.)	Berrien	MI	Bethpage	McDonald	MO
Bent's Fort	Bent	CO	Berros Creek	San Luis Obispo	CA	Betsey Lake	Grand Taverse	MI
Benvenue	Damphin	PA	Berry	Sangamon	IL	Bettsville	Seneca	OH
Benville	Jennings	IN	Berry Hill	Rockingham	NC	Beulah(c.h.)	Union	MA
Benwood	Marshall	WV	Berrysburg	Dauphin	PA	Beulah	Johnson	NC
Benazonia(c.h.)	Benzie	MI	Berry's Lick	Butler	KY	Beulahville	King William	VA
Beowawe	Lander	NV	Berry's Mill	Franklin	ME	Bevans	Sussex	NJ
Berdan	Greene	IL	Berrysville	Highland	OH	Beverly	Adams	IL
Berea	Franklin	KS	Berryton	Cass	IL	Beverly	Christian	KY
Berea	Madison	KY	Berryvale	Siskiyou	CA	Beverly	Essex	MA
Berea	Granville	NC	Berryville	Carroll	AR	Beverly	Macon	MO
Berea	Cuyahoga	OH	Berryville	Wayne	KY	Beverly	Burlington	NJ
Berea	Ritchie	WV	Berryville(c.h.)	Clarke	VA	Beverly	Anson	NC
Berea	McLeod	MN	Bertram	Linn	IA	Beverly	Washington	OH
Berea	Hudson	NJ	Bertrand	Berrien	MI	Beverly(c.h.)	Randolph	WV
Berea	Genesee	NY	Bertrandville	La Fayette	LA	Beverly Farms	Essex	MA
Bergen Point	Hudson	NJ	Berville	St. Clair	MI	Beverly Station	Platte	MO
Berger	Franklin	MO	Berwick	Warren	IL	Bevier	Macon	MO
Berger's Store	Pittsylvania	VA	Berwick	York	ME	Bevis Tavern	Hamilton	OH
Berges Gap	Wise	VA	Berwick	Seneca	OH	Bewleyville	Breckenridge	KY
Bergholtz	Niagra	NY	Berwick	Columbia	PA	Bible Grove	Clay	IL
Berkeley Spngs(c.h.)	Morgan	WV	Berzelia	Columbia	GA	Bible Grove	Scotland	MO
Berkey	Lucus	OH	Bessville	Bollinger	MO	Bickley's Mills	Russell	VA
Berkley	Madison	AL	Beta	Fulton	OH	Bicknell	Knox	IN
Berkley	Bristol	MA	Bethalto	Madison	IL	Biddeford	York	ME
Berkley's	Bristol	MA	Bethannia	Forsyth	NC	Biddeford Pool	York	ME
Berkshire	Berkshire	MA	Bethany	New Haven	CN	Bibwell's Bar	Butte	CA
Berkshire	Delaware	OH	Bethany	Jefferson	GA	Biehle	Perry	MO
Berkshire	Franklin	VT	Bethany	Parke	IN	Big Bar	Trinity	CA
Berlin	Ashley	AR	Bethany(c.h.)	Harrison	MO	Big Beaver	Oakland	MI
Berlin	Hartford	CN	Bethany	Genesee	NY	Big Bend	Polk	AR
Berlin	Sangamon	IL	Bethany	Butler	OH	Big Bend	Jewell	KS
Berlin	Clinton	IN	Bethany	Osborne	KS	Big Bend	Avoyelles	LA
Berlin	Hardin	IA	Bethany	Wayne	PA	Big Bend	Cottonwood	MN
Berlin	Bracken	KY	Bethany	York	SC	Big Bend	Venango	PA
Berlin	Worcester	MD	Bethany	Brooke	WV	Big Bend	Calhoun	WV
Berlin	Worcester	MA	Bethany Church	Iredell	NC	Big Bend	Waukesha	WI
Berlin	Ottawa	MI	Bethel	Fairfield	CN	Big Bottom	Independence	AR

PLACE NAMES OF THE UNITED STATES

PLACE	COUNTY	STATE	PLACE	COUNTY	STATE	PLACE	COUNTY	STATE
Big Bottom	Humpheys	TN	Big Thompson	Larimer	CO	Blackberry Plains	Fannin	TX
Big Brook	Oneida	NY	Big Timber	Riley	KS	Blackberry Ridge	Oceana	MI
Big Buffalo	Harrison	WV	Big Tree	Greene	PA	Blackberry Station	Kane	IL
Bigby Fork	Itawamba	MS	Big Tree Corners	Erie	NY	Black Bird	Newcastle	DE
Big Cabin	Cherokee Nation	IT	Big Trees	Calaveras	CA	Blackbird	Burt	NE
Big Cane	St. Landry	LA	Big Woods	Wright	MN	Black Brook	Clinton	NY
Big Clear Creek	Greenbrier	WV	Bijou Bason	El Paso	CO	Black Brook	Polk	WI
Big Clifty	Grayson	KY	Billerica	Middlesex	MA	Black Creek	Allegany	NY
Big Coon	Jackson	AL	Billings	Barry	MO	Black Creek	Wilson	NC
Big Cove Tannery	Fulton	PA	Billings	Dutchess	NY	Black Creek	Holmes	OH
Big Creek	Geneva	AL	Billingsly	Washington	AR	Black Creek	Luzerne	PA
Big Creek	Green	AR	Billingsville	Union	IN	Black Diamond	Contra Costa	CA
Big Creek	Forsyth	GA	Billingsville	Cooper	MO	Black Earth	Dane	WI
Big Creek	Clay	KY	Bill's Creek	Chase	KS	Blackfish	Crittenden	AR
Big Creek	Mecosta	MI	Biloxi	Harrison	MS	Blackfoot City	Deer Lodge	MT
Big Creek	Texas	MO	Bingamen	Marion	WV	Black Fork	Tucker	WV
Big Creek	Stokes	NC	Bingen	Northampton	PA	Black Hammer	Houston	MN
Big Creek	Steuben	NY	Bingham	Somerset	ME	Black Hawk	Gilpin	CO
Big Creek	Edgefield	SC	Bingham	Monroe	OH	Black Hawk	Concordia	LA
Big Creek	Cocke	TN	Bingham Canyon	Salt Lake	UT	Black Hawk	Carroll	MS
Big Creek	Monroe	WI	Bingham Centre	Potter	PA	Black Hawk	Beaver	PA
Big Dry Creek	Fresno	CA	Bingham Lake	Cottonwood	MN	Black Hawk	Sank	WI
Bigelow	Holt	MO	Bingham's Mills	Tioga	NY	Black Hawk Mills	Possey	IN
Big Falls	Alamance	NC	Binghamton	Solado	CA	Black Hawk Point	Gilpin	CO
Big Flats	Chemung	NY	Binghamton(c.h.)	Broome	NY	Black Heath	Chesterfield	VA
Big Flats	Adams	WI	Binghamton	Outagamie	WI	Black Horse	Harford	MD
Big Foot Prairie	McHenry	IL	Binkley's Bridge	Lancaster	PA	Black Horse	Chester	PA
Big Fork	Polk	AR	Birchardville	Susquehanna	PA	Blackinton	Berkshire	MA
Big Grove	Pottawattamie	IA	Birch Cooley	Renville	MN	Black Jack	Scott	AR
Bigg's Station	Butte	CA	Birch Lick	Jackson	KY	Black Jack	Douglas	KS
Biggsville	Henderson	IL	Birch River	Nicolas	WV	Black Jack	Hocking	OH
Big Hill	Labette	KS	Birch Run	Saginaw	MI	Black Jack	Robertson	TN
Big Hill	Madison	KY	Birch Run Ville	Chester	PA	Black Jack Grove	Hopkins	TX
Big Hollow	Greene	NY	Birch Tree	Shannon	MO	Black Jack Springs	Fayette	TX
Big Indian	Cass	IN	Birchwood	James	TN	Black Lake	Muskegon	MI
Big Island	Bedford	VA	Bird Hill	Carroll	MD	Blackleysville	Wayne	OH
Big Labette	Naosho	KS	Birdsall	Allegany	NY	Black Lick	Franklin	OH
Big Lake	Sherburne	MN	Birdsborough	Berks	PA	Black Lick Station	Indiana	PA
Bigler	Adams	PA	Bird's Bridge	Will	IL	Blackman's Mills	Sampson	NC
Big Like	Stanly	NC	Birdseye	Dubois	IN	Black Mingo	Williamsburg	SC
Big Lick	Roanoke	VA	Bird's Run	Guernsey	OH	Black Oak	Caldwell	MO
Big Meadows	Plumas	CA	Birdston	Navarro	TX	Black Oak	Hopkins	TX
Big Mound	Lee	OH	Birdsville	Livingston	KY	Black Oak Point	Hickory	MO
Big Muddy	Franklin	IL	Birk's City	Daviess	KY	Black Oak Ridge	Daviess	IN
Big Neck	Adams	IL	Birmingham	Schuyler	IL	Black Point	Marion	CA
Big North Fork	Fulton	AR	Birmingham	Van Buren	IA	Black River	Jefferson	NY
Big Oak Flat	Toulumne	CA	Burmingham	Marshall	KY	Black River	Lorain	OH
Big Patch	Grant	WI	Burmingham	Oakland	MI	Black River	King	WA
Big Pine	Inyo	CA	Burmingham	Burlington	NJ	Black River Chapel	New Hanover	NC
Big Plain	Madison	OH	Birmingham	Erie	OH	Black River Falls	Jackson	WI
Big Pond	Sanford	AL	Birmingham	Huntingdon	PA	Black Rock	Grant	WV
Big Pond	Bradford	PA	Birthright	Hopkins	TX	Black Rock	Baltimore	MD
Big Prairie	Newaygo	MI	Biscayne(c.h.)	Dade	FL	Black Rock	Fairfield	CN
Big Prairie	Wayne	OH	Bishop Creek	Mono	CA	Black's	Lawrence	TN
Big Rapids(c.h.)	Mecosta	MI	Bishop Hill	Henry	IL	Blacks and Whites	Nottoway	VA
Big Reedy	Edmonson	KY	Bishop's Head	Dorchester	MD	Blacksburg	Montgomery	VA
Big Renox	Cumberland	KY	Bishop's Station	Mason	IL	Black's Gap	Franklin	PA
Big River	Pierce	WI	Bishop's Store	Dodge	GA	Blackshear	Pierce	GA
Big Rock	Kand	IL	Bishop Street	Jefferson	NY	Black's Gap	Franklin	PA
Big Rock	Scott	IA	Bishopville	Worchester	MD	Blackshear	Pierce	GA
Big Rock	Harlon	KY	Bishopville	Morgan	OH	Black's Mills	Monmouth	NJ
Big Rock	Buchanan	IL	Bishopville	Sumter	SC	Blacksmith	Shawnee	KS
Big Run	Athens	OH	Bismarck	Wabaunsee	KS	Black Springs	Montgomery	AR
Big Spring	Jackson	NC	Bismarck	Eaton	MI	Black Stocks	Chester	SC
Big Spring	Comberland	PA	Bismarck	St. Francois	MO	Blackstone	Livingston	IL
Big Spring	Meigs	TN	Bismarck	Lebanon	PA	Blackstone	Worcester	MA
Big Spring	Adams	WI	Bismarck	Cuming	NE	Blacksville	Monongalia	WV
Big Spring Depot	Montgomery	VA	Bissell's	Geanga	OH	Black Swamp	Sandusky	OH
Big Springs	Douglas	KS	Bitter Creek	Carbou	WY	Black's Wells	Choctaw	MS
Big Springs	Chickasaw	MS	Biven's Grove	Marshall	IA	Blackville(c.h.)	Barnwell	SC
Big Springs	Logan	OH	Black Ash	Crawford	PA	Black Walnut	Ogle	IL
Big Stone Gap	Wise	VA	Black Bear	Klamath	CA	Black Walnut	Palo Alto	IA
Big Sycamore	Clay	WV	Blackberry	Kane	IL	Black Walunt	Wyoming	PA

PLACE NAMES OF THE UNITED STATES

PLACE	COUNTY	STATE	PLACE	COUNTY	STATE	PLACE	COUNTY	STATE
Black Walnut	Halifax	VA	Bloomfield	Greene	IN	Blue Grass	Scott	IA
Black Warrior	Saline	KS	Bloomfield	Davis	IA	Blue Hill	Hancock	ME
Black Water	Morgan	KY	Bloomfield	Nelson	KY	Blue Hill Falls	Hancock	ME
Blackwater	Sussex	DE	Bloomfield	Isabella	MI	Blue Island	Cook	IL
Blackwell's Station	St. Francois	MO	Bloomfield(c.h.)	Stoddard	MO	Blue Island(c.h.)	Saline	NE
Blackwoodtown	Camden	NJ	Bloomfield	Essex	NJ	Blue Knob	Blair	PA
Bladenburg	Bladen	NC	Bloomfield	Morrow	OH	Blue Lake	Muskegon	MI
Bladensburg	Prince George's	MD	Bloomfield	Crawford	PA	Blue Lakes	Lake	CA
Bladensburg	Knox	OH	Bloomfield	Essex	VT	Blue Lick	Franklin	AL
Bladen Springs	Choctaw	AL	Bloomfield	Laudoun	VA	Blue Lick	Clarke	IN
Blain	Perry	PA	Bloomfield	Walworth	WI	Blue Lick	Allen	OH
Blaine	Lawrence	KY	Bloomburgh	Sullivan	NY	Blue Lick Springs	Nicholas	KY
Blain's Cross Roads	Grainger	TN	Bloomburgh	Fayette	OH	Blue Mill	Jackson	MO
Blair	Union	DK	Bloomingdale	Clay	DA	Blue Mound	Livingston	MO
Blair	Randolph	IL	Bloomingdale	Du Page	IL	Blue Mound	Dane	WI
Blair	Barry	MI	Bloomingdale	Parke	IN	Blue Mounds	Linn	KS
Blair(c.h.)	Washington	NE	Bloomingdale	McPherson	KS	Blue Mountain	Calhoun	AL
Blair	Hancock	WV	Bloomingdale	Van Buren	MI	Blue Mountain	Izard	AR
Blairsburgh	Hamilton	IA	Bloomingdale	Passaic	NJ	Blue Mountain	Northampton	PA
Blair's Station	Doniphan	KS	Bloomingdale	Essex	NY	Blue Point	Suffolk	NY
Blairstown	Benton	IA	Bloomingdale	Jefferson	OH	Blue Point	Cherokee	AL
Blairsville(c.h.)	Union	GA	Bloomingdale	Luzerne	PA	Blue Pond	Cherokee	AL
Blairsville	Williamson	IL	Bloomingdale	Vernon	WI	Blue Rapids	Marshall	KS
Blairsville	Possey	IN	Blooming Grove	Franklin	IN	Blue Ridge	Shelby	IN
Blairsville	Indiana	PA	Blooming Grove	Linn	KS	Blue Ridge	Gilmer	GA
Blairsville	York	SC	Blooming Grove	Waseca	MN	Blue Ridge	Harrison	MO
Blair's Wharf	Prince George's	VA	Blooming Grove	Orange	NY	Blue Ridge	Henderson	NC
Blakeley	Scott	MN	Blooming Grove	Pike	PA	Blue Ridge	Botetourt	VA
Blakeley	Kitsap	WA	Blooming Grove	Navarro	TX	Blue River	Grant	WI
Blakely(c.h.)	Early	GA	Blooming Grove	Dane	WI	Blue Rock	Muskingum	OH
Blakely	Stokes	NC	Bloomingport	Randolph	IN	Blue Rock	Chester	PA
Blakesburgh	Wapello	IA	Blooming Prairie	Steele	MN	Blue Spring	Gordon	GA
Blake's Ferry	Randolph	AL	Blooming Rose	Phelps	MO	Blue Springs	Volusia	FL
Blakeville	Black Hawk	IA	Bloomingsburgh	Fulton	IN	Blue Springs	Jackson	MO
Blakeville	Cheshire	NH	Bloomington	Benton	AR	Blue Springs	Gage	NE
Blanche	Lincoln	TN	Bloomington(c.h.)	McLean	IL	Blue Stone	Tazewell	VA
Blanchard	Piscataquis	ME	Bloomington(c.h.)	Monroe	IN	Blue Stores	Columbia	NY
Blanchard	Centre	PA	Bloomington	Alleghany	MD	Blue Sulphur Spr-		
Blanchardville	La Fayegge	WI	Bloomington	Hennepin	MN	ings	Greenbrier	WV
Blanchester	Clinton	OH	Bloomington	Macon	MO	Blue Valley	York	NE
Blanco(c.h.)	Blanco	TX	Bloomington	Clinton	OH	Blue Wing	Granville	NC
Blancoe	Monona	IA	Bloomington	Clearfield	PA	Bluff	Fayette	TX
Bland	Bland	VA	Bloomington	Tipton	TN	Bluff City	Schuyler	IL
Blandinsville	McDonough	IL	Bloomington	Rich	UT	Bluff City	Livingston	MO
Blandon	Berks	PA	Bloomington	Grant	WI	Bluff Creek	Johnson	IN
Blandville	Marshall	KS	Bloomington Ferry	Hennepin	MN	Bluff Dale	Greene	IL
Blandville(c.h.)	Ballard	KY	Bloomsburgh(c.h.)	Columbia	PA	Bluff Point	Jay	IN
Blanford	Hampden	MA	Bloomsburgh	Halifax	VA	Bluff Point	Yates	NY
Blanket Hill	Armstrong	PA	Bloomsbury	Hunterdon	NJ	Bluff Point	Hickman	TN
Blauveltville	Rockland	NY	Bloomsdale	St. Genevieve	MO	Bluff Spring	Clay	AL
Blawenburgh	Somerset	NJ	Bloom Switch	Scioto	OH	Bluff Spring	Talbot	GA
Bleakwood	Newton	TX	Bloomville	Delaware	NY	Bluff Springs	Escambia	FL
Bledsoe	Crittenden	AR	Bloomville	Cumberland	PA	Bluffton	Yell	AR
Blecker	Fulton	NY	Bloomburgh	Tioga	PA	Bluffton(c.h.)	Wells	IN
Blenden	Ottawa	MI	Blossom Hill	Princess Anne	VA	Bluffton	Winneshick	IA
Bliss	Miller	MO	Blossom Prairie	Lamar	TX	Bluffton	Muskegon	MI
Blissfield	Lenawee	MI	Blossvale	Orcida	NY	Bluffton	Montgomery	MO
Blivin's Mills	McHenry	IL	Blount's Ferry	Columbia	FL	Bluffton	Allen	OH
Blockville	Pike	MO	Blountsville(c.h.)	Blount	AL	Bluffton	Beaufort	SC
Blockville	Chautauqua	NY	Blountsville	Henry	IN	Blumfield	Saginaw	MI
Blodget Mills	Cortland	NY	Blountsville(c.h.)	Sullivan	TN	Blumfield Junction	Saginaw	MI
Blodgett	Scott	MO	Blowing Rock	Watauga	NC	Blytheville	Jasper	MO
Blood's Depot	Steuben	NY	Blue Ball	Butler	OH	Boalsburgh	Centre	PA
Bloody Run	Redford	PA	Blue Bank	Rowan	KY	Boardman	Mahoning	OH
Bloom	Cook	IL	Blue Bell	Montgomery	PA	Boardman	St. Croix	WI
Bloom	Wood	OH	Blue Canyon	Placer	CA	Boar's Head	Rockingham	NH
Bloom Centre	Logan	OH	Blue Creek	Franklin	IN	Boatland	Fentress	TN
Bloomer	Sebastian	AR	Blue Creek	Adams	OH	Boaz	Graves	KY
Bloomer Centre	Moncalm	MI	Blue Eagle	Clay	MO	Boaz	Richland	WI
Blomery	Hamspire	WV	Blue Earth City(c.h.)	Faribault	MN	Bodenham	Giles	TN
Bloomfield	Sonoma	CA	Blue Eye	Stone	MO	Bodinesville	Lycoming	PA
Bloomfield	Hartford	CN	Blue Grass	Vermilion	IL	Body Camp	Bedford	VA
Bloomfield	Edgar	IL	Blue Grass	Fulton	IN	Boerne(c.h.)	Kendall	TX

PLACE	COUNTY	STATE	PLACE	COUNTY	STATE	PLACE	COUNTY	STATE
Boeuf Creek	Franklin	MO	Bono	Lawrence	IN	Botland	Nelson	KY
Bogard	Henry	MO	Bono	Washington	NE	Bouckville	Madison	NY
Boggstown	Shelby	IN	Bonsack's	Roanoke	VA	Bouknight's Ferry	Edgefield	SC
Boggsville	Roane	WV	Bontear	St. Francois	ME	Boulder(c.h.)	Boulder	CO
Boggy Depot	Choctaw N	IT	Bonus	Boone	IL	Boulder	Jefferson	MT
Bogue	Columbus	NC	Bonwell	Edgar	IL	Boulder Valley	Jefferson	MT
Bogue Chitto	Lincoln	MS	Boody	Macon	IL	Boundry	Jay	IN
Bohemia	La Crosse	WI	Booker's Mills	Tyler	WV	Boundbrook	Somerset	NJ
Bohon	Mercer	KY	Boone	Boone	AR	Bounty Land	Oconee	SC
Boiceville	Ulster	NY	Boone	Dallas	IA	Bourbon	Douglas	IL
Boiling Springs	Cumberland	PA	Boone(c.h.)	Watauga	NC	Bourbon	Marshall	IN
Boilston	Henderson	NC	Boone	Jasper	IL	Bourbon	Crawford	MO
Bois Brule	Perry	MO	Boone Furnace	Carter	KY	Bourbonnais Grove	Kankakee	IL
Bois D' Arc	Greene	MO	Boonesbrough(c.h.)	Boone	IA	Bourneville	Ross	OH
Bois City(c.h.)	Ada	ID	Boonsborough	Howard	MO	Bouser	Blackford	IN
Boistfort	Lewis	WA	Boonesborough	Uyalde	TX	Boutonville	Westchester	NY
Boke's Creek	Union	OH	Boone's Ferry	Tyler	TX	Boutte	St. Charles	IA
Boland's	Itawamba	MS	Booneville	Saber	AR	Bovina	Tama	IA
Bolckow	Andrew	MO	Booneville	Pueblo	CO	Bonvina	Warren	MS
Bold Spring	Franklin	GA	Booneville	Dallas	IA	Bonvina	Delaware	NY
Bold Spring	McLennan	TX	Booneville(c.h.)	Owsley	KY	Boniva Valley	Delaware	NY
Boles	Scott	AR	Booneville(c.h.)	Prentiss	MS	Boniva	Gibson	IN
Boles	Franklin	MO	Booneville	Yadkin	NC	Bovine	Gibson	IN
Bolesville	Pope	AR	Booneville	Clinton	PA	Bow	Merrimack	NH
Boligee	Greene	AL	Booneville	Lincoln	TN	Bowdoin	Sagadahoc	ME
Bolinas	Marin	CA	Boon Grove	Porter	IN	Bowdoin Centre	Sagadahoc	ME
Bolington	Loudoun	VA	Boon Hill	Johnston	NC	Bowdoinham	Sagadahoc	ME
Bolivar	Frederick	MD	Boonsborough	Washington	AR	Bowdon	Carroll	GA
Bolivar	Bolivar	MS	Boonsborough	Washington	MD	Bowdon	Cumberland	IL
Bolivar(c.h.)	Polk	MO	Boon's Creek	Washington	TN	Bowdon	Grenada	MS
Bolivar	Allegany	NY	Boon Spring	Clinton	IA	Bowensburgh	Hancock	IL
Bolivar	Tuscarawas	OH	Boonton	Morris	NJ	Bowen's Corners	Oswego	NY
Bolivar	Westmoreland	PA	Boonville(c.h.)	Warrick	IN	Bowen's Mills	Lawrence	MO
Bolivar	Hardman	TN	Boonville(c.h.)	Cooper	MO	Bowen's Prairie	Jones	IA
Bolling's Landing	Buckingham	VA	Boonville	Oneida	NY	Bowen Station	Kent	MI
Bolster's Mills	Cumberland	ME	Boot	Richland	IL	Bowenville	Carroll	GA
Bolton	Tolland	CN	Booth Bay	Lincoln	ME	Bowenville	Fauquier	VT
Bolton	Worcester	MS	Boothby Hill	Harford	MD	Bower	Clearfield	PA
Bolton	Harrison	NO	Booth Corner	Delaware	PA	Bower Hill	Washington	PA
Bolton	Warren	NY	Boothsville	Marion	WV	Bower's City	Carroll	ME
Bolton	Brunswick	NC	Bordertown	Burlington	NJ	Bower's Mills	Lawrence	MO
Bolton	Chittenden	VT	Border Plains	Webster	IA	Bower's Station	Berks	PA
Bolton's Depot	Hinds	MS	Bordley	Union	KY	Bowerston	Harrison	OH
Boltonville	Cobb	GA	Bordoville	Franklin	VT	Bowersville	Hart	GA
Boltonville	Iowa	IA	Borodino	Onondage	NY	Bowersville	Greene	OH
Boltonville	Orange	VT	Boscawen	Merrimack	NH	Bowerville	Jefferson	NE
Boltonville	Washington	WI	Boscobel	Westchester	NY	Bowling	Leon	TX
Bolt's Fork	Boyd	KY	Boscobel	Grant	WI	Bowling Brook	St. Genevieve	MO
Bomon's Bluff	Henderson	NC	Bosqueville	McLennan	TX	Bowling Green	Fayette	IL
Bombay	Franklin	NY	Bossardsville	Monroe	PA	Bowling Green(c.h.)	Clay	In
Bon Accord	Johnston	IA	Bostick	Jefferson	GA	Bowling Green(c.h.)	Warren	KY
Bonaparte	Van Buren	IA	Bostick's Mills	Richmond	NC	Bowling Green(c.h.)	Pike	MO
Bon Aqua	Hickman	TN	Boston	Thomas	GA	Bowling Green	Wood	OH
Bon Aqua	Franklin	VA	Boston	Wayne	IN	Bowling Green(c.h.)	Caroline	VA
Bonbrook	Franklin	WI	Boston	Howard	KS	Bowlusville	Clark	OH
Bonchea	St. Croix	WI	Boston	Nelson	KY	Bowman's Creek	Wyoming	PA
Bond's Station	Shelby	TN	Boston(c.h.)	Suffolk	MA	Bowmansville	Erie	NY
Bond's Village	Hampden	MA	Boston	Erie	NY	Bowmansville	Lancaster	PA
Bonduel	Shawanaw	WI	Boston	Allegheny	PA	Bowne	Kent	MI
Bondville	Bennington	VT	Boston	Bowie	TX	Boxborough	Middlesex	MA
Bone Camp	Madison	NC	Boston	Culpeper	VA	Boxford	Essex	MA
Bone Cave	Van Buren	TN	Boston Corner	Columbia	NY	Boxford	De Kalb	MO
Bone Creek	Ritchie	WV	Boston Mills	Linn	OR	Boxley	Appling	GA
Bone Gap	Edwards	IL	Boston Station	Pendleton	KY	Boxley	Hamilton	IN
Bonfil's Station	St. Louis	MO	Boston Store	Montgomery	IN	Box Spring	Talbot	GA
Bonham(c.h.)	Fannin	TX	Bost's Mills	Cabarrus	NC	Boxville	Union	KY
Bonhamme(c.h.)	Bonhamme	DA	Bostwick Lake	Kent	MI	Boyd	Dallas	MO
Bonn	Washington	OH	Boswell	Benton	IN	Boyd Lake	Piscantaquis	ME
Bonneau's Depot	Charleston	SC	Boswell	Mahoning	OH	Boyd's Corner	Putnam	NY
Bonner	Jackson	LA	Boswell	Fluvanna	VA	Boyd's Landing	Hardin	TN
Bonnet Carre	St. John Baptist	LA	Boswel's	Shelby	IA	Boyd's Mill	Wise	TX
Bonnie Brook	Butler	PA	Botany	Jefferson	IA	Boyd's Mills	Kosciusko	IN
Bonny Eagle	Cumberland	ME	Botavia	Roanoke	VA	Boyd's Station	Harrison	KY
Bono	Douglas	IL	Botetourt Springs					

PLACE NAMES OF THE UNITED STATES

PLACE	COUNTY	STATE	PLACE	COUNTY	STATE	PLACE	COUNTY	STATE
Boyd's Switch	Jackson	AL	Branch's Store	Duplin	NC	Brentwood	Rockingham	NH
Boydston's Mills	Kosciusko	IN	Branchville	St. Clair	AL	Brentwood	Suffolk	NY
Boydsville	Graves	KY	Branchville	Lincoln	AR	Brentwood	Williamson	TN
Boydton(c.h.)	Mecklenburgh	VA	Branchville	Prince George's	MD	Breslan	Suffolk	NY
Boyer River	Crawford	IA	Branchville	Linn	MO	Bretzville	Dubois	IN
Boyerstown	Becks	PA	Branchville	Sussex	NJ	Brevard(c.h.)	Transylvania	NC
Boykin's Depot	Southampton	VA	Branchville	Orangeburgh	SC	Brewer	Penobscot	ME
Boylan's Grove	Butler	IA	Branchville	Southampton	VA	Brewer's Mills	Marshall	KY
Boyler's Mill	Morgan	MO	Brandenburgh(c.h.)	Meade	KY	Brewersville	Jennings	IN
Boyleston	Henry	IA	Brandon	De Kalb	AL	Brewerton	Onondaga	NY
Boyleston Station	Norfolk	MS	Brandon	Buchanan	IA	Brewerton	Laurens	SC
Boylston	Worcester	MS	Brandon	Oakland	MI	Brewer Village	Penobscot	ME
Boylston Centre	Worcester	MS	Brandon	Douglas	MN	Brewerville	Randolph	IL
Boylston Centre	Oswego	NY	Brandon(c.h.)	Rankin	MS	Brewster	Barnstable	MA
Boyne	Charlevoix	MI	Brandon	Knox	OH	Brewster's Station	Putnam	NY
Boynton	Tazewell	IL	Brandon	Rutland	VT	Brewton	Escambia	AL
Bozeman(c.h.)	Gallatin	MT	Brandon	Prince George	VA	Brick Church	Guilford	NC
Bozrah	New London	CN	Brandon	Fond du Lac	WI	Brick Church	Giles	TN
Bozrahville	New London	CN	Brandon Church	Prince George	VA	Brickerville	Lancaster	PA
Braceville	Grundy	IL	Brandonville	Schuylkill	PA	Brickland	Lunenburgh	VA
Braceville	Trumbull	OH	Brandonville	Preston	WV	Brick Meeting		
Bracken	Huntington	IN	Brandt	Miami	OH	House	Cecil	MD
Brackney	Susquehanna	PA	Brandtwood	Starke	IN	Brick Mill	Blount	TN
Braddock's Field	Allegheny	PA	Brandy Camp	Elk	PA	Bricksburgh	Ocean	NJ
Braddyville	Page	IA	Brandy Station	Culpeper	VA	Bricksville	Merced	CA
Braden's Knobs	Bledsoe	TN	Brandywine	Prince George's	MD	Bridgeborough	Burlington	NJ
Braden Station	Fayette	TN	Brandywine Manor	Chester	PA	Bridge Creek	Carroll	MO
Bradenville	Westmoreland	PA	Brandywine Summit	Delaware	PA	Bridge Creek	Wasco	OR
Bradford	Coosa	AL	Branford	New Haven	CN	Bridgehampton	Suffolk	NY
Bradford	Stark	IL	Branson	San Diege	CA	Bridgeport	Jackson	AL
Bradford	Harrison	IN	Brant	Erie	NY	Bridgeport(c.h.)	Mono	CA
Bradford	Chickasaw	IA	Brant	Calumet	WI	Bridgeport	Fairfield	CN
Bradford	Bracken	KY	Brantford	Washington	KS	Bridgeport	Lawrence	IL
Bradford	Penobscot	ME	Brantford	Sherburne	MN	Bridgeport	Marion	IN
Bradford	Essex	MS	Brantingham	Lewis	NY	Bridgeport	Jackson	IA
Bradford	Merrimack	NH	Brashear	St. Mary's	LA	Bridgeport	Franklin	KY
Bradford	Steuben	NY	Brasher Falls	St. Lawrence	NY	Bridgeport	Frederick	MD
Bradford	Miami	OH	Brassfield	Wake	NC	Bridgeport	Warren	MO
Bradford	McKean	PA	Brasstown	Cherokee	NC	Bridgeport	Gloucester	NJ
Bradford	Orange	VT	Bratsberg	Fillmore	MN	Bridgeport	Madison	NY
Bradford Centre	Orange	VT	Brattleborough	Windham	VT	Bridgeport	Belmont	OH
Bradford Springs	Sumter	SC	Bratton	Nemaha	NE	Bridgeport	Polk	OR
Bradfordsville	Marion	KY	Bratton's Mills	Robertson	KY	Bridgeport	Montgomery	PA
Bradley	Lincoln	AR	Brattonsville	Armstrong	PA	Bridgeport	Cocke	TN
Bradley	Jackson	IL	Braxton	Braxton	WV	Bridgeport	Harrison	WV
Bradley	Allegan	MI	Bray's Mills	Bartholomew	IN	Bridgeport	Crawford	WI
Bradleyville	Taney	MO	Brazil	Clay	IN	Bridgeport Centre	Saginaw	MI
Bradrickville	Lawrence	OH	Brazito	Cole	MO	Bridgeton	Parke	IN
Bradshaw	Giles	TN	Brazoria(c.h.)	Brazoria	TX	Bridgeton(c.h.)	Cumberland	ME
Bradtville	Grant	WI	Brazos Santiago	Cameron	TX	Bridgeton	Newaygo	MI
Brady	Kalamazoo	MI	Breakabeen	Schoharie	NY	Bridgeton	Cumberland	NJ
Brady	Indiana	PA	Breakneck	Butler	PA	Bridgetown	Caroline	MD
Brady's	Richland	WI	Breathedsville	Washington	MD	Bridge Valley	Bucks	PA
Brady's Bend	Armstrong	PA	Breaux Bridge	St. Mattin's	LA	Bridgeville	Pickens	AL
Bradyville	Adams	OH	Breckinridge(c.h.)	Summit	CO	Bridgeville	Sussex	DE
Bradyville	Cannon	TN	Breckinridge	Caldwell	MO	Bridgeville	Gratiot	MI
Brafford's Store	Knox	KY	Breckinridge	Vernon	WI	Bridgeville	Warren	NJ
Braggs	Lowndes	AL	Breckville	Madison	MS	Bridgeville	Sullivan	NY
Braggville	Middlesex	MS	Bredinsburg	Venango	PA	Bridgeville	Mushingum	OH
Braidwood	Will	IL	Breeding's	Adair	KY	Bridgeville	Litchfield	CN
Brainard's	Warren	NJ	Breedsville	Van Buren	MI	Bridgewater	Arroostock	ME
Brainerd	Crow Wing	MN	Breese	Greene	IL	Bridgewater	Plymouth	MA
Brainerd	Rensselaer	NY	Breesport	Chemung	NY	Bridgewater	Washtenaw	MI
Braintree	Norfolk	MS	Breinigsville	Lehigh	PA	Bridgewater	Nodaway	MO
Braintree	Orange	VT	Bremen	Randolph	IL	Bridgewater	Grafton	NH
Braman's Corners	Schenectady	NY	Bremen	Marshall	IN	Bridgewater	Oneida	NY
Bramlette	Gallatin	KY	Bremen	Muhlenburgh	KY	Bridgewater	Burke	NC
Branch	Paulding	GA	Bremen	Fairfield	OH	Bridgewater	Williams	OH
Branch	Manitowoe	WI	Brenford	Kent	DE	Bridgewater	Bucks	PA
Branch Dale	Schuylkill	PA	Brenham(c.h.)	Washington	TX	Bridgewater	Windsor	VT
Branch Junction	Westmoreland	PA	Brenner	Doniphan	KS	Bridgewater	Rockingham	VA
Branchport	Yates	NY	Brentsville	Prince William	VA	Bridle Creek	Grayson	VA
Branch Store	Monomouth	NJ	Brentwood	Appling	GA	Bridport	Addison	VT

PLACE NAMES OF THE UNITED STATES

PLACE	COUNTY	STATE	PLACE	COUNTY	STATE	PLACE	COUNTY	STATE
Briensburgh	Marshall	KY	Broad Ripple	Marion	IN	Brooklyn	Susquehanna	PA
Brier Creek	Columbia	PA	Broad Run	Frederick	MD	Brooklyn	Halifax	VA
Briggsville	Luzerne	PA	Broad Run Station	Fanquier	VA	Brooklyn	Green	WI
Briggsville	Marquette	WI	Broad Shoals	Polk	TN	Brooklyn Village	Guyahoga	OH
Brigham City(c.h.)	Box Elder	UT	Broad Top	Huntington	PA	Brook Neal	Campbell	VA
Bright	Dearborn	IN	Broadway	Warren	NJ	Brooks	Adams	IA
Brighton	Sacramento	CA	Broadway	Union	OH	Brooks	Waldo	ME
Brighton	Maconpin	IL	Broadway Depot	Rockingham	VA	Brooks	Marion	OR
Brighton	La Grange	IN	Broadwell	Logan	IL	Brooks' Grove	Livingston	NY
Brighton	Washington	IA	Broadwell	Harrison	KY	Brookside	Osceola	MI
Brighton	Somerset	ME	Brock	Darke	OH	Brookside	Morris	NJ
Brighton	Montgomery	MD	Brockett's Bridge	Fulton	NY	Brookside	Oconto	WI
Brighton	Middlesex	MA	Brocktown	Pike	AR	Brook's Side	Fayette	GA
Brighton	Livingston	MI	Brockway	St. Clair	MI	Brookston	White	IN
Brighton	Polk	MO	Brockway	Stearns	MN	Brookston	Warren	NC
Brighton	Monroe	NY	Brockway Centre	St. Clair	MI	Brooks' Vale	New Haven	CN
Brighton	Lorain	OH	Brockway's Mills	Piscrataquis	ME	Brooksville	Blount	AL
Brighton	Beaufort	SC	Brockwayville	Jefferson	PA	Brooksville(c.h.)	Hernando	FL
Brighton	Kenosha	WI	Brocton	Chautauqua	NY	Brooksville	Addison	VT
Brighton Station	Lincoln	TN	Brodbecks	York	PA	Brook Vale	Prince William	VA
Bright Star	Lafayette	AR	Brodhead	Allgheny	PA	Brookville	Ogle	IL
Bright Star	Hopkins	TX	Brodhead	Green	WI	Brookville(c.h.)	Franklin	IN
Brightwood	Washington	DC	Brodheadsville	Monroe	PA	Brookville	Jefferson	IA
Brillion	Calumet	WI	Brodie's Landing	Decatur	TN	Brookville	Saline	KS
Brimfield	Peoria	IL	Broken Arrow	St. Clair	AL	Brookville(c.h.)	Bracken	KY
Brimfield	Noble	IN	Brokenburgh	Spottsylvanie	VA	Brookville	Montgomery	MD
Brimfield	Hampden	MA	Broken Kettle	Plymouth	IA	Brookville(c.h.)	Jefferson	PA
Brimfield	Portage	OH	Broken Straw	Chautaqua	NY	Brookville	St. Croix	WI
Brindletown	Burke	NC	Broken Sword	Crawford	OH	Broomall	Delaware	PA
Brinkerton	Clarion	PA	Bronson	Levy	FL	Broome Centre	Schoharie	NY
Brinkley	Monroe	AR	Bronson	Branch	MI	Broomtown	Cherokee	AL
Brinkleyville	Halifax	NC	Bronson's Prairie	Ranch	MI	Brosley	Cass	MO
Brinley's Station	Preble	OH	Bronxville	Westchester	NY	Botherton	St. Louis	MO
Brinsonville	Burke	GA	Brook	Newton	IN	Bothertown	Calumet	WI
Brinton	Champaign	OH	Brookdale(c.h.)	Rice	KS	Botzmanville	Warren	WI
Brinton	Alleheny	PA	Brookdale	Susquehanna	PA	Brower	Berks	PA
Briscoe	Sullivan	NY	Brookeland	Sabine	TX	Bower's MIlls	Randolph	NC
Bristersburg	Fauquier	VA	Brookfield	Fairfield	CN	Browne Hill	Wythe	VA
Bristoe Station	Prince William	VA	Brookfield	Shelby	IN	Brownfield	Oxford	ME
Bristol	Hartford	CN	Brookfield	Clinton	IA	Brownhelm	Lorain	OH
Bristol(c.h.)	Liberty	FL	Brookfield	Worcester	MA	Brown Hill	Crawford	PA
Bristol	Kendall	IL	Brookfield	Eaton	MI	Browning	Schuyler	IL
Bristol	Elkhart	In	Brookfield	Linn	MO	Browning	Carroll	IA
Bristol	Worth	IA	Brookfield	Carroll	NH	Browningsville	Bracken	KY
Bristol	Lincoln	ME	Brookfield	Madison	NY	Browington	Butler	PA
Bristol	Anne Arundel	MD	Brookfield	Trumbull	OH	Brownington	Orleans	VT
Bristol	Grafton	NH	Brookfield	Tioga	PA	Brownlow	Butler	KS
Bristol	Ontario	NY	Brookfield	Orange	VT	Brown Rock	Washington	KS
Bristol	Morgan	OH	Brookfield Centre	Fairfield	CN	Brownsborough	Madison	AL
Bristol	Bucks	PA	Brookfield Centre	Wankesha	WI	Brownsborough	Oldham	KY
Bristol(c.h.)	Bristol	RI	Brookhaven(c.h.)	Lincoln	MS	Brownsborough	Washington	TN
Bristol	Sullivan	TN	Brookhaven	Suffolk	NY	Brownsburgh	Rockbridge	VA
Bristol	Addison	VT	Brookland	Pottor	PA	Brown's Church	Cumberland	VA
Bristol	Kenosha	WI	Brooklandville	Baltimore	MD	Brown's Corners	Huntington	IN
Bristol Centre	Ontario	NY	Brooklin	Hancock	ME	Brown's Cove	Albemarle	VA
Bristol Station	Kendall	IL	Brookline	Jackson	LA	Brown's Creek	Harrison	WV
Bristolville	Trumbull	OH	Brookline	Norfolk	MS	Brownsdale	Mower	MN
Bristoria	Green	PA	Brookline	Hillsborough	NH	Brownsdale	Butler	PA
Bristow Station	Warren	KY	Brookline Station	Greene	MO	Brown's Landing	Butler	KY
British Hollow	Grant	WI	Brooklyn	Conecuh	AL	Brown's Mills	Davis	IA
Brittain	Rutherford	NC	Brooklyn	Alameda	CA	Brown's Mills	Muskegon	MI
Brittian's	Polaski	MO	Brooklyn(c.h.)	Windham	CN	Brown's Mills	Burlington	NJ
Britton	Woodruff	AR	Brooklyn	Schuyler	IL	Brown's Mills	Washington	OH
Britton's Neck	Marion	SC	Brooklyn	Morgan	IN	Brown's Mills	Franklin	PA
Britt's Landing	Perry	TN	Brooklyn	Poweshiek	IA	Brownsport Furnace	Decatur	TN
Broadallin	Fullton	NY	Brooklyn	Linn	KS	Brown's Station	Preble	OH
Broad Axe	Montgomery	PA	Brooklyn	Butler	KY	Brown's Store	Northumberland	VA
Broad Brook	Hartford	CN	Brooklyn	Anne Arndel	MD	Brown's Summit	Guilford	NC
Broad Creek	Queen Anne	MD	Brooklyn	Jackson	MI	Brownstown	Fayette	IL
Broad Creek Neck	Talbot	MD	Brooklyn	Hennepin	MN	Brownstown(c.h.)	Jackson	IN
Broad Ford	Fayette	PA	Brooklyn	Harrison	MO	Brownstown	Wayne	MI
Broadford	Smyth	VA	Brooklyn	Kings	NY	Brown's Valley	Montgomery	IN
Broad Mountian	Schuylikill	PA	Brooklyn	Cuyahoga	OH	Brown's Valley	Montgomery	IN

PLACE NAMES OF THE UNITED STATES

PLACE	COUNTY	STATE	PLACE	COUNTY	STATE	PLACE	COUNTY	STATE
Brownsville	Yuba	CA	Bryan(c.h.)	Williams	OH	Buck's Grove	Jackson	KS
Brownsville	Clear Creek	CO	Bryan(c.h.)	Brazos	TX	Buck Shoal	Halifax	VT
Brownsville	Paulding	GA	Bryan	Unintah	WY	Buckskin	Park	CO
Brownsville	Union	IN	Bryansville	York	PA	Buckskin	Gibson	IN
Brownsville(c.h.)	Edmonson	KY	Bryant	Fulton	IL	Buck's Mills	Hancock	ME
Brownsville	Piscataquis	ME	Bryant	Clinton	IA	Bucksport	Hancock	ME
Brownsville	Washington	MD	Bryant	Jefferson	NE	Bucksport Centre	Hancock	ME
Brownsville	Cass	MI	Bryantown	Charles	MD	Buck's Ranch	Plumas	CA
Brownsville	Houston	MN	Bryantsburgh	Jefferson	IN	Buckstown	Somerset	PA
Brownsville	Saline	MO	Bryant's Creek	Monroe	IN	Bucksville	Bucks	PA
Brownsville	Granville	NC	Bryant's Pond	Oxford	ME	Bucksville	Horry	SC
Brownsville	Licking	OH	Bryants's Station	Milam	TX	Buckton	Warren	VT
Brownsville	Linn	OR	Bucatunna	Wayne	MS	Buck Valley	Fulton	PA
Brownsville	Fayette	PA	Buchanan(c.h.)	Haralson	GA	Bucyrus	Lucas	IA
Brownsville	Marlborough	SC	Buchanan	Lawrence	KY	Bucyrus(c.h.)	Crawford	OH
Brownsville(c.h.)	Haywood	TN	Buchanan	Barrien	MI	Buda	Bureau	IL
Brownsville(c.h.)	Cameron	TX	Buchanan	Bollinger	MO	Budd's Creek	St. Mary's	MD
Brownsville	Windsor	VT	Buchanan	Granville	NC	Budd Town	Burlington	NJ
Browntown	Bradford	PA	Buchanan	Perry	OH	Buddville	Centre	PA
Brownville	Mitchell	IA	Buchanan	Allegheny	PA	Buel	Sanilac	MI
Brownville(c.h.)	Nemaha	NE	Buchanan	Botetourt	VA	Buel	Montgomery	NY
Brownville	Jefferson	NY	Butchtel	Isabella	MI	Buena	Van Wert	OH
Brownwood(c.h.)	Brown	TX	Buck	Lancaster	PA	Buena Vista	Amador	CA
Bruce	Barren	KY	Buck Branch	Jasper	MO	Buena Vista(c.h.)	Marion	GA
Bruceport	Chehalis	WA	Buck Creek	Bremer	IA	Buena Vista	Stephenson	IL
Bruce's Lake	Fulton	IN	Buck Creek	Greene	MS	Buena Vista	Clinton	IA
Brucston Mills	Preston	WV	Buck Creek	Richland	WI	Buena Vista	Prince George's	MD
Bruceville	Bullock	AL	Buck Eye	Yolo	CA	Buena Vista	Saginaw	MI
Bruceville	La Salle	IL	Buckeye	Garrard	KY	Buena Vista	Chickasaw	MS
Bruceville	Knox	IN	Buckeye Cottage	Perry	OH	Buena Vista	Steuben	NY
Bruceville	Carroll	MD	Buckeye Cove	Pocahontas	WV	Buena Vista	Duplin	NC
Bruin	Butler	PA	Buckeystown	Frederick	MD	Buena Vista	Tascarawas	OH
Bruin	Carter	KY	Buckfield	Oxford	ME	Buena Vista	Polk	OR
Bruington	King and Queen	VA	Buckannon(c.h.)	Upshur	WV	Buena Vista	Allegheny	PA
Bruin's Cross Roads	Parke	IN	Buck Head	Morgan	GA	Buena Vista	Greenville	SC
Brule River	Lake	MN	Buck Head	Fairfield	SC	Buena Vista	Carroll	TN
Brumfield Station	Boyle	KY	Buck Hollow	Franklin	VT	Buena Vista	Shelby	TX
Brumfieldville	Berks	PA	Buck Horn	Independence	AR	Buena Vista	Portage	WI
Brumley	Miller	MO	Buck Horn	Brown	IL	Buffalo	Sangamon	IL
Brunersburgh	Defiance	OH	Buck Horn	Mohaska	IA	Buffalo	Scott	IA
Brunnerville	Lancaster	PA	Buck Horn	Ohio	KY	Buffalo	Wilson	KS
Bruno	Monrgomery	KS	Buck Horn	Pendleton	WV	Buffalo	La Rue	KY
Brunot	Wayne	MO	Buckhorn	Webster	LA	Buffalo(c.h.)	Wright	MN
Brunswick(c.h.)	Glynn	GA	Buckhorn	Winston	MS	Buffalo	Dallas	MO
Brunswick	Peoria	IL	Buckhorn	Columbia	PA	Buffalo	Erie	NY
Brunswick	Lake	IN	Buckhorn	Nansemond	VA	Buffalo	Guernsey	OH
Brunswick	Cumberland	ME	Buckhorn	Adams	WI	Buffalo	Washington	PA
Brunswick	Kanabec	MN	Buckingham	Hartford	CN	Buffalo	Humphreys	TN
Brunswick	Chariton	MO	Buckingham	Tama	IA	Buffalo	Putnam	WV
Brunswick	Medina	OH	Buckingham	Bucks	PA	Buffalo	Putnam	WV
Brunswick	Essex	VT	Buckingham(c.h.)	Buckingham	VA	Buffalo	Buffalo	WI
Brush Creek	Perry	AL	Buckinn	Madison	IL	Buffalo Bluff	Putnam	FL
Brush Creek	Butte	CA	Buckland	Hartford	CN	Buffalo Cross Roads	Union	PA
Brush Creek	Fayette	IA	Buckland	Franklin	MA	Buffalo Ford	Randolph	NC
Brush Creek	Laclede	ME	Buckland	Gates	NC	Buffalo Forge	Rickbridge	VA
Brush Creek	Muskingum	OH	Buckland	Prince William	VA	Buffalo Fork	Kossuth	IA
Brush Creek	Beaver	PA	Buckley	Iroquois	IL	Buffalo Gap	Augusta	VA
Brushey	Choctaw Nation	IT	Buckley	Highland	OH	Buffalo Grove	Buchanan	IA
Brushland	Delaware	NY	Bucklin	Linn	MO	Buffalo Mills	Bedford	PA
Brush Prairie	McLeod	MN	Buckland	Hartford	CN	Buffalo Mills	Rockbridge	VA
Brush Prairie	Clark	WA	Buckland	Franklin	MA	Buffalo Paper Mill	Cleveland	NC
Brush Ran	Washington	PA	Buckland	Gates	NC	Buffalo Plains	Erie	NY
Bush's Mills	Franklin	NY	Buckland	Prince Williams	GA	Buffalo Pond	Washington	VA
Bush Valley	Indiana	PA	Buckley	Iroquois	IL	Buffalo Prairie	Rock Island	IL
Bushville	Bradford	PA	Buckley	Highland	OH	Buffalo Ridge	Washington	VA
Bushville	Wanshara	WI	Bucklin	Linn	MO	Buffalo Run	Centre	PA
Bushy Creek	Anderson	SC	Buckluxy	Choctaw Nation	IT	Buffalo Shoals	Wayne	WV
Bushy Fork	Douglas	IL	Buckinanville	Bucks	PA	Buffalo Valley	Putnam	TN
Bushy Prairie	La Grange	IN	Buck Mountain	Carbeu	PA	Buffaloville	Spencer	IN
Bushy Run	Pendleton	WV	Buckner's Station	Oldham	KY	Buford	Macoupin	IL
Busssels	Door	WI	Buckner's Station	Louisa	VA	Buford	Ohio	KY
Bruynswick	Ulster	NY	Buck Ridge	Tensas	LA	Buford	Highland	OH
Bryan	Saline	MO	Buck's	Columbiana	OH	Buford's	Bedford	VA

PLACE NAMES OF THE UNITED STATES

PLACE	COUNTY	STATE
Buford's Bridge	Barnwell	SC
Buford's Station	Giles	TN
Buhlsville	Gentry	MO
Bula	Goonhland	VA
Bulger	Washington	PA
Bullard's	Twiggs	GA
Bull City	Osborne	KS
Bull Creek	Georgetown	SC
Bull Creek	Wood	WV
Bullion	Elko	NV
Bullion(c.h.)	PiUte	UT
Bulliona	Alpine	CA
Bullitsville	Boone	KY
Bullock	Crenshaw	AL
Bullock Creek	Yoirk	SC
Bull Run	Knox	TN
Bull's Gap	Hawkins	TN
Bull's Head	Dutchess	NY
Bull's Mills	Christian	MO
Bulltown	Braxton	WV
Bullville	Orange	NY
Bumpass	Louisa	VA
Bunceton	Cooper	MO
Buncomb	Brown	KS
Buncombe	Pettis	MO
Buncombe	Union	MS
Buncombe	Johnson	IL
Bundy's Crossing	Oswego	NY
Bunker Hill	Macoupin	IL
Bunker Hill	Miami	IN
Bunker Hill	Lyon	KS
Bunker Hill	Russell	KS
Bunker Hill	Ingham	MI
Bunker Hill	Lewis	MO
Bunker Hill	Giles	TN
Bunker Hill	Bedford	VA
Bunker Hill	Grant	WI
Bunner's	Marion	WV
Bunn's Bluff	Orange	TX
Buras	Plaquemines	LA
Burbank	Kandiyohi	MN
Burbank	Wayne	OH
Burbois	Gasconade	MO
Burch's	Kent	MI
Burdett	Bates	MO
Burdett	Schuyler	NY
Burdick	Porter	IN
Burdickville	Leelenaw	MI
Bureau Junction	Bureau	IL
Burem's Store	Hawkin's	TN
Burford's Landing	Wilcox	AL
Bufordville	Cape Girardeau	MO
Bugaw Depot	New Hanover	NC
Burgess	Clinton	IA
Burgess	Dinwiddie	VA
Burget's Corner	Clinton	IN
Burgettstown	Washington	PA
Burgettsville	Shasta	CA
Burgh Hill	Trumbull	OH
Burk	Benton	OA
Burke	Caledonia	VT
Burke	Caledonia	VT
Burke's Garden	Tazewell	VA
Burke's Mills	Agusta	VA
Burkesville(c.h.)	Cumberland	KY
Burkesville	Nottaway	VA
Burkettville	Frederick	MD
Burkeville	Hempstead	AR
Burkeville	Newton	TX
Burk's Station	Fairfax	VA
Burksville	Monroe	IL
Burleson	Franklin	AL
Burlingame(c.h.)	Osage	KS
Burlingham	Sullivan	NY
Burlingham	Meigs	OH
Burlington	Hartford	CN
Burlington	Kane	IL
Burlington	Boone	AR
Burlington	Boulder	CO
Burlington	Carroll	IN
Burlington(c.h.)	Des Moines	IA
Burlington(c.h.)	Coffey	KS
Burlington(c.h.)	Boone	KY
Burlington	East Baton Rouge	LA
Burlington	Penobscot	ME
Burlington	Middlesex	MS
Burlington	Calhoun	MI
Burlington	Boone	MO
Burlington	Burlington	NJ
Burlington	Otsego	NY
Burlington	Lawrence	OH
Burlington	Bradford	PA
Burlington(c.h.)	Chittenden	VT
Burlington	Mineral	WV
Burlington	Racine	WI
Burlington Flats	Otsego	NY
Burnersville	Barbour	WV
Burnet(c.h.)	Burnet	TX
Burnett	Santa Clara	CA
Burnett	Vigo	IN
Burnett	Dodge	WI
Burnett's Creek	White	IN
Burnett Station	Dodge	WI
Burnettsville	Somerset	MD
Burney's Mills	Randolph	NC
Burnhamsville	Todd	MN
Burnham Village	Waldo	ME
Burning Springs	Wirt	WV
Burnip's Corner	Allegan	MI
Burns	Henry	IL
Burns	Shiawassee	MI
Burns	Allegany	NY
Burns	La Crosse	WI
Burnside	Hartford	CN
Burnside	Hancock	IL
Burnside	Clinton	IN
Burnside	Lapeer	MI
Burnside	Orange	NY
Burnside	Clearfield	PA
Burnside	Buffalo	WI
Burns' Mills	Bedford	PA
Burns' Station	Dickson	TN
Burnsville	Dallas	AL
Burnsville	Bartholomew	IN
Burnsville	Tishemingo	MS
Burnsville(c.h.)	Yancey	NC
Burnt Cabins	Fulton	PA
Burnt Chimney	Rutherford	NC
Burnt Corn	Monroe	AL
Burnt Hills	Saratoga	NY
Burnt Ordinary	James City	VA
Burnt Prairie	White	IL
Burnt Ranch	Trinity	CA
Burntville	Brunswick	VA
Burr	Vernon	WI
Burrageville	Worcester	MA
Burrell	Westmoreland	PA
Burrillville	Providence	RI
Burritt	Winnebago	IL
Burr Oak	winneshick	IA
Burr Oak	Jewell	KS
Burr Oak	Otoe	NE
Burr Oak	La Crosse	WI
Burrows	Carroll	IN
Burr's Mills	Jefferson	NY
Burrsville	Caroline	MD
Bursonville	Bucks	PA
Burton	Adams	IL
Burton	Geauga	OH
Burton	Washington	TX
Burton	Wetzel	WV
Burton	Grant	WI
Burtonsville	Montgomery	NY
Burtville	Pottor	PA
Burwood	San Joaaquin	CA
Busaco	Miami	IN
Bushberg	Jefferson	MO
Bush Hill	Randolph	NC
Bushkill	Pike	PA
Bushnell	McDonough	IL
Bushnell Centre	Montcalm	MI
Bushnell's Basin	Monroe	NY
Bushnellville	Greene	NY
Bush's Mill	Gallia	OH
Bush's Store	Laurel	KY
Bushville	Sullivan	NY
Bushy Fork	Person	NC
Businessburgh	Belmont	OH
Buskirk's Bridge	Washington	NY
Busseron	Knox	IN
Busseyville	Jefferson	WI
Busti	Howard	IA
Busti	Chautauqua	NY
Bustleton	Philadelphia	PA
Butcher Ranch	Placer	CA
Butler(c.h.)	Choctaw	AL
Butler(c.h.)	Taylor	GA
Butler	Montgomery	IL
Butler	De Kalb	IN
Butler	Keokuk	IA
Butler	Washington	KS
Butler	Pendleton	KY
Butler	Baltimore	MD
Butler	Branch	MI
Butler(c.h.)	Bates	MO
Butler	Johnson	NE
Butler	Richland	OH
Butler(c.h.)	Butler	PA
Butler	Johnson	TN
Butler	Freestone	TX
Butler	Milwaukee	WI
Butler Centre(c.h.)	Butler	NE
Butler Centre	Butler	NE
Butler's Landing(c.h.)	Clay	TN
Butler Springs	Butler	AL
Butlersville	Allen	KY
Butlerville	Pulaski	AR
Butlerville	Jennings	IN
Butlerville	Tama	IA
Butlerville	Warren	OH
Butte City	Deer Lodge	MT
Butte Creek	Clackamas	OR
Butte des Morts	Winnebago	WI
Butternuts	Otsego	NY
Butternut Valley	Blue Earth	MN
Butte Valley	Butte	CA
Butte Balley	Huerfano	CO
Butteville	Marion	OR
Butteville	Grundy	MO
Butztown	Northampton	PA
Buxton	York	ME
Buxton	Clinton	IL
Buyerstown	Lancaster	PA
Byberry	Philadelphia	PA
Byer's Station	Jackson	OH
Byersville	Livingston	NY
Byfield	Essex	MA
Byhalia	Marshall	MS

PLACE	COUNTY	STATE	PLACE	COUNTY	STATE	PLACE	COUNTY	STATE
Byhalia	Union	OH	Calcutta	Columbiana	OH	Calvert	Robertson	TX
Byington	Pike	OH	Caldwell	Appanoose	IA	Calverton	Suffolk	NY
Bynumville	Chariton	MO	Caldwell	Sumner	KS	Calverton Mills	Baltimore	MD
Byram	Hinds	MS	Caldwell	Essex	NJ	Calvert's	St. Francis	AR
Byrd's Springs	Jefferson	AR	Caldwell(c.h.)	Warren	NY	Calvin	Cass	MI
Byrne	Putnam	TN	Caldwell	Orange	NC	Calvin	Huntingdon	PA
Byrneville	Harrison	IN	Caldwell(c.h.)	Noble	OH	Calvin's Corners	Crawford	PA
Byromville	Dooly	GA	Caldwell(c.h.)	Burteson	TX	Calvy	Franklin	MO
Byron	Houston	GA	Caldwell Prairie	Racine	WI	Camac	Warren	GA
Byron	Ogle	IL	Caldwell's Store	Leon	TX	Camackville	Lee	IA
Byron	Humboldt	IA	Caleb's Valley	Stewart	TN	Camanche	Calaveras	CA
Byron	Woodson	KS	Caledonia(c.h.)	Pulaski	IL	Camargo	Douglas	IL
Byron	Oxford	ME	Caledonia	Binggold	IA	Camargo	Lancaster	PA
Byron	Shiawassee	MI	Caledonia	Kent	WA	Camargo	Lincoln	TN
Byron	Olmsted	MN	Caledonia(c.h.)	Houston	MN	Camas Valley	Douglas	OR
Byron	Osage	MO	Caledonia	Lowndes	MS	Camba	Jackson	OH
Byron	Genesee	NY	Caledonia	Washington	MO	Cambra	Luzerne	PA
Byron	Fond du Lac	WI	Caledonia	Livingston	NY	Cambria	San Luis Obispo	CA
Byron Centre	Kent	MI	Caledonia	Marion	OH	Cambria	Wayne	IA
Cabell(c.h.)	Cabell	WV	Caledonia	Elk	PA	Cambria	Niagara	NY
Caberey	Kankakee	IL	Caledonia	Busk	TX	Cambria	Cambria	PA
Cabin Creek	Lewis	KY	Caledonia	Goochland	VA	Cambria	Columbia	WI
Cabinet	Montgomery	PA	Caledonia Centre	Racine	WI	Cambria Mills	Hillsdale	MI
Cabin Hill	Delaware	PA	Caledonia Station	Boone	IL	Cambridge	Dallas	AL
Cabin Point	Surry	VA	Caledonia Station	Kent	MI	Cambridge(c.h.)	Henry	IL
Cable	Champaign	OH	Calera	Shelby	AL	Cambridge	Story	IA
Cable City	Deer Lodge	MT	Caler's Hill	Jackson	NC	Cambridge	Somerset	ME
Cabot	Washington	VT	Calf Creek	Searcy	AR	Cambridge	Porchester	MD
Cacapon Depot	Morgan	WV	Calhoun	Lowndes	AL	Cambridge	Middlesex	MA
Cacey's Station	Fulton	KY	Calhoun	Columbia	AR	Cambridge	Lenawee	MI
Cacharas	Huerfano	CO	Calhoun(c.h.)	Gordon	GA	Cambridge	Isanti	MN
Cache Creek	Yolo	CA	Calhoun	Richland	IL	Cambridge	Saline	MO
Cadaretta	Montgomery	MS	Calhoun	Harrison	IA	Cambridge	Washington	NY
Caddo Grove	Johnson	TX	Calhoun	McLean	Ky	Cambridge(c.h.)	Guernsey	OH
Cade's Cover	Blount	TN	Calhoun	Madison	MS	Cambridge	Lancaster	PA
Cadet	Washington	MO	Calhoun	Henry	MO	Cambridge	Lamoille	AT
Cadiz	Henry	IN	Calhoun	Transylvania	NC	Cambridge	Dane	WI
Cadiz(c.h.)	Trigg	KY	Calhoun	Barbour	WV	Cambridgeborough	Crawford	PA
Cadiz	Cattaraugus	NY	Calhoun's Mills	Abbeville	SC	Cambridgeport	Middlesex	MA
Cadiz(c.h.)	Harrison	OH	Calico	Sarber	AR	Cambridgeport	Windham	VT
Cadiz	Green	WI	California(c.h.)	Moniteau	MO	Camden(c.h.)	Wilcox	AL
Cadosia Valley	Delaware	NY	California	Branch	MI	Camden(c.h.)	Ouachita	AR
Cadron	Conway	AR	California	Moniteau	MO	Camden	Kent	DE
Cadwallader	Tuscarawas	OH	California	Hamilton	OH	Camden	Schuyler	IL
Cady	Macomb	MI	California	Washington	PA	Camden	Carroll	IN
Cady's Falls	Lamoille	VT	California House	Wirt	WV	Camden	Knox	ME
Cady's Tunnel	Bath	VA	Calistoga	Napa	CA	Camden	Hillsdale	MI
Cadyville	Clinton	NY	Calla	Pawnee	NE	Camden	Madison	MS
Cageville	Haywood	TN	Callaghan's	Alleghany	VA	Camden	Ray	MO
Cahaba	Dallas	AL	Callahan	Nassan	FL	Camden	Seward	NE
Cahoka	Clarke	MO	Callahan's Ranch	Siskiyon	CA	Camden(c.h.)	Camden	NJ
Cahto	Mendocino	CA	Callahan's Corners	Albany	NY	Camden	Oneida	NY
Cainsville	Harrison	MO	Calland's	Pittsylvania	VA	Camden(c.h.)	Kershaw	SC
Cain's	Gwinnett	GA	Callao	La Porte	IN	Camden(c.h.)	Benton	TN
Cain's	Lancaster	PA	Callao	Macon	NO	Camden(c.h.)	Camden	NC
Cain's Store	Pulaski	KY	Callaway	Josh Bell	KY	Camden Mills	Rock Island	IL
Cainsville	Wilson	TN	Callaway's	Franklin	VA	Camden Point	Platte	MO
Cainville	Rock	WI	Callensburgh	Clarion	PA	Cameron	Scriven	GA
Ca Ira	Cumberland	VA	Callicoon	Sullivan	NY	Cameron	Warren	IL
Cairo	Thomas	GA	Calhope(c.h.)	Sioux	IA	Cameron	Clinton	MO
Cairo(c.h.)	Putnam	IN	Calloway	Upshur	TX	Cameron	Steuben	NY
Cairo	Louisa	IA	Calmar	Winnishick	IA	Cameron	New Hanover	NC
Cairo	Henderson	KY	Calmus	Clinton	IA	Cameron	Monroe	OH
Cairo	Randolph	MO	Calu	Chester	PA	Cameron	Cameron	PA
Cairo	Greene	NY	Calno	Warren	NJ	Cameron(c.h.)	Milam	TX
Cairo	Stark	OH	Caloma	Marion	IA	Cameron	Marshall	WV
Cairo	Ritchie	WV	Calumet	Cook	IL	Cameron Mills	Steuben	NY
Calahaln	Davie	NC	Calumet	Houghton	MI	Camilla(c.h.)	Mitchell	GA
Calais	Washington	ME	Calumet Harbor	Fond du Lac	WI	Camilus	Ononodaga	NY
Calais	Monroe	OH	Calumet Village	Fond du Lac	WI	Campbell	Pulaski	AR
Calais	Washington	VT	Calvary	Decatur	GA	Campbell	Coles	IL
Calamine	Sharp	AR	Calvary	Morgan	OH	Campbell	Ionia	MI
Calcutta	Clay	IN	Calvary	Fond du Lac	Wi	Campbell(c.h.)	Campbell	VA

PLACE	COUNTY	STATE
Campbell Hall	Orange	NY
Campbell's Bridge	Marion	SC
Campbellsburgh	Washington	IN
Campbellsburgh	Henry	KY
Campbell's Mills	Windham	CN
Campbellsport	Portage	OH
Campbell's Station	Knox	TN
Campbellstown	Preble	OH
Campbellstown	Brown	IL
Campbellsville(c.h.)	Taylor	KY
Campbellsville	Yazoo	MS
Campbellsville	Giles	TN
Campbelton	Jackson	FL
Campbelton(c.h.)	Campbell	GA
Campbelton	Franklin	MO
Campbelton	Steuben	NY
Cambelton	Lebanon	PA
Cambellville	Sullivan	PA
Camp Call	Cleveland	NC
Camp Creek	Lancaster	NE
Camp Creek	Lane	OR
Camp Creek	Greene	Tn
Camp Creek	Floyd	VA
Camp Elkwater	Randolph	WV
Campello	Plymouth	MA
Camp Grant	Humboldt	CA
Camp Grove	Stark	IL
Camp Halleck	Elco	NV
Camp Hill	Cumberland	PA
Camp Izard	Marion	FL
Camp McDermitt	Humbolt	NV
Camp Melvin	Bexar	TX
Campobello	Spartanburgh	SC
Camp Point	Adams	IL
Camp Ridge	Williamsburgh	SC
Camp Run	Crawford	OH
Camp Spring	Lawrence	AL
Camp Stambaugh	Sweet Water	WY
Camp Station	De Kalb	AL
Camp Stockton	Presidio	TX
Campti	Natchitoches	LA
Campton	Coweta	GA
Campton	Kane	IL
Campton	Delaware	IA
Campton(c.h.)	Wolfe	KY
Campton	Grafton	NH
Campton Village	Grafton	NH
Camptonville	Yuba	CA
Camptown	Bradford	PA
Campville	Litchfield	CN
Campville	Tioga	NY
Camp Watson	Grant	OR
Can	Huron	MI
Cana	Jennings	IN
Canaan	Colusa	CA
Canaan	Litchfield	CN
Canaan	Jefferson	IN
Canaan	Somerset	ME
Canaan	Benton	MS
Canaan	Gasconade	MO
Canaan	Grafton	NH
Canaan	Columbia	NY
Canaan	Wayne	OH
Canaan	Wayne	PA
Canaan	Essex	VT
Canaan Centre	Columbia	NY
Canaan Four Crnrs	Columbia	NY
Canaan Valley	Litchfield	CN
Canaanville	Athens	OH
Canada Road	Somerset	ME
Canadensis	Monroe	PA
Canadice(c.h.)	Ontario	NY
Canajoharie	Montgomery	NY
Canal	Warrick	IN
Canal	Venango	PA
Canal Dover	Tuscarawas	OH
Canal Fulton	Stark	OH
Canal Lewisville	Coshocton	OH
Canal Winchester	Franklin	OH
Canandaigua	Lenawee	MI
Canandaigua	Ontario	NY
Canarsie	Kings	NY
Canaseraga	Allegany	NY
Canastota	Madison	NY
Canby	Clackamas	OR
Candia	Rockingham	NH
Candia Village	Rockingham	NH
Candor	Tioga	NY
Candor	Washington	PA
Caneadea	Allegany	NY
Cane Creek	Conway	AR
Cane Creek	Walker	GA
Cane Creek	Butler	MO
Cane Creek	Chatham	NC
Cane Hill	Cedar	MO
Cane Ridge	Claiborne	LA
Cane Spring Depot	Bullitt	KY
Cane Valley	Adair	KY
Caney	Nevada	AR
Caney	Howard	KS
Caney	Ozark	MO
Caney	Matagorda	TX
Caney Branch	Greene	TN
Caney Spring	Marshall	TN
Caneyville	Grayson	KY
Canfield	Fillmore	MN
Canfield(c.h.)	Mahoning	OH
Cannelton(c.h.)	Perry	IN
Cannelton	Kanawha	WV
Cannon City	Rice	MN
Cannon River Falls	Goodhue	MN
Cannonsburgh	Boyd	KY
Cannonsburgh	Kent	MI
Cannonsburgh	Hancock	OH
Cannonsburgh	Washington	PA
Cannon's Mill	Columbiana	OH
Cannon's Station	Fairfield	CN
Cannon's Store	Sevier	TN
Cannonsville	Delaware	NY
Canoe	Winnishick	IA
Canoe Camp	Tioga	PA
Canoe Creek	Blair	PA
Canoe Ridge	Jefferson	PA
Canoe Station	Escambia	AL
Canoga	Seneca	NY
Canoochee	Escambia	AL
Canterbury	Windham	CN
Canterbury	Kent	DE
Canterbury	Merrimack	NH
Canton	Lawrence	AR
Canton	Hartford	CN
Canton(c.h.)	Lincoln	DA
Canton(c.h.)	Cherokee	GA
Canton	Fulton	IL
Canton	Washington	IN
Canton	Jackson	IA
Canton	Trigg	KY
Canton	Oxford	ME
Canton	Norfolk	MA
Canton	Wayne	MI
Canton(c.h.)	Madison	MS
Canton	Lewis	MO
Canton	Stanton	NE
Canton	Salem	NJ
Canton(c.h.)	St. Lawrence	NY
Canton(c.h.)	Stark	OH
Canton	Bradford	PA
Canton(c.h.)	Van Zandt	TX
Canton	Marion	WV
Canton Centre	Hartford	CN
Canton Point	Oxford	ME
Cantrelle	St. James	LA
Cantrelle's Roads	McMinn	TN
Canville	Neosho	KS
Cany Hollow	Lee	VA
Canyon City(c.h.)	Fremont	CO
Canyon City(c.h.)	Grant	OR
Canyon Creek	Lewis & Clark	MT
Canyon Ferry	Meagher	MT
Capac	St. Clair	MI
Capay	Yolo	CA
Cape Eliz. Depot	Cumberland	ME
Cape Girardeau	Cape Birardeau	MO
Capell's Mills	Richmond	VA
Cape May(c.h.)	Cape May	NJ
Cape May	Cape May	NJ
Cape Neddick	York	ME
Cape Porpoise	York	ME
Caperville	Northampton	VA
Cape Vincent	Jefferson	NY
Capioma	Nemaha	KS
Capistrano	Los Angeles	CA
Caplinger's Mills	Cedar	MO
Capon Bridge	Hampshire	WV
Capon Iron Works	Hardy	
Capon Springs	Frederick	VA
Cappahosie	Gloucester	VA
Cappelu	St. Charles	MO
Capper's Spring	Frederick	VA
Capron	Boone	IL
Captina	Belmont	OH
Caput	Barton	MO
Carbon	Webster	IA
Carbon	Carbon	WY
Carbon Cliff	Rock Island	IL
Carbondale	Jackson	IL
Carbondale	Osage	KS
Carbondale	Luzerne	PA
Carbon Hill	Johnson	MO
Carbonvale	Kanawha	WV
Cardiff	Mitchell	IA
Cardiff	Onondaga	NY
Cardington	Morrow	OH
Cardsville	Calhoun	MS
Cardville	Washington	PA
Carey	Wyandot	OH
Caribou	Boulder	CO
Caribou	Aroostook	ME
Carimona	Fillmore	MN
Carl	Adams	IA
Carleton	Muskegon	MI
Carlin	Lander	'NV
Carlinville(c.h.)	Macoupin	IL
Carlisle	Sullivan	IN
Carlisle	Warren	IA
Carlisle(c.h.)	Nicholas	KY
Carlisle	Middlesex	MA
Carlisle	Eaton	MI
Carlisle	Schoharie	NY
Carlisle(c.h.)	Cumberland	PA
Carlisle Centre	Schoharie	NY
Carlisle Springs	Warren	OH
Carlisle Springs	Cumberland	PA
Carlisle Station	Warren	OH
Carlstadt	Bergen	NJ
Carlton	Pembina	DA
Carlton	Orleans	NY
Carlton	Kewaunee	WI
Carlton's Store	King and Queen	VA

PLACE NAMES OF THE UNITED STATES

PLACE	COUNTY	STATE	PLACE	COUNTY	STATE	PLACE	COUNTY	STATE
Calyle(c.h.)	Clinton	IL	Carson	Jefferson	AR	Cedar Lane	Greene	TN
Calyle	Allen	KS	Carson	Huerfano	CO	Cedar Mills	Renville	MN
Carmargo	Burleson	TX	Carson	Brown	KS	Cedar Mills	Adams	OH
Carmel	Hamilton	IN	Carson	Huron	OH	Cedar Mountain	Transylvania	NC
Carmel	Penobscot	ME	Carson City	Montcalm	MI	Cedar Plains	Morgan	AL
Carmel(c.h.)	Putnam	NY	Carson City(c.h.)	Ormsby	NV	Cedar Point	Chase	KS
Carmel	Highland	OH	Carson's Landing	Bolivar	MS	Cedar Point	Page	VA
Carmi(c.h.)	White	IL	Carter	Uintah	WY	Cedar Rapids	Linn	IA
Carmichael's	Greene	PA	Carter Camp	Potter	PA	Cedar Rock	Franklin	NC
Carnero	Saguache	CO	Carter Hill	Erie	PA	Cedar Run	Grand Traverse	MI
Carnesville(c.h.)	Franklin	GA	Carter's Bridge	Albemarle	VA	Cedar Springs	Cherokee	AL
Carney	Wyoming	PA	Cartersburgh	Hendricks	IN	Cedar Springs	Kent	MI
Caro(c.h.)	Tuscola	MI	Cartersburgh	Pittsylvania	VA	Cedar Springs	Clinton	PA
Carolina	Marion	SC	Carters Creek Stat.	Maury	TN	Cedar Springs	Spartansburgh	SC
Carolina	Falls	TX	Carter's Depot	Carter	TN	Cedartown(c.h.)	Polk	GA
Carolina Mills	Washington	RI	Carter's Furnace	Carter	TN	Cedar Tree	Hernando	FL
Carolina Seminary	Greene	NC	Carter's Mill	Moore	NC	Cedar Vale	Howard	KS
Caroline	Jefferson	NE	Carter's Mills	Patrick	VA	Cedar Valley	Black Haawk	IA
Caroline	Tomkins	NY	Carter's Store	Randolph	AL	Cedar Valley	Caldwell	NC
Caroline Centre	Tomkins	NY	Cartersville(c.h.)	Bartow	GA	Cedar Valley	Wayne	OH
Caroline Depot	Tomkins	NY	Cartersville	Tishemingo	MS	Cedar Valley	Utah	UT
Carondelet	St. Louis	MO	Cartersville	Darlington	SC	Cedar View	Sussex	VA
Carpenter	Lycoming	PA	Cartersville	Parker	TX	Cedarville	Siskiyon	CA
Carpenteria	Santa Barbara	CA	Cartersville	Cumberland	VA	Cedarville	Stephenson	IL
Carpenter's Eddy	Delaware	NY	Carthage	Tuscaloosa	AL	Cedarville	Allen	IN
Carpenter's Store	Rutherford	NC	Carthage	Hancock	IL	Cedarville	Pocahontas	IA
Carpenter's Store	Clinton	MO	Carthage	Rush	IN	Cedarville	Smith	KS
Carpentersville	Kane	IL	Carthage	Campbell	KY	Cedarville	Martin	MN
Carpentersville	Putnam	IN	Carthage	Leake	MS	Cedarville	Dade	MO
Carpentersville	Warren	NJ	Carthage	Jasper	MO	Cedarville	Cumberland	NJ
Carpentersville	Shannon	MI	Carthage	Jefferson	NY	Cedarville	Herkimer	NY
Carriage Point	Chicksaw N.	IT	Carthage	Moore	NC	Cedarville	Greene	OH
Carrick	Allegheny	PA	Carthage	Hamilton	OH	Cedarville	Chehalis	WA
Carrick's Ford	Tucker	WV	Carthage	Smith	TN	Cedar Wood	Harrison	IN
Carrick's Mills	Jackson	AL	Carthage	Panola	TX	Cedron	Clermont	OH
Carritunk	Somerset	ME	Cedar Creek	Scott	Ar	Celestine	Dubois	IN
Carrick's Ford	Tucker	WV	Cedar Creek	Dorchester	MD	Celina	Perry	IN
Carrick's Mill	Jackson	AL	Cedar Creek	Barry	MI	Celina	Dent	MO
Corritunk	Somerset	ME	Cedar Creek	Taney	MO	Celina(c.h.)	Mercer	OH
Carrizo(c.h.)	Zepata	TX	Cedar Creek	Ocean	NJ	Celina	Clay	TN
Carroll	Carroll	IN	Cedar Creek	Cumberland	NC	Centenary	Marion	SC
Carroll	Penobscot	ME	Cedar Creek	Greene	TN	Centenary	Buckingham	VA
Carroll	Baltimore	MD	Cedar Creek	Bastrop	TX	Center	Shelby	TX
Carroll	Coos	NH	Cedar Creek	Frederick	VA	Center	Monongalia	WV
Carroll	Fairfield	OH	Cedar Creek	Washington	WI	Center	Rock	WI
Carroll	Clinton	PA	Cedar Creek Land.	Perry	TN	Center Mills	Montgomery	VA
Carroll	Madison	TN	Cedar Dale	Sanilac	MI	Centerville(c.h.)	Appanoose	IA
Carroll City	Carroll	IA	Cedar Falls	Black Hawk	IA	Centerville	Davis	UT
Carrollton(c.h.)	Pickens	AL	Cedar Falls	Dunn	WI	Central	St. Louis	MO
Carrollton(c.h.)	Carroll	AR	Cedar Fork	Menomonede	MI	Central	Columbia	PA
Carrollton(c.h.)	Saginaw	MI	Cedar Fork	Union	TN	Central Bridge	Schoharie	NY
Carrollton(c.h.)	Carroll	GA	Cedar Fork	Caroline	VA	Central City(c.h.)	Gilpin	CO
Carrollton(c.h.)	Greene	IL	Cedar Grove	Jefferson	AL	Central City	Marion	IL
Carrollton	Hancock	IN	Cedar Grove	Walker	GA	Central City	Linn	IA
Carrollton(c.h.)	Carroll	IA	Cedar Grove	Franklin	IN	Central City	Anderson	KS
Carrollton(c.h.)	Carroll	KY	Cedar Grove	Grange	NC	Central City	Putnam	MO
Carrollton(c.h.)	Jefferson	LA	Cedar Grove	Kanfman	TX	Central City	Grant	NM
Carrollton	Carroll	MD	Cedar Grove	Sheboygan	WI	Central City	Salt Lake	UT
Carrollton	Fillmore	MN	Cedar Grove Mills	Rockbridge	VA	Central College	Franklin	OH
Carrollton(c.h.)	Carroll	GA	Cedar Hill	Jefferson	MI	Central Falls	Providence	RI
Carrollton(c.h.)	Carroll	MO	Cedar Hill	Albany	NY	Central Grove	Shawnee	KS
Carrollton	Cattarangus	NY	Cedar Hill	Anson	NC	Central House	Butte	CA
Carrollton(c.h.)	Carroll	OH	Cedar Hill	Fairfield	OH	Centralia	Marion	IL
Carrollton	Upshur	TX	Cedar Hill	Robertson	TN	Centralia	Nemaha	KS
Carrollton	Cowlitz	WA	Cedar Hill	Dallas	TX	Centralia	Boone	MO
Carrollton Station	Montgomery	OH	Cedar Junction	Missoula	MT	Centralia	Woods	SI
Carrolltown	Cambria	PA	Cedar Keys	Levy	FL	Centralia	Columbia	PA
Catt's	Lewis	KY	Cedar Lake	Lake	IN	Central Institute	Coosa	AL
Catt's	Hill	TX	Cedar Lake	Scott	MN	Central Lake	Antrim	MI
Cattsville	Livingston	KY	Cedar Lake	Atlantic	NJ	Central Park	Queens	NY
Cattsville	Isle of Wight	VA	Cedar Lake	Herkimer	NY	Central Square	Oswego	NY
Carrville	Washington	TN	Cedar Lake	Waushara	WI	Central Station	Doddridge	WV
Carryall	Paulding	OH	Cedar Landing	Meade	KY	Central Village	Windham	CN

PLACE	COUNTY	STATE	PLACE	COUNTY	STATE	PLACE	COUNTY	STATE
Central Village	Bristol	MS	Centre Valley	Lehigh	PA	Chambersburgh	Clarke	MO
Centre(c.h.)	Cherokee	AL	Centre View	Johnson	MO	Chambersburgh	Montgomery	OH
Centre	Schuyler	IL	Centre View	Monroe	OH	Chambrsbgh. (c.h.)	Franklin	PA
Centre	Howard	IN	Centre Village	Charlton	GA	Chambers Creek	Ellis	TX
Centre	Page	IA	Centre Village	Broome	NY	Chambers' Valley	Carroll	VA
Centre	Metcalf	KY	Centre Village	Delaware	OH	Chambersville	New CAstle	DE
Centre	Eaton	MI	Centreville(c.h.)	Bibb	AL	Chambersville	Indiana	PA
Centre	Texas	MO	Centreville	Montgomery	AR	Chamblissburgh	Bedford	VA
Centre	Guilford	NC	Centreville	Alameda	CA	Chamois	Osage	MO
Centre	Montgomery	OH	Centerville	Lake	CO	Champagnolle	Union	AR
Centre	Perry	PA	Centreville	New Castle	DE	Champion	Jefferson	NY
Centre Barnstead	Belknap	NH	Centreville	Boise	IA	Champlain	Clinton	NY
Centre Pelpre	Washington	OH	Centreville	Piatt	IL	Champlain	Hennepin	MN
Centre Bread	Morgan	OH	Centreville(c.h.)	Wayne	IN	Chanceford	York	PA
Centre Berlin	Beusselaer	NY	Centreville	Linn	KS	Chancellorville	Spottsylvania	VA
Centre Bridge	Bucks	PA	Centreville	Bourbon	KY	Chancey	Dodge	GA
Centre Brook	Middlesex	CN	Centreville	St. Mary's	LA	Chandallar	Keokeu	IA
Centre Brunswick	Bensselaer	NY	Centreville(c.h.)	Queen Anne	MD	Chandler's Valley	Warren	PA
Centreburgh	Knox	OH	Centreville	Barnstable	MA	Chandlersville	Mushkingum	OH
Centre Cambridge	Washington	NY	Centreville(c.h.)	St. Joseph	MI	Chandlersville	Cass	IL
Centre Caniseo	Steuben	NY	Centreville	Anoka	MN	Chaneysville	Bedford	PA
Centre Conway	Carroll	NH	Centreville	Amite	MS	Changewater	Warren	NJ
Centre Creek	Martin	MI	Centreville(c.h.)	Reynolds	ME	Channahatchee	Elmore	AL
Centre Creek	Jasper	MO	Centreville	Lancaster	NE	Channahon	Will	IL
Centre Cross	Essex	VA	Centreville	Hunterdon	NJ	Chantilly	Lincoln	ME
Centredale	Cedar	IA	Centerville	Allegany	NY	Chantilly	Fairfax	VA
Centredale	Providence	RI	Centreville	Montgomery	OH	Chapel	Howell	MO
Centre Effingham	Carroll	NH	Centreville	Washington	OR	Chapel Hill	Douglas	GA
Centrefield	Oldham	KY	Centreville	Crawford	PA	Chapel Hill	La Fayette	MO
Centrefield	Highland	OH	Centreville	Snohomish	WA	Chapel Hill	Monmouth	NJ
Centre Groton	New London	KY	Centreville	Laurens	SC	Chapel Hill	Orange	NC
Centre Grove	Shawnee	KS	Centreville	Kent	RI	Chapel Hill	Perry	OH
Centre Grove	Person	NC	Centreville(c.h.)	Hickman	TN	Chapel Hill	Marshall	TN
Centre Hall	Centre	PA	Centreville(c.h.)	Leon	TX	Chapel Hill	Washington	TX
Centre Harbor	Belkap	NH	Centreville	Fairfax	VA	Chapel Hill	Fluvanna	VA
Centre Hill	White	AR	Centreville Station	St. Clair	IL	Chapin	Morgan	IL
Centre Hill	Hartford	CN	Centreville Station	Sullivan	NY	Chapin	Franklin	OH
Centre Hill	Centre	PA	Centre White Creek	Washington	NY	Chapinville	Ontario	NY
Centre Lebanon	York	ME	Centropolis	Franklin	KS	Chapinville	Crawford	PA
Centre Lincolnville	Waldo	ME	Ceralvo	Ohio	KY	Chaplin	Windham	CN
Centre Lisle	Broome	NY	Ceres	Stanislaus	CA	Chaplin	Nelson	KY
Centre Lovell	Oxford	ME	Ceres	Clayton	OH	Chapman	Merrick	NE
Centre Mills	Centre	PA	Ceres	Allegany	NY	Chapman	Snyder	PA
Centre Montville	Waldo	ME	Ceresco	Calhoun	MI	Chapman Quarries	Northampton	PA
Centre Moreland	Wyoming	PA	Ceresco	McPhail	MN	Chapman's Creek	Dickinson	KS
Centre Ossipee	Carroll	NH	Ceresco	Saunders	NE	Chapmanville	Logan	WV
Centre Point	Sevier	AR	Cerro Gordo	Inyo	CA	Chappaqua	Westchester	NY
Centre Point	Knox	IL	Cerro Gordo(c.h.)	Holmes	FL	Chappell's Bridge	Newberry	SC
Centre Point	Brown	OH	Cerro Gordo	Piatt	IN	Chaptico	St. Mary's	MD
Centre Point	Clay	IN	Cerro Gordo	Randolph	IN	Chardon(c.h.)	Geauga	OH
Centre Point	Linn	IA	Cerro Gordo	Columbus	NC	Chariton(c.h.)	Lucas	IA
Centre Point	Monroe	KY	Cerro Gordo	Hardin	TN	Charlemont	Franklin	MA
Centre Point	Tallahatchee	MS	Cerulean Springs	Trigg	KY	Charlemont	Bedford	VA
Centreport	Suffolk	NY	Cesna	Wayne	IL	Charles City(c.h.)	Floyd	IA
Centreport	Berks	PA	Cessford	Cedar	OH	Charles City	Charles City	VA
Centre Ridge	Conway	AR	Ceylon	Greene	PA	Charles Riv. Village	Norfolk	MA
Centre Ridge	Woodson	KS	Chacahoula Statton	Terre Bonne	LA	Charleston	Franklin	SC
Centre Road Station	Crawford	PA	Chadd's Ford	Delaware	PA	Charleston	Yolo	CA
Centre Rutland	Rutland	VT	Chadwick's Mills	Oneida	NY	Charleston(c.h.)	Coles	IL
Centre Sandwich	Carroll	NH	Chagrin Falls	Cuyahoga	OH	Charleston	Coles	IL
Centre Sidney	Kennabec	ME	Chain Lake Centre	Martin	MN	Charleston	Lee	IA
Centre Square	Switzerland	IN	Chain of Rocks	Lincoln	MO	Charleston	Penobscot	ME
Centre Square	Montgomery	PA	Chalk Bluff	Marion	AL	Charleston(c.h.)	Talahatchee	MS
Centre Star	Landerdale	AL	Chalk Level	Pittsylvania	VA	Charleston(c.h.)	Mississippi	MO
Centre Stafford	Stafford	NH	Chalk Level	Harnett	NC	Charleston	Montgomery	NY
Centreton	Morgan	IN	Chalk Spring	Santa Rosa	FL	Charleston	Tioga	PA
Centreton	Salem	NJ	Chalmers	White	IN	Charleston(c.h.)	Charleston	SC
Centreton	Huron	OH	Chalybeate	Johnson	MO	Charleston	Bradley	TN
Centre Town	Cole	MO	Chalybos	Litchfield	CN	Charleston	Hopkins	TX
Centretown	Mercer	PA	Chamberlain	Allen	IN	Charleston Four Corners	Montgomery	NY
Centre Valley	Hendricks	IN	Chambers(c.h.)	Chambers	AL	Charlestown(c.h.)	Clarke	IN
Centre Valley	Cass	NE	Chambersburgh	Pike	IL	Charlestown	Cicil	MD
Centre Valley	Otsego	NY	Chambersburgh	Orange	IN			

PLACE NAMES OF THE UNITED STATES

PLACE	COUNTY	STATE	PLACE	COUNTY	STATE	PLACE	COUNTY	STATE
Charlestown	Middlesex	MA	Chehalis Point	Chehalis	WA	Cherryville	Northampton	PA
Charlestown	Sullivan	NH	Chelmsford	Middlesex	MA	Chesaning	Saginaw	MI
Charlestown	Portage	OH	Chelsea	Tama	IA	Chesapeake	Lawrence	MO
Charlestown	Luzerne	PA	Chelsea	Butler	KS	Chesapeake City	Cecil	MD
Charlestown	Washington	RI	Chelsea	Suffolk	MA	Cheshire	New Haven	CN
Charlestown	Jefferson	WV	Chelsea	Washtenaw	MI	Cheshire	Berkshire	MA
Charlestown	Calumet	WI	Chelsea	Delaware	PA	Cheshire	Allegan	MI
Charlestown	Bedford	PA	Chelsea(c.h.)	Orange	VT	Cheshire	Ontario	NY
Charlevoix(c.h.)	Charlevoix	MI	Cheltenham	St. Louis	MO	Cheshire	Gallia	OH
Charlie Hope	Brunswick	VA	Cheltenham	Montgomery	PA	Chesnut Bluff's	Dyer	TN
Charloe	Paulding	OH	Chemung	McHenry	IL	Chesnut Creek(c.h.)	Baker	AL
Charlotte	Clinton	IA	Chemung	Chemung	NY	Chesnut Fork	Bedford	VA
Charlotte	Washington	ME	Chemung Centre	Chemung	NY	Chesnut Grove	Shelby	KY
Charlotte(c.h.)	Eaton	MI	Chenango	Lawrence	PA	Chesnut Grove	Gallia	OH
Charlotte	Monroe	NY	Chenango	Brazoria	TX	Chesnut Grove	Lycoming	PA
Charlotte(c.h.)	Mecklenburgh	NC	Chenango Bridge	Broome	NY	Chesnut Hill	Washington	IN
Charlotte(c.h.)	Dickson	TN	Chenango Forks	Boome	NY	Chesnut Hill	Middlesex	MA
Charlotte	Chittenden	VT	Cheneyville	Rapids	LA	Chesnut Hill	Philadelphia	PA
Charlotte(c.h.)	Charlotte	VA	Chengwatana(c.h.)	Pine	MN	Chesnut Level	Lancaster	PA
Charlotteburgh	Passaic	NJ	Chenoa	McLean	IL	Chesnut Mound	Smith	TN
Charlottesville(c.h.)	Albemarle	VA	Chapachet	Providence	RI	Chesnut Ridge	St. Genevieve	MO
Charoltteville	Schoharie	NY	Chepstow	Washington	KS	Chesnut Ridge	Dutchess	NY
Charlton	Worcester	MA	Chepultepee	Blount	AL	Chesnut Ridge	Yadkin	NC
Charlton	Saratoga	NY	Chequist	Davis	IA	Chesnut Ridge	Lincoln	TN
Charlton City	Worcester	MA	Cheraw	Chesterfield	SC	Chest	Clearfield	PA
Charlton Depot	Worcester	MA	Cherino	Nacogdoches	TX	Chester	Jefferson	AL
Chartiers	Allgeheny	PA	Cherokee	Colbert	AL	Chester	Desha	AR
Chase	Johnson	IA	Cherokee	Butte	CO	Chester	Middlesex	CN
Chaseburgh	Vernon	WI	Cherokee(c.h.)	Cherokee	IA	Chester(c.h.)	Randolph	IL
Chase's Mills	St. Lawrence	NY	Cherokee	Lawrence	KY	Chester	Wayne	IN
Chase's Mills	Tioga	PA	Cherokee	San Saba	TX	Chester	Howard	IA
Chaseville	Otsego	NY	Cherokee City	Benton	AR	Chester	Jefferson	KS
Chaska(c.h.)	Carver	MN	Cherokee Mills	Cherokee	GA	Chester	Penobscot	ME
Chatata	Bradley	TN	Cherokee jound	Cherokee	KS	Chester	Hampden	MA
Chatawa	Pike	MS	Cherry Box	Shelby	MO	Chester	Eaton	MI
Chataugay	Franklin	NY	Cherry Camp	Harrison	WV	Chester	Olmsted	MN
Chateaugay Lake	Franklin	NY	Cherry Creek	Arapahoe	Co	Chester	Rockingham	NY
Chatfield	Fillmore	MN	Cherry Creek	Woodson	KS	Chester	Morris	NJ
Chatfield	Crawford	OH	Cherry Creek	Pontoloc	MS	Chester	Orange	NY
Chatfield	Navarro	TX	Cherry Creek	Chautauqua	NY	Chester	Meigs	OH
Chatham	Sanganon	IL	Cherryfield	Washington	ME	Chester	Delaware	PA
Chatham	Buchanan	IA	Cherryfield	Transylvania	NC	Chester	Windsor	VT
Chatham	Barnstable	MS	Cherry Flats	Tioga	PA	Chester	Chesterfield	VA
Chatham	Wright	MN	Cherry Fork	Adams	OH	Chester(c.h.)	Chester	SC
Chatham	Morris	NJ	Cherry Grove	Saline	AR	Chester Center	Hampden	MA
Chatham	Columbia	NY	Cherry Grove	Fillmore	MN	Chester Cross Roads	Geauga	OH
Chatham	Licking	OH	Cherry Grove	Schuyler	MO	Chesterfield	New London	CN
Chatham	Chester	PA	Cherry Grove	Platte	NE	Chesterfield	Macoupin	IL
Chatham Centre	Columbia	NY	Cherry Grove	Hamilton	OH	Chesterfield	Madison	IN
Chatham Centre	Medina	OH	Cherry Grove	Washington	TN	Chesterfield	Hampshire	MA
Chatham Hill	Smyth	VA	Cherry Grove	Rockingham	VA	Chesterfield	Cheshire	NH
Chatham Port	Barnstable	MS	Cherry Hill	Cecil	MD	Chesterfield(c.h.)	Chesterfield	SC
Chatham Run	Clinton	VA	Cherry Hill	Calhoun	MS	Chesterfield(c.h.)	Chesterfield	VA
Chatham Valley	Tioga	PA	Cherry Lane	Alleghany	NC	Chesterfield Factory	Cheshire	NH
Chatham Village	Columbia	NY	Cherry Lane	King William	VA	Chester Hill	Morgan	OH
Chatsworth	Livingston	IL	Cherry Point City	Edgar	IL	Chester Springs	Chester	PA
Chattahoochee	Gadsden	FL	Cherry Ridge	Union	LA	Chester Station	Dodge	WI
Chattan	Adams	IL	Cherry Ridge	Wayne	PA	Chesterton	Porter	IN
Chattanooga	Hamilton	IL	Cherry Run Depot	Morgan	WV	Chestertown(c.h.)	Kent	MD
Chatterton	King George	VA	Cherry Spring	Gillispie	TX	Chestertown	Warren	NY
Chattoogavile	Chattooga	GA	Cherrystone	Northampton	VA	Chester Valley	Chester	PA
Chaular	Monterey	CA	Cherry Tree	Venango	PA	Chesterville	Franklin	ME
Chaumong	Jefferson	NY	Cherry Vale	Montgomery	KS	Chesterville	Kent	MD
Chauncey	Tippercanoe	IN	Cherry Valley	Cross	AR	Chesterville	Pontotoc	MS
Chauncey	Athens	OH	Cherry Valley	Winnebago	IL	Chesterville	Morrow	OH
Chazy	Clinton	NY	Cherry Valley	Worcester	MA	Chesterville	Chester	PA
Cheat Mountain	Randolph	WV	Cherry Valley	Otsego	NY	Chest Springs	Cambria	PA
Chebanse	Iroquois	IL	Cherry Valley	Ashtabula	OH	Chetco	Curry	OR
Chebeague Island	Cumberland	ME	Cherry Valley	Washington	PA	Chetopah	Labette	KS
Cheboygan	Cheboygan	MI	Cherryville	Montgomery	KS	Cheviot	Hamilton	OH
Checo	Cherokee	KS	Cherryville	Crawford	MO	Chewalla	McNairy	TN
Checktowaga	Erie	NY	Cherryville	Hunterdon	NJ	Chewsville	Washington	MD
Cheesland	Augelina	TX	Cherryville	Gaston	NJ	Cheyevve City	Laramie	WY

PLACE	COUNTY	STATE	PLACE	COUNTY	STATE	PLACE	COUNTY	STATE
Cheyney	Delaware	PA	Choconut Centre	Broome	NY	City Point	Prince George	VA
Chicago(c.h.)	Cook	IL	Chocoville	Sebastian	AR	Civer	Fulton	IL
Chicago	Marion	KY	Chocowinity	Beaufort	NC	Civil Bend	Daviess	MO
Chicago	Douglas	NE	Choctaw Agency	Choctaw	IT	Clackamas	Clackamas	OR
Chichester	Merrimack	NH	Choctaw Agency	Oktibbeha	MS	Claiborne	Monroe	AL
Chickamauga	Hamilton	Tn	Choctow Bluff	Clarke	AL	Claiboune	Jasper	MS
Chickamauga Stat.	Hamilton	TN	Choctow Corner	Clarke	AL	Claire Springs	Cedar	MO
Chickaming	Berrien	MI	Choteau Creek	Bonhamme	DA	Clairville	Sonoma	CA
Chickasbogue	Mobile	AL	Christiana	New Castle	DE	Clanton	Baker	AL
Chickasaw	Franklin	AL	Christiana	Dakota	MN	Clanton	Madison	IA
Chickasaw(c.h.)	Chickasaw	IA	Christiana	Lancaster	PA	(c.h.)Claquato	Lewis	WA
Chicken Creek	Juab	UT	Christiana	Williamson	TN	Clara	Potter	PA
Chickies	Lancaster	PA	Christiana	Dane	WI	Clare	Clare	MI
Chick's Springs	Greenville	SC	Christiansburgh	Wapello	IA	Claremont	Richland	IL
Chico	Butte	CA	Christiansburgh	Shelby	KY	Claremont	Dodge	MN
Chicopee	Hampden	MA	Christiansburgh	Champaign	OH	Claremont	Nodaway	MO
Chicopee Falls	Hampden	MA	Christiansbgh.(c.h.)	Montgomery	VA	Claremont	Sullivan	NH
Chicora	Chicot	AR	Christiansville	Meeklenburgh	VA	Claremont	Allegheny	PA
Chikalah	Yell	AR	Christy's Prairie	Clay	IN	Calaremont Wharf	Surry	VA
Childersburgh	Talladega	AL	Chrome	Chester	PA	Clarence	Cedar	IA
Childress' Store	Montgomery	VA	Chrome Hill	Harford	MD	Clarence	Calhoun	MI
Childsville	Mitchell	NC	Chronicle	Catawba	NC	Clarence	Shelby	MO
Chilesburgh	Fayette	KY	Chuckatuck	Nansemond	VA	Clarence	Erie	NY
Chilesburgh	Caroline	VA	Chula Depot	Amelia	VA	Clarence Centre	Erie	NY
Chilhowee	Blount	TN	Chulafinnee	Cleburne	AL	Clarenceville	Queens	NY
Chilhowie	Johnson	MO	Chulahoma	Marshall	MS	Clarendon	Monroe	AR
Chili	Calaveras	CA	Chulasky	Northumberland	PA	Clarendon	Orleans	NY
Chili	Hancock	IL	Chunkey's Station	Newton	MS	Clarendon	Rutland	VT
Chili	Miami	IN	Church Creek	Dorchester	MD	Clarendon Centre	Calhoun	MI
Chili	Monroe	NY	Church Grove	Knox	TN	Clarendon Springs	Rutland	VT
Chili	Coshocton	OH	Church Hill	Christian	KY	Claridon	Geaugo	OH
Chillicothe	Peoria	IL	Church Hill	Queen Anne	MD	Clarinda(c.h.)	Page	IA
Chillicothe	Wapello	IA	Church Hill	Jefferson	MS	Clarington	Monroe	OH
Chillicothe(c.h.)	Livingston	IL	Church Hill	Trumbull	OH	Clarington	Forest	PA
Chillicothe	Ross	OH	Churchill	Ottawa	KS	Clarion(c.h.)	Wright	IA
Chillisquaque	Northcumberland	PA	Churchland	Norfolk	VA	Clarion	Sedgwick	KS
Chilmark	Dukes	MA	Church Road	Dinwiddie	VA	Clarion(c.h.)	Clarion	PA
Chilo	Clermount	OH	Church's Corners	Hilsdale	MI	Clark	Mercer	PA
Chilton(c.h.)	Calumet	WI	Churchtown	Columbia	NY	Clark Centre	Clark	IL
Chiltonville	Plymouth	MA	Churchtown	Lancaster	PA	Clark City	Clarke	MO
Chimney Point	Addison	VT	Church View	Middlesex	VA	Clarke Station	Lake	IN
Chimney Rock	Rutherford	NC	Churchville	Harford	MD	Clarkestown	Lycoming	PA
Chimney Rock	Trempeleau	WI	Churchville	Monroe	NY	Clarkesville(c.h.)	Habersham	GA
China	Kennebec	ME	Churchville	Augusta	VA	Clark's	Coshecton	OH
China	St. Clair	MI	Churubusco	Franklin	VA	Clarksborough	Gloucester	NJ
China Grove	Pike	AL	Churubusco	Whitley	IN	Clarksborough	St. Lawrence	NY
China Grove	Pike	MS	Churubusco	Clinton	NJ	Clarksburgh	Decatur	IL
China Grove	Rowan	NC	Cicero	Hamilton	IN	Clarksburgh	Montgomery	MD
China Grove	Williamsburg	SC	Cicero	Madison	MT	Clarksburgh	Marquette	MI
Chincoteague	Accomack	VA	Cicero	Onondaga	NY	Clarksburgh	Moniteau	MO
Chincotegue Island	Accomack	VA	Cicero	Difiance	OH	Clarksburgh	Monmouth	NJ
Chinese Cam	Tuolumue	CA	Cimarron	Morra	NM	Clarksburgh	Erie	NY
Chinkapin Hill	Sangamon	IL	Cincinnati	Washington	AR	Clarksburgh	Ross	OH
Chinkapin Roof	Jackson	KY	Cincinnati	Appanoose	IA	Clarksburgh	Indiana	PA
Chinook	Pacific	WA	Cincinnati	Walker	TX	Clarksburgh	Carroll	TN
Chipman's Point	Addison	VT	Cincinnati	Pawnee	NE	Clarksburgh(c.h.)	Harrison	WV
Chipmonk Cooley	Vernon	WI	Cincinnati(c.h.)	Hamilton	OH	Clark's Corner	Ashabula	OH
Chippenhook Spngs.	Rutland	VT	Cincinnatus	Cortland	NY	Clark's Creek	Grant	KY
Chippewa	New Castle	DE	Cinnaminson	Burlington	NJ	Clark's Factory	Delaware	NY
Chippewa	Wayne	OH	Circle	Vermillion	IL	Clark's FAlls	New London	CN
Chippewa City(c.h.)	Chippewa	MN	Circleville	Tazewell	IL	Clarksfield	Huron	OH
Chippewa City	Chippewa	WI	Circleville	Jackson	KS	Clark's Fork	Cooper	MO
Chippewa Falls	Pope	MN	Circleville	Orange	NY	Clark's Fork	York	SC
Chippewa Falls(c.h.)	Chippewa	WI	Circleville(c.h.)	Pickaway	OH	Clark's Gap	Loudoun	VA
Chippewa Lake	Mecosta	MI	Circleville	Williamson	TX	Clark's Green	Luzerne	Pa
Chisago City(c.h.)	Chisago	MN	Circleville	Loadoun	VA	Clark's Grove	Freeborn	MN
Chisago Lake	Chisago	MN	Cisco	Placer	CA	Clark's Hill	Tippacanoe	IN
Chismville	Saber	AR	Cistern	Fayette	TX	Clark's Mills	Oneida	NY
Chittenango	Madison	NY	Citico	Monroe	TN	Clark's Mills	Moore	NC
Chittenango Falls	Madison	NY	Citronelle	Mobile	AL	Clark's Mills	Mercer	PA
Chittenango Station	Madison	NY	City	Dutchess	NY	Clark's Mills	Lexington	SC
Chittenden	Rutland	VT	City Island	Westchester	NY	Clark's Mills	Manitowac	WI
Choconut	Susquehanna	PA	City Point	Platte	MO	Clarkson	Monroe	NY

PLACE NAMES OF THE UNITED STATES

PLACE	COUNTY	STATE	PLACE	COUNTY	STATE	PLACE	COUNTY	STATE
Clarkson	Columbiana	OH	Clayton Centre	Jefferson	NY	Clifton	Schuyler	MO
Clarkstown(c.h.)	Rockland	NY	Claytonville	Brown	KS	Clifton	Nemaha	NE
Clarksville(c.h.)	Johnson	AR	Claytonville	Clay	MO	Clifton	Passaic	NJ
Clarksville	El Dorado	CA	Claytonville	Transylvania	NC	Clifton	Colfax	NM
Clarksville	Hamilton	IN	Clay Village	Shelby	KY	Clifton	Monroe	NY
Clarksville	Butler	IA	Clayville	Oneida	NY	Clifton	Greene	OH
Clarksville	Howard	MD	Clear Branch	Washington	TN	Clifton	Luzerne	PA
Clarsville	Pike	MO	Clear Branch	Washington	VA	Clifton	Wayne	TN
Clarksville	Merrick	NE	Clear Creek	Marion	AR	Clifton	Bosque	TX
Clarksville	Coos	NH	Clear Creek	Monroe	IN	Clifton	Cache	UT
Clarksville	Hunterdon	NJ	Clear Creek	Alamakee	IA	Clifton	Mason	WV
Clarksville	Albany	NY	Clear Creek	Nemaha	KS	Clifton	Monroe	WI
Clarksville	Clinton	OH	Clear Creek	Cooper	MO	Clifton Dale	Essex	MA
Clarksville	Greene	PA	Clear Creek	Saunders	NE	Clifton Forge	Alleghany	VA
Clarksville(c.h.)	Montgomery	TN	Clear Creek	Chantaauqua	NY	Clifton Hill	Randolph	MO
Clarksville	Red River	TX	Clear Creek	Mecklenburgh	NC	Clifton Mills	Breckinridge	KY
Clarksville	Mecklenburgh	VA	Clear Creek	Fairfield	OH	Clifton Mills	Pierce	WI
Clarkton	Dunklin	MO	Clear Creek	Clackamas	OR	Clifton Park	Saratoga	NY
Clarktown	White	TN	Clear Creek	Greene	TN	Clifton Springs	Ontario	NY
Clarno	Green	WI	Clear Creek	Raleigh	WV	Clifton Station	Fairfax	VA
Claryville	Sullivan	NY	Clear Creek Falls	Winston	AL	Clifty	Madison	AR
Clanssville	Leigh	PA	Clear Creek Landing	Alexander	IL	Clifty	Decatur	IN
Clayerack	Columbia	NY	Clearfield	Powechiek	IA	Clifty	Todd	KY
Clay	Washington	IA	Clearfield(c.h.)	Clearfield	PA	Clifty	Fayette	WV
Clay	Webster	KY	Clearfield Bridge	Clearfield	PA	Clifty Dale	Maries	MO
Clay	Clarke	MO	Clear Fork	Bland	VA	Climax Prairie	Kalamazoo	MI
Clay	Onondaga	NY	Clear Lake	Steuben	IN	Clinesville	Catawba	NC
Clay	Jackson	OH	Clear Lake	Cerro Gordo	IA	Cline's Mills	Augusta	VA
Clay(c.h.)	Clay	WV	Clear Lake	Sherburne	MN	Clinton	Greene	AL
Clay Bank	Oceana	MI	Clear Pond	Marshall	KY	Clinton(c.h.)	Van Buren	AR
Clay Bank	Middlesex	NJ	Clear Port	Fairfield	OH	Clinton	Middlesex	CN
Clay Banks	Door	WI	Clear Spring	Clark	AR	Clinton(c.h.)	Jones	GA
Clay Brook	Madison	TN	Clear Spring	Graves	KY	Clinton(c.h.)	De Witt	IL
Clayburgh	Clinton	NY	Clear Spring	Washington	MD	Clinton	Vermillion	IN
Clay Centre(c.h.)	Clay	KS	Clear Spring	York	PA	Clinton	Clinton	IA
Clay City	Clay	IL	Clear Spring	Grainger	TN	Clinton	Douglas	KS
Clayford	Jones	IA	Clearview	Sullivan	MO	Clinton(c.h.)	Hickman	KY
Clay Hill	Marengo	AL	Clearville	Bedford	PA	Clinton	East Felicianan	LA
Clay Hill	Lincoln	GA	Clear Water	Sedwick	KS	Clinton	Kennebec	ME
Clay Hill	Wexford	MI	Clear Water	Antrim	MI	Clinton	Worcester	MA
Clay Hill	Titus	TX	Clear Water	Wright	MN	Clinton	Hinds	MS
Clay Lick	Licking	OH	Clear Water Harbor	Hillsborough	FL	Clinton(c.h.)	Henry	MO
Clay Lick	Franklin	PA	Cleaveland	Oswego	NY	Clinton(c.h.)	Stanton	NE
Clay Mills	Jones	IA	Cleaveland(c.h.)	Bradley	TN	Clinton	Hunterdon	NJ
Claymont	New Castle	DE	Cleburne	Johnson	TX	Clinton	Oneida	NY
Claypool	Warren	KY	Cleck's Mills	Bath	VA	Clinton(c.h.)	Sampson	NC
Clay's Grove	Lee	IA	Clemansville	Winnebnago	WI	Clinton	Summit	OH
Clay's Prairie	Edgar	IL	Clement	Clinton	IL	Clinton	Allegheny	PA
Claysville	Marshall	AL	Clementsville	Clay	TN	Clinton	Laurens	SC
Claysville	Washington	IN	Cleudenin	Kanawha	WV	Clinton(c.h.)	Anderson	TN
Claysville	Harrison	KY	Cleona	Brown	IN	Clinton(c.h.)	De Witt	TX
Claysville	Union	MS	Cleopatra	Mercer	MO	Clinton	Ohio	WV
Claysville	Boone	MO	Clermont	Marion	IN	Clinton	Rock	WI
Claysville	Guernsey	OH	Clermont	Fayette	IA	Clinton Corners	Dutchess	NY
Claysville	Washington	PA	Clermont	Columbia	NY	Clinton Corners	Wyoming	PA
Claysville	Mineral	WV	Clermont Mills	Harford	MD	Clintondale	Ulster	NY
Clayton(c.h.)	Barbour	AR	Clermontville	McKean	PA	Clinton Falls	Steele	MI
Clayton	Hempstead	AR	Cleveland(c.h.)	White	GA	Clinton Furnace	Monogalia	WV
Clayton	Contra Costa	CA	Cleveland	Henry	IL	Clinton Hollow	Dutchess	NY
Clayton	Kent	DE	Cleveland	Hancock	IN	Clinton Junction	Eaton	MI
Clayton(c.h.)	Rabun	GA	Cleveland	Fayette	KY	Clinton Lock	Parke	IN
Clayton	Adams	IL	Cleveland	Le Sueur	MN	Clinton Mills	Clinton	NY
Clayton	Hendricks	IN	Cleveland(c.h.)	Cuyahoga	OH	Clinton Point	Dutchess	NY
Clayton	Clayton	IA	Cleves	Hamilton	OH	Clinton Station	Hunterdon	NJ
Clayton	Harford	MD	Clifford	Bartholomew	IN	Clinton Station	Clinton	OH
Clayton	Lenawee	MI	Clifford	Lapeer	MI	Clinton Valley	Clinton	OH
Clayton	Fairbault	MN	Clifford	Susquehanna	PA	Clintonville	Kane	IL
Clayton	Gloucester	NJ	Clifton	Wilcox	AL	Clintonville	Bourbon	KY
Clayton	Jefferson	NY	Clifton	Iroquois	IL	Clintonville	Cedar	MO
Clayton	Johnston	NC	Clifton	Union	IN	Clintonville	Clinton	NY
Clayton	Montgomery	OH	Clifton	Louisa	IA	Clintonville	Franklin	OH
Clayton	Berks	PA	Clifton	Washington	KS	Clintonville	Venango	PA
Claytona	Noble	OH	Clifton	Penobscot	ME	Clitonville	Greenbrier	WV

PLACE	COUNTY	STATE
Clintonville	Waupace	WI
Clio	Babour	AL
Clio	Wayne	IA
Clio	Pulaski	KY
Clio	Genesee	MI
Clio	Marlborough	SC
Cliola	Adams	IL
Clipper Gap	Placer	CA
Clipper Mills	Butte	CA
Clipper Mills	Gallia	OH
Clitherall	Otter Tail	MN
Clockville	Madison	NY
Clokey	Washington	PA
Clonmell	Lancaster	PA
Clopton	Dale	AL
Closter	Bergen	NJ
Clouser's Mills	Montgomery	IN
Cloutarf	Dane	WI
Cloutierville	Natchitoches	LA
Clove	Sussex	NJ
Clove	Dutchess	NY
Clove Branch Junct.	Dutchess	NY
Clover Bend(c.h.)	Lawrence	AR
Clover Bottom	Jackson	KY
Clover Bottom	Franklin	MO
Clover Creek	Blair	PA
Clover Creek	Highland	VA
Cloverdale	Sonoma	CA
Cloverdale	Putnam	IN
Cloverdale	Howard	KS
Cloverdale	Benton	MO
Cloverdale	Botetourt	VA
Clover Dale	Doddridge	WV
Clover Depot	Halifaax	VA
Clover Green	Spottsylvania	VA
Clover Hill	Hunterdon	NJ
Clover Hill	Blonnet	TN
Cloverland	Clay	IN
Clover Orchard	Alamance	NC
Cloverport	Breckinridge	KY
Clover Valley	Washington	UT
Cloversville	Delaware	NY
Cloyd's Creek	Blount	TN
Clyde	Jasper	IA
Clyde	Wayne	NY
Clyde	Sandusky	OH
Clyde Mills	St. Clair	MI
Clyman	Dodge	WI
Clymer	Chantauqua	NY
Clymore	Labette	KS
Coal Bank	Trumball	OH
Coal Bluff	Washington	PA
Coalburgh	Trumbull	OH
Coalburgh	Kanawha	WV
Coal Centre	Linn	KS
Coal City	Venango	PA
Coal Creek	Boulder	CO
Coal Creek	Keokuk	IA
Coal Creek	Ottawa	KS
Coal Creek	Campbell	TN
Coal Dale	Perry	OH
Coalfield	Monroe	IA
Coal Fire	Pickens	AL
Coal Grove	Lawrence	OH
Coalmont	Huntington	PA
Coal Mountain	Forsyth	GA
Coal River Marshes	Raliegh	WV
Coal Run	Pike	KY
Coal Run	Washington	OH
Coalsmouth	Kanawha	WV
Coalton	Monroe	IA
Coalton	Boyd	KY
Coal Valley	Rock Island	IL
Coal Valley	Allgehany	PA
Coalville	Livingston	IL
Coalville(c.h.)	Summit	UT
Coalville	Lincoln	WV
Coast Fork	Lane	OR
Coast Range	Colasa	CA
Coatesville	Hendricks	IN
Coatesville	Chester	PA
Coatopa	Sumpter	AL
Coatsburgh	Adams	IL
Coatsville	Schnyler	MO
Cobalt	Middlesex	CN
Cobb	Randolph	IL
Cobb	Iowa	WI
Cobb River	Wasoca	MN
Cobb's Creek	Matthews	VA
Cobham	Warren	PA
Cobham	Albemarle	VA
Coblentz	Grundy	ME
Cobleskill	Schoharie	NY
Cob Moo Sa	Oceana	MI
Coburgh	Monmouth	NJ
Coburn's Corners	De Kalb	IN
Coburn's Store	Union	NC
Cocalico	Lancaster	PA
Cochercton	Sullivan	NY
Cochecton Centre	Sullivan	NY
Cocheselt	Plymouth	MA
Cochitunte	Middlesex	MA
Cochran	Puluski	GA
Cochran's Mills	Armstrong	PA
Cochransville	Chester	PA
Cochrauton	Marion	OH
Cochranton	Crawford	PA
Cockeysville	Baltimore	MD
Cockrum	De Soto	MS
Cocolamus	Juniata	PA
Coddle Creek	Cabarrus	NC
Codorus	York	PA
Cody's Mills	Kent	MI
Coelk	Livingston	LA
Coe Ridge	Covahaga	OH
Coe's Mills	Liberty	FL
Coesse	Whitley	IN
Coeymans	Albany	NY
Coeymans Hollow	Albany	NY
Coffadeliah	Neshoba	MS
Coffee	Clay	IN
Coffee Landing	Hardin	TN
Coffee Run	Huntingdon	PA
Coffeeville	Clark	IN
Coffeeville(c.h.)	Yalabusha	MS
Coffeeville	Upshur	TX
Coffeysburgh	Daviess	MO
Coffeyville	Montgomery	KS
Coffin's Summit	Dutchess	NY
Cogan House	Lycoming	PA
Cogan Station	Lycoming	PA
Cog Hill	McMinn	TN
Cohansey	Cumberland	NJ
Cohassett	Norfolk	MA
Cohocotah	Livingston	MI
Cohocton	Steuben	NY
Cohoes	Albany	NY
Coila	Washington	NY
Coinjock	Currituck	NC
Coitsville	Mahoning	OH
Cokerville	Monroe	AL
Cokeshury	Abbeville	SC
Colapauchee	Monroe	GA
Colbins	Greenwood	KS
Colburn	Tippecanoe	IN
Colbyville	Story	IA
Colchester	New Lendon	CN
Colchester	McDonough	IL
Colchester	Delaware	NY
Colchester	Chittenden	VT
Cold Brook	Herkimer	NY
Coldbrook Springs	Worcester	MA
Cold Creek	Bradford	PA
Colden	Erie	NY
Coldenham	Orange	NY
Cold Harbor	Hanover	VA
Cold Neck	Cooper	MO
Cold Spring	El Dorado	CA
Cold Spring	Fairfield	CN
Cold Spring	Shelby	IL
Cold Spring	Campbell	KY
Cold Spring	Berkshire	MA
Cold Spring	Cape May	NJ
Cold Spring	Putnam	NY
Cold Spring	Wayne	PA
Cold Spring	Bledsoe	TN
Cold Spring	San Jacinto	TX
Cold Spring	Jefferson	WI
Cold Spring City	Stearns	MN
Cold Spring Harbor	Suffolk	NY
Cold Springs	Edgefield	SC
Cold Streatu	Hampshire	WV
Coldwater	Franklin	IA
Coldwater	Callaway	KY
Coldwater	De Soto	MS
Cold Water	Cross	AR
Cold Water(c.h.)	Branch	MI
Cold Water	Wayne	MO
Cold Water	Monroe	NY
Cold Water	Mercer	OH
Cold Water	Doddridge	WV
Cold Well	White	AR
Cold Well	Union	SC
Coldwell's Store	Anderson	KY
Colebrook	Litchfield	CN
Colebrook	Coos	NH
Colebrook	Ashtabonia	OH
Colebrook	Lebanon	PA
Colebrookdale	Becks	PA
Colebrook River	Litchfield	CN
Colecamp	Benton	MO
Cole Creek	Fountain	IN
Cole Grove	McKean	PA
Colegrove's Point	Sutter	CA
Coleman	Midland	MI
Coleman's Depot	Randolph	GA
Colemansville	Harrison	KY
Colemanville	Lancaster	PA
Colerain	Franklin	MA
Colerain	Bertie	NC
Colerain	Belmont	OH
Colerain	Lancaster	PA
Colerain Forge	Huntingdon	PA
Colesburgh	Delaware	IA
Colesburgh	Potter	PA
Cole's Corners	De Kalb	IN
Cole's Creek	Columbia	PA
Cole's Ferry	Charoltte	VA
Cole's Mills	Putnam	NY
Cole's Mills	Randolph	NC
Colesville	Montgomery	MD
Colesville	Sussex	NJ
Colesville	Broome	NY
Colesville	Stokes	NC
Coleta	Clay	AL
Coleta	Whitesides	IL
Coleville	Mono	CA
Coleville	Bossier	LA
Coleville	Bates	MO

PLACE NAMES OF THE UNITED STATES

PLACE	COUNTY	STATE
Colfax	Placer	CA
Colfax	Fremont	CO
Colfax	Warren	IL
Colfax	Clinton	IN
Colfax	Jasper	IA
Colfax(c.h.)	Grant	LA
Colfax	Mason	MI
Colfax	Sullivan	MO
Colfax	Guilford	NC
Colfax	Fairfield	OH
Colfax	Huntingdon	PA
Colfax	Van Zandt	TX
Colfax	Dunn	WI
Collamer	Whitley	IN
Collamer	Onondaga	NY
Collamer	Cuyahoga	OH
Collamer	Chester	PA
College Corner	Jay	IN
College Corner	Butler	OH
College Grove	Williamson	TN
College Hill	Middlesex	MA
College Hill	Hamilton	OH
College Mound	Macon	MO
College Mound	Kaufman	TX
College of St. James	Washington	MD
College Point	Queens	NY
College Springs	Page	IA
Collegeville	Saline	AR
Collegeville	San Joaquin	CA
Collegeville	Montgomery	PA
Collettsville	Caldwell	NC
Colley	Sullivan	PA
Collier's Mill	Ocean	NJ
Collierstown	Rockbridge	VA
Colliersville	Otsego	NY
Colliersville	Shelby	TN
Collington	Prince George's	MD
Collingwood	Onondaga	NY
Collingwood	Fairfax	VA
Collins	Greenwood	KS
Collins	Erie	NY
Collinsburgh	Bossier	LA
Collins Centre	Erie	NY
Collins Depot	Hampden	MA
Collinsville	Etoway	AL
Collinsville	Solano	CA
Collinsville	Hartford	CN
Collinsville	Madison	IL
Collinsville	Lewis	NY
Collinsville	Butler	OH
Collinsville	Frederick	VA
Collinwood	Mecker	MN
Collomsville	Lycoming	PA
Colma	Hancock	IL
Colman	St. Louis	MO
Colmar	McDonough	IL
Colmar	Montgomery	PA
Colo	Story	IA
Cologne	Delaware	IN
Cologne	Mason	WV
Coloma	Cherokee	AL
Coloma	El Dorado	CA
Coloma	Parke	IN
Coloma	Woodson	KS
Coloma	Barrien	MI
Coloma	Carroll	MO
Coloma	Wanshara	WI
Colon	Saint Joseph	MI
Colona Station	Henry	IL
Colony	Knox	MO
Colora	Cecil	MD
Colorado	Lincoln	KS
Colorado City(c.h.)	El Paso	CO
Colosse	Oswego	NY
Colquit(c.h.)	Miller	GA
Coltharp's	Houston	TX
Colton	St. Lawrence	NY
Colton	Henry	OH
Colt's Neck	Monmouth	NJ
Columbia	Henry	AL
Columbia	Tuolumne	CA
Columbia	Tolland	CN
Columbia	Monroe	IL
Columbia	Fayette	IN
Columbia	Marion	IA
Columbia(c.h.)	Adair	KY
Columbia	Caldwell	LA
Columbia	Washington	ME
Columbia	Jackson	MI
Columbia(c.h.)	Marion	MS
Columbia(c.h.)	Boone	MO
Columbia	Coos	NH
Columbia	Warren	NJ
Columbia	Herkimer	NY
Columbia(c.h.)	Tyrrel	NC
Columbia	Hamilton	OH
Columbia	Columbia	OR
Columbia	Lancaster	PA
Columbia(c.h.)	Richland	SC
Columbia(c.h.)	Maury	TN
Columbia	Brazoria	TX
Columbia	Fluvanna	VA
Columbia Centre	Licking	OH
Columbia City(c.h.)	Whitley	IN
Columbia City	Columbia	OR
Columbia ' Roads	Bradford	PA
Columbia Farm	Venango	PA
Columbia Furnace	Shenandoah	VA
Columbiana(c.h.)	Shelby	AL
Columbiana	Columbiana	OH
Columbian Grove	Lunenburgh	VA
Columbia Station	Lorain	OH
Columbiaville	Lapeer	MI
Columbus	Hempstead	AR
Columbus	Madison	FL
Columbus(c.h.)	Muscogee	GA
Columbus	Adams	IL
Columbus(c.h.)	Bartholomew	IN
Columbus	Cherokee	KS
Columbus	Hickman	KY
Columbus	St. Clair	MI
Columbus(c.h.)	Lowndes	MS
Columbus	Johnson	MO
Columbus(c.h.)	Platte	NE
Columbus	Esmeralda	NV
Columbus	Burlington	NJ
Columbus	Chenango	NY
Columbus(c.h.)	Polk	NC
Columbus(c.h.)	Franklin	OH
Columbus	Warren	PA
Columbus(c.h.)	Colorado	TX
Columbus	Columbia	WI
Columbus City	Louisa	IA
Columbus Grove	Putnam	OH
Colusa(c.h.)	Colusa	CA
Comanche	Comanche	TX
Comann's Well	Sussex	VA
Comettsburgh	Beaver	PA
Comfort	Kerr	TX
Comly	Montour	PA
Commack	Suffolk	NY
Commerce	Conercuh	AL
Commerce	Oakland	MI
Commerce	Tunica	MS
Commerce(c.h.)	Scott	MO
Commerce	Wilson	TN
Commerce Mills	Polk	IA
Commiskey	Jennings	IN
Communia	Clayton	IA
Como	Dallas	AR
Como	Whitesides	IL
Como	Henry	TN
Como Depot	Panola	MS
Comorn	King George	VA
Company's Shops	Alamance	NC
Competine	Wapello	IA
Competition	Laclede	MO
Compromise	Champaign	IL
Compton	Los Angeles	CA
Comstock	Wapello	IA
Comstock	Kalamazoo	MI
Comstock's Landing	Washington	NY
Conaway	Tyler	WV
Conception	Nodaway	MO
Concord	Lawrence	AL
Concord	Susex	DE
Concord	Gadsden	FL
Concord	Pike	GA
Concord	Morgan	IL
Concord	Hancock	IA
Concord	Lewis	KY
Concord	Somerset	ME
Concord(c.h.)	Middlesex	MS
Concord	Jackson	MI
Concord	Dodge	MN
Concord	Calhoun	MS
Concord	Callaway	MO
Concord	Cass	NE
Concord(c.h.)	Merrimack	NH
Concord(c.h.)	Cabarrus	NC
Concord	Lake	OH
Concord	Franklin	PA
Concord	Knox	TN
Concord	Hardin	TX
Concord	Essex	VT
Concord	Jefferson	WI
Concord Church	Mercer	WV
Concord Depot	Campbell	VA
Concordia(c.h.)	Cloud	KS
Concord Station	Erie	PA
Concordville	Delaware	PA
Concrete	De Witt	TX
Condit	Delaware	OH
Coneburgh	Marion	KS
Conejos(c.h.)	Conejos	CO
Conemaugh	Cambria	PA
Conerly's	Pike	MS
Conestoga	Lancaster	PA
Conesus	Livingston	NY
Conesus Centre	Livingston	NY
Conesville	Muscatine	IA
Conesville	Schoharie	NY
Conewango	Cattaraugus	NY
Confederate X Rds.	Mushingum	OH
Confidence	Madison	IL
Confidence	Wayne	IA
Confidence	Somerset	PA
Congress	Wayne	OH
Congruity	Westmoreland	PA
Conklin Centre	Broome	NY
Conklingville	Saratoga	NY
Conklin Station	Broome	NY
Conlogue	Edgar	IL
Conloque	Jackson	IN
Conneaut	Ashtabula	OH
Conneautville	Crawford	PA
Connecticut Lake	Cross	NH
Connellsville(c.h.)	Fayette	PA
Conner's Creek	Wayne	MI

PLACE NAMES OF THE UNITED STATES

PLACE	COUNTY	STATE	PLACE	COUNTY	STATE	PLACE	COUNTY	STATE
Conner's Mills	Cooper	MO	Coon Rapids	Carroll	IA	Corinth	Grant	KY
Connersville	Fayette	IN	Coon's Corners	Crawford	PA	Corinth	Penobscot	ME
Connersville	Harrison	KY	Coon Creek	Jersey	IL	Corinth	Kent	MI
Connor's Mills	Floyd	VA	Coon Valley	Vernon	WI	Corinth	Alcorn	MS
Connor's Station	Wyandotte	KS	Cooper	Washington	ME	Corinth	Saratoga	NY
Connotton	Harrison	OH	Cooper	Kalamazoo	MI	Corinth	Orange	VT
Conn's Creek	Shelby	IN	Cooper(c.h.)	Delta	TX	Cork	Hillsborough	FL
Conococheague	Washington	MD	Cooperdale	Cambria	PA	Cork	Ashtabula	OH
Conover	Miami	OH	Cooper Hill	Izard	AR	Cornelia	Johnson	MO
Conowingo	Cecil	MD	Coopers	Franklin	VA	Cornell	Livingston	IL
Conquest	Cayuga	NY	Coopersburgh	Leigh	PA	Cornersville	Dorchester	MD
Conrad's Store	Rockingham	VA	Cooper's Gap	Rutherford	NC	Cornersville	Benton	MS
Conshohocken	Montgomery	PA	Cooper's Hill	Osage	MO	Cornersville	Hickory	MO
Constableville	Lewis	NY	Cooper's Mills	Lincoln	ME	Cornersville	Giles	TN
Constance	Boone	KY	Cooper's Plains	Steuben	NY	Coru Grove	Calhoun	AL
Constant	Cowley	KS	Cooperstown	Brown	IL	Corn Hill	Williamson	TX
Constantia	Oswega	NY	Cooperstown(c.h.)	Otsego	NY	Corning	Adams	IA
Constania	Delaware	OH	Cooperstown	Venango	PA	Corning	Nemaha	KS
Constantia Centre	Oswego	NY	Cooperstown	Manitowoe	WI	Corning	Holt	MO
Constantine	St. Joseph	MI	Coopersville	Wapello	IA	Corning(c.h.)	Steuben	NY
Constitution	Washington	OH	Coopersville	Ottawa	MI	Cornish	York	ME
Constitution	York	PA	Coopersville	Clinton	NY	Cornish	Sibley	MN
Consville	Henry	MO	Coopertown	Robertson	TN	Cornish Flat	Sullivan	NH
Contee's Station	Prince George's	MD	Coopertown	Harford	MD	Cornishville	Mercer	KY
Content	Colorado	TX	Coopwood	Winston	MS	Corn Planter	Warren	PA
Contoocook Village	Merrimack	NH	Coos	Coos	NH	Cornsville	Scott	VA
Contreras	Butler	OH	Coosa	Floyd	GA	Cornton	Windham	VT
Convent(c.h.)	St. James	LA	Coosawatchie	Beaufort	SC	Cornville	La Salle	IL
Convers	Clinton	MO	Coote's Store	Rockingham	VA	Cornville	Somerset	ME
Convis Centre	Calhoun	MI	Copake	Columbia	NY	Cornwall	Litchfield	CN
Conway	Conway	AR	Copake Iron Works	Columbia	NY	Cornwall	Madison	MO
Conway	Aroostook	ME	Cope	Morgan	IN	Cornwall	Orange	NY
Conway	Franklin	MA	Copeland	Dodge	GA	Cornwall	Lebanon	PA
Conway	Livingston	MI	Copenhagen	Caldwell	NC	Cornwall	Addison	VT
Conway	Leake	MS	Copenhagen	Lewis	NY	Cornwall Bridge	Litchfield	CN
Conway	Larclede	MO	Copenhagen	Caldwell	LA	Cornwall Hollow	Litchfield	CN
Conway	Carroll	NH	Copi	Johnson	OH	Cornwallis	Ritchie	WV
Conwaybrgh.(c.h.)	Horry	SC	Copley	Summit	OH	Cornwall Landing	Orange	NY
Conway's Landing	Mendocino	CA	Copley	Leigh	PA	Cornwallville	Greene	NY
Conyers(c.h.)	Rockdale	GA	Copopa	Lorain	OH	Corona	Coffey	KS
Conyersville	Henry	TN	Copperas Hill	Orange	VT	Corpus Christi(c.h.)	Nueces	TX
Conyngham	Luzerne	PA	Copper Creek	Rock Island	IL	Correctionville	Woodbury	IA
Coch's Bridge	New Castle	DE	Copper Falls Mine	Keweenaw	MI	Corrieville	Wabash	IL
Coody's Bluff	Cherokee Nation	IT	Copper Harbor	Keweenaw	MI	Corriganville	Alleghany	MD
Cookerly	Vigo	IN	Copper Hill	Hunterdon	NJ	Corry	Erie	PA
Cooksburgh	Albany	nY	Copper Hill	Floyd	VA	Corsica	Morrow	IN
Cooksburgh	Forest	PA	Copper Hill	Clay	AL	Corsica	Jefferson	PA
Cook's Corners	Franklin	NY	Copper Mines	Calaveras	CA	Corsicana	Barryy	MO
Cook's Ford	Jefferson	KS	Copperopolis	Calaveras	CA	Corsicana(c.h.)	Navarro	TX
Cook's Mills	Coles	IL	Copper Vale	Lassen	CA	Cortland	Jackson	IN
Cook's Station	Newaygo	MI	Copper Valley	Floyd	VA	Cortland Centre	Kent	MI
Cookstown	Burlington	NJ	Coquille	Coos	OR	Cortlanr Vill.(c.h.)	Cortland	NY
Cook's Valley	Wabashaw	MN	Coral	McHenry	IL	Corunna	De Kalb	IN
Cook's Valley	Chippewa	WI	Coral	Montcalm	MI	Corunna	Shawassee	MI
Cooksville	Howard	MD	Coral City	Trempealeau	WI	Corvallis	Missoula	MT
Cooksville	Noxubee	MS	Coral Hill	Barren	KY	Corvallis(c.h.)	Benton	OR
Cooksville	Putnam	TN	Coral Hill	Elko	NV	Corydon(c.h.)	Harrison	IN
Cool Bank	Pike	IL	Coralville	Johnson	IA	Corydon(c.h.)	Wayne	IA
Coolbauugh's	Monroe	PA	Coram	Suffolk	NY	Corydon	Warren	PA
Cooleysville	Steele	MN	Corbandale	Montgomery	TN	Corymbo	La Porte	IN
Cool Spring	Sussex	DE	Corbettsville	Broome	NY	Coshocton(c.h.)	Coshocton	OH
Cool Spring	Ohio	KY	Cotvotsn	Hennepin	MN	Cosmos	Renville	MN
Cool Spring	Iredell	NC	Cordaville	Worcester	MA	Cosmosa	Sedwick	KS
Cool Spring	Jefferson	PA	Cordelia	Solano	CA	Costigon	Bath	KY
Cool Spring	Henry	SC	Cordova	Rock Island	IL	Costilla	Costilla	CO
Coolville	Athens	OH	Cordova	Grant	KY	Cosumne	Sacramento	CA
Cool Well	Amherst	VA	Cordova	Talbot	MD	Cote Gelee	La Fayette	LA
Coomer	Lee	MS	Cordova	Le Suenr	MN	Cotile	Rapides	LA
Coon Creek	Anoka	MN	Corfu	Genesee	NY	Cotile Landing	Rapides	LA
Coon Creek	Barton	MO	Corinna	Penobscot	ME	Cottage	Hardin	IA
Coonewar	Lee	MS	Corinna	Wright	MN	Cottage	Cottarangus	NY
Coon Island	Washington	PA	Corinna Centre	Penobscot	ME	Cottage	Huntingdon	PA
Coon Prairie	Vernon	WI	Corinne	Box Elder	UT	Cottage Grove	Klamath	CA
			Corinth	Williamson	IL			

PLACE	COUNTY	STATE	PLACE	COUNTY	STATE	PLACE	COUNTY	STATE
Cottage Grove	Douglas	IL	Covelo	Mendocino	CA	Cram's Corner	Carroll	NH
Cottage Grove	Union	IN	Coventry	Tolland	CN	Cranberry	Allen	OH
Cottage Grove	Washington	MN	Coventry	Chenango	NY	Cranberry	Vanango	PA
Cottage Grove	Lane	OR	Coventry	Kent	RI	Cranberry Creek	Fulton	NY
Cottage Grove	Dane	WI	Coventry	Orleans	VT	Cranberry Forge	Mitchell	NC
Cottage Hill	Dubuque	IA	Coventry Centre	Kent	RI	Cranberry Isles	Hancock	ME
Cottage Hill	Muskingum	OH	Coventry Depot	Tolland	CN	Cranberry Plains	Carroll	VA
Cottage Home	Lincoln	NC	Coventryville	Chenango	NY	Cranberry Prairie	Mercer	OH
Cottage Inn	La Fayette	WI	Cove Point	Calvert	MD	Cranbury	Middlesex	NJ
Cottage Mills	Chattahoochee	GA	Covert	Van Buren	MI	Crandall	Lorain	OH
Cottageville	Jackson	WV	Covert	Seneca	NY	Crandell's Corners	Washington	NY
Cottle's Mills	Covington	AL	Cove Station	Huntingdon	PA	Cranesville	Montgomery	NY
Cottleville	St. Charles	MO	Covesville	Albemarie	VA	Cranesville	Preston	WV
Cotton Gin	Freestone	TX	Coveton	Barbour	WV	Cransford	Union	NJ
Cotton Gin Port	Monroe	MS	Coveville	Saratoga	NY	Cranston Prt. Works	Providence	RI
Cotton Grove	Henry	IA	Covington(c.h.)	Newton	GA	Crapo	Oscaola	GA
Cotton Hill	Sangamon	IL	Covington(c.h.)	Fountain	IN	Crary's Mills	St. Lawrence	NY
Cotton Hill	Dunklin	MO	Covington(c.h.)	Kenton	KY	Craryville	Columbia	NY
Cotton Hill	Fayette	WV	Covington(c.h.)	St. Tammany	LA	Crawford	Russell	AL
Cotton Plant	Marion	FL	Covington	Dakota	NE	Crawford	Oglethorpe	GA
Cotton Plant	Tippah	MS	Covington	Wyoming	NY	Crawford	Gallatin	IL
Cotton Plant	Lamar	TX	Covington	Richmond	NC	Crawford	Crawford	IA
Cotton's	Madison	MY	Covington	Miami	OH	Crawford	Washington	ME
Cotton Valley	Greene	NC	Covington	Tioga	PA	Crawford	ISabella	MI
Cottonville	Marshall	AL	Covington(c.h.)	Tipton	TN	Crawford	McLennan	TX
Cottonville	Jackson	IA	Covington	Hill	TX	Crawford House	Coos	NH
Cottonwood	Tehama	CA	Covington(c.h.)	Alleghany	VA	Crawford's Fork	Cass	MO
Cottonwood	Gallatin	IL	Covode	Indiana	PA	Crawfordsville	Crittenden	AR
Cottonwood	Brown	MN	Cowan	Delaware	IN	Crawfordsville	Crawford	IL
Cottonwood	Butler	NE	Cowan	Union	PA	Crawfordsville(c.h.)	Montgomery	IN
Cottonwd. Falls(c.h.)	Chase	KS	Cowan	Franklin	TN	Crawfordsville	Washington	IA
Cottonwood Grove	Bond	IL	Cowanesque Valley	Tioga	PA	Crawfordsville	Crawford	KS
Cottonwood Point	Pemiscot	MO	Cowan's Ford	Mecklenburgh	NC	Crawfordsville	Linn	OR
Cottonwood Springs	Lincoln	ME	Cowansville	Armstrong	PA	Crawfordsville(c.h.)	Wakula	FL
Cotuit Port	Barnstable	MA	Cowikee	Barbour	AL	Crawfordsville(c.h.)	Taliaferro	GA
Couchville	Davidson	TN	Cowle's Station	Macon	AL	Crawfordville	Lowndes	MS
Coudersport(c.h.)	Potter	PA	Cowlesville	Wyoming	NY	Creagerstown	Frederick	MD
Coultersville	Randolph	IL	Cowlitz	Lewis	WA	Cream Ridge	Livingston	MO
Coultersville	Butler	PA	Cowpasture Brigde	Alleghany	VA	Creek Agency	Creek Nation	IT
Council Bond	Crittendon	AR	Cow Run	Washington	NY	Creek Centre	Warren	NY
Council Bluffs(c.h.)	Pottawattomie	IA	Cowskin	Sedwick	Ks	Creek Locks	Ulster	NY
Council Grove(c.h.)	Morris	KS	Coxsackle	Greene	NY	Creekside	Indiana	PA
Council Hill	Jo Daviess	IL	Cox's Creek	Clayton	IA	Creelsborough	Russell	KY
Council Hill	Clayton	IA	Cox's Creek	Nelson	KY	Creighton	Iau qui Court	NE
Council Hill Station	Jo Daviess	IL	Cox's Mills	Wayne	IN	Creighton	Guernsey	OH
Counover	Winneshick	IA	Cox's Mills	Gilmer	WV	Cremona	Neosho	KS
Countsville	Lexington	SC	Coxville	Pitt	NC	Crescent	Saratoga	NY
County Line	Campbell	GA	Coyleville	Butler	PA	Crescent	Pike	PA
County Line	Tippecanoe	IN	Coytee	London	TN	Crescent City(c.h.)	Del Norte	CA
County Line	Eaton	MI	Coyville	Wilson	KS	Crescent City	Iroquois	IL
County Line	Niagara	NY	Crab Orchard	Williamson	IL	Crescent City	Pottawattamie	IA
County Line	Davie	NC	Crab Orchard	Lincoln	KY	Crescent Hill	Bates	MO
County Line	Northumberland	PA	Crab Orchard	Ray	MO	Crescent Mills	Plumas	CA
County Line	Lincoln	TN	Crab Orchard	Johnson	NE	Cresco	Howard	IA
County Line ' Roads	Charlotte	VA	Crab Tree	Haywood	NC	Cresskill	Bergen	NJ
Coupville	Island	WA	Crab Tree	Westmoreland	PA	Cresson	Cambria	PA
Courter	Miami	IN	Crabtree's Mills	Jackson	OH	Cressona	Schuylkill	PA
Courtland	Lawrence	AL	Cracow	Huron	MI	Crestline	Crawford	OH
Courtland	Nicollet	MN	Craftsbury	Orleans	VT	Creston	OGle	IL
Courtland	Panola	MS	Craggie Hope	Cheatham	TN	Creston	Union	IA
Courtland Station	De Kalb	IL	Craig	Perry	IL	Creswell	Jefferson	CO
Courtney	Grimes	TX	Craig	Switzerland	IN	Creswell	Spalding	GA
Coushatte Chute	Natchioches	LA	Craig	Holt	MO	Creswell	St. Clair	IL
Cousins	Ean Clair	WI	Craighead	Mecklenburgh	NC	Creswell	Jefferson	IN
Cove	Polk	AR	Craiglersville	Madison	VA	Creswell	Keokuk	IA
Cove	Union	OR	Craig's Ford	Campbell	TN	Creswell	Labette	KS
Cove City	Whitfield	GA	Craig's Mills	Washington	VA	Creswell	Caldwell	KY
Cove Creek	Etowah	AL	Craigsville	Orange	NY	Creswell	Antrim	MI
Cove Creek	Millard	UT	Craigsville	Gaston	NC	Creswell	Cortland	NY
Cove Creek	Wayne	WV	Craigsville	Armstrong	PA	Creswell	Jefferson	OH
Cove Dale	Hamilton	OH	Craigsville	Lancaster	SC	Creswell	Lancaster	PA
Coveland(c.h.)	Island	WA	Craigsville	Augusta	VA	Creswell(c.h.)	Houston	TX
Covell	McLean	IL	Crain's Creek	Moore	NC	Creswell	Milwaukee	WI

PLACE	COUNTY	STATE	PLACE	COUNTY	STATE	PLACE	COUNTY	STATE
Crete	Will	IL	Crosswicks	Burlington	NJ	Cumberland	Choctaw	MS
Crete	Saline	NE	Crotcher's Ferry	Dorchester	MD	Cumberland	Guernsey	OH
Crete	Indiana	PA	Crothersville	Jackson	IN	Cumberland(c.h.)	Cumberland	VA
Creve Coeur	St. Louis	NO	Croton	Lee	IA	Cumberland Centre	Cumberland	ME
Cribbs	Westmoreland	PA	Croton	Newaygo	MI	Cumberland City	Clinton	KY
Cridersville	Auglaize	OH	Croton	Hunterdon	NJ	Cumberland City	Houston	TN
Crigler's Mills	Ralls	MO	Croton	Delaware	NY	Cumberlnd. Curnace	Dixon	TN
Crisfield	Somerset	MD	Croton	Licking	OH	Cumberland Gap	Claiborne	TN
Crisman	Porter	IN	Croton Falls	Westchester	NY	Cumberland Hill	Providence	RI
Crisp's Cross Roads	Harrison	IN	Croton Landing	Westchester	NY	Cumberlnd In. Wks.	Stewart	TN
Crittenden	Franklin	IL	Crouse's Store	Dutchess	NY	Cumberland Valley	Bedford	PA
Crittenden	Cass	IN	Crow Creek		DA	Cuming City	Washington	NE
Crittenden	Grant	KY	Crowder's Mountain	Gaston	NC	Cumming(c.h.)	Forsyth	GA
Crittenden	Daviess	MO	Crow Lake	Stearns	MN	Cumming	Forsyth	GA
Crittenden	Erie	NY	Crowley	Greene	AR	Cummingsville	Goliad	TX
Crittenden Springs	Crittenden	KY	Crown City	Gallia	OH	Cummington	Hampshire	MA
Crockersville	Woodruff	AR	Crown Point(c.h.)	Lake	IN	Cummington W Vil.	Hampshire	MA
Crockett	Houston	TX	Crown Point	Essex	NY	Cummins	Lincoln	AR
Crockett's Bluff	Arkansas	AR	Crown Point Centre	Essex	NY	Commin's Creek	Ellis	TX
Croftsville	Woodruff	AR	Crownsville	Anne Arundel	MD	Cumminsville	Hamilton	OH
Croghan	Lewis	NY	Crow River	Meeker	MN	Cumru	Berks	PA
Cromwell	Middlesex	CN	Crow's Landing	Stanislaus	CA	Cunningham	Chariton	MO
Cromwell	Noble	IN	Croville	Warrick	IN	Cunningham's Mills	Ritchie	WV
Cromwell	Union	IA	Crow Wing(c.h.)	Crow Wing	MN	Cunningham's Stat.	Floyd	GA
Cromwell	Ohio	KY	Croxton	Jefferson	OH	Cunningham's Store	Person	NC
Crook	Boone	WV	Croyden	Sullivan	NH	Cupola	Chester	PA
Crooked Creek	Steuben	IN	Croyden	Morgan	UT	Curdsville	Daviess	KY
Crooked Creek	Stokes	NC	Croyden Flat	Sullivan	NH	Curdsville	Buckingham	VA
Crooked Creek	Tioga	PA	Cruger	Woodford	IL	Curenton's Bridge	Henry	AL
Crooked Fork	Morgan	TN	Crum Creek	Fulton	NY	Cureton's Store	Lancaster	SC
Crooked Hill	Montgomery	PA	Crum Elbow	Dutchess	NY	Curia	Independence	AR
Crooked Tree	Noble	OH	Crumley's	Henry	GA	Curlisville	Clarion	PA
Crooksville	Perry	OH	Crumpton	Queen Anne	MD	Curl's Wharf	Henrico	VA
Croom	Prince George's	MD	Cruso	Seneca	NY	Curran	Sangamon	IL
Cropper's Depot	Shelby	KY	Crystal	Tama	IA	Currant Creek	Fremont	CO
Cropsey	Gage	NE	Crystal	Mountain	MI	Curriersville	Moore	NC
Cropseyville	Rensselaer	NY	Crystal Hill	Montgomery	AR	Currie's Store	Caddo	LA
Cropwell	St. Clair	AL	Crystal Creek	Siskiyou	CA	Currituck(c.h.)	Currituck	NC
Crosbyville	Chester	SC	Crystal Lake	McHenry	IL	Currohee	Harbersham	GA
Cross	Ringgold	IA	Crystal Lake	Hancock	IA	Curry's Creek	Kendall	TX
Cross	Lyon	KS	Crystal Lake	Waupaca	WI	Curry's Run	Harrison	KY
Cross Anchor	Spartanburgh	SC	Crystal Spring	Yates	NY	Curryville	Pike	MO
Cross Anchor	Greene	TN	Crystal Spring	Copiah	MS	Curtin	Damphin	PA
Cross Creek Village	Washington	PA	Crystal Valley	Oceana	MI	Curtis' Corner	Androscoggin	ME
Cross Cut	Lawrence	PA	Cuba	Fulton	IL	Curtis' Mills	Tipton	IN
Cross Fork	Clinton	PA	Cuba	Owen	IN	Curtisville	Tipton	IN
Cross Hill	Kennebec	ME	Cuba	Republic	KS	Curtisville	Berkshire	MA
Cross Hill	Laurens	SC	Cuba	Crawford	MO	Curveton	Cass	IN
Cross Hollow	Benton	AR	Cuba	Alleghany	NY	Curwinsville	Clearfield	PA
Crossing	La Porte	IN	Cuba	Rutherford	NC	Cush	Clearfield	PA
Crossingville	Crawford	PA	Cuba	Clinton	OH	Cushing	Tuscaloosa	AL
Cross Keys	De Kalb	GA	Cuba	Ouachita	LA	Cushing	Knox	Me
Cross Keys	Camden	NJ	Cuba	Shelby	TN	Cushing	Polk	WI
Cross Keys	Union	SC	Cuba Landing	Humphreys	TN	Cusseta	Chambers	AL
Cross Keys	Rockingham	VA	Cuba Station	Sunter	AL	Cussetta(c.h.)	Chattahoochee	GA
Cross Kill Mills	Berks	PA	Cuba Creek	Jefferson	IL	Cusseta	Davis	TX
Crossland	Callaway	KY	Cub Hill	Baltimore	MD	Custar	Wood	OH
Cross Plains	Calhoun	AL	Cub Prairie	Jefferson	IL	Custard's	Crawford	PA
Cross Plains	Ripley	IN	Cucamongo	San Bernadino	CA	Cutchogue	Suffolk	NY
Cross Plains	Metcalf	KY	Cuckoo	Louisa	VA	Cuthand	Red River	TX
Cross Plains	Robertson	TN	Cuddebackville	Orange	NY	Cuthbert(c.h.)	Randolph	GA
Cross Plains	Dane	WS	Cuffey's Cove	Mendocino	CA	Cutler	Washington	ME
Cross River	Westchester	NY	Cuivre	Lincoln	MO	Cutler	Washington	OH
Cross Roads	Johnson	IL	Culdrum	Morrison	MN	Cuttingsville	Clackamas	OR
Cross Roads	Charles	MD	Cullen	Herkimer	NY	Cuttingsville	Rutland	VT
Cross Roads	Madison	OH	Culleoka	Maury	TN	Cut Off	Drew	AR
Cross Roads	York	PA	Culloden	Monroe	GA	Cuyahoga Falls	Summit	OH
Cross Timbers	Hickory	MO	Culpeper(c.h.)	Culpeper	VA	Cuyler	Cortland	NY
Cross Timbers	Ellis	TX	Culver's Station	Tippercanoe	IN	Cuylerville	Livingston	NY
Cross Village	Emmet	MI	Culverton	Hancock	GA	Cylon	St. Coix	Wi
Crossville	De Kalb	AL	Cumberland	Marion	IN	Cythiana	Posey	IN
Crossville	Gates	NC	Cumberland	Cumberland	ME	Cythiana	Harrison	KY
Crossville(c.h.)	Cumberland	TN	Cumberland(c.h.)	Alleghany	MD	Cythiana	Pike	OH

PLACE	COUNTY	STATE
Cypre-mont	St. Mary's	LA
Cypress	Monroe	AR
Cypress	Perry	TN
Cypress	Kenosa	WI
Cypress Creek	Desha	AR
Cypress Creek	Johnson	IL
Cypress Hill	Williamson	IL
Cypress Top	Harris	TX
Cyrus	Bosque	TX
Cyruston	Lincoln	TN
Dacada	Sheboygan	WI
Dacusville	Pickens	SC
Dadeville(c.h.)	Tallapoosa	AL
Dadeville	Dade	MO
Dagger's Springs	Botetourt	VT
Daggett's Mills	Tioga	PA
Dagsborough	Sussex	DE
Dahlonega(c.h.)	Lumpkin	GA
Dahlonega	Wapello	IA
Daileyville	Karnes	TX
Daingerfield	Titus	TX
Dairy	Washington	IA
Dairyland	Ulster	NY
Dakota	Stephenson	IL
Dakota(c.h.)	Dakota	NE
Dakota	Waushara	WI
Dakotah(c.h.)	Humbolt	IA
Dalby	Allamakee	IA
Dale	Spencer	IN
Dale	Campbell	KY
Dale	Wyoming	NY
Dale	Berks	PA
Dale City	Gutherie	IA
Daleville	Dale	AL
Daleville	Delaware	IN
Daleville	Landerdale	MS
Daleville	Luzerne	PA
Dalhoff	St. Charles	MO
Dallham's Creek	Logan	KY
Dallas	Polk	AR
Dallas	Paulding	GA
Dallas	Marion	IA
Dallas	Pulaski	KY
Dallas	Clinton	MI
Dallas	Webster	MO
Dallas(c.h.)	Gaston	NC
Dallas	Highland	OH
Dallas(c.h.)	Polk	OR
Dallas	Luzerne	PA
Dallas	Hamilton	TN
Dallas(c.h.)	Dallas	TX
Dallas	Marshall	WV
Dallasburgh	Warren	OH
Dallas Centre	Dalls	IA
Dallas City	Hancock	IL
Dallastown	York	PA
Dallies	Surry	VA
Dalmanutha	Guthrie	IA
Dalmatia	Northumberland	PA
Dalson	Clark	IL
Dalton (c.h.)	Whitfield	GA
Dalton	Wayne	IN
Dalton	Berkshire	MA
Dalton	Chariton	MO
Dalton	Coos	NH
Dalton	Bladen	NC
Dalton	Wayne	OH
Dalton	Luzerne	PA
Dalton's Corners	Wayne	MI
Damariscotta Mills	Lincoln	ME
Damascoville	Columbiana	OH
Damascus	Stephenson	IL
Damascus	Montgomery	MD
Damascus	Scott	MS
Damascus	Clackamas	OR
Damascus	Wayne	PA
Damascus	Spartanburg	SC
Dames' Quarter	Somerset	MD
Damiansville	Clinton	IL
Dan	Taylor	IA
Dana	Worcester	MA
Danborough	Bucks	PA
Danburgh	Wilkes	GA
Danbury (c.h.)	Fairfield	CT
Danbury	Grafton	NH
Danbury (c.h.)	Stokes	NC
Danby	Du Page	IL
Danby	Ionia	MI
Danby	Tompkins	NY
Danby	Rutland	VT
Danby Four Corners	Rutland	VT
Daneyville	Haywood	TN
Dandridge (c.h.)	Jefferson	TN
Dane	Dane	WI
Danforth	Johnson	IA
Danforth Station	Iroquois	IL
Daniel's Landing	Bladen	NC
Daniel's Springs	Cherokee N	IN
Danielsville (c.h.)	Madison	GA
Danielsville	Wayne	MO
Danielsville	Northampton	PA
Danielsville	Dickson	TN
Dannemora	Clinton	NY
Dansville	Ingham	MI
Dansville	Livingston	NY
Danube	Herkimer	NY
Danvers	McLean	IL
Danvers	Essex	MA
Danvers Centre	Essex	MA
Danversport	Essex	MA
Danville	Morgan	AL
Danville (c.h.)	Yell	AR
Danville	Contra Costa	CA
Danville (c.h.)	Vermilion	IL
Danville (c.h.)	Hendricks	IN
Danville	Des Moines	IO
Danville (c.h.)	Boyle	KY
Danville	Androscoggin	ME
Danville	Alcorn	MS
Daville (c.h.)	Montgomery	MO
Danville	Rockingham	NH
Danville	Warren	NJ
Danville	Knox	OH
Danville (c.h.)	Montour	PA
Danville	Benton	TN
Danville	Montgomery	TX
Danville	Caledonia	VT
Danville	Pittsylvania	VA
Danville	Dodge	WI
Darby	Delaware	PA
Darby Creek	Madison	OH
Darbyville	Pickaway	OH
Darcey's Store	Montgomery	MD
Dardanelle	Yell	AR
Daretown	Salem	NJ
Darien	Fairfield	CT
Darien (c.h.)	Mac Intosh	GA
Darien	Clark	IL
Darien	Kossuth	IA
Darien	Genesee	NY
Darien	Walworth	WI
Darien Centre	Genesee	NY
Darien Depot	Fairfield	CT
Dark Corner	Douglas	GA
Darke	Darke	OH
Darkesville	Berkeley	WV
Darkey Springs	White	TN
Darksville	Randolph	MO
Darlington	Montgomery	IN
Darlington	St. Helena	LA
Darlington	Harford	MD
Darlington	Richland	OH
Darlington	Beaver	PA
Darlington (c.h.)	La Fayette	WI
Darlington (c.h.)	Darlington	SC
Darlington Heights	Prince Edward	VA
Darnestown	Montgomery	MD
Darnstadt	St. Clair	IL
Darrtown	Butler	OH
Dartford (c.h.)	Green Lake	WI
Dartmouth	Bristol	MA
Darwin	Clark	IL
Darwin	Carroll	IN
Darwin	Meeker	MN
Darysaw	Jefferson	AR
Dassel	Meeker	MN
Dauphin	Dauphin	PA
Dauphine	Osage	MO
Davenport (c.h.)	Scott	IA
Davenport	Dade	MO
Davenport	Delaware	NY
Davenport Centre	Delaware	NY
Davidsburgh	York	PA
Davidson	Montgomery	OH
Davidson	Sullivan	PA
Davidson College	Mecklenburgh	NC
Davidson's Ferry	Fayette	PA
Davidson's River	Transylvania	NC
Davidsonville	Anne Arundel	MD
Davidsville	Somerset	PA
Davilla	Milam	TX
Davis	Stephenson	IL
Davisborough	Washington	GA
Davisburgh	Oakland	MI
Davis City	Decatur	IA
Davis Corners	Adams	WI
Davis Creek	Fayette	AL
Davis' Cross Roads	Cherokee	AL
Davis Grove	Montgomery	PA
Davis Mill	Alleghany	MD
Daivs' Mills	Benton	MS
Davis' Mills	Bedford	VA
Davison	Genesee	MI
Davistown	Greene	PA
Davisville	Calhoun	AL
Davisville	Yolo	CA
Davisville	Sanilac	MI
Davisville	Bucks	PA
Davisville	Washington	RI
Davisville	Wood	WV
Dawkin's Mills	Jackson	OH
Dawn	Livingston	MO
Dawn	Darke	OH
Dawson (c.h.)	Terrell	GA
Dawson	Sangamon	IL
Dawson's Mills	Richardson	NE
Dawson's Prairie	Kaufman	TX
Dawson's Station	Fayette	PA
Dawsonville (c.h.)	Dawson	GA
Dawsonville	Montgomery	MD
Dawnsonville	Greene	VA
Day	Saratoga	NY
Day Book	Yancey	NC
Day's Mills	Bibb	AL
Day's Store	Greene	PA
Daysville	Ogle	IL
Daysville	Todd	KY
Daysville	Oswego	NY
Daysville	Londoun	VA

PLACE NAMES OF THE UNITED STATES

PLACE	COUNTY	STATE	PLACE	COUNTY	STATE	PLACE	COUNTY	STATE
Dayton	Marengo	AL	De Pue	Bureau	IL	Dickinson's	Franklin	VA
Dayton	La Salle	IL	Deputy	Jefferson	IN	Dickson	Colbert	AL
Dayton	Tippecanoe	IN	Derby	New Haven	CT	Dickson	Benton	AR
Dayton	Bremer	IA	Derby	Perry	IN	Dickersonville	Niagara	NY
Dayton	Bourbon	KS	Derby	Orleans	VT	Dickeysville	Grant	WI
Dayton	Campbell	KY	Derby Line	Orleans	VT	Dickeyville	Aroostook	ME
Dayton	York	ME	Derinda	Jo Daviess	IL	Dickinson	Franklin	NY
Dayton	Howard	MD	De Roche	Clark	AR	Dickinson	Cumberland	PA
Dayton	Berrien	MI	Derry	Rockingham	NH	Dickinson Centre	Franklin	NY
Dayton	Hennepin	MN	Derry Church	Dauphin	PA	Dickson	Dickson	TN
Dayton	Cass	MO	Derry Depot	Rockingham	NH	Dicksonburg	Crawford	PA
Dayton (c.h.)	Lyon	NV	Derry Station	Westmoreland	PA	Dido	Choctaw	MS
Dayton	Middlesex	NJ	De Ruyter	Madison	NY	Dichlstadt	Scott	MO
Dayton	Cattarangus	NY	Des Arc	Prairie	AR	Difficult	Smith	TN
Dayton	Wake	NC	Deschutes	Wasco	OR	Dighton	Bristol	MA
Delta	McLean	IL	Deselm	Kankakee	IL	Dillard's Wharf	Surry	VA
Delta	Parke	IN	Deseret	Millard	UT	Dille's Bottom	Belmont	OH
Delta (c.h.)	Madison	LA	DES MOINES (c.h.)	Polk	IA	Dillingersville	Lehigh	PA
Delta	Eaton	MI	De Soto	Jackson	IL	Dillon	Taxewell	IL
Delta	Oneida	NY	De Soto	Dallas	IA	Dillon	Phelps	MO
Delta	Fulton	OH	De Sota	Johnson	KS	Dillon's Run	Hampshire	WV
Delta	York	PA	De Soto	Clark	MS	Dillsborough	Dearborn	IN
Delta Mills	Walla Walla	WA	De Soto	Jefferson	MO	Dillsburgh	York	PA
Delton	Sauk	WI	De Soto	Washington	NE	Dilworthtown	Chester	PA
Deming	Hamilton	IN	De Soto	Vernon	WI	Dimock	Susquehanna	PA
Democracy	Knox	OH	De Soto Front	De Soto	MS	Dimon	Leavenworth	KS
Democrat	Walker	AL	De Sotoville	Choctaw	AL	Dingman's Ferry	Pike	PA
Democrat	Buncombe	NC	Des Peres	St. Louis	MO	Dinsmore	Shelby	OH
Demopoiis (c.h.)	Marengo	AL	Des Plaines	Cook	IL	Dinsmore	Washington	PA
Demos	Belmont	OH	Detour	Chippewa	MI	Dinwiddie (c.h.)	Dinwiddie	VA
De Mossville	Pendleton	KY	Detroit	Sanford	AL	Diona	Coles	IL
Dempseytown	Venango	PA	Detroit	Pike	IL	Dirigo	Kennebec	ME
Denison (c.h.)	Crawford	IA	Detroit	Dickinson	KS	Dirt Town	Chattooga	GA
Denison	Herkimer	NY	Detroit	Somerset	ME	Disco	Macomb	MI
Denmark	Perry	IL	Detroit (c.h.)	Wayne	MI	Discord	Woodbury	IA
Denmark	Lee	IA	Detroit City	Becker	MN	Dismal	Sampson	NC
Denmark	Oxford	ME	Devall's Bluff (c.h.)	Prairie	AR	Dispatch	New Kent	VA
Denmark	Tuscola	MI	Devereaux Station	Hancock	GA	Disputanta	Prince George	VA
Denmark	Lewis	NY	De View	Woodruff	AR	Ditney Hill	Dubois	IN
Denmark	Ashtabula	OH	Dewart	Northumberland	PA	Dittmer's Store	Jefferson	MO
Denmark	Madison	TN	De Witt (c.h.)	Arkansas	AR	Divide	Anderson	KS
Denmark	Brown	WI	De Witt	De Witt	IL	Dividing Creek	Cumberland	NJ
Dennard's Bluff	Monroe	AL	De Witt (c.h.)	Clinton	IA	Dividing Ridge	Pendleton	KY
Denning	Uster	NY	De Witt	Clinton	MI	Dividing Ridge	Somerset	PA
Denning's	Carroll	MD	De Witt	Carroll	MO	Dix	Jefferson	IL
Dennis	Appanoose	IA	De Witt	Cuming	NE	Dixfield	Oxford	ME
Dennis	Barnstable	MA	De Witt	Onondaga	NY	Dixfield Centre	Oxford	ME
Dennis Mil's	St. Helena	LA	De Wittville	Chautauqua	NY	Dix Hills	Suffolk	NY
Dennison	Clark	IL	Dexter	Perry	IN	Dixie	Bossier	LA
Dennison	Ottawa	MI	Dexter	Dallas	IA	Dixie	Williamsburgh	SC
Dennison	Tuscarawas	OH	Dexter	Cowley	KS	Dixmont	Penobscot	ME
Dennis Port	Barstable	MA	Dexter	Penobscot	ME	Dixmont	Allegheny	PA
Dennisville	Cape May	NJ	Dexter	Washtenaw	MI	Dixmont Centre	Penobscot	ME
Denny	Warren	IL	Dexter	Jefferson	NY	Dixon	Solano	CA
Dennysville	Washington	ME	Dexter	Meigs	OH	Dixon	Dawson	GA
Dent	Hamilton	OH	D'Hanis	Medina	TX	Dixon (c.h.)	Lee	IL
Dent	Greene	PA	Dialton	Clark	OH	Dixon	Scott	IA
Denton (c.h.)	Caroline	MD	Diamond	Venango	PA	Dixon (c.h.)	Webster	KY
Denton	Wayne	MI	Diamond	Juab	UT	Dixon	Pulaski	MO
Denton (c.h.)	Denton	TX	Diamond Bluff	Pierce	WY	Dixon	Van Wert	OH
Dent's Run	Elk	PA	Diamond City (c.h.)	Meagher	MT	Dixon	Wyoming	PA
DENVER (c.h.)	Arapahoe	CO	Diamond Cross	Randolph	IL	Dixon's Springs	Trousdale	TN
Denver	Hancock	IL	Diamond Grove	Jasper	MO	Dixonville	Indiana	PA
Denver	Miami	IN	Diamond Hill	Anson	NC	Doaksville	Choctaw Nation	IN
Denver	Bremer	IA	Diamond Hill	Providence	RI	Dobb's Ferry	Westchester	NY
Denver	Newaygo	MI	Diamond Lake	Lake	IL	Dobson (c.h.)	Surry	SC
Denverton	Solano	CA	Diamond Mountain	White Pine	NV	Dobson (c.h.)	Surry	NC
Denville	Morris	NJ	Diamond Spring	El Dorado	CA	Doctor Town	Wayne	GA
Depanville	Jefferson	NY	Diamond Springs	Morris	KS	Doddsville	Schuyler	IL
De Pere	Brown	WI	Diana	Lewis	NY	Dodge	Guthrie	LA
De Peyster	St. Lawrence	NY	Diana Mills	Buckingham	VA	Dodge Centre	Dodge	MN
Deposit	Jefferson	KY	Dias Creek	Cape May	NJ	Dodge City	Steele	MN
Deposit	Broome	NY	Dickensonville	Russell	VA	Dodge's Corner's	Wankesha	WI

PLACE	COUNTY	STATE	PLACE	COUNTY	STATE	PLACE	COUNTY	STATE
Dodgeville	Des Moines	IA	Double Shoal	Cleveland	NC	Doyle's Mills	Juniata	PA
Dodgeville (c.h.)	Iowa	WI	Double Springs	Benton	AR	Doylesport	Barton	MO
Dodsonville	Jackson	AL	Double Springs	Oktibbeha	MS	Doyleston	St. Clair	MO
Dodsonville	Highland	OH	Double Springs	Putnam	TN	Doylestown (c.h.)	Bucks	PA
Doe Hill	Highland	VA	Double Springs	Tarrant	TX	Doylestown	Columbia	WI
Doe Run	Chester	PA	Double Wells	Warren	GA	Dracut	Middlesex	MA
Dog Creek	Putnam	OH	Doud Station	Van Furea	IA	Drady's	Wayne	GA
Dog Town	McMullen	TX	Dougherty's Station	Alameda	CA	Drake	Gasconade	MO
Doko	Fairfield	SC	Douglas	Coffee	GA	Drake's Branch	Charlotte	VA
Dolington	Bucks	PA	Douglas	Knox	IL	Drake's Creek	Madison	AR
Dolingville	Jefferson	PA	Douglas	Jackson	LA	Drake's Mills	Crawford	PA
Dolle's Mills	Bollinger	MO	Douglas	Allegan	MI	Drakestown	Morris	NJ
Dolten's Station	Cook	IL	Douglas	Gentry	MO	Drakesville	Davis	IA
Dona Ana	Dona Ana	NM	Douglas	Rockingham	NC	Drakesville	Morris	NJ
Donald	Washington	KS	Douglas Centre	Clay	IA	Dranesville	Fairfax	VA
Donaldson	Schuylkill	PA	Douglas Centre	Marquette	WI	Draper	Salt Lake	UT
Donaldsonville (c.h.)	Ascension	LA	Douglas City	Trinity	CA	Drapersville	Meeklenburgh	VA
Donally's Mills	Perry	PA	Douglass	Worcester	MA	Dravosburgh	Allegheny	PA
Donation	Huntingdon	PA	Douglass	Fayette	IA	Draw Bridge	Sussex	DE
Doncaster	Charles	MD	Douglass	Butler	KS	Draw Bridge	Dorchester	MD
Donegal	Westmoreland	PA	Douglass	Montgomery	PA	Drayton Plains	Oakland	MI
Donelan	Dubuque	IA	Douglass	Nacogdoches	TX	Drehersville	Schuylkill	PA
Donaldson	Marshall	IN	Douglassville	Berks	PA	Dresbach	Winona	MN
Donelson	Davidson	TN	Douglassville	Davis	TX	Dresden	Lincoln	ME
Donelton	Hunt	TX	Dousman	Waukesha	WI	Dresden	Pettis	MO
Donersville	Burnett	WI	Dover (c.h.)	Pope	AR	Dresden	Yates	NY
Dongola	Union	IL	Dover	Merced	CA	Dresden	Muskingum	OH
Doniphan	Doniphan	KS	Dover (c.h.)	Kent	DE	Dresden (c.h.)	Weakley	TN
Doniphan (c.h.)	Ripley	MO	Dover	Bureau	IL	Dresden	Navarro	TX
Don Juan	Perry	IN	Dover	Boone	IN	Dresden Mills	Lincoln	ME
Donley	Washington	PA	Dover	Lee	IA	Dresselville	Le Sueur	MN
Donaldsville	Abbeville	SC	Dover	Shawnee	KS	Dresserville	Cayuga	NY
Donneganna	Riley	KS	Dover	Mason	KY	Drewersburgh	Franklin	IN
Donnellson	Montgomery	IL	Dover (c.h.)	Piscataquis	ME	Drewryville	Southampton	VA
Donnelsville	Clark	OH	Dover	Norfolk	MA	Drew's Station	St. Bernard	LA
Doolittle's Mills	Perry	IN	Dover	La Fayette	MO	Drewsville	Cheshire	NH
Doon	Lyon	IA	Dover (c.h.)	Strafford	NH	Dreyspring	Montgomery	AL
Door Creek	Dane	WI	Dover	Morris	NJ	Driftwood	Cameron	PA
Door Village	La Porte	IN	Dover	Dutchess	NY	Dripping Springs	Hays	TX
Dora	Pike	AR	Dover	Craven	NC	Drum's	Luzerne	PA
Dora	Wabash	IN	Dover	Cuyahoga	OH	Drury	Rock Island	IL
Dora	Labette	KS	Dover	York	PA	Dry Branch	Franklin	MO
Doran	Mitchell	IA	Dover (ch.)	Stewart	TN	Dry Brook	Ulster	NY
Doraville	De Kalb	GA	Dover	Windham	VT	Dry Cove	Jackson	AL
Doraville	Broome	NY	Dover	Iowa	WI	Dry Creek	Lawrence	AL
Dorcheat	Columbia	AR	Dover Centre	Olmsted	MN	Dry Creek	Linn	IA
Dorchester	Macoupin	IL	Dover Furnace	Dutchess	NY	Dry Creek	Sedgwick	KS
Dorchester	Allamakee	IA	Dover Hill (c.h.)	Martin	IN	Dry Creek	Crawford	MO
Dorchester	Norfolk	MA	Dover Mines	Goochland	VA	Dryden	Tama	IA
Dorchester	Saline	NE	Dover Plains	Dutchess	NY	Dryden	Lapeer	MI
Dorchester	Grafton	NH	Dover South Mills	Piscataquis	ME	Dryden	Sibley	MN
Dorlan's Mills	Chester	PA	Dove's Creek	Elbert	GA	Dryden	Jefferson	NE
Dormansville	Albany	NY	Dove's Depot	Darlington	SC	Dryden	Tompkins	NY
Dorn's Gold Mines	Abbeville	SC	Dow	Cass	IN	Dry Fork	Barren	KY
Dornsife	Northumberland	PA	Dowagiac	Cass	MI	Dry Frok	Wise	VA
Dorn's Mill	Edgefield	SC	Dowdallville	Peoria	IL	Dry Grove	Hinds	MS
Dorr	Allegan	MI	Dowd's Landing	Coahoma	MS	Dry Hill	Jackson	IL
Dorrance	Luzerne	PA	Downer's Grove	Du Page	IL	Dry Hill	Lauderdale	TN
Dorret's Run	Hardin	KY	Downey	Cedar	IA	Dry Lake	Wright	IA
Dorrville	Washington	RI	Downey's Spring	Randolph	AR	Dry Mills	Cumberland	ME
Dorset	De Kalb	IL	Down Hill	Crawford	IN	Dry Ponds	Catawba	NC
Dorset	Ashtabula	OH	Downieville (c.h.)	Sierra	CA	Dry Ridge	Grant	KY
Dorset	Bennington	VT	Downing's Mills	Strafford	NH	Dry Ridge	Hamilton	OH
Dorset	Monroe	WI	Downingsville	Grant	KY	Dry Run	Scott	KY
Dorsey	Madison	IL	Downington	Meigs	OH	Dry Runn	Prentiss	MS
Dorseyville	Allegheny	PA	Downingtown	Chester	PA	Dry Runn	Franklin	PA
Dothen	Henry	AL	Downsville	Union	LA	Drytown	Amador	CA
Doty's Corner	Steuben	NY	Downsville	Washington	MD	Dryville	Berks	PA
Dotyville	Fond du Lac	WI	Downsville	Delaware	NY	Dry Wood	Vernon	MO
Double Bridge	Lunenburgh	VA	Downsville	Dunn	WI	Duane	Franklin	NY
Double Bridges	Lauderdale	TN	Doyle	Marion	KS	Duanesburgh	Schenectady	NY
Double Horn	Burnet	TX	Doyle	Columbia	WI	Dublin	Fayette	AL
Double Pipe Creek	Carroll	MD	Doylesburgh	Franklin	PA	Dublin (c.h.)	Laurens	GA

PLACE	COUNTY	STATE	PLACE	COUNTY	STATE	PLACE	COUNTY	STATE
Dublin	Wayne	IN	Dundaff	Susquehanna	PA	Durham	Bucks	PA
Dublin	Graves	KY	Dundarrach	Robeson	NC	Durham Centre	Middlesex	CT
Dublin	Harford	MD	Dundas	Richland	IL	Durham Hill	Waukesha	WI
Dublin	Harford	MD	Dundas	Rice	MN	Durham's	Orange	NC
Dublin	Cheshire	NH	Dundas	Pulaski	MO	Durhamville	Oneida	NY
Dublin	Franklin	OH	Dundas	Vinton	OH	Durhamville	Lauderdale	TN
Dublin	Bucks	PA	Dundas	Calumet	WI	Durlach	Lancaster	PA
Dublin	Pulaski	VA	Dundee	Kane	IL	Duroc	Benton	MO
Dublin Mills	Fulton	PA	Dundee	Monroe	MI	Dushore	Sullivan	PA
Dubois	Dodge	GA	Dundee	Franklin	MO	Dustin	De Kalb	IL
Dubois	Washington	IL	Dundee	Yates	NY	Dutch Creek	Washington	IA
Dubuquo (c.h.)	Dubuque	IA	Dundee	Tuscarawas	OH	Dutche's Creek	Yell	AR
Duchateau	Door	WI	Dundee	Fond du Lac	WI	Dutch Flat	Placer	CA
Duck Creek	Walker	GA	Dun Ellen	Middlesex	NJ	Dutch Hill	St. Clair	IL
Duck Creek	Warren	IL	Dungannon	Columbiana	OH	Dutch Hill	Crawford	PA
Duck Creek	Braxton	WV	Dun Glen	Humboldt	NV	Dutch Neck	Mercer	NJ
Duckers	Woodford	KY	Dunham	Washington	OH	Dutchtown	Cape Girardeau	MO
Duck Hill	Montgomery	MS	Dunkard	Greene	PA	Dutchville	Granville	NC
Duck Pond	Cumberland	ME	Dunkinsville	Adams	OH	Dutzow	Warren	MO
Duck Port	Madison	LA	Dunkirk	Jay	IN	Duvall's Landing	Greenup	KY
Duck River	Hickman	TN	Dunkirk	Calvert	MD	Duxbury	Plymouth	MA
Duck's Branch	Barnwell	SC	Dunkirk	Chautauqua	NY	Dwaar's Kill	Ulster	NY
Ducktown	Polk	TN	Dunkirk	Hanrdin	OH	Dwight	Livingston	IL
Dudley	Edgar	IL	Dunkirk	Dane	WI	Dyberry	Wayne	PA
Dudley	Wapello	IA	Dunkle's Store	Lawrence	MO	Dyckesville	Kewaunee	WI
Dudley	Worcester	MA	Dunklin	Greenville	SC	Dycusburgh	Crittenden	KY
Dudley	Wayne	NC	Dunlap	Harrison	IA	Dye	Martin	IN
Dudley	Huntingdon	PA	Dunlap	Hamilton	OH	Dyer	Lake	IN
Dudleytown	Jackson	IN	Dunlap (c.h.)	Sequatchie	TN	Dyer Brook	Aroostook	ME
Dudleyville	Bond	IL	Dunlapsville	Union	IN	Dyersburgh (c.h.)	Dyer	TN
Duelin	Benton	MN	Dunleith	Jo Daviess	IL	Dyer's Station	Gibson	TN
Due West	Abbeville	SC	Dunleith	Wayne	WV	Dyer's Store	Henry	VA
Duff	Dubois	IN	Dunlevy	Warren	OH	Dyersville	Dubuque	IA
Duffan	Earth	TX	Dunmore	Luzerne	PA	Dykeman's	Putnam	NY
Buffield	Charles	MD	Dunmore	Pocahontas	WV	Dyson's	Guernsey	OH
Duffield's	Jefferson	WV	Dunn	Moultrie	IL	Dyson's Mill	Edgefield	SC
Dugansville	Mercer	KY	Dunnings	Luzerne	PA	Dysortville	McDowell	NC
Dugansville	Grayson	TX	Dunningsville	Washington	PA			
Duggar's Ferry	Carter	TN	Dunnington	Hickman	TN	Eagle	Bremer	IA
Dug Hill	Carroll	MD	Dunningville	Allegan	MI	Eagle	Pottawatomie	KS
Dug Spur	Carroll	VA	Dunn's Rock	Transylvania	NC	Eagle	Clinton	MI
Dugway	Oswego	NY	Dunn's Store	Caroline	VA	Eagle	Harrison	MO
Dukedom	Weakley	TN	Dunnsville	Albany	NY	Eagle	Cass	NE
Dulaney's Valley	Baltimore	MD	Dunnsville	Essex	VA	Eagle	Wyoming	NY
Duluth	Gwinnett	GA	Dunnville	Dunn	WI	Eagle	Warren	PA
Duluth (c.h.)	St. Louis	MN	Dunreith	Henry	IN	Eagle	Waukesha	WI
Duluth	Wood	OH	Dunsfort	Washington	PA	Eagle Bend	Clay	KS
Dumas	Tippah	MS	Sunstable	Middlesex	MA	Eagle Bridge	Rensselaer	NY
Dumas Ferry	Anson	NC	Dunton	Cook	IL	Eagle City	Sibley	MN
Dumfries	Prince William	VA	Dupage	Will	IL	Eagle Cliff	Walker	GA
Dummerston	Windham	VT	Du Plain	Clinton	MI	Eagle Corners	Richalnd	WI
Dumontville	Fairfield	OH	Duplainville	Waukesha	WI	Eagle Creek	Bradley	AR
Dunbar	Washington	OH	Dupont	Jefferson	IN	Eagle Creek	Lyon	KS
Dunbar	Fayette	PA	Dupont	Putnam	OH	Eagle Creek	Clackamas	OR
Dunbarton	Merrimack	NH	Dupont	Wanpaca	WI	Eagle Foundry	Huntingdon	PA
Dunbarton	Adams	OH	Dupree's Old Store	Charlotte	VA	Eagle Furnace	Roane	TN
Dunbarton	Barnwell	SC	Duquoin	Perry	IL	Eagle Grove	Hart	GA
Duncan	Monroe	AR	Durand			Eagle Grove	Wright	IA
Duncan	Stark	IL	Durand (c.h.)	Pepin	WI	Eagle Harbor	Keweenaw	MI
Duncan	Mercer	KY	Durand Station	Winnebago	IL	Eagle Harbor	Orleans	NY
Duncan	Webster	MO	Durango	Dubuque	IA	Eagle Hill	Polk	AR
Duncan	Allegheny	PA	Durant	Cedar	IA	Eagle Hill	Owen	KY
Duncan Creek	Vernon	MO	Durant	Holmes	MS	Eagle Iron Works	Wythe	VA
Duncannon	Perry	PA	Durant's Neck	Perquimons	NC	Eagle Lake	Will	IL
Duncanon	Stephenson	IL	Durbin's Corners	Williams	OH	Eagle Lake	Colorado	TX
Duncan's Creek	Rutherford	NC	Durell	Bradford	PA	Eagle Lake City	Marshall	IN
Duncan's Falls	Muskingum	OH	Durgen's Creek	Lewis	MO	Eagle Landing	Pulaski	AR
Duncan's Mills	Sonoma	CA	Durham	Butte	CA	Eagle Mills	Fayette	AL
Duncan's Mills	Fulton	IL	Durham	Middlesex	CT	Eagle Mills	Rensselaer	NY
Duncan's Mills	Scott	VA	Durham	Hancock	IL	Eagle Mills	Iredell	NC
Duncan's Retreat	Kane	UT	Durham	Androscoggin	ME	Eagle Mills	Vinton	OH
Duncansville	Blair	PA	Durham	Strafford	NH	Eagle Pass (c.h.)	Maverick	TX
Duncombe	Webster	IA	Durham	Greene	NY	Eagle Point	Ogle	IL

PLACE NAMES OF THE UNITED STATES

PLACE	COUNTY	STATE
Eagle Point	Berks	PA
Eagle River (c.h.)	Keweenaw	MI
Eagle Rock	Oneida	ID
Eagle Rock	Wake	NC
Eagle Rock	Venango	PA
Eagle Salt Works	Churchill	NV
Eaglesfield	Clay	IN
Eagle's Mere	Sullivan	PA
Eagle Springs	Jefferson	IN
Eagle Springs	Coryell	TX
Eagle Station	Carroll	KY
Eagle Tannery	Wayne	TN
Eagletown	Hamilton	IN
Eagle Village	Wyoming	NY
Eagleville	Siskiyon	CA
Eagleville	Tolland	CT
Eagleville	Ashabula	OH
Eagleville	Montgomery	PA
Eagleville	Rutherford	TN
Eakin	Allegheny	PA
Eakle's Mills	Washington	MD
Earle	Vanderburgh	IN
Earle	Lucas	IA
Earle's	Muhlenburgh	KY
Earlesville	Spartanburg	SC
Earleton	Neosho	KS
Earley	Elk	PA
Earleysville	Albemarle	VA
Earlham	Madison	IA
Earlington	Hopkins	KY
Earlobion	Obion	TN
Earlville	La Salle	IL
Earlville	Delaware	IA
Earlville	Madison	NY
Earlville	Portage	OH
Earlville	Berks	PA
Early Grove	Marshall	MS
Earpsborough	Johnston	NC
Eartmon	Dodge	GA
East Abington	Plymouth	MA
Easta Boga	Talladega	AL
East Acworth	Sullivan	NH
East Albany	Orleans	VT
East Alburgh	Grand Isle	VT
Eastaloe	Pickens	SC
East Alton	Belknap	NH
East Amherst	Erie	NY
East Andover	Merrimack	NH
East Arcade	Wyoming	NY
East Arlington	Bennington	VT
East Ashford	Cattaraugus	NY
East Auburn	Androscoggin	ME
East Aurora	Erie	NY
East Avon	Livingston	NY
East Baldwin	Cumberland	ME
East Bangor	Penobscot	ME
East Barnard	Windsor	VT
East Beekmantown	Clinton	NY
East Bend	Ford	IL
East Bend	Yadkin	NC
East Benton	Kennebec	ME
East Benton	Luzerne	PA
East Berkshire	Tioga	NY
East Berkshire	Franklin	VT
East Berlin	Hartford	CT
East Berlin	Adams	PA
East Berne	Albany	NY
East Bethany	Genesee	NY
East Bethel	Windsor	VT
East Bethlehem	Washington	PA
East Blackstone	Worcester	MA
East Bloomfield	Ontario	NY
East Boston	Madison	NY
East Bowdoinham	Sagadahoc	ME
East Boyleston	Oswego	NY
East Bradford	Penobscot	ME
East Branch	Delaware	NY
East Brewster	Barnstable	MA
East Bridgewater	Plymouth	MA
½East Bridgewater	Susquehanna	PA
East Brimfield	Hampden	MA
East Brook	Lawrence	PA
East Brookfield	Worcester	MA
East Brookfield	Orange	VT
East Brooklyn	Poweshiek	IA
East Bucksport	Hancock	ME
East Burke	Caledonia	VT
East Burlington	Kane	IL
East Cabot	Washington	VT
East Calais	Washington	VT
East Cambridge	Middlesex	MA
East Cambridge	Lamoille	VT
East Canaan	Litchfield	CT
East Canaan	Grafton	NH
East Canton	Bradford	PA
East Carmel	Columbiana	OH
East Carlton	Orleans	NY
East Castle Rock	Dakota	MN
East Chain Lakes	Martin	MN
East Charlemont	Franklin	MA
East Charleston	Tioga	PA
East Charleston	Orlenas	VT
East Chatham	Columbia	NY
East Chatham	Tioga	PA
East Chester	West Chester	NY
East Clarence	Erie	NY
East Clarendon	Rutland	VT
East Claridon	Geauga	OH
East Clarksfield	Huron	OH
East Clarkson	Monroe	NY
East Cleveland	Cuyahoga	OH
East Cobleskill	Schoharie	NY
East Concord	Merrimack	NH
East Concord	Erie	NY
East Constable	Franklin	NY
East Corinth	Penobscot	ME
East Corinth	Orange	VT
East Cornwall	Litchfield	CT
East Coventry	Chester	PA
East Coventry	Orleans	VT
East Craftsbury	Orleans	VT
East Creek	Cape May	NJ
East Creek	Herkimer	NY
East Dayton	Tuscola	MI
East Deering	Hillsborough	NH
East De Kalb	St. Lawrence	NY
East Delavan	Walworth	WI
East Dennis	Barnstable	MA
East Derry	Rockingham	NH
East Dickinson	Franklin	NY
East Dimock	Susquehanna	PA
East Dixfield	Oxford	ME
East Dixmont	Penobscot	ME
East Dorset	Bennington	VT
East Douglass	Worcester	MA
East Dover	Piscataquis	ME
East Dover	Windham	VT
East Durham	Greene	NY
East Eddington	Penobscot	ME
East Eden	Hancock	
East Eden	Hancock	ME
East Eden	Erie	NY
East Elba	Genesee	NY
East Elma	Erie	NY
East Elmore	Lamoille	VT
East Enterprise	Switzerland	IN
Eastern	Franklin	IL
East Evans	Erie	NY
East Exeter	Penobscot	ME
East Fairfield	Columbiana	OH
East Fairfield	Franklin	VT
East Falmouth	Barnstable	MA
East Finley	Washington	PA
East Fishkill	Dutchess	NY
East Florence	Oneida	NY
Eastford	Windham	CT
East Fork	Montgomery	IL
East Fork	Metcalfe	KY
East Foxborough	Norfolk	MA
East Franklin	Franklin	VT
East Freedom	Blair	PA
East Freetown	Bristol	MA
East Fryeburgh	Oxford	ME
East Gaines	Orleans	NY
East Gainesville	Wyoming	NY
East Gallatin	Gallatin	MT
East Galway	Saratoga	NY
East Genoa	Caynga	NY
East Georgia	Franklin	VT
East German	Chenaugo	NY
East Germantown	Wayne	IN
East Gibson	Manitowoc	WI
East Gilead	Branch	MI
East Glastenbury	Hartford	CT
East Glenville	Schenectady	NY
East Gloucester	Essex	MA
East Granby	Hartford	CT
East Granger	Allegany	NY
East Granville	Hampden	MA
East Granville	Addison	VT
East Greenbush	Rensselaer	NY
East Greene	Chenango	NY
East Greene	Erie	PA
East Greensborough	Orelans	VT
East Greenville	Stark	OH
East Greenwich	Washington	NY
East Greenwich (c.h.)	Kent	RI
East Greenwood	Muskingum	OH
East Grove	Chemung	NY
East Groveland	Livingston	NY
East Guilford	Chenango	NY
East Haddam	Middlesex	CT
Eastham	Barnstable	MA
East Hamburg	Erie	NY
East Hamilton	Madison	NY
East Hampden	Penobscot	MA
East Hampstead	Rockingham	NH
East Hampton	Middlesex	CT
East Hampton	Cherokee	IA
East Hampton	Hampshire	MA
East Hampton	Suffolk	NY
East Hanover	Lebanon	PA
East Hardwick	Caledonia	VT
East Harlem	Cook	IL
East Harpswell	Cumberland	ME
East Hartford	Hartford	CT
East Harwich	Barnstable	MA
East Haven	New Haven	CT
East Haven	Essex	VT
East Haverhill	Essex	MA
East Haverhill	Grafton	NH
East Hebron	Oxford	ME
East Hebron	Potter	PA
East Hempfield	Lancaster	PA
East Hicotry	Forest	PA
East Highgate	Franklin	VT
East Holden	Penobscot	ME
East Holliston	Middlesex	MA
East Homer	Cortland	NY

PLACE	COUNTY	STATE	PLACE	COUNTY	STATE	PLACE	COUNTY	STATE
East Homer	Potter	PA	East Norwalk	Huron	OH	East Rodman	Jefferson	NY
East Houndsfield	Jefferson	NY	East Norway	Doniphan	KS	East Roxbury	Washington	VT
East Hubbardton	Rutland		East Norwich	Queens	NY	East Ramford	Oxford	ME
East Hubbardton	Rutland	VT	East Oasis	Wanshara	WI	East Rupert	Bennington	VT
East Hutchinson	McLeod	MN	Easton	Fairfield	CT	East Rush	Susquehanna	PA
East Jeffrey	Cheshire	NH	Easton	Leavenworth	KS	East Rush Creek	Perry	OH
East Java	Wyoming	NY	Easton	Aroostook	ME	East Rushford	Allegany	NY
East Jewett	Greene	NY	Easton (c.h.)	Talbot	MD	East Saginaw	Saginaw	MI
East Kendall	Orleans	NY	Easton	Bristol	MA	East St. Louis	St. Clair	IL
East Kent	Litchfield	CT	Easton	Ionia	MI	East Salamanca	Cattarangus	NY
East Killingly	Windham	CT	Easton	Buchanan	MO	East Salem	Washington	NY
East Kingston	Rockingham	NH	Easton	Washington	NY	East Salem	Juniata	PA
East Knox	Waldo	ME	Easton	Wayne	OH	East Salisbury	Essex	MA
East Lamoine	Hancock	ME	Easton (c.h.)	Northampton	PA	East Sandwich	Barnstable	MA
East Landaff	Grafton	NH	Easton	Monogalia	WV	East Sangerville	Piscataquis	ME
East Lansing	Tompkins	NY	Easton	Adams	WI	East Sandy	Venango	PA
East Laport	Jackson	NC	East Orange	Essex	NJ	East Sandy Creek	Oswego	NY
East Lebanon	Grafton	NH	East Orange	Schnyler	NY	East Schodack	Rensselaer	NY
East Lee	Berkshire	MA	East Orange	Delaware	OH	East Schuyler	Herkimer	NY
East Lempster	Sullivan	NH	East Orange	Orange	VT	East Scott	Cortland	NY
East Leon	Cattarangus	NY	East Orangeville	Wyoming	NY	East Setauket	Suffolk	NY
East Leroy	Calhoun	MI	East Orleans	Barnstable	MA	East Sharon	Norfolk	MA
East Lewistown	Mahoning	OH	East Orrington	Penobscot	ME	East Sharon	Potter	PA
East Lexington	Middlesex	MA	East Otis	Berkshire	MA	East Sharpsburgh	Blair	PA
East Liberty	Logan	OH	East Otisfield	Cumberland	ME	East Sheffield	Berkshire	MA
East Liberty	Fayette	PA	East Otto	Cattarangus	NY	East Shelburne	Franklin	MA
East Limington	York	ME	East Palermo	Waldo	ME	East Shelby	Orleans	NY
East Lincoln	Penobscot	ME	East Palermo	Oswego	NY	East Sheldon	Franklin	VT
East Line	Saratoga	NY	East Palestine	Columbiana	OH	East Smithfield	Bradford	PA
East Litchfield	Litchfield	CT	East Palmyra	Wayne	NY	East Somerville	Middlesex	MA
East Livermore	Androscoggin	ME	East Parsonfield	Yrok	ME	East Springfield	Sullivan	NH
East Liverpool	Columbiana	OH	East Paw Paw	De Kalb	IL	East Springfield	Otsego	NY
East Long Meadow	Hampden	MA	East Pembroke	Plymouth	MA	East Springfield	Jefferson	OH
East Lowell	Penobscot	ME	East Pembroke	Merrimack	NH	East Springfield	Erie	PA
East Lyme	New London	CT	East Pembroke	Genesee	NY	East Springhill	Bradford	PA
East Lyme	Cass	MO	East Penfield	Monroe	NY	East Steuben	Oneida	NY
East McDonough	Chenango	NY	East Pepin	Pepin	WI	East Stoneham	Oxford	ME
East Machias	Washington	ME	East Pepperell	Middlesex	MA	East Stoughton	Norfolk	MA
East Madison	Somerset	ME	East Peru	Oxford	ME	East Stroudsburgh	Monroe	PA
East Madison	Carroll	NH	East Pharsalia	Chenango	NY	East Sullivan	Hancock	ME
East Maine	Broome	NY	East Pike	Wyoming	NY	East Sullivan	Cheshire	NH
Eastman	Crawford	WI	East Pitcairn	St. Lawrence	NY	East Sumner	Oxford	ME
Eastmansville	Ottawa	MI	East Pittston	Kennebec	ME	East Sycamore	Hamilton	OH
East Marion	Suffolk	NY	East Plainfield	Sullivan	NH	East Taunton	Bristol	MA
East Marshfield	Plymouth	MA	East Plymouth	Ashtabula	OH	East Tawas	Iosco	MI
East Masonville	Delaware	NY	East Poestenskill	Rensselaer	NY	East Templeton	Worcester	MA
East Manch Chunk	Carbon	PA	East Point	Fulton	GA	East Thetford	Orange	VT
East Medway	Norfolk	MA	East Point	Johnson	KY	East Thompson	Windham	CT
East Melrose	Monroe	IA	East Poland	Androscoggin	ME	East Thorndike	Waldo	ME
East Meredith	Delaware	NY	Eastport	Freemont	IA	East Tilton	Belknap	NH
East Meredin	Steele	MN	Eastport	Washington	ME	East Toledo	Lucus	OH
East Middleborough	Plymouth	MA	Eastport	Tishemingo	MS	East Townsend	Huron	OH
East Middlebury	Addison	VT	East Porter	Niagara	NY	East Traverse Bay	Grand Traverse	MI
East Milan	Monroe	MI	East Portland	Multnomah	OR	East Tronpsburgh	Steuben	NY
East Monmouth	Kennebec	ME	East Poultney	Rutland	VT	East Troy	Bradford	PA
East Monroe	Highland	OH	East Prairieville	Rice	MN	East Troy	Walworth	WI
East Montpelier	Washington	VT	East Princeton	Worcester	MA	East Troy Lake	Walworth	WI
East Montville	Waldo	ME	East Providence	Prividence	RI	East Trumbull	Ashtabula	OH
East Moriches	Suffolk	NY	East Putnam	Windham	CT	East Turner	Androscoggin	ME
East Moultonborough	Carroll	NH	East Randolph	Norfolk	MA	East Union	Wayne	OH
East Nassau	Rensselaer	NY	East Randolph	Cattaraugus	NY	East Unity	Sullivan	NH
East New Market	Dorchester	MD	East Randolph	Orange	VT	East Varick	Seneca	NY
East Newport	Penobscot	ME	East Raymond	Cumberland	ME	East Vassalborough	Kennebec	ME
East New Portland	Somerset	ME	East Readfield	Kennebec	ME	East Venice	Cayuga	NY
East New Sharon	Franklin	ME	East Richford	Franklin	VT	East View	Hardin	KY
East New Vineyard	Franklin	ME	East Richland	Belmont	OH	Eastville (c.h.)	Northampton	VA
East New York	Kings	NY	East Ridge	Clearfield	PA	East Vincent	Chester	PA
East Nichols	Tioga	NY	East Ringgold	Pickaway	OH	East Virgil	Cortland	NY
East Nodoway	Adams	IA	East River	New Haven	CT	East Wakefield	Carroll	NH
East Northfield	Cook	IL	East Rochester	Strafford	NH	East Wales	Androscoggin	ME
East Northport	Waldo	ME	East Rochester	Columbiana	OH	East Wallingford	Rutland	VT
East Northwood	Rockingham	NH	East Rockaway	Queens	NY	East Walpole	Norfolk	MA
East North Yarmouth	Cumberland	ME	East Rockport	Cuyahoga	OH	East Wareham	Plymouth	MA

PLACE	COUNTY	STATE	PLACE	COUNTY	STATE	PLACE	COUNTY	STATE
East Warren	Washington	VT	Eddyville	Armstrong	PA	Edna	Cass	IA
East Washington	Sullivan	NH	Eden	Lincoln	Dak	Edneyville	Henderson	NC
East Waterborough	York	ME	Eden	Ellingham	GA	Edom	Rockingham	VA
East Waterford	Juniata	PA	Eden	Iroquois	IL	Edon	Williams	OH
East Watertown	Jefferson	NY	Eden	Hancock	IN	Edray	Pocahontas	WV
East Ware	Hillsborough	NH	Eden	Fayette	IA	Edsallville	Bradford	PA
East Westmoreland	Cheshire	NH	Eden	Atchison	KS	Edson	Chirpewa	WI
East Weymouth	Norfolk	MA	Eden	Hancock	ME	Edwards	Jefferson	KY
East Whately	Franklin	MA	Eden	Ingham	MI	Edwards	St. Lawrence	NY
East Wheatland	Will	IL	Eden	Faribault	MN	Edwards	Patrick	VA
East Wilson	Niagara	NY	Eden	Erie	NY	Edwards	Sheboygan	WI
East Wilton	Franklin	ME	Eden	Randolph	NC	Edwardsburgh	Cass	MI
East Windham	Cumberland	ME	Eden	McKean	PA	Edward's Depot	Hinds	MS
East Windham	Greene	NY	Eden	Laurens	SC	Edwardsport	Knox	IN
East Windsor	Hartford	CT	Eden	Weber	UT	Edward's Station	Peoria	IL
East Windsor	Berkshire	CT	Eden	Lamoille	VT	Edwardsville (c.h.)	Cleburne	AL
East Windsor	Berkshire	MA	Eden	Fond du Lac	WI	Edwardsville (c.h.)	Madison	IL
East Windsor Hill	Hartford	CT	Edenburgh	Shenandoah	VA	Edwardsville	Floyd	IN
East Winthrop	Kennebec	ME	Eden Mills	La Grange	IN	Edwardsville	Wyandotte	KS
East Woburn	Middlesex	MA	Eden Mills	Lamoille	VT	Edwardsville		
East Woodshull	Steuben	NY	Eden Prairie	Hennepin	MN	Edwardsville	St. Lawrence	KY
East Woodstock	Windham	CT	Eden's Ridge	Sullivan	TN	Edwardsville	Surry	NC
East Worcester	Otsego	NY	Edenton	Madison	KY	Edwardsville	Warren	OH
East Wrightstown	Brown	WI	Edenton	St. Lawrence	NY	Edwina	Monroe	OH
Eaton	Crawford	IL	Edenton (c.h.)	Chowan	NC	Eel River	Humboldt	
Eaton	Delaware	IN	Edenton	Clermont	OH	Eel River	Hamboldt	CA
Eaton	Madison	NY	Eden Valley	Erie	NY	Eel River	Allen	IN
Eaton (c.h.)	Preble	OH	Edenville	Marshall	IA	Effingham (c.h.)	Effingham	IL
Eaton	Wyoming	PA	Edenville	Midland	MI	Effingham	Atchison	KS
Eaton	Manitowoe	WI	Edenville	Orange	NY	Effingham	Carroll	NH
Eaton Centre	Carroll	NH	Edenville	Erie	PA	Effingham Falls	Carroll	NH
Eaton Rapids	Eaton	MI	Edes Falls	Cumberland	ME	Effingham Station	Marion	SC
Eaton's Cross Roads	London	TN	Edesville	Kent	MI	Effort	Monroe	PA
Eatonton (c.h.)	Putnam	GA	Edgard (c.h.)	St. John Baptist	LA	Efird's Mills	Stanley	NC
Eatontown	Monmouth	NJ	Edgar Prairie	Phelps	MO	Egan Canyon	Lander	NV
Eatonville	Herkimer	NY	Edgar Springs	Phelps	MO	Eggertsville	Erie	NY
Eau Claire	Berrien	MI	Edgartown (c.h.)	Dukes	MA	Egg Harbor	Door	WI
Eau Claire	Butler	PA	Edgecomb	Lincoln	ME	Egg Harbor City	Atlantic	NJ
Eau Claire (c.h.)	Eau Claire	WI	Edgefield (c.h.)	Edgefield	SC	Eggleston's Springs	Giles	VA
Eau Galle	Dunn	WI	Edgefield Junction	Davidson	TN	Egg's Point	Washington	MS
Eau Gallie	Brevard	FL	Edge Hill	Reynolds	MO	Eglantine	Van Buren	AR
Eau Pleine	Portage	WI	Edge Hill	King George	VA	Egypt	Effingham	GA
Ebenezer	Greene	MO	Edgemont	Delaware	PA	Egypt	Chckasaw	MS
Ebenezer	Erie	NY	Edgerton	El Paso	CO	Egypt	Monroe	NY
Ebenezer	Preble	OH	Edgerton	Johnson	KS	Egypt	Lehigh	PA
Ebenezer	Indiana	PA	Edgerton	Kent	MI	Egypt	Wharton	TX
Ebenezer	Knox	TN	Edgerton	Platte	MO	Egypt	Monroe	WV
Ebensburgh (c.h.)	Cambria	PA	Edgerton	Williams	OH	Egypt Depot	Chatham	NC
Eberhardt	White Pine	NV	Edgerton	Rock	WI	Egypt Mills	Cape Girardeau	MO
Eberie	Effingham	IL	Edgewood	Effingham	IL	Egypt Mills	Pike	PA
Eberly's Mill	Cumberland	PA	Edgewood	Harford	MD	Ehrenberg	Yuma	AZ
Echo	Dale	AL	Edgeworth	Sullivan	TN	Eighteen Mile	Pickens	SC
Echo	Armstrong	PA	Edgwood	Siskiyou	CA	Eight Mile Creek	Harrison	TX
Echo	Trousdale	TN	Edgwood	Buck's	PA	Eight Mile Grove	Cass	NE
Echo	Live Oak	TX	Edina (c.h.)	Knox	MO	Eighty-Eight	Barren	KY
Echo City	Summit	UT	Edinborough	Montgomery	NC	Eitzen	Honston	MN
Eckley	Carroll	OH	Edinborough	Erie	PA	Ekonk	Windham	CT
Eckley	Luzerne	PA	Edinburgh	Christian	IL	Ela	Lake	IL
Eckmansville	Adams	OH	Edinburgh	Johnson	IN	Elam	Delaware	PA
Ecleto	Karnew	TX	Edinburgh	Jones	IA	Elamsville	Patrick	VA
Econfina	Washington	FL	Edinburgh	Hillsdale	MI	Elba (c.h.)	Coffee	AL
Economy	Wayne	IN	Edinburgh	Leake	MS	Elba	Gallatin	IL
Economy	Macon	MO	Edinburgh	Grundy	MO	Elba	Winona	MN
Economy	Beaver	PA	Edinburgh	Mercer	NJ	Elba	Christian	MO
Economy	Hardin	TN	Edinburgh	Saratoga	NY	Elba	Genesee	NY
Ecorse	Wayne	MI	Edinburgh	Portage	OH	Elba	Washington	OH
Eddington	Penobscot	ME	Edinburgh	Lawrence	PA	Elbaville	Davie	NC
Eddington	Bucks	PA	Edinburgh (c.h.)	Hidalgo	TX	Elberfield	Warrick	IN
Eddytown	Yates	NY	Edington	Rock Island	IL	Elberton (c.h.)	Elbert	GA
Eddyville	Pope	IL	Edisto Island	Colleton	SC	Elbinsville	Bedford	PA
Eddyville	Wapello	IA	Edith	Shenandoah	VA	Elbow Spring	Barren	KY
Eddyville (c.h.)	Lyon	KY	Edmeston	Otsego	NY	Elbridge	Edgar	IL
Eddyville	Cattaraugus	NY	Edmonton (c.h.)	Metcalfe	KY	Elbridge	Onondaga	NY

PLACE	COUNTY	STATE
El Dara	Pike	IL
Eldena	Lee	IL
Elder's Ridge	Indiana	PA
Elderton	Armstrong	PA
Eldon	Wapello	IA
Eldora (c.h.)	Hardin	IA
El Dorado (c.h.)	Union	AR
El Dorado	El Dorado	CA
El Dorado	Saline	IL
El Dorado	Fayette	IA
El Dorado (c.h.)	Butler	KS
El Dorado	Clarke	MO
El Dorado	Colfax	NE
El Dorado	Preble	OH
El Dorado	Baker	OR
El Dorado	Blair	PA
El Dorado	Culpeper	VA
El Dorado	Fond du Lac	WI
El Dorado Mills	Fond du Lac	WI
Eldred	Saunders	NE
Eldred	Wayne	PA
Eldredgeville	Ford	IL
Eldredsville	Sullivan	PA
Eldridge	Walker	AL
Eldridge	Scott	IA
Eleroy	Stephenson	IL
Eleven Mile	Potter	PA
Elgin	Jackson	AR
Elgin	Kane	IL
Elgin	Fayette	IA
Elgin	Howard	KS
Elgin	Genesee	MI
Elgin	Wabashaw	MN
Elgin	Cattaraugus	NY
Elhi	Pierce	WA
Elida	Winnebago	IL
Elida	Allen	OH
Elimsport	Lycoming	PA
Elinor	Chase	KS
Elisabeth	Marshall	KS
Eliza	Mercer	IL
Eliza	Houston	TX
Elizabeth	Jo Daviess	IL
Elizabeth	Harrison	IN
Elizabeth (c.h.)	Union	NJ
Elizabeth	Allegheny	PA
Elizabeth	Denton	TX
Elizabeth City (c.h.)	Pasquotank	NC
Elizabeth Furnace	Augusta	VA
Elizabeth Port	Union	NJ
Elizabethton (c.h.)	Carter	TN
Elizabethtown (c.h.)	Hardin	IL
Elizabethtown	Bartholomew	IN
Elizabethtown	Anderson	KS
Elizabethtown (c.h.)	Hardin	KY
Elizabethtown	Otter Tail	MN
Elizabethtown (c.h.)	Colfax	NM
Elizabethtown (c.h.)	Essex	NY
Elizabethtown (c.h.)	Bladen	NC
Elizabethtown	Hamilton	OH
Elizabethtown	Lancaster	PA
Elizabethville	Pendleton	KY
Elizabethville	Dauphin	PA
Elizaville	Boone	IN
Elizaville	Fleming	KY
Elizaville	Columbia	NY
Elk	Decatur	IA
Elk	Saginaw	MI
Elk	Pocahontas	WV
Elk	Manitowoc	WI
Elkader (c.h.)	Clayton	IA
Elk City	Nez Perces	ID
Elk City	Montgomery	KS
Elk City	Barbour	WV
Elk Creek	Spencer	KY
Elk Creek	Texas	MO
Elk Creek	Otsego	NY
Elk Creek	Erie	PA
Elk Creek	Grayson	VA
Elk Creek	Trempealean	WI
Elk Cross Roads	Ashe	NC
Elk Dale	Chester	PA
Elk Falls (c.h.)	Howard	KS
Elk Grove	Sacramento	CA
Elk Grove	Cook	IL
Elk Grove	La Fayette	WI
Elkhart	Elkhart	IN
Elkhart	Polk	IA
Elkhart City	Logan	IL
Elk Head	Christian	MO
Elk Hill Mills	Goochland	VA
Elkhorn	Washington	IL
Elk Horn	Shelby	IA
Elk Horn	Lincoln	KS
Elk Horn	Lawrence	MO
Elk Horn	Polk	OR
Elk Horn (c.h.)	Walworth	WI
Elkhorn City	Douglas	NE
Elk Horn Grove	Carroll	IL
Elkin	Surry	NC
Elkinsville	Brown	IN
Elk Lake	Susquehanna	PA
Elkland	Tuscola	MI
Elkland	Webster	MO
Elkland	Tioga	PA
Elk Lick	Somerset	PA
Elk Mills	McDonald	MO
Elk Mills	Chester	PA
Elk Mound	Dunn	WI
Elko (c.h.)	Elko	NV
Elk Point (c.h.)	Union	Dak
Elkport	Clayton	IA
Elk Prairie	Jefferson	IL
Elk Rapids (c.h.)	Antrim	MI
Elk Ridge Landing	Howard	MD
Elk River	Clinton	IA
Elk River Station	Sherburne	MN
Elk River	Clay	WV
Elk Run	Tioga	PA
Elk Run	Fauquier	VA
Elk Shoals	Iredell	NC
Elk Spring	Warren	KY
Elkton	Crawford	IL
Elkton (c.h.)	Todd	KY
Elkton (c.h.)	Cecil	MD
Elkton	Hickory	MO
Elkton	Columbiana	OH
Elkton	Giles	TN
Elk Valley	Dakota	NE
Elkview	Chester	PA
Elkville	Jackson	IL
Elkville	Wilkes	NC
Ella	Pepin	WI
Ellaville (c.h.)	Schley	GA
Elleard	St. Louis	MO
Ellejoy	Blount	TN
Ellenborough	Ritchie	WV
Ellenborough	Grant	WI
Ellenburgh	Clinton	NY
Ellenburgh Centre	Clinton	NY
Ellenburgh Depot	Clinton	NY
Ellendale	Sussex	DE
Ellendale Forge	Dauphin	PA
Ellengowan	Baltimore	MD
Ellenorah	Gentry	MO
Ellensberg (c.h.)	Curry	
Ellensberg (c.h.)	Curry	OR
Ellenton	Palo Alto	IA
Ellenville	Ulster	NY
Ellerslie	Harris	GA
Ellerslie	Alleghany	MD
Ellerton	Frederick	MD
Ellery	Chautauqua	NY
Ellicott	Erie	NY
Ellicott City (c.h.)	Howard	MD
Ellicottsville (c.h.)	Cattaraugus	NY
Ellijay (c.h.)	Gilmer	GA
Ellington	Tolland	CT
Ellington (c.h.)	Hancock	IA
Ellington	Tuscola	MI
Ellington	Dodge	MN
Ellington	Chautauqua	NY
Ellingwood's Corner	Waldo	ME
Elliot	York	ME
Elliota	Fillmore	MN
Elliot Depot	York	ME
Elliott	San Joaquin	CA
Elliott	Grenada	MS
Elliottsburgh	Perry	PA
Elliott's Cross Roads	Morgan	OH
Elliott's Mill	Panola	MS
Elliotstown	Effingham	IL
Elliotsville	Monroe	MO
Ellis	Joaquin	CA
Ellis	Ellis	KS
Ellis	Portage	WI
Ellisburgh	Camden	NJ
Ellisburgh	Jefferson	NY
Ellisburgh	Potter	PA
Ellisdale	Ocean	NJ
Ellis Grove	Randolph	IL
Ellison	Warren	IL
Elliston	Grant	KY
Ellistown	Union	MS
Ellisville	Columbia	FL
Ellisville	Fulton	IL
Ellisville (c.h.)	Jones	MS
Ellisville	St. Louis	MO
Ellisville	Kewaunee	WI
Ellittsville	Monroe	IN
Ellsworth	Sarber	AR
Ellsworth	Litchfield	CT
Ellsworth	Vigo	IN
Ellsworth	Madison	IA
Ellsworth (c.h.)	Ellsworth	KS
Ellsworth (c.h.)	Hancock	ME
Ellsworth	Texas	MO
Ellsworth	Nye	NV
Ellsworth	Grafton	NH
Ellsworth	St. Lawrence	NY
Ellsworth	Mahoning	OH
Ellsworth (c.h.)	Pierce	WI
Ellwood	Hopkins	KY
Ellwood	Schuylkill	PA
Elm	Wayne	MI
Elm	Linn	MO
Elm	Fayette	PA
Elma	Erie	NY
Elma	Chehalis	WA
Elmay	Grant	IN
Elm Bluff	Dallas	AL
Elmendaro	Lyon	KS
Elmer	Salem	NJ
Elm Flat	Chautauqua	NY
Elm Grove	Adams	IL
Elm Grove	Franklin	MA
Elm Grove	Holt	MO
Elm Grove	Jefferson	NE

PLACE NAMES OF THE UNITED STATES

PLACE	COUNTY	STATE
Elm Grove	Ohio	WV
Elm Grove	Wankesha	WI
Elm Hall	Gratiot	MI
Elm Hill	Montgomery	KY
Elmhurst	Du Page	IL
Elmington	Nelson	VA
Elmira	Stark	OL
Elmira	Eaton	MI
Elmira (c.h.)	Chemung	NY
Elmira	Fulton	OH
Elmore	Peoria	IL
Elmore	Faribault	MN
Elmore	Richardson	NE
Elmore	Ottawa	OH
Elmore	Lamoille	VT
Elmore	Fond du Lac	WI
Elm Point	Bond	IL
Elmsford	Westchester	NY
Elm Springs	Washington	AR
Elm Springs	Washington	AR
Elm Springs	Butler	IA
Elm Store	Randolph	AR
Elm Tree	Crawford	MO
Elm Tree	Weakley	TN
Elm Wood	Carroll	AR
Elmwood	Peoria	IL
Elm Wood	Saline	MO
Elmwood	Cass	NE
Elo	Winnebago	WI
Elon	Ashley	AR
Elon	Allawakee	IA
Elora	Lincoln	TN
El Paso	Conway	AR
El Paso	El Paso	CO
El Paso	Woodford	IL
El Paso	Sedgwick	KS
El Paso	Barry	MO
El Paso (c.h.)	El Paso	TX
El Paso	Pierce	WI
El Rito	Rio Arriba	NM
Elrod	Ripley	IN
Elroy	Juneau	WI
Elsah	Jersey	IL
El Sanz	Hidalgo	TX
Elsie	Clinton	MI
Elsinor	McLean	IL
Elsinore	Allen	KS
Elston	Labette	KS
Elston	Richland	WI
Elston Station	Cole	MO
Eltham	Westmoreland	VA
Elton	Cattaraugus	NY
Elton	Walworth	WI
Elvaston	Hancock	IL
Elvira	Johnson	IL
Elvira	Clinton	IA
Elwell	Bradford	PA
Elwin	Macon	IL
Elwood	Will	IL
Elwood	Madison	IN
Elwood	Doniphan	KS
Elwood	Steele	MN
Elwood	Atlantic	NJ
Elwood	Suffolk	NY
Elwood	Fannin	TX
Ely	Warrick	IN
Ely	Linn	IA
Ely	Orange	VT
Elyria (c.h.)	Lorain	OH
Elysburgh	Northumberland	PA
Elysian	Le Sneur	MN
Elyton (c.h.)	Jefferson	AL
Emanuel	Bonhomme	Dak
Emaus	Lehigh	PA
Emaus	Bedford	VA
Embarrass	Waupaca	WI
Embden	Somerset	ME
Embreeville	Chester	PA
Embryville	Washington	TN
Emden	Logan	IL
Emerald	Adams	OH
Emerald	Anderson	KS
Emerald Grove	Rock	WI
Emerson	Mills	IA
Emerson	Marion	MO
Emerson	Otoe	NE
Emery	Fulton	OH
Emery	Monroe	WI
Emery's Mills	York	ME
Emigrant Gap	Placer	CA
Emigsville	York	PA
Emilie	Bucks	PA
Eminence	Logan	IL
Eminence	Morgan	IN
Eminence	Henry	KY
Eminence (c.h.)	Shannon	MO
Eminence	Schoharie	NY
Emison Station	Knox	IN
Emlenton	Venango	PA
Emma	Butler	AL
Emma	White	IL
Emmaton	Sacramento	CA
Emmaville	Fulton	PA
Emmaville	Salt Lake	UT
Emmett	Lake	IL
Emmett	Emmett	IA
Emmett	St. Clair	MI
Emmett	Dakota	NE
Emmett	Paulding	OH
Emmettsburgh	Deer Lodge	MT
Emmettsville	Ada	ID
Emmittsburgh (c.h.)	Palo Alto	IA
Emmittsburgh	Frederick	MD
Emmonsburgh	Herkimer	NY
Emmorton	Harford	MD
Emmorton	Richmond	VA
Emory (c.h.)	Rains	TX
Emory	Washington	VA
Empire	Wright	IA
Empire	Leelenaw	MI
Empire	Fillmore	NE
Empire	Fond du Lac	WI
Empire City	Clear Creek	CO
Empire City	Dakota	MN
Empire City	Ormsby	NV
Empire City (c.h.)	Coos	OR
Empire Iron Works	Trigg	KY
Empire Junction	Columbia	WI
Empire Prairie	Andrew	MO
Emporia (c.h.)	Lyon	KS
Emporium (c.h.)	Cameron	PA
Emuckfaw	Tallapoosa	AL
Enchanted Prairie	Coos	OR
Enders	Dauphin	PA
Endor	Will	IL
Energy	Clark	MS
Enfield	Hartford	CT
Enfield	White	IL
Enfield	Penobscot	ME
Enfield	Hampshire	MA
Enfield	Grafton	NH
Enfield	Tompkins	NY
Enfield	Halifax	NC
Enfield	King William	VA
Enfield Centre	Grafton	NH
Enfield Centre	Tompkins	NY
Engleman's Mills	Dade	MO
Englewood	Cook	IL
Englewood	Bergen	NJ
Englewood	Robertson	TX
English	Crawford	IN
English Centre	Lycoming	PA
English Lake	Stark	IN
English Prairie	McHenry	IL
English's Creek	Atlantic	NJ
English Settlement	Marion	IA
Englishtown	Monmouth	NJ
Englishville	Kent	MI
Ennall's Springs	Dorchester	MD
Ennisville	Huntingdon	PA
Enoch	Noble	OH
Enochsburgh	Franklin	IN
Enola	Iredell	NC
Enon	Bullock	AL
Enon	Fulton	IL
Enon	Perry	MS
Enon	Clark	OH
Enon College	Tronsdale	TN
Enon Grove	Heard	GA
Enon Valley	Lawrence	PA
Enoree	Spartanburgh	SC
Enosburgh	Franklin	VT
Enosburgh Falls	Franklin	VT
Ensley	Newaygo	MI
Enterline	Dauphin	PA
Enterprise	Etowah	AL
Enterprise	Lee	GA
Enterprise	Wayne	IL
Enterprise	Spencer	IN
Enterprise	Black Hawk	IA
Enterprise	Catahoula	LA
Enterprise	Winona	MN
Enterprise (c.h.)	Clark	MS
Enterprise	McDonald	MO
Enterprise	Lancaster	NE
Enterprise	Hocking	OH
Enterprise	Lancaster	PA
Enterprise	Morgan	UT
Enterprise	Vernon	WI
Enterprise Landing	Charleston	SC
Enterprise	Volusia	FL
Eola	Du Page	IL
Eola	Polk	OR
Ephraim	San Pete	UT
Ephraim	Door	WI
Ephratah	Fulton	NY
Ephratah	Lancaster	PA
Epperson	Marion	TX
Epping	Rockingham	NH
Epsom	Daviess	IN
Epsom	Merrimack	NH
Epworth	Dubuque	IA
Equality	Coosa	AL
Equality	Gallatin	IL
Equality	Saline	NE
Equality	Anderson	SC
Equinunk	Wayne	PA
Erastus	Banks	GA
Erata	Jones	MS
Ereildoun	Chester	PA
Erfurt	Jefferson	WI
Erhard's Grove	Otter Tail	MN
Erie	Weld	CO
Erie	Whitesides	IL
Erie	Lawrence	IN
Erie (c.h.)	Neosho	KS
Erie	Monroe	MI
Erie	McDonald	MO
Erie (c.h.)	Erie	PA

PLACE	COUNTY	STATE	PLACE	COUNTY	STATE	PLACE	COUNTY	STATE
Erie	London	TN	Eugene	Knox	IL	Ewingville	Mercer	NJ
Erie	Polk	TX	Eugene	Vermillion	IN	Excello	Macon	MO
Erieville	Madison	NY	Eugene	Ringgold	IA	Excello	Butler	OH
Erin	Meriweather	GA	Eugene	Shawnee	KS	Excelsior	Pueblo	CO
Erin	Washington	KS	Eugene City	Carroll	MO	Excelsior	Hennepin	MN
Erin	Calhoun	MS	Eugene City (c.h.)	Lane	OR	Excelsior	Morgan	MO
Erin	Chemung	NY	Euharley	Bartow	GA	Excelsior	Elko	NV
Erin	Houston	TN	Eulalia	Potter	PA	Excelsior	Northumberland	PA
Erin	St. Croix	WI	Eulia	Macon	TN	Excelsior	Richland	WI
Erin Shades	Henrico	VA	Eunice	Chicot	AR	Excelsior Mills	Jo Daviess	IL
Errol	Coos	NH	Euphemia	Preble	OH	Exchange	Marshall	KY
Ervin	Howard	IN	Eureka	De Kalb	AL	Exchange	Montour	PA
Ervin's Mills	Jackson	OH	Eureka	Cross	AR	Exeter	Scott	IL
Erving	Franklin	MA	Eureka (c.h.)	Humboldt	CA	Exeter	Clay	KS
Erwin	Schuyler	IL	Eureka	Woodford	IL	Exeter	Penobscot	ME
Erwin Centre	Steuben	NY	Eureka (c.h.)	Greenwood	KS	Exeter	Monroe	MI
Erwinna	Bucks	PA	Eureka	Clinton	MI	Exeter (c.h.)	Rockingham	NH
Erwinsville	Cleveland	NC	Eureka	St. Louis	MO	Exeter	Otsego	NY
Escatawpa	Washington	AL	Eureka	Lander	NV	Exeter	Luzerne	PA
Eschol	Perry	PA	Eureka	Sullivan	NY	Exeter	Washington	RI
Escoheag	Kent	RI	Eureka	Gallia	OH	Exter	Green	WI
Esconawba (c.h.)	Delta	MI	Eureka	Montgomery	PA	Exeter Mills	Penobscot	ME
Esdaile	Pierce	WI	Eureka	Winnebago	WI	Exeter Station	Berks	PA
Eskridge	Wabaumsee	KS	Eustis	Franklin	MO	Exira (c.h.)	Audubon	IA
Esofia	Vernon	WI	Eutaw (c.h.)	Greene	AL	Exonville	Wabaunsee	KS
Esom Hill	Trinity	TX	Eutaw	Limestone	TX	Experiment Mills	Monroe	PA
Esopus	Ulster	NY	Eva	Barry	MO	Express Ranch	Baker	OR
Esparanza	St. Johns	FL	Evans	Conway	AR	Exton	Chester	PA
Esperance	Schoharie	NY	Evans (c.h.)	Weld	CO	Eyer's Grove	Columbia	PA
Espy	Columbia	PA	Evans	Erie	NY	Eyota	Olmsted	MN
Espyville	Crawford	PA	Evansburgh	Coshocton	OH	Faber's Mills	Nelson	VA
Essex	Middlesex	CT	Evansburgh	Crawford	PA	Fabius	Onondaga	NY
Essex	Page	IA	Evans' Landing	Harrison	IN	Fabius	Hardy	WV
Essex	Essex	MA	Evans' Mills	Jefferson	NY	Fackler	Etowah	AL
Essex	Clinton	MI	Evansport	Defiance	OH	Factory Point	Bennington	VT
Essex	Essex	NY	Evanston	Cook	IL	Factory Village	Franklin	MA
Essex	Chittenden	VT	Evanston	Uintah	WY	Factoryville	Cass	NE
Essex Junction	Chittenden	VT	Evansville	Escambia	AL	Factoryville	Tioga	NY
Essexville	Bay	MI	Evansville	Washington	AR	Factoryville	Wyoming	PA
Esteina	Saunders	NE	Evansville	Randolph	IL	Fagleysville	Montgomery	PA
Estella	Ringgold	IA	Evansville (c.h.)	Vanderburg	IN	Fagundus	Warren	PA
Estell Flats	Carter	KY	Evansville	Douglas	MN	Furbank	Buchanan	IA
Estelville	Atlantic	NJ	Evansville	Ulster	NY	Fair Bluff	Columbus	NC
Estherville (c.h.)	Emmett	IA	Evansville	Columbia	PA	Fairburn	Campbell	GA
Estill's Fork	Jackson	AL	Evansville	Preston	WV	Fairbury	Livingston	IL
Estill Springs	Franklin	TN	Evansville	Rock	WI	Fairbury (c.h.)	Jefferson	NE
Estillville (c.h.)	Scott	VA	Evanswood	Waupaca	WI	Fairchild	Eau Claire	WI
Ethel	Mercer	IL	Evart	Osceola	MI	Fair Dale	Oswego	NY
Etlah	Franklin	MO	Eveland Grove	Mahaska	IA	Fairdale	Susquehanna	PA
Etna	Coles	IL	Eveline	Buchanan	MO	Fair Dealing	Marshall	KY
Etna	Penobscot	ME	Eve Mills	London	TN	Fairfax	Linn	IA
Etna	Fillmore	MN	Evendale	Juniata	PA	Fairfax	Osage	KS
Etna	Scotland	MO	Evening Shades (c.h.)	Sharp	AR	Fairfax	Highland	OH
Etna	Tompkins	NY	Everett	Cass	MO	Fairfax	Franklin	VT
Etna	Licking	OH	Evergreen (c.h.)	Conecuh	AL	Fairfax (c.h.)	Fairfax	VA
Etna	Allegheny	PA	Ever Green	Washington	AR	Fairfield (c.h.)	Fairfield	CT
Etna	Smith	TX	Evergreen	Santa Clara	CA	Fairfield (c.h.)	Wayne	IL
Etna	La Fayette	WI	Evergreen	Tama	IA	Fairfield	Franklin	IN
Etna Centre	Penobscot	ME	Evergreen	Avoyelles	LA	Fairfield (c.h.)	Jefferson	IA
Etna Green	Kosciusko	IN	Evergreen	Bradford	PA	Fairfield	Nelson	KY
Etna Mills	Siskiyou	CA	Evergreen	Appomattox	VA	Fairfield	Somerset	ME
Etna Mills	King William	VA	Everittstown	Hunterdon	NJ	Fairfield	St. Mary's	MD
Etter	Dakota	MN	Everton	Fayette	IN	Fairfield	Lenawee	MI
Etters	York	PA	Ewald	Faribault	MN	Fairfield	Benton	MO
Ettie	Tama	IA	Ewan's Mills	Gloucester	NJ	Fairfield	Herkimer	NY
Ettieville	Gentry	MO	Ewing	Franklin	IL	Fairfield	Hyde	NC
Ettrick	Trempealean	WI	Ewing	Jackson	IN	Fairfield	Greene	OH
Euchee	Meigs	TN	Ewing	Hocking	OH	Fairfield	Marion	OR
Euclid	Onondaga	NY	Ewing's Corner	Hancock	OH	Fairfield	Adams	PA
Euclid	Cuyahoga	OH	Ewing's Mills	Allegheny	PA	Fairfield	Bedford	TN
Eudora	Douglas	KS	Ewing's Neck	Cumberland	NJ	Fairfield(c.h.)	Freestone	TX
Eudora	Nodaway	MO	Ewington	Decatur	IN	Fairfield	Utah	UT
Eufaula	Barbour	AL	Ewington	Gallia	OH	Fairfield	Franklin	VT

PLACE NAMES OF THE UNITED STATES

PLACE	COUNTY	STATE	PLACE	COUNTY	STATE	PLACE	COUNTY	STATE
Fairfield	Rockbridge	VA	Fair View	Wilson	TX	Farmer	Defiance	OH
Fairfield	Rock	WI	Fair View	San Pete	UT	Farmer City	De Witt	IL
Fairfield Centre	De Kalb	IN	Fairview(c.h.)	Hancock	WV	Farmers	Sioux	IA
Fairfield Centre	Lycoming	PA	Fairview	Grant	WI	Farmers	Rowan	KY
Fairfield Corners	Somerset	ME	Fairview Village	Montgomery	PA	Farmers	Sanilac	MI
Fair Garden	Sevier	TN	Fairville	Saline	MO	Farmersburgh	Clayton	IA
Fair Grove	Greene	MO	Fairville	Wayne	NY	Farmers' Creek	Jackson	IA
Fair Grove	Tuscola	MI	Fairville	Chester	PA	Farmers' Creek	Lapeer	MI
Fair Grove	Davidson	NC	Fair Water	Fond du Lac	WI	Farmers' Fork	Richmond	VA
Fair Haven	New Haven	CN	Fair Weather	Adams	IL	Farmers' Grove	Southampton	VA
Fair Haven	Carroll	IL	Faison's Depot	Duplin	NC	Farmers' Grove	Green	WI
Fairhaven	Bristol	CN	Falcon	Nevada	AR	Farmers' Institute	Tippecanoe	IN
Fair Haven	St. Clair	MI	Falkland	Pitt	NC	Farmers' Mills	Putnam	NY
Fair Haven	Stearns	MN	Fallassburgh	Kent	MI	Farmers' Retreat	Dearborn	IN
Fair Haven	Cayuga	NY	Fall Brook	Tioga	PA	Farmers' Station	Owen	IN
Fair Haven	Preble	OH	Fall City	Dunn	WI	Farmers' Station	Clinton	OH
Fair Haven	Rutland	VT	Fall Creek	Marion	IN	Farmers' Valley	Hamilton	NE
Fair Hill	Cecil	MD	Fall Creek	Oconee	SC	Farmers' Valley	McKean	PA
Fair Hill	Rockingham	VA	Fall Creek	Bedford	TN	Farmer's Valley	Monroe	WI
Fair Hill	Marshall	WV	Fall Timber	Cambrin	PA	Farmersville	Lowndes	AL
Fairhope	Somerset	PA	Falling Creek	Lenoir	NC	Farmersville	Tulare	CA
Fairland	Shelby	IN	Falling Spring	Perry	PA	Farmersville	Posey	IN
Fairlee	Kent	MD	Falling Spring	Cumberland	TN	Farmersville	Mahaska	IA
Fairlee	Orange	VT	Falling Spring	Greenbrier	WV	Farmersville	Caldwell	KY
Fairmont(c.h.)	Martin	MN	Falling Waters	Berkeley	WV	Farmersville(c.h.)	Union	LA
Fairmont	Clarke	MO	Fallowfield	Crawford	PA	Farmersville	Livington	MO
Fairmont(c.h.)	Marion	WV	Fall River	Greenwood	KS	Farmersville	Cattaraugus	NY
Fair Mount	Gordon	GA	Fall River	Bristol	MA	Farmersville	Montgomery	OH
Fairmount	Vermillion	IL	Fall River	Columbia	Wi	Farmersville	Lancaster	PA
Fairmount	Grant	IN	Falls	Wyoming	PA	Farmersville	Collin	TX
Fairmount	Leavenworth	KS	Falls Branch	Washington	TN	Farmersville	Dodge	WI
Fairmount	Jefferson	KY	Fallsburgh	Sullivan	NY	Farmer Village	Seneca	NY
Fairmount	Somerset	IL	Fallsburgh	Licking	OH	Farm Hill	Olmstead	MN
Fair Mount	Hunterdon	NJ	Falls Church	Fairfax	VA	Farmingdale	Monmouth	NJ
Fair Mount	Onondaga	NY	Falls City(c.h.)	Richardson	NE	Farmingdale	Queens	NY
Fairmount Springs	Luzerne	PA	Falls City	Fayette	PA	Farmington	Washington	AR
Fair Oaks	San Marteo	CA	Fallsington	Bucks	PA	Farmington	San Josquin	CA
Fair Play	Randolph	AR	Falls Mill	Sullivan	NY	Farmington	Hartford	CN
Fair Play	El Dorada	CA	Falls Mills	Lincoln	WV	Farmington	Kent	DE
Fair Play(c.h.)	Park	CO	Falls of Blaine	Lawrence	KY	Farmington	Fulton	IL
Fair Play	Vanderburg	IN	Falls of Rough	Garyson	KY	Farmington	Van Buren	IA
Fair Play	Washington	MD	Fallston	Harford	MD	Farmington	Atchison	KS
Fair Play	Polk	MO	Falls Village	Litchfield	CN	Farmington	Graves	KY
Fair Play	Jefferson	OH	Fallulah	Madison	LA	Farmington(c.h.)	Franklin	ME
Fair Play	Park	CO	Falmouth	Rush	IN	Farmington	Cecil	MD
Fair Play	Oconee	SC	Falmouth(c.h.)	Pendleton	KY	Farmington	Oakland	MI
Fair Play	Grant	WI	Falmouth	Cumberland	ME	Farmington	Dakota	MN
Fair Point	Goodhue	MN	Falmouth	Barnstable	MS	Farmington(c.h.)	St. Fancois	MO
Fairport	Muscatine	IA	Falmouth	Lancaster	PA	Farmington	Stafford	NH
Fairport	De Kalb	MO	Falmouth	Stafford	VA	Farmington	Ontario	NY
Fairport	Monroe	NY	False Cape	Humbolt	CA	Farmington	Davie	NC
Fairport	Granville	NC	Falun	Saline	KS	Farmington	Trumbull	OH
Fairport	Cumberland	NJ	Fame	Greenwood	KS	Farmington	Fayette	PA
Fairview	Walker	AL	Fancy Creek	Clay	KS	Farmington	Marshall	TN
Fairview	Dallas	AR	Fancy Creek	Richland	WI	Farmington	Grayson	TX
Fairview	Lincoln	DA	Fancy Farm	Graves	KY	Farmington(c.h.)	Davis	UT
Fairview	Fulton	IL	Fancy Gap	Carroll	VA	Farmington	Marion	WV
Fairview	Randolph	IN	Fancy Grove	Bedford	VA	Farmington	Jefferson	WI
Fairview	Jones	IA	Fancy Hill	Iredell	NC	Farmington Centre	Tioga	PA
Fairview	Brown	KS	Fancy Hill	Rockbridge	VA	Farmington Centre	Polk	WI
Fairview	Christian	KY	Fandon	McDonough	IL	Farmington Falls	Franklin	ME
Fairview	Concordia	LA	Fanlight	Wetzel	WV	Farmland	Randolph	IN
Fairview	Washington	MD	Fannettsburgh	Franklin	PA	Farm Ridge	La Salle	IL
Fairview	Mason	MI	Fannin	Ranklin	MS	Farm's Village	Hartford	CN
Fairview	Fillmore	MN	Fanning	Doniphan	KS	Farmville	Woodford	IL
Fairview	St. Louis	MO	Farabee's Station	Washington	IN	Farmville	Pitt	NC
Fairview	Bergen	NJ	Faribault(c.h.)	Rice	MN	Farmville	Henderson	TN
Fairview	Cattaugus	NY	Farina	Fayette	IL	Farmville	Prince Edward	VA
Fairview	Buncombe	NC	Farley	Dubuque	IA	Farmwell	Loudon	VA
Fairview	Guernsey	OH	Farley	Platte	MO	Farnham	Erie	NY
Fairview	Erie	PA	Farlington	Crawford	KS	Farnham	Wood	OH
Fairview	Greenville	SC	Farlinville	Linn	KS	Farnham	Richmond	VA
Fairview	Anderson	TN	Farmdale	Franklin	KY	Farnham X Roads	Richmond	VA

PLACE NAMES OF THE UNITED STATES

PLACE	COUNTY	STATE	PLACE	COUNTY	STATE	PLACE	COUNTY	STATE
Farnumsville	Worcester	MA	Ferdinand	Mercer	IL	Fink's Creek	Lewis	WV
Farrandsville	Clinton	PA	Ferdinand	Dubois	IN	Finley Station	Cumberland	NJ
Farrarsville	Bibb	VA	Fergus Falls	Otter Tail	MN	Finleyville	Washington	PA
Farribaville	Sevier	AR	Ferguson	St. Louis	MO	Finney's Creek	Saline	MO
Farwell	Clare	MI	Ferguson's Corners	Yates	NY	Fir Cap	Sierra	CA
Fasset	Bradford	PA	Ferguson's Station	Allen	IN	Firebaugh	Fresno	CA
Fatama	Wilcox	AL	Fergusonville	Delaware	NY	Fire Island	Suffolk	NY
Faunsdale	Marengo	AL	FernandezdeTaos(ch)	Taos	NM	Fire Place	Suffolk	NY
Fauquier Wht. Sl.Sp.	Fauquier	VA	Fernandina(c.h.)	Nassau	FL	Fire Prairie	Jackson	MO
Fawn Grove	York	PA	Fern Creek	Jefferson	KY	Fire Broad	Rutherford	NC
Fawn River	St. Joseph	MI	Ferndale	Humbolt	CA	First Fork	Cameron	PA
Faxon	Sibley	MN	Fernland	Mobile	AL	Fish Creek	Steuben	IN
Fayette	Greene	IL	Fern Leaf	Mason	KY	Fish Creek	Jefferson	MT
Fayette	Fayette	IA	Fern Valley	Palo Alto	IA	Fish Creek	Oneida	NY
Fayette	Kennebec	ME	Ferris	Hancock	IL	Fish Creek	Door	WI
Fayette(c.h.)	Jefferson	MS	Ferris	Montcalm	MI	Fish Dam	Wake	NC
Fayette(c.h.)	Howard	MO	Ferrisburgh	Addison	VT	Fish Dam	Union	SC
Fayette	Seneca	NY	Ferrona	Clinton	NY	Fisher	Clarion	PA
Fayette	Allegheny	PA	Ferry	Mahaska	IA	Fisherman's Bay	Sonoma	CA
Fayette	La Fayette	WI	Ferry	Oceana	MI	Fisher's	Ontario	NY
Fayette(c.h.)	Fayette	AL	Ferry Point	Norfolk	VA	Fishersburgh	Madison	IN
Fayette City	Fayette	PA	Ferrysburgh	Ottawa	MI	Fisher's Ferry	Northumberland	PA
Fayette Corners	Fayette	TN	Ferry Village	Cumberland	ME	Fisher's Landing	Decatur	TN
Fayette Ridge	Kennebec	ME	Ferryville	St. Clair	AL	Fishersville	Merrimack	NH
Fayette Springs	Fayette	PA	Ferryville	Crawford	WI	Fishersville	Augusta	VA
Fayetteville(c.h.)	Washington	PA	Fertigs	Venango	PA	Fishersville	Jefferson	KY
Fayetteville(c.h.)	Fayette	GA	Fertile	Worth	IA	Fisherville	Dauphin	PA
Fayetteville	St. Clair	IL	Fertile Hill	Falls	TX	Fish Haul	King William	VA
Fayetteville	Lawrence	IN	Fertility	Lancaster	PA	Fish Haven	Rich	UT
Fayetteville	Clay	KS	Festina	Winneshiek	IA	Fish Hook	Pike	IL
Fayetteville	Johnson	MO	Fetherolffsville	Berks	PA	Fishing Creek	Dorchester	MD
Fayetteville	Onondaga	NY	Fetterman	Taylor	WV	Fishing Creek	Cape May	NJ
Fayetteville	Cumberland	NC	Fiatt	Fulton	IL	Fishing Creek	Columbia	PA
Fayetteville	Brown	OH	Fidalgo	Whatcom	WA	Fishkill	Dutchess	NY
Fayetteville	Franklin	PA	Fiddletown	Amador	CA	Fishkill on/Hudson	Dutchess	NY
Fayetteville(c.h.)	Lincoln	TN	Fidelity	Jersey	IL	Fishkill Plains	Dutchess	NY
Fayetteville	Fayette	TX	Fidelity	Pike	IN	Fish Lake	Elkhart	IN
Fayetteville(c.h.)	Windham	VT	Fidelity	Jasper	MO	Fish Point	Rockcastle	KY
Fayetteville(c.h.)	Fayette	WV	Fidelity	Miami	OH	Fish Pond	Tallapoosa	AL
Fayetteville	Walworth	WI	Fidelity	Pike	PA	Fish Rock	Mendocino	CA
Fayville	Worcester	MA	Field Bend	Pike	IL	Fish Springs	Inyo	CA
Fearing	Washington	OH	Fieldon	Jersey	IL	Fiskedale	Worcester	MA
Fern's Springs	Winton	MS	Fieldsborough	New Castle	DE	Fisk's Corners	Winnebago	WI
Feasterville	Bucks	PA	Field's Cross Roads	Milton	GA	Fisk's Mills	Sonoma	CA
Feasterville	Fairfield	SC	Fife's	Goochland	VA	Fitchburgh	Worcester	MA
Febing	Nemaha	NE	Fifteen Mile Grove	Tama	IA	Fitchburgh	Ingham	MI
Federal Hill	Harford	MD	Fig Grove	Coosa	AL	Fitchburgh	Dane	WI
Federal Point	Putnam	FL	Filer City	Manistee	MI	Fitchville	Huron	OH
Federalsburgh	Caroline	PA	Fillmore	Mongomery	IL	Fithian	Vermillion	IL
Federalton	Athens	OH	Fillmore	Putnam	IN	Fitts Hill	Franklin	IL
Feeding Hills	Hampton	MA	Fillmore	Dubuque	IA	Fitz Henry	Ogle	IL
Feed Spring	Harrison	OH	Fillmore	Bossier	IA	Fitz Henry	Westmoreland	PA
Feeburgh	Brown	OH	Fillmore	Barry	MI	Fitzpatrick's	Bullock	AL
Felchville	Windsor	VT	Fillmore	Fillmore	MN	Fitzwatertown	Montgomery	PA
Felicity	Clermont	OH	Fillmore	Andrew	MO	Fitzwilliam	Cheshire	NH
Fellowship	Burlington	NJ	Fillmore	Fillmore	NE	Fitzwilliam Depot	Cheshire	NH
Fellowsville	Preston	WV	Fillmore	Monmouth	NJ	Five Corners	Miami	IN
Felton	Santa Cruz	CA	Fillmore	Allegany	NY	Five Corners	Cayuga	NY
Felton	Kent	DE	Fillmore	Washington	OH	Five Forks	Stokes	NC
Felts	Ingham	MI	Fillmore	Centre	PA	Five Lakes	Lapeer	MI
Felt's Mills	Jefferson	NY	Fillmore	Sequatchie	TN	Five Mile	Hale	AL
Femme Osage	St. Charles	MO	Fillmore	Randolph	WV	Five Mile	Brown	OH
Fenner	Madison	NY	Fillmore	Washington	WI	Five Mile	Pickens	SC
Fennimore	Grant	WI	Fillmore City(c.h.)	Millard	UT	Five Mile House	Milwaukee	WI
Fenns	Shelby	IN	Fincastle	Brown	OH	Five Points	Gloucester	NJ
Fenn's Bridge	Jefferson	GA	Fincastle	Campbell	TN	Five Points	Pickaway	OH
Fenn's Mills	Allegan	MI	Fincastle(c.h.)	Botetonrt	VA	Flackville	St. Lawrence	NY
Fenton	Whitesides	IL	Finchford	Black Hawk	IA	Flagg Spring	Campbell	KY
Fenton	St. Louis	Mo	Findley(c.h.)	Hancock	OH	Flaggtown	Somerset	ME
Fenton	Wood	OH	Findley's Lake	Chautauqua	NY	Flag Pond	Washington	TN
Fentonville	Genesee	MI	Findley's Mills	Jackson	IL	Flag Pond	Bosque	TX
Fentonville	Chautauqua	NY	Fine	St. Lawrence	NY	Flag Springs	Andrew	MO
Fentriss	Guilford	NC	Fine Creek Mills	Powhatan	VA	Flagstaff	Somerset	ME
			Finksburgh	Carroll	MD			

PLACE	COUNTY	STATE	PLACE	COUNTY	STATE	PLACE	COUNTY	STATE
Flag Station	Ogle	IL	Flinty Branch	Yancey	NC	Fond du Lac	St. Louis	MN
Flanders	Morris	NJ	Flippin	Monroe	KY	Fond du Lac(c.h.)	Fond du Lac	WI
Flanders	Suffolk	NY	Flippo's	Caroline	VA	Foneswood	Richmond	VA
Flandreau	Brookins	DA	Floodwood	Athens	OH	Fonta Flora	Burke	NC
Flat	Pike	OH	Flora	Clay	IL	Fontanelle(c.h.)	Adair	IA
Flat Branches	Forsyth	NC	Flora Dale	Adams	PA	Fontania	Miami	KS
Flatbrook	Columbia	NY	Floral	Cowley	KS	Fontenoy	Brown	WI
Flatbrookville	Sussex	NJ	Floraville	St. Clair	IL	Foote	Iowa	IA
Flatbush	Kings	NY	Florence(c.h.)	Lauderdale	AL	Footville	Yadkin	NC
Flat Creek	Barry	MO	Florence	Pima	AZ	Footville	Rock	WI
Flat Creek	Montgomery	NY	Florence	Drew	AR	Forbestown	Butte	CA
Flat Creek	Bedford	TN	Florence	Stewart	GA	Ford	Genauga	OH
Flat Fork	Anson	NC	Florence	Pike	IL	Fordham	Westchester	NY
Flat Fork	Roane	WV	Florence	Switzerland	IN	Ford's Creek	Catahoula	LA
Flat Gap	Jefferson	TN	Florence	Benton	IA	Ford's Depot	Dinwiddle	VA
Flatlands	Kings	NY	Florence	Marion	KS	Ford's Ferry	Crittenden	KY
Flat Lick	Knox	KY	Florence	Boone	KY	Ford's Store	Hart	GA
Flatonia	Fayette	TX	Florence	Howard	MD	Fordsville	Ohio	KY
Flat River	St. Francois	MO	Florence	Hampshire	MS	Fordsville	Marion	MS
Flat River	Orange	NC	Florence	St. Joseph	MI	Fordtown	Sullivan	TN
Flat Rock	Talladega	AL	Florence	Morgan	MO	Fordyce	Greene	PA
Flat Rock	Crawford	IL	Florence	Douglas	NE	Forest	Livingston	IL
Flat Rock	Shelby	IN	Florence	Burlington	NJ	Forest	Scott	MS
Flat Rock	Neosho	KS	Florence	Oneida	NY	Forest	Clinton	NY
Flat Rock	Bourbon	KY	Florence	Erie	OH	Forest	Hardin	OH
Flat Rock	Henderson	NC	Florence	Washington	PA	Forest	Clearfield	PA
Flat Rock	Seneca	OH	Florence	Darlington	SC	Forest	Richland	WI
Flat Rock	Kershaw	SC	Florence	Williamson	TX	Forest Bay	Huron	MI
Flat Rock	Lewis	TN	Florence City	Idaho	ID	Forestburgh	Sullivan	NY
Flat Rock	Mason	WV	Florence Station	Stephenson	IL	Forest City	St. Francis	AR
Flat Shoals	Surry	NC	Florence Station	McCracken	KY	Forest City	Sierra	CA
Flat Shoals	Meriweather	GA	Florence Station	Rutherford	TN	Forest City	Mason	IL
Flat Top	Mercer	WV	Florenceville	Howard	IA	Forest City(c.h.)	Winnebago	IA
Flat Wood	Phelps	MO	Florid	Putnam	IL	Forest City	Muskegon	MI
Flatwoods	Fayette	PA	Florida	Madison	IN	Forest City	Mecker	MN
Flat Woods	Wayne	TN	Florida	Berkshire	MA	Forest City	Holt	MO
Flat Woods	Braxton	WV	Florida	Monroe	MO	Forest City	Missoula	MT
Fleecedale	Alleghany	PA	Florida	Orange	NY	Forest City	Sarpy	NE
Fleetville	Luzerne	PA	Florida	Henry	OH	Forest City	Utah	UT
Fleetwood	Berks	PA	Florin	Sacramento	CA	Forest Dale	Lawrence	OH
Fleming	Liberty	GA	Floris	Davis	IA	Forest Dale	Rutland	VT
Fleming	Livingston	MI	Florisant	St. Louis	MO	Forest Depot	Bedford	VA
Fleming	Cayuga	NY	Flourtown	Montgomery	PA	Forest Grove	Gloucester	NJ
Fleming	Washington	OH	Flower Creek	Pendleton	KY	Forest Grove	Washington	OR
Fleming	Centre	PA	Flower Creek	Oceana	MI	Forest Hill	Placer	CA
Flemingsburgh(c.h.)	Fleming	KY	Flowerdale	Richardson	NE	Forest Hill	Decatur	IN
Flemingsville	Tioga	NY	Flowerfield	St. Joseph	MI	Forest Hill	Lyon	KS
Fleminton	Marion	FL	Flower's Place	Smith	MS	Forest Hill	Harford	MD
Flemington(c.h.)	Hunterdon	NJ	Flowerville	White	IN	Forest Hill	Gratiot	MI
Flemington	Columbus	NC	Floyd	Floyd	IA	Forest Hill	Union	PA
Flemington	Clinton	PA	Floyd	Oneida	NY	Forest Hill	Monroe	WV
Flemington	Taylor	WV	Floyd(c.h.)	Floyd	VA	Forest Home	Amodor	CA
Flemingville	Linn	IA	Floyd's Creek	Adair	MO	Forest Home	Powechick	IA
Flemming's Ranch	Weld	CO	Floyd's Fork	Jefferson	KY	Forest Home	Franklin	KS
Fletcher	Miami	OH	Floyd's Knobs	Floyd	IN	Forest House	Potter	PA
Flint	Cherokee N	IT	Flukes	Botetourt	VA	Forest Lake	Washington	MN
Flint	Pike	IL	Flushing	Ringgold	IA	Forest Lake	Susquchanna	PA
Flint	Steuben	IN	Flushing	Genesee	MI	Forest Lake Centre	Susquchanna	PA
Flint	Mahaska	IA	Flushing	Queens	NY	Forest Mound	Wabashaw	MN
Flint(c.h.)	Genesee	MI	Flushing	Belmont	OH	Forest Oak	Montgomery	MD
Flint	Franklin	OH	Fiuvanna	Chautauqua	NY	Foreston	Ogle	IL
Flint Creek	Harrison	MS	Fly Creek	Cherokee	KS	Foreston	Howard	IA
Flint Creek	Ontario	NY	Fly Creek	Ostego	NY	Forest Port	Oncida	NY
Flint Factory	Madison	AL	Fly Mountain	Ulster	NY	Forest Station	Clayton	GA
Flint Hill	St. Charles	MO	Flynn's Lick	Jackson	TN	Forest Store	Douglas	MO
Flint Hill	Rappahannock	VA	Fly Summit	Washington	NY	Forestville	Hartford	CN
Flint Island	Meade	KY	Fogelsville	Lehigh	PA	Forestville	Madison	IN
Flint Ridge	Lancaster	SC	Folk's Station	Harrison	OH	Forestville	Delaware	IA
Flint River	Morgan	AL	Folkville	Morgan	AL	Forestville	Prince George's	MD
Flint's Mills	Washington	OH	Folsom City	Sacramento	CA	Forestville	Sanaliac	MI
Flint Stone	Alleghany	MD	Folsomdale	Wyoming	NY	Forestville	Fillmore	MN
Flintville	Lincoln	TN	Folsomville	Warrick	IN	Forestville	Chautauqua	NY
Flintville	Brown	WI	Fonda(c.h.)	Montgomery	NY	Forestville	Wake	NC

PLACE	COUNTY	STATE	PLACE	COUNTY	STATE	PLACE	COUNTY	STATE
Forestville	Marion	SC	Fort Henry	Randolph	MO	Foster	Bracken	KY
Forestville	Shenandoah	VA	Fort Hill	Lake	IL	Foster	Providence	RI
Forestville	Door	WI	Fort Howard	Brown	WI	Foster	Fond du Lac	WI
Forge Village	Middlesex	MA	Fort Hunter	Montgomery	NY	Fosterburgh	Madison	IL
Fork	Mecosta	MI	Fort Jennings	Putnam	OH	Foster Centre	Providence	RI
Forked River	Ocean	NJ	Fort Jessup	Sabine	LA	Fosterdale	Sullivan	NY
Forkland	Greene	AL	Fort Jones	Siskeyou	CA	Foster's	Tuscaloosa	AL
Forkland	Nottoway	VA	Fort Kearney	Kearney	NE	Foster's Crossings	Warren	OH
Fork Meeting House	Baltimore	MD	Fort Kent	Aroostook	ME	Foster's X Roads	Bledsoe	TN
Fork Mountain	Michell	NC	Fort Lamar	Madison	GA	Foster's Mills	Armstrong	PA
Forkner's Hill	Webster	MO	Fort Laramie	Laramie	WY	Foster's Ridge	Perry	IN
Forks	Columbia	PA	Fort Larned	Pawnee	KS	Fosterville	Cayyuga	NY
Forksburgh	Marion	WV	Fort Leavenworth	Leavenworth	KS	Fosterville	Rutherford	TN
Forks of Capon	Hampshire	WV	Fort Lee	Bergen	NJ	Fosterville	Anderson	TX
Forks of Elkhorn	Franklin	KY	Fort Lemhi	Lemhi	IA	Fostoria	Senca	OH
Forks of Pigeon	Hayward	NC	Fort Lincoln	Bourbon	KS	Fostoria	Blair	PA
Forks of Salmon	Klmath	CA	Fort Littleton	Fulton	PA	Foundryville	Columbia	PA
Forks' Station	Monroe	PA	Fort Lupton	Weld	CO	Fountain	El Paso	CO
Forkston	Wyoming	PA	Fort Lyon(c.h.)	Bent	CO	Fountain	Fountain	IN
Forksville	Onchita	LA	Fort Lyon	Benton	MO	Fountain	Fillmore	MN
Forksville	Sullivan	PA	Fort McKavett	Merad	TX	Fountain Bluff	Jackson	IL
Forksville	Mecklenburgh	VA	Fort Madison(c.h.)	Lee	IA	Fountain City	Buffalo	WI
Forktown	Wicomico	MD	Fort Meade	Polk	FL	Fountain Creek	Stephenson	IL
Fork Union	Fluvanna	VA	Fort Mill	York	SC	Fountain Creek	Maury	TN
Forrester	Sanilac	MI	Fort Miller	Washington	NY	Fountaindale	Winnebago	IL
Forsyth(c.h.)	Monroe	GA	Fort Mitchell	Russell	AL	Fountain Dale	Adams	PA
Forsyth(c.h.)	Taney	MO	Fort Montgomery	Orange	NY	Fountain Green	Hancock	IL
Forsythe	Macon	IL	Fort Motte	Orangeburgh	SC	Fountain Green	Harford	MD
Fort Albercrombie	Shyenne	DA	Fort Payne	De Kalb	AL	Fountain Head	Summer	TN
Fort Adams	Wilkinson	MS	Fort Pike	Orleans	LA	Fountain Hill	Ashley	AR
Fort Ancient	Warren	OH	Fort Plain	Warren	IA	Fountain Inn	Greenville	SC
Fort Ann	Washington	NY	Fort Plain	Montgomery	NY	Fountain Mills	Fayette	PA
Fort Arbuckle	Chickasaw Nat.	IT	Fort Quitman	El Paso	TX	Fountan Run	Monroe	KY
Fort Atkinson	Winneshiek	IA	Fort Randall(c.h.)	Todd	DA	Fountain Spring	Wood	WV
Fort Atkinson	Jefferson	WI	Fort Recovery	Mercer	OH	Fountain Station	Vigo	IN
Fort Baynard	Grant	NM	Fort Ridgely	Nicollet	MN	Fountaintown	Shelby	IN
Fort Benton(c.h.)	Choteau	MT	Fort Riley	Davis	KS	Fountainville	Bucks	PA
Fort Bidwell	Siskiyou	CA	Fort Ripley	Morrison	MN	Fourche	Perry	AR
Fort Blackmore	Scott	VA	Fort Ripley	Lawrence	IN	Fourche a Renault	Washington	MO
Fort Branch	Gibson	IN	Fort Ritner	Lawrence	IN	Four Corners	Huron	OH
Fort Bridger(c.h.)	Uintah	WY	Forts	Dallas	AL	Four Mile	Butler	KS
Fort Browder	Barbour	AL	Fort Scott(c.h.)	Bourbon	KS	Four Mile	Dunklin	MO
Fort Buffington	Cherokee	GA	Fort Selden	Dona Ana	NM	Four Mile Branch	Monroe	TN
Fort Buffort		DA	Fort Seneca	Seneca	OH	Four Mile Prairie	Perry	IL
Fort Calhoun	Washington	NE	Fort Shaw	Lewis and Clarke	MT	Four Crossing	Calaveras	CA
Fort Clark(c.h.)	Kinney	TX	Fort Sill	Choctaw Nation	IT	Four Towns	Oakland	MI
Fort Collins	Larimer	CO	Fort Simcoe	Klikitat	WA	Foust's Mills	Randolph	NC
Fort Colville(c.h.)	Stevens	WA	Fort Smith	Sebastian	AR	Fowler	Adams	IL
Fort Concho	Bexar	TX	Fort Snelling	Hennepin	MN	Fowler	Clinton	MI
Fort Covington	Franklin	NY	Fort's Station	Robertson	TN	Fowler	St. Lawrence	NY
Fort Covington Ctr.	Franklin	NY	Fort Stanton	Socorro	NM	Fowler	Trumbali	OH
Fort Craig	Socorro	NM	Fort Stephens	Kemper	MS	Fowler's	Brooke	WV
Fort Cummings	Grant	NM	Fort Sully	Buffalo	DA	Fowler's Knob	Nicholas	WV
Fort Dade	Hernando	FL	Fort Summit	Daviess	MO	Fowler's Landing	Humphreys	TN
Fort Davis	Presidio	TX	Fortsville	Saratoga	NY	Fowler's Mills	Geauga	OH
Fort Deposit	Lowndes	AL	Fort Taylor	Hernando	FL	Fowlersville	Rice	MN
Fort Dodge(c.h.)	Webster	IA	Fort Tongass		AL	Fowlersville	Columbia	PA
Fort Edward	Washington	NY	Fort Totten		DA	Fowlersville	Livingston	MI
Fort Faifield	Aroostook	ME	Fort Union	Mora	TX	Fowling Creek	Caroline	MD
Fort Foote	Prince George's	MD	Fort Valley	Houston	GA	Fox	Wells	IN
Fort Fred Steele	Carbon	WY	Fortville	Hancock	IN	Fox	Ray	MO
Fort Gaines(c.h.)	Clay	GA	Fort Wadsworth	Deuel	DA	Foxborough	Norfolk	MA
Fort Garland	Costilla	CO	Fort Wallace	Wallace	KS	Foxburgh	Clarion	PA
Fort Gay	Wayne	WV	Fort Washington	Prince George's	MD	Foxchase	Philadelphia	PA
Fort George	Duval	FL	Fort Washington	New York	NY	Fox Creek	Chase	KS
Fort Gibson	Cherokee Nation	IT	Fort Washita	Chickasaw Nat.	IT	Fox Creek	St. Louis	MO
Fort Gratiot	St. Clair	MI	Fort Wayne(c.h.)	Allen	IN	Foxcroft	Piscataquis	ME
Fort Griffin	Shackelford	TX	Fort Willopa	Chehalis	WA	Fox Lake	Lake	IL
Fort Halleck	Carbon	WY	Fort Worth(c.h.)	Tarrant	TX	Fox Lake	Dodge	WI
Fort Hamblin	Washington	UT	Fort Wrangle		AL	Fox River	Kenosha	WI
Fort Hamilton	Kings	NY	Forty Fort	Luzerne	PA	Foxville	Frederick	MD
Fort Hampton	Limestone	AL	Fort Zarah	Barton	KS	Frame's Mills	Braxton	WV
Fort Harker	Ellsworth	KS	Foscoro	Kewaunee	WI	Framingham	Middlesex	MA

PLACE NAMES OF THE UNITED STATES

PLACE	COUNTY	STATE	PLACE	COUNTY	STATE	PLACE	COUNTY	STATE
Frampton	Lawrence	OH	Franklin Furnace	Scioto	OH	Freeburgh	Houston	MN
Francesville	Pulaski	IN	Franklin Grove	Lee	IL	Freeburgh	Stark	OH
Francisco	Gibson	IN	Franklin Grove	Page	IA	Freeburgh	Snyder	PA
Francisco	Stokes	NC	Franklin Iron Works	Oneida	NY	Freedom	La Salle	IL
Francisoville	Jackson	MI	Franklin Mills	Des Moines	IA	Freedom	Owen	IN
Francis Creek	Manitowoc	WI	Franklin Mills	Fulton	PA	Freedom	Lucus	IA
Francistown	Hillsborough	NH	Franklin's X Roads	Hardin	KY	Freedom	Barren	KY
Franconia	Chicago	MN	Franklin Springs	Franklin	GA	Freedom	Waldo	ME
Franconia	Grafton	NH	Franklin Square	Columbiana	OH	Freedom	Carroll	MD
Franconia	Montgomery	PA	Franklin Station	Coshocton	OH	Freedom	La Cayette	MO
Frank	Seneca	OH	Franklinton	Henry	KY	Freedom	Carroll	NH
Frankenlust	Saginaw	MI	Franklinton(c.h.)	Washington	LA	Freedom	Portage	OH
Frankenmuth	Saginaw	MI	Franklinton	Schoharie	NY	Freedom	Beaver	PA
Frankford	Sussex	DE	Franklinton	Franklin	NC	Freedom	Washington	TN
Frankford	Mower	MN	Franklintown	York	PA	Freedom	Outagamie	WI
Frankford	Pike	MI	Franklinville	Carroll	MD	Freedom Centre	La Salle	IL
Frankford	Philadelphia	PA	Franklinville	Gloucester	NJ	Freedom Mills	Henry	OH
Frankford	Greenbrier	WV	Franklinville	Cattaraugus	NY	Freedom Plains	Dutchess	NY
Frankford	Franklin	AL	Franklinville	Randolph	NC	Freedom Station	Portage	OH
Frankfort	Franklin	IL	Franklinville	Huntingdon	PA	Freehold(c.h.)	Monmouth	NJ
Frankfort(c.h.)	Clinton	IN	Frank Pierce	Johnson	IA	Freehold	Greene	NY
Frankfort	Montgomery	IA	Frankstown	Blair	PA	Freehold	Warren	PA
Frankfort	Marshall	KS	Franskton	Madison	IN	Freehold	De Kalb	IL
Frankfort(c.h.)	Franklin	KY	Franktown(c.h.)	Douglas	CO	Freeland	Baltimore	MD
Frankfort	Waldo	ME	Franktown	Washoe	NV	Freelandville	Knox	IN
Frankfort	Benzie	MI	Franktown	Northampton	VA	Freeman	Clay	IA
Frankfort	L'Eau qui Cort	NE	Frankville	Winneshick	IA	Freeman	Franklin	ME
Frankfort	Herkimer	NY	Frankville	Alleghany	MD	Freeman	Licking	OH
Frankfort	Ross	OH	Frankville	Howell	MO	Freeman	Crawford	WI
Frankfort	Mineral	WV	Frankville	Clark	WI	Freemansburgh	Northampton	PA
Frankfort	Pepin	WI	Franksonia	Richland	IL	Freeman's Landing	Hancock	WV
Frankfort Hill	Herkimer	NY	Frasier	Macomb	MI	Freemanton	Effingham	IL
Frankfort Springs	Beaver	PA	Frazer	Buchanan	MO	Freeo	Quachita	AR
Frankfort Station	Will	IL	Frazer	Chester	PA	Freeport	Sacramento	CA
Frank Hill	Winona	MN	Frazeysburgh	Muskingum	OH	Freeport	Walton	FL
Franklin	Henry	AL	Frazier's Bottom	Putnam	WV	Freeport(c.h.)	Stephenson	IL
Franklin	Fulton	AR	Fraderica	Kent	DE	Freeport	Shelby	IN
Franklin	Sacramento	CA	Frederica	Glynn	GA	Freeport	Winnesc	hiIA
Franklin	New London	CN	Frederica	Bremer	IA	Freeport	Cumberland	ME
Franklin(c.h.)	Heard	GA	Frederick(c.h.)	Frederick	MD	Freeport	Queens	NY
Franklin	Morgan	IL	Frederick	Mahoning	OH	Freeport	Harrison	OH
Franklin(c.h.)	Johnson	IN	Frederick	Montgomery	PA	Freeport	Armstrong	PA
Franklin	Decatur	IA	Fredericksburgh	Washington	IN	Freeport	Cowlitz	WA
Franklin(c.h.)	Simpson	KY	Fredericksburgh	Chickasaw	IA	Freeshade	Middlesex	VA
Franklin(c.h.)	St. Mary's	LA	Fredricksburgh	Osage	MO	Free Soil	Fillmore	MN
Franklin	Hancock	ME	Fredricksburgh	Wayne	OH	Free Stone	Sonoma	CA
Franklin	Norfolk	MA	Fredricksburgh	Lebanon	PA	Freetown	Jackson	IN
Franklin	Oakland	MI	Fredricksburgh(c.h.)	Gillespie	TX	Freetown	Bristol	MA
Franklin	Renville	MN	Fredrecksburgh	Spottsylvania	VA	Freetown Corners	Cortland	NY
Franklin	Howard	MO	Frederick's Hall	Louisa	VA	Free Union	Albemarle	VA
Franklin	Merrimack	NH	Fredericksville	Schuyler	IL	Freeville	Tompkins	NY
Franklin	Essex	NJ	Fredericksville	Berks	PA	Freistadt	Ozankee	WI
Franklin	Delaware	NY	Fredericktown	Coffey	KS	Fremont	Steuben	IN
Franklin(c.h.)	Macon	NC	Fredericktown	Washington	KY	Fremont	Mahaska	IA
Franklin	Warren	OH	Fredrickstown(c.h.)	Madison	MO	Fremont	Lyon	KS
Franklin	Lane	OR	Fredrickstown	Knox	OH	Fremont	Shiawassee	MI
Franklin(c.h.)	Venango	PA	Fredrickstown	Washingtown	PA	Fremont	Freeborn	MN
Franklin(c.h.)	Williamson	TN	Fredie	Butler	MO	Fremont	Dodge	NE
Franklin	Cache	UT	Fredon	Sussex	NJ	Fremont	Rockingham	NH
Franklin	Franklin	VT	Fredonia	Chambers	AL	Fremont(c.h.)	Sandusky	OH
Franklin	Pierce	WA	Fredonia	Williamson	IL	Fremont	Chester	PA
Franklin(c.h.)	Pendleton	WV	Fredonia	Crawford	IN	Fremont	Waupace	WI
Franklin	Sheboygan	WI	Fredonia	Louisa	IA	Fremont Centre	Newaygo	MI
Franklin Centre	Lee	IA	Fredonia(c.h.)	Wilson	KS	Fremont Centre	Sullivan	NY
Franklin City	Norfolk	MA	Fredonia	Caldwell	KY	French Bar	Lewis and Clarke	MT
Franklin College	Davidson	TN	Fredonia	Washtenaw	MI	Frenchburgh	Menifee	KY
Franklin Corners	Erie	PA	Fredonia	Licking	OH	French Camp	Chotaw	MS
Franklin Crossing	Rock Island	IL	Fredonia	Mercer	PA	French Corral	Nevada	CA
Franklindale	Bradford	PA	Fredonia	Chautauqua	NY	French Creek	Chautauqua	NY
Franklin Depot	Southampton	VA	Fredonia	Ozaukee	WI	French Creek	Mercer	PA
Franklin Falls	Franklin	NY	Fredric	Monroe	IA	French Creek	Upsur	WV
Franklin Forks	Susquehanna	PA	Freeborn	Freeborn	MN	French Crk.Church	Bladen	NC
Franklin Furnace	Sessex	NJ	Freeburgh	St. Clair	IL	French Grove	Peria	IL

PLACE NAMES OF THE UNITED STATES

PLACE	COUNTY	STATE	PLACE	COUNTY	STATE	PLACE	COUNTY	STATE
French Gulch	Shasta	CA	Fulton	Jackson	IA	Gallon	Crawford	OH
French Gulch	Deer Lodge	MT	Fulton	Kalamazoo	MI	Galivant's Ferry	Horry	SC
French Hay	Hanover	VA	Fulton	Prentiss	MS	Gallant Green	Charles	MD
French Lake	Wright	MN	Fulton(c.h.)	Callaway	MO	Gallatia	Saline	IL
French Lick	Orange	IN	Fulton	Oswego	NY	Gallatin	Copiah	MS
French Mountain	Warren	NY	Fulton	Davie	NC	Gallatin(c.h.)	Daviess	MO
Frenchton	Missoula	MT	Fulton	Westmoreland	PA	Gallatin	Gallatin	MT
Frenchtown	Missoula	MT	Fulton	Clarendon	SC	Gallatin(c.h.)	Sumner	TN
Frenchtown	Hunterdon	NJ	Fulton	Landerdale	TN	Gallatinville	Columbia	NY
Frenchtown	Crawford	PA	Fulton	Refugio	TX	Gallaudet	Marion	IN
French Village	St. Clair	IL	Fulton	Rock	WI	Gallaway's Station	Osage	MO
French Village	St. Francois	MO	Fultonham	Schohorie	NY	Galley Rock	Pope	AR
Frenchville	Clearfield	PA	Fultonham	Muskingum	OH	Gallia Furnace(c.h.)	Gallia	OH
Frenchville	Trempealsean	WI	Fulton House	Lancaster	PA	Gallipolis	Gallia	OH
Fresh Pond	Suffolk	NY	Fulton Station	Fulton	KY	Gallitzin	Cambria	PA
Frewsburgh	Chautauqua	NY	Fultonville	Montogmery	NY	Galloway	La Salle	IL
Frey's Bush	Montgomery	NY	Funkhouse	Effingham	IL	Galloway Station	Osage	MO
Friar's Point(c.h.)	Coahoma	MS	Funk's Mills	Decatur	IA	Gallupville	Schoharie	NY
Frick's Gap	Walker	GA	Funkstown	Washington	MD	Galt	Sacramento	CA
Friedburgh	Forsyth	NC	Funny Louis	Catahoula	LA	Galt	Whitesides	IL
Friedens	Somerset	PA	Furnessville	Porter	IN	Galt's Mills	Amherst	VA
Friedensburgh	Schuylkill	PA	Fussville	Wausesha	WI	Galiun	Perry	IL
Friedensville	Lehigh	PA	Gabilan	Monterey	CA	Galva	Henry	IL
Friend Grove	Wabash	IL	Gadsden(c.h.)	Etowah	AL	Galveston	Cass	IN
Friendly Town	Perry	MO	Gadsden	Richland	SC	Galveston(c.h.)	Galveston	TX
Friendship	Ripley	IN	Gadsden	Madison	TN	Galway	Saratoga	NY
Friendship	Caldwell	KY	Gage's Lakes	Lake	IL	Galway	Fayette	TN
Friendship	KNox	ME	Gagetown	Tuscola	MI	Gamaliel	Monroe	KY
Friendship	Anne Arundel	MD	Gahanna	Franklin	OH	Gambier	Knox	OH
Friendship	Allehany	NY	Gaines	Orleans	NY	Gamble's	Alleghany	NC
Friendship	Guilford	NC	Gaines	Tioga	PA	Gamble's Store	Blount	TN
Friendship	Scioto	OH	Gainesborough(c.h.)	Jackson	TN	Game Hill	Franklin	AR
Friendship	Clarendon	SC	Gainesborough	Frederick	VA	Ganges	Richland	OH
Friendship	Dyer	TN	Gaines' Cross Roads	Rappahanock	VA	Gang Mills	Herkimer	NY
Friendship(c.h.)	Adams	WI	Gaines Farm	Henry	MO	Gansevoort	Saratoga	NY
Friendshipville	King Geroge	VA	Gaines Station	Genesee	MI	Gap	Walker	AL
Friendsville	Walbash	IL	Gainestown	Clarke	AL	Gap	Lancaster	PA
Friendsville	Medina	OH	Gainesville	Sumter	AL	Gap Civil(c.h.)	Alleghany	NC
Friendsville	Susquehanna	PA	Gainesville(c.h.)	Green	AR	Gap Creek	Ashe	NC
Friendsville	Blount	TN	Gainesville(c.h.)	Alachua	FL	Gap Creek	Knox	TN
Friendswood	Hendricks	IN	Gainesville(c.h.)	Hail	GA	Gap Grove	Lee	IL
Friendville	Saline	NE	Gainesville	Kent	MI	Gap Mills	Monroe	WV
Fritztown	Berks	PA	Gainesville	Hancock	MS	Gap Run	Carter	TN
Frizelburgh	Carroll	MD	Gainesville(c.h.)	Ozark	MO	Gapsville	Fulton	PA
Frog Level	Newberry	SC	Gainesville	Wyoming	NY	Garber's Mills	Washington	TX
Frohna	Perry	MO	Gainesville	Prince William	VT	Garden	Delta	MI
Frohtenac	Goodhue	MN	Gainesville Junction	Kemper	MS	Garden	Athens	OH
Frontier	Hillsdale	MI	Gainsville	Allen	KY	Garden City	Glue Earth	MN
Frontier	Clinton	NY	Gainsville(c.h.)	Cooke	TN	Garden Cottage	Pulaski	KY
Front Royal(c.h.)	Warren	VA	Galbriath's Store	Henry	MO	Garden Grove	Decatur	IA
Frost	Pocahontas	WV	Gale	Woodbury	IA	Garden Grove	Ralls	MO
Frostburgh	Jefferson	PA	Galen	Adams	IN	Garden Prairie	Boone	IL
Frost's Ranch	Douglas	CO	Galena(c.h.)	Jo Daviess	IL	Garden Prairie	Blue Earth	MN
Frost's STation	Fayette	PA	Galena	Floyd	IN	Garden Valley	Macon	GA
Fruitland	Mustegon	MI	Galena	Kent	MD	Garden Valley	Smith	TX
Fruitland	Burlington	NJ	Galena(c.h.)	Stone	MO	Gardenville	Erie	NY
Fruitport	Muskegon	MI	Galena	Dodge	NE	Gardenville	Bucks	PA
Frumet	Jefferson	MO	Galena	Humboldt	NV	Gardiner	Kennebec	ME
Fryburgh	Auglaize	OH	Galena	Delaware	OH	Gardiner	Douglas	OR
Fryburgh	Wright	IA	Gales	Sullivan	NY	Gardner	Grundy	IL
Fudgy's Creek	Cabell	WV	Galesburgh	Knox	IL	Gardner	Johnson	KS
Fulda	Spencer	IN	Galesburgh	Jasoer	IA	Gardner	Worcester	MA
Fulkerson	Scott	VA	Galesburgh	Neosho	KS	Gardner	Noble	OH
Fullen's	Greene	TN	Galesburgh	Kalamazoo	MI	Gardner's Corner	Beaufort	SC
Fullersburgh	Du Page	IL	Gale's Ferry	New London	CT	Gardner's Ford	Cleveland	NC
Fuller's Point	Coles	IL	Gales Town	Dorchester	MD	Gardner's Station	Weakley	TN
Fullerville Irn. Wrks	St. Lawrence	NY	Galesville	Washington	NY	Gard's Point	Wabash	IL
Fullwood's Store	Mecklenburgh	NC	Galesville	Douglas	OR	Garfield	La Salle	IL
Fulmer Valley	Allehany	NY	Galesville(c.h.)	Trempealeau	WI	Garfield	Mahoning	OH
Fulton	Sumter	AL	Galeville Mills	Ulster	NY	Garibaldi	Saguache	CO
Fulton	Hempstead	AR	Galien	Barrien	MI	Garibaldi	Keokuk	IA
Fulton	Whitesides	IL	Galigher	Guernsey	OH	Garibaldi	Tillamook	OR
Fulton	Fulton	IN	Galilee	Wayne	PA	Garland	Butler	AL

PLACE	COUNTY	STATE	PLACE	COUNTY	STATE	PLACE	COUNTY	STATE
Garlandville	Jasper	MS	Geneva	Allen	KS	Germantown	Montgomery	OH
Garman's Mills	Cambria	PA	Geneva	Lenawee	MI	Germantown	Philadelphia	PA
Garnavillo	Clayton	OH	Geneva	Freeborn	MN	German Valley	Morris	NJ
Garner	Cass	IL	Geneva	Ontario	NY	Germanville	Jefferson	IA
Garner	Hancock	IA	Geneva	Ashland	OH	Germany	Warren	PA
Garner's Station	Yalabusha	MS	Geneva	Walworth	WI	Gerrardstown	Berkeley	WV
Garnett(c.h.)	Anderson	KS	Genevia	Henderson	KY	Gery's	Bucks	PA
Garnettsville	Meade	KY	Genito	Powhatan	VA	Geryville	Bucks	PA
Garoga	Fulton	GA	Genoa	De Kalb	IL	Gethsomane	Darke	OH
Garrattsville	Otsego	NY	Genoa	Wayne	IA	Getty	Stearns	MN
Garretson's Landing	Jefferson	AR	Genoa	Livingston	MI	Gettysburgh	Darke	OH
Garrett	Meade	KY	Genoa	Platte	NE	Gettysburgh(c.h.)	Adams	PA
Garrett	Somerset	PA	Genoa(c.h.)	Douglas	NV	Getzville	Erie	NY
Garrettford	Delaware	PA	Genoa	Cayuga	NY	Ghent	Carroll	KY
Garrettsburgh	Christian	KY	Genoa	Ottawa	OH	Ghent	Columbia	NY
Garrettsville	Portage	OH	Genoa	Vernon	WI	Ghent's Station	Clinton	IN
Garrison Point	Walker	AL	Genoa Bluff	Iowa	IA	Gholson	Noxubee	MS
Garrison's	Putnam	NY	Gentryville	Spencer	IN	Gholsonville	Brunswick	VA
Garrisonville	Stafford	VA	Gentryville	Gentry	MO	Giard	Clayton	IA
Garrote	Tuolumne	CA	George Lake	Sterns	MN	Gibbon	Buffalo	NE
Garry Owen	Jefferson	IA	George's Creek	Pickens	SC	Gibbon's Landing	Perry	AR
Gartsides	St. Clair	IL	George's Mills	Sullivan	NH	Gibb's Cross Roads	Cumberland	NC
Garvin's	Sunflower	MS	George's Store	James	TN	Gibb's Cross Roads	Macon	TN
Gary's Store	Buckingham	VA	Georgesville	Franklin	OH	Gibbsville	Sheboygan	WI
Graysville	Prince George	VA	Georgetown	Pope	AR	Gibesonville	Hocking	OH
Gasconade City	Gasconade	MO	Georgetown	El Dorado	CA	Gibraltar	Lyons	IA
Gasconade Ferry	Gasconade	MO	Georgetown	Clear Creek	CO	Gibraltar	Wayne	MI
Gas Jet	Humbolt	CA	Georgetown	Fairfield	CN	Gibson	Glascock	GA
Gaskill's Corners	Tioga	NY	Georgetown(c.h.)	Sussex	DE	Gibson	Issaquena	MS
Gasport	Niagra	NY	Georgetown	Washington	DC	Gibson	Steuben	NY
Gassett's Station	Windsor	VT	Georgetown	Putnam	FL	Gibson	Pike	OH
Gaston	Sumter	AL	Georgetown(c.h.)	Quitman	GA	Gibson	Susquehanna	PA
Gatchellville	York	PA	Georgetown	Queida	IA	Gibsonburgh	Luzerne	PA
Gates	Newton	MO	Georgetown	Vermillion	IL	Gibson City	Ford	IL
Gates	Monroe	NY	Georgetown	Floyd	IN	Gibson's Station	Lake	IN
Gates' Mills	Cuyahoga	OH	Georgetown(c.h.)	Scott	KY	Gibson's Station	Guernsey	OH
Gatesville	Clay	GA	Georgetown	Sagadahoc	ME	Gibsonville	Sierra	CA
Gatesville	Clay	KS	Georgetown	Essex	MA	Gibsonville	Newton	MO
Gatesville(c.h.)	Gates	NC	Georgetown	Ottawa	MI	Gibsonville	Guilford	NC
Gatesville(c.h.)	Coryell	TX	Georgetown	Clay	MN	Gibsonville	Russell	VA
Gatewood	Ripley	MO	Georgetown	Pettis	MO	Giddings	Washington	TX
Gatlinburgh	Sevier	TN	Georgetown	Lewis and Clarke	MT	Gifford	Ingham	MI
Gauley Gridge	Fayette	WV	Georgetown	Jefferson	NE	Gila Bend	Lima	AZ
Gavers	Columbiana	OH	Georgetown	Burlington	NJ	Gilbert	Scott	IA
Gayhead	Greene	NY	Georgetown	Madison	NY	Gilbert	Monroe	PA
Galesville	Cherokee	AL	Georgetown(c.h.)	Brown	OH	Gilbert Hollow	Lexington	SC
Gaylord	Smith	KS	Georgetown	Beaver	PA	Gilbert's	Kane	IL
Gaylordsville	Litchfield	CN	Georgetown(c.h.)	Georgetown	SC	Gilbertsborough	Limestone	AL
Gaynorville	Decatur	IN	Georgetown	James	TN	Gilbert's Creek Stat.	Lincoln	KY
Gayoso(c.h.)	Pemiscot	MO	Georgetown(c.h.)	Williamson	TX	Gilbert's Mills	Paulding	OH
Gaysville	Windsor	VT	Georgetown	Lewis	WV	Gilbert's Mills	Owsego	NY
Gazelle	Siskiyou	CA	Georgetown	Grant	WI	Gilbertville	Montgomery	PA
Geary	Doniphan	KS	Georgeville	Kandiyohi	MN	Gilbertville	Black Hawk	IA
Geary	Clinton	MI	Georgeville	Gay	MO	Gilbertville	Worchester	MA
Geary	Westmoreland	PA	Georgia	Lawrence	IN	Gilbirdsport	Brown	IL
Gebhart's	Somerset	PA	Georgia	Franklin	VT	Gilboa	Schoharie	NY
Geddes	Omondaga	NY	Georgia City	Jasper	MO	Gilboa	Putnam	OH
Geetingsville	Clinton	IN	Georgiana	Butler	AL	Gilchirst	Pope	MN
Geiger's Mills	Berks	PA	Georgia Plains	Franklin	VT	Gilchirst Bridge	Marion	SC
Gem	Clayton	IA	Georgiaville	Providence	RI	Gilead	Tolland	CN
Gem	Baker	OR	German	Chenango	NY	Gilead	Calhoun	IL
General Wayne	Montgomery	PA	German	Darke	OH	Gilead	Miami	IN
Genesee	Waukesha	WI	German Gulch	Deer Lodge	MT	Gilead	Oxford	ME
Genesee Depot	Wankesha	WI	Germania	Potter	PA	Gilead	Branch	MI
Genesee Fork	Potter	PA	Germano	Harrison	OH	Gilead	Louis	MO
Genesee Village	Genesee	MI	German Settlement	Preston	WV	Giford	Tuscola	MI
Genesco	Henry	IL	Germanton	Stokes	NC	Gilford Village	Belknap	NH
Genesco	Cerro Gordo	IA	Germantown	Clinton	IL	Gilgal	Pike	IL
Genesco(c.h.)	Livingston	NY	Germantown	Mason	KY	Gill	Franklin	MS
Geneva(c.h.)	Geneva	AL	Germantown	Montgomery	MD	Gillem's Station	Dickson	TN
Geneva	Talbot	GA	Germantown	Henry	MO	Gillen's Landing	Phillips	AR
Geneva(c.h.)	Kane	IL	Germantown	Columbia	NY	Gillespie	Macoupin	IL
Geneva	Franklin	IA	Germantown	Columbia	NY	Gillespieville	Ross	OH

PLACE	COUNTY	STATE	PLACE	COUNTY	STATE	PLACE	COUNTY	STATE
Gillespieville	Kanawha	WV	Glenaloon	Moore	NC	Glenville	Panola	MS
Gillett	Oconto	WI	Glen Alta	Marion	GA	Glenville	Schenectady	NY
Gillett's Grove	Clay	IA	Glen Arbor	Leelenaw	MI	Glenville	Cuyahoga	OH
Gill Hall	Allegheny	PA	Glen Aubrey	Broome	NY	Glenville(c.h.)	Gilmer	WV
Gillisonville	Beaufort	SC	Glenbeulah	Sheboygan	WI	Glen White	Blair	PA
Gill's Mills	Rowan	KY	Glenbrook	Lake	CA	Glen Wild	Sullivan	NY
Gillsville	Hall	GA	Glenburn	Penobscot	ME	Glenwood(c.h.)	Mills	IA
Gillman	Iroquois	IL	Glen Carbon	Schuylkill	PA	Glenwood	Leavenworth	KS
Gilman	Marshall	IA	Glen Castle	Broome	NY	Glenwood	Aroostook	ME
Gilman	Hamilton	NY	Glencoe	Cook	IL	Glenwood(c.h.)	Pope	MN
Gilman's Depot	Sullivan	NY	Glencoe	Gallatin	KY	Glenwood	Schuyler	MO
Gilmanton	Belknap	NH	Glencoe(c.h.)	McLeod	MN	Glenwood	Sussex	NJ
Gilmanton Irn. Wks	Belknap	NH	Glencoe	Bolivar	MS	Glenwood	Erie	NY
Gilmantown	Buffalo	WI	Glencoe	St. Louis	MO	Glenwood	Susquehanna	PA
Gilmer	Lake	IL	Glencoe	Dodge	NE	Glidden	Carroll	IA
Gilmer(c.h.)	Upshur	TX	Glencoe	Belmont	OH	Glimpville	Landerdale	TN
Gilmer	Uintah	WY	Glencoe	Washington	OR	Glintonville	New Haven	CN
Gilmer's	Lowndes	AL	Glencoe	Buffalo	WI	Globe	Caldwell	NC
Gilmer's Store	Guilford	NC	Glencoe Mills	Columbia	NY	Globe Creek	Marshall	TN
Gilmore	Benzie	MI	Glen Cove	Queens	NY	Globe Village	Worcester	MA
Gilpin	Indiana	PA	Glendale	Pope	IL	Gloucester	Essex	MA
Gilpin's Point	Caroline	MD	Glen Dale	Daviess	IN	Gloucester(c.h.)	Gloucester	VA
Gilroy	Santa Clara	CA	Glendale	Jefferson	IA	Gloucester City	Camden	NJ
Gilson	Knox	IL	Glendale	Bourbon	KS	Glover	Orleans	VT
Gilson	Adams	NE	Glendale	Hardin	KY	Glover's Creek	Metcalf	KY
Gilsum	Cheshire	NH	Glendale	Berkshire	MA	Glover's Gap	Marion	WV
Ginger Hill	Washington	PA	Glendale	Van Buren	MI	Gloversville	Fulton	NY
Ginghamsburgh	Miami	OH	Glendale	McLeod	MN	Glymont	Charles	MD
Girard	Macoupin	IL	Glendale	Cass	NE	Glyndon	Crawford	PA
Girard(c.h.)	Crawford	KS	Glendale	Hamilton	OH	Gnadenbutten	Tuscarawas	OH
Girard	Richland	LA	Glendale	Cambria	PA	Goalby	St. Clair	IL
Girard	Branch	MI	Glendale	Monroe	WI	Godfrey	Madison	IL
Girard	Trumball	OH	Glendower	Algermarle	VA	Godfrey	Bourbon	KS
Girard	Erie	PA	Glen Easton	Marshall	WV	Godwinville	Bergin	NJ
Girard Manor	Schnylkill	PA	Gleneden	Lewis	WA	Goff's	Ritchie	WV
Girardsville	Schnylkill	PA	Glen Elder	Mitchell	KS	Goff's Falls	Hillsborough	NH
Girdletree Hill	Worcester	MD	Glenelg	Howard	MD	Goff's Mills	Steuben	NY
Gird's Creek	Missoula	MT	Glenford	Perry	OH	Goffstown	Hillsborough	NH
Gishe's Mills	Roanoke	VA	Glen Gardner	Hunterdon	NJ	Goffstown Centre	Hillsborough	NH
Givensville	McDonald	MO	Glengary	Berkeley	WV	Gogginsville	Franklin	VA
Givin	Mahaska	IA	Glen Grove	Douglas	CO	Goheenville	Armstrong	PA
Glade	Somerset	PA	Glen Hall	Tippercanoe	IN	Golconda(c.h.)	Pope	IL
Glade Creek	Ashe	NC	Glen Hall	Chester	PA	Goldonda	Humboldt	NV
Glade Creek	Gledsoe	TN	Glenham	Dutchess	NY	Golden City(c.h.)	Jefferson	CO
Glade Farms	Preston	WV	Glen Haven	Leelenaw	MI	Golden City	Barton	MO
Glade Hill	Franklin	VA	Glen Haven	Cortland	NY	Golden Corners	Wayne	OH
Glade Mills	Butler	PA	Glen Haven	Grant	WI	Golden Gate	Brown	MN
Gladen's Run	Bedford	PA	Glen Hope	Clearfield	PA	Golden Hill	Dorchester	MD
Glades	Morgan	TN	Glenloch	Chester	PA	Golden Hill	Wyoming	PA
Gladesborough	Randolph	NC	Glen Mills	Delaware	PA	Golden Lake	Wankesha	WI
Gladesborough	Carroll	VA	Glenmore	Ware	GA	Golden Pond	Trigg	KY
Glade Spring	Washington	VA	Glenmore	Oneida	NY	Golden Prairie	Delaware	IA
Gladesville	Preston	WV	Glenmore	Buckingham	PA	Golden Ridge	Aroostook	ME
Glad Tidings	Clackamas	OR	Glenn	Johnson	KS	Golden's Bridge	Westchester	NY
Glasco	Cloud	KS	Glenn	McKean	PA	Golden Springs	Anderson	SC
Glasco	Ulster	NY	Glenn's	Gloucester	VA	Golden Valley	Rutherford	NC
Glasford	Peoria	IL	Glenn Springs	Spartanburgh	SC	Goldfield	Wright	IA
Glasgow	New Castle	DE	Glenn's Valley	Marion	IN	Gold Hill	Storey	NV
Glasgow	Scott	IL	Glennville	Barbour	AL	Gold Hill	Rowan	NC
Glasgow	Jefferson	IA	Glenora	Yates	NY	Gold Hill	Buckingahm	VA
Glasgow(c.h.)	Barren	KY	Glen Park	Wyandotte	KS	Golding	Oceana	MI
Glasgow	Wabashaw	MN	Glen Riddle	Delaware	PA	Gold Mine	Marion	AL
Glasgow	Howard	ME	Glen Rock	Nenaha	NE	Gold Run	Placer	CA
Glasgow	Columbiana	OH	Glen Rock	York	PA	Goldsborough	Caroline	MD
Glasgow Junction	Barren	KY	Glen Roy	Howard	IA	Goldsborough(c.h.)	Wayne	NC
Glassborough	Gloucester	NJ	Glen Roy	Chester	PA	Goldville	Tallapoosa	AL
Glass River	Shiawassee	MI	Glensdale	Lewis	NY	Goliad(c.h.)	Goliad	TX
Glass Village	Pope	AR	Glen's Falls	Warren	NY	Golinde	Falls	TX
Glastenbury	Hartford	CN	Glen's Fork	Adair	KY	Gomber	Guernsey	OH
Glaze City	Canden	MO	Glen Union	Clinton	PA	Gomer	Allen	OH
Gleeson Station	Weakley	TN	Glen Valley	Trempealeau	WI	Gomeria	Republic	KS
Glen	Montgomery	NY	Glenville	Fairfield	CN	Gomer's Mills	Douglas	CO
Glen Allen	Henrico	VA	Glenville	Hartford	MD	Gonic	Stafford	NH

PLACE NAMES OF THE UNITED STATES

PLACE	COUNTY	STATE	PLACE	COUNTY	STATE	PLACE	COUNTY	STATE
Gonzales(c.h.)	Gonzales	TX	Goshen Springs	Rankin	MA	Grand Glade	Crawford	IL
Goochland	Rock Castle	KY	Goshenville	Chester	PA	Grand Glaze	Jackson	AR
Goochland(c.h.)	Goochland	VA	Gosport	Clarke	AL	Grand Gulf	Claiborne	MS
Gooch's Mill	Cooper	MO	Gosport	Owen	IN	Grand Haven(c.h.)	Ottawa	MI
Goodale's Corner	Penobscot	ME	Gosport	Marion	IA	Grand Island	Colusa	CA
Goodale's	Hanover	VA	Gouge's	Grant	KY	Grand Islnd St.(c.h.)	Hall	NE
Goodell's	St. Clair	ME	Gouglersville	Berks	PA	Grand Isle	Grand Isle	VT
Goodenow	Will	IL	Gouldsborough	Hancock	ME	Grand Junction	Greene	IA
Goodfield	Meigs	TN	Goldsborough	Luzerne	PA	Grand Junction	Hardeman	TN
Goodgion's Factory	Laurens	SC	Gouldsville	Washington	VT	Grand Lake	Chicot	AR
Good Ground	Suffolk	NY	Gourdin's Station	Williamsburg	SC	Grand Ledge	Eaton	MI
Good Harbor	Leelenaw	MI	Gourley's Bridge	Greene	TN	Grand Marsh	Adams	WI
Good Hope	McDonough	IL	Gouverneur	St. Lawrence	NY	Grand Meadow	Mower	MN
Good Hope	Leake	MS	Govanstown	Baltimore	MD	Grand Mound	Clinton	IA
Good Hope	Fayette	OH	Gowanda	Cattaraugus	NY	Grand Mound	Thurston	WA
Good Hope	Cumberland	PA	Gowdeysville	Union	SC	Grand Portage	Lake	MN
Good Hope	Milwaukee	WI	Gowdensville	Greenville		Grand Prairie	Brown	KS
Goodhue Centre	Goodhue	MN	Gower	Buchanan	MO	Grand Prairie	Plaquemine	LA
Gooding's Grove	Will	IL	Gower's Ferry	Cedar	IA	Grand Prairie	Lewis	WA
Good Intent	Washington	PA	Gowrie	Webster	IA	Grand Prairie	Green Lake	WI
Goodland	Newton	IN	Graafschap	Allegan	MI	Grand Rapids(c.h.)	Kent	MI
Goodland	Choctaw Nation	IT	Graceham	Frederick	MD	Grand Rapids(c.h.)	Wood	OH
Goodland	Lapeer	MI	Graddy Landing	Desha	AR	Grand Rapids	Wood	WI
Goodland	Knox	MO	Gradyville	Adair	KY	Grand River	Buffalo	DA
Goodlettsville	Davidson	TN	Graefenberg	Shelby	KY	Grand River	Wayne	IA
Goodman	Holmes	MS	Graefenberg	Adams	PA	Grand Bonde	Polk	OR
Goodrich	Genescee	MI	Graefenberg	Herkimer	NY	Grand Tower	Jackson	IL
Good's Mills	Rockingham	VA	Grafton	Yolo	CA	Grand Tunnell	Luzerne	PA
Good Spring	Giles	TN	Grafton	Jersey	IL	Grand Valley	Hamilton	OH
Good Thunder's Frd	Blue Earth	MN	Grafton	Howard	KS	Grand View	Edgar	IL
Good View	Buford	VA	Grafton	Oxford	ME	Grand View	Spencer	IN
Goodville	Lancaster	PA	Grafton	Worcester	MA	Grand View	Louisa	IA
Goodwin's Mills	York	ME	Grafton	Monroe	MI	Grand View	Hardin	KY
Goodwynsville	Dinwiddie	VA	Grafton	Grafton	NH	Grand View	Washington	OH
Goodyear's Bar	Sierra	CA	Grafton	Renssalaer	NY	Grandville	Kent	MI
Goole	Vernon	WI	Grafton	Lorain	OH	Granger	Allegany	NY
Goose Creek	Ritchie	WV	Grafton	Kane	UT	Granger	Fillmore	MN
Goose Island	Alexander	IL	Grafton	Windham	VT	Granger	Medina	OH
Goose Pond	Baker	IN	Grafton	Taylor	WV	Granite(c.h.)	Lake	CO
Gopher Prairie	Wabashaw	MN	Grafton	Ozaukee	WI	Granite Falls	Chippewa	MN
Gordon	Henry	IL	Grafton Centre	Grafton	NH	Granite Hall	Adams	PA
Gordon	Wilkinson	GA	Graham	Jefferson	IN	Granite Hill	Iredell	NC
Gordon	Darke	OH	Graham	Johnson	IA	Graniteville	Nevada	CA
Gordon	Schulkill	PA	Graham	Nodaway	MO	Graniteville	Middlesex	MA
Gordonsville	Logan	KY	Graham(c.h.)	Alamance	NC	Graniteville	Edgefield	SC
Gordonsville	Freeborn	MN	Graham Lake	Noble	MN	Grantly	Cleburne	AL
Gordonsville	Lancaster	PA	Graham's Forge	Wythe	VA	Grant	Pima	AR
Gordonsville	Smith	TN	Graham Station	Mason	WV	Grant	Park	CO
Gordonsville	Orange	VA	Graham's Turnout	Barnwell	SC	Grant	Vermilion	IL
Gordonville	Livingston	MO	Grahamsville	Sullivan	NY	Grant	Montgomery	IA
Gore	Hocking	OH	Grahamsville	Jackson	OH	Grant	Wabaunsee	KS
Goresville	Loudoun	VA	Grahampton	Glearfield	PA	Grant	Boone	KY
Gorham	Cumberland	ME	Grahamville	York	PA	Grant	Kent	MI
Gorham	Coos	NH	Grahamville	Beaufort	SC	Grant	Faribault	MN
Gorham	Fulton	OH	Grampian Hills	Clearfield	PA	Grant	Holt	MO
Gorham's Depot	Cocke	TN	Granada	Nemaha	KS	Grant	Nemaha	NE
Gorsuch's Mills	Baltimore	MD	Granbury(c.h.)	Hood	TX	Grant	Herkimer	NY
Goshen	Litchfield	CN	Granby	Hartford	CN	Grant	Hardin	OH
Goshen	Lincoln	GA	Granby	Hampshire	MA	Grant	Grant	OR
Goshen(c.h.)	Elkhart	IN	Granby	Nicollet	MN	Grant	Indiana	PA
Goshen	Oldham	KY	Granby	Newton	MO	Grant	Smith	TN
Goshen	Montgomery	MD	Granby	Essex	VT	Grant	Grayson	VA
Goshen	Hampshire	MS	Granby Centre	Oswego	NY	Grant	Portage	WI
Goshen	Mercer	MO	Granby City	Newton	MO	Grant(c.h.)	Grant	WV
Goshen	Sullivan	NH	Grand Bay	Mobile	AL	Grant Centre	Monona	IA
Goshen	Cape May	NJ	Grand Blane	Genesee	MI	Grant City	Sac	IA
Goshen(c.h.)	Orange	NY	Grand Bluff	Panola	TX	Grant City(c.h.)	Worth	ME
Goshen	Clermont	OH	Grand Cane	De Soto	LA	Grantfork	Madison	IL
Goshen	Lancaster	PA	Grand Chain	Pulaski	IL	Grantham	Sullivan	NH
Goshen	Lincoln	TN	Grand Chenier	Vermillion	LA	Grant Isle	Aroostock	ME
Goshen	Utah	UT	Grand Coteau	St. Landry	LA	Grantsborough	Craven	NC
Goshen Bridge	Rockbridge	VA	Grand Detour	Ogle	IL	Grantsburgh(c.h.)	Burnett	WI
Goshen Hill	Union	SC	Grand Forks	Pembina	DA	Grantsburgh	Johnson	IL

PLACE NAMES OF THE UNITED STATES

PLACE	COUNTY	STATE	PLACE	COUNTY	STATE	PLACE	COUNTY	STATE
Grantsburgh	Crawford	IN	Graysburgh	Northampton	NC	Green Castle	Fairfield	OH
Grant's Hill	Worth	ME	Graysburgh	Greenm	TN	Greencastle	Franklin	PA
Grant's Lick	Campbell	KY	Gray's Chapel	Jackson	AL	Green Centre	Noble	IN
Grant's Mills	Delaware	NY	Gray's Creek	Cumberland	NC	Green City	Weld	CO
Grant's Pass	Jackson	OR	Gray's Flat	Marion	WV	Green Cove Springs	Clay	FL
Grantsville	Alleghany	MD	Gray's Hill	Roane	TN	Green Creek	Cape May	NJ
Grantsville	Linn	MO	Gray's Landing	Green	PA	Greendale	Armstrong	PA
Grantsville	Tooele	UT	Grayson(c.h.)	Carter	KY	Greene	Jay	IN
Grantsville(c.h.)	Calhoun	WV	Grayson	Crittenden	AR	Greene	Androscoggin	ME
Grantville	Coweta	GA	Grayson Springs	Grayson	KY	Greene	Chenango	NY
Grantville	Jefferson	KS	Grayson Spr. Stat.	Grayson	KY	Greene	Lancaster	PA
Grantville	Norfolk	MA	Graysonville	Stanislaus	CA	Greene	Kent	RI
Grantville	Dauphin	PA	Graysonville	Clinton	MO	Greene Corner	Androscoggin	ME
Granville	Putnam	IL	Gray's Point	Lawrence	MO	Greenville(c.h.)	Greene	TN
Granville	Delaware	IN	Graysport	Grenada	MS	Greenfield	Colquitt	GA
Granville	Mahaska	IA	Gray's Summit	Franklin	MO	Greenfield	Greene	IL
Granville	Monroe	MO	Gray's Valley	Tioga	PA	Greenfield(c.h.)	Hancock	IN
Granville	Washington	NY	Graysville	Catoosa	GA	Greenfield	Adair	IA
Granville	Licking	OH	Graysville	Sullivan	IN	Greenfield	Howard	KS
Granville	Mifflin	PA	Graysville	Monroe	OH	Greenfield	Penobscot	ME
Granville	Jackson	TN	Graysville	Huntingdon	PA	Greenfield(c.h.)	Franklin	MA
Granville	Addison	VT	Graytown	Bexar	TX	Greenfield	Wayne	MI
Granville	Monongalia	WV	Grayville	White	IL	Greenfield(c.h.)	Dade	MO
Granville	Milwaukee	WI	Gray Willow	Kane	IL	Greenfield	Hillsborough	NH
Granville Centre	Bradford	PA	Greason	Cumberland	PA	Greenfield	Ulster	NY
Granville Corners	Hampden	MA	Greasy	Macoupin	IL	Greenfield	Highland	OH
Granville Summit	Bradford	PA	Greasy Creek	Floyd	VA	Greenfield	Erie	PA
Grape Grove	Greene	OH	Greasy Ridge	Lawrence	OH	Greenfield	Nelson	VA
Grape Island	Pleasants	WV	Great Barrington	Berkshire	MA	Greenfield	Milwaukee	WI
Grapeland	Faribault	MN	Great Bend	Jefferson	NY	Greenfield Centre	Saratoga	NY
Grapeville	Greene	NY	Great Bend	Meigs	OH	Greenfield Hill	Fairfield	CN
Grason	Andrew	MO	Great Bend	Susquehanna	PA	Greenfield Mills	Frederick	MD
Grasshopper Falls	Jefferson	KS	Great Bend Village	Susquehanna	PA	Greenford	Mahoning	OH
Grass Lake	Jackson	MI	Great Bridge	Norfolk	VA	Green Forest	Carroll	AR
Grassland	Harrison	WV	Great Crossing	Scott	KY	Green Garden	Will	IL
Grass Lick	Jackson	WV	Great Falls	Stafford	NH	Green Garden	Beaver	PA
Grass Valley	Nevada	CA	Great Mills	St. Mary's	MD	Green Grove	Madison	AL
Grassy Cove	Cumberland	TN	Great Neck	Queens	NY	Green Grove	Luzerne	PA
Grassy Creek	Livingston	MO	Great Oak	Palo Alto	IA	Green Hall	Jackson	KY
Grassy Creek	Yancey	NC	Great Pond	Hancock	ME	Green Haven	Dutchess	NY
Grassy Meadows	Greenbrier	WV	Great Valley	Cattaraugus	NY	Green Hill	Lauderdale	AL
Grassy Point	Wayne	MI	Great Works	Penobscot	ME	Green Hill	Stewart	GA
Grassy Point	Rockland	NY	Greble	Lebanon	PA	Green Hill	Warren	KY
Grassy Pond	Spartanburgh	SC	Greece	Monroe	NY	Green Hill	Wicomico	MD
Grater's Ford	Montgomery	PA	Greeley	Weld	CO	Green Hill	Rutherford	NC
Gratiot	Licking	OH	Greeley	Delaware	IA	Green Hill	Columbiana	OH
Gratiot	La Fayette	WI	Greeley	Anderson	KS	Green Hill	Wilson	TN
Gratis	Preble	OH	Green	Licking	OH	Green Hill	Campbell	VA
Grattan	Kent	MI	Greenback	Jefferson	AR	Greenhorn	Huerfano	CO
Gratz	Owen	KY	Green Bank	Burlington	NJ	Green Island	Albany	NY
Gratz	Damphin	PA	Green Bank	Lancaster	PA	Green Isle	Sibley	MN
Gravel Hill	Buckingham	VA	Green Bank	Porahontas	WV	Green Lake	Kandiyohi	MN
Gravella	Conecuh	AL	Green Bay	Clarke	IA	Greenland	Fayette	IL
Gravelly Spring	Landerdale	AL	Green Bay	Prince Edward	VA	Greenland	Outonagon	MI
Gravel Point	Texas	MO	Green Bay	Brown	WI	Greenland	Boone	MO
Gravel Ridge	Bradley	AR	Green Bottom	Cabell	WV	Greenland	Rockingham	NH
Gravel Run	Washtenaw	MI	Greenbrier	Limestone	AL	Greenland	Ross	OH
Gravel Spring	Frederick	VA	Greenbrier	Conway	AR	Greenland	Lancaster	PA
Gravel Switch	Marion	KY	Green Brier	Orange	IN	Greenland	Barnwell	SC
Gravelton	Wayne	MO	Green Brier	Monroe	OH	Greenland	Grant	WV
Gravel Run Mills	Baltimore	MD	Greenbrier	Northumberland	PA	Greenland Depot	Rockingham	NH
Gravesend	Kings	NY	Green Brier	Robertson	TN	Green Lane	Montgomery	PA
Graves' Mills	Madison	VA	Greenbrier Bridge	Greenbirer	WV	Greenleaf	Meeker	MN
Graveston	Knox	TN	Greenbush	Walker	GA	Green Level	Wake	NC
Gravesville	Herkimer	NY	Greenbush	Warren	IL	Green Mount	Lincoln	AR
Gravity	Taylor	IA	Greenbush	Penobscot	ME	Green Mount	Adams	PA
Gravois Coal Mines	St. Louis	MO	Green Bush	Alcona	MI	Greenmount	Rockingham	PA
Gravois Mills	Morgan	MO	Greenbush	Sheboygan	WI	Green Mountain	Marshall	IA
Gray	Cumberland	ME	Green Camp	Marion	OH	Green Oak	Fulton	IN
Gray	Herkimer	NY	Greencastle(c.h.)	Putnam	IN	Green Oak	Livingston	MI
Gray Eagle	Buncombe	NC	Greencastle	Jasper	IA	Green Park	Perry	PA
Gray Hawk	Jackson	KY	Green Castle	Warren	KY	Green Plain	Southampton	VA
Gray Rock	Titus	TX	Green Castle	Sullivan	MO	Green Point	Kings	NY

PLACE	COUNTY	STATE	PLACE	COUNTY	STATE	PLACE	COUNTY	STATE
Greenpoint	Bedford	PA	Guthrie Centre	Guthrie	IO	Hale's Mills	Fentross	TN
Green Pond	Pike	IL	Guthriesville	Chester	PA	Hale's Point	Lauderdale	TN
Green Pond	Colleton	SC	Guthriesville	York	SC	Haley's	Marion	AL
Greenport	Suffolk	NY	Guth's Stattion	Lehigh	PA	Haley's Station	Bedford	TN
Green Prairie	Morrison	MN	Guttenberg	Clayton	IO	Half Day	Lake	IL
Green Ridge	Pettis	MO	Guyandotte	Cabell	WV	Half Moon	Saratoga	NY
Green Ridge	Adams	PA	Guymard	Orange	NY	Half Moon	Centre	PA
Green River	Henry	IL	Guy's Mills	Crawford	PA	Halfmoon Bay	San Mateo	CA
Green Riber	Butler	KY	Guy's Store	Leon	TX	Half Moon Island	Roane	TN
Green River	Columbia	NY	Guysville	Athens	OH	Half Rock	Mercer	MO
Green River	Henderson	SC	Guyton	Effingham	GA	Half Way	Polk	MO
Green River	Windham	VT	Gwin Mine	Calaveras	CA	Half Way	Onondaga	NY
Green River City	Sweetwater	WY	Gwynedd	Montgomery	PA	Half Way	Montgomery	PA
Greensborough(c.h.)Hale		AL	Gypsum	Ontario	NY	Half Way Creek	La Crosse	WI
Greensborough	Craighead	AR	Gypsum Creek	McPherson	KS	Half Way House	Vermilion	IL
Greensborough(c.h.)Greene		GA				Half Way House	York	VA
Greensborough	Henry	IN	Hackberry	Floyd	IA	Half Way Prairie	Monroe	IA
Greensborough	Caroline	MD	Hackberry	Lavaca	TX	Halifax	Plymouth	MA
Greensborough(c.h.)Choctaw		MS	Hackensack (c.h.)	Bergen	NJ	Halifax (c.h.)	Halifax	NC
Greensborough(c.h.)Guilford		NC	Hacker's Creek	Lewis	WV	Halifax	Dauphin	PA
Greensborough	Greene	PA	Hacker's Valley	Webster	WV	Halifax	Windham	VT
Greensborough	Orleans	VT	Hackettstown	Warren	NJ	Halifax (c.h.)	Halifax	VA
Greensburgh	Clay	IL	Hackleman	Grant	IN	Hall	Morgan	IN
Greensburgh(c.h.)	Decatur	IN	Haddam (c.h.)	Middlesex	CT	Hall	York	PA
Greensburgh(c.h.)	Greene	KY	Haddam	Washington	KS	Hall Centre	Wayne	NY
Greensburgh(c.h.)	St. Helena	LA	Haddam Neck	Middlesex	CT	Halleck	Buchanan	MO
Greensburgh	Knox	MO	Haddock's Station	Jones	GA	Hallettsville (c.h.)	Lavaca	TX
Greensburgh	Mercer	NJ	Haddonfield	Camden	NJ	Hallock	Peoria	IL
Greensburgh	Trumbull	OH	Haddrell's	Charleston	SC	Hallock's Mills	Westchester	NY
Greensburgh(c.h.)	Westmoreland	PA	Haden's	Madison	AL	Hallowell	Kennebec	ME
Greensburgh X Rds	Sandusky	OH	Hadensville	Todd	KY	Hallsa's Ferry	Nodaway	MO
Green Sea	Horry	SC	Hadensville	Gooehland	VA	Hallsborough	Chesterfield	VA
Green's Fork	Wayne	IN	Hader	Goodhue	MN	Hall's Corners	Allen	IN
Greenside	Webster	IA	Hadley	Will	IL	Hall's Corners	Ontario	NY
Green's Landing	Hancock	ME	Hadley	Warren	KY	Hall's Gap Station	Lincoln	KY
Greensport	St. Clair	AL	Hadley	Hampshire	MA	Hall's Hill	Rutherford	TN
Green Spring	New Castle	DE	Hadley	Lapeer	MI	Hall's Mill	Bartow	GA
Green Spring	Seneca	OH	Hadley	Saratoga	NY	Hallsport	Allegany	NY
Green Spring	Cumberland	PA	Hadley	Mercer	PA	Hall's Valley	Morgan	OH
Green Spr. Furnace	Washington	PA	Hadley's Mills	Chatham	NC	Hallsville	Pike	AL
Green Spring Run	Hampshire	WV	Hadley Station	Lawrence	IL	Hallsville	De Witt	IL
Green Sulphur Sp'gs Greenbrier		WV	Hadlock	Northampton	VA	Hallsville	Bonne	MO
Greenton	La Fayette	MO	Hadlyme	New London	CT	Hallsville	Montgomery	NY
Green Top	Schuyler	MO	Hagaman's Mills	Montgomery	NY	Hallsville	Duplin	NC
Greentown	Howard	IN	Hagarstown	Fayette	IL	Hallsville	Ross	OH
Greentown	Stark	OH	Hagedorn's Mills	Saratoga	NY	Hallsville	Harrison	TX
Green Tree	Allegheny	PA	Hager's Grove	Shelby	MO	Halltown	Saline	IL
Green Tree	White	TN	Hagerstown	Wayne	IN	Halltown	Jefferson	WV
Greenup	Cumberland	IL	Hagerstown (c.h.)	Washington	MD	Halsellville	Chester	SC
Greenup(c.h.)	Greenup	KY	Hagersville	Bucks	PA	Halsey	Linn	OR
Gulf Mills	Montgomery	Pa	Hagley	Cass	IL	Halsey Valley	Tioga	NY
Gulf Summit	Broome	NY	Hagne	Warren	NY	Hambaugh's	Warren	VA
Gulf Lake	Barry	MI	Hague	Westmoreland	VA	Hamburgh	Perry	AL
Gully Branch	Coffee	GA	Haileborough	St. Lawrence	NY	Hamburgh (c.h.)	Ashley	AR
Gumborough	Sussex	DL	Hailsville	Montgomery	AL	Hamburgh	New London	CT
Gum Branch	Onslow	NC	Hainesburgh	Warren	NJ	Hamburgh	Calhoun	IL
Gum Creek	Dooley	GA	Hainesport	Burlington	NJ	Hamburgh	Franklin	IN
Gum Spring	Louisa	VA	Hainesville	Lake	IL	Hamburgh	Fremont	IA
Gum Sulphur	Rock Castle	KY	Hainesville	Clinton	MO	Hamburgh	Livingston	MI
Gum Tree	Chester	PA	Hainesville	Sussex	NJ	Hamburgh	Franklin	MI
Gunn City	Cass	MO	Hainesville	Berkeley	WV	Hamburgh	Franklin	MS
Gundrum	Pulaski	IN	Hair's Valley	Huntingdon	PA	Hamburgh	St. Charles	MO
Gunn Marsh	Allegan	MI	Halcott Centre	Greene	NY	Hamburgh	Sussex	NJ
Gunnison	San Pete	UT	Halcottsville	Delaware	NY	Hamburgh	Erie	NY
Guntersville (c.h.)	Marshall	AL	Haleyon Dale	Scriven	GA	Hamburgh	Fairfield	OH
Guntown	Lee	MI	Haldane	Ogle	IL	Hamburgh	Berks	PA
Gurleysville	Madison	AL	Hale	Ogle	IL	Hamburgh	Edgefield	SC
Gurleyville	Tolland	CN	Hale	Kossuth	IA	Hamburge	Hardin	TN
Gussettville	Live Oak	TX	Hale	Trempealeau	WI	Hamburgh	Shenandoah	VA
Gustavus	Trumbull	OH	Hale's Corners	Milwaukee	WI	Hamden	New Haven	CT
Guthrie	Lawrence	IN	Hale's Creek	Scioto	OH	Hamden	Delaware	NY
Guthrie	Guthrie	IO	Hale's Eddy	Delaware	NY	Hamel	Madison	IL
Guthrie	Todd	KY	Hale's Ford	Franklin	VA	Hamer	Paulding	OH

PLACE	COUNTY	STATE	PLACE	COUNTY	STATE	PLACE	COUNTY	STATE
Hamersville	Brown	OH	Hamrick's Station	Putnam	IN	Hardin	Clayton	IA
Hamilton	Park	CO	Ham's Prairie	Callaway	MO	Hardin	Ray	MO
Hamilton (c.h.)	Harris	GA	Hanby's Mills	Walker	AL	Hardin	Shelby	OH
Hamilton	Hancock	IL	Hancock	Harrison	IN	Hardin (c.h.)	Hardin	TX
Hamilton	Steuben	IN	Hancock	Hancock	ME	Hardin City	Hardin	IA
Hamilton	Marion	IA	Hancock	Washington	MD	Hardinsburgh	Washington	IN
Hamilton	Crawford	KS	Hancock	Berkshire	MA	Hardinsburgh (c.h.)	Breckinridge	KY
Hamilton	Boone	KY	Hancock	Houghton	MI	Hardinsville	Crawford	IL
Hamilton	Essex	MA	Hancock	Pulaski	MO	Hardison's Mills	Maury	TN
Hamilton	Allegan	MI	Hancock	Hillsborough	NH	Hardwick	Worcester	MA
Hamilton	Fillmore	MN	Hancock	Delaware	NY	Hardwick	Warren	NJ
Hamilton	Monroe	MI	Hancock	Addison	VT	Hardwick	Caledonia	VT
Hamilton	Caldwell	MO	Hancock	Waushara	WI	Hardwicksville	Nelson	VA
Hamilton	Gallatin	MT	Hancock's Bridge	Salem	NJ	Hardy	Dallas	AL
Hamilton (c.h.)	White Pine	NV	Handsborough	Harrison	MS	Hardy Station	Grenada	MS
Hamilton	Madison	NY	Handy	Fayette	AL	Hardyville	Mohave	AZ
Hamilton	Martin	NC	Handy	Fulton	OH	Hardyville	Hart	KY
Hamilton (c.h.)	Butler	OH	Hanerville	Dane	WI	Hareb	Bedford	VA
Hamilton	Jefferson	PA	Hanesville	Kent	MD	Hare's Corner	New Castle	DE
Hamilton	Shelby	TX	Haneyville	Lycoming	PA	Harewood	Baltimore	MD
Hamilton	Loudoun	VA	Hanford's Landing	Monroe	NY	Harford	Cortland	NY
Hamilton Square	Mercer	NJ	Hanging Rock	Lawrence	OH	Harford	Susquehanna	PA
Hamilton Station	Scott	MN	Hanging Rock	Hampshire	WV	Harford Furnace	Harford	MD
Hamlet	Mercer	IL	Hankins	Sullivan	NY	Harford Mills	Cortland	NY
Hamlet	Stark	IN	Hanley	Ottawa	MI	Hark	Shelby	IL
Hamlet	Chautauqua	NY	Hanlin Station	Washington	PA	Harker's Corners	Peoria	IL
Hamlin	McLean	IL	Hanly	Jessamine	KY	Harlan	Allen	IN
Hamlin	Brown	KS	Hannahatchee	Stewart	GA	Harlan (c.h.)	Shelby	IA
Hamlin	Monroe	MI	Hannahsville	Tucker	WV	Harlan (c.h.)	Harlan	KY
Hamlin	Monroe	NY	Hanna Station	La Porte	IN	Harlem	Winnebago	IL
Hamlin	Lebanon	PA	Hannersville	Davidson	NC	Harlem	Clay	MO
Hamlin (c.h.)	Lincoln	WV	Hannibal	Marion	MO	Harlem	New York	NY
Hamlin	Trempealean	WI	Hannibal	Oswego	NY	Harlem	Delaware	OH
Hamlin Grove	Audubon	IA	Hannibal	Monroe	OH	Harlem Spring	Carroll	OH
Hamlinton	Wayne	PA	Hannibal Centre	Oswego	NY	Harlemville	Columbia	NY
Hammersley's Fork	Clinton	PA	Hanover	Coosa	AL	Harlensburgh	Lawrence	PA
Hammond	Tangipahoa	LA	Hanover	New London	CT	Harleysville	Montgomery	PA
Hammond	Kent	MI	Hanover	Jo Daviess	IL	Harlingen	Somerset	NJ
Hammond	St. Lawrence	NY	Hanover	Jefferson	IN	Harmar	Washington	OH
Hammond	Barnwell	SC	Hanover	Washington	KS	Harmarville	Allegheny	PA
Hammond	Robertson	TX	Hanover	Oxford	ME	Harmon	Bracken	KY
Hammond	St. Croix	WI	Hanover	Howard	MD	Harmonsburgh	Crawford	PA
Hammondsburgh	Warren	IA	Hanover	Plymouth	MA	Harmony	McHenry	IL
Hammond's Creek	Tioga	PA	Hanover	Jackson	MI	Harmony	Clay	IN
Hammondsport	Steuben	NY	Hanover	Jefferson	MO	Harmony	Taylor	IA
Hammondsville	Jefferson	OH	Hanover	Grafton	NH	Harmony	Owen	KY
Hammonton	Atlantic	NJ	Hanover	Morris	NJ	Harmony	Somerset	ME
Hammonville	Hart	KY	Hanover	Licking	OH	Harmony	Fillmore	MN
Hamorton	Chester	PA	Hanover	York	PA	Harmony	Washington	MO
Hampden	Penobscot	ME	Hanover	Rock	WI	Harmony	Warren	NJ
Hampden	Geauga	OH	Hanover (c.h.)	Hanover	VA	Harmony	Chautauqua	NY
Hampden Corner	Penobscot	ME	Hanover Centre	Grafton	NH	Harmony	Clark	OH
Hampden Sidney College	Prince Edward	VA	Hanover Junction	York	PA	Harmony	Butler	PA
Hampshire	Kane	IL	Hanover Mills	Burlington	NJ	Harmony	Providence	RI
Hampshire	Maury	TN	Hanoverton	Columbiana	OH	Harmony	York	SC
Hampstead	Carroll	MD	Hanoverville	Northampton	PA	Harmony	Halifax	VA
Hampstead	Rockingham	NH	Hansel's	Dearborn	IN	Harmony	Mason	WV
Hampstead	King George	VA	Hansen	Oceana	MI	Harmony	Vernon	WI
Hampton (c.h.)	Calhoun	AR	Hanson	Hopkins	KY	Harmony Centre	Susquehanna	PA
Hampton	Windham	CT	Hanson	Plymouth	MA	Harmony Grove	Jackson	GA
Hampton	Rock Island	IL	Hansonville	Frederick	MD	Harmony Hill	Rusk	TX
Hampton (c.h.)	Franklin	IA	Hansonville	Russell	VA	Harmony Village	Middlesex	VA
Hampton	Dakota	MN	Happy Camp	Del Norte	CA	Harmsburg	Armstrong	PA
Hampton	Platte	MO	Happy Hollow	Wapello	IA	Harnedsville	Somerset	PA
Hampton	Rockingham	NH	Happy Home	Burke	NC	Harnett (c.h.)	Harnett	NC
Hampton	Washington	NY	Happy Valley	Harrison	MO	Harney	Caroll	MD
Hampton	Adams	PA	Happy Valley	Carter	TN	Harold	Montgomery	AR
Hampton	Carter	TN	Harbeson	Sussex	DE	Harp	De Witt	IL
Hampton	Hamilton	TX	Harbour Creek	Erie	PA	Harper	Logan	OH
Hampton (c.h.)	Elizabeth City	VA	Harbour's Mills	Putnam	WV	Harper's Cross Roads	Cheatham	NC
Hampton Falls	Rockingham	NH	Hardeeville	Beaufort	SC	Harper's Ferry	Allamakee	IA
Hamptonville	Yadkin	NC	Hardenburgh	Ulster	NY	Harper's Ferry	Henry	KY
			Hardin (c.h.)	Calhoun	IL	Harper's Ferry	Jefferson	WV

PLACE NAMES OF THE UNITED STATES

PLACE	COUNTY	STATE	PLACE	COUNTY	STATE	PLACE	COUNTY	STATE
Harpersfield	Delaware	NY	Harrisville	Lewis	NY	Harvard	Worcester	MA
Harpersfiled	Ashtabula	OH	Harrisville	Harrison	OH	Harvard	Delaware	NY
Harper's Mills	Pendleton	WV	Harrisville	Butler	PA	Harvey	Marquette	MI
Harpersville	Broome	NY	Harrisville	Bell	TX	Harvey	Dane	WI
Harpswell Centre	Cumberland	ME	Harrisville	Weber	UT	Harvey's	Greene	PA
Harrel	Montgomery	IL	Harrisville (c.h.)	Ritchie	WV	Hareysburgh	Fountain	IN'
Harreldsville	Butler	KY	Harrisville	Marquette	WI	Harveysburgh	Warren	OH
Harrell	Decatur	GA	Harrmann's Station	Dearborn	IN	Harvey's Mills	Jefferson	IA
Harrell's Store	New Hanover	NC	Harrodsburgh	Monroe	IN	Harvey's Store	Charlotte	VA
Harrellsville	Hertford	NC	Harrodsburgh (c.h.)	Mercer	KY	Harveyville	Wabaunsee	KS
Harriettsville	Noble	OH	Harshasville	Adams	OH	Harveyville	Luzerne	PA
Harrington	Kent	DE	Harshaville	Beaver	PA	Harwich	Barnstable	MA
Harrington	Washington	ME	Harshmansville	Montgomery	OH	Harwich Port	Barnstable	MA
Harrington	Harnett	NC	Hart (c.h.)	Oceana	MI	Harwinton	Litchfield	CT
Harris	Louisa	VA	Hartfield	Cahutauqua	NY	Harwood	Muskegon	MI
Harrisburgh (c.h.)	Poinsett	AR	Hartford (c.h.)	Hartford	CT	Hasbrouck	Sullivan	NY
Harrisburgh	Alameda	CA	Hartford	Saline	IL	Haskell	La Porte	IN
Harrisburgh	Lincoln	Dak	Hartford	Ohio	IN	Haskell Flats	Cattaraugus	NY
Harrisburgh (c.h.)	Saline	IL	Hartford	Warren	IA	Haskins	Wood	OH
Harrisburgh	Fayette	IN	Hartford	Lyon	KS	Haskinsville	Greene	KY
Harrisburgh	Lyon	KS	Hartford (c.h.)	Ohio	KY	Haskinville	Steuben	NY
Harrisburgh	Deer Lodge	MT	Hartford	Oxford	ME	Hasler	Lapeer	MI
Harrisburgh	Lewis	NY	Hartford	Van Buren	MI	Haslum	Appling	GA
Harrisburgh	Franklin	OH	Hartford	Todd	MN	Hassan	Hennepin	MN
Harrisburgh	Linn	OR	Hartford	Choctaw	MS	Hassan	Hancock	OH
Harrisburgh (c.h.)	Dauphin	PA	Hartford	Putnam	MO	Hastings	Mills	IA
Harrisburgh	Harris	TX	Hartford	Burlington	NJ	Hastings (c.h.)	Barry	MI
Harrisburgh	Washington	UT	Hartford	Washington	NY	Hastings (c.h.)	Dakota	MN
Harrisburgh Station	Madison		Hartford	Trumbull	OH	Hastings	Oswego	NY
Harrisburgh Station	Madison	TN	Hartford	Windsor	VT	Hastings	Richland	OH
Harris Creek	Kent	MI	Hartford	Washington	WI	Hastings Centre	Oswego	NY
Harris Creek	Amherst	VA	Hartford City (c.h.)	Blackford	IN	Hastings Landing	Calhoun	IL
Harris Depot	Cabarrus	NC	Hartford City	Mason	WV	Hastings-upon-		
Harris' Ferry	Wood	WV	Harthegig	Mercer	PA	Hudson	Westchester	NY
Harris Grove	Jefferson	IL	Hartland	Hartford	CT	Hatborough	Montgomery	PA
Harris Grove	Harrison	IA	Hartland	Worth	IA	Hatch	Kossuth	IA
Harris Hill	Erie	NY	Hartland	Somerset	ME	Hatchechubbee	Russell	AL
Harris Lot	Charles	MD	Hartland	Livingston	MI	Hatcher's Station	Quitman	GA
Harrison (c.h.)	Boone	AR	Hartland	Freeborn	MN	Hatch Hollow	Erie	PA
Harrison	Winnebago	IL	Hartland	Niagara	NY	Hatchsophka	Elmore	AL
Harrison	Delaware	IN	Hartland	Huron	OH	Hatchville	Barnstable	MA
Harrison	Cumberland	ME	Hartland	Windsor	VT	Hat Creek	Campbell	VA
Harrison	Dorchester	MD	Hartland	Waukesha	WI	Hatfield	Hampshire	MA
Harrison	Kandiyohi	MN	Hartland Four			Hatfield	Montgomery	PA
Harrison	Madison	MT	Corners	Windsor	VT	Hathaway	Lake	TN
Harrison	Westchester	NY	Hartleton	Union	PA	Haubstadt	Gibson	IN
Harrison	Hamilton	OH	Hartley	York	PA	Haught's Store	Dallas	TX
Harrison (c.h.)	James	TN	Hartleyville	Athens	OH	Hauppange	Suffolk	NY
Harrisonburgh (c.h.)	Catahoula	LA	Hart Lot	Onondaga	NY	Hansertown	Owen	IN
Harrisonburgh (c.h.)	Rockingham	VA	Hartman	Seward	NE	Havana (c.h.)	Mason	IL
Harrison City	Westmoreland	PA	Hartman	Columbia	WI	Havana	Montgomery	KS
Harrison Mills	Scioto	OH	Hartmonsville	Mineral	WV	Havana	Gentry	MO
Harrison's Creek	Bladen	NC	Hart's Corners	Westchester	NY	Havana	Schuyler	NY
Harrison's Mills	Crawford	MO	Hart's Creek	Lincoln	WV	Havana	Huron	OH
Harrison Square	Norfolk	MA	Hart's Falls	Reusselaer	NY	Havanna	Hale	AL
Harrison's Store	Shelby	TN	Hart's Grove	Ashtabula	OH	Havanna	Steele	MN
Harrison Station	Tallahatchie	MS	Hartshorn	Alamance	NC	Havelock	Cook	IL
Harrison Valley	Potter	PA	Hartstown	Crawford	PA	Havelock	Washington	PA
Harrisonville	Monroe	IL	Hartsville	Bartholomew	IN	Haven	Tama	IA
Harrisonville	Montgomery	KS	Hartsville	Berkshire	MA	Haverford	Delaware	PA
Harrisonville	Shelby	KY	Hartsville	Bucks	PA	Haverhill	Essex	MA
Harrisonville	Baltimore	MD	Hartsville	Darlington	SC	Haverhill (c.h.)	Grafton	NH
Harrisonville (c.h.)	Cass	MO	Hartsville	Trousdale	TN	Haverhill	Scioto	OH
Harrisonville	Gloucester	NJ	Hartsville (c.h.)	Wright	MO	Haverstraw	Rockland	NY
Harrisonville	Meigs	OH	Hartville	Stark	OH	Havilah (c.h.)	Kern	CA
Harrisonville	Fulton	PA	Hartwell (c.h.)	Hart	GA	Haviland Hollow	Putnam	NY
Harris Station	Limestone	AL	Hartwell	Hamilton	OH	Havilandsville	Harrison	KY
Harris Station	Obion	TN	Hartwellville	Shiawassee	MI	Havre de Grace	Harford	MD
Harristown	Macon	IL	Hartwick	Otsego	NY	Haw Branch	Onslow	NC
Harristown	Washington	IN	Hartwick Seminary	Otsego	NY	Haw Creek	Benton	MO
Harrisville	Randolph	IN	Hartwood	Sullivan	NY	Hawe's Cross Roads	Washington	TN
Harrisville (c.h.)	Alcona	MI	Hartwood	Stafford	VA	Hawesville (c.h.)	Hancock	KY
Harrisville	Cheshire	NH	Harvard	McHenry	IL	Hawk Creek	Chippewa	MN

PLACE	COUNTY	STATE	PLACE	COUNTY	STATE	PLACE	COUNTY	STATE
Hawk Eye	Fayette	IA	Hazleton	Gibson	IN	Helena	St. Lawrence	NY
Hawk Eye	Dixon	NE	Hazleton	Luzerne	PA	Helena (c.h.)	Karnes	TX
Hawkins	Jay	IN	Hazlettville	Kent	DE	Helena Station	Iowa	WI
Hawkinstown	Shenandoah	VA	Hazlewood	Ballard	KY	Helen Furnace	Clarion	PA
Hawkinsville (c.h.)	Pulaski	GA	Hazlewood	Webster	MO	Helenville	Jefferson	WI
Hawkinsville	Oneida	NY	Hazlewood	Chester	SC	Helham	Overton	TN
Hawkinsville	Sussex	VA	Hazlitt	Rock Island	IL	Helicon	Crenshaw	AL
Hawk Point	Lincoln	MO	Headland	Saunders	NE	Hellen	York	PA
Hawk's Nest	Fayette	WV	Head of Barren	Claiborne	TN	Hellen	Elk	PA
Hawley	Franklin	MA	Head of Elm	Montague	TX	Heller's Corner	Allen	IN
Hawley	Wayne	PA	Head of Tennessee	Rabun	GA	Hellertown	Northampton	PA
Hawley's Store	Sampson	NC	Head Quarters	Nicholas	KY	Hell Gate	Missoula	MT
Hawleysville	Page	IA	Headsville	Robertson	TX	Helmick	Coshocton	OH
Hawleyton	Broome	NY	Headsville	Mineral	WV	Helton	Ashe	NC
Hawleyville	Fairfield	CT	Head Waters	Highland	VA	Heltonville	Lawrence	IN
Haw Ridge	Dale	AL	Healdsburgh	Sonoma	CA	Helvetia	Waupaca	WI
Haw River	Alamance	NC	Healdville	Rutland	VT	Hematite	Jefferson	MO
Haw's Ford	Floyd	KY	Healing Spring	Davidson	NC	Hemlock	Cambria	PA
Hawthorn	Montgomery	IA	Healing Springs	Bath	VA	Hemlock City	Saginaw	MI
Hawthorne	Passaic	NJ	Hearne	Robertson	TX	Hemlock Grove	Meigs	OH
Hayden	Lassen	CA	Heart Prairie	Walworth	WI	Hemlock Hollow	Wayne	PA
Hayden Row	Middlesex	MA	Heartwellville	Bennington	VT	Hemlock Lake	Livingston	NY
Haydenville	Hampshire	MA	Heaslyville	Marshall	KS	Hempfield	Lancaster	PA
Haydenville	Hocking	OH	Heath	Franklin	MA	Hemphill (c.h.)	Sabine	TX
Hayes' Store	Madison	AL	Heathsville	Halifax	NC	Hemp's Creek	Catahoula	LA
Hayes' Store	Gloucester	VA	Heathsville (c.h.)	Northumberland	VA	Hempstead	Calloway	MO
Hayesville	Greene	AL	Heaton	Lee	IL	Hempstead	Queens	NY
Hayesville	Keokuk	IA	Hebbardsville	Henderson	KY	Hempstead	Austin	TX
Hayesville	Ashland	OH	Hebbardsville	Athens	OH	Henderson	Pike	AL
Hayesville (c.h.)	Clay	NC	Hebbertsburgh	Cumberland	TN	Henderson	Knox	IL
Hayesville	Chester	PA	Heber (c.h.)	Wasatch	UT	Henderson	Lucas	IA
Hayesville	Greene	TN	Hebron	Tolland	CT	Henderson (c.h.)	Henderson	KY
Hayfield	Crawford	PA	Hebron	Washington	GA	Henderson	Caroline	MD
Hayfield	Crawford	PA	Hebron	McHenry	IL	Henderson (c.h.)	Sibley	MN
Hayfield	Frederick	VA	Hebron	Porter	IN	Henderson	Webster	MO
Hay Market	Prince William	VA	Hebron	Adair	IA	Henderson	Jefferson	NY
Hay Meadow	Wilkes	NC	Hebron	Boone	KY	Henderson	Granville	NC
Haymond	Franklin	IN	Hebron	Oxford	ME	Henderson	Mercer	PA
Haynerville	Rensselaer	NY	Hebron	Nicollet	MN	Henderson (c.h.)	Rusk	TX
Haynes	Union	TN	Hebron	Jefferson	NE	Henderson's Mills	Marshall	KY
Haynesville	Claiborne	LA	Hebron	Grafton	NH	Henderson's Springs	Sevier	TN
Haynesville	Aroostook	ME	Hebron	Washington	NY	Henderson Station	Madison	TN
Hayneville (c.h.)	Lowndes	AL	Hebron	Licking	OH	Hendersonville (c.h.)	Henderson	NC
Haynie	Mills	IA	Hebron	Potter	PA	Hendersonville	Sumner	TN
Hays City (c.h.)	Ellis	KS	Hebron	Spartanburgh	SC	Hendricks	Otoe	NE
Hays' Store	Wake	NC	Hebron	Washington	UT	Hendricksburgh	Luzerne	PA
Haystack	Surry	NC	Hebron	Pleasants	WV	Hendrick's Store	Bedford	VA
Haysville	Dubois	IN	Hebron	Jefferson	WI	Hendrysburgh	Belmont	OH
Hayward	Freeborn	MN	Hebronville	Bristol	MA	Henley	Siskiyou	CA
Haywood	Alameda	CA	Becker	Monroe	IL	Hennepin (c.h.)	Putnam	IL
Haywood	Chatham	NC	Hecktown	Northampton	PA	Henniker	Merrimack	NH
Hazard	Cherokee	IA	Hecla	Whitley	IN	Henning	Bourbon	KS
Hazard (c.h.)	Perry	KY	Heela Works	Oneida	NY	Henning's Mills	Clermont	OH
Hazardville	Hartford	CT	Hector	Jay	IN	Henrietta	Jackson	MI
Hazelettville	Woodson	KS	Hector	Schuyler	NY	Henrietta	Nuckolls	NE
Hazel Green	Madison	TN	Hedgesville	Steuben	NY	Henrietta	Monroe	NY
Hazel Green	Grant	WI	Hedgesville	Berkeley	WV	Henrietta	Lorain	OH
Hazelton	Buchanan	IA	Hedwig's Hill	Mason	TX	Henrietta	Richland	WI
Hazelton	Shiawassee	MI	Heffren	Washington	IN	Henry	Marshall	IL
Hazelwood	Rice	MN	Hegarty's Cross Roads	Clearfield	PA	Henry	Ray	MO
Hazen	Cass	MO	Hegg	Trempealeau	WI	Henry	Sussex	VA
Hazle Barrens	Barry	MO	Hegins	Schuylkill	PA	Henry Clay Factory	New Castle	DE
Hazle Dell	Cumberland	IL	Heidlersburgh	Adams	PA	Henry's Cross Roads	Sevier	TN
Hazle Green	Delaware	IA	Heilmandale	Lebanon	PA	Henry's Fork	Roane	WV
Hazle Green	Wolfe	KY	Heistersburgh	Fayette	PA	Henry Station	Henry	TN
Hazle Green	Shiawassee	MI	Helena (c.h.)	Phillips	AR	Henrysville	Marshall	AL
Hazle Green	Laclede	MO	Helena	Lake	CO	Henrysville	Logan	KY
Hazle Grove	Lawrence	AR	Helena	Tama	IA	Henrysville	Monroe	PA
Hazlehurst	Appling	GA	Helena	Mason	KY	Henryville	Clarke	IN
Halehurst	Copiah	MI	Helena	Scott	MN	Henryville	Lawrence	TN
Halehurst	Laurel!		Helena (c.h.)	Lewis & Clarke	MT	Hensonville	Greene	NY
Halehurst	Copiah	MS	Helena	Johnson	NE	Hepler	Crawford	KS
Hazel Patch	Laurel	KY				Hepler	Schuylkill	PA

PLACE NAMES OF THE UNITED STATES

PLACE	COUNTY	STATE	PLACE	COUNTY	STATE	PLACE	COUNTY	STATE
Hepton	Kosciusko	IN	Hickory	Washington	PA	Highland	Moniteau	MO
Herbert	Kemper	MS	Hickory Barren	Greene	MO	Highland	Richardson	NE
Herbett	Neshoba	MS	Hicotry Branch	Posey	IN	Highland	Ulster	NY
Hereford	Baltimore	MD	Hicory Corners	Barry	MI	Highland	Highland	OH
Hereford	Berks	PA	Hicory Corners	Niagara	NY	Highland	Clackamas	OR
Herkimer (c.h.)	Herkimer	NY	Hickory Corners	Northumberland	PA	Highland	Bradford	PA
Hermaan	Ripley		Hictory Creek	Fayette	IL	Highland	Jackson	TN
Hermaan	Ripley	IN	Hickory Creek	Audrian	MO	Highland	Collin	TX
Herman	Dodge	WI	Hickory Flat	Chambers	AL	Highland	Ritchie	WV
Hermann (c.h.)	Gasconade	MO	Hickory Flat	Benton	MS	Highland	Iowa	WI
Hermansville	Coos	OR	Hickory Fork	Gloucester	VA	Highland Centre	Wapello	IA
Hermitage	Mendocino	CA	Hickory Grove	Crawford	GA	Highland Falls	Orange	NY
Hermitage	Point Coupee	LA	Hickory Grove	Massac	IL	Highland Grove	Jones	IA
Hermitage (c.h.)	Hickory	MO	Hickory Grove	Graves	KY	Highland Grove	Greenville	SC
Hermitage	Wyoming	NY	Hickory Grove	York	SC	Highland Home	Laurens	SC
Hermitage	Mercer	PA	Hickory Hill	Marion	IL	Highland Lake	Bradford	PA
Hermitage	Augusta	VA	Hickory Hill	Cole	MO	Highland Mills	Orange	NY
Hermon	Knox	IL	Hickory Hill	Chester	PA	Highland Park	Lake	IL
Hermon	Penobscot	ME	Hickory Hill	Cass	TX	Highlands	Monmouth	NJ
Hermon	St. Lawrence	NY	Hickory Plains	Prairie	AR	Highland Station	Doniphan	KS
Hermon Pond	Penobscot	ME	Hickory Ridge	Monroe	AR	Highland Station	Galveston	TX
Hermosilla	Pueblo	CO	Hickory Ridge	Hancock	IL	Highland Town	Grundy	IL
Hernando (c.h.)	De Sota	MS	Hickory Runn	Carbon	PA	Highlandville	Winnishiek	IA
Herndon	Greene	AR	Hickory Springs	Texas	MO	High Point	Walker	GA
Herndon	Burke	GA	Hickory Tavern	Harford	MD	High Point	Mercer	IL
Herndon	Montgomery	IL	Hickory Tavern	Catawba	NC	High Point	Decatur	IA
Herndon	Northumberland	PA	Hickory Town	Montgomery	PA	High Point	Moniteau	MO
Herndon	Fairfax	VA	Hickory Valley	Hardeman	TN	High Point	Guilford	NC
Heron Lake	Jackson	MN	Hicksburgh	Renville	MN	High Ridge	Fairfield	CT
Herrick	Bradford	PA	Hicksford (c.h.)	Greenville	VA	High Ridge	Jefferson	MO
Herrick Centre	Susquehanna	PA	Hicks' Mills	De Kalb	IL	High Shoals	Gaston	NC
Herrickville	Bradford	PA	Hicks Station	Prairie	AR	High Spire	Dauphin	PA
Herriman	Salt Lake	UT	Hicksville	Sacramento	CA	High Springs	Clark	AR
Herring	Allen	OH	Hicksville	Queens	NY	High Tower	Forsyth	GA
Herrington's Corners	Chemung	NY	Hicksville	Defiance	OH	Hightown	Highland	VA
Herrin's Prairie	Williamson	IL	Hick's Wharf	Matthews	VA	Highstown	Mercer	NJ
Herriottsville	Washington	PA	Hico	Benton	AR	High View	Frederick	VA
Hersey (c.h.)	Osceola	MI	Hico	Callaway	KY	Highville	Lancaster	PA
Herseyville	Monroe	WI	Hidalgo	Jasper	IL	Hika	Manitowoc	WI
Hersman's	Brown	IL	Hiester's Mill	Berks	PA	Hiko	Lincoln	NV
Hertford (c.h.)	Perquimons	NC	Higganum	Middlesex	CT	Hill	Grafton	NH
Herzhorn	Renville	MN	Higginsport	Jackson	IA	Hill	Mercer	PA
Heshbon	Indiana	PA	Ingginsport	Brown	OH	Hillabee	Clay	AL
Hesper	Winneshick	IA	Higginsville	Vermilion	IL	Hill Church	Berks	PA
Hesper	Douglas	KS	Higginsville	La Fayette	MO	Hillegass	Montgomery	PA
Hesperia	Oceana	MI	Higginsville	Oneida	NY	Hill Grove	Meade	KY
Hesperia	Fillmore	NE	High Blue	Cass	MO	Hill Grove	Darke	OH
Hesperian	Webster	IA	High Bluff	Dale	AL	Hill Grove	Pittsylvania	VA
Hess Road	Niagara	NY	High Bridge	Hunterdon	NJ	Hillham	Dubois	IN
Hessville	Harrison	WV	High Creek	Fremont	IA	Hillhouse	Lake	OH
Hester	Marion	MO	High Falls	Geneva	AL	Hillian's Store	Marshall	AL
Hester Mills	Meigs	TN	High Falls	Ulster	NY	Hilliard's	Allegan	MI
Hester's Store	Person	NC	High Forst	Olmstead	MN	Hilliards	Franklin	OH
Hetricks	York	PA	Highgate	Franklin	VT	Hilliardston	Nash	NC
Hetslersville	Darke	OH	Highgate Centre	Franklin	VT	Hills	Owen	KY
Heuvelton	St. Lawrence	NY	Highgate Springs	Franklin	VT	Hills	Washington	OH
Hewletts	Hanover	VA	High Grove	Nelson	KY	Hillsborough	Shelby	AL
Heyworth	McLean	IL	High Grove	Maries	MO	Hillsborough	Union	AR
Hiawassee (c.h.)	Towns	GA	High Health	Johnson	TN	Hillsborough	Weld	CO
Hiawatha (c.h.)	Brown	KS	High Hill	Leake	MS	Hillsborough (c.h.)	Montgomery	IL
Hibbetts	Carroll	OH	High Hill	Montgomery	MO	Hillsborough	Fountain	IN
Hibbsville	Appanoose	IA	High Hill	Muskingum	OH	Hillsborough	Henry	IA
Hibernia	Duval	FL	High Hill	Fayette	TX	Hillsborough	Fleming	KY
Hibernia	Morris	NJ	High Lake	Emmett	IA	Hillsborough	Caroline	MD
Hibernia	Dutchess	NY	High Lake	Wayne	PA	Hillsborough (c.h.)	Scott	MS
Hickman (c.h.)	Fulton	KY	Highland	Madison	IL	Hillsborough (c.h.)	Jefferson	MO
Hickman Mills	Jackson	MO	Highland	Clayton	IA	Hillsborough	Hillsborough	NH
Hickman's	Tuscaloosa	AL	Highland	Doniphan	KS	Hillsborough (c.h.)	Orange	NC
Hickory	Benton	AR	Highland	Lincoln	KY	Hillsborough (c.h.)	Highland	OH
Hickory	Lake	IL	Highland	Somerset	ME	Hillsborough (c.h.)	Washington	OR
Hickory	Van Buren	IA	Highland	Oakland	MI	Hillsborough (c.h.)	Coffee	TN
Hickory	Newton	MS	Higland	Fillmore	MN	Hillsborough (c.h.)	Hill	TX
Hickory	Lucas	OH	Highland	Tishemingo	MS	Hillsborough	Londoun	VA

PLACE	COUNTY	STATE	PLACE	COUNTY	STATE	PLACE	COUNTY	STATE
Hillsborough	Vernon	WI	Hobbysville	Spartanburgh	SC	Hollowtown	Highland	OH
Hillsborough			Hoboken	Hudson	NJ	Hollowville	Pike	GA
Bridge	Hillsborough	NH	Hochheim	De Witt	TX	Hollowville	Columbia	NY
Hillsborough Centre	Hillsborough	NH	Hockanum	Hartford	CT	Holly	Oakland	MI
Hillsdale	Rock Island	IL	Hockessin	New Castle	DE	Holly Grove	Walker	AL
Hillsdale	Mills	IA	Hocking	Athens	OH	Holly Grove	Madison	NC
Hillsdale	Miami	KS	Hockingport	Athens	OH	Holly Hill	Charleston	SC
Hillsdale (c.h.)	Hillsdale	MI	Hockley	Harris	TX	Holly Meadows	Tucker	WV
Hillsdale	Nemaha	NE	Hockley	Vernon	WI	Holly River	Braxton	WV
Hillsdale	Bergen	NJ	Hodgdon	Aroostook	ME	Holly Springs	Dallas	AR
Hillsdale	Columbia	NY	Hodgdon's Mills	Lincoln	ME	Holly Springs (c.h.)	Marshall	MS
Hillsdale	Guilford	NC	Hodgensville (c.h.)	La Rue	KY	Holly Springs	Jasper	TX
Hillsdale	Indiana	PA	Hodges	Abbeville	SC	Hollyville	Sussex	DE
Hill's Ferry	Stanislaus	CA	Hodge's Mill	Kendall	TX	Hollywood	Clark	AR
Hill's Fork	Adams	OH	Hodge's Prairie	Sebastain	AR	Hollywood	St. Mary's	MD
Hill's Grove	Sullivan	PA	Hoffman's Ferry	Schenectady	NY	Holman	Dearborn	IN
Hillside	Westmoreland	PA	Hogansburgh	Franklin	NY	Holman's Store	Warren	MO
Hill's Point	Dorchester	MD	Hogansville	Troup	GA	Holman Station	Scott	IN
Hill Spring	Morris	KS	Hogarth's Landing	St. John's	FL	Holmdel	Monmouth	NJ
Hill Spring	Henry	KY	Hog Branch	St. Helena	LA	Holmes	Boone	IN
Hill's Station	Rock Island	IL	Hog Creek	Allen	OH	Holmesburg	Philadelphia	PA
Hill's Station	Clermont	OH	Hoge	Leavenworth	KS	Holmes City	Douglas	MN
Hill's Store	Randolph	NC	Hogestown	Cumberland	PA	Holmes' Hole	Duke	MA
Hill's View	Westmoreland	PA	Hogg's Falls	Ohio	KY	Holmes' Mills	Jefferson	OH
Hillsville	Lawrence	PA	Hog Hollow	St. Louis	MO	Holmesville (c.h.)	Appling	GA
Hillsville (c.h.)	Carroll	VA	Hog Island	Surry	VA	Holmesville	Avoyelles	LA
Hilltown	Bucks	PA	Hog Mountain	Hall	GA	Holmesville	Pike	MS
Hill Valley	Huntingdon	PA	Hohokus	Bergen	NJ	Holmesville	Holmes	OH
Hilton	Sharpe	AR	Hokah	Houston	MN	Holmwood	Jewell	KS
Hilton	Taxewell	IL	Hokondauqua	Lehigh	PA	Holstein	Warren	MO
Hilton	Monroe	KY	Holaday's	Adair	IA	Holston	Washington	VA
Hilton	Sullivan	TN	Holbrook	Suffolk	NY	Holston Bridge	Scott	VA
Himrod's	Yates	NY	Holbrook	Greene	PA	Holston Furnace	Sullivan	TN
Hinckley	Pine	MN	Holbrook	Ritchie	WV	Holston Valley	Sullivan	TN
Hinckley			Holcombe	Burke	GA	Holt	Taylor	IA
Hinckley	Medina	OH	Holcomb's Rock	Bedford	VA	Holt	Ingham	MI
Hindsburgh	Orleans	NY	Holden	San Joaquin	CA	Holt	Clay	MO
Hindsville	Madison	AR	Holden	Butler	KS	Holt	Wood	OH
Hiner's Run	Clinton	PA	Holden	Penobscot	ME	Holt	Beaver	PA
Hinesberg	Fond du Lac	WI	Holden	Worcester	MA	Holton	Ripley	IN
Hinesburgh	Chittenden	VT	Holden	Goodhue	MN	Holton (c.h.)	Jackson	KS
Hine's Mills	Ohio	KY	Holden	Johnson	MO	Holt's Mills	Penobscot	ME
Hinesville (c.h.)	Liberty	GA	Holden	Millard	UT	Holt's Summit	Callaway	MO
Hingham	Plymouth	MA	Holiday's Cove	Hancock	WV	Holtsville	Suffolk	NY
Hingham	Sheboygan	WI	Holland	Shelby	IL	Holy Cross	Clay	MN
Hingham Centre	Plymouth	MA	Holland	Dubois	IN	Holy Cross	Ozaukee	WI
Hinkleton	Lancaster	PA	Holland	Hampden	MA	Holyoke	Hampden	MA
Hinkleville	Ballard	KY	Holland	Ottawa	MI	Home	Wayne	IL
Hinmansville	Oswego	NY	Holland	Hunterdon	NJ	Home	Jefferson	IN
Hinnaut's Mills	Johnson	NC	Holland	Erie	NY	Home	Van Buren	IA
Hinsdale	Du Page	IL	Holland	Lucas	OH	Home	Newaygo	MI
Hinsdale	Lee	IA	Holland	Bucks	PA	Home	Brown	MN
Hinsdale	Berkshire	MA	Holland	Orleans	VT	Home	Indiana	PA
Hinsdale	Cheshire	NH	Holland	Brown	WI	Home	Greene	TN
Hinsdale	Cattaraugus	NY	Holland Patent	Oneida	NY	Home	Trempealeau	WI
Hinton	Plymouth	IA	Hollands	Issequena	MS	Homeland	Culpeper	VA
Hiram	Oxford	ME	Holland's Store	Anderson	SC	Home Place	Plaquemine	LA
Hiram	Portage	OH	Hollandville	Kent	DE	Homer (c.h.)	Banks	GA
Hiramsburgh	Noble	OH	Holley	Orleans	NY	Homer	Champaign	IL
Hiseville	Barren	KY	Holliday	Macoupin	IL	Homer	Rush	IN
Hitchcock's Station	Washington	IN	Hollidaysburgh (c.h.)	Blair	PA	Homer	Hamilton	IA
Hitesville	Union	KY	Holling	Douglass	KS	Homer (c.h.)	Claiborne	LA
Hitt	Scotland	MO	Hollingsworth	Banks	GA	Homer	Calhoun	MI
Hivvihigna	Hillsborough	FL	Hollis	York	ME	Homer	Winona	MN
Hixton	Jackson	WI	Hollis	Hillsborough	NH	Homer	Atchison	MO
Hoag's Corner	Rensselaer	NY	Hollis Centre	York	ME	Homer	Cortland	NY
Hobart	Lake	IN	Hollister	Monterey	CA	Homer	Licking	OH
Hobart	Delaware	NY	Hollisterville	Wayne	PA	Homer	Potter	PA
Hobart's Mills	Sheboygan	WI	Holliston	Middlesex	MA	Homer (c.h.)	Angelina	TX
Hobbie	Luzerne	PA	Holloway's Store	Walker	TX	Homer Creek	Greenwood	KS
Hobbeville	Greene	IN	Hollowayville	Bureau	IL	Homerville (c.h.)	Clinch	GA
Hobb's Ferry	Giles	VA	Hollow Rock	Carroll	TN	Homerville	Medina	OH
Hobb's Station	Jefferson	KY	Hollow Square	Hale	AL	Homestead	Iowa	IA

PLACE	COUNTY	STATE	PLACE	COUNTY	STATE	PLACE	COUNTY	STATE
Homestead	Benzie	MI	Hopedale	Worcester	MA	Horse Creek	Greene	TN
Homestead	Burt	NE	Hopedale	Harrison	OH	Horse Head	Prince George's	MD
Homet's Ferry	Bradford	PA	Hope Falls	Hamilton	NY	Horseheads	Chemung	NY
Homewood	Cook	IL	Hope Farm	Moniteau	MO	Horseley's Landing	Nelson	VA
Homewood	Scott	MS	Hopefield	Crawford	KS	Horse Pasture	Henry	VA
Homewood	Beaver	PA	Hope Furnace	Vinton	OH	Horse Plains	Missoula	MT
Homewood	Monroe	WI	Hope Mills	Page	VA	Horse Prairie	Beaver Head	MT
Homeworth	Columbiana	OH	Hope Ridge	Monroe	OH	Horse Shoe Bend	Boise	IA
Hominy Creek	Buncombe	NC	Hope Station	Lexington	SC	Horse Shoe Bend	Scott	TN
Homowack	Ulster	NY	Hopeton	Merced	CA	Horse Shoe Bottom	Russell	KY
Honaker's Ferry	Warren	KY	Hope Valley	Washington	RI	Horse Shoe Run	Preston	WV
Honcut	Yuba	CA	Hopeville	Clarke	IA	Horsetown	Shasta	CA
Honduras	Wright	MO	Hopeville	Grant	WV	Horsham	Montgomery	PA
Honea Path	Anderson	SC	Hopewell	Mahaska	IA	Horton	Bremer	IA
Honek	Saline	KS	Hopewell	Somerset	MD	Horton's	Indiana	PA
Honeoye	Ontario	NY	Hopewell	Calhoun	MS	Hortonville	Red River	TX
Honcoye Falls	Monroe	NY	Hopewell	Mercer	NJ	Hortonville	Rutland	VT
Honesdale (c.h.)	Wayne	PA	Hopewell	Ontario	NY	Hortonville	Outagamie	WI
Honey Brook	Chester	PA	Hopewell	Mecklenburgh	NC	Hosensack	Lehigh	PA
Honey Creek	Henry	IN	Hopewell	Muskingum	OH	Hoskinsville	Noble	OH
Honey Creek	Pottawattomie	IA	Hopewell	Bedford	PA	Hosmer	Pike	IN
Honey Creek	McDonald	MO	Hopewell	York	SC	Host	Berks	PA
Honey Creek	Walworth	WI	Hopewell Academy	Warren	MO	Hotchkissville	Litchfield	CT
Honey Grove	Juniata	PA	Hopewell Centre	Ontario	NY	Hot Creek	Nye	NV
Honey Grove	Fannin	TX	Hopewell Centre	York	PA	Hotel	Bertie	NC
Honorville	Crenshaw	AL	Hopewell Cotton			Hot House	Fannin	GA
Hood River	Wasco	OR	Works	Chester	PA	Hot Springs	Hot Spring	AR
Hood's Fork	Johnson	KY	Hopewell Cross Roads	Harford	MD	Hot Springs	Bath	VA
Hood's Landing	Roane	TN	Hopwell Furnace	Washington	MD	Houcksville	Carroll ½	MD
Hood's Mills	Carroll	MD	Hopewell Junction	Dutchess	NY	Houcktown	Hancock	OH
Hoodsville	Monongalia	WV	Hopewell Springs	Monroe	TN	Houghton	Jo Daviess	IL
Hoodville	Hamilton	IL	Hopfield	Crittenden	AR	Houghton (c.h.)	Houghton	MI
Hooker	Shelby	IL	Hopkins	Allegan	MI	Houghton Creek	Allegany	NY
Hooker	Van Buren	MI	Hopkins	Nodaway	MO	Houghtonville	Windham	VT
Hooker	Gage	NE	Hopkins' Mill	Greene	PA	Houksville	Sevier	TN
Hooker	Butler	PA	Hopkins' Station	Allegan	MI	Houlka	Chickasaw	MS
Hooker	Trempealean	WI	Hopkins' Turnout	Richland	SC	Houlton (c.h.)	Aroostook	ME
Hooker	Trempealeau	WI	Hopkinsville (c.h.)	Christian	KY	Houma (c.h.)	Terre Bonne	LA
Hooker's Station	Fairfield	OH	Hopkinsville	Warren	OH	Housatonic	Berkshire	MA
Hookersville	Nicholas	WV	Hopkinsville	Gonzales	TX	House Creek	Wilcox	GA
Hookerton	Greene	NC	Hopkinton	Delaware	IA	Houserville	Centre	PA
Hookset	Merrimack	NH	Hopkinton	Middlesex	MA	House's Springs	Jefferson	MO
Hook's Point	Hamilton	IA	Hopkinton	Merrimack	NH	House's Store	Clay	KY
Hookstown	Baltimore	MD	Hopkinton	St. Lawrence	NY	Houseville	Lewis	NY
Hookstown	Beaver	PA	Hopkinton	Washington	RI	Houston (c.h.)	Winston	AL
Hooktown	Nicholas	KY	Hopkinton	St. Lawrence	NY	Houston (c.h.)	Suwannee	FL
Hoops Valley	Klamath	CA	Hopkinton	Washington	RI	Houston	Heard	GA
Hooper	Dodge	NE	Hoppenville	Montgomery	PA	Houston	Jackson	IN
Hooper	Broome	NY	Hopper	Washington	KS	Houston	Bourbon	KY
Hooper	Weber	UT	Hopper's Mills	Henderson	IL	Houston	Houston	MN
Hooper's Valley	Tioga	NY	Hoquiam	Chehalis	WA	Houston (c.h.)	Chickasaw	MS
Hoopersville	Dorchester	MD	Hord	Clay	IL	Houston (c.h.)	Texas	MO
Hooppole	Ross	OH	Horicon	Martin	MN	Houston	Shelby	OH
Hoosac Tunnel	Berkshire	MA	Horicon	Warren	NY	Houston	Allegheny	PA
Hoosick	Rensselaer	NY	Horicon	Dodge	WI	Houston (c.h.)	Harris	TX
Hoosick Falls	Rensselaer	NY	Horine Station	Jefferson	MO	Houston Station	Kent	DE
Hoover Hill	Randolph	NC	Horn	Jasper	IA	Houstonville	Champaign	IL
Hooversville	Anne Arundel	MD	Hornbrook	Bradford	PA	Houtzdale	Clearfield	PA
Hopatcong	Morris	NJ	Hornby	Steuben	NY	Howard	Conway	AR
Hop Btoom	Susquehanna	PA	Hornellsville	Steuben	NY	Howard	Taylor	GA
Hope	Vermilion	IL	Hornerstown	Ocean	NJ	Howard	Parke	IN
Hope	Bartholomew	IN	Hornitas	Mariposa	CA	Howard	Howard	KS
Hope	Dickinson	KS	Horn Lake	De Soto	MS	Howard	Piscataquis	ME
Hope	Knox	ME	Hornsby	Macoupin	IL	Howard	Muskegon	MI
Hope	Somerset	MD	Horn's Mills	Carroll	NH	Howard	Wright	MN
Hope	Midland	MI	Horn's Store	Grayson	KY	Howard	Nemeha	NE
Hope	Warren	NJ	Horntown	Accomack	VA	Howard	Warren	NJ
Hope	Franklin	OH	Horr's	Champaign	OH	Howard	Steuben	NY
Hope	Providence	RI	Horr's Ranch	Stanislaus	CA	Howard	Centre	PA
Hope	Lavaca	TX	Horse Branch	Ohio	KY	Howard	Bell	TX
Hope Centre	Hamilton	NY	Horse Cove	Macon	NC	Howard Centre	Howard	IA
Hope Church	Allegheny	PA	Horse Creek	Barton	MO	Howard City	Montcalm	MI
Hopedale	Taxewell	IL	Horse Creek	Ashe	NC	Howard's Grove	Sheboygan	WI

PLACE	COUNTY	STATE
Howard's Lick	Hardy	WV
Howard's Mills	Montgomery	KY
Howard's Mills	St. Clair	MO
Howard Springs	Cumberland	TN
Howardsville	Jo Daviess	IL
Howardsville	St. Joseph	MI
Howardsville	Albemarle	VA
Howardville	Floyd	IA
Howell (c.h.)	Livingston	MI
Howell's Depot	Orange	NY
Howellville	Delaware	PA
Howel's Cross Roads	Cherokee	AL
Howe's Cave	Schoharie	NY
Howe's Corners	Waushara	WI
Howe's Mill	Dent	MO
Howe's Valley	Hardin	KY
Howesville	Clay	IN
Howesville	Preston	WV
Howland	Penobscot	ME
Howland	Trumbull	OH
Howlet Hill	Onondaga	NY
Howlett	Sangamon	IL
Hoyleton	Washington	IL
Hoyt	Jackson	KS
Hozaddale	Warren	OH
Hubbard	Trumbull	OH
Hubbard	Marion	OR
Hubbardston	Worcester	MA
Hubbardston	Ionia	MI
Hubbardstown	Wayne	WV
Hubbardsville	Madison	NY
Hubbardton	Rutland	VT
Hubbleton	Jefferson	WI
Hubelsville	Huntingdon	PA
Hubertville	Robertson	TN
Hublersburgh	Centre	PA
Huckleberry	Echols	GA
Huddleston	Pike	AR
Hudson	McLean	IL
Hudson	Black Hawk	IA
Hudson	Penobscot	ME
Hudson	Middlesex	MA
Hudson	Lenawee	MI
Hudson	Bates	MO
Hudson	Hillsborough	NH
Hudson	Hudson	NJ
Hudson (c.h.)	Columbia	NY
Hudson	Summit	OH
Hudson	Jefferson	PA
Hudson (c.h.)	St. Croix	WI
Hudson City	Worth	MO
Hudsondale	Carbon	PA
Hudsonville	Breckinridge	KY
Hudsonville	Marshall	MS
Huerfano	Pueblo	CO
Huerfano Canyon	Huerfano	CO
Huff's Creek	Hancock	KY
Hugginsville	Gentry	MO
Hughes	Arapahoe	CO
Hughes	Schuylkill	PA
Hughesburgh	Habersham	GA
Hughesville	Charles	MD
Hughesville	Saginaw	MI
Hughesville	Lycoming	PA
Hughesville	Loudoun	VA
Hughsonville	Dutchess	NY
Huguenot	Orange	NY
Hulburton	Orleans	NY
Hull	Plymouth	MA
Hull Prairie	Wood	OH
Hull's	Athens	OH
Hull's Mills	Dutchess	NY
Hulmesville	Bucks	PA

PLACE	COUNTY	STATE
Hulton	Allegheny	PA
Humansville	Polk	MO
Humboldt	Humboldt	IA
Humboldt	Allen	KS
Humboldt	Marquette	MI
Humboldt	Pulaski	MO
Humboldt	Richardson	
Humboldt	Richardson	NE
Humboldt	Gibson	TN
Humboldt Basin	Baker	OR
Humburd	Clark	WI
Hume	Allegany	NY
Hummell's Wharf	Snyder	PA
Hummel's Store	Berks	PA
Hummelstown	Dauphin	PA
Humphrey	Platte	NE
Humphrey	Cattaraugus	NY
Humpreysville	Columbia	NY
Humphreysville	Luzerne	PA
Humphreyville	Holmes	OH
Hunlock Creek	Luzerne	PA
Hunnewell	Shelby	MO
Hunsucker's Store	Montgomery	NC
Hunter	Boone	IL
Hunter	Greene	NY
Hunter	Belmont	OH
Hunter's Bridge	Beaufort	NC
Hunter's Cave	Greene	PA
Hunter's Creek	Lapeer	MI
Hunter's Depot	Nelson	KY
Hunter's Gap	Lee	VA
Hunter's Land	Schoharie	NY
Hunter's Lodge	Fluvanna	VA
Hunter's Mills	Pickens	SC
Hunter's Mills	Fairfax	VA
Hunter's Point	Queens	NY
Hunter's Point	Wilson	TN
Hunter's Retreat	Montgomery	TX
Hunter's Run	Cumberland	PA
Hunterstown	Adams	PA
Huntersville	Hardin	OH
Huntersville	Lycoming	PA
Huntersville	Greenville	SC
Huntersville	Rutherford	TN
Huntersville (c.h.)	Pocahontas	WV
Huntertown	Allen	IN
Huntingburgh	Dubois	IN
Huntingdale	Henry	MO
Huntingdon (c.h.)	Huntingdon	PA
Huntingdon (c.h.)	Carroll	TN
Huntingdon Valley	Montgomery	PA
Huntington	Fairfield	CT
Huntington (c.h.)	Huntington	IN
Huntington	Hampshire	MA
Huntington	Suffolk	NY
Huntington	Lorain	OH
Huntington	Chittenden	VT
Huntington	Cabell	WV
Huntington Centre	Chittenden	VT
Huntington City	Prince Georges	MD
Huntingtown	Calvert	MD
Huntley Grove	McHenry	IL
Huntsburgh	Geauga	OH
Hunt's Corners	Cortland	NY
Hunt's Hollow	Livingston	NY
Hunt's Mills	Sussex	NJ
Hunt's Station	Knox	OH
Hunt's Station	Franklin	TN
Huntsville (c.h.)	Madison	AL
Huntsville (c.h.)	Madison	AR
Huntsville	Douglas	CO
Huntsville	Litchfield	CT
Huntsville	Schuyler	IL

PLACE	COUNTY	STATE
Huntsville	Madison	IN
Huntsville	Choctaw	MS
Huntsville (c.h.)	Randolph	MO
Huntsville	Sussex	NJ
Huntsville	Yadkin	NC
Huntsville	Logan	OH
Huntsville	Luzerne	PA
Huntsville (c.h.)	Scott	TN
Huntsville (c.h.)	Walker	TX
Huntsville	Weber	UT
Huntsville	Jackson	WV
Hurd	Clearfield	PA
Hurdle's Mills	Person	NC
Hurdtown	Morris	NJ
Hurffville	Camden	NJ
Hurlbut's Corners	Crawford	WI
Hurley	Ulster	NY
Hurlock	Dorchester	MD
Huron	Lawrence	IN
Huron	Des Moines	IA
Huron	Atchison	KS
Huron	Wayne	NY
Huron	Erie	OH
Huron City	Huron	MI
Huron Station	Wayne	MI
Hurricane	Montgomery	IL
Hurricane	Crittenden	KY
Hurricane	Warren	MS
Hurricane	Carroll	MO
Hurricane Bridge	Putnam	WV
Hurricane Creek	Lauderdale	MS
Hurriance Grove	Grant	WI
Hurricane Switch	Maury	TN
Hurt's Cross Roads	Maury	TN
Hurtville	Russell	AL
Hustisford	Dodge	WI
Hustontown	Fulton	PA
Hustonville	Lincoln	KY
Hutchinson	McLeod	MN
Hustchison's	Bourbon	KY
Huth	Franklin	IN
Hutsonville	Crawford	IL
Hutton	Coles	IL
Hutton's Switch	Alleghany	MD
Huttonsville	Randolph	WV
Hutton Valley	Howell	MO
Hyannis	Barstable	MA
Hyattstown	Montgomery	MD
Hyattsville	Garrard	KY
Hyattsville	Prince George's	MD
Hyco	McPherson	KS
Hyco	Halifax	VA
Hyde Park	Cook	IL
Hyde Park	Norfolk	MA
Hyde Park	Wabashaw	MN
Hyde Park	Dutchess	NY
Hyde Park	Luzerne	PA
Hyde Park	Cache	UT
Hyde Park (c.h.)	Lamoille	VT
Hydesburgh	Ralls	MO
Hyde's Mills	Iowa	WI
Hydesville	Humboldt	CA
Hydeville	Rutland	VT
Hyndsdale	Morgan	IN
Hyndeville	Schoharie	NY
Hyremansville	Lehigh	PA
Hyrum	Cache	UT
Iamton	Montgomery	OH
Iatan	Platte	MO
Iba	De Kalb	IN
Iberia	Brown	MN
Iberia	Miller	MO

PLACE NAMES OF THE UNITED STATES

PLACE	COUNTY	STATE	PLACE	COUNTY	STATE	PLACE	COUNTY	STATE
Iberia	Morrow	OH	Indian River	Washington	ME	Ireland	Lewis	WV
Iceland	Blue Earth	MN	Indian River	Lewis	NY	Ireland Corners	Albany	NY
Ichatucknee	Columbia	FL	Indian Rock	Botetourt	VA	Ireland Hill	Marion	AL
Ickesburgh	Perry	PA	Indian Run	Mercer	PA	Irene	Sioux	IA
Iconium	Appanoose	IA	Indian Springs	Nevada	CA	Irene	Mecklenburg	NC
Iconium	St. Clair	MO	Indian Springs	Butts	GA	Irisburgh	Henry	VA
Ida (c.h.)	Ida	IA	Indian Springs	Campbell	KY	Irish Grove	Atchison	MO
Ida	Monroe	MI	Indian Springs	Washington	MD	Irishtown	Mercer	PA
Idaho (c.h.)	Clear Creek	CO	Indian Town	Mason	MI	Iorna	Talladega	AL
Idaho	Adair	MO	Indian Valley	Floyd	VA	Irona	Clinton	NY
Idaho	Pike	OH	Indian Village	Noble	IN	Iron City	Iron	UT
Idaho City (c.h.)	Boise	ID	Industry	McDonough	IL	Iron Clad	Limestone	TX
Idaville	White	IN	Industry	Franklin	ME	Iron Creek	Austin	TX
Idaville	Adams	PA	Industry	Beaver	PA	Irondale	Washington	MO
Idell	Crawford	KS	Industry	Austin	TX	Irondale	Jefferson	OH
Iderbide	Wythe	VA	Ingall's Cross	Oswego	NY	Iron Furnace	Scioto	OH
Igon's Ferry	Hamilton	TN	Ingart Grove	Ringgold	IA	Iron Hill	Northampton	PA
Ijamsville	Frederick	MD	Ingham	Franklin	IA	Iron Hills	Jackson	IA
Ilchester Mills	Howard	MD	Ingham's Mills	Herkimer	NY	Ironia	Morris	NJ
Ilion	Herkimer	NY	Inglefield	Vanderburgh	IN	Iron Mountain	St. Francois	MO
Illawara	Carroll	LA	Ingleside	Hardin	TN	Iron Mountain	Rusk	TX
Illinois City	Rock Island	IL	Ingomar	Issaquena	MS	Iron Point	Perry	OH
Illinosi Grove	Marshall	IA	Ingraham	Clay	IL	Iron Ridge	Dodge	WI
Illiopolis	Sangamon	IL	Ingraham	Clinton	NY	Iron Rod	Madison	MT
Illyria	Fayette	IA	Inkermann	Hardy	WV	Iron Station	Lincoln	NC
Imlay	Lapeer	MI	Inkster	Wayne	MI	Ironton (c.h.)	Iron	MO
Imlay City	Lapeer	MI	Inland	Cedar	IA	Ironton (c.h.)	Lawrence	OH
Imlaystown	Manmouth	NJ	Inland	Benzie	MI	Ironton	Lehigh	PA
Imlertown	Bedford	PA	Inland	Summit	OH	Ironton	Sauk	WI
Increase	Warren	TN	Inland	Summit	OH	Ironville	Perry	AL
Independence	Autauga	AL	Inskip	Butte	CA	Ironwood	Liberty	TX
Independence (c.h.)	Inyo	CA	Intercourse	Sumter	AL	Iroquois	Iroquois	IL
Independence	Warren	IN	Intercourse	Lancaster	PA	Irvine (c.h.)	Estill	KY
Independence (c.h.)	Buchanan	IA	Inverness	Cumberland	NC	Irvine	Warren	PA
Independence (c.h.)	Montgomery	KS	Inverness	Columbiana	OH	Irving	Montgomery	IL
Independence	Kenton	KY	Inwood	Marshall	IN	Irving	Marshall	KS
Independence	Tangipahoa	LA	Inwood	New York	NY	Irving	Barry	MI
Independence	De Soto	MS	Ioka	Keokuk	IA	Irving	Kandiyohi	MN
Independence (c.h.)	Jackson	MO	Iola	Calhoun	FL	Irving	Chautauqua	NY
Independence	Allegany	NY	Iola	Marion	IA	Irving	Jackson	WI
Independence	Caswell	NC	Iola (c.h.)	Allen	KS	Irving College	Warren	TN
Independence	Cuyahoga	OH	Iola	Columbia	PA	Irvington	Washington	IL
Independence	Polk	OR	Iola	Grimes	TX	Irvington	Kossuth	IA
Independence	Washington	PA	Iola	Waupaca	WI	Irvington	Essex	NJ
Independence	Washington	TX	Ion	Allamakee	IA	Irvington	Westchester	NY
Independence (c.h.)	Grayson	VA	Iona	Cape Girardeau	MO	Irvington	Chesterfield	SC
Independence Centre	Jasper	IA	Iona	Fairfax	VA	Irwin	Audubon	IA
Independent Hill	Prince William	VA	Iona Island	Rockland	NY	Irwin	Neosho	KS
Indiana (c.h.)	Indiana	PA	Ione City	Nye	NV	Irwin	Union	OH
Indianapolis (c.h.)	Marion	IN	Ione Valley	Amador	CA	Irwin's Station	Westmoreland	PA
Indianapolis	Mahaska	IA	Ioni	Anderson	TX	Irwinton (c.h.)	Wilkinson	GA
Indian Bay	Monroe	AR	Ionia	Warren	IL	Irwinville (c.h.)	Irwin	GA
Indian Bottom	Letcher	KY	Ionia	Chickasaw	IA	Isaac's Camp	Doddridge	WV
Indian Camp	Guernsey	OH	Ionia	Jewell	KS	Isabella (c.h.)	Worth	GA
Indian Creek	Henry	AL	Ionia (c.h.)	Ionia	MI	Isabella	Ozark	MO
Indian Creek	Kent	MI	Ionia	Dixon	NE	Isabella	Chester	PA
Indian Creek	Monroe	MO	Ionia City	Pettis	MO	Isabella City	Isabella	MI
Indian Cree	Fayette	PA	Iowa Centre	Story	IA	Isadora	Worth	MO
Indian Creek	Washington	TN	Iowa City	Placer	CA	Isanti	Isanti	MN
Indian Creek	Monroe	WV	Iowa City (c.h.)	Johnson	IA	Ischua	Cattaraugus	NY
Indian Falls	Genesee	NY	Iowa City	Crawford	KS	Ishpeming	Marquette	MI
Indian Field	Knox	OH	Iowa Falls	Hardin	IA	Island	Clinton	PA
Indian Fields	Albany	NY	Iowa Point	Doniphan	KS	Island City	Owsley	KY
Indian Ford	Stoddard	MO	Iowaville	Van Buren	IA	Island City	Gentry	MO
Indian Ford	Rock	WI	Ipava	Fulton	IL	Island Creek	Jasper	IL
Indian Gulch	Mariposa	CA	Ipswich	Essex	MA	Island Creek	Jefferson	OH
Indian Lake	Hamilton	NY	Ira	Cayuga	NY	Island Falls	Aroostook	ME
Indian Mound	Stewart	TN	Ira	Rutland	VT	Island Pond	Essex	VT
Indianola	Vermilion	IL	Irasburgh (c.h.)	Orleans	VT	Isle La Motte	Grand Isle	VT
Indianola (c.h.)	Warren	IA	Irbyville	Fulton	GA	Isleborough	Hocking	OH
Indianola (c.h.)	Calhoun	TX	Iredell	Bosque	TX	Islip	Suffolk	NY
Indian Orchard	Hampden	MA	Ireland	Dubois	IN	Isola	Martin	IN
Indian Ridge	Currituck	NC	Ireland	Hampden	MA	Issequena	Goochland	VA

PLACE NAMES OF THE UNITED STATES

PLACE	COUNTY	STATE	PLACE	COUNTY	STATE	PLACE	COUNTY	STATE
Italy Hollow	Yates	NY	Jacksonville(c.h.)	Telfair	GA	Jasper(c.h.)	Walker	AL
Italy Hill	Yates	NY	Jacksonville(c.h.)	Morgan	IL	Jasper(c.h.)	Newton	AR
Itasca	Anoka	MN	Jacksonville	Chickasaw	IA	Jasper(c.h.)	Hamilton	FL
Ithaca(c.h.)	Gratiot	MI	Jacksonville	Neosho	KS	Jasper(c.h.)	Pickens	GA
Ithaca	Saunders	NE	Jacksonville	Shelby	KY	Jasper(c.h.)	Dubois	IN
Ithaca(c.h.)	Tompkins	NY	Jacksonville	Randolph	MO	Jasper	Jasper	MO
Ithaca	Darke	OH	Jacksonville	Burlington	NJ	Jasper	Steuben	NY
Ithaca	Richland	WI	Jacksonville	Tompkins	NY	Jasper	Pike	OH
Iuka(c.h.)	Marion	IL	Jacksonville(c.h.)	Jackson	OR	Jasper(c.h.)	Marion	TN
Iuka(c.h.)	Tishemingo	MS	Jacksonville	Lehigh	PA	Jasper(c.h.)	Jasper	TX
Ivesdale	Champaign	IL	Jacksonville	Cherokee	TX	Jasper City	Jasper	IA
Ives' Grove	Racine	WI	Jacksonville	Windham	VT	Jasper Mills	Fayette	OH
Ivor	Southampton	VA	Jacksonville	Lewis	WV	Jatt	Grant	LA
Ivy	Lyon	KS	Jacksonwald	Berks	PA	Java	Wyoming	NY
Ivy Depot	Albenarle	VA	Jack's Reef	Onondaga	NY	Java	Lucus	OH
Ivy Hill	Haywood	NC	Jacksville	Butler	PA	Java Village	Wyoming	NY
Ivy Log	Union	GA	Jacobsburgh	Belmont	OH	Jay	Franklin	ME
Ivy Mills	Delaware	PA	Jacob's Church	Shennandoah	VA	Jay	Saginaw	MI
Ivy Mills	Hickman	TN	Jacob's Creek	Westmoreland	PA	Jay	Harrison	MO
Ixonia Centre	Jefferson	WI	Jacob's Fork	Catawha	NC	Jay	Essex	NY
			Jacobstown	Burlington	NJ	Jay	Orleans	VT
Jactinto	Calusa	CA	Jadden	Grant	IN	Jay Hawk	Howard	KS
Jacinto	Alcorn	MS	Jaffrey	Cheshire	NH	Jayne's Store	Randolph	AR
Jacksborough(c.h.)	Campbell	TN	Jake's Prairie	Gasconade	MO	Jaynesville	Bremer	IA
Jacksbourgh(c.h.)	Jack	TX	Jalapa	Grant	IN	Jaynesville	Covington	MS
Jack's Fork	Texas	MO	Jalapa	Newberry	SC	Jaynesville	Conecuh	AL
Jackson	Clark	AL	Jalapa	Monroe	TN	Jaynesville	Darke	OH
Jackson(c.h.)	Amador	CA	Jamaica(c.h.)	Queens	NY	Jeanerett	Iberia	LA
Jackson(c.h.)	Butts	GA	Jamaica	Windham	VT	Jeansville	Luzerne	PA
Jackson	Adair	IA	Jamaica	Middlesex	VA	Jeannetville	Renville	MN
Jackson	Linn	KS	Jamaica Plain	Norfolk	PA	Jeddo	Allen	KS
Jackson(c.h.)	Breathitt	KY	James' Bayou	Mississippi	MO	Jeddo	St. Clair	MI
Jackson	East Felciana	LA	Jamesburgh	Middlesex	NJ	Jeddo	Orleans	NY
Jackson	Waldo	ME	James' Creek	Huntingdon	PA	Jeddo	Jefferson	OH
Jackson(c.h.)	Jackson	MI	James' Crossing	Jackson	KS	Jeddo	Luzerne	PA
Jackson(c.h.)	Jackson	MN	James' Fork	Sebastian	AR	Jeddo	Marquette	WI
Jackson(c.h.)	Hinds	MS	Jamesport	Daviess	MO	Jeddo	Marengo	AL
Jackson(c.h.)	Cape Girardeau	MO	Jamesport	Sufolk	NY	Jefferson(c.h.)	Jackson	GA
Jackson	Dakota	NE	James' Switch	Marion	IN	Jefferson	Cook	IL
Jackson	Carroll	NH	Jamestown	Conecuh	AL	Jefferson	Clinton	IN
Jackson(c.h.)	Northampton	NC	Jamestown	Tuolumne	CA	Jefferson(c.h.)	Greene	IA
Jackson(c.h.)	Jackson	OH	Jamestown	Boullder	CO	Jefferson	Douglas	KS
Jackson	Susquehanna	PA	Jamestown	Chattahoochee	GA	Jefferson	Jefferson	LA
Jackson(c.h.)	Madison	TN	Jamestown	Clinton	IL	Jefferson	Lincoln	ME
Jackson	Louisa	VA	Jamestown	Boone	IN	Jefferson	Frederick	MD
Jackson	Washington	WI	Jamestown(c.h.)	Russell	KY	Jefferson	Hillsdale	MI
Jackson(c.h.)	Jackson	WV	Jamestown	Ottawa	MI	Jefferson	Winona	MN
Jacksonborough	Butler	OH	Jamestown	Moniteau	MO	Jefferson	Coos	NH
Jacksonborough	Colleton	SC	Jamestown	Dodge	NE	Jefferson	Gloucester	NJ
Jackson Brook	Washington	ME	Jamestown	Chautauqua	NY	Jefferson	Schoharie	NY
Jacksonburgh	Wayne	IN	Jamestown	Guilford	NC	Jefferson(c.h.)	Ashe	NC
Jackson Centre	Shelby	OH	Jamestown	Greene	OH	Jefferson(c.h.)	Ashtabula	OH
Jackson Corners	Dutchess	NY	Jamestown	Mercer	PA	Jefferson	Marion	OR
Jackson Corners	Monroe	PA	Jamestown	Newport	RI	Jefferson	Greene	PA
Jackson Hall	Franklin	PA	Jamestown(c.h.)	Fentress	TN	Jefferson	Chesterfield	SC
Jacksonham	Lancaster	SC	Jamestown	Smith	TX	Jefferson	Rutherford	TN
Jackson Hill	Davidson	NC	Jamestown	Grant	WI	Jefferson(c.h.)	Marion	TX
Jacksonport(c.h.)	Jackson	AR	Jamestown	Onondaga	NY	Jefferson	Powhatan	VA
Jacksonport	Door	WI	Jamestown	Martin	NC	Jefferson(c.h.)	Jefferson	WI
Jackson's Corners	Sullivan	MO	Jamison	Plumas	CA	Jefferson Barrracks	St. Louis	ME
Jackson's Creek	Randolph	NC	Janelow	Lewis	WV	Jefferson City(c.h.)	Cole	MO
Jackson's Ferry	Wrthe	VA	Janesville	Lassen	CA	Jefferson City	Jefferson	MT
Jackson's Mills	Ocean	NJ	Janesville	Greenwood	KS	Jefferson Corners	Whitesides	IL
Jackson Springs	Jackson	NC	Janesville	Waseca	MN	Jefferson Furnace	Clarion	PA
Jackson Station	Tipton	IN	Janesville(c.h.)	Rock	WI	Jefferson Lake	Le Sneur	MN
Jackson Station	Daviess	MO	Janney's	Richland	WI	Jefferson Line	Clearfield	PA
Jackson Station	Seneca	OH	Jarett	Wilson	KS	Jefferson Station	York	PA
Jackson Store	Conecuh	AL	Jarratt's	Sussex	VA	Jeffersonton	Culpeper	VA
Jacksontown	Licking	OH	Jarrettown	Montgomery	PA	Jeffersontown	Jefferson	KY
Jackson Valley	Susquehanna	PA	Jarrett's	Sussex	VA	Jefferson Valley	Westchester	NY
Jacksonville(c.h.)	Calhoun	AL	Jarrettville	Harford	MD	Jeffersonville(c.h.)	Twiggs	GA
Jacksonville	Pulaski	AR	Jarnold's Valley	Raleigh	WV	Jeffersonville	Wayne	IL
Jacksonville(c.h.)	Duval	FL	Jasonville	Greene	IN	Jeffersonville	Clarke	IN

PLACE	COUNTY	STATE
Jeffersonville	Lee	IA
Jeffersonville	Cowley	KS
Jeffersonville	Montgomery	KY
Jeffersonville	Lamoille	VT
Jeffress Store	Nottaway	VA
Jeffrey's Creek	Marion	SC
Jeffries	Clearfield	PA
Jeffriesburgh	Franklin	MO
Jelloway	Knox	OH
Jena	Tuscaloosa	AL
Jena	Catahoula	LA
Jena	Falls	TX
Jenkins	Montgomery	PA
Jenkins' Bridge	Accomack	VA
Jenkins' Creek	Jasper	MO
Jenkins' Ferry	Grant	AR
Jenkins' Mills	Jefferson	NE
Jenkintown	Montgomery	PA
Jenksville	Tioga	NY
Jenner's Cross Roads	Somerset	PA
Jennerstown	Somerset	PA
Jennersville	Chester	PA
Jennieton	Iowa	WI
Jennings	Hamilton	FL
Jennings' Fork	Smitih	TN
Jennings' Ordinary	Nottaway	VA
Jenningsville	Wyoming	PA
Jenny	Marathon	WI
Jenny Lind	Sebastian	AR
Jenny Lind	Calaveras	CA
Jericho	Perry	AL
Jericho	Kane	IL
Jericho	Henry	KY
Jericho	Queens	NY
Jericho	Chittenden	VT
Jericho Centre	Chittenden	VT
Jerome	Howard	IN
Jerome	Appanoose	IA
Jerome	Hillsdale	MI
Jerome	Phelps	MO
Jerome	Westchester	NY
Jerome	Union	ON
Jeromesville	Ashland	OH
Jersey	Oakland	MI
Jersey	Licking	OH
Jersey City(c.h.)	Hudson	NJ
Jersey Mills	Lycoming	PA
Jersey Shore	Lycoming	PA
Jerseytown	Columbia	PA
Jerseyville(c.h.)	Jersey	IL
Jerseyville	Monmouth	NJ
Jerusalem	Albany	NY
Jerusalem	Davie	NC
Jerusalem	Monroe	OH
Jerusalem	Haywood	TN
Jerusalem(c.h.)	Southampton	VA
Jersualem Mills	Hartford	MD
Jessamine	Jessamine	KY
Jesse's Mills	Russell	VA
Jesse's Store	Shelby	KY
Jessup	Wayne	GA
Jessup	Buchanan	IA
Jessup's Station	Parke	IN
Jesuit's Bend	Plaquemine	LA
Jetersville	Amelia	VA
Jett's Creek	Breathitt	KY
Jewell	Jewell	KS
Jewett	Cumberland	IL
Jewett	Greene	NY
Jewett	Harrison	OH
Jewett Centre	Greene	NY
Jewett City	New London	CN
Jewett Mills	St. Croix	WI
Jimes	Jackson	OH
Joanna Furnace	Berks	PA
Jobe	Oregon	MO
Jobe	Monongalia	WV
Jobs	Madison	IL
Jobstown	Burlington	NJ
Joe's Lick	Madison	KY
Joetta	Hancock	IL
Johanesburgh	Washington	IL
John Day City	Grant	OR
John Day's Creek	Idaho	ID
John's Branch	Audrian	MO
Johnsburgh	McHenry	IL
Johnsburgh	Warren	NY
Johnsburgh	Somerset	PA
Johnson	Jones	IA
Johnson	Macon	MO
Johnson	Barnwell	SC
Johnson	Kane	UT
Johnson	Lemoille	VT
Johnsonburgh	Warren	NJ
Johnson City	Washington	TN
Johnsons	Christian	KY
Johnson's	Orange	NY
Johnsonsburgh	Wyoming	NY
Johnson's Corners	Summit	OH
Johnson's Creek	Carroll	IL
Johnson's Creek	Niagra	NY
Johnson's Creek	Jefferson	WI
Johnson's X Roads	Monroe	WV
Johnson's Fork	Magoffin	KY
Johnson's Grove	Haywood	TN
Johnson's Mills	Marion	AL
Johnson's Mills	Pitt	NC
Johnson's Point	Kaufman	TX
Johnson's Springs	Goochland	VA
Johnson's Station	Tarrant	TX
Johnson's Store	Anne Arundel	MD
Johnsontown	Northampton	VA
Johnsonville	Wayne	IL
Johnsonville	Jewell	KS
Johnsonville	Rensselaer	NY
Johnsonville	Trumbull	OH
Johnsonville	Northampton	PA
Johnsonville	Williamsburgh	SC
Johsonville	Humphreys	TN
Johnsonville	Sheboygan	WI
Johnston's Depot	Edgefield	SC
Johnston's Institute	Hays	TX
Johnstown	Cumberland	IL
Johnstown	Alleghany	MD
Johnstown	Barry	MI
Johnstown	Bates	MO
Johnstown(c.h.)	Fulton	NY
Johnstown	Licking	OH
Johnstown	Cambria	PA
Johnstown	Harrison	WV
Johnstown	Rock	WI
Johnstown Centre	Rock	WI
Johnsville	Bradley	AR
Johnsville	Frederick	MD
Johnsville	Ottawa	MI
Johnsville	Dutchess	NY
Johnsville	Montgomery	OH
Joliet(c.h.)	Will	IL
Joilett	Schuylkill	PA
Jolly	Monroe	OH
Jollytown	Greene	PA
Jollyville	Lee	IA
Jonas Ridge	Burke	NC
Jonathan's Creek	Haywood	NC
Jones' Bluff	Sumter	AL
Jonesborough	Jefferson	AL
Jonesborough(c.h.)	Craighead	AR
Jonesborough(c.h.)	Clayton	GA
Jonesborough(c.h.)	Union	IL
Jonesborough(c.h.)	Grant	IN
Jonesborough(c.h.)	Washington	ME
Jonesborough	Tippah	MS
Jonesborough	Moore	NC
Jonesborough	Washington	TN
Jonesborough	Brunswick	VA
Jonesburgh	Montgomery	MO
Jones' Chapel	Winston	AL
Jones' Corners	Holmes	OH
Jones' Creek	Newton	MO
Jones' Cross Roads	Tallapoosa	AL
Jones' Mills	Meriwether	GA
Jones' Mills	Westmoreland	PA
Jones' Mills	Coryell	TX
Jonesport	Washington	ME
Jones' Springs	Berkley	WV
Jones' Statton	Dearborn	IN
Jones' Station	Butler	OH
Jones' Station	Haywood	TN
Jones' Tan Yard	Callaway	MO
Jonestown	Lebannon	PA
Jonesville	Bartholomew	IN
Jonesville	Hillsdale	MI
Jonesville	Cass	MO
Jonesville	Saratoga	NY
Jonesville	Yardkin	NC
Jonesville	Union	SC
Jonesville	Harrison	TX
Jonesville	Chittenden	VT
Jonesville(c.h.)	Lee	VA
Joppa Village	Plymouth	MA
Jordan	Vermillion	IL
Jordan	Jay	IN
Jordan	Onondaga	NY
Jordan	Brazoria	TX
Jordan	Green	WI
Jordan's Chapel	Mercer	WV
Jordan's Grove	Randolph	IL
Jordan's Saline	Van Zandt	TX
Jordan Spring	Montgomery	TN
Jordan Station	Fulton	KY
Jordan Store	Williamson	TN
Jordan's Valley	Rutherford	TN
Jordan Valley	Baker	OR
Jordan Village	Owen	IN
Jordanville	Herkimer	NY
Jo's Branch	Wyoming	WV
Josco	Livingston	MI
Joseph's Mills	Tyler	WV
Joslyn	Rock Island	IL
Joy	Wayne	NY
Joy Creek	Washington	KS
Joyfield	Benzie	MI
Joyner's Depot	Wilson	NC
Juda	Green	WI
Judesville	Surry	NC
Judson	White	AR
Judson	Kankakee	IL
Judson	Blue Earth	MN
Judson	Sullivan	MO
Julesburgh	Weld	CO
Julian	San Diego	CA
Julian Furnace	Centre	PA
Julietta	Marion	IN
Julinstown	Burlington	NJ
Jumping Branch	Mercer	WV
Jumping Run	Alexander	NC
Junction	Pulaski	IL
Junction	Carlton	MN

PLACE NAMES OF THE UNITED STATES

PLACE	COUNTY	STATE
Junction	Madison	MT
Junction	Hunterdon	NJ
Junction	Rensselaer	NY
Junction	Paulding	OH
Junction	Lancaster	PA
Junction	Hanover	VA
Junction	Dane	WI
Junction City	Trinity	CA
Junction City	Mills	IA
Junction City(c.h.)	Davis	KS
Junction House	Lassen	CA
Juneau(c.h.)	Dodge	WI
Juniata	Pueblo	CO
Juniata	Perry	PA
Juniata	Seneca	NY
Juniata	Henderson	TN
Juno	Madison	AR
Jupiter	Madison	AR
Justice	Dixon	NE
Kabletown	Jefferson	WV
Kachu	King	WA
Kahle's	Clarion	PA
Kahama	Clarke	WA
Kalama	Cowlitz	WA
Kalamazoo	Kalamazoo	MI
Kalamo	Eaton	MI
Kalida	Woodson	KS
Kalida	Putnam	OH
Kanab	Summit	UT
Kansas	Kane	UT
Kanarraville	Iron	UT
Kanawha	Colusa	CA
Kanawha(c.h.)	Kanawha	WV
Kanawha Saline	Kanawha	WV
Kanawha Station	Wood	WV
Kandiyohi	Kandiyohi	MN
Kane	Greene	IL
Kane	Campbell	KY
Kane	McKean	PA
Kane City	Venango	PA
Kaneville	Kane	IL
Kankakee	Kankakee	IL
Kankakee	Starke	IN
Kannona	Steuben	NY
Kanosh	Millard	UT
Kansas	Walker	AL
Kansas	Edgar	IL
Kansas	Graves	KY
Kansas	Seneca	OH
Kansas	Jefferson	TN
Kansas City	Jackson	MI
Kansasville	Racine	WI
Kantz	Snyder	PA
Kaoline	Iron	ME
Kappa	Woodford	IL
Karrsville	Warren	NJ
Karthaus	Clearfield	PA
Kasey's	Bedford	VA
Kaseyville	Macon	MO
Kaskaskia	Randolph	IL
Kasoag	Oswego	NY
Kasota	Le Sueur	MN
Kasson	Vanderburgh	IN
Kasson	Madison	IA
Kasson	Leelenaw	MI
Kasson	Dodge	MN
Kasson	McKean	PA
Kasson	Barbour	WV
Kasson	Manitowoc	WI
Katahdin Iron Wks	Piscataquis	MI
Katonah	Westchester	NY
Kattelville	Broome	NY
Kaufman	Kaufman	TX
Kaukauna	Outagamie	WI
Kawkawlin	Bay	MI
Kaysville	Davis	UT
Kearney	Clay	MO
Kearney City(c.h.)	Kearney	NE
Keatchie	De Soto	LA
Keating	McKeon	PA
Keck's Centre	Fulton	NY
Keck's Church	Martin	IN
Kedron	Osage	KS
Keedysville	Washington	MD
Keefer's Corners	Albany	NY
Keffer's Store	Franklin	PA
Keffer's Bay	Grand Isle	VT
Keelersburgh	Wyoming	PA
Keelersburgh	Van Buren	MI
Keelville	Cherokee	KS
Keene	Jessamine	KY
Keene	Ionia	MI
Keene(c.h.)	Cheshire	NH
Keene	Essex	NY
Keene	Coshocton	OH
Keene	Portage	WI
Keene Flats	Essex	NY
Keeney's Settlement	Cortland	NY
Keeneyville	Tioga	PA
Keenville	Wayne	IL
Keeseville	Essex	NY
Keezletown	Rockingham	VA
Keith's	Noble	OH
Keighsburgh	Mercer	IL
Kekoskee	Dodge	WI
Kellersburgh	Armstrong	PA
Kellersville	Monroe	PA
Kellerville	Dubois	IN
Kelley	Mifflin	PA
Kelley's Island	Erie	OH
Kelley's Mills	Lawrence	OH
Kellis' Store	Kemper	MS
Kellogg	Jasper	IA
Kellogg's	Douglas	OR
Kelloggsville	Kent	MI
Kelloggsville	Cayuga	NY
Kelloggsville	Ashtabula	OH
Kellyburgh	Lycoming	PA
Kelly Point	Union	PA
Kelly's Corners	Lenawee	MI
Kelly's Creek	St. Clair	AL
Kelly's Station	Armstrong	PA
Kellysville	Delaware	PA
Kelsey	El Dorado	CA
Kelso	Dearborn	IN
Kelso	Sibley	MN
Kelso	Lincoln	TN
Kelton	Chester	PA
Kelton	Box Elder	UT
Kemblesville	Chester	PA
Kemp	Kaufman	TX
Kemper	Jersey	IL
Kemper City	Victoria	TX
Kemp's Creek	Cleburne	AL
Kempsville	Princess Anne	VA
Kemptown	Fredrick	MD
Kenansville(c.h.)	Duplin	NC
Kendaia	Seneca	NY
Kendall	Kendall	IL
Kendall	Van Buren	MI
Kendall	Orleans	NY
Kendall	Anson	NC
Kendall	Beaver	PA
Kendall Creek	McKean	PA
Kendall Mills	Orleans	NY
Kendall's Mills	Somerset	ME
Kendall's Store	Stanley	NC
Kendallville	Noble	IN
Kendrick's Creek	Sullivan	TN
Kenduskeag	Penobscot	ME
Kenesaw	Cobb	GA
Kennamer Cove	Marshall	AL
Kennard	Washington	NE
Kennard	Champaign	OH
Kennard	Mercer	PA
Kennebunk	York	ME
Kennebunk Depot	York	ME
Kennebunk Landing	York	ME
Kennebunkport	York	ME
Kennedale	Tuscaloosa	AL
Kennedy	Chautauqua	NY
Kennedy's	Brunswick	VA
Kenndeyville	Kent	MD
Kennekuk	Atchison	KS
Kenner	Jefferson	LA
Kenner	Matagorda	TX
Kennerdell	Venango	PA
Kennett(c.h.)	Dunklin	MO
Kennett's Square	Chester	PA
Kennon	Belmont	OH
Kennonsburgh	Noble	OH
Kenockee	St. Clair	MI
Kenosha(c.h.)	Kenosha	WI
Kensico	Westchester	NY
Kensington	Hartford	KN
Kensington	Oakland	MI
Kensington	Rockingham	NH
Kent	Litchfield	CN
Kent	Stephenson	IL
Kent	Jefferson	IN
Kent	Newton	MO
Kent	Putnam	NY
Kent	Portage	OH
Kent	Indiana	PA
Kentland(c.h.)	Newton	IN
Kenton	Kent	DE
Kenton	Kenton	KY
Kenton	Christian	MO
Kenton(c.h.)	Hardin	OH
Kenton	Obion	TN
Kenton Furnace	Greenup	KY
Kentontown	Robertson	KY
Kent's Hill	Kennebec	ME
Kentucky	Vermillion	IL
Kentucky Town	Grayson	TX
Kenyon	Goodhue	MN
Kenyon	Jackson	AR
Kenyonville	Orleans	NY
Keokuk	Lee	IA
Keokuk Junction	Adams	IL
Keosauqua(c.h.)	Van Buren	IA
Keowee	Oconee	SC
Kerby(c.h.)	Josephine	OR
Kerhonkson	Ulster	NY
Kerkhoven	Swift	MN
Kernerville	Forsyth	NC
Kerneysville	Jefferson	WV
Kernville	Kern	CA
Kerr's Station	Washington	PA
Kerr's Store	Clarion	PA
Kerrsville	Cumberland	PA
Kerrville(c.h.)	Kerr	TX
Kersey's	Elk	PA
Kershena	Shawanaw	WI
Kesler's Cross Lanes	Nicholas	WV
Kessler's	Northampton	PA
Keswick Depot	Albermarle	VA
Ketcham	Luzerne	PA
Ketchum's Corners	Saratoga	NY

PLACE NAMES OF THE UNITED STATES

PLACE	COUNTY	STATE	PLACE	COUNTY	STATE	PLACE	COUNTY	STATE
Ketchumville	Tioga	NY	King of Prussia	Montgomery	PA	Kirchhayn	Washington	WI
Kettle Creek	Potter	PA	King's	Barbour	AL	Kirkbyville	Taney	MO
Kewanee	Henry	IL	King's	Athens	OH	Kirkersville	Licking	OH
Kewanee	Lauderdale	MS	Kingsboro	Edgecombe	NC	Kirkland	Oneida	NY
Kewanna	Fulton	IN	Kingsborough	Fulton	NY	Kirkland Valley	Yavapai	AR
Kewaskum	Washington	WI	King's Bridge	Manitowoc	WI	Kirkmansville	Todd	KY
Kewaunee(c.h.)	Kewaunee	WI	Kingsbridgeville	Westchester	NY	Kirk's Cross Roads	Clinton	IN
Keyesport	Clinton	IL	Kingsbury	Whiteside	IL	Kirksey's	Callaway	KY
Key Port	Monmouth	NJ	Kingsbury	La Porte	IN	Kirk's Grove	Cherokee	AL
Keysburgh	Logan	KY	Kingsbury	Piscataquis	ME	Kirk's Mills	Lancaster	PA
Keystone	Douglas	CO	Kingsbury	Washington	NY	Kirksville	Madison	KY
Keystone	Wells	IN	King's Cave	Harrison	IN	Kirksville(c.h.)	Adair	MO
Keystone	Jackson	OH	King Creek	Roane	TN	Kirkville	Wapello	IA
Keystone	Perry	PA	King's Ferry	Nassau	FL	Kirkville	Onondaga	NY
Keystone	Charlotte	VA	King's Ferry	Cayuga	NY	Kirkwood	New Castle	DE
Keytesville(c.h.)	Chariton	MO	Kingsland	BErgen	NJ	Kirkwood	St. Louis	MO
Key West(c.h.)	Monroe	FL	King's Mountain	Gaston	NC	Kirkwood	Camden	NJ
Kezar Falls	York	ME	King's Point	Dade	MO	Kirkwood	Broome	NY
Kiantone	Chautauqua	NY	Kingsport	Sullivan	TN	Kirkwood	Shelby	OH
Kibbeville	Franklin	MS	King's River	Fresno	CA	Kirkwood	Lancaster	PA
Kickapoo	Peria	IL	King's Settlement	Chenango	NY	Kirkwood Centre	Broome	NY
Kickapoo	Anderson	TX	King's Station	Gibson	IN	Kirkland	Lake	OH
Kickapoo	Vernou	WI	Kingston	Autauga	AL	Kirwin	Phillips	KS
Kickapoo City	Leavenworth	KS	Kingston	Madison	AR	Kishacoquilas	Mifflin	PA
Kidder	Caldwell	MO	Kingston	Fresno	CA	Kishwaukee	Winnebago	IL
Kidder's Ferry	Seneca	NY	Kingston	Bartow	GA	Kiskiminitas	Armstrong	PA
Kiddville	Clark	KY	Kingston	De Kalb	IL	Kit Carson(c.h.)	Greenwood	CO
Kiddville	Ionia	MI	Kingston	Decatur	IN	Kittaning(c.h.)	Armstrong	PA
Kiddville	Sullivan	MO	Kingston	Des Moines	IA	Kittery	York	ME
Kidron	Coweta	GA	Kingston	Madison	KY	Kittery Depot	York	ME
Kidwell	Tyler	WV	Kingston	Somerset	MD	Kittery Point	York	ME
Kiel	Manitowoc	WI	Kingston	Plymouth	MA	Kittitass	Yakima	WA
Kienstra's Store	Adams	MS	Kingston	Tuscola	MI	Kittle River Station	Pine	MN
Kier	Buchanan	IA	Kingston	Adams	MS	Kittrell	Granville	NC
Kilbourn	Van Buren	IA	Kingston	Meeker	MN	Klamath	Siskiyou	CA
Kilbourn City	Columbia	WI	Kingston(c.h.)	Caldwell	MO	Klecknersville	Northampton	PA
Kildare	Juneau	WI	Kingston	Rockingham	NH	Kleinfeltersville	Lebanon	PA
Kilgore	Carroll	OH	Kingston	Somerset	NJ	Klikitat	Klikitat	WA
Kilgore	Venango	PA	Kingston(c.h.)	Ulster	NY	Kline's Grove	Northumberland	PA
Kilgour	Sullivan	NY	Kingston	Ross	OH	Klinesville	Hunterdon	NJ
Kilkenny	Le Sueur	MN	Kingston	Luzerne	PA	Klinesville	Berks	PA
Killawog	Broome	NY	Kingston(c.h.)	Washington	RI	Klingelhoeffer Lnd.	Perry	AR
Kilbourne	Delaware	OH	Kingston(c.h.)	Roane	TN	Klingerstown	Schuylkill	PA
Killbuck	Ogle	IL	Kingston	Green Lake	WI	Knap of Reeds	Granville	NC
Killian's Mills	Lincoln	NC	Kingston Centre	Delaware	OH	Knapp's Creek	Crawford	WI
Killinger	Dauphin	PA	Kingston Furnace	Washington	MO	Knappton	Pacific	WA
Killingly	Windham	CN	Kingston Mines	Peoria	IL	Knauer's	Berks	PA
Killingworth	Middlesex	CN	Kingstree(c.h.)	Williamsburgh	SC	Kniffin	Wayne	IA
Kill Mills	Warren	NJ	Kingsville	Ashtabula	OH	Knight's Ferry(c.h.)	Stanislaus	CA
Kilmarnock	Lancester	VA	Kingsville	Clarion	PA	Knight's Mill	Berrien	GA
Kilmoreville	Clinton	IN	Kingsville	Richland	SC	Knight's Prairie	Hamilton	IL
Kimball	Bosque	TX	King William(c.h.)	King William	VA	Knightstown	Henry	IN
Kimberton	Chester	PA	Kingwood	Hunterdon	NJ	Knightsville	Clay	IN
Kibolton	Guernsey	OH	Kingwood	Somerset	PA	Knob	Beaver	PA
Kimmel	Indiana	PA	Kingwood(c.h.)	Preston	WV	Knob	Tazewell	V A
Kimmers' Staud	Cumberland	TN	Kinlock	Lawrence	AL	Knob Creek	Harrison	IN
Kimmswick	Jefferson	MO	Kinmundy	Marion	IL	Knob Creek	Cleveland	NC
Kimulga	Talladega	AL	Kinney's 4 Corners	Oswego	NY	Knob Fork	Wetzel	WV
Kinard's Turnout	Newberry	SC	Kinnick Kinnick	St. Croix	WI	Knob Lick	Metcalfe	KY
Kincheloe	Harrison	WV	Kinsale	Westmoreland	VA	Knobnoster	Johnson	MO
Kinderhook	Van Buren	AR	Kinsman	Trumbull	OH	Knobsville	Fulton	PA
Kinderhook	Pike	IL	Kinston(c.h.)	Lenoir	NC	Knobsview	Crawford	MO
Kinderhook	Branch	MI	Kintnersville	Bucks	PA	Knott's Mills	PReston	WV
Kinderhook	Columbia	NY	Kinzers	Lancaster	PA	Knottsville	Daviess	KY
Kinderhook	Pickaway	OH	Kinzua	Warren	PA	Knottsville	Tyler	WV
Kinderkamack	Bergen	NJ	Kiomatia	Red River	TX	Knowersville	Albany	NY
King	Chattahoochee	GA	Kiowa	Douglas	CO	Knowlesville	Orleans	NY
King	Dubuque	IA	Kiowa	Jefferson	NE	Knowlton	Warren	NJ
King City	McPherson	KS	Kipp's Corners	Genesee	MI	Knowlton	Marathon	WI
King City	Gentry	MO	Kipton	Lorain	OH	Knowton's Landing	Desha	AR
Kingfield	Franklin	ME	Kirby	Wyandot	OH	Knox(c.h.)	Stark	IN
King George(c.h.)	King George	VA	Kirby	Greene	PA	Knox	Waldo	ME
Kingman	Penobscot	ME	Kirbyville	Gerks	PA	Knox	Albany	NY

PLACE	COUNTY	STATE	PLACE	COUNTY	STATE	PLACE	COUNTY	STATE
Knox	Knox	OH	Lackawack	Ulster	NY	La Grange	Lenoir	NC
Knox	Clarion	PA	Lackawanna	Luzerne	PA	La Grange	Lorain	OH
Knoxborough	Oneida	NY	Lackawaxen	Pike	PA	La Grange	Wyoming	PA
Knox Dale	Jefferson	PA	Lackamule	Polk	OR	La Grange	Fayette	TN
Knox Hill	Walton	FL	La Clair	De Kalb	IL	La Grange(c.h.)	Fayette	TX
Knoxville	Greene	AL	La Clede	Fayette	IL	La Grange	Grand Isle	VT
Knoxville	Lake	CA	Laclede	Linn	MO	La Grange	Walworth	WI
Knoxville(c.h.)	Crawford	GA	Lacon(c.h.)	Marshall	IL	La Grange	Bluff Brown	IL
Knoxville(c.h.)	Knox	IL	Lacon	Maries	MO	La Grangeville	Dutchess	NY
Knoxville(c.h.)	Marion	IA	Lacona	Warren	IA	La Gro	Wabash	IN
Knoxville	Pendleton	KY	Lacona	Jefferson	KY	Laguardo	Wilson	TN
Knoxville	Pendleton	KY	Lacona	Oswego	NY	La Harpe	Hancock	IL
Knoxville	Claiborne	LA	Laconia	Harrison	IN	Lahaska	Bucks	PA
Knoxville	Frederick	MD	Laconia(c.h.)	Belknap	NH	Laing's	Monroe	OH
Knoxville	Franklin	MS	La Conner	Whatcom	WA	Laingsburgh	Shiawassee	MI
Knoxville	Ray	MO	Lac-qui-parle	McPhail	MN	Lairdsville	Lycoming	PA
Knoxville	Jefferson	OH	La Crescent	Houston	MN	Lair's Station	Harrison	KY
Knoxville	Tioga	PA	La Crosse	Izard	AR	La Joya	Socorro	NM
Knoxville(c.h.)	Knox	TN	La Crosse	Hancock	IL	La Junta	Mora	NM
Knoxville	Cherokee	TX	La Crosse	La Porte	IN	Lake	Spencer	IN
Knoxville	Marshall	WV	La Crosse(c.h.)	La Crosse	WI	Lake	Newago	MI
Koch's	Wayne	OH	La Cneva	Mora	NM	Lake	Scott	MS
Kodiak		AL	La Cygne	Linn	KS	Lake	Washington	NY
Koeltztown	Osage	MO	Laddonia	Audrian	MO	Lake	Stark	OH
Kohlsville	Washington	WI	Laddsburgh	Bradford	PA	Lake	Luzerne	PA
Kokomo(c.h.)	Howard	IN	Ladiesburgh	Frederick	MD	Lake Addie	McLeod	MN
Konewodk	Yakimo	WA	Ladiga	Calhoun	AL	Lake Aurthur	Calcasieu	LA
Koniska	McLeod	MN	Ladoga	Montgomery	IN	Lake Butler(c.h.)	Bradford	FL
Koro	Winnebago	WI	Ladoga	Fond du Lac	WI	Lake Charles(c.h.)	Calcasieu	LA
Koronis	Mecker	MN	Ladonia	Fannin	TX	Lake City	Siskiyou	CA
Kortright	Delaware	NY	Ladora	Iowa	IA	Lake City(c.h.)	Columbia	FL
Kosciucko(c.h.)	Attala	MS	Ladore	Neosho	KS	Lake City	Starke	IN
Koskonoug	Rock	WI	La Due	Henry	MO	Lake City(c.h.)	Calhoun	IA
Kosse	Limestone	TX	Laenna	Logan	IL	Lake City	Iouia	MI
Kossuth	Washington	IN	La Farge	Vernon	WI	Lake City	Wabashaw	MN
Kossuth	Des Moines	IA	La Fargeville	Jefferson	NY	Lake Comfort	Hyde	NC
Kossuth	Alcorn	MS	La Fayette	Contra Costa	CA	Lake Como	Wayne	PA
Kossuth	Clarion	PA	La Fayette	Walker	GA	Lake Creek	Williamson	IL
Kossuth Centre	Kossuth	IA	La Fayette	Stark	IL	Lake Creek	Labette	KS
Koszta	Iowa	IA	La Fayette	Tippecanoe	IN	Lake Creek	Benton	MO
Kout's Station	Porter	IN	La Fayette	Linn	IA	Lake Creswell	Panola	MS
Krakow	Franklin	MO	La Fayette	Doniphan	KS	Lake Cystal	Blue Earth	MN
Kratzerville	Snyder	PA	La Fayette	Christian	KY	Lake Dora	Le Sueur	MN
Kreamer	Snyder	PA	La Fayette	Gratiot	MI	Lake Drummond	Norfolk	VA
Kreidersville	Northampton	PA	La Fayette	Sussex	NJ	Lake Elizabeth(c.h.)	Kandiyohi	MN
Kregeville	Monroe	PA	La Fayette	Onondaga	NY	Lake Eutice	Orange	FL
Krick's Mill	Berks	PA	La Fayette	Madison	OH	Lake Five	Washington	WI
Kripple Bush	Ulster	NY	La Fayette(c.h.)	Yam Hill	OR	Lake Forest	Lake	IL
Kroghville	Jefferson	WI	La Fayette	McKean	PA	Lake Fork	Ashland	OH
Kuckville	Orleans	NY	La Fayette	Washington	RI	Lake Fremont	Sherburne	MN
Kulpsville	Montgomery	PA	La Fayette(c.h.)	Maron	TN	Lake George	Warren	NY
Kunckle	Luzerne	PA	La Fayette	Upshur	TX	Lake Grove	Suffolk	NY
Kunkletown	Monroe	PA	La Fayette	Montgomery	PA	Lake Harbor	Muskegon	MI
Kutztown	Berks	PA	La Fayette	Chippewa	WI	Lake Harriod	Meeker	MN
Kyger	Gallia	OH	La Fayette Springs	La Fayette	MS	Lake Hill	Ulster	NY
Kylertown	Clearfield	PA	La Fayetteville	Dutchess	NY	Lake Johanna	Pope	MN
Kyle's Ford	Hancock	TN	Laflin	Bollinger	MO	Lakeland	Washington	MN
Kyserike	Ulster	NY	La Fontaine	Wabash	IN	Lake Landing	Hyde	NC
Kyte River	Ogle	IL	La Fontaine	Josh Bell	KY	Lake Lillian	Kandiyohi	MN
			Laforme's Store	Baxton	WV	Lake Linden	Houghton	MI
Lagaddie	Franklin	MO	La Fox	Kane	IL	Lake Maria	Green Lake	WI
Labadieville	Assumption	LA	La Grange(c.h.)	Union	OR	Lake Mill	Van Buren	MI
La Bajada	Santa Ana	NM	La Grange	Phillips	AR	Lake Mills	Winnebago	IA
La Belle	Lewis	MO	La Grange	Stanislaus	CA	Lake Mills	Jefferson	WI
Labette	Labette	KS	La Grange(c.h.)	Troup	GA	Lakenan	Shelby	MO
Lacelle	Clark	IA	La Grange(c.h.)	La Grange	IN	Lake Pleasant	Erie	PA
Lacey	Drew	AR	La Grange	Lucas	IA	Lake Point	Tooele	UT
Lacey	De Kalb	IL	La Grange	Morris	KS	Lakeport	Lake	CA
Lacey	Muscantine	IA	La Grange(c.h.)	Oldham	KY	Larissa	Winston	AL
Lacey Spring	Rockingham	VA	La Grange	Penobscot	ME	Larissa	Cherokee	TX
Lacey's Spring	Morgan	AL	La Grange	Cass	MI	Larkinsburgh	Clay	IL
Laceyville	Harrison	OH	La Grange	Lewis	MO	Larkin's Fork	Jackson	AL
Laceyville	Wyoming	PA	La Grange	Wyoming	NY	Larkinsville	Jackson	AL

PLACE NAMES OF THE UNITED STATES

PLACE	COUNTY	STATE	PLACE	COUNTY	STATE	PLACE	COUNTY	STATE
Larone	Somerset	ME	Lawler	Chickasaw	IA	Lebanon	St. Clair	IL
La Rose	Marshall	IL	Lawndale	Logan	IL	Lebanon(c.h.)	Boone	IN
Larrabee	Maintowoc	WI	Lawn Ridge	Marshall	IL	Lebanon	Van Buren	IA
Larry's Creek	Lycoming	PA	Lawrence	McHenry	IL	Lebanon(c.h.)	Marion	KY
La Rue	Benton	AR	Lawrence	Marion	IN	Lebanon	York	ME
Larue	Marion	OH	Lawrence	Fremont	IA	Lebanon(c.h.)	Laclede	MO
Larwill	Whitley	IN	Lawrence(c.h.)	Douglas	KS	Lebanon	Grafton	NH
La Salle	La Salle	IL	Lawrence	Essex	MA	Lebanon	Hunterdon	NJ
La Salle	Monroe	MI	Lawrence	Van Buren	MI	Lebanon	Madison	NY
La Salle	Niagra	NY	Lawrence	Newton	MS	Lebanon(c.h.)	Warren	OH
Las Animas	Bent	CA	Lawrence	Schuyler	NY	Lebanon	Linn	OR
Las Cruces	Santa Barbara	CA	Lawrence	Washington	OH	Lebanon(c.h.)	Lebanon	PA
Las Cruces	Dora Ana	NM	Lawrence	Washington	PA	Lebanon	Collin	TX
Lasellsville	Fulton	NY	Lawrence	Marquette	WI	Lebanon(c.h.)	Russell	VA
Lassen	Tehama	CA	Lawrenceburgh	Warren	IA	Lebanon Church	Allegheny	PA
Lassiter's Mills	Randolph	NC	Lawrenceburgh	Cloud	KS	Lebanon Church	Shenandoah	VA
Last Chance	Lucas	IA	Lawrencebgh.(c.h.)	Anderson	KY	Lebanon Junction	Bullitt	KY
Las Vegas(c.h.)	San Miguel	NM	Lawrenceburgh	Armstrong	PA	Lebanon Springs	Columbia	NY
Latham	Pike	OH	Lawrencebgh.(c.h.)	Lawrence	TN	Lebeck	Cedar	MO
Lathrop	San Joaquin	CA	Lawrenee Station	Mercer	NJ	Leboeuf	Erie	PA
Latimore	Adams	PA	Lawrenceville	Henry	AL	Le Claire	Scott	IL
Latonia Springs	Kenton	KY	Lawrenceville(c.h.)	Gwinnett	GA	Lecompton	Douglas	KS
Latrobe	El Dorado	CA	Lawrenceville(c.h.)	Lawrence	IL	Lecompton	Monroe	OH
Latrobe	Johnson	NE	Lawrenceville	Dearborn	IN	Leconte's Mills	Clearfield	PA
Latrobe	Westmoreland	PA	Lawrenceville	Mercer	NJ	Ledbetter	Washington	TX
Lattas	Ross	OH	Lawrenceville	St. Lawrence	NY	Lederachsville	Montgomery	PA
Lattasburgh	Wayne	OH	Lawrenceville	Tioga	PA	Ledge Dale	Wayne	PA
Lattner's	Douglas	IA	Lawrenceville(c.h.)	Brunswick	VA	Ledger	Mitchell	NC
Latty	Des Moines	IA	Lawson	Washington	MO	Ledyard	New London	CN
Lauback	Northampton	PA	Lawson Station	Ray	MO	Ledyard	Cayuga	NY
Laud	Whitley	IN	Lawsonville	Rockingham	NC	Lee	Warrick	IN
Lauderdale Station	Lauderdale	MS	Lawville Centre	Susquehanna	PA	Lee	Penobscot	ME
Laughlintown	Westmoreland	PA	Lawton	Clinch	GA	Lee	Berkshire	MA
Laur	Jefferson	IL	Lawton	Van Buren	MI	Lee	Strafford	NH
Laura	Miami	OH	Lawtonville	Burke	GA	Lee	Oneida	NY
Lauraville	Baltimore	MD	Lawtonville	Beaufort	NC	Lee	Athens	OH
Laurel	Sussex	DE	Lawyersville	Schoharie	NY	Lee Centre	Lee	IL
Laurel	Franklin	IN	Layman	Washington	OH	Lee Centre	Oneida	NY
Laurel	Clermont	OH	Layton	Sussex	NJ	Leechburgh	Johnston	NC
Laurel	Marshall	IA	Laytonia	Venango	PA	Leechburgh	Armstrong	PA
Laurel Bluff	Muhlenburgh	KY	Layton's Station	Fayette	PA	Leech Lake	Cass	MN
Laurel Bridge	Laurel	KY	Laytonville	Montgomery	MD	Leech's Corners	Mercer	PA
Laurel Creek	Clay	KY	Lazaretto Station	Delaware	PA	Leechville	Beaufort	NC
Laurel Creek	Lincoln	WV	Leacock	Lancaster	PA	Leeds	Androscoggin	ME
Laurel Factory	Prince George's	MD	Lead Hill	Marion	AR	Leeds	Hampshire	MA
Laurel Fork	Carroll	VA	Lead Mine	Tucker	WV	Leeds	Greene	NY
Laurel Gap	Greene	TN	Leadsville	Randolph	WV	Leeds	Washington	UT
Laurel Grove	Pittsylvania	VA	Leadvale	Jefferson	TN	Leeds	Columbia	WI
Laurel Hill	Neshoba	MS	Leaf Valley	Douglas	MN	Leeds Centre	Columbia	WI
Laurel Hill	Perry	MO	Leaksville	Greene	MS	Leeds Junction	Androscoggin	ME
Laurel Hill	Richmond	NC	Leaksville	Rockingham	NC	Leeds Point	Atlantic	NJ
Laurel Hill	De Kalb	TN	Leaksville	Page	VA	Leedston	Sterns	MN
Laurel Hill	Lunenburg	VA	Leaman Place	Lancaster	PA	Leedsville	Monmouth	NJ
Laurel Iron Works	Monongalia	WV	Leamon Corner	Hancock	IN	Leesburgh	Cherokee	AL
Laurel Junction	Wood	WV	Leanah	Estill	KY	Leesburgh	Sumter	FL
Laurel Mills	Rappahonnock	VA	Leasburgh	Crawford	MO	Leesburgh	Lemhi	ID
Laurel Point	Monongalia	WV	Leasburgh	Dona Ana	NM	Leesburgh	Kosciusko	In
Laurel Ridge	Kanawha	WV	Leasburgh	Caswill	NC	Leesburgh	Harrison	KY
Laurel Run	Luzerne	PA	Lea's Chapel	Person	NC	Leesburgh	Cumberland	NJ
Laurel Springs	Ashe	NC	Leasuresville	Butler	PA	Leesburgh	Highland	OH
Laurelton	Union	PA	Leathersville	Lincoln	GA	Leesburgh	Mercer	PA
Laurelville	Westmoreland	PA	Leatherwood	Guernsey	OH	Leesburgh	Washington	TN
Laurens	Otsego	NY	Leatherwood	Clarion	PA	Leesburgh(c.h.)	Loudoun	VA
Laurens(c.h.)	Laurens	SC	Leatherwood	Henry	VA	Lee's Creek	Crawford	AR
Laurens Hill	Laurens	GA	Leatherwood(c.h.)	Crawford	IN	Lee's Creek	Clinton	OH
Laurinburgh	Richmond	NC	Leatherwood(c.h.)	Leavenworth	KS	Lee's Cross Roads	Cumberland	PA
Laury's Station	Lehigh	PA	Leavenworth	Brown	MN	Leesport	Bucks	PA
Lavalle	Sank	WI	Leavenworth City	Leavenworth	KS	Lee's Summit	Jackson	MO
Lavansville	Somerset	PA	Leavitt	Carroll	OH	Leesville	Middlesex	CN
La Vega	Des Moines	IA	Leavittsburgh	Trumbull	OH	Leesville	Boone	IL
La Vergne	Rutherford	TN	Lebanon(c.h.)	De Kalb	AL	Leesville	Lawrence	IN
Lavernia	Wilson	TX	Lebanon	New London	CN	Leesville	Henry	MO
Lave Valley	Eldorado	CA	Lebanon	Kent	DE	Leesville	Schoharie	NY

PLACE	COUNTY	STATE	PLACE	COUNTY	STATE	PLACE	COUNTY	STATE
Leesville	Robeson	NC	Leon	Crenshaw	AL	Lewis	Essex	NY
Leesville	Carroll	OH	Leon	Whitesides	IL	Lewisberry	York	PA
Leesville	Lexington	SC	Leon(c.h.)	Decatur	IA	Lewisborough	Westchester	NY
Leesville	Campbell	VA	Leon	Cattaraugus	NY	Lewisburgh	Conway	AR
Leesville X Roads	Crawford	OH	Leon	Sampson	NC	Lewisburgh	Wayne	IA
Leetonia	Columbiana	OH	Leon	Ashland	OH	Lewisburgh	Preble	OH
Leetown	Jefferson	WV	Leon	Madison	VA	Lewisburgh(c.h.)	Union	PA
Leesdale	Allegheny	PA	Leon	Monroe	WI	Lewisburgh(c.h.)	Marshall	TN
Lee Valley	Hawkins	TN	Leona	Bradford	PA	Lewisburgh(c.h.)	Greenbrier	WV
Le Fever Falls	Ulster	NY	Leona	Leon	TX	Lewis Centre	Delaware	OH
Leghorn	Pottawatomie	KS	Leonardsburgh	Delaware	OH	Lewis Creek	Shelby	IN
Le Grand	Marshall	IA	Leonardsville	Madison	NY	Lewisport	Hancock	KY
Le Grand	Osborn	KS	Leonardtown(c.h.)	St. Mary's	MD	Lewis' Station	Escambia	AL
Lehi	Jefferson	AR	Leonardville	Monmouth	NJ	Lewis Station	Henry	MO
Lehi City	Utah	UT	Leoni	Jackson	MI	Lewis' Store	Spottsylvania	VA
Lehigh Gap	Carbon	PA	Leoni	Cannon	TN	Lewiston	Trinity	CA
Lehigh Tannery	Carbon	PA	Leonia	Bergen	NJ	Lewiston(c.h.)	Nez Perces	IA
Lehighton	Carbon	PA	Leonidas	St. Joseph	MI	Lewiston	Cherokee	KS
Lehigh Valley	Lehigh	PA	Leon Springs	Bexar	TX	Lewiston	Amdroscoggin	ME
Lehman	Luzerne	PA	Leopard	Chester	PA	Lewiston	Dakota	MN
Leicester	Worcester	MA	Leopold	Perry	IN	Lewiston	Niagara	NY
Leicester	Buncombe	NC	Leota Landing	Washington	MS	Lewiston	Columbia	WI
Leicester	Addison	VT	Leoti	Pike	IN	Lewiston Station	Columbia	WI
Leicester	Dane	WI	L'Erable	Iroquois	IL	Lewistown(c.h.)	Fulton	IL
Leidy	Clinton	PA	Le Raysville	Jefferson	NY	Lewistown	Frederick	MD
Leighs	Sunflower	MS	Le Raysville	Bradford	PA	Lewistown	Logan	OH
Leighton	Franklin	AL	Le Roy	Union	DA	Lewistown(c.h.)	Mufflin	PA
Leighton	Mahaska	IA	Leroy	Bremer	IA	Lewisville(c.h.)	La Fayette	AR
Leighton	Hennepin	MN	Le Roy	Coffey	KS	Lewisville	Henry	IN
Leighton's Corners	Carroll	NH	Le Roy	Mower	MN	Lewisville	Forsyth	NC
Leinbach's	Berks	PA	Le Roy	Barton	MO	Lewisville	Monroe	OH
Leipersville	Delaware	PA	Le Roy	Genesee	NY	Lewisville	Polk	OR
Leipsic	Kent	DE	Le Roy	Medina	OH	Lewisville	Chester	PA
Leipsic	Orange	IN	Le Roy	Bradford	PA	Lewisville	Denton	TX
Leipsic	Putnam	OH	Le Roy	Jackson	WV	Lewisville	King George	VA
Leitsville	Pickaway	OH	Leroy	Dodge	WI	Lexington	Santa Clara	CA
Leitersburgh	Washington	PA	Le Roy Station	Monroe	WI	Lexington(c.h.)	Oglethorpe	GA
Leithsville	Northampton	PA	Leroyville	Audubon	IA	Lexington(c.h.)	McLean	IL
Leland	La Salle	IL	Lesages	Cabel	WV	Lexington(c.h.)	Scott	IN
Leland	Leelenaw	MI	Leslie	Ingham	MI	Lexington(c.h.)	Washington	IA
Leled Lane	Tuscaloosa	AL	Leslie	Van Wert	OH	Lexington(c.h.)	Fayette	KY
Lemars	Plymouth	IA	Lesourdsville	Butler	OH	Lexington	Somerset	ME
Lementon	St. Clair	IL	Lesser Cross Roads	Somerset	NJ	Lexington	Middlesex	MA
Lemington	Essex	VT	Lester	Marion	IL	Lexington(c.h.)	Sanilac	MI
Lemon	Wyoming	PA	Lester	Black Hawk	TN	Lexington	Le Sueur	MN
Lemond	Steele	MN	Lester's	Giles	TN	Lexington(c.h.)	Holmes	MS
Lemont	Cook	IL	Lester's District	Burke	GA	Lexington(c.h.)	La Fayette	MO
Lemont	Centre	PA	Le Sueur(c.h.)	M N		Lexington	Greene	NY
Lemonweir	Juneau	WI	Letart	Mason	WV	Lexington(c.h.)	Davidson	NC
Lempster	Sullivan	NH	Letart Falls	Meigs	OH	Lexington	Richland	OH
Lena	Stephenson	IL	Letcher	Bath	VA	Lexington(c.h.)	Henderson	TN
Lena	Clay	IN	Letohatchee	Lowndes	AL	Lexington	Burleson	TX
Lenape	Leavenworth	KS	Letsinger	Roane	TN	Lexington(c.h.)	Rockbridge	VA
Lenape	Chester	PA	Letter Gap	Gilmer	WV	Lexington(c.h.)	Lexington	SC
Lenexa	Johnson	KS	Letts	Louisa	IA	Leyden	Cook	IL
Lenhartsville	Berks	PA	Letts Corner	Decatur	IN	Leyden	Franklin	MA
Lenni Mills	Delaware	PA	Lettsville	Daviess	IN	Leyden	Lewis	NY
Lenior(c.h.)	Caldwell	NC	Levan	Juab	UT	Leyden	Rock	WI
Lenora	Fillmore	MN	Levanna	Cayuga	NY	Leyden Centre	Cook	IL
Lenox	Kane	IL	Levanna	Brown	OH	Liberty	Omachita	AR
Lenox(c.h.)	Berkshire	MA	Levant	Penobscot	ME	Liberty	San Joaquin	CA
Lenox	Madison	NY	Levee	Montgomery	KY	Liberty	Union	DA
Lenox	Ashtabula	OH	Level	Warren	OH	Liberty	Adams	IL
Lenox Castle	Rockingham	NC	Level Green	Rockcastle	KY	Liberty(c.h.)	Union	IN
Lenox Furnace	Berkshire	MA	Level Land	Abbeville	SC	Liberty	Clarke	IA
Lenox Station	Warren	IL	Leverette	Franklin	MA	Liberty	Montgomery	KS
Lenoxville	Susquehanna	PA	Levering	Knox	OH	Liberty(c.h.)	Casey	KY
Lenz	Hennepin	MN	Levingood	Pendleton	KY	Liberty	Waldo	ME
Lenzburgh	St. Clair	IL	Lewes	Sussex	DE	Liberty	Jackson	MI
Leo	White	GA	Lewinsville	Fairfax	VA	Liberty(c.h.)	Amite	MS
Leo	Allen	IN	Lewis	Kendall	IL	Liberty(c.h.)	Clay	MO
Leo	Stanly	NC	Lewis	Vigo	IN	Liberty	Pawnee	NE
Leominster	Worcester	MA	Lewis(c.h.)	Cass	IA	Liberty	Sullivan	NY

PLACE	COUNTY	STATE	PLACE	COUNTY	STATE	PLACE	COUNTY	STATE
Liberty	Montgomery	OH	Lime Hill	Bradford	PA	Linden	Dallas	IA
Liberty	Tioga	PA	Lime Kiln	Frederick	MD	Linden	Genessee	MI
Liberty	De Kalb	TN	Limekiln	Berks	PA	Linden	Lycoming	PA
Liberty(c.h.)	Liberty	TX	Limeport	Lehigh	PA	Linden(c.h.)	Perry	TN
Liberty	Rich	UT	Limerick	Bureau	IL	Linden(c.h.)	Davis	TX
Liberty(c.h.)	Bedford	VA	Limerick	York	ME	Linden	Warren	VA
Liberty	Vernon	WI	Limerick	Jefferson	NY	Linden	Iowa	WI
Liberty Centre	Warren	IA	Limerick	Montgomery	PA	Linden Hall	Centre	PA
Liberty Centre	Henry	OH	Limerick Station	Montgomery	PA	Lindenville	Ashtabula	OH
Liberty Corner	Somerset	NJ	Lime Ridge	Columbia	PA	Lindenwood	Ogle	IL
Liberty Corners	Crawford	OH	Lime Ridge	Sank	WI	Linder	Jasper	IL
Liberty Corners	Bradford	PA	Lime Rock	Litchfield	CN	Lindersville	Adair	ME
Liberty Falls	Sullivan	NY	Lime Rock	Providence	RI	Lind Grove	Morchonse	LA
Liberty Farm	Clay	NE	Lime Rock	Outagamie	WI	Lindley	Grundy	MO
Liberty Furnace	Shenandoah	VA	Lime Spring	Howard	IA	Lindleytown	Steuben	NY
Liberty Grove	Cecil	MD	Limestone	Kanakakee	IL	Lindly's Mills	Washington	PA
Liberty Hall	Newberry	SC	Limestone	Washington	KS	Lindsborg(c.h.)	McPherson	KS
Liberty Hill	Dallas	AL	Limestone	Arrostook	ME	Lindsey(c.h.)	Ottawa	KS
Liberty Hill	New London	CN	Limestone	Hickory	MO	Lindsey	Sandusky	OH
Liberty Hill	Pike	GA	Limestone	Cattaraugus	NY	Lindsey's Mill	Trigg	KY
Liberty Hill	Iredell	NC	Limestone	Clarion	PA	Lindseyville	Worcester	MD
Liberty Hill	Williamson	TX	Limestone	Marshall	WV	Lindside	Monroe	WV
Liberty Landing	Clay	MO	Limestone Cove	Carter	TN	Line	Lyon	KS
Liberty Mills	Wabush	IN	Limestone Springs	Spartanburgh	SC	Line	Morehouse	LA
Liberty Mills	Orange	VA	Limestone Springs	Greene	TN	Line Creek	Bullock	AL
Liberty Pole	Vernon	WI	Limestoneville	Montour	PA	Line Creek	Pulaski	KY
Liberty Prairie	Madison	IL	Limington	York	ME	Line Creek	Oktibbeba	MS
Liberty Ridge	Grant	WI	Limitar	Socorro	NM	Line Creek	Laurens	SC
Liberty Springs	Van Buren	AR	Lincklean	Chenango	NY	Line Lexington	Montgomery	PA
Liberty Square	Lancaster	PA	Lincoln	Talladega	AL	Line Mountain	Northumberland	PA
Libertytown	Frederick	MD	Lincoln	Placer	CA	Line's Hollow	Crawford	PA
Libertyville	Lake	IL	Lincoln	Clay	DA	Lineville	Clay	AL
Libertyville	Jefferson	IA	Lincoln	Sussex	DE	Lineville	Venango	PA
Libertyville	St. Francois	MO	Lincoln(c.h.)	Logan	IL	Lineville Station	Crawford	PA
Libertyville	Sussex	NJ	Lincoln	Cass	IN	Linganore	Frederick	MD
Libertyville	Ulster	NY	Lincoln	Polk	IA	Linglestown	Dauphin	PA
Libary	Allegheny	PA	Lincoln	Penobscot	ME	Linkinson	Franklin	NY
Lick	Fannin	TX	Lincoln	Middlesex	MA	Linkwood	Dorchester	MD
Lick Creek	Union	IL	Lincoln(c.h.)	Mason	MI	Linlithgo	Columbia	NY
Lick Creek	Hickman	TN	Lincoln	Wabashaw	MN	Linn(c.h.)	Osage	MO
Licking	Texas	MO	Lincoln	Benton	MO	Linn Creek(c.h.)	Camden	MO
Licking Valley	Mushingum	OH	Lincoln	Deer Lodge	MT	Linneus	Aroostook	ME
Lickingville	Clarion	PA	Lincoln(c.h.)	Lancaster	ME	Linneus(c.h.)	Linn	MO
Lick Run	Hamilton	OH	Lincoln	Sussex	NJ	Linn Flat	Nacaogdoches	TX
Lick Run	Athens	OH	Lincoln	Wayne	NY	Linn Grove	Adams	IN
Licksville	Fredrick	MD	Lincoln	Gallia	OH	Linn's Valley	Kern	CA
Liddesdale	Columbia	AR	Lincoln	Polk	OR	Linnville	Lickling	OH
Light Steet	Columbia	PA	Lincoln	Lancaster	PA	Linwood	Osage	MO
Ligonier	Noble	IN	Lincoln	Addison	VT	Linton	Greene	IN
Ligonier	Vernon	MO	Lincoln	Loudoun	VA	Linton	Des Moines	IA
Ligonier	Westmoreland	PA	Lincoln	Kewaunee	WI	Linton	Triggs	KY
Likens	Crawford	IL	Lincoln Centre	Grundy	IA	Linton	Jefferson	OH
Lilesville	Anson	NC	Lincoln Centre	Lincoln	KS	Linton Mills	Coshocton	OH
Lillard's Mills	Marshall	TN	Lincoln Centre	Penobscot	ME	Linville	Rockingham	VA
Lillington	New Hanover	NC	Lincoln Centre	Polk	WI	Linwood	Pike	AL
Lilly	McLeon	IL	Lincoln City	Summit	CO	Linwood	Carroll	MD
Lilly	Scioto	OH	Lincoln Falls	Sullivan	PA	Linwood	Auoka	MN
Lilly Dale	Perry	IN	Lincoln Green	Johnson	IL	Linwood	Butler	NE
Lilly Pond	Wright	MN	Lincolnton(c.h.)	Lincoln	GA	Linwood	Davidson	NC
Lima	Adams	IL	Lincolnton(c.h.)	Lincoln	NC	Linwood	Hamilton	OH
Lima	La Grange	IN	Lincoln University	Chester	PA	Linwood	Bradley	TN
Lima	Fayette	IA	Lincolnville	Wabash	IN	Linwood	Cherokee	TX
Lima	Clay	KS	Lincolnville	Marion	KS	Linwood Station	Delaware	PA
Lima	Washtenaw	MI	Lincolnville	Pulaski	KY	Lionville	Chester	PA
Lima	Livingston	NY	Lincolnville	Waldo	ME	Lisbon	New London	CN
Lima(c.h.)	Allen	OH	Lincolnville	Crawford	PA	Lisbon	Union	AR
Lima	Delaware	PA	Lincolnia	Fairfax	VA	Lisbon	Kendall	IL
Lima Centre	Greenville	SC	Lind	Waupaca	WI	Lisbon	Noble	IN
Lima Centre	Rock	WI	Lindale	Osage	KS	Lisbon	Linn	IA
Limaville	Stark	OH	Linden	Marengo	AL	Lisbon	Claiborne	LA
Limber Lost	Adams	IN	Linden	St. Francis	AR	Lisbon	Androscoggin	ME
Lime Creek	Cerro Gordo	IA	Linden	San Joaquin	CA	Lisbon	Howard	MD
Lime Creek	McLennan	TX	Linden	Montgomery	IN	Lisbon	Sarpy	NE

PLACE	COUNTY	STATE
Lisbon	Grafton	NH
Lisbon	St. Lawrence	NY
Lisbon	Dallas	TX
Lisbon	Bedford	VA
Lisbon Centre	St. Lawrence	NY
Lisbon Falls	Androscoggin	ME
Lisburn	Cumberland	PA
Liscomb	Marshall	IA
Lisha's Kill	Albany	NY
Lisle	Du Page	IL
Lisle	Broome	NY
Lisle Station	Du Page	IL
Litchfield(c.h.)	Litchfield	CN
Litchfield	Montgomery	IL
Litchfield	Taylor	IA
Litchfield(c.h.)	Grayson	KY
Litchfield	Kennebec	ME
Litchfield	Hillsdale	MI
Litchfield(c.h.)	Meeker	MN
Litchfield	Herkimer	NY
Litchfield	Medina	OH
Litchfield	Bradford	PA
Litchfield Corners	Kennebec	ME
Liter	Morgan	IL
Lithgow	Dutchess	NY
Lithonia	De Kalb	GA
Lithopolis	Fairfield	OH
Litiz	Lancaster	PA
Little Black	Ripley	MO
Little Blue	Jackson	MI
Little Britain	Lancaster	PA
Little Canada	Ramsey	MN
Little Cedar	Mitchell	IA
Little Chucky	Grenne	TN
Little Chute	Outagamie	WI
Little Compton	Carroll	MO
Little Compton	Newport	RI
Little Cooley	Crawford	PA
Little Crab	Fentress	TN
Little Creek	Pike	KY
Little Creek Landing	Kent	DE
Little Detroit	Tazewell	IL
Little Doe	Johnson	TN
Little Eagle	Scott	KY
Little Elk	Benton	OR
Little Falls(c.h.)	Passaic	NJ
Little Falls	Herkimer	NY
Little Flat	Bath	KY
Little Gap	Carbon	PA
Little Genessee	Alleghany	NY
Little Georgetown	Berkely	WV
Little Giant	Howard	IN
Little Grant	Grant	WI
Little Gunpowder	Baltimore	MD
Little Hickman	Jessamine	KY
Little Hockhocking	Washington	OH
Little Indian	Cass	IL
Little Lake	Mendocino	CA
Little Lot	Hickman	TN
Little Marriack	Franklin	MO
Little Marsh	Tioga	PA
Little Meadows	Susquehanna	PA
Little Mount	Spencer	KY
Little Mountain	Newberry	SC
Little Neck	Queens	NY
Little Oak	Pike	AL
Little Oley	Berks	PA
Little Osage	Vernon	MO
Little Otter	Braxton	WV
Little Plymouth	King and Queen	VA
Little Port	Clayton	IA
Little Prairie	Walwoth	WI
Little Prairie Ronde	Cass	MI
Little Rest	Dutchess	NY
Little River	Cherokee	AL
Little River	Mendocino	CA
Little RIver	Allen	IN
Little River	Alexander	NC
Little River	Horry	SC
Little River	Floyd	VA
Little Riv. Acad.	Cumberland	NC
Little Rock(c.h.)	Pulaski	AR
Little Rock	Kendall	IL
Little Rock	Marion	SC
Little Sandusky	Wyandot	OH
Little Sandy	Jefferson	ME
Little Sewall Mt.	Greenbrier	WV
Little Sioux	Harrison	IA
Little's Mill	Richmond	NC
Little's Mills	Tyler	WV
Little Spring	Madison	AR
Littletown	Adams	PA
Little Sturgeon	Dorr	WI
Little Suamico	Oconto	WI
Little Sugar Loaf	Bladen	NC
Littlesville	Winston	AL
Little Toby	Clearfield	PA
Littleton	Arapahoe	CO
Littleton	Schuyler	IL
Littleton	Aroostook	ME
Littleton	Middlesex	MS
Littleton	Grafton	NH
Littleton	Morris	NJ
Littleton	Halifax	NC
Littleton	Sussex	VA
Little Traverse(c.h.)	Emmett	MI
Little Turkey	Chickasaw	IA
Little Utica	Onondaga	NY
Little Valley	Olmstead	MN
Little Walnut	Butler	KS
Little Warrior	Blout	AZ
Little Wildcat	Lewis	WV
Little Wind River	Sweetwater	WY
Little Wolf	Wanpaca	WI
Little Yadkin	Stokes	NC
Little York	Nevada	CA
Little York	Warren	IL
Little York	Washington	IN
Little York	Meade	KY
Little York	Greene	MO
Little York	Hunterdon	NJ
Little York	Cortland	NY
Little York	MOntgomery	OH
Littsville	Nodaway	MO
Litwalton	Lancaster	VA
Litzenberg	Lehigh	PA
Lively Grove	Washington	IL
Lively Oaks	Lancaster	VA
Live Oak	San Joaquin	CA
Live Oak	Suwannee	FL
Live Oak Store	Livingston	LA
Live Oak	Henry	TN
Livermore	Alameda	CA
Livermore	McLean	KY
Livermore	Androscoggin	ME
Livermore	Westmoreland	PA
Livermore Centre	Androscoggin	ME
Livermore Falls	Androscoggin	ME
Liverpool	Fulton	IL
Liverpool	Omondaga	NY
Liverpool	Medina	OH
Liverpool	Perry	PA
Liverpool(c.h.)	Sumter	AL
Livingston	Floyd	GA
Livingston	Clark	IL
Livingston	Appanoose	IA
Livingston	Essex	NJ
Livingston	Columbia	NY
Livingston(c.h.)	Overton	TN
Livingston(c.h.)	Polk	TX
Livingstonville	Schoharie	NY
Livonia	La Salle	IL
Livonia	Washington	IN
Livonia	Point Coupee	LA
Livonia	Sherburne	MN
Livonia	Livingston	ME
Livonia	Putnam	ME
Livonia Station	Livingston	NY
Lizemore's	Clay	WV
Lizzard	Pocahontas	IA
Llano(c.h.)	Llano	TX
Llewellyn	Schuylkill	PA
Lloyd	Tioga	PA
Lloyds	Essex	VA
Loachpapoka	Lee	AL
Loag	Lhester	PA
Lolachsville	Berks	PA
Lobelville	Perry	TN
Locharber	Omachita	LA
Lochiel	Union	PA
Loch Leven	Adams	MS
Lochleven	Lunenburgh	VA
Loch Lomond	Goochland	VA
Loch Sheldrake	Sullivan	NY
Lock	La Salle	IL
Lock	Knox	OH
Lock Berlin	Wayne	NY
Lockbourne	Franklin	OH
Locke	Elkhart	IN
Locke	Ingham	MI
Locke	Cayuga	NY
Lockeford	San Joaquin	CA
Locke's Mills	Oxford	ME
Lockhart	Lauderdale	MS
Lockhart(c.h.)	Caldwell	TX
Lockhart's	Jackson	WV
Lockhart's Run	Wood	WV
Lockhaven(c.h.)	Clinton	PA
Lockington	Shelby	OH
Lockland Station	Hamilton	OH
Lock No. 4	Washington	PA
Lockport	Will	IL
Lockport	Carroll	IN
Lockport	Henry	KY
Lockport(c.h.)	Niagra	NY
Lockport	Williams	OH
Lockport Station	Westmoreland	PA
Lockridge	Jefferson	IA
Locksburgh(c.h.)	Sevier	AR
Lock Seventeen	Tuscarawas	OH
Lock Spring	Ripley	IN
Lock Spring	Daviess	MO
Lock's Village	Franklin	MA
Locktown	Hunterdon	NJ
Lockville	Chatham	NC
Lockville	Fairfield	OH
Locust Bottom	Botetourt	VA
Locust Corner	Clermont	OH
Locust Cottage	Jefferson	AR
Locust Creek	Louisa	VA
Locust Gap	Northumberland	PA
Locust Grove	Henry	GA
Locust Grove	Williamson	IL
Locust Grove	Atchison	KS
Locust Grove	Callaway	KY
Locust Grove	Kent	MD
Locust Grove	Clarke	NO
Locust Grove	Lewis	NY
Locust Grove	Adams	OH

PLACE	COUNTY	STATE	PLACE	COUNTY	STATE	PLACE	COUNTY	STATE
Locust Grove	Fulton	PA	London	Atchison	MO	Long Reach	Tyler	WV
Locust Grove	Orange	VA	London	Nemaha	NE	Long Ridge	Fairfield	CN
Locust Hill	Knox	MO	London(c.h.)	Madison	OH	Long Ridge	Washington	NC
Locust Hill	Caswell	NC	London	Mercer	PA	Long Run	Jefferson	KY
Locust Hill	Washington	PA	London	Rusk	TX	Long Run	Licking	OH
Locust Hill	Middlesex	VA	London Bridge	Princess Anne	VA	Long Run	Armstrong	PA
Locust Lane	Winneshick	IA	Londonderry	Rockingham	NH	Long Run Station	Doddridge	WV
Locust Lane	Indiana	PA	Londonderry	Guernsey	OH	Long's Mills	Stone	MO
Locust Level	Stanly	NC	Londonderry	Chester	PA	Long's Mills	Randolph	NC
Locust Level	Halifax	VA	Londonderry	Windham	VT	Long's Stand	Crawford	PA
Locust Mills	Bracken	KY	London Grove	Chester	PA	Long Street	De Soto	LA
Locust Mound	Miller	MO	London Cedar	Martin	MN	Long Swamp	Berks	PA
Locust Mound	Washington	TN	London Cedar	Jackson	WV	Long Tom	Lane	OR
Locust Mount	Accomack	VA	London Elm	Howard	KS	Longton	Howard	KS
Locust Point	Ottawa	OH	London Elm	Cooper	MO	Longtown	Panola	MS
Locust Ridge	Brown	OH	London Elm	Henderson	TN	Long Valley	Lassen	CA
Locust Spring	Greene	TN	Lone Jack	Jackson	MO	Long View	Ashly	AR
Locust Valley	Queens	NY	Lone Oak	Rates	MO	Long Vimw	Christian	KY
Locust Valley	Lehigh	PA	Lone Oak	Hunt	TX	Long View	St. James	LA
Locustville	Accomack	VA	Lone Pine	Inyo	CA	Longview	Upshur	TX
Lodi	Clay	DA	Lone Pine	Washington	PA	Longville	Plumas	CA
Lodi	Coweta	GA	Lone Pine	Bedford	VA	Long Wassie	Oregon	MO
Lodi	Wabash	IN	Lone Pine	Portage	WI	Longwood	Pettis	MO
Lodi	Montgomery	MS	Lone Rock	Richland	WI	Longwood	Rockbridge	VA
Lodi	Newton	MO	Lone Star	Titus	TX	Lonsdale	Providence	RI
Lodi	Dakota	NE	Lone Tree	Bureau	IL	Loogootee	Martin	IN
Lodi	Bergen	NJ	Lone Tree	Cowley	KS	Looking-Glass	Douglas	AR
Lodi	Seneca	NY	Lone Tree(c.h.)	Merrick	NE	Lookout	Laramie	WY
Lodi	Medina	OH	Lone Tree	Greene	PA	Looney's Creek	Osage	MO
Lodi(c.h.)	Wilson	TX	Lone Tree	Collin	TX	Looneyville	Erie	NY
Lodi	Washington	VA	Lone Tree	Tyler	WV	Looniesville	McDonald	MO
Lodi	Columbia	WI	Lonetree Lake	Brown	MN	Loose Creek	Osage	MO
Lodi Centre	Seneca	NY	Lone Valley	Sanders	ME	Looxahoma	De Soto	MS
Lodore	Amelia	VA	Lone Well	Union	LA	Loraine	Adams	IL
Logan	Edgar	IL	Lone Willow	Martin	MN	Loramies	Shelby	OH
Logan	Bearborn	IN	Long	Vermillion	IL	Loran	Stephenson	IL
Logan	Harrison	IA	Long Bottom	Meigs	OH	Lordstown	Trumbull	OH
Logan	Lawrence	MO	Long Branch	Tatnall	GA	Lord's Valley	Pike	PA
Logan	Dodge	NE	Long Branch	Monroe	MO	Lordsville	Nansemond	VA
Logan	Schuyler	NY	Long Branch	Richardson	NE	Lordsville	Delaware	NY
Logan(c.h.)	Hocking	OH	Long Branch	Monmouth	NJ	Lorentz Store	Upshur	WV
Logan(c.h.)	Cache	UT	Long Branch	Franklin	VA	Lorettee	Houston	MN
Logan(c.h.)	Logan	WV	Long Corner	Howard	MD	Loretto	Marion	KY
Logan Mills	Clinton	PA	Long Creek	Decatur	IA	Loretto	Cambria	PA
Logan's Creek	Reynolds	MO	Long Creek Depot	Panola	MS	Loretto	Essex	VA
Logan's Ferry	Allegheny	PA	Long Dale	Alleghany	VA	Lorraine	Jefferson	NY
Logansport	Hamilton	IL	Long Eddy	Sullivan	NY	Los Alisos	Santa Barbara	CA
Logansport(c.h.)	Cass	IN	Long Falls Creek	McLean	KY	Los Angeles(c.h.)	Los Angeles	CA
Logansport	Butler	KY	Long Glade	Augusta	VA	Losantville	Randolph	IN
Logansport	De Soto	LA	Long Green Acad.	Baltimore	MD	Los Gatos	Santa Clara	CA
Logan's Store	Rutherford	NC	Long Grove	Lake	IL	Losh's Mills	Pottawattomie	IA
Logansville	Jefferson	IL	Long Grove	Scott	IA	Los Luceros	Rio Arriba	NM
Loganville	Logan	OH	Long Grove	Hardin	KY	Los Lunas	Valencia	NM
Loganville	York	PA	Long Hill	Stearns	MN	Los Nietos	Los Angeles	CA
Loganville	Sank	WI	Long Hill	Morris	NJ	Lostant	La Salle	IL
Log Cabin	Morgan	OH	Long Island	Jackson	AL	Lost Branch	Lincoln	MO
Loggy Bayou	Natchitoches	LA	Long Island City	Queens	NY	Lost Camp	Howell	MO
Log Town	Onachita	LA	Long Lake	Madison	IL	Lost Creek	Breathitt	KY
Lohmansville	Washington	MN	Long Lake	Hennepin	MN	Lost Creek	Union	TN
Loma	Conejos	CO	Long Lake	Hamilton	NY	Lost Creek	Harrison	WV
Lonax	Henderson	IL	Long Lane	Dallas	MO	Lostine	Cherokee	KS
Lombard	Du Page	IL	Long Marsh	Queen Anne	NY	Lost Island	Palo Alto	IA
Lombardville	Stark	IL	Long Meadow	Hampden	MA	Lost Mountain	Cobb	GA
Lombardville	Scioto	OH	Longmire	Washington	TN	Lost Mountain	Greene	TN
Lombardy	Columbia	GA	Longmire's Store	Edgefield	SC	Lost River	Hardy	WV
Lombardy Grove	Mecklenburgh	VA	Long Pine	Anson	SC	Lost Run	Breckinridge	KY
Lomira	Dodge	WI	Long Plain	Bristol	MA	Lot	Whitley	KY
Lonaconing	Alleghany	MD	Long Point	Livingston	IL	Lothair	Saunders	NE
Londenville	Albany	NY	Long Pond	Caldwell	KY	Lotridge	Athens	OH
London	Shelby	IN	Long Prairie	Sebastian	AR	Lottsburgh	Northumberland	VA
London	Sumner	KS	Long Prairie	Wayne	IL	Lott's Creek	Homboldt	IA
London(c.h.)	Laurel	KY	Long Prairie(c.h.)	Todd	MN	Lottsville	Warren	PA
London	Monroe	MI	Long Prairie	Fayette	TX	Louden City	Fayette	IL

PLACE	COUNTY	STATE	PLACE	COUNTY	STATE	PLACE	COUNTY	STATE
Loudesville	Albany	NY	Lowell Mills	Bartholomew	IN	Ludlow	Kenton	KY
Loudon	Merrimack	NH	Lowellville	Mahoning	OH	Ludlow	Hampden	MA
Loudon(c.h.)	Loudon	TN	Lower Bank	Burlington	NJ	Ludlow	McKean	PA
Loudon Centre	Merrimack	NH	Lower Bartlett	Carroll	NH	Ludlow	Windsor	VT
Loudon Ridge	Merrimack	NH	Lower Bern	Berks	PA	Ludlow Grove	Hamilton	OH
Loudonville	Ashland	OH	Lower Boise	Ada	IA	Ludlowville	Tomkins	NY
Loudsville	White	GA	Lower Gilmanton	Belknap	NH	Ludville	Pickens	GA
Loughboro	St. Francois	MO	Lower Heidelberg	Berks	PA	Lula	Montgomery	IL
Louina	Randolph	AL	Lower Lake(c.h.)	Lake	CA	Lumber City	Telfair	GA
Louisa(c.h.)	Lawrence	KY	Lower Lynxville	Crawford	WI	Lumber City	Clearfield	PA
Louisa(c.h.)	Louisa	VA	Lower Mahantango	Schuylkill	PA	Lumberland	Sullivan	NY
Louisburgh	Dallas	MO	Lower Merion	Montgomery	PA	Lumberman	Clark	WI
Louisburgh(c.h.)	Franklin	NC	Lower Newport	Washington	OH	Lumberport	Harrison	WV
Louisiana	Pike	MO	Lower Peach Tree	Wilcox	AL	Lumberton	Burlington	NJ
Louisville	Barbour	AL	Lower Providence	Montgomery	PA	Lumberton(c.h.)	Robeson	NC
Louisville(c.h.)	Jefferson	GA	Lower Salem	Washington	OH	Lumberton	Clinton	OH
Louisville(c.h.)	Clay	IL	Lower Saucon	Northampton	PA	Lumberville	Delaware	NY
Louisville(c.h.)	Pottawatomie	KS	Lower Sioux Agency	Redwood	MN	Lumberville	Bucks	PA
Louisville(c.h.)	Jefferson	KY	Lower Squankum	Monmouth	NJ	Lumberville	Iowa	WI
Louisville	Franklin	LA	Lower Valley	Hunterdon	NJ	Lummisville	Wayne	NY
Louisville	Carroll	MD	Lower Waterford	Caledonia	VT	Lumpkin(c.h.)	Stewart	GA
Louisville(c.h.)	Winston	MS	Lowe's Cross Roads	Sussex	DE	Luna Landing	Chicot	AR
Louisville	Lincoln	MO	Lowe's Station	Bourbon	KY	Lund's Station	Du Page	IL
Louisville	Missoula	MT	Low Gap	Scury	NC	Lundy's Lane	Erie	PA
Louisville	Cass	NE	Low Hampton	Washington	NY	Lunenburgh	Izard	AR
Louisville	St. Lawrence	NY	Lowhill	Lehigh	PA	Lunenburgh	Worcester	MA
Louisville	Stark	OH	Lowland	St. Clair	IL	Lunenburgh	Essex	VT
Louisville	Blount	TN	Lowman	Clemung	NY	Lunenburgh(c.h.)	Lunnenburgh	VA
Louisville	Dunn	WI	Lowmansville	Lawrence	KY	Luney's Creek	Grant	WV
Louisville Landing	St. Lawrence	NY	Low Moor	Clinton	OH	Luni	Wright	IA
Loutre	Audrian	MO	Lowndes	Wayne	MO	Luray	Henry	IN
Loutre Island	Montgomery	MO	Lowndesborough	Lowndes	AL	Luray(c.h.)	Page	VA
Lovejoy	Bureau	IL	Lowndesville	Abbeville	SC	Lusby's Mill	Owne	KY
Lovejoy's Station	Clayton	GA	Low Point	Woodford	IL	Lusk	Pope	IL
Lovelaceville	Ballard	KY	Lowry	Bedford	VA	Lusk's Springs	Parke	IN
Love Lake City	Macon	MO	Lowry City	St. Clair	MO	Luthersburgh	Clearfield	PA
Lovelady	Caldwell	NC	Lowville(c.h.)	Lewis	NY	Luther's Mills	Bradford	PA
Loveland	Pottawattomie	IA	Lowville	Erie	PA	Luthersville	Meriwether	GA
Loveland	Bladen	NC	Lowville	Columbia	WI	Lutherville	Baltimore	MD
Loveland	Clearmont	OH	Loxa	Coles	IL	Lutzton	Nodaway	MO
Lovell	Oxford	ME	Loyal	Carroll	GA	Luverne	Rock	MN
Lovell's Station	Erie	PA	Loyal	Clark	WI	Luxemburgh	Sterns	MN
Lovelton	Wyoming	PA	Loyal Hill	Greene	AR	Luzerne	Benton	IA
Lovely Dale	Knox	IN	Loyal Oak	Summit	OH	Luzerne	St. Clair	MO
Lovely Mount	Montgomery	VA	Loyalsock	Lycoming	PA	Luzerne	Luzerne	PA
Love's Mills	Washington	VA	Loyalton	Sierra	CA	Lycippus	Westmoreland	PA
Love Station	De Soto	MS	Loyalty	James	TN	Lycurgus	Allamakee	IA
Lovett	Jennings	IN	Loyal Valley	Mason	TX	Lydia	Scott	MN
Lovett's	Adams	OH	Loyd	Ulster	NY	Lydia	Darlington	SC
Lovettsville	Loudoun	VA	Loyd	Richland	WI	Lyell's Store	Richmond	VA
Loveville	New Castle	DE	Loydsville	Belmont	OH	Lykens	Dauphin	PA
Loveville	Centre	PA	Loy's Cross Roads	Union	TN	Lyle	Mower	MN
Lovilia	Monroe	PA	Loysville	Perry	PA	Lyles	Lancaster	PA
Lovilia	Hamilton	IL	Luana	Clayton	IA	Lylesford	Fairfield	SC
Loving Creek	Bedford	VA	Lubec	Washington	ME	Lyman	Pope	AR
Lovington(c.h.)	Nelson	VA	Lubec	Wood	WV	Lyman	York	ME
Lovington	Moultrie	IL	Lucas	Lucas	IA	Lyman	Grafton	NH
Lowden	Cedar	IA	Lucas	Henry	MO	Lyme	New London	CN
Lowe	Howard	KS	Lucas	Richland	OH	Lynchburgh	Jefferson	IL
Lowell	La Salle	IL	Lucas	Dunn	WI	Lynchburgh	Nodaway	MO
Lowell	Lake	IN	Lucasville	Scioto	OH	Lynchburgh	Highland	OH
Lowell	Henry	IA	Lucerne	Knox	OH	Lynchburgh	Sumter	SC
Lowell	Cherokee	KS	Lucesco	Westmoreland	PA	Lynchburgh	Lincoln	TN
Lowell	Garrard	KY	Lucinda Furnace	Clarion	PA	Lynchburgh	Harris	TX
Lowell	Penobscot	ME	Luck	Polk	WI	Lynchburgh	Campbell	VA
Lowell	Middlesex	MS	Luda	Onaachita	AR	Lynche's Lake	Williamsburgh	SC
Lowell	Kent	MI	Luda	Ogle	IL	Lynch's Creek	Marion	SC
Lowell	St. Louis	MO	Luddenville	Iroquois	IL	Lynch's Lake	Williamsburgh	SC
Lowell	Oneida	NY	Ludington	Mason	MI	Lynchwood	Kershaw	SC
Lowell	Washington	OH	Ludingtonville	Putnam	NY	Lynd	McPhail	MN
Lowell	Orleans	VT	Ludlow	Champaign	IL	Lyndeborough	Hillsborough	NH
Lowell	Snohomish	WA	Ludlow	Dubois	IN	Lyndon	Whitesides	IL
Lowell	Dodge	WI	Ludlow	Allamakee	IA	Lyndon	Osage	KS

PLACE	COUNTY	STATE	PLACE	COUNTY	STATE	PLACE	COUNTY	STATE
Lyndon	Jefferson	KY	McCleary	Noble	OH	McKune's Depot	Wyoming	PA
Lyndon	Aroostook	ME	McCleary	Beaver	PA	McLane	Erie	PA
Lyndon Centre	Caledonia	VT	McClelland	Franklin	NY	McLaughlin's Store	Westmoreland	PA
Lyndon Station	Ross	OH	McClellandsville	New Castle	DE	McLean	McLean	IL
Lyndonville	Orleans	NY	McClellandtown	Fayette	PA	McLean	Tompkins	NY
Lyndonville	Caledonia	VT	McClellan Gulch	Deer Lodge	MT	McLeansborgh(c.h.)	Hamilton	IL
Lynn	McDonough	IL	McClellanville	Charleston	SC	McLean's Corners	Crawford	PA
Lynn	Randolph	IN	McClintockville	Venango	PA	McLean's Station	Cherokee Nat.	IT
Lynn	Warren	IA	McCluney	Perry	OH	McLeansville	Guilford	NC
Lynn	Greenup	KY	McClure	Buchanan	VA	McLellan's Corners	Erie	PA
Lynn	Essex	MA	McClure Settlement	Broome	NY	McLemoresville	Carroll	TN
Lynn	St. Clair	MI	McClurg	Johnson	MO	McLeod's Station	Logan	KY
Lynn	Susquehanna	PA	McComb	Hancock	OH	McMath	Tuscaloosa	AL
Lynn	Clark	WI	McConnellsbg(c.h.)	Fulton	PA	McMillian	Knox	TN
Lynn Camp	Knox	KY	McConnell's Grove	Stephenson	IL	McMinnville	Yam Hill	OR
Lynn Camp	Marshall	WV	McConnellstown	Huntingdon	PA	McMinnville(c.h.)	Warren	TN
Lynn Centre	Henry	IL	McConnellville	Oneida	NY	McNairy Station	McNairy	TN
Lynne	Weber	UT	McConnellsvil.(c.h.)	Morgan	OH	McNeeley's Ridge	Clark	AR
Lynnfield	Essex	MA	McConnellsville	York	SC	McNutt(c.h.)	Leflore	MS
Lynnfield Centre	Essex	MA	McCordsville	Hancock	IN	McPaul	Fremont	IA
Lynnport	Lehigh	PA	McCoy's Station	Decatur	IN	McPherson	Coles	IL
Lynnville	Henry	AL	McCoy's Station	Jefferson	OH	McRae	Telfair	GA
Lynnville	Morgan	IL	McCoysville	Juniata	PA	McSherrystown	Adams	PA
Lynnville	Warrick	IN	McCray's Store	Alamance	NC	McSherrysville	York	PA
Lynnville	Jasper	IA	McCullock's Mills	Junianta	PA	Mc's Ville	Shelby	TN
Lynnville	Graves	KY	McCutchanville	Vanderburgh	IN	McVeytown	Mifflin	PA
Lynnville	Lehigh	PA	McCutchenville	Wyandot	OH	McVill	Armstrong	PA
Lynnville	Henry	AL	McDaniel's	Gallia	OH	McVille	Telfair	GA
Lynnville	Morgan	IL	McDonald	Hardin	OH	McWilliamstown	Chester	PA
Lynnville	Warrick	IN	McDonald's Mill	Montgomery	VA	McZena	Ashland	OH
Lynnville	Jasper	IA	McDonaldsville	Stark	OH	Mabbettsville	Dutchess	NY
Lynnville	Graves	KY	McDonough	New Castle	DE	Mabee's	Jackson	OH
Lynnville	Lehigh	PA	McDonough(c.h.)	Henry	GA	Mabry's Ferry	Stone	MO
Lynnville	Giles	TN	McDonough	Chenango	NY	Mace	Montgomery	IN
Lynnwood	Rockingham	VA	McDowell	Yavapai	AZ	Macedon	Wayne	NY
Lyon	Wabashaw	MN	McDowell	Highland	VA	Macedon	Mercer	OH
Lyon	Laclede	MO	McElhattan	Clinton	PA	Macedon Centre	Wayne	NY
Lyona	Dickinson	KS	McElroy	Doddridge	WV	Macedonia	Hamilton	IL
Lyons	Cook	IL	McEwen's Station	Humphreys	TN	Macedonia	Pottawattomie	IA
Lyons	Greene	IN	McEwensville	Northcumberland	PA	Macedonia	Clinton	OH
Lyons	Clinton	IA	McFadden	York	NE	Macedonia	Bradford	PA
Lyons	Ionia	MI	McFarland's	Lunnenburgh	VA	Macedonia Depot	Summit	OH
Lyons	Burt	NE	McGaheysville	Rockingham	VA	Macfarland	Dane	WI
Lyons(c.h.)	Wayne	NY	McGarvey's	Clearfield	PA	Machias(c.h.)	Washington	ME
Lyons	Fulton	OH	McGehee Landing	Bolivar	MS	Machias	Cattaraugus	NY
Lyons	Fayette	TX	McGill	Paulding	OH	Machias Port	Washington	ME
Lyons	Walworth	WI	McGoingle's Station	Butler	OH	Machirville	Mason	WV
Lyonsdale	Lewis	NY	McGrawsville	Miami	IN	Mackerel Corner	Carroll	NH
Lyon's Falls	Lewis	NY	McGrawville	Cortland	NY	Mackey's Grove	Boone	IA
Lyon's Mill	Clinton	MI	McGregor	Clayton	OH	Mackinaw	Tazewell	IL
Lyon's Station	Fayette	IN	McHenry	McHenry	IL	Mackinaw(c.h.)	Mackinaw	MI
Lyon's Station	Berks	PA	McIndoe's Falls	Caledonia	VT	Mackinaw City	Cheboygan	MI
Lyonsville	Cook	IL	McIntire	Wilkinson	GA	Mack's	Carroll	IA
Lyon Valley	Lehigh	PA	McIntosh(c.h.)	Liberty	GA	Macksville	Harrison	TX
Lyra	Scioto	OH	McIntyre	Dutchess	NY	Macksville	Pendleton	WV
Lysander	Onondaga	NY	McKay	Ashland	OH	Macksville	Piatt	IL
Lystle City	Iowa	IA	McKean	Erie	PA	Macksville	Washington	KY
			McKeansburgh	Schuylkill	PA	Macksville	Outagamie	WI
			McKean's Old Stand	Westmoreland	PA	Macomb(c.h.)	Macomb	MI
McAfee	Mercer	KY	McKee(c.h.)	Jackson	KY	Macomb	St. Lawrence	NY
McAfee Valley	Sussex	NJ	McKeen	Clark	IL	Macomb	Grayson	TX
McAlvey's Fort	Huntingdon	PA	McKee's Gap	Blair	PA	Macon(c.h.)	Bibb	GA
McAllister's Roads	Montgomery	TN	McKee's Half Falls	Snyder	PA	Macon	Macon	IL
McAllisterville	Juniata	PA	McKeesport	Allegheny	PA	Macon	Lenawee	MI
McArthur(c.h.)	Vinton	OH	McKenny's Mill	Rockbridge	VA	Macon(c.h.)	Noxubee	MI
McBean Depot	Richmond	GA	McKenzie	Carroll	TN	Macon	Fayette	TN
McBride's Mill	Watauga	NC	McKinley	Marengo	AL	Macon City(c.h.)	Macon	MO
McCainsville	Morris	NJ	McKinley's Landing	Henderson	KY	Macon Depot	Warren	NC
McCall	Hancock	IL	McKinney(c.h.)	Collin	TX	Macon Station	Hale	AL
McCall's Ferry	York	PA	McKinstry's Mills	Carroll	MD	Macoupin Station	Macoupin	IL
McCameron	Martin	IN	McKnight's POint	Humbolt	IA	Macungie	Lehigh	PA
McCandless	Butler	PA	McKnightstown	Adams	PA	Madalin	Dutchess	NY
McCanleyville	Wilkin	MN	McKownville	Albany	NY	Madawaska	Aroostook	ME

PLACE	COUNTY	STATE	PLACE	COUNTY	STATE	PLACE	COUNTY	STATE
Maddensville	Huntingdon	PA	Mahamet	Champaign	IL	Manchester	Sumter	SC
Madeira	Hamilton	OH	Mahomet	Burnet	TX	Manchester(c.h.)	Coffee	TN
Madelia(c.h.)	Watonwan	MN	Mahoning	Indiana	PA	Manchester(c.h.)	Bennington	VT
Madely	Portage	WI	Mahopac	Oakland	MI	Manchester	Chesterfield	VA
Maderia	Clearfield	PA	Mahopac	Putnam	NY	Manchester	Green Lake	WI
Madison(c.h.)	St. Francis	AR	Mahapac Falls	Putnam	NY	Manchester Bridge	Dutchess	NY
Madison(c.h.)	Madison	FL	Mahwah	Bergen	NJ	Manchester Centre	Ontario	NY
Madison	New Haven	CN	Maiden Creek	Berks	PA	Mandana	Onondaga	NY
Madison(c.h.)	Morgan	GA	Maiden Rock	Pierce	WI	Mandarin	Duval	FL
Madison	Richland	IL	Maidsville	Monongalia	WV	Mandeville	St. Tammany	LA
Madison(c.h.)	Jefferson	IN	Maine	Waseca	MN	Mandeville	Carroll	MO
Madison	Jones	IA	Maine	Columbia	PA	Mangohick	King William	VA
Madison	Greenwood	KS	Maine	Broome	NY	Mangum	Richmond	NC
Madison	Somerset	ME	Maine	Marathon	WI	Manhasset	Queens	NY
Madison	Livingston	MI	Maine Prairie	Solano	CA	Manhattan	Putnam	IN
Madison	Mower	MN	Mainesburgh	Tioga	PA	Manhattan	Keokuk	IA
Madison	Monroe	MO	Mainville	Cook	IL	Manhattan(c.h.)	Riley	KS
Madison	Gallatin	MT	Mainville	Warren	OH	Manhattanville	New York	NY
Madison	Rockingham	SC	Mainville	Columbia	PA	Manheim	Lancaster	PA
Madison	Lake	OH	Majenica	Huntington	IN	Manilla	Rush	IN
Madison	Westmoreland	PA	Majority Point(c.h.)	Cumberland	IL	Manistee(c.h.)	Manistee	MI
Madison	Davidson	TN	Malade City(c.h.)	Oneida	ID	Manito	Mason	IL
Madison(c.h.)	Dane	WI	Makauda	Jackson	IL	Manitowoc(c.h.)	Manitowoe	WI
Madison(c.h.)	Madison	VA	Malaga	Gloucester	NJ	Manitowoc Rapids	Manitowoc	WI
Madisonburgh	Wayne	OH	Malaga	Monroe	OH	Mankato(c.h.)	Blue Earth	MN
Madisonburgh	Centre	PA	Malakoff	Henderson	TX	Manlius	Bureau	IL
Madison Centre	Somerset	ME	Malcom	Poweshick	IA	Manlius	Allegan	MI
Madison Mills	Madison	VA	Malden	Bureau	IL	Manlius	Onondaga	NY
Madison Mills	Fayette	OH	Malden	Middlesex	MA	Manlius Centre	Omondaga	NY
Madison Run Stat.	Orange	VA	Malden	Ulster	NY	Manlius Station	Onondaga	MY
Madison Springs	Madison	GA	Malden Bridge	Columbia	NY	Manlyville	Henry	TN
Madison Station	Madison	AL	Mallet Creek	Medina	OH	Manborough	Amelia	VA
Madisonville(c.h.)	Hopkins	KY	Mallory	Oswego	NY	Manning(c.h.)	Clarendon	SC
Madisonville	St. Tammany	LA	Malma	De Kalb	IL	Mann's Choice	Bedford	PA
Madisonville	Ralls	MO	Malone	Clinton	IA	Mannsville	Taylor	KY
Madisonville	Hamilton	OH	Malone(c.h.)	Franklin	NY	Mannsville	Jefferson	MY
Madisonville	Luzerne	PA	Malta	De Kalb	IL	Mannsville	Perry	PA
Madisonville(c.h.)	Monroe	TN	Malta	Saratoga	MY	Manville	Brown	KS
Madisonville(c.h.)	Madison	TX	Malta	Morgan	OH	Manville	Sumter	SC
Madonaville	Monroe	IL	Malta Bend	Saline	MO	Manny(c.h.)	Sabine	LA
Madrid	Franklin	ME	Maltaville	Saratoga	NY	Manomin	Anoka	MN
Madrid	St. Lawrence	NY	Malton	Plymouth	IA	Manor	Lancaster	PA
Madrid Springs	St. Lawrence	MY	Malugin Grove	Lee	IL	Manor Dale	Westmoreland	PA
Madura	Clay	KS	Malvern	Mills	IA	Manor Hill	Huntingdon	PA
Maeystown	Monroe	IL	Malvern	Carroll	OH	Manor Kill	Schoharie	NY
Magalia	Butte	CA	Mamaroneck	Westchester	NY	Manor Station	Westmoreland	PA
Magazine	Saber	AR	Manack	Lowness	AL	Manorsvil'e	Armstrong	PA
Magee's Corners	Seneca	NY	Manada Hill	Dauphin	PA	Manorville	Suffolk	NY
Magnolia(c.h.)	Columbia	AR	Manahawkin	Ocean	NJ	Manquin	King William	VA
Magnolia	Kent	DE	Manahapan	Monmouth	NJ	Mansfield	Tolland	CN
Magnolia	Pulaski	GA	Manamuskin	Cumberland	NJ	Mansfield	Piatt	IL
Magnolia	Putnam	IL	Manannah	Meeker	MN	Mansfield	Parke	IN
Magnolia	Crawford	IN	Manassas	Prince William	VA	Mansfield	Linn	KS
Magnolia(c.h.)	Columbia	AR	Manatawny	Berks	PA	Mansfield(c.h.)	De Soto	LA
Magnolia	La Rue	KY	Manatee(c.h.)	Manatee	FL	Mansfield	Bristol	MA
Magnolia	Harford	MD	Manayunk	Philadelphia	PA	Mansfield	Dutchess	MY
Magnolia	Pike	MS	Manchaug	Worcester	MA	Mansfield(c.h.)	Richland	OH
Magnolia	Moniteau	MO	Manchester	Hartford	CN	Mansfield	Rioga	PA
Magnolia	Duplin	NC	Manchester	Scott	IL	Mansfield	Tarrant	TX
Magnolia	Stark	OH	Manchester	Dearborn	IN	Mansfield Centre	Tolland	CN
Magnolia	Houston	TN	Manchester	Delaware	IA	Mansfield Depot	Tolland	CN
Magnolia	Anderson	TX	Manchester(c.h.)	Clay	KY	Mansfield Valley	Allegheny	PA
Magnolia	Morgan	WV	Manchester	Kennebec	ME	Manson	Calhoun	IA
Magnolia	Rock	WI	Manchester	Carroll	MD	Mansura	Avoyelles	LA
Magnolia Centre	Lawrence	MO	Manchester	Essex	MA	Manteno	Kankakee	IL
Magnolia Mills	Duval	FL	Manchester	Washtenaw	MI	Manteno	Shelby	IA
Magnolia Springs	Jasper	TX	Manchester	St. Louis	MO	Manteo(c.h.)	Dare	NC
Maguire's Store	Washington	AR	Manchester	Hillsborough	NH	Manti	Fremont	OH
Mahalasville	Morgan	IN	Manchester	Ocean	NJ	Manti(c.h.)	San Pete	UT
Mahanoy	Northcumberland	PA	Manchester	Ontario	NY	Manton	Maries	MO
Mahanoy City	Schuylkill	PA	Manchester	Cumberland	MC	Manton	Providence	RI
Mahonoy Plane	Schuylkill	PA	Manchester	Adams	OH	Mantorville(c.h.)	Dodge	MN
Maharg	Butler	PA	Manchester	York	PA	Mantua	Gloucester	NJ

PLACE	COUNTY	STATE	PLACE	COUNTY	STATE	PLACE	COUNTY	STATE
Mantua	Portage	OH	Marbut's	Giles	TN	Marionville	Lawrence	MO
Mantua	Collin	TX	Marcella Falls	Lawrence	TN	Marionville	Forest	PA
Mantua Station	Portage	OH	Marcelline	Adams	IL	Mariposa(c.h.)	Mariposa	CA
Manville	Mobile	AL	Marcellon	Columbia	WI	Marisa	St. Clair	IL
Manville	Jefferson	IN	Marcellus	Cass	MI	Marits	Morrow	OH
Manville	Providence	RI	Marcellus	Onondaga	NY	Mark	Defiance	OH
Manzana	Valencia	NM	Marcellus Falls	Onondaga	NY	Marked Poplar	Washington	NC
Maple	Ionia	MI	Marchand	Indiana	PA	Markelsville	Perry	PA
Maple	Brown	OH	Marco	Greene	IN	Markesan	Green Lake	WI
Maple Creek	Dodge	NE	Marcus	Cherokee	IA	Market Lake	Oneida	ID
Maple Creek	Carroll	TN	Marcy	La Grange	IN	Markham Station	Fanquier	VA
Maple Glen	Scott	MN	Marcy	Fairfield	OH	Markle	Huntington	IN
Maple Grove	Edwards	IL	Marcy	Waukesha	WI	Markleeville	Alpine	CA
Maple Grove	Aroostook	ME	Mardisville	Talladega	AL	Markleville	Madison	IL
Maple Grove	Barry	MI	Marengo	McHenry	IL	Markleysburgh	Fayette	PA
Maple Grove	Hennepin	MN	Marengo	Crawford	IN	Marksborough	Warren	NJ
Maple Grove	Otsego	NY	Marengo(c.h.)	Iowa	IA	Marksville(c.h.)	Avoyelles	LA
Maple Grove	Fayette	PA	Marengo	Calhoun	MI	Marksville	Page	VA
Maple Grove	Manitowoc	WI	Marengo	Wayne	NY	Mark West	Sonoma	CA
Maple Hill	Wabaunsee	KS	Marengo	Morrow	OH	Marlborough	Hartford	CN
Maple Hill	Montcalm	MI	Marengo	Jackson	WI	Marlborough	Middlesex	MA
Maple Hill	Oswego	NY	Margaretta Furnace	York	PA	Marlborough	Cheshire	NH
Maple Hill	Lycoming	PA	Margarettsville	Northampton	NC	Marlborough	Monmouth	NJ
Maple Lake	Wright	MN	Margarettville	Delaware	NY	Marlborough	Ulster	NY
Maple Landing	Monona	IA	Mariah Hill	Spencer	IN	Marlborough	Pitt	NC
Maple Lawn	Monroe	WV	Marianna	Phillips	AR	Marlborough	Stark	OH
Maple Plain	Hennepin	MN	Marianna(c.h.)	Jackson	FL	Marlborough	Chester	PA
Maple Rapids	Clinton	MI	Maria Stein	Mercer	OH	Marlborough	Carroll	TN
Maple Ridge	Isanti	MN	Mariaville	Schenectady	NY	Marlborough	Windham	VT
Maple Ridge	Tioga	PA	Maricopa Wells	Pima	AZ	Marlborough Depot	Cheshire	NH
Maple River	Blue Earth	MN	Marietta(c.h.)	Cobb	GA	Marlette	Sanilac	MI
Maples	Allen	IN	Marietta	Fulton	IL	Marlin(c.h.)	Falls	TX
Maple's Mill	Fulton	IL	Marietta	Shelby	IN	Marlow	Cheshire	NH
Maple Springs	La Fayette	MS	Marietta	Marshall	IA	Marlsville	Bladen	NC
Maple Springs	Wilkes	NC	Marietta	Prentiss	MS	Marlton	Burlington	NJ
Maple Springs	Red River	TX	Marietta	Onondaga	NY	Marmiton	Bourbon	KS
Maple Springs	Dunn	WI	Marietta(c.h.)	Washington	OH	Maroa	Macon	IL
Maple Street	Niagara	NY	Marietta	Lancaster	PA	Marple	Delaware	PA
Mapplesville	Baker	AL	Marietta	Greenville	SC	Marquand	Madison	MO
Mapleton	Monroe	IA	Marietta	Crawford	WI	Marquette(c.h.)	Marquette	MI
Mapleton	Bourbon	KS	Marilla	Erie	NY	Marquette	Green Lake	WI
Mapleton	Grand Traverse	MI	Marindal	Yankton	DA	Marr	Luzerne	PA
Mapleton	Blue Earth	MN	Marine	Madison	IL	Marriottsville	Howard	MD
Mapleton	Stark	OH	Marine	Lewis	KY	Marron	Clearfield	PA
Mapleton	Waukesha	WI	Marine City	St. Clair	MI	Marrowbone	Moultrie	IL
Mapleton Depot	Huntingdon	PA	Marine Mills	Washington	MN	Marrowbone	Cumberland	KY
Mapletown	Greene	PA	Mariner's Harbor	Richmond	NY	Mars	Bibb	AL
Mapleville	Dodge	NE	Marinette	Oconto	WI	Mars Bluff	Marion	SC
Mapleville	Providence	RI	Marion(c.h.)	Perry	AL	Marscilles	La Salle	IL
Maplewood	Middlesex	MA	Marion(c.h.)	Crittenden	AR	Marscilles	McPhail	MN
Maple Works	Clark	WI	Marion	Hartford	CN	Marsh	Chester	PA
Maquoketa	Jackson	IA	Marion(c.h.)	Williamson	IL	Marshall(c.h.)	Searcy	AR
Maquon	Knox	IL	Marion(c.h.)	Grant	IN	Marshall(c.h.)	Clark	IL
Marak	Brown	KS	Marion(c.h.)	Linn	IA	Marshall	Henry	IA
Maramec	Phelps	MO	Marion	Douglas	KS	Marshall	Bath	KY
Marathon	Lapeer	MI	Marion(c.h.)	Crittenden	KY	Marshall(c.h.)	Calhoun	MI
Marathon	Cortland	NY	Marion	Union	LA	Marshall	McPhail	MN
Marathon	Clermont	OH	Marion	Washington	ME	Marshal(c.h.)	Saline	NY
Marathon City	Marathon	WI	Marion	Plymouth	MA	Marshall	Oneida	NY
Marble	Madison	AR	Marion	Livingston	MI	Marshall(c.h.)	Madison	NC
Marble	Brown	IN	Marion	Olmsted	MN	Marshall	Highland	OH
Marble	Waupaca	WI	Marion	Cole	MO	Marshall(c.h.)	Harrison	TX
Marble Creek	Iron	ME	Marion	Wayne	NY	Marshall	Dane	WI
Marble Dale	Litchfield	CN	Marion(c.h.)	McDowell	NC	Marshall College	Cabell	WV
Marblehead	Essex	MA	Marion(c.h.)	Marion	OH	Marshall Hall	Charles	MD
Marblehead	Ottawa	OH	Marion	Newton	OR	Marshall Prairie	Newton	AR
Marble Hill(c.h.)	Bollinger	MO	Marion	Franklin	PA	Marshall's Creek	Monroe	PA
Marbel Ridge	Sauk	WI	Marion	Agelina	TX	Marshall's Ferry	Grainger	TN
Marble Rock	Floyd	IA	Marion(c.h.)	Smyth	VA	Marshallsville	Macon	GA
Marble Salt Works	Cherokee Nat.	IT	Marion	Marion	SC	Marshallton	Chester	PA
Marbletown	Fulton	IL	Marion Centre(c.h.)	Marion	KS	Marshalltown(c.h.)	Marshall	IA
Marbletown	Ulster	NY	Marion Station	Lauderdale	MS	Marsh Creek	Whitley	KY
Marble Valley	Coosa	AL	Marionville	Yell	AR	Marshfield	Warren	IN

PLACE	COUNTY	STATE
Marshfield	Plymouth	MA
Marshfield(c.h.)	Webster	MO
Marshfield	Erie	NY
Marshfield	Athens	OH
Marshfield	Tioga	PA
Marshfield	Washington	VT
Mars Hill	Aroostook	ME
Marshland	Richmond	NY
Marshland	Bonbomme	DA
Marshville	Oceana	MI
Marshville	Montgomery	NY
Marston's Mills	Barnstable	MA
Martell	Pierce	WI
Martha Furnace	Centre	PA
Marthasville	Warren	MO
Marthaville	Natchitoches	LA
Martickville	Lancaster	PA
Martin	Turner	DA
Martin	Allegan	MI
Martin	Green	WI
Martindale	Coffey	KS
Martindale	Mecklenburgh	NC
Martindale Depot	Columbia	NY
Martinez(c.h.)	Contra Costa	CA
Martin's Bluff	Clark	WA
Martinsburgh	Butte	CA
Martinsburgh	Pike	IL
Martinsburgh	Washington	IN
Martinsburgh	Keokuk	IA
Martinsburgh	Johnson	KS
Martinsburgh	Monroe	KY
Martinsburgh	Audrian	MO
Martinsburgh	Lewis	NY
Martinsburgh	Knox	OH
Martinsburgh	Blair	PA
Martinsburgh(c.h.)	Berkeley	WV
Martin's Corner	Chester	PA
Martin's Creek	Sharpe	AR
Martin's Ferry	Northampton	PA
Martin's Ferry	Belmont	OH
Martin's Lime Kilns	Stokes	NC
Martin's Station	Pulaski	VA
Martin's Store	Hamilton	IL
Martinstown	Putnam	MO
Martinsville	Clark	IL
Martinsville(c.h.)	Morgan	IN
Martinsville	Wayne	MI
Martinsville	Copiah	MS
Martinsville	Harrison	MO
Martinsville	Adams	NE
Martinsville	Somerset	NJ
Martinsville	Niagara	NY
Martinsville	Clinton	OH
Martinsville	Lancaster	PA
Martinsville	Nacogdoches	TX
Martinsville(c.h.)	Henry	VA
Martinville	Grant	WI
Martzville	Cayuga	NY
Martz	Clay	IN
Marvel	Bates	MO
Marvin	Pocahontas	IA
Marvin	Henry	MO
Marvin	Chautauqua	NY
Marydell	Caroline	MD
Maryland	Otsego	NY
Marylandline	Baltimore	MD
Marysburgh	Le Sueur	MN
Marysville(c.h.)	Yuba	CA
Marysville	Vermilion	IL
Marysville	Clark	IN
Marysville	Marion	IA
Marysville(c.h.)	Marshall	KS
Marysville	St. Clair	MI
Marysville(c.h.)	Union	OH
Marysville	Perry	PA
Marysville	Campbell	VA
Marysville	Fond du Lac	WI
Marysville(c.h.)	Nodaway	MO
Marysville(c.h.)	Blount	TN
Masardis	Aroostook	ME
Mascoutah	St. Clair	IL
Mashapaug	Tolland	CN
Mashpee	Barnstable	MA
Mashulaville	Noxubee	MS
Mason	Effingham	IL
Mason	Washington	MD
Mason(c.h.)	Ingham	MI
Mason	Hillsborough	NH
Mason	Warren	OH
Mason	Tipton	TN
Mason(c.h.)	Mason	TX
Mason	Mason	WV
Mason and Dixon	Franklin	PA
Mason City	Mason	IL
Mason City	Cerro Gordo	IA
Mason Creek	McLean	KY
Mason's Depot	Amherst	VA
Masontown	Fayette	PA
Masontown	Preston	WV
Mason Valley	Esmeralda	NV
Mason Village	Hillsborough	NH
Masonville	Delaware	NY
Masonville	Daviess	KY
Masonville	Burlington	NJ
Masonville	Delaware	NY
Maspeth	Queens	NY
Massac Creek	Massac	IL
Massack	McCracken	KY
Massanatton	Page	VA
Massena	St. Lawrence	NY
Massey's X Roads	Kent	MD
Massie's Mills	Nelson	VA
Massillon	Cedar	IA
Massillon	Stark	OH
Mastersonville	Lancaster	PA
Mastersville	McLennan	TX
Masterton	Monroe	OH
Masthope	Pike	PA
Mast Yard	Merrimack	NH
Matagorda(c.h.)	Matagorda	TX
Matamoras	Pike	PA
Matanzas	St. John's	FL
Matawan	Monmouth	NJ
Matfield Green	Chase	KS
Matherton	Ionia	MI
Mathews	Montgomery	AL
Mathews	Knox	ME
Matoaca	Chesterfield	VA
Matoax	Amelia	VA
Mattapan	Norfolk	MA
Mattapoisett	Plymouth	MA
Mattawamkeag	Penobscot	ME
Mattawan	Van Buren	MI
Matteawan	Dutchess	NY
Matthews(c.h.)	Matthews	VA
Matthews' Store	Howard	MD
Mathews	Jackson	MO
Mattison	Cook	IL
Mattison	Branch	MI
Mattituck	Suffolk	NY
Mattoon	Coles	IL
Matville	Raliegh	WV
Mauch Chunk(c.h.)	Carbon	PA
Mauckport	Harrison	IN
Maumee City	Lucas	OH
Maumelle	Pulaske	AR
Manne's Store	Franklin	MO
Maurertown	Shenandoah	VA
Mauricetown	Cumberland	NJ
Mauston(c.h.)	Jeneau	WI
Maxatawny	Berks	PA
Maxey	Oglethorpe	GA
Maxfield	Penobscot	ME
Maximo	Stark	OH
Maxinkukee	Marshall	IN
Max Meadows	Wythe	VA
Maxon's Mills	McCracken	KY
Maxville	Perry	OH
Maxville	Dyer	TN
Maxville	Buffalo	WI
Maxville	Delaware	OH
Maxwell's Creek	Mariposa	CA
May	Tuscola	MI
May	Martin	MN
May	Lancaster	PA
Mayberry	Carroll	MD
May Day	Riley	KS
Mayesville	Sumter	SC
Mayfield	Santa Clara	CA
Mayfield	Hancock	GA
Mayfield(c.h.)	Graves	KY
Mayfield	Grand Traverse	MI
Mayfield	Fulton	NY
Mayfield	Cuyahoga	OH
Mayhew's Station	Sacramento	CA
Mayhew's Station	Lowndes	MS
May Hill	Adams	OH
Maynard	Middlesex	MA
Maynard's Cove	Jackson	AL
Maynardsville	Calhoun	IL
Maynardville(c.h.)	Union	TN
Mayo Forge	Patrick	VA
Mayport	Duval	FL
Maysfield	Milam	TX
May's Landing(c.h.)	Atalantic	NJ
May's Lick	Mason	KY
May Spring	Grainger	TN
Maysville	Benton	AR
Maysville	Pike	IL
Maysville	Franklin	IA
Maysville(c.h.)	Mason	KY
Maysville(c.h.)	De Kalb	MO
Maysville	Columbiana	OH
Maysville	Mercer	PA
Mayton	Washington	KS
Maytown	Lancaster	PA
Mayview	Champaign	IL
Mayview	La Fayette	MO
Mayville(c.h.)	Chautauqua	NY
Mayville	Dodge	WI
Maywood	Cook	IL
Maywood	Benton	MN
Mazeppa	Wabashaw	MN
Mazo Maine	Dane	WI
Mazon	Grundy	IL
Mead Corners	Crawford	PA
Meade	Macomb	MI
Meadow	Millard	UT
Meadow Bluff	Greenbrier	WV
Meadow Creek	Whitley	KY
Meadow Creek	Madison	MT
Meadow Dale	Highland	VA
Meadow Gap	Huntingdon	PA
Meadows of Dan	Patrick	VA
Meadow Valley	Plumas	CA
Meadowville	Umatilla	OR
Meadowville	Barbour	WV
Mead's Basin	Passaic	NJ
Mead's Creek	Steuben	NY

PLACE	COUNTY	STATE	PLACE	COUNTY	STATE	PLACE	COUNTY	STATE
Mead's Mills	Wayne	MI	Melissadale	Butler	PA	Mercer(c.h.)	Mercer	PA
Meadville	Barry	MI	Melita	Alameda	CA	Mercer's Bottom	Mason	WV
Meadville	Franklin	MS	Mellenbruch	Jackson	IN	Mercersburgh	Franklin	PA
Meadville	Linn	MO	Mellenville	Columbia	NY	Mercer's Gap	Brown	TX
Meadville(c.h.)	Crawford	PA	Melleray	Dubuque	IA	Mercerville	Gallia	OH
Meadville	Halifax	VA	Mellington	Kendall	IL	Merchantville	Camden	NJ
Meagsville	Jackson	TN	Mellonville	Orange	FL	Merchantville	Steuben	NY
Means	Harrison	OH	Mellow Valley	Clay	AL	Mercury	Madison	IN
Mebanesville	Almance	NC	Mellwood	Prince George's	MD	Mercyville	Macon	MO
Mecca	Trumball	OH	Melmore	Seneca	OH	Meredith	Cloud	KS
Mechanicsburgh	Sangamon	IL	Meloy	Washington	PA	Meredith	Delaware	NY
Mechanicsburgh	Henry	IN	Melpine	Muscatine	IA	Meredith	Venango	PA
Mechanicsburgh	Champaign	OH	Melrose	Clark	IL	Meredith Centre	Belknap	NH
Mechanicsburgh	Cumberland	PA	Melrose	Middlesex	MA	Meredith's Tavern	Marion	WV
Mechanicsburgh	Bland	VA	Melrose	Stearns	MN	Meredosia	Morgan	IL
Mechanic's Falls	Ancroscoggin	ME	Melrose	St. Louis	MO	Meriden	New Haven	CN
Mechanic's Grove	Lancaster	PA	Melrose	Robeson	NC	Meriden	La Salle	IL
Mechanicstown	Frederick	ME	Melrose	Nacogloches	TX	Meriden(c.h.)	Steele	MN
Mechanicstown	Carroll	OH	Melrose	Rockingham	VA	Meriden	Sullivan	NH
Mechanic's Valley	Cecil	MD	Melrose	Jackson	WI	Meriden	Sutter	CA
Mechanicsville	Vanderburgh	IN	Melton	Lincoln	AR	Meriden(c.h.)	Lauderdale	MS
Mechanicsville	Cedar	IA	Melton's Mill	Tallapoosa	AL	Meridian(c.h.)	Jefferson	ME
Mechanicsville	St. Mary's	MD	Meltonsville	Marshall	AL	Meridian	Cayuga	NY
Mechanicsville	St. Charles	MO	Melvern	Osage	KS	Meridian(c.h.)	Bosque	TX
Mechanicsville	Saratoga	NY	Melville	Chattooga	GA	Meridianville	Marion	AL
Mechanicsville	Ashabula	OH	Melville	Leelenaw	MI	Mermaid	New Castle	DE
Mechanicsville	Bucks	PA	Melville	Monroe	WI	Mermenton	St. Laudry	LA
Mechanicsville	Smuter	SC	Melvin Village	Carroll	NH	Meroa	Mitchell	IA
Mechanicsville	Rutland	VT	Memory	Taylor	IA	Merom	Sullivan	IN
Mechum's River	Albermarle	VA	Memphis	Pickens	AL	Merriam	Noble	IN
Mecklenburgh	Schuyler	NY	Memphis	Clarke	IN	Merrick	Queens	NY
Mecosta	Mecosta	MI	Memphis	Macomb	MI	Merrillon	Jackson	WI
Medarysville	Pulaski	IN	Memphis(c.h.)	Scotland	ME	Merrill's Store	Caroline	VA
Mederville	Clayton	IA	Memphis	Onondaga	NY	Merrillsville	St. Clair	MI
Medfield	Norfolk	MA	Memphis	Clinton	OH	Merrillsville	Franklin	NY
Medford	Piscataquis	ME	Memphis(c.h.)	Shelby	TN	Merrilltown	Travis	TX
Medford	Middlesex	MA	Memphis Junction	Warren	KY	Merrillville	Lake	IN
Medford	Steele	MN	Menallen	Adams	PA	Merrimac	Jefferson	IA
Medford	Burlingham	NJ	Menardville(c.h.)	Menard	TX	Merrimack	Hillsborough	NH
Medford Centre	Piscataquis	ME	Menasha	Winnebago	WI	Merrimack	Sauk	WI
Media(c.h.)	Delaware	PA	Menchville	Warwick	VA	Merrimack Point	Monroe	IL
Mediapolis	Des Moines	IA	Mendham	Morris	NJ	Merrillsville	Franklin	NY
Medicine	Sullivan	MO	Mendocino	Mendocino	CA	Merrilltown	Travis	TX
Medicine Bow	Carbon	WY	Mendon	El Dorado	CA	Merrillville	Lake	IN
Medina	Jefferson	KS	Mendon	Adams	IL	Merrimac	Jefferson	IA
Medina	Lenawee	MI	Mendon	Worcester	MA	Merrimack	Hillsborough	NH
Medina	Orleans	NY	Mendon	St. Joseph	MI	Merrimack	Sauk	WI
Medina(c.h.)	Medina	OH	Mendon	Monroe	NY	Merrimack Point	Monroe	IL
Medina	Outagamie	WI	Mendon	Mercer	OH	Merrimack Station	St. Louis	ME
Medo	Blue Earth	MN	Mendon	Westmoreland	PA	Merritt	Yolo	CA
Medo	Bell	TX	Mendon	Cache	UT	Merritt	Scott	IL
Medoc	Jasper	MO	Mendon	Rutland	VT	Merritt's Bridge	Lexington	SC
Medon	Madison	TN	Mendon Centre	Monroe	NY	Merrittstown	Fayette	PA
Medora	Macoupin	IL	Mendota	La Salle	IL	Merrow Station	Tolland	CN
Medora	Jackson	IN	Mendota	Labette	KS	Merryall	Bradford	PA
Medora	Warren	IA	Mendota	Dakota	MN	Merry Oaks	Chatham	NC
Medora	Osage	MO	Mendota	Putnam	MO	Mershon's X Roads	Laurel	KY
Medusa	Albany	NY	Menckaune	Oconto	WI	Merton	Steele	MN
Medway	Penobscot	ME	Mento Park	San Meteo	CA	Merton	Waukesha	WI
Medway	Norfolk	MA	Mento Park	Middlesex	NJ	Mertztown	Berks	PA
Medway	Greene	NY	Menno	Mifflin	PA	Merwinsburgh	Monroe	PA
Medway	Clark	OH	Menomonee(c.h.)	Menomonee	ME	Meshack's Creek	Monre	KY
Medybemps	Washington	ME	Menomonee Falls	Waukesha	WI	Meshannon	Centre	PA
Meeker	Washington	WI	Menoti	Buren Vista	IA	Meshoppen	Wyoming	PA
Meeker's Grove	La Fayette	WI	Mentor	Bremer	IA	Mesilla(c.h.)	Dona Ana	NM
Meeme	Manitowoc	WI	Mentor	Lake	OH	Mesopotamia	Trumbull	OH
Meeting Street	Edgefield	SC	Menzie	Franklin	IA	Messengerville	Cortland	NY
Mehoopany	Wyoming	PA	Mequon River	Ozaukee	WI	Messongo	Accomack	VA
Meig's Creek	Morgan	OH	Merced	Merced	CA	Metamora(c.h.)	Woodford	IL
Meigsville	Morgan	OH	Merced Falls	Merced	CA	Metamora	Franklin	IN
Meinecke	San Joaquin	CA	Mercer	Somerset	ME	Metamora	Lapeer	MI
Melburn	Williams	OH	Mercer	Mercer	MO	Metamora	Fulton	OH
Melissa	Ozark	MO	Mercer	Mercer	OH	Metedeconk	Ocean	NJ

PLACE	COUNTY	STATE	PLACE	COUNTY	STATE	PLACE	COUNTY	STATE
Methuen	Essex	MA	Middlefield	Otsego	NY	Midway	Spencer	IN
Metomen	Fond du Lac	WI	Middlefield	Geauga	OH	Midway	Crawford	KS
Metropolis Cty(c.h.)	Massac	IL	Middlefield Centre	Otsego	NY	Midway	Woodford	KY
Metuchen	Middlesex	NJ	Middleford	Sussex	DE	Midway	Hinds	MS
Metz	Steuben	IN	Middle Fork	Clinton	IN	Midway	Boone	MI
Metz	Vernon	MO	Middle Fork	Jackson	KY	Midway	Erie	NY
Mexico	Miami	IN	Middle Fork	Hocking	OH	Midway	Davidson	NC
Mexico	Oxford	ME	Middle Fork	Randolph	WV	Midway	Guernsey	OH
Mexico(c.h.)	Audrian	MO	Middle Granville	Washington	NY	Midway	Washington	PA
Mexico	Oswego	NY	Middle Grove	Fulton	IL	Midway	Barnwell	SC
Mexico	Wyandot	OH	Middle Grove	Monroe	MO	Midway	Greene	TN
Mexico	Juniata	PA	Middle Grove	Saratoga	NY	Midway	Madison	TX
Meyerhoeffer's Str	Rockingham	VA	Middle Haddam	Middlesex	CN	Midway	Wasatch	UT
Meyer's Dale	Somerset	PA	Middle Hope	Orange	NY	Mier	Wabash	IL
Meyer's Mills	Somerset	PA	Middle Island	Suffolk	NY	Mier	Grant	IN
Meyerstown	Lebanon	PA	Middle Lake	Nicollette	MN	Mifflin	Crawford	IN
Meyersville	De Witt	TX	Middle Lancaster	Butler	PA	Mifflin	Ashland	OH
Miami	Miami	IN	Middle Point	Van Wert	OH	Mifflin	Henderson	TN
Miami	Saline	MO	Middleport	Iroquois	IL	Mifflin	Iowa	WI
Miami	Hamilton	OH	Middleport	Niagara	NY	Mifflinburgh	Union	PA
Miamisburgh	Montgomery	OH	Middleport	Meigs	OH	Mifflinville	Franklin	OH
Miami Station	Carroll	MO	Middleport	Schuylkill	PA	Mifflinville	Columbia	PA
Miamiville	Clermont	OH	Middleport	Webster	WV	Mikesville	Columbia	FL
Miami Village	Miami	KS	Middle River	Banks	GA	Milam	Sabine	TX
Mianus	Fairfield	CN	Middle River	Madison	IA	Milan	Rock Island	IL
Micanopy	Alachua	FL	Middle Saluda	Greenville	SC	Milan	Ripley	IL
Micklen	Jackson	MO	Middlesex	Yates	NY	Milan	Lucas	IA
Micco	Creek Nat.	IT	Middlesex	Washington	VT	Milan	Washtenaw	MI
Miccosukee	Leon	FL	Middlesex Village	Middlesex	MA	Milan(c.h.)	Sullivan	MO
Michaelsville	Hartford	MD	Middle Spring	Cumberland	PA	Milan	Coos	NH
Micham	Leelenaw	MI	Middle Sprite	Fulton	NY	Milan	Dutchess	NY
Michigan Bar	Sacramento	CA	Middlesworth	Shelby	IL	Milan	Erie	OH
Michigan Bluff	Placer	CA	Middleton	Lake	CA	Milan	Bradford	PA
Michigan Centre	Jackson	MI	Middleton	Ada	ID	Milan Depot	Gibson	TN
Michigan City	La Porte	IN	Middleton	Essex	MA	Milanville	Wayne	PA
Michigantown	Clinton	IN	Middleton	Stafford	NH	Milburn	Ballard	KY
Michigan Valley	Osage	KS	Middleton	Washington	OR	Mile Creek	Muskegon	MI
Middagh's	Northampton	PA	Middleton	Rutherford	TN	Mile Creek	Pickens	SC
Middle Bass	Ottawa	OH	Middleton	Leon	TX	Milesburgh	Centre	PA
Middleborough	Plymouth	MS	Middleton	Dane	WI	Miles Grove	Erie	PA
Middlebourne	Guernsey	OH	Middleton Station	Hardeman	TN	Miles Point	Carroll	MO
Middleborne(c.h.)	Tyler	WV	Middletown(c.h.)	Middlesex	CN	Miles Pond	Essex	VT
Middle Branch	Stark	OH	Middletown	New Castle	DE	Miles Station	Macoupin	IL
Middlebrook	Montgomery	MD	Middletown	Logan	IL	Milestown	St. Mary's	MD
Middlebrook	Iron	MO	Middletown	Henry	IN	Milestown	Philadelphia	PA
Middlebrook	Augusta	VA	Middletown	Des Moines	IA	Mile Strip	Madison	NY
Middleburg	Clay	FL	Middletown	Jefferson	KY	Milford	Lassen	CA
Middleburgh	Washington	IA	Middletown	Frederick	MD	Milford	New Haven	CN
Middleburgh	Casey	KY	Middletown	Ingham	MI	Milford	Kent	DE
Middleburgh	Carroll	MD	Middletown	Montgomery	NJ	Milford	Iroquois	IL
Middleburgh	Richardson	NE	Middletown	Monmouth	NJ	Milford	Kosciusko	IN
Middleburgh	Schoharie	NY	Middletown	Orange	NY	Milford	Dickinson	IA
Middleburgh	Cnyahoga	OH	Middletown	Hyde	NC	Milford	Riley	KS
Middleburgh(c.h.)	Snyder	PA	Middletown	Butler	OH	Milford	Bracken	KY
Middleburgh	Hardeman	TN	Middletown	Damphin	PA	Milford	Penobscot	ME
Middleburgh	Loudonn	VA	Middletown	Rutland	VT	Milford	Worcester	MA
Middlebury	New Haven	CN	Middletown	Frederick	VA	Milford	Oakland	MI
Middlebury	Elkhart	IN	Middletown Centre	Susquehanna	PA	Milford	Brown	MN
Middlebury	Grundy	MO	Middle Valley	Morris	NJ	Milford	Barton	MO
Middlebury	Summit	OH	Middle Valley	Wayne	PA	Milford(c.h.)	Seward	NE
Middlebury(c.h.)	Addison	VT	Middleville	Barry	MI	Milford	Hillsborough	NH
Middlebury	Iowa	WI	Middleville	Sussex	NJ	Milford	Hunterdon	NJ
Middlebury Centre	Tioga	PA	Middleville	Herkimer	NY	Milford	Otsego	NY
Middlebush	Somerset	NJ	Middleway	Jefferson	WV	Milford	Clermont	OH
Middle Creek	Hancock	IL	Midland	Hardin	IA	Milford(c.h.)	Pike	PA
Middle Creek	Chase	KS	Midland(c.h.)	Midland	MI	Milford	Ellis	TX
Middle Creek	Gallatin	MT	Midothian	Chesterfield	VA	Milford	Caroline	VA
Middle Creek	Noble	OH	Mid Prairie	Louisa	IA	Milford	Jefferson	WI
Middle Creek	Snyder	PA	Midville	Burke	GA	Milford Centre	Union	OH
Middle Fabius	Scotland	MO	Midway	Bullock	AL	Milford Mills	Chester	PA
Middlefield	Middlesex	CN	Midway	Hot Spring	AR	Milford Square	Bucks	PA
Middlefield	Buchanan	IA	Midway	Alameda	CA	Milfordton	Knox	OH
Middlefield	Hampshire	MA	Midway	Fulton	IL	Mill	Fayette	IA

PLACE NAMES OF THE UNITED STATES

PLACE	COUNTY	STATE	PLACE	COUNTY	STATE	PLACE	COUNTY	STATE
Millard	Adair	MO	Millerton(c.h.)	Fresno	CA	Millville	Worcester	MA
Millard	Walworth	WI	Millerton	Dutchess	MN	Millville	Wabashaw	MN
Millbach	Lebanon	PA	Millerville	Douglas	MN	Millville	Ray	MO
Mill Bend	Hawkins	TN	Mill Falls	Marion	WV	Millville	Cumberland	NJ
Millborough Springs	Bath	VA	Millfield	Athens	OH	Millville	Orleans	NY
Millbrae	San Matoe	CA	Mill Ford	Cherokee	AL	Millville	Butler	OH
Millbridge	Washington	ME	Mill Gap	Highland	VA	Millville	Columbia	PA
Mill Brook	St. Francis	AR	Mill Green	Harford	MD	Millville	Spartanburgh	SC
Mill Brook	Litchfield	CN	Millgrove	Blackford	IN	Millville	Lincoln	TN
Millbrook	Kendall	IL	Mill Grove	Poweshick	IA	Millville	Cache	UT
Millbrook	Mecosta	MI	Mill Grove	Erie	NY	Millville	Westmoreland	VA
Millbrook	Warren	NJ	Mill Grove	Morgan	OH	Millville	Grant	WI
Millbrook	Dutchess	NY	Mill Hall	Clinton	PA	Millville Depot	Pike	PA
Mill Brook	Wayne	OH	Millheim	Centre	PA	Millway	Lancaster	PA
Mill Brook	Washington	TN	Millheim	Austin	TX	Millwood	Kosciusko	IN
Millbrook	Frederick	VA	Mill Hill	Cabarrus	NC	Millwood	Leavenworth	KS
Millburgh	Barrien	MI	Mill Hollow	Luzerne	PA	Millwood	Grayson	KY
Millburn	Lake	IL	Millhousen	Decatur	IN	Millwood	Lincoln	MO
Millburn	Essex	NJ	Millican	Brazos	TX	Millwood	Knox	OH
Millburnton	Greene	TN	Milligan	Tuscarawas	OH	Millwood	Westmoreland	PA
Millbury	Worcester	MA	Milliken's Bend	Madison	LA	Millwood	Washington	TN
Millbury	Wood	OH	Millin	Burke	GA	Millwood	Collin	TX
Mill City	Clear Creek	CO	Millington	Middlesex	CN	Millwood	Clarke	VA
Mill City	Humbolt	NV	Millington	Kent	MD	Milmine	Piatt	IL
Mill City	Wyoming	PA	Millington	Franklin	MA	Milner	Randolph	AL
Mill Creek	Izard	AR	Millington	Tuscola	MI	Milner	Pike	GA
Mill Creek	Bourbon	KS	Millington	Morris	NJ	Milner's Corners	Hancock	IN
Mill Creek	Calvert	MD	Millington	Albemarle	VA	Milnersville	Guernsey	OH
Mill Creek	Kent	MI	Mill Plain	Fairfield	CN	Milnesville	Augusta	VA
Mill Creek	Huntingdon	PA	Mill Point	Sullivan	TN	Milo	Pike	AL
Mill Creek	Salt Lake	UT	Mill Point	Pocahontas	WV	Milo	Bureau	IL
Mill Creek	Berkeley	WV	Millport	Sanford	AL	Milo	Delaware	IA
Mill Creek	Richland	WI	Millport	Washington	IN	Milo	Piscataquis	ME
Milldale	Warren	VA	Millport	Knox	MO	Milo	Barry	MI
Milledgeville(c.h.)	Baldwin	GA	Mill Port	Chemung	NY	Milo	Defiance	OH
Milledgeville	Carroll	IL	Millport	Columbiana	OH	Milo	Wetzel	WV
Milledgeville	Appanoose	IA	Millport	Potter	PA	Milo Centre	Yates	NY
Milledgeville	Lincoln	KY	Mill River	Berkshire	MS	Milor	Sebastian	AR
Milledgeville	Montgomery	NC	Mill River	Henderson	NC	Milpitas	Santa Clara	CA
Milledgeville	Mercer	PA	Mill Rock	Jackson	IA	Milquatay	San Diego	CA
Millegeville	McNairy	TN	Mill Run	Fayette	PA	Milroy	Knox	IL
Millen's Bay	Lawrence	OH	Millry	Washington	AL	Milroy	Rush	IN
Miller Grove	Hopkins	TX	Mills	Jackson	WI	Milroy	Mifflin	PA
Miller's	Lawrence	OH	Millsborough	Sussex	DE	Milroy	Calaveras	CA
Millersburgh	Mercer	IL	Millsborough	Washington	PA	Milton	Calaveras	CA
Millsburgh	Elkhart	IN	Mills Centre	Brown	WI	Milton	Litchfield	CN
Millsburgh	Iowa	IA	Mills' Corners	Fulton	NY	Milton	Sussex	DE
Millersburgh	Bourbon	KY	Mill Shoals	White	IL	Milton(c.h.)	Santa Rosa	FL
Millersburgh	Rice	MN	Mill Site	Douglas	MN	Milton	Pike	IL
Millersburgh	Calloway	MO	Mill's Mill	Allegany	NY	Milton	Wayne	IN
Millersburgh(c.h.)	Holmes	OH	Mills' Prairie	Edwards	IL	Milton	Van Buren	IA
Millersburgh	Dauphin	PA	Mill Spring	St. Louis	MO	Milton	Trimble	KY
Miller's Camp Br.	Raleigh	WV	Mill Spring	Polk	NC	Milton	Norfolk	MA
Miller's Corners	Ontario	NY	Mill Spring	Jefferson	TN	Milton	Macomb	MI
Miller's Creek	Black Hawk	IA	Mill Springs	Wayne	KY	Milton	Randolph	MO
Miller's Creek	Estill	KY	Millstadt	St. Clair	IL	Milton	Saunders	NE
Miller's Eddy	Armstrong	PA	Mill Station	Lapeer	MI	Milton	Stafford	NH
Miller's Falls	Franklin	MA	Millstone	Somerset	NJ	Milton	Morris	NJ
Miller's Grove	Woodson	KS	Millstone Point	Washington	MD	Milton	Ulster	NY
Miller's Mill	Davidson	NC	Milltown	Chambers	AL	Milton	Caswell	NC
Miller's Mills	Herkimer	NY	Mill Town	Berrien	GA	Milton	Mahoning	OH
Miller's Place	Suffolk	NY	Milltown	Crawford	IN	Milton	Northumberland	PA
Millersport	Fairfield	OH	Milltown	Adair	KY	Milton	Rutherford	TN
Miller's Station	Lake	IN	Milltown	Washington	ME	Milton	Chittenden	VT
Miller's Station	Crawford	PA	Milltown	Middlesex	NJ	Milton	Rock	WI
Miller's Tavern	Essex	VA	Milltown	Chester	PA	Milton Centre	Saratoga	NY
Millerstown	Champaign	OH	Millview	Sullivan	PA	Milton Centre	Wood	OH
Millerstown	Perry	PA	Mill Village	Sullivan	PA	Milton Junction	ROck	WI
Millerstown Station	Perry	PA	Mili Village	Erie	PA	Milton Mills	Stafford	NH
Millersville	Russell	KY	Millville	Shasta	CA	Milton Plantation	Oxford	ME
Millersville	Anne Arundel	MD	Millville	Henry	IN	Miltonsburgh	Monroe	OH
Millersville	Cape Girardeau	MO	Millville	Clayton	IA	Milton Station	Coles	IL
Millersville	Lancaster	PA	Millville	Woodford	KY	Milton Station	Wayne	OH

PLACE NAMES OF THE UNITED STATES

PLACE	COUNTY	STATE	PLACE	COUNTY	STATE	PLACE	COUNTY	STATE
Milville	Rusk	TX	Minonk	Woodford	IL	Mohawk Valley	Plumas	CA
Milwaukee	Luzerne	PA	Minooka	Grundy	IL	Mohawk Village	Cochocton	OH
Milwaukee(c.h.)	Milwaukee	WI	Minorsville	Scott	KY	Mohegan	Providence	RI
Mimosa	Hendricks	IN	Minot	Androscoggin	ME	Mohican	Ashland	OH
Mimosa	Republic	KS	Minster	Auglaize	OH	Mohn's Store	Berks	PA
Mims	Barnwell	SC	Minta	Indiana	PA	Mohontongo	Juiata	PA
Mim's Store	Marion	TX	Mint Hill	Osage	MO	Mohrsville	Berks	PA
Mina	Chautauqua	NY	Mint Hill	Mecklenburgh	NC	Moingona	Boone	IA
Minaville	Montgomery	NY	Mintonville	Casey	KY	Moira	Franklin	NY
Minburn	Dallas	IA	Mint Spring	Wright	MO	Mokelumne	San Joaquin	CA
Miney	Tanney	MO	Mint Spring	Augusta	VA	Mokelumne Hl.(c.h.)	Calaveras	CA
Minden(c.h.)	Webster	LA	Mirablie	Caldwell	MO	Mokena	Will	IL
Minden	Sanilac	MI	Miracle Run	Monongalia	WV	Moksee(c.h.)	Yakima	WA
Minden	Benton	MN	Miranda	Rowan	NC	Molalla	Clackamas	OR
Minden	Lawrence	MO	Miser's Station	Bount	TN	Mole Hill	Ritchie	WV
Minden	Montgomery	NY	Misha Mokwa	Buffalo	WI	Moline	Rock Island	IL
Mindoro	La Crosse	WI	Mishawaka	St. Joseph	IN	Moline	Allegan	MI
Mine Kill Falls	Schoharie	NY	Mishicot	Manitowoc	WI	Molino	Escambia	FL
Mine La Motte	Madison	MO	Mission	Shawnee	KS	Molino	Escambia	FL
Mineola	Queens	NY	Mission Creek	Wabanusee	KS	Molino	Union	MS
Miner	La Salle	IL	Mission Creek	Pawnee	NE	Molino	Oswego	NY
Mineral	Bureau	IL	Misson San Jose	Alameda	CA	Molino	Lincoln	TN
Mineral	Athens	OH	Misson Valley	Victoria	TX	Moltown	Berks	PA
Mineral City	White Pine	NV	Mississip.City(c.h.)	Harrison	MS	Moluncus	Aroostook	ME
Mineral Mill	Elco	NV	Missoula(c.h.)	Missoula	MT	Momence	Kankakee	IL
Mineral Point	Anderson	KS	Missouri City	Clay	MO	Mona	Mitchell	OH
Mineral Point	Washington	MO	Misouriton	St. Charles	MO	Mona	Juab	UT
Mineral Point	Tuscarawas	OH	Missouri Valley	Harrison	IA	Monagan	St. Clair	MO
Mineral Point	Cambria	PA	Mitchell	Lawrence	IN	Monches	Waukesha	WI
Mineral Point	Iowa	WI	Mitchell	Mitchell	IA	Monclova	Lucas	OH
Mineral Ridge	Boone	IA	Mitchell	Autrim	MI	Monclova	Morgan	WV
Mineral Ridge	Mahoning	OH	Mitchellsburgh	Boyle	KY	Mondamin	Harrison	IA
Mineral Ridge	Hempstead	AR	Mitchell's Creek	Tioga	PA	Mondovi	Buffalo	WI
Mineral Springs	Hempstead	AR	Mitchell's Mills	Indiana	PA	Monee	Will	IL
Mineral Springs	Bonbomme	DA	Mitchell's Salt Wks	Jefferson	OH	Money Creek	Houston	MN
Mineral Springs	Mower	MN	Mitchell's Station	Culpepper	VA	Mongaup	Sullivan	NY
Mineral Springs	Schoharie	NY	Mitchellsville	Saline	IL	Mongaup Valley	Sullivan	NY
Mineral Springs	Adams	OH	Mitchellsville	Steuben	NY	Mongoquinong	La Grange	IN
Mineral Wells	Wood	WV	Mitchellsville	Sumner	TN	Monhergan Island	Lincoln	ME
Miner's Delight	Sweetwater	WY	Mitchellville	Polk	IA	Monie	Somerset	MD
Minersville	Henry	IL	Mitchellville	Prince George's	MD	Monitor	Alpine	CA
Minersville	Christian	MO	Mitchellville	Harrison	MO	Monitor	Tippecanoe	IN
Minersville	Meigs	OH	Mitchie	Monroe	IL	Monitor	Marion	OR
Minersville	Schuylkill	PA	Mittineague	Hampdon	MA	Monk's Store	Sampson	NC
Minersville	Beaver	UT	Mixersville	Franklin	IN	Monkton	Addison	VT
Minerva	Marshall	IA	Mixville	Ballard	MO	Monkton Mills	Baltimore	MD
Minerva	Mason	KY	Moberly	Randolph	MO	Monkton Ridge	Addison	VT
Minerva	Essex	NY	Mobile(c.h.)	Mobile	AL	Monmouth(c.h.)	Warren	IL
Minerva	Stark	OH	Mobley Pond	Scriven	GA	Monmouth	Adams	IN
Minetto	Oswego	NY	Moccasin	Effingham	IL	Monmouth	Jackson	IA
Mineville	Essex	NY	Mockeson	Lawrence	TN	Monmouth	Crawford	KS
Mingo	Bates	MO	Mock's Mill	Washington	VA	Monmouth	Kennebec	ME
Mingo	Champaign	OH	Mocksville(c.h.)	Davie	NC	Monmouth	Polk	OR
Mingo Flat	Randolph	WV	Modale	Harrison	IA	Monmouth	Rockbridge	VA
Ming Springs	Wright	MO	Mode	Shelby	IL	Monmouth Junction	Middlesex	NJ
Mingville	Wright	MO	Model City	Cass	MI	Monocracy	Montgomery	MD
Minier	Tazewell	IL	Modena	Stark	IL	Monocracy	Berks	PA
Mining	Morgan	MO	Modena	Mercer	MO	Monon	White	IN
Minisink	Orange	NY	Modena	Ulster	NY	Monona	Clayton	IA
Minneapolis(c.h.)	Hennepin	MN	Modena	Buffalo	WI	Monongahela City	Washington	PA
Minnega	Sedwick	KS	Modesto	Stanislaus	CA	Monroe	Tuscaloosa	AL
Minneola	Goodhue	MN	Modest Town	Accomack	VA	Monroe	Fairfield	CN
Minnequa	Bradford	PA	Moe	Douglas	MN	Monroe(c.h.)	Walton	GA
Minnereka	Mower	MN	Moffat's Station	Marion	TN	Monroe	Jasper	IA
Minneska	Cowley	KS	Moffatt's Creek	Augusta	VA	Monroe(c.h.)	Onachita	LA
Minneska	Wabashaw	MN	Moffettsville	Anderson	SC	Monroe	Waldo	ME
Minnesota City	Winona	MN	Moffitt's Grove	Guthrie	IA	Monroe	Franklin	MA
Minnesota Crossing	Renville	MN	Moffitt's Mills	Randolph	NC	Monroe(c.h.)	Monroe	MI
Minnesota Junction	Dodge	WI	Moffitt's Store	Columbia	NY	Monroe	Perry	MS
Minnesota Lake	Fairbault	MN	Mogadore	Summit	OH	Monroe	Platte	NE
Minnetonka	Hennepin	MN	Mohave City(c.h.)	Mohave	AZ	Monroe	Grafton	NH
Minnetrista	Hennepin	MN	Mohawk	Herkimer	NY	Monroe	Sussex	NJ
Minnora	Calhoun	WV	Mohawk Hill	Lewis	NY	Monroe	Orange	NY

PLACE	COUNTY	STATE	PLACE	COUNTY	STATE	PLACE	COUNTY	STATE
Monroe(c.h.)	Union	NC	Montezuma	McNairy	TN	Monument	El Paso	CO
Monroe	Butler	OH	Montfort	Grant	WI	Monument	Pike	IL
Monroe	Overton	TN	Montgomery(c.h.)	Montgomery	AL	Monument	Barnstable	MA
Monroe	Rusk	TX	Montgomery	Kane	IL	Monument House	Baltimore	MD
Monroe	Sevier	UT	Montgomery	Montgomery	KS	Moodna	Orange	NY
Monroe(c.h.)	Green	WI	Montgomery	Trigg	KY	Moodus	Middlesex	CN
Monroe Centre	Ogle	IL	Montgomery	Grant	LA	Moody's Mills	Paulding	GA
Monroe Centre	Waldo	ME	Montgomery	Hampden	MA	Moodyville	Greene	KY
Monroe Centre	Grand Traverse	MI	Montgomery	Le Sueur	MN	Mooers	Clinton	NY
Monroe Centre	Ashtabula	OH	Montgomery	Orange	NY	Mooers Forks	Clinton	NY
Monroe City	Monroe	IL	Montgomery	Montgomery	NC	Mooers' Prairie	Wright	MN
Monroe City	Monroe	MO	Montgomery	Hamilton	OH	Moon	Allegheny	PA
Monroe Draft	Greengrier	WV	Montgomery(c.h.)	Morgan	TN	Mooney	Jackson	IN
Monroe Forge	Lebanon	PA	Montgomery(c.h.)	Montgomery	TX	Moon Lake	Coahama	MS
Monroe Furnace	Jackson	OH	Montgomery	Franklin	VT	Moons	Fayette	OH
Monroe Mills	Monroe	IN	Montgomery Centre	Franklin	VT	Moon's Ranch	Tehama	CA
Monroe Mills	Knox	OH	Montgomery City	Park	CO	Moorefield	Switzerland	IN
Monroeton	Rockingham	NC	Montgomery City	Montgomery	MO	Moorefield	Nicholas	KY
Monroeton	Bradford	PA	Montgomery's Ferry	Perry	PA	Moorefield	Harrison	OH
Monroeville(c.h.)	Monroe	AL	Montgomery Spr.	Montgomery	VA	Moorefield (c.h.)	Hardy	WV
Monroeville	Allen	IN	Montgomery Square	Montgomery	PA	Moore's	Tyler	WV
Monroeville	Salem	NJ	Montgomery's Stat.	Daviess	IN	Mooresborough	Cleveland	NC
Monroeville	Huron	OH	Monticello(c.h.)	Drew	AR	Mooresburgh	Montour	PA
Monroeville	Allegheny	PA	Monticello	Napa	CA	Mooresburgh	Hawkins	TN
Monroe Works	Orange	NY	Monticello(c.h.)	Jefferson	FL	Moore's Creek	New Hanover	NC
Monrovia	Morgan	IN	Monticello(c.h.)	Jasper	GA	Moore's Creek	Monroe	WS
Monrovia	Frederick	MD	Monticello(c.h.)	Piatt	IL	Moore's Flat	Nevada	CA
Monsey	Rockland	NY	Monticello(c.h.)	White	IN	Moore's Hill	Dearborn	IN
Monson	Piscataquis	ME	Monticello	Jones	IA	Moore's Mill	Dutchess	NY
Monson	Hampden	MA	Monticello	Johnson	KS	Moore's Ordinary	Prince Edward	VA
Montague	Franklin	MA	Monticello(c.h.)	Wayne	KY	Moore's Prairie	Jefferson	IL
Montague	Muskegon	MI	Monticello(c.h.)	Aroostook	ME	Moore's Salr Works	Jefferson	OH
Montague	Sussex	NJ	Monticello(c.h.)	Lawrence	MS	Moore's Station	Butte	CA
Montague(c.h.)	Montague	TX	Monticello	Wright	MN	Moore's Store	Clay	TN
Montague	Essex	VA	Monticello(c.h.)	Lewis	MO	Moore's Store	Shenandoah	VA
Montague City	Franklin	MA	Monticello	Sullivan	NY	Moorestown	Burlington	NJ
Montalto	Franklin	PA	Monticello	Guilford	NC	Moorestown	Northhampton	PA
Montana	Boone	IA	Monticello	Armstrong	PA	Mooresville	Limestone	AL
Montana	Labette	KS	Monticello(c.h.)	Fairfield	SC	Mooresville	Morgan	IN
Montana	Beaver Head	MT	Monticello(c.h.)	Cowlitz	WA	Mooresville	Livingston	MO
Montana	Warren	NJ	Monticello	Green	WI	Mooresville	Iredell	NC
Montandon	Northumberland	PA	Montmorence	Barnwell	SC	Mooresville	Monongalia	WV
Montauk	Dent	MO	Montmorency	Tippecanoe	IN	Moore's Vineyard	Bartholomew	IN
Montaview	Montgomery	KY	Montongo	Drew	AR	Mooreville	Itawamba	MS
Montclair	Essex	NJ	Montowese	New Haven	CN	Moorhead	Allegheny	PA
Monte	Los Angeles	CA	Montpelier	Blackford	IN	Moorhead	Freestone	TX
Montello(c.h.)	Marquette	WI	Montpelier	Adair	KY	Moorheadville	Erie	PA
Monterey(c.h.)	Monterey	CA	Montpelier	Chickasaw	MS	Mooringsport	Caldo	LA
Monterey	Calhoun	IL	Montpelier	Williams	OH	Moorland	Wayne	OH
Monterey	Pulaski	IN	Montpelier	Rich	UT	Moorman's River	Albemarle	VA
Monterey	Davis	IA	Montpelier(c.h.)	Washington	VT	Moorton	Kent	DE
Monterey	Owen	KY	Montpelier	Hanover	VA	Moorville	Tama	IA
Monterey	Berkshire	MA	Montpelier	Kewaunee	WI	Moose Meadow	Tolland	KN
Monterey	Allegan	MI	Montra	Shelby	OH	Moose River	Somerset	ME
Monterey	Richardson	NE	Montreal	Nelson	VA	Mooshaunee	Moore	NC
Monterey	Clermont	OH	Montrose	Lee	IA	Moosup	Windham	CN
Monterey	Berks	PA	Montrose	Montgomery	MD	Mora(c.h.)	Mora	NM
Monterey	Abbeville	SC	Montrose	Genessee	MI	Moral	Shelby	IN
Monterey(c.h.)	Highland	VA	Montrose	Wright	MN	Morales	Jackson	TX
Monterey	Waukesha	WI	Montrose	Jasper	MS	Moravia	Appanoose	IA
Montesano(c.h.)	Chehalis	WA	Montrose	Henry	MO	Moravia	Caynga	NY
Montevallo	Shelby	AL	Montrose	Westchester	NY	Moravia	Lawrence	PA
Montevallo	Vernon	MO	Montrose	Summit	OH	Mordansville	Columbia	PA
Montevideo(c.h.)	Chippewa	MN	Montrose(c.h.)	Susquehanna	PA	Morean Station	Saratoga	NY
Monte Vista	Choctaw	MS	Montrose Depot	Susquehanna	PA	Moreauville	Avoyelles	LA
Montez	Cass	IN	Montrose (c.h.)	Westermoreland	VA	Morehead(c.h.)	Rowan	KY
Montezuma	Tuolumne	CA	Monturesville	Lycoming	PA	Morehead City	Carteret	NC
Montezuma	Summit	CO	Montvale Springs	Blount	TN	Morehouseville	Hamilton	NY
Montezuma	Macon	GA	Montville	New London	CN	Moreland	Pope	AR
Montezuma	Pike	IL	Montville	Waldo	ME	Moreland	Lycoming	PA
Montezuma	Parke	IN	Montville	Berkshire	MA	Morell's Mill	Sullivan	TN
Montezuma(c.h.)	Poweshiek	IA	Montville	Morris	NJ	Morenci	Lenawee	MI
Montezuma	Cayuga	NY	Montville	Geanga	OH	Moresville	Delaware	NY

PLACE NAMES OF THE UNITED STATES

PLACE	COUNTY	STATE	PLACE	COUNTY	STATE	PLACE	COUNTY	STATE
Moretown	Washington	VT	Morrisonville	Christian	IL	Motier	Pendleton	KY
Moretz Mills	Watauga	NC	Morrisonville	Clinton	NY	Motley	Lancaster	PA
Morgan	Lake	CA	Morris Ridge	Harrison	NO	Mott	Angelina	TX
Morgan(c.h.)	Calhoun	GA	Morris Run	Tioga	PA	Mott Haven	Westchester	NY
Morgan	Montgomery	KS	Morris Station	Quitman	GA	Mottomosa	Atasosa	TX
Morgan	Pendleton	KY	Morristown	Henry	IL	Mott's Bridge	Clarendon	SC
Morgan	Marquette	MI	Morristown	Shelby	IN	Mott's Corner	Tompkins	NY
Morgan	Ashtabula	OH	Morristown	Rice	MN	Mottville	St. Joseph	MI
Morgan(c.h.)	Morgan	UT	Morristown	Cass	MO	Mottville	Onondaga	NY
Morgan	Orleans	VT	Morrisville(c.h.)	Madison	NY	Moulton(c.h.)	Lawrence	AL
Morganfield(c.h.)	Union	KY	Morrisville	Wake	NC	Moulton	Shelby	IL
Morgan's Fork	Franklin	MS	Morris Town	Moore	NC	Moulton	Appanose	IA
Morgan's Glade	Preston	WV	Morristown	Belmont	OH	Moulton	Auglaize	OH
Morgan's Mills	Union	NC	Morristown(c.h.)	Hamblen	TN	Moulton	Lavaca	TX
Morgan Spring	Perry	AL	Morristown	Lamoile	VT	Moultonborough	Carroll	NH
Morgansville	Morgan	OH	Morrisville	Calhoun	AL	Moultonville	Madison	IL
Morganton(c.h.)	Fannin	GA	Morrisville(c.h.)	Madison	NY	Moultonville	Carroll	NH
Morganton(c.h.)	Burke	NC	Morrisville	Wake	NC	Moultrie(c.h.)	Colquitt	GA
Morgantown	Morgan	IN	Morrisville	Clinton	OH	Moultrie	Columbiana	OH
Morgantown	Morgan	IN	Morrisville	Bucks	PA	Mound	Madison	LA
Morgantown(c.h.)	Butler	KY	Morrisville	Lamoile	VT	Mound City	Crittenden	AR
Morgantown	Berks	PA	Morrisville	Fanquier	VA	Mound City(c.h.)	Pulaski	IL
Morgantown	London	TN	Morrisville	Dane	WI	Mound City(c.h.)	Linn	KS
Morgantown(c.h.)	Monongalia	WV	Morro	San Luis Obispo	CA	Mound City	Holt	MO
Morgan Valley	Wyoming	WV	Morrosenian	Robeson	NC	Mound Place	Coahoma	MS
Morganville	Dade	GA	Morrow	Warren	OH	Mound Prairie	Houston	MN
Morganville	Hillsdale	MI	Morrow's Station	Clayton	GA	Mounds	Vernon	MO
Morganville	Monmouth	NJ	Morrowville	Jefferson	AL	Mound Springs	Jackson	WI
Morganville	Genesee	NY	Morse	Johnson	OH	Mound Station	Brown	IL
Morganville	Polk	TX	Morse's	Grave	KY	Moundsville(c.h.)	Marshall	WV
Morganza	St. Mary's	MD	Morse's Mill	Jefferson	MO	Mound Valley	Labette	KS
Morganzia	Point Coupee	LA	Morseville	Schoharie	NY	Moundville	Marquette	WI
Moriah	Essex	NY	Morsston	Sullivan	NY	Mount Adams	Arkansas	AR
Moriah Centre	Essex	NY	Morton	Tazewell	IL	Mount Ariel	Allen	KY
Morian	Colfax	NE	Morton	Putnam	IN	Mount Etna	Berks	PA
Moriches	Suffolk	NY	Morton	Scott	MS	Mountain	Berks	PA
Morley	Mecosta	MI	Morton	Delaware	PA	Mountain	Morgan	UT
Morley	Scott	MO	Morton's Corners	Erie	NY	Mountain	Monroe	WI
Morley	St. Lawrence	NY	Morton's Store	Alamance	NC	Mountain City	Elko	NV
Morman Island	Sacramento	CA	Mortonsville	Clinton	IN	Mountain City	Hays	TX
Morman Mills	Burnet	TX	Mortonsville	Woodford	KY	Mountain Cove	Fayette	WV
Morning Sun	Louisa	IA	Mortonville	Chester	PA	Mountain Creek	Catawba	NC
Morning Sun	Preble	OH	Morven	Auson	NC	Mountain Creek	Cumberland	PA
Mornington	Webster	MO	Morven	Amelia	VA	Mountain Creek	Warren	TN
Morning View	Kenton	KY	Moscow	Sanford	AL	Mountain Eagle	Centre	PA
Morning View	Belmont	OH	Moscow	Union	IL	Mountain Falls	Frederick	VA
Moro	Monroe	AR	Moscow	Rush	IN	Mountain Grove	Bath	VA
Moro	Madison	IL	Moscow	Muscatine	IA	Mountain Hill	Harris	GA
Moro	Aroostook	ME	Moscow	Hickman	KY	Mountain Home	Lawrence	AL
Moro Bay	Bradley	AR	Moscow	Hillsdale	ME	Mountain Home	Marion	AR
Morocco	Newton	IN	Moscow	Freeborn	MN	Mountain Home	Monroe	PA
Moroni	San Pete	UT	Moscow	Kemper	MS	Mountain Home	Bell	TX
Morrell	Huntingdon	PA	Moscow	Livingston	NY	Mountain Home	Hardy	WV
Morrill	Brown	KS	Moscow	Clermont	OH	Mountain House	Yam Hill	OR
Morrill	Jackson	KY	Moscow	Luzerne	PA	Mountain Lake	Cottonwood	MN
Morrill	Waldo	ME	Moscow	Fayette	TN	Mountain Lake	Bradford	PA
Morris	Litchfield	CN	Moscow	Polk	TX	Mountain Lake	Giles	VA
Morris(c.h.)	Grundy	IL	Moscow	Iowa	WI	Mountain Ranch	Calaveras	CA
Morris	Ripley	IN	Moscow Mills	Morgan	OH	Mountain Spring	Carroll	AR
Morris	Stevens	MN	Mosel	Sheboygan	WI	Mountain Spring	Martin	IN
Morris	Otsego	NY	Moselle	Franklin	MO	Mountain Top	Luzerne	PA
Morris	Hanover	VA	Moselin	Berks	PA	Mountain Valley	Luzerne	PA
Morrisania	Westchester	NY	Mosherville	Hillsdale	MI	Mountain View	Santa Clara	CA
Morris Corners	Crawford	PA	Mosherville	Saratoga	MY	Mountain View	Passaic	NJ
Morris Cross Roads	Fayette	PA	Mosiertown	Crawford	PA	Mountainville	Hunterdon	NJ
Morrisdale	Clearfield	PA	Mosinee	Marathon	WI	Mountainville	Lehigh	PA
Morris Hill	Alleghany	VA	Moss Bluff	Liberty	TX	Mount Airy	Carroll	MD
Morrison(c.h.)	Whitesides	IL	Mossing Ford	Charlotte	VA	Mount Airy	Randolph	MO
Morrison	Gasconade	MO	Moss Point	Jackson	MS	Mount Airy	Surry	NC
Morrison	Luzerne	PA	Moss Run	Washington	OH	Mount Airy	Hamilton	OH
Morrison	Warren	TN	Mossville	Peoria	IL	Mount Airy	Washington	PA
Morrison	Brown	WI	Mossy Creek	Jefferson	TN	Mount Airy	Bledsoe	TN
Morrison's Tan Yd	Mecklenburgh	NC	Mossy Creek	Augusta	VA	Mount Airy	Pittsylvania	VA

PLACE NAMES OF THE UNITED STATES

PLACE	COUNTY	STATE	PLACE	COUNTY	STATE	PLACE	COUNTY	STATE
Mount Algor	Jackson	IA	Mount Hope	Cass	NE	Mount Pleasant	Marshall	MS
Mount Alvis	Blount	AL	Mount Hope	Morris	NJ	Mount Pleasant	Gentry	MO
Mount Andrew	Barbour	AL	Mount Hope	Orange	NY	Mount Pleasant	Cass	NE
Mount Athos	Campbell	VA	Mount Hope	Holmes	OH	Mount Pleasant	Hunterdon	NJ
Mount Auburn	Christian	IL	Mount Hope	Lancaster	PA	Mount Pleasant	Oswego	NY
Mount Auburn	Shelby	IN	Mount Hope	Grant	WI	Mount Pleasant	Cabarrus	NC
Mount Auburn	Benton	IA	Mount Hor	Bracken	KY	Mount Pleasant	Jefferson	OH
Mount Auburn	Middlesex	MA	Mount Horeb	Dane	WI	Mount Pleasant	Westmoreland	PA
Mount Ayr(c.h.)	Ringgold	IA	Mount Ida(c.h.)	Montgomery	AR	Mount Pleasant	Laurens	SC
Mount Bethel	Northampton	PA	Mount Ida	Grant	WI	Mount Pleasant	Maury	TN
Mount Blanchard	Hancock	OH	Mount Idaho	Nez Perces	IA	Mt Pleasant(c.h.)	Titus	TX
Mount Blanco	Meigs	OH	Mount Jackson	Lawrence	PA	Mount Pleasant	San Pete	UT
Mount Bullion	Mariposa	CA	Mount Jackson	Shenandoah	VA	Mount Pleasant	Spottsylvania	VA
Mount Calm	Limestone	TX	Mount Jefferson	Lee	AL	Mt Pleasant Mills	Snyder	PA
Mount Carmel	New Haven	CN	Mount Joy	Scott	IA	Mount Polk	Calhoun	AL
Mount Carmel(c.h.)	Wabash	IL	Mount Joy	Lancaster	PA	Mount Pulaski	Logan	IL
Mount Carmel	Franklin	IN	Mount Joy	Union	SC	Mount Prospect	Crawford	IN
Mount Carmel	Carroll	IA	Mount Judea	Newton	AR	Mount Read	Monroe	NY
Mount Carmel	Crawford	KS	Mount Kisco	Westchester	NY	Mount Repose	Clermont	OH
Mount Carmel	Fleming	KY	Mount Landing	Essex	VA	Mount Riga	Dutchess	NY
Mount Carmel	Baltimore	MD	Mount Laurel	Burlington	NJ	Mount Rock	Cumberland	PA
Mount Carmel	Covington	MS	Mount Laurel	Halifax	VA	Mount Rozell	Limestone	AL
Mount Carmel	Clermont	OH	Mount Lebanon	Bienville	LA	Mount Royal	York	PA
Mount Carmel	Northumberland	PA	Mount Lebanon	Columbia	NY	Mount Salem	Sussex	NJ
Mount Carmel	Wilson	TN	Mount Lebanon	Allegheny	PA	Mount Salem	Putnam	WV
Mount Carmel	Smith	TX	Mount Liberty	Brown	IN	Mount Savage	Carter	KY
Mount Carmel	Halifax	VA	Mount Liberty	Knox	OH	Mount Savage	Alleghany	MD
Mount Carrick	Monroe	OH	Mount Meigs	Montgomery	AL	Mount Shasta	Siskiyou	CA
Mount Carroll(c.h.)	Carroll	IL	Mount Meridian	Putnam	IN	Mount Sherman	La Rue	KY
Mount Chesnut	Butler	PA	Mount Meridian	Augusta	VA	Mount Sidney	Agusta	VA
Mt.Clemens(c.h.)	Macomb	MI	Mount Moriah(c.h.)	Nevada	AR	Mount Sinai	Suffolk	NY
Mount Clifton	Washington	KS	Mount Moriah	Kent	DE	Mount Solon	Agusta	VA
Mount Clifton	Shenandoah	VA	Mount Moriah	Brown	IN	Mount Sterling	Chotaw	AL
Mount Clinton	Rockingham	VA	Mount Moriah	Harrison	MO	Mount Sterling(c.h.)	Brown	IL
Mount Comfort	Hancock	IN	Mount Morris	Ogle	IL	Mount Sterling	Switzerland	IN
Mount Crawford	Rockingham	VA	Mount Morris	Livingston	NY	Mount Sterling	Van Buren	IA
Mount Croghan	Chesterfield	SC	Mount Morris	Greene	PA	Mount Sterling	Bourbon	KS
Mount Deseret	Hancock	ME	Mount Morris	Waushara	WI	Mount Sterling(c.h.)	Montgomery	KY
Mount Eaton	Wayne	OH	Mount Morris Stat.	Genesee	MI	Mount Sterling	Madison	OH
Mount Eden	Alameda	CA	Mount Moarne	Irdell	NC	Mount Sterling	Crawford	WI
Mount Eden	Spencer	KY	Mount Murphy	Pocahontas	WV	Mount Storm	Grant	WV
Mount Elba	Lincoln	AR	Mount Nebo	Miami	KS	Mount Summit	Henry	IN
Mount Enterprise	Cedar	MO	Mount Nebo	Yardkin	NC	Mount Sumner	Jo Daviess	IL
Mount Enterprise	Rusk	TX	Mount Nebo	Lancaster	PA	Mount Sylvan	Smith	TN
Mount Eolia	Towns	GA	Mount Niles	St. Clair	AL	Mount Tabor	Forsyth	NC
Mount Ephraim	Camden	NJ	Mount Olive	Coosa	AL	Mount Tabor	Vernon	WI
Mount Ephraim	Noble	OH	Mount Olive(c.h.)	Izard	AR	Mount Tizah	Person	NC
Mount Eric	Wayne	IL	Mount Olive	Macoupin	IL	Mount Top	York	PA
Mount Etna	Huntington	IN	Mount Olive	Wayne	NC	Mount Ula	Rowan	NC
Mount Etna	Adams	IA	Mount Olive	Clermont	OH	Mount Union	Stark	OH
Mount Florence	Jefferson	KS	Mount Olive	Shenandoah	VA	Mount Union	Huntingdon	PA
Mount Freedom	Pendleton	WV	Mount Olivet(c.h.)	Robertson	KY	Mount Upton	Chenango	NY
Mount Gallagher	Laurens	SC	Mount Orab	Brown	OH	Mount Vernon(c.h.)	Washington	AL
Mount Gilead	Mason	KY	Mount Palatine	Putnam	IL	Mount Vernon(c.h.)	Jefferson	CO
Mount Gilread	Montgomery	NC	Mount Parnel	Franklin	PA	Mount Vernon(c.h.)	Montgomery	GA
Mount Gilread(c.h.)	Morrow	OH	Mount Parthenon	Newton	AR	Mount Vernon(c.h.)	Jefferson	IL
Mount Gilread	Loudoun	VA	Mount Perry	Perry	OH	Mount Vernon(c.h.)	Posey	IN
Mount Healthy	Bartholomew	IN	Mount Pinson	Jefferson	AL	Mount Vernon	Linn	IA
Mount Healthy	Hamilton	OH	Mount Pisgah	La Grange	IN	Mount Vernon(c.h.)	Rock Castle	KY
Mount Healthy	Somerset	PA	Mount Pisgah	Clermont	OH	Mount Vernon	Kennebec	ME
Mount Herbron	Greene	AL	Mount Pisgah	Clay	TN	Mount Vernon	Somerset	MD
Mount Heron	Darke	OH	Mount Pisgah	Monroe	WI	Mount Vernon	Macomb	MI
Mount Hilliard	Bullock	AL	Mount Pleasant	Monroe	AL	Mount Vernon(c.h.)	Lawrence	MO
Mount Holly(c.h.)	Burlington	NJ	Mount Pleasant	Carroll	AR	Mount Vernon	Hillsborough	NH
Mount Holly	Clermont	OH	Mount Pleasant	New Castle	DE	Mount Vernon	Westchester	NY
Mount Holly	Rutland	VT	Mount Pleasant	Gadsden	FL	Mount Vernon	Rowan	NC
Mount Holly Spr.	Cumberland	PA	Mount Pleasant	Wayne	GA	Mount Vernon(c.h.)	Knox	OH
Mount Hope	Lawrence	AL	Mount Pleasant	Union	IL	Mount Vernon	Chester	PA
Mount Hope	Tolland	CN	Mount Pleasant	Perry	IN	Mount Vernon	Providence	RI
Mount Hope	De Kalb	IN	Mt Plmasant(c.h.)	Henry	IA	Mount Vernon	Monroe	TN
Mount Hope	Delaware	IA	Mount Pleasant	Atchison	KS	Mount Vernon	Dane	WI
Mount Hope	Copiah	MS	Mount Pleasant	Frederick	MD	Mt Vernon Forge	Rockingham	VA
Mount Hope	La Fayette	MO	Mt Pleasant(c.h.)	Isbella	MI	Mt Vernon Tannery	Frederick	VA

PLACE	COUNTY	STATE
Mount Victory	Hardin	OH
Mount View	Benton	MO
Mountville	Troup	GA
Mountville	Effingham	IL
Mountville	Lancaster	PA
Mountville	Londoun	Va
Mount Vinco	Buckingham	VA
Mount Vision	Otsego	NY
Mount Vitio	Bullitt	KY
Mount Washington	Bullitt	KY
Mount Washington	Baltimore	MD
Mount Washington	Hamilton	OH
Mount Washington	Alleghany	PA
Mount Willing	Edgefield	SC
Mount Wolf	York	PA
Mount Zion	Hancock	GA
Mount Zion	Macon	IL
Mount Zion	Van Buren	IA
Mount Zion	Grant	KY
Mount Zion	Simpson	MS
Mount Zion	Leganon	PA
Mount Zion	Tipton	TN
Mount Zion	Campbell	VA
Mount Zion	Juneau	WI
Mouse Creek	McMinn	TN
Mouse's	Grant	WV
Mouth of Indian	Monreo	WV
Mouth of Laurel	Lewis	KY
Mouth of Pond	Pike	KY
Mouth of Scary	Putnam	WV
Mouth of Seneca	Pendleton	WV
Mouth of Wilson	Grayson	VA
Mouth of Wolf	Clay	TN
Mouth Short Creek	Boone	WV
Moweaqua	Shelby	IL
Mower City	Mower	MN
Mowersville	Franklin	PA
Mowry's Mills	Bedford	PA
Mowersville	Franklin	PA
Moyer's Store	Bucks	PA
Muchinippe	Logan	OH
Mud Bridge	Cabell	WV
Mud Creek	St. Clair	IL
Mud Crek	Eaton	MI
Muddy Creek	Pueblo	CO
Muddy Creek	Lancaster	PA
Muddy Creek	Preston	WV
Muddy Creek Forks	York	PA
Muddy Fork	Clark	IN
Muddy Lake	Livingston	MO
Mud Lick	Jefferson	IN
Mud Lick	Monroe	KY
Mud Lick	Chatham	NC
Muhlenburgh	Luzerne	PA
Muir	Ionia	MI
Muirkirk	Prince George's	MD
Muirton	Grundy	MO
Mukiteo	Snohomish	WA
Mukwonago	Wankesha	WI
Mulberry	Clinton	IN
Mulberry	Bates	MO
Mulberry	Wilkes	NC
Mulberry	Clermont	OH
Mulberry	York	PA
Mulberry	Lincoln	TN
Mulberry Corners	Geauga	OH
Mulberry Gap	Hancock	TN
Mulberry Grove	Harris	GA
Mulberry Grove	Bond	IL
Mulberry Grove	Crawford	KS
Muldon	Monroe	MS
Mule Creek	Cumberland	IL
Mulford	Cook	IL

PLACE	COUNTY	STATE
Mulkeyton	Franklin	IL
Mull Grove	Catawba	NC
Mullica Hill	Gloucester	NJ
Mullin's	Baker	AL
Mullin's Depot	Marion	SC
Mulloy's	Robertson	TN
Mumford	Monroe	NY
Mummasburgh	Adams	PA
Mumre Lund	Kandiyohi	MN
Muncie(c.h.)	Delaware	IN
Muncie	Wyandotte	KS
Muncie	Vernon	WI
Muney	Lycoming	PA
Muncy Bottom	Sullivan	PA
Muncy Station	Lycoming	PA
Mundy	Genesee	MI
Mumford	Talladega	AL
Munfordsville(c.h.)	Hart	KY
Mungen	Wood	OH
Munger's Mill	Reynolds	MO
Mungerville	Shiawassee	MI
Munising	Schoolcraft	MI
Munna	Chotaw Nation	IT
Munnsville	Coshocton	OH
Munntown	Washington	PA
Munonville	Cheshire	NH
Munster	Cambria	PA
Munsville	Madison	NY
Munterville	Wapello	IA
Murdock	Warren	OH
Murdocksville	Washington	PA
Murtressborgh(c.h.)	Jackson	IL
Murtreesborough	Hartford	NC
Murtreesborgh(c.h.)	Rutherford	TN
Murphey(c.h.)	Cherokee	NC
Murphey's Creek	Lewis	WV
Murhpree's Valley	Blout	VA
Murphy's	Calaveras	CA
Murphysborgh(c.h.)	Jackson	IL
Murphy's Mill	Wood	WV
Murphysville	Mason	KY
Murray	Wells	IN
Murray	Clark	IA
Murray(c.h.)	Callaway	KY
Murray	Orleans	NY
Murraysville	Jackson	WV
Murrayville	Morgan	IL
Murrinsville	Butler	PA
Murrysville	Westmoreland	PA
Muscatine(c.h.)	Muscatine	IA
Muscle Fork	Chariton	MO
Musceoda	Grant	WI
Musconetcong	Warren	NJ
Muscotah	Atchison	KS
Muse's Bottom	Jackson	WV
Museville	Pittsylvania	VA
Mush Creek	Greenville	SC
Muskego Centre	Waukesha	WI
Muskegon(c.h.)	Muskegon	MI
Muskootink	Chsago	MN
Musson	Iberville	LA
Mutual	Champaign	OH
Myerhoeffer's Store	Rockingham	VA
Myers	Howard	MO
Myersburgh	Bradford	PA
Myer's Valley	Pottawatomie	KS
Myersville	Vermillion	IL
Myersville	Frederick	MD
Myersville	Williamsburgh	SC
Myra	Washington	WI
Myrickville	Bristol	MA
Myron	Allamakee	IA
Myrtle	Knox	MO

PLACE	COUNTY	STATE
Myrtle Creek	Douglas	OR
Mystic	New London	CN
Mystic Bridge	New London	CN
Mystic River	New London	CN
Naches	Houston	TX
Nachusa	Lee	IL
Nacogdoches(c.h.)	Nacogdoches	TX
Nacoochec	White	GA
Naff's	Franklin	VA
Nahant	Essex	MA
Nahama	Delta	MI
Nahunta	Wayne	NC
Nail's Creek	Banks	GA
Nairn	Scioto	OH
Namaqua	Larimer	CO
Nanaupa	Fond de Lac	WI
Nancy	Pottawatomie	KS
Nanjemoy	Charles	MD
Nankin	Wayne	MI
Nankin	Ashland	OH
Nannie	Floyd	GA
Nansemond	Nansemond	VA
Nanticoke	Wicomico	MD
Nanticoke	Luzerne	PA
Nantucket(c.h.)	Nantucket	MA
Nanuet	Rockland	NY
Nanomi	Walker	GA
Napa City(c.h.)	Nappa	CA
Napanock	Ulster	NY
Naperville	Du Page	IL
Naples	Scott	IL
Naples	Cumberland	ME
Naples	Ontario	NY
Napoleon(c.h.)	Desha	AR
Napoleon	Ripley	IN
Napoleon	Gallatin	KY
Napoleon	Jackson	MI
Napoleon	La Fayette	MO
Napoleon(c.h.)		M O
Napoli	Cattaraugus	NY
Narragausett	Washington	RI
Narragansett Pier	Washington	RI
Narraguagus	Washington	ME
Narrows Bridge	Daviess	KY
Narrowsburgh	Sullivan	NY
Narrows Creek	Macon	MO
Nash Depot	Vanderburgh	IN
Nashtotah Mission	Waukesha	WI
Nashport	Muskingham	OH
Nashua	Chickasaw	IA
Nashua	Hillsborough	NH
Nashville	El Dorado	CA
Nashville(c.h.)	Berrien	GA
Nashville(c.h.)	Washington	IL
Nashville(c.h.)	Brown	IN
Nashville	Barry	MI
Nashville	Barton	MO
Nashville	Chautauqua	NY
Nashville(c.h.)	Nash	NC
Nashville	Holmes	OH
Nashville(c.h.)	Davidson	TN
Nashville Centre	Martin	MN
Nason's Mille	York	ME
Nasonville	Wood	WI
Nassau	Nassau	FL
Natchez	Martin	IN
Natchez(c.h.)	Natchitoches	LA
Natchitoches(c.h.)	Natchitoches	LA
Natic	Middlesex	MA
Natic	Kent	RI
National	Clayton	IA
National City	San Diego	CA

PLACE NAMES OF THE UNITED STATES

PLACE	COUNTY	STATE	PLACE	COUNTY	STATE	PLACE	COUNTY	STATE
Nat'l Milit'y Asylum	Kennebec	ME	Nelson	Tioga	PA	New Albany	Bradford	PA
Nat'l Milit'y Asylum	Montgomery	OH	Nelson	Hardin	TN	New Albion	Cattaraugus	NY
Natividad	Monterey	CA	Nelson	Buffalo	WI	New Alexander	Columbia	OH
Natrona	Mason	IL	Nelson Furnace	Nelson	KY	New Alexanderia	Jefferson	OH
Natrona	Mason	IL	Nelson Point	Flumas	CA	New Alexandria	Westmoreland	PA
Natrona	Allegheny	PA	Nelsonville	Franklin	AL	New Alsace	Dearborn	IN
Natural Bridge	Jefferson	NY	Nelsonville	Charleviox	MI	New Alstead	Cheshire	NH
Natural Bridge	Rockbridge	VA	Nelsonville	Marion	MO	New Amsterdan	Harrison	IN
Naubuc	Hartford	CN	Nelsonville	Athens	OH	New Amsterdan	La Crosse	WI
Naugart	Marathon	WI	Nelsonville	Portage	WI	New Anhalt	Burleson	TX
Naugatuck	New Haven	CN	Nelta Boc	Sevier	AR	New Antioch	Clinton	OH
Naubrightville	Morris	NJ	Nemaha City	Nemaha	NE	Newark	New CAstle	DE
Naumburgh	Lewis	NY	Nenno	Washington	WI	Newark	Kendall	IL
Nautrill	Black Hawk	IA	Neodesha	Wilson	KS	Newark	Greene	IN
Nauvoo	Hancock	IL	Neodesha	Wilson	KS	Newark	Wilson	KS
Nauvoo	Tioga	PA	Neoga	Cumberland	IL	Newark	Worcester	MD
Nauvarino	Onondaga	NY	Neola	Pottawattomie	IA	Newark	Gratiot	MI
Navarre	Stark	OH	Neosho	Allen	KS	Newark	Knox	MO
Navarro Ridge	Mendocino	CA	Neosho(c.h.)	Newton	MO	Newark(c.h.)	Essex	NJ
Navasink	Monmouth	NJ	Neosho	Dodge	WI	Newark	Wayne	NY
Navasota	Grimes	TX	Neosho Falls(c.h.)	Woodson	KS	Newark(c.h.)	Licking	OH
Navan	Winneshick	IA	Neosho Rapids	Lyon	KS	Newark	White	TN
Navidad	Jackson	TX	Nepaug	Lithfield	CN	Newark	Caledonia	VT
Nayatt Point	Bristol	RI	Neperan	Westchester	NY	Newark	Wirt	WV
Naylor	Lowndes	GA	Nepeuskun	Winnebago	WI	Newark Valley	Tioga	NY
Nazareth	Northampton	PA	Neponset	Bureau	IL	New Ashford	Berkshire	MA
Neabsco Mills	Prince William	VA	Neposet Village	Norfolk	MA	New Athens	St. Clair	IL
Nealery's Corner	Penobscot	ME	Neptawah	Sumner	KS	New Athens	Harrison	OH
Nealsville	McDowell	NC	Neptune	Mercer	OH	New Athens	Clarion	PA
Nearman	Wyandotte	KS	Neptune	Richland	WI	New Auburn	Sibley	MN
Neath	Bradford	PA	Ner-noh-tah-he	Cherokee Nat.	IT	Newaygo(c.h.)	Newaygo	MI
Neatsville	Adair	KY	Nero	Isabella	MI	New Baden	Clinton	IL
Nebett's Landing	Bolivar	MS	Nero	Washington	NE	New Baltimore	Wayne	IL
Nebo	Hopkins	KY	Nero	Manitowoc	WI	New Baltimore	Mascomb	MI
Nebo	Laclede	MO	Nesbit's Station	De Soto	MS	New Baltimore	Greene	NY
Nebraska	Scott	AR	Nescopeck	Luzerne	PA	New Baltimore	Stark	OH
Nebraska	Jennings	IN	Neshaminy	Bucks	PA	New Baltimore	Somerset	PA
Nebraska	Pickaway	OH	Neshanic	Somerset	NJ	New Baltimore	Fanquier	VA
Nebraska	Forest	PA	Neshannock Falls	Lawrence	PA	New Barden	Tippah	MS
Nebraska	Jefferson	TN	Neshkoro	Marquette	WI	New Bavaria	Henry	OH
Nebraska	Appomattox	VA	Nesquehoning	Carbon	PA	New Bedford	Bureau	IL
Nebraska City(c.h.)	Otoe	NE	Nestocton	Tillamook	OR	New Bedford	Bristol	MA
Neccedah	Juneau	WI	Nestorville	Barbour	WV	New Bedford	Monmouth	NJ
Needham	Norfolk	MA	Nestarus	Tillamook	OR	New Bedford	Coshecton	OH
Needham's Station	Johnson	IN	Netaawaka	Jackson	KS	New Bedford	Lawrence	PA
Needy	Clackamas	OR	Netherland	Overton	TN	New Bellsville	Brown	IN
Needy's Landing	Cape Giradeau	MO	Nettle Carrier	Overton	TN	Newberg	Yam Hill	OR
Neelyville	Morgan	IL	Nettle Lake	Williams	OH	New Berlin	Sangamon	IL
Neenab	Winnebago	WI	Nettle Ridge	Patrick	VA	New Berlin	Chenango	NY
Neersville	Loudoun	VA	Nettleton	Marion	MO	New Berlin	Stark	OH
Neese's Store	Fayette	TX	Nettletonville	Caldwell	MO	New Berlin	Union	PA
Neff	Randolph	IN	Neuchatel	Nemaha	KS	New Berlin	Waukesha	WI
Neffs	Lehigh	PA	Neutral City	Cherokee	KS	New Berlin Centre	Chenango	NY
Neff's Mills	Huntingdon	PA	Nevada	Livingston	IL	Newborn	Hale	AL
Neffsville	Lancaster	PA	Nevada	Tipton	IN	Newborn	Jersey	IL
Negaunee	Marquette	MI	Nevada(c.h.)	Story	IA	Newborn	Bartholomew	IN
Negro Foot	Hanover	VA	Nevada	Mercer	KY	Newborn	Marion	IA
Negro Hill	White	AR	Nevada	Mower	MN	Newborn	Dyer	TN
Nehalem	Clatsop	OR	Nevada(c.h.)	Vernon	MO	Newborn(c.h.)	Pulaski	VA
Neil's Creek	Jefferson	IN	Nevada	Wyandot	OH	New Berne or		
Neil's Creek	Steuben	NY	Nevada City(c.h.)	Nevada	CA	Newborn(c.h.)	Craven	NC
Neilsville(c.h.)	Clark	WI	Nevada City	Madison	MT	Newberry	Greene	IN
Nekama	Winnebago	WI	Nevada Mills	Steuben	IN	Newberry	Lycoming	PA
Nekoma	Henry	IL	Neversink	Sullivan	NY	Newberry(c.h.)	Newberry	SC
Nellie	Ashley	AR	Neville	Wionna	MN	Newberrytown	York	PA
Nelly's Ford	Nelson	VA	Neville	Clermont	OH	New Bethlehem	Clarion	PA
Nelson	Lee	IL	Nevin	Highland	OH	New Bloomfield	Callaway	MO
Nelson	Vigo	IN	Nevinville	Adams	IA	New Bloomfld(c.h.)	Perry	PA
Nelson	Munlenburg	KY	New Alba	Winneshick	IA	New Bloomfieldton	Marion	OH
Nelson	Kent	MI	New Albany(c.h.)	Floyd	IN	New Boston	Windham	CN
Nelson	Cheshire	NH	New Albany	Wilson	KS	New Boston	Lee	IA
Nelson	Madison	NY	New Albany(c.h.)	Union	MS	New Boston	Berkshire	MA
Nelson	Portage	OH	New Albany	Mahoning	OH	New Boston	Wayne	MI

PLACE NAMES OF THE UNITED STATES

PLACE	COUNTY	STATE
New Boston	Winona	MN
New Boston	Macon	MO
New Boston	Hillsborough	NH
New Boston	Henry	TN
New Braintree	Worcester	MA
New Branch	Monmouth	NJ
New Braunfells(c.h.)	Comal	TX
New Bremen	Cook	IL
New Bremen	Auglaize	OH
New Bridge	Lumpkin	GA
New Bridge	Bergen	NJ
New Bridge	Franklin	PA
New Bridgeport	Bedford	PA
New Bridgeville	York	PA
New Brighton	Richmond	NY
New Brighton	Beaver	PA
New Brighton	Fanquier	VA
New Britian	Hartford	CN
New Britian	Bucks	PA
New Britton	Hamilton	IN
New Brunswk(c.h.)	Middlesex	NJ
New Buda	Decatur	IA
New Buena Vista	Bedford	PA
New Buffalo	Berrien	MI
New Buffalo	Perry	PA
Newburgh	Franklin	AL
Newburgh	Izard	AR
Newburgh	Macon	IL
Newburgh	Warrick	IN
Newburgh	Mitchell	IA
Newburgh	Jefferson	KY
Newburgh	Penobscot	ME
Newburgh	Charles	MD
Newburgh	Cass	MI
Newburgh	Fillmore	MN
Newburgh	Macon	MO
Newburgh(c.h.)	ORange	NY
Newburgh	Cuyahoga	OH
Newburgh	Cumberland	PA
Newburgh	Preston	WV
Newburgh	Washington	WI
Newburgh Centre	Penobscot	ME
New Burlington	Clinton	OH
New Burlington	Delaware	IN
Newbury	Wabaunsee	KS
Newbury	Tuscola	MI
Newbury	Merrimack	NH
Newbury	Orange	VT
Newbury Centre	Orange	VT
Newburyport	Essex	MA
New California	Union	OH
New California	Grant	WI
New California	Macon	MO
New Canaan	Fairfield	CN
New Canton	Hawkins	TN
New Canton	Buckingham	VA
New Carlisle	St. Joseph	IN
New Carthage	Madison	LA
New Casco	Cumberland	ME
New Casco	Allegan	MI
New Cassel	Fond du Lac	WI
Newcastle	Placer	CA
New Castle(c.h.)	New Castle	DE
Newcastle(c.h.)	Henry	IN
Newcastle(c.h.)	Henry	KY
New Castle	Lincoln	ME
New Castle	Gentry	MO
Newcastle	Dixon	NE
Newcastle	Rockingham	NH
New Castle	Westchester	NY
New Castle	Coshocton	CH
Newcastle(c.h.)	Lawrence	PA
New Castle	Hardeman	TN
Newcastle(c.h.)	Craig	VA
New Centreville	Oswage	NY
New Centreville	Chester	PA
New Centreville	St. Croix	WI
New Chambersbgh	Columbia	OH
New Chester	Adams	PA
New Chester	Adams	WI
New Chicago	Neosho	KS
New Church	Accomack	VA
New Clifton	Monroe	WI
New Cocln	Milwaukee	WI
New Columbta	Massac	IL
New Columbia	Union	PA
New Colubus	Owen	KY
New Columbus	Luzerne	PA
Newcomb	Champaign	IL
Newcomb	Essex	NY
New Cornerstone	Tuscarawas	OH
New Concord	Columbia	NY
New Concord	Muskingum	OH
New Concord	Delaware	IN
New Corwin	Highland	OH
New Corydon	Jay	IN
New Creek(c.h.)	Mineral	WV
New Cumberland	Grant	IN
New Cumberland	Tuscarawas	OH
New Cumberland	Cumberland	PA
New Cumberland	Hancock	WV
New Dale	Wetzel	WV
New Danville	Lancaster	PA
New Danville	Rusk	TX
New Derry	Westmoreland	PA
New Diggins	La Fayette	WI
New Douglas	Madison	IL
New Dorp	Richmond	NY
New Dover	Union	OH
New Dublin	Scott	MN
New Dungens.(c.h.)	Clallam	WA
New Durham	Hudson	NJ
New Eagle Mills	Grant	KY
New Egypt	Ocean	NJ
New Elizabeth	Hendricks	IN
Newell	Burena Vista	IA
Newell's Run	Washington	OH
Newellsville	Marion	Or
New England	Athens	OH
New England	Wood	WI
New England Village	Worcester	MA
New Enterprise	Bedford	PA
New Era	De Kalb	IN
New Era	Bradford	PA
New Eureka	Jackson	KS
New Fairfield	Fairfield	CN
Newfane	Niagra	NY
Newfane	Fond du Lac	WI
Newfield	York	ME
Newfield	Gloucester	NJ
Newfield	Tompkins	NY
New Florence	Montgomery	MO
New Florence	Westmoreland	PA
New Forestville	Anson	NC
Newfoundland	Elliot	KY
Newfoundland	Morris	NJ
Newfoundland	Wayne	PA
New Fountain	Medina	TX
New Franken	Brown	WI
New Frankfort	Saline	ME
New Franklin	Wayne	IL
New Franklin	Stark	OH
New Freedom	York	PA
New Freeport	Greene	PA
New Galilee	Beaver	PA
New Garden	Wayne	IN
New Garden	Ray	MO
New Garden	Guilford	NC
New Garden	Columbiana	OH
New Garden	Chester	PA
New Garden	Russell	VA
New Gascony	Jefferson	AR
New Genesee	Whitesides	IL
New Geneva	Fayette	PA
New Geneve	Jackson	WV
New Germantown	Hunterdon	NJ
New Germantown	Perry	PA
New Glarus	Green	WI
New Gloucester	Cumberland	ME
New Goshen	Vigo	IN
New Grenada	Fulton	PA
New Gretna	Burlington	NJ
New Gilford	Coshocton	OH
New Hackensack	Dutchess	NY
New Hagerstown	Carroll	OH
New Hamburgh	Scott	IA
New Hamburgh	Dutchess	NY
New Hamburgh	Mercer	PA
New Hampden	Highland	VA
New Hampshire	Auglaize	OH
New Hampton	Madison	IL
New Hampton	Belknap	NH
New Hampton(c.h.)	Chickasaw	IA
New Hampton	Hunterdon	NJ
New Hampton	Orange	NY
New Hampton	Montgomery	PA
New Harmony	Sangamon	IL
New Harmony	Possey	IN
New Harmony	Pike	MO
New Harmony	Brown	OH
New Harmony	Washington	UT
New Harrisburgh	Wabash	IN
New Harrisburgh	Carroll	OH
New Hartford	Litchfield	CN
New Hartford	Pike	IL
New Hartford	Butler	IA
New Hartford	Winona	MN
New Hartford	Oneida	NY
Newharts	Northampton	PA
New Haven(c.h.)	New Haven	CN
New Haven	Gallatin	IL
New Haven	Allen	IN
New Haven	Nelson	KY
New Haven	Macomb	MI
New Haven	Franklin	MO
New Haven	Oswego	NY
New Haven	Huron	OH
New Haven	Addison	VT
New Haven	Mason	WV
New Haven	Adams	WI
New Haven Centre	Gratiot	MI
New Hebron	Addison	VT
Hew Hebron	Crawford	IL
New Hill	Wake	NC
New Holland	Wabash	IN
New Holland	Pickaway	OH
New Holland	Lancaster	PA
New Holstein	Calumet	WI
New Home	Montcalm	MI
New Home	Pawnee	NE
New Hope	Madison	AL
New Hope	Wabash	IL
New Hope	Nelson	KY
New Hope	Caroline	MD
New Hope	Lincoln	MO
New Hope	Cayuga	NY
New Hope	Iredell	NC
New Hope	Brown	OH
New Hope	Bucks	PA

PLACE	COUNTY	STATE
New Hope	Augusta	VA
New Hope	Portage	WI
New Hope Academy	Randolph	NC
New Hope Mills	Graville	NC
New House	York	SC
New Hudson	Oakland	MI
New Hudson	Allegany	NY
New Hurley	Ulster	NY
New Hyde Park	Queens	NY
New Iberia(c.h.)	Iberia	LA
New Idria	Fresno	CA
Newington	Hartford	CN
Newington	Rockingham	NH
Newington Junction	Hartford	CN
New Interest	Randolph	WV
New Ipwich	Hillsborough	NH
New Jasper	Greene	OH
New Jersualem	Berks	PA
New Kent(c.h.)	New Kent	VA
New Kingston	Delaware	NY
New Kingstown	Cumberland	PA
Newkirk Mills	Fulton	NY
New Knoxville	Auglaize	OH
New Lancaster	Tipton	IN
New Lancaster	Miami	KS
New Lebanon	De Kalb	IL
New Lebanon	Sullivan	IN
New Lebanon	Columbia	NY
New Lebanon	Montgomery	OH
New Lebanon	Mercer	PA
New Lebanon Centre	Columbia	NY
New Lebanon Springs	Columbia	NY
New Lenox	Will	IL
New Lenox	Berkshire	MA
New Lexington	Tucaloosa	AL
New Lexington (c.h.)	Perry	OH
New Lexington	Somerset	PA
New Liberty	Pope	IL
New Liberty	Scott	IA
New Liberty	Owen	KY
New Light	Wake	NC
New Limerick	Aroostook	ME
New Lisbon	Henry	IN
New Lisbon	Burlington	NJ
New Lisbon	Otsego	NY
New Lisbon (c.h.)	Columbiana	OH
New Lisbon	Juneau	WA
New London (c.h.)	New London	CN
New London	Howard	IN
New London	Henry	IA
New London	Frederick	MD
New London (c.h.)	Randiyohi	MN
New London (c.h.)	Ralls	MO
New London	Merrimack	NH
New London	Oneida	NY
New London	Haron	OH
New London	Chester	PA
New London	Campbell	VA
New London	Waupaca	WS
New Lyme	Ashtabala	OH
New Madison	Wabash	IN
New Madison	Darke	OH
New Madrid (c.h.)	New MAdrid	MO
New Mahoning	Carbon	PA
Newman	Douglas	IL
Newman	Jefferson	KS
Newman	Sanilac	MC
Newmanville	Clarion	PA
New Marion	Ripley	IN
New Market	Madison	AL
New Market	Sebastian	AR
New Market	Monroe	GA
New Market	Gallatin	IL
New Market	Marion	KY
New Market	Frederick	MD
New Market	Scott	MN
New Market	Platte	MO
New Market	Rockingham	NH
New Market	Middlesex	NJ
New Market	Highland	OH
New Market	Abbeville	SC
New Market	Jefferson	TN
New Market	Shenandoah	VA
New Marlborough	Berkshire	MA
New Martinsburgh	Fayette	OH
New Martinvil.(c.h.)	Wetzel	WV
New Maysville	Putnam	IN
New Melle	St. Charles	MO
New Memphis	Clinton	IL
New Metamora	Washington	OH
New Michigan	Livingston	IL
New Middleton	Smith	TN
New Middletown	Harrison	IN
New Middletown	Mahoning	OH
New Milford	Litchfield	CN
New Milford	Winnebago	IL
New Milford	Orange	NY
New Milford	Portage	OH
New Milford	Susquehanna	PA
New Millport	Clearfield	PA
New Milton	Doddridge	WV
New Minden	Washington	IL
New Mollis	Outagamie	WS
New Monmouth	Monmouth	NJ
New Moon	Cherokee	AL
New Moorefield	Clark	OH
New Moscow	Coshocton	OH
New Mount Pleasant	Jay	IN
New Mount Pleasant	Monroe	PA
New Munich	Stearns	MN
Newnan(c.h.)	Coweta	GA
New Offenburgh	St. Genevieve	MO
New Ohio	Broome	NY
New Oregon(c.h.)	Howard	IL
New Oregon	Erie	NY
New Orleans(c.h.)	Orleans	LA
New Oxford	Adams	PA
New Palestine	Cooper	MO
New Palestine	Clermont	OH
New Platz	Ulster	NY
New Paris	Elkhart	IN
New Paris	Preble	OH
New Paris	Bedford	PA
New Petersburgh	Highland	OH
New Petersburgh	Jefferson	PA
New Philadelphia	McDonough	IL
New Philadelphia	Washington	IN
New Phil.(c.h.)	Tuscarawas	OH
New Pittsburgh	St. Clair	IL
New Pittsburgh	Randolph	IN
New Pittsburgh	Wayne	OH
New Pleasant Grove	Huntingdon	PA
New Plymouth	Vinton	OH
New Point	Decatur	IN
Newport	New Castle	DE
Newport	Lake	IL
Newport(c.h.)	Vermillion	IN
Newport	Johnson	IA
Newport	Neosho	KS
Newport(c.h.)	Campbell	KY
Newport	Winn	LA
Newport	Penobscot	ME
Newport	Charles	MD
Newport	Monroe	MI
Newport	Washington	MN
Newport(c.h.)	Sullivan	NH
Newport	Cumberland	NJ
Newport	Herkimer	NY
Newport	Carteret	NC
Newwport	Washington	OH
Newport	Benton	OR
Newport	Perry	PA
Newport(c.h.)	Newport	RI
Newport(c.h.)	Cocke	TN
Newport	San Jacinto	TX
Newport	Orleans	VT
Newport	Giles	VA
New Portage	Summit	OH
Newport Centre	Orleans	VT
New Portland	Somerset	ME
Newport News	Warwick	VA
Newportville	Bucks	PA
New Preston	Litchfield	CN
New Prosspect	Winston	MS
New Prospect	Spartanburgh	SC
New Prospect	Fond du Lac	WI
New Providence	Pike	AL
New Providence	Clarke	IN
New Providence	Hardin	IA
New Providence	Osage	MO
New Providence	Union	NJ
New Providence	Lancaster	PA
New Providence	Lancaster	PA
New Providence	Montgomery	CA
New Republic	Monterey	CA
New Richland	Waseca	MN
New Richland	Logan	OH
New Richmong	Montgomery	IN
New Richmond	Clermont	OH
New Richmond	Crawford	PA
New Richmond	Raliegh	WV
New Richmnd	St. Croix	WI
New Ringgold	Schuylkill	PA
New River	Fayette	AL
New River	Ascension	LA
New River	Huron	MI
New River	Alleghany	NC
New River Depot	Pulaski	VA
New Rochelle	Westchester	NY
New Rochester	Wood	OH
New Rome	Adams	WI
New Ross	Montgomery	AL
New Rumley	Harrison	OH
New Russia	Essex	NY
New Rutland	La Salle	IL
Newry	Oxford	ME
Newry	Blair	PA
Newry	Vernon	WI
News	Calhoun	IL
New Salem	Pike	IL
New Salem	Albany	NY
New Salem	Randolph	NC
New Salem	Fairfield	OH
New Salem	Fayette	PA
New Salem	Rusk	TX
New Salem	Harrison	IN
New Salisbury	Harrison	IN
New Santa Fe	Jackson	MO
New Scandinavia	Republic	KS
New Scotland	Albany	NY
New Scottsville	Beaver	PA
New Ferry	Halifax	VA
New Sharon	Mahaska	IA
New Sharon	Franklin	ME
New Sharon	Monmouth	NJ
New Sheffield	Beaver	PA

PLACE	COUNTY	STATE	PLACE	COUNTY	STATE	PLACE	COUNTY	STATE
New Shoreham	Newport	RI	New Village	Warren	NJ	Nisbet Lycoming	P A	
New Site	Tallapoosa	AL	Newville	Colusa	CA	Nishnabotna	Atchison	MO
New Smyrna	Volusia	FL	Newville	De Kalb	IN	Niskayunna	Schenectady	NY
New Somerset	Jefferson	OH	Newville	Herkimer	NY	Nittany	Centre	PA
Newson's Depot	Southampton	VA	Newville	Richland	OH	Niven	Susquehanna	PA
New Springfield	Mahoniag	OH	Newville	Cumberland	PA	Niverville	Columbia	NY
New Springville	Richmond	VA	Newville	Vernon	WI	Nixon	De Witt	IL
New Stanton	Westmoreland	PA	New Vineyard	Frankln	MO	Nixon's Store	Marengo	AL
Newstead zzzzzzzzz	Christianzzzzzzzzz	KY	New Virginia	Warren	IA	Noah	Shelby	IN
New Stirling	Irdell	NC	New Washington	Clarke	IN	Noank	New London	CN
New Store	Buckingham	VA	New Washington	Crawford	OH	Noble	Richland	IL
New Straitsville	Perry	OH	New Washington	Clearfield	PA	Noble	Noble	IN
New Sweden	Aroostook	ME	New Washington	Marshall	WV	Noble Centre	Branch	MI
New Texas	Allegheny	PA	New Waterford	Columbiana	OH	Noblesvborough	Lincoln	ME
Newton(c.h.)	Dale	AL	New Waverly	Cass	IN	Noblestown	Allegheny	PA
Newton(c.h.)	Baker	GA	Newway	Licking	OH	Noblesville(c.h.)	Hamilton	IN
Newton(c.h.)	Jasper	IL	New Wells	Cape Gir.	MO	Nobleville	Noble	OH
Newton(c.h.)	Jasper	IA	New Westville	Preble	OH	Nobob	Barren	KY
Newton	Sedwick	KS	New Wilmington	Lawrence	PA	Nochway	Randolph	GA
Newton	Middlesex	MA	New Winchester	Hendricks	IN	Nockenut	Guadalupe	TX
Newton	Calhoun	MI	New Windsor	Mercer	IL	Nodaway	Andrew	MO
Newton	Newton	MS	New Windsor	Carroll	MD	Nadaway Mills	Page	IA
Newton	Burt	NE	New Woodstook	Madison	NY	Nohart	Richardson	NE
Newton	Rockingham	NH	New York	Wayne	IA	Nokesville	Prince William	LA
Newton(c.h.)	Sussex	NJ	New York(c.h.)	New York	NY	Nokomis	Montogomery	IL
Newton(c.h.)	Catawba	NC	New York Mills	Oneida	NY	Nolensville	Williamson	TN
Newton	Newton	TX	New Zion	Clarendora	SC	Nolin	Hardin	KY
Newton	Cache	UT	Ney	De Kalb	IL	Nolo	Indiana	PA
Newton	King and Queen	VA	Ney	DiDefiance	OH	Nominy Grove	Westmoreland	VA
Newton	Roane	WV	Niagara Falls	Niagara	NY	Non Intervention	Lunenburgh	VA
Newton	Vernon	WI	Niangua	Webster	MO	Nonpariel	Knox	OH
Newton Academy	Monroe	AL	Niantic	New London	CN	Nooseneck Hill	Kent	RI
Newtonburgh	Manitowoc	WI	Niantic	Macon	IL	Nopal	McMullen	TX
Newton Centre	Middlesex	MA	Nicasio	Marin	CA	Nora	Jo Daviess	IL
Newton Depot	Rockingham	NH	Nicholas(c.h.)	Nicholas	WV	Nora	Berks	PA
Newton Factory	Newton	GA	Nicholas(c.h.)	Jessamine	KY	Nora	Dane	WI
Newton Falls	Trumbull	OH	Nichols	Montgomery	MD	Nora Springs	Floyd	IA
Newton Grove	Sampson	NC	Nichols	Tioga	NY	Norbeck	Montgomery	MD
Newton Hamilton	Mifflin	PA	Nichols	Marion	SC	Norborne	Carroll	MO
Newton Highlands	Middlesex	MA	Nicholson	Wyoming	PA	Nord	Butte	CA
Newtonia	Newton	MO	Nicholson's Store	Chotaw	AL	Nordsk	Dallas	IA
Newton Lower Falls	Middlesex	MA	Nicholsville	Cleveland	NC	Norfolk	Litchfield	CN
Newton's Retreat Z.	Tippecanoe	IN	Nicholsonville	Cleveland	NC	Norfolk	Norfolk	MA
Newton Stewart	Orange	IN	Nicholville	Clermont	OH	Norfolk(c.h.)	Madison	NE
Newtonsville	Clermont	OH	Nickerson	Dodge	NE	Norfolk	St. Lawrence	NY
Newton Upper Falls	Middlesex	MA	Nicojack	Marion	TN	Norfolk(c.h.)	Norfolk	VA
Newtonville	Albany	NY	Nicolaus	Sutter	CA	Normal	McLean	IL
New Topia	Barbour	AL	Nicollet	Nicollet	MN	Normanda	Tipton	IN
Newtown	El Dorado	VA	Nicanza	Miami	IN	Normandy	St. Louis	MO
Newtown	Fairfield	CN	Nile	Brown	MN	Normandy	Bedford	TN
Newtown	Fountain	IN	Nile	Allegany	NY	Norman Ridge	Calhoun	WV
Newtown	Scott	KY	Niles	Cook	IL	Norman's Kill	Albany	NY
Newtown	Worchester	MD	Niles	Van Buren	IA	Normanville	Doniphan	KS
Newtown	Putnam	MO	Niles	Berrien	MI	Norridgewock(c.h.)	Somerset	ME
Newtown	Queens	NY	Niles	Cayuga	NY	Norris	Fulton	IL
Newtown	Bucks	PA	Niles	Trumbull	OH	Norris Creek	Lincoln	TN
Newtown	Bucks	PA	Niles	Manitowoc	WI	Norris City	White	IL
Newtown	Kng and Queen	VA	Niles Centre	Cook	IL	Norris Fork	Henry	MO
New Town Landing	Warren	MS	Nile's Valley	Tioga	PA	Norisstown	Pope	AR
Newtown Mills	Forest	PA	Nilwood	Macoupin	IL	Norristown	Carroll	OH
Newtown Square	Delaware	PA	Nimisila	Summit	OH	Norristown(c.h.)	Montgomery	PA
Newtown Steph.bgh	Frederick	VA	Nine Mile	Allen	IN	Norrisville	Hartford	MD
New Trenton	Franklin	IN	Nine Points	Lancaster	PA	Norrisville	Crawford	PA
New Trier	Dakota	MN	Ninescha	Cowley	KS	Norrisville	Caledonia	VT
New Tripoli	Lehigh	PA	Nine Times	Pickens	SC	Norritonville	Montgomery	PA
New Troy	La Fayette	FL	Ninety-Six	Abbeville	SC	Norseland	Nicollet	MN
New Ulm(c.h.)	Brown	MN	Nineveh	Johnson	IN	North Abington	Plkymouth	MA
New Ulm	Austin	TX	Ninevey	Adair	MO	North Acton	York	ME
NewUpton	Gloucester	VA	Nineveh	Broome	NY	North Adams	Berkshire	MA
New Ulrecht	Kings	NY	Nineveh	Greene	PA	North Adams	Hillsdale	MI
New Vernon	Morris	NJ	Nineveh	Warren	PA	North Alfred	York	ME
New Vienna	Dubuque	IA	Niobrara(c.h.)	L'Eau qui Court	NE	New Amherst	Hampshire	MA
New Vienna	Clinton	OH	Nippenose	Lycoming	PA	Northampton(c.h.)	NHampshire	MA

PLACE NAMES OF THE UNITED STATES

PLACE	COUNTY	STATE	PLACE	COUNTY	STATE	PLACE	COUNTY	STATE
Northampton	Fulton	NY	North Buckfield	Oxford	ME	North Egremont	Berkshire	MA
North Andover	Essex	MA	North Bcksport	Hancock	ME	Northeim	Manitowoc	WI
North And.Depot	Essex	MA	North Bucksport	Hancock	ME	North Elba	Essex	NY
North Anson	Somerset	ME	North Buena Vista	Clayton	IA	North Elk	Republic	KS
North Appleton	Knox	ME	North Burns	Huron	MI	North Elk Grove	La Fayette	WI
North Argyle	Washington	NY	North Bryon	Kent	MI	North Ellsworth	Hancock	ME
North Ashford	Windham	CN	Morth Cambridge	Middlesex	MA	North English	Iowa	IA
North Attleborough	Bristol	MA	North Cambridge	Middlesex	MA	North Enosburgh	Franklin	VT
North Auburn	Androscoggin	ME	NorthCambridge	Washington	NY	Northern Junction	Milwaukee	WI
North Aurelius	Ingham	MI	North Camden	Loraine	OH	Northern Depot	Boone	IN
North Aurora	Kane	IL	North Cameron	Steuben	NY	North Evans	Erie	NY
North Baldwin	Cumberland	ME	North Canton	Hartford	CN	North Fairfax	Franklin	VT
North Bangor	Penobscot	ME	North Canyonville	Douglas	OR	North Fairfield	Somerset	ME
North Bangor	Franklin	NY	North Cape	Racine	WI	North Fairfield	Huron	OH
North Barnstead	Belknap	NH	North Carmel	Penobscot	ME	North Falmouth	Barnstable	MA
North Barrier	Cabarrus	NC	North Carver	Plymouth	MA	North Farmington	Franklin	ME
North Barrington	Strafford	NH	North Castine	Hancock	ME	North Farmington	Oakland	MI
North Barton	Tioga	NY	North Castle	Westchester	NY	North Fayette	Kennebec	ME
North Bass Island	Ottawa	OH	North Cedar	Jackson	KS	North Fayston	Washington	VT
North Bay	Oncida	NY	North Charlestown	Sullivan	NH	North Fenton	Broome	NY
North Bay	Door	WI	North Chatham	Barnstable	MA	North Ferrisburgh	Addison	VT
North Belgrade	Kennebec	ME	North Chatham	Colmbia	NY	Northfield	Litchfield	CN
North Bellingham	Norfolk	MA	North Chelmsford	Middlesex	MA	Northfield	Boone	IN
North Bend	Stark	IN	North Chelsea	Suffolk	MA	Northfield	Des Moines	IA
North Bend	Dodge	NE	North Chemung	Chemung	NY	Northfield	Washington	ME
North Bend	Jackson	WI	North Chester	Hampden	MA	Northfield	Rice	MN
North Bennington	Bennington	NY	North Chester	Windsor	VT	Northfield	Summit	OH
North Benson	Shelby	KY	North Chesterville	Franklin	ME	Northfield	Washington	VT
North Benton	Mahoning	OH	North Chichester	Merimack	NH	Northfield Depot	Merrimack	NH
North Bergen	Genesee	NY	North Chili	Monroe	NY	Northfield Farms	Franklin	MA
North Berne	Fairfield	OH	North Clarendon	Rutland	VT	Northford	New Haven	CN
North Berwick	York	ME	North Clarkson	Monroe	NY	North Fork	Mason	KY
North Bethel	Oxford	ME	North Clayton	Miami	OH	North Fork	Ashe	NC
North Beverly	Essex	MA	North Clove	Dutchess	NY	North Franklin	Delaware	NY
North Billerica	Middlesex	MA	North Clymer	Chautauqua	NY	North Fryebrugh	Oxford	ME
North Blanford	Hampden	MA	North Cohasset	Norfolk	MA	North Gage	Oneida	NY
North Blenheim	Schoharie	NY	North Cohocton	Steuben	NY	North Galway	Saratoga	NY
North Bloomfield	Nevada	CA	North Colebrook	Litchfield	CN	North Garden	Albemarle	VA
North Bloomfield	Ontario	NY	North Colesville	Broome	NY	North Georgetown	Columbiana	OH
North Blue Hill	Hancock	ME	North Columbia	Nevada	CA	North Granby	Hartford	CN
North Bolton	Warren	NY	North Columbus	Franklin	OH	North Grantham	Sullivan	NH
North Bothbay	Lincoln	ME	North Copake	Columbia	NY	North Granville	Washington	NY
Northborough	Worcester	MA	North Conway	Carroll	NH	North Gray	Cumberland	ME
North Boscawen	Merrimack	NH	North Cornville	Somerset	ME	North Greece	Monroe	NY
North Boston	Erie	NY	North Cornwall	Litchfield	CN	North Greenfield	Logan	OH
North Bradford	Penobscot	ME	North Cove	McDowell	NC	North Greenfield	Saratoga	NY
North Branch	Cook	IL	North Coventry	Chester	PA	North Greenwich	Washington	NY
North Branch	Baltimore	MD	North Craftsbury	Orleans	VT	North Grosv. Dale	Windham	CN
North Branch	Lapeer	MI	North Creek	Phillips	AR	North Grafton	Grafton	NH
North Branch	Isanti	MN	North Cutler	Washington	ME	North Grove	Miami	IN
North Branch	Otoe	NE	Northcutt	Linn	MO	North Guilford	New Haven	CN
North Branch	Hillsborough	NH	North Dana	Worcester	MA	North Hadley	Hampshire	MA
North Branch	Somerset	NJ	North Danville	Caledonia	VT	North Hamdend	Delaware	NY
North Branch	Sullivan	NY	North Dartmouth	Bristol	MA	North Hamlin	Monroe	NY
North Branch	Jacson	WI	North Deer Isle	Hancock	ME	North Hammond	St. Lawrence	NY
North Branch Depot	Somerset	NJ	North Derby	Orleans	VT	North Hampton	Peoria	IL
North Brch Station	Chicago	MN	North Dighton	Bristol	MA	North Hampton	Rockingham	NH
North Branford	New Haven	CN	North Dixmont	Penobscot	ME	North Hampton	Clark	OH
Northbridge	Worcester	MA	North Dorchester	Grafton	NH	North Hancock	Hancock	ME
Northbridge	Worcester	MA	North Dorset	Bennington	VT	North Hannigan	Oswego	NY
North Bridgeton	Cumberland	ME	North Dover	Cuyahoga	OH	North Harpersfield	Delaware	NY
North Bridgewater	Plymouth	MA	North Dunbarton	Merrimack	NH	North Harpswell	Cumberland	ME
North Bridgewater	Oneida	NY	North Duxbury	Washington	VT	North Hartland	Niagara	NY
North Bristol	Trumbull	OH	North Eagle	Clinton	MI	North Hartland	Windsor	VT
North Broadalbin	Fulton	NY	Northeast	Cecil	MD	North Harwich	Barnstable	MA
North Broadalbin	Fulton	NY	North East	Erie	PA	North Hatfield	Hampshire	MA
North Brook	Lincoln	NC	North East Centre	Dutchess	NY	North Haven	New Haven	CN
North Brook	Linciln	NC	North Eastham	Barstable	MA	North Haven	Knox	ME
North Brook	Chester	PA	Northeast Harbor	Hancock	ME	North Haverhill	Grafton	NH
North Brookfield	Worcester	MA	North Easton	Bristol	MA	North Hebron	Washington	NY
North Brookfield	Madison	NY	North Easton	Washington	NY	North Hector	Schuyler	NY
North Brooklin	Hancock	ME	North Eaton	Lorain	OH	North Heidelberg	Berks	PA
North Brooksville	Hanck	ME	North Edgecomb	Licoln	ME	North Henderson	Mercer	IL

PLACE NAMES OF THE UNITED STATES

PLACE	COUNTY	STATE
North Hermon	Penobscot	ME
North Hero(c.h.)	Grand Isle	VT
North Hogan	Ribley	IN
North Hoosick	Rensselaer	NY
North Hope	Butler	PA
North Hudson	Essex	NY
North Huron	Wayne	NY
North Hyde Park	Lemoille	VT
North Industry	Stark	OH
North Irving	Barry	MI
North Isleborough	Waldo	ME
North Jackson	Mahoning	OH
North Jackson	Susquehanna	PA
North Jasper	Steuben	NY
North Java	Wyoming	NY
North Jay	Franklin	ME
North Judson	Stark	IN
North Kenneb. Port	York	ME
North Kingston	De Kalb	IL
North Kortright	Delaware	NY
North La Crosse	La Crosse	WI
North Lake	Waukesha	WI
North Landgrove	Bennington	VT
North Lansing	Tompkins	NY
North Lawrence	St. Lawrence	NY
North Lebanon	York	ME
North Leeds	Androscoggin	ME
North Leeds	Columbia	WI
North Leominster	Worchester	MA
North Leverett	Franklin	MA
North Lewisburgh	Champaign	OH
North Liberty	St. Joseph	IN
North Liberty	Johnson	IA
North Chesterville	Franklin	ME
North Chichester	Merrimack	NH
North Chili	Monroe	NY
North Clarendon	Rutland	VT
North Clarkson	Monroe	NY
North Clayton	Miami	OH
North Clove	Dutchmss	NY
North Clymer	Chautauqua	NY
North Cohasset	Norfolk	MA
North Cohocton	Steuben	NY
North Colebrook	Litchfield	CN
North Colesville	Broome	NY
North Columbia	Nevada	CA
North Columbus	Franklin	OH
North Copake	Columbia	NY
North Conway	Carroll	NH
North Cornville	Somerset	ME
North Cornwall	Litchfield	CN
North Cove	McDowell	NC
North Coventry	Chester	PA
North Craftsbury	Orleans	VT
North Creek	Phillips	AR
North Cutler	Washington	ME
Northcutt	Linn	MO
North Dana	Worchester	MA
North Danville	Caledonia	VT
North Dartmouth	Bristol	MA
North Deer Isle	Hancock	ME
North Derby	Orleans	VT
North Dighton	Bristol	MA
North Dixmont	Penobscot	ME
North Dorchester	Grafton	NH
North Dorset	Bennington	VT
North Dover	Cuyahoga	OH
North Dunbarton	Merrimack	NH
North Duxbury	Washington	VT
North Eagle	Clinton	MI
Northeast	Cecil	MD
North East	Erie	PA
North East Centre	Dutchess	NY
North Eastham	Barstable	MA
Northeast Harbor	Hancock	ME
North Easton	Bristol	MA
North Easton	Washington	NY
North Eaton	Lorain	OH
North Edgecomb	Licoln	ME
North Egremont	Berkshire	MA
Northeim	Manitowoc	WI
North Elba	Essex	NY
North Elk	Republic	KS
North Elk Grove	La Fayette	WI
North Ellsworth	Hancock	ME
North English	Iowa	IA
North Enosburgh	Franklin	VT
Northern Junction	Milwaukee	WI
Northern Depot	Boone	IN
North Evans	Erie	NY
North Fairfax	Franklin	VT
North Fairfield	Somerset	ME
North Fairfield	Huron	OH
North Falmouth	Barnstable	MA
North Farmington	Franklin	ME
North Farmington	Oakland	MI
North Fayette	Kennebec	ME
North Fayston	Washington	VT
North Fenton	Broome	NY
North Ferrisburgh	Addison	VT
Northfield	Litchfield	CN
Northfield	Boone	IN
Northfield	Des Moines	IA
Northfield	Washington	ME
Northfield	Rice	MN
Northfield	Summit	OH
Northfield	Washington	VT
Northfield Depot	Merrimack	NH
Northfield Farms	Franklin	MA
Northford	New Haven	CN
North Fork	Mason	KY
North Fork	Ashe	NC
North Franklin	Delaware	NY
North Fryebrugh	Oxford	ME
North Gage	Oneida	NY
North Galway	Saratoga	NY
North Garden	Albemarle	VA
North Georgetown	Columbiana	OH
North Granby	Hartford	CN
North Grantham	Sullivan	NH
North Granville	Washington	NY
North Gray	Cumberland	ME
North Greece	Monroe	NY
North Greenfield	Logan	OH
North Greenfield	Saratoga	NY
North Greenwich	Washington	NY
North Grosv. Dale	Windham	CN
North Grafton	Grafton	NH
North Grove	Miami	IN
North Guilford	New Haven	CN
North Hadley	Hampshire	MA
North Hamdend	Delaware	NY
North Hamlin	Monroe	NY
North Hammond	St. Lawrence	NY
North Hampton	Peoria	IL
North Hampton	Rockingham	NH
North Hampton	Clark	OH
North Hancock	Hancock	ME
North Hannigal	Oswego	NY
North Harpersfield	Delaware	NY
North Harpswell	Cumberland	ME
North Hartland	Niagara	NY
North Hartland	Windsor	VT
North Harwich	Barnstable	MA
North Hatfield	Hampshire	MA
North Haven	New Haven	CN
North Haven	Knox	ME
North Haverhill	Grafton	NH
North Hebron	Washington	NY
North Hector	Schuyler	NY
North Heidelberg	Berks	PA
North Henderson	Mercer	IL
North Hermon	Penobscot	ME
North Hero(c.h.)	Grand Isle	VT
North Hogan	Ribley	IN
North Hoosick	Rensselaer	NY
North Hope	Butler	PA
North Hudson	Essex	NY
North Huron	Wayne	NY
North Hyde Park	Lemoille	VT
North Industry	Stark	OH
North Irving	Barry	MI
North Isleborough	Waldo	ME
North Jackson	Mahoning	OH
North Jackson	Susquehanna	PA
North Jasper	Steuben	NY
North Java	Wyoming	NY
North Jay	Franklin	ME
North Judson	Stark	IN
North Kenneb. Port	York	ME
North Kingston	De Kalb	IL
North Kortright	Delaware	NY
North La Crosse	La Crosse	WI
North Lake	Waukesha	WI
North Landgrove	Bennington	VT
North Lansing	Tompkins	NY
North Lawrence	St. Lawrence	NY
North Lebanon	York	ME
North Leeds	Androscoggin	ME
North Leeds	Columbia	WI
North Leominster	Worchester	MA
North Leverett	Franklin	MA
North Lewisburgh	Champaign	OH
North Liberty	St. Joseph	IN
North Liberty	Johnson	IA
North Liberty	Knox	OH
North Liberty	Mercer	PA
North Lima	Mahoning	OH
North Limington	York	ME
North Lincklaen	Chenango	NY
North Cinneus	Aroostook	ME
North Lisbon	Grafton	NH
North Litchfield	Herkimer	NY
North Littleton	Grafton	NH
North Livermore	Androscoggin	ME
North Londonderry	Rockberry	NH
North Lovell	Oxford	ME
North Lubec	Washington	ME
North Lyme	New London	CN
North Lynderborough	Hillsborough	NH
North McGregor	Clayton	IA
North Madison	New Haven	CN
North Madison	Jefferson	IN
North Madison	Somerset	ME
North Madison	Lake	OH
North Manchester	Hartford	CN
North Manlius	Onomdaga	NY
North Mariaville	Hancock	ME
North Marshfield	Plymouth	MA
North Middleborough	Plymouth	MA
North Middletown	Bourbon	KY
North Milford	Penobscot	ME
North Mills	Page	IA
North Monmouth	Kennebec	ME
North Monroe	Waldo	ME
North Monroe	Grafton	NH
North Montpelier	Washington	NY

PLACE	COUNTY	STATE
North Mountain	Berkeley	WV
North Mount Pleasant	Marshall	MS
North Nassau	Rensselaer	NY
North Newberg	Shiawassee	MI
North Newburgh	Penobscot	ME
North Newbury	Geauga	OH
North New Castle	Lincoln	ME
North Newfield	York	ME
North Newport	Penobscot	ME
North N. Portland	Somerset	ME
North Newry	Oxford	ME
North New Salem	Franklin	MS
North Norfolk	Litchfield	CN
North Norwich	Chenango	NY
North Oakfield	Genesee	NY
North Oakland	Butler	PA
North Ogden	Weber	UT
North Orange	Franklin	MA
North Orwell	Bradford	PA
North Oxford	Worcester	MA
North Palermo	Waldo	ME
North Paris	Oxford	MA
North Parma	Monroe	NY
North Parsonfield	York	ME
North Pembroke	Plymouth	MA
North Pembroke	Genesee	NY
North Penn	Schuylkill	PA
North Penobscot	Hancock	ME
North Perry	Washington	ME
North Petersburgh	Renssalaer	NY
North Pharsalia	Chenango	NY
North Pine Grove	Clairion	PA
North Pitcher	Chenango	NY
North Pittston	Kennebec	ME
North Plains	Ionia	MI
North Plato	Kane	IL
North Platte(c.h.)	Lincoln	NE
North Plympton	Plymouth	MA
North Point	Pulaski	AR
North Point	Holt	MO
North Pomfret	Windsor	VT
Northport	Waldo	ME
Northport(c.h.)	Leelenaw	ME
Northport	Suffolk	NY
Northport	Waupaca	WI
North Powder	Union	OR
North Pownal	Cumberland	ME
North Pownal	Bennington	VT
North Prairie	Knox	IL
North Prairie	dMorrison	MN
North Prairie Station	Waukesha	WI
North Prescott	Hampshire	MA
North Raisinville	Monroe	MI
North Randolph	Orange	VT
North Raymond	Cumberland	ME
North Raynham	Bristol	MA
North Reading	Schuyler	NY
North Rehoboth	Bristol	MA
North Richmond	Cheshire	NH
North Richmond	Ashtabula	OH
North Ridge	Niagara	NY
North Rigdeville	Lorain	OH
North Ridgeway	Orleans	NY
North River	Tuscaloosa	AL
North River	Marion	MO
North River	Warren	NY
North River Mills	Hampshire	WV
North Robinson	Crawford	OH
North Rome	Bradford	PA
North Rose	Wayne	NY
North Royalton	Cuyahoga	OH
North Rumford	Oxford	ME
North Rush	Monroe	NY
North Russel	St. Lawrence	NY
North Rutland	Worcester	MA
North Salem	Hendricks	IN
North Salem	Linn	MO
North Salem	Rockingham	NH
North Salem	Westchester	NY
North Sanbornton	Belknap	NH
North San Diego(c.h.)	San Diego	CA
North Sandwich	Barnstable	MA
North Sandwich	Carroll	NH
North Sandy	Mercer	PA
North Sanford	Broome	NY
North San Juan	Nevada	CA
North Santee	Georgetown	SC
North Savern	Owen	KY
North Scituate	Plymouth	MA
North Scituate	Providence	RI
North Scriba	Oswego	NY
North Searsmont	Waldo	ME
North Searsport	Waldo	NE
Northport	Waupaca	WI
North Powder	Union	OR
North Pownal	Cumberland	ME
North Pownal	Bennington	VT
North Prairie	Knox	IL
North Prairie	dMorrison	MN
North Prairie Stion	Waukesha	WI
North Prescott	Hampshire	MA
North Raisinville	Monroe	MI
North Randolph	Orange	VT
North Raymond	Cumberland	ME
North Raynham	Bristol	MA
North Reading	Schuyler	NY
North Rehoboth	Bristol	MA
North Richmond	Cheshire	NH
North Richmond	Ashtabula	OH
North Ridge	Niagara	NY
North Rigdeville	Lorain	OH
North Ridgeway	Orleans	NY
North River	Tuscaloosa	AL
North River	Marion	MO
North River	Warren	NY
North River Mills	Hampshire	WV
North Robinson	Crawford	OH
North Rome	Bradford	PA
North Rose	Wayne	NY
North Royalton	Cuyahoga	OH
North Rumford	Oxford	ME
North Rush	Monroe	NY
North Russel	St. Lawrence	NY
North Rutland	Worcester	MA
North Salem	Hendricks	IN
North Salem	Linn	MO
North Salem	Rockingham	NH
North Salem	Westchester	NY
North Sanbornton	Belknap	NH
North S. Diego(c.h.)	San Diego	CA
North Sandwich	Barnstable	MA
North Sandwich	Carroll	NH
North Sandy	Mercer	PA
North Sanford	Broome	NY
North San Juan	Nevada	CA
North Santee	Georgetown	SC
North Savern	Owen	KY
North Scituate	Plymouth	MA
North Scituate	Providence	RI
North Scriba	Oswego	NY
North Searsmont	Waldo	ME
North Searsport	Waldo	NE
North Sedgwick	Hancock	ME
North Sewickly	Beaver	PA
North Shapleigh	York	MI
North Sheffield	Ashtabula	OH
North Sheldon	Franklin	VT
North Shenango	Crawford	PA
North Shrewsb.	Rutland	VA
Northside	Goochland	VA
North Sidney	Kennebec	ME
North's Landing	Switzerland	IN
North's Mills	Mercer	PA
North Smithfield	Bradford	PA
North Solon	Cuyahoga	OH
worth Somerville	Middlesex	MA
North Sparta	Livingston	NY
North Spencer	Worchester	MA
North Springfield	Greene	MO
North Springfield	Summit	OH
North Springfield	Erie	PA
North Springfield	Windsor	VT
North Springs	Jackson	TN
North Stamford	Fairfield	CN
North Star	Atchison	MO
North Star	Darke	OH
North Star	Allegheny	PA
North Star	Crawford	WI
North Stephentn.	Rensselaer	NY
North Sterling	Caynga	NY
North Stockholm	St. Lawrence	NY
North Stoaunton	New London	CN
North Stoughton	Norfolk	MA
North Stafford	Stafford	NH
North Sudbury	Middlesex	MA
North Sutton	Merrimack	NH
North Swansea	Bristol	MA
North Tarrytown	Westchester	NY
N. Taycheeday	Fon du Lac	WI
North Thetford	Orange	VT
North Tisbury	Dukes	MA
North Topeka	Shawnee	KS
North Towanda	Bradford	PA
North Troy	Orleans	VT
North Truro	Barnstable	MA
North Tunbridge	Orange	VT
North Turner	Androscoggin	ME
N. Turner Bridge	Androscoggin	ME
Northumberland	Coos	NH
Northumberland	Saratoga	NY
Northumberland	Northumberland	PA
North Underhill	Chittenden	VT
North Union	Knox	ME
North Uniontn.	Highland	OH
North Unity	Leelenaw	MI
Northup	Gallia	OH
North Urbana	Steuben	NY
North Uxbridge	Worcester	MA
North Vassaib	Kennebec	ME
North Virnon	Shiawassee	MI
North Victory	Cayuga	NY
North Vienna	Kennebec	ME
North View	Mecklenburg	VA
Northville	Litchfield	CN
Northville	La Salle	IL
Northville	Greene	IA
Northville	Wayne	MI
Northville	Fulton	NY
Northville	Erie	PA
North Vineland	Cumberland	NJ
North Volney	Oswego	NY
North Wakefield	Carroll	NH
North Walden	Caledona	VT
N. Waldoborough	Lincoln	MO
North Wales	Montgomery	PA
North Walton	Delaware	NY
Northward	Greenwood	KS
North Warren	Knox	ME

PLACE	COUNTY	STATE	PLACE	COUNTY	STATE	PLACE	COUNTY	STATE
North Warren	Winona	MN	Norwood	Stanly	NC	Oakfuskee	Cleburne	AL
N. Washington	Chickasaw	IA	Norwood	Hamilton	OH	Oak Glen	Steele	MN
N. Washington	Knox	PA	Norwood	Chester	PA	Oak Grove	Carroll	AR
N. Washington	Hardin	OH	Norwood	Nelson	VA	Oak Grove	Sussex	DE
N. Washington	Westmoreland	PA	Norwood Park	Cook	IL	Oak Grove	McLean	IL
N. Waterborough	York	ME	Norwoodville	Sevier	AR	Oak Grove	Christian	KY
North Wayne	Kennebec	ME	Nossville	Huntingdon	PA	Oak Grove	Prince George's	MD
North Weare	Hillsborough	NH	Nostasulga	Macon	AL	Oak Grove	Livingston	MI
North West	Williams	OH	Notre Dame	St. Joseph	IN	Oak Grove	Anoka	MN
N.W. Bridgewater	Plymouth	MA	Nottawa	St. Joseph	MI	Oak Grove	Jackson	MO
North Western	Oneida	NY	Nottingham	Wells	IN	Oak Grove	Jackson	MO
N. Wethersfield	Wyoming	NY	Nottingham	Prince George's	MD	Oak Grove	Hunterdon	NJ
North Weymouth	Norfolk	MA	Nottingham	Rockingham	NH	Oak Grove	Union	NC
North Wharlton	Pottor	WV	Nottingham	Cuyahoga	OH	Oak Grove	Marion	SC
North Whitefield	Lincoln	ME	Nottingham	Chester	PA	Oak Grove	Jefferson	TN
North Whitehall	Lehigh	PA	Nottoway(c.h.)	Nottaway	VA	Oak Grove Furnace	Westmoreland	PA
North Williston	Chittenden	VT	Nova	Ashland	OH	Oak Grove	Seward	NE
N. Wilmington	Middlesex	MA	Novelty	Knox	MO	Oakham	Worcester	MA
North Wilna	Jefferson	NV	Novi	Oakland	MI	Oak Harbor	Ottawa	OH
North Wilton	Fairfield	CN	Nuckellsville	Grayson	VA	Oak Hill	Newton	GA
North Windham	Windham	CN	Nueccs	Nuecss	TX	Oak Hill	Clay	KS
North Windham	Cumberland	ME	Nugent's Grove	Linn	IA	Oak Hill	Cumberland	ME
North Windham	Windham	VT	Nulhegan	Essex	VT	Oak Hill	Oakland	MI
North Windsor	Dane	WI	Null's Mills	Fayette	IN	Oak Hill	Gasconade	MO
North Winfield	Herkimer	NY	Numa	Parke	IN	Oak Hill	Greene	NY
North Winterp.	Waldo	ME	Numa	Appanoose	IA	Oak Hill	Granville	NC
North Woburn	Middlesex	MA	Numidia	Columbia	PA	Oak Hill	Jackson	OH
North Wolfb.	Carroll	NH	Nunda	McHenry	IL	Oak Hill	Lancaster	PA
Northwood(c.h.)	Worth	IA	Nunda	Freeborn	MN	Oak Hill	Overton	TN
Northwood	Logan	OH	Nunda	Livingston	NY	Oak Hill	Travis	TX
Northwd Ctre.	Rockingham	NH	Nunda Station	Livingston	NY	Oak Hill	Fayette	WV
Northwood Nrws	Rockingham	NH	Nunica	Ottawa	MI	Oak Hill	Jefferson	WI
North Woodstock	Windham	CN	Nunna	Choctaw Nat.	IT	Oakhumpka	Sumter	FL
North Woodstock	Oxford	ME	Nursey Hill	Dent	MO	Oakburst	Miller	MO
North Woodstock	Grafton	NH	Nusery Hill	Otoe	NE	Oakington	Hartford	MD
North Woodville	Penobscot	ME	Nuzums	Marion	WV	Oakland	Wilcox	AL
North Yam Hill	O R		Nyzack	Rockland	NY	Oakland	Alameda	CA
North Yarmouth	Cumberland	ME	Nyce's	Pike	NY	Oakland	Coles	IL
Norton	Kankakee	IL				Oakland	Spencer	IN
Norton	Bristol	MA	Oak	Pope	IL	Oakland	Jewell	KS
Norton	Delaware	OH	Oak	Pulaski	IN	Oakland	Marshall	KY
Norton Hill	Greene	NY	Oak	Marion	IA	Oakland	Alleghany	MD
Norton Mills	Essex	VT	Oak	Wayne	MI	Oakland	Oakland	MI
Norton's Bluff	McCracken	KY	Oakella	Iroquois	IL	Oakland	Yalabusha	MS
Nortonville	Clarke	IA	Oak Bower	Hart	GA	Oakland	Laclede	MO
Nortonville	Hopkins	KY	Oak Centre	Fond du Lac	WI	Oakland	Burt	NE
Norval	Harnet	NC	Oak Creek	Milwaukee	WI	Oakland	Livingston	NY
Norvell	Jackson	MS	Oakdale	Livingston	IL	Oakland	Clinton	OH
Norwalk	Fairfield	CN	Oakdale	Jennings	IN	Oakland	Douglas	OR
Norwalk	Warren	IA	Oakdale	Worcester	MA	Oakland	Armstrong	PA
Norwalk	fManistee	ME	Oak Dale	Washington	MN	Oakland	Fayette	TN
Norwalk(c.h.)	Huron	OH	Oak Dale	Hunterdon	NJ	Oakland	Colorado	TX
Norway	La Salle	IL	Oakdale	Delaware	PA	Oakland(c.h.)	Mason	WA
Norway	Republic	KS	Oakdale	Rockbridge	VA	Oakland	Jefferson	WI
Norway	Oxford	ME	Oakdale Station	Suffolk	NY	Oakland City	Gibson	IN
Norway	Goodhue	MN	Oakdale Station	Alleghany	PA	Oakland X-Roads	Westmoreland	PA
Norway	Herkimer	NY	Oakdam	Vanderburgh	IN	Oakland Mills	Henry	IA
Norway	Chester	PA	Oak Farm	Brown	IN	Oakland Mills	Nicholas	KY
Norway	Racine	WI	Oakfield	Audubon	IA	Oakland Mills	Howard	MD
Norway Lake	Kandiyohi	MN	Oakfield	Kent	MI	Oakland Mills	Guernsey	OH
Norweigian	Watonwan	MN	Oakfield	Franklin	MO	Oakland Mills	Juanita	PA
Norwich(c.h.)	New London	CN	Oakfield	Genesee	NY	Oaklandon	Marion	IN
Norwich	Hampshire	MA	Oakfield	Perry	OH	Oakland Station	Warren	KY
Norwich(c.h.)	Chenango	NY	Oakfield	Fond du Lac	WI	Oakland Valley	Franklin	IA
Norwich	Muskingham	OH	Oakfield Centre	Fond du Lac	WI	Oakland Valley	Orange	NY
Norwich	McKean	PA	Oak Flat	Pendleton	WV	Oak Lawn	Providence	RI
Norwich	Windsor	VT	Oakford	Howard	IN	Oak Lawn	Shelby	TN
Norwich Town	New London	CN	Oakford	Daviess	KY	Oak Level	Cleburne	AL
Norwood	Lucas	IA	Oakford	Bucks	PA	Oak Level	Henry	VA
Norwood	Franklin	KS	Oak Forest	Franklin	IN	Oakley	Montgomery	AL
Norwood	Charleviox	MI	Oak Forest	Iredell	NC	Oakley	Macon	IL
Norwood	Carter	MO	Oak Forest	Greene	PA	Oakley	Franklin	LA
Norwood	Bergen	NJ	Oak Forest	Cumberland	VA	Oakley	Saginaw	MI

PLACE NAMES OF THE UNITED STATES

PLACE	COUNTY	STATE	PLACE	COUNTY	STATE	PLACE	COUNTY	STATE
Oakley	New Hanover	NC	Ocean View	Sussex	DE	Okemos	Ingham	MI
Oakley	Hamilton	OH	Oceanville	Hancock	ME	Okmulkee	Creek Nation	IT
Oakley	Susquehanna	PA	Oceola	St. Joseph	IN	Okoboji	Dickinson	IA
Oakley	Mecklenburgh	VA	Oceola(c.h.)	Clarke	IA	Okolona	Chickasaw	MS
Oakley	Greene	WI	Oceola	Greene	KY	Okolona	Henry	OH
Oakley Depot	Charleston	SC	Oceola	Fond du Lac	WI	Okolona	Carter	TN
Oakley Mills	Atchison	KS	Oceola Centre	Livingston	MI	Okonoko	Hampshire	WV
Oak Orchard	Orleans	NY	Ocheltree	Johnson	KS	Ola	Lucas	IA
Oak Orchard	Frederick	MD	Ochesee	Calhoun	FL	Olamon	Penobscot	ME
Oak Park	Cook	IL	Ocona Lufty	Swain	NC	Olathe(c.h.)	Johnson	KS
Oak Park	Madison	VA	Oconee	Washington	GA	Olcott	Niagra	NY
Oak Point	Clark	IL	Oconee Station	Shelby	IL	Old Alexandira	Lincoln	MO
Oak Point	Van Buren	IA	Oconomowoc	Waukesha	WI	Old Bridge	Middlesex	NJ
Oak Point	Wilson	TN	Oconto(c.h.)	Oconto	WI	Old Church	Hanover	VA
Oak Point	Jefferson	AL	Oconto Falls	Oconto	WI	Old Cotton Grove	Madison	TN
Oak Ridge	Jefferson	AL	Ocoya	Livingston	IL	Old Creek	San Luis Obispo	CA
Oak Ridge	Menard	IL	Ocracoke	Hyde	NC	Oldenburgh	Franklin	IN
Oak Ridge	Winona	MN	Octagon	Tippecanoe	IN	Old Farm	Lawrence	IL
Oak Ridge	Cape Girardean	MO	Octavia	Early	GA	Old Field	Livingston	LA
Oak Ridge	Guilford	NC	Octararo	Lancaster	PA	Old Forge	Luzerne	PA
Oak Ridge	Hancock	OH	Oddville	Harrison	KY	Old Fort	McDowell	NC
Oak Row	Richmond	VA	Odell	Livingston	IL	Old Furnace	Gaston	NC
Oak Run	Hancock	OH	Odenton	Anne Arundel	MD	Oldham's X-Roads	Westmoreland	VA
Oak's	Orange	NC	Odessa	New Castle	DE	Old Hickory	Conway	AR
Oaks	Montgomery	PA	Odessa	Schuyler	NY	Old Hickory	Wayne	OH
Oaks	Sauk	WI	Odin	Marion	IL	Old Hickory	Botetourt	VA
Oak's Corners	Ontario	NY	Ofahoma	Leake	MS	Old Line	Lancaster	PA
Oak Shade	Lancaster	PA	O'Fallon	St. Charles	MO	Old Mines	Washington	MO
Oak Spring	Daviess	IA	O'Fallon Depot	St. Clair	IL	Old Mission	Winneshick	IA
Oak Springs	Rutherford	NC	Offutt's X-Roads	Montgomery	MD	Old Misson	Grand Traverse	MI
Oak Springs	Anoka	MN	Ogden	Champaign	IL	Old Monroe	Lincoln	MO
Oaksville	Otsego	NY	Ogden	Henry	IN	Old Point Comfort	Elizabeth	VA
Oaktown	Knox	IN	Ogden	Dubuque	IA	Old Richmond	Forsyth	SC
Oak Valley	Schuyler	IL	Ogden	Boone	IA	Old Ripley	Bond	IL
Oakville	Lawrence	AL	Ogden	Riley	KS	Old Store	Chesterfield	SC
Oakville	Jefferson	AR	Ogden	Monroe	NY	Old Town	Phillips	AR
Oakville	Napa	CA	Ogden	Clinton	OH	Old Town	Penobscot	ME
Oakville	New Haven	CN	Ogden	Weber	UT	Old Town	Alleghany	MD
Oakville	St. Mary's	MD	Ogden Centre	Lenawee	MI	Old Town	Forsyth	NC
Oakville	Monroe	MI	Ogden City(c.h.)	Weber	UT	Oldtown	Claiborne	TN
Oakville	Cumberland	PA	Ogdensburgh	Sussex	NY	Old Westbury	Queens	NY
Oakville	Shelby	TN	Ogdensburgh	Tioga	PA	Olean	Ripley	IN
Oakville	Live Oak	TX	Ogdensburgh	Waupaca	WI	Olean	Cattaraugus	NY
Oakville	Appomattox	VA	Ogden's Landing	Ballard	KY	Olema	Marin	CA
Oakway	Oconee	SC	Ogdensville	Cook	TN	Olena	Henderson	IL
Oak Well	Hawkins	TN	Ogee	Blount	AL	Olena	Huron	OH
Oakwood	Vermillion	IL	Ogeechee	Scriven	GA	Oleopolis	Venango	PA
Oakwood	Linn	KS	Ogemaw	Iocho	MI	Oley	Berks	PA
Oakwood	Oakland	MI	Ogle	Butler	PA	Olin	Iredell	NC
Oakwood	Paulding	OH	Oglesby	La Salle	IL	Olin	Adams	WI
Oakwood	Montgomery	TN	Oglethorpe(c.h.)	Macon	GA	Olin	Scott	AR
Oak Woods	Fleming	KY	Ogunquit	York	ME	Olive	Lawrence	IL
Oaky Streak	Butler	AL	Ohio	Bureau	IL	Olive	Marshall	KY
Oasis	Johnson	IA	Ohio	Madison	IA	Olive	Clinton	MI
Oasis	Waushara	WI	Ohio	Herkimer	NY	Olive	Ulster	NY
Oatlands	Loudoun	VA	Ohio Mill	Ottawa	MI	Olive Branch	De Soto	MS
Oatmeal	Burnet	TX	Ohioville	Ulster	NY	Olive Branch	Lancaster	NE
O'Bannon	Jefferson	KY	Ohioville	Beaver	PA	Olive Branch	Union	NC
Oberle's Corners	Carver	MN	Ohiowa	Fillmore	MN	Olive Branch	Clermont	OH
Oberlin	Lorain	OH	Ohl's Town	Trumbull	OH	Olive Bridge	Ulster	NY
Oblong	Crawford	IL	Oil City	Venango	PA	Oliveburgh	Jefferson	PA
Oblong	Dutchess	NY	Oil Creek	Perry	IN	Olive Green	Noble	OH
O'Brien	O'Brien	IA	Oll Creek	Crawford	PA	Olive Hill	Wayne	IN
Ocate	Mora	NM	Oil Diggins	Trumbull	OH	Olive Hill	Carter	KY
Ocala(c.h.)	Marion	FL	Oil Mill Village	Hillsborough	NH	Olive Hill	Hardin	TN
Occoquan	Prince William	VA	Oil Rock	Wirt	WV	Oliver's	Anderson	TN
Ocean	Alleghany	MD	Oil Springs	Johnson	KY	Olivesburgh	Richland	OH
Oceana(c.h.)	Wyoming	VA	Oil Trough	Independence	AR	Olivet	Union	IA
Oceanic	Monmouth	NJ	Oil Works	Greenup	KY	Olivet	Osage	KS
Ocean Grove	Monmouth	NJ	Okaman	Waseca	MN	Olivet	Eaton	MI
Ocean Port	Monmouth	NJ	Okaw	Washington	IL	Olivet	Armstrong	PA
Ocean Springs	Jackson	MS	Okenana	Butler	OH	Olivet	Pierce	WI
Ocean View	Sonoma	CA	Okee	Columbia	WI	Olivet	Blair	PA

PLACE NAMES OF THE UNITED STATES

PLACE	COUNTY	STATE	PLACE	COUNTY	STATE	PLACE	COUNTY	STATE
Olivia	Blair	PA	Ontario	Vernon	WI	Ore Banks	Buckingham	VA
Olmstead	Logan	KY	Ontonagon(c.h.)	Ontonagon	MI	Orefield	Lehigh	PA
Olmstead Falls	Franklin	VT	Onward	Cass	IN	Oregon	Jefferson	OR
Olmsted	Cuyahoga	OH	Onyx	Yell	AR	Oregon(c.h.)	Ogle	IL
Olmstedville	Essex	NY	Oolteway	James	TN	Oregon	Clarke	IN
Olney(c.h.)	Richland	IL	Oostburgh	Sheboygan	WI	Oregon(c.h.)	Holt	MO
Olney	Montgomery	MD	Optika(c.h.)	Lee	AL	Oregon	Chautauqua	NY
Olney	Philadelphia	PA	Opelausas(c.h.)	St. Landry	LA	Oregon	Warren	OH
Olneyville	Providence	RI	Opequan	Lancaster	NE	Oregon	Lancaster	PA
Olnstee	Baker	FL	Opheim	Henry	IL	Oregon	Lincoln	TN
Olnstee Creek	Pike	IL	Ophir	Cherokee	GA	Oregon	Dane	WI
Olympia(c.h.)	Thurston	WA	Ophir	Washoe	NV	Oregon City(c.h.)	Clackamas	OR
Olympian Springs	Bath	KY	Ophir	Tooele	UT	Oregon Hill	Lycoming	PA
Olympus	Overton	TN	O'Plain	Lake	IL	Oregon House	Yuba	CA
Olyphant	Luzerne	PA	Oporto	St. Joseph	MI	Oregonia	Tucaloosa	AL
Omandi	Dakota	NE	Oppelo	Perry	AR	Ore Hill	Litchfield	CN
Omaha	Gallatin	IL	Oppenhiem	Fulton	NY	Orell	Jefferson	KY
Omaha	Putnam	IL	Opposition	Lawrence	AR	Oreville	Dutchess	NY
Omaha(c.h.)	Douglas	NE	Owuawka(c.h.)	Henderson	IL	Orford	Tama	IA
Omaha Agency	Blackbird	NE	Ora	Jackson	IL	Orford	Grafton	NH
Omaha Barracks	Douglas	NE	Oral	Scott	MN	Orfordville	Grafton	NH
Omaha City	Douglas	ME	Ora Labor	Lunnenburgh	Va	Organ Spring	Washington	IN
Omar	Jefferson	NY	Oral Oaks	Lunnenburgh	VA	Orient	Adair	IA
Omard	Sanilac	MI	Oramel	Allegany	NY	Orient	Aroostook	ME
Omega	Nevada	CA	Oran	Fayette	IA	Orient	Suffolk	NY
Omega	Marion	IL	Oran	Onondaga	NY	Orhula	Winnebago	WI
Omega	Hamilton	IN	Orange	New Haven	CN	Orion	Pike	AL
Omega	Hart	KY	Orange	Cherokee	GA	Orion	Henry	MO
Omega	Pike	OH	Orange	Fayette	IN	Orion	Richland	WI
Omega	Upshur	TX	Orange	Clinton	IA	Oriskany	Oneida	NY
Omega	Halifax	VA	Orange	Fleming	KY	Oriskany Falls	Oncida	NY
Omena	Leelenaw	MI	Orange	Franklin	MA	Orizaba	Tippah	MS
Omnia	Cowley	KS	Orange	Ionia	MI	Orkney Springs	Shenandoah	VA
Omph Ghent	Madison	IL	Orange	Essex	NJ	Orland	Cook	IL
Omro	Winnebago	WI	Orange	Schuyler	NY	Orland	Steuben	IN
Onalaska	La Crosse	WI	Orange	Mahoning	OH	Orland	Hancock	ME
Onancock	Accomack	VA	Orange	Luzerne	PA	Orlando(c.h.)	Orange	FL
Onawa City(c.h.)	Monona	IA	Orange(c.h.)	Orange	TX	Orlando	Sherbune	MN
Onberg	Indiana	PA	Orange	Orange	VT	Orlean	Fanquier	VA
O'Neals's	Amite	MS	Orange	Juneau	WI	Orleans(c.h.)	Klamath	CA
O'Neal's Mills	Troup	GA	Orangeburgh	Mason	KY	Orleans	Morgan	IL
Oneco	Windham	CN	Orangeburgh(c.h.)	Orangeburgh	SC	Orleans	Orange	IN
Oneida	Knox	IL	Orange City	Sioux	IA	Orleans	Appanoose	IA
Oneida	Kosciusko	IN	Orange(c.h.)	Orange	VA	Orleans	Barnstable	MA
Oneida	Madison	NY	Orange Factory	Orange	NC	Orleans	Ionia	MI
Oneida	Brown	WI	Orange Grove	Dallas	AL	Orleans	Polk	ME
Oneida Castle	Oneida	NY	Orange Hill	Washington	FL	Orleans	Ontario	NY
Oneida Lake	Madison	NY	Orange Lake	Orange	NY	Orleans X-Roads	Morgan	WV
Oneida Mills	Carroll	OH	Orange Lodge	Orange	FL	Orleans 4 Corners	Jefferson	NY
Oneida Valley	Madison	NY	Orange Mills	St. John's	FL	Ormanville	Wapello	IA
Onekama	Manistee	MI	Orangeport	Niagara	NY	Orme's Store	Bledsoe	TN
Oneonta	Otsego	NY	Orange Springs	Marion	FL	Ormsby	Alleghany	PA
Oneota	St. Louis	MN	Orange Station	Delaware	OH	Orneville	Piscataquis	ME
Oneyville	Davidson	TN	Orange Valley	Essex	NY	Oro	Chesterfield	SC
Onion Creek	Travis	TX	Orangeville	Stephenson		Oro City	Placer	CA
Onion River	Sheboygan	WI	Orangeville	Orange	IN	Oro City	Lake	CO
Onisbo	Sacramento	CA	Orangeville	Baltimore	MD	Orodell	Union	OR
Ono	Lebanon	PA	Orangeville	Branch	MI	Oro Fino	Siskiyou	CA
Ono	Pierce	WI	Orangeville	Wyoming	NY	Orono	Penobscot	ME
Onondaga	Ingham	MI	Orangeville	Trumbull	OH	Orono(c.h.)	Sherburne	MN
Onondaga	Onondaga	NY	Orangeville	Columbia	PA	Oronoco	Olmsted	MN
Onondaga Castle	Onondaga	NY	Orangeville	Fannin	TX	Oronoco	Amhearst	VA
Onondaga Valley	Onondaga	NY	Orangeville Mills	Barry	MI	Oroville(c.h.)	Butte	CA
Onota	Schoolcraft	MI	Ora Creek	Grant	WI	Orrington	Penobscot	ME
Onoville	Cattaraugus	NY	Orbisonia	Huntingdon	PA	Orr's Island	Cumberland	ME
Onsley	Loundes	GA	Orchard	Mitchell	IA	Orrstown	Franklin	PA
Onslow(c.h.)	Onslow	NC	Orchard Grove	Lake	IN	Orrsville	Armstrong	PA
Ontario	Knox	IL	Orchard Mine	Peoria	IL	Orrville	Dallas	AL
Ontario	La Grange	IN	Orcutt Creek	Bradford	PA	Orrville	Wayne	OH
Ontario	Story	IA	Orcuttville	Neosho	KS	Orth	Montgomery	IN
Ontario	Jackson	KS	Ord	Neosho	KS	Ortonville	Oakland	MI
Ontario	Wayne	NY	Ordino	Marquette	WI	Orville	Ellis	TX
Ontario	Richland	OH	Oreana	Humbolt	NV	Orville	Pope	IL

PLACE	COUNTY	STATE	PLACE	COUNTY	STATE	PLACE	COUNTY	STATE
Orwell	Oswego	NY	Osyka	Pike	MS	Overton	Cooper	MO
Orsell	Bradford	PA	Ottay	San Diego	Ca	Overton	Bradford	PA
Orwell	Addison	VT	Ottego	Ottsego	NY	Ovid	Madison	IN
Orwigsburgh	Schuylkill	PA	Othello	Olmstead	MN	Ovid	Taylor	IA
Orwin	Schuylkill	PA	Otho	Webster	IA	Ovid	Clinton	MI
Osaga	Bourbon	KS	Otis	Hancock	ME	Ovid(c.h.)	Senecca	NY
Osage	Carroll	AR	Otis	Berkshire	MA	Ovid	Franklin	OH
Osage	Franklin	IL	Ottisco	Clarke	IN	Ovid	Rich	UT
Osage(c.h.)	Mitchell	IA	Ottisco	Ironia	MI	Ovid Centre	Senecca	NY
Osage	Crawford	MO	Ottisco	Waseca	MN	Owaneco	Christian	IL
Osage	Otoe	NE	Ottisco Valley	Onondaga	NY	Owaneco	Sullivan	MO
Osage Bluff	Cole	MO	Otisfield	Cumberland	ME	Owaneco	Cayuga	NY
Osage City	Osage	KS	Otisville	Franklin	IA	Owasco Lake	Cayuga	NY
Osage Mission	Neosho	KS	Otisville	Genesee	MI	Owatonna(c.h.)	Steele	MN
Osakis	Douglas	MN	Otisville	Orange	NY	Owego(c.h.)	Tioga	NY
Osanippa	Chambers	AL	Otley	Marion	IA	Owego	Shawanaw	WI
Osawatomie	Miami	KS	Oto	Talladega	AL	Owen	Winnebago	IL
Osborn	Rock Island	IL	Oto	Woodbury	IA	Owensbor.(c.h.)	Daviess	KY
Osborn	Neosho	KS	Otoe Agency	Gage	NE	Owensboro' Junct.	Munlenburg	KY
Osborn	De Kalb	MO	Otranto	Mitchell	*ia	Owensburgh	Greene	IN
Osborn	Greene	OH	Otsdawa	Otsego	NY	Owen's X-Roads	Madison	AL
Osborne Hollow	Broome	NY	Otsego	Fayette	IA	Owen's Grove	Cerro Gordo	IA
Osborne's Mills	Kanawha	WV	Otsego	Allegan	MI	Owensville	Saline	AR
Osborn's Bridge	Fulton	NY	Otsego	Wright	MN	Owensville	Gibson	IN
Osborn's Ford	Scott	VA	Otsego	Ray	MO	Owensville	Gasconade	MO
Osborn's Gap	Wise	VA	Otsego	Muskingum	OH	Owensville	Clermont	OH
Osborn's Store	I;ssaquena	MS	Otsego	Columbia	WI	Owensville(c.h.)	Robertson	TX
Oscar	Armstrong	PA	Otselic	Chenango	NY	Owenton(c.h.)	Owen	KY
Osceola(c.h.)	Mississippi	Ar	Ottawa(c.h.)	La Salle	IL	Owing's Mills	Baltimore	MD
Osceola	Stark	IL	Ottawa	Clarke	IA	Owingsville(c.h.)	Bath	KY
Osceola(c.h.)	St. CLair	MO	Ottawa	Le Sueur	MN	Owl Hill	Cumberland	TN
Osceola(c.h.)	Polk	NE	Ottowa(c.h.)	Franklin	KS	Owl Prairie	Daviess	IN
Osceola	Lewis	NY	Ottowa(c.h.)	Putnam	OH	Owl Run	Fauquier	VA
Osceola	Tioga	PA	Ottowa	Waukesha	WI	Owesso	Shiawassee	MI
Osceola Mills	Clearfield	PA	Ottawa Lake	Monroe	MI	Oxbow	Putnam	IL
Osceola Mills(c.h.)	Polk	WI	Otter Creek	Levy	FL	Oxbow	Jefferson	NY
Osuma	Cherokee Nation	IT	Otter Creek	Jersey	IL	Oxen Hill	Prince George's	MD
Osgood	Ripley	IN	Otter Creek	Jackson	IA	Oxford	Calhoun	AL
Oshaukuta	Columbia	WI	Otter Creek	Clay	KS	Oxford	New Haven	CN
Oshawa	Osage	MO	Otter Creek	Jackson	MI	Oxford	Newton	GA
Oshkosh(c.h.)	Winnebago	WI	Otter Creek	Wayne	MO	Oxford	Henry	IL
Oshtemo	Kalamazoo	MI	Otter Creek	Rutherford	NC	Oxford(c.h.)	Benton	IN
Oskaloosa	Clay	IL	Otter Creek	Eau Claire	WI	Oxford	Johnson	IA
Oskaloosa(c.h.)	Mahaska	IA	Otter Hill	Bedford	VA	Oxford	Sumner	KS
Oskaloosa(c.h.)	Jefferson	KS	Otter Lake	Pottawatomie	KS	Oxford	Scott	KY
Oslo	Manitowoc	WI	Otter River	Worcester	MA	Oxford	Oxford	ME
Osman's	Adams	OH	Otter Tail City	Otter Trail	MN	Oxford	Talbot	MD
Osnaburgh	Stark	OH	Otterville	Buchanan	IA	Oxford	Worcester	MA
Oso	Fayette	TX	Otterville	Cooper	MO	Oxford	Oakland	MI
Osprey	Monroe	IA	Otterville	Bedford	VA	Oxford(c.h.)	Isanti	MN
Ossco	Hillsdale	MI	Otto	Fulton	IL	Oxford(c.h.)	La Fayette	MS
Ossco	Hennepin	MN	Otto	Clarke	IN	Oxford	Worth	MO
Ossco	Trempealeau	WI	Otto	Pope	MN	Oxford	Chenango	NY
Ossian	Wells	IN	Otto	Cattaraugus	NY	Oxford	Butler	OH
Ossian	Livingston	NY	Ottobine	Rockingham	VA	Oxford(c.h.)	Granville	NC
Ossineke	Alpena	MI	Ottokee	Fulton	OH	Oxford	Chester	PA
Ossipee(c.h.)	Carroll	NH	Ottsville	Bureau	IL	Oxford	Cache	UT
Ossipee Mills	York	ME	Ottsville	Bucks	PA	Oxford	Doddridge	WV
Ossian	Livingston	NY	Ottumwa(c.h.)	Wapello	IA	Oxford	Marquette	WI
Ostend	McHenry	IL	Ottumwa	Coffey	KS	Oxford Church	Philadelphia	PA
Ostend	Clearfield	PA	Otway	Scioto	OH	Oxford Depot	Orange	NY
Osterville	Barnstable	MA	Otwell	Pike	IN	Oxford Mills	Jones	IA
Osterville	Caldwell	MO	Onaquaga	Broome	NY	Oxford Valley	Bucks	PA
Ostrander	Delaware	OH	Ouleout	Delaware	NY	Oyster	Lewis	MO
Oswahldville	Lehigh	PA	Our Town	Sheboygan	WI	Oyster Bay	Queens	NY
Oswayo	Potter	PA	Ousleie's Gap	Cabell	WV	Oysterville(c.h.)	Pacific	WA
Oswego	Kendall	IL	Outlaw's Bridge	Duplin	NC	Ozan	Hempstead	AR
Oswego	Kosciusko	IN	Outville	Licking	OH	Ozark	Dale	AL
Oswego(c.h.)	Labette	KS	Overbrook	Montgomery	PA	Ozark	Jackson	IA
Oswego(c.h.)	Oswego	NY	Overisel	Allegan	MI	Ozark(c.h.)	Franklin	AR
Oswego	Clackamas	OR	Overfield	Barbour	WV	Ozark(c.h.)	Christian	MO
Oswego Centre	Oswego	NY	Overpeck's Station	Butler	OH	Ozark	Allen	KS
Oswego Falls	Oswego	NY	Overton	Lincoln	NV	Ozark	Monroe	OH

PLACE	COUNTY	STATE	PLACE	COUNTY	STATE	PLACE	COUNTY	STATE
Ozaukee(c.h.)	Ozaukee	WI	Palma	Marshall	KY	Papineau	Iroquois	IL
Ozawkie	Jefferson	KS	Palmer	Christian	IL	Papinsville	Bates	MO
Ozro Falls	Howard	KS	Palmer	Polk	IA	Paraclifta	Sevier	AR
			Palmer	Hampden	MA	Paradise	Stanislaus	CA
Paces	Metcalf	KY	Palmer's Springs	Mecklenburg	VA	Paradise	Coles	IL
Pacherco	Contra Costa	CA	Palmersville	Allegheny	PA	Paradise	Muhlenburgh	KY
Pacific	Franklin	MO	Palmetto	Pickens	AL	Paradise	Clay	MO
Pacific	Franklin	NC	Palmetto	Campbell	GA	Paradise	Lancaster	PA
Pacific	Columbia	WI	Palmetto	Darlington	SC	Paradise	Cache	UT
Pacific City	Mills	IA	Palmetto	Bedford	TN	Paradise Valley	Humbolt	NV
Pacific Junction	Mills	IA	Palmetto Home	Yazoo	MS	Paradise Valley	Monroe	PA
Packard	Vinton	OH	Palmyra	Macoupin	IL	Paragon	Morgan	IN
Packer	Jefferson	PA	Palmyra	Harrison	IN	Paragonah	Iron	UT
Packer's Prairie	Douglas	MN	Palmyra	Warren	IA	Paraje	Socorro	NM
Pack's Ferry	Monroe	WV	Palmyra	Somerset	ME	Parallel	Riley	KS
Packsville	Clarendon	SC	Palmyra	Lenawee	MI	Pardee	Atchison	KS
Packwaukee	Marquette	WI	Palmyra(c.h.)	Marion	MO	Pardeeville	Columbia	WI
Pacolett Depot	Spartanburgh	SC	Palmyra	Otoe	NE	Parham's Store	Sussex	VA
Pactolus	Pitt	NC	Palmyra	Burlington	NJ	Paris(c.h.)	Edgar	IL
Paddock's Grove	Madison	IL	Palmyra	Wayne	NY	Paris	Jennings	IN
Paddy's Run	Butler	OH	Palmyra	Halifax	NC	Paris	Linn	IA
Padonia	Brown	KS	Palmyra	Portage	OH	Paris(c.h.)	Bourbon	KY
Padoria	Crawford	IL	Palmyra	Lebanon	PA	Paris(c.h.)	Monroe	MO
Padua	McClean	IL	Palmyra(c.h.)	Fluvanna	VA	Paris	Mecosta	MI
Paducah(c.h.)	McCracken	KY	Palmyra	Jefferson	WI	Paris	Oneida	NY
Page City	Page	IA	Palo	Marion	AL	Paris	Anson	NC
Pagetown	Morrow	OH	Palo	Linn	IA	Paris	Stark	OH
Pageville	Barren	KY	Palo	Ionia	MI	Paris	Washington	PA
Pahaquarry	Warren	NJ	Palo Alto	Louisa	IA	Paris(c.h.)	Henry	TN
Paincourtville	Assuption	LA	Palo Alto	Neosho	KS	Paris(c.h.)	Lamar	TX
Paine's Hollow	Herkimer	NY	Palo Alto	Chickasaw	MS	Paris	Rich	UT
Paine's Point	Ogle	IL	Palo Alto	Onslow	NC	Paris	Fanquier	VA
Painesville(c.h.)	Lake	OH	Palo Alto	Seneca	OH	Paris	Kenosha	WI
Paint	Highland	OH	Palo Alto	Schuylkill	PA	Parisville	Oswego	NY
Paint Creek	Washtenaw	MI	Palo Alto	Lawrence	TN	Parisville	St. Lawrence	NY
Paint Creek	Kanawha	WV	Palo Alto	Highland	VA	Parisville Centre	St. Lawrence	NY
Painted Post	Steuben	NY	Paloma	Adams	IL	Paris Landing	Henry	TN
Painter Creek	Darke	OH	Palo Pinto(c.h.)	Palo Pinto	TX	Parisville	Portage	OH
Painterhood	Howard	KS	Palos	Cook	IL	Park	Greene	IN
Painter's Bridge	Chester	PA	Paloma	Cook	IL	Park	Barren	KY
Paintersville	Greene	OH	Pamilia 4 Corners	Jefferson	NY	Park	St. Joseph	MI
Paint Lick	Garrard	KY	Pamilico	Craven	NC	Park	Lancaster	NE
Paintsville(c.h.)	Johnson	KY	Pamphu's Depot	Appomattox	VA	Park City	Sedwick	KS
Paint Valley	Holmes	OH	Pana	Christian	IL	Parker	Yuma	AZ
Paisley	Ottoe	NE	Panaca	Lincoln	NV	Parker	Randolph	IN
Pajarito	Bernalillo	NM	Panama	Lancaster	NE	Parker	Montgomery	KS
Palarm Bayou	Pulaski	AR	Panama	Chautauqua	NY	Parker's Bluff	Anderson	TX
Palatine	Cook	IL	Pana Maria	Karnes	TX	Parkersburgh	Richland	IL
Palatine	Salem	NJ	Panamore Hill	Scriven	GA	Parkersburgh	Montgomery	IN
Palatine	Marion	WV	Pancoastburgh	Fayette	OH	Parkersburgh	Butler	IA
Palatine Bridge	Montgomery	NY	Pandora	Johnson	TN	Parkersburgh(c.h.)	Wood	WV
Palenville	Greene	NY	Pan Handle	Brooke	WV	Parker's Head	Sagadahoe	ME
Palermo	Edgar	OH	Panoche	Fresno	CA	Parker's Lake	Hennepin	MN
Palermo	Doniphan	KS	Panola(c.h.)	Panola	MS	Parker's Landing	Armstrong	PA
Palermo	Waldo	MO	Panola Station	Woodford	IL	Parker's Mills	Houston	TX
Palermo	Osewgo	NY	Panora(c.h.)	Panola	MS	Parker's Mills	Ritchie	WV
Palermo Centre	Waldo	ME	Pantego	Beaufort	NC	Parker's Settlement	Possey	IN
Palestine	Crawford	IL	Panther Creek	Daviess	KY	Parker's Store	Hart	GA
Palestine	St. Francis	AR	Panther Creek	Yadkin	NC	Parker's Store	Giles	TN
Palestine	Columbia	AR	Panther Creek	Hancock	TN	Parkersville	Morris	KS
Palestine	Kosciusko	IN	Panther Rock	Forest	PA	Parkersville	Bates	MO
Palestine	Johnson	IA	Panther Spings	Hamblen	TN	Parkersville	Chester	PA
Palestine	Sunmer	KS	Panton	Addison	VT	Parkesburgh	Chester	PA
Palestine	Washington	LA	Paola(c.h.)	Miami	KS	Parkerton	Lamar	TX
Palestine	Pickaway	OH	Paloli(c.h.)	Paloli	IN	Parkison's Landing	Hardin	IL
Palestine	Lewis	TN	Paloli	Orange	IN	Park Lane	Litchifield	CN
Palestine	Greenbrier	WV	Paloli	Chester	PA	Parkman	Ceanga	OH
Palestine(c.h.)	Anderson	TX	Paloli	Dane	WI	Parkman	Piscataquis	ME
Palisade	Lander	NY	Papakating	Sussex	NY	Park Ridge	Cook	IL
Palisades	Rockland	NY	Papalote	Bee	TX	Park Ridge	Bergen	NJ
Pallas	Green	MO	Pa Pa Me	Oceana	MI	Parks	Scott	AR
Pall Mall	Fentress	TN	Paper Mills	Baltimore	MD	Park's	Edgefield	SC
Palm	Montgomery	PA	Papillion	Sarpy	NE	Park's Corners	Boone	IL

PLACE	COUNTY	STATE	PLACE	COUNTY	STATE	PLACE	COUNTY	STATE
Park's Creek	Bradford	PA	Patterson	Hardin	OH	Peaksville	Henry	GA
Park's Grove	St. Clair	MO	Patterson	Juiata	PA	Peaksville	Bedford	VA
Park's Mills	Franklin	OH	Patterson's Bluff	Sarber	AR	Peapack	Somerset	NJ
Park's Store	Jackson	AL	Patterson's Depot	Mineral	WV	Pea Ridge	Benton	AR
Parksville	Boyle	KY	Patterson's Mills	Ionia	MI	Pea Ridge	Kemper	MS
Parksville	Sullivan	NY	Patterson's Mills	Washington	PA	Pearisburgh(c.h.)	Giles	VA
Parksville	Polk	TN	Patterson's Store	Alamance	NC	Pearl	Pike	IL
Parkton	Baltimore	MD	Pattersonville	St. Mary's	LA	Pearl City	Madison	MS
Parkville	Shasha	CA	Patton	Bollinger	MO	Pearl Creek	Wyoming	NY
Parkville	Parke	IN	Pattonsburgh	Daviess	MO	Pearlington	Hancock	MS
Parkville	St. Joseph	MI	Patton's Home	Rutherford	NC	Pearson's Corner	Kent	DE
Parkviile	Platte	MO	Pattonsville	Scott	VA	Peart's Eddy	Armstrong	PA
Parkville	Kings	NY	Pattonsville	Lemar	TX	Peasleeville	Clinton	NY
Parkwood	Indiana	PA	Patty's Mill	Lyon	KS	Pebble Creek	Dodge	NE
Parma	Jackson	MI	Patuxent	Anne Arundel	MD	Pecan Point	Mississippi	AR
Parma Centre	Monroe	NY	Paul	Benton	IA	Pecatonica	Winnebago	IL
Parmitchie	Alcon	MS	Paulding(c.h.)	Jasper	MA	Peck	Sanilac	MI
Parmleysville	Wayne	KY	Paulding(c.h.)	Paulding	OH	Pecksburgh	Hendricks	IN
Parnassus	Westmoreland	PA	Paulina	Warren	NJ	Peck's Run	Upshur	WV
Parnassus	Marlborough	SC	Paulinville	Yuba	Ca	Peckville	Luzerne	PA
Parnassus	Augusta	VA	Paulsborough	Gloucester	NJ	Peconic	Suffolk	NY
Parowan(c.h.)	Iron	UT	Paul's X-Roads	Essex	VA	Peculiar	Cass	MO
Parrish	Franklin	IL	Paul's Valley	Chocotaw Nat.	IT	Pedee	Cedar	IA
Parrish	Des Moines	IA	Paulton	Westmoreland	PA	Pedee	Green	WI
Parrottsville	Cocke	TN	Paulville	Adair	MO	Peden	Kempet	MS
Parryville	Wayne	KY	Paupac	Pike	PA	Pendlar's Hill	Chatham	NC
Parshallville	Livingston	MI	Pavia	Bedford	PA	Pedricktown	Salem	NJ
Parsippany	Morris	NJ	Pavilion	Kendall	IL	Pee Dee	Anson	NC
Parsonfield	York	ME	Pavilion	Wabaunsee	KS	Pee Dee	Marion	SC
Paron's	Labette	KS	Pavilion	Kalamazoo	MI	Peekskill	Westchester	NY
Parson's Seminary	Travis	TX	Pavilion Centre	Genesee	NY	Peeled Oak	Bath	KY
Partello	Calhoun	MI	Pawlet	Rutland	VT	Peel Tree	Barbour	WV
Partlow's	Spottsylvania	VA	Pawling	Dutchess	NY	Pee Pee	Pike	OH
Partridge	Letcher	KY	Pawling	Chester	PA	Perrysville(c.h.)	McDowell	WV
Partirdge Island	Delaware	NY	Pawnee	Sangamon	IL	Pegram's Station	Cheatham	TN
Parscagoula	Jackson	MS	Pawnee	Bourbon	KS	Pekin(c.h.)	Tazewell	IL
Pascoag	Providence	RI	Pawnee City(c.h.)	Pawnee	NE	Pekin	Washington	IN
Paskack	Bergen	NJ	Pawnee Station	Bourbon	KS	Pekin	Jessamine	KY
Paso Robles	San Luis Obispo	CA	Paw Paw	Miami	IN	Pekin	Niagara	NY
Passadumkeag	Penobscot	ME	Pawselin	Wabashaw	MN	Pekin	Montgomery	NC
Passasic	Passasic	NJ	Pawtucket	Providence	RI	Pekin	Putnam	TN
Pass Christian	Harrison	MS	Pawtucket	Providence	RI	Pekin	Clark	WA
Passe de Terre	Stevens	MN	Pawtuxett	Wakulla	FL	Pelahatchee		
Pass Patansy	King George	VA	Paxinos	Northumberland	PA	Depot	Rankin	MS
Passumpsic	Caledonla	VT	Paxton(c.h.)	Ford	IL	Peletier's Mills	Carteret	NC
Pastoria	Jefferson	AR	Paxton	Harrison	KY	Pelham	Hampshire	MA
Pataskala	Licking	OH	Paxton	Worcester	MA	Pelham	Hillsborough	NH
Patch Grove	Grant	WI	Paxton	Dauphin	PA	Pelham	Westchester	NY
Patchin	Erie	NY	Paxton's	Sullivan	IN	Pelham	Caswell	NC
Patchinsville	Clearfield	PA	Paxtonville	Snyder	PA	Pelham	Grundy	TN
Patchogue	Suffolk	NY	Pay Down	Maries	MO	Penham	Boulder	CO
Paterson(c.h.)	Passaic	NJ	Payetteville	Ada	OH	Pella	Boulder	CO
Patesville	Hancock	KY	Payne	Paulding	OH	Pella	Dearborn	IN
Patmos	Mahoning	OH	Payne's Corners	Trubull	OH	Pella	Marion	IA
Patoka	Marion	IL	Payne's Depot	Scott	KY	Pella	Shawanaw	WI
Patoka	Gibson	IN	Paynesville	Stearns	MN	Pellania	Massac	IL
Patrick(c.h.)	Patrick	VA	Paynesville	Pike	MO	Pellville	Hancock	KY
Patricksburgh	Owen	IN	Paynesville	Milwaukee	WI	Pemaquid	Lincoln	MO
Patrick Springs	Patrick	VA	Paynesville	Meade	KY	Pemberton	Burlington	NJ
Patriot	Switzerland	IN	Payson	Adams	IL	Pemberville	Wood	OH
Partiot	Decatur	IA	Payson	Utah	UT	Pembina(c.h.)	Pembina	DA
Partiot	Gallia	OH	Peabody	Essex	MA	Pembroke	Christian	KY
Partiot	Wayne	TN	Peace Creek(c.h.)	Polk	FL	Pembroke	Washington	ME
Partroon	Shelby	TX	Peace Dale	Washington	RI	Pembroke	Plymouth	MA
Pattagumpus	Penbscot	ME	Peacham	Caledonia	VT	Pembroke	Merrimack	NH
Patten	Penbscot	ME	Peach Bottom	York	VA	Pembroke	Genesee	NY
Pattenburgh	Hunterdon	NJ	Peach Creek	Washington	KS	Pembroke	Giles	VA
Patten's Mills	Washington	OH	Peacher's Mills	Montgomery	TN	Pence's Mills	Warren	OH
Patten's Mills	Washington	NY	Peachland	Osage	MO	Pendarvis	Wayne	GA
Patterson	Nevada	CA	Peach Orchard	Lawrence	KY	Pendell	Butler	KS
Patterson	Wayne	MO	Peachville	Butler	PA	Pendleton	Arkansas	AR
Patterson	Putnam	NY	Peacock's Store	Columbus	SC	Pendleton	Madison	IN
Patterson	Caldwell	NC	Peak's Hill	Calhoun	AL	Pendleton	Henry	KY

PLACE NAMES OF THE UNITED STATES

PLACE	COUNTY	STATE	PLACE	COUNTY	STATE	PLACE	COUNTY	STATE
Pendleton	Warren	MO	Perch River	Jefferson	NY	Pescadero	San Mateo	CA
Pendleton	Niagara	NY	Percival	Fremont	IA	Peshitgo	Oconto	WI
Pendleton	Putnam	OH	Percy	Carbon	WY	Pesotum	Champaign	IL
Pendleton(c.h.)	Umatilla	OR	Perdenales	Travis	TX	Petaluma	Sonoma	CA
Pendleton	Anderson	SC	Perdido Station	Baldwin	AL	Peterborough	Hillsborough	NH
Pendleton Centre	Niagara	NY	Perin's Mills	Braxton	WV	Peterborough	Madison	NY
Pendleton Factory	Anderson	SC	Perkinsville	Madison	IN	Peter's	San Joaquin	CA
Pendleton Hill	Windham	CN	Perkinsville	Winston	MS	Petersburgh	Klamath	CA
Penfield	Greene	GA	Perkinsville	Steuben	NY	Petersburgh	Menard	IL
Penfield	Monroe	NY	Perkinsville	Burke	NC	Petersburgh(c.h.)	Pike	IN
Penfield	Lorain	OH	Perkinsville	Windsor	VT	Petersburgh	Leavenworth	KS
Penfield	Clearfield	PA	Perkinsville	Goochland	VA	Petersburgh	Boone	KY
Penbrook	Franklin	VA	Perkimenville	Montgomery	PA	Petersburgh	Monroe	KY
Penick	Marion	KY	Perote	Bullock	AL	Petersburgh	Jackson	MN
Peninsula	Summit	OH	Perrine	Mercer	PA	Petersburgh	Cape May	NJ
Penllyn	Montgomery	PA	Perrineville	Monmouth	NJ	Petersburgh	Rensselaer	NY
Penn(c.h.)	Osborne	KS	Perrinsville	Wayne	MI	Petersburgh	Mahoning	OH
Penn	Lancaster	PA	Perry(c.h.)	Houston	GA	Petersburgh	Butler	PA
Pennellville	Oswego	NY	Perry	Pike	IL	Petersburgh	Lincoln	TN
Penn Hall	Centre	PA	Perry	Dallas	IA	Petersburgh	Lavaca	TX
Penn Haven	Cabon	PA	Perry	Jefferson	KS	Petersburgh	Millard	UT
Penninger	Union	IL	Perry	Washington	ME	Petersburgh	Dinwiddle	VA
Pennington	Mercer	NJ	Perry	Shiawassee	MI	Peter's Creek	Stokes	NC
Pennington	Houston	TX	Perry	Ralls	MO	Peter's Creek	Lancaster	PA
Pennington Point	McDonough	IL	Perry	Wyoming	NY	Petersham	Worcester	MS
Pennington's Mills	Pulaski	AR	Perry	Lake	OH	Peter's Landing	Perry	TN
Penningtonville	Chester	PA	Perry	Forest	PA	Peterson(c.h.)	Clay	IA
Penn Line	Crawford	PA	Perry	Dane	WI	Peterson	Fillmore	MN
Penn Mine	Keweenaw	MI	Perry Centre	Wyoming	NY	Peterson	Morgan	UT
Penn Run	Indiana	PA	Perry City	Schuyler	NY	Peterstown	Monroe	WV
Pennsborough	Ritchie	WV	Perrydale	Polk	OR	Petersville	Frederick	MD
Pennsburgh	Montgomery	PA	Perrymansville	Harford	MD	Petersville	Northampton	PA
Penn's Creek	Snyder	PA	Perryopolis	Fayette	PA	Petit Jean	Yell	AR
Penn's Grove	Salem	NJ	Perry's Bridge	Vermillion	LA	Petra	Saline	MO
Penn's Park	Bucks	PA	Perrysburgh	Miami	IN	Petroleum Centre	Venango	PA
Penn's Square	Montgomery	PA	Perrysburgh(c.h.)	Wood	OH	Petrolia	Humbolt	CA
Penn's Station	Westmoreland	PA	Perry's Mills	Montgomery	AL	Petroliopolis	Los Angeles	CA
Penn's Store	Patrick	VA	Perry's Mills	Clinton	NY	Petrolium	Vernon	WE
Pennsville	Salem	NJ	Perry Springs	Pike	IL	Pettis	Crawford	PA
Pennsville	Morgan	NJ	Perrysville	Vermillion	IN	Pettisville	Fulton	OH
Pennsville	Fayete	PA	Perrysville	Allegheny	PA	Pettit	Tippercanoe	IN
Pennsville	Jay	IN	Perrysville	Washington	RI	Pettysville	Livingston	MI
Pennsville	Sullivan	MO	Perrysville	Licking	OH	Pevely	Jefferson	MO
Penn Van(c.h.)	Yates	NY	Perryville	Perry	AL	Pewamo	Ionia	MI
Penobscot	Hancock	ME	Perryville(c.h.)	Perry	MO	Pewaukee	Waukesha	WI
Penola	Caroline	VA	Perryville	Boyle	KY	Pewee Valley	Oldham	KY
Pensacola(c.h.)	Escambia	FL	Perryville	Cecil	MD	Peytona	Montgomery	MO
Pensaukie	Oconto	WI	Perryville	Hunterdon	NJ	Peytona	Boone	WV
Pentonville	Salem	NJ	Perryville	Madison	NY	Peyton's	Adams	IL
Pent Water	Oceana	MI	Perryville	Ashland	OH	Peytonsburgh	Cumberland	KY
Pentz	Butte	CA	Perryville	Decatur	TN	Peytonsburgh	Pittsylvania	KY
Peoa	Summit	UT	Persia	Cattaraugus	NY	Peyton's Creek	Smith	TN
Peola Mills	Madison	VA	Persia	Hawkins	TN	Peytonsville	Little River	AR
Peoli	Tuscarawas	OH	Personville	Venango	PA	Peytonsville	Williamson	TN
Peoria(c.h)	Peoria	dIL	Personville	Limestone	TX	Pharisburgh	Union	OH
Peoria	Mahaska	IA	Perth	Jefferson	MS	Pharsalia	Chenango	NY
Peoria	Franklin	KS	Perth	Fulton	NY	Pheasant Branch	Dane	WI
Peoria	Wyoming	NY	Perth Amboy	Middlesex	NJ	Phelps	Lawrence	MO
Peoria	Linn	OR	Peru	La Salle	IL	Phelps	Ontario	NY
Peoria	Hill	TX	Peru(c.h.)	Miami	IN	Phelps	Atchison	ME
Peoria City	Polk	IA	Peru	Madison	IA	Phelps Mills	Clinton	PA
Peosta	Dubuque	IA	Peru	Howard	KS	Phenix	Ashtabula	OH
Peotone	Will	IL	Peru	Oldham	KY	Phenix	Kent	RI
Pepacton	Delaware	NY	Peru	Oxford	ME	Philadelphia	Hancock	IN
Pepacton	Delaware	NY	Peru	Berkshire	MA	Philadelphia	Marion	MO
Pepin	Pepin	WI	Peru	Nemaha	NE	Philadelphia(c.h.)	Neshoba	MS
Pepperell	Middlesex	MA	Peru	Clinton	NY	Philadelphia	Jefferson	NY
Peppertown	Franklin	IN	Peru	Huron	OH	Philadelphia	Philadelphia	PA
Pepperville	Butler	NE	Peru	Bennington	VT	Philadelphia	London	TN
Pequabuck	Litchfield	CN	Peru	Hardy	WV	Philander	Gentry	MO
Pequea	Lancaster	PA	Peru	Dunn	WI	Philanthropy	Butler	OH
Peralta	Valencia	NM	Peru Mills	Juniata	PA	Philippi(c.h.)	Barbour	WV
Perch Lake	Blue Earth	MN	Peruville	Tomkins	NY	Philipsburgh	Deer Lodge	MT

PLACE	COUNTY	STATE	PLACE	COUNTY	STATE	PLACE	COUNTY	STATE
Philipsburgh	Jefferson	OH	Pierron	Madison	IL	Pickneyville(c.h.)	Perry	IL
Philipsburgh	Centre	PA	Pierson	Montcalm	MI	Pine	Linn	OR
Philip's Mills	Indiana	PA	Pierson	Montcalm	MI	Pine Apple	Wilcox	AL
Philips	Franklin	ME	Pierz	Morrison	MN	Pine Bend	Dakota	MN
Phillip's Bayou	Phillips	AR	Piffard	Livingston	NY	Pine Bluff(c.h.)	Jefferson	AR
Phillipsburgh	Laclede	MO	Pigeon Cove	Essex	MA	Pine Bluff	Caliaway	KY
Phillips Creek	Allegheny	NY	Pigeon Creek	Butler	AL	Pine Bluff	Chickasaw	MS
Phillipsport	Sullivan	NY	Pigeon Creek Centre	Jackson	WI	Pine Bluff	Pulaski	MO
Phillip's Store	Surry	VA	Pigeon Forge	Sevier	TN	Pine Bluff	Warren	TN
Phillipston	Worcester	MA	Pigeon Hill	Union	AR	Pine Bluff	Dane	WI
Phillipstown	White	IL	Pigeon River	Lake	MN	Pine Bluff	Laramine	WY
Philmont	Columbia	NY	Pigeon River	Haywood	NC	Pine Brook	Morris	NJ
Philo	Champaign	IL	Pigeon Run	Campbell	VA	Pine Bush	Orange	NY
Philo	Muskingum	OH	Pigeon Roost	Choctaw	MS	Pine City	Pine	MN
Philomath	Benton	OH	Pig River	Franklin	VA	Pine Creek	Butte	CA
Philomont	Loudoun	VA	Pike	Muscatine	IA	Pine Creek	Calhoun	MI
Philopolis	Baltimore	MD	Pike	Wyoming	NY	Pine Creek	Laclede	MO
Phil Sheridan	Wallace	KS	Pike	Perry	OH	Pine Creek	Schuyler	NY
Phippsburgh	Sagadahoc	ME	Pike	Bradford	PA	Pine Creek	Tioga	PA
Phoenicia	Ulster	NY	Pike Creek	Carter	MO	Pine Creek	Lamar	TX
Phoenix	Yavapai	AZ	Pike Mills	Potter	PA	Pine Flats	Indiana	PA
Phoenix	Douglas	IL	Pike Pond	Sullivan	NY	Pine Glen	Centre	PA
Phoenix	Baltimore	MD	Pike Rapids	Morrison	MN	Pine Grove	AMador	CA
Phoenix	Keweenaw	MI	Pike Road	Montgomery	AL	Pine Grove	Douglas	CO
Phoenix	Oswego	NY	Pike Run	Washington	PA	Pine Grove	Clarke	KY
Phoenix	Jackson	OR	Pike's Peak	Brown	IN	Pine Grove	Prince George's	MD
Phoenix	Armstrong	PA	Pike's Peak	Deer Lodge	MT	Pine Grove	Tuscola	MI
Phoenix	Abbeville	SC	Pike Station	Wayne	OH	Pine Grove	Esmeralda	NV
Phoenix Mills	Otsego	NY	Pikesville	Baltimore	MD	Pine Grove	Schuyler	NY
Phoenixville	Windham	CN	Piketon(c.h.)	Pike	KY	Pine Grove	Montgomery	NC
Phoenixville	Chester	PA	Piketon	Stoddard	MO	Pine Grove	Gallia	OH
Piasa	Macoupin	IL	Piketon	Pike	OH	Pine Grove	Schulkill	PA
Picacho	Monterey	CA	Pike Township	Berks	PA	Pine Grove	Henderson	TX
Pickard's Mills	Clinton	IN	Pikeville(c.h.)	Marion	AL	Pine Grove	Wetzel	WV
Pickens(c.h.)	Pickens	SC	Pikeville	Pike	IN	Pine Grove	Brown	WI
Pickens Station	Holmes	MS	Pikeville	Wayne	NC	Pine Grove Mills	Van Buren	MI
Pickensville	Pickens	AL	Pikeville	Darke	OH	Pine Grove Mills	Centre	PA
Pickensville	Pickens	SC	Pikeville(c.h.)	Putnam	FL	Pine Hill	Wilcox	AL
Pickerel	Greene	MO	Piland's Store	Ozark	MO	Pine Hill	Ashley	AR
Pickereltown	Logan	OH	Pilatka(c.h.)	Putnam	FL	Pine Hill	Rock Castle	KY
Pickering	Nodaway	MO	Pilcher	Belmont	OH	Pine Hill	Sanilac	MI
Pickering	Chester	PA	Pile Falls	Fayette	AL	Pine Hill	Shannon	MO
Pickerington	Fairfield	OH	Pilgrim's Rest	Fayette	AL	Pine Hill	Ulster	NY
Pickwick	Winona	MN	Pillar Point	Jefferson	NY	Pine Hill	York	PA
Picolata	St. John's	FL	Pillow	Dauphin	PA	Pine Hill	Washington	RI
Picture Rocks	Lycoming	PA	Pilot	Vermillion	IL	Pine Hill	Rusk	TX
Piedmont	Mineral	WV	Pilot	Montgomery	VA	Pine Hill	Jackson	WI
Piedmont	Uintah	WY	Pilot Centre	Kankakee	IL	Pine House Depot	Edgefield	SC
Piadmont Springs	Burke	NC	Pilot Grove	Newton	IN	Pine Iron Works	Berks	PA
Piedmont Station	Fanquier	VA	Pilot Grove	Lee	IA	Pine Island	Goodhue	MN
Piedra Blanca	San Luis Obispo	CA	Pilot Grove	Faribault	MN	Pine Island	Orange	NY
Pierce	Will	IL	Pilot Grove	Cooper	MO	Pine Knob	Iowa	WI
Pierce	Callaway	MO	Pilot Grove	Grayson	TX	Pine Knot	Campbell	TN
Pierce(c.h.)	Pierce	NE	Pilot Hill	Fulton	AR	Pine Lake	Fulton	NY
Pierce	Stark	OH	Pilot Hill	El Dorada	CA	Pine Land	Meigs	TN
Pierce	Armstrong	PA	Pilot Hill	Washington	TN	Pine Level	Montgomery	AL
Pierce	Kewaunee	WI	Pilot Knob	Crawford	IL	Pine Level	Manatee	FL
Pierce City(c.h.)	Shoshone	ID	Pilot Knob	Todd	KY	Pine Level	Johnston	NC
Pierce City	Lawrence	MO	Pilot Knob	Iron	MO	Pine Log	Bartow	GA
Pierce's	Goochland	VA	Pilot Knob	Greene	TN	Pine Meadow	Litchfield	CN
Pierce Station	Weakley	TN	Pilot Knob	Adams	WI	Pine Mills	Muscatine	IA
Pierceton	Kosciusko	IN	Pilot Mound	Boone	IA	Pine Mountain	Campbell	TN
Piercetown	Anderson	SC	Pilot Mound	Fillmore	MN	Pine Plains	Dutchess	NY
Pierceville(c.h.)	Hernando	FL	Pilot Mountain	Stokes	NC	Pine Ridge	Winn	LA
Pierceville	De Kalb	IL	Pilot Point	Denton	TX	Pine Ridge	Lexington	SC
Pierceville	Ripley	IN	Pilot Rock	Cherokee	IA	Pine River	Lake	MI
Pierceville	Van Buren	IA	Pilot Rock	Umatilla	OR	Pine River	Waushara	WI
Pierceville	Wyoming	PA	Pilot Village	Yavapai	AZ	Pine Run	Genessee	NI
Pierceville	Grafton	NH	Pimento	Vigo	IN	Pine's Bridge	Westchester	NY
Pierceville	Rockland	NY	Pinckney	Livingston	MI	Pine Springs	Rowan	KY
Pierpont	Ashtabula	OH	Pinckney	Warren	MO	Pine Station	Clinton	PA
Pierrepont	St. Lawrence	NY	Pinckney	Lewis	NY	Pine Summit	Columbia	PA
Pierrepont Manor	Jefferson	NY	Pickneyville	Clay	AL	Pinetown	Cherokee	TX

PLACE NAMES OF THE UNITED STATES

PLACE	COUNTY	STATE	PLACE	COUNTY	STATE	PLACE	COUNTY	STATE
Pine Township	Armstrong	PA	Pittsburgh	Shiawassee	MI	Plants	Miegs	OH
Pine Tree	Chesterfield	SC	Pittsburgh	Hickory	MO	Plantsville	Hartford	CN
Pine Tree	Upshur	TX	Pittsburgh	Coos	NH	Plantsville	Morgan	OH
Pine Tucky	Perry	AL	Pittsburgh	Upshur	TX	Plaquemine(c.h.)	Deerville	LA
Pine Valley	Yalabusha	MS	Pitt's X Roads	Bledsoe	TN	Plaquemine Brulee	St. Landry	LA
Pine Valley	Chemung	NY	Pittsfield(c.h.)	Pike	IL	Platea	Eric	PA
Pine Valley	Washington	UT	Pittsfield	Somerset	ME	Platea	Iroquois	IL
Pine Village	Warren	IN	Pittsfield	Berkshire	MA	Platea	Pulaski	KY
Pine View	Faquier	VA	Pittsfield	Merrimack	NH	Platea	McLeod	MN
Pineville	Izard	AR	Pittsfield	Otsego	NY	Platea	Texas	MO
Pineville	Marion	GA	Pittsfield	Lorain	OH	Platea	Lorain	OH
Pineville	Pike	IL	Pittsfield	Warren	PA	Platt	Taylor	IA
Pineville(c.h.)	Josh Bell	KY	Pittsfield	Rutland	VT	Platt	Benzie	MI
Pineville	Mecklenburgh	NC	Pittsfield	Hillsdale	MI	Platte City(c.h.)	Platte	MO
Pineville	Bucks	PA	Pittsford	Monroe	NY	Plattekill	Ulster	NY
Pine Wood	Hickman	TN	Pitts' Grove	Salem	NJ	Platte River	Buchanan	MO
Pine Woods	Madison	NY	Pitts' Point	Bullitt	KY	Platteville	Taylor	IA
Piney Creek	Carroll	MD	Pittston	Kennebec	ME	Platteville	Saunders	NE
Piney Creek	Alleghany	NC	Pittstown	Hunterdon	NJ	Platteville	Grant	WI
Piney Flats	Sullivan	TN	Pittstown	Rensscleaer	NY	Plateford	Sarpy	NE
Piney Grove	Prince George	VA	Pittsville	Wicomico	MD	Platsburgh	Winston	MS
Piney Point	Saint Mary's	MD	Pittsville	Johnson	MO	Plattsburgh(c.h.)	Clinton	MO
Pingree Grove	Kane	IL	Pittsville	Venango	PA	Plattsburgh(c.h.)	Clinton	NY
Pinhook Landing	Meigs	TN	Pittsville	Fort Bend	TX	Plattsburgh	Clark	OH
Pink Hill	Jackson	MO	Pittsylvania(c.h.)	Pittsylvania	VA	Plattsmouth(c.h.)	Cass	NE
Pink Hill	Lenoir	NC	Placerville(c.h.)	El Dorado	CA	Plattsville	Fairfield	CN
Pinkleyville	Oregon	MI	Placerville	Boise	ID	Plattsville	Shelby	OH
Pink Prairie	Henry	IL	Plain	Wayne	OH	Plattsville	Kendall	IL
Pinnebog	Huron	MI	Plain	Greenville	SC	Plattville	Cambria	PA
Pinnellville	Jones	MS	Plain	Sauk	WI	Pleasant	Switzerland	IN
Pino	Placer	CA	Plain City	Weber	UT	Pleasant	Kent	MI
Pin Oak	Wayne	IL	Plainfield	Windham	KY	Pleasant	Calibourne	PA
Pin Oak	Dubuque		Plainfield	Will	IL	Pleasant Brook	Otsego	NY
Pin Oak	Warren	MO	Plainfield	Hendricks	IN	Pleasant Corners	Franklin	OH
Pin Oak	Fayette	TX	Plainfield	Bremer	IA	Pleasant Corners	Carbon	PA
Pinos Altos(c.h.)	Grant	NM	Plainfield	Hampshire	MS	Pleasant Creek	Barbour	WV
Pinson	Madison	TN	Plainfield	Livingston	MI	Pleasant Dale	Seward	NE
Pinto	Iron	UT	Plainfield	Sullivan	NH	Pleasant Dale	Hampshire	WV
Piny	Clarion	PA	Plainfield	Union	NJ	Pleasant Farm	Miller	MO
Pioche(c.h.)	Lincoln	NV	Plainfield	Coshocton	OH	Pleasant Gap	Cherokee	AL
Pioneer	Greene	IL	Plainfield	Cumberland	PA	Pleasant Gap	Bates	MO
Pioneer	Deer Lodge	MT	Plainfield	Washington	VT	Pleasant Gap	Pittsylvania	VA
Pioneer	Jefferson	NE	Plainfield	Waushara	WI	Pleasant Green	Stark	IL
Pioneer	Williams	OH	Plain Grove	Lawrence	PA	Pleasant Green	Cooper	MO
Pioneer	Venango	PA	Plainsberg	Merced	CA	Pleasant Green	Pickens	AL
Pioneer Mills	Cabarrus	NC	Plainsborough	Middlesex	NJ	Pleasant Grove	Wayne	IL
Pioneerville	Boise	ID	Plains of Dura	Sumter	GA	Pleasant Grove	Jasper	IN
Piper City	Ford	IL	Plainsville	Luzerne	PA	Pleasant Grove	Des Moines	IA
Piper's Gap	Carroll	VA	Plain View	Macoupin	IL	Pleasant Grove	Greenwood	KS
Pipersville	Bucks	PA	Plain View	Wabashaw	MN	Pleasant Grove	Olmsted	MN
Pipersville	Jefferson	WI	Plain View	King and Queen	VA	Pleasant Grove	Morris	NJ
Pipestone	Berrien	MI	Plainville	Hartford	CN	Pleasant Grove	Alamance	NC
Piqua	Miami	OH	Plainville	Daviess	IN	Pleasant Grove	Belmount	OH
Pireway Ferry	Columbus	NC	Plainville	Norfolk	MA	Pleasant Grove	Lancaster	PA
Piscataway	Prince George's	MD	Plainville	Onondaga	NY	Pleasant Grove	Bedford	TN
			Plainville	Hamilton	OH	Pleasant Grove	Utah	UT
Pisgah	Butler	OH	Plainville	Adams	WI	Pleasant Grove	Lunnenburgh	VA
Pisgah	Giles	TN	Plainwell	Allegan	MI	Pleasant Grove	Sutter	CA
Pishon's Ferry	Kennebec	ME	Plaistow	Rockingham	NH	Pleasant Grove Crk.	Sutter	CA
Pitcairn	St. Lawrence	NY	Plane No. Four	Fredrick	MD	Pleasant Hall	Franklin	PA
Pitcher	Chennango	NY	Plank Road	Wayne	MI	Pleasant Hill	Dallas	AL
Pitcher Springs	Chenango	NY	Plank Road	Onondaga	OH	Pleasant Hill	Franklin	AR
Pitcherville	Jo Daviess	IL	Plank Road	Belmont	OH	Pleasant Hill	New Castle	DE
Pit Hole City	Venango	PA	Plank Road	York	PA	Pleasant Hill	Talbot	GA
Pitman	Randolph	AR	Plano	Tulare	CA	Pleasant Hill	Pike	IL
Pitman Grove	Gloucester	NJ	Plano	Kendall	IL	Pleasant Hill	Montgomery	IN
Pitts	Warren	MO	Plano	Collin	TX	Pleasant Hill	Cedar	IA
Pittsborough	Hendricks	IN	Plantation No. 14	Washington	ME	Pleasant Hill	Mercer	KY
Pittsborough(c.h.)	Calhoun	MS	Planter's	Phillips	AR	Pleasant Hill	De Soto	LA
Pittsborough(c.h.)	Chatham	NC	Planter's Landing	Nachitoches	LA	Pleasant Hill	De Soto	MS
Pittsburgh	Johnson	AR	Plantersville	Dallas	AL	Pleasant Hill	Cass	MO
Pittsburgh	Carroll	IN	Plantersville	Grimes	TX	Pleasant Hill	Saline	NE
Pittsburgh	Van Buren	IA	Plantersville	Lunnenburgh	VA	Pleasant Hill	Northampton	NC

PLACE	COUNTY	STATE	PLACE	COUNTY	STATE	PLACE	COUNTY	STATE
Pleasant Hill	Miami	OH	Pleasant Valley	Chittenden	VT	Po	Allen	IN
Pleasant Hill	Lane	OR	Pleasant Valley	Fairfax	VA	Poage's Mill	Roanoke	VA
Pleasant Hill	Lancaster	SC	Pleasant Valley	Monongalia	WV	Poast Town	Butler	OH
Pleasant Hill	Cumberland	TN	Pleasant Valley	St. Coix	WI	Pocahontas(c.h.)	Randolph	AR
Pleasant Hill	Preston	WV	Pleasant Valley Mills	Nicholas	KY	Pocahontas	Bend	IL
Pleasant Home	Owen	KY	Pleasant View	Schuyler	IL	Pocahontas	Pocahontas	IA
Pleasant Home	Putnam	MO	Pleasant View	Creek Nation	IT	Pocahontas	Cape Girardeau	MO
Pleasant Hope	Polk	MO	Pleasant View	Madison	IA	Pocahontas	Somerset	PA
Pleasant Lake	Steuben	IN	Pleasant View	Cherokee	KS	Pocahontas	Hardeman	TN
Pleasant Mills	Adams	IL	Pleasant View	Whitley	KY	Pocahontas Centre	Pocahontas	IA
Pleasant Mills	Atlantic	NJ	Pleasant View	Ray	MO	Pocasset	Barnstable	MA
Pleasant Mound	Bond	IL	Pleasant View	Juniata	PA	Pocataligo	Kanawha	WV
Pleasant Mound	Laurens	SC	Pleasant View	Cheatham	TN	Poe	Medina	OH
Pleasant Mound	Montgomery	TN	Pleasant View	Jackson	WV	Poe	Beaver	PA
Pleasant Mounds	Blue Earth	MN	Pleasantville	Sullivan	IN	Poestenkill	Rensselaer	NY
Pleasant Mount	Panola	MS	Pleasantville	Marion	IA	Poheta	Saline	KS
Pleasant Mount	Miller	MO	Pleasantville	Harford	MD	Pohocco	Saunders	NE
Pleasant Mount	Wayne	PA	Pleasantville	Westchester	NY	Poindexter's Store	Louisa	VA
Pleasant Oaks	Brunswick	VA	Plesantville	Fairfield	OH	Point a la		
Pleasanton	Alameda	CA	Pleasantville	Venango	PA	Hache(c.h.)	Plaquemine	LA
Pleasanton	Decatur	IA	Pleasureville	Henry	KY	Point Bluff	Adams	WI
Pleasanton	Linn	KS	Pleito	Monterey	CA	Point Caswell	New Hanover	NC
Pleasanton	Manistee	MI	Plenitude	Anderson	TX	Point Cedar	Clark	AR
Pleasanton	Prentiss	MS	Plesis	Jefferson	NY	Point Coupee(c.h.)	Point Coupee	LA
Pleasanton	Athens	OH	Plimpton	Holmes	OH	Point Douglas	Washington	MN
Pleasanton(c.h.)	Atacosa	TX	Pliny	Saline	KS	Point Eastern	Caroline	VA
Pleasant Park	Carroll	MO	Plover	Portage	WI	Point Hope	Grayson	VA
Pleasant Plain	Jefferson	OH	Plowboy	Shawnee	KS	Point Isabel	Grant	IN
Pleasant Plain	Warren	OH	Plowden's Mills	Sumter	SC	Point Isabel	Clermont	OH
Pleasant Plain	Warren	OH	Plocuemin	Somerset	NJ	Point Isabel	Comeron	TX
Pleasant Plain	Independence	AR	Plum	Venago	PA	Point Jefferson	Morehouse	LA
Pleasant Plains	Sangamon	IL	Plum Bayou	Jefferson	AR			
Pleasant Plains	Dutchess	NY	Plum City	Pierce	WI			
Pleasant Plains	Sullivan	TN	Plum Creek	Jefferson	KS	Point Lookout	St. Mary's	MD
Pleasant Prairie	Pond	IL	Plum Creek	Caldwell	TX	Point Michael	Plaquemine	LA
Pleasant Prairie	Muscatine	IA	Plumer	Venango	PA	Point of Rocks	Frederick	MD
Pleasant Prairie	Martin	MN	Plum Grove	Butler	KS	Point of Rocks	Uintah	WY
Pleasant Prairie	Polk	MO	Plum Hill	Washinton	IL	Point of Timber	Contra Costa	CA
Pleasant Prairie	Konosha	WI	Plum Hollow	Fremont	IA	Point Peninsula	Jefferson	NY
Pleasant Retreat	White	GA	Plummer's			Point Peter	Searcy	AR
Pleasant Retreat	Scotland	MO	Landing	Fleming	KY	Point Peter	Oglethorpe	GA
Pleasant Retreat	McDowell	NC	Plummer's Mills	Fleming	KY	Point Pleasant	Vermillion	IL
Pleasant Ridge	Greene	IL	Plummerville	Robeson	NC	Point Pleasant	Hardin	IA
Pleasant Ridge	Rock Island	IL	Plummerville	Frederick	MD	Point Pleasant	Ohio	KY
Pleasant Ridge	Greene	IN	Plum River	Jo Daviess	IL	Point Pleasant	New Madrid	MO
Pleasant Ridge	Leavenworth	KS	Plumsteadville	Bucks	PA	Point Pleasant	Ocean	NJ
Pleasant Ridge	Daviess	KY	Plum Valley	Sierra	CA	Point Pleasant	Clermont	OH
Pleasant Ridge	Harrison	MO	Plum Valley	Texas	MO	Point Pleasant	Bucks	PA
Pleasant Ridge	Hamilton	OH	Plumville	Indiana	PA	Point Pleasant	Upshur	TX
Pleasant Ridge	Princess Anne	VA	Plunkett	Sullivan	PA	Point Pleasant(c.h.)	Mason	WV
Pleasant Ridge	Clark	WI	Plymouth	Litchfield	CN	Point Remove	Conway	AR
Pleasant Run	Pottawatomie	KS	Plymouth	Hancock	IL	Point Truth	Scott	VA
Pleasant Run	Stanton	NE	Plymouth(c.h.)	Marshall	IN	Pointville	Burlington	NJ
Pleasant Run	Hamilton	OH	Plymouth	Wayne	MI	Pojuaque	Santa Fe	NM
Pleasant Run	Hunterdon	OH	Plymouth	Cerro Gordo	IA	Pokagon	Cass	MI
Pleasant Shade	Greenville	VA	Plymouth	Lyon	KS	Poland	Clay	IN
Pleasant Site	Franklin	AL	Plymouth	Penobscot	ME	Poland	Androscoggin	ME
Pleasant Unity	Westmoreland	PA	Plymouth(c.h.)	Plymouth	MS	Poland	Herkimer	NY
Pleasant Vale	Pike	IL	Plymouth	Wayne	MI	Poland	Mahoning	OH
Pleasant Valley	Pike	IL	Plymouth	Christian	MO	Poland Centre	Chautauqua	NY
Pleasant Valley	El Dorado	CA	Plymouth(c.h.)	Grafton	NH	Pole Grove	Jackson	WI
Pleasant Valley	Litchfield	CN	Plymouth	Chenango	NY	Polk	Ashland	OH
Pleasant Valley	Jo Daviess	IL	Plymouth(c.h.)	Washington	NC	Polk	Venango	PA
Pleasant Valley	Scott	IA	Plymouth	Richland	OH	Polk Bayou	Independence	AR
Pleasant Valley	Cowley	KS	Plymouth	Luzerne	PA	Polk City	Polk	IA
Pleasant Valley	Berrien	MI	Plymouth	Windsor	VT	Polk Patch	Warrick	IN
Pleasant Valley	Sherburne	MN	Plymouth	Sheboygan	WI	Polk Run	Clarke	IN
Pleasant Valley	Wright	MO	Plymouth			Polk Store	Phillips	AR
Pleasant Valley	Sussex	NJ	Centre(c.h.)	Plymouth	IA	Polksville	Hall	GA
Pleasant Valley	Dutchess	NY	Plymouth Meeting	Montgomery	PA	Polksville	Smith	MS
Pleasant Valley	Morgan	OH	Plymouth Rock	Winneshick	IA	Polksville	Warren	NJ
Pleasant Valley	Bucks	PA	Plymton	Plymouth	MA	Polksville	Columbia	PA
Pleasant Valley	Lancaster	SC	Plymton Station	Plymouth	MA	Pollard(c.h.)	Escambia	AL

PLACE NAMES OF THE UNITED STATES

PLACE	COUNTY	STATE
Pollinger	Madison	MT
Pollock	Clarion	PA
Pollocksville	Jones	NC
Polo	Ogle	IL
Polo	Caldwell	MO
Polsgrove	Carroll	IL
Polsgrove's Store	Franklin	KY
Pomaria	Newberry	SC
Pomeroy	Calhoun	PA
Pomeroy	Wyandotte	KS
Pomeroy	Chester	PA
Pomeroy(c.h.)	Meigs	OH
Pomfret	Windham	CN
Pomfret	Windsor	VT
Pomfret Landing	Windham	CN
Pomme de Terre	Grant	ME
Pomo	Mendocino	CA
Pomona	Franklin	KS
Pomona	Cumberland	TN
Pomonakey	Charles	MD
Pompanoosuc	Windsor	VT
Pompei	Gratiot	MI
Pompey	Onondaga	NY
Pompey Centre	Onondaga	NY
Pompton	Passaic	NJ
Pompton Plains	Morris	NJ
Ponama	Newaygo	MI
Ponca(c.h.)	Dixon	NE
Ponce de Leon	Holmes	FL
Ponchatoula	Tangipahoa	LA
Pond	St. Louis	MO
Pond Creek	Campbell	KY
Pond Eddy	Sullivan	NY
Ponder's Mill	Montgomery	AL
Pond Grove	Benton	IN
Pond Run	Scoito	OH
Pond Spring	Walker	GA
Pond Spring	Williamson	TX
Pond's Shop	Southampton	VA
Pond Valley	Howard	IA
Poney Hollow	Tompkins	NY
Ponka Agency	Todd	DA
Ponona	Plymouth	IA
Pontiac(c.h.)	Livingston	IL
Pontiac(c.h.)	Oakland	MI
Pontiac	Erie	NY
Pontiac	Huron	OH
Pontiac	Kent	RI
Pontoosuc	Hancock	IL
Pontotoc(c.h.)	Pontotoc	MS
Pontotoc	Balstrop	TX
Ponville	Wilson	TN
Pool	Lapeer	MI
Poolesville	Montgomery	MD
Poolsville	Warren	IN
Poolville	Madison	NY
Poolville	Harlan	KY
Poor Fork	Harlan	KY
Poor's Mills	Waldo	ME
Poor Valley	Hawkins	TN
Pope's Depot	Panola	MS
Pope's Mills	St. Lawrence	NY
Pope Valley	Napa	CA
Poplar	Crawford	OH
Popular Bluff	Ashley	AR
Popular Bluff(c.h.)	Butler	MO
Popular Branch	Currituck	NC
Popular Creek	Montgomery	MS
Popular Flat	Lewis	KY
Popular Grove	Phillips	AR
Popular Grove	Boone	IL
Popular Grove	Howard	IN
Popular Grove	Owen	KY
Popular Hill	McDonald	MO
Popular Hill	Anson	NC
Popular Hill	Giles	VA
Popular Mount	Greenville	VA
Popular Plains	Fleming	KY
Popular Ridge	Cayuga	NY
Popular Ridge	Darke	OH
Popular Run	Blair	PA
Popular Spring	Henderson	TN
Popular Springs	Hall	GA
Popular Spings	Howard	MD
Poquetanuck	Hartford	CN
Poquonock Bridge	New London	CN
Porche's Prairie	Chariton	MO
Portage	Kalamazoo	MI
Porta e	Wood	OH
Portage	Cambria	PA
Portage	Box Elder	UT
Portage Centre	Hancock	OH
Portage City(c.h.)	Columbia	WI
Portage Des Sioux	St. Charles	MO
Portage Lake	Aroostook	ME
Portageville	Wyoming	NY
Port Alleghany	McKean	PA
Port Allen	Louisa	IA
Port Andrew	Richland	WI
Port Angeles	Clallam	Wa
Port Austin(c.h.)	Huron	MI
Port Blanchard	Luzerne	PA
Port Bryon	Rock Island	IL
Port Byron	Cayuga	NY
Port Carbon	Schuylkill	PA
Port Chester	Westchester	NY
Port Clinton	Ottawa	OH
Port Clinton	Schuylkill	PA
Port Colden	Warren	NJ
Port Conway	King George	VA
Port Crane	Broome	NY
Port Crescent	Huron	MI
Port Deposit	Cecil	MD
Port Dickinson	Broome	NY
Port Discovery	Jefferson	WA
Port Edwards	Wood	WI
Port Elizabeth	Cumberland	NJ
Porter	Oxford	ME
Porter	Midland	MI
Porter	Jefferson	PA
Porterfield	Venango	PA
Porter's	Carroll	MD
Porter's Corners	Saratoga	NY
Porter's X Roads	Porter	IN
Porter's Falls	Wetzel	WV
Porter's Sideling	York	PA
Porter Station	Porter	IN
Porter Station	Henry	TN
Portersville	De Kalb	AL
Portersville	Tulare	CA
Portersville	Dubois	IN
Portersville	Perry	OH
Portersville	Butler	PA
Portersville	Tipton	TN
Port Ewen	Ulster	NY
Port Gibson(c.h.)	Claiborne	MS
Port Gibson	Ontario	NY
Port Haywood	Mathews	VA
Port Henry	Essex	NY
Port Homer	Jefferson	OH
Port Hope	Huron	MI
Port Hope	Columbia	WI
Port Hudson	East Feliciana	LA
Port Hudson	Franklin	MO
Port Huron(c.h.)	St. Clair	MI
Port Jackson	Montgomery	NY
Port Jefferson	Suffolk	NY
Port Jervis	Orange	NY
Port Kennedy	Montgomery	PA
Port Kent	Essex	NY
Portland	Dallas	AL
Portland	Middlesex	CN
Portland	Whitesides	IL
Portland(c.h.)	Jay	IN
Portland	Cerro Gordo	IA
Portland(c.h.)	Cumberland	ME
Portland	Ionia	MI
Portland	Callaway	MO
Portland	Chautauqua	NY
Portland	Preston	WV
Portland Mills	Parke	IN
Portland Station	Jefferson	OH
Portlandville	Otsego	NY
Port Lavaca	Calhoun	TX
Port Leyden	Lewis	NY
Port Louisa	Louisa	IA
Port Ludlow	Jefferson	WA
Port Madison(c.h.)	Kitsap	WA
Port Matilda	Centre	PA
Port Monmouth	Monmouth	NJ
Port Murry	Warren	NJ
Port Ontario	Oswego	NY
Port Oram	Morris	NJ
Port Orange	Volusia	FL
Port Orchard	Kitnap	WA
Port Orford	Curry	OR
Port Penn	New Castle	DE
Port Perry	Alleghany	PA
Port Providence	Montgomery	PA
Port Republic	Calvert	MD
Port Republic	Atlantic	NJ
Port Republic	Rockingham	VA
Port Richmond	Wapello	IA
Port Richmond	Richmond	NY
Port Royal	Henry	KY
Port Royal	Juiata	PA
Port Royal	Beaufort	SC
Port Royal	Montgomery	TN
Port Sanilac	Sanilac	MI
Port Sheldon	Ottawa	MI
Portsmouth	Ray	MI
Portsmouth(c.h.)	Rockingham	NH
Portsmouth	Careret	NC
Portsmouth(c.h.)	Scioto	OH
Portsmouth	Norfolk	VA
Port Sullivan	Milam	TX
Port Tobacco(c.h.)	Charles	MD
Port Townsend(c.h.)	Jefferson	WA
Port Treverton	Snyder	PA
Portuguee	Shasta	CA
Port Union	Butler	OH
Portville	Cattaraugus	NY
Port Washington	Queens	NY
Port Washington	Tuscarawas	OH
Port William	Clinton	OH
Port Wine	Sierra	CA
Poseyville	Posey	IN
Post Creek	Chemung	NY
Post Mill Village	Orange	VT
Post Oak	Calhoun	AR
Post Oak	Yalabusa	MS
Post Oak	Lincoln	MO
Post Oak Springs	Roane	TN
Poston	Ripley	IN
Postville	Allamakee	IO
Potatoe Creek	Montgomery	IN
Potecasi	Northampton	NC
Potomac	Vermilion	IL
Potomac	Prince William	VA
Potosi	Livingston	IL

PLACE NAMES OF THE UNITED STATES

PLACE	COUNTY	STATE	PLACE	COUNTY	STATE	PLACE	COUNTY	STATE
Potosi	Stevens	MN	Prairie Bluff	Wilcox	AL	Preston	Chenango	NY
Potosi(c.h.)	Washington	MO	Praireburgh	Linn	IA	Preston	Hamilton	OH
Potosi	Grant	WI	Prairie Centre	Prairie	AR	Preston	Wayne	PA
Potsdam	St. Lawrence	NY	Prairie Centre	La Salle	IL	Preston Bluff	Arkansas	AR
Potsdam	Miami	OH	Prairie City	McDonough	IL	Prestonburgh(c.h.)	Floyd	KY
Potsdam Junction	St. Lawrence	NY	Prairie City	Jasper	IA	Preston Hollow	Albany	NY
Pottamie	Ottawa	MI	Prairie City	Bates	MO	Preston Station	Fillmore	MN
Potter	Yates	NY	Prairie City	Grant	OR	Prestonville	Cameron	PA
Potter	Wood	OH	Prairie Creek	Vigo	IN	Prestonville	Rhea	TN
Potter Hill	Rensselaer	NV	Prairie Creek	Martin	MN	Prewitt's Ferry	Desha	AR
Potter Hill	Washington	RI	Prairie Depot	Wood	OH	Priam	Blackford	IN
Potter Place	Merrimack	NH	Prairie du Chien	Neosho	KS	Price	Mercer	OH
Pottersburgh(c.h.)	Lincoln	KS	Prairie du Chien(c.h.)	Crawford	WI	Price's Branch	Montgomery	MO
Pottersburgh	Union	OH	Prairie Du Rocher	Randolph	IL	Price's Creek	De Witt	TX
Potter's Corners	Crawford	PA	Prairie du Sac	Sauk	WI	Price's Landing	Scott	MO
Potter's Hollow	Albany	NY	Prairie Edge	Montgomery	IN	Price's Store	Rockingham	NC
Potter's Landing	Caroline	MD	Prairie Farm	Barron	WI	Pricetown	Highland	OH
Potter's Mills	Dale	AL	Prairie Grove	Washington	AR	Pricetown	Berks	PA
Potter's Mills	Calumet	WI	Prairie Grove	Clarke	IA	Priceville	Wayne	PA
Pottersville	Howell	MO	Prairie Hall	Macon	IL	Prickley Pear	Jefferson	MT
Pottersville	Cheshire	NH	Prairie Hill	Boone	IA	Pride's Point	Bolivar	MA
Pottersville	Hunterdon	NJ	Prairie Hill	Chariton	MO	Prillaman's	Franklin	VA
Pottersville	Warren	NY	Prairie Hill	Shelby	IL	Primrose	Lee	IA
Potter Valley	Mendocino	CA	Prairie Home	Republic	KS	Primrose	Lewis	MO
Potterville	Eaton	MI	Prairie Home	Cooper	MO	Primrose	Douglas	NE
Potterville	Bradford	PA	Prairie Home	Montgomery	TX	Primrose	Williams	OH
Pott's Grove	Northumberland	PA	Prairie Landing	Desha	AR	Primrose	Dane	WI
Pottstown	Montgomery	PA	Prairie Lea	Caldwell	TX	Prince Edward(c.h.)	Prince Edw'd	VA
Pottsville(c.h.)	Schuylkill	PA	Prairie Mills	Muscatine	IA	Prince Fredericktown(c.h.)	Calvert	MD
Poughkeepsie	Sharp	AR	Prairie Park	Nodway	MO	Prince George(c.h)	Prince George	VA
Poughkeepsie(c.h.)	Dutchess	NY	Prairie Plains	Grimes	TX	Prince of Wales	Breckinridge	KY
Poughquag	Dutchess	NY	Prairie Pond	De Kalb	IL	Prince's Bay	Richmond	NY
Poultney	Rutland	VA	Prairie Station	Monroe	MS	Princess Anne(c.h.)	Somerset	MD
Pound	Wise	VA	Prairieton	Vigo	IN	Princess Anne(c.h.)	Princess Anne	VA
Poundridge	Westchester	NY	Prairie Town	Madison	IL	Princeton	Jackson	AL
Powar's Store	Casey	KY	Prairieville	Barry	MI	Princeton(c.h.)	Dallas	AR
Poway	San Diego	CA	Prairieville	Brown	MN	Princeton	Colusa	CA
Powder Spring Gap	Grainger	TN	Prairieville	Pike	MO	Princeton	Bureau	IL
Powder Springs	Cobb	GA	Pratt	Whitesides	IL	Princeton(c.h.)	Gibson	IN
Powell	McDonald	MO	Pratt	Clay	IN	Princeton	Scott	IA
Powell	Delaware	OH	Pratt	Shelby	OH	Princeton	Franklin	KS
Powell Grove	Bowie	TX	Prattsburgh	Talbot	GA	Princeton(c.h.)	Caldwell	KY
Powell's Mills	Pike	KY	Pratt's Corner	Franklin	ME	Princeton	Washington	ME
Powell's Point	Currituck	NC	Pratt's Fork	Athens	OH	Princeton	Worcester	MA
Powellsville	Scoito	OH	Pratt's Hollow	Madison	NY	Princeton(c.h.)	Milie Lacs	MN
Powellton	Harrison	TX	Pratt's Junction	Worchester	MA	Princeton(c.h.)	Mercer	MO
Powellton	Brunswick	VA	Prattsville	Saline	AR	Princeton	Green Lake	WI
Powellville	Coweta	GA	Prattsville	Greene	NY	Princeton	Peoria	IL
Powellville	Wicomico	MD	Prattsville(c.h.)	Autauga	AL	Princeville	Peoria	IL
Powel's Creek	Dauphin	PA	Preakness	Passaic	NJ	Princeville	Cloud	KS
Powelton	Richmond	NC	Preble	Cortland	NY	Prince William	Carroll	IN
Powelton	Centre	PA	Pre-emtion	Mercer	IL	Principio	Cecil	MD
Powers	Terrel	GA	Prentice	Morgan	IL	Prine	Wasco	OR
Powers	Jay	IN	Prentiss	Penobscot	ME	Prior Creek	Vernon	MO
Power's Shop	Laurens	NC	Prentiss	Bolivar	MA	Prior's Station	Polk	GA
Powersville	Houston	GA	Prentiss Vale	McKean	PA	Privateer	Sumter	SC
Powersville	Bracken	KY	Prescott(c.h.)	Yavapai	AZ	Proctor(c.h.)	Lee	KY
Powhatan	Lawrence	AR	Prescott	Shelby	IN	Proctor	Morgan	MO
Powhatan	Baltimore	MD	Prescott	Adams	IA	Proctor	Wetzel	WV
Powhatan	Richmond	NC	Prescott	Linn	KS	Proctor's Creek	Chesterfield	VA
Powhatan(c.h.)	Powhatan	VA	Prescott	Hampshire	MA	Proctorsville	Windsor	VT
Powhatan Point	Belmont	OH	Prescott	Pierce	WI	Proctorville	Caldwell	MO
Powl's Valley	Dauphin	PA	President	Venango	PA	Profile House	Grafton	NH
Pownal	Cumberland	ME	Presidio	Presidio	TX	Progress	Dauphin	PA
Pownal Centre	Bennington	VT	Presque Isle	Aroostook	ME	Promise City	Wayne	IA
Poygan	Winnebago	WI	Preston	New London	CN	Prompton	Shelby	AL
Poynett	Columbia	WI	Preston(c.h.)	Webster	GA	Propell	Shelby	AL
Prag	Manitowoc	WI	Preston	Randolph	IL	Prophetstown	Whitesides	IL
Prairie	YOlo	CA	Preston	Jackson	IA	Prospect	New Haven	CN
Prairie	Mower	MN	Preston	Caroline	MD	Prospect	Madison	IN
Prairie	Clinton	MO	Preston	Jasper	MO	Prospect	Waldo	ME
Prairie	Houston	TX	Preston(c.h.)	Fillmore	MN	Prospect	Harford	MD
Prairie Bird	Adair	MO						

PLACE NAMES OF THE UNITED STATES

PLACE	COUNTY	STATE
Prospect	Oneida	NY
Prospect	Marion	OH
Prospect	Butler	PA
Prospect	Burleson	TX
Prospect	Prince Edward	VA
Prospect Bluff	White	AR
Prospect Ferry	Waldo	ME
Prospect Grove	Scotland	MO
Prospect Hall	Bladen	NC
Prospect Harbor	Hancock	ME
Prospect Hill	Linn	IA
Prospect Hill	Washington	KS
Prospect Hill	Clay	MO
Prospect Hill	Caswell	NC
Prospect Hill	Fairfax	VA
Prospect Hill	Waukesha	WI
Prospect Lake	Van Buren	MI
Prospect Plains	Middlesex	NJ
Prospect Station	Chautauqua	NY
Prospect Station	Giles	TN
Prospect Valley	Harrison	WV
Prospectville	Montgomery	PA
Prosper	Fillmore	MN
Prosperity	Franklin	IL
Prosperity	Madison	IN
Prosperity	Lawrence	KY
Prosperity	Moore	NC
Prosperity	Washington	PA
Protection	Erie	NY
Provement	Leelenaw	MI
Providence	Pickens	AL
Providence	Scarcy	AR
Providence	Bureau	IL
Providence	Webster	KY
Providence	Boone	MO
Providence	Saratoga	NY
Providence	Luzerne	PA
Providence(c.h.)	Providence	RI
Providence	Cache	UT
Providence Forge	New Kent	VA
Provincetown	Barnstable	MA
Proviso	Cook	IL
Provo City	Utah	UT
Prunty's	Henry	VA
Pruntytown(c.h.)	Taylor	WV
Pryorsburgh	Graves	KY
Pryorsburgh	Graves	KY
Pryor's Creek	Choctaw Nation	IT
Pryor's Store	Douglas	MO
Pubelo(c.h.)	Pueblo	CO
Pugh	Belmont	CO
Pughtown	Chester	PA
Pulaski	Hancock	IL
Pulaski	Pulaski	IN
Pulaski	Davis	IA
Pulaski	Jackson	MI
Pulaski(c.h.)	Oswego	NY
Pulaski	Williams	OH
Pulaski	Lawrence	PA
Pulaski(c.h.)	Giles	TN
Pulaskiville	Morrow	OH
Pulsifer	Shawanaw	WI
Pulley's Mills	Williamson	IL
Pultney	Steuben	NY
Pultneyville	Wayne	NY

Providence	Cache	VA
Providence Forge	New Kent	VA
Provincetown	Barnstable	MA
Proviso	Cook	IL
Provo City	Utah	UT
Prunty's	Henry	VA
Pruntytown(c.h.)	Taylor	WV
Pryorsburgh	Graves	KY

PLACE	COUNTY	STATE
Pryorsburgh	Graves	KY
Pryor's Creek	Choctaw Nation	IT
Pryor's Store	Douglas	MO
Pubelo(c.h.)	Pueblo	CO
Pugh	Belmont	PA
Pughtown	Chester	IL
Pulaski	Hancock	IN
Pulaski	Pulaski	IA
Pulaski	Davis	MI
Pulaski	Jackson	NY
Pulaski(c.h.)	Oswego	OH
Pulaski	Williams	PA
Pulaski	Lawrence	TN
Pulaski(c.h.)	Giles	OH
Pulaskiville	Morrow	WI
Pulsifer	Shawanaw	IL
Pulley's Mills	Williamson	NY
Pultney	Steuben	NY
Pultneyville	Wayne	NY
Pulver's Corners	Dutchess	WA
Pumphrey's Landing	Lewis	NC
Pungo Creek	Beaufort	VA
Pungateague	Accomack	MO
Punjaub	St. Genevieve	CA
Punta Arenas	Mendocino	PA
Punxatawney	Jefferson	PA
Purcell	Bedford	IN
Purcell's	Knox	VA
Purcellville	Loudoun	NY
Purchase	Westchester	PA
Purchase Line	Indiana	TN
Purdy(c.h.)	McNairy	NY
Purdy Creek	Steuben	NY
Purdy's Station	Westchester	WV
Purgitsville	Hampshire	NC
Purlear's Creek	Wilkes	NC
Purley	Caswell	WV
Pursley	Tyler	NY
Purvis	Sullivan	AL
Pushmataha	Choctaw	OH
Put in Bay	Ottawa	CT
Putnam	Windham	IA
Putnam	Fayette	NY
Putnam	Washington	OH
Putnam	Muskingum	IN
Putnamville	Putnam	VT
Putney	Windham	PA
Putneyville	Armstrong	MD
Pylesville	Harford	IN
Pyrmont	Carroll	OH
Pyrmont	Montgomery	
Quacken Kill	Rensselaer	NY
Quaker Bottom	Lawrence	OH
Quaker Hill	Vermillion	IN
Quaker Hill	Dutchess	NY
Quaker Springs	Saratoga	NY
Quaker Street	Schenectady	IN
Quakertown	Union	NJ
Quakertown	Hunterdon	PA
Quakertown	Bucks	KY
Quality Valley	Butler	NC
Quallatown	Jackson	MD
Quantico	Wicomico	MO
Quapaw	Newton	IA
Quarry	Marshall	TN
Quarrysville	Hawkins	CT
Quarrysville	Tolland	MO
Quarrytown	St. Genevieve	NY
Quarryville	Ulster	PA
Quarryville	Lancaster	MT
Quartz Creek	Missoula	

PLACE	COUNTY	STATE
Quasqueton	Buchanan	IA
Quechee	Windsor	VT
Queen City	Coffee	KS
Queen City	Schuyler	MO
Queens	Queens	NY
Queensbury	Warren	NY
Queenstown	Queen Anne	MD
Queensville	Jennings	IN
Queen Valley	Reno	KS
Quenemo	Osage	KS
Quicksand	Johnson	TX
Quiet Dell	Harrison	WV
Quimby	Barry	MI
Quincy (c.h.)	Plumas	CA
Quincy (c.h.)	Gadsden	FL
Quincy (c.h.)	Adams	IL
Quincy	Owen	IN
Quincy (c.h.)	Adams	IA
Quincy	Greenwood	KS
Quincy	Lewis	KY
Quincy	Norfolk	MA
Quincy	Branch	MI
Quincy	Olmsted	MN
Quincy	Monroe	MS
Quincy	Hickory	MO
Quincy	Logan	OH
Quincy	Franklin	PA
Quincy	Gibson	TN
Quincy	Adams	WI
Quincy Point	Norfolk	MA
Quindaro	Qyandotte	KS
Quinn	Macomb	MI
Quinney	Calumet	WI
Quinn's Grove	Ringgold	IA
Quinton	Salem	NJ
Quitman	Van Buren	AR
Quitman (c.h.)	Brooks	GA
Quitman	Clark	MS
Quitman	Nodaway	MO
Quitman (c.h.)	Wood	TX
Quito	Butler	KS
Quogue	Suffolk	NY
Quonochontaug	Washington	RI
Rabbit Town	Calhoun	AL
Rabbittsville	Logan	KY
Raccoon	Laurel	KY
Raccoon	Washington	PA
Raccoon Ford	Culpeper	VA
Raccoon Valley	Union	TN
Raceland	La Fourche	LA
Racine	Newton	MO
Racine	Meigs	OH
Racine	Ohio	WV
Racine (c.h.)	Racine	WI
Racoon	Marion	IL
Racoon	Preston	WV
Radersburgh (c.h.)	Jefferson	MT
Radford Furnace	Pulaski	VA
Radfordsville	Perry	AL
Radical	Madison	GA
Radical City	Montgomery	KS
Radnor	Delaware	OH
Radnor	Delaware	PA
Raglesville	Daviess	IN
Rahway	Union	NJ
Raif Branch	Montgomery	AL
Rail Road	York	PA
Rail Road Flat	Calaveras	CA
Rainbow	Hartford	CT
Rainey Creek	Camden	MO
Rainey's Creek	Coryell	TX
Rainier	Columbia	OR

PLACE NAMES OF THE UNITED STATES

PLACE	COUNTY	STATE
Rainsborough	Highland	OH
Rainsburgh	Bedford	PA
Rainsville	Warren	IN
Raisin Centre	Lenawee	MI
Raleigh	Saline	IL
Raleigh	Rush	IN
Raleigh	Union	KY
Raleigh (c.h.)	Smith	MS
Raleigh (c.h.)	Wake	NC
Raleigh	Shelby	TN
Raleigh (c.h.)	Raleigh	WV
Rally Hill	Boone	AR
Ralston	Grant	NM
Ralston	Lycoming	PA
Ralston's Station	Weakley	TN
Ramapo Works	Rockland	NY
Ramer	Montgomery	AL
Ramer	McNairy	TN
Ramey	Johnson	MO
Ramsaytown	Yancey	NC
Ramsey	Sumter	AL
Ramsey	Fayette	IL
Ramsey's	Bergen	NJ
Rancho	Gonzales	TX
Rancocas	Burlington	NJ
Randall	Jefferson	AR
Randall	Allen	IN
Randall	Hamilton	IA
Randall	Saginaw	MI
Randall	Montgomery	NY
Randall	Cuyahoga	OH
Randall	Smith	TX
Randall	Monongalia	WV
Randallstown	Baltimore	MD
Randallsville	Madison	NY
Randellsville	Christian	IL
Randolph	Bibb	AL
Randolph	La Fayette	AR
Randolph	McLean	IL
Randolph	Randolph	IN
Randolph	Riley	KS
Randolph	Metcalfe	KY
Randolph	Norfolk	MA
Randolph	Randolph	MO
Randolph	Dakota	NE
Randolph	Coos	NH
Randolph	Cattaraugus	NY
Randolph	Portage	OH
Randolph	Coos	OR
Randolph	Crawford	PA
Randolph	Tipton	TN
Randolph	Orange	VT
Randolph Centre	Broome	NY
Randolph Centre	Columbia	WI
Rangeley	Franklin	ME
Ranger	Perry	IN
Rankin's Depot	Cocke	TN
Ransom	Hillsdale	MI
Ransom	Luzerne	PA
Ransom's Bridge	Nash	NC
Ransomville	Niagara	NY
Rantoul	Champaign	IL
Rantoul	Calumet	WI
Rapid Ann Station	Culpeper	VA
Rapids	Niagara	NY
Rapids	Portage	OH
Rapids City	Rock Island	IL
Rappahannock Academy	Caroline	VA
Rapp's Mill	Rockbridge	VA
Rarden	Scioto	OH
Raritan	Henderson	IL
Raritan	Somerset	NJ
Rathboneville	Steuben	NY
Rathbun	Sheboygan	WI
Rattlesnake	Lane	OR
Rauch's Gap	Clinton	PA
Raught's Mills	Forest	PA
Ravanna	Mercer	MO
Ravena City	Los Angeles	CA
Ravenna	Muskegon	MI
Ravenna (c.h.)	Portage	OH
Raven Rock	Hunterdon	NJ
Raven's Eye	Fayette	WV
Raven's Nest	Washington	VA
Raven Stream	Scott	MN
Ravenwood	Cook	IL
Ravenswood	Queens	NY
Ravenswood	Jackson	WV
Rawley Springs	Rockingham	VA
Rawling's Springs (c.h.)	Carbon	WY
Rawling's Station	Alleghany	MD
Rawlingsville	De Kalb	AL
Rawlinsville	Lancaster	PA
Rawson	Aroostook	ME
Rawson	Cattaraugus	NY
Rawson	Hancock	OH
Rawsonville	Wayne	MI
Rawsonville	Lorain	OH
Ray	Bedford	TN
Ray Centre	Macomb	MI
Raymertown	Rensselaer	NY
Raymilton	Venango	PA
Raymond	Champaign	IL
Raymond	Black Hawk	IA
Raymond	Cumberland	ME
Raymond	Stearns	MN
Raymond (c.h.)	Hinds	MS
Raymond	Rockingham	NH
Raymond	Racine	WI
Raymond City	Putnam	WV
Raymonds	Union	OH
Raymonds	Potter	PA
Raymondsville	Texas	MO
Raymondville	St. Lawrence	NY
Raynham	Bristol	MA
Raynold	Montcalm	MI
Rays	Jackson	OH
Ray's Crossing	Shelby	IN
Ray's Hill	Bedford	PA
Raysville	Henry	IN
Raytown	Jackson	MO
Rayville (c.h.)	Richland	LA
Rayville	Baltimore	MD
Rayville	Ray	MO
Raywick	Marion	KY
Raywood	Union	NC
Read	Clayton	IA
Readfield	Kennebec	ME
Readfield	Waupaca	WI
Readfield Depot	Kennebec	MO
Readfield Depot	Kennebec	ME
Reading	Livingston	IL
Reading	Lyon	KS
Reading	Middlesex	MA
Reading	Hillsdale	MI
Reading	Pike	MO
Reading	Schuyler	NY
Reading	Hamilton	OH
Reading (c.h.)	Berks	PA
Reading	Windsor	VT
Reading Centre	Schuyler	NY
Readington	Hunterdon	NJ
Readsborough	Bennington	VT
Readstown	Vernon	WI
Readsville	Callawya	MO
Readville Station	Norfolk	MA
Readyville	Rutherford	TN
Ream's Chapel	Hart	KY
Ream's Station	Dinwiddie	VA
Reamstown	Lancaster	PA
Reaville	Hunterdon	NJ
Rebecca	Lancaster	NE
Rebersburgh	Centre	PA
Rebucks	Northumberland	PA
Recklesstown	Burlington	NJ
Rectortown Station	Fanquier	VA
Rectorville	Hamilton	IL
Red Apple	Marshall	AL
Red Bank	Monmouth	NJ
Red Bank	Halifax	VA
Red Bank Furnace	Clarion	PA
Red Bank Furnace	Armstrong	PA
Red Banks	Marshall	MS
Red Banks	Robeson	NC
Red Beach	Washington	ME
Red Bluff	Jefferson	AL
Red Bluff (c.h.)	Tehama	CA
Red Bluff	Coffee	GA
Red Brick	Sullivan	NY
Red Bridge	Ingham	MI
Red Bud	Randolph	IL
Red Clay	Whitfield	GA
Red Cloud	Webster	NE
Red Creek	Jackson	MS
Red Creek	Wayne	NY
Red Creek	Tucker	WV
Redden	Sussex	DE
Redding	Fairfield	CT
Redding	Ringgold	IA
Redding Ridge	Fairfield	CT
Red Falls	Greene	NY
Redfield	Dallas	IA
Redfield	Carver	MN
Redfield	Oswego	NY
Redford	Wayne	MI
Redford	Clinton	NY
Red Fork	Desha	AR
Red Haw	Ashland	OH
Red Hill	Marshall	AL
Red Hill	Hardin	KY
Red Hill	Mitchell	NC
Red Hill	Montgomery	PA
Red Hill	Albemarle	VA
Red Hook	Dutchess	NY
Red House	Morgan	IN
Red House	Cattaraugus	NY
Red House	Charlotte	VA
Red House Shoals	Putnam	WV
Redington	Northampton	PA
Red Jacket	Erie	NY
Redkey	Jay	IN
Red Land	Pike	AR
Redland	Montgomery	MD
Red Lane	Pontotoc	MS
Red Land	Adams	PA
Red Lion	New Castle	DE
Red Lion	Warren	OH
Red Mound	Henderson	TN
Red Mountain	Orange	NC
Red Mountain City	Deer Lodge	MT
Red Mouth	Richland	LA
Red Oak	Fayette	GA
Red Oak	Choctaw N.	IN
Red Oak (c.h.)	Montgomery	IA
Red Oak	Cedar	IA
Red Oak	Grayson	KY
Red Oak	Brown	OH

PLACE	COUNTY	STATE
Red Oak	Ellis	TX
Red Red Oak Grove	Charlotte	VA
Red Oak Junction	Montgomery	IA
Red Plains	Yadkin	NC
Red River	Kewannee	WI
Red River Iron Works	Estill	KY
Red River Landing	Point Coupee	LA
Red River Mills	Logan	KY
Red Rock	Marion	IA
Red Rock	Lincoln	KS
Red Rock	Columbia	NY
Red Rock	Luzerne	PA
Red Rock	Bastrop	TX
Red Run	Lancaster	PA
Red Shoals	Stokes	NC
Red Stone	Cloud	KS
Red Stone	Nicollet	MN
Redstone	Fayette	PA
Red Sulphur Springs	Monroe	WV
Red Wing (c.h.)	Goodhue	MN
Redwood	Jefferson	NY
Redwood City (c.h.)	San Mateo	CA
Redwood Falls (c.h.)	Redwood	MN
Reed	Oceana	MI
Reed Creek	Hart	GA
Reed Creek	Randolph	NC
Reeder's Mills	Harrison	IA
Reed Island	Wythe	VA
Reed Level	Covington	AL
Reedsburgh	Wayne	OH
Reedsburgh	Sauk	WI
Reed's Corners	Ontario	NY
Reed's Creek	Lawrence	AR
Reed's Ferry	Hillsborough	NH
Reed's Gap	Juniata	PA
Reed's Landing	Pulaski	AR
Reed's Landing	Wabashaw	MN
Reed's Mills	Vinton	OH
Reed's Springs	Stone	MO
Reed's Station	Yuba	CA
Reedsville	Meigs	OH
Reedsville	Mifflin	PA
Reedsville	Preston	WV
Reedsville	Manitowoc	
Reedsville	Manitowoc	WI
Reedtown	Seneca	OH
Reedy	Jackson	WV
Reedy Creek	Davidson	NC
Reedy Creek	Marion	SC
Reedy Ripple	Wirt	WV
Reedyville	Butler	KY
Reedyville	Roane	WV
Reelsville	Putnam	IN
Reem's Creek	Buncombe	NC
Reese Hill	Reynolds	MO
Reese Mill	Etowah	AL
Reese's Mill	Boone	IN
Reese's Mills	Iowa	WI
Reeseville	Chester	PA
Reeseville	Dodge	WI
Reeson	Chippewa	MN
Reesville	Clinton	OH
Reeves' Landing	Arkansas	AR
Reeves' Station	Gordon	GA
Reeves' Station	Butler	MO
Reevesville	Colleton	SC
Reform	Pickens	AL
Reform	Jefferson	AR
Reform	Callaway	Mo
Refugio (c.h.)	Refugio	TX
Regnier's Mills	Washington	OH
Rego	Orange	IN
Rehoboth	Wilcox	AL
Rehoboth	Bristol	MA
Rehoboth	Perry	OH
Rehoboth	Edgefield	SC
Rehoboth	Lunenburgh	VA
Rehrersburgh	Berks	PA
Rei	Ripley	IN
Reidenbach's Store	Lancaster	PA
Reid's	Paulding	OH
Reidsburgh	Clarion	PA
Reidsville (c.h.)	Tatnall	GA
Reidsville	Albany	NY
Reidsville	Rockingham	NC
Reidsville	Spartanburgh	SC
Reiffsburgh	Wells	IN
Reiley	Butler	OH
Reiner City	Schuylkill	PA
Reinersville	Morgan	OH
Reinhold's Station	Lancaster	PA
Reinholdsville	Lancaster	PA
Reisterstown	Baltimore	MD
Reiter	Washington	KS
Relfe	Phelps	MO
Relf's Bluff	Lincoln	AR
Remington	Jasper	'N
Remington	Allegheny	PA
Remsen	Oneida	NY
Remson's Corners	Medina	OH
Renault	Monroe	IL
Reno	Hendricks	IN
Reno	Leavenworth	KS
Reno	Pope	MN
Reno (c.h.)	Washoe	NE
Reno	Venango	PA
Renovo	Clinton	PA
Renrock	Noble	OH
Rensselaer (c.h.)	Jasper	IN
Rensselaer Falls	St. Lawrence	NY
Rensselaerville	Albany	NY
Renterville	Escambia	AL
Renwick	Lee	GA
Repose	Haralson	GA
Republic	Vadkin	NC
Republic	Seneca	OH
Republican	Choctaw	MS
Republican	Darke	OH
Republican City	Clay	KS
Republican Grove	Halifax	VA
Resaca	Gordon	GA
Resaca	Duplin	NC
Reserve	Miami	IN
Reserve	Erie	NY
Reservoir	Mercer	OH
Rest	Iowa	IA
Retreat	Jackson	IN
Retreat	Franklin	VA
Retreat	Vernon	WI
Reveille	Ney	NE
Revere	Suffolk	MA
Revilee (c.h.)	Sarber	AR
Rexford Flats	Saratoga	NY
Rexville	Ripley	IN
Rexville	Steuben	NY
Reyburn	Hot Spring	AR
Reynale's Basin	Niagara	NY
Reynolds	Taylor	GA
Reynolds	White	IN
Reynolds	Schuylkill	PA
Reynoldsburgh	Johnson	IL
Reynoldsburgh	Franklin	OH
Reynoldson	Gates	NC
Reynoldsville	Schuyler	NY
Reynoldsville	Jefferson	PA
Rhea	Lawrence	AR
Rhea's Mills	Washington	AR
Rheatown	Greene	TN
Rhine	Sheboygan	WI
Rhinebeck	Dutchess	NY
Rhinecliff	Dutchess	NY
Rhineland	Montgomery	MO
Rialto	Chatham	NC
Rice Depot	Prince Edward	VA
Riceford	Houston	MN
Rice Lake	Dodge	MN
Rice's Landing	Greene	PA
Rice's Store	Westmoreland	VA
Riceville	Mitchell	IA
Riceville	Saline	NE
Riceville	Crawford	PA
Riceville	McMinn	TN
Riceville	Pittsylvanias	VA
Rich	Atchison	MO
Richardson	St. Joseph	IN
Richardson	Osage	KS
Richardson's	Montgomery	TN
Richardson's Landing	Meade	KY
Richardsonville	Chariton	MO
Richardsonville	Edgefield	SC
Richardsville	Dekalb	AL
Richardsville	Jefferson	PA
Richardsville	Culpeper	VA
Richborough	Bucks	PA
Richburgh	Allegany	NY
Rich Creek	Logan	WV
Richfield	Adams	IL
Richfield	Fayette	IA
Richfield	Genesee	MI
Richfield	Hennepin	MN
Richfield	Otsego	NY
Richfield	Summit	OH
Richfield	Juniata	PA
Richfield (c.h.)	Sevier	UT
Richfield	Washington	WI
Richfield Springs	Otsego	NY
Richford	Tioga	NY
Richford	Franklin	VT
Richford	Waushara	WI
Rich Fountain	Osage	MO
Rich Hill	Bates	MO
Rich Hill	Knox	OH
Richland	Sacramento	CA
Richland	Union	Dak
Richland	Stewart	GA
Richland	Sangamon	IL
Richland	Rush	IN
Richland	Kcokuk	IA
Richland	Shawnee	KS
Richland	Kalamazoo	MI
Richland	Pulaski	MO
Richland	Colfax	NE
Richland	Oswego	NY
Richland	Tazewell	VA
Richland Centre	Bucks	PA
Richland Centre (c.h.)	Richland	WI
Richland City	Richland	WI
Richland Crossing	NBavarro	TX
Richland Grove	Mercer	IL
Richland Mill	Stafford	VA
Richland's	Onslow	NC
Richald Station	Lebanon	PA
Richland Station	Sumner	TN
Richlandtown	Bucks	PA
Richland Valley	Haywood	NC
Richman Falls	Raleigh	WV

PLACE NAMES OF THE UNITED STATES

PLACE	COUNTY	STATE	PLACE	COUNTY	STATE	PLACE	COUNTY	STATE
Richmond	Dallas	AL	Ridgely	Caroline	MD	Ringwood	Halifax	NC
Richmond	Little River	AR	Ridgely	Dodge	NE	Ringwood Furnace	Passaic	NJ
Richmond	McHenry	IL	Ridge Mills	Oneida	NY	Rinosa	Kankakee	IL
Richmond	Wayne	IN	Ridge Prairie	St. Clair	IL	Rio	Coweta	GA
Richmond	Washington	IA	Ridge Prairie	St. Clair	IL	Rio	Knox	IL
Richmond	Franklin	KS	Ridge Road	Niagara	NY	Rio	Hart	KY
Richmond (c.h.)	Madison	KY	Ridge's Creek	Montgomery	NC	Rio	Kemper	MS
Richmond	Madison	LA	Ridge Spring	Pitt	NC	Rio	Columbia	WI
Richmond	Sagadahoe	ME	Ridgeview	Westmoreland	PA	Rio Colorado	Taos	NM
Richmond	Berkshire	MA	Ridgeville	Randolph	IN	Rio Grande	Cape May	NJ
Richmond	Macomb	MI	Ridgeville	Warren	OH	Rio Grande	Gallia	OH
Richmond	Winona	MN	Ridgeville	Colleton	SC	Rio Grande		
Richmond (c.h.)	Ray	MO	Ridgeville	Mineral	WV	City (c.h.)	Starr	TX
Richmond	Cheshire	NH	Ridgeville	Monroe	WI	Rio Mimbres	Grant	NM
Richmond (c.h.)	Richmond	NY	Ridgeville Corners	Henry	OH	Rio Seco	Butte	CA
Richmond	Jefferson	OH	Ridgeway	Gallatin	IL	Rio Vista	Solano	CA
Richmond	Northampton	PA	Ridgeway	Winnishiek	IA	Ripley	Brown	IL
Richmond	Bedford	TN	Ridgeway	Osage	KS	Ripley	Somerset	ME
Richmond (c.h.)	Fort Bend	TX	Ridgeway	Lenawee	MI	Ripley (c.h.)	Tippah	MS
Richmond	Cache	UT	Ridgeway	Winena	MN	Ripley	Chantauqua	NY
Richmond	Chittenden	VT	Ridgeway	Orleans	NY	Ripley	Brown	OH
Richmond (c.h.)	Henrico	VA	Ridgeway	Warren	NC	Ripley (c.h.)	Lauderdale	TN
Richmond	Walworth	WI	Ridgeway	Hardin	OH	Ripley Landing	Jackson	WV
Richmond Centre	Ashtabula	OH	Ridgeway	Fairfield	SC	Ripley's	Tyler	WV
Richmond Corner	Sagadahoe	ME	Ridgeway	Bastrop	TX	Ripley's Mills	Craig	VA
Richmond Dale	Ross	OH	Ridgeway	Henry	VA	Ripleyville	Huron	OH
Richmond Hill	Yadkin	NC	Ridgeway	Iowa	WI	Ripon	Labette	KS
Richmond Hill	Susquehanna	PA	Ridgewood	Bergen	NJ	Ripon	Fond du Lac	WI
Richmond Mills	Ontario	NY	Ridgewood	Queens	NY	Rippey	Greene	IA
Richmond Switch	Washington	RI	Ridgeley	Platte	MO	Rippon	Jefferson	WV
Richmondville	Sanilac	MI	Ridgway (c.h.)	Elk	PA	Rippon's Hall	York	VA
Richmondville	Schoharie	NY	Ridott	Stephenson	IL	Ripton	Addison	VT
Rich Patch	Alleghany	VA	Riegelsville	Bucks	PA	Ripyville	Anderson	KY
Rich Pond Grove	Warren	KY	Rienza	Mecosta	MI	Risdon	St. Clair	IL
Rich Square	Northampton	NC	Rienzi	Alcorn	MS	Rish's Store	Lexington	SC
Rich Valley	Wabash	IN	Rifton Glen	Ulster	NY	Rising Fawn	Dade	GA
Rich Valley	Montgomery	KY	Riga	Lenawee	MI	Rising Sun (c.h.)	Ohio	IN
Rich Valley	Dakota	MN	Riga	Monroe	NY	Rising Sun	Polk	IA
Richview	Washington	IL	Rigdon	Madison	IN	Rising Sun	Cecil	MD
Richville	Tuscola	MI	Riggsbee's Store	Chatham	NC	Rising Sun	Crawford	WI
Richville	Douglas	MO	Rigg's Cross Roads	Williamson	TN	Risingville	Steuben	NY
Richville	St. Lawrence	KY	Riggston	Scott	IL	Ritchey	Newton	MO
Richville	St. Lawrence	NY	Riggsville	Izard	AR	Ritchieville	Dinwiddie	VA
Richville	Addison	VT	Riker's Hollow	Steuben	NY	Rittersville	Lehigh	PA
Richwood	Union	OH	Riley	McHenry	IL	River	Dane	WI
Richwood	Dodge	WI	Riley	Vigo	IN	River aux Vases	St. Genevieve	MO
Richwoods	Delaware	IN	Riley	Clinton	MI	River Bend	Clinton	MI
Richwoods	Washington	MO	Riley Centre	Riley	KS	Riverdale	Clay	KS
Rickardsville	Dubuque	IA	Riley Centre	St. Clair	MI	Riverdale	Westchester	NY
Rickoe's Bluff	Gadsden	FL	Riley's Station	Marion	KY	Riverdale	Hamilton	OH
Rickreall	Polk	OR	Rileyville	Wayne	PA	Riverdale	Weber	UT
Riddicksville	Hertford	NC	Rimer	Armstrong	PA	River Edge	Bergen	NJ
Riddlesburgh	Bedford	PA	Rimersburgh	Clarion	PA	River Falls	Pierce	WI
Riddle's Cross Roads	Butler	PA	Rinard	Wayne	OH	Riverhead (c.h.)	Suffolk	NY
Riddlesville	Washington	GA	Rinard's Mills	Monroe	OH	Riverhead	Jackson	WI
Riddleville	Karnes	TX	Rindge	Cheshire	NH	River Point	Steele	MN
Rider's Mills	Columbia	NY	Rinehart	Anglaize	OH	River Point	Kent	RI
Rider's Mills Station	Columbia	NY	Ring	Winnebago	WI	River Raisin	Washtenaw	MI
Ridge	St. Mary's	MD	Ringgold	Cherokee	AL	Riverside	San Bernardino	CA
Ridge	Carroll	MO	Ringgold (c.h.)	Catoosa	GA	River Side	New Haven	CT
Ridge	Livingston	NY	Ringgold	La Grange	IN	Riverside	Clay	Dak
Ridge	Noble	OH	Ringgold	Ringgold	IA	Riverside	Cook	IL
Ridge	Edgefield	SC	Ringgold	Bienville	LA	Riverside	Kane	IL
Ridge	Colorado	TX	Ringgold	Washington	MD	Riverside	Kennebec	ME
Ridgebury	Fairfield	CT	Ringgold	Morgan	OH	Riverside	Burt	NE
Ridgebury	Orange	NY	Ringgold	Jefferson	PA	Riverside	Burlington	NJ
Ridgebury	Bradford	PA	Ringgold	Montgomery	TN	Riverside	Broome	NY
Ridgedale	Polk	IA	Ringgold	Pittsylvania	VA	Riverside	Buncombe	NC
Ridge Farm	Vermilion	IL	Ringoes	Hunterdon	NJ	Riverside	Northumberland	PA
Ridgefield	Fairfield	CT	Ringo's Point	Adair	MO	River Side	Cocke	TN
Ridgefield	McHenry	IL	Ringtown	Schuylkill	PA	River Side	Pacific	WA
Ridgefield Station	Fiarfield	CT	Ringville	Hampshire	MA	River Styx	Medina	OH
Ridgeland	Henry	OH	Ringwood	McHenry	IL	Riversville	Amherst	VA

PLACE NAMES OF THE UNITED STATES

PLACE	COUNTY	STATE
Riverton	Litchfield	CT
Riverton	Fremont	IA
Riverton	Wicomico	MD
Riverton	Mason	MI
Riverton	Burlington	NJ
Riverton	Warren	VA
River Vale	Lawrence	IN
River Vale	Bergen	NJ
River View	Jefferson	KY
Rives	Richland	OH
Rives Junction	Jackson	MI
Rivesville	Marion	WV
Rixeyville	Culpeper	VA
Rix's Mills	Muskingum	OH
Roachton	Wood	OH
Road House Station	Greene	IL
Roadside	Rockingham	VA
Roadstown	Cumberland	NJ
Roadville	Charleston	SC
Roan Mountain	Carter	TN
Roann	Wabash	IN
Roanoke	Randolph	AL
Roanoke	Huntingdon	IN
Roanoke	Howard	MO
Roanoke	Suffolk	NY
Roanoke	Martin	NC
Roanoke	Putnam	OH
Roan's Prairie	Grimes	TX
Roaring Branch	Lycoming	PA
Roaring Creek	Columbia	PA
Roaring Creek	Randolph	WV
Roaring Creek	Jackson	WI
Roaring Gap	Wilkes	NC
Roaring River	Barry	MO
Roaring Run	Botetourt	VA
Roaring Spring	Trigg	KY
Roaring Spring	Blair	PA
Robard's Station	Henderson	KY
Robbinston	Washington	ME
Robbinsville	Mercer	NJ
Robbinsville	Red River	TX
Rob Camp	Claiborne	TN
Robella	Allegheny	PA
Roberson's Cross Roads	Bledsoe	TN
Roberts' Landing	St. Clair	MI
Robertson's	Anderson	TN
Robertson's Mill	Stone	MO
Robertson's Station	Harrison	KY
Robertsonville	Hardin	KY
Robertsonville	Calhoun	MS
Robertsonville	Sullivan	NY
Robertsville	Litchfield	CT
Robertsville	Franklin	MO
Robertsville	Stark	OH
Robertsville	Anderson	TN
Robeson	Brunswick	NC
Robeson	Berks	PA
Robesonia Furnaces	Berks	PA
Robeystown	Prince George's	MD
Robin	Benton	IA
Robin's Nest	Peoria	IL
Robinson (c.h.)	Crawford	IL
Robinson	Brown	KS
Robinson	Ottawa	MI
Robinson	Brown	WI
Robinson Creek	Pike	KY
Robinson's Mills	Menard	IL
Robisonville	Bedford	PA
Rob Roy	Jefferson	AR
Rob Roy	Fountain	IN
Robtown	Pickaway	OH
Roby's Corner	Merrimack	NH
Rochdale	Worcester	MA
Roche-a-Cri	Adams	WI
Rochelle	Ogle	IL
Rochelle	Madison	VA
Rocheport	Boone	MO
Rochester	Sangamon	IL
Rochester (c.h.)	Fulton	IN
Rochester	Cedar	IA
Rochester	Neosho	KS
Rochester	Butler	KY
Rochester	Plymouth	MA
Rochester	Oakland	MI
Rochester (c.h.)	Olmsted	MN
Rochester	Andrew	MO
Rochester	Madison	MT
Rochester	Strafford	NH
Rochestor (c.h.)	Monroe	NY
Rochester	Beaver	PA
Rochester	Windsor	VT
Rochester	Racine	WI
Rochester Depot	Lorain	OH
Rochester Mills	Wabash	IL
Rochester Mills	Indiana	PA
Rock	Pope	IL
Rock	Cerro Gordo	IA
Rock	Cowley	KS
Rock	Plymouth	MA
Rock	Schuylkill	PA
Rockabema	Aroostook	ME
Rockaway	Morris	NJ
Rockaway	Queens	NY
Rock Bluff	Liberty	FL
Rock Bluff	Cass	NE
Rock Bottom	Middlesex	MA
Rockbridge	Greene	IL
Rock Bridge	Monroe	KY
Rockbridge	Ozark	MO
Rockbridge	Hocking	OH
Rockbridge	Richland	WI
Rockbridge	Rockbridge	VA
Rockbridge Baths	Rockbridge	VA
Rock Butte	Douglas	CO
Rock Camp	Lawrence	OH
Rock Castle	Patrick	VA
Rock Castle	Mason	WV
Rock Cave	Upshur	WV
Rock City	Dutchess	NY
Rock City Falls	Saratoga	NY
Rock Creek	Clark	AR
Rock Creek	Butte	CA
Rock Creek	Owyhee	ID
Rock Creek	Carroll	IL
Rock Creek	Mitchell	IA
Rock Creek	Lyon	KS
Rock Creek	Alamance	NC
Rock Creek	Stephens	WA
Rock Creek	Iredell	NC
Rock Cut	Dubuque	IA
Rock Dale	Owen	KY
Rock Dale	Baltimore	MD
Rockdale	Chenango	NY
Rockdale	Lehigh	PA
Rock Dale Mills	Berkshire	MA
Rockdale Mills	Jefferson	PA
Rock Dam	Falls	TX
Rock Dell	Olmsted	MN
Rock Elm	Pierce	WI
Rock Elm Centre	Pierce	WI
Rockfall	Middlesex	CT
Rock Falls	Whitesides	IL
Rock Falls	Huron	MI
Rock Falls	Dunn	WI
Rock Farm	Russell	VA
Rockfield	Carroll	IN
Rockfield	Warren	KY
Rock Fish	Duplin	NC
Rockfish Depot	Nelson	VA
Rockford (c.h.)	Coosa	AL
Rockford (c.h.)	Winnebago	IL
Rockford	Jackson	IN
Rockford	Floyd	IA
Rockford	Bourbon	KS
Rockford	Kent	MI
Rockford	Wright	MN
Rock Ford	Lincoln	MO
Rockford	Surry	NC
Rockford	Blount	TN
Rockford	Harrison	WV
Rock Grove	Stephenson	IL
Rock Grove City	Floyd	IA
Rock Hall	Kent	MD
Rock Haven	Meade	KY
Rock Hill	St. Louis	MO
Rock Hill	York	SC
Rockhold's	Whitley	KY
Rockhouse (c.h.)	Menifee	KY
Rock House	Hocking	OH
Rock House Paairie	Buchanan	MO
Rockingham (c.h.)	Richmond	NC
Rockingham	Windham	VT
Rock Island (c.h.)	Rock Island	IL
Rock Island	Perry	IN
Rock Island	White	TN
Rock Lake	Wayne	PA
Rockland	New Haven	CT
Rockland	New Castle	DE
Rockland	Lake	IL
Rockland (c.h.)	Knox	ME
Rockland	Ontonagon	MI
Rockland	Esmeralds	NV
Rockland	Sullivan	NY
Rockland	Venango	PA
Rockland	Providence	RI
Rockland Lake	Rockland	NY
Rockland Mills	Metcalfe	KY
Rock Lick	Breckinridge	KY
Rock Lick	Marshall	WV
Rocklin	Placer	CA
Rock Mills	Randolph	AL
Rock Mills	Anderson	SC
Rock Mills	Rappahannock	VA
Rock Oak	Athens	OH
Rock Point	Jackson	OR
Rock Point	Beaver	PA
Rockport (c.h.)	Hot Spring	AR
Rockport	Pike	IL
Rockport (c.h.)	Spencer	IN
Rockport	Ohio	KY
Rockport	Knox	ME
Rockport	Essex	MA
Rockport	Copiah	MS
Rockport (c.h.)	Atchison	MO
Rockport	Cuyahoga	OH
Rockport	Carbon	PA
Rockport	Refugio	TX
Rockport	Wood	WV
Rock Prairie	Dade	MO
Rock Prairie	Rock	WI
Rock Rapids	Lyon	IA
Rock Rift	Delaware	NY
Rock River	Rock	WI
Rock Run	Stephenson	IL
Rocksburgh	Warren	NJ
Rock Spring	Chickasaw	IA
Rock Spring	Walker	GA
Rock Spring	Washington	MO

PLACE NAMES OF THE UNITED STATES

PLACE	COUNTY	STATE	PLACE	COUNTY	STATE	PLACE	COUNTY	STATE
Rock Spring	Orange	NC	Rohrersville	Washington	MD	Rose	Oakland	MI
Rock Spring	Centre	PA	Rohrsburgh	Columbia	PA	Rose	Wayne	NY
Rock Spring	Patrick	VA	Rokeby	Morgan	OH	Roseberry	Knox	TN
Rock Springs	Cecil	MD	Roland	White	IL	Roseboom	Otsego	NY
Rock Stream	Yates	NY	Roland	Story	IA	Rose Bud	White	AR
Rockton	Winnebago	IL	Roland	Centre	PA	Rose Bud	Pope	IL
Rockton	Clearfield	PA	Rolesville	Wake	NC	Roseburgh (c.h.)	Douglas	OR
Rockton	Vernon	WI	Rolfe (c.h.)	Pocahontas	IA	Roseburgh	Perry	PA
Rock Valley	Redwood	MN	Rolla (c.h.)	Phelps	MO	Rosecrans	Lake	IL
Rock View	Wyoming	WV	Rollersville	Sandusky	OH	Rosecrans	Clinton	PA
Rockville	Jefferson	AL	Rollin	Lenawee	MI	Rosecrans	Manitowoe	WI
Rockville	Tolland	CT	Rolling Fork	Pope	MN	Rose Creek	Mower	MN
Rockville	Kankakee	IL	Rolling Fork	Issaquena	MS	Rose Creek	Jefferson	NE
Rockville (c.h.)	Parke	IN	Rolling Hill	Charlotte	VA	Rosedale	Parke	IN
Rockville	Miami	KS	Rolling Home	Randolph	MO	Rosedale	Iberville	LA
Rockville	Knox	ME	Rolling Prairie	Marion	AR	Rosedale	Bolivar	MS
Rockville (c.h.)	Montgomery	MD	Rolling Prairie	La Porte	IN	Rosedale	Pasquotank	NC
Rockville	Norfolk	MA	Rolling Prairie	Dodge	WI	Rosedale	Madison	OH
Rockville	Stearns	MN	Rolling Stone	Winona	MN	Rosedale	Greene	PA
Rocville	Bates	MO	Rollingsburgh	Monroe	WV	Rosedale	Russell	VA
Rockville	Chester	PA	Rollinsville	Gilpin	CO	Rosefield	Peoria	IL
Rockville	Washington	RI	Rollinsville	Gilpin	CO	Rosefield	Catahoula	LA
Rockville	Kane	UT	Rollo	Iosco	MI	Rose Grove	Hamilton	IA
Rockville	Hanover	VA	Roma	Starr	TX	Rose Head (c.h.)	Taylor	FL
Rockville	Grant	WI	Romance	Marshall	IL	Rose Hill	Covington	AL
Rockville Centre	Queens	NY	Romance	Vernon	WI	Rose Hill	Ouachita	AR
Rockwall	Kaufman	TX	Rome	Covington	AL	Rose Hill	Jasper	IL
Rockwell	Cerro Gordo	IA	Rome (c.h.)	Floyd	GA	Rose Hill	Kosciusko	IN
Rockwood	Randolph	IL	Rome	Peoria	IL	Rose Hill	Mercer	KY
Rockwood	Fulton	NY	Rome	Perry	IN	Rose Hill	Neosho	KS
Rockwood	Roane	TN	Rome	Henry	IA	Rose Hill	Amite	MS
Rocky Bar (c.h.)	Alturas	ID	Rome	Kennebec	ME	Rose Hill	Johnson	MO
Rocky Brook	Washington	RI	Rome	Lenawee	MI	Rose Hill	Seneca	NY
Rocky Comfort (c.h.)	Little River	AR	Rome	Winston	MS	Rose Hill	Darke	OH
Rocky Comfort	Newton	MO	Rome (c.h.)	Oneida	NY	Rose Hill	Harris	TX
Rocky Ford	Seriven	GA	Rome	Ashtabula	OH	Rose Hill	Lee	VA
Rocky Ford	Pontotoc	MS	Rome	Bradford	PA	Rose Lake	Martin	MN
Rocky Fork	Licking	OH	Rome	Smith	TN	Roselle	Union	NJ
Rocky Gap	Bland	VA	Rome	Jefferson	WI	Rosemary	Desha	AR
Rocky Glade	Iron	MO	Rome City	Noble	IN	Rosemond	Christian	IL
Rocky Head	Dale	AL	Romeo	Macomb	MI	Rose Mount	Warren	IA
Rocky Hill	Hartford	CT	Romeo	Greene	TN	Rosemount	Dakota	MN
Rocky Hill (c.h.)	Lincoln	KS	Romine's Mills	Harrison	WV	Rosendale	Andrew	MO
Rocky Hill	Somerset	NJ	Romney	Tippecanoe	IN	Rosendale	Ulster	NY
Rocky Hill	Jackson	OH	Romney (c.h.)	Hampshire	WV	Rosendale	Fond du Lac	WI
Rocky Hill	Fayette	WV	Romulus	Tuscaloosa	AL	Rosenhayn	Cumberland	NJ
Rocky Hill Station	Elmonson	KY	Romulus	Wayne	MI	Rose Point	Lawrence	PA
Rocky Mount	Meriwether	GA	Romulus	Seneca	NY	Rose's Valley	Lycoming	PA
Rocky Mount	Bossier	LA	Romulus Centre	Seneca	NY	Rose Vale	Clay	KS
Rocky Mount	Miller	MO	Rondo	La Fayette	AR	Roseville	Franklin	AR
Rocky Mount	Edgecombe	NC	Rondo	Polk	MO	Roseville	Placer	CA
Rocky Mount (c.h.)	Franklin	VA	Rondout	Ulster	NY	Roseville	Warren	IL
Rocky Point	New Hanover	NC	Roney	Hickory	MO	Roseville	Parke	IN
Rocky Ridge	Frederick	MD	Ronkonkoma	Suffolk	NY	Roseville	Barren	KY
Rocky River	Warren	TN	Rono	Perry	IN	Roseville	Macomb	MI
Rocky Run	McLeod	MN	Rook's Creek	Livingston	IL	Roseville	Kandivohi	MN
Rocky Run	Columbia	WI	Root	Allen	IN	Roseville	Muskingum	OH
Rocky Springs	Claiborne	MS	Root	Montgomery	NY	Rosewood	Cleburne	AL
Rocky Station	Lee	VA	Root Creek	Milwaukee	WI	Rosewood	Harrison	IN
Rodman	Jeferson	NY	Root River	Mower	MN	Rosiclare	Hardin	IL
Rodney	Jefferson	MS	Rootstown	Portage	OH	Rosindale	Bladen	NC
Rodney	Gallia	OH	Rootville	Antrim	MI	Roslin	Cumberland	NC
Ro-Ellen	Dyer	TN	Roperville	Gage	NE	Roslindale	Norfolk	MA
Roesburgh	Grant	IN	Rosalia	Butler	KS	Roslyn	Queens	NY
Roesville	Queen Anne	MD	Rosaryville	Prince George's	MD	Ross	Lake	IN
Rogers	Ritchie	WV	Rosby's Rock	Marshall	WV	Ross	Kent	MI
Roger's Store	Osage	MO	Roscoe	Winnebago	IL	Ross	Butler	OH
Rogersville	Launderdale	AL	Roscoe	Goodhue	MN	Ross	Anderson	TN
Rogersville	Henry	IN	Roscoe	St. Clair	MO	Ross Corners	York	ME
Rogersville	Tuscarawas	OH	Roscoe	Coshocton	OH	Rosseau	Morgan	OH
Rogersville	Greene	PA	Roscoe Centre	Goodhue	MN	Ross Fork	Oneida	ID
Rogersville (c.h.)	Hawkins	TN	Roscommon	Monroe	PA	Ross Grove	De Kalb	IL
			Rose	Woodson	KS	Rossie	St. Lawrence	NY

PLACE	COUNTY	STATE	PLACE	COUNTY	STATE	PLACE	COUNTY	STATE
Rossland	Monroe	PA	Roxalana	Roane	WV	Rural Retreat	Wythe	VA
Rosston	Armstrong	PA	Roxana	Sussex	DE	Rural Ridge	Allegheny	PA
Rossville	Vermilion	IL	Roxana	Eaton	MI	Rural Shade	Navarro	TX
Rossville	Clinton	IN	Roxanna	Paulding	GA	Rural Vale	Lapeer	MI
Rossville	Allamakee	IA	Roxborough (c.h.)	Person	NC	Rural Valley	Armstrong	PA
Rossville	Shawnee	KS	Roxbury	Litchfield	GT	Rush	Jo Daviess	IL
Rossville	Baltimore	MD	Roxbury	Oxford	ME	Rush	Monroe	NY
Rossville	Richmond	NY	Roxbury	Delaware	NY	Rush	Tuscarawas	OH
Rossville	Darke	OH	Roxbury	Morgan	OR	Rush	Susquehanna	PA
Rossville	York	PA	Roxbury	Franklin	PA	Rushbottom	Holt	MO
Rossville	Chester	SC	Roxbury	Washington	VT	Rush City	Chicago	MN
Rossville	Fayette	TN	Roxbury	Dane	WI	Rush Creek	Union	OH
Rossville	Fayette	TX	Roxbury Mills	Howard	MD	Rush Creek	Navarro	TX
Rostraver	Westmoreland	PA	Roxobel	Bertie	NC	Rushford	Fillmore	MN
Roswell	Cobb	GA	Roxton	Lamar	TX	Rushford	Allegany	NY
Rotherwood	Hawkins	TN	Roayal Centre	Cass	IN	Rush Four Corners	Susquehanna	PA
Rothrock's Mills	Harrison	IN	Royal Oak	Talbot	MD	Rush Lake	Palo Alto	IA
Rothsville	Lancaster	PA	Royal Oak	Oakland	MI	Rush Rake	Otter Tail	MN
Rothville	Chariton	MO	Royal Oak	Paulding	OH	Rush River	Sibley	MN
Rotterdam	Jewell	KS	Royalston	Worcester	MA	Rush Run	Jefferson	OH
Roubidoux	Texas	MO	Royalton	Boone	IN	Rush Run	Ritchie	WV
Rough and Ready	Nevada	CA	Royalton	Russell	KY	Rushsylvania	Logan	OH
Rough and Ready	Anderson	KY	Royalton	Siagara	NY	Rushtown	Northumberland	PA
Rough and Ready	Schuylkill	PA	Royalton	Fairfield	OH	Rushville (c.h.)	Schuyler	IL
Rough and Ready Furnace	Stewart	TN	Royalton	Crawford	PA	Rushville (c.h.)	Bush	IN
Rough Creek	Breckinridge	KY	Royalton	Windsor	VT	Rushville	Buchanan	MO
Rough Creek	Laurel	KY	Royalton	Waupaca	WI	Rushville	Yates	NY
Roulette	Potter	PA	Royer's Ford	Montgomery	PA	Rushville	Fairfield	OH
Round Bottom	Monroe	OH	Royerton	Delaware	IN	Rushville	Susquehanna	PA
Round Bottom	Wayne	WV	Roysfield	Somerset	NJ	Rushville	Rockingham	VA
Round Grove	Whitesides	IL	Royston	Pike	AR	Rusk	Surry	NC
Round Grove	Scott	IA	Rozetta	Henderson	IL	Rusk (c.h.)	Cherokee	TX
Round Grove	Washington	KS	Rubens	Jewell	KS	Russell	Lucas	IA
Round Grove	Lawrence	MO	Rubicon	Dodge	WI	Russell	Russell	KS
Round Head	Hardin	OH	Ruby	St. Clair	MI	Russell	Hampden	MA
Round Hill	Fairfield	CT	Ruby Valley	Elko	NV	Russell	St. Lawrence	NY
Round Hill	Orange	NC	Ruckersville	Tippah	MS	Russell	Geanga	OH
Round Hill	Adams	PA	Ruckersville	Tippah	MS	Russell	Sheboygan	WI
Round Hill	Loudoun	VA	Ruckersville	Elbert	GA	Russell Hill	Wyoming	PA
Round Island	Clinton	PA	Ruckersville	Tippah	MS	Russell Place	Kershaw	SC
Round Knob	Putnam	WV	Ruckersville	Green	VA	Russellsburgh	Warren	PA
Round Lake	Branch	MI	Ruckerville	Clark	KY	Russell's Hill	Shannon	MO
Round Lake	Saratoga	NY	Rucksville	Lehigh	PA	Russell's Mills	Parke	IN
Round Lake	Gonzales	TX	Rudd	Floyd	IA	Russell's Place	Lawrence	OH
Round Mountain	Blanco	TX	Ruddel's Mills	Bourbon	KY	Russell's Station	Highland	OH
Round Pond	Lincoln	ME	Rudd's Mills	Monroe	WI	Russellville (c.h.)	Franklin	AL
Round Prairie	Todd	MN	Rudolph	Le Sucur	MN	Russellville	Pope	AR
Round Prairie	Todd	MO	Rudyville	Hidalgo	TX	Russellville	Monroe	GA
Round Prairie	Vernon	MO	Ruff Creek	Greene	PA	Russellville	Lawrence	IL
Round Rock	Williamson	TX	Ruffin	Rockingham	NC	Russellville	Putnam	IN
Round Top	Wilson	TN	Ruggles	Ashland	OH	Russellville (c.h.)	Logan	KY
Round Top	Fayette	TX	Rulo	Richardson	NE	Russellville	Cole	MO
Round Valley	Plumas	CA	Ruma	Randolph	IL	Russellville	Brown	OH
Rouse's Point	Clinton	NY	Rumburg	Siskiyou	CA	Russellville	Chester	PA
Rouseville	Venango	PA	Rumford	Oxford	ME	Russellville	Hamblen	TN
Rousseau	Brown	WI	Rumford Centre	Oxford	ME	Russellville	Fayette	WV
Rover	Yell	AR	Rumford Point	Oxford	ME	Russia	Herkimer	NY
Rowan Mills	Rowan	NC	Rummerfield Creek	Bradford	PA	Russia	Shelby	OH
Rowaytopn	Fairfield	CT	Rumney	Grafton	NH	Russiaville	Howard	IN
Rowe	Franklin	MA	Rumsey	McLean	KY	Rust Creek Valley	Washington	IN
Rowes	Crawford	WI	Rundell's	Crawford	PA	Rutersville	Fayette	TX
Pump	Orangeburgh	SC	Running Creek	Douglas	CO	Ruth	Texas	MO
Rupert	Columbia	PA				Rutherford Depot	Gibson	TN
Rowland	Isabella	MI	Rupert	Bennington	VT	Rutherford Park	Bergen	NJ
Rowland	Pike	PA	Rural	Rock Island	IL	Rutherfordton (c.h.)	Rutherford	NC
Rowland Mills	Hunterdone	NJ	Rural	Linn	IA	Ruther Glen	Caroline	VA
Rowlandsville	Cecil	MD	Rural	Waupaca	WI	Rutland	Humboldt	IA
Rowlesburgh	Preston	WV	Rural Dale	Grundy	MO	Rutland	Harrison	KY
Rowletta	Pettis	MO	Rural Dale	Muskingum	OH	Rutland	Anne Arundel	MD
Rowlett's Depot	Hart	KY	Rural Dale	Upshur	WV	Rutland	Worcester	MA
Rowley	Essex	MA	Rural Hill	Jefferson	NY	Rutland	Martin	MN
Rows	Ashland	OH	Rural Hill	Wilson	TN	Rutland	Jefferson	NY
Roxabell	Ross	OH	Rural Retreat	Coles	IL	Rutland	Meigs	OH

PLACE NAMES OF THE UNITED STATES

PLACE	COUNTY	STATE
Rutland	Tioga	PA
Rutland(c.h.)	Rutland	VT
Rutland	Dane	WI
Rutledge(c.h.)	Crenshaw	AL
Rutledge	Morgan	GA
Rutledge(c.h.)	Grainger	TN
Ryan	Kewaunee	WI
Ryan Creek	Winston	AL
Ryan's Well	Prentiss	AL
Rye	Rockingham	NH
Rye	Westchester	NY
Rye Cove	Scott	VA
Ryegate	Caledonia	VT
Ryerson's Station	Greene	PA
Rye Valley	Baker	OR
Rye Valley	Smyth	VA
Ryeland's Depot	Greenville	VA
Rynex's Corners	Schenectady	NY
Sabbatus	Androscoggin	ME
Sabbath Rest	Blair	PA
Sabbot Island	Goochland	VA
Sabetha	Nemaha	KS
Sabillisville	Frederick	MD
Sabina	Clinton	OH
Sabinal	Socorro	NM
Sabine	Uvalde	TX
Sabine	Marion	IN
Sabine Pass	Jefferson	TX
Sabinstown	Sabine	TX
Sabinsville	dTioga	PA
Sabula	Jackson	IA
Sacaton	Yuma	AZ
Saccarappa	Cumberland	ME
Sac City(c.h.)	Sac	IA
Sacket's Harbor	Jefferson	NY
Saco	York	ME
Sacramento	Sacarmento	CA
Sacramento	White	IL
Sacramento	McLean	KY
Sacremento	Wright	MO
Sacremento	Schulkill	PA
Sacremento City(c.h.)	Sacramento	CA
Sacred Heart	Renville	MN
Sadawaga	Windham	VT
Saddle River	Bergen	NJ
Saddler's Creek	Anderson	SC
Sadawa	Randolph	IL
Sadsburyville	Lehigh	PA
Saegerstown	Chester	PA
Safe Harbor	Lancaster	PA
Sagetown	Henderson	IL
Sageville(c.h.)	Hamilton	NY
Sag Harbor	Suffolk	NY
Saginaw(c.h.)	Saginaw	MI
Sago	Muskingham	OH
Sago	Upshur	WV
Sagone	Du Page	IL
Saguche(c.h.)	Saguache	CA
Saidora	Mason	IL
Sailora' Mills	Wayne	IL
Sailor's Rest	Montgomery	TN
Saint Albans	Hancock	IL
Saint Albans	Somerset	ME
Saint Albans(c.h.)	Franklin	VT
Saint Alban's Bay	Franklin	VT
Saint Andrew's	Orange	NY
Saint Andrew's Bay	Washington	FL
Saint Anna	Calumet	WI
Saint Anne	Kankakee	IL
Saint Annie	Pulaski	MO
Saint Ansgar	Mitchell	IA
Saint Anthony's Falls	Hennepin	MN
Saint Aubert's	Callaway	MO
Saint Augusta	Sterns	MN
Saint Augustine(c.h.)	St. John's	FL
Saint Augustine	Knox	IL
Saint Augustine	Cecil	MD
Saint Augustine	Cambria	PA
Saint Benedict	Doniphen	KS
Saint Bernard(c.h.)	St. Bernard	LA
Saint Bernice	Vermillion	IN
Saint Bethlehem	Montgomery	TN
Saint Bonifacius	Hennepin	MN
Saint Bridget	Marshall	KS
Saint Bonifacius	Cambria	PA
Saint Catherine	Linn	MO
Saint Charles	Arkansas	AR
Saint Charles	Puelbo	CO
Saint Charles	Kane	IL
Saint Charles	Madiosn	IA
Saint Charles(c.h.)	St. Charles	LA
Saint Charles	Saginaw	MI
Saint Charles	Winona	MN
Saint Charles	Winona	MN
Saint Charles(c.h.)	St. Charles	MO
Saint Charles	Cuming	NE
Saint Charles	Butler	OH
Saint Charles	Rich	UT
Saint Clair	St. Clair	MI
Saint Clair	Monona	IA
Saint Clair	Franklin	MO
Saint Clair	Columbiana	OH
Saint Clair	Schuylkill	PA
Saint Clairsville(c.h.)	Belmont	OH
Saint Clairsville	Bedford	PA
Saint Clement's Bay	St. Mary's	MD
Saint Cloud	Heard	GA
Saint Cloud(c.h.)	Stearns	MN
Saint Cloud	Scott	MO
Saint Cloud	Fond du Lac	WI
Saint Croix Falls	Polk	WI
Saint David	Fulton	IL
Saint Dennis	Baltimore	MD
Saint Derion	Nemaha	NE
Saint Donatus	Jackson	IA
Saint Elmo	Mobile	AL
Saint Elmo	Fayette	IL
Saint Elmo	Chistian	KY
Saint Elmo	Alleghany	PA
Saint Francis	Anoka	MN
Saint Francis Station	Milwaukee	WI
Saint Francisville	Lawrence	IL
Saint Francisville(c.h.)	W. Feliciana	LA
Saint Francisville	Clark	MO
Saint Francis Xavier	Hamilton	IL
Saint Frederick	Nemaha	NE
Saint Gabriel	Iberville	LA
Saint Genevieve(c.h.)	St. Genevieve	MO
Saint Geroge	Kankakee	IL
Saint George	Pottawatomie	KS
Saint George	Knox	ME
Saint George	McLeod	MN
Saint George(c.h.)	Washington	UT
Saint George	Chittenden	VT
Saint George(c.h.)	Tucker	WV
Saint George's	New Castle	De
Saint George's	Colleton	SC
Saint Helen(c.h.)	Columbia	OR
Saint Helena	Napa	CA
Saint Helena	Cedar	NE
Saint Henry	Dubois	IN
Saint Henry	Le Sueur	MN
Saint Henry's	Mercer	OH
Saint Hubertus	Le Sueur	WI
Saint Inigoes	St. Mary's	MD
Saint Jocob	Madison	IL
Saint James(c.h.)	Manitou	MI
Saint James	Watonwan	MN
Saint James	Phelps	MO
Saint James(c.h.)	Cedar	NE
Saint James	Suffolk	NY
Saint John	Lincoln	AR
Saint John	Colusa	CA
Saint John	Perry	IL
Saint John	Lake	IN
Saint John	Harrison	IA
Saint John	Putnam	MO
Saint John	Hertford	NC
Saint John's	Kandiyohi	MN
Saint John's	Auglaize	OH
Saint John's	Stewart	TN
Saint Johnsburgh	Niagra	NY
Saint Johnsbury(c.h.)	Caledonia	VT
Saint Jonsville	Montgomery	NY
Saint Joseph	Lincoln	NE
Saint Joseph	Pembina	DA
Saint Joseph	Vanderburgh	IN
Saint Joseph	Barrien	MI
Saint Joseph	Sterns	MN
Saint Joseph(c.h.)	Buchanan	MO
Saint Joseph	Susquehanna	PA
Saint Joseph's	Champaign	IL
Saint Joseph's(c.h.)	Tensas	LA
Saint Joseph's Collete	Perry	OH
Saint Joseph's Hill	Clake	IN
Saint Lawrmnce	Scott	MN
Saint Lawrence	Jefferson	NY
Saint Lawrence	Chatham	NC
Saint Lawrence	Cambria	PA
Saint Lawrence	Washington	WI
Saint Leger	Ozark	MO
Saint Leon	Dearborn	IN
Saint Leonard's	Calvert	MD
Saint Louis	Sierra	CA
Saint Louis	Miami	KS
Saint Louis	Gratiot	MI
Saint Louis(c.h.)	St. Louis	MO
Saint Louis	Jefferson	MT
Saint Louis	Marion	OR
Saint Louis Xing	Bartholomew	IN
Saint Louisville	Licking	OH
Saint Lucie(c.h.)	Brevard	FL
Saint Magdalene	Ripley	IN
Saint Margaret's	Anne Arundel	MD
Saint Marie	Jasper	IL
Saint Mark's	Wakulla	FL
Saint Mark's	Randolph	IL
Saint Martin's	Worcester	MD
Saint Martin's	Morgan	MO
Saint Martin's	Brown	OH
Saint Martin's	Milwaukee	WI
Saint Martinville(c.h.)	St. Martin's	LA
Saint Mary's	Huerfano	CO
Saint Mary's	Camden	GA
Saint Mary's	Vigo	IN
Saint Mary's	Warren	IA
Saint Mary's	Marion	KY
Saint Mary's	St. Genevieve	MO
Saint Mary's	Auglaiz	OH

PLACE NAMES OF THE UNITED STATES

PLACE	COUNTY	STATE
Saint Mary's	Elk	PA
Saint Mary's	Refugio	TX
Saint Mary's(c.h.)	Pleasants	WV
Saint Mary's	Monroe	WI
Saint Mary's Mission	Pottawotomie	KS
Saint Matthew's	Jefferson	KY
Saint Matthew's	Orangeburgh	SC
Saint Maurice	Decantur	IN
Saint Maurice	Winn	LA
Saint Meinrad	Spencer	IN
Saint Michael's	Talbot	MD
Saint Michael's	Wright	MN
Saint Morgan	Madison	IL
Saint Nazians	Manitowoc	WI
Saint Nicholas	Duval	FL
Saint Nicholas	Atchison	KS
Saint Nicholas	Schuylkill	PA
Saint Oloff	Otter Tail	MN
Saint Omer	Coles	IN
Saint Omer	Decatur	IN
Saint Paris	Champaign	OH
Saint Paul	Madison	AR
Saint Paul	Decatur	IN
Saint Paul	Lee	IA
Saint Paul	Montgomery	KS
Saint Paul(c.h.)	Ramsey	MN
Saint Paul	Webster	MO
Saint Paul	Howard	NE
Saint Paul's	Robeson	NC
Saint Paul's	Pickaway	OH
Saint Peter(c.h.)	Necollet	MN
Saint Peter's	Franklin	IN
Saint Peter's	St. Laundry	LA
Saint Peter's	St. Charles	MO
Saint Peter's	Chester	PA
Saint Petersburgh	Clarion	PA
Saint Rose	Grant	WI
Saint Sebald	Clayton	IA
Saint Sophia	Plauemine	LA
Saint Stephens	Washington	AL
St. Stephen's Church	King and Queen	VA
Saint Stephen's Depot	Charleston	SC
Saint Tammany's	Mecklenburgh	VA
Saint Thomas(c.h.)	Lincoln	NV
Saint Thomas	Cole	MO
Saint Thomas	Franklin	PA
Saint Vrain	Weld	CO
Saint Wendell's	Posey	IN
Sakeville	Randolph	IL
Salado	Bell	TX
Salamanca	Cattaraugus	NY
Salamonia	Jay	IN
Sale Creek	Hamilton	TN
Salem	Lee	AL
Salem	New London	CN
Salem	Walker	GA
Salem(c.h.)	Marion	IL
Salem(c.h.)	Washington	IN
Salem	Henry	IA
Salem	Livingston	KY
Salem	Franklin	ME
Salem	Dorchester	MD
Salem(c.h.)	Essex	MA
Salem	Washtenaw	MI
Salem	Olmstead	MN
Salem	Benton	MS
Salem(c.h.)	Dent	MO
Salem	Richardson	NE
Salem	Rockingham	NH
Salem(c.h.)	Salem	NJ
Salem(c.h.)	Washington	NY
Salem	Forsyth	NC
Salem	Columbiana	OH
Salem(c.h.)	Marion	OR
Salem	Snyder	PA
Salem	Newton	TX
Salem(c.h.)	Roanoke	VA
Salem	Kenosha	WI
Salem Centre	Steuben	IN
Salem Centre	Westchester	NY
Salem Centre	Meigs	OH
Salem Chapel	Forsyth	NC
Salem Church	Randolph	NC
Salem X Roads	Westmoreland	PA
Salem Depot	Rockingham	NH
Salem Fauquier	Fauquier	VA
Salem Grove	Alexandar	NC
Salesville	Montgomery	PA
Salfordville	Guernsey	OH
Salina	Kankakee	IL
Salina	Fulton	IN
Salina	Harrison	IN
Salina	Jefferson	IA
Salina	Onondaga	NY
Salina(c.h.)	Saline	KS
Salina	Athens	OH
Salina	Westmoreland	PA
Salina	Sevier	UT
Salina	Monterey	CA
Salina	Bienville	LA
Salina	Washtenaw	MI
Salina	Mercer	MO
Salina City	Saline	MO
Salina Mines	Gallatin	IL
Saline Valley	Saline	KS
Salineville	Columbiana	OH
Salisbury	Litchfield	CN
Salisbury	Sangamon	IL
Salisbury(c.h.)	Wicomico	MD
Salisbury	Essex	MA
Salisbury	Chariton	MO
Salibury	Merrimack	NH
Salibury	Lancaster	PA
Salibury(c.h.)	Rowan	NC
Salibury	Lancaster	PA
Salibury	Addison	VT
Salisbury Centre	Herkimer	NY
Salisbury Cove	Hancock	ME
Salisbury Mills	Orange	NY
Salladyburgh	Lycoming	PA
Salmon Brook	Aroostook	ME
Salmon City(c.h.)	Lemhi	ID
Salmon Falls	El Dorado	CA
Salmon Falls	Stafford	NH
Salmon River	Oswego	NY
Salmona	Taylor	KY
Salona	Clinton	PA
Sal Soda	Crenshaw	AL
Salt Creek	Porter	IN
Salt Creek	Perry	KY
Salt Creek	Chariton	MO
Salt Creek	Holmes	OH
Salt Creek	Polk	OR
Salt Creek(c.h.)	Juab	UT
Salt Creek	Amherst	VA
Salter's Depot	Williamsburgh	SC
Saltillo	Lee	MS
Saltillo	Lancaster	NE
Saltillo	Holmes	OH
Saltillo	Huntingdon	PA
Saltillo	Hardin	TN
Saltillo	Hopkins	TX
Saltilloville	Washington	IN
Salt Lake City(c.h.)	Salt Lake	UT
Salt Lick	Clearfield	PA
Salt Lick Bridge	Braxton	WV
Salt Marsh	Republic	KS
Saltpete Cave	Gotetourt	VA
Salt Point	Dutchess	NY
Salt River	Isbella	MI
Salt Road	Douglas	MO
Saltsburgh	Indiana	PA
Salt Springs	Douglas	GA
Salt Springs	Howard	KS
Salt Sulphur Springs	Monroe	WV
Saltville	Washington	VA
Salubria	Ada	ID
Salubrity	Pickens	SC
Saluda	Jefferson	IN
Saluda(c.h.)	Middlesex	VA
Saluda Oldtown	Newberry	SC
Salunga	Lancaster	PA
Saluria	Calhoun	TX
Saint Stephens	Washington	AL
St. Stephen's Church	King and Queen	VA
Saint Stephen's Depot	Charleston	SC
Saint Tammany's	Mecklenburgh	VA
Saint Thomas(c.h.)	Lincoln	NV
Saint Thomas	Cole	MO
Saint Thomas	Franklin	PA
Saint Vrain	Weld	CO
Saint Wendell's	Posey	IN
Sakeville	Randolph	IL
Salado	Bell	TX
Salamanca	Cattaraugus	NY
Salamonia	Jay	IN
Sale Creek	Hamilton	TN
Salem	Lee	AL
Salem	New London	CN
Salem	Walker	GA
Salem(c.h.)	Marion	IL
Salem(c.h.)	Washington	IN
Salem	Henry	IA
Salem	Livingston	KY
Salem	Franklin	ME
Salem	Dorchester	MD
Salem(c.h.)	Essex	MA
Salem	Washtenaw	MI
Salem	Olmstead	MN
Salem	Benton	MS
Salem(c.h.)	Dent	MO
Salem	Richardson	NE
Salem	Rockingham	NH
Salem(c.h.)	Salem	NJ
Salem(c.h.)	Washington	NY
Salem	Forsyth	NC
Salem	Columbiana	OH
Salem(c.h.)	Marion	OR
Salem	Snyder	PA
Salem	Newton	TX
Salem(c.h.)	Roanoke	VA
Salem	Kenosha	WI
Salem Centre	Steuben	IN
Salem Centre	Westchester	NY
Salem Centre	Meigs	OH
Salem Chapel	Forsyth	NC
Salem Church	Randolph	NC
Salem X Roads	Westmoreland	PA
Salem Depot	Rockingham	NH
Salem Fauquier	Fauquier	VA
Salem Grove	Alexandar	NC
Salesville	Montgomery	PA
Salfordville	Guernsey	OH
Salina	Kankakee	IL

PLACE	COUNTY	STATE	PLACE	COUNTY	STATE	PLACE	COUNTY	STATE
Salina	Fulton	IN	Salvisa	Mercer	KY	Sandwich	Barnstable	MA
Salina	Harrison	IN	Salyersville(c.h.)	Magoffin	KY	Sandwich	Carroll	NH
Salina	Jefferson	IA	Salzburgh	Bay	MI	Sandy	Columbiana	OH
Salina	Onondaga	NY	Samantha	Highland	OH	Sandy	Jackson	WV
Salina(c.h.)	Saline	KS	Samaria	Johnson	IN	Sandy Beach	Cumberland	ME
Salina	Athens	OH	Samish	Whatcom	WA	Sandy Creek	Oswego	NY
Salina	Westmoreland	PA	Sammonsville	Fulton	NY	Sandy Creek	Randolph	NC
Salina	Sevier	UT	Samson Creek	Harrison	MO	Sandy Creek	Crawford	PA
Salina	Monterey	CA	Sam's Creek	Carroll	MD	Sandy Cross	Oglethorpe	GA
Salina	Bienville	LA	Samsonville	Ulster	NY	Sandy Flat	Greenville	SC
Salina	Washtenaw	MI	Samsonville	Jackson	OH	Sandy Ford	Madison	FL
Salina	Mercer	MO	Samsville	Edwards	IL	Sandy Grove	Chatham	NC
Salina City	Saline	MO	Samuel's Depot	Nelson	KY	Sandy Hill	Carroll	GA
Salina Mines	Gallatin	IL	San Anders	Milan	TX	Sandy Hill	Worcester	MD
Saline Valley	Saline	KS	San Andreas	Calaveras	CA	Sandy Hill(c.h.)	Washington	NY
Salineville	Columbiana	OH	San Antonia	Monterey	CA	Sandy Hill	Perry	PA
Salisbury	Litchfield	CN	San Antonio	Socorro	NM	Sandy Hill	Henry	TN
Salisbury	Sangamon	IL	San Antonio(c.h.)	Bexar	TX	Sandy Hook	Fairfield	CN
Salisbury(c.h.)	Wicomico	MD	San Augustine(c.h.)	San Augustine	TX	Sandy Hook(c.h.)	Elliot	KY
Salisbury	Essex	MA	San Bartolo(c.h.)	Zapata	TX	Sandy Hook	Harford	MD
Salisbury	Chariton	MO	San Benito	Monterey	CA	Sandy Hook	Monmouth	NJ
Salibury	Merrimack	NH	San			Sandy Hook	Rappahannock	VA
Salibury	Lancaster	PA	Bernardino(c.h.)	C A		Sandy Lake	Mercer	PA
Salibury(c.h.)	Rowan	NC	Sanborn	Niagara	NY	Sandy Level	Pittsylvania	VA
Salibury	Lancaster	PA	Sanbornton	Belkhap	NH	Sandy Mush	Buncombe	NC
Salibury	Addison	VT	San Buenaventura	Santa Barbara	CA	Sandy Plains	Patarick	VA
Salibury Centre	Herkimer	NY	Sanburn	Johnson	IL	Sandy Point	Waldo	ME
Salisbury Cove	Hancock	ME	Sancelito	Marin	CA	Sandy Point	Brazoria	TX
Salisbury Mills	Orange	NY	Sand Bank	Oswego	NY	Sandy Ridge	Henry	GA
Salladyburgh	Lycoming	PA	Sand Beach	Huron	MI	Sandy Spring	Montgomery	MD
Salmon Brook	Aroostook	ME	Sandborn	Knox	IN	Sandy Springs	Grant	AR
Salmon City(c.h.)	Lemhi	ID	Sand Brook	Hunterdon	NJ	Sandyville	Warren	IA
Salmon Falls	El Dorado	CA	Sandburg	Sullivan	NY	Sandyville	Tuscarawas	OH
Salmon Falls	Stafford	NH	Sand Creek	Scott	MN	Sanel	Mendocino	CA
Salmon River	Oswego	NY	Sand Creek	Saunders	NE	San Elizario	El Paso	TX
Salmona	Taylor	KY	Sand Cut	Wayne	PA	San Fmlipe	Santa Clara	CA
Salona	Clinton	PA	Sandefer's Store	Carroll	KY	San Felipe	Austin	TX
Sal Soda	Crenshaw	AL	Sander's Hill	Montgomery	NC	Sanford	Pima	AZ
Salt Creek	Porter	IN	Sanderson(c.h.)	Baker	FL	Sanford	York	ME
Salt Creek	Perry	KY	Sanders' Store	Carteret	NC	Sanford	Broome	NY
Salt Creek	Chariton	MO	Sandersville(c.h.)	Baker	FL	Sanford's Corners	Jefferson	NY
Salt Creek	Holmes	OH	Sand Fly	Bastrop	TX	Sanfordville	Cherokee	KS
Salt Creek	Polk	OR	Sandford	Vigo	IN	San Francisco(c.h.)	San Francisco	CA
Salt Creek(c.h.)	Juab	UT	Sandford	Midland	MI	San Gabriel	Los Angeles	CA
Salt Creek	Amherst	VA	Sand Fork	Gallia	OH	San Gabriel	Milam	TX
Salter's Depot	Williamsburgh	SC	Sand Fork	Gilmer	WV	Sangamon Station	Macon	IL
Saltillo	Lee	MS	Sandgate	Bennington	VT	Saugerville	Piscataquis	ME
Saltillo	Lancaster	NE	Sand Hill	Lewis	KY	Saugerville	Augusta	VA
Saltillo	Holmes	OH	Sand Hill	Scotland	MO	San Gregoria	San Mateo	CA
Saltillo	Huntingdon	PA	Sand Hollow	Morgan	OH	San Jacinto	San Diego	CA
Saltillo	Hardin	TN	San Diego(c.h.)	San Diego	CA	San Jacinto	Jennings	IN
Saltillo	Hopkins	TX	San Diego	Nueces	TX	San Jacinto	Houston	MN
Saltilloville	Washington	IN	Sandiges	Amhearst	VA	San Jose(c.h.)	Santa Clara	CA
Salt Lake City(c.h.)	Salt Lake	UT	Sandisfield	Berkshire	MA	San Jose	Mason	IL
Salt Lick	Clearfield	PA	Sand Lake	Lake	IL	San Jose	San Miguel	NM
Salt Lick Bridge	Braxton	WV	Sand Lake	Kent	MI	San Juan	Monterey	CA
Salt Marsh	Republic	KS	Sand Lake	Kandiyohi	MN	San Juan	Rio Arriba	NM
Saltpete Cave	Gotetourt	VA	Sandoval	Marion	IL	San Leandro(c.h.)	Alameda	CA
Salt Point	Dutchess	NY	Sandown	Rockingham	NH	San Lorenzo	Alameda	CA
Salt River	Isbella	MI	Sand Patch	Somerset	PA	San Luis(c.h.)	Costilla	CO
Salt Road	Douglas	MO	Sand Point	Volusia	FL	San Luis		
Saltsburgh	Indiana	PA	Sand Rock	Cherokee	AL	Obispo(c.h.)	San Luis Obispo	CA
Salt Springs	Douglas	GA	Sand Run	Upshur	WV	San Luis Ranch	Merced	CA
Salt Springs	Howard	KS	Sand Spring	Delaware	IA	San Luis Rey	San Diego	CA
Salt Sulphur Springs	Monroe	WV	Sand Springs	Webster	MO	San Marcial	Socorro	NM
Saltville	Washington	VA	Sandstone	Jackson	MI	San Marcos	San Luis Obispo	CA
Salubria	Ada	ID	Sand Stone	Vernon	MO	San Marcos(c.h.)	Hays	TX
Salubrity	Pickens	SC	Sandt's Eddy	Northampton	PA	San Marino	Dinwiddle	VA
Saluda	Jefferson	IN	Sandusky	Lee	IA	San Mateo	San Mateo	CA
Saluda(c.h.)	Middlesex	VA	Sandusky	Cattaraugus	NY	Sannemin	Livingston	IL
Saluda Oldtown	Newberry	SC	Sandusky(c.h.)	Erie	OH	San Pablo	Contra Costa	CA
Salunga	Lancaster	PA	Sandusky	Sauk	WI	San Patricio	San Patricio	TX
Saluria	Calhoun	TX	Sandwich	De Kalb	IL	San Pedro	Houston	TX

PLACE NAMES OF THE UNITED STATES

PLACE	COUNTY	STATE	PLACE	COUNTY	STATE	PLACE	COUNTY	STATE
San Pierre	Stark	IN	Saukville	OZaukee	WI	Schoharie(c.h.)	Schoharie	NY
San Quentin	Marin	CA	Saulsburgh	Huntingdon	PA	Schonberg	Warren	IA
San Rafeal(c.h.)	Marin	CA	Saulsbury	Hardeman	TN	School	White	IL
San Saba(c.h.)	San Saba	TX	Sault de Ste Maria	Chippewa	MI	Schoolcraft	Kalamazoo	MI
Santa Ana	Los Angeles	CA	Saumsville	Shenandoah	VA	Schooley's		
Santa Barbara(c.h.)	Santa Barbara	CA	Saunders' Creek	Simpson	MS	Mountain	Morris	NJ
Santa Clara	Santa Clara	CA	Sauners' Ferry	Garrard	KY	Schooley's Station	Boss	OH
Santa Claus	Spencer	CA	Saundersville	Worcester	MA	School House		
Santa Cruz(c.h.)	Sant Cruz	CA	Saundersville	Sumner	TN	Station	San Mateo	CA
Santa Fe	Alexandar	IL	Sanquoit	Oneida	NY	Schoolings	La Fayette	MO
Santa Fe	Miami	IN	Sauvie's Island	Columbia	OR	Schrealenburgh	Bergen	NJ
Santa Fe	Monroe	MO	Savage	Howard	MD	Schroon Lake	Essex	NY
Santa Fe(c.h.)	Santa Fe	NM	Savanna	Carroll	IL	Schroon River	Essex	NY
Santa Fe	Maury	TN	Savannah(c.h.)	Chatham	GA	Schulzville	Dutchess	NY
Santa Margarita	San Luis Obispo	CA	Savannah	Davis	IA	Schulzville	Luzerne	PA
Santa Maria	Santa Barbara	CA	Savannah	Pottawatomie	KS	Schumacker's Store	St. Charles	ME
Santaquin	Utah	UT	Savannah(c.h.)	Andrew	MO	Schuyler	Cass	jO
Santa Rosa(c.h.)	Sonoma	CA	Savannah	Wayne	NY	Schuyler(c.h.)	Colifax	NE
Santa Rosa	Daviess	MO	Savannah	Ashland	OH	Schuyler's Falls	Clinton	NY
Santee Agency	L'Eau aui Court	NE	Savannah(c.h.)	Hardin	TN	Schuyler's Lake	Otsego	NY
Santiago	Sherburne	MN	Savannah	Red River	TX	Schuylersville	Saratoga	NY
Santuck	Union	SC	Saverton	Ralls	MO	Schuylkill	Chester	PA
San Ysidro	Santa Clara	CA	Savill	Orange	NY	Schuylkill Haven	Schuylkill	PA
Sappington	St. Louis	MO	Savona	Steuben	NY	Schwenk's Store	Montgomery	PA
Sarahsville	Williamson	IL	Savoy	Champaign	IL	Science Hill	Randolph	NC
Sarahsville	Noble	OH	Savoy	Berkshire	MA	Scio	Washeenaw	MI
Saranac	Ionia	MI	Saw Dust	Columbia	GA	Scio	Alleghany	NY
Saranac	Clinton	NY	Saw Mill	Seneca	OH	Scio	Harrison	OH
Saranac Lake	Franklin	NY	Sawpit	Plumas	CA	Scio	Linn	OR
Sarassa	Arkansas	AR	Sawyer	Berrien	MI	Sciola	Montgomery	IA
Saratoga	Santa Clara	CA	Sawyer's Bar	Klamath	CA	Sciota	McDonough	IL
Saratoga	Randolph	IN	Sawyer's Mills	Seneca	OH	Schiota	Clinton	NY
Saratoga	Howard	IA	Sawyersville	Randolph	NC	Schioto	Schioto	OH
Saratoga	Winona	MN	Saxapahaw	Alamance	NC	Scioto	Monroe	PA
Saratoga Springs	Saratoga	NY	Saxenbrugh	Butler	PA	Scioto Furnace	Scioto	OH
Sarcoxie	Jasper	MO	Saxeville	Waushara	WI	Sciotoville	Scioto	OH
Sardinia	Pike	IL	Saxon	Henry	IL	Scipio	Jennings	IN
Sardinia	Decatur	IN	Saxon	Meigs	OH	Scipio	Anderson	KS
Sardinia	Erie	NY	Saxonville	Middlesex	MA	Scipio	Cayuga	NY
Sardinia	Brown	OH	Saxton	Bedford	PA	Scipio	Millard	UT
Sardis	Mason	KY	Saxton's River	Windham	VT	Scipioville	Cayuga	NY
Sardis	Panola	MS	Saybrook	Middlsex	CN	Scitico	Hartford	CN
Sardis	Monroe	OH	Saybrook	Clay	DA	Scituate	Plymouth	MA
Sardis	Westmoreland	PA	Saybrook	McClean	IL	Scooba	Bumper	MS
Sardis	Fayette	TN	Saybrook	Ashtabula	OH	Scootch Bush	Montgomery	NY
Sardis	Harrison	WV	Salorsburgh	Monroe	PA	Scotch Grove	Jones	IA
Sarecta	Duplin	NC	Sayville	Suffolk	NY	Scotch Hill	Clarion	PA
Sarapta	Calhoun	MS	Scales' Diggings	Sierra	CA	Scotch Plains	Union	NJ
Sargent	McKean	PA	Scales Mound	Jo Daviess	IL	Scoth Ridge	Wood	OH
Sargentville	Buena Vista	IA	Scalp Level	Cambria	PA	Scotchtown	Orange	NY
Sargentville	Hancock	ME	Scandia	Stevens	MN	Scotia	Schenetady	NY
Sartwell	McKean	PA	Scandinavia	Waupaca	WI	Scotland	Windham	CN
Sarverville	Butler	PA	Scarborough	Scriven	GA	Scotland	Greene	IN
Sarvis Point	Webster	MO	Scarborough	Cumberland	ME	Scotland	Plymouth	MA
Sarvis Spring	Phelps	MO	Scarborough	Westchester	NY	Scotland	Franklin	PA
Sasabi Flat	Pima	AZ	Scarlet's MIll	Berks	PA	Scotland Neck	Halifax	NC
Sassras	Kent	MI	Scarsdale	Westchester	NY	Scott	La Grange	IN
Sassafras Fork	Granville	NC	Scenery Hill	Washington	PA	Scott	Kenton	KY
Satartil	Yazoo	MS	Schellsburgh	Bedford	PA	Scott	Kenton	KY
Satilla Mills	Camden	GA	Schenectady(c.h.)	Schenctady	NY	Scott	Cortland	NY
Satsop	Chehalis	WA	Schenevus	Otsego	NY	Scott	Adams	OH
Satterfield	Mercer	PA	Schenley Station	Armstrong	PA	Scott	Sheboygan	WI
Satterlee's Mills	Mecosta	MI	Schereville	Lake	IN	Scott Centre	Fayette	IA
Satter's	Comal	TX	Schereville	Brown	WI	Scott Landing	Jefferson	KS
Saturn	Whitley	IN	Schleisingerville	Washington	WE	Scott River	Sisiyou	CA
Saugatuck	Fairfield	CN	Schlensburgh	St. Charles	MO	Scotts	Wasco	OR
Sasugatuck	Allegan	MI	Schlichter	Bucks	PA	Scottsborough(c.h.)	Jackson	AL
Saugerties	Ulster	NY	Schnocksville	Lehigh	PA	Scottsburgh	Livingston	NY
Saugus	Essex	MS	Schneider	Schuylkill	PA	Scottsburgh	Douglas	OR
Saugus Centre	Essex	MS	Schnellville	Dubois	IN	Scottsburg	Halifax	VA
Sasuk City	Stearns	MN	Schodack Centre	Rensselaer	NY	Scott's Hill	Henderson	TN
Sauk City	Sauk	WI	Schoeneck	Lancaster	PA	Scottsville	Bibb	AL
Sauk Rapids(c.h.)	Benton	MN	Schoffner's Corners	Jefferson	PA	Scottsville	Floyd	IN

PLACE NAMES OF THE UNITED STATES

PLACE	COUNTY	STATE	PLACE	COUNTY	STATE	PLACE	COUNTY	STATE
Scottsville(c.h.)	Allen	KY	Sellersburgh	Clarke	IN	Seymour	Ontagamie	WI
Scottsville	Sullivan	MO	Seller's Landing	Hardin	IL	Seymoursville	Grant	WV
Scottsville	Monroe	NY	Sellersville	Bucks	PA	Shabbonas Grove	De Kalb	IL
Scottsville	Wyoming	PA	Sell's Station	Adams	PA	Shabonier	Fayette	IL
Scottsville	Harrison	TX	Selma(c.h.)	Dallas	AL	Shackelford	Henderson	TX
Scottsville	Albemarle	VA	Selma	Drew	AR	Shack's Mills	Buchanan	VA
Scotts Town	Lawrence	OH	Slema	McLean	IL	Shade	Athens	OH
Scottville	Macoupin	IL	Selma	Delaware	IN	Shade Furnace	Somerset	PA
Scottville	Ashe	PA	Selma	Wayne	OA	Shade Gap	Huntingdon	PA
Scranton Station	Greene	IA	Selma	Johnston	NC	Shade Mills	Alleghany	MD
Screven	Appling	GA	Selma	Clark	OH	Shadesville	Grant	IN
Scriba	Oswega	NY	Selma	Bexar	TX	Shade Valley	Juniata	PA
Sccroggsfield	Carroll	OH	Selma	Alleghany	VA	Shadeville	Franklin	OH
Scuffletown	Henderson	KY	Seminary	Onachita	AR	Shadwell	Albemarle	VA
Scuppernong	Washington	NC	Sempronius	Cayugn	NY	Shady	Johnson	TN
Scyeue	Dallas	TX	Sempronius	Austin	TX	Shady Grove	Taylor	FL
SChytheville	Merrimack	NH	Senatobia	De Soto	MS	Shady Grove	Crittenden	KY
Seabeck	Kitsap	WA	Seneca	La Salle	IL	Shady Grove	Washington	LA
Seaboard	Northampton	NC	Seneca	Crocker	IA	Shady Grove	Jasper	MS
Seabright	Monmouth	NJ	Seneca(c.h.)	Nemaha	KS	Shady Grove	Franklin	PA
Seabrook	Rockingham	NH	Seneca	Montgomery	MD	Shady Grove	Franklin	PA
Seafield	White	IN	Seneca	Lenawee	MI	Shady Grove	Franklin	VA
Seaford	Sussex	DE	Seneca	Newton	MO	Shady Hill	Henderson	TN
Seal	Wyandot	OH	Seneca	Schuyler	NY	Shady Plain	Armstrong	PA
Seal Cove	Hancock	ME	Seneca	Venango	PA	Shaefferstown	Lebanon	PA
Seale's Station(c.h.)	Russell	AL	Seneca	Crawford	WI	Shaff's Gridge	Somerset	PA
Seapo(c.h.)	Republic	KS	Seneca Castle	Ontario	NY	Shaftsbury	Bennington	VT
Searight's	Fayette	PA	Seneca Falls	Seneca	NY	Shaker Village	Merrimack	NH
Searsborough	Poweshick	IA	Senecaville	Guernsey	OH	Shakers	Albany	NY
Searsburgh	Schuyler	NY	Senex	McLean	IL	Shakleford's	King and Queen	VA
Searsburgh	Bennington	VT	Sennet	Cayugna	NY	Shakopee(c.h.)	Scott	MN
Searsmont	Waldo	MO	Senoia	Coweta	GA	Shaler's Mills	Knox	OH
Searsport	Waldo	MO	Sentinel	Juneau	WI	Shalersville	Portage	OH
Searsville	San Mateo	CA	Sentinel Prairie	Polk	MO	Shallotte	Brunswick	NC
Searsville	Orange	NY	Sequoyah	Cherokee Nat.	IT	Shambling's Mills	Roane	WV
Seatco	Thurston	WA	Serbin	Bastrop	TX	Shamburgh	Venango	PA
Seatcon	Fayette	IA	Serena	La Salle	IL	Shamokin	Northampton	PA
Seattle(c.h.)	King	WA	Serena	Stafford	VA	Shamokin Dam	Snyder	PA
Sea View	Northampton	VA	Sereno	Columbia	PA	Shamong	Burlington	NJ
Seaville	Cape May	NJ	Sergeant Bluffs	Woodbury	IA	Shamrock	Callaway	MO
Sebago	Cumberland	ME	Sergeantsville	Hunterdon	NJ	Shanandoah	Richland	OH
Sebago	Linn	MO	Service	Beaver	PA	Shaudaken	Ulster	NY
Sebastopol	Sonoma	CA	Setauket	Suffolk	NY	Shandsville	Pope	IL
Sebec	Picataquis	ME	Setzler's Store	Chester	PA	Shane	Baltimore	MD
Sebewa	Ionia	MI	Sebastopol	Koscinsko	IN	Shane's Xing	Mercer	OH
Sebewaing	Huron	MI	Seven Fountains	Shenandoah	VA	Shanesville	Tuscarawas	OH
Sebree	Webster	KY	Seven Islands	Fluvanna	VA	Shanesville	Berks	PA
Sechlersville	Jackson	WI	Seven Mile	Butler	OH	Shanghai	Howard	IN
Secillia	Calhoun	MI	Seven Mile Ford	Smyth	VA	Shanghai	Berkeley	WV
Second Creek	Greenbrier	WV	Seven Mile House	Erie	OH	Shanksville	Somerset	PA
Secor	Woodford	IL	Seven Stars	Adams	PA	Shannock Mills	Washington	RI
Sedalia(c.h.)	Pettis	MO	Seventy-Eight	Johason	IA	Shannon	Carroll	IL
Sedan	De Kalb	IN	Seventy-Six	Clinton	KY	Shannon	Lee	MS
Sedan	Howard	KS	Seventy-Six	Beaver	PA	Shannondale	Montgomery	IN
Sedan	Hampshire	WV	Seventy-Six Centre	Washington	IA	Shannon Hill	Goochland	VA
Sedge's Garden	Forsyth	NC	Seven Valleys	York	PA	Shannonville	Montgomery	PA
Sedgewick	Decatur	IA	Severance	Domiphan	KS	Shapleigh	York	ME
Seekonk	Bristol	MA	Sevierville(c.h.)	Sevier	TN	Shark River	Monmouth	NJ
Seely Creek	Chemung	NY	Seville	Fullton	IL	Sharlow	Bourbon	KS
Seelyville	Vigo	IN	Seville	Madison	VA	Sharon	Litchfield	CN
Sego	Perry	OH	Sewanee	Franklin	VA	Sharon	Taliaferro	GA
Seguin(c.h.)	Guadalupe	TX	Seward	Seward	NE	Sharon	Henry	IL
Seiad Valley	Siskiyou	CA	Sewee	Meigs	TN	Sharon	Delaware	IN
Seiberlingville	Lehigh	PA	Sewellsville	Belmont	OH	Sharon	Warren	IA
Seidersville	Northampton	PA	Sewickly	Alleghany	PA	Sharon	Norfolk	MA
Seigfried's Bridge	Northampton	PA	Sewicklyville	Belmont	OH	Sharon	Le Sueur	MN
Seisholtzville	Berks	PA	Sexton's Creek	Clay	KY	Sharon	Schoharie	NY
Selah	Yakima	WA	Sextonville	Richland	KY	Sharon	Noble	OH
Selbysport	Alleghany	MD	Seymour	New Haven	CN	Sharon	Mercer	PA
Selbyville	Sussex	DE	Seymour	Jackson	IN	Sharon	Windsor	VT
Selden	Suffolk	DE	Seymour	Wayne	IA	Sharon	Bland	VA
Seldin's Grove	Snyder	PA	Seymour	Hart	KY	Sharon	Chehalis	WA
Selkirk	Marion	GA	Seymour	Allegany	NY	Sharon	Walworth	WI

PLACE	COUNTY	STATE
Sharon Centre	Schoharie	NY
Sharon Centre	Medina	OH
Sharon Centre	Potter	PA
Sharon Grove	Toid	KY
Sharon Springs	Schoharie	NY
Sharon Station	Dutchess	NY
Sharonville	Hamilton	OH
Sharp Corners	Milwaukee	WI
Sharpsburg	Coweta	GA
Sharpsburgh	Cross	AR
Sharpsburgh	Washington	MD
Sharpsburgh	Allegheny	PA
Sharp's Chapel	Union	TN
Sharp's Cross Roads	Independence	AR
Sharp's Mills	Harrison	IN
Sharpsville	Tipton	IN
Sharpsville	Washington	KY
Sharpsville	Mercer	PA
Sharpsville Furnace	Mercer	PA
Sharptown	Wicomico	MD
Sharptown	Salem	NJ
Shartlesville	Berks	PA
Shasta(c.h.)	Shasta	CA
Shattickville	Franklin	MA
Shauck's	Morrow	OH
Shaumburgh	Cook	IL
Shave Head	Cass	MI
Shaver's Creek	Huntingdon	PA
Shavertown	Delaware	NY
Shavwanaw(c.h.)	Shawanaw	WI
Shawangunk	Ulster	NY
Shawhan	Bourbon	KY
Shaw Hill	Crawford	WI
Shawnee	Johnson	KS
Shawnee	Niagara	NY
Shawnee	Monroe	PA
Shawnee Mission	Johnson	KS
Shawnee Mound	Tippecanoe	IN
Shawnee Mound	Henry	MO
Shawneetown(c.h.)	Gallatin	IL
Shawneetown	Cape Girardeau	MO
Shawnee Village	Mississippi	AR
Shawn's Cross Roads	Johnson	TN
Shaw's Flats	Tuolumne	CA
Shaw's Landing	Crawford	PA
Shaw's Mills	Guilford	NC
Shaw's Point	Macoupin	IL
Shawsville	Clearfield	PA
Shawsville	Montgomery	VA
Shawyer's Mills	Tazewell	VA
Sheakleyville	Mercer	PA
Shearer's X Roads	Westmoreland	PA
Sheboygan(c.h.)	Sheboygan	WI
Sheboygan Falls	Sheboygan	WI
Shedd's	Linn	OR
Shed's Corners	Madison	NY
Sheenwater	Erie	NY
Sheepscott Bridge	Lincoln	ME
Sheffield	Fayette	AL
Sheffield	Bureau	IL
Sheffield	Dubuque	IA
Sheffield	Berkshire	MA
Sheffield	Lorain	OH
Sheffield	Warren	PA
Sheffield	Caledonia	VT
Sheffield Depot	Warren	PA
Shekomeko	Dutchess	NY
Shelbina	Shelby	MO
Shelburn	Sullivan	IN
Shelburne	Franklin	MA
Shelburne	Coos	NH
Shelburne	Chittenden	VT
Shelburne Falls	Franklin	MA
Shelby	Shelby	ID
Shelby	Ocenan	MI
Shelby	Orleans	MI
Shelby(c.h.)	Cleveland	NC
Shelby(c.h.)	Richland	OH
Shelby	Austin	TX
Shelby	La Crosse	WI
Shelby Basin	Orleans	NY
Shelby City	Boyle	KY
Shelby Iron Works	Shelby	AL
Shelby Springs	Shelby	AL
Shelbyville(c.h.)	Shelby	IL
Shelbyville(c.h.)	Shelby	IN
Shelbyville(c.h.)	Shelby	KY
Shelbyvile	Blue Earth	MN
Shelbyville(c.h.)	Shelby	MO
Shelbyville(c.h.)	Bedford	TN
Shelbyville(c.h.)	Shelby	TX
Shelbyville(c.h.)	Shelby	CA
Sheldon	Sacramento	IL
Sheldon	Iroquois	IN
Sheldon	Allen	KS
Sheldon	Sedgwick	MN
Sheldon	Houston	NY
Sheldon	Wyoming	VT
Sheldon	Franklin	WI
Sheldon	Monroe	IL
Sheldon's Grove	Schuyler	PA
Sheldonville	Norfolk	NY
Sheldrake	Seneca	MO
Shell City	Vernon	MS
Shell Mound	Sunflower	IA
Shell Rock	Butler	MN
Shell Rock	Freedom	IA
Shell Rock Falls	Cerro Gordo	IA
Shellsburgh	Benton	PA
Shelocta	Indiana	NY
Shelter Island	Suffolk	SC
Shelton	Fairfield	GA
Sheltonville	Forsyth	IA
Shenandoah	Page	PA
Shenandoah	Schuylkill	VA
Shenandoah Iron Works	Page	MI
Shepardsville	Clinton	MD
Shepard's Store	Anne Arundel	OH
Shepherdstown	Belmont	PA
Shepherdstown	Cumberland	WV
Shepherds-town(c.h.)	Jefferson	KY
Sheperdville(c.h.)	Bulitt	MD
Shepperdville	Wicomico	VA
Sherando	Augusta	MA
Sherborn	Middlesex	NY
Sherburne	Chenango	VA
Sherburne	Rutland	NY
Sherburne 4 Corners	Chenango	KY
Sherburne Mills	Fleming	IL
Sherburneville	Kankakee	AR
Sheridan(c.h.)	Grant	AR
Sheridan	Placer	IL
Sheridan	La Salle	IN
Sheridan	Hamilton	IA
Sheridan	Van Buren	MI
Sheridan	Montcalm	MO
Sheridan	Macon	MT
Sheridan	Madison	NE
Sheridan	Nemaha	NV
Sheridan	Douglas	NY
Sheridan	Chautauqua	OH
Sheridan	Putnam	OR
Sheridan	Yam Hill	
Sheridan	Lebanan	PA
Sheridan Coal Works	Lawrence	OH
Sherman(c.h.)	Marion	AR
Sherman	Santa Clara	CA
Sherman	Fairfield	CN
Sherman	Sangamon	IL
Sherman	Jennings	IN
Sherman	Powechick	IA
Sherman	Grant	KY
Sherman	Aroostook	ME
Sherman(c.h.)	Wexford	MI
Sherman	Blue Earth	MO
Sherman	St. Louis	MO
Sherman	Nemaha	NE
Sherman	Chautauqua	NY
Sherman	Summit	OH
Sherman	Marathon	WI
Sherman	Albany	SY
Sherman(c.h.)	Grayson	TX
Sherman City	Cherokee	KS
Sherman City	Isabella	MI
Sherman Mills	Aroostook	ME
Sherman's Dale	Perry	PA
Shermantown	White Pine	NV
Shermanville	Casey	KY
Sherman Wells	Venango	PA
Sherodsville	Carroll	OH
Sherrand	Marshall	WV
Sherrett	Armstrong	PA
Shmrrill's Ford	Catawba	NC
Sherrill's Mount	Dubuque	IA
Sherwood	Branch	MI
Sherwood	Jasper	MO
Sherwood	Cayuga	NY
Sherwood	Calumet	WI
Sherwood's Mills	Mason	WA
Sherwood Valley	Mendocino	CA
Sheshequin	Bradford	PA
Shibley's Point	Adair	MO
Shickshinny	Luzerne	PA
Shields	Jackson	IN
Shields	Belmont	OH
Shieldsbor-ough(c.h.)	Hancock	MS
Shieldsville	Rice	MN
Shiloh	Marengo	AL
Shiloh	Van Buren	AR
Shiloh	St. Clair	IL
Shiloh	Cedar	IA
Shiloh	Cathaway	KY
Shiloh	Cumberland	NJ
Shiloh	Richland	OH
Shiloh	Camden	NC
Shiloh	Sumter	SC
Shiloh	Montgomery	TN
Shiloh	Hunt	TX
Shiloh	King George	VA
Shiloh Academy	Lamar	TX
Shiloh Hill	Randolph	IS
Shimerville	Lehigh	PA
Shinbone	Fayette	PA
Shin Creek	Sullivan	NY
Shingle Creek	St. Lawrence	NY
Shinglehouse	Potter	PA
Shingle Springs	El Dorado	CA
Shinn's Point	Johnson	IL
Shinnston	Harrison	WV
Shiocton	Outagamie	WI
Shipman	Macoupin	IL
Shippensburgh	Cumberland	PA
Shippensville	Clarion	PA
Shippingsport	Beaver	PA

PLACE	COUNTY	STATE	PLACE	COUNTY	STATE	PLACE	COUNTY	STATE
Shiremantown	Cumberland	PA	Siam	Taylor	IA	Silver Spring	Wilson	TN
Shirland	Winnebago	IL	Sibley	Sibley	MN	Silver Springs	ALcorn	MS
Shirland	Alleghany	PA	Sibley	Jackson	MO	Silver Star	Madison	MT
Shirley	Covington	AL	Sicily	Highland	OH	Silver Street	Newberry	SC
Shirley	McLean	IL	Sideling Hill	Fulton	PA	Silverton	Ocean	NJ
Shirley	Cloud	KS	Side View	Montgomery	KY	Silverton	Marion	OR
Shirley	Piscataquis	ME	Sidney	Marshall	AL	Silverville	Lawrence	IN
Shirley	Middlesex	MA	Sidney	Champaign	IL	Simmon's Bluff	Wilson	TN
Shirley	Erie	NY	Sidney(c.h.)	Fremont	IA	Simmonsville	Craig	VA
Shirley	Tyler	WV	Sidney	Coffey	KS	Simonville	Windsor	VT
Shirley Mills	Piscataquis	ME	Sidney	Kennebec	ME	Simonton's Mills	Iredell	NC
Shirleysburgh	Huntingdon	PA	Sidney	Montcalm	MI	Simpson	Adams	IA
Shirley Village	Middlesex	MA	Sidney	Ralls	MO	Simpson's	Floyd	VA
Shivelton	Platte	MO	Sidney	Cheyenne	NE	Simpson's Corner	Penobscot	ME
Shoal Creek	Saber	AR	Sidney	Hunterdon	NJ	Simpson's Creek	Taylor	WV
Shoal Creek	Livingston	MO	Sidney	Delaware	NY	Simpson's Mills	Laurens	SC
Shoal Creek St.	Clinton	IL	Sidney	Venango	PA	Iimpson's Mills	White	TN
Shoal Ford	Limestone	AL	Sidney(c.h.)	Shelby	OH	Simpson's Store	Washington	PA
Shoals	Martin	IN	Sidney Centre	Delaware	NY	Simpsonville	Shelby	KY
Shoalsburgh	Newton	MO	Sidney Plains	Delaware	NY	Simpsonville	Howard	MD
Shobe's Grove	Franklin	IA	Sidonsburgh	York	PA	Simpsonville	Upshur	TX
Shockeysville	Frederick	VA	Siegle's Store	Lincoln	NC	Simsbury	Hartford	CN
Shoe Heel	Robeson	NC	Sierra	Vernon	WI	Sim's Creek	Dade	MO
Shoemakers	Monroe	PA	Sierra City	Sierra	CA	Simsport	Avoyelles	LA
Shoemakersville	Berks	PA	Sierra Valley	Sierra	CA	Sinclairville	Chatauuqua	NY
Shoemakertown	Montgomery	PA	Sigel	Shelby	IL	Sineath's	Charleston	SC
Shoenersville	Lehigh	PA	Sigel	Clayton	IA	Singer's Glen	Rockingham	VA
Shohola	Pike	PA	Sigel	Douglas	KS	Sing Sing	westchester	NY
Shokan	Ulster	NY	Sigel	Pettis	MO	Sinkin	Sahnnon	MO
Shokokon	Henderson	IL	Sigel	Jefferson	MO	Sinking Creek	Craig	VA
Shoneytown	Putnam	MO	Siglerville	Mifflin	PA	Sinking Fork	Christian	KY
Shongo	Allegany	NY	Sigourney(c.h.)	Keokuk	IA	Sinking Spring	Highland	OH
Shoo Fly	Johnson	IA	Sikeston	Scott	MO	Sinking Spring	Berks	PA
Shootman	Carroll	MO	Siloam	Greene	GA	Sinking Spring	Sevier	TN
Shop Creek	Montgomery	IL	Siloam	Okibbeha	MS	Sinking Valley	Blair	PA
Shopiere	Rock	WI	Siloam	Madison	NY	Sink's Grove	Monroe	WV
Shop Spring	Wilson	TN	Silver Bow	Deer Lodge	MT	Sinnamahoning	Cameron	PA
Shopville	Pulaski	KY	Silver Brook	Schuylkill	PA	Sinnett's Mills	Ritchie	WV
Shoreham	Addison	VT	Silver City(c.h.)	Owyhee	ID	Sinsinawa Mound	Grant	WI
Short Bend	Depot	MO	Silver City	Lewis and Clarke	MT	Sioux City(c.h.)	Woodbury	IA
Short Creek	Marshall	AL	Silver City	Lyon	NV	Sioux Falls(c.h.)	Minnehaha	DA
Short Creek	Grayson	KY	Silver City	Grant	NM	Sioux Rapids	Buena Vista	IA
Short Creek	Harrison	OH	Silver City	Juab	UT	Sioux Valley	Union	DA
Short Creek	Brooke	WV	Silver Creek	Stephenson	IL	Sipes' Mill	Fulton	PA
Shorter's Depot	Macon	AL	Silver Creek	Chase	KS	Sipestown	Lehigh	PA
Short Falls	Merrimack	NH	Silver Creek	Madison	KY	Sipesville	Somerset	PA
Short Mountain	Dauphin	PA	Silver Creek	Allegan	MI	Sipsey Turnpike	Tuscaloosa	VA
Short Mountain	Cannon	TN	Silver Creek	Wright	MN	Sir John's Run	Morgan	WV
Shortsville	Ontario	NY	Silver Creek	Lawrence	MS	Sissiton Agency		DA
Short Tract	Allegany	NY	Silver Creek	Cedar	MO	Sissonville	Kanawha	WV
Shoshone	Alturas	ID	Silver Creek	Burt	NE	Sisterdale	Kendall	TX
Shotwell	Franklin	MO	Silver Creek	Chantauqua	NY	Sistersville	Tyler	WV
Shoustown	Allegheny	PA	Silver Creek	Hardin	OH	Sitka(c.h.)		AK
Shovel Mount	Burnet	TX	Silver Creek	Schuylkill	PA	Sitka	Martin	IN
Shreve	Wayne	OH	Silver Dale	Cowley	KS	Sitka	Newaygo	MI
Shreveport(c.h.)	Caddo	LA	Silver Glen	Kane	IL	Siuslaw	Lane	OR
Shrewsbury	Worcester	MA	Silver Glen	Merrick	NE	Siverly	Vinton	OH
Shrewsbury	Monmouth	NJ	Silver Hill	Prince George's	MD	Six Corners	Ottawa	MI
Shrewsbury	York	PA	Silver Hill	Wetzel	WV	Six Mile	Jennings	IN
Shrewsbury	Rutland	VT	Silver Lake	Koscinusko	IN	Six Mile Falls	Penobscot	ME
Shrewsbury	Kanawha	WV	Silver Lake	Worth	IA	Six Mile Run	Somerset	NJ
Shrub Oak	Westchester	NY	Silver Lake	Shawnee	KS	Six Mile Run	Bedford	PA
Shubuta	Clark	MS	Silver Lake	McLeod	MN	Six Oaks	Olmsted	MN
Shuey's Mills	Green	WI	Silver Lake	Perry	MO	Six Points	Butler	PA
Shueyville	Johnson	IA	Silver Lake	Clinton	NY	Six Roads	Bedford	PA
Shufordville	Henderson	NC	Silver Lake	Susquehanna	PA	Sixteen Mile Stand	Hamilton	OH
Shullsburgh	La Fayette	WI	Silver Mountain(c.h.)	Alpine	CA	Skaneateles	Onondaga	NY
Shunk	Sullivan	PA	Silver Peak	Esmeralda	NV	Skeel's X Roads	Mercer	OH
Shunpike	Columbia	NY	Silver Run	Talladega	AL	Skiddy	Morris	KS
Shuqualak	Noxubee	MS	Silver Run	Carroll	MD	Skinner	Campbell	GA
Shusban	Washington	NY	Silver Run	Meigs	OH	Skinner	Bay	MI
Shuttesbury	Franklin	MA	Silver Spring	Lancaster	PA	Skinner	Green	WI
Shutter's Corners	Schoharie	NY				Skinner's Eddy	Wyoming	PA

PLACE	COUNTY	STATE	PLACE	COUNTY	STATE	PLACE	COUNTY	STATE
Skinquarter	Chesterfield	VA	Smithfield Summitt	Bradford	PA	Smyrna Mills	Aroostook	ME
Skipanon	Clatsop	OR	Smith Cove	Davie	NC	Snachwine	Putnam	IL
Skippack	Montgomery	PA	Smith Lake	Wright	MN	Snake Prairie	Bastrop	TX
Skippirville	Dale	AL	Smithland	Shelby	IN	Snake Root	McDowell	VA
Skipton	Talbot	MD	Smithland	Woodbury	IA	Snapping Shoals	Newton	GA
Skipwith's Landing	Issaquena	MS	Smithland	Woodbury	IA	Snead's Ferry	Onslow	NC
Skokomish	Mason	WA	Smithland	Jackson	KS	Snedkekerville	Bradford	PA
Skookumchick	Lewis	WA	Smithland(c.h.)	Livingston	KY	Sneedville(c.h.)	Hancock	TN
Skowhegan	Somerset	ME	Smithport(c.h.)	McKean	PA	Sneedville	San Augustine	TX
Skull Valley	Yavapai	AZ	Smith River	Del Norte	CA	Snelling(c.h.)	Hancock	TN
Slabtown	Boone	IN	Smith Road	Medina	OH	Snelling's Ranch	Merced	CA
Slack	Mason	KY	Smith's Basin	Washington	NY	Snibar	La Fayette	MO
Slack Water	Lancaster	PA	Smithsborough	Tioga	NY	Snicarte	Mason	IL
Sladesburgh	Crawford	WI	Smithsburgh	Washington	MD	Snickersville	Loudoun	VA
Sladesville	Hyde	NC	Smith's Corners	Oceana	MI	Snidersville	Outagamie	WI
Slanesville	Hampshire	WV	Smith's Creek	St. Clair	MI	Snipe's Store	Chatham	NC
Slash	Grant	IN	Smith's Creek	Washington	VA	Snoddy's Mills	Fountain	IL
Slate	Jennings	IN	Smith's X Roads	Rhea	TN	Snohomish(c.h.)	Snohomish	WA
Slate Creek	Idaho	ID	Smith's Ferry	Beaver	PA	Snoqualmie	King	WA
Slate Creek	Josephine	OR	Smith's Ford	Cabarrus	NC	Snow Camp	Alamance	NC
Slate Cut	Clarke	IN	Smith's Ford	Union	NC	Snow Creek	Iredell	NC
Slateford	Northampton	PA	Smith's Gap	Hampshire	WV	Snow Creek	Smith	TN
Slate Hill	Orange	NY	Smith's Grove	Warren	KY	Snow Creek	Franklin	VA
Slate Hill	York	PA	Smith's Landing	Atlantic	NJ	Snowdoun	Montgomery	AL
Slate Lick	Armstrong	PA	Smith's Landing	Clermont	OH	Snow Falls	Oxford	ME
Slate Mills	Rappahannock	VA	Smith's Mills	Henderson	KY	Snow Hill	Catoosa	GA
Slatersville	Weber	UT	Smith's Mills	Passaic	NJ	Snow Hill	Randolph	IN
Slaterville	Tompkins	NY	Smith's Mills	Chautauqua	NY	Snow Hill(c.h.)	Worcester	MD
Slaterville	Providence	RI	Smith's Mills	Clearfield	PA	Snow Hill	St. Charles	MO
Slatington	Lehigh	PA	Smithson's Valley	Comal	TX	Snow Hill	Titus	TX
Slaughter	Kent	DE	Smith's Ranch	Sonoma	CA	Snow Hill(c.h.)	Greene	NC
Slaughter	King	WA	Smith's Ridge	Fairfield	CN	Snow Hill	Surry	VA
Slaughtersville	Webster	KY	Smith's Station	Lee	AL	Snow Hill	Nicholas	WV
Slavanger	McPhail	MN	Smith's Station	Hinds	MS	Snow Shoe	Centre	PA
Sleepy Creek Bridge	Morgan	WV	Smith's Station	York	PA	Snowville	Pulaski	VA
Slick Rock	Barren	KY	Smith's Turn Out	York	PA	Snyder	Dallas	IA
Slifer	Union	PA	Smithville Station	Wayne	OH	Snyder's Grove	Woodbury	IA
Sligo	Montgomery	MD	Smithton	St. Clair	IL	Snydersville	Monroe	PA
Sligo	Clarion	PA	Smithton	Pettis	MO	Snydertown	Northcumberland	PA
Slippery Ford	El Dorado	CA	Smithton	Worth	MO	Social Circle	Walton	GA
Slippery Rock	Butler	PA	Smithton	Doddridge	WV	Society Hill	Macon	AL
Sloan	Woodbury	IA	Smithtown	Suffolk	NY	Society Hill	Darlington	SC
Sloan's Point	Adair	MO	Smithtown Branch	Suffolk	NY	Socorro(c.h.)	Socorro	NM
Sloan's Station	Jefferson	OH	Smith Valley	Schuyler	NY	Soda Bar	Palo Alto	IA
Sloansville	Schoharie	NY	Smithville	Lawrence	AR	Soda Springs	Linn	OR
Sloatsburgh	Rockland	NY	Smithville	Peoria	IL	Soda Springs	Oneida	ID
Slocum's Grove	Muckegon	MI	Smithville	Monroe	IN	Soddy	Hamilton	TN
Slocumville	Washington	RI	Smithville	Caroline	MD	Sodorus	Champaign	IL
Small Point	Sagadahoc	ME	Smithville	Worcester	MA	Sodus	Berrien	MI
Smartt's Station	Warren	TN	Smithville	Wayne	MI	Sodus	Wayne	NY
Smartville	Yuba	CA	Smithville	Monroe	MS	Sodus Centre	Wayne	NY
Smead	Lyon	IA	Smithville	Clay	MO	Sodus Point	Wayne	NY
Smicksburgh	Indiana	PA	Smithville	Burlington	NJ	Soldier	Montana	IA
Smiley	Susquehana	PA	Smithville	Jefferson	NY	Soldiers' Grove	Crawford	WI
Smileytown	Spencer	KY	Smithville	Wayne	OH	Soledad	Monterey	CA
Smith	Dade	GA	Smithville(c.h.)	Burnswick	SC	Solemn Grove	Moore	NC
Smith City	Pettis	MO	Smithville	Lancaster	PA	Solo	Davidson	NC
Smithdale	Livingston	IL	Smithville(c.h.)	De Kalb	TN	Solomon City	Saline	KS
Smithdale	Amite	MS	Smithville Flats	Chenango	NY	Solomon Rapids	Mitchell	KS
Smithfield	Fulton	IL	Smithville South	Queens	NY	Solomon's Island	Calvert	MD
Smithfield	Butler	KS	Smithwick Mills	Burnet	TX	Solon	Johnson	IA
Smithfield	Henry	KY	Smitten	INdiana	PA	Solon	Somerset	ME
Smithfield	Somerset	ME	Smoky Ordinary	Brunswick	VA	Solon	Leelenaw	MI
Smithfield	Wabasyaw	MN	Smootsdell	Hendricks	IN	Solon	Otoe	NE
Smithfield	Jasper	MO	Smyrna	Kent	DE	Solon	Cortland	NY
Smithfield(c.h.)	Johnston	NC	Smyrana	Cobb	GA	Solon	Cuyahogn	OH
Smithfield	Jefferson	OH	Smyrana	Clarke	IA	Solon	White	TN
Smithfield	Fayette	PA	Smyrana	Aroostook	ME	Solon Mills	McHenry	IL
Smithfield	Providence	RI	Smyrana	Ionia	MI	Solsberry	Greene	IN
Smithfield	Polk	TX	Smyrana	Chenango	NY	Somerfield	Somerset	PA
Smithfield	Cache	UT	Smyrana	Harrison	OH	Somers	Tolland	CN
Smithfield(c.h.)	Isle of Wight	VA	Smyrana	Lancaster	PA	Somers	Westchester	NY
			Smyrana	Rutherford	TN	Somers	Kenosha	WI

PLACE NAMES OF THE UNITED STATES

PLACE	COUNTY	STATE	PLACE	COUNTY	STATE	PLACE	COUNTY	STATE
Somerset	Saline	IL	South Barre	Orleans	VT	South Leeds	Andoscoggin	ME
Somerset	Wabash	IN	South Barton	Orleans	VT	South Levant	Penobscot	ME
Somerset(c.h.)	Pulaski	KY	South Beddington	Washington	ME	South Lewiston	Androscoggin	ME
Somerset	Bristol	MS	South Belmont	Waldo	ME	South Liberty	Waldo	ME
Somerset	Hillsdale	MI	South Bend	Lincoln	AR	South Liberty	Adams	OH
Somerset	Monroe	MO	South Bend(c.h.)	St. Joseph	IN	South Lincoln	Middlesex	MA
Somerset	Perry	OH	South Bend	Blue Earth	MN	South Lima	Livngston	NY
Somerset(c.h.)	Somerset	PA	South Bend	Cass	NE	South Limington	York	ME
Somerset	Atasosa	TX	South Bend	Armstrong	PA	South Litchfield	Kennebec	ME
Somerset	Windham	VT	South Bend	Trempealeau	WI	South Litchfield	Bradford	PA
Somerset	St. Croix	WI	South Berlin	Rensslaer	NY	South Livermore	Androscoggin	ME
Somerset Furnace	Somerset	PA	South Berne	Albany	NY	South Livonia	Livingston	NY
Somerset Mills	Somerset	ME	South Berwick	York	ME	South Londonderry	Windham	VT
Somers' Point	Atlantic	NJ	South Berwick Junction	York	ME	South Lyme	New London	CN
Somersville	Contra Costa	CA	South Bethany	Bartholomew	IN	South Lyndeborough	Hillsborough	NH
Somerton	Belmount	OH	South Bethlehem	Northampton	PA	South Lyon	Oakland	MI
Somerton	Philadephia	PA	South Bloomfield	Pickaway	OH	South Malden	Middlesex	MA
Somerville(c.h.)	Morgan	AL	South Bloomingville	Hocking	OH	South Manchester	Hartford	CN
Somerville	Tolland	CN	South Bolivar	Allegany	NY	South Martin	Martin	IN
Somerville	Gibson	IN	South Bombay	Franklin	NY	South Meriden	New Haven	CN
Somerville	Lincoln	ME	Southborough	Worcester	MA	South Merrimack	Hillsborough	NH
Somerville	Middlesex	MA	South Boston	Ionia	MI	South Middleborough	Plymouth	MA
Somerville	Somerset	NJ	South Boston Depot	Halifax	VA	South Milford	La Grange	IN
Somerville	St. Lawrence	NY	South Bradford	Stueben	NY	South Milford	Worcester	MA
Somerville	Butler	OH	South Braintree	Norfolk	MA	South Mills	Camden	NC
Somerville(c.h.)	Fayette	TN	South Branch	Somerset	NJ	South Milton	Stafford	NH
Somerville	Fauguier	VA	South Branch	Bradford	PA	South Moluncus	Aroostook	ME
Somonauk	De Kalb	IL	South Branch Depot	Hampshire	WV	South Monmouth	Kennebec	ME
Sonestown	Sullivan	PA	Southbridge	Worcester	MA	South Montville	Waldo	ME
Sonnan	Cambira	PA	South Bridgeton	Cumberland	ME	South Natick	Middlesex	MA
Sononia	Sonoma	CA	South Bristol	Lincoln	ME	South New Berlin	Chenango	NY
Sonota(c.h.)	Tuolumne	CA	South Grove	De Kalb	IL	South Newburgh	Penobscot	ME
Sonora	Hancock	IL	South Groveland	Essex	MA	South Newbury	Merrymack	NH
Sonora	Hardin	KY	South Hardley	Hamshire	MA	South Newcastle	Gallia	OH
Sonora	Chickasaw	MS	South Hadley Falls	Hampshire	MA	South New Market	Rockingham	NH
Sonora	Steuben	NY	South Halifax	Windham	VT	South Nestead	Erie	NY
Sonora	Muskingham	OH	South Hamilton	Madison	NY	South Norfolk	Litchfield	CN
Sopchoppy	Wakulla	FL	South Hampton	Gallatin	IL	South Norridgewock	Somerset	ME
Soquel	Santa Cruz	CA	South Hampton	Rockingham	NH	South Northfield	Cook	IL
Sorghotown	Daviess	KY	South Hancock	Hancock	ME	South Oil City	Venango	PA
Sorrel Horse	Montgomery	PA	South Hannibal	Oswego	NY	Southold	Suffolk	NY
Soudersburg	Lancaster	PA	South Hanover	Plymouth	MS	South Olive	Noble	OH
Shoulder's Station	Montgomery	PA	South Hanson	Plymouth	MA	South Onondaga	Onondaga	NY
Sour Spring	Cladwell	TX	South Hartford	Washington	NY	South Orange	Essex	NJ
South Abington	Plymouth	MA	South Harwick	Otsego	NY	South Orleans	Barstable	MA
South Acton	York	ME	South Harwich	Barnstable	MA	South Orrington	Penobscot	ME
South Acton	Middlesex	MA	South Haven	New Haven	CN	South Osborn	Outagamie	WI
South Acworth	Sullivan	NH	South Haven	Van Buren	MI	South Otselic	Chenango	NY
South Addison	Steuben	NY	South aaven	Suffolk	NY	South Owego	Gioga	NY.
South Alabanna	Genesee	NY	South Hermitage	Lancaster	PA	South Oxford	Chenango	NY
South Albany	Orleans	VT	South Hero	Grand Isle	VT	South Paris	Oxford	ME
South Albion	Kennebec	ME	South Hill	Bradford	PA	South Parsonfield	York	ME
South Albion	Oswego	NY	South Hill	Mecklenburgh	VA	South Pass	Union	IL
South Amboy	Middlesex	NJ	South Hinesburgh	Chittenden	VT	South Pass	Lancaster	NE
South Amenia	Dutchess	NY	South Hingham	Plymouth	MA	South Pass City(c.h.)	Sweetwater	WY
South America	Saline	IL	South Holland	Cook	IL	South Peacham	Caledonia	VT
Southampton	Suffolk	NH	South Hope	Knox	ME	South Pendleton	Hamilton	OH
Southampton	Hampshire	MA	South Howard	Steuben	NY	South Penobscot	Hancock	OH
Southampton Mills	Somerset	PA	South Hume	Whitesides	IL	South Perry	Hocking	OH
South Andover	Oxford	ME	Southington	Hartford	CN	South Plattsburgh	Clinton	NY
South Argyle	Washington	NY	Southington	Trumbull	OH	South Plymouth	Plymouth	MA
South Arkansas	Lake	CO	South Jackson	Jackson	MI	South Plymouth	Chenango	NY
South Arlington	Montgomery	OH	South Jefferson	Lincoln	ME	South Plymouth	Fayette	MO
South Ashfield	Franklin	MA	South Jefferson	Schoharie	NY	South Point	Fraklin	MO
South Atkinson	Piscataquis	ME	South Killingly	Windham	CN	South Point	Gaston	NC
South Attleborough	Bristol	MA	South Kingston	Rockingham	NH	South Point	Lawrence	OH
South Auburn	Androscoggin	ME	South Kirkland	Lake	OH	South Point	Androscoggin	ME
South Auburn	Susquehanna	PA	South Korkright	Delaware	NY	South Pomfret	Windsor	VT
South Avon	Livingston	NY	South Lancaster	Worcester	MA	South Point	Lawrence	OH
South Ballston	Saratoga	NY	South Lansing	Tompkins	NY			
South Bangor	Buckingham	VA	South Lebanon	Warren	OH			
South Barnstead	Belknap	NH	South Lee	Berkshire	MA	Southport	Fairfield	CN

PLACE	COUNTY	STATE	PLACE	COUNTY	STATE	PLACE	COUNTY	STATE
Southprot	Peoria	IL	South Wardsborough	Windham	VT	Spartanburgh(c.h.)	Spartanb'gh	SC
Southport	Marion	IN	South Warren	Bradford	PA	Spartansburgh	Crawford	PA
Southport	Lincoln	ME	South Warsaw	Allen	OH	Spart Station	Gallatin	KY
Southport	Chemung	NY	South Washington	New Hanover	NC	Spavinaw	Benton	AR
Southport	Naury	TN	South Waterford	Oxford	ME	Speakeville	Lavaca	TX
South Portsmouth	Newport	WY	South Ware	Hillsborough	NH	Spears	Jessamine	KY
South Prairie	Henderson	IL	South Wellfleet	Barnstable	MA	Spearsville	Brown	IN
South Pultney	Steuben	NY	South West	Warren	PA	Speedsville	Tomkins	NY
South Quay	Nansemond	VA	South West City	McDonald	MO	Speedsville	Madison	KY
South Randolph	Norfolk	MA	South Westerlo	Albany	NY	Speedwell	Madison	KY
South Reading	Windsor	VT	South West Harbor	Hancock	ME	Speedwell	Claiborne	TN
South Richland	Oswego	NY	South Weston	Aroostook	ME	Speedwell	Wythe	VA
South Ridge	Ashtabula	OH	South West Oswego	Oswego	NY	Speer	Blue Earth	MN
South Riley	Clinton	MI	South Westport	Bristol	MA	Speer's Ferry	Scott	VA
South River	Anne Arundel	MD	South Weymouth	Norfolk	MA	Speight's Bridge	Greene	NC
South River	Middlesex	NJ	South Whecolci	Caledonia	VT	Spencer	Will	IL
South Robbinston	Washington	ME	South Whitehall	Lehigh	PA	Spencer(c.h.)	Owen	IN
South Royalston	Worchester	MA	South Whitley	Whitley	IN	Spencer	Clay	IA
South Royalton	Windsor	VT	Southwick	Hampden	MA	Spencer	Worcester	MA
South Rutland	Jefferson	NY	South Wilbraham	Hampden	MA	Spencer	Lawrence	MO
South Ryegate	Caledonia	VT	South Williamstown	Berkshire	MA	Spencer	Tioga	NY
South Saint George	Knox	ME	South Willow Creek	Lee	IL	Spencer	Davidson	NC
South Salem	Westchester	NY	South Wilson	Niagra	NY	Spencer	Medina	OH
South Salem	Ross	OH	South Wilton	Saratoga	NY	Spencer(c.h.)	Van Buren	TN
South San Diego	San Diego	CA	South Windham	Windham	CN	Spencer(c.h.)	Roane	WV
South Sandisfield	Berkshrie	MA	South Windham	Cumberland	ME	Spencer Brook	Isanti	MN
South Sand Lake	Rensselaer	NY	South Windham	Windham	VT	Spencerburgh	Pike	IL
South Sandwich	Barnstable	MA	South Windsor	Hartford	CN	Spencer Creek	Antrim	MI
South Sanford	York	ME	South Windsor	Kennebec	ME	Spencer Grove	Benton	IA
South Sangerville	Piscataquis	ME	South Winn	Penobscot	ME	Spencerport	Monroe	NY
South Schodack	Rensselaer	NY	South Wolfborough	Carroll	NH	Spencer's Mill	Kent	MI
South Schron	Essex	NY	South Woodbury	Washington	VT	Spencer's Springs	Tioga	NY
South Scituate	Plymouth	MA	South Woodstock	Windham	CN	Spencer's Shop	Crawford	AR
South Scituate	Providence	RI	South Woodstock	Windsor	VT	Spencer's Station	Guernsey	OH
South Scriba	Oswega	NY	South Worcester	Otsego	NY	Spencertown	Columbia	NY
South Seaville	Cape Mill	NJ	South Worthington	Hampshire	MA	Spencerville	De Kalb	IN
South Sebec	Piscataquis	ME	South Wright	Hillsdale	MI	Spencerville	Montgomery	MD
South Seekonk	Bristol	MA	South Yarmouth	Barnstable	MA	Spencerville	Allen	OH
South Shaftsbury	Bennington	VT	Spade's Depot	Ripley	IN	Speonk	Suffolk	NY
South Side	Bent	CO	Spadra	Johnson	AR	Sperry	Des Moines	IA
South Side	Richmond	NY	Spafford	Onondaga	NY	South Bristol	Ontario	NY
South Sodus	Wayne	NY	Spadra	Los Angeles	CA	South Brookfield	New Haven	CN
South Solon	Somerset	ME	Spafford	La Fayette	WI	South Brookfield	Madison	NY
South Solon	Madison	OH	Spaffor's Grove	Hamilton	NE	South Brooks	Waldo	ME
South Somerset	Niagara	NY	Spauldingville	Knox	IN	South Brooksville	Hancock	ME
South Starksborough	Addison	VT	Spangville	Berks	PA	Southbury	New Haven	CN
South Sterling	Wayne	PA	Spanish Bar	Clear Creek	CO	South Butler	Butler	AL
South Stockton	Chautauqua	NY	Spanishburgh	Mercer	WV	South Butler	Branch	MI
South Stoddard	Cheshire	NH	Spanish Flat	El Dorado	CA	South Butler	Wayne	NY
South Strafford	Orange	VT	Spanish Fork	Utah	UT	South Butte	Sutter	CA
South Sudbury	Middlesex	MA	Spanish Hollow	Wasco	OR	South Byron	Genesee	NY
South Sunapee	Sullivan	NH	Spanish Peaks	Huerfano	CO	South Cabot	Washington	VT
South Sutton	Merrimack	NH	Spanish Ranch	Plumas	CA	South Cairo	Greene	NY
South Tamworth	Carroll	NH	Spark's Hill	Hardin	IL	South Camden	Hillsdale	MI
South Thomaston	Knox	ME	Sparksville	Jackson	IN	South Cameron	Steuben	NY
South Thompson	Geauga	OH	Sparland	Marshall	IL	South Canaan	Litchfield	CN
South Trenton	Oneida	NY	Sparrow Bush	Orange	NY	South Carrollton	Muhlenburg	KY
South Troupsburgh	Steuben	NY	Sparta	Conecuh	AL	South Carthage	Franklin	ME
South Troy	Wabashaw	MN	Sparta(c.h.)	Hancock	GA	South Carver	Plymouth	MA
South Tumbridge	Orange	VT	Sparta	Randolph	IL	South Casco	Cumberland	ME
South Union	Logan	KY	Sparta	Deerborn	IN	South Cass	Ionia	MI
South Vallejo	Solano	CA	Sparta(c.h.)	Bienville	LA	South Cedar	Jahkson	KS
South Valley	Otsega	NY	Sparta	Chicksaw	MS	South Champion	Jmfferson	NY
South Vassalborough	Kennebec	ME	Sparta	Sussex	NJ	South Charleston	Clark	OH
Southville	Litchfield	CN	Sparta	Edgecombe	NC	South Charlestown	Sullivan	NH
Southville	St. Lawrence	NY	Sparta	Morrow	OH	South Chatham	Barnstable	MA
South Vineland	Cumberland	NJ	Sparta	Washington	PA	South Chelmsford	Middlesex	MA
South Walden	Caledonia	VT	Sparta(c.h.)	White	TN	South Chesterville	Franklin	ME
South Wales	Erie	NY	Sparta	Caroline	VA	South Chicago	Cook	IL
South Wallingford	Rutland	VA	Sparta(c.h.)	Monroe	WI	South China	Kennebec	ME
South Walpole	Norfolk	MA	Sparta Centre	Kent	MI	South Cleveland	Whitely	IN
			Spartanburgh	Randolph	IN	South Climax	Kalamazoo	MI
						South Colton	St. Lawrence	NY

PLACE NAMES OF THE UNITED STATES

PLACE	COUNTY	STATE	PLACE	COUNTY	STATE	PLACE	COUNTY	STATE
South Columbia	Coos	NH	Spoonville	Clark	AR	Springfield Store	Queens	NY
South Columbia	Herkimer	NY	Sporting Hill	Lancaster	PA	Spring Forge	York	PA
South Corinth	Penobscot	ME	Sportswood	Middlesex	NJ	Spring Garden	Cherokee	AL
South Corinth	Saratoga	NY	Sporttsville	Henderson	KY	Spring Garden	Jefferson	IL
South Cortland	Cortland	NY	Spottsylvania(c.h.)	Spottsylvania	VA	Spring Garden	Lancaster	PA
South Cottonwood	Salt Lake	UT	Spout Spring	Appomattox	VA	Spring Garden	Pittsylvania	VA
South Coventy	Tolland	CN	Spout Springs	Harnett	NC	Spring Garden	Sauk	WI
South Creek	Dixon	NE	Spragg's	Greene	PA	Spring Garden	Warren	IL
South Creek	Beauford	NC	Spragueville	Jackson	IA	Spring Garden	Linn	IA
South Creek	Bradford	PA	Spraker's Basin	Montgomery	NY	Spring Garden	Houston	MN
South Danbury	Grafton	NH	Sparkle's MIlls	Jefferson	PA	Spring Garden	Dallas	MO
South Danby	Tomkins	NY	Spread Eagle	Chester	PA	Spring Garden	Rowan	NC
South Dansville	Steuben	NY	Spring	Jasper	MO	Spring Garden	Lancaster	PA
South Danville	Caledoni	VT	Spring	Crawford	PA	Spring Grove	Surry	VA
South Dartmouth	Bristol	MA	Spring Arbor	Jackson	MI	Spring Hill	Hempstead	AR
South Dayton	Cattarugus	NY	Spring Bay	Woodford	IL	Spring Hill	Whitesides	IL
South Dedham	Norfolk	MA	Spring Bluff	Lake	IL	Spring Hill	Decatur	IN
South Deerfield	Franklin	MA	Spring Bluff	Choctaw Nation	IT	Spring Hill	Johnson	KS
South Deerfield	Rockingham	NY	Spring Bluff	Adams	WI	Spring Hill	Barstable	MA
South Deer Isle	Hançock	ME	Springborough	Warren	OH	Spring Hill	Sterns	MN
South Dennis	Barnstable	MA	Spring Branch	Butler	KS	Spring Hill	Benton	MS
South Dorset	Bennington	VT	Spring Branch	Comal	TX	Spring Hill	Livingston	MO
South Dover	Piscataquis	ME	Spring Brook	Jackson	IA	Spring Hill	Bradford	PA
South Dover	Dutchess	NY	Spring Brook	Gratiot	MI	Spring Hill	Sumter	SC
South Durham	Androscoggin	ME	Spring Brook	Erie	NY	Spring Hill	Maury	TN
South Durham	Greene	NY	Spring Brook	Luzerne	PA	Spring Hill	Navarro	TX
South Duxbury	Plymouth	MA	Spring Church	Armstrong	PA	Spring Hill	Mecklenburgh	VA
South Eaton	Bristol	MA	Spring City	San Pete	UT	Spring Hill Academy	Henry	TN
South Eaton	Washington	NY	Spring Creek	Phillips	AR	Spring Hill Depot	Henry	KY
South Eaton	Northampton	PA	Spring Creek	Pike	IL	Springhill Furnace	Fayette	PA
South Eaton	Wyoming	PA	Spring Creek	Tama	IA	Sprtng Hills	Champaign	OH
South Edmenston	Otsego	NY	Spring Creek	Oceana	MI	Spring Hollow	Laclede	MO
South Edwards	St. Lawrence	NY	Spring Creek	Goodhue	MN	Spring Hope	Bedford	PA
South Effingham	Carroll	NH	Spring Creek	Phelps	MO	Spring House	Montgomery	PA
South Egremont	Berkshire	MA	Spring Creek	Johnson	NE	Spring Lake	Bremer	IA
South Elkhorn	Fayette	KY	Spring Creek	Madison	NC	Spring Lake	Williams	OH
South Elliot	York	ME	Spring Creek	Rockinghams	VA	Spring Lake	Waushara	WI
South English	Keokuk	IA	Spring Creek	Adams	WI	Spring Lick	Grayson	KY
Southern	Marshall	AL	Spring Dale	Cedar	IA	Spring Meadow	Bedford	PA
South Evansville	Berks	PA	Springdale	Leavenworth	KS	Spring Mills	Oakland	MI
South Exeter	Penobscot	ME	Springdale	Mason	KY	Spring Mills	Allegany	NY
Southfield	Berkshire	MA	Springdale	La Fayette	MS	Spring Mills	Richland	OH
Southfield	Oakland	MI	Spring Dale	Hamilton	OH	Spring Mills	Centre	PA
South Flint	Des Moines	IA	Spring Dale	Allegheny	PA	Spring Mills	Appomattox	VA
South Florence	Franklin	AL	Springdale	Claiborne	TN	Spring Mountain	Coshocton	OH
Southford	New Haven	CN	Springdale	Kane	UT	Spring Place(c.h.)	Murray	GA
Southfork	Owsley	KY	Spring Dale	Dane	WI	Spring Place	Marshall	TN
South Fork	Ashe	NC	Springerton	White	IL	Springport	Jackson	MI
South Foster	Providence	RI	Springfield(c.h.)	Conway	AR	Springport	Henry	KY
South Framingham	Middlesex	MA	Springfield	Bonhomme	DA	Spring Prairie	Walworth	WI
South Franklin	Forfolk	MA	Springfield(c.h.)	Saugamon	IL	Spring Ranch	Clay	NE
South Freeport	Cumberland	ME	Springfield	Franklin	IN	Spring Ridge	Caddo	LA
South Galway	Saratoga	NY	Springfield	Keokuk	IA	Spring River Falls	Cherokee	KS
South Gardiner	Kennebec	ME	Springfield	Linn	KS	Spring Run	Franklin	PA
South Gaston	Halifax	NC	Springfield(c.h.)	Washington	KY	Springs	Suffolk	NY
South Gate	Franklin	IN	Springfield(c.h.)	Livingston	LA	Spring Side	Pottawatomie	KS
South Georgetown	Washington	WI	Springfield	Pennobscot	ME	Spring's Station	Brown	IL
South Germantown	Washington	WI	Springfield(c.h.)	Hampden	MA	Spring Station	Woodford	KY
South Gibson	Susquehanna	PA	Springfield	Oakland	MI	Springtown	Benton	AR
South Gibba	Scoharie	NY	Springfield(c.h.)	Greene	MO	Springtown	Warren	NJ
South Glastenbury	Hartford	CN	Springfield	Sullivan	NH	Springtown	Bucks	PA
South Glens Falls	Sacatoga	VY	Springfield	Union	NJ	Springvale	Humboldt	IA
South Glover	Orleans	VT	Springfield	Otsego	NY	Springvale	York	ME
Outh Granby	Osewga	NY	Springfield(c.h.)	Clark	OH	Spring Vale	Isanti	MN
South Granville	Washington	NY	Springfield	Lane	OR	Spring Vale	Fairfax	VA
South Greece	Monroe	NY	Springfield	Bradford	PA	Spring Valley	Colusa	CA
Sperryville	Rappahonnock	VA	Springfield	Windsor	VT	Spring Valley	Douglas	CA
Spiceland	Henry	IN	Springfield(c.h.)	Robertson	TN	Spring Valley	Marion	IN
Spilville	Winneshiek	IA	Springfield(c.h.)	Limestone	TX	Spring Valley	Decatur	IA
Spinnerstown	Bucks	PA	Springfield	Hampshire	WV	Spring Valley	Fillmore	MN
Spirit Lake(c.h.)	Dickinson	IA	Springfield	Walworth	WI	Spring Valley	Adair	MO
Spokan Bridge	Stevens	WA	Springfield Centre	Otsego	NY	Spring Valley	Bergen	NJ
Spooner's Corners	Otsego	NV	Springfield Furnace	Blair	PA	Spring Valley	Rockland	NY

PLACE	COUNTY	STATE	PLACE	COUNTY	STATE	PLACE	COUNTY	STATE
Spring Valley	Greene	OH	Stanhope	Sussex	NJ	Station Creek	Covington	MS
Spring Valley	Grayson	VA	Stanhope	Nash	SC	Station Creek	Coryell	TX
Spring Valley	Pierce	WI	Stanley	Morris	NJ	Station Fifteen	Harrison	OH
Springville	St. Clair	AL	Stanley	Putnam	OH	Statler's Run	Monongalia	WV
Springville	Coles	IL	Stanley Corners	Ontario	NY	Stauton	Macoupin	IL
Springville	Lawrence	IN	Stanley's Creek	Gaston	NC	Staunton	Clay	IN
Springville	Linn	IA	Stannard	Caledonia	VT	Stauton(c.h.)	Augusta	VA
Springville	Washington	KS	Stanton	New Castle	DE	Staunton	Fayette	OH
Springville	Lenawee	MI	Stanton	Montgomery	IA	Stamton's Mills	Somerset	PA
Springville	Jefferson	MT	Stanton(c.h.)	Powell	KY	Steamboat Rock	Hardin	IA
Springville	Erie	NY	Stanton	Miami	KS	Steamburgh	Cattaraugus	NY
Springville	Wayne	OH	Stanton(c.h.)	Montcalm	MI	Steamburgh	Ashtabula	OH
Springville	Multomay	OR	Stanton	Goodhue	MN	Steamburgh	Crawford	PA
Springville	Susquehanna	PA	Stanton(c.h.)	Stanton	NE	Steam Corner	Fountain	IN
Springville	Henry	TN	Stanton	Hunterdon	NJ	Steam Corners	Morrow	OH
Springville	Utah	UT	Stanton	Jefferson	PA	Steam Mill	Warren	PA
Springville	Tazewell	VA	Stanton Copper			Stebbinsville	Oceana	MI
Springville	Vernon	WI	Mines	Franklin	MO	Stedman	Chautanqua	NY
Springville		IA	Stanton Depot	Haywood	CN	Steedman's	Lexington	SC
Springwater	Winneshick		Stantonsburgh	Wilson	NC	Steegall's Landing	Roane	TN
Springwater	Livingston	NY	Stantonville	McNairy	TN	Steele Centre	Steele	MN
Spring Water	Waushara	WI	Stanwich	Farifield	CN	Steele's	Rush	IN
Sprout Brook	Montgomery	NY	Stanwix	Oneida	NY	Steele's Depot	St. Clair	AL
Sprout Creek	Dutchess	NY	Stanwood	Cedar	IA	Steele's Mills	Randolph	IL
Sprouce	Indiana	PA	Stanwood	Leavenworth	KS	Steele's Tavern	Augusta	VA
Spruce Creek	Huntingdon	PA	Stanwood	Mecosta	MI	Steeleville	Chester	VA
Spruce Hill	Douglas	MN	Stapleton	Chickasaw	IA	Steelville(c.h.)	Crawford	ME
Spruce Hill	Highland	VA	Stapleton	Meade	KY	Steel Works	Dauphin	PA
Spruce Hill	Juniata	PA	Stapleton	Richmond	NY	Steen's Creek	Rankin	MS
Spruce Pine	Franklin	AL	Stapleton	Morgan	TN	Steen's Prairie	Maries	MO
Spruce Vale	Columbian	OH	Stapleton	Amherst	VA	Steep Falls	Cumberland	ME
Sprys Landing	Kent	MD	Stapleton Mills	Amherst		Steer Creek	Gilmer	VA
Spurgeon	Pike	IN	Star	Omachita	AR	Stegall's Depot	Bartow	GA
Spurlockville	Lincoln	WV	Star	Rush	IN	Steilacoom		
Spuyten Duyvil	Westchester	NY	Star	Marion	IA	City(c.h.)	Pierce	WA
Squak	King	WA	Star	Warren	PA	Stiensburgh	Bucks	PA
Squam Village	Monmouth	NJ	Star	Lavace	TX	Stelapolis	Iowa	IA
Square Corner	Adams	PA	Star	Vernon	WI	Stella	Graitot	MI
Square Pond	Tolland	CN	Star City	Pulaski	IN	Stelton	Middlesex	NJ
Squaw Creek	Boise	ID	Stark	Butts	GA	Stevidio	Darke	OH
Squaw Grove	De Kalb	IL	Stark	Somerset	ME	Stembersville	Carbon	PA
Squiresville	Owen	KY	Stark	Chisago	MN	Stemton	Northampton	PA
Staatsburgh	Dutchess	NY	Stark	Coos	NH	Stephens	Oglethorpe	GA
Stablersville	Baltimore	MD	Starke	Bradford	FL	Stephens	Boone	MO
Staceyville	Mitchell	IA	Starkesville	Lamar	TX	Stephensburgh	Hardin	KY
Stafford	Tolland	CN	Starkey	Yates	NY	Stepensburgh	Morris	NJ
Stafford	Genesee	NY	Starksborough	Addison	VT	Stephens' Chapel	Bledsoe	TN
Stafford	Monroe	IA	Starkville(c.h.)	Lee	GA	Stephenson's Depot	Fredrick	VA
Stafford	Ford Bend	TX	Starkville(c.h.)	Aktibbeha	MS	Stephensport	Breckinridge	KY
Stafford(c.h.)	Stafford	VA	Star of the West	Pike	AR	Stephen's Pottery	Baldwin	GA
Stafford Springs	Tolland	CN	Star Place	Panola	MS	Stephensville	Wilkinson	GA
Stafford Store	Stafford	VA	Star Prairie	St. Croix	WI	Steppensville(c.h.)	Erath	TX
Staffordville	Tolland	CN	Starr's Point	Benton	OR	Stephensville	Outagamie	WI
Staffordville	Clark	WI	Starrville	Smith	TX	Stephentown	Rensselaer	NY
Stagville	Orange	NC	Starneca	Wayne	PA	Stepney	Fairfield	CN
Stablestown	Westmoreland	PA	State Bridge	Oneida	NY	Stepney Depot	Fairfield	CN
Stairfield	Clinton	MO	Stateburgh	Sumter	NC	Sterling	Windham	CN
Stamford	Fairfield	CN	State Centre	Marshall	IA	Sterling	Whitesides	IL
Stamford	Delaware	NY	State Farm	Providence	RI	Sterling	Jackson	IA
Stamford	Bennington	VT	Stateley's Run	Grant	KY	Sterling	Rice	KS
Stamper's Creek	Orange	IN	State Line	Columbia	AR	Sterling	Worcester	MA
Stamping Burches	Floyd	VA	State Line	Heard	GA	Sterling	Madison	MT
Stamping Ground	Scott	KY	State Line	Warren	IN	Sterling	Johnson	NE
Stanard's Corners	Allegany	NY	State Line	Berkshire	MA	Sterling	Cayuga	NY
Stanardsville(c.h.)	Greene	VA	State Line	Freeborn	MN	Sterling	Wayne	PA
Stanchfield	Isanti	MN	State Line	Cass	MO	Sterling Bush	Lewis	NY
Standing Pine	Leake	MS	State Line	Franklin	PA	Sterling Centre	Blue Earth	MN
Standing Stone	Bradford	PA	State Line Mills	McKean	PA	Sterling Hill	Windham	CN
Standish	Cumberland	ME	State Line Station	Wayne	MS	Sterling Run	Cameron	PA
Stanford	McLean	IL	Statenville	Echols	GA	Sterlington	Ouachita	LA
Stanford	Monroe	IN	State Road	Chemung	NY	Sterling Valley	Cayuga	NY
Stanford	Marshall	IA	State Road	Surry	NC	Sterlingville	Jefferson	NY
Stanford(c.h.)	Lincoln	KY	Statesville(c.h.)	Iredell	NC			
Stanfordville	Dutchess	NY	Statesville	Wilson	TN			

PLACE	COUNTY	STATE	PLACE	COUNTY	STATE	PLACE	COUNTY	STATE
Sternerton	Montgomery	KS	Stockdale	Miami	IN	Stoney Creek	Washtenaw	MI
Sterrettania	Erie	PA	Stockertown	Northampton	PA	Stoney Creek	Somerset	PA
Sterrett's Gap	Perry	PA	Stockholm	Sussex	NY	Stoney Creek	Carter	TN
Stetson	Penobscot	ME	Stockholm	St. Lawrence	NY	Stoney Creek		
Stettin	Marathon	WI	Stockholm	Pepin	WI	Warehouse	Sessex	VA
Steuben	Washington	ME	Stockholm Depot	St. Lawrence	NY	Stony Fork	Watauga	NC
Steuben	Oneida	NY	Stockport	Columbia	NY	Stony Fork	Tioga	PA
Steuben	Huron	OH	Stockport	Morgan	OH	Stony Man	Page	VA
Steubenville	Wayne	KY	Stockport	Delaware	NY	Stony Point	White	AR
Steubenville(c.h.)	Jefferson	OH	Stocksville	Buncombe	NC	Stony Point	Sonoma	CA
Stevens	Lancaster	PA	Stockton	Balwin	AL	Stony Point	Jefferson	IN
Stevensborough	Red River	TX	Stockton(c.h.)	San Joaquin	CA	Stony Point	East Baton Rouge	LA
Stevensburgh	Culpeper	VA	Stockton(c.h.)	Clinch	GA	Stony Point	Jackson	MO
Stevenson's Mills	Wayne	MO	Stockton	Jo Davies	IL	Stony Point	Rockland	NY
Stevenson's Mills	Wayne	PA	Stockton	Owen	IN	Stony Point	Alexander	NC
Stevenson Station	Baltimore	MD	Stockton	Mascatine	IA	Stony Point	Crawford	PA
Stevens' Plains	Cumberland	ME	Stockton	Waldo	ME	Stony Point	Anderson	SC
Steven's Point(c.h.)	Portage	WI	Stockton	Worcester	MD	Stony Point	Hawkins	TN
Stevenstown	Crawford	KS	Stockton	Winona	MN	Stony Point	Albemarle	VA
Stevenstown	La Crosse	WI	Stockton(c.h.)	Cedar	MO	Stony Point Mills	Cumberland	VA
Stevensville	Missoula	MT	Stockton	Hunterdon	NJ	Stony Ridge	Wood	OH
Stevensville	Sullivan	NY	Stockton	Chautauqua	NY	Stony Rum	Oakland	MI
Stevensville	Bradford	PA	Stockton	Luzerne	PA	Stony Run	Berks	PA
Stevensville	King and Queen	VA	Stockton	Loudon	TN	Storeville	Anderson	SC
Steward	Erie	PA	Stockton	Tooele	UT	Storm Lake	Buena VIsta	IA
Stewart	Stewart	TN	Stockton	Portage	WI	Stormville	Dutchess	NY
Stewart	Green	WI	Stockwell	Tippecanoe	IN	Stormville	Mornroe	PA
Stewarton	Fayette	PA	Stoddard	Cheshire	NH	Storrs	Hamilton	OH
Stewart's Run	Venango	PA	Stoddard	Vernon	WI	Story City	Story	IA
Stewart's Station	Hale	AL	Stoddartsville	Luzerne	PA	Stottville	Columbia	NY
Stewartstown	Coos	NH	Stoker	Davis	UT	Stouchsburgh	Berks	PA
Stewartstown	York	PA	Stokes' Bridge	Oneida	NY	Stoughstown	Cumberland	PA
Stewartstown	Monongalia	WV	Stokes' Bridge	Darlington	SC	Stoughton	Norfolk	MA
Stewartsville	Posey	IN	Stokes' Mound	Carroll	MO	Stoughton	Dane	WI
Stewartsville	Grant	KY	Stone Arabia	Montgomery	NY	Stoutland	Camden	MO
Stewartsville	De Kalb	MO	Stone Bank	Waukesha	WI	Stout's	Adams	OH
Stewartsville	Warren	NJ	Stone Bluffs	Fountain	IN	Stout's	Northampton	PA
Stewartsville	Westmoreland	PA	Stoneborough	Mercer	PA	Stouts' Mills	Gilmer	WV
Stewartsville	Olmsted	MN	Stone Chruch	Genesee	NY	Stoutsville	Fairfield	OH
Stice's Shoal	Cleveland	NC	Stone Church	Northampton	PA	Stover	Dallas	AR
Sticklerville	Sullivan	MO	Stone Creek	Tuscarawas	OH	Stow	Oxford	ME
Stickleyville	Lee	VA	Stone Fort	Saline	IL	Stow	Middlesex	MA
Stiflesville	Crawford	IL	Stoneham	Middlesex	MA	Stowe	Lamoille	VT
Stiles	Davies	IA	Stoneham	Warren	PA	Stowell's Corners	Jefferson	NY
Stiles	Oconto	WI	Stone House	Lawrence	KY	Stoyestown	Somerset	PA
Stilesborough	Bartow	GA	Stone House	Morgan	MO	Strabane	Washington	PA
Stilesville	Hendricks	IN	Stone House Hotel	Prince William	VA	Strafford	Greene	MO
Still Pond	Kent	MD	Stone Lick	Clermont	OH	Strafford	Strafford	NH
Still River	Worcester	MA	Stone Mills	Jefferson	IL	Strafford	Orange	VT
Still Valley	Warren	NJ	Stone Mountain	Jefferson	NY	Strafford Blue Hills	Strafford	NY
Stillwater	Shasta	CA	Stone Mountain	De Kalb	GA	Strafford Corner	Stafford	NH
Stillwater	Mitchell	IA	Stone Mountain	McDowell	NC	Straight Fork	Scott	KY
Stillwater(c.h.)	Washington	MN	Stone Moutain	Carroll	VA	Straight Fork	Scott	TN
Stillwater	Sussex	NJ	Stoner	Clarke	KY	Straighstone	Pittsylvania	VA
Stillwater	Saratoga	NY	Stone Ridge	Ulster	NY	Strait Creek	Highland	VA
Stillwater	Columbia	PA	Stoner's Prairie	Dane	WI	Strait's Corners	Tioga	NY
Stillwell	Hancock	IL	Stonersville	Carroll	MD	Strait's Lake	Oakland	MI
Stillwell	La Porte	IN	Stonersville	Berks	PA	Straitsville	Perry	OH
Stillwell	Monroe	IN	Stone's Bay	Onslow	NC	Stranger	Leavenworth	KS
Stinesville	Lehigh	PA	Stone's Prairie	Adams	IL	Stranger's Home	Lawrence	AR
Stinson	Outahamie	WI	Stoneville	Rockingham	NC	Strasburgh	Tuxarawas	OH
Stip's Hill	Franklin	IN	Stonewall	Scott	KY	Strasburgh	Lancaster	PA
Stirling	Montgomery	GA	Stonewall	Harrison	MS	Strasburgh	Shenandoah	VA
Stirrup Grove	Macoupin	IL	Stonewall	Freestone	TX	Strata	Montgomery	AL
Stissing	Dutchess	NY	Stoney Brook	Suffolk	NY	Stratford	Fairfield	CN
Stittville	Oneida	NY	Stoney Hill	Gasconade	MO	Stratford	Coos	CN
Stockbridge	Henry	GA	Stoney Point	Bourbon	KY	Stratford	Fulton	NY
Stockbridge	Berkshire	MA	Stonington	New London	CN	Stratham	Rockingham	NH
Stockbridge	Ingham	MI	Stonington	Christian	IL	Stratton	Windham	NY
Stockbridge	Madison	NY	Stono	St. Francois	MO	Stratton's Falls	Delaware	NY
Stockbridge	Windsor	VT	Stony Bluff	Jefferson	TN	Strattonville	Clarion	PA
Stockbridge	Calmnet	WI	Stoney Brook	Morris	NJ	Straughn's Station	Henry	IN
Stock Creek	Scott	VA	Stoney Creek	New Haven	CN	Strausstown	Cass	MO

PLACE	COUNTY	STATE	PLACE	COUNTY	STATE	PLACE	COUNTY	STATE
Strausstown	Berks	PA	Sugar Creek	Walworth	WI	Summerville	Calhoun	AR
Strawberry	Washington	KS	Sugar Grove	Sarber	AR	Summerville(c.h.)	Chattooga	GA
Strawberry Plains	Jefferson	TN	Sugar Grove	Kane	IL	Summerville	Peroia	IL
Strawberry Point	Clayton	IA	Sugar Grove	Tippecanoe	IN	Summerville	Cass	MI
Strawberry Valley	Yuba	CA	Sugar Grove	Butler	KY	Summerville(c.h.)	Harnett	NC
Strawbridge	York	PA	Sugar Grove	Watauga	NC	Summerville	Union	OR
Strawtown	Hamilton	IN	Sugar Grove	Fairfield	OH	Summerville	Jefferson	PA
Strayhorn	De Soto	MS	Sugar Grove	Warren	PA	Summerville	Charleston	SC
Streator	La Salle	IL	Sugar Grove	Pendleton	WV	Summit	Blout	AL
Street Road	Chester	PA	Sugar Grove	Vernon	WI	Summit	Plumas	CA
Streetsborough	Portage	OH	Sugar Hill	Hall	GA	Summit	Cook	IL
Stribling Springs	Augusta	VA	Sugar Hill	Grafton	NH	Summit	De Kalb	IN
Strickland	Chester	PA	Sugar Hill	Schuyler	NY	Summit	Muscatine	IA
Strickland's Ferry	Androscoggin	ME	Sugar Hill	McDowell	NC	Summit	Leavenworth	KS
Strickling	Burnet	TX	Sugar Hill	Perry	TN	Summit	Jefferson	KY
Stringtown	Richland	IL	Sugar Hill	Panola	TX	Summit	Washtenaw	MI
Stringtown	Cole	MO	Sugar Lake	Crawford	PA	Summit	Jackson	MN
String Town	Pickaway	OH	Sugar Lake	Fort Bend	TX	Summit	Pike	MS
Stringtown	Wilson	TN	Sugar Loaf	Sebastian	AR	Summit	Madison	MT
Stroderville	Cape Girardeau	MO	Sugar Loaf	Boulder	CO	Summit	Union	NJ
Strode's Mills	Mifflin	PA	Sugar Loaf	Ford	IL	Summit	Schoharie	NV
Stronach	Manistee	MI	Sugar Loaf	Orange	NY	Summit	Summit	OH
Strong	Franklin	ME	Sugar Notch	Luzerne	PA	Summit	Benton	OR
Strong's Prairie	Adams	WI	Sugar Pine	Tuolumne	CA	Summit	Cambria	PA
Strongstown	Indiana	PA	Sugar Run	Bradford	PA	Summit	Kent	RI
Strongsville	Cuyahoga	OH	Sugartown	Chester	PA	Summit	Iron	UT
Strother	Fairfield	SC	Sugartree	Guernsey	OH	Summit	Waukesha	WI
Stroudsburgh(c.h.)	Monroe	PA	Sugar Tree RIdge	Highland	OH	Summit Bridge	New Castle	DE
Struther's Station	Mahoning	OH	Sugar Valley	Gordon	GA	Summit Hill	Carbon	PA
Stryker	Williams	OH	Sugar Valley	Clinton	PA	Summit Mills	Somerset	PA
Stuar	Adair	IA	Suggsville	Clarke	AL	Summit Point	Jeferson	WV
Stuart's Draft	Augusta	VA	Suisun City(c.h.)	Solano	CA	Summit Station	Onondaga	NY
Stuart's Mills	Christian	KY	Suitsville	Prince George's	MD	Summit Station	Licking	OH
Stuckeysville	Bedford	PA	Sullivan(c.h.)	Moultrie	IL	Summit Station	Schuylkill	PA
Stump Knob	Johnson	TN	Sullivan(c.h.)	Sullivan	IN	Summitville	Madison	IN
Sturbrige	Worchester	MA	Sullivan	Hancock	ME	Summitville	Lee	IA
Sturgeion	Fulton	IN	Sullivan	Franklin	MO	Summitville	Columbiana	OH
Sturgeion Bay(c.h.)	Door	WI	Sullivan	Cheshire	NH	Summitville	Coffee	TN
Sturgeionville	Brunswick	VA	Sullivan	Ashland	OH	Summum	Fulton	IL
Sturgis	St. Joseph	MI	Sullivan	Tioga	PA	Sumner	Lawrence	IL
Stuyvesant	Columbia	NY	Sullivan	Jefferson	WI	Sumner	Rush	IN
Stuyvesant Falls	Columbia	NY	Sullivan Centre	Livingston	IL	Sumner	Oxford	ME
Suamico	Brown	WI	Sullivanville	Chemung	NY	Sumner(c.h.)	Sumner	KS
Sublett	Adair	MO	Sulphur Bluff	Hopkins	TX	Sumner	Gratiot	MI
Sublett	Lee	IL	Sulphur Fork	Henry	KY	Sumner	Freeborn	MN
Sublett's Tavern	Powhatan	VA	Sulphur Hill	Shelby	IN	Sumnersville	Texas	MO
Sublimity	Pulaski	KY	Sulphur Lick	Monroe	KY	Sumneytown	Montgomery	PA
Sublimity	Marion	OR	Sulphur Rock	Indipendence	AR	Sumpter(c.h.)	Trinity	TX
Sub Rosa	Franklin	AR	Sulphur Springs	Crawford	OH	Sumption Prairie	St. Joseph	IN
Sucarnoochee	Kemper	MS	Sulphur Springs	Williamson	IL	Sumter	Moultre	IL
Success	Suffolk	NY	Sulphur Springs	Henry	IN	Sumter	McLeod	MN
Sucasunny	Morris	NJ	Sulphur Springs	Montgomery	NC	Sumter(c.h.)	Sumter	FL
Sudbury	Middlesex	MA	Sulphur Springs	Rhea	TN	Sumterville	Sumter	AL
Sudbury	Rutland	VT	Sulphur			Sumterville(c.h.)	Sumter	FL
Sudlersville	Queen Anne	MD	Springs(c.h.)	Hopkins	TX	Sun	St. Tammany	LA
Sudley	Anne Arundel	MD	Sulphur Springs			Sunapee	Sullivan	NH
Sue City	Macon	MO	Landing	Jefferon	MO	Sunbeam	Mercer	IL
Suez	Santa Barbara	CA	Sulphur Well	Shelby	TN	Sunburgh	Kandiyohi	MN
Suez	Mercer	IL	Sumac	Bollinger	MO	Sunbury	Livingston	IL
Suffern	Rockland	IL	Sumner Dale	Jefferson	NY	Sunbury	Gates	NC
Suffield	Hartford	CN	Summmerfield	Chautauqua	NY	Sunbury	Delaware	OH
Suffield	Portage	OH	Summerfield	Dallas	AL	Sunbury(c.h.)	Northumberland	PA
Suffolk	Suffolk	NY	Summerfield	St. Clair	IL	Suncliff	Indiana	PA
Suffolk(c.h.)	Nansemond	VA	Summerfield	Guilford	NC	Suncook	Merrimack	NH
Sugar Branch	Switzerland	IN	Summerfield	Noble	OH	Sunderland	Franklin	MA
Sugar Bush	Outagamie	WI	Summerfield	Grayson	VA	Sunderland	Bennington	VT
Sugar Creek	Benton	AR	Summerfield	Madison	OH	Sunderlinville	Potter	PA
Sugar Creek	Vermillion	IL	Summerford	Madison	OH	Sunfield	Eaton	PA
Sugar Creek	Hancock	IN	Summer Hill	Pike	IL	Sun Hill	Wyomin	WV
Sugar Creek	Jasper	IA	Summer Hill	Cayuga	NY	Sunman	Ripley	IN
Sugar Creek	Gallatin	KY	Summer Hill	Cambria	PA	Sunny Dale	Pickens	SC
Sugar Creek	Gallatin	KY	Summers	Rockbridge	VA	Sunny Side	Chicot	AR
Sugar Creek	Claiborne	LA	Summerset	Warren	IA	Sunny Side	Spalding	GA
			Summerton	Graitot	MI			

PLACE	COUNTY	STATE	PLACE	COUNTY	STATE	PLACE	COUNTY	STATE
Sunny Side	Marion	IN	Swanton	Butler	OH	Sylvan	Hancock	IL
Sunny Side	Buchanan	IA	Swanton	Alleghany	MD	Sylvan Hill	Meeker	MN
Sunny Side	Wright	MO	Swanton	Fulton	OH	Sylvania	Scriven	GA
Sunny Side	Washington	NC	Swanton	Franklin	VT	Sylvania	Parke	IN
Sunny Side	Allegheny	PA	Swanton Centre	Franklin	VT	Sylvania	Dade	MO
Sunny Side	Cumberland	VA	Swanton Junction	Franklin	VT	Sylvania	Lucus	OH
Sunny Slope	Lawrence	TN	Swanville	Jefferson	IN	Sylvania	Bradford	PA
Sunol	Alameda	CA	Swanville	Waldo	ME	Sylvania	Racine	WI
Sunolghen	Alameda	CA	Swanwick	Perry	IL	Sylvania	Dutchess	NY
Sun Prairie	Dane	WI	Swanzey	Cheshire	NH	Sylvania Lodge	Newton	MO
Sun Rise	Bath	PA	Swathmore	Delaware	PA	Sylvarena	Smith	MA
Sunrise City	Chisago	MN	Swatswood	Sussex	NJ	Symco	Waupaca	WI
Sun River	Lewis and Clarke	MT	Swatwout	San Jacinto	TX	Symmes	Hamilton	OH
Sunshine	Montgomery	MD	Swatara	Schuylkill	PA	Symmes' Corner	Butler	OH
Sunville	Venango	PA	Swartara Station	Dauphin	PA	Syosset	Queens	NY
Superior	Missoula	MT	Sweadel	McPhearson	KS	Syracuse	Kosciusko	IN
Superior(c.h.)	Douglas	WI	Swede Grove	Meeker	MN	Syracuse	Morgan	MO
Suplee	Chester	PA	Sweden	Oxford	ME	Syracuse(c.h.)	Onondaga	NY
Supply	Brunswick	NC	Sweden	Monroe	NY	Syracuse	Meigs	OH
Surgeion's Hall	Alleghany	PA	Sweden	Potter	PA			
Surgionsville	Hawkins	TN	Sweden Valley	Potter	PA			
Surrency	Appling	GA	Swedesobrough	Gloucester	NJ	Taberg	Oneida	NY
Surrey	Portage	WI	Swedesburgh	Henry	IA	Tabernacle	Tipton	TN
Surry	Hancock	ME	Swede's Forest	Redwood	MN	Taberville	St. Clair	MO
Surry(c.h.)	Surry	VA	Swedona	Mercer	IL	Table Bluff	Humboldt	CA
Susanville(c.h.)	Lassen	CA	Sweede Point	Boone	IA	Table Grove	Fulton	IL
Suspension	Bullock	AL	Sweedlin Hill	Pendleton	WV	Table Mountain	Pickens	SC
Suspension Bridge	Neagara	NY	Sweet Air	Baltimore	MD	Table Rock	Izard	AR
Susquehana	Dauphin	PA	Sweek Chalybeate	Allegahany	VA	Table Rock	Sierra	CA
Susquehanna Depot	Susquehanna	PA	Sweet Hall	King William	VA	Table Rock	Pawnee	NB
Sussex	Waukesha	WI	Sweet Home	Nodaway	MO	Table Rock	Adams	PA
Sussex(c.h.)	Sussex	VA	Sweet Home	Iredell	NC	Table Rock	Raleigh	WV
Sutersville	Westmoreland	PA	Sweet Home	Lavaca	TX	Tabo	La Fayette	MO
Sutherland	Dinwiddie	VA	Sweetland	Nevada	CA	Tabor	Fremont	IO
Sutherland Falls	Rutland	VT	Sweetland Centre	Muscatine	IA	Tabor	Saline	NB
Sutherland Springs	Wilson	TX	Sweetser's	Grant	IN	Tabor	Roane	TN
Sutter Creek	Amador	CA	Sweet Springs	Monroe	WV	Tacoleechee	Benton	MS
Sutter Station	Sutter	CA	Sweet Valley	Luzerne	PA	Tacoma	Pierce	WA
Sutton	Worcester	MA	Sweet Water	Monroe	TN	Tacony	Philadelphia	PA
Sutton	Clay	NE	Sweet Water	Menard	IL	Tadmer	Montgomery	OH
Sutton	Merrimack	NH	Sweetwaver	Esmeralda	NV	Taff	Rice	MN
Sutton	Caledonia	VT	Sweet Water	Gwinnett	GA	Taffe(c.h.)	Wayne	NB
Sutton's Bay	Leelenaw	MI	Sweet Wine	Hamilton	OH	Tafton	Pike	PA
Sutton's Corners	Crawford	PA	Swift Creek Bridge	Craven	NC	Taftsville	Windsor	VT
Sutton's Station	Robertson	TX	Swift Island	Montgomery	NC	Taghkanick	Columbia	NY
Suwanee	Suwanee	FL	Swift Lake	Meeker	MN	Tahlequah(c.h.)	Cherokee Nat., Ind.
Suwanee	Gwinnett	GA	Swift River	Hampshire	MA		Territory	
Suwanee Shoals	Columbia	FL	Swingleville	Washington	TN	Taho	El Dorado	CA
Swain	Allegany	NY	Swit's City	Greene	IN	Tahoe	Placer	CA
Swainsborough(c.h.)	Emanuel	GA	Switzler	Monroe	MO	Talbottom(c.h.)	Talbot	GA
Swale	Steuben	NY	Swoope's Depot	Augusta	VA	Talbott's Mills	Jefferson	TN
Swallow Bluff	Dectur	TN	Sybertsville	Luzerne	PA	Talbotville	Chester	PA
Swampseett	Essex	MA	Sycamore	Colusa	CA	Talcott	Charlotte	VA
Swan	Noble	IN	Sycamore(c.h.)	De Kalb	IL	Talcottville	Tolland	CN
Swan	Vinton	OH	Sycamore	Howard	KS	Talking Rock	Pickens	GA
Swan City(c.h.)	Slaine	NE	Sycamore	Wyandot	OH	Talladega(c.h.)	Talladega	AL
Swan Creek	Warren	IL	Sycamore	Cheatham	TN	Tallahassee(c.h.)	Leon	FL
Swan Creek	Saginaw	MI	Sycamore	Calhoun	WV	Tallahoma	Lucas	IO
Swan Creek	Gallia	OH	Sycamore Dale	Harrison	WV	Tallapoosa	Harralson	GA
Swander's Xing	Shelby	OH	Sycamore Grove	Putnam	WV	Talley Cavey	Allegheny	PA
Swangstown	Cleveland	NC	Sycamore Springs	Butler	KS	Talleyrand	Keokuk	IO
Swan Lake	Arkansas	AR	Syndnorsville	Franklin	VA	Talley Springs	Montgomery	KS
Swan Lake	Lincoln	DA	Syene	Dane	WI	Tallmadge	Ottawa	MI
Swannano	Buncombe	NC	Sykes' Mills	Elmore	AL	Tallmadge	Summitt	OH
Swann's Station	Moore	NC	Sykesville	Carroll	MD	Tallman	Rockland	NY
Swan Pond	Knox	KY	Sykesville	Burlington	NJ	Tallmansville	Upshur	WV
Swan Quarter	Hyde	NC	Sykesville	Talladega	AL	Tallula	Menard	IL
Swan River	Morrison	MN	Sykesville	Izard	AR	Tallulah	Habersham	GA
Swansborough	Onslow	NC	Sylarsville	Monroe	AR	Tallulah	Madison	LA
Swansea	Bristol	MA	Syliman	Shcuylkill	PA	Tallulah(c.h.)	Issaquena	MS
Swan's Island	Hancock	ME	Sylvan	Washtenaw	MI	Tally Ho	Granville	NC
Swansonville	Pittsylvania	VA	Sylvan	Franklin	PA	Talmage	Baldwin	GA
Swan Station	Erie	PA	Sylvan	Richland	WI	Tama City	Tama	IO

PLACE NAMES OF THE UNITED STATES

PLACE	COUNTY	STATE	PLACE	COUNTY	STATE	PLACE	COUNTY	STATE
Tamaqua	Schuylkill	PA	Taylorsville	Bartow	GA	Tennessee Ridge	Houston	TN
Tamarac	Crawford	PA	Taylorsville	Bartholomew	IN	Tennessee River St.	Stewart	TN
Tamarack	Montcalm	MC	Taylorsville	Fayette	IO	Tennille	Washington	GA
Tamarack	Trempealeau	WS	Taylorsville(c.h.)	Spencer	KY	Tensaw	Baldwin	AL
Tamaroa	Perry	IL	Taylorsville	Montgomery	OH	Tenth Legion	Rockingham	VA
Tamola Station	Kemper	MS	Taylorsville	Bucks	PA	Terre Bonne	Terre Bonne	LA
Tamorack	Will	IL	Taylorsville(c.h.)	Johnson	TN	Terre Coupee	St. Joseph	IN
Tampa(c.h.)	Hillsborough	FL	Taylorsville	Hanover	VA	Terre Haute	Henderson	IL
Tampico	Whitesides	IL	Taylorsville(c.h.)	Christian	IL	Terre Haute(c.h.)	Vigo	IN
Tampico	Jackson	IN	Taylorsville(c.h.)	Alexander	NC	Terre Haute	Decatur	IO
Tampico	Oktibbeha	MS	Taymouth	Saginaw	MI	Terre Haute	Putnam	MO
Tampico	Darke	OH	Tazewell(c.h.)	Claiborne	TN	Terre Haute	Champaign	OH
Tampico	Grainger	TN	Tazewell(c.h.)	Tazewell	VA	Terre Hill	Lancaster	PA
Tanworth	Carroll	NH	T.B.	Prince George's	MD	Terrene	Bolivar	MS
Tamworth Iron Works	Carroll	NH	Teachey's	Duplin	NC	Terry	Hinds	MS
Taneytown	Carroll	MD	Teague's Mills	Hardeman	TN	Terry	Carroll	TN
Tangapaho	St. Helena	LA	Tebeanville	Ware	GA	Terrysville	Litchfield	CN
Tanktown	Delaware	OH	Tecolote	San Miguel	NM	Terrytown	Bradford	PA
Tanne Hill	Tuscaloosa	AL	Tecumseh	Shawnee	KN	Terryville	De Witt	TX
Tanners	Gilmer	WV	Tecumseh	Warren	KY	Tess Corners	Waukesha	WS
Tanner's Falls	Wayne	PA	Tecumseh	Lenawee	MI	Tetersburgh	Tipton	IN
Tannersville	Greene	NY	Tecnmseh(c.h.)	Johnson	NB	Tentopolis	Effingham	IL
Tannersville	Monroe	PA	Tedrow	Fulton	OH	Tewkesbury	Middlesex	MA
Tannery	Indiana	PA	Teegardin	Columbiana	OH	Texana(c.h.)	Jackson	TX
Taos	Cole	MO	Teekalet	Kitsap	WA	Texas	Union	DA
Tappahannock (c.h.)	Essex	VA	Tehama	Tehama	CA	Texas	Washington	KY
Tappan	Harrison	OH	Tehichipa	Kern	CA	Texas	Oswego	NY
Tappantown	Rockland	NY	Tehuacana	Limestone	TX	Texas	Henry	OH
Taraborough(c.h.)	Edgecombe	NC	Tekamah(c.h.)	Burt	NB	Texas	Lycoming	PA
Tardyville	Union	MS	Tekonsha	Calhoun	MI	Texas	Tucker	WV
Tarentum	Allegheny	PA	Telegraph City	Calaveras	CA	Texas City	Saline	IL
Tariffville	Hartford	CN	Telford	Bucks	PA	Texas Valley	Cortland	NY
Tar Heel	Bladen	NC	Tell City	Perry	IN	Thacker's Creek	Blount	AL
Tarkeo	Decatur	IN	Teller's Corners	Crawford	WS	Thaxton's	Bedford	VA
Tarkio	Page	IO	Tellico Plains	Monroe	TN	Thayer	Union	IO
Tarlton	Pickaway	OH	Teloga Springs	Chattooga	GA	Thayer	Neosho	KS
Tarrant	Hopkins	TX	Temecula	San Diego	CA	Thebes	Alexander	IL
Tarr Farm	Venango	PA	Temperance	Telfair	GA	The Corner	Ulster	NY
Tarrytown	Crawford	AR	Temperance Hall	De Kalb	TN	The Dalles(c.h.)	Wasco	OR
Tarrytown	Westchester	NY	Temperance Hill	Monroe	MS	The Forks	Somerset	ME
Tassinong	Porter	IN	Temperance Hill	Marion	SC	The Glen	Warren	NY
Tate Creek	Braxton	WV	Temperance Mount	Simpson	KY	The Grove	Cook	IL
Tate's Station	Montgomery	TN	Temperanceville	Belmont	OH	The Grove	Caroline	VA
Tatesville	Bedford	PA	Temperanceville	Allegheny	PA	The Narrows	Crawford	AR
Taunton(c.h.)	Bristol	MS	Temperanceville	Accomack	VA	Theo. Seminary	Fairfax	VA
Taverner's Woods	Talbot	MD	Temple	Hillsborough	NH	The Plains	Fauquier	VA
Tawas City(c.h.)	Ioaco	MI	Temple	Berks	PA	Theresa	Jefferson	NY
Tawawa	Shelby	OH	Temple Hills	Barren	KY	Theresa	Dodge	WI
Taxahau	Lancaster	SC	Templeman's X-Rds	Westmorel'd	VA	The Rock	Upson	GA
Taycheedah	Fond du Lac	WS	Temple Mills	Franklin	ME	The Rock	Mercer	WV
Taylor	Ogle	IL	Temple of Health	Abbeville	SC	The Square	Cayuga	NY
Taylor	Harford	MD	Templeton	Worcester	MS	Thetford	Orange	VT
Taylor	Cortland	NY	Templeton	Prince George	VA	Thetford Centre	Genessee	MI
Taylor	Red River	TX	Templeville	Queen Anne	MD	Thetford Centre	Orange	VT
Taylor Centre	Wayne	MI	Tenafly	Bergen	NJ	Thibodeaux(c.h.)	La Fourche	LA
Taylor Hill	Franklin	IL	Tenallytown	Washington	DC	Thistle	Taney	MQ
Taylor's	Sumter	SC	Tenant's Harbor	Knox	ME	Thivener	Galia	OH
Taylor's Bridge	Sussex	DE	Tenhassen	Martin	MN	Thomas	Oceana	MI
Taylor's Creek	St. Francis	AR	Ten Island	Calhoun	AL	Thomas	Harrison	MO
Taylor's Creek	Liberty	GA	Ten Mile	Fulton	AR	Thomasborough	Champaign	IL
Taylor's Creek	Hamilton	OH	Ten Mile	Campbell	KY	Thomas' Run	Harford	MD
Taylor's Depot	LaFayette	MS	Ten Mile	Macon	MO	Thomas Station	Bullock	AL
Taylor's Falls	Chisago	MN	Ten Mile	Douglas	OR	Thomaston	Litchfield	CN
Taylor's Island	Dorchester	MD	Ten Mill	Washington	PA	Thomaston(c.h.)	Knox	ME
Taylor's Mills	Randolph	WV	Ten Mill	Lincoln	WV	Thomaston	Upson	GA
Taylor's Stand	Crawford	PA	Ten Mile Bottom	Venango	PA	Thomastown	Lake	MS
Taylor's Station	Franklin	OH	Ten Mile House	Clinton	IO	Thomastown	Kowley	KS
Taylor's Store	Franklin	VA	Ten Mile House	Milwaukee	WS	Thomastown(c.h.)	Thomas	GA
Taylorstown	Washington	PA	Ten Mile Lake	Otter Tail	MN	Thomastown	Oregon	MO
Taylorstown	Loudoun	VA	Ten Mile Stand	Meigs	TN	Thomasville	Davidson	NC
Taylorsvilln	Plumas	CA	Tennant	Santa Clara	CA	Thomasville	York	PA
			Tennessee	McDonough	IL	Thomasville	Cheatham	TN
			Tennessee Colony	Anderson	TX	Thompson	Windham	CN

PLACE	COUNTY	STATE	PLACE	COUNTY	STATE	PLACE	COUNTY	STATE
Thompson	Columbia	GA	Tiffin(c.h.)	Seneca	OH	Todd's	Morgan	OH
Thompson	Geauga	OH	Tigerville	Terre Boone	LA	Todd's	Shelby	IL
Thompson	Susquehanna	PA	Tilden	Randolph	IL	Todd's Point	Shelby	IL
Thompson	Washington	WI	Tilden	Hancock	ME	Todd's Point	Shelby	KY
Thompson's X-Rds	Louisa	VA	Tillamook(c.h.)	Tillamook	OR	Todd's Valley	Placer	CA
Thompson's River	Missoula	MT	Tillatoba	Yalabusha	MS	Toddsville	Otsego	NY
Thompson's Station	Williamson	TN	Tiller's Ferry	Kershaw	SC	Token Creek	Dane	WI
Thompsontown	Juiata	PA	Tilton	Whitefield	GA	Toland's Prairie	Washington	WI
Thompsonville	Carrol	AR	Tilton	Poweshiek	IA	Toledo(c.h.)	Tama	IA
Thompsonville	Hartford	CN	Tilton	Fleming	KY	Toledo	Chase	KS
Thompsonville	Pulaski	KY	Tilton	Belknap	NH	Toledo(cc.h.)	Lucas	OH
Thompsonville	Sullivan	NY	Timber Cove	Sonoma	CA	Toledo	Benton	OR
Thompsonville	Rockingham	NC	Timber Creek	Marshall	IA	Tolersville	Louisa	VA
Thompsonville	Washington	PA	Timber Creek	Riley	KS	Tolesborough	Lewis	KY
Thompsonville	Gonzales	TX	Timber Creek	Hunt	TX	Toleston	Lake	IN
Thompsonville	Racine	WI	Timber Hill	Labette	KS	Tolland(c.h.)	Tolland	CN
Thomson	McDuffie	GA	Timber Ridge	Union	SC	Tolland	Hampden	MA
Thomson	Carlton	MN	Timber Ridge	Greene	TN	Tolona	Champaign	IL
Thomson	Carroll	IL	Timber Ridge	Rockbridge	VA	Tomah	Monroe	WI
Thoms' Run	Greene	PA	Timberville	Dodge	NE	Tomaha	Red River	TX
Thornburg	Spottsylvania	VA	Timberville	Padding	OH	Tomahawk	Searcy	AR
Thornbury	Chester	PA	Timberville	Rockingham	PA	Tomahawk Springs	Berkeley	WV
Thorndale Iron Wks	Chester	PA	Timbuctoo	Yuba	CA	Tomales	Martin	CA
Thorndike	Waldo	ME	Time	Pike	IL	Tom's Run	Lycoming	PA
Thorndike	Hampden	MS	Timmonsville	Darlington	SC	Tomhannock	Rensselaer	NY
Thorndike	Cabell	WV	Tindell	Grundy	MO	Tomkin's Cove	Rockland	NY
Thorn Grove	Knox	TN	Tingley	Union	IA	Tomkin's	Jackson	MI
Thorn Hill	Marion	AL	Tinker Run	Westmoreland	PA	Tompkin's Corners	Chemng	NY
Thorn Hill	Onondaga	NY	Tinker's Knob	Botetourt	VA	Tompkinsville(c.h.)	Monroe	KY
Thorn Hill	Grainger	TN	Tinmouth	Rutland	VT	Tompkinsville	Richmond	NY
Thornhill	Orange	VA	Tinney's Grove	Ray	MO	Tompkinsville	Luzerne	PA
Thornleigh	Pettis	MO	Tinton Falls	Monmouth	NJ	Tompson's Station	Audrian	MO
Thornton	Cook	IL	Tioga	Neosho	KS	Tom's Book	Shenandoah	VA
Thornton	St. Clair	MI	Tioga	Tioga	PA	Tom's Creek	Surry	NC
Thornton	Grafton	NH	Tioga Centre	Tioga	NY	Tom's River	Ocean	NJ
Thornton	Delaware	PA	Tioga Valley	Bradford	PA	Tonawanda	Erie	NY
Thornton	Taylor	WV	Tionesta(c.h.)	Forest	PA	Tongaloo	Madison	MS
Thornton's Bluff	Etowah	AL	Tionus	Bibb	AL	Tonganoxie	Leavenworth	KS
Thornton's Depot	Fairfax	VA	Tippecanoe	Harrison	OH	Tonica	La Salle	IL
Thornton's Ferry	Hillsborough	NH	Tippecanoe	Fayette	PA	Tontogany	Wood	OH
Thorntown	Boone	IN	Tippercance City	Miami	OH	Tontzville	Miami	KS
Thornville	Lapeer	MI	Tippecanoetown	Marshall	IN	Tooele(c.h.)	Tooele	UT
Thornville	Perry	OH	Tipp's Branch	Pawnee	NE	Toolesborough	Louisa	IA
Thoroughfare	Prince Williams	VA	Tipton	Lenawee	MI	Toomsborough	Wilkinson	GA
Three Bridges	Hunterdon	NJ	Tipton(c.h.)	Tipton	IN	Toomsuba	Landerdale	MS
Three Grove	Cass	NE	Tipton(c.h.)	Cedar	IA	Tooner's Station	Hardeman	TN
Three Locusts	Marion	OH	Tipton	Moniteau	MO	Topeka	Mason	IL
Three Mile Bay	Jefferson	NY	Tipton	Lancaster	NE	Topeka(c.h.)	Shawnee	KS
Three Notch	Bullock	AL	Tipton	Blair	PA	Topin's Grove	Jackson	WV
Three Oaks	Berrien	MI	Tipton Grove	Hardin	IA	Topsail Sound	New Hanover	NC
Three Rivers	Hampden	MA	Tiptonville(c.h.)	Lake	TN	Topsfield	Washington	ME
Three Rivers	St. Joseph	MI	Tiptown	Monroe	IL	Topsfield	Essex	MA
Three Runs	Clearfield	PA	Tirade	Walworth	WI	Topsham	Sagadahoc	ME
Three Sprtngs	Hart	KY	Tiro	Crawford	OH	Topton	Berks	PA
Three Springs	Huntingdon	PA	Tishemingo	Chickasaw Nation	IT	Toquerville(c.h.)	Kane	UT
Three Tons	Montgomery	PA	Tiskilwa	Bureau	IL	Torah	Stearns	MN
Throopville	Cayuga	NY	Titusville	Ripley	IN	Torch	Athens	OH
Thurlow	Delaware	PA	Titusville	Mercer	NJ	Torch Lake	Antrim	MI
Thurman	Warren	NY	Titusville	Crawford	PA	Tordenskjold	Otter Tail	MN
Thurman	Gallia	OH	Tiverton	Newport	RI	Toronto	Jefferson	AR
Thurston	Steuben	NY	Tiverton 4 Corners	Newport	RI	Toronto	Vermillion	IN
Thurston	Buckingham	VA	Tivoli	Dubuque	IA	Toronto	Clinton	IA
Tibbatt's X Roads	Campbell	KY	Tivoli	Blue Earth	MN	Toronto	Woodson	KS
Tibby Station	Lowndes	MS	Tivoli	Dutchess	NY	Toronto	Miller	MO
Tiblow	Wyandotte	KS	Tivoli	Lycoming	PA	Torrance	Grenada	MS
Tickfaw	Tangipahoa	LA	Tobacco Port	Stewart	TN	Torresdale	Philadelphia	PA
Tick Ridge	Wayne	WV	Tobacco Stick	Dorchester	MD	Torringford	Litchfield	CN
Ticonderoga	Essex	NY	Toboso	Linking	OH	Torrington	Litchfield	CN
Ticonic	Monoma	IA	Toboxky	Choctaw Nation	IT	Toto	Stark	IN
Tidioute	Warren	PA	Toby Creek	Marion	SC	Tottenville	Richmond	NY
Tierra Amarilla	Rio Arriba	NM	Tobyhanna Mills	Monroe	PA	Totty's Bend	Hickman	TN
Tiffany	Rock	WI	Toccopola	Pontotoc	MS	Touchet	Walla-Walla	WA
Tiffin	Johnson	IA	Todd	Huntingdon	PA	Tough Kenamon	Chester	PA

PLACE NAMES OF THE UNITED STATES

PLACE	COUNTY	STATE	PLACE	COUNTY	STATE	PLACE	COUNTY	STATE
Toulon(c.h.)	Stark	IL	Tremont	Schuylkill	PA	Troy	Davis	IA
Towanda	McKlean	IL	Trempealeau	Trempealeau	WI	Troy(c.h.)	Dohiphan	KS
Towanda	Butler	KS	Trent	Muskegon	MI	Troy	Woodford	KY
Towanda(c.h.)	Bradford	PA	Trenton	Jackson	AL	Troy	Waldo	ME
Towash	Hill	TX	Trenton	Phillips	AR	Troy	Oakland	MI
Tower City	Schuylkill	PA	Trenton(c.h.)	Dade	GA	Troy	Winona	MN
Tower Hill	Shelby	IL	Trenton	Clinton	IL	Troy	Cheshire	NH
Tower Hill	Delaware	IA	Trenton	Randolph	IN	Troy(c.h.)	Lincoln	MO
Tower Hill	Appomattox	VA	Trenton	Henry	IA	Troy(c.h.)	Rensselaer	NY
Towerville	Crawford	WI	Trenton	Todd	KY	Troy(c.h.)	Montgomery	NC
Towlesville	Steuben	NY	Trenton	Onachita	LA	Troy(c.h.)	Miami	OH
Town Bluff	Tyler	TX	Trenton	Baltimore	MD	Troy	Bradford	PA
Town Chester	Kanawha	WV	Trenton	Wayne	MI	Troy	Kershaw	SC
Town Creek	Lawarence	AL	Trenton	Freeborn	MN	Troy(c.h.)	Obion	TN
Town Creek	Gilmer	GA	Trenton	Smith	MS	Troy	Orleans	VT
Towners	Putnam	NY	Trenton(c.h.)	Grundy	MO	Troy	Gilmer	WV
Townersville	Granville	NC	Trenton(c.h.)	Mercer	NJ	Troy	Walworth	WI
Town Hill	Luzerne	PA	Trenton	Oneida	NY	Troy	Waldo	ME
Town Line	Erie	NY	Trenton(c.h.)	Jones	NC	Troy Grove	La Salle	IL
Town Line	Luzerne	PA	Trenton	Butler	OH	Troy Mills	Linn	IA
Towns	Telfair	GA	Trenton(c.h.)	Gibson	TN	Troy Mills	Adair	MO
Townsbury	Warren	NJ	Trenton	Pierce	WI	Troy's Store	Randolph	NC
Townsend	Newcastle	DE	Trenton Falls	Oneida	NY	Truckee	Nevada	CA
Townsend	Middlesex	MA	Tresckow	Cabon	PA	Truckee Meadows	Washoe	NV
Townsend	Schuyler	NY	Tres Pino's	Monterey	CA	Trumansburgh	Tompkins	NY
Townsend	Sandusky	OH	Trevilian's Depot	Louisa	VA	Trumansburgh Ldg	Seneca	NY
Townsend Harbor	Middlesex	MA	Trevorton	Northumberalnd	PA	Trumbaursville	Bucks	PA
Townsend Inlet	Cape May	NJ	Trexlertown	Lehigh	PA	Trumbull	Fairfield	CN
Townsend's Mills	Gilmer	WV	Trezevant	Carroll	TN	Trumbull	Ashtabula	OH
Townsend Station	Huron	OH	Triadelphia	Montgomery	MD	Trumbull Corners	Tompkins	NY
Townsendville	Seneca	NY	Triadelphia	Morgan	OH	Trumbull Long Hill	Fairfield	CN
Townshend	Windham	VT	Triadelphia	Ohio	WV	Trundles' X Roads	Sevier	TN
Townsville	Butler	KY	Triana	Madison	AL	Trunkeyville	Forest	PA
Townsville	Crawford	PA	Triangle	Broome	NY	Truro	Knox	IL
Townville	Anderson	SC	Tribe's Hill	Montgomery	NY	Truro	Barnstable	MA
Towsontown(c.h.)	Baltimore	MD	Tribulation	McDonald	MO	Trussville	Jefferson	AL
Tracy	Barren	KY	Trigg Furnace	Trigg	KY	Trust	Osage	KS
Tracy City	Marion	TN	Trim Belle	Pierce	WI	Truxton	Bureau	IL
Tracy Creek	Broome	NY	Trimble	Athens	OH	Truxton	Cortland	NY
Tracy's Landing	Anne rundel	MD	Trinidad	Klamath	CA	Tryon	Polk	NC
Trade	Johnson	Tw	Trinidad(c.h.)	Los Animas	CO	Tryonville	Crawford	PA
Trade Lake	Burnett	WI	Trinity	Trinity	CA	Tualitin	Washington	OR
frader's Hill(c.h.)	Charlton	GA	Trinity	Catahoula	LA	Tubac	Pima	AZ
Traderville	Madison	OH	Trinity Centre	Trinity	CA	Tuckahoe	Cape May	NJ
Trafalgar	Johnson	IN	Trinity College	Randolph	NC	Tuckahoe	Westchester	NY
Trail Ridge	Clay	FL	Trinity Mills	Dallas	TX	Tuckaleechee Cove	Blount	TN
Trail Run	Monroe	OH	Trinity Springs	Martin	IN	Tucker's Creek	Wirth	WV
Trammel	Sumner	TN	Trinity Station	Morgan	AL	Tucksville	Luzerne	PA
Tranquility	Appanoose	IA	Trion	Tuscaloosa	AL	Tucker's X Roads	Wilson	TN
Tranquility	Sussex	NJ	Trion	Jefferson	TN	Tucker's Mills	Limestone	TX
Tranquility	Adams	OH	Trion Factory	Chattooga	GA	Tuckersville	Morgan	MO
Tranquilia	Washington	AR	Tripoli	Bremer	IA	Tuckerton	Burlington	NJ
Transfer	Mercer	PA	Trippville	Vernon	WI	Tuckerton	Berks	PA
Transfer	Sibley	MN	Trimph	La Salle	IL	Tucson(c.h.)	Pima	AR
Transit	Hamilton	OH	Trinne	Williamson	TN	Tuftonborough	Carroll	NH
Transitville	Tippecanoe	IN	Trivoli	Peoria	IL	Tugalo	Oconee	SC
Trap Hill	Wilkes	NC	Trostville	Saginaw	MI	Tuggleville	Trigg	KY
Trappe	Talbot	MD	Trotwood	Montgomery	OH	Tug River	McDowell	WV
Trask	Grant	IN	Troubleson	Rockingham	NC	Tukannon	Walla-Walla	WA
Traveller's Repose	Pocahontas	WV	Troup	Smith	TX	Tulaip	Snohomish	WA
Traveller's Rest	Coosa	AL	Troupsburgh	Steuben	NY	Tule	Tulare	CA
Traveller's Rest	Owsely	KY	Trout Creek	Meagher	MT	Tulin	Cabarrus	NC
Traveller's Rest	Greenville	SC	Trout Creek	Delaware	NY	Tulip	Dallas	AR
Travers des Sioux	Nicollet	MN	Troutona	Lycoming	PA	Tullahoma	Coffee	TN
Traverse City(c.h.)	Grand Traverse	MI	Trout River	Franklin	NY	Tullamore	Tazewell	IL
Travis	Austin	TX	Trout Run	Lycoming	PA	Tullvania	Macon	MO
Travisville	Fentress	TN	Trout Run	Hardy	WV	Tully	Onondaga	NY
Traylorsville	Henry	VA	Troutville	Botetourt	VA	Tully	Van Wert	OH
Treasure City	White Pine	NV	Troutville	Clearfield	VA	Tullystown	Bucks	PA
Tremont	Tazewell	IL	Troxelville	Snyder	PA	Tully Valley	Onondaga	NY
Tremont	Hancock	ME	Troy(c.h.)	Pike	AL	Tulpehocken	Berks	PA
Tremont	Westchester	NY	Troy	Madison	IL	Tumble	Hunterdon	NJ
Tremont	Clark	OH	Troy	Perry	IN	Trumbling Shoals	Laurens	SC

PLACE NAMES OF THE UNITED STATES

PLACE	COUNTY	STATE	PLACE	COUNTY	STATE	PLACE	COUNTY	STATE
Tumwater	Thurson	WA	Twiggs	Pleasantw	WV	Unadilla Centre	Otsego	NY
Tunbridge	Orange	VT	Twiggsville	Twiggs	VA	Unadilla Forks	Otsego	NY
Tunkhannock(c.h.)	Wyoming	PA	Twin Bridges	Madison	MT	Uncasville	New London	CN
Tunnel	Washington	OH	Twin Corners	Cass	IN	Uncle Sam	Lake	CA
Tunnel City	Monroe	WI	Twin Falls	Greenwood	KS	Underhill	Chittenden	VT
Tunnel Hill	Whitfield	GA	Twin Grove	Oakland	NE	Underhill Centre	Chittenden	VT
Tunnel Hill	Oconee	SC	Twin Grove	Green	WI	Underwood	Hopkins	KY
Tunnelton	Lawrence	IN	Twin Lakes	Calhoun	MN	Unger's Store	Morgan	WV
Tunnelton	Indiana	PA	Twin Lakes	Carlton	MN	Union	Greeene	AL
Tunnelton	Preston	WV	Twin Mound	Douglas	KS	Union	Merced	CA
Tunstalls	New Kent	VA	Twin Mountain	Coos	NH	Union	Tolland	CN
Tuolumne City	Stanislaus	CA	Twin River	Nyce	NV	Union	McHenry	IL
Tupelo(c.h.)	Lee	MS	Twinsburgh	Summit	OH	Union	Pike	IN
Tupper's Plains	Meigs	OH	Twin Sisters	Blanco	TX	Union	Hardin	IA
Tuque	Warren	MO	Twin Spring	Winneshick	IA	Union	Chase	KS
Turbotville	Northumberland	PA	Twin Springs	Linn	KS	Union	Boone	KY
Turin	Saline	AR	Twinville	Knox	TN	Union	Knox	ME
Turin	Coweta	GA	Two Bayons	Onachity	AR	Union	Houston	MN
Turin	Lewis	NY	Two Mile Branch	Smyth	VA	Union	Cass	MI
Turkey	Monmouth	NJ	Two Rivers	Morrison	MN	Union	Newton	MS
Turkey Cove	Lee	VA	Two Rivers	Manitowoc	WI	Union(c.h.)	Franklin	MO
Turkey Creek	Dooley	GA	Two Rocks	Sonoma	CA	Union	Cass	NE
Turkey Creek	Steuben	IN	Two Taverns	Adams	PA	Union	Carroll	NJ
Turkey Creek	Bourbon	KS	Tyman's Store	Spottsylvania	VA	Union	Union	NJ
Turkey Foot	Somerset	PA	Tyaskin	Wicomico	jD	Union	Broome	NY
Turkey Foot	Scott	KY	Tye River Depot	Nelson	VA	Union	Montgomery	OH
Turlock	Stanislaus	CA	Tyler	Winnebago	IL	Union	Union	OR
Turkey Town	Etowa	AL	Tyler(c.h.)	Smith	TX	Union	York	PA
Turman's Creek	Sullivan	IN	Tyler Mountain	Kanawha	WV	Union	Maury	TN
Turnback	Dade	MO	Tyler's	Brown	KS	Union	Salt Lake	UT
Turnbull	Dickson	TN	Tyler's	Clearfield	PA	Union(c.h.)	Monroe	WV
Turner	Du Page	IL	Tylersburgh	Clarion	PA	Union	Rock	WI
Turner	Androscoggin	ME	Tyler's Port	Montgomery	PA	Union Bridge	Carroll	MD
Turner	Marion	OR	Tylersville	Clinton	PA	Unionburg	Harrison	IA
Turner's	Clay	IN	Tylersville	Laurens	SC	Union Centre	Cumberland	IL
Turner's	Franklin	MS	Tymochtee	Wydandot	OH	Union Centre	Jackson	IA
Turner's	Orange	NY	Tyner	Hamilton	TN	Union Centre	Howard	KS
Turnersburgh	Iredell	NC	Tyner City	Marshall	IN	Union Centre	Le Sueuer	MN
Turner's Falls	Fraklin	MA	Tynersborough	Middlesex	MA	Union Centre	Broome	NY
Turner's Point	Kaufman	TX	Tyre	Sanilac	MI	Union Centre	Juneau	WI
Turnersport	Manistee	MI	Tyre	Seneca	NY	Union Church	Jefferson	MS
Turner's Store	Somerset	PA	Tyringham	Berkshire	MA	Union Church	Albany	NY
Turnersville	Camden	NJ	Tyro	Poweshciek	IA	Union Church	Racine	WI
Turnersville	Crawford	PA	Tyro	Marshall	MS	Union City	Perry	AR
Turnersville	Robertson	TN	Tyro	Monroe	IA	Union City	Randolph	IN
Turnersville	Tolland	CN	Tyrone	Livingston	MI	Union City	Union	IA
Tunrersville	Jasper	MS	Tyrone	Schuyler	NY	Union City	Rice	KS
Turney's Station	Clinton	MO	Tyrone	Coshocton	OH	Union City	Branch	MI
Turnpike	Buncombe	NC	Tyrone	Blair	PA	Union City	Atchison	MO
Turnwood	Ulster	NY	Tyson Furnace	Windsor	VT	Union City	Erie	PA
Turtle Creek	Allegheny	PA	Tyson's Mills	Webster	IA	Union Corner	Northcumberland	PA
Turtle Lake	Otter Tail	MN				Union Corners	Livingston	NY
Turtle Point	McKean	PA	Uchee	Russell	Al	Union Cross Roads	Union	LA
Turtle Rock	Floyd	VA	Uchee Anna(c.h.)	Walton	FL	Union Dale	Susquehanna	PA
Tuscaloosa(c.h.)	Tuscaloosa	AL	Udina	Kane	IL	Union Deposit	Dauphin	PA
Tucarawas	Tuscarawas	OH	Uhlerstown	Bucks	PA	Union Depot	Sullivan	TN
Tuscarota	Elko	NV	Uhlersville	Northampton	PA	Union Falls	Clinton	NY
Tuscarora	Livingston	NY	Uhricksville	Tuscarawas	OH	Union Fiat	Stevens	WA
Tuscarona	Schuylkill	PA	Uintah	Weber	UT	Union Forge	Leannon	PA
Tuscarora Valley	Bradford	PA	Ukiah(c.h.)	Mendocino	CA	Union Furnace	Patrick	VA
Tuscola(c.h)	Douglas	IL	Ulah	Henry	IL	Union Grove	Whitesides	IL
Tuscumbia(c.h.)	Colbert	AL	Ulin	Pulaski	IL	Union Grove	Page	IA
Tuscumbia(c.h.)	Miller	MO	Ulman's Ridge	Miller	MO	Union Grove	Gentry	MO
Tuskegee(c.h.)	Macon	AL	Ulster	Floyd	IA	Union Grove	Delaware	NY
Tusquitee	Clay	NC	Ulster	Bradford	PA	Union Grove	Iredell	NC
Tustenuggee	Columbia	PA	Ulster Park	Ulster	NY	Union Grove	Racine	WI
Tustin	Waushara	WI	Ulsterville	Ulster	NY	Union Hall	Franklin	WI
Tuthill	Ulster	NY	Ultima Thule	Sevier	AR	Union Hill	Kankekee	IL
Tuttle's Corners	Sussex	NJ	Ulysses	Butler	NE	Union Hill	Ringgold	IA
Tuttle's X Roads	Caldwell	NC	Ulysses	Potter	PA	Union Hill	Monroe	NY
Twelve Mile	Cass	IN	Umatilla	Umatilla	OR	Union Home	Clinton	MI
Twenty Mile Stand	Warren	OH	Umadilla	Livingston	MI	Union House	Sacramento	CA
26 Mile House	Stanislaus	CA	Unadilla	Otsego	NY	Union Lakes	Rice	MN

PLACE	COUNTY	STATE	PLACE	COUNTY	STATE	PLACE	COUNTY	STATE
Union Mting	Baltimore	MD	Upper Aquebogue	Suffolk	NY	Vail X Rds	Morrow	OH
Union Mills	La Porte	IN	Upper Bern	Berks	PA	Vail's Gate	Orange	NY
Union Mills	Mahaska	IA	Upper Black Eddy	Bucks	PA	Vail's Mills	Fulton	NY
Union Mills	Carroll	MD	Upper Blue Licks	Fleming	KY	Vailatie	Columbia	NY
Union Mills	Tippah	MS	Upper Clear Lake	Lake	CA	Valcour	Clinton	NY
Union Mills	Platte	MO	Upperco	Blatimore	MD	Valdosta(c.h.)	Lowndes	GA
Union MIlls	Fluvanna	PA	Upper X Roads	Harford	MD	Valeene	Orange	IN
Union Mills	Pleasants	WV	Upper Darby	Delaware	PA	Vale Mills	Giles	TN
Union Mills	Iowa	WI	Upper Dublin	Montgomery	PA	Valentine	La Grange	IN
Union Pier	Berrien	MI	Upper Falls	Baltimore	MD	Valhalla	Westchester	NY
Union Plains	Brown	OH	Upper Fails	Windsor	VT	Valhermoso Springs	Morgan	AL
Union Point	Greene	OH	Upper Falls of Coal	Canawha	WV	Vallejo	Solano	CA
Union Point	Union	IL	Upper Gloucester	Cumberland	ME	Valley	Washington	OH
Unionport	Jefferson	OH	Upper Grove	Hancock	IA	Valley	Douglas	NE
Union Prairie	Allamakee	IA	Upper Jay	Essex	NY	Valley	Columbiana	OH
Union Ridge	Brown	IL	Upper Lehigh	Luzerne	PA	Valley	Clarion	PA
Union Ridge	Butler	IA	Upper Ltsle	Broome	NY	Valley	Gaudalupe	TX
Union Ridge	Sullivan	MO	Upper Madawaska	Aroostook	ME	Valley	Vernon	WI
Union Ridge	Clark	WA	Upper Mahontago	Schuylkill	PA	Valley Bend	Randolph	WV
Union Society(c.h.)	Greene	NY	Upper Marlb.(c.h.)	Prince George's	MD	Valley Brook	Osage	KS
Union Springs	Dodge	MN	Upper Middletown	Fayette	PA	Valley City	Harrison	IN
Union Springs	Bullock	AL	Upper Ochoco	Casco	OR	Valley City	Neosho	KS
Union Springs	Cayuga	NY	Upper Providence	Delaware	PA	Valley Creek	Chester	PA
Union Square	Oswego	NY	Upper Red Hook	Dutchess	NY	Valley Crucis	Watauga	NC
Union Square	Montgomery	PA	Upper St. Clair	Alleghany	PA	Valley Falls	Rensselaer	NY
Union Star	Breckinridge	KY	Upper Stillwater	Penobscot	ME	Valley Falls	Providence	RI
Union Star	De Kalb	MO	Upper Strasburgh	Franklin	PA	Valley Falls	Spartanburgh	SC
Union Station	Licking	OH	Upper Tract	Pendleton	WV	Valley Falls	Marion	WV
Union Station	Lancaster	PA	Upper Trappe	Somerset	MD	Valley Farm	Linn	IA
Uniontown	Perry	AL	Upper Tygart	Carter	KY	Valley Ford	Meigs	OH
Uniontown	Delaware	IA	Upperville	Susquehanna	PA	Valley Forge	Chester	PA
Uniontown	Union	KY	Upton	Van Buren	IA	Valley Furnace	Barbour	WV
Uniontown	Carroll	MD	Upton	Oxford	ME	Valley Grove	Ohio	WV
Uniontown	Perry	MO	Upton	Worcester	MA	Valley Head	De Kalb	AL
Uniontown	Belmont	OH	Upton	Franklin	PA	Valley Junction	Polk	IA
Uniontown(c.h.)	Fayette	PA	Uptonville	Hardin	KY	Valley Junction	Hamilton	OH
Union Valley	Cortland	NY	Urban	Butler	NE	Valley Mills	Marion	IN
Union Village	Orange	VT	Urban	Northumberland	PA	Valley Mills	Madison	NY
Unionville	Hartford	CN	Urbana(c.h.)	Champaign	OH	Valley Mills	Bosque	TX
Unionville	Monroe	GA	Urbana	Middlesex	VA	Valley Mills	Wood	WV
Unionville	Monroe	IN	Urbanna	Benton	IA	Valley Oak	Pulaski	KY
Unionville	Appanoose	IA	Urbana City	Monroe	IA	Valley Point	Preston	WV
Unionville	Frederick	MD	Urieville	Kent	MD	Valley Stream	Queens	NY
Unionville	Tuxcola	MI	Urmeyville	Johnson	IN	Valley Town	Cherokee	NC
Unionville(c.h.)	Putnam	MO	Ursa	Adams	IL	Valley Town	Cherokee	NC
Unionville	Lewis and Clark	MT	Ursina	Somerset	PA	Vallicita	Calaveras	CA
Unionville	Gloucester	NJ	Usquepaugh	Washington	RI	Vallonia	Jackson	IN
Unionville(c.h.)	Humbolt	NV	Utah	Warren	IL	Vallonia Springs	Broome	NY
Unionville	Orange	NY	Utah	Indiana	PA	Valmont	Boulder	CO
Unionville	Lake	OH	Utahville	Clearfield	PA	Valparaiso(c.h.)	Porter	IN
Unionville	Chester	PA	Ute Creek	Colfax	NM	Valton	Sauk	WI
Unionville(c.h.)	Union	SC	Utica	La Salle	IL	Vanatta	Licking	OH
Unionville	Bedford	TN	Utica	Clarke	IN	Van Buren(c.h.)	Crawford	AR
Unionville	Orange	VA	Utica	Van Buren	IA	Van Buren	De Kalb	IL
Unionville Centre	Union	OH	Utica	Daviess	KY	Van Buren	Jackson	IA
Uniopolis	Auglaize	OH	Utica	Macomb	MI	Van Buren	Aroostook	ME
Unison	Loundon	VA	Utica	Winona	MN	Van Buren(c.h.)	Crawford	AR
Unitia	Loundon	TN	Utica	Hinds	MS	Van Buren	Onondaga	NY
Unity	Waldo	ME	Utica	Livingston	MO	Van Buren	Hancock	OH
Unity	Montgomery	MD	Utica(c.h.)	Oneida	NY	Van Buren	Washington	PA
Unity	Sullivan	NH	Utica(c.h.)	Licking	OH	Van Buren Furnace	Shenandoah	VA
Unity	Columbiana	OH	Utica	Venango	PA	Van Camp	Columbia	PA
Unity	Pacific	WA	Utica	Dane	WI	Van Camp	Wetzel	WV
Unityville	Lycoming	PA	Utica	Dane	MD	Vanceburgh(c.h.)	Lewis	KY
Unityville	Lycoming	PA	Utica Mills	Frederick	WA	Vanceford	Alleghany	PA
University of VA	Algemarle	VA	Utsaladdy	Island	TX	Vancefort	Alleghany	PA
Ununda	Brown	KS	Uvalde(c.h.)	Uvalde	PA	Vance's Ferry	Orangeburgh	SC
Upatoie	Muscogee	GA	Uwchland	Chester	MA	Vanceville	Washington	PA
Updegraff's	Jefferson	OH	Uxbridge	Worcester	CA	Vancil's Point	Macoupin	IL
Upland	Grant	IN	Vaca	Solano	CA	Vancleave's	Jackson	MS
Upland	Mason	WV	Vacaville	Solano	LA	Vancil's Point	Macoupin	IL
Uplands	Deleware	PA	Vacherie Roads	St. Jame	MS	Vancleave's	Jackson	MS
Upper Alton	Madison	IL	Vaiden	Carroll	IA	Vancouver(c.h.)	Clark	WA
			Vail	Crawford				

PLACE	COUNTY	STATE	PLACE	COUNTY	STATE	PLACE	COUNTY	STATE
Vandalia(c.h.)	Fayette	IL	Vermillion	Nemaha	KS	Victory	Essex	VT
Vandalia	Owen	IN	Vermillion	Oswego	NY	Victory	Vernon	WI
Vandalia	Jasper	IA	Vermillion	Erie	OH	Victory Mills	Saratoga	NY
Vandalia	Cass	MI	Vermillion Lake	St. Louis	MN	Vidalia(c.h.)	Concordia	LA
Vandalia	Audrian	MO	Vermillionville	La Salle	IL	Vidalia(c.h.)	Dooly	GA
Vandalia	Cattaraugus	NY	Vermillionvtlle(c.h.)	La Fayette	LA	Vienna(c.h.)	Johnson	IL
Vandalia	Montgomery	OH	Vermont	Fulton	IL	Vienna	Scott	IN
Vanderbuilt	Lander	NV	Vermont	Cooper	MO	Vienna	Marshall	IA
Vandergriff's	Knox	TN	Vermont	Chautaqua	NY	Vienna	Pottawatomie	KS
Van Deusenville	Berkshire	MA	Vermontville	Eaton	MI	Vienna	Clarke	KS
Vandeve	Craven	NC	Vernal	Greene	MS	Vienna	Jackson	LA
Vandyke	New Castle	DE	Vernon(c.h.)	Sanford	AL	Vienna	Kennebec	ME
Van Dyke's Mill	Spencer	KY	Vernon	Tolland	CN	Vienna	Dorchester	MD
Van Dyne	Fond du Lac	WI	Vernon	Kent	DE	Vienna(c.h.)	Maries	MO
Van Etten	Chemung	NY	Vernon	Troup	GA	Vienna	Warren	NJ
Van Hill	Hawkins	TX	Vernon(c.h.)	Jennings	IN	Vienna	Forsyth	NC
Van Hiseville	Ocean	NJ	Vernon	Van Buren	IA	Vienna	Trumbull	OH
Van Hook's Store	Person	NC	Vernon(c.h.)	Jackson	LA	Vienna	Fairfax	VA
Van Horn	Clinton	OH	Vernon	Shiawassee	MI	Vienna	Walworth	WI
Van Horn	Carroll	MO	Vernon	Dodge	MN	Vienna X Roads	Clark	OH
Van Hornesville	Herkimer	NY	Vernon	Madison	MS	Vigod	Ross	OH
Vanlue	Hancock	OH	Vernon	Sussex	NJ	Village Creek	Allamakee	IA
Van Metre	Dallas	IA	Vernon	Oneida	NY	Village Creek	Delaware	PA
Vannatterville	Lincoln	WV	Vernon	Trumbull	OH	Village Springs	Blount	AL
Vannoy's Mills	Pike	MO	Vernon	Marion	OR	Villanova	Chautauqua	NY
Van's Valley	Delaware	OH	Vernon	Wyoming	PA	Villanow	Walker	GA
Van Vechten	Schenectady	NY	Vernon	Hickman	TN	Villa Rica	Carroll	GA
Vanville	Chippewa	WI	Vernon	Windup	VT	Villa Ridge	Pulaski	IL
Van Wagner	Dutchess	NY	Vernon	Waukesha	WI	Villa Platte	St. Laundry	LA
Van Wert	Polk	GA	Vernon Centre	Blue Earth	MN	Villisca	Montgomery	IA
Van Wert(c.h.)	Van Wert	OH	Vernon Depot	Tolland	CN	Villula	Russell	AL
Van Wert	Juniata	PA	Vernon Hill	Halifax	VA	Vina	Tehama	CA
Varick	Seneca	NY	Vernona	Poweshiek	IA	Vincennes(c.h.)	Knox	IN
Variety Mills	Nelson	VA	Vernona	Boone	KY	Vincennes	Lee	IA
Varna	Marshall	IL	Vernona	Lee	MS	Vincent	St. Clair	ME
Varna	Thomkins	NY	Vernona	Lawrence	MO	Vincent	Washington	OH
Varnell's Station	Whitfield	GA	Vernona	Oneida	NY	Vincent	Chester	PA
Varysburgh	Wyoming	NY	Vernona	Westmoreland	PA	Vincentown	Burlington	NJ
Vasa	Goodhue	MN	Vernona	Marshall	TN	Vine Grove	Hardin	KY
Vasalborough	Kennebec	ME	Vernona	Dane	WI	Vine Grove	Washington	TX
Vassar(c.h.)	Tuscola	MI	Vernona Mills	Huron	MI	Vineland	Jefferson	MO
Vaughn	Yazoo	MS	Verplank	Westcester	NY	Vineland	Cumberland	NJ
Vaughnsville	Putnam	OH	Verrees Mills	Philadelphia	PA	Vinemount	Bollinger	MO
Veazie	Penobscot	ME	Versailles	Brown	IL	Vine's Mills	Worth	GA
Vedder	Calhoun	IL	Versailles(c.h.)	Ripley	IN	Vine's Springs	Ripley	IN
Vega	Jefferson	OH	Versailles(c.h.)	Woodford	KY	Vine Valley	Yates	NY
Velasco	Brazoria	TX	Versailles(c.h.)	Morgan	MO	Vinewood	Clarke	KY
Velp	Brown	FL	Versailles	Cattaraugus	NY	Vineyard	Bradley	AR
Venango	Crawford	PA	Versailles	Darke	OH	Vineyard	Tama	IA
Venedocia	Van Wert	OH	Versailles	Rutherford	TN	Vineyard Grove	Dukes	MA
Veni	Effingham	IL	Versailles	Orange	VT	Vineyard Haven	Dukes	MA
Venice	Madison	IL	Vervilla	Warren	TN	Vineyard Hill	Adams	OH
Venice	Cayuga	NY	Vesper	Onondaga	NY	Vineyard Hill	Kanawha	WV
Venice	Erie	OH	Vesta	Johnson	NE	Vineyard Mills	Huntindon	PA
Venice	Washington	PA	Vestal	Broome	NY	Viney Grove	Washington	AR
Venice Centre	Cayuga	NY	Vestal Centre(c.h.)	Broome	NY	Vining Station	Cobb	GA
Ventura	Ottawa	MI	Veto	Washington	OH	Vinland	Douglas	KS
Venus	Madison	IA	Vevay(c.h.)	Warren	MS	Vinland	Winnebago	WI
Vera	Fayette	IL	Vibbard	Ray	MO	Vinton(c.h.)	Benton	IA
Vera Cruz	Wells	IN	Vicar	Russell	VA	Vinton	Riley	KS
Vera Cruz	Douglas	MO	Vickery's Creek	Forsyth	GA	Vinton	Bates	MO
Vera Cruz	Lehigh	PA	Vickeryville	Montcalm	MI	Vinton	Gallia	OH
Verbank	Dutchess	NY	Vicksburgh	Jewell	KS	Vinton Station	Vinton	OH
Verdi	Wilson	KS	Vicksville	Southampton	VA	Viola	Mercer	IL
Verdi	Washoe	NV	Victor	Iowa	IA	Viola	Linn	IA
Verdierville	Orange	VA	Victor	Clinton	MI	Viola	Howard	KS
Verdigris Falls	Greenwood	KS	Victor	Ontario	NY	Viola	Warren	TN
Verdon	Hanover	VA	Victor Center	De Kalb	IL	Viola	Richland	WI
Vergennes	Jackson	IL	Victoria	Coffee	IL	Viola Station	Graves	KY
Vergennes	Kent	MI	Victoria	Jefferson	AR	Violy	Blount	AL
Vergennes	Addison	VT	Victory	Mason	MI	Viona	Humbolt	IA
Vermillion(c.h.)	Clay	DA	Victory	Cayuga	NY	Virden	Macoupin	IL
Vermillion	Edgar	IL	Victory	Essex	VT	Virgil	Greenwood	KS

PLACE NAMES OF THE UNITED STATES

PLACE	COUNTY	STATE	PLACE	COUNTY	STATE	PLACE	COUNTY	STATE
Virgil	Cortland	NY	Wagontown	Chester	PA	Walkerville	Greene	IL
Virgil City	Cedar	MO	Wagram	Licking	OH	Wallace	Fountain	IN
Virgil City	Kane	UT	Wahaghbonsey	Mills	IA	Wallace	Steuben	KY
Virginia	Douglas	CO	Wahalak Station	Kemper	MS	Wallace	Duplin	NC
Virginia	Union	DA	Wahjamega	Tuscola	MI	Wallace	Chester	PA
Virginia	Cass	IL	Wahoo	Saunders	NE	Wallaceburgh	Hempstead	AR
Virginia	Bates	MO	Wah-Wah	Butler	KS	Wallace's X Roads	Anderson	TN
Virginia	Dallas	TX	Wah Wah Sink	Shawnee	KS	Walaceton	Clearfield	PA
Virginia City(c.h.)	Madison	MT	Wailesborough	Bartholomew	IN	Wallaceville	Wayne	MI
Virginia City(c.h.)	Storey	NV	Waite	Washington	ME	Wallaceville	Venango	PA
Viriginia Grove	Louisa	IA	Waitesville	Jefferson	WI	Walla Walla(c.h.)	Walla Walla	WA
Virginia Mines	Franklin	MO	Waitsfield	Washington	VT	Walled Lake	Oakland	MI
Virginia Ranch	Siskiyou	CA	Wait's River	Orange	VT	Wallen	Allen	IN
Virginville	Berks	PA	Wakarusa	Elkhart	IN	Waller	Rose	OH
Viroqua	Vernon	WI	Wakarus	Shawnee	KS	Wall Hill	Marshall	MS
Vislia(c.h.)	Tulare	CA	Wakatomica	Coshocton	OH	Wallingford	New Haven	CN
Visalia	Kenton	KY	Wakefield	Richland	IL	Wallingford	Will	IL
Vischer's Ferry	Saratoga	NY	Wakefield	Clay	KS	Wallingford	Rutland	VT
Vista	Westchester	NY	Wakefield	Carroll	MD	Walling's Ferry	Rusk	TX
Vista Ridge	Carroll	LA	Wakefield	Middlesex	MA	Wallin's Creek	Harlan	KY
Vistula	Elkhart	IN	Wakefield	Carroll	NH	Wallisville(c.h.)	Chambers	TX
Vivian	Waseca	MN	Wakefield	Wake	NC	Wall Lake	Otter Tail	MN
Voak	Yates	NY	Wakefield	Lancaster	PA	Wallpack Centre	Sussex	NJ
Vogansville	Lancaster	PA	Wakefield	Washington	RI	Wall Rose	Beaver	PA
Volant	Lawrence	PA	Wakefield	Outagamie	WI	Wallsville	Luzerne	PA
Volcano	Amador	CA	Wakefield Station	Sussex	VA	Wallula	Walla Walla	WA
Volcano	Wood	WV	Wakeman	Huron	OH	Walnford	Monmouth	NJ
Volcano	Jefferson	IN	Wakeshma	Kalamazoo	MI	Walnut	Bureau	IL
Volga	Jefferson	IN	Walbridge	Pulaski	IL	Walnut	Marshall	IN
Volinia	Cass	MI	Walcott	Green	AR	Walnut	Butler	KS
Volney	Allamakee	IA	Walden	Orange	NY	Walnut	Juniata	PA
Volney	Oswego	NY	Walden	Caledonia	VT	Walnut Bottom	Cumberland	PA
Volo	Lake	IL	Waldenburgh	Macomb	MI	Walnut City	Appanoose	IA
Volo	Bell	TX	Walden's	Rappahonnock	VA	Walnut Cove	Stokes	NC
Voluntown	Windham	CN	Walden's Creek	Sevier	TN	Walnut Creek	Contra Costa	CA
Volusia	Volusia	FL	Waldingsfield	Kanawaha	WV	Walnut Creek	Fremont	IA
Volusai	Chautauqua	NY	Waldo	Talladega	AL	Walnut Creek	Crawford	KS
Von	Humbolt	IA	Waldo	Alachua	FL	Walnut Creek	Buncombe	NC
Voorheesville	Albany	NY	Waldo	Waldo	ME	Walnut Creek	Holmes	OH
Vosburgh	Wyoming	PA	Waldo	Webster	MO	Walnut Creek St.	Pottawattomie	IA
Vriesland	Ottawa	MI	Waldo	Marion	OH	Walnut Fork	Jones	IA
			Waldo	Josephine	OR	Walnut Grove	Blount	AL
Wabash	Wayne	IL	Waldoborough	Lincoln	ME	Walnut Grove	Independence	AR
Wabash(c.h.)	Wabash	IN	Waldron(c.h.)	Scott	AR	Walnut Grove	Sacramento	CA
Wabashaw(c.h.)	Wabashaw	MN	Waldron	Platte	MO	Walnut Grove	Walton	GA
Wabaunsee	Wabaunsee	KS	Waldrop's Mills	Jefferson	AL	Walnut Grove	McDounough	IL
Wachusett Village	Worcester	MA	Waldwick	Iowa	WI	Walnut Grove	Scott	IA
Waco	Franklin	AL	Wales	Ogle	IL	Walnut Grove	Caldwell	KY
Waco	Madison	KY	Wales	Worth	IA	Walnut Grove	Martin	MN
Waco(c.h.)	McLennan	TX	Wales	Androscoggin	ME	Walnut Grove	Leake	MS
Waconda	Marion	OR	Wales	Hampden	MA	Walnut Grove	Greene	MO
Wacousta	Humbolt	IA	Wales	St. Clair	MI	Walnut Grove	Morris	NJ
Wacousta	Clinton	MI	Wales	Erie	NY	Walnut Grove	Hardin	TN
Wadaloup	Grundy	IA	Wales	Callia	OH	Walnut Hill	Tallapoosa	AL
Waddam's Centre	Stephenson	IL	Wales	San Pete	UT	Walnut Hill	La Fayette	AR
Waddington	St. Lawrence	NY	Wales Centre	Erie	NY	Walnut Hill	Marion	IL
Wade	Washington	OH	Walesville	Oneida	NY	Walnut Hill	Mashall	IN
Wade's	Bedford	VA	Walhain	Kewaunee	WI	Walnut Hill	Bourbon	KS
Wadesborough	Calloway	KY	Walhalla	Pembina	DA	Walnut Hill	Fayette	KY
Wadesborough(c.h.)	Anson	NC	Walhalla(c.h.)	Oconee	SC	Walnut Hill	Buchanan	MO
Wadesburgh	Cass	MO	Walhonding	Coshcoton	OH	Walnut Hill	Ashe	NC
Wadestown	Monomgalia	WV	Walker	Centre	PA	Walnut Hill	Sequatchie	TN
Wadesville	Possey	IN	Walker	Wood	WV	Walnut Hill	Panola	TX
Wadesville	Clarke	VA	Walker's	Columbia	AR	Walnut Hill	Lee	VA
Wadesville	Wood	WV	Walker's Church	Appomattox	VA	Walnut Hills	Hamilton	OH
Wadhams' Mills	Essex	NY	Walker's Ford	Amherst	VA	Walnut Lake	Fairbault	MN
Wadeville	Navarro	TX	Walker's Mills	Allegheny	PA	Walnut Lick	Gallatin	KY
Wading River	Burlington	NJ	Walkerstown	Forsyth	NC	Walnut Ridge	Lawrence	AR
Wadley's Falls	Stafford	NH	Walkersville	Frederick	MD	Walnut Run	Madison	OH
Wadsworth	Washoe	NE	Walkersville	Union	NC	Walnut Shade	Tarney	MO
Waggoner's Ripple	Adams	OH	Walkersville	Lewis	WV	Walnut Tree	Yell	AR
Wagner	Clayton	OH	Walkerton	St. Joseph	IN	Walnut Valley	Warren	NJ
Wagon Landing	Polk	WI	Walker Valley	Ulster	NY	Walnut Valley	Sequatchie	TN

PLACE NAMES OF THE UNITED STATES

PLACE	COUNTY	STATE	PLACE	COUNTY	STATE	PLACE	COUNTY	STATE
Walpole	Norfolk	MA	Warren	Cloud	KS	Waseca	Waseca	MN
Walpole	Cheshire	NH	Warren	Knox	ME	Waseca	Otter Tail	MN
Walshville	Montgomery	IL	Warren	Baltimore	MO	Washburn	Woodford	IL
Walterborough(c.h.)	Collecton	SC	Warren	Worcester	MS	Washburn	Franklin	OH
Walter Hill	Rutherford	TN	Warren	Macomb	MI	Washburn	Barry	MO
Waltham	Hancock	ME	Warren	Marion	MO	Washburn	Grant	WI
Waltham	Middlesex	MA	Warren	Grafton	NH	Washington(c.h.)	Hempstead	AR
Waltham	Mower	MN	Warren	Herkimer	NY	Washington	Nevada	CA
Walthourville	Liberty	GA	Warren	Bristol	RI	Washington	Litchfield	CN
Walton	Cass	IN	Warren(c.h.)	Trumbull	OH	Washington(c.h.)	Washington	DC
Walton	Boone	KY	Warren(c.h.)	Warren	PA	Washington(c.h.)	Wilkes	GA
Walton	Delaware	NY	Warren	Fannin	TX	Washington(c.h.)	Idaho	ID
Walton	Roane	WV	Warren	Washington	VT	Washington	Tazewell	IL
Walton Mills	Washington	MO	Warren	Albemarle	VA	Washington	Mason	KY
Walton's Ford	Habersham	GA	Warren	Wood	WV	Washington(c.h.)	Daviess	IN
Walts Mills	Westmoreland	PA	Warren	St. Coix	WI	Washington	Washington	IA
Waltz	Wabash	IN	Warren Centre	Bradford	PA	Washington(c.h.)	Washington	KS
Walworth	Walworth	WI	Warren Grove	Jasper	IA	Washington	Mason	KY
Wamego	Pottawattomie	KS	Warrenham	Bradford	PA	Washington	St. Laundry	LA
Wampsville	Madison	NY	Warren Mills	Monroe	WI	Washington	Knox	ME
Wampum's	Lawrence	PA	Warren Plains	Warren	NC	Washington	Berkshire	MA
Wamsley's	Adams	OH	Warrensburgh(c.h.)	Johnson	MO	Washington	Macomb	MI
Wanamie	Luzerne	PA	Warrensburgh	Warren	NY	Washington	Fillmore	MN
Wanamiga	Goodhue	MN	Warrensburgh	Greene	TN	Washington	Franklin	MO
Wanatah	Laporte	IN	Warrensburgh	Washington	UT	Washington	Washington	NV
Waneka	Dunn	WI	Warren's Corners	Niagara	NY	Washington	Nye	NV
Wanship	Summit	UT	Warren's Corners	Door	Wi	Washington	Sullivan	NH
Wapakonetta(c.h.)	Auglaize	OH	Warren Summitt	Grafton	NH	Washington	Warren	NJ
Wapatoe	Washington	OR	Warrensville	Du Page	IL	Washington	Dutchess	NY
Wapecau	Grundy	IL	Warrensville	Cuyahoga	OH	Washington	Guernsey	OH
Wapella	De Witt	IL	Warrensville	Lycoming	PA	Washington(c.h.)	Beaufort	NC
Wapello(c.h.)	Louisa	IA	Warren Tavern	Chester	PA	Washington(c.h.)	Washington	PA
Wapping	Hartford	CN	Warrenton	Marshall	AL	Washington(c.h.)	Rhea	TN
Wappinger's Falls	Dutchess	NY	Warrenton(c.h.)	Warren	GA	Washington	Washington	TX
Wapwallopen	Luzerne	PA	Warrenton	Jefferson	OH	Washington	Washington	TX
Waquoit	Barnstable	MA	Warrenton(c.h.)	Warren	MO	Washington	Orange	VT
Waranancoke	King William	VA	Warrenton(c.h.)	Warren	NC	Washington(c.h.)	Rappahannock	VA
Warburgh	Callway	KY	Warrenton(c.h.)	Fauquier	VA	Washington Centre	Whitely	IN
War Creek	Hancock	TN	Warrenville	Laclede	MO	Washington Corners	Alameda	CA
Ward District	Boulder	CO	Warrneville	Somerset	NJ	Washington Gulch	Deer Lodge	MT
Wardena	Fayette	IA	War Ridge	Hancock	TN	Washington Harbor	Door	WI
Wardensville	Hardy	WV	Warrington	Escambia	FL	Washington Heights	Cook	IL
Wardsborough	Windham	VT	Warrington	Hancock	IN	Washington Hollow	Dutchess	NY
Ward's Corners	Buchanan	IA	Warrington	Bucks	PA	Washington Mills	Oneida	NY
Ward's Iron Works	Johnson	TN	Warrior Creek	Wilkes	NC	Washington Prairie	Winneshick	IA
Wardville	Chowan	NC	Warrior's Mark	Huntingdon	PA	Washingtonville	Mahoning	OH
Ware	Hampshire	MA	Warsaw	Milton	GA	Washingtonville	Montour	PA
War Eagle	Madison	AR	Warsaw	Hancock	IL	Washoe City	Washoe	NV
Wareham	Plymouth	MA	Warsaw(c.h.)	Kosciusko	IN	Washta	Cherokee	IA
Warehouse Point	Hartford	CN	Warsaw(c.h.)	Gallatin	KY	Wasioga	Dodge	MN
Warfield	Lawrence	KY	Warsaw	Wayne	OH	Waskey's Mills	Botetourt	VA
Warfieldburgh	Carroll	MD	Warsaw	Franklin	LA	Wassaic	Dutchess	NY
Warfordsburgh	Fulton	PA	Warsaw	Rice	MN	Wassonville	Washington	IA
War Gap	Hawkins	TN	Warsaw	Duplin	NC	Wastedo	Goodhue	MN
Warm Fork	Oregon	MO	Warsaw(c.h.)	Benton	MO	Wastaga	Knox	IL
Warminster	BUcks	PA	Warsaw(c.h.)	Wyoming	NY	Watab	Benton	MN
Warminster	Nelson	VA	Warsaw	Coshocton	OH	Watauga Falls	Watauga	NC
Warm Springs	Meriwether	GA	Warsaw	Jefferson	PA	Watanwon	Blue Earth	MN
Warm Springs	Deer Lodge	MT	Warsaw(c.h.)	Richmond	VA	Watchemoket	Providence	RI
Warm Springs	Madison	NC	Wartburg(c.h.)	Morgan	TN	Watch Hill	Washington	RI
Warner	Merrimack	NH	Warthen's Store	Washington	GA	Waterborough	York	ME
Warner's	Onondaga	NY	Wartrace Depot	Bedford	TN	Waterborough Ctre.	York	ME
Warner's Landing	Vernon	WI	Warwick	Worth	GA	Waterburgh	Tompkins	NY
Warner's Ranch	San Diego	CA	Warwick	Cecil	MD	Waterbury	New Haven	CN
Warnerville	Meriwether	GA	Warwick	Franklin	MA	Waterbury	Anne Arundel	MD
Warnerville	Schoharie	NY	Warwick	Orange	NY	Waterbury	Washington	VT
Warnock	Belmont	OH	Warwick	Chester	PA	Waterbury Centre	Washington	VT
Warpole	Wyandot	OH	Warwick	Kent	RI	Water Cuare	Beaver	PA
Warren(c.h.)	Bradley	AR	Warwock(c.h.)	Warwock	VA	Wateree	Richland	SC
Warren	Litchfield	CN	Warwick Neck	Kent	RI	Waterford	New London	CN
Warren	Jo Daviess	CN	Warwick's X Roads	Union	TN	Waterford	Spencer	KY
Warren	Huntingdon	IN	War Woman	Raburn	GA	Waterford	Oxford	ME
Warren	Lee	IA	Wasco	Wasco	OR	Waterford	Oakland	MI

PLACE	COUNTY	STATE	PLACE	COUNTY	STATE	PLACE	COUNTY	STATE
Waterford	Dakota	MN	Watson	Atchison	MO	Wayne	Du Page	IL
Waterford	Marshall	MS	Watson	Beaver Head	MT	Wayne	Henry	IA
Waterford	Saratoga	NY	Watson	Lewis	NY	Wayne	Kennebec	ME
Waterford	Washington	OH	Watson Creek	Fillmore	MN	Wayne	Wayne	MI
Waterford	Erie	PA	Watson's Station	Seneca	OH	Wayne	Steuben	NY
Waterford	Caledonia	VT	Watsontown	Northumberland	PA	Wayne	Wayne	OH
Waterford	Loudoun	VA	Watsonville	Ssant Cruz	CA	Wayne	Wayne	OH
Waterford	Racine	WI	Watt	Indiana	PA	Wayne	Erie	PA
Waterford Mills	Elkhart	IN	Watterson's Ferry	Clairion	PA	Wayne	Washington	WI
Waterford Works	Camden	NJ	Watts	Sangamon	IL	Wayne(c.h.)	Wayne	WV
Water Lick	Warren	VA	Wattsburgh	Erie	PA	Wayne Centre	Wayne	NY
Waterloo	Lauderdale	AL	Watt's Flats	Chautauqua	NY	Wayne Centre	Crawford	PA
Waterloo	San Joaquin	CA	Wattsville	Carroll	OH	Wayne City	Wayne	IL
Waterloo(c.h.)	Monroe	IL	Waubeck	Linn	IA	Wayne 4 Corners	Steuben	NY
Waterloo	De Kalb	IN	Waubeck	Pepin	WI	Wayne Furnace	Wayne	TN
Waterloo(c.h.)	Seneca	NY	Wauncoma	Fayette	IA	Waynesbor.(c.h.)	Burke	GA
Waterloo	Lawrence	OH	Wauconda	Lake	IL	Waynesbor.(c.h.)	Wayne	MS
Waterloo	Juainta	PA	Wauconsta	Fond du Lac	WI	Waynesborough	Franklin	PA
Waterloo	Laurens	SC	Wauatchie	Hamilton	TN	Waynesbor.(c.h.)	Wayne	TN
Waterloo	Fauquier	VA	Waukau	Winnebago	WI	Waynesborough	Augusta	VA
Waterloo	Jefferson	WI	Waukecheon	Shawanaw	WI	Waynesborough	Decatur	IN
Waterloo Mills	Orange	NY	Waukeenah	Jefferson	FL	Waynesborough	Lincoln	KY
Waterman	Parke	IN	Waukee Station	Dallas	IA	Waynesborough	Stark	OH
Waterman	Wright	IA	Waukegan(c.h.)	Lake	IL	Waynesbor.(c.h.)	Greene	PA
Waterman's Mills	Suffolk	NY	Waykesh(c.h.)	Waukesha	WI	Waynesfield	Anglaize	OH
Water Mill	Suffolk	NY	Waukokii	Fillmore	MN	Waynesville(c.h.)	Wayne	GA
Waterport	Orleans	NY	Waukon(c.h.)	Allamakee	IA	Waynesville	De Witt	IL
Water Proof	Tensas	PA	Waumandee(c.h.)	Buffalo	WI	Waynesville	Bartholomew	IN
Waterside	Bedford	PA	Waukon(c.h.)	Waupaca	WI	Waynesville(c.h.)	Pulaski	MO
Water Street	Huntingdon	PA	Waupecong	Miami	IN	Waynesville(c.h.)	Haywood	NC
Waterville	Carroll	MD	Waupun	Fond du Lac	WI	Waynesville	Warren	OH
Watertown	Litchfield	CN	Wauregan	Windham	CN	Waynetown	Montgomery	IN
Watertown	Rock Island	IL	Wausau(c.h.)	Marathon	WI	Waynewood	Marion	IN
Watertown	Floyd	IA	Wauseon(c.h.)	Fulton	OH	Waynmanville	Upson	GA
Watertown	Middlesex	MI	Waushara	Lyon	KS	Wayside	Mecklenburgh	VA
Watertown	Tuxcola	MI	Wautiska	Saunders	NE	Wayside	Brown	WI
Watertown	Carver	MN	Wautoma(c.h.)	Waushara	WI	Way's Station	Bryan	GA
Watertown(c.h.)	Jefferson	NY	Waveland	Montgomery	IN	Wayzata	Hennepin	MN
Watertown	Washington	OH	Waveland	Pottawattomie	IA	Wea	Tippecanoe	IN
Watertown	Wilson	TN	Waveland	Shawnee	KS	Weare	Oceana	MI
Watertown	Jefferson	WI	Waveland	Rockingham	VA	Weare	Hillsborough	NH
Waatervale	Onondaga	NY	Waverly	Morgan	IL	Wear's Valley	Sevier	TN
Water Valley	Yalabusha	MS	Waverly	Morgan	IN	Weatherford(c.h.)	Parker	TX
Water Valley	Erie	NY	Waverly(c.h.)	Bremer	IA	Weatherly	Carbon	PA
Water Village	New Haven	CN	Waverly	Caldwell	LA	Weathersfield	Windsor	VT
Waterville	Carroll	NH	Waverly	Baltimore	MD	Weathersfield Ctr.	Windsor	VT
Waterville	Allamakee	IA	Waverly	Middlesex	MA	Weatogue	Hartford	CN
Waterville	Marshall	KS	Waverly	Van Buren	MI	Weaver	Wabashaw	MN
Waterville	Kennebec	ME	Waverly	Martin	MN	Weaver's Station	Darke	OH
Waterville	Le Sueur	MN	Waverly	La Fayette	MO	Weaversville	Northampton	PA
Waterville	Oncida	NY	Waverly	Lancaster	NE	Weaversville	Fanquier	VA
Waterville	Lucas	OH	Waverly	Essex	NJ	Weaverton	Wayne	KY
Waterville	Lycoming	PA	Waverly	Tioga	NY	Weaverville(c.h.)	Trinity	CA
Waterville	Lamoille	VT	Waverly(c.h.)	Pike	OH	Weaw	Humphreys	TN
Waterville	Waukesha	WI	Waverly	Luzerne	PA	Webber's Falls	Cherokee Nat.	IT
Watervliet	Berrien	MI	Waverly	Walker	TX	Webberville	Ingham	MI
Watervliet Centre	Albany	NY	Waverly(c.h.)	HUmphreys	TN	Webberville	Travis	TX
Wathena	Doniphan	KS	Waverly Hall	Harris	GA	Webbs	Greene	KY
Wathkins(c.h.)	Schuyler	NY	WaverlyHeights	Montgomery	PA	Webb's Ford	Rutherford	NC
Watkins	Union	OH	Waverly Mills	Wright	MN	Webb's Mills	Cumberland	ME
Watkinsville(c.h.)	Clarke	GA	Waverly Station	Sussex	VA	Webb's Mills	Chemung	NY
Watopa	Wabashaw	MN	Wawaka	Noble	IN	Webb's Mills	Ritchie	WV
Watrousville	Tuscola	MI	Wawarsing	Ulster	NY	Webb's Prairie	Franklin	IL
Watseka(c.h.)	Schuyler	NY	Wawayanda	Sussex	NJ	Webbville	Lawrence	KY
Watkins	Union	OH	Wawahachie(c.h.)	Ellis	TX	Weber	Jackson	OH
Watkinsville(c.h.)	Clarke	GA	Wayland	Schuyler	IL	Webertown	Highland	OH
Watopa	Wabashaw	MN	Wayland	Middlesex	MA	Webster	Hancock	IL
Watrousville	Tuscola	MI	Wayland	Allegan	MI	Webster	Wayne	IN
Wateska(c.h.)	Iroquois	IL	Wayland Depot	Sheuben	NY	Webster	Keokuk	IA
Watson	Effingham	IL	Waylandsburgh	Culpeper	VA	Webster	Brekinridge	KY
Watson	Prince George's	MD	Wayland Springs	Lawrence	TN	Webster	Androscoggin	ME
Watson	Allegan	MI	Waymansville	Bartholomew	IN	Webster	Worcester	MA
Watson	Marshall	MS	Waymart	Wayne	PA	Webster	Winston	MA

PLACE NAMES OF THE UNITED STATES

PLACE	COUNTY	STATE	PLACE	COUNTY	STATE	PLACE	COUNTY	STATE
Webster	Oregon	MO	Wellsburgh	Page	IA	West Barre	Fulton	OH
Webster	Dodge	NE	Wellsburgh	St. Charles	MO	West Batavia	Genesee	NY
Webster	Merrimack	NH	Wellsburgh	Chemung	NY	W.Bat Rouge(c.h.)	West Baton Rouge	LA
Webster	Monroe	NY	Wellsburgh(c.h.)	Brooke	WV	West Beaver	Columbiana	OH
Webster	Darke	OH	Wells Corner	Orange	NY	West Becket	Berkshire	MA
Webster(c.h.)	Jackson	NC	Wells Depot	York	ME	West Bedford	Coshocton	OH
Webster	Westmoreland	PA	Wells' Mills	Appanoose	IA	West Bend	Palo Alto	IA
Webster	Roane	TN	Wells' Mills	Richardson	NE	West Bend	Powell	KY
Webster	Taylor	WV	Wells Spring	Campbell	TN	West Bend(c.h.)	Washington	WI
Webster(c.h.)	Webster	WV	Wells River	Orange	VT	West Bergen	Genesee	NY
Webster(c.h.)	Hamilton	IA	Wells Tannery	Fulton	PA	West Berkshire	Franklin	VT
Webster Groves	St. Louis	ME	Wellsville	Franklin	KS	West Berlin	Worcester	MA
Webster Place	Elbert	GA	Wellsville	Lenawee	MI	West Berne	Albany	NY
Webster's Crossing	Livingston	NY	Wellsville	Montgomery	MO	West Bethany	Genessee	NV
Webster's Mills	Fulton	PA	Wellsville	Allegany	NY	West Bethel	Oxford	ME
Wedowee(c.h.)	Randolph	AL	Wellsville	Columbiana	OH	West Bingham	Potter	PA
Weedsport	Cayuga	NY	Wellsville	York	PA	West Bloomfield	Ontario	NY
Weehawken	Hudson	NJ	Wellsville	Cache	UT	West Blue	Fillmore	NE
Week's Mills	Kennebec	ME	Well Water	Buckinham	VA	West Blue	Mond	IA
Weeksville	Southampton	VA	Wellwood	Haywood	TN	West Bolton	Chittenden	VT
Weelaunee	Jefferson	FL	Welshfield	Geauga	OH	Westborough	Worcester	MA
Weeping Water	Cass	NE	Welsh Run	Franklin	PA	Westborough	Clinton	OH
Weesatch	Goliad	TX	Welton	Clinton	IA	West Bowdoin	Sagadahoc	ME
Weesaw	Berrien	MI	Weltonville	Tioga	NY	West Boxford	Essex	MA
Weewokaville	Talladega	AL	Wendell	Franklin	MA	West Boylston	Worcester	MA
Wegatchie	St. Lawrence	NY	Wenks	Adams	PA	West Braintree	Orange	VT
Wegdal	Chippewa	MN	Wennersville	Lehigh	PA	West Branch	Cedar	IA
Wegee	Belmount	OH	Wenonna	Bay	MI	West Branch	Oneida	NY
Wehoga	Calhoun	AL	Wenona Station	Marshall	IL	West Branch	Richland	WI
Weidasville	Lehigh	PA	Wentwoth	Mitchell	IA	West Brattleborough	Windham	VT
Weimer	Wood	TX	Wentworth	Grafton	NH	West Brewster	Barnstable	MA
Weir's Bridge	Belknap	NH	Wentworth(c.h.)	Rockingham	SC	West Bridgeton	Cumberland	ME
Weisburgh	Dearborn	IN	Wentworth's Local	Coos	NH	West Bridgewater	Plymouth	MA
Weisenburgh	Lehigh	PA	Wentzville	St. Charles	MO	West Brighton	Monroe	NY
Weiser	Ada	ID	Wecosville	Lehigh	PA	West Brook	Middlesex	CN
Weisesburgh	Baltimore	MD	Wesley	Montgomery	IN	West Brook	Delaware	NY
Weishample	Schuylkill	PA	Wesley	Hickman	KY	West Brook	Bladen	NC
Weissport	Carbon	PA	Wesley	Washington	ME	Westbrook	Blanco	TX
Weister	Vernon	WI	Wesley	Washington	OH	West Brookfield	Stark	OH
Wekiva	Orange	FL	Wesley	Venango	PA	West Brookfield	Stark	OH
Weklaka	Putnam	FL	Wesley	Austin	TX	West Brooksville	Washington	PA
Welch Glade	Webster	WV	Wesley Station	Kossurth	IA	West Brownsville	Washington	PA
Welch's Creek	Butler	KY	Wesleyville	Erie	PA	West Brunswick	Cumberland	ME
Welchville	Oxford	ME	Wesson	Copiah	MS	West Buena Vista	Gibson	IN
Weld	Weid	CO	West	Wetzel	WV	West Buffalo	Williams	OH
Weldon	Karen	CA	West Action	Middlesex	MA	West Burke	Caledonia	VT
Weldon	Redwood	MN	West Addison	Steuben	NY	West Burlington	Otsego	NY
Weldon	Maries	MO	West Addison	Addison	VT	West Burlington	Bedford	PA
Weldon	Seware	NE	West Albany	Wabashaw	MN	Westbury	Cayuga	NY
Weldon	Halifax	NC	West Albany	Albany	NY	West Butler	Wayne	NY
Weldon	Houston	TX	West Alexander	Washington	PA	West Butte	Sutter	CA
Well	Fairbault	MN	West Alexandria	Preble	OH	West Buxton	York	ME
Wellborn	Suwannee	FL	West Almond	Allegany	NY	West Cairo	Allen	OH
Wellborn	Brazos	TX	West Alton	Belknap	NH	West Camden	Knox	ME
Weller	Monroe	IA	West Amboy	Oswego	NY	West Camden	Oneida	NY
Wellersburgh	Somerset	PA	West Amesbury	Essex	MA	West Camp	Ulster	NY
Wellerville	Crawford	OH	West Andover	Merrimack	NH	West Campbell	Ironia	MI
Wellesley	Norfolk	MA	West Andover	Ashtabula	OH	West Campton	Grafton	NH
Wellflect	Barnstable	MA	West Appleton	Knox	ME	West Canana	Madison	OH
Wellington	Sumner	KS	West Arlington	Bennington	VT	West Candor	Tioga	NY
Wellington	Piscataquis	ME	West Ashford	Windham	CN	West Carlisle	Coshocton	OH
Wellington	La Fayette	MO	West Athens	Somerset	ME	West Carrollton	Montgomery	OH
Wellington	Esmeralda	NV	West Auburn	Androscoggin	ME	West Casco	Allegen	MI
Wellington	Lorain	OH	West Auburn	Susquehanna	PA	West Castleton	Rutland	VA
Wells	York	ME	West Avon	Hartford	CN	West Casco	Allegan	MI
Wells	Attala	MS	West Baden	Orange	IN	West Castleton	Rutland	VA
Wells	Elko	NV	West Baldwin	Cumberland	ME	West Charleston	Penobscot	ME
Wells	Hamilton	NY	West Baltimore	Montgomery	OH	West Charlotte	Chittenden	VT
Wells	Bradford	PA	West Bangor	Franklin	NY	West Charlton	Saratoga	NY
Wells	Rutland	VT	West Bangor	York	PA	West Chatham	Barnstable	MA
Wellsborough(c.h.)	Tioga	PA	West Barnet	Caledonia	VT	West Chazy	Clinton	NY
Wells' Bridge	Otsego	NY	West Barnstable	Barnstable	MA	West Chehalem	Yam Hill	OR
Wellsburgh	Wells	IN	West Barre	Orleans	NY	West Chelmsford	Middlesex	MA

PLACE NAMES OF THE UNITED STATES

PLACE	COUNTY	STATE	PLACE	COUNTY	STATE	PLACE	COUNTY	STATE
West Chenango	Broome	NY	Westerville	Franklin	OH	Westham Locks	Henrico	VA
West Cheshire	New Haven	CN	West Exeter	Otsego	NY	West Hamden	Penobscot	ME
Westchester	New London	CN	West Fairfield	Westmoreland	PA	West Hampstead	Rockingham	NH
Westchester	Jay	IN	West Fairlee	Orange	VT	West Hampton	Hampshire	MA
West Chester	Wabashaw	MN	West Fairview	Cumberland	PA	West Hampton	Suffolk	NY
West Chester	Westchester	NY	West Falls	Erie	NY	West Hanover	Plymouth	MA
West Chester	Butler	OH	West Falmouth	Cumberland	ME	West Hanover	Dauphin	PA
West Chester	Chester	PA	West Farmingdale	Kennebec	ME	West Harpswell	Cumberland	ME
West Chesterfield	Hampshire	MA	West Farmington	Ontario	NY	West Hartford	Hartford	CN
West Chesterfield	Cheshire	NH	West Farms	Westchester	NY	West Hartford	Ralls	MO
West Claremont	Sullivan	NH	West Fayette	Seneca	NY	West Hartford	Windsor	VT
West Clarksville	Allegahany	NY	Westfield	Clark	IL	West Hartland	Hartford	CN
West Colesville	Broome	NY	Westfield	Worth	IA	West Hartland	Barnstalbe	MA
West Columbia	Mason	WV	Westfield	Aroostook	ME	West Haven	New Haven	CN
West Concord	Merrimack	NH	Westfield	Hampden	MA	West Haven	Shiawassee	MI
West Conesville	Schoharie	NY	Westfield	Pope	MN	West Haven	Rutland	VT
West Constable	Franklin	NY	Westfield	Union	NJ	West Haverford	Delaware	PA
West Copake	Columbia	NY	Westfield	Chautauqua	NY	West Hawley	Franklin	MA
West Corinna	Penobscot	ME	Westfield	Stokes	NC	West Hayden	Franklin	OH
West Corinth	Orange	VT	Westfield	Morrow	OH	West Hebron	Washington	NY
West Cornville	Somerset	MO	Westfield	Tioga	PA	West Henniker	Merrimack	NH
West Cornwall	Litchfield	CN	Westfield	Orleans	VT	West Henrietta	Monroe	NY
West Cornwall	Addison	VT	Westfield	Marquette	WI	West Hickory	Forest	PA
West Covington	Tioga	PA	West Finley	Washington	PA	West Hoboken	Hudson	NJ
West Creek	Lake	IN	West Fitchburg	Worcester	MA	West Hoosick	Rensselaer	NY
West Creek	Republic	KS	West Florence	Preble	OH	West Hope	Henry	OH
West Creek	Ocean	NJ	Westford	Windham	CN	West Hopkinton	Merrimack	NH
West Cumberland	Cumberland	ME	Westford	Middlesex	MA	West Hurley	Ulster	NY
West Damascus	Wayne	PA	Westford	Otsega	NY	West Independence	Hancock	OH
West Danby	Tompkins	NY	Westford	Chittenden	VT	West Irving	Tama	IA
West Danvers	Essex	MA	Westford	Dodge	WI	West Jasper	Steuben	NY
West Danville	Caledonia	VT	West Fork	Washington	AR	West Jefferson	Madison	OH
West Davenport	Delaware	NY	West Fork	Crawford	IN	West Jersey	Stark	IL
West Day	Saratoga	NY	West Fork	Monona	IA	West Jordan	Sal Lake	UT
West Dayton	Webster	IA	West Fork	Howell	MO	West Junius	Seneca	NY
West Dacatur	Clearfield	PA	West Fork	Overton	TN	West Kendall	Orleans	NY
West Dedham	Norfolk	MA	West Fork Furnace	Floyd	VA	West Kill	Greene	NY
West Deering	Hillsborough	NH	West Fort Ann	Washington	NY	West Killingly	Windham	CN
West Deer Isle	Hancock	ME	West Foxborough	Norfolk	MA	West Kinderhook	Tipton	IN
West Dennis	Barstable	MA	West Franklin	Bradford	PA	West Kortright	Delaware	NY
West Derby	Orleans	VT	West Freedom	Clarion	PA	West La Fayette	Coshocton	OH
West Dover	Piscataquis	ME	West Freehold	Monmouth	NJ	West Lake	Kandiyohi	MN
West Dresden	Lincoln	ME	West Friendship	Howard	MD	West Lancaster	Fayette	OH
West Dryden	Tompkins	NY	West Fulton	Schoharie	NY	Westland	Hdancock	IN
West Dublin	Fulton	PA	West Galway	Fulton	NY	West Laurens	Otsego	NY
West Dudley	Worchester	MA	West Gardiner	Kennebec	ME	West Lebanon	Warren	IN
West Dummerston	Windham	VT	West Garland	Penboscot	ME	West Lebanon	York	ME
West Durham	Androscoggin	ME	West Geneva	Van Buren	MI	West Lebanon	Grafton	NH
West Duxbury	Plymouth	MA	West Georgia	Franklin	VT	West Lebanon	Columbia	NY
West Earl	Lancaster	PA	West Gloucester	Cumberland	ME	West Lebanon	Wayne	OH
West Eaton	Madison	NY	West Cloucester	Essx	MA	West Lebanon	Indiana	PA
West Eau Claire	Eau Claire	WI	West Glover	Orleans	VT	West Leeds	Androscoggin	ME
West Eden	Hancock	ME	West Gorham	Cumberland	ME	West Lenox	Susquehanna	PA
West Edmeston	Otsego	NY	West Goshen	Litchfield	CN	West Leroy	Calhoun	MI
West Elizabeth	Allegheny	PA	W Gouldsbor.	Hancock	ME	West Levant	Penobscot	ME
West Elkton	Preble	OH	West Granby	Hartford	CN	West Leyden	Lewis	NY
West Ellsworth	Hancock	MO	W Granville Crns.	Washington	NY	West Liberty	Howard	IN
West Embden	Somerset	ME	West Granville	Hampden	MA	West Liberty	Muscatine	IA
West End	Bedford	PA	West Granville	Milwaukee	WI	West Liberty(c.h.)	Morgan	FL
West Enfield	Penobscot	ME	West Great Works	Penobscot	ME	West Liberty	Putnam	MO
West Enfield	Grafton	NH	West Greece	Monroe	NY	West Libery	Logan	OH
West Enosburgh	Franklin	VT	West Greene	Erie	PA	West Liberty	Butler	PA
West Epping	Rockingham	NH	West Greenfield	Saratoga	NY	West Lima	Richland	WI
Westerlo	Albany	NY	West Green Lake	Green Lake	WI	West Lodi	Seneca	OH
Westerly	Washington	RI	W Greenwich Ctr.	Kent	RI	West Louisville	Daviess	KY
Western	Saline	NE	West Greenwood	Crawford	PA	West Lubec	Washington	ME
Western College	Linn	IA	West Groton	Middlesex	MA	West Lyons	Cook	IL
Western Park	Howard	KS	West Groton	Tompkins	NY	West Macedon	Wayne	NY
Western Port	Alleghany	MD	West Grove	Davis	IA	West Magnolia	Rock	WI
Western Saratoga	Union	IL	West Grove Station	Chester	PA	West Manchester	Preble	OH
Western Star	Summitt	OH	West Halifax	Windham	VT	West Mansfield	Bristol	MA
Westernville	Oneida	NY	West Hallock	Peoria	IL	West Mansfield	Logan	OH
Westerville	Dacatur	IA	West Hanburgh	Erie	NY	West Marlborough	Windham	VT

PLACE NAMES OF THE UNITED STATES

PLACE	COUNTY	STATE	PLACE	COUNTY	STATE	PLACE	COUNTY	STATE
West Martinsburgh	Lewis	NY	Westonburgh	Crittenden	KY	West Rutland	Rutland	VT
West Medford	Middlesex	MA	West Oneonta	Otsego	NY	West Saint Paul	Dakota	MN
West Medway	Norfolk	MA	West Ossipee	Carroll	NH	West Salem	Edwards	IL
West Meredith	Delaware	NY	West Otis	Berkshire	MA	West Salem	Wayne	OH
West Meriden	New Haven	CN	Westover	Somerset	MD	West Salem	Mercer	PA
West Middleburgh	Logan	OH	Westover's	Clearfield	PA	West Salem	La Crosse	WI
West Middlesex	Mercer	PA	West Overton	Westmoreland	PA	West Salisbury	Merrimack	NH
West Middleton	Dane	WI	West Paris	Oxford	ME	West Salisbury	Addison	VT
West Middletown	Washington	PA	West Parsonfield	York	ME	West Sand Lake	Rensslaer	NY
West Milan	Monroe	MI	West Pawlet	Rutland	VT	West Sandwich	Barnstable	MA
West Milford	Passaic	NJ	West Pembroke	Washington	ME	West Schuyler	Herkimer	NY
West Milford	Harrison	WV	West Penn	Schuylkill	PA	West Scituate	Plymouth	MA
West Milbury	Worcester	MA	West Pensaukie	Oconto	WI	West Sebewa	Ionia	MI
West Mill Grove	Wood	OH	West Perth	Fulton	NY	West Seneca	Erie	NY
West Milton	Stafford	NH	West Peru	Oxford	ME	West Seneca Centre	Erie	NY
West Milton	Saratoga	NY	West Peterborough	Hillsborough	NH	West Shelby	Orleans	NY
West Milton	Miami	OH	Westphalia	Clinton	MI	Westside	Crawford	IA
West Milton	Union	PA	Westphalia	Oswate	MO	West's Mills	Franklin	ME
West Milton	Chittenden	VT	West Pike	Potter	PA	West's Mill	Seward	NE
West Minot	Androsoggin	ME	West Pittsfield	Somerset	ME	West Somers	Westchester	NY
Westminster	Windham	CN	West Pittsfield	Berkshire	MA	West Somerset	Niagra	NY
Westminster(c.h.)	Carroll	MD	West Plains(c.h.)	Howell	MO	West Sonora	Preble	OH
Westminister	Worcester	MA	West Plattsburgh	Clinton	NY	West Spring Creek	Warren	PA
Westminister	Guilford	NC	West Plymouth	Grafton	NY	West Springfield	Hampden	MA
Westminister	Allen	OH	West Point	White	AR	West Springfield	Sullivan	NH
Westminister	Windham	VT	West Point	Calaveras	CA	West Springfield	Erie	PA
Westminister Depot	Worcester	MA	West Point	Troup	GA	West's Station	Holmes	MS
Westminster West	Windham	VT	West Point	Hancock	IL	West Stafford	Tolland	CN
West Mitchell	Mitchell	IA	West Point	Tippecanoe	IN	West Stephentown	Rensslaer	NY
West Monroe	Oswego	NY	West Point	Lee	IA	West Sterling	Worcester	MA
West Monterey	Clarion	PA	West Point	Hardin	KY	West Stewartstown	Coos	NH
Westmore	Orleans	VT	West Point	Lowndes	MS	West Stockbridge	Berkshire	MA
Westmoreland	Pottawatomie	KS	West Point	Bares	MO	W. Stockbridge Ctr.	B'kshire	MA
Westmoreland	Cheshire	NJ	West Point	Orange	NY	West Stockholm	St. Lawrence	NY
Westmoreland	Oneida	NY	West Point	Cuming	NE	West Suffield	Hartford	CN
Westmoreland Dpt.	Cheshire	NH	West Point	Columbiana	OH	West Sumner	Oxford	ME
West Mount Vernon	Kennebec	MO	West Point	Lawrence	TN	West Sutton	Worchester	MA
West Nanticoke	Luzerne	PA	West Point	Rio Virgin	UT	West Swanzey	Cheshire	NH
West Newart	Tioga	NY	West Point	King William	VA	West Taghkanick	Columbia	NY
West New Brighton	Richmond	NY	West Point	Columbia	WI	West Thompson	Windham	CN
West Newbury	Essex	MA	West Poland	Androscoggin	ME	West Thornton	Grafton	NH
West Newbury	Orange	VT	Westport	Fairfield	CN	West Tisbury	Dukes	MA
West Newfield	York	ME	Westport	Decatur	IN	West Topsham	Orange	VT
West Newfield	Orleans	VT	Westport	Oldham	KY	West Town	Orange	NY
West Newport	Orleans	VT	Westport	Lincoln	ME	West Townsend	Middlesex	MA
West Newton	Marion	IN	Westport	Bristol	MS	West Townshend	Windham	VT
West Newton	Middlesex	MS	Westport	Jackson	MO	West Township	Albany	NY
West Newton	Nicollet	MN	Westport	Cheshire	NH	West Trenton	Hancock	ME
West Newton	Allen	OH	Westport	Essex	NY	West Troupsburgh	Steuben	NY
West Newton	Westmoreland	PA	Westport	Clatsop	OR	West Troy	Waldo	ME
West Norfolk	Litchfield	CN	Westport	Clinton	PA	West Troy	Albany	NY
West Northfield	Cook	IL	Westport	Dane	WI	West Union(c.h.)	Fayette	IA
West Northfield	Franklin	MA	Westport Point	Bristol	MA	West Union	Owen	KY
West Norwalk	Fairfield	CN	West Potsday	St. Lawrence	NY	West Union	Cass	MO
West Nottingham	Rockingham	RI	West Pownal	Cumberland	ME	West Union	Steuben	NY
West Novi	Oakland	MI	West Prairie	Linn	IA	West Union(c.h.)	Adams	OH
West Odgen	Lenawee	MI	West Prairie	Dunklin	MO	West Union(c.h.)	Doddridge	WV
West Olive	Ottawa	MI	West Prairie	Vernon	WI	West Unity	Williams	OH
Weston	Fairfield	CN	West Providence	Saratoga	NY	West Upton	Worcester	MA
Weston	McLeon	IL	Westralia	Montgomery	KS	West Vale	Middlesex	MA
Weston	NIcholas	KY	West Randolph	Orange	VT	West Valley	Cattaraugus	NY
Weston	Aroostook	ME	West Redding	Fairfield	CN	West Valley	Armstrong	PA
Weston	Middlesex	MA	West Richfield	Summit	OH	West Vienna	Oneida	NY
Weston	Lenawee	MI	West Richmondville	Schoharie	NY	West View	Cuyahoga	OH
Weston	Platte	MO	West River	Anne Arundel	MD	West View	Allegheny	PA
Weston	Somerset	NJ	West Rochester	Windsor	VT	Westville	Dale	AL
Weston	Schuyler	NY	West Rosendale	Fond du Lac	WI	Westville	New Haven	CN
Weston	Wood	OH	West Roxbury	Norfolk	MA	Westville	La Porte	IN
Weston	Umatilla	OR	West Romney	Grafton	NH	Westville(c.h.)	Simpson	MS
Weston	Collin	TX	West Rupert	Bennington	VT	Westville	Chartion	MO
Weston	Cache	UT	West Rush	Monroe	NY	Westville	Gloucester	NJ
Weston	Windsor	VT	West Rushville	Fairfield	OH	Westville	Otsego	NY
Weston(c.h.)	Lewis	WV	West Rutland	Worcester	MA	Westville	Champaign	OH

PLACE NAMES OF THE UNITED STATES

PLACE	COUNTY	STATE	PLACE	COUNTY	STATE	PLACE	COUNTY	STATE
Westville Centre	Franklin	NY	Wheatland	Keosha	WI	White Hall	Baltimore	MD
West Vincent	Chester	PA	Wheatland Centre	Hillsdale	MI	Whitehall	Nuskegon	MI
West Walworth	Wayne	NY	Wheatland Furnace	Mercer	PA	Whitehallville	Bucks	PA
West Wardsborough	Windham	VT	Wheatland Mills	Lancaster	PA	Whitehaven	Wicomico	MD
West Wareham	Plymouth	MA	Wheaton(c.h.)	Du Page	IL	White Haven	Erie	NY
West Warren	Bradford	PA	Wheaton	Montgomery	MD	White Haven	Luzerne	PA
West Warren	Worcester	MA	Wheatonville	Warrick	IN	White Haven	Shelby	TN
West Washington	Knox	ME	Wheat Ridge	Adams	OH	Whitehead's Store	Pittsylvania	VA
West Waterford	Caledonia	VT	Wheat Sheaf	Philadelphia	PA	White Horn	Hawkins	TN
West Waterville	Kennebec	ME	Wheatville	Miami	IN	White Horse	Chester	PA
West Watson	Allegan	MI	Wheatville	Genesee	NY	White Horse	Greenville	SC
West Webster	Monroe	NY	Wheatville	Titus	TX	White Horse	Hunterdon	NJ
West Whiteland	Chester	PA	Wheatville	Crawford	WI	White House	Randolph	NC
West Williamsfield	Ashtabula	OH	Wheeler	Potter	IN	White House	Lucas	OH
West Willington	Tolland	CN	Wheeler	Grratiot	MI	White House	Mecklenburgh	VA
West Wilton	Hillsborough	NH	Wheeler	Steuben	NY	White House Station	Hunterdon	NJ
West Windham	Rockingham	NY	Wheeler	Mercer	PA	White Lake	Oakland	MI
West Windham	Bradford	PA	Wheelersburgh	Scoito	OH	White Lake	Sullivan	NY
West Windham	Eaton	MI	Wheeler's Grove	Pottawattomie	IA	Whiteland	Johnson	IN
West Windsor	Broome	NY	Wheeler Station	Lawrence	AL	Whiteley	Greene	PA
West Windsor	Richland	OH	Wheelersville	Northampton	NC	Whiteleysburgh	Caroline	MD
West Winfield	Herkimer	NY	Wheeling	Cook	IL	White Lick	Boone	IN
West Winsted	Litchfield	CN	Wheeling	Delaware	IN	White Lick	Laurel	KY
West Winterprot	Waldo	ME	Wheeling	Marion	IA	White Marsh	Montgomery	PA
Westwood	Bergin	NY	Wheeling	Winn	LA	White Mills	Hardin	KY
Westwood	Erie	NY	Wheeling	Rice	MN	White Mills	Jewell	KS
West Woodstock	Windham	CN	Wheeling	Livingston	MO	White Mound	Jewell	KS
West Woodville	Clermont	OH	Wheeling(c.h.)	Ohio	WV	White Mound	Sauk	WI
West Worthington	Hampshire	MA	Wheelock	Choctaw Nation	IT	White Mt. Home	Coos	NH
West Wrentham	Norfolk	MA	Wheelock	Robertson	TX	White Oak	Jefferson	AR
West Yarmouth	Barnstable	MA	Wheelock	Caledonia	VT	White Oak	Columbia	GA
West Yorkshire	Cattaraugus	NY	Whetham	Clinton	PA	White Oak	Columbia	IL
West Zanesville	Muskingham	OH	Whetstone	Morrow	OH	White Oak	Montgomery	IL
Wetazug	Pulaski	IL	Whetstone Agency		DA	White Oak	Mahaska	IA
Wet Glaze	Camden	MO	Whig Valley	Holt	MO	White Oak	Ingam	MI
Wetheredville	Baltimore	MD	Whigville	Noble	OH	White Oak	Lancaster	PA
Wethersfield	Hartford	CN	Whilden's Factory	Greenville	SC	White Oak	Hopkins	TX
Wethersfield	Henry	IL	Whippany	Moris	NJ	White Oak	Richie	WV
Wethersfield	Wyoming	NY	Whippoorwill	Laurel	KY	White Oak Gap	Pulaski	KY
Wethersfield Springs	Wyoming	NY	Whistler	Mobile	AL	White Oak Springs	Barbour	AL
Wetmore	Nemaha	KS	Whitaker's	Edgecombe	NC	White Oak Springs	Brown	IL
Wetmore	Pike	OH	Whitcomb	Franklin	IN	White Oak Springs	Lee	VA
Wetumpka(c.h.)	Elmore	Al	White Ash	Allegheny	PA	White Oak Springs	La Fayette	WI
Wever	Lee	OH	White Bear Centre	Pope	MN	White Pigeon	Keokuk	IA
Weverton	Washington	MD	White Bear Lake	Ramsey	MN	White Pigeon	St. Joseph	MI
Weverton	Washington	MD	White Bird	Idaho	ID	White Pine	Lycoming	PA
Weverton	Warren	NY	White Bluff	Dallas	AL	White Plains	Calhoun	AL
We Wo Ka	Seninnole	IT	White Bluffs	Dickson	fN	White Plains	Calhoun	AL
Wexford	Wexford	MI	White Breast	Lucas	IA	White Plains	Greene	GA
Wexford	Allegheny	PA	White Church	Wyandotte	KS	White Plains	Christian	KY
Weyauwega	Waupace	WI	White Church	Erie	PA	White Plains(c.h.)	Westchester	NY
Weybridge Falls	Addison	VT	White Cloud	Mills	IA	White Plains	Cleveland	NC
Weymouth	Norfolk	MA	White Cloud	Doniphan	KS	White Plains	Chesterfield	SC
Weymouth	Atlantic	NJ	White Cloud	Nodaway	MO	White Plains	Putnam	TN
Weymouth	Medina	OH	White Cottage	Muskingham	OH	White Plains	Brunswick	VA
Whalan	Fillmore	MN	White Cottage	Greene	PA	White Pond	Barbour	AL
Whaleysville	Worcester	MD	White Cottage	Jackson	IN	White Pond	Barnwell	SC
Whallonsburgh	Essex	NY	White Creek	Washington	NY	White Post	Clarke	VA
Wharton	Potter	PA	White Creek	Adams	WI	White River	Desha	AR
Wharton(c.h.)	Wharton	TX	White Cross	Orange	NC	White River	Muskegon	MI
Whatonsburgh	Wydot	OH	White Day	Monomgalia	WV	White River	King	WA
What Cheer	Kiokuk	IA	White Deer Mills	Union	PA	White River Jnct.	Windsor	VT
Whateon(c.h.)	Whatcom	WI	White Earth	Becker	MN	White Road	Forsyth	NC
Wately	Franklin	MA	White Eyes Plains	Coshocton	OH	White Rock	Ogle	IL
Wheatfield	Sangamon	IL	Whitefield	Lincoln	ME	White Rock	Republic	KS
Wheatfield	Yuba	CO	Whitefield	Oktibbeha	MS	White Rock	Cumberland	ME
Wheatland	El Paso	CO	Whitefield	Coos	NH	White Rock	Huron	MI
Wheatland	Knox	IN	Whiteford Centre	Monroe	MI	White Rock	Elko	NV
Wheatland	Clinton	IA	White Gate	Giles	VA	White Rock	Hunt	TX
Wheatland	Rice	MN	Whitehall	Yankton	DA	White Rock Prairie	McDonald	MO
Wheatland	Hickory	MO	White Hall	Greene	IL	White Salmon	Klikitat	WA
Wheatland	Yam Hill	OR	White Hall	Owen	IN	White Sand	Lawrence	MS
Wheatland	Loudoun	VA	White Hall	Madison	KY	Whitesborough	Harrison	IA

PLACE	COUNTY	STATE	PLACE	COUNTY	STATE	PLACE	COUNTY	STATE
Whitesborough	Grayson	TX	Wittle's Mills	Mecklenburgh	VA	Williamson	Wayne	NY
Whitesborough	Madison	AL	Wichita(c.h.)	Sedgwick	KS	Willamsonville	Door	WI
Whitesburgh(c.h.)	Harrison	IA	Wick	Tyler	WV	Williamsport(c.h.)	Warren	IN
Whitesburgh	Letcher	KY	Wickenburgh	Yavapai	AZ	Williamsport	Washington	MD
Whitesburgh	Genesee	MI	Wickford	Washington	RI	Williamsport	Pickaway	OH
Whitesburgh	Armstrong	PA	Wickle's Store	Macon	NC	Williamsport(c.h.)	Lycoming	PA
Whitesburgh	Hamblen	TN	Wickliffe	Crawford	IN	Williamsport(c.h.)	Naury	TN
White's Corner	Waldo	ME	Wickliffe	Jackson	IA	Williamsport	Grant	WV
White's Corners	Erie	NY	Wickliffe	Lake	OH	Williams' Station	Escambia	AL
White's Creek	Wayne	WV	Wicomico Church	Northumberland	VA	Williams' Store	Casey	KY
Whiteside	Marion	TN	Wiconisco	Dauphia	PA	Williamston(c.h.)	Martin	NC
White Shoals	Lee	VA	Wideman's	Abbeville	SC	Williams' Store	Westmoreland	PA
White's Mills	Logan	WV	Wiess Bluff	Jasper	TX	Williamston	Anderson	SC
White Spring	Hamilton	FL	Wilbar	Wilkes	NC	Williamston	Chickasaw	IA
White's Station	Calhoun	MI	Wilborn	Madison	IL	Williamston	Jefferson	KS
White's Station	Shelby	TN	Wilbraham	Manpden	MS	Williamston	Grant	KY
White's Store	Chennango	NY	Wilbur	Ulster	NY	Williamston	Berkshire	MA
White's Tannery	Monroe	PA	Wilbur	Douglas	OR	Williamston	Ingham	MI
Whitestone	Queens	NY	Wilcox	Elk	PA	Williamston	Lewis	MO
Whitestown	Boone	IN	Wilcox Wharf	Charles City	VA	Williamston	Camden	NJ
Whitestown	Oneida	NY	Wildbrier	Chester	PA	Williamston	Osewgo	NY
Whitestown	Butler	PA	Wild Cat	Carroll	IN	Williamston	Hancock	OH
White Sulphus	Scott	KY	Wild Cat	Riley	KS	Williamston	Dauphin	PA
White Sulphur	Delaware	OH	Wild Cat	Whitley	KY	Williamston	Orange	VT
White Sulphur Spr.	Jefferson	AR	Wild Cat	Lancaster	SC	Williamston	Wood	WV
White Sulphur Spr.	Meriwether	GA	Wilderness	Spottsylvania	VT	Williamsville	Sanganmon	IL
White Sulphur Spr.	Catahoula	LA	Wiley	Green	PA	Williamsville	Cass	MI
White Sulphur Spr.	Greenbrier	WV	Wiley's Cove	Searcy	AR	Williamsville	Richarson	NE
White's Valley	Wayne	PA	Wiley Station	Darke	OH	Williamsville	Erie	NY
Whitesville	Harris	GA	Wileysville	Steuben	NY	Williamsville	Elk	PA
Whitesville	Montgomery	IN	Wilkesbarre(c.h.)	Luzerne	PA	Williamsville	Windham	VT
Whitesville	Daviess	KY	Wilkesborough(c.h.)	Wilkes	NC	Williamsville	Bath	VA
Whitesville	Andrew	MO	Wilkesville	Vinton	OH	Williamsville	Hampden	MA
Whitesville	Allegany	NY	Wilkins	Allegheny	PA	Willmantic	Windham	CN
Whitesville(c.h.)	Columbus	NC	Wilkinsburgh	Allegheny	PA	Willington	Tolland	CN
Whitesville	Halifax	VA	Wilkinson's Shop	Amelia	VA	Willington	Abbeville	SC
White Swan	Charles Mix	DA	Wilkins Run	Licking	OH	Willink	Erie	NY
Whiteville	Marion	AR	Willamette Forks	Lane	OR	Willisburgh	Washington	KY
Whiteville	Hardeman	TN	Willard	Greene	MO	Willis Station	Fayette	TN
White Water	Pike	AL	Willard	Seneca	NY	Williston	Erie	NY
White Water	Fayette	GA	Willard	Box Elder	UT	Williston	Potter	PA
White Water	Wayne	IN	Willard's Landing	Union	IL	Williston	Barnwell	SC
White Water	Butler	KS	Willet	Cortland	NY	Williston	Chittenden	VT
Whitewater	Walworth	WI	Willet	Indiana	PA	Willistown Inn	Chester	PA
White Water Falls	Winona	MN	Willet	Green	WI	Wilmer	Kandiyohi	MN
White Willow	Kendall	IL	Willettville	Highland	OH	Willmathsville	Adair	MO
Whiting	Escambia	AL	Willey	Carroll	NY	Willoughby	Butler	IA
Whiting	Lake	IN	Willey	Preston	WV	Willoughby	Lake	OH
Whiting	Jackson	KS	Willey's Station	Christian	IL	Willoughby Lake	Orleans	VT
Whiting	Washington	ME	William Penn	Montgomery	PA	Willow	Jo Daviess	IL
Whiting	Ocean	NJ	Williams	Hamilton	IA	Willow Branch	Hancock	IN
Whiting	Addison	VT	Williams	Christian	KY	Willow Brook	Dutchess	NY
Whitingham	Windham	VT	Williams	Bay	MI	Willow Creek	Lee	IL
Whiting Station	Addison	VT	Williamsburgh	Jefferson	FL	Willow Creek	Clay	IA
Whitinsville	Worcester	MA	Williamsburgh	Wayne	IN	Willow Creek	Blue Earth	MN
Whitley(c.h.)	Whitley	KY	Williamsburgh	Wapello	IA	Willow Creek	Gallatin	MT
Whitley's Point	Moultrie	IL	Williamsburgh	Franklin	KS	Willow Dale	Ida	IA
Whitleyville	Jackson	TN	Williamsburgh	Piscaquais	ME	Willowdale	Chester	PA
Whitlock	Halifax	VA	Williamsburgh	Dorchester	MD	Willowdale	Sulivan	NY
Whitman	Lowndes	AL	Williamsburgh	Hampshire	MA	Willow Grove	Montgomery	PA
Whitman	Walla-Walla	WA	Williamsburgh	Grand Traverse	MI	Willow Grove	Shelby	TX
Whitmell	Pittsylvania	VA	Williamburgh(c.h.)	Covington	MS	Willow Hill	Jasper	IL
Whitmire's	Newberry	SC	Williamsburgh	Calloway	MO	Willow Hole	Madison	TX
Whitmore Lake	Washtenaw	MI	Williamsburgh	Kings	NY	Willow Island	Plesants	WV
Whitney	Boulder	CO	Williamsburgh	Iredell	NC	Willow Ranch	Siskiyou	CA
Whitney's X-ing	Allegany	NY	Williamsburgh	Clermont	OH	Willow Shade	Metcalfe	KY
Whitney's Point	Broome	NY	Williamsburgh	Blair	PA	Willow Spring	Cook	IL
Whitneyville	Cass	IA	Williamsburgh(c.h.)	James City	VA	Willow Spring	Russell	VA
Whitneyville	Washington	ME	Williamsburgh	Trempealeau	WI	Willow Spring	Douglas	KS
Whittier	Lake	IL	Williams Centre	Williams	OH	Willow Springs	Howell	MO
Whittington	Hot Spring	AR	Williamsfield	Ashtabula	OH	Willow Springs	Jackson	OR
Whittle	Washington	GA	Williams' Grove	Clearfield	PA	Willow Springs	Columbia	PA
Whittlesey	Medina	OH	William's Mill	Roane	TN	Willow Street	Lancaster	PA

PLACE	COUNTY	STATE
Willow Tree	Greene	PA
Willow Tree	Mason	WV
Willow Valley	Greenwood	KS
Willow Wood	Lawrence	OH
Willsborough	Essex	NY
Wills' Creek	Coshocton	OH
Willseyville	Tioga	NY
Willshire	Van Wert	OH
Will's Ridge	Floyd	VA
Wilmarth	Elk	PA
Wilmette	Cook	IL
Wilmington	Walker	AL
Wilmington	Union	Ar
Wilmington	Los Angeles	CA
Wilmington	New Castle	DE
Wilmington	Will	IL
Wilminton	Dearborn	IN
Wilmington	Osage	KS
Wilmington	Middlesex	MA
Wilmington	Houston	MN
Wilmington	Essex	NY
Wilmington(c.h.)	New Hanover	NC
Wilmington(c.h.)	Clinton	OH
Wilmington	Windham	VT
Wilmington	Pluvanna	VA
Wilmore	Cambria	PA
Wilmot	Noble	IN
Wilmot	Merrimack	NH
Wilmot	Stark	OH
Wilmot	Bradford	PA
Wilmot	Kenosha	WI
Wilmot Flat	Merrimack	NH
Wilna	Jefferson	NY
Wilna	Harford	MD
Wilseyville	Defiance	OH
Wilson	Yavapai	AZ
Wilson	Montgomery	IA
Wilson	Adair	MO
Wilson	Otoe	NE
Wilson	Niagara	NY
Wilson(c.h.)	Wilson	NC
Wilson	Adams	OH
Wilsonburgh	Richland	IL
Wilsonburgh	Harrison	WV
Wilson Creek	Tioga	NY
Wilson Grove	Fayette	OH
Wilson's	Anderson	TN
Wilson's Xing	Rockiangham	NY
Wilson's X Roads	Hempstead	AR
Wilson's Depot	Dinwiddie	VA
Wilson's Landing	Charles City	VA
Wilson's Mills	Oxford	ME
Wilson's Mills	Johnston	NC
Wilson's Mills	Cuyahoga	OH
Wilson's Mills	Venango	PA
Wilson's Store	Dallas	AL
Wilson's Store	Stokes	NC
Wilsonville	Shelby	AL
Wilsonville	Windham	CN
Wilsonville	Spencer	KY
Wilsonville	Highland	VA
Wilton	Pike	AR
Wilton	Fairfield	CN
Wilton	Franklin	ME
Wilton(c.h.)	Waseca	MN
Wilton	Hillsborough	NH
Wilton	Saratoga	NY
Wilton(c.h.)	Granville	NC
Wilton	Ellis	TX
Wilton	Monroe	WI
Wilton Junction	Muscatine	IA
Winamac(c.h.)	Pulaski	IN
Winameg	Fulton	OH
Winchendon	Worcester	MA
Winchester(c.h.)	Randolph	IN
Winchester(c.h.)	Scott	IL
Winchester	Van Buren	IA
Winchester(c.h.)	Clarke	KY
Winchester	Jefferson	KS
Winchester	Middlesex	MD
Winchester	Wayne	MS
Winchester	Clarke	MO
Winchester	Cheshire	NH
Winchester	Union	NC
Winchester	Guernsey	OH
Winchester	Fayette	TX
Winchester(c.h.)	Franklin	TN
Winchester(c.h.)	Frederick	VA
Winchester	Winnebago	WE
Winchester Centre	Litchfield	CN
Windermere	Tolland	CN
Windfall	Tipton	IN
Wind Gap	Northampton	PA
Windham	Windham	CN
Windham	Cumberland	ME
Windham	Rockingham	NH
Windham	Portage	OH
Windham	Bradford	PA
Windham	Windham	VT
Windham Centre	Greene	NY
Windham Centre	Bradford	PA
Windham Depot	Rockingham	NH
Windham Station	Portage	OH
Windham Summit	Bradford	PA
Windom	Cottonwood	MN
Wind Ridge	Greene	PA
Windsor	Sonoma	CA
Windsor	Hartford	CN
Windsor	Shelby	IL
Windsor	Randolph	IN
Windsor	Ottawa	KS
Windsor	Kennebec	ME
Windsor	Berkshire	MA
Windsor	Eaton	MI
Windsor	Henry	MO
Windsor	Mercer	NJ
Windsor	Broome	NY
Windsor	Ashtabula	OH
Windsor(c.h.)	Bertie	NC
Windsor	York	PA
Windsor	Barnwell	SC
Windsor	Windsor	VT
Windsor	Dane	WI
Windsor Castle	Berks	PA
Windsor Locks	Hartford	CN
Windsor Station	Isle of Wight	VA
Windsorville	Hartford	CN
Winesburgh	Holmes	OH
Winfield	Du Page	IL
Winfield	Columbia	GA
Winfield	Lake	IN
Winfield	Henry	IA
Winfield(c.h.)	Cowley	KS
Winfield(c.h.)	Winn	LA
Winfield	Carroll	MD
Winfield	Ingham	MI
Winfield	Herkimer	NY
Winfield	Tuscarawas	OH
Winfield	Union	PA
Winfield	Scott	TN
Winfield(c.h.)	Putnam	WV
Wingos Station	Graves	KY
Wingville	Baker	OR
Winhall	Bennington	VT
Winn	Penobscot	ME
Winn	Isabella	MI
Winnebago	Winnebago	IL
Winnebago	Dakota	NE
Winnebago Agency	Blue Earth	MN
Winnebago City	Faribault	MN
Winnebago Depot	Winnebago	IL
Winneconne	Winnebago	WI
Winnegance	Sagadahoc	ME
Winnnemucca	Humbolt	NV
Winnetka	Cook	IL
Winnipauk	Fairfield	CN
Winnsborough(c.h.)	Franklin	LA
Winnsborough(c.h.)	Fairfield	SC
Winnton	Gozales	TX
Winona	Henry	IA
Winona	Trimble	KY
Winona(c.h.)	Winona	MN
Winona(c.h.)	Montgomery	MS
Winona	Pitt	NC
Winona	Columbiana	OH
Wionooski	Sheboygan	WI
Winooski Falls	Chittenden	VT
Winslow	Stephenson	IL
Winslow	Pike	IN
Winslow	Kennebec	ME
Winslow	De Kalb	MO
Winslow	Camden	NJ
Winsor	Kane	UT
Winspear	Erie	NY
Winsted	Litchfield	CN
Winsted Lake	McLead	MN
Winston	Estill	KY
Winston	Dent	MO
Winston	Forsyth	NC
Winter Harbor	Hancock	ME
Winterpock	Chesterfield	VA
Winterpock	Waldo	ME
Winterround	Shelby	IN
Winterrowd	Effingham	IL
Winterset(c.h.)	Madison	IA
Winter's Station	Sandusky	OH
Wintersville	Decature	IN
Wintersville	Sullivan	MO
Wintersville	Jefferson	OH
Wintersville	Berks	PA
Winterton	Sullivan	NY
Winterville	Oglethorpe	GA
Winthrop	Middlesex	CN
Winthrop	Buchanan	IA
Winthrop	Kennebec	ME
Winthrop	Suffolk	MA
Winthrop	Buchanan	MO
Winton(c.h.)	Hertford	NC
Winton Place	Hamilton	OH
Wiota	Isbella	MI
Wiota	La Fayette	WI
Wiretown	Ocean	NJ
Wirt	Jefferson	IN
Wirt(c.h.)	Wirt	WV
Wirt Centre	Allegany	NY
Wirtonia	Cherokee	KS
Wiscasset(c.h.)	Lincoln	ME
Wiscoy	Winona	MN
Wiscoy	Allehany	NY
Wisdom's Store	Harris	GA
Wise(c.h.)	Wise	GA
Wiseville	Accmack	VA
Wistar	Clinton	PA
Withamsville	Clermont	OH
Withers' Mills	Marion	MO
Witherup's	Venango	PA
Wiktoka	Winona	MN
Witt	Montgomery	IL
Wittenberg	Alexander	NC

PLACE NAMES OF THE UNITED STATES

PLACE	COUNTY	STATE	PLACE	COUNTY	STATE	PLACE	COUNTY	STATE
Wittenberg	Alexander	NC	Woodbury	Wood	OH	Woodstock	Oxford	ME
Wittenberg	Somerset	PA	Woodbury	Bedford	PA	Woodstock	Howard	MD
Wittenburg	Perry	MO	Woodbury(c.h.)	Cannon	TN	Woodstock	Lenawee	MI
Witten's	Monroe	OH	Woodbury	Hill	TX	Woodstock	Grafton	NH
Wittman	Talbot	MD	Woodbury	Washinton	VT	Woodstock	Ulster	NY
Wittsburgh(c.h.)	Cross	AR	Woodcock	Crawford	PA	Woodstock	Champaign	OH
Witt's Foundry	Hamblin	TN	Woodensburgh	Baltimore	MD	Woodstock(c.h.)	Windsor	VT
Witt's Mills	Orangeburgh	SC	Woodford	Bennington	VT	Woodstock	Richland	WI
Witt Springs	Searcy	AR	Woodford	Barbour	WV	Woodstock(c.h.)	Shennandoah	VA
Woburn	Bond	IL	Woodford's	Alpine	CA	Woodstock Valley	Windham	CN
Woburn	Jackson	KS	Woodford's	Cumberland	ME	Woodstown	Salem	NJ
Woburn	Middlesex	MA	Wood Grove	Morgan	OH	Wrightstown	Burlington	NJ
Wolcott	New Haven	CN	Woodhaven	Queens	NY	Wrightstown	Bucks	PA
Wolcott	White	IN	Woodhull	Henry	IL	Wrightstown	Brown	WI
Wolcott	Scott	IA	Woodhull	Fond du Lac	WI	Wrightstown(c.h.)	Johnson	GA
Wolcott	Wayne	NY	Woodington	Darke	OH	Wrightsville	Greene	IL
Wolcott	Lamoille	VT	Wood Lake	Montcalm	MI	Wrightsville	York	PA
Wolcottsville	Niagara	NY	Woodland	Putnam	FL	Wrightsville	Jackson	WI
Wolcottsville	Litchfield	NY	Woodland	St. Joseph	IN	Wulstenville	Fremont	CO
Wolcottsville	La Grange	IN	Woodland	East Felicianna	LA	Wurtemburghd	Lawrence	PA
Wolcottsville	Independence	AR	Woodland	Talbot	MD	Wurtsborough	Sullivan	NY
Wolf Bayou	Independence	AR	Woodland	Barry	MI	Wyaconda	Scotlan	MO
Wolfborough	Carroll	NJ	Woodland	Wabashaw	MN	Wyalusing	Grant	WI
Wolfborough Centre	Carroll	NH	Woodland	Pulaski	MO	Wyandot	Wyandot	OH
Wolf Branch	Coffee	AL	Woodland	Ulster	NY	Wyandotte	Tippecanoe	IN
Wolf Creek	Pike	AR	Woodland	Northampton	NC	Wyandotte(c.h.)	Wyandotte	KS
Wolf Creek	Williamson	IL	Woodland	Union	OH	Wyandotte	Wayne	MI
Wolf Creek	Marshall	IN	Woodland	Clearfield	PA	Wyanet	Burnette	IL
Wolf Creek	Tama	IA	Woodland	Robertson	TX	Wyatt's Store	Mariposa	CA
Wolf Creek	Meade	KY	Woodland	Dodge	WI	Wyattville	Winona	MN
Wolf Creek	Wright	MO	Woodland Mills	Obion	TN	Wyckoff	Bergen	NJ
Wolf Creek	Cherokee	NC	Woodlands	Marshall	WV	Wye Mills	Talbot	MD
Wolf Creek	Mercer	PA	Woodlawn	Onachita	AR	Wykertown	Sussex	NJ
Wolf Creek	Scott	TN	Wood Lawn	Jefferson	IL	Wyliesburgh	Charlotte	VA
Wolf Creek	Monroe	WV	Woodlawn	Cecil	MD	Wynant	Shelby	OH
Wolfdale	Woodbury	IA	Woodlawn	Monroe	MO	Wynantskill	Rensselaer	NY
Wolf Glade	Carroll	VA	Wood Lawn	Carroll	VA	Wynn	Franklin	IN
Wolf Hill	Albany	NY	Woodleaf	Rowan	NC	Wynnville	Blount	AL
Wolf Island	Mississippi	MO	Woodman	Grant	WI	Wyocena	Columbia	WI
Wolf Lake	Noble	IN	Woodmansie	Burlington	NJ	Wyoming	Kent	DE
Wolf Run	Lycoming	PA	Wood Ridge	Albemarle	VA	Wyoming	Stark	IL
Wolf's Store	Centre	PA	Wood River	Hall	NE	Wyoming	Jones	IA
Wolf Summit	Harrison	WV	Wood River	Burnett	WI	Wyoming	Marshall	KS
Wolfsville	Frederick	MD	Woodrow	Washington	PA	Wyoming	Bath	KY
Wolfsville	Union	NC	Woodruff's	Sparanburgh	SC	Wyoming	Chisago	MN
Wolftown	Madison	VA	Woods	Panola	TX	Wyoming	Otoe	NE
Wolf Trap	Halifax	VA	Woodsborough	Frederick	MD	Wyoming	Wyoming	NY
Wollaston	Norfolk	MA	Wood's Corners	Ionia	MI	Wyoming	Luzerne	PA
Womelsdorf	Berks	PA	Wood's Cross	Davis	UT	Wyoming	Washington	RI
Wonders	Nacogdoches	TX	Wood's X Roads	Gloucester	VA	Wyoming	Iowa	WI
Wonewoc	Juneau	WI	Woodsdale	Person	NC	Wyoming	Albany	WY
Wood	Orange	NY	Woodsdale	Butler	OH	Wysox	Bradford	PA
Wood	Wood	WI	Wood's Falls	Clinton	NY	Wythe Depot	Shelby	TN
Woodard's	Fillmore	NE	Woodsfield(c.h.)	Monroe	OH	Wytheville(c.h.)	Wyathe	VA
Woodard's Landing	Chehalis	WA	Woodsfork	Wright	MO			
Woodbank	Marion	IN	Wood's Hill	Roane	TN	Xenia	Clay	IL
Woodberry	Baltimore	MD	Wood's Hole	Barnstable	MA	Xenia	Miami	IN
Woodbine	Harrison	IA	Woodside	San Mateo	CA	Xenia	Dallas	IA
Woodbine	Carroll	MD	Woodside	Kent	ME	Xenia	Bourbon	KS
Woodborne	Sullivan	NY	Woodside	Sangamon	IL	Xenia	Nodaway	MO
Woodbridge	San Joaquin	CA	Woodside	Queens	NY	Xenia	Sarpy	NE
Woodbridge	Middlesex	NJ	Woodside	St. Croix	WI	Xenia(c.h.)	Greene	OH
Woodburn	Macoupin	IL	Wood's Mills	St. Francois	MO	Xenia	York	PA
Woodburn	Allen	IN	Woodson	Morgan	IL			
Woodburn	Warren	KY	Woodsonville	Hart	KY	Yadkin College	Davidson	NC
Woodbury	Litchfield	CN	Wood's Run	Allegheny	PA	Yadkinville(c.h.)	Yadkin	NC
Woodbury	Meriwether	GA	Wood's Station	Jefferson	AL	Yakima	Yakima	WA
Woodbury	Cumberland	IL	Wood's Station	Butler	OH	Yale	Jasper	IL
Woodbury	Hancock	IN	Woodstock	Tuscaloosa	AL	Yalesville	New Haven	CN
Woodbury	Butler	KY	Woodstock	Windham	CN	Yancy	Phelps	MO
Woodbury	Washington	MN	Woodstock	Cherokee	GA	Yancy Mills	Phelps	MO
Woodbury(c.h.)	Gloucester	NJ	Woodstock(c.h.)	McHenry	IL	Yanceyville(c.h.)	Caswell	NC
Woodbury	Queens	NY	Woodstock	Jefferson	KS			

PLACE	COUNTY	STATE
Yanckee Hill	Butte	CA
Yankee Hollow	Jo Daviess	IL
Yankee Jim's	Placer	CA
Yankee Ridge	Coshocton	OH
Yankee Settlement	Clayton	IA
Yankee Spring	Barry	MI
Yankeetown	Warrick	IN
Yankeetown	Crawford	WI
Yankton(c.h.)	D A	
Yantic	New London	CN
Yaphank	Suffolk	NY
Yarborough	Floyd	GA
Yarmouth	Mercer	NJ
Yarmouth	Barnstable	MA
Yarmouth Port	Barnstable	MA
Yates	Orleans	NY
Yates City	Knox	IL
Yatesville	Morgan	IL
Yatesville	Calhoun	IA
Yatesville	Schuylkill	PA
Yatesville	Lunenburgh	VA
Yatton	Washington	IA
Yazoo	Harrison	IA
Yazoo City(c.h.)	Yazoo	MS
Yeater's Mills	Doddridge	WV
Yellow Bluff	Duval	FL
Yellow Branch	Campbell	VA
Yellow Bud	Ross	OH
Yellow Creek	Stephenson	IL
Yellow Creek	Josh Bell	KY
Yellow Creek	Beford	PA
Yellow Creek	Dickson	TN
Yeloow Head	Kankakee	IL
Yellow House	Berks	PA
Yellow Medicine	Redwood	MN
Yellow River	Gwinnett	GA
Yellow Spring	Blair	PA
Yellow Spring	Hampshire	WV
Yellow Springs	Green	OH
Yellow Stone	La Fayette	WI
Yellow Store	Hawkins	TN
Yellow Sulphur Spr.	Montgomery	VA
Yellville(c.h.)	Marion	AR
Yelm	Thurston	WA
Yelverton	Hardin	OH
Yelvington	Daviess	KY
Yemassee	Beaufort	SC
Yew	Wayne	MI
Yocony	Itawamba	MS
Yocumtown	York	PA
Yocumville	Klamath	CA
Yohogany	Westmoreland	PA
Yokum Station	Lee	VA
Yolo(c.h.)	Yolo	CA
Yoncalla	Douglas	OR
Yongesborough	Lee	AL
Yonkers	Wstchester	NY
York	Walker	AL

PLACE	COUNTY	STATE
York	Clark	IL
York	Delaware	IA
York	York	ME
York	Washtenaw	MI
York	Union	OH
York(c.h.)	York	PA
York	Dane	WI
York Centre	Iowa	IA
York Centre	Steuben	IN
York Collegiate In.	Alexander	NC
York Funace	York	PA
York Neck	Adams	IL
York Prairie	Cedar	IA
York Road	Carroll	MD
Yorkshire	Cattaraugus	NY
Yorkshire Centre	Cattaraugus	NY
York Station	Sumter	AL
York Sulphur	Adams	PA
Yorktown	Bureau	IL
Yorktown	Delaware	IN
Yorktown	Salem	NJ
Yorktown	Westchester	NY
Yorktown	De Witt	TX
Yorktown(c.h.)	York	VA
Yorkville	Mendocino	CA
Yorkville(c.h.)	Kendall	IL
Yorkville	Dearborn	IN
Yorkville	Kalamazoo	MI
Yorkville	New York	NY
Yorkville	Bladen	NC
Yorkville	Jefferson	OH
Yorkville(c.h.)	York	SC
Yorkville	Gibson	TN
Yorkyville	Racine	WI
Yosemite	Mariposa	CA
You Bet	Nevada	CA
Yough	Boone	IA
Young America	Warren	IL
Young America	Carver	MN
Young Ameria	Washington	WI
Young America	Steuben	NY
Young Hickory	Muskingham	OH
Young Hickory	Washington	WI
Young's Creek	Orange	IN
Young's Creek	Whitley	KY
Young's Creek	Audrian	MO
Young's X Roads	Granville	SC
Young's Mills	Guilford	NC
Young's Mills	Monroe	OH
Youngsport	Bell	TX
Young's Settlement	Bastrop	TX
Young's Store	Laurens	SC
Young's Store	Franklin	VA
Youngstown	Warren	IL
Younstown	Vigo	IN
Youngstown	Niagara	NY
Youngstown	Mahoning	OH
Youngstown	Westmoreland	PA

PLACE	COUNTY	STATE
Youngstown	Tallapoosa	AL
Youngstown	Sullivan	NY
Youngstown	Adams	OH
Youngstown	Warren	PA
Young Womanstwn	Clinton	PA
Yountsville	Montgomery	IN
Yountville	Napa	CA
Ypsilanti(c.h.)	Washtenaw	MI
Yreka(c.h.)	Siskiyou	CA
Yuba	Grand Traverse	MI
Yuba	Richland	WI
Yuba City(c.h.)	Sutter	CA
Yucatan	Houston	MN
Zackville	Wirt	WV
Zaleski	Vinton	OH
Zanesfield	Logan	OH
Zanesville	Wells	IN
Zanesville(c.h.)	Muskingham	OH
Zanzenburgh	Kerr	TX
Zarah	Barton	KS
Zabulon(c.h.)	Pike	GA
Zeeland	Ottawa	MI
Zeiglerville	Montgomery	PA
Zileinople	Butler	PA
Zem Zem	Lake	CA
Zena	Polk	OR
Zenas	Jennings	IN
Zeno	Muskingham	OH
Zeno	York	SC
Zevely	Whitfield	GA
Zif	Wayne	IL
Zig	Adair	MO
Zilwaukee	Saginaw	MI
Zimmerman	Greene	OH
Zinsburgh	Madison	IN
Zion	Henderson	KY
Zion	Cecil	MD
Zion	Yadkin	NC
Zion	Centre	PA
Zion	Bucks	PA
Zion's	Stearns	MN
Zion's Grove	Schuylkill	PA
Zion's Mills	Lee	VA
Zion Station	Grant	KY
Zionsville	Boone	IN
Zoar	Cedar	IA
Zoar	Franklin	MA
Zoar	Tuscarawas	OH
Zoar	Winnebago	WI
Zoar Station	Tuscarawas	OH
Zollarsville	Washington	PA
Zumbro Falls	Wabashaw	MN
Zumbrota	Goodhue	MN
Zuni Station	Goodhue	MN
Zuni Station	Isle of Wight	VA
Zwingle	Dubuque	IA

WHOLISTIC SOCIETY

If you subscribe to the Wholistic Research principles as explained on page 17 of this book, then you are invited to become a member of the Wholistic Society. Send one dollar for a special certificate suitable for framing. We will also send you a registration form so that we may add your name to this distinguished honor society.

Wholistic Society
P.O. Box 16422
Salt Lake City, UT 84116

CHAPTER 29

AMERICAN TOWNSHIPS — MINOR CIVIL DIVISIONS

In the United States there are two uses of the word township. In the section on Land Records, we pointed out that for surveying purposes the land is divided in a grid system, one subdivision of which is called a township. Except for finding specific places, they are of little value in research. However, in many states the counties are divided into political subdivisions called townships where records are kept. In these states when information is not available at the county level it may be available at the township level.

Townships often keep vital records, census records, tax lists, etc., that can be of value in your research. Although it is not always true, there are occasions when probate, property and military records are kept at the township level. This is more true the further east you go. In Massachusetts and New York, for example, many records are kept at the township level.

Below is an alphabetical listing of the political townships along with its county and state. You will note that in many states the same township name is found in more than one county.

This 112-page comprehensive listing is a designation of *modern* townships, so defunct townships or townships which merged with others will not be listed. Often the researcher will know the name of the township but not what county the township is in. This section will help you find that out.

Those who wish to see this information in map form should consult Andriot Associates Township Atlas.

TOWNSHIPS OF THE UNITED STATES

TOWNSHIP	COUNTY	STATE	TOWNSHIP	COUNTY	STATE	TOWNSHIP	COUNTY	STATE
			Acme	Hettinger	ND	Adams	Carroll	IN
			Acoma	McLeod	MN	Adams	Cass	IN
	—A—		Acme	Whatcom	WA	Adams	Morgan	IN
			Acorn	Polk	AR	Adams	Parke	IN
Aastad	Otter Tail	MN	Acton	York	ME	Adams	Ripley	IN
Abbeville	Abbeville	SC	Acton	Middlesex	MA	Adams	Warren	IN
Abbot	Piscataquis	ME	Acton	Meeker	MN	Adams	Dallas	IA
Abbott	Potter	PA	Acton	Walsh	ND	Adams	Delaware	IA
Abbotts Creek	Davidson	NC	Acworth	Sullivan	NH	Adams	Keokuk	IA
Abbotts Creek	Forsyth	NC	Ada	Kent	MI	Adams	Mahaska	IA
Abbotts	Bladen	NC	Ada	Dickey	ND	Adams	Wapello	IA
Abercrombie	Richland	ND	Ada	Perkins	SD	Adams	Nemaha	KS
Aberdeen	Brown	SD	Adair	Adair	IA	Adams	Arenac	MI
Abilene	Caddo	OK	Adair	Camden	MO	Adams	Hillsdale	MI
Abington	Plymouth	MA	Adair	Mayes	OK	Adams	Houghton	MI
Abington	Mercer	IL	Adams Creek	Wagoner	OK	Adams	Mower	MN
Abington	Wayne	IN	Adams	Bershire	MA	Adams	De Kalb	MO
Abington	Lackawanna	PA	Adams	Adams	WI	Adams	Harrison	MO
Abington	Montgomery	PA	Adams	Decatur	IN	Adams	Gage	NB
Aboite	Allen	IN	Adams	Hamilton	IN	Adams	Walsh	ND
Abrams	Oconto	WI	Adams	Madison	IN	Adams	Champaign	OH
Achilles	Rawlins	KS	Adams	Green	WI	Adams	Clinton	OH
Achushnet	Bristol	MA	Adams	Jackson	WI	Adams	Coshocton	OH
Ackley	Langlade	WI	Adams	La Salle	IL	Adams	Drake	OH
Acme	Grand Traverse	MI	Adams	Allen	IN	Adams	Defiance	OH

TOWNSHIPS OF THE UNITED STATES

TOWNSHIP	COUNTY	STATE	TOWNSHIP	COUNTY	STATE	TOWNSHIP	COUNTY	STATE
Adams	Guernsey	OH	Aitkin	Aitkin	MN	Alden	Saint Louis	MN
Adams	Monroe	OH	Akan	Richland	WI	Alden	Hettinger	ND
Adams	Muskingum	OH	Akeley	Hubbard	MN	Alden	Hand	SD
Adams	Seneca	OH	Akers	Carter	OK	Alderson	Pittsburg	OK
Adams	Washington	OH	Akra	Pembina	ND	Aldine	Norton	KS
Adams	Harper	OK	Akron	Peoria	IL	Aldrich	Wadena	MN
Adams	Butler	PA	Akron	Tuscola	MI	Aleppo	Allegheny	PA
Adams	Cambria	PA	Akron	Big Stone	MN	Aleppo	Greene	PA
Adams	Snyder	PA	Akron	Wiklin	MN	Alex	McKenzie	ND
Adams	Grant	SD	Alabam	Madison	AR	Alex	Grady	OK
Adams	Miner	SD	Alabama	Genesee	NY	Alexander	Washington	ME
Addie	Griggs	ND	Alabama	Nevada	AR	Alexander	Genesee	NY
Addison	Washington	ME	Alabaster	Losco	MI	Alexander	Cheyenne	KS
Addison	Steuben	NY	Alaiedon	Ingham	MI	Alexander	Rush	KS
Addison	Addison	VT	Alameda	Alameda	CA	Alexander	Benton	MO
Addison	Washington	WI	Alamo	Kalamazoo	MI	Alexander	Athens	OH
Addison	Du Page	IL	Alamo	Lincoln	NV	Alexander	Pierce	ND
Addison	Shelby	IN	Alamota	Lane	KS	Alexander	Stutsman	ND
Addison	Oakland	MI	Alango	Saint Louis	MN	Alexandria	Grafton	NH
Addison	Knox	NB	Alaska	Beltrami	MN	Alexandria	Jefferson	NY
Addison	Cass	ND	Alba	Henry	IL	Alexandria	Leavenworth	KS
Addison	Gallis	OH	Alba	Jackson	MN	Alexandria	Douglas	MN
Addison	Somerset	PA	Alban	Portage	WI	Alexandria	Divide	ND
Adel	Dallas	IA	Alban	Grant	SD	Alexandria	Hunterdon	NJ
Adelaide	Bowman	ND	Albano	Stafford	KS	Alexis	Butler	NB
Adell	Sheridan	KS	Albany	Carroll	NH	Alfalfa	Blaine	OK
Adin-Lookout	Modoc	CA	Albany	Orleans	VT	Alfalfa	Grant	OK
Adler	Nelson	ND	Albany	Green	WI	Alfalfa	Tillman	OK
Adrian	Monroe	WI	Albany	Pepin	WI	Alford	Berkshire	MA
Adrian	Jackson	KS	Albany	Nevada	AR	Alfordville	Robeson	NC
Adrian	Lenawee	MI	Albany	Whiteside	IL	Alfred	York	ME
Adrian	Watonwan	MN	Albany	Stearns	MN	Alfred	Allegany	NY
Adrian	La Moure	ND	Albany	Harlan	NB	Alfsborg	Sibley	MN
Adrian	Edmunds	SD	Albany	Bryan	OK	Algansee	Branch	MI
Advance	Pembina	ND	Albany	Berks	PA	Algernon	Custer	NB
Advance	Texas	OK	Albany	Bradford	PA	Algoma	Winnebago	WI
Aetna	Logan	IL	Albee	Saginaw	MI	Algoma	Kent	MI
Aetna	Barber	KS	Albert Lea	Freeborn	MN	Algona	Kossuth	IA
Aetna	Mecosta	MI	Albert	Montmorency	MI	Alger	Mountrail	ND
Aetna	Missoukee	MI	Albert	Benson	ND	Algonquin	Mc Henry	IL
Aetna	Pipestone	MN	Alberta	Benton	MN	Alhambra	Madison	IL
Afton	Chenago	NY	Albertha	Dickey	ND	Aliceton	Ransom	ND
Afton	Fulton	AR	Albertson	Duplin	NC	Alila	Tulare	CA
Afton	De Kalb	IL	Albion	Kennebec	ME	Aline	Alfalfa	OK
Afton	Cherokee	IA	Albion	Dickey	ND	Alisal	Monterey	CA
Afton	Howard	IA	Albion	Orleans	NY	Alix	Fulton	AR
Afton	Sedgwick	KS	Albion	Oswego	NY	Allamuchy	Warren	NJ
Afton	Washington	MN	Albion	Dane	WI	Allegan	Allegan	MI
Afton	Ward	ND	Albion	Jackson	WI	Allegany Indian Reservation	Cattaraugus	NY
Afton	Ottawa	OK	Albion	Trempealeau	WI	Allegany	Cattaraugus	NY
Afton	Brookings	SD	Albion	White	AR	Allegany	Potter	PA
Afton	Sanborn	SD	Albion	Noble	IN	Alleghany	Davidson	NC
Aqassiz	Lac Qui Parle	MN	Albion	Butler	IA	Alleghany	Ransom	ND
Aqawam	Hampden	MA	Albion	Howard	IA	Allegheny	Blair	PA
Aqder	Marshall	MN	Albion	Barton	KS	Allegheny	Butler	PA
Agency	Wapello	IA	Albion	Reno	KS	Allegheny	Cambria	PA
Agency	Osage	KS	Albion	Republic	KS	Allegheny	Somerset	PA
Agency	Muskogee	OK	Albion	Calhoun	MI	Allegheny	Venago	PA
Agency	Buchanan	MO	Albion	Wright	MN	Allegheny	Westmoreland	PA
Agency	Roberts	SD	Albion	Bon Homme	SD	Allen Grove	Mason	IL
Agenda	Ashland	WI	Albion	Saint Louis	MN	Allen	Allegany	NY
Agnes City	Lyon	KS	Albright	Alamance	NC	Allen	Pope	AR
Agnes	Grand Forks	ND	Albright	Chatham	NC	Allen	La Salle	IL
Agram	Morrison	MN	Albug	Grand Isle	VT	Allen	Miami	IL
Ahnapee	Kewaunee	WI	Alcester	Union	SD	Allen	Noble	IN
Ahoskie	Hertford	NC	Alcona	Rooks	KS	Allen	Harrison	IA
Aid	Lawrence	OH	Alcona	Alcona	MI	Allen	Polk	IA
Aiken	Aiken	SC	Alda	Hall	NB	Allen	Warren	IA
Ainsworth	Langlade	WI	Alden	Erie	NY	Allen	Jewell	KS
Airport	Saint Louis	MO	Alden	Polk	WI	Allen	Kingman	KS
Aitkin Northeast	Aitkin	MN	Alden	Mc Henry	IL	Allen	Hillsdale	MI
Aitkin Northwest	Aitkin	MN	Alden	Hardin	IA	Allen	Worth	MO
Aitkin Southeast	Aitkin	MN	Alden	Freeborn	MN			

TOWNSHIPS OF THE UNITED STATES

TOWNSHIP	COUNTY	STATE
Allen	Kidder	ND
Allen	Drake	OH
Allen	Hancock	OH
Allen	Ottawa	OH
Allen	Union	OH
Allen	Murray	OK
Allen	Pontotoc	OK
Allen	Northampton	PA
Allendale	Ottawa	MI
Allendale	Hoke	NC
Allendale	Grand Forks	ND
Allendale	Allendale	SC
Allens Grove	Scott	IA
Allenstown	Merrimack	NH
Allensville	Person	NC
Allent	Beadle	SD
Alliance	Clay	MN
Alliance	Moody	SD
Alligator	Tyrrell	NC
Alligator	Chesterfield	SC
Allin	Mc Lean	IL
Allis	Presque Isle	MI
Allison	Lawrence	IL
Allison	Lyon	IA
Allison	Osceola	IA
Allison	Decatur	KS
Allison	Garfield	OK
Allison	Clinton	PA
Allison	Brown	SD
Allodium	Graham	KS
Allouez	Brown	WI
Allouez	Keweenaw	MI
Alloway	Salem	NJ
Alluwe	Nowata	OK
Alma	Allegany	NY
Alma	Buffalo	WI
Alma	Jackson	WI
Alma	Crawford	AR
Alma	Marion	IL
Alma	Marion	KS
Alma	Wabaunsee	KS
Alma	Marshall	MN
Alma	Harlan	NB
Alma	Cavalier	ND
Almelo	Norton	KS
Almena	Barron	WI
Almena	Norton	KS
Almena	Van Buren	MI
Almer	Tuscola	MI
Almira	Benzie	MI
Almon	Shawano	WI
Almond	Allegany	NY
Almond	Portage	WI
Almond	Big Stone	MN
Almond	Stanly	NC
Almont	Lapeer	MI
Alna	Lincoln	ME
Aloha	Cheboygan	MI
Alpaugh	Tulare	CA
Alpena	Alpena	MI
Alpena	Jerauld	SD
Alpha	Hand	SD
Alpha	Kent	MI
Alpine	Stone	MO
Alpine		PA
Alsace	Berks	PA
Alstead	Cheshire	NH
Alta	Harvey	KS
Alta	Barnes	ND
Alta Vista	Lincoln	MN
Altamont	Franklin	NY
Altamont	Avery	NC
Altamont	Devel	SD
Alto	Fond du Lac	WI
Alto	Lee	IL
Alto	Roberts	SD
Alton	Penobscot	ME
Alton	Belknap	NH
Alton	Madison	IL
Alton	Waseca	MN
Alton	Brookings	SD
Altona	Clinton	NY
Altona	Pinestone	MN
Altona	Kingfisher	OK
Altoona	Beadle	SD
Altory	Decatur	KS
Alturas	Modoc	CA
Alva	Woods	OK
Alvin	Forest	WI
Alvwood	Itasca	MN
Amador	Chisago	MN
Amanda	Allen	OH
Amanda	Fairfield	OH
Amanda	Hancock	OH
Amaqua	Boone	IA
Amber	Mason	MI
Amber	Grady	OK
Amberg	Marinetta	WI
Amberley	Hamilton	OH
Amboy	Oswego	NY
Amboy	San Beradino	CA
Amboy	Lee	IL
Amboy	Hillsdale	MI
Amboy	Cottonwood	MN
Amboy	Fulton	OH
Ambrose	Divide	ND
Amelia	Calhoun	SC
Amenia	Dutchess	NY
Amenia	Cass	ND
America	Plymouth	IA
America	Brule	SD
American	Allen	OH
American	Sacramento	CA
American	Lyon	KS
Americus	Grand Forks	ND
Americus	Athens	OH
Ames	Essex	MA
Amesbury	Essex	MA
Amherst	Hancock	ME
Amherst	Hamshire	MA
Amherst	Hillsborough	NH
Amherst	Erie	NY
Amherst	Portage	WI
Amherst	Cherokee	IA
Amherst	Fillmore	MN
Amherst	Lorain	OH
Amiret	Lyon	MN
Amity	Aroostook	ME
Amity	Allegany	NY
Amity	Clark	AR
Amity	Livingston	IL
Amity	Page	IA
Amity	Bottineau	ND
Amity	Berks	PA
Amity	Erie	PA
Amity		WI
Amnicon	Douglas	WI
Amo	Cottonwood	MN
Amor	Ottertail	MN
Amor	Bowman	ND
Amor	Hancock	IA
Amsterdam	Montgomery	NY
Amsterdam	Mc Lean	ND
Amwell	Washington	PA
Anaheim	Orange	CA
Analy	Sonoma	CA
Anamoose	Mc Henry	ND
Anchor	Mc Lean	IL
Ancram	Columbia	NY
Andalusia	Rock Island	IL
Anderson Creek	Harnett	NC
Anderson	Burnett	WI
Anderson	Iron	WI
Anderson	Benton	AR
Anderson	Mendocino	CA
Anderson	Clark	IL
Anderson	Madison	IN
Anderson	Perry	IN
Anderson	Rush	IN
Anderson	Warrick	IN
Anderson	Mills	IA
Anderson	McDonald	MO
Anderson	New Madrid	MO
Anderson	Phelps	NB
Anderson	Caswell	NC
Anderson	Barnes	ND
Anderson	Hamilton	OH
Anderson	Anderson	SC
Anderson (No. 5)	Williamsburg	SC
Anderson	Perkins	SD
Andes	Delaware	NY
Andover	Tolland	CT
Andover	Oxford	ME
Andover	Essex	MA
Andover	Merrimack	NH
Andover	Allegany	NY
Andover	Windsor	VT
Andover	Henry	IL
Andover	Polk	MN
Andover	Sussex	NJ
Andover	Ashtabula	OH
Andover	Day	SD
Andrea	Wilkin	MN
Andrews	Mc Lean	ND
Andrews	Georgetown	SC
Angelica	Allegany	NY
Angelica	Shawano	WI
Angelo	Monroe	WI
Angels	Calaveras	CA
Angora	Saint Louis	MN
Angus	Polk	MN
Anina	Jerauld	SD
Aniwa	Shawano	WI
Ann Arbor	Washtenaw	MI
Ann	Cottonwood	MN
Ann Lake	Kanabec	MN
Anna	Ward	ND
Annawan	Henry	IL
Annieville	Lawrence	AR
Annin	Mc Kean	PA
Annin	Lyman	SD
Annsville	Oneida	NY
Annville	Lebanon	PA
Ansel	Cass	MN
Ansley	Custer	NB
Anson	Somerset	ME
Anson	Chippewa	WI
Ansonia	New Haven	CT
Ansonville	Anson	NC
Antelope Creek	McKenzie	ND
Antelope Lake	Pierce	ND
Antelope Springs	Morgan	CO
Antelope	Los Angeles	CA
Antelope	Mono	CA
Antelope	Franklin	NB
Antelope	Harlan	NB
Antelope	Holt	NB
Antelope	Richland	ND
Antelope	Logan	OK
Antelope	Perkins	SD
Antelope	Spink	SD
Antelope Valley	Deuel	SD
Anthony	Harper	KS

TOWNSHIPS OF THE UNITED STATES

TOWNSHIP	COUNTY	STATE	TOWNSHIP	COUNTY	STATE	TOWNSHIP	COUNTY	STATE
Anthony	Norman	MN	Argentine	Fall River	SD	Ash Flat	Coal	OK
Anthony	Lycoming	PA	Argo	Brookings	SD	Ash Grove	Iroquois	IL
Anthony	Montour	PA	Argonne	Forest	WI	Ash Grove	Shelby	IL
Antigo	Langlade	WI	Argonne	Adams	ND	Ash Grove	Franklin	NB
Antioch	Garland	AR	Argyle	Washington	NY	Ash Hill	Butler	MO
Antioch	Hot Spring	AR	Argyle	Lafayette	WI	Ash Lake	Lincoln	MN
Antioch	White	AR	Argyle	Sanilac	MI	Ash Rock	Rooks	KS
Antioch	Lake	IL	Arietta	Hamilton	NY	Ash	Monroe	MI
Antioch	Wexford	MI	Arion	Cloud	KS	Ash	Barry	MO
Antioch	Hoke	NC	Arispie	Bureau	IL	Ash	Clark	SD
Antioch	Wilkes	NC	Arizona	Burt	NB	Ash	Pennington	SD
Antis	Blair	PA	Arkansas	Little River	AR	Ash Valley	Pawnee	KS
Antler	Bottineau	ND	Arkinda	Little River	AR	Ashburnham	Worcester	MA
Antlers	Pushmataha	OK	Arkwright	Chautauqua	NY	Ashby	Middlesex	MA
Antonie	Pine	AR	Arland	Barron	WI	Asheboro	Randolph	NC
Antrim	Hillsborough	NH	Arlee	Lake	MT	Asherville	Mitchell	KS
Antrim	Shiawassee	MI	Arlington Heights	Hamilton	OH	Asherville	Buncombe	NC
Antrim	Watonwan	MN	Arlington	Middlesex	MA	Ashfield	Franklin	MA
Antrim	Wyandot	OH	Arlington	Bennington	VT	Ashford	Windham	CT
Antrim	Franklin	PA	Arlington	Columbia	WI	Ashford	Cattaraugus	NY
Antwerp	Jefferson	NY	Arlington	Woodbury	IA	Ashford	Fond du Lac	WI
Antwerp	Van Buren	MI	Arlington	Reno	KS	Ashippum	Dodge	WI
Aplin	Perry	AR	Arlington	Van Buren	MI	Ashkum	Iroquois	IL
Apolacon	Susquehanna	PA	Arlington	Sibley	MN	Ashland	Aroostook	ME
Appanoose	Hancock	IL	Arlington	Phelps	MO	Ashland	Middlesex	MA
Appanoose	Franklin	KS	Arlington	Washington	NB	Ashland	Grafton	NH
Apple Creek	Cape Girardeau	MO	Arlone	Pine	MN	Ashland	Chemung	NY
Apple Creek	Burleigh	ND	Armada	Macomb	MI	Ashland	Greene	NY
Apple Glenn	Benton	AR	Armada	Buffalo	NB	Ashland	Ashland	WI
Apple River	Jo Daviess	IL	Armagh	Mifflin	PA	Ashland	Lawrence	AR
Apple River	Polk	WI	Armenia	Juneau	WI	Ashland	Cass	IL
Applegate	Lyman	SD	Armenia	Bradford	PA	Ashland	Morgan	IN
Appleton	Knox	ME	Armourdale	Towner	ND	Ashland	Riley	KS
Appleton	Clark	KS	Armstead	Beaverhead	MT	Ashland	Newaygo	MI
Appleton	Swift	MN	Armstrong Creek	Forest	WI	Ashland	Dodge	MN
Appleton	Saint Clair	MO	Armstrong Grove	Emmet	IA	Ashland	Saunders	NB
Appomattox	Potter	SD	Armstrong	Oconto	VT	Ashland	Stutsman	ND
Arago	Hubbard	MN	Armstrong	Vanderburgh	IN	Ashland	Clarion	PA
Arapaho	Custer	OK	Armstrong	Indiana	PA	Ashley	Independence	AR
Arapahoe	Blaine	OK	Armstrong	Lycoming	PA	Ashley	Washington	IL
Arapahoe	Blaine	OK	Armstrong	Nowata	OK	Ashley	Stearns	MN
Ararat	Susquehanna	PA	Arna	Pine	MN	Ashley	Pike	MO
Arbo	Itasca	MN	Arna	Benson	ND	Ashmore	Coles	IL
Arbor	Rawlins	KS	Amegard	McKenzie	ND	Ashtabula	Ashtabula	OH
Arbor Vitae	Vilas	WI	Arnold	Custer	NB	Ashtabula	Barnes	ND
Arcada	Gratiot	MI	Aroma	Kankakee	IL	Ashton	Lee	IL
Arcade	Wyoming	NY	Aripin	Wood	WI	Ashton	Monona	IA
Arcade	Phillips	KS	Argyle	Penobscot	ME	Ashton	Sherman	NB
Arcade	Faulk	SD	Arrington	Wayne	IL	Ashwaubenon	Brown	WI
Arcadia	Wayne	NY	Arrow Rock	Saline	MO	Assumption	Christian	IL
Arcadia	Trempealeau	WI	Arrowhead	Saint Louis	MN	Assyria	Barry	MI
Arcadia	Carroll	IA	Arrowhead	Perkins	SD	Aston	Delaware	PA
Arcadia	Lapeer	MI	Arrowsic	Saqadahoc	ME	Astoria	Fulton	IL
Arcadia	Manistee	MI	Arrowsmith	McLean	IL	Asylum	Bradford	PA
Arcadia	Iron	MO	Arroyo Grande	San Luis Obispo	CA	Atascadero	San Luis Obispo	CA
Arcadia	Valley	NB	Artesia	Iroquois	IL	Atchison	Clinton	MO
Arcadia	Davidson	NC	Arthur	Chippewa	WI	Atchison	Nodaway	MO
Archer	Harrison	OH	Arthur	Clare	MI	Athelstane	Marinette	WI
Archey Valley	Van Buren	AR	Arthur	Kanabec	MN	Athelstane	Clay	KS
Arcola	Douglas	IL	Arthur	Traverse	MN	Athens	Somerset	ME
Arctander	Kandiyohi	MN	Arthur	Pitt	NC	Athens	Greene	NY
Arden	Little River	AR	Arthur	Cass	ND	Athens	Windham	VT
Ardenhurst	Itasca	MN	Artichoke	Big Stone	MN	Athens	Izard	AR
Ardoch	Walsh	ND	Artichoke	Potter	SD	Athens	Ringgold	IA
Arela	Tuscola	MI	Arundel	York	ME	Athens	Jewell	KS
Arena	Iowa	WI	Arvard	Woods	OK	Athens	Calhoun	MI
Arena	Mendocino	CA	Arveson	Kittson	MN	Athens	Isanti	MN
Arena	Lac Qui Parle	MN	Arvilla	Grand Forks	ND	Athens	Gentry	MO
Arena	Potter	SD	Arvon	Barga	MI	Athens	Williams	ND
Arenac	Arenac	MI	Arvonia	Osage	KS	Athens	Athens	OH
Arenzville	Cass	IL	Asbury	Gallatin	IL	Athens	Harrison	OH
Argenta	Lander	NV	Ash Coulee	Stark	ND	Athens	Ellis	OK
Argentine	Genessee	MI	Ash Creek	Ellsworth	KS	Athens	Bradford	PA

TOWNSHIPS OF THE UNITED STATES

TOWNSHIP	COUNTY	STATE
Athens	Crawford	PA
Athensville	Greene	IL
Atherton	Wilkin	MN
Athol	Worcester	MA
Athol	Spink	SD
Athol	Sequayah	OK
Atkins	Towner	ND
Atkinson	Piscataquis	ME
Atkinson	Rockingham	NH
Atkinson	Henry	IL
Atkinson	Carlton	MN
Atkinson	Holt	NB
Atkinson	Rusk	WI
Atlanta	Logan	IL
Atlanta	Rice	KS
Atlanta	Becker	MN
Atlantic	Cass	IA
Atlantic	Carteret	NC
Atlantic	Dare	NC
Atlas	Pike	IL
Atlas	Genesee	MI
Atolia	San Bernardino	CA
Attica	Wyoming	NY
Attica	Sedgwick	KS
Attica	Lapeer	MI
Attleboro	Bristol	MA
Atwater	Portage	OH
Atwell	Rowan	NC
Atwood	Rawlins	KS
Atwood	Kidder	ND
Au Gres	Arenac	MI
Au Sable	Losco	MI
Au Sable	Roscommon	MI
Au Train	Alger	MI
Aubbeenaubbee	Fulton	IN
Auborn	Noble	OK
Aubry	Johnson	KS
Auburn	Worcester	MA
Auburn	Rockingham	NH
Auburn	Chippewa	WI
Auburn	Fond du Lac	WI
Auburn	Lincoln	AR
Auburn	Clark	IL
Auburn	Sangamon	IL
Auburn	Fayette	IA
Auburn	Shawnee	KS
Auburn	Crawford	OH
Auburn	Geauga	OH
Auburn	Tuscarawas	OH
Auburn	Susquehanna	PA
Auburn	Wood	WI
Auburnadle	Montgomery	IL
Audubon	Audubon	IA
Audubon	Becker	MN
Auglaize	Camden	MO
Auglaize	Laclede	MO
Auglaize	Allen	OH
Auglaize	Paulding	OH
Augsburg	Marshall	MN
Augusta	Oneida	NY
Augusta	Woodruff	AR
Augusta	Hancock	IL
Augusta	Des Moines	IA
Augusta	Butler	KS
Augusta	Washtenaw	MI
Augusta	Lac Qui Parle	MN
Augusta	Carroll	OH
Augustine	Logan	KS
Ault	Saint Louis	MN
Aurdal	Otter Tail	MN
Aurelius	Cayuga	NY
Aurelius	Ingham	MI
Aurelius	Washington	OH
Aurena	Mc Lean	ND
Aurora	Hancock	ME
Aurora	Erie	NY
Aurora	Florence	WI
Aurora	Taylor	WI
Aurora	Waushara	WI
Aurora	Kane	IL
Aurora	Cloud	KS
Aurora	Steele	MN
Aurora	Lawrence	MO
Aurora	Benson	ND
Aurora	Portage	OH
Aurora	Aurora	SD
Aurora	Brookings	SD
Ausable	Clinton	NY
Austerlitz	Columbia	NY
Austin	Conway	AR
Austin	Macon	IL
Austin	Mecosta	MI
Austin	Sanilac	MI
Austin	Mower	MN
Austin	Cass	MO
Austin	Lander	NV
Austin	Mountrail	ND
Austin	Ellis	OK
Austin	Greenville	SC
Austinburg	Ashtabula	OH
Austintown	Mahoning	OH
Automba	Carlton	MN
Autry	Noble	OK
Aux Sable	Grundy	IL
Auxvasse	Callaway	MO
Ava	Oneida	NY
Avena	Fayette	IL
Avenal	Kings	CA
Averasboro	Harnett	NC
Averill	Essex	Vt
Avery Creek	Buncombe	NC
Avery	Hancock	IA
Avery	Humboldt	IA
Avery	Montmorency	MI
Avilla	Comanche	KS
Avoca	Steuben	NY
Avoca	Pottawatomie	OK
Avoca	Livingston	IL
Avon Lake	Lorain	OH
Avon Springs	Potter	SD
Avon	Hartford	CT
Avon	Franklin	ME
Avon	Norfolk	MA
Avon	Livingston	NY
Avon	Rock	WI
Avon	Lake	IL
Avon	Coffey	KS
Avon	Sumner	KS
Avon	Oakland	MI
Avon	Stearns	MN
Avon	Grand Forks	ND
Avon	Lorain	OH
Avon	Bon Homme	SD
Ayden	Pitt	NC
Ayer	Middlesex	MA
Ayers	Champaign	IL
Ayr	Adams	NE
Ayr	Cass	ND
Ayr	Fulton	PA
Aztalan	Jefferson	WI

—B—

TOWNSHIP	COUNTY	STATE
Babylon	Suffolk	NY
Bachelor	Greenwood	KS
Back Creek	Randolph	NC
Back Swamp	Robeson	NC
Backus	Rosecommon	MI
Bacon	Vernon	MO
Bad Lands	Pennington	SD
Bad Nation	Mellette	SD
Badger	Webster	IA
Badger	Polk	MN
Badger	Vernon	MO
Badger	La Moure	ND
Badger	Davison	SD
Badger	Kingsbury	SD
Badoura	Hubbard	MN
Badus	Lake	SD
Baer	Hettinger	ND
Bagley	Oconto	WI
Bagley	Otsego	MI
Bailey	Nash	NC
Bailey	Lyman	SD
Baileys Harbor	Door	WI
Baileyville	Washington	ME
Bain	Garland	AR
Bainbridge	Chenango	NY
Bainbridge	Schuyler	IL
Bainbridge	Dubois	IN
Bainbridge	Berrien	MI
Bainbridge	Geauga	OH
Baker	Izard	AR
Baker	Lafayette	AR
Baker	Randolph	AR
Baker	Morgan	IN
Baker	Guthrie	IA
Baker	Howard	IA
Baker	O'Brien	IA
Baker	Osceola	IA
Baker	Crawford	KS
Baker	Gore	KS
Baker	Linn	MO
Baker	Stevens	MN
Baker	Kidder	ND
Baker	White Pine	NV
Baker	Davison	SD
Baker	Kingsbury	SD
Baker	Whatcom	WA
Bakersfield	Franklin	VT
Bakersville	Mitchell	NC
Bala	Riley	KS
Bald Bluff	Henderson	IL
Bald Eagle	Clinton	PA
Bald Hill	Jefferson	IL
Bald Hill	Okmulgee	OK
Bald Knob	White	AR
Bald Mountain	Washoe	NV
Bald Mountain	Watauga	NC
Balderson	Marshall	KS
Baldoc	Allendale	SC
Baldwin	Cumberland	ME
Baldwin	Chemung	NY
Baldwin	Saint Croix	WI
Baldwin	Delta	MI
Baldwin	Iosco	MI
Baldwin	Sherburne	MN
Baldwin	Chatham	NC
Baldwin	Barnes	ND
Baldwin	Allegheny	PA
Balkan	Saint Louis	MN
Baldy Mesa	San Bernardino	CA
Bale	Ransom	ND
Bales	Pottawatomie	OK
Balfour	McHenry	ND
Balko	Beaver	OK
Ball Bluff	Aitkin	MN
Ball Hill	Griggs	ND
Ball	Benton	AR

TOWNSHIPS OF THE UNITED STATES

TOWNSHIP	COUNTY	STATE	TOWNSHIP	COUNTY	STATE	TOWNSHIP	COUNTY	STATE
Ball	Sangamon	IL	Barkley	Jasper	IN	Barton	Newaygo	MI
Ballard	Adair	OK	Barksdale	Bayfield	WI	Barton	Pierce	ND
Ballston	Saratoga	NY	Barlow	Washington	OH	Barton	Tioga	NY
Ballville	Sandusky	OH	Barnard	Windsor	VT	Barton	Orleans	VT
Balmont	Iroquois	IL	Barnes	Bayfield	WI	Barto	Roseau	MN
Balsam	Aitkin	MN	Barnes	Woodruff	AR	Barton City	Barton	MO
Balsam	Itasca	MN	Barnes	Buena Vista	IA	Barton Creek	Wake	NC
Balsam	Polk	WI	Barnes	Washington	KS	Bashaw	Washburn	WI
Balta	Pierce	ND	Barnes	Cass	ND	Bashaw	Brown	MN
Baltimore	Windson	VT	Barneston	Gage	NE	Basin	Boyd	NE
Baltimore	Henry	IA	Barnesville	Clay	MN	Bass Brook	Itasca	MN
Baltimore	Barry	MI	Barnet	Caledonia	VT	Bass Lake	Sawyer	WI
Bamberg	Bamberg	SC	Barnett	Van Buren	AR	Bass Lake	Washburn	WI
Bancroft	Aroostook	ME	Barnett	De Witt	IL	Bass Little	Sebastian	AR
Bancroft	Freeborn	MN	Barnett	Roseau	MN	Bass River	Burlington	NJ
Bancroft	Cuming	NE	Barnett	Forest	PA	Bassett	Saint Louis	MN
Bandon	Renville	MN	Barnett	Jefferson	PA	Bassettville	Decatur	KS
Bandy	Catawba	NC	Barney	Richland	ND	Bastress	Lycoming	PA
Bangor	Franklin	NY	Barnhill	Wayne	IL	Batavia	Genesee	NY
Bangor	La Crosse	WI	Barnitz	Custer	OK	Batavia	Boone	AR
Bangor	Marshall	IA	Barnstable	Barnstable	MA	Batavia	Kane	IL
Bangor	Bay	MI	Barnstead	Belknap	NH	Batavia	Branch	MI
Bangor	Van Buren	MI	Barnwell	Barnwell	SC	Batavia	Clermont	OH
Bangor	Pope	MN	Baroda	Berrien	MI	Bateman	Jackson	AR
Bangor	Brookings	SD	Barnum	Carlton	MN	Bates	Iron	MI
Banks	Fayette	IA	Baron	Adair	OK	Bates	Greenville	SC
Banks	Antrim	MI	Barr Butte	Williams	ND	Bates	Brown	SD
Banks	Carbon	PA	Barr	Macoupin	IL	Bates	Hand	SD
Banks	Indiana	PA	Barr	Daviess	IN	Bath	Grafton	NH
Banner	Pratt	KS	Barr	Cambria	PA	Bath	Steuben	NY
Banner	Rush	KS	Barre	La Crosse	WI	Bath	Cerro Gordo	IA
Banner	Smith	KS	Barraque	Jefferson	AR	Bath	Mason	IL
Banner	Ashley	AR	Barre	Worcester	MA	Bath	Franklin	IN
Banner	Saline	AR	Barre	Orleans	NY	Bath	Beaufort	NC
Banner	Effingham	IL	Barre	Washington	VT	Bath	Clinton	MI
Banner	Fulton	IL	Barree	Huntington	PA	Bath	Freeborn	MN
Banner	Woodbury	IA	Barren Fork	Izard	AR	Bath	Allen	OH
Banner	Dickinson	KS	Barren Fork	Ozark	MO	Bath	Greene	OH
Banner	Harper	KS	Barren	Independence	AR	Bath	Summit	OH
Banner	Jackson	KS	Barren	Jackson	AR	Bath	Brown	SD
Banner	Stevens	KS	Barren	Franklin	IL	Bathgate	Pembina	ND
Banner	Johnston	NC	Barrett	Thomas	KS	Baton Rouge	Chester	SC
Banner	Cavalier	ND	Barrett	Monroe	PA	Batson	Johnson	AR
Banner	Mountrail	ND	Barrett	Beadle	SD	Battle Creek	Lincoln	KS
Banner	Caddo	OK	Barrett	Perkins	SD	Battle Creek	Calhoun	MI
Banner	Dewey	OK	Barrie	Richland	ND	Battle Hill	McPherson	KS
Banner	Garfield	OK	Barringer	Iredell	NC	Battle Plain	Rock	MN
Banner	Grant	OK	Barrington	Stafford	NH	Battle	Ida	IA
Banner	Kingfisher	OK	Barrington	Yates	NY	Battle	Beltrami	MN
Banner	Pawnee	??	Barrington	Bristol	RI	Battleboro	Windham	VT
Banner	Beadle	SD	Barrington	Cook	IL	Battleview	Burke	ND
Banner	Hyde	SD	Barron	Barron	WI	Baucum	Jackson	OK
Banner	Jones	SD	Barronett	Washburn	WI	Baughman	Wayne	OH
Banner	Tripp	SD	Barry	Pike	IL	Baugo	Elkhart	IN
Bantry	Mc Henry	ND	Barry	Barry	MI	Bauzite	Saline	AR
Bar Harbor	Hancock	ME	Barry	Pine	MN	Baxter	Garland	AR
Bar X	Roger Mills	OK	Barry	Schuylkill	PA	Baxter	Lac Qui Parle	MN
Baraboo	Sauk	WI	Barsness	Pope	MN	Bay De Noc	Delta	MI
Baraga	Baraga	MI	Barstow	San Bernardino	CA	Bay Lake	Crow Wing	MN
Barbecue	Harnett	NC	Bart	Lancaster	PA	Bay Mills	Chippewa	MI
Barber	Logan	AR	Bartelme	Shawano	WI	Bay	Charlevoix	MI
Barber	Faribault	MN	Bartholomew	Drew	AR	Bay	Ottawa	OH
Barberton	Summit	OH	Bartholomew	Lincoln	AR	Bayboro	Horry	SC
Barclay	Osage	KS	Bartlett	Carroll	NH	Bayfield	Bayfield	WI
Barclay	Cass	MN	Bartlett	Todd	MN	Bayliss	Pope	AR
Barden	Ward	ND	Bartlett	Shannon	MO	Bayou Meto	Arkansas	AR
Barham	Franklin	AR	Bartlett	Ramsey	ND	Bayou	Ashley	AR
Baring	Washington	ME	Bartley	Griggs	ND	Bayou	Baxter	AR
Bark River	Delta	MI	Bartlow	Henry	OH	Bayou	Ozark	??
Barker	Broome	NY	Barton	Washington	WI	Baytown	Washington	MN
Barclay	Black Hawk	IA	Barton	Arkansas	AR	Bayview	Bayfield	WI
Barkers Creek	Jackson	NC	Barton	Gibso	IN	Bazaar	Chase	KS
Barkhamsted	Litchfield	CT	Barton	Worth	IA	Bazetta	Trumbull	OH

TOWNSHIPS OF THE UNITED STATES

TOWNSHIP	COUNTY	STATE	TOWNSHIP	COUNTY	STATE	TOWNSHIP	COUNTY	STATE
Bazile	Antelope	NE	Beaver Island	Stokes	NC	Bedford	Monroe	MI
Bazine	Ness	KS	Beaver	Clark	WI	Bedford	Lincoln	MO
Beach	Golden Valley	ND	Beaver	Marinette	WI	Bedford	Coshocton	OH
Beacon Falls	New Haven	CT	Beaver	Polk	WI	Bedford	Meigs	OH
Beale	Juniata	PA	Beaver	Carroll	AR	Bedford	Bedford	PA
Beals	Washington	ME	Beaver	Saline	AR	Bedminster	Somerset	NJ
Bean Blossom	Monroe	IN	Beaver	Searcy	AR	Bedminster	Bucks	PA
Bear Bluff	Jackson	WI	Beaver	Iroquois	IL	Bee Branch	Chariton	MO
Bear Butte	Meade	SD	Beaver	Newton	IN	Bee Ridge	Knox	MO
Bear Creek	Sauk	WI	Beaver	Pulaski	IN	Beech Creek	Ashley	AR
Bear Creek	Waupaca	WI	Beaver	Boone	IA	Beech Creek	Greene	IN
Bear Creek	Lee	AR	Beaver	Butler	IA	Beech Creek	Clinton	PA
Bear Creek	Searcy	AR	Beaver	Dallas	IA	Beech Glenn	Madison	NC
Bear Creek	Sevier	AR	Beaver	Grundy	IA	Beech Mountain	Avery	NC
Bear Creek	Christian	IL	Beaver	Gauthrie	IA	Beech Springs	Spartanburg	SC
Bear Creek	Hancock	IL	Beaver	Humboldt	IA	Beech	Miller	AR
Bear Creek	Poweshiek	IA	Beaver	Polk	IA	Beecher	Marinette	WI
Bear Creek	Hamilton	KS	Beaver	Barton	KS	Beekman	Dutchess	NY
Bear Creek	Emmet	MI	Beaver	Cheyenne	KS	Beekmantown	Clinton	NY
Bear Creek	Clearwater	MN	Beaver	Cowley	KS	Beemer	Cuming	NE
Bear Creek	Henry	MO	Beaver	Decatur	KS	Beetown	Grant	WI
Bear Creek	Montgomery	MO	Beaver	Lincoln	KS	Beggs	Okmulgee	OK
Bear Creek	Chatham	NC	Beaver	Phillips	KS	Behestian	Ouachita	AR
Bear Creek	Dickey	ND	Beaver	Rawlins	KS	Beisigi	Adams	ND
Bear Creek	Logan	OK	Beaver	Republic	KS	Bejou	Mahnomen	MN
Bear Creek	Luzerne	PA	Beaver	Scott	KS	Belcher	Prairie	AR
Bear Den	McKenzie	ND	Beaver	Smith	KS	Belchertown	Hampshire	MA
Bear Grove	Fayette	IL	Beaver	Wichita	KS	Belews Creek	Forsyth	NC
Bear Grove	Cass	IA	Beaver	Bay	MI	Belfast	Allegany	NY
Bear Grove	Guthrie	IA	Beaver	Newaygo	MI	Belfast	Murray	MN
Bear Lake	Barron	WI	Beaver	Aitkin	MN	Belfast	Fulton	PA
Bear Lake	Kalkaska	MI	Beaver	Fillmore	MN	Belford	Richland	ND
Bear Lake	Manistee	MI	Beaver	Roseau	MN	Belford	Aurora	SD
Bear Park	Norman	MN	Beaver	Taney	MO	Belgium	Ozaukee	WI
Bear Valley	San Bernardino	CA	Beaver	Buffalo	NE	Belgium	Polk	MN
Bear Wallow	Logan	AR	Beaver	Nance	NE	Belgrade	Kennebec	ME
Bearcreek	Jay	IN	Beaver	Benson	NE	Belgrade	Nicollet	MN
Beard	Alfalfa	OK	Beaver	Mahoning	OH	Belgrade	Washington	MO
Bearden	Marion	AR	Beaver	Noble	OH	Belknap	Pottawattamie	IA
Beardon	Okfuskee	OK	Beaver	Pike	OH	Belknap	Presque Isle	MI
Beardstown	Cass	IL	Beaver	Beaver	OK	Bell Creek	Burt	NE
Bearfield	Perry	OH	Beaver	Caddo	OK	Bell Plain	Marshall	IL
Beargrass	Martin	NC	Beaver	Cotton	OK	Bell	Bayfield	WI
Bearhouse	Ashley	AR	Beaver	Haskell	OK	Bell	Reno	KS
Bearhouse	Drew	AR	Beaver	Kay	OK	Bell	Rice	KS
Bearinger	Presque Isle	MI	Beaver	Clarion	PA	Bell	Cass	ND
Bearville	Itasca	MN	Beaver	Columbia	PA	Bell	Clearfield	PA
Beatie	Benton	AR	Beaver	Crawford	PA	Bell	Jefferson	PA
Beatty	Saint Louis	MN	Beaver	Jefferson	PA	Bell	Westmoreland	PA
Beatty	Nye	NV	Beaver	Snyder	PA	Bell	Colleton	SC
Beaucoup	Washington	IL	Beaver	Miner	SD	Bellair	Appanoose	IA
Beauford	Blue Earth	MN	Beaverdam	Cherokee	NC	Belle Creek	Goodhue	MN
Beaufort	Carteret	NC	Beaverdam	Haywood	NC	Belle Fourhe-Cheyenne		
Beaufort	Beaufort	SC	Beaverdam	Richmond	NC	River Valley	Meade	SD
Beaugrand	Cheboygan	MI	Beaverdam	Watauga	NC	Belle Plain	Norton	KS
Beaulieu	Mahnomen	MN	Beaverhill	Iroquois	IL	Belle Plain	Shawano	WI
Beaulieu	Pembina	ND	Beaverton	Gladwin	MI	Belle Plain	Benton	IA
Beaumont	Riverside	CA	Beecaria	Clearfield	PA	Belle Plain	Sumner	KS
Beauvais	Saint Genevieve	Mo	Beck	McIntosh	OK	Belle Plaine	Scott	MN
Beaver Bay	Lake	MN	Beck	Perkins	SD	Belle Plaine	Spink	SD
Beaver Brook	Washburn	WI	Becker	Cass	MN	Belle Prairie	Livingston	IL
Beaver Creek	Hamilton	IL	Becker	Sherburne	MN	Belle Prairie	Rush	KS
Beaver Creek	Crawford	MI	Becker	Roberts	SD	Belle Prairie	Morrison	MN
Beaver Creek	Rock	MN	Becket	Berkshire	MA	Belle Prairie	Fillmore	NE
Beaver Creek	Jones	NC	Beckwourth	Plumas	CA	Belle Prairie	Beadle	SD
Beaver Creek	Wilkes	NC	Beddington	Washington	ME	Belle River	Douglas	MN
Beaver Creek	Steele	ND	Bedford	Middlesex	MA	Belle	Holt	NE
Beaver Creek	Green	OH	Bedford	Hillsborough	NH	Belle	Woods	OK
Beaver Creek	Tripp	SD	Bedford	Westchester	NY	Belle	Edmunds	SD
Beaver Dam	Dodge	WI	Bedford	Cross	AR	Bellefonte	Boone	AR
Beaver Dam	Butler	MO	Bedford	Wayne	IL	Belleview	Washington	MO
Beaver Dam	Cumberland	NC	Bedford	Taylor	IA	Belleview	Miner	SD
Beaver Falls	Renville	MN	Bedford	Calhoun	MI	Belleville	San Bernardino	CA

TOWNSHIPS OF THE UNITED STATES

TOWNSHIP	COUNTY	STATE	TOWNSHIP	COUNTY	STATE	TOWNSHIP	COUNTY	STATE
Belleville	Saint Clair	IL	Bennington	Ottawa	KS	Benzinger	Elk	PA
Belleville	Chautauqua	KS	Bennington	Shiawassee	MI	Benzonia	Benzie	MI
Belleville	Republic	KS	Bennington	Mower	MN	Beotia	Spink	SD
Belleville	Essex	NJ	Bennington	Licking	OH	Beowawe	Eureka	NV
Bellevue	Brown	WI	Bennington	Morrow	OH	Bergen	Genesee	NY
Bellevue	Jackson	IA	Bennington	Bryan	OK	Bergen	Marathon	WI
Bellevue	Eaton	MI	Benona	Oceana	MI	Bergen	Vernon	WI
Bellevue	Morrison	MN	Bensalem	Moore	NC	Bergen	Mc Leod	MN
Bellevue	Huron	OH	Bensalem	Bucks	PA	Bergen	Nelson	ND
Bellevue	Sandusky	OH	Benson	Hamilton	NY	Bereley Heights	Union	NJ
Bellflower	McLean	IL	Benson	Rutland	VT	Berkeley	Ocean	NJ
Bellingham	Norfork	MA	Benson	Swift	MN	Berkley	Bristol	MA
Bellmont	Franklin	NY	Bentinck	Bottineau	ND	Berkshire	Tioga	NY
Bellmore	Stone	AR	Bentley	Conway	AR	Berkshire	Franklin	VT
Bellville	Pocahontas	IA	Bentley	Gladwin	MI	Berkshire	Delaware	OH
Belmond	Wright	IA	Bentley	Atoka	OK	Berland	Ononagon	MI
Belmont	Waldo	ME	Benton	Kennebec	ME	Berlin	Hartford	CT
Belmont	Middlesex	MA	Benton	Grafton	NH	Berlin	Worcester	MA
Belmont	Belknap	NH	Benton	Yates	NY	Berlin	Rensselaer	NY
Belmont	Lafayette	WI	Benton	Lafayette	WI	Berlin	Washington	VT
Belmont	Portage	WI	Benton	Faulkner	AR	Berlin	Green Lake	WI
Belmont	Warren	IA	Benton	Fulton	AR	Berlin	Marathon	WI
Belmont	Kingman	KS	Benton	Mono	CA	Berlin	Bureau	IL
Belmont	Phillips	KS	Benton	Franklin	IL	Berlin	Harper	KS
Belmont	Rooks	KS	Benton	Lake	IL	Berlin	Ionia	MI
Belmont	Woodson	KS	Benton	Elkhart	IN	Berlin	Monroe	MI
Belmont	Jackson	MN	Benton	Monroe	IN	Berlin	Saint Clair	MI
Belmont	Traill	ND	Benton	Benton	IA	Berlin	Steele	MN
Belmont	Douglas	SD	Benton	Cass	IA	Berlin	Cass	ND
Belmont	Spink	SD	Benton	Des Moines	IA	Berlin	Wells	ND
Beloit	Rock	WI	Benton	Fremont	IA	Berlin	Camden	NJ
Beloit	Mitchell	KS	Benton	Keokuk	IA	Berlin	Delaware	OH
Belpre	Edwards	KS	Benton	Lucas	IA	Berlin	Erie	OH
Belpre	Washington	OH	Benton	Ringgold	IA	Berlin	Holmes	OH
Belton	Flathead	MT	Benton	Taylor	IA	Berlin	Knox	OH
Belton	Anderson	SC	Benton	Wayne	IA	Berlin	Mahoning	OH
Belvedere	Los Angeles	CA	Benton	Atchison	KS	Berlin	Roger Mills	OK
Belvidere	Lamoille	VT	Benton	Butler	KS	Berlin	Wayne	PA
Belvidere	Buffalo	WI	Benton	Hodgeman	KS	Bern	Marathon	WI
Belvidere	Boone	IL	Benton	Berrien	MI	Bern	Athens	OH
Belvidere	Monona	IA	Benton	Cheboygan	MI	Bern	Berks	PA
Belvidere	Montcalm	MI	Benton	Eaton	MI	Bernadotte	Fulton	IL
Belvidere	Goodhue	MN	Benton	Carver	MN	Bernadotte	Nicollet	MN
Belvidere	Warren	NJ	Benton	Adair	MO	Bernard	Hughes	OK
Belvidere	Perquimans	NC	Benton	Andrew	MO	Bernards	Somerset	NJ
Belvidere	Jackson	SD	Benton	Atchison	MO	Bernardston	Franklin	MA
Belvoir	Pitt	NC	Benton	Cedar	MO	Berne	Albnay	NY
Belvoir	Sampson	NC	Benton	Crawford	MO	Berne	Fairfield	OH
Belvue	Pottawatomie	KS	Benton	Davies	MO	Berreman	Jo Daviess	IL
Bement	Piatt	IL	Benton	Douglas	MO	Berrien	Berrien	MI
Bemidji	Betrami	MN	Benton	Holt	MO	Berry	Dane	WI
Ben Lomond	Sevier	AR	Benton	Howell	MO	Berry	Wayne	IL
Ben Wade	Pope	MN	Benton	Knox	MO	Berry	Grant	OK
Benedict	Faulkner	AR	Benton	Linn	MO	Berryhill	Mecklenburg	NC
Benedict	Sanborn	SD	Benton	Newton	MO	Bertha	Todd	MN
Benedicta	Aroostook	ME	Benton	Osage	MO	Berthold	Ward	ND
Benezette	Elk	PA	Benton	Polk	MO	Bertram	Linn	IA
Bengal	Clinton	MI	Benton	Wayne	MO	Bertrand	Berrien	MI
Benkelman	Cheyenne	KS	Benton	Hocking	OH	Berwick	York	ME
Benicia	Solano	CA	Benton	Monroe	OH	Berwick	Warren	IL
Benner	Centre	PA	Benton	Ottawa	OH	Berwick	Nemaha	KS
Bennett Bayou	Fulton	AR	Benton	Paulding	OH	Berwick	Newton	MO
Bennett Springs	Barnwell	SC	Benton	Pike	OH	Berwick	McHenry	ND
Bennett	Douglas	WI	Benton	Beaver	OK	Berwick	Adams	PA
Bennett	Clay	AR	Benton	Ellis	OK	Berwyn	Cook	IL
Bennett	Kingman	KS	Benton	Columbia	PA	Berwyn	Custer	NE
Bennett	Fillmore	NE	Benton	Lackawanna	PA	Berwyn	Cartar	OK
Bennezette	Butler	IA	Benton	McCook	SD	Beseman	Carlton	MN
Bennington	Hillsborough	NH	Benton	Minnehaha	SD	Bessemer	Gogebic	MI
Bennington	Wyoming	NY	Benton	Spink	SD	Bessie	Washita	OK
Bennington	Bennington	VT	Bentonsville	Johnston	NC	Bethania	Forsyth	NC
Bennington	Marshall	IL	Bentru	Grand Forks	ND	Bethany	New Haven	CT
Bennington	Black Hawk	IA	Benville	Beltrami	MN	Bethany	Genesee	NY

TOWNSHIPS OF THE UNITED STATES

TOWNSHIP	COUNTY	STATE	TOWNSHIP	COUNTY	STATE	TOWNSHIP	COUNTY	STATE
Bethany	Osborne	KS	Big Creek	White	IN	Binghampton	Barnes	ND
Bethany	Gartiot	MI	Big Creek	Black Hawk	IA	Binghamton	Bromme	NY
Bethany	Harrison	MO	Big Creek	Ellis	KS	Birch Cooley	Renville	MN
Bethany	Iredell	NC	Big Creek	Neosho	KS	Birch Creek	Chippewa	WI
Bethea	Dillon	SC	Big Creek	Russell	KS	Birch Creek	Pine	MN
Bethel	Fairfield	CT	Big Creek	Oscoda	MI	Birch Lake	Cass	MN
Bethel	Oxford	ME	Big Creek	Cass	MO	Birch Run	Saginaw	MI
Bethel	Sullivan	NY	Big Creek	Henry	MO	Birch	Lincoln	WI
Bethel	Windsor	VT	Big Creek	Madison	MO	Birch	Beltrami	MN
Bethel	McDonough	IL	Big Creek	Ozark	MO	Birch Tree	Shannon	MO
Bethel	Posey	IN	Big Creek	Taney	MO	Birchdale	Todd	MN
Bethel	Fayette	IA	Big Creek	Stokes	NC	Birchwood	Washburn	WI
Bethel	Branch	MI	Big Falls	Rusk	WI	Bird City	Cheyenne	KS
Bethel	Shelby	MO	Big Flat	Baxter	AL	Bird Island	Renville	MN
Bethel	Bladen	NC	Big Flats	Chemung	NY	Bird	Conway	AR
Bethel	Perquimans	NC	Big Flats	Adams	WI	Bird	Jackson	AR
Bethel	Pitt	NC	Big Fork	Montgomery	AR	Bird	Macoupin	IL
Bethel	Towner	ND	Big Fork	Polk	AR	Birdsall	Allegany	NY
Bethel	Clark	OH	Big Grove	Kendall	IL	Biringham	Schuyler	IL
Bethel	Miami	OH	Big Grove	Benton	IA	Biringham	Chester	PA
Bethel	Monroe	OH	Big Grove	Johnson	IA	Biringham	Delaware	PA
Bethel	Armstrong	PA	Big Hill	Osage	OK	Birnamwood	Shawano	WI
Bethel	Berks	PA	Big Island	Marion	OH	Birtsell	Foster	ND
Bethel	Delaware	PA	Big Lake	Mississippi	AR	Biscoe	Montgomery	NC
Bethel	Fulton	PA	Big Lake	Sherburne	MN	Bishop	Effingham	IL
Bethel	Lebanon	PA	Big Lick	Stanly	NC	Bishop	Major	OK
Bethel	York	SC	Big Meadow	Williams	ND	Bishopville	Lee	SC
Bethel	Clay	SD	Big Mound	Wayne	IL	Bismarck	Hot Springs	AR
Bethesda	York	SC	Big Prairie	Newaygo	MI	Bismarck	Presque Isle	MI
Bethlehem	Litchfield	CT	Big Prairie	New Madrid	MO	Bismarck	Sibley	MN
Bethlehem	Grafton	NH	Big Rapids	Mecosta	MI	Bismarck	Cuming	NE
Bethlehem	Albany	NY	Big River	Mendocino	CA	Bismark	Platte	NE
Bethlehem	Cass	IN	Big River	Jefferson	MO	Bison	Perkings	SD
Bethlehem	Clark	IN	Big River	Saint Francois	MO	Biwabik	Saint Louis	MN
Bethlehem	Henry	MO	Big Rock	Pulaski	AR	Bixby	Tulsa	OK
Bethlehem	Hunterdon	NJ	Big Rock	Kane	IL	Bjornson	McHenry	ND
Bethlehem	Coshocton	OH	Big Sioux	Union	SD	Black Bear	Noble	OK
Bethlehem	Stark	OH	Big Spring	Benton	AR	Black Brook	Clinton	NY
Bethlehem	Northampton	PA	Big Spring	Izard	AR	Black Brook	Polk	WI
Bettina	Beckham	OK	Big Spring	Shelby	IL	Black Butte	Hettinger	ND
Beulah	Cass	MN	Big Spring	Seneca	OH	Black Creek	Outagamie	WI
Beulah	Johnston	NC	Big Springs	Union	SD	Black Creek	Shelby	MO
Beulah	Davison	SD	Big Springs	Marion	AR	Black Creek	Wilson	NC
Beulah	Hanson	SD	Big Stone	Big Stone	MN	Black Creek	Mercer	OH
Bevent	Marathon	WI	Big Stone	Grant	SD	Black Creek	Luzerne	PA
Beverly Hills	Los Angeles	CA	Big Stone	Williams	ND	Black Creek	Lexington	SC
Beverly	Sebastain	AR	Big Timber	Rush	KS	Black Dog	Osage	OK
Beverly	Adams	IL	Big Valley	Lassen	CA	Black Dog	Lyman	SD
Bevier	Macon	MO	Big Woods	Marshall	MN	Black Earth	Dane	WI
Bexley	Franklin	OH	Bigelow	Marshall	KS	Black Fish	Saint Francis	AR
Bible Grove	Clay	IL	Bigelow	Nobles	MN	Black Fork	Scott	AR
Bicker	Mountrail	ND	Bigelow	Holt	MO	Black Hammer	Houston	MN
Bidwell	Modoc	CA	Bigfork	Itasca	MN	Black Hawk	Rock Island	IL
Big Apple	Oregon	MO	Bigger	Jennings	IN	Black Hawk	Black Hawk	IA
Big Bend	Rusk	WI	Biggs	Butte	CA	Black Hawk	Grundy	IA
Big Bend	Republic	KS	Biggsville	Henderson	IL	Black Hawk	Jefferson	IA
Big Bend	Chippewa	MN	Bigheart	Osage	OK	Black Jack	Richmond	NC
Big Bend	Mountrail	ND	Bigler	Clearfield	PA	Black Lick	Indiana	PA
Big Bend	Ransom	ND	Biglick	Hancock	OH	Black Loam	La Moure	ND
Big Bottom	Independence	AR	Bilby	Hughes	OK	Black Mountain	Buncombe	NC
Big Bow	Stanton	KS	Billerica	Middlesex	MA	Black Oak	Craighead	AR
Big Buffalo	Jackson	SD	Billings	Gladwin	MI	Black Oak	Crittenden	AR
Big Creek	Cleburne	AR	Billings	Cavalier	ND	Black Oak	Franklin	AR
Big Creek	Craighead	AR	Billmore	Oregon	MO	Black Oak	Mahaska	IA
Big Creek	Fulton	AR	Bilodeau	Wells	ND	Black Pond	Oregon	MO
Big Creek	Hot Spring	AR	Bingham	Somerset	ME	Black River	Independence	AR
Big Creek	Lee	AR	Bingham	Hancock	IA	Black River	Lawrence	AR
Big Creek	Marion	AR	Bingham	Clinton	MI	Black River	Pennington	MN
Big Creek	Phillips	AR	Bingham	Huron	MI	Black River	Butler	MO
Big Creek	Searcy	AR	Bingham	Leelanau	MI	Black River	Reynolds	MO
Big Creek	Sharp	AR	Bingham	Orange	NC	Black River	Wayne	MO
Big Creek	Sebastian	AR	Bingham	Traill	ND	Black River	Cumberland	NC
Big Creek	White	AR	Bingham	Potter	PA	Black River	Harnett	NC

TOWNSHIPS OF THE UNITED STATES

TOWNSHIP	COUNTY	STATE
Black Rock	Lawrence	AR
Black Swamp	Florence	SC
Black Tail	Williams	ND
Black	Posey	IN
Black	Somerset	PA
Black	Tripp	SD
Black Wolf	Winnebago	WI
Black Wolf	Ellsworth	KS
Blackberry	Kane	IL
Blackberry	Itasca	MN
Blackburn	Jefferson	OK
Blackburn	Pawnee	OK
Blackgum	Sequoyah	OK
Blackhoof	Carlton	MN
Blackhawk-Piedmont-Ellsworth	Meade	SD
Blackland	Howard	AR
Blacklick	Cambria	PA
Blackman	Jackson	MI
Blackpipe	Mellette	SD
Blacks	Yolo	CA
Blackstock	Chester	SC
Blackstone	Worcester	MA
Blackville	Barnwell	SC
Blackwater	Cooper	MO
Blackwater	Pettis	MO
Blackwater	Saline	MO
Blackwater	Mc Lean	ND
Blackwell	Forest	WI
Blackwell	Kay	OK
Bladenboro	Bladen	NC
Blain	Bottineau	ND
Blaine	Aroostook	ME
Blaine	Burnett	WI
Blaine	Ida	IA
Blaine	Wright	IA
Blaine	Clay	KS
Blaine	Harper	KS
Blaine	Lane	KS
Blaine	Marion	KS
Blaine	Ottawa	KS
Blaine	Smith	KS
Blaine	Benzie	MI
Blaine	Adams	NE
Blaine	Antelope	NE
Blaine	Cuming	NE
Blaine	Kearney	NE
Blaine	Garfield	OK
Blaine	Washington	PA
Blaine	Clark	SD
Blaine	Jerauld	SD
Blair	Clay	IL
Blair	Grand Traverse	MI
Blair	Washington	NE
Blairsburg	Hamilton	IA
Blairstown	Warren	NJ
Blake	Colleton	SC
Blakely	Scott	MN
Blakely	Gage	NE
Blanchard	Lafayette	WI
Blanchard	Traill	ND
Blanchard	Hancock	OH
Blanchard	Hardin	OH
Blanchard	Putnam	OH
Blanchard	Spokane	WA
Blandford	Hampden	MA
Blandinsville	McDonough	IL
Blanset	Scott	AR
Bleecker	Fulton	NY
Blendon	Ottawa	MI
Blendon	Franklin	OH
Blendon	Davison	SD
Blenheim	Schoharie	NY
Blind Lake	Cass	MN
Blinsmon	Moody	SD
Bliss	Emmet	MI
Blissfield	Lenawee	MI
Blissville	Jefferson	IL
Blocker	Edgefield	SC
Blom	Deuel	SD
Bloom	Richland	WI
Bloom	Cook	IL
Bloom	Clay	KS
Bloom	Ford	KS
Bloom	Osborne	KS
Bloom	Nobles	MN
Bloom	Stutsman	ND
Bloom	Fairfield	OH
Bloom	Morgan	OH
Bloom	Scioto	OH
Bloom	Seneca	OH
Bloom	Wood	OH
Bloom	Clearfield	PA
Bloomenfield	Stutsman	ND
Bloomer	Chippewa	WI
Bloomer	Sebastian	AR
Bloomer	Montcalm	MI
Bloomer	Marshall	MN
Bloomfield	Hartford	CT
Bloomfield	Essex	VT
Bloomfield	Walworth	WI
Bloomfield	Waushara	WI
Bloomfield	Nevada	CA
Bloomfield	Johnson	IL
Bloomfield	Lagrange	IN
Bloomfield	Clinton	IA
Bloomfield	Davis	IA
Bloomfield	Polk	IA
Bloomfield	Winneshiek	IA
Bloomfield	Mitchell	KS
Bloomfield	Sheridan	KS
Bloomfield	Huron	MI
Bloomfield	Missaukee	MI
Bloomfield	Oakland	MI
Bloomfield	Fillmore	MN
Bloomfield	Essex	NJ
Bloomfield	Traill	ND
Bloomfield	Jackson	OH
Bloomfield	Logan	OH
Bloomfield	Trumbull	OH
Bloomfield	Bedford	PA
Bloomfield	Crawford	PA
Bloomfield	Grand Forks	ND
Blooming Grove	Orange	NY
Blooming Grove	Dane	WI
Blooming Grove	Franklin	IN
Blooming Grove	Waseca	MN
Blooming Grove	Richland	OH
Blooming Grove	Pike	PA
Blooming Prairie	Steele	MN
Blooming Prairie	Divide	ND
Blooming Valley	Roseau	MN
Blooming Valley	Divide	ND
Blooming Valley	Grant	SD
Bloomingdale	Du Page	IL
Bloomingdale	Van Buren	MI
Bloomington City	McLean	IL
Bloomington	Grant	WI
Bloomington	San Bernardino	CA
Bloomington	McLean	IL
Bloomington	Monroe	IN
Bloomington	Decatur	IA
Bloomington	Muscatine	IA
Bloomington	Butler	KS
Bloomington	Buchanan	MO
Bloomington	Franklin	NE
Bloomington	Greer	OK
Bloomsburg	Columbia	PA
Bloss	Tioga	PA
Blount	Vermillion	IL
Blowers	Otter Tail	MN
Blowing Rock	Watauga	NC
Blue Ash	Hamilton	OH
Blue Bayou	Howard	AR
Blue Butte	McKenzie	ND
Blue Cane	Greene	AR
Blue Creek	Adams	IN
Blue Creek	Paulding	OH
Blue Earth City	Faribault	MN
Blue Grass	Beaver	OK
Blue Grass	Scott	IA
Blue Hill	Mitchell	KS
Blue Hill	Sherburne	MN
Blue Hill	McLean	ND
Blue Lake	Kalkaska	MI
Blue Lake	Muskegon	MI
Blue Mound	Macon	IL
Blue Mound	McLean	IL
Blue Mound	Linn	KS
Blue Mound	Livingston	MO
Blue Mound	Vernon	MO
Blue Mound	Wagoner	OK
Blue Mounds	Dane	WI
Blue Mounds	Pope	MN
Blue Mountain	Logan	AR
Blue Mountain	Stone	AR
Blue Rapids City	Marshall	KS
Blue Rapids	Marshall	KS
Blue Ridge	Howard	AR
Blue Ridge	Piatt	IL
Blue Ridge	Henderson	NC
Blue Ridge	Watauga	NC
Blue Ridge	Williams	ND
Blue River	Harrison	IN
Blue River	Henry	IN
Blue River	Johnson	IN
Blue Rock	Muskingum	OH
Blue Springs	Gage	NE
Blue River	Hancock	IN
Blue Springs	Hoke	NC
Blue	Pottawatomie	KS
Blue	Jackson	MO
Blue Valley	Pottawatomie	KS
Blueberry	Wadena	MN
Bluebird	La Moure	ND
Bluehill	Hancock	ME
Bluff Creek	Monroe	IA
Bluff Springs	Cass	IL
Bluff	Sumner	KS
Bluff	Grant	OK
Bluffdale	Greene	IL
Bluffton	Yell	AR
Bluffton	Winneshiek	IA
Bluffton	Otter Tail	MN
Bluffton	Beaufort	SC
Blumfield	Saginaw	MI
Blythe	Boone	AR
Blythe	Marion	AR
Blythe	Schuylkill	PA
Boardman	Clayton	IA
Boardman	Kalkaska	MI
Boardman	Mahoning	OH
Boardman	Medina	OH
Boas	Lawrence	AR
Bob Ward	Crittenden	AR
Bodcaw	Hempstead	AR
Bodie	Mono	CA
Boeuf	Franklin	MO
Boeuf	Gasconade	MO

TOWNSHIPS OF THE UNITED STATES

TOWNSHIP	COUNTY	STATE	TOWNSHIP	COUNTY	STATE	TOWNSHIP	COUNTY	STATE
Bogansville	Union	SC	Boone	Douglas	MO	Bowling Green	Licking	OH
Bogard	Daviess	IN	Boone	Franklin	MO	Bowling Green	Marion	OH
Bogard	Henry	MO	Boone	Greene	MO	Bowling	Rock Island	IL
Boggs	Armstrong	PA	Boone	Maries	MO	Bowman	Cleveland	AR
Boggs	Centre	PA	Boone	Texas	MO	Bowman	Sullivan	MO
Boggs	Clearfield	PA	Boone	Wright	MO	Bowman	Bowman	ND
Bogle	Gentry	MO	Boone	Davidson	NC	Bowman	Roger Mills	OK
Bogue	Columbus	NC	Boone	Watauga	NC	Bowman	Orangeburg	SC
Bogus Brook	Mille Lacs	MN	Boone	Caddo	OK	Bowne	Kent	MI
Bogy	Jefferson	AR	Boone	Oklahoma	OK	Bowstring	Itasca	MN
Bohannon	Madison	AR	Boons Lick	Howard	MO	Box	Cedar	MO
Bohemia	Ontonagon	MI	Boonton	Morris	NJ	Boxborough	Middlesex	MA
Bohemia	Knox	NE	Boonville	Oneida	NY	Boxford	Essex	MA
Bohemia	Saunders	NE	Boonville	Cooper	MO	Bosville	Marshall	MN
Bohnsack	Traill	ND	Boonville	Yadkin	NC	Boy Lake	Cass	MN
Boiling Springs	Cleveland	NC	Booth	Palo Alto	IA	Boy River	Cass	MN
Boiling Springs	Lexington	SC	Boothbay Harbor	Lincoln	ME	Boyd	Burleigh	ND
Bois Blanc	Mackinac	MI	Boothbay	Lincoln	ME	Boyd	Transylvania	NC
Bois Brule	Perry	MO	Bordeaux	McCormick	SC	Boyd	Dewey	OK
Bois d' Arc	Hemstead	AR	Bordentown	Burlington	NJ	Boyer	Crawford	IA
Bois d' Arc	Montgomery	IL	Border	Divide	ND	Boyer	Harrison	IA
Bokchito	Bryan	OK	Bordulac	Foster	ND	Boyer Valley	Sac	IA
Bokes Creek	Logan	OH	Borego	San Diego	CA	Boyesen	Bowman	ND
Bokoshe	LeFlore	OK	Borgholm	Mille Lacs	MN	Boylston	Worcester	MA
Boles	Tulsa	OK	Borough	Beaver	PA	Boylston	Oswego	NY
Boles	Franklin	MO	Boscawen	Merrimack	NH	Boyne Valley	Charlevoix	MI
Bolivar	Allegany	NY	Boscobel	Grant	WI	Boynton	Tazewell	IL
Bolivar	Jefferson	AR	Bossko	Roberts	SD	Bozrah	New London	CT
Bolivar	Poinsett	AR	Boston	Erie	NY	Braceville	Grundy	IL
Bolivar	Benton	IN	Boston	Franklin	AR	Braceville	Trumbull	OH
Bolo	Washington	IL	Boston	Madison	AR	Brackett	McDowell	NC
Bolton	Tolland	CT	Boston	Newton	AR	Bradbury	Mille Lacs	MN
Bolton	Worcester	MA	Boston	Washington	AR	Braden	Le Flore	OK
Bolton	Warren	NY	Boston	Wayne	IN	Bradford	Penobscot	ME
Bolton	Chittenden	VT	Boston	Ionia	MI	Bradford	Merrimack	NH
Bolton	Cowley	KS	Boston	Summit	OH	Bradford	Steuben	NY
Bolton	Columbus	NC	Boughton	Nevada	AR	Bradford	Orange	VT
Bombay	Franklin	NY	Boulder Junction	Vilas	WI	Bradford	Rock	WI
Bon Homme	Bon Homme	SD	Boulder	Linn	IA	Bradford	Lee	IL
Bonaparte	Van Buren	IA	Boulware	Gasconade	MO	Bradford	Chickasaw	IA
Bonaville	McPherson	KS	Bourbois	Gasconade	MO	Bradford	Isanti	MN
Bond	Lawrence	IL	Bourbon	Douglas	IL	Bradford	Wilkin	MN
Bondin	Murray	MN	Bourbon	Marsahll	IN	Bradford	Clearfield	PA
Bone Creek	Butler	NE	Bourbon	Boone	MO	Bradford	McKean	PA
Bone Lake	Polk	WI	Bourbon	Callaway	MO	Bradley	Grady	OK
Bonetrail	Williams	ND	Bourbon	Knox	MO	Bradley	Greenwood	SC
Bonhomme	Saint Louis	MO	Bourbonnais	Kankakee	IL	Bradley	Penobscot	ME
Bonilla	Beadle	SD	Bourland	Jefferson	OK	Bradley	Lincoln	WI
Bonne Femme	Howard	MO	Bourne	Barnstable	MA	Bradley	Van Buren	AR
Bono	Lawrence	IN	Bourret	Gladwin	MI	Bradley	Monterey	CA
Bonpas	Richland	IL	Bovina	Delaware	NY	Bradley	Jackson	IL
Bonus	Boone	IL	Bovine	Outagamie	WI	Bradley	Quachita	AR
Boomer	Pottawattamie	IA	Bovine	Jones	SD	Bradshaw	Clay	AR
Boomer	Wilkes	NC	Bow Creek	Phillips	KS	Bradshaw	Mitchell	NC
Boon Hill	Johnston	NC	Bow Creek	Rooks	KS	Brady	Kalamazoo	MI
Boon Lake	Renville	MN	Bow Creek	Sheridan	KS	Brady	Saginaw	MI
Boon Station	Alamance	NC	Bow	Merrimack	NH	Brady	Garvin	OK
Boon	Warrick	IN	Bowbells	Burke	ND	Brady	Williams	OH
Boon	Wexford	MI	Bowden	Madison	AR	Brady	Butler	PA
Boone	Logan	AR	Bowdie	Edmunds	SD	Brady	Clarion	PA
Boone	Union	AR	Bowdoin	Sagadahoc	ME	Brady	Clearfield	PA
Boone	Boone	IL	Bowdoinham	Sagadahoc	ME	Brady	Huntingdon	PA
Boone	Cass	IN	Bowdre	Douglas	IL	Brady	Lycoming	PA
Boone	Crawford	IN	Bowden	Mississippi	AR	Bradys Bend	Armstrong	PA
Boone	Debois	IN	Bowen	Sargent	ND	Bragg	Ouachita	AR
Boone	Harrison	IN	Bowerbank	Piscataquis	ME	Braggadocio	Pemiscot	MO
Boone	Madison	IN	Bowie	Chicot	AR	Brainard	Brown	SD
Boone	Porter	IN	Bowie	Desha	AR	Braintree	Norfolk	MA
Boone	Dallas	IA	Bowlan	Shannon	MO	Braintree	Orange	VT
Boone	Hamilton	IA	Bowlesville	Gallatin	IL	Braintrim	Wyoming	PA
Boone	Hancock	IA	Bowling Green	Fayette	IL	Bramhall	Hyde	SD
Boone	Wright	IA	Bowling Green	Chariton	MO	Brampton	Delta	MI
Boone	Crawford	MO	Bowling Green	Pettis	MO	Brampton	Sargent	ND

TOWNSHIPS OF THE UNITED STATES

TOWNSHIP	COUNTY	STATE	TOWNSHIP	COUNTY	STATE	TOWNSHIP	COUNTY	STATE
Branch	Mason	MI	Bridge Creek	Eau Claire	WI	Bristol	Worth	IA
Branch	Schuylkill	PA	Bridge Creek	Ouachita	AR	Bristol	Fillmore	MN
Branchburg	Somerset	NJ	Bridgehampton	Sanilac	MI	Bristol	Sherman	NE
Branchville	Orangeburg	SC	Bridgeport	Fairfield	CT	Bristol	Trumbull	OH
Brandenburg	Richland	ND	Bridgeport	Crawford	WI	Bristow	Randolph	AR
Brander	Bottineau	ND	Bridgeport	Lawrence	IL	Bristow	Boyd	NE
Brandon	Franklin	NY	Bridgeport	Mono	CA	Bristow	Creek	OK
Brandon	Rutland	VT	Bridgeport	Nevada	CA	Britt	Hancock	IA
Brandon	Jackson	IA	Bridgeport	Saginaw	MI	Brittian	Hettinger	ND
Brandon	Oakland	MI	Bridgeport	Warren	MO	Britton	Oklahoma	OK
Brandon	Douglas	MN	Bridges	Ozark	MO	Brittons Neck	Marion	SC
Brandon	Madison	MT	Bridgeton	Newaygo	MI	Britts	Robeson	NC
Brandon	Renville	ND	Bridgeton	Bucks	PA	Broad River	Buncombe	NC
Brandon	Minnehaha	SD	Bridgewater	McCook	SD	Broad River	Lexington	SC
Brandrup	Wilkin	MN	Bridgewater	Litchfield	CT	Broad River	York	SC
Brandsvold	Polk	MN	Bridgewater	Arookstook	ME	Broad Top	Bedford	PA
Brandt	Polk	MN	Bridgewater	Plymouth	MA	Broadalbin	Fulton	NY
Brandt	Deuel	SD	Bridgewater	Grafton	NH	Broadbay	Forsyth	NC
Brandywine	Hancock	IN	Bridgewater	Oneida	NY	Broadland	Beadle	SD
Brandywine	Shelby	IN	Bridgewater	Windsor	VT	Broadlawn	Steele	ND
Branford	New Haven	CT	Bridgewater	Adair	IA	Broadview	Griggs	ND
Branson	Taney	MO	Bridgewater	Washtenaw	MI	Broadway	Anderson	SC
Brant	Erie	NY	Bridgewater	Rice	MN	Broadwell	Logan	IL
Brant	Saginaw	MI	Bridgewater	Somerset	NJ	Brockway	Jackson	WI
Brantford	Washington	KS	Bridgewater	Williams	OH	Brockway	Saint Clair	MI
Brantford	Hamlin	SD	Bridgewater	Susquehanna	PA	Brockway	Stearns	MN
Brasher	Saint Lawrence	NY	Bridgton	Cumberland	ME	Broe	Benson	ND
Brassfirld	Granville	NC	Bridprot	Addison	VT	Brogden	Wayne	NC
Brasstown	Clay	NC	Briggs	Cherokee	OK	Brogdon	Johnston	OK
Bratton	Adams	OH	Briggsville	Yell	AR	Broken Bow	Custer	NE
Bratton	Miffin	PA	Brighton	Franklin	NY	Brokenstraw	Warren	PA
Brawley	Scott	AR	Brighton	Marathon	WI	Bronson	Branch	MI
Bray	Pennington	MN	Brighton	Cass	IA	Bronson	Huron	OH
Brazeau	Oconto	WI	Brighton	Washington	IA	Brook Park	Pine	MN
Brazeau	Perry	MO	Brighton	Sacramento	CA	Brookbank	Mountrail	ND
Brazil	Clay	IN	Brighton	Macoupin	IL	Brookdale	Rush	KS
Brea	Orange	CA	Brighton	Monroe	NY	Brooke	Buena Vista	IA
Breckenridge	Greene	AR	Brighton	Kenosha	WI	Brooken	Haskell	OK
Breckenridge	Jackson	AR	Brighton	Livingston	MI	Brookfield	Fairfield	CT
Breckenridge	Wilkin	MN	Brighton	Nicollet	MN	Brookfield	Worcester	MA
Breckenridge	Caldwell	MO	Brighton	Essex	VT	Brookfield	Carroll	NH
Brecknock	Berks	PA	Brighton	Beaver	PA	Brookfield	Madison	NY
Brecknock	Lancaster	PA	Brighton	Lorain	OH	Brookfield	Orange	VT
Breed	Oconto	WI	Brightwater	Benton	AR	Brookfield	Waukesha	WI
Breen	Dickinson	MI	Brightwood	Richland	ND	Brookfield	La Salle	IL
Brease	Clinton	IL	Briley	Montmorency	MI	Brookfield	Clinton	IA
Breitung	Dickson	MI	Brillian	Ward	ND	Brookfield	Worth	IA
Breitung	Saint Louis	MN	Brillion	Calumet	WI	Brookfield	Eaton	MI
Bremen	Lincoln	ME	Brimer	Barnes	ND	Brookfield	Huron	MI
Bremen	Cook	IL	Brimfield	Hampden	MA	Brookfield	Renville	MN
Bremen	Delaware	IA	Brimfield	Peoria	IL	Brookfield	Linn	MO
Bremen	Pine	MN	Brimfield	Portage	OH	Brookfield	Noble	OH
Bremen	Wells	ND	Bringham	Iowa	WI	Brookfield	Trumbull	OH
Brenham	Kiowa	KS	Brinkley	Monroe	AR	Brookfield	Tioga	PA
Brenna	Grand Forks	ND	Brinkleyville	Halifax	NC	Brookfield	McCook	SD
Brent	Sequoyah	OK	Brinton	Pottawatomie	OK	Brookhaven	Suffolk	NY
Brenton	Ford	IL	Brisbane	Grant	ND	Brooking	Jackson	MO
Brentwood	Rockingham	NH	Brislet	Polk	MN	Brookings	Brookings	SD
Bressia	Noble	OK	Bristol	Day	SD	Brookland	Craighead	AR
Brenton	Washington	MO	Bristol	Bucks	PA	Brooklin	Hancock	ME
Bretton	Hughes	SD	Bristol	Morgan	OH	Brookline	Norfork	MA
Brevard	Transylvania	NC	Bristol	Aurora	SD	Brookline	Hillsborough	NH
Brevator	Saint Louis	MN	Bristol	Hartford	CT	Brookline	Windham	VT
Brevort	Mackinac	MI	Bristol	Lincoln	ME	Brookline	Greene	MO
Brewer	Penobscot	ME	Bristol	Grafton	NH	Brooklyn	Windham	CT
Brewer	Arkansas	AR	Bristol	Ontario	NY	Brooklyn	Green	WI
Brewer	Howard	AR	Bristol	Bristol	RI	Brooklyn	Green Lake	WI
Brewer	Pike	AR	Bristol	Addison	VT	Brooklyn	Washburn	WI
Brewer	Muskogee	OK	Bristol	Dane	WI	Brooklyn	Alameda	CA
Brewington	Clarendon	SC	Bristol	Kenosha	WI	Brooklyn	Lee	CA
Brewster	Barnstable	MA	Bristol	Faulkner	AR	Brooklyn	Schuyler	IL
Briar Creek	Columbia	PA	Bristol	Kendall	IL	Brooklyn	Williams	ND
Brick	Ocean	NJ	Bristol	Green	IA	Brooklyn	Susquehanna	PA

TOWNSHIPS OF THE UNITED STATES

TOWNSHIP	COUNTY	STATE	TOWNSHIP	COUNTY	STATE	TOWNSHIP	COUNTY	STATE
Brooklyn	Lincoln	SD	Bruce	Cavalier	ND	Buck Prairie	Lawrence	MO
Brooks	Waldo	ME	Brule	Douglas	WI	Buck Range	Howard	AR
Brooks	Newaygo	MI	Brule	Brule	SD	Buck Shoal	Yadkin	NC
Brooks	Greenwood	SC	Brule	Lyman	SD	Buck Swamp	Wayne	NC
Brookside	Clinton	IL	Brule	Union	SD	Buck	Edgar	IL
Brooksville	Hancock	ME	Bruner	Christian	MO	Buck	Hardin	OH
Brookville	Ogle	IL	Bruno	Butler	KS	Buck	Luzerne	PA
Brookville	Franklin	IN	Bruno	Pine	MN	Buckeye	Stephenson	IL
Brookville	Redwood	MN	Brunson	Tripp	SD	Buckeye	Hardin	IA
Broome	Schoharie	NY	Brunswick Hills	Medina	OH	Buckeye	Dickinson	KS
Broomfield	Isabella	MI	Brunswick	Cumberland	ME	Buckeye	Ellis	KS
Brothersfield	Turner	SD	Brunswick	Rensselaer	NY	Buckeye	Ottawa	KS
Brothersvalley	Somerset	PA	Brunswick	Essex	VT	Buckeye	Gladwin	MI
Brothertown	Calumet	WI	Brunswick	Eau Claire	WI	Buckeye	Shannon	MO
Broughton	Livingston	IL	Brunswick	Kanabec	MN	Buckeye	Kidder	ND
Brouillitts Creek	Edgar	IL	Brunswick	Chariton	MO	Buckeye	Spokane	WA
Brower	Randolph	NC	Brunswick	Medina	OH	Buckfield	Oxford	ME
Brown Marsh	Bladen	NC	Brush Creek	Washington	AR	Buckhart	Christian	IL
Brown Springs	Hot Springs	AR	Brush Creek	Fairibault	MN	Buckheart	Fulton	IL
Brown	Mc Henry	ND	Brush Creek	Douglas	MO	Buckhorn	Baxter	AR
Brown	Clay	AR	Brush Creek	Gasconade	MO	Buckhorn	Sevier	AR
Brown	Monroe	AR	Brush Creek	Wright	MO	Buckhorn	Brown	IL
Brown	Champaign	IL	Brush Creek	Yancey	NC	Buckhorn	Harnett	NC
Brown	Hancock	IN	Brush Creek	Adams	OH	Buckhorn	Wake	NC
Brown	Hendricks	IN	Brush Creek	Highland	OH	Buckingham	Tama	IA
Brown	Montgomery	IN	Brush Creek	Jefferson	OH	Buckingham	Bucks	PA
Brown	Morgan	IN	Brush Creek	Muskingum	OH	Buckingham	Wayne	PA
Brown	Ripley	IN	Brush Creek	Scioto	OH	Buckland	Franklin	MA
Brown	Washington	IN	Brush Creek	Fulton	PA	Bucklin	Ford	KS
Brown	Linn	IA	Brushvalley	Indiana	PA	Bucklin	Linn	MO
Brown	Clark	KS	Brushy Creek	Anderson	SC	Bucklin	Slope	ND
Brown	Manistee	MI	Brushy Fork	Watauga	NC	Bucklucksy	Pittsburg	OK
Brown	Douglas	MO	Brushy Lake	Cross	AR	Buckman	Morrison	MN
Brown	Carroll	OH	Brushy Mound	Macoupin	IL	Bucks	Tuscarawas	OH
Brown	Darke	OH	Brushy Mountain	Wilkes	NC	Bucks	Horry	SC
Brown	Delaware	OH	Brushy	Scott	AR	Buckskin	Ross	OH
Brown	Franklin	OH	Brushy	Saline	IL	Buckskin	Grant	ND
Brown	Knox	OH	Brussels	Door	WI	Bucksport	Hancock	ME
Brown	Miami	OH	Brutus	Cayuga	NY	Bucyrus	Adams	ND
Brown	Paulding	OH	Bryan	Boone	AR	Bucyrus	Crawford	OH
Brown	Vinton	OH	Bryan	Greene	AR	Buel	Sanilac	MI
Brown	Bryan	OK	Bryan	Izard	AR	Buena Vista	Portage	WI
Brown	Comanche	OK	Bryan	Jackson	AR	Buena Vista	Richland	WI
Brown	Jefferson	OK	Bryan	Stone	AR	Buena Vista	Schuyler	IL
Brown	Muskogee	OK	Bryan	Douglas	MO	Buena Vista	Clayton	IA
Brown	Seminole	OK	Bryan	Surry	NC	Buena Vista	Jasper	IA
Brown	Stephens	OK	Bryan	Griggs	ND	Buena Vista	Saginaw	MI
Brown	Lycoming	PA	Bryan	Williams	OH	Buena Vista	Atlantic	NJ
Brown	Mifflin	PA	Bryan	Coal	OK	Buena Vista	Bowman	ND
Brownfield	Oxford	ME	Bryan	Cotton	OK	Buffalo Hart	Sagamon	IL
Brownhelm	Lorain	OH	Bryan	Grant	OK	Buffalo Prairie	Rock Island	IL
Browning	Taylor	WI	Bryan	Lincoln	OK	Buffalo	Buffalo	WI
Browning	Franklin	IL	Bryan	Mayes	OK	Buffalo	Marquette	WI
Browning	Schuyler	IL	Bryan	Okmulgee	OK	Buffalo	Craighead	AR
Brownington	Orleans	VT	Bryan	Charles Mix	SD	Buffalo	Marion	AR
Browns Creek	Red Lake	MN	Bryant	Saline	AR	Buffalo	Ogle	IL
Browns Creek	Jewell	KS	Bryant	Graham	KS	Buffalo	Buchanan	IA
Browns Grove	Pawnee	KS	Bryant	Fillmore	NE	Buffalo	Kossuth	IA
Browns Valley	Big Stone	MN	Bryant	Logan	ND	Buffalo	Linn	IA
Brownstown	Jackson	IN	Bryant	Edmunds	SD	Buffalo	Scott	IA
Brownstown	Wayne	MI	Bryant	Faulk	SD	Buffalo	Winnebago	IA
Brownsville	Union	IN	Bryant	Roberts	SD	Buffalo	Barton	KS
Brownsville	Houston	MN	Bucephalia	Foster	ND	Buffalo	Cloud	KS
Brownsville	Fayette	PA	Buchanan	Outagamie	WI	Buffalo	Jewell	KS
Brownville	Piscataquis	ME	Buchanan	Jefferson	IA	Buffalo	Wright	MN
Brownville	Jefferson	NY	Buchanan	Page	IA	Buffalo	Dunklin	MO
Broxton	Colleton	SC	Buchanan	Berrien	MI	Buffalo	McDonald	MO
Bruce	La Salle	IL	Buchanan	Atchison	MO	Buffalo	Morgan	MO
Bruce	Benton	IA	Buchanan	Douglas	MO	Buffalo	Newton	MO
Bruce	Chippewa	MI	Buchanan	Sullivan	MO	Buffalo	Pike	MO
Bruce	Macomb	MI	Buchanan	Stutsman	ND	Buffalo	Franklin	NE
Bruce	Todd	MN	Buchanan Valley	Emmons	ND	Buffalo	Cass	ND
Bruce	Guilford	NC	Buck Creek	Hancock	IN	Buffalo	Noble	OH

TOWNSHIPS OF THE UNITED STATES

TOWNSHIP	COUNTY	STATE	TOWNSHIP	COUNTY	STATE	TOWNSHIP	COUNTY	STATE
Buffalo	Beckham	OK	Burlington	Des Moines	IA	Bushy Fork	Person	NC
Buffalo	Garfield	OK	Burlington	Coffey	KS	Busseron	Knox	IN
Buffalo	Harper	OK	Burlington	Calhoun	MI	Busti	Chautauqua	NY
Buffalo	Latimer	OK	Burlington	Lapeer	MI	Butler Grove	Montgomery	IL
Buffalo	Noble	OK	Burlington	Becker	MN	Butler	Wayne	NY
Buffalo	Butler	PA	Burlington	Ward	ND	Butler	Clark	WI
Buffalo	Perry	PA	Burlington	Burlington	NJ	Butler	Lonoke	AR
Buffalo	Union	PA	Burlington	Alamance	NC	Butler	Randolph	AR
Buffalo	Washington	PA	Burlington	Licking	OH	Butler	Vermilion	IL
Buffalo	Kershaw	SC	Burlington	Bradford	PA	Butler	De Kalb	IN
Buffalo	Jones	SD	Burnett	Dodge	WI	Butler	Franklin	IN
Buffalo	Marshall	SD	Burnett	Pope	AR	Butler	Miami	IN
Buffalo	Minnehaha	SD	Burnett	Santa Clara	CA	Butler	Butler	IA
Buffalo	Spink	SD	Burnett	Antelope	NE	Butler	Calhoun	IA
Buffington	Indiana	PA	Burnett	Pottawatomie	OK	Butler	Jackson	IA
Buford Bridge	Bamberg	SC	Burney	Love	OK	Butler	Scott	IA
Buford	Baxter	AR	Burnham	Waldo	ME	Butler	Kiowa	KS
Buford	Union	NC	Burnham	Pawnee	OK	Butler	Branch	MI
Buford	Williams	ND	Burnhamville	Todd	MN	Butler	Otter Tail	MN
Buford	Lancaster	SC	Burningtown	Macon	NC	Butler	Harrison	MO
Bug Hill	Columbus	NC	Burns	Allegany	NY	Butler	Pemiscot	MO
Buh	Morrison	MN	Burns	La Crosse	WI	Butler	Saint Clair	MO
Bull Butte	Williams	ND	Burns	Henry	IL	Butler	Platte	NE
Bull Creek	Tripp	SD	Burns	Shiawassee	MI	Butler	Columbiana	OH
Bull Head	Greene	NC	Burns	Anoka	MN	Butler	Drake	OH
Bull Moose	Cass	MN	Burns	Dorchester	SC	Butler	Knox	OH
Bull Moose	Wells	ND	Burnside	Trempealeau	WI	Butler	Mercer	OH
Bull Pond	Allendale	SC	Burnside	Johnson	IL	Butler	Montgomery	OH
Bull Swamp	Lexington	SC	Burnside	Webster	IA	Butler	Richland	OH
Bullard	Prairie	AR	Burnside	Lapeer	MI	Butler	Stark	OH
Bullard	Wadena	MN	Burnside	Goodhue	MN	Butler	Adams	PA
Bullion	Golden Valley	ND	Burnside	Centre	PA	Butler	Butler	PA
Bullocks Creek	York	SC	Burnstown	Brown	MN	Butler	Luzerne	PA
Bullskin	Fayette	PA	Burnsville	Anson	NC	Butler	Schuylkill	PA
Bunch Creek	Noble	OK	Burnsville	Yancey	NC	Butler	Greenville	SC
Bunch	Adair	OK	Burnt Creek	Burleigh	ND	Butler	Day	SD
Buncombe	Sioux	IA	Burnt Prairie	White	IL	Butler	Sanborn	SD
Bungo	Cass	MN	Burnt Swamp	Robeson	NC	Butman	Gladwin	MI
Bunker Hill	Macoupin	IL	Burntwood	Rawlins	KS	Butte	Sierra	CA
Bunker Hill	Ingham	MI	Burr Oak	Mitchell	IA	Butte	Siskiyou	CA
Bunker	Kidder	ND	Burr Oak	Winneshiek	IA	Butte	Sutter	CA
Bunkerville	Clark	NV	Burr Oak	Doniphan	KS	Butte	Boyd	NE
Bunn	Dallas	AR	Burr Oak	Jewell	KS	Butte	McLean	ND
Burbank	Kandiyohi	MN	Burr Oak	Saint Joseph	MI	Butte	Hughes	SD
Burdell	Osceola	MI	Burr Oak	Lincoln	MO	Butte	Lyman	SD
Burdette	Mississippi	AR	Burr Oak	Beadle	SD	Butte	Melletta	SD
Burdette	Hand	SD	Burr	Grant	OK	Butte Valley	Benson	ND
Burdick	Morris	KS	Burrell	Decatur	IA	Butterfield	Hot Springs	AR
Burdick	Perkins	SD	Burrell	Armstrong	PA	Butterfield	Missaukee	MI
Burdine	Texas	MO	Burrell	Indiana	PA	Butterfield	Watonwan	MN
Bureau	Bureau	IL	Burrillville	Providence	RI	Butterfield	Barry	MO
Burg	Howard	AR	Burris Fork	Moniteau	MO	Butternut Valley	Blue Earth	MN
Burg	Divide	ND	Burritt	Winnebago	IL	Butternuts	Otsego	NY
Burgaw	Pender	NC	Burrows	Platte	NE	Butterwood	Halifax	NC
Burgess	Bond	IL	Burrton	Harvey	KS	Button	Ford	IL
Burk	Minnehaha	SD	Burt	Kossuth	IA	Buxton	York	ME
Burke	Franklin	NY	Burt	Alger	MI	Buxton	Traill	ND
Burke	Caledonia	VT	Burt	Cheboygan	MI	Buzzle	Beltrami	MN
Burke	Dane	WI	Burt	Ward	ND	Byars	McClain	OK
Burke	Little River	AR	Burtchville	Saint Clair	MI	Byersville	McClean	ND
Burke	Pipestone	MN	Burton	Adams	IL	Bygland	Polk	MN
Burke	Mountrail	ND	Burton	Mc Henry	IL	Byram	Sussex	NJ
Burke	Gregory	SD	Burton	Genesee	MI	Byrd	Cape Girardeau	MO
Burleene	Todd	MN	Burton	Yellow Medicine	MN	Byrd	Brown	OH
Burleigh	Iosco	MI	Burton	Howard	MO	Byrd	Oxford	ME
Burlingame	Osage	KS	Burton	Geauga	OH	Byron	Genesee	NY
Burlington	Hartford	CT	Burton	McIntosh	OK	Byron	Fond de Lac	WI
Burlington	Penobscot	ME	Buse	Otter Tail	MN	Byron	Monroe	WI
Burlington	Middlesex	MA	Bush	Boyd	NE	Byron	Ogle	IL
Burlington	Otsego	NY	Bush	Eddy	ND	Byron	Buchanan	IA
Burlington	Racine	WI	Bushnell	McDonough	IL	Byron	Stafford	KS
Burlington	Kane	IL	Bushnell	Montcalm	MI	Byron	Kent	MI
Burlington	Carroll	IN	Bushkill	Northampton	PA	Byron	Cass	MN

TOWNSHIPS OF THE UNITED STATES

TOWNSHIP	COUNTY	STATE	TOWNSHIP	COUNTY	STATE	TOWNSHIP	COUNTY	STATE
Byron	Waseca	MN	California	Branch	MI	Campbell	La Crosse	WI
Byron	Cavalier	ND	Calistoga	Napa	CA	Campbell	Lawrence	AR
Byron	Alfalfa	OK	Callahan	Siskiyou	CA	Campbell	Searcy	AR
			Callahan	Renville	ND	Campbell	Santa Clara	CA
			Callao	Macon	MO	Campbell	Jennings	IN
—C—			Callaway	Becker	MN	Campbell	Warrick	IN
			Callaway	Saint Charles	MO	Campbell	Ionia	MI
Cable	Alamance	NC	Callicoon	Sullivan	NY	Campbell	Wilkin	MN
Cable	Bayfield	WI	Callison	Greenwood	SC	Campbell	Douglas	MO
Cabanal	Carroll	AR	Calmar	Winneshiek	IA	Campbell	Greene	MO
Cabot	Washington	VT	Calm Lake	Wexford	MI	Campbell	Polk	MO
Cache	Clay	AR	Caln	Chester	PA	Campbell	Emmons	ND
Cache	Greene	AR	Calton	Blaine	OK	Campbell	Hettinger	ND
Cache	Jackson	AR	Calumet	Fond du Lac	WI	Campbell	Sequoyah	OK
Cache	Lawrence	AR	Calumet	Cook	IL	Campbell	Hand	SD
Cache	Monroe	AR	Calumet	Lake	IN	Campobello	Spartanburg	SC
Cache	Woodruff	AR	Calumet	Houghton	MI	Campton	Grafton	NH
Cache	Johnson	IL	Calumet	Pike	MO	Campton	Kane	IL
Cache	Caddo	OK	Calumet	Canadian	OK	Camptonville	Yuba	CA
Cache	Cotton	OK	Calvary	Clarendon	SC	Canaan	Litchfield	CT
Cachevelle	Yolo	CA	Calvert	Grant	AR	Canaan	Grafton	NH
Caddo	Clark	AR	Calvey	Franklin	MO	Canaan	Columbia	NY
Caddo	Montgomery	AR	Calvin	Jewell	KS	Canaan	Essex	VT
Caddo	Bryan	OK	Calvin	Cass	MI	Canaan	Henry	IA
Caddo	Caddo	OK	Calvin	Hughes	OK	Canaan	Gasconade	MO
Cadillac	Corson	SD	Calwood	Callaway	MO	Canaan	Athens	OH
Cadiz	Green	WI	Calzona	San Bernardino	CA	Canaan	Masison	OH
Cadiz	Harrison	OH	Camanche	Clinton	IA	Canaan	Morrow	OH
Cadogan	Armstrong	PA	Camargo	Douglas	IL	Canaan	Wayne	OH
Cadron	Cleburne	AR	Cambria	Niagara	NY	Canaan	Wayne	PA
Cadron	Faulkner	AR	Cambria	Saline	KS	Canada	Lebette	KS
Cadron	Van Buren	AR	Cambria	Hillsdale	MI	Canada	Jackson	NC
Cadron	White	AR	Cambria	Blue Earth	MN	Canadian	Mississippi	AR
Cady	Saint Croix	WI	Cambria	Cambria	PA	Canadian	Blaine	OK
Cahokia	Macoupin	IL	Cambria	Brown	SD	Canadian	Cleveland	OK
Cain	Fountain	IN	Camarillo	Ventura	CA	Canadian	Pittsburg	OK
Cains	Florence	SC	Cambridge	Somerset	ME	Canadice	Ontario	NY
Cairo	Greene	NY	Cambridge	Coos	NH	Canajoharie	Montgomery	NY
Cairo	Renville	MN	Cambridge	Washington	NY	Canal	Lyon	NV
Cairo	Randolph	MO	Cambridge	Lamoille	VT	Canal	Uenago	PA
Calabasas	Los Angeles	CA	Cambridge	Henry	IL	Canandaigus	Ontario	NY
Calahaln	Davie	NC	Cambridge	Lenawee	MI	Canby	Modoc	CA
Calais	Washington	VT	Cambridge	Isanti	MN	Candeadea	Allegany	NY
Calamus	Dodge	WI	Cambridge	Saline	MO	Candia	Rockingham	NH
Calwell	Appanoose	IA	Cambridge	Guernsey	OH	Cando	Towner	ND
Caldwell	Sumner	KS	Cambridge	Crawford	PA	Candor	Tioga	NY
Caldwell	Missaukee	MI	Camden	Knox	ME	Candor	Otter Tail	MN
Caldwell	Callaway	MO	Camden	Oneida	NY	Cane Greek	Butler	MO
Caldwell	Catawba	NC	Camden	Schuyler	IL	Cane Creek	Mitchell	NC
Caledonia	Livingston	NY	Camden	Hillsdale	MI	Cane Creek	Lancaster	SC
Caledonia	Columbia	WI	Camden	Carver	MN	Cane Hill	Washington	AR
Caledonia	Racine	WI	Camden	De Kalb	MO	Cane River	Yancey	NC
Caledonia	Trempealeau	WI	Camden	Ray	MO	Cane	White	AR
Caledonia	Waupaca	WI	Camden	Lorain	OH	Canetuck	Pender	NC
Caledonia	Boone	IL	Cameron	Steuben	NY	Caney Fork	Pike	AR
Caledonia	O'Brien	IA	Cameron	Wood	WI	Caney Fork	Jackson	NC
Caledonia	Alcona	MI	Cameron	Audubon	IA	Caney	Little River	AR
Caledonia	Kent	MI	Cameron	Murray	MN	Caney	Montgomery	AR
Caledonia	Shiawassee	MI	Cameron	Hall	NE	Caney	Nevada	AR
Caledonia	Houston	MN	Cameron	Le Flore	OK	Caney	Woodruff	AR
Caledonia	Traill	ND	Cameron	Ward	ND	Caney	Montgomery	KS
Calera	Bryan	OK	Camillus	Onondaga	NY	Caney	Atoka	OK
Calf Creek	Searcy	AR	Camp Branch	Cass	MO	Caney	Osage	OK
Calhoun	Prairie	AR	Camp Branch	Warren	MO	Caneyville	Chautauqua	KS
Calhoun	Calhoun	IA	Camp Creek	Rutherford	NC	Canfield	Burleigh	ND
Calhoun	Harrison	IA	Camp Creek	Pike	OH	Canfield	Mahoning	OH
Calhoun	Cheyenne	KS	Camp Keltner	Texas	OK	Canisteo	Steuben	NY
Caliente	Lincoln	NV	Camp Lake	Swift	MN	Canisteo	Dodge	MN
California	Cleburne	AR	Camp Point	Adams	IL	Canistota	McCook	SD
California	Faulkner	AR	Camp Release	Lac Qui Parle	MN	Cannon Ball	Hettinger	ND
California	Madison	AR	Camp	Polk	IA	Cannon City	Rice	MN
California	Starke	IN	Camp	Renville	MN	Cannon Falls	Goodhue	MN
California	Coffey	KS	Campbell	Steuben	NY	Cannon	Kent	MI

TOWNSHIP	COUNTY	STATE	TOWNSHIP	COUNTY	STATE	TOWNSHIP	COUNTY	STATE
Cannon	Kittson	MN	Carlton	Chicot	AR	Carter	Carter	MO
Cannon (No. 10)	Newberry	SC	Carlton	Tama	IA	Carter	Burke	ND
Cannonball	Grant	ND	Carlton	Barry	MI	Carter	Tripp	SD
Canoe Creek	Rock Island	IL	Carlton	Hand	SD	Carterville	Florence	SC
Canoe	Winneshiek	IA	Carlyle	Clinton	IL	Carthage	Franklin	ME
Canoe	Indiana	PA	Carlyle	Allen	KS	Carthage	Hancock	IL
Canosia	Saint Louis	MN	Carlyle	Beadle	SD	Carthage (No. 1)	Moore	NC
Canova	Miner	SD	Carman	Henderson	IL	Carthage	Athens	OH
Canteen	Saint Clair	IL	Carmel	Penobscot	ME	Carthage	Texas	OK
Canterbury	Windham	CT	Carmel	Putnam	NY	Carthage	Miner	SD
Canterbury	Merrimack	NH	Carmel	Eaton	WI	Cartoogechaye	Mascon	NC
Canton	Hartford	CT	Carmel	Jackson	OK	Cartwright	Sagamon	IL
Canton	Oxford	ME	Carmi	White	IL	Carver	Plymouth	MA
Canton	Norfork	MA	Carmi	Pratt	KS	Carvers Bay (No. 6)	Georgetown	SC
Canton	Buffalo	WI	Carmichael	Dillon	SC	Carvers Creek	Bladen	NC
Canton	Saint Lawrence	NY	Carneiro	Ellsworth	KS	Carvers Creek	Cumberland	NC
Canton	Fulton	IL	Carns	Dorchester	SC	Cary	Wood	WI
Canton	Benton	IA	Caroga	Fulton	NY	Cary	Wake	NC
Canton	Kingman	KS	Carolina	Pitt	NC	Casa	Perry	AR
Canton	McPherson	KS	Caroline	Tompkins	NY	Cascade	Dubuque	IA
Canton	Wayne	MI	Caroline	Lonoke	AR	Cascade	Kent	MI
Canton	Fillmore	MN	Carp Lake	Emmet	MI	Cascade	Olmsted	MN
Canton	Lewis	MO	Carp Lake	Ontonagon	MI	Cascade	Lycoming	PA
Canton	Stark	OH	Carpenter	Clay	AR	Casco	Cumberland	ME
Canton	Blaine	OK	Carpenter	Jasper	IN	Casco	Kewaunee	WI
Canton	Bradford	PA	Carpenter	Itasca	MN	Casco	Allegan	MI
Canton	Washington	PA	Carpenter	Steele	ND	Casco	Saint Clair	MI
Canton	Lincoln	SD	Carpio	Ward	ND	Case	Presque Isle	MI
Canton	Potter	SD	Carr Creek	Mitchell	KS	Case	Cleveland	OK
Cantonment	Blaine	OK	Carr	Clark	IN	Caseville	Huron	MI
Canville	Necshu	KS	Carr	Jackson	IN	Casey	Washburn	WI
Capa	Jones	SD	Carr	Durham	NC	Casey	Clark	IL
Capay	Yolo	CA	Carr	Tillman	OK	Casey	Ranson	ND
Cape Elizabeth	Cumberland	ME	Carr	Potter	SD	Caseyville	Saint Clair	IL
Cape Fear	Chatham	NC	Carrier Mills	Saline	IL	Cash	Slope	ND
Cape Fear (No. 3)	Lee	NC	Carringan	Marion	IL	Cash	Perkins	SD
Cape Fear	New Hanover	NC	Carrington	Foster	ND	Cashel	Swift	MN
Cape Girardeau	Cape Girardeau	MO	Carroll	Coos	NH	Cashiers	Jackson	NC
Cape Vincent	Jefferson	NY	Carroll	Chautauqua	NY	Casner	Jefferson	IL
Capel	Sioux	IA	Carroll	Ouachita	AR	Casnovia	Muskegon	MI
Capioma	Nemaha	KS	Carroll	Vermilion	IL	Cass	Fulton	IL
Capital	Sangamon	IL	Carroll	Carroll	IA	Cass	Clay	IN
Capital	Hutchinson	SD	Carroll	O'Brien	IA	Cass	Dubois	IN
Capitola	Spink	SD	Carroll	Tama	IA	Cass	Greene	IN
Capps Creek	Barry	MO	Carroll	Platte	MO	Cass	La Porte	IN
Carbon	Huntingdon	PA	Carroll	Reynolds	MO	Cass	Ohio	IN
Carbondale	Jackson	IL	Carroll	Texas	MO	Cass	Pulaski	IN
Carbondale	Ward	ND	Carroll	Slope	ND	Cass	Sullivan	IN
Carbondale	Lackawanna	PA	Carroll	Ottawa	OH	Cass	White	IN
Cardington	Morrow	OH	Carroll	Perry	PA	Cass	Boone	IA
Carey	Iron	WI	Carroll	Washington	PA	Cass	Cass	IA
Cargile	Van Buren	AR	Carroll	York	PA	Cass	Cedar	IA
Caribou	Kittson	MN	Carroll	Charles Mix	SD	Cass	Clayton	IA
Caribou	Morton	ND	Carrollton	Cattaraugus	NY	Cass	Guthrie	IA
Carimona	Fillmore	MN	Carrollton	Boone	AR	Cass	Hamilton	IA
Carl	Adams	IA	Carrollton	Carroll	AR	Cass	Harrison	IA
Carl	Grant	ND	Carrollton	Greene	IL	Cass	Jones	IA
Carl	McPherson	SD	Carrollton	Carroll	IN	Cass	Shelby	IA
Carlin	Elko	NV	Carrollton	Saginaw	MI	Cass	Wapello	IA
Carlinville	Macoupin	IL	Carrollton	Fillmore	MO	Cass	Douglas	MO
Carlisle	Middlesex	MA	Carrollton	Carroll	MO	Cass	Greene	MO
Carlisle	Schoharie	NY	Carrs	Greene	NC	Cass	Stone	MO
Carlisle	Lonoka	AR	Carryall	Paulding	OH	Cass	Texas	MO
Carlisle	Otter Tail	MN	Carson Lake	Mississippi	AR	Cass	Hancock	OH
Carlisle	Lorain	OH	Carson	Portage	WI	Cass	Muskingum	OH
Carlisle	Kay	OK	Carson	Fayette	IL	Cass	Richland	OH
Carlisle	Pembina	ND	Carson	Pottawattamie	IA	Cass	Oklahoma	OK
Carlisle	Brown	SD	Carson	Cottonwood	MN	Cass	Huntingdon	PA
Carlock	Gregory	SD	Carson	Noble	OK	Cass	Schuylkill	PA
Carlos	Douglas	MN	Carson	Grant	ND	Cassel	Marathon	WI
Carlston	Freeborn	MN	Carsonville	Becker	MN	Casselton	Cass	ND
Carlton	Orleans	NY	Carter	Ashley	AR	Cassian	Oneida	WI
Carlton	Kewaunee	WI	Carter	Spencer	IN	Cassville	Grant	WI

TOWNSHIP	COUNTY	STATE	TOWNSHIP	COUNTY	STATE	TOWNSHIP	COUNTY	STATE
Castalia	Nash	NC	Cecil	Haywood	NC	Cedar	Woods	OK
Castalia	Charles Mix	SD	Cecil	Bottineau	ND	Cedar	Mineral	MT
Castanea	Clinton	PA	Cecil	Washington	PA	Cedar	Adams	ND
Castile	Wyoming	NY	Cedar Bluff	Oregon	MO	Cedar	Hand	SD
Castine	Hancock	ME	Cedar Butte	Adams	ND	Cedar Valley	Blaine	OK
Castle Butte	Pennington	SD	Cedar Butte	Pennington	SD	Cedar Valley	Saint Louis	MN
Castle Butte	Perkins	SD	Cedar Creek	Crawford	AR	Cedarbend	Roseau	MN
Castle Grove	Jones	IA	Cedar Creek	Marion	AR	Cedarburg	Ozaukee	MI
Castle Hill	Aroostook	ME	Cedar Creek	Allen	IN	Cedarbutte	Mellette	SD
Castle Rock	Grant	WI	Cedar Creek	Lake	IN	Cedarville	Crawford	AR
Castle Rock	Dakota	MN	Cedar Creek	Muskegon	MI	Cedarville	Modoc	CA
Castle Rock	Hettinger	ND	Cedar Creek	Wexford	MI	Cedarville	Menominee	MI
Castle	McPherson	KS	Cedar Creek	Taney	MO	Cedarville	Greene	OH
Castle	Okfuskee	OK	Cedar Creek	Wayne	MO	Cedarville	Woodward	OK
Castleton	Rutland	VT	Cedar Creek	Cumberland	NC	Cedron	Lincoln	KS
Castleton	Reno	KS	Cedar Creek	Slope	ND	Celina	Rawlins	KS
Castleton	Barry	MI	Cedar Creek	Lancaster	SC	Cement	Canadian	OK
Castlewood	Hamlin	SD	Cedar Falls	Conway	AR	Centennial	Lyon	IA
Castor	Madison	MD	Cedar Falls	Black Hawk	IA	Center Creek	Martin	MN
Castor	Stoddard	MO	Cedar Fork	Wake	NC	Center Grove	Dickinson	IA
Castoria	San Joaquin	CA	Cedar Grove	Essex	NJ	Center Grove	Guilford	NC
Castroville	Monterey	CA	Cedar Grove	Orange	NC	Center Harbor	Belknap	NH
Caswell	Forest	WI	Cedar Grove	Randolph	NC	Center Point	Howard	AR
Caswell	Calhoun	AR	Cedar Grove	Comanche	OK	Center Post	Cleburne	AR
Caswell	Pender	NC	Cedar Island	Carteret	NC	Center	Outagamie	WI
Cataba Island	Ottawa	OH	Cedar Lake	Barron	WI	Center	Rock	WI
Catalina	Los Angeles	CA	Cedar Lake	Scott	MN	Center	Montogmery	AR
Cataloochee	Haywood	NC	Cedar Lake	Bennett	SD	Center	Polk	AR
Catawba Springs	Lincoln	NC	Cedar Mills	Meeker	MN	Center	Pope	AR
Catawba	Price	WI	Cedar Rapids	Rusk	WI	Center	Prairie	AK
Catawba	Catawba	NC	Cedar Rock (No. 8)	Franklin	NC	Center	Sebastian	AR
Catawba	York	SC	Cedar Springs	Abbeville	SC	Center	Washington	AR
Catawissa	Columbia	PA	Cedar	Carroll	AR	Center	Sacramento	CA
Catharine	Schuyler	NY	Cedar	Polk	AR	Center	Benton	IN
Catharine	Blair	PA	Cedar	Scott	AR	Center	Boone	IN
Cathay	Wells	ND	Cedar	Knox	IL	Center	Clinton	IN
Catherine	Ellis	KS	Cedar	Benton	IA	Center	Dearborn	IN
Catheys Creek	Transylvania	NC	Cedar	Black Hawk	IA	Center	Delaware	IN
Catholic Point	Canway	AR	Cedar	Calhoun	IA	Center	Gibson	IN
Catlin	Chemung	NY	Cedar	Cherokee	IA	Center	Grant	IN
Catlin	Vermillion	IL	Cedar	Floyd	IA	Center	Greene	IN
Catlin	Marion	KS	Cedar	Greene	IA	Center	Hancock	IN
Cato	Cayuga	NY	Cedar	Jefferson	IA	Center	Hendricks	IN
Cato	Manitowoc	WI	Cedar	Johnson	IA	Center	Howard	IN
Cato	Montcalm	MI	Cedar	Lee	IA	Center	Jennings	IN
Cato	Ramsey	ND	Cedar	Lucas	IA	Center	LaPorte	IN
Caton	Steuben	NY	Cedar	Mahaska	IA	Center	Lake	IN
Catoosa	Rogers	OK	Cedar	Mitchell	IA	Center	Marion	IN
Catskill	Greene	NY	Cedar	Monroe	IA	Center	Marshall	IN
Cattaraugus Indian Reservation	Cattaraugus	NY	Cedar	Muscatine	IA	Center	Martin	IN
Cattaraugus Indian Reservation	Chautaugua	NY	Cedar	Pocahontas	IA	Center	Porter	IN
			Cedar	Sac	IA	Center	Posey	IN
Cattaraugus Indian Reservation	Erie	NY	Cedar	Van Buren	IA	Center	Ripley	IN
Cattron	Potter	SD	Cedar	Washington	IA	Center	Rush	IN
Cauthron	Logan	AR	Cedar	Barber	KS	Center	Saint Joseph	IN
Cauthron	Scott	AR	Cedar	Chase	KS	Center	Starke	IN
Cavalier	Pembina	ND	Cedar	Jackson	KS	Center	Union	IN
Cave	Sharp	AR	Cedar	Smith	KS	Center	Vanderburgh	IN
Cave	Franklin	IL	Cedar	Wilson	KS	Center	Wayne	IN
Cavendish	Windsor	VT	Cedar	Osceola	MI	Center	Allamakee	IA
Cavour	Beadle	SD	Cedar	Marshall	MN	Center	Appanoose	IA
Caw Caw	Calhoun	SC	Cedar	Martin	MN	Center	Calhoun	IA
Cawker	Mitchell	KS	Cedar	Boone	MO	Center	Cedar	IA
Cayuta	Schuyler	NY	Cedar	Callaway	MO	Center	Clinton	IA
Cazenovia	Madison	NY	Cedar	Cedar	MO	Center	Decatur	IA
Cazenovia	Woodford	IL	Cedar	Dade	MO	Center	Dubuque	IA
Ceasar Creek	Deerborn	IN	Cedar	Pettis	MO	Center	Emmer	IA
Ceasar Creek	Greene	OH	Cedar	Nance	NE	Center	Fayette	IA
Ceaser (No. 11)	Cleveland	NC	Cedar	Antelope	NE	Center	Henry	IA
Cearnarvon	Berks	PA	Cedar	Buffalo	NE	Center	Jefferson	IA
Cearnarvon	Lancaster	PA	Cedar	Caddo	OK	Center	Madison	IA
			Cedar	Custer	OK	Center	Mills	IA
			Cedar	Logan	OK	Center	Monona	IA

TOWNSHIP	COUNTY	STATE	TOWNSHIP	COUNTY	STATE	TOWNSHIP	COUNTY	STATE
Center	O'Brien	IA	Center	Oconee	SC	Chandler	Comanche	OK
Center	Pocahontas	IA	Center	Aurora	SD	Chandler	Grady	OK
Center	Pottawattamie	IA	Centerview	Johnson	MO	Chandler	Lincoln	OK
Center	Shelby	IA	Centerville	Washington	ME	Chandler	Adams	ND
Center	Sioux	IA	Centerville	Allegany	NY	Chandlerville	Cass	IL
Center	Wapello	IA	Centerville	Manitowoc	WI	Channahon	Will	IL
Center	Winnebago	IA	Centerville	Yell	AR	Chapel Hill	Orange	NC
Center	Atchison	KS	Centerville	Linn	KS	Chapel	Howell	MO
Center	Chautauqua	KS	Centerville	Neosho	KS	Chapin	Saginaw	MI
Center	Clark	KS	Centerville	Leelanau	MI	Chaplin	Windham	CT
Center	Cloud	KS	Centerville	Anderson	SC	Chapman	Aroostook	ME
Center	Decatur	KS	Centerville	Faulk	SD	Chapman	Clay	KS
Center	Dickinson	KS	Centerville	Turner	SD	Chapman	Ottawa	KS
Center	Doniphan	KS	Central Cabarrus			Chapman	Merrick	NE
Center	Hodgeman	KS	(No. 11)	Cabarrus	NC	Chapman	Saunders	NE
Center	Jewell	KS	Central	Franklin	MO	Chapman	Clinton	PA
Center	Kiowa	KS	Central	Bond	IL	Chapman	Snyder	PA
Center	Lyon	KS	Central	Barton	MO	Charbon	McKenzie	ND
Center	Marion	KS	Central Point	Goodhue	MN	Chardon	Geauga	OH
Center	Marshall	KS	Central Point	Day	SD	Chariton	Appanoose	IA
Center	Mitchell	KS	Central Lake	Antrim	MI	Chariton	Lucas	IA
Center	Nemaha	KS	Central	Jefferson	MO	Chariton	Chariton	MO
Center	Ness	KS	Central	Madison	MO	Chariton	Howard	MO
Center	Norton	KS	Central	Perry	MO	Chariton	Macon	MO
Center	Ottawa	KS	Central	Knox	NE	Chariton	Randolph	MO
Center	Pottawatomie	KS	Central	Merrick	NE	Chariton	Schuyler	MO
Center	Pratt	KS	Central	Bladen	NC	Charlemont	Franklin	MA
Center	Reno	KS	Central	Nelson	ND	Charles City	Floyd	IA
Center	Rice	KS	Centralia	Marion	IL	Charleston	Penobscot	ME
Center	Riley	KS	Centralia	Boone	MO	Charleston	Montgomery	NY
Center	Rush	KS	Centre	Berks	PA	Charleston	Orleans	VT
Center	Russell	KS	Centre	Perry	PA	Charleston	Coles	IL
Center	Smith	KS	Centre	Snyder	PA	Charleston	Lee	IA
Center	Stevens	KS	Centreville	Saint Clair	IL	Charleston	Clark	IN
Center	Wilson	KS	Centropolis	Franklin	KS	Charleston	Washington	KS
Center	Woodson	KS	Ceres	Stanislaus	CA	Charleston	Kalamazoo	MI
Center	Emmet	MI	Ceres	McKean	PA	Charleston	Swain	NC
Center	Crow Wing	MN	Ceresco	Blue Earth	MN	Charleston	Lorain	OH
Center	Buchanan	MO	Cerro Gordo	Piatt	IL	Charleston	Chester	PA
Center	Dade	MO	Cerro Gordo	Lac Qui Parie	MN	Charleston	Tioga	PA
Center	Greene	MO	Cerro Gordo	Columbus	NC	Charlestown	Sullivan	NH
Center	Hickory	MO	Cessna	Hardin	OH	Charlestown	Washington	PA
Center	Knox	MO	Chadboun	Columbus	NC	Charlestown	Calumet	WI
Center	McDonald	MO	Chadwick	Christian	MO	Charlestown	Redwood	MN
Center	Ralls	MO	Chagrin Falls	Cuyahoga	OH	Charlestown	Portage	OH
Center	Saint Clair	MO	Chagrin	Lake	OH	Charlevoix	Charlevoix	MI
Center	Vernon	MO	Chain Lake	Ramsey	ND	Charlotte	Washington	ME
Center	Buffalo	NE	Chalk Bluff	Clay	AR	Charlotte	Chautauqua	NY
Center	Butler	NE	Chalk Level	Saint Clair	MO	Charlotte	Chittenden	VT
Center	Hall	NE	Chalky Butte	Slope	ND	Charlotte	Livingston	IL
Center	Phelps	NE	Chalmers	McDonough	IL	Charlotte	Bates	MO
Center	Saunders	NE	Chalybeats Springs	Stone	AR	Charlotte (No. 1)	Mecklenburg	NC
Center	Chatham	NC	Chamberian	Brule	SD	Charlton	Saratoga	NY
Center	Stanly	NC	Chambers	Holt	NE	Charlton	Worcester	MA
Center	Richland	ND	Chambersburg	Pike	IL	Charlton	Otsego	MI
Center	Carroll	OH	Chambersburg	Iredell	NC	Charrette	Warren	MO
Center	Columbinana	OH	Champagnolle	Calhoun	AR	Charter Oak	Crawford	IA
Center	Guernsey	OH	Champaign City	Champaign	IL	Chartiers	Washington	PA
Center	Mercer	OH	Champaign	Champaign	IL	Chase Lake	Stutsman	ND
Center	Monroe	OH	Champion	Jefferson	NY	Chase	Oconto	WI
Center	Morgan	OH	Champion	Marquette	MI	Chase	Lake	MI
Center	Noble	OH	Champion	Wilkin	MN	Chaseley	Wells	ND
Center	Williams	OH	Champion	Douglas	MO	Chaska	Carver	MN
Center	Wood	OH	Champion	Williams	ND	Chassell	Houghton	MI
Center	Harper	OK	Champion	Trumbull	OH	Chateaugay	Franklin	NY
Center	Haskell	OK	Champlain	Clinton	NY	Chatfield	Fillmore	MN
Center	Kingfisher	OK	Champlin	Hennepin	MN	Chatfield	Bottineau	ND
Center	Mayes	OK	Chanarambie	Murray	MN	Chatfield	Crawford	OH
Center	Woodward	OK	Chance	Adair	OK	Chatham	Barnstable	MA
Center	Beaver	PA	Chance	Perkins	SD	Chatham	Carroll	NH
Center	Butler	PA	Chanceford	York	PA	Chatham	Columbia	NY
Center	Greene	PA	Chandler	Charlevoix	MI	Chatham	Sangamon	IL
Center	Indiana	PA	Chandler	Huron	MI	Chatham	Wright	MN

TOWNSHIP	COUNTY	STATE	TOWNSHIP	COUNTY	STATE	TOWNSHIP	COUNTY	STATE
Chatham	Morris	NJ	Cheshire	Gallia	OH	Chilhowee	Johnson	MO
Chatham	Medine	OH	Chest	Cambria	PA	Chili	Monroe	NY
Chatham	Tioga	PA	Chest	Clearfield	PA	Chili	Hancock	IL
Chatsworth	Livingston	IL	Chester	Middlesex	CT	Chillicothe	Peoria	IL
Chattaroy	Spokane	WA	Chester	Hampden	MA	Chillicothe	Livingston	MO
Chattooga	Oconee	SC	Chester	Penobscot	ME	Chilmark	Dukes	MA
Chaudion	Perkins	SD	Chester	Rockingham	NH	Chilton	Calumet	WI
Chautaugua	Chautaugua	NY	Chester	Orange	NY	Chilton	Hettinger	ND
Chazy	Clinton	NY	Chester	Warren	NY	Chimney Rock	Trempealeau	WI
Chebanse	Iroquois	IL	Chester	Windsor	VT	Chimney Rock	Rutherford	NC
Checotah	McIntosh	OK	Chester	Dodge	WI	China Grove	Rowan	NC
Cheek Creek	Montgomery	NC	Chester	Arkansas	AR	China	Kennebec	ME
Cheeks	Orange	NC	Chester	Crawford	AR	China	Lee	IL
Cheektowaga	Erie	NY	Chester	Dallas	AR	China	Saint Clair	MI
Cheever	Dickinson	KS	Chester	Logan	IL	Chino	Butte	CA
Chelmsford	Middlesex	MA	Chester	Wabash	IN	Chino	San Bernardino	CA
Chelsea	Kennebec	ME	Chester	Wells	IN	Chinquapin (No. 6)	Jones	NC
Chelsea	Orange	VT	Chester	Howard	IA	Chinquepin	Aiken	SC
Chelsea	Taylor	WI	Chester	Poweshiek	IA	Chinquepin	Lexington	SC
Chelsea	Butler	KS	Chester	Eaton	MI	Chippewa Falls	Pope	MN
Chelsea	Fillmore	NE	Chester	Otsego	MI	Chippewa	Ashland	WI
Chelsea	Rogers	OK	Chester	Ottawa	MI	Chippewa	Chippewa	MI
Cheltenham	Montgomery	PA	Chester	Polk	MN	Chippewa	Isabella	MI
Chemung	Chemung	NY	Chester	Wabasha	MN	Chippewa	Mecosta	MI
Chemung	McHenry	IL	Chester	Saunders	NE	Chippewa	Wayne	OH
Chenango	Broome	NY	Chester	Grand Forks	ND	Chippewa	Beaver	PA
Cheney Grove	McLean	IL	Chester	Morris	NJ	Chisago Lake	Chisago	MN
Cheney	Spokane	WA	Chester	Clinton	OH	Chittenden	Rutland	VT
Chengwatana	Pine	MN	Chester	Geauga	OH	Chocolay	Marquette	MI
Cheoah	Graham	NC	Chester	Mergs	OH	Choconut	Susquehanna	PA
Chenoa	McLean	IL	Chester	Morrow	OH	Chocowinity	Beaufort	NC
Cheguest	Van Buren	IA	Chester	Wayne	OH	Choctaw	Lincoln	AR
Cheraw	Cherfield	SC	Chester	Delaware	PA	Choctaw	Van Buren	AR
Cherokee	Benton	AR	Chester	Chester	SC	Choctaw	Oklahoma	OK
Cherokee	Sharp	AR	Chester	Douglas	SD	Cholame	Monterey	CA
Cherokee	Cherokee	IA	Chester	Lake	SD	Cholame	San Luis Obispo	CA
Cherokee	Cherokee	KS	Chester	Spokane	WA	Choteau Creek	Charles Mix	SD
Cherokee	Montgomery	KS	Chesterfield	Hamshire	MA	Choteau	Mayes	OK
Cherokee	Payne	OK	Chesterfield	Cheshire	NH	Chouteau	Madison	IL
Cherokee	Wagoner	OK	Chesterfield	Essex	NY	Chouteau	Clay	MO
Cherokee	Cherokee	SC	Chesterfield	Macoupin	IL	Chrisp	White	AR
Cherokee	Spartanburg	SC	Chesterfield	Macomb	MI	Christ Church	Charleston	SC
Cherry Creek	Chautauqua	NY	Chesterfield	Burlington	NJ	Christian	Independence	AR
Cherry Creek	Cheyenne	KS	Chesterfield	Fulton	OH	Christian	Dane	WI
Cherry Creek	Buffalo	NE	Chesterville	Franklin	ME	Christiana	Vernon	WI
Cherry Grove	Carroll	IL	Chestina	Kidder	ND	Christiana	Jackson	MN
Cherry Grove	Wexford	MI	Chestnut Hill	Ashe	NC	Christiania	Burleigh	ND
Cherry Grove	Goodhue	MN	Chestnut	Knox	IL	Christie	Adair	OK
Cherry Grove	Warren	PA	Chestnuthill	Monroe	PA	Christy	Lawrence	IL
Cherry Hill	Perry	AR	Chestonia	Antrim	MI	Churchhill	Ogemaw	MI
Cherry Hill	Camden	NJ	Chetek	Barron	WI	Cirero	Onondego	NY
Cherry Lake	Eddy	ND	Chetopa	Neosho	KS	Cicero	Outagamie	WI
Cherry Lane	Alleghany	NC	Chetopa	Wilson	KS	Cicero	Cook	IL
Cherry Ridge	Wayne	PA	Cheyenne	Barton	KS	Cicero	Tipton	IN
Cherry	Montgomery	KS	Cheyenne	Lane	KS	Cimarron	Gray	KS
Cherry	Saint Louis	MN	Cheyenne	Roger Mills	OK	Cimarron	Meade	KS
Cherry	McKenzie	ND	Cheyenne	Pennington	SD	Cimarron	Morton	KS
Cherry	Butler	PA	Chicago City	De Page	IL	Cimarron	Blaine	OK
Cherry	Sullivan	PA	Chicago	Stutsman	ND	Cimarron	Kingfisher	OK
Cherry	Jerauld	SD	Chichester	Merrimack	NH	Cimarron	Lincoln	OK
Cherry Valley	Otsego	NY	Chick Springs	Greenville	SC	Cimarron	Major	OK
Cherry Valley	Winnebago	IL	Chickasaw	Chickasaw	IA	Cimarron	Pawnee	OK
Cherry Valley	Lake	MI	Chickasaw	Pontotoc	OK	Cimarron	Payne	OK
Cherry Valley	Carroll	MO	Chickasawba	Mississippi	AR	Cincinnati	Pike	IL
Cherry Valley	Ashtabula	OH	Chickasha	Grady	OK	Cincinnati	Tazewell	IL
Cherryfield	Washington	ME	Chickaskia	Harper	KS	Cincinnati	Harrison	IA
Cherryhill	Indiana	PA	Chickaskia	Kingman	KS	Cincinnatus	Cortland	NY
Cherrytree	Venango	PA	Chickaskia	Sumner	KS	Cinnaminson	Burlington	NJ
Cherryville	Gaston	NC	Chicod	Pitt	NC	Cinque Hommes	Perry	MO
Chesaning	Saginaw	MI	Chicog	Washburn	WI	Circleville	Pickaway	OH
Cheshire	New Haven	CT	Chief	Mahnomen	MN	City Point	Jackson	WI
Cheshire	Berkshire	MA	Chikaming	Berrien	MI	City	Orangeburg	SC
Cheshire	Allegan	MI	Childstown	Turner	SD	Civil Bend	Union	SD

TOWNSHIPS OF THE UNITED STATES

TOWNSHIP	COUNTY	STATE	TOWNSHIP	COUNTY	STATE	TOWNSHIP	COUNTY	STATE
Claiborne	Izard	AR	Clay	White	AR	Clayton	Adams	IL
Claibourne	Union	OH	Clay	Bartholomew	IN	Clayton	Woodford	IL
Clam Falls	Polk	WI	Clay	Carroll	IN	Clayton	Clayton	IA
Clam Union	Missaukee	MI	Clay	Cass	IN	Clayton	Taylor	IA
Clara	Nelson	ND	Clay	Dearborn	IN	Clayton	Norton	KS
Clara	Potter	PA	Clay	Decatur	IN	Clayton	Arenac	MI
Clare	Saint Lawrence	NY	Clay	Hamilton	IN	Clayton	Mower	MN
Clare	Moody	SD	Clay	Hendricks	IN	Clayton	Saint Louis	MO
Claremount	Richland	IL	Clay	Howard	IN	Clayton	Johnston	NC
Claremount	Dodge	MN	Clay	Kosciusko	IN	Clayton	Burke	ND
Claremount	Brown	SD	Clay	Lagrange	IN	Clayton	Perry	OH
Clarence	Barton	KS	Clay	Miami	IN	Clayton	Payne	OK
Clarence	Calhoun	MI	Clay	Morgan	IN	Clayton	Hutchinson	SD
Clarendon	Orleans	NY	Clay	Owen	IN	Clear Creek	Eau Claire	WI
Clarendon	Rutland	VT	Clay	Pike	IN	Clear Creek	Drew	AR
Clarendon	Calhoun	MI	Clay	Saint Joseph	IN	Clear Creek	Hot Spring	AR
Clarendon	Williamsburg	SC	Clay	Spencer	IN	Clear Creek	Sevier	AR
Claridon	Geauga	OH	Clay	Wayne	IN	Clear Creek	Huntington	IN
Clairdon	Marion	OH	Clay	Clay	IA	Clear Creek	Monroe	IN
Clarion	Bureau	IL	Clay	Grundy	IA	Clear Creek	Jasper	IA
Clarion	Clarion	PA	Clay	Hardin	IA	Clear Creek	Johnson	IA
Clark Fork	Cooper	MO	Clay	Harrison	IA	Clear Creek	Keokuk	IA
Clark	Clay	AR	Clay	Jones	IA	Clear Creek	Ellsworth	KS
Clark	Green	AR	Clay	Marion	IA	Clear Creek	Marion	KS
Clark	Logan	AR	Clay	Polk	IA	Clear Creek	Nemaha	KS
Clark	Pike	AR	Clay	Shelby	IA	Clear Creek	Pottawatomie	KS
Clark	Johnson	IN	Clay	Washington	IA	Clear Creek	Stafford	KS
Clark	Montgomery	IN	Clay	Wayne	IA	Clear Creek	Cooper	MO
Clark	Perry	IN	Clay	Webster	IA	Clear Creek	Vernon	MO
Clark	Tama	IA	Clay	Butler	KS	Clear Creek	Henderson	NC
Clark	Marion	KS	Clay	Reno	KS	Clear Creek	Mecklenburg	NC
Clark	Mackinac	MI	Clay	Saint Clair	MI	Clear Creek	Saunders	NE
Clark	Aitkin	MN	Clay	Adair	MO	Clear Creek	Ashland	OH
Clark	Faribault	MN	Clay	Andrew	MO	Clear Creek	Fairfield	OH
Clark	Atchison	MO	Clay	Atchison	MO	Clear Creek	Warren	OH
Clark	Chariton	MO	Clay	Clark	MO	Clear Creek	Payne	OK
Clark	Cole	MO	Clay	Douglas	MO	Clear Fork	Marshall	KS
Clark	Lincoln	MO	Clay	Dunklin	MO	Clear Lake City	Cerro Gordo	IA
Clark	Wright	MO	Clay	Gasconade	MO	Clear Lake	Polk	WI
Clark	Dixon	NE	Clay	Greene	MO	Clear Lake	Mississippi	AR
Clark	Union	NJ	Clay	Harrison	MO	Clear Lake	Sangamon	IL
Clark	Brown	OH	Clay	Holt	MO	Clear Lake	Steuben	IN
Clark	Clinton	OH	Clay	Lafayette	MO	Clear Lake	Cerro Gordo	IA
Clark	Coshocton	OH	Clay	Linn	MO	Clear Lake	Hamilton	IA
Clark	Holmes	OH	Clay	Monroe	MO	Clear Lake	Sherburne	MN
Clark	Dewey	OK	Clay	Ralls	MO	Clear Lake	Burleigh	ND
Clark	Douglas	SD	Clay	Saline	MO	Clear Lake	Kidder	ND
Clark	Pope	AR	Clay	Shelby	MO	Clear Lake	Devel	SD
Clark	Searcy	AR	Clay	Sullivan	MO	Clear Lake	Edmunds	SD
Clark	Faulk	SD	Clay	Guilford	NC	Clear Lake	Minnehaha	SD
Clark	Perkins	SD	Clay	Renville	ND	Clear Water	Mountrail	ND
Clarks Creek	Morris	KS	Clay	Sherman	NE	Clearfield	Juneau	WI
Clarksburg	Berkshire	MA	Clay	Auqlaize	OH	Clearfield	Griggs	ND
Clarksburg	Yolo	CA	Clay	Gallia	OH	Clearfield	Butler	PA
Clarksburg	Shelby	IL	Clay	Highland	OH	Clearfield	Cambria	PA
Clarksfield	Huron	OH	Clay	Knox	OH	Clearspring	Lagrange	IN
Clarkson	Monroe	NY	Clay	Montgomery	OH	Clearwater	Kalkaska	MI
Clarkson	Payne	OK	Clay	Muskingum	OH	Clearwater	Wright	MN
Clarkstown	Rockland	NY	Clay	Ottawa	OH	Clearwater	Antelope	NE
Clarksville	Coos	NH	Clay	Scioto	OH	Clearwater	Miner	SD
Clarksville	Allegany	NY	Clay	Tuscarawas	OH	Cleary	Burke	ND
Clarksville	Merrick	NE	Clay	Alfalfa	OK	Cleburne	Monroe	AR
Clarksville	Davie	NC	Clay	Butler	PA	Cleburne	Phillips	AR
Clarno	Green	WI	Clay	Huntingdon	PA	Clement	Clinton	IL
Clarno	Lake	SD	Clay	Lancaster	PA	Clement	Gladwin	MI
Classen	Morton	ND	Claybanks	Door	WI	Clement	Dickey	ND
Clatonia	Gage	NE	Claybanks	Oceana	MI	Clemmonsville	Forsyth	NC
Claverack	Columbia	NY	Clayton	Jefferson	NY	Cleo	Major	OK
Clay Center	Clay	KS	Clayton	Crawford	WI	Cleon	Manistee	MI
Clay City	Clay	IL	Clayton	Polk	WI	Cleons	Scott	IA
Clay	Onondage	NY	Clayton	Winnebago	WI	Clermont	Columbia	NY
Clay	Bradley	AR	Clayton	Cleburne	AR	Clermont	Fayette	IA
Clay	Howard	AR	Clayton	Desha	AR	Clermont	Adams	ND

TOWNSHIP	COUNTY	STATE	TOWNSHIP	COUNTY	STATE	TOWNSHIP	COUNTY	STATE
Cleveland Run	Cheyenne	KS	Clinton	Boone	IN	Coal Creek	Wagoner	OK
Cleveland	Chippewa	WI	Clinton	Cass	IN	Coalfield	Divide	ND
Cleveland	Jackson	WI	Clinton	Decatur	IN	Coal	Scott	AR
Cleveland	Marathon	WI	Clinton	Elkhart	IN	Coal	Vernon	MO
Cleveland	Taylor	WI	Clinton	La Porte	IN	Coal	Jackson	OH
Cleveland	Clay	AR	Clinton	Putnam	IN	Coal	Perry	OH
Cleveland	Fulton	AR	Clinton	Vermillion	IN	Coal	Northumberland	PA
Cleveland	Little River	AR	Clinton	Clinton	IA	Coal Valley	Rock Island	IL
Cleveland	Lonoke	AR	Clinton	Franklin	IA	Cobb	Franklin	AR
Cleveland	Miller	AR	Clinton	Linn	IA	Cobb	McIntosh	OK
Cleveland	Ouachita	AR	Clinton	Pocahontas	IA	Cobleskill	Schoharie	MY
Cleveland	Phillips	AR	Clinton	Ringgold	IA	Coburn	Ransom	ND
Cleveland	White	AR	Clinton	Sac	IA	Cochecton	Sullivan	NY
Cleveland	Elkhart	IN	Clinton	Wayne	IA	Cockrell	Chariton	MO
Cleveland	Whitley	IN	Clinton	Douglas	KS	Coe	Rock Island	IL
Cleveland	Davis	IA	Clinton	Rawlins	KS	Coe	Isabella	MI
Cleveland	Lyon	IA	Clinton	Lenawee	MI	Coddle Creek	Iredell	NC
Cleveland	Barton	KS	Clinton	Macomb	MI	Codorus	York	PA
Cleveland	Lane	KS	Clinton	Oscoda	MI	Cody	Mellette	SD
Cleveland	Marshall	KS	Clinton	Rock	MN	Coeymans	Albany	NY
Cleveland	Stafford	KS	Clinton	Saint Louis	MN	Coffey	White	AR
Cleveland	Leelanau	MI	Clinton	Clinton	MO	Coffins Grove	Delaware	IA
Cleveland	Le Sueur	MN	Clinton	Douglas	MO	Cogan House	Lycoming	PA
Cleveland	Callaway	MO	Clinton	Henry	MO	Cohasset	Norfolk	MA
Cleveland	Johnston	NC	Clinton	Texas	MO	Cohoctah	Livingston	MI
Cleveland	Rowan	NC	Clinton	Divide	ND	Cohocton	Steuben	NY
Cleveland	Walsh	ND	Clinton	Hunterdon	NJ	Coin	Carroll	AR
Cleveland	Cuming	NE	Clinton	Franklin	OH	Coitsville	Mahoning	OH
Cleveland	Holt	NE	Clinton	Fulton	OH	Cokato	Wright	MN
Cleveland	Knox	NE	Clinton	Knox	OH	Cokato	Logan	ND
Cleveland	Cimarron	OK	Clinton	Seneca	OH	Cokesburg	Greenwood	SC
Cleveland	Dewey	OK	Clinton	Shelby	OH	Cokey	Edgecombe	NC
Cleveland	Columbia	PA	Clinton	Vinton	OH	Colbert	Bryan	OK
Cleveland	Greenville	SC	Clinton	Wayne	OH	Colbert	McClain	OK
Cleveland	Bon Homme	SD	Clinton	Custer	OK	Colbert	Spokane	WA
Cleveland	Brule	SD	Clinton	Butler	PA	Colburn	Adams	WI
Cleveland	Edmunds	SD	Clinton	Lycoming	PA	Colburn	Chippewa	WI
Cleveland	Hamlin	SD	Clinton	Venango	PA	Colby	Clark	WI
Cliff	Custer	NE	Clinton	Wayne	PA	Colchester	New London	CT
Clifford	Butler	KS	Clinton	Wyoming	PA	Colchester	Delaware	NY
Clifford	Susquehanna	PA	Clinton	Miner	SD	Colchester	Chittenden	VT
Clifton Park	Saratoga	NY	Clintonia	De Witt	IL	Colchester	McDonough	IL
Clifton	Penobscot	ME	Cliquot	Polk	MO	Cold Spring	Cattaraugus	NY
Clifton	Saint Lawrence	NY	Clitheral	Otter Tail	MN	Cold Spring	Shelby	IL
Clifton	Grant	WI	Clontarf	Swift	MN	Cold Spring	Phelps	MO
Clifton	Monroe	WI	Cloud	Alfalfa	OK	Cold Spring	Lebanon	PA
Clifton	Pierce	WI	Clough	Morrison	MN	Cold Spring	Jefferson	WI
Clifton	Faulkner	AR	Clover Leaf	Pennington	MN	Cold Springs	Kalkaska	MI
Clifton	Washington	KS	Clover	Bayfield	WI	Coldbrook	Warren	IL
Clifton	Wilson	KS	Clover	Henry	IL	Colden	Erie	NY
Clifton	Lyon	MN	Clover	Clearwater	MN	Coldwater	Cross	AR
Clifton	Randolph	MO	Clover	HUbbard	MN	Coldwater	Comanche	KS
Clifton	Traverse	MN	Clover	Mahnomen	MN	Coldwater	Branch	MI
Clifton	Ashe	NC	Clover	Pine	MN	Coldwater	Isabella	MI
Clifton	Cass	ND	Clover	Jefferson	PA	Coldwater	Cass	MO
Clifton	Lackawanna	PA	Cloverdale	Sonoma	CA	Coldwater	Grant	OK
Clifton	Beadle	SD	Cloverdale	Putnam	IN	Coldwater	Butler	IA
Clifton	Spink	SD	Cloverland	Douglas	WI	Coldwell	White	AR
Clifty	Carroll	AR	Cloverland	Vilas	WI	Cole Hill	Chesterfield	SC
Clifty	Bartholomew	IN	Clow	Kittson	MN	Cole	Sebastian	AR
Climax	Kalamazoo	MI	Cloyd Valley	Edmunds	SD	Cole	Benton	MO
Climax	Williams	ND	Clyde	Iowa	WI	Colebrook	Litchfield	CT
Clines	Catawba	NC	Clyde	Whiteside	IL	Colebrook	Coos	NH
Clinton Falls	Steele	MN	Clyde	Allegan	MI	Colebrook	Ashtabula	OH
Clinton	Middlesex	CT	Clyde	Saint Clair	MI	Colebrook	Clinton	PA
Clinton	Kennebec	ME	Clyde	Haywood	NC	Colebrookdale	Berks	PA
Clinton	Worcester	MA	Clyde	Beadle	SD	Colegate	Steele	ND
Clinton	Clinton	NY	Clymon	Dodge	WI	Coleman	Washington	KS
Clinton	Dutchess	NY	Clymer	Chautauqua	NY	Coleman	Holt	NE
Clinton	Barron	WI	Clymer	Tioga	PA	Colerain	Bertie	NC
Clinton	Rock	WI	Coachella	Riverside	CA	Colerain	Belmont	OH
Clinton	Vernon	WI	Coal Creek	Montgomery	IN	Colerain	Hamilton	OH
Clinton	De Kalb	IL	Coal Creek	Pawnee	OK	Colerain	Ross	OH

TOWNSHIPS OF THE UNITED STATES

TOWNSHIP	COUNTY	STATE
Colerain	Bedford	PA
Colerain	Lancaster	PA
Coleridge	Randolph	NC
Colesville	Broome	NY
Coleville	Burke	ND
Colfax	Dunn	WI
Colfax	Champaign	IL
Colfax	Newton	IN
Colfax	Boone	IA
Colfax	Dallas	IA
Colfax	Grundy	IA
Colfax	Page	IA
Colfax	Pocahontas	IA
Colfax	Webster	IA
Colfax	Cloud	KS
Colfax	Marion	KS
Colfax	Wilson	KS
Colfax	Benzie	MI
Colfax	Huron	MI
Colfax	Mecosta	MI
Colfax	Oceana	MI
Colfax	Wexford	MI
Colfax	Kandiyohi	MN
Colfax	Atchinson	MO
Colfax	Daviess	MO
Colfax	De Kalb	MO
Colfax	Harrison	MO
Colfax	Rutherford	NC
Colfax	Richland	ND
College	Linn	IA
College	Knox	OH
College	Centre	PA
Collegeville	Stearns	MN
Colley	Sullivan	PA
Collier	Greene	AR
Collier	Allegheny	PA
Colliers	Edgefield	SC
Collins	Erie	NY
Collins	Drew	AR
Collins	Story	IA
Collins	McLeod	MN
Collins	Saint Clair	MO
Collins	Buffalo	NE
Collins	Dorchester	SC
Collins	Edgefield	SC
Collins	Clark	SD
Collinsville	Madison	IL
Collinsville	Rogers	OK
Collinsville	Tulsa	OK
Collinwood	Meeker	MN
Colly	Bladen	NC
Collyer	Trego	KS
Colman	Moody	SD
Coloma	Waushara	WI
Coloma	El Dorado	CA
Coloma	Whiteside	IL
Coloma	Berrien	MI
Colome	Tripp	SD
Colon	Saint Joseph	MI
Colona	Henry	IL
Colonie	Albany	NY
Colony	Adams	IA
Colony	Delaware	IA
Colony	Greeley	KS
Colony	Knox	MO
Colorado	Lincoln	KS
Colquhoun	Renville	ND
Colrain	Franklin	MA
Colton	Saint Lawrence	NY
Colton	San Bernardino	CA
Colts Neck	Monmouth	NJ
Columbia Falls	Washington	ME
Columbia	Tolland	CT
Columbia	Washington	ME
Columbia	Coos	NH
Columbia	Herkimer	NY
Columbia	Randolph	AR
Columbia	Dubois	IN
Columbia	Fayette	IN
Columbia	Gibson	IN
Columbia	Jennings	IN
Columbia	Whitley	IN
Columbia	Tama	IA
Columbia	Wapello	IA
Columbia	Ellsworth	KS
Columbia	Jackson	MI
Columbia	Tuscola	MI
Columbia	Van Buren	MI
Columbia	Polk	MN
Columbia	Boone	MO
Columbia	Flathead	MT
Columbia	Pender	NC
Columbia	Randolph	NC
Columbia	Tyrrell	NC
Columbia	Eddy	ND
Columbia	Knox	NE
Columbia	Hamilton	OH
Columbia	Lorain	OH
Columbia	Meigs	OH
Columbia	Kingfisher	OK
Columbia	Bradford	PA
Columbia	Brown	SD
Columbia	Whatcom	WE
Columbus City	Louisa	IA
Columbus	Chenango	NY
Columbus	Columbia	WI
Columbus	Adams	IL
Columbus	Bartholomew	IN
Columbus	Luce	MI
Columbus	Saint Clair	MI
Columbus	Anoka	MN
Columbus	Johnson	MO
Columbus	Polk	NC
Columbus	Platte	NE
Columbus	Warren	PA
Colusa	Colusa	CA
Colville	Benton	AR
Colvin	Saint Louis	MN
Colvin	Eddy	ND
Comanche	Barton	KS
Combs	Carroll	MO
Comfort	Kanabec	MN
Comins	Oscoda	MI
Cominto	Drew	AR
Commerce	Oakland	MI
Commerce	Scott	MO
Commercial	Cumberland	NJ
Commonwealth	Florence	WI
Como	Marshall	MN
Como	New Madrid	MO
Como	Hand	SD
Competine	Wapello	IA
Compromise	Champaign	IL
Compton	Yell	AR
Compton	Los Angeles	CA
Compton	Otter Tail	MN
Comstock	Kalamazoo	MI
Comstock	Marshall	MN
Comstock	Custer	NE
Conata	Pennington	SD
Concord	Middlesex	MA
Concord	Erie	NY
Concord	Essex	VT
Concord	Jefferson	WI
Concord	Adams	IL
Concord	Bureau	IL
Concord	Iroquois	IN
Concord	De Kalb	IN
Concord	Elkhart	IN
Concord	Dubuque	IA
Concord	Hancock	IA
Concord	Hardin	IA
Concord	Louisa	IA
Concord	Woodbury	IA
Concord	Ford	KS
Concord	Ottawa	KS
Concord	Jackson	MI
Concord	Dodge	MN
Concord	Clinton	MO
Concord	Pemiscot	MO
Concord	Saint Louis	MO
Concord	Washington	MO
Concord (No. 12)	Cabarrus	NC
Concord	Iredell	NC
Concord	Randolph	NC
Concord	Dixon	NE
Concord	Champaign	OH
Concord	Delaware	OH
Concord	Fayette	OH
Concord	Highland	OH
Concord	Lake	OH
Concord	Miami	OH
Concord	Ross	OH
Concord	Butler	PA
Concord	Delaware	PA
Concord	Erie	PA
Concord	Clarendon	SC
Concord	Sumter	SC
Concord	Lake	SD
Concordia	Des Moines	IA
Conde	Spink	SD
Condit	Champaign	IL
Condon	Tripp	SD
Conemaugh	Cambria	PA
Conemaugh	Indiana	PA
Conemaugh	Somerset	PA
Conestoga	Lancaster	PA
Conesus	Livingston	NY
Conesville	Schoharie	NY
Conewago	Adams	PA
Conewago	Dauphin	PA
Conewago	York	PA
Conewango	Cattaraugus	NY
Conewango	Warren	PA
Congaree	Lexington	SC
Congress	Morrow	OH
Congress	Wayne	OH
Conklin	Broome	NY
Conklin	Stutsman	ND
Conkling	Pawnee	KS
Conley	Holt	NE
Conneaut	Astabula	OH
Conneaut	Crawford	PA
Conneaut	Erie	PA
Connellsville	Fayette	PA
Connelly	Wilkin	MN
Connersville	Fayette	IN
Connewango	Caddo	OK
Connoquenessing	Butler	PA
Connor	Slope	ND
Cono	Buchanan	IA
Conoconnara	Halifax	NC
Conover	Vilas	WI
Conoy	Lancaster	PA
Conquest	Cayuga	NY
Conrad Hill	Davidson	NC
Constable	Franklin	NY
Constantia	Oswego	NY
Constantine	Saint Joseph	MI

TOWNSHIPS OF THE UNITED STATES

TOWNSHIP	COUNTY	STATE	TOWNSHIP	COUNTY	STATE	TOWNSHIP	COUNTY	STATE
Contentnea Nack	Lenoir	NC	Cornie	Union	AR	Court House	Chesterfield	SC
Convenience	Pope	AR	Corning	Steuben	NY	Courtenay	Stutsman	ND
Convis	Calhoun	MI	Corning	Lincoln	WI	Courtland	Nicollet	MN
Conway	Franklin	MA	Corning	Tehama	CA	Courtland	Republic	KS
Conway	Carroll	NH	Corning	Rooks	KS	Courtland	Kent	MI
Conway	Sumner	KS	Cornish	York	ME	Courtland	Columbia	WI
Conway	Livingston	MI	Cornish	Sullivan	NH	Courtois	Crawford	MO
Conway	Horry	SC	Cornish	Aitkin	MN	Cove City	Crawford	AR
Conyngham	Columbia	PA	Cornish	Sibley	MN	Cove Creek	Washington	AR
Conyngham	Luzerne	PA	Cornplanter	Venango	PA	Cove Creek	Watauga	NC
Cook	Sac	IA	Cornville	Somerset	ME	Cove	Polk	AR
Cook	Decatur	KS	Cornwall	Litchfield	CT	Cove	Stone	AR
Cook	Westmoreland	PA	Cornwall	Orange	NY	Coventry	Tolland	CT
Cooke	Cumberland	PA	Cornwall	Addison	VT	Coventry	Chenango	NY
Cooks Valley	Chippewa	WI	Cornwall	Henry	IL	Coventry	Kent	RI
Cookson	Cherokee	OK	Cornwall	Spink	SD	Coventry	Orleans	VT
Cool Spring	LaPorte	IN	Coronaca	Greenwood	SC	Coventry	Summit	OH
Cool Spring	Iredell	NC	Coronado	Kingfisher	OK	Covert	Seneca	NY
Coolbaugh	Monroe	PA	Corsicana	Barry	MO	Covert	Osborne	KS
Coolidge	Hamilton	KS	Cortland	De Kalb	IL	Covert	Van Buren	MI
Coolin	Towner	ND	Cortlandt	Westchester	NY	Covington	Wyoming	NY
Coolspring	Mercer	PA	Cortlandt	Edmunds	SD	Covington	Washington	IL
Coon Creek	Lyon	MN	Cortlandville	Cortland	NY	Covington	Baraga	MI
Coon Island	Butler	MO	Corvallis (No. 3)	Ravalli	MT	Covington	Clearfield	PA
Coon	Vernon	WI	Corwin	Logan	IL	Covington	Lackawanna	PA
Coon	Buena Vista	IA	Corwin	Ida	IA	Covington	Tioga	PA
Coon Valley	Sac	IA	Corwin	Stutsman	ND	Cow Castle	Orangeburg	SC
Cooper Gap	Polk	NC	Corwith	Otsego	MI	Cow Creek	Williams	ND
Cooper	Washington	ME	Corydon	Wayne	IA	Cow Lake	Jackson	AR
Cooper	Sangamon	IL	Corydon	McKean	PA	Cowan	Wayne	MO
Cooper	Monona	IA	Cosmo	Kearney	NE	Cowanshannock	Armstrong	PA
Cooper	Webster	IA	Cosmos	Meeker	MN	Cowee	Macon	NC
Cooper	Kalamazoo	MI	Cosumnes	Ed Dorado	CA	Coweta	Wagoner	OK
Cooper	Gentry	MO	Cote Sans Dessein	Callaway	MO	Cowlington	Le Flore	OK
Cooper	Clearfield	PA	Cottage Grove	Dana	WI	Cox Creek	Clayton	IA
Cooper	Montour	PA	Cottage Grove	Allen	KS	Coxsackie	Greene	NY
Cooper	Kingfisher	OK	Cottage Hill	Marshall	KS	Coyle	Murray	OK
Cooper	Kiowa	OK	Cottage	Saline	IL	Crab Creek	Henderson	NC
Cooper	Aurora	SD	Cotterell	Dodge	NE	Crab Orchard (No. 7)	Mecklenburg	NC
Coopers	Nash	NC	Cotton Grove	Davidson	NC	Crabtree	Haywood	NC
Cooperstown	Manitowoc	WI	Cotton Hill	Sagamon	IL	Crabtree	Yancey	NC
Cooperstown	Brown	IL	Cotton Hill	Dunklin	MO	Craftsbury	Orleans	VT
Cooperstown	Griggs	ND	Cotton Plant	Woodruff	AR	Craig	Van Buren	AR
Coosawhatchie	Jasper	SC	Cotton	Switzerland	IN	Craig	Switzerland	IN
Cooter	Pemiscott	MO	Cotton	Saint Louis	MN	Craig	Burt	NE
Copake	Columbia	NY	Cottonwood Lake	McHenry	ND	Cranberry Isles	Hancock	ME
Copeland	Gray	KS	Cottonwood Lake	Edmunds	SD	Cranberry	Alleghany	NC
Copley	Knox	IL	Cottonwood	Yolo	CA	Cranberry	Avery	NC
Copley	Clearwater	MN	Cottonwood	Cumberland	IL	Cranberry	Crawford	OH
Copley	Summit	OH	Cottonwood	Chase	KS	Cranberry	Butler	PA
Cora	Smith	KS	Cottonwood	Brown	MN	Cranberry	Venango	PA
Coral	McHenry	IL	Cottonwood	Powell	MT	Cranbury	Middlesex	NJ
Corcoran	Kings	CA	Cottonwood	Mountrail	ND	Crandon	Spink	SD
Cordelia	Bottineau	ND	Cottonwood	Adams	NE	Crandon	Forest	WI
Cordell	Washita	OK	Cottonwood	Nance	NE	Crane Creek	Lincoln	AR
Cordova	Rock Island	IL	Cottonwood	Phelps	NE	Crane Creek	Logan	AR
Cordova	Le Sueur	MN	Cottonwood	Butte	SD	Crane Creek	Mason	IL
Corinna	Penobscot	ME	Cottonwood	Clark	SD	Crane Creek	Barry	MO
Corinna	Wright	MN	Cottonwood	Fall River	SD	Crane Creek	Mountrail	ND
Corinne	Stutsman	ND	Cottonwood Valley	Mellette	SD	Crane	Paulding	OH
Corinth	Penobscot	ME	Cottrellville	Saint Clair	MI	Crane	Wyandot	OH
Corinth	Saratoga	NY	Couch	Oregon	MO	Cranford	Union	NJ
Corinth	Orange	VT	Couderay	Sawyer	WI	Cranmoor	Wood	WI
Corinth	Humboldt	IA	Coulee	Ramsey	ND	Crate	Chippewa	MN
Corinth	Osborne	KS	Coulee	Spokane	WA	Cranens	Franklin	AR
Corliss	Otter Tail	MN	Council Creek	Nance	NE	Cravens	Latimer	OK
Cormant	Beltrami	MN	Council Grove	Morris	KS	Crawford	Washington	ME
Cormorant	Becker	MN	Council Grove	Oklahoma	OK	Crawford	Orange	NY
Corn Creek	Mellette	SD	Council Hill	Jo Daviess	IL	Crawford	Washington	AR
Cornell	Delta	MI	Council House	Ottawa	OK	Crawford	Yell	AR
Cornell	Cass	ND	Council	Lee	AR	Crawford	Madison	IA
Corner	Custer	NE	County Line	Howard	AR	Crawford	Washington	IA
Corner	Anderson	SC	Court House	Camden	NC	Crawford	Cherokee	KS

TOWNSHIP	COUNTY	STATE	TOWNSHIP	COUNTY	STATE	TOWNSHIP	COUNTY	STATE
Crawford	Crawford	KS	Cross Creek	Jefferson	OH	Cuming	Dodge	NE
Crawford	Buchanan	MO	Cross Creek	Washington	PA	Cumming	Ogemaw	MI
Crawford	Osage	MO	Cross Hill	Laurens	SC	Cummings	Lycoming	PA
Crawford	Currituck	NC	Cross Keys	Union	SC	Cummington	Harris	MA
Crawford	Slope	ND	Cross Plains	Hutchinson	SD	Cummins	Pocahontas	IA
Crawford	Antelope	NE	Cross Plains	Dane	WI	Comru	Berks	PA
Crawford	Coshocton	OH	Cross Roads	Martin	NC	Cunningham	Champaign	IL
Crawford	Wyandot	OH	Cross Roads	Wilson	NC	Cunningham	Chariton	MO
Crawford	Clinton	PA	Cross Timbers	Hickory	MO	Cunningham	Person	NC
Cream Ridge	Livingston	MO	Cross	Buffalo	WI	Cunningham	Potter	SD
Credit River	Scott	MN	Cross	Carroll	AR	Curlew	Morton	ND
Creel	Ramsey	ND	Cross	Grady	OK	Curlew	Tripp	SD
Creek	De Witt	IL	Cross	Kay	OK	Curran	Sangamon	IL
Creek	Sumner	KS	Cross Village	Emmet	MI	Curran	Jackson	WI
Creek	Creek	OK	Croton	Newaygo	MI	Current	Dent	MO
Creek	Okfuskee	OK	Crouch	Hamilton	IL	Current	Texas	MO
Creek	Wagoner	OK	Crow Lake	Stearns	MN	Current River	Randolph	AR
Creighton	Knox	NE	Crow Lake	Jerauld	SD	Current River	Ripley	MO
Cremerville	McLean	ND	Crow River	Stearns	MN	Currituck	Hyde	NC
Crescent	Oneida	WI	Crow	Jerauld	SD	Curry	Sullivan	IN
Crescent	Del Norte	CA	Crow Wing Lake	Hubbard	MN	Curtin	Centre	PA
Crescent	Pottawattamie	IA	Crow Wing	Crow Wing	MN	Curtis	Alcona	MI
Crescent	Iroquois	IL	Crowders Mountain	Gaston	NC	Cusator	Stutsman	ND
Crescent	Logan	OK	Crowell	Major	OK	Cushing	Knox	ME
Crescent	Allegheny	PA	Crowfoot	Mountrail	ND	Cushing	Morrison	MN
Crescent	Whatcom	WA	Crowley	Greene	AR	Cushman	Independence	AR
Cresco	Kossuth	IA	Crown Hill	Kidder	ND	Cussewago	Crawford	PA
Cresson	Cambria	PA	Crown Point	Essex	NY	Custer	Will	IL
Crest Forest	San Bernardino	CA	Croydon	Sullivan	NH	Custer	Decatur	KS
Creston	Union	IA	Croyle	Cambria	PA	Custer	Mitchell	KS
Creston	Ashe	NC	Cruger	Woodford	IL	Custer	Antrim	MI
Creston	Platte	NE	Crutcho	Oklahoma	OK	Custer	Mason	MI
Creswell	Cowley	KS	Crystal Bay	Lake	MN	Custer	Sanilac	MI
Crete	Will	IL	Crystal Falls	Iron	MI	Custer	Lyon	MN
Creve Coeur	Saint Louis	MO	Crystal Lake	Barron	WI	Custer	Morton	ND
Crittenden	Champaign	IL	Crystal Lake	Marquette	WI	Custer	Antelope	NE
Crittenden	Cherokee	OK	Crystal Lake	Benzie	MI	Custer	Custer	NE
Croatan	Dare	NC	Crystal Lake	Wells	ND	Custer	Beadle	SD
Crocker	Polk	IA	Crystal Lake	Aurora	SD	Custer	Corson	SD
Crockery	Ottawa	MI	Crystal Plains	Smith	KS	Custer	Whatcom	WA
Crockett	Arkansas	AR	Crystal Spring	Kidder	ND	Cut Bank	Bottineau	ND
Crockett	Marion	AR	Crystal	Aroostook	ME	Cut Off	Miller	AR
Crocus	Towner	ND	Crystal	Washburn	WI	Cutler	Franklin	KS
Crofte	Burleigh	ND	Crystal	Hancock	IA	Cutler	Washington	ME
Croghan	Lewis	NY	Crystal	Tama	IA	Cutler	Juneau	WI
Croke	Traverse	MN	Crystal	Norton	KS	Cuyahoga Falls	Summit	OH
Cromer (No. 4)	Newberry	SC	Crystal	Phillips	KS	Cuyler	Cortland	NY
Cromwell	Middlesex	CT	Crystal	Montcalm	MI	Cyclone	McDonald	MO
Cromwell	Clay	MN	Crystal	Oceana	MI	Cylon	Saint Croix	WI
Cromwell	Burleigh	ND	Crystal	Pembina	ND	Cynthian	Shelby	OH
Cromwell	Huntingdon	PA	Cuba	Allegany	NY	Cypert	White	AR
Crook	Drew	AR	Cuba	Lake	IL	Cypress	Faulkner	AR
Crook	Hamilton	IL	Cuba	Becker	MN	Cypress	Phillips	AR
Crooked Creek	Lonoke	AR	Cuba	Barnes	MO	Cypress	Harrison	MO
Crooked Creek	Marion	AR	Cucamonga	San Bernardino	CA	Cypress	Cavalier	ND
Crooked Creek	Cumberland	IL	Cuffeys Cove	Mendocino	CA	Cypress	Lee	SC
Crooked Creek	Jasper	IL	Cuivre	Audrain	MO	Cypress Creek	Bladen	NC
Crooked Creek	Meade	KS	Cuivre	Pike	MO	Cypress Creek	Duplin	NC
Crooked Creek	Houston	MN	Cuivre	Saint Charles	MO	Cypress Creek (No. 9)	Franklin	NC
Crooked Creek	Bollinger	MO	Culdrum	Morrison	MN	Cypress Creek (No. 4)	Jones	NC
Crooked Creek	McDowell	NC	Cullen	Pulaski	MO	Cypress Ridge	Monroe	AR
Crooked Creek	Pennington	SD	Cullowhee	Jackson	NC			
Crooked Lake	Cass	MN	Culpepper	Van Buren	AR	—D—		
Crooked River	Ray	MO	Culver	Ottawa	KS			
Crooks	Renville	MN	Culver	Saint Louis	MN	Dabney	Vance	NC
Crookston	Polk	MN	Cumberland	Cumberland	ME	Dabney	Beckham	OK
Cropsey	McLean	IL	Cumberland	Providence	RI	Dafter	Chippewa	MI
Crosby	White	AR	Cumberland	Barron	WI	Dagget Brook	Crow Wing	MN
Crosby	Pine	MN	Cumberland	Adams	PA	Daggett	Menominee	MI
Crosby	Hamilton	OH	Cumberland	Greene	PA	Dague	Texas	OK
Crosby	Comanche	OK	Cumberland Valley	Bedford	PA	Dahlgren	Hamilton	IL
Cross Anchor	Spartanburg	SC	Cuming City	Washington	NE	Dahlgren	Carver	MN
Cross Creek	Cumberland	NC	Cuming	Cuming	NE	Dahlonega	Wapello	IA

TOWNSHIP	COUNTY	STATE	TOWNSHIP	COUNTY	STATE	TOWNSHIP	COUNTY	STATE
Dailey	Mille Lacs	MN	Danville	Blue Earth	MN	Dayton	Butler	IA
Dailey	Dixon	NE	Danville	Montgomery	MO	Dayton	Cedar	IA
Dairyland	Douglas	WI	Danville	Rockingham	NH	Dayton	Newaygo	MI
Dakota	Stephenson	IL	Danville	Steuben	NY	Dayton	Tuscola	MI
Dakota	Humboldt	IA	Danville	Caledonia	VT	Dayton	Hennipin	MN
Dakota	Adams	ND	Darby	Madison	OH	Dayton	Cass	MO
Dakota	Waushara	WI	Darby	Pickaway	OH	Dayton	Newton	MO
Dalbo	Isanti	MN	Darby	Union	OH	Dayton	Lake	MT
Dale	Lyon	IA	Darby	Delaware	PA	Dayton	Nelson	ND
Dale	O'Brien	IA	Dardanelle	Yell	AR	Dayton	Lyon	NV
Dale	McLean	IL	Dardenne	Saint Charles	MO	Dayton	Cattaraugus	NY
Dale	Kingman	KS	Darien	Fairfield	CT	Dayton	Lincoln	SD
Dale	Cottonwood	MN	Darien	Genesee	NY	Dayton	Marshall	SD
Dale	Atchison	MO	Darien	Walworth	WI	Dayton	Richland	WI
Dale	Burke	ND	Darling	Morrison	MN	Dayton	Waupaca	WI
Dale	Ellis	OK	Darling	Muskogee	OK	Dazey	Barnes	ND
Dale	Jerauld	SD	Darling Spring	Adams	ND	De Bastrop	Ashley	AR
Dale	Kay	OK	Darlington	Harvey	KS	De Gray	Hughes	SD
Dale	Outagamie	WI	Darlington	Canadian	OK	De Kalb	De Kalb	IL
Dalen	Bottineau	ND	Darlington	Beaver	PA	De Kalb	Saint Lawrence	NY
Dallas	Calhoun	AR	Darlington	Charles Mix	SD	De Pere	Brown	WI
Dallas	Dallas	IA	Darlington	Clark	SD	De Peyster	Saint Lawrence	NY
Dallas	Marion	IA	Darnen	Stevens	MN	De Roan	Hemstead	AR
Dallas	Taylor	IA	Darmouth	Bristo	MA	De Roche	Hot Spring	AR
Dallas	Huntington	IN	Darwin	Clark	IL	De Ruyter	Madison	NY
Dallas	Clinton	MI	Darwin	Meeker	MN	De Smit	Kingsbury	SD
Dallas	De Kalb	MO	Darysaw	Grant	AR	De Soto	Marion	AK
Dallas	Saint Clair	MO	Dash	Towner	ND	De Soto	Jackson	IL
Dallas	Harrison	MO	Dassel	Meeker	MN	De Soto	Dallas	IA
Dallas	Gaston	NC	Date	Texas	MO	De Soto	Washington	NE
Dallas	Crawford	OH	Daugherty	Beaver	PA	De Vaul	Morton	ND
Dallas	Luzerne	PA	Davenport City	Scott	IA	De View	Woodruff	AR
Dallas	Barron	WI	Davenport	Delaware	NY	De Witt	Clinton	IA
Dallas City	Hancock	IL	Davenport	Cass	ND	De Witt	De Witt	IL
Dalton	Wayne	IN	David City	Butler	NE	De Witt	Clinton	MI
Dalton	Berkshire	MA	Davidson	Randolph	AR	De Witt	Divide	ND
Dalton	Muskegon	MI	Davidson	Sharp	AR	De Witt	Onondaga	NY
Dalton	Coos	NH	Davidson	Iredell	NC	De Witt	Perkins	SD
Damariscotta	Lincoln	ME	Davidson	Sullivan	PA	Dead Lake	Otter Tail	MN
Damascus	Henry	OH	Davis Creek	Valley	NE	Dead Lake	Crow Wing	MN
Damascus	Wayne	PA	Davis	Grant	AR	Dean	La Moure	ND
Damon	Latimer	OK	Davis	Van Buren	AR	Dean	Cambria	PA
Dan Emmet	Knox	OH	Davis	Fountain	IN	Dear Lake	Stutsman	ND
Dan River	Caswell	NC	Davis	Starke	IN	Dearborn	Beadle	SD
Dana	Emmons	ND	Davis	Kittson	MN	Debing	Mountrail	ND
Danbury	Fairfield	CT	Davis	Caldwell	MO	Deblois	Washington	ME
Danby	Ionia	MI	Davis	Henry	MO	Decatur	Benton	AR
Danbury	Stokes	NC	Davis	Lafayette	MO	Decatur	Decatur	IA
Danbury	Merrimack	NH	Davis	Carteret	NC	Decatur	Macon	IL
Danbury	Emmons	ND	Davis	Pottawatomie	OK	Decatur	Marion	IN
Danbury	Ottawa	OH	Davison	Genesse	MI	Decatur	Van Buren	MI
Danby	Tompkins	NY	Dawson	McLean	IL	Decatur	Burt	NE
Danby	Rutland	VT	Dawson	Greene	IA	Decatur	Otsego	NY
Dane Prairie	Otter Tail	MN	Dawson	Phelps	MO	Decatur	Lawrence	OH
Dane	Major	OK	Dawson	Dewey	OK	Decatur	Washington	OH
Dane	Dane	WI	Dawson	Tulsa	OK	Decatur	Clearfield	PA
Daneville	Turner	SD	Dawt	Ozark	MO	Decatur	Mifflin	PA
Danforth	Iroquois	IL	Day	Montcalm	MI	Decatur	Green	WI
Danforth	Washington	ME	Day	Saratoga	NY	Decker	Richland	IL
Danforth	Pine	Mn	Day	Ellis	OK	Decker	Knox	IN
Daniels	Burnett	WI	Day	Clark	SD	Decorah	Winneshiek	IA
Danielson	Meeker	MN	Day	Marathon	WI	Decoria	Blue Earth	MN
Danley	Faulkner	AR	Days Creek	Miller	AR	Decorah	Dunn	ND
Dannemora	Clinton	NY	Days Creek	York	ME	Dedham	Hancock	ME
Danneville	Divide	ND	Dayton	Sebastian	AR	Dedham	Norfolk	MA
Danton	Richland	ND	Dayton	Chickasaw	IA	Deep Creek	Clinton	IA
Danube	Herkimer	NY	Dayton	Iowa	IA	Deep Creek (No. 4)	Edgecombe	NC
Danvers	Essex	MA	Dayton	Webster	IA	Deep Creek	Yadkin	NC
Danver	McLean	IL	Dayton	Wright	IA	Deep Creek	Slope	ND
Danville	Yell	AR	Dayton	Phillips	KS	Deep Creek	Major	OK
Danville	Des Moines	IA	Dayton	Saline	KS	Deep Creek	Spokane	WA
Danville	Worth	IA	Dayton	La Salle	IL	Deep Fork	Oklahoma	OK
Danville	Vermilion	IL	Dayton	Bremer	IA	Deep River	Middlesex	CT

TOWNSHIP	COUNTY	STATE	TOWNSHIP	COUNTY	STATE	TOWNSHIP	COUNTY	STATE
Deep River	Poweshiek	IA	Delafield	Waukesha	WI	Denmark	Emmet	IA
Deep River	Arenac	MI	Delafield	Jackson	MN	Denmark	Lee	IA
Deep River	Guilford	NC	Delana	Humboldt	IA	Denmark	Tuscola	MI
Deep River (No. 4)	Lee	NC	Delanco	Burlington	NJ	Denmark	Washington	MN
Deep River (No. 5)	Moore	NC	Delaney	Corson	SD	Denmark	Ward	ND
Deep River	McHenry	ND	Delano	Sedgwick	KS	Denmark	Ashtabula	OH
Deepwater	Bates	MO	Delano	Schuykill	PA	Denning	Ulster	NY
Deepwater	Henry	MO	Delapre	Lincoln	SD	Denning	Franklin	IL
Deepwater	McLean	ND	Delavan	Walworth	WI	Dennis	Barnstable	MA
Deer	Roseau	MN	Delavan	Tazewell	IL	Dennis	Cape May	NJ
Deer Creek	Mills	IA	Delavan	Fairbault	MN	Dennison	Luzerne	PA
Deer Creek	Webster	IA	Delaware	Sullivan	NY	Dennysville	Washington	ME
Deer Creek	Worth	IA	Delaware	Logan	AR	Dent	Lawrence	AR
Deer Creek	Tazewell	IL	Delaware	Delaware	IN	Dent	Woodruff	AR
Deer Creek	Carroll	IN	Delaware	Hamilton	IN	Dent	San Joaquin	CA
Deer Creek	Cass	IN	Delware	Ripley	IN	Dent	Cheyenne	KS
Deer Creek	Miami	IN	Delaware	Delaware	IA	Dent	Iron	MO
Deer Creek	Allen	KS	Delaware	Polk	??	Dent	Pottawatomie	OK
Deer Creek	Phillips	KS	Delaware	Sac	IA	Denton	Scott	AR
Deer Creek	Otter Tail	MN	Delaware	Jefferson	KS	Denton	Roscommon	MI
Deer Creek	Bates	MO	Delaware	Leavenworth	KS	Denver	Richland	IL
Deer Creek	Henry	MO	Delaware	Wyandotta	KS	Denver	Isabella	MI
Deer Creek	Madison	OH	Delaware	Sanilac	MI	Denver	Newaygo	MI
Deer Creek	Pickaway	OH	Delaware	Grant	MN	Denver	Rock	MN
Deer Creek	Custer	OK	Delaware	Shannon	MO	Denver	Sargent	ND
Deer Creek	Oklahoma	OK	Delaware	Hunterdon	NJ	Denver	Adams	NE
Deer Creek	Mercer	PA	Delaware	Defiance	OH	Denver	Kingsbury	SD
Deer Creek	Outagamie	WI	Delaware	Delaware	OH	Denverton	Solano	CA
Deer Creek	Taylor	WI	Delaware	Hancock	OH	Denville	Morris	NJ
Deer Isle	Hancock	ME	Delaware	Caddo	OK	Departee	Independence	AR
Deer Park	La Salle	IL	Delaware	Juniata	PA	Depew	Creek	OK
Deer Park	Pennington	MN	Delaware	Mercer	PA	Deposit	Delaware	NY
Deer Park	Hamilton	OH	Delaware	Northumberland	PA	Deptford	Gloucester	NJ
Deer Park	Spokane	WA	Delaware	Pike	PA	Derby	New Haven	CT
Deer River	Itasca	MN	Delaware	Lincoln	SD	Derby	Orleans	VT
Deerfield	Franklin	MA	Delger	Wells	ND	Derinda	Jo Daviess	IL
Deerfield	Rockingham	NH	Delhi	Delaware	NY	Derry	Rockingham	NH
Deerfield	Oneida	NY	Delhi	Delaware	IA	Derry	Pike	IL
Deerfield	Dane	WI	Delhi	Osborne	KS	Derry	Dauphin	PA
Deerfield	Waushara	WI	Delhi	Ingham	MI	Derry	Mifflin	PA
Deerfield	Fulton	IL	Delhi	Redwood	MN	Derry	Montour	PA
Deerfield	Lake	IL	Delhi	Golden Valley	ND	Derry	Westmoreland	PA
Deerfield	Chickasaw	IA	Delhi	Hamilton	OH	Derrynane	Le Sueur	MN
Deerfield	Kearney	KS	Delhi	Beckham	OK	Des Arc	Prairie	AR
Deerfield	Isabella	MI	Delight	Custer	NE	Des Arc	White	AR
Deerfield	Lapeer	MI	Dell Grove	Pine	MN	Des Lacs	Ward	ND
Deerfield	Lenawee	MI	Dell Prairie	Adams	WI	Des Moines	Murray	MN
Deerfield	Livingston	MI	Dell Rapids	Minnehaha	SD	Des Moines	Boone	IA
Deerfield	Mecosta	MI	Dellona	Sauk	WI	Des Moines	Dallas	IA
Deerfield	Cass	MN	Delmar	Chippewa	WI	Des Moines	Jasper	IA
Deerfield	Steele	MN	Delmar	Carroll	AR	Des Moines	Jefferson	IA
Deerfield	Vernon	MO	Delmar	Tioga	PA	Des Moines	Lee	IA
Deerfield	Cumberland	NJ	Delmore	McPherson	KS	Des Moines	Pocahontas	IA
Deerfield	Morgan	OH	Deloit	Holt	NE	Des Moines	Polk	IA
Deerfield	Portage	OH	Delran	Burlington	NJ	Des Moines	Van Buren	IA
Deerfield	Ross	OH	Delta	Bayfield	WI	Des Moines	Jackson	MN
Deerfield	Warren	OH	Delta	Eaton	MI	Des Moines	Clark	MO
Deerfield	Tioga	PA	Delta	Whatcom	WA	Detour	Chippewa	MI
Deerfield	Warren	PA	Delton	Sauk	WI	Detroit	Somerset	ME
Deerhead	Barber	KS	Delton	Cottonwood	MN	Detroit	Pike	IL
Deerhorn	Wilkin	MN	Dement	Ogle	IL	Detroit	Becker	MN
Deering	Hillsborough	NH	Deming	Whatcom	WA	Detroit	Woodward	ND
Deering	McHenry	ND	Democrat	Carroll	IN	Dettman	Morton	ND
Deerpark	Orange	NY	Dempster	Hamlin	SD	Devoe	Faulk	SD
Deerwood	Crow Wing	MN	Demun	Randolph	AR	DeVillo	Richland	ND
Deerwood	Kittson	MN	Denbigh	McHenry	ND	DeVol	Cotton	OK
Defiance	Defiance	OH	Denhoff	Sheridan	ND	Dewald	Nobles	MN
Degnan	Latimer	OK	Denison	Lawrence	IL	Deweese (No. 9)	Mecklenburg	??
Degognia	Jackson	IL	Denison	Crawford	IA	Dewey	Burnett	WI
De Groat	Ramsey	ND	Denison	Spokane	WA	Dewey	Portage	WI
Dehlen	Nelson	ND	Denmark	Oxford	ME	Dewey	Rush	WI
Dekalb	Grant	AR	Denmark	Lewis	NY	Dewey	Modoc	CA
Dekorra	Columbia	WI	Denmark	White	AR	Dewey	La Porte	IN

TOWNSHIP	COUNTY	STATE	TOWNSHIP	COUNTY	STATE	TOWNSHIP	COUNTY	STATE
Dewey	Roseau	MN	Dobson	Poinsett	AR	Douglas	Rioquois	IL
Dewey	Walsh	ND	Dobson	Surry	NC	Douglas	Jackson	KS
Dewey	Oklahoma	OK	Doby	Harper	OK	Douglas	Stafford	KS
Dewey	Roger Mills	OK	Dochouquet	Auglaize	OH	Douglas	Dakota	MN
Dewey	Hyde	SD	Dodd City	Marion	AR	Douglas	McLean	ND
Dewhurst	Clark	WI	Dodds	Jefferson	IL	Douglas	Saunders	NE
Dewitt	Carroll	MO	Dodds	Nelson	ND	Douglas	Worcester	MA
Dexter	Penobscot	ME	Dodge	Boone	IA	Douglas	Clarendon	SC
Dexter	Wood	WI	Dodge	Dubuque	IA	Douglas	Hyde	SD
Dexter	Cowley	KS	Dodge	Guthrie	IA	Douglas	Marquette	WI
Dexter	Washtenaw	MI	Dodge	Union	IA	Douglass	Butler	KS
Dexter	Mower	MN	Dodge	Ford	KS	Douglass	Montcalm	MI
Dexter	Richland	ND	Dodge	Trempealeau	WI	Douglass	Berks	PA
Dexter	Codington	SD	Dodgeville	Iowa	WI	Douglass	Montgomery	PA
Deyo	Comanche	OK	Dodson	Highland	OH	Dover	Hot Spring	AR
Dials	Laurens	SC	Dog Bluff	Horry	SC	Dover	Pope	AR
Diamond Bluff	Pierce	WI	Dog Ear	Tripp	SD	Dover	Fayette	IA
Diamond Creek	Chase	KS	Dogden	McLean	ND	Dover	Pocahontas	IA
Diamond Hill	Abbeville	SC	Dogwood Neck	Horry	SC	Dover	Bureau	IL
Diamond Lake	Dickinson	IA	Dogwood	White	AR	Dover	Shawnee	KS
Diamond Lake	Lincoln	MN	Dolan	Cass	MO	Dover	Norfolk	MA
Diamond Springs	El Dorado	CA	Dollymount	Traverse	MN	Dover	Lake	MI
Diamond	Sebastian	AR	Dolphin	Knox	NE	Dover	Lenawee	MI
Diamond	Cherokee	IA	Dolson	Clark	IL	Dover	Otsego	MI
Diamond	Haskell	OK	Dolton	Turner	SD	Dover	Olmsted	MN
Diamond Valley	Morris	KS	Donald	Franklin	AR	Dover	Lafayette	MO
Diana	Lewis	NY	Donegal	Butler	PA	Dover	Vernon	MO
Diane	Sanborn	SD	Donegal	Washington	PA	Dover	Griggs	ND
Dick Johnson	Clay	IN	Donegal	Westmoreland	PA	Dover	Morris	NJ
Dickens	Gregory	SD	Doniphan	Ripley	MO	Dover	Ocean	NJ
Dickerson	Johnson	AR	Doniphan	Hall	NE	Dover	Dutchess	NY
Dickerson	Lewis	MO	Donnelly	Marshall	MN	Dover	Athens	OH
Dickinson	Broome	NY	Donnelly	Stevens	MN	Dover	Fulton	OH
Dickinson	Franklin	NY	Doon	Lyon	IA	Dover	Tuscarawas	OH
Dickinson	Cumberland	PA	Dor	Smith	KS	Dover	Union	OH
Dickson	Benton	AR	Dora	Crawford	AR	Dover	York	PA
Dickson	Manistee	MI	Dora	Moultrie	IL	Dover	Windham	VT
Dieter	Roseau	MN	Dora	Otter Tail	MN	Dover	Buffalo	WI
Dighton	Bristol	MA	Dorchester	Grafton	NH	Dover	Racine	WI
Dighton	Lane	KS	Dorchester	Macoupin	IL	Dover-Foxcroft	Piscataquis	ME
Dill	Kiowa	OK	Dorchester	Dorchester	SC	Dovray	Murray	MN
Dillard	Howard	AR	Dorman	Lyman	SD	Dovre	Barron	WI
Dillion	Beaverhead	MT	Dorr	McHenry	IL	Dovre	Kandiyohi	MN
Dillon	Tazewell	IL	Dorr	Allegan	MI	Dovre	Slope	ND
Dillon	Phelps	MO	Dorrance	Luzerne	PA	Dow	Pittsburg	OK
Dillsbora	Jackson	NC	Dorset	Ashtabula	OH	Dowell	Lawrence	AR
Dimmick	La Salle	IL	Dorset	Bennington	VT	Dowling	Knox	NE
Dimock	Susquehanna	PA	Dortch	Lonoke	AR	Downe	Cumberland	NJ
Dimond	Burke	ND	Dota	Independence	AR	Downers Grove	Du Page	IL
Dingman	Pike	PA	Doty	Oconto	WI	Downey	Los Angeles	CA
Dinsmore	Shelby	OH	Double Shoals (No. 9)	Cleveland	NC	Downieville	Sierra	CA
Dinuba	Tulare	CA	Dougherty	Cerro Gordo	IA	Downs	McLean	IL
Dirigo	Grant	OK	Douglas Grove	Custer	NE	Downs	Sumner	KS
Dismal	Sampson	NC	Douglas	San Joaquin	CA	Downs	Kingfisher	OK
District	Berks	PA	Douglas	Adams	IA	Dows	Cass	ND
Divernon	Sangamon	IL	Douglas	Appanoose	IA	Doyal	Saint Clair	MO
Divide	Golden Valley	ND	Douglas	Audubon	IA	Doyle	Clarke	IA
Divide	Buffalo	NE	Douglas	Bremer	IA	Doyle	Marion	KS
Divide	Phelps	NE	Douglas	Coone	IA	Doyle	Schoolcraft	MI
Divide	Dickey	NE	Douglas	Clay	IA	Doyle	Caddo	OK
Dix	Ford	IL	Douglas	Harrison	IA	Doyle	Barron	WI
Dix	Schuyler	NY	Douglas	Ida	IA	Doylesport	Barton	MO
Dixfield	Oxford	ME	Douglas	Madison	IA	Doylestown	Bucks	PA
Dixmont	Penobscot	ME	Douglas	Mitchell	IA	Dracut	Middlesex	MA
Dixon	Monroe	AR	Douglas	Montgomery	IA	Dragoon	Osage	KS
Dixon	Lee	IL	Douglas	Page	IA	Drake	Macon	MO
Dixon	Sumner	KS	Douglas	Polk	IA	Drakesville	Davis	IA
Dixon	Logan	ND	Douglas	Sac	IA	Drammen	Lincoln	MN
Dixon	Blaine	OK	Douglas	Shelby	IA	Drammen	Eau Claire	WI
Dixon	Preble	OH	Douglas	Union	IA	Draper	Jones	SD
Dixon	Gregory	SD	Douglas	Webster	IA	Draper	Sawyer	WI
Dixon	Hamlin	SD	Douglas	Clark	IL	Drayton	Pembina	ND
Dixville	Coos	NH	Douglas	Effingham	IL	Draytonville	Cherokee	SC

TOWNSHIPS OF THE UNITED STATES

TOWNSHIP	COUNTY	STATE	TOWNSHIP	COUNTY	STATE	TOWNSHIP	COUNTY	STATE
Dreher	Wayne	PA	Dunbar	Fayette	PA	Eagan	Dakota	MN
Dresbach	Winona	MN	Dunbar	Sargent	ND	Eagle Chief	Alfalfa	OK
Dresden	Chickasaw	IA	Dunbar	Marinette	WI	Eagle Creek	Gallatin	IL
Dresden	Decatur	KS	Dunbarton	Marrimack	NH	Eagle Creek	Lake	IN
Dresden	Kingman	KS	Duncan	Monroe	AR	Eagle Creek	Scott	MN
Dresden	Lincoln	ME	Duncan	Mercer	IL	Eagle Grove	Wright	IA
Dresden	Pettis	MO	Duncan	Houghton	MI	Eagle Harbor	Keweenaw	MI
Dresden	Cavalier	ND	Duncan	Sullivan	MO	Eagle Lake	Aroostook	ME
Dresden	Washington	NY	Duncan	Tioga	PA	Eagle Lake	Otter Tail	MN
Drexel	Burke	NC	Duncan	Spokane	WA	Eagle Mills	Iredell	NC
Driftwood	Jackson	IN	Duncans Creek	Rutherford	NC	Eagle Point	Ogle	IL
Driftwood	Rawlins	KS	Dundee	Kane	IL	Eagle Point	Marshall	MN
Driftwood	Alfalfa	OK	Dundee	Monroe	MI	Eagle Point	Chippewa	WI
Driftwood	Woods	OK	Dundee	Walsh	ND	Eagle	Bradley	AR
Driggs	Logan	AR	Dunham	McHenry	IL	Eagle	Faulkner	AR
Driscoll	Burleigh	ND	Dunham	Washington	OH	Eagle	Lonoke	AR
Drum Creek	Montgomery	KS	Dunkard	Greene	PA	Eagle	Polk	AR
Drummer	Ford	IL	Dunkel	Jones	SD	Eagle	Black Hawk	IA
Drummond	Chippewa	MI	Dunkirk	Chautauqua	NY	Eagle	Kosuth	IA
Drummond	Bayfield	WI	Dunkirk	Dane	WI	Eagle	Kossuth	IA
Drumore	Lancaster	PA	Dunklin	Greenville	SC	Eagle	Sioux	IA
Drury	Rock Island	IL	Dunleith	Jo Daviess	IL	Eagle	La Salle	IL
Dry Creek	Howell	MO	Dunn	Otter Tail	MN	Eagle	Boone	IN
Dry Creek	Maries	MO	Dunn (No. 1)	Franklin	NC	Eagle	Barber	KS
Dry Fork	Carroll	AR	Dunn	Dane	WI	Eagle	Harper	KS
Dry Fork	Williams	ND	Dunn	Dunn	WI	Eagle	Kingman	KS
Dry Grove	McLean	IL	Dunnigan	Yolo	CA	Eagle	Sedgwick	KS
Dry Lake	Ramsey	ND	Dunnington	Jefferson	AR	Eagle	Clinton	MI
Dry Wood Lake	Roberts	SD	Dunns Rock	Transylvania	NC	Eagle	Macon	MO
Dry Point	Shelby	IL	Dunnstable	Clinton	PA	Eagle	Richland	ND
Dry Run	Dallas	AR	Dunstable	Middlesex	MA	Eagle	Wyoming	NY
Dry Wells	Nash	NC	Du Page	Will	IL	Eagle	Brown	OH
Dryden	Lapeer	MI	Deplain	Clinton	MI	Eagle	Hancock	OH
Dryden	Sibley	MN	Dupont	Waupaca	WI	Eagle	Vinton	OH
Dryden	Tompkins	NY	Durand	Winnebago	IL	Eagle	McCurtain	OK
Dryden	Harmon	OK	Durand	Beltrami	MN	Eagle	Pawnee	OK
Dryden	Fall River	SD	Durand	Pepin	WI	Eagle	Payne	OK
Drywood	Bourbon	KS	Durbin	Cass	Nd	Eagle	Woods	OK
Drywood	Vernon	MO	Durham	Washington	AR	Eagle	Brule	SD
Drytown	Izard	AR	Durham	Butte	CA	Eagle	Hyde	SD
Duane	Franklin	NY	Durham	Middlesex	CT	Eagle	Meade	SD
Duanesburg	Schenectady	NY	Durham	Hancock	IL	Eagle	Richland	WI
Dublin	Cheshire	NH	Durham	Marion	KS	Eagle	Waukesha	WI
Dublin	Swift	MN	Durham	Ottawa	KS	Eagle Valley	Todd	MN
Dublin	Mercer	OH	Durham	Androscoggin	ME	Eagles Nest	Morton	ND
Dublin	Huntingdon	PA	Durham	Durham	NC	Eagleswood	Ocean	NJ
Dublin	Fulton	PA	Durham	Stutsman	ND	Earl	La Salle	IL
Du Bois	Washington	IL	Durham	Strafford	NH	Earl	Jefferson	OK
Dubuque	Dubuque	IA	Durham	Greene	NY	Earl	Berks	PA
Duck Creek	Madison	IN	Durham	Bucks	PA	Earl	Lancaster	PA
Duck Creek	Wilson	KS	Dustin	Holt	NE	Earlboro	Potawatomie	OK
Duck Creek	Stoddard	MO	Dustin	Hughes	OK	Earling	Lyman	SD
Duck Creek	Adams	ND	Dutch Creek	Yell	AR	Easby	Cavalier	ND
Duckett	Howard	AR	Dutch Creek	Washington	IA	Easley	Macon	MO
Ducor	Tulare	CA	Dutch Mills	Washington	AR	Eason	Pottawatomie	OK
Dudley	Henry	IN	Dutchville	Granville	NC	East Allen	Northampton	PA
Dudley	Haskell	KS	Dulton	Grady	OK	East Alma	Cavalier	ND
Dudley	Worcester	MA	Duty	Lawrence	AR	East Amwell	Hunterdon	NJ
Dudley	Clearwater	MN	Duval	Jasper	MO	East Bay	Grand Traverse	MI
Dudley	Hardin	OH	Duxbury	Plymouth	MA	East Bend	Champaign	IL
Dudley	Aurora	SD	Duxbury	Washington	VT	East Bend	Yadkin	NC
Dudley	Fall River	SD	Dwight	Livingston	IL	East Benton	Christian	MO
Dudley Lake	Jefferson	AR	Dwight	Huron	MI	East Benton	Webster	MO
Duell	Perkins	SD	Dwight	Richland	ND	East Bethlehem	Washington	PA
Due West	Abbeville	SC	Dyberry	Wayne	PA	East Bloomfield	Ontario	NY
Duerr	Richland	ND	Dyer Brook	Aroostook	ME	East Boone	Bates	MO
Duke	Harnett	NC	Dyer	Crawford	AR	East Boyer	Crawford	IA
Duke	Jackson	OK	Dyer	Saline	AR	East Bradford	Chester	PA
Duluth	Saint Louis	MN	Dyess	Mississippi	AR	East Branch	Marion	KS
Dumarce	Marshall	SD	Dysartsville	McDowell	NC	East Brandywine	Chester	PA
Dummer	Coos	NH				East Bridgewater	Plymouth	MA
Dummerston	Windham	VT				East Brookfield	Worcester	MA
Dunbar	Faribault	MN	—E—			East Brunswick	Middlesex	NJ

— 804 —

TOWNSHIP	COUNTY	STATE	TOWNSHIP	COUNTY	STATE	TOWNSHIP	COUNTY	STATE
East Brunswick	Schuylkill	PA	East Machias	Washington	ME	Eastover	Cumberland	NC
East Buffalo	Union	PA	East Mahoning	Indiana	PA	Easttown	Chester	PA
East Caln	Chester	PA	East Manchester	York	PA	Eaton Rapids	Eaton	MI
East Cameron	Northumberland	PA	East Marlborough	Chester	PA	Eaton	Lawrence	AR
East Carroll	Cambria	PA	East McKinley	Caddo	OK	Eaton	Eaton	MI
East Chain	Martin	MN	East Mead	Crawford	PA	Eaton	Kearney	NE
East Cheney	Spokane	WA	East Millinocket	Penobscot	ME	Eaton	Carroll	NH
East Chillisquaque	Northumberland	PA	East Montpelier	Washington	VT	Eaton	Madison	NY
East China	Saint Clair	MI	East Nantmeal	Chester	PA	Eaton	Lorain	OH
East Choteau	Douglas	SD	East Nelson	Moultrie	IL	Eaton	Wyoming	PA
East Cocalico	Lancaster	PA	East Newman	Nance	NE	Eau Galle	Dunn	WI
East Cooper	Stafford	KS	East Norriton	Montgomery	PA	Eau Galle	Saint Croix	WI
East Coventry	Chester	PA	East Norwegian	Schuylkill	PA	Eau Pleine	Marathon	WI
East Custer	Custer	NE	East Nottingham	Chester	PA	Eau Pleine	Portage	WI
East Dallas	Webster	MO	East Oakland	Coles	IL	Ebbs Chapel (No. 7)	Madison	NC
East Deer	Allegheny	PA	East Orange	Sioux	IA	Ebenezer	Florence	SC
East Des Moines	Mahaska	IN	East Otto	Cattaraugus	NY	Ebenezer	York	SC
East Donegal	Lancaster	PA	East Park	Marshall	MN	Eaton	Brown	WI
East Drumore	Lancaster	PA	East Pen	Carbon	PA	Eaton	Clark	WI
East Earl	Lancaster	PA	East Pennsboro	Cumberland	PA	Eaton	Manitowoc	WI
East Eldorado	Saline	IL	East Pikeland	Chester	PA	Echo	Antrim	MI
East Fairfield	Crawford	PA	East Providence	Benford	PA	Echo	Yellow Medicine	MN
East Fallowfield	Chester	PA	East River	Page	IA	Eckelson	Barnes	ND
East Fallowfield	Crawford	PA	East Rockhill	Bucks	PA	Eckford	Calhoun	MI
East Finley	Washington	PA	East Rondell	Brown	SD	Eckles	Beltrami	MN
East Fishkill	Dutchess	NY	East Saint Clair	Bedford	PA	Ecklund	Burleigh	ND
East Fork	Faulkner	AR	East Saint Louis	Saint Clair	IL	Eckvoll	Marshall	MN
East Fork	Clinton	IL	East Saline	Sheridan	KS	Economy	McLean	ND
East Fork	Montgomery	IL	East Sanford (No. 5)	Lee	NC	Econtuchka	Seminole	OK
East Fork	Haywood	NC	East Side	Mille Lacs	MN	Ecore Fabre	Ouachita	AR
East Fork	Benson	ND	East Six	Slope	ND	Eddington	Penobscot	ME
East Fork	Williams	ND	East Spokane	Spokane	WA	Eddy	Clearwater	MN
East Fork	Douglas	NV	East Sullivan	Sharp	AR	Eddy	Eddy	ND
East Franklin	Armstrong	PA	East Taylor	Cambria	PA	Eden Lake	Stearns	MN
East Fulton	Callaway	MO	East	Montgomery	IA	Eden	Alameda	CA
East Galena	Jo Daviess	IL	East	Carroll	OH	Eden	Ness	KS
East Goshen	Chester	PA	East Troy	Walworth	WI	Eden	Sumner	KS
East Granby	Hartford	CT	East Turkey Creek	Washita	OK	Eden	Benton	IA
East Greenbush	Rensselaer	NY	East Union	Wayne	OH	Eden	Carroll	IA
East Greenwick	Cloucester	NJ	East Union	Schuylkill	PA	Eden	Clinton	IA
East Greenwick	Kent	RI	East Valley	Marshall	MN	Eden	Decatur	IA
East Grove	Lee	IL	East Vincent	Chester	PA	Eden	Fayette	IA
East Haddam	Middlesex	CT	East Walnut	Canadian	OK	Eden	Marshall	IA
East Hale	Thomas	KS	East Washington	Rice	KS	Eden	Sac	IA
East Hamilton	Ellis	KS	East Waterloo	Black Hawk	IA	Eden	Winnebago	IA
East Hampton	Middlesex	CT	East Wheatfield	Indiana	PA	Eden	La Salle	IL
East Hampton	Suffolk	NY	East Whiteland	Chester	PA	Eden	Lagrange	IN
East Hanover	Morris	NJ	East Windsor	Hartford	CT	Eden	Lake	MI
East Hanover	Dauphin	PA	East Windsor	Mercer	NJ	Eden	Mason	MI
East Hanover	Lebanon	PA	Eastampton	Burlington	NJ	Eden	Brown	MN
East Hanson	Brown	SD	Eastatoe	Transylvania	NC	Eden	Pipestone	MN
East Hartford	Hartford	CT	Eastbrook	Hancock	ME	Eden	Polk	MN
East Haven	New Haven	CT	Eastchester	Westchester	NY	Eden	Walsh	ND
East Haven	Essex	VT	Easter	Roberts	SD	Eden	Antelope	NE
East Hempfield	Lancaster	PA	Eastern	Franklin	IL	Eden	Erie	NY
East Hess	Gray	KS	Eastern	Otter Tail	MN	Eden	Licking	OH
East Hibbard	Kearney	KS	Eastern	Knox	NE	Eden	Seneca	OH
East Hopewell	York	PA	Eastford	Windham	CT	Eden	Wyandot	OH
East Howellsville	Robeson	NC	Eastham	Barnstable	MA	Eden	Payne	OK
East Huntingdon	Westmoreland	PA	Easthampton	Hampshire	MA	Eden	Lancaster	PA
East James	Stone	MO	Eastlake	Lake	OH	Eden	Buffalo	SD
East Keating	Clinton	PA	Eastman	Foster	NE	Eden	Clark	SD
East Kingston	Rockingham	NH	Eastman	Crawford	WI	Eden	Codington	SD
East Lackawannock	Mercer	PA	Eastman	Fairfield	CT	Eden	Hyde	SD
East Lake Lillian	Kandiyohi	MN	Easton	Leavenworth	KS	Eden	Lincoln	SD
East Lake	Dare	NC	Easton	Bristol	MA	Eden	Marshall	SD
East Lampeter	Lancaster	PA	Easton	Aroostook	ME	Eden	Lamoille	VT
East Lancaster	Keokuk	IA	Easton	Ionia	MI	Eden	Fond du Lac	WI
East Lincoln	Logan	IL	Easton	Steele	ND	Eden	Iowa	WI
East Line	Elko	NV	Easton	Grafton	NH	Eden Valley	Renville	ND
East Longmeadow	Hampden	MA	Easton	Washington	NY	Edendale	Steele	ND
East Lucas	Johnson	IA	Easton	Adams	WI	Edens	Gregory	SD
East Lyme	New London	CT	Easton	Marathon	WI	Edenton (No. 1)	Chowan	NC

TOWNSHIPS OF THE UNITED STATES

TOWNSHIP	COUNTY	STATE	TOWNSHIP	COUNTY	STATE	TOWNSHIP	COUNTY	STATE
Edenville	Midland	MI	Elba	Genesse	NY	Elk Prairie	Jefferson	IL
Edford	Henry	IL	Elba	Dodge	WI	Elk Rapids	Antrim	MI
Edgar	Edger	IL	Elberta	Woods	OK	Elk River	Clinton	IA
Edgar	Clay	NE	Elbow Lake	Grant	MN	Elk River	McDonald	MO
Edgartown	Dukes	MA	Elbridge	Edgar	IL	Elk River	Sherburne	MN
Edgecomb	Lincoln	ME	Elbridge	Oceana	MI	Elk	Buena Vista	IA
Edgefield	McCormick	SD	Elbridge	Onondaga	NY	Elk	Clayton	IA
Edgemont	Sheridan	ND	Elcho	Langlade	WI	Elk	Delaware	IA
Edgemont	Delaware	PA	Elden	Dickey	ND	Elk	Jackson	IL
Edgerton	Hanson	SD	Elder	Cambria	PA	Elk	Cloud	KS
Edgewater Park	Burlington	NJ	Elderon	Marathon	WI	Elk	Osaga	KS
Edgewater	Sawyer	WI	Eldon	Benson	ND	Elk	Rawlins	KS
Edgewood	Siskiyou	CA	Eldora City	Hardin	IA	Elk	Lake	MI
Edgington	Rock Island	IL	Eldora	Hardin	IA	Elk	Sanilac	MI
Edinburg	Penobscot	ME	Eldora	Surry	NC	Elk	Nobles	MN
Edinburg	Saratoga	NY	Eldorado	Benton	AR	Elk	Stoddard	MO
Edinburg	Portage	OH	Eldorado	Benton	IA	Elk	Ashe	NC
Edison	Swift	MN	Eldorado	McDonough	IL	Elk	Watauga	NC
Edison	Middlesex	NJ	Eldorado	Stevens	MN	Elk	Wilkes	NC
Edison	Minnehaha	SD	Eldorado	Montgomery	NC	Elk	McKenzie	ND
Edisto Island	Charleston	SC	Eldorado	Traill	ND	Elk	Saunders	NE
Edisto	Orangeburg	SC	Eldorado	Clay	NE	Elk	Gloucester	NJ
Edmeston	Otsego	NY	Eldorado	Harian	NE	Elk	Noble	OH
Edmond	Oklahoma	OK	Eldorado	Jackson	OK	Elk	Vinton	OH
Edmunds	Stutsman	ND	Eldorado	Fond du Lac	WI	Elk	Beckham	OK
Edna	Cass	IA	Eldred	Cass	ND	Elk	Oklahoma	OK
Edna	Otter Tail	MN	Eldred	Jefferson	PA	Elk	Chester	PA
Edna	Barnes	ND	Eldred	Lycoming	PA	Elk	Clarion	PA
Edna	Lyman	SD	Eldred	McKean	PA	Elk	Tioga	PA
Edneyville	Henderson	NC	Eldred	Monroe	PA	Elk	Warren	PA
Edson	Chippewa	WI	Eldred	Schuylkill	PA	Elk	Spokane	WA
Edward	Wichita	KS	Eldred	Warren	PA	Elk	Price	WI
Edwards	Ogemaw	MI	Eldridge	Laciede	MO	Elkader	Logan	KS
Edwards	Kandiyohi	MN	Eldridge	Stutsman	ND	Elkhart	Polk	IA
Edwards (No. 1)	Ravalli	MT	Elevation	Johnston	NC	Elkhart	Logan	IL
Edwards	Wilkes	NC	Eleven Point	Randolph	AR	Elkhart	Elkhart	IN
Edwards	Saint Lawrence	NY	Elgin	Lyon	IA	Elkhart	Noble	IN
Edwardsville	Madison	IL	Elgin	Plymouth	IA	Elkhart	Bates	MO
Eel River	Allen	IN	Elgin	Kane	IL	Elkhorn	San Joaquin	CA
Eel River	Hendricks	IN	Elgin	Wabasha	MN	Elkhorn	Plymouth	IA
Eel	Cass	IN	Elgin	Cavalier	ND	Elkhorn	Webster	IA
Effingham	Carroll	NH	Elgin	Antelope	NE	Elkhorn	Brown	IL
Effingham	Florence	SC	Elida	Potter	SD	Elkhorn	Carroll	IL
Effington	Otter Tail	MN	Elim	Custer	NE	Elkhorn	Lincoln	KS
Egan	Mountrail	ND	Eliot	Louisa	IA	Elkhorn	Divide	ND
Egan	Moody	SD	Eliot	York	ME	Elkhorn	Cuming	NE
Egeland	Day	SD	Elixir	Boone	AR	Elkhorn	Dodge	NE
Egelston	Muskegon	MI	Eliza	Mercer	IL	Elkhorn	Warren	MO
Egg Creek	McHenry	ND	Elizabeth City	Pasquotank	NC	Elkin	Surry	NC
Egg Harbor	Atlantic	NJ	Elizabeth	Jo Daviess	IL	Elkland	Tuscola	MI
Egg Harbor	Door	WI	Elizabeth	Otter Tail	MN	Elkland	Sullivan	PA
Eglon	Clay	MN	Elizabeth	Lawrence	OH	Elkland	Tioga	PA
Egremont	Berkshire	MA	Elizabeth	Miami	OH	Elkmount	Grand Forks	ND
Egypt	Ashley	AR	Elizabeth	Allegheny	PA	Elko	Elko	NV
Egypt	Carroll	MO	Elizabeth	Lancaster	PA	Elkrun	Columbiana	OH
Egypt	Yancey	NC	Elizabeth	Orangeburg	SC	Elkton	Clay	MN
Eidsvild	Lyon	MN	Elizabethtown	Bladen	NC	Elkton	Brookings	SD
Eidsvild	Bottineau	ND	Elizabethtown	Essex	NY	Ell	Hancock	IA
Eileen	Bayfield	WI	Elk Creek	Jasper	IA	Ellenboro	Grant	WI
Eisenstein	Price	WI	Elk Creek	Republic	KS	Ellenburg	Clinton	NY
El Cajon	San Diego	CA	Elk Creek	Wright	MO	Ellendale	Alexander	NC
El Dorado	Union	AR	Elk Creek	Golden Valley	ND	Ellendale	Dickey	ND
El Dorado	Butler	KS	Elk Creek	Custer	NE	Ellery	Chautauqua	NY
El Monte	Los Angeles	CA	Elk Creek	Erie	PA	Ellicott	Chautauqua	NY
El Paso	White	AR	Elk Falls	Elk	KS	Ellicottville	Cattaraugus	NY
El Paso	Woodford	IL	Elk Fork	Pettis	MO	Ellijay	Macon	NC
El Paso	Pierce	WI	Elk Grove	Cook	IL	Elling	Pierce	ND
El Reno	Canadian	OK	Elk Grove	Lafayette	WI	Ellington	Tolland	CT
Eia	Lake	IL	Elk Horn	McDonald	MO	Ellington	Palo Alto	IA
Elba	Knox	IL	Elk Lake	Grant	MN	Ellington	Hancock	IA
Elba	Gratiot	MI	Elk Lick	Somerset	PA	Ellington	Adams	IL
Elba	Lapeer	MI	Elk Mound	Dunn	WI	Ellington	Tuscola	MI
Elba	Winona	MN	Elk Point	Union	SD	Ellington	Dodge	MN

TOWNSHIPS OF THE UNITED STATES

TOWNSHIP	COUNTY	STATE	TOWNSHIP	COUNTY	STATE	TOWNSHIP	COUNTY	STATE
Ellington	Chautauqua	NY	Elmira	Codington	SD	Empire	Cass	ND
Ellington	Outagamie	WI	Elmo	Otter Tail	MN	Empire	McLean	IL
Ellinwood	Barton	KS	Elmore	Daviess	IN	Empire	Ellsworth	KS
Elliot	San Joaquin	CA	Elmore	Fairbault	MN	Empire	Harper	KS
Elliott	Ransom	ND	Elmore	Garvin	OK	Empire	McPherson	KS
Elliott	Sanborn	SD	Elmore	Lamoille	VT	Empire	Leelanau	MI
Ellis	Cross	AR	Elms	Bottineau	ND	Empire	Dakota	MN
Ellis	Hardin	IA	Elmwood Place	Hamilton	OH	Empire	Andrew	MO
Ellis	Ellis	KS	Elmwood	Boone	AR	Empire	Fond du Lac	WI
Ellis	Cheboygan	MI	Elmwood	Peoria	IL	Emporia	Lyon	KS
Ellisburg	Jefferson	NY	Elmwood	Leelanau	MI	Encinitas	San Diego	CA
Ellison	Warren	IL	Elmwood	Tuscola	MI	Endy	Stanly	NC
Elliston	Tripp	SD	Elmwood	Clay	MN	Enfield	Hartford	CT
Ellisville	Fulton	IL	Elmwood	Saline	MO	Enfield	White	IL
Ellisville	Williams	ND	Elmwood	Golden Valley	ND	Enfield	Penobscott	ME
Ellisville	Faulk	SD	Elmwood	Beaver	OK	Enfield	Halifax	NC
Elloree	Orangeburg	SC	Elmwood	Edgefield	SC	Enfield	Grafton	NH
Ellsborough	Murray	MN	Elon	Ashley	AR	Enfield	Tompkins	NY
Ellsburg	Saint Louis	MN	Elora	Pembrina	ND	Engelter	Morton	ND
Ellsbury	Barnes	NE	Elrod	Clark	SD	Enger	Steele	ND
Ellston	Gregory	SD	Elroy	Faulk	SD	Englemann	Saint Clair	IL
Ellsworth	Logan	AR	Elsah	Jersay	IL	Englewood	Clark	KS
Ellsworth	Emmet	IA	Elsinboro	Salem	NJ	Englewood	Perkins	SD
Ellsworth	Hamilton	IA	Elsinore	Riverside	CA	English River	Keokuk	IA
Ellsworth	Ellsworth	KS	Elsmore	Allen	KS	English River	Washington	IA
Ellsworth	Lake	MI	Elsworth	McKenzie	ND	English	Iowa	IA
Ellsworth	Meeker	MN	Elverum	Pierce	ND	English	Lucas	IA
Ellsworth	Antelope	NE	Elvira	Johnson	IL	English	Jersey	IL
Ellsworth	Grafton	NH	Elvira	Buffalo	SD	Enid	Garfield	OK
Ellsworth	Mahoning	OH	Elwood	Vermilion	IL	Eno	Orange	NC
Ellsworth	Pierce	WI	Elwood	Barber	KS	Enoch	Noble	OH
Elm	Allen	KS	Ely	Marquette	MI	Enola	Faulkner	AR
Elm	Pratt	KS	Ely	White Pine	NV	Enosburg	Franklin	VT
Elm	Putnam	MO	Ely	Lorain	OH	Ensign	Delta	MI
Elm	Dickey	ND	Elyria	Valley	NE	Ensign	Renville	ND
Elm	Grant	ND	Elyria	Lorain	OH	Ensley	Newaygo	MI
Elm	Antelope	NE	Elysian	Le Sueur	MN	Enstrom	Roseau	MN
Elm	Gage	NE	Elysian	Bottineau	NE	Enterprise	Ford	KS
Elm	Sherman	NE	Elzas	Emmons	ND	Enterprise	Reno	KS
Elm Creek	Marshall	KS	Emanuel	Bon Homme	SD	Enterprise	Missaukee	MI
Elm Creek	Morris	KS	Emarald	Paulding	OH	Enterprise	Jackson	MN
Elm Creek	Saline	KS	Emardville	Red Lake	MN	Enterprise	Linn	MO
Elm Creek	Martin	MN	Embarrass	Edgar	IL	Enterprise	Nelson	ND
Elm Creek	Buffalo	NE	Embarrass	Saint Louis	MN	Enterprise	Valley	NE
Elm Grove	Calhoun	IA	Embden	Somerset	ME	Enterprise	Faulk	SD
Elm Grove	Louisa	IA	Emerald	Saint Croix	WI	Enterprise	Moody	SD
Elm Grove	Tazewell	IL	Emerald	Faribault	MN	Enterprise	Roberts	SD
Elm Grove	Labette	KS	Emerson	Columbia	AR	Enterprise	Oneida	WI
Elm Grove	Grand Forks	ND	Emerson	Gratiot	MI	Ephrata	Lancaster	PA
Elm Grove	Payne	OK	Emerson	Dixon	NE	Ephratah	Fulton	NY
Elm Mills	Garber	KS	Emerson	Harian	NE	Eppards Point	Livingston	IL
Elm River	Wayne	IL	Emerson	Faulk	SD	Epping	Rockingham	NH
Elm River	Houghton	MI	Emery	McCook	SD	Epps	Butler	MO
Elm River	Traill	ND	Emery	Price	WI	Epsom	Merrimack	NH
Elm Springs	Washington	AR	Eminence	Logan	IL	Equality	Gallatin	IL
Elm Store	Randolph	AR	Eminence	Woodson	KS	Equality	Red Lake	MN
Elm Tree	McKenzie	ND	Eminence	Shannon	MO	Equality	Miller	MO
Elma	Richland	ND	Emma	White	IL	Equality	Williams	ND
Elma	Erie	NY	Emma	Harvey	KS	Erdahl	Grant	MN
Elmdale	Ward	ND	Emmet	Nevada	AR	Erhards Grove	Otter Tail	MN
Elmdale	Morrison	MN	Emmet	Emmet	IA	Ericson	Renville	MN
Elmer	Oscoda	MI	Emmet	McDonough	IL	Erie	Whiteside	IL
Elmer	Sanilac	MI	Emmet	Renville	MN	Erie	Miami	IN
Elmer	Pipeston	MN	Emmet	Holt	NE	Erie	Neosho	KS
Elmer	Saint Louis	MN	Emmet	Union	SD	Erie	Sedgwick	KS
Elmer	Jefferson	OK	Emmet	Dodge	WI	Erie	Monroe	MI
Elmerdaro	Lyon	KS	Emmet	Marathon	WI	Erie	Becker	MN
Elmhurst	Lackawanna	PA	Emmetsburg	Palo Alto	IA	Erie	McDonald	MO
Elmira	Solano	CA	Emmett	Norton	KS	Erie	Cass	ND
Elmira	Stark	IL	Emmett	Pottawatomie	KS	Erie	Ottawa	OH
Elmira	Otsego	MI	Emmett	Calhoun	MI	Erienna	Grundy	IL
Elmira	Olmsted	MN	Emmett	Saint Clair	MI	Erick	Beckham	OK
Elmira	Chemung	NY	Emmons	Davidson	NC	Erin Prairie	Saint Croix	WI

TOWNSHIPS OF THE UNITED STATES

TOWNSHIP	COUNTY	STATE
Erin	Hancock	IA
Erin	Stephenson	IL
Erin	Rice	MN
Erin	Chemung	NY
Erin	Washington	WI
Ernest	Dade	MO
Errol	Coos	NH
Ervin	Howard	IN
Ervin	Traill	ND
Erving	Jewell	KS
Erving	Franklin	MA
Erwin	Gogebic	MI
Erwin	Steuben	NY
Esbon	Jewell	KS
Escanaba	Delta	MI
Escondido	San Diego	CA
Esculapia	Benton	AR
Esmen	Livingston	IL
Esmeralda	Esmeralda	NV
Esmond	Benson	ND
Esmond	Kingsburg	SD
Esopus	Ulster	NY
Espanola	Spokane	WA
Esparto	Yolo	CA
Espelie	Marshall	MN
Esperance	Schoharie	NY
Essex	Middlesex	CT
Essex	Kankakee	IL
Essex	Stark	IL
Essex	Essex	MA
Essex	Clinton	MI
Essex	Essex	NY
Essex	Chittenden	VT
Estabrook	Foster	ND
Estella	Chippewa	WI
Estelline	Hamlin	SD
Esther	Polk	MN
Estherville	Emmet	IA
Estherville	Burleigh	ND
Etiwanda	San Bernardino	CA
Etna	Siskiyou	CA
Etna	Kosciusko	IN
Etna	Hardin	IA
Etna	Penobscot	ME
Etna	Licking	OH
Etna-Troy	Whitley	IN
Ettrick	Trempealeau	WI
Eubank	Texas	OK
Euchee	Creek	OK
Euclid	Polk	MN
Eudora	Douglas	KS
Eufaula	McIntosh	OK
Eugene	Vermillion	IN
Eugene	Carroll	MO
Eulalia	Potter	PA
Eureka	Humboldt	CA
Eureka	Nevada	CA
Eureka	Adair	IA
Eureka	Sac	IA
Eureka	Barton	KS
Eureka	Cheyenne	KS
Eureka	Greenwood	KS
Eureka	Kingman	KS
Eureka	Mitchell	KS
Eureka	Rice	KS
Eureka	Saline	KS
Eureka	Montcalm	MI
Eureka	Dokota	MN
Eureka	Ward	ND
Eureka	Valley	NE
Eureka	Eureka	NV
Eureka	Aurora	SD
Eureka	Brookings	SD
Eureka	Polk	WI
Eustis	Franklin	ME
Eutaw	Berkeley	SC
Eutaw	Orangeburg	SC
Evan	Kingman	KS
Evangeline	Charlevoix	MI
Evans	Marshall	IL
Evans	Erie	NY
Evanston	Cook	IL
Evansville	Douglas	MN
Evart	Osceola	MI
Eveline	Charlevoix	MI
Evening Shade	Greene	AR
Everest	Cass	ND
Everett	Woodson	KS
Everett	Newaygo	MI
Everett	Cass	MO
Everett	Burt	NE
Everett	Dodge	NE
Everglade	Stevens	MN
Evergreen	Cheyenne	KS
Evergreen	Montcalm	MI
Evergreen	Sanilac	MI
Evergreen	Becker	MN
Evergreen	Ward	ND
Evergreen	Langlade	WI
Evergreen	Washburn	WI
Everidge	Choctaw	OK
Everts	Otter Tail	MN
Evesham	Burlington	NJ
Ewing	Boone	AR
Ewing	Franklin	IL
Ewing	Marquetta	MI
Ewing	Holt	NE
Ewing	Mercer	NJ
Ewington	Jackson	MN
Ewoldt	Carroll	IA
Excel	Marshall	MN
Excelsior	Dickinson	IA
Excelsior	Kalkaska	MI
Excelsior	Kidder	ND
Excelsior	Kingfisher	OK
Excelsior	Sauk	WI
Exeter	Tulare	CA
Exeter	Clay	KS
Exeter	Penobscot	ME
Exeter	Monroe	MI
Exeter	Barry	MO
Exeter	Fillmore	NE
Exeter	Rockingham	NH
Exeter	Otsego	NY
Exeter	Berks	PA
Exeter	Luzerne	PA
Exeter	Wyoming	PA
Exeter	Washington	RI
Exeter	Green	WI
Exira	Audubon	IA
Exline	Spink	SD
Extra	Ashley	AR
Eyota	Olmstead	MN

—F—

TOWNSHIP	COUNTY	STATE
Fabius	Davis	IA
Fabius	Saint Joseph	MI
Fabius	Knox	MO
Fabius	Marion	MO
Fabius	Schuyler	MO
Fabius	Onondago	NY
Fahlum	Kandiyohi	MN
Fair	Platte	MO
Fair	Hutchinson	SD
Fair Bluff	Columbus	NC
Fair Haven	Rutland	VT
Fair Oaks	Cross	AR
Fair Valley	Morton	ND
Fairbank	Buchanan	IA
Fairbank	Sullivan	IN
Fairbank	Saint Louis	MN
Fairbanks	Delta	MI
Fairbanks	Renville	ND
Fairbanks	Shawano	WI
Fairchild	Eau Claire	WI
Fairfax	Linn	IA
Fairfax	Osage	KS
Fairfax	Polk	MN
Fairfax	Osage	OK
Fairfax	Gregory	SD
Fairfax	Franklin	VT
Fairfield	Fairfield	CT
Fairfield	Buena Vista	IA
Fairfield	Cedar	IA
Fairfield	Fayette	IA
Fairfield	Grundy	IA
Fairfield	Jackson	IA
Fairfield	Jefferson	IA
Fairfield	Palo Alto	IA
Fairfield	Bureau	IL
Fairfield	De Kalb	IN
Fairfield	Franklin	IN
Fairfield	Tippecanoe	IN
Fairfield	Somerset	ME
Fairfield	Lenawee	MI
Fairfield	Shiawassee	MI
Fairfield	Crow Wing	MN
Fairfield	Swift	MN
Fairfield	Carroll	MO
Fairfield	Hyde	NC
Fairfield	Grand Forks	ND
Fairfield	Clay	NE
Fairfield	Harian	NE
Fairfield	Cumberland	NJ
Fairfield	Herkimer	NY
Fairfield	Butler	OH
Fairfield	Columbiana	OH
Fairfield	Highland	OH
Fairfield	Huron	OH
Fairfield	Madison	OH
Fairfield	Tuscarawas	OH
Fairfield	Washington	OH
Fairfield	Crawford	PA
Fairfield	Lycoming	PA
Fairfield	Westmoreland	PA
Fairfield	Beadle	SD
Fairfield	Franklin	VT
Fairfield	Spokane	WA
Fairfield	Sauk	WI
Fairgrove	Tuscola	MI
Fairhaven	Carroll	IL
Fairhaven	Bristol	MA
Fairhaven	Huron	MI
Fairhaven	Stearns	MN
Fairhope	Somerset	PA
Fairland	Lyman	SD
Fairlee	Orange	VT
Fairmont	Martin	MN
Fairmont	Robeson	NC
Fairmont	Fillmore	NE
Fairmount	Pike	IL
Fairmount	Grant	IN
Fairmount	Butler	KS
Fairmount	Leavenworth	KS
Fairmount	Richland	ND

TOWNSHIP	COUNTY	STATE	TOWNSHIP	COUNTY	STATE	TOWNSHIP	COUNTY	STATE
Fairmount	Luzerne	PA	Falls	Sumner	KS	Fawn Lake	Todd	MN
Fairplain	Montcalm	MI	Falls	Hocking	OH	Fawn River	Saint Joseph	MI
Fairplay	Saline	AR	Falls	Muskingum	OH	Fawn	Allegheny	PA
Fairplay	Greene	IN	Falls	Bucks	PA	Fawn	York	PA
Fairplay	Marion	KS	Falls	Wyoming	PA	Faxon	Sibley	MN
Fairview	Independence	AR	Fallsburg	Sullivan	NY	Fay	Burke	ND
Fairview	Allamakee	IA	Fallsbury	Licking	OH	Fayal	Saint Louis	MN
Fairview	Jasper	IA	Fallstown	Iredell	NC	Fayette	Calhoun	AR
Fairview	Jones	IA	Falmouth	Cumberland	ME	Fayette	Decatur	IA
Fairview	Monana	IA	Falmouth	Barnstable	MA	Fayette	Fayette	IA
Fairview	Osceola	IA	Falsen	McHenry	ND	Fayette	Linn	IA
Fairview	Shelby	IA	Falun	Saline	KS	Fayette	Livingston	IL
Fairview	Fulton	IL	Falun	Roseau	MN	Fayette	Vigo	IN
Fairview	Fayette	IN	Fancher	Ramsey	IL	Fayette	Kennebec	ME
Fairview	Barton	KS	Fancy Creek	Sangamon	IL	Fayette	Hillsdale	MI
Fairview	Butler	KS	Fancy Creek	Riley	KS	Fayette	Seneca	NY
Fairview	Cowley	KS	Fannett	Franklin	PA	Fayette	Lawrence	OH
Fairview	Ford	KS	Fanny	Polk	MN	Fayette	Juniata	PA
Fairview	Jefferson	KS	Farden	Hubbard	MN	Fayette	Potter	SD
Fairview	Labette	KS	Fargo	Seward	KS	Fayette	Lafayette	WI
Fairview	Republic	KS	Fargo	Cass	ND	Fayetteville	Saint Clair	IL
Fairview	Rooks	KS	Farina	Hettinger	ND	Fayston	Washington	VT
Fairview	Rush	KS	Farland	McKenzie	ND	Fearing	Washington	OH
Fairview	Russell	KS	Farley	Polk	MN	Featherstone	Goodhue	MN
Fairview	Stafford	KS	Farm Island	Aitkin	MN	Federal Point	New Hanover	NC
Fairview	Cass	MN	Farm Ridge	La Salle	IL	Feeley	Itasca	MN
Fairview	Lyon	MN	Farmer	Rice	KS	Felch	Dickinson	MI
Fairview	Caldwell	MO	Farmer	Wabaunsee	KS	Felix	Grundy	IA
Fairview	Henry	MO	Farmer	Defiance	OH	Felix	Grundy	IL
Fairview	Livingston	MO	Farmer Creek	Jackson	IA	Felker	Benton	AR
Fairview	Buncombe	NC	Farmers	Fulton	IL	Fell	Lackawanna	PA
Fairview	Rolette	ND	Farmers	Franklin	NE	Fellowship	Greenwood	SC
Fairview	Holt	NE	Farmersburg	Clayton	IA	Felson	Pembina	ND
Fairview	Grant	OK	Farmersville	Cattaraugus	NY	Felton	Clay	MN
Fairview	Major	OK	Farming	Stearns	MN	Femme Osage	Saint Charles	MO
Fairview	Butler	PA	Farmingdale	Kennebec	ME	Fence	Florence	WI
Fairview	Erie	PA	Farmington	Hartford	CT	Fenner	Madison	NY
Fairview	Luzerne	PA	Farmington	Cedar	IA	Fennimore	Grant	WI
Fairview	Mercer	PA	Farmington	Van Buren	IA	Fenter	Grant	AR
Fairview	York	PA	Farmington	Fulton	IL	Fenter	Hot Spring	AR
Fairview	Greenville	SC	Farmington	Republic	KS	Fenton	Kossuth	IA
Fairview	Clay	SD	Farmington	Rooks	KS	Fenton	Genesee	MI
Fairview	Corson	SD	Farmington	Stafford	KS	Fenton	Murray	MN
Fairview	Faulk	SD	Farmington	Washington	KS	Fenton	Whiteside	IL
Fairview	Hand	SD	Farmington	Franklin	ME	Fenton	Broome	NY
Fairview	Hanson	SD	Farmington	Oakland	MI	Fentress	Guilford	NC
Fairview	Lincoln	SD	Farmington	Olmsted	MN	Ferdinand	Dubois	IN
Fairview	Mellette	SD	Farmington	Davie	NC	Ferdinand	Essex	VT
Fairview	Pennington	SD	Farmington	Walsh	ND	Fergus Falls	Otter Tail	MN
Fairview	Potter	SD	Farmington	Strafford	NH	Ferguson	Yell	AR
Fairville	Wells	ND	Farmington	Ontario	NY	Ferguson	Saint Louis	MO
Faison	Duplin	NC	Farmington	Trumbull	OH	Ferguson	Centre	PA
Faithorn	Menominee	MI	Farmington	Clarion	PA	Ferguson	Clearfield	PA
Falconer	Grand Forks	ND	Farmington	Tioga	PA	Fermanagh	Juniata	PA
Falk	Clearwater	MN	Farmington	Warren	PA	Fermory	Saint Louis	MN
Falkland	Pitt	NC	Farmington	Day	SD	Fern	Hubbard	MN
Fall Creek	Adams	IL	Farmington	Grant	SD	Fern	Caddo	OK
Fall Creek	Hamilton	IN	Farmington	Lake	SD	Fern	Florence	WI
Fall Creek	Henry	IN	Farmington	Jefferson	WI	Fern Valley	Palo Alto	IA
Fall Creek	Madison	IN	Farmington	La Crosse	WI	Ferndale	Whatcom	WA
Fall Creek	Yadkin	NC	Farmington	Polk	WI	Ferrells	Nash	NC
Fall Lake	Lake	MN	Farmington	Washington	WI	Ferris	Montcalm	MI
Fall River Northeast	Fall River	SD	Farmington	Waupaca	WI	Ferris	Addison	VT
Fall River Southwest	Fall River	SD	Farmvale	Williams	ND	Ferrisbrug	Oceana	MI
Fall River	La Salle	IL	Farmville	Pitt	NC	Ferry	Grand Forks	ND
Fall River	Greenwood	KS	Farrington	Jefferson	IL	Fertile	Worth	IA
Fall River	Wilson	KS	Farris	Stone	AR	Fertile	Mountrail	ND
Fallbrook	San Diego	CA	Farris	Atoka	OK	Fertile	Walsh	ND
Falling Creek	Lenoir	NC	Faucett	Halifax	NC	Fertile Valley	Divide	ND
Falling Spring	Oregon	MO	Faucette (No. 5)	Alamance	NC	Fideliey	Jersey	IL
Fallowfield	Washington	PA	Faulk Southwest	Faulk	SD	Field	Jefferson	IL
Falls	Cerro Gordo	IA	Faulkner	Polk	AR	Field	Saint Louis	MN
Falls	Chase	KS	Fawn Creek	Montgomery	KS	Field	Nelson	ND

TOWNSHIPS OF THE UNITED STATES

TOWNSHIP	COUNTY	STATE	TOWNSHIP	COUNTY	STATE	TOWNSHIP	COUNTY	STATE
Fieldon	Watonwan	MN	Flat Creek	Perkins	SD	Fondulac	Tazewell	IL
Fields Creek	Henry	MO	Flat River	Person	NC	Fontana	San Bernardino	CA
Fife Lake	Grand Traverse	MI	Flat Rock	Bartholomew	IN	Foote	Gray	KS
Fifield	Price	WI	Flat Rock	Kershaw	SC	Foothills	Burke	ND
Filer	Manistee	MI	Flathead	Flathead	MT	Foothills	Spokane	WA
Filley	Gage	NE	Flatrock	Henry	OH	Foraker	Osage	OK
Fillmore	Ventura	CA	Flats	Macon	NC	Forbes	Hoh	MO
Fillmore	Iowa	IA	Flatwoods	Ripley	MO	Fontanelle	Washington	NE
Fillmore	Montgomery	IL	Fleener	Lee	AR	Forbes	Charles Mix	SD
Fillmore	Allegan	MI	Fleming	Cayuga	NY	Forbush	Yadkin	NC
Fillmore	Fillmore	MN	Fleming	Aitkin	MN	Ford River	Delta	MI
Fillmore	Bollinger	MO	Fleming	Pike	MN	Ford	Ford	KS
Fillmore	Divide	ND	Flemington	Polk	MO	Ford	Kanabec	MN
Findlay	Allegheny	PA	Fletchall	Worth	MO	Ford	Taylor	WI
Findley	Douglas	MO	Fletcher	Lonoke	AR	Forde	Nelson	ND
Findley	Mercer	PA	Fletcher	Mississippi	AR	Fordham	Clark	SD
Fine Lakes	Saint Louis	MN	Fletcher	Franklin	VT	Fordyce	Dallas	AR
Fine	Saint Lawrence	NY	Flint River	Des Moines	IA	Fort Calhoun	Washington	NE
Fines Creek	Haywood	NC	Flint Rock	Perkins	SD	Forest	Sierra	CA
Finlayson	Pine	MN	Flint	Benton	AR	Forest	Winnebago	IA
Finley	Scott	IN	Flint	Pike	IL	Forest	Clinton	IN
Finley	Decatur	KS	Flint	Genesee	MI	Forest	Cheboygan	MI
Finley	Christian	MO	Flint	Stutsman	ND	Forest	Genesee	MI
Finley	Webster	MO	Flom	Norman	MN	Forest	Missaukee	MI
Finley	Steele	ND	Floodwood	Saint Louis	MN	Forest	Rice	MN
Finley	Pushmataha	OK	Flora	Boone	IL	Forest	Holt	MO
Finley	Juneau	WI	Flora	Dickinson	KS	Forest	Kingfisher	OK
Finn	Logan	ND	Flora	Renville	MN	Forest	Pottawatomie	OK
Fir	Montgomery	AR	Florance	Foster	ND	Forest	Fond du Lac	WI
Firesteel	Aurora	SD	Florence Lake	Burleigh	ND	Forest	Richland	WI
Firesteel	Dewey	SD	Florence	Benton	IA	Forest	Saint Croix	WI
First Saint James			Florence	Stephenson	IL	Forest	Vernon	WI
Goose Creek	Berkeley	SC	Florence	Will	IL	Forest City	Howard	IA
First Saint James			Florence	Saint Joseph	MI	Forest City	Mason	IL
Goose Creek	Charleston	SC	Florence	Goodhue	MN	Forest City	Meeker	MN
First Saint Johns Berkeley	Berkeley	SC	Florence	Burlington	NJ	Forest City	Potter	SD
First Faint Stephens	Berkeley	SC	Florence	Oneida	NY	Forest Home	Antrim	MI
Fischbein	Bowman	ND	Florence	Erie	OH	Forest Lake	Washington	MN
Fish Lake	Chisago	MN	Florence	Williams	OH	Forest Lake	Susquehanna	PA
Fish Pond	Bambera	SC	Florence	Florence	SC	Forest Prairie	Meeker	MN
Fishdam	Union	SC	Florence	Hamlin	SD	Forest River	Walsh	ND
Fisher	Fremont	IA	Florence	Hand	SD	Forestburg	Sullivan	NY
Fisher	Polk	MN	Florence	Florence	WI	Forester	Sanilac	MI
Fisher	Grant	ND	Florida	Parke	IN	Forestport	Oneida	NY
Fishing Creek	Granville	NC	Florida	Berkshire	MA	Forestville	Fillmore	MN
Fishing Creek	Warren	NC	Florida	Yellow Medicine	MN	Forestville	Door	WI
Fishing River	Clay	MO	Florida	Montgomery	NY	Fork	Mecosta	MI
Fishing River	Ray	MO	Floris	Beaver	OK	Fork	Marshall	MN
Fishingcreek	Columbia	PA	Florissant	Saint Louis	MO	Fork	Warren	NC
Fishkill	Dutchess	NY	Flowerfield	Saint Joseph	MI	Fork	Wayne	NC
Fitchburg	Dane	WI	Flowing	Clay	MN	Fork	Anderson	SC
Fitchville	Huron	OH	Floyd	Floyd	IA	Fork	Lexington	SC
Fitzhugh	Pontotoc	OK	Floyd	O'Brien	IA	Fork Mountain	Mitchell	NC
Fitzwilliam	Cheshire	NH	Floyd	Sioux	IA	Forks	Northampton	PA
Five Creeks	Clay	KS	Floyd	Woodbury	IA	Forks	Sullivan	PA
Five Mile	Newton	MO	Floyd	Warren	IL	Forkston	Wyoming	PA
Five Mile	Spokane	WA	Floyd	Putnam	IN	Forman	Sargent	ND
Flag	Stone	AR	Floyd	Oneida	NY	Forney Creek	Swain	NC
Flagg	Ogle	IL	Floyd	Horry	SC	Forrest	Livingston	IL
Flambeau	Price	WI	Floyd (No. 6)	Newberry	SC	Forrester	Ness	KS
Flambeau	Rusk	WI	Floyd	Sanborn	SD	Forreston	Ogle	IL
Flambeau	Vilas	WI	Flushing	Genessee	MI	Forsyth	Marquette	MI
Flandreau	Moody	SD	Flusing	Belmont	OH	Fort Ann	Washington	NY
Flanningan	Hamilton	IL	Flynn	Sanilac	MI	Fort Bragg Military		
Flasher	Morton	ND	Flynn	Blaine	OK	Reservation	Hoke	NC
Flat Branch	Shelby	IL	Flynn	Garfield	OK	Fort Calhoun	Washington	NE
Flat Butte	Pennington	SD	Fogleman	Crittenden	AR	Fort Cobb	Caddo	OK
Flat Creek	Lawrence	AR	Foldahl	Marshall	MN	Fort Covington	Franklin	NY
Flat Creek	Barry	MO	Folden	Otter Tail	MN	Fort Edward	Washington	NY
Flat Creek	Pettis	MO	Folker	Clark	MO	Fort Fairfield	Aroostook	ME
Flat Creek	Stone	MO	Folly Island	Charleston	SC	Fort Gratiot	Saint Clair	MI
Flat Creek	Buncombe	NC	Folsom	Traverse	MN	Fort Kent	Arookstook	ME
Flat Creek	Lancaster	SC	Fond du Lac	Fond du Lac	WI	Fort Mill	York	SC

TOWNSHIPS OF THE UNITED STATES

TOWNSHIP	COUNTY	STATE	TOWNSHIP	COUNTY	STATE	TOWNSHIP	COUNTY	STATE
Fort Osage	Jackson	MO	Francis	Pontotoc	OK	Franklin	Ness	KS
Fort Ransom	Ransom	ND	Franconia	Grafton	NH	Franklin	Trego	KS
Fort Ripley	Crow Wing	MN	Franconia	Chisago	MN	Franklin	Washington	KS
Fort Russell	Madison	IL	Franconia	Montgomery	PA	Franklin	Norfolk	MA
Fort Steuben	Jefferson	OH	Francure	White	AR	Franklin	Hancock	ME
Fort	Marshall	SD	Frankenlust	Bay	MI	Franklin	Clare	MI
Fort Winnebago	Columbia	WI	Frankenmuth	Saginaw	MI	Franklin	Houghton	MI
Fortier	Yellow Medicine	MN	Frankford	Mower	MN	Franklin	Lenawee	MI
Fortun	Burke	ND	Frankford	Sussex	NJ	Franklin	Wright	MN
Fortuna	Humboldt	CA	Frankfort	Montgomery	IA	Franklin	Dent	MO
Forward	Wells	ND	Frankfort	Franklin	IL	Franklin	Greene	MO
Forward	Allegheny	PA	Frankfort	Will	IL	Franklin	Grundy	MO
Forward	Butler	PA	Frankfort	Waldo	ME	Franklin	Howard	MO
Fossum	Norman	MN	Frankfort	Wright	MN	Franklin	Laciede	MO
Foster	Randolph	AR	Frankfort	Knox	NE	Franklin	Miller	MO
Foster	Madison	IL	Frankfort	Herkimer	NY	Franklin	Newton	MO
Foster	Marion	IL	Frankfort	Spink	SD	Franklin	Macon	NC
Foster	Ogemaw	MI	Frankfort	Marathon	WI	Franklin	Rowan	NC
Foster	Big Stone	MN	Frankfort	Pepin	WI	Franklin	Sampson	NC
Foster	Faribault	MN	Franklin	Calhoun	AR	Franklin	Surry	NC
Foster	Luzerne	PA	Franklin	Carroll	AR	Franklin	Steele	ND
Foster	McKean	PA	Franklin	Desha	AR	Franklin	Butler	NE
Foster	Schuylkill	PA	Franklin	Drew	AR	Franklin	Fillmore	NE
Foster	Providence	RI	Franklin	Grant	AR	Franklin	Franklin	NE
Foster	Beadle	SD	Franklin	Howard	AR	Franklin	Gloucester	NJ
Foster	Hutchinson	SD	Franklin	Izard	AR	Franklin	Hunterdon	NJ
Foster	Perkins	SD	Franklin	Little River	AR	Franklin	Somerset	NJ
Foster	Clark	wI	Franklin	Marion	AR	Franklin	Warren	NJ
Fountain Bluff	Jackson	IL	Franklin	Stone	AR	Franklin	Delaware	NY
Fountain Creek	Iroquois	IL	Franklin	Union	AR	Franklin	Franklin	NY
Fountain Green	Hancock	IL	Franklin	New London	CT	Franklin	Adams	OH
Fountain Prairie	Pipestone	MN	Franklin	Allamakee	IA	Franklin	Brown	OH
Fountain Prairie	Columbia	WI	Franklin	Appanoose	IA	Franklin	Clermont	OH
Fountain	Ottawa	KS	Franklin	Bremer	IA	Franklin	Columbiana	OH
Fountain	Fillmore	MN	Franklin	Cass	IA	Franklin	Coshocton	OH
Fountain	Pitt	NC	Franklin	Clarke	IA	Franklin	Darke	OH
Fountain	Edmunds	SD	Franklin	Decatur	IA	Franklin	Franklin	OH
Fountain	Juneau	WI	Franklin	Des Moines	IA	Franklin	Fulton	OH
Four Lakes	Spokane	WA	Franklin	Fremont	IA	Franklin	Harrison	OH
Four Mile	Polk	IA	Franklin	Greene	IA	Franklin	Jackson	OH
Four Mile	Wayne	IL	Franklin	Lee	IA	Franklin	Licking	OH
Four Mile	Morris	KS	Franklin	Linn	IA	Franklin	Mercer	OH
Four Mile	Barnwell	SC	Franklin	Marion	IA	Franklin	Monroe	OH
Fourche Lafave	Perry	AR	Franklin	Monona	IA	Franklin	Morrow	OH
Fowler	Meade	KS	Franklin	Monroe	IA	Franklin	Portage	OH
Fowler	Trumbull	OH	Franklin	O'Brien	IA	Franklin	Richland	OH
Fowler	McCurtain	OK	Franklin	Polk	IA	Franklin	Ross	OH
Fowler	Saint Lawrence	NY	Franklin	Story	IA	Franklin	Shelby	OH
Fox Creek	Harrison	MO	Franklin	Washington	IA	Franklin	Summit	OH
Fox Lake	Martin	MN	Franklin	De Kalb	IL	Franklin	Tuscarawas	OH
Fox Lake	Dodge	WI	Franklin	De Kalb	IN	Franklin	Warren	OH
Fox River	Davis	IA	Franklin	Floyd	IN	Franklin	Wayne	OH
Fox	Black Hawk	IA	Franklin	Grant	IN	Franklin	Adams	PA
Fox	Jasper	IL	Franklin	Harrison	IN	Franklin	Beaver	PA
Fox	Kendall	IL	Franklin	Hendricks	IN	Franklin	Bradford	PA
Fox	Carroll	OH	Franklin	Henry	IN	Franklin	Butler	PA
Fox	Elk	PA	Franklin	Johnson	IN	Franklin	Carbon	PA
Fox	Sullivan	PA	Franklin	Kosciusko	IN	Franklin	Chester	PA
Foxborough	Norfolk	MA	Franklin	Marion	IN	Franklin	Columbia	PA
Foxholm	Ward	ND	Franklin	Montgomery	IN	Franklin	Erie	PA
Foxhome	Wilkin	MN	Franklin	Owen	IN	Franklin	Fayette	PA
Foxton	Clark	SD	Franklin	Pulaski	IN	Franklin	Greene	PA
Foyil	Rogers	OK	Franklin	Putnam	IN	Franklin	Huntingdon	PA
Fragrant Hill	Dickinson	KS	Franklin	Randolph	IN	Franklin	Luzerne	PA
Frailey	Schuylkill	PA	Franklin	Ripley	IN	Franklin	Lycoming	PA
Fram	Wells	ND	Franklin	Washington	IN	Franklin	Snyder	PA
Framingham	Middlesex	MA	Franklin	Wayne	IN	Franklin	Susquehanna	PA
Framnas	Stevens	MN	Franklin	Bourbon	KS	Franklin	Westmoreland	PA
Frances	Burleigh	ND	Franklin	Edwards	KS	Franklin	York	PA
Francestown	Hillsborough	NH	Franklin	Franklin	KS	Franklin	Bon Homme	SD
Francis	Cleburne	AR	Franklin	Johnson	KS	Franklin	Jerauld	SD
Francis	Holt	NE	Franklin	Lincoln	KS	Franklin	Lake	SD
Francis	Harmon	OK	Franklin	Marshall	KS	Franklin	Jackson	WI

TOWNSHIP	COUNTY	STATE	TOWNSHIP	COUNTY	STATE	TOWNSHIP	COUNTY	STATE
Franklin	Kewaunee	WI	Freeport	Cumberland	ME	Fruitland	Muskegon	MI
Franklin	Manitowoc	WI	Freeport	Harrison	OH	Fruitport	Muskegan	MI
Franklin	Sauk	WI	Freeport	Greene	PA	Fruitville	Currituck	NC
Franklin	Vernon	WI	Freesoil	Mason	MI	Fry	Tulsa	OK
Franklinton (No. 4)	Franklin	NC	Freetown	Bristol	MA	Fryburg	Billings	ND
Franklinville	Cattaraugus	NY	Freetown	Cortland	NY	Freyburg	Oxford	ME
Frankinville	Randolph	NC	Freistatt	Lawrence	MO	Fugit	Decatur	IN
Franklyn	Brown	SD	Frelinghuysen	Warren	NJ	Fuller	Codington	SD
Franks	Saint Francis	AR	Fremont	Santa Clara	CA	Fullerton	Orange	CA
Franks	Woodruff	AR	Fremont	Benton	IA	Fullerton	Nance	NE
Frankstown	Blair	PA	Fremont	Bremer	IA	Fulton	Fulton	AR
Frankville	Winneshiek	IA	Fremont	Buchanan	IA	Fulton	Polk	AR
Franzen	Marathon	WI	Fremont	Butler	IA	Fulton	Fountain	IA
Fraser	Bay	MI	Fremont	Cedar	IA	Fulton	Muscatine	IA
Fraser	Martin	MN	Fremont	Clarke	IA	Fulton	Webster	IA
Fraser	Colleton	SC	Fremont	Fayette	IA	Fulton	Whiteside	IL
Frazer	Allegheny	PA	Fremont	Hamilton	IA	Fulton	Schoharie	NY
Frazier	Divide	ND	Fremont	Johnson	IA	Fulton	Gratiot	MI
Freda	Grant	ND	Fremont	Page	IA	Fulton	Davie	NC
Fredenberg	Saint Louis	MN	Fremont	Winneshiek	IA	Fulton	Fulton	OH
Frederic	Crawford	MI	Fremont	Lake	IL	Fulton	Lancaster	PA
Frederick	Schuyler	IL	Fremont	Steuben	IN	Fulton	Clarendon	SC
Frederick	Divide	ND	Fremont	Lyon	KS	Fulton	Sumter	SC
Frederick	Brown	SD	Fremont	Isabella	MI	Fulton	Rock	WI
Fredericksburg	Chickasaw	IA	Fremont	Saginaw	MI	Funks Grove	McLean	IL
Frederika	Bremer	IA	Fremont	Sanilac	MI	Furlow	Lonoke	AR
Fredlund	Perkins	SD	Fremont	Tuscola	MI	Furr	Stanly	NC
Fredon	Sussex	NJ	Fremont	Winona	MN			
Fredonia	Plymouth	IA	Fremont	Cavalier	ND			
Fredonia	Calhoun	MI	Fremont	Rockingham	NH	—G—		
Fredonia	Ozaukee	WI	Fremont	Sullivan	NY			
Freeborn	Freeborn	MN	Fremont	Steuben	NY	Gabbs	Nye	NV
Freeborn	Dunklin	MO	Fremont	Moody	SD	Gaddy	Robeson	NC
Freeborn	Eddy	ND	Fremont	Clark	WI	Gaeland	Gove	KS
Freeburg	Saint Clair	IL	Fremont	Waupaca	WI	Gail Lake	Crow Wing	MN
Freedom	Polk	AR	French Broad	Buncombe	NC	Gaines	Genesse	MI
Freedom	Hamilton	IA	French Creek	Allamakee	IA	Gaines	Kent	MI
Freedom	Palo Alto	IA	French Creek	Chautauqua	NY	Gaines	Tioga	PA
Freedom	Carroll	IL	French Creek	Mercer	PA	Gaines	Orleans	NY
Freedom	La Salle	IL	French Lick	Orange	IN	Gainesville	Wyoming	NY
Freedom	Bourbon	KS	French Lake	Wright	MN	Gainsboro	Independence	AR
Freedom	Ellis	KS	French	Lafayette	AR	Gaither	Boone	AR
Freedom	Phillips	KS	French	Adams	IN	Galatia	Saline	IL
Freedom	Republic	KS	French	Saint Louis	MN	Gale	Marion	KS
Freedom	Waldo	ME	Frenchcreek	Venago	PA	Gale	Trempealeau	WI
Freedom	Washtenaw	MI	Frenchs Creek	Bladen	NC	Galen	Wayne	NY
Freedom	Waseca	MN	Frenchtown	Monroe	MI	Galena	La Porte	IN
Freedom	Lafeyette	MO	Frenchtown	Mineral	MT	Galena	Martin	MN
Freedom	Ward	ND	Frenchtown	Antelope	NE	Galena	Jasper	MO
Freedom	Carroll	NH	Frenchville	Aroostook	ME	Galena	Dixon	NE
Freedom	Cattaraugus	NY	Freshwater	Ramsey	ND	Galena	Woods	OK
Freedom	Henry	OH	Frettim	Kidder	ND	Gales	Redwood	MN
Freedom	Potage	OH	Friberg	Otter Tail	MN	Gales	Aurora	SD
Freedom	Wood	OH	Fried	Stutsman	ND	Galesburg City	Knox	IL
Freedom	Adams	PA	Friends Creek	Macon	IL	Galesburg	Knox	IL
Freedom	Blair	PA	Friendship	Greene	AR	Galesburg	Kingman	KS
Freedom	Faulk	SD	Friendship	Knox	ME	Galesburg	Traill	ND
Freedom	Forest	WI	Friendship	Emmet	MI	Galien	Berrien	MI
Freedom	Outagamie	WI	Friendship	Yellow Medicine	MN	Galivants Ferry	Horry	SC
Freedom	Sauk	WI	Friendship	Guilford	NC	Galla Creek	Pope	AR
Freehold	Monmouth	NJ	Friendship	Texas	OK	Galla Rock	Yell	AR
Freehold	Warren	PA	Friendship	Clarendon	SC	Gallagher	Clinton	PA
Freeland	Lac Qui Parie	MN	Friendship	Allegany	NY	Gallatin	Clay	MO
Freeman	Pope	AR	Friendship	Fond du Lac	WI	Gallatin	Columbia	NY
Freeman	Woodruff	AR	Frisco	Canadian	OK	Gallipolis	Gallia	OH
Freeman	Clay	IA	Frisco	McCurtain	OK	Gallitzin	Cambria	PA
Freeman	Clare	MI	Frisco	Texas	OK	Galloway	Atlantic	NJ
Freeman	Freeborn	MN	Frohn	Beltrami	MN	Galt	Rice	KS
Freeman	Richland	ND	Fritzlen	Woods	OK	Galva	Ida	IA
Freeman	Spokane	WA	Fristoe	Benton	MO	Galva	Henry	IL
Freeman	Crawford	WI	Frog Creek	Washburn	WI	Galway	Saratoga	NY
Freeo	Ouachita	AR	Frost	Clare	MI	Gamble	Lycoming	PA
Freeport	Stephenson	IL	Fruitland	Muscatine	IA	Ganeer	Kankakee	IL

TOWNSHIPS OF THE UNITED STATES

TOWNSHIP	COUNTY	STATE	TOWNSHIP	COUNTY	STATE	TOWNSHIP	COUNTY	STATE
Ganges	Allegan	MI	Garfield	Clark	SD	Geneva	Midland	MI
Gans	Sequoyah	OK	Garfield	Clay	SD	Geneva	Van Buren	MI
Gantt	Greenville	SC	Garfield	Douglas	SD	Geneva	Freeborn	MN
Gap Civil	Alleghany	NC	Garfield	Hamlin	SD	Geneva	Fillmore	NE
Gap Springs	Polk	AR	Garfield	Roberts	SD	Geneva	Ontario	NY
Gap	Montgomery	AR	Garfield	Spink	SD	Geneva	Ashtabula	OH
Garberville	Humboldt	CA	Garfield	Jackson	WI	Geneva	Whatcom	WA
Garborg	Richland	ND	Garfield	Polk	WI	Geneva	Walworth	WI
Gardar	Pembina	ND	Garland	Arkansas	AR	Genoa	De Kalb	IL
Garden	Woodruff	Ar	Garland	Benton	AR	Genoa	Livingston	MI
Garden	Boone	IA	Garland	Hempstead	AR	Genoa	Lance	NE
Garden	Cherokee	KS	Garland	Miller	AR	Genoa	Cayuga	NY
Garden	Harper	KS	Garland	Saint Francis	AR	Genoa	Delaware	OH
Garden	Harvey	KS	Garland	Penobscot	ME	Genoa	Vernon	WI
Garden	Delta	MI	Garland	Beaver	OK	Gentilly	Polk	MN
Garden	Polk	MN	Garland	Garfield	OK	Gentry	Benton	AR
Garden City	Finney	KS	Garland	Brown	SD	George	Harper	OK
Garden City	Blue Earth	MN	Garnavillo	Clayton	IA	George	Dorchester	SC
Garden Grove	Decatur	IA	Garner	Union	AR	Georges Creek	Barnwell	SC
Garden Hill	Wayne	IL	Garner	White	AR	Georges	Fayette	PA
Garden Plain	Whiteside	IL	Garner	Pottawattamie	IA	Georgetown	El Dorado	CA
Garden Plain	Sedgwick	KS	Garner	Golden Valley	ND	Georgetown	Vermillion	IL
Garden Prairie	Brown	SD	Garner	Johnson	OK	Georgetown	Essex	MA
Garden Valley	Jackson	WI	Garness	Red Lake	MN	Georgetown	Sagadahoc	ME
Gardiner	Ulster	NY	Garness	Burke	ND	Georgetown	Floyd	MI
Gardner	Sangamon	IL	Garnet	Divide	ND	Georgetown	Ottawa	MI
Gardner	Johnson	KS	Garrett	Douglas	IL	Georgetown	Clay	MN
Gardner	Wilson	NC	Garrett	Cimarron	OK	Georgetown	Madison	NY
Gardner	Cass	ND	Garrett	Johnston	OK	Georgetown (No. 3)	Georgetown	SC
Gardner	Buffalo	NE	Garrettsville	Portage	OH	Georgetown	Polk	WI
Gardner	Door	WI	Garrison	Crow Wing	MN	Georgetown	Price	WI
Garfield	Benton	AR	Garrison	Christian	MO	Georgeville (No. 9)	Cabarrus	NC
Garfield	Calhoun	IA	Garvey	Woodward	OK	Georgia	Nevada	AR
Garfield	Clay	IA	Garvin	Anderson	SC	Georgia	Grant	SD
Garfield	Hancock	IA	Gasconade	Laciede	MO	Georgia	Franklin	VT
Garfield	Ida	IA	Gasconade	Wright	MO	Georgiana	Sacramento	CA
Garfield	Kossuth	IA	Gascoyne	Bowman	ND	Geranium	Valley	NE
Garfield	Lyon	IA	Gaskill	Jefferson	PA	Gerber	Stutsman	ND
Garfield	Mahaska	IA	Gasman	Ward	ND	Gerlack	Washoe	NV
Garfield	Montgomery	IA	Gasper	Preble	OH	German Flatts	Herkimer	NY
Garfield	Plymouth	IA	Gaston	Montgomery	AR	German	Grundy	IA
Garfield	Pocahontas	IA	Gaston	Northampton	NC	German	Kossuth	IA
Garfield	Sioux	IA	Gastonia	Gaston	NC	German	Richland	IL
Garfield	Grundy	IL	Gate	McLean	ND	German	Bartholomew	IN
Garfield	Clay	KS	Gate	Beaver	OK	German	Marshall	IN
Garfield	Decatur	KS	Gates	Monroe	NY	German	Saint Joseph	IN
Garfield	Dickinson	KS	Gates	Eddy	ND	German	Vanderburgh	IN
Garfield	Ellsworth	KS	Gatesville	Gates	NC	German	Smith	KS
Garfield	Finney	KS	Gatesville	Wagoner	OK	German	Dickey	ND
Garfield	Jackson	KS	Gatewood	Ripley	MO	German	Chenango	NY
Garfield	Kiowa	KS	Gay Head	Dukes	MA	German	Auglaize	OH
Garfield	Morris	KS	Gay	Taylor	IA	German	Clark	OH
Garfield	Norton	KS	Gayville	Yankton	SD	German	Fulton	OH
Garfield	Ottawa	KS	Geck	Morton	ND	German	Harrison	OH
Garfield	Pawnee	KS	Geddes	Onondage	NY	German	Montgomery	OH
Garfield	Rush	KS	Gem	Bowman	ND	German	Fayette	PA
Garfield	Smith	KS	Gem	Brown	SD	German	Hutchinson	SD
Garfield	Wabaunsee	KS	Genesee Falls	Wyoming	NY	Germania	Todd	MN
Garfield	Bay	MI	Genesee	Whiteside	IL	Germania	Stutsman	ND
Garfield	Clare	MI	Genesse	Genesse	MI	Germania	Shawano	WI
Garfield	Grand Traverse	MI	Genesee	Allegany	NY	Germantown	Clinton	IL
Garfield	Kalkaska	MI	Genesse	Potter	PA	Germantown	Cottonwood	MN
Garfield	Mackinac	MI	Geneseo	Cerro Grodo	IA	Germantown	Wells	ND
Garfield	Newaygo	MI	Geneseo	Tama	IA	Germantown	Columbia	NY
Garfield	Lac Qui Parie	MN	Geneseo	Henry	IL	Germantown	Codington	SD
Garfield	Polk	MN	Geneseo	Livingston	NY	Germantown	Turner	SD
Garfield	Traill	ND	Geneseo	Roberts	SD	Germantown	Juneau	WI
Garfield	Antelope	NE	Genessee	Kandiyohi	MN	Germantown	Washington	WI
Garfield	Buffalo	NE	Genessee	Waukesha	WI	Germanville	Livingston	IL
Garfield	Cuming	NE	Geneva	Franklin	IA	Germany	Adams	PA
Garfield	Custer	NE	Geneva	Kane	IL	Germfask	Schoolcraft	MI
Garfield	Phelps	NE	Geneva	Jennings	IN	Gerrard	Towner	ND
Garfield	Harper	OK	Geneva	Allen	KS	Gerrish	Roscommon	MI

TOWNSHIPS OF THE UNITED STATES

TOWNSHIP	COUNTY	STATE	TOWNSHIP	COUNTY	STATE	TOWNSHIP	COUNTY	STATE
Gerry	Chautauqua	NY	Gladden	Dent	MO	Godfrey	Polk	MN
Gervais	Red Lake	MN	Glade Creek	Alleghany	NC	Goebel	Oregon	MO
Getchell	Barnes	ND	Glade	Warren	PA	Goetz	Chippewa	WI
Getty	Stearns	MN	Gladstone	Henderson	IL	Goewey	Osceola	IA
Gettysburg	Graham	KS	Gladstone	La Moure	ND	Goethe	Hampton	SC
Gettysburg	Potter	SD	Gladwin	Gladwin	MI	Goffstown	Hillsborough	NH
Ghent	Columbia	NY	Glaize	Jackson	AR	Gold Creek	Powell	MT
Ghylin	Burleigh	ND	Grand Rapids	La Moure	ND	Gold Hill	Gallatin	IL
Giard	Canyon	IA	Grandview	La Moure	ND	Gold Hill (No. 7)	Cabarrus	NC
Gibbon	Buffalo	NE	Glasgow	Wabasha	MN	Gold Hill	Rowan	NC
Gibbs	Burleigh	ND	Glass	Jackson	AR	Gold Lake	Steele	ND
Gibbs	Johnston	OK	Glassy Mountain	Greenville	SC	Gold Mine (No. 7)	Franklin	NC
Gibraltar	Door	WI	Glastonbury	Hartford	CT	Gold Run	Humboldt	NV
Gibson	Washington	IN	Glaze	Miller	MO	Gold	Bureau	IL
Gibson	Bay	MI	Gleghorn	Clay	AR	Golden Belt	Lincoln	KS
Gibson	Mercer	OH	Glen	Aitkin	MN	Golden City	Barton	MO
Gibson	Cameron	PA	Glen	La Moure	ND	Golden Glen	La Moure	ND
Gibson	Susquehanna	PA	Glen	Montgomery	NY	Golden Lake	Mississippi	AR
Gibson	Manitowoc	WI	Glen	Edmunds	SD	Golden	Oceana	MI
Gid	Izard	AR	Glen Arbor	Leelanau	MI	Golden	Walsh	ND
Giddy Swamp	Aiken	SC	Glen Elder	Mitchell	KS	Golden	Holt	NE
Gifford	Hot Springs	AR	Glen Haven	Grant	WI	Golden Valley	Roseau	MN
Gilbert Hollow	Lexington	SC	Glenburn	Penobscot	ME	Golden Valley	Rutherford	NC
Gilbert	Hand	SD	Glenburn	Lackawanna	PA	Golden Valley	Williams	ND
Gilboa	Benton	IN	Glencoe	Butler	KS	Golden Wealth	Sioux	ND
Gilboa	Schoharie	NY	Glencoe	Trego	KS	Goldfield	Bowman	ND
Gilby	Grand Fords	ND	Glencoe	McLeod	MN	Goldsberry	Howell	MO
Gilchrist	Pope	MN	Glencoe	Payne	OK	Goldsboro	Wayne	NC
Gilead	Oxford	ME	Glencoe	Buffalo	WI	Goldsby	McClain	OK
Gilead	Branch	MI	Glendale	Los Angeles	CA	Gomer	Caldwell	MO
Gilead	Morrow	OH	Glendale	Saline	KS	Gonzales	Monterey	CA
Giles	Cleburne	AR	Glendale	Logan	ND	Good Hope	Itasca	MN
Gilford	Tusicola	MI	Glendale	Hamilton	OH	Good Hope	Norman	MN
Gilford	Belknap	NH	Glendale	Hand	SD	Good Hope	Hocking	OH
Gilkerson	Craighead	AR	Glendale	Monroe	WI	Good Luck	Williams	ND
Gilkey	Yell	AR	Glendo	Perkins	SD	Good	Harper	OK
Gilkey	Rutherford	NC	Glendorado	Benton	MN	Goodar	Ogemaw	MI
Gill	Sullivan	IN	Glenfield	Foster	ND	Goode	Franklin	IL
Gill	Clay	KS	Glengary	Fillmore	NE	Goodfarm	Grundy	IL
Gill	Franklin	MA	Glenila	Cavalier	ND	Goodhue	Goodhue	MN
Gill	Cass	ND	Glenmore	La Moure	ND	Goodlan	Itasca	MN
Gillam	Jasper	IN	Glenmore	Brown	WI	Goodland	Lapeer	MI
Gillespie	Macoupin	IL	Glenn Springs	Spartanburg	SC	Goodland	Orangeburg	SC
Gillett Grove	Clay	IA	Glenpool	Tulsa	OK	Goodman	Marinette	WI
Gillett	Oconto	WI	Glenrose	Noble	OK	Goodrich	Crawford	IA
Gillford	Wabasha	MN	Glenview	Burleigh	ND	Goodrich	Taylor	WI
Gillis Bluff	Butler	MO	Glenvil	Clay	NE	Goodridge	Pennington	MN
Gills Creek	Lancaster	SC	Glenville	Schenectady	NY	Goodrum	Lonoke	AR
Gilman	Osceola	IA	Glenwood	Mills	IA	Goodsprings	Clark	NV
Gilman	Nemaha	KS	Glenwood	Winneshiek	IA	Goodwell	Newaygo	MI
Gilman	Pierce	WI	Glenwood	Phillips	KS	Goodwell	Texas	OK
Gilmanton	Benton	MN	Glenwood	Pope	MN	Goodwill	Roberts	SD
Gilmanton	Belknap	NH	Glenwood	Schuyier	MO	Goodwin	Saint Francis	AR
Gilmanton	Buffalo	WI	Glenwood	McDowell	NC	Goodwin	Plumas	CA
Gilmer	Adams	IL	Glenwood	Walsh	ND	Goodwin	Deuel	SD
Gilmer	Guilford	NC	Glenwood	Gage	NE	Goose Creek	Piatt	IL
Gilmore	Benzie	MI	Glenwood	Clay	SD	Goose Creek	Union	NC
Gilmore	Isbella	MI	Glenwood	Deuel	SD	Goose Lake	Modoc	CA
Gilmore	McHenry	ND	Glenwood	Saint Croix	WI	Goose Lake	Grundy	IL
Gilmore	Greene	PA	Glick	Kiowa	KS	Goose Lake	Charles Mix	SD
Gilpin	Armstrong	PA	Glidden	Carroll	IA	Goose Nest	Martin	NC
Gilroy	Santa Clara	CA	Glisson	Duplin	NC	Goose Prairie	Clay	MN
Gilstrap	Adams	ND	Globe	Caldwell	NC	Gooseneck	Divide	ND
Gilsum	Cheshire	NH	Glocester	Providence	RI	Gordon	Todd	MN
Gingles	Ashland	WI	Gloucester	Transylvania	NC	Gordon	Cavalier	ND
Girard	Macoupin	IL	Gloucester	Camden	NJ	Gordon	Ashland	WI
Girard	Branch	MI	Glover	Colleton	SC	Gordon	Douglas	WI
Girard	Otter Tail	MN	Glover	Edmunds	SD	Gore	Sumner	KS
Girard	Clearfield	PA	Glover	Orleans	VT	Gore	Huron	MI
Girard	Erie	PA	Glyndon	Clay	MN	Gore	Grant	OK
Girhans	Dorchester	SC	Gnesen	Saint Louis	MN	Goreville	Johnson	IL
Glacier	Stutsman	ND	Godair	Pemiscot	MO	Gorham	Cumberland	ME
Glacier	Whatcom	WA	Godfrey	Madison	IL	Gorham	Coos	NH

TOWNSHIP	COUNTY	STATE	TOWNSHIP	COUNTY	STATE	TOWNSHIP	COUNTY	STATE
Gorham	Ontario	NY	Grand	Hand	SD	Granite Rock	Redwood	MN
Gorham	Fulton	OH	Grand Blanc	Genesee	MI	Granite	Sacramento	CA
Gorman	Otter Tail	MN	Grand Chute	Outagamie	WI	Granite	Phillips	KS
Gorman	McHenry	ND	Grand Detour	Ogle	IL	Granite	Morrison	MN
Gorton	Grant	MN	Grand Forks	Polk	MN	Granite	Greer	OK
Gorton	Union	SC	Grand Forks	Grand Forks	ND	Grant	Newton	AR
Goshen Hill	Litchfield	CT	Grand Harbor	Ramsey	ND	Grant	Adams	IA
Goshen	Hampshire	MA	Grand Haven	Ottawa	MI	Grant	Boone	IA
Goshen	Sullivan	NH	Grand Island	Alger	MI	Grant	Buena Vista	IA
Goshen	Washington	AR	Grand Island	Erie	NY	Grant	Carroll	IA
Goshen	Muscatine	IA	Grand Isle	Aroostook	ME	Grant	Cass	IA
Goshen	Stark	IL	Grand Isle	Grand Isle	VT	Grant	Cerro Gordo	IA
Goshen	Clay	KS	Grand Lake	Saint Louis	MN	Grant	Clinton	IA
Goshen	Orange	NY	Grand Meadow	Cherokee	IA	Grant	Dallas	IA
Goshen	Auglaize	OH	Grand Meadow	Clayton	IA	Grant	Franklin	IA
Goshen	Belmont	OH	Grand Meadow	Mower	MN	Grant	Greene	IA
Goshen	Champaign	OH	Grand Meadow	Minnehaha	SD	Grant	Grundy	IA
Goshen	Clermont	OH	Grand Pass	Saline	MO	Grant	Guthrie	IA
Goshen	Hardin	OH	Grand Plain	Marshall	MN	Grant	Hardin	IA
Goshen	Mahoning	OH	Grand Prairie	Jefferson	IL	Grant	Ida	IA
Goshen	Tuscarawas	OH	Grand Prairie	Nobles	MN	Grant	Kossuth	IA
Goshen	Clearfield	PA	Grand Prairie	Barnes	ND	Grant	Linn	IA
Goshen	Addison	VT	Grand Prairie	Platte	NE	Grant	Lyon	IA
Gosnold	Dukes	MA	Grand Prairie	Marion	OH	Grant	Monona	IA
Gould	Lincoln	AR	Grand Rapids	La Salle	IL	Grant	Montgomery	IA
Gould	Cass	MN	Grand Rapids	Kent	MI	Grant	O'Brien	IA
Gouldsboro	Hancock	ME	Grand Rapids	Itasca	MN	Grant	Page	IA
Gourley	Menominee	MI	Grand Rapids	Wood	OH	Grant	Plymouth	IA
Gouverneur	Saint Lawrence	NY	Grand Rapids	Wood	WI	Grant	Pocahontas	IA
Gove	Gove	KS	Grand River	Adair	IA	Grant	Poweshiek	IA
Gowdeysville	Cherokee	SC	Grand River	Decatur	IA	Grant	Ringgold	IA
Gowen	Latimer	OK	Grand River	Madison	IA	Grant	Sioux	IA
Gower	Cedar	IA	Grand River	Wayne	IA	Grant	Story	IA
Gower	Webster	IA	Grand River	Sedgwick	KS	Grant	Tama	IA
Gowrie	Chippewa	MN	Grand River	Bates	MO	Grant	Taylor	IA
Grace	Grand Forks	ND	Grand River	Cass	MO	Grant	Union	IA
Grace	Codington	SD	Grand River	Daviess	MO	Grant	Winnebago	IA
Graceland	Caddo	OK	Grand River	De Kalb	MO	Grant	Woodbury	IA
Gracemont	Big Stone	MN	Grand River	Livingston	MO	Grant	Wright	IA
Graceville	Pender	NC	Grand River	Bowman	ND	Grant	Lake	IL
Grady	Kidder	ND	Grand River	Perkins	SD	Grant	Vermilion	IL
Graf	Yolo	CA	Grand Tower	Jackson	IL	Grant	Benton	IN
Grafton	McHenry	IL	Grand Valley	Dickey	ND	Grant	De Kalb	IN
Grafton	Worcester	MA	Grand Valley	Beaver	OK	Grant	Greene	IN
Grafton	Sibley	MN	Grand Valley	Texas	OK	Grant	Newton	IN
Grafton	Walsh	ND	Grand Valley	Corson	SD	Grant	Barton	KS
Grafton	Fillmore	NE	Grand View	Caddo	OK	Grant	Clay	KS
Grafton	Grafton	NH	Grandby	Oswego	NY	Grant	Cloud	KS
Grafton	Rensseiaer	NY	Grandfield	Eddy	ND	Grant	Cowley	KS
Grafton	Lorain	OH	Grandfield	Haakon	SD	Grant	Crawford	KS
Grafton	Miner	SD	Grandview Heights	Franklin	OH	Grant	Decatur	KS
Grafton	Windham	VT	Grandview	Louisa	IA	Grant	Dickinson	KS
Grafton	Ozaukee	WI	Grandview	Edgar	IL	Grant	Douglas	KS
Graham	Johnson	IA	Grandview	Ford	KS	Grant	Harper	KS
Graham	Jefferson	IN	Grandview	Morris	KS	Grant	Jackson	KS
Graham	Graham	KS	Grandview	Lyon	MN	Grant	Jewell	KS
Graham	Benton	MN	Grandview	Washington	OH	Grant	Lincoln	KS
Graham (No. 6)	Alamance	NC	Grandview	Cherokee	OK	Grant	Marion	KS
Graham	Carter	OK	Grandview	Brule	SD	Grant	Neosho	KS
Graham	Clearfield	PA	Grandview	Douglas	SD	Grant	Norton	KS
Graham Lake	Nobles	MN	Grandview	Harding	SD	Grant	Osage	KS
Grail	McKenzie	ND	Grandview	Hutchinson	SD	Grant	Osborne	KS
Grainbelt	Bowman	ND	Grandview	Jackson	SD	Grant	Ottawa	KS
Grainfield	Gove	KS	Grandview	Jones	SD	Grant	Pawnee	KS
Grainfield	Towner	ND	Grandville	Jasper	IL	Grant	Pottawatomie	KS
Granada	Nemaha	KS	Grange	Woodbury	IA	Grant	Rawlins	KS
Granby	Hartford	CT	Grange	Pipestone	MN	Grant	Reno	KS
Granby	Hampshire	MA	Grange	Deuel	SD	Grant	Republic	KS
Granby	Nicollet	MN	Granger	Allegany	NY	Grant	Riley	KS
Granby	Newton	MO	Granger	Medina	OH	Grant	Russell	KS
Granby	Essex	VT	Granite City	Madison	IL	Grant	Sedgwick	KS
Grand	Marion	OH	Granite Falls	Chippewa	MN	Grant	Sherman	KS
Grand	Ellis	OK	Granite Ledge	Benton	MN	Grant	Washington	KS

TOWNSHIPS OF THE UNITED STATES

TOWNSHIP	COUNTY	STATE	TOWNSHIP	COUNTY	STATE	TOWNSHIP	COUNTY	STATE
Grant	Cheboygan	MI	Grassy Creek	Ashe	NC	Green	Pottawatomie	KS
Grant	Clare	MI	Grassy Fork	Jackson	IN	Green	Alpena	MI
Grant	Grand Traverse	MI	Grassy	Cleburne	AR	Green	Mecosta	MI
Grant	Huron	MI	Gratiot	Lafayette	WI	Green	Hickory	MO
Grant	Iosco	MI	Gratis	Preble	OH	Green	Lawrence	MO
Grant	Keweenaw	MI	Gratt	Pratt	KS	Green	Livingston	MO
Grant	Mason	MI	Grattan	Kent	MI	Green	Nodaway	MO
Grant	Mecosta	MI	Grattan	Itasca	MN	Green	Platte	MO
Grant	Newaygo	MI	Grattan	Holt	NE	Green	Barnes	ND
Grant	Oceana	MI	Gravel Hill	White	AR	Green	Saunders	NE
Grant	Saint Clair	MI	Gravelly Hill	Yell	AR	Green	Sussex	NJ
Grant	Washington	MN	Graves	Spokane	WA	Green	Adams	OH
Grant	Caldwell	MO	Gravois	Saint Louis	MO	Green	Ashland	OH
Grant	Clark	MO	Gray	Lonoke	AR	Green	Brown	OH
Grant	Dade	MO	Gray	White	AR	Green	Clinton	OH
Grant	Dallas	MO	Gray	White	IL	Green	Fayette	OH
Grant	De Kalb	MO	Gray	Cumberland	ME	Green	Gallia	OH
Grant	Harrison	MO	Gray	Pipestone	MN	Green	Hamilton	OH
Grant	Nodaway	MO	Gray	Stutsman	ND	Green	Harrison	OH
Grant	Putnam	MO	Gray	Greene	PA	Green	Hocking	OH
Grant	Stone	MO	Grayling	Crawford	MI	Green	Mahoning	OH
Grant	Webster	MO	Grays Creek	Cumberland	NC	Green	Monroe	OH
Grant	Randolph	NC	Grayson	Jefferson	OK	Green	Ross	OH
Grant	Richland	ND	Great Barrington	Berkshire	MA	Green	Scioto	OH
Grant	Antelope	NE	Great Bend	Barton	KS	Green	Shelby	OH
Grant	Buffalo	NE	Great Bend	Cottonwood	MN	Green	Summit	OH
Grant	Cuming	NE	Great Bend	Susquehanna	PA	Green	Wayne	OH
Grant	Custer	NE	Great Bend	Spink	SD	Green	Forest	PA
Grant	Franklin	NE	Great Cypress	Barnwell	SC	Green	Indiana	PA
Grant	Gage	NE	Great Oak	Palo Alto	IA	Green Valley	Solano	CA
Grant	Kearney	NE	Great Scott	Saint Louis	MN	Green Valley	Becker	MN
Grant	Custer	OK	Great Swamp	Wayne	NC	Green Valley	Holt	NE
Grant	Dewey	OK	Great Valley	Cattaraugus	NY	Green Valley	Woods	OK
Grant	Garfield	OK	Greatstone	McLean	ND	Green Valley	Miner	SD
Grant	Kingfisher	OK	Greece	Monroe	NY	Green Valley	Marathon	WI
Grant	Indiana	PA	Greeley	Audubon	IA	Green Valley	Shawano	WI
Grant	McCook	SD	Greeley	Shelby	IA	Greenacres	Spokane	WA
Grant	Lincoln	SD	Greeley	Saline	KS	Greenbrier	Independence	AR
Grant	Roberts	SD	Greeley	Sedgwick	KS	Greenbrier	Greene	IA
Grant	Clark	WI	Greely	Ward	ND	Greenburgh	Westchester	NY
Grant	Dunn	WI	Green Bay	Clarke	IA	Greenbush	Warren	IL
Grant	Monroe	WI	Green Bay	Lee	IA	Greenbush	Penobscot	ME
Grant	Portage	WI	Green Bay	Brown	WI	Greenbush	Alcona	MI
Grant	Rusk	WI	Green Bluff	Spokane	WA	Greenbush	Clinton	MI
Grant	Shawano	WI	Green Brook	Somerset	NJ	Greenbush	Mille Lacs	MN
Grant	Johnson	AR	Green Camp	Marion	OH	Greenbush	Ward	ND
Grant Center	Grant	SD	Green Creek	Sandusky	OH	Greenbush	Sheboygan	WI
Grant Valley	Beltrami	MN	Green Garden	Will	IL	Greencastle	Marshall	IA
Grantham	Wayne	NC	Green Garden	Ellsworth	KS	Greencastle	Putnam	IN
Grantham	Sullivan	NH	Green Grove	Clark	WI	Greendale	Midland	MI
Grantsburg	Johnson	IL	Green Hill	Rutherford	NC	Greendale	Richland	ND
Grantsburg	Burnett	WI	Green Island	Albany	NY	Greene	Iowa	IA
Grantsville	Linn	MO	Green Isle	Sibley	MN	Greene	Mercer	IL
Granville	Putnam	IL	Green Lake	Grand Traverse	MI	Greene	Woodford	IL
Granville	Hampden	MA	Green Lake	Kandiyohi	MN	Greene	Jay	IN
Granville	Kittson	MN	Green Lake	Green Lake	WI	Greene	Morgan	IN
Granville	Washington	NY	Green Meadow	Norman	MN	Greene	Parke	IN
Granville	McHenry	ND	Green Mountain	Yancey	NC	Greene	Saint Joseph	IN
Granville	Platte	NE	Green Oak	Livingston	MI	Greene	Harper	KS
Granville	Licking	OH	Green Prairie	Morrison	MN	Greene	Sumner	KS
Granville	Mercer	OH	Green Ridge	Pettis	MO	Greene	Androscoggin	ME
Granville	Bradford	PA	Green River	Henderson	NC	Greene	Polk	MO
Granville	Mifflin	PA	Green River	Stark	ND	Greene	Worth	MO
Granville	Addison	VT	Green Sea	Horry	SC	Greene	Guilford	NC
Grape Grove	Ray	MO	Green	Fremont	IA	Greene	Ransom	ND
Grass	Spencer	IN	Green	Wapello	IA	Greene	Chenango	NY
Grass Lake	Jackson	MI	Green	Grant	IN	Greene	Clark	OH
Grass Lake	Kanabec	MN	Green	Hancock	IN	Greene	Trumbull	OH
Grass Lake	Burleigh	ND	Green	Madison	IN	Greene	Beaver	PA
Grass Valley	Nevada	CA	Green	Marshall	IN	Greene	Clinton	PA
Grasshopper	Atchison	KS	Green	Noble	IN	Greene	Erie	PA
Grassland	Renville	ND	Green	Randolph	IN	Greene	Franklin	PA
Grassy Creek (Nos. 1 & 2)	Mitchell	NC	Green	Wayne	IN	Greene	Greene	PA

TOWNSHIP	COUNTY	STATE	TOWNSHIP	COUNTY	STATE	TOWNSHIP	COUNTY	STATE
Greene	Mercer	PA	Greenwood	Baxter	AR	Grouse Creek	Lyman	SD
Greene	Pike	PA	Greenwood	Poinsett	AR	Grout	Gladwin	MI
Greenfield	Craighead	AR	Greenwood	El Dorado	CA	Grove Lake	Pope	MN
Greenfield	Monroe	AR	Greenwood	Kossuth	IA	Grove Park	Polk	MN
Greenfield	Poinsett	AR	Greenwood	Christian	IL	Grove	Newton	AR
Greenfield	Calhoun	IA	Greenwood	McHenry	IL	Grove	Cass	IA
Greenfield	Jones	IA	Greenwood	Franklin	KS	Grove	Davis	IA
Greenfield	Warren	IA	Greenwood	Phillips	KS	Grove	Humboldt	IA
Greenfield	Grundy	IL	Greenwood	Oxford	ME	Grove	Pottawattamie	IA
Greenfield	Adair	IN	Greenwood	Clare	MI	Grove	Shelby	IA
Greenfield	Lagrange	IN	Greenwood	Oceana	MI	Grove	Taylor	IA
Greenfield	Orange	IN	Greenwood	Osceola	MI	Grove	Worth	IA
Greenfield	Elk	KS	Greenwood	Saint Clair	MI	Grove	Jasper	IL
Greenfield	Rooks	KS	Greenwood	Wexford	MI	Grove	Adair	IN
Greenfield	Franklin	MA	Greenwood	Clearwater	MN	Grove	Reno	KS
Greenfield	Penobscot	ME	Greenwood (No. 1)	Lee	NC	Grove	Shawnee	KS
Greenfield	Wabasha	MN	Greenwood (No. 6)	Moore	NC	Grove	Stearns	MN
Greenfield	Griggs	ND	Greenwood	Steuben	NY	Grove	Harnett	NC
Greenfield	Traill	ND	Greenwood	Ellis	OK	Grove	Allegany	NY
Greenfield	Hillsborough	NH	Greenwood	Clearfield	PA	Grove	Cameron	PA
Greenfield	Saratoga	NY	Greenwood	Columbia	PA	Grove	Greenville	SC
Greenfield	Fairfield	OH	Greenwood	Crawford	PA	Groveland	Essex	MA
Greenfield	Gallia	OH	Greenwood	Juniata	PA	Groveland	La Salle	IL
Greenfield	Huron	OH	Greenwood	Perry	PA	Groveland	Tazewell	IL
Greenfield	Lackawanna	PA	Greenwood	Greenwood	SC	Groveland	McPherson	KS
Greenfield	Blair	PA	Greenwood	McCormick	SC	Groveland	Oakland	MI
Greenfield	Erie	PA	Greenwood	Tripp	SD	Groveland	Livingston	NY
Greenfield	Brown	SD	Greenwood	Taylor	WI	Groveland	Spink	SD
Greenfield	La Crosse	WI	Greenwood	Vernon	WI	Grovena	Moody	SD
Greenfield	Monroe	WI	Greer	Warrick	IN	Grover	Baxter	AR
Greenfield	Sauk	WI	Gregg	Morgan	IN	Grover	Franklin	AR
Greenhills	Hamilton	OH	Gregg	Centre	PA	Grover	Wayne	IL
Greenland	Washington	AR	Gregg	Union	PA	Grover	Johnson	MO
Greenland	Ontonagon	MI	Gregg	Aiken	SC	Grover	Renville	ND
Greenland	Barnes	ND	Gregory	Conway	AR	Grover	Marinette	WI
Greenland	Rockingham	NH	Gregory	Mahnomen	MN	Grover	Taylor	WI
Greenland	McCook	SD	Greig	Lewis	NY	Grow	Anoka	MN
Greenleaf	Washington	KS	Grenora	Williams	ND	Grow	Rusk	WI
Greenleaf	Sanilac	MI	Grenville	Day	SD	Grubbs	Jackson	AR
Greenleaf	Meeker	MN	Gresham	Cimmarron	OK	Grugan	Clinton	PA
Greenleaf	Hand	SD	Grey Cloud Island	Washington	MN	Guelph	Sumner	KS
Greenport	Columbia	NY	Grey Eagle	Todd	MN	Guenther	Marathon	WI
Greens Creek	Jackson	NC	Grey	Cavalier	ND	Guilderland	Albany	NY
Greens Creek	Polk	NC	Gridley	Butte	CA	Guildhall	Essex	VT
Greensboro	Henry	IN	Gridley	McLean	IL	Guilford	New Haven	CT
Greensboro	Orleans	VT	Griffin	Conway	AR	Guilford	Piscataquis	ME
Greensburg	Putnam	OH	Griffin	Pope	AR	Guilford	Monroe	IA
Greensburg	Knox	MO	Griffin	Stutsman	ND	Guilford	Jo Daviess	IL
Greensfork	Randolph	IN	Griffins	Martin	NC	Guilford	Hendricks	IN
Greenup	Cumberland	IL	Griffins	Nash	NC	Guilford	Wilson	KS
Greenvale	Dakota	MN	Grifton	Pitt	NC	Guilford	Chenango	NY
Greenview	Siskiyou	CA	Griggs	Saint Francis	AR	Guilford	Medina	OH
Greenview	Steele	ND	Griggs	Van Buren	AR	Guilford	Franklin	PA
Greenville	Bureau	IL	Griggs	Ida	IA	Guilford	Windham	VT
Greenville	Floyd	IN	Griggsville	Pike	IL	Guinda	Yolo	CA
Greenville	Piscataquis	ME	Grilley	McHenry	ND	Guion	Izard	AR
Greenville	Pitt	NC	Grim	Gladwin	MI	Guittard	Marshall	KS
Greenville	La Moure	ND	Grimes	Cerro Gordo	IA	Gulf	Chatham	NC
Greenville	Hillsborough	NH	Grimesland	Pitt	NC	Gulich	Clearfield	PA
Greenville	Greene	NY	Grimstad	Roseau	MN	Gull Lake	Washburn	WI
Greenville	Orange	NY	Grinnell	Poweshiek	IA	Gulledge	Anson	NC
Greenville	Darke	OH	Grinnell	Gove	KS	Gully	Polk	MN
Greenville	Somerset	PA	Grisham	Montgomery	IL	Gum Log	Pope	AR
Greenville	Greenville	SC	Griswold	New London	CT	Gum Neck	Tyrrell	NC
Greenville	Outagamie	WI	Grosselle	Wayne	MI	Gum Pond	Arkansas	AR
Greenway	Itasca	MN	Grosse Pointe	Wayne	MI	Gum Springs	White	AR
Greenwich	Fairfield	CT	Groton	New London	CT	Gum Woods	Lonoke	AR
Greenwich	Cumberland	NJ	Groton	Middlesex	MA	Gunkel	Cass	ND
Greenwich	Gloucester	NJ	Groton	Grafton	NH	Gunplain	Allegan	MI
Greenwich	Warren	NJ	Groton	Tompkins	NY	Gurney	Iron	WI
Greenwich	Washington	NY	Groton	Erie	OH	Gustavas	Trumbull	OH
Greenwich	Huron	OH	Groton	Brown	SD	Gustin	Alcona	MI
Greenwich	Berks	PA	Groton	Caledonia	VT	Guthrie	Izard	AR

TOWNSHIPS OF THE UNITED STATES

TOWNSHIP	COUNTY	STATE	TOWNSHIP	COUNTY	STATE	TOWNSHIP	COUNTY	STATE
Guthrie	White	AR	Halley	Desha	AR	Hammond	Polk	MN
Guthrie	Lawrence	IN	Hallie	Chippewa	WI	Hammond	Saint Lawrence	NY
Guthrie	Hubbard	MN	Hallock	Peoria	IL	Hammond	Aiken	SC
Guthrie	Callaway	MO	Hallock	Kittson	MN	Hammond	Saint Croix	WI
Guthrie	Logan	OK	Halls	Sampson	NC	Hammonton	Atlantic	NJ
Gutschmiedt	Logan	ND	Halsellville	Chester	SC	Hampden	Coffey	KS
Guttenberg	Hudson	NJ	Halsey	Marathon	WI	Hampden	Hampden	MA
Guyan	Gallia	OH	Halstad	Norman	MN	Hampden	Penobscot	ME
Guymon	Texas	OK	Halstead	Harvey	KS	Hampden	Kittson	MN
Gwaltneys	Alexander	NC	Ham Lake	Anoka	MN	Hampden	Cumberland	PA
Gypsum Creek	McPherson	KS	Hambden	Geauga	OH	Hampden	Columbia	WI
Gypsum	Saline	KS	Hamblen	Brown	IN	Hampshire	Clinton	IA
Gypsum	Sedgwick	KS	Hamburg	Livingston	MI	Hampshire	Kane	IL
			Hamburg	Jackson	NC	Hampton Falls	Rockingham	NH
			Hamburg	Dickey	ND	Hampton	Lee	AR
—H—			Hamburg	Wells	ND	Hampton	Marion	AR
			Hamburg	Erie	NY	Hampton	Windham	CT
Haag	Logan	ND	Hamburg	Marathon	WI	Hampton	Rock Island	IL
Haaland	Wells	ND	Hamburg	Vernon	WI	Hampton	Rush	KS
Hackberry	Labette	KS	Hamden	New Haven	CT	Hampton	Bay	MI
Hackberry	Garfield	OK	Hamden	Becker	MN	Hampton	Dakota	MN
Hackberry	Texas	OK	Hamden	Delaware	NY	Hampton	Davidson	NC
Hackett	Price	WI	Hamel	Madison	IL	Hampton	Rockingham	NH
Hackettstown	Warren	NJ	Hamer	Highland	OH	Hampton	Washington	NY
Haddam	Middlesex	CT	Hamerly	Renville	ND	Hampton	Sussex	NJ
Haddam	Washington	KS	Hamilton	Lonoke	AR	Hampton	Allegheny	PA
Haddon	Sullivan	IN	Hamilton	Decatur	IA	Hamptonburgh	Orange	NY
Haddon	Camden	NJ	Hamilton	Franklin	IA	Hamre	Beltrami	MN
Haddon	Dewey	OK	Hamilton	Hamilton	IA	Hancock	Plymouth	IA
Hadley	Lafayette	AR	Hamilton	Lee	IL	Hancock	Hancock	IL
Hadley	Pike	IL	Hamilton	Deleware	IN	Hancock	Osborne	KS
Hadley	Hampshire	MA	Hamilton	Jackson	IN	Hancock	Berkshire	MA
Hadley	Lapeer	MI	Hamilton	Sullivan	IN	Hancock	Hancock	ME
Hadley	Saint Louis	MO	Hamilton	Essex	MA	Hancock	Houghton	MI
Hadley	Chatham	NC	Hamilton	Clare	MI	Hancock	Carver	MN
Hadley	Saratoga	NY	Hamilton	Gratiot	MI	Hancock	Hillsborough	NH
Hagali	Beltrami	MN	Hamilton	Van Buren	MI	Hancock	Delaware	NY
Hagar	Berrien	MI	Hamilton	Caldwell	MO	Hancock	Bon Homme	SD
Hagel	Pierce	ND	Hamilton	Harrison	MO	Hancock	Addison	VT
Hagen	Clay	MN	Hamilton	Martin	NC	Hancock	Waushara	WI
Hagener	Cass	IL	Hamilton	Pembina	ND	Handy	Livingston	MI
Hague	Warren	NY	Hamilton	Fillmore	NE	Haney	Crawford	WI
Hague	Clark	SD	Hamilton	Atlantic	NJ	Hanford	Kings	CA
Hahanaman	Whiteside	IL	Hamilton	Mercer	NJ	Hangaard	Clearwater	MN
Haight	Ontonagon	MI	Hamilton	Madison	NY	Hanging Grove	Jasper	IN
Haines	Marion	IL	Hamilton	Franklin	OH	Hanna	Henry	IL
Haines	Centre	PA	Hamilton	Jackson	OH	Hanna	La Porte	IN
Hainesport	Burlington	NJ	Hamilton	Lawrence	OH	Hanna	McIntosh	OK
Halbert	Martin	IN	Hamilton	Warren	OH	Hannah	Florence	SC
Halcott	Greene	NY	Hamilton	Okmulgee	OK	Hannibal	Iswego	NY
Halden	Saint Louis	MN	Hamilton	Adams	PA	Hanover	Allamakee	IA
Hale	Garland	AR	Hamilton	Franklin	PA	Hanover	Crawford	IA
Hale	Jones	IA	Hamilton	McKean	PA	Hanover	Cook	IL
Hale	Warren	IL	Hamilton	Monroe	PA	Hanover	Jo Daviess	IL
Hale	McLeod	MN	Hamilton	Tioga	PA	Hanover	Jefferson	IN
Hale	Hardin	OH	Hamilton	Charles Mix	SD	Hanover	Lake	IN
Hale	Caddo	OK	Hamilton	Marshall	SD	Hanover	Shelby	IN
Hale	Trempealeau	WI	Hamilton	La Crosse	WI	Hanover	Lincoln	KS
Haley	Bowman	ND	Hamiltonban	Adams	PA	Hanover	Washington	KS
Half Moon Lake	Mississippi	AR	Hamlet	Renville	ND	Hanover	Plymouth	MA
Halfmoon	Saratoga	NY	Hamlin	Audubon	IA	Hanover	Oxford	ME
Halfmoon	Centre	PA	Hamlin	Brown	KS	Hanover	Jackson	MI
Halifax	Plymouth	MA	Hamlin	Eaton	MI	Hanover	Wexford	MI
Halifax	Halifax	NC	Hamlin	Mason	MI	Hanover	Adams	NE
Halifax	Dauphin	PA	Hamlin	Lac Qui Parie	MN	Hanover	Gage	NE
Halifax	Windham	VT	Hamlin	Nelson	ND	Hanover	Grafton	NH
Hall	Bureau	IL	Hamlin	Monroe	NY	Hanover	Morris	NJ
Hall	Dubois	IN	Hamlin	McKean	PA	Hanover	Chautauqua	NY
Hall	Gates	NC	Hamlin	Hamlin	SD	Hanover	Ashland	OH
Hall	Sargent	ND	Hammel	Taylor	WI	Hanover	Butler	OH
Hall	Anderson	SC	Hammer	Yellow Medicine	MN	Hanover	Columbiana	OH
Hall	Perkins	SD	Hammer	Ramsey	ND	Hanover	Licking	OH
Hallet	Hodgeman	KS	Hammond	Spencer	IN	Hanover	Beaver	PA

TOWNSHIP	COUNTY	STATE	TOWNSHIP	COUNTY	STATE	TOWNSHIP	COUNTY	STATE
Hanover	Lehigh	PA	Harmony	Chautauqua	NY	Harrison	Kosciusko	IN
Hanover	Luzerne	PA	Harmony	Clark	OH	Harrison	Miami	IN
Hanover	Northampton	PA	Harmony	Morrow	OH	Harrison	Morgan	IN
Hanover	Washington	PA	Harmony	Beaver	PA	Harrison	Owen	IN
Hanraty	Coal	OK	Harmony	Forest	PA	Harrison	Pulaski	IN
Hansen	Wood	WI	Harmony	Susquehanna	PA	Harrison	Spencer	IN
Hanson	Plymouth	MA	Harmony	Clarendon	SC	Harrison	Union	IN
Hanson	Ransom	ND	Harmony	Edmunds	SD	Harrison	Vigo	IN
Hanson	Sequoyah	OK	Harmony	Fall River	SD	Harrison	Wayne	IN
Hanson	Hanson	SD	Harmony	Jerauld	SD	Harrison	Wells	IN
Hansonville	Lincoln	MN	Harmony	Spink	SD	Harrison	Chautauqua	KS
Hantho	Lac Qui Parie	MN	Harmony	Price	WI	Harrison	Franklin	KS
Happy Camp	Siskiyou	CA	Harmony	Rock	WI	Harrison	Greeley	KS
Happy	Graham	KS	Harmony	Vernon	WI	Harrison	Jewell	KS
Haram	Bottineau	ND	Harnett	New Hanover	NC	Harrison	Nemaha	KS
Harbison	Dubois	IN	Harp	De Witt	IL	Harrison	Norton	KS
Harborcreek	Erie	PA	Harper	Cleveland	AR	Harrison	Rice	KS
Hardeeville	Jasper	SC	Harper	Harper	KS	Harrison	Wallace	KS
Hardenburgh	Ulster	NY	Harper	McPherson	KS	Harrison	Cumberland	ME
Hardesty	Texas	OK	Harper	Slope	ND	Harrison	Macomb	MI
Hardin	Faulkner	AR	Harper	Dewey	OK	Harrison	Kandiyohi	MN
Hardin	Greene	IA	Harpersfield	Delaware	NY	Harrison	Daviess	MO
Hardin	Hardin	IA	Harpersfield	Ashtabula	OH	Harrison	Grundy	MO
Hardin	Johnson	IA	Harpswell	Cumberland	ME	Harrison	Mercer	MO
Hardin	Pottawattamie	IA	Harrell	Mitchell	NC	Harrison	Moniteau	MO
Hardin	Webster	IA	Harrellsville	Hertford	NC	Harrison	Scotland	MO
Hardin	Pike	IL	Harrietstown	Franklin	NY	Harrison	Vernon	MO
Hardin	Clinton	MO	Harriett	Burleigh	ND	Harrison	Ward	ND
Harding	Emmons	ND	Harrington	Washington	ME	Harrison	Buffalo	NE
Harding	Ramsey	ND	Harris	Stone	AR	Harrison	Buffalo	NE
Harding	Morris	NJ	Harris	Fulton	IL	Harrison	Hall	NE
Harding	Lucas	OH	Harris	Saint Joseph	IN	Harrison	Hayes	NE
Harding	Lincoln	WI	Harris	Menominee	MI	Harrison	Knox	NE
Hardscrabble	Williams	ND	Harris	Itasca	MN	Harrison	Sherman	NE
Hardwick	Worcester	MA	Harris	Ripley	MO	Harrison	Gloucester	NJ
Hardwick	Warren	NJ	Harris (No. 2)	Franklin	NC	Harrison	Hudson	NJ
Hardwick	Caledonia	VT	Harris	Stanly	NC	Harrison	Westchester	NY
Hardy	Lee	AR	Harris	Ottawa	OH	Harrison	Carroll	OH
Hardy	Sharp	AR	Harris	Johnston	OK	Harrison	Champaign	OH
Hardy	Holmes	OH	Harris	Muskogee	OK	Harrison	Darke	OH
Hardyston	Sussex	NJ	Harris	Centre	PA	Harrison	Gallia	OH
Harford	Cortland	NY	Harris	Marquette	WI	Harrison	Hamilton	OH
Harford	Susquehanna	PA	Harrisburg	Van Buren	IA	Harrison	Henry	OH
Haring	Wexford	MI	Harrisburg	Saline	IL	Harrison	Knox	OH
Harkers Island	Carteret	NC	Harrisburg (No. 1)	Cabarrus	NC	Harrison	Licking	OH
Harlan	Fayette	IA	Harrisburg	Lewis	NY	Harrison	Logan	OH
Harlan	Page	IA	Harrison	Hot Spring	AR	Harrison	Montgomery	OH
Harlan	Shelby	IA	Harrison	Union	AR	Harrison	Muskingum	OH
Harlan	Decatur	KS	Harrison	Union	AR	Harrison	Paulding	OH
Harlan	Smith	KS	Harrison	White	AR	Harrison	Perry	OH
Harlan	Warren	OH	Harrison	Adair	IA	Harrison	Pickaway	OH
Harleesville	Dillon	SC	Harrison	Benton	IA	Harrison	Preble	OH
Harlem	Stephenson	IL	Harrison	Boone	IA	Harrison	Ross	OH
Harlem	Winnebago	IL	Harrison	Harrison	IA	Harrison	Scioto	OH
Harlem	Sargent	ND	Harrison	Koosuth	IA	Harrison	Van Wert	OH
Harlem	Delaware	OH	Harrison	Lee	IA	Harrison	Vinton	OH
Harlowe	Carteret	NC	Harrison	Mehaska	IA	Harrison	Dewey	OK
Harmar	Allegheny	PA	Harrison	Osceola	IA	Harrison	Grady	OK
Harmon	Washington	AR	Harrison	Winnebago	IL	Harrison	Kingfisher	OK
Harmon	Lee	IL	Harrison	Bartholomew	IN	Harrison	Kiowa	OK
Harmon	Sumner	KS	Harrison	Blackford	IN	Harrison	Potter	PA
Harmon	Morton	ND	Harrison	Boone	IN	Harrison	Allegheny	PA
Harmon	Roberts	SD	Harrison	Cass	IN	Harrison	Bedford	PA
Harmonius	Burke	ND	Harrison	Clay	IN	Harrison	Hand	SD
Harmony	Hancock	IL	Harrison	Daviess	IN	Harrison	Spink	SD
Harmony	Posey	IN	Harrison	Dearborn	IN	Harrison	Calumet	WI
Harmony	Union	IN	Harrison	Delaware	IN	Harrison	Grant	WI
Harmony	Stevens	KS	Harrison	Elkhart	IN	Harrison	Lincoln	WI
Harmony	Somerset	ME	Harrison	Fayette	IN	Harrison	Marathon	WI
Harmony	Fillmore	MN	Harrison	Harrison	IN	Harrison	Waupaca	WI
Harmony	Washington	MO	Harrison	Henry	IN	Harriston	Walsh	ND
Harmony	Cass	ND	Harrison	Howard	IN	Harristown	Macon	IL
Harmony	Warren	NJ	Harrison	Knox	IN	Harrisville	Alcona	MI

TOWNSHIPS OF THE UNITED STATES

TOWNSHIP	COUNTY	STATE	TOWNSHIP	COUNTY	STATE	TOWNSHIP	COUNTY	STATE
Harrisville	Cheshire	NH	Hatton	Clare	MI	Hazard	Sherman	NE
Harrisville	Medina	OH	Haugen	Aitkin	MN	Hazel Dell	Pottawattamie	IA
Harrold	Hughes	SD	Havana	Mason	IL	Hazel Green	Delaware	IA
Hart Lake	Hubbard	MN	Havana	Steele	MN	Hazel Green	Grant	WI
Hart	Warrick	IN	Havana	Deuel	SD	Hazel Grove	Burleigh	ND
Hart	Oceana	MI	Havelock	Chippewa	MN	Hazel Hill	Johnson	MO
Hart	Winona	MN	Havelock	Hettinger	ND	Hazel Run	Yellow Medicine	MN
Hart	Wright	MO	Haven	Reno	KS	Hazel	Montgomery	AR
Hart	Bowman	ND	Haven	Sherburne	MN	Hazel	Williams	ND
Hart	Roberts	SD	Haven	Foster	ND	Hazel	Tillman	OK
Harter	Clay	IL	Haverford	Delaware	PA	Hazelhurst	Oneida	WI
Hartford	Sebastian	AR	Haverhill	Olmstead	MN	Hazelton	Barber	KS
Hartford	Hartford	CT	Haverhill	Grafton	NH	Hazelton	Shiawassee	MI
Hartford	Iowa	IA	Haverstraw	Rockland	NY	Hazelton	Aitkin	MN
Hartford	Adams	IN	Haw Creek	Knox	IL	Hazelton	Kittson	MN
Hartford	Oxford	ME	Haw Creek	Bartholomew	IN	Hazelton	Emmons	ND
Hartford	Van Buren	MI	Haw Creek	Morgan	MO	Hazelwood	Webster	MO
Hartford	Todd	MN	Haw River (No. 4)	Alamance	NC	Hazelwood	Chester	SC
Hartford	Pike	MO	Haw River	Chatham	NC	Hazen	Prairie	AR
Hartford	Washington	NY	Hawes	Alcona	MI	Hazle	Luzerne	PA
Hartford	Licking	OH	Hawk Creek	Renville	MN	Hazlet	Monmouth	NJ
Hartford	Trumbull	OH	Hawk Point	Lincoln	MO	Hazleton	Buchanan	IA
Hartford	Minnehaha	SD	Hawkeye	Osborne	KS	Hazlip	Creek	OK
Hartford	Windsor	VT	Hawkeye	Divide	ND	Headrick	Jackson	OK
Hartford	Washington	WI	Hawkeye Valley	McKenzie	ND	Healdsburg	Sonoma	CA
Hartland	Hartford	CT	Hawkins	Rusk	WI	Healing Spring	Davidson	NC
Hartland	Worth	IA	Hawksnest	Wells	ND	Healing Springs	Cleburne	AR
Hartland	McHenry	IL	Hawley	Franklin	MA	Hearlds Prairie	White	IL
Hartland	Kearney	KS	Hawley	Clay	MN	Heath	Franklin	MA
Hartland	Somerset	ME	Hawthorne	White	IL	Heath	Allegan	MI
Hartland	Livingston	MI	Hawthorne	Mineral	NV	Heath	Jefferson	PA
Hartland	Freeborn	MN	Hawthorne	Douglas	WI	Heaths Creek	Pettis	MO
Hartland	Niagara	NY	Hawtree	Warren	NC	Heaton	McLean	ND
Hartland	Huron	OH	Hay Brook	Kanabec	MN	Heavener	Le Flore	OK
Hartland	Beadle	SD	Hay Creek	Goodhue	MN	Heber	Cleburne	AR
Hartland	Kinsburg	SD	Hay Creek	Burleigh	ND	Hebron	Tolland	CT
Hartland	Windsor	VT	Hay Fork	Trinity	CA	Hebron	Kossuth	IA
Hartland	Pierce	WI	Hay River	Dunn	WI	Hebron	McHenry	IL
Hartland	Shawano	WI	Hay	Gladwin	MI	Hebron	Oxford	ME
Hartley	O'Brien	IA	Hay	Cavalier	ND	Hebron	Cheboygan	MI
Hartley	Union	PA	Haycock	Bucks	PA	Hebron	Williams	ND
Hartsell	White	AR	Hayes	Buena Vista	IA	Hebron	Grafton	NH
Hartsgrove	Ashtabula	OH	Hayes	Crawford	IA	Hebron	Washington	NY
Hartsugg	Van Buren	AR	Hayes	Ida	IA	Hebron	Potter	PA
Hartsville	Steuben	NY	Hayes	Clay	KS	Hebron	Orangeburg	SC
Hartwick	Ocseola	MI	Hayes	Dickinson	KS	Hebron	Jefferson	WI
Hartwick	Otsego	NY	Hayes	Franklin	KS	Hecla	Brown	SD
Hartzell	Oklahoma	OK	Hayes	McPherson	KS	Hector	Mississippi	AR
Harvard	Worcester	MA	Hayes	Mitchell	KS	Hector	Renville	MN
Harvard	Clay	NE	Hayes	Reno	KS	Hector	Schuyler	NY
Harve	Faulkner	AR	Hayes	Stafford	KS	Hector	Potter	PA
Harvel	Montgomery	IL	Hayes	Cherlevoix	MI	Hectors Creek	Harnett	NC
Harvey	Cowley	KS	Hayes	Clare	MI	Hegbert	Swift	MN
Harvey	Smith	KS	Hayes	Otsego	MI	Hegins	Schuylkill	PA
Harvey	Meeker	MN	Hayes	Swift	MN	Hegne	Norman	MN
Harvey	Cavalier	ND	Hayes	Custer	NE	Hegton	Grand Forks	ND
Harwich	Barnstable	MA	Hayes	Kearney	NE	Heidelberg	Berks	PA
Harwinton	Litchfield	CT	Hayesville	Clay	NC	Heidelberg	Lebanon	PA
Harwood	Champaign	IL	Hayesville (No. 5)	Franklin	NC	Heidelberg	Lehigh	PA
Haskell	Saline	AR	Hayfield	Dodge	MN	Heidelberg	York	PA
Haskell	Haskell	KS	Hayfield	Crawford	PA	Heier	Mahnomen	MN
Haskell	Coal	OK	Hayland	Mille Lacs	MN	Height of Land	Becker	MN
Haskell	Tillman	OK	Hayland	Divide	ND	Heimdal	Wells	ND
Haslett	Gates	NC	Haynes	Alcona	MI	Helen	McLeod	MN
Hassan	Hennepin	MN	Haynes	Kidder	ND	Helena	Antrim	MI
Hassan Valley	McLeod	MN	Haynesville	Aroostook	ME	Helena	Scott	MN
Hastings	Barry	MI	Haynesville	Pratt	KS	Helena	Griggs	ND
Hastings	Bottineau	ND	Hays	Green	AR	Helena	Alfalfa	OK
Hastings	Oswego	NY	Hayti	Pemiscot	MO	Helendale	Richland	ND
Hasty	Newton	AR	Hayti	Hamlin	SD	Helga	Hubbard	MN
Hartfield	Montgomery	PA	Hayward	Freeborn	MN	Helgeland	Polk	MN
Hartfield	Hampshire	MA	Hayward	Sawyer	WI	Hellam	York	PA
Hatteras	Dare	NC	Haywood	Clay	AR	Heller (No. 11)	Newberry	SC

TOWNSHIPS OF THE UNITED STATES

TOWNSHIP	COUNTY	STATE	TOWNSHIP	COUNTY	STATE	TOWNSHIP	COUNTY	STATE
Helt	Vermillion	IN	Herman	Washington	NE	Higginson	White	AR
Helton	Ashe	NC	Herman	Lake	SD	High Forest	Olmsted	MN
Helvetia	Madison	IL	Herman	Dodge	WI	High Lake	Emmet	IA
Helvetia	Waupaca	WI	Herman	Shawano	WI	High Market	Lewis	NY
Hematite	Iron	MI	Herman	Sheboygan	WI	High Point	Decatur	IA
Hemem	Adams	ND	Hermon	Penobscot	ME	High Point	Guilford	NC
Hemet	Riverside	CA	Hermon	Saint Lawrence	NY	High Prairie	Leavenworth	KS
Hemlock	Columbia	PA	Hermosa	Custer	SD	High Prairie	Webster	MO
Hempfield	Mercer	PA	Heron Lake	Jackson	MN	High Shoals	Rutherford	NC
Hempfield	Westmoreland	PA	Herrick	Shelby	IL	Highgate	Franklin	VT
Hempstead	Rockingham	NH	Herrick	Knox	NE	Highgrove	Riverside	CA
Hempstead	Nassau	NY	Herrick	Bradford	PA	Highland Center	Ramsey	ND
Henden	Miner	SD	Herrick	Susquehanna	PA	Highland Grove	Clay	MN
Henderson	Hot Spring	AR	Herrick	Deuel	SD	Highland	Sharp	AR
Henderson	Union	AR	Herring	Yell	AR	Highland	San Bernardino	CA
Henderson	Knox	IL	Herrings	Sampson	NC	Highland	Clayton	IA
Henderson	Wexford	MI	Hersey	Aroostook	ME	Highland	Greene	IA
Henderson	Sibley	MN	Hersey	Osceola	MI	Highland	Guthrie	IA
Henderson	Vance	NC	Hersey	Nobles	MN	Highland	O'Brien	IA
Handerson	Cavalier	ND	Herford	Perquimans	NC	Highland	Palo Alto	IA
Henderson	Clark	NV	Herzog	Ellis	KS	Highland	Tama	IA
Henderson	Jefferson	NY	Hesper	Winneshiek	IA	Highland	Union	IA
Henderson	Huntingdon	PA	Hesper	Benson	ND	Highland	Wapello	IA
Henderson	Jefferson	PA	Hesperia	San Bernardino	CA	Highland	Washington	IA
Hendersonville	Henderson	NC	Heth	Saint Francis	AR	Highland	Winneshiek	IA
Hendren	Clark	WI	Heth	Harrison	IN	Highland	Grundy	IL
Hendricks	Shelby	IN	Hettinger	Adams	ND	Highland	Franklin	IN
Hendricks	Chautauqua	KS	Hewett	Clark	WI	Highland	Greene	IN
Hendricks	Mackinac	MI	Hewitt	Carter	OK	Highland	Vermillion	IN
Hendricks	Lincoln	MN	Hewitt	Marathon	WI	Highland	Clay	KS
Hendrickson	Hubbard	MN	Heyward	Colleton	SC	Highland	Harvey	KS
Hendrickson	McHenry	ND	Hiawatha	Brown	KS	Highland	Jewell	KS
Hendrum	Norman	MN	Hiawatha	Schoolcraft	MI	Highland	Kiowa	KS
Henery	Golden Valley	ND	Hibler	Edgefield	SC	Highland	Lincoln	KS
Hennepin	Putnam	IL	Hickey	Johnson	AR	Highland	Morris	KS
Hennessey	Kingfisher	OK	Hickman	Mississippi	AR	Highland	Norton	KS
Henniker	Merrimack	NH	Hickman	Scott	AR	Highland	Washington	KS
Henning	Otter Tail	MN	Hickman	Marshall	SD	Highland	Oakland	MI
Henrietta	Jackson	MI	Hickory Grove	Newton	AR	Highland	Osceola	MI
Henrietta	Hubbard	MN	Hickory Grove	Jasper	IA	Highland	Osceola	MI
Henrietta	La Moure	ND	Hickory Grove	Scott	IA	Highland	Wabasha	MN
Henrietta	Monroe	NY	Hickory Grove	Benton	IN	Highland	Lewis	MO
Henrietta	Lorain	OH	Hickory Grove	Warren	MO	Highland	Oregon	MO
Henrietta	Richland	WI	Hickory Grove	Grant	WI	Highland	Cass	ND
Henry Clay	Fayette	PA	Hickory Hill	Wayne	IL	Highland	Adams	NE
Henry	Plymouth	IA	Hickory Mountain	Chatham	NC	Highland	Gage	NE
Henry	Van Buren	IA	Hickory Plain	Prairie	AR	Highland	Sullivan	NY
Henry	Marshall	IL	Hickory Point	Macon	IL	Highland	Defiance	OH
Henry	Fulton	IN	Hickory Ridge	Cross	AR	Highland	Muskingum	OH
Henry	Henry	IN	Hickory Ridge	Phillips	AR	Highland	Caddo	OK
Henry	Ottawa	KS	Hickory Ridge	Okfuskee	OK	Highland	Adams	PA
Henry	Vernon	MO	Hickory	Carroll	AR	Highland	Chester	PA
Henry	Wood	OH	Hickory	Schuyler	IL	Highland	Clarion	PA
Henry	Okmulgee	OK	Hickory	Butler	KS	Highland	Elk	PA
Henry	Payne	OK	Hickory	Pennington	MN	Highland	Greenville	SC
Henry	Brown	SD	Hickory	Holt	MO	Highland	Brown	SD
Henry	Codington	SD	Hickory	Catawba	NC	Highland	Brule	SD
Henryville	Renville	MN	Hickory	Love	OK	Highland	Charles Mix	SD
Hensley	Champaign	IL	Hickory	Grant	OK	Highland	Day	SD
Hensley	Johnson	IN	Hickory	Nowata	OK	Highland	Jones	SD
Henton	Arkansas	AR	Hickory	Forest	PA	Highland	Lincoln	SD
Hepburn	Lycoming	PA	Hickory	Lawrence	PA	Highland	Minnehaha	SD
Herburg	Traill	ND	Hickory	Mercer	PA	Highland	Perkins	SD
Herd	Stone	AR	Hicksville	Phillips	AR	Highland	Douglas	WI
Herdland	Clay	IA	Hicksville	Defiance	OH	Highland	Iowa	WI
Herdon	Craighead	AR	Hico	Benton	AR	Highlanding	Pennington	MN
Herdon	Rawlins	KS	Hidden	Stutsman	ND	Highlands	Macon	NC
Hereford	Berks	PA	Hiddenwood	Ward	ND	Highlands	Orange	NY
Hereim	Roseau	MN	Hidewood	Deuel	SD	Highmore	Hyde	SD
Herkimer	Marshall	KS	Higdem	Polk	MN	Highpoint	Ness	KS
Herkimer	Herkimer	NY	Higgins	Conway	AR	Hightowers	Caswell	NC
Herman	Saint Louis	MN	Higgins	Roscommon	MI	Highwater	Cottonwood	MN
Herman	Sargent	ND	Higgins	McDowell	NC	Hiland	Hand	SD

TOWNSHIPS OF THE UNITED STATES

TOWNSHIP	COUNTY	STATE	TOWNSHIP	COUNTY	STATE	TOWNSHIP	COUNTY	STATE
Hilburn	Madison	AR	Hoberg	Lawrence	MO	Holst	Clearwater	MN
Hiles	Forest	WI	Hocking	Fairfield	OH	Holt Creek	Holt	NE
Hiles	Wood	WI	Hodgdon	Aroostook	ME	Holt	Adams	ND
Hill City	Graham	KS	Hodges	Stevens	MN	Holt	Gage	NE
Hill Lake	Aitkin	MN	Hodges	Greenwood	SC	Holton	Muskegon	MI
Hill River	Polk	MN	Hoff	Pope	MN	Holton	Tillman	OK
Hill	Independence	AR	Hoffiund	Williams	ND	Holton	Marathon	WI
Hill	Johnson	AR	Hoffman	Bottineau	ND	Holway	Taylor	WI
Hill	Pope	AR	Hoffman	McPherson	SD	Holy Cross	Clay	MN
Hill	Pulaski	AR	Hogan	Franklin	AR	Holyoke	Carlton	MN
Hill	Ogemaw	MI	Hogan	Pope	AR	Homan	Miller	AR
Hill	Kittson	MN	Hogan	Dearborn	IN	Home Brook	Cass	MN
Hill	Carroll	MO	Hogan	Mayes	OK	Home Lake	Norman	MN
Hill	Cass	ND	Hogback	Transylvania	NC	Home	Nemaha	KS
Hill	Knox	NE	Hoerauf	Grant	ND	Home	Montcalm	MI
Hill	Merrimack	NH	Hokah	Houston	MN	Home	Newaygo	MI
Hill	Price	WI	Holabird	Hyde	SD	Home	Brown	MN
Hilliar	Knox	OH	Holbrook	Norfork	MA	Home	Turner	SD
Hillman	Montmorency	MI	Holcomb	Dunklin	MO	Homen	Bottineau	ND
Hillman	Kanabec	MN	Holden	Penobscot	ME	Homer	Mono	CA
Hillman	Morrison	MN	Holden	Worcester	MA	Homer	Benton	IA
Hillsboro	Montgomery	IL	Holden	Goodhue	MN	Homer	Buchanan	IA
Hillsboro	Traill	ND	Holden	Adams	ND	Homer	Will	IL
Hillsboro	Grady	OK	Holden	Hand	SD	Homer	Calhoun	MI
Hillsboro	Dillon	SC	Holderness	Grafton	NH	Homer	Midland	MI
Hillsboro	Vernon	WI	Holding	Stearns	MN	Homer	Winona	MN
Hillsborough	Orange	NC	Holdrege	Phelps	NE	Homer	Bates	MO
Hillsborough	Hillsborough	NH	Holfrod	Marshall	OK	Homer	Stutsman	ND
Hillsborough	Somerset	NJ	Holland	Saline	AR	Homer	Cortland	NY
Hillsdale	Hillsdale	MI	Holland	Sioux	IA	Homer	Medina	OH
Hillsdale	Winona	MN	Holland	Shelby	IL	Homer	Morgan	OH
Hillsdale	Eddy	ND	Holland	Dickinson	KS	Homer	Potter	PA
Hillsdale	Wells	ND	Holland	Hampden	MA	Homer	Day	SD
Hillsdale	Columbia	NY	Holland	Missaukee	MI	Homestead	Chase	KS
Hillsdale	Faulk	SD	Holland	Ottawa	MI	Homestead	Benzie	MI
Hillsgrove	Sullivan	PA	Holland	Kandiyohi	MN	Homestead	Otter Tail	MN
Hillside	Union	NJ	Holland	Pemiscot	MO	Homestead	Blaine	OK
Hillside	Edmunds	SD	Holland	Hunterdon	NJ	Homestead	Richland	ND
Hilltown	Bucks	PA	Holland	Erie	NY	Homestead	Florence	WI
Hillyard	Macoupin	IL	Holland	Douglas	SD	Homewood	Franklin	KS
Hilmore	Lyman	SD	Holland	Orleans	VT	Hominy	Osage	OK
Hilt	Siskiyou	CA	Holland	Brown	WI	Hon	Scott	AR
Hilton Head	Beaufort	SC	Holland	La Crosse	WI	Honea Path	Anderson	SC
Hilton	Iowa	IA	Holland	Sheboygan	WI	Honey Creek	Delaware	IA
Hilton	Ward	ND	Hollenback	Luzerne	PA	Honey Creek	Iowa	IA
Hinckley	Pine	MN	Hollis	Peoria	IL	Honey Creek	Henry	MO
Hinckley	Medina	OH	Hollis	York	ME	Honey Creek	Adams	IL
Hindman	Monroe	AR	Hollis	Hillsborough	NH	Honey Creek	Crawford	IL
Hingham	Plymouth	MA	Hollis	Harmon	OK	Honey Creek	Howard	IN
Hines	Beltrami	MN	Hollister	San Benito	CA	Honey Creek	Vigo	IN
Hinesburg	Chittenden	VT	Holliston	Middlesex	MA	Honey Creek	White	IN
Hinsdale	Berkshire	MA	Hollow Creek	Lexington	SC	Honey Creek	Sauk	WI
Hinsdale	Cheshire	NH	Hollow	Bladen	NC	Honey Lake	Lassen	CA
Hinsdale	Cattaraugus	NY	Holloway	Person	NC	Honey Point	Macoupin	IL
Hinton	Mecosta	MI	Holly Creek	Howard	AR	Honeybrook	Chester	PA
Hiram	Oxford	ME	Holly Grove	Gates	NC	Honeycutts	Sampson	NC
Hiram	Cass	MN	Holly Hill	Orangeburg	SC	Honner	Redwood	MN
Hiram	Portage	OH	Holly Springs	Dallas	AR	Hooker	Laclede	MO
Hire	McDonough	IL	Holly Springs	Wake	NC	Hooker	Dixon	NE
Hittle	Tazwell	IL	Holly	Van Buren	AR	Hooker	Gage	NE
Hiwassee	Clay	NC	Holly	Oakland	MI	Hooker	Texas	OK
Hixon	Clark	WI	Holly	Murray	MN	Hookerton	Greene	NC
Hixson	Stone	AR	Holly	Pender	NC	Hooksett	Merrimack	NH
Hixton	Jackson	WI	Hollywood	Carver	MN	Hooper	Dodge	NE
Hoaglin	Van Wert	OH	Holman	Osceola	IA	Hoopers Creek	Henderson	NC
Hoard	Clark	WI	Holmdel	Monmouth	NJ	Hoosick	Rensselaer	NY
Hobart	Lake	IN	Holmes City	Douglas	MN	Hoosier	Clay	IL
Hobart	Rooks	KS	Holmes	Menominee	MI	Hoosier	Kingman	KS
Hobart	Otter Tail	MN	Holmes	Crawford	OH	Hoover	Benton	AR
Hobart	Barnes	ND	Holmes	Sheridan	ND	Hope	La Salle	IL
Hobart	Garfield	OK	Holmsville	Becker	MN	Hope	Dickinson	KS
Hobart	Kiowa	OK	Holmwood	Jewell	KS	Hope	Knox	ME
Hobart	Brown	WI	Holsclaw	Tripp	SD	Hope	Barry	MI

TOWNSHIPS OF THE UNITED STATES

TOWNSHIP	COUNTY	STATE	TOWNSHIP	COUNTY	STATE	TOWNSHIP	COUNTY	STATE
Hope	Midland	MI	Hovey	Armstrong	PA	Huggins	Tripp	SD
Hope	Lincoln	MN	How	Oconto	WI	Hughes	Nodaway	MO
Hope	Cavalier	ND	Howard Center	Howard	IA	Hughes	Slope	ND
Hope	Warren	NJ	Howard	Conway	AR	Hughes	Bayfield	WI
Hope	Hamilton	NY	Howard	Howard	IA	Hughesville	Pettis	MO
Hope	Stephens	OK	Howard	Story	IA	Hugo	Steele	ND
Hope (No. 1)	Williamsburg	SC	Howard	Tama	IA	Hulbert	Chippewa	MI
Hope	Lyman	SD	Howard	Wayne	IA	Hulbert	Cherokee	OK
Hopedale	Worcester	MA	Howard	Howard	IN	Hulbert	Hand	SD
Hopedale	Tazewell	IL	Howard	Parke	IN	Hulen	Comanche	OK
Hopeton	Woods	OK	Howard	Washington	IN	Hulen	Cotton	OK
Hopewell	Green	AR	Howard	Elk	KS	Hull	Plymouth	MA
Hopewell	Marshall	IL	Howard	Labette	KS	Hull	Marathon	WI
Hopewell	Cumberland	NJ	Howard	Cass	MI	Hull	Portage	WI
Hopewell	Mercer	NJ	Howard	Bates	MO	Humboldt	Humboldt	IA
Hopewell	Ontario	NY	Howard	Gentry	MO	Humboldt	Coles	IL
Hopewell	Licking	OH	Howard	Grant	ND	Humboldt	Allen	KS
Hopewell	Mercer	OH	Howard	Steuben	NY	Humboldt	Marquette	MI
Hopewell	Muskingum	OH	Howard	Knox	OH	Humboldt	Clay	MN
Hopewell	Perry	OH	Howard	Centre	PA	Humboldt	Minnehaha	SD
Hopewell	Seneca	OH	Howard	Charles Mix	SD	Humboldt	Brown	WI
Hopewell	Ellis	OK	Howard	Meade	SD	Hume	Whiteside	IL
Hopewell	Beaver	PA	Howard	Miner	SD	Hume	Huron	MI
Hopewell	Bedford	PA	Howard	Chippewa	WI	Hume	Slope	ND
Hopewell	Cumberland	PA	Howards Creek	Lincoln	NC	Hume	Allegany	NY
Hopewell	Huntingdon	PA	Howe	Grant	ND	Humphrey	Platte	NE
Hopewell	Washington	PA	Howe	Le Flore	OK	Humphry	Cattaraugus	NY
Hopewell	York	PA	Howe	Forest	PA	Hungerford	Plymouth	IA
Hopewell	Aiken	SC	Howe	Perry	PA	Hunlock	Luzerne	PA
Hopewell	Anderson	SC	Howell	Johnson	AR	Hunt City	Jasper	IL
Hopkins	Whiteside	IL	Howell	Livingston	MI	Hunt	Scott	AR
Hopkins	Allegan	MI	Howell	Howell	MO	Hunter	Edger	IL
Hopkins	Nodaway	MO	Howell	Monmouth	NJ	Hunter	Jackson	MN
Hopkins	Middlesex	MA	Howell	Towner	ND	Hunter	Cass	ND
Hopkinton	Merrimack	NH	Howell	Hand	SD	Hunter	Greene	NY
Hopkinton	Saint Lawrence	NY	Howes	Cass	ND	Hunter	Choctaw	OK
Hopkinton	Washington	RI	Howie	Mountrail	ND	Hunter	Tillman	OK
Hopper	Aurora	SD	Howland	Penobscot	ME	Hunter	Laurens	SC
Hopping	McClain	OK	Howland	Trumbull	OH	Hunter	Sawyer	WI
Horicon	Warren	NY	Hoyleton	Washington	IL	Hunters Mill	Gates	NC
Hornby	Steuben	NY	Hubbard	Hubbard	MN	Huntersville	Wadena	MN
Hornellsville	Steuben	NY	Hubbard	Polk	MN	Huntersville (No. 15)	Macklenburg	NC
Horet	Beltrami	MN	Hubbard	Trumbull	OH	Huntington Beach	Orange	CA
Hornor	Phillips	AR	Hubbard	Dodge	WI	Huntington	Huntington	IN
Horse Creek	Ashe	NC	Hubbard	Rusk	WI	Huntington	Hampshire	MA
Horse Creek	Perkins	SD	Hubbardston	Worcester	MA	Huntington	Suffolk	NY
Horsehead	Johnson	AR	Hubbardton	Rutland	VT	Huntington	Brown	OH
Horsehead	Chemung	NY	Hubble	Cape Girardeau	MO	Huntington	Gallia	OH
Horseshoe Valley	McLean	ND	Hubley	Schuylkill	PA	Huntington	Lorain	OH
Horsham	Montgomery	PA	Hudgin	Cleveland	AR	Huntington	Ross	OH
Horton	Osceola	IA	Hudgins	Perkins	SD	Huntington	Adams	PA
Horton	Ogemaw	MI	Hudson	Newton	AR	Huntington	Luzerne	PA
Horton	Stevens	MN	Hudson	McLean	IL	Huntington	Chittenden	VT
Horton	Elk	PA	Hudson	La Porte	IN	Huntley	Edmunds	SD
Hortonia	Outagamie	WI	Hudson	Middlesex	MA	Huntly	Marshall	MN
Hosmer	Edmunds	SD	Hudson	Penobscot	ME	Huntsburg	Geauga	OH
Hot House	Cherokee	NC	Hudson	Charlevoix	MI	Huntsville	Schuyler	IL
Hot Springs	Garland	AR	Hudson	Lenawee	MI	Huntsville	Reno	KS
Hot Springs	Madison	MT	Hudson	Mackinac	MI	Huntsville	Polk	MN
Hot Springs (No. 6)	Madison	NC	Hudson	Douglas	MN	Huntsville	Rockingham	NC
Hough	New Madrid	MO	Hudson	Bates	MO	Hurlbut	Logan	IL
Houghton	Keweenaw	MI	Hudson	Macon	MO	Hurley	Stone	MO
Houlton	Aroostook	ME	Hudson	Caldwell	NC	Hurley	Renville	ND
Hounsfield	Jefferson	NY	Hudson	Dickey	ND	Hurley	Ulster	NY
House Creek	Wake	NC	Hudson	Hillsborough	NH	Hurley	Turner	SD
House Creek	Pawnee	OK	Hudson	Summit	OH	Huron	Des Moines	IA
Houston	Perry	AR	Hudson	Edmunds	SD	Huron	Huron	MI
Houston	Adams	IL	Hudson	Saint Croix	WI	Huron	Wayne	MI
Houston	Smith	KS	Hueneme	Ventura	CA	Huron	Cavalier	ND
Houston	Houston	MN	Huey	Calhoun	AR	Huron	Wayne	NY
Houston	Le Flore	OK	Huff	Independence	AR	Huron	Erie	OH
Houstonia	Pettis	MO	Huff	Spencer	IN	Huron	Pennington	SD
Hoven	Potter	SD	Huggins	Gentry	MO	Hurricane	Saline	AR

TOWNSHIPS OF THE UNITED STATES

TOWNSHIP	COUNTY	STATE	TOWNSHIP	COUNTY	STATE	TOWNSHIP	COUNTY	STATE
Hurricane	Cleveland	AR	Independent	Valley	NE	Iosco	Stutsman	ND
Hurricane	Franklin	AR	Index	Cass	MO	Iota Flat	Ward	ND
Hurricane	Greene	AR	Indian Bayou	Lonoke	AR	Iowa City	Johnson	IA
Hurricane	Fayette	IL	Indian Creek	Mills	IA	Iowa Lake	Emmet	IA
Hurricane	Carroll	MO	Indian Creek	Story	IA	Iowa	Allamakee	IA
Hurricane	Lincoln	MO	Indian Creek	White	IL	Iowa	Benton	IA
Hurricane	Ashe	NC	Indian Creek	lawrence	IN	Iowa	Cedar	IA
Huss	Roseau	MN	Indian Creek	Monroe	IN	Iowa	Crawford	IA
Hustisford	Dodge	WI	Indian Creek	Pulaski	IN	Iowa	Dubuque	iA
Huston	Blair	PA	Indian Creek	Anderson	KS	Iowa	Iowa	IA
Huston	Centre	PA	Indian Creek	Monroe	MO	Iowa	Jackson	IA
Huston	Clearfield	PA	Indian Creek	Hettinger	ND	Iowa	Marshall	IA
Hutchinson	McLeod	MN	Indian Creek	Jackson	SD	Iowa	Washington	IA
Hutsonville	Crawford	IL	Indian Grove	Livingston	IL	Iowa	Wright	IA
Hutton	Coles	IL	Indian Hill	McCormick	SC	Iowa	Doniphan	KS
Hutton Valley	Howell	MO	Indian Lake	Nobles	MN	Iowa	Rooks	KS
Hyde Park	Wabasha	MN	Indian Lake	Hamilton	NY	Iowa	Sherman	KS
Hyde Park	Dutchess	NY	Indian Land	Lancaster	SC	Iowa	Benson	ND
Hyde Park	Lamoille	VT	Indian Point	Knox	IL	Iowa	Holt	NE
Hydro	Caddo	OK	Indian Prairie	Wayne	IL	Iowa	Lincoln	OK
			Indian Springs	Wayne	NC	Iowa	Logan	OK
—I—			Indian	Plumas	CA	Iowa	Beadle	SD
			Indian	Pike	MO	Iowa	Douglas	SD
Ibsen	Richland	ND	Indian	Payne	OK	Ipswich	Essex	MA
Icard	Burke	NC	Indian (No. 11)	Williamsburg	SC	Ipswich	Edmunds	SD
Ida	Monroe	MI	Indian Village	Tama	IA	Ira	Saint Clair	MI
Ida	Douglas	MN	Indian Woods	Bertie	NC	Ira	Cayuga	NY
Idaho	Mountrail	ND	Indiahoma	Comanche	OK	Ira	Rutland	VT
Ideal	Crow Wing	MN	Indiana	Marion	IA	Irasburg	Orleans	VT
Ideal	McKenzie	ND	Indiana	Graham	KS	Irene	Yankton	SD
Ideal	Tripp	SD	Indiana	Lincoln	KS	Irishtown	Clinton	IL
Idun	Aitkin	MN	Indiana	Allegheny	PA	Iron Duff	Haywood	NC
Illini	Macon	IL	Indianfields	Tuscola	MI	Iron Mound	Logan	OK
Illinois	Pope	AR	Indiantown	Bureau	IL	Iron Range	Itasca	MN
Illinois	Washington	AR	Indio	Riverside	CA	Iron River	Iron	MI
Illinois	Sangamon	IL	Industrial	Saint Louis	MN	Iron River	Bayfield	WI
Illinois	Nemaha	KS	Industry	McDonough	IL	Iron	Iron	MO
Illinois	Rush	KS	Industry	Franklin	ME	Iron	Saint Francois	MO
Illinois	Sedgwick	KS	Industry	Phelps	NE	Irondale	Crow Wing	MN
Illinois	Sumner	KS	Ingalls	Gray	KS	Irondequoit	Monroe	NY
Illinois	Nelson	ND	Ingallston	Menominee	MI	Ironton	Lincoln	NC
Illinois	Hyde	SD	Ingersoll	Midland	MI	Ironton	Sauk	WI
Illyria	Fayette	IA	Ingham	Franklin	IA	Ironwood	Gogebic	MI
Imlay	Lapeer	MI	Ingham	Ingham	MI	Iroquois	Iroquois	IL
Imlay	Pennington	SD	Inglewood	Los Angeles	CA	Iroquois	Newton	IN
Impark	Benson	ND	Ingram	Randolph	AR	Iroquois	Kingsbury	SD
Independence	Baxter	AR	Ingram	Mills	IA	Irvine	Benson	ND
Independence	Lee	AR	Ingrams	Johnston	NC	Irving	Montgomery	IL
Independence	Marion	AR	Inguadona	Cass	MN	Irving	Brown	KS
Independence	Pope	AR	Inkster	Grand Forks	ND	Irving	Barry	MI
Independence	Appanoose	IA	Inland	Cedar	IA	Irving	Kandiyohi	MN
Independence	Hamilton	IA	Inland	Benzie	MI	Irving	Jackson	WI
Independence	Jasper	IA	Inland	Clay	NE	Irvington	Kossuth	IA
Independence	Palo Alto	IA	Inlet	Hamilton	NY	Irvington	Washington	IL
Independence	Saline	IL	Inman	Otter Tail	MN	Irvington	Essex	NJ
Independence	Doniphan	KS	Inman	Holt	NE	Irwin	Woodward	OK
Independence	Montgomery	KS	Inola	Rogers	OK	Irwin	Venago	PA
Independence	Osborne	KS	Institute	Lenoir	NC	Irwin	Tripp	SD
Independence	Washington	KS	Interior	Ontonagon	MI	Isabel	Fulton	IL
Independence	Oakland	MI	Interior	Jackson	SD	Isabel	Benson	ND
Independence	Dunklin	MO	Inverness	Cheboygan	MI	Isabella	Isabella	MI
Independence	Macon	MO	Inwood	Schoolcraft	MI	Isabelle	Pierce	WI
Independence	Nodaway	MO	Iola	Allen	KS	Isanti	Isanti	MN
Independence	Schuyler	MO	Iola	Waupaca	WI	Isbel	Scott	KS
Independence	Warren	NJ	Iona	Murray	MN	Isbell	Lonoke	AR
Independence	Allegany	NY	Iona	Todd	MN	Ischua	Cattaraugus	NY
Independence	Washington	OH	Iona	Lyman	SD	Ishpeming	Marquette	MI
Independence	Beaver	PA	Ionia	Jewell	KS	Island Creek	Duplin	NC
Independence	Washington	PA	Ionia	Ionia	MI	Island Creek	Jefferson	OH
Independence	Day	SD	Ionia	Lee	SC	Island Falls	Aroostook	ME
Independence	Douglas	SD	Ions Creek	Yell	AR	Island Grove	Sangamon	IL
Independence	Perkins	SD	Iosco	Livingston	MI	Island Grove	Gage	NE
Independent	Barton	KS	Iosco	Waseca	MN	Island Lake	Lyon	MN

TOWNSHIPS OF THE UNITED STATES

TOWNSHIP	COUNTY	STATE	TOWNSHIP	COUNTY	STATE	TOWNSHIP	COUNTY	STATE
Island Lake	Mahnomen	MN	Jackson	Taylor	IA	Jackson	Clinton	MO
Island Park	Ransom	ND	Jackson	Van Buren	IA	Jackson	Dallas	MO
Island	Sebastian	AR	Jackson	Warren	IA	Jackson	Daviess	MO
Isle Au Haut	Knox	ME	Jackson	Washington	IA	Jackson	Douglas	MO
Isle Harbor	Mille Lacs	MN	Jackson	Wayne	IA	Jackson	Gentry	MO
Isle La Motte	Grand Isle	VT	Jackson	Webster	IA	Jackson	Greene	MO
Islesborough	Waldo	ME	Jackson	Winneshiek	IA	Jackson	Grundy	MO
Isley	Ransom	ND	Jackson	Effingham	IL	Jackson	Jasper	MO
Islip	Suffolk	NY	Jackson	Will	IL	Jackson	Johnson	MO
Israel	Preble	OH	Jackson	Allen	IN	Jackson	Linn	MO
Italy	Yates	NY	Jackson	Bartholomew	IN	Jackson	Livingston	MO
Itasca	Sherman	KS	Jackson	Blackford	IN	Jackson	Macon	MO
Itasca	Clearwater	MN	Jackson	Boone	IN	Jackson	Maries	MO
Ithaca	Tompkins	NY	Jackson	Brown	IN	Jackson	Monroe	MO
Ithaca	Richland	WI	Jackson	Carroll	IN	Jackson	Nodaway	MO
Iuka	Marion	IL	Jackson	Cass	IN	Jackson	Osage	MO
Iuka	Pratt	KS	Jackson	Clay	IN	Jackson	Ozark	MO
Ivanhoe	Finney	KS	Jackson	Clinton	IN	Jackson	Polk	MO
Ivanhoe	Renville	ND	Jackson	De Kalb	IN	Jackson	Putnam	MO
Ivanhoe	Ellis	OK	Jackson	Dearborn	IN	Jackson	Randolph	MO
Ivey	Franklin	AR	Jackson	Decatur	IN	Jackson	Reynolds	MO
Ivy Hill	Haywood	NC	Jackson	Dubois	IN	Jackson	Saint Clair	MO
Ivy	Lyon	KS	Jackson	Elkhart	IN	Jackson	Saint Genevieve	MO
Ivy	Buncombe	NC	Jackson	Fayette	IN	Jackson	Shannon	MO
Ixonia	Jefferson	WI	Jackson	Fountain	IN	Jackson	Shelby	MO
			Jackson	Greene	IN	Jackson	Sullivan	MO
—J—			Jackson	Hamilton	IN	Jackson	Texas	MO
			Jackson	Hancock	IN	Jackson	Webster	MO
Jack Creek	Emmet	IA	Jackson	Harrison	IN	Jackson	Nash	NC
Jackman	Somerset	ME	Jackson	Howard	IN	Jackson	Northampton	NC
Jacks Creek	Yancey	NC	Jackson	Huntington	IN	Jackson	Union	NC
Jacks	Laurens	SC	Jackson	Jackson	IN	Jackson	Sargent	ND
Jackson Hill	Davidson	NC	Jackson	Jay	IN	Jackson	Hall	NE
Jackson	Boone	AR	Jackson	Kosciusko	IN	Jackson	Carroll	NH
Jackson	Calhoun	AR	Jackson	Madison	IN	Jackson	Ocean	NJ
Jackson	Cleveland	AR	Jackson	Miami	IN	Jackson	Washington	NY
Jackson	Crittenden	AR	Jackson	Morgan	IN	Jackson	Allen	OH
Jackson	Dallas	AR	Jackson	Newton	IN	Jackson	Ashland	OH
Jackson	Little River	AR	Jackson	Orange	IN	Jackson	Auglaize	OH
Jackson	Monroe	AR	Jackson	Owen	IN	Jackson	Brown	OH
Jackson	Nevada	AR	Jackson	Parke	IN	Jackson	Champaign	OH
Jackson	Newton	AR	Jackson	Porter	IN	Jackson	Clermont	OH
Jackson	Pope	AR	Jackson	Putnam	IN	Jackson	Coshocton	OH
Jackson	Randolph	AR	Jackson	Randolph	IN	Jackson	Crawford	OH
Jackson	Sharp	AR	Jackson	Ripley	IN	Jackson	Darke	OH
Jackson	Union	AR	Jackson	Rush	IN	Jackson	Franklin	OH
Jackson	White	AR	Jackson	Shelby	IN	Jackson	Guernsey	OH
Jackson	Adair	IA	Jackson	Spencer	IN	Jackson	Hancock	OH
Jackson	Benton	IA	Jackson	Starke	IN	Jackson	Hardin	OH
Jackson	Boone	IA	Jackson	Steuben	IN	Jackson	Highland	OH
Jackson	Bremer	IA	Jackson	Sullivan	IN	Jackson	Jackson	OH
Jackson	Butler	IA	Jackson	Tippecanoe	IN	Jackson	Knox	OH
Jackson	Calhoun	IA	Jackson	Washington	IN	Jackson	Mahoning	OH
Jackson	Clarke	IA	Jackson	Wayne	IN	Jackson	Monroe	OH
Jackson	Crawford	IA	Jackson	Wells	IN	Jackson	Montgomery	OH
Jackson	Des Moines	IA	Jackson	White	IN	Jackson	Muskingum	OH
Jackson	Greene	IA	Jackson	Anderson	KS	Jackson	Noble	OH
Jackson	Guthrie	IA	Jackson	Edwards	KS	Jackson	Paulding	OH
Jackson	Hardin	IA	Jackson	Geary	KS	Jackson	Perry	OH
Jackson	Harrison	IA	Jackson	Jewell	KS	Jackson	Pickaway	OH
Jackson	Henry	IA	Jackson	Lyon	KS	Jackson	Pike	OH
Jackson	Jackson	IA	Jackson	McPherson	KS	Jackson	Preble	OH
Jackson	Jones	IA	Jackson	Osborne	KS	Jackson	Putnam	OH
Jackson	Keokuk	IA	Jackson	Riley	KS	Jackson	Richland	OH
Jackson	Lee	IA	Jackson	Sumner	KS	Jackson	Sandusky	OH
Jackson	Linn	IA	Jackson	Waldo	ME	Jackson	Seneca	OH
Jackson	Lucas	IA	Jackson	Scott	MN	Jackson	Shelby	OH
Jackson	Madison	IA	Jackson	Andrew	MO	Jackson	Stark	OH
Jackson	Monroe	IA	Jackson	Buchanan	MO	Jackson	Union	OH
Jackson	Montgomery	IA	Jackson	Callaway	MO	Jackson	Van Wert	OH
Jackson	Poweshiek	IA	Jackson	Camden	MO	Jackson	Vinton	OH
Jackson	Sac	IA	Jackson	Carter	MO	Jackson	Wood	OH
Jackson	Shelby	IA	Jackson	Clark	MO	Jackson	Wyandot	OH

TOWNSHIP	COUNTY	STATE	TOWNSHIP	COUNTY	STATE	TOWNSHIP	COUNTY	STATE
Jackson	Coal	OK	Jasper	Crittenden	AR	Jefferson	Huntington	IN
Jackson	Cotton	OK	Jasper	Adams	IA	Jefferson	Jay	IN
Jackson	Washington	OK	Jasper	Carroll	IA	Jefferson	Kosciusko	IN
Jackson	Butler	PA	Jasper	Wayne	IL	Jefferson	Miami	IN
Jackson	Cambria	PA	Jasper	Midland	MI	Jefferson	Morgan	IN
Jackson	Columbia	PA	Jasper	Camden	MO	Jefferson	Newton	IN
Jackson	Dauphin	PA	Jasper	Dallas	MO	Jefferson	Noble	IN
Jackson	Greene	PA	Jasper	Jasper	MO	Jefferson	Owen	IN
Jackson	Huntingdon	PA	Jasper	Ozark	MO	Jefferson	Pike	IN
Jackson	Lebanon	PA	Jasper	Ralls	MO	Jefferson	Pulaski	IN
Jackson	Luzerne	PA	Jasper	Taney	MO	Jefferson	Putnam	IN
Jackson	Lycoming	PA	Jasper	Steuben	NY	Jefferson	Sullivan	IN
Jackson	Mercer	PA	Jasper	Fayette	OH	Jefferson	Switzerland	IN
Jackson	Monroe	PA	Jasper	Hanson	SD	Jefferson	Tipton	IN
Jackson	Northumberland	PA	Java	Wyoming	NY	Jefferson	Washington	IN
Jackson	Perry	PA	Jay	Franklin	ME	Jefferson	Wayne	IN
Jackson	Snyder	PA	Jay	Martin	MN	Jefferson	Wells	IN
Jackson	Susquehanna	PA	Jay	Essex	NY	Jefferson	Whitley	IN
Jackson	Tioga	PA	Jay	Elk	PA	Jefferson	Chautauqua	KS
Jackson	Venango	PA	Jay	Orleans	VT	Jefferson	Cheyenne	KS
Jackson	York	PA	Jeddo	Knox	MO	Jefferson	Dickinson	KS
Jackson	Bon Homme	SD	Jeff Davis	Little River	AR	Jefferson	Geary	KS
Jackson	Charles Mix	SD	Jeff	Oregon	MO	Jefferson	Jackson	KS
Jackson	Sanborn	SD	Jefferson	Boone	AR	Jefferson	Jefferson	KS
Jackson	Adams	WI	Jefferson	Calhoun	AR	Jefferson	Rawlins	KS
Jackson	Burnett	WI	Jefferson	Desha	AR	Jefferson	Republic	KS
Jackson	Washington	WI	Jefferson	Independence	AR	Jefferson	Lincoln	ME
Jacksonport	Door	WI	Jefferson	Izard	AR	Jefferson	Cass	MI
Jacksonville	Chickasaw	IA	Jefferson	Jackson	AR	Jefferson	Hillsdale	MI
Jacksonville	Onslow	NC	Jefferson	Jefferson	AR	Jefferson	Houston	MN
Jacobs Fork	Catawba	NC	Jefferson	Little River	AR	Jefferson	Andrew	MO
Jacobs	Hughes	OK	Jefferson	Marion	AR	Jefferson	Cedar	MO
Jacobs	Ashland	WI	Jefferson	Newton	AR	Jefferson	Clark	MO
Jacumba	San Diego	CA	Jefferson	Ouachita	AR	Jefferson	Cole	MO
Jadis	Roseau	MN	Jefferson	Saline	AR	Jefferson	Daviess	MO
Jaffrey	Cheshire	NH	Jefferson	Sevier	AR	Jefferson	Grundy	MO
Jamaica	Vermillion	IL	Jefferson	White	AR	Jefferson	Harrison	MO
Jamaica	Windham	VT	Jefferson	Adair	IA	Jefferson	Johnson	MO
James Bayou	Mississippi	MO	Jefferson	Allamakee	IA	Jefferson	Linn	MO
James Creek	Marion	AR	Jefferson	Bremer	IA	Jefferson	Maries	MO
James Cross Roads	Florence	SC	Jefferson	Buchanan	IA	Jefferson	Monroe	MO
James Hill	Mountrail	ND	Jefferson	Butler	IA	Jefferson	Nodaway	MO
James Island	Charleston	SC	Jefferson	Clayton	IA	Jefferson	Osage	MO
James R. Bush	Phillips	AR	Jefferson	Dubuque	IA	Jefferson	Polk	MO
James River Valley	Dickey	ND	Jefferson	Fayette	IA	Jefferson	Saint Louis	MO
James	Scott	AR	Jefferson	Greene	IA	Jefferson	Scotland	MO
James	Pottawattamie	IA	Jefferson	Harrison	IA	Jefferson	Shelby	MO
James	Saginaw	MI	Jefferson	Henry	IA	Jefferson	Wayne	MO
James	Stone	MO	Jefferson	Johnson	IA	Jefferson	Madison	MT
Jamesport	Davies	MO	Jefferson	Lee	IA	Jefferson	Ashe	NC
Jamestown	Howard	IA	Jefferson	Louisa	IA	Jefferson	Guilford	NC
Jamestown	Steuben	IN	Jefferson	Madison	IA	Jefferson	Pierce	ND
Jamestown	Ottawa	MI	Jefferson	Mahaska	IA	Jefferson	Knox	NE
Jamestown	Blue Earth	MN	Jefferson	Marshall	IA	Jefferson	Coos	NH
Jamestown	Guilford	NC	Jefferson	Polk	IA	Jefferson	Morris	NJ
Jamestown	Newport	RI	Jefferson	Poweshiek	IA	Jefferson	Schoharie	NY
Jamestown	Grant	WI	Jefferson	Ringgold	IA	Jefferson	Adams	OH
Jamesville	Martin	NC	Jefferson	Shelby	IA	Jefferson	Ashtabula	OH
Jamesville	Yankton	SD	Jefferson	Taylor	IA	Jefferson	Brown	OH
Janes Creek	Randolph	AR	Jefferson	Warren	IA	Jefferson	Clinton	OH
Janesburg	Grant	ND	Jefferson	Wayne	IA	Jefferson	Coshocton	OH
Janesville	Greenwood	KS	Jefferson	Massac	IL	Jefferson	Crawford	OH
Janesville	Waseca	MN	Jefferson	Stephenson	IL	Jefferson	Fayette	OH
Janesville	Rock	WI	Jefferson	Adams	IN	Jefferson	Franklin	OH
Janette Lake	Saint Louis	MN	Jefferson	Allen	IN	Jefferson	Greene	OH
Janke	Logan	ND	Jefferson	Boone	IN	Jefferson	Guernsey	OH
Japton	Madison	AR	Jefferson	Carroll	IN	Jefferson	Jackson	OH
Jaqua	Cheyenne	KS	Jefferson	Cass	IN	Jefferson	Knox	OH
Jarbidge	Elko	NV	Jefferson	Dubois	IN	Jefferson	Logan	OH
Jarvis	Madison	IL	Jefferson	Elkhart	IN	Jefferson	Madison	OH
Jarvis	Grant	OK	Jefferson	Grant	IN	Jefferson	Mercer	OH
Jason	Greene	NC	Jefferson	Greene	IN	Jefferson	Montgomery	OH
Jasper	Crawford	AR	Jefferson	Henry	IN	Jefferson	Muskingum	OH

TOWNSHIP	COUNTY	STATE	TOWNSHIP	COUNTY	STATE	TOWNSHIP	COUNTY	STATE
Jefferson	Noble	OH	Joachim	Jefferson	MO	Jones	Beltrami	MN
Jefferson	Preble	OH	Jobe	Oregon	MO	Jones	Major	OK
Jefferson	Richland	OH	Jobs Cabin	Wilkes	NC	Jones	Elk	PA
Jefferson	Ross	OH	Jocko	Flathead	MT	Jones	Gregory	SD
Jefferson	Scioto	OH	Jocko	Lake	MT	Jonesboro	Craighead	AR
Jefferson	Tuscarawas	OH	Joe Burleson	Marion	AR	Jonesboro	Washington	ME
Jefferson	Williams	OH	Johannesdale	Logan	ND	Jonesboro (No. 2)	Lee	NC
Jefferson	Caddo	OK	Johannisburg	Washington	IL	Jonesfield	Saginaw	MI
Jefferson	Coal	OK	Johnny Clem	Licking	OH	Jonesport	Washington	ME
Jefferson	Cotton	OK	Johns Island	Charleston	SC	Jonesville	Union	SC
Jefferson	Ellis	OK	Johns River	Caldwell	NC	Joplin	Jasper	MO
Jefferson	Washington	OK	Johns	Appanoose	IA	Jordan	Monona	iA
Jefferson	Woods	OK	Johnsburg	Warren	NY	Jordan	Whiteside	IL
Jefferson	Woodward	OK	Johnson	Clay	AR	Jordan	Jasper	IN
Jefferson	Berks	PA	Johnson	Little River	AR	Jordan	Warren	IN
Jefferson	Butler	PA	Johnson	Logan	aR	Jordan	Antrim	MI
Jefferson	Dauphin	PA	Johnson	Saint Francis	AR	Jordan	Fillmore	MN
Jefferson	Fayette	PA	Johnson	Scott	AR	Jordan	Hickory	MO
Jefferson	Greene	PA	Johnson	Sharp	AR	Jordan	Ripley	MO
Jefferson	Lackawanna	PA	Johnson	Union	AR	Jordan	Adams	ND
Jefferson	Mercer	PA	Johnson	Washington	AR	Jordan	Clearfield	PA
Jefferson	Somerset	PA	Johnson	Plymouth	IA	Jordan	Lycoming	PA
Jefferson	Washington	PA	Johnson	Webster	IA	Jordan	Northumberland	PA
Jefferson	Chesterfield	SC	Johnson	Christian	IL	Jordan	Tripp	SD
Jefferson	Bon Homme	SD	Johnson	Clark	IL	Jordan	Green	WI
Jefferson	McCook	SD	Johnson	Clinton	IN	Jordan Valley	Pawnee	OK
Jefferson	Moody	SD	Johnson	Crawford	IN	Joshua	Fulton	IL
Jefferson	Spink	SD	Johnson	Gibson	IN	Josie	Holt	NE
Jefferson	Union	SD	Johnson	Knox	IN	Joubert	Douglas	SD
Jefferson	Green	WI	Johnson	Lagrange	IN	Joy	White	AR
Jefferson	Jefferson	WI	Johnson	La Porte	IN	Joyfield	Benzie	MI
Jefferson	Monroe	WI	Johnson	Ripley	IN	Jubilee	Peoria	IL
Jefferson	Vernon	WI	Johnson	Scott	IN	Judkins	Warren	NC
Jeffersonville	Clark	IN	Johnson	Ness	KS	Judson	Blue Earth	MN
Jeffreys	Florence	SC	Johnson	Polk	MN	Judson	Williams	ND
Jenkins	Mitchell	IA	Johnson	Carter	MO	Julien	Dubuque	IA
Jenkins	Crow Wing	MN	Johnson	Maries	MO	Jump River	Taylor	WI
Jenkins	Barry	MO	Johnson	Oregon	MO	Junction City	Trinity	CA
Jenkins	Luzerne	PA	Johnson	Polk	MO	Junction	Greene	IA
Jenks	Tulsa	OK	Johnson	Ripley	MO	Junction	Osage	KS
Jenks	Forest	PA	Johnson	Scotland	MO	Juniata	Tuscola	MI
Jenner	Somerset	PA	Johnson	Washington	MO	Juniata	Adams	NE
Jennings	Crawford	IN	Johnson	Wells	ND	Juniata	Bedford	PA
Jennings	Fayette	IN	Johnson	Champaign	OH	Juniata	Blair	PA
Jennings	Owen	IN	Johnson	Dewey	OK	Juniata	Huntingdon	pA
Jennings	Scott	IN	Johnson	McClain	OK	Juniata	Perry	PA
Jennings	Decatur	KS	Johnson	Florence	SC	Junius	Seneca	NY
Jennings	Putnam	OH	Johnson (No. 12)	Williamsburg	SC	Jupiter	Kittson	MN
Jennings	Van Wert	OH	Johnson	Lamoille	VT			
Jenny Lind	Calaveras	CA	Johnson	Marathon	WI			
Jericho	Chittenden	VT	Johnsonville	Redwood	MN		**—K—**	
Jerome	Gove	KS	Johnsonville	Harnett	NC			
Jerome	Midland	MI	Johnston	Macon	MO	Kadoka	Jackson	SD
Jerome	Union	OH	Johnston	Trumbull	OH	Kampeska	Codington	SD
Jersey	Jersey	IL	Johnston	Edgefield	SC	Kalamazoo	Kalamazoo	MI
Jersey	Licking	OH	Johnston	Providence	RI	Kalamo	Eaton	MI
Jerusalem	Yates	NY	Johnstown	Barry	MI	Kalevala	Carlton	MN
Jerusalem	Davie	NC	Johnstown	Grand Forks	ND	Kalkaska	Kalkaska	MI
Jerusalem	Lucas	OH	Johnstown	Fulton	NY	Kalispell	Flathead	MT
Jessenland	Sibley	MN	Johnstown	Polk	WI	Kalmar	Olmsted	MN
Jessieville	Garland	AR	Johnstown	Rock	WI	Kanabec	Kanabec	MN
Jessup	Susquehanna	PA	Joliet	Will	IL	Kanaranzi	Rock	MN
Jester	Greer	OK	Joliet	Platte	NE	Kandiyohi	Kandiyohi	MN
Jesup	Lawrence	AR	Joliette	Pembina	ND	Kandiyohi	Burke	ND
Jeter	Choctaw	OK	Jonas Ridge	Burke	NC	Kandota	Todd	MN
Jevne	Aitkin	MN	Jonathan Creek	Moultrie	IL	Kane	Benton	IA
Jewell	Little River	AR	Jonathans Creek	Haywood	NC	Kane	Pottawattamie	IA
Jewett	Greene	NY	Jones	Greene	AR	Kane	Greene	IL
Jewett	Jackson	SD	Jones	Newton	AR	Kane	Bottineau	ND
Jim Fork	Sebastian	AR	Jones	Scott	AR	Kaneville	Kane	IL
Jim Henry	Miller	MO	Jones	Stone	AR	Kankakee	Kankakee	IL
Jim River Valley	Stutsman	ND	Jones	Union	IA	Kankakee	Jasper	IN
Jo Daviess	Faribault	MN	Jones	Morton	KS	Kankakee	La Porte	IN

TOWNSHIP	COUNTY	STATE	TOWNSHIP	COUNTY	STATE	TOWNSHIP	COUNTY	STATE
Kannapolis (No. 4)	Cabarrus	NC	Kenesaw	Adams	NE	Kilbuck	Allegheny	PA
Kansas City	Adams	ND	Kenmare	Ward	ND	Kildare	Swift	MN
Kansas	Edgar	IL	Kennady	Le Flore	OK	Kildare	Kay	OK
Kansas	Woodford	IL	Kennan	Price	WI	Kildare	Juneau	WI
Kanwaka	Douglas	KS	Kennebec	Monona	IA	Kilfoil	Custer	NE
Kaolin	Iron	MO	Kennebec	Lyman	SD	Kilgore	Clay	AR
Kapioma	Atchison	KS	Kennebunk	York	ME	Kilkenny	Le Sueur	MN
Karlsruhe	McHenry	ND	Kennebunkport	York	ME	Kilkenny	Coos	NH
Karoma	Alfalfa	OK	Kennedy	Hettinger	ND	Kill Creek	Osborne	KS
Karthaus	Clearfield	PA	Kennedy	Blaine	OK	Killbuck	Holmes	OH
Kaskaskia	Fayette	IL	Kennedy	Allegheny	PA	Killbuck	Wayne	OH
Kasota	Le Sueur	MN	Kennedy	Charles Mix	SD	Killingly	Windham	CT
Kassel	Hutchinson	SD	Kennekeet	Dare	NC	Killingworth	Middlesex	CT
Kasson	Leelanau	MI	Kenneth	Sheridan	KS	Kilso	Traill	ND
Kathio	Mille Lacs	MN	Kenneth	Chester	PA	Kimball	Saint Clair	MI
Kaukauna	Outagamie	Wi	Kenney	Perry	AR	Kimball	Jackson	MN
Kaw	Jefferson	KS	Kenockee	Saint Clair	MI	Kimball	Brule	SD
Kaw	Wabaunsee	KS	Kennison	La Moure	ND	Kimball	Iron	WI
Kaw	Jackson	MO	Kensal	Stutsman	ND	Kimberly	Aitkin	MN
Kaw	Kay	OK	Kensett	White	AR	Kimbrough	Lincoln	AR
Kawkawlin	Bay	MI	Kensett	Worth	IA	Kimeo	Washington	KS
Kaylor	Hutchinson	SD	Kensington	Walsh	ND	Kimmell	Bedford	PA
Kearney	Antrim	MI	Kensington	Rockingham	NH	Kimshew	Butte	CA
Kearney	Clay	MO	Kent	Litchfield	CT	Kinards	Greenwood	SC
Kearny	Hudson	NJ	Kent	Stephenson	IL	Kinder Cape	Girardeau	MO
Keating	McKean	PA	Kent	Warren	IN	Kinderhook	Pike	IL
Keating	Potter	PA	Kent	Dickey	ND	Kinderhook	Branch	MI
Keaton	Arkansas	AR	Kent	Putnam	NY	Kinderhook	Columbia	NY
Kechi	Sedgwick	KS	Kent	Edmunds	SD	King City	Monterey	CA
Kedron	Woodbury	IA	Kentner	Dickey	ND	King City	McPherson	KS
Keeler	Van Buren	MI	Kenton	Cimarron	OK	King Mountain	York	SC
Keen	McKenzie	ND	Kentucky	Madison	AR	King Prairie	Barry	MO
Keene	Adams	IL	Kentucky	Newton	AR	King	Johnson	AR
Keene	Ionia	MI	Kentucky	Saline	AR	King	Winnebago	IA
Keene	Clay	MN	Kentucky	White	AR	King	Christian	IL
Keene	Essex	NY	Kentucky	Jefferson	KS	King	Polk	MN
Keene	Coshocton	OH	Kenyon	Goodhue	MN	King	Oregon	MO
Keener	Jasper	IN	Keokuk	Lee	IA	King	Stephen	OK
Keesee	Marion	AR	Keokuk	Wapello	IA	King	Bedford	PA
Keeter	Marion	AR	Keowee	Garfield	OK	King	Tripp	SD
Keevil	Monroe	AR	Keowee	Oconee	SC	King	Lincoln	WI
Keg Creek	Pottawattamie	IA	Kerkhoven	Swift	MN	Kingery	Thomas	KS
Kego	Cass	MN	Kern	Hettinger	ND	Kingfield	Franklin	ME
Keith	Wayne	IL	Kernersville	Forsyth	NC	Kingfisher	Kingfisher	OK
Keith	Alfalfa	OK	Kerr	Champaign	IL	Kinghurst	Itasca	MN
Keithsburg	Mercer	IL	Kerrick	Pine	MN	Kingman	Kingman	KS
Keller	Burke	ND	Kerton	Fulton	IL	Kingman	Renville	MN
Kelley	Ripley	MO	Kertsonville	Polk	MN	Kings Creek	Caldwell	NC
Kelleys Island	Erie	OH	Kettle River	Pine	MN	Kings Mountain (No. 4)	Cleveland	NC
Kelliher	Beltrami	MN	Kewanee	Henry	IL	Kings River	Carroll	AR
Kellogg	Jasper	IA	Kewaskum	Washington	WI	Kings River	Madison	AR
Kellogg	Beadle	SD	Key West	Coffey	KS	Kings (No. 7)	Williamsburg	SC
Kelly	Warren	IL	Keyapaha	Tripp	SD	Kingsburg	Washington	NY
Kelly	Carter	MO	Keyser	De Kalb	IN	Kingsland	Cleveland	AR
Kelly	Cooper	MO	Keystone	Scott	IN	Kingsley	Griggs	ND
Kelly	Union	PA	Keystone	Polk	MN	Kingsley	Forest	PA
Kelly	Bayfield	WI	Keystone	Dickey	ND	Kingston	De Kalb	IL
Kellyville	Creek	OK	Keystone	Bayfield	WI	Kingston	Plymouth	MA
Kelsey	El Dorado	CA	Keysville	Pawnee	KS	Kingston	Tuscola	MI
Kelsey	Saint Louis	MN	Keytesville	Chariton	MO	Kingston	Meeker	MN
Kelso	San Bernardino	CA	Kiamichi	Pushmataha	OK	Kingston	Caldwell	MO
Kelso	Dearborn	IN	Kiantone	Chauauqua	NY	Kingston	Washington	MO
Kelso	Sibley	MN	Kickapoo	Peoria	IL	Kingston	Sargent	ND
Kelso	Scott	MO	Kickapoo	Leavenworth	KS	Kingston	Rockingham	NH
Kemp	Bryan	OK	Kickapoo	Mountrail	ND	Kingston	Ulster	NY
Kenansville	Duplin	NC	Kickapoo	Lincoln	OK	Kingston	Delaware	OH
Kendall	Kendall	IL	Kickapoo	Vernon	WI	Kingston	Luzerne	PA
Kendall	Hamilton	KS	Kidder	Caldwell	MO	Kingston	Green Lake	WI
Kendall	Kearney	KS	Kidder	Carbon	PA	Kingston	Juneau	WI
Kendall	Orleans	NY	Kidder	Day	SD	Kingstree (No. 16)	Williamsburg	SC
Kendall	Lafayette	WI	Kiester	Faribault	MN	Kingsville	Johnson	MO
Kendrick	Greene	IA	Kilborn	Grant	SD	Kingsville	Ashtabula	OH
Kenduskeag	Penobscot	ME	Kilbourne	Mason	IL	Kingwood	Hunterdon	NJ

TOWNSHIP	COUNTY	STATE	TOWNSHIP	COUNTY	STATE	TOWNSHIP	COUNTY	STATE
Kinkaid	Jackson	IL	Koger	Dorchester	SC	Lake Sarah	Murray	MN
Kinloss	Walsh	ND	Kohlmeier	Rolette	ND	Lake Shore	Lac Qui Parie	MN
Kinmundy	Marion	IL	Kokomo	Beaver	OK	Lake Sinai	Brookings	SD
Kinnickinnic	Saint Croix	WI	Kolls	Jones	SD	Lake Stay	Lincoln	MN
Kinross	Chippewa	MI	Komensky	Jackson	WI	Lake Tomahawk	Oneida	WI
Kinsley	Edwards	KS	Konawa	Seminole	OK	Lake	Greene	AR
Kinsman	Trumbull	OH	Kortright	Delaware	NY	Lake	Perry	AR
Kinston	Lenoir	NC	Kosciusko	Day	SD	Lake	Phillips	AR
Kintire	Redwood	MN	Koshkonong	Jefferson	WI	Lake	Siskiyou	CA
Kinyon	Cass	ND	Kosoma	Pushmataha	OK	Lake	Cerro Gordo	IA
Kiowa	Barber	KS	Kossuth	Manitowoc	WI	Lake	Clay	IA
Kiowa	Kiowa	KS	Kottke Valley	McHenry	ND	Lake	Humboldt	IA
Kiowa	Harper	OK	Koylton	Tuscola	MI	Lake	Monona	IA
Kiowa	Pittsburg	OK	Kregero	Chippewa	MN	Lake	Muscatine	IA
Kiowa	Roger Mills	OK	Kragnes	Clay	MN	Lake	Pocahontas	IA
Kirby	Northampton	NC	Krain	Stearns	MN	Lake	Pottawattamie	IA
Kirby	Dillon	SC	Krakow	Presque Isle	MI	Lake	Wright	IA
Kirby	Caledonia	VT	Kranzburg	Codington	SD	Lake	Clinton	IL
Kirk	McCurtain	OK	Kratka	Pennington	MN	Lake	Allen	IN
Kirkelie	Ward	ND	Kremlin	Garfield	OK	Lake	Kosciusko	IN
Kirkland	Adams	IN	Kroeber	Logan	ND	Lake	Newton	IN
Kirkland	Oneida	NY	Kronenwetter	Marathon	WI	Lake	Harper	KS
Kirklin	Clinton	IN	Kroschel	Kanabec	MN	Lake	Harvey	KS
Kirksey	Greenwood	SC	Kugler	Saint Louis	MN	Lake	Scott	KS
Kirkwood	Belmont	OH	Kulm	Hutchinson	SD	Lake	Benzie	MI
Kirkwood	Broome	NY	Kully Chaha	Le Flore	OK	Lake	Berrien	MI
Kirtland	Lake	OH	Kunze	Hettinger	ND	Lake	Huron	MI
Kirwin	Phillips	KS	Kurtz	Clay	MN	Lake	Lake	MI
Kiskiminetas	Armstrong	PA	Kyseth	Dunn	ND	Lake	Macomb	MI
Kittanning	Armstrong	PA				Lake	Menominee	MI
Kittery	York	ME				Lake	Missaukee	MI
Kittrell	Vance	NC	—L—			Lake	Roscommon	MI
Klacking	Ogemaw	MI				Lake	Roseau	MN
Klamath	Del Norte	CA	La Belle	Lewis	MO	Lake	Wabasha	MN
Klamath	Humboldt	CA	La Belle	Marshall	SD	Lake	Buchanan	MO
Kline	Schuylkill	PA	La Clede	Fayette	IL	Lake	Vernon	MO
Klingstrup	Ramsey	ND	La Crescent	Houston	MN	Lake	Barnes	ND
Knapp	Jackson	WI	La Crosse	Rush	KS	Lake	Cass	ND
Kniest	Carroll	IA	La Crosse	Jackson	MN	Lake	Hall	NE
Knife Falls	Carlton	MN	La Fave	Scott	AR	Lake	Holt	NE
Knife Lake	Kanabec	MN	La Follette	Barnett	WI	Lake	Phelps	NE
Knife River	Mountrail	ND	La Font	New Madrid	MO	Lake	Pershing	NV
Knight Prairie	Hamilton	IL	La Garde	Mahnomen	MN	Lake	Ashland	OH
Knight	Vanderburgh	IN	La Grand	Douglas	MN	Lake	Logan	OH
Knight	Iron	WI	La Grange	Lafayette	AR	Lake	Lorain	OH
Knob Creek (No. 10)	Cleveland	NC	La Grange	Stanislaus	CA	Lake	Stark	OH
Knob	Clay	AR	La Grange	Harrison	IA	Lake	Wood	OH
Knobs	Yadkin	NC	La Grange	Cass	MI	Lake	Comanche	OK
Knobview	Crawford	MO	La Grange	Dutchess	NY	Lake	Luzerne	PA
Knowles	Beaver	OK	La Grange	Monroe	WI	Lake	Mercer	PA
Knowlton	Warren	NJ	Lake Hamilton	Garland	AR	Lake	Wayne	PA
Knowlton	Marathon	WI	Lake Hanska	Brown	MN	Lake	Florence	SC
Knox	Clarke	IA	Lake Hattie	Hubbard	MN	Lake	Aurora	SD
Knox	Pottawattamie	IA	Lake Hendricks	Brookings	SD	Lake	Clark	SD
Knox	Knox	IL	Lake Henry	Stearns	MN	Lake	Codington	SD
Knox	Jay	IN	Lake Hester	McHenry	ND	Lake	Corson	SD
Knox	Waldo	ME	Lake Hill	Pennington	SD	Lake	Roberts	SD
Knox	Albany	NY	Lake Holcombe	Chippewa	WI	Lake	Spink	SD
Knox	Benson	ND	Lake Ibsen	Benson	ND	Lake	Tripp	SD
Knox	Columbiana	OH	Lake Ida	Norman	MN	Lake	Marinette	WI
Knox	Guernsey	OH	Lake Jessie	Itasca	MN	Lake	Price	WI
Knox	Holmes	OH	Lake Johanna	Pope	MN	Lake Valley	El Dorado	CA
Knox	Jefferson	OH	Lake Landing	Hyde	NC	Lake Valley	Traverse	MN
Knox	Vinton	OH	Lake Lillian	Kandiyohi	MN	Lake View	Becker	MN
Knox	Clarion	PA	Lake Luzerne	Warren	NY	Lake View	Burke	ND
Knox	Clearfield	PA	Lake Marshall	Lyon	MN	Lake View	Lake	SD
Knox	Jefferson	PA	Lake Mary	Douglas	MN	Lake Villa	Lake	IL
Knox	Price	WI	Lake Mills	Jefferson	WI	Lake Washington	Eddy	ND
Knoxville	Marion	IA	Lake Park	Becker	MN	Lake Williams	Kidder	ND
Knoxville	Ray	MO	Lake Pleasant	Hamilton	NY	Lake Williams	McLean	ND
Knute	Polk	MN	Lake Pleasant	Red Lake	MN	Lakefield	Luce	MI
Kochville	Saginaw	MI	Lake Prairie	Marion	IA	Lakefield	Saginaw	MI
Koehler	Cheboygan	MI	Lake Prairie	Nicollet	MN	Lakeland	Barron	WI

TOWNSHIP	COUNTY	STATE	TOWNSHIP	COUNTY	STATE	TOWNSHIP	COUNTY	STATE
Lakeline	Lake	OH	Lane	Warrick	IN	Lafayette	Onondage	NY
Lakemore	Summit	OH	Lane	Greenwood	KS	Lafayette	Coshocton	OH
Lakeport	Woodbury	IA	Lane	Smith	KS	Lafayette	Medina	OH
Lakeport	Hubbard	MN	Lanes Creek	Union	NC	Lafayette	McKean	PA
Lakeside	Aitkin	MN	Lanesboro	Anson	NC	Lafayette	Lyman	SD
Lakeside	Cottonwood	MN	Lanesborough	Berkshire	MA	Lafayette	Chippewa	WI
Lakeside	Creek	OK	Lanesburgh	Le Sueur	MN	Lafayette	Monroe	WI
Lakeside	Meade	SD	Lanesville	Sangamon	IL	Lafayette	Walworth	WI
Lakeside	Douglas	WI	Langberg	Browman	ND	Lafferty	Izard	AR
Laketon	Muskegon	MI	Langdon	Reno	KS	Lafoon	Faulk	SD
Laketon	Brookings	SD	Langdon	Cavalier	ND	Lagoon	Pawnee	OK
Laketown	Allegan	MI	Langdon	Sullivan	NH	Lagrange	Penobscot	ME
Laketown	Carver	MN	Langhei	Pope	MN	Lagrange	Bond	IL
Laketown	Polk	WI	Langlade	Langlade	WI	Lagrange	Lorian	OH
Lakeview	Carlton	MN	Langley	Ellsworth	KS	Largo	Wabash	IN
Lakeville	Dickinson	IA	Langley	Aiken	SC	Laguna Beach	Orange	CA
Lakeville	Plymouth	MA	Langola	Benton	MN	Laing	Rawlins	KS
Lakeville	Grand Forks	ND	Langor	Beltrami	MN	Laird	Houghton	MI
Lakewood	Shelby	IL	L'Anguille	Phillips	AR	Laird	Phelps	NE
Lakewood	Saint Louis	MN	L'Anguille	Saint Francis	AR	Lake Alice	Hubbard	MN
Lakewood	Ocean	NJ	Lanier	Preble	OH	Lake Andrew	Kandiyohi	MN
Lakewood	Oconto	??	L'Anse	Baraga	MI	Lake Bett	Martin	MN
Lakin	Barton	KS	Lansford	Bottineau	ND	Lake Benton	Lincoln	MN
Lakin	Harvey	KS	La Grange	Walworth	WI	Lake Byron	Beadle	SD
Lakin	Kearney	KS	La Grue	Arkansas	AR	Lake City	Craighead	AR
Lakin	Morrison	MN	La Harpe	Hancock	IL	Lake City	Modoc	CA
Lakota	Nelson	ND	La Moille	Bureau	IL	Lake City	Calhoun	IA
Lallie	Benson	ND	La Monte	Pettis	MO	Lake City	Barber	KS
Lamar City	Barton	MO	La Mars	Richland	ND	Lake City	Florence	SC
Lamar	Madison	AR	La Moure	Pembina	ND	Lake Creek	Calhoun	IA
Lamar	Yell	AR	La Plata	Macon	MO	Lake Creek	Pettis	MO
Lamar	Barton	MO	La Pointe	Ashland	WI	Lake Creek	Pennington	SD
Lamar	Clinton	PA	La Prairie	Marshall	IL	Lake East	Lake	MN
Lamard	Wayne	IL	La Prairie	Clearwater	MN	Lake Edwards	Crow Wing	MN
Lamartine	Fond du Lac	WI	La Prairie	Spink	SD	Lake Elizabeth	Kandiyohi	MN
Lamb	Scott	AR	La Prairie	Rock	WI	Lake Emma	Hubbard	MN
Lambert	Red Lake	MN	La Roche	Charles Mix	SD	Lake Eunice	Becker	MN
Lamberton	Redwood	MN	La Salle	La Salle	IL	Lake Flat	Pennington	SD
Lamine	Cooper	MO	La Salle	Monroe	MI	Lake Fork	Logan	IL
Lammers	Beltrami	MN	La Valle	Sauk	WI	Lake Fremont	Martin	MN
Lamoine	McDonough	IL	La Valley	Lincoln	SD	Lake George	Hubbard	MN
Lamoine	Hancock	ME	Labette	Labette	KS	Lake George	Stearns	MN
Lamoni	Decatur	IA	Lac Qui Parle	Lac Qui Parie	MN	Lake George	McHenry	ND
Lamont	Hamilton	KS	Lacey	Thomas	KS	Lake George	Warren	NY
Lamont	Sheridan	ND	Lacey	Ocean	NJ	Lake George	Charles Mix	SD
Lamont	Grant	OK	Lacey	Kingfisher	OK	Lake Grove	Mahnomen	MN
Lamont	Lafayette	WI	Lack	Juniata	PA	Lansing	Allamakee	IA
Lamotte	Crawford	IL	Lacawannock	Mercer	PA	Lansing	Ingham	MI
Lamotte	Sanilac	MI	Lackawaxen	Pike	PA	Lansing	Mower	MN
Lampton	Walsh	ND	Lacon	Marshall	IL	Lansing	Towner	ND
Lamro	Tripp	SD	Lacrosse	Izard	AR	Lansing	Tompkins	NY
Lanark	Rooks	KS	Ladd	Bowman	ND	Lansing	Brown	SD
Lanark	Portage	WI	Ladore	Neosho	KS	Laona	Winnebago	IL
Lancaster	Crawford	AR	Laenna	Logan	IL	Laona	Roseau	MN
Lancaster	Stephenson	IL	Lafayette	Crawford	AR	Laona	Forest	WI
Lancaster	Huntington	IN	Lafayette	Lonoke	AR	Lapeer	Lapeer	MI
Lancaster	Jefferson	IN	Lafayette	Ouachita	AR	Lapeer	Cortland	NY
Lancaster	Wells	IN	Lafayette	Scott	AR	Lapile	Union	AR
Lancaster	Atchison	KS	Lafayette	Allamakee	IA	Laporte	Sullivan	PA
Lancaster	Worcester	MA	Lafayette	Bremer	IA	Larchwood	Lyon	IA
Lancaster	Coos	NH	Lafayette	Keokuk	IA	Larimer	Somerset	PA
Lancaster	Erie	NY	Lafayette	Story	IA	Larimore	Grand Forks	ND
Lancaster	Fairfield	OH	Lafayette	Coles	IL	Lark	Grant	ND
Lancaster	Butler	PA	Lafayette	Ogle	IL	Larkin	Midland	MI
Lancaster	Lancaster	pA	Lafayette	Allen	IN	Larkin	Nobles	MN
Land O'Lake	Vilas	WI	Lafayette	Floyd	IN	Larkinsburg	Clay	IL
Land	Grant	MN	Lafayette	Madison	IN	Larned	Pawnee	KS
Land	McHenry	ND	Lafayette	Owen	IN	Larrabee	Gove	KS
Landaff	Grafton	NH	Lafayette	Chautauqua	KS	Larrabee	Foster	nD
Landgrove	Bennington	VT	Lafayette	Gratiot	MI	Larrabee	Waupaca	WI
Landing Creek	Gregory	SD	Lafayette	Nicollet	MN	Las Vegas	Clark	NV
Landsford	Chester	SC	Lafayette	Clinton	MO	Latan	Spokane	WA
Lane Town	Jerauld	SD	Lafayette	Sussex	NJ	Lathrop	Clinton	MO

TOWNSHIPS OF THE UNITED STATES

TOWNSHIP	COUNTY	STATE	TOWNSHIP	COUNTY	STATE	TOWNSHIP	COUNTY	STATE
Lathrop	Susquehanna	PA	Le Sueur	Kingsbury	SD	Leeper	Murray	OK
Latimore	Adams	PA	Leacock	Lancaster	PA	Leepertown	Bureau	IL
Latona	Walsh	ND	Lead Hill	Christian	MO	Lees Creek	Crawford	AR
Latty	Paulding	OH	Leaf Lake	Otter Tail	MN	Lees Creek	Washington	AR
Laughery	Ripley	IN	Leaf Mountain	Otter Tail	MN	Lees Mills	Washington	NC
Lauramie	Tippecanoe	IN	Leaf Mountain	Burke	ND	Lees	Logan	KS
Laurel Creek	Watauga	NC	Leaf River	Ogle	IL	Lees	Columbus	NC
Laurel Hill	Scotland	NC	Leaf River	Wadena	MN	Leesburg	Union	OH
Laurel	Franklin	IN	Leaf Valley	Douglas	MN	Leesville	Henry	MO
Laurel	Ashe	NC	Leake	Nevada	AR	Leesville	Wake	NC
Laurel (No. 2)	Madison	NC	Leaksville	Rockingham	NC	Leet	Allegheny	PA
Laurel	Hocking	OH	Leasburg	Caswell	NC	Lehigh	Marion	KS
Laurens	Otsego	NY	Leavenworth	Brown	MN	Lehigh	Carbon	PA
Laurens	Laurens	SC	Leavitt	Oceana	MI	Lehigh	Lackawanna	PA
Lausanne	Carbon	PA	Lebanon	New London	CT	Lehigh	Northampton	PA
Lave Creek	Sharp	AR	Lebanon	Saint Clair	IL	Lehigh	Wayne	PA
Lavell	Saint Louis	MN	Lebanon	York	ME	Lehman	Luzerne	PA
Laverne	Harper	OK	Lebanon	Clinton	MI	Lehman	Pike	PA
Lawn Ridge	Cheyenne	KS	Lebanon	Cooper	MO	Leicester	Worcester	MA
Lawn	Harper	KS	Lebanon	Laclede	MO	Leicester	Buncombe	NC
Lawndale	McLean	IL	Lebanon	Durham	NC	Leicester	Clay	NE
Lawrence North	Lawrence	SD	Lebanon	McHenry	ND	Leicester	Livingston	NY
Lawrence Park	Erie	PA	Lebanon	Hunterdon	NJ	Leicester	Addison	VT
Lawrence South	Lawrence	SD	Lebanon	Madison	NY	Leiding	Saint Louis	MN
Lawrence	Lawrence	AR	Lebanon	Meigs	OH	Leidy	Clinton	PA
Lawrence	Montgomery	AR	Lebanon	Wayne	PA	Leigh	Morrison	MN
Lawrence	Lawrence	IL	Lebanon	Dodge	WI	Leighton	Allegan	MI
Lawrence	Marion	IN	Lebanon	Waupaca	WI	Lein	Burleigh	ND
Lawrence	Cloud	KS	Lecompton	Douglas	KS	Leipzig	Grant	ND
Lawrence	Osborne	KS	Ledyard	New London	CT	Leland	Leelanau	MI
Lawrence	Van Buren	MI	Ledyard	Kossuth	IA	Lemay	Saint Louis	MO
Lawrence	Grant	MN	Ledyard	Cayuga	NY	Lemington	Essex	VT
Lawrence	Itasca	MN	Lee Center	Lee	IL	Lemley (No. 10)	Mecklenburg	NC
Lawrence	Cumberland	NJ	Lee Creek	Adair	OK	Lemmon	Adams	ND
Lawrence	Mercer	NJ	Lee	Boone	AR	Lemmons	Clay	AR
Lawrence	Saint Lawrence	NY	Lee	Cleveland	AR	Lemon Cove	Tulare	CA
Lawrence	Lawrence	OH	Lee	Garland	AR	Lemon	Butler	OH
Lawrence	Stark	OH	Lee	Johnson	AR	Lemon	Wyoming	PA
Lawrence	Tuscarawas	OH	Lee	Pope	AR	Lemond	Steele	MN
Lawrence	Washington	OH	Lee	Sacramento	CA	Lemont	Cook	IL
Lawrence	Comanche	OK	Lee	Adair	IA	Lemonweir	Juneau	WI
Lawrence	Clearfield	PA	Lee	Buena Vista	IA	Lemoore	Kings	CA
Lawrence	Tioga	PA	Lee	Franklin	IA	Lempster	Sullivan	NH
Lawrence	Charles Mix	SD	Lee	Madison	IA	Lena	Oconto	WI
Lawrence	Roberts	SD	Lee	Polk	IA	Lenapah	Nowata	OK
Lawrence	Whatcom	WA	Lee	Brown	IL	Lenoir	Caldwell	NC
Lawrence	Brown	WI	Lee	Fulton	IL	Lenora	Norton	KS
Lawrence	Rusk	WI	Lee	Berkshire	MA	Lenora	Griggs	ND
Lawrenceburg	Dearborn	IN	Lee	Penobscot	ME	Lenox	Iowa	IA
Lawrie	Logan	OK	Lee	Allegan	MI	Lenox	Warren	IL
Laws (No. 2)	Williamsburg	SC	Lee	Calhoun	MI	Lenox	Berkshire	MA
Lawton	Blaine	OK	Lee	Midland	MI	Lenox	Macomb	MI
Lawton	Comanche	OK	Lee	Aitkin	MN	Lenox	Madison	NY
Lawton	Hampton	SC	Lee	Beltrami	MN	Lenox	Ashtabula	OH
Layton	Pottawattamie	IN	Lee	Norman	MN	Lenox	Susquehanna	PA
Layton	McHenry	ND	Lee	Platte	MO	Lenroot	Sawyer	WI
Le Baron	Logan	OK	Lee	Nelson	ND	Lent	Chisago	MN
Le Boeuf	Erie	PA	Lee	Strafford	NH	Lentner	Shelby	MO
Le Claire	Scott	IA	Lee	Oneida	NY	Lenton	Stutsman	ND
Le Grand	Marshall	IA	Lee	Athens	OH	Lenzburg	Saint Clair	IL
Le Gette	Marion	SC	Lee	Carroll	OH	Leda	Adams	WI
Le Ray	Blue Earth	MN	Lee	Monroe	OH	Leola	Codington	SD
Le Ray	Jefferson	NY	Lee	Florence	SC	Leon	Cattaraugus	NY
Le Roy	Bremer	IA	Lee	Roberts	SD	Leon	Monroe	WI
Le Roy	Boone	IL	Leech Lake	Cass	MN	Leon	Waushara	WI
Le Roy	Coffey	KS	Leech	Wayne	IL	Leon	Decatur	IA
Le Roy	Calhoun	MI	Leeds	Androscoggin	mE	Leon	Clearwater	MN
Le Roy	Osceola	MI	Leeds	Murray	MN	Leon	Goodhue	MN
Le Roy	Mower	MN	Leeds	Benson	ND	Leonard	Cass	ND
Le Roy	Genesee	NY	Leeds	Columbia	WI	Leonardsville	Traverse	MN
Le Roy	Lake	SD	Leef	Madison	IL	Leoni	Jackson	MI
Le Sauk	Stearns	MN	Leelanau	Leelanau	MI	Leonidas	Saint Joseph	MI
Le Sieur	New Madrid	MO	Leenthrop	Chippewa	MN	Leopoid	Perry	IN

TOWNSHIP	COUNTY	STATE	TOWNSHIP	COUNTY	STATE	TOWNSHIP	COUNTY	STATE
Leota	Norton	KS	Leyden	Lewis	NY	Liberty	Saline	KS
Leota	Nobles	MN	Libby	Aitkin	MN	Liberty	Woodson	KS
Leoti	Wichita	KS	Liberal	Lyon	IA	Liberty	Waldo	ME
Leroy	Audubon	IA	Liberal	Seward	KS	Liberty	Jackson	MI
Leroy	Benton	IA	Libert	Siskoyou	CA	Liberty	Wexford	MI
Leroy	Ingham	MI	Liberty Grove	Richland	ND	Liberty	Beltrami	MN
Leroy	Barton	MO	Liberty Grove	Door	WI	Liberty	Itasca	MN
Leroy	Lake	OH	Liberty	Carroll	AR	Liberty	Polk	MN
Leroy	Bradford	PA	Liberty	Dallas	AR	Liberty	Adair	MO
Leroy	Dodge	WI	Liberty	Independence	AR	Liberty	Barry	MO
Leshara	Saunders	NE	Liberty	Lee	AR	Liberty	Bollinger	MO
Leslie	Ingham	MI	Liberty	Marion	AR	Liberty	Callaway	MO
Leslie	Todd	MN	Liberty	Ouachita	AR	Liberty	Cape Girardeau	MO
Leslie	Carroll	MO	Liberty	Pope	AR	Liberty	Clay	MO
Lessor	Polk	MN	Liberty	Saline	AR	Liberty	Cole	MO
Lessor	Shawano	WI	Liberty	Stone	AR	Liberty	Crawford	MO
Lester	Craighead	AR	Liberty	Van Buren	AR	Liberty	Daviess	MO
Lester	Black Hawk	IA	Liberty	White	AR	Liberty	Grundy	MO
Lester	Okfuskee	OK	Liberty	San Joaquin	CA	Liberty	Holt	MO
Lesterville	Reynolds	MO	Liberty	Clinton	IA	Liberty	Iron	MO
Letart	Meigs	OH	Liberty	Cherokee	IA	Liberty	Knox	MO
Letcher	Sanborn	SD	Liberty	Clarke	IA	Liberty	Macon	MO
Letterkenny	Franklin	PA	Liberty	Dubuque	IA	Liberty	Madison	MO
Leval	Nelson	ND	Liberty	Hamilton	IA	Liberty	Marion	MO
Levan	Jackson	IL	Liberty	Jefferson	IA	Liberty	Phelps	MO
Levant	Penobscot	ME	Liberty	Johnson	IA	Liberty	Pulaski	MO
Levant	Grand Forks	ND	Liberty	Keokuk	IA	Liberty	Putnam	MO
Levee	Pike	IL	Liberty	Lucas	IA	Liberty	Faint Francois	MO
Level Cross	Randolph	NC	Liberty	Marion	IA	Liberty	Saline	MO
Leven	Pope	MN	Liberty	Marshall	IA	Liberty	Schuyler	MO
Leverett	Franklin	MA	Liberty	Mitchell	IA	Liberty	Stoddard	MO
Leverney	Montgomery	AR	Liberty	O'Brien	IA	Liberty	Sullivan	MO
Levey	Sac	IA	Liberty	Plymouth	IA	Liberty	Washington	MO
Levis	Clark	WI	Liberty	Ringgold	IA	Liberty	Randolph	NC
Lewis Fork	Wilkes	NC	Liberty	Scott	IA	Liberty	Yadkin	NC
Lewis	Scott	AR	Liberty	Warren	IA	Liberty	Mountrail	ND
Lewis	Pottawattamie	IA	Liberty	Woodbury	IA	Liberty	Ransom	ND
Lewis	Clay	IN	Liberty	Wright	IA	Liberty	Fillmore	NE
Lewis	Gove	KS	Liberty	Adams	IL	Liberty	Gage	NE
Lewis	Mille Lacs	MN	Liberty	Effingham	IL	Liberty	Kearney	NE
Lewis	Holt	MO	Liberty	Carroll	IN	Liberty	Valley	NE
Lewis	New Madrid	MO	Liberty	Crawford	IN	Liberty	Warren	NJ
Lewis	Bottineau	ND	Liberty	Delaware	IN	Liberty	Sullivan	NY
Lewis	Clay	NE	Liberty	Fulton	IN	Liberty	Adams	OH
Lewis	Essex	NY	Liberty	Grant	IN	Liberty	Butler	OH
Lewis	Lewis	NY	Liberty	Hendricks	IN	Liberty	Clinton	OH
Lewis	Brown	OH	Liberty	Henry	IN	Liberty	Crawford	OH
Lewis	Atoka	OK	Liberty	Howard	IN	Liberty	Darke	OH
Lewis	Lycoming	PA	Liberty	Parke	IN	Liberty	Delaware	OH
Lewis	Northumberland	PA	Liberty	Porter	IN	Liberty	Fairfield	OH
Lewis	Union	PA	Liberty	Saint Joseph	IN	Liberty	Guernsey	OH
Lewis	Essex	VT	Liberty	Tipton	IN	Liberty	Hancock	OH
Lewisboro	Westchester	NY	Liberty	Wabash	IN	Liberty	Hardin	OH
Lewiston	Fulton	IL	Liberty	Warren	IN	Liberty	Henry	OH
Lewiston	Niagara	NY	Liberty	Wells	IN	Liberty	Highland	OH
Lewiston	Columbia	WI	Liberty	White	IN	Liberty	Jackson	OH
Lewisville	Forsyth	NC	Liberty	Barton	KS	Liberty	Knox	OH
Lewisville	Chester	SC	Liberty	Clark	KS	Liberty	Licking	OH
Lexington	McLean	IL	Liberty	Coffey	KS	Liberty	Logan	OH
Lexington	Scott	IN	Liberty	Decatur	KS	Liberty	Mercer	OH
Lexington	Clark	KS	Liberty	Dickinson	KS	Liberty	Putnam	OH
Lexington	Johnson	KS	Liberty	Elk	KS	Liberty	Ross	OH
Lexington	Middlesex	MA	Liberty	Geary	KS	Liberty	Seneca	OH
Lexington	Sanilac	MI	Liberty	Hamilton	KS	Liberty	Trumbull	OH
Lexington	Le Sueur	MN	Liberty	Harper	KS	Liberty	Union	OH
Lexington	Lafayette	MO	Liberty	Jackson	KS	Liberty	Van Wert	OH
Lexington	Davidson	NC	Liberty	Kingman	KS	Liberty	Washington	OH
Lexington	Greene	NY	Liberty	Labette	KS	Liberty	Wood	OH
Lexington	Stark	OH	Liberty	Linn	KS	Liberty	Blaine	OK
Lexington	Cleveland	OK	Liberty	Marion	KS	Liberty	Cleveland	OK
Lexington	Lexington	SC	Liberty	Montgomery	KS	Liberty	Grant	OK
Leyden	Cook	IL	Liberty	Osborne	KS	Liberty	Haskell	OK
Leyden	Franklin	MA	Liberty	Republic	KS	Liberty	Pawnee	OK

TOWNSHIPS OF THE UNITED STATES

TOWNSHIP	COUNTY	STATE	TOWNSHIP	COUNTY	STATE	TOWNSHIP	COUNTY	STATE
Liberty	Woods	OK	Limestone	Lincoln	MN	Lincoln	Edwards	KS
Liberty	Woodward	OK	Limestone	Buncombe	NC	Lincoln	Ellsworth	KS
Liberty	Adams	PA	Limestone	Duplin	NC	Lincoln	Franklin	KS
Liberty	Bedford	PA	Limestone	Lycoming	PA	Lincoln	Grant	KS
Liberty	Centre	PA	Limestone	Montour	PA	Lincoln	Jackson	KS
Liberty	McKean	PA	Limestone	Union	PA	Lincoln	Kiowa	KS
Liberty	Mercer	PA	Limestone	Warren	PA	Lincoln	Linn	KS
Liberty	Montour	PA	Limestone	Cherokee	SC	Lincoln	Marshall	KS
Liberty	Susquehanna	PA	Limestone	Orangeburg	SC	Lincoln	Neosho	KS
Liberty	Tioga	PA	Limestone	Fall River	SD	Lincoln	Norton	KS
Liberty	Orangeburg	SC	Limington	York	ME	Lincoln	Osage	KS
Liberty	Beadle	SD	Lincklean	Chenango	NY	Lincoln	Ottawa	KS
Liberty	Brown	SD	Lincoln Heights	Hamilton	OH	Lincoln	Pawnee	KS
Liberty	Corson	SD	Lincoln	Madison	AR	Lincoln	Pottawatomie	KS
Liberty	Day	SD	Lincoln	Newton	AR	Lincoln	Pratt	KS
Liberty	Edmunds	SD	Lincoln	Adair	IA	Lincoln	Reno	KS
Liberty	Hutchinson	SD	Lincoln	Adams	IA	Lincoln	Republic	KS
Liberty	Lyman	SD	Lincoln	Audubon	IA	Lincoln	Rice	KS
Liberty	Perkins	SD	Lincoln	Appanoose	IA	Lincoln	Russell	KS
Liberty	Grant	WI	Lincoln	Black Hawk	IA	Lincoln	Sedgwick	KS
Liberty	Manitowoc	WI	Lincoln	Buena Vista	IA	Lincoln	Sherman	KS
Liberty	Outagamie	WI	Lincoln	Calhoun	IA	Lincoln	Smith	KS
Liberty	Vernon	WI	Lincoln	Cass	IA	Lincoln	Stafford	KS
Libertyville	Lake	IL	Lincoln	Cerro Gordo	IA	Lincoln	Washington	KS
Lick Creek	Little River	AR	Lincoln	Clay	IA	Lincoln	Penobscot	ME
Lick Creek	Davis	IA	Lincoln	Clinton	IA	Lincoln	Middlesex	MA
Lick Creek	Van Buren	IA	Lincoln	Dallas	IA	Lincoln	Arenac	MI
Lick Creek	Ozark	MO	Lincoln	Emmet	IA	Lincoln	Berrien	mI
Lick Mountain	Conway	AR	Lincoln	Grudy	IA	Lincoln	Clare	MI
Lick	Jackson	OH	Lincoln	Hamilton	IA	Lincoln	Huron	MI
Licking Creek	Fulton	PA	Lincoln	Harrison	IA	Lincoln	Isabella	MI
Licking	Crawford	IL	Lincoln	Iowa	IA	Lincoln	Midland	MI
Licking	Blackford	IN	Lincoln	Johnson	IA	Lincoln	Newaygo	MI
Licking	Licking	OH	Lincoln	Shelby	IN	Lincoln	Osceola	MI
Licking	Muskingum	OH	Lincoln	Buchanan	IA	Lincoln	Blue Earth	MN
Licking	Clarion	PA	Lincoln	Kossuth	IA	Lincoln	Marshall	MN
Lida	Otter Tail	MN	Lincoln	Lucas	IA	Lincoln	Washington	MN
Liddell	Clay	AR	Lincoln	Madison	IA	Lincoln	Andrew	MO
Lien	Grant	MN	Lincoln	Mahaska	IA	Lincoln	Atchison	MO
Lien	Roberts	SD	Lincoln	Monona	IA	Lincoln	Caldwell	MO
Lighting Creek	Adams	ND	Lincoln	Montgomery	IA	Lincoln	Christian	MO
Ligonier	Westmoreland	PA	Lincoln	O'Brien	IA	Lincoln	Clark	MO
Lilesville	Anson	NC	Lincoln	Page	IA	Lincoln	Dallas	MO
Lillehoff	Ramsey	ND	Lincoln	Plymouth	IA	Lincoln	Daviess	MO
Lilley	Newaygo	MI	Lincoln	Pocahontas	IA	Lincoln	Douglas	MO
Lillian	Custer	NE	Lincoln	Polk	IA	Lincoln	Grundy	MO
Lillington	Harnett	NC	Lincoln	Pottawattamie	IA	Lincoln	Harrison	MO
Lily Town	Day	SD	Lincoln	Poweshiek	IA	Lincoln	Holt	MO
Lima	Adams	IL	Lincoln	Ringgold	IA	Lincoln	Jasper	MO
Lima	Carroll	IL	Lincoln	Scott	IA	Lincoln	Lawrence	MO
Lima	Lagrange	IN	Lincoln	Shelby	IA	Lincoln	Nodaway	MO
Lima	Washtenaw	MI	Lincoln	Sioux	IA	Lincoln	Putnam	MO
Lima	Cass	MN	Lincoln	Story	IA	Lincoln	Saint Louis	MO
Lima	Beaverhead	MT	Lincoln	Tama	IA	Lincoln	Stone	MO
Lima	Livingston	NY	Lincoln	Union	IA	Lincoln	Powell	MT
Lima	Licking	OH	Lincoln	Warren	IA	Lincoln	Pembina	ND
Lima	Grant	WI	Lincoln	Winnebago	IA	Lincoln	Antelope	NE
Lima	Pepin	WI	Lincoln	Winneshiek	IA	Lincoln	Cuming	NE
Lima	Rock	WI	Lincoln	Worth	IA	Lincoln	Franklin	NE
Lima	Sheboygan	WI	Lincoln	Wright	IA	Lincoln	Gage	NE
Lime Creek	Cerro Gordo	IA	Lincoln	Ogle	IL	Lincoln	Kearney	NE
Lime Creek	Washington	IA	Lincoln	Hendricks	IN	Lincoln	Knox	NE
Lime Lake	Murray	MN	Lincoln	La Porte	IN	Lincoln	Grafton	NH
Lime	Blue Earth	MN	Lincoln	Newton	IN	Lincoln	Madison	NY
Limerick	York	ME	Lincoln	Saint Joseph	IN	Lincoln	Morrow	OH
Limerick	Montgomery	PA	Lincoln	White	IN	Lincoln	Alfalfa	OK
Limeston	Clarion	PA	Lincoln	Anderson	KS	Lincoln	Blaine	OK
Limestone	Franklin	AR	Lincoln	Butler	KS	Lincoln	Caddo	OK
Limestone	Kankakee	IL	Lincoln	Cloud	KS	Lincoln	Comanche	OK
Limestone	Peoria	IL	Lincoln	Coffey	KS	Lincoln	Dewey	OK
Limestone	Jewell	KS	Lincoln	Crawford	KS	Lincoln	Garfield	OK
Limestone	Aroostook	ME	Lincoln	Decatur	KS	Lincoln	Okfuskee	OK
Limestone	Alger	MI	Lincoln	Dickinson	KS	Lincoln	Oklahoma	OK

TOWNSHIPS OF THE UNITED STATES

TOWNSHIP	COUNTY	STATE	TOWNSHIP	COUNTY	STATE	TOWNSHIP	COUNTY	STATE
Lincoln	Seminole	OK	Linton	Ward	ND	Little Robe	Dewey	OK
Lincoln	Bedford	PA	Linton	Coshocton	OH	Little Robe	Ellis	OK
Lincoln	Huntingdon	PA	Linville	Avery	NC	Little Rock Creek	Mitchell	NC
Lincoln	Somerset	PA	Linville	Burke	NC	Little Rock	Kendall	IL
Lincoln	Providence	RI	Linwood	Anoka	MN	LIttle Rock	Nobles	MN
Lincoln	Bon Homme	SD	Linwood	Butler	NE	Little Sauk	Todd	MN
Lincoln	Brown	SD	Linwood	Portage	WI	Little Sioux	Harrison	IA
Lincoln	Clark	SD	Lipp	Emmons	ND	Little Sioux	Woodbury	IA
Lincoln	Corson	SD	Lippert	Stutsman	ND	Little Suamico	Oconto	WI
Lincoln	Douglas	SD	Lisbon	New London	CT	Little Texas	Craighead	AR
Lincoln	Hyde	SD	Lisbon	Kendall	IL	Little Texas	Scott	AR
Lincoln	Jones	SD	Lisbon	Androscoggin	ME	Little	Harper	OK
Lincoln	Lincoln	SD	Lisbon	Yellow Medicine	MN	Little Traverse	Emmet	MI
Lincoln	McPherson	SD	Lisbon	Sampson	NC	Little Valley	McPherson	KS
Lincoln	Perkins	SD	Lisbon	Grafton	NH	Little Valley	Cattaraugus	NY
Lincoln	Potter	SD	Lisbon	Saint Lawrence	NY	Little Walnut	Butler	KS
Lincoln	Spink	SD	Lisbon	Davison	SD	Little Wolf	Waupaca	WI
Lincoln	Tripp	SD	Lisbon	Juneau	WI	Little York	Nevada	CA
Lincoln	Addison	VT	Lisbon	Waukesha	WI	Littlefield	Emmet	MI
Lincoln	Adams	WI	Liscomb	Marshall	IA	Littleton	Aroostook	ME
Lincoln	Bayfield	WI	Lisle	De Page	IL	Littleton	Middlesex	MA
Lincoln	Buffalo	WI	Lisle	Broome	NY	Littleton	Halifax	NC
Lincoln	Burnett	WI	Lismore	Nobles	MN	Littleton	Grafton	NH
Lincoln	Eau Claire	WI	Liston	Woodbury	IA	Littleton	Schuyler	NH
Lincoln	Forest	WI	Litchfield	Litchfield	CT	Litaker	Rowan	NC
Lincoln	Kewaunee	WI	Litchfield	Kennebec	ME	Litteral	Washington	AR
Lincoln	Monroe	WI	Litchfield	Hillsdale	MI	Live Oak	Drew	AR
Lincoln	Polk	WI	Litchfield	Meeker	MN	Lively Grove	Washington	IL
Lincoln	Trempealeau	WI	Litchfield	Hillsborough	NH	Livepool	Fulton	IL
Lincoln	Vilas	WI	Litchfield	Herkimer	NY	Livermore Falls	Androscoggin	ME
Lincoln	Wood	WI	Litchfield	Medina	OH	Livermore	Androscoggin	ME
Lincoln Valley	Divide	ND	Litchfield	Bradford	PA	Liverpool	Columbiana	OH
Lincolnton	Lincoln	NC	Litchville	La Moure	ND	Liverpool	Medina	OH
Lincolnville	Waldo	ME	Little Beaver	Lawrence	PA	Liverpool	Perry	PA
Lind	Roseau	MN	Little Black	Randolph	AR	Livingston	Otsego	MI
Lind	Grand Forks	ND	Little Black	Taylor	WI	Livingston	Essex	NJ
Lind	Waupaca	WI	Little Blue	Washington	KS	Livingston	Columbia	NY
Lindaas	Traill	ND	Little Blue	Adams	NE	Livonia	Sherburne	MN
Lindahl	Williams	ND	Little Britain	Lancaster	PA	Lizard	Pocahontas	IA
Linden Grove	Saint Louis	MN	Little Buffalo	Jackson	SD	Lianos	Sherman	KS
Linden	Winnebago	iA	Little Caney	Chautauqua	KS	Lloyd	Dickinson	IA
Linden	Brown	MN	Little Coharie	Sampson	NC	Lloyd	Ulster	NY
Linden	Christian	MO	Little Compton	Newport	RI	Livonia	Livingston	NY
Linden	Cavalier	ND	Little Deep	McHenry	ND	Loam	Cavalier	ND
Linden	Iowa	WI	Little Egg Harbor	Ocean	NJ	Loami	Sangamon	IL
Linder	Greene	IL	Little Elk	Todd	MN	Loch Arbour Village	Monmouth	nJ
Linder	McLean	ND	Little Falls	Morrison	MN	Locke	Elkhart	IN
Lindina	Juneau	WI	Little Falls	Herkimer	NY	Locke	Ingham	MI
Lindley	Mercer	MO	Little Falls	Monroe	WI	Locke	Rowan	NC
Lindley	Steuben	NY	Little	Passaic	NJ	Locke	Cayuga	NY
Lindsay	Tulare	CA	Little Grant	Grant	WI	Lockhart	Pike	IN
Lindsay	Garvin	OK	Little Lake	Mendocino	CA	Lockhart	Norman	MN
Lindsey	Benton	MO	Little Machinaw	Tazewell	IL	Lockland	Hamilton	OH
Lingo	Macon	MO	Little Mahanoy	Northunberland	PA	Lockport	Will	IL
Linn Creek	Van Buren	AR	Little Oak	Corson	SD	Lockport	Haskell	KS
Linn	Cedar	IA	Little Pine	Crow Wing	MN	Lockport	Saint Joseph	MI
Linn	Dallas	IA	Little Prairie	Pemiscot	MO	Lockport	Niagara	NY
Linn	Linn	IA	Little Rice	Oneida	WI	Lockridge	Jefferson	IA
Linn	Warren	IA	Little River	Little River	AR	Lockwood	Dade	MO
Linn	Woodford	IL	Little River	Mississippi	AR	Lockwood	Renville	ND
Linn	Washington	KS	Little River	Poinsett	AR	Lockwood	Roberts	SD
Linn	Audrain	MO	Little River	Reno	KS	Lockwoods Folly	Brunswick	NC
Linn	Cedar	MO	Little River	Pemiscot	MO	Loco	Stephen	OK
Linn	Christian	MO	Little River	Alexander	NC	Locust Bayou	Calhoun	AR
Linn	Dent	MO	Little River	Caldwell	NC	Locust Creek	Linn	MO
Linn	Monteau	MO	Little River	Montgomery	NC	Locust Grove	Stone	AR
Linn	Osage	MO	Little River (No. 10)	Moore	NC	Locust Grove	Fremont	IA
Linn	Hand	SD	Little River	Orange	NC	Locust Grove	Jefferson	IA
Linn	Walworth	WI	Little River	Transylvania	NC	Locust Hill	Caswell	NC
Linneus	Aroostook	ME	Little River	Wake	NC	Locust	Christian	IL
Linsell	Marshall	MN	Little River	Cleveland	OK	Locust	Columbia	PA
Linton	Allamakee	IA	Little River	Horry	SC	Loda	Iroquois	IL
Linton	Vigo	IN	Little River	Oconto	WI	Loda	Reno	KS

TOWNSHIP	COUNTY	STATE	TOWNSHIP	COUNTY	STATE	TOWNSHIP	COUNTY	STATE
Lodema	Pembina	ND	Logan	Blaine	OK	Long Lake	Grand Traverse	MI
Lodgepole	Perkins	SD	Logan	Garfield	OK	Long Lake	Crow Wing	MN
Lodi	Washtenaw	MI	Logan	Kingfisher	OK	Long Lake	Watonwan	MN
Lodi	Mower	MN	Logan	Blair	PA	Long Lake	Burleigh	ND
Lodi	Seneca	NY	Logan	Clinton	PA	Long Lake	Hamilton	NY
Lodi	Athens	OH	Logan	Huntingdon	PA	Long Lake	Florence	WI
Lodi	spink	SD	Logan	Beadle	SD	Long Lake	Washburn	WI
Lodi	Columbia	WI	Logan	Clark	SD	Long Point	Livingston	IL
Lodomillo	Clayton	IA	Logan	Hand	SD	Long Prairie	Todd	MN
Logan Center	Grand Forks	ND	Logan	Hughes	SD	Long Prairie	Mississippi	MO
Logan Store	Rutherford	NC	Logan	Jerauld	SD	Long Rapids	Alpena	MI
Logan	Baxter	AR	Logan	Minnehaha	SD	Long	Blaine	OK
Logan	Benton	AR	Logan	Potter	SD	Long	Sequoyah	OK
Logan	Independence	AR	Logan	Sanborn	SD	Long Valley	Mendocino	CA
Logan	Logan	AR	Logansport	Logan	KS	Long X	McKenzie	ND
Logan	Calhoun	IA	Lohnes	Benson	ND	Longfellow	McLean	ND
Logan	Clay	IA	Lola	Cherokee	KS	Longmeadow	Hampden	MA
Logan	Ida	IA	Loleta	Humboldt	CA	Longrun	Ozark	MO
Logan	Lyon	IA	Lomax	Henderson	IL	Longswamp	Berks	PA
Logan	Marshall	IA	Lomira	Dodge	WI	Longton	Elks	KS
Logan	Sioux	IA	Lon Norris	Sebastian	AR	Longview	Ashley	AR
Logan	Winnebago	IA	London Britain	Chester	PA	Longview	Foster	ND
Logan	Peoria	IL	London Grove	Chester	PA	Longwood	Pettis	MO
Logan	Dearborn	IN	London	Sumner	KS	Longwood	Kay	OK
Logan	Fountain	IN	London	Monroe	MI	Longwood	Clark	WI
Logan	Pike	IN	London	Freeborn	MN	Lonoke	Lonoke	AR
Logan	Allen	KS	Londonderry	Rockingham	NH	Looking Glass	Clinton	IL
Logan	Barton	KS	Londonderry	Guernsey	OH	Lookout	Ellis	KS
Logan	Butler	KS	Londonderry	Bedford	PA	Loomer	Fall River	SD
Logan	Comanche	KS	Londonderry	Chester	PA	Loon Lake	Cass	MN
Logan	Decatur	KS	Londonderry	Dauphin	PA	Looney	Polk	MO
Logan	Dickinson	KS	Londonderry	Windham	VT	Looney	Harmon	OK
Logan	Edwards	KS	Lone Elm	Anderson	KS	Lopatcong	Warren	NJ
Logan	Gray	KS	Lone Grove	Fayette	IL	Loquemont	McLean	ND
Logan	Lincoln	KS	Lone Grove	Carter	OK	Lorain	Nobles	MN
Logan	Marion	KS	Lone Hill	Hot Springs	AR	Lorain	Polk	wI
Logan	Marshall	KS	Lone Mound	Caddo	OK	Loraine	Henry	IL
Logan	Meade	KS	Lone Oak	Bates	MO	Loramie	Shelby	OH
Logan	Mitchell	KS	Lone Pine	Lincoln	AR	Loran	Stephenson	IL
Logan	Ottawa	KS	Lone Pine	Itasca	MN	Lorance	Bollinger	MO
Logan	Pawnee	KS	Lone Rock	Baxter	AR	Lordsburg	Bottineau	ND
Logan	Phillips	KS	Lone Rock	Caddo	OK	Lordstown	Trumbull	OH
Logan	Pratt	KS	Lone Rock	Moody	SD	Loretta	Grand Forks	ND
Logan	Rawlins	KS	Lone Star	Rush	KS	Lorraine	Dickey	ND
Logan	Rooks	KS	Lone Star	Wagoner	OK	Lorraine	Jefferson	NY
Logan	Sheridan	KS	Lone Star	Gregory	SD	Los Angeles	Los Angeles	CA
Logan	Sherman	KS	Lone Star	Tripp	SD	Lost Creek	Vigo	IN
Logan	Smith	KS	Lone Tree	Clay	IA	Lost Creek	Wayne	MO
Logan	Washington	KS	Lone Tree	McPherson	KS	Lost Creek	Platte	NE
Logan	Mason	MI	Lone Tree	Pottawatomie	KS	Lost Grove	Webster	IA
Logan	Ogemaw	MI	Lone Tree	Chippewa	MN	Lost Island	Palo Alto	IA
Logan	Aitkin	MN	Lone Tree	Golden Valley	ND	Lost River	Martin	IN
Logan	Grant	MN	Lone Tree	Clay	NE	Lost Springs	Marion	KS
Logan	Reynolds	MO	Lone Tree	Merrick	NE	Lostcreek	Miami	OH
Logan	Wayne	MO	Lone Tree	Charles Mix	SD	Lostwood	Mountrail	ND
Logan	Burleigh	ND	Lone Tree	Perkins	SD	Lotts Creek	Kossuth	IA
Logan	Adams	NE	Lone Tree	Tripp	SD	Lotts Creek	Ringgold	IA
Logan	Antelope	NE	Long Acre	Beaufort	NC	Loud	Montmorency	MI
Logan	Buffalo	NE	Long Beach	Los Angeles	CA	Loudon	Fayette	IL
Logan	Burt	NE	Long Beach	Ocean	NJ	Loudon	Merrimack	NH
Logan	Clay	NE	Long Branch	Saline	IL	Loudon	Carroll	OH
Logan	Cuming	NE	Long Crane	Abbeville	SC	Loudon	Seneca	OH
Logan	Dixon	NE	Long Creek	Boone	AR	Louisburg	Montgomery	KY
Logan	Dodge	NE	Long Creek	Carroll	AR	Louisburg (No. 10)	Franklin	NC
Logan	Franklin	NE	Long Creek	Searcy	AR	Louisville	Clay	IL
Logan	Gage	NE	Long Creek	Decatur	IA	Louisville	Pottawatomie	KS
Logan	Kearney	NE	Long Creek	Macon	IL	Louisville	Red Lake	MN
Logan	Knox	NE	Long Creek (No. 11)	Mecklenburg	NC	Louisville	Scott	MN
Logan	Sherman	NE	Long Creek	Pender	NC	Louisville	Saint Lawrence	NY
Logan	Gloucester	NJ	Long Creek	Divide	ND	Loup City	Sherman	NE
Logan	Clark	NV	Long Hill	Surry	NC	Loup Ferry	Nance	NE
Logan	Auglaize	OH	Long Hollow	Roberts	SD	Loup	Buffalo	NE
Logan	Beaver	OK	Long Island	Phillips	KS	Loup	Custer	NE

TOWNSHIPS OF THE UNITED STATES

TOWNSHIP	COUNTY	STATE	TOWNSHIP	COUNTY	STATE	TOWNSHIP	COUNTY	STATE
Loup	Merrick	NE	Lower Turkey Foot	Somerset	PA	Lyman	York	ME
Loup	Platte	NE	Lower Tyrone	Fayette	PA	Lyman	Burleigh	ND
Louriston	Chippewa	MN	Lower Windsor	York	PA	Lyman	Grafton	NH
Loutre	Audrain	MO	Lower Yoder	Cambria	PA	Lyme	New London	CT
Loutre	Montgomery	MO	Lowery	Stutsman	ND	Lyme	Grafton	NH
Love	Vermilion	IL	Lowhill	Lehigh	PA	Lyme	Jefferson	NY
Lovejoy	Iroquois	IL	Lowland	Mountrail	ND	Lyme	Huron	OH
Lovelace	Wilkes	NC	Lowndes	Colleton	SC	Lynch	Texas	MO
Lovelady	Burke	NC	Lowndesville	Abbeville	SC	Lynch	Boyd	NE
Lovelady	Caldwell	NC	Lowrance	Murray	OK	Lynch	Florence	SC
Loveland	Tillman	OK	Lowry Town	Walworth	SD	Lynchburg	Mason	IL
Lovell	Jones	IA	Lowville	Lewis	NY	Lynchburg	Lee	SC
Lovell	Dickey	ND	Lowville	Murray	MN	Lynd	Lyon	MN
Lovells	Crawford	MI	Lowville	Columbia	WI	Lyndeborough	Hillsborough	NH
Lovett	Jennings	IN	Loyal	McKenzie	ND	Lynden	Stearns	MN
Lovington	Moultrie	IL	Loyal	Clark	WI	Lynden	Whatcom	WA
Low Gap	Johnson	AR	Loyalhanna	Westmoreland	PA	Lyndhurst	Bergen	NJ
Low Gap	Newton	AR	Loyalsock	Lycoming	PA	Lyndon	Whiteside	IL
Lowe	Moultrie	IL	Loyalton	Sierra	CA	Lyndon	Washtenaw	MI
Lowe	Washington	KS	Loyalton	Edmunds	SD	Lyndon	Cattaraugus	NY
Lowe	Kay	OK	Lubec	Washington	ME	Lyndon	Caledonia	VT
Lowe	Noble	OK	Lucas	Crittenden	AR	Lyndon	Juneau	WI
Lowe	Deuel	SD	Lucas	Effingham	IL	Lyndon	Sheboygan	WI
Lowell	Cherokee	KS	Lucas	Lyon	MN	Lynn Grove	Jasper	IA
Lowell	Rooks	KS	Lucas	Potter	SD	Lynn Lane	Tulsa	OK
Lowell	Oxford	ME	Lucas	Dunn	WI	Lynn	Sioux	IA
Lowell	Penobscot	ME	Luce	Spencer	IN	Lynn	Henry	IL
Lowell	Kent	MI	Lucile	Grady	OK	Lynn	Knox	IL
Lowell	Polk	MN	Luck	Polk	WI	Lynn	Posey	IN
Lowell	Kearney	NE	Lucy	Burke	ND	Lynn	Saint Clair	MI
Lowell	Marshall	SD	Ludell	Rawlins	KS	Lynn	McLeod	MN
Lowell	Potter	SD	Ludington	Eau Claire	WI	Lynn	Wells	ND
Lowell	Orleans	VT	Ludlow	San Bernadino	CA	Lynn	Clay	NE
Lowell	Dodge	WI	Ludlow	Allamakee	IA	Lynn	Hardin	OH
Lower Allen	Cumberland	PA	Ludlow	Champaign	IL	Lynn	Kingfisher	OK
Lower Alloways Creek	Salem	NJ	Ludlow	Hampden	MA	Lynn	Lehigh	PA
Lower Alsace	Berks	PA	Ludlow	Aroostook	ME	Lynn	Day	SD
Lower Augusta	Northumberland	PA	Ludlow	Washington	OH	Lynn	Lincoln	SD
Lower Chanceford	York	PA	Ludlow	Windsor	VT	Lynn	Moody	SD
Lower Chichester	Delaware	PA	Lukin	Lawrence	IL	Lynn	Clark	WI
Lower Conetoe	Edgecombe	NC	Lulu	Mitchell	KS	Lynne	Oneida	WI
Lower Creek	Burke	NC	Lumber Bridge	Robeson	NC	Lynnfield	Essex	MA
Lower Creek	Caldwell	NC	Lumber	Cameron	PA	Lynnville	Ogle	IL
Lower Fishing Creek	Edgecombe	NC	Lumberland	Sullivan	NY	Lyon	Hamilton	IA
Lower Fork	Burke	NC	Lumberton	Robeson	NC	Lyon	Lyon	IA
Lower Frankford	Cumberland	PA	Lumberton	Burlington	NJ	Lyon	Cherokee	KS
Lower Frederick	Montgomery	PA	Lummi Island	Whatcom	WA	Lyon	Cloud	KS
Lower Gwynedd	Montgomery	PA	Lund	Douglas	MN	Lyon	Decatur	KS
Lower Heidelberg	Berk	PA	Lund	Ward	ND	Lyon	Dickinson	KS
Lower Hominy	Buncombe	NC	Lund	White Pine	NV	Lyon	Geary	KS
Lower Macumgie	Lehigh	PA	Lund	Lyman	SD	Lyon	Oakland	MI
Lower Mahanoy	Northumberland	PA	Lunenburg	Izard	AR	Lyon	Roscommon	MI
Lower Makefield	Bucks	PA	Lunenburg	Worcester	MA	Lyon	Franklin	MO
Lower Merion	Montgomery	PA	Lunenburg	Essex	VT	Lyon	Knox	MO
Lower Mifflin	Cumberland	PA	Lunsford	Pointsett	AR	Lyon	Lewis	MO
Lower Milford	Lehigh	PA	Lura	Faribault	MN	Lyon	Stutsman	ND
Lower Moreland	Montgomery	PA	Lura	Grant	SD	Lyon	Brule	SD
Lower Mount Bethel	Northampton	PA	Luray	Ruswell	KS	Lyons	Mills	IA
Lower Nazareth	Northampton	PA	Lurgan	Franklin	PA	Lyons	Cook	IL
Lower North	Sharp	AR	Luther	Oklahoma	OK	Lyons	Ionia	MI
Lower Oxford	Chester	PA	Luverne	Kossuth	IA	Lyons	Lyon	MN
Lower Paxton	Dauphin	PA	Luverne	Rock	MN	Lyons	Wadena	MN
Lower Pottsgrove	Montgomery	PA	Luxemburg	Stearns	MN	Lyons	Wayne	NY
Lower Providence	Montgomery	PA	Luxemburg	Kewaunee	WI	Lyons	Calhoun	SC
Lower Red Lake	Beltrami	MN	Luzerne	Fayette	PA	Lyons	Minnehaha	SD
Lower Salford	Montgomery	PA	Lycoming	Lycoming	PA	Lyons	Walworth	WI
Lower Saucon	Northampton	PA	Lyda	Macon	MO	Lyonsdale	Lewis	NY
Lower Southampton	Bucks	PA	Lykens	Crawford	OH	Lyra	Blue Earth	MN
Lower Surrounded Hill	Prairie	AR	Lykens	Dauphin	PA	Lysander	Onondage	NY
Lower Swatar	Dauphin	PA	Lyle	Mower	MN			
Lower Towamensing	Carbon	PA	Lyman Northeast	Lyman	SD		—M—	
Lower Town Creek	Edgecombe	NC	Lyman South	Lyman	SD			
Lower	Cape May	NJ	Lyman	Ford	IL	Mable	Griggs	ND

TOWNSHIP	COUNTY	STATE	TOWNSHIP	COUNTY	STATE	TOWNSHIP	COUNTY	STATE
Macdoel	Siskiyou	CA	Madison	Harrison	MO	Maine Prairie	Stearns	MN
Macedon	Wayne	NY	Madison	Jasper	MO	Maine	Linn	IA
Macedonia	Pottawattamie	IA	Madison	Johnson	MO	Maine	Cook	IL
Macedonia	Summit	OH	Madison	Mercer	MO	Maine	Grundy	IL
Machias	Washington	ME	Madison	Polk	MO	Maine	Otter Tail	MN
Machias	Cattaraugus	NY	Madison	Madison	MT	Maine	Adams	ND
Machiasport	Washington	ME	Madison	Guilford	NC	Maine	Broome	NY
Machire	Haskell	OK	Madison	Rockingham	NC	Maine	Marathon	WI
Mackford	Green Lake	WI	Madison	Hettinger	ND	Maine	Outagamie	WI
Mackinaw	Tazewell	IL	Madison	Fillmore	NE	Makanda	Jackson	IL
Mackinaw	Cheboygan	MI	Madison	Carroll	NH	Makee	Allamakee	IA
Macomb City	McDonough	IL	Madison	Middlesex	NJ	Malaga	Monroe	OH
Macomb	McDonough	IL	Madison	Madison	NY	Malaka	Jasper	IA
Macomb	Macomb	MI	Madison	Butler	OH	Malcolm	McLean	ND
Macomb	Saint Lawrence	NY	Madison	Clark	OH	Malcom	Poweshiek	IA
Macon	Bureau	IL	Madison	Columbiana	OH	Malibu	Los Angeles	CA
Macon	Harvey	KS	Madison	Fairfield	OH	Mallard Creek	Mecklenburg	NC
Macon	Lenawee	MI	Madison	Fayette	OH	Mallory	Clayton	IA
Macon	Franklin	NE	Madison	Franklin	OH	Malmo	Aitkin	MN
Macsville	Grant	MN	Madison	Guernsey	OH	Malone	Tazewell	IL
Macville	Aitkin	MN	Madison	Hancock	OH	Malone	Franklin	NY
Mad River	Humboldt	CA	Madison	Highland	OH	Malta	De Kalb	IL
Mad River	Trinity	CA	Madison	Jackson	OH	Malta	Big Stone	MN
Mad River	Champaign	OH	Madison	Lake	OH	Malta	Saratoga	NY
Mad River	Clark	OH	Madison	Licking	OH	Malta	Morgan	OH
Mad River	Montgomery	OH	Madison	Montgomery	OH	Maltby	Perkins	SD
Madawaska	Aroostook	ME	Madison	Muskingum	OH	Malung	Roseau	MN
Madbury	Strafford	NH	Madison	Perry	OH	Malvern	Mills	IA
Madreia	Hamilton	OH	Madison	Pickaway	OH	Mamakating	Sullivan	NY
Madelia	Watonwan	MN	Madison	Richland	OH	Mamaroneck	Westchester	NY
Madeline	Lassen	CA	Madison	Sandusky	OH	Mammoth Spring	Fulton	AR
Madge	Harmon	OK	Madison	Scioto	OH	Mammoth	Mono	CA
Madge	Washburn	WI	Madison	Vinton	OH	Mamre	Kandiyohi	??
Madison	Grant	AR	Madison	Williams	OH	Manalapan	Monmouth	NJ
Madison	Howard	AR	Madison	Washington	OK	Manannah	Meeker	MN
Madison	New Haven	CT	Madison	Armstrong	PA	Mancelona	Antrim	MI
Madison	Buchanan	IA	Madison	Clarion	PA	Manchester	Dallas	AR
Madison	Butler	IA	Madison	Columbia	PA	Manchester	Hartford	CT
Madison	Clarke	IA	Madison	Lackawanna	PA	Manchester	Boone	IL
Madison	Fremont	IA	Madison	Edmunds	SD	Manchester	Dearborn	IN
Madison	Hancock	IA	Madison	Grant	SD	Manchester	Essex	MA
Madison	Johnson	IA	Madison	Dane	WI	Manchester	Kennebec	ME
Madison	Jones	IA	Madrid	Franklin	ME	Manchester	Washtenaw	MI
Madison	Lee	IA	Madrid	Saint Lawrence	NY	Manchester	Freeborn	MN
Madison	Madison	IA	Magazine	Yell	AR	Manchester	Cumberland	NC
Madison	Mahaska	IA	Magness	Independence	AR	Manchester	Ocean	NJ
Madison	Polk	IA	Magness	Lonoke	AR	Manchester	Ontario	NY
Madison	Poweshiek	IA	Magnet	Hot Spring	AR	Manchester	Adams	OH
Madison	Winneshiek	IA	Magnolia	Columbia	AR	Manchester	Morgan	OH
Madison	Richland	IL	Magnolia	Harrison	IA	Manchester	Grant	OK
Madison	Allen	IN	Magnolia	Putnam	IL	Manchester	Wayne	PA
Madison	Carroll	IN	Magnolia	Rock	MN	Manchester	York	PA
Madison	Clinton	IN	Magnolia	Duplin	NC	Manchester	Sumter	SC
Madison	Daviess	IN	Magnolia	Abbeville	SC	Manchester	Kingsbury	SD
Madison	Dubois	IN	Magnolia	Rock	WI	Manchester	Bennington	VT
Madison	Jay	IN	Magor	Hancock	IA	Manchester	Green Lake	WI
Madison	Jefferson	IN	Maguire	Tillman	OK	Manchester	Jackson	WI
Madison	Montgomery	IN	Mahanoy	Schuylkill	PA	Mandan	Ward	ND
Madison	Morgan	IN	Mahnomen Southeast	Mahnomen	MN	Mandt	Chippewa	MN
Madison	Pike	IN	Mahomet	Champaign	IL	Maneys Neck	Hertford	NC
Madison	Putnam	IN	Mahoning	Armstrong	PA	Manfred	Lac Qui Parie	MN
Madison	Saint Joseph	IN	Mahoning	Carbon	PA	Manfred	Wells	ND
Madison	Tipton	IN	Mahoning	Lawrence	PA	Mangan	Comanche	OK
Madison	Washington	IN	Mahoning	Montour	PA	Mangum	Durham	NC
Madison	Greenwood	KS	Mahto	Corson	SD	Mangum	Greer	OK
Madison	Lincoln	KS	Mahtowa	Carlton	MN	Manhattan Borough	New York	NY
Madison	Riley	KS	Mahwan	Bergen	NJ	Manhattan	Will	IL
Madison	Somerset	ME	Maiden Rock	Pierce	WI	Manhattan	Riley	KS
Madison	Lenawee	MI	Maidencreek	Berks	PA	Manheim	Herkimer	NY
Madison	Lac Qui Parie	MN	Maidstone	Essex	VT	Manheim	Lancaster	PA
Madison	Cedar	MO	Main Shore	Greene	AR	Manheim	York	PA
Madison	Clark	MO	Main	Columbia	PA	Manilla	Cavalier	ND
Madison	Grundy	MO	Maine Prairie	Solano	CA	Manistee	Manistee	MI

TOWNSHIPS OF THE UNITED STATES

TOWNSHIP	COUNTY	STATE	TOWNSHIP	COUNTY	STATE	TOWNSHIP	COUNTY	STATE
Manistique	Schoolcraft	MI	Mapleton	Cass	ND	Marion	Jennings	IN
Manito	Mason	IL	Mapleton	Minnehaha	SD	Marion	Lawrence	IN
Manitou	Mountrail	ND	Maplewood	Otter Tail	MN	Marion	Owen	IN
Manitowish Waters	Vilas	WI	Maplewood	Essex	NJ	Marion	Pike	IN
Manitowoc Rapids	Manitowoc	WI	Maquoketa	Jackson	IA	Marion	Putnam	IN
Manitowoc	Manitowoc	WI	Maquon	Knox	IL	Marion	Shelby	IN
Mankato	Blue Earth	MN	Marathon	Lapeer	MI	Marion	Bourbon	KS
Manlius	Bureau	IL	Marathon	Cortland	NY	Marion	Doniphan	KS
Manlius	La Salle	IL	Marathon	Marathon	WI	Marion	Douglas	KS
Manlius	Allegan	MI	Marble City	Newton	AR	Marion	Lincoln	KS
Manlius	Onondaga	NY	Marble	Madison	AR	Marion	Nemaha	KS
Mann	Bedford	PA	Marble	Saline	AR	Marion	Plymouth	MA
Mannford	Creek	OK	Marble	Lincoln	MN	Marion	Charlevoix	MI
Manning	Clarendon	SC	Marble	Saunders	NE	Marion	Livingston	MI
Manning	Dillon	SC	Marble	Sequoyah	OK	Marion	Osceola	MI
Mannings	Nash	NC	Marblehead	Essex	MA	Marion	Saginaw	MI
Mannington	Salem	NJ	Marbletown	Ulster	NY	Marion	Sanilac	MI
Manns	Stutsman	ND	Marboe	Sargent	ND	Marion	Olmsted	MN
Manor	Armstrong	PA	Marceline	Linn	MO	Marion	Buchanan	MO
Manor	Lancaster	PA	Marcell	Itasca	MN	Marion	Cole	MO
Mansfield	Tolland	CT	Marcellon	Columbia	WI	Marion	Dade	MO
Mansfield	Bristol	MA	Marcellus	Cass	MI	Marion	Daviess	MO
Mansfield	Iron	MI	Marcellus	Onondage	NY	Marion	Grundy	MO
Mansfield	Freeborn	MN	Marcus	Cherokee	IA	Marion	Harrison	MO
Mansfield	Barnes	ND	Marcy	Boone	IA	Marion	Jasper	MO
Mansfield	Burlington	NJ	Marcy	Oneida	NY	Marion	Mercer	MO
Mansfield	Warren	NJ	Marella	Cimarron	OK	Marion	Monroe	MO
Mansfield	Cattaraugus	NY	Marena	Hodgeman	KS	Marion	Newton	MO
Manston	Wilkin	MN	Marengo	Iowa	IA	Marion	Polk	MO
Manteno	Kankakee	IL	Marengo	McHenry	IL	Marion	Saint Francois	MO
Manter	Stanton	KS	Marengo	Calhoun	MI	Marion	McDowell	NC
Mantorville	Dodge	MN	Marengo	Ashland	WI	Marion	Bowman	ND
Mantrap	Hubbard	MN	Marenisco	Gogebic	MI	Marion	Franklin	NE
Mantua	Monroe	IA	Margaretta	Erie	OH	Marion	Wayne	NY
Mantua	Gloucester	NJ	Margaret	Ward	ND	Marion	Allen	OH
Mantua	Portage	OH	Mariaville	Hancock	ME	Marion	Clinton	OH
Manyaska	Martin	MN	Marie Saline	Ashley	AR	Marion	Fayette	OH
Maple Creek	Outagamie	WI	Marie	Madison	IL	Marion	Hancock	OH
Maple Falls	Whatcom	WA	Marie	Emmons	ND	Marion	Hardin	OH
Maple Forest	Crawford	MI	Marietta New	Washington	OH	Marion	Henry	OH
Maple Grove	Barry	MI	Marietta	Marshall	IA	Marion	Hocking	OH
Maple Grove	Manistee	MI	Marietta	Robeson	NC	Marion	Marion	OH
Maple Grove	Saginaw	MI	Marietta	Saunder	NE	Marion	Mercer	OH
Maple Grove	Becker	MN	Marietta	Whatcom	WA	Marion	Morgan	OH
Maple Grove	Crow Wing	MN	Marietta	Crawford	WI	Marion	Noble	OH
Maple Grove	Barron	WI	Marilla	Manistee	MI	Marion	Pike	OH
Maple Grove	Manitowoc	WI	Marilla	Erie	NY	Marion	Dewey	OK
Maple Grove	Shawano	WI	Marindahl	Yankton	SD	Marion	Beaver	PA
Maple Hill	Wabaunsee	KS	Marion	Bradley	AR	Marion	Berks	PA
Maple Lake	Wright	MN	Marion	Drew	AR	Marion	Butler	PA
Maple Plain	Barron	WI	Marion	Lawrence	AR	Marion	Centre	PA
Maple Ridge	Alpena	MI	Marion	Ouachita	AR	Marion	Marion	SC
Maple Ridge	Delta	MI	Marion	Phillips	AR	Marion	Turner	SD
Maple Ridge	Beltrami	MN	Marion	Sebastian	AR	Marion	Grant	WI
Maple Ridge	Isanti	MN	Marion	White	AR	Marion	Juneau	WI
Maple River	Carroll	IA	Marion	Clayton	IA	Marion	Waushara	WI
Maple River	Emmet	MI	Marion	Davis	IA	Mariposa	Jasper	IA
Maple River	Cass	ND	Marion	Franklin	IA	Mariposa	Saunders	NE
Maple Shade	Burlington	NJ	Marion	Hamilton	IA	Marissa	Saint Clair	IL
Maple	Ida	IA	Marion	Henry	IA	Mark	Defiance	OH
Maple	Monona	IA	Marion	Lee	IA	Markey	Roscommon	MI
Maple	Cowley	KS	Marion	Linn	IA	Marks Creek	Richmond	NC
Maple	Cass	MN	Marion	Marshall	IA	Marks Creek	Wake	NC
Maple	Dickey	ND	Marion	Plymouth	IA	Mariar	Jerauld	SD
Maple	Dodge	NE	Marion	Washington	IA	Marlboro	Delaware	OH
Maple	Canadian	OK	Marion	Lee	IL	Marlboro	Stark	OH
Maple	Douglas	WI	Marion	Ogle	IL	Marlboro	Monmouth	NJ
Maple Valley	Buena Vista	IA	Marion	Allen	IN	Marlboro	Windham	VT
Maple Valley	Montcalm	MI	Marion	Boone	IN	Marlborough	Hartford	CT
Maple Valley	Oconto	WI	Marion	Decatur	IN	Marlborough	Cheshire	NH
Maplehurst	Taylor	WI	Marion	Dubois	IN	Marlborough	Ulster	NY
Mapleton	Aroostook	ME	Marion	Hendricks	IN	Marlborough	Montgomery	PA
Mapleton	Blue Earth	MN	Marion	Jasper	IN	Marlette	Sanilac	MI

TOWNSHIPS OF THE UNITED STATES

TOWNSHIP	COUNTY	STATE
Marlow	Cheshire	NH
Marmaton	Allen	KS
Marmaton	Bourbon	KS
Maroa	Macon	IL
Marple	Delaware	PA
Marquand	Madison	MO
Marquette	McPherson	KS
Marquette	Mackinac	MI
Marquette	Marquette	MI
Marquette	Green Lake	WI
Marquis	McKenzie	ND
Marrowbone	Moultrie	IL
Marrs Hill	Washington	AR
Marrs	Posey	IN
Mars Hill	Lafayette	AR
Mars Hill	Aroostook	ME
Mars Hill	Madison	NC
Marseilles	Wyandot	OH
Marsh Creek	Mahnomen	MN
Marsh Grove	Marshall	MN
Marsh	Surry	NC
Marsh	Barnes	ND
Marshall	White	AR
Marshall	Louisa	IA
Marshall	Marshall	IA
Marshall	Pocahontas	IA
Marshall	Taylor	IA
Marshall	Clark	IL
Marshall	Lawrence	IN
Marshall	Calhoun	MI
Marshall	Mower	MN
Marshall	Platte	MO
Marshall	Saline	MO
Marshall	Madison	NC
Marshall	Williams	ND
Marshall	Clay	NE
Marshall	Oneida	NY
Marshall	Highland	OH
Marshall	Garfield	OK
Marshall	Logan	OK
Marshall	Kiowa	OK
Marshall	Allegheny	PA
Marshall	Spokane	WA
Marshall	Richland	WI
Marshall	Rusk	WI
Marshallberg	Carteret	NC
Marshan	Dakota	MN
Marshell	Independence	AR
Marshfield	Plymouth	MA
Marshfield	Washington	ME
Marshfield	Lincoln	MN
Marshfield	Perkins	SD
Marshfield	Washington	VT
Marshfield	Fond du Lac	WI
Marshfield	Wood	WI
Marshville	Union	NC
Marston Moor	Stutsman	ND
Martell	Pierce	WI
Martha	Jackson	OK
Martic	Lancaster	PA
Martin	Conway	AR
Martin	Pope	AR
Martin	Crawford	IL
Martin	McLean	IL
Martin	Kiowa	KS
Martin	Smith	KS
Martin	Allegan	MI
Martin	Rock	MN
Martin	Sheridan	ND
Martin	Walsh	ND
Martin	Hall	NE
Martin	Harmon	OK
Martin	Muskogee	OK
Martin	Anderson	SC
Martin	Perkins	SD
Martinsburg	Pike	IL
Martinsburg	Renville	MN
Martinsburg	Lewis	NY
Martinsville	Clark	IL
Martinton	Iroquois	IL
Martiny	Mecosta	MI
Mary Ann	Licking	OH
Mary	Norman	MN
Maryland	Ogle	IL
Maryland	Ward	ND
Maryland	Otsego	NY
Marysland	Swift	MN
Marysville	Yuba	CA
Marysville	Marshall	KS
Marysville	Miami	KS
Marysville	Wright	MN
Masardis	Aroostook	ME
Mascoutah	Saint Clair	IL
Mashpee	Barnstable	MA
Mason City	Cerro Gordo	IA
Mason City	Mason	IL
Mason	Yell	AR
Mason	Cerro Gordo	IA
Mason	Taylor	IA
Mason	Effingham	IL
Mason	Arenac	MI
Mason	Cass	MI
Mason	Murray	MN
Mason	Marion	MO
Mason	Lawrence	OH
Mason	Hillsborough	NH
Mason	Bayfield	WI
Mason Valley	Benton	AR
Mason Valley	Lyon	NV
Masonboro	New Hanover	NC
Masonville	Delta	MI
Masonville	Delaware	NY
Massena	Cass	IA
Massena	Saint Lawrence	NY
Massie	Warren	OH
Massillon	Cedar	IA
Massillon	Wayne	IL
Massillon	Stark	OH
Mastodon	Iron	MI
Matawan	Monmouth	NJ
Matchwood	Ontonagon	MI
Matfield	Chase	KS
Mathews	Kingsbury	SD
Mathewson	Canadian	OK
Mathias	Alger	MI
Matney	Baxter	AR
Matoy	Bryan	OK
Mattapoisett	Plymouth	MA
Mattawankeag	Penobscot	ME
Matteson	Branch	MI
Matteson	Waupaca	WI
Matthews	Faulkner	AR
Matthews	Chatham	NC
Mattison	Haakon	SD
Mattole	Humboldt	CA
Mattoon	Coles	IL
Maumee	Searcy	AR
Maumee	Allen	IN
Maumelle	Craighead	AR
Maumelle	Perry	AR
Maurice River	Cumberland	NJ
Max	Itasca	MN
Maxatawny	Berks	PA
Maxey	Crawford	AR
Maxfield	Bremer	IA
Maxfield	Penobscot	ME
Maxton	Robeson	NC
Maxville	Buffalo	WI
Maxwell	Sangamon	IL
Maxwell	Lac Qui Parie	MN
Maxwell	Pontotoc	OK
May Day	Riley	KS
May	Christian	IL
May	Lee	IL
May	Cass	MN
May	Washington	MN
May	Platte	MO
May	Kearney	NE
Mayberry	Hamilton	IL
Mayberry	Montour	PA
Maybinton	Newberry	SC
Maydell	Clark	SD
Mayesville	Sumter	SC
Mayfield	De Kalb	IL
Mayfield	Grand Traverse	MI
Mayfield	Lapeer	MI
Mayfield	Pennington	MN
Mayfield	Laciede	MO
Mayfield	Hall	NE
Mayfield	Fulton	NY
Mayfield	Yankton	SD
Mayhew Lake	Benton	MN
Mayland	Ward	ND
Maynard	Middlesex	MA
Mayo	Rockingham	NC
Mayville	Houston	MN
Mayville	Traill	ND
Mayville	Clark	WI
Maywood	Benton	MN
Maza	Towner	ND
Mazarn	Garland	AR
Mazarn	Montgomery	AR
Mazeppa	Wabasha	MN
Mazeppa	Grant	SD
Mazie	Mayes	OK
Mazomanie	Dane	WI
Mazon	Grundy	IL
McAdoo	Barber	KS
McAllaster	Logan	KS
McAlmond	Mountrail	ND
McArthur	Logan	OH
McCalmont	Jefferson	PA
McCamish	Johnson	KS
McCandless	Allegheny	PA
McCauleyville	Wilkin	MN
McClellan	Jefferson	IL
McClellan	Newton	IN
McClellan	Pratt	KS
McClellan	Benson	ND
McClure	Holt	NE
McClure	Lyman	SD
McClusky	Sheridan	ND
McCormack Lake	Saint Louis	MN
McCracken	Christian	MO
McCrea	Marshall	MN
McCredie	Callaway	MO
McCulley	Emmons	ND
McCulley	Boyd	NE
McDaniels	McIntosh	OK
McDaniels	Sampson	NC
McDavit	Saint Louis	MN
McDermitt	Humboldt	NV
McDonald	Hardin	OH
McDonald	Barry	MO
McDonald	Jasper	MO
McDonaldsville	Norman	MN
McDonough	Chenango	NY
McDowell	Barry	MO
McElroy	Pawnee	OK

TOWNSHIPS OF THE UNITED STATES

TOWNSHIP	COUNTY	STATE	TOWNSHIP	COUNTY	STATE	TOWNSHIP	COUNTY	STATE
McFall	Arkansas	AR	Meade	Mason	MI	Melvern	Osage	KS
McGahan	Mountrail	ND	Meadow Brook	Cass	MN	Melville	Audubon	IA
McGavock	Mississippi	AR	Meadow Lake	Nevada	CA	Melville	Renville	MN
McGinnis	McLean	ND	Meadow Lake	Barnes	ND	Melville	Alamance	NC
McGregor	Aitkin	MN	Meadow	Clay	IA	Melville	Foster	ND
McHenry	McHenry	IL	Meadow	Plymouth	IA	Melville	Grant	ND
McHenry	Foster	ND	Meadow	Wadena	MN	Melvin	Nelson	ND
McHenry	Lycoming	PA	Meadow	Johnston	NC	Menallen	Adams	PA
McHue	Independence	AR	Meadow	McHenry	ND	Menallen	Fayette	PA
McIlroy	Franklin	AR	Meadow	Perkins	SD	Menash	Winnebago	WI
McIntosh	Spokane	WA	Meadowbrook	Sawyer	WI	Mendenhall	Newberry	SC
McIntyre	Lycoming	PA	Meadowlands	Saint Louis	MN	Mendham	Morris	NJ
McJester	Cleburne	AR	Meadows	Wilkin	MN	Mendon	Clayton	IA
McKean	Licking	OH	Meadows	Stokes	NC	Mendon	Adams	IL
McKean	Erie	PA	Meat Camp	Watauga	NC	Mendon	Saint Joseph	MI
McKee	Adams	IL	Mecan	Marquette	WI	Mendon	Chariton	MO
McKendree	Vermilion	IL	Mecca	Riverside	CA	Mendon	Monroe	NY
McKennon	Johnson	AR	Mecca	Trumbull	OH	Mendon	Rutland	VT
McKenzie	Burleigh	ND	Mechanic Falls	Androscoggin	ME	Mendota	La Salle	IL
McKey	Sequoyah	OK	Mechanic	Holmes	OH	Menlo	Thomas	KS
McKinley	Emmet	MI	Mechanicsburg	Sangamon	IL	Menno	Marion	KS
McKinley	Huron	MI	Mechanicsville	Lee	SC	Menno	Mifflin	PA
McKinley	Cass	MN	Meckling	Clay	SD	Meno	Major	OK
McKinley	Kittson	MN	Mecosta	Mecosta	MI	Menoken	Shawnee	KS
McKinley	Douglas	MO	Medary	Brookings	SD	Menoken	Burleigh	ND
McKinley	Polk	MO	Medary	La Crosse	WI	Menominee	Jo Daviess	IL
McKinley	Stone	MO	Meddybemps	Washington	ME	Menominee	Menominee	MI
McKinley	Ward	ND	Medfield	Norfolk	MA	Menominee	Menominee	WI
McKinley	Stark	OH	Medford	Reno	KS	Menomonie	Dunn	WI
McKinley	Garfield	OK	Medford	Piscataquis	ME	Mentor	Cheboygan	MI
McKinley	Lincoln	OK	Medford	Steele	MN	Mentor	Oscoda	MI
McKinley	Woods	OK	Medford	Burlington	NJ	Mentor	Divide	ND
McKinley	Marshall	SD	Medford	Walsh	ND	Mentor	Lake	OH
Mckinley	Polk	WI	Medford	Grant	OK	Mentor	Clark	WI
Mckinley	Taylor	WI	Medford	Taylor	WI	Mentz	Cayuga	NY
McKinney	Renville	ND	Meina	Henderson	IL	Menz	Sioux	ND
McKinnon	Foster	ND	Meina	Jerauld	SD	Meramec	Crawford	MO
McLain	Muskogee	OK	Medicine Hill	McLean	ND	Meramec	Dent	MO
McLaren	Conway	AR	Medicine Lodge	Barber	KS	Meramec	Franklin	MO
McLauchlin	Hoke	NC	Medicine	Rooks	KS	Meramec	Jefferson	MO
McLaughlin	Corson	SD	Medicine	Livingston	MO	Meramec	Phelps	MO
McLean	Shelby	OH	Medicine	Mercer	MO	Meramec	Saint Louis	MO
McLeansboro	Hamilton	IL	Medicine	Putnam	MO	Mercer	Adams	IA
McMaster	Comanche	OK	Medina	Peoria	IL	Mercer	Mercer	IL
McMillan	Luce	MI	Medina	Warren	IN	Mercer	Somerset	ME
McMillan	Ontonagon	MI	Medina	Lenawee	MI	Mercer	McLean	ND
McMillan	Marathon	WI	Medina	Medina	OH	Mercer	Butler	PA
McMillen	McDonald	MO	Medina	Dane	WI	Mercer	Iron	WI
McMillen	Florence	SC	Medo	Blue Earth	MN	Mercier	Brown	SD
McMurtrey	Douglas	MO	Medora	Reno	KS	Meredith	Cloud	KS
McNeal	Woodward	OK	Medora	Billings	ND	Meredith	Wake	NC
McNeely	Tripp	SD	Medway	Norfolk	MA	Meredith	Belknap	NH
McNeil	Columbia	AR	Medway	Penobscot	ME	Meredith	Delaware	NY
McNeills	Moore	NC	Meeme	Manitowoc	WI	Meriden	New Haven	CT
McNett	Lycoming	PA	Meenon	Burnett	WI	Meriden	La Salle	IL
McPherson Central	McPherson	SD	Mehoopany	Wyoming	PA	Meriden	Steele	MN
McPherson West	McPherson	SD	Mehurin	Lac Qui Parie	MN	Meridian	Clinton	IL
McPherson	McPherson	KS	Meigs	Adams	OH	Meridian	McPherson	KS
McPherson	Pratt	KS	Meigs	Muskingum	OH	Meridian	Ingham	MI
McPherson	Sherman	KS	Meigsville	Morgan	OH	Meridian	Roger Mills	OK
McPherson	Blue Earth	MN	Mekinock	Grand Forks	NC	Meriwether	Edgefield	SC
McPherson	Stephen	OK	Mellen	Menominee	MI	Merrill	Aroostook	ME
McRae	White	AR	Mellette Central	Mellette	SD	Merrill	Newaygo	MI
McTier	Aiken	SC	Mellette	Spink	SD	Merrill	Hettinger	ND
Meacham	Marion	IL	Melrose	Grundy	IA	Merrill	Lincoln	WI
Mead	Merrick	NE	Melrose	Adams	IL	Merrimac	Essex	MA
Mead	Belmont	OH	Melrose	Clark	IL	Merrimac	Sauk	WI
Mead	Warren	PA	Melrose	Charlevoix	MI	Merrimack	Hillsborough	NH
Mead	Spokane	WA	Melrose	Stearns	MN	Merrimon	Carteret	NC
Mead	Clark	WI	Melrose	Steele	ND	Merritt	Bay	MI
Meade Center	Meade	KS	Melrose	Grant	SD	Merritt	Beckham	OK
Meade North	Meade	SD	Melrose	Jackson	WI	Merry Green	Grant	AR
Meade	Huron	MI	Melton	Jefferson	AR	Merry Hill	Bertie	NC

TOWNSHIPS OF THE UNITED STATES

TOWNSHIP	COUNTY	STATE	TOWNSHIP	COUNTY	STATE	TOWNSHIP	COUNTY	STATE
Mertilla	Meade	KS	Middlefield	Geauga	OH	Milford	Lagrange	IN
Merton	Steele	MN	Middlefork	Vermillion	IL	Milford	Geary	KS
Merton	Clark	SD	Middlefork	Worth	MO	Milford	Worcester	MA
Merton	Waukesha	WI	Middleport	Iroquois	IL	Milford	Penobscot	ME
Meshoppen	Wyoming	PA	Middlesex	Yates	NY	Milford	Oakland	MI
Mesopotamia	Trumbull	OH	Middlesex	Butler	PA	Milford	Brown	MN
Mesquite	Clark	NV	Middlesex	Cumberland	PA	Milford	Barton	MO
Metal	Franklin	PA	Middlesex	Washington	VT	Milford	Hillsborough	NH
Metamora	Woodford	IL	Middleton	Essex	MA	Milford	Otsego	NY
Metamora	Lepeer	MI	Middleton	Lafayette	MO	Milford	Butler	OH
Metamore	Franklin	IN	Middleton	Strafford	NH	Milford	Defiance	OH
Meteor	Sawyer	WI	Middleton	Columbiana	OH	Milford	Knox	OH
Methuen	Essex	MA	Middleton	Wood	OH	Milford	Bucks	PA
Metomen	Fond du Lac	WI	Middleton	Sumter	SC	Milford	Juniata	PA
Metz	Presque Isle	MI	Middleton	Turner	SD	Milford	Pike	PA
Metz	Vernon	MO	Middleton	Dane	WI	Milford	Somerset	PA
Mexico	Oxford	ME	Middletown Springs	Rutland	VT	Milford	Beadle	SD
Mexico	Oswego	NY	Middletown	Middlesex	CT	Milford	Jefferson	WI
Meyer	Menominee	MI	Middletown	Jackson	MN	Military	Winneshiek	IA
Meyer	Pierce	ND	Middletown	Monmouth	NJ	Milks Grove	Iroquois	IL
Miami	Cass	IN	Middletown	Delaware	NY	Mill Bayou	Arkansas	AR
Miami	Miami	KS	Middletown	Bucks	PA	Mill Creek	Ashley	AR
Miami	Reno	KS	Middletown	Delaware	PA	Mill Creek	Franklin	AR
Miami	Carroll	MO	Middletown	Susquehanna	PA	Mill Creek	Izard	AR
Miami	Saline	MO	Middletown	Newport	RI	Mill Creek	Lincoln	AR
Miami	Clermont	OH	Mididleville	Wright	MN	Mill Creek	Madison	AR
Miami	Greene	OH	Midland	Lyon	IA	Mill Creek	Newton	AR
Miami	Hamilton	OH	Midland	Midland	MI	Mill Creek	Polk	AR
Miami	Logan	OH	Midland	Saint Louis	MO	Mill Creek	Scott	AR
Miami	Montgomery	OH	Midland	Cabarrus	NC	Mill Creek	Sevier	AR
Mica	Spokane	WA	Midland	Pembina	ND	Mill Creek	Fountain	IN
Michigamme	Marquette	MI	Midland	Gage	NE	Mill Creek	Bourbon	KS
Michigan City	Nelson	ND	Midland	Merrick	NE	Mill Creek	Pottawatomie	KS
Michigan	Clinton	IN	Midland	Pontotoc	OK	Mill Creek	Wabaunsee	KS
Michigan	La Porte	IN	Midland	Hand	SD	Mill Creek	Washington	KS
Michigan	Scott	KS	Midway	Hot Spring	AR	Mill Creek	Morgan	MO
Michigan	Grand Forks	ND	Midway	Cottonwood	MN	Mill Creek	Coshocton	OH
Michigan	Valley	NE	Midway	Saint Louis	MN	Mill Creek	Williams	OH
Mickinock	Roseau	MN	Midway	Davidson	NC	Mill Creek	Lycoming	PA
Micro	Johnston	NC	Midway	Stutsman	ND	Mill Creek	Mercer	PA
Middle Branch	Osceola	MI	Midway	Bamberg	SC	Mill Shoals	White	IL
Middle Creek	Miami	KS	Midway	Clarendon	SC	Mill Spring	Wayne	MO
Middle Creek	Wake	NC	Mifflin	Ashland	OH	Mill	Baxter	AR
Middle Fork	Ringgold	IA	Mifflin	Franklin	OH	Mill	Grant	IN
Middle Fork	Macon	MO	Mifflin	Pike	OH	Mill	Tuscarawas	OH
Middle Fork	Forsyth	NC	Mifflin	Richland	OH	Milladore	Wood	IN
Middle Inlet	Marinette	WI	Mifflin	Wyandot	OH	Millboro	Tripp	SD
Middle Paxton	Dauphin	PA	Mifflin	Columbia	PA	Millbrook	Peoria	IL
Middle River	Marshall	MN	Mifflin	Dauphin	PA	Millbrook	Graham	KS
Middle Smithfield	Monroe	PA	Mifflin	Lycoming	PA	Millbrook	Mecosta	MI
Middle Taylor	Cambria	PA	Mifflin	Iowa	WI	Millbrook	Aiken	SC
Middle	Franklin	AR	Mikado	Alcona	MI	Millbury	Worcester	MA
Middle	Hendricks	IN	Mikesell	Rawlins	KS	Millcreek	Union	OH
Middle	Chowan	NC	Mikkelson	La Moure	ND	Millcreek	Clarion	PA
Middle	Cape May	NJ	Milaca	Mille Lacs	MN	Millcreek	Erie	PA
Middle	Orangeburg	SC	Milam	Macon	IL	Millcreek	Lebanon	PA
Middleberg	Grandy	OK	Milan	Coos	NH	Millen	Alcona	MI
Middleborough	Plymouth	MA	Milan	Dutchess	NY	Miller	Cleveland	AR
Middleburg-Nutbush	Vance	NC	Milan	De Kalb	IL	Miller	Franklin	AR
Middleburg	Schoharie	NY	Milan	Allen	IN	Miller	Woodbury	IA
Middlebury	New Haven	CT	Milan	Monroe	MI	Miller	La Salle	IL
Middlebury	Elkhart	IN	Milan	Erie	OH	Miller	Dearborn	IN
Middlebury	Shiawassee	MI	Milan	Spokane	WA	Miller	Dallas	MO
Middlebury	Wyoming	NY	Millberry Grove	Bond	IL	Miller	Douglas	MO
Middlebury	Knox	OH	Milbridge	Washington	ME	Miller	Gentry	MO
Middlebury	Tioga	PA	Milburn	Custer	NE	Miller	Maries	MO
Middlebury	Addison	VT	Milburn	Essex	NJ	Miller	Marion	MO
Middlecreek	Snyder	PA	Miles	Centre	PA	Miller	Phelps	MO
Middlecreek	Somerset	PA	Milford	New Haven	CT	Miller	Scotland	MO
Middlefield	Middlesex	CT	Milford	Crawford	IA	Miller	Knox	NE
Middlefield	Buchanan	IA	Milford	Dickinson	IA	Miller	Knox	OH
Middlefield	Hampshire	MA	Milford	Story	IA	Miller	Kay	OK
Middlefield	Otsego	NY	Milford	Iroquois	IL	Miller	Seminole	OK

TOWNSHIPS OF THE UNITED STATES

TOWNSHIP	COUNTY	STATE	TOWNSHIP	COUNTY	STATE	TOWNSHIP	COUNTY	STATE
Miller	Huntingdon	PA	Mineral Springs	Moore	NC	Mitchell	Cross	AR
Miller	Perry	PA	Mineral Springs	Richmond	NC	Mitchell	Mitchell	IA
Miller	Hand	SD	Mineral Springs	Slope	ND	Mitchell	Nemaha	KS
Miller	Marshall	SD	Mineral	Sevier	AR	Mitchell	Rice	KS
Millers	Alexander	NC	Mineral	Plumas	CA	Mitchell	Alcona	MI
Millersburg	Mercer	IL	Mineral	Bureau	IL	Mitchell	Wilkin	MN
Millerville	Douglas	MN	Mineral	Cherokee	KS	Mitchell	Davidson	SD
Millett	Allendale	SC	Mineral	Barry	MO	Mitchell	Sheboygan	WI
Millgove	Steuben	IN	Mineral	Jasper	MO	Mitchells	Bertie	NC
Millington	Tuscola	MI	Mineral	Venango	PA	Mitcheltree	Martin	IN
Millinocket	Penobscot	ME	Minerva	Marshall	IA	Moapa	Clark	NV
Millis	Norfolk	MA	Minerva	Clearwater	MN	Moccasin	Effingham	IL
Mills River	Henderson	NC	Minerva	Essex	NY	Mocksville	Davie	NC
Mills	Bond	IL	Minetto	Oswego	NY	Model	Mountrail	ND
Mills	Midland	MI	Mingo	Bates	MO	Modell	Norton	KS
Mills	Ogemaw	MI	Mingo	Sampson	NC	Modena	Edmunds	SD
Millsfield	Coos	NH	Mingo	Williamsburg	SC	Modena	Buffalo	WI
Millshoal	Macon	NC	Mingona	Barber	KS	Medesto	Stanislaus	CA
Millstadt	Saint Clair	IL	Minisink	Orange	NY	Moe	Douglas	MN
Millston	Jackson	WI	Minneha	Sedgwick	KS	Moffatt	Arenac	MI
Millstone	Monmouth	NJ	Minnehaha	Bowman	ND	Mohawk	Montgomery	NY
Millstone	Elk	PA	Minneiska	Wabasha	MN	Mohican	Ashland	OH
Milltown	Hutchinson	SD	Minneola	Goodhue	MN	Moira	Franklin	NY
Milltown	Polk	WI	Minneota	Jackson	MN	Mokelumne Hill	Calaveras	CA
Millville	Clayton	IA	Minnesota Falls	Yellow Medicine	MN	Molan	Hutchinson	SD
Millville	Worcester	MA	Minnesota Lake	Faribault	MN	Moland	Clay	MN
Millville	Grant	WI	Minnesota	Burke	ND	Moline	Rock Island	IL
Milwood	Stearns	MN	Minnesota	Roberts	SD	Moline	McKenzie	ND
Millwood	Lincoln	MO	Minnewaska	Pope	MN	Molitor	Taylor	WI
Millwood	Guernsey	OH	Minnewaukan	Ramsey	ND	Moltke	Presque Isle	MI
Milnor	Sargent	ND	Minnie Lake	Barnes	ND	Moltke	Sibley	MN
Milo	Delaware	IA	Minnie	Beltrami	MN	Momence	Kankakee	IL
Milo	Bureau	IL	Minnie	Grant	ND	Momence	Fillmore	NE
Milo	Piscatauqis	ME	Minocqua	Oneida	WI	Mona	Ford	IL
Milo	Mille Lacs	MN	Minong	Washburn	WI	Monaghan	York	PA
Milo	Yates	NY	Minonk	Woodford	IL	Monclova	Lucas	OH
Milroy	Jasper	IN	Minot	Androscoggin	ME	Mondamin	Hand	SD
Milton	Du Page	IL	Minto	Cavalier	ND	Monday Creek	Perry	OH
Milton	Jefferson	IN	Minton	Holt	MO	Mondovi	Buffalo	WI
Milton	Butler	KS	Mintonsville	Gates	NC	Monee	Will	IL
Milton	Marion	KS	Mirabile	Caldwell	MO	Monegaw	Saint Clair	MO
Milton	Norfolk	MA	Mirage	Rawlins	KS	Monett	Barry	MO
Milton	Oxford	ME	Mirage	Kearney	NE	Money Creek	McLean	IL
Milton	Antrim	MI	Mishicot	Manitowoc	WI	Money Creek	Houston	MN
Milton	Cass	MI	Missabe Mountain	Saint Louis	MN	Monico	Oneida	WI
Milton	Dodge	MN	Mission Creek	Wabaunsee	KS	Moniteau	Howard	MO
Milton	Caswell	NC	Mission Creek	Pine	MN	Moniteau	Randolph	MO
Milton	Strafford	NH	Mission Hill	Yankton	SD	Monitor	Bay	MI
Milton	Saratoga	NY	Mission	San Bernardino	CA	Monkton	Addison	VT
Milton	Ashland	OH	Mission	La Salle	IL	Monmouth	Jackson	IA
Milton	Jackson	OH	Mission	Brown	KS	Monmouth	Warren	IL
Milton	Mahoning	OH	Mission	Neosho	KS	Monmouth	Shawnee	KS
Milton	Wayne	OH	Mission	Shawnee	KS	Monmouth	Kennebec	ME
Milton	Wood	OH	Mission	Crow Wing	MN	Monon	White	IN
Milton	Le Flore	OK	Mission	Lake	MT	Monona	Clayton	IA
Milton	Chittenden	VT	Mission	Benson	ND	Monongahela	Greene	PA
Milton	Buffalo	WI	Mission	Corson	SD	Monroe	Mississippi	AR
Milton	Rock	WI	Mississinawa	Darke	OH	Monroe	Sevier	AR
Miltona	Douglas	MN	Mississippi	Crittenden	AR	Monroe	Fairfield	CT
Milwood	Stearns	MN	Mississippi	Desha	AR	Monroe	Benton	IA
Mina	Chautauqua	NY	Mississippi	Sebastian	AR	Monroe	Butler	IA
Mina	Mineral	NV	Mississippi	Jersey	IL	Monroe	Fremont	IA
Minco	Benson	ND	Mississippi	Mississippi	MO	Monroe	Johnson	IA
Minden	Pottawattamie	IA	Missouri Ridge	Williams	ND	Monroe	Linn	IA
Minden	Sanilac	MI	Missouri	Clark	AR	Monroe	Madison	IA
Minden	Benton	MN	Missouri	Montgomery	AR	Monroe	Mahaska	IA
Minden	Montgomery	NY	Missouri	Nevada	AR	Monroe	Monroe	IA
Mine Creek	Hempstead	AR	Missouri	Pike	AR	Monroe	Ringgold	IA
Mine Hill	Morris	NJ	Missouri	Brown	IL	Monroe	Shelby	IA
Mine La Motte	Madison	MO	Missouri	Boone	MO	Monroe	Wayne	IA
Miner	Miner	SD	Missouri	Chariton	MO	Monroe	Ogle	IL
Mineral Point	Iowa	WI	Missouri	Burleigh	ND	Monroe	Adams	IN
Mineral Springs	Howard	AR	Missouri	Noble	OK	Monroe	Allen	IN

TOWNSHIPS OF THE UNITED STATES

TOWNSHIP	COUNTY	STATE	TOWNSHIP	COUNTY	STATE	TOWNSHIP	COUNTY	STATE
Monroe	Carroll	IN	Mont	Williams	ND	Moodys	Cherokee	OK
Monroe	Clark	IN	Mont Vernon	Hillsborough	NH	Mooers	Clinton	NY
Monroe	Delaware	IN	Montague	Franklin	MA	Moon Lake	Stutsman	ND
Monroe	Grant	IN	Montague	Muskegon	MI	Moon	Allegheny	PA
Monroe	Howard	IN	Montague	Sussex	NJ	Moon	Newberry	SC
Monroe	Jefferson	IN	Montague	Lewis	NY	Mooney	Phillips	AR
Monroe	Kosciusko	IN	Montana	Jewell	KS	Mooney	Polk	MO
Monroe	Madison	IN	Montana	Labette	KS	Moonshine	Big Stone	MN
Monroe	Morgan	IN	Montana	Buffalo	WI	Moord	Slope	ND
Monroe	Pike	IN	Montcalm	Montcalm	MI	Moore Park	Itasca	MN
Monroe	Pulaski	IN	Montclair	Essex	NJ	Moore	Barber	KS
Monroe	Putnam	IN	Montebello	Los Angeles	CA	Moore	Marion	KS
Monroe	Randolph	IN	Montebello	Hancock	IL	Moore	Sanilac	MI
Monroe	Washington	IN	Montello	Marquette	WI	Moore	Stevens	MN
Monroe	Anderson	KS	Monterey	Monterey	CA	Moore	Oregon	MO
Monroe	Franklin	MA	Monterey	Berkshire	MA	Moore	Shannon	MO
Monroe	Waldo	ME	Monterey	Allegan	MI	Moore	Ransom	ND
Monroe	Monroe	MI	Monterey	Cuming	NE	Moore	Cleveland	OK
Monroe	Newaygo	MI	Monterey	Putnam	OH	Moore	Muskogee	OK
Monroe	Lyon	MN	Montevallo	Vernon	MO	Moore	Pottawatomie	OK
Monroe	Andrew	MO	Montezuma	Pike	IL	Moore	Northampton	PA
Monroe	Daviess	MO	Montezuma	Gray	KS	Moore	Charles Mix	SD
Monroe	Lincoln	MO	Montford Cove	McDowell	NC	Moore	Lyman	SD
Monroe	Livingston	MO	Montgomery	Hot Spring	AR	Moorefield	Independence	AR
Monroe	Monroe	MO	Montgomery	Monroe	AR	Moorefield	Clark	OH
Monroe	Nodaway	MO	Montgomery	Crawford	IL	Moorefield	Harrison	OH
Monroe	Guilford	NC	Montgomery	Woodford	IL	Mooreland	Woodward	OK
Monroe	Union	NC	Montgomery	Gibson	IN	Moores Prairie	Jefferson	IL
Monroe	Towner	ND	Montgomery	Jennings	IN	Moorestown	Burlington	NJ
Monroe	Platte	NE	Montgomery	Owen	IN	Mooresville	Livingston	MO
Monroe	Grafton	NH	Montgomery	Le Sueur	MN	Mooreton	Richland	ND
Monroe	Gloucester	NJ	Montgomery	Hickory	MO	Moorhead	Clay	MN
Monroe	Middlesex	NJ	Montgomery	Montgomery	MO	Moorland	Muskegon	MI
Monroe	Orange	NY	Montgomery	Wright	MO	Moose Creek	Clearwater	MN
Monroe	Adams	OH	Montgomery	Somerset	NJ	Moose Lake	Beltrami	MN
Monroe	Allen	OH	Montgomery	Orange	NY	Moose Lake	Carlton	MN
Monroe	Ashtabula	OH	Montgomery	Ashland	OH	Moose Lake	Cass	MN
Monroe	Carroll	OH	Montgomery	Franklin	OH	Moose River	Somerset	ME
Monroe	Clermont	OH	Montgomery	Marion	OH	Moose River	Marshall	MN
Monroe	Coshocton	OH	Montgomery	Wood	OH	Moose	Roseau	MN
Monroe	Darke	OH	Montgomery	Franklin	PA	Moraine	Grand Forks	ND
Monroe	Guernsey	OH	Montgomery	Indiana	PA	Moraine	Montgomery	OH
Monroe	Harrison	OH	Montgomery	Montgomery	PA	Moral	Shelby	IN
Monroe	Henry	OH	Montgomery	Franklin	VT	Moran	Mackinac	MI
Monroe	Holmes	OH	Monticello City	Jones	IA	Moran	Todd	MN
Monroe	Knox	OH	Monticello	Piatt	IL	Moran	Richland	ND
Monroe	Licking	OH	Monticello	Johnson	KS	Moran	Spokane	WA
Monroe	Logan	OH	Monticello	Aroostook	ME	Moranville	Roseau	MN
Monroe	Madison	OH	Monticello	Wright	MN	Moravia	Cayuga	NY
Monroe	Miami	OH	Monticello	Lafayette	WI	Moravian Falls	Wilkes	NC
Monroe	Muskingum	OH	Montier	Shannon	MO	Morcom	Saint Louis	MN
Monroe	Perry	OH	Montmorency	Whiteside	IL	Moreau	Saratoga	NY
Monroe	Pickaway	OH	Montmorency	Montmorency	MI	Moreau	Cole	MO
Monroe	Preble	OH	Montour	Schuyler	NY	Moreau	Montieau	MO
Monroe	Putnam	OH	Montour	Columbia	PA	Moreau	Morgan	MO
Monroe	Richland	OH	Montpelier	Muscatine	IA	Moreau	Perkins	SD
Monroe	Le Flore	OK	Montpelier	Edmunds	SD	Morehead	Carteret	NC
Monroe	Bedford	PA	Montpelier	Kewaunee	WI	Morehead	Guilford	NC
Monroe	Bradford	PA	Montpiler	Stutsman	ND	Morehouse	Hamilton	NY
Monroe	Clarion	PA	Montrose	Ashley	AR	Moreland	Pope	AR
Monroe	Cumberland	PA	Montrose	Lee	IA	Moreland	Scott	MO
Monroe	Juniata	PA	Montrose	Genesee	MI	Moreland	Lycoming	PA
Monroe	Snyder	PA	Montrose	Cavalier	ND	Moretown	Washington	VT
Monroe	Wyoming	PA	Montrose	McCook	SD	Morgan	Cleburne	AR
Monroe	Bon Homme	SD	Montrose	Dane	WI	Morgan	Franklin	AR
Monroe	Turner	SD	Montserrat	Johnson	MO	Morgan	Lawrence	AR
Monroe	Adams	WI	Monture	Powell	MT	Morgan	Sharp	AR
Monroe	Green	WI	Montville	Waldo	ME	Morgan	Crawford	IA
Monrovia	Los Angeles	CA	Montville	Morris	NJ	Morgan	Decatur	IA
Monson	Hampden	MA	Montville	Geauga	OH	Morgan	Franklin	IA
Monson	Piscataquis	ME	Montville	Medina	OH	Morgan	Harrison	IA
Monson	Traverse	MN	Monument	Logan	KS	Morgan	Woodbury	IA
Mont Sandals	Sebastain	AR	Moody	Marion	SC	Morgan	Coles	IL

TOWNSHIP	COUNTY	STATE	TOWNSHIP	COUNTY	STATE	TOWNSHIP	COUNTY	STATE
Morgan	Harrison	IN	Morton	Ottawa	KS	Mount Holly	Burlington	NJ
Morgan	Owen	IN	Morton	Pawnee	KS	Mount Holly	Rutland	VT
Morgan	Porter	IN	Morton	Sedgwick	KS	Mount Hope	McLean	IL
Morgan	Thomas	KS	Morton	Wallace	KS	Mount Hope	Orange	NY
Morgan	Redwood	MN	Morton	Mecosta	MI	Mount Hope	Spokane	WA
Morgan	Mercer	MO	Morton	Alamance	NC	Mount Hope	Grant	WI
Morgan	Rowan	NC	Morton	Burleigh	ND	Mount Ida	Grant	WI
Morgan	Rutherford	NC	Morton	Boyd	NE	Mount Joy	Adams	PA
Morgan	Traill	ND	Morton	Knox	NE	Mount Joy	Lancaster	PA
Morgan	Ashtabula	OH	Morton	Day	SD	Mount Laurel	Burlington	NJ
Morgan	Butler	OH	Morven	Anson	NC	Mount Lebanon	Allegheny	PA
Morgan	Gallia	OH	Mosalem	Dubuque	IA	Mount Morris	Ogle	IL
Morgan	Knox	OH	Moscow	Muscatine	IA	Mount Morris	Genesee	MI
Morgan	Morgan	OH	Moscow	Stevens	KS	Mount Morris	Morrison	MN
Morgan	Scioto	OH	Moscow	Somerset	ME	Mount Morris	Livingston	NY
Morgan	Carter	OK	Moscow	Hillsdale	MI	Mount Morris	Waushara	WI
Morgan	Ellis	OK	Moscow	Freeborn	MN	Mount Olive	Izard	AR
Morgan	Murray	OK	Moscow	Cavalier	ND	Mount Olive	Macoupin	IL
Morgan	Greene	PA	Moscow	Iowa	WI	Mount Olive	Morris	NJ
Morgan	Cherokee	SC	Mosel	Sheboygan	WI	Mount Pisgah	White	AR
Morgan	Jones	SD	Moseley Hall	lenoir	NC	Mount Pleasant	Scott	AR
Morgan	Orleans	VT	Mosher	Mellette	SD	Mount Pleasant	Searcy	AR
Morgan	Oconto	WI	Mosinee	Marathon	WI	Mount Pleasant	Henry	IA
Morganton	Burke	NC	Mosley	Murray	OK	Mount Pleasant	Whiteside	IL
Moriah	Essex	NY	Mosquito	Christian	IL	Mount Pleasant	Delaware	IN
Morken	Clay	MN	Moss Creek	Carroll	MO	Mount Pleasant	Atchison	KS
Morlan	Graham	KS	Moss	Edgefield	SC	Mount Pleasant	Labette	KS
Morley	Scott	MO	Motley	Morrison	MN	Mount Pleasant	Wabasha	MN
Morning Star	Mecklenburg	NC	Mott	Siskiyou	CA	Mount Pleasant	Bates	MO
Morning Sun	Louisa	IA	Mott	Franklin	IA	Mount Pleasant	Cass	MO
Morningside	Lyman	SD	Motts	Florence	SC	Mount Pleasant	Lawrence	MO
Moro	Bradley	AR	Mottville	Saint Joseph	MI	Mount Pleasant	Scotland	MO
Moro	Calhoun	AR	Moulton	Murray	MN	Mount Pleasant	Cabarrus	NC
Moro	Madison	IL	Moulton	Auglaize	OH	Mount Pleasant	Rolette	ND
Morrill	Brown	KS	Moultonborough	Carroll	NH	Mount Pleasant	Westchester	NY
Morrill	Waldo	ME	Mound City	Crittenden	AR	Mount Pleasant	Jefferson	OH
Morrill	Morrison	MN	Mound City	Linn	KS	Mount Pleasant	Adams	PA
Morris	Arkansas	AR	Mound Prairie	Jasper	IA	Mount Pleasant	Columbia	PA
Morris	Litchfield	CT	Mound Prairie	Houston	MN	Mount Pleasant	Washington	PA
Morris	Grundy	IL	Mound	Effingham	IL	Mount Pleasant	Wayne	PA
Morris	Seward	KS	Mound	McDonough	IL	Mount Pleasant	Westmoreland	PA
Morris	Sumner	KS	Mound	Warren	IN	Mount Pleasant	Clark	SD
Morris	Stevens	MN	Mound	McPherson	KS	Mount Pleasant	Green	WI
Morris	Sullivan	MO	Mound	Miami	KS	Mount Pleasant	Racine	WI
Morris	Texas	MO	Mound	Phillips	KS	Mount Pulaski	Logan	IL
Morris	Ramsey	ND	Mound	Rock	MN	Mount Rose	Bottineau	ND
Morris	Morris	NJ	Mound	Bates	MO	Mount Rushmore	Pennington	SD
Morris	Otsego	NY	Mound	Slope	ND	Mount Sterling	Brown	IL
Morris	Knox	OH	Mound	Payne	OK	Mount Tabor	Rutland	VT
Morris	Okmulgee	OK	Mound Valley	Labette	KS	Mount Tirzah	Person	NC
Morris	Clearfield	PA	Mound Valley	Caddo	OK	Mount Ulla	Rowan	NC
Morris	Greene	PA	Mounds	Creek	OK	Mount Valley	Winnebago	IA
Morris	Huntingdon	PA	Moundville	Vernon	MO	Mount Vernon	Benton	AR
Morris	Tioga	PA	Moundville	Marquette	WI	Mount Vernon	Faulkner	AR
Morris	Washington	PA	Mount Airy	Surray	NC	Mount Vernon	Searcy	AR
Morris	Shawano	WI	Mount Auburn	Christian	IL	Mount Vernon	Black Hawk	IA
Morrison	Aitkin	MN	Mount Ayr	Ringgold	IA	Mount Vernon	Cerro Gordo	IA
Morrison	Brown	WI	Mount Ayr	Osborne	KS	Mount Vernon	Jefferson	IL
Morristown	Saint Lawrence	NY	Mount Calm	Fulton	AR	Mount Vernon	Kennebec	ME
Morristown	Lamoille	VT	Mount Carleton	Spokane	WA	Mount Vernon	Winona	MN
Morristown	Rice	MN	Mount Carmel	Cavalier	ND	Mount Vernon	Lawrence	MO
Morristown	Morris	NJ	Mount Carmel	Northumberland	PA	Mount Vernon	Davison	SD
Morro	San Luis Obispo	CA	Mount Carmel	McCormick	SC	Mount View	Towner	ND
Morrow	Washington	AR	Mount Carroll	Carroll	IL	Mount Washington	Berkshire	MA
Morrow	Adair	MO	Mount Clio	Lee	SC	Mount Zion	Macon	IL
Morrow	Macon	MO	Mount Crogham	Chesterfield	SC	Mount Zion	Clarendon	SC
Morse Bluff	Saunders	NE	Mount Desert	Hancock	ME	Mountain City	Elko	NV
Morse	Itasca	MN	Mount Erie	Wayne	IL	Mountain Creek	Catawba	NC
Morse	Saint Louis	MN	Mount Forest	Bay	MI	Mountain Grove	Wright	MO
Morse	Okfuskee	OK	Mount Gilead	Cabarrus	NC	Mountain Home	Baxter	AR
Morse	Ashland	WI	Mount Gilead	Montgomery	NC	Mountain Lake	Cottonwood	MN
Morton	Page	IA	Mount Haley	Midland	MI	Mountain Park	Kiowa	OK
Morton	Tazewell	IL	Mount Hermon	Pasquotank	NC	Mountain	Cleburne	AR

TOWNSHIP	COUNTY	STATE	TOWNSHIP	COUNTY	STATE	TOWNSHIP	COUNTY	STATE
Mountain	Crawford	AR	Murphysboro	Jackson	IL	Nashville	Nash	NC
Mountain	Faulkner	AR	Murray	Newton	AR	Nashville	Forest	WI
Mountain	Franklin	AR	Murray	Alameda	CA	Nashwauk	Itasca	MN
Mountain	Howard	AR	Murray	Marshall	KS	Nashua	Ogle	IL
Mountain	Logan	AR	Murray	Murray	MN	Nassau	Sioux	IA
Mountain	Pike	AR	Murray	Greene	MO	Nassau	Rensselaer	NY
Mountain	Polk	AR	Murray	Orleans	NY	Natick	Middlesex	MA
Mountain	Scott	AR	Murray	Coal	OK	National	San Diego	CA
Mountain	Van Buren	AR	Murrels Inlet	Georgetown	SC	Natoma	Osborne	KS
Mountain	Yell	AR	Murrietta	Riverside	CA	Natura	Okmulgee	OK
Mountain	El Dorado	CA	Murry	Rusk	WI	Naugatuck	New Haven	CT
Mountain	Siskiyou	CA	Muscatine	Muscatine	IA	Naughton	Burleigh	ND
Mountain	Saline	IL	Muscoda	Grant	WI	Nauvoo	Hancock	IL
Mountain	Barry	MO	Muse	Le Flore	OK	Navan	Corson	SD
Mountain	McDonald	MO	Muskegon	Muskegon	MI	Navarino	Shawano	WI
Mountain	Jackson	NC	Muskingum	Muskingum	OH	Navajo	Jackson	OK
Mountain	McCurtain	OK	Muskingum	Washington	OH	Neal	Mississippi	AR
Mountain View	Kiowa	OK	Muskego	Renville	ND	Neave	Darke	OK
Mountain View	Whatcom	WA	Musselfork	Chariton	MO	Nebish	Beltrami	MN
Mountrail	Mountrail	ND	Mussey	Saint Clair	MI	Nebo	McDowell	NC
Mouse Riven	McHenry	ND	Mussman	Jones	SD	Nebo	Bowman	ND
Mouzon	Williamsburg	SC	Mustang	Canadian	OK	Nebraska	Page	IA
Moville	Woodbury	IA	Mustang	Oklahoma	OK	Nebraska	Livingston	IL
Moweaqua	Shelby	IL	Myatt	Fulton	AR	Necedah	Juneau	WI
Moyer	Swift	MN	Myatt	Howell	MO	Neche	Pembina	ND
Moylan	Marshall	MN	Myers	Grundy	MO	Nedrose	Ward	ND
Moyock	Currituck	NC	Myrick	Johnston	OK	Needham	Johnson	IN
Mud Lake	Marshall	MN	Myron	Faulk	SD	Needham	Norfolk	MA
Mud Springs	Dorado	CA	Myrtle	Knox	MO	Needles	San Bernardino	CA
Muddy Fork	Howard	AR	Myrtle	Oregon	MO	Neely	Butler	MO
Muddy Fork	Pike	AR	Myrtle	Mountrail	ND	Neenah	Winnebago	WI
Muddycreek	Butler	PA	Myrtle	Custer	NE	Negaunee	Marquette	MI
Mudgett	Mille Lacs	MN				Neills Creek	Harnett	NC
Mueller	Schoolcraft	MI				Nekimi	Winnebago	WI
Muhlenberg	Pickaway	OH		—N—		Nekoma	Cavalier	ND
Muhlenberg	Berks	PA				Neligh	Antelope	NE
Mukwa	Waupaca	WI	Naausay	Kendall	IL	Neligh	Cuming	NE
Mukwonaga	Waukesha	WI	Nabisco	Beaver	OK	Nelson	Clay	AR
Mulberry	Franklin	AR	Nabisco	Texas	OK	Nelson	Lee	IL
Mulberry	Johnson	AR	Nachusa	Lee	IL	Nelson	Kent	MI
Mulberry	Clay	KS	Nadeau	Menominee	MI	Nelson	Watonwan	MN
Mulberry	Ellsworth	KS	Nags Head	Dare	NC	Nelson	Barnes	ND
Mulberry	Caldwell	NC	Nahant	Essex	MA	Nelson	Cheshire	NH
Mulberry	Wikes	NC	Nahma	Delta	MI	Nelson	Kent	??
Muldrow	Sequoyah	OK	Nahunta	Wayne	NC	Nelson	Clark	NV
Mulhall	Logan	OK	Namakago	Bayfield	WI	Nelson	Madison	NY
Mullally	Harlan	NE	Nameoki	Madison	IL	Nelson	Portage	OH
Mullen	Boyd	NE	Nance	Beadle	SD	Nelson	Tioga	PA
Mullen	Jones	SD	Nansen	Richland	ND	Nelson	Buffalo	WI
Mullet	Cheboygan	MI	Nantahala	Macon	NC	Nelson Park	Marshall	MN
Mullica	Atlantic	NJ	Nantahala	Swain	NC	Nemaha	Nemaha	KS
Mulligan	Brown	MN	Nanticoke	Broome	NY	Nemaha	Gage	NE
Munch	Pine	MN	Nantucket	Nantucket	MA	Neodesha	Wilson	KS
Muncrief	McClain	OK	Napa	Napa	CA	Neoga	Cumberland	IL
Muncy Creek	Lycoming	PA	Napdi	Cattaraugus	NY	Nepeuskun	Winnebago	WI
Muncy	Lycoming	PA	Naperville	Du Page	IL	Neola	Pottawattamie	IA
Mundy	Genesee	MI	Napier	Bedford	PA	Neponset	Bureau	IL
Munising	Alger	MI	Naples	Ontario	NY	Neosho	Cherokee	KS
Munro	Cheboygan	MI	Naples	Grady	OK	Neosho	Coffey	KS
Munroe Falls	Summit	OH	Naples	Buffalo	WI	Neosho	Labette	KS
Munson	Henry	IL	Napoleon	Jackson	MI	Neosho	Morris	KS
Munson	Stearns	MN	Napoleon	Henry	OH	Neosho	Newton	MO
Munson	Geauga	OH	Narcissa	Ottawa	OK	Neosho Falls	Woodson	KS
Munson	Eddy	ND	Naron	Pratt	KS	Neptune	Monmouth	NJ
Munster	Cambria	PA	Narragansett	Washington	RI	Nereson	Roseau	MN
Murdo	Jones	SD	Narrows	Macon	MO	Nesbit	Polk	MN
Murdock	Douglas	IL	Nasewaupee	Door	WI	Nescatunga	Comanche	KS
Murdock	Butler	KS	Nash	Nelson	ND	Nescopeck	Luzerne	PA
Murdock	Ellis	OK	Nash	Muskogee	OK	Neshannock	Lawrence	PA
Murfreesboro	Hertford	NC	Nashville	Howard	AR	Nesheim	Nelson	ND
Murfreesboro	Cherokee	NC	Nashville	Washington	IL	Neshkoro	Marquette	WI
Murphy	Mayes	OK	Nashville	Martin	MN	Ness	Saint Louis	MN
Murphys	Calaveras	CA	Nashville	Barton	MO	Ness	Pierce	ND

TOWNSHIPS OF THE UNITED STATES

TOWNSHIP	COUNTY	STATE	TOWNSHIP	COUNTY	STATE	TOWNSHIP	COUNTY	STATE
Nessel	Chisago	MN	New Haven	Shiawassee	MI	New Vernon	Mercer	PA
Nesson Valley	Williams	ND	New Haven	Olmsted	MN	New Vineyard	Franklin	ME
Nester	Roscommon	MI	New Haven	Franklin	MO	New Windsor	Orange	NY
Netawaka	Jackson	KS	New Haven	Huron	OH	New Wine	Dubuque	IA
Nether Providence	Delaware	PA	New Haven	Oswego	NY	New York	Caldwell	MO
Nett River	Koochiching	MN	New Haven	Addison	VT	New Zion	Clarendon	SC
Nettle Creek	Grundy	IL	New Haven	Adams	WI	Newark	Webster	IA
Nettleton	Craighead	AR	New Haven	Dunn	WI	Newark	Wilson	KS
Neuchatel	Nemaha	KS	New Holstein	Calument	WI	Newark	Gratiot	MI
Neuse River	Wake	NC	New Bates	Bates	MO	Newark	Kearney	NE
Neuse	Lenoir	NC	New Home	Williams	ND	Newark	Licking	OH
Neva	Langlade	WI	New Hope	Izard	AR	Newark	Marshall	SD
Nevada	Nevada	CA	New Hope	Newton	AR	Newark	Caledonia	VT
Nevada	Livingston	IL	New Hope	Union	IA	Newark	Rock	WI
Nevada	Palo Alto	IA	New Hope	Chatham	NC	Newark Valley	Tioga	NY
Nevada	Story	IA	New Hope	Iredell	NC	Newberg	Cass	MI
Nevada	Ness	KS	New Hope	Perquimans	NC	Newbern	Dickinson	KS
Nevada	Mower	MN	New Hope	Randolph	NC	Newberry	Lagrange	IN
Neversink	Sullivan	NY	New Hope	Wayne	NC	Newberry	Miami	OH
Neville	Allegheny	PA	New Hope	Morton	ND	Newberry	York	PA
Nevins	Vigo	IN	New Hope	Orangeburg	SC	Newberry	Newberry	SC
Nevis	Hubbard	MN	New Hope	Brown	SD	Newbold	Oneida	WI
New Albany	Story	IA	New Hope	Portage	WI	Newborg	Bottineau	ND
New Albany	Floyd	IN	New Hudson	Allegany	NY	Newbre	Ramsey	ND
New Albion	Cattaraugus	NY	New Independence	Saint Louis	MN	Newburg	Izard	AR
New Ashford	Berkshire	MA	New Ipswich	Hillsborough	NH	Newburg	Mitchell	IA
New Athens	Saint Clair	IL	New Jasper	Greene	OH	Newburg	Pike	IL
New Auburn	Sibley	MN	New Lebanon	Columbia	NY	Newburg	Fillmore	MN
New Avon	Redwood	MN	New Lenox	Will	IL	Newburg	Hughes	OK
New Baltimore	Greene	NY	New Light	Wake	NC	Hewburgh	Penobscot	ME
New Braintree	Worcester	MA	New Limerick	Aroostook	ME	Newburgh	Steele	ND
New Bremen	Lewis	NY	New Lisbon	Stoddard	MO	Newburgh	Orange	NY
New Berlin	Sangamon	IL	New Lisbon	Otsego	NY	Newbury	Wabaunsee	KS
New Berlin	Chenango	NY	New London	New London	CT	Newbury	Essex	MA
New Bethel	Rockingham	NC	New London	Henry	IA	Newbury	Stutsman	ND
New Boston	Mercer	IL	New London	Kandiyohi	MN	Newbury	Merrimack	NH
New Boston	Hillsborough	NH	New London	Merrimack	NH	Newbury	Geauga	OH
New Boston	Scotio	OH	New London	Huron	OH	Newbury	Orange	VT
New Britain	Hartford	CT	New London	Chester	PA	Newby	Creek	OK
New Britain	Bucks	PA	New Lyme	Ashtabula	OH	Newcastle	Fulton	IN
New Buda	Decatur	IA	New Lyme	Monroe	WI	Newcastle	Lincoln	ME
New Buffalo	Berrien	MI	New Madrid	New Madrid	MO	Newcastle	Dixon	NE
New Canaan	Fairfield	CT	New Maine	Marshall	MN	Newcastle	Coschocton	OH
New Castle	Wilkes	NC	New Market	Scott	MN	Newcomb	Saline	AR
New Castle	Rockingham	NH	New Market	Randolph	NC	Newcomb	Champaign	IL
New Castle	Westchester	NY	New Market	Highland	OH	Newcomb	Essex	NY
New Castle	Scuyikill	PA	New Marlborough	Berkshire	MA	Newell	Buena Vista	IA
New Chester	Adams	WI	New Milford	Litchfield	CT	Newell	Vermilion	IL
New City	Towner	ND	New Milford	Susquehanna	PA	Newfane	Niagara	NY
New Denmark	Brown	WI	New Oregon	Howard	IA	Newfane	Windham	VT
New Diggings	Lafayette	WI	New Paltz	Ulster	NY	Newfield	York	ME
New Dooey	Pine	MN	New Philadelphia	Tuscarawas	OH	Newfield	Oceana	MI
New Durham	La Porte	IN	New Portland	Somerset	ME	Newfield	Tompkins	NY
New Durham	Strafford	NH	New Prairie	Pope	MN	Newfields	Rockingham	NH
New Douglas	Madison	IL	New Prairie	Ward	ND	Newington	Hartford	CT
New England	Hettinger	ND	New Richland	Waseca	MN	Newington	Rockingham	NH
New Fairfield	Fairfield	CT	New River	Watauga	NC	Newkirk	Lake	MI
New Folden	Marshall	MN	New River	Churchill	NV	Newkirk	Kay	OK
New Garden	Wayne	IN	New Rockford	Rockford	ND	Newland	Pasquotank	NC
New Garden	Chester	PA	New Salem	McDonough	IL	Newland	Ramsey	ND
New Glarus	Green	WI	New Salem	Pike	IL	Newlin	Alamance	NC
New Gloucester	Cumberland	ME	New Salem	Franklin	MA	Newlin	Chester	PA
New Gottland	McPherson	KS	New Salem	Union	NC	Newman	Stanislaus	CA
New Hampton	Chickasaw	IA	New Scandia	Washington	MN	Newman	Douglas	IL
New Hampton	Belknap	NH	New Scotland	Albany	NY	Newman	Ward	ND
New Hanover	Burlington	NJ	New Sewickley	Beaver	PA	Newman	Saunders	NE
New Hanover	Montgomery	PA	New Sharon	Franklin	ME	Newman	Spokane	WA
New Hartford	Litchfield	CT	New Shoreham	Washington	RI	Newmansville	Cass	IL
New Hartford	Winona	MN	New Solum	Marshall	MN	Newmarket	Rockingham	NH
New Hartford	Oneida	NY	New Sweden	Aroostook	ME	Newport Beach	Orange	CA
New Haven	New Haven	CT	New Sweden	Nicollet	MN	Newport	Penobscot	ME
New Haven	Gallatin	IL	New Tennessee	Perry	AR	Newport	Johnson	IA
New Haven	Gratiot	MI	New Trier	Cook	IL	Newport	Lake	IL

TOWNSHIPS OF THE UNITED STATES

TOWNSHIP	COUNTY	STATE	TOWNSHIP	COUNTY	STATE	TOWNSHIP	COUNTY	STATE
Newport	Barton	MO	Nininger	Dakota	MN	Nore	Itasca	MN
Newport	Carteret	NC	Ninnekah	Grady	OK	Norfolk	Litchfield	CT
Newport	McHenry	ND	Ninnescah	Cowley	KS	Norfolk	Norfolk	MA
Newport	Sullivan	NH	Ninnescah	Kingman	KS	Norfolk	Renville	MN
Newport	Herkimer	NY	Ninnescah	Pratt	KS	Norfolk	Saint Lawrence	NY
Newport	Washington	OH	Ninnescah	Reno	KS	Norland	Lyon	MN
Newport	Luzerne	PA	Ninnescah	Sedgwick	KS	Norma	Barnes	ND
Newport	Marshall	SD	Niobrara	Knox	NE	Normal	McLean	IL
Newport	Orleans	VT	Nipomo	San Luis Obispo	CA	Normal	McHenry	ND
Newport	Columbia	WI	Nippawalla	Barber	KS	Norman	Grudy	IL
Newry	Oxford	ME	Nippenose	Lycoming	PA	Norman	Manistee	MI
Newry	Freeborn	MN	Nishnabotna	Atchison	MO	Norman	Pine	MN
Newstead	Erie	NY	Nishnabotny	Crawford	IA	Norman	Yellow Medicine	MN
Newton Grove	Sampson	NC	Niskayuna	Schenectaby	NY	Norman	Dent	MO
Newton	Faulkner	AR	Niven	Cleveland	AR	Norman	Traill	ND
Newton	Buchanan	IA	Niven	Jefferson	AR	Norman	Cleveland	OK
Newton	Carroll	IA	Nix	Dallas	AR	Normandy	Saint Louis	MO
Newton	Jasper	IA	Nixon	De Witt	IL	Normania	Yellow Medicine	MN
Newton	Winnebago	IA	Nixon	Ramsey	ND	Normania	Benson	ND
Newton	Whiteside	IL	Nixonton	Pasquotank	NC	Normanna	Saint Louis	MN
Newton	Jasper	IN	Noble	Cass	IA	Normanna	Cass	ND
Newton	Harvey	KS	Noble	Richland	IL	Norphlet	Union	AR
Newton	Calhoun	MI	Noble	Cass	IN	Norridgewock	Somerset	ME
Newton	Mackinac	MI	Noble	Joy	IN	Norrie	Marathon	WI
Newton	Otter Tail	MN	Noble	La Porte	IN	Norris	Mellette	SD
Newton	Shannon	MO	Noble	Noble	IN	North Abington	Lackawanna	PA
Newton	Catawaba	NC	Noble	Rush	IN	North Albemarle	Stanly	NC
Newton	Rockingham	NH	Noble	Shelby	IN	North Allis	Presque Isle	MI
Newton	Sussex	NJ	Noble	Wabash	IN	North Andover	Essex	MA
Newton	Licking	OH	Noble	Dickinson	KS	North Annville	Lebanon	PA
Newton	Miami	OH	Noble	Ellsworth	KS	North Attleborough	Bristol	MA
Newton	Muskingum	OH	Noble	Marshall	KS	North Beaver	Lawrence	PA
Newton	Pike	OH	Noble	Norton	KS	North Bend	Starke	IN
Newton	Trumbull	OH	Noble	Branch	MI	North Bend	Jackson	WI
Newton	Lackawanna	PA	Noble	Ozark	MO	North Benton	Dallas	MO
Newton	Manitowoc	WI	Noble	Cass	ND	North Bergen	Hudson	NJ
Newton	Marquette	WI	Noble	Valley	NE	North Berwick	York	ME
Newtonia	Newton	MO	Noble	Auglaize	OH	North Bethlehem	Washington	PA
Newtown	Fairfield	CT	Noble	Defiance	OH	North Big Rick	Sharp	AR
Newtown	Livingston	IL	Noble	Noble	OH	North Bloomfield	Morrow	OH
Newtown	Bucks	PA	Noble	Cleveland	OK	North Branch	Lapeer	MI
Newtown	Delaware	PA	Noble	Garfield	OK	North Branch	Isanti	MN
Newville	De Kalb	IN	Noble	Noble	OK	North Branch	Wyoming	PA
Niagara	Grand Forks	ND	Nobleboro	Lincoln	ME	North Branford	New Haven	CT
Niagara	Niagara	NY	Noblesville	Hamilton	IN	North Brook	Lincoln	NC
Niagara	Marinette	WI	Nockamixon	Bucks	PA	North Brookfield	Worcester	MA
Niangua	Webster	MO	Nodaway	Adams	IA	North Brown	Edwards	KS
Niantic	Macon	IL	Nodaway	Page	IA	North Brunswick	Middlesex	NJ
Nichols	Conway	AR	Nodaway	Taylor	IA	North Bryant	Edmunds	SD
Nichols	Saint Louis	MN	Nodaway	Andrew	MO	North Buffalo	Armstrong	PA
Nichols	Tioga	NY	Nodaway	Holt	MO	North Campbell	Greene	MO
Nicholson	Fayette	PA	Nodaway	Nodaway	MO	North Canaan	Litchfield	CT
Nicholson	Wyoming	PA	Nogosek	Stutsman	ND	North Castle	Westchester	NY
Nickerson	Pine	MN	Nokay Lake	Crow Wing	MN	North Catawba	Caldwell	NC
Nickerson	Dodge	NE	Nokomis	Buena Vista	IA	North Cedar	Saunders	NE
Nicodemus	Graham	KS	Nokomis	Montgomery	IL	North Cement	Caddo	OK
Nicolaus	Sutter	CA	Nokomis	Oneida	WI	North Centre	Columbia	PA
Nicollet	Nicollet	MN	Noland	Hempstead	AR	North Choctaw	Lincoln	OK
Nidaros	Otter Tail	MN	Noltimier	Barnes	ND	North Cimarron	Logan	OK
Nile	Scioto	OH	Nooksack	Whatcom	WA	North Clinton	Sampson	NC
Niles	Floyd	IA	Noonan	Ramsey	ND	North Cobb	Caddo	OK
Niles	Cook	IL	Nora	Jo Daviess	IL	North Codorus	York	PA
Niles	Delaware	IN	Nora	Clearwater	MN	North College Hill	Hamilton	OH
Niles	Berrien	MI	Nora	Pope	MN	North Collins	Erie	NY
Niles	Cayuga	NY	Nora	La Moure	ND	North Cornwall	Lebanon	PA
Nilsen	Wilkin	MN	Norden	Pennington	MN	North Cove	McDowell	NC
Nilwood	Macoupin	IL	Norden	La Moure	ND	North Coventry	Chester	PA
Nimishillen	Stark	OH	Norden	Deuel	SD	North Creek	Lincoln	OK
Nine Mile Prairie	Callaway	MO	Norden	Hamlin	SD	North Dansville	Livingston	NY
Nine Mile	Spokane	WA	Nordick	Wilkin	MN	North Detroit	Brown	SD
Nineveh	Johnson	IN	Nordland	Aitkin	MN	North East	Erie	PA
Nineveh	Adair	MO	Nordland	Marshall	SD	North Elba	Essex	NY
Nineveh	Lincoln	MO	Nordmore	Foster	ND	North Elk	Washita	OK

TOWNSHIPS OF THE UNITED STATES

TOWNSHIP	COUNTY	STATE	TOWNSHIP	COUNTY	STATE	TOWNSHIP	COUNTY	STATE
North Enid	Garfield	OK	North Shade	Gratiot	MI	Norton	Jefferson	KS
North Fayette	Allegheny	PA	North Shenango	Crawford	PA	Norton	Bristol	MA
North Fork	Baxter	AR	North Smithfield	Providence	RI	Norton	Winona	MN
North Fork	Marion	AR	North Star	Gratiot	MI	Norton	Walsh	ND
North Fork	Pope	AR	North Star	Brown	MN	Norton	Summit	OH
North Fork	Delaware	IA	North Star	Burke	ND	Norton	Essex	VT
North Fork	Gallatin	IL	North Stonington	New London	CT	Norvell	Jackson	MI
North Fork	Stearns	MN	North Strabane	Washington	PA	Norwalk	Fairfield	CT
North Fork	Barton	MO	North Sugar Creek	Randolph	MO	Norwalk	Pottawattamie	IA
North Fork	Ashe	NC	North Towanda	Bradford	PA	Norwalk	Huron	OH
North Fork	Watauga	NC	North	Lake	IN	Norway Lake	Kandiyohi	MN
North Fork	Beckham	OK	North	Marshall	IN	Norway Lake	Wells	ND
North Fox	Lincoln	OK	North	Labette	KS	Norway	Humboldt	IA
North Franklin	Franklin	NE	North	Wallace	KS	Norway	Winnebago	IA
North Franklin	Washington	PA	North	Woodson	KS	Norway	Wright	IA
North Galloway	Christian	MO	North	Pennington	MN	Norway	Republic	KS
North Germany	Wadena	MN	North	Dade	MO	Norway	Oxford	ME
North Greenbush	Rensselaer	NY	North	Harrison	OH	Norway	Dickinson	MI
North Hampton	Rockingham	NH	North Union	Sharp	AR	Norway	Fillmore	MN
North Hanover	Burlington	NJ	North Union	Fayette	PA	Norway	Kittson	MN
North Harmony	Chautauqua	NY	North Union	Schuylkill	PA	Norway	Traill	ND
North Harrison	Boone	AR	North Versailles	Allegheny	PA	Norway	Herkimer	NY
North Haven	New Haven	CT	North Viking	Benson	ND	Norway	Clay	SD
North Haven	Knox	ME	North Whitakers	Nash	NC	Norway	Lincoln	SD
North Hayes	Reno	KS	North Whitehall	Lehigh	PA	Norway	Roberts	SD
North Heidelberg	Berks	PA	North Wichita	Lincoln	OK	Norway	Turner	SD
North Hempstead	Nassau	NY	North Wilkesboro	Wilkes	NC	Norway	Racine	WI
North Henderson	Mercer	IL	North Woodbury	Blair	PA	Norwegian Grove	Otter Tail	MN
North Hero	Redwood	MN	North Yarmouth	Cumberland	ME	Norwegian	Schuylkill	PA
North Hero	Grand Isle	VT	Northampton	Rooks	KS	Norwell	Plymouth	MA
North Homestead	Barton	KS	Northampton	Fulton	NY	Norwich	New London	CT
North Hopewell	York	PA	Northampton	Summit	OH	Norwich	Missaukee	MI
North Hudson	Essex	NY	Northampton	Bucks	PA	Norwich	Newaygo	MI
North Huntingdon	Westmoreland	PA	Northampton	Somerset	PA	Norwich	McHenry	ND
North Keokuk	Lincoln	OK	Northborough	Worcester	MA	Norwich	Chenango	NY
North Kingstown	Washington	RI	Northbridge	Worcester	MA	Norwich	Franklin	OH
North Lancaster	Grant	WI	Northeast Madison	Perry	PA	Norwich	Huron	OH
North Las Vegas	Clark	NV	Northeast	Adams	IL	Norwich	McKean	PA
North Lathram	Caddo	OK	Northeast	Orange	IN	Norwich	Windsor	VT
North Lebanon	Sharp	AR	Northeast	Dutchess	NY	Norwood Park	Cook	IL
North Lebanon	Lebanon	PA	Northern	Franklin	IL	Norwood	Norfolk	MA
North Lemmon	Adams	ND	Northern	Beltrami	MN	Norwood	Charlevoix	MI
North Letchfield	Montgomery	IL	Northfield Center	Summit	OH	Norwood	Hamilton	OH
North Loma	Cavalier	ND	Northfield	Cook	IL	Norwood	Langlade	WI
North Londonderry	Lebanon	PA	Northfield	Franklin	MA	Notla	Cherokee	NC
North Loup	Valley	NE	Northfield	Washington	ME	Nottawa	Isabella	MI
North Mahoning	Indiana	PA	Northfield	Washtenaw	MI	Nottawa	Saint Joseph	MI
North Manheim	Schuylkill	PA	Northfield	Rice	MN	Nottingham	Wells	IN
North Middleton	Cumberland	PA	Northfield	Ramsey	ND	Nottingham	Rockingham	NH
North Moniteau	Cooper	MO	Northfield	Merrimack	NH	Nottingham	Harrison	OH
North Morgan	Dade	MO	Northfield	Summit	OH	Nottingham	Washington	PA
North Muddy	Jasper	IL	Northfield	Washington	VT	Nottinghill	Ozark	MO
North Newton	Cumberland	PA	Northfield	Jackson	WI	Notwata	Nowata	OK
North Norwich	Chenango	NY	Northfork	McKenzie	ND	Novato	Marin	CA
North Okaw	Coles	IL	Northland	Polk	MN	Novesta	Tuscola	MI
North Ottawa	Grant	MN	Northland	Saint Louis	MN	Novi	Oakland	MI
North Otter	Macoupin	IL	Northland	Ransom	ND	Nowata	Nowata	OK
North Palmyra	Macoupin	IL	Northmoreland	Wyoming	PA	Noxen	Wyoming	PA
North Plains	Ionia	MI	Northport	Waldo	ME	Noyes	Clinton	PA
North Prairie	McHenry	ND	Northumberland	Coos	NH	Numa	Grant	OK
North Providence	Providence	RI	Northumberland	Saratoga	NY	Numedal	Pennington	MN
North Randall	Thomas	KS	Northville	La Salle	IL	Nunda	McHenry	IL
North Reading	Middlesex	MA	Northville	Wayne	MI	Nunda	Cheboygan	MI
North Red River	Kittson	MN	Northville	Spink	SD	Nunda	Freeborn	MN
North Rich	Anderson	KS	Northwest Angle	Lake of the Woods	MN	Nunda	Livingston	NY
North River	Shelby	MO	Northwest	Stone	AR	Nunda	Lake	SD
North Riverside	Potter	SD	Northwest	Orange	IN	Nutbush	Warren	NC
North Roscoe	Hodgeman	KS	Northwest	Brunswick	NC	Nutley	Essex	NJ
North Salem	Linn	MO	Northwest	Dickey	ND	Nutley	Day	SD
North Salem	Westchester	NY	Northwest	Williams	OH	Nutty Combe	Cheyenne	KS
North Seminole	Lincoln	OK	Northwood	Grand Forks	ND			
North Seward	Stafford	KS	Northwood	Rockingham	NH			
North Sewickley	Beaver	PA	Norton	Kankakee	IL			

—O—

TOWNSHIPS OF THE UNITED STATES

TOWNSHIP	COUNTY	STATE	TOWNSHIP	COUNTY	STATE	TOWNSHIP	COUNTY	STATE
Oacoma	Lymnan	SD	Oakley	Logan	KS	Ohio	Monroe	OH
Oak Bar	Siskiyou	CA	Oakport	Clay	MN	Ohio	Ellis	OK
Oak Bluff	Clay	AR	Oakville	Grand Forks	ND	Ohio	Allegheny	PA
Oak Bluffs	Dukes	MA	Oakwood	Vermilion	IL	Ohio	Hand	SD
Oak Creek	Borrineau	ND	Oakwood	Wabasha	MN	Oil Creek	Crawford	PA
Oak Creek	Butler	NE	Oakwood	Walsh	ND	Oil Fields	Wilson	NC
Oak Creek	Saunders	NE	Oakwood	Montgomery	OH	Oil	Perry	IN
Oak Creek	Sherman	NE	Oakwood	Brookings	SD	Oil Trough	Independence	AR
Oak Dale	Howard	IA	Oasis	Waushara	WI	Oilcreek	Venango	PA
Oak Forest	Lee	AR	Oawala	Rogers	OK	Ojai	Ventura	CA
Oak Grove	Lonoke	AR	Oberlin	Decatur	KS	Ojibwa	Sawyer	WI
Oak Grove	Benton	IN	Oberon	Benson	ND	Okaton	Jones	SD
Oak Grove	Anoka	MN	Obids	Ashe	NC	Okaw	Shelby	IL
Oak Grove	Durham	NC	Oblong	Crawford	IL	Okawville	Washington	IL
Oak Grove	Franklin	NE	O'Brien	Beltrami	MN	O'Kean	Randolph	AR
Oak Grove	Barron	WI	O'Bryan	Woods	OK	Okemah	Okfuskee	OK
Oak Grove	Dodge	WI	Ocean	Monmouth	NJ	Oketo	Marshall	KS
Oak Grove	Pierce	WI	Ocean	Ocean	NJ	Okfuskee	Okfuskee	OK
Oak Gulch	Day	SD	Oceanside	San Diego	CA	Oklahoma	Oklahoma	OK
Oak Hill	Crawford	MO	Oceola	Livingston	MI	Okoboji	Dickinson	IA
Oak Hill	Granville	NC	Ocheyedan	Osceola	IA	Ola	Brule	SD
Oak Hollow	Hutchinson	SD	Oconee	Shelby	IL	Olathe	Johnson	KS
Oak Lake	Brookings	SD	Oconee	Platte	NE	Old Fort	McDowell	NC
Oak Lawn	Crow Wing	MN	Oconeechee	Northampton	NC	Old Hickory	Conway	AR
Oak Level	Nash	NC	Oconomowoc	Waukesha	WI	Old Lycoming	Lycoming	PA
Oak Park	Cook	IL	Oconto	Oconto	WI	Old Lyme	New London	CT
Oak Park	Marshall	MN	Ocqueoc	Presque Isle	MI	Old Orchard Beach	York	ME
Oak Ridge	Guilford	NC	Ocracoke	Hyde	NC	Old Richmond	Forsyth	NC
Oak Run	Madison	OH	Octavia	La Flore	OK	Old Ripley	Bond	IL
Oak	Mills	IA	Odee	Meade	KS	Old River	Jefferson	AR
Oak	Smith	KS	Odell	Livingston	IL	Old Saybrook	Middlesex	CT
Oak	Stearns	MN	Odell	Harper	KS	Old Town	Forsyth	NC
Oak	Canadian	OK	Odell	Cabarrus	NC	Oldfield	Christian	MO
Oak Valley	Elk	KS	Odell	Coos	NH	Oldfields	Ashe	NC
Oak Valley	Otter Tail	MN	Odell	Marshall	OK	Oldmans	Salem	NJ
Oak Valley	Bottineau	ND	Odessa	Jewell	KS	Olds	Greene	NC
Oak View	Logan	OK	Odessa	Rice	KS	Oldtown	McLean	IL
Oakaloosa	Clay	IL	Odessa	Ionia	MI	Olean	Cattaraugus	NY
Oakdale	Stanislaus	CA	Odessa	Big Stone	MN	Olean	Spink	SD
Oakdale	Washington	IL	Odessa	Ramsey	ND	Oleta	Ells	OK
Oakdale	Antelope	NE	Odessa	Buffalo	NE	Oley	Berks	PA
Oakdale	Noble	OK	Odessa	Edmunds	SD	Olga	Cavalier	ND
Oakdale	Washita	OK	Odin	Marion	IL	Olin	Iredell	NC
Oakdale	Monroe	WI	Odin	Watonwan	MN	Olio	Woodford	IL
Oakes	Choctaw	OK	Odin	McHenry	ND	Olive Hill	Person	NC
Oakfield	Audubon	IA	O'Fallon	Saint Clair	IL	Olive	Clinton	IA
Oakfield	Aroostook	ME	Ogallah	Trego	KS	Olive	Madison	IL
Oakfield	Kent	MI	Ogden	Champaign	IL	Olive	Elkhart	IN
Oakfield	Genesee	NY	Ogden	Riley	KS	Olive	Saint Joseph	IN
Oakfield	Fond du Lac	WI	Ogden	Lenawee	MI	Olive	Decatur	KS
Oakham	Worcester	MA	Ogema	Pine	MN	Olive	Clinton	MI
Oakhill	Barnes	SD	Ogema	Price	WI	Olive	Ottawa	MI
Oakland	Alameda	CA	Ogemaw	Ogemaw	MI	Olive	Butler	NE
Oakland	Franklin	IA	Ogle	Muskogee	OK	Olive	Ulster	NY
Oakland	Louisa	IA	Ogle	Somerset	PA	Olive	Meigs	OH
Oakland	Schuyler	IL	O'Hara	Allegheny	PA	Olive	Noble	OH
Oakland	Clay	KS	Ohio Grove	Mercer	IL	Olive	Creek	OK
Oakland	Cloud	KS	Ohio	Madison	IA	Olive	Garfield	OK
Oakland	Kennecec	ME	Ohio	Bureau	IL	Olive Springs	Crawford	AR
Oakland	Oakland	MI	Ohio	Bartholomew	IN	Oliver	Scott	AR
Oakland	Freeborn	MN	Ohio	Crawford	IN	Oliver	Huron	MI
Oakland	Mahnomen	MN	Ohio	Spencer	IN	Oliver	Kalkaska	MI
Oakland	Chatham	NC	Ohio	Warrick	IN	Oliver	Taney	MO
Oakland	Mountrail	ND	Ohio	Franklin	KS	Oliver	Williams	ND
Oakland	Burt	NE	Ohio	Morris	KS	Oliver	Adams	OH
Oakland	Butler	PA	Ohio	Ness	KS	Oliver	Ellis	OK
Oakland	Susquehanna	PA	Ohio	Saline	KS	Oliver	Jefferson	PA
Oakland	Venango	PA	Ohio	Sedgwick	KS	Oliver	Mifflin	PA
Oakland	Burnett	WI	Ohio	Stafford	KS	Oliver	Perry	PA
Oakland	Douglas	WI	Ohio	Mississippi	MO	Olivet	Osage	KS
Oakland	Jefferson	WI	Ohio	Herkimer	NY	Olivia	McHenry	ND
Oaklawn	Greenville	SC	Ohio	Clermont	OH	Olmsted	Cuyahoga	OH
Oakley	Macon	IL	Ohio	Gallia	OH	Olney	Richland	IL

TOWNSHIP	COUNTY	STATE	TOWNSHIP	COUNTY	STATE	TOWNSHIP	COUNTY	STATE
Olney	Nobles	MN	Orange	Norton	KS	Ortley	Roberts	SD
Olson	Towner	ND	Orange	Pawnee	KS	Orton	Wadena	MN
Olustee	Jackson	OK	Orange	Franklin	MA	Ortonville	Big Stone	MN
Olvey	Boone	AR	Orange	Ionia	MI	Orvil	Logan	IL
Oma	Iron	WI	Orange	Kalkaska	MI	Orwell	Otter Tail	MN
Omaha	Boone	AR	Orange	Douglas	MN	Orwell	Oswego	NY
Omaha	Gallatin	IL	Orange	Adams	ND	Orwell	Ashtabula	OH
Omega	Carroll	AR	Orange	Grafton	NH	Orwell	Bradford	PA
Omega	O'Brien	IA	Orange	Schuyler	NY	Orwell	Addison	VT
Omega	Marion	IL	Orange	Ashland	OH	Osage	Benton	AR
Omega	Kingfisher	OK	Orange	Carroll	OH	Osage	Carroll	AR
Omnia	Cowley	KS	Orange	Delaware	OH	Osage	Newton	AR
Omphghent	Madison	IL	Orange	Hancock	OH	Osage	Mitchell	IA
Omro	Yellow Medicine	MN	Orange	Meigs	OH	Osage	La Salle	IL
Omro	Winnebago	WI	Orange	Shelby	OH	Osage	Allen	KS
Onalaska	La Crosse	WI	Orange	Columbia	PA	Osage	Bourbon	KS
Onamia	Mille Lacs	MN	Orange	Orangeburg	SC	Osage	Crawford	KS
Onarga	Iroquois	IL	Orange	Orange	VT	Osage	Labette	KS
Onawa	Monona	IA	Orange	Juneau	WI	Osage	Miami	KS
One Road	Roberts	SD	Orangetown	Rockland	NY	Osage	Becker	MN
O'Neal	San Joaquin	CA	Orangeville	Orange	IN	Osage	Bates	MO
O'Neal	Greenville	SC	Orangeville	Barry	MI	Osage	Camden	MO
O'Neals	Johnston	NC	Orangeville	Wyoming	NY	Osage	Cole	MO
Oneco	Stephenson	IL	Orchard Park	Erie	NY	Osage	Crawford	MO
Oneida	Delaware	IA	Orchard	Wayne	IL	Osage	Dent	MO
Oneida	Tama	IA	Ord	Antelope	NE	Osage	Henry	MO
Oneida	Eaton	MI	Ord	Valley	NE	Osage	Laclede	MO
Oneida	Kearney	NE	Ordway	Brown	SD	Osage	Miller	MO
Oneida	Huntingdon	PA	Oregon	Washington	IA	Osage	Morgan	MO
Oneida	Sanborn	SD	Oregon	Ogle	IL	Osage	Saint Clair	MO
Oneida	Outagamie	WI	Oregon	Clark	IN	Osage	Vernon	MO
O'Neil	Faulk	SD	Oregon	Starke	IN	Osage	Lincoln	OK
Oneka	Washington	MN	Oregon	Lepeer	MI	Osago	Nelson	ND
Onekama	Manistee	??	Oregon	Wayne	PA	Osakis	Douglas	MN
Oneonta	Otsego	NY	Oregon	Dane	WI	Osawatomie	Miami	KS
Oneota	Brown	SD	Orel	Wayne	IL	Osborn	Sumner	KS
Onondage	Ingham	MI	Orford	Grafton	NH	Osborn	Garfield	OK
Onondage	Onondage	NY	Orient	Adair	IA	Osborn	Mountrail	ND
Onota	Alger	MI	Orient	Aroostook	ME	Osborn	Outagamie	WI
Onstad	Polk	MN	Orient	Osceola	MI	Osborne	Pipestone	MN
Ontario	San Bernardino	CA	Orient	Faulk	SD	Oscar	Otter Tail	MN
Ontario	Knox	IL	Orienta	Bayfield	WI	Osceola City	Clarke	IA
Ontario	Ramsey	ND	Orion	Fulton	IL	Osceola	Clarke	IA
Ontario	Wayne	NY	Orion	Oakland	MI	Osceola	Franklin	IA
Ontario	Hand	SD	Orion	Olmsted	MN	Osceola	Stark	IL
Ontelaunee	Berks	PA	Orion	Richland	WI	Osceola	Houghton	MI
Ontonagon	Ontonagon	MI	Oriska	Barnes	ND	Osceola	Osceola	MI
Ontwa	Cass	MI	Orland	Cook	IL	Ocseola	Renville	MN
Oolagah	Rogers	OK	Orland	Hancock	ME	Osceola	Saint Clair	MO
Opdahl	Hamlin	SD	Orland	Lake	SD	Osceola	Lewis	NY
Ophir	La Salle	IL	Orlando	Cheyenne	KS	Osceola	Tioga	PA
Ophir	Powell	MT	Orlando	Logan	OK	Osceola	Brown	SD
Ophir	Montgomery	NC	Orleans	Winneshiek	IA	Osceola	Grant	SD
Oppenheim	Fulton	NY	Orleans	Orange	IN	Osceola	Fond du Lac	WI
Opportunity	Spokane	WA	Orleans	Barnstable	MA	Osceola	Polk	WI
Ops	Walsh	ND	Orleans	Ionia	MI	Osco	Henry	IL
Optima	Texas	OK	Orleans	Harlan	NE	Oscoda	Iosco	MI
Oquawka	Henderson	IL	Orleans	Jefferson	NY	Osford	Cavalier	ND
Ora	Jackson	IL	Orlien	Ward	ND	Oshawa	Nicollet	MN
Ora	Nelson	ND	Ormonds	Greene	NC	Oshkosh	Yellow Medicine	MN
Oran	Fayette	IA	Oro Grande	San Bernardino	CA	Oshkosh	Winnebago	WI
Oran	Logan	IL	Orono	Muscatine	IA	Oshkosk	Wells	ND
Orange	Orange	CA	Orono	Penobscot	ME	Oshtemo	Kalamazoo	MI
Orange	New Haven	CT	Oronoco	Olmsted	MN	Oskaloosa	Mahaska	IA
Orange	Black Hawk	IA	Oronoko	Berrien	MI	Oskaloosa	Jefferson	KS
Orange	Clinton	IA	Orosi	Tulare	CA	Oslo	Brookings	SD
Orange	Guthrie	IA	Oroville	Butte	CA	Osloe	Mountrail	ND
Orange	Clark	IL	Orrick	Ray	MO	Osnabrock	Cavalier	ND
Orange	Knox	IL	Orrington	Penobscot	ME	Osnaburg	Stark	OH
Orange	Fayette	IN	Orrock	Sherburne	MN	Osolo	Elkhart	IN
Orange	Noble	IN	Orrum	Robeson	NC	Ossian	Livingston	NY
Orange	Rush	IN	Orthel	Hancock	IA	Ossineke	Alpena	MI
Orange	Lincoln	KS	Orthell	Williams	ND	Ossining	Westchester	NY

TOWNSHIP	COUNTY	STATE	TOWNSHIP	COUNTY	STATE	TOWNSHIP	COUNTY	STATE
Ossipee	Carroll	NH	Ouachita	Montgomery	AR	Pacific Grove	Monterey	CA
Ostby	Bottineau	ND	Ouachita	Polk	AR	Pacific	Humboldt	CA
Oswayo	Potter	PA	Oulu	Bayfield	WI	Pacific	Columbia	WI
Oswegatchie	Saint Lawrence	NY	Overfield	Wyoming	PA	Pacolet	Spartanburg	SC
Oswego	Kendall	IL	Overisel	Allegan	MI	Packard Springs	Carroll	AR
Oswego	Labette	KS	Overland	Morris	KS	Packer	Carbon	PA
Oswego	Oswego	NY	Overland	Ramsey	ND	Packwaukee	Marquette	WI
Otego	Fayette	IL	Overton	Clark	NV	Pactolus	Pitt	NC
Otego	Otesgo	NY	Overton	Bradford	PA	Paddock	Otter Tail	MN
Oteneagen	Itasca	MN	Ovid	Branch	MI	Paddock	Gage	NE
Otho	Webster	IA	Ovid	Clinton	MI	Paddock	Holt	NE
Otis	Berkshire	MA	Ovid	La Moure	ND	Paden	Okfuskee	OK
Otis	Hancock	ME	Ovid	Seneca	NY	Padonia	Brown	KS
Otis	McLean	ND	Owanka	Pennington	SD	Page	Mille Lacs	MN
Otisco	Ionia	MI	Owasco	Cayuga	NY	Page	Cass	ND
Otisco	Waseca	MN	Owasso	Tulsa	OK	Page	Le Flore	OK
Otisco	Onondage	NY	Owatonna	Steele	MN	Pageland	Chesterfield	SC
Otisfield	Cumberland	ME	Owattonna	Potter	SD	Pahapesto	Tripp	SD
Oto	Woodbury	IA	Owego	Livingston	IL	Pahaquarry	Warren	NJ
Otoe	Lincoln	OK	Owego	Ransom	ND	Pahrump	Nye	NV
Otoe	Noble	OK	Owego	Tioga	NY	Painesville	Lake	OH
Otoe	Pawnee	OK	Owen	Dallas	AR	Paint Creek	Allamakee	IA
Otranto	Mitchell	IA	Owen	Lincoln	AR	Paint	Fayette	OH
Otrey	Big Stone	MN	Owen	Poinsett	AR	Paint	Highland	OH
Otsego Lake	Otsego	MI	Owen	Saline	AR	Paint	Holmes	OH
Otsego	Steuben	IN	Owen	Cerro Gordo	IA	Paint	Madison	OH
Otsego	Allegan	MI	Owen	Winnebago	IL	Paint	Ross	OH
Otsego	Wright	MN	Owen	Clark	IN	Paint	Wayne	OH
Otsego	Otsego	NY	Owen	Clinton	IN	Paint	Clarion	PA
Otsego	Columbia	WI	Owen	Jackson	IN	Paint	Somerset	PA
Otselic	Chenango	NY	Owen	Warrick	IN	Painted Woods	Burleigh	ND
Ottawa Hills	Lucas	OH	Owen	Kay	OK	Painter	Comanche	OK
Ottawa	La Salle	IL	Owens	Saint Louis	MN	Painterhood	Elk	KS
Ottawa	Franklin	KS	Owl Creek	Woodson	KS	Pajaro	Monterey	CA
Ottawa	Ottawa	KS	Owls Head	Knox	ME	Palacky	Ellsworth	KS
Ottawa	Le Sueur	MN	Owosso	Shiawassee	MI	Palarm	Faulkner	AR
Ottawa	Putnam	OH	Oxford	New Haven	CT	Palatine	Cook	IL
Ottawa	Ottawa	OK	Oxford	Johnson	IA	Palatine	Montgomery	NY
Ottawa	Waukesha	WI	Oxford	Jones	IA	Palatine	Aurora	SD
Otter Creek	Crawford	IA	Oxford	Henry	IL	Palermo	Grundy	IA
Otter Creek	Jackson	IA	Oxford	Johnson	KS	Palermo	Waldo	ME
Otter Creek	Linn	IA	Oxford	Sumner	KS	Palermo	Mountrail	ND
Otter Creek	Lucas	IA	Oxford	Worcester	MA	Palermo	Oswego	NY
Otter Creek	Tama	IA	Oxford	Oxford	ME	Palestine	Bradley	AR
Otter Creek	Jersey	IL	Oxford	Oakland	MI	Palestine	Story	IA
Otter Creek	La Salle	IL	Oxford	Isanti	MN	Palestine	Woodford	IL
Otter Creek	Ripley	IN	Oxford	Granville	NC	Palestine	Sumner	KS
Otter Creek	Vigo	IN	Oxford	Warren	NJ	Palestine	Cooper	MO
Otter Creek	Greenwood	KS	Oxford	Chenango	NY	Palisade	Minnehaha	SD
Otter Creek	Edgecombe	NC	Oxford	Butler	OH	Palm Springs	Riverside	CA
Otter Creek	Grant	ND	Oxford	Coshocton	OH	Palmer	Hampden	MA
Otter Creek	Dixon	NE	Oxford	Delaware	OH	Palmer	Sherburne	MN
Otter Creek	Kiowa	OK	Oxford	Erie	OH	Palmer	Divide	ND
Otter Creek	Mercer	PA	Oxford	Guernsey	OH	Palmer	Putnam	OH
Otter Creek	Dunn	WI	Oxford	Tuscarawas	OH	Palmer	Washington	OH
Otter Creek	Eau Claire	WI	Oxford	Adams	PA	Palmer	Northampton	PA
Otter Tail	Otter Tail	MN	Oxford	Hamlin	SD	Palmville	Roseau	MN
Otter	Saline	AR	Oxford	Marquette	WI	Palmyra	Warren	IA
Otter	Warren	IA	Oxnard	Ventura	CA	Palmyra	Lee	IL
Otter	Cowley	KS	Oyster Bay	Nassau	NY	Palmyra	Knox	IN
Otter	Ellis	OK	Ozan	Hempstead	AR	Palmyra	Douglas	KS
Otter	Garfield	OK	Ozark	Anderson	KS	Palmyra	Somerset	ME
Otter	Harper	OK	Ozark	Barry	MO	Palmyra	Lenawee	MI
Otter	Kingfisher	OK	Ozark	Barton	MO	Palmyra	Renville	MN
Otterville	Cooper	MO	Ozark	Lawrence	MO	Palmyra	Halifax	NC
Otto	Kankakee	IL	Ozark	Oregon	MO	Palmyra	Wayne	NY
Otto	Oceana	MI	Ozark	Texas	MO	Palmyra	Portage	OH
Otto	Otter Tail	MN	Ozark	Webster	MO	Palmyra	Pike	PA
Otto	Cattaraugus	NY	Ozawkie	Jefferson	KS	Palmyra	Wayne	PA
Otto	McKean	PA				Palmyra	Brown	SD
Ottumwa	Coffey	KS		—P—		Palmyra	Jefferson	WI
Ouachita	Bradley	AR				Palo Alto	Santa Clara	CA
Ouachita	Hot Spring	AR	Pablo	Lake	MT	Palo Alto	Jasper	IA

TOWNSHIPS OF THE UNITED STATES

TOWNSHIP	COUNTY	STATE
Palo Verde	Riverside	CA
Palos	Cook	IL
Pamelia	Jefferson	NY
Pamplin	Sioux	ND
Pana	Christian	IL
Panaca	Lincoln	NV
Panoche	San Benito	CA
Panola	Woodford	IL
Pantego	Beaufort	NC
Panther Branch	Wake	NC
Panther Creek	Cass	IL
Panton	Addison	VT
Paola	Miami	KS
Paoli	Orange	IN
Papineau	Iroquois	IL
Paraclifta	Sevier	AR
Paradise	Crawford	IA
Paradise	Coles	IL
Paradise	Rooks	KS
Paradise	Russell	KS
Paradise	Grand Traverse	MI
Paradise	Eddy	ND
Paradise	Payne	OK
Paradise	Lancaster	PA
Paradise	Monroe	PA
Paradise	York	PA
Paradise Valley	Humboldt	NV
Paris Mountain	Greenville	SC
Paris	Howard	IA
Paris	Edgar	IL
Paris	Linn	KS
Paris	Oxford	ME
Paris	Huron	MI
Paris	Stutsman	ND
Paris	Oneida	NY
Paris	Portage	OH
Paris	Stark	OH
Paris	Union	OH
Paris	Grant	WI
Paris	Kenosha	WI
Parish Grove	Benton	IN
Parish	Oswego	NY
Parishville	Saint Lawrence	NY
Park Hill	Cherokee	OK
Park	Scott	AR
Park	Sedgwick	KS
Park	Ottawa	MI
Park	Saint Joseph	MI
Park	Pine	MN
Park	Pembina	ND
Park	Kingfisher	OK
Park	Hand	SD
Park	Whatcom	WA
Parke	Clay	MN
Parker	Nevada	AR
Parker	Clark	IL
Parker	Montgomery	KS
Parker	Morris	KS
Parker	Marshall	MN
Parker	Morrison	MN
Parker	Butler	PA
Parker	Turner	SD
Parkers Prairie	Otter Tail	MN
Parkland	Douglas	WI
Parkman	Piscataquis	MN
Parkman	Geauga	OH
Parkman	Ellis	OK
Parks	Montgomery	AR
Parks	Stephen	OK
Parks	Armstrong	PA
Parkton	Robeson	NC
Parkville	Perquimans	NC
Parma	Jackson	MI
Parma	Monroe	NY
Parnell	Sheridan	KS
Parnell	Polk	MN
Parnell	Traverse	MN
Parnell	Brookings	SD
Parrish	Langlade	WI
Parshall	Mountrail	ND
Parsippany-Troy Hills	Morris	NJ
Parson Creek	Linn	MO
Parsonfield	York	ME
Parsons	Alfalfa	OK
Partridge	Woodford	IL
Partridge	Pine	MN
Pasadena	Los Angeles	CA
Pascoe	Okulgee	OK
Pascola	Pemiscot	MO
Paso Robles	San Luis Obispo	CA
Passaic	Morris	NJ
Passadumkeag	Penobscot	ME
Passport	Ward	ND
Pastoria	Jefferson	AR
Patch Grove	Grant	WI
Patent Gate	McKenzie	ND
Patoka	Marion	IL
Patoka	Crawford	IN
Patoka	Dubois	IN
Patoka	Gibson	IN
Patoka	Pike	IN
Paton	Green	IA
Patten	Penobscot	ME
Patten	Aurora	SD
Patterson	Stanislaus	CA
Patterson	Greene	IL
Patterson	Alamance	NC
Patterson	Caldwell	NC
Patterson	Putnam	NY
Patterson	Darke	OH
Patterson	Garfield	OK
Patterson	Jefferson	OK
Patterson	Woods	OK
Patterson	Beaver	PA
Patton	Ford	IL
Patton	Centre	PA
Paulding	Paulding	OH
Paulson	Towner	ND
Paupack	Wayne	PA
Pavilion	Kalamazoo	MI
Pavilion	Genesee	NY
Paw Creek	Mecklenburg	NC
Paw Paw	De Kalb	IL
Paw Paw	Wabash	IN
Paw Paw	Elk	KS
Paw Paw	Van Buren	MI
Paw Paw	Sequoyah	OK
Pawlet	Turland	VT
Pawling	Dutchess	NY
Pawnee Rock	Barton	KS
Pawnee	Sangamon	IL
Pawnee	Bourbon	KS
Pawnee	Pawnee	KS
Pawnee	Smith	KS
Pawnee	Lincoln	OK
Pawnee	Pawnee	OK
Pawnee	Payne	OK
Paxton	Logan	KS
Paxton	Pratt	KS
Paxton	Worcester	MA
Paxton	Redwood	MN
Paxton	Ross	OH
Payne	Clay	AR
Payne	Gove	KS
Payne	Sedgwick	KS
Payne	Saint Louis	MN
Paynesville	Stearns	MN
Payson	Adams	IL
Pea Ridge	Brown	IL
Peabody	Marion	KS
Peabody	Bottineau	ND
Peace	Kanabec	MN
Peace	Kidder	ND
Peaceful Valley	Slope	ND
Peach Botton	York	PA
Peach Orchard	Ford	IL
Peacham	Caledonia	VT
Peachtree	Monterey	CA
Peacock	Lake	MI
Peaine	Charlevoix	MI
Peak Creek	Ashe	NC
Pearces Mill	Cumberland	NC
Pearl Creek	Beadle	SD
Pearl Lake	La Moure	ND
Pearl	Pike	IL
Pearl	Golden Valley	ND
Pearl	Hand	SD
Pearl	McCook	SD
Pease	Belmont	OH
Pebble	Dodge	NE
Pebble	Pike	OH
Pecan	Mississippi	AR
Pecatonica	Winnebago	IL
Peck	Langlade	WI
Peculiar	Cass	MO
Pee Dee and Choppee	Georgetown	SC
Pee Dee	Chesterfield	SC
Pee Dee	Florence	SC
Pee Pee	Pike	OH
PeeDee	Montgomery	NC
Peeksville	Ashland	WI
Peeples	Hampton	SC
Peggs	Cherokee	OK
Pekin	Tazewell	IL
Pelan	Kittson	MN
Pelham	Hampshire	MA
Pelham	Caswell	NC
Pelham	Hillsborough	NH
Pelham	Westchester	NY
Pelican Lake	Grant	MN
Pelican	Crow Wing	MN
Pelican	Otter Tail	MN
Pelican	Ramsey	ND
Pelican	Codington	SD
Pelican	Oneida	WI
Pella	Ford	IL
Pella	Shawano	WI
Pemberton	Burlington	NJ
Pembina	Mahnomen	MN
Pembina	Pembina	ND
Pembine	Marinette	WI
Pembroke	Kankakee	IL
Pembroke	Plymouth	MA
Pembroke	Washington	ME
Pembroke	Robeson	NC
Pembroke	Merrimack	NH
Pembroke	Genesee	NY
Pembrook	Edmunds	SD
Pemiscot	Pemiscot	MO
Pence	Iron	WI
Pencil Bluff	Montgomery	AR
Pendleton	Jefferson	IL
Pendleton	Saint Francois	MO
Pendleton	Niagara	NY
Pendleton	Anderson	SC
Penfield	Monroe	NY
Penfield	Lorain	OH
Peninsula	Grand Traverse	MI
Penn Forest	Carbon	PA

TOWNSHIPS OF THE UNITED STATES

TOWNSHIP	COUNTY	STATE	TOWNSHIP	COUNTY	STATE	TOWNSHIP	COUNTY	STATE
Penn Hills	Allegheny	PA	Perry	Buchanan	IA	Persia	Cattaraugus	NY
Penn	Guthrie	IA	Perry	Davis	IA	Persifer	Knox	IL
Penn	Jefferson	IA	Perry	Jackson	IA	Perth	Walsh	ND
Penn	Johnson	IA	Perry	Plymouth	IA	Perth	Fulton	NY
Penn	Madison	IA	Perry	Tama	IA	Peru	Dubuque	IA
Penn	Shelby	IL	Perry	Pike	IL	Peru	La Salle	IL
Penn	Stark	IL	Perry	Allen	IN	Peru	Miami	IN
Penn	Jay	IN	Perry	Boone	IN	Peru	Berkshire	MA
Penn	Parke	IN	Perry	Clay	IN	Peru	Oxford	ME
Penn	Saint Joseph	IN	Perry	Clinton	IN	Peru	Clinton	NY
Penn	Osborne	KS	Perry	Delaware	IN	Peru	Huron	OH
Penn	Cass	MI	Perry	Lawrence	IN	Peru	Morrow	OH
Penn	McLeod	MN	Perry	Marion	IN	Peru	Bennington	VT
Penn	Sullivan	MO	Perry	Martin	IN	Peru	Dunn	WI
Penn	Highland	OH	Perry	Miami	IN	Peshtigo	Marinette	WI
Penn	Morgan	OH	Perry	Monroe	IN	Pesotum	Champaign	IL
Penn	Woods	OK	Perry	Noble	IN	Petaluma	Sonoma	CA
Penn	Woodward	OK	Perry	Tippecanoe	IN	Peter Creek	Cleburne	AR
Penn	Berks	PA	Perry	Vanderburgh	IN	Peters Creek	Stokes	NC
Penn	Butler	PA	Perry	Wayne	IN	Peters	Kingman	KS
Penn	Centre	PA	Perry	Woodson	KS	Peters	Franklin	PA
Penn	Chester	PA	Perry	Washington	ME	Peters	Washington	PA
Penn	Clearfield	PA	Perry	Shiawassee	MI	Peterborough	Hillsborough	NH
Penn	Cumberland	PA	Perry	Lac Qui Parle	MN	Petersburg	Jackson	MN
Penn	Huntingdon	PA	Perry	Saint Francois	MO	Petersburg	Nelson	ND
Penn	Lancaster	PA	Perry	Cavalier	ND	Petersburg	Rensselaer	NY
Penn	Lycoming	PA	Perry	Wyoming	NY	Petersham	Worcester	MA
Penn	Perry	PA	Perry	Allen	OH	Peterson	Clay	IA
Penn	Snyder	PA	Perry	Ashland	OH	Peterson	Stutsman	ND
Penn	Westmoreland	PA	Perry	Brown	OH	Petersville	Kidder	ND
Penn	York	PA	Perry	Carroll	OH	Petit	Conway	AR
Penn	Williamsburg	SC	Perry	Columbiana	OH	Petit Jean	Logan	AR
Pennfield	Calhoun	MI	Perry	Coshocton	OH	Petit Jean	Perry	AR
Pennington	Bradley	AR	Perry	Fayette	OH	Pettibone	Kidder	ND
Pennsauken	Camden	NJ	Perry	Franklin	OH	Pettis	Adair	MO
Pennsbury	Chester	PA	Perry	Gallia	OH	Pettis	Platte	MO
Pennsville	Salem	NJ	Perry	Hocking	OH	Pettus	Lonoke	AR
Pennsylvania	Mason	IL	Perry	Lake	OH	Petty	Lawrence	IL
Peno	Pike	MO	Perry	Lawrence	OH	Pewaukee	Waukesha	WI
Peno	Hyde	SD	Perry	Licking	OH	Pharsalia	Chenango	NY
Peno	Pennington	SD	Perry	Logan	OH	Phatcono	Warren	NJ
Penobscot	Hancock	ME	Perry	Monroe	OH	Phelman	Emmons	ND
Pensacola	Yancey	NC	Perry	Montgomery	OH	Phelps	Ontario	NY
Pensaukee	Oconto	WI	Perry	Morrow	OH	Phelps	Vilas	WI
Pentland	Luce	MI	Perry	Muskingum	OH	Phenix	Henry	IL
Pentwater	Oceana	MI	Perry	Pickaway	OH	Pherrin	Williams	ND
Peone	Spokane	WA	Perry	Pike	OH	Philadelphia	Cass	IL
Peoples	Boone	IA	Perry	Putnam	OH	Philadelphia	Jefferson	NY
Peoria City	Peroia	IL	Perry	Richland	OH	Philadelphus	Robeson	NC
Peoria	Peoria	IL	Perry	Shelby	OH	Philipstown	Putnam	NY
Peoria	Franklin	KS	Perry	Stark	OH	Phillips	Garland	AR
Peoria	Knox	NE	Perry	Tuscarawas	OH	Phillips	White	IL
Peoria	Ottawa	OK	Perry	Wood	OH	Phillips	Franklin	ME
Peotone	Will	IL	Perry	McClain	OK	Phillips	Coal	OK
Pepin	Wabasha	MN	Perry	Armstrong	PA	Phillipsburg	Phillips	KS
Pepin	Pepin	WI	Perry	Berks	PA	Phillipsburg	Laclede	MO
Pepperell	Middlesex	MA	Perry	Clarion	PA	Phillipsburg	Warren	NJ
Pepperton	Stevens	MN	Perry	Fayette	PA	Phillipston	Worcester	MA
Pequannock	Morris	NJ	Perry	Greene	PA	Philo	Champaign	IL
Pequea	Lancaster	PA	Perry	Jefferson	PA	Phipps	Codington	SD
Perche	Boone	MO	Perry	Lawrence	PA	Phippsburg	Sagadahoc	ME
Percy	Kittson	MN	Perry	Mercer	PA	Phoenix	Pope	AR
Pere Marquette	Mason	MI	Perry	Snyder	PA	Phoenix	Greenwood	SC
Perham	Aroostook	ME	Perry	Davison	SD	Piasa	Jersey	IL
Perham	Otter Tail	MN	Perry	Lincoln	SD	Piatt	Lycoming	PA
Perinton	Monroe	NY	Perry	Dane	WI	Pickard	Sheridan	ND
Perkins	Payne	MO	Perrysburg	Cattaraugus	NY	Pickaway	Shelby	IL
Perkins	Erie	OH	Perrysburg	Wood	OH	Pickaway	Pickaway	OH
Perkiomen	Montgomery	PA	Perryton	Mercer	IL	Pickens	Cleburne	AR
Perris	Riverside	CA	Pershing	Jackson	IN	Pickens	Edgefield	SC
Perry Lake	Crow Wing	MN	Pershing	McKenzie	ND	Pickerel Lake	Freeborn	MN
Perry	Johnson	AR	Pershing	Burt	NE	Pickering	Bottineau	ND
Perry	Perry	AR	Pershing	Taylor	WI	Pickford	Chippewa	MI

TOWNSHIPS OF THE UNITED STATES

TOWNSHIP	COUNTY	STATE	TOWNSHIP	COUNTY	STATE	TOWNSHIP	COUNTY	STATE
Pickney	Union	SC	Pin Oak	Madison	IL	Pioneer	Corson	SD
Picton	Towner	ND	Pinckney	Warren	MO	Pioneer	Faulk	SD
Piehl	Oneida	WI	Pinckney	Lewis	NY	Pioneer	Spokane	WA
Pierce	Page	IA	Pinconning	Bay	MI	Pipe Creek	Madison	IN
Pierce	De Kalb	IL	Pine City	Pine	MN	Pipe Creek	Miami	IN
Pierce	Washington	IN	Pine Creek	Ogle	IL	Pipestem Valley	Stutsman	ND
Pierce	Lawrence	MO	Pine Creek	Ozark	MO	Pipestone	Berrien	MI
Pierce	Stone	MO	Pine Creek	Clinton	PA	Piru	Ventura	CA
Pierce	Texas	MO	Pine Creek	Mellette	SD	Piscataway	Middlesex	NJ
Pierce	Barnes	ND	Pine Grove	Van Buren	MI	Picairn	Saint Lawrence	NY
Pierce	Clermont	OH	Pine Grove	Schuylkill	PA	Pitcher	Cherokee	IA
Pierce	Kewaunee	WI	Pine Grove	Warren	PA	Pitcher	Chenango	NY
Piercefield	Saint Lawrence	NY	Pine Grove	Calhoun	SC	Pitman	Montgomery	IL
Pierceville	Finney	KS	Pine Grove	Portage	WI	Pitt	Wyandot	OH
Piermont	Grafton	NH	Pine Island	Goodhue	MN	Pittsburg	Coos	NH
Pierpont	Ashtabula	OH	Pine Lake	Cass	MN	Pittsburg	Johnson	AR
Pierrepont	Saint Lawrence	NY	Pine Lake	Clearwater	MN	Pittsburg	Mitchell	KS
Pierson	Vigo	IN	Pine Lake	Otter Tail	MN	Pittsfield	Pike	IL
Pierson	Montcalm	MI	Pine Lake	Pine	MN	Pittsfield	Somerset	ME
Pierz	Morrison	MN	Pine Lake	Oneida	WI	Pittsfield	Washtenaw	MI
Pigeon Grove	Iroquois	IL	Pine Level	Johnston	NC	Pittsfield	Merrimack	NH
Pigeon	Baxter	AR	Pine Log	Benton	AR	Pittsfield	Otsego	NY
Pigeon	Vanderburgh	IN	Pine Mountain	Faulkner	AR	Pittsfield	Lorian	OH
Pigeon	Warrick	IN	Pine Plains	Dutchess	NY	Pittsfield	Warren	PA
Pigeon	Haywood	NC	Pine Point	Becker	MN	Pittsfield	Rutland	VT
Pigeon	Trempealeau	WI	Pine Ridge	Monroe	AR	Pittsfield	Brown	WI
Pike Bay	Cass	MN	Pine River	Gratiot	MI	Pittsford	Butler	IA
Pike City	Pike	AR	Pine River	Cass	MN	Pittsford	Hillsdale	MI
Pike Creek	Morrison	MN	Pine River	Lincoln	WI	Pittsford	Monroe	NY
Pike	Muscatine	IA	Pine Rock	Ogle	IL	Pittsford	Rutland	VT
Pike	Livingston	IL	Pine Swamp	Ashe	NC	Pittsgrove	Salem	NJ
Pike	Jay	IN	Pine	Cleburne	AR	Pittston	Kennebec	ME
Pike	Marion	IN	Pine	Benton	IN	Pittston	Luzerne	PA
Pike	Ohio	IN	Pine	Porter	IN	Pittstown	Rensselaer	NY
Pike	Warren	IN	Pine	Warren	IN	Pixley	Clay	IL
Pike	Lyon	KS	Pine	Montcalm	MI	Placerville	El Dorado	CA
Pike	Saint Louis	MN	Pine	Ripley	MO	Plain Center	Charles Mix	SD
Pike	Carter	MO	Pine	Stone	MO	Plain Grove	Lawrence	PA
Pike	Stoddard	MO	Pine	Allegheny	PA	Plain	Kosciusko	IN
Pike	Wyoming	NY	Pine	Armstrong	PA	Plain	Renville	ND
Pike	Brown	OH	Pine	Clearfield	PA	Plain	Franklin	OH
Pike	Clark	OH	Pine	Columbia	PA	Plain	Stark	OH
Pike	Coshocton	OH	Pine	Crawford	PA	Plain	Wayne	OH
Pike	Fulton	OH	Pine	Indiana	PA	Plain	Wood	OH
Pike	Knox	OH	Pine	Lycoming	PA	Plain View	Sampson	NC
Pike	Madison	OH	Pine	Mercer	PA	Plainfield	Windham	CT
Pike	Perry	OH	Pine Valley	Clark	WI	Plainfield	Will	IL
Pike	Stark	OH	Pinecreek	Jefferson	PA	Plainfield	Hampshire	MA
Pike	Berks	PA	Pinegrove	Venango	PA	Plainfield	Iosco	MI
Pike	Bradford	PA	Pineville	McDonald	MO	Plainfield	Kent	MI
Pike	Clearfield	PA	Pineville	Mecklenburg	NC	Plainfield	Sullivan	NH
Pike	Potter	PA	Pineville	Alleghany	NC	Plainfield	Otsego	NY
Pikeville	Wayne	NC	Piney Creek	Ashe	NC	Plainfield	Northampton	PA
Pilesgrove	Salem	NJ	Piney Fork	Sharp	AR	Plainfield	Brule	SD
Pilgrim	Dade	MO	Piney Grove	Sampson	SC	Plainfield	Washington	VT
Pillsbury	Swift	MN	Piney	Carroll	AR	Plainfield	Waushara	WI
Pilot Grove	Montgomery	IA	Piney	Cleburne	AR	Plains	Luzerne	PA
Pilot Grove	Hancock	IL	Piney	Johnson	AR	Plainsboro	Middlesex	NJ
Pilot Grove	Faribault	MN	Piney	Oregon	MO	Plainview	Phillips	KS
Pilot Grove	Cooper	MO	Piney	Pulaski	MO	Plainview	Wabasha	MN
Pilot Grove	Moniteau	MO	Piney	Texas	MO	Plainview	Stutsman	ND
Pilot Knob	Washington	IL	Piney	Clarion	PA	Plainview	Tripp	SD
Pilot Knob	Harper	KS	Pingree	Stutsman	ND	Plainville	Hartford	CT
Pilot Mound	Boone	IA	Pink Hill	Lenoir	NC	Plainville	Rooks	KS
Pilot Mound	Fillmore	MN	Pinora	Lake	MI	Plainville	Norfolk	MA
Pilot Mound	Griggs	ND	Pioche	Lincoln	NV	Plaistow	Rockingham	NH
Pilot Rock	Johnson	AR	Pioneer	Cedar	IA	Plank	Keokuk	IA
Pilot	Cherokee	IA	Pioneer	Graham	KS	Plankinton	Aurora	SD
Pilot	Iowa	IA	Pioneer	Rice	KS	Plano	Hanson	SD
Pilot	Kankakee	IL	Pioneer	Rush	KS	Planters	Chicot	AR
Pilot	Vermilion	IL	Pioneer	Missaukee	MI	Plateau	Perkins	SD
Pilot	Surry	NC	Pioneer	Barry	MO	Plato	Sioux	IA
Pilsen	Bayfield	WI	Pioneer	Washington	OH	Plato	Kane	IL

TOWNSHIP	COUNTY	STATE	TOWNSHIP	COUNTY	STATE	TOWNSHIP	COUNTY	STATE
Plato	Hand	SD	Pleasant	Grant	IN	Pleasant View	Holt	NE
Platte Lake	Crow Wing	MN	Pleasant	Johnson	IN	Pleasant View	Texas	OK
Platte	Taylor	IA	Pleasant	La Porte	IN	Pleasant View	Beadle	SD
Platte	Union	IA	Pleasant	Porter	IN	Pleasant View	Potter	SD
Platte	Benzie	MI	Pleasant	Steuben	IN	Pleasant View	Tripp	SD
Platte	Morrison	MN	Pleasant	Switzerland	IN	Pleasantdale	Rush	KS
Platte	Andrew	MO	Pleasant	Wabash	IN	Pleasanton	Manistee	MI
Platte	Buchanan	MO	Pleasant	Butler	KS	Pleassanton	Alaleda	CA
Platte	Clay	MO	Pleasant	Coffey	KS	Plevna	Reno	KS
Platte	Clinton	MO	Pleasant	Harvey	KS	Pliny	Aitkin	MN
Platte	Buffalo	NE	Pleasant	Lincoln	KS	Plover	Marathon	WI
Platte	Butler	NE	Pleasant	Smith	KS	Plover	Portage	WI
Platte	Dodge	NE	Pleasant	Northampton	NC	Plowden Mills	Clarendon	SC
Platte	Charles Mix	SD	Pleasant	Cass	ND	Plum Bayou	Jefferson	AR
Plattekill	Ulster	NY	Pleasant	Brown	OH	Plum Branch	McCormick	SC
Platteville	Grant	WI	Pleasant	Clark	OH	Plum Creek	Kossuth	IA
Plattin	Jefferson	MO	Pleasant	Fairfield	OH	Plum Creek	Mitchell	KS
Platts Springs	Lexington	SC	Pleasant	Franklin	OH	Plum Creek	Butler	NE
Plattsburgh	Clinton	NY	Pleasant	Hancock	OH	Plum Grove	Butler	KS
Plattville	Mills	IA	Pleasant	Hardin	OH	Plum Hill	Washington	IL
Plaza	Mountrail	ND	Pleasant	Henry	OH	Plum Lake	Vilas	WI
Plaza	Spokane	WA	Pleasant	Knox	OH	Plum	Phillips	KS
Pleasant Gap	Bates	MO	Pleasant	Logan	OH	Plum	Venango	PA
Pleasant Grove	Des Moines	IA	Pleasant	Madison	OH	Plumas	Plumas	CA
Pleasant Grove	Floyd	IA	Pleasant	Marion	OH	Plumb	Wabaunsee	KS
Pleasant Grove	Mahaska	IA	Pleasant	Perry	OH	Plumcreek	Armstrong	PA
Pleasant Grove	Marion	IA	Pleasant	Putnam	OH	Plumer	Divide	ND
Pleasant Grove	Coles	IL	Pleasant	Seneca	OH	Plumlee	Newton	AR
Pleasant Grove	Greenwood	KS	Pleasant	Van Wert	OH	Plummer	Brule	SD
Pleasant Grove	Pawnee	KS	Pleasant	Warren	PA	Plumstead	Bucks	PA
Pleasant Grove	Olmsted	MN	Pleasant	Clark	SD	Plumsted	Ocean	NJ
Pleasant Grove	Alamance	NC	Pleasant	Hanson	SD	Plunketts Creek	Lycoming	PA
Pleasant Grove	Johnston	NC	Pleasant	Hutchinson	SD	Plymouth	Plymouth	IA
Pleasant Grove	Randolph	NC	Pleasant	Jerauld	SD	Plymouth	Russell	KS
Pleasant Grove	Brule	SD	Pleasant	Lincoln	SD	Plymouth	Plymouth	MA
Pleasant Hill	Izard	AR	Pleasant	Lyman	SD	Plymouth	Penobscot	ME
Pleasant Hill	Newton	AR	Pleasant Vale	Pike	IL	Plymouth	Wayne	MI
Pleasant Hill	Pike	IL	Pleasant Valley	Carroll	IA	Plymouth	Washington	NC
Pleasant Hill	Ellis	KS	Pleasant Valley	Cerro Gordo	IA	Plymouth	Grand Forks	ND
Pleasant Hill	Winona	MN	Pleasant Valley	Fayette	IA	Plymouth	Grafton	NH
Pleasant Hill	Cass	MO	Pleasant Valley	Grundy	IA	Plymouth	Chenango	NY
Pleasant Hill	Sullivan	MO	Pleasant Valley	Johnson	IA	Plymouth	Ashtabula	OH
Pleasant Hill	Kidder	ND	Pleasant Valley	Scott	IA	Plymouth	Richland	OH
Pleasant Hill	Lancaster	SC	Pleasant Valley	Webster	IA	Plymouth	Luzerne	PA
Pleasant Lake	Benson	ND	Pleasant Valley	Jo Daviess	IL	Plymouth	Montgomery	PA
Pleasant Lake	Aurora	SD	Pleasant Valley	Cowley	KS	Plymouth	Windsor	VT
Pleasant Mound	Bond	IL	Pleasant Valley	Decatur	KS	Plymouth	Juneau	WI
Pleasant Mound	Blue Earth	MN	Pleasant Valley	Finney	KS	Plymouth	Rock	WI
Pleasant Prairie	Martin	MN	Pleasant Valley	Ford	KS	Plymouth	Sheboygan	WI
Pleasant Prairie	Eddy	ND	Pleasant Valley	Pawnee	KS	Plympton	Plymouth	MA
Pleasant Prairie	Spokane	WA	Pleasant Valley	Saline	KS	Poarch	Beckham	OK
Pleasant Prairie	Kenosha	WI	Pleasant Valley	Wilson	KS	Pocasset	Grady	OK
Pleasant Ridge	Fulton	AR	Pleasant Valley	Mower	MN	Pocket	Lee	NC
Pleasant Ridge	Lee	IA	Pleasant Valley	Wright	MO	Pocola	Le Flore	OK
Pleasant Ridge	Livingston	IL	Pleasant Valley	Williams	ND	Pocono	Monroe	PA
Pleasant Ridge	Pawnee	KS	Pleasant Valley	Dodge	NE	Pocopson	Chester	PA
Pleasant Ridge	Barry	MO	Pleasant Valley	Dutchess	NY	Pocotaligo	Jasper	SC
Pleasant Ridge	Corson	SD	Pleasant Valley	Potter	PA	Poe	Ringgold	IA
Pleasant Run	Lawrence	IN	Pleasant Valley	Aurora	SD	Poe	McKenzie	ND
Pleasant Springs	Dane	WI	Pleasant Valley	Clay	SD	Poestenkill	Rensselaer	NY
Pleasant	Appanoose	IA	Pleasant Valley	Gregory	SD	Poff	Cleburne	AR
Pleasant	Cass	IA	Pleasant Valley	Hand	SD	Pohlitz	Roseau	MN
Pleasant	Hardin	IA	Pleasant Valley	Hughes	SD	Pohocco	Saunders	NE
Pleasant	Lucas	IA	Pleasant Valley	Marshall	SD	Point De Luce	Arkansas	AR
Pleasant	Monroe	IA	Pleasant Valley	Perkins	SD	Point Pleasant	Warren	IL
Pleasant	Pottawattamie	IA	Pleasant Valley	Tripp	SD	Point Roberts	Whatcom	WA
Pleasant	Poweshiek	IA	Pleasant Valley	Eau Claire	WI	Point	Woodruff	AR
Pleasant	Union	IA	Pleasant Valley	Saint Croix	WI	Point	Posey	IN
Pleasant	Wapello	IA	Pleasant View	Macon	IL	Point	Northumberland	PA
Pleasant	Winneshiek	IA	Pleasant View	Cherokee	KS	Pointe Aux Barque	Huron	MI
Pleasant	Wright	IA	Pleasant View	Emmet	MI	Pokagon	Cass	MI
Pleasant	Fulton	IL	Pleasant View	Norman	MN	Pokegama	Pine	MN
Pleasant	Allen	IN	Pleasant View	Grand Forks	ND	Poland	Greene	AR

TOWNSHIPS OF THE UNITED STATES

TOWNSHIP	COUNTY	STATE	TOWNSHIP	COUNTY	STATE	TOWNSHIP	COUNTY	STATE
Poland	Buena Vista	IA	Poplar Tent	Cabarrus	NC	Portsmouth	Carteret	NC
Poland	Androscoggin	ME	Poplar	Cass	MN	Portsmouth	Newport	RI
Poland	Chautauqua	NY	Poplar	Mitchell	NC	Portville	Cattaraugus	NY
Poland	Mahoning	OH	Poplar	McLean	ND	Porum	Muskogee	OK
Polar	Langlade	WI	Popple Grove	Mahnomen	MN	Posen	Presque Isle	MI
Polk Centre	Pennington	MN	Popple River	Forest	WI	Posen	Yellow Medicine	MN
Polk	Calhoun	AR	Popple	Clearwater	MN	Posey	Clay	IN
Polk	Montgomery	AR	Poppleton	Kittson	MN	Posey	Fayette	IN
Polk	Newton	AR	Port Austin	Huron	MI	Posey	Franklin	IN
Polk	Benton	IA	Port Byron	Rock Island	IL	Posey	Harrison	IN
Polk	Bremer	IA	Port Edwards	Wood	WI	Posey	Rush	IN
Polk	Jefferson	IA	Port Emma	Dickey	ND	Posey	Switzerland	IN
Polk	Shelby	IA	Port Hope	Beltrami	MN	Posey	Washington	IN
Polk	Taylor	IA	Port Huron	Saint Clair	MI	Post Oak	Johnson	MO
Polk	Wapello	IA	Port Louisa	Louisa	IA	Post	Allamakee	IA
Polk	Macoupin	IL	Port Sheldon	Ottawa	MI	Poteau	La Flore	OK
Polk	Huntington	IN	Port Washington	Ozaukee	WI	Potosi	Linn	KS
Polk	Marshall	IN	Port Wing	Bayfield	WI	Potosi	Grant	WI
Polk	Monroe	IN	Portage Des Sioux	Saint Charles	MO	Potsdam	Dickey	ND
Polk	Washington	IN	Portage Lake	Aroostook	ME	Potsdam	Saint Lawrence	NY
Polk	Adair	MO	Portage	Porter	IN	Pottawatomie	Coffey	KS
Polk	Atchison	MO	Portage	Saint Joseph	IN	Pottawatomie	Franklin	KS
Polk	Cass	MO	Portage	Houghton	MI	Pottawatomie	Pottawatomie	KS
Polk	Christian	MO	Portage	Mackinac	MI	Pottawatomie	Oklahoma	OK
Polk	Dade	MO	Portage	Saint Louis	MN	Potter	Polk	AR
Polk	De Kalb	MO	Portage	New Madrid	MO	Potter	Barnes	ND
Polk	Madison	MO	Portage	Livingston	NY	Potter	Yates	NY
Polk	Nodaway	MO	Portage	Hancock	OH	Potter	Beaver	PA
Polk	Ray	MO	Portage	Ottawa	OH	Potter	Centre	PA
Polk	Saint Clair	MO	Portage	Summit	OH	Poughkeepsie	Dutchess	NY
Polk	Sullivan	MO	Portage	Woods	OH	Poultney	Rutland	VT
Polk	Crawford	OH	Portage	Cambria	PA	Pound Ridge	Westchester	NY
Polk	Jefferson	PA	Portage	Cameron	PA	Pound	Marinette	WI
Polk	Monroe	PA	Portage	Potter	PA	Powell	Craighead	AR
Polk	Washington	WI	Portage	Brown	SD	Powell	Comanche	KS
Polkton	Ottawa	MI	Portal	Burke	ND	Powell	Marquette	MI
Polkville	Cleveland	NC	Porter	Crawford	AR	Powell	Edmunds	SD
Pollard	Clay	AR	Porter	Porter	IN	Power Lake	Mountrail	ND
Pollocksville	Jones	NC	Porter	Cheyenne	KS	Powers	Cass	MN
Polo	Carroll	AR	Porter	Oxford	ME	Powers	Mountrail	ND
Polonia	Roseau	MN	Porter	Cass	MI	Poweshiek	Jasper	IA
Polson	Lake	MT	Porter	Midland	MI	Powhatan	Pocahontas	IA
Pomfret	Windham	CT	Porter	Van Buren	MI	Powhattan	Brown	KS
Pomfret	Chautauqua	NY	Porter	Christian	MO	Pownal	Cumberland	ME
Pomfret	Windsor	VT	Porter	Dickey	ND	Pownal	Bennington	VT
Pomme de Terre	Grant	MN	Porter	Niagara	NY	Poygan	Winnebago	WI
Pomona	Jackson	IL	Porter	Delaware	OH	Poyner	Black Hawk	IA
Pomona	Franklin	KS	Porter	Scioto	OH	Poynor	Ripley	MO
Pomona View	La Moure	ND	Porter	Muskogee	OK	Poysippi	Waushara	WI
Pompey	Onondaga	NY	Porter	Wagoner	OK	Prairie Center	Walsh	ND
Pomroy	Itasca	MN	Porter	Clarion	PA	Prairie Center	Clay	SD
Pomroy	Lanabec	MN	Porter	Clinton	PA	Prairie Center	Spink	SD
Ponca City	Dixon	NE	Porter	Huntingdon	PA	Prairie City	McDonough	IL
Ponca	Newton	AR	Porter	Jefferson	PA	Prairie Creek	Dubuque	IA
Ponca	Dixon	NE	Porter	Lycoming	PA	Prairie Creek	Logan	IL
Ponca	Lincoln	OK	Porter	Pike	PA	Prairie Creek	Vigo	IN
Ponce de Leon	Stone	MO	Porter	Schuylkill	PA	Prairie Creek	Hall	NE
Pond Creek	Greene	MO	Porter	Rock	WI	Prairie Creek	Merrick	NE
Pond Mountain	Ashe	NC	Porterfield	Marinette	WI	Prairie Creek	Nance	NE
Pontiac	Livingston	IL	Porterville	Tulare	CA	Prairie Dog	Decatur	KS
Pontiac	Oakland	MI	Portland	Ashley	AR	Prairie Dog	Sheridan	KS
Pontiac	Ozark	MO	Portland	Middlesex	CT	Prairie Dog	Harlan	NE
Pontiac	Cass	ND	Portland	Cerro Gordo	IA	Prairie du Chien	Crawford	WI
Ponto Lake	Cass	MN	Portland	Kossuth	IA	Prairie du Long	Saint Clair	IL
Pontoosuc	Hancock	IL	Portland	Plymouth	IA	Prairie du Sac	Sauk	WI
Pony Gulch	Wells	ND	Portland	Whiteside	IL	Prairie Farm	Barron	WI
Pope	Fayette	IL	Portland	Ionia	MI	Prairie Green	Iroquois	IL
Poplar Bluff	Butler	MO	Portland	Chautauqua	NY	Prairie Grove	Washington	AR
Poplar Branch	Currituck	NC	Portland	Erie	OH	Prairie Home	Cooper	MO
Poplar Grove	Boone	IL	Portland	Deuel	SD	Prairie Island	Merrick	NE
Poplar Grove	Roseau	MN	Portland	Dodge	WI	Prairie Lake	Saint Louis	MN
Poplar Point	Martin	NC	Portland	Monroe	WI	Prairie Lake	Barron	WI
Poplar River	Red Lake	MN	Portsmouth	Bay	MI	Prairie Ronde	Kalamazoo	MI

TOWNSHIP	COUNTY	STATE	TOWNSHIP	COUNTY	STATE	TOWNSHIP	COUNTY	STATE
Prairie Springs	Jackson	IA	Preble	Fillmore	MN	Providence	Lancaster	PA
Prairie	Arkansas	AR	Preble	Cortland	NY	Providence	Orangeburg	SC
Prairie	Ashley	AR	Preemption	Mercer	IL	Providence	Sumter	SC
Prairie	Boone	AR	Prentice	Price	WI	Provincetown	Barnstable	MA
Prairie	Carroll	AR	Prescott	Adams	IA	Proviso	Cook	IL
Prairie	Craighead	AR	Prescott	Faribault	MN	Provo	Fall River	SD
Prairie	Franklin	AR	Prescott	Renville	ND	Prussia	Adair	IA
Prairie	Hot Spring	AR	Presho	Lyman	SD	Pukwana	Brule	SD
Prairie	Johnson	AR	President	Venango	PA	Pulaski	Lonoke	AR
Prairie	Lonoke	AR	Presque Isle	Presque Isle	MI	Pulaski	Jackson	MI
Prairie	Madison	AR	Presque Isle	Vilas	WI	Pulaski	Morrison	MN
Prairie	Marion	AR	Preston Lake	Renville	MN	Pulaski	Walsh	ND
Prairie	Newton	AR	Preston	New London	CT	Pulaski	Williams	OH
Prairie	Saint Francis	AR	Preston	Plymouth	IA	Pulaski	Beaver	PA
Prairie	Searcy	AR	Preston	Richland	IL	Pulaski	Lawrence	PA
Prairie	Sebastian	AR	Preston	Fillmore	MN	Pulaski	Oconee	SC
Prairie	Washington	AR	Preston	Jasper	MO	Pulaski	Faulk	SD
Prairie	Yell	AR	Preston	Platte	MO	Pulaski	Iowa	WI
Prairie	Davis	IA	Preston	Ransom	ND	Pulawski	Presque Isle	MI
Prairie	Delaware	IA	Preston	Chenango	NY	Pulteney	Steuben	NY
Prairie	Fremont	IA	Preston	Wayne	PA	Pultney	Belmont	OH
Prairie	Keokuk	IA	Preston	Brookings	SD	Pumpkin Bend	Woodruff	AR
Prairie	Kossuth	IA	Preston	Adams	WI	Purcell	Mountrail	ND
Prairie	Mahaska	IA	Preston	Trempealeau	WI	Purdy	Madison	AR
Prairie	Crawford	IL	Pretty Creek	Grant	ND	Purdy	Barry	MO
Prairie	Edgar	IL	Price Creek	Yancey	NC	Pure Water	Mellette	SD
Prairie	Hancock	IL	Price	Washington	AR	Pursley	Grady	OK
Prairie	Shelby	IL	Price	Rockingham	NC	Pusheta	Auglaize	OH
Prairie	Henry	IN	Price	Jefferson	OK	Putah	Yolo	CA
Prairie	Kosciusko	IN	Price	Monroe	PA	Put-in-Bay	Ottawa	OH
Prairie	La Porte	IN	Price	Langlade	WI	Putnam	Windham	CT
Prairie	Tipton	IN	Prices Chapel	Sequoyah	OK	Putnam	Fayette	IA
Prairie	Warren	IN	Primrose	Steele	ND	Putnam	Linn	IA
Prairie	White	IN	Primrose	Dane	WI	Putnam	Fulton	IL
Prairie	Jewell	KS	Princeton	Dallas	AR	Putnam	Anderson	KS
Prairie	Wilson	KS	Princeton	Scott	IA	Putnam	Stafford	KS
Prairie	Wyandotte	KS	Princeton	Bureau	IL	Putnam	Livingston	MI
Prairie	Audrain	MO	Princeton	White	IN	Putnam	Washington	NY
Prairie	Bates	MO	Princeton	Worcester	MA	Putnam	Tioga	PA
Prairie	Carroll	MO	Princeton	Washington	ME	Putnam Valley	Putnam	NY
Prairie	Franklin	MO	Princeton	Mille Lacs	MN	Putney	Brown	SD
Prairie	Howard	MO	Princeton	Mercer	NJ	Putney	Windham	VT
Prairie	Jackson	MO	Princeton	Green Lake	WI	Pymatuning	Mercer	PA
Prairie	Lincoln	MO	Princetown	Schenectady	NY	Pymosa	Cass	IA
Prairie	McDonald	MO	Princeville	Peoria	IL			
Prairie	Montgomery	MO	Prior	Big Stone	MN	—Q—		
Prairie	Pettis	MO	Privateer	Sumter	SC			
Prairie	Randolph	MO	Proctor	Crittenden	AR	Quaker Gap	Stokes	NC
Prairie	Schuyler	MO	Proctor	Rutland	VT	Quaker Meadow	Burke	NC
Prairie	La Moure	ND	Progress	Wells	ND	Qualla	Jackson	NC
Prairie	Phelps	NE	Progressive	McIntosh	ND	Quanah	Comanche	OK
Prairie	Franklin	OH	Progressive	Tripp	SD	Quapaw	Ottawa	OK
Prairie	Holmes	OH	Promised Land	Craighead	AR	Quarry	Jersey	IL
Prairie	Canadian	OK	Promised Land	Lawrence	AR	Quartz	Plumas	CA
Prairie	Grant	OK	Prophetstown	Whiteside	IL	Quartz	Greer	OK
Prairie	Union	SD	Prospect	New Haven	CT	Queen	Polk	MN
Prairie Valley	Grady	OK	Prospect	Butler	KS	Queensborough	Queens	NY
Prairie View	Phillips	KS	Prospect	Waldo	ME	Queensbury	Warren	NY
Prairie View	Wilkin	MN	Prospect	Ramsey	ND	Quemahoning	Somerset	PA
Prairie View	Corson	SD	Prospect	Marion	OH	Quewhiffle	Hoke	NC
Prairieton	Christian	IL	Prospect	Mellette	SD	Quincy	Adams	IA
Prairieton	Vigo	IN	Prosper	Davison	SD	Quincy	Adams	IL
Prairieville	Barry	MI	Prosperity	Renville	ND	Quincy	Greenwood	KS
Prairieville	Brown	MN	Protection	Comanche	KS	Quincy	Branch	MI
Prairieville	Pike	MO	Providence	Buena Vista	IA	Quincy	Houghton	MI
Prathers Creek	Alleghany	NC	Providence	Hardin	IA	Quincy	Olmsted	MN
Pratt	McHenry	ND	Providence	Lac Qui Parle	MN	Quincy	Franklin	PA
Pratt	Hyde	SD	Providence	Mecklenburg	NC	Quincy	Adams	WI
Pratt	Lyman	SD	Providence	Pasquotank	NC	Quindaro	Wyandotte	KS
Pratt	Bayfield	WI	Providence	Randolph	NC	Quinlan	Major	OK
Prattsburg	Steuben	NY	Providence	Rowan	NC	Quinn	Pennington	SD
Prattsville	Green	NY	Providence	Saratoga	NY	Quinnebaugh	Burt	NE
Preble	Adams	IN	Providence	Lucas	OH	Quinton	Salem	NJ

TOWNSHIP	COUNTY	STATE	TOWNSHIP	COUNTY	STATE	TOWNSHIP	COUNTY	STATE
Quinton	Pittsburg	OK	Ransom	Hillsdale	MI	Red Colony	Sevier	AR
Quiring	Beltrami	MN	Ransom	Nobles	MN	Red Eye	Wadena	MN
Quiver	Mason	IL	Ransom	Columbus	NC	Red Fish	Mellette	SD
			Ransom	Sargent	ND	Red Fork	Desha	AR
			Ransom	Lackawanna	PA	Red Fork	Tulsa	OK
—R—			Rantoul	Champaign	IL	Red Hill	Ouachita	AR
			Rantoul	Calumet	WI	Red Hill	Mitchell	NC
Rabbit Lake	Crow Wing	MN	Rapho	Lancaster	PA	Red Hook	Dutchess	NY
Raber	Chippewa	MI	Rapid River	Kalkaska	MI	Red House	Cattaraugus	NY
Raber	Hughes	SD	Rapidan	Blue Earth	MN	Red Iron Lake	Marshall	SD
Raccoon	Marion	IL	Rapids	Linn	IA	Red Lake Falls	Red Lake	MN
Raccoon	Parke	IN	Rarden	Scioto	OH	Red Lake	Logan	ND
Raccoon	Gallia	OH	Raritan	Henderson	IL	Red Lake	Brule	SD
Raccoon	Beaver	PA	Raritan	Hunterdon	NJ	Red Lick	Johnson	AR
Racine	Mower	MN	Raritan	Barnes	ND	Red Mound	Seminole	OK
Racine	Day	SD	Raritan	Day	SD	Red Oak	Cedar	IA
Radisson	Sawyer	WI	Rascoe	La Moure	ND	Red Oak	Montgomery	IA
Radnor	Peoria	IL	Rat Lake	Mountrail	ND	Red Oak	Lawrence	MO
Radnor	Delaware	OH	Rathbone	Steuben	NY	Red Oak	Nash	NC
Radnor	Delaware	PA	Ratliff	Johnson	OK	Red Oak	Latimer	OK
Raeford	Hoke	NC	Ratliffe	Choctaw	OK	Red Oak	Barnwell	SC
Raft Swamp	Robeson	NC	Rauville	Codington	SD	Red Point	Texas	OK
Rafting Creek	Sumter	SC	Ravanna	Mercer	MO	Red River	Little River	AR
Raglan	Harrison	IA	Ravenna	Muskegon	MI	Red River	Miller	AR
Rahn	Schuylkill	PA	Ravenna	Dakota	MN	Red River	Searcy	AR
Rail Prairie	Morrison	MN	Ravenna	Portage	OH	Red River	Stone	AR
Railroad	Starke	IN	Ravenna	Sanborn	SD	Red River	Van Buren	AR
Rainbow	Williams	ND	Ravinia	Brown	SD	Red River	White	AR
Rainbow	Perkins	SD	Rawdon	Ellis	OK	Red River	Tillman	OK
Rainey	Washita	OK	Rawles	Mills	IA	Red River	Kewaunee	WI
Rainy Butte	Slope	ND	Rawlins	Jo Daviess	IL	Red Rock	Marion	IA
Rainy Creek	Pennington	SD	Ray	Franklin	IN	Red Rock	Mower	MN
Raisin	Lenawee	MI	Ray	Morgan	IN	Red Rock	Noble	OK
Raisinville	Monroe	MI	Ray	Macomb	MI	Red Rock	Minnehaha	SD
Raleigh	Saline	IL	Ray	La Moure	ND	Red Springs	Robeson	NC
Raleigh	Wake	NC	Rayburn	Armstrong	PA	Red Springs	Shawano	WI
Raleigh	Grant	ND	Raymond	Monroe	AR	Red Vermillion	Nemaha	KS
Ralpho	Northumberland	PA	Raymond	Champaign	IL	Red Wing	McKenzie	ND
Ramapo	Rockland	NY	Raymond	Montgomery	IL	Redbank	Armstrong	PA
Rames	Tripp	SD	Raymond	Rice	KS	Redbank	Clarion	PA
Ramona	San Diego	CA	Raymond	Cumberland	ME	Reddies River	Wilkes	NC
Ramsey	Kossuth	IA	Raymond	Stearns	MN	Redding	Fairfield	CT
Ramsey	Fayette	IL	Raymond	Cass	ND	Redding	Jackson	IN
Ramsey	Anoka	MN	Raymond	Knox	NE	Redding	Clare	MI
Ramsey	McCook	SD	Raymond	Rockingham	NH	Reddish	Lewis	MO
Ramseytown	Yancey	NC	Raymond	Clark	SD	Redelm	Ziebach	SD
Randall	Kenosha	WI	Raymond	Racine	WI	Redfield	Oswego	NY
Ranleman	Randolph	NC	Raymore	Cass	MO	Redfield	Spink	SD
Randol	Cape Girardeau	MO	Rayne	Indiana	PA	Redford	Wayne	MI
Randolph	Desha	AR	Raynham	Bristol	MA	Redland	Cleveland	AR
Randolph	McLean	IL	Read	Clayton	IA	Redland	Hempstead	AR
Randolph	Ohio	IN	Read	Butler	NE	Redland	Nevada	AR
Randolph	Tippecanoe	IN	Reade	Cambria	PA	Redland	Sequoyah	OK
Randolph	Norfolk	MA	Readfield	Kennebec	ME	Redlands	San Bernardino	CA
Randolph	Kennebec	ME	Reading	Calhoun	IA	Redmond	Mountrail	ND
Randolph	Dakota	MN	Reading	Sioux	IA	Redpath	Traverse	MN
Randolph	Saint Francois	MO	Reading	Livingston	IL	Redstone	Miner	SD
Randolph	McKenzie	ND	Reading	Lyon	KS	Redstripe	Stone	AR
Randolph	Coos	NH	Reading	Middlesex	MA	Redwood Falls	Redwood	MN
Randolph	Morris	NJ	Reading	Hillsdale	MI	Redwood	Santa Clara	CA
Randolph	Cattaraugus	NY	Reading	Butler	NE	Redwood	Sonoma	CA
Randolph	Montgomery	OH	Reading	Schuyler	NY	Ree Heights	Hand	SD
Randolph	Portage	OH	Reading	Hamilton	OH	Ree	Ward	ND
Randolph	Crawford	PA	Reading	Perry	OH	Ree	Charles Mix	SD
Randolph	Orange	VT	Reading	Adams	PA	Reed Keathly	Yell	AR
Randolph	Columbia	WI	Reading	Windsor	VT	Reed	Washington	AR
Raney	La Moure	ND	Readington	Hunterdon	NJ	Reed	Will	IL
Raney	Greer	OK	Readmond	Emmet	MI	Reed	Cass	ND
Range	Madison	OH	Readsboro	Bennington	VT	Reed	Seneca	OH
Range	Texas	OK	Recovery	Mercer	OH	Reed	Garfield	OK
Rangeley	Franklin	ME	Rector	Saline	IL	Reed	Dauphin	PA
Ranger	Slope	ND	Red Bluff	Tehama	CA	Reeder	Anderson	KS
Rankin	Perry	AR	Red Cedar	Dunn	WI	Reeder	Kiowa	KS

TOWNSHIPS OF THE UNITED STATES

TOWNSHIP	COUNTY	STATE	TOWNSHIP	COUNTY	STATE	TOWNSHIP	COUNTY	STATE
Reeder	Missaukee	MI	Rice Lake	Saint Louis	MN	Richland	Story	IA
Reeder	Adams	ND	Rice Lake	Ward	ND	Richland	Tama	IA
Reeder	Newberry	SC	Rice Lake	Barron	WI	Richland	Wapello	IA
Reeds Creek	Lawrence	AR	Rice River	Aitkin	MN	Richland	Warren	IA
Reedsburg	Sauk	WI	Rice	Ringgold	IA	Richland	La Salle	IL
Reedy Creek	Davidson	NC	Rice	Jo Daviess	IL	Richland	Marshall	IL
Reems Creek	Buncombe	NC	Rice	Clearwater	MN	Richland	Shelby	IL
Reeve	Franklin	IA	Rice	Sandusky	OH	Richland	Benton	IN
Reeve	Daviess	IN	Rice	Luzerne	PA	Richland	De Kalb	IN
Reeves	Marion	SC	Riceland	Freeborn	MN	Richland	Fountain	IN
Rehoboth	Bristol	MA	Riceville	Becker	MN	Richland	Fulton	IN
Reid	Marathon	WI	Rich Grove	Pulaski	IN	Richland	Grant	IN
Reidsville	Rockingham	NC	Rich Hill	Livingston	MO	Richland	Greene	IN
Reidville	Spartanburg	SC	Rich Hill	Muskingum	OH	Richland	Jay	IN
Reilly	Nemaha	KS	Rich Mountain	Polk	AR	Richland	Madison	IN
Reilly	Schuylkill	PA	Rich Square	Northampton	NC	Richland	Miami	IN
Reily	Butler	OH	Rich	Cook	IL	Richland	Monroe	IN
Reine	Roseau	MN	Rich	Anderson	KS	Richland	Rush	IN
Reiner	Pennington	MN	Rich	Lapeer	MI	Richland	Steuben	IN
Reis	Polk	MN	Rich	Cass	ND	Richland	Whitley	IN
Reliance	Lyman	SD	Rich Valley	McLeod	MN	Richland	Butler	KS
Relief	Independence	AR	Rich Valley	Benson	ND	Richland	Cowley	KS
Remer	Cass	MN	Rich Valley	Jones	SD	Richland	Ford	KS
Remington	Wood	WI	Richards	Comanche	OK	Richland	Hamilton	KS
Remsen	Plymouth	IA	Richardson	Randolph	AR	Richland	Harvey	KS
Remsen	Oneida	NY	Richardson	Morrison	MN	Richland	Jewell	KS
Rendsville	Stevens	MN	Richardson	Butler	NE	Richland	Kingman	KS
Renfrow	Grant	OK	Richardville	Kittson	MN	Richland	Labette	KS
Renfrow	Kay	OK	Richburg	Bottineau	ND	Richland	Marshall	KS
Rennert	Robeson	NC	Richfield	Adams	IL	Richland	Miami	KS
Reno	Leavenworth	KS	Richfield	Morton	KS	Richland	Ottawa	KS
Reno	Reno	KS	Richfield	Genesee	MI	Richland	Pratt	KS
Reno	Iosco	MI	Richfield	Roscommon	MI	Richland	Rawlins	KS
Reno	Pope	MN	Richfield	Otsego	NY	Richland	Republic	KS
Reno	Washoe	NV	Richfield	Henry	OH	Richland	Rooks	KS
Reno	Canadian	OK	Richfield	Lucas	OH	Richland	Strafford	KS
Reno	Grant	OK	Richfield	Summit	OH	Richland	Kalamazoo	MI
Reno Valley	Pierce	ND	Richfield	Spink	SD	Richland	Missaukee	MI
Rensselaerville	Albany	NY	Richfield	Adams	WI	Richland	Montcalm	MI
Renville	Bottineau	ND	Richfield	Washington	WI	Richland	Ogemaw	MI
Republic	Marquette	MI	Richfield	Wood	WI	Richland	Saginaw	MI
Republic	Greene	mO	Richford	Tioga	NY	Richland	Rice	MN
Republican City	Harlan	BE	Richford	Franklin	VT	Richland	Barton	MO
Republican	Jefferson	IN	Richford	Wasushara	WI	Richland	Douglas	MO
Republican	Clay	KS	Richhill	Greene	PA	Richland	Gasconade	MO
Roseburg	Clark	WI	Richill	Greene	PA	Richland	Macon	MO
Reserve	Parke	IN	Richland Center	Slope	ND	Richland	Morgan	MO
Reserve	Kingfisher	OK	Richland Grove	Mercer	IL	Richland	Ozark	MO
Reserve	Allegheny	PA	Richland	Crawford	AR	Richland	Putnam	MO
Resort	Emmet	MI	Richland	Desha	AR	Richland	Scott	MO
Reuben	Harlan	NE	Richland	Jefferson	AR	Richland	Stoddard	MO
Revilee	Logan	AR	Richland	Lee	AR	Richland	Vernon	MO
Rex	Lyman	SD	Richland	Little River	AR	Richland	Beaufort	NC
Rexino	Kidder	ND	Richland	Madison	AR	Richland	Randolph	NC
Reyno	Randolph	AR	Richland	Monroe	AR	Richland	Burke	ND
Reynolds	Greene	AR	Richland	Newton	AR	Richland	Saunders	NE
Reynolds	Lee	IL	Richland	Searcy	AR	Richland	Oswego	NY
Reynolds	Montcalm	MI	Richland	Washington	AR	Richland	Allen	OH
Reynolds	Todd	MN	Richland	Yell	AR	Richland	Belmont	OH
Reynoldson	Gates	NC	Richland	Adair	IA	Richland	Clinton	OH
Rhame	Bowman	ND	Richland	Carroll	IA	Richland	Darke	OH
Rheas Mill	Washington	AR	Richland	Chickasaw	IA	Richland	Defiance	OH
Rheiderland	Chippewa	MN	Richland	Decatur	IA	Richland	Fairfield	OH
Rhine	Sheboygan	WI	Richland	Delaware	IA	Richland	Guernsey	OH
Rhinebeck	Dutchess	NY	Richland	Dickinson	IA	Richland	Holmes	OH
Rhinehart	Polk	MN	Richland	Franklin	IA	Richland	Logan	OH
Rhoades	Mckenzie	ND	Richland	Guthrie	IA	Richland	Marion	OH
Rhoades	Gregory	SD	Richland	Jackson	IA	Richland	Vinton	OH
Rhoda	Charles Mix	SD	Richland	Jasper	IA	Richland	Wyandot	OH
Rialto	San Bernardino	CA	Richland	Jones	IA	Richland	Beckham	OK
Rib Falls	Marathon	WI	Richland	Keokuk	IA	Richland	Stephens	OK
Rib Lake	Taylor	WI	Richland	Lyon	IA	Richland	Tillman	OK
Rib Mountain	Marathon	WI	Richland	Mahaska	IA	Richland	Allegheny	PA
			Richland	Sac	IA			

TOWNSHIPS OF THE UNITED STATES

TOWNSHIP	COUNTY	STATE	TOWNSHIP	COUNTY	STATE	TOWNSHIP	COUNTY	STATE
Richland	Bucks	PA	Ridgeville	Henry	OH	Riverdale	Buffalo	NE
Richland	Cambria	PA	Ridgeville	Lorain	OH	Riverhead	Suffolk	NY
Richland	Clarion	PA	Ridgeville	Monroe	WI	Riverside	Riverside	CA
Richland	Venango	PA	Ridgeway	Gallatin	IL	Riverside	Fremont	IA
Richland	Barnwell	SC	Ridgeway	Osage	KS	Riverside	Lyon	IA
Richland	Beadle	SD	Ridgeway	Lenawee	MI	Riverside	Adams	IL
Richland	Brookings	SD	Ridgeway	Orleans	NY	Riverside	Cook	IL
Richland	Brown	SD	Ridgeway	Iowa	WI	Riverside	Trego	KS
Richland	Brule	SD	Ridgway	Elk	PA	Riverside	Sedgwick	KS
Richland	Clark	SD	Ridley	Delaware	PA	Riverside	Missaukee	MI
Richland	Codington	SD	Ridott	Stephenson	IL	Riverside	Lac Qui Parie	MN
Richland	Edmunds	SD	Rietbrock	Marathon	WI	Riverside	Steele	ND
Richland	Jones	SD	Rifle	Hettinger	ND	Riverside	Burt	NE
Richland	Richland	WI	Riga	Lenawee	MI	Riverside	Gage	NE
Richland	Rusk	WI	Riga	McHenry	ND	Riverside	Burlington	NJ
Richlands	Onslow	NC	Riga	Monroe	NY	Riverside	Brown	SD
Richman	Wayne	IA	Riggin	Benson	ND	Riverside	Clay	SD
Richmond Borough	Richmond	NY	Riley	Yell	AR	Riverside	Corson	SD
Richmond	McHenry	IL	Riley	Ringgold	IA	Riverside	Hand	SD
Richmond	Franklin	KS	Riley	McHenry	IL	Riverside	Mellette	SD
Richmond	Nemaha	KS	Riley	Vigo	IN	Riverton	Clay	IA
Richmond	Berkshire	MA	Riley	Clinton	MI	Riverton	Floyd	IA
Richmond	Sagadahoc	ME	Riley	Saint Clair	MI	Riverton	Fremont	IA
Richmond	Macomb	MI	Riley	Putnam	OH	Riverton	Mason	MI
Richmond	Marquette	MI	Riley	Sandusky	OH	Riverton	Clay	MN
Richmond	Osceola	MI	Rimertown	Cabarrus	NC	Riverview	Ellis	KS
Richmond	Winona	MN	Rindge	Cheshire	NH	Riverview	McKenzie	ND
Richmond	Howard	MO	Rinehart	Dickinson	KS	Riverview	Moody	SD
Richmond	Ray	MO	Ring Thunder	Millette	SD	Riverview	Oconto	WI
Richmond	Cheshire	NH	Ringgold	Jefferson	PA	Rives	Jackson	MI
Richmond	Ontario	NY	Ringle	Marathon	WI	Rivoli	Mercer	IL
Richmond	Ashtabula	OH	Rio	Knox	IL	Roane	Lafayette	AR
Richmond	Huron	OH	Rio Vista	Solano	CA	Roanoke Rapids	Halifax	NC
Richmond	Berks	PA	Ripley	Butler	IA	Roanoke	Randolph	AR
Richmond	Crawford	PA	Ripley	Brown	IL	Roanoke	Woodford	IL
Richmond	Tioga	PA	Ripley	Montgomery	IN	Roanoke	Northampton	NC
Richmond	Washington	RI	Ripley	Rush	IN	Roanoke	Warren	NC
Richmond	Chittenden	VT	Ripley	Somerset	ME	Roaring Brook	Lackawanna	PA
Richmond	Shawano	WI	Ripley	Dodge	MN	Roaring Creek	Avery	NC
Richmond	Saint Croix	WI	Ripley	Morrison	MN	Roaring River	Barry	MO
Richmond	Walworth	WI	Ripley	Chautauqua	NY	Roaringcreek	Columbia	PA
Richmondville	Schoharie	NY	Ripley	Holmes	OH	Roark	Gasconade	MO
Richview	Washington	IL	Ripley	Huron	OH	Roasting Ear	Stone	AR
Richville	Logan	ND	Ripon	San Joaquin	CA	Robb	Posey	IN
Richwood	Jersey	IL	Ripon	Fon du Lac	WI	Robberson	Greene	MO
Richwood	Becker	MN	Rippys	Cleveland	NC	Robbinston	Washington	ME
Richwood	McDonald	MO	Ripton	Addison	VT	Robersonville	Martin	NC
Richwood	Richland	WI	Risley	Marion	KS	Roberts	Jefferson	AR
Richwoods	Jackson	AR	Rison	Cleveland	AR	Roberts	Marshall	IL
Richwoods	Lawrence	AR	Ritters	Moore	NC	Roberts	Wilkin	MN
Richwoods	Lonoke	AR	River Bend	Gaston	NC	Roberts	Jasper	SC
Richwoods	Sharp	AR	River Edge	Cuyahoga	OH	Robeson	Berks	PA
Richwoods	Stone	AR	River Falls	Pennington	MN	Robins	Fall River	SD
Richwoods	Peoria	IL	River Falls	Pierce	WI	Robinson	Crawford	IL
Richwoods	Miller	MO	River Forest	Cook	IL	Robinson	Posey	IN
Richwoods	Washington	MO	River	Bradley	AR	Robinson	Brown	KS
Ricks	Christain	IL	River	Calhoun	AR	Robinson	Ottawa	MI
Ridenhour	Stanly	NC	River	Grant	AR	Robinson	Kidder	ND
Rider	Mayes	OK	River	Logan	AR	Robinson	Allegheny	PA
Ridge	Shelby	IL	River	Ouachita	AR	Robinson	Washington	PA
Ridge	Barber	KS	River	Pawnee	KS	Roc Roe	Monroe	AR
Ridge	Dickinson	KS	River	Red Lake	MN	Roc Roe	Prairie	AR
Ridge	Carroll	MO	River	Jackson	NC	Rochelle Park	Bergen	NJ
Ridge	Van Wert	OH	River	Cleveland	NC	Rochester	Cedar	IA
Ridge	Wyandot	OH	River	Warren	NC	Rochester	Sangamon	IL
Ridge	Williamsburg	SC	River	Blaine	OK	Rochester	Fulton	IN
Ridgebury	Bradford	PA	River	Kingfisher	OK	Rochester	Kingman	KS
Ridgefield	Fairfield	??	River	Mayes	OK	Rochester	Plymouth	MA
Ridgefield	Huron	OH	River Vale	Bergen	NJ	Rochester	Olmsted	MN
Ridgeland	Iroquois	IL	Riverbank	Stanislaus	CA	Rochester	Andrew	MO
Ridgeland	Corson	SD	Riverdale	Kossuth	IA	Rochester	Cass	ND
Ridgeley	Dodge	NE	Riverdale	Watonwan	MN	Rochester	Ulster	NY
Ridgely	Nicollet	MN	Riverdale	Kickey	ND	Rochester	Lorain	OH

TOWNSHIPS OF THE UNITED STATES

TOWNSHIP	COUNTY	STATE
Rochester	Beaver	PA
Rochester	Windsor	VT
Rochester	Racine	WI
Rock Branch	Norton	KS
Rock Creek	Searcy	AR
Rock Creek	Jasper	IA
Rock Creek	Carroll	IL
Rock Creek	Hancock	IL
Rock Creek	Bartholomew	IN
Rock Creek	Carroll	IN
Rock Creek	Huntington	IN
Rock Creek	Wells	IN
Rock Creek	Butler	KS
Rock Creek	Coffey	KS
Rock Creek	Cowley	KS
Rock Creek	Jefferson	KS
Rock Creek	Nemaha	KS
Rock Creek	Pottawatomie	KS
Rock Creek	Wabaunsee	KS
Rock Creek	Pine	MN
Rock Creek	Guilford	NC
Rock Creek	Wilkes	NC
Rock Creek	Saunders	NE
Rock Creek	Pottowatomie	OK
Rock Creek	Stephens	OK
Rock Creek	Miner	SD
Rock Creek Valley	Spokane	WA
Rock Dell	Olmsted	MN
Rock Elm	Pierce	WI
Rock Falls	Holt	NE
Rock Falls	Phelps	NE
Rock Falls	Kay	OK
Rock Falls	Lincoln	WI
Rock Grove	Floyd	IA
Rock Grove	Stephenson	IL
Rock Hill	Burleigh	ND
Rock Island	Rock Island	IL
Rock Island	Williams	ND
Rock Island	Canadian	OK
Rock Island	Grant	OK
Rock Lake	Lyon	MN
Rock Lake	Towner	ND
Rock Lake	Spokane	WA
Rock Mills	Anderson	SC
Rock Prairie	Dade	MO
Rock River	Alger	MI
Rock Run	Stephenson	IL
Rock	Cherokee	IA
Rock	Lyon	IA
Rock	Mitchell	IA
Rock	Sioux	IA
Rock	Woodbury	IA
Rock	Marshall	KS
Rock	Pipestone	MN
Rock	Jefferson	MO
Rock	Benson	ND
Rock	Grant	ND
Rock	Ellis	OK
Rock	Noble	OK
Rock	Rock	WI
Rock	Wood	WI
Rockaway	Morris	NJ
Rockbridge	Greene	IL
Rockbridge	Richland	WI
Rockdale	Crawford	PA
Rockdale	Hand	SD
Rockefeller	Northumberland	PA
Rockfish	Cumberland	NC
Rockfish	Duplin	NC
Rockford	Floyd	IA
Rockford	Pottawattamie	IA
Rockford	Winnebago	IL
Rockford	Sedgwick	KS
Rockford	Wright	MN
Rockford	Caldwell	MO
Rockford	Carroll	MO
Rockford	Surry	NC
Rockford	Renville	ND
Rockford	Gage	NE
Rockford	Perkins	SD
Rockingham	Richmond	NC
Rockingham	Windham	VT
Rockland	Plymouth	MA
Rockland	Ontonagon	MI
Rockland	Sullivan	NY
Rockland	Berks	PA
Rockland	Venango	PA
Rockland	Brown	WI
Rockland	Manitowoc	WI
Rockport	Essex	MA
Rockport	Knox	ME
Rocksbury	Pennington	MN
Rockton	Winnebago	IL
Rockvale	Ogle	IL
Rockville	Kankakee	IL
Rockville	Rice	KS
Rockville	Stearns	MN
Rockville	Bates	MO
Rockville	Sherman	NE
Rockwell	Norton	KS
Rockwell	Norman	MN
Rockwood	Hubbard	MN
Rockwoo	Wadena	MN
Rocky Ford	Mellette	SD
Rocky Fork	Boone	MO
Rocky Grove	Aiken	SC
Rocky Grove	Orangeburg	SC
Rocky Hill	Hartford	CT
Rocky Mount	Edgecombe	NC
Rocky Mount	Nash	NC
Rocky Mountain	Sequoyah	OK
Rocky Point	Pender	NC
Rocky Run	Hancock	IL
Rocky Springs	Montgomery	NC
Rocky Springs	Aiken	SC
Rodgers	Barnes	ND
Rodman	Jefferson	NY
Rogers	Sebastian	AR
Rogers	Ford	IL
Rogers	Presque Isle	MI
Rogers	Cass	MN
Roland	Webster	IA
Roland	Bottineau	ND
Roland	Sequoyah	OK
Rolla	Morton	KS
Rolla	Phelps	MO
Rolland	Isabella	MI
Roller Ridge	Benton	AR
Rollin	Lenawee	MI
Rolling Forks	Pope	MN
Rolling Green	Martin	MN
Rolling Green	Ward	ND
Rolling Green	Corson	SD
Rolling Prairie	Morris	KS
Rolling Prairie	Foster	ND
Rolling	Langlade	WI
Rollingstone	Winona	MN
Rollinsford	Strafford	NH
Rollis	Marshall	MN
Roloff	McIntosh	ND
Rome	Jones	IA
Rome	Jefferson	IL
Rome	Kennebec	ME
Rome	Kenawee	MI
Rome	Faribault	MN
Rome	Ashtabula	OH
Rome	Athens	OH
Rome	Lawrence	OH
Rome	Bradford	PA
Rome	Crawford	PA
Rome	Davison	SD
Rome	Deuel	SD
Rome	Whatcom	WA
Rome	Adams	WI
Romine	Marion	IL
Romness	Griggs	ND
Romulus	Wayne	MI
Romulus	Seneca	NY
Ronald	Ionia	MI
Roodhouse	Greene	IL
Rooks Creek	Livingston	IL
Roome	Polk	MN
Roosevelt	Pocahontas	IA
Roosevelt	Decatur	KS
Roosevelt	Beltrami	MN
Roosevelt	Crow Wing	MN
Roosevelt	Renville	ND
Roosevelt	Burnett	WI
Roosevelt	Taylor	WI
Root	Adams	IN
Root	Montgomery	NY
Rootstown	Portage	OH
Roque Bluffs	Washington	ME
Rosalia	Butler	KS
Rosamond	Christian	IL
Roscoe	Davis	IA
Roscoe	Winnebago	IL
Roscoe	Reno	KS
Roscoe	Goodhue	MN
Roscoe	Saint Clair	MO
Roscommon	Roscommon	MI
Rose Creek	Perry	AR
Rose Creek	Republic	KS
Rose Dell	Rock	MN
Rose Grove	Hamilton	IA
Rose Hill	Johnson	MO
Rose Hill	Duplin	NC
Rose Hill	Foster	ND
Rose Hill	Logan	OK
Rose Hill	Hand	SD
Rose Lake	Osceola	MI
Rose	Shelby	IL
Rose	Oakland	MI
Rose	Ogemaw	MI
Rose	Stutsman	ND
Rose	Wayne	NY
Rose	Carroll	OH
Rose	Payne	OK
Rose	Jefferson	PA
Rose	Lyman	SD
Rose	Waushara	WI
Rose Valley	Stafford	KS
Roseboom	Otsego	NY
Rosebud	Polk	MN
Rosebud	Barnes	ND
Rosebud	Mellette	SD
Rosedale	Jersey	IL
Rosedale	Mahnomen	MN
Rosedale	Clark	SD
Rosedale	Hanson	SD
Rosedale	Tripp	SD
Rosefield	Peoria	IL
Rosefield	Eddy	ND
Rosefield	Turner	SD
Roseglen	McLean	ND
Rosehill	Cottonwood	MN
Roseland	Kandiyohi	MN
Roseland	Burke	ND
Roseland	Adams	NE

TOWNSHIPS OF THE UNITED STATES

TOWNSHIP	COUNTY	STATE	TOWNSHIP	COUNTY	STATE	TOWNSHIP	COUNTY	STATE
Roseland	Tripp	SD	Round Springs	Mitchell	KS	Rush Springs	Grady	OK
Roselle	Carroll	IA	Round Top	Stutsman	ND	Rush	Jo Daviess	IL
Rosemary	Barnwell	SC	Round Valley	Mendocino	CA	Rush	Rooks	KS
Rosemeade	Ransom	ND	Roundhead	Hardin	OH	Rush	Shiawassee	MI
Rosemont	McLean	ND	Rountree	Montgomery	IL	Rush	Buchanan	MO
Rosemount	Dakota	MN	Rouse	Charles Mix	SD	Rush	Monroe	NY
Rosendal	Griggs	ND	Rover	Yell	AR	Rush	Champaign	OH
Rosendale	Watonwan	MN	Rovohl	Thomas	KS	Rush	Scioto	OH
Rosendale	Ulster	NY	Rowe	Franklin	MA	Rush	Tuscarawas	OH
Rosendale	Fond du Lac	WI	Rowe	Lyman	SD	Rush	Centre	PA
Roseneath	Halifax	NC	Rowell	Cleveland	AR	Rush	Dauphin	PA
Rosette	Edmunds	SD	Rowell	Marion	SC	Rush	Northumberland	PA
Roseville	Logan	AR	Rowland	Robeson	NC	Rush	Schuylkill	PA
Roseville	Warren	IL	Rowley	Essex	MA	Rush	Susquehanna	PA
Roseville	Grant	MN	Roxand	Eaton	MI	Rushcreek	Logan	OH
Roseville	Kandiyohi	MN	Rosboro	Person	NC	Rushford	Walsh	ND
Roseville	Traill	ND	Roxbury	Litchfield	CT	Rushford	Allegany	NY
Rosewell	Miner	SD	Roxbury	Oxford	ME	Rushford	Winnebago	WI
Rosewood	Chippewa	MN	Roxbury	Cheshire	NH	Rushseba	Chisago	MN
Rosie	Independence	AR	Roxbury	Morris	NJ	Rushville	Schuyler	IL
Rosing	Morrison	MN	Roxbury	Delaware	NY	Rushville	Rush	IN
Ross Lake	Crow Wing	MN	Roxbury	Washington	VT	Rushville	Phillips	KS
Ross	Franklin	IA	Roxbury	Dane	WI	Rushville	Ward	ND
Ross	Fremont	IA	Roxobel	Bertie	NC	Rusk	Day	SD
Ross	Taylor	IA	Roy	Potter	SD	Rusk	Burnett	WI
Ross	Edgar	IL	Royal Oak	Oakland	MI	Rusk	Rusk	WI
Ross	Pike	IL	Royal	White	AR	Rusland	Wells	ND
Ross	Vermilion	IL	Royal	Ford	KS	Russell Springs	Logan	KS
Ross	Clinton	IN	Royal	Lincoln	MN	Russell	Lafayette	AR
Ross	Lake	IN	Royal	Ramsey	ND	Russell	White	AR
Ross	Cherokee	KS	Royal	Antelope	NE	Russell	Lawrence	IL
Ross	Osborne	KS	Royalston	Worcester	MA	Russell	Putnam	IN
Ross	Kalamazoo	MI	Royalton	Berrien	MI	Russell	Russell	KS
Ross	Roseau	MN	Royalton	Pine	MN	Russell	Hampden	MA
Ross	Mountrail	ND	Royalton	Niagara	NY	Russell	Saint Lawrence	NY
Ross	Butler	OH	Royalton	Fulton	OH	Russell	Camden	MO
Ross	Greene	OH	Royalton	Windsor	VT	Russell	Macon	MO
Ross	Jefferson	OH	Royalton	Waupaca	WI	Russell	Geauga	OH
Ross	Wood	OH	Rozetta	Henderson	IL	Russell	La Moure	ND
Ross	Allegheny	PA	Rubicon	Greene	IL	Russell	Bayfield	WI
Ross	Luzerne	PA	Rubicon	Huron	MI	Russell	Lincoln	WI
Ross	Forest	WI	Rubicon	Dodge	WI	Russell	Sheboygan	WI
Rossford	Wood	OH	Rubin	Nelson	ND	Russia	Polk	MN
Rossie	Saint Lawrence	NY	Ruby	Chippewa	WI	Russia	Herkimer	NY
Rossville	Shawnee	KS	Rudd	Floyd	IA	Russia	Lorain	OH
Rossville	Chester	SC	Ruddell	Independence	AR	Rust	Montmorency	MI
Rost	Jackson	MN	Rudolph	Wood	WI	Ruth	Stone	MO
Rostraver	Westmoreland	PA	Rudy	Crawford	AR	Rutherford	Martin	IN
Rotate	Rawlins	KS	Rudyard	Chippewa	MI	Rutherfordton	Rutherford	NC
Rotterdam	Schenectady	NY	Ruella	Harper	KS	Rutland	Humboldt	IA
Roubidoux	Pulaski	MO	Ruffin	Rockingham	NC	Rutland	Woodbury	IA
Roubidoux	Texas	MO	Ruggles	Ashland	OH	Rutland	Kane	IL
Rough & Ready	Nevada	CA	Rugh	Nelson	ND	Rutland	La Salle	IL
Roulette	Potter	PA	Rumford	Oxford	ME	Rutland	Montgomery	KS
Round Grove	Livingston	IL	Rumley	Harrison	OH	Rutland	Worcester	MA
Round Grove	White	IN	Rumney	Grafton	NH	Rutland	Barry	MI
Round Grove	McLeod	MN	Runeburg	Becker	MN	Rutland	Martin	MN
Round Grove	Macon	MO	Running Bird	Mellette	SD	Rutland	Sargent	ND
Round Grove	Marion	MO	Running Lake	Randolph	AR	Rutland	Jefferson	NY
Round Grove	Alfalfa	OK	Running Water	Bon Homme	SD	Rutland	Meigs	OH
Round Grove	Kay	OK	Rupert	Bennington	VT	Rutland	Tioga	PA
Round Lake	Becker	MN	Rural	Rock Island	IL	Rutland	Lake	SD
Round Lake	Jackson	MN	Rural	Shelby	IL	Rutland	Rutland	VT
Round Lake	McHenry	ND	Rural	Jefferson	KS	Rutland	Dane	WI
Round Lake	Sawyer	WI	Rural	Kingman	KS	Rutledge	De Witt	IL
Round Mound	Osborne	KS	Rusco	Buffalo	NE	Ruyle	Jefsey	IL
Round Mountain	?????	??	Ruscombmanor	Berks	PA	Ryals	McIntosh	OK
Round Mountain	Nye	NV	Rush Creek	Fairfield	OH	Ryan	Sumner	KS
Round Prairie	Benton	AR	Rush Lake	Palo Alto	IA	Ryan	La Moure	ND
Round Prairie	Jefferson	IA	Rush Lake	Otter Tail	MN	Ryan	Schuylkill	PA
Round Prairie	Todd	MN	Rush Lake	Pierce	ND	Ryder	Ward	ND
Round Prairie	Callaway	MO	Rush River	Saint Croix	WI	Rye	Grand Forks	ND
Round Prairie	Williams	ND	Rush River	Cass	ND	Rye	Rockingham	NH

TOWNSHIP	COUNTY	STATE	TOWNSHIP	COUNTY	STATE	TOWNSHIP	COUNTY	STATE
Rye	Westchester	NY	Saint Francois	Wayne	MO	Salado	Independence	AR
Rye	Perry	PA	Saint George	Knox	ME	Salamanca	Cherokee	KS
Ryegate	Caledonia	VT	Saint George	Chittenden	VT	Salamanca	Cattaraugus	NY
Ryno	Custer	NE	Saint George	Pottawatomie	KS	Salamonie	Huntington	IN
			Saint George	Benton	MN	Salem Chapel	Forsyth	NC
			Saint Germain	Vilas	WI	Salem	Greene	AR
—S—			Saint Helena	Nape	CA	Salem	Saline	AR
			Saint Helena	Beaufort	SC	Salem	New London	CT
Sac	Sac	IA	Saint Ignance	Macinac	MI	Salem	Henry	IA
Sac	Dade	MO	Saint Jacob	Madison	IL	Salem	Carroll	IL
Sacramento	Sacramento	CA	Saint James Santee	Berkeley	SC	Salem	Knox	IL
Sacred Heart	Renville	MN	Saint James Santee	Charleston	SC	Salem	Marion	IL
Saddle Brook	Bergen	NJ	Saint James	Charlevoix	MI	Salem	Delaware	IN
Saddle Butte	Golden Valley	ND	Saint James	Watonwan	MN	Salem	Pulaski	IN
Saddle Mountain	Comanche	OK	Saint James	Mississippi	MO	Salem	Steuben	IN
Saddletree	Robeson	NC	Saint James	Phelps	MO	Salem	Allen	KS
Sadie	Sequoyah	OK	Saint James	Clarendon	SC	Salem	Cowley	KS
Sadorus	Champaign	IL	Saint Joe	Searcy	AR	Salem	Greenwood	KS
Sadsbury	Chester	PA	Saint John	Lake	IN	Salem	Sedgwick	KS
Sadsbury	Crawford	PA	Saint John	Stafford	KS	Salem	Allegan	MI
Sadsbury	Lancaster	PA	Saint John	New Madrid	MO	Salem	Washtenaw	MI
Sagamore Hills	Summit	OH	Saint Johns	Harrison	IA	Salem	Cass	MN
Sage	Izard	AR	Saint Johns	Kandiyohi	MN	Salem	Olmsted	MN
Sage	Gladwin	MI	Saint Johns	Franklin	MO	Salem	Daviess	MO
Saginaw	Saginaw	MI	Saint Johns	Hertford	NC	Salem	Dunklin	MO
Sago	Itasca	MN	Saint Johnsbury	Caledonia	VT	Salem	Lewis	MO
Sagola	Dickinson	MI	Saint Johnsville	Montgomery	NY	Salem	Perry	MO
Saint Agatha	Aroostook	ME	Saint Joseph	Saint Croix	WI	Salem	Granville	NC
Saint Albans	Hancock	IL	Saint Joseph	Champaign	IL	Salem	Pasquotank	NC
Saint Albans	Somerset	ME	Saint Joseph	Allen	IN	Salem	Franklin	NE
Saint Albans	Licking	OH	Saint Joseph	Berrien	MI	Salem	Rockingham	NH
Saint Albans	Franklin	VT	Saint Joseph	Kittson	MN	Salem	Washington	NY
Saint Andrews	Walsh	ND	Saint Joseph	Stearns	MN	Salem	Auglaize	OH
Saint Andrews	Charleston	SC	Saint Joseph	Pembina	ND	Salem	Champaign	OH
Saint Anna	Wells	ND	Saint Joseph	Williams	OH	Salem	Columbiana	OH
Saint Anne	Kankakee	IL	Saint Lawrence	Scott	MN	Salem	Highland	OH
Saint Ansgar	Mitchell	IA	Saint Lawrence	Hand	SD	Salem	Jefferson	OH
Saint Armand	Essex	NY	Saint Lawrence	Waupaca	WI	Salem	Meigs	OH
Saint Aubert	Callaway	MO	Saint Louis	Pottawatomie	OK	Salem	Monroe	OH
Saint Augusta	Stearns	MN	Saint Marie	Green Lake	WI	Salem	Muskingum	OH
Saint Bernard	Platte	NE	Saint Mark	Clarendon	SC	Salem	Ottawa	OH
Saint Bernard	Hamilton	OH	Saint Martin	Stearns	MN	Salem	Shelby	OH
Saint Bridget	Marshall	KS	Saint Mary	Hancock	IL	Salem	Tuscarawas	OH
Saint Charles	Floyd	IA	Saint Mary	Waseca	MN	Salem	Warren	OH
Saint Charles	Kane	IL	Saint Mary	McLean	ND	Salem	Washington	OH
Saint Charles	Saginaw	MI	Saint Marys	Mills	IA	Salem	Wyandot	OH
Saint Charles	Winona	MN	Saint Marys	Adams	IN	Salem	Clarion	PA
Saint Charles	Saint Charles	MO	Saint Marys	Pottawatomie	KS	Salem	Luzerne	PA
Saint Charles	Cuming	NE	Saint Marys	Perry	MO	Salem	Mercer	PA
Saint Charles	Gregory	SD	Saint Marys	Wake	NC	Salem	Wayne	PA
Saint Charles	Lee	SC	Saint Marys	Ward	ND	Salem	Westmoreland	PA
Saint Clair	Benton	IA	Saint Marys	Auglaize	OH	Salem	McCook	SD
Saint Clair	Monona	IA	Saint Mathias	Crow Wing	MN	Salem	Turner	SD
Saint Clair	Saint Clair	IL	Saint Matthews	Wake	NC	Salem	Kenosha	WI
Saint Clair	Saint Clair	MI	Saint Michael & Saint			Salem	Pierce	WI
Saint Clair	Butler	OH	Phllip	Charleston	SC	Salford	Montgomery	PA
Saint Clair	Columbiana	OH	Saint Michael	Madison	MO	Salina	Kankakee	IL
Saint Clair	Westmoreland	PA	Saint Olaf	Otter Tail	MN	Salina	Onondaga	NY
Saint Clere	Pottawatomie	KS	Saint Onge	Lawrence	SD	Saline	Cleburne	AR
Saint Cloud	Stearns	MN	Saint Paul	Stutsman	ND	Saline	Cleveland	AR
Saint Croix Falls	Polk	WI	Saint Paul	Claredon	SC	Saline	Drew	AR
Saint Croix	Hettinger	ND	Saint Pauls	Robeson	NC	Saline	Hempstead	AR
Saint Dennis & Saint			Saint Pauls	Charleston	SC	Saline	Hot Spring	AR
Thomas	Berkeley	SC	Saint Regis Indian			Saline	Howard	AR
Saint Ferdinand	Saint Louis	MO	Reservation	Franklin	NY	Saline	Pike	AR
Saint Francis	Clay	AR	Saint Rose	Clinton	IL	Saline	Salle	AR
Saint Francis	Green	AR	Saint Thomas	Pembina	ND	Saline	Sevier	AR
Saint Francis	Lee	AR	Saint Thomas	Franklin	PA	Saline	Madison	IL
Saint Francis	Phillips	AR	Saint Vincent	Conway	AR	Saline	Ellis	KS
Saint Francis	Effingham	IL	Saint Vincent	Kittson	MN	Saline	Washtenaw	MI
Saint Francois	Butler	MO	Saint Wendel	Stearns	MN	Saline	Cooper	MO
Saint Francois	Madison	mO	Sainte Genevieve	Sainte Genevieve	MO	Saline	Miller	MO
Saint Francois	Saint Francois	MO	Sainte Marie	Jasper	IL	Saline	Perry	MO

TOWNSHIPS OF THE UNITED STATES

TOWNSHIP	COUNTY	STATE	TOWNSHIP	COUNTY	STATE	TOWNSHIP	COUNTY	STATE
Saline	Ralls	MO	San Gebriel	Los Angeles	CA	Sandycreek	Venango	PA
Saline	Sainte Genevieve	MO	San Gorgonio	Riverside	CA	Sandyston	Sussex	NJ
Saline	Jefferson	OH	San Jacinto	Riverside	CA	Sandywoods	Scott	MO
Saline	McHenry	ND	San Joaquin	Sacramento	CA	Saneca	Plumas	CA
Saline	Alfalfa	OK	San Jose	Los Angeles	CA	Sanel	Mendocino	CA
Saline	Harper	OK	San Jose	Santa Clara	CA	Sanford	York	ME
Saline	Mayes	OK	San Juan	Orange	CA	Sanford	Grant	MN
Saling	Audrain	MO	San Juan	San Benito	CA	Sanford	Broome	NY
Salisbury	Litchfield	CT	San Luis Obispo	San Luis Obispo	CA	Sangamon	Piatt	IL
Salisbury	Sangamon	IL	San Miguel	San Luis Obispo	CA	Sangamon	Edmunds	SD
Salisbury	Essex	MA	San Rafael	Marin	CA	Sangamon Valley	Cass	IL
Salisbury	Chariton	MO	San Simeon	San Luis Obispo	CA	Sangerfield	Oneida	NY
Salisbury	Rowan	NC	Sanborn	Alpena	MI	Sangerville	Piscataquis	ME
Salisbury	Merrimack	NH	Sanborn	Ashland	WI	Sanilac	Sanilac	MI
Salisbury	Herkimer	NY	Sanbornton	Belknap	NH	Sanner	Potter	SD
Salisbury	Meigs	OH	Sand Beach	Huron	MI	Sans Bois	Haskell	OK
Salisbury	Lancaster	PA	Sand Creek	Union	IA	Santa Ana	Orange	CA
Salisbury	Lehigh	PA	Sand Creek	Bartholomew	IN	Santa Ana	De Witt	IL
Salisbury	Addison	VT	Sand Creek	Decatur	IN	Santa Clara	Santa Clara	CA
Sallisaw	Sequoyah	OK	Sand Creek	Jennings	IN	Santa Clara	Franklin	NY
Salmon Falls	El Dorado	CA	Sand Creek	Meade	KS	Santa Cruz	Santa Cruz	CA
Salo	Aitkin	MA	Sand Creek	Norton	KS	Santa Fe	Clinton	IL
Salonia	Latimer	OK	Sand Creek	Scott	MN	Santa Fe	Pawnee	KS
Salt Creek	Davis	IA	Sand Creek	Slope	ND	Santa Fe	Noble	OK
Salt Creek	Tama	IA	Sand Creek	Holt	NE	Santa Margarita	San Luis Obispo	CA
Salt Creek	Mason	IL	Sand Creek	Beadle	SD	Santa Monica	Los Angeles	CA
Salt Creek	Decatur	IN	Sand Creek	Dunn	WI	Santa Paula	Ventura	CA
Salt Creek	Franklin	IN	Sand Hill	Scotland	MO	Santa Rosa	Sonoma	CA
Salt Creek	Jackson	IN	Sand Hill	Lenoir	NC	Santee	Knox	NE
Salt Creek	Monroe	IN	Sand Hill	Moore	NC	Santee	Clarendon	SC
Salt Creek	Chautauqua	KS	Sand Lake	Itasca	MN	Santee	Georgetown	SC
Salt Creek	Lincoln	KS	Sand Lake	Rensselaer	NY	Santiago	Sherburne	MN
Salt Creek	Mitchell	KS	Sand Lake	Burnett	WI	Santuc	Union	SC
Salt Creek	Reno	KS	Sand Lake	Sawyer	WI	Sappa	Decatur	KS
Salt Creek	Chariton	MO	Sand Point	Crawford	AR	Sappa	Harlan	NE
Salt Creek	Hocking	OH	Sand Prairie	Tazewell	IL	Sapulpa	Creek	OK
Salt Creek	Holmes	OH	Sand Ridge	Jackson	IL	Saranac	Clinton	NY
Salt Creek	Muskingum	OH	Sand Spring	Pope	AR	Saratoga	Howard	AR
Salt Creek	Pickaway	OH	Sanders	Pennington	MN	Saratoga	Santa Clara	CA
Salt Creek	Wayne	OH	Sandgate	Bennington	VT	Saratoga	Howard	IA
Salt Fork	Saline	MO	Sandisfield	Berkshire	MA	Saratoga	Grundy	IL
Salt Fork	Grant	OK	Sandnes	Yellow Medicine	MN	Saratoga	Marshall	IL
Salt Lick	Perry	OH	Sandoun	Ranson	ND	Saratoga	Pratt	KS
Salt Pond	Saline	MO	Sandoval	Marion	IL	Saratoga	Winona	MN
Salt River	Adair	MO	Sandown	Rockingham	NH	Saratoga	Wilson	NC
Salt River	Audrain	MO	Sands	Marquette	MI	Saratoga	La Moure	ND
Salt River	Knox	MO	Sandstone	Jackson	MI	Saratoga	Holt	NE
Salt River	Pike	MO	Sandstone	Pine	MN	Saratoga	Saratoga	NY
Salt River	Ralls	MO	Sandsville	Polk	MN	Srartoga	Faulk	SD
Salt River	Randolph	MO	Sandusky	Crawford	OH	Saratoga	Wood	WI
Salt River	Schuyler	MO	Sandusky	Richland	OH	Sarcoxie	Jefferson	KS
Salt River	Shelby	MO	Sundusky	Sandusky	OH	Sarcoxie	Jasper	MO
Salt Rock	Marion	OH	Sandwich	De Kalb	IL	Sardinia	Erie	NY
Salt Spring	Randolph	MO	Sandwich	Barnstable	MA	Sargeant	Mower	MN
Salt Springs	Greenwood	KS	Sandwich	Carroll	NH	Sargent	Douglas	IL
Saltese	Mineral	MT	Sandy Creek	Franklin	NC	Sargent	Texas	MO
Saltlick	Fayette	PA	Sandy Creek	Vance	NC	Sargent	Sargent	ND
Saluda	Jefferson	IN	Sandy Creek	Warren	NC	Sargent	Custer	NE
Saluda	Polk	NC	Sandy Creek	Oswego	NY	Sarnia	Nelson	ND
Saluda	Greenville	SC	Sandy Creek	Mercer	PA	Sarona	Washburn	WI
Saluda	Lexington	SC	Sandy Grove	Clarendon	SC	Sartoria	Buffalo	NE
Sammy Swamp	Clarendon	SC	Sandy Hook	Cimarron	OK	Sassafras Fork	Granville	NC
Sampit	Georgetown	SC	Sandy Lake	Mercer	PA	Sauble	Lake	MI
Sampsell	Livingston	MO	Sandy Mush	Buncombe	NC	Saugatuck	Allegan	MI
Sampson	Chippewa	WI	Sandy Point	Le Flore	OK	Saugerties	Ulster	NY
San Antonia	Los Angeles	CA	Sandy Ridge	Union	NC	Saugus	Essex	MA
San Antonio	Monterey	CA	Sandy Run	Cleveland	NC	Sauk Centre	Stearns	MN
San Andreas	Calaveras	CA	Sandy Run	Calhoun	SC	Sauk Prairie	Ward	ND
San Ardo	Monterey	CA	Sandy Run	Lexington	SC	Sauk Rapids	Benton	MN
San Bernardino	San Bernardino	CA	Sandy	Saint Louis	MN	Sauk Valley	Williams	ND
San Diego	San Diego	CA	Sandy	Stark	OH	Saukville	Ozaukee	WI
San Franado	Los Angeles	CA	Sandy	Tuscarawas	OH	Saulston	Wayne	NC
San Francisco	Carver	MN	Sandy	Clearfield	PA	Saunemin	Livingston	IL

TOWNSHIPS OF THE UNITED STATES

TOWNSHIP	COUNTY	STATE
Sauratown	Stokes	NC
Sausalito	Marin	CA
Sauter	Walsh	ND
Savanna	Carroll	IL
Savanna	Pittsburg	OK
Savanna	Becker	MN
Savannah	Jackson	NC
Savannah	Butler	NE
Savannah	Wayne	NY
Savannah	Anderson	SC
Saverton	Ralls	MO
Saville	Perry	PA
Savo	Brown	SD
Savoy	Berkshire	MA
Sawlog	Hodgeman	KS
Sawmill	Pawnee	KS
Sawyer	Ward	ND
Saxeville	Waushara	WI
Saxon	Iron	WI
Saybrook	Ashtabula	OH
Saylor	Polk	IA
Sayre	Beckham	OK
Scales Mound	Jo Daviess	IL
Scandia	Republic	KS
Scandia	Polk	MN
Scandia	Bottineau	ND
Scandia Valley	Morrison	MN
Scandinavia	Harlan	NE
Scandinavia	Deuel	SD
Scandinavia	Waupaca	WI
Scarborough	Cumberland	ME
Scarsdale	Westchester	NY
Scenic	Pennington	SD
Schafer	McKenzie	ND
Schaghticoke	Rensselaer	NY
Schauburg	Cook	IL
Schiller	McHenry	ND
Schleswig	Manitowoc	WI
Schley	Lincoln	NE
Schneider	Buffalo	NY
Schodack	Rensselaer	NY
Schoepke	Oneida	WI
Schoharie	Schoharie	NY
School Creek	Clay	NE
Schoolcraft	Houghton	MI
Schoolcraft	Kalamazoo	MI
Schoolcraft	Hubbard	MN
Schriever	Gregory	SD
Schroeppel	Oswego	NY
Schroon	Essex	NY
Schulter	Okmulgee	OK
Schultz	Grant	ND
Schultz	Aiken	SC
Schurz	Mineral	NV
Schuyler Falls	Clinton	NY
Schuyler	Herkimer	NY
Schuylkill	Chester	PA
Schuylkill	Schuylkill	PA
Scio	Allegany	NY
Scio	Washtenaw	MI
Sciota	McDonough	IL
Sciota	Shiawassee	MI
Sciota	Dakota	MN
Scioto	Delaware	OH
Scioto	Jackson	OH
Scioto	Pickaway	OH
Scioto	Pike	OH
Scioto	Ross	OH
Scipio	Allen	IN
Scipio	LaPorte	IN
Scipio	Hillsdale	MI
Scipio	Cayuga	NY
Scipio	Meigs	OH
Scipio	Seneca	OH
Scituate	Plymouth	MA
Scituate	Providence	RI
Scopus	Bollinger	MO
Scorio	Williams	ND
Scotch Cap	Perkins	SD
Scotch Grove	Jones	IA
Scotch Irish	Rowan	NC
Scotch Plains	Union	NJ
Scotia	Humboldt	CA
Scotia	Bottineau	ND
Scotland Neck	Halifax	NC
Scotland	McDonough	IL
Scotland	Bon Homme	SD
Scotland	Day	SD
Scott Creek	Jackson	NC
Scott River	Siskiyou	CA
Scott	Lonoke	AR
Scott	Mississippi	AR
Scott	Montgomery	AR
Scott	Poinsett	AR
Scott	Sharp	AR
Scott	Buena Vista	IA
Scott	Fayette	IA
Scott	Floyd	IA
Scott	Franklin	IA
Scott	Fremont	IA
Scott	Hamilton	IA
Scott	Henry	IA
Scott	Johnson	IA
Scott	Madison	IA
Scott	Mahaska	IA
Scott	Montgomery	IA
Scott	Poweshiek	IA
Scott	Champaign	IL
Scott	Ogle	IL
Scott	Kosciusko	IN
Scott	Montgomery	IN
Scott	Steuben	IN
Scott	Vanderburgh	IN
Scott	Bourbon	KS
Scott	Lincoln	KS
Scott	Linn	KS
Scott	Scott	KS
Scott	Stevens	MN
Scott	Taney	MO
Scott	Adams	ND
Scott	Buffalo	NE
Scott	Holt	NE
Scott	Sherman	NE
Scott	Cortland	NY
Scott	Adams	OH
Scott	Brown	OH
Scott	Marion	OH
Scott	Sandusky	OH
Scott	Allegheny	PA
Scott	Columbia	PA
Scott	Lackawanna	PA
Scott	Lancaster	PA
Scott	Wayne	PA
Scott	Brown	WI
Scott	Burnett	WI
Scott	Columbia	WI
Scott	Crawford	WI
Scott	Lincoln	WI
Scott	Monroe	WI
Scott	Sheboygan	WI
Scott Valley	Siskiyou	CA
Scottville	Macoupin	IL
Scovil	Jones	SD
Scoville	Ransom	ND
Scrambler	Otter Tail	MN
Scranton	Greene	IA
Scranton	Osage	KS
Scranton	Bowman	ND
Scriba	Oswego	NY
Scrubgrass	Venango	PA
Scuffletown	Laurens	SC
Scuppenong	Tyrrell	NC
Scuppernong	Washington	NC
Sea Level	Carteret	NC
Seaboard	Northampton	NC
Seabrook	Rockingham	NH
Seal Beach	Orange	CA
Seal	Pike	OH
Seal	Logan	ND
Sealy	Logan	ND
Searchlight	Clark	NV
Searcy	Cross	AR
Searcy	Phillips	AR
Searsburg	Bennington	VT
Searsmont	Waldo	ME
Searsport	Waldo	ME
Seavey	Aitkin	MN
Seay	Blaine	OK
Sebago	Cumberland	ME
Sebec	Piscatauqis	ME
Sebewa	Ionia	MI
Sebewaing	Huron	MI
Secaucus	Hudson	NJ
Second Saint Jones Goose Creek	Berkeley	SC
Second Saint James Goose Creek	Charleston	SC
Second Saint John Berkeley	Berkeley	SC
Second Saint Stephens	Berkeley	SC
Secord	Gladwin	MI
Sedalia	Pettis	MO
Sedan	Chautauqua	KS
Sedgwick	Harvey	KS
Sedgwick	Hancock	ME
Seelonk	Bristol	MA
Seely	Guthrie	IA
Seely	Faribault	MN
Sefton	Fayette	IL
Segar	Washita	OK
Seif	Clark	WI
Seiling	Dewey	OK
Seim	Perkins	SD
Seivert	Cavalier	ND
Selby	Bureau	IL
Self Creek	Pike	AR
Selma	Wexford	MI
Selma	Cottonwood	MN
Selma	Johnston	NC
Selz	Emmons	ND
Semiahmoo	Whatcom	WA
Seminary	Fayette	IL
Sempronius	Cayuga	NY
Senachwine	Putnam	IL
Seneca Falls	Seneca	NY
Seneca	Kossuth	IA
Seneca	McHenry	IL
Seneca	Lenawee	MI
Seneca	Christian	MO
Seneca	Newton	MO
Seneca	Ontario	NY
Seneca	Monroe	OH
Seneca	Noble	OH
Seneca	Seneca	OH
Seneca	Oconee	SC
Seneca	Crawford	WI
Seneca	Green Lake	WI
Seneca	Shawano	WI
Seneca	Wood	WI
Seney	Schoolcraft	MI

TOWNSHIPS OF THE UNITED STATES

TOWNSHIP	COUNTY	STATE	TOWNSHIP	COUNTY	STATE	TOWNSHIP	COUNTY	STATE
Sennett	Cayuga	NY	Sharon	Potter	PA	Shenango	Lawrence	PA
Sentinel	Golden Valley	ND	Sharon	Hutchinson	SD	Shenango	Mercer	PA
Serena	La Salle	IL	Sharon	Windsor	VT	Shenford	Ransom	ND
Sergeant	McKean	PA	Sharon	Portage	WI	Shepherd	Crawford	AR
Sergius	Bottineau	ND	Sharon	Walworth	WI	Shepherd	Walsh	ND
Settlers	Sioux	IA	Sharonville	Hamilton	OH	Sherborn	Middlesex	MA
Sevastopol	Door	WI	Sharpes	Alexander	NC	Sherbrooke	Steele	ND
Seven Hickory	Coles	IL	Sharpesburg	Iredell	NC	Sherburne	Chenango	NY
Seven Mile Creek	Juneau	WI	Shaw	Saline	AR	Sherburne	Rutland	VT
Severance	Sibley	MN	Shaw	Edgefield	SC	Sheridan	Carroll	IA
Severdrup	Minnehaha	SD	Shawangunk	Ulster	NY	Sheridan	Cherokee	IA
Severn	Stutsman	ND	Shawnee	Gallatin	IL	Sheridan	Poweshiek	IA
Severs	Okmulgee	OK	Shawnee	Fountain	IN	Sheridan	Scott	IA
Seward	Kendall	IL	Shawnee	Cherokee	KS	Sheridan	Sioux	IA
Seward	Winnebago	IL	Shawnee	Johnson	KS	Sheridan	Logan	IL
Seward	Kosciusko	IN	Shawnee	Wyandotte	KS	Sheridan	Cherokee	KS
Seward	Seward	KS	Shawnee	Bates	MO	Sheridan	Cowley	KS
Seward	Nobles	MN	Shawnee	Cape Girardeau	MO	Sheridan	Crawford	KS
Seward	Schoharie	NY	Shawnee	Henry	MO	Sheridan	Linn	KS
Seward	Logan	OK	Shawnee	Allen	OH	Sheridan	Ottawa	KS
Sewickley	Westmoreland	PA	Shawneehaw	Watauga	NC	Sheridan	Sheridan	KS
Seymour	New Haven	CT	Shaws Point	Macoupin	IL	Sheridan	Washington	KS
Seymour	Eau Claire	WI	Shaws	Aiken	SC	Sheridan	Calhoun	MI
Seymour	Lafayette	WI	Shawswick	Lawrence	IN	Sheridan	Clare	MI
Seymour	Outagamie	WI	Shealey	Ward	ND	Sheridan	Huron	MI
Shabbona	De Kalb	IL	Sheboygan Falls	Sheboygan	WI	Sheridan	Mason	MI
Shade	Somerset	PA	Sheboygan	Sheboygan	WI	Sheridan	Mecosta	MI
Shady Grove	Greene	AR	Sheets	Slope	ND	Sheridan	Newaygo	MI
Shady Grove	Searcy	AR	Sheffield	Tippecanoe	IN	Sheridan	Redwood	MN
Shady Grove	Davie	NC	Sheffield	Berkshire	MA	Sheridan	Dallas	MO
Shafer	Chisago	MN	Sheffield	Ashtabula	OH	Sheridan	Daviess	MO
Shafter	Fayette	IL	Sheffield	Lorain	OH	Sheridan	Jasper	MO
Shaftsbury	Bennington	VT	Sheffield	Warren	PA	Sheridan	La Moure	ND
Shahan	Wagoner	OK	Sheffield	Caledonia	VT	Sheridan	Clay	NE
Shaler	Allegheny	PA	Sheffields	Moore	NC	Sheridan	Holt	NE
Shalersville	Portage	OH	Shelburne	Franklin	MA	Sheridan	Phelps	NE
Shallotte	Brunswick	NC	Shelburne	Lyon	MN	Sheridan	Chautauqua	NY
Shamokin	Northumberland	PA	Shelburne	Coos	NH	Sheridan	Garfield	OK
Shamong	Burlington	NJ	Shelburne	Chittenden	VT	Sheridan	Major	OK
Shamrock	Aitkin	MN	Shelby	Shelby	IA	Sheridan	Colleton	SC
Shamrock	Callaway	MO	Shelby	Jefferson	IN	Sheridan	Codington	SD
Shamrock	Holt	NE	Shelby	Ripley	IN	Sheridan	Dunn	WI
Shanagolden	Ashland	WI	Shelby	Shelby	IN	Sherley	Ripley	MO
Shandaken	Ulster	NY	Shelby	Tippecanoe	IN	Sherlock	Finney	KS
Shannon	Carroll	IL	Shelby	Macomb	MI	Sherman	Johnson	AR
Shannon	Atchison	KS	Shelby	Oceana	MI	Sherman	Fairfield	CT
Shannon	Pottawatomie	KS	Shelby	Blue Earth	MN	Sherman	Calhoun	IA
Shannon	Robeson	NC	Shelby	Cleveland	NC	Sherman	Hardin	IA
Shannon	Creek	OK	Shelby	Orleans	NY	Sherman	Jasper	IA
Shannon	Wagoner	OK	Shelby	Brown	SD	Sherman	Kossuth	IA
Shaokatan	Lincoln	MN	Shelby	La Crosse	WI	Sherman	Monona	IA
Shapleigh	York	ME	Shelbyville	Shelby	IL	Sherman	Montgomery	IA
Sharlow	Stutsman	ND	Sheldon	Iroquois	IL	Sherman	Pocahontas	IA
Sharon Springs	Wallace	KS	Sheldon	Houston	MN	Sherman	Sioux	IA
Sharon	Litchfield	CT	Sheldon	Wyoming	NY	Sherman	Story	IA
Sharon	Appanoose	IA	Sheldon	Ellis	OK	Sherman	Mason	IL
Sharon	Audubon	IA	Sheldon	Beaufort	SC	Sherman	Clay	KS
Sharon	Clinton	IA	Sheldon	Franklin	VT	Sherman	Crawford	KS
Sharon	Johnson	IA	Sheldon	Monroe	WI	Sherman	Decatur	KS
Sharon	Fayette	IL	Shell Creek	Platte	NE	Sherman	Dickinson	KS
Sharon	Barber	KS	Shell Knob	Barry	MO	Sherman	Ellsworth	KS
Sharon	Norfolk	MA	Shell Lake	Becker	MN	Sherman	Grant	KS
Sharon	Washtenaw	MI	Shell River	Wadena	MN	Sherman	Leavenworth	KS
Sharon	Le Sueur	MN	Shell Rock	Butler	IA	Sherman	Ottawa	KS
Sharon	Mecklenburg	NC	Shell Rock	Greenwood	KS	Sherman	Pottawatomie	KS
Sharon	Steele	ND	Shell Rock	Freeborn	MN	Sherman	Riley	KS
Sharon	Buffalo	NE	Shell	Mountrail	ND	Sherman	Sedgwick	KS
Sharon	Hillsborough	NH	Shellsburg	Benton	IA	Sherman	Washington	KS
Sharon	Schoharie	NY	Shelly	Norman	MN	Sherman	Aroostook	ME
Sharon	Franklin	OH	Shelter Island	Suffolk	NY	Sherman	Gladwin	MI
Sharon	Medina	OH	Shelton	Fairfield	CT	Sherman	Huron	MI
Sharon	Noble	OH	Shelton	Knox	MO	Sherman	Iosco	MI
Sharon	Richland	OH	Shelton	Buffalo	NE	Sherman	Isabella	MI

TOWNSHIP	COUNTY	STATE	TOWNSHIP	COUNTY	STATE	TOWNSHIP	COUNTY	STATE
Sherman	Keweenaw	MI	Shocco	Warren	NC	Silver Lake	Desha	AR
Sherman	Mason	MI	Shohola	Pike	PA	Silver Lake	Dickinson	IA
Sherman	Newaygo	MI	Shooks	Beltrami	MN	Silver Lake	Palo Alto	IA
Sherman	Osceola	MI	Shooting Creek	Clay	NC	Silver Lake	Worth	IA
Sherman	Saint Joseph	MI	Shoreham	Addison	VT	Silver Lake	Shawnee	KS
Sherman	Redwood	MN	Shores	Franklin	AR	Silver Lake	Martin	MN
Sherman	Cass	MO	Short Bend	Dent	MO	Silver Lake	Wells	ND
Sherman	Dallas	MO	Short Creek	Burke	ND	Silver Lake	Adams	NE
Sherman	De Kalb	MO	Short Creek	Harrison	OH	Silver Lake	Becker	MN
Sherman	Harrison	MO	Short Mountain	Logan	AR	Silver Lake	Summit	OH
Sherman	Putnam	MO	Shotley	Beltrami	MN	Silver Lake	Susquehanna	PA
Sherman	Bottineau	ND	Shrewsbury	Worcester	MA	Silver Spring	Cumberland	PA
Sherman	Antelope	NE	Shrewsbury	Monmouth	NJ	Silver	Cherokee	IA
Sherman	Cuming	NE	Shrewsbury	Lycoming	PA	Silver	Carlton	MN
Sherman	Gage	NE	Shrewsbury	Sullivan	PA	Silverdale	Cowley	KS
Sherman	Kearney	NE	Shrewsbury	York	PA	Silverlake	Hutchinson	SD
Sherman	Platte	NE	Shrewsbury	Rutland	VT	Silverton	Pennington	MN
Sherman	Chautauqua	NY	Shullsburg	Lafayette	WI	Silverton	Hamilton	OH
Sherman	Huron	OH	Shuman	Sargent	ND	Silverton	Aiken	SC
Sherman	Kingfisher	OK	Shutesbury	Franklin	MA	Silvesta	Walsh	ND
Sherman	Brookings	SD	Shyne	Pennington	SD	Silveyville	Solano	CA
Sherman	Corson	SD	Sibley Butte	Burleigh	ND	Simi	Ventura	CA
Sherman	Faulk	SD	Sibley	Cloud	KS	Simpson Creek	Horry	SC
Sherman	Clark	WI	Sibley	Crow Wing	MN	Simpson	Grant	AR
Sherman	Dunn	WI	Sibley	Sibley	MN	Simpson	Johnson	IL
Sherman	Iron	WI	Sibley	Kidder	ND	Simpson	Johnson	MO
Sherman	Sheboygan	WI	Sibley Trail	Barnes	ND	Simpson	Stark	ND
Shermanville	Sherman	KS	Sicily	Gage	NE	Simpson	Dewey	OK
Sherrill	Texas	MO	Sickle	Dewey	OK	Simpson	McIntosh	OK
Sherry	Wood	WI	Sickles	Caddo	OK	Simpsonville	Rockingham	NC
Sherwood	Branch	MI	Sidell	Vermilion	IL	Sims	Grant	IN
Sherwood	Clark	WI	Sidney	Freemont	IA	Sims	Arenac	MI
Sheshequin	Bradford	PA	Sidney	Champaign	IL	Sims	Morton	ND
Shetek	Murray	MN	Sidney	Kennebec	ME	Simsbury	Hartford	CT
Shevlin	Clearwater	MN	Sidney	Montcalm	MI	Sinclair	Jewell	KS
Sheyenne	Richland	ND	Sidney	Towner	ND	Sinclair	Clearwater	MN
Shiawassee	Shiawassee	MI	Sidney	Delaware	NY	Sinclair	Stutsman	ND
Shible	Swift	MN	Sidney	Perkins	SD	Single	Wexford	MI
Shields	Lake	IL	Sidney	Fremont	IA	Sinking	Dent	MO
Shields	Grant	ND	Sidonia	Mountrail	ND	Sinnott	Marshall	MN
Shields	Holt	NE	Sierra	Sierra	CA	Sioux Agency	Yellow Medicine	MN
Shields	Dodge	WI	Sigel	Shelby	IL	Sioux City	Woodbury	IA
Shields	Marquette	WI	Sigel	Huron	MI	Sioux Creek	Barron	WI
Shieldsville	Rice	MN	Sigel	Brown	MN	Sioux Falls	Minnehaha	SD
Shiley	Pawnee	KS	Sigel	Chippewa	WI	Sioux Rapids	Buena Vista	IA
Shiloh	Randolph	AR	Sigel	Wood	WI	Sioux	Clay	IA
Shiloh	Grundy	IA	Signal Hill	Los Angeles	CA	Sioux	Lyon	IA
Shiloh	Edgar	IL	Signal	Charles Mix	SD	Sioux	Monona	IA
Shiloh	Jefferson	IL	Sigourney	Keokuk	IA	Sioux	Plymouth	IA
Shiloh	Neosho	KS	Sikes	Mountrail	ND	Sioux	Sioux	IA
Shiloh	Camden	NC	Siloam Springs	Howell	MO	Sioux	McKenzie	ND
Shiloh	Iredell	NC	Siloam	Randolph	AR	Sioux	Lyman	SD
Shiloh	Sumter	SC	Siloam	Surry	NC	Sioux Trail	Divide	ND
Shiloh Valley	Saint Clair	IL	Silver Brook	Carlton	MN	Sioux Valley	Jackson	MN
Shimer	Comanche	KS	Silver Cliff	Marinette	WI	Sioux Valley	Union	SD
Shine	Greene	NC	Silver Creek	Ida	IA	Siren	Burnett	WI
Shingobee	Cass	MN	Silver Creek	Mills	IA	Sisseton	Marshall	SD
Shipman	Macoupin	IL	Silver Creek	Pottawattamie	IA	Sisseton	Roberts	SD
Shippen	Cameron	PA	Silver Creek	Stephenson	IL	Sisson	Howell	MO
Shippen	Tioga	PA	Silver Creek	Clark	IN	Sitka	Clark	KS
Shippensburg	Cumberland	PA	Silver Creek	Cowley	KS	Six Mile Grove	Swift	MN
Shirland	Winnebago	IL	Silver Creek	Harper	KS	Six Mile	Franklin	AR
Shirley	Cloud	KS	Silver Creek	Cass	MI	Six Mile	Logan	AR
Shirley	Middlesex	MA	Silver Creek	Lake	MN	Six Mile	Franklin	IL
Shirley	Piscataquis	ME	Silver Creek	Wright	MN	Sixpound	Warren	NC
Shirley	Grady	OK	Silver Creek	Randolph	MN	Skagen	Roseau	MN
Shirley	Huntingdon	PA	Silver Creek	Burke	NC	Skanawan	Lincoln	WI
Shoal Creek	Logan	AR	Silver Creek	Burt	NE	Skandia	Marquette	MI
Shoal Creek	Bond	IL	Silver Creek	Dixon	NE	Skandia	Murray	MN
Shoal Creek	Newton	MO	Silver Creek	Merrick	NE	Skandia	Barnes	ND
Shoal Creek	Cherokee	NC	Silver Creek	Greene	OH	Skane	Kittson	MN
Shoal	Clinton	MO	Silver Creek	Sanborn	SD	Skaneateles	Onondaga	NY
Shoals	Surry	NC	Silver Hill	Davidson	NC	Skedee	Pawnee	OK

TOWNSHIPS OF THE UNITED STATES

TOWNSHIP	COUNTY	STATE	TOWNSHIP	COUNTY	STATE	TOWNSHIP	COUNTY	STATE
Skelton	Warrick	IN	Smoky Hill	McPherson	KS	Somo	Lincoln	WI
Skelton	Carlton	MN	Smoky Hill	Saline	KS	Somonauk	De Kalb	IL
Skeleton	Garfield	OK	Smoky Hollow	Cass	MN	Songer	Clay	IL
Skeleton	Kingfisher	OK	Smoky	Sherman	KS	Sonoma	Sonoma	CA
Skiatook	Tulsa	OK	Smoky View	Saline	KS	Sonora	Hancock	IL
Skinnersville	Washington	NC	Smolan	Saline	KS	Soo	Chippewa	MI
Skippack	Montgomery	PA	Smyrna	Pope	AR	Soo	Burke	ND
Skowhegan	Somerset	ME	Smyrna	Jefferson	IN	Sorenson	Towner	ND
Skree	Clay	MN	Smyrna	Aroostook	ME	Sorkness	Mountrail	ND
Skull	Butler	NE	Smyrna	Carteret	NC	Sorrento	Hancock	ME
Skyeston	Wells	ND	Smyrna	Robeson	NC	South Abington	Lackawanna	PA
Slater	Cass	MN	Smyrna	Chenango	NY	South Albemarie	Stanly	NC
Slayton	Murray	MN	Snake Bite	Bertie	NC	South Annville	Lebanon	PA
Sledgeville	Texas	OK	Snake Creek	McLean	ND	South Arm	Charlevoix	MI
Sleepy Hollow	Aiken	SC	Snake Spring Valley	Bedford	PA	South Beaver	Beaver	PA
Sletten	Polk	MN	Sni-A-Bar	Jackson	MO	South Bend	Barton	KS
Slim Butte	Fall River	SD	Sin-A-Bar	Lafayette	MO	South Bend	Blue Earth	MN
Slippery Rock	Butler	PA	Snow Creek	Mitchell	NC	South Bend	Armstrong	PA
Slippery Rock	Lawrence	PA	Snow Creek	Stokes	NC	South Benton	Dallas	MO
Sloan	Woodbury	IA	Snow Creek	Nowata	OK	South Berwick	York	ME
Slocum	Luzerne	PA	Snow Hill	Lincoln	MO	South Bloomfield	Morrow	OH
Slope Center	Slope	ND	Snow Hill	Greene	NC	South Branch	Crawford	MI
Smackover	Ouachita	AR	Snow Shoe	Centre	PA	South Branch	Wexford	MI
Smackover	Union	AR	Snow	McLean	ND	South Branch	Watonwan	MN
Smalley	Monroe	AR	Snyder	Blair	PA	South Branch	Nance	NE
Smallwood	Jasper	IL	Snyder	Jefferson	PA	South Bristol	Lincoln	ME
Smart	Stone	AR	Soap Creek	Davis	IA	South Bristol	Ontario	NY
Smelser	Grant	WI	Socastee	Horry	SC	South Brown	Edwards	KS
Smiley	Pennington	MN	Sodus	Berrien	MI	South Brunswick	Middlesex	NJ
Smith Creek	Warren	NC	Sodus	Lyon	MN	South Buffalo	Armstrong	PA
Smith River	Del Norte	CA	Sodus	Wayne	NY	South Burlington	Chittenden	VT
Smith	Cleveland	AR	Sodville	Ford	KS	South Canaan	Wayne	PA
Smith	Cross	AR	Soldier	Crawford	IA	South Cedar	Saunders	NE
Smith	Dallas	AR	Soldier	Monona	IA	South Cement	Caddo	OK
Smith	Lincoln	AR	Soldier	Jackson	KS	South Centre	Columbia	PA
Smith	Montgomery	AR	Soldier	Shawnee	KS	South Choctaw	Lincoln	OK
Smith	Saline	AR	Solebury	Bucks	PA	South Cimarron	Logan	OK
Smith	Greene	IN	Soledad	Los Angeles	CA	South Clinton	Sampson	NC
Smith	Posey	IN	Soledad	Monterey	CA	South Cottonwood	Wells	ND
Smith	Whitley	IN	Solem	Douglas	MN	South Coventry	Chester	PA
Smith	Thomas	KS	Solen	Sioux	ND	South Creek	Lincoln	OK
Smith	Carroll	MO	Soler	Roseau	MN	South Creek	Bedford	PA
Smith	Dade	MO	Solomon Rapids	Mitchell	KS	South Creek	Jones	SD
Smith	Laclede	MO	Solomon	Cloud	KS	South Crouch	Hamilton	IL
Smith	Worth	MO	Solomon	Graham	KS	South Detroit	Brown	SD
Smith	Duplin	NC	Solomon	Norton	KS	South Dixon	Lee	IL
Smith	Towner	ND	Solomon	Phillips	KS	South Dresden	Cavalier	ND
Smith	Belmont	OH	Solomon	Saline	KS	South Elk	Washita	OK
Smith	Mahoning	OH	Solomon	Sheridan	KS	South Fayette	Allegheny	PA
Smith	Washington	PA	Solon Springs	Dodge	WI	South Fillmore	Montgomery	IL
Smith	Brule	SD	Solon	Somerset	ME	South Flannigan	Hamilton	IL
Smith Valley	Lyon	NV	Solon	Kent	MI	South Fork	Fulton	AR
Smithfield	Fayette	IA	Solon	Leelanau	MI	South Fork	Montgomery	AR
Smithfield	De Kalb	IN	Solon	Cortland	NY	South Fork	Delaware	IA
Smithfield	Johnson	NC	Solway	Saint Louis	MN	South Fork	Jackson	IA
Smithfield	Madison	NY	Somer	Champaign	IL	South Fork	Wayne	IA
Smithfield	Jefferson	OH	Somerford	Madison	OH	South Fork	Christian	IL
Smithfield	Bradford	PA	Somers	Tolland	CT	South Fork	Kanabec	MN
Smithfield	Huntingdon	PA	Somers	Wilkes	NC	South Fork	Audrain	MO
Smithfield	Monroe	PA	Somers	Westchester	NY	South Fork	Howell	MO
Smithfield	Providence	RI	Somers	Preble	OH	South Fork	Monroe	MO
Smiths Bridge	Monroe	NC	Somers	Kenosha	WI	South Fork	Forsyth	NC
Smiths	Robeson	NC	Somerset	Jackson	IL	South Fork	Tyrrell	NC
Smithton	Saint Clair	IL	Somerset	Bristol	MA	South Fork	Adams	ND
Smithton	Pettis	MO	Somerset	Hillsdale	MI	South Fork	Rusk	WI
Smithtown	Suffolk	NY	Somerset	Steele	MN	South Fox	Lincoln	OK
Smithville	Brunswick	NC	Somerset	Mercer	MO	South Franklin	Washington	PA
Smithville	Chenango	NY	Somerset	Niagara	NY	South Galloway	Christian	MO
Smithville	Abbeville	SC	Somerset	Belmont	OH	South Grove	De Kalb	IL
Smoky Butte	Divide	ND	Somerset	Somerset	PA	South Hackensack	Bergen	NJ
Smoky Creek	Burke	NC	Somerset	Washington	PA	South Hadley	Hampshire	MA
Smoky Hill	Ellis	KS	Somerset	Saint Croix	WI	South Hampton	Rockingham	NH
Smoky Hill	Geary	KS	Somes Bar	Siskiyou	CA	South Hanover	Dauphin	PA

TOWNSHIPS OF THE UNITED STATES

TOWNSHIP	COUNTY	STATE
South Harbor	Mille Lacs	MN
South Harrison	Boone	AR
South Harrison	Gloucester	NJ
South Haven	Sumner	KS
South Haven	Van Buren	MI
South Haven	Van Buren	ND
South Heart	Stark	ND
South Heidelberg	Berks	PA
South Hero	Grand Isle	VT
South Homer	Champaign	IL
South Homestead	Barton	KS
South Huntingdon	Westmoreland	PA
South Hurricane	Fayette	IL
South Keokuk	Lincoln	OK
South Kingstown	Washington	RI
South Lancaster	Grant	WI
South Lathram	Caddo	OK
South Lebanon	Sharp	AR
South Lebanon	Lebanon	PA
South Litchfield	Montgomery	IL
South Londonderry	Lebanon	PA
South Loup	Hall	NE
South Macon	Macon	IL
South Mahoning	Indiana	PA
South Manheim	Schuylkill	PA
South Meadow	Williams	ND
South Middleton	Cumberland	PA
South Mills	Camden	NC
South Minnewaukan	Ramsey	ND
South Moline	Rock Island	IL
South Moniteau	Cooper	MO
South Moran	Spokane	WA
South Morgan	Dade	MO
South Muddy	Jasper	IL
South Newton	Cumberland	PA
South Ottawa	La Salle	IL
South Otter	Macoupin	IL
South Palmyra	Macoupin	IL
South Park	Allegheny	PA
South Platte	Hall	NE
South Point	Gaston	NC
South Pymatuning	Mercer	PA
South Randali	Thomas	KS
South Red River	Kittson	MN
South River	Marion	MO
South River	Sampson	NC
South Riverside	Potter	SD
South Rock Island	Rock Island	IL
South Roscoe	Hodgeman	KS
South Ross	Vermilion	IL
South Salem	Greenwood	KS
South Seminole	Lincoln	OK
South Seward	Stafford	KS
South Sharps Creek	McPherson	KS
South Shenango	Crawford	PA
South Strabane	Washington	PA
South Sugar Creek	Randolph	MO
South Thomaston	Knox	ME
South Tow	Yancey	NC
South	Madison	IA
South	Dade	MO
South	Hamilton	IL
South Twigg		AR
South Union	Sharp	PA
South Union	Fayette	NY
South Valley	Cattaraugus	ND
South Valley	Rolette	PA
South Versailes	Allegheny	ND
South Viking	Benson	MO
South West	Barton	NC
South Westfield	Surry	IL
South Wheatland	Macon	NC
South Whitakers	Nash	PA
South Whitehall	Lehigh	OK
South Wichita	Lincoln	OK
South Williams	Columbus	NC
South Windsor	Hartford	CT
South Woodbury	Bedford	PA
Southhall	Dallas	AR
Southampton	Hampshire	MA
Southampton	Burlington	NJ
Southampton	Suffolk	NY
Southampton	Bedford	PA
Southampton	Cumberland	PA
Southampton	Franklin	PA
Southampton	Somerset	PA
Southborough	Worcester	MA
Southbridge	Worcester	MA
Southbrook	Cottonwood	MN
Southbury	New Haven	CT
Southeast	Putnam	NY
Southeast	Orange	IN
Southeast	Oakland	MI
Southfield	Hartford	CT
Southington	Hartford	CT
Southington	Trumbull	OH
Southold	Suffolk	NY
Southport	Lincoln	ME
Southport	Chemung	NY
Southside	Kearney	KS
Southside	Wright	MN
Southwest Harbor	Hancock	ME
Southwest Madison	Perry	PA
Southwest	Crawford	IL
Southwest	Lenoir	NC
Southwest	Sargent	ND
Southwest	Warren	PA
Southwick	Hampden	MA
Spade	Knox	NE
Spadra	Johnson	AR
Spafford	Onondaga	NY
Spalding	Menominee	MI
Spalding	Aitkin	MN
Spang	Itasca	MN
Spangle	Spokane	WA
Spanish Lake	Saint Louis	MO
Sparks	Washoe	NV
Sparta	Knox	IL
Sparta	Dearborn	IN
Sparta	Noble	IN
Sparta	Kent	MI
Sprata	Chippewa	MN
Sparta	Christian	MO
Sparta	Edgecombe	NC
Sparta	Knox	NE
Sparta	Sussex	NJ
Sparta	Livingston	NY
Sparta	Crawford	PA
Sparta	Monroe	WI
Spartanburg	Spartanburg	SC
Spaulding	Union	IA
Spaulding	Saginaw	MI
Spaulding	Bryan	OK
Speairs		MI
Speaker	Sanilac	MI
Spearville	Ford	KS
Speedwell	Saint Clair	MO
Speedwell	Wells	ND
Speedwell	Harper	OK
Speermoore	Greene	NC
Speights Bridge	Spokane	WA
Spence		MN
Spencer Brook	Isanti	IA
Spencer	Clay	IN
Spencer	De Kalb	IN
Spencer	Harrison	IN
Spencer	Jennings	IN
Spencer	Worcester	MA
Spencer	Kent	MI
Spencer	Aitkin	MN
Spencer	Douglas	MO
Spencer	Pike	MO
Spencer	Ralls	MO
Spencer	Ward	ND
Spencer	Boyd	NE
Spencer	Tioga	NY
Spencer	Allen	OH
Spencer	Guernsey	OH
Spencer	Lucas	OH
Spencer	Medina	OH
Spencer	Marathon	WI
Sperry	Clayton	IA
Spice Valley	Lawrence	IN
Spiceland	Henry	IN
Spider Lake	Sawyer	WI
Spink	Union	SD
Spirit Lake	Dickinson	IA
Spirit Lake	Kingsbury	Sd
Spirit Mound	Clay	SD
Spirit	Price	WI
Spiritwood	Stutsman	ND
Spiro	Le Flore	OK
Split Rock	Carlton	MN
Split Rock	Minnehaha	SD
Spooner	Washburn	WI
Spotted Horse	Arthur	NE
Sprague	New London	CT
Sprigg	Adams	OH
Spring Arbor	Jackson	MI
Spring Bank	Dixon	NE
Spring Bay	Woodford	IL
Spring Brook	Sheridan	KS
Spring Brook	Kittson	MN
Spring Brook	Lackawanna	PA
Spring Brook	Dunn	WI
Spring Butte	Adams	ND
Spring Coulee	Mountrail	ND
Spring Creek	Lee	AR
Spring Creek	Phillips	AR
Spring Creek	Bleck Hawk	IA
Spring Creek	Mahaska	IA
Spring Creek	Tama	IA
Spring Creek	Pike	IL
Spring Creek	Coffey	KS
Spring Creek	Cowley	KS
Spring Creek	Greenwood	KS
Spring Creek	Lane	KS
Spring Creek	Pottawatomie	KS
Spring Creek	Saline	KS
Spring Creek	Becker	MN
Spring Creek	Norman	MN
Spring Creek	Dent	MO
Spring Creek	Douglas	MO
Spring Creek	Howell	MO
Spring Creek	Maries	MO
Spring Creek	Ozark	MO
Spring Creek	Phelps	MO
Spring Creek	Shannon	MO
Spring Creek	Madison	NC
Spring Creek	Barnes	ND
Spring Creek	Custer	NE
Spring Creek	Logan	OK
Spring Creek	Oklahoma	OK
Spring Creek	Elk	PA
Spring Creek	Warren	PA
Spring Creek	Moody	SD
Spring Garden	Jefferson	IL
Spring Garden	York	PA
Spring Green	Sauk	WI
Spring Grove	Greene	AR
Spring Grove	Linn	IA
Spring Grove	Warren	IL
Spring Grove	Houston	MN
Spring Grove	McHenry	ND

TOWNSHIP	COUNTY	STATE	TOWNSHIP	COUNTY	STATE	TOWNSHIP	COUNTY	STATE
Spring Grove	Harlan	NE	Springettsbury	York	PA	Spruce Valley	Marshall	MN
Spring Grove	Roberts	SD	Springfield	Cedar	IA	Spurr	Baraga	MI
Spring Grove	Green	WI	Springfield	Kossuth	IA	Squaw Grove	De Kalb	IL
Spring Hill	Drew	AR	Springfield	Winneshiek	IA	Squaw	Warren	??
Spring Hill	Stearns	MN	Springfield	Sangamon	IL	Squaw Valley	Siskiyou	CA
Spring Hill	Scotland	NC	Springfield	Allen	IN	Stacy	Carteret	NC
Spring Hill	Lee	SC	Springfield	Franklin	IN	Stacyville	Mitchell	IA
Spring Hill	Hand	SD	Springfield	Lagrange	IN	Stacyville	Penobscot	ME
Spring Hollow	Laclede	MO	Springfield	La Porte	IN	Stafford	Tolland	CT
Spring Lake	Tazewell	IL	Springfield	Penobscot	ME	Stafford	De Kalb	IN
Spring Lake	Ottawa	MI	Springfield	Kalkaska	MI	Stafford	Greene	IN
Spring Lake	Scott	MN	Springfield	Oakland	MI	Stafford	Stafford	KS
Spring Lake	Ward	ND	Springfield	Cottonwood	MN	Stafford	Roseau	MN
Spring Lake	Hand	SD	Springfield	Henry	MO	Stafford	Renville	ND
Spring Lake	Hanson	SD	Springfield	Towner	ND	Stafford	Ocean	NJ
Spring Lake	Hyde	SD	Springfield	Sullivan	NH	Stafford	Genesee	NY
Spring Lake	Kingsbury	SD	Springfield	Burlington	NJ	Stambaugh	Iron	MI
Spring Lake	Pierce	WI	Springfield	Union	NJ	Stamford	Fairfield	CT
Spring Point	Cumberland	IL	Springfield	Otsego	NY	Stamford	Delaware	NY
Spring Prairie	Clay	MN	Springfield	Clark	OH	Stamford	Bennington	VT
Spring Prairie	Walworth	WI	Springfield	Gallia	OH	Stampers Creek	Orange	IN
Spring Ranch	Clay	NE	Springfield	Hamilton	OH	Stanchfield	Isanti	MN
Spring River	Randolph	AR	Springfield	Jefferson	OH	Standing Stone	Bradford	PA
Spring River	Lawrence	AR	Springfield	Lucas	OH	Standish	Cumberland	ME
Spring River	Lawrence	MO	Springfield	Mahoning	OH	Standish	Arenac	MI
Spring Rock	Clinton	IA	Springfield	Muskingum	OH	Stanfold	Barron	WI
Spring	Jefferson	AR	Springfield	Richland	OH	Stanford	Clay	IL
Spring	Lincoln	AR	Springfield	Ross	OH	Stanford	Isanti	MN
Spring	Searcy	AR	Springfield	Summit	OH	Stanford	Dutchess	NY
Spring	Cherokee	IA	Springfield	Williams	OH	Stanley	Arkansas	AR
Spring	Boone	IL	Springfield	Bradford	PA	Stanley	Lyon	MN
Spring	Butler	KS	Springfield	Bucks	PA	Stanley	Cass	ND
Spring	Harper	KS	Springfield	Delaware	PA	Stanley	Barron	WI
Spring	Alfalfa	OK	Springfield	Erie	PA	Stannard	Ontonagon	MI
Spring	Woods	OK	Springfield	Fayette	PA	Stannard	Caledonia	VT
Spring	Berks	PA	Springfield	Huntingdon	PA	Stanton	Plymouth	IA
Spring	Centre	PA	Springfield	Mercer	PA	Stanton	Champaign	IL
Spring	Crawford	PA	Springfield	Montgomery	PA	Stanton	Linn	KS
Spring	Perry	PA	Springfield	York	PA	Stanton	Miami	KS
Spring	Snyder	PA	Springfield	Bon Homme	SD	Stanton	Ottawa	KS
Spring	Hand	SD	Springfield	Windsor	VT	Stanton	Stanton	KS
Spring	Spink	SD	Springfield	Dane	WI	Stanton	Houghton	MI
Spring Valley	Clinton	IA	Springfield	Jackson	WI	Stanton	Wilkes	NC
Spring Valley	Dallas	IA	Springfield	Marquette	WI	Stanton	Antelope	NE
Spring Valley	Monona	IA	Springfield	Saint Croix	WI	Stanton	Fillmore	NE
Spring Valley	Cherokee	KS	Springhill	Hemstead	AR	Stanton	Dunn	WI
Spring Valley	McPherson	KS	Springhill	Wilson	NC	Stanton	Saint Croix	WI
Spring Valley	Fillmore	MN	Springhill	Fayette	PA	Stantonsburg	Wilson	NC
Spring Valley	Shannon	MO	Springhill	Greene	PA	Staples	Todd	MN
Spring Valley	Dickey	ND	Springport	Jackson	MI	Stapleton	Chickasaw	IA
Spring Valley	Greene	OH	Springport	Sayuga	NY	Star Lake	Otter Tail	MN
Spring Valley	Clark	SD	Springvale	Humboldt	IA	Star Prairie	Saint Croix	WI
Spring Valley	Gregory	SD	Springvale	Pratt	KS	Star Prairie	Tripp	SD
Spring Valley	McCook	SD	Springvale	Emmet	MI	Star	Coffey	KS
Spring Valley	Turner	SD	Springvale	Isanti	MN	Star	Antrim	MI
Spring Valley	Rock	WI	Springvale	Barnes	ND	Star	Pennington	MN
Springbrook	Williams	ND	Springvale	Logan	OK	Star	Bowman	ND
Springbrook	Washburn	WI	Springvale	Columbia	WI	Star	Clay	SD
Springcreek	Miami	OH	Springvale	Fond du Lac	WI	Star Valley	Gregory	SD
Springdale	Washington	AR	Springville	Wexford	MI	Star Valley	Tripp	SD
Springdale	Cedar	IA	Springville	Susquehanna	PA	Starbuck	Bottineau	ND
Springdale	Sumner	KS	Springville	Adams	WI	Stark	Brown	MN
Springdale	Manistee	MI	Springwater	Rock	MN	Stark	Hickory	MO
Springdale	Redwood	MN	Springwater	Livingston	NY	Stark	Coos	NH
Springdale	Valley	NE	Springwater	Waushara	WI	Stark	Herkimer	NY
Springdale	Hamilton	OH	Spruce Creek	Huntingdon	PA	Stark	Vernon	WI
Springdale	Allegheny	PA	Spruce Grove	Becker	MN	Starkey	Logan	ND
Springdale	Lincoln	SD	Spruce Grove	Beltrami	MN	Starkey	Yates	NY
Springdale	Roberts	SD	Spruce Hill	Douglas	MN	Starks	Somerset	ME
Springdale	Dane	WI	Spruce Hill	Juniata	PA	Starksboro	Addison	VT
Springer	Logan	OK	Spruce	Roseau	MN	Starr Hill	Washington	AR
Springer	Oklahoma	OK	Spruce	Bates	MO	Starr	Cloud	KS
Springer	Ransom	ND	Spruce	Oconto	WI	Starr	Hocking	OH

TOWNSHIP	COUNTY	STATE
Starr	Grady	OK
Starr	Hutchinson	SD
State Center	Marshall	IA
State Line	Sherman	KS
State Line	Sherman	MN
Stately	Brown	SC
Statesbury	Sumter	NC
Statesville	Iredell	NC
Statesville	Goodhue	MN
Staton		IL
Staunton	Macoupin	IL
Staunton	Miami	OH
Staunton		ND
Stavanger	Traill	ND
Stave	Mountrail	ND
Steady Run	Keokuk	IA
Stecoah	Graham	NC
Steel Creek	Mecklenburg	NC
Steel Creek	Holt	NE
Steele	Conway	AR
Steele	Lafayette	AR
Steele	Daviess	IN
Steele		NC
Steele	Rowan	NC
Steeles	Richmond	IN
Steen	Knox	MN
Steenerson	Beltrami	MN
Steer Pen	Chesterfield	SC
Steiber	Burleigh	ND
Stella	Alfalfa	OK
Stella	Cleveland	OK
Stella	Oneida	WI
Stella	Marshall	SD
Stena		OK
Stephens	Tillman	OK
Stephenson	Menominee	MI
Stephenson	Marinette	WI
Stephenson	Rensselaer	NY
Stephenton	Windham	CT
Sterling	Whiteside	IL
Sterling		IN
Sterling	Crawford	IN
Sterling	Hodgeman	KS
Sterling	Rice	KS
Sterling	Worcester	MA
Sterling	Blue Earth	MN
Sterling	Burleigh	ND
Sterling	Cayuga	NY
Sterling	Brown	OH
Sterling	Wayne	PA
Sterling	Brookings	SD
Sterling	Polk	WI
Sterling	Vernon	WI
Sterlings	Robeson	NC
Stetson	Penobscot	ME
Stettin	Marathon	WI
Steuben	Marshall	IN
Steuben	Steuben	IN
Steuben	Warren	ME
Steuben	Washington	ME
Steuben	Oneida	NY
Steuben	Crawford	PA
Steubenville	Jefferson	OH
Stevens	Stevens	MN
Stevens	Ravalli	MT
Stevens	Ramsey	ND
Stevens	Bradford	PA
Stevens	Spokane	WA
Stevenson	Marion	IL
Stevenson	Morton	ND
Stewardson	Potter	PA
Stewart	Barnes	ND
Stewart	Kidder	ND
Stewart	Fayette	PA
Stewart	Tripp	SD
Stewarts Creek	Harnett	NC
Stewarts Creek	Surry	NC
Stewartstown	Coos	NH
Stewartsville	Scotland	NC
Stickney	Cook	IL
Stickney	Aurora	SD
Stiles	Oconto	WI
Stillwater	Washington	MN
Stillwater	Bowman	ND
Stillwater	Sussex	NJ
Stillwater	Saratoga	NY
Stillwater	Payne	OK
Stilwell	Adair	OK
Stilwell		WI
Stinnett	Washburn	WI
Stirton	Stutsman	ND
Stites	Saint Clair	IL
Stock	Harrison	OH
Stock	Noble	OH
Stockbridge	Berkshire	MA
Stockbridge	Ingham	MI
Stockbridge	Madison	NY
Stockbridge	Windsor	VT
Stockbridge	Calumet	WI
Stockholm	Crawford	IA
Stockholm	Aroostook	ME
Stockholm	Wright	MN
Stockholm	Saint Lawrence	NY
Stockholm	Grant	SD
Stockholm	Pepin	WI
Stocking	Saunders	NE
Stockland	Iroquois	IL
Stockport	Columbia	NY
Stockton Springs	Waldo	ME
Stockton	San Joaquin	CA
Stockton	Jo Daviess	IL
Stockton	Greene	IN
Stockton	Rooks	KS
Stockton	Chautauqua	NY
Stockton	Portage	WI
Stoddard	Cheshire	NH
Stohrville	Harper	KS
Stokes Bridge	Lee	SC
Stokes Mound	Carroll	MO
Stokes	Itasca	MN
Stokes	Roseau	MN
Stokes	Logan	OH
Stokes	Madison	OH
Stokes	Wagoner	OK
Stone Bluff	Bottineau	ND
Stone Creek		NJ
Stone Harbor	Cape May	NJ
Stone Lake	Washburn	WI
Stone	Major	OK
Stone View	Divide	ND
Stonefort	Saline	IL
Stoneham	Middlesex	MA
Stoneham	Oxford	ME
Stoneham	Chippewa	MN
Stonelick	Clermont	OH
Stonewall	Johnson	AR
Stonewall	Hoke	NC
Stonewall	Pontotoc	OK
Stoney Brook	Saint Louis	MN
Stoney Creek	Randolph	IN
Stonington	New London	CT
Stonington	Christian	IL
Stonington	Hancock	ME
Stony Battery	Newberry	SC
Stony Brook	Grant	MN
Stony Brook		SD
Stony Butte	Lyman	SD
Stone Creek	Henry	IN
Stony Creek	Madison	IN
Stony Creek	Caswell	NC
Stony Creek	Nash	NC
Stony Creek	Warren	NC
Stony Creek	Wayne	NC
Stony Creek	Williams	ND
Stony Fork	Watauga	NC
Stony Point	Rockland	NY
Stony Run	Yellow Medicine	MN
Stonycreek	Cambria	PA
Stonycreek	Somerset	PA
Stookey	Saint Clair	IL
Storden	Cottonwood	MN
Storlie	Cavalier	ND
Storm Lake	Buena Vista	IA
Stoughton	Norfolk	MA
Stow Creek	Cumberland	NJ
Stow	Middlesex	MA
Stow	Oxford	ME
Stow		MN
Stowe Prairie	Todd	MN
Stowe	Allegheny	PA
Stowe	Lamoille	VT
Straban	Adams	PA
Strabane	Grand Forks	ND
Strafford	Strafford	NH
Strafford	Orange	VT
Strafford		KS
Straight Creek	Jackson	KS
Straight River	Hubbard	MN
Straits	Carteret	NC
Strand	Norman	MN
Strandahl	Williams	ND
Stranger	Leavenworth	KS
Stratford	Fairfield	CT
Stratford	Coos	NH
Stratford	Fulton	NY
Stratford	Garvin	OK
Stratham	Rockingham	NH
Strathmore	Tulare	CA
Stratton	Edgar	IL
Stratton	Texas	OK
Stratton	Windham	VT
Strasburg	Lancaster	PA
Strauss	Cotton	OK
Strawberry	Fulton	AR
Strawberry	Izard	AR
Strawberry	Lawrence	AR
Strawberry	Sharp	AR
Strawberry	Washington	KS
Streeter	Stutsman	ND
Streeter	Roger Mills	OK
Streetsboro	Portage	OH
Strege	McHenry	ND
Strehlow	Hettinger	ND
Strickland	Rusk	WI
Strike Axe	Osage	OK
Stringtown	Atoka	OK
Stronach	Manistee	MI
Strong	Chase	KS
Strong	Franklin	ME
Strong	Stutsman	ND
Stronghurst	Henderson	IL
Strongs Prairie	Adams	WI
Strool	Perkins	SD
Stroud	Monroe	PA
Stuart	Adair	IA
Stuart	Guthrie	IA
Stuart	Holt	NE
Stuart	Hughes	OK
Stuart	Rusk	WI
Stubbs	Rusk	WI
Stump Sound	Onslow	NC
Stuntz	Saint Louis	MN
Sturbridge	Worcester	MA
Sturgeon Bay	Door	WI
Sturgeon Lake	Pine	MN
Sturgeon	Saint Louis	MN
Sturgis	Saint Joseph	MI
Stuyvesant	Columbia	NY
Suamica	Brown	WI
Sublette	Lee	IL
Success	Coos	NH

TOWNSHIPS OF THE UNITED STATES

TOWNSHIP	COUNTY	STATE	TOWNSHIP	COUNTY	STATE	TOWNSHIP	COUNTY	STATE
Sudbury	Middlesex	MA	Sulphur	Garland	AR	Sumter	Sumter	SC
Sudbury	Rutland	VT	Sulphur	Miller	AR	Sumter	Williamsburg	SC
Suez	Mercer	IL	Sulphur	Pope	AR	Sun City	Barber	KS
Suffield	Hartford	CT	Sulphur	McCurtain	OK	Sun Prairie	McCook	SD
Suffield	Portage	OH	Sulsun	Solano	CA	Sun Prairie	Dane	WI
Sugar Bush	Becker	MN	Summerfield	Le Flore	OK	Sunapee	Sullivan	NH
Sugar Bush	Beltrami	MN	Summerfield	Clare	MI	Sunbury	Livingston	IL
Sugar Camp	Cleburne	AR	Summerfield	Monroe	MI	Sundal	Norman	MN
Sugar Camp	Oneida	WI	Summerhill	Cayuga	NY	Sunderland	Franklin	MA
Sugar Creek	Benton	AR	Summerhill	Cambria	PA	Sunderland	Bennington	VT
Sugar Creek	Greene	AR	Summerhill	Crawford	PA	Sundown	Redwood	MN
Sugar Creek	Logan	AR	Summers	Thomas	KS	Sundre	Ward	ND
Sugar Creek	Cedar	IA	Summerset	Adair	IA	Sunfield	Eaton	MI
Sugar Creek	Powesheik	IA	Summit Lake	Noble	MN	Sunfish	Pike	OH
Sugar Creek	Clinton	IL	Summit	Boone	AR	Sunny Slope	Bowman	ND
Sugar Creek	Boone	IN	Summit	Marion	AR	Sunny Slope	Creek	OK
Sugar Creek	Clinton	IN	Summit	Adair	IA	Sunnyside	Wilkin	MN
Sugar Creek	Hancock	IN	Summit	Clay	IA	Sunnyside	Pennington	SD
Sugar Creek	Montgomery	IN	Summit	Marion	IA	Sunnyvale	Santa Clara	CA
Sugar Creek	Parke	IN	Summit	O'Brien	IA	Sunrise	Chisago	MN
Sugar Creek	Shelby	IN	Summit	Effingham	IL	Sunsbury	Monroe	OH
Sugar Creek	Vigo	IN	Summit	Chautauqua	KS	Sunshine	Slope	ND
Sugar Creek	Miami	KS	Summit	Cloud	KS	Superior	Dickinson	IA
Sugar Creek	Barry	MO	Summit	Decatur	KS	Superior	McPherson	KS
Sugar Creek	Harrison	MO	Summit	Marion	KS	Superior	Osage	KS
Sugar Creek	Allen	OH	Summit	Jackson	MI	Superior	Chippewa	MI
Sugar Creek	Greene	OH	Summit	Mason	MI	Superior	Washtenaw	MI
Sugar Creek	Putnam	OH	Summit	Beltrami	MN	Superior	Mineral	MT
Sugar Creek	Stark	OH	Summit	Steele	MN	Superior	Eddy	ND
Sugar Creek	Tuscarawas	OH	Summit	Bates	MO	Superior	Williams	OH
Sugar Creek	Wayne	OH	Summit	Callaway	MO	Superior	Douglas	WI
Sugar Creek	Walworth	WI	Summit	Burleigh	ND	Supply	Woodward	OK
Sugar Ford	Macon	NC	Summit	Richland	ND	Surprise Valley	Mellette	SD
Sugar Grove	Dallas	IA	Summit	Burt	NE	Surry	Hancock	ME
Sugar Grove	Kane	IL	Summit	Butler	NE	Surrey	Clare	MI
Sugar Grove	Mercer	PA	Summit	Schoharie	NY	Surrey	Ward	ND
Sugar Grove	Warren	PA	Summit	Monroe	OH	Surry	Cheshire	NH
Sugar Hill	Grafton	NH	Summit	Butler	PA	Susquehanna	Cambria	PA
Sugar Island	Chippewa	MI	Summit	Crawford	PA	Susquehanna	Dauphin	PA
Sugar Loaf	Boone	AR	Summit	Erie	PA	Susquehanna	Juniata	PA
Sugar Loaf	Cleburne	AR	Summit	Potter	PA	Susquehanna	Lycoming	PA
Sugar Loaf	Saint Clair	IL	Summit	Somerset	PA	Susquehanna	Hutchinson	SD
Sugar Loaf	Rooks	KS	Summit	Lake	SD	Sutter	Sutter	CA
Sugar Loaf	Alexander	NC	Summit	Roberts	SD	Sutton	Lane	KS
Sugar Ridge	Clay	IN	Summit	Douglas	WI	Sutton	Worcester	MA
Sugarcreek	Armstrong	PA	Summit	Juneau	WI	Sutton	Clay	NE
Sugarloaf	Marion	AR	Summit	Langlade	WI	Sutton	Merrimack	NH
Sugarloaf	Sebastian	AR	Summit	Waukesha	WI	Sutton	Meigs	OH
Sugarloaf	Columbia	PA	Sumner	Bremer	IA	Sutton	Muskogee	OK
Sugarloaf	Luzerne	PA	Sumner	Buchanan	IA	Sutton	Caledonia	VT
Sugartree	Carroll	MO	Sumner	Iowa	IA	Suttons Bay	Leelanau	MI
Sullivan	Livingston	IL	Sumner	Webster	IA	Suttons	Williamsburg	SC
Sullivan	Moultrie	IL	Sumner	Winneshiek	IA	Svea	Kittson	MN
Sullivan	Grant	KS	Sumner	Kankakee	IL	Svea	Barnes	ND
Sullivan	Hancock	ME	Sumner	Warren	IL	Sverdrup	Otter Tail	MN
Sullivan	Muskegon	MI	Sumner	Osborne	KS	Sverdrup	Griggs	ND
Sullivan	Polk	MN	Sumner	Phillips	KS	Swain	Clay	AR
Sullivan	Ramsey	ND	Sumner	Reno	KS	Swampscott	Essex	MA
Sullivan	Cheshire	NH	Sumner	Sumner	KS	Swan Creek	Saginaw	MI
Sullivan	Madison	NY	Sumner	Oxford	ME	Swan Creek	Fulton	OH
Sullivan	Ashland	OH	Sumner	Gratiot	MI	Swan Island	Hancock	ME
Sullivan	Tioga	PA	Sumner	Fillmore	MN	Swan Lake	Emmet	IA
Sullivan	Laurens	SC	Sumner	Guilford	NC	Swan Lake	Pocahontas	IA
Sullivan	Jefferson	WI	Sumner	Garfield	OK	Swan Lake	Stevens	MN
Sullivans Island	Charleston	SC	Sumner	Spink	SD	Swan Lake	Caddo	OK
Sullivant	Ford	IL	Sumner	Barron	WI	Swan Lake	Turner	SD
Sully	Tripp	SD	Sumner	Jefferson	WI	Swan Quarter	Hyde	NC
Sulphur Springs	Benton	AR	Sumner	Trempealeau	WI	Swan River	Morrison	MN
Sulphur Springs	Howard	AR	Sumpter	Cumberland	IL	Swan	Warren	IL
Sulphur Springs	Montgomery	AR	Sumpter	Wayne	MI	Swan	Noble	IN
Sulphur Springs	Searcy	AR	Sumpter	Sauk	WI	Swan	Smith	KS
Sulphur Springs	Yell	AR	Sumter	Bradley	AR	Swan	Taney	MO
Sulphur Springs	Rutherford	NC	Sumter	McLeod	MN	Swan	Holt	NE

TOWNSHIPS OF THE UNITED STATES

TOWNSHIP	COUNTY	STATE
Swan	Vinton	OH
Swannanoa	Buncombe	NC
Swansboro	Onslow	NC
Swansea	Bristol	MA
Swanton	Lucas	OH
Swanton	Franklin	VT
Swanton	Waldo	ME
Swanville	Morrison	MN
Swanville	Cheshire	NH
Swanzey	Dauphin	PA
Swatara	Lebanon	PA
Swatara	Mississippi	AR
Swayne	Kossuth	IA
Swea	Riley	KS
Swede Creek	Meeker	MN
Swede Grove	Yellow Medicine	MN
Swede Prairie	La Moure	ND
Swede	Oxford	ME
Sweden	Monroe	NY
Sweden	Potter	PA
Sweden	Redwood	MN
Swedes Forest	Morton	ND
Sweet Briar	Clark	MO
Sweet Home	Pipestone	MN
Sweet	Hutchinson	SD
Sweet	Muscatine	IA
Sweetland	Lake	MI
Sweetwater	Clay	NC
Sweetwater	Swift	MN
Swenoda	Edgecombe	NC
Swift Creek	Pitt	NC
Swift Creek	Wake	NC
Swift Creek	Burnett	WI
Swiss	Monroe	OH
Switzerland	De Kalb	IL
Sycamore	Butler	KS
Sycamore	Montgomery	KS
Sycamore	Hamilton	OH
Sycamore	Wyandot	OH
Sycamore	Allendale	SC
Sycamore	Ransom	ND
Sydna	Stutsman	ND
Sydney	Stone	AR
Sylamore	Jackson	NC
Sylva	Oxceola	MI
Sylvan	Washtenaw	MI
Sylvan	Cass	MN
Sylvan	Richland	WI
Sylvan	Scott	MO
Sylvania	Lucas	OH
Sylvania	Potter	PA
Sylvania	Green	WI
Sylvester	Reno	KS
Sylvia	Lyman	SD
Sylvia	Edgar	IL
Symmes	Hamilton	OH
Symmes	Lawrence	OH
Synnes	Stevens	MN
Syracuse	Hamilton	KS

—T—

TOWNSHIP	COUNTY	STATE
Taber	Saint Clair	MO
Tabernacle	Randolph	NC
Tabernacle	Burlington	NJ
Table Mound	Dubuque	IA
Table Mountain	Harding	SD
Table Rock	Sierra	CA
Table Rock	Siskiyou	CA
Tabler	Grady	OK
Tabor	Polk	MN
Tabor	Bon Homme	SD
Tacoma	Bottineau	ND
Taft	Burleigh	ND
Taft	Taylor	WI
Taghkanic	Columbia	NY
Tahoe	Douglas	NV
Tainter	Dunn	WI
Talala	Rogers	OK
Talbert	Edgefield	SC
Talbot	Bowman	ND
Taliaferro	Marshall	OK
Talinhina	La Flore	OK
Talkington	Sangamon	??
Talladega	Jefferson	AR
Talleyrand	Wilson	KS
Tallmadge	Ottawa	MI
Tallmadge	Summit	OH
Tally Ho	Granville	NC
Taloga	Morton	KS
Taloga	Dewey	OK
Taloka	Haskell	OK
Tama	Des Moines	IA
Tama	Tama	IA
Tamalco	Bond	IL
Tamarac	Marshall	MN
Tamico	Whiteside	IL
Tamworth	Faulk	SD
Tanberg	Wilkin	MN
Tanner	Kidder	ND
Tans Bay	Florence	SC
Tansem	Clay	MN
Tanworth	Carroll	NH
Taopin	Minnehaha	SD
Tappan	Phillips	AR
Tappen	Kidder	ND
Tara	Swift	MN
Tara	Traverse	MN
Tarboro	Edgecombe	NC
Tarkio	Page	IA
Tarkio	Atchison	MO
Tate	Scott	AR
Tate	Saline	IL
Tate	Clermont	OH
Tatman	Ward	ND
Tatums	Columbus	NC
Tavern	Pulaski	MO
Tawas	Iosco	MI
Taylor Butte	Adams	ND
Taylor Creek	Hardin	OH
Taylor	Columbia	AR
Taylor	Craighead	AR
Taylor	Nevada	AR
Taylor	Allamakee	IA
Taylor	Appanoose	IA
Taylor	Benton	IA
Taylor	Dubuque	IA
Taylor	Harrison	IA
Taylor	Marshall	IA
Taylor	Ogle	IL
Taylor	Greene	IN
Taylor	Harrison	IN
Taylor	Howard	IN
Taylor	Owen	IN
Taylor	Traverse	MN
Taylor	Greene	MO
Taylor	Grundy	MO
Taylor	Shelby	MO
Taylor	Sullivan	MO
Taylor	Wilson	NC
Taylor	Sargent	ND
Taylor	Cortland	NY
Taylor	Union	OH
Taylor	Cleveland	OK
Taylor	Blair	PA
Taylor	Centre	PA
Taylor	Fulton	PA
Taylor	Lawrence	PA
Taylor	Hanson	SD
Taylor	Tripp	SD
Taylors Bridge	Sampson	NC
Taylorsville	Alexander	NC
Taylorsville	Christian	IL
Taylorville	Saginaw	MI
Taymouth	Saginaw	NJ
Teaneck	Bergen	NJ
Tebernacle	Aiken	SC
Tebo	Henry	MO
Tecoma	Elko	NV
Tecumseh	Shawnee	KS
Tecumseh	Lenawee	MI
Teddy	Towner	ND
Tegner	Kittson	MN
Teien	Kittson	MN
Tekonsha	Calhoun	MI
Telfer	Burleigh	ND
Telico	Sant Francis	AR
Tell	Emmons	ND
Tell	Huntingdon	PA
Temescal	Riverside	CA
Temple	Franklin	ME
Temple	Hillsborough	NH
Templeton	San Luis Obispo	CA
Templeton	Worcester	MA
Templeton	Atchison	MO
Ten Lake	Beltrami	MN
Ten Mile Lake	Lac Qui Parle	MN
Ten Mile River	Mendocino	CA
Ten Mile	Miami	KS
Ten Mile	Macon	MO
Ten Mile	Whatcom	WA
Tenhassen	Martin	MN
Tennant	Siskiyou	CA
Tennessee	Grant	AR
Tennessee	McDonough	IL
Tepee Butte	Hettinger	ND
Tepee	Texas	OK
Terre Haute	Henderson	IL
Terra Noire	Clark	AR
Terrabonne	Red Lake	MN
Terry	Finney	KS
Terry	Bradford	PA
Tete Des Morts	Jackson	IA
Tetonka	Spink	SD
Tewaukon	Sargent	ND
Tewksbury	Middlesex	MA
Tewksbury	Hunterdon	NJ
Texas	Craighead	AR
Texas	Lee	AR
Texas	De Witt	IL
Texas	Kalamazoo	MI
Texas	Dent	MO
Texas	Crawford	OH
Texas	Cotton	OK
Texas	Washita	OK
Texas	Wayne	PA
Texas	Marathon	WI
Texhoma	Texas	OK
Texola	Beckham	OK
Thacker	Lawrence	AR
Thain	Grant	ND
Thayer	Oregon	MO
Thelma	Burleigh	ND
Theresa	Jefferson	NY
Theresa	Beadle	SD
Theresa	Dodge	WI
Thermal	Riverside	CA
Thetford	Genesee	MI
Thetford	Orange	VT

TOWNSHIPS OF THE UNITED STATES

TOWNSHIP	COUNTY	STATE	TOWNSHIP	COUNTY	STATE	TOWNSHIP	COUNTY	STATE
Theif Lake	Marshall	MN	Tilton	Belknap	NH	Tonkawa	Kay	OK
Thingvalla	Pembina	ND	Timber Creek	Marshall	IA	Tonopah	Nye	NV
Third Creek	Gasconade	MO	Timber Creek	McKenzie	ND	Tonti	Marion	IL
Third River	Itasca	MN	Timber Creek	Nance	NE	Tontitown	Washington	AR
Thomas	Johnston	OK	Timber	Peoria	IL	Topeka	Shawnee	KS
Thomas	Ellsworth	KS	Timberhill	Bourbon	KS	Topsail	Pender	NC
Thomas	Saginaw	MI	Timberlake	Lake	OH	Topsfield	Essex	MA
Thomas	Ripley	MO	Timbo	Stone	AR	Topsham	Sagadahoc	ME
Thomaston	Litchfield	CT	Timmonsville	Florence	SC	Topsham	Orange	VT
Thomaston	Knox	ME	Timothy	Crow Wing	MN	Toqua	Big Stone	MN
Thomastown	Wadena	MN	Tingley	Ringgold	IA	Torch Lake	Antrim	MI
Thomasville	Davidson	NC	Tinicum	Bucks	PA	Torch Lake	Houghton	MI
Thompson	Pike	AR	Tinicum	Delaware	PA	Tordenskjold	Otter Tail	MN
Thompson	Windham	CT	Tinmouth	Rutland	VT	Torning	Swift	MN
Thompson	Guthrie	IA	Tintah	Traverse	MN	Torning	Ward	ND
Thompson	Jo Daviess	IL	Tioga	Neosho	KS	Toronto	Woodson	KS
Thompson	Schoolcraft	MI	Tioga	Williams	ND	Torrey Lake	Brule	SD
Thompson	Kittson	MN	Tioga	Tioga	NY	Torrey	Cass	MN
Thompson	Alamance	NC	Tioga	Tioga	PA	Torrey	Yates	NY
Thompson	Robeson	NC	Tionesta	Forest	PA	Torrington	Litchfield	CT
Thompson	Sullivan	NY	Tipler	Florence	WI	Totten	Lonoke	AR
Thompson	Delaware	OH	Tippecanoe	Henry	IA	Toulon	Stark	IL
Thompson	Geauga	OH	Tippecanoe	Carroll	IN	Towamencin	Montgomery	PA
Thompson	Seneca	OH	Tippecanoe	Kosciusko	IN	Towamensing	Carbon	PA
Thompson	Fulton	PA	Tippecanoe	Marshall	IN	Towanda	Mclean	IL
Thompson	Susquehanna	PA	Tippecanoe	Pulaski	IN	Towanda	Butler	KS
Thomson	Carlton	MN	Tippecanoe	Tippecanoe	IN	Towanda	Phillips	KS
Thomson	Scotland	MO	Tipton	Tulare	CA	Towanda	Bradford	PA
Thordenskjold	Barnes	ND	Tipton	Cass	IN	Tower Hill	Shelby	IL
Thorn	Perry	OH	Tipton	Hardin	IA	Tower	Cass	ND
Thornapple	Barry	MI	Tisbury	Dukes	MA	Town Creek	Brunswick	NC
Thornapple	Rusk	WI	Tisdale	Cowley	KS	Townsend	Middlesex	MA
Thornbury	Chester	PA	Titsworth	Logan	AR	Townsend	Huron	OH
Thornbury	Delaware	PA	Tittabawassee	Saginaw	MI	Townsend	Sandusky	OH
Thorncreek	Whitley	IN	Tiverton	Coshocton	OH	Townsend	Windham	VT
Thorndike	Waldo	ME	Tiverton	Newport	RI	Townsend	Oconto	WI
Thornfield	Ozark	MO	Toad Lake	Becker	MN	Townsville	Vance	NC
Thornton	Cook	IL	Tobacco Garden	McKenzie	ND	Tracy	Lyman	SD
Thornton	Buffalo	NE	Tobacco	Gladwin	MI	Trade Lake	Burnett	WI
Thornton	Grafton	NH	Tobin	Perry	IN	Trail Creek	Harrison	MO
Thorp	Clark	SD	Tobin	Scotland	MO	Trail	Dewey	OK
Thorp	Clark	WI	Tobin	Davison	SD	Trail	Perkins	SD
Thorpe	Hubbard	MN	Toboyne	Perry	PA	Trap Hill	Wilkes	NC
Thorson	Burke	ND	Toby	Clarion	PA	Transit	Sibley	MN
Three Buttes	Grant	ND	Tobyhanna	Monroe	PA	Traskwood	Saline	AR
Three Lakes	Redwood	MN	Tod	Crawford	OH	Traverse	Nicollet	MN
Three Lakes	Oneida	WI	Todd	Hubbard	MN	Tredyffrin	Chester	PA
Three Miles	Bamberg	SC	Todd	Fulton	PA	Trego	Washburn	WI
Three Oaks	Berrien	MI	Todd	Huntingdon	PA	Trelipe	Cass	MN
Three Rivers	Spink	SD	Todds Point	Shelby	IL	Tremont	Solano	CA
Throop	Cayuga	NY	Toe River	Avery	NC	Tremont	Tazewell	IL
Thunder Hawk	Corson	SD	Tohee	Lincoln	OK	Tremont	Buchanan	MO
Thunder Lake	Cass	MN	Toisnot	Wilson	NC	Tremont	Schuylkill	PA
Thurman	Warren	NY	Toivola	Saint Louis	MN	Tremont	Hancock	ME
Thurston	Steuben	NY	Toledo	Tama	IA	Trempealeau	Trempealeau	WI
Ti	Pittsburg	OK	Toledo	Chase	KS	Trent	Lenoir	NC
Tiber	Walsh	ND	Tolgen	Ward	ND	Trenton	Henry	IA
Ticonderoge	Essex	NY	Tolland	Tolland	CT	Trenton	Edwards	KS
Tiffany	Eddy	ND	Tolland	Hampden	MA	Trenton	Hancock	ME
Tiffany	Dunn	WI	Tolono	Champaign	IL	Trenton	Grundy	MO
Tiffin	Adams	OH	Tom	Benton	MO	Trenton	Jones	NC
Tiffin	Defiance	OH	Tomah	Monroe	WI	Trenton	Williams	ND
Tiffin	Seneca	OH	Tomahawk	Searcy	AR	Trenton	Oneida	NY
Tiger Fork	Shelby	MO	Tomahawk	Lincoln	WI	Trenton	Delaware	OH
Tiger	Creek	OK	Tomales	Marin	CA	Trenton	Brookings	SD
Tiger	Okmulgee	OK	Tomlinson	Logan	AR	Trenton	Dodge	WI
Tilden	Cherokee	IA	Tomlinson	Scott	AR	Trenton	Pierce	WI
Tilden	Osborne	KS	Tompkins	Jackson	MI	Trenton	Washington	WI
Tilden	Marquette	MI	Tompkins	Delaware	NY	Tre Pinos	San Benito	CA
Tilden	Polk	MN	Tompkins	Warren	NY	Triangle	Durham	NC
Tilden	Berks	PA	Tonawanda	Erie	NY	Triangle	Broome	NY
Tilden	Chippewa	WI	Tonganoxie	Leavenworth	KS	Tribune	Greeley	KS
Tilly	Greer	OK	Tonkawa	Caddo	OK	Trier	Cavalier	ND

TOWNSHIPS OF THE UNITED STATES

TOWNSHIP	COUNTY	STATE
Trimbelle	Pierce	WI
Trimble	Athens	OH
Trinity Center	Trinity	CA
Trinity	Randolph	NC
Trinity	Randolph	MO
Triplett	Chariton	WI
Tripp	Bayfield	ND
Triumph	Ramsey	NE
Triumph	Custer	NE
Triumph	Warren	PA
Triumph	Warren	IL
Trivoli	Peoria	IL
Trivoli	Ellsworth	KS
Trona	San Bernardino	CA
Trondhjem	Otter Tail	MN
Trotter	Carroll	MO
Troupsburg	Steuben	NY
Trout Lake	Chippewa	MI
Trout Lake	Itasca	MN
Trowbridge	Allegan	MI
Troy Grove	La Salle	IL
Troy	Mississippi	AR
Troy	Clarke	IA
Troy	Iowa	IA
Troy	Monroe	IA
Troy	Wright	IA
Troy	Will	IL
Troy	De Kalb	IN
Troy	Fountain	IN
Troy	Perry	IN
Troy	Reno	KS
Troy	Waldo	ME
Troy	Newaygo	MI
Troy	Pipestone	MN
Troy	Renville	MN
Troy	Montgomery	NC
Troy	Divide	ND
Troy	Cheshire	NH
Troy	Ashland	OH
Troy	Athens	OH
Troy	Delaware	OH
Troy	Geauga	OH
Troy	Morrow	OH
Troy	Richland	OH
Troy	Wood	OH
Troy	Bradford	PA
Troy	Crawford	PA
Troy	Greenwood	SC
Troy	Day	SD
Troy	Grant	SD
Troy	Orleans	VT
Troy	Saint Croix	WI
Troy	Sauk	WI
Troy	Walworth	WI
Truax	Williams	ND
True	Rusk	WI
Trumbull	Fairfield	CT
Trumbull	Ashtabula	OH
Trumbull	Knox	IL
Truro	Barnstable	MA
Truro	Franklin	OH
Truro	Aurora	SD
Truxton	Cortland	NY
Trygg	Burleigh	ND
Tryon	Polk	NC
Tryon	Union	AR
Tubal		NC
Tuckahoe	Jones	NC
Tuftonboro	Carroll	NH
Tugaloo	Oconee	SC
Tulare	San Joaquin	CA
Tulare	Tulare	CA
Tulare	Spink	SD
Tule Lake	Modoc	CA
Tule Lake	Siskiyou	CA
Tullahassee	Wagoner	OK
Tuller	Ransom	ND
Tully	Onondaga	NY
Tully	Marion	OH
Tully	Van Wert	OH
Tulpehocken	Berks	PA
Tumuli	Otter Tail	MN
Tumbridge	De Witt	IL
Tunbridge	Orange	VT
Tunkhannock	Monroe	PA
Tunkhannock	Wyoming	PA
Tunnel Hill	Johnson	IL
Tunsberg	Chippewa	MN
Turbett	Juniata	PA
Turbut	Northumberland	PA
Turin	Marquette	MI
Turin	Lewis	NY
Turkey Creek	Stone	AR
Turkey Creek	Kosciusko	IN
Turkey Creek	Barber	KS
Turkey Creek	McPherson	KS
Turkey Creek	Mitchell	KS
Turkey Creek	Franklin	NE
Turkey Creek	Harlan	NE
Turkey Creek	Lee	SC
Turkey	Sampson	NC
Turkey	Williamsburg	SC
Turkey Valley	Yankton	SD
Turlock	Stanislaus	CA
Turman	Sullivan	IN
Turnback	Lawrence	MO
Turnbull	McClain	OK
Turnbull	Bladen	NC
Turner	Androscoggin	ME
Turner	Arenac	MI
Turner	Aitkin	MN
Turner	Murry	OH
Turner	McIntosh	OK
Turner	Turner	SD
Turnersburg	Iredell	NC
Turney	Texas	OK
Turtle Creek	Todd	MN
Turtle Creek	Shelby	OH
Turtle Creek	Warren	OH
Turtle Lake	Beltrami	MN
Turtle Lake	Cass	MN
Turtle Lake	McLean	ND
Turtle Lake	Barron	WI
Turtle River	Beltrami	MN
Turtle River	Grand Forks	ND
Turtle	Rock	WI
Turton	Spink	SD
Tuscarawas	Coshocton	OH
Tuscarawas	Stark	OH
Tuscarora	Cheboygan	MI
Tuscarora	Pierce	ND
Tuscarora	Steuben	NY
Tuscarora	Bradford	PA
Tuscarora	Juniata	PA
Tuscarora	Perry	PA
Tuscola	Douglas	IL
Tuscola	Tuscola	MI
Tuskahoma	Pushmataha	OK
Tusquittee	Clay	NC
Tusten	Sullivan	NY
Tustin	Orange	CA
Tuttle	Kidder	ND
Tuttle	Grady	OK
Tuxedo	Orange	NY
Twelve Mile Lake	Emmet	IA
Twelve Mile	Williams	ND
Twelvemile	Madison	MO
Twelvemile	San Bernardino	CA
Twenty-nine Palms	San Bernardino	CA
Twig	Hamilton	IL
Twin Butte	Divide	ND
Twin Butte	Corson	SD
Twin Grove	Greenwood	KS
Twin Groves	Jasper	MO
Twin Hill	Towner	ND
Twin Lake	Hancock	IA
Twin Lake	Benson	ND
Twin Lake	Sanborn	SD
Twin Lakes	Calhoun	IA
Twin Lakes	Carlton	MN
Twin Mound	Rooks	KS
Twin	Darke	OH
Twin	Preble	OH
Twin	Ross	OH
Twin	Harding	SD
Twin	Benson	ND
Twin Tree	Benson	ND
Twin Valley	McKenzie	ND
Twinsburg	Summit	OH
Twist	Cross	AR
Two Creeks	Manitowoc	WI
Two Inlets	Becker	MN
Two Mile	Grant	ND
Two Rivers	Morrison	MN
Two Rivers	Manitowoc	WI
Tyler	Perry	AR
Tyler	Prairie	AR
Tyler	Hickory	MO
Tyler	Spokane	WA
Tycheedah	Fond du Lac	WI
Tymochtee	Wyandot	OH
Tyngsborough	Middlesex	MA
Tynsid	Polk	MN
Tyre	Seneca	NY
Tyringham	Berkshire	MA
Tyro	Yellow Medicine	MN
Tyro	Davidson	NC
Tyrol	Griggs	ND
Tyrone	Franklin	IL
Tyrone	Kent	MI
Tyrone	Livingston	MI
Tyrone	La Sueur	MN
Tyrone	Williams	ND
Tyrone	Schuyler	NY
Tyrone	Adams	PA
Tyrone	Blair	PA
Tyrone	Perry	PA
Tyronza	Crittenden	AR
Tyronza	Cross	AR
Tyronza	Poinsett	AR
Tyson	Stanly	NC
Tywappity	Mississippi	MO
Tywappity	Scott	MO

—U—

TOWNSHIP	COUNTY	STATE
Udell	Appanoose	IA
Udolpho	Mower	MN
Ukiah	Mendocino	CA
Ulen	Clay	MN
Ulster	Floyd	IA
Ulster	Ulster	NY
Ulster	Bradford	PA
Ulysses	Butler	NE
Ulysses	Tompkins	NY
Ulysses	Potter	PA
Umpire	Howard	AR
Unadilla	Livingston	MI
Unadilla	Otsego	NY
Underhill	Chittenden	VT
Underhill	Oconto	WI
Underwood	Redwood	MN
Union Center	Elk	KS

TOWNSHIPS OF THE UNITED STATES

TOWNSHIP	COUNTY	STATE	TOWNSHIP	COUNTY	STATE	TOWNSHIP	COUNTY	STATE
Union City	Allamakee	IA	Union	Worth	IA	Union	Harrison	MO
Union Grove	Whiteside	IL	Union	Effingham	IL	Union	Iron	MO
Union Grove	Meeker	MN	Union	Fulton	IL	Union	Jasper	MO
Union Grove	Iredell	NC	Union	Livingston	IL	Union	Laclede	MO
Union Prairie	Allamakee	IA	Union	Adams	IN	Union	Lewis	MO
Union	Ashley	AR	Union	Benton	IN	Union	Lincoln	MO
Union	Baxter	AR	Union	Boone	IN	Union	Marion	MO
Union	Conway	AR	Union	Clark	IN	Union	Monroe	MO
Union	Crawford	AR	Union	Clinton	IN	Union	Nodaway	MO
Union	Faulkner	AR	Union	Crawford	IN	Union	Perry	MO
Union	Fulton	AR	Union	De Kalb	IN	Union	Polk	MO
Union	Garland	AR	Union	Delaware	IN	Union	Pulaski	MO
Union	Greene	AR	Union	Elkhart	IN	Union	Putnam	MO
Union	Independence	AR	Union	Fulton	IN	Union	Randolph	MO
Union	Izard	AR	Union	Gibson	IN	Union	Ripley	MO
Union	Jackson	AR	Union	Hendricks	IN	Union	Sainte Genevieve	MO
Union	Lee	AR	Union	Howard	IN	Union	Scotland	MO
Union	Marion	AR	Union	Huntington	IN	Union	Stone	MO
Union	Nevada	AR	Union	Jasper	IN	Union	Sullivan	MO
Union	Newton	AR	Union	Johnson	IN	Union	Washington	MO
Union	Ouachita	AR	Union	La Porte	IN	Union	Webster	MO
Union	Perry	AR	Union	Madison	IN	Union	Worth	MO
Union	Prairie	AR	Union	Marshall	IN	Union	Wright	MO
Union	Randolph	AR	Union	Miami	IN	Union	Madison	MT
Union	Saline	AR	Union	Montgomery	IN	Union	Pender	NC
Union	Stone	AR	Union	Ohio	IN	Union	Randolph	NC
Union	Van Buren	AR	Union	Parke	IN	Union	Robeson	NC
Union	White	AR	Union	Perry	IN	Union	Rutherford	NC
Union	Humboldt	CA	Union	Porter	IN	Union	Wilkes	NC
Union	San Joaquin	CA	Union	Randolph	IN	Union	Grand Forks	ND
Union	Tollard	CT	Union	Rush	IN	Union	Butler	NE
Union	Adair	IA	Union	Saint Joseph	IN	Union	Dodge	NE
Union	Adams	IA	Union	Shelby	IN	Union	Knox	NE
Union	Appanoose	IA	Union	Tippecanoe	IN	Union	Phelps	NE
Union	Benton	IA	Union	Union	IN	Union	Saunders	NE
Union	Black Hawk	IA	Union	Vanderburgh	IN	Union	Humboldt	NV
Union	Boone	IA	Union	Wells	IN	Union	Hunterdon	NJ
Union	Calhoun	IA	Union	White	IN	Union	Ocean	NJ
Union	Carroll	IA	Union	Whitley	IN	Union	Union	NJ
Union	Cass	IA	Union	Anderson	KS	Union	Broome	NY
Union	Cerro Gordo	IA	Union	Barton	KS	Union	Ashland	OH
Union	Crawford	IA	Union	Butler	KS	Union	Auglaize	OH
Union	Dallas	IA	Union	Clay	KS	Union	Belmont	OH
Union	Davis	IA	Union	Dickinson	KS	Union	Brown	OH
Union	Delaware	IA	Union	Doniphan	KS	Union	Butler	OH
Union	Des Moines	IA	Union	Jefferson	KS	Union	Carroll	OH
Union	Fayette	IA	Union	Kingman	KS	Union	Champaign	OH
Union	Floyd	IA	Union	Kiowa	KS	Union	Clermont	OH
Union	Guthrie	IA	Union	McPherson	KS	Union	Clinton	OH
Union	Hardin	IA	Union	Pottawatomie	KS	Union	Fayette	OH
Union	Harrison	IA	Union	Rawlins	KS	Union	Hancock	OH
Union	Jackson	IA	Union	Republic	KS	Union	Highland	OH
Union	Johnson	IA	Union	Rice	KS	Union	Knox	OH
Union	Kossuth	IA	Union	Rush	KS	Union	Lawrence	OH
Union	Louisa	IA	Union	Sedgwick	KS	Union	Licking	OH
Union	Lucas	IA	Union	Sheridan	KS	Union	Logan	OH
Union	Madison	IA	Union	Sherman	KS	Union	Madison	OH
Union	Mahaska	IA	Union	Stafford	KS	Union	Mercer	OH
Union	Marion	IA	Union	Washington	KS	Union	Miami	OH
Union	Mitchell	IA	Union	Knox	ME	Union	Morgan	OH
Union	Monroe	IA	Union	Branch	MI	Union	Muskingum	OH
Union	O'Brien	IA	Union	Grand Traverse	MI	Union	Pike	OH
Union	Plymouth	IA	Union	Isabella	MI	Union	Putnam	OH
Union	Polk	IA	Union	Houston	MN	Union	Ross	OH
Union	Poweshiek	IA	Union	Barton	MO	Union	Scioto	OH
Union	Ringgold	IA	Union	Benton	MO	Union	Tuscarawas	OH
Union	Shelby	IA	Union	Bollinger	MO	Union	Union	OH
Union	Story	IA	Union	Cass	MO	Union	Van Wert	OH
Union	Union	IA	Union	Clark	MO	Union	Warren	OH
Union	Van Buren	IA	Union	Crawford	MO	Union	Canadian	OK
Union	Warren	IA	Union	Daviess	MO	Union	Garfield	OK
Union	Wayne	IA	Union	Dunklin	MO	Union	Grady	OK
Union	Woodbury	IA	Union	Franklin	MO	Union	Kingfisher	OK

TOWNSHIPS OF THE UNITED STATES

TOWNSHIP	COUNTY	STATE
Union	Lincoln	OK
Union	Payne	OK
Union	Washita	OK
Union	Woodward	OK
Union	Adams	PA
Union	Bedford	PA
Union	Berks	PA
Union	Centre	PA
Union	Clearfield	PA
Union	Crawford	PA
Union	Erie	PA
Union	Fulton	PA
Union	Huntingdon	PA
Union	Jefferson	PA
Union	Lawrence	PA
Union	Lebanon	PA
Union	Luzerne	PA
Union	Mifflin	PA
Union	Schuylkill	PA
Union	Snyder	PA
Union	Tioga	PA
Union	Union	PA
Union	Washington	PA
Union	Orangeburg	SC
Union	Union	SC
Union	Brule	SD
Union	Butte	SD
Union	Davison	SD
Union	Day	SD
Union	Edmunds	SD
Union	Faulk	SD
Union	Gregory	SD
Union	Harding	SD
Union	Hyde	SD
Union	Jones	SD
Union	McCook	SD
Union	Meade	SD
Union	Moody	SD
Union	Spink	SD
Union	Sanborn	SD
Union	Burnett	WI
Union	Door	WI
Union	Eau Claire	WI
Union	Pierce	WI
Union	Rock	WI
Union	Vernon	WI
Union	Waupaca	WI
Union Vale	Dutchess	NY
Union Valley	Perry	AR
Unique	Slope	ND
Unity	Piatt	IL
Unity	Waldo	ME
Unity	Rowan	NC
Unity	Sullivan	NH
Unity	Columbiana	OH
Unity	Westmoreland	PA
Unity	Clark	WI
Unity	Trempealeau	WI
Upland	San Bernardino	CA
Upland	Divide	ND
Upper Allen	Cumberland	PA
Upper Arlington	Franklin	OH
Upper Augusta	Northumberland	PA
Upper Bern	Berks	PA
Upper Burrell	Westmoreland	PA
Upper Chichester	Delaware	PA
Upper Conetoe	Edgecombe	NC
Upper Creek	Burke	NC
Upper Darby	Delaware	PA
Upper Deerfield	Cumberland	NJ
Upper Dublin	Montgomery	PA
Upper Fairfield	Lycoming	PA
Upper Fishing Creek	Edgecombe	NC
Upper Fork	Burke	NC
Upper Frankford	Cumberland	PA
Upper Frederick	Montgomery	PA
Upper Freehold	Monmouth	NJ
Upper Gwynedd	Montgomery	PA
Upper Hanover	Montgomery	PA
Upper Hominy	Buncombe	NC
Upper Leacock	Lancaster	PA
Upper Little River	Harnett	NC
Upper Loutre	Montgomery	MO
Upper Macungie	Lehigh	PA
Upper Mahanoy	Northumberland	PA
Upper Mahantango	Schuylkill	PA
Upper Makefield	Bucks	PA
Upper Merion	Montgomery	PA
Upper Mifflin	Cumberland	PA
Upper Milford	Lehigh	PA
Upper Moreland	Montgomery	PA
Upper Mount Bethel	Northampton	PA
Upper Nazareth	Northampton	PA
Upper North	Sharp	AR
Upper Oxford	Chester	PA
Upper Paxton	Dauphin	PA
Upper Penns Neck	Salem	NJ
Upper Pittsgrove	Salem	NJ
Upper Pottsgrove	Montgomery	PA
Upper Providence	Delaware	PA
Upper Providence	Montgomery	MO
Upper Red Lake	Beltrami	SD
Upper Red Owl	Meade	PA
Upper St. Clair	Allegheny	PA
Upper Salford	Montgomery	PA
Upper Saucon	Lehigh	PA
Upper Southampton	Bucks	AR
Upper Surrounded Hill	Prairie	NC
Upper Town Creek	Edgecombe	AR
Upper	Crawford	AR
Upper	Sebastian	NC
Upper	Chowan	NJ
Upper	Cape May	OH
Upper	Lawrence	PA
Upper Tulpehocken	Berks	PA
Upper Turkeyfoot	Somerset	PA
Upper Tyrone	Fayette	PA
Upper Uwchlan	Chester	PA
Upper Yoder	Cambria	WI
Upham	Langlade	ME
Upton	Oxford	MA
Upton	Worcester	MO
Upton	Texas	IA
Urbana	Monroe	IL
Urbana	Champaign	NY
Urbana	Steuben	OH
Urbana	Champaign	MN
Urness	Douglas	IL
Ursa	Adams	KS
Ursula	Kiowa	IL
Ustick	Whiteside	IA
Utica	Chickasaw	IL
Utica	La Salle	IN
Utica	Clark	MN
Utica	Winona	SD
Utica	Yankton	WI
Utica	Crawford	WI
Utica	Winnebago	PA
Uwchlan	Chester	NC
Uwharrie	Montgomery	MA
Uxbridge	Worcester	ND
Uxbridge	Barnes	

—V—

TOWNSHIP	COUNTY	STATE
Vacaville	Solano	CA
Vail	Redwood	MN
Vail	Perkins	SD
Vale	Burke	ND
Valhalla	Wells	ND
Valle	Jefferson	MO
Vallejo	Solano	CA
Vallers	Lyon	MN
Valley Brook	Osage	KS
Valley Center	Pawnee	KS
Valley Center	Sedgwick	KS
Valley Spring	Stutsman	ND
Valley Town	Cherokee	NC
Valley	Armstrong	PA
Valley	Cleburne	AR
Valley	Garland	AR
Valley	Hot Spring	AR
Valley	Madison	AR
Valley	Ouachita	AR
Valley	Pope	AR
Valley	Washington	AR
Valley	Guthrie	IA
Valley	Page	IA
Valley	Polk	IA
Valley	Pottawattamie	IA
Valley	Stark	IL
Valley	Barber	KS
Valley	Comanche	KS
Valley	Ellsworth	KS
Valley	Hodgeman	KS
Valley	Kingman	KS
Valley	Kiowa	KS
Valley	Lincoln	KS
Valley	Linn	KS
Valley	Miami	KS
Valley	Morris	KS
Valley	Osborne	KS
Valley	Phillips	KS
Valley	Pratt	KS
Valley	Reno	KS
Valley	Rice	KS
Valley	Scott	KS
Valley	Sheridan	KS
Valley	Smith	KS
Valley	Allegan	MI
Valley	Marshall	MN
Valley	Macon	MO
Valley	Dickey	ND
Valley	Kidder	ND
Valley	Brown	NE
Valley	Buffalo	NE
Valley	Knox	NE
Valley	Guernsey	OH
Valley	Scioto	OH
Valley	Canadian	OK
Valley	Grant	OK
Valley	Pawnee	OK
Valley	Woods	OK
Valley	Chester	PA
Valley	Montour	PA
Valley	Beadle	SD
Valley	Day	SD
Valley	Douglas	SD
Valley	Hughes	SD
Valley	Hutchinson	SD
Valley	Hyde	SD
Valley	Tripp	SD
Valley View	Grant	ND
Valleyford	Spokane	WA
Valverde	Sumner	KS
Van Buren	Crawford	AR
Van Buren	Newton	AR
Van Buren	Union	AR
Van Buren	Jackson	IA

TOWNSHIP	COUNTY	STATE	TOWNSHIP	COUNTY	STATE	TOWNSHIP	COUNTY	STATE
Van Buren	Keokuk	IA	Venus	Madison	AR	Vesta	Walsh	ND
Van Buren	Lee	IA	Verdery	Greenwood	SC	Vestal	Broome	NY
Van Buren	Van Buren	IA	Verdi	Lincoln	MN	Veteran	Chemung	NY
Van Buren	Brown	IN	Verdi	Washoe	NV	Vevay	Ingham	MI
Van Buren	Clay	IN	Verdier	Colleton	SC	Vian	Sequoyah	OK
Van Buren	Daviess	IN	Verdigre	Knox	NE	Vickers	Perkins	SD
Van Buren	Fountain	IN	Verdigris	Wilson	KS	Vicksburg	Jewell	KS
Van Buren	Grant	IN	Verdigris	Antelope	NE	Victor	San Bernardino	CA
Van Buren	Kosciusko	IN	Verdigris	Holt	NE	Victor	De Kalb	IL
Van Buren	Lagrange	IN	Verdigris	Rogers	OK	Victor	Osborn	KS
Van Buren	Madison	IN	Verdon	Aitkin	MN	Victor	Clinton	MI
Van Buren	Monroe	IN	Vergennes	Jackson	IL	Victor	Wright	MN
Van Buren	Pulaski	IN	Vergennes	Kent	MI	Victor	Towner	ND
Van Buren	Shelby	IN	Vermilion Lake	Saint Louis	MN	Victor	McClain	OK
Van Buren	Aroostook	ME	Vermilion	Appanoose	IA	Victor	Marshall	SD
Van Buren	Wayne	MI	Vermilion	Ashland	OH	Victor	Roberts	SD
Van Buren	Saint Louis	MN	Vermilion	Erie	OH	Victoria	Jefferson	AR
Van Buren	Jackson	MO	Vermillion	La Salle	IL	Victoria	Cass	IA
Van Buren	Newton	MO	Vermillion	Vermillion	IN	Victoria	Knox	IL
Van Buren	Wright	MO	Vermillion	Marshall	KS	Victoria	Ellis	KS
Van Buren	Renville	ND	Vermillion	Dakota	MN	Victoria	Rice	KS
Van Buren	Onondaga	NY	Vermillion	Clay	SD	Victoria	McLean	ND
Van Buren	Darke	OH	Vermillion	Miner	SD	Victoria	Custer	NE
Van Buren	Hancock	OH	Vermont	Fulton	IL	Victory	Guthrie	IA
Van Buren	Montgomery	OH	Vermont	Edmunds	SD	Victory	Mason	MI
Van Buren	Putnam	OH	Vermont	Dane	WI	Victory	Cayuga	NY
Van Buren	Shelby	OH	Vermontville	Eaton	MI	Victory	Venango	PA
Van Hook	Mountrail	ND	Verner	Sargent	ND	Victory	Essex	VT
Van Horn	Carroll	MO	Vernon Center	Blue Earth	MN	Vidette	Fulton	AR
Van Meter	Dallas	IA	Vernon Springs	Howard	IA	Viding	Clay	MN
Van Meter	Dickey	ND	Vernon	Sutter	CA	Vienna	Marshall	IA
Van Metre	Jones	SD	Vernon	Tolland	CT	Vienna	Grundy	IL
Van Order	Hyde	SD	Vernon	Lake	IL	Vienna	Johnson	IL
Van	Major	OK	Vernon	Dubuque	IA	Vienna	Scott	IN
Van Wyck	Whatcom	WA	Vernon	Humboldt	IA	Vienna	Pottawatomie	KS
Vance Creek	Barron	WI	Vernon	Palo Alto	IA	Vienna	Kennebec	ME
Vance	Vermilion	IL	Vernon	Van Buren	IA	Vienna	Genesee	MI
Vance	Lenoir	NC	Vernon	Wright	IA	Vienna	Montmorency	MI
Vance	Union	NC	Vernon	Hancock	IN	Vienna	Rock	MN
Vance	Orangeburg	SC	Vernon	Jackson	IN	Vienna	Forsyth	NC
Vanceboro	Washington	ME	Vernon	Jennings	IN	Vienna	Oneida	NY
Vandalia	Fayette	IL	Vernon	Washington	IN	Vienna	Trumbull	OH
Vandenbroek	Outagamie	WI	Vernon	Cowley	KS	Vienna	Dale	WI
Vanderbilt	San Bernardino	CA	Vernon	Isabella	MI	Vieregg	Merrick	NE
Vang	Ward	ND	Vernon	Shiawassee	MI	View	Williams	ND
Vann	Muskogee	OK	Vernon	Dodge	MN	Vigo	Knox	IN
Vanville	Burke	ND	Vernon	Clark	MO	Viking	Marshall	MN
Varennes	Anderson	SC	Vernon	Kidder	ND	Viking	Richland	ND
Varick	Seneca	NY	Vernon	Walsh	ND	Viking	Traill	ND
Varner	Ripley	MO	Vernon	Sussex	NJ	Viking	Perkins	SD
Vasa	Goodhue	MN	Vernon	Oneida	NY	Vilas	Langlade	WI
Vassalborough	Kennebec	ME	Vernon	Clinton	OH	Village	Columbia	AR
Vassar	Tuscola	MI	Vernon	Crawford	OH	Village	Jackson	AR
Vaughn	Independence	AR	Vernon	Scioto	OH	Village	Van Buren	IA
Vaugine	Jefferson	AR	Vernon	Trumbull	OH	Villard	Todd	MN
Veale	Daviess	IN	Vernon	Kay	OK	Villard	McHenry	ND
Veasey	Drew	AR	Vernon	Crawford	PA	Villemont	Jefferson	AR
Veazie	Penobscot	ME	Vernon	Beadle	SD	Villenova	Chautauqua	NY
Veblen	Marshall	SD	Vernon	Grant	SD	Vinalhaven	Knox	ME
Vega	Marshall	MN	Vernon	Windham	VT	Vincennes	Knox	IN
Veldt	Marshall	MN	Vernon	Waukesha	WI	Vincent	Grady	OK
Velva	McHenry	ND	Verona	Hancock	ME	Vine Prairie	Crawford	AR
Velvet Ridge	White	AR	Verona	Huron	MI	Vinegar Hill	Jo Daviess	IL
Venango	Butler	PA	Verona	Faribault	MN	Vineland	Polk	MN
Venango	Crawford	PA	Verona	Adams	NE	Vineyard	Washington	AR
Venango	Erie	PA	Verona	Oneida	NY	Vineyard	Lawrence	MO
Venedy	Washington	IL	Versailles	Brown	IL	Vinita	Kingman	KS
Venice	Los Angeles	CA	Vershire	Orange	VT	Vinland	Winnebago	WI
Venice	Madison	IL	Vesper	Lincoln	KS	Vinton	Benton	IA
Venice	Shiawassee	MI	Vessey	Harding	SD	Vinton	Valley	NE
Venice	Cayuga	NY	Vest	Scotland	MO	Vinton	Vinton	OH
Venice	Seneca	OH	Vesta	Clark	KS	Viola	Audubon	IA
Ventura	Ventura	CA	Vesta	Redwood	MN	Viola	Osceola	IA

TOWNSHIPS OF THE UNITED STATES

TOWNSHIP	COUNTY	STATE	TOWNSHIP	COUNTY	STATE	TOWNSHIP	COUNTY	STATE
Viola	Sac	IA	Wagendorf	Hettinger	ND	Wall	Monmouth	NJ
Viola	Lee	IL	Wagener	Oconee	SC	Wall	Stephens	OK
Viola	Sedgwick	KS	Wager	Benton	AR	Wall	Jackson	SD
Viola	Olmsted	MN	Wagner	Clayton	IA	Wallace	Benton	AR
Viola	Jerauld	SD	Wagner	Aitkin	MN	Wallace	Franklin	AR
Violet Hill	Izard	AR	Wagner	Marinette	WI	Wallace	Little River	AR
Violet	Fairfield	OH	Wahee	Marion	SC	Wallace	Stone	AR
Virden	Macoupin	IL	Wahehe	Charles Mix	SD	Wallace	La Salle	IL
Virgil	Kane	IL	Wahkonsa	webster	IA	Wallace	Wallace	KS
Virgil	Vernon	MO	Wahnena	Cass	MN	Wallace	Kidder	ND
Virgil	Cortland	NY	Wahoo	Saunders	NE	Wallace	Chester	PA
Virgil	Jones	SD	Waite Hill	Lake	OH	Wallace	Snohomish	WA
Virginia	Warren	IA	Waite	Washington	ME	Wallaceburg	Hempstead	AR
Virginia	Cass	IL	Waitsfield	Washington	VT	Walle	Grand Forks	ND
Virginia	Pemiscot	MO	Wakarusa	Douglas	KS	Wallingford	New Haven	CT
Virginia	Towner	ND	Wake Forest	Wake	NC	Wallingford	Rutland	VT
Virginia	Storey	NV	Wakeeney	Trego	KS	Wallkill	Orange	NY
Virginia	Coshocton	OH	Wakefield	Middlesex	MA	Walls	Lonoke	AR
Virginia	Union	SD	Wakefield	Gogebic	MI	Walls	Traverse	MN
Viroquo	Vernon	WI	Wakefield	Stearns	MN	Walls	Douglas	MO
Visalia	Tulare	CA	Wakefield	Dixon	NE	Walnut Corner	Greene	AR
Vista	San Diego	CA	Wakefield	Carroll	NH	Walnut Creek	Mitchell	KS
Vivian	Waseca	MN	Wakeman	Huron	OH	Walnut Creek	Macon	MO
Vivian	Sargent	ND	Wakenda	Carroll	MO	Walnut Creek	Edgecombe	NC
Vivian	Lyman	SD	Wakeshma	Kalamazoo	MI	Walnut Creek	Holmes	OH
Volga	Clayton	IA	Wakita	Grant	OK	Walnut Grove	Knox	IL
Volga	Brookings	SD	Wakpala	Corson	SD	Walnut Grove	McDonough	IL
Volin	Yankton	SD	Walburg	Cass	ND	Walnut Grove	Neosho	KS
Volinia	Cass	MI	Walcott	Rice	MN	Walnut Grove	Granville	NC
Volney	Oswego	NY	Walcott	Richland	ND	Walnut Grove	Wilkes	NC
Voltaire	Sherman	KS	Walden	Cass	MN	Walnut Grove	Knox	NE
Voltaire	McHenry	ND	Walden	Pope	MN	Walnut Grove	Woods	OK
Voluntown	New London	CT	Walden	Caledonia	VT	Walnut Grove	Greenwood	SC
Voorhees	Stevens	KS	Waldo	Columbia	AR	Walnut Grove	Spartanburg	SC
Voorhees	Camden	NJ	Waldo	Livingston	IL	Walnut Grove	Douglas	SD
Vrooman	Perkins	SD	Waldo	Russell	KS	Walnut Hill	Ashe	NC
			Waldo	Waldo	ME	Walnut Lake	Desha	AR
			Waldo	Richland	ND	Walnut Lake	Faribault	MN
—W—			Waldo	Marion	OH	Walnut	Benton	AR
			Waldoboro	Lincoln	ME	Walnut	Lee	AR
Waasa	Saint Louis	MN	Waldro	Brule	SD	Walnut	Montgomery	AR
Wabana	Itasca	MN	Waldron	Platte	MO	Walnut	Newton	AR
Wabash	Clark	IL	Waldron	Grady	OK	Walnut	Adair	IA
Wabash	Adams	IN	Waldwick	Iowa	WI	Walnut	Appanoose	IA
Wabash	Fountain	IN	Wales	Hampden	MA	Walnut	Dallas	IA
Wabash	Gibson	IN	Wales	Androscoggin	ME	Walnut	Fremont	IA
Wabash	Jay	IN	Wales	Saint Clair	MI	Walnut	Jefferson	IA
Wabash	Parke	IN	Wales	Erie	NY	Walnut	Madison	IA
Wabash	Tippecanoe	IN	Walhalla	Pembina	ND	Walnut	Palo Alto	IA
Wabash	Darke	OH	Walker Creek	Lafayette	AR	Walnut	Polk	IA
Wabaunsee	Wabaunsee	KS	Walker	Faulkner	AR	Walnut	Wayne	IA
Wabedo	Cass	MN	Walker	Franklin	AR	Walnut	Bureau	IL
Wabeno	Forest	WI	Walker	White	AR	Walnut	Marshall	IN
Waccamaw	Brunswick	NC	Walker	Hancock	IL	Walnut	Montgomery	IN
Waccamaw	Columbus	NC	Walker	Jasper	IN	Walnut	Atchison	KS
Wachter	McPherson	SD	Walker	Rush	IN	Walnut	Barton	KS
Wacker	McPherson	SD	Walker	Anderson	KS	Walnut	Bourbon	KS
Waco	Sedgwick	KS	Walker	Ellis	KS	Walnut	Brown	KS
Waconda	Caddo	OK	Walker	Cheboygan	MI	Walnut	Butler	KS
Waconia	Carver	MN	Walker	Henry	MO	Walnut	Cowley	KS
Wacousta	Humboldt	IA	Walker	Moniteau	MO	Walnut	Crawford	KS
Wacouta	Goodhue	MN	Walker	Vernon	MO	Walnut	Jewell	KS
Waddams	Stephenson	IL	Walker	Platte	NE	Walnut	Marshall	KS
Waddington	Saint Lawrence	NY	Walker	Garvin	OK	Walnut	Pawnee	KS
Wade	Clinton	IL	Walker	Center	pA	Walnut	Phillips	KS
Wade	Jasper	IL	Walker	Huntingdon	PA	Walnut	Reno	KS
Wade	Aroostook	ME	Walker	Juniata	PA	Walnut	Saline	KS
Wadena	Wadena	MN	Walker	Schuylkill	PA	Walnut	Adair	MO
Wadesboro	Anson	NC	Walker	Corson	SD	Walnut	Bates	MO
Wadmalaw	Charleston	SC	Walkerville	Greene	IL	Walnut	Greene	MO
Wadsworth	Stutsman	ND	Wall Lake	Wright	IA	Walnut	Madison	NC
Wadsworth	Washoe	NV	Wall Lake	Minnehaha	SD	Walnut	Fairfield	OH
Wadsworth	Medina	OH	Wall	Ford	IL	Walnut	Gallia	OH

TOWNSHIP	COUNTY	STATE	TOWNSHIP	COUNTY	STATE	TOWNSHIP	COUNTY	STATE
Walnut	Pickaway	OH	Warner	Clark	WI	Washington	Benton	AR
Walnut	Caddo	OK	Warren	Litchfield	CT	Washington	Bradley	AR
Walnut	Noble	OK	Warren	Bremer	IA	Washington	Conway	AR
Walpack	Sussex	NJ	Warren	Carroll	IA	Washington	Fulton	AR
Walpole	Norfolk	MA	Warren	Keokuk	IA	Washington	Grant	AR
Walpole	Cheshire	NH	Warren	Lucas	IA	Washington	Independence	AR
Walsh Center	Walsh	ND	Warren	Poweshiek	IA	Washington	Jefferson	AR
Walshtown	Yankton	SD	Warren	Story	IA	Washington	Ouachita	AR
Walshville	Montgomery	IL	Warren	Wayne	IA	Washington	Sevier	AR
Walshville	Walsh	ND	Warren	Jo Daviess	IL	Washington	Sharp	AR
Walter	Lac Qui Parie	MN	Warren	Lake	IL	Washington	Stone	AR
Walters	Stutsman	ND	Warren	Clinton	IN	Washington	Van Buren	AR
Waltham	La Salle	IL	Warren	Huntington	IN	Washington	Alameda	CA
Waltham	Hancock	ME	Warren	Marion	IN	Washington	Nevada	CA
Waltham	Mower	MN	Warren	Putnam	IN	Washington	Yolo	CA
Waltham	Kay	OK	Warren	Saint Joseph	IN	Washington	Litchfield	CT
Waltham	Addison	VT	Warren	Warren	IN	Washington	Adair	IA
Walton	Harvey	KS	Warren	Morris	KS	Washington	Adams	IA
Walton	Labette	KS	Warren	Worcester	MA	Washington	Appanoose	IA
Walton	Rooks	KS	Warren	Knox	ME	Washington	Black Hawk	IA
Walton	Sumner	KS	Warren	Midland	MI	Washington	Bremer	IA
Walton	Eaton	MI	Warren	Winona	MN	Washington	Buchanan	IA
Walton	Washington	MO	Warren	Camden	MO	Washington	Buena Vista	IA
Walton Village	Delaware	NY	Warren	Marion	MO	Washington	Butler	IA
Waltz	Wabash	IN	Warren	Cass	ND	Washington	Carroll	IA
Walworth	Becker	MN	Warren	Grafton	NH	Washington	Cass	IA
Walworth	Wayne	NY	Warren	Somerset	NJ	Washington	Chickasaw	IA
Walworth	Walworth	WI	Warren	Herkimer	NY	Washington	Clarke	IA
Wamduska	Nelson	ND	Warren	Belmont	OH	Washington	Clinton	IA
Wamego	Pottawatomie	KS	Warren	Jefferson	OH	Washington	Crawford	IA
Wanagan	Golden Valley	ND	Warren	Trumbull	OH	Washington	Dallas	IA
Wanamingo	Goodhue	MN	Warren	Tuscarawas	OH	Washington	Des Moines	IA
Wanda	Adams	NE	Warren	Washington	OH	Washington	Dubuque	IA
Wang	Renville	MN	Warren	Bradford	PA	Washington	Franklin	IA
Wanger	Marshall	MN	Warren	Franklin	PA	Washington	Fremont	IA
Wano	Cheyenne	KS	Warren	Bristol	RI	Washington	Greene	IA
Wano	La Moure	ND	Warren	Colleton	SC	Washington	Grundy	IA
Wantage	Sussex	NJ	Warren	Clark	SD	Washington	Harrison	IA
Wapella	De Witt	IL	Warren	Sanborn	SD	Washington	Iowa	IA
Wapello	Louisa	IA	Warren	Washington	VT	Washington	Jackson	IA
Wappanocca	Crittenden	AR	Warren	Saint Croix	WI	Washington	Jasper	IA
Wappinger	Dutchess	NY	Warren	Waushara	WI	Washington	Johnson	IA
Wapsinonoc	Muscatine	IA	Warren Valley	Noble	OK	Washington	Jones	IA
War Creek	Jones	SD	Warrensburg	Johnson	MO	Washington	Keokuk	IA
War Eagle	Benton	AR	Warrensburg	Warren	NY	Washington	Lee	IA
War Eagle	Madison	AR	Warrensville	Cuyahoga	OH	Washington	Linn	IA
Ward	Johnson	AR	Warrenton	Marshall	MN	Washington	Lucas	IA
Ward	Lonoke	AR	Warrenton	Warren	NC	Washington	Marion	IA
Ward	Yell	AR	Warrington	Bucks	PA	Washington	Marshall	IA
Ward	Clarke	IA	Warrington	York	PA	Washington	Montgomery	IA
Ward	Randolph	IN	Warriorsmark	Huntingdon	PA	Washington	Page	IA
Ward	Todd	MN	Warsaw	Hancock	IL	Washington	Plymouth	IA
Ward	Ravalli	MT	Warsaw	Goodhue	MN	Washington	Polk	IA
Ward	Burke	ND	Warsaw	Rice	MN	Washington	Pottawattamie	IA
Ward	Allegany	NY	Warsaw	Duplin	NC	Washington	Poweshiek	IA
Ward	Hocking	OH	Warsaw	Jefferson	PA	Washington	Ringgold	IA
Ward	Tioga	PA	Warsaw	Wyoming	NY	Washington	Shelby	IA
Ward	Edgefield	SC	Warwick	Franklin	MA	Washington	Sioux	IA
Ward	Moody	SD	Warwick	Benson	ND	Washington	Story	IA
Wards Grove	Jo Daviess	IL	Warwick	Orange	NY	Washington	Taylor	IA
Wards	Aiken	SC	Warwick	Tuscarawas	OH	Washington	Van Buren	IA
Wardsboro	Windham	VT	warwick	Bucks	PA	Washington	Wapello	IA
Ware	Hampshire	MA	Warwick	Chester	PA	Washington	Warren	IA
Ware	Boyd	NE	Warwick	Lancaster	PA	Washington	Washington	IA
Ware	Grant	OK	Wascott	Douglas	WI	Washington	Wayne	IA
Wareham	Plymouth	MA	Washburn	Logan	AR	Washington	Webster	IA
Waring	Ness	KS	Washburn	Sebastian	AR	Washington	Winneshiek	IA
Warlick	Cleveland	NC	Washburn	Aroostook	ME	Washington	Carroll	IL
Warm Springs	Randolph	AR	Washburn	Barry	MO	Washington	Tazewell	IL
Warminster	Bucks	PA	Washburn	Griggs	ND	Washington	Will	IL
Warner	Antrim	MI	Washburn	Bayfield	WI	Washington	Adams	IN
Warner	Merrimack	NH	Washburn	Clark	WI	Washington	Allen	IN
Warner	Brown	SD	Washington Lake	Sibley	MN	Washington	Blackford	IN

TOWNSHIPS OF THE UNITED STATES

TOWNSHIP	COUNTY	STATE	TOWNSHIP	COUNTY	STATE	TOWNSHIP	COUNTY	STATE
Washington	Boone	IN	Washington	Franklin	MO	Washington	Stark	OH
Washington	Brown	IN	Washington	Greene	MO	Washington	Tucsarawas	OH
Washington	Carroll	IN	Washington	Grundy	MO	Washington	Union	OH
Washington	Cass	IN	Washington	Harrison	MO	Washington	Van Wert	OH
Washington	Clark	IN	Washington	Jackson	MO	Washington	Warren	OH
Washington	Clay	IN	Washington	Johnson	MO	Washington	Wood	OH
Washington	Clinton	IN	Washington	Laclede	MO	Washington	Garfield	OK
Washington	Daviess	IN	Washington	Lafayette	MO	Washington	Grady	OK
Washington	Dearborn	IN	Washington	Mercer	MO	Washington	Love	OK
Washington	Decatur	IN	Washington	Monroe	MO	Washington	Armstrong	PA
Washington	Delaware	IN	Washington	Nodaway	MO	Washington	Berks	PA
Washington	Elkhart	IN	Washington	Osage	MO	Washington	Butler	PA
Washington	Gibson	IN	Washington	Pettis	MO	Washington	Cambria	PA
Washington	Grant	IN	Washington	Ripley	MO	Washington	Clarion	PA
Washington	Greene	IN	Washington	Saint Clair	MO	Washington	Dauphin	PA
Washington	Hamilton	IN	Washington	Saint Louis	MO	Washington	Erie	PA
Washington	Harrison	IN	Washington	Stone	MO	Washington	Fayette	PA
Washington	Hendricks	IN	Washington	Vernon	MO	Washington	Franklin	PA
Washington	Jackson	IN	Washington	Webster	MO	Washington	Greene	PA
Washington	Knox	IN	Washington	Beaufort	NC	Washington	Indiana	PA
Washington	Kosciusko	IN	Washington	Guilford	NC	Washington	Jefferson	PA
Washington	La Porte	IN	Washington	Grand Forks	ND	Washington	Lawrence	PA
Washington	Marion	IN	Washington	Franklin	NE	Washington	Lehigh	PA
Washington	Miami	IN	Washington	Hall	NE	Washington	Lycoming	PA
Washington	Monroe	IN	Washington	Harlan	NE	Washington	Northampton	PA
Washington	Morgan	IN	Washington	Knox	NE	Washington	Northumberland	PA
Washington	Newton	IN	Washington	Sherman	NE	Washington	Schuylkill	PA
Washington	Noble	IN	Washington	Sullivan	NH	Washington	Snyder	PA
Washington	Owen	IN	Washington	Bergen	NJ	Washington	Westmoreland	PA
Washington	Parke	IN	Washington	Burlington	NJ	Washington	Wyoming	PA
Washington	Pike	IN	Washington	Gloucester	NJ	Washington	York	PA
Washington	Porter	IN	Washington	Mercer	NJ	Washington	McCormick	SC
Washington	Putnam	IN	Washington	Morris	NJ	Washington	Aurora	SD
Washington	Randolph	IN	Washington	Warren	NJ	Washington	Bon Homme	SD
Washington	Ripley	IN	Washington	Dutchess	NY	Washington	Clark	SD
Washington	Rush	IN	Washington	Auglaize	OH	Washington	Douglas	SD
Washington	Shelby	IN	Washington	Belmont	OH	Washington	Hyde	SD
Washington	Starke	IN	Washington	Brown	OH	Washington	Jones	SD
Washington	Tippecanoe	IN	Washington	Carroll	OH	Washington	Orange	VT
Washington	Warren	IN	Washington	Clermont	OH	Washington	Door	WI
Washington	Washington	IN	Washington	Clinton	OH	Washington	Eau Claire	WI
Washington	Wayne	IN	Washington	Columbiana	OH	Washington	Green	WI
Washington	Whitley	IN	Washington	Coshocton	OH	Washington	La Crosse	WI
Washington	Anderson	KS	Washington	Darke	OH	Washington	Rusk	WI
Washington	Brown	KS	Washington	Defiance	OH	Washington	Sauk	WI
Washington	Chautauqua	KS	Washington	Fayette	OH	Washington	Shawano	WI
Washington	Crawford	KS	Washington	Franklin	OH	Washington	Vilas	WI
Washington	Doniphan	KS	Washington	Guernsey	OH	Washita	Custer	OK
Washington	Jackson	KS	Washington	Hancock	OH	Washita	Roger Mills	OK
Washington	Jewell	KS	Washington	Hardin	OH	Wasioja	Dodge	MN
Washington	Nemaha	KS	Washington	Harrison	OH	Wasta	Pennington	SD
Washington	Republic	KS	Washington	Henry	OH	Watab	Benton	MN
Washington	Saline	KS	Washington	Highland	OH	Waskish	Beltrami	MN
Washington	Sherman	KS	Washington	Hocking	OH	Watalula	Franklin	AR
Washington	Smith	KS	Washington	Holmes	OH	Watauga	Watauga	NC
Washington	Wabaunsee	KS	Washington	Jackson	OH	Watauga	Corson	SD
Washington	Washington	KS	Washington	Lawrence	OH	Watensaw	Prairie	AR
Washington	Berkshire	MA	Washington	Licking	OH	Water Creek	Hempstead	AR
Washington	Knox	ME	Washington	Logan	OH	Water Creek	Marion	AR
Washington	Gratiot	MI	Washington	Lucas	OH	Water Valley	Randolph	AR
Washington	Macomb	MI	Washington	Mercer	OH	Waterboro	York	ME
Washington	Sanilac	MI	Washington	Miami	OH	Waterbury	New Haven	CT
Washington	La Sueur	MN	Washington	Monroe	OH	Waterbury	Redwood	MN
Washington	Buchanan	MO	Washington	Montgomery	OH	Waterbury	Washington	VT
Washington	Carroll	MO	Washington	Morrow	OH	Wateree	Kershaw	SC
Washington	Cedar	MO	Washington	Muskingum	OH	Waterford	Stanislaus	CA
Washington	Clark	MO	Washington	Paulding	OH	Waterford	New London	CT
Washington	Clay	MO	Washington	Pickaway	OH	Waterford	Fulton	IA
Washington	Dade	MO	Washington	Preble	OH	Waterford	Clay	IA
Washington	Dallas	MO	Washington	Richland	OH	Waterford	Clinton	IA
Washington	Daviess	MO	Washington	Sandusky	OH	Waterford	Oxford	ME
Washington	De Kalb	MO	Washington	Scioto	OH	Waterford	Oakland	MI
Washington	Douglas	MO	Washington	Shelby	OH	Waterford	Dakota	MN

TOWNSHIP	COUNTY	STATE	TOWNSHIP	COUNTY	STATE	TOWNSHIP	COUNTY	STATE
Waterford	Ward	ND	Waverly	Bremer	IA	Wayne	McClain	OK
Waterford	Camden	NJ	Waverly	Cheboygan	MI	Wayne	Armstrong	PA
Waterford	Saratoga	NY	Waverly	Van Buren	MI	Wayne	Clinton	PA
Waterford	Washington	OH	Waverly	Martin	MN	Wayne	Crawford	PA
Waterford	Erie	PA	Waverly	Lincoln	MO	Wayne	Dauphin	PA
Waterford	Caledonia	VT	Waverly	Franklin	NY	Wayne	Erie	PA
Waterford	Racine	WI	Waverly	Codington	SD	Wayne	Greene	PA
Waterloo	Allamakee	IA	Waverly	Marshall	SD	Wayne	Lawrence	PA
Waterloo	Black Hawk	IA	Waverly	Spokane	WA	Wayne	Mifflin	PA
Waterloo	Fayette	IN	Wawarsing	Ulster	NY	Wayne	Schuylkill	PA
Waterloo	Lyon	KS	Wa-Watam	Emmet	MI	Wayne	Hanson	SD
Waterloo	Jackson	MI	Wawayanda	Orange	NY	Wayne	Lake	SD
Waterloo	Cavalier	ND	Wawina	Itasca	MN	Wayne	Minnehaha	SD
Waterloo	Seneca	NY	Waxhaw	Lancaster	SC	Wayne	Lafayette	WI
Waterloo	Athens	OH	Wayandotte	Ottawa	OK	Wayne	Washington	WI
Waterloo	Laurens	SC	Waybridge	Addison	VT	Waynesfield	Lucas	OH
Waterloo	Grant	WI	Wayland	Middlesex	MA	Waynesville	De Witt	IL
Waterloo	Jefferson	WI	Wayland	Allegan	MI	Waynesville	Haywood	NC
Waterman	O'Brien	IA	Wayland	Chariton	MO	Waynoka	Woods	OK
Watersment	Gogebic	MI	Wayland	Steuben	NY	Wayside	Spokane	WA
Watertown	Litchfield	CT	Wayne	Henry	IA	Wayzetta	Mountrail	ND
Watertown	Middlesex	MA	Wayne	Jones	IA	Wea	Tippecanoe	IN
Watertown	Jefferson	NY	Wayne	Mitchell	IA	Wea	Miami	KS
Watertown	Clinton	MI	Wayne	Monroe	IA	Wealthwood	Aitkin	MN
Watertown	Sanilac	MI	Wayne	De Page	IL	Weare	Oceana	MI
Watertown	Tuscola	MI	Wayne	Allen	IN	Weare	Hillsborough	NH
Watertown	Carver	MN	Wayne	Bartholomew	IN	Weathersfield	Trumbull	OH
Watertown	Washington	OH	Wayne	Fulton	IN	Weathersfield	Windsor	VT
Watertown	Jefferson	WI	Wayne	Hamilton	IN	Weaublea	Hickory	MO
Waterville	Marshall	KS	Wayne	Henry	IN	Weaver	Franklin	AR
Waterville	Le Sueur	MN	Wayne	Huntington	IN	Weaver	Humboldt	IA
Waterville	Lucas	OH	Wayne	Jay	IN	Weaver	Tripp	SD
Waterville	Lamoille	VT	Wayne	Kosciusko	IN	Weaverville	Trinity	CA
Waterville	Pepin	WI	Wayne	Marion	IN	Webb Lake	Burnett	WI
Waterville Valley	Grafton	NH	Wayne	Montgomery	IN	Webb	Reynolds	MO
Watervliet	Berrien	MI	Wayne	Noble	IN	Webb	Herkimer	NY
Watkins	Dent	MO	Wayne	Owen	IN	Webb	Dewey	OK
Watkins	Vance	NC	Wayne	Randolph	IN	Webber	Jefferson	IL
Watkins	Noble	OK	Wayne	Starke	IN	Webber	Lake	MI
Watonga	Blaine	OK	Wayne	Tippecanoe	IN	Weber	Sargent	ND
Watopa	Wabasha	MN	Wayne	Wayne	IN	Weber	McPherson	SD
Watova	Nowata	OK	Wayne	Doniphan	KS	Webster	Hamilton	IA
Watson	Effingham	IL	Wayne	Edwards	KS	Webster	Madison	IA
Watson	Allegan	MI	Wayne	Kennebec	ME	Webster	Polk	IA
Watson	Cass	ND	Wayne	Cass	MI	Webster	Webster	IA
Watson	Lewis	NY	Wayne	Bollinger	MO	Webster	Harrison	IN
Watson	Lycoming	PA	Wayne	Buchanan	MO	Webster	Wayne	IN
Watson	Warren	PA	Wayne	Bottineau	ND	Webster	Smith	KS
Watsonville	Santa Cruz	CA	Wayne	Custer	NE	Webster	Wilson	KS
Watterstown	Grant	WI	Wayne	Passaic	NJ	Webster	Worcester	MA
Watts	Perry	PA	Wayne	Steuben	NY	Webster	Androscoggin	ME
Waubay	Day	SD	Wayne	Adams	OH	Webster	Penobscot	ME
Waubeek	Pepin	WI	Wayne	Ashtabula	OH	Webster	Washtenaw	MI
Waubonsie	Ringgold	IA	Wayne	Auglaize	OH	Webster	Rice	MN
Waucedah	Dickinson	MI	Wayne	Belmont	OH	Webster	Jackson	NC
Wauconda	Lake	IL	Wayne	Butler	OH	Webster	Ramsey	ND
Wauhillau	Adair	OK	Wayne	Champaign	OH	Webster	Dodge	NE
Waukechon	Shawano	WI	Wayne	Clermont	OH	Webster	Sherman	NE
Waukegan	Lake	IL	Wayne	Clinton	OH	Webster	Merrimack	NH
Waukenabo	Aitkin	MN	Wayne	Columbiana	OH	Webster	Monroe	NY
Waukesha	Waukesha	??	Wayne	Darke	OH	Webster	Wood	OH
Waukomis	Garfield	OK	Wayne	Fayette	OH	Webster	Woodward	OK
Waukon	Norman	MN	Wayne	Jefferson	OH	Webster	Day	SD
Waumandee	Buffalo	WI	Wayne	Knox	OH	Webster	Huges	SD
Waupaca	Waupaca	WI	Wayne	Monroe	OH	Webster	Vernon	WI
Wauponsee	Grundy	IL	Wayne	Montgomery	OH	Wedington	Washington	AR
Waupun	Fond du Lac	WI	Wayne	Muskingum	OH	Weehawken	Hudson	NJ
Wausau	Marathon	WI	Wayne	Noble	OH	Weesaw	Berrien	MI
Wausaukee	Marinette	WI	Wayne	Pickaway	OH	Weigel	Logan	ND
Wautoma	Waushara	WI	Wayne	Scioto	OH	Weimer	Jackson	MN
Wauzeka	Crawford	WI	Wayne	Tuscarawas	OH	Weimer	Barnes	ND
Waveland	Yell	AR	Wayne	Warren	OH	Weirgor	Sawyer	WI
Waveland	Pottawattamie	IA	Wayne	Wayne	OH	Weisenberg	Lehigh	PA

TOWNSHIPS OF THE UNITED STATES

TOWNSHIP	COUNTY	STATE	TOWNSHIP	COUNTY	STATE	TOWNSHIP	COUNTY	STATE
Weiser	Kidder	ND	West Bend	Palo Alto	IA	West Howellsville	Robeson	NC
Wekiwa	Tulsa	OK	West Bend	Washington	WI	West Jefferson	Ashe	NC
Welborn	Conway	AR	West Benton	Christain	MO	West Jersey	Stark	IL
Welch Creek	Columbus	NC	West Benton	Newton	MO	West Keating	Clinton	PA
Welch	Goodhue	MN	West Benton	Webster	MO	West Kewaunee	Kewaunee	WI
Welch	Cape Girardeau	MO	West Bethlehem	Washington	PA	West Lakeland	Washington	MN
Welcome	Sioux	IA	West Bloomfield	Ontario	NY	West Lampeter	Lancaster	PA
Weld	Franklin	ME	West Bloonfield	Oakland	MI	West Lancaster	Keokuk	IA
Weld	Stutsman	ND	West Blue	Adams	NE	West Lebanon	Lebanon	PA
Welda	Anderson	KS	West Blue	Fillmore	NE	West Lincoln	Logan	IL
Weldon	Benzie	MI	West Boone	Bates	MO	West Lincoln	Mitchell	IA
Weldon	Halifax	NC	West Boylston	Worcester	MA	West Lucas	Johnson	IA
Weldon	Halifax	OK	West Bradford	Chester	PA	West Mahanoy	Schuylkill	PA
Weleetka	Okfuskee	OK	West Branch	Sioux	IA	West Mahoning	Indiana	PA
Weller	Henry	IL	West Branch	Marion	KS	West Manchester	York	PA
Weller	Richland	OH	West Branch	Dickinson	MI	West Manheim	York	PA
Wellesley	Norfolk	MA	West Branch	Marquette	MI	West Marlborough	Chester	PA
Wellfleet	Barnstable	MA	West Branch	Missaukee	MI	West Marshland	Burnett	WI
Wellington	Sumner	KS	West Branch	Ogemaw	MI	West McKinley	Caddo	OK
Wellington	Piscataquis	ME	West Branch	Potter	PA	West Mead	Crawford	PA
Wellington	Alpena	MI	West Brandywine	Chester	PA	West Milford	Passaic	NJ
Wellington	Renville	MN	West Bridgewater	Plymouth	MA	West Monroe	Oswego	NY
Wellington	Bottineau	ND	West Brookfield	Worcester	MA	West Nantmeal	Chester	PA
Wellington	Lorain	OH	West Brunswick	Schuylkill	PA	West New York	Hudson	NJ
Wellington	Minnehaha	SD	West Buffalo	Union	PA	West Newbury	Essex	MA
Wellington	Monroe	WI	West Caln	Chester	PA	West Newman	Nance	NE
Wells Bayou	Lincoln	AR	West Cameron	Northumberland	PA	West Newton	Nicollet	MN
Wells	Appanoose	IA	West Carroll	Cambria	PA	West Norriton	Montgomery	PA
Wells	Marshall	KS	West Center	Stevens	KS	West Norway	Wells	ND
Wells	York	ME	West Cherry	Montgomery	KS	West Nottingham	Chester	PA
Wells	Delta	MI	West Chillisquaque	Northumberland	PA	West Ontario	Wells	ND
Wells	Marquette	MI	West Cocalico	Lancaster	PA	West Orange	Essex	NJ
Wells	Tuscola	MI	West Cooper	Stafford	KS	West Paris	Oxford	ME
Wells	Rice	MN	West Cornwall	Lebanon	PA	West Peculiar	Cass	MO
Wells	Wells	ND	West Creek	Lake	IN	West Penn	Schuylkill	PA
Wells	Elko	NV	West Dallas	Webster	MO	West Perry	Snyder	PA
Wells	Hamilton	NY	West Deer	Allegheny	PA	West Pike Run	Washington	PA
Wells	Jefferson	OH	West Deerfield	Lake	IL	West Pikeland	Chester	PA
Wells	Blaine	OK	West Deptford	Gloucester	NJ	West Plains	Meade	KS
Wells	Bradford	PA	West Des Moines	Mahaska	IA	West Point	Calaveras	CA
Wells	Fulton	PA	West Dolan	Cass	MO	West Point	Butler	IA
Wells	Rutland	VT	West Donegal	Lancaster	PA	West Point	Lee	IA
Wells	Monroe	WI	West Doniphan	Ripley	MO	West Point	Stephenson	IL
Wellsford	Kiowa	KS	West Earl	Lancaster	PA	West Point	White	IN
Wellston	Jackson	OH	West End	Richland	ND	West Point	Bates	MO
Wellston	Lincoln	OK	West Fairlee	Orange	VT	West Point	Brule	SD
Wellsville	Columbiana	OH	West Fallowfield	Chester	PA	West Pottsgrove	Montgomery	PA
Welton	Clinton	IA	West Fallowfield	Crawford	PA	West Prairie	Poinsett	AR
Wendall	Thomas	KS	West Finley	Washington	PA	West Providence	Bedford	PA
Wendell	Franklin	MA	West Fork	Washington	AR	West Riverside	Riverside	CA
Wenham	Essex	MA	West Fork	Franklin	IA	West Rockhill	Bucks	PA
Wentworth	Rockingham	NC	West Fork	Monona	IA	West Rondell	Brown	SD
Wentworth	Grafton	NH	West Fork	Woodbury	IA	West Rutland	Rutland	VT
Wentworth	Lake	SD	West Franklin	Armstrong	PA	West Sadsbury	Chester	PA
Wergeland	Yellow Medicine	MN	West Fulton	Callaway	MO	West Saint Clair	Bedford	PA
Wescott	Shawano	WI	West Galena	Jo Daviess	IL	West Salem	Mercer	PA
Weskan	Wallace	KS	West Gardiner	Kennebec	ME	West Saline	Sheridan	KS
Wesley	Kossuth	IA	West Goshen	Chester	PA	West Sanford	Lee	NC
Wesley	Will	IL	West Greenwich	Kent	RI	West Seneca	Erie	NY
Wesley	Washington	ME	West Grove	Davis	IA	West Shenango	Crawford	PA
Wesley	Washington	OH	West Hale	Thomas	KS	West Side	Crawford	IA
Wesley	Faulk	SD	West Hamilton	Ellis	KS	West Sparta	Livingston	NY
Wesley	Beadle	SD	West Hanover	Dauphin	PA	West Spokane	Spokane	WA
Wessington	Union	AR	West Hanson	Brown	SD	West Springfield	Hampden	MA
Wesson	Lackawanna	PA	West Hartford	Hartford	CT	West Stockbridge	Berkshire	MA
West Abington	Wabasha	MN	West Hartford	New Haven	CT	West Sullivan	Sharp	AR
West Albany	Allegany	NY	West Haven	Rutland	VT	West Sweden	Polk	WI
West Almond	Hunterdon	NJ	West Hemlock	Montour	PA	West Taylor	Cambria	PA
West Amwell	Benson	ND	West Hempfield	Lancaster	PA	West Tisbury	Dukes	MA
West Antelope	Swift	MN	West Heron Lake	Jackson	MN	West	Montgomery	IA
West Bank	Williams	ND	West Hess	Gray	KS	West	Effingham	IL
West Bank	Sagadahoc	ME	West Hibbard	Kearney	KS	West	McLean	IL
West Bath	Benson	ND	West Hope	Cavalier	ND	West	Marshall	IN
West Bay	Snyder	PA						
West Beaver								

TOWNSHIPS OF THE UNITED STATES

TOWNSHIP	COUNTY	STATE	TOWNSHIP	COUNTY	STATE	TOWNSHIP	COUNTY	STATE
West	New Madrid	MO	Westmore	Orleans	VT	Wheatland	Vernon	WI
West	Columbiana	OH	Westmoreland	Cheshire	NH	Wheatley	Saint Francis	AR
West	Huntingdon	PA	Westmoreland	Oneida	NY	Wheaton	Barry	MO
West Traverse	Emmet	MI	Westola	Morton	KS	Wheaton	Bottineau	ND
West Turin	Lewis	NY	Weston	Fairfield	CT	Wheaton	Hand	SD
West Turkey Creek	Washita	OK	Weston	Middlesex	MA	Wheaton	Chippewa	WI
West Union	Fayette	IA	Weston	Aroostook	ME	Wheeler	Van Buren	AR
West Union	Norton	KS	Weston	Platte	MO	Wheeler	Lyon	IA
West Union	Todd	MN	Weston	Wood	OH	Wheeler	Sac	IA
West Union	Custer	NE	Weston	Kay	OK	Wheeler	Gratiot	MI
West Union	Steuben	NY	Weston	Marshall	SD	Wheeler	Grant	ND
West Valley	Marshall	MN	Weston	Windsor	VT	Wheeler	Steuben	NY
West Vincent	Chester	PA	Weston	Clark	WI	Wheeless	Cimarron	OK
West Walnut	Canadian	OK	Weston	Dunn	WI	Wheeling	Cook	IL
West Warwick	Kent	RI	Weston	Marathon	WI	Wheeling	Rice	MN
West Washington	Rice	KS	Westover	Jones	SD	Wheeling	Livingston	MO
West Wheatfield	Indiana	PA	Westphalia	Shelby	IA	Wheeling	Belmont	OH
West Whiteland	Chester	PA	Westphalia	Anderson	KS	Wheeling	Guernsey	OH
West Windsor	Mercer	NJ	Westphalia	Clinton	MI	Wheelock	Williams	ND
West Windsor	Windsor	VT	Westport Island	Lincoln	ME	Wheelock	Caledonia	VT
Westampton	Burlington	NJ	Westport	Fairfield	CT	Whetstone	Adams	ND
Westboro	Taylor	WI	Westport	Dickinson	IA	Whetstone	Crawford	OH
Westborough	Worcester	MA	Westport	Bristol	MA	Whetstone	Gregory	SD
Westbrook	Middlesex	CT	Westport	Pope	MN	Whiskey Run	Crawford	IN
Westbrook	Cottonwood	MN	Westport	Essex	NY	Whitby	Bottineau	ND
Westbrooks	Sampson	NC	Westport	Brown	SD	White Ash	Renville	ND
Westburg	Buchanan	IA	Westport	Dane	WI	White Bear Lake	Pope	MN
Westby	Divide	ND	Westside	Nobles	MN	White Bear	Ramsey	MN
Westchester	Porter	IN	Westside	Phelps	NE	White Bread	Caddo	OK
Westerheim	Lyon	MN	Westtown	Chester	PA	White Breast	Warren	IA
Westerlo	Albany	NY	Westville	Adair	OK	White Butte	Perkins	SD
Westerly	Washington	RI	Westville	Franklin	NY	White Cloud	Mills	IA
Western Mound	Macoupin	IL	Westmore	Norfolk	MA	White Cloud	Nodaway	MO
Western Prong	Columbus	NC	Westwood	Lassen	CA	White Creek	Washington	NY
Western	Henry	IL	Weta	Jackson	SD	White Deer	Union	PA
Western	Logan	KS	Wethersfield	Hartford	CT	White Eagle	Conway	AR
Western	Otter Tail	MN	Wethersfield	Henry	IL	White Earth	Becker	MN
Western	Wells	ND	Wethersfield	Wyoming	NY	White Earth	Mountrail	ND
Western	Knox	NE	Wetmore	Nemaha	KS	White Eyes	Coshocton	OH
Western	Oneida	NY	Wetmore	McKean	PA	White Hall	Greene	IL
Westerville	Custer	NE	Wetumka	Hughes	OK	White Hill	Perkins	SD
Westfall	Pike	PA	Wexford	Wexford	MI	White Lake	Oakland	MI
Westfield	Fayette	IA	Weyauwega	Waupaca	WI	White Lake	Slope	ND
Westfield	Plymouth	IA	Weymouth	Norfolk	MA	White Lake	Aurora	SD
Westfield	Bureau	IL	Weymouth	Atlantic	NJ	White Mound	Jewell	KS
Westfield	Clark	IL	Wharton Creek	Madison	AR	White Oak Springs	Lafayette	WI
Westfield	Aroostook	ME	Wharton	Potter	PA	White Oak	Cleveland	AR
Westfield	Dodge	MN	Wharton	Fayette	PA	White Oak	Franklin	AR
Westfield	Surry	NC	Whately	Franklin	MA	White Oak	Sebastain	AR
Westfield	Steele	ND	Whearfield	Niagara	NY	White Oak	El Dorado	CA
Westfield	Union	NJ	Wheatfield	Clinton	IL	White Oak	Mahaska	IA
Westfield	Chautauqua	NY	Wheatfield	Jasper	IN	White Oak	Warren	IA
Westfield	Orleans	VT	Wheatfield	Ingham	MI	White Oak	McLean	IL
Westfield	Medina	OH	Wheatfield	Grand Forks	ND	White Oak	Ingham	MI
Westfield	Morrow	OH	Wheatfield	Perry	PA	White Oak	Hubbard	MN
Westfield	Tioga	PA	Wheatland	Yuba	CA	White Oak	Harrison	MO
Westfield	Marquette	WI	Wheatland	Carroll	IA	White Oak	Henry	MO
Westfield	Sauk	WI	Wheatland	Bureau	IL	White Oak	Bladen	NC
Westford	Middlesex	MA	Wheatland	Fayette	IL	White Oak	Carteret	NC
Westford	Martin	MN	Wheatland	Will	IL	White Oak	Haywood	NC
Westford	Kidder	ND	Wheatland	Barton	KS	White Oak	Jones	NC
Westford	Otsego	NY	Wheatland	Dickinson	KS	White Oak	Onslow	NC
Westford	Chittenden	VT	Wheatland	Ellis	KS	White Oak	Polk	NC
Westford	Dodge	WI	Wheatland	Ford	KS	White Oak	Wake	NC
Westford	Richland	WI	Wheatland	Hillsdale	MI	White Oak	Highland	OH
Westhampton	Hampshire	MA	Wheatland	Mecosta	MI	White Pigeon	Saint Joseph	MI
Westland	Kiowa	KS	Wheatland	Sanilac	MI	White Pine	Aitkin	MN
Westland	Guernsey	OH	Wheatland	Rice	MN	White Plains	Cherokee	SC
Westline	Redwood	MN	Wheatland	Hickory	MO	White Post	Pulaski	IN
Westmark	Phelps	NE	Wheatland	Cass	ND	White River	Independence	AR
Westminster	Reno	KS	Wheatland	Monroe	NY	White River	Izard	AR
Westminster	Worcester	MA	Wheatland	Day	SD	White River	Madison	AR
Westminster	Windham	VT	Wheatland	Keosha	WI	White River	Marion	AR

- 884 -

TOWNSHIP	COUNTY	STATE
White River	Prairie	AR
White River	Washington	AR
White River	Woodruff	AR
White River	Gibson	IN
White River	Hamilton	IN
White River	Johnson	IN
White River	Randolph	IN
White River	Muskegon	MI
White River	Barry	MO
White River	Lyman	SD
White River	Ashland	WI
White Rock	Franklin	AR
White Rock	Ogle	IL
White Rock	Lane	KS
White Rock	Republic	KS
White Rock	Smith	KS
White Rock	McDonald	MO
White Rock	Noble	OK
White Rock	Roberts	SD
White Store	Anson	NC
White Swan	Charles Mix	SD
White	Ashley	AR
White	Newton	AR
White	Pike	AR
White	Polk	AR
White	Kingman	KS
White	Saint Louis	MN
White	Benton	MO
White	Macon	MO
White	Pierce	ND
White	Warren	NJ
White	McCurtain	OK
White	Beaver	PA
White	Cambria	PA
White	Indiana	PA
White	Marshall	SD
White Water	Oconee	SC
Whitebead	Garvin	OK
Whitebreast	Lucas	IA
Whited	Kanabec	MN
Whitefield	Marshall	IL
Whitefield	Lincoln	ME
Whitefield	Kandiyohi	MN
Whitefield	Coos	NH
Whitefish	Chippewa	MI
Whitefish	Flathead	MT
Whiteford	Monroe	MI
Whiteford	Marshall	MN
Whitehall	Muskegon	MI
Whitehall	Washington	NY
Whitehall	Franklin	OH
Whitehall	Lehigh	PA
Whitehead	Alleghany	NC
Whitehorse	Woods	OK
Whiteley	Greene	PA
Whitemarsh	Montgomery	PA
Whites Creek	Bladen	NC
Whites	Bertie	NC
Whiteside	Beadle	SD
Whitestone Hill	Sargent	ND
Whitestone	Dickey	ND
Whitestone	Oneida	NY
Whitestown	Vernon	WI
Whiteville	Baxter	AR
Whiteville	Cleveland	AR
Whiteville	Jefferson	AR
Whiteville	Columbus	NC
Whitewater	Dubuque	IA
Whitewater	Franklin	IN
Whitewater	Grand Traverse	MI
Whitewater	Winona	MN
Whitewater	Bollinger	MO
Whitewater	Cape Girardeau	MO
Whitewater	Hamilton	OH
Whitewater	Walworth	WI
Whitewoman	Wichita	KS
Whitewood	Kingsbury	SD
Whiting	Jackson	KS
Whiting	Washington	ME
Whiting	Bowman	ND
Whiting	Addison	VT
Whitingham	Windham	VT
Whitley	Crawford	AR
Whitley	Moutrie	IL
Whitman	Plymouth	MA
Whitman	Macon	IL
Whitmore	Macon	MI
Whitney	Arenac	MI
Whitney	Perkins	SD
Whitneyville	Washington	ME
Whitpain	Montgomery	PA
Whittemore	Kossuth	IA
Whitteron	Bottineau	ND
Whittier	Los Angeles	CA
Whittington	Garland	AR
Whitton	Mississippi	AR
Wiccacanee	Northampton	NC
Wichita	Sedgwick	KS
Wichita	Comanche	OK
Wickliffe	Lake	OH
Wiconisco	Dauphin	PA
Widner	Knox	IN
Wien	Marathon	WI
Wilber	Iosco	MI
Wilberton	Fayette	IL
Wilbraham	Hampden	MA
Wilbur	McKenzie	ND
Wilbur	Brule	SD
Wilburn	Cleburne	AR
Wilburn	Ford	KS
Wilcox	Hancock	IL
Wilcox	Trego	KS
Wilcox	Newaygo	MI
Wilcox	Roger Mills	OK
Wild Cat	Elk	KS
Wild Cat	Riley	KS
Wild Cherry	Fulton	AR
Wild Horse	Graham	KS
Wild Rice	Norman	MN
Wild Rose	Burleigh	ND
Wildcat	Tipton	IN
Wilders	Johnston	NC
Wiley	Randolph	AR
Wileys Cove	Searcy	AR
Wilkes-Barre	Luzerne	PA
Wilkesboro	Wilkes	NC
Wilkesville	Vinton	OH
Wilkins	Allegheny	PA
Wilkinson	Cass	MN
Wilkinson	Rusk	WI
Will	Will	IL
Willard	Rusk	WI
Willet	Cortland	NY
Willey	Sargent	ND
William Hamilton	Hyde	SD
William	Chatham	NC
Williams Creek	Jones	SD
Williams	Lonoke	AR
Williams	Colusa	CA
Williams	Calhoun	IA
Williams	Hamilton	IA
Williams	Sangamon	IL
Williams	Bay	MI
Williams	Aitkin	MN
Williams	Benton	MO
Williams	Stone	MO
Williams	Wayne	MO
Williams	Columbus	NC
Williams	Martin	NC
Williams	Kidder	ND
Williams	Nelson	ND
Williams	Dauphin	PA
Williams	Northampton	PA
Williamsboro	Vance	NC
Williamsburg	Franklin	KS
Williamsburg	Hampshire	MA
Williamsburg	Rockingham	NC
Williamsburg	Phelps	NE
Williamsburg	Clermont	OH
Williamsfield	Ashtabula	OH
Williamson	Wayne	NY
Williamson	Scotland	NC
Williamsons	Shawnee	KS
Williamsport	Martin	NC
Williamston	Anderson	SC
Williamstown	Berkshire	MA
Williamstown	Ingham	MI
Williamstown	Oswego	NY
Williamstown	Orange	VT
Williamstown	Dodge	WI
Willimantic	Piscataquis	ME
Willing	Allegany	NY
Willingboro	Burlington	NJ
Willington	Tolland	CT
Willis	Poinsett	AR
Willis	Ward	ND
Willis	Marshall	OK
Williston	Williams	ND
Williston	Barnwell	SC
Williston	Chittenden	VT
Willistown	Chester	PA
Willmar	Kandiyohi	MN
Willoughby	Lake	OH
Willow Bar	Cimarron	OK
Willow Branch	Piatt	IL
Willow Creek	Lee	IL
Willow Creek	McHenry	ND
Willow Creek	Tripp	SD
Willow Fork	Moniteau	MO
Willow Hill	Jasper	IL
Willow Lake	Redwood	MN
Willow Lake	Steele	ND
Willow Lake	Brule	SD
Willow Ranch	Modoc	CA
Willow Springs	Douglas	KS
Willow Springs	Howell	MO
Willow Springs	Tulsa	OK
Willow Springs	Lafayette	WI
Willow	Dallas	AR
Willow	Cherokee	IA
Willow	Crawford	IA
Willow	Monona	IA
Willow	Woodbury	IA
Willow	Griggs	ND
Willow	Antelope	NE
Willow	Caddo	OK
Willow	Greer	OK
Willow	Orangeburg	SC
Willow	McPherson	SD
Willow	Richland	WI
Willow Vale	Bottineau	ND
Willow Valley	Saint Louis	MN
Willowbank	La Moure	ND
Willowdale	Dickinson	KS
Willowdale	Holt	NE
Willowick	Lake	OH
Wills	La Porte	IN
Wills	Guernsey	OH
Willsboro	Essex	NY
Willshire	Van Wert	OH

TOWNSHIPS OF THE UNITED STATES

TOWNSHIP	COUNTY	STATE	TOWNSHIP	COUNTY	STATE	TOWNSHIP	COUNTY	STATE
Wilma	Pine	MN	Winchester	Cheshire	NH	Winsor	Clearwater	MN
Wilmington	Union	AR	Winchester	Adams	OH	Winsted	McLeod	MN
Wilmington	Will	IL	Winchester	Vilas	WI	Winston	Forsyth	NC
Wilmington	De Kalb	IN	Winchester	Winnebago	WI	Winter Harbor	Hancock	ME
Wilmington	Wabaunsee	KS	Windam	Bradford	PA	Winter	Sawyer	WI
Wilmington	Middlesex	MA	Windemere	Pine	MN	Winterfield	Clare	MI
Wilmington	Houston	MN	Windham	Windham	CT	Winterport	Waldo	ME
Wilmington	New Hanover	NC	Windham	Cumberland	ME	Winters	Yolo	CA
Wilmington	Essex	NY	Windham	Rockingham	NH	Winterset	Russell	KS
Wilmington	Lawrence	PA	Windham	Greene	NY	Winterville	Pitt	NC
Wilmington	Mercer	PA	Windham	Windham	??	Winthrop	Kennebec	ME
Wilmington	Windham	VT	Windham	Portage	OH	Winthrop	Suffolk	ME
Wilmot	Nobles	MN	Windham	Wyoming	PA	Winton	Hertford	NC
Wilmot	Ashley	AR	Windom	Mower	MN	Wiota	Lafayette	WI
Wilmot	Cheboygan	MI	Windor	Brookings	SD	Wirt	Itasca	MN
Wilmot	Merrimack	NH	Windsor Locks	Hartford	CT	Wirt	Allegany	NY
Wilmot	Bradford	PA	Windsor	Hartford	CT	Wiscasset	Lincoln	ME
Wilna	Jefferson	NY	Windsor	Fayette	IA	Wisconsin	Jackson	MN
Wilson Creek	Caldwell	NC	Windsor	Shelby	IL	Wiscoy	Winona	MN
Wilson Mills	Johnston	NC	Windsor	Cowley	KS	Wisdom	Beaverhead	MT
Wilson	Clay	AR	Windsor	Berkshire	MA	Wise	Isabella	MI
Wilson	Faulkner	AR	Windsor	Kennebec	ME	Wise	McLean	ND
Wilson	Fulton	AR	Windsor	Eaton	MI	Wise	Edgefield	SC
Wilson	Pope	AR	Windsor	Traverse	MN	Wiser	Cass	ND
Wilson	Stone	AR	Windsor	Henry	MO	Wishart	Park	MO
Wilson	Yell	AR	Windsor	Bertie	NC	Wishart	Polk	MO
Wilson	Osceola	IA	Windsor	Stutsman	ND	Wishart	Robeson	NC
Wilson	De Witt	IL	Windsor	Hillsborough	NH	Wismer	Marshall	SD
Wilson	Ellsworth	KS	Windsor	Broome	NY	Wisner	Franklin	IA
Wilson	Lane	KS	Windsor	Ashtabula	OH	Wisner	Tuscola	MI
Wilson	Marion	KS	Windsor	Lawrence	OH	Wisner	Cuming	NE
Wilson	Rice	KS	Windsor	Morgan	OH	Wister	Le Flore	OK
Wilson	Alpena	MI	Windsor	Berks	PA	Withee	Clark	WI
Wilson	Charlevoix	MI	Windsor	York	PA	Witt	Montgomery	IL
Wilson	Cass	MN	Windsor	Aiken	SC	Witten	Tripp	SD
Wilson	Winona	MN	Windsor	Windsor	VT	Wittenberg	Alexander	NC
Wilson	Adair	MO	Windsor	Dane	WI	Wittenberg	Hutchinson	SD
Wilson	Audrain	MO	Winfield	Scott	IA	Wittenberg	Shawano	WI
Wilson	Dallas	MO	Winfield	Du Page	IL	Wittich	Franklin	AR
Wilson	Gentry	MO	Winfield	Lake	IN	Wolcott	New Haven	CT
Wilson	Greene	MO	Winfield	Osborne	KS	Wolcott	Wayne	NY
Wilson	Grundy	MO	Winfield	Montcalm	MI	Wolcott	Lamoille	VT
Wilson	Putnam	MO	Winfield	Renville	MN	Wold	Traill	ND
Wilson	Wilson	NC	Winfield	Stutsman	ND	Wolf Butte	Adams	ND
Wilson	Burleigh	ND	Winfield	Union	NJ	Wolf Creek	Pike	AR
Wilson	Niagara	NY	Winfield	Herkimer	NY	Wolf Creek	Woodbury	IA
Wilson	Clinton	OH	Winfield	Butler	PA	Wolf Creek	Mercer	PA
Wilson	Atoka	OK	Winfield	Sauk	WI	Wolf Creek	Hutchinson	SD
Wilson	Carter	OK	Winfred	Lake	SD	Wolf Island	Mississippi	MO
Wilson	Choctaw	OK	Winfrey	Crawford	AR	Wolf Lake	Becker	MN
Wilson	Harper	OK	Wing River	Wadena	MN	Wolf Pit	Richmond	NC
Wilson	McCurtain	OK	Wing	Burleigh	ND	Wolf River	Doniphan	KS
Wilson	Allendale	SC	Winger	Polk	MN	Wolf River	Langlade	WI
Wilson	Perkins	SD	Wingfield	Geary	KS	Wolf River	Winnebago	WI
Wilson	Tripp	SD	Wingville	Grant	WI	Wolf	Seminole	OK
Wilson	Dunn	WI	Winhall	Bennington	VT	Wolf	Lycoming	PA
Wilson	Eau Claire	WI	Winn	Penobscot	ME	Wolfeboro	Carroll	NH
Wilson	Lincoln	WI	Winnebago City	Faribault	MN	Wolford	Crow Wing	MN
Wilson	Rusk	WI	Winnebago	Winnebago	IL	Wolford	Pierce	ND
Wilson	Sheboygan	WI	Winnebago	Houston	MN	Wolfscrape	Duplin	NC
Wilsons Creek	Avery	NC	Winneconne	Winnebago	WI	Wolsey	Beadle	SD
Wilton	Fairfield	CT	Winner	Williams	ND	Wolverton	Wilkin	MN
Wilton	Muscatine	IA	Winona	Carroll	AR	Womble	Montgomery	AR
Wilton	Will	IL	Winona	Logan	KS	Wonewoc	Juneau	WI
Wilton	Franklin	ME	Winona	Winona	MN	Wood Lake	Yellow Medicine	MN
Wilton	Waseca	MN	Winona	Shannon	MO	Wood Lake	Benson	ND
Wilton	Hillsborough	NH	Winona	Grant	ND	Wood River	Madison	IL
Wilton	Saratoga	NY	Winslow	Washington	AR	Wood River	Custer	NE
Wilton	Monroe	WI	Winslow	Stephenson	IL	Wood River	Hall	NE
Winchendon	Worcester	MA	Winslow	Kennebec	ME	Wood River	Burnett	WI
Winchester	Litchfield	CT	Winslow	Camden	NJ	Wood	Clark	IN
Winchester	Middlesex	MA	Winslow	Jefferson	PA	Wood	Douglas	MO
Winchester	Norman	MN	Winsor	Huron	MI	Wood	Wright	MO

TOWNSHIPS OF THE UNITED STATES

TOWNSHIP	COUNTY	STATE
Wood	Emmons	ND
Wood	Garfield	OK
Wood	Huntingdon	PA
Wood	Wood	WI
Woodberry	Slope	ND
Woodbine	Jo Daviess	IL
Woodboro	Oneida	WI
Woodbridge	New Haven	CT
Woodbridge	Hillsdale	MI
Woodbridge	Middlesex	NJ
Woodbury	Litchfield	CT
Woodbury	Woodbury	IA
Woodbury	Cumberland	IL
Woodbury	Stutsman	ND
Woodbury	Orange	NY
Woodbury	Bedford	PA
Woodbury	Blair	PA
Woodbury	Marion	SC
Woodbury	Washington	VT
Woodcock	Crawford	PA
Woodford	Bennington	VT
Woodhull	Shiawassee	MI
Woodhull	Steuben	NY
Woodington	Lenoir	NC
Woodland	Yolo	CA
Woodland	Decatur	IA
Woodland	Carroll	IL
Woodland	Fulton	IL
Woodland	Aroostook	ME
Woodland	Barry	MI
Woodland	Wright	MN
Woodland	Burlington	NJ
Woodland	Logan	OK
Woodland	Clark	SD
Woodland	Sauk	WI
Woodlawn	Monroe	MO
Woodlawn	Kidder	ND
Woodman	Grant	WI
Woodmohr	Chippewa	MN
Woodrow	Beltrami	MN
Woodrow	Cass	MN
Woodrow	Ellis	OK
Woodruff	Spartanburg	SC
Woodruff	Oneida	WI
Woods	Chippewa	MN
Woodsdale	Person	NC
Woodside	Sangamon	IL
Woodside	Otter Tail	MN
Woodside	Polk	MN
Woodside	Oregon	MO
Woodstock	Windham	CT
Woodstock	Wright	IA
Woodstock	Schuyler	IL
Woodstock	Oxford	ME
Woodstock	Lenawee	MI
Woodstock	Grafton	NH
Woodstock	Ulster	NY
Woodstock	Windsor	VT
Woodville	Greene	IL
Woodville	Penobscot	ME
Woodville	Waseca	MN
Woodville	Bertie	NC
Woodville	Platte	NE
Woodville	Sandusky	OH
Woodville	Calumet	WI
Woodward	Wells	ND
Woodward	Woodward	OK
Woodward	Clearfield	PA
Woodward	Clinton	PA
Woodward	Lycoming	PA
Woolwich	Sagadahoc	ME
Woolwich	Gloucester	NJ
Woonsocket	Sanborn	SD

TOWNSHIP	COUNTY	STATE
Wooster	Wayne	OH
Woosung	Ogle	IL
Worcester	Otsego	NY
Worcester	Montgomery	PA
Worcester	Washington	VT
Worcester	Price	WI
Worden	Clark	WI
Workman	Aitkin	MN
Worth	Boone	IA
Worth	Cook	IL
Worth	Woodford	IL
Worth	Boone	IN
Worth	Sanilac	MI
Worth	Jefferson	NY
Worth	Butler	PA
Worth	Centre	PA
Worth	Mercer	PA
Worth	Hanson	SD
Worthen	Hampshire	MA
Worthington	Noble	MN
Worthington	Richland	OH
Wortman	Tripp	SD
Wouri	Saint Louis	MN
Wray	Jefferson	OK
Wrenshall	Carlton	MN
Wrentham	Norfolk	MA
Wright	Pottawattamie	IA
Wright	Greene	IN
Wright	Hillsdale	MI
Wright	Ottawa	MI
Wright	Marshall	MN
Wright	Dickey	ND
Wright	Schoharie	NY
Wright	Jefferson	OK
Wright	Luzerne	PA
Wright	Tripp	SD
Wright	Greene	IL
Wrights	Greene	PA
Wrightstown	Bucks	PA
Wrightstown	Brown	WI
Writing Rock	Divide	ND
Wyaconda	Clark	MO
Wyacondah	Davis	IA
Wyalusing	Bradford	PA
Wyalusing	Grant	WI
Wyandotte	Wyandotte	KS
Wyandotte	Pennington	MN
Wyandotte	Perkins	SD
Wyanet	Bureau	IL
Wyanett	Isanti	MN
Wyard	Foster	ND
Wyckoff	Bergen	NJ
Wycough	Independence	AR
Wye	Perry	AR
Wykeham	Todd	MN
Wylie	Red Lake	MN
Wyman	Washington	AR
Wymore	Gage	NE
Wyndmere	Richland	ND
Wynne	Cross	AR
Wyocena	Columbia	WI
Wyoming	Jones	IA
Wyoming	Lee	IL
Wyoming	Chisago	MN
Wyoming	Holt	NE
Wyoming	Hamilton	OH
Wyoming	Iowa	WI
Wyoming	Waupaca	WI
Wysox	Carroll	IL
Wysox	Bradford	PA
Wythe	Hancock	IL

—X—

TOWNSHIP	COUNTY	STATE
Xenia	Clay	IL
Xenia	Greene	OH

—Y—

TOWNSHIP	COUNTY	STATE
Yadkin College	Davidson	NC
Yadkin	Stokes	NC
Yadkin Valley	Caldwell	NC
Yale	Valley	NE
Yanceyville	Caswell	NC
Yankee Springs	Barry	MI
Yarmouth	Barnstable	MA
Yarmouth	Cumberland	ME
Yates	McLean	IL
Yates	Lake	MI
Yates	Orleans	NY
Yeager	Hughes	OK
Yell	Benton	AR
Yell	Boone	IA
Yell	Webster	IA
Yellow Bank	Lac Qui Parle	MN
Yellow Creek	Chariton	MO
Yellow Creek	Linn	MO
Yellow Creek	Graham	NC
Yellow Creek	Columbiana	OH
Yellow Springs	Des Moines	IA
Yellowhead	Kankakee	IL
Yellowstone	McKenzie	ND
Yellowstone	Woods	OK
Yemassee	Beaufort	SC
Yeopim	Chowan	NC
Yermo	San Bernardino	CA
Yocum	Carroll	AR
Yoder	Reno	KS
York	Lonoke	AR
York	Iowa	IA
York	Pottawattamie	IA
York	Tama	IA
York	Carroll	IL
York	Clark	IL
York	Du Page	IL
York	Benton	IN
York	Dearborn	IN
York	Elkhart	IN
York	Noble	IN
York	Steuben	IN
York	Switzerland	IN
York	Stafford	KS
York	York	ME
York	Washtenaw	MI
York	Fillmore	MN
York	Putnam	MO
York	Benson	ND
York	Livingston	NY
York	Athens	OH
York	Belmont	OH
York	Darke	OH
York	Fulton	OH
York	Medina	OH
York	Morgan	OH
York	Sandusky	OH
York	Tuscarawas	OH
York	Union	OH
York	Van Wert	OH
York	York	PA
York	York	SC
York	Day	SD
York	Hand	SD
York	Clark	WI
York	Dane	WI
York	Green	WI
Yorkshire	Cattaraugus	NY

TOWNSHIPS OF THE UNITED STATES

TOWNSHIP	COUNTY	STATE	TOWNSHIP	COUNTY	STATE	TOWNSHIP	COUNTY	STATE
Yorktown	Henry	IL	Yreka	Siskiyou	CA	Zella	Comanche	OK
Yorktown	Dickey	ND	Yuba	Sutter	CA	Zerbe	Northumberland	PA
Yorktown	Westchester	NY	Yucaipa	San Bernardino	CA	Zero	Adams	NE
Yorkville	Racine	WI	Yucatan	Houston	MN	Zickrick	Jones	SD
Young America	Edgar	IL	Yukon	Canadian	OK	Zif	Wayne	IL
Young America	Carver	MN				Zillwaukee	Saginaw	MI
Young Hickory	Fulton	IL		—Z—		Zinc	Boone	AR
Young	Dickey	ND				Zion	Lake	IL
Young	Indiana	PA	Zane	Logan	OH	Zion	Stearns	MN
Young	Jefferson	PA	Zanesville	Montgomery	IL	Zion	Towner	ND
Youngs	Laurens	SC	Zanesville	Muskingum	OH	Zion	Orangeburg	SC
Youngsville	Franklin	NC	Zeandale	Riley	KS	Zuma	Rock Island	IL
Ypsilanti	Washtenaw	MI	Zeeland	Ottawa	MI	Zumbro	Wabasha	MN
Ypsilanti	Stutsman	ND	Zell	Faulk	SD	Zumbrota	Goodhue	MN

ASSOCIATION OF GENEALOGICAL EDITORS

Do you do any of the following?:

- Edit a genealogical magazine?
- Edit a genealogical newspaper?
- Edit a quarterly genealogical publication?
- Edit a genealogical newsletter?
- Edit a family organization publication?
- Edit a occassionally for other geneaological publications?

Then you are invited to become a member of the Association of Genealogical Editors (AGE)! Send one dollar for membership application and information.

Association of Genealogical Editors
P.O. Box 16422
Salt Lake City, UT 84116

Section V
MAPS, FORMS, GLOSSARY

ANALYSIS REPORT

HUSBAND

DATE BORN	PLACE
DATE CHR.	PLACE
DATE MARR.	PLACE
DATE DIED	PLACE
DATE BUR.	PLACE
HUS' FATHER	
HUS' MOTHER	

HUSB'S OTHER WIVES

OCCUPATION(S)

SOURCES OF INFORMATION

WIFE

DATE BORN	PLACE
DATE CHR.	PLACE
DATE DIED	PLACE
DATE BUR.	PLACE
WIFE'S FATHER	
WIFE'S MOTHER	

WIFE'S OTHER HUSBANDS

(USE REVERSE SIDE IF NECESSARY)

SEX M/F	CHILDREN (IN ORDER OF BIRTH)	DATE BORN PLACE BORN	DATE MARRIED PLACE MARRIED	MARRIED TO	DATE DIED PLACE DIED
	1				
	2				
	3				
	4				
	5				
	6				
	7				
	8				
	9				
	10				

FAMILY GROUP SHEET

Enter all data in this order:

NAMES: Ronald Allan Bremer
DATES: 2 May 1937
PLACES: Southgate, Los Angeles, Calif.

INSTRUCTIONS

Only Ten Dollars Per Problem

Type or print all information. Choose any one ancestral research problem or family anywhere in the world. Do not use any other papers or forms. Be sure and send all that you know about this problem. No actual research will be conducted. Specific research suggestions and techniques relative to the problem indicated will be made on a separate piece of paper.

Your Name _____

Address _____

City & State _____

Zip Code _____

Please complete this form and mail it together with your check for 20.00 dollars to:

Genealogy Book Club
P.O. Box 4064
Wofford Heights, CA 93285

CHAPTER 30

MAPS & MIGRATIONS

Before the Civil War everyone traveled the same way, one foot in front of the other. After the Civil War almost everyone traveled by train; however, it must be remembered that covered wagons were still being used during the great depression. Most of those early people traveled in groups. They traveled not only as families but whole congregations, communities, and organizations, therefore, when searching migrations there are some special rules you must follow.

1. Always start with the county of destination; never start with the departure point, it can lead to serious errors.

2. You must always find the exact county of departure; just knowing the state can be misleading.

3. You will be most successful if you do a general search of county of destination.

Since most people came in groups, Social Histories of the county are a very good source of information such as; wills, church records, and diaries, especially of leading citizens.

The first line of most original land deeds will tell you where the people came from.

Warning—even though documents like census records may give you the state of origin, unless you know the exact county of origin you can be led astray. Remember, that you must always look for sources in the county of destination, and trace backward. Moving too quickly can lead to road blocks that are hard to overcome.

Enclosed is a list of the main migration trails

Main Migration Trails

1. Augusta Cherokee Trail—often called the Traders' Trail.
2. Augusta and Savannah Trail.
3. Alabama and Mobile Trail.
4. Alabama, Choctaw and Natchez Trail—From Great South Trail to Vicksburg.
5. Augusta and St. Augustine Trail.
6. Atascosita Road—Eastward through Columbus, San Felipe and Liberty, crossing Neches River, and turning north to Nacogdoches.
7. Boliver and Memphis Trail—Memphis east to join Chickasaw Trail.
8. Black Fox Trail—cut off from Cisca and St. Augustine Trail to join Tennessee, Ohio and the Great Lakes Trail.
9. Buffalo Trace—New Albany, Ind., Vincennes, Centralia & Kaskaskia, Ill.
10. Boston—New York Post Road—Boston, Providence, New London, N.Y.
11. Boston to Hartford.
12. Braddock's Road—or Nemacolin's Path—from Alexandria, Va., through Cumberland, Md. to Fort Pitt (Pittsburgh).
13. Bay Road—Boston to Tauton.
14. Butterfield Overland Stage Rt.—from St. Louis, passengers and mail on Pacific Railroad to Tipton, Mo., transferred to Stage coaches, continued via Springfield, Mo., to Ft. Smith, Ark, meeting stage from Memphis and Little Rock, to Stringtown and Atoka, Ok, crossed Red River at Colbert's Ferry, and then to Gainsville, west a little south of Middle Concho River, to Horsehead Crossing, following the Pecos River to El Paso and San Diego.
15. Big Medicine Trail—Williston to Ft. Bridger.
16. Chickasaw Trail—from Boliver—Memphis Trail to Lower Harpeth Trail.
17. Cisca and St. Augustine Trail—Nashville to Atlanta to St. Augustine.
18. Cumberland and Ohio Falls Trail—Nashville to Louisville.
19. Catawba Trail—Old South Carolina State Road to North—to Cumberland Gap.
20. Chicago and Dubuque Highway—from Chicago to Dubuque, Ia, going north and east to Northern Wisc. near northern part of Lake Michigan.
21. Coast Path—Boston to tip of Cape Cod. Boston to Plymouth.

22. Cumberland Trace—from Tennessee, Ohio and Great Lakes Trail to Nashville.
23. California Trail—follow route of Butterfield Overland Trail to Preston's Ford to Cross Red River, north and west of Butterfield Trail to Ft. Belknap and Camp Cooper, west toward Big Springs, to Pecos River, following route of Butterfield.
24. Chisholm Trail—Nueces River, San Antonio, San Marcos, Austin, Georgetown, near Hillsboro, Ft. Worth, Red River crossing, Ft. Sill, Anadarko to Abilene.
25. John Chisum Trail—followed southern part of Butterfield Trail to Pope's Crossing and then to Pecos River to Roswell, N.M.
26. Chihauhau Road.
27. Caddo Trail—from Port Caddo to Pittsburg, Texas.
28. Cherokee Trail—Southwest of Walling at Cherokee Village, north to Gilmer, Tx, to old Ft. Sherman, southwest of Mt. Pleasant.
29. Cimmarron Trail—Santa Fe to St. Joseph.
30. El Camino Real—from Saltillo, Mex to Eagle Pass, San Antonio, Bastrop, Madisonville, Midway, Crockett to Nacogodoches, La. Also known as Royal Road.
31. Federal Road—South Carolina to Montgomery to Natchez.
32. Fremont's Route—Ft. Vancouver to Sacramento.
33. Fort Miami Trail—Maysville, Ky. to Ft. Miami (on western tip of Lake Erie).
34. Forbes Road—Philadelphia, Middletown, Carlisle, New Cumberland to Pittsburg. Also called Old Trading Path, Old State Rd, Lancaster Road.
35. Gila Trail—El Paso to Yuma to Los Angeles (California Trail).
36. Grand Pass—Albany to Montreal.
37. Great South Trail—Nashville to Mobile.
38. Great Trail—Pittsburg, north and west to Ft. Detroit. A western Expansion of Braddock's Road.
39. Great Indian Warpath—(Warrior's Trading Path)—began near Philadelphia crossed the Susquehanna near Harrisburg, passed westerly and southwesterly between mountain ranges and along valleys of the Shenandoah to the upper tributaries of the Tennessee River, Cumberland Gap to Chattanooga.
40. Goodnight—loving Trail—began approximately at Fredericksburg, west to Horsehead Crossing on Pecos River, followed Pecos into N.M., continued northward to Cheyenne, Wyoming.
41. Hastings Cut-Off—Salt Lake City to Sacramento.
42. Hudson River—Lake Champlain Trail—connected N.Y. and early roads of Canada into St. Lawrence Valley. Also known as Lake Shore Trail.
43. Hurreras Road—(1805) from Mexico to Laredo to Nueces River, to Frio, to San Antonio.
44. Iroquois-Mohawk Trail—Albany to Buffalo, N.Y.
45. Jackson's Military Road—Nashville to Madison.
46. Jacksonville and Appalachee Bay Trail—from Jacksonville to Old Trading Path of the South.
47. Kanawha Branch of the Great Indian Warpath—Chillicothe, Ohio to Gallipolis, Ohio to Charleston, W. Va., north of Briscoe into Great Indian Warpath.
48. Kellog Trail—from Terre Haute to junction of Chicago-Dubuque Trail.
49. Kennebunk Road—Boston to Portland and Augusta, Me. and northward.
50. King's Path—Philadelphia to N.Y. City. (Old Post Road or Kings Highway).
51. Lower Immigrant Trail—San Antonio to El Paso.
52. Lower Harpeth Trail—from Chickasaw Trail to Nashville.
53. Lower Creek Trading Path—from Augusta to Macon.
54. Lower Cherokee Trader's Path—joining Great Indian Warpath, Spartanburg.
55. La Fayette Road—from Vincennes north to join Old Chicago Road.
56. Labadie Trail—a contraband trail, older than El Camino Real, and was almost parallel to El Camino Real, about 50 miles southward.
57. La Bahia Road—began at Goliad, east to La Grange, Washington-on-the Trinity to El Camino Real.
58. Lake Shore Trail—connected N.Y. and early roads of Canada into St. Lawrence Valley. (Hudson River-Lake Champlain Trail).
59. Multan Road—Great Falls to Spokane.
60. Macon and Montgomery Trail.
61. Mobile and Natchez Trail.
62. Memphis, Pototoc and Mobile Trail—Pototoc is in Northern, Miss.
63. Mowhawk-Iroquois Trail—Albany to Buffalo, N.Y.
64. Michigan Road—Indianapolis, South Bend, to Chicago-Dubuque Road, on to Michigan.
65. Mormon Trail—from St. Joseph, Omaha, following the North Platte River to Salt Lake City.
66. Northern Trail—Bozeman, Mont. to Baker City, Oregon.
67. Natchez to Lower Greeks—Natchez, Miss. to Ala.—Mobile Trail.
68. Natchez—New Orleans Trail.
69. National Road—often referred to as the Cumberland Road—Philadelphia, Baltimore, Frederick,

Cumberland, Wheeling, Columbus, Richmond, Ind., Indianapolis, Terre Haute, to St. Louis.

70. Natchez Trace—Memphis to Chickasaw towns about Pototoc in Northern Mississippi and connecting with all sections of Southern U.S. to Natchez, Miss.

71. New York Post Road—Boston, Providence, New London, New York.

72. Old San Antonio Road—San Antonio to Natchez.

73. Old South Carolina State Road to the North—from Charleston to Catawba Trail.

74. Occaneechi Path—led from Bermuda Hundred on James River and Petersburg, Va. to trading town of Occaneechi on Roanoke River thru what is now Raleigh, Charlotte, N.C. to Columbia, S.C. to Augusta.

75. Old Chicago Road—Indianapolis to Chicago.

76. Old Trading Path of the South—Mobile, Pensacola, Tallahassee to Pecatonia Trail.

77. Old Connecticut Path—Boston to Albany, N.Y.

78. Old Roebuck Road—Dedham, Mass., Walpole, Foxboro to Providence, R.I.

79. Old Trading Path of Pennsylvania—Philadelphia, Middletown, Carlisle, N. Cumberland to Pittsburgh.

80. Oregon Trail—Also known as Overland Trail—through Neb., Wyo., Idaho to Portland, Ore. At Granger, Wyo. and again Southern Idaho, this trail branched southward through Utah and Nevada to San Francisco.

81. Old Spanish Trail—From Florida to Mexico with route to San Diego.

82. Opelousa Route—Opelousa, La., to Orange, Texas, Richmond, Columbus.

83. Old Comanche Road—east of Nacodoches, north of El Camino Real, crossed the Brazos, Leon, Colorado River about 50 miles north of San Antonio, ending western side of Guadalupe River.

84. Pamunkey-New River Trail—from the Kanawha Branch of Great Indian Warpath to Occaneechi Path.

85. Pecatonica Trail—from Junction of Chicago—Quincy Road to Northern Wisconsin near Lake Michigan.

86. Pony Express—from St. Joseph, Mo. to Salt Lake City to Sacramento.

87. Royal Road—See El Camino Real.

88. Southern St. Augustine—Appalachee Trail—Pecatonica Trail to St. Augustine and branches off to Tampa and then curves to Atlantic Ocean.

89. Savannah and Jacksonville Trail—joins a trail from Charleston, S.C., then Savannah to Jacksonville, joining trail to St. Augustine.

90. Southern Trail—from Memphis, across the Mississippi River, across Arkansas, Oklahoma, into Texas, N. Mexico, Arizona, Nevada curving north to Los Angeles. Part of this route follows what is now Route 66. One Branch follows the old Butterfield State Line and another follows route of the Southern Pacific Railway.

91. Santa Fe Trail—from Independence, Mo. to Santa Fe. The safer route went by Ranton, NM.

92. Southwestern Trail through Arkansas—this trail connects with road from St. Louis, south to Fredericksburg, and Poplar Bluff, Mo., and enters Arkansas at Corning, on to Pocahontas, Newport, Searcy, Little Rock, Malvern, Arkadelphia, Prescott, Hope, Fulton (crossing Red River at Fulton), to Texarkana.

93. Sedalia Trail—Nueces River to vicinity of Bastrop, Cameron, Dallas, crossing at Colbert's Ferry, to Ft. Gibson, Okla., Neosho, Mo., to Sedalia and on to Quincy, Ill.

94. Stage Line from Monroe, La. to Shreveport, San Antonio, on to El Paso.

95. St Antonio-El Paso Trail—followed Chihuahua Trail to Leon Springs to Ft. Davis, to Ft. Hancock, to El Paso.

96. Scioto Trail—Warrior's Path.

97. Tennessee, Ohio, and Great Lakes Trail—Chattanooga, Maysville, Ky., joins the Ft. Miami Trail.

98. Trammill's Trace—early trail from Texarkana, taking wide arc to south of Jefferson, east of Marshall, south to Redland, Nacogdoches, to Galveston (traded with Jean Lafitte).

99. Unicoi Turnpike—Black Fox Trail to Augusta to Cherokee Trail.

100. Tombigbee and Arkansas River Trail—Macon, Georgia, Birmingham to Greenville, Miss., crossing the Mississippi to the Arkansas River.

101. Vincennes and Indianapolis Road.

102. Warrior's Path of Kentucky—led from the Carolinas and Georgia, through Cumberland Gap to Chillicothe, Ohio, on to Lake Erie at Toledo. (part of this Trail is often called Wilderness Road, which began at Block House, Virginia, crossed the Powell Mountains, climbed Cumberland Gap to the Plateau of Central Kentucky).

103. Wilmington, Highpoint and Northern Trail—Wilmington, S.C. to Salisbury, N.C. to Great Indian Warpath.

104. Western Trail—Nueces River, San Antonio, almost due north to northwesternly course to Dodge City, Kansas.

105. Wilderness Road—Richmond, Virginia to Louisville.

The United States Department of the Interior, Geological Survey, Provides sets of topographic maps to a substantial number of cooperating repositories throughout the United States and Canada. These maps are, in general, for the use of the public.

The maps, especially the 7½ minute series, are invaluable to genealogists who are searching for the particular location where their ancestors lived, or for searching for the location of the cemetery where they might be buried.

Free indexes and price lists by individual states may be obtained by writing to: (East of Mississippi River) Branch of Distribution, U.S. Geological Survey, 1200 East Eads St., Arlington, VA 22202. (West of Mississippi) Branch of Distribution, U.S. Geological Survey, Box 25286 Federal Center, Denver, CO 80225.

ALASKA

University of Alaska
Elmer E. Rasmuson Library
310 Tanana Drive
Fairbanks, AK 99701

Ketchikan Public Library
629 Dock Street
Ketchikan, AK 99901

Matanuska-Susitna Comm. Coll.
University of Alaska
P.O. Box 899
Palmer, AK 99645

ALABAMA

Special Collections Dept.
Ralph Brown Draugh Library
Auburn University
Auburn, AL 36830

Dept. of Geography-Geology
Jacksonville State Univ.
Jacksonville, AL 36265

University of Alabama
Dept. of Anthropology
P.O. Box 6135
University, AL 35486

ARKANSAS

Arkansas College
Batesville, AR 72501

Univ. of Central Arkansas
Geography Department
Old Main, Room M-36
Conway, AR 72032

Mullins Library
Reference Department
University of Arkansas
Fayetteville, AR 72701

Magale Library
Southern State College
Southern Arkansas Univ.
Magnolia, AR 71753

Dean B. Ellis Library
Arkansas Room
P.O. Box 2040
State University, AR 72467

ARIZONA

Library, Govt. Documents
Northern Arizona University
P.O. Box 6022
Flagstaff, AZ 86011

Library & Archives
3rd Floor Capitol
Phoenix, AZ 85007

Director of Learning Res.
Yavipai College
Prescott, AZ 86301

Map Service
University Library
Arizona State University
Tempe, AZ 85281

University of Arizona
University Library
Map Collection
Tucson, AZ 85721

CALIFORNIA

Reference Libraries
Alameda Free Library
1433 Oak St.
Alameda, CA 94501

Dept. of Geography Library
Cabrillo College
6500 Soquel Drive
Aptos, CA 95003

Documents Dept. Library
Humboldt State University
Arcata, CA 9521

Map Room
General Library
Univ. of California
Berkeley, CA 94720

Map Dept.
University Library
Calif. State Univer-Chico
Chico, CA 95929

Government Publications
Honnold Library
Claremont College
Claremont, CA 91711

Librarian
West Hills College
300 Cherry Lane
Coalinga, CA 93210

Map Librarian
Cupertino Library
10400 Torre Ave.
Cupertino, CA 95014

Map Collection
University Library
Univ. of California-Davis
Davis, CA 95616

Map Librarian
Henry Madden Library
Calif. State Univ-Fresno
Fresno, CA 93740

William T. Boyce Library
Fullerton College
321 E. Chapman Ave.
Fullerton, CA 92634

Reference Dept.
Calif. State Univ. Library
2580 Hillary St.
Hayward, CA 94541

Map Collection Library
University of Calif-Irvine
Irvine, CA 92664

Map Section, C-075
Central University Library
Univ. of Calif. San Diego
La Jolla, CA 92093

Library
West Hills College
457 "C" St.
Lemoore, CA 93245

Documents Librarian
Long Beach Public Library
101 Pacific Avenue
Long Beach, CA 90802

Calif. State Univer-Los Angeles
Dept. Geog. & Urban Studies
5151 State University Dr.
Los Angeles, CA 90032

Los Angeles Public Library
Acquisitions/Serials
361 S. Anderson St.
Los Angeles, CA 90033

UCLA Geology-Geophysics Lib.
4697 Geology Bldg.
405 Hilgard Rd.
Los Angeles, CA 90024

UCLA Map Library
University of California
Los Angeles, CA 90024

Geog. Map Library
Dept. of Geography
California State University
Northridge, CA 91330

History & Literature Dept.
Oakland Public Library
125 - 14th St.
Oakland, CA 94612

Merritt College Library
12500 Campus Drive
Oakland, CA 94619

Palm Springs Public Library
300 S. Sunrise Way
Palm Springs, CA 92262

Palo Alto City Library
1213 Newell Road
Palo Alto, CA 94303

Geology Library
California Institute of Tech.
Pasadena, CA 91125

Documents Librarian
Pasadena Public Library
285 E. Walnut St.
Pasadena, CA 91101

Documents Librarian
Conta Costa County Library
1750 Oak Park Blvd.
Pleasant Hill, CA 94523

Library
Diablo Valley College
Pleasant Hill, CA 94523

Library Serials Unit

California State Poly. Univ.
3801 W. Temple Ave.
Pomona, CA 91768

Pomona Public Library
TSD — Documents
625 S. Garer Ave.
Pomona, CA 91766

Irvine Map Library
Armacost Library
University of Redlands
Redlands, CA 92373

Documents Librarian
Richmond Public Library
Richmond, CA 94804

L. A. County Public Library
Special Materials Unit
8800 Valley Blvd.
Rosemead, CA 91770

Map Section, General Library
University of California
P.O. Box 5900
Riverside, CA 92507

Government Publications
California State Library
P.O. Box 2037
Sacramento, CA 95809

Library, Soc. Sci. Ref. Dept.
California State Univ.
2000 Jed Smith Drive
Sacramento, CA 95819

Map Collection
University Library
San Diego State University
San Diego, CA 92182

San Diego Public Library
Science & Industry Section
820 "E" St.
San Diego, CA 92101

Library
Calif. Academy of Science
Golden Gate Park
San Francisco, CA 94118

Mechanics Institute Library
57 Post St.
San Francisco, CA 94104

J. D. Randall, Jr. Museum
199 Museum Way
San Francisco, CA 94114

Documents Dept.
San Francisco State Univ.
Civic Center
San Francisco, CA 94102

Geography Dept.-Map Library
San Francisco State Univ.
1600 Holloway Ave.
San Francisco, CA 94132

Documents & Maps Dept.
Calif. Polytechnic State
University Library
San Luis obispo, CA 93407

Library
Contra Costa College
2600 Mission Bell Dr.
San Pablo, CA 94806

Map & Imagery Laboratory
Library
University of California
Santa Barbara, CA 93106

Santa Clara Public Library
2635 Homestead Road
Santa Clara, CA 95051

Orradre Library
Documents Dept.
University of Santa Clara
Santa Clara, CA 95053

Map Collection
University Library
University of California
Santa Cruz, CA 95064

Government Documents Dept.
Federal Division
Stanford Univ. Libraries
Stanford, CA 94305

Sunnyvale Public Library
665 W. Olive Ave.
Sunnyvale, CA 94086

Goleman Library
San Joaquin Delta College
5151 Pacific Ave.
Stockton, CA 95207

Stockton Public Library
605 N. El Dorado
Stockton, CA 95202

JFK Library
Ref. Dept.
505 Santa Clara St.
Vallejo, CA 94590

COLORADO

Map Library
University of Colorado
Boulder, CO 80309

Tutt Library
Colorado College
Colorado Springs, CO 80903

Learning Resources Center
Pikes Peak Community College
5675 S. Academy Blvd.
Colorado Springs, CO 80906

Map Colletion — Library
Univ. of Colo.-Colo. Springs
Colorado Springs, CO 80907

Documents Div.
Denver Public Library
1357 Broadway
Denver, CO 80203

Library
Fort Lewis College
Durange, CO 81301

The Libraries
Colorado State University
Fort Collins, CO 80523

Map Room
Arthur Lakes Library
Colorado School of Mines
Golden, CO 80401

Technical Library
Bendix-Grand Junc. Operations
P.O. Box 1569
Grand Junction, CO 81501

Map Service
James A. Michener Library
Univ. of Northern Colorado
Greeley, CO 80609

Dov. Nat. Sc. & Mathematics
Geology Dept.
Western State College of CO
Gunnison, CO 81230

Library
Southern Colo. State College
Pueblo, CO 81001

CONNECTICUT

Tech. & Business Dept.
Bridgeport Public Library
925 Broad St.
Bridgeport, CT 06603

Arch. Hist. & Gen.
Connecticut State Library
231 Capital Ave.
Hartford, CT 06115

Ref. & Gen. Reading Dept.
Hartford Public Library
500 Main St.
Hartford, CT 06103

Dept. of Earth & Env. Science
Wesleyan University
Middleton, CT 06457

Free Public Library
133 Elm St.
New Haven, CT 06510

Reference Map Librarian
So. Conn. State College
501 Crescent St.
New Haven, CT 86515

Geology Library
Yale University
210 Whitney Ave. P.O. Box 6666
New Haven, CT 06511

The Ferguson Library
Stamford Public Library
96 Broad St.
Stamford, CT 06901

Map Room
Univ. of Conn. Library
Storrs, CT 06268

DISTRICT OF COLUMBIA

The Public Library
Documents Desk
901 "G" St., NW
Washington, DC 20001

Cartographic Dept.
National Geographic Society
17th & "M" Sts., NW
Washington, DC 20036

Map Library
Metro Wash. Council of Govts.
1875 Eye St., Suite 200
Washington, DC 20036

Library, Serials Dept.
George Washington University
Washington, DC 20052

Geography and Map Div.
Library of Congress
Washington, DC 20540

DELAWARE

Reference Dept.
Newark Free Library
750 E. Delaware Ave.
Newark, DE 19711

Government Documents
Morris Library
University of Delaware
Newark, DE 19711

Wilmington Inst. Free Library
& New Castle County Free Lib.
Wilmington, DE 19801

FLORIDA

Library, Documents Div.
Florida Atlantic Univ.
Boca Raton, FL 33432

Documents Librarian
Dupon - Ball Library
Stetson University
Deland, FL 32720

Map Library
Univ. of Florida Libraries
Gainsville, FL 32611

Reference-Maps Dept.
University of North Florida
Box 17605
Jacksonville, FL 32216

Special Collection Dept.

FL Internat'l Univ. Library
Tamiami Trail, at 252
Miami, FL 33199

Florida Collection
Miami-Dade Public Library
One Biscayne Blvd.
Miami, FL 33132

Business-Sci-Tech-Dept.
Orlando Public Library
10 North Rosalind
Orlando, FL 32801

Maps Librarian
John C. Pace Library
Univ. of West Florida
Pensacola, FL 32504

Library
Seminole Junior College
Sanford, FL 32771

Maps Division
R. M. Strozier Library
Florida State University
Tallahassee, FL 32306

Govt. Documents Dept.
Library
Univ. of South Florida
Tampa, FL 33620

Mills Memorial Library
Rollins College
Winter Park, FL 32789

GEORGIA

Dept. of Geology
Emory University
Atlanta, GA 30222

Gift & Exchange Dept.
Prince Gilber Mem. Library
GA Institute of Technology
Atlanta, GA 30332

Map Dept. W. R. Pullen Lib.
Georgia State University
104 Decatur St., SE
Atlanta, GA 30303

Map Room, Science Library
University of Georgia
Athens, GA 30602

Library
West Georgia College
Carrollton, GA 30118

Govt. Documents D120A
Simon Schwob Mem. Library
Columbus College
Columbus, GA 31907

The E. Louise Patten Library
Piedmont College
Demorest, GA 30535

Library
South Georgia College
Douglas, GA 31533

Library
Southern Technical Institute
534 Clay St.
Marietta, GA 30060

Library
Georgia Southern College
Statesboro, GA 30458

Library
Valdosta State College
Valdosta, GA 31698

HAWAII

Library, Govt. Documents Dept.
University of Hawaii at Hilo
P.O. Box 1357
Hilo, HI 96720

Map Collection
University of Hawaii Library
2550 The Mall
Honolulu, HI 96822

IOWA

Map Librarian
University Library
Iowa State University
Ames, IA 50010

Govt. Documents & Maps
Library
University of Northern Iowa
Cedar Falls, IA 50613

Public Library
Council Bluffs, IA 51501

Govt. Publications Dept.
Cowles Library
Drake University
Des Moines, IA 50311

State Library
Historical Building
Des Moines, IA 50319

Carnegie-Stout Public Library
Dubuque, IA 52001

Wahlert Memorial Library
Loras College
1450 Alta Vista
Dubuque, IA 52001

Library, Govt. Documents
Grinnel College
Grinnell, IA 50112

Geology Library
University of Iowa
136 Trowbridge
Iowa City, IA 52242

Ottumwa Public Library
125 N. Court St.
Ottumwa, IA 52501

IDAHO

Map Reference Dept.
Boise State Univ. Library
1910 College Blvd.
Boise, ID 83725

Documents Library
University of Idaho
Moscow, ID 83843

Documents Division
Idaho State Univ. Library
Pocatello, ID 83209

Pocatello Public Library
Pocatello, ID 83201

Documents Dept.
Learning Resources Center
Ricks College
Rexburg, ID 83440

ILLINOIS

Public Library
Aurora, IL 60506

Map Room, Science Library
So. Illinois University
Carbondale, IL 62901

Booth Library
Eastern Illinois University
Charleston, IL 61920

Govt. Publications Dept.
Chicago Public Library
425 N. Michigan Ave.
Chicago, IL 60611

The John Crerar Library
35 W. 33rd St.
Chicago, IL 60616

Dept. of Geology Library
Field Museum of Natural Hist.
Roosevelt Rd. & Lake Shore Dr.
Chicago, IL 60605

Map Librarian
Loyola Univ. of Chicago
6525 N. Sheridan Rd.
Chicago, IL 60626

Map Librarian
University of Chicago
1100 E. 57th St.
Chicago, IL 60637

Library - Map Section
Univ. of Illinois-Chicago
P.O. Box 8198
Chicago, IL 60680

Map Library - Rm. 222
William Morris Davis Hall

Northern Illinois University
Dekalb, IL 60115

Map Dept., Lovejoy Library
Southern Illinois University
Edwardsville, IL 62025

Adult Services
Gail Borden Public Library
Elgin, IL 60121

Dept. of Geology
Principia College
Elsah, IL 62028

Map Curator
The University Library
Northwestern Univ.
Evanston, IL 60201

Dept. of Geology
Knox College
Galesburg, IL 61401

Benner Lib. & Res. Center
Olivet Nazarene College
P.O. Box 592
Kankakee, IL 60901

Map Library
Dept. of Geography
Western Illinois University
Macomb, IL 61455

Documents Library
Monmouth College
Monmouth, IL 61462

Milner Library, Map Room
Illinois State Univ.
Normal, IL 61761

Peoria Public Library
107 NE Monroe
Peoria, IL 61602

Loring Map Library
Augustana College
639 - 38th St.
Rock Island, IL 61201

Documents Unit
Illinois State Library
Centennial Bldg.
Springfield, IL 62756

Map & Geography Library
418 Univ. Lib., Univ. of Ill.
1408 West Gregory Dr.
Urbana, IL 61801

INDIANA

Geography & Map Library
Indiana University
Kirkwood Hall 307
Bloomington, IN 47405

Allen County Public Library
900 Webster St.
P.O. Box 2270

Fort Wayne, IN 46801

Walter E. Helmke Library
In. Univ.-Purdue University
Fort Wayne, IN 46805

Library
Indiana University
The NW Campus,
3400 Broadway
Gary, IN 46408

Library - Documents Dept.
De Pauw University
Box 137
Greencastle, IN 46135

Hanover College
Geology Dept.
Map Library
Hanover, IN 47243

Indiana State Library
Serials Section
140 N. Senate Ave.
Indianapolis, IN 46204

University Library at Iupui
Attn: Serials
815 West Michigan St.
Indianapolis, IN 46202

Map Collection
Dept. of Library Service
Ball State University
Muncie, IN 47306

Indiana University
Southeast Library
4201 Grant Line Rd., Box 679
IVS Library/Reference
New Albany, IN 47150

Microtext Reading Room
Memorial Library
University of Notre Dame
Notre Dame, IN 46556

Library
St. Joseph's College
Rensselaer, IN 47978

Map Library
Wildman Science Library
Box E-72 Earlham College
Richmond, IN 47374

Geology-Geography Dept.
Indiana State University
Terre Haute, IN 47809

Mollering Library
Map Room
Valparaiso University
Valparaiso, IN 46383

Map Collection
Prudue Univ. Libraries
Stewart Center
W. Lafayette, IN 47907

KANSAS

Document Librarian
The University of Kansas
Spencer Research Library
Lawrence, KS 66045

Hutchinson Public Library
901 N. Main St.
Hutchinson, KS 67501

Library
Documents Division
Kansas State University
Manhattan, KS 66506

State Libraries of Kansas
3rd Floor; State House Bldg.
Topeka, KS 66612

Wichita Public Library
223 South Main
Wichita, KS 67202

KENTUCKY

Dept. of Geology & Geography
Berea College
C.P.O. 1105
Berea, KY 40403

Library
North Kentucky University
Highland Heights, KY 41076

Geology Library
100 Bowman Hall
University of Kentucky
Lexington, KY 40506

Library, Ref. Dept.
Belknap Campus
University of Louisville
Louisville, KY 40208

LOUISIANA

Map Rm., School of Geoscience
Louisiana State University
Univ. Stat., 313 Geol. Bldg.
Baton Rouge, LA 70803

Federal Documents
Earl K. Long Library
University of New Orleans
New Orleans, LA 70122

New Orleans Public Library
Business and Science Div.
New Orleans, LA 70140

Toulane University
Documents Dept.
Howard-Tilton Mem. Library
New Orleans, LA 70118

Prescott Memorial Library
Louisiana Tech. University
Ruston, LA 71212

Louisana State University
8515 Youree St.
Shreveport, LA 71115

Magale Library
Centenary College
Shreveport, LA 71104

MASSACHUSETTS

Amherst College Library
Amherst, MA 01002

Serials Dept.
Univ. of Mass. Library
Amherst, MA 01002

Babson College
Curator, Map & Globe
Babson Park, MA 02157

Boston Athenaeum
10½ Beacon St.
Boston, MA 02108

Boston Public Library
Map Section
Boston, MA 02117

Documents Division
Joseph P. Healey Library
Univ. of Massachusetts-Boston
Boston, MA 02125

Massachusetts State Library
442 State House
Boston, MA 02133

Library
Bridgewater State College
Bridgewater, MA 02324

Library
Mass. Maritime Academy
Div. of State Colleges
Buzzards Bay, MA 02532

Map Room
Harvard University Library
Cambridge, MA 02138

MIT Libraries
Serial Journal Room 14 E-210
Mass. Institute of Technology
Cambridge, MA 02139

Haverhill Public Library
99 Mian St.
Haverhill, MA 01830

Lowell City Library
401 Merrimack Street
Lowell, MA 01852

University of Lowell
Reference Dept.
O'Leary Library South Campus
Lowell, MA 01854

Tufts University
Geology Dept., Lane Hall
Medford, MA 02155

Free Public Library
Box C-902
New Bedford, MA 02740

Forbes Library
20 West St.
Northampton, MA 01063

Smith College
Dept. of Geology
Clark Science Center
Northampton, MA 01063

Map Curator - The Library
Salem State College
Salem, MA 01970

Dept. of Geology
Mt. Holyoke College
South Hadley, MA 01075

Documents Section
City Library
220 State St.
Springfield, MA 01103

Dept. of Geology
Wellesley College
Wellesley, MA 02181

Dept. of Geology
Williams College
Williamstown, MA 01267

Woods Hole Oceanographic Inst.
Data Library McLean Lab.
Quisset Campus
Wood Hole, MA 02543

Map Curator
Graduate School of Geography
Clark University
Worcester, MA 01610

Free Public Library
Technology Div.
Worcester, MA 01608

MARYLAND

John Hopkins University
Milton E. Eisenhower Library
Map Room (Attn: Mrs. Sack)
Baltimore, MD 21218

Maryland Historical Society
201 W. Monument St.
Prints & Photographs Dept.
Baltimore, MD 21201

Documents Librarian
Enoch Pratt Free Library
400 Cathedral St.
Baltimore, MD 21201

Library
Univ. of Maryland
5401 Wilkins Ave.
Baltimore, MD 21228

Documents Map Room

McKeldin Library
University of Maryland
College Park, MD 20742

Jerome Franpton Library
Frostburg State College
Frostburg, MD 21533

Blackwell Library
Salisbury State College
Salisbury, MD 21801

MAINE

Maine State Library
Cultural Bldg.
Station #64
Augusta, ME 04333

Periodical Dept.
Bangor Public Library
145 Harlow St.
Bangor, ME 04401

Library
Bowdoin College
Brunswick, ME 04011

Dept. of Geology
University of Maine
Preble Hall
Farmington, ME 04938

Dept. of Geography
University of Maine
Ft. Kent, ME 04743

University Librarian
College Avenue
University of Maine
Gorham, ME 04038

Library
Bates College
Lewiston, ME 04240

Tri-State Reg'l Doc. Depos.
Raymond H. Fogler Library
University of Maine
Orono, ME 04473

Public Library
Portland, ME 04101

Colby College
Dept. of Geology
Waterville, ME 04901

MICHIGAN

Stockwell Memorial Library
Albion College
602 East Cass St.
Albion, MI 49224

Library
Grand Valley State College
College Landing
Allendale, MI 49401

Monteith Library

Alma College
Alma, MI 48801

Map Room
825 Harlan Hatcher Grad. Lib.
University of Michigan
Ann Arbor, MI 48109

Map Dept.
James White Library
Andrews University
Berrian Springs, MI 49104

History & Travel Dept.
Detroit Public Library
5201 Woodward Ave.
Detroit, MI 48202

Map Librarian
Wayne State University
G. Flint Purdy Library
Detroit, MI 48202

Library
Documents Dept.
Michigan State University
East Lansing, MI 48859

Grand Rapids Public Library
Michigan Room
60 Library Plaza NE
Grand Rapids, MI 48859

Michigan Technological Univ.
Library; Map Librarian
Houghton, MI 49931

Western Michigan University
Waldo Library
Map Library
Kalamazoo, MI 49008

Documents & Map Dept.
Olson Library
Northern Michigan University
Marquette, MI 49855

Library - Documents Dept.
Central Michigan University
Mt. Pleasant, MI 48859

Eastern Michigan University
University Library
Map Library
Ypsilanti, MI 48197

MINNESOTA

Bemidji State College
Dept. of Geography
Bemidji, MN 56601

Documents Librarian
Duluth Public Library
520 W. Superior St.
Duluth, MN 55802

Map Library
Dept. of Geography
University of Minnesota

Duluth, MN 55812

Map Library
S. 76 Wilson Library
University of Minnesota
Minneapolis, MN 55455

Memorial Library
Mankato State College
Box 19
Mankato, MN 56001

Geology Map Library
Geology Dept.
Carleton College
Northfield, MN 55057

Map Section
Learning Resources Services
St. Cloud State University
St. Cloud, MN 56301

James Jerome Hill Ref. Libr.
4th & Market Sts.
St. Paul, MN 55102

Map Library
Minnesota Historical Society
690 Cedar St.
St. Paul, MN 55101

Dept. of Geography
Gustavus Adolphus College
St. Peter, MN 56082

MISSOURI

Depository Librarian
S.E. Missouri State Univ.
Cape Girardeau, MO 63701

Geology Library
201 Geology Bldg.
University of Missouri
Colubmia, MO 65201

Kansas City Public Library
Librarian - Documents Div.
311 East 12th St.
Kansas City, MO 64106

Linda Hall Library
Documents Div.
5109 Cherry St.
Kansas City, MO 64110

Dept. of Geology
Univ. of Missouri - Rolla
Rolla, MO 65401

Documents Librarian
SW Missouri State University
901 S. National Ave.
Springfield, MO 65802

Mercantile Library
Box 633
St. Louis, MO 63188

St. Louis Public Library
1301 Olive St.

St. Louis, MO 63103

St. Louis University
Pius XII Memorial Library
3655 W. Pine, Serial Dept.
St. Louis, MO 63108

Earth & Planetary Science Lib.
Washington University
St. Louis, MO 63130

MISSISSIPPI

Dept. of Geology
University of Southern Miss.
Southern Station, Box 5051
Hattisburg, MS 39406

Acquisitions Dept.
Mitchell Memorial Library
Mississippi State University
State College, MS 39762

The Library
Documents Dept.
University of Mississippi
University, MS 38677

MONTANA

Librarian/Documents
Eastern Montana College
Billings, MT 59101

Documents Librarian
Montana State University
Library
Bozeman, MT 59717

Library - Documents Div.
Montana College of Mineral
 Science & Technology,
Pork St.
Butte, MT 59701

Library
Montana Historical Society
225 N. Roberts St.
Helena, MT 59601

Lewistown Carnegie
Public Library
701 West Main
Lewistown, MT 59457

Mansfield Library
Documents Div.
Univ. of Montana
Missoula, MT 59812

NORTH CAROLINA

Serials & Documents Librarian
Gardner-Webb College Library
P.O. Box 836
Boiling Springs, NC 28017

Map Library
Geography Dept.
Appalachian State University
Boone, NC 28607

Map Division
Carrie Rich Memorial Library
Campbell College
Buies Creek, NC 27506

John N. Couch Library
Dept. of Botany
Univ. of North Carolina
Chapel Hill, NC 27514

Geology Library
Mitchell Hall 029A
Univ. of North Carolina
Chapel Hill, NC 27514

Univ. of North Carolina
Library, Documents Section
Univ. of NC at Charlotte
Charlotte, NC 28223

Reference Librarian
Western Carolina University
Library
Cullowhee, NC 28723

Documents Librarian
Duke University Library
Durham, NC 27706

Map Librarian
Jackson Library
UNC at Greensboro
Greensboro, NC 27412

Dept. of Geography
East Carolina University
Greenville, NC 27834

Documents Librarian
The D. H. Hill Library
North Carolina State Library
Raleigh, NC 27650

North Carolina State Museum
Box 27647
Raleigh, NC 27611

Library
Catawba College
Salisbury, NC 28144

Director of Learning Resourc.
Mitchell Community College
Statesville, NC 28677

Documents Librarian
Univ. of NC - Wilmington
Wilmington, NC 28406

Wake Forest Univ. Library
Z. Smith Reynolds Library
Box 7777, Reynolds Sta.
Winston-Salem, NC 27109

NORTH DAKOTA

Map Collection
Library
N. D. State Univ.
Fargo, ND 58102

Geology Library
326 Leonard Hall
Univ. of North Dakota
Grand Forks, ND 58202

Division of Science
Minot State College
Minot, ND 58701

NEBRASKA

Library
Midland College
Fremont, NE 68025

Univ. of Nebraska Libraries
Acquisition Dept.
Serials Section
Lincoln, NE 68588

Documents Librarian
W. Dale Clark Library
215 S. 15th St.
Omaha, NE 68102

Univ. Library; Documents D347
Univ. of Nebraska at Omaha
60th & Dodge St.
Omaha, NE 68182

NEW HAMPSHIRE

State Library
Concord, NH 03301

Library - Map Room
University of New Hampshire
Durham, NH 03824

Baker Library - Map Room
Dartmouth College
Hanover, NH 03755

Librarian
New England College
Henniker, NH 03242

Dept. of Geography
Map Repository
Keene State College
Keene, NH 03431

Reference Librarian
Geisel Library
Saint Anselm's College
Manchestger, NH 03102

Nashua Public Library
2 Court St.
Nashua, NH 03060

NEW JERSEY

Public Library, Govt. Doc. Div.
Science & Tech. Dept.
11 S. Broad St.
Elizabeth, NJ 07202

Free Public Library
Documents Div.
472 Jersey Ave.

Jersey City, NJ 07302

Burlington County Library
Mt. Holly, NJ 08060

U.S. Documents Div.
Newark Public Library
5 Washington St.
Newark, NJ 07102

Reference Dept. Dana Library
Rutgers University
185 University Ave.
Newark, NJ 07102

Government Publications
Rutgers University
Lib. of Sci. & Med.
P.O. Box 1029
Piscataway, NJ 08854

Plainfield Public Library
8th St. at Park Ave.
Plainfield, NJ 07060

Documents Dept.
Library
Stockton State College
Pomona, NJ 08240

Documents Division
Firestone Library
Princeton University
Princeton, NJ 08540

Map Curator
Monmouth County Library
State Highway No. 35
Shrewsbury, NJ 07701

Delaware River Basin Comm.
Library
P.O. Box 7360
Trenton, NJ 08628

Documents Librarian
New Jersey State Library
185 West State St.
Trenton, NJ 08625

NEW MEXICO

Map Coordinator
University of New Mexico
Library
Albuquerque, NM 87131

Map Collection, Spec. Coll.
New Mexico State Univ. Libr.
Box 3475
La Cruces, NM 88003

Donnelly Library
New Mexico Highlands Univ.
Las Vegas, NM 87701

New Mexico State Library
P.O. Box 1629
Santa Fe, NM 87503

Lab. of Anthropology Library
Museum of New Mexico
P.O. Box 2087
Santa Fe, NM 87503

NEVADA

Nevada State Library
Documents Desk
401 N. Carson St.
Carson City, NV 89701

Mines Library
Getchnell Library
Univ. of Nevada - Reno
Reno, NV 89557

Documents Librarian
Univ. of Nevada, Las Vegas
4505 Maryland Parkway
Las Vegas, NV 89154

NEW YORK

New York State Library
Govt. Documents Unit, GEC
Empire State Plaza
Albany, NY 12230

State Univ. of NY Albany
Univ. Library, Gov. Pubs. Dept.
1400 Washington Ave.
Albany, NY 12222

New York State Museum &
 Science Service Library
State Education Bldg. Annex
Albany, NY 12234

Herrick Memorial Library
Alfred University
Alfred, NY 14802

Science Library
Harpur College of State Univ.
 of New York
Binghamton, NY 13901

Map Librarian
Drake Memorial Library
State Univ. of NY - Brockport
Brockport, NY 14420

Brooklyn College
Dept. of Geology
Bedford Ave. & Ave. H
Brooklyn, NY 11210

Brooklyn Public Library
History Div.
Grand Army Plaza
Brooklyn, NY 11238

Librarian, Ref. Dept.
Pratt Institute Library
200 Willoughby Ave.
Brooklyn, NY 11205

Buffalo & Erie County Public
 Library, Doc. Div.

Lafayette Square
Buffalo, NY 14203

State Univ. of NY at Buffalo
University Libraries
Buffalo, NY 14260

Dept. of Geology
Hamilton College
Clinton, NY 13323

Dept. Earth & Envir. Sciences
Queens College
Flushing, NY 11367

State University College
Documents Librarian
Milne Library
Geneseo, NY 14454

Library
Hobart & Wm. Smith Colleges
Geneva, NY 14456

Documents Librarian
Fofstra Univ.
Hempstead L.I., NY 11550

Map Librarian
Cornell University Library
Ithaca, NY 14853

Acqusitions Librarian
York Coll., City Univ. of NY
150 14 Jamaica Ave.
Jamaica, NY 11432

Geology Map Depository
Sojourner Truth Library
State Univ. College
New Paltz, NY 12561

Library - Serials Unit
Amer. Museum of Nat. History
Central Park West at 79th St.
New York, NY 10024

Dept. of Earth & Plane. Sci.
College of the City of N.Y.
Convent Ave. & 138th St.
New York, NY 10031

Columbia University Map Rm.
Herbert Lehman Library
420 W. 118th St.
New York, NY 10027

Governments Documents Div.
Hunter College Library
695 Park Ave.
New York, NY 10021

NY Public Library - Div. MP
Grand Central Station
P.O. Box 2238
New York, NY 10017

School of Visual Arts
Attn: Lowell Bodger
209 E. 23rd St.
New York, NY 10010

Documents Librarian
Feinberg Library
State Univ. College
Plattsburgh, NY 12901

State University College
Crumb Library
Potsdam, NY 13676

Library
Vassar College
Poughkeepsie, NY 12601

Univ. of Rochester Map Center
Rush Rhees Library
University of Rochester
Rochester, NY 14627

Main Library
Documents Section
State Univ. of NY-Stony Brook
Stony Brook, NY 11794

Schaffer Library
Union College
Schenectady, NY 12308

Bird Library
Geography, Area Studies
Syracuse University
Syracuse, NY 13210

Library, Serials Dept.
Rensselaer Polytechnic Inst.
Troy, NY 12181

Utica Public Library
303 Genesee St.
Utica, NY 13501

OHIO

Akron Public Library
55 S. Main St.
Akron, OH 44326

Nelsonville Public Library
Athens Branch
65 North Court St.
Athens, OH 45701

Map Librarian
Ohio University
Athens, OH 45701

Map Library
BGSU Libraries
Bowling Green, OH 43403

Map Library
The Public Library
8th & Vine Sts.
Cincinnati, OH 45202

University of Cincinnati
Geology/Geography Library
103 Old Tech Bldg.
Cincinnati, OH 45221

Sears Library, Geology Coll.
10900 Euclid Ave.

Case Western Reserve Univ.
Cleveland, OH 44106

Map Collection
Cleveland Public Library
325 Superior Ave.
Cleveland, OH 44114

Cleveland State University
Library, Map Collection
1860 East 22nd St.
Cleveland, OH 44115

Ohio State Univ. Libraries
Serial Division
1858 Neil Ave.
Columbus, OH 43210

Columbus & Ohio Division
Public Library
28 South Hamilton Road
Columbus, OH 43213

State Library of Ohio
Documents Section
65 So. Front St.
Columbus, OH 43215

Dayton Museum of Natl. Hist.
2629 Ridge Ave.
Dayton, OH 45414

Dayton Public Library
215 E. 3rd St.
Dayton, OH 45402

Reference Dept.
Wright State University
Dayton, OH 45431

Library
Acquisitions Dept.
Ohio Wesleyan University
Delaware, OH 43015

Chalmers Memorial Library
Kenyon College
Gambier, OH 43022

Wm. Howard Doane Library
Geology Map Div.
Denison University
Granville, OH 43023

Map Library
406 McGilvrey Hall
Kent State University
Kent, OH 44242

Office of Librarian
Marietta College
Marietta, OH 45750

Science Library
Miami University
Oxford, OH 45056

Warder Memorial Library
Reference Dept.
137 E. High St.
Springfield, OH 45501

Dept. of Geology
Wittenberg University
Springfield, OH 45501

Toledo Public Library
Science & Technology Dept.
325 Michigan St.
Toledo, OH 43624

University of Toledo Library
Gov't Documents Div.
Toledo, OH 43606

Dept. of Earth Sciences
Antioxh College
Yellow Springs, OH 45387

The Public Library
of Youngstown & Mahoning Co.
Science & Industry Div.
Youngstown, OH 44503

OKLAHOMA

Map Dept.
Central State University
Edmond, OK 73034

Museum of The Great Plains
P.O. Box 68
Lawton, OK 73502

Geology Library
Univ. of Oklahoma
830 Van Vleet Oval Rm. 103
Norman, OK 73019

Metropolital Library System
Documents Dept.
131 N.W. Third
Oklahoma City, OK 73102

Oklahoma Historical Society
Historical Bldg.
Oklahoma City, OK 73105

Map Collection
Edmond Low Library
Oklahoma State Univ.
Stillwater, OK 74074

Tulsa City-County Library
Business & Technology Dept.
400 Civic Center
Tulsa, OK 74103

OREGON

Library
So. Oregon State College
Ashland, OR 97520

Library
Central Oregon Comm. Coll.
College Way
Bend, OR 97701

Oregon State University
Library, Documents Div.
Corvallis, OR 97331

University of Oregon Library
Map Room
165 Con Con Hall
Eugene, OR 97403

Librarian
Oregon Inst. of Technology
Oretech Branch P.O.
Klamath Falls, OR 97601

Reference Librarian
Walter M. Pierce Library
Eastern Oregon College
LaGrande, OR 97850

Dept. of Social Science
Western Oregon State College
Monmouth, OR 97361

Portland State University
Library-Serial Documents Div.
P.O. Box 1151
Portland, OR 97207

Oregon State Library
Documents Section
State Library Bldg.
Salem, OR 97310

PENNSYLVANIA

Linderman Library No. 30
Lehigh University
Bethlehem, PA 18015

Library
Moravian College
Bethlehem, PA 18018

Geology Dept. Library
Bryn Mawr College
Bryn Mawr, PA 19010

Library
Dickinson College
Carlisle, PA 17013

Geography Dept., Map Library
Clarion State College
Clarion, PA 16214

Lafayette College
Skillman Library
Acquisitions Dept.
Easton, PA 18042

ESSC Library
Documents Dept.
East Stroudsburg, State Coll.
East Stroudsburg, PA 18301

Edinboro State College
Dept. of Earth Sciences
Edinboro, PA 16412

Map Collection Gen. Library
State Library of Penn.
Box 1601
Harrisburg, PA 17105

Library
Juniata College
Huntingdon, PA 16652

Reference Dept.
Indiana University of PA
Rhodes R. Stabley Library
Indiana, PA 15701

Cambria County Library
248 Main St.
Johnstown, PA 15901

Map Librarian
Kutztown State College
Rohrbach Library
Kutztown, PA 19530

Bucknell University
Ellen Clarke Bertrand Lib.
Lewisburg, PA 17837

Geoscience Dept.
Lock Haven State College
Lock Haven, PA 17745

Allegheny College
Dept. of Geology
Meadville, PA 16335

Map Collection
Dept. of Geography
Millersville State College
Millersville, PA 17551

Reference Librarian
New Castle Public Library
106 East North St.
New Castle, PA 16101

Map Collection
Free Library of Philadelphia
Logan Square
Philadelphia, PA 19103

LaSalle College
Dept. of Geology
Philadelphia, PA 19141

Temple University Library
Documents Room
Philadelphia, PA 19122

Geology Map Library
Hayden Hall
University of Pennsylvania
Philadelphia, PA 19104

Government Documents Section
Carnegie Libr. of Pittsburg
4400 Forbes Ave.
Pittsburgh, PA 15213

University of Pittsburgh
Documents Ofc. G-8
Hillman Library
Pittsburgh, PA 15260

Northland Public Library
Attn: Carol W. Inglis

300 Cumberland Road
Pittsburgh, PA 15237

Public Library
Scranton, PA 18503

Shippensburg State College
Ezra Lehman Memorial Lib.
Shippensburg, PA 17257

Reference Dept.
Swarthmore College Library
Swarthmore, PA 19081

Map Librarian, Ref. Dept.
Pattee Library
Penn. State University
University Park, PA 16802

Warren Public Library
205 Market St.
P.O. Box 489
Warren, PA 16365

Francis Harvey Green Library
Documents & Maps Librarian
West Chester State College
West Chester, PA 19380

Reference Librarian
Osterhout Free Library
71 So. Franklin
Wilkes-Barre, PA 18701

RHODE ISLAND

Brown University Library
Documents Division
Providence, RI 02912

Reference Dept.
Providence Public Library
150 Empire St.
Providence, RI 02903

SOUTH CAROLINA

Daniel Library
The Citadel
Serials & Documents
Charleston, SC 29409

Map Library
University of South Carolina
Columbia, SC 29208

Geology Dept.
Furman University
Greenville, SC 29613

SOUTH DAKOTA

Documents Dept.
H. M. Briggs Library
South Dakota State Univ.
Brookings, SD 57007

S. Dak. School of Mines
& Tech.
Devereaux Library
Rapid City, SD 57701

Gifts & Exchange (Geology)
I. D. Weeks Library
Univ. of South Dakota
Vermillion, SD 57069

TENNESSEE

Felix G. Woodward Library
Austin Peay State Univ.
Clarksville, TN 37040

Documents Librarian
Jere Whitson Memorial Lib.
Tennessee Tech. University
Cookeville, TN 38501

Carson-Newman College
Map Library
Dept. of Geology
Jefferson City, TN 37760

Map Library
East Tenn. State Univ.
Johnson City, TN 37614

Map Library
Dept. of Geography
University of Tennessee
Knoxville, TN 37916

Physical Science Dept.
Univ. of Tennessee - Martin
Martin, TN 38237

Memphis Public Library &
Information Center, Doc. Sec.
1850 Peabody Ave.
Memphis, TN 38104

Engineering Library
Memphis State University
Memphis, TN 38152

Tennessee State Library
State Library Section
403 7th Ave., North
Nashville, TN 37219

Joint University Libraries
Science Library-Map Room
Nashville, TN 37203

TEXAS

Geology Dept.
Sul. Ross State University
Alpine, TX 79830

Dept. of Geology
Univ. of Texas-Arlington
Box 19049
Arlington, TX 76019

Central Serials Record
General Libraries
Univ. Texas at Austin
Austin, TX 78712

Map Library
Library

Texas A & M University
College Station, TX 77843

Dallas Public Library
Attn: Map Librarian
1515 Young St.
Dallas, TX 75201

Map Library
Southern Methodist University
Science/Engineering Library
Dallas, TX 75275

North Texas State University
Library
Documents Dept.
Denton, TX 76203

The Library Annex-Maps Sect.
Univ. of Texas at El Paso
El Paso, TX 79968

Fort Worth Public Library
300 Taylor St.
Fort Worth, TX 76102

Document Librarian
Rosenberg Library
2310 Sealy
Galveston, TX 77550

Houston Public Library
500 McKinney Ave.
Governmnet Documents Section
Houston, TX 77002

William Marsh Rice Univ.
Fondren Lib.-Gifts & Exch.
P.O. Box 1892
Houston, TX 77001

Univ. of Houston Libraries
Gifts and Exchange Section
4800 Calhoun Blvd.
Houston, TX 77004

Social Science Librarian
Sam Houston State Univ.
Huntsville, TX 77340

Library, Documents Dept.
Texas Tech. University
P.O. Box 4079
Lubbock, TX 79409

Midland Public Library
301 W. Missouri
P.O. Box 1191
Midland, TX 79702

Library-Documents Dept.
Stephen F. Austin State Univ.
Nacogdoches, TX 75961

Senior Reference Librarian
University of Texas-Dallas
P.O. Box 643
Richardson, TX 75080

Documents Librarian-Map Coll.

Trinity Univ. Library
715 Stadium Drive
San Antonio, TX 78284

Baylor University Library
Documents Dept.
Box 6307, B U Station
Waco, TX 76703

UTAH

Library
Southern Utah State College
Cedar City, UT 84720

Utah State Univ.-Merrill Lib.
Learning Resources Program
Documents UMC 30
Logan, UT 84322

Documents Dept.
Stewart Library 2901
Weber State College
Ogden, UT 84408

Documents & Map Section
Lee Library
Brigham Young University
Provo, UT 84602

Map Section
Salt Lake City Public Libr.
209 East 5th South
Salt Lake City, UT 84111

University of Utah
Government Documents Library
Salt Lake City, UT 84112

VIRGINIA

Map Librarian
Virginia Polytechnic Inst. &
  State Univ., Library
Blacksburg, VA 24061

Library
Bridgewater College
Bridgewater, VA 22812

Public Documents
Alderman Library
Univ. of Virginia
Charlottesville, VA 22901

Documents Librarian
Chesapeake Public Library
300 Cedar Rd.
Chesapeake, VA 23320

Geography Program
George Mason University
4400 University Drive
Fairfax, VA 22030

Librarian
Virginia Institute of Marine
  Science
Gloucester Point, VA 23062

Library

Hampden-Sidney College
Hampden Sidney, VA 23943

Madison Memorial Library
James Madison University
Harrisonburg, VA 22807

Dept. of Geology
Virginia Military Institute
Lexington, VA 24450

Geography & Geology Dept.
Christopher Newport College
Newport News, VA 23606

University Library
Documents Dept.
Old Dominion University
Norfolk VA 23508

Radford University
Dept. of Geography
Radford, VA 24142

Federal Documents Librarian
Virginia State Library
11th & Capitol Sts.
Richmond, VA 23219

Acquisitions Dept.
Earl Gregg Swem Library
College of William & Mary
Williamsburg, VA 23185

John Cook Wyllie Library
Clinch Valley College of the
  University of Virginia
Wise, VA 24293

VERMONT

Guy W. Bailey Library
Map Room
University of Vermont
Burlington, VT 05401

Middlebury College
Map Library Dept.-Geography
Warner Science Hall
Middlebury, VT 05753

Vermont Dept. of Libraries
Law & Document Unit
Montpelier, VT 05602

Gov't. Documents Librarian
Henry Prescott Chaplin Lib.
Norwich University
Northfield, VT 05663

WASHINGTON

Bellevue Public Library
11501 Main St.
Bellevue, WA 98004

Western Washington University
Map Library
Arntzen Hall 101
Bellingham, WA 98225

Library, Documents Section
Central Washington Univ.
Ellensburg, WA 98926

Documents Center
Washington State Library
Olympia, WA 98504

The Science & Engineering Lib.
Washington State University
Pullman, WA 99164

Documents Librarian
Seattle Public Library
1000 4th Ave.
Seattle, WA 98104

Map Section
Univ. of Wash. Libraries
FM-25
Seattle, WA 98195

Reference Dept.
Spokane Public Library
West 906 Main Ave.
Spokane, WA 99201

References Support Services
Robert A. L. Mortvedt Libr.
Pacific Lutheran University
Tacoma, WA 98447

Tacoma Public Library
Business & Technology Dept.
Tacoma, WA 98402

University of Puget Sound
Dept. of Geology
Tacoma, WA 98416

Document Librarian
Penrose Memorial Library
Whitman College
Walla Walla, WA 99362

WISCONSIN

Government Documents
Seeley G. Mudd Library
Lawrence University
Appleton, WI 54911

Reference Librarian
Beloit College Libraries
Beloit, WI 53511

Geography Dept., Map Library
Wisconsin State University
Eau Claire, WI 54701

Gov't Publications Dept.
Library Learning Center
Univ. of Wisc.-Green Bay
Green Bay, WI 54302

Library — Documents
Wisconsin State University
LaCrosse, WI 54601

Parkside Library
Univ. of Wisconsin-Parkside

Kenosha, WI 53141

Wisconsin State Historical Soc.
Manuscripts & Maps Section
816 State St.
Madison, WI 53706

Map Library, Science Hall
University of Wisconsin
550 N. Park St.
Madison, WI 53706

University of Wisconsin Center
Manitowoc County
705 Viebahn St.
Manitowoc, WI 54220

Milwaukee Public Library
Documents
814 W. Wisconsin Ave.
Milwaukee, WI 53233

AGS Collection of the Univ.
of Wisconsin-Milwaukee
Golda Meir Lib.
P.O. Box 399
Milwaukee, WI 53210

The Univ. of Wisc.-Milwaukee
Dept. of Geography
Map Library
Milwaukee, WI 53211

Dept. of Geology
Univ. of Wisc. — Oshkosh
Oshkosh, WI 54901

Karrmann Library
Gov't Publications
Univ. of Wisconsin-Platteville
Platteville, WI 53818

Dept. of Geography
University of Wisconsin
Stevens Point, WI 54481

WEST VIRGINIA

Learning Resource Center
Mesa Academy
Airport Rd.
Beckley, WV 25801

Library
W. Virginia State College
Institute, WV 25112

Library, Map Room
West Virginia University
Morgantown, WV 26506

WYOMING

Western History Librarian
Casper College
125 College Drive
Casper, WY 82601

Natrona County Public Library
307 East Second St.
Casper, WY 82601

Wyoming State Library
Supreme Ct. & State Libr. Bldg.
Cheyenne, WY 82001

Information Services Library
George Amos Memorial Library
412 South Gillette Ave.
Gillette, WY 82716

Documents Librarian
The Library
The Univ. of Wyoming
Laramie, WY 82071

Librarian
Central Wyoming College
Riverton, WY 82501

Librarian, Kooi Library
Sheridan College
Sheridan, WY 82801

CANADA

Alberta

Map & Air Photo Division
Univ. of Calgary Library
Calgary, Alberta
Canada T2N 1N4

University Map Collection
University of Alberta
Dept. of Geography, Edmonton
Alberta, Canada T6G 2H4

British Columbia

Simon Fraser Univ. Library
Acquisition Div. - Serials
Burnaby, British Columbia
Candad V5A 1S6

Library, Map Division
Univ. of British Columbia
1956 Main Mall
Vancouver, BC, Canada V6T 1Y3

Manitoba

References Services
University of Manitoba
Elizabeth DaFoe Library

Winnipeg 19 Manitoba, Canada

Nova Scotia

Map Collection
Dalhousie University Library
Halifax, Nova Scotia
Canada B3H 4J3

Ontario

Map Library
York University
4700 Kelle St., Downsview
Ontario, Canada

The Univ. of Western Ontario
Map Curator, Dept. Geography
Social Science Center
London, Ont. Canada N6A 5C2

Carleton University
Map Library
D299 Loeb Bldg.
Ottawa, Canada K1S 5B6

Map Library
University Toronto
130 St. George St.
Toronto, Ont., Canada M5S 1A5

University Map Library
University of Waterloo
Waterloo, Ontario,
Canada N2L 3G1

Quebec

La Cartotheque
Bibliotheque Generale
Universite Laval
Quebec, Canada

La Cartotheque
Universite Du Quebec
300 Avenue Des Ursulines
Quebec, Canada G1K 7P4

Map & Air Photo Library
524 Burnside Hall, McGill Univ.
805 Shebrooke St. West
Montreal, Que. H3A 2K6 Canada

Univ. of Montreal
Library, Dept. of Geology
P.O. Box 6128 Montreal
Quebec, Canada H3C 3J7

Saskatchewan

Map Library C215, FAC of ART
Attn: Mrs. S. S. Qureshi
University of Regina
Regina, Sask. S4S 0A2 Canada

North American
Tribal Map

PHYSIOGRAPHIC DIAGRAM
Adapted from a map compiled by
Erwin Raisz, 1954

"Physiographic Diagram adapted from a map compiled by Erwin Raisz, 1954," sheet number 59 in the *United States National Atlas*, U.S. Geological Survey, Washington, D.C., 1958. Scale, approx. 1:17,000,000. Dimensions 8 x 12 inches. Printed map in color on paper.

DISTRIBUTION OF PRINCIPAL INDIAN TRAILS AND PATHS ABOUT 1600

H.R.FRIIS '66

"Map of the United States showing the principal paths of diffusion of population: 1800-1815." Scale 1:7,000,000. Dimensions 20 x 30 inches.

PRINCIPAL PATHS OF DIFFUSION OF POPULATION: 1800–1815

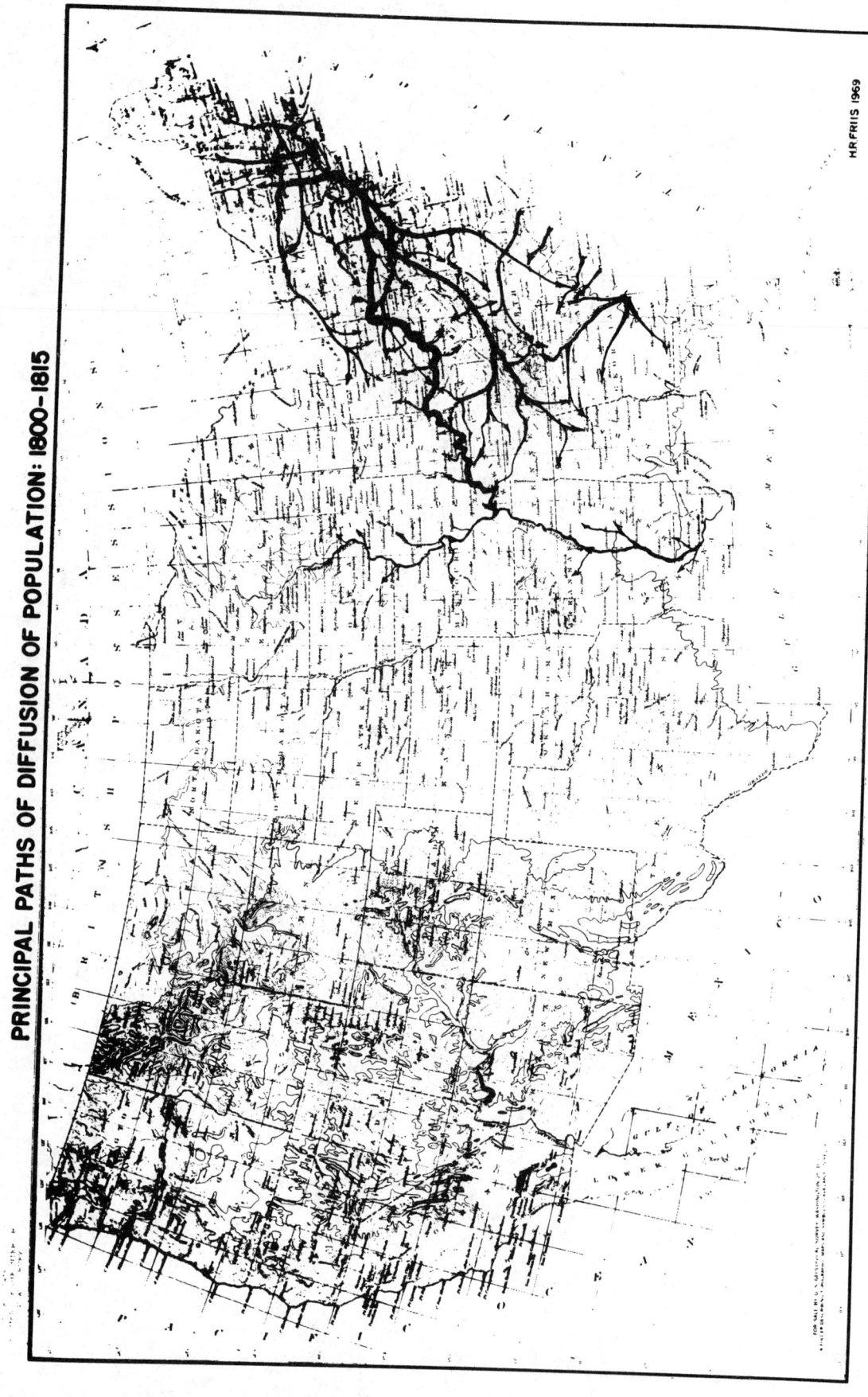

H R FRIIS 1969

"Map of the United States showing the distribution of principal Indian trails and paths about 1600." Scale: 1:7,000,000. Dimensions 20 x 30 inches.

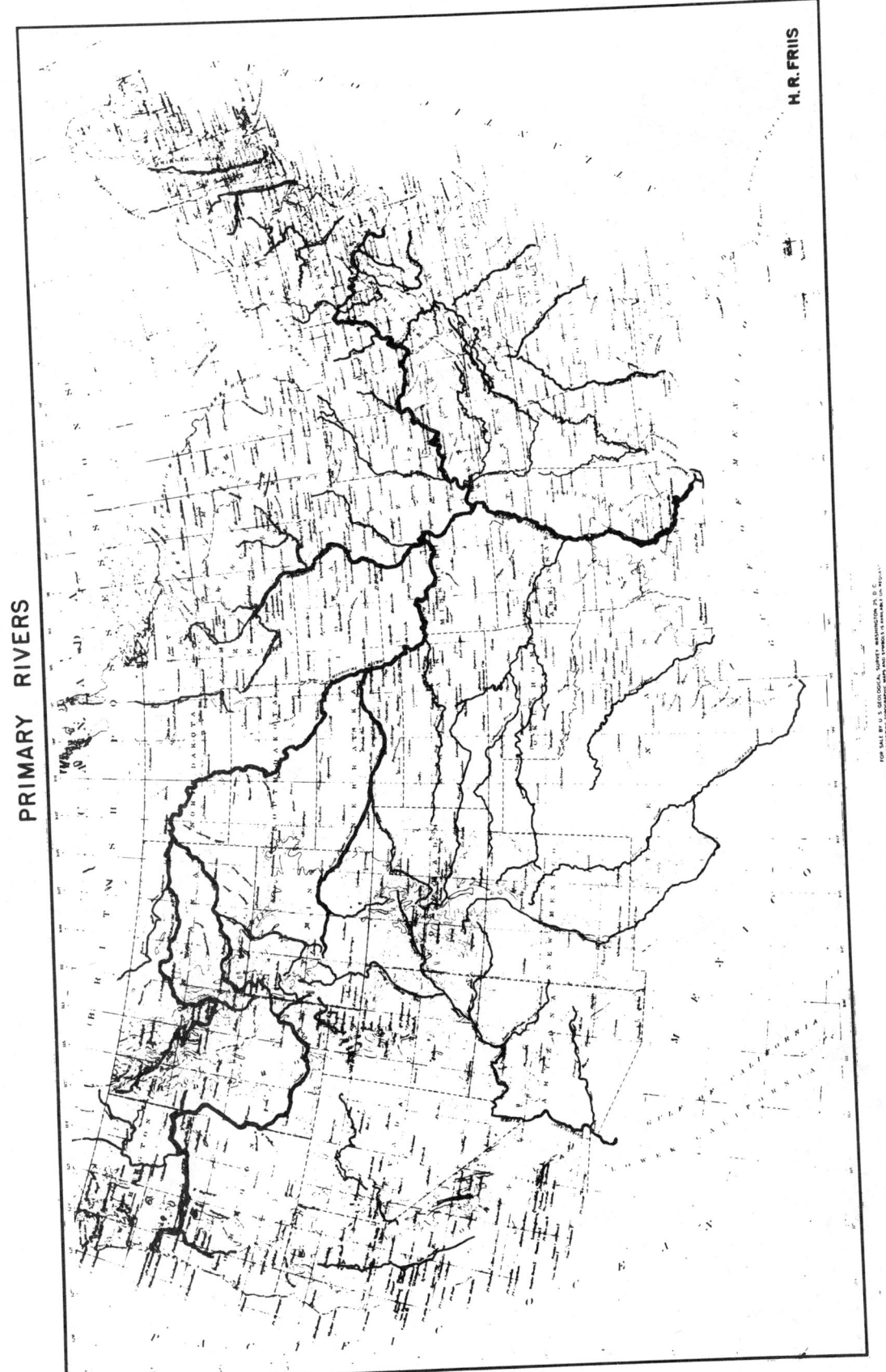

PRIMARY RIVERS

H. R. FRIIS

"Map of the United States showing the primary rivers." Scale 1:7,000,000. Dimensions 20 x 30 inches.

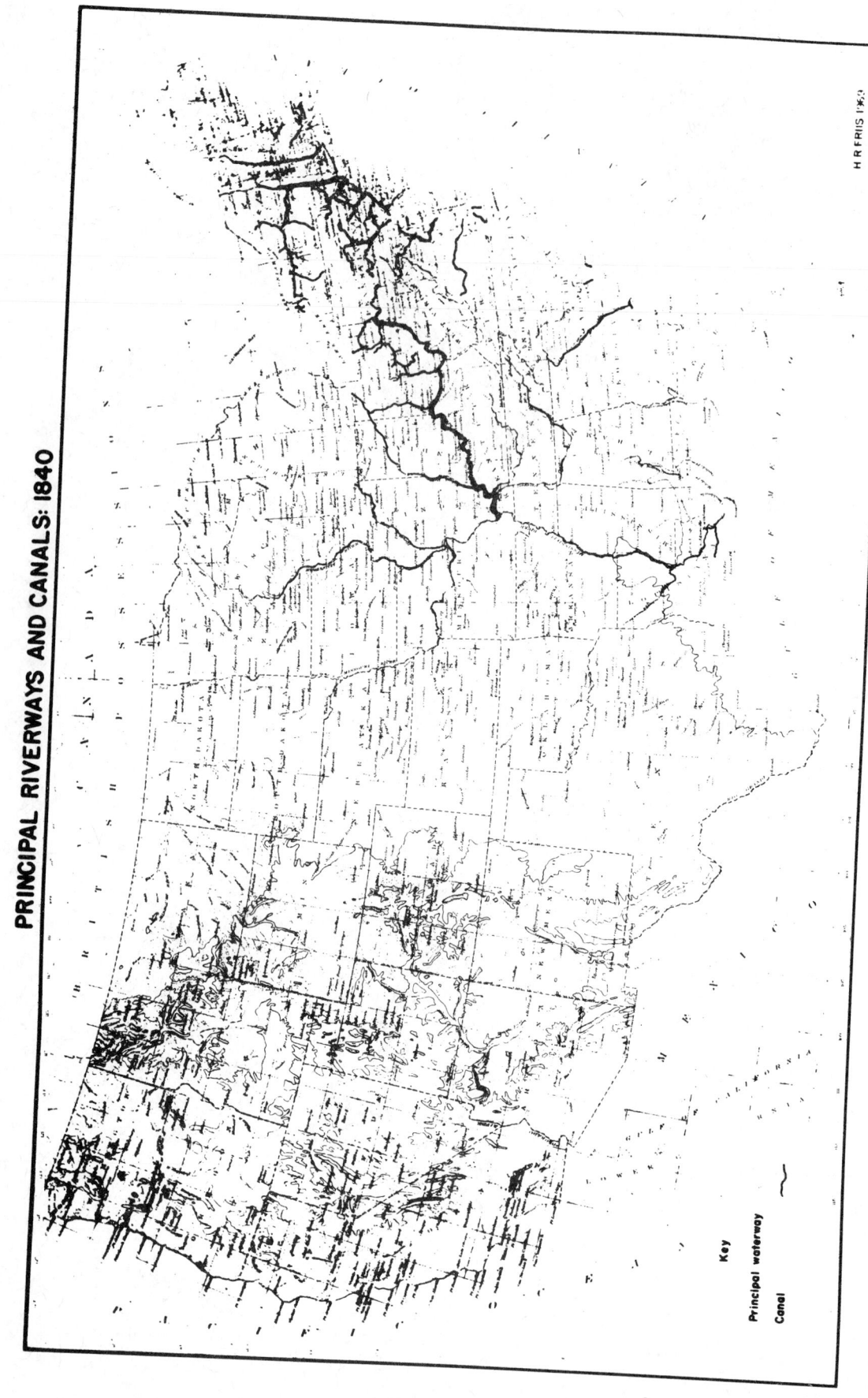

PRINCIPAL RIVERWAYS AND CANALS: 1840

Key

Principal waterway

Canal

H R FRIIS 1962

"Map of the United States showing riverways and canals: 1840." Scale 1:7,000,000. Dimensions 20 x 30 inches. Annotated printed map in color on paper.

BRITISH POSSESSIONS

CANADA

VIRGINIA
(Ceded 1784)

Disputed

MASS.

VT. & N.Y.
(Adjusted 1791)

N.H.

NEW
YORK

VIRGINIA
(Ceded
1784)

AND MASS.
(Ceded
1785)

NEW YORK
AND MASS.
(Adjusted 1786)

MASS.

CONN.

R.I.

VIRGINIA
(Ceded 1784)

AND CONN.
(Ceded 1786)

(Ceded
1800)

PENNSYLVANIA

N.J.

VIRGINIA

MD.

DEL.

L O U I S I A N A

(Spanish)
(Ceded by Spain
to France 1800)

(Ceded 1784)

VIRGINIA

NORTH CAROLINA
(Ceded 1790)

NORTH
CAROLINA

SOUTH CAROLINA (Ceded 1787)

SOUTH
CAROLINA

GEORGIA
(Ceded 1802)

GEORGIA

Claimed by Spain

F L O R I D A

(Spanish)

Claims

Treaty Line, 1783

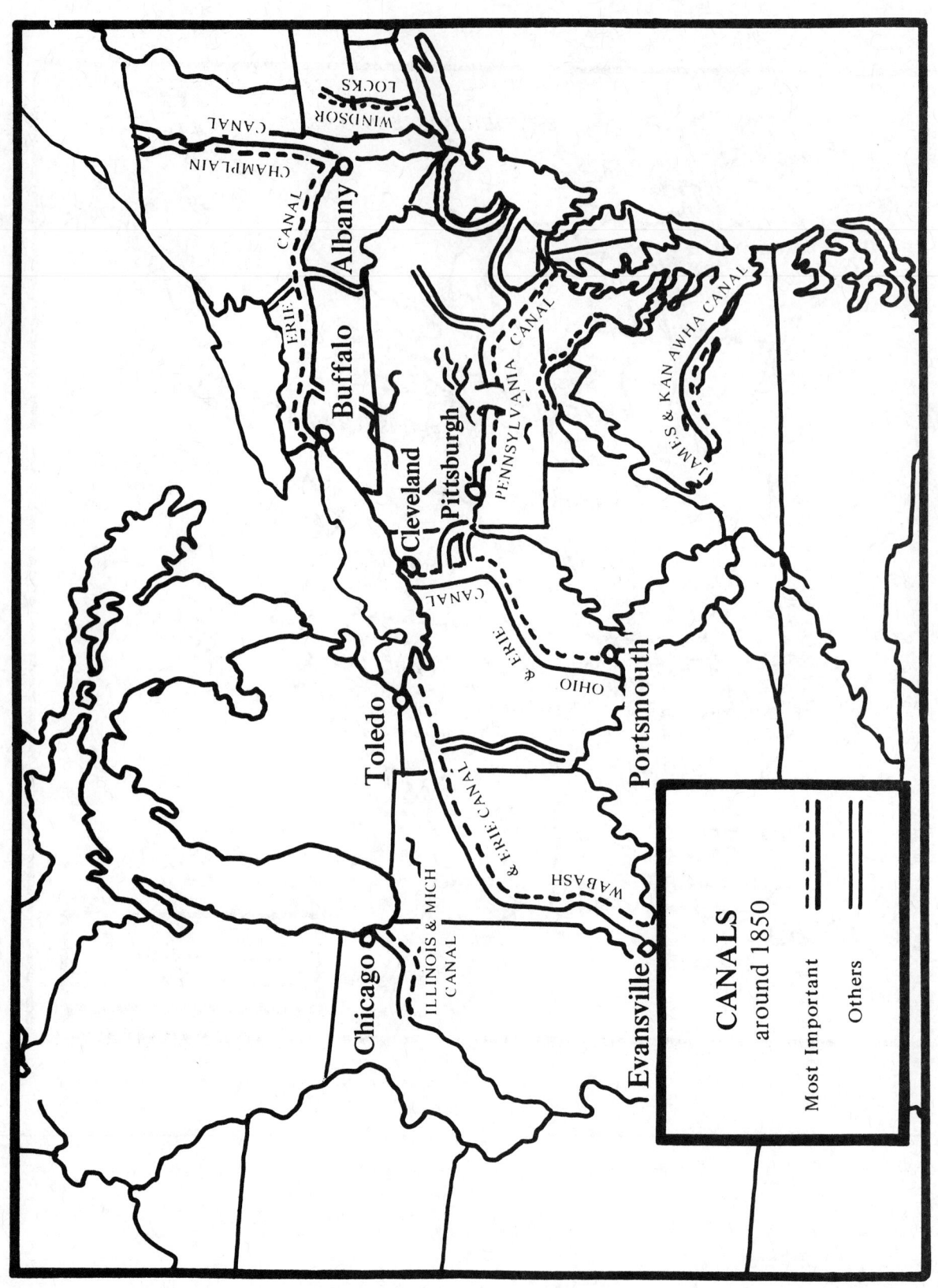

CANALS
around 1850

Most Important

Others

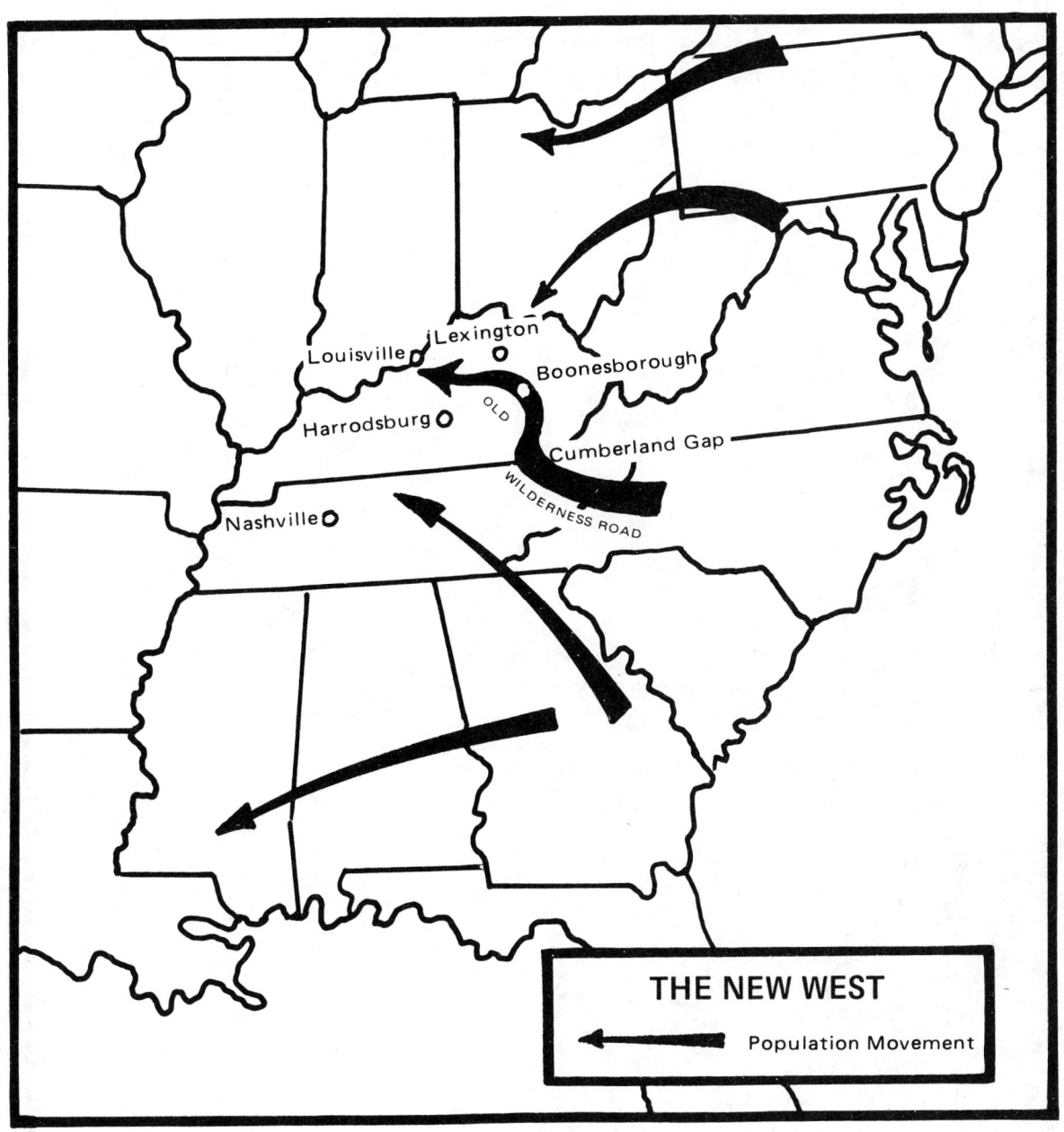

Louisville ¡Lexington
Boonesborough
Harrodsburg
OLD
Cumberland Gap
Nashville
WILDERNESS ROAD

THE NEW WEST

Population Movement

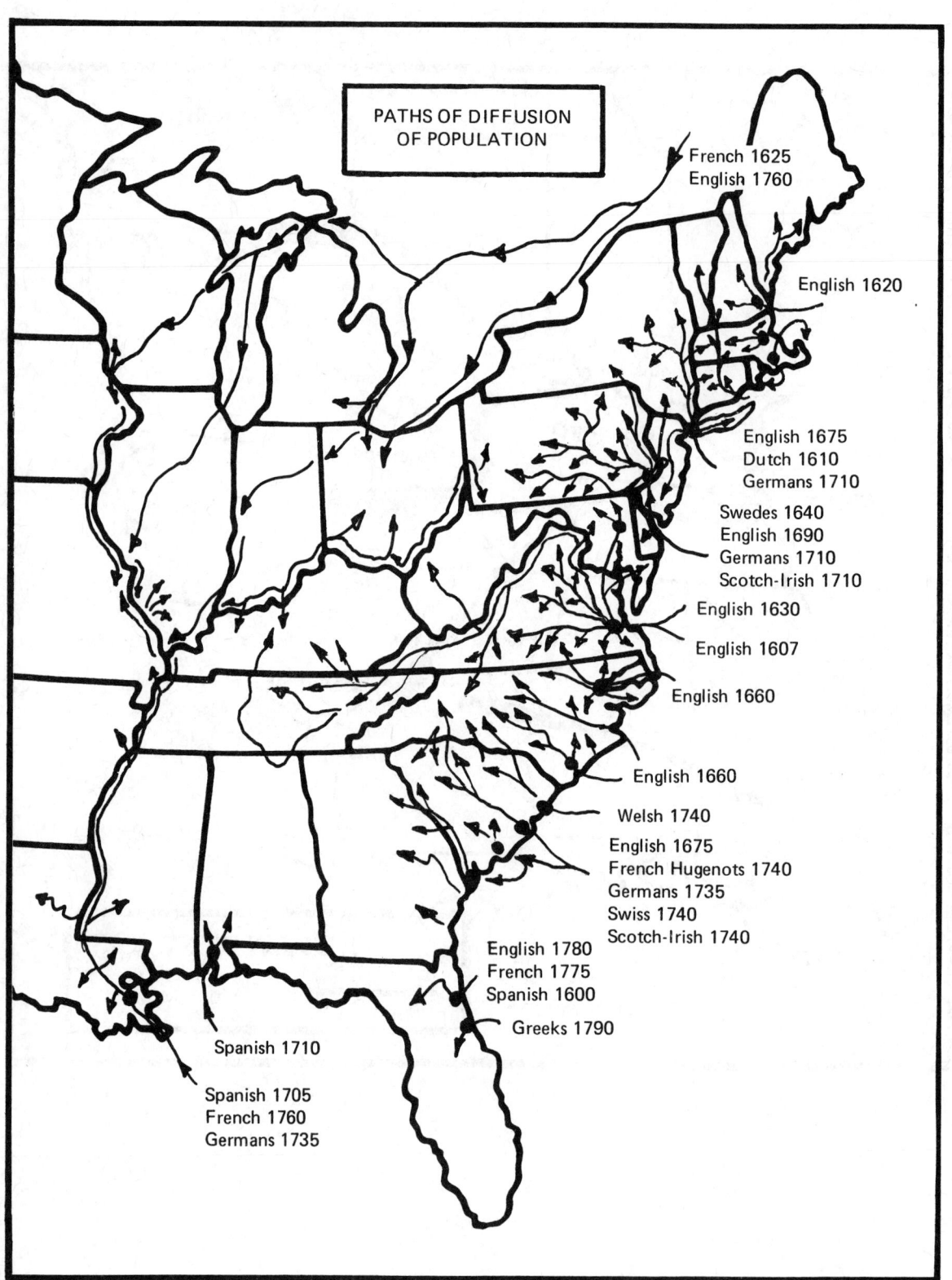

PATHS OF DIFFUSION
OF POPULATION

French 1625
English 1760

English 1620

English 1675
Dutch 1610
Germans 1710

Swedes 1640
English 1690
Germans 1710
Scotch-Irish 1710

English 1630

English 1607

English 1660

English 1660

Welsh 1740

English 1675
French Hugenots 1740
Germans 1735
Swiss 1740
Scotch-Irish 1740

English 1780
French 1775
Spanish 1600

Greeks 1790

Spanish 1710

Spanish 1705
French 1760
Germans 1735

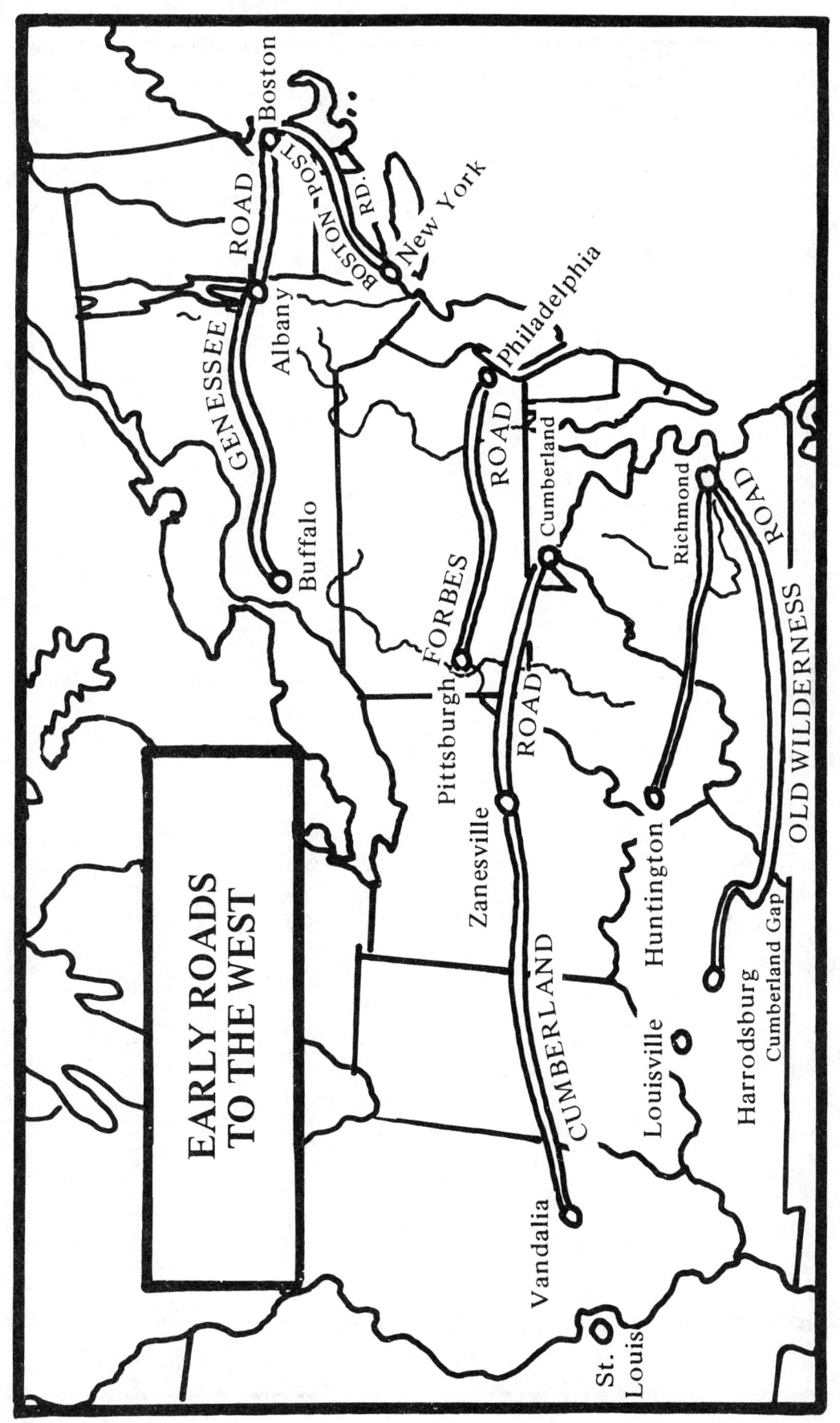

EARLY ROADS TO THE WEST

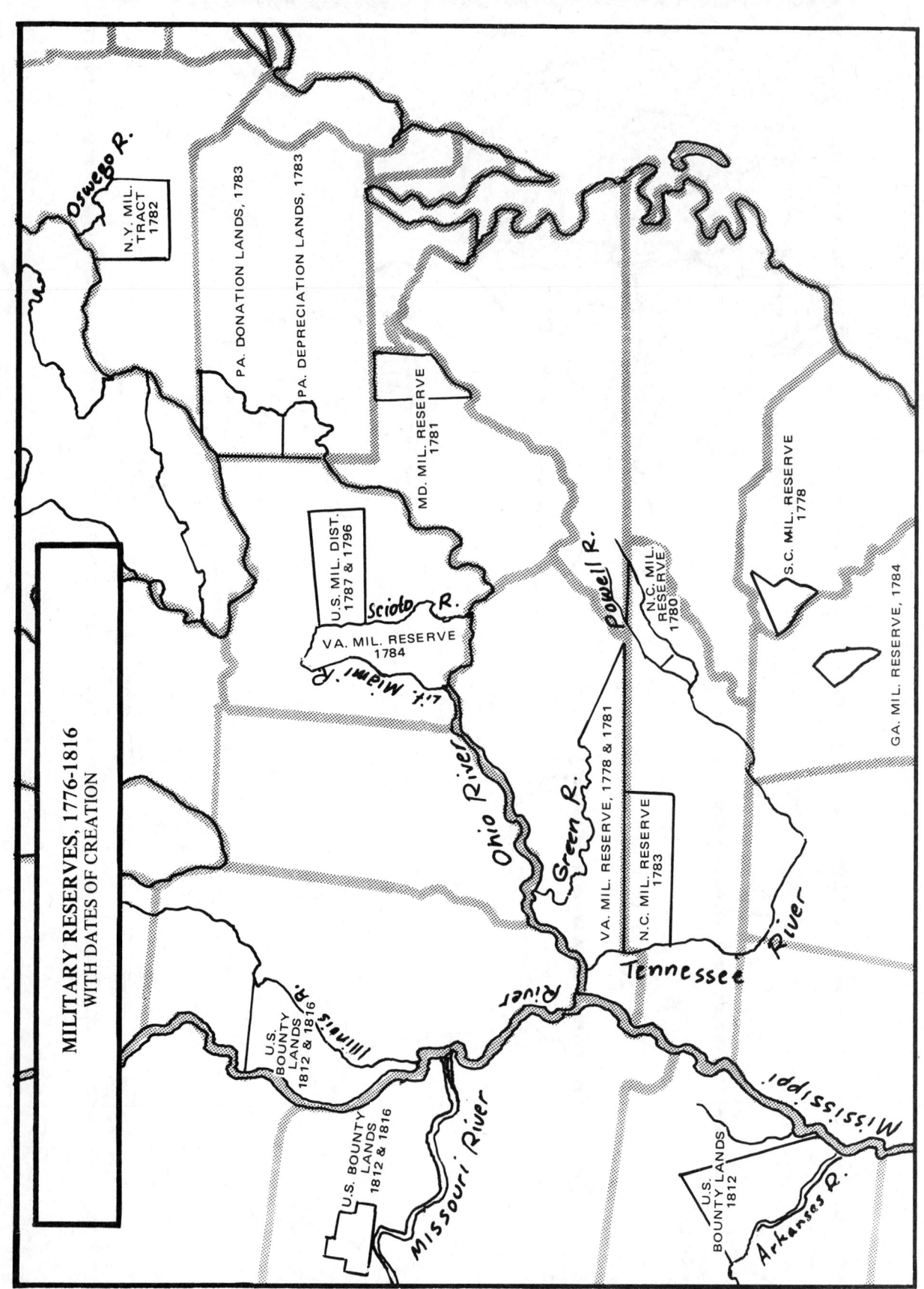

MILITARY RESERVES, 1776-1816
WITH DATES OF CREATION

Oswego R.

N.Y. MIL. TRACT 1782

PA. DONATION LANDS, 1783

PA. DEPRECIATION LANDS, 1783

MD. MIL. RESERVE 1781

U.S. MIL. DIST. 1787 & 1796

Scioto R.

VA. MIL. RESERVE 1784

Lit. Miami R.

Powell R.

N.C. MIL. RESERVE 1780

S.C. MIL. RESERVE 1778

GA. MIL. RESERVE, 1784

Ohio River

Green R.

VA. MIL. RESERVE, 1778 & 1781

N.C. MIL. RESERVE 1783

Tennessee River

River

U.S. BOUNTY LANDS 1812 & 1816

Illinois R.

U.S. BOUNTY LANDS 1812 & 1816

Missouri River

Mississippi

U.S. BOUNTY LANDS 1812

Arkansas R.

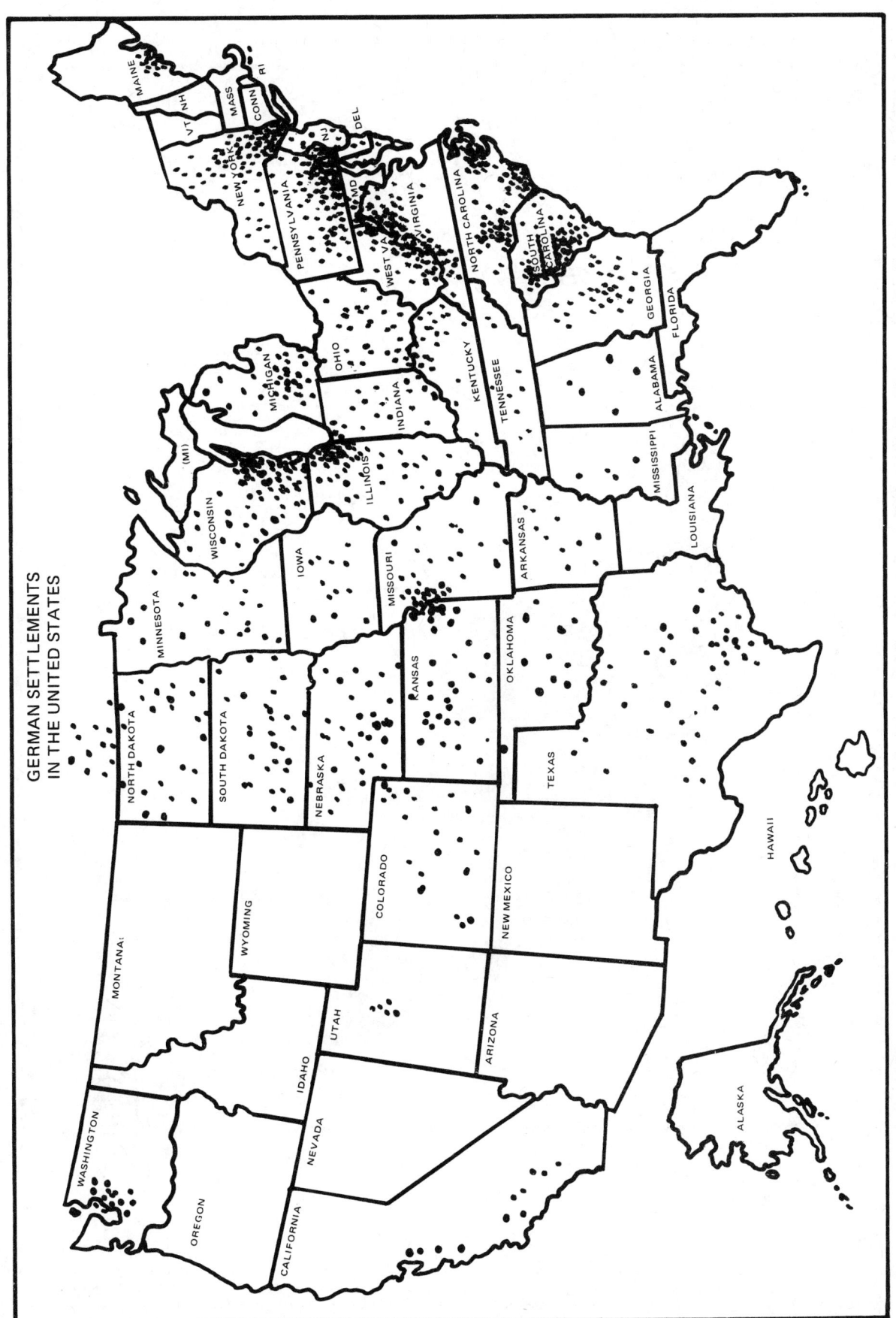

GERMAN SETTLEMENTS
IN THE UNITED STATES

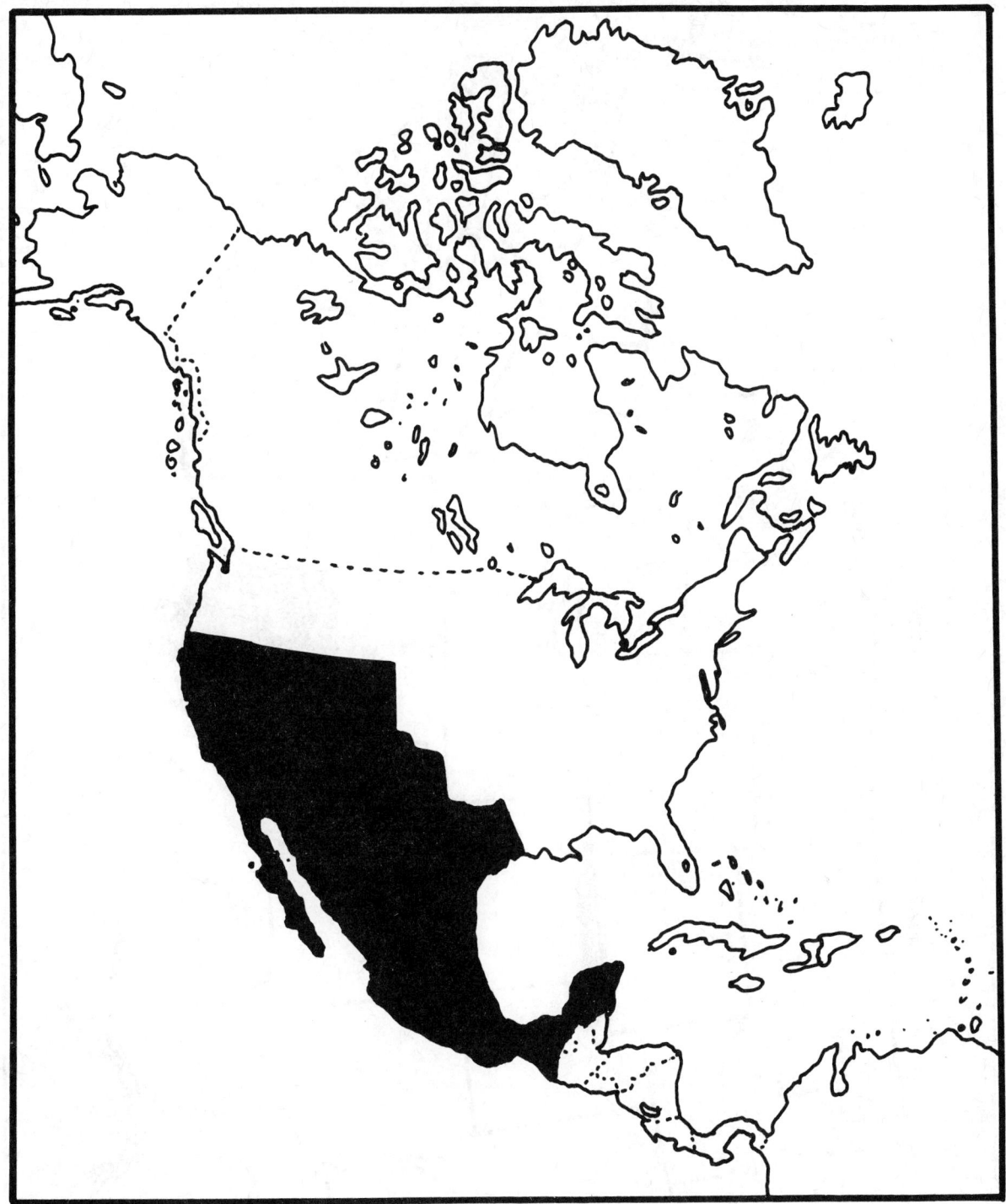

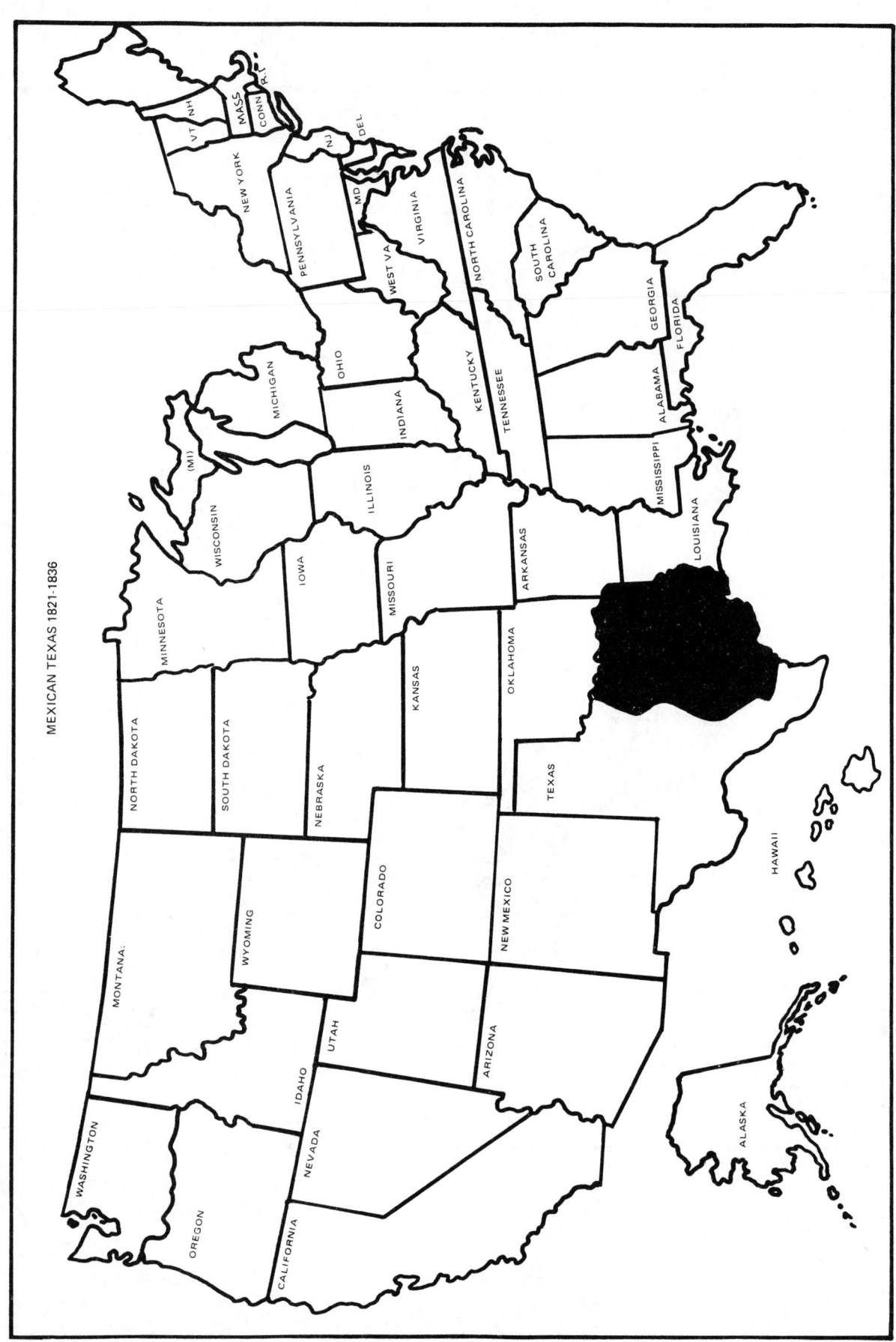

MEXICAN TEXAS 1821-1836

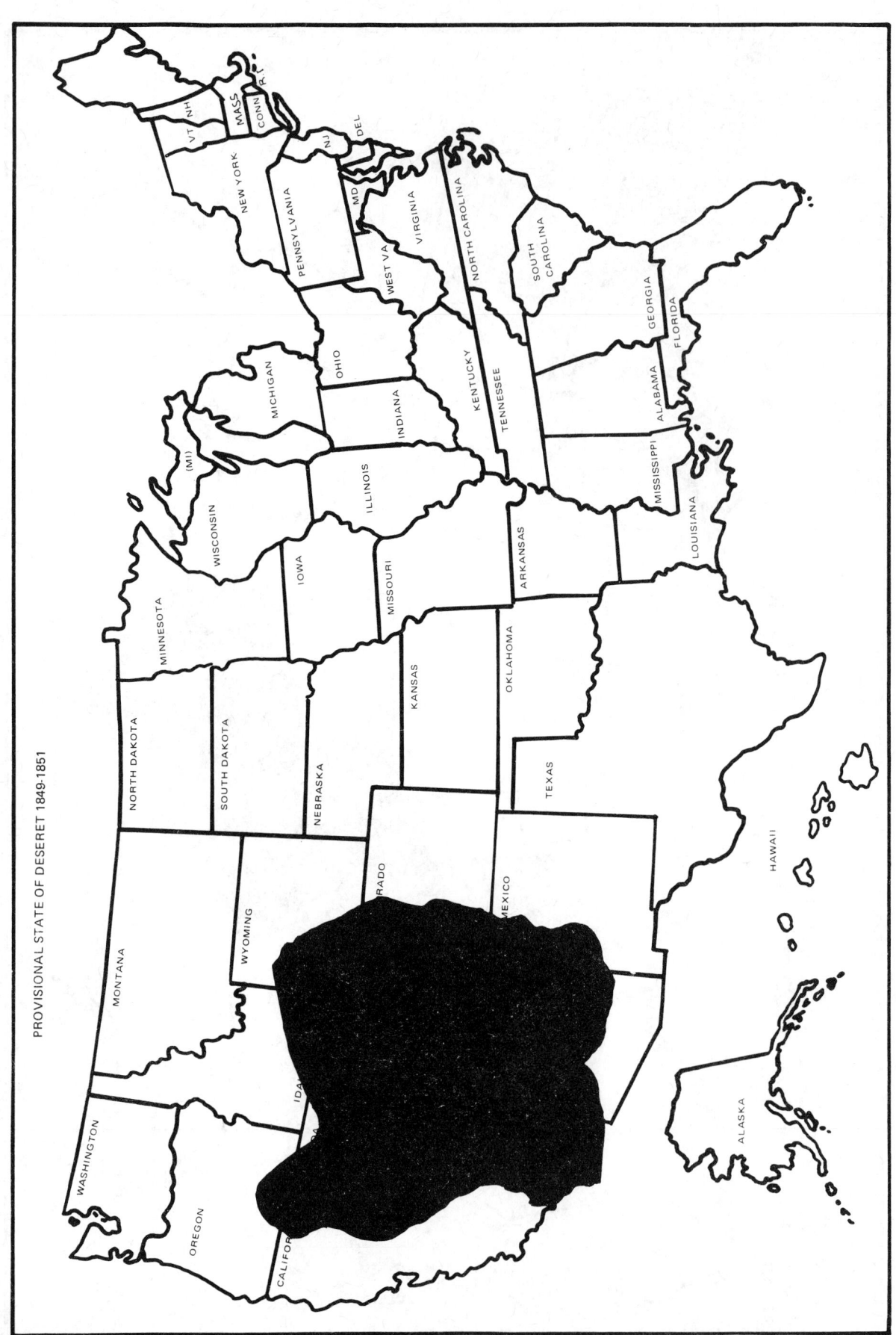

PROVISIONAL STATE OF DESERET 1849-1851

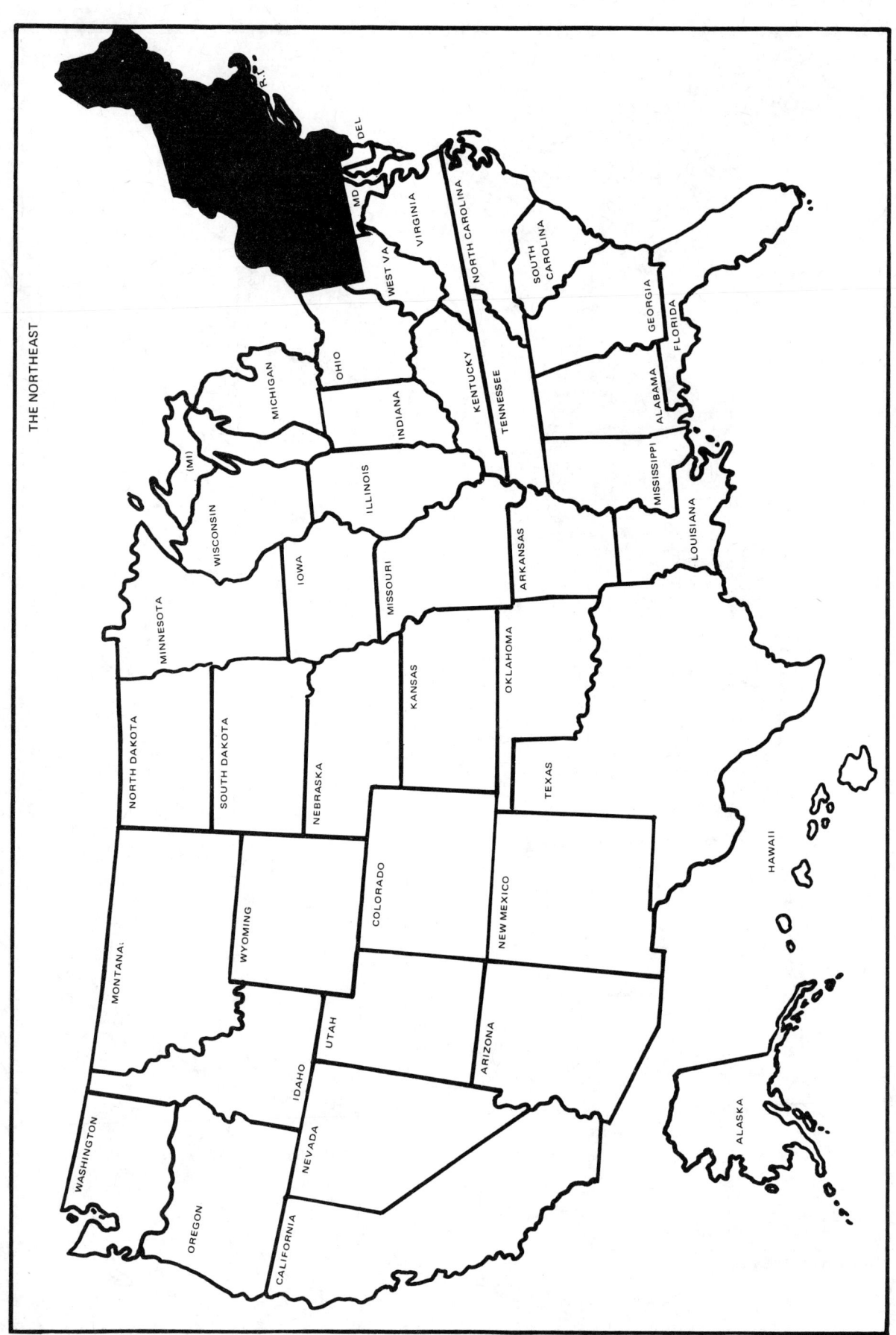

THE NORTHEAST

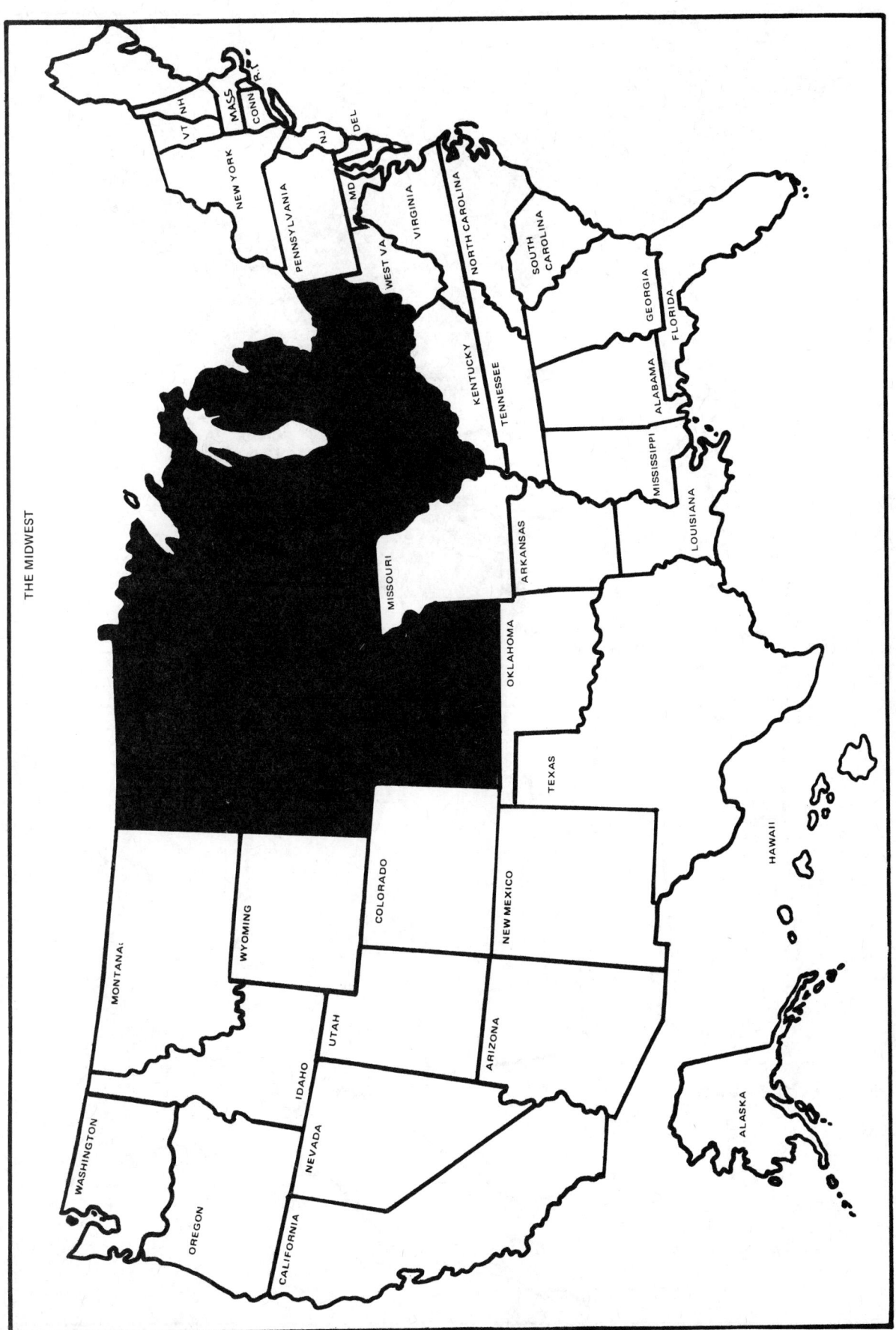

THE MIDWEST

WASHINGTON
OREGON
CALIFORNIA
NEVADA
IDAHO
MONTANA
UTAH
WYOMING
ARIZONA
COLORADO
NEW MEXICO
TEXAS
OKLAHOMA
MISSOURI
ARKANSAS
LOUISIANA
MISSISSIPPI
ALABAMA
TENNESSEE
KENTUCKY
GEORGIA
FLORIDA
SOUTH CAROLINA
NORTH CAROLINA
VIRGINIA
WEST VA
MD
PENNSYLVANIA
DEL
NJ
NEW YORK
VT
NH
MASS
CONN
R.I.
ALASKA
HAWAII

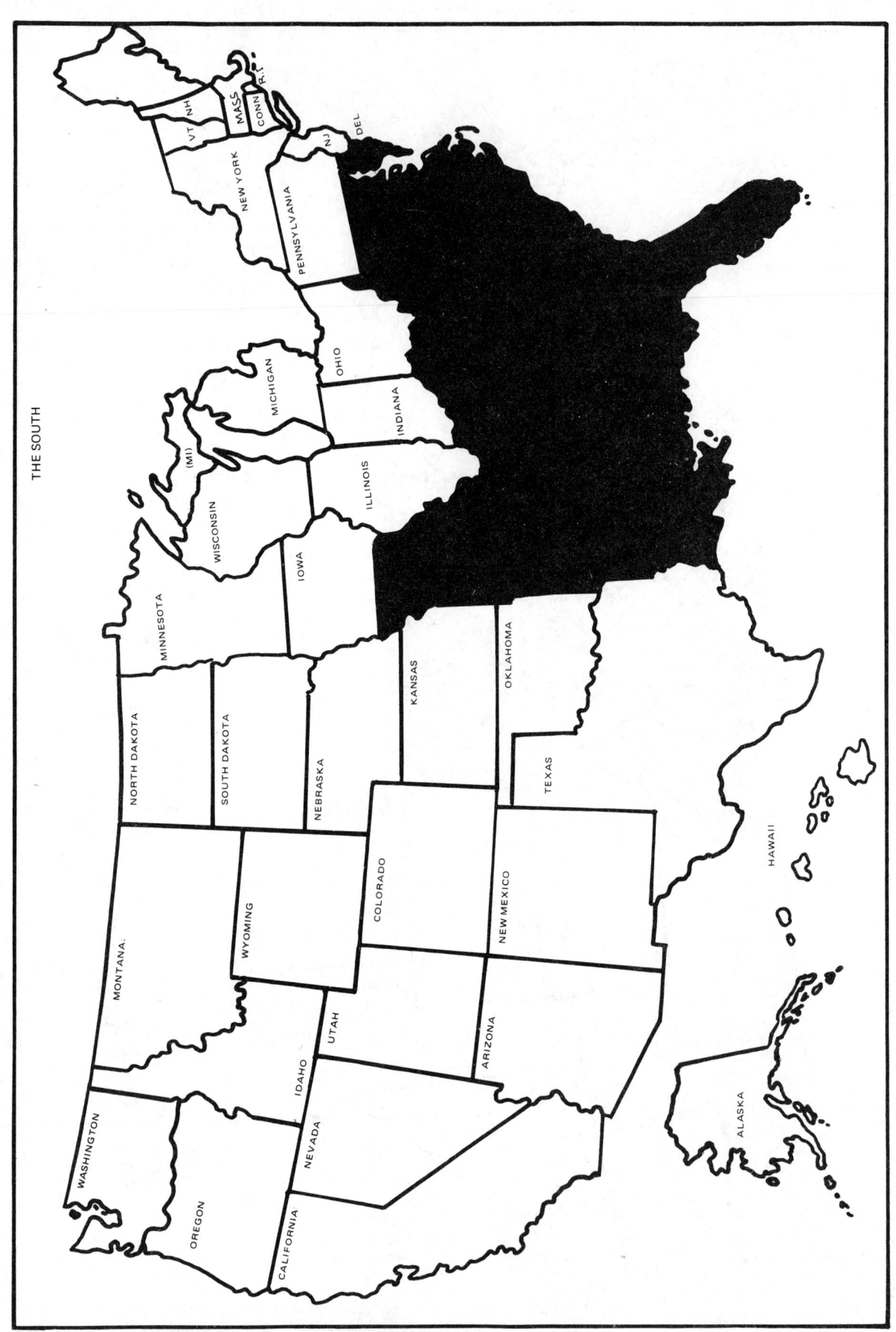

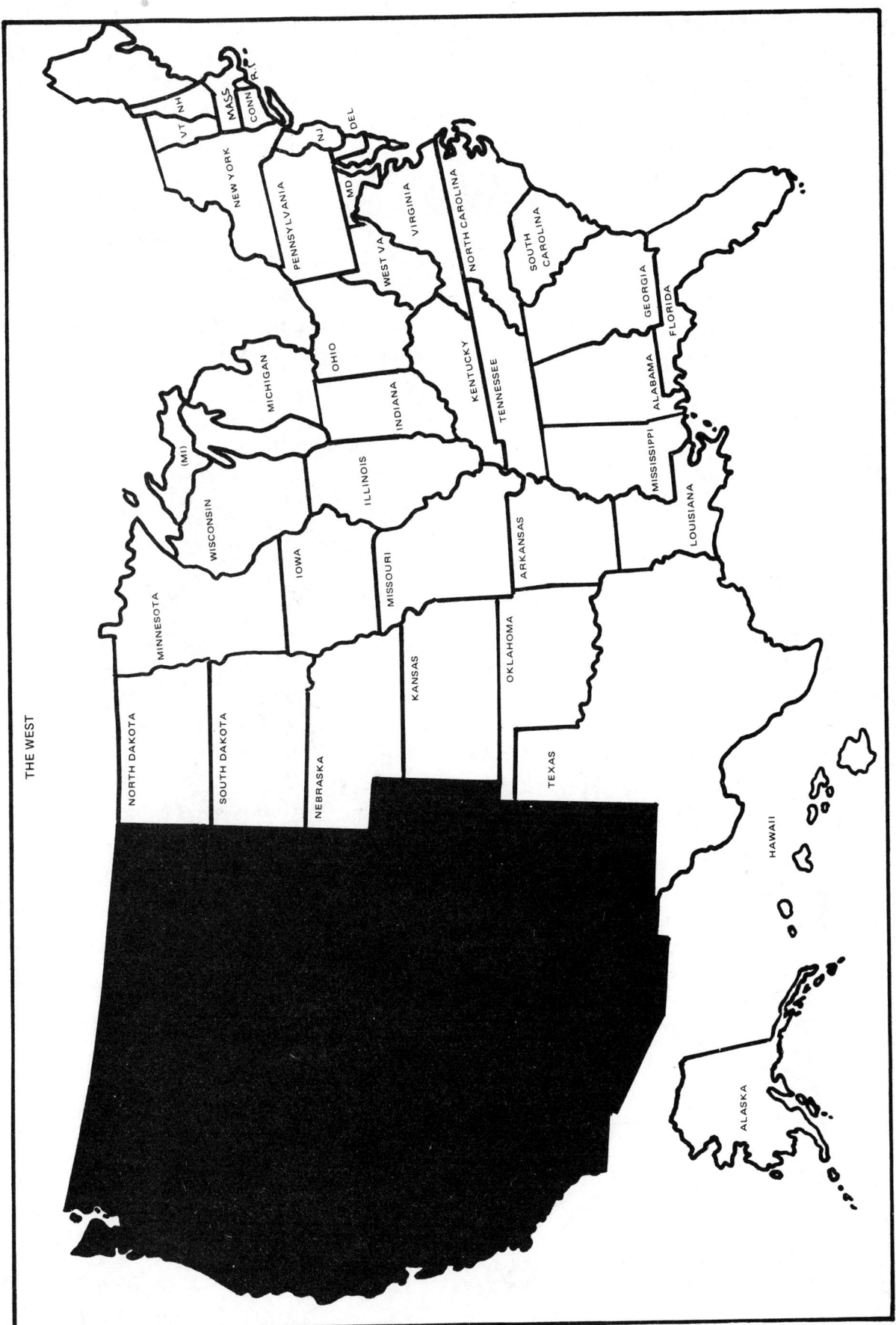

THE WEST

NORTH DAKOTA

SOUTH DAKOTA

NEBRASKA

KANSAS

OKLAHOMA

TEXAS

MINNESOTA

IOWA

MISSOURI

ARKANSAS

LOUISIANA

WISCONSIN

(MI)

MICHIGAN

ILLINOIS

INDIANA

OHIO

MISSISSIPPI

ALABAMA

TENNESSEE

KENTUCKY

WEST VA.

PENNSYLVANIA

NEW YORK

VT NH

MASS.

CONN. R.I.

NJ

DEL

MD

VIRGINIA

NORTH CAROLINA

SOUTH CAROLINA

GEORGIA

FLORIDA

HAWAII

ALASKA

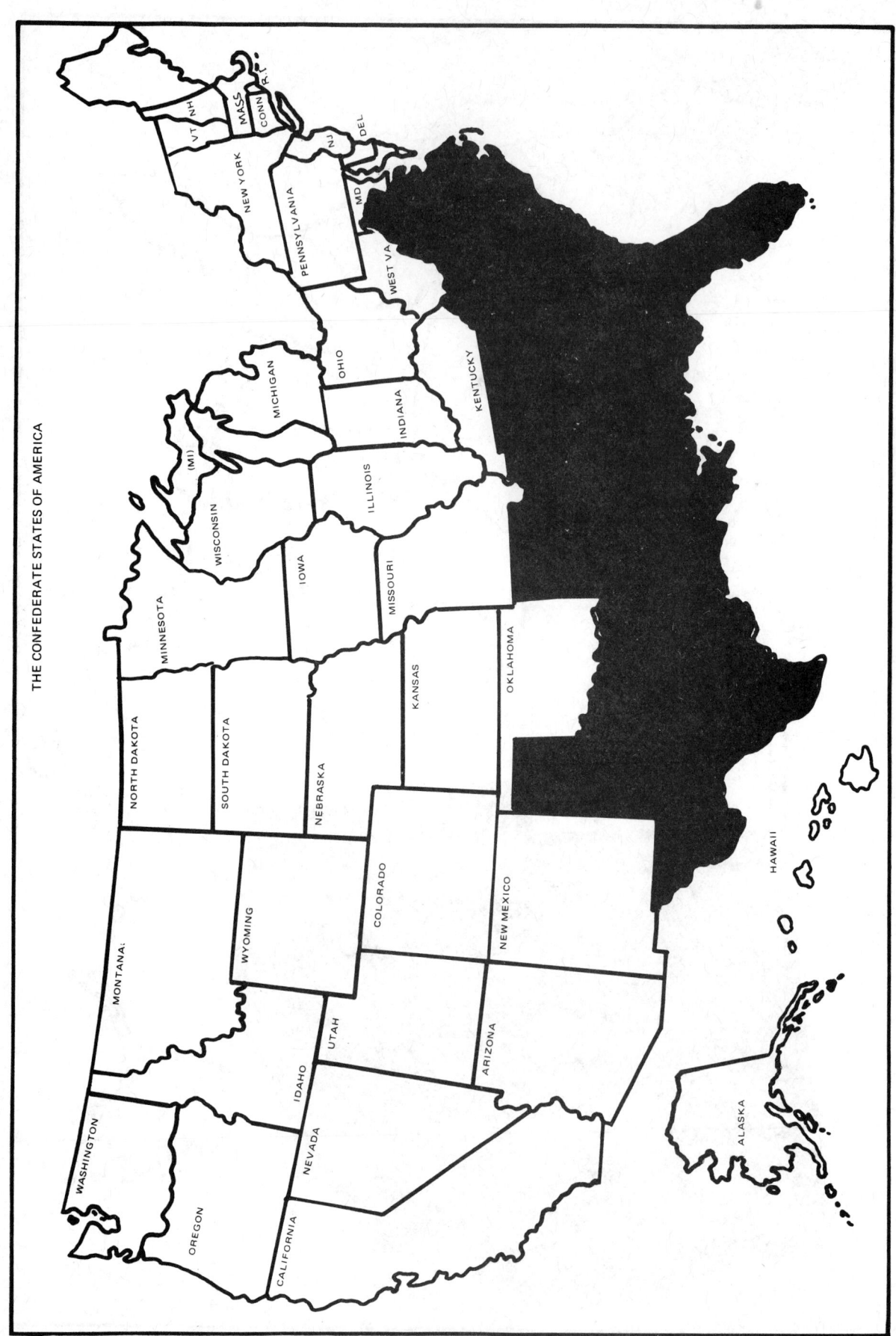

THE CONFEDERATE STATES OF AMERICA

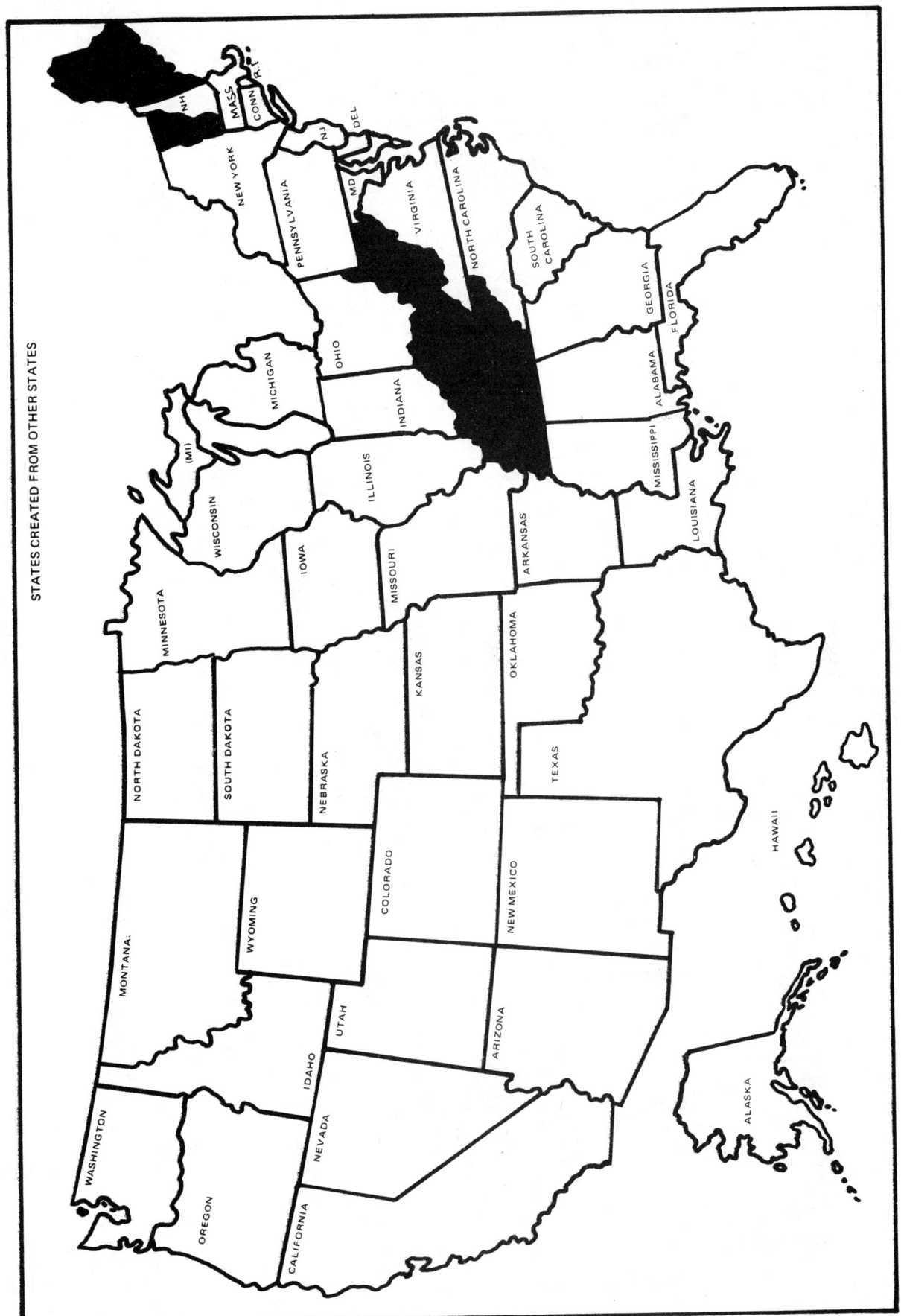

STATES CREATED FROM OTHER STATES

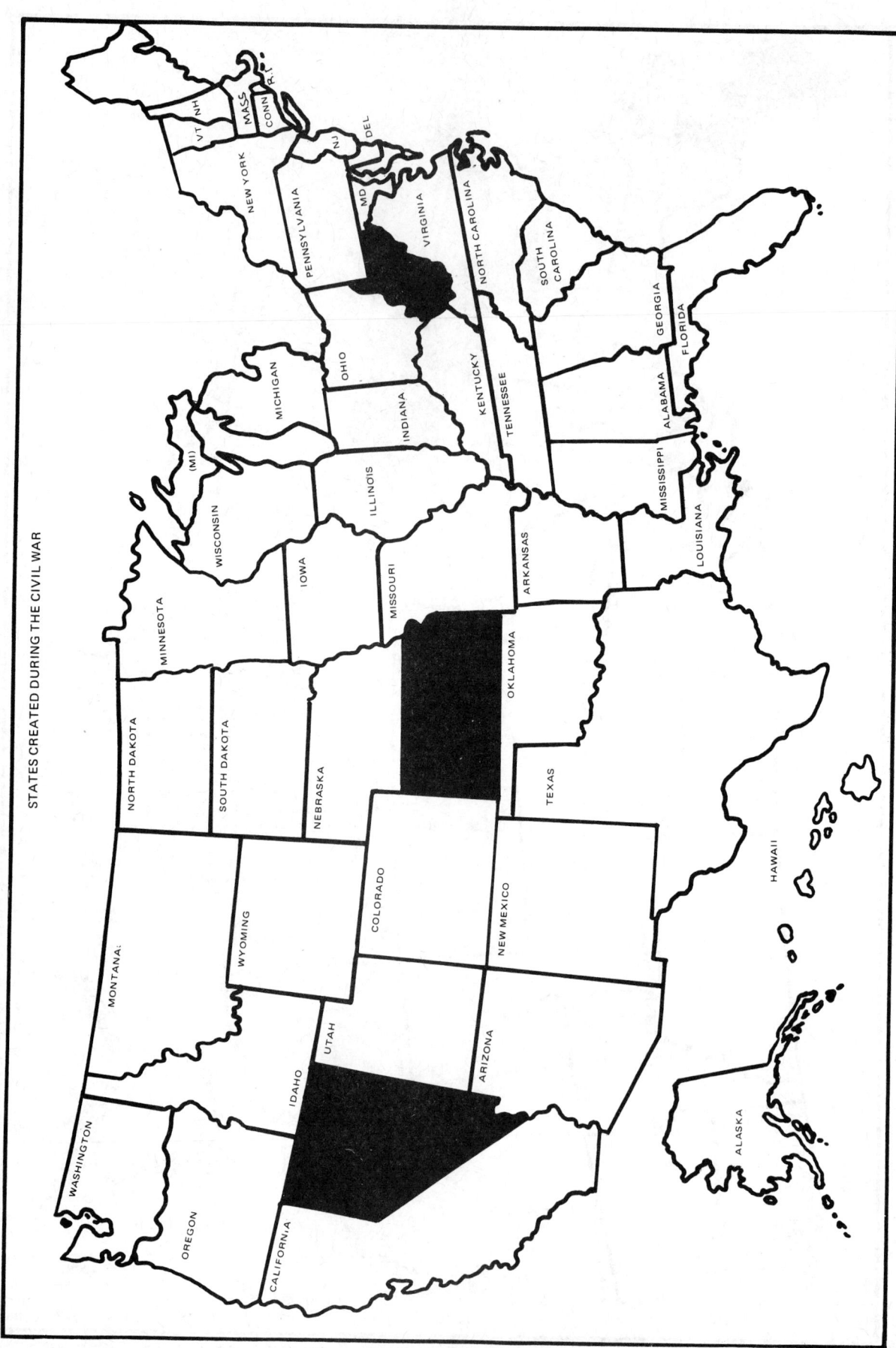

STATES CREATED DURING THE CIVIL WAR

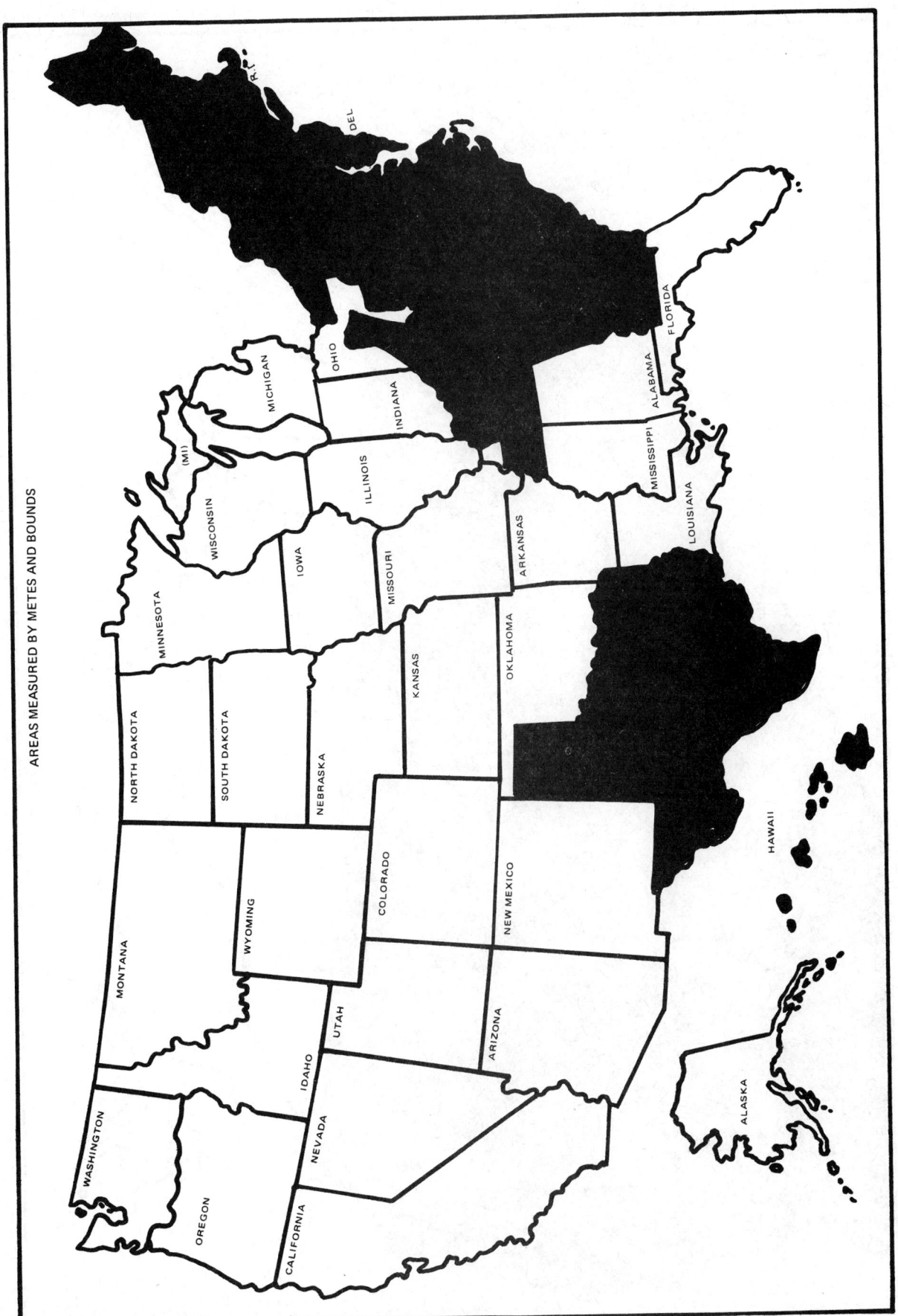

AREAS MEASURED BY METES AND BOUNDS

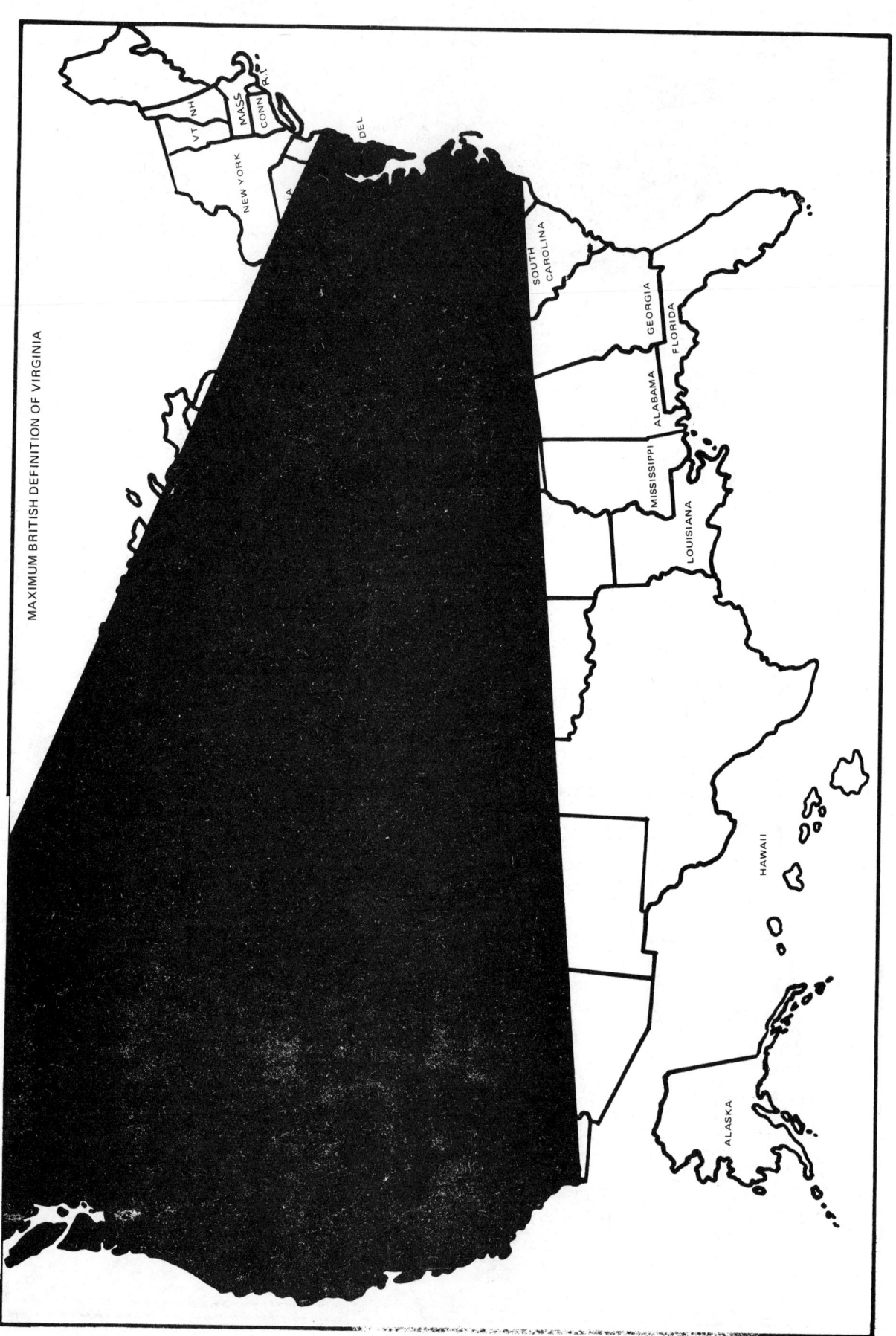

MAXIMUM BRITISH DEFINITION OF VIRGINIA

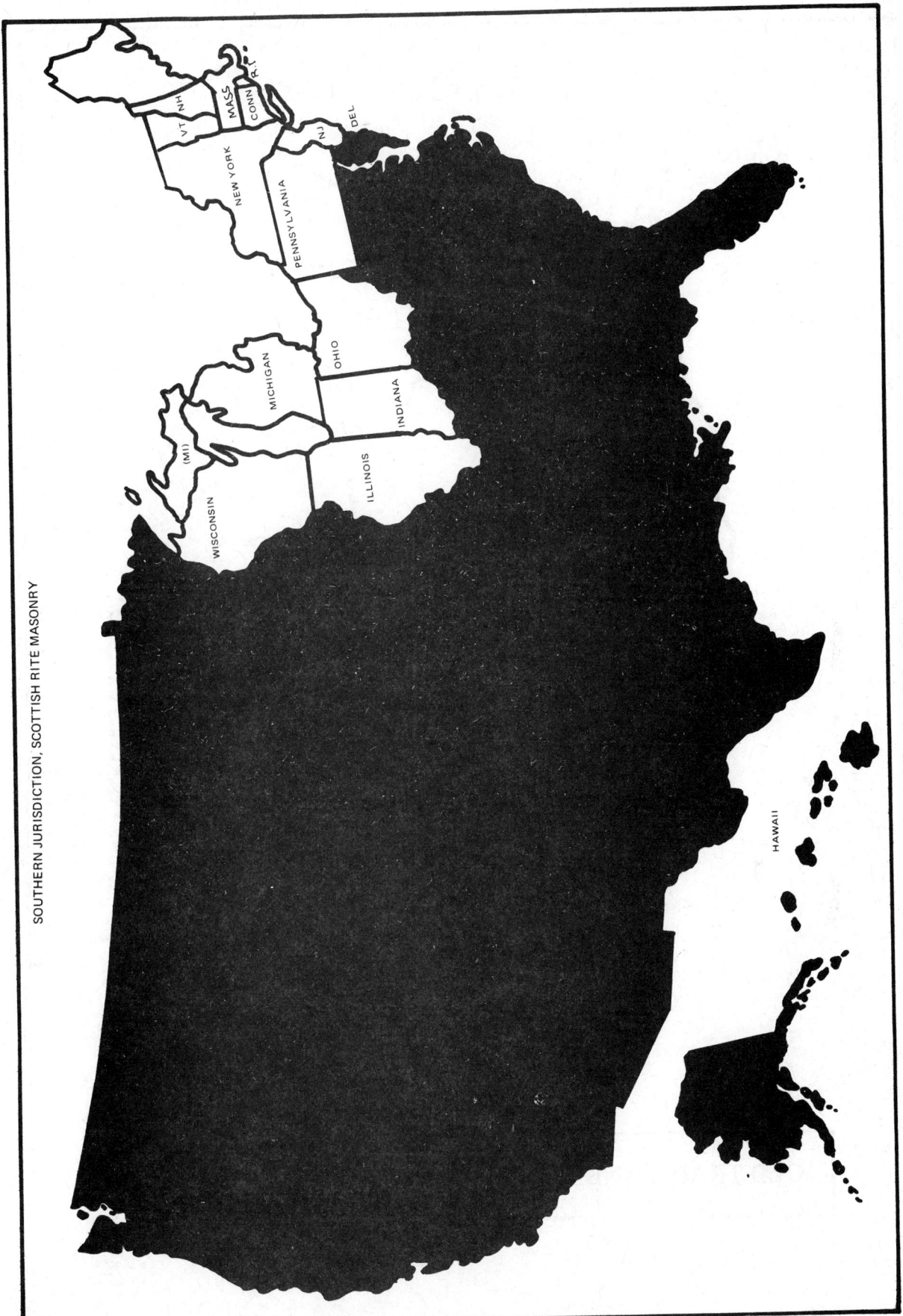

SOUTHERN JURISDICTION, SCOTTISH RITE MASONRY

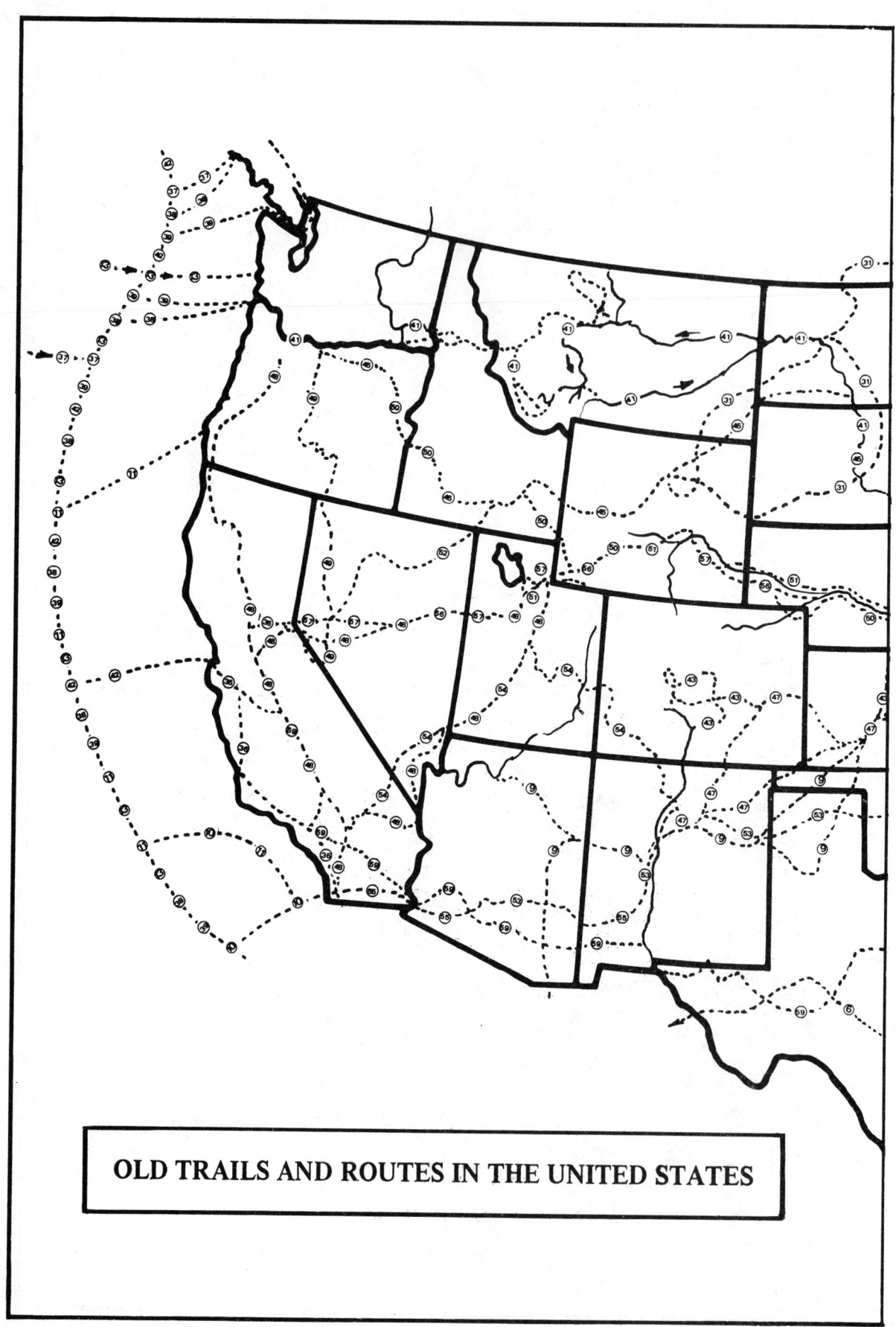

OLD TRAILS AND ROUTES IN THE UNITED STATES

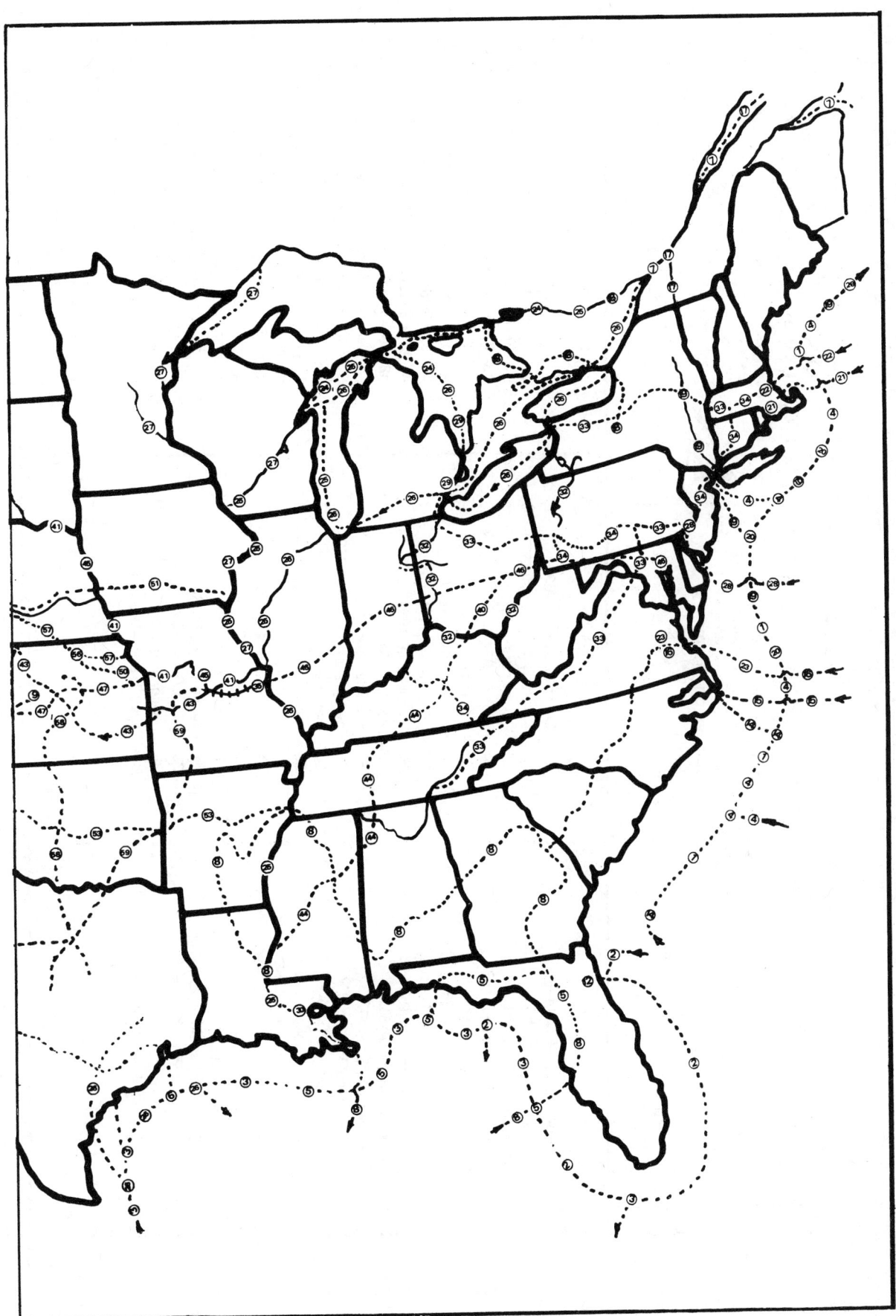

DESCRIPTION OF OLD TRAILS AND ROUTES IN THE UNITED STATES

Most of these trails had been used by buffalo, indian, trapper and trader before the dates assigned on this map.

1—John Cabot 1497-1498
2—Ponce de Leon 1513
3—Alvarez de Pineda 1519
4—Giovanni Verrazano 1524
5—Panfilo de Narvaez 1528
6—Cabeza de Vaca 1528-1536
7—Jacques Cartier 1534-1543
8—Hernando de Soto 1539-1542
9—Coronado 1540-1542
10—Juan Cabrillo 1542
11—Bartolome Ferrelo 1543
12—St. Augustine 1565
13—Sir Francis Drake 1578-1580
14—Grenville and Lane 1585
15—Raleigh's Lost Colony 1587
16—Jamestown 1607
17—Quebec 1608
18—Governor Samuel
      de Champlain 1611-1616
19—Henry Hudson 1603
20—Captain John Smith 1614

21—Plymouth Colony 1620
22—Massachusetts Bay Colony 1629
23—Williamsburg 1632
24—Nicolet 1634
25—Marquette and Joliet 1673
26—Sieur de la Salle 1679-1687
27—Father Hennepin 1680
28—William Penn 1681
29—Detroit 1701
30—New Orleans 1718
31—The Verendryes 1742-1743
32—Celeron de Bienville 1749
33—Five Important Indian
      Trails in 1750
34—Five Main Post Roads in 1769
35—St. Louis 1763
36—Father Serra 1769
37—Captain Cook 1778
38—Robert Gray 1792
39—Sir George van Couver 1792
40—Zane's Trace 1796

41—The Lewis and Clark
      Expedition 1804-1806
42—Nikolai Rezanov 1806
43—Zebuloh Pike 1806-1807
44—The Natches Trace 1806
45—The Astor Party 1810-1812
46—The National Road 1806-1807
47—The Santa Fe Trail 1824
48—Jedediah Smith 1822-1831
49—James C. Fremont 1842-1844
50—The Oregon Trail 1843
51—The Mormon Road 1846-1847
52—The California Trail 1849
53—The Arkansas Route 1849
54—The Old Spanish Trail 1785
55—The Gila River Route 1846-1849
56—The Pony Express 1860-1861
57—The Overland Stage 1859-1869
58—The Chisholm Trail 1867-1887
59—Butterfield's Southern
      Stage 1858-1861

National Atlas

SEPARATE SALES EDITIONS

Mail this ORDER FORM to:

Customers east of the Mississippi River	Customers west of the Mississippi River
BRANCH OF DISTRIBUTION, EASTERN REGION **U.S. GEOLOGICAL SURVEY** **1200 SOUTH EADS STREET** **ARLINGTON, VIRGINIA 22202**	**BRANCH OF DISTRIBUTION, CENTRAL REGION** **U.S. GEOLOGICAL SURVEY** **BOX 25286, FEDERAL CENTER** **DENVER, COLORADO 80225**

FROM: Name _____

Street Address _____

_____
City   State   Zip Code

PREPAYMENT REQUIRED Remittance payable to U.S. Geological Survey
List prices given include cost of surface transportation.

	OFFICE USE DO NOT WRITE IN THIS SPACE
Customer Order No.	
Date	
Total Maps Ordered	
Amount Enclosed $ _____ Check ___ Money Order ___	

DISCOUNT On an order amounting to Three Hundred Dollars or more, a 30% discount is allowed. No other discount is applicable.

SURCHARGE For transmittal of maps outside of the United States (except for Canada and Mexico), a surcharge of 25 percent of the net bill will be added to cover surface transportation. Special service will be charged at full cost of service.

Selected National Atlas maps have been published in separate sales editions. They are general reference and thematic maps covering topics of current interest. The scale varies from 1:7,500,000 for a full sheet size map to 1:17,000,000 and 1:34,000,000 when there are more than one map to a sheet. The General Reference Sectional Maps divide the country into 21 sections at a scale of 1:2,000,000. Sheet size is 19 by 28 inches.

FOR PROMPT, ACCURATE SHIPMENT PLEASE FILL IN MAILING LABEL ON LAST PAGE ▶

Quantity	Sheet No.	Subject	Unit Price
_____	2	United States General Reference (1973) ....$1.50 *Shows populated places, transportation routes, and highest elevation in each State. Insets show Alaska and the principal islands of Hawaii.*	
_____	56	United States, shaded relief (1969) $1.50	
_____	58	Alaska, shaded relief (1969) ....$1.50 *Text on landforms, geology and other features of the United States.*	

Quantity	Sheet No.	Subject	Unit Price
_____	59	Physiography and Physiographic Divisions (1968 Edition) *Four maps of the conterminous United States showing physiographic regions and provinces, physical division, and a physiographic diagram. One map showing topographic relief with insets for Alaska and the principal islands of Hawaii.*	1.50
_____	61	Land-Surface Form (1965 Edition)...................... *Map of Alaska. Text of classes of land-surface form in the United States with map showing physical subdivisions.*	$1.00
_____	62	Classes of Land-Surface Form (1964 Edition)........... *Map of conterminous United States with inset showing principal islands of Hawaii. (Text and data for Alaska shown on sheet No. 61.)*	$1.50
_____	69	Tectonic Features (1968 Edition)...................... *Map of Alaska. Text on tectonic maps of the United States.*	$1.50
_____	70	Tectonic Features (1967 Edition)...................... *Map of conterminous United States with inset showing principal islands of Hawaii. (Text and data for Alaska on sheet No. 69.)*	$1.50
_____	74	Geology (1966 Edition)................................ *Map of conterminous United States with insets showing Alaska and principal islands of Hawaii.*	$1.50
_____	89	Potential Natural Vegetation of Alaska and Hawaii (1966). *Maps of Alaska and principal islands of Hawaii. Text on potential natural vegetation with explanation of symbols.*	$1.50
_____	90	Potential Natural Vegetation (1966 Edition)........... *Maps of conterminous United States showing forests and grasslands.*	$1.50
_____	94-95	Monthly Sunshine (1965 Edition) .... Thirteen maps on one sheet. Total hours of sunshine for each month, total hours of sunshine during the year at selected locations.	$1.00
_____	97	Annual Sunshine, Evaporation, and Solar Radiation (1969). *Three maps showing mean annual sunshine, mean annual pan evaporation, and mean May-October evaporation. Five maps showing annual solar radiation, and solar radiation for January, April, July, and October.*	$1.00
_____	106	Monthly Average Temperature. (1965 Edition) .... Thirteen maps on one sheet. Average temperature for each month, mean monthly average temperature for the year at selected locations.	$1.00

Quantity	Sheet No.	Subject	Unit Price
_____	110	**Monthly Minimum Temperature** (1965 Edition)............$1.00 *Thirteen maps on one sheet. Mean minimum temperature for each month, mean monthly minimum temperature for the year at selected locations.*	
_____	117	**Surface Water** (1966 Edition) ....$1.00 *Four maps on conterminous United States showing normal monthly distribution of runoff, maximum and minimum annual runoff, and coefficient of variation. Data not available for Hawaii and Alaska. Text on water resources.*	
_____	142	**Territorial Growth** (1969 Edition)....................$1.50 *Fourteen maps on one sheet show territorial growth from 1775 to 1920; and United States and outlying areas: 1960.*	
_____	182	**Major Forest Types** (1967 Edition)....................$1.50 *Information shown by colors on map of conterminous United States with insets showing Alaska and the principal islands of Hawaii.*	
_____	270	**Population Distribution, Urban and Rural; 1960** ....$1.00 *Map of Conterminous United States. Insets show Alaska and principal islands of Hawaii.* (Also see sheet 420)	
_____	272	**Federal Lands** (1968 Edition) ....$1.50 *Principal lands administered or held in trust by Federal agencies: January 1, 1968.*	
_____	276	**Congressional Districts for the 94th Congress** (1975)....$1.00 *Map of conterminous United States with insets showing Alaska and principal islands of Hawaii; text and number of repre- sentatives by States.*	
_____	418	**Population** (1970).....................................$1.50 Four maps on one sheet showing Population Trends 1940-1970; Population Density 1970; Percent Change in Total Population 1960-1970; Percent of Population Urban 1970.	
_____	420	**Population Distribution, Urban and Rural; 1970**..........$1.00 *Map of Conterminous United States. Insets show Alaska and principal islands of Hawaii.*	

GENERAL REFERENCE   1:2,000,000 Scale Sectional Maps

Quantity	Sheet No.	Subject	Unit Price
_____	6-7	**Northeastern States** (1972).....................$1.50 includes Maine, New Hampshire, Vermont, New York, Massachusetts, Connecticut, Rhode Island.	

GENERAL REFERENCE 1:2,000,000 Scale Sectional Maps

Quantity	Sheet No.	Subject	Unit Price
_____	8-9	Middle Atlantic States (1972)..................$1.50 includes Pennsylvania, New Jersey, Delaware, Maryland, Virginia, West Virginia, Ohio.	
_____	10-11	Southeastern States (1972)....................$1.50 includes North Carolina, South Carolina, Georgia,	
_____	12-13	Florida (1972).................................$1.50	
_____	14-15	Southern Mississippi Valley States (1972).......$1.50 includes Alabama, Mississippi, Louisiana, Arkansas, Tennessee.	
_____	16-17	Central Mississippi Valley States (1972).......$1.50 includes Indiana, Illinois, Iowa, Missouri, Kentucky.	
_____	18-19	Northern Great Lakes States (1972).............$1.50 includes Michigan, Wisconsin, Minnesota.	
_____	20-21	Northern Plains States (1972)..................$1.50 includes North Dakota, South Dakota, Montana, Wyoming.	
_____	22-23	Central Plains States (1973)...................$1.50 includes Nebraska, Colorado, Kansas.	
_____	24-25	Southern Plains States (1973)..................$1.50 includes Oklahoma, Texas.	
_____	26-27	Southern Texas (1973)..........................$1.50	
_____	28-29	Arizona and New Mexico (1973)..................$1.50	
_____	30-31	Southern California (1973).....................$1.50	
_____	32-33	Central Pacific States (1972)..................$1.50 includes Northern California, Nevada, Utah.	
_____	34-35	Northwestern States (1973)....................$1.50 includes Idaho, Washington, Oregon.	
_____	36	Hawaiian Islands (1972).......................$1.50	
_____	37	Southeastern Alaska (1972)....................$1.50	

GENERAL REFERENCE   1:2,000,000 Scale Sectional Maps

Quantity	Sheet No.	Subject	Unit Price
_____	38-39	Central Alaska (1973)..........................$1.50	
_____	40-41	Northern Alaska (1973)..........................$1.50	
_____	42-43	Southwestern Alaska (1973).....................$1.50	
_____	44-45	Aleutian Islands (1973).......................$1.50	

USE SPACE BELOW FOR OTHER MAPS

------   ----------------------------------   ------   ----------------------------------
------   ----------------------------------   ------   ----------------------------------
------   ----------------------------------   ------   ----------------------------------
------   ----------------------------------   ------   ----------------------------------
------   ----------------------------------   ------   ----------------------------------
------   ----------------------------------   ------   ----------------------------------
------   ----------------------------------   ------   ----------------------------------
------   ----------------------------------   ------   ----------------------------------
------   ----------------------------------   ------   ----------------------------------

U. S. DEPARTMENT OF THE INTERIOR—GEOLOGICAL SURVEY

for PROMPT, ACCURATE SHIPMENT PLEASE FILL IN THE FOLLOWING LABEL
Please PRINT or TYPEWRITE

FROM:

BRANCH OF DISTRIBUTION
EASTERN REGION
U.S. GEOLOGICAL SURVEY
1200 SOUTH EADS STREET
ARLINGTON, VIRGINIA 22202

TO:

Name_____

Street Address_____

City_____State_____ Zip Code___

CHAPTER 31

FEDERAL FORMS

When seeking information from the federal Government certain forms and procedures must be used.

Enclosed are the most often used Federal Forms. Additional copies are available from the various agencies concerned at no charge. These do not apply to state or private agencies. Copies may be made of the forms in this book to be used for the purpose intended. Following this procedure will allow you to leave this book intact.

The 1920 and Later Census; Confidential

The personal data contained in the 1920 and later Censuses is confidential under Title 13, United States Code. The confidentiality of these records applies on an individual basis to names and addresses, as well as to personal data.

We are not, therefore, permitted to furnish information showing names of all persons found living in any household on the census dates. The information we can furnish is limited to the name and personal data of the individual for whom the authority is received. Names of parents or other head of household may be shown, but the names of all persons in the household cannot be listed without the authority to do so for each.

Our policy on genealogy requests is to charge one search fee of $12.00 for each family and provide a transcript of personal data (name, relationship, age and place of birth) for one member of the family. The full schedule requires an additional $4.00 for each individual whose personal data is requested.

This information is taken from a letter written by the United States Department of Commerce, Bureau of the Census, Personal Census Service Branch, Pittsburg, Kansas 66762, to Mr. Ron Bremer.

 General
Services
Administration

National Archives
and
Records Service   Washington, DC 20408

October 20, 1982

Dear

This is in response to your letter of September 5, 1982, concerning pre-1906 passport applications. Enclosed is a reference report which, we hope, will explain our holdings. Also enclosed is a form letter which furnishes additional information. This letter is used in most of our responses regarding passports.

Please contact us if we can be of any further assistance.

Sincerely,

RONALD E. SWERCZEK
Legislative and Diplomatic Branch
Civil Archives Division

Enclosures

 General Services Administration   National Archives and Records Service Washington, DC 20408

Date

Reply to
Attn of NNFD

Subject

To

1. ( ) We cannot undertake extensive searches of the indexes, but we can make them available for your use in our index room.

2. ( ) We are unable to locate any record of an application.

3. ( ) We cannot conduct a search without more specific information. If possible, please provide the full name and approximate date of travel on the back of this form and return it to us.

4. ( ) Passport applications dated 1906-1925 are in the custody of the General Branch, Civil Archives Division, National Archives and Records Service, Washington, DC 20409. We have referred a copy of your inquiry to that office.

5. ( ) Passport records dated after 1925 are in the custody of the Passport Office, Department of State, 1425 K Street, N.W., Washington, DC 20520. You must provide name, date of birth, and as much other information as you can. In addition, you should include a copy of a death certificate or a letter from the applicant granting permission for the search.

6. ( ) We do not have passport applications for foreign citizens who traveled or emigrated to the United States.

7. ( ) We have located an application for _____
from _____, dated _____.
We can provide a copy for _____.
To order please send a check or money order, payable to the National Archives Trust Fund (NNFD), to the Cashier, National Archives and Records Service, Washington, DC 20408.

ORDER BLANKS CORRECTLY FILLED IN HELP TO SPEED PROCESSING OF YOUR ORDER

Microfilm publication numbers (preceded by an "M" or "T") are assigned to each microfilm publication. Please enter microfilm publication number and roll number in the proper column. As we accept orders for individual rolls as well as for complete microfilm publications, we must know which rolls you wish to purchase.

The price of each roll of film is $15.00. The introduction to this catalog contains an explanation of our pricing policy.

Sample of Correctly Completed Form

MICRO. PUB. NUMBER	ROLL NUMBER	PRICE
T624	1138	$15
T1270	89	$15

Additional order forms are available upon request

The price of microfilm was raised to $17 per roll on August 9, 1982

MICROFILM ORDER *(Prices subject to change)*		MICRO. PUB. NUMBER	ROLL NUMBER	PRICE
TO	Cashier National Archives Trust Fund Board Washington, DC 20408			
Please send me the microfilm listed in this order. Enclosed is ☐ CHECK ☐ MONEY ORDER for $ _____ or charge my ☐ VISA ☐ MASTER CHARGE				
ACCOUNT NUMBER EXPIRATION DATE				
SIGNATURE				
FROM	Name			
	Address (Number and street)			
	City, State and ZIP Code		**TOTAL PRICE**	

NATIONAL ARCHIVES TRUST FUND BOARD

NATF Form 36 (8-79)

MICROFILM ORDER *(Prices subject to change)*		MICRO. PUB. NUMBER	ROLL NUMBER	PRICE
TO	Cashier National Archives Trust Fund Board Washington, DC 20408			
Please send me the microfilm listed in this order. Enclosed is ☐ CHECK ☐ MONEY ORDER for $ _____ or charge my ☐ VISA ☐ MASTER CHARGE				
ACCOUNT NUMBER EXPIRATION DATE				
SIGNATURE				
FROM	Name			
	Address (Number and street)			
	City, State and ZIP Code		**TOTAL PRICE**	

NATIONAL ARCHIVES TRUST FUND BOARD

NATF Form 36 (8-79)

ORDERING INSTRUCTIONS

Microfilm publication numbers (preceded by an "M" or "T") are assigned to each microfilm publication. Please enter microfilm publication number and roll number in the proper column. As we accept orders for individual rolls as well as for complete microfilm publications, we must know which rolls you wish to purchase.

Effective August 9, 1982, the price of microfilm is $17 per roll. Orders postmarked before that date will be filled at $15 per roll. To order, complete the form below and send with check, money order, or purchase order payable to the "National Archives Trust Fund (NEPS)" to Cashier (NJC) National Archives Trust Fund, Washington, DC 20408.

Sample of Correctly Completed Form

MICRO. PUB. NUMBER	ROLL NUMBER	PRICE
M653	20	
M704	12	

Additional order forms are available upon request

MICROFILM ORDER (Prices subject to change)		MICRO PUB NUMBER	ROLL NUMBER	PRICE
TO	Cashier National Archives Trust Fund Board Washington, DC 20408			
Please send me the microfilm listed in this order. Enclosed is ☐ CHECK ☐ MONEY ORDER for $ or charge my ☐ VISA ☐ MASTER CHARGE				
ACCOUNT NUMBER EXPIRATION DATE				
SIGNATURE				
FROM	Name			
	Address (Number and street)			
	City, State and ZIP Code			**TOTAL PRICE**

NATIONAL ARCHIVES TRUST FUND BOARD

Dear Patron:

Your order for military or passenger arrival records is being returned because it was not prepaid or we received insufficient payment.

Effective September 1, 1981, the cost of furnishing reproductions from military and passenger arrival records in response to mail inquiries was increased to $5.00 for each record ordered. We are also asking that your requests for reporductions from these records be pre-paid. *Billing for this service has been discontinued.* You may continue to use existing copies of NATF Form 26 (order and Billing for Copies of Veterans Records) and NATF Form 40 (Order and Billing for Copies of Passenger Arrival Records) until the supply is exhausted. The $3.00 fee for reproductions which appears on some of the older forms should be disregarded.

Please Make your check or money order payable to:

NATF 26

NATF 40

National Archives Trust Fund (NNMS)

National Archives Trust Fund (NNIR)

Mail Completed form with payment to:

Cashier (NJC)
National Archives Trust Fund
8th & Pennsylvania Avenue, N.W.
Washington, DC 20408

THANK YOU FOR YOUR COOPERATION

Date Received (NNMS)

ORDER FOR COPIES
OF VETERANS RECORDS

NJC Use

INSTRUCTIONS FOR COMPLETING THIS FORM

Submit a separate set of forms for each veteran. Do NOT remove any of the pages of this 3-part set. A payment of $5.00 is required for EACH file checked in Block 1. **PREPAYMENT IS REQUIRED.** Make check payable to **National Archives Trust Fund (NNMS).**

Mail completed form with payment to:

Cashier (NJC)
National Archives Trust Fund
8th & Pennsylvania Avenue, N.W.
Washington, DC 20408

AMOUNT ENCLOSED ▶

☐ ORDER FILLED
☐ Partial ☐ Complete

1. CHECK RECORD DESIRED	REQUIRED MINIMUM IDENTIFICATION OF VETERAN
	Items 2, 3, 4, 5 (and 6, when applicable) MUST be completed or your order cannot be serviced.

☐ PENSION

☐ BOUNTY-LAND WARRANT APPLICATION *(Service before 1856 only)*

☐ MILITARY

2. VETERAN *(Give last, first, and middle names)*

3. BRANCH OF SERVICE IN WHICH HE SERVED
☐ Army ☐ Navy ☐ Marine Corps

4. STATE FROM WHICH SERVED

5. WAR IN WHICH, OR DATES BETWEEN WHICH HE SERVED

6. IF SERVICE WAS CIVIL WAR
☐ Union ☐ Confederate

PLEASE PROVIDE THE FOLLOWING INFORMATION, IF KNOWN

7. UNIT IN WHICH HE SERVED *(Name of regiment or number, company, etc., name of ship)*

8. IF SERVICE WAS ARMY, ARM IN WHICH HE SERVED
☐ Infantry ☐ Cavalry ☐ Artillary

If other, specify:

9. KIND OF SERVICE
☐ Volunteers ☐ Regulars

10. Pension or Bounty Land File No.

11. DATE OF BIRTH

12. PLACE OF BIRTH *(City, County, State, etc.)*

13. NAME OF WIDOW OR OTHER CLAIMANT

14. DATE OF DEATH

15. PLACE OF DEATH *(City, County, State, etc.)*

17. PLACE(S) VETERAN LIVED AFTER SERVICE

16. IF VETERAN LIVED IN A HOME FOR SOLDIERS, GIVE LOCATION *(City & State)*

18. YOUR NAME & ADDRESS

Print or type your name and address within the block below.

[Zip Code]

Do NOT write below — Space is for our reply to you.

☐ RECORD FILE ENCLOSED
☐ Pension $5   ☐ Bounty Land $5   ☐ Military $5

NUMBER OF FILES FROM WHICH COPIES WERE REPRODUCED

☐ WE WERE UNABLE TO COMPLETE YOUR ORDER

☐ REQUIRED MINIMUM IDENTIFICATION OF VETERAN WAS NOT PROVIDED. Please complete items 2 (give full name), 3, 4, and 5, and resubmit. Your order and remittance are returned to you.

☐ A SEARCH WAS MADE BUT THE RECORDS YOU REQUESTED WERE NOT FOUND.
☐ Pension
☐ Bounty Land
☐ Military

When we do not find a record for a veteran, this does not mean that he did not serve. You may be able to obtain information about him from the State archives.

☐ Your order and your remittance are returned to you.

☐ Because extended search time was involved, a formal refund must be issued by the US Treasury, which will take 6–8 weeks for processing.

REFUND AUTHORIZING SIGNATURE *(Complete Name)*

REFUND AMOUNT ▶

☐ We found _____ pension or bounty land files and _____ military service files of the same name (or similar variations). You may order copies by returning the enclosed, marked forms.

☐ See attached forms/leaflets/information sheet.

☐ Other: _____

19. NUMBER OF THESE BLANK FORMS YOU WOULD LIKE SENT TO YOU	SEARCHER	FILE DESIGNATION
	DATE	

NATIONAL ARCHIVES TRUST FUND BOARD

NATF Form 26 (Rev. 5-82)

CUSTOMER

TYPES OF RECORDS THAT CAN BE ORDERED WITH THIS FORM

PENSION APPLICATION FILES based on United States (not State) service before World War I. Pension files usually include an official statement of the veteran's military service, as well as information of a personal nature. Pensions based on military service for the Confederate States of America were authorized by some Southern States but not by the Federal Government until 1959. Inquiries about State pensions should be addressed to the State archives or equivalent agency at the capital of the veteran's State of residence after the war.

BOUNTY-LAND WARRANT APPLICATION FILES based on United States (not State) service before 1856. Documents in a bounty-land warrant application file are similar to those in a pension application file. In addition, these files usually give the veteran's age and place of residence at the time the application was made.

MILITARY SERVICE RECORDS based on service in the United States Army (officers who served before June 30, 1917; enlisted men who served before October 31, 1912); Navy (officers who served before 1903; enlisted men who served before 1886); Marine Corps (officers and enlisted men who served before 1896); and Confederate armed forces (officers and enlisted men, 1861-65). In addition to persons who served in regular forces raised by the Federal Government, volunteers fought in various wars chiefly in the Federal Government's interest from the Revolutionary War through the Phillipine Insurrection, 1775-1902.

Compilations of information concerning most military service performed by individuals in volunteer organizations during the nineteenth and early twentieth century are available, but such records were not compiled for Regular Army officers who served before 1863 and for Regular Army enlisted men and Navy and Marine Corps personnel who served during most of the nineteenth century. Records pertaining to such service are scattered among many files and vary in content, but we can furnish information on the military careers of individuals who served in these organizations. Because of Department of Defense restrictions on personnel records, we cannot provide photocopies of files pertaining to military service that ended less than 75 years ago; however, we are usually able to provide certain unrestricted information from these files. Military service records rarely contain family information.

The record of an individual's service in any one organization is entirely separate from his record of service in another organization. We are ordinarily unable to accurately establish the identity of individuals of the same name who served in different organizations. If you know that an individual served in more than one organization and you desire copies of all of the military service records, submit a separate form for the service record in each organization.

IMPORTANT INFORMATION

When you send more than one form at a time, each form may be handled separately and you may not receive all of your replies at the same time.

When because of the size of a pension or bounty-land warrant application file, we are unable to provide copies of all documents, we send copies of the documents we think will be most useful to you. You may order copies of all documents in a file by making a specific request. We will notify you of the cost of the copies. We will also advise you of the cost of reproducing any military service records that cannot be furnished for the $5.00 fee. Prepayment is required.

Often there are many files for veterans of the same or nearly the same name. If there are **five or fewer files** for men with the same name as the individual in whom you are interested, we will examine all the relevant files and compare their contents with the information that you have provided us. If the veteran's identity seems obvious, we will furnish you a copy of the file we think is the correct one.

If there are more than five files, we will not make a file-by-file check to see if the information in the numerous files matches that provided for the veteran in whom you are interested. In such cases, we suggest that you visit the National Archives and examine the various files, or hire a professional researcher to examine the files for you. We do not maintain a list of persons who do research for a fee; however many researchers advertise their services in genealogical periodicals, usually available in libraries.

More information about the availability of records pertaining to military service may be found in our free genealogical information leaflets and forms. These may be requested by writing to:

Reference Services Branch (NNIR)
Washington, DC 20408

NATIONAL ARCHIVES TRUST FUND BOARD

NATF Form 26 BACK (5-82)

ORDER AND BILLING FOR COPIES OF PASSENGER ARRIVAL RECORDS

Please follow instructions below.
Submit a separate set of order forms for each passenger arrival. Do not remove any of the sheets of this 3 part set. You will be billed $3.00 for each list reproduced. **Do not mail payment with your order.** This form will be returned to you and serves as your bill when we fill your order.

Date received

Mail the complete set of this order to ▶ **Passenger Arrival Records (NNCC), Washington, DC 20408**

IDENTIFICATION OF ENTRY

	NAME OF IMMIGRANT OR NAMES OF MEMBERS OF IMMIGRANT FAMILY	AGE	SEX
DATE OF ARRIVAL			
PORT OF ENTRY			
WHERE NATURALIZED *(if known)*			
SHIP NAME *(or carrier line)*			
PASSENGER'S COUNTRY OF ORIGIN			

NOTE

The National Archives has customs passenger lists dating back to 1820 with a few as early as 1787. Lists prior to 1820 that are not at the National Archives may be on file at the port of entry or the State archives in the State where the port is located. The **Morton Allan Directory of European Passenger Steamship Arrivals** may be useful in determining the name and arrival date of ships arriving at New York, 1890—1930, and Philadelphia, Baltimore, and Boston, 1904—1926.

Please fill in as much of the information called for above as possible. We will advise you if the information is inadequate to enable us to locate the entry you are seeking.

We do not maintain a list of persons who do research for a fee; however, many researchers advertise their services in genealogical periodicals, usually available in libraries.

YOUR NAME & ADDRESS

Type or print legibly
PRESS HARD

Name
Number & Street
City & State
(Zip code)

DO NOT WRITE BELOW - SPACE IS FOR REPLY TO YOU

ARRIVAL DATE	PORT	SHIP

☐ THIS IS YOUR BILL — RECORD ENCLOSED ▶

MICROFILM PUBLICATION	make check or money order payable to NATF (NNCC)
ROLL	PAGE	AMOUNT DUE ▶ $

☐ WE WERE UNABLE TO COMPLETE YOUR ORDER — RECORD SEARCHED FOR BUT NOT FOUND ▶

RECORDS SEARCHED

MICROFILM PUBLICATION	SEARCHER

☐ SEE REVERSE

ROLL	PAGE	DATE SEARCHED

☐ A SEARCH WAS NOT MADE FOR THE REASON INDICATED:

☐ 1. Our index to New York passenger arrivals covers the periods 1820 — 1846 and 1897 — 1943. We regret that we cannot undertake a page-by-page search of the lists for the period between 1847 — 1896, inclusive.

☐ 2. Masters of vessels departing from U.S. ports were not required to list the names of passengers. Therefore, we would not have a list for the passenger you have cited.

☐ 3. Our holdings of passenger lists do not include any for Pacific coast ports. The San Francisco passenger lists were destroyed by fires in 1851 and 1940. (Consult the two works by Louis J. Pasmussen, **San Francisco Ship Passenger Lists**, 4 vols., 1965; and **Railway Passenger Lists of Overland Trains to San Francisco and the West**, 1 vol., 1966.)

☐ 4. Overland arrivals into the U.S. from Canada and Mexico are not documented in passenger list records.

☐ 5. Justice Department restrictions prohibit us from making searches in Immigration and Naturalization records less than 50 years old. We suggest that you direct an inquiry to: District Director, Immigration and Naturalization Service, New York, NY 10007.

NUMBER OF BLANK ORDER FORMS YOU WOULD LIKE SENT TO YOU ▶

NATIONAL ARCHIVES TRUST FUND BOARD

NATF FORM 40 (12-79)

Important Immigration Records Now Available for Sale on Microfilm

All restrictions have been lifted on access to name indexes to passenger arrivals and passenger and crew lists in the custody of the National Archives. The Immigration and Naturalization Service (INS), at the request of the National Archives and Records Service, agreed to the release of "Passenger Arrival Records, 1883-1954," previously subject to a 50 year restriction.

The agreement opens 6,055 rolls of microfilm to researchers, making a total of 11,476 rolls of INS microfilm available.

Of particular interest are the following eight titles, comprising a total of 888 rolls that have never before been available to researchers. These newly released publications reproduce extensive name indexes for passengers arriving at major ports in the eastern United States:

Index (Soundex) to Passenger Lists of Vessels Arriving at Baltimore, 1897-July 1952. T520. 43 rolls. $731.00*

Index to Passengers Arriving at Gulfport, [MS] August 27, 1904- August 28, 1954. T523. 1 roll. $17.00

Index to Passengers Arriving at New Bedford, [MA] July 1, 1902 - November 18, 1954. T522. 2 rolls. $34.00

Index to Passenger Lists of Vessels Arriving at New Orleans, 1900-1952. T618. 22 rolls. $374.00

Index (Soundex) to Passenger Lists of Vessels Arriving at New York, July 1, 1902 - December 31, 1943. T621. 756 rolls. $12,852.00

Index (Soundex) cards, Ship Arrivals at Philadelphia, January 1, 1883- June 28, 1948. T526. 61 rolls. $1,037.00

Index to Passengers Arriving at Portland, Maine, January 29, 1893 - November 22, 1954. T524. 1 roll. $17.00

Index to Passengers Arriving at Providence, Rhode Island, June 18, 1911- October 5, 1954. T518. 2 rolls. $34.00

A catalog describing microfilm publications of passenger arrivals, crew lists, and indexes will be published in the fall of 1982. The catalog will contain both detailed descriptions of the records and roll-by-roll listings for most publications. For a copy please write to: Publications Sales Branch (NEPS), National Archives and Records Service, Washington, DC 20408 or call (202) 523-3181

---

*Prices quoted reflect increase to $17 per roll effective August 9, 1982.

July 1982

PASSENGER LISTS IN THE NATIONAL ARCHIVES

☐ 1. We found several entries for persons of the same name arriving at the same port during the same period. Additional information, such as age, occupation, etc., will help in resolving this problem.

☐ 2. We found the requested information on the passenger index, but we regret that the corresponding passenger list is missing. A copy of the index card is enclosed.

☐ 3. We are unable to locate the passenger list for the ship listed and have found no entry on the passenger index for the requested party at that port.

☐ 4. We examined the passenger list for the requested ship and were unable to find an entry for the requested passenger.

☐ 5. The register of ship arrivals did not show any entry for the ship named.

☐ 6. Our only passenger lists for the cited port do not cover the date that you have requested, and we were unable to find an entry on the index to the lists we have.

☐ 7. You may find some help in the book **Irish and Scotch-Irish Ancestral Research** by Margaret Dickson Falley (1962). It is a guide to genealogical records and repositories in Ireland and is normally available in larger libraries.

☐ 8. Passports are issued to persons leaving the U.S., not arriving but early arrivals are frequently documented in passenger lists, which are described in the enclosed leaflet.

☐ 9. The National Archives has abstracts of Naturalization proceedings for the New England States (1787 — 1906) and the District of Columbia (1802 — 1926). For information about citizenship granted elsewhere before September 27, 1906, send inquiries to the clerk of the Federal, State, or other court that issued the naturalization certificate. The Immigration and Naturalization Service, Washington, DC 20536, can furnish information on naturalizations that occurred after September 26, 1906.

☐ 10. It should be noted that the passenger lists in our custody do not represent a complete collection. Some passenger lists of the 19th century were either lost or destroyed by dampness, fire, and other causes before records of this type were deposited in the National Archives.

PASSENGER LISTS AND INDEXES

M-334   A Supplemental Index to Passenger Lists of Vessels Arriving at Atlantic and Gulf Coast Ports (Excluding New York) 1820-1874

M-575   Copies of Lists of Passengers Arriving at Miscellaneous Ports on the Atlantic and Gulf Coasts and at Ports on the Great Lakes, 1820-1873

M-326   Index to Passenger Lists of Vessels Arriving at Baltimore, 1833-1866

M-327   Index to Passenger Lists of Vessels Arriving at Baltimore, 1820-1897 (Federal Passenger Lists)

T-790   Boox Indexes, Boston Passenger Lists, 1899

T-521   Index to Passenger Lists of Vessels Arriving at Boston, 1902-1906

T-843   Passenger Lists of Vessels Arriving at Boston, 1891-1919

T-944   Passenger Lists of Vessels Arriving at New Bedford, 1902

M-261   Index to Passenger Lists of Vessels Arriving at New York, 1820-1846

M-360   Index to Passenger Lists of Vessels Arriving at Philadelphia, 1800-1906

M-425   Passenger Lists of Vessels Arriving at Philadelphia, 1800-1882

T-840   Passenger Lists of Vessels Arriving at Philadelphia, 1883-1919

T-943   Passenger Lists of Vessels Arriving at Savannah, 1906

REFERENCE REPORT

INQUIRY: Passport records

REPORT: Since 1789 the Department of State has issued passports to U.S. citizens traveling abroad. The Department did not, however, have sole authority to do so until section 23 of an act of August 18, 1856 (11 Stat. 60), for the first time regulated the issuance of passports.

Except for two periods during wartime, American citizens were not required to have a passport for travel abroad until World War II. Passports were required for a short time during the Civil War (August 19, 1861-March 17, 1862) and during World War I. Executive Order No. 2285 of December 15, 1915, stated that all persons leaving the United States should have passports, and an act of May 22, 1918 (40 Stat.559), made it unlawful for American citizens to travel abroad without a valid passport. This law lapsed with the formal termination of war in 1921. On June 21, 1941, the act of 1918 was revived (55 Stat.252), and, since that date, U.S. citizens have been required to have passports for foreign travel.

State Department passport records in the National Archives include applications dated October 27, 1795-November 30, 1812; February 22, 1830-November 15, 1831; and May 13, 1833-December 31, 1905; emergency applications submitted abroad, 1877-1907; originals and copies of passports, 1794-1901; and applications for special (diplomatic) passports, 1829-1897.

Finding aids for these records are incomplete. There is an alphabetical card index for applications dated 1850-1852 and 1860-1880. For the years 1810-1817 and 1834-1906 there are also registers and indexes which vary in arrangement. Some are chronological and some are alphabetical by the first one or two letters of the applicant's surname.

RONALD E. SWERCZEK
Diplomatic Branch
Civil Archives Division

General Services Administration   National Archives and Records Service

WORLD WAR I REGISTRATION CARD REQUEST

Return this form to: ARCHIVES BRANCH, FARC 1559 ST. JOSEPH AVENUE
                         EAST POINT, GEORGIA 30344 PHONE: 404/763-7477

ATTENTION:

More than 24,000,000 World War I Selective Service records are on file at
our Center. They are filed by state and by draft board. To search this
large file we must have the full name of the person and their city and/or
county at the time of registration. For the cities listed below, a home
street address or other specific location information (such as ward) is
required.

Please complete this form and return it to us. For each card required,
complete a separate request form and enclose $~~0.00~~. Make check payable
to: NATIONAL ARCHIVES TRUST FUND. $5.00

REGISTRANT DATA   (COMPLETED BY REQUESTOR)

Full name of Registrant   Birthdate

Home Address at time of registration (street, city, county)   Birthplace (city, county & state)
                              and state

Draft Board Location (city, county, board no. and street address)   Registration Date

Name of Wife or nearest relative at time of registration   Occupation at the time of reg.

SIGNATURE OF REQUESTOR: DATE:

ADDRESS:

CITIES FOR WHICH A STREET ADDRESS OR OTHER SPECIFIC INFORMATION IS REQUIRED

CALIFORNIA	LOUISIANA	NEW YORK	WISCONSIN
Los Angeles	New Orleans	Albany	Milwaukee
San Francisco		Buffalo	
	MARYLAND	New York City	
DISTRICT OF COLUMBIA	Baltimore	Syracuse	
Washington			
	MASSACHUSETTS	OHIO	
GEORGIA	Boston	Cincinnati	
Atlanta		Cleveland	
	MINNESOTA		
ILLINOIS	Minneapolis	PENNSYLVANIA	
Chicago	St. Paul	Luzerne County	
		Philadelphia	
INDIANA	MISSOURI	Pittsburgh	
Indianapolis	Kansas City		
	St. Louis	RHODE ISLAND	
KENTUCKY		Providence	
Louisville	NEW JERSEY		
	Jersey City	WASHINGTON	
	Newark	Seattle	

UNITED STATES DEPARTMENT OF JUSTICE
Immigration and Naturalization Service

Form approved
OMB No. 043-R0570

Fee Stamp

APPLICATION FOR
VERIFICATION OF INFORMATION FROM
IMMIGRATION AND NATURALIZATION SERVICE
RECORDS

TYPE OR PRINT THE NAME AND MAILING ADDRESS OF THE PERSONS TO WHOM IN-
FORMATION OR COPIES OF RECORD SHOULD BE RETURNED IN THE BOX BELOW:

NAME	
STREET ADDRESS	
CITY, STATE ZIP CODE	

PERSON CONSENTING

NAME AND ADDRESS

SIGNATURE OF PERSON CONSENTING

1. CHECK TYPE OF VERIFICATION REQUESTED:	2. STATE PURPOSE FOR WHICH DESIRED	3. NUMBER OF COPIES DESIRED, IF ANY:
☐ AGE OR DATE OF BIRTH		
☐ NATURALIZATION OR CITIZENSHIP		
☐ GENEALOGICAL INFORMATION	2A. NAMES OF BENEFICIARIES	4. IF INFORMATION IS FOR SOCIAL SECURITY BENEFITS, SHOW SOCIAL SECURITY NUMBER:
☐ OTHER (CERTIFICATE OF BIRTH DATA, ETC.)		

DATA FOR IDENTIFICATION OF THE RECORD TO BE VERIFIED

5. FAMILY NAME GIVEN NAME	MIDDLE NAME	6. ALIEN REGISTRATION NUMBER
7. OTHER NAMES USED, IF ANY	8. NAME USED AT TIME OF ENTRY INTO UNITED STATES	
9. PLACE OF BIRTH	10. DATE OF BIRTH	11. PORT ABROAD FROM WHICH LEFT FOR UNITED STATES
12. PORT OF ENTRY INTO UNITED STATES	13. DATE OF ENTRY	14. NAME OF VESSEL OR OTHER MEANS OF ENTRY

GIVE THE FOLLOWING INFORMATION FOR VERIFICATION OF NATURALIZATION OR CERTIFICATE OF CITIZENSHIP

15. NAME ON CERTIFICATE	16. CERTIFICATE NUMBER	17. DATE ISSUED
18. ADDRESS WHEN CERTIFICATE WAS ISSUED	19. NAME AND LOCATION OF NATURALIZATION COURT OR IMMI-GRATION OFFICE ISSUING CERTIFICATE OF CITIZENSHIP	

20. SIGNATURE OF APPLICANT

DO NOT COMPLETE THIS BLOCK —
RESERVED FOR GOVERNMENT USE ONLY

THE RECORDS OF THE IMMIGRATION AND NATURALIZATION SERVICE REFLECT THE FOLLOWING:
VERIFICATION OF INFORMATION REQUESTED WAS MADE ON THE DATE SHOWN AT RIGHT

DATE:

☐ LAWFUL ADMISSION FOR PERMANENT RESIDENCE ON _____ AT _____

☐ NATURALIZATION INFORMATION AS SHOWN ABOVE IS CORRECT

☐ NATURALIZATION IN (COURT) _____ ON (DATE) _____

AT (LOCATION) _____

☐ DATE OF BIRTH _____

☐ ARRIVAL RECORD DATED _____ SHOWED SUBJECT'S AGE AT TIME TO BE _____

☐ UNABLE TO IDENTIFY ANY RECORD

☐ COPIES ATTACHED AS REQUESTED

SIGNATURE _____

TITLE _____

PRIVACY ACT IDENTIFICATION (WHEN REQUIRED)	☐ IDENTITY ESTABLISHED IN PERSON	Approved By:	DATE
	DOCUMENTS ATTACHED ☐ G-652 Affidavit ☐ OTHER (List)		

FORM G-641 (REV. 6-20-80)N

UNITED STATES DEPARTMENT OF JUSTICE
IMMIGRATION AND NATURALIZATION SERVICE

APPLICATION FOR VERIFICATION OF INFORMATION FROM
IMMIGRATION AND NATURALIZATION SERVICE RECORDS

INSTRUCTIONS

Failure to comply with instructions may make it necessary to reject your application.

1. APPLICATION. Form G-641 shall be used where it is requested that verification of age or date of birth, naturalization or citizenship and genealogical information be provided, in letter form, to a person or organization. The form shall also be used for any other requests where the information is to be furnished directly to another Government agency or Court. This application must be accompanied by a fee of $5.00.

Note: Verification of naturalization or citizenship records will not be returned to the subject of the record.

2. IDENTIFICATION OF THE RECORD. The personal data requested in Items 5 thru 19 should relate to the individual from whose record the information is sought. It should be complete and as accurate as possible.

3. CONSENT REQUIRED. The subject of a Service record may consent in writing to another person's obtaining information to which the subject would be entitled. A block is provided in the application form where such consent is shown.

4. IDENTIFICATION OF REQUESTER. Service regulations implementing the Privacy Act of 1974, P.L. 93-597, require that a United States citizen or an alien lawfully admitted for permanent residence who is seeking access to records about himself, or consenting to disclosure from records about himself, shall establish his identity before access or disclosure may be granted. Such an individual appearing in person may identify himself by showing a document bearing a photograph (such as an Alien Registration Card, Form I-151, Citizen Identification Card, Form I-197, Naturalization Certificate, or passport); or two items which bear his name and address (such as driver's license or credit card). By mail, such an individual shall identify himself by signature, address, date and place of birth, alien or employee identification number (if any), and one other identifier such as a photocopy of a document bearing name, address, and signature. If the above mentioned identification is not available, Form G-652, Privacy Act Affidavit of Identity, or similar Department of Justice form may be used. Identification is not required if the information requested is contained in a public record such as a naturalization proceeding.

5. FEES. (a) **Basic Charges.** A fee of $5.00 shall be charged for the filing of each application. The fee is not returnable. When the information requested relates to two or more persons a separate form shall be filed on each individual with accompanying fee.

(b) **Certifications.** A fee of $3.00 is required for each certification of a record under seal. (See instruction No. 8). A fee of $1.00 is required for each certification of a record not under seal.

(c) **Manner of submission.** If this application is mailed, DO NOT SEND CASH, ALL FEES MUST BE SUBMITTED IN THE EXACT AMOUNT. Attach a check or a United States postal money order (or, if outside the United States, an international money order) made payable to "Immigration and Naturalization Service, Department of Justice." An applicant residing in the U.S. Virgin Islands shall make his remittance payable to "Commissioner of Finance of the Virgin Islands," and if residing in Guam, to "Treasurer, Guam." Personal checks are accepted subject to collectibility. An uncollectible check will render the application and any documents issued pursuant thereto invalid. A charge of $5.00 will be imposed if a check in payment of a fee is not honored by the bank on which it is drawn.

6. NATURALIZATION RECORDS. This Service does not maintain records of naturalization prior to September 27, 1906. These records are maintained by the court in which the person was naturalized and may be obtained directly from the clerk of court. Records of naturalization created on and after September 27, 1906 may also be obtained directly from the clerk of the court in which the person was naturalized. Do not use this form unless a verification of naturalization prior to September 27, 1906 is desired for official purposes, such as applying for a U.S. passport or qualifying for old age assistance, etc. Direct requests for genealogical or other personal information to the clerk of the court in which the person was naturalized.

7. ARRIVAL RECORDS. Records of arrival are not available from this Service prior to 1891. Some passenger lists of the Bureau of Customs dating from 1820 are maintained by the General Reference Section, the National Archives, Washington, D.C. 20408. Inquiries concerning these records should not be made on this form nor submitted to this Service but should be forwarded directly to that agency with sufficient information for an adequate search, i.e., approximate dates of travel, name under which the person arrived, name of vessel, and port of entry and embarkation.

This Service has records of arrivals at the port of New York since June 16, 1897, and at certain other ports since 1891. Our records of arrivals prior to July 1, 1924, do not contain birthdates but merely show age at time of entry.

OVER

FORM G-641 (REV. 11-12-77) N

8. CERTIFICATES OF NATURALIZATION RECORDS. Section 343(e) of the Immigration and Nationality Act authorizes the Attorney General to make and issue certifications of any part of the naturalization records of any court, or of any certificate of naturalization or citizenship, for use in complying with any statute, state or federal, or in any judicial proceeding. If such certification is required, block No. 1 should contain a listing of the specific information desired followed by the phrase: "in certification form" or the phrase: "in certification form under seal." If the space provided is insufficient, attach an additional sheet of paper. If the certification is required for use in complying with a statute, the relevant statute should be cited or described clearly in block No. 2. If a certification is required for use in a judicial proceeding, attach a separate sheet of paper, listing the title and character of the proceedings, the court in which it is pending and the specific use to which the certification will be put.

9. CERTIFICATE OF BIRTH DATA FROM IMMIGRATION AND NATURALIZATION RECORDS. A Certificate of Birth Data may be issued for a fee of $5.00 to foreign-born children under twenty-one years of age who:

(a) Have been admitted to the United States for permanent residence, whether or not they have since become naturalized, or

(b) Are citizens of the United States and have been issued a Certificate of Citizenship by the Service.

The parent, guardian, or other adult having a legitimate interest in a person who is under fourteen years of age may file an application on such person's behalf. A person between the ages of 14 and 21 may apply for such a certification on his own behalf.

Where documentary evidence is presented to show the child's name has been legally changed, the certification may be issued in the child's new name.

10. PRIVACY ACT INFORMATION. The authority for collecting the information requested on this form is contained in 8 U.S.C. 1103(a). Submission of the information solicited, including the social security number, is voluntary. The purpose for which the information is solicited is to identify the records or information which is to be verified according to applicant's request. Failure to provide any or all of the solicited information may result in delay or inability to make the requested verification.

4-744 (Rev. 11-4-81)

U.S. Department of Justice

Federal Bureau of Investigation

Washington, D.C. 20535

Request No. _____

Dear Requester:

      This is to acknowledge receipt by FBI Headquarters of your recent Freedom of Information-Privacy Acts (FOIPA) request and to advise you we will comply with your request according to Title 5, United States Code, Section 552 (a)(6)(A)(i) and other Federal statutes and regulations. Additional information, if needed, will be requested by separate letter.

      A search of the indices to our records will be made to determine if we have the information you seek. If the search fails to locate record(s) pertaining to your request, you will be notified. If the search locates a record(s) which may be responsive to your request, it will be retrieved and processed according to the provisions of the FOIPA.

      Your request has been assigned the number indicated above. Please use this number in all correspondence with us.

Sincerely yours,

James K. Hall

Chief
Freedom of Information-
  Privacy Acts Section
Records Management Division

DEPARTMENT OF HEALTH, EDUCATION, AND WELFARE
SOCIAL SECURITY ADMINISTRATION
BALTIMORE, MARYLAND 21235

REFER TO:
IDP-62

Dear

This is in further response to your inquiry concerning release of
information from our records.

With reference to your inquiry concerning release of information for
genealogical purposes, information regarding deceased individuals is
available from our records. The only exception is that information
about a decedent may be withheld if disclosure would be a clearly
unwarranted invasion of personal privacy of a living person. In
this event an exemption of the Freedom of Information Act would
apply [5 U.S.C. 552 (b)(6)].

Additionally, because disclosure of information under these circumstances
is permissible only if the individual is deceased, we will require that
the requester submit evidence of death. A public record of death will
meet this requirement.

Fees for providing information will be determined in accordance with
the Department of Health, Education and Welfare regulations implementing
the Freedom of Information Act (45 CFR 5.1 et seq.).

I hope this information is helpful to you.

Sincerely yours,

Harry Over
Director, Bureau of
Data Processing

Social Security
Request For Letter Forwarding Information

From: Bureau of Data Processing
       Baltimore, Maryland 21235

Refer to:

Date:

Records of the Social Security Administration are confidential under the law and generally may be used only for social security and related purposes. Therefore, we cannot disclose whereabouts information to you.

Because there are situations in which it would be proper to offer assistance, we have a service by which we will attempt to forward a letter. Since letter forwarding is not related in any way to a social security program, the use of this service must necessarily be limited so that it does not interfere with our regular program activities. For this reason we cannot accept all letter forwarding requests. Moreover, the service is available only to inform a person of a matter of considerable significance of which he or she is unaware and about which he or she would undoubtedly want to be informed. Requests concerning business propositions are not acceptable for forwarding.

There is no charge for forwarding letters which have a humanitarian purpose. However, we must charge a $3.00 fee when the letter is to inform the missing person of money or property due him or her. This fee is usually not refundable.

The Social Security Administration does not normally maintain the current addresses of people, except for those receiving benefits. We usually forward a letter in care of the employer who most recently reported earnings for the missing person. Therefore, we cannot assure you that the letter will be delivered or that you will receive a reply. In any event, we cannot forward a second letter.

Your request may meet our letter forwarding criteria. If you would like us to consider forwarding a letter for you, please fill in your responses to the items checked on the other side of this form and return it to us with your original letter. Include the letter to be forwarded in an unsealed envelope. We must read the letter to ensure that it contains nothing which could prove embarrassing to the missing person if read by a third party. Documents or money cannot be forwarded.

Enclosure

(See Reverse Side)

Department of Health, Education, and Welfare
Social Security Administration

Form SSA-L963 (3-77)

IF YOU WISH US TO CONSIDER FORWARDING A LETTER, PLEASE RETURN THIS FORM TO US WITH YOUR RESPONSE(S) TO THE CHECKED ITEM(S) AND RETURN YOUR ORIGINAL LETTER.

1	Give the missing person's social security number OR date/place of birth and both parents' names.	2	What is your relationship to the missing person?

3	Describe property or specify the amount of money due the missing person.	4	Why do you want to contact the missing person? Be specific.

5	Are assets due because of a policy or plan of which the missing person at one time had knowledge? If no, explain.	6	Will the assets be lost to the missing person by operation of law within a limited period of time? Specify.

7	When monetary considerations are involved, we require a $3.00 fee per letter to help defray the cost of our records search. This fee is ordinarily not refundable. Make your check payable to the Social Security Administration.	8	We need the letter to be forwarded in a plain unsealed envelope addressed only with the missing person's name. It must say nothing which might embarrass the missing person if accidentally read by a third party.

9	When did the missing person disappear?	10	

DATE:_____19____

REFER TO MAIL LOG #____

DEAR

Your request for photocopies regarding_____

_____

( ) Is enclosed.

( ) Is complete. Your order cost $____. Enclosed is a bill in the
amount to cover your order. Please return _____ copy with your
payment. Make CHECK or MONEY ORDER payable to: THE NATIONAL ARCHIVES
TRUST FUND.

( ) Is not complete (see STATUS INFORMATION below).

_____

_____

STATUS INFORMATION

( ) We don't have enough information for a proper search. We need_____

_____

( ) We have made a proper search and found no records for _____

_____

( ) We have located _____

_____

( ) OTHER: _____

_____

REQUESTOR'S NAME AND ADDRESS

THIS PORTION OF THIS FORM WILL SERVE AS A REQUEST IF COMPLETED AND RETURNED TO THIS CENTER

SECTION I - INFORMATION NEEDED TO LOCATE RECORDS

NAME USED DURING SERVICE (Last, first, and middle)	SOCIAL SECURITY NO.	DATE OF BIRTH	PLACE OF BIRTH

ACTIVE SERVICE, PAST AND PRESENT

BRANCH OF SERVICE	DATES OF ACTIVE SERVICE		Check one		SERVICE NUMBER DURING THIS PERIOD
	DATE ENTERED	DATE RELEASED	OFFICER	ENLISTED	

SECTION II - REQUEST

☐ I request the informational data available under FOIA. I realize that a fee may be applicable.

☐ Please verify the following additional data to ensure that NPRC has identified the correct veteran's record:

IDENTIFICATION OF REQUESTER (Check appropriate box)	RELEASE AUTHORIZATION, IF REQUIRED (Read second-to-last paragraph on front side)
☐ NEXT OF KIN (relationship): ☐ OTHER (specify):	I hereby authorize release of the requested information/documents to the person indicated at left. *SIGNATURE OF VETERAN OR NEXT OF KIN*
SIGNATURE OF REQUESTER	*(If signed by other than veteran, show relationship to veteran):*

REQUESTS SHOULD BE SUBMITTED TO: **Director** **National Personnel Records Center** **9700 Page Boulevard** **St. Louis, Missouri 63132**	COMPLETE RETURN ADDRESS OF REQUESTER (Please type or print clearly)
	NAME
	NUMBER AND STREET
	CITY, STATE AND ZIP CODE
	TELEPHONE NO. (Include area code)

R6-7231 (REV. 9/81) BACK

GENEALOGICAL STATEMENT

Past experience indicates that documents issued to the veteran at time of discharge (or issued to his/her next of kin, if individual died in service) usually contain information suitable for genealogical purposes. Such documents usually are still in the possession of the veteran or his/her next of kin. Every effort should be made to contact the veteran or the next of kin, if individual is deceased, to obtain genealogical information before contacting this Center. We must caution that genealogical requests have a low priority at this Center as our primary function is to process requests relating to veterans' claims for benefits. As a result, our answer to a request for genealogical information should not be anticipated for several weeks. (Also, please note that biographical sketches, though similar to genealogical requests, are not provided by this Center.)

When information cannot be obtained from the veteran or next of kin, this Center is permitted to honor a request only to the limits of the Freedom of Information Act (FOIA), as amended in 1974. Under the provisions of FOIA, we may release certain items of information to the general public. Only the following items are releasable to the general public, regardless of whether or not FOIA is cited in the request:

> name
> age (date of birth)
> salary
> photographs
> source of commission
> duty status
> office telephone number
> military and civilian educational level
> decorations and awards (including a copy of the citation, if available)
> present and past duty assignments (including geographical location)
> future assignments which have been finalized
> records of court-martial trials (unless classified)
> marital status
> education/schooling
> rank/grade
> serial/service number
> date of rank/grade
> promotion sequence number
> dependents (including name, sex and age)

If the written consent of the veteran or his/her next of kin (if veteran is deceased) can be obtained, then we will verify additional items such as name of father and/or mother, home address, or comparable information needed to establish that we have identified the person in question. For purposes of release authorization, the next of kin is defined as any of the following: widow or widower, son, daughter, father, mother, brother or sister.

A fee is applicable for researching, processing, and photocopying certain types of genealogical requests. We are unable to predict the exact cost of this service in advance. If your request is determined to be a chargeable inquiry, you will be billed upon completion of the response.

6NCP

NATIONAL PERSONNEL RECORDS CENTER
(Military Personnel Records)
9700 Page Boulevard
St. Louis, Missouri 63132

R6-7231 (REV. 9/81)

GENERAL SERVICES ADMINISTRATION

THE LIBRARY OF CONGRESS

WASHINGTON, D.C. 20540

PHOTODUPLICATION SERVICE

October 1, 1981

PHOTOREPRODUCTION OF CATALOG CARDS

Rates for photoreproduction of 3" x 5" catalog cards from the Library's Main Catalog for routine reference use:

	Photocopy*	16mm Negative Microfilm
Per card..................................	$ .12	$ .04
Minimum per item**........................	5.00	5.00
Minimum charge per order.................	7.00	10.00
Packaging and mailing fee (U.S.) minimum..	1.80	1.80
Spool and box for microfilm..............		.60

*Regular production xerox prints on sulphite paper are generally furnished. Untrimmed photocopies, several cards grouped on a sheet, may be supplied on small orders at our Laboratory's discretion.

**All cards under the author or subject must be ordered and the minimum item charge applied to each author or subject.

NOTE: Please consult the Photoduplication Service for requests for more than 2,000 cards, for cards from other catalogs, for other sizes, and for reproductions on heavy duty card stock. Considerations affecting costs are size, color uniformity, paper clips, staples, rubber bands, guide cards, etc.

ORDER FOR PHOTODUPLICATION TO

THE LIBRARY OF CONGRESS
PHOTODUPLICATION SERVICE

WASHINGTON, D. C. 20540

Job Number

25-15 (rev 3/70)

MAKE CHECK OR MONEY ORDER PAYABLE TO

CHIEF, PHOTODUPLICATION SERVICE, LIBRARY OF CONGRESS

Name ....

Signature ....

Address ....

Date of Request

....

Customer's Order No.

PS...
Deposit Account No.

Mail ☐ Pick Up ☐

Type of reproduction

☐ Electrostatic Positive Prints (Xerox)   ☐ Photostat   ☐ Microfilm   ☐ Photograph   ☐ ....

	☐ Negative	☐ Positive
Exp. @ $		
Exp. @ $		
Exp. @ $		

Special Instructions:

Spools and boxes
for microfilm ....@ $.......   ....

Packaging and
mailing ....

Delivered to:

Date

TOTAL COST ....

FOR PROMPT, ACCURATE SHIPMENT will you please fill in the following mailing label—Please PRINT or typewrite.

THE LIBRARY OF CONGRESS
PHOTODUPLICATION SERVICE
10 FIRST STREET, S.E.
WASHINGTON, D. C. 20540
———
OFFICIAL BUSINESS
PENALTY FOR PRIVATE USE 8300

POSTAGE AND FEES PAID
LIBRARY OF CONGRESS

U.S.MAIL

Name ....

Address ....

City and state ....

PAYMENT INSTRUCTIONS

Payment in advance is generally, required. However, upon receipt of a formal purchase order from a domestic public library, university, or governmental organization, photoduplicates may be prepared and an invoice issued. A billing fee of $2.00 is added to each order that is not prepaid or chargeable to a deposit account having sufficient funds with this Photoduplication Service. Orders cannot be charged to accounts maintained with the Library's Cataloging Distribution Service, the Superintendent of Documents, or other offices. Coupons or stamps are not acceptable. Do not send cash through mail.

Remittances should be payable to Library of Congress, Photoduplication Service, by check or money order and sent with the order.

Foreign Countries - Remittances must be in one of the following three forms:

        1) Bank draft payable in dollars and drawn on a bank in the U. S.
        2) International money order
        3) UNESCO Book Coupons

OTHER FORMS OF PAYMENT ARE NOT ACCEPTABLE.

If payment cannot be sent with the order, forward your order to us and let us know when and how payment will be made. When your remittance is received, we will proceed with the order.

The Library of Congress
Photoduplication Service
10 First Street, S.E.
Washington, D. C. 20540

ORDER FORM

Customer's Telephone Numbers

Area Code | Home | Area Code | Office

MasterCard   VISA

Mail to:
Superintendent of Documents
US Government Printing Office
Dept. 33
Washington, DC 20402

Date ....   Your Order Number ....

Credit Card No.

Expiration Date Month/Year

Customer's Name and Address

ZIP

FOR OFFICE USE ONLY

Quantity		Charges
_____ Publications		_____
_____ Subscriptions		_____
Special Shipping Charges		_____
International Handling		_____
Special Charges		_____
OPNR		_____
_____ UPNS		
_____ Balance Due		
_____ Discount		
_____ Refund	GPO Form 3868 (R 8 81)	

Deposit Account Number

Stock Number (Non-Subscriptions)	Quantity	Unit of Issue	List ID (Subs)	☐ Publication	Title of ☐ Subscription	Unit Price	Total

An order from this catalog automatically places you on our mailing list to receive the next issue.

Total Enclosed $

Ship To: (If different from above)

ZIP

Y 2

Unit of issue	Explanation
EA	Each single copy
KT	Kit of multiple items in a special container
PD	Pad containing multiple sheets
PK	Package containing multiple copies
SE	Set of multiple items
SU	Subscription

Information Concerning Your Order

Unless otherwise noted, prices are for single copies, and all prices are subject to change without notice. Payment is required in advance of shipment of publications. You may order using check or money order drawn on a bank located in Canada, the United States, or United States Possessions, in Canadian or U.S. dollars. Make checks/money orders payable to the Superintendent of Documents. Checks returned by the bank as uncollectible are subject to a penalty of up to 10 percent of the amount of the check, with a minimum charge of five dollars ($5.00). You may also order, by using your VISA, MasterCard, or Superintendent of Documents Prepaid Deposit Account. Do not send currency (bills or coins) or postage stamps.

Shipping is by non-priority mail or United Parcel Service (UPS). First class and airmail services are available for an additional charge if requested. Please contact us in advance for rates if you desire this service (202–783–3238) and indicate on your order if you desire special postage.

DISCOUNTS:

With the exception of certain publications and subscriptions, a discount of 25% from the domestic price is allowed on orders of 100 or more units of issue mailed to a single address. A discount of 25% from the domestic price is also applicable on orders from bookdealers, for orders of any quantity, mailed to the dealer's business address. (The maximum discount allowable is 25%).

INTERNATIONAL CUSTOMERS:

Mailing regulations require special handling for orders mailed to addresses outside the United States or its possessions for which we charge an additional 25% of the domestic price. Payment is required in advance by one of the methods stated above. You may also remit by UNESCO coupons or by International Postal Money Order, made payable to the Superintendent of Documents. Foreign currency and foreign checks will not be accepted. All orders must be in English. International customers are allowed the same discounts stated above.

Orders are sent via surface mail unless otherwise requested. Should you desire airmail service, please contact us in advance by letter, telephone (202–783–3238), or Telex (#710–822–9413; ANSWERBACK USGPO WSH) for the total cost of your order.

TO ORDER, USE FORM ON REVERSE SIDE

1. *A separate order form must be used for ordering each of the following: publications, subscription services, and single issues of a subscription.*

2. Type or print your complete name and address, home and office telephone numbers, date, order number (if any), Deposit Account Number (if applicable), VISA or MasterCard number and expiration date (if applicable), in proper places at the top of the form. If order is to be shipped to another location, enter address at bottom of form.

3. When ordering publications, type or print the stock number, unit of issue (see front), quantity, title, price, and total payment enclosed. Allow 4 weeks for delivery (longer for International Orders).

4. When ordering a subscription service, type or print the quantity, title, price, List ID (when available), and total payment enclosed. Allow 2–6 weeks, plus mailing time, for processing. All subscriptions are for one year, unless otherwise noted. Subscribers will be notified by mail in ample time to renew.

5. When ordering a specific single issue of a subscription, type or print the complete title of the subscription, List ID (when available), single copy price, and all data pertaining to the requested issue (issue date, volume number, issue number, etc.). Allow 4 weeks for delivery (longer for International Orders).

6. Mail original of form to Superintendent of Documents, Washington, DC 20402.

7. Orders and inquiries can be placed with our order/information desk (202-783-3238) from 8:00 A.M. to 4:30 P.M., Eastern Time.

Superintendent of Documents
United States Government Printing Office

Washington, D.C. 20402

OFFICIAL BUSINESS
Penalty for private use, $300

FORM BC-600
(6-1-81)

U.S. DEPARTMENT OF COMMERCE
BUREAU OF THE CENSUS

Form Approved:
O.M.B. No. 0607-0117

APPLICATION FOR SEARCH OF CENSUS RECORDS

PURPOSE FOR WHICH RECORD IS TO BE USED (MUST BE STATED HERE) *(See Instruction 1)*

RETURN TO: U.S. Department of Commerce, Bureau of the Census, PITTSBURG, KANSAS 66762

DO NOT USE THIS SPACE

CASE NO.

$ _____ (Fee)

☐ Money Order
☐ Check
☐ Other

| FULL NAME OF PERSON WHOSE CENSUS RECORD IS REQUESTED *(Print or type)* | FIRST NAME | MIDDLE NAME | MAIDEN NAME *(If any)* | PRESENT LAST NAME | NICKNAMES |

DATE OF BIRTH *(If unknown – estimate)* | PLACE OF BIRTH *(City, county, State)* | RACE | SEX

FULL NAME OF FATHER *(Stepfather, guardian, etc.)*

FULL MAIDEN NAME OF MOTHER *(Stepmother, etc.)*

Please give FULL name of husband or wife of person whose record is requested.

FIRST MARRIAGE *(Name of husband or wife)* | YEAR MARRIED *(Approximate)*

SECOND MARRIAGE *(Name of husband or wife)* | YEAR MARRIED *(Approximate)*

GIVE PLACE OF RESIDENCE AT EACH DATE LISTED BELOW

CENSUS DATE	NUMBER AND STREET *(Very important)*	CITY, TOWN, TOWNSHIP *(Precinct, beat, etc.)*	COUNTY AND STATE	NAME OF PERSON WITH WHOM LIVING *(Head of household)*	RELATIONSHIP
JUNE 1, 1900 *(See Instruction 2)*					
APRIL 15, 1910 *(See Instruction 3)*					
JAN. 1, 1920 *(See Instruction 2)*					
APRIL 1, 1930 *(See Instruction 3)*					
APRIL 1, 1940 *(See Instruction 3)*					
APRIL 1, 1950 *(See Instruction 3)*					
APRIL 1, 1960 *(See Instructions 3 and 9)*					
APRIL 1, 1970 *(See Instructions 3 and 9)*					

● If the census information is to be sent to someone other than the person whose record is requested, give the name and address, including Zip code, of the other person or agency.

● This authorizes the Bureau of the Census to send the record to: *(See Instruction 4)*

▶ FEE REQUIRED: See Instructions 5, 6, and 7 on the reverse side.

A check or money order (DO NOT SEND CASH) payable to "Commerce – Census," must be sent with the application. This fee covers the cost of a search of not more than two census years about one person only.

Fee required ....$ 12.00

—— extra copies @ $2.00 each ...$ ——

—— full schedules @ $4.00 each . $ ——

TOTAL amount enclosed ➤ $ ——

I certify that information furnished about anyone other than the applicant will not be used to the detriment of such person or persons by me or by anyone else with my permission.

SIGNATURE – Do not print
(Read Instruction 8 carefully before signing)

PRESENT ADDRESS | NUMBER AND STREET

CITY | STATE | ZIP CODE

IF SIGNED ABOVE BY MARK (X), TWO WITNESSES MUST SIGN HERE

SIGNATURE

SIGNATURE

NOTICE – Intentionally falsifying this application may result in a fine of $10,000 or five years imprisonment, or both (title 18, U.S. Code, section 1001).

GENERAL INFORMATION

The Application on the reverse side of this sheet is for use in requesting a search of the census records and **an official** copy of the personal information found which includes age, place of birth, and citizenship. This application should be filled in and mailed to **BUREAU OF THE CENSUS, PITTSBURG, KANSAS 66762,** together with a money order or check payable to "Commerce – Census."

Birth certificates, including delayed birth certificates, are not issued by the Bureau of the Census but by the Health Department or similar agency of the State in which the birth occurred. In most Federal Censuses, the census takers obtained the age and place of birth of individuals. Copies of these census records often are accepted as evidence of age, citizenship, and place of birth for employment, social security benefits, insurance, and other purposes. *Since the place* *of birth and citizenship were obtained only on a sample basis during the 1960 and 1970 Censuses, this information will not be shown on transcripts for those years.*

Census records for **1900** and prior years have been transferred to the National Archives and Records Service, Washington, D.C. 20408, and are considered public records. Requests for information from these Censuses should be addressed to that agency.

If you authorize the Bureau of the Census to send your record to someone other than yourself, attention is called to the possibility that the information shown in the census record may not agree with that given in your application. The record must be copied exactly as it appears and will be sent as you direct regardless of what it shows.

INSTRUCTIONS FOR COMPLETING THIS FORM

► 1. Purpose

The purpose for which the information is desired must be shown so that a determination may be made under 13 U.S.C. 8(a) that the record is required for a proper use. The statement of purpose also provides a basis for determining which census records would best serve such purpose and thereby, save the expense of additional searches.

► 2. Censuses 1900–1920

A system for filing names by sound is available for these census years. Information can be furnished in many instances when only the following information is given:

The name of the person about whom the information is desired.

The name of the city or county and State where the person resided.

The name of the head of the household with whom this person was living on the various dates of these censuses.

Additional information **such as the names of brothers and sisters is helpful if it can be furnished.**

► 3. Censuses – years 1910–1930–1940–1950–1960–1970

If residing in a city at the time these censuses were taken, it is necessary to furnish the house number, the name of the street, city, county, and State and the name of the parent or other head of household with whom residing at the time of the census. If residing in a small town or a rural area, give all available information as to cross-streets, road names, township, district, precinct, or beat, etc. If the district or township is unknown, give the distance from the nearest town and the direction, also the rural route number.

► 4. Confidential information given to other than person to whom it relates

(a) Census information for the years 1900 and on is confidential and ordinarily will not be furnished to another person unless the person to whom it relates authorizes this in the space provided or there is other proper authorization as indicated in 4(b), 4(c), and 4(d) hereof.

(b) Minor children

Information regarding a child who has not reached legal age may be obtained upon the written request of either parent or the legal guardian.

(c) Mentally incompetent persons

Information regarding persons who are mentally incompetent may be obtained upon the written request of the legal representative supported by a certified copy of the court order naming such legal representative.

(d) Deceased persons

If the record requested relates to a deceased person, the application must be signed by (1) a blood relative in the immediate family (parent, brother, sister, or child), (2) the surviving wife or husband, (3) the administrator or executor of the estate, or (4) a beneficiary by will, or insurance. In all cases involving deceased persons, a certified copy of the death certificate must be furnished, and the relationship to the deceased must be stated on the application. Legal representatives must also furnish a certified copy of the court order naming such legal representatives; and beneficiaries must furnish legal evidence of such beneficiary interest.

► 5. Fee required

The $12.00 fee is for a search in regular turn, based on the date the request is received, of not more than two suggested censuses about one person only. The time required to complete a search depends upon the number of cases on hand at the particular time and the difficulty encountered in searching a particular case. The normal processing time would require from two to four weeks.

Not more than two censuses will be searched and the results furnished for one fee. Should it be necessary to search more than two censuses to find the record, you will be notified to send another fee before further searches are made. Tax monies are not available for the furnishing of this information. Accordingly, even though the information is not found, if a search has been made, the fee cannot be returned.

► 6. Additional copies of Census information

Additional copies of this information furnished will be prepared at a cost of $2.00 for each additional copy. Fill in the amount of money enclosed and the number of extra copies desired in the spaces provided.

► 7. Full schedules (For Genealogy)

Upon request, a full schedule will be furnished. There is an additional charge of $4.00 for each full schedule requested. The full schedule is the complete one-line entry of personal data recorded for the individual. The name of the head of household may also be shown, but the names of other persons will not be listed.

► 8. Signature

In general, the signature should be the same as that shown on the line captioned "full name of person whose census record is requested." When the application is for the census record concerning another person, the authority of the requester must be furnished as set forth in instruction 4 above.

► 9. 1960–1970 Censuses

Since the place of birth and citizenship were obtained only on a sample basis during the 1960 and 1970 Censuses, this information will not be shown on transcripts.

FORM BC-600 6-1-81

GLOSSARY

A (no period)—ante (L.), before.

A (no period)—argon.

a.—about; accepted; acre; active; adjective; afternoon; aged; alto; annus (L.) year; answer; ante (L.), before; are (metric system); assists (baseball); at.

A.—Academician; Academy; Alberta (Canada); America; American; Artillery.

A.A.—Associate in, or of, Arts.

A.A.A.—Agricultural Adjustment Administration; Amateur Athletic Association; American Automobile Association.

A.A.A.L.—American Academy of Arts and Letters.

A.A.A.S.—American Association for the Advancement of Science.

A.A.C.—Anno Ante Christum (L.), in the year before Christ

A.A.G.—Assistant Adjutant-General

A.A.P.S.S.—American Academy of Political and Social Science.

a.a.r.—against all risks

A.A.S.—Fellow (L. Socius) of the American Academy of Arts and Sciences.

A.A.S.L.H.—American Association for State and Local History, Nashville, Tennessee.

A.A.S.S.—Fellow (L. Socuis) of the American Antiquarian Society.

A.A.U.—Amateur Athletic Union.

ab.—about; (times) at bat (baseball).

A.B.—able-bodied seaman; Artuim Baccalaureus (L.), Bachelor of Arts.

Abatement—Means reduction or decrease; when applied to the payment of claims from a fund which is insufficient to pay claims in full, it means a proportionate reduction of the claims.

abbr. or abbrev.—abbreviated; abbreviation.

A.B.C.—Argentina, Brazil, and Chile.

A.B.C.F.M.—American Board of Commissioners for Foreign Missions.

abd.—abdicated

abduction—(Criminal law) is the offense of taking away a female or child by violence or fraud.

Aber. or Aberd.—Aberdeen.

Abeyance—is a state of being undetermined or held in suspension.

A.B.F.M.—American Board of Foreign Missions.

ab init.—ab initio (L.), from the beginning.

ab initio—From the beginning

Ab initio—(Latin "from the beginning") signifies a transaction or document from its inception; thus, a marriage may be held to be unlawful ab initio or an insurance policy valid ab initio.

abl.—ablative.

Abortion—Is the criminal miscarriage of a child.

Abp.—Archbishop.

abr.—abridged; abridgment.

abs.—abstract.

A.B.S.—American Bible Society

absol.—absolute; absolutely

abs. re.—absente reo (L.), the defendant being absent

abst.—abstract

Abstract—An extraction of the pertinent information usually all that is of genealogical value, from a will or other probate document.

Abstract of Title—A genealogical type of history of a piece of property which shows all of the owners from the beginning also any liabilities charges to which the same may be subject.

abt.—about.

Abys.—Abyssinia

ac.—account.

a.c.—account current; alternating current.

A.C.—Alpine Club; ante Christum (L.), before Christ; Army-Corps; Athletic Club; Automobile Club.

A.C.A.—Associate of the Institute of Chartered Accountants (Brit.).

acad.—academy.

acc.—acceptance; account; accusative.

accel.—accelerando (It.), increasing in speed (music).

acct.—account

Accord and satisfaction—is an agreement between two persons that settles a claim or a lawsuit.

Accounts—A common-law action or statement of receipts and disbursements and the recovery of any balance due; also the writ by which it is bought. A report of executor or Administrator.

Accredited genealogist.—certification by the Genealogical Society, Salt Lake City, Utah.

Acknowledgment—is the certificate of a notary or

another officer having the authority to administer oaths attesting that the person who executed a document declared that the document was his free act and deed.

Acquittal—in the law of contracts, means a release or discharge from an obligation in the law of crime, it means the deliverance of a person from a charge of guilt.

act.—active.

Act Book:—A court record of day by day entries of official grants of probates and admons.

actg.—acting.

actiones in personam—Personal actions

Act of God—(Also known as Force Majeure) is an event caused exclusively by the violence of nature and which man is powerless to prevent.

ad. (pl. ads.)—advertisement.

A.D.—(Anno Domini) the year of our Lord. After the birth of Christ.

a.D. ausser Dienst—formerly employed in that capacity (profession), or in retirement.

a.d.—after date; ante diem (L.), before the day.

A.D.—anno Domini (L.), in the year of our Lord.

A.D.C.—Aide-de-Camp.

Adel.—Adelaide (Australia).

Ademption—is the cancellation of a legacy because an act of the testator is interpreted as an intention to revoke the legacy.

ad eund.—ad eundem (gradum) (L.), to the same degree or rank.

ad faciedum—to do.

ad fin.—ad finem (L.), to or at the end.

ad hoc.—For this; (for this special purpose).

ad inf.—ad infinitum (L.), to infinity.

ad infinitum—Indefinitely; forever.

ad init.—ad initium (L.), to or at the being.

ad int.—ad interim (L.), in the meantime.

adj.—adjective.

Adj. or Adjt.—Adjutant.

Adj Gen or Adjt. Gen.—Adjutant-General.

Adjective law—refers to rules of procedure or practice. (see substantive law).

Adjudication—ordinarily means the pronouncing or a judgment or decree in a litigated case. When used in bankruptcy proceedings the terms refers to the order of a bankruptcy court declaring that the debtor is a bankrupt person.

Adjuster—usually refers to a person who is employed to make a settlement; an adjuster is most frequently employed by an insurance company.

ad lib.—ad libitum (L.), at pleasure, as one wishes, to the amount desired.

ad litem—For the suit; for the litigation. (a guardian ad litem is a person appointed to prosecute or defend a suit for a person incapacitated by infancy or incompetency.)

ad loc.—ad locum (L.), to or at the place.

adm.—admission

Adm.—Admiral; Admiralty.

administration—(Intestate) probate without a will.

Administrative Law—is that branch of law which governs procedure before various agencies of the government.

Administrator (Administratrix), de bonis non—A person appointed by the court to carry out the administration of an estate. Administratrix is feminine. One who is appointed to succeed an administrator who died before completing his trust.

Administratrix—A woman administrator

Admiralty—designates the branch of law which regulates maritime matters.

admix.—administratrix.

admr.—administrator.

admrx or admx.—administratrix.

Adolescence—the stage between childhood and man or womanhood beginning with puberty.

Adopt—to accept as one's own the child of another.

Adoption—is (1) the act of one who takes another's child into his own family and treats him as his own (assuming all the responsibilities of parenthood and giving the child all the privileges of his own child) and (2) the act of a court which creates between two persons the relationship of parent and child.

ad quod damnum.—To what damage; what injury. (A phrase used to describe the plaintiff's money loss or the damages that he claims.)

ad respondendum.—To answer

ad satisfaciendum.—To satisfy

Adult—a person grown to maturity.

Adultry—a crime in most states, is the voluntary sexual intercourse with a person other than the offender's husband or wife.

adv.—ad valorem; adverb; adverbial; adverbially; adversus (L.), against, advertisement; advertising; advocate.

Adv.—Advent.

ad Val.—ad valorem.

ad valorem—According to value.

Adverse possession—is a method of acquiring title to real estate by occupancy for a specified number of years, sometimes called "squatters title" (see Chapter 16, "Real Property Law").

Advocate—refers to a lawyer who pleads for another person in court.

advt.—advertisement.

a.e. ausserehelich—illegitimate

ae—age(s)

A.E.F.—American Expeditionary Forces.

A.E.I.O.U.—Austria est imperare orbi universo (L.), it is given to Austria to rule the whole earth.

A.E. & P.—Ambassador Extraordinary and Plenipotentiary.

aet.—aged (years of age).

aet. or actat.—aetatis (L.), of age, aged.

ae—aetatis (L.), of age, aged.

AF. or A.F.—Anglo-French.

A.F.A.M. or A.F. & A.M.—Ancient Free and Accepted Masons.

A.F.C.—Air Force Cross (Brit.).

aff.—affectionate; affirmative; affirmatively.

Affiant—a person making an affidavit, also called a deponent.

Affidavit—is a written statement sworn to before a

notary public or another officer having the authority to administer oaths.

Affinity—Relationship by marriage between the husband and the blood relations of the wife, and between the wife and the blood relations of the husband.

afft.—Affidavit.

Afgh. or Afghan—Afghanistan.

A.F.L. or A.F. of L.—American Federation of Labor.

aft.—after

A.F.M.—Air Force Medal (Brit.).

A.F. of L.—See. A.F.L.

Afr.—Africa; African.

a fortiou—With stronger reason; much more.

aft.—Afternoon

Ag (no period)—Argentum (L.), silver.

A.G.—Accredited Genealogist

A.G.—Adjutant-General; Agent-General; Aktiengesellscfagt. (G.), stock company (business); Attorney-General.

a.g.b.—any good brand.

Age—the period that has elapsed since an individual's birth.

agcy.—agency

aggregatio menium—Meeting of minds.

agric.—agricultural; agriculture.

agt.—agent.

A.H.—Anno Hejirae (L.), in the year of or from the Hejira (A.D. 622).

A.H.A.—American Historical Association, Washington, D.C.

a.h.l.—ad hunc locum (L.), to or at this place.

A.H.S.—anno humanae solutis (L.), in the year of human salvation.

a.h.v.—ad hanc vocem (L.), at this word.

A.I.—American Institute.

A.I.A.—American Institute of Architects.

A.I.G.—Adjutant-Inspector-General; Assistant Inspector-General.

A.I.N.A.—Associate of the Institution of Naval Architects (Brit.).

Al (no period)—aluminium.

AL. or A.L.—Anglo-Latin.

A.L.A.—American Library Association.

A.L.A.—American Library Association; Authors' League of America.

Ala.—Alabama.

Alas.—Alaska.

Alb.—Albania; Albert.

ald.—alderman.

Alex.—Alexander.

Alf.—Alfred.

alg.—algebra.

Alg.—Algeria; Algernon; Alg :s.

Alias, Alius, Ais—An assumed name formerly, before, at another time.

alias dictus—Otherwise called.

alibi—In another place; elsewhere

alien—a foreigner

alii.—Others.

aliunde—From another place; from without (as evidence outside the document).

alius.—Another.

alliance—an ethnic insurance union or association.

almanac—a calendar of dates.

Almanacs—A regular publication giving statistical and general information.

alter ego.—The other self.

alt.—alternate; altitude; alto.

Alta.—Alberta (Canada).

alumnus.—A foster child.

A.M.—Albert Medal (Brit.); anno mundi (L.), in the year of the world; ante meridiem (L.), before noon; Artium Magistu (L.), Master of Arts; Ave Maria (L.), Hail, Mary.

A.M.A.—American Medical Association.

Am.—America; American.

Amb.—Ambassador.

Ambulance chasing—refers to the unlawful and unethical conduct of a lawyer in the solicitation by him of claims arising out of personal injuries.

A.M.D.G.—ad majorem Dei ptoriam (L.), for the greater glory of God.

A.M.E.—African Methodist Episcopal.

A mensa et thoro—is a divorce by means of which the parties are merely separated; it should be distinguished from a divorce a vinculo, which effects a complete dissolution of the marriage freely translated "a mensa et thoro" refers to a divorce from bed and board; "a vinculo" means the breaking of the bonds or chains (of matrimony).

a mensa et thoro.—From bed and board.

amer—america(n)

Amer.—America; American.

American Lineage Specialist—one who prepares papers for applicants seeking admission to hereditary patriotic societies.

A.M.I.C.E.—Associate Member of the Institution of Civil Engineers. (Brit.).

amicus curiae.—Friend of the court.

Amicus curiae—(Latin, literally "a friend of the court") generally means a person who has no legal right to appear in a court proceeding but who is allowed by the court to introduce argument, authority, or evidence, because he has a corollary or collateral interest in the proceeding.

A.M.I.E.E.—Associate Member of the Institution of Electrical Engineers. (Brit.).

amp.—amperage; ampere.

Amst.—Amsterdam

amt.—amount.

an—anno (L.), in the year.

A.N.A.—Associate of the National Academy.

anal.—analogous; analogy; analysis; analytic; analytical.

analysis—separation and study.

anat.—anatomical; anatomy.

anc.—ancient

anc—ancestor(s)

Ancestor—1. One from whom another is descended in a direct line of descent. 2. By statutory law any person of lineal or collateral relationship from whom property has been derived by descent.

And.—Andrew.

Ang.—Anglice.

Angl.—Anglican; Anglice.

animo—With intention, disposition, design, will.

animus.—Mind; intention.

animus furandi.—The intention to steal.

animus revertendi.—An intention of returning.

animus revocandi.—An intention to revoke.

Animus testandi.—An intention to make a testament or will.

ann.—anni (L.), years; annual; annuity.

Annuity—A yearly payment of a certain sum of money.

Anniversary—An annual celebration of an event.

anno Domini (A.D.)—In the year of the Lord.

annot.—annotated.

anon.—anonymous.

ans.—answer

ant.—Antiquary; antonym.

Ant.—Anthony; Antiqua.

Ante.—Before.

Ante Cessor—a predecessor or ancestor.

ante litem motam.—Before suit brought.

Ante-Nuptial Contract—Legal agreement before marriage concerning property rights.

anth.—anthology.

anthrop. or anthropol.—anthropological; anthropology.

Anthropology—the science which studies the human being racially and culturally.

anticedent—one from whom you are descended.

antiq.—antiquary; antiquities; antiquity.

Antiquarian—one who studies antiquities.

Antw.—Antwerp.

Ao.—Account of.

A.O.F.—Ancient Order of Foresters.

A.O.H.—Ancient Order of Hibernians.

aor.—Aorist.

A.O.S.S.—Fellow (L. Sovius) of the American Oriental Society.

a.p.—assessment paid.

A.P.—Associated Press.

A.P.A.—American Pharmaceutical Association; American Philological Association; American Protective Association.

Apoc.—Apocalypse; Aprocrypha.

Apocr.—Apocrypha.

app.—apparent; apparently; appendix; appointed.

Appalachian—mountain range from Quebec to Alabama.

appar.—apparent; apparently.

Appeal—Resort to a higher court to redress supposed error or injustice of lower court.

appellate court—a court of appeals.

Appointment of Attorney—Docket listing attorneys appointed by courts for any purpose, but usually to represent defendants in criminal cases.

Appraisal—Estimated worth of property by one with ability or authorized by the court if an estate is involved.

Apprentice—A person, usually a minor, bound in due form of law to a master, to learn from him his art, trade, or business, and to serve him during the time of his apprenticeship.

Apprenticeship—see civil records.

approx.—approximately.

appx.—appendix.

Apr.—April

A.P.R.C.—anno post Roman conditam (L.), in the year after the founding of Rome (in 753 B.C.).

a priori—From what goes before; from the cause to the effect.

A.P.S.—American Peace Society; American Philosophical Society.

apt. (pl. apts.).—apartment.

apx.—appendix.

aq.—aqua (L.), water

aq. dest.—aqua destillata (L.), distilled water.

A.Q.M.G.—Assistant Quartermaster-General.

Ar (no period)—Argon.

ar.—arrival; arrived; arrives.

Ar.—Arabic

a.r.—all risks

A.R.—Anno regni (L.), in the year of the reign.

A.R.A.—Associate of the Royal Academy.

Arab.—Arabia; Arabic.

Aram.—Aramaic

A.R.A.M.—Associate of the royal Academy of Music.

&—and

Arbitration—means the submission for determination of a disputed matter to one or more unofficial persons (as distinguished from an official tribunal like a court) who makes a decision or award with respect to the disputed matter. Arbitration is becoming a popular method of settling business disputes; businessmen have formed an organization known as the American Arbitration Association which puts at the disposal of businessmen a panel of arbitrators whom the parties to a dispute may use to make an arbitration and or decision.

A.R.C.—American Red Cross.

arch.—Archaic; archaism; archipelago; architect; architectural; architecture.

Arch.—Archibald

Archaeol.—Archaeological; archaelogy.

Archd.—Archdeacon; Archduke.

Archives—Includes material about the archive and the holdings of the archive.

A.R.C.M.—Associate of the Royal College of Music.

A.R.C.O.—Associate of the Royal College of Organists.

A.R.C.S.—Associate of the Royal College of Surgeons.

A.R.E.—Associate of the Royal Society of Painter-Etchers.

Arg.—Argentina.

arguendo.—In the course of the argument.

A.R.I.B.A.—Associate of the Royal Institute of British Architects.

Arising out of and in the course of employment—is a phrase used, in connection with Workmen's Compensation Laws, to classify an injury incident to employment.

arith.—Arithmetic; arithmetical.

Ariz.—Arizona

Ark.—Arkansas.

Arm.—Armenian; Armoric.

armigerous—entitled to bear arms.

Armor.—Armoric.

Armorial—pertaining to heraldic bearings.

Arr.—Arranged; arrival; arrived; arrives.

A.R.R.—anno regni Regis, or Reginae (L.), in the year of the reign of the King. or the Queen.

Arraignment—is the bringing of a person accused of a crime before a court to be advised of the charge against him and to state his answer to the charge.

Arrest—is the act of depriving a person of his liberty by legal authority.

Arrest of judgment—is the act of staying or postponing a judgment.

A.R.S.A.—Associate of the Royal Scottish Academy.

Arson—is the crime of burning, setting fire to, a building. In various states this crime is specifically defined as first-, second-, or third-, degree arson. For example, in some states "arson in the first degree involves setting fire at night to a house or other structure in which there is a human being. "Arson in the second degree" may be setting fire to a house during the day or setting fire to a building, in which there is no human being, at night. "Arson in the third degree" may be setting fire to a vessel, vehicle, or other structure or even setting fire to personal property valued at more than $25.00.

art.—Article; artillery; artist.

Articles of agreement—consists of a written statement of the terms of an agreement.

A.R.W.S.—Associate of the Royal Water-Colour Society.

As (no period)—Arsenic.

As.—Asia; Asiatic.

As. or A.S.—Anglo-Saxon.

a.s.—at sight.

A.S.—Anno salutis (L.), in the year of salvation.

A.S.A.—American Statistical Association.

A.S.A.A.—Associate of the Society of Accountants and Auditors (London).

A.S.C.E.—American Society of Civil Engineers.

ascendent—an ancestor

ascent—back to an ancestor.

Ascetic—an individual who denies himself sensous pleasures.

A.S.G.B.—Aeronautical Society of Great Britain.

A.S.M.E.—American Society of Mechanical Engineers.

assd.—assigned.

assignee—one to whom an assignment is made.

assignment—to transfer or appoint.

assn.—association.

assoc.—associate; associated; association.

Associate—a colleague or companion.

asst.—assistant.

A.S.S.U.—American Sunday-School Union.

assumpsit.—He undertook; he promised.

* (asterisk) — geboren—born

* (asterisk) — unehelich geboren—born (illegit-

imate).

Astr.—Astronomer; astronomical; astronomy.

Astrol.—Astrologer; astrological; astrology.

Astron.—Astronmer; astronomical; astronomy.

Atl.—Atlantic

ats.—at suit of.

Asylum—a place for lunatics and orphans.

Atlas—a volume of maps bound together.

Attachments—Process of siezing chattels or taking title to real property by virtue of a writ; frequently used to satisfy judgment or to guarantee appearance at trial.

Attest—To witness the execution of a written instrument at the request of him who makes it, and subscribe the same as a witness.

Attestation of a will—is the act of witnessing the execution of a will.

Attorney-at-law—is an officer of the court and a member of the bar who is authorized to conduct legal proceedings in behalf of others and to give legal advice.

Attorney-in-fact—identifies a person, not necessarily a member of the bar, authorized by another to act in his place and stead.

A.T.S.—American Tract Society.

att.—attorney

attrib.—attribute; attributive; attributively.

atty.—attorney

at. wt.—atomic weight.

Au (no period)—aurum (L.), gold.

A.U.C.—ab urbe condita or anno urbis conditae (L.), in the year since the founding of the city (of Rome, in 753 B.C.).

aud.—auditor

Aud-Gen.—Auditor-General.

Auditor—Court-appointed officer who examines accounts (usually in equity cases).

Aufl.—Auflage (G.), edition.

aug.—augmentative.

Aug.—August; Augustus.

Aunt—a father or mothers' sister, but applied also to an uncle's marriage partner.

Aus.—Austria, Austrian.

Ausg.—Ausgabe (G.), edition

†† ausgest orben—line is extinct

Aust.—Austria; Austrian.

Aust.-Hung.—Austria-Hungary

Austral—Australasia; Australasian; Australia; Australian.

Authentic—Proven, correct, true.

Auth. Ver.—Authorized Version.

Auto—"I"

autobiography—a life story written by the individual concerned.

Autocrat—one with absolute power.

Autogenic—originating with oneself.

aux. or auxil.—auxiliary

av.—avenue; average; avoirdupois.

a.v.—ad valorem; annos vixit (L.), he, or she, lived (so many years.)

A.V.—Artillery Volunteers; Authorized Version

A.V.C.—Army Veterinary Corps.

avdp.—avoirdupois.

ave.—avenue.

Averment—is a statement of facts in legal pleadings.

Avia—Grandmother or ancestress.

a vinculo matrimonii—From the bonds of marriage.

avoir.—avoirdupois

Avus—Grandfather or ancestor.

A.W.L.—absent with leave.

A.W.O.L.—absent without leave.

ax.—axiom.

Ayer's—N.W. Ayer and Son's Directory of Newspapers and Periodicals.

Azer.—Azerbaijan.

—B—

B.A.—Bachelor of Arts.

Bachelor—a celibate or unmarried man.

Bail—The process of obtaining the release of a person under arrest by assuming responsibility for his appearance at the time and place specified; also refers to money pledged to guarantee this appearance.

Bailee—names one to whom property is entrusted; it has nothing to do with criminal bail (see bailment).

Bailiff—usually refers to a sheriff or his deputy or a court attendant who is a representative of the sheriffs office.

Bailment—is the delivery of personal property by one person in trust to another (a bailee) to carry out a special purpose and with the understanding that the goods will be redelivered when the purpose of the bailment is carried out.

Banns—a public announcement, especially in church, of a proposed marriage.

Banns of Matrimony—A public announcement of an intended marriage, required by the English law to be made in a church or chapel, during service, on three consecutive Sundays before the marriage is celebrated. The object is to afford an opportunity for any person to interpose an objection if he knows of any impediment or other just cause why the marriage should not take place. The publication of the banns may be dispensed with by procuring a special license to marry.

Baptism—ceremonial purification by immersion, bathing or sprinkling with water, generally accompied by namegiving.

basic jurisdiction—usually that government agency which has to do with recording land transactions.

basline—an imaginary line running east and west as used in surveying.

Bastardy bonds—Money pledged to court to guarantee that bastards do not become public charges; usually paid by putative father.

Battle Abbey—Virginia State Historical Society, Richmond, Virginia.

bayou—sluggish or slow moving water.

B.C.—before Christ.

B.d. Band—volume

bdt—birth date(s)

bef—before

begraben—buried

behoof—use or benefit.

Bench warrant—is a process issued by a court in session for the arrest of a person.

bet—between

bequeath—to give or leave by a will.

Bequest—A gift by will of personal property; a legacy. A testamentary gift of real or personal property.

betroth—a pledge or contract to marry.

Bez Bezirk—district

Bibliography—a list of sources about a certain subjust or author.

bicentennial—pertaining to two hundred.

biennial—every two years.

Bigamy—the crime or offense of having in a monogamous society, two wives or husbands at the same time.

Bill—is the formal declaration in a complaint or written statement; it is also the draft of a legislative act (before it becomes law).

Bill of attainder—was formerly a legislative act in which a person was pronouned guilty of crime, usually treason, without trial or conviction. It is prohibited by the Constitution of the United States.

Bills of cost—A certified, itemized statement of the amount of costs in an action or suit.

Bill of indictment—(same as indictment) is a formal written document accusing a person of having committed a crime.

Bill of lading—is written evidence of a contract for delivery of goods by freight.

Bill of particulars—is a written statement of the details of a claim for which a suit is brought.

Bill of Rights—consists of the first ten amendments of the federal Constitution and guarantees rights and privileges to individuals.

Bill of Sale—Legal document showing the exchange of property with all of the conditions recorded.

Bill payable.—In commercial parlance, is an obligation which is owed by the person keeping a ledger account.

Bill Receivable—In commercial parlance, is an account owing to the person keeping the ledger account.

bimonthly—every two months.

Biography—collected personal journals, collected life histories.

Biology—the science which investigates living organisms.

Bi-Parental—derived from two parents.

birth—nativity or entrance into life.

Bi-Sexual—having the organs of both sexes in one person.

Bishop's Transcripts—see vital records

Blackmail—Is a term usually used as the equivalent of the term extortion; it is the extraction of money as something else of value in return for silence or for refraining from performing some act.

blood-relative—a relative or kinsman.

blue belly—a northerner.

Blue Book—American Blue Book (a directory of funeral parlors).

blue nose—native of Nova Scotia or New Brunswick.

B.L.W.—Bounty Land Warrant

bog—a marsh or swamp.

bona fide (Latin)—means "in good faith" without deceit or fraud.

bona fide—in good faith.

bona vacantia—Vacant goods. (Personal property that no one claims which escheats to the state.)

Bond—a writing under seal by which a person binds himself to pay a certain sum on or before a future day appointed. usually a condition is added that the writer shall do (or refrain from doing) a certain act on or before a time specified obligation shall be void, but otherwise shall remain in full force.

Bondman—one who is in servitude to another, as an immigrant who bound himself to the person who paid his passage to this county. Also one who acted as surety for administrators or executors of wills.

bondsman—A person who is bound to insure the performance of a specified act.

Book value—Applied to corporate stock, designates the value shown after deducting the liabilities from the assets.

borough—town

boundary—a limiting line or edge.

Bounty land—Land or value received for military service given by the government. This was usually land, because it was more available than cash. Land donated by a government for volunteer services rendered.

bp—birthplace(s)

B.P.O.E.—Benevolent and Protective Order of Elks.

bpt—baptised

Braddock's road—trail from Baltimore to Pittsburgh.

brand—a mark of identification burned into the side of an animal to show ownership.

Breach of the peace—is a catchall phrase used in criminal law to describe the offense of disturbing the public peace by any riotous or unlawfull act.

Breasts—the mammary glands of women and female animals.

Breed—to procreate or beget

briarpatch child—born out of wedlock

Bribery—is a crime of offering, giving, or receiving anything of value to infulence the action of a public official.

Bride—a women about to be, or newly married.

Brief—is a written or printed document prepared by counsel and addressed to a court; it is a basis for an argument in support of a litigant's postion.

bro—brother(s)

brook—stream, smaller than a river.

Brother-German—a male born of the same parents as another person.

B.S.—Bachelor of Science.

Bullinger's—Bullinger's Postal and Shipping Guide for the United States and Canada; conatining Post Offices and Railroad Stations with the Railroad or Steamer Line on which every place, or the nearest communicating point, is located; and the list of Railroads and Water Lines with their terminal points.

bur—buried

Burden of proof—is the duty to establish in dispute in a lawsuit.

Burglary—is the crime of breaking and entering the house of another at night with intent to commit a felony in the house. Various states have modified the foregoing common-law definition in order to cover breaking into and entering a house under different circumstances and have labelled burglary myerious degrees. Thus, in some instances, the crime of "burglary in the first degree" is committed by the burglar who enteres a house at night armed with a dangerous weapon or assisted by confederates; "burglary in the second degree" may be committed during the day by a person who simply breaks and enters the house of another; and "burglary in the third degree" may be committed by a person who commits the crime and then breaks out of the building that is, he is already in the building and does not break in to commit the burglary, but he does break out of the building.

Burial—interment of a body in the earth or in a crypt or tomb.

Burial Ground—a place for the burial of the dead.

Business Enterprises—records of a specific business organization.

Bust—a sculptured representation, photograph or painting of a person from the waist upwards.

Bylaws—Are regulations, ordinances, rules, or laws adopted by an association or corporation for its internal government.

—C—

C—Roman numeral for 100.

Ca—about

cabinet-maker—early furniture maker who also built coffins.

Caelebs, Coelebs—Bachelor

cadastral—tax map or property survey.

Cadastral Map—A farm atlas map or map showing the names of property owners or taxpayers on the specific place on the maps; also showing churches, cemeteries, schools.

Calendars and Chronology—works dealing with dates and calendars. A research index, register, or log. Refers to a list of cases (sometimes called a "trail list") to be tried during a particular term of court.

Call Number—The number which identifies a book and its location on the library shelves.

Canal—a water way.

Canon—A law, rule, or ordiance of the church. An ecciesiastical law or statute.

Cannon, Cannon Law—A rule, law or statute of a church.

Canuck—French Canadian.

capias.—Take; arrest. (A form of writ directing an arrest.)

Capias (Latin)—Is the general name for a class of writs which require a court officer to take (the body of) the defendant into custody, that is, arrest him.

capias ad satisfaciendum.—(ca. sa.). Arrest to satisfy. (A form of writ.)

Capital crime—describes a crime for which the maximum penalty is death.

Capital stock—describes the amount of stock authorized by a corporate charter.

Capt—Captain

Caput Capitis—Head, chief

Card Catalog—Card index of library holdings in a library.

Carnal knowledge—Is a phrase used in connection with criminal charges, such as rape, and signifies sexual intercourse.

Carrier,—Common, is one who undertakes to transport persons or property for hire.

Case history—pertaining to research for an individual or family.

Case law—Signifies that branch of law established by court decisions, as distinguished from statutes or other sources of law.

Castration—removal of the sex glands or testicles.

Causa mortis (Latin)—means "in contemplation of approaching death."

causa mortis.—By reason of death.

Cause of action—is a person's right to bring a lawsuit against another.

Cavalier—a knight, or an adherent of Charles I of England. A royalist during the revolution.

Caveat—A warning notice issued by an interested person to a probate court that no action is to be taken in granting a probate without his case being heard.

caveat.—Let him beware; a warning.

Caveat emptor—Let the buyer beware.

Caveat emptor (Latin)—means "let the buyer beware."

Caveat venditor (Latin)—means "let the seller beware.

Cease and desist—Is a type of order usually issued by federal regulatory agencies, such as the Federal Trade Commission, to require an individual or a firm to discontinue a practice which is considered objectionable. If the order is not obeyed, the government agency applies to a court for an order requiring the person to "cease and desist" and the violation of such a court order is punishable as a contempt of court.

Cem—Cemetery

Cen—Census

cepit et asportavit.—He took and carried away.

Cer—Certificate

Certificate of incorporation—is the instrument by which a private corporation is formed. It is sometimes called a "charter," although originally a charter was a direct legislative grant which gave a corporation the right to exist.

Certiorari (Latin "to be made certain")—refers to a legal proceeding by which a court reviews the decision of a lower court or governmental agency.

certiorari.—To be informed of; to be made certain in regard to.

cestui (pl. cesuis).—Beneficiaries. (Pronounced "setty.")

cestui que trust.—He who benefits by the trust.

Cestui que trust (latin)—means "the beneficiary of a trust."

cestui que use.—He who benefits by the use.

cestui que vie.—He whose life measures the duration of the estate.

Cemetery—a burial ground, generally unconnected with a church.

Census—An official counting or enumeration of the people of a state or nation, with statistics of wealth, commerce, education, etc.

Centenarian—a person aged 100 years and upwards.

centennial—one hundred.

century—one hundred years.

Ceremony—a formal rite or observance.

Certificate—an authorized or attested statement of fact.

Certified Copy—A copy of a document, signed and certified as a true copy by the officer to whose custody the original is entrusted.

certified genealogist—rating given by Board of Certification in Washington D.C.

C.F.—Confessed fornicator

C.G.—certified genealogist

Ch—Child(ren)

Chambers—refers to the private office of a judge.

Chancellor—Judge in Court of Chancery

Chancery Clerk—Custodian of wills, deeds and probate records in some states, as in Mississippi.

Chancery Court—court of equity

Chancery Proceeding—see court records

Chapelry—A subdivision of a parish, with its own chapel and sometimes its separate register of christenings, marriages and burials.

Charter—See certificate of incorporation.

Chattel—Personal property.

Character—ideals or sentiments which make a person's actions comparatively stable.

Check-off system—refers to the deduction of union dues by an employer from employee's pay.

Chicago road—trail from Chicago to Detroit.

Child—a very young person or descendant.

Children—are one's offspring while they are young. One remains a son or a daughter lifelong. One does not remain a child lifelong unless death precludes adulthood. "Grown children" and "married children" are contradicitons.)

Chose in action—Is the right to personal property which has not been reduced to possession. Most intangible property rights, such as checks, promissory notes, claims for damage, etc., are choses in action.

Christen—to name and baptize into a Christian community.

Christian—Official church naming of a child to enter the name on the church roster.

Chromosome—a gene-carrying body taking part in the cell division of the fertilized ovum.

Church Directories—lists of religious groups or leaders.

Church History—history of religious groups and organizations.

Church Records—records created by the church; minutes, accounts, pew arrangements, etc. (Does not include baptisms, marriages or burials—see vital records).

Churchwarden Accounts—See church records.

Churchyard—area surrounding a church, generally used as a burial ground.

Circa, Cir Ca—about or approximately. A certain year.

Circuit Clerk—Custodian of marriage records in some states, for instance, Mississippi.

Circuit court—A court which meets in various places.

Circumstantial—secondary or less relevant.

Circumstantial evidence—Is evidence of facts or circumstances from which the existence or non-existence of a fact may be inferred. For example, if one of the points in issue in a lawsuit was whether John Jones was at a certain house at a certain time, the facts that his car was seen in front of the house and his gloves were found, which the inference could be drawn that, he was at the house at the time in question, even though there was no direct proof of his being seen there.

Citation—Is an order or notice by which a person is directed to appear in a proceeding.

Citizenship—records dealing with citizenship lists.

city—metropolitan area or town.

City directory—usually an annual alphabetical listing of inhabitants.

civil—having to do with contracts.

civiliter mortuus.—Civilly dead.

Civil Law or Court—Those laws or courts regulating private matters between individuals or groups of them.

Civil Records—miscellaneous records created by civil authorities.

Civ W—Civil War

Clan—a group of families having in theory a remote common ancestor.

Clean hands—Is an equitable doctrine that a person is not entitled to relief if he has been guilty of unjust or unfair conduct.

Clergyman—Authority in a church.

Clerk of court—Signifies an officer who has charge of the records and proceeding of court.

Clerk of Ordinary—Custodian of marriage records in Georgia.

Client's—The person who employs an attorney-at-law.

Closed case history file—the completed research records on one given family.

C.L.S.C.—Chautauqua Literary and Scientific Circle

Co—County

Coat of Arms—an authorized heraldic diploma of nobility.

Codicil—An instrument made subsequently to a will, and modifying it in some respects. A codicil must be executed in the same manner as the will itself, and forms a part of it, superseding it so far as inconsistent with it. There may be any number of codicils.

Col—Colonel

Coel—Single, unmarried

Cognomen—Surname

Co-Heir—one of several heirs having a right by will or settlement.

Collateral Ancestors—A phrase sometimes used to designate uncles and aunts, and other collateral antecessors, who are not strictly ancestors.

Collateral (lines or ancestors)—Pertaining to brothers, and sisters, of direct line ancestors, including aunts, uncles, cousins, nephews, and all kinsmen who are not in the direct line of ancestors or descendents.

Collateral Lines—Persons descended from uncles or aunts, great-uncles, great-aunts, etc.

Colonial—pre-revolutionary era.

Comity of States—designates the practice or courtesy by which the courts of one state recognize the laws and judicial decisions of another state.

Commercial Directories—see directories

Commitment—In criminal law, is the act of sending a person to prison. The word may also refer to the warrant or order of the court which directs that a person be taken to a prison or another institution.

Committee of an incompetent person—or a lunatic refers to a person who, by order of the court, is given the custody of the person and the estate of one who has been adjudged incompetent.

Common law—refers to the ancient, unwritten law which originated in England. It also refers to that body of law in the United States which is derived from judicial decisions based on usage and customs of antiquity and on principles recognized in the English common law.

Common Law Marriage—Mutual Agreement of marriage by the couple without benefit of a ceremony and not by legal terms.

compiled—published works.

Conception—the beginning of pregnancy.

Confederate—southern states.

Confirmation—A church rite (at age of puberty) which places the person on the church membership records. The completion of the probate of a testament by the executors.

Conformist—one who complies with established rule or custom.

Congenital—existing at the time of birth and usually inherited.

Conjunx, Conjus—Wife

Consanguineous—related by birth, or of the same blood.

Consanguinity—Blood relationship, descended from a common ancestor

Conscience—a person's system of accepted principles or moral conduct.

Consensus, non concubitus, facit nuptias vel matri-

monium.—Consent, not cohabitation, constitutes nuptials or marriage.

Consort—Royal Spouse — wife.

Constitution—a totality, of factors, hereditary and acquired, establishing a person's physical condition and development.

consortium (pl. consortia).—A union of lots or chances; (a lawful marriage).

Contemporary—At the same time or a designated time as in living at the same time or records made right when an event took place.

contra.—Against.

Contra bonos mores.—Against good morals.

Contraception—the prevention by artifical or oral methods, of conception in the human female.

contra pacem.—against the peace.

Conubuim—Marriage

copied—transcribed or imitated.

coram non judice.—In presence of a person not a judge. (A suit brought and determined in a court having no jurisdiction over the matter is said to be coram non judice, and the judgment is void.)

Cpl—Corporal

corpus.—Body

Corpus, Corporis—A body or group

corpus delicti.—The body of the offense; the essence of the crime.

corpus juris.—A body of law.

corpus juris civilis.—The body of the civil law.

Corpse—a dead human body.

Corr—Correspond(ence).

Cortege—a funeral procession.

Countess—wife of an earl or count.

county—unit of government above minor civil divisions and below that of the state. A genealogical division.

Courtesan—a court mistress or prostitute.

Court of Ordinary—Custodian of wills and deeds in Georgia.

Court Records—records kept by civil and criminal courts; court dockets, calendars, etc.

Cousin (German)—the son or daughter of an aunt or uncle.

Cousins—share an identical relationship to a common progenitor. Siblings share their parents; in logic (though not in common parlance), they are cousins. First cousins share their grandparents; second cousins share their great-grandparents. Cousins one or two generations apart are said to be once or twice removed.

C.P.—Common pleas court.

Cra—Church records archives.

Creed Registers—See civil records.

Cremate—to reduce to ashes by burning.

criminal—having to do with laws.

Crowd—an indeterminate number of persons, generally presenting some unity of feeling and purpose.

Crypt—A burial room or vault beneath a church.

C.S.A.—Confederate States of America, or Army.

C.S.N.—Confederate State Navy.

Cujus est solum, ejus est usque ad coelum.—Whose the soil is, his it is up to the sky.

Culture—the educated and refined side of civilization.

Cumberland Gap—pass through the Allegheny Mountains located in north-eastern Tennessee.

sum testamento annexo (c.t.a.)—With the will annexed. (Describes an administrator who operates under a will rather than in intestacy.)

Curator—an administrator of another person's affairs.

Custody—safe-keeping or guardianship.

Custom—ykbit or usage.

—**D**—

D—Roman numeral for 500.

d.A. der Altere—the older (elder), sen.

Daguerrotype—an early method of taking pictures by sunlight on glass plates or silverised copper.

damnum absque injuria.—Damage without injury. (Damage without legal wrong.)

D.A.R.—Daughters of the American Revolution.

Darvinism—the theory of evolution propounded by Charles Robert Darvin (1809-1882) in his Origin of Species.

datum (pl. data)—A thing given; a date.

dau—daughter(s)

Daughter—a female child.

Daughter-in-law—a son's wife.

Day—the period from sunrise to sunset.

D.C.C—dictionary card catalog.

D.D.—Doctor of Divinity.

ddt—death date(s)

Dea—Deacon

de bonis non administratis.—Of the goods not administered. Frequently abbreviated to de bonis non.

de bono et malo.—For good and ill.

Dead—without life.

Death—extinction of life.

Debenture—an acknowledgement of a debt, with a guarantee or repayment.

decedent—a deceased or dead person.

decennial—ten

Decessit—Deceased or died.

Decessit Sine Prole (D.S.P.)—Died without issue or died childless.

Decessit Vita Matris (D.V.M.)—Died during Mother's lifetime.

Decessit Vita Patris (D.V.P.)—Died during Father's lifetime.

Declaration—The first pleading on the part of the plaintiff in a lawsuit; usually states the specific complaints alleged against the defendant.

Declaration of Intention—In naturalization cases, the declaration filed by alien seeking to become a citizen; these were required until the 1950's and include such information as country of origin, method of arrival, age, and occupation.

Deed—A sealed instrument in writing, duly executed and delivered, by which one person conveys land, tenements, or hereditaments to another.

deed of gift—a gift, or seal or personal property, to a heir before the death of the grantor.

deed of partition—deed by persons holding property jointly.

deed of trust—a deed which creates a trust.

de facto.—In fact; in deed; actually.

defendant—one who is sued or charged with a crime or wrong.

Degenerate—a person of low social behavior.

de jure.—Of right; lawful.

Delinquent—generally a young offender against accepted social or legal values.

De minimis non curat lex.—The law does not concern itself with trifles.

Demurrer—Statement by defendant admitting truth of plaintiff's allegations are not sufficient to make demurring party answer them or not sufficient to require answers or to allow cause to proceed.

Denizen—An adopted or naturalized citizen; a person having permission to reside in a foreign country.

Denization—The act of making a foreigner a citizen. The act of naturalizing a citizen.

denomination—church or religion.

de novo.—Anew; afresh.

Deposition—Testimony of witness taken by interrogation but not in court. Testimony under oath for court records.

Deposition—The testimony of a witness taken upon interrogatories, not in open court, but in pursuance of a commission to take testimony issued by a court, or under a general law on the subject, and reduced to writing and duly authenticated, and intended to be used upon the trail of an action in court.

depository—a records storehouse or archive.

desc—descendant(s)

descent—forward or from an ancestor.

Descendants or Progency—Children, grandchildren, great-grandchildren, etc. opposite of ancestors, direct blood line children.

Description—describing the city, its streets, buildings, etc.

Description and Travel—description of an area larger than a city.

de son tort.—Of his own wrong.

devise—a gift of land by a will, to become effective at the death of the donor.

Devisee—The person to whom lands or other real property are devised or given by will.

Devisor—The decedent who made the will.

Dewey Decimal System—Method of cataloging books in a library.

Dexit—Said, say

Dexter—relating to the right hand or side.

Dialect—a variation of language or speech pecular to an area or social group.

Diary—a personal record of thoughts and events.

Die, Diem, Dies—Day

dies non.—Not a day (on which the business of the courts can be carried on).

Diocese—The territorial extent of a bishop's jurisdiction. The circuit of every bishop's jurisdiction.

directional finder—document locater or equivalent.

Directories—Contains a list of persons or organizations usually gives an address.

Dishonour—discredit or disgrace.

Distaff—the maternal side.

District Land Office — plat book—a book of maps showing the location of the land of all patentees.

div—divorced

Divine—having a sacred or holy nature.

Divorce—dissolution of a marriage by law.

Dixie—the southern states.

d.j. der j Ungere—the younger (jun.)

D.N.B.—Dictionary of National Biography.

Docket—Outline of case prepared by clerk of court; gives dates of major pre-trial, trial, and post-trial actions. A generic term which also includes specialized dockets, such as juvenile, officers, auditors, and masters.

Document—an official or legal paper containing information or instructions.

document file—a repository for all research sources.

Domestic—related to household affairs.

donatio mortis causa—A gift by reason of death.

Donation (Lands)—Vand given by the government for services. A gift or gratuity. Bounty land, in Texas, donated to veterans of the Alamo, Goliad, San Antonio, and Harrisburg. These lands could not be sold during the life of the grantee. Later, veterans of Confederate service were also awarded land for their service.

Dormant—in a quiesant state.

Dowager—Title given to a widow, usually to distinguish her from the wife of her husband's heir.

Dower—that portion of, or interest in, the real estate of a deceased husband which the law gives to his widow during her life. A widow's life interest in one-third of the lands and tenements which her deceased husband acquired during the marriage.

down east—New England.

dowry—Possessions of a woman before marriage.

dt—date(s)

dtr—daughter(s)

Ducal—pertaining to a duke.

duces tecum.—You bring with you.

Duchess—the wife or widow of a duke.

dum bene se gessert.—While he shall conduct himself well; during good behavior.

durante minore aetate.—During minority.

durante viduitate.—During widowhood.

Dynasty—a line, generally of kings, of the same ancestry.

—E—

Earl—rank between a marquis and a viscount.

ebd. Ebenda—at the same place.

Eccentric—a person of singular or abnormal habits.

eccesiastical—church or faith.

e converso.—Conversely; on the other hand.

Education—instruction and discipline in relational thinking.

Effeminate—having the characteristics or behavior of women.

Ego—relating to oneself.

Electorate—voter registration lists and election

records.

Elegy—A funeral or mourning song.

Elope—to run away clandestinely

Eloquent—having the power or gift of impressive language.

Emancipate—to free from servitude or slavery.

Emasculate—to deprive of male qualities.

Embryo—feotus in initial stages of gestation.

Emigrant—One who leaves his native country to live somewhere else.

emigration—to leave a country.

Emigration and Immigration—ship passenger lists, ship arrivlas and departures, list of emigrants.

Enbalm—to preserve a dead body by the use of balm, oil, spices, or antiseptic agents.

enclosure file—see document file.

Encyclopedias and Dictionaries—

Engender—to beget or breed.

enl—enlist(ed)

Ens—Ensign

Entainment—Limited inheritance, to specific succession of heirs.

Entomb—to inter or bury.

Enumeration—The census record as taken by the enumerator.

Enumerator—One officially appointed to take a census.

Eped—Christened

es instanti—Upon the instant.

Epigraph—an inscription, generally on a building or mausoleum, and often in verse.

Epitaph—an inscription on a monument or tomb, commemorating the dead.

erratum (pl. errata).—Error.

err. Errechnet—Calculated; approximated.

escheat—the reversion of property to the state when the heirs are unknown.

Esquire—originally a shield-bearer or one of two attendants on a knight, but now often a courtesy title used instead of "Mr."

Estate—The aggregate of property of all kinds which a person leaves to be divided at his death.

Estate Sale — Sale Bill—The sale of one's estate, usually personal property, made by his executor or administrator in the settlement of the estate after his death; lists items, buyer, and prices.

Estreats—A copy or extract from the book of estreats, that is, the rolls of any court in which the fines, recognizances, etc., imposed or taken by that court upon or from the accused are set down, and which are to be levied by the bailiff or other officer of the court.

et al (et alii)—And others. Use of this phrase in deeds may indicate an estate settlement including a complete list of heirs.

et alli (et al.)—And others.

et alius (et al.)—And another.

et cetera (etc.).—And other things.

ethnic—nationality or race.

et uxor (et ux.).—And wife.

Et Uxor, Et ux—and wife.

et vir.—And husband.

Eunuch—a castrated human male.

ev. evangelisch—Evangelical

Evidence—Any species or mode of proof which is presented through the means of witnesses, records, documents, concrete objects, etc., for the purpose either of establishing or disproving any alleged fact.

ex cathedra—From the chair.

Exception—Objection to a decisin made by the court.

ex contractu.—(Arising) from the contract.

exch—exchange

ex delicto.—(Arising) from a tort.

Execution—A writ putting into effect a final judgment of the court, such as signing sealing acknowledging, and delivering the instrument. It should be distinguished from the mere signing of an instrument which in and of itself may be incomplete execution. In court practice, execution refers to proceedings to enforce a judgement. In the case of a money judgment, it is a direction to the sheriff to take the necessary steps to collect the judgment.

Executor (Executrix)—A person appointed by the testator to execute his will, or to see its provisions carried into effect his decease. The executor is the personal representative of the testator. Executrix is feminine.

Executrix—A women who has been appointed by will to execute such will or testament.

ex gratia.—As a matter of favor.

ex necessitate legis.—From legal necessity.

ex officio.—From office; by virtue of his office.

ex parte.—On one side only; by or for one party.

Expatriate—to banish or deport from one's native land.

ex post facto.—After the act.

ex rel (short for ex relatione).—On information of; on behalf of a party or parties.

extract—full and complete copy.

—**F**—

f—father

Fact—anything actually true.

F.A.G.S.—Fellows American Genealogical Society.

F. & A.M.—Free and Accepted Masons.

F & I W—French and Indian War

fam(s)—family(ies)

Familial—refering or relating to the family.

Family—a group of individuals, ideally consisting of parents, children and grandchildren.

family group record—form for recording a singular family hisotry or event.

Family Tradition—Family information passed by word of mouth from generation to generation.

Father—a male parent.

federal—national.

Federal Road—trail from Baltimore to Natchez.

Fee Simple—Complete ownership of land clear or unencumbered.

Fee Tail—ownership of land upon conditions.

Feet of Fine—The bottom part of an indenture retained by the record office.

felonice.—Feloniously.

Feminine—having female characteristics.

feme covert.—A married woman.

Feme sole.—A single woman (including one who has been married but whose marriage has been dissolved by death or divorce).

feral natural.—Of a wild nature.

ff.—pages following.

F.F.V.—First Families of Virginia.

fiat.—Let it be done. (A short order or warrant of a judge, commanding that something shall be done).

fieri.—To be made up; to become.

fieri facias.—Cause to be made.

Files—Papers accompanying a case or action, usually including writs, complaints, answers and bonds.

Filia—Daughter

Filial—befitting a son or daughter

filuis nullius.—The son of nobody; a bastard.

filuis populi.—A son of the people.

final certificate—document given to former aliens upon becoming citizens.

Fine—Sum of money paid at end of a case, usually as a penalty.

First Generation.—Is one's own generation. The third generation in either direction is prefixed grand (e.g. grandfather, grandaunt, grandson). The fourth generation in either direction is prefixed great-grand (e.g. great-granduncle, great-granddaughter.

1/h—1st husband

first papers—declaration of intention to be naturalized.

1/w—first wife

flagrante delicto.—In the very act of committing the crime.

Floruit—"Flourished" or living (used with a date)

F.N.—free negro.

Folio—In probate usage—a leaf or several leaves, pages or documents, numbered, but not necessarily corresponding with page numbers. A folio may contain as many as 15 to 20 pages or documents.

foll—following

footstone—a stone placed at the foot of a grave.

Forbear—an ancestor

Forbes Road—trail from Philadelphia to Pittsburgh

Foster—to rear or nourish

Foster child—a young person reared or nourished as one's own.

fr—from

(?) fraglich—questionable or doubtful

Frater—Brother

fraternal—a male union or gang. brotherly.

Freeholder—one entitled to vote and hold office as a landowner

Freeman—In modern legal phraseology, it is the appellation of a member of a city or borough having the right of suffrage, or a member of any municipal corporation invested with full civic rights

0—0 freie Verbindung—common law marriage; illegitimate union

Friend—a person attached to another by esteem or affection

Ft. Wayne—public library of Ft. Wayne and Allen County, Indiana

funeral parlor—mortuary.

—G—

G.A.R.—Grand Army of the Republic.

Gazeteer—A list of Geographical names countries, cities, rivers, etc.

Gazetteers—list of geographic names

gch—grandchild(ren)

gdau(s)—granddaughter(s)

geb. geboren—born

x^x^x gefallen—killed in action

Gemelli—Twins

gen—genealogy

Genealogical Societies—exist to facilitate pro genitological research which must precede genealogical writing unless the writing is being done by the common progenitor himself. (Alex Haley's Roots was written as a genealogy of Kunta Kinte; Haley's findings of the African was a classic piece of progenitorship.) Genealogists and their societies should, in the interests of cogency, be renamed progenitologists and progenitological societies.

Genealogist—one who is qualified to investigate ancestral descent and construct a pedigree based to the fullest possible extent on primary sources.

Genealogy—Is the identification of the descendants of a common progenitor and/or the families of those descendants. Takes the form "Abraham begat Isaac." A progenitology takes the form "Jacob was a son of Isaac." Ancient books such as the Bible often contain both.

general search—research in the basic jurisdiction or that agency which records property records.

Generation—Either a degree of removal in computing descents, or a single succession of living beings in natural descent. Average period between one generation and another (about 33 years).

Generosus—of noble birth

Genital—regarding generation or the organs of generation.

Gentleman—a man of good breeding and refined character.

Gentry—People classed between nobility and farmers

Genus—Ancestry

G.E.R.M.S.—Genealogical Research: Methods and Sources.

0/0 geschieden—divorced

gesch. geschieden—divorced

Gestation—the carrying of young in the womb.

gest. gestorben—died

† gestorben—died

getauft—baptized

getauft—christened (christening register)

get. getauft—Christened

Given Name—First names given at birth

glebe—land belonging to a Parish Church.

Gm Gemeinde—community; parish

gmo—grandmother(s)

Goodman, Goodwife—A householder of the working class, not rich

G.P.A.I.—Genealogical Periodical Annual Index.

gpar—grandparent(s)

gr—great

Grandchildren and Great-grandchildren—ought to be called third or fourth generation descendants when they become adults. The terms grandson, granddaughter, great-grandson, and great-granddaughter are correct.

Grand Jury minutes—Skeletal record of witnesses, testimony before grand jury; record of grand jury action.

Grant—A general term applicable to all transfers of real property.

Grantee—The person to whom a grant is made. A person who buys or receives property.

Grantor—A person by whom a grant or conveyance is made.

Grange—an American agricultural society.

grayback—a southern soldier.

Great—more distant in relationship by one generation; used in compounds such as great-grandfather.

great lakes—Superior, Michigan, Huron, Erie, and Ontario.

Great Road—trail from Pennsylvania (down the Shenandoah Valley) to Louisville.

G.R.S.—Genealogical Record Search

G.S.A.—General Services Administration

gson—grandson(s)

Guardian—A guardian is a person lawfully invested with the power and charged with the duty, of taking care of the person and managing the property and rights of another person, who, for some peculiarity of status, or defect of age, understanding, or self-control, is considered incapable of administering his own affairs.

Guardian and Ward—non-court records pertaining to guardianship

Guide—The Researcher's Guide to American Genealogy.

—H—

h—husband

habeas corpus.—You have the body.

habendum clause.—Clause in deed that defines extent of ownership by grantee.

habere facias possessionem.—That you cause to have possession. (A writ of ejectment.)

habere facias seisinam.—That you cause to have seisin. (A writ to give possession.)

Handybook—Handy Book for Genealogists.

Handbook.—Manuèls, etc.

headright—colonial system of granting 50 acres to each immigrant.

headstone—the stone at the head of a grave.

Hearsay Evidence—A term applied to that species of testimony given by a witness who relates, not what he knows personally, but what others have told him, or what he had heard said by others.

Hearsay evidence is that which does not derive its value solely from the credit of the witness, but rests mainly on the veracity and competency of other persons. The very nature of the evidence shows its weakness, and it is admitted only in specified cases from necessity. Hearsay evidence is second-hand evidence, as distinguished from original evidence; it is the repetition at second-hand of what would be original evidence if given by the person who originally made the statement.

heir heiraten—marry

Heir-apparent—a person next in line of succession to a title or estate

Heir, Heiress—An heir at common law is a person who succeeds, by the rules of law, to an estate in lands, tenements, or hereditaments, upon the death of his ancestor, by descent and right of relationship. (Man or Woman-Heiress)

Heirloom—an article of personal property which descends to an heir.

Heraldry—a decorative shorthand for identification of clans, families, national figures, churchmen and institutions. Coat of arms. Work dealing with coats of arms and heraldry.

hereditaments—any property which may be transmitted by law of descent.

Heredity—the transmission of physical and mental charteristics to offspring.

Heritage—something inherited or to be inherited.

hist—history

Historical Records Survey (W.P.A.)—government inventory of various records during the great depression and war years.

History—History of a specific area, also broken down chronologically.

H.J. (Hic Jacet)—here lies.

H.J.S. (Hic Jacet Sepultus)—here lies buried

holograph—an instrument hand-written by the person from whom it eminates and need not be witnessed.

homestead—land granted to settlers.

Homosexual—a male who is sexually attracted to another male.

Honor—respect and dignity

honorarium (pl honoraria).—An honorary fee or gift; compensation from gratitude.

H.S. (Hic Sepultus)—here is buried

H.S. (Hic Situs)—here lies

Hubbard's Trace—trail from Chicago to southern Illinois.

Huguenot—French Protestant.

Human—having the characteristics of man or mankind

Hundred—A land division which was also used in the early colonies. A land division used in England.

Husband—a married man or spouse

Husbandman—A farmer

—I—

idem sonans.—Having the same sound (as names sounding alike but spelled differently).

iden—identity; identify

Ident-Ident Slip:—A brief, identifying designation, usually on a page or small slip of paper proceeding the will or other document that follows, giving the name, place and wd or wp date, or one or more of these.

Ignorantia legis neminem excusat.—Ignorance of the law excuses no one.

Illegitimate—born out of wedlock.

illicitum collegium.—An unlawful association.

Immigrant—A person coming into a new country to live.

immigration—entrance into a foreign country.

immigrant aid society—societies dedicated to assisting immigrants.

Immoral—not influenced by moral principles.

Impotentia excusat legem.—Impossibility is an excuse in law.

Imperial—pertaining to an empire or emperor.

imprimis—in the first place—as in old wills.

imprint—any printed or typed work.

in bonis.—In goods; among possessions.

Incest—sexual intercourse by near relatives, within the degrees of consanguinity prohibited by law.

incompetency—not legally capable is the lack of legal qualification or ability to discharge a required duty; it is also the condition of a person who is mentally unable or unfit to manage his own affairs.

indebitatus assumpsit.—Being indebted, be promised, or undertook. (An action in which plaintiff alleges defendant is indebted to him.)

Indenture—A deed to which two or more persons are parties, and in which these enter into reciprocal or corresponding grants or obligations towards each other. In early days a written contract torn in half so that the parts had to match.

indentured servant—a system of colonial immigration where individuals served from 5 to 7 years as a servant to pay for their passage to America.

Index—Alphabetical or chronological listing of cases or parties referred to in a given record series; as used here, usually compiled at the time the records were created and intended to be used with them.

indicia.—Marks; signs.

Indictment—Is a written accusation in criminal case found and presented by grand jury.

indiscriminate—a system of surveying in the state-land-states.

Individual—one person, or peculiar to one being.

Inebriate—a habitual drunkard.

in esse.—In being; existence.

in extremis.—In extremity (in the last illness).

Infant—A person not of full age; a minor, in most places under twenty-one years of age.

info—information

informant—one who gives data.

infra—Below.

in fraudem legis.—In circumvention of law.

in futuro.—In the future.

Inherit—to possess by will or descent.

Inheritance—that which is received by will or descent.

Inhumatus, Inhumata—unburied

in loco parentis.—In the place of a parent.

inn—lodge or hotel.

Innholders and Retailers—Provisioners to whom Court of General Sessions granted licenses, particularly to serve liquor.

Innubus, Innupta—unmarried

innuendo.—Meaning.

in pari delicto.—In equal fault.

in personam.—A remedy where the proceedings are against the person, as contradistinquished from those against a specific thing.

in praesenti.—At present; at once; now.

Inquest—Coroner's investigation into a death.

in re.—In the matter.

in rem.—A remedy where the proceedings are against the thing, as distinguished from those against the person.

in rerum natura.—In nature; in life; in existence.

Inseminate—the approach of spermatozoon to the ovum.

in specie.—In the smae, or like, form. (To decreé performance in specie is to decree specific performance.)

in statu quo.—In the condition in which it was.

int—intentions of mar.

Intellect—the faculty of thought and reason.

inter.—Among; between.

Intercourse—sexual contact or communication.

interim.—In the meantime.

Interred—buried

in terrorem.—In terror.

inter vivos.—Between the living.

Intestate—Without making a will. A person is said to die intestate when he dies without making a will, or dies, without leaving anything to testify what his wishes were with respect to the disposal of his property after his death.

in toto.—In the whole; completely.

intra.—Within; inside.

in transitu.—In transit; in course of transfer.

Inventory—An account, catalogue, or schedule made by an executor or administrator, of all the goods and chattels, and sometimes the real property of a deceased person.

I.O.F.—Independent Order of Foresters.

I.O.O.F.—Independent Order of Odd Fellows.

I.O.R.—Independent Order of Rechabites.

I.O.R.M.—Improved Order of Red Men.

ipse dixit.—He himself said (it). (An assertion made but not proved.)

ipso facto.—By the fact itself.

i.r. im Ruhestand—in retirement

Iroquis Trail—trail from Albany to Buffalo (Mohawk Valley)

Issue—Offspring, children; sometimes in genealogy used loosely to indicate any blood relationship of later generations.

Item, It., ITM—Also likewise; a charge in an account, in wills.

ita est.—So it is.

Jahrg. Jahrgang—year

Journal—A daily book; a book in which entries are

made or events recorded from day to day. A diary; an account of daily transactions and events. Daily accounting of court proceeding replace extended. Records in some countries in the 1950's.

—J—

jubilee—pertaining to 50 years.
judicial—pertaining to courts.
jura personarum.—Rights of persons.
jura rerum.—Rights of things.
jurat.—Portion of affidavit in which officer administering the oath certifies that it was sworn to before him.
jure divino.—By divine right.
jure uxoris.—In his wife's right.
jurisdiction—the extent or territory of authority, by which courts act.
Jury Bills—Costs for maintaining jury (in this usage, distinct from grand jury bill, or finding of sufficient evidence to prosecute).
jus (pl. jura).—Law; laws collectively.
jus accrescendi.—The right of survivorship.
jus ad rem.—A right to a thing.
jus civile.—Civil law.
jus commune.—The common law; the common right.
jus gentium.—The law of nations; international law.
jus habendi.—The right to have a thing.
jus proprietatis.—Right of property.
Justice of Peace (J.P.)—Justice of the Peace.

—K—

kath. katholisch—Catholic
KB. Kirchenbuch—parish register, church book.
K. of C.—Knights of Columbus.
K.K.K.—Ku Klux Klan.
K. of P.—Knights of Pythias.
Kindred—Relatives by blood; affinity by blood or marriage.
kinfolk—cousin or relative.
Kings and Rulers—works dealing with the genealogy of the ruling class.
King's Highway—trail from Boston to Charleston.
Kr. Kreis—County

—L—

L.—Roman numeral for 50.
Lady—A woman of good breeding and refined character.
Lake Champlain Route—trail from Albany to Montreal.
Land and Property—deeds, land grants and surveys, mortgages, title abstracts fee books, and rent rolls.
Land Patent—Public lands assigned to individuals in writing similar to a deed but not transacted with money.
Land Warrant—a negotiable government certificate entitling the holder to a specified quantity of public land.
Land Warranty-lease and release—a type of conveyance used in England and early colonial land records.

law—legal rules or principles.
Laws and Legislation—legal measures and procedures.
Lay Subsidies—see civil records or taxation.
L.C.—Library of Congress.
L.D.S.—Latter-day Saints.
Lease—a contract renting land or property for a specified period. One who leases from another.
Leasehold—Property held by a lease.
leasor—one who leases to another.
Lecher—a man of lewd or lustful habits.
Legacy—Property left to a person in a will or that which is due him. A bequest or gift of personal property by last will and testament.
Legatee;—A person named in a will as one to whom the testator wishes to bequeath certain property, money or personal possessions.
Legitimate—born in lawful wedlock.
Lesbian—a woman who is sexually attracted to another women.
lessee—person to whom a lease is given.
lessor—one who grants a lease or sells land.
Letters of Administration—The instrument by which an administrator is authorized to administer the goods or estate of a deceased person.
Letters Testamentary—An instrument granted by the proper officer to the executor of a will, authorizing him to act as executor.
levari facias.—Cause to be levied; a writ of execution.
lex loci.—Law of the place (where the cause of action arose).
lex loci rei sitae.—The law of the place where a thing is situated.
lex mercatoria.—The law merchant.
Liber—Book or volume
Liborum—Children
Library of Congress System—The system used in the library of congress and also by many librarians.
License—Permission to sell liquor, granted by General Sessions. A legal permit.
lien—a claim against property.
life insurance—started in American before the revolution.
Lineage—descendants in a line from an ancestor or progenitor.
Lineal—That which comes in a line; especially a direct line, as from father to son. Collateral relationship is not called "lineal," though the expression "collateral line," is not unusual.
lis pendens—pending suits of court cases.
lis pendens.—Litigation pending; a pending suit.
List of entries—List of cases formally entered on to court docket or records.
litigation—concerning a law suit.
liv—lived; living
locus delicti.—The place of the crime or tort.
locus in quo.—The place in which.
Locus, Locorum—Location
locus sigilii (L.S.)—The place for the seal.
log—see calendar

Longevity—prolonged life

Love—devoted attachment to one of the opposite sex.

Loyalist—People in America who stayed loyal to the British during the Revolutionary War.

l.p.m.s.—legitimatus per matrimonium subsequens German: durch nachfolgende Eke anerkannt. Legitimized by subsequent marriage.

L.S.D.—(librae, solidi, denarii) pounds, shillings, pence.

Lt.—Lieutenant

Lust—inordinate carnal desires.

luth. lutherisch—Lutheran

—M—

m—marriage; married

mdt—marriage date

Magna—Great

Magna Carta—The "Great Charter" which granted freedoms and rights to citizens in England.

Maj—Major

mala fides.—Bad faith.

mala in se.—Wrongs in themselves; (acts morally wrong).

mala praxis.—Malpractice.

mala prohibita—Prohibited wrongs or offenses.

malo animo—With evil intent.

malum in se.—Evil in itself.

Man—an adult male.

mandamus.—We command.

mannl. mannlich—male

Manors—see civil records or court records.

manu forti.—With a strong hand; (forcible entry).

Manumission—The freeing of a slave.

Maps—single maps of an area.

Marita—Wife

Mariti, Maritus—Husband

Marriage—legal union between two individuals of opposite sexes, the aims of which are procreation and friendship.

Marriage Contract—an agreement entered into before or after marriage for the purpose of regulating the rights of property of husband and wife, and their children.

Marriage License—A license or permission granted by public authority to persons who intended to intermarry. By statute in some jurisdictions, it is made an essential prerequisite to the lawful solemnization of the marriage.

Marriage Portion—Dowry; a sum of money or other property which is given to or settled on a woman on her marriage.

Marriage Settlement—A written agreement in the nature of a converyance, called a "settlement," which is made in contemplation of a proposed marriage and in consideration thereof, either by the parties about to intermarry, or one of them, or by a parent or relation on their behalf, by which the title to certain property is settled, i.e. fixed or limited to a prescribed course of succession; the object being, usually to provide for the wife and children. Thus, the estate might be limited to the husband and issue, or to the wife and issue, or to the husband and wife for their joint lives, remainder to the survivor for life, remainder over to the issue, or otherwise. Such settlements may also be made after marriage, in which case they are called "post-nuptial."

M/1—married first

Masculine—having manly characteristics.

Master—Officer of court, appointed by judge to handle specialized and/or technical matters assigned to him; a master examines causes, takes accounts, computes damages, and reports findings to help to facilitate decisions in equity cases.

Mater—Mother

Maternal—That which belongs to, or comes from, the mother; as maternal authority, maternal relation, maternal estate, maternal line.

Matriarch—an influential mother of a family or tribe.

Matrimony—state of wedlock.

Mausoleum—an imposing tomb.

Medical and Health Records—hospital records, physicians and midwife records excluding births, marriages and deaths.

Memoir—a brief biographical sketch.

Memorial(s)—anything intended to commemorate a person or event. Land records found in South Carolina, in the nature of an abstract of title. All purchasers were required to file memorials at one time.

menn. mennonitisch—Mennonite

Menopause—the change of life in a woman.

mens rea.—Guilty mind.

Menses—the monthly discharge from the uterus of the female.

Mensis—Month

Mesne conveyances—legal conveyance of land, as a deed, in South Carolina.

Menstruate—to discharge the menses.

Mental reports—Reports of psychiatrists concerning mental condition of accused in criminal cases.

Messuage—A dwelling house with adjacent lands and buildings

Metizo—Mixed ancestry of Indian and European bloods.

Mex W—Mexican War

M.I.—Monumental Inscription

Microfilm—Photographic reproduction on film of something printed that is reduced for ease in moving and storage.

Midwife—a woman who assists another at the birth of a child.

Midwifery—the practice of obstetrics.

Migration, Internal—records of internal migraion and population trends.

Military Records—military pensions, service files, muster rolls, enlistment and discharge papers.

Minor—a person who has not attained legal age.

Minorities—racial or religious minorities within an area.

Miscarriage—a premature and immature birth.

Miss—title of an unmarried woman.

Mistress (abbreviated Mrs.):—a courtesy title given to a married woman.

Misogamy—hatred of marriage.

Mittimus—Order of court or magistrate to sheriff commanding him to take the person herein named to jail and to the jailer commanding him to keep the prisoner until further notice.

Mo—mother

Monies paid into court—Record of money paid to court for use as recognizance, surety, bonds, and similar purposes.

moiety—about one-half (in wills or deeds).

Monogamy—the state of being married to one person at a time.

Monogenesis—descent of an organism from a single cell.

Monogenism—the theory of descent from an original human pair.

Monogynous—mating with a single female.

Monthly Meeting—Quaker meetings and/or records; records taken at the monthly meeting are called by the same name.

Monument—Large tombstone.

Monumental Inscriptions—see vital records.

Moral—relating to the good conduct of man in his environment.

Morale—the mental state which causes one or more persons to face an ordeal or emergency with spirit.

Morganatic—applied to a marriage between a man of high or royal state and a woman of lower station (e.g. the late British Duke of Windsor—formerly King Edward VIII—and Mrs. Wallis Simpson.)

Morgue—a mortuary used particularly for the temporary retention of people who have died by unnatural means.

Mors, MS, Mortis—Manuscript. Death

Mortality Schedules—Death information taken with the censuses of 1860, 1879, 1880.

Mortgage—the conveyance of property in security of a loan.

Mortician—a person who undertakes to dispose of the dead by burial or cremation.

Mortuary—a building designed for the temporary reception of the dead.

Motions—Applications made for consideration and hearing of a certain point, made to a court for an order.

Mother—a female parent.

Mother-in-Law—the mother of a wife or husband.

Motto—a short phrase added to armorial bearings.

Mourn—to lament or grieve over the death of a loved one.

mov—moved

Mr.—abbreviation for Master informerly Master (formerly Master of Arts,) now a courtesy title given to a man.

Mulato—Mixed white and negro parentage.

Muniments—Evidence, written or otherwise, proving title to property.

Mummy—a dead body preserved by embalming.

Murder—a homicide with premeditated intent. Is the killing with malice aforethought of one human being by another.

—N—

Names, Geographical—geographical names and their origin.

Names, Personal—meaning of names.

Nat—Born

Nata—Daughter

Naturalise—to give an alien or foreigner the rights of a native.

Naturalization—records dealing with a person becoming a citizen.

Naval records—see military records.

Ne: Nee—Born (after a female name) indicates her maiden name as in Mary Nee Jones — Jones is the maiden name.

Neanderthal—denoting a man of the earliest long-headed European race, extinct over 50,000 years ago.

Nephew—the son of a brother or sister.

Nepos Nepotis—Grandson

Neptis—Granddaughter

Newspapers—for actual newspapers, not for vital statistics that are clipped out.

Niece—the dauthter of a brother or sister.

nihil dicit.—He says nothing. (Judgment against defendant who does not put in a defense to the complaint.)

nil debet.—He owes nothing.

nisi prius—Unless before. (The phrase is used to denote the forum where the trail was held as distinguished from the appellate court.)

Nobility—a class holding special rank or privilege, generally hereditary.

Noble—distinguished by birth, rank, deeds, or character.

nolle prosequi.—To be unwilling to follow up, or to prosecute. (A formal entry on the record by the plaintiff or the prosecutor that he will no further prosecute the case.)

nolo contendere.—I will not contest it.

Nomen—Name

Nomenclature—a system of naming.

Nonage—legal infancy.

Nonagenarian—a person aged 90 years and upwards.

non compos mentis.—Not of sound mind.

Noncupative Will—One made verbally with witnesses to record it.

Non-Entries—Writs issued in cases which were satisfied or dropped before coming to court.

non est factum.—It is not his deed.

non obstante.—Notwithstanding

non prosequitur (non pros.).—He does not follow up, or pursue, or prosecute. (If the plaintiff fails to take some step that he should, the defendant may enter a judgment of non pros. against him.)

Notary, Notary Public—An officially authorized person with right to draw up or attest documents.

Notice—Court documents notifying parites of suits, appearances, and other official matters.

Nothus—Illegitimate

nudum pactum.—A nude pact. (A contract without consideration.)

nul tiel record.—No such record.

nul tort.—No wrong done.

nulla bona.—No goods. (Wording of return to a writ of fieri facias.)

nunc pro tunc.—Now for then.

Nuncupative Will—A will which depends merely upon oral evidence, having been declared or dictated by the testator in his last sickness before a sufficient number of witnesses, and afterwards reduced to writing.

Nupt, Nupta, Nuptial—Marriage

Nurse—a person trained for the care of the young, sick or aged.

N.X.N.—No Christian name.

Nymphomaniac—a female with an exaggerated desire for varied sexual intercourse.

—O—

obiter dictum.—Remark by the way.

Obituary—a biographical sketch of a deceased person.

Obstetrics—the practice of midwifery.

Ob. Unm—Died unmarried.

Occupations—freemens records, records of members of guilds.

Octaroon—One-eighth negro blood.

Octogenarian—a person aged 80 years and upwards.

Officers—Court-appointed person who determines causes between parties or renders decisions in a judicial capacity.

Offspring or issue—are one's sons and daughters (i.e., immediate progency).

Old—of advanced age.

onus probandi.—The burden of proof.

Oppiddani—Inhabitants of a town.

Optimas—Aristocrat

opus (pl. opera).—Work; labor.

Ordinary—A probate judge in some states.

ore tenus.—By word of mouth; orally.

Origin—parentage, birth or nationality.

Orphan—A child bereaved by the death of both father and mother, or less commonly, of either parent.

Orphans Court—In some states this is the same as a probate court, handling all probate matters.

Orphans and Orphanages—non-court records concerning orphans.

Ostracise—to exclude from society.

Ovum—the embryo after fertilization; also the female egg cell.

—P—

P—page

Pace—a unit of measurement equal to a step or stride. Actual length varies from 30 to 40 inches.

P.A.C.S.—Provisional Army of the Confederate States.

Pageant—a display of people in costume and in procession, usually illustrating history or tradition.

Palatinate—A province of northern Germany from which many people came to America.

Paleography—studies of ancient and modern handwriting.

par—parent(s)

Parchment—part of a sheep or goatskin prepared for use as a manuscript.

Parent—a father or mother.

Parentage—the idenity or relationship of father and mother to children.

pari delicto.—In equal guilt.

Parish—a subdivision of a county or town for ecclesiastical or civil administration. Catholic Division of church groups by area in early days.

Parish Registers—see vital records.

Parochia—Parish

Parochial—Pertaining to a parish.

Parrish Clerk—Custodian of wills, deeds, marriages, divorces, and civil court records in Louisiana.

particeps criminis.—An accomplice in the crime.

Partition—To divide into severalty; as to partition an estate among several heirs. When the owners themselves cannot agree, partition is used as a form of a legal action, whereby the court compels the land to be divided between the co-owners or directs that the land be sold and the proceeds of the sale be divided between or among the owners.

Parson—Clergyman

Passim—Confusedly, Indiscriminately.

Patent—(1) an instrument conveying title to public lands to private ownership. (2) a grant made by the government to an inventor giving him the exclusive right to make, use, and sell his invention for a specified period.

Paternal—That which belongs to the father or comes from him.

pater familias.—The father(head) of a family.

Paternity—the relation of a father to his progeny.

Patriarch—a ruler and father of a family or tribe.

Patronimic—A name formed by using prefixes and/or suffixes to show parent/child relationships as in Anderson or son of Ander or O'Nielson son of Niel.

Peculiar—A court, usually limited in jurisdiction to one or a few parishes, with possible adjacent chapelries or hamlets, having probate jurisdictions within itself. If a testator resided within the jurisdiction of a peculiar, his will may be more readily found. However, he may have had property elsewhere, so that his will may be found in the records of a court of larger jurisdiciton.

peculium.—Private property.

Pedigree—Recorded ancestry or line of descent. A chart showing lines of ancestry.

pendente lite.—Pending the suit; during the litigation.

Pension—Money given by the government for a person's military serive. Non-military pensions.

per annum.—By the year.

per autre vie.—For another's lifetime. (See also pur antre vie.)

per capita.—By the head; as individuals. (In a distribution of an estate, if the descendants take per capita, they take share and share alike regardless of family lines of decent.)

per centum (per cent).—By the hundred.

per contra.—In opposition.

per curiam.—By the court.

per diem.—By the day.

Perigrinus—A traveler or foreigner.

Periodicals—magazines, newsletters, etc.

per se.—By itself; taken alone.

Person—an individual human being.

Personal—relating to one person.

Personal Property—Property of a personal or movable nature, as opposed to property of a local or immovabvle character, (such as land or houses) the latter being called "real property."

Per Stirpes—An estate left to a group.

per stirpes.—By stems or root; by representation. (In a distribution of an estate, if distribution is per stirpes, descendants take by virtue of their representation of an ancestor, not as individuals.)

Petition—A written application to a court requesting its action in some matter.

Petition and Records—As used in a naturalization case, the complete record including petitions to become a citizen affidavits of witnesses, certificate of arrival, final decision on petition, admission to citizenship; includes all documents except preliminary declaration of intention.

Photograph—a picture made by the chemical action of light on a sensitive plate or film.

Photostate—Copy of material made by photo graphy.

Pipe Rolls—see civil records.

Pleading—Process performed by parties in a suit, alternately presenting written statements of their contention, responding to preceding contentions.

Poll—a register of persons kept for a specific purpose.

Poll Books—see taxation.

Polygamy—the practice of having more than one wife at the same time.

Poor Law—see civil records.

Portrait—a picture or likeness, usually painted in oils, of an individual.

poss—possibly

Postal Guides—lists of cities and towns with their post office designation.

Posterity—Whether one is alive or dead, one's posterity grows greater (like Abraham's) unless and until the line becomes extinct (like Shakespeare's). Whether one is alive or dead, one's ancestry is fixed, however far back it may be traceable. One can be deprived of descendants; one cannot be deprived of progenitors.

Posthumous—born after the death of the father.

post-mortem.—After death.

post-obit.—To take affect after death.

Power of Attorney—To vest in another certain powers to act in one's behalf. Extent and limits usually detailed in writing of the power.

praecipe or precipe.—Command. (A written order to the clerk of the court to issue a writ.)

Pre-Emption—An official right to purchase property before anyone else.

Pregnant—fertile, or with child.

Prerogative Court—In Maryland, they have records of probate which were recorded in the counties prior to 1777. If county records were burned look for some record in Prerogative Court.

Presentment—Writing containing the accusation presented by grand jury and representing to the court that a public offense has been committed, that it is triable in the county, and that there is ground for believing a particular individual has committed the crime. It lacks, however, the formality of a bill of indictment.

prima facie.—At first sight; on the face of it.

Primogenitor—the earliest ancestor.

Primogeniture—the position of being the first-born child, or the right of the eldest son to inherit to the exclusion of others.

Prius—before, prior to.

pro.—For

pro—probate(d)

prob—probably

Probate—The proof before a competent officer or tribunal that an instrument offered is the last will and testament of a person deceased as it purports and is alleged to be; also an officially authenticated copy of a will so proved. Proved-Tried-Approved.

Probate Act—A short record found at the end of most wills giving the date the will was proved, and the name or names of the person or persons to whom court authorization was given to execute the terms of the will, normally the executor, executrix or executors named in the will.

Probate court—Any matters pertaining to the settlement of a will or an estate.

Probate Records—wills, testaments, administra tions.

prochein ami.—Next friend.

pro confesso.—As confessed.

Procreate—tp beget children.

Procurer—a person who obtains or supplies women for immoral purposes.

pro forma.—As a matter of form.

Progenitors—are one's parents, one's grand parents, one's great-grandparents, etc. In the direct line. Ancestor, oppoiste of descendant.

Progenitorship—Is the logical opposite of genealogy. The former, seeking ancestry, proceeds backward in time; the latter, seeking posterity, proceeds forward in time.

Progeny—descendants or offspring.

pro hac vice.—For this occasion.

Promiscuous—not limited to one individual or class.

Propagate—to reproduce by generation.

Proprietor—an owner of property.

pro rata.—According to the rate or proportion.

Prostitute—a person who for reward or gain gratifies the lust of various persons of the opposite or same sex.

prot. protestantisch—Protestant

pro tanto.—For so much; to that extent.

Protege—one under the protection or partronage of another.

pro tempore (pro tem.)—For the time being; temporarily.

Prothonotary—A chief clerk or court registrar.

Prove—deposition of witnesses to a will or deed, who state that they saw testator or grantor sign the instrument which has been presented to the court.

Proxy—May be either a person or a written instrument. As a person. A proxy is one deputized to reprensent another person at a meeting, such as a stockholders' meeting or a ceremony, such as marriage. When it is a written instrument, a proxy is a document which appoints a person to act at a meeting or similar event.

Puberty—the earliest age at which a person is capable of reproduction.

Public Domain—Government owned lands.

publici juris.—Of public right.

pur autre vie.—For, or during, the life of another.

Putative—Supposed, guessed at, reputed means "commonly reputed," as in the case of a man who is commonly known as the father of an illegitimate child; he is said to be the "putative father" of the child.

Pvt—Private

p.V. polnische Verwaltung—Polish Administration

—Q—

Quadrangle Map—A tract of land on an atlas sheet.

quaere.—Query; question; doubt. (This word indicated that a particular rule, decision, or statement that follows it, is open to question.)

quantum.—How much; the amount.

quantum merrit.—As much as he deserved.

quantum valebant.—As much as they were (reasonably) worth (in absence of agreement as to value).

quare.—Wherefore

quare clausum fregit.—Wherefore he broke the close. (A form of trespass on another's land.)

Quarter Sessions—see court records.

quasi.—As if; as it were. (Indicates that one subject resembles another, but that there are also intrinsic differences between them. Thus, we speak of quasi contracts, quasi torts, etc.)

quid pro quo.—What for what; something for something, (A term denoting the consideration for a contract.)

Quit Claim Deed—Deed giving all rights of grantor at signing.

quo warranto.—By what right or authority.

quoad hoc.—As to this.

quod Computet.—That he account.

Quod Vide (Q.V.)—See reference, which see.

—R—

Race—descendants of a common ancestor.

Rape—carnal knowledge of a female without her consent. Is a crime committed by a man who has sexual intercourse with a woman (not his wife) without her consent. The crime of statutory rape differs from rape in that the offender has intercourse with a female under a stated age (for example, 16 or 18 or 21), either with or without her consent.

Ravish—to rape or violate.

re—regarding

Real Property—A general term for lands, tenements, and hereditaments; property which, on the death of the owner intestate, passes to the heir.

Realty—Relating to land, not personal property.

rec—record(s)

Rector—A clergyman with management duties as well as spiritual.

Recognizance—Obligation entered into before some court with condition to perform some particular act; as to appear in court, keep the peace, pay a debt, and the like.

Record—As used here, the extended account of a case, including a prose summary of the proceeding, but generally lacking substantive summaries of testimony and evidence.

reductio ad absurdum.—Reduced to the absurd.

ref. reformiert—Reformed

ref—reference

Reference—a quoted passage in a printed book or original manuscript.

Regal—relating to a king or royalty.

rel—relatives/related

Relative—a person connected by blood or affinity.

Relic—an object surviving from the past.

Relict, Relicta (Relictus)—A woman or man survivor of a decedent, widow, or widower.

rem—remove

Remand—The sending of a case back to a lower court by a higher court.

Removal Orders—see civil records.

Renunciation—Act of repudiating or giving up of an administratorship or executorship.

Repatriation—As used in naturalization cases, losing citizenship through marriage to an alien.

Replica—a facsimile or exact copy.

Representative—the head of a family by right of primogeniture.

req.—request(ed)

Requiem—the celebration of Holy Eucharist for the soul of a dead person.

res—reside(d)(ence)

res.—A thing; an object; the subject matter.

res gestae.—Things done; transactions.

res ipsa loquitur.—the thing speaks for itself.

resjudicata.—A matter adjudicated.

Return—The certificate of an officer stating what he has done about the execution of a writ and filing said document properly indorsed in the clerk's office.

Return Day—Day named in writ by which an officer is required to return it.

Rev—Reverend

Revolutionary Pensions—Applications by Revolutionary War veterans for pensions, C. 1820; include important information about applicants finances.

Rev W—Revolutionary War
Rite—a custom or religious practice.
Royal—pertaining to a crowned head of state or his family.
Royal Descent, Families of—families of nobility and kings.
Rural—relating to the country.

—S—

s—son(s)
S. Seite—page
s. siehe—see
Sacra—Sacred
Sacrament—a ceremony observed in a Christian church
Sacred—spiritual or holy.
Sacrosanct—secure against desecration.
Salt Lake Library—The library of the Genealogical society of the Church of Jesus Christ of Latter-day Saints.
Salt System—A system of making four cards for each book for the catalog under the headings of subject, author, location, and title.
Sanctify—to consecrate
Sanction—express permission or authorization.
Sarcophagus—a coffin hewn from a single stone.
Savage—an uncivilized person.
Schedule—A tabulated list as in a census record.
Schools—alumi lists; registration lists.
scienter.—Knowingly
scilicet (SS. or ss.)—To wit. (sc. is not used in legal papers).
scintilla.—A spark; the least particle.
scire facias.—Cause to know, give notice. (A writ used to revive a judgment that has expired.)
Scire Facias (Latin "do you cause to know")—Process to revive either judgment or the original action. Designates a writ requiring a person to show why a record should not be annulled.
Scrivener—a person who draws up contracts or documents.
Scroll—a writing formed into a roll.
Sculpture—an object carved of solid material, or modelled from clay or other material.
se defendendo.—In self-defense; in defending oneself.
Sec., Security—The father, neighbor or cousin was named security if the bride or groom was a minor.
Secular—temporal or wordly.
Seized of—Property possessed by law.
Seizen—Taking legal possession.
Self—the individual person.
semper.—Always
semper paratus.—Always ready. (A plea by which the defendant alleges that he has always been ready to perform what is demanded of him.)
Senile—degenerating physically and mentally as a result of old age.
Sensual—depending on the senses only.
Sentence—Judgment formally pronounced in criminal cases.
Sepulta—Buried
Seriatim.—Severally; separately.

Session Book—List of cases heard in a given period or court session; more, skeletal than docket; similar to trial calendar.
Settlement—A disposition of property for the benefit of some person or persons, usually through the medium of trustees.
Settlement Papers—see civil records.
Sex—distinction between male and female organisms.
Sgt.—Sergeant
Shame—emotion caused by knowledge of loss of honor.
Shield—essutchion on which are placed bearing in coats of arms.
Shipping—agreement and crew lists, merchant marine records, etc.
Shroud—a cloth or garment for a dead person.
sib—sibling(s)
Sibling—a blood relative.
Sic—Appears as shown, often used in parenthesis to indicate an error, strange name or mistake in spelling, quotation.
sigillum.—A seal.
simplex obligato.—A simple obligation.
Sinister—relating to the left hand or side.
Sin—transgression against moral or divine law.
Sine—Without
Sine Anno—Without year.
sine dic.—Without day. (Without a specified day being assigned for a future meeting or hearing.)
Sine Loco—Without place.
Sine Prole—Without children.
sis—sister
Sister-German—a female born of the same parents as another person.
situs.—Situation; location.
Social—affecting public interest or relating to society.
Societies—works dealing with genealogical or historical organizations.
Society—the community or people in general.
sol—soldier(s)
Solemn—grave or impressive.
Solicitor—one legally qualified to counsel or represent another.
Son—a male child.
Son-in-Law—the husband of one's daughter.
Sovereign—a king or ruler.
Souvenir—a keepsake or memento.
Sperm—fertilizing semen or fluid of the male.
Spermatozoon—generative cell present in semen and capable of fertilizing the female germ cell or ovum.
Spiritual—applicable to the spirit or mind.
Spouse—a husband or wife, but generally the latter.
stare decisis.—To abide by decided cases.
Statistics—non-census statistics.
status quo.—State in which (the existing state of things at any given date.) See in statu quo.
Sterile—unable to have children.
Sterilise—to render incapable of having offspring.
Stigma—a mark of disgrace.
Strain—definable line of descent.

sub judice.—Under consideration.

sub modo.—Under a qualification; in a qualified way.

sub nom.—Under the name.

Subscribe—to sign or write at the end of a document.

succession—A will in Louisiana.

sui juris.—Of his own right; (having legal capacity to act for himself).

Suicide—the act of killing oneself intentionally.

Summons—Writ notifying person to appear in court on a given day.

supersedeas.—That you supersede. (A writ commanding a stay of the proceeding.)

Supplementary Documents—Will-related documents; such as inventories, allegations, depositions, summones, etc.

supra.—Above

Surety—One who signs for or guarantees another's debts.

Surname—A last name, inherited or family name; as opposed to a given name or a christian name.

Surrogate—In the state of New York and some other states, a judicial officer who has jurisdiction over the probate of will and settlement of estates, and often has the power to appoint and supervise guardians of infants and other incompetent persons. The use of surrogate in this sense arose from the fact that these matters were formerly under ecclesiastical jurisdiction and were managed by the surrogates of the Bishops. (Surrogate originally was a deputy of an ecclesiastical judge or bishop).

Surveyors; measures—
1 link—7.92 inches
1 chain—100 links—66 feet
10 square chain—1 acre
1 pole—1 rod or 16.5 feet
1 section—1 square mile—640 acres
1 township—36 square miles—23,040 acres
1 range—1 tier of township
1 league—4,428.4 acres
1 labor—177.14 acres

Survivor—a person who outlivves another.

S.v. Sohn von—son of

Syphilis—a contagious veneral disease.

†* totgeboren—stillborn

—T—

Taboo—prohibited or proscribed.

Taxation—Tax rolls, records, assessment rolls, lay subsidy rolls.

Temporal—transient or secular.

terminus a quo.—The starting point.

terr—territory

Testament—Official declaration of disposal of property after death. A will.

Testate—One dying after having made a written will is said to have died testate.

Tesator—The person who writes or dictates to another (usually a lawyer), his or her wishes regarding the disposition of property after his or her decease.

Testatrix—A woman who makes a will; a woman who dies leaving a will; a female testator.

Testimony—an affirmation or solemn declaration.

Tib—Temple (records) index bureau.

Title—an appellation denoting position or rank. In the law of property, is the evidence of a person's right to possession and ownership of property.

Tomb—a grave or receptacle for the dead.

Topographic Map—Maps made by the government of all of the areas in the united States, showing the geography and locations of many landmarks including cemeteries.

Town—A small unit of land divisions, sometimes comparable to a village, sometimes like the townships in most places.

Township—A land division, sometimes of an odd size and shape and other times a specific unit of square miles.

trad—tradition

Tradition—belief or custom transmitted orally.

Transcribe—to copy a manuscript.

Trial Calendar—List of cases scheduled for trial in a given term (similar to session book).

Trustee—a person to whom duties are confidently relegated.

T.v. Tochter von—daughter of

twp—township

—U—

u.d. und der—and of

ultra vires.—Without power; beyond the powers of.

Uncle—a father or a mother's brother, but also applied to an aunt's marriage partner.

Undertaker—a person who makes arrangements for a funeral.

unehel unehelich—illegitimate

Unfaithful—not adhering to the marriage vows.

Union—marriage

unk—unknown

unm—unmarried

Urn—a container for the ashes of a dead person after cremation.

Uterine—born of the same mother, but different fathers.

Ux., Uxor., Vixor, VX.—Wife

—V—

v. von—of (if part of a name, it *usually* signified nobility).

Vagina—canal between external oriface and uterus.

Vault—a subterrainian burial place.

Vellum—part of a calf's skin prepared for use as a manuscript.

Venire—order by court to sheriff to summon a jury.

venire facias.—That you cause to come; (a kind of summons).

ver—verify

verh. verheiratet—married

Verba fortuis accipiuntur contra proferentem.—Words are to be taken most strongly against the one using them.

⁰⁰ verheiratet—married (also: X is used)

⁰ verlobt—engaged

Vestry Minutes—see civil records.
versus (v.s. v.)—Against
vi et armis.—By force and arms.
via.—A road; a right of way; by way of.
vic—vicinity
vice versa.—On the contrary; on opposite sides.
Videlicet (viz.)—(contraction of videre and licet). It is easy to see; (that is to say; namely).
Vidua—Widow, Relict.
Vignette—a portrait or photograph showing only head or quarterlength likeness against a shaded background.
Virgin—a female with unruptured hymen.
virtute officii.—By virtue of his office.
viva voce.—By the living voice; by word of mouth.
Visitations, Heraldic—lists of coats of arms which contain the specific names of the individual who claimed them.
Vital—essential to life.
Vital Records—official documents relating to births, deaths, and marriages, baptisms, christenings, banns burials.
Voir dire.—To speak the truth. (Denotes a preliminary examination to determine the competency of a witness.)
vol—volume
VR.—Vital Records

—W—

w—wife
Wanton—a lewd or libidinous person.
Ward—a pupil or minor in the care of a guardian.
Warrant—Means to assure that certain facts are true. Writ requiring sheriff to arrest a person and to bring him to court on a given day for an offense with which person is charged. Usually government right to property given to veterans.
Warrantee Deed—A guaranteed deed.
WD -wd—Will dated. The date a will was written.
Wealthy—rich or affluent.
Wedding—a nuptial ceremony.
Wedlock—the married state.

Weekly meeting (Yearly meeting)—Quaker meeting (see monthly meeting)
weibl. weiblich—female
wid—widow(er)
Wife—a married woman or spouse.
Will—The legal declaration of a person's mind as to the manner he would have his property or estate disposed of after his death. A will or testament may be nuncupative (oral) or written. In the U.S. any type of property may be disposed of by will.
Witness—one who attests another person's signature, or who gives evidence or proof.
Witness book—Record of witnesses in given court session.
Woman—an adult female.
Womb—the uterus or female organ of conception and gestation.
WWI—World War I
WWII—World War II
Worship—religious adoration.
WP wp—Will proved. The date a will was probated or proved.
Wreath—a garland of flowers.
Writ—Legal notice. Designates a court order directed to the sheriff or another public officer requiring the performance of a certain act.
Wwe. Witwe—widow
Wwer Witwer—widower

—Y—

Year—the time taken by one revolution of the earth (approximately 365¼ days).
Yearbooks—yearly publications about statistics, geography and happenings of localities.
Yeoman—A man who owned property in England, one who was of a class of land owners.
Youth—a young man.
yr—year
1812 W—War of 1812
... unbekannte Angabe—unknown declaration.
†x×x an im Kampfe erlittenen Wunden gestorben—died of wounds (battle).

INDEX

Addendum:

1. County (Cemetery) Maps - Soil Conservation Service, P.O. Box 2890, Washington, D.C 20013.
2. Comprehensive listing of morticians - National Directory of Morticians, P.O. Box 20, Chagrin Falls, OH 44022.
3. Comprehensive listing of monument makers - American Monument Assoc. 6902 N. High Street, Worthington, OH 43085.
4. Civil War Organizations -Civil War Round Table Assoc., P.O. Box 7388 Little Rock, AR 72217.
5. Surname Changes - The German-American Connection by Heinz Moos Publishing Co., Inc., Rotunda Office Center, 711 W. Fortieth St., Baltimore, MD 21211.